The Heritage of WORLD Civilizations

SECOND EDITION

Albert M. Craig *Harvard University*

William A. Graham *Harvard University*

Donald Kagan *Yale University*

Steven Ozment *Harvard University*

Frank M. Turner *Yale University*

Macmillan Publishing Company

New York

Copyright © 1990 by Macmillan Publishing Company,
a division of Macmillan, Inc.

Printed in the United States of America

A portion of this book previously appeared in *The Western
Heritage* by Donald Kagan, Steven Ozment, and Frank M.
Turner.

Earlier edition copyright © 1986 by Macmillan Publishing
Company

Macmillan Publishing Company
866 Third Avenue, New York, New York 10022

Collier Macmillan Canada, Inc.

Library of Congress Cataloging in Publication Data

The Heritage of world civilizations / Albert M. Craig . . . [et al.].—
  2nd ed.
     p.   cm.
    Includes bibliographical references.
    Contents: v. 1. To 1600 — v. 2. Since 1500.
    ISBN 0-02-325491-2 (set).
    1. Civilization—History.   I. Craig, Albert M.
CB69.H45   1990   89-12994
909—dc20   CIP

Printing: 1 2 3 4 5 6 7 8   Year: 0 1 2 3 4 5 6 7 8 9

Acquisitions Editor: Eben Ludlow
Developmental Editor: Johnna Barto
Production Supervisor: J. Edward Neve
Production Manager: Richard C. Fischer
Text Designer: Andrew P. Zutis
Cover Designer: Eileen Burke
Photo Researchers: Barbara and John Schultz

This book was set in Orion typeface by York Graphic Services,
Inc., printed and bound by Rand McNally and Company.
The cover was printed by: Lehigh Press.

Preface

Today, more than during any previous era of history, we live in a time of interaction and interdependence of nations around the entire globe. More people with differing cultural heritages and religious outlooks live more closely together than in any other period. Economic, political, and military developments in one part of the world quickly affect millions of people in other parts. The common problems of environmental pollution, overpopulation, and urban sprawl affect every continent. The vast expansion of markets for products as diverse as oil, electronics, and fast food have changed the standard of living virtually everywhere. Furthermore, never before in human history have fervent adherents of so many of the major religious traditions lived in such close proximity throughout the world. No people or nation today can live without an awareness of its place in what has rapidly become a global village.

The current situation is itself the result of a major historical development—the close of the European era of world history. Between approximately 1500 and the middle of the twentieth century Europeans and their colonists in North America and elsewhere dominated the world scene through the strength of their political organization, economic productivity, and military might. That era came to an end during the third quarter of this century as the nations of Asia, the Near East, and Africa achieved new positions on the world scene. Their new political independence, their control over strategic natural resources (especially oil), the expansion of their economies (particularly those of the nations on the Pacific rim of Asia), and their control over nuclear weapons have changed the shape of world affairs in virtually every respect. Because of these developments Europe and the United States now play a lesser role in world affairs than they did a half century ago or even a quarter century ago.

As citizens of the world, we confront political and economic relationships virtually unimagined even half a century ago. These conditions demand that we learn and teach history from a global perspective. It is the goal of this volume to provide just that perspective. It is our hope that students—and teachers for that matter—who now live in the global village may, through the study of the various world civilizations, better understand and appreciate other citizens of that village.

On this transformed world stage the students who read this book will spend their lives. It is our hope that through the exploration of the diverse world civilizations they may enter that world better informed and more culturally sensitive. We have aimed not merely to describe the several civilizations, but also to convey an inner sense of what each civilization meant to those who have lived in it. For that reason we have paid very special attention to the emergence of the major religious traditions of world civilizations. These represent on the one hand the most ancient roots of those civilizations and on the other the most relevant factors in contemporary human interaction.

We are also quite aware of the vast array of new tools and concepts that historians have brought to bear on the treatment of history. Our coverage has attempted to introduce students to the various aspects of social and intellectual history as well as to the more traditional political and diplomatic coverage. We firmly believe that only through an appreciation of all pathways to understanding of the past can the real heritage of world civilizations be achieved.

Changes in Second Edition

In undertaking this second edition we have attempted to make a number of major revisions to aid both teachers and students.

❏ Much more extensive coverage of topics in social history with special emphasis on women and the family.
❏ Extensively revised and expanded sections on African history in Chapters 7, 11, 15, 22, 31, and 37.
❏ A new statement regarding Neo-Confucian philosophy in Chapter 9 and a new section on women in warrior society Japan in Chapter 10.
❏ A new section on Meso-American civilization in Chapter 21.
❏ An extensively revised chapter (Chapter 23) that integrates the seventeenth-century European scientific revolution with the eighteenth-century Enlightenment.
❏ A completely new chapter (Chapter 27) on the history of North America during the nineteenth century.
❏ New sections incorporating the twentieth-century history of the United States in Chapters 34 and 36.
❏ Extensively revised treatment of the world since 1945 in Chapters 36 and 37.

Pedagogical Elements

We have concentrated our efforts on improving the pedagogy to make the text more accessible to all students.

❏ *Part Essays* open each of the seven major sections of the book. These serve to preview the coverage in the subsequent chapters while highlighting major trends and movements.
❏ *Part Timelines* show the major events that occurred in five different civilizations during the same period. These provide quick reference for events occurring concurrently in the Middle East, Africa, East Asia, Europe, and the Americas.
❏ *Chapter Outlines* display major headings and subheadings on the opening page of each chapter. A quick glance helps to organize material before reading the chapter and provides a quick review after completing the chapter.
❏ *Primary Source Documents* include selections from sacred books, poems, philosophy, political manifestos, and travel accounts. They will aid both teachers and students to experience the general character of the major civilizations. Along with the photographs, they convey the experiences and voices of even ancient societies with immediacy and concreteness.
❏ *In World Perspective Sections* serve as chapter conclusions and place the materials of each chapter into an integrated worldview.
❏ *Color Portfolios* include photographs accompanied by interpretive essays that are organized around

the major world religions: Judaism, Christianity, Islam, Buddhism, Hinduism, and contemporary religious revival.

We should note that most scholarship on China uses the Wade-Giles system of romanizaton for Chinese names and terms. In order that students may be able to move easily from the present text to advanced works of scholarship in Chinese history, we have used the Wade-Giles system throughout. China today, however, uses another system known as pinyin. Virtually all Western newspapers have adopted it. Therefore, for Chinese history since 1949 (See Chapter 37) we have included the pinyin spellings in parentheses after the Wade-Giles.

Also, we have followed the most accurate currently accepted English transliteration of Arabic words. For example, today *Koran* is being replaced by the more accurate *Qur'an*; similarly *Muhammad* is preferable to *Mohammed* and *Muslim* to *Moslem*. We have not tried to distinguish the letters *'ayn* and *hamza*: both are rendered by a simple apostrophe ('), as in *shi'ite*.

With regard to Sanskritic transliteration, we have not distinguished linguals and dentals, and both palatal and lingual "s" are rendered "sh," as in *Shiva* and *Upanishad*.

Teaching Supplements

To help ease the burden of teaching such a comprehensive course as world civilization, we have made available several very useful supplements.

❏ INSTRUCTOR'S MANUAL. Prepared by Perry Rogers, Ph. D., Ohio State University, this item includes summary and multiple choice questions for each part essay; chapter summaries, outline of key points and concepts, identification questions, multiple choice and essay questions to be used for tests, and a suggested list of relevant films and videos.
❏ COMPUTERIZED TEST BANK. The test items are also available on computer disk which allows the instructor to choose different configurations of questions as well as add original questions. The result is greater flexibility in the administration of tests.
❏ MAP TRANSPARENCIES. A number of maps from the text have been computer colorized and are available as full-color acetates. These transparencies provide strong visual support during lectures.
❏ COMPUTERIZED STUDY GUIDE. Students may review their comprehension of the text presentation by answering questions included on a computer disk.

Acknowledgments

In developing this second edition of *The Heritage of World Civilizations*, we are grateful to the many scholars and teachers who responded to our surveys and who read the manuscript and offered valuable insights. We wish to acknowledge the following academic reviewers:

Sarah J. Adams, *University of Charleston*
David Bard, *Concord College*
Gerald W. Berkley, *University of Hawaii at Manoa*
Richard M. Berthold, *University of New Mexico*
Charmarie J. Blaisdell, *Northeastern University*
C. Dewey Caldwell, *U. of Hawaii, Honolulu Community College*
Richard J. Carey, *Chaminade University of Honolulu*
Daniel Crecelius, *California State University, Los Angeles*
Allen Cronenburg, *Auburn University*
Elton L. Daniel, *University of Hawaii, Honolulu*
Lawrence E. Daxton, *University of Southern Colorado*
Wayne A. DeJohn, *St. Ambrose University*
Samuel E. Dicks, *Emporia State University*
Joel Epstein, *Olivet College*
John D. Fair, *Auburn University at Montgomery*
Harvey M. Feinberg, *Southern Connecticut State University*
Peter J. Frederick, *Wabash College*
Richard Geiger, *St. Ambrose University*
Stephen S. Gosch, *University of Wisconsin, Eau Claire*

C. Wilfred Griggs, *Brigham Young University*
Roland L. Guyotte, *University of Minnesota, Morris*
Edward S. Haynes, *Winthrop College*
John M. Hirschfield, *St. Mary's College of Maryland*
Sarah Hughes, *Hampton University*
Gregory C. Kozlowski, *DePaul University*
Dennis E. Lawther, *West Liberty State College*
Donald L. Layton, *Indiana State University, Terre Haute*
Robert L. Lembright, *James Madison University*
Richard D. Lewis, *St. Cloud State University*
William G. Morris, *Midland College*
John P. Mueller, *Aims Community College*
William O. Oldson, *Florida State University, Tallahassee*
Richard V. Pierard, *Indiana State University, Terre Haute*
Philip F. Riley, *James Madison University*
Anthony W. Snyder, *Brookdale Community College*
David B. Stenzel, *California State University, Stanislaus*
Janet D. Stone, *Armstrong State College*
Teddy J. Uldricks, *University of North Carolina at Asheville*
James Weland, *Bentley College*
Allan M. Winkler, *Miami University (of Ohio)*

We are especially grateful to Theodore M. Ludwig of Valparaiso University who offered many helpful suggestions on the essays that accompany the color sections.

About the Authors

ALBERT M. CRAIG is the Harvard-Yenching Professor of History at Harvard University where he has taught since 1959. A graduate of Northwestern University, he took his Ph.D. at Harvard University. He has studied at Strasbourg University, and at Kyoto and Tokyo universities in Japan. He is the author of *Chóshú in the Meiji Restoration* (1961), and, with others, of *East Asia, Tradition and Transformation* (1978). He is the editor of *Japan, A Comparative View* (1973) and co-editor of *Personality in Japanese History* (1970). At present he is engaged in research on the thought of Fukuzawa Yukichi. For eleven years (1976–1987) he was the director of the Harvard-Yenching Institute. In 1988 he was awarded the Order of the Rising Sun by the Japanese government.

WILLIAM A. GRAHAM is Professor of the History of Religion and Islamic Studies at Harvard University. He has taught there for sixteen years in the Department of Near Eastern Languages and Civilizations and currently chairs the Committee on the Study of Religion. He is the author of *Divine Word and Prophetic Word in Early Islam* (1977), which was awarded the American Council of Learned Societies prize for the "Best First Book in the History of Religions" in 1977–1978. His most recent book is *Beyond the Written Word: Oral Aspects of Scripture in the History of Religion* (1987). He studied for his B.A. in comparative literature (Classics, German, French) as a Morehead Scholar at the University of North Carolina in Chapel Hill, and for the A.M. and Ph.D. degrees in the comparative study of religion as a Woodrow Wilson and Danforth Graduate Fellow at Harvard University. He is the recipient of John Simon Guggenheim (1981) and Alexander von Humboldt (1982) research fellowships.

DONALD KAGAN received the A.B. degree in history from Brooklyn College, the M.A. in classics from Brown University, and the Ph.D. in history from Ohio State University. During 1958–1959 he studied at the American School of Classical Studies as a Fulbright Scholar. Richard M. Colgate Professor at Yale University, where he has taught since 1969, he has received three awards for undergraduate teaching at Cornell and Yale. He is the author of *The Great Dialogue* (1965), a history of Greek political thought, a four volume history of the Peloponnesian War: *The Origins of the Peloponnesian War* (1969), *The Archidamian War* (1974), *The Peace of Nicias and the Sicilian Expedition* (1981), *The Fall of the Athenian Empire* (1987), and he has just completed a biography of Pericles. With Brian Tierney and L. Pearce Williams he is the editor of *Great Issues in Western Civilization*, a collection of readings in the same subject. He is currently Dean of Yale College.

STEVEN OZMENT is Professor of History at Harvard University. He is the author of *The Reformation in the Cities: The Appeal of Protestantism in Sixteenth Century Germany and Switzerland* (1975); *The Age of Reform, 1250–1550: An Intellectual and Religious History of Late Medieval and Reformation Europe* (1980), winner of the Schaff Prize and nominated for the 1981 American Book Award; *When Fathers Ruled: Family Life in Reformation Europe* (1983); *Magdalena and Balthasar: An Intimate Portrait of Life in Sixteenth Century Europe* (1986). Mr. Ozment's new book, *Three Behaim Boys: Growing Up in Early Modern Germany*, will appear in 1990.

FRANK M. TURNER is Professor of History at Yale University. He also serves as University Provost. He received his B.A. degree at the College of William and Mary and his Ph.D. from Yale. He has received the Yale College Award for Distinguished Undergraduate Teaching. He has directed a National Endowment for the Humanities Summer Institute. His scholarly research has received the support of fellowships from the National Endowment for the Humanities and the Guggenheim Foundation. He is the author of *Between Science and Religion: The Reaction to Scientific Naturalism in Late Victorian England* (1974) and *The Greek Heritage in Victorian Britain* (1981). The latter study received the British Council Prize of the Conference on British Studies and the Yale Press Governors Award. He has also contributed numerous articles to journals and has served in the editorial advisory boards of *The Journal of Modern History, Isis,* and *Victorian Studies.*

Brief Contents

Detailed Contents

The Coming of Civilization

Empires and Cultures of the Ancient World

Consolidation and Interaction of World Civilizations: 500–1500

Enlightenment and Revolution in the West

Toward the Modern World

Global Conflict and Detente

Documents

Maps

Color Plates

The Coming of Civilization

THE way of life of prehistoric cavepeople differed immensely from that of today's civilized world. Yet the few millennia in which we have been civilized are but a tiny fraction of the long span of human existence. Especially during the recent millennia, changes in our culture have far outpaced changes in our bodies. We live a highly organized and often sedentary life but still retain the emotional make-up and motor reflexes of primitive men and women.

Homo sapiens—modern man—first appeared about 100,000 years ago. Since then, the pace of human control over the environment has constantly accelerated. It took tens of thousands of years to learn to use fire and to make stone tools, to domesticate the dog, and to master the rudiments of agriculture. It took another seven to nine thousand years to develop cities, systems of writing, and then, bronze and iron. Several hundred years later occurred the great religious and philosophical revolutions of the ancient world, followed by the empires of China, India, Iran, and Rome that straddled the B.C.–A.D. divide.

Now, two thousand years later, humans have unlocked the power of the atom, walked on the moon, and broken the genetic code. The pace of new discoveries continues to quicken. If we compare the invention of writing late in the fourth millennium B.C. with the breaking of the genetic code, the latter was far more complex, but the former may have been more difficult.

The timetable for the development of river valley civilizations varied. The Near Eastern cultures began earlier, followed by India and China. But the parallelism in stages of development is remarkable. First came agriculture and pottery, then cities, writing, and bronze, and, finally, iron and empire. Does the logic of nature dictate that once agriculture develops, cities will arise in alluvial river valleys favorable to intensive cultivation? Was it inevitable that the firing of clay to produce pots would reduce metallic oxides and lead to the discovery of smelting? Did the formation of the aristocratic and priestly classes, who controlled the resources of cities, automatically lead to record keeping and writing?

That is to say, did agriculture set in motion a train of similar events in widely separated river valleys? Or, is diffusion a more likely cause? Is it not conceivable that contacts between the early civilizations were more numerous than we now imagine? The earliest written languages—the Sumerian cuneiform, the Egyptian hieroglyphs, and the Chinese ideographs—probably had independent origins. They are too dissimilar to be the result of diffusion. But what of seeds, bronze, and iron? Might not migrating peoples or wandering merchants have carried these over long distances? Both hypotheses — diffusion and independent origins — are plausible. However, in the absence of evidence, a definitive answer cannot be given. Little remains even of the material culture of the men and women of these earliest civilizations. Understanding their lives is like reconstructing a dinosaur from a broken tooth and a fragment of jawbone.

In or near the same river valleys that saw the birth of civilization occurred the religious and philosophical revolutions that permanently marked the world thereafter: monotheistic Judaism, from which would later develop the world religions of Christianity and Islam; Hinduism and Buddhism in South Asia; and the philosophies of China and Greece. The simultaneity of their appearance was striking. The Hebrew prophets, Buddha, Confucius, and Socrates, if not all contemporaries, were grouped within a few hundred years of each other in the first millennium B.C. Most founders of the great religions based their teachings on intensely personal religious experiences, on experiences that cannot be analyzed in historical terms. Yet, we can examine their historical contexts and can note certain similarities.

The coming of the bronze and iron ages — and we speak of bronze and iron partly as a shorthand for many complex developments — led to a series of political and spiritual crises across the world of the early civilizations. The founders of the great religions and philosophies responded to these crises with new visions of man's place in the universe, and with new and more universal ethics. It is their greater universalism that distinguishes the world religions from those centered more narrowly on a particular tribe or people. Of course, all religions spring from a common human impulse, and treat the questions of how to live and what life means in the face of death. But Buddhism, Christianity, and Islam differed from the Shinto of Japan, the religions of the Egyptians or Mayas, or even the Zoroastrianism of ancient Iran, in contending that their answers were true for all peoples and times. It was this universalism that made them missionary religions.

Similarly, the philosophies of China and Greece were more universal than previous systems of thought. Confucianism eventually spread to Korea, Japan, and Vietnam, countries whose customs were quite different from those of China. It became the basis for laws in these countries because its ethics transcended particular Chinese institutions.

Greek ideas played an equivalent role in the West. They joined Judaic concepts to form Christianity. The gospel according to Saint John starts: "In the beginning was the Word (*logos*), and the Word was with God, and the Word was God." In Greek, *logos* means something like "Universal Principle" or "Reason." Universal Greek conceptions also lay at the base of the Roman law code (*ius gentium*) used to govern provinces with different peoples and widely varying customs. This last example also says something about the transition from the older civilizations to the empires of the ancient world. These empires, to be sure, were built by armies, not philosophies. But for their leaders to govern, for their bureaucracies to function, they had to have philosophies and laws. ❏

A Sumerian wall plaque carved in relief. It shows Ur-Nanshe, ruler of Lagash (2494–2465 B.C.). The upper portion shows him carrying a basket of bricks for building a temple; in the lower he sits among his children. The plaque is covered with inscriptions in a very old form of Sumerian writing.

1 The Birth of Civilization

"Prehistory": Early Human Beings and Their Culture

Scientists estimate that the earth may be as many as six billion years old, that creatures very much like humans may have appeared three to five million years ago, and that our own species of human beings goes back at least one hundred thousand years. Humans are different from other animals in that they are capable of producing and passing on a culture. *Culture* may be defined as the ways of living built up by a group and passed on from one generation to another. It may include behavior, material things, ideas, institutions, and religious faith. The source of human creativity is our large and convoluted brain. We create ideas and institutions. We formulate our thoughts in speech, allowing us to transmit our culture to future generations. We also can bring together our fingers and thumb, enabling us to make and hold tools. The combination of speech and material invention was necessary for the development of human culture.

The anthropologist designates early human cultures by their tools. The earliest period is the Paleolithic (from Greek, "old stone") Age. In this immensely long period (from perhaps 600,000 to 10,000 B.C.), people were hunters, fishers, and gatherers, but not producers, of food. They learned to make and use tools of stone and of perishable materials like wood, to make and control fire, and to pass on what they learned in language. In the regions where civilization ultimately was born, people depended on nature for their food and were very vulnerable to attacks from wild beasts and to natural disasters. Because their lives were often "solitary, poor, nasty, brutish, and short," as Thomas Hobbes put it, their responses to troubles may have been rooted in fear of the unknown. Their fear concerned the uncertainties of human life or the overpowering forces of nature. Such fear is often one element in

3

Paleolithic cave painting from Dordogne in France. Deep in caves in southern France and northern Spain are wall paintings of hundreds of animals—bison, deer, horses, and oxen. They are shown in remarkable realism. Often they are shown as hunted by men, sometimes with a spear sticking in them. [Bettmann Archive.]

human recourse to magic as an effort to coerce—or to religion to propitiate—superhuman forces often thought to animate or direct the natural world.

But preliterate human beings are, and were, also much closer to nature than more civilized peoples. This closeness to nature seems to be another primary reason for the evidence of religious faith and practice, as well as magic, that goes as far back as archaeology can take us. Fear or awe, exultation, gratitude, and empathy with the natural world must all have figured in the cave art and in the ritual practices, such as burial, that we find evidenced at Paleolithic sites around the globe. Human life itself is a kind of miracle. The concern in all known societies with life's major transitions—birth, puberty, marriage, and death—was probably a source of "rites of passage" among the earliest human beings as well. For example, the many figurines of pregnant women (or goddesses?) that have been found at prehistoric sites might have been used in rites aimed at ensuring fertility or successful childbirth. However, given the sparse evidence, all we can say is that the sense that there is more to the world than meets the eye— in other words, the religious response to the world—seems to be as old as humankind.

The style of life and the level of technology of the Paleolithic period could support only a sparsely settled society. If the hunters were too numerous, the available game would not suffice. In Paleolithic times, people were subject to the same natural and ecological constraints that today maintain a balance between wolves and deer in Alaska.

Human life in the Paleolithic Age easily lent itself to division of labor by sex. The men engaged in hunting, fishing, making tools and weapons, and fighting against other families, clans, and tribes. The women, less mobile because of frequent childbearing, smaller in stature, and less strong and swift than the men, gathered nuts, berries, and wild grains; wove baskets; and made clothing. Women gathering food probably discovered how to plant and care for seeds. This knowledge eventually made possible the Age of Agriculture—the Neolithic revolution.

Of the early Paleolithic societies, only a few developed into Neolithic or New Stone Age agricultural societies, and anthropologists and archaeologists disagree on why that revolutionary development occurred. In many areas, right into our own time, some isolated portions of humankind have been content to continue to live in the "Stone Age" unless compelled by more advanced cultures to change. The reasons for the shift to agriculture by late Paleolithic groups are unclear. In the past, some scientists thought that climatic change—a drop in temperature and rainfall—forced people to be inventive and to seek new ways of acquiring food. But newer evidence suggests that there was little climatic variation in Neolithic times. Other theories focus on the human element: a possible growth in population, an increased sense of territoriality, and a resulting interference with the pursuit of herds for hunting.

However it happened, some ten thousand years ago parts of what we now call the Near East began to shift from a hunter–gatherer culture to a settled agricultural one. People began to use precisely carved stone tools, so we call this period the Neolithic (from Greek, "new stone") Age. Animals as well as food crops were domesticated. The important invention of pottery made it possible to store surplus liquids, just as the invention of baskets had earlier made it possible to store dry foods. Cloth came to be made from flax and wool. Crops required constant care from planting to harvest, so the Neolithic people built permanent buildings, usually in clusters near the best fields.

The agricultural revolution may not, however, have produced an immediate population explosion. Anthropologists suggest that village living produced a much greater incidence of disease, there being no provision for the disposal of human and animal waste. The Neolithic villages also provided attractive targets for raiders.

Still, agriculture provided a steadier source of food and a greater production of food in a given area. It thus provided the basis for a denser population over time. It was a major step in the human control of nature, and it was a vital precondition for the emergence of civilization. The earliest Neolithic societies appeared in the Near East about 8000 B.C., in China about 4000 B.C., and in India by at least 3600 B.C.. The Neolithic revolution in the Near East and India was based on wheat, in China on millet and rice; in Meso-America, several millennia later, it would be based on corn.

Neolithic villages and their culture, gradually having grown from and having replaced Paleolithic culture, could be located on almost any kind of terrain. But beginning about four thousand years before the Christian era, people began to settle in substantive numbers in the river-watered lowlands of Mesopotamia, Egypt, northern China, and northwestern India. Here a new style of life evolved: an urban society and civilization. The shift was accompanied by the gradual introduction of new technologies and by the invention of writing.

Again, we do not know why people first chose to live in cities, with their inherent disadvantages: overcrowding, epidemics, wide separation from sources of

MAP 1-1   THE FOUR GREAT RIVER VALLEY CIVILIZATIONS TO CA. 1000 B.C.
By CA. *2000* B.C. *urban life was established along the Tigris-Euphrates in Mesopotamia, the Nile in Egypt, the Indus and Ganges in India, and the Yellow River in China.*

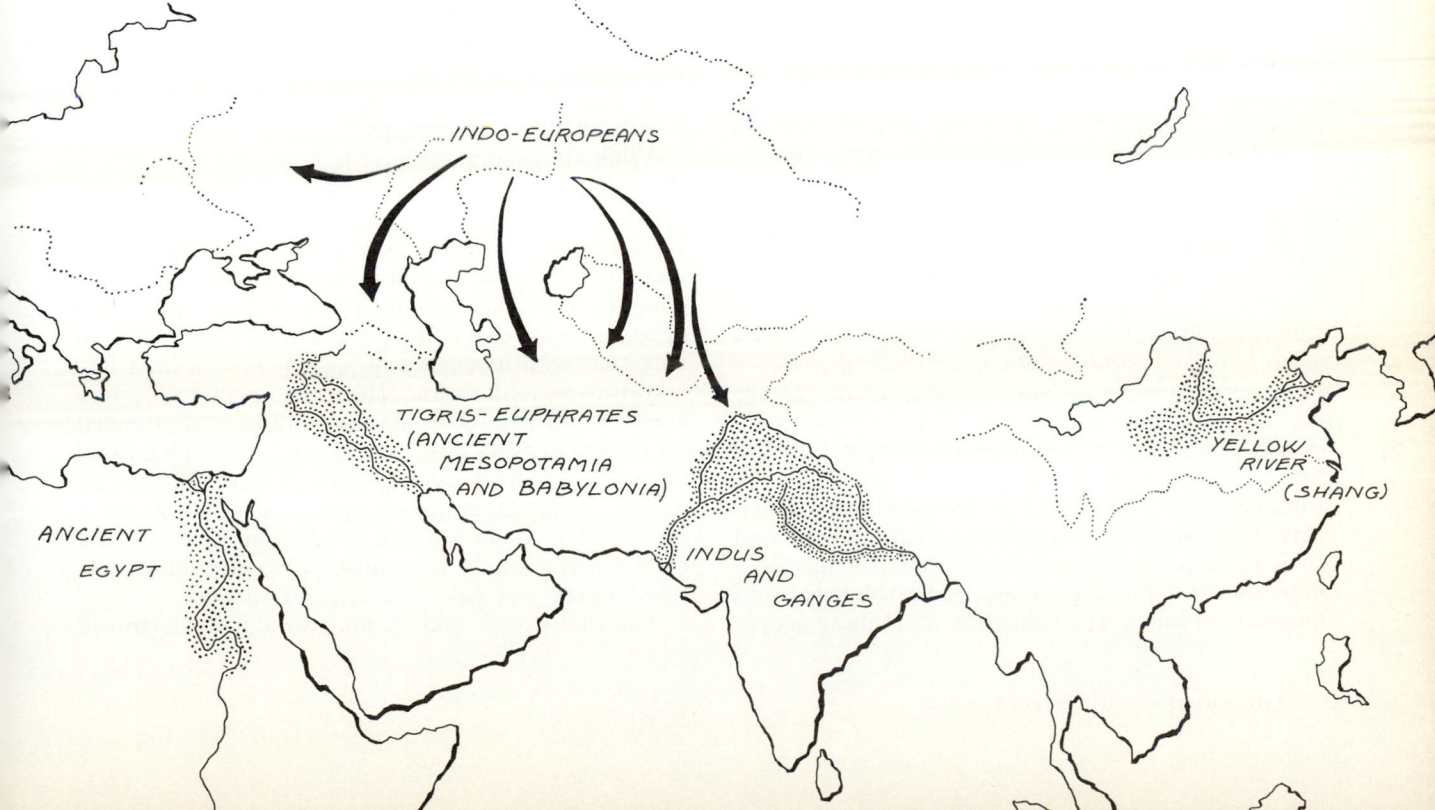

food and raw materials, and the concentration of wealth that permitted organized warfare. Perhaps cities were created because, to quote the Greek philosopher Aristotle, "Man is by nature a political animal." Perhaps they arose merely because they offered more possibilities for amusement, occupational choice, and enrichment than had the Neolithic villages. In any event, by about 3000 B.C., when the invention of writing gave birth to history, urban life was established in the valleys of the Tigris and Euphrates rivers in Mesopotamia (modern Iraq) and of the Nile in Egypt. Somewhat later, urban life arose in the Indus valley of India and the Yellow River basin of China. The development of urban centers by no means meant the disappearance of numerous outlying peasant agricultural villages. Nevertheless, with the coming of cities, writing, and metals, humankind had attained civilization.

Early Civilizations in the Near East

Civilization, then, is a form of human culture in which many people live in urban centers, have mastered the art of smelting metals, and have developed a method of writing. The rich alluvial plains where civilization began made possible the production of unprecedented surpluses of food—but only if there was an intelligent management of the water supply. Proper flood control and irrigation called for the control of the river by some strong authority capable of managing the distribution of water. This control and management required careful observation and record keeping. The first use of writing may have been to record the behavior of the river and the astronomical events that gave clues about it. It was also used by the powerful individuals (the kings) who dominated the life of the river valleys to record their possessions, by priests to record omens and religious texts, by merchants and artisans to record business transactions, and by others to record acts of government, laws, and different kinds of literature.

This widely varied use of writing reflects the complex culture of the urban centers in the river valleys. Commerce was important enough to support a merchant class. Someone discovered how to smelt tin and copper to make a stronger and more useful material—bronze—which replaced stone in the making of tools and weapons: The importance of this technological development is reflected in the term *Bronze Age*. The great need for record keeping created a class of scribes, because the picture writing and complicated scripts of these cultures took many years to learn and could not be mastered by many. To deal with the gods, temples were built, and many priests attended and administered them. The collection of all these people

into cities gave the settlements an entirely new character. Unlike Neolithic villages, they were communities established for purposes other than agriculture. The city was an administrative, religious, manufacturing, entertainment, and commercial center.

The logic of nature pointed in the direction of the unification of an entire river valley. As a result, these civilizations in time produced unified kingdoms under powerful monarchs who often came to be identified with divinity. The typical king in a river-valley civilization was regarded either as a god or as the delegate of a god. Around him developed a rigid class structure. Beneath the monarch was a class of hereditary military aristocrats and a powerful priesthood. Below them were freemen, mostly peasants, and at the bottom were serfs or slaves. Most of the land was owned or controlled by the king, the nobility, and the priests. These were conservative cultures of numerous peasant villages and a few urban centers. Such cultural patterns took form early and changed only slowly and grudgingly.

The Fertile Crescent:
Mesopotamian Civilization

The first civilization appears to have arisen in the valley of the Tigris and Euphrates rivers: Mesopotamia (the term means land "between the rivers" in Greek). Its founders seem to have been a people called Sumerians, who controlled the southern part of the valley (Sumer) close to the head of the Persian Gulf by the dawn of history, around 3000 B.C. (see Map 1.2). At first, city-states about one hundred square miles in size dotted the landscape. Ur, Erech, Lagash, and Eridu are examples of such cities that archaeologists have revealed to us. Quarrels over water rights and frontiers led to incessant fighting, and in time, stronger towns conquered weaker ones and expanded to form larger units, usually kingdoms.

While the Sumerians were fighting with their neighbors and among themselves for supremacy in the south, a people, called Semites, from the Arabian Desert on the west had been moving into Mesopotamia north of Sumer. Their language and society were different from those of the Sumerians, but they soon absorbed Sumerian culture and established their own kingdom, with its capital at Akkad, near a later city known to us as Babylon. The most famous Akkadian king was Sargon, who conquered Sumer and extended his empire in every direction. Legends grew up around his name, and he is said to have conquered the "cedar forests" of Lebanon, far to the west near the coast of the Mediterranean Sea. He ruled about 2340 B.C. and established a family, or dynasty, of Semitic kings that ruled Sumer and Akkad for two centuries.

External attack and internal weakness destroyed

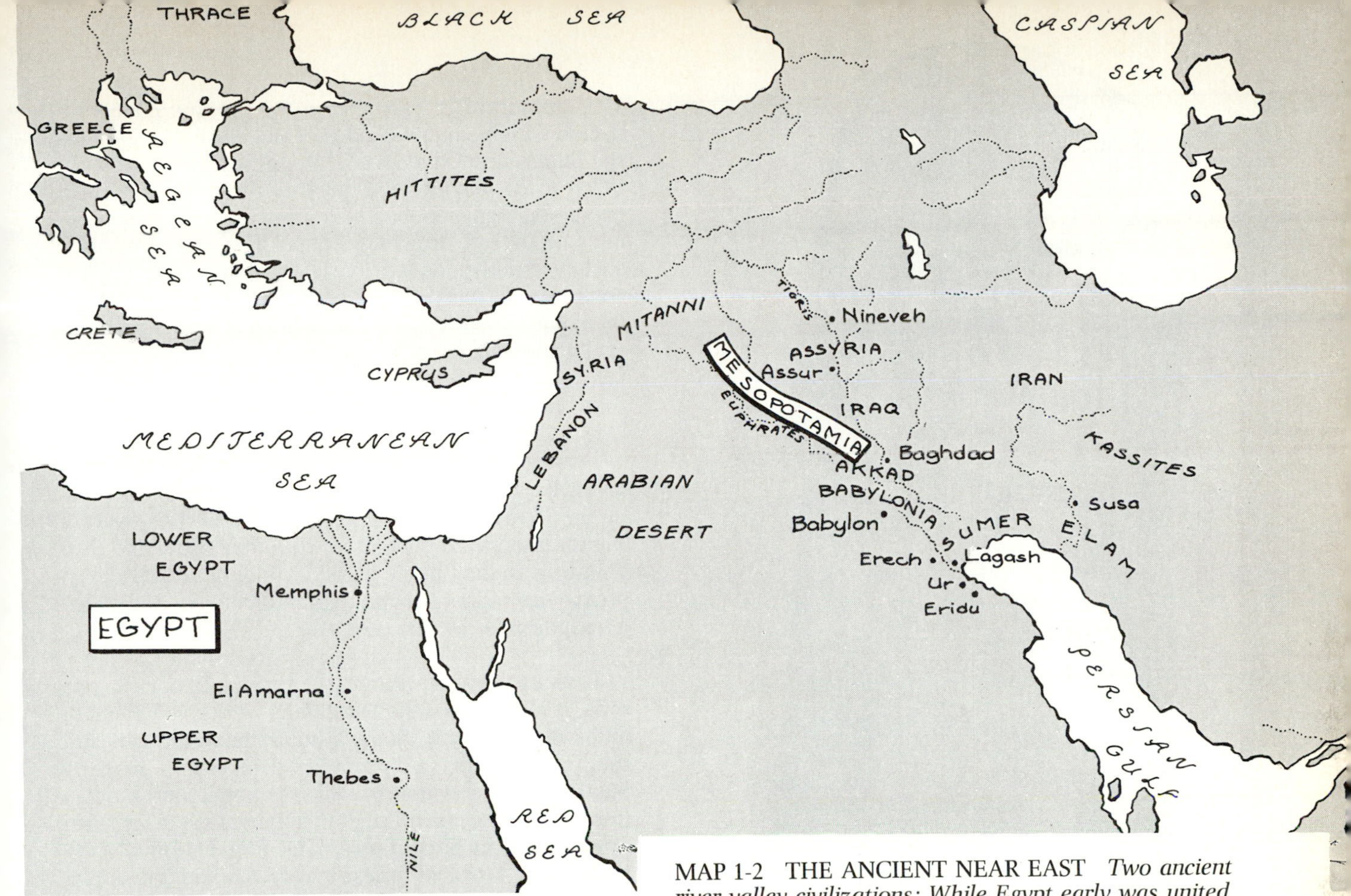
THRACE
BLACK SEA
CASPIAN SEA
GREECE
AEGEAN SEA
HITTITES
CRETE
CYPRUS
MEDITERRANEAN SEA
MITANNI
SYRIA
LEBANON
TIGRIS
Nineveh
ASSYRIA
Assur
MESOPOTAMIA
EUPHRATES
IRAQ
IRAN
Baghdad
AKKAD
KASSITES
BABYLONIA
ARABIAN
DESERT
Babylon
SUMER
Susa
ELAM
Erech
Lagash
Ur
Eridu
LOWER EGYPT
Memphis
EGYPT
El Amarna
UPPER EGYPT
Thebes
NILE
RED SEA
PERSIAN GULF

MAP 1-2 THE ANCIENT NEAR EAST *Two ancient river valley civilizations: While Egypt early was united into a single state, Mesopotamia was long divided into a number of city states.*

In Mesopotamia inscriptions on stone like this one are much less common than those on clay. This stele records the deeds of Enkhegal, king of Lagash, one of the earliest Sumerian city states. Before the rise of Akkad, Lagash dominated much of Mesopotamia. [Copyrighted by University Museum, University of Pennsylvania.]

Akkad. About 2125 B.C., the city of Ur in Sumer revolted and became the dominant power, and this Third Dynasty of Ur established a large empire of its own. About 2000 B.C., however, it was swept aside by another Semitic invasion, which ended Sumerian rule forever. Thereafter, Semites ruled Mesopotamia, but the foundations of their culture were Sumerian. The Semites changed much of what they inherited; but in law, government, religion, art, science, and all other areas of culture, their debt to the Sumerians was enormous.

The fall of the Third Dynasty of Ur (CA. 2100–2000 B.C.) put an end to the Sumerians as an identifiable group. The Sumerian language survived only in writing, as a kind of sacred language known only to priests and scribes, preserving the cultural heritage of Sumer. For about a century after the fall of Ur, dynastic chaos reigned, but about 1900 B.C., a Semitic people called the Amorites gained control of the region, establishing their capital at Babylon. The high point of this Amorite, or Old Babylonian, dynasty came more than a hundred years later under its most famous king, Hammurabi (CA. 1792–1750 B.C.)

Hammurabi is best known for the law code connected with his name. Codes of law existed as early as the Sumerian period, and Hammurabi's plainly owed much to earlier models, but it is the fullest and best preserved legal code we have from ancient Mesopotamia, or indeed, from anywhere. The code reveals a society strictly divided in class: There were nobles, commoners, and slaves, and the law did not treat them equally. In general, punishments were harsh, literally applying the principle "an eye for an eye, a tooth for a tooth." The prologue to the code makes it clear that law and justice came from the gods through the king.

About 1600 B.C., the Babylonian kingdom fell apart under the impact of invasions from the north and east by the Hittites and the Kassites. The Hittites were a raiding party who plundered what they could and then withdrew to their home in Asia Minor. The Kassites, a people from the Iranian plateau, stayed and ruled Mesopotamia for five centuries.

GOVERNMENT. From the earliest historical records, it is clear that the Sumerians were ruled by monarchs in some form. Some scholars have thought that they could detect a "primitive democracy" in early Sumer, but the evidence, which is poetic and hard to interpret, shows no more than a limited check on royal power even in early times. The first historical city-states had kings or priest-kings who led the army, administered the economy, and served as judges and as intermediaries between their people and the gods. At first, the kings were thought of as favorites and representatives of the gods; later, on some occasions and for relatively short periods, they instituted cults that worshiped them as divine. This union of church and state (to use modern terminology) in the person of the king reflected the centralization of power typical of Mesopotamian life. The economy was managed from the center by priests and kings and was planned very carefully. Each year, the land was surveyed, fields were assigned to specific farmers, and the amount of seed to be used was designated. The government estimated the size of the crop and planned its distribution even before it was planted.

This process required a large and competent staff, the ability to observe and record natural phenomena, a good knowledge of mathematics, and , for all of this,

The code of Hammurabi. This is a cast of the stele on which is inscribed in cuneiform characters the law code issued by the Babylonian king Hammurabi (CA. 1792–1750 B.C.). In the relief at the top the king stands before the sun god and receives the law from him. The original stele is in the Louvre in Paris. [Courtesy of the Oriental Institute, University of Chicago.]

Hammurabi Creates a Code of Law in Mesopotamia

Hammurabi's Babylonian empire stretched from the Persian Gulf to the Mediterranean Sea. Building on earlier laws, Hammurabi compiled one of the great ancient codes. It was discovered about seventy-five years ago in what is now Iran. Hammurabi, like other rulers before and after, represented himself and his laws as under the protection and sponsorship of all the right gods. Property was at least as sacred as persons, and the eye-for-an-eye approach characterizes the code. Here are a few examples from it.

LAWS

If a son has struck his father, they shall cut off his hand.

If a seignior has destroyed the eye of a member of the aristocracy, they shall destroy his eye.

If he has broken another seignior's bone, they shall break his bone.

If he has destroyed the eye of a commoner or broken the bone of a commoner, he shall pay one mina of silver.

If he has destroyed the eye of a seignior's slave or broken the bone of a seignior's slave, he shall pay one-half his value.

If a seignior has knocked out a tooth of a seignior of his own rank, they shall knock out his tooth.

If he has knocked out a commoner's tooth, he shall pay one-third mina of silver. . . .

EPILOGUE

I, Hammurabi, the perfect king,
was not careless (or) neglectful of the black-headed (people),
whom Enlil had presented to me,
(and) whose shepherding Marduk had committed to me;
I sought out peaceful regions for them;
I overcame grievous difficulties; . . .
With the mighty weapon which Zababa and Inanna entrusted to me,
with the insight that Enki allotted to me,
with the ability that Marduk gave me,
I rooted out the enemy above and below;
I made an end of war;
I promoted the welfare of the land;
I made the peoples rest in friendly habitations; . . .
The great gods called me,
so I became the beneficent shepherd whose scepter is righteous. . . . ❑

James B. Pritchard, *Ancient Near Eastern Texts*, 3rd ed. (Princeton: Princeton University Press, 1969), pp. 164–180.

---

a system of writing. The Sumerians invented the writing system known as *cuneiform* (from the Latin *cuneus*, "wedge"). The name comes from the wedge-shaped stylus with which they wrote on clay tablets; the writing also came to be used in beautifully cut characters in stone. Sumerians also began the development of a sophisticated system of mathematics. The calendar they invented had twelve lunar months. To make it agree with the solar year and to make possible accurate designation of the seasons, they introduced a thirteenth month about every three years.

RELIGION. The Sumerians and their Semitic successors believed in gods in the shape of humans who were usually identified with some natural phenomenon. They were pictured as frivolous, quarrelsome, selfish, and often childish, differing from humans only in their greater power and their immortality. They each appear to have begun as a local deity. The people of Mesopotamia had a negative and gloomy picture of

the afterworld as a "land of no return." Their religion dealt with problems of this world, and they employed prayer, sacrifice, and magic to achieve their ends. Expert knowledge was required to reach the perfection in wisdom and ritual needed to influence the gods, so the priesthood flourished. A high percentage of the cuneiform writing that we now have is devoted to religious texts: prayers, incantations, curses, and omens.

It was important to discover the will and intentions of the gods, and the Sumerians sought hints in several places. The movements of the heavenly bodies were an obvious evidence of divine action, so astrology was born. They also sought to discover the divine will by examining the entrails of sacrificial animals for symbolic signs in their particular features. All of this religious activity required numerous scribes to keep records, as well as learned priests to interpret them.

Religious thought, in the form of myth, played a large part in the literature and art of Mesopotamia. A *myth* (from the Greek, "story" or "plot") is a narrative that deals with truths about relationships between the human and the transcendent. In the poetic language of myth, the Sumerians and their successors told tales of the creation of the world, of a great flood that almost destroyed human life, of an island paradise from which the god Enki was expelled for eating forbidden plants, of a hero named Gilgamesh who tried to gain immortality, and many more.

Religion was also the inspiration for the most interesting architectural achievement in Mesopotamia: the ziggurat. The ziggurat was an artificial stepped mound surmounted by a temple. It may have been a symbolic representation of the cosmic mountain that many cultures have thought lies at the center of the world. Neighbors and successors of the Sumerians adopted the style, and the eroded remains of many of these monumental structures, some partly restored, still dot the Iraqi landscape.

SOCIETY. We have a very full and detailed picture of the way people in ancient Mesopotamia conducted their lives and of the social conditions in which they lived during the reign of Hammurabi. More than fifty royal letters, many business contracts, and especially the Code of Hammurabi are the sources of our knowledge. We find that society was legally divided into three classes: nobles, commoners, and slaves. Punishment for crimes committed against freemen was harsher than for those against slaves, and crimes committed against nobles were considered more serious than those against commoners.

Slaves were chiefly captives from wars, although some native Babylonians were enslaved for committing certain crimes, such as kicking one's mother or striking an elder brother. Parents could sell their children into slavery or pledge themselves and their entire family as surety for a debt. In case of default, they

Sumerian statuettes from Tell Asmar. The tallest figure in this collection of gods, priests, and worshipers is the god Abu, the "lord of vegetation." The group was found buried beside the altar of a temple at a site near modern Baghdad dating from 3000–2500 B.C. [Courtesy of the Oriental Institute, University of Chicago.]

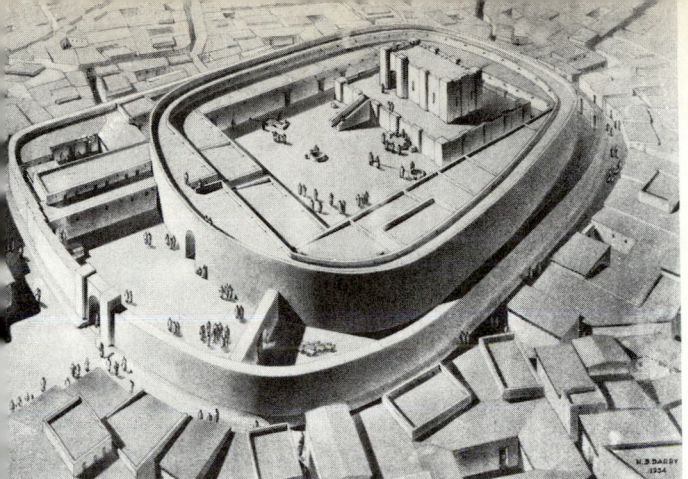

Reconstruction of the temple oval at Khafaje. The remains of this temple complex (not far from Baghdad in modern Iraq) have made a probable reconstruction possible. It reveals an elaborate religious establishment of the early third millenium B.C. that was even earlier than the ziggurat at Ur and the major pyramids of Egypt. [H. D. Darby. Courtesy of the Oriental Institute, University of Chicago.]

would all become slaves of the creditor for a stated period of time. Some slaves worked for the king and the state, others for the temple and the priests, and still others for private citizens. Their tasks varied accordingly. Most of the temple slaves appear to have been women, who were probably used to spin and weave and grind flour. The royal slaves did the heavy work of building palaces, canals, and fortifications. Private owners used their slaves chiefly as domestic servants. Some female slaves were used as concubines.

Laws against fugitive slaves or slaves who denied their masters were harsh, but in some respects, Mesopotamian slavery appears enlightened compared to other slave systems in history. Slaves could engage in business and, with certain restrictions, hold property. They could marry free men or women, and the result-

KEY EVENTS AND PEOPLE IN MESOPOTAMIAN HISTORY

CA. 3500 B.C.	Sumerians arrive
CA. 2800–2340 B.C.	Sumerian city-states: early dynastic period
CA. 2340 B.C.	Sargon establishes Semitic dynasty at Akkad
CA. 2125–2027 B.C.	Third Dynasty of Ur
CA. 1900 B.C.	Amorites at Babylon
1792–1750 B.C.	Reign of Hammurabi
CA. 1600 B.C.	Invasion by Hittites and Kassites

ing children would be free. A slave who acquired the necessary wealth could buy his or her own freedom. Children of a slave by the master might be allowed to share in his property after his death.

The Nile Valley: Egyptian Civilization

While a great civilization arose in the valley of the Tigris and Euphrates, another, no less important, emerged in Egypt. The center of Egyptian civilization was the Nile River. From its source in central Africa, the Nile runs north some four thousand miles to the Mediterranean, with long navigable stretches broken by several cataracts. Ancient Egypt included the 750 miles of the valley from the First Cataract northward to the sea and was shaped like a long-necked funnel with two distinct parts. Upper (southern) Egypt was the stem, consisting of the narrow valley of the Nile. The broad, triangular delta, which branches out about 150 miles from the sea, formed the mouth of the funnel, or Lower Egypt (see Map 1.1). The Nile alone made life possible in the almost rainless desert that surrounded it. Each year, the river flooded and covered the land, and when it receded, it left a fertile mud that could produce two crops a year. The construction and maintenance of irrigation ditches to preserve the river's water, with careful planning and organization of planting and harvesting, produced an agricultural prosperity unmatched in the ancient world.

The Nile also served as a highway connecting the long, narrow country and encouraging its unification. Upper and Lower Egypt were, in fact, already united into a single kingdom at the beginning of our historical record, about 3100 B.C. Nature helped protect and isolate the ancient Egyptians from outsiders. The cataracts, the sea, and the desert made it difficult for foreigners to reach Egypt for friendly or hostile purposes. Egypt knew far more peace and security than Mesopotamia. This security, along with the sunny, predictable climate, gave Egyptian civilization a more optimistic outlook than the civilizations of the Tigris–Euphrates, which were always in fear of assault from storm, flood, earthquake, and hostile neighbors.

The more than three-thousand-year span of ancient Egyptian history is traditionally divided into thirty-one royal dynasties. They range from the first, founded by Menes, the unifier of Upper and Lower Egypt, to the last, established by Alexander the Great, who conquered Egypt in 322 B.C. The dynasties are conventionally arranged into periods (see table on page 16). The unification of Egypt was vital, for even more than in Mesopotamia, the entire river valley required the central control of irrigation. By the time of the Third Dynasty, the king had achieved full supremacy and had imposed internal peace and order; his kingdom enjoyed great prosperity. The capital was at Memphis in Lower Egypt, just above the delta. The king was no mere representative of the gods but a god himself. The land was his own personal possession, and the people were his servants.

Nothing better illustrates the extent of royal power than the three great pyramids built as tombs by the kings of the Fourth Dynasty. The largest, that of Khufu, was originally 481 feet high and 756 feet long on each side; it was made up of 2,300,000 stone blocks

Pharaoh Menkaure and his queen. This Fourth Dynasty monarch built the third and smallest of the great pyramids at Giza. The frontality of the two figures and the extension of the left foot of each in this slate sculpture from Giza are typical of Egyptian statues. (About 2550 B.C.) [Courtesy of the Museum of Fine Arts, Boston; MFA Expedition Fund.]

averaging 2.5 tons each. It was said by the much later Greek historian Herodotus to have taken 100,000 men twenty years to build. The pyramids are remarkable not only for the technical skill that was needed to build them but even more for what they tell us of the royal power. They give evidence that the Egyptian kings had enormous wealth, the power to concentrate so much effort on a personal project, and the confidence to undertake one of such a long duration. There were earlier pyramids and many were built later, but those of the Fourth Dynasty were never surpassed.

THE OLD KINGDOM. In the Old Kingdom, royal power was absolute. The pharaoh, as he was later called (the term originally meant "great house" or "palace"), governed his kingdom through his family and appointed officials removable at his pleasure. The peasants were carefully regulated, their movement was limited, and they were taxed heavily, perhaps as much as one fifth of what they produced. Luxury accompanied the king in life and death, and he was raised to a remote and exalted level by his people. Such power and eminence could not be sustained long by force alone. The Egyptians worked for the king and obeyed him because he was a living god on whom their life, safety, and prosperity depended. He was the direct source of law and justice, so no law codes were needed.

In such a world, government was merely one aspect of religion, and religion dominated Egyptian life. The gods of Egypt had many forms: animals, humans, and natural forces. In time, Re, the sun god, came to have a special dominant place, but for centuries, there seems to have been little clarity or order in the Egyptian pantheon. Unlike the Mesopotamians, the Egyptians had a rather precise idea of an afterlife. They took great care to bury their dead according to their custom and supplied the grave with things that the departed would need for a pleasant life after death. The king and some nobles had their bodies preserved as mummies. Their tombs were beautifully decorated with paintings and religious texts useful in the next life; food and furnishings were provided at burial and even after. Some royal tombs were equipped with full-sized ships for the voyage to heaven. At first only kings were thought to achieve eternal life; then nobles were included; finally, all Egyptians could hope for immortality. The dead had to be properly embalmed, and the proper spells had to be written and spoken.

The Egyptians developed a system of writing not much later than the Sumerians. Though the idea may have come from Mesopotamia, the form of their script was independent. It began as picture writing and later combined pictographs with sound signs to produce a difficult and complicated script that the Greeks called *hieroglyphics* ("sacred carvings"). Though much of

The Sphinx. The great Sphinx is located at Giza, near modern Cairo. It seems to have been associated with the pyramid of Khafre, a king who ruled Egypt some time after 2600 B.C. The origin of the colossal lion with the head of a man is unknown, but the face is thought to be a likeness of the pharaoh himself. [Hirmer Foto-archiv München.]

what we have is preserved on wall paintings and carvings, most of Egyptian writings was done with pen and ink on a fine paper made from the papyrus reed found in the delta. Egyptian literature was more limited in depth and imagination than the Mesopotamian writings. Hymns, myths, magical formulas, tales of travel, and "wisdom literature," or bits of advice to help one get on well in the world, have been preserved. But nothing as serious and probing as the story of Gilgamesh was produced in the more optimistic world of Egypt.

THE MIDDLE KINGDOM. The power of the kings of the Old Kingdom waned as priests and nobles gained more independence and influence. The governors of the regions of Egypt, called *nomes*, gained hereditary claim to their offices, and their families acquired large estates. About 2200 B.C., the Old Kingdom collapsed and gave way to the decentralization and disorder of the First Intermediate Period (CA. 2200–2052 B.C.). Finally, the nomarchs (governors) of Thebes in Upper Egypt gained control of the country and established the Middle Kingdom in about 2052 B.C.

The rulers of the Twelfth Dynasty restored the pharaoh's power over the whole of Egypt, though they could not completely control the nobles who ruled the nomes. Still, they brought order, peace, and prosperity to a troubled land. They encouraged trade and extended Egyptian power and influence northward toward Palestine and southward toward Ethiopia. Though they moved the capital back to the more defensible site at Memphis, they gave great prominence to Amon, a god especially connected with Thebes. He became identified with Re, emerging as Amon-Re, the main god of Egypt.

The kings of this period seem to have emphasized their role in doing justice. In their statues, they are often shown as burdened with care, presumably concern for their people. Tales of the period place great emphasis on the king as interested in right and in the welfare of his people. Much later, in the New Kingdom, ethical concerns appeared, as they had in the law codes of Mesopotamia, but the divine status of the kings gave them a strong religious tinge.

THE NEW KINGDOM (THE EMPIRE). The Middle Kingdom disintegrated in the Thirteenth Dynasty with the resurgence of the power of the local nobility. About 1700 B.C., Egypt suffered an invasion. Tradition speaks of a people called the Hyksos who came from the east and conquered the Nile Delta. They seem to

Akhnaton Intones New Hymns to Aton, the One God

These hymns were composed in the reign of Amenhotep IV (1367–1350 B.C.), or Akhnaton, as he called himself after instituting a religious revolution in Egypt.

Thou makest the Nile in the Nether World,
Thou bringest it as thou desirest,
To preserve alive the people of Egypt
For thou hast made them for thyself,
Thou lord of them all, who weariest thyself for them;
Thou lord of every land, who risest for them.
Thou Sun of day, great in glory,
All the distant highland countries,
Thou makest also their life,
Thou didst set a Nile in the sky.
When it falleth for them,
It maketh waves upon the mountains,
Like the great green sea,
Watering their fields in their towns.

How benevolent are thy designs, O lord of eternity!
There is a Nile in the sky for the strangers
And for the antelopes of all the highlands that go about
    upon their feet.
But the Nile, it cometh from the Nether World for
    Egypt.

Thou didst make the distant sky in order to rise
    therein,
In order to behold all that thou hast made,
While thou wast yet alone
Shining in thy form as living Aton,
Dawning, glittering, going afar and returning.
Thou makest millions of forms
Through thyself alone;
Cities, villages, and fields, highways and rivers,
All eyes see thee before them,
For thou art Aton of the day over the earth,
When thou hast gone away,
And all men, whose faces thou hast fashioned
In order that thou mightest no longer see thyself
    alone;

[Have fallen asleep, so that not] one [seeth] that which
    thou hast made,
Yet art thou still in my heart.

REVELATION TO THE KING

There is no other that knoweth thee
Save thy son Akhnaton.
Thou hast made him wise
In thy designs and in thy might.

UNIVERSAL MAINTENANCE

The world subsists in thy hand,
Even as thou hast made them
When thou hast risen they live,
When thou settest they die;
For thou art length of life of thyself,
Men live through thee.

The eyes of men see beauty
Until thou settest.
All labour is put away
When thou settest in the west.
When thou risest again
[Thou] makest [every hand] to flourish for the king
And [prosperity] is in every foot,
Since thou didst establish the world,
And raise them up for thy son,
Who came forth from thy flesh,
The king of Upper and Lower Egypt,
Living in Truth, Lord of the Two Lands,
Nefer-khepru-Re, Wan-Re [Akhnaton],
Son of Re, living in Truth, lord of diadems,
Akhnaton, whose life is long;
[And for] the chief royal wife, his beloved,
Mistress of the Two Lands, Nefer-nefru-Aton,
    Nofretete,
Living and flourishing for ever and ever.   ❑

James H. Breasted, *The Dawn of Conscience* (New York: Charles Scribners' Sons, 1933, 1961), p. 137.

have been a collection of Semitic peoples from the area of Palestine and Syria at the eastern end of the Mediterranean. Egyptian nationalism reasserted itself in about 1575 B.C., when a dynasty from Thebes drove out the Hyksos and reunited the kingdom. In reaction to the humiliation of the Second Intermediate Period, the pharaohs of the Eighteenth Dynasty, the most prominent of whom was Thutmose III (1490–1436 B.C.), created an absolute government based on a powerful army and an Egyptian empire extending far beyond the Nile valley.

From the Hyksos, the Egyptians learned new military techniques and obtained new weapons. To these they added determination, a fighting spirit, and an increasingly military society. They pushed the southern frontier back a long way and extended Egyptian power farther into Palestine and Syria and beyond to the upper Euphrates River. They were not checked until they came into conflict with the powerful Hittite empire of Asia Minor. Both powers were weakened by the struggle, and though Egypt survived, it again became the victim of foreign invasion and rule, as one

Akhnaton worshiping Aton. The scene curved into this stone stele shows Eighteenth-Dynasty Pharaoh Akhnaton (1367–1350 B.C.) paying homage to the newly enthroned god, Aton, the disk of the sun. [Library of the Egyptian Museum, Cairo.]

was the growth in power of the priests of Amon and the threat it posed to the position of the king. When young Amenhotep IV (1367–1350 B.C.) came to the throne before the middle of the fourteenth century B.C., he was apparently determined to resist the priesthood of Amon. He was supported by his family and advisers and ultimately made a clean break with the worship of Amon-Re. He moved his capital from Thebes, the center of Amon worship, and built an entirely new city about three hundred miles to the north at a place now called El Amarna. Its god was Aton the physical disk of the sun, and the new city was called Akhtaton. The king changed his own name to Akhnaton, "It pleases Aton." The new god was different from any that had come before him, for he was believed to be universal, not merely Egyptian. Unlike the other gods, he had no cult statue but was represented in painting and relief sculpture by the symbol of the sun disk.

The universal claims for Aton led to religious intolerance of the worshipers of the other gods. Their temples were shut down, and the name of Amon-Re was chiseled from the monuments on which it was carved. The old priests, of course, were deprived of their posts and privileges, and the people who served the pharaoh and his god were new, sometimes even foreign. The new religion, moreover, was more remote than the old. Only the pharaoh and his family worshiped Aton directly, and the people worshiped the pharaoh. Akhnaton's interest in religious reform apparently led him to ignore foreign affairs, which proved disastrous. The Asian possessions of Egypt fell away. This imperial decline and its economic consequences presumably caused further hostility to the new religion. When the king died, a strong counterrevolution swept away the work of his lifetime.

His chosen successor was soon put aside and replaced by Tutankhamon (1347–1339 B.C.), the young husband of one of the daughters of Akhnaton, the beautiful Nefertiti. The new pharaoh restored the old religion and wiped out as much as he could of the memory of the worship of Aton. He restored Amon to the center of the Egyptian pantheon, abandoned El Amarna, and returned the capital to Thebes. There, he and his successors built his magnificent tomb, which remained remarkably intact until its discovery in 1922. The end of the El Amarna age restored power to the priests of Amon and to the military officers. A general named Horemhab became king (1335–1308? B.C.), restored order, and recovered much of the lost empire. He referred to Akhnaton as "the criminal of Akhtaton" and erased his name from the records. Akhnaton's city and memory disappeared for over three thousand years, to be rediscovered only by chance about a century ago.

For the rest of its independent history, Egypt returned to its traditional culture, but its mood was more

foreign empire after another took possession of the ancient kingdom.

The Eighteenth Dynasty, however, witnessed an interesting religious change. One of the results of the successful imperial ventures of the Egyptian pharaohs

CA. 3100–2700 B.C.	Early Dynastic Period (I–II)
2700–2200 B.C.	Old Kingdom (III–VI)
2200–2052 B.C.	First Intermediate Period (VII–X)
2052–1786 B.C.	Middle Kingdom (XI–XII)
1786–1575 B.C.	Second Intermediate Period (XIII–XVII)
CA. 1700 B.C.	Hyksos invasion
1575–1087 B.C.	New Kingdom (or Empire) (XVIII–XX)
1087–30 B.C.	Post-Empire (XXI–XXXI)

pessimistic. The Book of the Dead, a product of this late period, was a collection of spells whereby the dead could get safely to the next world without being destroyed by a hideous monster. Egypt itself would soon be devoured by powerful empires, and the Pharaonic civilization would pass from history forever.

Ancient Near Eastern Empires

In the time of the Eighteenth Dynasty in Egypt, new groups of peoples had established themselves in the Near East: the Kassites in Babylonia, the Hittites in Asia Minor, and the Mitannians in northern Mesopotamia. They all spoke languages in the Indo-European group, which includes Greek, Latin, Sanskrit, Persian, Celtic, and the Germanic languages and is thought to have originated in the Ukraine (now the southwestern Soviet Union) or to the east of it. The Kassites and the Mitannians were warrior peoples who ruled as a minority over more civilized folk and absorbed their culture without changing it.

THE HITTITES. The Hittites arrived in Asia Minor about 2000 B.C., and by about 1500 B.C., they had established a strong, centralized government with a capital at Hattusas (near Ankara, the capital of modern Turkey). Between 1400 and 1200 B.C., the Hittites contested Egypt's control of Palestine and Syria. They were strong enough to achieve a dynastic marriage with the daughter of the powerful Nineteenth Dynasty pharaoh Ramses II, in about 1265 B.C. By 1200 B.C., the Hittite kingdom was gone, swept away by the arrival of new, mysterious Indo-Europeans. However, Neo-Hittite centers flourished in Asia Minor and Mesopotamia for a few centuries longer.

In most respects, the Hittites reflected the influence of the dominant Mesopotamian culture of the region, but their government resembled more closely what we know of other Indo-European cultures. Their kings did not claim to be divine or even to be the chosen representatives of the gods. In the early period, the king's power was checked by a council of nobles, and the assembled army had to ratify his succession to the throne. The Hittites appear to have been responsible for a great technological advance, the smelting of iron. They also played an important role in transmitting the ancient cultures of Mesopotamia and Egypt to the Greeks, who lived on their frontiers.

THE ASSYRIANS. The fall of the Hittites was followed shortly by the formation of empires that dominated the Near East's ancient civilizations and even extended them to new areas. The first of these empires was established by the Assyrians, whose homeland was in the valleys and hills of northern Mesopotamia along, and to the east of, the Tigris River. They had a series of capitals, of which the great city of Nineveh is perhaps best known (modern Mosul, Iraq). They spoke a Semitic language and, from early times, were a part of the culture of Mesopotamia. Akkadians, Sumerians, Amorites, and Mitannians had dominated Assyria in turn.

The Hittites' defeat of Mitanni liberated the Assyrians and prepared the way for their greatness from earlier than 1000 B.C. By 665 B.C., they had come to control everything from the southern frontier of Egypt, through Palestine, Syria, and much of Asia Minor, down to the Persian Gulf in the southeast. They succeeded in part because they made use of iron weapons. Because iron was more common than copper and tin, it was possible for them to arm more men cheaply. The Assyrians were also fierce, well disciplined, and cruel. Their cruelty was calculated, at least in part, to terrorize real and potential enemies, for the Assyrians boasted of their brutality.

Unlike earlier empires, the Assyrian Empire systematically and profitably exploited the area it held. The Assyrians employed different methods of control, ranging from the mere collection of tribute, to the sta-

CA. 1400–1200 B.C.	Hittite Empire
CA. 1100 B.C.	Rise of Assyrian power
732–722 B.C.	Assyrian conquest of Palestine–Syria
671 B.C.	Assyrian conquest of Egypt
612 B.C.	Destruction of Assyrian capital at Neneveh
612–539 B.C.	Neo-Babylonian (Chaldaean) Empire

A late Hittite war chariot. The Hittites were probably the earliest major users of iron implements and of the horse. This relief, now in the Ankara museum, shows a pair of horse-drawn Hittite fighters oblivious to the defeated enemy below. It is from the eighth century B.C.*, by which time the formerly unified empire had been succeeded by several scattered Hittite groups. [AHM.]*

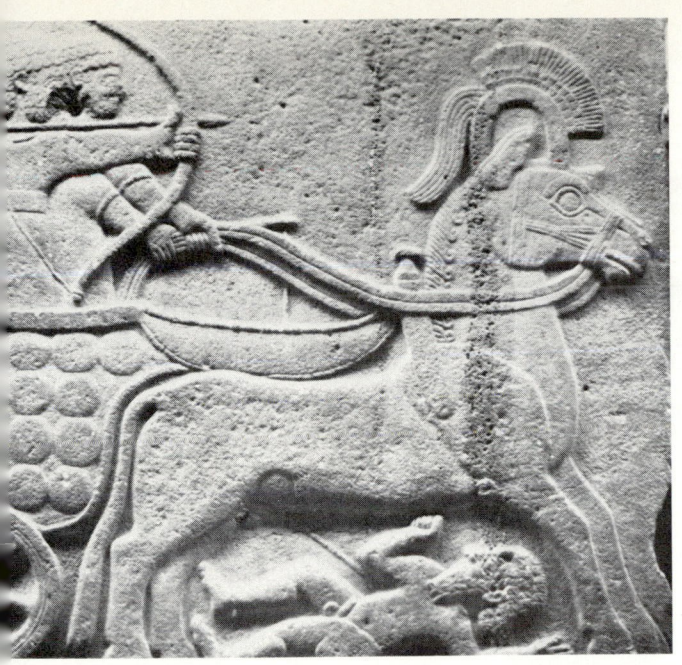

tioning of garrisons in conquered territory, to removing entire populations from their homelands and scattering them elsewhere, as they did to the people of the kingdom of Israel. Because of their military and administrative skills, they were able to hold vast areas even as they absorbed the teachings of the older cultures under their sway.

In addition to maintaining their own empire, the Assyrians had to serve as a buffer of the civilized Middle East against the barbarians on its frontiers. In the seventh century B.C., the task of fighting off the barbarians so drained the overextended Assyrians that the empire fell because of internal revolution. A new dy-

An Assyrian palace. This is a reconstruction drawing of the palace complex of King Sargon II (722–705 B.C.*) at Khorsabad (in modern Iraq). [Charles Altman. Courtesy of the Oriental Institute, University of Chicago.]*

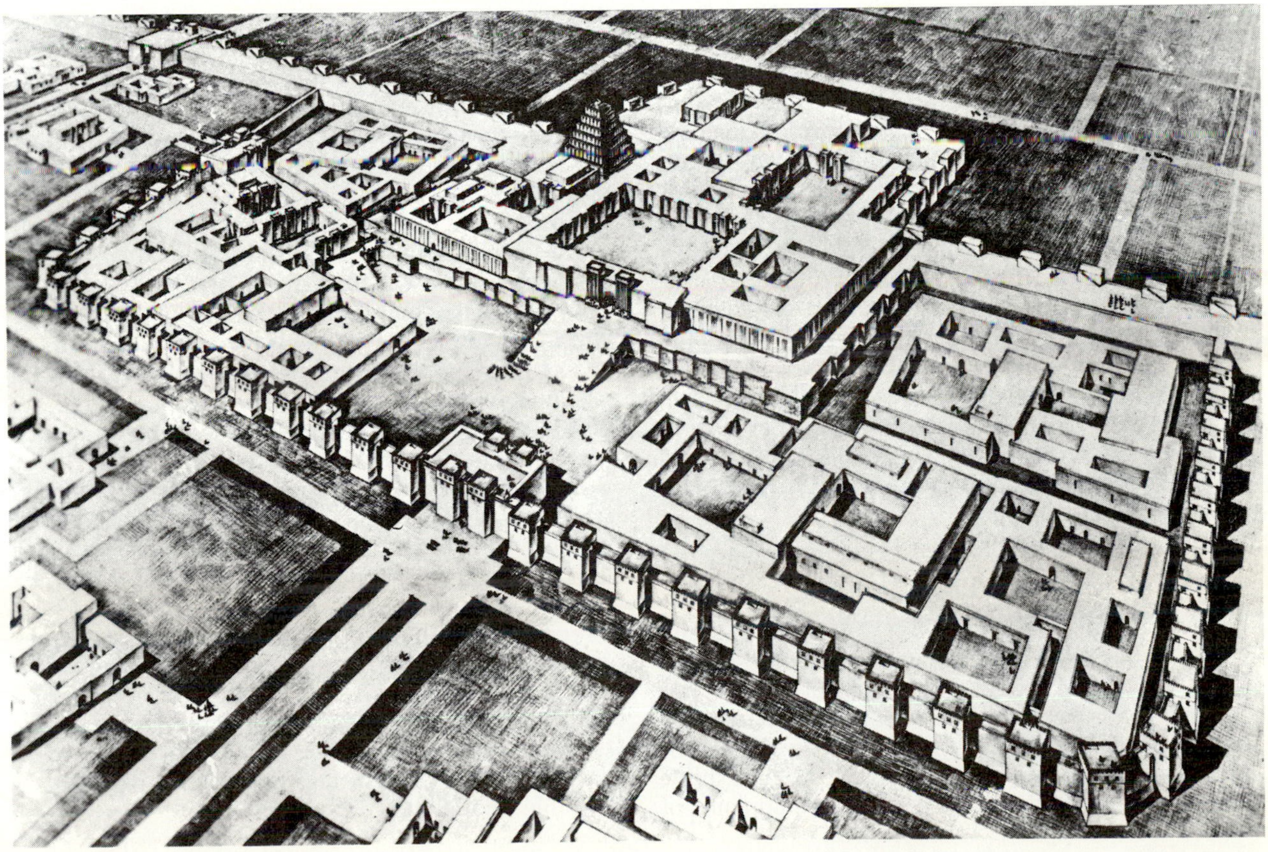

nasty in Babylon joined with the rising kingdom of Media to the east (in modern Iran) to defeat the Assyrians and destroy Nineveh in 612 B.C. The successor kingdoms, the Chaldean or Neo-Babylonian and the Median, did not last long; they were swallowed, by 539 B.C., by yet another great eastern empire, that of the Persians.

Early Indian Civilization

To the east of Mesopotamia, beyond the Iranian plateau and the mountains of Baluchistan, the Asian continent bends sharply southward into the southern oceans. This great triangular projection of Asia south of the massive mountain barrier of the Himalaya is known today as the *Indian subcontinent.* From sites well north in modern Pakistan and Afghanistan to the southern tip of India and Sri Lanka (Ceylon), archaeologists have unearthed evidence of diverse Paleolithic cultures. The latest of these probably existed side by side with the many Neolithic and Bronze Age sites also found on the subcontinent.

The earliest Neolithic pottery and agricultural hunting tools, together with evidence of settled life, have been dated as early as about 5500 B.C. These are in present-day Pakistan in the foothills of Sind and Baluchistan. The Neolithic revolution thus came to the subcontinent somewhat later than in the Near East. Some used to believe that it was imported from the west, but today scholars think that it was of independent origin in much, if not all, of the subcontinent.

The beginning of identifiable civilization in India was unusual, in that the initial breakthrough to literate, urban culture in the Indus valley lasted only a few hundred years. The Aryan culture that replaced the Indus civilization was foreign and bore little relation or resemblance to it. It centered on a different part of northern India, first the extreme northwest (Gandhara, the Punjab), then the plains west of the upper Ganges, and then along the Ganges itself. Although this Aryan culture provided the base for all later Indian civilization, it existed for nearly a millennium without taking up writing or building large cities. Because of the different character of these two cultures, we shall look at each separately.

The Harappan Civilization on the Indus River

The first breakthrough to civilization in the subcontinent came in the region of modern Pakistan. Here, there emerged a culture boasting Bronze age tools, developed cities, a writing system, and diversified social and economic organization. As one might expect, this civilization flourished on the fertile floodplains of one of the two largest river systems of the subcontinent, the Indus and its tributaries. Several sizable rivers flow west and south out of the Himalaya in Kashmir and the Punjab (*Panjab,* "five rivers") to merge into the single stream of the Indus as it crosses Sind to empty into the Indian Ocean. (The second great river system of the subcontinent, the Ganges and its tributaries, also rises in the Himalaya but flows south and east to the Bay of Bengal on the opposite side of the subcontinent.) The Indus culture is sometimes also called *Harappan,* from the name of the site, Harappa, where archaeologists first discovered it. Until the excavations began in the 1920s, no one knew of its existence. Today, two cities, Harappa and Mohenjo-Daro, and numerous lesser towns of this culture have been unearthed and studied.

Of the four great river-valley civilizations that mark the beginnings of literate, urban culture, the Indus is the one about which we know the least. Our relative ignorance is due to two factors.

First, this civilization disappeared as a living cultural tradition sometime before the middle of the second millennium B.C. It was once commonly assumed that this culture was destroyed by invading steppe peoples from the northwest, the Indo-European-speaking tribes who migrated in the second millennium B.C. from the Eurasian steppelands west, south, and eastward into new territories. (The groups that entered India and, at about the same time, Iran, are known as Aryans.) Now scholars recognize that there is no firm evidence to support this hypothesis, and without new evidence, the true cause of the passing of Indus civilization must remain one of history's unsolved mysteries.

Second, although we have many Indus inscriptions (mostly small stamp seals cut into soapstone), no one has been able to decipher them. Many scholars think that the Indus language was a Dravidian tongue, which would place it in the same family as some languages still spoken in the subcontinent, the most important of which is Tamil in southern India. Until it can be read, we have no self-testimony of the Indus peoples to guide us. Without the patient, still-unfolding work of modern archaeologists, this once great and widely dispersed civilization would have remained a wholly "vanished" culture. Now, however, we know that it flourished for at least five hundred years, and perhaps longer, before it passed from history's stage forever. Although material remains do not give us access to the history of the rise and fall of the Indus society, or to its precise institutions, they do yield indisputable evidence of a high culture. We can make some educated guesses about the Indus civilization, based on archaeological data and inferences from later Indian life and culture.

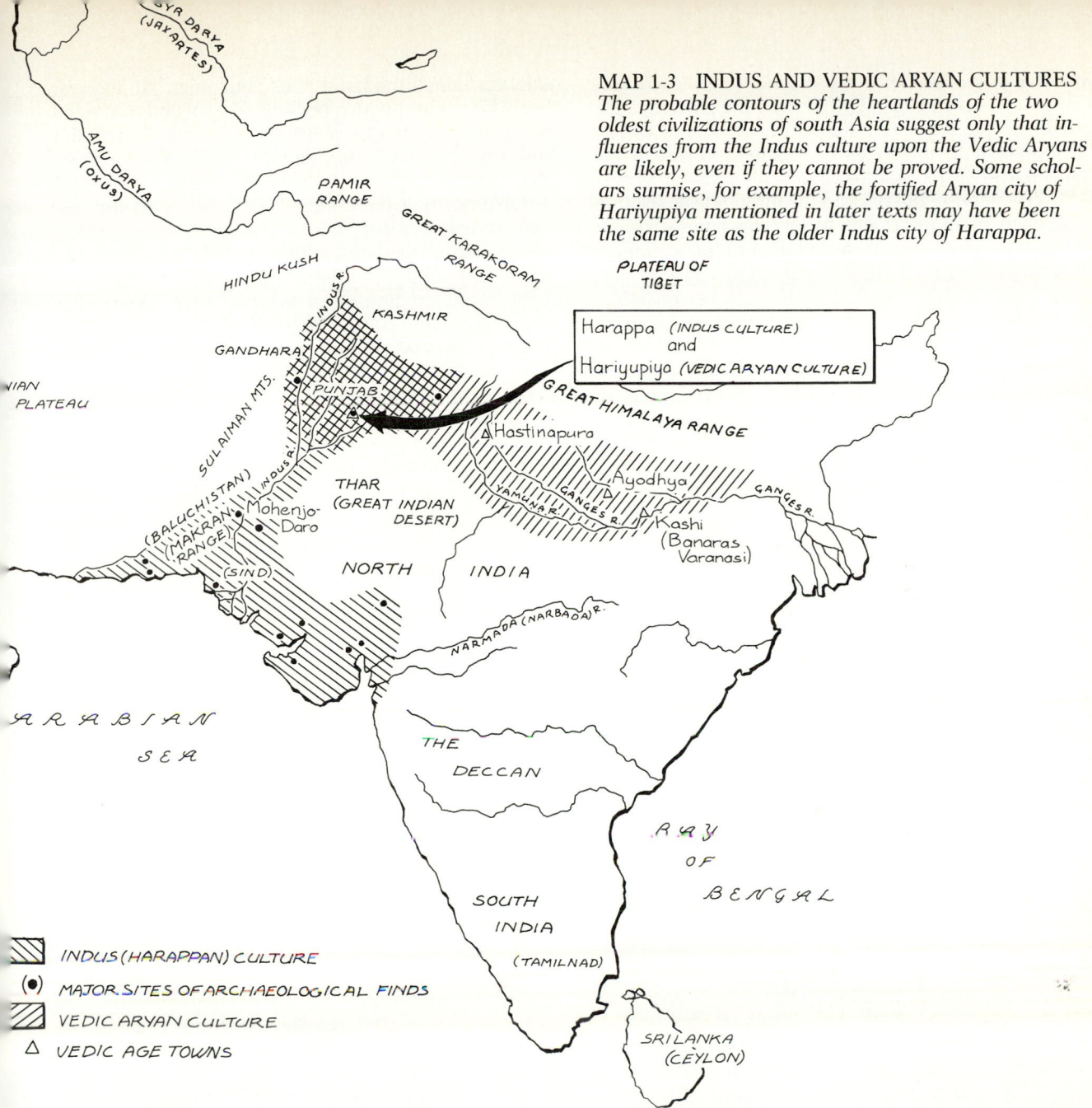

MAP 1-3 INDUS AND VEDIC ARYAN CULTURES
The probable contours of the heartlands of the two oldest civilizations of south Asia suggest only that influences from the Indus culture upon the Vedic Aryans are likely, even if they cannot be proved. Some scholars surmise, for example, the fortified Aryan city of Hariyupiya mentioned in later texts may have been the same site as the older Indus city of Harappa.

Harappa (INDUS CULTURE)
and
Hariyupiya (VEDIC ARYAN CULTURE)

⧄ INDUS (HARAPPAN) CULTURE
(•) MAJOR SITES OF ARCHAEOLOGICAL FINDS
⧄ VEDIC ARYAN CULTURE
△ VEDIC AGE TOWNS

GENERAL CHARACTER. The Indus or Harappan civilization covered an area many times larger than either of its contemporaries, Middle Kingdom Egypt and Third Dynasty Ur. Yet this vast territory was united in a culture of remarkable homogeneity, as the archaeological finds tell us. The similarities in city layouts, building construction, weights and measures, seal inscriptions, artifacts, and even the size of the burnt brick used in all the Indus towns for buildings and floodwalls point to the unusual uniformity of this civilization. Such uniformity suggests a strong, perhaps centralized, government, an integrated economic system, and good internal communications.

The Indus culture is thought to have remained strikingly unchanged over the centuries that it endured (probably from about 2250 to 1750 B.C., although some scholars argue for as long as 2500–1500 B.C.). Change does not seem to have been prized. Because the main cities and towns lay in river lowlands subject to periodic flooding, they had to be rebuilt numerous times in

Indus history. The excavations show that each new level of construction closely followed the pattern of the previous one. Similarly, we find no evidence of any development in the Indus pictographic script in the more than two thousand stamp seals thus far uncovered. Stability, regularity, and traditionalism seem to have been hallmarks of this society. Such unusual continuity has led scholars to speculate that Indus civilization may have flourished under a single conservative, theocratic, priestly state rather than a more unstable, secular state or states dominated by a royal court.

THE CITIES. The major sites at Harappa and Mohenjo-Daro appear to have been two centers of Indus culture. Each probably had a population of at least thirty-five thousand and was meticulously laid out on a similar plan. On the western side of the city stood a large, walled citadel on a raised rectangular platform about 800 by 1400 feet in size; east of this platform lay the town proper, which was laid out on a careful north-south–east-west grid of main avenues, some of which were 30 feet wide. The citadel appar-

ently contained the main public buildings. An impressively large bath, with a brick-lined pool and columned porticos, has been excavated at Mohenjo-Daro, and both sites have buildings tentatively identified as temples.

Each city boasted a large granary for food storage. Cemeteries were laid out on the periphery of each. The town "blocks" formed by the main avenues were crisscrossed by small, less rigidly planned lanes, off which opened private houses of various sizes, sometimes more than one story. The typical house was built around a central courtyard and presented only blank walls to the outside lanes. This arrangement is recalled by houses in many Near Eastern and Indian cities today.

Perhaps the most striking feature of these cities, however, was a complex system of covered drains and sewers. Private houses were serviced by wells, bathrooms, and latrines, and the great bath at Mohenjo-Daro was filled from its own large well. The drainage system that served these facilities in the Indus towns was an engineering feat unrivaled in the ancient world

Ancient Mohenjo-Daro, like most cities of the Indus Valley civilization, was built principally of mud brick. The structures are laid on straight lines; streets cross each other at right angles. The impression is one of order, prosperity, and civic discipline.

Stone torso from Mohenjo-Dara. [Borromeo/Art Resource.]

until the time of the Romans, nearly two thousand years later.

ECONOMIC LIFE. The Indus state had an economy based on a thriving agriculture. Wheat and barley were the main crops; peas, lentils, sesame, and cotton were also important. Whether artificial irrigation or only flood control was used is not known, but indications are that the whole Indus region was more densely vegetated and productive than it is today. Cattle, dogs, goats, sheep, and fowl were raised, and elephants and water buffalo were known and possibly tamed for work as well. Cotton weaving, metalworking, and wheel-driven pottery making were practiced. Trade contacts abroad are indicated by Indus stamp seals found in Mesopotamia; the "Melukka" region mentioned in ancient Akkadian texts as a source of ivory, precious stones, and other wares may have been the Indus basin.

Excavations in the Persian Gulf indicate that the island of Bahrain may have been a staging point for Indus-Mesopotamian sea trade. Metals and semiprecious stones were apparently imported from present-day Iran and Afghanistan, as well as from central Asia, modern Rajasthan, and Mysore in peninsular India, and perhaps from Arabia. There are also indications from shared drawing motifs that these trade contacts resulted in cultural borrowings.

MATERIAL CULTURE. Without literary remains, we must look to pottery, tools, sculpture, ornaments, and other objects unearthed at Indus sites to glean some idea of arts, crafts, and technology. The chief evidence of creative art is found in the fine bronze and stone statues that have been recovered. We find also an accomplished mastery of design and production techniques in various artifacts: copper and bronze tools and vessels, impressive black-on-red painted pottery, dressed stonework, stone and terra-cotta figurines and toys, silver vessels and ornaments, gold jewelry, and dyed woven fabric. The numerous flat stamp seals of stone are our major source, along with some pottery painting and small copper-tablet engravings, for both the Indus script and portrayals of animals, humans, and what are thought to be divine or semidivine beings.

Such handiwork shows the Indus capabilities at their best. Unfortunately, no monumental or wall art, beyond some decorative brickwork, has been found in the excavations. There are no friezes, mosaics, or large-scale sculpture. In general, the range of art and artifacts seems limited by comparison with that of ancient Egypt or Mesopotamia.

RELIGION. The Indus remains give us somewhat more to speculate about in the religious realm. The elaborate bath facilities suggest practices like the ritual bathing and water purification rites that are so important in Indian life even in the present day. Later Hindu (and possibly even elements of Indo-Aryan) polytheism and image worship may also have historical links with Indus ideas and practices. This possibility is suggested by the stone images from the so-called "temples" of Mohenjo-Daro and the far more common terra-cotta figurines found at many sites. Later symbols important to Hindus, such as the pipal tree or the swastika sign, are also found on Indus artifacts.

Among the most common images, the large number of male animals—above all, the humped bull—might be symbols of power and fertility or may conceivably indicate some kind of animal worship. Other animals depicted are the tiger, the snake, and a unicornlike animal. The recurring figure of a male with a leafy headdress and horns, often seated in a posture associated later in India with yogic mediation, has been likened to the Aryan "Lord of All Creatures." This figure merges with the major god Shiva in Hindu piety. Such a comparison is strengthened by some pictures in which the seated figure has three faces and an erect phallus, both common elements of Shiva iconography.

The many terra-cotta figurines of females, often pregnant or carrying a child, could be a prefiguration of the goddess (Devi, Durga, and so on) who, as the consort of Shiva, is widely worshiped in India today. Similar female images have been found in other prehistoric cultures, but their actual significance is purely conjectural. If goddess worship did exist in the Indus culture, this may be one of the elements of pre-Aryan religion that survived in folk tradition; it reemerged

This terra-cotta suggests links with later Hindu image worship. [Borromeo/Art Resource.]

over a millennium later, after 500 B.C., as a prominent feature of Hindu culture. Other aspects of Indus religion—the burial customs, for example—do not seem to have later Hindu analogies. However, they remind

us that the Indus peoples, like all others, had their own ways of coming to terms with the mysteries of birth, life, and death, even if we can only guess at what these were.

THE PASSING OF INDUS CIVILIZATION. This distant culture has thus far kept more secrets than it has revealed. Its ruins tell us that sometime in the early second millennium B.C., it went into decline. Some think that it was destroyed by abnormal flooding or changes in the course of the Indus even before the first Aryan invaders arrived. These warlike peoples probably first appeared in the upper Indus area about 1800 B.C. They later swept with their horse-drawn chariots in successive waves across the northern plains of the subcontinent as far as the Ganges valley. As we have indicated, the culture that they established across much of northern India exhibits little trace of clear Indus survivals. The sacred texts of this culture, the Vedas, refer only occasionally either to enemies whose strongholds were destroyed with the help of the gods, or to "dark," "snub-nosed," small and ugly "slaves" brought under subjection by the conquerors.

The Indus civilization remains too much in the shadows of prehistory for its full influence to be seen. Even the common theory that India's Dravidian-speaking people are descendants of the Indus peoples remains to be proved. Still, these forgotten predecessors of the Aryans probably made significant contributions to later life in the subcontinent in ways yet to be discovered.

The Vedic Aryan Civilization of North India

By comparison with the Indus civilization, we know much more about the Aryan culture that effectively "refounded" Indian civilization. Unlike the Indus culture, that of the Indo-Aryans was not an urban civilization. It left behind neither city ruins nor substantial

Indus stone stamp seals. Note the familiar humped bull of India. [Borromeo/EPA.]

artifacts beyond tools, weapons, and pottery. But the Vedas did survive, and we give the name *Vedic* to the early Aryan culture of northern India because the Vedic texts are virtually the exclusive source of our knowledge of it. Although the latest portions of the Vedas date from perhaps 500 B.C., the oldest may go back to 1700 B.C. Because these texts are not historical, but ritual, priestly, and speculative works, they tell us little about specific events. But the Vedas do offer evidence for some general inferences about religion, society, values, and thought in early Aryan India.

Veda, which means "knowledge," is the collective term for the texts still recognized today by most Indians as the holiest sources of their tradition. In Hindu perspective, Veda is the eternal wisdom realized by the most ancient seers and preserved over thousands of years by generations of professional reciters in unbroken oral transmission. We speak of "the Vedas" in the plural to refer to the four major compilations of Vedic ritual texts and the explanatory and speculative texts associated with each. The most significant of the four main collections for the history of the early Aryans is the collection of 1,028 religious hymns known as the Rig Veda, which contains the oldest materials. The latest Rigvedic hymns date from CA. 1000 B.C., the oldest from perhaps 1700–1200 B.C., when the Aryans spread across the northern Indian plains as far as the upper reaches of the Ganges.

Aryan is a different kind of term. The second-millennium invaders of northern India called themselves *Aryas* to distinguish themselves from the peoples that they conquered. Vedic Sanskrit, the language of the invaders, gave this word to later Sanskrit as a term for "noble," or "free-born" *(arya)*. The word is found also in old Iranian texts (*Iran* is itself a name derived from the Old Persian equivalent of *Arya*). It seems to have been originally the name of peoples who migrated out of the steppeland between eastern Europe and central Asia into Europe, Greece, Anatolia, the Iranian plateau, and India in the second and first millennia B.C. Those who moved into India can thus be more precisely designated *Vedic Aryans*, or *Indo-Aryans*.

In the nineteenth century, *Aryan* was the term applied to the widespread language group known more commonly today as *Indo-European*. To this widely distributed family belong Greek, Latin, and the Romance languages, the Germanic languages, the Slavic tongues, and the Indo-Iranian languages of Persian and Sanskrit and their derivatives. The common basis of all these Indo-European tongues is evident in similar names for both family relations (*father, mother,* and so on) and divine beings (for example, Latin *deus,* and Sanskrit *deva,* "god"). The perverse misuse of *Aryan* in Nazi Germany referred to a white "master race." This term is now usually restricted to linguistic use for the Indo-Iranian branch of the Indo-

Hymn to a Rigvedic Goddess

Here we see the personification of a natural phenomenon, the night, as a goddess whom worshipers can petition. Such hymns make up the Rigveda collection and mirror the close relationship of nature and the transcendent world in the Vedic Aryan world view.

TO NIGHT

With all her eyes the goddess Night looks forth
    approaching many a spot:
She hath put all her glories on.

Immortal, she hath filled the waste, the goddess
    hath filled height and depth:
She conquers darkness with her light.

The goddess as she comes hath set the Dawn her
    sister in her place:
And then the darkness vanishes.

So favour us this night, O thou whose pathways we
    have visited
As birds their nest upon the tree.

The villagers have sought their homes, and all that
    walks and all that flies,
Even the falcons fain for prey.

Keep off the she-wolf and the wolf; O Night, keep
    the thief away:
Easy be thou for us to pass.

Clearly hath she come nigh to me who decks the
    dark with richest hues:
O morning, cancel it like debts.

These have I brought to thee like kine. O Night,
    thou child of heaven, accept
This laud as for a conqueror. ❑

Rig Veda (10.127)

From *Hinduism,* ed. by L. Renou (New York: George Braziller, 1962), p. 71.

Hymn to Indra

This hymn celebrates especially the greatest deed ascribed to Indra, the slaying of the dragon Vritra to release the waters needed by people and livestock. Whether these are the rain or the dammed-up rivers is difficult to say. This victory also symbolizes the victory of the Aryans over the dark-skinned Dasas *and the very creation of the world from the dragon's body. Note the sexual and rain imagery. The* kadrukas *may be the bowls used for soma in the sacrifice. The* vajra *is Indra's thunderbolt; the name* Dasa *for the lord of the waters is also that used for the peoples defeated by the Aryans and for all enemies of Indra, of whom the* Pani *tribe are one.*

Indra's heroic deeds, indeed, will I proclaim, the first ones which the wielder of the vajra accomplished. He killed the dragon, released the waters, and split open the sides of the mountains.

He killed the dragon lying spread out on the mountain; for him Tvashtar fashioned the roaring vajra. Like bellowing cows, the waters, gliding, have gone down straightway to the ocean.

Showing off his virile power he chose soma; from the three *kadrukas* he drank of the extracted soma. The bounteous god took up the missile, the vajra; he killed the first-born among the dragons.

When you, O Indra, killed the first-born among the dragons and further overpowered the wily tricks (*māyā*) of the tricksters, bringing forth, at that very moment, the sun, the heaven and the dawn—since then, indeed, have you not come across another enemy.

Indra killed Vritra, the greater enemy, the shoulderless one, with his mighty and fatal weapon, the vajra. Like branches of a tree lopped off with an axe, the dragon lies prostrate upon the earth. . . .

Over him, who lay in that manner like a shattered reed flowed the waters for the sake of man. At the feet of the very waters, which Vritra had [once] enclosed with his might, the dragon [now] lay [prostrate]. . . .

With the Dāsa as their lord and with the dragon as their warder, the waters remained imprisoned, like cows held by the Pani. Having killed Vritra, [Indra] threw open the cleft of waters which had been closed.

You became the hair of a horse's tail, O Indra, when he [Vritra] struck at your sharp-pointed vajra—the one god (*eka deva*) though you were. You won the cows, O brave one, you won soma; you released the seven rivers, so that they should flow. . . .

Indra, who wields the vajra in his hand, is the lord of what moves and what remains rested, of what is peaceful and what is horned. He alone rules over the tribes as their king; he encloses them as does a rim the spokes. ☐

Rig Veda 1.32

Wm. Theodore de Bary et al., *Sources of Indian Tradition* (New York, 1963).

European family (Sanskrit, Persian, and so on), or to historical use for the particular peoples who invaded northern India and the Iranian plateau in the second millennium B.C.

THE "ARYANIZING" OF NORTH INDIA. The Vedic Aryans were seminomadic warriors who reached India via the mountain passes of the Hindu Kush, in modern Afghanistan. Theirs was probably a gradual migration of rather small tribal groups. These Aryans were horsemen and cattle herders rather than farmers and city builders. They, like their Iranian relatives, left their mark not in their material culture but in the changes that their conquest of new territory brought to existing society: a new language, a new social organization, new techniques of warfare, and new religious forms and ideas.

Without documentation, we can piece together only the broad outlines of the early Aryans' gradual subjugation of northern India and their equally gradual shift from pastoral nomadism to settled agriculture and animal husbandry. We know that they penetrated first into the area of the Punjab and the Indus valley (CA. 1800–1500 B.C.), presumably in search of grazing lands for their cattle and other livestock. They would have exploited their military superiority (based on the use of horses, chariots, and copper–bronze weaponry) to overcome the Indus peoples or their successors in these regions.

Echoes of such conflict seem to occur in some Rig-vedic hymns. One thinks especially here of those in which the god Indra is hailed as the warrior who smashes the fortifications of enemies (possibly the conquest of the Indus citadels?) and slays the great serpent who had blocked the rivers (possibly the destruction of the dams used to control the rivers of the Indus area for agriculture?). Where some later Rigvedic hymns speak of human rather than divine warriors, actual historical events may lie behind the legends. An example is the late hymn that praises the king of a tribe called the *Bharatas*—whence the modern name of India, *Bharat,* "land of the Bharatas."

Hymn to the Lord of Creatures

Here we have the creation of the world depicted as a Vedic sacrifice in which the primeval male principle, Purusha, is sacrificed by the gods as priests, apparently as an offering to himself. This paradox can occur in part because the figure Purusha is a blend of aspects of the male principle (Viraj in the text was originally a female principle of creative power), the god Agni, and the power of the sacrifice itself. The hymn is a late one, and its reference to the creation of the four social classes of humankind is the first such mention in an Indian text (Brāhmans formed the priestly class; Rajānyas, the warriors; Vaishyas, the merchant or commoner groups; and Shūdras, the serf or servant class). These became and remained in later India the four major categories of the social order (note that the warriors were later called Kshatriyas).

Thousand-headed Purusha, thousand-eyed, thousand-footed—he, having pervaded the earth on all sides, still extends ten fingers beyond it.

Purusha alone is all this—whatever has been and whatever is going to be. Further, he is the lord of immortality and also of what grows on account of food.

Such is his greatness; greater, indeed, than this is Purusha. All creatures constitute but one quarter of him, his three quarters are the immortal in the heaven.

With his three quarters did Purusha rise up; one quarter of him again remains here. With it did he variously spread out on all sides over what eats and what eats not.

From him was Virāj born, from Virāj there evolved Purusha. He, being born, projected himself behind the earth as also before it.

When the gods performed the sacrifice with Purusha as the oblation, then the spring was its clarified butter, the summer the sacrificial fuel, and the autumn the oblation.

The sacrificial victim, namely, Purusha, born at the very beginning, they sprinkled with sacred water upon the sacrificial grass. With him as oblation the gods performed the sacrifice, and also the Sādhyas [a class of semidivine beings] and the rishis [ancient seers].

From that wholly offered sacrificial oblation were born the verses [rc] and the sacred chants; from it were born the meters (chandas); the sacrificial formula was born from it.

From it horses were born and also those animals who have double rows [i.e., upper and lower] of teeth; cows were born from it, from it were born goats and sheep.

When they divided Purusha, in how many different portions did they arrange him? What became of his mouth, what of his two arms? What were his two thighs and his two feet called?

His mouth became the brāhman; his two arms were made into the rājanya; his two thighs the vaishyas; from his two feet the shūdra was born.

The moon was born from the mind; from the eye the sun was born; from the mouth Indra and Agni; from the breath (prāna) the wind (vāyu) was born.

From the navel was the atmosphere created, from the head the heaven issued forth; from the two feet was born the earth and the quarters (the cardinal directions) from the ear. Thus did they fashion the worlds.

Seven were the enclosing sticks in this sacrifice, thrice seven were the fire-sticks made, when the gods, performing the sacrifice, bound down Purusha, the sacrificial victim.

With this sacrificial oblation did the gods offer the sacrifice. These were the first norms (dharma) of sacrifice. These greatnesses reached to the sky wherein live the ancient Sādhyas and gods. ❑

Rig Veda 19.90

Wm. Theodore de Bary et al., *Sources of Indian Tradition* (New York, 1963).

In what may be called the Rigvedic period (CA. 1700–1000 B.C.), the newcomers settled in the Punjab and beyond, where they took up agriculture as well as stockbreeding. The Thar desert blocked any southward expansion, so their subsequent movement was to the east. How far they penetrated before 1000 B.C. is not clear, but their main locus remained the Punjab and the plains west of the Yamuna River (northwest of modern Delhi). Then, between about 1000 and 500 B.C., these Aryan Indians (for no longer can we speak of them as a foreign people) spread across the Doab, the "two-rivers" plain formed between the Yamuna and the Ganges, and beyond. They cleared (probably by burning) the heavy forests that covered this area at that time and settled here. They also moved further northeast to the Himalayan foothills and southeast along the Ganges, in what was to be the cradle of subsequent Indian civilization. In this age, the importance of the Punjab receded sharply.

This later Vedic period (CA. 1000–500 B.C.) is often referred to as the Brahmanic age because of the dominance of the priestly religion of the Brahman class attested in later Vedic commentaries called the *Brahmanas* (CA. 1000–800 or 600 B.C.). This age is sometimes also called the *epic age*, because it provided the setting for the two classical Indian epics, the *Mahabharata* and the *Ramayana.* Both were composed much later, probably only in the period CA. 400 B.C.–A.D. 200, but they contain older materials and refer to dimly remembered events of earlier times. The *Mahabharata*, the longest epic poem in the world, centers on the power struggle of two Aryan clans in the area to the north and west of modern Delhi, perhaps around 900 B.C. The *Ramayana* tells of the legendary and dramatic adventures of King Rama, whose travels may at one level recall the movement of northern Indian culture into southern India about the end of the Brahmanic period. Both epics evidence the complex cultural mixing of Aryan, Indus, and other earlier subcontinent peoples.

By about A.D. 200, this mixing would give rise to a distinguishable "Indian" civilization over most of the subcontinent. Its basis was clearly Aryan, but its language, society, and religion had assimilated much that was non-Aryan. Harappan culture vanished, but elements of it and other regional cultures played their part in the formation of Indian culture as we know it.

VEDIC ARYAN SOCIETY. The Aryans brought with them a society apparently characterized by patrilineal family descent and inheritance. The masculine orientation of the society is reflected in its overwhelmingly male gods. The patriarchal family was the basic unit of society. Marriage seems to have been monogamous, and widows could remarry.

Related families formed larger kin groups. The largest social grouping was the tribe, which was ruled by a tribal leader, or *raja* ("king" in Sanskrit, and a cognate of the latin *rex*), whose power was shared with a tribal council. In early Vedic days, the ruler was chosen for his prowess and was never a priest-king. His chief function was to lead in battle; he had originally no sacred authority. Alongside him was a chief priest, who looked after the often elaborate sacrifices on which religious life centered. We do not know if the king originally acted as the judge in legal matters, although by late Vedic, or Brahmanic, times he performed this function with the help of the priests. In the Brahmanic period, the power of the priestly class increased along with that of the king, who was now a heredity ruler claiming divine qualities sanctioned by the priestly establishment.

Although there were probably identifiable groups of warriors and priests, Aryan society seems originally to have distinguished only two basic grades of society: the noble and the common. The *Dasas*, the darker, conquered peoples, came to form a third group (together with those who intermarried with them) of the socially excluded. Over time, a more rigid set of social classes, four in number, evolved. By the late Rigvedic period, these four divisions, or *varnas*, had become so basic as to be sanctioned explicitly in religious theory. These four classes (excluding the non-Aryan *Dasas*) were the priestly (*brahman*), the warrior/noble (*Kshatriya*), the peasant/tradesman (*Vaishya*), and the servant (*Shudra*) groups, a division that has continued in theory to the present as a general way of organizing the far more numerous subgroups known as *castes* (see Chapter 7). It was, of course, only the members of the three upper classes who were full participants in the various spheres of social, political, and religious life. This isolation of the lowest groups foreshadowed the rigidity of caste distinctions that would later become a basic element in Indian life.

MATERIAL CULTURE. The early, seminomadic Aryans had little in the way of impressive material culture. They did not build cities or even monuments as far as we know. A gray-painted pottery is one of the few physical remains of their culture. They lived simply in wood and thatch or, later, mud-walled dwellings, measured wealth in cattle (presaging the later importance of the cow in Hindu India?), and had developed craftsmanship in carpentry and bronze metalworking. Iron probably was not known in India before 1000 B.C. Gold was used for ornamentation. Wool provided the basic textiles, and alongside stockbreeding, some cultivation, especially of grains, was practiced. Intoxicating drink was well known, both the *soma* used in religious rites and a kind of mead.

Music seems to have been a highly developed art and pastime; singing and dancing are mentioned in the texts, as are various musical instruments. Gambling appears to have been a popular and frequent vice. Betting on chariot racing may have attracted the more affluent, but it is dicing above all that we hear of in Vedic and epic texts. One of the few secular pieces among the Vedic hymns is a "Gambler's Lament," which closes with a plea to the dice: "Take pity on us. Do not bewitch us with your fierce magic. . . . Let no one be trapped by the brown dice!"

The Brahmanic age has left us only a few more material remains. It was still not a time of developed urban culture, even in the mud-brick towns that now were growing up as new lands were burned clear for cultivation and village settlements. There were now established kingdoms with fixed capitals, and trade was growing, especially along the Ganges, although we have no mention of a true coinage system. Specialized groups of craftsmen—goldsmiths, basketmakers, weavers, potters, and entertainers—are mentioned in the later texts.

We do not know when writing was introduced or developed. To judge from references to its common use by around 500 B.C. it may have been about 700 B.C.

The evidence shows that Indian goods were again finding their way to Mesopotamia in this period. This suggests that writing may have been reintroduced in the subcontinent through this trade connection. Yet so highly developed was the oral tradition of Veda transmission among the Brahman class, that writing continued to be scorned as an unworthy medium for the sacred texts of the Veda.

RELIGION. The most important contributions of Vedic India to later history were religious. In the Vedas, we can glimpse the broad outlines and development of Vedic-Brahmanic religion over the thousand years following the arrival of the first Aryans in the subcontinent. However, they tell us only about the public cult and domestic rituals of the Aryan upper classes, not about popular traditions of the masses. We can surmise that among the latter, many Harappan and other non-Aryan practices and ideas continued to flourish. Apparently non-Aryan elements are visible occasionally even in the Vedic texts themselves—especially later ones such as the Upanishads (after CA. 800 B.C.)—in their emphasis on fertility and female deities, ritual pollution and ablutions, and the transmigration of the soul after death.

The central Vedic cult, which was controlled by priests serving a military aristocracy, was dominant until the middle of the first millennium B.C. By this time other, perhaps older, religious forms were evidently asserting themselves among the populace.

The increasing ritual formalism of Brahmanic religion generated challenges in both religious practice and speculative thought. It culminated in the rise and spread of the Buddhist, Jain, and Hindu traditions (see Chapter 2).

The earliest Indo-Aryans seem to have worshiped numerous gods, who most often embodied or were associated with powers of nature. We see vestiges of this in the Rigvedic hymns, which are addressed to anthropomorphic gods. Despite their human form, these gods are commonly linked to one or more natural phenomena: the sky, the clouds, or the sun. Whether the human aspect of what may once have been deified natural forces was due to a gradual divinizing or mythologizing of the ancient human heroes, we cannot say. But the deities we encounter in the Rig Veda are comparable to those of Greek religion. They are also probably distantly related to the latter; note, for example, the similar names of the Aryan father-god Dyaus and the Greek father-god Zeus, which point to a common Indo-European source. In Vedic India, however, unlike in Greece, the father-god had receded in importance before the rising cult of his children. Chief among them was Indra, god of war and the storm. A rowdy god not unlike the old Norse Thor, he led his heavenly warriors across the sky to slay dragons or other enemies with his thunderbolt in his hand.

Also of major importance was Varuna, who may have connections with the later Iranian god Ahura Mazda and Uranus, Greek god of the heavens. Varuna was more remote from human affairs than Indra. He was depicted as an imperial or regal figure who sat on his heavenly throne and guarded the cosmic order, *Rta*, which is both the law of nature and the universal moral law or truth. As the god whose great holiness commanded awe and demanded righteous behavior, Varuna had characteristics of a supreme, omnipresent divinity.

Another god whose central place in the Vedas stands out is Agni, the god of fire (his name, which is the word for "fire" in Sanskrit, is related to Latin *ignis*, "fire," and thus to our *ignite*). He had diverse roles. He was the god who mediated between earth and heaven through the offering of the fire sacrifice; thus, he was the god of the sacrifice and the priests; and he was also the god of the hearth and hence the home. Like the elusive flame, he was a mysterious deity about whose form and presence in all earthly fires there is much speculation in the Rig Veda.

Many other gods could be mentioned: Soma, the god of the hallucinogenic soma plant and drink; Ushas, the goddess of dawn (one of very few feminine deities); Yama, god of the dead; Rudra, the archer and storm god; Vishnu, a solar deity; and the sun god Surya. A major characteristic of the Vedic hymns is that when any single god is addressed, he or she is praised as possessing a wide variety of powers. Many of these powers may normally have been associated with other deities, but this did not bar attributing them also to the god the worshiper was addressing.

The focus of Vedic religious life was sacrifice to the gods. In the sacrificial ritual, the sacrificers seem to have experienced the presence of the gods to whom they made their offering.

The drinking of soma juice was a prominent sacrificial ritual that greatly enhanced the subjective experience of the participants. There seems to have been no emphasis on thanksgiving or expiation of guilt through sacrifice. The recurring theme is the desire for the good things of this life: prosperity, health, victory, and the like. Fire sacrifices were particularly important, on both a large, public and private, domestic scale. There were also exclusively royal rituals, such as that of the elaborate and seldom-performed horse sacrifice.

By Brahmanic times, there had emerged considerable mystical and speculative interpretation of the sacrifice in which sacrificer, sacrificial animal, and god were all identified with one another. Even the creation of the world is described in one Rigvedic hymn as the sacrifice of a primordial being to himself by the lesser gods. The late Vedic texts also emphasize magical and

CA. 2250–1750 B.C. (2500–1500?)	Indus (Harappan) civilization
CA. 1800–1500 B.C.	Aryan peoples invade northwest India
CA. 1500–1000 B.C.	Rigvedic period: Composition of Rigvedic hymns; Punjab as center of Indo-Aryan civilization
CA. 1000–500 B.C.	Later Vedic period: Doab as center of Indo-Aryan civilization
CA. 1000–800/600 B.C.	Composition of Brahmanas and other Vedic texts
CA. 800–500 B.C.	Composition of major Upanishads
CA. 700–500 B.C.	Probable introduction of writing
CA. 400 B.C.–A.D. 200	Composition of great epics, the *Mahabharata* and *Ramayana*

cosmic aspects of ritual and sacrifice. Indeed, some of the Brahmanas indicate that only through the exact performance of the sacrifice is the world order maintained.

The word *Brahman* was originally used to designate the ritual utterance, and it came to refer also to the generalized divine power present in the sacrifice. In the Upanishads, some of the latest Vedic texts and the ones most concerned with speculation about the universe, *Brahman* is extended to refer to the Absolute, the transcendent principle of reality. As the guardian of ritual and the master of the sacred word, the priest was known throughout the Vedic Aryan period by a related word, *Brahmana*, for which the English is *Brahman*. Echoes of these associations were to lend force in later Hindu tradition to the special status of the Brahman caste groups as the highest class of society. We shall see this in Chapter 7 when we take up the Indian story once more.

Early Chinese Civilization

Neolithic Origins in the Yellow River Valley

Agriculture began in China about 4000 B.C. in the basin of the southern bend of the Yellow River. This is the northernmost of East Asia's four great river systems. The others are the Yangtze in central China, the West River in southern China, and the Red River in what is today northern Vietnam. All drain eastward into the Pacific Ocean. In recent millennia, the Yellow River has flowed through a deforested plain, cold in winter and subject to periodic droughts. But in 4000 B.C., its climate was warmer, with forested highlands in the west and swampy marshes to the east. The bamboo rat that today can be found only in semitropical Southeast Asia lived along the Yellow River.

The chief crop of China's agricultural revolution was millet. A second agricultural development focusing on rice may have occurred on the Huai River between the Yellow River and the Yangtze near the coast. In time, wheat entered China from the west. The early Chinese cleared land and burned its cover to plant millet and cabbage and later, rice and soybeans. When the soil became exhausted, the fields were abandoned, and sometimes early villages were abandoned, too. The tools were of stone: axes, hoes, spades, and sickle-shaped knives. The early Chinese domesticated pigs, sheep, cattle, dogs, and chickens. Game was also plentiful, and hunting continued to be important to the village economy. In excavated village garbage heaps of ancient China are found the bones of deer, wild cattle, antelopes, rhinoceros, hares, and marmots. Grain was stored in pottery painted in bold, geometric designs of red and black. This pottery gave way later to a harder, thin black pottery, made on a potter's wheel, that spread west along the Yellow River and south to the Yangtze. The tripodal shapes of Neolithic pots prefigure later Chinese bronzes.

The earliest cultivators lived in wattle-and-daub pit-dwellings with wooden support-posts and sunken, plastered floors. Their villages were located in isolated clearings along the slopes of river valleys. Archaeological finds of weapons and the remains of earthen walls suggest tribal warfare between villages. Of the religion of these people, little is known, though some evidence indicates the worship of ancestral spirits. They practiced divination by applying heat to a hole drilled in the shoulder bone of a steer or the undershell of a tortoise, and interpreting the resulting cracks in the bone. They buried their dead in cemeteries with jars of food. Tribal leaders wore rings and beads of jade.

The Early Bronze Age: The Shang

The traditional history of China tells of three ancient dynasties:

2205–1766 B.C.	Hsia
1766–1050 B.C.	Shang
1050–256 B.C.	Chou

Until early in this century, modern historians saw the first two as legendary. Then, in the 1920s, archaeological excavations at "the wastes of Yin" near present-day An Yang discovered the ruins of a walled city that had been a late Shang capital. Other Shang cities have been discovered more recently. The ruins contained the archives of the department of divination of the Shang court, with thousands on thousands of "oracle bones" incised with archaic Chinese writing. The names of kings on the bones fit almost perfectly those of the traditional historical record. The recognition that the Shang actually existed has led historians to suggest that the Hsia may also have been an actual dynasty. Perhaps the Hsia was a late Neolithic black-pottery kingdom; perhaps it already had bronze and represents the earliest, still missing stage of Chinese writing.

The characteristic political institution of Bronze Age China was the city-state. The largest was the Shang capital, which, frequently moved, lacked the monumental architecture of Egypt or Mesopotamia. The walled city contained public buildings, altars, and the residences of the aristocracy and was surrounded by a sea of Neolithic tribal villages. By late Shang times, several such cities were spotted across the north China plain. The Shang king possessed political, economic, social, and religious authority. When he died, he was sometimes succeeded by a younger brother and sometimes by a son. The rulers of other city-states acknowledged his authority.

The military aristocracy went to war in chariots, supported by levies of foot soldiers. Their weapons were spears and powerful compound bows. Accounts tell of armies of three or four thousand troops, and of a battle involving thirteen thousand. The Shang fought against barbarian tribes and, occasionally, against other city-states in rebellion against their rule. Captured prisoners were enslaved.

One feature of Shang civilization was its system of writing. Scribes at the Shang court kept records on strips of bamboo, which have not survived. But there are inscriptions on bronzes as well as on the oracle bones. Some bones contain the question put to the oracle, the answer, and the outcome of the matter. Representative questions were: Which ancestor is causing the king's earache? If the king goes hunting at Ch'i, will there be a disaster? Will the king's child be a son? If the king sends his army to attack an enemy, will

MAP 1-4 BRONZE-AGE CHINA DURING THE SHANG DYNASTY, 1766–1050 B.C. *An Yang was a capital toward the end of the Shang dynasty. Loyang was the capital of the Eastern Chou.*

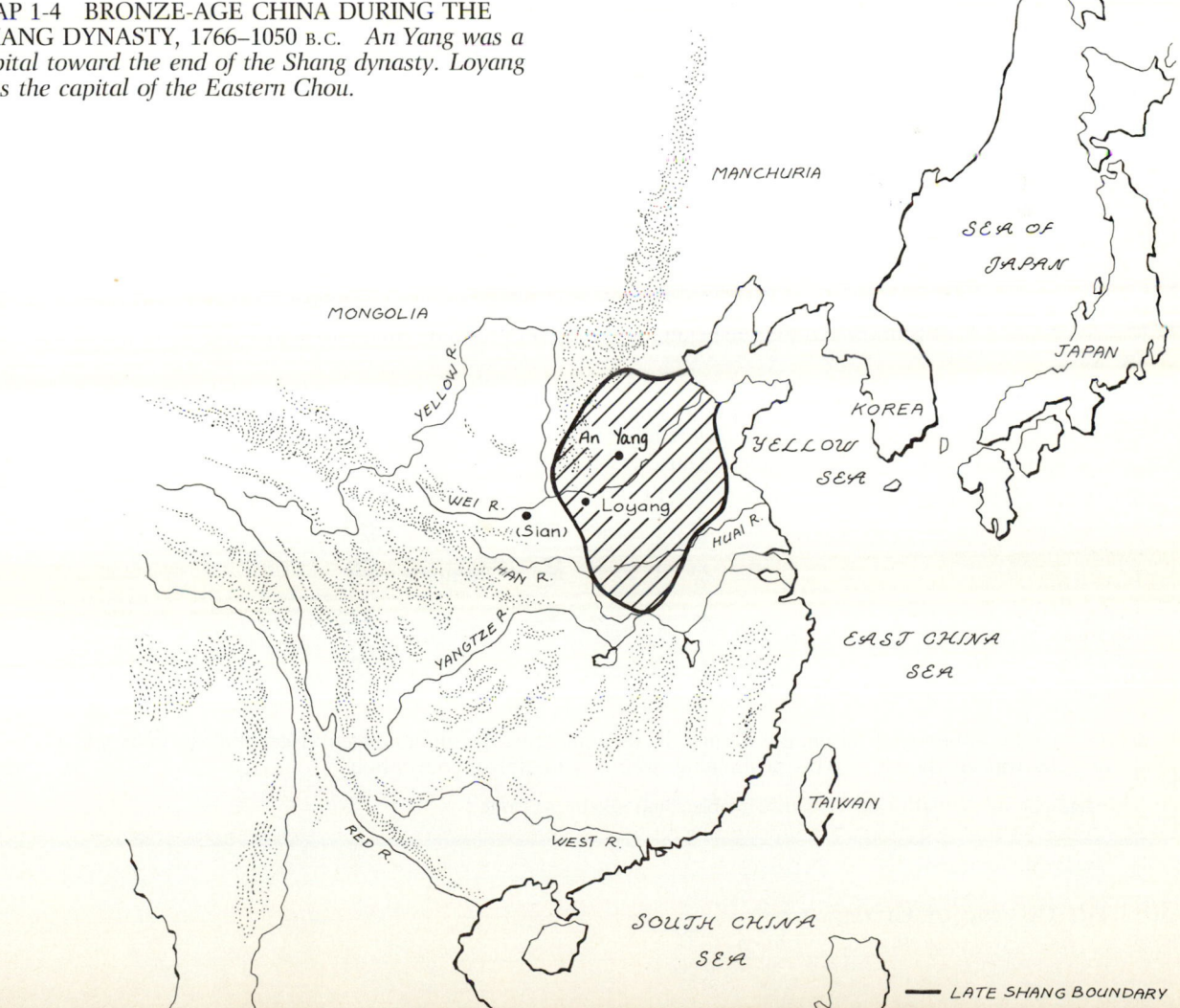

— LATE SHANG BOUNDARY

Chinese Writing

The Chinese system of writing dates back at least to the Shang dynasty (1766–1050 B.C.), when animal bones and tortoise shells (the so-called oracle bones) were incised for the purpose of divination. About half of the three thousand characters used in Shang times have been deciphered. These evolved over the centuries into the fifty thousand characters found in the largest dictionaries. But even today only about three thousand or four thousand are in common use. A scholar may know twice that number.

Characters developed from little pictures. Note the progressive stylization. By 200 B.C., the writing had become standardized and close to the modern form of the printed character.

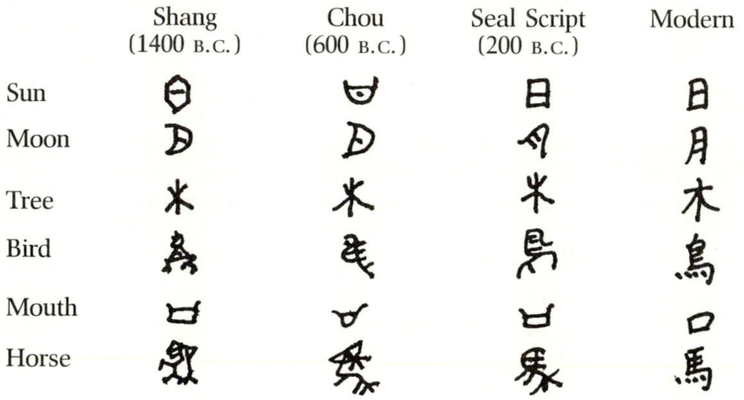

	Shang (1400 B.C.)	Chou (600 B.C.)	Seal Script (200 B.C.)	Modern
Sun				
Moon				
Tree				
Bird				
Mouth				
Horse				

Other characters combined two pictures to express an idea. The following examples use modern characters:

Sun 日 + moon 月 = bright 明

Mouth 口 + bird 鳥 = to chirp 鳴

Woman 女 + child 子 = good 好

Tree 木 + sun 日 = east 東

It was a matter of convention that the sun behind a tree meant the rising sun in the east and not the setting sun in the west.

Characters were formed several other ways. In one, a sound element was combined with a meaning element. Chinese has many homonyms, words with the same sound. The character 台, for example, is read *tai* and means "elevation" or "to raise up." But in spoken Chinese, there are other words with the same sound that mean "moss," "trample," a "nag," and "idle." Thus

Tai 台 + grass 艹 = moss 苔

Tai 台 + foot 足 = trample 跆

Tai 台 + horse 馬 = a nag 駘

Tai 台 + heart 心 = idle 怠

In each case the sound comes from the 台, and the meaning from the other element. Note that the 台 may be at the bottom, the top, or the right. This positioning, too, is a matter of convention. ❑

Calligraphy by Teruko Craig. (Otherwise table composed by A. Craig.)

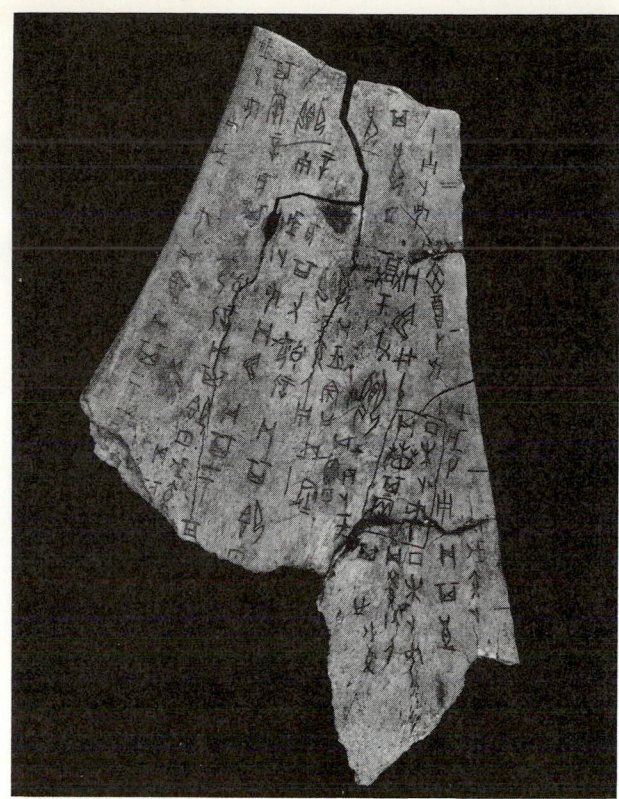

Inscribed oracle bone from the Shang Dynasty city of An Yang. [Columbia University.]

ated with cosmology. The Shang people observed the movements of the planets and stars and reported eclipses. Celestial happenings were seen as omens from the gods above. The chief cosmologists also recorded events at the court. The Shang calendar had a month of 30 days and a year of 360 days. Adjustments were made periodically by adding an extra month. The calendar was used by the king to tell his people when to sow and when to reap.

A second mark of Shang civilization was the mastery of bronze technology. Bronze appeared in China about 2000 B.C., a thousand years later than in Mesopotamia and five hundred years after India. Because Shang methods of casting were more advanced than those of Mesopotamia, and because the designs emerge directly from the preceding black-pottery culture, an independent origin is likely. Bronze was used for weapons, armor, and chariot fittings, and for a variety of ceremonial vessels of amazing fineness and beauty.

A third feature of Shang society, and indeed of all early river valley civilizations, was that as humans gained freedom from nature through agriculture and bronze technology, they abandoned the rough equality of primitive society and used their new powers to create a rigidly stratified society in which the many were compelled to serve the few. A monopoly of bronze weapons enabled aristocrats to exploit other groups. A hierarchy of class defined life in the Chinese city-state. The king and the officials of his court lived within the walled city. Their houses were spacious, built above the ground with roofs supported by rows of wooden pillars, resting on foundation stones. Their lifestyle was, for ancient times, opulent. They wore fine clothes, feasted at banquets, and drank wine from bronze vessels. In contrast, a far larger population of agricultural workers lived outside the city in cramped pit dwellings. Their life was meager and hard. Archaeological excavations of their underground hovels have uncovered only pottery pots.

Nowhere was the gulf between the royal lineage and the baseborn more apparent than in the Shang institution of human sacrifice. One Shang tomb 39 feet long, 26 feet wide, and 26 feet deep contained the de-

the deity help him? Was a sacrifice acceptable to ancestral deities? What we know of Shang religion is based on the bones.

The Shang Chinese believed in a supreme "Deity Above," who had authority over the human world. There were also lesser natural deities—the sun, moon, earth, rain, wind, and the six clouds—who served at the court of the Deity Above. Even the Shang king sacrificed not to the Deity Above, but to his ancestors, who interceded with the Deity Above on the king's behalf. Kings, while alive at least, were not divine but were the high priests of the state. In Shang times, as later, religion in China was closely associ-

The Languages of East Asia

The two main language families in East Asia today are the Sinitic and the Ural-Altaic. These are as different from each other as they are from European tongues. The Sinitic languages are Chinese, Vietnamese, Thai, Burmese, and Tibetan. Within Chinese are several mutually unintelligible dialects. Standard Chinese, based on the Peking dialect, is further from Cantonese than Spanish is from French. Ural-Altaic languages are spoken to the east, north, and west of China. They include Japanese, Korean, Manchurian, Mongolian, the Turkic languages, and, in Europe, Finnish and Hungarian.

Human Sacrifice During the Shang

By the seventh century B.C., human sacrifices were less frequent but still happened. A poem composed when Duke Mu of the state of Ch'in died in 631 casts doubt on whether religious belief or the honor of it all made the victims go gladly to the grave. Were human feelings different, Professor K. C. Chang has asked, a thousand years earlier during the Shang? Note the identification of Heaven with "that blue one," the sky.

"Kio" sings the oriole
As it lights on the thorn-bush.
Who went with Duke Mu to the grave?
Yen-hsi of the clan Tsu-chu.
Now this Yen-hsi
Was the pick of all our men;
But as he drew near the tomb-hole
His limbs shook with dread.
That blue one, Heaven,
Takes all our good men.
Could we but ransom him
There are a hundred would give their lives

"Kio" sings the oriole
As it lights on the mulberry-tree.
Who went with Duke Mu to the grave?
Chung-hang of the clan Tsu-chu.
Now this Chung-hang
Was the sturdiest of all our men;
But as he drew near the tomb-hole
His limbs shook with dread.
That blue one, Heaven,
Takes all our good men.
Could we but ransom him
There are a hundred would give their lives. ❑

The Book of Songs, trans. by Arthur Waley (New York: Grove Press, 1960).

capitated bodies of humans, horses, and dogs, as well as ornaments of bone, stone, and jade. When a king died, hundreds of slaves or prisoners of war, together, at times, with those who had served the king during his lifetime, might be buried with him. Sacrifices also were made when a palace or an altar was built.

The Later Bronze Age: The Western Chou

To the west of the area of Shang rule, in the Wei valley near the present-day city of Sian, lived the Chou people. The Wei River is a tributary of the Yellow River.

They were less civilized, closer to the Neolithic black-pottery culture, but more warlike than the Shang. According to the oracle bones, they had relations with the Shang, sometimes friendly, sometimes hostile. In 1050 B.C., the Shang were weakened by campaigns against nomads in the north and rebellious tribes in the east. According to the traditional historical record, the last Shang kings had become weak, cruel, and tyrannical. The Chou seized the opportunity, made alliances with disaffected city-states, and swept in, conquering the Shang.

In most respects, the Chou continued the Shang pattern of life and rule. The agrarian-based city-state continued to be the basic unit of society. It is estimated that there were about two hundred in the eighth century B.C. The hierarchy of classes was not unlike that of the Shang: kings and lords, officials and warriors, peasants, and slaves. Slaves were used primarily as domestic servants. Because the Chou were culturally backward, they assimilated the culture of the Shang. Ideographic writing developed without interruption. Bronze ceremonial vessels continued to be cast, though Chou vessels lack the fineness that set the Shang above the rest of the Bronze Age world.

The Chou kept their capital in the west but set up a secondary capital at Loyang, along the southern bend of the Yellow River. They appointed their kinsmen or other aristocratic allies to rule in other city-states. Blood or lineage ties were essential to the Chou pattern of rule. The Chou king was the head of the senior branch of the family. He performed the sacrifices to the Deity Above for the entire family. The rankings of the lords of other princely states—which, for want of better terms, are usually translated into the titles of English feudal nobility: duke, marquis, earl, viscount, and baron—reflected their degree of closeness to the senior line of Chou kings.

One difference between the Shang and the Chou was in the nature of political legitimacy. The Shang rulers, descended from shamanistic rulers, had an inbuilt religious authority and needed no theory to justify their rule. But the Chou, having conquered the Shang, needed a rationale for why they, and not the Shang, were the rightful rulers. Their argument was that Heaven (the name for the supreme being that gradually replaced the "Deity Above" during the early Chou), appalled by the wickedness of the last Shang king, had withdrawn its mandate to rule, awarding the mandate, instead, to the Chou. This concept of the mandate of Heaven was subsequently invoked by every dynasty in China down to the twentieth century.

A Chou Dynasty Bronze Bell. Hung from the ring at the top, the bell was rung with a wooden mallet. This bell has bosses, decorative panels, and is inscribed with a text. It rests on a brocade cushion. [National Palace Museum, Taiwan, R.O.C.]

In the beginning, Heaven was both cosmological and anthropomorphic. The ideograph for Heaven 天 is related to that for man 人. In the later Chou, although Heaven continued to have a moral will, it became less anthropomorphic and more a metaphysical force.

The Iron Age: The Eastern Chou

In 771 B.C., the Wei valley capital of the Western Chou was overrun by barbarians. In Chinese tradi-

tion, the event provided the equivalent of "crying wolf." The last Western Chou king was so infatuated with a favorite concubine that he repeatedly lit the bonfires that signaled a barbarian attack. His concubine would clap her hands in delight at the sight of the army assembled in martial splendor. But the army tired of the charade, and when invaders actually came, the king's beacons were ignored. The king was killed and the Chou capital sacked. The heir to the throne, with some members of the court, escaped to the secondary capital at Loyang, two hundred miles to the east and just south of the bend in the Yellow River.

The first phase of the Eastern Chou is sometimes called the Spring and Autumn period after the classic history by that name that treats the 722–481 year span. After their flight to Loyang, the Chou kings were never able to reestablish their old authority. Loyang remained a center of culture and ritual observances. But by the early seventh century B.C., its political power was nominal: Kinship and religious ties to the Chou house had worn thin, and it no longer had the military strength to reimpose its rule. During the seventh and sixth centuries in China, the political configuration was an equilibrium of many little principalities on the north-central plain surrounded by larger, wholly autonomous territorial states along the borders of northern China. The larger states consolidated the areas within their borders, absorbed tribal peoples, and expanded, conquering states on their periphery.

To defend themselves against the more aggressive territorial states, and in the absence of effective Chou authority, the smaller states entered into defensive alliances. The earliest alliance, of 681 B.C., was directed against the half-barbarian state of Ch'u (pronounced "chew"), which straddled the Yangtze in the south. Princes and lords of smaller states elected as their hegemon (or military overlord) the lord of a northern territorial state and pledged him their support. At the formal ceremony that established the alliance, a bull was sacrificed. The hegemon and then the other lords smeared its blood on their mouths and before the gods swore oaths to uphold the alliance. That the oaths were not always upheld can be surmised from the Chinese expression "to break an oath while the blood is still wet on one's lips."

During the next two centuries, alliances shifted and hegemons changed. At best, the alliances only slowed down the pace of military aggrandizement.

The second phase of the Eastern Chou is known as the Warring States period after a chronicle of the same name treating the years from 401 to 256 B.C. By the fifth century, all defensive alliances had broken down. Strong states swallowed their weaker neighbors. The border states grew in size and power. Interstate stability disappeared. By the fourth century, only eight or nine great territorial states remained as contenders.

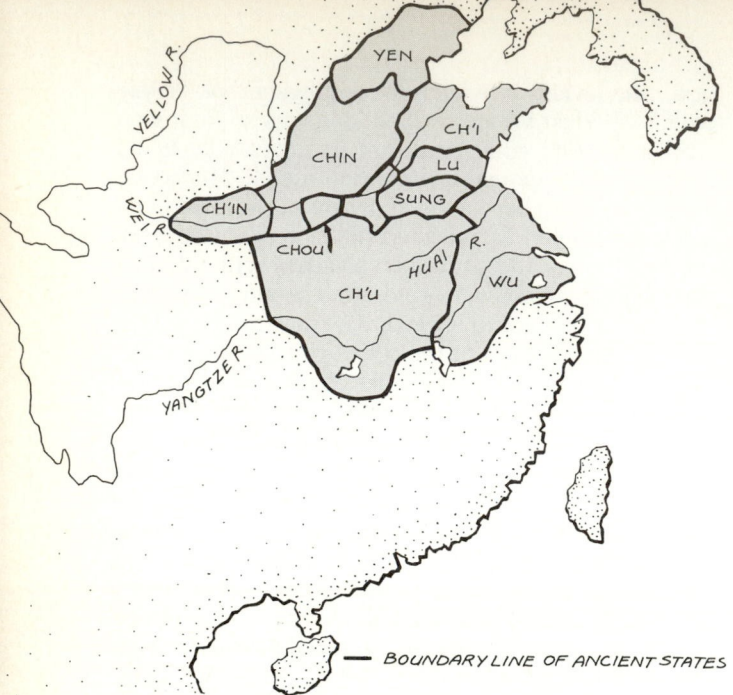

MAP 1-5   EARLY IRON-AGE TERRITORIAL STATES IN CHINA DURING THE SIXTH CENTURY B.C. *After the fall of the Western Chou in 771 B.C., north China divided into territorial states that became increasingly independent of the later Chou kings.*

EARLY CHINA

4000 B.C.	Neolithic agricultural villages
1766 B.C.	Bronze Age city-states, aristocratic charioteers, pictographic writing
771 B.C.	Iron Age territorial states
500 B.C.	Age of philosophers
221 B.C.	China is unified

The only question was which one would defeat the others and go on to unify China.

Three basic changes in Chinese society contributed to the rise of large territorial states. One was the expansion of population and agricultural lands. The walled cities of the Shang and Western Chou had been like oases in the wilds, bounded by plains, marshes, and forests. Game was plentiful; thus, hunting, along with sheep and cattle breeding, supplemented agriculture. But in the Eastern Chou as the population grew, the wilds began to disappear, the economy became almost entirely agricultural, and hunting became an aristocratic pastime. Friction arose over boundaries as states began to abut. These changes accelerated in the late sixth century B.C. after the start of the Iron Age. Iron tools cleared new lands and plowed deeper, raising yields and increasing agricultural surpluses. Irrigation and drainage canals became important for the first time. Serfs gave way to farmers who bought and sold land. By the third century B.C., China had about twenty million people, making it the most populous country in the world, a distinction that it has never lost.

A second development was the rise of commerce. The roads built for war were used by merchants. Goods were transported by horses, oxcarts, riverboats, and by the camel, which entered China in the third century B.C. The products of one region were traded for those of another. Copper coins joined bolts of silk and precious metals as media of exchange. Rich merchants rivaled in lifestyle the landowning lower nobility. New outer walls were added to cities to provide for expanded quarters for merchants. The bronze bells and mirrors, clay figurines, lacquer boxes, and musical instruments found in late Chou tombs give ample evidence that the material and artistic culture of China leaped ahead during this period despite its endemic wars.

A third change that doomed the city-state was the rise of a new kind of army. The war chariots of the old aristocracy, practical only on level terrain, gave way to cavalry armed with crossbows. Most of the fighting was done by conscript foot soldiers. The armies of the territorial states numbered in the hundreds of thousands. The old nobility gave way to professional commanders. The old aristocratic etiquette, which governed behavior even in battle, gave way to military tactics that were bloody and ruthless. Prisoners were often massacred.

Change also affected government. The lords of the new territorial states began to style themselves as kings, taking the title that previously only the Chou royalty had enjoyed. At some courts, the hereditary nobility began to decline, supplanted by ministers appointed for their knowledge of statecraft. To survive, the new states had to transform their agricultural and commercial wealth into military strength. To collect taxes, conscript soldiers, and administer the affairs of state required records and literate officials. Academies were established to fill the need. Beneath the ministers, a literate bureaucracy developed. Its members were referred to as *shih,* a term that had once meant "warrior" but gradually came to mean "scholar-bureaucrat." The *shih* were of mixed social origins, including the petty nobility, literate members of the old warrior class, landlords, merchants, and rising commoners. From this class came the philosophers who created the "one hundred schools" and transformed the culture of China.

Suggested Readings

GENERAL PREHISTORY

V. GORDON CHILDE, *What Happened in History* (1946).
   A pioneering study of human prehistory and history

before the Greeks from an anthropological point of view.

D. C. JOHNSON AND M. R. EDEY, *Lucy: The Beginning of Mankind* (New York, 1981). An account of man's African origins.

CHARLES L. REDMAN, *The Rise of Civilization* (San Francisco, 1978). An attempt to use the evidence provided by anthropology, archaeology, and the physical sciences to illuminate the development of early urban society.

NEAR EAST

CYRIL ALDRED, *Akhenaten, Pharaoh of Egypt: A New Study* (London, 1968). A judicious and critical biography of the enigmatic pharaoh.

HENRI FRANKFORT, *Ancient Egyptian Religion: An Interpretation* (New York, 1948). A brief but masterful attempt to explore the religious conceptual world of ancient Egyptians in intelligible and interesting terms.

HENRI FRANKFORT et al., *Before Philosophy* (1949). A brilliant examination of the mind of the ancients from the Stone Age to the Greeks.

ALAN GARDINER, *Egypt of the Pharaohs* (Oxford, 1961). A sound narrative history.

O. R. GURNEY, *The Hittites* (Harmondsworth, 1954). A good general survey.

W. W. HALLO AND W. K. SIMPSON, *The Ancient Near East: A History* (New York, 1971). A fine survey of Egyptian and Mesopotamian history.

THORKILD JACOBSEN, *The Treasures of Darkness: A History of Mesopotamia Religion* (New Haven, 1976). A superb and sensitive re-creation of the spiritual life of Mesopotamian peoples from the fourth to the first millennium B.C.

SAMUEL N. KRAMER, *The Sumerians: Their History, Culture and Character* (Chicago, 1963). A readable general account of Sumerian history.

A. T. OLMSTEAD, *History of Assyria* (New York, 1923). A good narrative account.

JAMES B. PRITCHARD (ed.), *Ancient Near Eastern Texts Relating to the Old Testament* (Princeton, 1969). A good collection of documents in translation with useful introductory material.

G. ROUX, *Ancient Iraq* (New York, 1964). A good recent account of ancient Mesopotamia.

W. F. SAGGS, *The Greatness That Was Babylon* (New York, 1962). An excellent narrative account of Mesopotamian history.

W. F. SAGGS, *Everyday Life in Babylonia and Assyria* (London, 1965).

K. C. SEELE, *When Egypt Ruled the East* (Chicago, 1965). A study of Egypt in its imperial period.

B. G. TRIGGER et al., *Ancient Egypt: A Social History* (Cambridge, 1982).

JOHN A. WILSON, *Culture of Ancient Egypt* (Chicago, 1956). A fascinating interpretation of the civilization of ancient Egypt.

INDIA

D. P. AGRAWAL, *The Archaeology of India* (London, 1982). A fine survey of the problems and data. Detailed, but with excellent summaries and brief general discussions of major issues.

B. AND R. ALLCHIN, *The Birth of Indian Civilization: India and Pakistan before* 500 B.C. (Harmondsworth, 1968). A one-volume summary of prehistoric India from an archaeological perspective.

W. T. DE BARY et al., comp., *Sources of Indian Tradition* (1958. 2nd rev. ed. 2 vols. New York, 1988). A fine anthology of original texts in translation from all periods of Indian civilization.

A. L. BASHAM, *The Wonder That Was India*, 2nd rev. ed. (New York, 1963). Chapters 1 and 2 provide a readable and carefully done introduction to ancient India through the Aryan culture. Still the classic general work.

E. C. L. DURING CASPERS, "Summer, Coastal Arabia and The Indus Valley in Protoliterate and Early Dynastic Eras," *JESHO* 22, 2 (1979): 121–35.

C. CHAKRABORTY, *Common Life in the Rigveda and Atharvaveda–an Account of the Folklore in the Vedic Period* (Calcutta, 1977). An interesting attempt to reconstruct everyday life in the Vedic period from the principal Vedic texts.

G. L. POSSEHL, ed. *Harappan Civilization: A Contemporary Perspective* (New Delhi, 1982). Many helpful articles on recent developments in Indus research, including urbanization, the Indus script, trade relations, decline and demise of this culture.

D. D. KOSAMBI, *Ancient India: A History of its Culture and Civilization* (New York, Toronto, and London, 1965). The most readable survey history of India to the fourth century A.D. See chapters 2–4 on prehistoric, Indus, and Aryan culture.

W. D. O'FLAHERTY, *The Rig Veda: An Anthology* (Harmondsworth, England, 1981). An excellent selection of vedic texts of different kinds in prosaic but very careful translation with helpful notes on the texts.

J. E. SCHWARTZBERG, ed. *A Historical Atlas of South Asia* (Chicago, 1978). The definitive reference work for matters of historical geography. Includes chronological tables and substantive essays.

R. L. SINGH, ed. *India: A Regional Geography* (Banaras, 1971). An excellent reference source for each of the major regions of the subcontinent.

CHINA

K. C. CHANG, *Shang Civilization* (1980).

K. C. CHANG, *Art, Myth, and Ritual, The Path to Political Authority in Ancient China* (1984). A study of the relation between shamans, gods, agricultural production, and political authority during the Shang and Chou dynasties.

K. C. CHANG, *The Archeology of Ancient China*, 4th ed. (1986). The standard work on the subject.

D. HAWKES, *Ch'u Tz'u, The Songs of the South* (1985). Chou poems from the southern state of Ch'u, superbly translated.

C. Y. HSU, *Ancient China in Transition: An Analysis of Social Mobility 722–222* B.C. (1965).

X. Q. LI, *Eastern Zhou and Qin Civilizations* (1986). This work includes fresh interpretations based on new archaeological finds.

A Torah Scroll. Such a scroll is used in the Synagogue and symbolizes the Judaic commitment to the life of the Law. [Jewish Museum/Frank J. Darmstaedter.]

2 The Four Great Revolutions in Thought and Religion

Between 800 B.C. and 300 B.C., four philosophical or religious revolutions occurred that shaped the subsequent history of the world. The names of many of those involved in these revolutions are world-famous; for example, Socrates, Plato, Aristotle, the Buddha, Isaiah, and Confucius. All occurred in or near the four heartland areas in which the river valley civilizations (described in Chapter 1) had appeared one-and-a-half or more millennia earlier. The transition from the early river-valley civilizations to the intellectual and spiritual breakthroughs of the middle of the first millennium B.C. are schematized, oversimply, in the chart below.

The most straightforward case is that of China. Both geographically and culturally, its philosophical breakthrough grew directly out of the earlier river-valley civilization. There was no such continuity anywhere else in the world. The natural barrier of the central Asian steppes, mountain ranges, and deserts allowed China to develop its own unique culture relatively undisturbed and uninfluenced by outside forces.

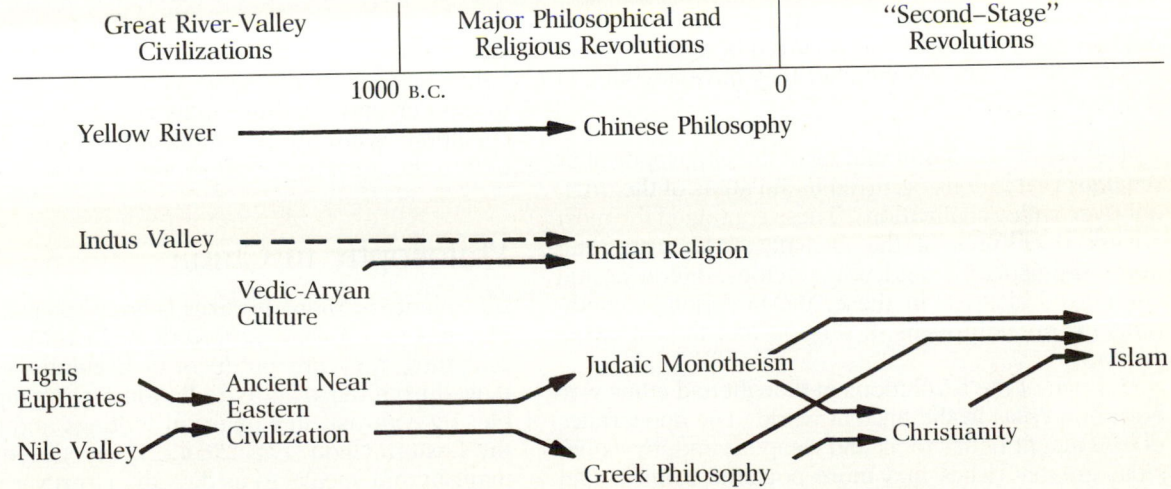

Great River-Valley Civilizations	Major Philosophical and Religious Revolutions	"Second–Stage" Revolutions

37

The sharpest contrast with China is the Indian sub-continent, where there was neither geographical nor cultural continuity. By the middle of the second millennium B.C., the Indus civilization had collapsed. It was replaced by the culture of the Indo-Aryan warriors who swept in from the northwest. Absorbing many particulars from the earlier tradition, they built a new civilization on the plains further east along the mighty Ganges. The great tradition of Indian thought and religion emerged after 600 B.C. from this Ganges civilization.

In southwest Asia and along the shores of the Mediterranean, the transition was more complex than in either the Chinese or the Indian case. No direct line of development can be traced from the Nile civilization of ancient Egypt or the civilization of the Tigris-Euphrates river valley to Greek philosophy or Judaic monotheism. Rather, the ancient river-valley civilizations evolved into a complex amalgam that we call ancient Near Eastern civilization. This cosmopolitan culture included diverse older religious, mythical, and cosmological traditions, as well as newer mystery cults. The Greeks and the ancient Hebrews were two among many outside peoples who invaded this region, settled down, and both absorbed and contributed to the composite civilization.

Judaic monotheism and Greek philosophy—representing very different outgrowths of this amalgam—were important in their own right. They have continued as vital elements in Western and Near Eastern civilizations. But their greatest influence occurred some centuries later when they joined to help shape, first, Christianity and then, Islam. When we talk of the major cultural zones in world history since the mid-first millennium A.D., they are the Chinese, the Indian, the Western-Christian, and the Islamic. But the latter two were formed much later than the Chinese and the Indian. They represent a second-stage formation of which the first stage was the Judaic and the Greek.

Before turning to a brief consideration of each of the original breakthroughs that occurred between 800 and 300 B.C., we might ask whether they have anything in common.

1. It is not accidental that all of the philosophical or religious revolutions occurred in the areas of the original river-valley civilizations. These contained the most advanced cultures of the ancient world. They had more sophisticated agriculture, cities, literacy, and specialized classes. In these, the material preconditions for breakthroughs in religion and thought were present.
2. Each of the revolutions in thought and ethos was born of a crisis in the ancient world. The appearance of iron meant better tools and weapons and, by extension, greater riches and more powerful armies. Old societies began to change and then to disintegrate. Old aristocratic and priestly codes of behavior broke down, producing a demand for more universalized rules of behavior, that is to say, for ethics. The very relation of humans to nature or to the universe seemed to be changing. This predicament led to new visions of social and political order. There is more than an accidental similarity between the Jewish Messiah, the Chinese sage-king, and Plato's philosopher-king. Each was a response to a crisis in a society of the ancient world. Each would rejoin ethics to history and restore order to a troubled society.
3. It is notable how few philosophical and religious revolutions there have been. They can be counted on the fingers of one hand. The reason is not that humans' creativity dried up after 300 B.C., but that subsequent breakthroughs and advances tended to occur within the original traditions, which, absorbing new energies, continued to evolve.
4. After the first- and second-stage transformations, much of the cultural history of the world is of the spread of cultures derived from these original heartlands to ever wider spheres. Christianity spread to northern and eastern Europe, the Americas, and parts of Asia; Buddhism to central, southeastern, and eastern Asia; Confucianism to Korea, Vietnam, and Japan; and Islam to Africa, southeastern Europe, and southern, central, and southeastern Asia. Sometimes the spread occurred by movements of people; in other cases, some areas were like dry grasslands needing only the spark of the new ideas to ignite them.
5. Once a cultural pattern was set, it usually endured. Each major culture was resistant to the others and only rarely was one displaced. Even in modern times, although the culture of modern science and the learning associated with it has penetrated into every cultural zone, it has reshaped—and is reshaping, rather than displacing—the major cultures. Only Confucianism crumbled at the touch of science, and even its ethos is far from dead today. One reason for the endurance of these major cultures is that they were not only responses to particular crises, but also attempts to answer universal questions concerning the human condition: What are human beings? What is our relation to the universe? How should we relate to others?

Philosophy in China

The beauty of Shang bronzes is breathtaking, but they also have an archaic strangeness. Like Mayan stone sculpture, they are products of a culture so far removed from our own as to be almost incomprehensible. By contrast, in Confucian writings and poetry of the Eastern Chou (771–256 B.C.), we encounter a humanism that speaks to us directly. However much the philosophies of these centuries grew out of the earlier matrix of archaic culture, they mark a break with it and the beginning of what we think of today as the Chinese tradition.

The background of the philosophical revolution in China was the disintegration of the old Chou society (see Chapter 1 for details). New territorial states took the place of the many Chou city-states. Ruthless, upstart, peasant armies, augmented by an early Iron Age cavalry, began to replace the old nobles, who had gone to war in chariots. A rising merchant class disrupted the formerly stable agricultural economy. As the old etiquette crumbled, as the old rituals lost their force, a search began for new principles by which to re-create a peaceful society and new rules by which to live.

Of the four great revolutions in thought of the first millennium B.C., the Chinese was more akin, perhaps, to the Greek than to the religious transformations of India or to Judaic monotheism. Just as Greece had a gamut of philosophies, so in China there were the "one hundred schools." (When Mao Tse-tung said in 1956, "Let the one hundred flowers bloom"— encouraging a momentary easing of intellectual repression—he was referring to the creative era of Chou philosophy.) Whereas Greek thought was speculative and more concerned with the world of nature, Chinese thought was sociopolitical and more practical. Even the Taoist sages, who were inherently apolitical, found it necessary to offer a political philosophy. Chinese thought also had far greater staying power than Greek thought. Only a few centuries after the glory of Athens, Greek thought was submerged by Christianity. It became the handmaiden of theology and did not reemerge as an independent force until the Renaissance. In contrast, Chinese philosophy, though challenged for a time by Buddhism, remained dominant down to the early twentieth century. How were these early philosophies able to maintain such a grip on China when the cultures of every other part of the world fell under the sway of religions?

Part of the answer is that most Chinese philosophy was not without a religious dimension. But it was another kind of religion with assumptions quite different from those of the West. In the Christian or Islamic worldview, there is a God who, however concerned with humankind, is not of this world. This worldview leads to dualism, the distinction between an other-world, which is supernatural, and this world, which is natural.

In the Chinese worldview, the two spheres are not separate: The cosmos is seen as a single, continuous sphere, which includes heaven, earth, and man. Heaven is above. Earth is below. Man, represented by the emperor, stands in between and regulates or harmonizes the cosmological forces of heaven and earth by the power of his virtue and by performing the sacrifices. The forms that this cosmology took under the last Manchu dynasty can be seen today in the city of Peking: The Temple of Heaven is in the south, the Temple of Earth is in the northeast, and the Imperial Palace is, symbolically at least, in between. To say that the emperor's sacrifices at the Temple of Heaven were secular (and, therefore, not religious) or religious

The Temple of Heaven. The three-storied "Temple of Prayer for a Good Harvest" is a part of the "Temple of Heaven" to the south of Peking. Once sacrosanct, it is now popular with tourists. On the second terrace, a banner proclaims that "Marxism and Leninism will endure for 10,000 years." [Magnum Photos, Inc., photograph by Rene Burri.]

(and not secular) misses the point. It projects our own dualistic assumptions onto China. Similarly, when we speak of the Taoist sage becoming one with nature, it is not the nature of a twentieth-century natural scientist; it is a nature that contains metaphysical and cosmological forces of a kind that our worldview might label as religious.

Most of the one hundred schools—if, in fact, there were that many—are unknown today. Many works disappeared in the book burning of the Ch'in dynasty (256–221 B.C.). But apart from the three major schools of Confucianism, Taoism, and Legalism, enough have survived to convey a sense of the vitality and creativity of Chou thought:

1. *Rhetoricians.* This school taught the arts of persuasion to be used in diplomatic negotiations. Its principal work instructed the rulers of territorial states by using historical anecdote. A practical work, it was popular for its humor and lively style.
2. *Logicians.* This school taught logic and relativity. For example, one proposition was "The south has no limit and has a limit." Another was "A white horse is not a horse": The concept of *horse* is not the same as the concept of *white horse*.
3. *Strategists. The Art of War* by Sun-tzu became the classic of military science in China and is studied today by guerrillas and in military academies around the world. It praises the general who wins victories without battles but also talks of organizing states for war, of supply, of spies, and of propaganda.
4. *Cosmologists.* This school described the functions of the cosmos in terms of *yin* and *yang*, the complementary negative and positive forces of nature, and in terms of the five elements (metal, wood, earth, fire, and water). Its ideas were later absorbed by other schools.
5. *Mohists.* Mo-tzu (470–391 B.C.) was an early critic of Confucius. His goals were peace, wealth, and the increase of population. He taught an ethic of universal love—to overcome a selfish human nature. He preached discipline and austerity and was critical of whatever lacked utility, including music, other arts, elaborate funerals, wasteful rites, and, above all, war. To achieve his goals, Mo-tzu argued for a strong state: Subjects must obey their rulers, who, in turn, must obey Heaven. Heaven would punish evil and reward good. To promote peace, Mo-tzu organized his followers into military units to aid states that were attacked.

Confucianism

Confucius was born in 551 B.C. in a minor state in northeastern China. As he received an education in

Confucius. Depicted wearing the robes of a scholar of a later age. [*National Palace Museum, Taiwan, Republic of China.*]

writing, music, and rituals, he probably belonged to the lower nobility, or the knightly class. His father died when Confucius was young, so he may have known privation. He made his living by teaching students. He traveled with his disciples from state to state, seeking a ruler who would put his ideas into practice. His ideas, however, were rejected as impractical—though he may once have held a minor position. He died in 479 B.C., honored as a teacher but a failure in his own eyes. The name Confucius is the Latinized form of K'ung Fu-tzu, or Master K'ung as he is known in China.

We know of Confucius only through the *Analects*, his sayings collected by his disciples, or perhaps by their disciples. They are mostly in the form of "The Master said," followed by his words. The picture that emerges is of a man of moderation, propriety, optimism, good sense, and wisdom. In an age of cruelty and superstition, he was humane and rational. He was upright. He demanded much of others and more of himself. Asked about death, he replied, "You do not understand even life. How can you understand

Confucius Defines the Gentleman

For over two thousand years in China, the cultural ideal was the gentleman, who combined knowledge of the ancient sages with an inner morality and outer propriety.

The Master said, "I never enlighten anyone who has not been driven to distraction by trying to understand a difficulty or who has not got into a frenzy trying to put his ideas into words.

"When I have pointed out one corner of a square to anyone and he does not come back with the other three, I will not point it out to him a second time."

The Master said, "Yu, shall I tell you what it is to know. To say you know when you know, and to say you do not when you do not, that is knowledge."

The Master said, "Is it not a pleasure, having learned something, to try it out at due intervals? Is it not a joy to have friends come from afar? Is it not gentlemanly not to take offence when others fail to appreciate your abilities?"

Someone said, "Repay an injury with a good turn. What do you think of this saying?" The Master said, "What, then, do you repay a good turn with? You repay an injury with straightness, but you repay a good turn with a good turn."

Lin Fang asked about the basis of the rites. The Master said, "A noble question indeed! With the rites, it is better to err on the side of frugality than on the side of extravagance; in mourning, it is better to err on the side of grief than on the side of formality."

The Master said, "I suppose I should give up hope. I have yet to meet the man who is as fond of virtue as he is of beauty in women."

The Master said, "The gentleman agrees with others without being an echo. The small man echoes without being in agreement."

The Master said, "The gentleman is at ease without being arrogant; the small man is arrogant without being at ease."

The Master said, "There is no point in seeking the views of a gentleman who, though he sets his heart on the Way, is ashamed of poor food and poor clothes." ❑

Confucius, *The Analects*, trans. by D. C. Lau (Penguin Books, 1979), 86, 65, 59, 129, 67, 134, 122, 123, 73.

---

death?"[1] Asked about how to serve the spirits and the gods—in which he did not disbelieve he answered, "You are not able even to serve man. How can you serve the spirits?"

Confucius described himself as a transmitter and a conservator of tradition, not an innovator. He idealized the early Shang and Chou kings as paragons of virtue. He particularly saw early Chou society as a golden age. He sought the secrets of this golden age in its writings. Some of these, along with later texts, became the Confucian classics, which through most of subsequent Chinese history had an authority not unlike Scripture in the West. Five of the thirteen classics were the following:

1. *The Book of Changes* (also known as the *Classic of Divination*). A handbook for diviners, this book was later seen as containing metaphysical truths about the universe.
2. *The Book of History*. This book contains documents and speeches from the early Chou, some au-

thentic. Chinese tradition holds that it was edited by Confucius. It was interpreted as the record of sage-kings.
3. *The Book of Poetry*. This book contains some three hundred poems from the early Chou. Representing a sophisticated literary tradition, it includes love songs, as well as poems of friendship, ritual, and politics. All were given a political or moral reading in later times.
4. *The Book of Rites*. This book includes both rituals and rules of etiquette. Rites were important to Confucians, both as a support for proper behavior and because they were seen as corresponding to the forces of nature.
5. *The Spring and Autumn Annals*, a brief record of the major occurrences from 722 to 481 B.C. in the state where Confucius was born. Chinese tradition held that this book was edited by Confucius and reflected his moral judgments on past historical figures.

Basing his teachings on these writings, Confucius' solution to the turmoil of his own age was a return to the good old ways of the early Chou. When asked

[1] This quotation and all quotations from Confucius in this passage are from Confucius, *The Analects*, trans. by D. C. Lau (Penguin Books, 1979).

about government, he said, "Let the ruler be a ruler, the subject a subject, the father a father, the son a son." (The other three of the five Confucian relationships were husband–wife, older brother–younger brother, and friend–friend.) If everyone fulfilled the duties of his or her status, then harmony would prevail. Confucius understood the fundamental truth that the well-being of a society depends on the morality of its members. His vision was of an unbroken social harmony extending from the individual family member below to the monarch above.

But a return to the early Chou was impossible. China was undergoing a dynamic transition from hundreds of small city-states to a few large territorial states. New, specialized classes were appearing. Old rituals no longer worked. In this situation, it was not enough just to stress basic human relationships. The genius of Confucius was to transform the old aristocratic code into a new ethics that could be practiced by any educated Chinese. His reinterpretation of the early Chou tradition can be seen in the concept of the *chun-tzu*. This term literally meant the son of the ruler or the aristocrat. Confucius redefined it to mean a person of noble behavior, a person with the inner virtues of humanity, integrity, righteousness, altruism, and loyalty, and an outward demeanor and propriety to match.

This redefinition was not unlike the change in the meaning of *gentleman* in England from one who is gentle-born to one who is gentle-behaved. But whereas *gentleman* remained a fairly superficial category in the West, in China it went deeper. Confucius saw ethics as grounded in nature. The true gentleman was in touch with his own basic nature, which, in turn, was a part of the cosmic order. Confucius expressed this saying: "Heaven is the author of the virtue that is in me." Confucius' description of his own passage through life goes far beyond the question of good manners: "At fifteen I set my heart on learning; at thirty I took my stand; at forty I came to be free from doubts; at fifty I understood the Decree of Heaven; at sixty my ear was attuned; at seventy I followed my heart's desire without overstepping the line."

Confucius often contrasted the gentleman with the small or common person. The gentleman, educated in the classics and cultivating the Way, understands moral action. The common people, in contrast, "can be made to follow a path but not to understand it." Good government for Confucius depended on the appointment to office of good men, who would serve as examples for the multitude: "Just desire the good yourself and the common people will be good. The virtue of the gentleman is like wind; the virtue of the small man is like grass. Let the wind blow over the grass and it is sure to bend." Beyond the gentleman was the sage-king, who possessed an almost mystical virtue and

Mencius, who taught that human nature is good. [*Bettmann Archives.*]

power. For Confucius, the early Chou kings were clearly sages. But Confucius wrote, "I have no hopes of meeting a sage. I would be content if I met someone who is a gentleman."

Confucianism was not adopted as the official philosophy of China until the second century B.C., during the Han dynasty. But two other important Confucian philosophers had appeared in the meantime. Mencius (370–290 B.C.) represents the idealistic extension of Confucius' thought. His interpretation became orthodox for most of subsequent history. He is famous for his argument that humans tend toward the good just as water runs downward. All that education need do, therefore, is uncover and cultivate that innate goodness. And just as humans are good, so does Heaven possess a moral will. The will of Heaven is that a government should see to the education and the well-being of its people. The rebellion of a people against its government is the primary evidence that Heaven has withdrawn its mandate. At times in Chinese history, only lip service was paid to a concern for the people. In fact, rebellions occurred more often against weak governments than against harsh ones. But the idea that government ought to care for the people became a permanent part of the Confucian tradition.

The other influential Confucian philosopher was Hsun-tzu (300–237 B.C.), who represents a tough-minded extension of Confucius' thought. Hsun-tzu felt Heaven was amoral, indifferent to whether China was ruled by a tyrant or a sage. He felt human nature was

Taoism

LAO-TZU TELLS OF THE WAY OF THE SAGE

The way that can be spoken of
Is not the constant way;
The name that can be named
Is not the constant name.
The nameless was the beginning of heaven
    and earth;
The named was the mother of the myriad
    creatures.

The spirit of the valley never dies.
This is called the mysterious female.
The gateway of the mysterious female
Is called the root of heaven and earth.
Dimly visible, it seems as if it were there,
Yet use will never drain it.

There is a thing confusedly formed,
Born before heaven and earth.
Silent and void

It stands alone and does not change,
Goes round and does not weary.
It is capable of being the mother of the world.
I know not its name
So I style it "the way."

When the way prevails in the empire, fleetfooted
horses are relegated to ploughing the fields; when
the way does not prevail in the empire, war-horses
breed on the border.

One who knows does not speak; one who speaks
does not know.

Therefore the sage puts his person last and it comes
first,
Treats it as extraneous to himself and it is preserved.
Is it not because he is without thought of self that
he is able to accomplish his private ends?   ❑

Lao-tzu, *Tao Te Ching*, trans. by D. C. Lau (Penguin Books, 1963).

CHUANG-TZU COMPARES GOVERNMENTAL OFFICE TO A DEAD RAT

When Hui Tzu was prime minister of Liang, Chuang Tzu set off to visit him. Someone said to Hui Tzu, "Chuang Tzu is coming because he wants to replace you as prime minister!" With this Hui Tzu was filled with alarm and searched all over the state for three days and three nights trying to find Chuang Tzu. Chuang Tzu then came to see him and said, "In the south there is a bird called the Yuan-ch'u—I wonder if you've ever heard of it? The Yuan-ch'u rises up from the South Sea and flies to the North Sea, and it will rest on nothing but the Wu-t'ung tree, eat nothing but the fruit of the Lien, and drink only from springs of sweet water. Once there was an owl who had gotten hold of a half-rotten old rat, and as the Yuan-ch'u passed by, it raised its head, looked up at the Yuan-ch'u, and said, 'Shoo!' Now that you have this Liang state of yours, are you trying to shoo me?"   ❑

The Complete Works of Chuang-tzu, trans. by B. Watson (Columbia University Press, 1968), p. 188.

bad, or, at least, that desires and emotions, if un-checked, led to social conflict. So he placed a great emphasis on etiquette and education as restraints on an unruly human nature. He emphasized good institutions, including punishments and rewards, as a means for shaping behavior. These ideas exerted a powerful influence on thinkers of the Legalist school.

Taoism

It is often said that the Chinese have been Confucian while in office and Taoist (pronounced "Dah-oh-ist") in their private lives. Taoism offered a refuge from the burden of social responsibilities. The classics of the school are the *Lao-tzu*, dating from the fourth century B.C., and the *Chuang-tzu*, dating from about a century later.

The central concept is the Tao, or Way. It is mysterious and cannot be named. It is the creator of the universe, the sustainer of the universe, and the process or flux of the universe. The Tao functions on a cosmic, not a human, scale. As the *Lao-tzu* put it, "Heaven and Earth are ruthless, and treat the myriad creatures as straw dogs; the sage [in accord with the Tao] is ruthless, and treats the people as straw dogs."[2]

What does it mean to be a sage? How does a human join in the rhythms of nature? The answer given by the *Lao-tzu* is by regaining or returning to an original simplicity. Various similes are used to describe this state: "to return to the infinite," "to return to being a babe," or "to return to being the uncarved block." To attain this state, one must "learn to be without learning." Knowledge is bad because it creates distinctions, because it leads to the succession of ideas and images

[2]All quotations from the *Lao-tzu* are from Lao Tzu, *Tao Te Ching*, trans. by D. C. Lau (Penguin Books, 1963).

Lao-Tzu, the founder of Taoism, as imagined by a later artist. [Freer Gallery of Art, Washington, DC.]

that interfere with participation in the Tao. One must also learn to be without desires beyond the immediate and simple needs of nature: "The nameless uncarved block is but freedom from desire."

If the sage treats the people as straw dogs, it would appear that he is beyond good and evil. But elsewhere in the *Lao-tzu*, the sage is described as one who "excels in saving people." If not a contradiction, this is at least a paradox. The resolution is that the sage is clearly beyond morality, but is not immoral or even amoral. Quite to the contrary, by being in harmony with the Tao the sage is impeccably moral—as one who clings to the forms of morality or makes morality a goal could never be. So in the *Lao-tzu*, it is written, "Exterminate benevolence, discard rectitude, and the people will again be filial; exterminate ingenuity, discard profit, and there will be no more thieves and bandits."

In this formulation, we also see the basis for the political philosophy of Taoism, which can be summed up as "not doing" *(wu wei)*. What this means is something between "doing nothing" and "being, but not acting." In this concept, there is some overlap with Confucianism. The Confucian sage-king exerts a moral force by dint of his internal accord with nature. If a Confucian sage were perfect, he could rule without doing. Confucius said, "If there was a ruler who

achieved order without taking any action, it was, perhaps, [the sage emperor] Shun. There was nothing for him to do but to hold himself in a respectful posture and to face due south." In Taoism, all true sages had this Shun-like power to rule without action: "The way never acts yet nothing is left undone. Should lords and princes be able to hold fast to it, the myriad creatures will be transformed of their own accord." Or, says the *Lao-tzu*, "I am free from desire and the people of themselves become simple like the uncarved block." The sage acts without acting, and "when his task is accomplished and his work is done, the people will say, 'It happened to us naturally.'"

Along with the basic Taoist prescription of becoming one with the Tao are two other assumptions or principles. One is that any action pushed to an extreme will initiate a countervailing reaction in the direction of the opposite extreme. The other is that too much government, even good government, can become oppressive by its very weight. As the *Lao-tzu* put it, "The people are hungry; It is because those in authority eat up too much in taxes that the people are hungry. The people are difficult to govern; it is because those in authority are too fond of action that the people are difficult to govern." Elsewhere, the same idea was expressed in even homelier terms: "Govern a large state as you would cook small fish," that is, without too much stirring.

Legalism

The third great current in classical Chinese thought, and by far the most influential in its own age, was Legalism. Like the philosophers of other schools, the Legalists were anxious to end the wars that plagued China. True peace, they felt, required a united country, and to this end, they advocated a strong state. They favored conscription and looked on war as a means of extending state power.

The Legalists did not seek a model in the distant past. In ancient times, said one, there were fewer people and more food, so it was easier to rule; different conditions require new principles of government. Nor did the Legalists model their state on a heavenly order of values. Human nature is selfish, argued both of the leading Legalists, Han Fei-tzu (d. 233 B.C.) and Li Ssu (d. 208 B.C.). It is human to like rewards or pleasure and to dislike punishments or pain. If laws are severe and impartial, if what strengthens the state is rewarded and what weakens the state is punished, then a strong state and a good society will ensure.

Legalism

HAN FEI-TZU ARGUES FOR THE EFFICACY OF PUNISHMENTS

Now take a young fellow who is a bad character. His parents may get angry at him, but he never makes any change. The villagers may reprove him, but he is not moved. His teachers and elders may admonish him but he never reforms. The love of his parents, the efforts of the villagers, and the wisdom of his teachers and elders—all the three excellent disciplines are applied to him, and yet not even a hair on his shins is altered. It is only after the district magistrate sends out his soldiers and in the name of the law searches for wicked individuals that the young man becomes afraid and changes his ways and alters his deeds. So while the love of parents is not sufficient to discipline the children, the severe penalties of the district magistrate are. This is because men became naturally spoiled by love, but are submissive to authority. . . .

That being so, rewards should be rich and certain so that the people will be attracted by them; punishments should be severe and definite so that the people will fear them; and laws should be uniform and steadfast so that the people will be familiar with them. Consequently, the sovereign should show no wavering in bestowing rewards and grant no pardon in administering punishments, and he should add honor to rewards and disgrace to punishments—when this is done, then both the worthy and the unworthy will want to exert themselves. . . .

HAN FEI-TZU ATTACKS CONFUCIANISM

There was once a man of Sung who tilled his field. In the midst of his field stood the stump of a tree, and one day a hare, running at full speed, bumped into the stump, broke its neck, and died. Thereupon the man left his plow and kept watch at the stump, hoping that he would get another hare. But he never caught another hare, and was only ridiculed by the people of Sung. Now those who try to rule the people of the present age with the conduct of government of the early kings are all doing exactly the same thing as that fellow who kept watch by the stump. . . .

Those who are ignorant about government insistently say: "Win the hearts of the people." If order could be procured by winning the hearts of the people, then even the wise ministers Yi Yin and Kuan Chung would be of no use. For all that the ruler would need to do would be just to listen to the people. Actually, the intelligence of the people is not to be relied upon any more than the mind of a baby. If the baby does not have his head shaved, his sores will recur; if he does not have his boil cut open, his illness will go from bad to worse. However, in order to shave his head or open the boil someone has to hold the baby while the affectionate mother is performing the work, and yet he keeps crying and yelling incessantly. The baby does not understand that suffering a small pain is the way to obtain a great benefit.

Now, the sovereign urges the tillage of land and the cultivation of pastures for the purpose of increasing production for the people, but they think the sovereign is cruel. The sovereign regulates penalties and increases punishments for the purpose of repressing the wicked, but the people think the sovereign is severe. Again, he levies taxes in cash and in grain to fill up the granaries and treasuries in order to relieve famine and provide for the army, but they think the sovereign is greedy. Finally, he insists upon universal military training without personal favoritism, and urges his forces to fight hard in order to take the enemy captive, but the people think the sovereign is violent. These four measures are methods for attaining order and maintaining peace, but the people are too ignorant to appreciate them. ❏

From W. T. de Bary et al., *Sources of Chinese Tradition* (New York: Columbia University Press, 1968), 146–147, 144, 142, 143.

Laws, therefore, should contain incentives for loyalty and bravery in battle, and for obedience, diligence, and frugality in everyday life. The Legalists despised merchants as parasites and approved of productive farmers. They particularly despised the purveyors of doctrines different from their own and were critical of rulers who honored the philosophers while ignoring their philosophies.

Legalism was the philosophy of the state of Ch'in, which destroyed the Chou in 256 B.C. and unified China in 221 B.C.. Because Ch'in laws were cruel and severe, and because Legalism put human laws above an ethics modeled on Heaven, later generations of Chinese have execrated its doctrines. They saw it, not without justification, as a philosophy that consumed its founders: Han Fei-tzu became an official of the Ch'in state but was eventually poisoned in a prison cell by Li Ssu, who was jealous of his growing influence. Li Ssu, too, though he became prime minister of Ch'in, was killed in 208 B.C. in a political struggle with a court eunuch. Yet, for all of the abuse heaped on the Legalist doctrines, their legacy of criminal laws became a vital part of subsequent dynastic China.

Religion in India

By the mid-first millennium B.C., new social and religious forms took shape in the Indian subcontinent. A tradition was created that drew on both the older traditions of the Aryan ruling and priestly elites, and non-Aryan ideas and practices. This tradition took its "classical" shape only much later, sometime in the early Christian era. We can call it *Indian*, as distinct from the earlier Rigvedic-Brahmanic culture (described in Chapter 1), in that its fundamental institutions and ideas came to prevail at all levels of society in virtually every part of the subcontinent.

Despite staggering internal diversity and divisions, and long periods of foreign rule, this Indian culture has survived for at least two thousand years as a coherent tradition of historical heritage, social organization, and religious worldview.

"Indian" and "Hindu"

Indian culture and tradition include more than is commonly implied by the word *Hindu* today. Earlier, *Hindu* was simply a word for *Indian*. It came from the Indo-Iranian name for the Indus and was originally the term used by outsiders, like the ancient Persians and the Greeks, to refer to the people or the land of the subcontinent. Even invading Muslims, and then invading Western Christians, used *Hindu* to characterize the most prominent religious and social institutions of India as a whole. The concept of *transmigration*, the sacredness of the Vedas and of the cow, the worship of Shiva or Vishnu, and the caste system head the list of

MAP 2-1   HEARTLANDS OF INDIAN CULTURE
Major ancient and modern cities of the subcontinent and their locations relative to major rivers are shown. Note that while north India is thought of as the cradle of Vedic and classical Indian religion and culture, the south was the locus, especially in the post Gupta period but also earlier, of important, long-lived regional dynasties, major religious movements, and brilliant artistic traditions.

such "Hindu" institutions. Yet not all Indians in the past twenty-five hundred years have accepted all of these and other related institutions. Most obviously, Indian Buddhists, Jains, Muslims, Sikhs, and Christians have rejected at least some of them.

We cannot say exactly when the typical aspects of Hindu society and religious life as we know it today were "in place." Some argue that it was only after A.D. 200 (or even 400), rather than sometime in the latter half of the first millennium B.C. However we date the beginning of "Hindu" religion and culture, we must remember that such usage lumps together an immense diversity of social, racial, linguistic, and religious groups. It is totally inaccurate to think of *Hindu* as a term for any single or uniform religious community.

Indian, on the other hand, commonly refers today to all the native inhabitants of the subcontinent, including Muslims, Sikhs, and Christians (who belong to traditions considerably younger than the Buddhist, Jain, or Hindu). In this book, we shall on occasion use the term *Indian* in this inclusive sense when referring to the subcontinent as a geographic or political whole, or to its peoples. However, for the period before the arrival of Muslim culture (CA. A.D. 1000), *Indian* will be used here to refer to the distinctively Indian tradition of thought and culture that began with the flowering of Upanishadic speculation and Buddhist and Jain thought around the middle of the first millennium B.C. This "Indian" tradition achieved its classical formulation in the Hindu society and religion of the first millennium A.D. However, the Jains of India and the Buddhists of wider Asia were also its legitimate heirs.

The Historical Background

We saw in Chapter 1 how, in the later Vedic or Brahmanic period, a priest-centered cult dominated among the upper classes of Aryanized northern Indian society. Apparently, by the sixth century B.C., this ritualistic cult had grown so extreme in its basically magical approach to ritual and piety that it had become an elite, esoteric cult to which most people had little or no access. The elaborate animal sacrifices on behalf of Aryan rulers were an economic burden upon the peasants of the countryside, whose livestock provided the victims. Such sacrifices were also largely irrelevant to the religious concerns of peasant and town-dweller alike. New, ascetic tendencies placed in question the basic values and practices of the older Aryan religion. Skepticism in religious matters accompanied social and political upheavals during the seventh and sixth centuries B.C.

The latest Vedic texts themselves reflect a reaction against excessive emphasis on the power of sacrifice and ritual formulas, accumulation of worldly wealth and power, and hope for an afterlife in some kind of paradise. The treatises of the Brahmanas (CA. 1000–800 B.C.) deal with the ritual application of the old Vedic texts, the explanation of Vedic rites and mythology, and the theory of the sacrifice. They had focused early on control of the sacred power *(Brahman)* present in sacrificial ritual, but now they gave ever greater attention to acquiring this power through knowledge instead of ritual acts.

This tendency became central in the Upanishads (CA. 800–500 B.C.) treatises, which proposed meditations on the meaning of ritual and the nature of Brahman. These texts carried to new levels of subtlety previous Vedic theorizing about the origin and nature of reality and the relation of thought and action to ultimate truth. The principal ideas that would guide all later Indian tradition are first clearly visible in the Upanishads, and in the thought and institutions of the

The major Hindu Gods of the cardinal directions. Hinduism has traditionally seen the absolute (Brahman) as manifest in a vast array of gods and goddesses as well as in nature. [Diana L. Eck.]

early Jain and Buddhist movements (fifth century B.C.). The Upanishadic thinkers represent the culmination of the Vedic-Brahmanic tradition in many ways. The Jain and Buddhist traditions, on the other hand, were but the most enduring of a series of sixth- and fifth-century B.C. religious movements that explicitly rejected much of the Vedic-Brahmanic tradition of sacrificial ritualism and class distinction.

Both the Upanishadic sages and the early Jains and Buddhists shared a number of ideas and concerns that signaled the "coming of age" of Indian thought. Their thinking and piety influenced not only all later Indian intellectual thought, but, through the spread of the Buddhist tradition, much of the intellectual and religious life of East and Southeast Asia as well. Thus, the middle centuries of the first millennium B.C. in India began a religious and philosophical revolution that ranks alongside those of Chinese philosophy and reli-

These sunnyasis, *or "renouncers," in the city of Benares have given up homes and families for a life of poverty, discipline, and meditation.* [Diana L. Eck.]

gion, Judaic monotheism, and Greek philosophy as a turning point in the history of civilization.

The Upanishadic Worldview

In the Upanishads, we see two new emphases. These are already evident in two sentences from the prayer of one of the earliest Upanishadic thinkers, who said, "From the unreal lead me to the Real. . . . From death lead me to immortality." The first request points to the Upanishadic focus on speculation about the nature of things, the quest for ultimate truth. Here ritual takes a back seat to meditation; knowledge, not the sacred word or act, has become the ultimate source of power.

The second new emphasis reflects a new concern with life after death. The old Vedic ideal of living a full and upright life so as to attain an afterlife in some kind of heaven of the fathers, among the gods, is no longer seen as an adequate ideal or goal. Immortality is now interpreted in terms not of afterlife but of escape from all existence—earthly, heavenly, or any other. These two Upanishadic emphases gave birth to a series of ideas that were to change the shape of Indian thought forever. Together they provide the key to its basic worldview.

THE NATURE OF REALITY. The quest for knowledge by the sages of the Upanishads concentrated on the nature of the individual self (*Atman*) and its rela-

tion to ultimate reality, or *Brahman*. The gods now take a lesser place as only one part of the total scheme of things. They are themselves subject to the laws of existence and not to be put on the same plane with the transcendent Absolute. Prayer and sacrifice to particular gods for their help is one thing; realization of Brahman is something altogether different. The latter is possible only through the action of the mind, not the bodily acts of ritual.

The culmination of the Upanishadic speculation is the recognition that the way to the Absolute is through the Self. Through contemplation, Atman-Brahman is recognized not as some divine being that can be addressed as a deity, but as the very principle of Reality itself: the unborn, unmade, unchanging Infinite. Of this Reality, all that can be said is that it is "neither this nor that," because the Ultimate cannot be conceived of nor described in finite terms. Beneath or behind the impermanence of ordinary reality is the changeless Brahman, to which the immortal self of every being belongs. The difficulty is recognizing this Self, and with it the Absolute, while one is caught in the realm of normal existence.

A second, related focus of Upanishadic inquiry was into the nature of "normal" existence. The realm of life is seen to be ultimately impermanent, ever in change. What seems such "solid" things—the physical world, our bodies and personalities, worldly success—are revealed in the Upanishads to be finally insubstantial,

Discussions of Brahman and Atman from the Upanishads

A REPORT OF THE SAGE SANDILYA'S STATEMENT ABOUT THE IDENTITY OF ATMAN AND BRAHMAN

"Verily, this whole world is Brahman. Tranquil, let one worship it as that from which he came forth, as that into which he will be dissolved, as that in which he breathes. Now, verily, a person consists of purpose. According to the purpose which a person has in this world, thus does he become on departing hence. So let him form for himself a purpose. He who consists of mind, whose body is life, whose form is light, whose conception is truth, whose soul [*atman*] is space, containing all odors, containing all tastes, encompassing this whole world, the unspeaking, the unconcerned—this Soul of mine within the heart is smaller than a grain of rice, or a barley-corn, or a mustard-seed, or a grain of millet; or the kernel of a grain of millet; this Soul of mine within the heart is greater than the earth, greater than the atmosphere, greater than the sky, greater than these worlds. Containing all works, containing all desires, containing all odors, containing all tastes, encompassing this whole world, the unspeaking, the unconcerned—this Soul of mine within the heart, this is Brahman. Into him I shall enter on departing hence. If one would believe this, he would have no more doubt."—Thus used Sandilya to say. . . .

Chandogya Upanishad 3.14

THE YOUNG BRAHMAN, SHEVETAKETU, IS INSTRUCTED IN THE IDENTITY OF ATMAN AND BRAHMAN BY HIS FATHER:

"These rivers, my dear, flow, the eastern toward the east, the western toward the west. They go just from the ocean to the ocean. They become the ocean itself. As there they know not 'I am this one,' 'I am that one'— even so, indeed, my dear, all creatures here, though they have come forth from Being, know not 'We have come forth from Being.' Whatever they are in this world, whether tiger, or lion, or wolf, or boar, or worm, or fly, or gnat, or mosquito, that they become. That which is the finest essence—this whole world has that as its soul. That is Reality. That is Atman. That art thou, Shevetaketu." ❑

Chandogya Upanishad 6.10

Selections taken with minor changes from Robert Ernest Hume (trans.), *The Thirteen Principal Upanishads*, 2nd ed. rev. (London: Oxford University Press, 1931), pp. 209–210, 246–247.

impermanent, and ephemeral. Even happiness is passing. Existence is neither satisfying nor lasting in any fundamental sense. Only Brahman is enduring, eternal, unchanging—the unmoved ground of existence. In this, there is already a marked tendency toward the eventual emphasis of the Buddhists on impermanence and suffering as the fundamental facts of existence as we know it.

LIFE AFTER DEATH. The new understanding of immortality that emerges in the Upanishads is related to these basic perceptions about the Self, the Absolute, and the world of existence. It runs, as we noted, counter to the older Vedic Aryan concept of an immortal existence either in heaven or in hell after this life is done. The Upanishadic sages developed the concept of existence as a ceaseless cycle of existence, a never-ending alternation between life and death. This idea was not only to have major implications for Indian speculative thought; it was also to become the basic assumption of all Indian thought and religious life.

The idea of the endless cycle of renewed existence, which Indians refer to as *samsara,* is only superficially to be compared to or translated as our idea of "transmigration" of souls. For Indians, it is the key to the nature of reality as we can know it. Furthermore, it is a fact that is not promising or liberating, but suffocating or burdensome. In the Indian context, *samsara* refers to the terrifying prospect of endless "redeath" as the normal lot of all beings in this world, whether animals, plants, humans, or gods. This is the fundamental problem posed for all later Indian thought. It is the problem to which the great Indian thinkers of the mid-first millennium B.C., from the sages of the Upanishads to the Buddha, addressed themselves most centrally.

KARMA. The key to the solution of the dilemma of *samsara* lies in the concept of *karma,* which in Sanskrit literally means "work" or "action." At base, it is the concept that every action has its inevitable effects, soon or later, and that as long as there is action of mind or body, there is continued effect, and hence continued existence. Good deeds bring good results, perhaps even rebirth in a heaven or as a god, and evil ones bring evil consequences, whether in this life or in rebirth in the next, whether in the everyday world or in the lower worlds of hell. Because of the fundamental impermanence of everything in existence (heavens and hells included), the good as well as the evil is temporary. The flux of existence knows only movement, change, endless cause and effect far transcending a mere human life span, or even a mere world eon.

THE SOLUTIONS. Working from the ruthless analysis of existence posed in the Upanishads and taken as the starting point of all later Indian thought, the solution to the problem of *samsara* that was worked out in the Indian tradition is of two kinds. The first alternative or strategy involves maximizing good actions and minimizing bad actions, in order to achieve the best possible rebirth in one's next round of existence. The second is different; it involves "release" *(moksha)* from existence: escaping all karmic effects by escaping action itself.

The first strategy has been followed by the great masses of Hindus, Buddhists, and Jains over the centuries. It has been characterized by Franklin Edgerton as the "ordinary norm," as opposed to the "extraordinary norm," which has been the path of only the select elite, the greatest seekers of Upanishadic truth, Jain asceticism, or the Buddhist "middle path." Essentially, the ordinary norm involves a life lived according to some code of social responsibility. The most significant codes for Indian history are those recognized by most Hindus, Buddhists, and Jains over the centuries. On the other hand, the seekers of the "extraordinary norm" are usually involved in some kind of ascetic discipline aimed at withdrawal from the karmic cycle al-

Thai monks receiving food from a Buddhist lay couple. Feeding the monks is a meritorious act. [Magnum/ Hiraji Kubota.]

together—and the consequent release *(moksha)* from cause and effect, good and evil, birth and rebirth. These two characteristic Indian responses to the problem posed by *samsara* show how the fundamental forms of Indian thought and piety took shape in the middle and later first millennium B.C.

SOCIAL RESPONSIBILITY: *DHARMA* AS IDEAL. The "ordinary norm" or ideal of life in the various traditions of Indian religiousness can be summarized as life lived according to *dharma*. Although *dharma* has many meanings in Indian usage, its most common is similar to that of the Vedic Aryan concept of *Rta* (see Chapter 1). In this sense, *dharma* means "the right (order of things)," "moral law," "right conduct," or even "duty." It includes the cosmic order (compare the Chinese *Tao*) as well as the right conduct of political, commercial, social, and religious affairs and individual moral responsibility. For most people—those we might call the laity, as distinguished from monks and ascetics—life according to *dharma* is the life of moral action that will lead to a better birth in the next round of existence.

Life according to *dharma* has several implications. First, it accepts action in the world of *samsara* as necessary and legitimate. Second, it demands acceptance of the responsibilities appropriate to one's sex, one's class and caste group, one's stage in life, and one's other particular circumstances. Third, it allows for legitimate self-interest: One's duty is to do those things that acquire merit for one's eternal *atman* and to avoid those that involve demerit, or evil consequences. Fourth, rebirth in heaven, in paradise, is the highest goal attainable through the life of *dharma*. However (fifth), all achievement in the world of *dharma* (which is also the world of *samsara*), even the attainment of heaven, is ultimately impermanent and is subject to change.

ASCETIC DISCIPLINE: *MOKSHA* AS IDEAL. For those who have the mental and physical capacity to abandon the world of ordinary life and to find freedom from *samsara*, the implications for living are in direct contrast to those of the "ordinary norm." First, action is viewed as negative, whether it is good or bad, for action only produces more action, more *karma*, more rebirth. Second, nonaction is achieved only by withdrawal from "normal" existence. The person seeking release *(moksha)* from *samsara* has to move beyond the usual responsibilities of family and society. Most often, this removal involves becoming some kind of "renouncer"—whether a homeless Hindu hermit, yogi, or wanderer, or a Jain or Buddhist monk. Third, this renunciation of the world and its goals demands selflessness, or absence of ego. One must give up the desires and attachments that the self normally needs to function in the world. Fourth, the highest goal is not rebirth in heaven at all, but *moksha*, "release" from all rebirth and redeath. Finally, *moksha* is lasting, permanent. Its realization means no more becoming, no more existence, no more suffering in the realm of *samsara*. Permanence, eternity, transcendence, and freedom from suffering are its attributes.

SEEKERS OF THE "EXTRAORDINARY NORM." The ideas that led persons to seek the "extraordinary norm" appeared in fullest form first in the Upanishads. These ideas were particularly congenial to an increasing number of persons who abandoned both the ritualistic religious practices and the society of class distinctions and material concerns around them. It is noteworthy that many of these seekers were of warrior-noble *(Kshatriya)*, not Brahman, birth. They took up the wandering or hermit existence of the ascetic, seeking in yogic meditation and self-denial or even self-torture to gain spiritual powers. The higher seekers tried to transcend the body and bodily existence in order to realize the Absolute.

In the sixth century B.C., a number of teachers of new ideas appeared, especially in the lower Ganges basin, in the area of Magadha (modern Bihar). Most of them rejected traditional forms of religiousness as well as the authority of the Vedas in favor of one or another kind of ascetic discipline as the true spiritual path. Two of these teachers acquired sufficient followings so that their ideas and practice became the foundations of new and lasting traditions of piety and faith, those of the Jains and the Buddhists.

Mahavira and the Jain Tradition

The Jains trace their tradition to one Vardhamana, known as Mahavira ("the great hero"), who lived about 540–468 B.C. Mahavira is held by his followers to have been the final *Jina* ("victor" over *samsara*) or *Tirthankara* ("ford maker," one who finds the way across the waters of existence), in a line of twenty-four great teachers who have appeared in the latter, degenerative half of the present-world time cycle. The Jains (or *Jainas*, "adherents of the *Jina*") see in Mahavira a human teacher, not a god. He found and taught the

Jain Comments on Samsara and the Monastic Virtues

The following two selections from a later Jain writing give some idea of how vividly the suffering of the self in the many forms of existence it undergoes is conceived of (Selection 1) and how totally Jain ascetics should fight all selfishness and self-pity as they undertake the stern discipline that will rid them of karmic accretions (Selection 2).

From clubs and knives, stakes and maces, breaking my limbs,
An infinite number of times I have suffered without hope.
By keen-edged razors, by knives and shears,
Many times I have been drawn and quartered, torn apart and skinned.
Helpless in snares and traps, a deer,
I have been caught and bound and fastened, and often I have been killed. . . .
A tree, with axes and adzes by the carpenters
An infinite number of times I have been felled, stripped of my bark, cut up, and sawn into planks. . . .
Ever afraid, trembling, in pain and suffering,
I have felt the utmost sorrow and agony. . . .
In every kind of existence I have suffered
Pains which have scarcely known reprieve for a moment.
—*Uttaradhyayana* 19.61–64, 71, 74

If another insult him, a monk should not lose his temper,
For that is mere childishness—a monk should never be angry.
If he hears words harsh and cruel, vulgar and painful,
He should silently disregard them, and not take them to heart.
Even if beaten he should not be angry, or even think sinfully,
But should know that patience is best, and follow the Law.

. . . .

When his limbs are running with sweat, and grimed with dust and dirt
In the heat of summer, the wise monk will not lament his lost comfort.
He must bear it all to wear out his karma, and follow the noble, the supreme Law.
Until his body breaks up, he should bear the filth upon it.
—*Uttaradhyayana* 2.24–37

From W. T. de Bary et al., *Sources of Indian Tradition* (New York: Columbia University Press, 1958), pp. 59–60, 64–65.

Jain monks honoring Bahubali, the first person in the present cosmic cycle to achieve enlightenment. The small image is a replica of the huge statue of Bahubali, the foot of which the monk in the background is touching reverently. [Magnum/Alex Webb.]

way to extricate the self, or soul, from the bonds of the material world and its accumulations of karma.

In the Jain view, there is no beginning or end to phenomenal existence, only innumerable, ceaseless cycles of generation and degeneration. The universe is alive from end to end with an infinite number of souls, all of which are immortal, omniscient, and pure in their essence. But all are caught in the web of *samsara*, whether as animals, gods, humans, plants, or even inanimate stones or fire. *Karma* here takes on a quasi-material form: Any thought, word, or deed attracts karmic matter that clings to and encumbers the soul. The greatest amounts come from evil acts, especially those done out of hate, greed, or cruelty to any other being.

Mahavira's path to release focused on the elimination of evil thoughts and acts, especially those harmful to others. His radical ascetic practice aimed at destroying one's karmic defilements and, ultimately, all actions leading to further karmic bondage. At the age of thirty, Mahavira entered on the radical self-denial

of a wandering ascetic and eventually gave up even clothing altogether (the latter a practice followed today by a relatively small sect of Jain mendicants). After a dozen years of self-deprivation and yogic meditative discipline, he attained enlightenment. Then, for some thirty years, he went about teaching his discipline to others. At the age of seventy-two, he chose to fast to death in order to burn out the last karmic residues, an action that has been emulated by some of the most advanced of Jain ascetics down to the present day.

It would, however, be very wrong to think of the entire Jain tradition in terms only of the extreme ascetic practices of some Jain mendicants. (Such practices can involve the attempt to avoid hurting even the tiniest organisms by wearing cloth masks and drinking only strained water.) Monks are bound basically by the five great vows that they share with other monastic traditions like the Buddhist and the Christian: not to kill, steal, lie, engage in sexual activity, or own anything.

Most Jains are not monks. Today, as in earlier centuries, there is a thriving lay community of perhaps three million Jains, most in western India (Gujarat and Rajasthan). Laypersons of both sexes have close ties to the monks (also of both sexes), whom they support with gifts and food. Many Jain laypersons spend some time during their life as a monk or in retreat with monks.

Jains tend to be merchants because of their aversion to farming and other occupations that involve harming plants or animals. They are vegetarians and regard *ahimsa*, "noninjury" to any being, as the paramount rule. In this latter emphasis, they have had great influence on Indian values. For example, Mahatma Gandhi, who came from a Jain area, seems to have been influenced by them in his adoption of *ahimsa* as a central tenet of his thought. Jains are known, in addition, for their hospitals—not only for humans, but also for animals. Compassion is for them, as for Buddhists, the great virtue. The merit of serving the "extraordinary-norm" seekers who adopt the mendicant life and of living a life according to the high standards of the community provides a goal even for those who as laypersons are following the "ordinary norm."

The Buddha

It can be argued that India's greatest contribution to world civilization was precisely the tradition of faith that eventually withered away in the subcontinent itself. The Buddhist tradition remains one of the greatest universalist forms of faith in the world today, but numbers only small minorities in India proper. Yet that is where it was born, where it received its fundamental shape, and where it left its mark on Hindu and Jain religion and culture. Like the two other great universalist traditions, Christianity and Islam, it traces its origins to a single figure who has loomed larger than life in the community of the faithful over the centuries.

This figure is Siddhartha Gautama, known as the "sage of the Shakya tribe" and, above all, as the Buddha, or the "enlightened/awakened one." A contemporary of Mahavira, Gautama was also born of a *Kshatriya* family (CA. 566 B.C.) in apparently comfortable if not, as the legend has it, royal circumstances. His people lived near the border of modern Nepal in the Himalayan foothills. The traditional story of how Gautama came to be the teacher of the "Middle Path" to release from *samsara* begins with his sheltered life of ease as a young married prince.

At the age of twenty-nine, Gautama suddenly realized the reality of aging, sickness, and death as the human lot. Revolted at his previous delight in sensual pleasures and even his wife and child, he abandoned his home and family to seek an answer to the dilemma of the endless cycle of mortal existence. After this "Great Renunciation," he studied first with renowned teachers and then took up extreme ascetic disciplines of penance and self-mortification. Still finding no answer, Gautama turned finally to intense yogic meditation under a pipal tree in the place near Varanasi (Banaras) known as Gaya. In one historic night, he moved through different levels of trance, during which he realized all of his past lives, the reality of the cycle of existence of all beings, and how to stop the karmic outflows that fuel suffering existence. At this point, he became the Buddha; that is, he achieved full enlightenment—the omniscient consciousness of reality as it is. Having realized the truth of suffering existence, he committed himself to the goal of gaining release for all beings.

From the time of the experience under the Bodh Tree, or "enlightenment tree," Gautama devoted the last of his earthly lives before his final release to teaching others his "Middle Path" between asceticism and sensual indulgence. This path has been the core of

An early Indian carving showing the chakra, *or wheel of the Dharma, the Buddha's teaching, adored by humans and gods. The tree is the Bo-tree under which Gautama attained enlightenment and became the Buddha. [Diana L. Eck.]*

Buddhist faith and practice ever since. It begins with realizing the "four noble truths"—(1) all life is *dukkha*, or suffering; (2) the source of suffering is desiring; (3) the cessation of desiring is the way to end suffering; (4) and the path to this end is eightfold: right understanding, thought, speech, action, livelihood, effort, mindfulness, and concentration. The key idea of the Buddhist teaching, or *dharma*, is that everything in the world of existence is causally linked. The essential fact of existence is *dukkha:* All existing is suffering; for no pleasure, however great, is permanent (here we see the Buddhist variation on the central Indian theme of

The "Turning of the Wheel of the Dharma": Basic Teachings of the Buddha

The following are selections from the sermon said to have been the first preached by the Buddha. It was directed at five of his former companions, with whom he had practiced extreme austerities. When he had abandoned asceticism to mediate under the Bodh Tree, they had left him. This sermon is said to have made them the first to follow him. Because it set in motion the Buddha's teaching, or dharma, *on earth, it is usually described as "Setting in Motion the Wheel of* Dharma.*" The text is from the Dhammacakkappavattana-sutta.*

Thus have I heard. The Blessed One was once living in the Deer Park at Isipatana (the Resort of Seers) near Bārānasi (Benares). There he addressed the group of five bhikkhus.

"Bhikkhus, these two extremes ought not to be practiced by one who has gone forth from the household life. What are the two? There is devotion to the indulgence of sense-pleasures, which is low, common, the way of ordinary people, unworthy and unprofitable; and there is devotion to self-mortification, which is painful, unworthy and unprofitable.

"Avoiding both these extremes, the Tathāgata has realized the Middle Path: it gives vision, it gives knowledge, and it leads to calm, to insight, to enlightenment, to Nibbāna. And what is that Middle Path . . . ? It is simply the Noble Eight-fold Path, namely, right view, right thought, right speech, right action, right livelihood, right effort, right mindfulness, right concentration. This is the Middle Path realized by the Tathāgata, which gives vision, which gives knowledge, and which leads to calm, to insight, to enlightenment, to Nibbāna. . . .

"The Noble Truth of suffering *(Dukkha)* is this: Birth is suffering; aging is suffering; sickness is suffering; death is suffering; sorrow and lamentation, pain, grief and despair are suffering; association with the unpleasant is suffering; dissociation from the pleasant is suffering; not to get what one wants is suffering—in brief, the five aggregates of attachment are suffering.

"The Noble Truth of the origin of suffering is this: It is this thirst (craving) which produces re-existence and re-becoming, bound up with passionate greed. It finds fresh delight now here and now there, namely, thirst for non-existence (self-annihilation).

"The Noble Truth of the Cessation of suffering is this: It is the complete cessation of that very thirst, giving it up, renouncing it, emancipating oneself from it, detaching oneself from it.

"The Noble Truth of the Path leading to the Cessation of suffering is this: It is simply the Noble Eightfold Path. . . .

"'This is the Noble Truth of Suffering (Dukkha)': such was the vision, the knowledge, the wisdom, the science, the light, that arose in me with regard to things not heard before. 'This suffering, as a noble truth, should be fully understood.' . . .

"'This is the Noble Truth of the Cessation of suffering': such was the vision . . . 'This Cessation of suffering, as a noble truth, should be realized.' . . .

"'This is the Noble Truth of the Path leading to the Cessation of suffering': such was the vision, . . . 'This Path leading to the Cessation of suffering, as a noble truth, has been followed (cultivated).' . . .

"As long as my vision of true knowledge was not fully clear . . . regarding the Four Noble Truths, I did not claim to have realized the perfect Enlightenment that is supreme in the world with its gods, . . . in this world with its recluses and brāhmanas, with its princes and men. But when my vision of true knowledge was fully clear . . . regarding the Four Noble Truths, then I claimed to have realized the perfect Enlightenment that is supreme in the world with its gods, in this world with its recluses and brāhmanas, with its princes and men. And a vision of true knowledge arose in me thus: My heart's deliverance is unassailable. This is the last birth. Now there is no more rebecoming (rebirth)."

This the Blessed One said. The group of five bhikkhus was glad, and they rejoiced at his words. ❑
(Samyutta-nikāya, LVI, II)

From Walpola Rahula, *What the Buddha Taught* (New York: Grove Press, 1974). pp. 92–94.

samsara). *Dukkha* comes from desire, from craving, from attachment to self.

Thus, Buddhist discipline focuses on the moral "eightfold path" and the cardinal virtue of compassion for all beings with the intent of eliminating the selfish desiring that is literally the root of *samsara* and its unavoidable suffering. The Buddha himself had attained this goal. When he died (CA. 486 B.C.) after a life of teaching others how to reach it, he passed from the round of existence forever. In Buddhist terminology, he attained *nirvana*, the extinguishing of continued karmic bondage. This attainment was to become the starting point for the growth and eventual spread of the Buddhist *dharma*, which was to take on diverse and far different forms in its long history.

Like the Jain movement, the Buddhist movement involved not only followers who were willing to renounce marriage and normal occupations to become part of the Buddha's communities of monks or nuns, but also laypersons who would strive to live by the high moral standards of the tradition and support those who were willing and able to strive as mendicants to realize full release. Like the Jain tradition, the Buddhist tradition encompassed from the start seekers of both the "extraordinary" and the "ordinary" norm in their present lives. This dual community has remained characteristic of all forms of Buddhism wherever it is practiced. Certainly, we shall have occasion later to see how varied these forms have been historically. But however much the essentially a-theistic, a-ritualistic, and pragmatic basic tradition was later modified and added to, so that popular Buddhism would encompass even theistic devotion to a divinized Buddha and other enlightened beings, the fundamental vision of a humanly attainable wisdom that leads to compassion and release remained.

The varying visions of Upanishadic, Jain, and Buddhist thought have proved durable, albeit in very different ways and degree in India itself, as we have noted. The emergence of "Hindu" tradition was to draw on all three of these revolutionary strands in Indian thought and to integrate their fundamental ideas about the universe, human life, morality, and society into the cultic and mythic strands of Brahmanic and popular Indian practice.

The Religion of the Jews

The world of the ancient Near East, both in Egypt and in the lands east of the Mediterranean across to the Iranian plateau, was a polytheistic world. Everywhere people worshiped local or regional gods and goddesses. Some of these deities were associated with natural places and phenomena, such as mountains or animals, the sky or the earth. For example, Shamash

in Mesopotamia and Re in Egypt were both sun gods. Others were tribal or local deities, such as Marduk in Babylonia, or Atum, the patron god of the Egyptian city of On (Heliopolis). Still others represented elemental powers of this world or the next, as was the case with Baal, the ancient fertility god of the Canaanite peoples, and Ishtar, whom the Sumerians worshiped as a goddess of love and the Assyrians as a goddess of war. Furthermore, from our perspective,

MAP 2-2 ANCIENT PALESTINE *The Hebrews established a unified kingdom in Palestine under Kings David and Solomon in the tenth century B.C. After the death of Solomon, however, the kingdom was divided into two parts—Israel in the north and Judah, with its capital Jerusalem, in the south. North of Israel were the great commercial cities of Phoenicia.*

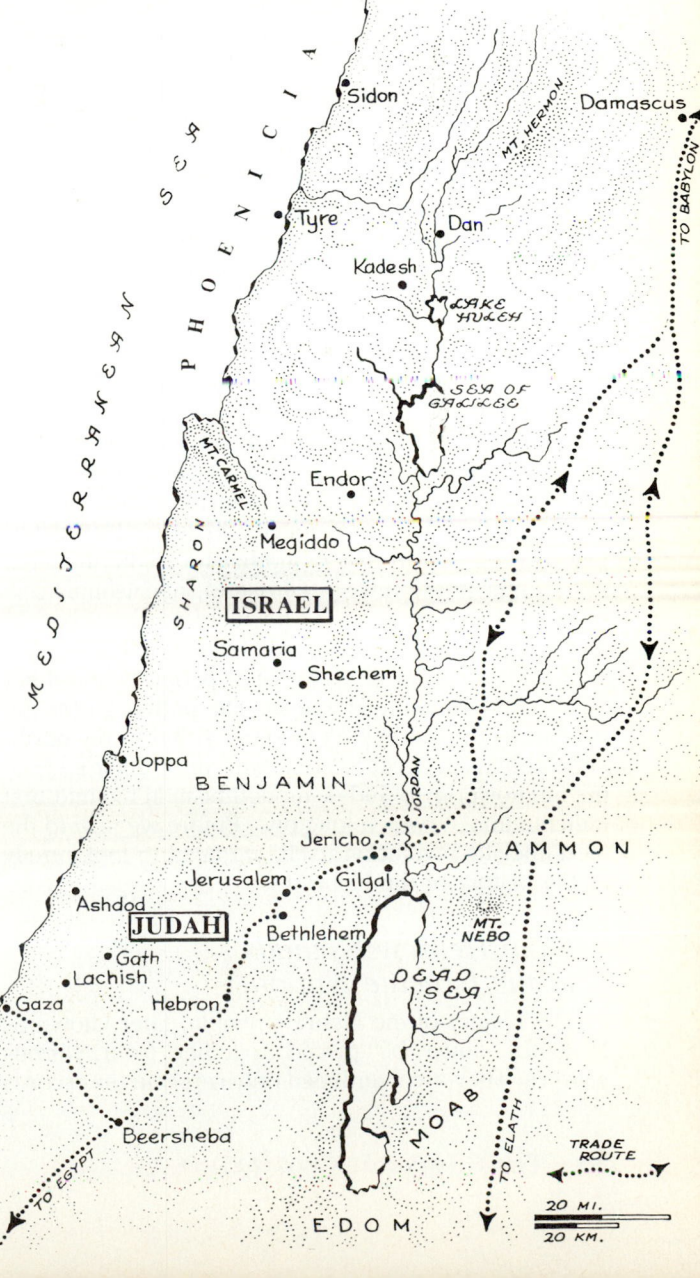

the gods were represented, by and large, as arbitrary and amoral beings who were often no more affected by the actions of human beings than were the natural forces that some of them represented.

If the gods were many and diverse, so too were the religious traditions of the ancient Near Eastern world. Even the major traditions of religious thought in Egypt and Mesopotamia did not offer comprehensive interpretations of human life that linked history and human destiny to a transcendent or eternal realm of meaning beyond this world—or at least no one such interpretation was able to spread and become dominant in this highly pluralistic, religiously fragmented world.

Out of this polytheistic and pluralistic world came the great tradition of monotheistic faith represented historically in the Jewish, Christian, and Islamic communities. This tradition traces its origin not to any of the great imperial cultures of the ancient Near Eastern world, but to the small nation of the Israelites. Although they were only a tiny tribal people whose external fortunes were at the mercy of the ebb and flow of the great dynasties and empires of the first millennium B.C., their impact on the global history of civilization was far greater than that of their giant neighbors. For all the glories of the great civilizations of the Fertile Crescent and the Nile valley, it was the Israelites, not the Babylonians or the Egyptians, who founded a tradition that significantly affected later history. This tradition was ethical monotheism.

Monotheism (faith in a single, all-powerful God who is the sole creator, sustainer, and ruler of the universe) may well be older than the Hebrews, but it made its first clear appearance with them. Their emphasis on the moral demands and ethical responsibilities placed on the individual and the community by the one God was first definitively linked to human history itself (and the Divine plan for that history). This historically based ethical and monotheistic tradition culminated later in the Jewish, Christian, and Islamic religions, but its direction had been set much earlier.

The beginnings of the tradition lie far back in the early history of an obscure tribal people whom later history knows as the Hebrews. The path from the appearance of this group as nomadic tribes in the northern Arabian peninsula, sometime after 2000 B.C., to the full flowering of Judaic monotheism in the mid-first millennium B.C. was a long one. Before we turn to the monotheistic revolution itself, we need to look briefly at the history of the Hebrews.

From Hebrew Nomads to the Israelite Nation

The history of the Hebrew people, later known as Israelites, must be pieced together from various sources. They are mentioned only rarely in the records of their ancient Near Eastern neighbors, so we must rely chiefly on their own accounts as compiled in the Hebrew Bible (or Old Testament, in Christian terminology). It was not intended as a history in our sense; rather, it is a complicated collection of historical narrative, wisdom literature, poetry, law, and religious witness. Scholars of an earlier day in the West tended to discard the Bible as a source for historians, but the most recent trend is to take it seriously while using it cautiously and critically. Although its earliest written portions go back at most only to the ninth century B.C. (it came to be fixed in the form in which it is known today only in the second century A.D.), it contains much older oral materials in its earliest parts. These allow us at least some glimpses of the earliest history of the Hebrew tribe.

We need not reject the tradition that the patriarch Abraham came from Ur in Mesopotamia and wandered west with his Hebrew clan to tend his flocks in the land along the eastern shore of the Mediterranean that became known to later history as Palestine. Such

Moses and the Burning Bush, a fresco from a synagogue in Syria from CA. A.D. 250. *The burning bush episode symbolizes divine-human encounter in Western monotheism. [Art Resource.]*

God's Purpose with Israel

In the first selection here, God, speaking through the prophet Jeremiah (fl. 626–586 B.C.), says that Jerusalem will be given over to the Babylonians. But he goes on to assure the Jews that he will also "gather them" together again and restore the "everlasting covenant" when he brings them again to Palestine. Such words provided the exiles in Babylon with an interpretation of their fate that helped them hold to their faith even in a foreign land. In the second selection, we hear the unknown prophetic voice of, so-called Second Isaiah, which dates from about 540 B.C. Here God addresses Israel as his suffering servant and promises to comfort and restore the Israelites as "a light to the nations." Such prophetic promises reflect the self-understanding of Israel with regard both to the tragedies of their history and to their special role as God's chosen instrument in his larger plan of salvation for all the nations of the earth.

The word of the LORD came to Jeremiah: "Behold, I am the LORD, the God of all flesh; is anything too hard for me? Therefore, thus says the LORD: Behold, I am giving this city into the hand of the Chalde'ans and into the hand of Nebuchadnez'zar king of Babylon, and he shall take it. . . . For the sons of Israel and the sons of Judah have done nothing but evil in my sight from their youth; the sons of Israel have done nothing but provoke me to anger by the work of their hands, says the LORD.

"Now therefore thus says the LORD, the God of Israel, concerning this city of which you say, 'It is given into the hand of the king of Babylon by sword, by famine, and by pestilence': Behold, I will gather them from all the countries to which I drove them in my anger and my wrath and in great indignation; I will bring them back to this place, and I will make them dwell in safety. And they shall be my people, and I will be their God. I will give them one heart and one way, that they may fear me for ever, for their own good and the good of their children after them. I will make with them an everlasting covenant, that I will not turn away from doing good to them; and I will put the fear of me in their hearts, that they may not turn from me. I will rejoice in doing them good, and I will plant them in this land in faithfulness, with all my heart and all my soul."

Jeremiah 32:26–41

Behold my servant, whom I uphold,
my chosen, in whom my soul delights;
I have put my Spirit upon him,
  he will bring forth justice to the nations.
He will not cry or lift up his voice, or make it
heard in the street;
a bruised reed he will not break,
  and a dimly burning wick he will not quench;
  he will faithfully bring forth justice.
He will not fail or be discouraged
  till he has established justice in the earth;
  and the coastlands wait for his law.

Isaiah 42:1–4

From *The Oxford Annotated Bible with the Apocrypha: Revised Standard Version*, ed. by H. G. May and B. M. Metzger (New York: Oxford University Press, 1965).

a movement would be in accord with what we know of a general migration of seminomadic tribes from Mesopotamia westward after about 1950 B.C. Any precise dating of the arrival of the Hebrews in the region of Palestine is impossible, but it may have been as early as 1900 B.C. or as late as 1600 B.C.

It is, however, with the patriarchal figure of Moses, at about the beginning of the thirteenth century B.C., that the Hebrews come onto the stage of history with greater clarity. Some of Abraham's people had settled down in the Palestinian area, but others apparently had wondered farther westward, into Egypt, perhaps with the Hyksos invaders (see Chapter 1). As the biblical narrative tells it, they had, by about 1400 B.C., become a settled but subject and even enslaved people there. Under the leadership of Moses, a segment of the Egyptian Israelites left the land of Egypt in search of a new homeland in the region to the east from which Abraham's descendants had come. The Children of Israel may then have wandered in the Sinai Desert and elsewhere for several decades before reaching Canaan, the province of Palestine that is described in the Bible as their promised homeland. The Bible presents this experience as the key event in Israel's history: the forging of the covenant, or mutual pact, between God, or *Yahweh*, and his people. We interpret the events of this Exodus period as the time that the Israelites emerged as a nation, a people with a sense of community and common purpose.

By about 1200 B.C., they had carved out a new Palestinian homeland for themselves at the expense of the Canaanite inhabitants of the area. After perhaps two centuries of consolidation and an existence as a loose federation of tribes, the now-settled nation reached its peak as a monarchy under kings David and Solomon in the tenth century B.C. But the sons of Solomon could not maintain the unity of the kingdom, and it split into two parts in the ninth century B.C.: Israel in the north of Palestine, and Judah, with its capital at Jerusalem, in the south.

The rise of the great empires around them brought disaster to the Israelites. The northern kingdom fell to the Assyrians in 722 B.C.; its people were scattered and, according to tradition, lost forever. These were the so-called ten lost tribes. Only the kingdom of Judah, with its seat at Jerusalem, remained, and hereafter we may call the Israelites Jews. In 586 B.C., Judah was defeated by the Neo-Babylonian king Nebuchadnezzar II. He destroyed the center of the Jewish cult, the great temple built by Solomon, and carried off the cream of the Jewish nation as exiles to be resettled in Babylon. There, in the "Babylonian Captivity" of the Exile, without a temple, the Jews managed still to cling to their traditions and faith. After the new Persian dynasty of the Achaemenids defeated the Babylonians in 539 B.C., they were allowed to return and resettle in their homeland. Many, but not all, of the exiles did return, and by about 516 B.C., a second temple was erected in a restored Jerusalem after the Exile.

The new Judaic state continued to be dominated by foreign peoples in the following centuries, but it was able to maintain its religious and national identity and occasionally to assert itself. However, it was again destroyed and its people dispersed after the destruction of Jerusalem by the Romans, in A.D. 70 and again in A.D. 132. By this time, however, the Jews had developed a religious worldview that would far exceed and long outlive that of any Judaic national state.

The Monotheistic Revolution

The fate of this small nation would be of little interest were it not for its unique religious achievement. It developed a tradition of faith that amounted to a revolution in ways of thinking about the human condition, the meaning of life and history, and the nature of the divine. It was not the overt history of the Judaic state down to its catastrophic end in A.D. 132 that was to have lasting historical importance, but what the Jews made of that history and how they interpreted it. The revolutionary character of this interpretation lay in its uniquely moralistic understanding of human life and history and the uncompromising monotheism on which this understanding was based.

At the root of this monotheistic tradition stands the figure of Abraham. Not only Jews but also Christians and Muslims look to him as the symbolic founder of their monotheistic faith. It is likely that the Hebrews in Abraham's time were much like other primitive tribal peoples in their religious attitudes. For them, the world must have been alive with many supernatural or divine powers: ancestral spirits, personifications or masters of the forces of nature, and divinities associated with particular places. Abraham probably conceived of his Lord simply as the most powerful of many divinities whom people might worship. But for the strength of his faith in God, the later biblical account recognizes him as the "Father of the Faithful," the first of the Hebrew patriarchs to enter into a covenant, or mutual pact, with God. In this covenant, Abraham promised to serve only this God, and this God prom-

A highly speculative reconstruction of Solomon's Temple, based on biblical accounts of its construction. [Bettmann Archive.]

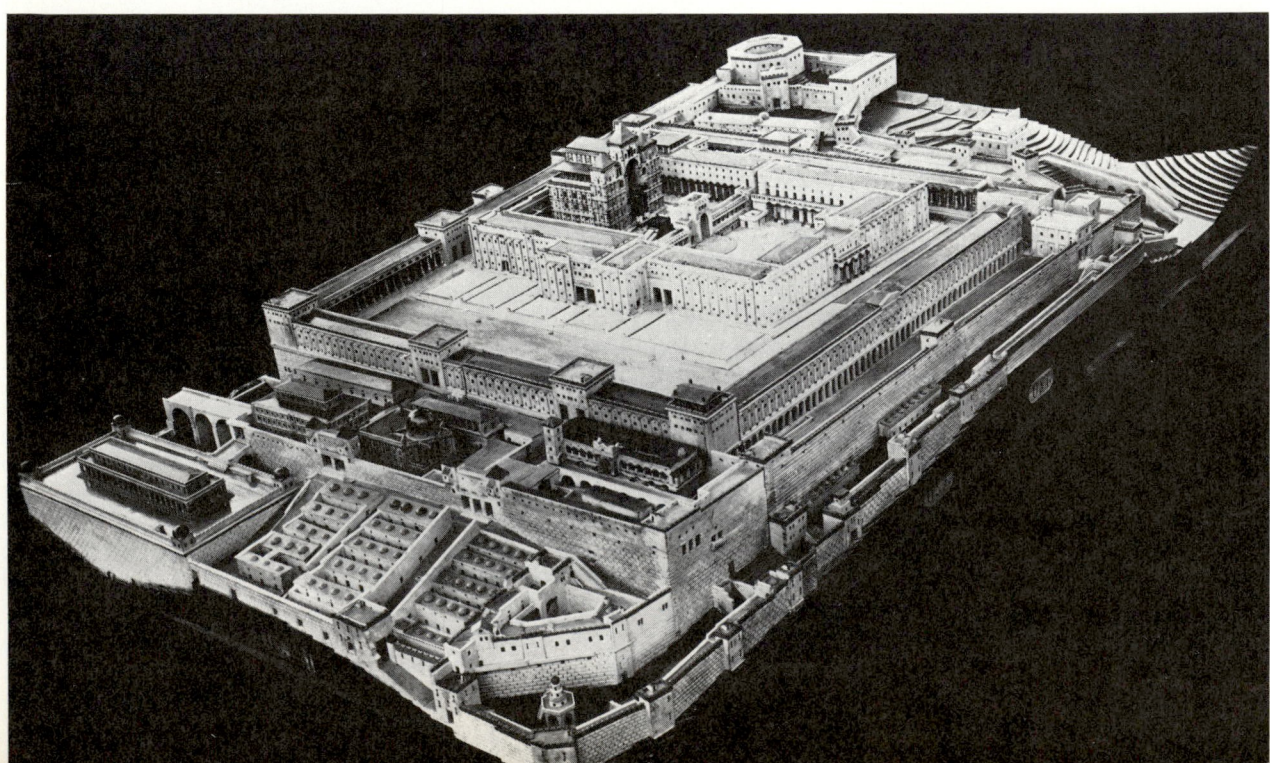

"The Wailing Wall" of Temple Mount, Jerusalem. This site is believed to be the remains of the Temple and is a focal point for Jewish pilgrimage and prayer. [*James Casson.*]

ised in turn to bless Abraham's descendants and guide them as his special people.

As is the case with the faith of Abraham, it is difficult to say how much the Mosaic covenant at Sinai actually represented the achievement of an exclusively monotheistic faith. A notion of the supremacy of Yahweh is reflected in the biblical emphasis on the Israelites' rejection of all other gods at this time—and on their subsequent victory, through Yahweh's might, over the Canaanites. Certainly, the covenant event was the decisive one in making of the Israelites a people united and identified by their special relationship to God. At Sinai, they received both God's holy Law (the Torah) and his promise of protection and guidance as long as they kept the law. This covenant was the necessary first step in the monotheistic revolution that came to full fruition several hundred years later. From Sinai forward, the Israelites looked on themselves as God's chosen people among the nations, and on their history as the history of the mighty acts of God.

The monotheistic revolution may thus be said to have begun with Abraham or Moses. Historically, we can trace it primarily from the division of the Israelite kingdom into two parts in 922 B.C. After this there arose men and women who were known as the *prophets*. Inspired messengers of God, prophets were sent to call people back from the worship of false gods to the worship of the one true God, and from increasing immorality and injustice to obedience to God's commandments.

Here we cannot trace the colorful history of the great and lesser prophets of Israel. The important point is that their activity was directly tied to the crucial events of Israelite history in the middle centuries of the first millennium B.C. In the biblical interpretation of these events, we can see the consolidation of the Judaic religious tradition in process. This consolidation, even amidst the political disintegration of the Israelite kingdom, was largely the result of the activities of the prophets. Their concern with purifying the faith and the morality of their people focused in particular on two ideas that proved central to Judaic monotheism.

The first was the significance of history in the Divine plan. Calling on the Jews' awareness of the covenant made at Sinai, the prophets saw in Israel's past and present troubles the hand of God punishing them for failing in their covenant duties. Their prophecies of coming disaster at the hands of enemies were based on the conviction that unless Israel changed its ways, more punishment would follow. But they were not only prophets of doom. When the predicted disasters came, their vision extended to seeing Israel the "suffering servant" among the nations, the people who, by their trials, would purify other nations and bring them also eventually to God. Here the nationalistic, particularistic focus of previous Israelite religion gave way to a universal, and therefore more complete, monotheism: Yahweh is God of all, even the Babylonians or Assyrians.

The second idea, or set of ideas, centered on the nature of Yahweh. The prophets saw in him the transcendent ideal of justice and goodness. From this view followed naturally the demand for justice and goodness in his worshipers, both individually and collectively. God was a righteous God who expected righteousness from human beings. No longer could he be understood only as the object of a sacrificial cult: He was a moral God who demands fairness and goodness, not blood offerings and empty prayers. A corollary of God's goodness was his love for his people, as especially the prophet Hosea (late eighth century B.C.) emphasized. However much he might have to punish them for their sins, God would eventually lead them back to him and his favor.

In the linking of the Lord of the Universe to history and to morality lay the heart of the breakthrough to true ethical monotheism. The Almighty Creator was seen as actively concerned with the actions and fates of his human creatures as exemplified in Israel. This concern was reflected in his involvement in history; history took on transcendent meaning. God had created humankind for an ultimately good purpose: They were called upon to be just and good like their Creator, for they were involved in the fulfillment of his divine purpose. Most concretely, this would come in the restoration of Israel as a people purified of their sins: "I will put my law within them, and I will write it upon their hearts; and I will be their God, and they shall be my people" (Jeremiah 31:33).

However, even after the Exile, the full realization of the prophecied days of peace and blessedness under God's rule clearly still had not come. The Jews were scattered now from Egypt to Babylonia, and their homeland remained in the control of stronger powers. Out of this context developed the late prophetic concept that the culmination of history would come in a future Messianic age. Faith and morality were now tied to human destiny, even without the still later Jewish idea that a day of judgment would end the golden age of the Messiah. The significance of these ideas, some of which may have come from the Jews' encounter with Zoroastrian traditions in the Exile, did not stop with Judaic religion. They went on to play a key role in similar Christian and Muslim ideas of a Messianic deliverer, resurrection of the body, and a life after death.

Alongside the prophets, the other key element in the monotheistic revolution of the Jews was the Law itself. The law is embodied in the five books of Torah (the Pentateuch, or "five books" of Genesis, Exodus, Leviticus, Numbers, and Deuteronomy). The central place of the Law in Jewish life was reestablished, after a period of decline, by King Josiah of Judah shortly before the fall of Jerusalem and the Exile. Its presence and importance in Judaic faith enabled the Jews to survive the loss of the Temple and its priestly cult even in exile, thereby fixing the Torah even over Jerusalem as the ultimate earthly focus of faith in God. Its centrality for the Jewish nation was reaffirmed after the reestablishment of the Temple, by Ezra and Nehemiah, in the fifth century B.C.

In the second century B.C., the enduring role of the Torah was ensured by its physical compilation, together with the books of the prophets and other writings, into the Holy Scriptures, or the Bible. Here we have the record of the Jews' long road to the recognition of God's law for his people, as well as the actual Law of the Torah itself. A holy, authoritative, divinely revealed scripture as an element of Judaic monotheism had revolutionary consequences, not only for Jews, but also for Christians and Muslims. In many ways, it put the seal on the monotheistic revolution that had made the sovereignty and righteousness of God the focal point of faith. It thereby affirmed the meaning of human action and human history for the faithful through the tangible historical record of God's law and Israel's historical experience.

A rabbi in Jerusalem reading from Torah in morning prayer. [Bettmann Archive.]

CA. 1000–961 B.C.	Reign of King David
CA. 961–922 B.C.	Reign of King Solomon
722 B.C.	Assyrian conquest of Israel (northern kingdom)
586 B.C.	Destruction of Jerusalem; fall of Judah (southern kingdom); Babylonian Captivity
539 B.C.	Restoration of temple; return of exiles

In the evolution of Judaic monotheistic faith, we see the beginning of one of the major religious traditions of world civilization. For the first time, in the Jews we find a nation defined not primarily by dynastic, linguistic, or geographical considerations, but above all by shared religious faith and practice. This was something new in human history. It was to have still greater effects in later times when not only Judaic but also Christian and Muslim tradition would change the face of major portions of the world.

Greek Philosophy

Different approaches and answers to many of the same concerns were offered by ancient Greek thought. Calling attention, even this early, to some of those differences will help to point up the distinctive outlook of the Greeks and of the later cultures of Western civilization that have drawn heavily on it.

Greek ideas had much in common with the ideas of earlier peoples. The gods of the Greeks had most of the characteristics of the Mesopotamian deities; magic and incantations played a part in Greek lives; and their law was usually connected with divinity. Many, if not most, Greeks in the ancient world must have lived their lives with notions not very different from those held by other peoples. But the surprising thing is that some Greeks developed ideas that were strikingly different and, in so doing, set a part of humankind on an entirely new path. As early as the sixth century B.C., some Greeks living in the Ionian cities of Asia Minor raised questions and suggested answers about nature that produced an intellectual revolution. In speculating about the nature of the world and its origin, they made guesses that were completely naturalistic and made no reference to supernatural powers. One historian of Greek thought put the case particularly well:

In one of the Babylonian legends it says: "All the lands were sea. . . . Marduk bound a rush mat upon the face of the waters, he made dirt and piled it beside the rush mat." What Thales did was to leave Marduk out. He, too, said that everything was once water. But he thought that earth and everything else had been formed out of water by a natural process, like the silting up of the Delta of the Nile. . . . It is an admirable beginning, the whole point of which is that it gathers together into a coherent picture a number of observed facts without letting Marduk in.[3]

Thales was the first Greek philosopher. His putting of the question of the world's origin in a naturalistic form as early as the sixth century B.C. may have been the beginning of the unreservedly rational investigation of the universe, and so the beginning of both Western philosophy and Western science.

The same relentlessly rational approach was used even in regard to the gods themselves. In the same century as Thales, Xenophanes of Colophon expressed the opinion that humans think that the gods were born and have clothes, voices, and bodies like themselves. If oxen, horses, and lions had hands and could paint like human beings, they would paint gods in their own image; the oxen would draw gods like oxen and the horses like horses. Thus black people believed in flat-nosed, black-faced gods, and the Thracians in gods with blue eyes and red hair.[4] In the fifth century B.C., Protagoras of Abdera went so far in the direction of agnosticism as to say, "About the gods I can have no knowledge either that they are or that they are not or what is their nature."[5]

This rationalistic, skeptical way of thinking carried over into practical matters as well. The school of medicine led by Hippocrates of Cos (about 400 B.C.) attempted to understand, diagnose, and cure disease without any attention to supernatural forces or beings. One of the Hippocratics wrote of the mysterious disease epilepsy: "It seems to me that the disease is no more divine than any other. It has a natural cause, just as other diseases have. Men think it divine merely because they do not understand it. But if they called everything divine which they do not understand, why, there would be no end of divine things."[6] By the fifth century B.C., too, it was possible for the historian Thucydides to analyze and explain the behavior of humans in society completely in terms of human nature and chance, leaving no place for the gods or supernatural forces.

The same absence of divine or supernatural forces characterized Greek views of law and justice. Most

---

[3] Benjamin Farrington, *Greek Science* (London: Penguin, 1953), p. 37.

[4] Frankfort et. al., pp. 14–16.

[5] Hermann Diels, *Fragmente der Vorsokratiker*, 5th ed., by Walther Kranz (Berlin: Weidmann, 1934–1938), Frg. 4.

[6] Ibid., Frgs. 14–16.

Greeks, of course, liked to think in a vague way that law came ultimately from the gods. In practice, however, and especially in the democratic states, they knew very well that laws were made by humans and should be obeyed because they represented the expressed consent of the citizens. Law, according to the fourth century B.C. statesman Demosthenes, is "a general covenant of the whole State, in accordance with which all men in that State ought to regulate their lives."[7]

The statement of these ideas, so different from any that came before the Greeks, opens the discussion of most of the issues that appear in the long history of civilization and that remain major concerns in the modern world: What is the nature of the universe and how can it be controlled? Are there divine powers, and if so, what is humanity's relationship to them? Are law and justice human, divine, or both? What is the place in human society of freedom, obedience, and reverence? These and many other problems were confronted and intensified by the Greeks.

Reason and the Scientific Spirit

The rational spirit characteristic of Greek geometric pottery and even of many Greek myths blossomed in the sixth century B.C. into the intellectual examination of the physical world and the place of humankind in it that we call philosophy. It is not surprising that the first steps along this path were taken in Ionia, which was on the fringe of the Greek world and therefore in touch with foreign ideas and the learning of the East. The Ionians were among the first to realize that the Greek account of how the world was created and maintained and of the place of humans in it was not universally accepted. Perhaps this realization helped spark the first attempts at disciplined philosophical inquiry.

We have already met Thales of Miletus, who lived early in the sixth century B.C. He believed that the earth floated on water and that water was the primary substance. This was not a new idea; what was new was the absence of any magical or mythical elements in the explanation. Thales observed, as any person can, that water has many forms: liquid, solid, and gaseous. He saw that it could "create" land by alluvial deposit and that it is necessary for all life. These observations he organized by reason into a single explanation that accounted for many phenomena without any need for the supernatural. The first philosopher thus set the tone for future investigations. Greek philosophers assumed that the world was knowable, rational, and simple.

The search for fundamental rational explanations of phenomena was carried forward by another

[7] Against Aristogeiton, 16.

Thales of Miletus, the first Greek philosopher. His explanation for the origin of the world was based on reason and the observation of nature without any need for the supernatural. [Bettmann Archive.]

Milesian, Anaximander. He imagined that the basic element was something undefined, "unlimited." The world emerged from it as the result of an interaction of opposite forces—wet and dry, hot and cold. He pictured the universe in eternal motion, with all sensible things emerging from the "unlimited," then decaying and returning to it. He also argued that human beings originated in water and had evolved to the present state through several stages, including that of a fish.

Anaximenes, another Milesian who flourished about 546 B.C., believed air to be primary. It took different forms because of the purely physical processes of rarefaction and condensation.

Heraclitus of Ephesus, who lived near the end of the sixth century B.C., carried the dialogue further. His famous saying, "All is motion," raised important problems. If all is constantly in motion, it would appear that nothing ever really exists. Yet Heraclitus believed that the world order was governed by a guiding principle, the Logos, and that though phenomena changed, the Logos did not. *Logos* has several meanings, among them "word," "language," "speech," and "reason." So when Heraclitus said that the physical world was governed by Logos, he implied that it could be explained by reason. In this way, speculations about the physical world, what we would call natural

The Atomists' Account of the Origin of the World Order

Leucippus and Democritus were Greek thinkers of the fifth century B.C. *who originated the theory that the world is entirely material, made up of atoms and the void, moving through space without external guidance. They provided a fundamental explanation of things that was purely natural, without divine or mythical intervention. Their view was passed on and later influenced such Renaissance scientists as Galileo.*

The world-orders arise in this way. Many bodies of all sorts of shapes "split off" from the infinite into a great void where, being gathered together, they give rise to a single vortex, in which, colliding and circling in all sorts of ways, they begin to separate apart, like to like. Being unable to circle in equilibrium any longer because of their congestion, the light bodies go off into the outer void like chaff, while the rest "remain together" and, becoming entangled, unite their motions and produce first a spherical structure.

This stands apart like a "membrane," containing in itself all sorts of bodies; and, because of the resistance of the middle, as these revolve the surrounding membrane becomes thin as contiguous bodies continually flow together because of contact with the vortex. And in this way the earth arose, the bodies which were carried to the middle remaining together. Again, the surrounding membrane increases because of the acquisition of bodies from without; and as it moves with the vortex, whatever it touches it adds to itself. Certain of these, becoming entangled, form a structure at first very watery and muddy; but afterward they dry out, being carried about with the rotation of the whole, and ignite to form the substance of the heavenly bodies.

Certainly the atoms did not arrange themselves in order by design or intelligence, nor did they propound what movements each should make. But rather myriad atoms, swept along through infinite time or myriad paths by blows and their own weight, have come together in every possible way and tried out every combination that they could possibly create. So it happens that, after roaming the world for aeons of time in making trial of every combination and movement, at length they come together—those atoms whose sudden coincidence often becomes the origin of mighty things: of earth and sea and sky and the species of living things. ❑

The first selection is from Diogenes Laertius 9.31; the second is from Lucretius, *De Rerum Naturae* 5.419–431. Both are cited in and translated by J. M. Robinson, *An Introduction to Early Greek Philosophy* (Boston: Houghton Mifflin, 1968), pp. 206, 208–209.

science, soon led the way toward even more difficult philosophical speculations about language, about the manner of human thought, and about knowledge itself.

In opposition to Heraclitus, Parmenides of Elea and his pupil Zeno argued that change was only an illusion of the senses. Reason and reflection showed that reality was fixed and unchanging because it seemed evident that nothing could be created out of nothingness. Such fundamental speculations were carried forward by Empedocles of Acragas, who spoke of four basic elements: fire, water, earth, and air. Like Parmenides, he thought that reality was permanent but not immobile, for the four elements were moved by two primary forces, Love and Strife, or, as we might be inclined to say, attraction and repulsion.

This theory was clearly a step on the road to the atomic theory of Leucippus of Miletus and Democritus of Abdera. They believed that the world consisted of innumerable tiny, solid particles that could not be divided or modified and that moved about in the void. The size of the atoms and the arrangement in which they were joined with others produced the secondary qualities that the senses could perceive, such as color and shape. These qualities—unlike the atoms themselves, which were natural—were merely conventional. Anaxagoras of Clazomenae, an older contemporary and a friend of Pericles, had previously spoken of tiny fundamental particles called *seeds*, which were put together on a rational basis by a force called *nous*, or "mind." Thus, Anaxagoras suggested a distinction between matter and mind. The atomists, however, regarded "soul," or "mind," as material and believed that everything was guided by purely physical laws. In the arguments of Anaxagoras and the atomists, we have the beginning of the philosophical debate between materialism and idealism that has continued through the ages.

These discussions interested very few, and, in fact, most Greeks were suspicious of such speculations. A far more influential debate was begun by a group of professional teachers who emerged in the mid-fifth century B.C. and whom the Greeks called *Sophists*. They traveled about and received pay for teaching practical techniques such as rhetoric, a valuable skill in democracies like Athens. Others claimed to teach wisdom and even virtue. They did not speculate about

The Sophists: From Rational Inquiry to Skepticism

The rational spirit inherent in Greek thought was carried to remarkable and dangerous extremes by the Sophists in the fifth century B.C. They questioned even the nature, the existence, and the origin of the gods, subjecting these matters to rational analysis.

Concerning the gods, I do not know whether they exist or not. For many are the obstacles to knowledge: the obscurity of the subject and the brevity of human life.

Prodicus says that the ancients worshiped as gods the sun, the moon, rivers, springs, and all things useful to human life, simply because of their usefulness—just as the Egyptians deify the Nile. For this reason bread is worshiped as Demeter, wine as Dionysus, water as Poseidon, fire as Hephaestus, and so on for each of the things that are useful to men.

There was a time when the life of man was disorderly and bestial and subject to brute force; when there was no reward for the good and no punishment for the bad. At that time, I think, men enacted laws in order that justice might be absolute ruler and have arrogance as its slave; and if anyone did wrong he was punished. Then, when the laws prohibited them from doing deeds of violence, they began to do them secretly. Then, I think, some shrewd and wise man invented fear of the gods for mortals, so that there might be some deterrent to the wicked even if they did or said or thought something in secret. Therefore he introduced the divine, saying that there is a god, flourishing with immortal life, hearing and seeing with his mind, thinking of all things and watching over them and having a divine nature; who will hear everything that is said among mortals and will be able to see all that is done. And if you plan any evil in secret it will not escape the notice of the gods, for they are of surpassing intelligence. In speaking thus he introduced the prettiest of teachings, concealing the truth under a false account. And in order that he might better strike fear into the hearts of men he told them that the gods dwell in that place which he knew to be a source of fears to mortals—and of benefits too—namely, the upper periphery where they saw lightnings and heard the dreaded rumblings of thunder and saw the starry body of the heaven, the beauteous embroidery of that wise craftsman Time, where the bright glowing mass of the sun moves and whence dark rains descend to earth. With such fears did he surround men, and by means of them he established the deity securely in a place befitting his dignity, and quenched lawlessness. Thus, I think, did some man first persuade mortals to believe in a race of gods. ❑

The first selection is from Diogenes Laertius 9.51; the next two are from Sextus Empiricus, *Against the Schoolmasters* 9.18, 9.54. All are cited in and translated by J. M. Robinson, *An Introduction to Early Greek Philosophy* (Boston: Houghton Mifflin, 1968), pp. 269–270.

the physical universe, but applied reasoned analysis to human beliefs and institutions. This human focus was characteristic of fifth-century thought, as was the central problem that the Sophists considered: They discovered the tension and even the contradiction between nature and custom, or law. The more traditional among them argued that law itself was in accord with nature, and this view fortified the traditional beliefs of the *polis*, the Greek city-state.

Others argued, however, that laws were merely conventional and not in accord with nature. The law was not of divine origin but merely the result of an agreement among people. It could not pretend to be a positive moral force, but merely had the negative function of preventing people from harming each other. The most extreme Sophists argued that law was contrary to nature, a trick whereby the weak control the strong. Critias went so far as to say that the gods themselves had been invented by some clever man to deter people from doing what they wished. Such ideas attacked the theoretical foundations of the *polis* and helped provoke the philosophical responses of Plato and Aristotle in the next century.

Political and Moral Philosophy

Like thinkers in other parts of the world around the middle of the first millennium B.C., some Greeks were vitally concerned with the formulation of moral principles for the governance of the state and the regulation of individual life, as well as more abstract problems of the nature of existence and transcendence. Nowhere is the Greek concern with ethical, political, and religious issues clearer than in the philosophical tradition that began with Socrates in the latter half of the fifth century B.C. That tradition continued with Socrates' pupil Plato and Plato's pupil Aristotle. Aristotle also had great interest in and made great contributions to the scientific understanding of the physical world, but he is perhaps more important for his impact on later Western and Islamic metaphysics.

Portfolio I: Judaism

Monotheism, the belief in a unique God who is the creator of the universe and its all-powerful ruler, first became a central and lasting element in religion among the Hebrews, later called Israelites and also Jews. Their religion, more than the many forms of polytheistic worship that characterized the ancient world, demanded moral rectitude and placed ethical responsibilities both on individuals and on the community as a whole. Their God had a divine plan for human history and the behavior of his chosen people was linked to it. This vision of the exclusive worship of the true God, obedience to the laws governing the community that derive from Him, and a strong ethical responsibility was connected to humanity's historical experience in this world. Ultimately it gave rise to three great religions: Judaism, Christianity, and Islam.

At the beginning of this tradition stands Abraham, recognized as the founder of their faith by all three of its branches. According to the story recorded in the Torah, this first of the Hebrew patriarchs entered into a covenant with God in which Abraham promised to worship only this God, who in turn promised to make Abraham's descendants his own chosen people—chosen to worship Him, obey His laws, and to undertake a special set of moral responsibilities. The covenant was renewed with Moses at Mount Sinai. God freed the Israelites from bondage, promised them the land of Canaan (later called Palestine and part of which is now Israel), and gave them the Law (the Torah), including the ten commandments, by which they were to guide their lives. As long as they lived by his law he would give them his guidance and protection.

In time the Israelites formed themselves into a kingdom which remained unified from about 1000 B.C. to 922 B.C. In the period after its division men and women called prophets emerged. These people, thought to be inspired by God, recalled the Israelites from their lapses into idolatry and immorality. Even as the kingdom was disintegrating and the Israelites falling under the control of alien empires, the prophets preached social reform and a return to more Godly ways. At the center of their vision was the place in history, in the fulfillment of God's plan for mankind. The prophets saw Israel's misfortune as punishment for failing to keep the covenant in many ways and predicted disaster if the Israelites did not change their ways. When disasters came, the Jewish kingdoms captured, the people enslaved and exiled, they interpreted Israel's status as a chosen people to mean that their sufferings were part of a process whereby they would become "a light unto the nations" leading other nations to the true worship of God. By this time, at the latest, the God of the Israelites was understood not only as the single God worshipped by the Jews but as the universal God for all humanity.

It was the prophets, too, who gave full expression to the Jews' belief that God was righteous and demanded righteousness from his people. At the same time, he was also a God of love; although he might need to punish his people for their sins, he would one day reward them with divine favor. Traditional Jewish belief expects that the Messiah, or "Anointed One," will someday come and establish God's kingdom on earth. He will be a descendant of King David who will restore the kingdom of Israel and rebuild the sanctuary in Jerusalem destroyed, finally, by the Romans. He will introduce an age of universal brotherhood in which all nations will acknowledge the true God and the righteous of past generations will be restored to life.

The Jews are very much "the people of the Book," and the foremost of their sacred writings is the Bible, consisting of the Five Books of Moses (the Torah), the books of the prophets, and other writings. Its heart is the Torah, the source of law. Over the centuries new experiences required the interpretation of the law to fit new circumstances, and this was accomplished by the oral law, no less sacred than the written law. Compilations of interpretation and commentary by wise and learned teachers were brought together to form the Talmud.

The destruction of their temple by the Romans in A.D. 70 hastened the scattering of the Jews throughout the empire. Thereafter almost all Jews lived in the Diaspora (dispersion), without a homeland, a political community, a national or religious center until the establishment of the Jewish state of Israel in 1948. However most Jews still live in other countries. A dominant experience for modern Judaism was the Holocaust, the culmination of centuries of persecution, when Hitler and the Nazis killed some six million Jews in a deliberate attempt to destroy the entire people in Europe. In spite of that the Jewish people and their religion live on in Israel and in many other countries.

The adherents of Judaism are divided into several groups who hold significantly different views about the place of tradition and the traditional law in the modern world. Perhaps all of them, however would give assent to the saying of Hillel, the great Talmudic teacher of the first century B.C.: "What is distasteful to you do not to your fellow man. This is the Law, all the rest is commentary. Now go and study."

I-1   The Ruins of Masada. *Masada was a fortress overlooking the Dead Sea in Israel. It was the last place the Jews held out in their rebellion against the imposition of Roman rule. The 1,000 Jewish zealots—men, women and children—held out for almost two years before the capture of the stronghold in 73 A.D. [Erich Lessing/Magnum.]*

I-2 Israel's Bondage in Egypt. *The biblical story of The Israelites' slavery in Egypt, their liberation by Moses and the renewal of Israel's covenant with God is a critical part of the history of the Jews and their religion. This scene is painted on a wall of the tomb of Rechmire in Thebes about 1450 B.C. Rechmire was the Vizier, or minister, of the pharaohs Thutmose III and Amenophis II. It shows a construction gang of slaves directed by an overseer doing the kind of work the Israelites were compelled to perform. [Erich Lessing/Magnum.]*

I-3 Exile of the Israelites. *In 722 B.C. the northern part of Jewish Palestine, the Kingdom of Israel, was conquered by the Assyrians. Its people were driven from their homeland and exiled all over the vast Assyrian Empire. This wall carving in low relief comes from the palace of the Assyrian King Sanherib at Nineveh. It shows the exiled Jews with their cattle and baggage going into exile. [Erich Lessing/Magnum.]*

I-4   Reconstruction of the Temple of Jerusalem. *This is a model of a reconstruction of the Temple at Jerusalem. It was originally erected by King Solomon in the tenth century* B.C. *to be the religious center of the kingdom and the symbol of Jewish unity. It was finally destroyed by Titus, the son of the Roman Emperor Vespasian in 70* A.D. *as part of the crushing of a Jewish rebellion. [Art Resource.]*

I-5   The Prophet Ezekiel. *This wall painting from a Jewish synagogue in the ancient Syrian city of Dura-Europus depicts the prophet Ezekiel's vision of the valley of the dry bones. Ezekiel's prophecies of the resurrection of Israel and the restoration of the Temple encouraged the Jews during their Babylonian captivity. [Princeton University Press.]*

I-6 The Jews Under Islam. *This painting from an Ottoman Turkish manuscript of the late sixteenth century shows the founder of Islam, the Prophet Muhammad, ordering the execution of Jews refusing to embrace Islam. Later in the history of Islam the Jews were tolerated as a "people of the book" [the Bible].* [Chester Beatty Library, Dublin, Ireland.]

I-7 Jews in Medieval France. *This French miniature painting from the mid-thirteenth century shows a debate between Jews and Christians, probably before the French King Saint Louis who presided over a similar debate.* [Biblioteque National, Paris.]

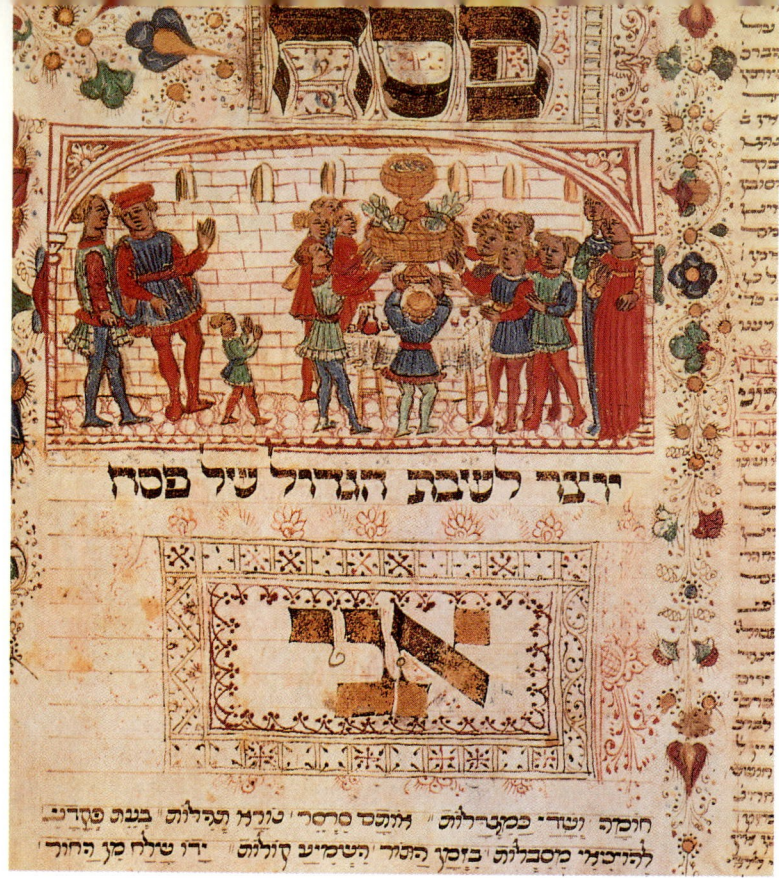

I-8 Passover in Renaissance Italy. *The Jews were scattered all over Europe by the end of the middle ages. This illumination from a Hebrew manuscript in Italy in 1466 shows a part of the Passover ceremony celebrating the escape from Egyptian bondage. [Reproduced by courtesy of the board of British Library.]*

I-9 Jews in Fifteenth Century Germany. *This illumination from a Hebrew manuscript in the State and University Library of Hamburg shows the houses of the Jewish quarter of the city. They are crowded together in the lower part of the town near the defensive walls. [Staats and Universitätsbibliothek, Hamburg.]*

I-10   The Portuguese Synagogue in Amsterdam. *After the expulsion of the Jews from
Spain and Portugal in the fifteenth century,
they sought sanctuary in many countries.
The Dutch Republic, extraordinarily tolerant of different religions, provided a welcome haven for many. This painting by
Emanuel de Witte, done about 1680, shows
the impressive interior of the Portuguese
Synagogue in Amsterdam. [Rijksmuseum,
Amsterdam.]*

I-11   Napoleon and the
Jews. *The Enlightenment
and the French Revolution
brought emancipation from
many of the old laws dis-
criminating against Jews.
Napoleon carried the ideas
of these movements to the
territories he conquered.
This bit of Napoleonic
propaganda shows the
emperor holding out his
hand to the Jews, as represented by the Jewish
woman at his feet while
rabbis express their thanks.
He holds the new laws
governing the Jews under
French rule, and his arm
rests on the Ten Com-
mandments. [Bibliotheque
National, Paris.]*

I-12 Russian Persecution of the Jews. *This painting,* After the Pogrom, *done by the Polish painter Maurycy Minkowski in 1910, shows a group of Jews in the aftermath of a pogrom, an organized persecution of Jews that often became a massacre. Such activities were frequently encouraged by the Russian government and were especially frightful in the late nineteenth and early twentieth centuries. [Jewish Museum/ Art Resource.]*

I-13 Nazi Anti-Jewish Propaganda. *Hitler's Nazi movement in Germany had a virulent, racist, doctrine of hostility towards the Jews as a fundamental doctrine. This propaganda poster printed during the Second World War shows the emblems of Great Britain, the United States, and the Soviet Union, the allied coalition fighting Germany and its allies. Behind them is a crude caricature of a Jew; the legend on the poster reads: "Behind the enemy the Jew." Hitler's hatred of the Jews lead to the Holocaust in which some six million Jews were murdered. [Bildarchiv Preussischer Kulturbesitz.]*

The starting point for all three of the philosophical giants of Hellenic political and moral philosophy was the social and political reality of the Greek city-state, or *polis*. The greatest crisis for the *polis* was the Great Peloponnesian War (435–404 B.C.), which is discussed in Chapter 4. Probably the most complicated response to this crisis may be found in the life and teachings of Socrates (469–399 B.C.). Because he wrote nothing, our knowledge of him comes chiefly from his disciples Plato and Xenophon and from later tradition. Although as a young man he was interested in speculations about the physical world, Socrates later turned to the investigation of ethics and morality. As Cicero put it, he brought philosophy down from the heavens.

Socrates was committed to the search for truth and for the knowledge about human affairs that he believed could be discovered by reason. His method was to go among men, particularly those reputed to know something, like craftsmen, poets, and politicians, to question and cross-examine them. The result was always the same: Those he questioned might have technical information and skills but seldom had any knowledge of the fundamental principles of human behavior. It is understandable that Athenians so exposed should be angry with their examiner, and it is not surprising that they thought Socrates was undermining the beliefs and values of the *polis*. Socrates' unconcealed contempt for democracy, which seemingly relied on ignorant amateurs to make important political decisions without any certain knowledge, created further hostility. Moreover, his insistence on the primacy of his own individualism and his determination to pursue philosophy even against the wishes of his fellow citizens reinforced this hostility and the prejudice that went with it.

But Socrates, unlike the Sophists, did not accept pay for his teaching; he professed ignorance and denied that he taught at all. His individualism, moreover, was unlike the worldly hedonism of some of the Sophists. It was not wealth or pleasure or power that he urged people to seek, but "the greatest improvement of the soul." He differed also from the more radical Sophists in that he denied that the *polis* and its laws were merely conventional. He thought, on the contrary, that they had a legitimate claim on the citizen, and he proved it in the most convincing fashion. In 399 B.C., he was condemned to death by an Athenian jury on the charges of bringing new gods into the city and of corrupting the youth. His dialectical inquir-

Socrates (469–399 B.C.) *changed the main focus of Greek philosophy from speculations about the physical world to the investigation of ethics and morality.* [New York Public Library.]

ies had angered many important people, and his criticism of democracy must have been viewed with suspicion. He was given a chance to escape, but in Plato's *Crito* we are told of his refusal because of his veneration of the laws.

Socrates' career set the stage for later responses to the travail of the *polis*; he recognized its difficulties and criticized its shortcomings. Although he turned away from an active political life, he did not abandon the idea of the *polis*. He fought as a soldier in its defense, obeyed its laws, and sought to put its values on a sound foundation by reason.

THE CYNICS. One branch of Socratic thought—the concern with personal morality and one's own soul, the disdain of worldly pleasure and wealth, and the withdrawal from political life—was developed and then distorted almost beyond recognition by the Cynic school. Antisthenes (CA. 455–CA. 360 B.C.), a follower of Socrates, is said to have been its founder, but its most famous exemplar was Diogenes of Sinope (CA. 400–CA. 325 B.C.). Socrates disparaged wealth and worldly comfort, so Diogenes wore rags and lived in a tub. He performed shameful acts in public and made his living by begging, in order to show his rejection of convention. He believed that happiness lay in satisfy-

Plato Reports the Claims of the Sophist Protagoras

Plato (CA. 429–347 B.C.) *remains to many the greatest of the ancient philosophers. Protagoras, the famous Sophist from Leontini in Sicily, came to Athens in 427 B.C. and created great excitement. In the following passage from the dialogue* Protagoras, *Plato's spokesman, Socrates, introduces a young man who wishes to benefit from Protagoras' skills.*

When we were all seated, Protagoras said: Now that the company are assembled, Socrates, tell me about the young man of whom you were just now speaking.

I replied: I will begin again at the same point, Protagoras, and tell you once more the purport of my visit: this is my friend Hippocrates, who is desirous of making your acquaintance; he would like to know what will happen to him if he associates with you. I have no more to say.

Protagoras answered: Young man, if you associate with me, on the very first day you will return home a better man than you came and better on the second day than on the first, and better every day than you were on the day before.

When I heard this, I said: Protagoras, I do not at all wonder at hearing you say this; even at your age, and with all your wisdom, if any one were to teach you what you did not know before, you would become better no doubt: but please to answer in a different way—I will explain how by an example. Let me suppose that Hippocrates, instead of desiring your acquaintance, wished to become acquainted with the young man Zeuxippus of Heraclea, who has lately been in Athens, and he had come to him as he has come to you, and had heard him say, as he heard you say, that every day he would grow and become better if he associated with him: and then suppose that he were to ask him, "In what shall I become better, and in what shall I grow?"—Zeuxippus would answer, "In painting." And suppose that he went to Orthagoas the Theban, and heard him say the same thing, and asked him, "In what shall I become better day by day?" he would reply, "In flute-playing." Now I want you to make the same sort of answer to this young man and to me, who am asking questions on his account. When you say that on the first day on which he associates with you he will return home a better man, and on every day will grow in like manner,—in what, Protagoras, will he be better? and about what?

When Protagoras heard me say this, he replied: You ask questions fairly, and I like to answer a question which is fairly put. If Hippocrates comes to me he will not experience the sort of drudgery with which other Sophists are in the habit of insulting their pupils; who, when they have just escaped from the arts, are taken and driven back into them by these teachers, and made to learn calculation, and astronomy, and geometry, and music (he gave a look at Hippias as he said this); but if he comes to me, he will learn that which he comes to learn. And this is prudence in affairs private as well as public; he will learn to order his own house in the best manner, and he will be able to speak and act for the best in the affairs of the state. ❑

Plato, *Protagoras*, trans. by Benjamin Jowett in *The Dialogues of Plato*, Vol. 1 (New York: Random House, 1937), pp. 88–89.

ing natural needs in the simplest and most direct way. Because actions to this end, being natural, could not be indecent, they could and should be done publicly.

Socrates questioned the theoretical basis for popular religious beliefs; the Cynics ridiculed all religious observances. As Plato said, Diogenes was Socrates gone mad. Beyond that, the way of the Cynics contradicted important Socratic beliefs. Socrates, unlike traditional aristocrats like Theognis, believed that virtue was not a matter of birth but of knowledge and that people do wrong only through ignorance of what is virtuous. The Cynics, on the contrary, believed that virtue is an affair of deeds and does not need a store of words and learning. Wisdom and happiness come from pursuing the proper style of life, not from philosophy. The Cynics moved even further from Socrates by abandoning the concept of the *polis* entirely. When Diogenes was asked about his citizenship, he answered that he was *kosmopolites*, a citizen of the world. The Cynics plainly had turned away from the past, and their views anticipated those of the Hellenistic Age.

PLATO. Plato (429–347 B.C.) was by far the most important of Socrates' associates and is a perfect example of the pupil who becomes greater than his master. He was the first systematic philosopher and therefore the first to place political ideas in their full philosophical context. He was also a writer of genius, leaving us twenty-six philosophical discussions. Almost all are in the form of dialogues, which somehow make the examination of difficult and complicated philosophical problems seem dramatic and entertaining.

Born of a noble Athenian family, Plato looked forward to an active political career until he was discouraged by the excesses of the Thirty Tyrants and the execution of Socrates by the restored democracy. Twice he made trips to Sicily in the hope of producing a model state at Syracuse under the tyrants Dionysius I and II, but without success. In 386 B.C., Plato founded the Academy, a center of philosophical investigation and a school for training statesmen and citizens that had a powerful impact on Greek thought and lasted until it was closed by the Emperor Justinian in the sixth century A.D.

Like Socrates, Plato firmly believed in the *polis* and its values. Its virtues were order, harmony, and justice, and one of its main objects was to produce good people. Like his master, and unlike the radical Sophists, Plato thought that the *polis* was in accord with nature. He accepted Socrates' doctrine of the identity of virtue and knowledge and made it plain what that knowledge was: *episteme*, science, a body of true and unchanging wisdom open to only a few philosophers, whose training, character, and intellect allowed them to see reality. Only such people were qualified to rule; they themselves would prefer the life of pure contemplation but would accept their responsibility and take their turn as philosopher kings. The training of such men required a specialization of function and a subordination of the individual to the community. This specialization would lead to Plato's definition of justice: that each man should do only that one thing to which his nature is best suited.

Plato saw quite well that the *polis* of his day suffered from terrible internal stress, class struggle, and factional divisions. His solution, however, was not that of some Greeks, that is, conquest and resulting economic prosperity. For Plato, the answer was in moral and political reform. The way to harmony was to destroy the causes of strife: private property, the family—anything, in short, that stood between the individual citizen and devotion to the *polis*.

The concern for the redemption of the *polis* was at the heart of Plato's system of philosophy. He began by asking the traditional questions: What is a good man, and how is he made? The goodness of a human being was a theme that belonged to moral philosophy, and when it became a function of the state, the question became part of political philosophy. Because goodness depended on knowledge of the good, it required a theory of knowledge and an investigation of what the knowledge was that was required for goodness. The answer must be metaphysical and so required a full examination of metaphysics. Even when the philosopher knew the good, however, the question remained of how the state could bring its citizens to the necessary comprehension of that knowledge. The answer required a theory of education. Even purely logical and metaphysical questions, therefore, were subordinate to the overriding political questions. In this way, Plato's need to find a satisfactory foundation for the beleaguered *polis* contributed to the birth of systematic philosophy.

ARISTOTLE. Aristotle (384–322 B.C.) was a pupil of Plato's who owed much to the thought of his master, but his very different experience and cast of mind led him in some new directions. He was born in northern Greece, the son of the court doctor of neighboring Macedon. As a young man, he came to study at the Academy, where he stayed until Plato's death. Then he joined a Platonic colony at Assos in Asia Minor, and from there, he moved to Mytilene. In both places, he carried on research in marine biology, and biological interests played a large part in all his thoughts. In 342 B.C., Philip, the king of Macedon, appointed him tutor to his son, the young Alexander (see Chapter 4). In 336, he returned to Athens, where he founded his own school, the Lyceum, or the Peripatos, as it was also called based on the covered walk within it. In later years, its members were called *Peripatetics*. On the death of Alexander in 323 B.C., the Athenians rebelled from Macedonian rule, and Aristotle found it wise to leave. He died at Chalcis in Euboea in the following year.

The Lyceum was a very different place from the Academy. Its members took little interest in mathematics and were concerned with gathering, ordering, and analyzing all human knowledge. Aristotle wrote dialogues on the Platonic model, but none survived. He and his students also prepared many collections of information to serve as the basis for scientific works, but of these only the *Constitution of the Athenians*, one of 158 constitutional treatises, remains. Almost all of what we posses is in the form of philosophical and scientific studies, whose loose organization and style suggest that they were lecture notes. The range of subjects treated is astonishing, including logic, physics, astronomy, biology, ethics, rhetoric, literary criticism, and politics.

In each field, the method is the same. Aristotle began with observation of the empirical evidence, which in some cases was physical and in others was common opinion. To this body of information he applied reason and discovered inconsistencies or difficulties. To deal with these, he introduced metaphysical principles to explain the problems or to reconcile the inconsistencies. His view on all subjects, like Plato's, was teleological; that is, both Plato and Aristotle recognized purposes apart from and greater than the will of the individual human being. Plato's purposes, however, were contained in the Ideas, or Forms—transcendental concepts outside the experience of most people. For Aristotle, the purposes of most things were easily inferred by observation of their behavior in the world. Aristotle's most striking characteristics are his moderation and common sense. His epistemology finds room for both reason and experience; his metaphysics gives meaning and reality to both mind and body; his ethics aims at the good life, which is the contemplative life, but recognizes the necessity for moderate wealth, comfort, and pleasure.

All these qualities are evident in Aristotle's political thought. Like Plato, he opposed the Sophists' assertion that the *polis* was contrary to nature and the result of mere convention. His response was to apply the teleology that he saw in all nature to politics as well. In his view, matter existed to achieve an end, and it developed until it achieved its form, which was its end. There was constant development from matter to form, from potential to actual. Therefore, human primitive instincts could be seen as the matter out of which the human's potential as a political being could be realized. The *polis* made individuals self-sufficient and allowed the full realization of their potentiality. It was therefore natural. It was also the highest point in the evolution of the social institutions that serve the human need to continue the species: marriage, household, village, and finally, *polis*. For Aristotle, the purpose of the *polis* was neither economic nor military but moral: "The end of the state is the good life" (*Politics* 1280b), the life lived "for the sake of noble actions" (1281a), a life of virtue and morality.

Characteristically, Aristotle was less interested in the best state—the utopia that required philosophers to rule it—than in the best state practically possible, one that would combine justice with stability. The constitution for that state he called *politeia*, not the best constitution, but the next best, the one most suited to and most possible for most states. Its quality was moderation, and it naturally gave power to neither the rich nor the poor but to the middle class, which must also be the most numerous. The middle class possessed many virtues: Because of its moderate wealth, it was free of the arrogance of the rich and the malice of the poor. For this reason, it was the most stable class. The stability of the constitution also came from it being a mixed constitution, blending in some way the laws of democracy and of oligarchy. Aristotle's scheme was unique because of its realism and the breadth of its vision.

All the political thinkers of the fourth century B.C. recognized that the *polis* was in danger, and all hoped to save it. All recognized the economic and social troubles that threatened it. Isocrates, a contemporary of Plato and Aristotle, urged a program of imperial conquest as a cure for poverty and revolution. Plato saw the folly of solving a political and moral problem by purely economic means and resorted to the creation of utopias. Aristotle combined the practical analysis of political and economic realities with the moral and political purposes of the traditional defenders of the *polis*. The result was a passionate confidence in the virtues of moderation and of the middle class and the proposal of a constitution that would give it power. It is ironic that the ablest defense of the *polis* came soon before its demise.

The concern with an understanding of nature in a purely rational, scientific way remained strong through the fifth century B.C., culminating in the work of the formulators of the atomic theory, Democritus and Leucippus, and in that of the medical school founded by Hippocrates of Cos. In the mid-fifth century, however, men like the Sophists and Socrates turned their attention to humankind and to ethical, political, and religious questions. This latter tradition of inquiry led, by way of Plato, Aristotle (in his metaphysical thought), and the Stoics, to Christianity and had, as well, a substantial impact on Judaic and Islamic thought. The former tradition of thought, following a line from the natural philosophers, the Sophists, Aristotle (in his scientific thought), and the Epicureans, had to wait until the Renaissance in Western Europe to exert an influence. Since the eighteenth century, this line of Greek thought has been the more influential force in Western civilization. It may not be too much to say that since the Enlightenment of that century, the Western world has been engaged in a debate between the two strands of the Greek intellectual tradition. As Western influence has spread over the world in recent times, that debate has become of universal importance, for other societies have not seen cause to separate the religious and philosophical from the scientific and physical realms as radically as has the modern West.

Suggested Readings

CHINA

W. T. deBary et al., *Sources of Chinese Tradition* (1960). A reader in China's philosophical and historical literature. It should be consulted for the later periods as well as for the Chou.

H. G. Creel, *What is Taoism? And Other Studies in Chinese Cultural History* (1970).

Y. L. Fung (D. Bodde, ed.), *A Short History of Chinese Philosophy* (1948). A survey of Chinese philosophy from its origins down to recent times.

D. C. Lau (trans.), *Lao Tzu, Tao Te Ching* (1963).

D. C. Lau (trans.), *Confucius, The Analects* (1979).

F. W. Mote, *Intellectual Foundations of China* (1971).

B. I. Schwartz, *The World of Thought in Ancient China* (1985).

A. Waley, *Three Ways of Thought in Ancient China* (1956). An easy yet sound introduction to Confucianism, Taoism, and Legalism.

B. Watson (trans.), *Basic Writings of Mo Tzu, Hsun Tzu, and Han Fei Tzu* (1963).

B. Watson (trans.), *The Complete Works of Chuang Tzu* (1968).

H. Welch, *Taoism, The Parting of the Way* (1967).

INDIA

W. T. deBary et al., *Sources of Indian Tradition* (1958). 2 vols. Vol. I: *From the Beginning to* 1800, ed. and rev. Ainslie T. Embree. (New York, 1988). Excellent selections from a wide variety of Indian texts, with good introductions to chapters and individual selections.

A. L. Basham, ed. *A Cultural History of India* (Delhi, Oxford, etc., 1975). A fine collection of historical-survey essays by a variety of scholars. Relevant here is Part I, "The Ancient Heritage" (Chapters 2–16).

A. L. Basham. *The Wonder That Was India*, rev. ed. (New York, 1963). Chapter VII, "Religion," is a superb introduction to the Vedic-Aryan, Brahmanic, Hindu, Jain, and Buddhist traditions of thought.

W. N. Brown. *Man in the Universe: Some Continuities in Indian Thought* (Berkeley, 1970). A superb and brief reflective summary of major patterns in Indian thinking.

T. J. Hopkins, *The Hindu Religious Tradition* (Belmont, CA, 1971). A first-rate, thoughtful introduction to Hindu religious ideas and practice.

W. Rahula, *What the Buddha Taught*, 2nd ed. (New York, 1974). A clear, concise, and readable introduction to Buddhist thought from a traditionalist Theravadin viewpoint, with primary-source selections.

R. H. Robinson and W. L. Johnson, *The Buddhist Religion: A Historical Introduction*, 3rd ed. (Belmont, CA, 1982). An excellent first text on the Buddhist tradition, its thought, development, and diffusion.

R. C. Zaehner, *Hinduism* (New York, 1966). One of the best general introductions to central Indian religious and philosophical ideas.

ISRAEL

J. Bright. *A History of Isreal* (1968). 2nd ed. (Philadelphia, 1972). One of the standard scholarly introductions to biblical history and literature.

W. D. Davies and L. Finkelstein, eds., *The Cambridge History of Judaism: Vol. I: Introduction; The Persian Period* (Cambridge, 1984). Excellent essays on diverse aspects of the exilic period and later.

J. Neusner, *The Way of Torah: An Introduction to Judaism* (North Scituate, MA, 1979). A sensitive introduction to the Judaic tradition and faith.

L. W. Schwarz, ed., *Great Ages and Ideas of the Jewish People* (New York, 1956). Especially interesting is the first section, "The Biblical Age," by Yehezkel Kaufmann.

GREECE

J. Burnet, *Early Greek Philosophy* (1963). Stresses the rational aspect of Greek thought and its sharp break with mythology.

F. M. Cornford, *From Religion to Philosophy* (1912). Emphasizes the elements of continuity between myth and religion on the one hand and Greek philosophy on the other.

B. Farrington, *Greek Science* (1953). A lively interpretation of the origins and character of Greek scientific thought.

G. B. Kerferd, *The Sophistic Movement* (Cambridge, 1981). An excellent description and analysis.

J. Lear, *Aristotle: the Desire to Understand* (Cambridge, 1988). A brilliant yet comprehensible introduction to the work of the philosopher.

J. M. Robinson, *An Introduction to Early Greek Philosophy* (1968). A valuable collection of the main fragments of, and ancient testimony to the works of, the early philosophers, with excellent commentary.

G. Vlastos, *The Philosophy of Socrates* (New York, 1971). A splendid collection of essays illuminating the problems presented by this remarkable man.

G. Vlastos, *Platonic Studies*, 2nd ed. (Princeton, 1981). A similar collection on the philosophy of Plato.

Empires and Cultures of The Ancient World

THE LAST five hundred years before the beginning of the Christian era and the two centuries that followed saw the appearance of great empires in Iran, India, and China, and of the Roman Empire in the West. Though each arose in response to local conditions, they had common features. Each replaced a confusion of local sovereign units, whether aristocratic family domains, smaller territorial states, tribal confederacies, or city-states, with vast centralized monarchies. Each had the large, efficient armies needed to conquer and control new lands. They all created well-organized bureaucracies to regulate their widespread empires and built extensive roads to ease communication and transportation. They all systematically imposed and collected taxes to pay for the armies and bureaucracies, for the construction of roads and defenses, and for the splendor of their imperial courts and palaces.

The military, political, and economic unification of vast territories produced considerable periods of relative peace and prosperity. There is evidence of communication and trade even between the Romans and the distant eastern empires of India and China. Imperial unification also had cultural consequences. The imposition of a single rule over different peoples in a far-flung empire encouraged the use of a common tongue, at least as a second language, which assisted the formation of a common culture. The Greeks, the Romans, the Hindus, and the Chinese produced great works in a variety of literary genres, such as epic poetry, history, and philosophy, which set a stamp on their own societies and served as the basis for later cultural developments. In all four areas, the wealth and patronage of the monarchs, the general prosperity of their empires, and the desire for splendor gave great impetus to such arts as painting, sculpture, and architecture.

The rise of these empires also brought important developments in religion. The Iranian conquests under the Achaemenid dynasty spread the religion of Zarathushtra (Zoroaster) throughout the Persian Empire, and the quasi-monotheistic faith had a powerful and broad influence before the tide of Islam swept over it in the seventh century A.D. In India in the third century B.C., under the Mauryan king Ashoka, Buddhism took on a missionary character and spread across Asia to the east and west. In the first century B.C., it came to China, where it competed not only with traditional Confucianism but also with a new form of Taoism that had taken on a more mysterious and otherworldly character during the Later Han period. In Greece, as the city-states gave way to the great empires of Philip and Alexander of Macedon and their Hellenistic successors, a largely amoral paganism gave way to such quasi-religious philosophies as Stoicism. In the Roman Empire that succeeded the

Hellenistic kingdoms, Christianity ultimately overcame all competitors to become the official religion by the end of the fourth century A.D. These religious movements stressed morality, and most of them were more otherworldly than their predecessors, placing greater emphasis on escape from the pain and troubles of this world and the search for personal immortality.

Such developments seem to have had some connection with the loss of prosperity, the increase of warfare, both internal and external, and the collapse of stability. None of the great empires could avoid a cycle of growth and decline. There was never enough wealth to sustain the cost of empire beyond a limited period of time. Taxes rose beyond the citizens' capacity to pay, and bureaucracies became bloated and ineffective. More and more depended on the central government, but talented leadership was not always available. The attractions of civilization drew the envy of vigorous barbarians outside the empires, even as internal problems and diminished willingness to fight reduced the capacity of the empires to resist. The Achaemenids fell victim to Alexander the Great, but the rule of his Hellenistic successors was brief. The Parthians, who succeeded to the old Persian Empire, were never able to impose the same imperial and cultural unity. In India, the Mauryan Empire did not long survive the death of its gentle king Ashoka, giving way to local uprisings and barbarian assaults from central Asia. Both China and Rome, weakened by internal struggles, gave way to barbarian assaults and saw the collapse of central authority. In both cases, the conquering tribes were themselves conquered by the religions of their victims, Buddhism in China and Christianity in Rome. In India, China, and Rome, moreover, the cultural achievements of the great empires would later serve as the basis for new advances in civilization. ❑

	EUROPE	NEAR EAST/INDIA
3000 B.C.	*ca. 2500–1100* Minoan Civilization on Crete *ca. 1600–1100* Mycenaean Civilization on Greek mainland	*ca. 3000* Emergence of cililization along the Nile River *ca. 2300* Emergence of Harappan Civilization in Indus Valley *2276–2221* Sargon of Akkad creates the first Mesopotamian Empire *ca. 2000* Epic of Gilgamesh *1750* Hammurabi's Code
1500 B.C.	*ca. 1100–800* Greek "Dark Ages" *800* Etruscan civilization begins in Italy *ca. 750–550* Rise of the "polis" *594* Solon's legislation at Athens *509* Foundation of the Roman Republic *508* Democracy established in Athens	*ca. 1500* Aryan peoples migrate into N.W. India *960–933* Rule of Hebrew King Solomon *ca. 628–551* Traditional dates of Zarathustra *ca. 537–486* Siddhartha Gautama *559–529* Cyrus the Great creates the Persian Empire
500 B.C.	*480–479* Persian invasion of Greece *478* Foundation of Delian League/Athenian Empire *431–404* Peloponnesian Wars *338* Battle of Chaeronia; Macedonian conquest of Greece *336–323* Career of Alexander the Great	*ca. 540–468* Vardhamana Mahavira, founder of Jain tradition *334* Alexander begins conquest of the Near East; invades India in 327 *321–181* Mauryan Empire in India *ca. 300* Foundation of Seleucid dynasty in Anatolia, Syria, and Mesopotamia; Ptolemaic dynasty in Egypt
300 B.C.	*265* Rome rules all of Italy *146* Rome destroys Carthage; rules all of Western Mediterranean *44–31* Civil Wars destroy Republic *31* Rome rules Mediterranean *31 B.C.–A.D. 14* Principate of Augustus	*269–232* Mauryan Emperor, Ashoka, patronizes Buddhism *247 B.C.–A.D. 224* Parthian dynasty controls Persia *180 B.C.–A.D. 320* India politically divided
A.D. 1	*91–180* The Good Emperors rule Rome *180–284* Breakdown of the Pax Romana *306–337* Constantine reigned *313* Edict of Milan *325* Council of Nicaea *380* Theodosius makes Christianity the official imperial religion *ca. 400–500* The Germanic Invasions *426 The City of God*, by Augustine *476* The last Western Emperor is deposed	*30* Crucifixion of Jesus *70* Romans destroy the Temple at Jerusalem *ca. 224* Fall of Parthians, rise of Sasanids in Persia *ca. 320–500* Gupta Dynasty in India *ca. 400* Chandra Gupta (r. 375–415) conquers western India; increases trade with Near East and China *ca. 450* The Huns invade India

EAST ASIA	AFRICA	THE AMERICAS
ca. 3000 Neolithic cultures in China *ca. 3000* Jōmon Neolithic cultures in Japan *1766* Bronze Age city-states and writing in China *ca. 1600–1050* Shang Civilization in China	*ca. 3000* Practice of agriculture spreads from Nile River Valley to the Sudan *ca. 2000* Ivory and gold trade between Kush (Nubia) and Egypt *ca. 1500* Practice of agriculture spreads from the Sudan to Abyssinia and the savannah region.	*ca. 3000* Maize already domesticated in the Mexican peninsula
1027–771 Western Zhou Dynasty, China *ca. 771* Iron Age territorial states in China *771–256* Chou dynasty in China *ca. 551–479* Confucius in China	*750* Kushite King Kashta conquers Upper Egypt; founds 25th Egyptian dynasty *ca. 720* Kushite king Piankhy completes conquest of Egypt and reigns as king of Kush and Egypt *ca. 600* Meroitic period of Kushan Civilization begins	*ca. 1500* B.C.–A.D. *300* Olmec Civilization on Gulf Coast of Mexico *ca. 1000* Practice of agriculture and village communities in American Southwest; enclosed ceremonial centers in eastern North America
ca. 500–200 Rise of Mohist, Taoist and Legalist schools of thought in China *403–321* Period of the Warring States in China *ca. 300* Jōmon Neolithic Culture in Japan replaced by Yayoi Culture		
221 Ch'in Emperor unites all of China *207* End of Ch'in dynasty *206* B.C.–A.D. *8* Former Han Dynasty in China *ca. 179–104* Han philosopher, Dong Zhong Shu *ca. 145–90* Han historian, Sima Qian *141–187* Emperor Wu Ti of China reigned	*25* Romans sack Kushite capital of Napata *100* B.C.–A.D. *1* Probable first Indonesia migrations to East African coast	*ca. 300* Mexican sun temple Atetello at Teothuican *ca. 164* Oldest Mayan monuments
9–25 Interregnum of Wang Mang in China *25–220* The Later Han Dynasty, China *ca. 220–590* Spread of Buddhism in China *221–280* Three Kingdoms Era in China *ca. 300–500* Barbarian invasions of China *ca. 300–680* Archaic Yamato State in Japan	*ca. 200* Camel first used for trans-Saharan transport *ca. 200–900* Expansion of Bantu people *ca. 250* Aksum (Ethiopia) controls the Red Sea Trade *ca. 300–400* Rise of Kingdom of Ghana *ca. 350* Kush ceases to exist	*ca. 300* Disappearance of Olmec civilization *ca. 300–1500* Mayan civilization, Central America *ca. 300–900* Classic period of Teotihucacán civilization, Mexico

Olive harvest. This scene on an Attic jar from late in the sixth century B.C. shows how olives, one of Athen's most important crops, were harvested. [Reproduced by courtesy of the Trustees of the British Museum.]

3 The Rise of Greek Civilization

About 2000 B.C., Greek-speaking peoples settled the lands surrounding the Aegean Sea and established a style of life and formed a set of ideas, values, and institutions that spread far beyond the Aegean corner of the Mediterranean Sea. Preserved and adapted by the Romans, Greek culture powerfully influenced the society of Western Europe in the Middle Ages and dominated the Byzantine Empire in the same period. The civilization emerging from this experience spread across Europe and in time crossed the Atlantic to the Western Hemisphere.

At some time in their history, the Greeks of the ancient world founded cities on every shore of the Mediterranean Sea, and pushing on through the Dardanelles, they placed many settlements on the coasts of the Black Sea in southern Russia and as far east as the approaches to the Caucasus Mountains. The center of Greek life, however, has always been the Aegean Sea and the lands in and around it. This location at the eastern end of the Mediterranean very early put the Greeks in touch with the more advanced and earlier civilizations of the Near East: Egypt, Asia Minor, Syria–Palestine, and the rich culture of Mesopotamia. A character in one of Plato's dialogues says, "Whatever the Greeks have acquired from foreigners they have, in the end, turned into something finer."[1] This proud statement indicates at least that the Greeks were aware of how much they had learned from other civilizations.

The Bronze Age on Crete and on the Mainland to CA. 1150 B.C.

One source of Greek civilization was the culture of the large island of Crete in the Mediterranean. With

---

[1] *Epinomis*, 987 d.

Greece to the north, Egypt to the south, and Asia to the east, Crete was a cultural bridge between the older civilizations and the new one of the Greeks.

The Minoans

The Bronze Age came to Crete not long after 3000 B.C. In the third and second millenia B.C., a civilization arose that powerfully influenced the islands of the Aegean and the mainland of Greece. This civilization has been given the name *Minoan*, after Minos, the legendary king of Crete.

On the basis of pottery styles and the excavated levels where the pottery and other artifacts are found, scholars have divided the Bronze Age on Crete into three major divisions with some subdivisions. Dates for Bronze Age settlements on the Greek mainland, for which the term *Helladic* is used, are derived from the same chronological scheme.

During the Middle and Late Minoan periods in the cities of eastern and central Crete, a civilization developed that was new and unique in its character and its beauty. Its most striking feature is presented by the palaces uncovered at such sites as Phaestus, Haghia Triada, and, most important, Cnossus. The palace design and the paintings show the influence of Syria, Asia Minor, and Egypt, but the style and quality are unique to Crete.

Along with palaces, paintings, pottery, jewelry, and other valuable objects, writing of three distinct kinds was found and one of these proved to be an early form of Greek. The script was written on clay tablets like those found in Mesopotamia. They were preserved accidentally, being hardened in a great fire that destroyed the palace. They reveal an organization centered on the palace, in which the king ruled and was served by an extensive bureaucracy, which kept remarkably detailed records. This sort of organization is typical of what we find in the Near East but nothing like what we will see among the Greeks, yet the inventories were written in a form of Greek. Why should Minoans, who were not Greek, write in a language not their own? This question raises the larger one of what the relationship was between Crete and the Greek mainland in the Bronze Age. It leads us to an examination of mainland, or Helladic, culture.

The Mycenaeans

In the third millennium B.C., most of the Greek mainland, including many of the sites of later Greek cities, was settled by people who used metal, built some impressive houses, and traded with Crete and the islands of the Aegean. The names they gave to places—names that were sometimes preserved by later invaders—make it clear that they were not Greeks and that they spoke a language that was not Indo-European.

Not long after the year 2000 B.C., many of the Early Helladic sites were destroyed by fire, some were abandoned, and still others appear to have yielded peacefully to an invading people. This invasion probably signaled the arrival of the Greeks.

The invaders succeeded in establishing control of the entire mainland, and the shaft graves cut into the rock at the royal palace-fortress of Mycenae show that they prospered and sometimes became very rich. At Mycenae and all over Greece, there was a smooth transition between the Middle and Late Helladic periods. At Mycenae, the richest finds come from the period after 1600 B.C. The city's wealth and power reached their peak during this time, and the culture of the whole mainland during the Late Helladic period goes by the name *Mycenaean*.

The excavation of Mycenaean sites reveals a culture influenced by, but very different from, the Minoan culture. Mycenae and Pylos, like Cnossus, were built some distance from the sea. It is plain, however, that defense against attack was foremost in the minds of the founders. Both cities were built on hills in a position commanding the neighboring territory. The Mycenaean people were warriors, as their art, architecture, and weapons reveal. The success of their campaigns and the defense of their territory required strong central authority, and all available evidence shows that the kings provided it. Their palaces, in which the royal family and its retainers lived, were located within the walls; most of the population lived outside the walls. The palace walls were usually covered with paintings, like those on Crete, but instead of peaceful scenery and games, the Mycenaean murals depicted scenes of war and boar hunting.

About 1500 B.C., the already impressive shaft graves were abandoned in favor of *tholos* tombs. These were large, beehivelike chambers cut into the hillside, built of enormous, well-cut, fitted stones, approached by an unroofed passage (*dromos*) cut horizontally into the side of the hill. The lintel block alone of one of these tombs weighs over a hundred tons. Only a strong king whose wealth was great, whose power was unquestioned, and who commanded the labor of many could undertake such a project. His wealth had to come from plundering raids, piracy, and trade. Some of this trade went westward to Italy and Sicily, but most of it was with the islands of the Aegean, the coastal towns of Asia Minor, and the cities of Syria, Egypt, and Crete. The Mycenaeans sent pottery, olive oil, and animal hides in exchange for jewels and other luxuries.

Tablets containing Mycenaean writing have been found all over the mainland; the largest and most useful collection was found at Pylos. The tablets reveal a world very similar to the one shown by the records at Cnossus. The king, whose title was *wanax*, held a

MAP 3-1   THE AEGEAN AREA IN THE BRONZE AGE   *The Bronze Age in the
Aegean area lasted from about 1900 to about 1100 B.C. Its culture on Crete is called
Minoan and was at its height about 1900–1400 B.C. Bronze Age Helladic culture on the
mainland flourished from about 1600 to 1200 B.C.*

royal domain, appointed officials, commanded servants, and kept a close record of what he owned and what was owed to him. This evidence confirms all the rest: the Mycenaean world was made up of a number of independent, powerful, and well-organized monarchies. These Greek invaders inhabited a flourishing Crete until the end of the Bronze Age, and there is good reason to believe that at the height of Mycenaean power (1400–1200 B.C.), Crete was part of the Mycenaean world.

These were prosperous and active years for the Mycenaeans. Their cities were enlarged, their trade grew, and they even established commercial colonies in the east. They are mentioned in the archives of the Hittite kings of Asia Minor. They are also named as marauders of the Nile Delta in the Egyptian records, and sometime about 1250 B.C. they probably sacked the city of Troy on the coast of northwestern Asia Minor, giving rise to the epic poems of Homer, the *Iliad* and the *Odyssey* (see Map 3.1). Around the year

1200 B.C., however, the Mycenaean world showed signs of great trouble, and by 1100 B.C., it was gone: its palaces were destroyed, many of its cities abandoned, and its art, its pattern of life, its system of writing buried and forgotten.

The Greeks themselves believed in a legend that told of the Dorians, a rude people from the north who spoke a different Greek dialect from that of the Mycenaean peoples. The Dorians joined with one of the Greek tribes, the Heraclidae, in an attack on the southern Greek peninsula of Peloponnesus, which was repulsed. One hundred years later they returned and gained full control. This legend of "the return of the Heraclidae" has been identified by modern historians with the Dorian invasion, the incursion from the north into Greece of a less civilized Greek people speaking the Dorian dialect.

The Greek "Middle Ages" to CA. 750 B.C.

The immediate effects of the Dorian invasion were disastrous for the inhabitants of the Mycenaean world. The palaces and the kings and bureaucrats who managed them were destroyed. The wealth and organization that had supported the artists and the merchants were likewise swept away by a barbarous people who did not have the knowledge or social organization to maintain them. Many villages were abandoned and never resettled. Some of their inhabitants probably turned to a nomadic life, and many perished.

Another result of the invasion was the spread of the Greek people eastward from the mainland to the Aegean islands and the coast of Asia Minor. The Dorians themselves, after occupying most of the Peloponnesus, swept across the Aegean to occupy the southern islands and the southern part of the Anatolian coast.

These migrations made the Aegean a Greek lake, but trade with the old civilizations of the Near East was virtually ended by the fall of the advanced Minoan and Mycenaean civilizations. Nor was there much trade between different parts of Greece. The Greeks were forced to turn inward, and each community was left largely to its own devices. This happened at a time when the Near East was also in disarray, and no great power arose to impose its ways and its will on the helpless people who lived about the Aegean. These circumstances allowed the Greeks time to recover from their disaster and to create their unique style of life.

The Age of Homer

For a picture of society in these "dark ages," the best source is Homer. His epic poems, the *Iliad* and the *Odyssey*, tell of the heroes who captured Troy, men of the Mycenaean age, but the world described in those poems clearly is a different one. Homer's heroes are not buried in *tholos* tombs but are cremated; they worship gods in temples, whereas the Mycenaeans had no temples; they have chariots but do not know their proper use in warfare. The poems of Homer are the result of an oral tradition that went back into the Mycenaean age. Through the centuries, bards sang tales of the heroes who fought at Troy, using verse arranged in rhythmic formulas to aid the memory. In this way, some very old material was preserved until the poems were finally written, no sooner than the eighth century B.C., but the society these old oral poems describe seems to be that of the tenth and ninth centuries B.C.

In the Homeric poems, the power of the kings is much smaller than that of the Mycenaean rulers. The ability of the kings to make important decisions was limited by the need to consult the council of nobles. The nobles felt free to discuss matters in vigorous language and in opposition to the king's wishes. In the *Iliad*, Achilles does not hesitate to address Agamemnon, the "most kingly" commander of the Trojan expedition, in these words: "thou with face of dog and heart of deer . . . folk devouring king." Such language may have been impolite, but it was not treasonous. The king, on the other hand, was free to ignore the council's advice, but it was risky to do so.

The right to speak in council was limited to noblemen (males only), but the common people could not be ignored. If a king planned a war or a major change of policy during a campaign, he would not fail to call the common soldiers to an assembly, where they could listen and express their feelings by acclamation, even though they could not take part in the debate. The evidence of Homer shows that even in these early times the Greeks, unlike their predecessors and contemporaries, practiced some forms of limited constitutional government.

Homeric society, nevertheless, was sharply divided into classes, the most important division being the one between nobles and commoners. We do not know the origin of the distinction, but we cannot doubt that at this time Greek society was aristocratic. Birth determined noble status, and wealth usually accompanied it. Below the nobles were the peasants, the landless laborers, and the slaves. We cannot tell whether the peasants owned the land they worked outright and so were free to sell it or if they worked a hereditary plot that belonged to their clan and was therefore not theirs to dispose of as they chose. It is clear, however, that the peasants worked hard to make a living.

Far worse was the condition of the hired agricultural laborer. The slave, at least, was attached to a family household and so was protected and fed. In a

Odysseus Addresses Nobles and Commoners: Homeric Society

The Iliad *was probably composed about 750 B.C. In this passage, Odysseus is trying to stop the Greeks at Troy from fleeing to their ships and returning to their homes. The difference in his treatment of nobles and commoners is striking.*

Whenever he found one that was a captain and a man of mark, he stood by his side, and refrained him with gentle words: "Good sir, it is not seemly to affright thee like a coward, but do thou sit thyself and make all thy folk sit down. For thou knowest not yet clearly what is the purpose of Atreus' son; now is he but making trial, and soon he will afflict the sons of the Achaians. And heard we not all of us what he spake in the council? Beware lest in his anger he evilly entreat the sons of the Achaians. For proud is the soul of heaven-fostered kings; because their honour is of Zeus, and the god of counsel loveth them."

But whatever man of the people he saw and found him shouting, him he drave with his sceptre and chode him with loud words: "Good sir, sit still and hearken to the words of others that are thy betters; but thou art no warrior, and a weakling, never reckoned whether in battle or in council. In no wise can we Achaians all be kings here. A multitude of masters is no good thing; let there be one master, one king, to whom the son of crooked-counselling Kronos hath granted it . . . " ❏

Homer, *The Iliad*, trans. by A. Lang, W. Leaf, and E. Myers (New York: Random House, n.d.), pp. 24–25.

world where membership in a settled group gave the only security, the free laborers were desperately vulnerable. Slaves were few in number and were mostly women, who served as maids and concubines. Some male slaves worked as shepherds. Few, if any, worked in agriculture, which depended on free labor throughout Greek history.

The Homeric poems hold up a mirror to this society, and they reflect an aristocratic code of values that powerfully influenced all future Greek thought. In classical times, Homer was the schoolbook of the Greeks. They memorized his text, settled diplomatic disputes by citing passages in it, and emulated the behavior and

cherished the values they found in it. Those values were physical prowess, courage; fierce protection of one's family, friends, and property; and above all, one's personal honor and reputation. Returning home after his wanderings, Odysseus ruthlessly kills all the suitors of his wife because they have used up all his wealth, wooed his wife, scorned his son, and so dishonored him. Speed of foot, strength, and, most of all, excellence at fighting in battle are what make a man great, yet Achilles leaves the battle and allows his fellow Greeks to be slain and almost defeated because Agamemnon has wounded his honor by taking away his battle prize. He returns not out of a sense of duty to

Jumpers painted on a Greek cup. Athletics were an important part of Greek culture. The Gods were honored with contests, and physical training was essential for young males. Here, the jumpers are using weights to improve their performance.

the army but because his dear friend Patroclus has been killed. In each case, the hero seeks to display the highest virtue of Homeric society, *arētē*—manliness, courage in the most general sense, and the excellence proper to a hero.

This quality was best revealed in a contest, or *agon*. Homeric battles are not primarily group combats but a series of individual contests between great champions. One of the prime forms of entertainment is the athletic contest, and the funeral of Patroclus is celebrated by such a contest. The central ethical idea in Homer can be found in the instructions that the father of Achilles gives to his son when he sends him off to fight at Troy: "Always be the best and distinguished above others." The father of another Homeric hero has given his son exactly the same orders and has added to them the injunction "do not bring shame on the family of your fathers who were by far the best in Ephyre and in wide Lycia." Here in a nutshell we have the chief values of the aristocrats of Homer's world: to vie for individual supremacy in *arētē* and to defend and increase the honor of the family. They would remain prominent aristocratic values long after Homeric society was only a memory.

The *Polis*

The characteristic Greek institution was the *polis*. The attempt to translate that word as "city-state" is misleading, for it says both too much and too little. All Greek *poleis* began as little more than agricultural villages or towns, and many stayed that way, so the word *city* is inappropriate. All of them were states, in the sense of being independent political units, but they were much more than that. The *polis* was thought of as a community of relatives; all its citizens, who were theoretically descended from a common ancestor, belonged to subgroups, such as fighting brotherhoods (*phratries*), clans, and tribes. They worshiped the gods in common ceremonies.

Aristotle argued that the *polis* was a natural growth and that man (explicitly male; Greek women were not full participants in the life on the *polis*) was by his nature "an animal who lives in a *polis*." Man alone has the power of speech and from it derives the ability to distinguish good from bad and right from wrong, "and the sharing of these things is what makes a household and a *polis*." A man who is incapable of sharing these things or who is so self-sufficient that he has no need of them is not a man at all, but either a wild beast or a god. Without law and justice, man is the worst and most dangerous of the animals. With them he can be the best, and justice exists only in the *polis*. These high claims were made in the fourth century B.C., hundreds of years after the *polis* came into existence, but they

accurately reflect an attitude that was present from the first.

Development of the Polis

Originally the word *polis* referred only to a citadel, an elevated, defensible rock to which the farmers of the neighboring area could retreat in case of attack. The Acropolis in Athens and the hill called Acrocorinth in Corinth are examples. For some time, such high places and the adjacent farms comprised the *polis*. The towns grew gradually and without planning, as the narrowness and the winding, disorderly character of their streets show. For centuries, they had no city walls. Unlike the city-states of the Near East, they were not placed for commercial convenience on rivers or the sea, nor did they grow up around a temple to serve the needs of priests and to benefit from the needs of worshipers. The availability of farmland and of a natural fortress determined their location. They were placed either well inland or far enough away from the sea to avoid piratical raids. Only later and gradually did the *agora* appear. It grew to be not only a marketplace but also a civic center and the heart of the Greeks' remarkable social life, which was distinguished by conversation and argument carried on in the open air.

Some *poleis* probably came into existence early in the eighth century B.C. The institution was certainly common by the middle of that century, for all the colonies that were established by the Greeks in the years after 750 B.C. took the form of the *polis*. Once the new institution had been fully established, true monarchy disappeared. Vestigial kings survived in some places, but they were almost always only ceremonial figures without power. The original form of the *polis* was an aristocratic republic dominated by the nobility through its council of nobles and its monopoly of the magistracies.

The Hoplite Phalanx

A new military technique was crucial to the development of the *polis*. In earlier times, the brunt of the fighting had been carried on by small troops of cavalry and individual "champions" who first threw their spears and then came to close quarters with swords. Toward the end of the eighth century B.C., however, the hoplite phalanx came into being. It remained the basis of Greek warfare thereafter.

The hoplite was a heavily armed infantryman who fought with a sword and a pike about nine feet long. These soldiers were formed into a phalanx in close order, usually at least eight ranks deep. So long as the hoplites fought bravely and held their ground, there would be few casualties and no defeat, but if they gave way, the result was usually a rout. All depended on the discipline, strength, and courage of the individual

The hoplite phalanx. This vase painting from the so-called "Chigi" vase is the earliest surviving picture of the new style of close-order, heavily armed infantry adopted by the Greeks toward the end of the eighth century B.C. *Notice the large circular shields, helmets, greaves, body armor, raised spears, and the close order of the soldiers. The flute player provides music to help keep the soldiers in step. [Hirmer Fotoarchiv München.]*

soldier. At its best, the phalanx could withstand cavalry charges and defeat infantries not as well protected or disciplined. Until defeated by the Roman legion, it was the dominant military force in the eastern Mediterranean.

The usual hoplite battle in Greece was between the armies of two *poleis* quarreling over a piece of land. One army invaded the territory of the other at a time when the crops were almost ready for harvest. The defending army had no choice but to protect its fields. If the army was beaten, its fields were captured or destroyed and its people might starve. In every way, the phalanx was a communal effort that relied not on the extraordinary actions of the individual but on the courage of a considerable portion of the citizens.

The phalanx and the *polis* arose together, and both heralded the decline of the kings. The phalanx, however, was not made up only of aristocrats. Most of the hoplites were farmers working relatively small holdings. The immediate beneficiaries of the royal decline were the aristocrats, but because the existence of the *polis* depended on the small farmers, their wishes could not for long be wholly ignored. The rise of the hoplite phalanx created a bond between the aristocrats and the peasants who fought in it, and this bond helps to explain why class conflicts were muted for some time. It also guaranteed, however, that the aristocrats, who dominated at first, would not always be unchallenged.

Expansion of the Greek World

From the middle of the eighth century B.C. until well into the sixth, the Greeks vastly expanded the territory they controlled, their wealth, and their contacts with other peoples in a burst of colonizing activity that placed *poleis* from Spain to the Black Sea. A century earlier, a few Greeks had established trading posts in Syria. There they had learned new techniques in the art and crafts and much more from the older civilizations of the Near East. About 750 B.C., they borrowed a writing system from one of the Semitic scripts and added vowels to create the first true alphabet. The new Greek alphabet was easier to learn than any earlier writing system and made possible the widely literate society of classical Greece.

The Greek Colony

Syria and its neighboring territory were too strong to penetrate, so the Greeks settled the southern coast of Macedonia and the Chalcidic peninsula (see Map 3.2). These regions were sparsely settled, and the natives were not well enough organized to resist the Greek colonists. Southern Italy and eastern Sicily were even more inviting areas. Before long, there were so many Greek colonies in Italy and Sicily that the Romans called the whole region *Magna Graecia* ("Great Greece"). The Greeks also put colonies in Spain and southern France. In the seventh century B.C., Greek colonists settled the coasts of the northeastern Mediterranean, the Black Sea, and the straits connecting them. About the same time, they established settlements on the eastern part of the northern African coast. The Greeks now had outposts throughout the Mediterranean world.

Only powerful pressures like overpopulation and land hunger drove thousands of Greeks from their homes to found new *poleis*. Most colonies, though independent, were friendly with their mother cities. Each might ask the other for aid in time of trouble and expect to receive a friendly hearing, although neither was obliged to help.

Colonization had a powerful influence of Greek life. By relieving the pressure of a growing population, it was a safety valve that allowed the *poleis* to escape civil wars. By emphasizing the differences between the Greeks and the new peoples they met, colonization gave the Greeks a sense of cultural identity and fostered a Panhellenic ("all-Greek") spirit that led to the establishment of a number of common religious festivals. The most important ones were at Olympia, Delphi, Corinth, and Nemea.

Colonization also encouraged trade and industry. The influx of new wealth from abroad and the increased demand for goods from the homeland stimulated a more intensive use of the land and an emphasis on crops for export, chiefly the olive and the wine grape. The manufacture of pottery, tools, weapons, and fine artistic metalwork as well as perfumed oil, the soap of the ancient Mediterranean world, was likewise encouraged. New opportunities allowed some men, sometimes outside the nobility, to become wealthy and important. These newly enriched men became a troublesome element in the aristocratic *poleis*, for they had an increasingly important part in the life of their states but were barred from political power, religious privileges, and social acceptance by the ruling aristocrats. These conditions soon created a crisis in many states.

The Tyrants (CA. 700–500 B.C.)

The crisis produced by the new economic and social conditions usually led to or intensified factional divisions within the ruling aristocracy. In the years between 700 and 550 B.C., the result was often the establishment of a tyranny.

The founding tyrant was usually a member of the ruling aristocracy who either had a personal grievance or led an unsuccessful faction. He often rose to power because of his military ability and support of the politically powerless group of the newly wealthy and of the poor peasants as well. When he took power, he often expelled many of his aristocratic opponents and divided at least some of their land among his supporters. He pleased his commercial and industrial supporters by destroying the privileges of the old aristocracy and by fostering trade and colonization.

The tyrants presided over a period of population growth that saw an increase especially in the number of city-dwellers. They responded with a program of public works that included improvement of the drainage systems, care for the water supply, the construction and organization of marketplaces, the building and strengthening of city walls, and the erection of temples. They introduced new local festivals and elaborated the old ones. They were active in the patronage of the arts, supporting poets and artisans with gratifying results. All this activity contributed to the tyrant's popularity, to the prosperity of his city, and to his self-esteem.

In most cases, the tyrant's rule was secured by a personal bodyguard and by mercenary soldiers. An

MAP 3-2 PHOENICIAN AND GREEK COLONIZATION *Most of the coast line of the Mediterranean and Black Seas was populated by Greek or Phoenician colonies. The Phoenicians were a commercial people who planted their colonies in North Africa, Spain, Sicily, and Sardinia, chiefly in the ninth century* B.C. *The height of Greek colonization came later, between about 750 and 550* B.C.

armed citizenry, necessary for an aggressive foreign policy, would have been dangerous, so the tyrants usually pursued a program of peaceful alliances with other tyrants abroad and avoided war.

By the end of the sixth century B.C., tyranny had disappeared from the Greek states and did not return again in the same form or for the same reasons. The last tyrants were universally hated for the cruelty and repression they employed. They left bitter memories in their own states and became objects of fear and hatred everywhere.

From a longer perspective, however, it is clear that the tyrants made important contributions to the development of Greek civilization. They put an end, for a time, to the crippling civil wars that threatened the

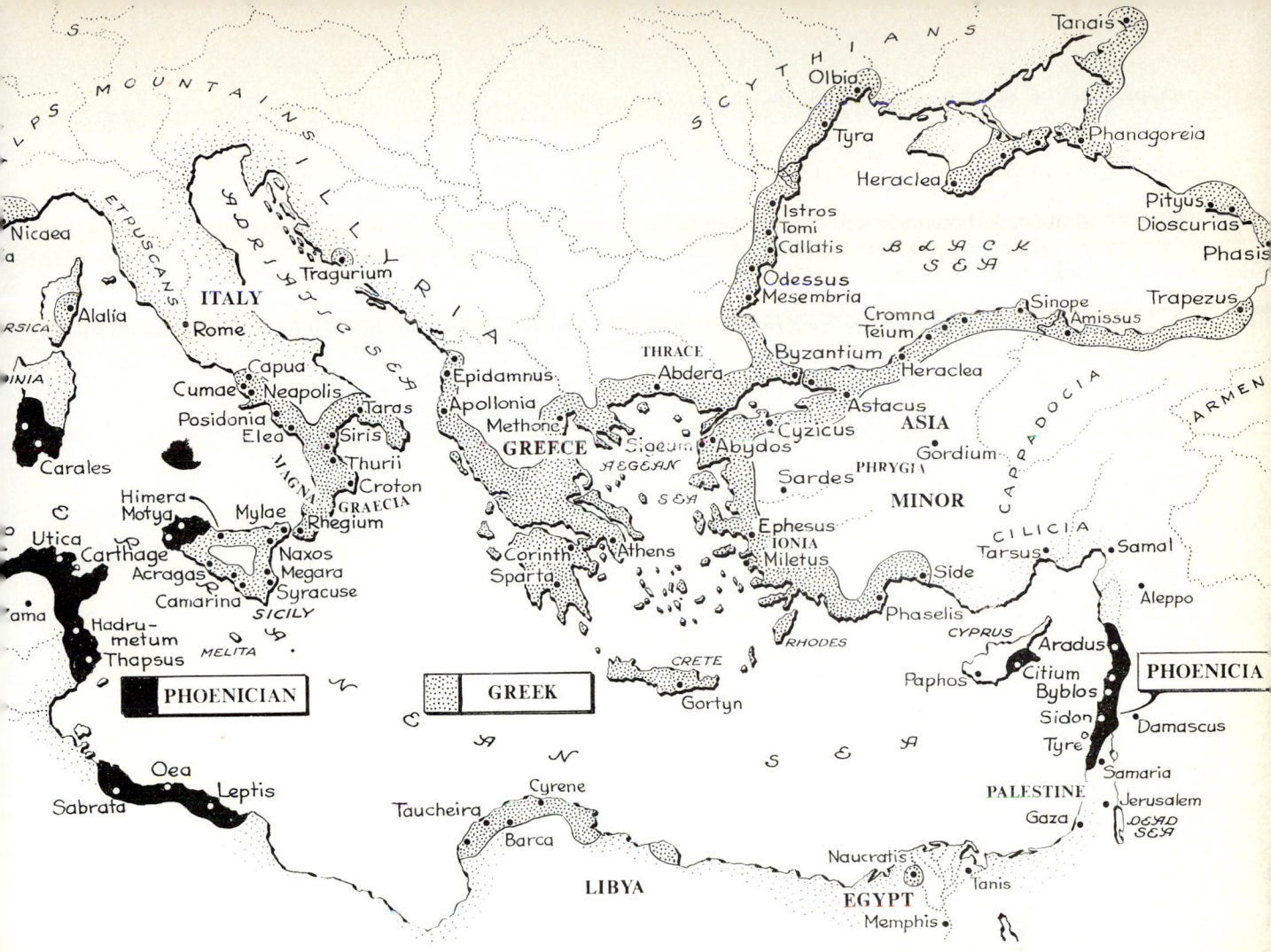

survival of the aristocratic *poleis.* In general, they reduced the warfare between the states. They encouraged the economic changes that were necessary for the future prosperity of Greece. They increased the degree of communication with the rest of the Mediterranean world and made an enormous contribution to the cultivation of crafts and technology, as well as of the arts and literature. Most important of all, they broke the grip of the aristocrats and put the productive powers of the most active and talented of its citizens fully at the service of the *polis.*

Society and Culture in Archaic Greece

Styles of Life

As the "dark ages" came to an end, the features that would distinguish Greek society thereafter took

CHRONOLOGY OF THE RISE OF GREECE	
CA. 2900–1150 B.C.	Minoan period
CA. 1900 B.C.	Probable date of the arrival of the Greeks on the mainland
CA. 1600–1150 B.C.	Mycenaean period
CA. 1250 B.C.	Sack of Troy (?)
CA. 1200–1150 B.C.	Destruction of Mycenaean centers in Greece
CA. 1100–750 B.C.	Dark Ages
CA. 750–500 B.C.	Major period of Greek colonization
CA. 725 B.C.	Probable date of Homer
CA. 700 B.C.	Probable date of Hesiod
CA. 700–500 B.C.	Major period of Greek tyranny

shape. The role of the artisan and the merchant grew more important as contact with the non-Hellenic world became easier, but the great majority of people continued to make their living from the land. Wealthy aristocrats with large estates, powerful households, families, and clans, however, led very different lives from those of the poorer peasants and the independent farmers who had smaller and less fertile fields.

PEASANTS. Peasants rarely leave a record of their thoughts or activities, and we have no such record from ancient Greece. The poet Hesiod (CA. 700 B.C.), however, who presented himself as a small farmer, was certainly no aristocrat. From his *Works and Days* we get some idea of the life of such a farmer. The crops included grain, chiefly barley but also wheat; grapes for wine; olives for food, but chiefly for oil, used for cooking, lighting, and washing; green vegetables, especially the bean; and some fruit. Sheep and goats provided milk and cheese. The Homeric heroes had great herds of cattle and ate lots of meat, but by Hesiod's time land fertile enough to provide fodder for cattle was needed to grow grain. He and small farmers like him tasted meat chiefly from sacrificial animals at festivals.

These farmers worked hard to make their living. Although Hesiod had the help of oxen and mules and one or two hired helpers for occasional labor, his life was one of continuous toil. The hardest work came in October, at the start of the rainy season, the time for the first plowing. The plow was light and easily broken, and the work of forcing the iron tip into the earth was back-breaking, though Hesiod had a team of oxen to pull his plow. Not every farmer was so fortunate,

Hesiod's Farmer's Almanac

Hesiod was a farmer and poet who lived in a village in Greece about 700 B.C. His poem Works and Days *contains wisdom on several subjects, but its final section amounts to a farmer's almanac, taking readers through the year and advising them on just when each activity is demanded. Hesiod painted a picture of a very hard life for Greek farmers. In the following passage he talks about one of the few times when the farmer is free from toil, during the hottest part of summer.*

But when House-on-Back, the snail, crawls from
    the ground up
the plants, escaping the Pleiades, it's no longer time
  for vine-digging;
time rather to put an edge to your sickles, and rout out
  your helpers.
Keep away from sitting in the shade or lying in bed till
  the sun's up
in the time of the harvest, when the sunshine scorches
  your skin dry.
This is the season to push your work and bring home
  your harvest;
get up with the first light so you'll have enough to live
  on.
Dawn takes away from work a third part of the work's
  measure.
Dawn sets a man well along on his journey, in his
  work also,
dawn, who when she shows, has numerous people
  going their ways; dawn who puts the yoke upon
  many oxen.
    But when the artichoke is in flower, and the clam-
      orous cricket
sitting in his tree lets go his vociferous singing, that
  issues
from the beating of his wings, in the exhausting season
  of summer,

then is when goats are at their fattest, when the wine
  tastes best,
women are most lascivious, but the men's strength
  fails them
most, for the star Seirios shrivels them, knees and
  heads alike,
and the skin is all dried out in the heat; then, at that
  season,
one might have the shadow under the rock, and the
  wine of Biblis,
a curd cake, and all the milk that the goats can give
  you,
the meat of a heifer, bred in the woods, who has never
  borne a calf,
and of baby kids also. Then, too, one can sit in the
  shadow
and drink the bright-shining wine, his heart satiated
  with eating
and face turned in the direction where Zephyros blows
  briskly,
make three libations of water from a spring that keeps
  running forever
and has no mud in it; and pour wine for the fourth
  libation. ❑

Hesiod, *Works and Days*, trans. by Richmond Lattimore (Ann Arbor: 1959), University of Michigan Press, pp. 87, 89.

Theognis of Megara Gives Advice to a Young Aristocrat

Theognis was born about 500 B.C. and lived to see his native city Megara torn by social upheaval and civil war. His poems present the political and ethical ideas of the Greek aristocracy.

Do not consort with bad men, but always hold to the good. Eat and drink with them, whose power is great, sit with them and please them. You will learn good from good men, but if you mingle with the bad you will lose such wisdom as you already have. Therefore consort with the good and one day you will say that I give good advice to my friends.

We seek thoroughbred rams, asses, and horses, Cyrnus, and a man wants offspring of good breeding. But in marriage a good man does not decline to marry the bad daughter of a bad father, if he gives him much wealth. Nor does the wife of a bad man refuse to be his bedfellow if he be rich, preferring wealth to goodness. For they value possessions and a good man marries a woman of bad stock and the bad a woman of good. Wealth mixes the breed. So do not wonder, son of Polypaus, that the race of your citizens is obscured since bad things are mixed with good.

It is easier to beget and rear a man than to put good sense into him. No one has ever discovered a way to make a fool wise or a bad man good. If God had given the sons of Asclepius the knowledge to heal the evil nature and mischievous mind of man, great and frequent would be their pay. If thought could be made and put into a man, the son of a good man would never become bad, since he would obey good counsel. But you will never make the bad man good by teaching.

The best thing the gods give to men, Cyrnus, is judgment; judgment contains the ends of everything. O happy is the man who has it in his mind; it is much greater than destructive insolence and grievous satiety. There are no evils among mortals worse than these—for every evil, Cyrnus, comes out of them. ❑

Trans. By Donald Kagan in *Sources in Greek Political Thought*, ed. by D. Kagan (New York: Free Press, 1965), pp. 39–40.

and the cry of the crane that announced the time of year to plow "bites the heart of the man without oxen."

Autumn and winter were the time for cutting wood, building wagons, and making tools. Late winter was the time to tend to the vines, May the time to harvest the grain, July to winnow and store it. Only at the height of summer's heat did Hesiod allow for rest, but when September came, it was time to harvest the grapes. No sooner was that task done than the cycle started again. The work went on under the burning sun and in the freezing cold.

Hesiod wrote nothing of pleasure or entertainment. Less austere farmers than Hesiod gathered at the blacksmith's shop for warmth and companionship in winter, and even he must have taken part in religious rites and festivals that were accompanied by some kind of entertainment, but the life of the peasant farmers was hard and their pleasures few.

ARISTOCRATS. Most aristocrats were rich enough to employ many hired laborers, sometimes sharecroppers and sometimes even slaves, to work their extensive lands and were therefore able to enjoy leisure for other activities. The center of aristocratic social life was the drinking party, or *symposion*. This activity was not a mere drinking bout, meant to remove inhibi-

tions and produce oblivion. The Greeks, in fact, almost always mixed their wine with water, and one of the goals of the participants was to drink as much as the others without becoming drunk.

The *symposion* was a carefully organized occasion, with a "king" chosen to set the order of events and to determine that night's mixture of wine and water. Only men took part, and they ate and drank as they reclined on couches along the walls of the room. The sessions began with prayers and libations to the gods. Usually there were games, such as dice or *kottabos*, in which wine was flicked from the cups at different targets. Sometimes dancing girls or flute girls offered entertainment. Frequently, the aristocratic participants provided their own amusements with songs, poetry, or even philosophical disputes. Characteristically, these took the form of contests, with some kind of prize for the winner, for aristocratic values continued to emphasize competition and the need to excel, whatever the arena.

This aspect of aristocratic life appears in the athletic contest that became widespread early in the sixth century B.C. The games included running events; the long jump; the discus and javelin throws; the *pentathlon*, which included all of these; boxing; wrestling; and the chariot race. Only the rich could afford to raise, train, and race horses, so the chariot race was a special preserve of aristocracy. Wrestling, however, was also especially favored by the nobility, and the *palaestra* where they practiced became an important social center for the aristocracy. The contrast between the hard, drab life of the peasants and the leisured and lively one of the aristocrats could hardly be greater.

Culture

RELIGION. Like most ancient peoples, the Greeks were polytheists, and religion played an important part in their lives. A great part of Greek art and literature was closely connected with religion, as was the life of the *polis* in general. The Greek pantheon consisted of the twelve gods who lived on Mount Olympus: Zeus, the father of the gods; his wife, Hera; his brother, Poseidon, god of the seas and earthquakes; his sisters, Hestia, goddess of the hearth, and Demeter, goddess of agriculture and marriage; and his children— Aphrodite, goddess of love and beauty; Apollo, god of the sun, music, poetry, and prophecy; Ares, god of war; Artemis, goddess of the moon and the hunt; Athena, goddess of wisdom and the arts; Hephaestus, god of fire and metallurgy; and Hermes, messenger of the gods who was connected with commerce and cunning.

On the one hand, these gods were seen as behaving very much like mortals, with all the human foibles, except that they were superhuman in these as well as in their strength and immortality. On the other hand, Zeus, at least, was seen as being a source of human justice, and even the Olympians were understood to be subordinate to the Fates. Each *polis* had one of the Olympians as its guardian deity and worshiped the god in its own special way, but all the gods were Panhellenic. In the eighth and seventh centuries B.C., common shrines were established at Olympia for the worship of Zeus, at Delphi for Apollo, at the Isthmus of Corinth for Poseidon, and at Nemea once again for Zeus. Each held athletic contests in honor of its god, to which all Greeks were invited and for which a sacred truce was declared.

The worship of these deities did not involve great emotion. It was a matter of offering prayer, libations, and gifts in return for protection and favors from the god during the lifetime of the worshiper. There was no hope of immortality for the average human and little moral teaching. Most Greeks seem to have held to the commonsense notion that justice lay in paying one's debts; that civic virtue consisted of worshiping the state deities in the traditional way, performing the required public services, and fighting in defense of the state; and that private morality meant to do good to one's friends and harm to one's enemies.

In the sixth century B.C., the influence of the cult of Apollo at Delphi and of his oracle there became very great. The oracle was the most important of several that helped satisfy human craving for a clue to the future. The priests of Apollo preached moderation; their advice was exemplified in the two famous sayings identified with Apollo: "Know thyself" and "Nothing in excess." Humans need self-control *(sophrosynē)*. Its opposite is arrogance *(hybris)*, which is brought on by

The temple of Apollo at Delphi. The shrine of Apollo at Delphi was one of the oldest and holiest religious sites in Greece. For centuries pilgrims came from all over the Mediterranean to consult the god's oracle there. [Alinari-SCALA.]

The god Dionysus dancing with two maenads, who were female followers of him. The vase decoration is by a painter who worked between about 559 and 525 B.C. [Photograph Bibliothèque Nationale, Paris.]

excessive wealth or good fortune. *Hybris* leads to moral blindness and finally to divine vengeance. This theme of moderation and the dire consequences of its absence was central to Greek popular morality and appears frequently in Greek literature.

The somewhat cold religion of the Olympian gods and of the cult of Apollo did little to attend to human fears, hopes, and passions. For these needs, the Greeks turned to other deities and rites. Of these, the most popular was Dionysus, a god of nature and fertility, of the grape vine and drunkenness and sexual abandon. In some of his rites, the god was followed by maenads, female devotees who cavorted by night, ate raw flesh, and were reputed to tear to pieces any creature they came across.

POETRY. The great changes sweeping through the Greek world were also reflected in the poetry of the sixth century B.C. The lyric style, whether sung by a chorus or by one singer, predominated. Sappho of Lesbos, Anacreon of Teos, and Simonides of Cous composed personal poetry, often speaking of the pleasure

and agony of love. Alcaeus of Mytilene, an aristocrat driven from his city by a tyrant, wrote bitter invective.

Perhaps the most interesting poet of the century from a political point of view was Theognis of Megara. An aristocrat who lived through a tyranny, an unusually chaotic and violent democracy, and an oligarchy that restored order but that ended the rule of the old aristocracy. Theognis was the spokesman for the old, defeated aristocracy of birth. He divided everyone into two classes, the noble and the base; the former were good, the latter bad. Those nobly born had to associate only with others like themselves if they were to preserve their virtue; if they mingled with the base, they became base. Those born base, on the other hand, could never become noble. Only nobles could aspire to virtue, and only nobles possessed the critical moral and intellectual qualities, respect or honor, and judgment. These qualities could not be taught; they were innate. Even so, nobles had to be carefully guarded against corruption by wealth or by mingling with the base. Intermarriage between the noble and the base was especially condemned. These were the ideas of the unreconstructed nobility, whose power had been destroyed or reduced in most Greek states by this time. These ideas remained alive in aristocratic hearts throughout the next century and greatly influenced later thinkers, Plato, again, among them.

The Major City-States

Generalization about the *polis* becomes difficult not long after its appearance, for though the states had much in common, some of them developed in unique ways. Sparta and Athens, which became the two most powerful Greek states, had especially unusual histories.

Sparta

At first, Sparta seems not to have been strikingly different from other *poleis*, but about 725 B.C., the pressure of population and land hunger led the Spartans to launch a war of conquest against their western neighbor, Messenia. This First Messenian War gave the Spartans as much land as they would ever need, and the reduction of the Messenians to the status of serfs, or Helots, meant that the Spartans did not even have to work the land that supported them.

The turning point in Spartan history came with the Second Messenian War, a rebellion of the Helots, assisted by Argos and some other Peloponnesian cities, about 650 B.C. The war was long and bitter and at one point threatened the existence of Sparta. After the revolt had been put down, the Spartans were forced to reconsider their way of life. They could not expect to keep down the Helots, who outnumbered them perhaps ten to one, and still maintain the old free-and-easy habits typical of most Greeks. Faced with the choice of making drastic changes and sacrifices or abandoning their control of Messenia, the Spartans chose to introduce fundamental reforms that turned their city forever after into a military academy and camp.

SOCIETY. The new system that emerged late in the sixth century B.C. exerted control over each Spartan from birth, when officials of the state decided which infants were physically fit to survive. At the age of seven, the Spartan boy was taken from his mother and turned over to young instructors who trained him in athletics and the military arts and taught him to endure privation, to bear physical pain, and to live off the country, by theft if necessary. At twenty the Spartan youth was enrolled in the army and lived in barracks with his companions until the age of thirty. Marriage was permitted, but a strange sort of marriage it was, for the Spartan male could visit his wife only infrequently and by stealth. At thirty, he became a full citizen, an "equal," and was allowed to live in his own house with his wife, though he took his meals at a public mess in the company of fifteen comrades. His food, a simple diet without much meat or wine, was provided by his own plot of land, which was worked by Helots. Military service was required until the age of sixty; only then could the Spartan retire at last to his home and family.

This educational program extended to the women, too. They were not given military training, but female infants were examined for fitness to survive in the same way as males. Girls were given gymnastic training, were permitted greater freedom of movement than among other Greeks, and were equally indoctrinated with the idea of service to Sparta. The entire system was designed to change the natural feelings of devotion to wife, children, and family into a more powerful commitment to the *polis*. Privacy, luxury, and even comfort were sacrificed to the purpose of producing soldiers whose physical powers, training, and discipline made them the best in the world. Nothing that might turn the mind away from duty was permitted. The very use of coins was forbidden lest it corrupt the desires of Spartans. Neither family nor money was allowed to interfere with the only ambition permitted to a Spartan male: to win glory and the respect of his peers by bravery in war.

GOVERNMENT. The Spartan constitution was mixed, containing elements of monarchy, oligarchy, and democracy. There were two kings, whose power was limited by law and also by the rivalry that usually existed between the two royal houses.

The oligarchic element was represented by a king and a council of elders consisting of twenty-eight men over sixty, who were elected for life. These elders had important judicial functions, sitting as a court in cases involving the kings. They also were consulted before

MAP 3-3 ATTICA AND VICINITY *Citizens of all towns in Attica were also citizens of Athens. Sparta's region, Laconia, was in the Peloponnesus. Near-by states were members of the Peloponnesian League under Sparta's leadership.*

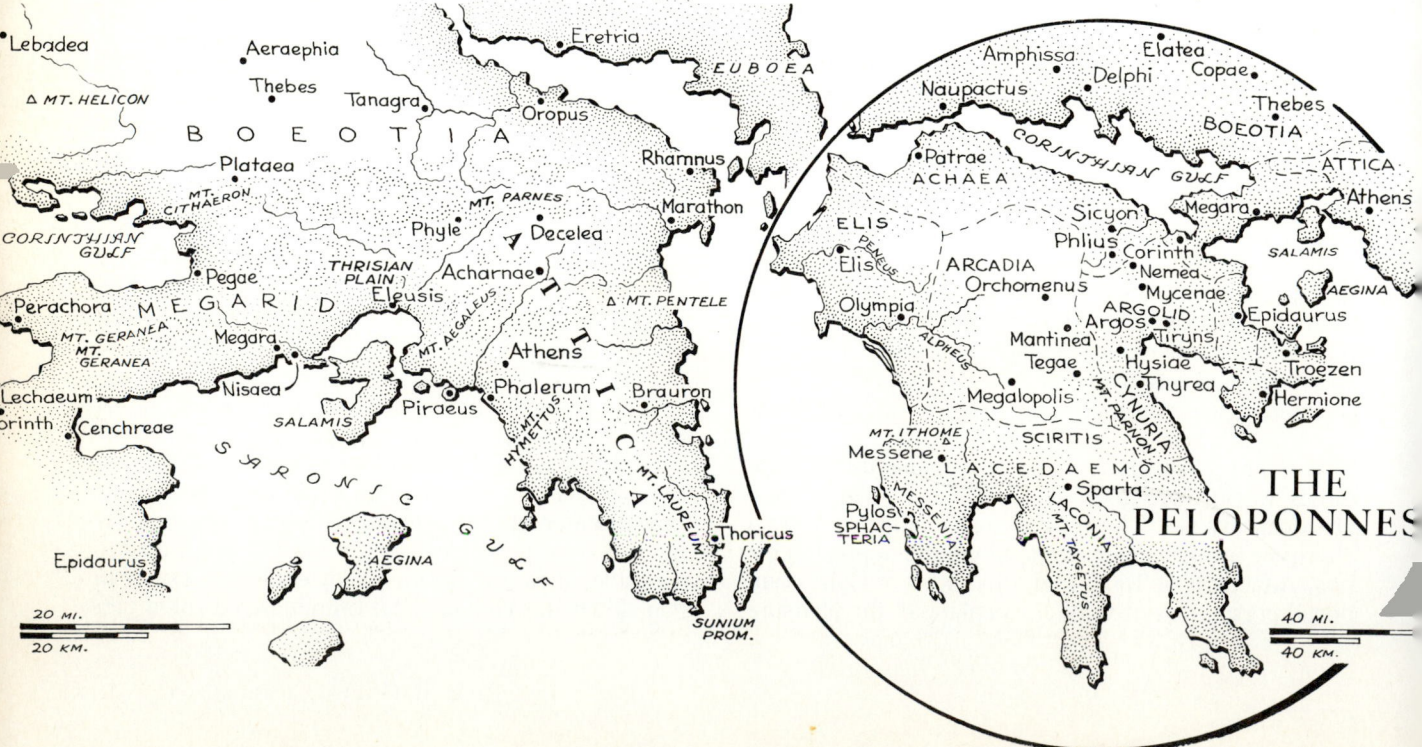

any proposal was put before the assembly of Spartan citizens. In a traditional society like Sparta's, they must have had considerable influence.

The Spartan assembly consisted of all males over thirty. Theoretically, they were the final authority, but because, in practice, debate was carried on by magis-

Tyrtaeus Describes Excellence: Code of the Citizen Soldier

The military organization of citizen soldiers for the defense of the polis *and the idea of the* polis *itself, which permeated Greek political thought, found echoes in Greek lyric poetry. A major example is this poem by Tyrtaeus, a Spartan poet who wrote about 625* B.C. *It gives important evidence on the nature of warfare in the phalanx and the values taught by the* polis.

I would not say anything for a man nor take
    account of him
      for any speed of his feet or wrestling skill he
      might have,
not if he had the size of a Cyclops and strength to
    go with it,
      not if he could outrun Bóreas, the North Wind
      of Thrace,
not if he were more handsome and gracefully
    formed than Tithónos,
      or had more riches than Midas had, or Kinyras
      too,
not if he were more of a king than Tantalid Pelops,
    or had the power of speech and persuasion
    Adrastos had,
not if he had all splendors except for a fighting
    spirit.
      For no man ever proves himself a good man in
      war unless he can endure to face the blood
      and the slaughter,
      go close against the enemy and fight with his
      hands.
Here is courage, mankind's finest possession, here
    is
      the noblest prize that a young man can
      endeavor to win,
and it is a good thing his city and all the people
    share with him
      when a man plants his feet and stands in the
      foremost spears
relentlessly, all thought of foul flight completely
    forgotten,
      and has well trained his heart to be steadfast
      and to endure,
and with words encourages the man who is
    stationed beside him.
      Here is a man who proves himself to be valiant
      in war.
With a sudden rush he turns to flight the rugged
    battalions
      of the enemy, and sustains the bearing waves
      of assault.

And he who so falls among the champions and loses
    his sweet life,
      so blessing with honor his city, his father, and
      all his people,
with wounds in his chest, where the spear that he
    was facing has transfixed
      that massive guard of his shield, and gone
      through his breastplate as well,
why, such a man is lamented alike by the young
    and the elders,
      and all his city goes into mourning and grieves
      for his loss.
His tomb is pointed out with price, and so are his
    children,
      and his children's children, and afterward all
      the race that is his.
His shining glory is never forgotten, his name is
    remembered,
      and he becomes an immortal, though he lies
      under the ground,
when one who was a brave man has been killed by
    the furious War God
      standing his ground and fighting hard for his
      children and land.
But if he escapes the doom of death, the destroyer
    of bodies,
      and wins his battle, and bright renown for the
      work of his spear,
all men give place to him alike, the youth and the
    elders,
      and much joy comes his way before he goes
      down to the dead.
Aging he has reputation among his citizens. No one
    tries to interfere with his honors or all he
    deserves;
all men withdraw before his presence, and yield
    their seats to him,
      and youth, and the men of his age, and even
      those older than he.
Thus a man should endeavor to reach this high
    place of courage
      with all his heart, and, so trying, never be
      backward in war. ❑

Greek Lyrics, trans. by Richmond Lattimore (Chicago: University of Chicago Press, 1949, 1950, 1955), pp. 14–15.

trates, elders, and kings alone, and because voting was usually by acclamation, the assembly's real function was to ratify decisions already taken or to decide between positions favored by the leading figures. In addition, Sparta had a unique institution, the board of ephors. This consisted of five men elected annually by the assembly. Originally they appear to have been intended to check the power of the kings, but gradually they acquired other important functions: they controlled foreign policy, oversaw the generalship of the kings on campaign, presided at the assembly, and guarded against rebellion by the Helots.

By about 550 B.C., the Spartan system was well established, and its limitations had been made plain. Suppression of the Helots required all the effort and energy that Sparta had. The Spartans could expand no further, but they could not allow unruly independent neighbors to cause unrest that might inflame the Helots.

When the Spartans defeated Tegea, their northern neighbor, they imposed an unusual peace. Instead of taking away land and subjecting the defeated state, Sparta left the Tegeans their land and their freedom. In exchange, they required the Tegeans to follow the Spartan lead in foreign affairs and to supply a fixed number of soldiers to Sparta on demand. This became the model for Spartan relations with the other states in the Peloponnesus, and soon Sparta was the leader of an alliance that included every Peloponnesian state but Argos; modern scholars have named this alliance the Peloponnesian League. It provided the Spartans with the security they needed, and it also made Sparta the most powerful *polis* in Hellenic history. By 500 B.C., Sparta and the league had given the Greeks a force capable of facing mighty threats from abroad.

Athens

In the seventh century B.C., Athens was a typical aristocratic *polis*. The aristocrats held the most and best land and dominated religious and political life. There was no written law, and decisions were rendered by powerful nobles on the basis of tradition and, most likely, self-interest. The state was governed by the Areopagus, a council of nobles deriving its name from the hill where it held its sessions. Annually, the council elected nine magistrates who joined the Areopagus after their year in office. Because they served for only a year, were checked by their colleagues, and looked forward to a lifetime as members of the Areopagus after their terms were ended, it is plain that the aristocratic council was the true master of the state.

In the seventh century B.C., the peaceful life of Athens experienced some disturbances, which were caused in part by quarrels within the nobility and in part by the beginnings of an agrarian crisis.

The root of Athens' troubles were agricultural. Many Athenians worked family farms, from which they obtained most of their living. It appears that they planted wheat, the staple crop, year after year without rotating fields or using sufficient fertilizer. In time, this procedure exhausted the soil and led to bad crops. To survive, the farmer had to borrow from a wealthy neighbor to get through the year. In return, he promised one sixth of the next year's crop. The arrangement was marked by the deposit of an inscribed stone on the entailed farm. Bad harvests persisted, and soon the debtor had to pledge his wife and children and himself as surety for the loans needed for survival. As bad times continued, many Athenians defaulted and were enslaved. Some were even sold abroad. Revolutionary pressures grew among the poor, who began to demand the abolition of debt and a redistribution of the land.

SOLON AND REFORM. The circumstances might easily have brought about class warfare and tyranny, but the remarkable conciliatory spirit of Athens intervened. In the year 594 B.C., as tradition has it, the Athenians elected Solon, a successful general and talented poet, with extraordinary powers to legislate and revise the constitution. Immediately, he attacked the agrarian problem by canceling current debts and forbidding future loans secured by the person of the borrower. He helped bring back many Athenians enslaved abroad as well as freeing those in Athens enslaved for debt. This program was called the "shaking off of burdens." It did not, however, solve the fundamental economic problem, and Solon did not redistribute the land. In the short run, therefore, he did not put an end to the economic crisis, but his other economic actions had profound success in the long run. He forbade the export of wheat and encouraged that of olive oil. This policy had the effect of making wheat more available in Attica and encouraging the cultivation of olive oil and wine as cash crops. By the fifth century B.C., this form of agriculture had become so profitable that much Athenian land was diverted from grain production to the cultivation of cash crops, and Athens became dependent on imported wheat.

Solon also changed the Athenian standards of weights and measures to conform with those of Corinth and Euboea and the cities of the East. This change also encouraged commerce and turned Athens in the direction that would lead to great prosperity in the fifth century. He also encouraged industry by offering citizenship to foreign artisans, and his success is reflected in the development of the outstanding Attic pottery of the sixth century.

Solon also significantly changed the constitution. All male adults whose fathers were citizens were citizens, too, and to their number he added immigrants who were offered citizenship. All these Athenian citizens were divided into four classes on the basis of wealth, measured by annual agricultural production.

Men whose property produced five hundred measures were called five-hundred-measure men, and those producing three hundred measures were called cavalry; these two classes alone could hold office and sit on the Areopagus.

Producers of two hundred measures were called owners of a team of oxen; they were allowed to serve as hoplites. They could be elected to the council of four hundred chosen by all the citizens, one hundred from each tribe. Solon seems to have meant this council to serve as a check on the Areopagus and to prepare any business that needed to be put before the assembly.

The last class, producing less than two hundred measures, were the *thetes*. They voted in the popular assembly for the magistrates and the council members and on any other business brought before them by the magistrates. They also sat on a new popular court established by Solon. At first, this court must have had little power, for most cases continued to be heard in the country by local barons and in Athens by the aristocratic Areopagus. But the new court was recognized as a court of appeal, and by the fifth century B.C., almost all cases came before the popular courts.

PISISTRATUS THE TYRANT. Solon's efforts to avoid factional strife failed. Within a few years, contention reached such a degree that no magistrates could be chosen. Out of this turmoil emerged the first Athenian tyranny. Pisistratus, a nobleman, faction leader, and military hero, seized power firmly. His rule rested on the force provided by mercenary soldiers. He engaged in great programs of public works, urban improvement, and religious piety. Temples were built and religious centers expanded and improved. New religious festivals were introduced, such as the one dedicated to Dionysus, the god of fertility, wine, and ecstatic religious worship imported from Phrygia in Asia Minor. Old ones, like the Great Panathenaic festival, were amplified and given greater public appeal. Poets and artists were supported to add cultural luster to the court of the tyrant.

Pisistratus aimed at increasing the power of the central government at the expense of the nobles. The festival of Dionysus and the Great Panathenaic festival helped fix attention on the capital city, as did the new temples and the reconstruction of the Agora as the center of public life. Circuit judges were sent out into the country to hear cases, another feature that weakened the power of the local barons. All this time, Pisistratus made no formal change in the Solonian constitution. Assembly, councils, and courts met; magistrates and councils were elected; Pisistratus merely saw to it that his supporters were chosen. The intended effect was to blunt the sharp edge of tyranny with the appearance of constitutional government, and it worked. The rule of Pisistratus was remembered as popular and mild. The unintended effect was to give the Athenians more experience in the procedures of self-government and a growing taste for it.

INVASION BY SPARTA. Pisistratus was succeeded by his oldest son, Hippias, who followed his father's ways at first. In 514 B.C., however, brother Hipparchus was murdered as a result of a private quarrel. Hippias became nervous, suspicious, and harsh. At last, one of the noble clans exiled by the sons of Pisistratus, the Alcmaeonids, won favor with the influential oracle at Delphi and used its support to persuade Sparta to attack the Athenian tyranny. Led by their ambitious king, Cleomenes I, the Spartans marched into Attica in 510 B.C. and deposed Hippias, who went into exile to the Persian court. The tyranny was over.

The Spartans must have hoped to leave Athens in friendly hands, and indeed Cleomenes' friend Isagoras held the leading position in Athens after the withdrawal of the Spartan army. However, he was not unopposed. Clisthenes of the restored Alcmaeonid clan was his chief rival who, however, lost out in the political struggle among the noble factions. Isagoras seems to have tried to restore a version of the pre-Solonian aristocratic state. As part of his plan, he carried through a purification of the citizen lists, removing those who had been enfranchised by Solon or Pisistratus and any others thought to have a doubtful claim. Clisthenes then took an unprecedented action by turning to the people for political support and won it with a program of great popular appeal. In response, Isagoras called in the Spartans again; Cleomenes arrived and allowed the expulsion from Athens of Clisthenes and a large number of his supporters. But the Athenian political consciousness, ignited by Solon and kept alive under Pisistratus, was fanned by the popular appeal of Clisthenes. The people would not hear of an aristocratic restoration and drove out the Spartans and Isagoras with them. Clisthenes and his allies returned, ready to put their program into effect.

CLISTHENES, THE FOUNDER OF DEMOCRACY. A central aim of Clisthenes' reforms was to diminish the influence of traditional localities and regions in Athenian life, for these were an important source of power for the nobility and of factions in the state.

Clisthenes immediately enrolled the disenfranchised who had supported him in the struggle with Isagoras. Ten new tribes replaced the traditional four. The composition of each tribe guaranteed that no region would dominate any of them. Because the tribes had common religious activities and fought as regimental units, the new organization would also increase devotion to the *polis* and diminish regional divisions and personal loyalty to local barons.

A new council of five hundred was invented to replace the Solonian council of four hundred. Final authority in all things rested with the assembly composed of all adult male Athenian citizens. Debate was free and open; any Athenian could submit legislation, offer amendments, or argue the merits of any question. It is fair to call Clisthenes the father of Athenian democracy. He did not alter the property qualifications of Solon, but his enlargement of the citizen rolls, his diminution of the power of the aristocrats, and his elevation of the role of the assembly, with its effective and manageable council, all give him a firm claim to that title.

As a result of the work of Solon, Pisistratus, and

Aristogeiton and Harmodius were Athenian aristocrats who were slain while assassinating Hipparchos, brother of the tyrant Hippias. After the overthrow of the Pisistratids, the Athenians erected a famous statue to honor their memory. This is a Roman Copy. [Alinari-SCALA.]

CA. 725–710 B.C.	First Messenian War
CA. 650–625 B.C.	Second Messenian War
632 B.C.	Cylon tries to establish a tyranny at Athens
621 B.C.	Draco publishes legal code at Athens
594 B.C.	Solon institutes reforms at Athens
CA. 560–550 B.C.	Sparta defeats Tegea: Beginning of Peloponnesian League
546–527 B.C.	Pisistratus reigns as tyrant at Athens (main period)
510 B.C.	Hippias, son of Pisistratus, deposed as tyrant of Athens
CA. 508–501 B.C.	Clisthenes institutes reforms at Athens

Clisthenes, Athens entered the fifth century B.C. well on the way to prosperity and democracy. It was much more centralized and united than it had been, and was ready to take its place among the major states that would lead the defense of Greece against the dangers that lay ahead.

The Persian Wars

The Greeks' period of fortunate isolation and freedom at last came to an end. In the middle of the sixth century B.C., these Greek cities of Asia Minor came under the control of Lydia and its king, Croesus (CA. 560–546 B.C.). The Lydian rule seems not to have been very harsh, but the Persian conquest of Lydia in 546 B.C. brought a subjugation that was less pleasant.

The Persians required their subjects to pay tribute and to serve in the Persian army. They ruled the Greek cities through local individuals, who governed their cities as "tyrants." The Ionians had been moving in the direction of democracy and were not pleased with monarchical rule, but most of the "tyrants" were not harsh. The Persian tribute was not excessive, and there was general prosperity.

The Ionian Rebellion

The Ionian Greeks, nevertheless, preferred to be free and when the opportunity for liberty came they seized upon it. The private troubles of the ambitious tyrant of Miletus, Aristagoras, started the Ionian rebellion of 499 B.C. He had urged a Persian expedition against the island of Naxos; when it failed, he feared the consequences and organized the rebellion. To gain support, he overthrew the tyrannies and proclaimed democratic constitutions. Then he turned to the mainland states for help. As the most powerful Greek state, Sparta was naturally the first stop, but the Spartans would have none of Aristagoras' promises of easy victory and great wealth.

Aristagoras next sought help at Athens, and there the assembly agreed and voted to send a fleet of twenty ships to help the rebels. The Athenians were related to the Ionians and had close ties of religion and tradition with the rebels. The Athenian expedition was strengthened by five ships from Eretria in Euboea, which participated out of gratitude for past favors.

In 498 B.C., the Athenians and their allies made a swift march and a surprise attack on Sardis, the old capital of Lydia and now the seat of the satrap, and burned it. This caused the revolt to spread throughout the Greek cities of Asia Minor outside Ionia, but the Ionians could not follow it up. The Athenians withdrew and took no further part, and gradually the Persians imposed their will. In 495 B.C., they defeated the Ionian fleet at Lade, and in the next year, they wiped out Miletus. Many men were killed; others were transported to the Persian Gulf, and the women and children were enslaved. The Ionian rebellion was over.

The War in Greece

In 490 B.C., the Persians launched an expedition directly across the Aegean to punish Athens, to restore Hippias, and to gain control of the Aegean Sea (see Map 3.3). The resistance was led by Miltiades, an Athenian and an outstanding soldier who had fled from Persian service after earning the anger of Darius (reigned 521–486 B.C.). His knowledge of the Persian army and his distaste for submission to Persia made him an ideal leader. He led the army to Marathon in Attica and won a decisive victory. The battle at Marathon (490 B.C.) was of enormous importance to the future of Greek civilization. A Persian victory would have destroyed Athenian freedom, and the conquest of all the mainland Greeks would have followed. The greatest achievements of Greek culture, most of which lay in the future, would have been impossible under Persian rule. The Athenian victory, on the other hand, made a positive contribution to those achievements. It instilled in the Athenians a sense of confidence and price in their *polis*, and themselves.

For the Persians, Marathon was only a small and temporary defeat, but it was annoying. Internal troubles, however, prevented swift revenge. In 481 B.C., Darius' successor, Xerxes (reigned 486–465 B.C.), gathered an army of at least 150,000 men and a navy of more than six hundred ships for the conquest of Greece. The Greeks did not make good use of the

Greek hoplite attacking a Persian soldier. The contrast between the Greek's heavy metal body armor, large shield, and long spear and the cloth and leather garments of the Persian gives some indication of the reason for the ultimate Greek victory. This Attic red-figure vase is said to be from the island of Rhodes and was made about 475 B.C. [Metropolitan Museum of Art, New York; Rogers Fund, 1906.]

discovered a rich vein of silver in the state mines, and Themistocles persuaded them to use the profits to increase their fleet. By 480 B.C., Athens had over two hundred ships, the backbone of the navy that defeated the Persians.

As the Persian army gathered south of the Hellespont, only thirty-one Greek states out of hundreds were willing to fight. They were led by Sparta, Athen, Corinth, and Aegina. In the spring of 480 B.C., Xerxes launched his invasion. The Persian strategy was to march into Greece, destroy Athens, defeat the Greek army, and add the Greeks to the number of Persian subjects. The huge Persian army needed to keep in touch with the fleet for supplies. If the Greeks could defeat the Persian navy, the army could not remain in Greece long. Themistocles knew that the Aegean was subject to sudden devastating storms that might damage or destroy the enemy fleet. His strategy was to delay the Persian army and then to bring on the kind of naval battle he might hope to win.

The Greek League, founded specifically to resist this Persian invasion, met at Corinth as the Persians were ready to cross the Hellespont. The league chose Sparta as leader on land and sea and sent a force to Tempe to try to defend Thessaly. Tempe proved to be indefensible, so the Greeks retreated and took up new positions at Thermopylae (the "hot gates") on land and off Artemisium at sea. The opening between the mountains and the sea at Thermopylae was so narrow that it might be held by a smaller army against a much larger one. The Spartans sent their king, Leonidas, with three hundred of their own citizens and enough allies to make a total of about nine thousand. The Greeks may have intended to hold only long enough to permit the Athenians to evacuate Athens, or to force a sea battle, or they may have hoped to hold Thermopylae until the Persians were discouraged enough to withdraw. Perhaps they thought of all these possibilities, for they were not mutually contradictory.

Severe storms wrecked a large number of Persian ships while the Greek fleet waited safely in their protected harbor. Then Xerxes attacked Thermopylae, and for two days the Greeks butchered his best troops without serious loss to themselves. On the third day, however, a traitor showed the Persians a mountain trail that permitted them to attack the Greeks from behind. Many allies escaped, but Leonidas and his three hundred Spartans all died. At about the same time, the Greek and Persian fleets fought an indecisive battle, and the fall of Thermopylae forced the Greek navy to withdraw.

If an inscription discovered in 1959 is authentic, Themistocles had foreseen this possibility, and the Athenians had begun to evacuate their homeland and move to defend Salamis. The fate of Greece was decided in the narrow waters to the east of the island.

delay, but Athens was an exception. Themistocles had become its leading politician, and he had always wanted to turn Athens into a naval power. The first step was to build a fortified port at Piraeus during his archonship in 493 B.C. A decade later, the Athenians

CA. 560–546 B.C.	Greek cities of Asia Minor conquered by Croesus of Lydia
546 B.C.	Cyrus of Persia conquers Lydia and gains control of Greek cities
499–494 B.C.	Greek cities rebel (Ionian rebellion)
490 B.C.	Battle of Marathon
480–479 B.C.	Xerxes' invasion of Greece
480 B.C.	Battles of Thermopylae, Artemisium, and Salamis
479 B.C.	Battles of Plataea and Mycale

Themistocles persuaded the reluctant Peloponnesians to stay by threatening to remove all the Athenians and settle anew in Italy. The Spartans knew that they and the other Greeks could not hope to win without the aid of the Athenians. The Greek ships were fewer, slower, and less maneuverable than those of the Persians, so the Greeks put soldiers on their ships and relied chiefly on hand-to-hand combat. The Persians lost more than half their ships and retreated to Asia with a good part of their army, but the danger was not over yet. The Persian general Mardonius spent the winter in central Greece, and in the spring, he unsuccessfully tried to win the Athenians away from the Greek League. The Spartan regent, Pausanias, then led the largest Greek army up to that time to confront Mardonius in Boeotia. At Plataea, in the summer of 479 B.C., Mardonius died in battle, and his army fled toward home. Meanwhile, the Ionian Greeks urged King Leotychidas, the Spartan commander of the fleet, to fight the Persian fleet at Samos. At Mycale, on the coast nearby, Leotychidas destroyed the Persian camp and its fleet offshore. The Persians fled the Aegean and Ionia. For the moment, at least, the Persian threat was gone.

The Rise of Greek Civilization in World Perspective

Hellenic civilization, a unique cultural experience, is at the root of Western civilization. It has powerfully influenced the peoples of the modern world. Itself influenced by the great Bronze-Age civilization of Crete, it emerged from the collapse of the Bronze-Age civilization on the Greek mainland that we call Myce-naean. These earlier civilizations resembled others in Egypt, Mesopotamia, Palestine–Syria, China, India, and elsewhere more than they did the Hellenic version that sprang from them. They had highly developed urban lives; a system of writing; strong, centralized monarchical systems of government ruling over tightly organized, large bureaucracies; hierarchical social systems; professional standing armies—and a regular system of taxation to support all this. To a greater or lesser degree, (more in Egypt, less in China), these early civilizations tended toward cultural stability and uniformity. The striking fact about the emergence of Hellenic civilization was its sharp departure from this pattern of development. The collapse of the Myce-naean world produced a harsh drop in the level of material well-being for the Greeks. It also caused a decline in the cultural level. Cities were swept away and replaced by small farm villages. Trade was all but ended, and communications not only between the Greeks and other peoples, but even among the Greeks themselves, were sharply curtailed. The art of writing was lost for more than three centuries. The matrix of Hellenic civilization was a dark age in which a small number of poor, isolated, illiterate people were ignored by the rest of the world and let alone to develop their own kind of society.

During the three and a half centuries from about 1100 to 750 B.C., the Greeks set the foundations for their great achievements. The crucial unit in the new Greek way of life was the *polis*, the Hellenic city-state. There were hundreds of them, ranging in size from a few thousand inhabitants to hundreds of thousands. Each city-state evoked a kind of loyalty and attachment by its citizens that made the idea of dissolving one's own *polis* into a larger unit unthinkable. The result was a dynamic, many-faceted, competitive, sometimes chaotic society in which rivalry for excellence and victory had the highest value.

This competitive quality marks Greek life throughout its history. Its negative aspect was constant warfare among the states. Its positive side was its extraordinary achievement in literature and art, where competition, sometimes formal and organized, spurred on poets and artists.

The *poleis* were republics. Class distinctions were less marked and less important than in other civilizations, partly because the Greeks were so poor and the differences in wealth among them were relatively small. The introduction of a new mode of fighting, the hoplite phalanx, had further leveling effects upon a class system, for it placed the safety of the state in the hands of the average farmer. Armies were made up of unpaid citizen-soldiers, who returned to their farms after a campaign. As a result, political control was shared with a relatively large portion of the people, and participation in political life was highly valued.

Even when the art of writing was newly acquired from western Semites (perhaps the Phoenicians), there was no bureaucracy, for there were no kings, and not much economic surplus to support them. Most states imposed no regular taxation. There was no separate caste of priests and little concern with any life after death. In this varied, dynamic, secular, and remarkably free context there arose a speculative natural philosophy based on observation and reason. Greek ideas formed the root of modern natural science and philosophy.

Expanded contact and trade with the rest of the world increased the wealth of many Greek cities and brought in valuable new information and ideas. Greek art was powerfully shaped by Egyptian and Near Eastern models that were always adapted and changed rather than copied. Changes often produced social and economic strain, leading to the overthrow of traditional aristocratic regimes by tyrants. Because monarchic rule was anathema to the Greeks, these regimes were temporary. They were usually replaced by oligarchies of greater or lesser breadth, but in Athens the destruction of the tyranny brought the world's first democracy. Sparta, on the other hand, developed a uniquely stable government that avoided tyranny and impressed the other Greeks.

The Greeks' time of independent development, untroubled by external forces, came to an end in the sixth century when Iran's powerful Achaemenid dynasty conquered the Greek cities of Asia Minor. When the Persian kings tried to conquer the Greek mainland, however, the leading states managed to put their quarrels aside and unite against the common enemy. Their determination to preserve their freedom carried them to victory over tremendous odds.

Suggested Readings

A. ANDREWES, *Greek Tyrants* (New York, 1963). A clear and concise account of tyranny in early Greece.

A. ANDREWES, *The Greeks* (London, 1967). A thoughtful general survey.

JOHN BOARDMAN, *The Greeks Overseas* (Harmondsworth, England, 1964). A study of the relations between the Greeks and other peoples.

A. R. BURN, *The Lyric Age of Greece* (New York, 1960). A discussion of early Greece that uses the evidence of poetry and archaeology to fill out the sparse historical record.

A. R. BURN, *Persia and the Greeks*, 2nd ed. (London, 1984). A thorough narrative and analysis of the conflict between the Persians and the Greeks down to 479 B.C.

J. B. BURY AND R. MEIGGS, *A History of Greece*, 4th ed. (London and New York, 1975). A thorough and detailed one-volume narrative history.

J. CHADWICK, *The Mycenaean World* (Cambridge, 1976). A readable account, by a man who helped decipher Mycenaean writing.

E. R. DODDS, *The Greeks and the Irrational* (1955). An excellent account of the role of the supernatural in Greek life and thought.

V. EHRENBERG, *The Greek State* (1964). A good handbook of constitutional history.

V. EHRENBERG, *From Solon to Socrates* (1968). An interpretive history that makes good use of Greek literature to illuminate politics.

J. V. FINE, *The Ancient Greeks* (1983). An excellent survey that discusses historical problems and the evidence that gives rise to them.

M. I. FINLEY, *World of Odysseus*, rev. ed. (1965). A fascinating attempt to reconstruct Homeric society.

M. I. FINLEY, *Early Greece* (1970). A succinct interpretive study.

W. G. FORREST, *The Emergence of Greek Democracy* (1966). A lively interpretation of Greek social and political developments in the archaic period.

W. G. FORREST, *A History of Sparta*, 950–192 B.C. (1968). A brief but shrewd account.

P. GREEN, *Xerxes at Salamis* (1970). A lively and stimulating history of the Persian wars.

C. HIGNETT, *A History of the Athenian Constitution* (1952). A scholarly account, somewhat too skeptical of the ancient sources.

C. HIGNETT, *Xerxes' Invasion of Greece* (1963). A valuable account, but too critical of all sources other than Herodotus.

S. HOOD, *The Minoans* (1971). A sketch of Bronze Age civilization on Crete.

D. KAGAN, *The Great Dialogue: A History of Greek Political Thought from Homer to Polybius* (1965). A discussion of the relationship between the Greek historical experience and political theory.

G. S. KIRK, *The Songs of Homer* (1962). A discussion of the Homeric epics as oral poetry.

H. D. F. KITTO, *The Greeks* (1951). A personal and illuminating interpretation of Greek culture.

W. K. LACEY, *The Family in Ancient Greece* (Ithaca, 1984).

H. L. LORIMER, *Homer and the Monuments* (1950). A study of the relationship between the Homeric poems and the evidence of archaeology.

H. MICHELL, *Sparta* (1952). A study of Spartan institutions.

O. MURRAY, *Early Greece* (1980). A lively and imaginative account of the early history of Greece to the end of the Persian War.

D. L. PAGE, *History and the Homeric Iliad*, 2nd ed. (1966). A well-written and interesting, if debatable, attempt to place the Trojan War in a historical setting.

G. M. A. RICHTER, *Archaic Greek Art* (1949).

CARL ROEBUCK, *Ionian Trade and Colonization* (1959). An introduction to the history of the Greeks in the east.

B. SNELL, *Discovery of the Mind* (1960). An important study of Greek intellectual development.

A. M. SNODGRASS, *The Dark Age of Greece* (Chicago, 1972). A good examination of the archaeological evidence.

C. G. STARR, *Origins of Greek Civilization* 1100–650 B.C. (1961). An interesting interpretation based largely on archaeology and especially on pottery styles.

C. G. STARR, *The Economic and Social Growth of Early Greece*, 800–500 B.C. (1977).

EMILY VERMEULE, *Greece in the Bronze Age* (1972). A study of the Mycenaean period.

A. G. WOODHEAD, *Greeks in the West* (1962). An account of the Greek settlements in Italy and Sicily.

W. J. WOODHOUSE, *Solon the Liberator* (1965). A discussion of the great Athenian reformer.

D. C. YOUNG, *The Olympic Myth of Greek Athletics* (Chicago, 1984). A lively challenge to the orthodox view that Greek athletes were amateurs.

The striding god from Artemisium. This bronze statue dating about 460 B.C. was found in the sea near Artemisium, the northern tip of the large Greek island of Euboea. Exactly whom he represents is not known. Some have thought him to be Poseidon holding a trident; others believe that he is Zeus hurling a thunderbolt. In either case he is a splendid representative of the early classical period of Greek sculpture and therefore now lives at the Athens archaeological museum. [Bettmann Archive.]

4 Classical and Hellenistic Greece

Classical Greece

The Greeks' remarkable victory over the Persians in 480–479 B.C. won them another period of freedom and autonomy, a time when they carried their political and cultural achievement to its height. In Athens, especially, the victory produced a great sense of confidence and ambition. Spartan withdrawal from active leadership against the Persians left a vacuum that was filled by the Delian League, which soon turned into the Athenian Empire.

At the same time as it tightened its hold over the Greek cities in and around the Aegean Sea, Athens developed an extraordinarily democratic constitution at home. Fears and jealousies of this new kind of state and empire created a split in the Greek world that led to a series of major wars. These wars impoverished Greece and left it vulnerable to conquest. In 338 B.C. Philip of Macedon conquered the Greek states, putting an end to the age of the *polis*.

The Delian League

The unity of the Greeks had shown strain even in the life-and-death struggle against the Persians. Within two years of the Persian retreat, the unity gave way almost completely and yielded to a division of the Greek world into two spheres of influence, dominated by Sparta and Athens. The need of the Ionian Greeks to obtain and defend their freedom from Persia and the desire of many Greeks to gain revenge and financial reparation for the Persian attack brought on the split.

Sparta had led the Greeks to victory, and it was natural to look to the Spartans to continue the campaign. But Sparta was ill suited to the task, which required a long-term commitment and continuous naval action far from the Peloponnesus.

The emergence of Athens as the leader of a Greek coalition against Persia was a natural development.

PAEONIA

ILLYRICUM

M A C E D O N I A

THRACE

Philippi
Abdera
Maronea

Amphipolis · Eion
· Pella
Thessalonica
Stagira

THASOS

Pactye
Cardia

CHALCIDICE

SAMOTHRACE
IMBROS

Sestos
Lampsacus

Methone
Pydna
Olynthus
Potidaea
Torone
Scione

MT.
OLYMPUS

MT.
ATHOS

LEMNOS

Abydos
Elaeus
Troy

GRANICUS

EPIRUS

Dodona

TROAD

PHR

CORCYRA

PENEIUS
Larisa

THESSALY

Ambracia
Pherae
Thysalus

MT. PELIUM

AEGEAN

Methymna

Adra-
mytt

AEOLIS

Mytilene

CAIC

Atarne

Anactorium
Sollium
ACAR-
NANIA
AETOLIA
Heraclae
Elatea
LOCRIS
Amphissa
Naupactus
MT. PARNASSUS
DELPHI

THERMOPYLAE
Oreus
ARTEMESIUM
PEPARETHUS

SKYROS

LESBOS

Phocaea
Cyme
Magn

LEUCAS

CEPHALLENIA

Chaeronea
BOEOTIA
Coronea Delium
Thespiae
Leuctra
Plataea

Chalcis
Eretria

EUBOEA

Oropus

CHIOS
Chios

Erythrae

Clazomen
Teos
Colophon

ACHAEA
ELIS
Sicyon
Corinth
ARCADIA
Elis
Nemea
Olympia
Cleonae
Mantinea
Argos

Megara
Decelea
ATHENS
Piraeus
SAL-
AMIS
ATTICA
Thoricus
Laureum

Carystus

ANDROS

Notium
Ephe

SAMOS

ZACYNTHUS

Megalopolis
Tegea
MT.
DIDYMA
Epidaurus
Hermione

AEGINA

KEOS
TENOS

SYROS

ICARIA

Miletus

Messene
LACONIA

MESSENIA
SPARTA
PELOPONNESUS
Pylos
MT.
TAYGETUS
Gythium

CYNTHOS

DELOS
MYKONOS

Halicarnassu

PAROS

NAXOS

IONIAN

SERIPHOS
SIPHNOS

AMORGUS
COS

SEA

SIKINOS
MELOS
IOS
PHOLEGANDROS

ASTYPALAEA CNIDUS

CAPE
TAENARUS
CAPE
MALEA
CYTHERA

CRETAN
SEA

CARPATHOS

100 MI.

100 KM.

Cnossus
Tylissus

MEDITERRANEAN

CRETE
Gortyna

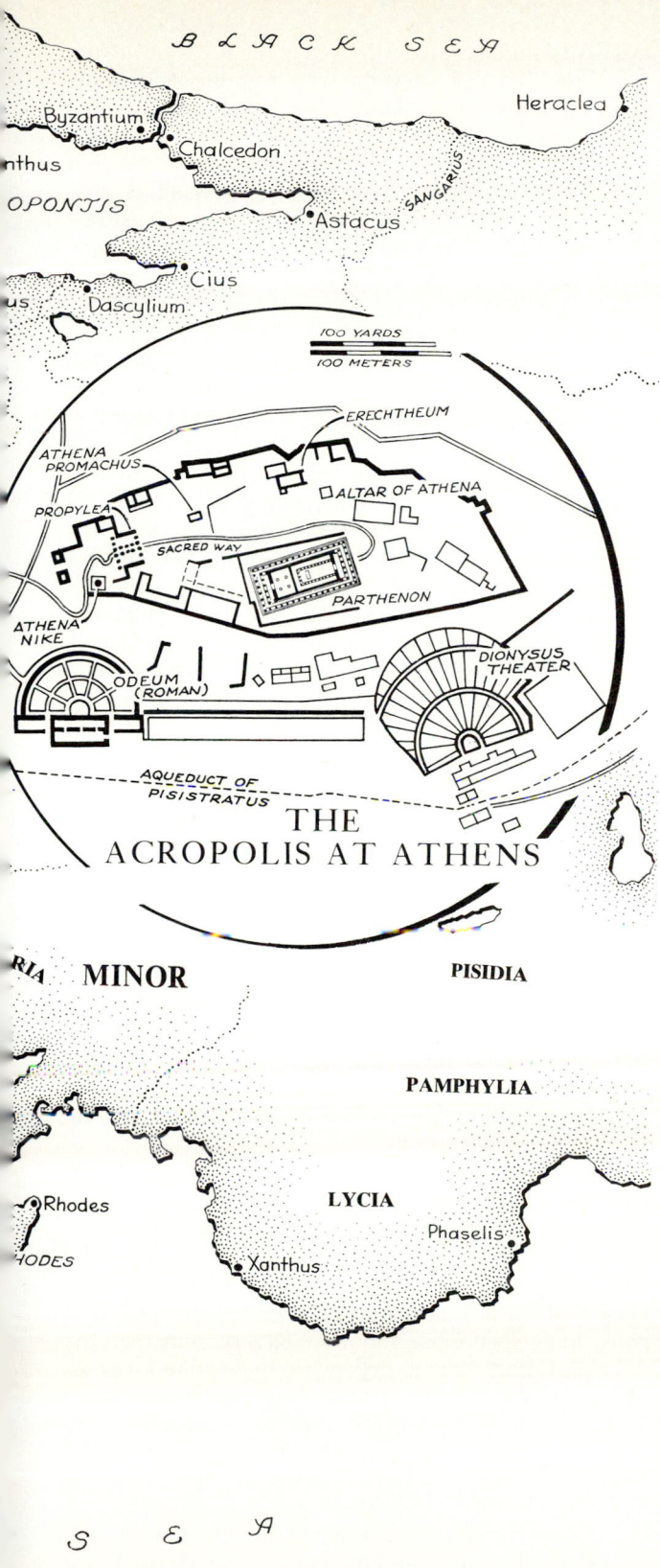

BLACK SEA

Byzantium
Chalcedon
nthus
OPONTIS
Astacus
SANGARIUS
Heraclea
Cius
Dascylium

THE ACROPOLIS AT ATHENS

100 YARDS
100 METERS

ERECHTHEUM
ATHENA PROMACHUS
ALTAR OF ATHENA
PROPYLEA
SACRED WAY
ATHENA NIKE
PARTHENON
ODEUM (ROMAN)
DIONYSUS THEATER
AQUEDUCT OF PISISTRATUS

RIA MINOR
PISIDIA
PAMPHYLIA
Rhodes
HODES
LYCIA
Xanthus
Phaselis

S E A

MAP 4-1   CLASSICAL GREECE   *Greece in the classical period* (CA. 480–338 B.C.) *centered on the Aegean Sea. Although there were important Greek settlements in Italy, Sicily, and all around the Black Sea, the area shown in this general reference map embraced the vast majority of Greek states. The inset shows the location of the major monuments still visible on the Athenian Acropolis of the classical period.*

Athens had become the leading naval power in Greece, and the same motives that had led Athens to support the Ionian revolt moved it to try to drive the Persians from the Aegean and the Hellespont. The Ionians were at least as eager for the Athenians to take the helm as the Athenians were to accept the responsibility and opportunity.

In the winter of 478–477 B.C., the islanders, the Greeks from the coast of Asia Minor, and some from other Greek cities on the Aegean met with the Athenians on the sacred island of Delos. Here, they swore oaths of alliance. As a symbol that the alliance was meant to be permanent, they dropped lumps of iron into the sea; the alliance was to hold until these rose to the surface.

The aims of this new Delian League were to free those Greeks who were under Persian rule, to protect all against a Persian return, and to obtain compensation from the Persians by attacking their lands and taking booty. League policy was determined by a vote of the assembly, in which each state, including Athens, had one vote. Athens, however, was clearly designated leader.

From the first, the league was remarkably successful. The Persians were driven from Europe and the Hellespont, and the Aegean was cleared of pirates. Some states were forced into the league or were prevented from leaving. The members approved coercion because they believed it was necessary for the common safety. In 467 B.C., a great victory over the Persians at the Eurymedon River in Asia Minor routed the Persians and added a number of cities to the league.

Cimon, son of Miltiades, the hero of Marathon, became the leading Athenian soldier and statesman soon after the Persian war. Themistocles appears to have been driven from power by a coalition of his enemies. Ironically, the author of the Greek victory over Persia of 480 B.C. was ostracized and ended his days at the court of the Persian king. Cimon, who was to dominate Athenian politics for almost two decades, pursued a policy of aggressive attacks on Persia and friendly relations with Sparta. In domestic affairs, Cimon was conservative. He accepted the democratic constitution of Clisthenes, which appears to have become somewhat more limited after the Persian war. Defending this constitution and this foreign policy,

Cimon led the Athenians and the Delian League to victory after victory. His own popularity grew with success.

The First Peloponnesian War

In 465 B.C., the island of Thasos rebelled from the league. After a siege of more than two years Cimon forced an end to the rebellion. The revolt of Thasos had an important influence on the development of the Delian League, on Athenian politics, and on relations between Athens and Sparta. It is the first recorded instance in which Athenian interests alone seemed to have determined league policy, a significant step in the evolution of the Delian League into the Athenian empire. When Cimon returned to Athens from Thasos, he was charged with taking bribes not to conquer Macedonia, although that was not part of his assignment. He was acquitted and the trial was proved to be only a device by which his political opponents tried to reduce his influence.

The democratic opposition's program at home was to undo the gains made by the conservative council called the Areopagus and to bring about further changes in the direction of democracy. Abroad, the enemies of Cimon wanted to break with Sparta and contest its claim to leadership over the Greeks. They intended at least to establish the independence of Athens and its alliance. The head of this faction was Ephialtes. His supporter, and the man chosen to be the public prosecutor of Cimon, was Pericles, a member of a distinguished Athenian family. He was still a young man, and his defeat in court did not do lasting damage to his career.

When the Thasians began their rebellion, they asked Sparta to invade Athens the next spring. The ephors agreed. An earthquake, accompanied by a rebellion of the Helots that threatened the survival of Sparta, prevented the invasion. The Spartans asked their allies, the Athenians among them, for help. In Athens, Ephialtes urged the Athenians "not to help or restore a city that was a rival to Athens but to let Sparta lie low and be trampled underfoot." However, Cimon persuaded them to send help. The results were disastrous. The Spartans sent the Athenian troops home for fear of "the boldness and revolutionary spirit of the Athenians." While Cimon was in the Peloponnesus, helping the Spartans, Ephialtes stripped the Areopagus of almost all its power. In the spring of 461 B.C., Cimon was exiled, and Athens made an alliance with Argos, Sparta's traditional enemy. Almost overnight, Cimon's domestic and foreign policies had been overturned.

The new regime at Athens was confident and ambitious. When Megara, getting the worst of a border dispute with Corinth, withdrew from the Peloponnesian League, the Athenians accepted the Megarians as allies. This alliance gave Athens a great strategic advantage, for Megara barred the way from the Peloponnesus to Athens. The alliance also brought on the First Peloponnesian War, for Sparta resented the defection of Megara to Athens. The early years of the war brought Athens great success. The Athenians conquered Aegina and gained control of Boeotia. At one moment, Athens was supreme and invulnerable, controlling the states on its borders and dominating the sea (see Map 4.1).

In 454 B.C., however, the tide turned. In that year, a disastrous defeat struck an Athenian fleet that had gone to aid an Egyptian rebellion against Persia. The great loss of men, ships, and prestige caused rebellions in the empire, forcing Athens to make a truce in Greece in order to subdue Athens' allies in the Aegean. In 449 B.C., the Athenians ended the war against Persia. In 446 B.C., the war on the Greek mainland broke out again. Rebellions in Boeotia and Megara removed Athens' land defenses and brought a Spartan invasion. Rather than fight, Pericles, the commander of the Athenian army, agreed to a peace of thirty years. By the terms of the agreement, he abandoned all Athenian possessions on the continent. In return, the Spartans gave formal recognition to the Athenian empire. From then on, Greece was divided into two power blocs: Sparta and its alliance on the mainland and Athens ruling its empire in the Aegean.

The Athenian Empire

After the Egyptian disaster, the Athenians moved the Delian League's treasury to Athens and began to keep one sixtieth of the annual revenues for themselves. Because of the peace with Persia, there seemed no further reason for the allies to pay tribute. In spite of Athenian propaganda, nothing could cloak the fact that Athens was becoming the master and its allies mere subjects. By 445 B.C., only Chios, Lesbos, and Samos were autonomous and provided ships. All the other states paid tribute.

The change from alliance to empire came about because of the pressure of war and rebellion and in large measure because the allies were unwilling to see to their own defense. The empire was not universally unpopular and had many friends among the lower classes and the democratic politicians. Nevertheless, it came to be seen more and more as a tyranny. But the Athenians had come to depend on the empire for prosperity and security. The Thirty Years' Peace of 445 B.C. had recognized the empire, and the Athenians were determined to defend it at any cost.

Athenian Democracy

Even as the Athenians were tightening their control over their allies at home, they were evolving the freest government the world had ever seen. This extension of

MAP 4-2 THE ATHENIAN EMPIRE ABOUT 450 B.C. *The Empire at its fullest extent shortly before 450 B.C. We see Athens and the independent states that provided manned ships for the imperial fleet but paid no tribute, dependent states who paid tribute, and states allied to but not actually in the Empire.*

the Athenian democracy took place chiefly under the guidance of Pericles, who succeeded to the leadership of the democratic faction after the assassination of Ephialtes in 462 B.C. Legislation was passed making the hoplite class eligible for the archonship. In practice, no adult male was thereafter prevented from serving on the basis of property class. Pericles himself proposed the law introducing pay for jury members, opening that important duty to the poor. Circuit judges were reintroduced, making swift impartial justice available even to the poorest residents in the countryside.

Finally, Pericles himself introduced a bill limiting citizenship to those who had two citizen parents. From a modern perspective, this measure might be seen as a step away from democracy, and, in fact, it would have barred Cimon and one of Pericles' ancestors. In Greek terms, however, it was quite natural. Democracy was defined in terms of those who held citizenship, and

because citizenship had become a valuable commodity, the decision to limit it must have won a large majority. Participation in government in all the Greek states was denied to slaves, resident aliens, and women.

Within the citizen body, however, the extent of the democracy was remarkable. Every decision of the state had to be approved by the popular assembly—a collection of the people, not their representatives. Every judicial decision was subject to appeal to a popular court of not fewer than 51 and as many as 1,501 citizens, chosen from an annual panel of jurors widely representative of the Athenian male population. Most officials were selected by lot, without regard to class. The main elected officials, such as the generals and the imperial treasurers, were generally nobles and almost always rich men, but the people were free to choose others. All public officials were subject to scrutiny before taking office, could be called to account and re-

Thucydides Reports Pericles on Athenian Democracy

Pericles (CA. 495–429 B.C.) *delivered this speech after the first campaigning season of the Great Peloponnesian War, probably late in the winter of 431* B.C. *It is the most famous statement of the ideals of the Athenian imperial democracy.*

Our constitution does not copy the laws of neighbouring states; we are rather a pattern to others than imitators ourselves. Its administration favours the many instead of the few; this is why it is called a democracy. If we look to the laws, they afford equal justice to all in their private differences; if to social standing, advancement in public life falls to reputation for capacity, class considerations not being allowed to interfere with merit; nor again does poverty bar the way, if a man is able to serve the state, he is not hindered by the obscurity of his condition. The freedom which we enjoy in our government extends also to our ordinary life. There, far from exercising a jealous surveillance over each other, we do not feel called upon to be angry with our neighbour for doing what he likes, or even to indulge in those injurious looks which cannot fail to be offensive, although they inflict no positive penalty. But all this ease in our private relations does not make us lawless as citizens. . . . Our public men have, besides politics, their private affairs to attend to, and our ordinary citizens, though occupied with the pursuits of industry, are still fair judges of public matters; for, unlike any other nation, regarding him who takes no part in these duties not as unambitious but as useless, we Athenians are able to judge at all events if we cannot originate, and instead of looking on discussion as a stumbling-block in the way of action, we think it an indispensable preliminary to any wise action at all. . . .

In short, I say that as a city we are the school of Hellas; while I doubt if the world can produce a man, who where he has only himself to depend upon, is equal to so many emergencies, and graced by so happy a versatility as the Athenian. ❑

Thucydides, *The Peloponnesian War*, trans. by Richard Crawley (New York: Random House, 1951), pp. 104–106.

moved from office during their tenure, and were held to a compulsory examination and accounting at the end of their term. There was no standing army, no police force, open or secret, and no way to coerce the people.

If Pericles was elected to the generalship fifteen years in a row and thirty times in all, it was not because he was a dictator but because he was a persuasive speaker, a skillful politician, a respected general, an acknowledged patriot, and a man patently incorruptible. When he lost the people's confidence, they did not hesitate to depose him from office. In 443 B.C., however, after the removal of his chief rival, he stood at the height of his power. He had been persuaded by the defeat of the Athenian fleet in the Egyptian campaign and the failure of Athens' continental campaigns that its future lay in a conservative policy of retaining the empire in the Aegean and living at peace with the Spartans. It was in this direction that he led Athens' imperial democracy in the years after the First Peloponnesian War.

The Women of Athens

Greek society, like most cultures, was dominated by men. This was true of the democratic city of Athens

A klepsydra, or juror's water clock. The Athenians used water clocks to time speeches in their law courts. The clock shown here was found in the Athenian Agora and is now in the Royal Ontario Museum, Toronto. The mark XX shows that it holds two choes (about 6.5 liters); the six minutes that it would take to empty was the time alloted for rebuttal speeches in suits of a certain magnitude. [Agora Excavations, American School of Classical Studies at Athens.]

in the great days of Pericles, in the fifth century B.C., no less than in other Greek cities. Nonetheless, the position of women in classical Athens has been the subject of much controversy. The bulk of the evidence—coming from the law, from philosophical and moral writings, and from information about the conditions of daily life and the organization of society—shows that women were excluded from most aspects of public life. They could not vote, take part in the political assemblies, hold public office, or take any direct part in politics. Male citizens of all classes had these public responsibilities and opportunities.

The same sources show that, in the private aspects of life, women were always under the control of a male guardian: a father, a husband, or, failing these, an appropriate male relative. Women married young, usually between the ages of twelve and eighteen, whereas their husbands were typically over thirty; hence, they were always in a relationship like that of a daughter to a father. Marriages were arranged; the woman normally had no choice of husband, and her dowry was controlled by a male relative. Divorce was difficult for a woman to obtain, for she needed the approval of a male relative who was then willing to serve as her guardian after the dissolution of the marriage. In case of divorce, the dowry returned with the woman but was controlled by her father or the appropriate male relative.

The main function and responsibility of a respectable Athenian woman of a citizen family was to produce male heirs for the household (*oikos*) of her husband. If, however, her father's *oikos* lacked a male heir, the daughter became an *epikleros*, the "heiress" to the family property. In that case, she was required by law to marry the next of kin on her father's side in order to produce the desired male offspring. In the Athenian way of thinking, women were "lent" by one household to another for purposes of bearing and raising a male heir to continue the existence of the *oikos*.

Because the pure and legitimate lineage of the offspring was important, women were carefully segregated from men outside the family and were confined to the women's quarters in the house. Men might seek sexual gratification outside the house with prostitutes of high or low style, frequently recruited from abroad. But respectable women stayed home to raise the children, cook, weave cloth, and oversee the management of the household. The only public function of women was an important one in the various rituals and festivals of the state religion. Apart from these activities, Athenian women were expected to remain home, quiet and unnoticed. Pericles told the widows and mothers of the Athenian men who died in the first year of the Peloponnesian War only this: "Your great glory is not to fall short of your natural character, and the greatest glory of women is to be least talked about by men, whether for good or bad."

The picture derived from these sources is largely accurate, but it does not fit well with what we learn from the evidence of the pictorial art, the tragedy and

Medea Bemoans the Condition of Women

In 431 B.C., Euripides (CA. 485–406 B.C.) presented his play Medea *at the Dionysiac festival in Athens. The heroine is a foreign woman who has unusual powers, but in the speech that follows, she describes the fate of women in terms that appear to give an accurate account of the condition of women in fifth-century B.C. Athens.*

Of all things which are living and can form a
   judgment
We women are the most unfortunate creatures.
Firstly, with an excess of wealth it is required
For us to buy a husband and take for our bodies
A master; for not to take one is even worse.
And now the question is serious whether we take
A good or bad one; for there is no easy escape
For a woman, nor can she say no to her marriage.
She arrives among new modes of behavior and
   manners,
And needs prophetic power, unless she has learned
   at home,
How best to manage him who shares the bed with her.
And if we work out all this well and carefully,

And the husband lives with us and lightly bears his
   yoke,
Then life is enviable. If not, I'd rather die.
A man, when he's tired of the company in his
   home,
Goes out of the house and puts an end to his
   boredom
And turns to a friend or companion of his own age.
But we are forced to keep our eyes on one alone.
What they say of us is that we have a peaceful time
Living at home, while they do the fighting in war.
How wrong they are! I would very much rather
   stand
Three times in the front of battle than bear
   one child. ❑

Euripides, *Medea* in *Four Tragedies*, trans. by Rex Warner, (Chicago: University of Chicago Press, 1955), pp. 66–67.

478–477 B.C.	Delian League founded
CA. 474–462 B.C.	Cimon leading politician
467 B.C.	Victory over Persians at Eurymedon River
465–463 B.C.	Rebellion of Thasos
462 B.C.	Ephialtes murdered; Pericles rises to leadership
461 B.C.	Cimon ostracized
461 B.C.	Reform of Areopagus
CA. 460 B.C.	First Peloponnesian War begins
454 B.C.	Athens defeated in Egypt; crisis in the Delian League
449 B.C.	Peace with Persia
445 B.C.	Thirty Years' Peace ends First Peloponnesian War

comedy, and the mythology of the Athenians. These often show women as central characters and powerful figures in both the public and the private spheres. The Clytemnestra in Aeschylus' tragedy *Agamemnon* arranges the murder of her royal husband and establishes the tyranny of her lover, whom she dominates. The terrifying and powerful Medea negotiates with kings. We are left with an apparent contradiction clearly revealed by a famous speech in Euripides' tragedy *Medea*. (See the document on page 105.)

The picture that Medea paints of women subjected to men accords well with much of the evidence, but we must take note of the fact that the woman who complains of women's lot is the powerful central figure in a tragedy bearing her name. This tragedy was produced at state expense before most of the Athenian population, and was written by a man who was one of Athens' greatest poets and dramatists. Medea is a cause of terror to the audience and, at the same time, an object of their pity and sympathy as a victim of injustice. She is anything but the creature "least talked about by men, whether for good or for bad." There is reason to believe that the role played by Athenian women may have been more complex than their legal status might suggest.

The Great Peloponnesian War

In the decade after the Thirty Years' Peace of 445 B.C., the willingness of each side to respect the new arrangements was tested and not found wanting.

About 435 B.C., however, a dispute arose in a remote and unimportant part of the Greek world, plunging the Greeks into a long and disastrous war that shook the foundations of their civilization. On one side stood Sparta and the Peloponnesian League, on the other Athens and its Empire.

The Spartan strategy was traditional: to invade the enemy's country and threaten the crops, forcing the enemy to defend them in a hoplite battle. Such a battle the Spartans were sure to win, because they had the better army and they and their allies outnumbered the Athenians at least two to one. Any ordinary *polis* would have yielded or fought and lost, but Athens had an enormous navy, an annual income from the empire, a vast reserve fund, and long walls that connected the fortified city with the fortified port of Piraeus.

A foundry is depicted on an Attic vase of the fifth century B.C. Greek skill in metal work reached a high level of achievement by the fifth century. The major practical use for the skill was in weapons of war, but artistic applications, especially in bronze, were also important. Here we see an artisan stroking a furnace to maintain the high but carefully controlled temperature needed in his work.

The Athenians' strategy was to allow devastation of the land to prove that Athens was invulnerable. At the same time, the Athenians launched seaborne raids on the Peloponnesian coast to show that the allies of Sparta could be hurt. Pericles expected that within a year or two, three at most, the Peloponnesians would become discouraged and make peace, having learned their lesson. If the Peloponnesians held out, Athenian resources were inadequate to continue for more than four or five years without raising the tribute in the empire and running an unacceptable risk of rebellion. The plan required restraint and the leadership only a Pericles could provide.

Ten years of war (431–421 B.C.) led to a stalemate concluded by the Peace of Nicias. The peace was for fifty years and guaranteed the status quo, with a few exceptions. Neither side carried out all its commitments, and several of Sparta's allies refused to ratify the peace.

In 415 B.C. Alcibiades, a young and ambitious leader, persuaded the Athenians to attack Sicily to bring it under their control. In 413 B.C., the entire expedition was destroyed. The Athenians lost some two hundred ships, about forty-five hundred of their own men, and almost ten times as many allies. It was a disaster perhaps greater than the defeat of the Athenian fleet in the Egyptian campaign some forty years earlier. It shook Athenian prestige, reduced the power of Athens, provoked rebellions, and brought the wealth and power of Persia into the war on Sparta's side.

It is remarkable that the Athenians were able to continue fighting in spite of the disaster. They survived a brief oligarchic coup in 411 B.C. and won several important victories at sea as the war shifted to the Aegean. As their allies rebelled, however, and were sustained by fleets paid for by Persia, the Athenians saw their financial resources shrink and finally disappear. When their fleet was caught napping at Aegospotami in 405 B.C., they could not build another. The Spartans—under Lysander, a clever and ambitious general who was responsible for obtaining Persian support—cut off the food supply through the Hellespont, and the

Athenians were starved into submission. In 404 B.C., they surrendered unconditionally; the city walls were dismantled, Athens was permitted no fleet, and the empire was gone. The Great Peloponnesian War was over.

The Struggle for Greek Leadership

THE HEGEMONY OF SPARTA. The collapse of the Athenian empire created a vacuum of power in the Aegean and opened the way for Spartan leadership, or hegemony. Fulfilling the contract that had brought them the funds to win the war, the Spartans handed the Greek cities of Asia Minor back to Persia. Under the leadership of Lysander, the Spartans went on to make a complete mockery of their promise to free the Greeks by stepping into the imperial role of Athens in the cities along the European coast and the islands of the Aegean. In most of the cities, Lysander installed a board of ten local oligarchs loyal to him and supported them with a Spartan garrison. Tribute brought in an annual revenue almost as great as that which the Athenians had collected.

Limited manpower, the Helot problem, and traditional conservatism all made Sparta less than an ideal state to rule a maritime empire. Some of Sparta's allies, especially Thebes and Corinth, were alienated by the increasing arrogance of Sparta's policies. In 404 B.C., Lysander installed an oligarchic government in Athens whose outrageous behavior earned them the title "Thirty Tyrants." Democratic exiles took refuge in Thebes and Corinth and created an army to challenge the oligarchy. Sparta's conservative king, Pausanias, replaced Lysander, arranging a peaceful settlement and ultimately the restoration of democracy. Thereafter, Athenian foreign policy remained under Spartan control, but otherwise Athens was free.

In 405 B.C., Darius II of Persia (reigned 424–405 B.C.) died and was succeeded by Artaxerxes II. His younger brother, Cyrus, contested his rule and received Spartan help in recruiting a Greek mercenary army to help him win the throne. They marched inland as far as Mesopotamia, where they defeated the Persians at Cunaxa in 401 B.C., but Cyrus was killed. The Greeks were able to march back to the Black Sea and safety; their success revealed the potential weakness of the Persian Empire.

The Greeks of Asia Minor had supported Cyrus and were now afraid of Artaxerxes' revenge. The Spartans accepted their request for aid and sent an army into Asia, attracted by the prospect of prestige, power, and money. In 396 B.C., the command was given to Sparta's new king, Agesilaus (444–360 B.C.). His personality and policy dominated Sparta throughout its period of hegemony and until his death in 360 B.C. Hampered by his lameness and his disputed claim to the throne, he seems to have compensated for both by always ad-

THE GREAT PELOPONNESIAN WAR

435 B.C.	Civil war at Epidamnus
432 B.C.	Sparta declares war on Athens
431 B.C.	Peloponnesian invasion of Athens
421 B.C.	Peace of Nicias
415–413 B.C.	Athenian invasion of Sicily
405 B.C.	Battle of Aegospotami
404 B.C.	Athens surrenders

vocating aggressive policies and providing himself with opportunities to display his bravery in battle.

Agesilaus collected much booty and frightened the Persians. They sent a messenger with money and promises of further support to friendly factions in all the likely states. By 395 B.C., Thebes was able to organize an alliance that included Argos, Corinth, and a resurgent Athens. The result was the Corinthian War (395–387 B.C.), which put an end to Sparta's Asian adventure. In 394, the Persian fleet destroyed Sparta's maritime empire. Meanwhile the Athenians took advantage of events to rebuild their walls, enlarge their navy, and even to recover some of their lost empire in the Aegean. The war ended when the exhausted Greek states accepted a peace dictated by the Great King of Persia.

The Persians, frightened by the recovery of Athens, turned the management of Greece over to Sparta. Agesilaus broke up all alliances except the Peloponnesian League. He interfered with the autonomy of other *poleis* by using the Spartan army, or the threat of its use, to put friends in power within them. Sparta reached a new level of lawless arrogance in 382 B.C., when it seized Thebes during peacetime without warning or pretext. In 379, a Spartan army made a similar attempt on Athens. That action persuaded the Athenians to join with Thebes, which had rebelled from Sparta a few months earlier, to wage war on the Spartans. In 371 B.C., the Thebans, led by their great generals Pelopidas and Epaminondas, defeated the Spartans at Leuctra. The Thebans encouraged the Arcadian cities of the central Peloponnesus to form a federal league, freed the Helots, and helped them found a city of their own. They deprived Sparta of much of its farmland and of the men who worked it and hemmed it in with hostile neighbors. Sparta's popula-tion had shrunk so that it could put fewer than two thousand men into the field at Leuctra. Sparta's aggressive policies had led to ruin. The Theban victory brought the end of Sparta as a power of the first rank.

THEBAN HEGEMONY. Victorious Thebes had a democratic constitution, control over Boeotia, and two outstanding and popular generals. These were the basis for Theban power after Leuctra. Pelopidas died in a successful attempt to gain control of Thessaly. Epaminondas consolidated his work, and Thebes was soon dominant over all Greece north of Athens and the Corinthian Gulf. The Thebans challenged the reborn Athenian empire in the Aegean.

All this activity provoked resistance, and by 362 B.C., Thebes faced a Peloponnesian coalition as well as Athens. Epaminondas once again led a victorious Boeotian army into the Peloponnesus at Mantinea but he died in the fight, and the loss of its two great leaders ended Thebes' dominance.

THE SECOND ATHENIAN EMPIRE. Athens had organized the Second Athenian Confederation in 378 B.C. It was aimed at resisting Spartan aggression in the Aegean, and its constitution was careful to avoid the abuses of the Delian League. But the Athenians soon began to repeat those abuses, although this time they did not have the power to put down resistance. When the collapse of Sparta and Thebes and the restraint of Persia removed any reason for voluntary membership, Athens' allies revolted. By 355 B.C., Athens had to abandon most of the empire. After two centuries of almost continuous warfare, the Greeks returned to the chaotic disorganization of the time before the founding of the Peloponnesian League.

THE SPARTAN AND THEBAN HEGEMONIES

404–403 B.C.	Thirty Tyrants rule at Athens
401 B.C.	Expedition of Cyrus, rebellious prince of Persia; Battle of Cunaxa
400–387 B.C.	Spartan War against Persia
398–360 B.C.	Reign of Agesilaus at Sparta
395–387 B.C.	Corinthian War
382 B.C.	Sparta seizes Thebes
378 B.C.	Second Athenian Confederation founded
371 B.C.	Thebans defeat Sparta at Leuctra; end of Spartan hegemony
362 B.C.	Battle of Mantinea; end of Theban hegemony

The Culture of Classical Greece

The repulse of the Persian invasion released a flood of creative activity in Greece rarely if ever matched anywhere at any time.

The Fifth Century B.C.

The century and a half between the Persian retreat and the conquest of Greece by Philip of Macedon (479–338 B.C.) produced achievements of such quality as to justify that era's designation as the Classical Period. Ironically, we often use the term *classical* to suggest calm and serenity, but the word that best describes the common element present in Greek life, thought, art, and literature in this period is *tension.* It was a time in which conflict among the *poleis* continued and intensified as Athens and Sparta gathered most of them into two competing and menacing blocs.

The Parthenon at Athens. This temple to Athena Parthenos (Athena the Maiden) was built under the direction of Pericles between 447 and 432 B.C., using funds from the treasury of the Delian League. It is generally thought to be the finest of all Greek temples. Built in the Doric order, with many subtle refinements, and crowning the Acropolis, it gave visible evidence of the greatness of Athens. [Greek National Tourist Organization, New York.]

The victory over the Persians brought a sense of exultation in the capacity of humans to accomplish great things and of confidence in the divine justice that brought arrogant pride low. But these feelings conflicted with a sense of unease as the Greeks recognized that the fate that had met Xerxes awaited all those who reached too far. Another source of tension was the conflict between the soaring hopes and achievements of individuals and the claims and limits put on them by their fellow citizens in the *polis*. These forces were at work throughout Greece, but we know them best and they had the most spectacular results in Athens in its Golden Age, the time between the Persian and Peloponnesian wars.

ATTIC TRAGEDY. Nothing reflects these concerns better than the appearance of Attic tragedy as the major form of Greek poetry in the fifth century B.C. The tragedies were presented as part of public religious observations in honor of the god Dionysus.

The whole affair was very much a civic occasion. Each poet who wished to compete submitted his work to the archon. Each offered three tragedies, which might or might not have a common subject, and a satyr play (a comic choral dialogue with Dionysus) to close. The archon chose the best three competitors and awarded them each three actors and a chorus. The actors were paid by the state, and the chorus was provided by a wealthy citizen selected by the state to perform this service as *choregos*, for the Athenians had no direct taxation to support such activities. Most of the tragedies were performed in the theater of Dionysus on the south side of the Acropolis, and as many as thirty thousand Athenians could attend. Prizes and honors were awarded to the author, the actor, and the *choregos* voted best by a jury of Athenians chosen by lot. On rare occasions, the subject of the play might be a contemporary or historical event, but almost always it was chosen from mythology. Before Euripides, it always dealt solemnly with serious questions of religion, politics, ethics, morality, or some combination of these.

ARCHITECTURE AND SCULPTURE. The great architectural achievements of Periclean Athens, just as much as Athenian tragedy, illustrate the magnificent

The porch of the maidens on the Erechtheum. This is a uniquely designed Ionic temple built on the Athenian Acropolis near the Parthenon between about 421 and 409 B.C. It housed the shrines of three different gods and presented special architectures in the porch facing the Parthenon. In place of the usual fluted columns it uses statues of young girls taking part in a religious festival as columns. (Columns made from the draped female figure are called caryatids.) [Greek National Tourist Organization, New York.]

results of the union and tension between religious and civic responsibilities on the one hand and the transcendent genius of the individual artist on the other. Beginning in 448 B.C. and continuing down to the outbreak of the Great Peloponnesian War, Pericles undertook a great building program on the Acropolis. The funds were provided by the income from the empire. The buildings were temples to honor the city's gods and a fitting gateway to the temples.

Pericles' main purpose seems to have been to represent visually the greatness and power of Athens, but in such a way as to emphasize intellectual and artistic achievement, civilization rather than military and naval power. It was as though these buildings were tangible proof of Pericles' claim that Athens was "the school of Hellas," that is, the intellectual center of all Greece.

HISTORY.   The fifth century B.C. produced the first prose literature in the form of history. Herodotus, born shortly before the Persian wars, deserves his title of the "father of history," for his account of the Persian wars goes far beyond all previous chronicles, genealogies, and geographical studies. His history attempts to explain human actions and to draw instruction from them.

Herodotus accepted the evidence of legends and oracles, although not uncritically, and often explained human events in terms of divine intervention. Human arrogance and divine vengeance are key forces that help explain the defeat of Croesus by Cyrus as well as Xerxes' defeat by the Greeks. Yet the *History* is typical of its time in celebrating the crucial role of human intelligence as revealed by Miltiades at Marathon and Themistocles at Salamis. Nor was Herodotus unaware of the importance of institutions. There is no mistaking his pride in the superiority of the Greek *polis* and the discipline it inspired in its citizen soldiers and his pride in the superiority of the Greeks' voluntary obedience to law over the Persians' fear of punishment.

Thucydides, the historian of the Peloponnesian wars, was born about 460 B.C. and died a few years after the end of the Great Peloponnesian War. He was very much a product of the late fifth century, reflecting the influence of the scientific attitude of the Hippocratic school of medicine as well as the secular, human-centered, skeptical rationalism of the Sophists. Hippocrates of Cos was a contemporary of Thucydides who was part of a school of medical writers and practitioners. They did important pioneer work in medicine and scientific theory, placing great emphasis on the need to combine careful and accurate observation with reason to make possible the understanding, prognosis, treatment, and cure of a disease.

In the same way, Thucydides took great pains to achieve factual accuracy and tried to use his evidence to discover meaningful patterns of human behavior. He believed that human nature was essentially unchanging, so that a wise person equipped with the understanding provided by history might accurately foresee events and thus help to guide them. He believed, however, that only a few had the ability to understand history and put its lessons to good use. He thought that even the wisest could be foiled by the intervention of chance, which played a great role in human affairs. Thucydides focused his interest on politics, and in that area, his assumptions about human nature do not seem unwarranted. His work has proved to be, as he had hoped, "a possession forever." Its

The theater at Epidaurus. This theater, built in the fourth century B.C., is one of the best preserved of ancient Greek theaters. Epidaurus, a city in the eastern Peloponnesus, was the site of the Sanctuary of Asclepius, the hero and god of healing. The sick and crippled came there, as to Lourdes in modern times, to be healed. The religious festivals there included theatrical performances that drew large crowds. [Greek National Tourist Organization, New York.]

description of the terrible civil war between the two basic kinds of *polis* is a final and fitting example of the tension that was the source of both the greatness and the decline of classical Greece.

The Fourth Century B.C.

Historians often speak of the Great Peloponnesian War as the crisis of the *polis* and of the fourth century as the period of its decline. But the Greeks of the fourth century B.C. did not know that their traditional way of life was on the verge of destruction. Some looked to the past and tried to shore up the weakened structure of the *polis*; others tended toward despair and looked for new solutions; and still others averted their gaze from the public arena altogether. All of these responses are apparent in the literature, philosophy, and art of the period.

DRAMA. The tendency of some to avert their gaze from the life of the *polis* and to turn inward to everyday life, the family, and their own individuality is apparent in the poetry of the fourth century B.C. Tragedy proved to be a form whose originality was confined to the fifth century B.C.. No tragedies written in the fourth century B.C. have been preserved, and it was common to revive the great plays of the previous century. Some of the late plays of Euripides (CA. 484–406 B.C.), in fact, seem less like the tragedies of Aeschylus and Sophocles than forerunners of later forms such as the New Comedy (CA. 325–260 B.C.). Plays of Euripides like *Helena*, *Andromeda*, and *Iphigenia in Tauris* are more like fairy tales, tales of adventure, or love stories than tragedies. Euripides was less interested in cosmic confrontations of conflicting principles than in the psychology and behavior of individual human beings. His plays, which rarely won first prize when first produced for Dionysian festival competitions, became increasingly popular in the fourth century B.C. and after.

Comedy was introduced into the Dionysian festival early in the fifth century B.C. Such poets as Cratinus, Eupolis, and the great master of the genre called Old Comedy, Aristophanes (CA. 450–CA. 385 B.C.), the only one from whom we have complete plays, wrote political comedies filled with scathing invective and satire against such contemporary figures as Pericles, Cleon, Socrates, and Euripides. The fourth century B.C., however, produced what is called Middle Comedy, which turned away from political subjects and personal invective toward a comic-realistic depiction of daily life, plots of intrigue, and mild satire of domestic situations. Significantly, the role of the chorus, which in some way represented the *polis*, was very much diminished. These trends all continued and were carried even further in the New Comedy, whose leading playwright, Menander (342–291 B.C.), completely abandoned mythological subjects in favor of domestic

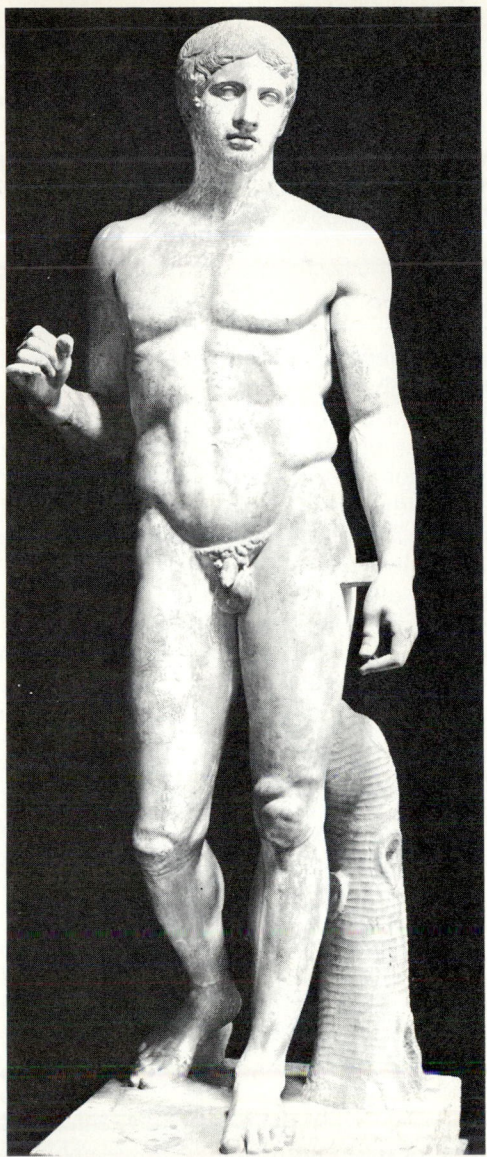

The Doryphorus ("The spear-bearer"). The young man portrayed is an athlete prepared to throw a javelin. The original, of which this is a Roman copy, was a bronze statue by the great Greek sculptor Polycleitus, who worked during the middle of the fifth century B.C. This statue was found at Pompeii and is now in the museum at Naples. [Alinari/SCALA.]

tragicomedy. His gentle satire of the foibles of ordinary people and his tales of lovers temporarily thwarted before a happy and proper ending would not be unfamiliar to viewers of modern situation comedies.

SCULPTURE. The same movement away from the grand, the ideal, and the general and toward the ordinary, the real, and the individual is apparent in the development of Greek sculpture. To see these developments, one has only to compare the statue of the *Striding God of Artemisium* (CA. 460 B.C.), thought to be either Zeus on the point of releasing a thunderbolt or Poseidon about to throw his trident or the *Doryphoros* of Polycleitus (CA. 450–440 B.C.) with the *Hermes* of Praxiteles (CA. 340–330 B.C.) or the *Apoxyomenos* attributed to Lysippus (CA. 330 B.C.).

Emergence of the Hellenistic World

The term *Hellenistic* was coined in the nineteenth century to describe the period of three centuries during which Greek culture spread far from its homeland to Egypt and far into Asia. The new civilization formed in this expansion was a mixture of Greek and Oriental elements, although the degree of mixture varied from time to time and place to place. The Hellenistic world was larger than the world of classical Greece, and its major political units were much larger than the city-states, though these persisted in different forms. The new political and cultural order had its roots in the rise to power of a Macedonian dynasty that conquered Greece and the Persian Empire in the space of two generations.

The Macedonian Conquest

The quarrels among the Greeks brought on defeat and conquest by a new power that suddenly rose to eminence in the fourth century B.C., the kingdom of Macedon. The Macedonians inhabited the land to the north of Thessaly, and through the centuries, they had unknowingly served the vital purpose of protecting the Greek states from barbarian tribes further to the north. By Greek standards, Macedon was a backward, semibarbaric land. It had no *poleis* and was ruled loosely by a king in a rather Homeric fashion. He was chosen partly on the basis of descent, but the acclamation of the army gathered in assembly was required to make him legitimate. Quarrels between pretenders to the throne and even murder to achieve it were not uncommon. A council of nobles checked the royal power and could reject a weak or incompetent king.

Hampered by constant wars with the barbarians, internal strife, loose organization, and lack of money, Macedon played no great part in Greek affairs up to the fourth century B.C. The Macedonians were of the same stock as the Greeks and spoke a Greek dialect, and the nobles, at least, thought of themselves as Greeks. The kings claimed descent from Heracles and the royal house of Argos. They tried to bring Greek culture into their court and won acceptance at the Olympic games. If a king could be found with the ability to unify this nation, it was bound to play a greater part in Greek affairs.

PHILIP OF MACEDON. That king was Philip II (359–336 B.C.), who, while still under thirty, took advantage of his appointment as regent to overthrow his infant nephew and make himself king. Like many of his predecessors, he admired Greek culture. Between 367 and 364 B.C., he had been a hostage in Thebes, where he learned much about Greek politics and warfare under the tutelage of Epaminondas. His natural talents for war and diplomacy and his boundless ambition made him the ablest king in Macedonian history. Using both diplomatic and military means, he was able to pacify the tribes on his frontiers and to make his own hold on the throne firmer. Then he began to undermine Athenian control of the northern Aegean. He took Amphipolis, which gave him control of the Strymon valley and of the gold and silver mines of Mount Pangaeus. The income allowed him to found new cities, to bribe politicians in foreign towns, and to reorganize his army into the finest fighting force in the world.

THE INVASION OF GREECE. So armed, Philip turned south toward central Greece. His conquests

Mosaic of a lion hunt from Pella, which became the royal capital of Macedon at the end of the fifth century B.C. The city developed rapidly under Philip II. [Bettmann Archive.]

Demosthenes Denounces Philip of Macedon

Demosthenes (384–322 B.C.) was an Athenian statesman who urged his fellow citizens and other Greeks to resist the advance of Philip of Macedon (CA. 358–317 B.C.). The following is from the speech we call the First Philippic, delivered probably in 351 B.C.

Do not imagine, that his empire is everlastingly secured to him as a god. There are those who hate and envy him, Athenians, even among those that are most friendly; and all feelings that are in other men belong, we may assume, to his confederates. But now they are cowed, having no refuge through your tardiness and indolence, which I say you must abandon forthwith. For you see, Athenians, the case, to what pitch of arrogance the man has advanced, who leaves you not even the choice of action or inaction, but threatens and uses (they say) outrageous language, and, unable to rest in possession of his conquests, continually widens their circle, and whilst we dally and delay, throws his net all around us. When then, Athenians, when will ye act as becomes you? In what event? In that of necessity, I suppose. And how should we regard the events happening now? Methinks, to freemen the strongest necessity is the disgrace of their condition. Or tell me, do ye like walking about and asking one another:—is there any news? Why, could there be greater news than a man of Macedonia subduing Athenians, and directing the affairs of Greece? Is Philip dead? No, but he is sick. And what matters it to you? Should anything befall this man, you will soon create another Philip, if you attend to business thus. For even he has been exalted not so much by his own strength, as by our negligence. ❑

Demosthenes, *The Olynthiac and Other Public Orations of Demosthenes*, trans. by C. R. Kennedy (London: George Bell and Sons, 1903), pp. 62–63.

threatened the vital interest of Athens, which still had a formidable fleet of three hundred ships.

The Athens of 350 B.C. was not the Athens of Pericles. It had neither imperial revenue nor allies to share the burden of war on land or sea, and its own population was smaller than in the fifth century. The Athenians, therefore, were reluctant to go on expeditions themselves or even to send out mercenary armies under Athenian generals, for they must be paid out of taxes or contributions from Athenian citizens.

The leading spokesman against these tendencies and the cautious foreign policy that went with them was Demosthenes (384–322 B.C.), one of the greatest orators in Greek history. He was convinced that Philip was a dangerous enemy to Athens and the other Greeks and spent most of his career urging the Athenians to resist Philip's encroachments. He was right, for beginning in 349 B.C., Philip attacked several cities in northern and central Greece and firmly planted Macedonian power in those regions. The king of "barbarian" Macedon was elected president of the Pythian Games at Delphi, and the Athenians were forced to concur in the election.

The years between 346 B.C. and 340 B.C. were spent in diplomatic maneuvering, each side trying to win strategically useful allies. At last, Philip attacked Perinthus and Byzantium, the life line of Athenian commerce, and in 340, he besieged both cities and declared war. The Athenian fleet saved both, so in the following year Philip marched into Greece. Demosthenes performed wonders in rallying the Athenians and winning Thebes over to the Athenian side, but in 338, Philip defeated the allied forces at Chaeronea in Boeotia in a great battle whose decisive blow was a cavalry charge led by the eighteen-year-old son of Philip, Alexander.

THE MACEDONIAN GOVERNMENT OF GREECE. The Macedonian settlement of Greek affairs was not as harsh as many had feared, although in some cities the friends of Macedon came to power and killed or exiled their enemies. Demosthenes continued to be free or engage in politics, and Athens was not attacked on the condition that it give up what was left of its empire and follow the lead of Macedon. The rest of Greece was arranged in such a way as to remove all dangers to Philip's rule. To guarantee his security, Philip placed garrisons at Thebes, Chalcis, and Corinth; these came to be known as the fetters of Greece. In 338 B.C., Philip called a meeting of the Greek states to form the federal league of Corinth. The constitution provided for autonomy, freedom from tribute and garrisons, and suppression of piracy and civil war. The league delegates would make foreign policy, in theory without consulting their home governments or Philip. All this was a facade; not only was Philip of Macedon president of the league, but he was its ruler. The defeat at Chaeronea meant the end of Greek freedom and autonomy. Though its form and internal life continued for some time, the *polis* had lost control of its own affairs and the special conditions that had made it unique.

Philip's choice of Corinth as the seat of his new confederacy was not made out of convenience or by accident. It was at Corinth that the Greeks had gathered to resist a Persian invasion almost 150 years earlier, and

Alexander the Great. This Hellenistic marble portrait comes from Pergamum in Asia Minor and is dated about 200 B.C. [Hirmer Fotoarchiv München.]

it was there in 337 B.C. that Philip announced his intention to invade Persia in a war of liberation and revenge as leader of the new league. In the spring of 336 B.C., as he prepared to begin the campaign, Philip was assassinated.

In 1977, a mound was excavated at the Macedonian village of Vergina. The extraordinarily rich finds and associated buildings have led many scholars to conclude that this is the royal tomb of Philip II. If they are right, and the evidence seems persuasive, Philip richly deserved so distinguished a resting place. He found Macedon a disunited kingdom of semibarbarians, despised and exploited by the Greeks; at his death, Macedon was a united kingdom, master and leader of the Greeks, rich, powerful, and ready to undertake the invasion of Asia. The completion of this task was left to Philip's first son, Alexander III (356–323 B.C.), later called Alexander the Great, who came to the throne at the age of twenty.

Alexander the Great

Along with his throne, the young king Alexander inherited his father's plan to invade Persia. The idea was daring, for Persia's empire was vast and its re-

MAP 4-3   ALEXANDER'S CAMPAIGNS   *The route taken by Alexander the Great in his conquest of the Persian Empire, 334–323 B.C. Starting from the Macedonian capital at Pella, he reached the Indus valley before being turned back by his own restive troops. He died of fever in Mesopotamia.*

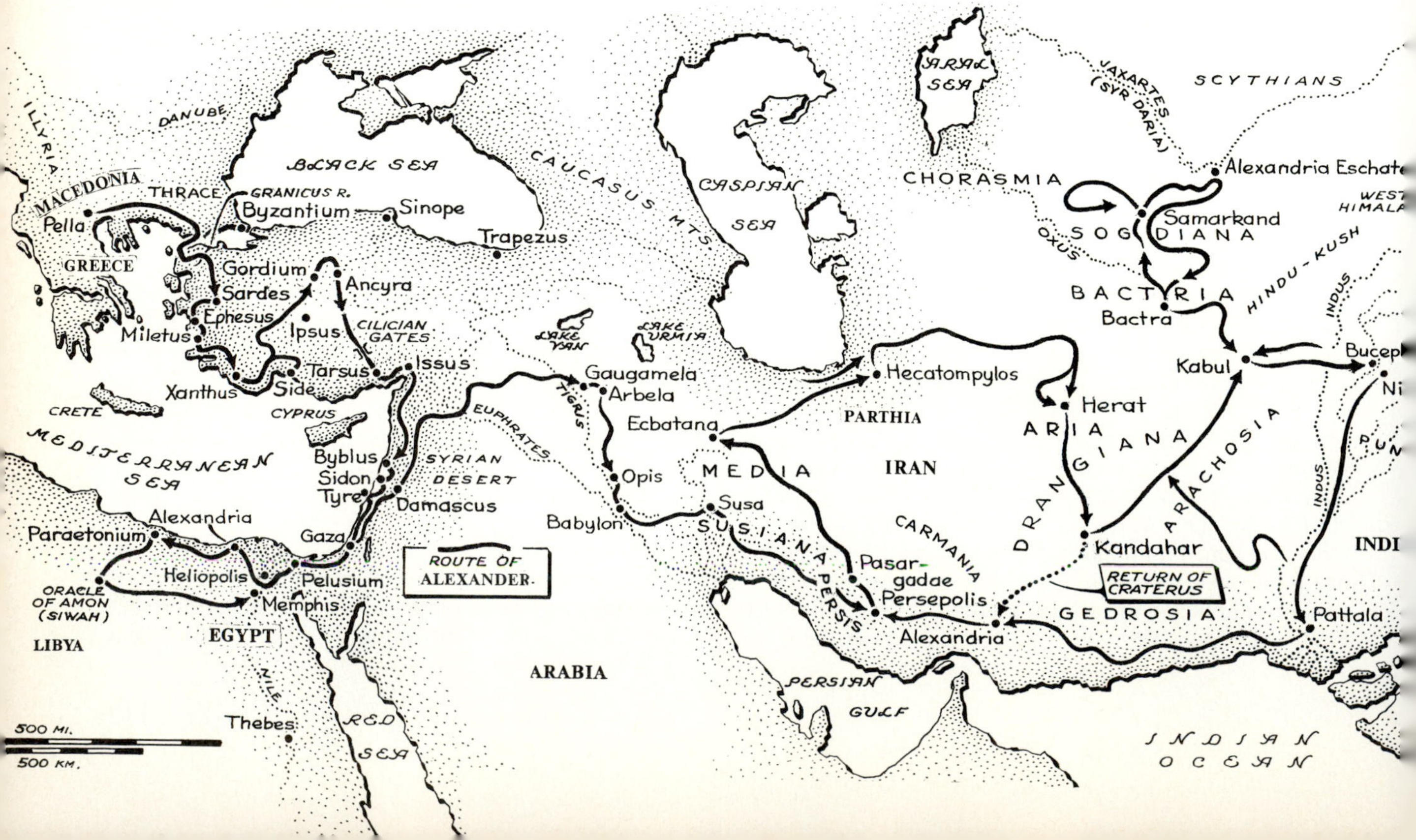

sources enormous, but the usurper Cyrus and his Greek mercenaries had shown its vulnerability by penetrating deep into the Persian Empire at the beginning of the fourth century B.C.

THE CONQUEST OF PERSIA AND BEYOND. In 334 B.C., Alexander crossed the Hellespont into Asia. His army consisted of about thirty thousand infantry and five thousand cavalry; he had no navy and little money. These facts determined his early strategy: he aimed to seek quick and decisive battles to gain money and supplies from the conquered territory. He moved along the coast so as to neutralize the Persian navy by depriving it of ports.

Alexander met the Persian forces of Asia Minor at the Granicus River, where he won a smashing victory in characteristic style (see Map 4.3). He led a cavalry charge across the river into the teeth of the enemy on the opposite bank, almost losing his life in the process and winning the devotion of his soldiers. That victory

Arrian Describes Alexander's Actions at a Tragic Drinking Party

Arrian lived in the second century A.D., *almost five hundred years after Alexander the Great, but his* Anabasis *is the best ancient source of information about Alexander's career. In 328* B.C., *Alexander's expedition had reached Samarkand. By now he had adopted a number of Persian customs and had begun to reduce the distinction between Macedonians and Persians. The older Macedonians, in particular, were resentful, and the following passage describes a drinking bout in which a quarrel arose between Alexander and one of the most distinguished Macedonian veterans.*

When the drinking-party on this occasion had already gone on too long (for Alexander had now made innovations even in regard to drinking, by imitating too much the custom of foreigners), and in the midst of the carouse a discussion had arisen about the Dioscuri, how their procreation had been taken away from Tyndareus and ascribed to Zeus, some of those present, in order to flatter Alexander, maintained that Polyleuces and Castor were in no way worthy to compare with him and his exploits. Such men have always destroyed and will never cease to ruin the interests of those who happen to be reigning. In their carousal they did not even abstain from comparing him with Heracles, saying that envy stood in the way of the living receiving the honours due to them from their associates. It was well known that Clitus had long been vexed at Alexander for the change in his style of living in excessive imitation of foreign customs, and at those who flattered him with their speech. At that time also, being heated with wine, he would not permit them either to insult the deity or, by depreciating the deeds of the ancient heroes, to confer upon Alexander this gratification which deserved no thanks. He affirmed Alexander's deeds were neither in fact at all so great or marvellous as they represented in their laudation; nor had he achieved them by himself, but for the most part they were the deeds of the Macedonians. The delivery of this speech annoyed Alexander; and I do not commend it, for I think, in such a drunken bout, it would have been sufficient if, so far as he was personally concerned, he had kept silence, and not committed the error of indulging in the same flattery as the others. But when some even mentioned Philip's actions without exercising a just judgment, declaring that he had performed nothing great or marvellous, they herein gratified Alexander; but Clitus being then no longer able to contain himself, began to put Philip's achievements in the first rank, and to depreciate Alexander and his performances. Clitus being now quite intoxicated, made other depreciatory remarks and even vehemently reviled him, because after all he had saved his life, when the cavalry battle had been fought with the Persians at the Granicus. Then indeed, arrogantly stretching out his right hand, he said, "This hand, O Alexander, preserved you on that occasion." Alexander could now no longer endure the drunken insolence of Clitus; but jumped up against him in a great rage. He was however restrained by his boon companions. As Clitus did not desist from his insulting remarks, Alexander shouted out a summons for his shield-bearing guards to attend him; but when no one obeyed him, he said that he was reduced to the same position as Darius, when he was led about under arrest by Bessus and his adherents, and that he now possessed the mere name of king. Then his companions were no longer able to restrain him; for according to some he leaped up and snatched a javelin from one of his confidential body-guards; according to others, a long pike from one of his ordinary guards, with which he struck Clitus and killed him. ❏

Arrian, *The Anabasis of Alexander*, trans. by E. J. Chinnock in *The Greek Historians*, ed. by F. R. B. Godolphin, Vol. 2 (New York: Random House, 1942), pp. 507–508.

left the coast of Asia Minor open, and Alexander captured the coastal cities, thus denying them to the Persian fleet.

In 333 B.C., Alexander marched inland to Syria, where he met the main Persian army under King Darius at Issus. Alexander himself led the cavalry charge that broke the Persian line and sent Darius fleeing into central Asia Minor. He continued along the coast and captured previously impregnable Tyre after a long and ingenious siege, putting an end to the threat of the Persian navy. He took Egypt with little trouble and was greeted as liberator, pharaoh, and son of Re (the Egyptian god whose Greek equivalent was Zeus). At Tyre, Darius sent Alexander a peace offer, yielding his entire empire west of the Euphrates River and his daughter in exchange for an alliance and an end to the invasion. But Alexander aimed at conquering the whole empire and probably whatever lay beyond that.

In the spring of 331 B.C., Alexander marched into Mesopotamia. At Gaugamela, near the ancient Assyrian city of Nineveh, he met Darius, ready for a last stand. Once again, Alexander's tactical genius and personal leadership carried the day. The Persians were broken and Darius fled once more. Alexander entered Babylon, again hailed as liberator and king. In January of 330 B.C., he came to Persepolis, the Persian capital, which held splendid palaces and the royal treasury. This bonanza ended his financial troubles and put a vast sum of money into circulation, with economic consequences that lasted for centuries. After a stay of several months, Alexander burned Persepolis to dramatize the completion of Hellenic revenge for the Persian invasion and the destruction of the native Persian dynasty.

The new regime could not be secure while Darius lived, so Alexander pursued him eastward. Just south of the Caspian Sea, he came upon the corpse of Darius, killed by Darius' relative Bessus. The Persian nobles around Darius had lost faith in him and had joined in the plot. The murder removed Darius from Alexander's path, but now had to catch Bessus, who proclaimed himself successor to Darius. The pursuit of Bessus (who was soon caught), a great curiosity, and a longing to go as far as he could and see the most distant places took Alexander to the frontier of India.

Near Samarkand, in the land of the Scythians, he founded the city of Alexandria Eschate ("Furthest Alexandria"), one of the many cities bearing his name that he founded as he traveled. As a part of his grand scheme of amalgamation and conquest, he married the Bactrian princess Roxane and enrolled thirty thousand young Bactrians for his army. These were to be trained and sent back to the center of the empire for use later.

In 327 B.C., Alexander took his army through the Khyber Pass in an attempt to conquer the lands around

THE RISE OF MACEDON

359–336 B.C.	Reign of Philip II
338 B.C.	Battle of Chaeronea; Philip conquers Greece
338 B.C.	Founding of League of Corinth
336–323 B.C.	Reign of Alexander III, the Great
334 B.C.	Alexander invades Asia
333 B.C.	Battle of Issus
331 B.C.	Battle of Gaugamela
330 B.C.	Fall of Persepolis
327 B.C.	Alexander reaches Indus Valley
323 B.C.	Death of Alexander

the Indus River (modern Pakistan). He reduced its king, Porus, to vassalage but pushed on in the hope of reaching the river called Ocean that the Greeks believed encircled the world. Finally, his weary men refused to go on. By the spring of 324 B.C., the army was back at the Persian Gulf and celebrated in the Macedonian style, with a wild spree of drinking.

THE DEATH OF ALEXANDER. Alexander was filled with plans for the future: for the consolidation and organization of his empire; for geographical exploration; for building new cities, roads, and harbors; perhaps even for further conquests in the west. There is even some evidence that he asked to be deified and worshiped as a god, although we cannot be sure if he really did so or what he had in mind if he did. In June of 323 B.C., he was overcome by a fever and died in Babylon at the age of thirty-three. His memory has never faded, and he soon became the subject of myth, legend, and romance. From the beginning, estimates of him have varied. Some have seen in him a man of grand and noble vision who transcended the narrow limits of Greek and Macedonian ethnocentrism and aimed at the brotherhood of humankind in a great world state. Others have seen him as a calculating despot, given to drunken brawls, brutality, and murder.

The truth is probably in between. Alexander was one of the greatest generals the world has seen; he never lost a battle or failed in a siege, and with a modest army, he conquered a vast empire. He had rare organizational talents, and his plan for creating a multinational empire was the only intelligent way of proceeding. He established many new cities—seventy, according to tradition—mostly along trade routes. These cities had the effect of encouraging commerce and prosperity as well as introducing Hellenic civilization into new areas. It is hard to know if the vast new empire could have been held together, but Alexander's death proved that only he could have succeeded.

Nobody was prepared for Alexander's sudden death in 323 B.C., and affairs were further complicated by a weak succession: Roxane's unborn child and Alexander's weak-minded half-brother. His able and loyal Macedonian generals at first hoped to preserve the empire for the Macedonian royal house, and to this end, they appointed themselves governors of the various provinces of the empire. However, the conflicting ambitions of these strong-willed men led to prolonged warfare among various combinations of them, in which three of the original number were killed, and all of the direct members of the Macedonian royal house were either executed or murdered. With the murder of Roxane and her son in 310 B.C., there was no longer any focus for the enormous empire, and in 306 and 305, the surviving governors proclaimed themselves kings of their various holdings.

Three of these Macedonian generals founded dynasties of significance in the spread of Hellenistic culture:

Ptolemy I (367?–283 B.C.)	Founder of the Thirty-first Dynasty in Egypt, the Ptolemies, of whom Cleopatra, who died in 30 B.C., was the last
Seleucus I (358?–280 B.C.)	Founder of the Seleucid dynasty in Mesopotamia
Antigonus I (382–301 B.C.)	Founder of the Antigonid dynasty in Asia Minor and Macedon

For the first seventy-five years or so after the death of Alexander, the world ruled by his successors enjoyed considerable prosperity. The vast sums of money he and they put into circulation greatly increased the level of economic activity. The opportunities for service and profit in the east attracted many Greeks and relieved their native cities of some of the pressure of the poor. The opening of vast new territories to Greek trade, the increased demand for Greek products, and the new availability of things wanted by the Greeks, as well as the conscious policies of the Hellenistic kings, all helped the growth of commerce. The new prosperity, however, was not evenly distributed. The urban Greeks, the Macedonians, and the hellenized natives who made up the upper and middle classes lived lives of comfort and even luxury, but the rural native peasants did not. During prosperous times, these distinctions were bearable, although even then there was tension between the two groups.

After a while, however, the costs of continuing wars, inflation, and a gradual lessening of the positive effects of the introduction of Persian wealth all led to economic crisis. The kings bore down heavily on the middle classes, who, however, were skilled in avoiding their responsibilities. The pressure on the peasants and the city laborers became great, too, and they responded by slowing down their work and even by striking. In Greece, economic pressures brought clashes between rich and poor, demands for the abolition of debt and the redistribution of land, and even, on occasion, civil war.

These internal divisions, along with the international wars, weakened the capacity of the Hellenistic kingdoms to resist outside attack, and by the middle of the second century B.C., they were all gone, except for Egypt. The two centuries between Alexander and the Roman conquest, however, were of great and lasting importance. They saw the formation into a single political, economic, and cultural unit of the entire eastern Mediterranean coast and of Greece, Egypt, Mesopotamia, and the old Persian Empire. The period also saw the creation of a new culture that took root, at least in the urban portions of that vast area, one that deserves to be differentiated from the earlier one of the Greek city-states: Hellenistic culture.

Hellenistic Culture

The career of Alexander the Great marked a significant turning point in the thought of the Greeks as it was represented in literature, philosophy, religion, and art. His conquests and the establishment of the successor kingdoms put an end once and for all to the central role of the *polis* in Greek life and thought.

Deprived of control of their foreign affairs, their important internal arrangements determined by a foreign monarch, the postclassical cities lost the kind of political freedom that was basic to the old outlook. They were cities, perhaps—in a sense, even city-states—but not *poleis*. As time passed, they changed from sovereign states to municipal towns merged in military empires. Never again in antiquity would there be either a serious attack on or a defense of the *polis*, for its importance was gone. For the most part, the Greeks after Alexander turned away from political solutions for their problems and sought instead personal responses to their hopes and fears, particularly in religion, philosophy, and magic. The confident, sometimes arrogant, humanism of the fifth century B.C. gave way to a kind of resignation to fate, a recognition of helplessness before forces too great for humans to manage.

Philosophy

These developments are noticeable in the changes that overtook the established schools of philosophy as well as in the emergence of two new and influential groups of philosophers, the Epicureans and the Stoics. Athens' position as the center of philosophical studies was reinforced, for the Academy and the Lyceum continued in operation, and the new schools were also located in Athens. The Lyceum turned gradually away from the universal investigations of its founder, Aristotle, even from his scientific interests, to become a center chiefly of literary and especially historical studies.

The Academy turned even further away from its tradition. It adopted the systematic Skepticism of Pyrrho of Elis, and under the leadership of Arcesilaus and Carneades, the Skeptics of the Academy became skilled at pointing out fallacies and weaknesses in the philosophies of the rival schools. They thought that nothing could be known and so consoled themselves and their followers by suggesting that nothing mattered. It was easy for them, therefore, to accept conventional morality and the world as it was. The Cynics, of course, continued to denounce convention and to advocate the crude life in accordance with nature, which some of them practiced publicly to the shock and outrage of respectable citizens. Neither of these views had much appeal to the middle-class city-dweller of the third century B.C., who sought some basis for choosing a way of life now that the *polis* no longer provided one ready-made.

THE EPICUREANS. Epicurus of Athens (342–271 B.C.) formulated a new teaching, which was embodied in the school he founded in his native city in 306. His philosophy conformed to the new mood in that its goal was not knowledge but human happiness, which he believed could be achieved if one followed a style of life based on reason. He took sense perception to be the basis of all human knowledge. The reality and reliability of sense perception rested on the acceptance of the physical universe described by the atomists, Democritus and Leucippus, in which atoms were continually falling through the void and giving off images that were in direct contact with the senses. These falling atoms could swerve in an arbitrary, unpredictable way to produce the combinations seen in the world; Epicurus thereby removed an element of determinism that existed in the Democritean system. When a person died, the atoms that composed the body dispersed so that the person had no further existence or perception and therefore nothing to fear after death. Epicurus believed that the gods existed but that they took no interest in human affairs. This belief amounted to a practical atheism, and Epicureans were often thought to be atheists.

The purpose of Epicurean physics was to liberate people from their fear of death, the gods, and all nonmaterial or supernatural powers. Epicurean ethics were hedonistic, that is, based on the acceptance of pleasure as true happiness. But pleasure for Epicurus was chiefly negative: the absence of pain and trouble. The goal of the Epicureans was *ataraxia*, the condition of being undisturbed, without trouble, pain, or responsibility. Ideally, a man should have enough means to allow him to withdraw from the world and avoid business and public life; Epicurus even advised against marriage and children. He preached a life of genteel, restrained selfishness, which might appeal to intellectual men of means, but was not calculated to be widely attractive.

THE STOICS. Soon after Epicurus began teaching in his garden in Athens, Zeno of Citium in Cyprus (335–263 B.C.) established the Stoic school, which derived its name from the *Stoa Poikile*, or Painted Portico, in the Athenian Agora, where Zeno and his disciples walked and talked beginning about 300 B.C.

Like the Epicureans, the Stoics sought the happiness of the individual. Quite unlike them, the Stoics held a philosophy almost indistinguishable from religion. They believed that humans must live in harmony within themselves and in harmony with nature; for the Stoics, god and nature were the same. The guiding principle in nature was divine reason (Logos), or fire. Every human had a spark of this divinity, and after death, it returned to the eternal divine spirit. From time to time, the world was destroyed by fire, from which a new world arose. The aim of humans, and the definition of human happiness, was the virtuous life, life lived in accordance with natural law, "when all actions promote the harmony of the spirit dwelling in the individual man with the will of him who orders the universe."[1] To live such a life required the knowledge possessed only by the wise, who knew what was good, what was evil, and what was neither, but "indifferent." Good and evil were dispositions of the mind or soul: prudence, justice, courage, temperance, and so on were good, whereas folly, injustice, cowardice, and the like were evil. Life, health, pleasure, beauty, strength, wealth, and so on were neutral, morally indifferent, for they did not contribute either to happiness or to misery. Human misery came from an irrational mental contraction, from passion, which was a disease of the soul. The wise sought freedom from passion *(apatheia)*, because passion arose from things that were morally indifferent.

[1] Diogenes Laertius, *Life of Zeno*

Politically, the Stoics fit well into the new world. They thought of it as a single *polis* in which all men were children of god. Although they did not forbid political activity, and many Stoics took part in political life, withdrawal was obviously preferable because the usual subjects of political argument were indifferent. Because the Stoics aimed at inner harmony of the individual, because their aim was a life lived in accordance with the divine will, and because their attitude was fatalistic and their goal a form of apathy, they fit in well with the reality of post-Alexandrian life. In fact, the spread of Stoicism made simpler the task of creating a new political system that relied not on the active participation of the governed, but merely on their docile submission.

Literature

The literature of the Hellenistic period reflects the new intellectual currents and, even more, the new conditions of literary life and the new institutions created in that period. The center of literary production in the third and second centuries B.C. was the new city of Alexandria in Egypt. There the Ptolemies, the kings of Egypt during that time, founded the museum, a great research institute where scientists and scholars were supported by royal funds, and the library, which contained almost half a million volumes, or papyrus scrolls. In the library were the works making up the great body of past Greek literature of every kind, much of which has since been lost. The Alexandrian scholars saw to it that what they judged to be the best works were copied; they edited and criticized these works from the point of view of language, form, and content and wrote biographies of their authors. Much of their work was valuable and is responsible for the preservation of most of ancient literature. Some of it is dry, petty, quarrelsome, and simply foolish. At its best, however, it is full of learning and perception.

The scholarly atmosphere of Alexandria naturally gave rise to work in the field of history and its ancillary discipline, chronology. Eratosthenes (CA. 275–195 B.C.) established a chronology of important events dating from the Trojan War, and others undertook similar tasks. Contemporaries of Alexander, such Ptolemy I, Aristobulus, and Nearchus, wrote what were apparently sober and essentially factual accounts of his career. Most of the work done by Hellenistic historians is known to us only in fragments cited by later writers, but it seems in general to have emphasized sensational and biographical detail rather than the rigorous impersonal analysis of a Thucydides.

Architecture and Sculpture

The opportunities open to architects and sculptors were greatly increased by the advent of the Hellenistic monarchies. There was plenty of money, the royal

The stoa of Attalus, Athens. Many Hellenistic kings sought to glorify their reigns by embellishing Athens in recognition of the city's intellectual fame. This two-story gallery of colonnaded shops was built by Attalus II, king of Pergamum (160–138 B.C.) in the Athenian agora, or marketplace. It was reconstructed by American archaelogists and is now a museum. [AHM.]

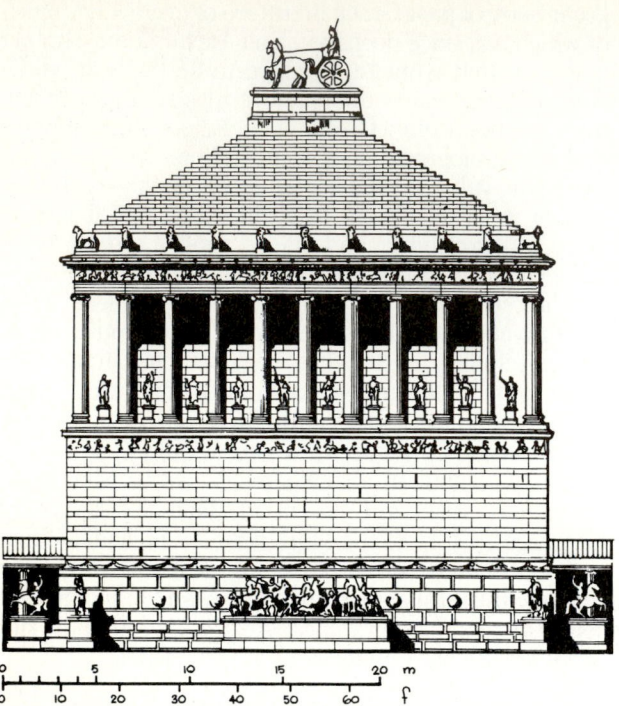

need for conspicuous display, the need to build and beautify new cities, and a growing demand from the well-to-do for objects of art. The new cities were usually laid out on the gridiron plan introduced in the fifth century by Hippodamus of Miletus. Temples were built on the classical model, and the covered portico or *stoa* became a very popular addition to the *agoras* of the Hellenistic towns.

Sculpture reflected the cosmopolitan nature of the Hellenistic world, for leading sculptors accepted commissions wherever they were attractive, and the result was a certain uniformity of style, although Alexandria, Rhodes, and the kingdom of Pergamum in Asia Minor developed their own characteristic styles. For the most part, Hellenistic sculpture carried forward the tendencies of the fourth century B.C., moving away from the balanced tension and idealism of the fifth century toward a sentimental, emotional, and realistic mode. These qualities are readily apparent in the statue of the *Dying Gaul* dedicated by Attalus I, king of Pergamum, in about 225 B.C.

Mathematics and Science

Among the most spectacular and remarkable intellectual developments of the Hellenistic age were those that came in mathematics and science. It is not too much to say that the work done by the Alexandrians formed the greater part of the scientific knowledge available to the Western world until the scientific revolution of the sixteenth and seventeenth centuries A.D.

Euclid's *Elements* (written early in the third century B.C.) remained the textbook of plane and solid

The Mausoleum. This is a conjectural reconstruction of the tomb of King Mausolus of Caria in Asia Minor, which gave us the word "mausolem." It was built at Halicarnassus in 353 B.C. by the widow, Queen Artemisia, and later made its way into Hellenistic lists of wonders of the world. [World Architecture; An Illustrated History, Trewin Copplestone, General Editor (London: Hamlyn, 1963), p. 54.]

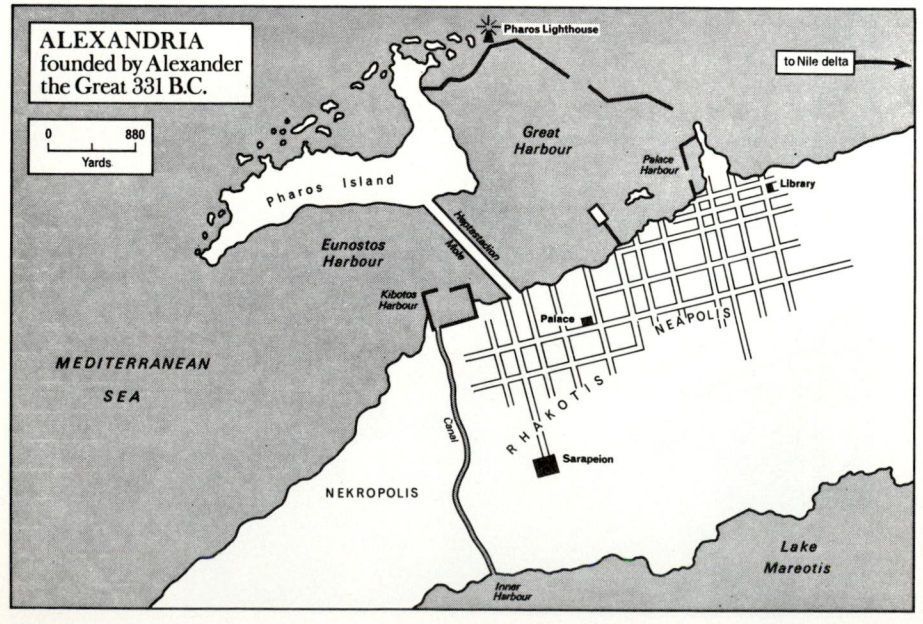

Map of Alexandria. Alexander the Great was given to founding new cities along the major trade routes in his newly conquered provinces, and several of these he allowed to be named for himself, but this one in Egypt was the only one to remain a place of consequence. His Macedonian successors, the Ptolemies, made it the capital of their Egyptian kingdom and also a center of Hellenistic culture; its library and museum were famous centers of learning and scholarship, and its lighthouse, the Pharos, was a marvel of construction to the ancient world. [Michael Grant, Ancient History Atlas (New York: Macmillan, 1971), p. 42.]

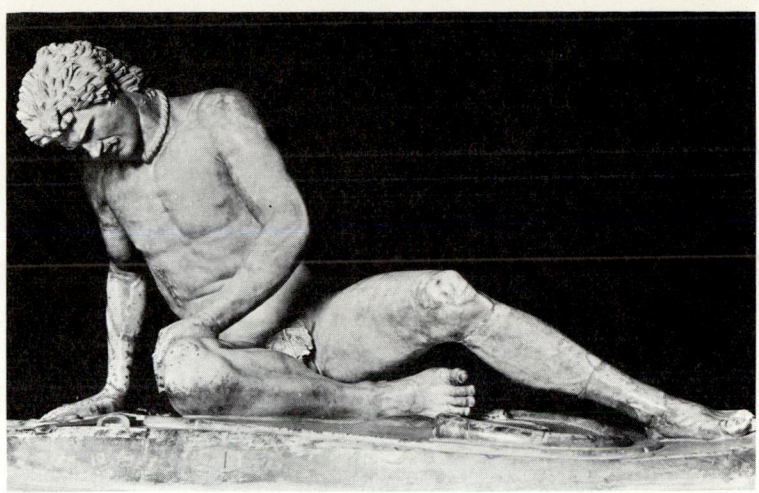

The Dying Gaul. This is a Roman copy of one of a group originally dedicated at the temple of Athena at Pergamum by Attalus I about 230 B.C. It is now in the Museo Capitolino, Rome. [Bettmann Archive.]

geometry until just recently. Archimedes of Syracuse (CA. 287–212 B.C.) made further progress in geometry, as well as establishing the theory of the lever in mechanics and inventing hydrostatics. The advances in mathematics, when added to the availability of Babylonian astronomical tables, allowed great progress in the field of astronomy. As early as the fourth century, Heraclides of Pontus (CA. 390–310 B.C.) had argued that Mercury and Venus circulate around the sun and not the earth, and he appears to have made other suggestions leading in the direction of a heliocentric the-

ory of the universe. Most scholars, however, give credit for that theory to Aristarchus of Samos (CA. 310–230 B.C.), who asserted that the sun, along with the other fixed stars, did not move and that the earth revolved around the sun in a circular orbit and rotated on its axis while doing so.

The heliocentric theory ran contrary not only to the traditional view codified by Aristotle but to what seemed to be common sense. However, Hellenistic technology was not up to proving the theory, and, of course, the planetary orbits are not circular. The helio-

Plutarch Cites Archimedes and Hellenistic Science

Archimedes (CA. 287–211 B.C.) was one of the great mathematicians and physicists of antiquity. He was a native of Syracuse in Sicily and a friend of its king. Plutarch discusses him in the following selection and reveals much about the ancient attitude toward applied science.

Archimedes, however, in writing to King Hiero, whose friend and near relation he was, had stated that given the force, any given weight might be moved, and even boasted, we are told, relying on the strength of demonstration, that if there were another earth, by going into it he could remove this. Hiero being struck with amazement at this, and entreating him to make good this problem by actual experiment, and show some great weight moved by a small engine, he fixed accordingly upon a ship of burden out of the king's arsenal, which could not be drawn out of the dock without great labour and many men; and, loading her with many passengers and a full freight, sitting himself the while

far off, with no great endeavour, but only holding the head of the pulley in his hand and drawing the cords by degrees. . . . Yet Archimedes possessed so high a spirit, so profound a soul, and such treasures of scientific knowledge, that though these inventions had now obtained him the renown of more than human sagacity, he yet would not deign to leave behind him any commentary or writing on such subjects; but, repudiating as sordid and ignoble the whole trade of engineering, and every sort of art that lends itself to mere use and profit, he placed his whole affection and ambition in those purer speculations where there can be no reference to the vulgar needs of life. . . . ❏

Plutarch, "Marcellus," in *Lives of the Noble Grecians and Romans*, trans. by John Dryden, revised by A. H. Clough (New York: Random House, n.d.), pp. 376–378.

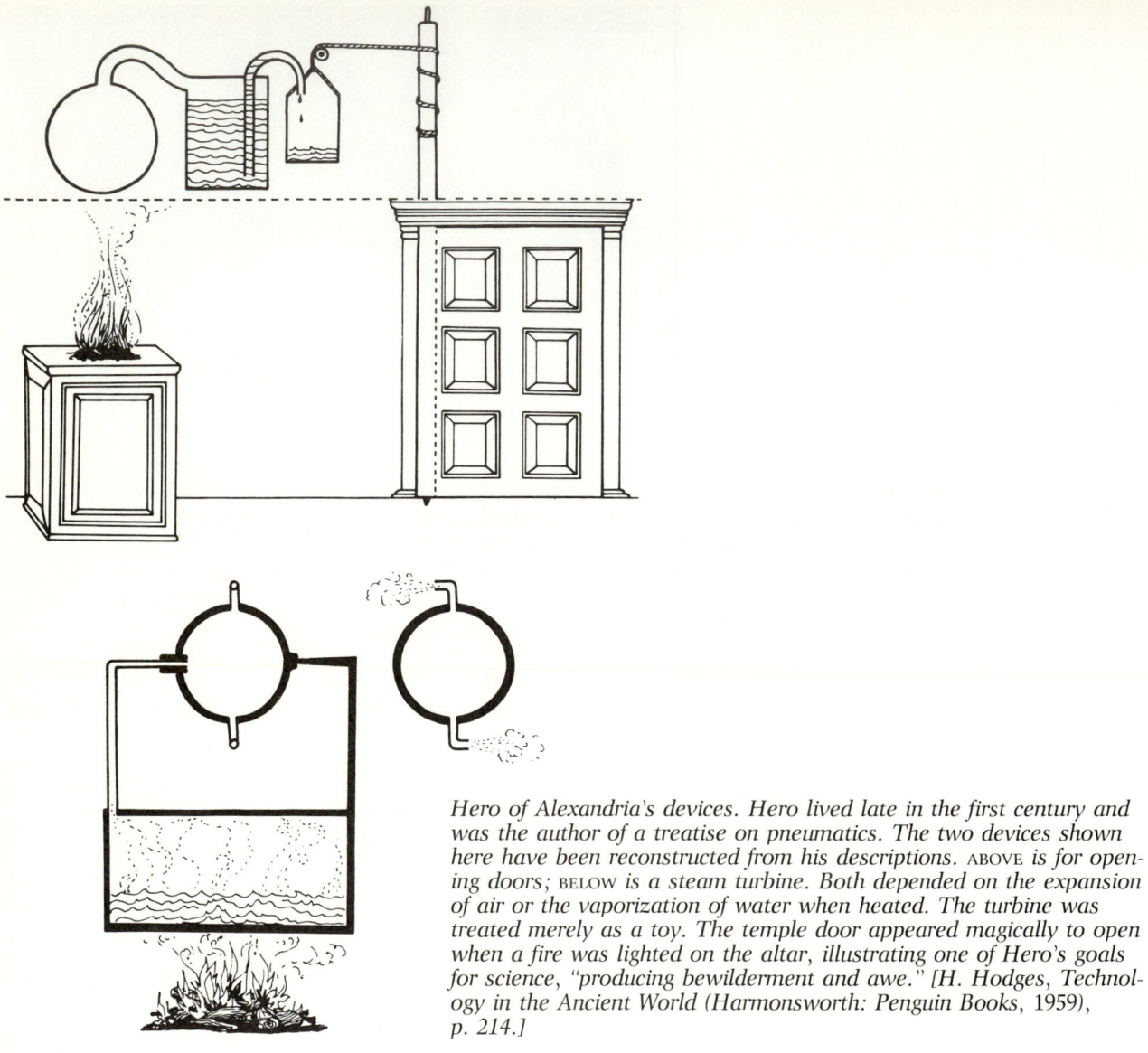

Hero of Alexandria's devices. Hero lived late in the first century and was the author of a treatise on pneumatics. The two devices shown here have been reconstructed from his descriptions. ABOVE is for opening doors; BELOW is a steam turbine. Both depended on the expansion of air or the vaporization of water when heated. The turbine was treated merely as a toy. The temple door appeared magically to open when a fire was lighted on the altar, illustrating one of Hero's goals for science, "producing bewilderment and awe." [H. Hodges, Technology in the Ancient World (Harmonsworth: Penguin Books, 1959), p. 214.]

centric theory did not, therefore, take hold. Hipparchus of Nicaea (b. CA. 190 B.C.) constructed a model of the universe on the geocentric theory, employing an ingenious and complicated model that did a very good job of accounting for the movements of the sun, the moon, and the planets. Ptolemy of Alexandria (second century A.D.) adopted Hipparchus' system with a few improvements, and it remained dominant until the work of Copernicus, in the sixteenth century A.D.

Hellenistic scientists made progress in mapping the earth as well as the sky. Eratosthenes of Cyrene (CA. 275–195 B.C.) was able to calculate the circumference of the earth within about two hundred miles and wrote a treatise on geography based on mathematical and physical reasoning and the reports of travelers. In spite of the new data that were available to later geographers, Eratosthenes' map (see Map 4.4) was in many ways more accurate than the one constructed by Ptolemy that became standard in the Middle Ages.

The Achievement of the Classical and Hellenistic Ages in World Perspective

The Classical Age of Greece was a period of unparalleled achievement. It carried forward the tradition of rational, secular speculation in natural philosophy and science, but turned its attention more to human questions in medicine and ethical and political philosophy.

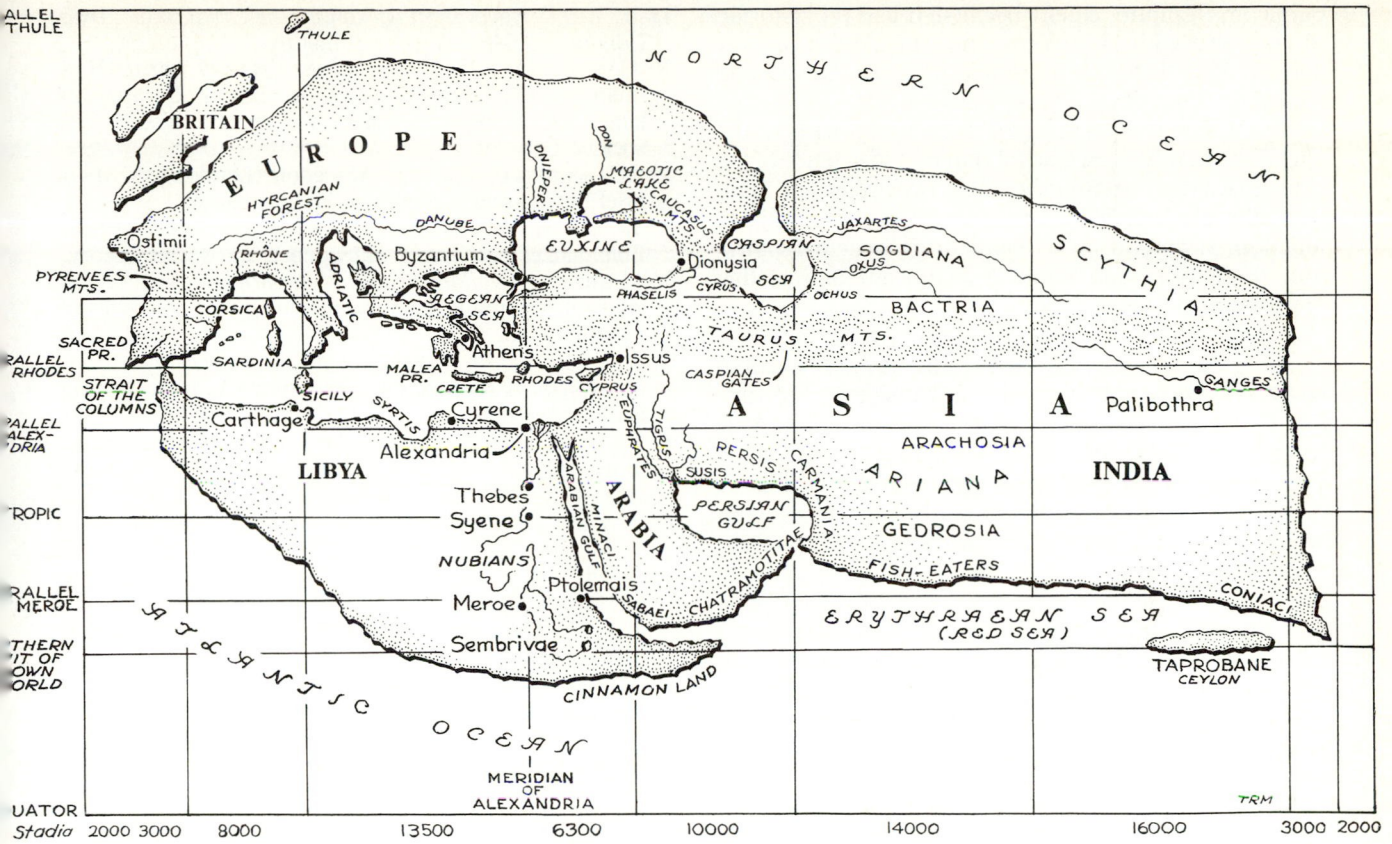

MAP 4-4 THE WORLD ACCORDING TO ERATOSTHENES *Eratosthenes of Alexandria* (CA. *275–195 B.C.) was a Hellenistic geographer. His map, reconstructed here, was remarkably accurate for its time. The world was divided by lines of "latitude" and "longitude," thus anticipating our global divisions.*

While the rest of the world continued to be characterized by monarchical, hierarchical, command societies, in Athens democracy was carried as far as it would go before modern times. Although limited to adult males of native parentage, Athenian citizenship granted full and active participation in every decision of the state without regard to wealth or class. Democracy disappeared with the end of Greek autonomy late in the fourth century B.C. When it returned in the modern world more than two millennia later, it was broader but shallower. Democratic citizenship did not again imply the active direct participation of every citizen in the government of the state.

It was in this democratic imperial Athens that the greatest artistic, literary, and philosophical achievements took place. Many of the literary genres and forms that are vital in the modern world arose and were developed during this time. Analytical, secular history, tragedy and comedy, the philosophical dialogue, an organized system of logic, and logical philosophical treatise on almost every aspect open to

human thought, were among the achievements of the Classical Age. A naturalistic style of art evolved that placed human beings, first as they ideally might look, and then as they really looked. This approach dominated Greek and Roman art until the fall of the Roman Empire when it largely disappeared. It rose again to have a powerful effect on the Italian Renaissance and, through it, on the modern world.

These Hellenic developments, it should be clear, diverge sharply from the experience of previous cultures and of contemporary ones in the rest of the world. To a great degree, they sprang from the unique political experience of the Greeks, which avoided monarchies and great, extended, land empires but was based on independent city states. That unique experience came to an end with the Macedonian conquest, which ultimately made the Greeks subject to or part of some great national state or empire and brought an end to the Classical period.

The Hellenistic Age speaks to us less fully and vividly than that of classical Greece or of the Roman Republic and Empire, chiefly because it had no historian to compare with Herodotus and Thucydides or Livy and Tacitus. We lack a continuous, rich, lively, and meaningful narrative. This deficiency should not obscure the great importance of the achievements of the age. The literature, art, scholarship, and science of the period deserve attention in their own right. In addition, the Hellenistic Age performed a vital civilizing function. It spread the Greek culture over a remarkably wide area and made a significant and lasting impression on much of it.

Greek culture also adjusted to its new surroundings to a degree, unifying and simplifying its cultural cargo so as to make it more accessible to outsiders. The various Greek dialects gave way to a version of the Attic tongue, the *koinē*, or common language. In the same way, the scholarship of Alexandria established canons of literary excellence and the scholarly tools with which to make the great treasures of Greek culture understandable to later generations. The union of thought and belief introduced in this period also made understanding and accord more likely among peoples who were very different. When the Romans came into contact with Hellenism, they were powerfully impressed by it, and when they conquered the Hellenistic world, they became, as Horace said, captives of its culture.

The conquests of Alexander and the Hellenistic civilization that came with them greatly affected the conquered societies and their neighbors. The Seleucid successors of Alexander ruled some parts of the old Persian Empire for almost two centuries after his death, and Hellenistic culture continued to influence the urban upper classes for some time.

The Hellenistic influence reached even further under another group of Greeks who broke away from the Seleucids to form the Indo-Greek people of Bactria. By the second century B.C., they controlled parts of northern India. The legacy of Hellenism in the East can be seen reflected in art as far as China. In the West, of course, the legacy was more complete and influential, powerfully shaping the nature of the Roman culture that would ultimately dominate the entire Mediterranean world and make important contacts beyond it.

Suggested Readings

M. AUSTIN AND P. VIDAL-NAQUET, *The Economic and Social History of Classical Greece* (Berkeley, 1977). A combination of documents and explanation.

E. BARKER, *Political Philosophy of Plato and Aristotle* (1959). A sober and reliable account.

H. I. BELL, *Egypt from Alexander the Great to the Arab Conquest* (1948). A general history.

P. CARTLEDGE, *Agesilaus and the Crisis of Sparta* (Baltimore, 1987). More than a biography of the Spartan king, it is a complex discussion of Spartan history and society.

G. CAWKWELL, *Philip of Macedon* (London, 1978). A brief but learned account of Philip's career.

J. K. DAVIES, *Democracy and Classical Greece* (1978). Emphasizes archeological evidence and social history.

V. EHRENBERG, *The People of Aristophanes* (1962). A study of Athenian society as reveled by the comedies of Aristophanes.

J. R. ELLIS, *Philip II and Macedonian Imperialism* (London, 1976). A study of the career of the founder of Macedonian power.

J. R. LANE FOX, *Alexander the Great* (1973). An imaginative account that does more justice to the Persian side of the problem than is usual.

PETER GREEN, *Alexander the Great* (1972). A lively biography.

N. G. L. HAMMOND AND G. T. GRIFFITH, *A History of Macedonia*, vol. 2, 550–336 B.C. (1979). A thorough account of Macedonian history that focuses on the careers of Philip and Alexander.

W. JAEGER, *Demosthenes* (1938). A good biography of the Athenian statesman.

D. KAGAN, *The Outbreak of the Peloponnesian War* (1969). A study of the period from the foundation of the Delian League to the coming of the Peloponnesian War that argues that war could have been avoided.

D. KAGAN, *The Archidamian War* (1974). A history of the first ten years of the Peloponnesian War.

D. KAGAN, *The Peace of Nicias and the Sicilian Expedition* (1981). A history of the middle period of the Peloponnesian War.

D. KAGAN, *The Fall of the Athenian Empire* (Ithaca, 1987). The last period of the war.

H. D. F. KITTO, *Greek Tragedy* (1966). A good introduction.

B. M. W. KNOX, *The Heroic Temper: Studies in Sophoclean Tragedy* (1964). A brilliant analysis of tragic heroism.

D. M. LEWIS, *Sparta and Persia* (Leiden, 1977). A valuable discussion of relations between Sparta and Persia in the fifth and fourth centuries B.C.

G. E. R. LLOYD, *Greek Science After Aristotle* (1974).

A. A. LONG, *Hellenistic Philosophy: Stoics, Epicureans, Sceptics* (1974). An account of Greek science in the Hellenistic and Roman periods.

R. MEIGGS, *The Athenian Empire* (1972). A fine study of the rise and fall of the empire, making excellent use of inscriptions.

H. W. PARKE, *Festivals of the Athenians* (Ithaca, 1977). A fine discussion of the religious practices of the Athenians.

J. J. POLLITT, *Art and Experience in Classical Greece* (1972). A scholarly and entertaining study of the relationship between art and history in classical Greece, with excellent illustrations.

J. J. Pollitt, *Art in the Hellenistic Age* (Cambridge, 1986). An extraordinary analysis that places the art in its historical and intellectual context.

M. I. Rostovtzeff, *Social and Economic History of the Hellenistic World*, 3 vols. (1941). A masterpiece of synthesis by a great historian.

D. M. Schaps, *Economic Rights of Women in Ancient Greece* (Edinburgh, 1981).

B. S. Strauss, *Athens After the Peloponnesian War* (Ithaca, 1987). An excellent discussion of Athens' recovery and of the nature of Athenian society and politics in the fourth century B.C.

W. W. Tarn, *Alexander the Great*, 2 vols. (1948). The first volume is a narrative account; the second a series of detailed studies.

W. W. Tarn and G. T. Griffith, *Hellenistic Civilization* (1961). A survey of Hellenistic history and culture.

A. E. Taylor, *Socrates* (1953). A good, readable account.

V. Tcherikover, *Hellenistic Civilization and the Jews* (1970). A fine study of the impact of Hellenism on the Jews.

F. W. Walbank, *The Hellenistic World* (1981).

T. B. L. Webster, *Hellenistic Poetry and Art* (1961). A clear survey.

A. E. Zimmern, *The Greek Commonwealth* (1961). A study of political, social, and economic conditions in fifth-century Athens.

A patrician with portraits of his ancestors. Roman patricians took great pride in their lineage and would not marry outside their own group. [German Archaelogical Institute, Rome.]

5 Rome: From Republic to Empire

The achievement of the Romans was one of the most remarkable accomplishments in human history. The descendants of the inhabitants of a small village in central Italy ruled the entire Italian peninsula, then the entire Mediterranean coastline. They conquered most of the Near East and finally much of continental Europe. They ruled this vast empire under a single government that provided considerable peace and prosperity for centuries. At no time before the Romans or since has that area been united, and rarely, if ever, has it enjoyed a stable peace. But Rome's legacy was not merely military excellence and political organization. The Romans adopted and transformed the intellectual and cultural achievements of the Greeks and combined them with their own outlook and historical experience. They produced the Graeco-Roman tradition in literature, philosophy, and art that served as the core of learning for the Middle Ages and the inspiration for the new paths taken in the Renaissance. That tradition remains at the heart of Western civilization to this day.

Prehistoric Italy

The culture of Italy developed late. Paleolithic settlements gave way to the Neolithic mode of life only about 2500 B.C. The Bronze Age came about 1500 B.C., and about 1000 B.C., Italy began to be infiltrated by bands of new arrivals from across the Adriatic Sea and around its northern end. The invaders were warlike people who imposed their language and social organization on almost all of Italy. Their bronze work was better than their predecessors', and soon they made weapons, armor, and tools of iron. They cremated their dead and put the ashes in tombs stocked with weapons and armor. Before 800 B.C., people living in this style occupied the highland pastures of the Apennines. These tough mountain people—Umbrians,

MAP 5-1 ANCIENT ITALY *This map of the Italian peninsula and its neighbors in antiquity shows the major cities and towns, as well as a number of geographical regions and the locations of some of the Italic and non-Italic peoples of the area.*

Sabines, Samnites, Latins, and others—spoke a set of closely related languages that we call *Italic*.

They soon began to challenge the earlier settlers for control of the tempting western plains. Other peoples lived in Italy in the ninth century B.C., but the Italic speakers and three peoples who had not yet arrived— the Etruscans, the Greeks, and the Celts—would shape its future.

The Etruscans

The Etruscans exerted the most powerful external influence on the Romans. Their civilization arose in Etruria (now Tuscany), west of the Apennines between the Arno and Tiber rivers, about 800 B.C. (see Map 5.1). Their origin is far from clear, but their tomb architecture, resembling that of Asia Minor, and their practice of divining the future by inspecting the livers of sacrificial animals point to an eastern origin.

The Etruscans brought civilization with them. Their settlements were self-governing, fortified city-states, of which twelve formed a loose religious confederation. At first, these cities were ruled by kings, but they were replaced by an aristocracy of the agrarian nobles, who ruled by means of a council and elected annual magistrates. The Etruscans were a military ruling class that dominated and exploited the native Italians, who worked their land and mines and served as infantry in their armies. This aristocracy accumulated considerable wealth through agriculture, industry, piracy, and a growing commerce with the Carthaginians and the Greeks.

The Etruscans' influence on the Romans was greatest in religion. They imagined a world filled with gods and spirits, many of them evil. To deal with such demons, the Etruscans evolved complicated rituals and powerful priesthoods. Divination by sacrifice and omens in nature helped discover the divine will, and careful attention to precise rituals directed by priests helped please the gods. After a while, the Etruscans,

Terracotta figures from an Etruscan sarcophagus of the late sixth century B.C. The dead couple are shown reclining as for a banquet. Museo de Villa Giulia, Rome. [Photo by Robert Emmett Bright. Rapho Guilumette.]

The Tiber island at Rome. This island in the Tiber made the river fordable at its location and therefore helped determine the location of the city of Rome. Later bridges kept the crossing a popular one, as shown in this eighteenth-century etching by G.B. Piranesi.

influenced by the Greeks, worshiped gods in the shape of humans and built temples for them.

The Etruscan aristocracy remained aggressive and skillful in the use of horses and war chariots. In the seventh and sixth centuries B.C., they expanded their power in Italy and across the sea to Corsica and Elba. They conquered Latium (a region that included the small town of Rome) and Campania, where they became neighbors of the Greeks of Naples.

Royal Rome

In the sixth century B.C., Rome came under Etruscan control. Led by their Etruscan kings, the Roman army, equipped and organized like the Greek phalanx, gained control of most of Latium. They achieved this success under an effective political and social order that gave extraordinary power to the ruling figures in both public and private life.

Government

To their kings, the Romans gave the awesome power of *imperium*, the right to issue commands and to enforce them by fines, arrests, and corporal or even capital punishment. The kingship was elective and the office appears to have tended to remain in the same family. The Senate, however, had to approve the candidate, and the *imperium* was formally granted by a vote of the people in assembly. The basic character of Roman government was already clear: Great power was granted to executive officers, but it had to be approved by the Senate and was derived ultimately from the people. Ostensibly the Senate had neither executive nor legislative power; it met only when summoned by the king and then only to advise him. In reality, its authority was great, for the senators, like the king, served for life. The Senate, therefore, had continuity and experience, and as it was composed of the most powerful men in the state, it could not lightly be ignored.

In early Rome, citizenship required descent from Roman parents on both sides. All citizens were organized into the third branch of government, an assembly made up of thirty groups. It met only when summoned by the king; he determined the agenda, made proposals, and recognized other speakers, if any. For the most part, the assembly was called to listen and approve. Voting was not by head but by group; a majority within each group determined its vote, and the decisions were made by majority vote of the groups. Group voting was typical of all Roman assemblies in the future.

The Family

The center of Roman life was the family. At its head stood the father, whose power and authority within the family resembled those of the king within the state. Over his children, he held broad powers analogous to *imperium* in the state, for he had the right to sell his children into slavery, and he even had the power of life and death over them. Over his wife he had less power; he could not sell or kill her. As the king's power was more limited in practice than in theory, so it was with the father. His power to dispose of his children was limited by consultation with the family, by public opinion, and, most of all, by tradition. The wife could not be divorced except for stated serious offenses, and even then she had to be convicted by a court made up of her male blood relatives. The Roman woman had a respected position and the main responsibility for managing the household. The father was the chief priest of the family. He led it in daily prayers to the dead that reflected the ancestor worship central to the Roman family and state.

Clientage

Clientage was one of Rome's most important institutions. The client was "an inferior entrusted, by custom or by himself, to the protection of a stranger more powerful than he, and rendering certain services and observances in return for this protection."[1] The Romans spoke of a client as being in the *fides*, or trust, of his patron, so that the relationship always had moral implications. The patron provided his client with protection, both physical and legal; he gave him economic assistance in the form of a land grant, the opportunity to work as a tenant farmer or a laborer on the patron's land, or simply handouts. In return, the client would fight for his patron, work his land, and support him politically. These mutual obligations were enforced by public opinion and tradition. When early custom was codified in the mid-fifth century B.C., one of the twelve tablets of laws announced: "Let the patron who has defrauded his client be accursed."

In the early history of Rome, patrons were rich and powerful whereas clients were poor and weak. But as time passed, it was not uncommon for rich and powerful members of the upper classes to become clients of even more powerful men, chiefly for political purposes.

[1] E. Badian, *Foreign Clientelae* (264–70 B.C.) (Oxford: 1958), p. 1.

Because the client–patron relationship was hereditary and sanctioned by religion and custom, it was to play a very important part in the life of the Roman Republic.

Patricians and Plebeians

In the royal period, Roman society was divided in two by a class distinction based on birth. The upper class was composed of the patricians, the wealthy men who held a monopoly of power and influence. They alone could conduct the religious ceremonies in the state, sit in the Senate, or hold office, and they formed a closed caste by forbidding marriage outside their own group. The plebeians must originally have been the poor and dependent men who were small farmers, laborers, and artisans, the clients of the nobility.

As Rome and its population grew in various ways, families who were rich but outside the charmed circle gained citizenship. From very early times, therefore, there were rich plebeians, and incompetence and bad luck must have produced some poor patricians. The line between the classes and the monopoly of privileges remained firm, nevertheless, and the struggle of the plebeians to gain equality occupied more than two centuries of republican history.

The Republic

Roman tradition tells us that the republic replaced the monarchy at Rome suddenly in 509 B.C. as the result of a revolution sparked by the outrageous behavior of the last kings and led by the noble families.

Its Constitution

The Roman constitution was an unwritten accumulation of laws and customs that had won respect and the force of law over time. The Romans were a conservative people, so they were never willing to deprive their chief magistrates of the great powers exercised by the monarchs.

THE CONSULS. The Romans elected two patricians to the office of consul and endowed them with *imperium.* They were assisted by two financial officials called *quaestors*, whose number ultimately reached eight. Like the kings the consuls led the army, had religious duties, and served as judges. They retained the visible symbols of royalty—the purple robe, the ivory chair, and the lictors (minor officials) bearing rods and axe who accompanied them—but their power was limited legally and institutionally as well as by custom.

The vast power of the consulship was granted not for life but only for a year. Each consul could prevent any action by his colleague by simply saying no to his proposal, and the religious powers of the consuls were shared with others. Even the *imperium* was limited,

Polybius Summarizes the Roman Constitution

Polybius (CA. 203–120 B.C.) was a Greek from the city of Megalopolis, an important member of the Achaean League. As a hostage in Rome, he became a friend of influential Romans and later wrote a history of Rome's conquest of the Mediterranean lands. He praised the Roman constitution as an excellent example of a "mixed constitution" and as a major source of Roman success.

As for the Roman constitution, it had three elements, each of them possessing sovereign powers: and their respective share of power in the whole state had been regulated with such a scrupulous regard to equality and equilibrium, that no one could say for certain, not even a native, whether the constitution as a whole were an aristocracy or democracy or despotism. . . .

. . . .

The result of this power of the several estates for mutual help or harm is a union sufficiently firm for all emergencies, and a constitution than which it is impossible to find a better. For whenever any danger from without compels them to unite and work together, the strength which is developed by the State is so extraordinary, that everything required is unfailingly carried out by the eager rivalry shown by all classes to devote their whole minds to the need of the hour, and to secure that any determination come to should not fail for want of promptitude; while each individual works, privately and publicly alike, for the accomplishment of the business in hand. Accordingly, the peculiar constitution of the State makes it irresistible, and certain of obtaining whatever it determines to attempt. . . . For when any one of the three classes becomes puffed up, and manifests an inclination to be contentious and unduly encroaching, the mutual interdependency of all the three, and the possibility of the pretensions of any one being checked and thwarted by the others, must plainly check this tendency: and so the proper equilibrium is maintained by the impulsiveness of the one part being checked by its fear of the other. . . . ❏

Polybius, *Histories*, Vol. 1, trans. by E. S. Shuckburgh (Bloomington: Indiana University Press, 1962), pp. 468, 473–474.

---

for though the consuls had full powers of life and death while leading an army, within the sacred boundary of the city of Rome the citizens had the right to appeal to the popular assembly all cases involving capital punishment. Besides, after their one year in office, the consuls would spend the rest of their lives as members of the Senate. It was a most reckless consul who failed to ask the advice of the Senate or who failed to follow it when there was general agreement.

The many checks on consular action tended to prevent initiative, swift action, and change, but this was just what a conservative, traditional, aristocratic republic wanted. Only in the military sphere did divided counsel and a short term of office create important problems. The Romans tried to get around the difficulties by sending only one consul into the field or, when this was impossible, allowing the consuls sole command on alternate days. In really serious crises, the consuls, with the advice of the Senate, could appoint a single man, the *dictator*, to the command and could retire in his favor. The *dictator's* term of office was limited to six months, but his own *imperium* was valid both inside and outside the city without appeal. These devices worked well enough in the early years of the republic, when Rome's battles were near home, but longer wars and more sophisticated opponents revealed the system's weaknesses and required significant changes.

Long campaigns prompted the invention of the proconsulship in 325 B.C., whereby the term of a consul serving in the field was extended. This innovation contained the seeds of many troubles for the constitution.

The introduction of the office of *praetor* also helped provide commanders for Rome's many campaigns. The basic function of the praetors was judicial, but they also had *imperium* and served as generals. By the end of the republic, there were eight praetors, whose annual terms, like the consuls', could be extended for military commands when necessary.

At first, the consuls classified the citizens according to age and property, the bases of citizenship and assignment in the army. After the middle of the fifth century B.C., two censors were elected to perform this duty. They conducted a census and drew up the citizen rolls, but this was no job for clerks. The classification fixed taxation and status, so that the censors had to be men of reputation, former consuls. The censors soon acquired additional powers. By the fourth century, they compiled the roll of senators and could strike senators from that roll not only for financial reasons but for moral reasons as well. As the prestige of the office grew, becoming a censor came to be considered the ultimate prize of a Roman political career.

THE SENATE AND THE ASSEMBLY. The end of the monarchy increased the influence and power of the Senate. It became the single continuous deliberative body in the Roman state. Its members were leading patricians, often leaders of clans and patrons of many clients. The Senate soon gained control of finances and of foreign policy. Its formal advice was not lightly ignored either by magistrates or by popular assemblies.

The most important assembly in the early republic was the centuriate assembly. In a sense, it was the Roman army acting in a political capacity, and its basic unit was the century, theoretically 100 fighting men classified according to their weapons, armor, and equipment. Because each man equipped himself, the organization was by classes according to wealth.

THE STRUGGLE OF THE ORDERS. The laws and constitution of the early republic clearly reflected the class structure of the Roman state, for they gave to the patricians almost a monopoly of power and privilege. The plebeians undertook a campaign to achieve political, legal, and social equality, and this attempt, which succeeded after two centuries of intermittent effort, is called the *struggle of the orders.*

The most important source of plebeian success was the need for their military service. Rome was at war almost constantly, and the patricians were forced to call on the plebeians to defend the state. According to tradition, the plebeians, angered by patrician resistance to their demands, withdrew from the city and camped on the Sacred Mount. There they formed a plebeian tribal assembly and elected plebeian tribunes to protect them from the arbitrary power of the magistrates. They declared the tribune inviolate and sacrosanct, and anyone laying violent hands on him was accursed and liable to death without trial. By extension of his right to protect the plebeians, the tribune gained the power to veto any action of a magistrate or any bill in a Roman assembly or the Senate. The plebeian assembly voted by tribe, and a vote of the assembly was binding on plebeians. They tried to make their decisions binding on all Romans but could not do so until 287 B.C.

The next step was for the plebeians to obtain access to the laws, and by 450 B.C., the Twelve Tables codified early Roman custom in all its harshness and simplicity. In 445 B.C., plebeians gained the right to marry patricians. The main prize was consulship. The patricians did not yield easily, but at last, in 367 B.C., the Licinian-Sextian Laws provided that at least one consul could be a plebeian. Before long plebeians held other offices, even the dictatorship and the censorship. In 300 B.C., they were admitted to the most important priesthoods, the last religious barrier to equality. In 287 B.C., the plebeians completed their triumph. They once again withdrew from the city and secured the passage of a law whereby decisions of the plebeian assembly bound all Romans and did not require the approval of the Senate.

It might seem that the Roman aristocracy had given

THE RISE OF THE PLEBEIANS TO EQUALITY IN ROME

509 B.C.	Kings expelled—republic founded
450–449 B.C.	Laws of the Twelve Tables published
445 B.C.	Plebeians gain right of marriage with patricians
367 B.C.	Licinian-Sextian Laws open consulship to plebeians
300 B.C.	Plebeians attain chief priesthoods
287 B.C.	Laws passed by Plebeian Assembly made binding on all Romans

way under the pressure of the lower class, but the victory of the plebeians did not bring democracy. An aristocracy based strictly on birth had given way to an aristocracy more subtle, but no less restricted, based on a combination of wealth and birth. The significant distinction was no longer between patrician and plebeian but between the *nobiles*—a relatively small group of wealthy and powerful families, both patrician and plebeian, whose members attained the highest offices in the state—and everyone else.

These same families dominated the Senate, whose power became ever greater. It remained the only continuous deliberative body in the state, and the pressure of warfare gave it experience in handling public business. Rome's success brought the Senate prestige and increased its control of policy and confidence in its capacity to rule. The end of the struggle of the orders brought domestic peace under a republican constitution dominated by a capable, if narrow, senatorial aristocracy. This outcome satisfied most Romans outside the ruling group because Rome conquered Italy and brought many benefits to its citizens.

The Conquest of Italy

Not long after the fall of the monarchy in 509 B.C., a coalition of Romans, Latins, and Italian Greeks defeated the Etruscans and drove them out of Latium for good.

GALLIC INVASION OF ITALY. At the beginning of the fourth century B.C., the Romans were the chief power in central Italy, but a disaster struck. In 387 B.C., the Gauls, barbaric Celtic tribes from across the Alps, defeated the Roman army and captured, looted, and burned Rome. The Gauls sought plunder, not conquest, so they extorted a ransom from the Romans and returned to their homes in the north. Rome's power appeared to have been wiped out.

When the Gauls left, some of Rome's allies and old enemies tried to take advantage of its weakness, but by about 350 B.C., the Romans had recovered their leadership of central Italy and were more dominant than ever. Their success in turning back new Gallic raids added still more to their power and prestige. As the Romans tightened their grip on Latium, the Latins became resentful. In 340 B.C., they demanded independence from Rome or full equality, and when the Romans refused, they launched a war of independence that lasted until 338. The victorious Romans dissolved the Latin League, and their treatment of the defeated opponents provided a model for the settlement of Italy.

ROMAN POLICY TOWARD THE CONQUERED. The Romans did not destroy any of the Latin cities or their people, nor did they treat them all alike. Some in the vicinity of Rome received full Roman citizenship; others farther away gained municipal status, which gave them the private rights of intermarriage and com-merce with Romans but not the public rights of voting and holding office in Rome. They retained the rights of local self-government and could obtain full Roman citizenship if they moved to Rome. They followed Rome in foreign policy and provided soldiers to serve in the Roman legions.

Still other states became allies of Rome on the basis of treaties, which differed from city to city. Some were given the private rights of intermarriage and commerce with Romans and some were not; the allied states were always forbidden to exercise these rights with one another. Some, but not all, were allowed local autonomy. Land was taken from some but not from others, nor was the percentage always the same. All the allies supplied troops to the army, in which they fought in auxiliary battalions under Roman officers, but they did not pay taxes to Rome.

On some of the conquered land, the Romans placed colonies, permanent settlements of veteran soldiers in the territory of recently defeated enemies. The colo-

The Via Latina, here shown not far outside Rome, is one of the network of military roads that went from Rome into the Italian country. They enabled Roman legions to move swiftly to enforce their control of the peninsula—and, conversely, also served as convenient avenues of invasion. The Via Latina is thought to be the earliest of these great roads, dating to the fourth century B.C [Fototeca Unione.]

nists retained their Roman citizenship and enjoyed home rule, and in return for the land they had been given, they served as a kind of permanent garrison to deter or suppress rebellion. These colonies were usually connected to Rome by a network of military roads built as straight as possible and so durable that some are used even today. They guaranteed that a Roman army could swiftly reinforce an embattled colony or put down an uprising in any weather.

The Roman settlement of Latium reveals even more clearly than before the principles by which Rome was able to conquer and dominate Italy for many centuries. The excellent army and the diplomatic skill that allowed Rome to separate its enemies help explain its conquests. The reputation for harsh punishment of rebels and the sure promise that such punishment would be delivered, made unmistakably clear by the presence of colonies and military roads, help account for the slowness to revolt. But the positive side, represented by Rome's organization of the defeated states, is at least as important. The Romans did not regard the status given each newly conquered city as permanent. They held out to loyal allies the prospect of improving their status, even of achieving the ultimate prize, full Roman citizenship. In so doing, the Romans gave their allies a stake in Rome's future and success and a sense of being colleagues, though subordinate ones, rather than subjects. The result, in general, was that most of Rome's allies remained loyal even when put to the severest test.

DEFEAT OF THE SAMNITES. The next great challenge to Roman arms came in a series of wars with a tough mountain people of the southern Appenines, the Samnites. Some of Rome's allies rebelled, and soon the Etruscans and Gauls joined in the war against Rome. But most of the allies remained loyal. In 295 B.C., at Sentinum, the Romans defeated an Italian coalition, and by 280, they were masters of central Italy. Their power extended from the Po valley south to Apulia and Lucania.

The victory over the Samnites brought the Romans into direct contact with the Greek cities of southern Italy, which they soon conquered. By 265 B.C., Rome ruled all Italy as far north as the Po River, an area of 47,200 square miles.

Rome and Carthage

Rome's acquisition of coastal territory and its expansion to the toe of the Italian boot brought it face to face with the great naval power of the western Mediterranean, Carthage (see Map 5.2). Late in the ninth century B.C., the Phoenician city of Tyre had planted a colony on the coast of northern Africa near modern Tunis, calling it the New City, or Carthage. In the sixth century B.C., the conquest of Phoenicia by the Assyri-

ans and the Persians made Carthage independent and free to exploit its very advantageous situation.

The city was located on a defensible site and commanded an excellent harbor that encouraged commerce. The coastal plain grew abundant grain, fruits, and vegetables. An inland plain allowed sheep herding. The Phoenician settlers conquered the native inhabitants and used them to work the land. Beginning in the sixth century B.C., the Carthaginians expanded their domain to include the coast of northern Africa west beyond the Straits of Gibraltar and eastward into Libya. Overseas, they came to control the southern part of Spain, Sardinia, Corsica, Malta, the Balearic Islands, and western Sicily. The people of these territories, though originally allies, were all reduced to subjection like the natives of the Carthaginian home territory; and they all served in the Carthaginian army or navy and paid tribute. Carthage also profited greatly from the mines of Spain and from the absolute monopoly of trade Carthage imposed on the western Mediterranean.

Early contacts between Rome and Carthage had been few but not unfriendly, but Rome's new proximity to Sicily brought conflict. Roman intervention in the Sicilian city of Messana in 264 B.C. produced the first Punic War (the Romans called the Carthaginians by their ancestral name, Phoenicians; in Latin the name is *Poeni* or *Puni*).

THE FIRST PUNIC WAR (264–241 B.C.). The war in Sicily soon settled into a stalemate. At last, the Romans built a fleet to cut off supplies to the besieged Carthaginian cities at the western end of Sicily. When Carthage sent its own fleet to raise the siege, the Romans destroyed it. In 241 B.C., Carthage signed a treaty giving up Sicily and the islands between Italy and Sicily and agreed to pay a war indemnity in ten annual installments, to keep its ships out of Italian waters, and not to recruit mercenaries in Italy. Neither side was to attack the allies of the other. Rome had earned Sicily, and Carthage could well afford the indemnity.

The treaty did not bring peace to Carthage, even for the moment. A rebellion broke out among the Carthaginian mercenaries, newly recruited from Sicily and demanding their pay. In 238 B.C., while Carthage was still in danger, Rome seized Sardinia and Corsica and demanded that Carthage pay an additional indemnity. This was a harsh and cynical action by the Romans; even the historian Polybius, a great champion of Rome, could find no justification for it. The Romans were moved, no doubt, by the fear of giving Carthage a base so near Italy, but their action was unwise. It undid the calming effects of the peace of 241 B.C. and angered the Carthaginians without preventing them from recovering their strength to seek vengeance in the future.

The harbor of the ancient city of Carthage, near modern Tunis in North Africa, as reconstructed by an artist. [Radio Times Hulton Picture Library.]

THE SECOND PUNIC WAR (218–202 B.C.). After 241 B.C., Carthage recovered strength by building a rich empire in Spain while Rome looked on with some concern. In 221 B.C. Hannibal (247–182 B.C.) took command of Carthaginian forces in Spain while still a young man of twenty-five. A few years before his accession, Rome had received an offer from the people of the Spanish town of Saguntum to become the friends of Rome. The Romans accepted, thereby taking on the responsibilities of friendship with a foreign state. At first, Hannibal was careful to avoid interfering with the friends of Rome, but the Saguntines, confident of Rome's protection, began to interfere with some of the Spanish tribes allied with Hannibal.

Finally, the Romans sent an embassy to Hannibal, warning him to let Saguntum alone and repeating the injunction not to cross the Ebro. The Romans probably expected Hannibal to yield as his predecessors had, but they misjudged their man. Hannibal ignored Rome's warning, besieged Saguntum, and took the town

MAP 5-2 THE WESTERN MEDITERRANEAN AREA DURING THE RISE OF ROME *This map covers the theater of the conflicts between the growing Roman dominions and those of Carthage in the third century B.C. The Carthaginian empire stretched westward from the city (in modern Tunisia) along the North African coast and into southern Spain.*

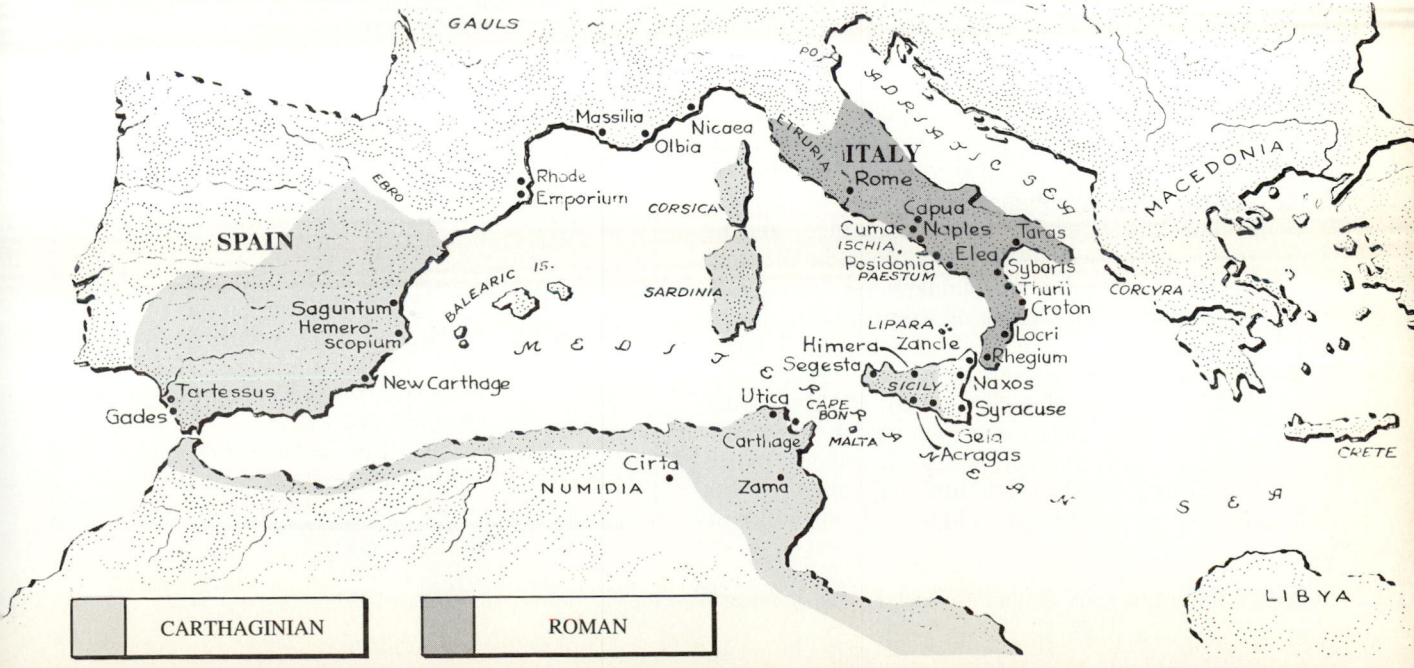

On hearing of Saguntum's fall, the Romans sent an ultimatum to Carthage demanding the surrender of Hannibal. Carthage refused, and Rome declared war in 218 B.C. Rome's policy between the wars had been the worst possible combination of approaches. Rome had insulted and injured Carthage by the annexation of Sardinia in 238 B.C., and had repeatedly provoked and insulted Carthage by interventions in Spain. But Roman policy took no measures to prevent the construction of a powerful and dangerous Punic Empire or even to build defenses against a Punic attack from Spain. Hannibal saw to it that the Romans paid the price for their blunders. By September of 218 B.C., he was across the Alps. His army was weary, bedraggled, and greatly reduced, but he was in Italy and among the friendly Gauls.

Hannibal defeated the Romans at the Ticinus River and crushed the joint consular armies at the Trebia River. In 217 B.C., he outmaneuvered and trapped another army at Lake Trasimene. Hannibal's first victory brought him reinforcements of fifty thousand Gauls, and his second confirmed that his superior generalship could defeat the Roman army. The key to success, however, would be defection by Rome's allies.

Sobered by their defeats, the Romans elected Quintus Fabius Maximus (CA. 275–203 B.C.) dictator. He understood that Hannibal could not be beaten by the usual tactics and that the Roman army, decimated and demoralized, needed time to recover. His strategy was to avoid battle while following and harassing Hannibal's army. When the Roman army had recovered and Fabius could fight Hannibal on favorable ground, only then would the Romans fight.

In 216 B.C., Hannibal marched to Cannae in Apulia to tempt the Romans into another open fight. The Romans could not allow him to ravage the country freely, so they sent off an army of some eighty thousand men to meet him. Almost the entire Roman army was killed or captured. It was the worst defeat in Roman history; Rome's prestige was shattered, and most of its allies in southern Italy, as well as Syracuse in Sicily, now went over to Hannibal. In 215 B.C., Philip V, king of Macedon, made an alliance with Hannibal and launched a war to recover his influence on the Adriatic. For more than a decade, no Roman army would dare face Hannibal in the open field, and he was free to roam over all Italy and do as he pleased.

Hannibal had neither the numbers nor the supplies to besiege such walled cities as Rome and the major allies, nor did he have the equipment to take them by assault. To win the war in Spain, the Romans appointed Publius Cornelius Scipio (237–183 B.C.), later called Scipio Africanus, to the command in Spain with proconsular *imperium*. This was such a breach of tradition as to be almost unconstitutional, for Scipio was not yet twenty-five and had held no high office. But he

Portrait of Hannibal (247–183 B.C), *the great Carthaginian general from a bust in the National Museum in Naples. [Erving Galloway.]*

was a general almost as talented as Hannibal. In 209 B.C., he captured the main Punic base in Spain, New Carthage. His skillful and tactful treatment of the native Iberians won them away from the enemy and over to his own army. Within a few years, young Scipio had conquered all Spain and had deprived Hannibal of hope of help from that region.

In 204 B.C., Scipio landed in Africa, defeated the Carthaginians, and forced them to accept a peace

THE PUNIC WARS

264–241 B.C.	First Punic War
238 B.C.	Rome seizes Sardinia and Corsica
221 B.C.	Hannibal takes command of Punic army in Spain
218–202 B.C.	Second Punic War
216 B.C.	Battle of Cannae
209 B.C.	Scipio takes New Carthage
202 B.C.	Battle of Zama
149–146 B.C.	Third Punic War
146 B.C.	Destruction of Carthage

whose main clause was the withdrawal of Hannibal and his army from Italy. Hannibal had won every battle but lost the war, for he had not counted on the determination of Rome and the loyalty of its allies. Hannibal's return inspired Carthage to break the peace and to risk all in battle. In 202 B.C., Scipio and Hannibal faced each other at the battle of Zama. The generalship of Scipio and the desertion of Hannibal's mercenaries gave the victory to Rome. The new peace terms reduced Carthage to the status of a dependent ally of Rome. The Second Punic War ended the Carthaginian command of the western Mediterranean and Carthage's term as a great power. Rome ruled the seas and the entire Mediterranean coast from Italy westward.

THE NEW IMPERIAL SYSTEM. The Roman conquest of territory overseas presented a new problem. Instead of following the policy they had pursued in Italy, the Romans made Sicily a province and Sardinia and Corsica another. It became common to extend the term of the governors of these provinces beyond a year. The governors were unchecked by colleagues and exercised full *imperium*. New magistracies, in effect, were thus created free of the limits put on the power of officials in Rome. The new populations were neither Roman citizens nor allies; they were subjects who did not serve in the army but paid tribute instead. The old practice of extending citizenship and with it loyalty to Rome stopped at the borders of Italy. Rome collected the new taxes by "farming" them out at auction to the highest bidder. At first, the tax collectors were natives from the same province, later Roman allies, and finally Roman citizens below senatorial rank who became powerful and wealthy by squeezing the provincials hard. These innovations were the basis for Rome's imperial organization in the future; in time they strained the constitution and traditions of Rome to such a degree as to threaten the existence of the republic.

After the First Punic War, Carthage sent the general Hamilcar to Spain where he built a strong and profitable colony. He befriended the local Iberians and enrolled their men in his army.

Hamilcar's successor, his son-in-law Hasdrubal, pursued the same policies. His success alarmed the Romans, and they imposed a treaty in which he promised not to take an army north across the Ebro River in Spain, although Punic expansion in Spain was well south of that river at the time of the treaty. Even though the agreement preserved the appearance of Rome's giving orders to an inferior, the treaty gave equal benefits to both sides. If the Carthaginians agreed to accept the limit of the Ebro to their expansion in Spain, the Romans would not interfere with that expansion.

The Republic's Conquest of the Hellenistic World

THE EAST. By the middle of the third century B.C., the eastern Mediterranean had reached a condition of stability. It was based on a balance of power among the three great kingdoms, and even lesser states had an established place. That equilibrium was threatened by the activities of two aggressive monarchs, Philip V of Macedon (221–179 B.C.), and Antiochus III of the Seleucid kingdom (223–187 B.C.). Philip and Antiochus moved swiftly, the latter against Syria and Palestine, the former against cities in the Aegean, in the Hellespontine region, and on the coast of Asia Minor.

The threat that a more powerful Macedon might pose to Rome's friends and, perhaps, even to Italy was enough to persuade the Romans to intervene. In 200 B.C., the Romans sent an ultimatum to Philip, ordering him not to attack any Greek city and to pay reparations to Pergamum. These orders were meant to provoke, not prevent, war, and Philip refused to obey. Two years later, the Romans sent out a talented young general, Flaminius, who demanded that Philip withdraw from Greece entirely. In 197 B.C., with Greek support, he defeated Philip in the hills of Cynoscephalae in Thessaly, bringing an end to the Second Macedonian War (the first had been fought while the Romans were still occupied with Carthage, from 215 to 205 B.C.). The Greek cities freed from Philip were made autonomous, and in 196 B.C., Flaminius proclaimed the freedom of the Greeks.

Soon after the Romans withdrew from Greece, they came into conflict with Antiochus, who was expanding his power in Asia and on the European side of the Hellespont. On the pretext of freeing the Greeks from Roman domination, he landed an army on the Greek mainland. The Romans routed Antiochus at Thermopylae and quickly drove him from Greece, and in 189 B.C., they crushed his army at Magnesia in Asia Minor. The peace of Apamia in the next year deprived Antiochus of his elephants and his navy and imposed a huge indemnity on him. Once again, the Romans took no territory for themselves and left a number of Greek cities in Asia free. They continued their policy of regarding Greece, and now Asia Minor, as a kind of protectorate in which they could intervene or not as they chose.

In 179 B.C., Perseus succeeded Philip V as king of Macedon. He tried to gain popularity in Greece by favoring the democratic and revolutionary forces in the cities. The Romans, troubled by this threat to stability, launched the Third Macedonian War (172–168 B.C.), and in 168, Aemilius Paullus defeated Perseus at Pydna. The peace imposed by the Romans reveals a change in policy and a growing harshness. It divided

Macedon into four separate republics, whose citizens were forbidden to intermarry or even to do business across the new national boundaries.

The new policy reflected a change in Rome from the previous relatively gentle one to the stern and businesslike approach favored by the conservative censor Cato (234–149 B.C.). The new harshness was applied to allies and bystanders as well as to defeated opponents. Leaders of anti-Roman factions in the Greek cities were punished severely.

When Aemilius Paullus returned from his victory, he celebrated a triumph that lasted three days, during which the spoils of war, royal prisoners, and great wealth were paraded through the streets of Rome behind the proud general. The public treasury benefited to such a degree that the direct property tax on Roman citizens was abolished. Part of the booty went to the general and part to his soldiers. New motives were thereby introduced into Roman foreign policy, or, perhaps, old motives were given new prominence. Foreign campaigns could bring profit to the state, rewards to the army, and wealth, fame, honor, and political power to the general.

THE WEST. Harsh as the Romans had become toward the Greeks, they were even worse in their treatment of the people of the Iberian Peninsula, whom they considered barbarians. The Romans committed dreadful atrocities, lied, cheated, and broke treaties in their effort to exploit and pacify the natives, who fought back fiercely in guerrilla style. From 154 to 133 B.C., the fighting waxed, and it became hard to recruit Roman soldiers to fight in the increasingly ugly war. At last, in 134, Scipio Aemilianus took the key city of Numantia by siege, burned it to the ground, and put an end to the war in Spain.

Roman treatment of Carthage was no better. Although Carthage lived up to its treaty with Rome faithfully and posed no threat, some Romans refused to abandon their hatred and fear of the traditional enemy. Cato is said to have ended all his speeches in

the Senate with the same sentence, "Ceterum censeo delendam esse Carthaginem" ("Besides, I think that Carthage must be destroyed"). At last, the Romans took advantage of a technical breach of the peace to destroy Carthage. In 146 B.C., Scipio Aemilianus took the city, plowed up its land, and put salt in the furrows as a symbol of the permanent abandonment of the site. The Romans incorporated it as the province of Africa, one of six Roman provinces, including Sicily, Sardinia–Corsica, Macedonia, Hither Spain, and Further Spain.

Civilization in the Early Roman Republic: The Greek Influence

Among the most important changes wrought by Roman expansion overseas were those in the Roman style of life and thought brought about by close and continued association with the Greeks of the Hellenistic world. Attitudes toward the Greeks themselves ranged from admiration for their culture and history to contempt for their constant squabbling, their commercial practices, and their weakness. Such Roman aristocrats as the Scipios surrounded themselves with Greek intellectuals, like the historian Polybius and the philosopher Panaetius. Conservatives such as Cato might speak contemptuously of the Greeks as "Greeklings" (Graeculi), but even he learned Greek and absorbed Greek culture.

Before long, the education of the Roman upper classes was bilingual. In addition to the Twelve Tables, young Roman nobles studied Greek rhetoric, literature, and sometimes philosophy. These studies even had an effect on education and the Latin language. As early as the third century B.C., Livius Andronicus, a liberated Greek slave, translated the Odyssey into Latin. It became a primer for young Romans and put Latin on the road to becoming a literary language.

Religion

Roman religion was influenced by the Greeks almost from the beginning; the Romans identified their own gods with Greek equivalents and incorporated Greek mythology into their own. For the most part, however, Roman religious practice remained simple and Italian, until the third century B.C. brought important new influences from the east. In 205, the Senate approved the public worship of Cybele, the Great Mother goddess from Phrygia. Hers was a fertility cult accompanied by ecstatic, frenzied, and sensual rites that shocked and outraged conservative Romans to such a degree that they soon banned the cult to Romans. Similarly, the Senate banned the worship of Dionysus, or Bacchus, in 186 B.C. In the second century B.C., interest in Babylonian astrology also grew,

ROMAN ENGAGEMENT OVERSEAS

215–205 B.C.	First Macedonian War
200–197 B.C.	Second Macedonian War
196 B.C.	Proclamation of Greek freedom by Flaminius at Corinth
189 B.C.	Battle of Magnesia; Antiochus defeated in Asia Minor
172–168 B.C.	Third Macedonian War
168 B.C.	Battle of Pydna
154–133 B.C.	Roman wars in Spain
134 B.C.	Numantia taken

Plutarch Describes a Roman Triumph

In 168 B.C., *Lucius Aemilius Paullus defeated King Perseus in the battle of Pydna, bringing an end to the Third Macedonian War. For his great achievement, the Senate granted Paullus the right to celebrate a triumph, the great honorific procession granted only for extraordinary victories and eagerly sought by all Roman generals. Plutarch described the details of Paullus' triumph.*

The people erected scaffolds in the forum, in the circuses, as they call their buildings for horseraces, and in all other parts of the city where they could best behold the show. The spectators were clad in white garments; all the temples were open, and full of garlands and perfumes; the ways were cleared and kept open by numerous officers, who drove back all who crowded into or ran across the main avenue. This triumph lasted three days. On the first, which was scarcely long enough for the sight, were to be seen the statues, pictures, and colossal images which were taken from the enemy, drawn upon two hundred and fifty chariots. On the second was carried in a great many wagons the finest and richest armour of the Macedonians, both of brass and steel, all newly polished and glittering; the pieces of which were piled up and arranged purposely with the greatest art, so as to seem to be tumbled in heaps carelessly and by chance. . . .

. . . .

On the third day, early in the morning, first came the trumpeters, who did not sound as they were wont in a procession or solemn entry, but such a charge as the Romans use when they encourage the soldiers to fight. Next followed young men wearing frocks with ornamented borders, who led to the sacrifice a hundred and twenty stalled oxen, with their horns gilded, and their heads adorned with ribbons and garlands; and with these were boys that carried basins for libation, of silver and gold.

. . . .

After his children and their attendants came Perseus himself, clad all in black, and wearing the boots of his country, and looking like one altogether stunned and deprived of reason, through the greatness of his misfortunes. Next followed a great company of his friends and familiars, whose countenances were disfigured with grief, and who let the spectators see, by their tears and their continual looking upon Perseus, that it was his fortune they so much lamented, and that they were regardless of their own.

. . . .

. . . After these were carried four hundred crowns, all made of gold, sent from the cities by their respective deputations to Aemilius, in honour of his victory. Then he himself came, seated on a chariot magnificently adorned (a man well worthy to be looked at, even without these ensigns of power), dressed in a robe of purple, interwoven with gold, and holding a laurel branch in his right hand. All the army, in like manner, with boughs of laurel in their hands, divided into their bands and companies, followed the chariot of their commander; some singing verses, according to the usual custom, mingled with raillery; others, songs of triumph and the praise of Aemilius's deeds; who, indeed, was admired and accounted happy by all men, and unenvied by every one that was good; except so far as it seems the province of some god to lessen that happiness which is too great and inordinate, and so to mingle the affairs of human life that no one should be entirely free and exempt from calamities; but, as we read in Homer, that those should think themselves truly blessed whom fortune has given an equal share of good and evil. ❑

Plutarch, "Aemilius Paullus," in *Lives of the Noble Grecians and Romans*, trans. by John Dryden, revised by A. H. Clough (New York: Random House, n.d.), pp. 340–341.

---

and the Senate's attempt in 139 to expel the "Chaldaeans," as the astrologers were called, did not prevent the continued influence of their superstition.

Education

Human society depends on the passing on from generation to generation of the knowledge, skills, and values needed for life in any particular community. A system of education, whether formal or informal, is essential to each culture and reveals its character even as it tries to stamp that character on its children. The education provided in the early centuries of the Roman Republic reflected the limited, conservative, and practical nature of that community of plain farmers and soldiers.

Education was entirely the responsibility of the family, the father teaching his own son at home. It is not clear whether in early times girls received any education, though they certainly did later on. The boys learned to read, write, and calculate, and they learned the skills of farming. They memorized the laws of the Twelve Tables, Rome's earliest code of law; learned how to perform religious rites; heard stories of the great deeds of early Roman history and particularly those of their ancestors; and engaged in the physical training appropriate for potential soldiers. This course of study was practical, vocational, and moral. It aimed at making the boys moral, pious, patriotic, law-abiding, and respectful of tradition.

In the third century B.C., the Romans came into contact with the Greeks of southern Italy, and this contact produced momentous changes in Roman education. Greek teachers came to Rome and introduced the study of language, literature, and philosophy, as well as the idea of a liberal education, or what the Romans called *humanitas*, the root of our concept of the humanities. The aim of education changed from the practical, vocational goals of earlier times to an emphasis on broad intellectual training, critical thinking, an interest in ideas, and the development of a well-rounded person.

The first need was to learn Greek, for Rome did not yet have a literature of its own. For this purpose, schools were established where the teacher, called a *grammaticus*, taught his students the Greek language and its literature, especially the poets and particularly Homer. Hereafter, educated Romans were expected to be bilingual. After the completion of this elementary education, Roman boys of the upper classes studied rhetoric—the art of speaking and writing well—with Greeks who were expert in those arts. For the Greeks, rhetoric was a subject of less importance than philosophy. But the more practical Romans took to it avidly,

for it was of great use in legal disputes and was becoming ever more valuable in political life.

Some Romans, however, were powerfully attracted to Greek literature and philosophy. The Roman aristocrat Scipio Aemilianus, who finally defeated and destroyed Carthage, surrounded himself and his friends with such Greek thinkers as the historian Polybius and the philosopher Panaetius. Other Romans, such as Cato the Elder, were more conservative and opposed the new learning on the grounds that it would weaken Roman moral fiber. They were able on more than one occasion to pass laws expelling philosophers and teachers of rhetoric. But these attempts to go back to older ways failed. The new education suited the needs of the Romans of the second century B.C., who found themselves changing from a rural to an urban society, and who were being thrust into the sophisticated world of Hellenistic Greeks.

By the last century of the Roman Republic, the new Hellenized education had become dominant. Latin literature had come into being along with Latin translations of Greek poets, and these formed part of the course of study, but Roman gentlemen were expected to be bilingual, and Greek language and literature were still central to the curriculum. Many schools were established, and the number of educated people grew, extending beyond the senatorial class to the equestrians and outside Rome to the cities of Italy.

Though the evidence is limited, we can be sure that girls of the upper classes were educated similarly to boys, at least through the earlier stages. They were

Cato Educates His Son

Marcus Porcius Cato (234–149 B.C.) *was a remarkable Roman who rose from humble origins to the highest offices in the state. He stood as the firmest defender of the old Roman traditions at a time when Hellenic ideas were strongly influential. In the following passage, Plutarch tells how Cato attended to his son's education.*

After the birth of his son, no business could be so urgent, unless it had a public character, as to prevent him from being present when his wife bathed and swaddled the babe. For the mother nursed it herself, and often gave suck also to the infants of her slaves, that so they might come to cherish a brotherly affection for her son. As soon as the boy showed signs of understanding, his father took him under his own charge and taught him to read, although he had an accomplished slave, Chilo by name, who was a schoolteacher, and taught many boys. Still, Cato thought it not right, as he tells us himself, that his son should be scolded by a slave, or have his ears tweaked when he was slow to

learn, still less that he should be indebted to his slave for such a priceless thing as education. He was therefore himself not only the boys' reading-teacher, but his tutor in law, and his athletic trainer, and he taught his son not merely to hurl the javelin and fight in armour and ride the horse, but also to box, to endure heat and cold, and to swim lustily through the eddies and billows of the Tiber. His History of Rome, as he tells us himself, he wrote with his own hand and in large characters, that his son might have in his own home an aid to acquaintance with his country's ancient traditions. ❑

Plutarch, *Cato Major*, 20, trans. by Bernadotte Perrin (London and New York: Loeb Classical Library, William Heinemann, 1914).

probably taught by tutors at home rather than going to school, as was the increasing fashion among boys in the late republic. Young women did not study with philosophers and rhetoricians, for they were usually married by the age the men were pursuing their higher education. Still, some women found ways to continue their education. Some became prose writers and others poets. By the first century A.D., there were apparently enough learned women to provoke the complaints of a crotchety and conservative satirist:

Still more exasperating is the woman who begs as soon as she sits down to dinner, to discourse on poets and poetry, comparing Virgil with Homer; professors, critics, lawyers, auctioneers—even another woman—can't get a word in. She rattles on at such a rate that you'd think that all the pots and pans in the kitchen were crashing to the floor or that every bell in town was clanging. All by herself she makes as much noise as some primitive tribe chasing away an eclipse. She should learn the philosopher's lesson: "moderation is necessary even for intellectuals." And, if she still wants to appear educated and eloquent, let her dress as a man, sacrifice to men's gods and bathe in the men's baths. Wives shouldn't try to be public speakers; they shouldn't use rhetorical devices; they shouldn't read all the classics—there should be some things women don't understand. I myself cannot understand a woman who can quote the rules of grammar and never make a mistake and cites obscure, long-forgotten poets—as if men cared about such things. If she has to correct somebody let her correct her girl friends and leave her husband alone.[2]

In the late republic, Roman education, though still entirely private, became more formal and organized. From the ages of seven to twelve, boys went to elementary school accompanied by a Greek slave called a *paedagogus* (whence our term *pedagogue*) who looked after his physical well-being and his manners, and who improved his ability in Greek conversation. At school, the boy learned to read and write, using a wax tablet and a stylus, and to do simple arithmetic with the aid of an abacus and pebbles *(calculi)*. Discipline was harsh and corporal punishment frequent. From twelve to sixteen, boys went to a higher school, where the *grammaticus* undertook to provide a liberal education, using Greek and Latin literature as his subject matter. In addition, he taught dialectic, arithmetic, geometry, astronomy, and music. Sometimes he included the elements of rhetoric, especially for those boys who would not go on to a higher education.

At sixteen, some boys went on to advanced study in rhetoric. The instructors were usually Greek, and they

trained their charges by requiring them to study models of fine speech of the past and by having them write, memorize, and declaim speeches suitable for different occasions. Sometimes the serious student attached himself to some famous public speaker and followed him about to learn what he could.

Sometimes a rich and ambitious Roman would support a Greek philosopher in his own home so that his son could converse with him and acquire the learning and polish thought necessary for the fully cultured gentleman. Some, like the great orator Cicero (106–43 B.C.), undertook what we might call postgraduate study by traveling abroad to study with great teachers of rhetoric and philosophy in the Greek world. One consequence of this whole style of education was to broaden the Romans' understanding through the careful study of a foreign language and culture. It made them a part of the older and wider culture of the Hellenistic world, a world that they had come to dominate and needed to understand.

Roman Imperialism

Rome's expansion in Italy and overseas was accomplished without a grand general plan. The new territories were acquired as a result of wars that the Romans believed were either defensive or preventive. Their foreign policy was aimed at providing security for Rome on Rome's terms, but these terms were often unacceptable to other nations and led to continued conflict. Whether intended or not, Rome's expansion brought the Romans an empire, and with it, power, wealth, and responsibilities.

The republican constitution, which had served Rome well during its years as a city-state and had been well adapted to the mastery of Italy, would be severely tested by the need to govern an empire beyond the seas. Roman society and the Roman character had maintained their integrity through the period of expansion in Italy. But these would be tested by the temptations and strains presented by the wealth and the complicated problems presented by an overseas empire.

The Aftermath of Conquest

War and expansion changed the economic, social, and political life of Italy. Before the Punic wars, most Italians owned their own farms, which provided most of the family's needs. Some families owned larger holdings, but their lands chiefly grew grain, and they used the labor of clients, tenants, and hired workers rather than slaves. Fourteen years of fighting in the Second Punic War did terrible damage to much Italian farmland. Many veterans returning from the wars found it impossible or unprofitable to go back to their

[2]Juvenal, *Satires* 6.434–456, trans. by Roger Killian, Richard Lynch, Robert J. Rowland, and John Sims, cited by Sarah B. Pomeroy in *Goddesses, Whores, Wives, and Slaves* (New York: Schocken Books, 1975), p. 172.

MAP 5-3 ROMAN DOMINIONS OF THE LATE REPUBLIC *The Roman Republic's conquest of Mediteranean lands—and beyond—until the death of Julius Caesar
is shown here. Areas conquered before Tiberius Gracchus (ca. 133 B.C.) are distinguished from later ones and from client areas owing allegiance to Rome.*

farms. Some moved to Rome, where they could find
work as occasional laborers, but most stayed in the
country to work as tenant farmers or hired hands. No
longer landowners, they were also no longer eligible
for the army. Often the land they abandoned was gathered into large parcels by the wealthy. They converted
these large units, later called *latifundia*, into large
plantations for growing cash crops—grain, olives, and
grapes for wine—or into cattle ranches.

The upper classes had plenty of capital to stock and
operate these estates because of profits from the war
and from exploiting the provinces. Land was cheap,
and slaves conquered in war provided cheap labor. By
fair means and foul, large landholders obtained large
quantities of public land and forced small farmers from
it. These changes separated the people of Rome and
Italy more sharply into rich and poor, landed and landless, privileged and deprived. The result was political, social, and ultimately constitutional conflict that
threatened the existence of the republic.

The Gracchi

By the middle of the second century B.C., the problems caused by Rome's rapid expansion troubled per-

ceptive Roman nobles. The fall in status of the peasant
farmers made it harder to recruit soldiers and came to
present a political threat as well. The patron's traditional control over his clients was weakened by their
flight from their land. Even those former landowners
who worked on the land of their patrons as tenants or
hired hands were less reliable. The introduction of the
secret ballot in the 130s made them even more independent.

In 133 B.C., Tiberius Gracchus tried to solve these
problems. He became tribune for 133 B.C. on a program of land reform. The program aroused great hostility. When Tiberius put it before the tribal assembly,
one of the tribunes interposed his veto. Unwilling to
give up, he put his bill before the tribal assembly
again. Again it was vetoed, so Tiberius, strongly supported by the people, had the offending tribune removed from office, thereby violating the constitution.

Tiberius then proposed a second bill, harsher than
the first and more appealing to the people, for he had
given up hope of conciliating the Senate. There could
be no compromise: Either Tiberius or the Roman constitution must go under.

Tiberius understood the danger that he would face

if he stepped down from the tribunate, so he announced his candidacy for a second successive term, another blow at tradition. At the elections, a riot broke out, and a mob of senators and their clients killed Tiberius and some three hundred of his followers and threw their bodies into the Tiber River. The Senate had put down the threat to its rule, but at the price of the first internal bloodshed in Roman political history.

The tribunate of Tiberius Gracchus brought a permanent change to Roman politics. Heretofore, Roman political struggles had generally involved struggles for honor and reputation between great families or coalitions of such families. Fundamental issues were rarely at stake. The revolutionary proposals of Tiberius, however, and the senatorial resort to bloodshed created a new situation. Tiberius' use of the tribunate to challenge senatorial rule encouraged imitation in spite of his failure. From then on, Romans could pursue a political career that was not based solely on influence within the aristocracy; pressure from the people might be an effective substitute. In the last century of the republic, such politicians were called *populares*, whereas those who supported the traditional role of the Senate were called *optimates* ("the best men").

The tribunate of Gaius Gracchus (brother of Tiberius) was much more dangerous than that of Tiberius

Appian Discusses Rome's Agrarian Crisis and the Proposal of Tiberius Gracchus

The changes that the second century B.C. had brought to Rome produced economic, social, political, and constitutional problems that demanded attention. The senatorial government was slow to move toward their solution, and the first major attempt at reform was undertaken in 133 B.C. by the tribune Tiberius Gracchus. Appian, a historian who lived in the second century A.D., described the situation.

The Romans, as they subdued the Italian nations successively in war, seized a part of their lands and built towns there, or established their own colonies in those already existing, and used them in place of garrisons. Of the land acquired by war they assigned the cultivated part forthwith to settlers, or leased or sold it. Since they had no leisure as yet to allot the part which then lay desolated by war (this was generally the greater part), they made proclamation that in the meantime those who were willing to work it might do so for a share of the yearly crops—a tenth of the grain and a fifth of the fruit. From those who kept flocks was required a share of the animals, both oxen and small cattle. They did these things in order to multiply the Italian race, which they considered the most laborious of peoples, so that they might have plenty of allies at home. But the very opposite thing happened; for the rich, getting possession of the greater part of the undistributed lands, and being emboldened by the lapse of time to believe that they would never be dispossessed, and adding to their holdings the small farms of their poor neighbors, partly by purchase and partly by force, came to cultivate vast tracts instead of single estates, using for this purpose slaves as laborers and herdsmen, lest free laborers should be drawn from agriculture into the army. The ownership of slaves itself brought them great gain from the multitude of their progeny, who increased because they were exempt from military service. Thus the powerful ones became enormously rich and the race of slaves multiplied throughout the country, while the Italian people dwindled in numbers and strength, being oppressed by penury, taxes, and military service. If they had any respite from these evils they passed their time in idleness, because the land was held by the rich, who employed slaves instead of freemen as cultivators.

. . . .

At length Tiberius Sempronius Gracchus, an illustrious man, eager for glory, a most powerful speaker, and for these reasons well known to all, delivered an eloquent discourse, while serving as tribune, concerning the Italian race, lamenting that a people so valiant in war, and blood relations to the Romans, were declining little by little in pauperism and paucity of numbers without any hope of remedy. He inveighed against the multitude of slaves as useless in war and never faithful to their masters, and adduced the recent calamity brought upon the masters by their slaves in Sicily, where the demands of agriculture had greatly increased the number of the latter; recalling also the war waged against them by the Romans, which was neither easy nor short, but long-protracted and full of vicissitudes and dangers. After speaking thus he again brought forward the law, providing that nobody should hold more than 500 jugera of the public domain. But he added a provision to the former law, that the sons of the present occupiers might each hold one-half that amount, and that the remainder should be divided among the poor by triumvirs, who should be changed annually. ❑

Appian, *Roman History*, trans. by Horace White (London and New York: William Heinemann and the Macmillan Company, 1913), pp. 5–7.

because all the tribunes of 123 B.C. were Gaius' supporters, so there could be no veto, and a recent law permitted the reelection of tribunes. Gaius developed a program of such breadth as to appeal to a variety of groups. First, he revived the agrarian commission, which had been allowed to lapse. Because there was not enough good public land left to meet the demand, he proposed to establish new colonies: two in Italy and one on the old site of Carthage. Among other popular acts, he put through a law stabilizing the price of grain in Rome, which involved building granaries to guarantee an adequate supply.

Gaius broke new ground in appealing to the equestrian order in his struggle against the Senate. The equestrians (so called because they served in the Roman cavalry) were neither peasants nor senators. A highly visible minority of them were businessmen who supplied goods and services to the Roman state and collected its taxes. Almost continuous warfare and the need for tax collection in the provinces had made many of them rich. Most of the time, these wealthy men had the same outlook as the Senate; generally they used their profits to purchase land and to try to reach senatorial rank themselves. Still, they had a special interest in Roman expansion and in the exploitation of the provinces. Toward the latter part of the second century B.C., they came to have a clear sense of group interest and they began to exert political influence.

In 129 B.C., Pergamum became a new Roman province called Asia. Gaius put through a law turning over to the equestrian order the privilege of collecting its revenue. The equestrians were now given reality as a class, as a political unit that might be set against the Senate, and they might be formed into a coalition to serve Gaius' purposes.

Gaius easily won reelection as tribune for 122 B.C. He aimed at giving citizenship to the Italians, both to solve the problem that their dissatisfaction presented and to add them to his political coalition. But the common people did not want to share the advantages of Roman citizenship, and the Senate seized on this proposal as a way of driving a wedge between Gaius and his supporters.

The Romans did not reelect Gaius in 121 B.C., and he stood naked before his enemies. A hostile consul provoked an incident that led to violence. The Senate invented an extreme decree ordering the consuls to see to it that no harm came to the republic; in effect, this decree established martial law. Gaius was hunted down and killed, and a senatorial court condemned and, without trial, put to death some three thousand of his followers.

Marius and Sulla

For the moment, the senatorial oligarchy had fought off the challenge to its traditional position. Be-fore long, however, it faced more serious dangers arising from troubles abroad. The first grew out of a dispute over the succession to the throne of Numidia, a client kingdom of Rome's near Carthage. The victory of Jugurtha (d. 104 B.C.), who became king of Numidia, and his massacre of Roman and Italian businessmen in Numidia gained Roman attention. Although the Senate was reluctant to become involved, pressure from the equestrians and the people forced the declaration of what became known as the Jugurthine War in 111 B.C.

As the war dragged on, the people, sometimes with good reason, suspected the Senate of taking bribes from Jugurtha. They elected Gaius Marius (157–86 B.C.) to the consulship for 107, and the assembly, usurping the role of the Senate, assigned him to the province of Numidia. This action was significant in several ways: Marius was a *novus homo*, a "new man," that is, the first in the history of his family to reach the consulship. Although a wealthy equestrian, he had been born in the town of Arpinum and was outside the closed circle of the old Roman aristocracy. His earlier career had won him a reputation as an outstanding soldier and something of a political maverick.

Marius quickly defeated Jugurtha, but Jugurtha escaped and guerrilla warfare continued. Finally, Marius' subordinate, Lucius Cornelius Sulla (138–78 B.C.), trapped Jugurtha and brought the war to an end. Marius celebrated the victory, but Sulla, an ambitious but impoverished descendant of an old Roman family, resented being cheated of the credit he thought he deserved. Soon rumors circulated crediting Sulla with the victory and diminishing Marius' role. Thus were the seeds planted for a personal rivalry and mutual hostility that would last until Marius' death.

While the Romans were fighting Jugurtha, a far greater danger threatened Rome from the north. In 105 B.C., two barbaric tribes, the Cimbri and the Teutones, had come down the Rhone valley and crushed a Roman army at Arausio (Orange). To meet the danger, the Romans elected Marius to his second consulship when these tribes threatened again. From 104, he served five consecutive terms until 100 B.C., when the crisis was over.

While the barbarians were occupied elsewhere, Marius used the time to make important changes in the army. He began using volunteers for the army, mostly the dispossessed farmers and rural proletarians whose problems had not been solved by the Gracchi. They enlisted for a long term of service and looked on the army not as an unwelcome duty but as an opportunity and a career. They became semiprofessional clients of their general and sought guaranteed food, clothing, shelter, and booty from victories. They came to expect a piece of land as a form of mustering-out pay or veteran's bonus when they retired. Volunteers

Sculptured portrait of Sulla, the first Roman to seize control of the republic by force. [Staatliche Antikensammlungen und Glyptothek, Munich. Studio Koppermann.]

were most likely to enlist with a man who was a capable soldier and who was influential enough to obtain what he needed for them. They looked to him rather than to the state for their rewards. He, on the other hand, had to obtain these favors from the Senate if he was to maintain his power and reputation.

Marius' innovation created both the opportunity and the necessity for military leaders to gain enough power to challenge civilian authority. The promise of rewards won these leaders the personal loyalty of their troops, and that loyalty allowed them to frighten the Senate into granting their demands.

The War against the Italian Allies (90–88 B.C.)

For a decade, Rome took no action to deal with Italian discontent. In frustration, the Italians revolted and established a separate confederation with its own capital and its own coinage.

Employing the traditional device of divide and conquer, the Romans immediately offered citizenship to those cities that remained loyal and soon made the same offer to the rebels if they laid down their arms.

Even then, hard fighting was needed to put down the uprising, and by 88 B.C., the war against the allies was over. All the Italians became Roman citizens with the protections that citizenship offered, but they retained local self-government and a dedication to their own municipalities that made Italy flourish. The passage of time blurred the distinction between Romans and Italians and forged them into a single nation.

Sulla's Dictatorship

During the war against the allies, Sulla had performed well, and he was elected consul for 88 B.C. A champion of senatorial control, he fought and won a civil war against Marius and his friends. He now held all power and had himself appointed dictator, not in the traditional sense, but for the express purpose of reconstituting the state. He had enough power and influence to make himself the permanent ruler of Rome. Yet, he was traditional enough to want a restoration of senatorial government, reformed in such a way as to prevent the misfortunes of the past.

Sulla retired to a life of ease and luxury in 79 B.C. He could not, however, undo the effect of his own example: a general using the loyalty of his own troops to take power and to massacre his opponents, as well as innocent people. These actions proved to be more significant than his constitutional arrangements.

The Fall of the Republic

Pompey, Crassus, Caesar, and Cicero

Within a year of Sulla's death, his constitution came under assault. To deal with armed threats to its powers, the Senate violated the constitution by ignoring Sulla's rigid rules for holding office, which had been meant to guarantee experienced, loyal, and safe commanders.

Crassus and Pompey were ambitious men whom the Senate feared. Both demanded special honors and election to the consulship for the year 70 B.C. They both won election and repealed most of Sulla's constitution. This opened the way for further attacks on senatorial control and for collaboration between ambitious generals and demagogic tribunes.

In 67 B.C., a special law gave Pompey *imperium* for three years over the entire Mediterranean and fifty miles in from the coast. He also was given the power to raise great quantities of troops and money to rid the area of pirates. His power was then extended to fight a war that had broken out in Asia Minor. When he returned to Rome in 62 B.C., he had more power, prestige, and popular support than any Roman in history. The Senate and his personal enemies had reason to fear that he might emulate Sulla and establish his own rule.

Rome had not been quiet in Pompey's absence. Crassus was the foremost among those who had reason to fear Pompey's return. Although rich and influential, he did not have the confidence of the Senate, a firm political base of his own, or the kind of military glory needed to rival Pompey. During the 60s, therefore, he allied himself with various popular leaders. The ablest of these men was Gaius Julius Caesar (100–44 B.C.), a descendant of an old but politically obscure patrician family that claimed descent from the kings and even from the goddess Venus.

The chief opposition to Crassus' candidates for the consulship for 63 B.C. came from Cicero (106–43 B.C.), a "new man" from Marius' home town of Arpinum. He had made a spectacular name as the leading lawyer in Rome. He wanted to unite the stable elements of the state—the Senate and the equestrians—in a harmony of the orders. This program did not appeal to the senatorial oligarchy, but the Senate preferred him to Catiline, a dangerous popular politician thought to be linked with Crassus. Cicero and Antonius were elected consuls for 63 B.C., Catiline running third.

Cicero soon learned of a plot hatched by Catiline. Catiline had run in the previous election on a platform of cancellation of debts, which appealed to discontented elements in general but especially to the heavily indebted nobles and their many clients. Made desperate by defeat, Catiline planned to stir up rebellions around Italy, to cause confusion in the city, and to take it by force. Quick action by Cicero defeated Catiline.

The First Triumvirate

Toward the end of 62 B.C., Pompey landed at Brundisium and, to general surprise, disbanded his army, celebrated a great triumph, and returned to private life. He had achieved amazing things for Rome and simply wanted the Senate to approve his excellent arrangements in the east and to make land allotments to his veterans. But the Senate was jealous and fearful of overmighty individuals and refused his requests. In this way, Pompey was driven to an alliance with his natural enemies, Crassus and Caesar, because all three found the Senate standing in the way of what they wanted.

In 60 B.C. Caesar returned to Rome from his governorship of Spain. He wanted the privilege of celebrating a triumph but the Senate refused. Caesar then performed a political miracle: He reconciled Crassus with Pompey and gained the support of both for his own ambitions. So was born the First Triumvirate, an informal agreement among three Roman politicians, each seeking his private goals, that further undermined the future of the republic.

Portrait bust of Pompey the Great. This portrait, like others, illustrates the Roman preference for realistic portrayal of public figures. [Frank Brown Collection.]

Portrait of Julius Caesar. The sculpture is in the Naples museum. [Alinari/SCALA.]

146

Suetonius Describes Caesar's Dictatorship

Suetonius (CA. A.D. 69–CA.140) wrote a series of biographies of the emperors, from Julius Caesar to Domitian. In the following selection, he described some of Caesar's actions during his dictatorship in the years 46–44 B.C.

His other words and actions, however, so far outweigh all his good qualities, that it is thought he abused his power, and was justly cut off. For he not only obtained excessive honours, such as the consulship every year, the dictatorship for life, and the censorship, but also the title of emperor, and the surname of Father of His Country, besides having his statue amongst the kings, and a lofty couch in the theatre. He even suffered some honours to be decreed to him, which were unbefitting the most exalted of mankind; such as a gilded chair of state in the senate-house and on his tribunal, a consecrated chariot, and banners in the Circensian procession, temples, altars, statues among the gods, a bed of state in the temples, a priest, and a college of priests dedicated to himself, like those of Pan; and that one of the months should be called by his name. There were, indeed, no honours which he did not either assume himself, or grant to others, at his will and pleasure. In his third and fourth counsulship, he used only the title of the office, being content with the power of dictator, which was conferred upon him with the consulship; and in both years he substituted other consuls in his room, during the last three months; so that in the intervals he held no assemblies of the people, for the election of magistrates, excepting only tribunes and ediles of the people; and appointed officers, under the name of præfects, instead of the prætors, to administer the affairs of the city during his absence. The office of consul having become vacant, by the sudden death of one of the consuls the day before the calends of January [the 1st Jan.], he conferred it on a person who requested it of him, for a few hours. Assuming the same license, and regardless of the customs of his country, he appointed magistrates to hold their offices for terms of years. He granted the insignia of the consular dignity to ten persons of prætorian rank. He admitted into the senate some men who had been made free of the city, and even natives of Gaul, who were semi-barbarians. He likewise appointed to the management of the mint, and the public revenue of the state, some servants of his own household; and entrusted the command of three legions, which he left at Alexandria, to an old catamite of his, the son of his freed-man Rufinus.

He was guilty of the same extravagance in the language he publicly used, as Titus Ampius informs us; according to whom he said, "The republic is nothing but a name, without substance or reality. Sulla was an ignorant fellow to abdicate the dictatorship. Men ought to consider what is becoming when they talk with me, and look upon what I say as a law." ❑

Suetonius, *The Lives of the Twelve Caesars*, trans. by Alexander Thompson, revised by T. Forster (London: George Bell and Sons, 1903), pp. 45–47.

The Dictatorship of Julius Caesar

Caesar's efforts were retarded with election to the consulship for 59 B.C. The triumvirate program was quickly enacted, and Caesar got the extraordinary command that would give him a chance to earn the glory and power with which to rival Pompey: the governship of Illyricum and Gaul for five years.

Caesar was now free to seek the military success he craved. By 56 B.C., he had conquered most of Gaul, but he had not yet consolidated his victories firmly. He therefore sought an extension of his command, but quarrels between Crassus and Pompey so weakened the Triumvirate that the Senate was prepared to order Caesar's recall. To prevent the dissolution of his base of power, Caesar persuaded Crassus and Pompey to meet with him at Luca in northern Italy to renew the coalition. Caesar was now free to return to Gaul and finish the job.

By the time he was ready to return to Rome, however, the Triumvirate had dissolved, and a crisis was at hand. At Carrhae, in 53 B.C., Crassus died trying to conquer the Parthians, successors to the Persian Empire. Soon, Pompey broke with Caesar and joined the Senate in opposing him.

Early in January of 49 B.C., the more extreme faction in the Senate had its way and ordered Pompey to defend the state and Caesar to lay down his command by a specified day. For Caesar, this meant exile or death, so he ordered his legions to cross the Rubicon River, the boundary of his province. This action was the first act of the civil war.

In 45 B.C., Caesar defeated the last of the enemy forces under Pompey's sons at Munda in Spain. The war was over, and Caesar, in Shakespeare's words, bestrode "the narrow world like a Colossus."

Caesar's innovations generally sought to make rational and orderly what was traditional and chaotic. Another general tendency of his reforms in the political area was the elevation of the role of Italians and even provincials at the expense of the old Roman families, most of whom were his political enemies.

Caesar made few changes in the government of Rome, but his own monopoly of military power made the whole structure a sham. He treated the Senate as his creature, sometimes with disdain. His enemies were quick to accuse him of aiming at monarchy. A senatorial conspiracy gathered strength under the leadership of Gaius Cassius Longinus and Marcus Junius Brutus and included some sixty senators in all. On March 15, 44 B.C., Caesar entered the Senate, characteristically without a bodyguard, and was stabbed to death. The assassins regarded themselves as heroic tyrannicides and did not have a clear plan of action after the tyrant was dead. No doubt they simply expected the republic to be restored in the old way, but things had gone too far for that. There followed instead thirteen years of more civil war, at the end of which the republic received its final burial.

The Second Triumvirate and the Emergence of Octavian

Caesar's heir was his grandnephew, Octavian, a youth of eighteen. He joined Marcus Antonius and Lepidus, two of Caesar's officers, in the Second Triumvirate to fight the assassins, who called themselves "tyrannicides." The new triumvirs defeated the enemy in a great battle at Philippi in 42 B.C., but they soon quarreled among themselves. Octavian gained control of the western part of the empire. Antonius, together with Cleopatra, queen of Egypt, ruled the east. In 31 B.C., the forces of Octavian crushed the fleet and army of Antony and Cleopatra at Actium, putting an end to the conflict.

The CIVIL wars were over, and at the age of thirty-two, Octavian was absolute master of the Mediterranean world. His power was enormous, but so too was the task before him. He had to restore peace, prosperity, and confidence, and all of these required the establishment of a constitution that would reflect the new realities without offending unduly the traditional republican prejudices that still had so firm a grip on Rome and Italy.

Rome: From Republic to Empire in World Perspective

The history of the Roman republic reflects almost as sharp a departure from the common experience of ancient civilizations as that of the Greek city-states. A monarchy in its earliest known form, Rome quite early expelled its king, abandoned the institution of monarchy, and established an aristocratic republic somewhat like the *poleis* of the Greek dark ages. Unlike the Greeks, however, the Romans continued to be in touch with foreign neighbors, including the far more civilized urban monarchies of the Etruscans, but they clung faithfully to their republican institutions. For a long time, the Romans remained a nation of farmers and herdsmen, to whom trade was relatively unimportant, especially outside Italy.

Over time, the caste distinctions between patricians and plebeians became unimportant, giving way to distinctions based on wealth. Distinctions led to an aristocracy of noble families, who held the highest elected offices in the state. The nobles enhanced their power by their military service. The Roman republic from the first found itself engaged in almost continuous warfare with its neighbors. Wars were waged either in defense of its own territory, in fights over disputed territory, or in defense of other cities or states who were friends and allies of Rome.

In both their domestic and foreign relations, the Romans were a very legalistic people who placed great importance on traditional behavior encoded into laws. Although backed by the powerful authority of the magistrates at home and the potent Roman army abroad, the laws were based on experience, common sense, and equity. Aimed at stability and fairness, Roman law succeeded well enough that few people who lived under it wanted to do away with it. Roman law grew during the imperial period and even beyond. During the European Middle Ages, it played an important part in the revival of the West and continued to exert an influence into modern times.

The force of Roman arms, the high quality of Roman roads and bridges, and the pragmatic character of Roman law helped create something unique: an empire ruled by a republic, first a large one including

THE FALL OF THE ROMAN REPUBLIC

133 B.C.	Tribunate of Tiberius Gracchus
123–122 B.C.	Tribunate of Gaius Gracchus
111–105 B.C.	Jugurthine War
104–100 B.C.	Consecutive consulships of Marius
90–88 B.C.	War against the Italian allies
70 B.C.	Consulship of Crassus and Pompey
60 B.C.	Formation of First Triumvirate
58–50 B.C.	Caesar in Gaul
53 B.C.	Crassus killed in Battle of Carrhae
49 B.C.	Caesar crosses Rubicon; civil war begins
46–44 B.C.	Caesar's dictatorship
45 B.C.	End of civil war
43 B.C.	Formation of Second Triumvirate
42 B.C.	Triumvirs defeat Brutus and Cassius at Philippi
31 B.C.	Octavian and Agrippa defeat Antony at Actium

all of Italy, and later one that commanded the shores of the entire Mediterranean (and quite a distance inland in many places). Rome controlled an area comparable to some of the empires of the east with an effective power equal to those of the kings and emperors of China, India, and Iran. It acquired that territory, wealth, and power in a state managed by annual magistrates elected by the male Roman citizens and by an aristocratic senate, which recognized popular assemblies and a published, impersonal code of law. Rome achieved its greatness with an army of citizens and allies, without a monarchy or a regular bureaucracy.

The temptations and responsibilities of governing a vast and rich empire, however, finally proved too much for the republican constitution. Trade grew, and with it a class of merchants and financiers called equestrians, which was neither aristocratic nor agricultural but increasingly powerful. The influx of masses of slaves captured in war undermined the small farmers who had been the backbone of the Roman state and its army. As many of them were forced to leave their farms, they moved to the cities, chiefly to Rome, where they had no productive role.

Conscripted armies of farmers serving relatively short terms gave way to volunteer armies of landless men serving as professionals and expecting to be rewarded with gifts of land or money. The generals of these armies were not annual magistrates controlled by the Senate and the constitution but ambitious military leaders seeking glory and political advantage. The result was civil war and the destruction of the republic. The conquest of a vast empire moved the Romans away from their unusual historical traditions toward the more familiar path of empire trodden by rulers in Egypt, Mesopotamia, China, India, and Iran.

Suggested Readings

F. E. ADCOCK, *The Roman Art of War Under the Republic* (1940). An analysis of Roman military procedures.

E. BADIAN, *Foreign Clientelae* (1958). A brilliant study of the Roman idea of a client–patron relationship extended to foreign affairs.

E. BADIAN, *Roman Imperialism in the Late Republic*, 2nd ed. (1968).

A. H. BERNSTEIN, *Tiberius Sempronius Gracchus: Tradition and Apostacy* (1978). A new interpretation of Tiberius' place in Roman politics.

R. BLOCH, *Origins of Rome* (1960). A good account of the most generally accepted point of view.

P. A. BRUNT, *Social Conflicts in the Roman Republic* (1971).

B. CAVEN, *The Punic Wars* (1980).

T. CORNELL AND J. MATTHEWS, *Atlas of the Roman World* (1982). Much more than the title indicates, this book presents a comprehensive view of the Roman world in its physical and cultural setting.

D. C. EARL, *The Moral and Political Tradition of Rome* (1967).

R. M. ERRINGTON, *The Dawn of Empire: Rome's Rise to Power* (1972). An account of Rome's conquest of the Mediterranean.

M. GELZER, *Caesar: Politician and Statesman*, trans. by P. Needham (1968). The best biography of Caesar.

E. GJERSTAD, *Legends and Facts of Early Roman History* (1962). An unorthodox but interesting account of early Rome.

E. S. GRUEN, *The Last Generation of the Roman Republic* (1973). An interesting but controversial interpretation of the fall of the republic.

E. S. GRUEN, *The Hellenistic World and the Coming of Rome* (1984). A new interpretation of Rome's conquest of the eastern Mediterranean.

W. V. HARRIS, *War and Imperialism in Republican Rome*, 327–70 B.C. (Oxford, 1975). An analysis of Roman attitudes and intentions concerning imperial expansion and war.

L. P. HOMO, *Primitive Italy and the Beginning of Roman Imperialism* (1967). A study of early Roman relations with the peoples of Italy.

F. B. MARSH, *A History of the Roman World from 146 to 30 B.C.*, 3rd ed., rev. by H. H. Scullard (1963). An excellent narrative account.

J. C. MEYER, *Pre-Republican Rome* (1983).

C. NICOLET, *The World of the Citizen in Republican Rome* (1980).

M. PALLOTTINO, *The Etruscans*, 6th ed. (1974). Makes especially good use of archaeological evidence.

E. T. SALMON, *Roman Colonization Under the Republic* (1970).

E. T. SALMON, *The Making of Roman Italy* (1980). The story of Roman expansion on the Italian peninsula.

H. H. SCULLARD, *A History of the Roman World 753–146 B.C.*, 4th ed. (1980). An unusually fine narrative history with useful critical notes.

H. H. SCULLARD, *From the Gracchi to Nero*, 5th ed. (1982). A work of the same character and quality.

A. N. SHERWIN-WHITE, *Roman Citizenship* (1939). A useful study of the Roman franchise and its extension to other peoples.

R. E. SMITH, *Cicero the Statesman* (1966). A sound biography.

D. STOCKTON, *Cicero: A Political Biography* (1971). A readable and interesting study.

D. STOCKTON, *The Gracchi* (1979). An interesting analytic narrative.

L. R. TAYLOR, *Party Politics in the Age of Caesar* (1949). A fascinating analysis of Roman political practices.

B. H. WARMINGTON, *Carthage* (1960). A good survey.

G. WILLIAMS, *The Nature of Roman Poetry* (1970). An unusually graceful and perceptive literary study.

Equestrian statue of Emperor Marcus Aurelius in a setting in Rome arranged in the sixteenth century by Michelangelo. This is the only remaining equestrian statue of an emperor and had enormous influence on sculptors after it was discovered during the Renaisance. [Copyright by Leonard von Matt.]

6 Imperial Rome

The fall of the Roman Republic put an end to an unusual chapter in the history of civilization. Examples of nonmonarchical governments lasting for more than a relatively short time are few. And the experience of a republic lasting for almost five hundred years, as well as ruling a vast empire, has no parallel. The transition toward the more typical organization of vast territories into an imperial monarchy was difficult. The early generations of Romans after the collapse of the old order continued to think in republican terms; many of their members longed simply for a restoration of the republic.

The years of Augustus' rule were crucial in making the transition, because he skillfully maintained the appearance of republican institutions that helped mask the monarchical reality. The passage of time made such deception less necessary. Hard times and chaos in the third century revealed more clearly the basically military foundations of the rule of the increasingly autocratic emperors. In the first century, emperors began to be declared divine upon their deaths, and by the second century they were worshipped as gods during their lifetime, just like the rulers of ancient Egypt, China, Japan, and most other early empires. The basis for all this, however, was established during the years in which Augustus ruled Rome.

The Augustan Principate

If the problems facing Octavian after the Battle of Actium were great, so too were his resources for addressing them. He was the master of a vast military force, the only one in the Roman world, and he had loyal and capable assistants. Yet the memory of Julius Caesar's fate was still clear in Octavian's mind, and its lesson was that it was dangerous to flaunt unprecedented powers and to disregard all republican traditions.

Octavian's constitutional solution proved to be successful and lasting, subtle and effective. Behind all the republican trappings and the apparent sharing of authority with the Senate, the government of Octavian, like that of his successors, was a monarchy. All real power, both civil and military, lay with the ruler, whether he was called by the unofficial title of "first citizen" *(princeps)*, like Octavian, who was the founder of the regime, or "emperor" *(imperator)*, like those who followed.

On January 13, 27 B.C., he put forward a new plan in dramatic style, coming before the Senate to give up all his powers and provinces. In what was surely a rehearsed response, the Senate begged him to reconsider, and at last he agreed to accept the provinces of Spain, Gaul, and Syria with proconsular power for military command and to retain the consulship in Rome. The other provinces would be governed by the Senate as before. Because his were the border provinces containing twenty of the twenty-six legions, his true power was undiminished, but the Senate responded with almost hysterical gratitude, voting him many honors. Among them was the semireligious title "Augustus," which carried implications of veneration, majesty, and holiness. From this time on, historians speak of Rome's first emperor as Augustus and of his regime as the Principate. This would have pleased him, for it helps conceal the novel, unrepublican nature of the regime and the naked power on which it rested.

Administration

Augustus made important changes in the government of Rome, Italy, and the provinces. Most of these had the effect of reducing inefficiency and corruption, eliminating the threat to peace and order by ambitious individuals, and reducing the distinction between Romans and Italians, senators and equestrians. Augustus controlled the elections and saw to it that promising young men, whatever their origin, served the state as administrators and provincial governors. In this way, equestrians and Italians who had no connection with the Roman aristocracy entered the Senate in great numbers. For all his power, Augustus was careful always to treat the Senate with respect and honor.

The Augustan period was one of great prosperity, based on the wealth that Augustus had brought in by the conquest of Egypt, on the great increase in commerce and industry made possible by general peace and a vast program of public works, and on a strong return to successful small farming on the part of Augustus' resettled veterans.

The union of political and military power in the hands of the *princeps* made it possible for him to in-

Emperor Augustus (27 B.C.–A.D. 14). *This statue, now in the Vatican, stood in the villa of Augustus's wife Livia. The figures on the elaborate breastplate are all of symbolic significance. At the top, for example, Dawn in her chariot brings in a new day under the protective mantle of the sky god; in the center Tiberius, Augustus's future successor, accepts the return of captured Roman standards from a barbarian prince; and at the bottom is Mother Earth with a horn of plenty. [Copyright by Leonard von Matt.]*

stall rational, efficient, and stable government in the provinces for the first time.

The Army and Defense

The main external problem facing Augustus—and one that haunted all his successors—was the northern frontier. In A.D. 9, a revolt broke out, led by the German tribal leader Herrmann, or Arminius, as the Romans called him. He ambushed and destroyed three Roman legions under the general Varus as they marched through the Teutoburg Forest. The aged Au-

The Emperor Augustus Writes His Testament

Emperor Augustus wrote a record of his achievements to be read, engraved, and placed outside his mausoleum after his death. The following selections are from that document.

13. The temple of Janus Quirinus, which our ancestors desired to be closed whenever peace with victory was secured by sea and by land throughout the entire empire of the Roman people, and which before I was born is recorded to have been closed only twice since the founding of the city, was during my principate three times ordered by the senate to be closed.

. . . .

34. In my sixth and seventh consulships, after I had put an end to the civil wars, having attained supreme power by universal consent, I transferred the state from my own power to the control of the Roman senate and people. For this service of mine I received the title of Augustus by decree of the senate, and the doorposts of my house were publicly decked with laurels, the civic crown was affixed over my doorway, and a golden shield was set up in the Julian senate house, which, as the inscription on this shield testifies, the Roman senate and people gave me in recognition of my valor, clemency, justice, and devotion. After that time I excelled all in authority, but I possessed no more power than the others who were my colleagues in each magistracy.

35. When I held my thirteenth consulship, the senate, the equestrian order, and the entire Roman people gave me the title of "father of the country" and decreed that this title should be inscribed in the vestibule of my house, in the Julian senate house, and in the Augustan Forum on the pedestal of the chariot which was set up in my honor by decree of the senate. At the time I wrote this document I was in my seventy-sixth year. ❑

Augustus, *Res Gestae*, trans. by N. Lewis and M. Reinhold, in *Roman Civilization*, Vol. 2 (New York: Columbia University Press, 1955), pp. 13, 19.

---

gustus abandoned the campaign, leaving a problem of border defense that caused great trouble for his successors.

Under Augustus, the armed forces achieved true professional status. Enlistment, chiefly by Italians, was for twenty years, but the pay was relatively good and there were occasional bonuses and the promise of a pension on retirement in the form of money or a plot of land. Together with the auxiliaries from the provinces, these forces formed a frontier army of about 300,000 men. In normal times, this number was barely enough to hold the line. The Roman army permanently based in the provinces played a vital role in bringing Roman culture to the natives. The soldiers spread their language and customs, often marrying local women and settling down in the area of their service. They attracted merchants, who often became the nuclei of new towns and cities that became centers of Roman civilization. As time passed, the provincials on the frontiers became Roman citizens and helped strengthen Rome's defenses against the barbarians outside.

Soldiers of the élite Praetorian Guard, which was originally formed by Augustus into the personal bodyguard of the princeps. They numbered nine thousand and earned twice the salary of legionary soldiers. [Musée du Louvre, Paris. Giraudon.]

Religion and Morality

A century of political strife and civil war had undermined many of the foundations of traditional Roman society. Augustus thought it desirable to try to repair the damage, and he undertook a program aimed at preserving and restoring the traditional values of the family and religion in Rome and Italy. He introduced laws curbing adultery and divorce and encouraging early marriage and the procreation of legitimate children.

Augustus also worked at restoring the dignity of formal Roman religion, building many temples, reviving old cults, and reorganizing and invigorating the priestly colleges, and he banned the worship of newly introduced foreign gods. During his lifetime, he did not accept divine honors, though he was deified after his death, and as with Julius Caesar, a state cult was dedicated to his worship.

Civilization of the Ciceronian and Augustan Ages

The high point of Roman culture came in the last century of the republic and during the Principate of Augustus. Both periods reflected the dominant influence of Greek culture, especially in its Hellenistic mode. The education of Romans of the upper classes was in Greek rhetoric, philosophy, and literature, which also served as the models for Roman writers and artists. Yet in spirit and sometimes in form, the art and writing of both periods show uniquely Roman qualities, though each in different ways.

The Late Republic

CICERO. The towering literary figure of the late republic was Cicero. He is most famous for his orations delivered in the law courts and in the Senate. Together with a considerable body of his private letters, these orations provide us with a clearer and fuller insight into his mind than into that of any other figure in antiquity. We see the political life of his period largely through his eyes. He also wrote treatises on rhetoric, ethics, and politics that put Greek philosophical ideas into Latin terminology and at the same time changed them to suit Roman conditions and values.

Cicero's own views combined the teachings of the Academy, the Stoa, and other Greek schools to provide support for his moderate and conservative practicality. He believed in a world governed by divine and natural law that human reason could perceive and human institutions reflect. He looked to law, custom, and tradition to produce both stability and liberty. His literary style, as well as his values and ideas, was an

important legacy for the Middle Ages and, reinterpreted, for the Renaissance.

HISTORY. The last century of the republic produced some historical writing, much of which is lost to us. Sallust (86–35 B.C.) wrote a history of the years 78–67 B.C., but only a few fragments remain to remind us of his reputation as the greatest of republican historians. His surviving work consists of two pamphlets on the Jugurthine War and on the Catilinarian conspiracy of 63 B.C. They reveal his Caesarean and antisenatorial prejudices and the stylistic influence of Thucydides.

Julius Caesar (100–44 B.C.) wrote important treatises on the Gallic and civil wars. They are not fully rounded historical accounts but chiefly military narratives written from Caesar's point of view and with propagandist intent. Their objective manner (Caesar always referred to himself in the third person) and their direct, simple, and vigorous style make them persuasive even today, and they must have been most effective with their immediate audience.

LAW. The period from the Gracchi to the fall of the republic was important in the development of Roman law. Before that time, Roman law was essentially national and had developed chiefly by means of juridical decisions, case by case, but contact with foreign peoples and the influence of Greek ideas forced a change. From the last century of the republic on, the edicts of the praetors, which interpreted and even changed and added to existing law, had increasing importance in developing the Roman legal code. Quite early, the edicts of the magistrates who dealt with foreigners developed the idea of the *jus gentium*, or law of peoples, as opposed to that arising strictly from the experience of the Romans. In the first century B.C., the influence of Greek thought made the idea of *jus gentium* identical with that of the *jus naturale*, or natural law, taught by the Stoics. It was this view of a world ruled by divine reason that Cicero enshrined in his treatise on the laws, *De Legibus*.

POETRY. The time of Cicero was also the period of two of Rome's greatest poets, Lucretius and Catullus, each representing a different aspect of Rome's poetic tradition. The Hellenistic poets and literary theorists saw two functions for the poet, as entertainer and as teacher. They thought the best poet combined both roles, and the Romans adopted the same view. When Naevius and Ennius wrote epics on Roman history, they combined historical and moral instruction with pleasure. Lucretius (CA. 99–CA. 55 B.C.) pursued a similar path in his epic poem *De Rerum Natura (On the Nature of Things)*. In it, he set forth the scientific and philosophical ideas of Epicurus and Democritus with the zeal of a missionary trying to save society from fear and superstition. He knew that his doctrine might be bitter medicine to the reader: "That is why I have tried to administer it to you in the dulcet strain of poesy, coated with the sweet honey of the Muses."[1]

Catullus (CA. 84–CA. 54 B.C.) was a poet of a thoroughly different kind. He wrote poems that were personal, even autobiographical. In imitation of the Alexandrians, he wrote short poems filled with learned allusions to mythology, but he far surpassed his models in intensity of feeling. He wrote of the joys and pains of love, he hurled invective at important contemporaries like Julius Caesar, and he amused himself in witty poetic exchanges with others. He offered no moral lessons and was not interested in Rome's glorious history and in contemporary politics. In a sense, he is an example of the proud, independent, pleasure-seeking nobleman who characterized part of the aristocracy at the end of the republic.

The Age of Augustus

The spirit of the Augustan Age, the Golden Age of Roman literature, was quite different, reflecting the new conditions of society. The old aristocratic order, with its system of independent nobles following their own particular interests, was gone. So was the world of poets of the lower orders, receiving patronage from any of a number of individual aristocrats. Augustus replaced the complexity of republican patronage with a simple scheme in which all patronage flowed from the *princeps*, usually through his chief cultural adviser, Maecenas (d. 8 B.C.).

The major poets of this time, Vergil and Horace, had lost their property during the civil wars. The patronage of the *princeps* allowed them the leisure and the security to write poetry and at the same time made them dependent on him and limited their freedom of expression. They wrote on subjects that were useful for his policies and that glorified him and his family, but they were not mere propagandists. It seems evident that for the most part they were persuaded of the virtues of Augustus and his reign and sang its praises with some degree of sincerity. Because they were poets of genius, they were also able to maintain a measure of independence in their work.

VERGIL. Vergil (70–19 B.C.) was the most important of the Augustan poets. His first important works, the *Eclogues* or *Bucolics*, are pastoral idylls in a somewhat artificial mode. The subject of the *Georgics*, however, was suggested to Vergil by Maecenas. The model here was the early Greek poet Hesiod's *Works and Days*, but the mood and purpose of Vergil's poem are far different. It is, to be sure, a didactic account of

---

[1]I, Lucretius, *De Rerum Natura*, lines 93lff.

A mosaic showing Vergil reading from the Aenead to the Muses of Epic and Tragedy. [Giraudon.]

the agricultural life, but it is also a paean to the beauties of nature and a hymn to the cults, traditions, and greatness of Italy. All this, of course, served the purpose of glorifying Augustus' resettlement of the veterans of the civil wars on Italian farms and his elevation of Italy to special status in the empire.

Vergil's greatest work is the *Aeneid*, a long national epic that succeeded in placing the history of Rome in the great tradition of the Greeks and the Trojan War. Its hero, the Trojan warrior Aeneas, personifies the ideal Roman qualities of duty, responsibility, serious purpose, and patriotism. As the Roman's equivalent of Homer, Vergil glorified not the personal honor and excellence of the Greek epic heroes but the civic greatness represented by Augustus and the peace and prosperity that he and the Julian family had given to imperial Rome.

HORACE. Horace (65–8 B.C.) was the son of a freed man and fought on the republican side until its defeat at Philippi. He was won over to the Augustan cause by the patronage of Maecenas and by the attractions of the Augustan reforms. His *Satires* are genial and humorous. His great skills as a lyric poet are best revealed in his *Odes*, which are ingenious in their adaptation of Greek meters to the requirements of Latin verse. Two of the *Odes* are directly in praise of Augustus, and many of them glorify the new Augustan order, the imperial family, and the empire.

OVID. The darker side of Augustan influence on the arts is revealed by the career of Ovid (43 B.C.–

A.D. 18). He wrote light and entertaining love elegies that reveal the sophistication and the loose sexual code of a notorious sector of the Roman aristocracy. Their values and way of life were contrary to the seriousness and family-centered life that Augustus was trying to foster. Ovid's *Ars Amatoria*, a poetic textbook on the art of seduction, angered Augustus and was partly responsible for the poet's exile in A.D. 8 to Tomi on the Black Sea.

Ovid tried to recover favor, especially with his *Fasti*, a poetic treatment of Roman religious festivals, but to no avail. His most popular work is the *Metamorphoses*, a kind of mythological epic that turns Greek myths into charming stories in a graceful and lively style. Ovid's fame did not fade with his exile and death, but his fate was an effective warning to later poets.

HISTORY. The achievements of Augustus and his emphasis on tradition and on the continuity of his regime with the glorious history of Rome encouraged both historical and antiquarian prose works. A number of Augustan writers wrote scholarly treatises on history and geography in Greek. By far the most important and influential prose writer of the time, however, was Livy (59 B.C.–A.D. 17), an Italian from Padua. His *History of Rome* was written in Latin and treated the period from the legendary origins of Rome until 9 B.C. Only a fourth of his work is extant; of the rest, we have only pitifully brief summaries. He based his history on earlier accounts, chiefly the Roman annalists, and made no effort at original research. His great achievement was in telling the story of Rome in a continuous and impressive narrative. Its purpose was moral—setting up historical models as examples of good and bad behavior—and, above all, patriotic. He glorified Rome's greatness and connected it with Rome's past, just as Augustus tried to do.

ARCHITECTURE AND SCULPTURE. The visual arts revealed the same tendencies as other aspects of Roman life under Augustus. Augustus was the great patron of the visual arts, as he was of literature. He embarked on a building program that beautified Rome, glorified his reign, and contributed to the general prosperity and his own popularity. He filled the Campus Martius with beautiful new buildings, theaters, baths, and basilicas; the Roman Forum was rebuilt; and Augustus built a forum of his own. At its heart was the temple of Mars the Avenger to commemorate Augustus' victory and the greatness of his ancestors. On Rome's Palatine Hill, he built a splendid tem-

Aerial view of Pompeii, an Italian town on the Bay of Naples destroyed by the volcanic eruption of nearby Mt. Vesuvius which buried it in volcanic ash. This eruption was witnessed by the Younger Pliny and is described in his letters. The ruins of Pompeii were accidentally rediscovered in the 18th century and have now been largely excavated, revealing a prosperous and pleasant town of moderate size with an active local political life. [Fotocielo.]

Tacitus Gives a Provincial View of the Imperial Peace

Tacitus (A.D. 55–CA. 115) *was a Roman senator. He is most famous as historian of Rome for the period* A.D. 14–68, *but the following selection comes from a eulogy for his father-in-law,* Agricola (A.D. 40–93). *It gives an insight into the Roman Empire viewed critically.*

The Britons, . . . convinced at length that a common danger must be averted by union, had, by embassies and treaties, summoned forth the whole strength of all their states. More than 30,000 armed men were now to be seen, and still there were pressing in all the youth of the country, with all whose old age was yet hale and vigorous, men renowned in war and bearing each decorations of his own. Meanwhile, among the many leaders, one superior to the rest in valour and in birth, Galgacus by name, is said to have thus harangued the multitude gathered around him and clamouring for battle:—

"Whenever I consider the origin of this war and the necessities of our position, I have a sure confidence that this day, and this union of yours, will be the beginning of freedom to the whole of Britain. To all of us slavery is a thing unknown; there are no lands beyond us, and even the sea is not safe, menaced as we are by a Roman fleet. And thus in war and battle, in which the brave find glory, even the coward will find safety. Former contests, in which, with varying fortune, the Romans were resisted, still left in us a last hope of succour, inasmuch as being the most renowned nation of Britain, dwelling in the very heart of the country and out of sight of the shores of the conquered, we could keep even our eyes unpolluted by the contagion of slavery. To us who dwell on the uttermost confines of the earth and of freedom, this remote sanctuary of Britain's glory has up to this time been a defence. Now, however, the furthest limits of Britain are thrown open, and the unknown always passes for the marvellous. But there are no tribes beyond us, nothing indeed but waves and rocks, and the yet more terrible Romans, from whose oppression escape is vainly sought by obedience and submission. Robbers of the world, having by their universal plunder exhausted the land, they rifle the deep. If the enemy be rich, they are rapacious; if he be poor, they lust for dominion; neither the east nor the west has been able to satisfy them. Alone among men they covet with equal eagerness poverty and riches. To robbery, slaughter, plunder, they give the lying name of empire; they make a solitude and call it peace." ❑

Tacitus, *Agricola,* in *Complete Works of Tacitus,* trans. by A. J. Church and W. Brodribb (New York: Random House, 1942), pp. 694–695.

ple to his patron god, Apollo. This was one of the many temples he constructed in pursuit of his religious policy.

Most of the building was influenced by the Greek classical style, which aimed at serenity and the ideal type. The same features were visible in the portrait sculpture of Augustus and his family. The greatest monument of the age is the Altar of Peace *(Ara Pacis)* dedicated in 9 B.C. Set originally in an open space in the Campus Martius, its walls still carry a relief. Part of it shows a procession in which Augustus and his family appear to move forward, followed in order by the magistrates, the Senate, and the people of Rome. There is no better symbol of the new order.

Peace and Prosperity: Imperial Rome (A.D. 14–180)

The central problem for Augustus' successors was the position of the ruler and his relationship to the ruled. Augustus tried to cloak the monarchical nature of his government, but his successors soon abandoned all pretense. The rulers came to be called *imperator*—from which comes our word *emperor*—as well as *Caesar.* The latter title signified connection with the imperial house, and the former indicated the military power on which everything was based. Because Augustus was ostensibly only the "first citizen" of a restored republic and his powers were theoretically voted him by the Senate and the people, he could not legally name his successor. In fact, he plainly designated his heirs by favors lavished on them and by giving them a share in the imperial power and responsibility.

Tiberius (emperor A.D. 14–37),[2] his immediate successor, was at first embarrassed by the ambiguity of his new role, but soon the monarchical and hereditary nature of the regime became patent. Gaius (Caligula, A.D. 37–41), Claudius (A.D. 41–54), and Nero (A.D. 54–68) were all descended from either Augustus or his wife, Livia, and all were elevated because of that fact.

---

[2]Dates for the emperors give the years of each reign.

WALL OF ANTONINUS
WALL OF HADRIAN

NORTH

SEA

BRITAIN

HIBERNIA

ATLANTIC

RHINE

ELBE

ODER

VISTULA

Cologne

GERMANIA (INF.)

G E R M A N I A

OCEAN

S A R M

LUGDUNENSIS

SEINE

LOIRE

GERMANIA (SUP.)

GAUL

RAETIA

DANUBE

NOR-ICUM

PANNONIA (SUP.)

(INF.)

DNIESTER

PRUTH

AQUITANIA

CISALPINE GAUL

DACIA

TARRACONENSIS

NARBONENSIS

DUERO

EBRO

RHÔNE

PO

DALMATIA

(SUP.)

DANUBE

(INF.)

Bl

LUSITANIA

SPAIN

CORSICA

ITALY

MOESIA

THRACE

Byzant

BAETICA

Rome

BALEARIC IS.

SARDINIA

Apollonia

MACEDONIA

ASIA

M E D I T

ILLYRIA

GREECE

P

MAURETANIA

Carthage

E

R

SICILY

ACHAEA

CRETE

R

A

N

E

A

N

S

E

A

A F R I C A

AFRICA

NUMIDIA

CYRENAICA

LIBYA

T R MILLER

14 A.D.— *DEATH OF AUGUSTUS*

14–98 A.D.— *ACQUISITIONS,*
AUGUSTUS TO TRAJAN

98–117 A.D.— *ACQUISITIONS*
DURING THE REIGN OF TRAJAN

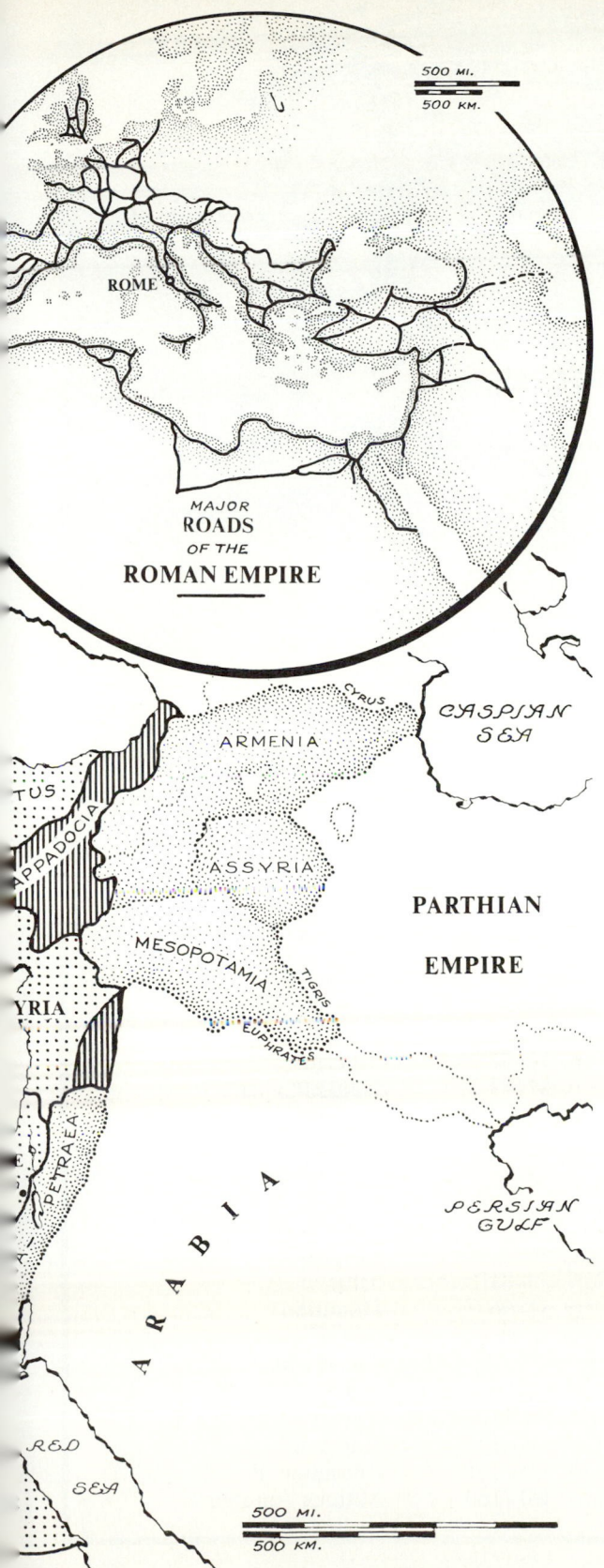

MAP 6-1 PROVINCES OF THE ROMAN EMPIRE TO A.D. 117 *The growth of the Empire to its greatest extent is here shown in three states—at the death of Augustus in B.C. 14, at the death of Nerva in 98, and at the death of Trajan in 117. The division into provinces is also indicated. The inset outlines the main roads that tied the far-flung empire together.*

In A.D. 41, the naked military basis of imperial rule was revealed when the Praetorian Guard dragged the lame, stammering, and frightened Claudius from behind a curtain and made him emperor. In A.D. 68, the frontier legions learned what the historian Tacitus called "the secret of Empire . . . that an emperor could be made elsewhere than at Rome." Nero's incompetence and unpopularity, and especially his inability to control his armies, led to a serious rebellion in Gaul in A.D. 68. The year 69 saw four different emperors assume power in quick succession as different Roman armies took turns placing their commanders on the throne.

Vespasian (A.D. 69–79) emerged victorious from the chaos, and his sons, Titus (A.D. 79–81) and Domitian (A.D. 81–96), carried forward his line, the Flavian dynasty. Vespasian was the first emperor who did not come from the old Roman nobility. He was a tough soldier who came from the Italian middle class. A good administrator and a hard-headed realist of rough wit, he resisted all attempts by flatterers to find noble ancestors for him. On his deathbed, he is said to have ridiculed the practice of deifying emperors by saying, "Alas, I think I am becoming a god."

The assassination of Domitian put an end to the Flavian dynasty. Because Domitian had no close relative who had been designated as successor, the Senate put Nerva (A.D. 96–98) on the throne to avoid chaos. He was the first of the five "good emperors," who included Trajan (A.D. 98–117), Hadrian (A.D. 117–138), Antoninus Pius (A.D. 138–161), and Marcus Aurelius (A.D. 161–180). Until Marcus Aurelius, none of these emperors had sons, so they each followed the example set by Nerva of adopting an able senator and establishing him as successor. This rare solution to the problem of monarchical succession was, therefore, only a historical accident. The result, nonetheless, was almost a century of peaceful succession and competent rule, which ended when Marcus Aurelius allowed his incompetent son, Commodus (A.D. 180–192), to succeed him, with unfortunate results.

There was, of course, some real opposition to the imperial rule. It sometimes took the form of plots against the life of the emperor. Plots and the suspicion of plots led to repression, the use of spies and paid informers, book burning, and executions. The opposition consisted chiefly of senators who looked back to republican liberty for their class and who found justifi-

Masada. In A.D. *70, Titus, the son of Emperor Vespasian, crushed the Jewish rebellion against Roman occupation of Palestine that had been raging since 66. He destroyed the Temple, plundered Jerusalem, and killed many survivors of the siege. The most determined resisters fled to the rocky fortress of Masada where they held out for years. When the Romans finally built a rampart that brought them to the summit, the resisters committed suicide rather than yield to them. [Israel Government Tourist Office, New York.]*

cation in the Greek and Roman traditions of tyrannicide as well as in the precepts of Stoicism. Plots and repression were most common under Nero and Domitian. From Nerva to Marcus Aurelius, however, the emperors, without yielding any power, again learned to enlist the cooperation of the upper class by courteous and modest deportment.

The Administration of the Empire

From an administrative and cultural standpoint, the empire was a collection of cities and towns that had little to do with the countryside. Roman policy during the Principate was to raise urban centers to the status of Roman municipalities with the rights and privileges attached to them. The Romans enlisted the upper classes of the provinces in their own government, spread Roman law and culture, and won the loyalty of the influential people.

As the efficiency of the bureaucracy grew, so did the number and scope of its functions and therefore its size. The importance and autonomy of the municipalities shrank as the central administration took a greater part in local affairs. The provincial aristocracy came to regard public service in their own cities as a burden rather than an opportunity; the price paid for the increased efficiency offered by centralized control was the loss of the vitality of the cities throughout the empire.

Augustus' successors, for the most part, accepted

his conservative and defensive foreign policy. Trajan was the first emperor to take the offensive in a sustained way. Between A.D. 101 and 106, he crossed the Danube and, after hard fighting, established the new

RULERS OF THE EARLY EMPIRE

27 B.C.–A.D. 14	Augustus
	The Julio-Claudian Dynasty
A.D. 14–37	Tiberius
A.D. 37–41	Gaius (Caligula)
A.D. 41–54	Claudius
A.D. 54–68	Nero
A.D. 69	Year of the Four Emperors
	The Flavian Dynasty
A.D. 69–79	Vespasian
A.D. 79–81	Titus
A.D. 81–96	Domitian
	The "Good Emperors"
A.D. 96–98	Nerva
A.D. 98–117	Trajan
A.D. 117–138	Hadrian
A.D. 138–161	Antoninus Pius
A.D. 161–180	Marcus Aurelius

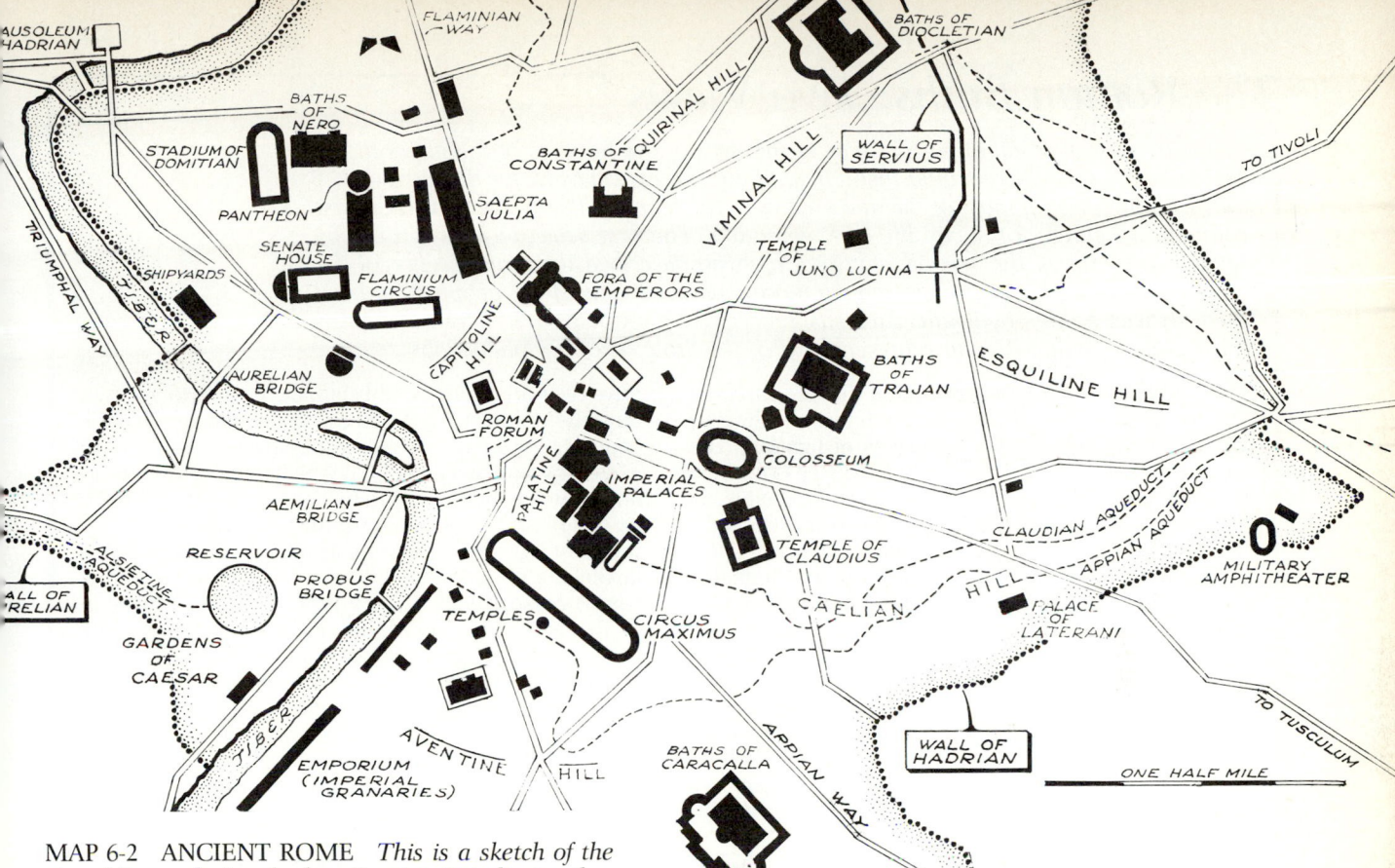

Map labels (clockwise from top):

FLAMINIAN WAY · BATHS OF DIOCLETIAN · MAUSOLEUM HADRIAN · BATHS OF NERO · STADIUM OF DOMITIAN · BATHS OF QUIRINAL HILL · WALL OF SERVIUS · TO TIVOLI · PANTHEON · SAEPTA JULIA · BATHS OF CONSTANTINE · VIMINAL HILL · SENATE HOUSE · FLAMINIUM CIRCUS · TEMPLE OF JUNO LUCINA · SHIPYARDS · FORA OF THE EMPERORS · ESQUILINE HILL · TRIUMPHAL WAY · TIBER · CAPITOLINE HILL · BATHS OF TRAJAN · AURELIAN BRIDGE · ROMAN FORUM · COLOSSEUM · AEMILIAN BRIDGE · PALATINE HILL · IMPERIAL PALACES · CLAUDIAN AQUEDUCT · APPIAN AQUEDUCT · MILITARY AMPHITHEATER · ALSIETINE AQUEDUCT · WALL OF AURELIAN · RESERVOIR · PROBUS BRIDGE · TEMPLE OF CLAUDIUS · CAELIAN HILL · PALACE OF LATERANI · GARDENS OF CAESAR · TEMPLES · CIRCUS MAXIMUS · TIBER · EMPORIUM (IMPERIAL GRANARIES) · AVENTINE HILL · BATHS OF CARACALLA · APPIAN WAY · WALL OF HADRIAN · TO TUSCULUM · ONE HALF MILE

MAP 6-2 ANCIENT ROME *This is a sketch of the city of Rome during the late Empire. It indicates the seven hills on and around which the city was built, as well as the major walls, bridges, and other public sites and buildings. The Forum is between the Capitoline and Palatine hills.*

province of Dacia between the Danube and the Carpathian Mountains. He was tempted, no doubt, by its important gold mines, but he probably was also pursuing a new general strategy: to defend the empire more aggressively by driving wedges into the territory of threatening barbarians. The same strategy dictated the invasion of the Parthian Empire in the east (A.D. 113–117). Trajan's early success was astonishing, and he established three new provinces in Armenia, Assyria, and Mesopotamia, but his lines were overextended. Rebellions sprang up, and the campaign crumbled. Trajan was forced to retreat and died before getting back to Rome.

Hadrian returned to the traditional policy, keeping Dacia but abandoning the eastern provinces. Hadrian's reign marked an important shift in Rome's frontier policy. The Roman defense became rigid, and initiative passed to the barbarians. Marcus Aurelius was compelled to spend most of his reign resisting dangerous attacks in the east and on the Danube frontier, and these attacks put enormous pressure on the human and financial resources of the empire.

The Culture of the Early Empire

LITERATURE. In Latin literature, the years between the death of Augustus and the time of Marcus Aurelius are known as the Silver Age, and as the name implies, work of high quality—although probably not of so high a quality as in the Augustan era—was produced. In contrast to the hopeful, positive optimists of the Augustans, the writers of the Silver Age were gloomy, negative, and pessimistic. In the works of the former period, praise of the emperor, his achievements, and the world abound; in the latter, criticism and satire lurk everywhere.

Some of the most important writers of the Silver Age came from the Stoic opposition and reflected its hostility to the growing power and personal excesses of the emperors.

The writers of the second century appear to have turned away from contemporary affairs and even recent history. Historical writing was about remote periods, so there was less danger of irritating imperial sensibilities. Scholarship was encouraged, but we hear little of poetry, especially about any dealing with dangerous subjects.

In the third century A.D., romances written in Greek became popular and provide further evidence of the

The Roman Baths: Two Views

Public baths played an important part in the lives of the Romans of the imperial period. The finest architects built them, beautifully and expensively, for the citizens not only of Rome, but of most of the major cities in the empire. The baths served as vast community centers for social life and recreation. The first selection was written by Lucian, a writer of the second century A.D., *who described the magnificence of the baths. The second selection presents a more jaundiced view of the people who used them. It was written by Lucius Annaeus Seneca* (CA. 4 B.C.–A.D. 65), *who was Nero's tutor and a leading Roman representative of the Stoic school of philosophy.*

The building suits the magnitude of the site, accords well with the accepted idea of such an establishment, and shows regard for the principles of lighting. The entrance is high, with a flight of broad steps of which the tread is greater than the pitch, to make them easy to ascend. On entering, one is received into a public hall of good size, with ample accommodations for servants and attendants. On the left are the lounging rooms, also of just the right sort for a bath, attractive, brightly lighted retreats. Then, besides them, a hall, larger than need be for the purposes of a bath, but necessary for the reception of richer persons. Next, capacious locker rooms to undress in, on each side, with a very high and brilliantly lighted hall between them, in which are three swimming pools of cold water; it is finished in Laconian marble, and has two statues of white marble in the ancient style, one of Hygeia, the other of Aesculapius.

On leaving this hall, you come into another which is slightly warmed instead of meeting you at once with fierce heat; it is oblong, and has an apse on each side. Next to it, on the right, is a very bright hall, nicely fitted up for massage, which has on each side an entrance decorated with Phrygian marble, and receives those who come in from the exercising floor. Then near this is another hall, the most beautiful in the world, in which one can stand or sit with comfort, linger without danger, and stroll about with profit. It also is refulgent with Phrygian marble clear to the roof. Next comes the hot corridor, faced with Numidian marble. The hall beyond it is very beautiful, full of abundant light and aglow with color like that of purple hangings. It contains three hot tubs.

When you have bathed, you need not go back through the same rooms, but can go directly to the cold room through a slightly warmed chamber. Everywhere there is copious illumination and full indoor daylight. . . . Why should I go on to tell you of the exercising floor and of the cloak rooms? . . . Moreover, it is beautiful with all other marks of thoughtfulness—with two toilets, many exits, and two devices for telling time, a water clock that makes a bellowing sound and a sundial. ❑

Lucian, *Hippias, or the Bath*, in N. Lewis and M. Reinhold, *Roman Civilization*, Vol. 2 (New York: Columbia University Press, 1955), pp. 227–228.

I live over a bathing establishment. Picture to yourself now the assortment of voices, the sound of which is enough to sicken one. When the stronger fellows are exercising and swinging heavy leaden weights in their hands, when they are working hard or pretending to be working hard, I hear their groans; and whenever they release their pent-up breath, I hear their hissing and jarring breathing. When I have to do with a lazy fellow who is content with a cheap rubdown, I hear the slap of the hand pummeling his shoulders, changing its sound according as the hand is laid on flat or curved. If now a professional ball player comes along and begins to keep score, I am done for. Add to this the arrest of a brawler or a thief, and the fellow who always likes to hear his own voice in the bath, and those who jump into the pool with a mighty splash as they strike the water. In addition to those whose voices are, if nothing else, natural, imagine the hair plucker keeping up a constant chatter in his thin and strident voice, to attract more attention, and never silent except when he is plucking armpits and making the customer yell instead of yelling himself. It disgusts me to enumerate the varied cries of the sausage dealer and confectioner and of all the peddlers of the cook shops, hawking their wares, each with his own peculiar intonation. ❑

Seneca, *Moral Epistles*, in N. Lewis and M. Reinhold, *Roman Civilization*, Vol. 2 (New York: Columbia University Press, 1955), p. 228.

tendency of writers of the time to seek and provide escape from contemporary realities.

ARCHITECTURE. The prosperity and relative stability of the first two centuries of imperial Rome allowed for the full development of the Roman contribution to architecture. To the fundamental styles of buildings developed by the Greeks, the Romans added little; the great public bath and a new, free-standing kind of amphitheater were the main innovations.

The main contribution of the Romans lay in the great size of the structures they could build and in the advances in engineering that made these large structures possible. While keeping the basic post-and-lintel construction used by the Greeks, the Romans added to it the principle of the semicircular arch, borrowed from the Etruscans. They also made good use of concrete, a building material first used by the Hellenistic Greeks and fully developed by the Romans. The new principle, sometimes combined with the new material, allowed progress over the old style. The arch combined with the post and lintel produced the great Colosseum built by the Flavian emperors. When used internally in the form of vaults and domes, the arch permitted great buildings like the baths, of which the most famous and best preserved are those of the later emperors Caracalla and Diocletian.

One of Rome's most famous buildings, the Pantheon, begun by Augustus' friend Agrippa and rebuilt by Hadrian, is a good example of the combination of all these elements. Its portico of Corinthian columns is of Greek origin, but its rotunda of brick-faced concrete with its domed ceiling and relieving arches is thoroughly Roman. The new engineering also made possible the construction of more mundane but more useful structures like bridges and aqueducts.

The Colosseum at Rome. The Romans called this building the Flavian Amphitheatre because it was built by three successive emperors of the Flavian family—begun by Vespasian, dedicated in A.D. 80 by his son Titus, and finished by his younger son Domitian. How it acquired its present name is uncertain; this may derive either from its enormous size or from its proximity to a colossal statue of Emperor Nero. It is said to have been built by prisoners taken in the Jewish War, and could seat 50,000 spectators for the animal hunts, gladiatorial combats, mock sea battles, and other spectacles that took place in it. [Fototeca Unione.]

The Pantheon at Rome. A temple, with baths and water gardens, was built on this spot by Agrippa in 27–25 B.C. Destroyed by fire, it was rebuilt in its present form by Emperor Hadrian between A.D. 117 and 125 and then repaired by Septimus Severus in about 200. [Italian Government Travel Office, New York.]

SOCIETY. Seen from the harsh perspective of human history, the first two centuries of the Roman Empire deserve their reputation of a "golden age," but by the second century, troubles had arisen, troubles that foreshadowed the difficult times ahead. The literary efforts of the time reveal a flight from the present and from reality and the public realm to the past, to romance, and to private pursuits. Some of the same aspects may be seen in the more prosaic world of everyday life, especially in the decline of vitality in local government.

In the first century A.D., members of the upper classes vied with one another for election to municipal office and for the honor of doing service to their communities. By the second century, much of their zeal had disappeared, and it became necessary for the emperors to intervene to correct abuses in local affairs and even to force unwilling members of the ruling classes to accept public office. The reluctance to serve was caused largely by the imperial practice of holding magistrates and councilmen personally and collectively responsible for the revenues due. There were even some instances of magistrates' fleeing to avoid their office, a practice that became widespread in later centuries.

All of these difficulties reflected the presence of more basic problems. The prosperity brought by the end of civil war and the influx of wealth from the east, especially Egypt, could not sustain itself beyond the first half of the second century. There also appears to have been a decline in population for reasons that remain mysterious. The cost of government kept rising as the emperors were required to maintain a costly standing army, to keep the people in Rome happy with "bread and circuses," to pay for an increasingly numerous bureaucracy, and, especially in the reign of Marcus Aurelius, to wage expensive wars to defend the frontiers against dangerous and determined barbarian enemies.

The ever-increasing need for money compelled the emperors to raise taxes, to press hard on their subjects, and to bring on inflation by debasing the coinage. These were the elements that were to bring on the desperate crises that ultimately destroyed the empire, but under the able emperors, from Trajan to Marcus Aurelius, the Romans met the challenge successfully.

Life in Imperial Rome: The Apartment House

The civilization of the Roman Empire depended on the vitality of its cities, of which no more than three or four had a population of more than 75,000, the typical city having about 20,000 inhabitants. The population of Rome, however, was certainly greater than 500,000, and some scholars think it was more than a million. People coming to it for the first time found it overwhelming and were either thrilled or horrified by its size, bustle, and noise.

The rich lived in elegant homes called *domus*, single-storied houses with plenty of space, an open central courtyard, and several rooms designed for specific and different purposes, such as dining, sitting, or sleeping, in privacy and relative quiet. Though only a small portion of Rome's population lived in them, these houses took up as much as a third of the city's space. Public space for temples, markets, baths, gymnasiums, theaters, forums, and governmental buildings took up another quarter of Rome's territory.

This left less than half of Rome's area to house the mass of its inhabitants. Inevitably, as the population grew, it was squeezed into multiple dwellings that grew increasingly tall. Most Romans during the imperial period lived in apartment buildings called *insulae* ("islands") that rose to a height of five or six stories and sometimes even more. The most famous of them, the Insula of Febiala, seems to have "towered above the Rome of the Antonines like a skyscraper."[3]

These buildings were divided into separate apartments *(cenicula)* of undifferentiated rooms, the same plan on each floor. The apartments were cramped and uncomfortable. They had neither central heating nor an open fireplace; heat and fire for cooking came from small, portable stoves or braziers. The apartments were hot in summer, cold in winter, and stuffy and smoky when the stoves were lit. There was no plumbing, so tenants needed to go into the streets to wells or fountains for water and to public baths and latrines, or to less well-regulated places, to perform some natural functions. The higher up one lived, the more difficult these trips, so chamber pots and commodes were kept in the rooms. These receptacles were emptied into vats on the staircase landings or in the alleys outside, or on occasion, the contents, and even the containers, were tossed out the window. Roman satirists complained of the discomforts and dangers of walking the streets beneath such windows, and Roman law tried to find ways to assign responsibility for the injuries done to dignity and person.

In spite of these difficulties, the attractions of the city and the shortage of space caused rents to rise, making life in these buildings expensive as well as uncomfortable. Conditions were also dangerous. The houses were lightly built of concrete and brick, far too high for the limited area of their foundations, so they often collapsed. Laws limiting the height of buildings were not always obeyed and did not, in any case, always prevent disaster. The satirist Juvenal did not exaggerate much when he wrote, "We inhabit a city held up chiefly by slats, for that is how the landlord patches up the cracks in the old wall, telling the tenants to sleep peacefully under the ruin that hangs over their heads."

Even more serious was the threat of fire. The floors were supported by wooden beams, and the rooms were lit by torches, candles, and oil lamps. They were heated by braziers. Fires broke out easily and, without running water, were not easily put out; once started, they usually led to disaster.

[3] J. Carcopino, *Daily Life in Ancient Rome* (New Haven, 1940), p. 26.

When we consider the character of these apartments and compare them with the attractive public places in the city, we can easily understand why the people of Rome spent most of their time out of doors.

The Rise of Christianity

The story of how Christianity emerged, spread, survived, and ultimately conquered the Roman Empire is one of the most remarkable in history. Its origin among poor people from an unimportant and remote province of the empire gave little promise of what was to come. Christianity faced the hostility of the established religious institutions of its native Judaea and had to compete not only against the official cults of Rome and the highly sophisticated philosophies of the educated classes but also even against other "mystery" religions like the cults of Mithra, Isis, and Osiris, and many others. The Christians also faced the opposition of the imperial government and suffered formal persecution, yet Christianity achieved toleration and finally exclusive command as the official religion of the empire.

Jesus of Nazareth

An attempt to understand this amazing outcome must begin with a discussion of Jesus of Nazareth, though there are many problems in arriving at a clear picture of his life and teachings. The most important evidence is in the Gospel accounts. The authors of the Gospels believed that Jesus was the son of God and that he came into the world to redeem humanity and to bring immortality to those who believed in him and followed his way; to the Gospel writers, Jesus' resurrection was striking proof of his teachings. At the same time, the Gospels regard Jesus as a figure in history, and they recount events in his life as well as his sayings.

There is no reason to doubt that Jesus was born in the province of Judaea in the time of Augustus and that he was a most effective teacher in the tradition of the Jewish prophets. This tradition promised the coming of a Messiah (in Greek, *christos*—so *Jesus Christ* means "Jesus the Messiah"), the redeemer who would make Israel triumph over its enemies and establish the kingdom of God on earth. In fact, Jesus seems to have insisted that the Messiah would not establish an earthly kingdom but, at the Day of Judgment, would bring an end to the world as human beings knew it. On that day, God would reward the righteous with immortality and happiness in heaven and condemn the wicked to eternal suffering in hell. Until that day, which his followers believed would come very soon, Jesus taught the faithful to abandon sin and worldly concerns; to follow him and his way; to follow the moral code de-

Mark Describes the Resurrection of Jesus

Belief that Jesus rose from the dead after his crucifixion (about A.D. 30) was and is central to traditional Christian doctrine. The record of the Resurrection in the Gospel of Mark, written a generation later (toward A.D. 70), is the earliest we have. The significance to most Christian groups revolves about the assurance given them that death and the grave are not final and that, instead, salvation for a future life is possible. The appeal of these views was to be nearly universal in the West during the Middle Ages. The Church was commonly thought to be the means of implementing the promise of salvation; hence the enormous importance of the Church's sacramental system, its rules, and its clergy.

And when evening had come, since it was the day of Preparation, that is, the day before the sabbath, Joseph of Arimathea, a respected member of the council, who was also himself looking for the kingdom of God, took courage and went to Pilate, and asked for the body of Jesus. And Pilate wondered if he were already dead; and summoning the centurion, he asked him whether he was already dead. And when he learned from the centurion that he was dead, he granted the body to Joseph. And he bought a linen shroud, and taking him down, wrapped him in the linen shroud, and laid him in a tomb which had been hewn out of the rock; and he rolled a stone against the door of the tomb. Mary Magdalene and Mary the mother of Jesus saw where he was laid.

And when the sabbath was past, Mary Magdalene, and Mary the mother of James, and Salome, bought spices, so that they might go and anoint him. And very early on the first day of the week they went to the tomb when the sun had risen. And they were saying to one another, "Who will roll away the stone for us from the door of the tomb?" And looking up, they saw that the stone was rolled back; for it was very large. And entering the tomb, they saw a young man sitting on the right side, dressed in a white robe; and they were amazed. And he said to them, "Do not be amazed; you seek Jesus of Nazareth, who was crucified. He has risen, he is not here, see the place where they laid him. But go, tell his disciples and Peter that he is going before you to Galilee; there you will see him, as he told you." And they went out and fled from the tomb; for trembling and astonishment had come upon them; and they said nothing to any one, for they were afraid. ❑

Gospel of Mark 15:42–47; 16:1–8, Revised Standard Version of the Bible (New York: Thomas Nelson and Sons, 1946 and 1952).

---

scribed in the Sermon on the Mount, which preached love, charity, and humility; and to believe in him and his divine mission.

Jesus had success and won a considerable following, especially among the poor. This success caused great suspicion among the upper classes. His novel message and his criticism of the current religious practices connected with the temple at Jerusalem and its priests provoked the hostility of the religious establishment. A misunderstanding of the movement made it easy to convince the Roman governor that Jesus and his followers might be dangerous revolutionaries. He was put to death in Jerusalem by the cruel and degrading device of crucifixion, probably in A.D. 30. His followers believed that he was resurrected on the third day after his death, and that belief became a critical element in the religion that they propagated throughout the Roman Empire and beyond.

Although the new belief spread quickly to the Jewish communities of Syria and Asia Minor, there is reason to believe that it might have had only a short life as a despised Jewish heresy had it not been for the conversion and career of Saint Paul.

Paul of Tarsus

Paul (A.D. ?5–?67) was born Saul, a citizen of the Cilician city of Tarsus in Asia Minor. Even though he was trained in Hellenistic culture and was a Roman citizen, he was a zealous member of the Jewish sect known as the Pharisees, the group that was most strict in its insistence on adherence to the Jewish law. He took a vigorous part in the persecution of the early Christians until his own conversion outside Damascus about A.D. 35. The great problem facing the early Christians was their relationship to Judaism. If the new faith was a version of Judaism, then it must adhere to the Jewish law and seek converts only among Jews. James, called the brother of Jesus, was a conservative who held to that view, whereas the Hellenist Jews tended to see it as a new and universal religion.

Paul, converted and with his new name, supported the position of the Hellenists and soon won many converts among the gentiles. Paul believed it important that the followers of Jesus be evangelists (messengers), to spread the gospel ("good news") of God's gracious gift. He taught that Jesus would soon return for the

Day of Judgment, and it was important that all should believe in him and accept his way. Faith in Jesus as the Christ was necessary but not sufficient for salvation, nor could good deeds alone achieve it. That final blessing of salvation was a gift of God's grace that would be granted to some but not to all.

Organization

Paul and the other apostles did their work well, and the new religion spread throughout the Roman Empire and even beyond its borders. It had its greatest success in the cities and for the most part among the poor and uneducated. The rites of the early communities appear to have been simple and few. Baptism by water removed original sin and permitted participation in the community and its activities. The central ritual was a common meal called the *agape* ("love feast"), followed by the ceremony of the *eucharist* ("thanksgiving"), a celebration of the Lord's Supper in which unleavened bread was eaten and unfermented wine

The Catacomb of the Jordani in Rome. The early Christians built miles of tunnels, called catacombs, in Rome. They were used as underground cemeteries and as refuges from persecution. [Leonard von Matt.]

drunk. There were also prayers, hymns, and readings from the Gospels.

At first, the churches had little formal organization. Soon, it appears, affairs were placed in the hands of boards of *presbyters* ("elders") and *deacons* ("those who serve"). By the second century A.D., as their numbers grew, the Christians of each city tended to accept the authority and leadership of bishops (*episkopoi*, or "overseers"), who were elected by the congregation to lead them in worship and supervise funds. As time passed, bishops extended their authority over the Christian communities in outlying towns and the countryside. The power and almost monarchical authority of the bishops was soon enhanced by the doctrine of Apostolic Succession, which asserted that the powers that Jesus had given his original disciples were passed on from bishop to bishop by the rite of ordination.

The bishops kept in touch with one another, maintained communications between different Christian communities, and prevented doctrinal and sectarian splintering, which would have destroyed Christian unity. They maintained internal discipline and dealt with the civil authorities. After a time, they began the practice of coming together in councils to settle difficult questions, to establish orthodox opinion, and even to expel as heretics those who would not accept it. It seems unlikely that Christianity could have survived the travails of its early years without such strong internal organization and government.

The Persecution of Christians

The new faith soon incurred the distrust of the pagan world and of the imperial government. The Christians' refusal to worship the emperor was judged to be treason. The privacy and secrecy of Christian life and worship ran counter to a traditional Roman dislike of any private association, especially any of a religious nature, and the Christians thus earned the reputation of being "haters of humanity." Claudius expelled them from the city of Rome, and Nero tried to make them scapegoats for the great fire that struck the city in A.D. 64. By the end of the first century, "the name alone"—that is, simple membership in the Christian community—was a crime.

Most persecutions in this period, however, were instituted not by the government but by mob action. But even this adversity had its uses. It weeded out the weaklings among the Christians, brought greater unity to those who remained faithful, and provided the Church with martyrs around whom legends could grow that would inspire still greater devotion and dedication.

The Emergence of Catholicism

The great majority of Christians never accepted complex, intellectualized opinions, but held to what even then were traditional, simple, conservative beliefs. This body of majority opinion and the Church that enshrined it came to be called *Catholic*, which means "universal." Its doctrines were deemed orthodox, whereas those holding contrary opinions were heretics.

The need to combat heretics, however, compelled the orthodox to formulate their own views more clearly and firmly. By the end of the second century, an orthodox canon had been shaped that included the Old Testament, the Gospels, and the Epistles of Paul, among other writings. The process was not completed for at least two more centuries, but a vitally important start had been made. The orthodox declared the Church itself to be the depository of Christian teaching and the bishops to be its receivers. They also drew up creeds, brief statements of faith to which true Christians should adhere. In the first century, all that was required of one to be a Christian was to be baptized, to partake of the eucharist, and to call Jesus the Lord. By the end of the second century, an orthodox Christian—that is, a member of the Catholic church—was required to accept its creed, its canon of holy writings, and the authority of the bishops. The loose structure of the apostolic Church had given way to an organized body with recognized leaders able to define its faith and to exclude those who did not accept it.

Rome as a Center of the Early Church

During this same period, the Church in the city of Rome came to have special prominence. Besides having the largest single congregation of Christians, Rome also benefited from the tradition that both Jesus' apostles Peter and Paul were martyred there. Peter, moreover, was thought to be the first bishop of Rome, and the Gospel of Matthew (16:18) reported Jesus' statement to Peter: "Thou art Peter [in Greek, *Petros*] and upon this rock [in Greek, *petra*] I will build my church." Because of the city's early influence and because of the Petrine doctrine derived from the Gospel of Matthew, later bishops of Rome claimed supremacy in the Catholic church, but as the era of the "good emperors" came to a close, this controversy was far in the future.

The Crisis of the Third Century

The pressure on Rome's frontiers, already serious in the time of Marcus Aurelius, reached massive proportions in the third century A.D. In the east, the frontiers were threatened by a new power arising in the old Persian Empire. In A.D. 224, a new Iranian dynasty, the Sassanians, seized control from the Parthians and brought new vitality to Persia. They soon recovered Mesopotamia and made raids deep into Roman provinces.

Barbarian Invasions

On the western and northern frontiers, the pressure came not from a well-organized rival empire but from an ever-increasing number of German tribes. These tough barbarians were always eager for plunder and were much attracted by the civilized delights they knew existed beyond the frontier of the Rhine and Danube rivers.

The most aggressive of the Germans in the third century A.D. were the Goths. Centuries earlier, they had wandered from their ancestral home near the Baltic Sea into the area of southern Russia. In the 220s and 230s they began to put pressure on the Danube frontier, and by about A.D. 250, they were able to penetrate into the empire and overrun the Balkan provinces. The need to meet this threat and the one

Emperor Valerian (253–260) surrendering to Shapur I. This is a relief carved into a rock near the ancient Persian city of Persepolis. It commemorates the victory in 260 over the Romans by Shapur I of the Sassanid dynasty of Persian kings. Kneeling before Shapur is the chained Roman emperor, who soon died in captivity. [AHM.]

posed by the Persian Sassanids in the east made the Romans weaken their western frontiers, and other Germanic peoples—the Franks and the Alemanni—broke through in those regions. There was a considerable danger that Rome would be unable to meet this challenge.

Rome's perils were caused, no doubt, by the unprecedentedly numerous and simultaneous attacks against it, but Rome's internal weakness encouraged these attacks. The pressure on the frontiers and epidemics of plague in the time of Marcus Aurelius forced the emperor to resort to the conscription of slaves, gladiators, barbarians, and brigands.

Septimius Severus (emperor A.D. 193–211) and his successors played a crucial role in the transformation of the character of the Roman army. Septimius was a military usurper who owed everything to the support of his soldiers. He meant to establish a family dynasty, in contrast to the policy of the "good emperors" of the second century A.D., and he was prepared to make Rome into an undisguised military monarchy. Septimius drew recruits for the army increasingly from peasants of the less civilized provinces, and the result was a barbarization of Rome's military forces.

Economic Difficulties

These changes were a response to the great financial needs caused by the barbarian attacks. Inflation had forced Commodus (ruled A.D. 180–192) to raise the soldiers' pay, but the Severan emperors had to double it to keep up with prices, which increased the imperial budget by as much as 25 per cent. The emperors resorted to inventing new taxes, debasing the coinage, and even to selling the palace furniture, to raise money. Even then, it was hard to recruit troops, and the new style of military life introduced by Septimius—with its laxer discipline, more pleasant duties, and greater opportunity for advancement, not only in the army but in Roman society—was needed to attract men into the army. The policy proved effective for a short time but could not prevent the chaos of the late third century.

The same forces that caused problems for the army did great damage to society at large. The shortage of workers reduced agricultural production. As external threats distracted the emperors, they were less able to preserve domestic peace. Piracy, brigandage, and the neglect of roads and harbors all hampered trade. So, too, did the debasement of the coinage and the inflation in general. Imperial exactions and confiscations of the property of the rich removed badly needed capital from productive use.

More and more, the government was required to demand services that had been given gladly in the past. Because the empire lived on a hand-to-mouth basis, with no significant reserve fund and no system of credit financing, the emperors were led to compel the people to provide food, supplies, money, and labor. The upper classes in the cities were made to serve as administrators without pay and to meet deficits in revenue out of their own pockets. Sometimes these demands caused provincial rebellions, as in Egypt and Gaul. More typically, they caused peasants and even town administrators to flee to escape their burdens. The result of all these difficulties was to weaken Rome's economic strength when it was most needed.

The Social Order

The new conditions caused important changes in the social order. The Senate and the traditional ruling class were decimated by direct attacks from hostile emperors and by economic losses. Their ranks were filled by men coming up through the army. The whole state began to take on an increasingly military appearance. Distinctions among the classes by dress had been traditional since the republic, but in the third and fourth centuries A.D. they developed to the point where the people's everyday clothing was a kind of uniform that precisely revealed their status. Titles were assigned to ranks in society as to ranks in the army. The most important distinction was the one formally established by Septimius Severus, which drew a sharp line between the *honestiores* (senators, equestrians, the municipal aristocracy, and the soldiers) and the lower classes, or *humiliores*. Septimius gave the *honestiores* a privileged position before the law. They were given lighter punishments, could not be tortured, and alone had the right of appeal to the emperor.

As time passed, it became more difficult to move from the lower order to the higher, another example of the growing rigidity of the late Roman Empire. Peasants were tied to their lands, artisans to their crafts, soldiers to the army, merchants and shipowners to the needs of the state, and citizens of the municipal upper class to the collection and payment of increasingly burdensome taxes. Freedom and private initiative gave way before the needs of the state and its ever-expanding control of its citizens.

Civil Disorder

Commodus was killed on the last day of A.D. 192, and the succeeding year was like the year A.D. 69: Three emperors ruled in swift succession, Septimius Severus emerging, as we have seen, to establish firm rule and a dynasty. The death of Alexander Severus, the last of the dynasty, in A.D. 235 brought on a half century of internal anarchy and foreign invasion.

The empire seemed on the point of collapse, but two able soldiers, Claudius II Gothicus (A.D. 268–270) and Aurelian (A.D. 270–275), drove back the barbarians and stamped out internal disorder. The soldiers who followed Aurelian on the throne were good fighters and made significant changes in Rome's system of defense. They built heavy walls around Rome, Athens, and other cities that could resist barbarian attack. They drew back their best troops from the frontiers, relying chiefly on a newly organized heavy cavalry and a mobile army near the emperor's own residence. Hereafter, the army was composed largely of mercenaries who came from among the Germans. The officers gave personal loyalty to the emperor rather than to the empire. These officers became a foreign, hereditary caste of aristocrats that increasingly supplied high administrators and even emperors. In effect, the Roman people hired an army of mercenaries, only technically Roman, to protect them.

The Tetrarchs. This porphyry sculpture on the corner of the church of San Marco in Venice depicts Emperor Diocletian (284–305) and his three imperial colleagues. They are in battle dress and clasp one another to express solidarity. This fourth-century sculpture was part of the booty brought back by the Venetians from their capture of Constantinople during the Fourth Crusade about nine hundred years later. [AHM.]

The Late Empire

The Fourth Century and Imperial Reorganization

The period from Diocletian (A.D. 284–305) to Constantine (A.D. 306–337) was one of reconstruction and reorganization after a time of civil war and turmoil. Diocletian was from Illyria (now Yugoslavia), a man of undistinguished birth who rose to the throne through the ranks of the army. He knew that he was not a great general and that the job of defending and governing the entire empire was too great for one man. He therefore decreed the introduction of the tetrarchy, the rule of the empire by four men with power divided on a territorial basis (see Map 6.3).

DIOCLETIAN. Diocletian was recognized as the senior Augustus, but each tetrarch was supreme in his own sphere. The Caesars were recognized as successors to each half of the empire, and their loyalty was enhanced by marriages to daughters of the Augusti. It was a return, in a way, to the happy precedent of the "good emperors," who chose their successors from the ranks of the ablest men, and it seemed to promise orderly and peaceful transitions instead of assassinations, chaos, and civil war.

CONSTANTINE. In 305, Diocletian retired and compelled his coemperor to do the same. But his plan for a smooth succession failed completely. In 310, there were five Augusti and no Caesars. Out of this chaos, Constantine, son of Constantius, produced order. In 324, he defeated his last opponent and made himself sole emperor, uniting the empire once again; he reigned until 337.

The emperor was a remote figure surrounded by carefully chosen high officials. He lived in a great palace and was almost unapproachable. Those admitted to his presence had to prostate themselves before him and kiss the hem of his robe, which was purple and had golden threads going through it. The emperor was addressed as *dominus* ("lord"), and his right to rule was not derived from the Roman people but from God. All this remoteness and ceremony had a double purpose: to enhance the dignity of the emperor and to safeguard him against assassination.

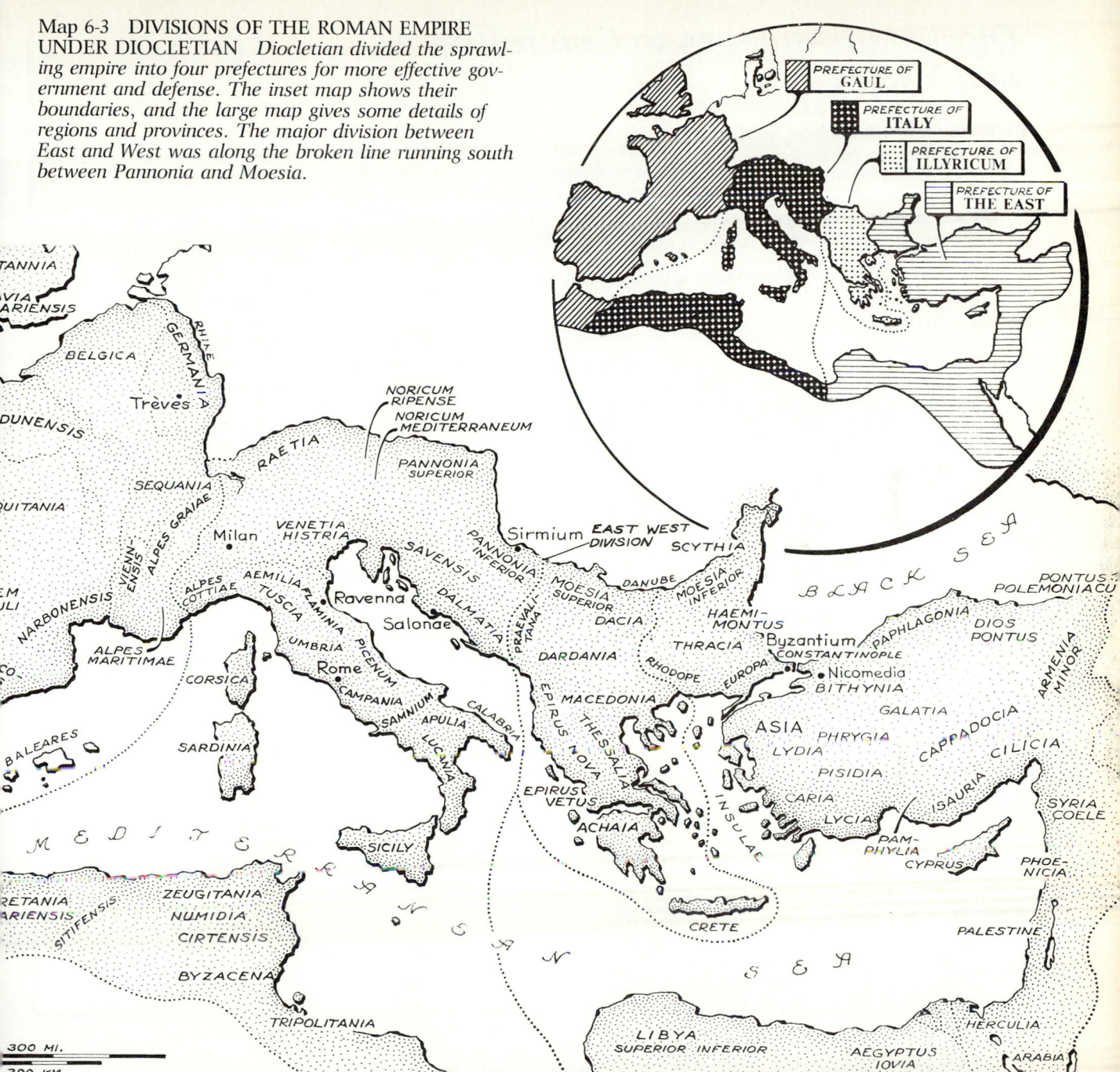

Map 6-3 DIVISIONS OF THE ROMAN EMPIRE UNDER DIOCLETIAN *Diocletian divided the sprawling empire into four prefectures for more effective government and defense. The inset map shows their boundaries, and the large map gives some details of regions and provinces. The major division between East and West was along the broken line running south between Pannonia and Moesia.*

PREFECTURE OF **GAUL**

PREFECTURE OF **ITALY**

PREFECTURE OF **ILLYRICUM**

PREFECTURE OF **THE EAST**

300 MI.

300 KM

Constantine erected the new city of Constantinople on the site of ancient Byzantium on the Bosporus, which leads to both the Aegean and the Black seas, and made it the new capital of the empire. Its strategic location was excellent for protecting the eastern and Danubian frontiers, and, surrounded on three sides by water, it was easily defended. Until its fall to the Turks in 1453, it served as the bastion of civilization, the pre-

server of classical culture, a bulwark against barbarian attack, and the greatest city in Christendom.

The autocratic rule of the emperors was carried out by a civilian bureaucracy, which was carefully separated from the military service to reduce the chances of rebellion by anyone combining the two kinds of power.

The operation of the entire system was supervised by a vast system of spies and secret police, without

Diocletian Attempts to Control Prices and Wages

Rome's troubles in the third century A.D. caused serious economic problems. Debased currency and vast government expenditures produced a runaway inflation. In an attempt to control it, Diocletian took the unprecedented step of issuing a decree that put ceilings on prices and wages throughout the empire in the year 301. In spite of the most drastic penalties prescribed by the decree, it was widely evaded. After a time, its failure was acknowledged, and the decree was at last revoked.

Who does not know that wherever the common safety requires our armies to be sent, the profiteers insolently and covertly attack the public welfare, not only in villages and towns, but on every road? They charge extortionate prices for merchandise, not just fourfold or eightfold, but on such a scale that human speech cannot find words to characterize their profit and their practices. Indeed, sometimes in a single retail sale a soldier is stripped of his donative and pay. Moreover, the contributions of the whole world for the support of the armies fall as profits into the hands of these plunderers, and our soldiers appear to bestow with their own hands the rewards of their military service and their veterans' bonuses upon the profiteers. The result is that the pillagers of the state itself seize day by day more than they know how to hold.

Aroused justly and rightfully by all the facts set forth above, and in response to the needs of mankind itself, which appears to be praying for release, we have decided that maximum prices of articles for sale must be established. We have not set down fixed prices, for we do not deem it just to do this, since many provinces occasionally enjoy the good fortune of welcome low prices and the privilege, as it were, of prosperity. Thus, when the pressure of high prices appears anywhere—may the gods avert such a calamity!—avarice . . . will be checked by the limits fixed in our statute and by the restraining curbs of the law.

It is our pleasure, therefore, that the prices listed in the subjoined schedule be held in observance in the whole of our Empire. And every person shall take note

that the liberty to exceed them at will has been ended, but that the blessing of low prices has in no way been impaired in those places where supplies actually abound. . . . Moreover, this universal edict will serve as a necessary check upon buyers and sellers whose practice it is to visit ports and other provinces. For when they too know that in the pinch of scarcity there is no possibility of exceeding the prices fixed for commodities, they will take into account in their calculations at the time of sale the localities, the transportation costs, and all other factors. In this way they will make apparent the justice of our decision that those who transport merchandise may not sell at higher prices anywhere.

It is agreed that even in the time of our ancestors it was the practice in passing laws to restrain offenses by prescribing a penalty. For rarely is a situation beneficial to humanity accepted spontaneously; experience teaches that fear is the most effective regulator and guide for the performance of duty. Therefore it is our pleasure that anyone who resists the measures of this statute shall be subject to a capital penalty for daring to do so. And let no one consider the statute harsh, since there is at hand a ready protection from danger in the observance of moderation. . . . We therefore exhort the loyalty of all, so that a regulation instituted for the public good may be observed with willing obedience and due scruple, especially as it is seen that by a statute of this kind provision has been made, not for single municipalities and peoples and provinces but for the whole world. . . . ❑

"Diocletian's Edict on Maximum Prices," from the *Corpus Inscriptionum Latinarum*, Vol. 3, in N. Lewis and M. Reinhold, *Roman Civilization*, Vol. 2 (New York: Columbia University Press, 1955), pp. 465–466.

whom the increasingly rigid totalitarian organization could not be trusted to perform. In spite of these efforts, the system was filled with corruption and inefficiency.

The cost of maintaining a 400,000-man army as well as the vast civilian bureaucracy, the expensive imperial court, and the imperial taste for splendid buildings put a great strain on an already weak economy. Diocletian's attempts at establishing a uniform and reliable currency failed and merely led to increased inflation. To deal with it, he resorted to price control

with his Edict of Maximum Prices in 301. For each product and each kind of labor a maximum price was set, and violations were punishable by death. The edict failed despite the harshness of its provisions.

Peasants unable to pay their taxes and officials unable to collect them tried to escape, and Diocletian resorted to stern regimentation to keep all in their places and at the service of the government. The terror of the third century had turned many peasants into *coloni*, tenant farmers who fled for protection to the *villa* ("country estate") of a larger and powerful land-

Arch of Constantine. The triumphal arch was a characteristic Roman imperial structure, and examples are found throughout the empire. This one at Rome was dedicated by Constantine in 315 in celebration of his victory over Maxentius at the Milvian Bridge.

In the distance, through the center arch, note some remaining arches of a first-century aqueduct, the Aqua Claudia.

Such structures as this arch and the aqueduct illustrate a significant point: With control of their diverse and far-flung empire continually at stake, as an adjunct of its administration, maintenance, safety, and amusement the Romans were immensely practical—almost compulsive—builders and engineers. Their bridges and aqueducts, temples and altars, triumphal arches and columns, theatres and arenas, palaces and villas, roads and government buildings, baths and public housing, harbor facilities, defensive walls, and fortresses were to be found all over the Mediterranean world and set standards that long challenged the West. [Alinari/SCALA.]

owner. They were tied to the land, as were their descendants, as the caste system hardened.

DIVISION OF THE EMPIRE. The peace and unity established by Constantine did not last long. His death was followed by a struggle for succession that was won by Constantius II (ruled 337–361). His death left the empire to his young cousin Julian (361–363), called by the Christians "the Apostate" because of his attempt to stamp out Christianity and restore paganism. Julian undertook a campaign against Persia, with the aim of putting a Roman on the throne of the Sassanids and ending the Persian menace once and for all. He penetrated deep into Persia but was killed in battle. His death put an end to the expedition and to the pagan revival.

The Germans in the west took advantage of the eastern campaign to attack along the Rhine River and the upper Danube River, but even greater trouble was brewing along the middle and upper Danube (see Map 6.4). That territory was occupied by the eastern Goths, the Ostrogoths. They were being pushed hard by their western cousins, the Visigoths, who in turn had been driven from their home in the Ukraine by the fierce Huns, a nomadic people from central Asia. The Emperor Valentinian (364–375) saw that he could not defend the empire alone and appointed his brother Valens (364–378) as coruler. Valentinian made his own headquarters at Milan and spent the rest of his life fighting successfully against the Franks and the Alemanni in the west. Valens was given control of the east. The empire was once again divided in two. The

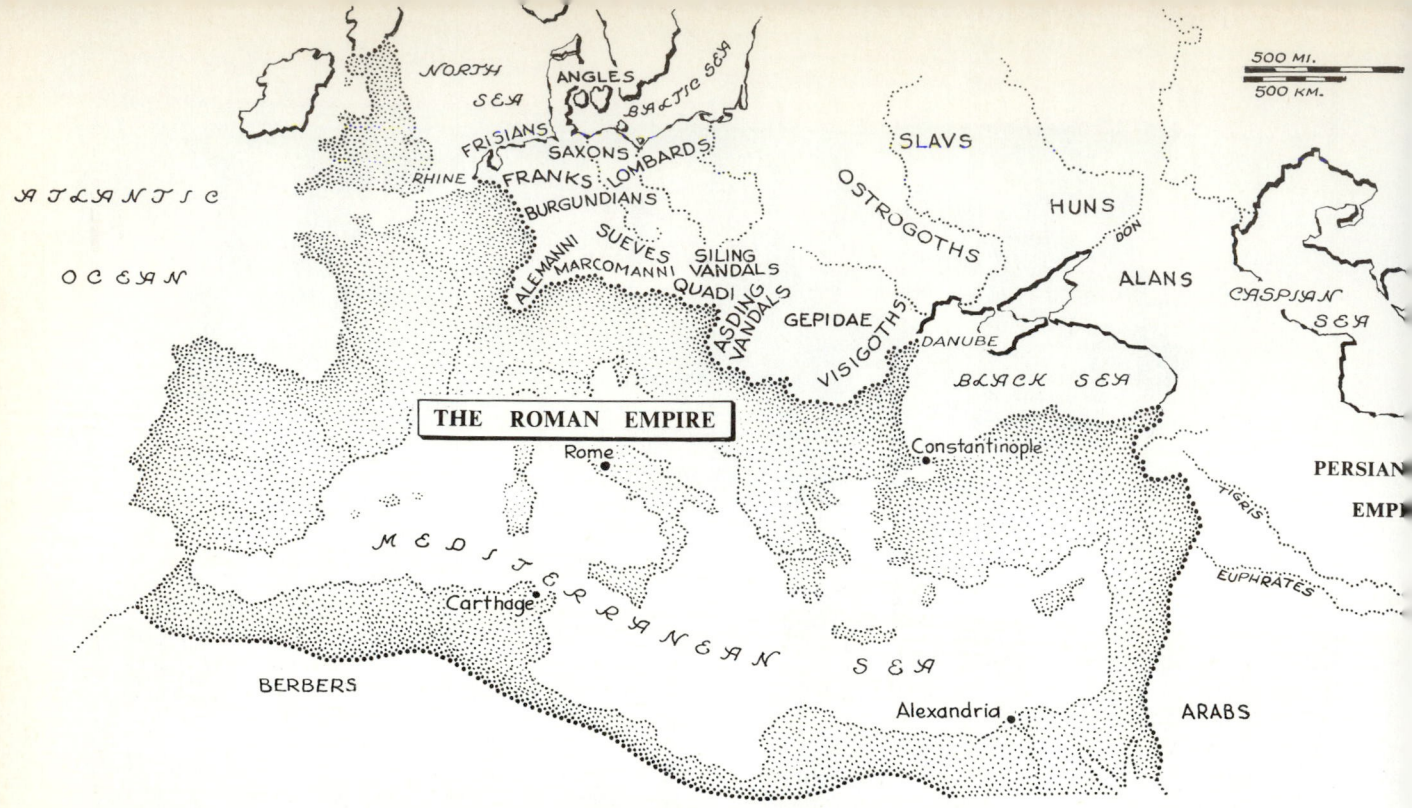

MAP 6-4 THE EMPIRE'S NEIGHBORS *In the fourth century the Roman Empire was nearly surrounded by ever more threatening neighbors. The map shows who these so-called barbarians were and where they lived before their armed contact with the Romans.*

two emperors maintained their own courts, and the two halves of the empire became increasingly separate and different. Latin was the language of the west and Greek of the east.

In 376, the hard-pressed Visigoths asked and received permission to enter the empire to escape the Huns. Contrary to the bargain, the Goths kept their weapons and began to plunder the Balkan provinces. Valens attacked the Goths and died, along with most of his army, at Adrianople in Thrace in 378. Theodosius (379–395), an able and experienced general, was named coruler in the east. He tried to unify the empire again, but his death in 395 left it divided and weak.

For the future, the two parts of the empire went their separate and different ways. The west became increasingly rural as barbarian invasions continued and grew in intensity. The *villa*, a fortified country estate, became the basic unit of life. There, *coloni* gave their services to the local magnate in return for economic assistance and protection from both barbarians and imperial officials. Many cities shrank to no more than tiny walled fortresses ruled by military commanders and bishops. The upper classes moved to the country and asserted ever greater independence of imperial authority. The failure of the central authority to maintain the roads and the constant danger from robber

bands sharply curtailed trade and communications, forcing greater self-reliance and a more primitive style of life. The new world emerging in the west by the fifth century and after was increasingly made up of isolated units of rural aristocrats and their dependent laborers. The only institution providing a high degree of unity was the Christian Church. The pattern for the early Middle Ages in the west was already formed.

In the east, the situation was quite different. Constantinople became the center of a vital and flourishing culture that we call *Byzantine* and that lasted until the fifteenth century. Because of its defensible location, the skill of its emperors, and the firmness and strength of its base in Asia Minor, it was able to deflect and repulse barbarian attacks. A strong navy allowed commerce to flourish in the eastern Mediterranean and, in good times, far beyond. Cities continued to prosper, and the emperors made their will good over the nobles in the countryside. The civilization of the Byzantine Empire was a unique combination of classical culture, the Christian religion, Roman law, and eastern artistic influences. While the west was being overrun by barbarians, the Roman Empire, in altered form, persisted in the east. While Rome shrank to an insignificant ecclesiastical town, Constantinople flourished as the seat of empire, the "New Rome," and the Byzantines called themselves "Romans." When we contemplate

Ammianus Marcellinus Describes the People Called Huns

Ammianus Marcellinus was born about A.D. 330 in Syria, where Greek was the language of his well-to-do family. After a military career and considerable travel, he lived in Rome and wrote an encyclopedic Latin history of the empire, covering the years A.D. 96–378 and giving special emphasis to the difficulties of the fourth century. Here he described the Huns, one of the barbarous peoples pressing on the frontiers.

The people called Huns, barely mentioned in ancient records, live beyond the sea of Azof, on the border of the Frozen Ocean, and are a race savage beyond all parallel. At the very moment of birth the cheeks of their infant children are deeply marked by an iron, in order that the hair, instead of growing at the proper season on their faces, may be hindered by the scars; accordingly the Huns grow up without beards, and without any beauty. They all have closely knit and strong limbs and plump necks; they are of great size, and low legged, so that you might fancy them two-legged beasts or the stout figures which are hewn out in a rude manner with an ax on the posts at the end of bridges.

They are certainly in the shape of men, however uncouth, and are so hardy that they neither require fire nor well-flavored food, but live on the roots of such herbs as they get in the fields, or on the half-raw flesh of any animal, which they merely warm rapidly by placing it between their own thighs and the backs of their horses.

They never shelter themselves under roofed houses, but avoid them, as people ordinarily avoid sepulchers as things not fit for common use. Nor is there even to be found among them a cabin thatched with reeds; but they wander about, roaming over the mountains and the woods, and accustom themselves to bear frost and hunger and thirst from their very cradles. . . .

There is not a person in the whole nation who cannot remain on his horse day and night. On horseback they buy and sell, they take their meat and drink, and there they recline on the narrow neck of their steed, and yield to sleep so deep as to indulge in every variety of dream.

And when any deliberation is to take place on any weighty matter, they all hold their common council on horseback. They are not under kingly authority, but are contented with the irregular government of their chiefs, and under their lead they force their way through all obstacles. . . . ❏

Ammianus Marcellinus, *Res Gestae*, trans. by C. D. Yonge (London: George Bell and Son, 1862), pp. 312–314.

the decline and fall of the Roman Empire in the fourth and fifth centuries, we are speaking only of the west. A form of classical culture persisted in the Byzantine east for a thousand years more.

The Triumph of Christianity

RELIGIOUS CURRENTS IN THE EMPIRE. In the troubled times of the fourth and fifth centuries, people sought powerful, personal deities who would bring them safety and prosperity in this world and immortality in the next. Paganism was open and tolerant, and it was by no means unusual for people to worship new deities alongside the old and even to intertwine elements of several to form a new amalgam by the device called *syncretism.*

Christianity's success owed something to the same causes as accounted for the popularity of other cults, which are often spoken of as its rivals. None of them, however, attained Christianity's universality, and none appears to have given the early Christians and their leaders as much competition as the ancient philosophies or the state religion.

IMPERIAL PERSECUTION. By the third century, Christianity had taken firm hold in the eastern provinces and in Italy. As times became bad and the Christians became more numerous and visible popular opinion blamed disasters, natural and military, on the Christians. About 250, the Emperor Decius (249–251) invoked the aid of the gods in his war against the Goths and required that all citizens worship the state gods publicly. True Christians could not obey, and Decius instituted a major persecution. Many Christians, even some bishops, yielded to threats and torture, but others held out and were killed. Valerian (253–260) resumed the persecutions, partly in order to confiscate the wealth of rich Christians. His successors, however, found other matters more pressing, and the persecution lapsed until the end of the century.

Diocletian was not generous toward unorthodox intellectual or religious movements, and his own effort to bolster imperial power with the aura of divinity boded ill for the church, yet he did not attack the Christians for almost twenty years. In 303, however, he launched the most serious persecution inflicted on the

Christians in the Roman Empire. The persecution horrified many pagans, and the plight and the demeanor of the martyrs often aroused pity and sympathy. For these reasons, as well as the incapacity of any large ancient state to carry out a program of terror with the thoroughness of modern totalitarian governments, the Christians and their church survived to enjoy what they must have considered a miraculous change of fortune. In 311, Galerius, who had been one of the most vigorous persecutors, was influenced, perhaps by his Christian wife, to issue an edict of toleration permitting Christian worship.

The victory of Constantine and his emergence as sole ruler of the empire changed the condition of Christianity from a precariously tolerated sect to the religion favored by the emperor and put it on the path to becoming the official and only legal religion in the empire.

CHRISTIANITY BECOMES THE STATE RELIGION. The sons of Constantine continued to favor the new religion, but the succession of Julian the Apostate posed a new threat. Though he refrained from persecution, he tried to undo the work of Constantine by withdrawing the privileges of the Church, removing Christians from high offices, and attempting to introduce a new form of pagan worship. His reign, however, was short, and his work did not last.

In 394, Theodosius forbade the celebration of pagan cults and abolished the pagan religious calendar. At the death of Theodosius, Christianity was the official religion of the Roman Empire.

The favored position of the Church attracted converts for the wrong reasons and diluted the moral excellence and spiritual fervor of its adherents. The problem of the relationship between church and state arose, presenting the possibility that religion would become subordinate to the state, as it had been in the classical world and in earlier civilizations. In the east, that is what happened to a considerable degree. In the west, the weakness of the emperors prevented such a development and permitted Church leaders to exercise remarkable independence. In 390, Ambrose, bishop of Milan, excommunicated Emperor Theodosius for a massacre he had carried out, and the emperor did humble penance. This act provided an important precedent for future assertions of the Church's autonomy and authority, but it did not put an end to secular interference and influence in the Church by any means.

ARIANISM AND THE COUNCIL OF NICEA. Internal divisions proved to be even more troubling as new heresies emerged. The most important and the most threatening was Arianism, founded by a priest named Arius of Alexandria (CA. 280–336) in the fourth century. Arius' view did away with the mysterious con-

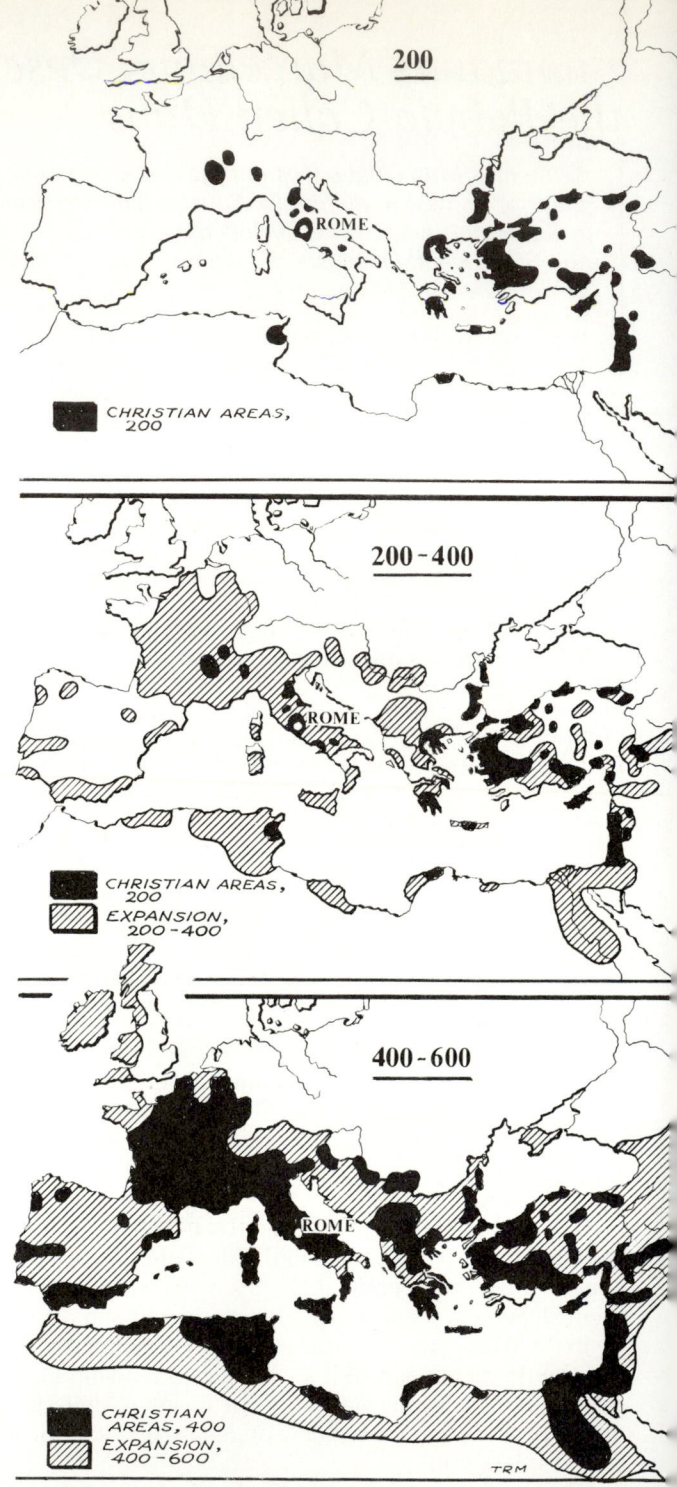

MAP 6-5 THE SPREAD OF CHRISTIANITY *Christianity grew swiftly in the third, fourth, fifth, and sixth centuries—especially after the conversion of the emperors in the fourth century. By 600, on the eve of the birth of Mohammed's new Moslem religion, Christianity was dominant throughout the Mediterranean world and most of Western Europe.*

The Council at Nicea Creates the Test of Religious Orthodoxy

In 325, Emperor Constantine called a general council of leading Christians at Nicea in Asia Minor in an attempt to end the quarreling over the question of the Trinity. The Nicene Creed was the result. Adherence to it became a test of orthodoxy, and those rejecting it were declared heretics.

We believe in one God, the Father Almighty, maker of all things visible and invisible; and in one Lord Jesus Christ, the Son of God, the only-begotten of his Father, of the substance of the Father, God of God, Light of Light; very God of very God, begotten not made, being of one substance with the Father, By whom all things were made, both which be in heaven and in earth. Who for us men and for our salvation came down [from heaven] and was incarnate and was made man. He suffered and the third day he rose again, and as- cended into heaven. And he shall come again to judge both the quick and the dead. And [we believe] in the Holy Ghost. And whosoever shall say that there was time when the Son of God was not, or that before he was begotten he was not, or that he was made of things that were not, or that he is of a different sub- stance or essence [from the Father] or that he is a crea- ture, or subject to change or conversion—all that so say, the Catholic and Apostolic Church anathematizes them. ❑

"The Nicene Creed," from *The Seven Ecumenical Councils*, trans. by A. C. McGiffort and E. C. Richardson (New York: Library of the Nicene and Post-Nicene Fathers, 2nd Series, 1900, Vol. 14), p. 3.

---

cept of the Trinity, the difficult doctrine that holds that God is three persons (the Father, the Son, and the Holy Spirit) and at the same time one in substance and essence.

Athanasius (CA. 293–373), later bishop of Alexan- dria, saw the Arian view as an impediment to any ac- ceptable theory of salvation, to him the most impor- tant religious question. He adhered to the old Greek idea of salvation as involving the change of sinful mor- tality into divine immortality through the gift of "life." Only if Jesus were both fully human and fully God could the transformation of humanity to divinity have taken place in him and be transmitted by him to his disciples. "Christ was made man," he said, "that we might be made divine."

To deal with the growing controversy, Constantine called a council of Christian bishops of Nicea, not far from Constantinople, in 325. For the emperor, the question was essentially political, but for the dispu- tants, salvation was at stake. At Nicea, the view ex- pounded by Athanasius won out, became orthodox, and was embodied in the Nicene Creed. But Arianism persisted and spread. Some later emperors were either Arians or sympathetic to that view. Some of the most successful missionaries to the barbarians were Arians, with the result that many of the German tribes who overran the empire were Arians. The Christian emper- ors hoped to bring unity to their increasingly decentral- ized realms by imposing the single religion, and over time, it did prove to be a unifying force, but it also introduced new divisions where none had existed before.

REIGNS OF SELECTED LATE EMPIRE RULERS (ALL DATES ARE A.D.)

180–192	Commodus
193–211	Septimius Severus
222–235	Alexander Severus
249–251	Decius
253–260	Valerian
253–268	Gallienus
268–270	Claudius II Gothicus
270–275	Aurelian
284–305	Diocletian
306–337	Constantine
324–337	Constantine sole emperor
337–361	Constantius II
361–363	Julian the Apostate
364–375	Valentinian
364–378	Valens
379–395	Theodosius

Arts and Letters in the Late Empire

The art and literature of the late empire reflect the con- fluence of pagan and Christian ideas and traditions as well as the conflict between them. Much of the litera- ture is polemical and much of the art is propaganda.

The salvation of the empire from the chaos of the third century was accomplished by a military revolu- tion based on and led by provincials whose origins were in the lower classes. They brought with them the fresh winds of cultural change, which blew out not only the dust of classical culture but much of its substance as well. Yet the new ruling class was not interested in leveling but wanted instead to establish itself as a new aristocracy. It thought of itself as effecting a great restoration rather than a revolution and sought to restore classical culture and absorb it. The confusion and uncertainty of the times were tempered in part, of course, by the comfort of Christianity, but the new ruling class sought order and stability—ethical, literary, and artistic—in the classical tradition as well.

The Preservation of Classical Culture

One of the main needs and accomplishments of this period was the preservation of classical culture and the discovery of ways to make it available and useful to the newly arrived ruling class. The great classical authors were reproduced in many copies, and their works were transferred from perishable and inconvenient papyrus rolls to sturdier codices, bound volumes that were as easy to use as modern books. Scholars also digested long works like Livy's *History of Rome* into shorter versions and wrote learned commentaries and compiled grammars. Original works by pagan writers of the late empire were neither numerous nor especially distinguished.

Christian Writers

Of Christian writings, on the other hand, the late empire saw a great outpouring. There were many examples of Christian apologetics in poetry as well as in prose, and there were sermons, hymns, and biblical commentaries. Christianity could also boast important scholars. Jerome (348–420), thoroughly trained in both the east and the west in classical Latin literature and rhetoric, produced a revised version of the Bible in Latin, commonly called the Vulgate, which became the Bible used by the Catholic church.

Probably the most important eastern scholar was Eusebius of Caesarea (CA. 260–CA. 340). He wrote apologetics, an idealized biography of Constantine, and a valuable attempt to reconstruct the chronology of important events in the past. His most important contribution, however, was his *Ecclesiastical History*, an attempt to set forth the Christian view of history. He saw all of history as the working out of God's will. All of history, therefore, had a purpose and a direction, and Constantine's victory and the subsequent unity of empire and Church were its culmination.

The closeness and also the complexity of the relationship between classical pagan culture and that of the Christianity of the late empire is nowhere better displayed than in the career and writings of Augustine (354–430), bishop of Hippo in north Africa. He was born at Carthage and was trained as a teacher of rhet-oric. His father was a pagan, but his mother was a Christian and hers was ultimately the stronger influence. He passed through a number of intellectual way stations before his conversion to Christianity. His training and skill in pagan rhetoric and philosophy made him peerless among his contemporaries as a defender of Christianity and as a theologian. His greatest works are his *Confessions*, an autobiography describing the road to his conversion, and *The City of God*. The latter was a response to the pagan charge that Rome's sack by the Goths in 410 was caused by the abandonment of the old gods and the advent of Christianity. The optimistic view held by some Christians that God's will worked its way in history and was easily comprehensible needed further support in the face of this disaster.

Augustine sought to separate the fate of Christianity from that of the Roman Empire. He contrasted the secular world, the City of Man, with the spiritual, the City of God. The former was selfish, the latter unselfish; the former evil, the latter good. Augustine argued that history was moving forward, in the spiritual sense, to the Day of Judgment, but that there was no reason to expect improvement before then in the secular sphere. The fall of Rome was neither surprising nor important, for all states, even a Christian Rome, were part of the City of Man and therefore corrupt and mortal. Only the City of God was immortal, and it, consisting of all the saints on earth and in heaven, was untouched by earthly calamities.

Augustine believed that faith is essential and primary—a thoroughly Christian view—but that it is not a substitute for reason, the foundation of classical thought. Instead, faith is the starting point for and the liberator of human reason, which continues to be the means by which people can understand what is revealed by faith. His writings constantly reveal the presence of both Christian faith and pagan reason—and the tension between them, a legacy he left to the Middle Ages.

The Problem of the Decline and Fall of the Empire in the West

Whether important to Augustine or not, the massive barbarian invasions of the fifth century put an end to effective imperial government in the West. For centuries, people have speculated about the causes of the collapse of the ancient world. Every kind of reason has been put forward, and some suggestions seem to have nothing to do with reason at all. Soil exhaustion, plague, climatic change, and even poisoning caused by lead water pipes have been suggested as reasons for Rome's decline in population, vigor, and the capacity to defend itself. Some blame the institution of slavery and the failure to make advances in science and technology that they believe resulted from it. Others blame excessive government interference in the economic life of the empire; others, the destruction of the urban middle class, the carrier of classical culture.

Perhaps a plausible explanation can be found that is more simple and obvious. It might begin with the observation that the growth of so mighty an empire as Rome's was by no means inevitable. Rome's greatness had come from conquests that provided the Romans with the means to expand still further, until there were not enough Romans to conquer and govern any more peoples and territory. When pressure from outsiders grew, the Romans lacked the resources to advance and defeat the enemy as in the past. The tenacity and success of their resistance for so long were remarkable. Without new conquests to provide the immense wealth needed for the defense and maintenance of internal prosperity, the Romans finally yielded to unprecedented onslaughts by fierce and numerous attackers.

To blame the ancients and the institution of slavery for the failure to produce an industrial and economic revolution like that of the later Western world, one capable of producing wealth without taking it from another, is to stand the problem on its head. No one yet has a satisfactory explanation for those revolutions, so it is improper to blame any institution or society for not achieving what has been achieved only once in human history, in what are still mysterious circumstances.

Imperial Rome in World Perspective

Perhaps we would do well to think of the decline of Rome as Gibbon did:

The decline of Rome was the natural and inevitable effect of immoderate greatness. Prosperity ripened the principle of decay; the cause of the destruction multiplied with the extent of conquest; and, as soon as time or accident had removed the artificial supports, the stupendous fabric yielded to the pressure of its own weight. The story of the ruin is simple and obvious; and instead of inquiring why

Imperial Rome. This is a model of a reconstruction of the city of Rome during the imperial period. At the left is the Circus Maximus; on the lower right is the Colosseum; and the Forum is just above the exact center of the picture. The model is in the Museo della Civiltà Romana. [Bettmann Archive.]

the Roman Empire was destroyed, we should rather be surprised that it had subsisted so long.[4]

This explanation allows us to see the Roman Empire as one among several great empires around the world that had similar experiences.

Out of the civil wars and chaos that brought down the republic, Augustus brought unity, peace, order, and prosperity. As a result, he was regarded with almost religious awe and attained more military and political power than any Roman before him. He ruled firmly but with moderation. He tried to limit military adventures and the costs they incurred. He supported public works that encouraged trade and communication in the empire. He tried to restore and invigorate the old civic pride, in which he had considerable success, and private morality based on family values. In this latter goal, he was less successful. He patronized the arts in such a way as to beautify Rome and glorify his reign. On his death, he was able to pass on the regime to his family, the Julio-Claudians.

For almost two hundred years, with a few brief interruptions, the empire was generally prosperous, peaceful, and well-run, but problems were growing. Management of the many responsibilities assumed by the government required the growth of a large bureaucracy. This placed a heavy and increasing burden on the treasury, required higher taxes, and stifled both civic spirit and private enterprise. Pressure from barbarian tribes on the frontiers required a large standing army, which was also very costly and led to further rises in taxation.

In the late empire, Rome's rulers resorted to many devices for dealing with their problems, which included putting down internal military rebellions led by generals from different parts of the empire. More and more, the emperors' rule and their safety depended on the loyalty of the army, so they courted the soldiers' favor with gifts of various kinds. This only increased the burden of taxes; the rich and powerful found ways to avoid their obligations, making the load on everyone else all the heavier. The government's control over the lives of its people became ever greater and the society more rigid as people tried to flee to escape the crushing load of taxes. Many measures were tried: inflating the currency, fixing farmers to the soil as serfs, building walls to keep the barbarians out, bribing barbarian tribes to fight for Rome against other barbarians; but ultimately they all failed.

It is especially instructive to look at Rome from the perspective of the historians who discern a "dynastic cycle" in China (see Chapter 8). The development of the Roman Empire, although by no means the same as the Chinese, fits the same pattern fairly well. Like the Former Han Dynasty in China, the Roman Empire in the West fell, leaving disunity, insecurity, disorder, and poverty. Like similar empires in the ancient world, it had been unable to sustain its "immoderate greatness."

Suggested Readings

J. ·P. V. D. Balsdon, *Roman Women* (1962).

T. Barnes, *The New Empire of Diocletian and Constantine* (1982).

P. Brown, *Augustine of Hippo* (1967). A splendid biography.

P. Brown, *The World of Late Antiquity*, A.D. 150–750 (1971). A brilliant and readable essay.

J. Burckhardt, *The Age of Constantine the Great* (1956). A classic work by the Swiss cultural historian.

J. Carcopino, *Daily Life in Ancient Rome*, trans. by E. O. Lorimer (1940).

C. M. Cochrane, *Christianity and Classical Culture* (1957). A study of intellectual change in the late empire.

S. Dill, *Roman Society in the Last Century of the Western Empire* (1958).

E. R. Dodds, *Pagan and Christian in an Age of Anxiety* (1965). An original and perceptive study.

E. Gibbon, *The History of the Decline and Fall of the Roman Empire*, 7 vols., ed. by J. B. Bury, 2nd ed. (1909–1914). One of the masterworks of the English language.

T. Rice Holmes, *Architect of the Roman Empire*, 2 vols. (1928–1931). An account of Augustus' career in detail.

A. H. M. Jones, *The Later Roman Empire*, 3 vols. (1964). A comprehensive study of the period.

D. Kagan (ed.), *The End of the Roman Empire: Decline or Transformation?*, 2nd ed. (1978). A collection of essays discussing the problem of the decline and fall of the Roman Empire.

M. L. W. Laistner, *The Greater Roman Historians* (1963). Essays on the major Roman historical writers.

J. Lebreton and J. Zeiller, *History of the Primitive Church*, 3 vols. (1962). From the Catholic viewpoint.

H. Lietzmann, *History of the Early Church*, 2 vols. (1961). From the Protestant viewpoint.

F. Lot, *The End of the Ancient World and the Beginnings of the Middle Ages* (1961). A study that emphasizes gradual transition rather than abrupt change.

E. N. Luttwak, *The Grand Strategy of the Roman Empire* (1976). An original and fascinating analysis by a keen student of modern strategy.

R. MacMullen, *Enemies of the Roman Order* (1966). An original and revealing examination of opposition to the emperors.

R. MacMullen, *Paganism in the Roman Empire* (1981).

---

[4]Edward Gibbon, *Decline and Fall of the Roman Empire*, ed. by J. B. Bury, 2nd ed., Vol. 4 (London, 1909), pp. 173–174.

R. MacMullen, *Roman Social Relations, 50 B.C. to A.D. 284* (1981).

F. B. Marsh, *The Founding of the Roman Empire* (1959).

F. Millar, *The Roman Empire and Its Neighbors*, 2nd ed. (1981).

A. Momigliano (ed.), *The Conflict Between Paganism and Christianity* (1963). A valuable collection of essays.

H. M. D. Parker, *A History of the Roman World from A.D. 138 to 337* (1969). A good survey.

M. I. Rostovtzeff, *Social and Economic History of the Roman Empire*, 2nd ed. (1957). A masterpiece whose main thesis has been much disputed.

E. T. Salmon, *A History of the Roman World, 30 B.C. to A.D. 138* (1968). A good survey.

C. G. Starr, *Civilization and the Caesars* (1965). A study of Roman culture in the Augustan period.

R. Syme, *The Roman Revolution* (1960). A brilliant study of Augustus, his supporters, and their rise to power.

L. R. Taylor, *The Divinity of the Roman Empire* (1931). A study of the imperial cult.

A Bodhisattva statue from the Peshawar valley in India (2nd century A.D.). It probably represents the beginning of the Bodhisattva image as an important theme of Buddhist art. While the clothing is that of a contemporary Kushan or Indian nobleman, the stiff, fan-like folds of the skirt and the facial carving reflect Greco-Roman influence. [Bettmann Archive.]

7 Africa, Iran, and India before A.D. 200

After our initial look at the several birthplaces of civilization and the great revolutions in thought and religion of the first millennium B.C., we have focused on the Greek, Hellenistic, and Roman world that gave birth to Western European civilization and its modern offshoots. In Chapters 7 and 8, we take up the continuing story of ancient civilization in the world's two largest continents, Asia and Africa, during the centuries surrounding the beginning of the Christian era.

In this chapter, we shall look first at the prehistory and early history of Africa, with focus upon its principal civilized state of Kush, the successor empire to Pharaonic Egypt in ancient Nubia. Then we shall turn to the major civilizations of Iran and India from about 500 B.C. to A.D. 200. Three main themes will occupy us, all of which are primarily important in the Asian world. However, they are not wholly absent from the African scene, especially since the history of north Africa and Egypt continued to be bound up with that of the rest of the Mediterranean and western Asia.

One theme of the period from about 600 B.C. to A.D. 200 is the rise of centralized empires on a new and unprecedented scale, from the Mediterranean to China. While Africa did not produce an empire comparable to those of Rome, Iran, India, or China in this period, the vigorous Kushite kingdom of the upper Nile entered a new and lengthy phase of imperial expansion. The prosperity of this age carried on Pharaonic Egyptian culture in new ways. In Babylonia and Iran, the Achaemenids, an Aryan dynasty from the southwestern part of the Iranian plateau, founded the greatest empire yet seen in world history (CA. 539–330 B.C.). In northeast India, centered on the state of Magadha in the Ganges basin, a local dynasty known as the Mauryans founded the first great Indian empire (CA. 321–CA. 185 B.C.). Both of these empires, like their Roman and Chinese counterparts, developed sophisticated bureaucracies, professional armies, and strong communication systems.

A second theme of this period is the increasing contact and interaction of major civilizations. Africa is again something of an exception; yet, throughout this era, the peoples of its northern and eastern peripheries were in regular, largely commercial, contact with the rest of the Mediterranean-western Asian world—and to a lesser degree with the lands to the east. In Asia, these centuries saw the first sustained contact among the major centers of culture from the Mediterranean to China. These centers of civilization had already had some links of trade and travel, but the flourishing of the empires of Rome, Iran, India, and China increased and secured these links. These vast empires created new markets for diverse goods, both material and human (such as slaves, soldiers, and artisans); new security along major trade routes; new impetus for both diplomacy and conquest abroad; and a generally wider interest in the world beyond the empires' own frontiers.

The conquest (334–323 B.C.) by Alexander the Great of the Persian Empire, including modern Afghanistan and northwest India, was the most dramatic contribution of the age to new contact among diverse cultures, races, and religious traditions. His conquests ended the Achaemenid dynasty and, in the east, allowed the rising Mauryan power to extend its control over all of north India. The Hellenes and steppe peoples of northeast Iran and Central Asia, who ruled first post-Alexandrine Iran and then post-Mauryan India down to the third century A.D., inherited a world with horizons irrevocably larger than their original homelands.

A third theme of this period is the rise, spread, and consolidation of major religious traditions that would have considerable effect on later history from Africa to China. The evolution of Judaism in the Second Temple and early Diaspora periods as well as the rise and spread of early Christianity and diverse Hellenistic cults were of considerable importance to the history of north and northeast Africa and western Asia (see Chapter 6). Also important was the rise of Han Confucianism and classical Taoist thought in China (see Chapters 2, 8). Here we will emphasize the origins and growth in Iran of Zoroastrian religious practice and thought. We also take note of both the gradual emergence of an identifiable Hindu tradition and the important expansion of the Buddhist movement in India—and its spread abroad, especially into southeast Asia and China.

AFRICA

The Continent and Its Early Civilization

Africa has figured thus far only in our consideration of the ancient Mediterranean world. This belies its early importance to the history of civilization, since the origins of the human species may lie over one and one half million years ago in the Africa continent. A search for the cradle of humankind would take us first to east Africa, where archaeological research of recent decades has given us evidence of hominid society nearly two million years ago. This has prompted the hypothesis that the other continents were peopled by dispersion from this area.

However geographically isolated the majority of the African continent was from the earliest major civilizations of Eurasia, it was never entirely cut off from the rest of the world. Most obviously, above the great divide of the Sahara, Egypt was always oriented to the Mediterranean, into which its great river emptied. In Chapter 1, we saw how the Nile valley produced one of the earliest civilized cultures as early as the fourth millennium B.C. Similarly, the north African coast was also oriented to Eurasia, and we have noted its ancient sea links across the Mediterranean in Greek, Hellenistic, and Roman times. It was a place where Berber-speaking peoples mixed with other Mediterraneans like the Phoenicians. Here a powerful Carthagenian Punic state arose that later fell prey to the imperialism of the upstart Roman state (see Chapter 5).

We turn now away from the Mediterranean to other centers of early culture in Africa in the first millennium B.C. To place these in the larger African geographical context and to introduce the continent as a whole, we must first note the special physical attributes that have controlled the history of African civilization in greater measure than that of most other continents.

Physical Considerations

Africa is huge and geologically massive. Its more than thirty million square kilometers compose one fifth of the Earth's entire land mass. It is three and one-half times the size of the continental United States and second only to Asia in total area. Its massiveness is evident in its lack of natural harbors and islands, the generally steep escarpments that surmount its narrow coasts, and its unusually high relief (the average continental elevation is 660 meters). The vast size and sharp physical variations, from high mountains to swamplands and deserts, have made rapid long-distance movement and communication difficult, consequently both were channeled along certain corridors (such as the Rift valley of East Africa, or the Niger or Zambezi river valley). The continent's high relief has made access to, as well as egress from, its interior difficult. All of Africa's major rivers (the Niger, Congo [Zaïre], Nile, Zambezi and Orange) lie largely in plateau basins and are navigable in these inland reaches but not across the cataracts and falls that they traverse before they reach the coastlands.

Africa is a continent that straddles the equator, and the special character of various regions is due in considerable part to climatic considerations. As a whole, its climate is unusually hot. North and south of the equator, dense rainforests dominate an west–east band of tropical territory from the southern coasts of West Africa across the Congo or Zaire basin to the Kenyan highlands. (Note, however, that the tropical rainforests cover only about five per cent of Africa's total surface area.) North and south of this band (and in the Kenyan highlands), the lush rainforests give way to broad grassy plains and open woodlands known as *savannah*. These in turn pass into steppeland and semidesert (the *sahel*), and finally true desert as one moves farther from the equator. Despite high rainfall and humidity in its western and central equatorial regions (except in the eastern highlands) and along its Indian-Ocean coasts, Africa contains two of the world's greatest and driest desert regions. The Sahara ("the Desert": Arabic *al-Sahra*') is the world's largest desert and has historically been the major factor hindering contact between the Mediterranean world and sub-Saharan Africa. The Kalahari is its smaller but still vast counterpart in southwest Africa. It partially cuts off the south African plateau and coastal regions from much of central Africa.

These physical factors have played a major role in the regionalization of African history. Even so, both cultural and linguistic diffusion show that, despite natural barriers, Africa's peoples have not been as internally isolated or compartmentalized as once was thought.

Other natural factors are of importance to Africa's history. The soils of Africa are typically tropical in character, which means devoid of much humus, or vegetable mold, and generally easily leached of their mineral and nutrient contents. Thus, they are easily exhausted and not highly productive for extended periods. Water shortage is also a perennial problem for agriculture in most of Africa, and a potent factor in its history past and recent. Crop pests and insects such as the tsetse fly, mosquito, and locust have also been enemies of both farming and pastoralism in Africa. On the other hand, abundant animal life has from early on made hunting or fishing an important way of survival in Africa.

The great mineral wealth of Africa has been very influential in shaping human activity throughout the continent. Salt was a very important trading commodity among Africans for centuries in various parts of the continent. For example, salt was an important focus of the trans-Sahara trade between the western Sudan and north Africa from as early as the first millennium A.D. Iron was even earlier a major trading commodity between forest and savannah zones. Copper, mined in only limited areas on the continent, was also a much-sought-after commodity. For centuries, gold was a significant trading commodity within the continent as well as an export. The ancient Egyptians sought the gold of Nubia; later, gold from west and central Africa was in demand in north Africa, the Mediterranean world, and the Indian Ocean sphere.

Finally, we should note that by convention Africa is divided into at least seven major regions:

1. north Africa, including all the Mediterranean coastal regions from modern Morocco through modern Libya and the northern regions of the Sahara;
2. Nilotic Africa (i.e., the lands of the Nile), roughly the area of the modern states of Egypt and Sudan;
3. the Sudan, the broad belt of sahel and savannah below the Sahara, which stretches from the Atlantic east across the entire continent, over the upper Nile to the Red Sea;
4. west Africa, including the desert, sahel, and savannah of the western Sudan as far east as the Lake Chad basin, and the woodland coastal regions from Cape Verde to Cameroon;
5. east Africa, from the Ethiopian highlands (a high, fertile plateau cut off by desert to its south and north) and "the Horn of Africa" south over modern Kenya and Tanzania—an area split north to south by the great Rift valley;
6. central Africa, the region north of the Kalahari, stretching from the Chad basin in the north over the Zaïre basin southeast to Lakes Tanganyika and Malawi and down to the Zambezi river (or, sometimes, the Limpopo river) in the southeast;
7. south Africa, from the Kalahari desert and Zambezi (or the Limpopo) south to the Cape of Good Hope.

Early Culture outside of Egypt

Unlike that of other continents, African history has not been one of major empires and a few major centers of cultural diffusion. This has been true especially south of the Sahara because this vast region was relatively isolated from events and cultures in Asia and

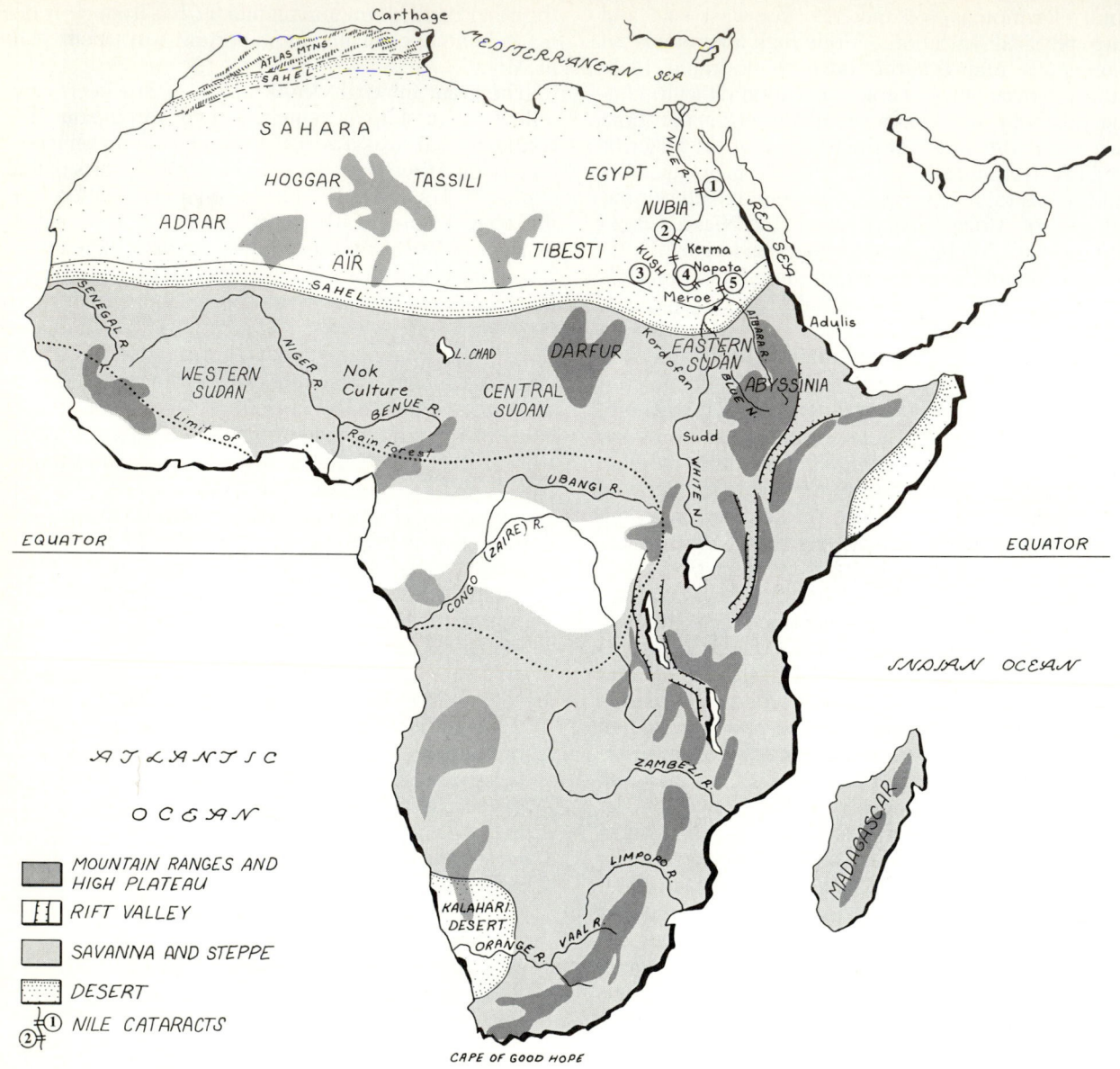

MAP 7-1   AFRICA: MAJOR PHYSICAL FEATURES.   *Showing the principal physical zones and waterways of the continent, as described in the text.*

Europe until after A.D. 1000. The chief cause of this relative isolation was the increasing dessication of the once well-watered northern third of the continent from about 2500 B.C. By 1000 B.C., this process was advanced enough to make the Sahara an immense east–west expanse of largely uninhabitable desert separating the greater part of the African continent from the Mediterranean coastal rim and Near Eastern centers of early civilization.

This is not, however, to imply that regular contacts between sub-Saharan Africa and the Mediterranean world in ancient times ceased. We know, for example, that a number of north–south routes across the western and central Sahara were traversed by horses and carts or chariots long before the coming of the camel.

Well before the Christian era, the peoples of the upper Nile, the Abyssinian plateau (modern Ethiopia), and the coastal areas of East Africa below the Horn maintained contacts with Egypt, south Arabia, and likely with India and Indonesia via the Indian Ocean. We have learned from archaeology that sub-Saharan Africa had extensive settled cultures before the Christian era, most notably in the Sudanic regions below the Sahara.

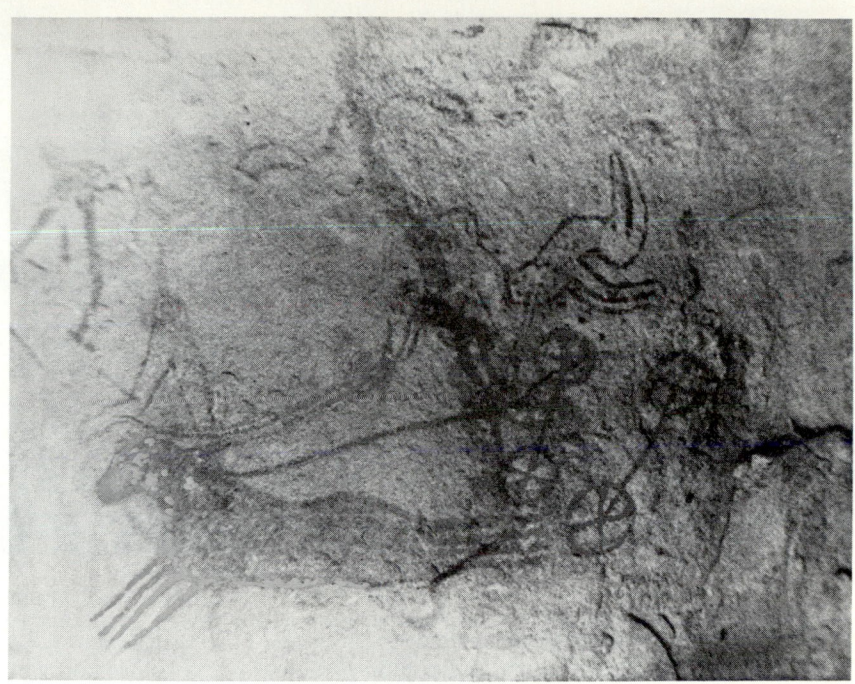

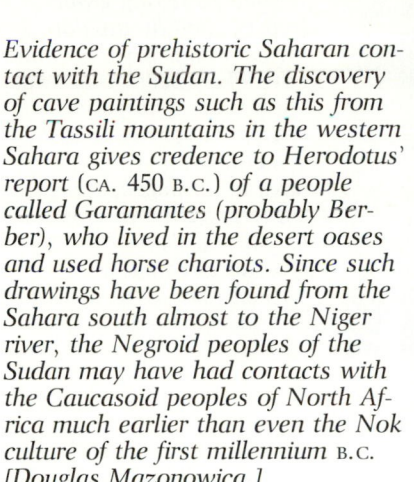

Evidence of prehistoric Saharan contact with the Sudan. The discovery of cave paintings such as this from the Tassili mountains in the western Sahara gives credence to Herodotus' report (CA. 450 B.C.) of a people called Garamantes (probably Berber), who lived in the desert oases and used horse chariots. Since such drawings have been found from the Sahara south almost to the Niger river, the Negroid peoples of the Sudan may have had contacts with the Caucasoid peoples of North Africa much earlier than even the Nok culture of the first millennium B.C. [Douglas Mazonowica.]

NEOLITHIC SUDANIC CULTURES. In the first millennium B.C., the very advanced civilization of the Kushites occupied the Nile basin on the eastern end of the great sub-Saharan belt of the Sudan. Other less advanced and preliterate, but still complex, agricultural communities of neolithic and early iron-age culture dotted its central and western reaches. Scholars surmise that these sub-Saharan peoples had once been spread farther north, in the formerly arable Saharan lands that they apparently shared with the largely nomadic Berber-speaking peoples of contemporary west-Saharan and north Africa.

Evidence for previously settled cultures in what is now uninhabitable desert comes from archaeological finds in the southwestern Sahara; they have revealed an ancient agricultural civilization with as many as two hundred towns in modern Mauritania. The most popular theory is that these towns may have been associated with trade in commodities such as salt, and that progressive dessication forced the trading centers and the agriculturalists south. They took with them the techniques of settled agriculture, especially those based on cereal grains, and of animal husbandry, as they spread into the savannah below the desert and sahel. They also domesticated new crops using their old techniques. Augmented ultimately by the knowledge of ironworking (whether passed on from north Africa or from the Nilotic kingdom of Kush), these people were able to effect an agricultural revolution. This led to considerable population growth in the more fertile of the Sudanic regions—notably those regions near the great river basins of the Niger and Senegal—and the Lake Chad basin. (A similar spread of agricultural techniques and cattle and sheep raising seems to have occurred down the Rift Valley of the east African highlands.) This agricultural revolution, effected by some time in the first millennium B.C., provided the basis for the growth of new culture centers in the sub-Saharan regions.

RACIAL DIFFERENTIATION. The changes in African food production, the subsequent development of local settled cultures, and even larger patterns of civilization have been linked by some to the apparent differences in appearance of African populations. In historical times, lighter skinned, Caucasoid African peoples have predominated in the Sahara, north Africa, and Egypt, while darker skinned, Negroid peoples have been the majority in the rest of Africa.[1] (The Greeks called all of the black peoples of Africa of whom they knew *Ethiopians*, "those with burnt skins." The Arabs termed all of Africa south of the Sahara and of Egypt *Bilad al-Sudan*, "the Land of the Blacks," and from this we get the term *Sudan*.) Other, yellowish-brown

[1] Note, however, that actual distribution of skin color in the past is very hard to determine; there is even sharp disagreement as to whether the ancient Egyptians were more "white" or more "black." See the discussions in G. Mokhtar, ed., *Ancient Civilizations of Africa*, vol. 2 of UNESCO General History of Africa (London, 1981), pp. 27–83.

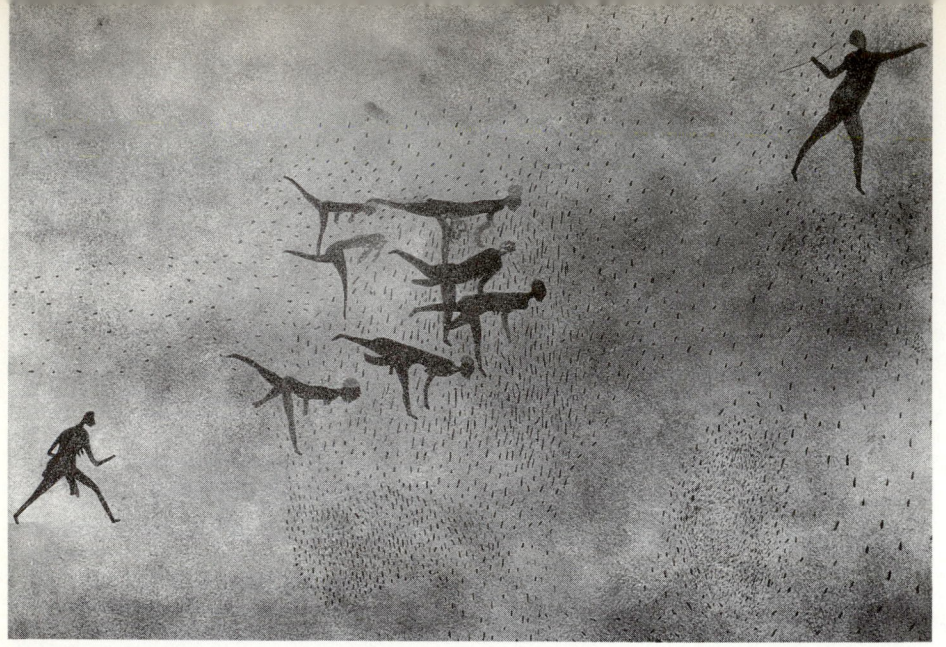

A Stone Age Saharan rock painting. *One scholar believes this strikingly beautiful painting represents women gathering grain (represented by the dots, presumably). If so, it would have likely been wild grain unless cereal crops were cultivated very early here— something for which we have no evidence. Whether gathering grain or engaged in graceful dance, the figures here remind us of the ancient human presence in the once-green Saharan regions.*

peoples occur in smaller numbers in sub-Saharan, especially southern, Africa, largely as more isolated, small herding or hunter-gatherer groups. These peoples are known as the Khoikhoi and San—the "Hottentots" and "Bushmen" of traditional European usage—or, collectively, the Khoisan; they survive in greatest number in the Kalahari region today.

Some theories have attempted to link differences of color or racial type to the development and spread of everything from agriculture or cattle herding to ironworking or state-building in Africa. However, none of these theories is tenable, if only because the concept of race itself is a problematic one. As many scholars have pointed out, long periods of relative isolation of different human populations in prehistory led to differing common gene pools in different areas. Yet always, especially in more recent times, the mixing of different gene pools produced constant change. In Africa, the various populations were so mixed that most Africans might even best be considered to belong to one large race, regardless of color or other physical attributes.[2] Thus, one should not make too much out of the obvious color differences in Africa. These differences have resulted from differing gene pools and, perhaps, some climatic adaptation. We do not know at what point in prehistory such factors led to differentiation between the Caucasoid peoples of northern Africa, the Negroid peoples of the Sudan and regions further south, and the "brown" peoples of the more southern areas. All these types are found in an infinite variety of mixtures in most areas of Africa today.

[2]Philip Curtin, et al., *African History* (London, 1978), pp. 14–16.

THE NOK CULTURE. Whatever their earlier history, we know that in the first millennium B.C. the Negroid peoples of the Sudan developed and refined techniques for settled agriculture. The result changed the face of sub-Saharan Africa, where previously small groups of hunter-gatherers had predominated. With the advent of early iron technology, these settled peoples were able to develop societies larger and more complex than had existed before.

One of the most impressive neolithic cultures in the Sudanic regions was located in west Africa on the central Nigerian plateau of Jos. Archaeological digs have yielded evidence of the agriculturalist and cattle-herding Nok culture, named for the village of the first find. Stone tools, iron implements, and highly artistic terracotta sculpture dated between 900 B.C. and A.D. 200 have been found here. Two aspects of this culture are of particular interest. The first is the fact that the Nok people had entered the Iron Age. They had learned the relatively difficult art of smelting iron as early as 500 B.C. and thus represent perhaps the earliest iron-age culture in west Africa. A major unanswered question is whether this technique reached the Jos plateau from the Kushite culture of the upper Nile (see below) via the central and eastern Sudan, or from the north African world via the Sahara. In either case, we have here evidence of contacts among early identifiable cultures in the African continent.

The second distinctive aspect is their extraordinarily highly developed sculptural art, most vividly seen in the magnificent burial or ritual masks they produced. The apparent continuities of Nok sculptural traditions with those of other, later west African cultures to the south suggest that this culture had an important impact on later west African life. These continuities pro-

Prehistoric West African sculpture from Nok. Magnificent terra-cotta heads recovered from Nok culture sites such as Igbo-Ukwu reveal that the prehistoric civilization of the western Sudan had highly developed artistic tastes and techniques. The style of the head shown here suggests that such terra-cotta castings may have had wooden prototypes. [National Museum of African Art, Smithsonian Institution.]

vide good indication that ancient communities of some sophistication laid a basis upon which later, better-known Sudanic civilizations must have built. We shall return to these in Chapter 11.

The Successor to Egyptian Empire: The Kingdom of Kush

When we move east across the Sudan to the upper Nile basin, just above the first cataract, we find the land of Kush, in lower Nubia. By comparison with the western or central Sudan, this eastern region had earlier and more frequent contact with ancient Near Eastern culture through its intercourse with Pharaonic Egypt down the Nile valley. It was here that an Egyptianized segment of the Negroid peoples of Nubia built the earliest-known literate and politically unified civilization in Africa outside of Egypt.

THE NAPATAN EMPIRE. As early as 2000 B.C., Kerma, a Kushite town above the third cataract, was a major trading outpost for the Middle-Kingdom Egyptians. From this and other Sudanic settlements, a stream of building materials, ivory, slaves, mercenaries, and especially gold flowed north down the Nile. After the Hyksos invasions, in New Kingdom times, Kush came under stronger Egyptian cultural influence as well as political and military domination. By the tenth century B.C., as the later Pharaonic dynasties grew weak, Kush went from being a provincial border territory of the Egyptian state to emergence as a virtually independent kingdom. Nonetheless, the royal line that ruled at the new Kushite capital of Napata was culturally heavily Egyptian; indeed, they saw themselves as Egyptian. Their kings practiced the Pharaohs' custom of marrying their own sisters—a practice known to many kingship institutions around the world. They buried their royalty embalmed in pyramids in traditional Egyptian style. They used Egyptian protocol and titles. In the eighth century B.C., they conquered Egypt proper and ruled it for about a century as the Twenty-fifth pharaonic Dynasty. This Kushite dynasty was driven out of Egypt only by the iron-equipped military might of Assyria around the middle of the seventh century B.C.

THE MEROITIC EMPIRE. Forced back above the lower cataracts of the Nile by the Assyrians and kept there by the Persians, the Kushite kingdom became increasingly isolated from Egypt and the Mediterranean world and developed in its own distinctive ways. Invaded by an Egyptian army in 591 B.C., Napata itself was sacked. This led to a relocation of the capital farther south in the prosperous city of Meroe, bringing the seat of rule closer to the geographical center of the Kushite domains. By this time, the Kushite kings had extended their sway westward into Kordofan, south above the confluence of the Blue and the White Nile, and southeast to the edges of the Abyssinian plateau. Meroe now became the kingdom's densely populated political and cultural capital. In the sixth century B.C. Meroe was the center of a flourishing iron industry, from which iron smelting may first have been dispersed west and south to the sub-Saharan world. Certainly the Kushites traded widely to the west across the Sudan. The Meroitic empire enjoyed a long and

The Kushite Conquest of Memphis

The following text is taken from a granite pillar that the Kushite king Piankhi had erected near Napata to commemorate his conquest of Egypt in the decade before 750 B.C. It describes the siege and capture of Memphis.

When day broke, at early morning, his majesty reached Memphis. When he had landed on the north of it, he found that the water had approached to the walls, the ships mooring at (the walls of) Memphis. Then his majesty saw that it was strong, and that the wall was raised by a new rampart, and battlements manned with mighty men. There was found no way of attacking it. Every man told his opinion among the army of his majesty, according to every rule of war. Every man said: "Let us besiege it—; lo, its troops are numerous." Others said: "Let a causeway be made against it; let us elevate the ground to its walls. Let us bind together a tower; let us erect masts and make the spars into a bridge to it. We will divide it on this (plan) on every side of it, on the high ground and ——— on the north of it, in order to elevate the ground at its walls, that we may find a way for our feet."

Then his majesty was enraged against it like a panther; he said: "I swear, as Re loves me, as my father, Amon (who fashioned me), favors me, this shall befall it, according to the command of Amon . . . I will take it like a flood of water. I have commanded . . . " Then he sent forth his fleet and his army to assault the harbor of Memphis; they brought to him every ferryboat, every (cargo) boat, every (transport), and the ships, as many as there were, which had moored in the harbor of Memphis, with the bow-rope fastened among its houses. (There was not) a citizen who wept, among all the soldiers of his majesty.

His majesty himself came to line up the ships, as many as there were. His majesty commanded his army: "Forward against it! Mount the walls! Penetrate the houses over the river. If one of you gets through upon the wall, let him not halt before it (so that) the (hostile) troops may not repulse you . . . "

Then Memphis was taken as (by) a flood of water, a multitude of people were slain therein, and brought as living captives to the place where his majesty was. ❑

From J. H. Breasted, *Ancient Records of Egypt* (Chicago: 1906), vol. 4, pars, 861 ff. Reprinted in Basil Davidson, *The African Past* (New York: Grosset and Dunlap, 1964, 1967), pp. 51–52.

prosperous life before it began to decline, apparently about A.D. 100. It came to an end in the fourth century at the hands of the rival trading state of Aksum on the Abyssinian plateau (see Chapter 11).

CULTURE AND ECONOMY. The heyday of Meroitic [i.e., of Meroe] culture was from about the middle of the third century B.C. to the first century A.D. The kingdom was middleman for the varied African goods in demand in the Mediterranean and Near East: animal skins, ebony and ivory, gold, oils and perfumes, and slaves. The Kushites traded with the Hellenistic-Roman world, south Arabia, and India, and in this regard were truly a part of the larger international world. Economically, the Kushite lands between the Nile and the Red Sea were a major source of gold for Egypt and the ancient Mediterranean world. They shipped quality iron to Aksum and the Red Sea. Cattle breeding and other forms of animal husbandry were of special importance, while agriculture along the banks of the Nile and more widely afield by irrigation was the other mainstay of the economy. Cotton cultivation in Kush preceded that of Egypt and may well have been an early export product of the kingdom.

Pyramid tombs of the kings of Kush. These pyramids at Gebel Barkal in Upper Nubia, the heartland of Kush, date from the first century B.C. The Meroites may have transferred the royal cemetery here from Meroe, which is farther south along the Nile, when they became increasingly active in the northern part of their realm, which stretched beyond Aswan in Ptolemaic times. For example, they inflicted a substantial, if temporary, defeat on the Romans in the Aswan area in 24 B.C. [Oriental Institute, University of Chicago]

A Temple Ram of Ancient Meroe. *This finely chiseled granite statue stands before the ruins of a Meroitic temple at the site of Naqa. Such statues were apparently associated with temples dedicated especially to the worship of Amun Re, who, like the god Khnum, is commonly depicted as a Ram-headed deity.*

This was an era of prosperity. Many monuments were built, including royal pyramids and the storied palace and walls of the capital. Fine pottery and jewelry were produced. Meroitic culture is especially renowned for its two kinds of pottery: one turned on wheels was the product of an all-male industry attuned apparently to market demands, and another made exclusively by hand by women was used largely domestically. This latter kind of pottery seems to have come out of an older tradition of African pottery craft that is found well outside the region of Kush—an indication of ancient traditions shared in varied regions of Africa.

RULE AND ADMINISTRATION. The political system of the Meroitic empire, like the Pharaonic, was apparently traditionalist and stable over many centuries. The system did, however, have features that distinguished it from its Egyptian models. The king seems to have ruled strictly by customary law, presumably as interpreted by the priests. His actions were limited by firm taboos; according to some Greek accounts, violation of those taboos could lead to enforced royal suicide. There was also a royal election system, commented on by Herodotus and other Greek authors. Diodorus of Sicily says that the priests would present several outstanding candidates for king, and from this group the god would choose the new sacred king (by what oracular mechanism, we are not told). The priests apparently considered the king to be a living god—a practice known both in ancient Egypt and many other African societies. A Kushite inscription on the coronation of a new king tells us, however, that King Aspelta (reigned 593–568 B.C.) was elected to succeed his brother from among his other royal brothers by twenty-four high officials and military leaders.

From this we see that royal succession was not from father to son, but within the royal family. Other inscriptions tell us that the succession was often through the maternal rather than the paternal line. The role of the queen mother in the election appears to have been crucial—another parallel if not a direct link to African practices elsewhere. Indeed, the queen mother seems to have adopted formally her son's wife upon his succession. By the second century B.C., a woman had become sole monarch, initiating a long line of queens, or "Candaces" (*Kandake*, from the Meroitic word for queen mother).

We know very little of Meroitic administration. The empire seems to have been under the autocratic rule of the royal sovereign, perhaps on the Egyptian model. He or she presided over a central administration run by a number of high officials: chiefs of the treasury, seal bearers, chiefs of granaries, army commanders, and chiefs of scribes and archives. The various provinces had to be delegated to princes who must have functioned with considerable autonomy, given the likely slow communication over the vast and difficult terrain of the upper Nile and eastern Sudanic region.

SOCIETY AND RELIGION. We know little of the social structure outside the circle of the palace—the ruling class of monarch and relatives, priests, courtiers, and provincial nobility. We do find mention of slaves, most commonly female domestics, but also male laborers who were drawn largely from prisoners of war. We can presume that cattle breeders, farmers, traders, craftsmen, and minor government functionar-

Herodotus Mentions "the Ethiopians" of Meroitic Kush

[CA. 430 B.C.] I went as far as Elephantine [Aswan] to see what I could with my own eyes, but for the country still further south I had to be content with what I was told in answer to my questions. The most I could learn was that beyond Elephantine the country rises steeply; and in that part of the river boats have to be hauled along by the ropes—one rope on each side—much as one drags an ox. If the rope parts, the boat is gone in a moment, carried away by the force of the stream. These conditions last over a four days' journey, the river all the time winding greatly, like the Maeander, and the distance to be covered amounting to twelve *schoeni*. After this one reaches a level plain, where the river is divided by an island named Tachompso.

South of Elephantine the country is inhabited by Ethiopians who also possess half of Tachompso, the other half being occupied by Egyptians. Beyond the island is a great lake, and round its shores live nomadic tribes of Ethiopians. After crossing the lake one comes again to the stream of the Nile, which flows into it. At this point one must land and travel along the bank of the river for forty days, because sharp rocks, some showing above the water and many just awash, make the river impracticable for boats. After the forty days' journey on land one takes another boat and in twelve days reaches a big city named Meroë, said to be the capital city of the Ethiopians. The inhabitants worship Zeus and Dionysus alone of the Gods, holding them in great honor. There is an oracle of Zeus there, and they make war according to its pronouncements, taking from it both the occasion and the object of their various expeditions. ❑

From the translation of *The Histories* of Herodotus by Aubrey de Sélincourt, Penguin Books, 1954, as cited by Basil Davidson, *The African Past* (New York: Grosset and Dunlap, 1964, 1967), pp. 52–53.

EARLY AFRICAN CIVILIZATIONS

CA. 10,000 B.C.	Dessication of Saharan region begins
CA. 3000–2000 B.C.	Relatively rapid dessication of Saharan region
CA. 2000–1000 B.C.	Increasing Egyptian influence in Nubia
CA. 1000–900 B.C.	Kushite kingdom with capital at Napata becomes independent of Egypt
751–663 B.C.	Kushite kings Piankhy and Taharqa rule all Egypt
CA. 600–500 B.C.	Meroe becomes new Kushite capital
CA. 500 B.C.–A.D. 330	Meroitic kingdom of Kush (height of Meroitic Kushite power CA. 250–B.C.–A.D. 50)
CA. 500 B.C.–A.D. 500(?)	Nok Culture flourishes on Jos plateau in western Sudan (modern central Nigeria)
CA. A.D. 1–100	Rise of Aksum as trading power on Ethiopian (Abyssinian) plateau
CA. A.D. 330	Kush conquered by Aksumites

ies formed an intermediate class or classes between the slaves and the rulers.

In religious matters, we have no direct records of actual Kushite practices, but it is clear that they closely followed Egyptian traditions in their worship for a number of centuries. To judge from the great temples dedicated to him, Amon seems to have been the highest god for the earlier kings; and his priests had considerable influence. By the third century B.C., however, gods unknown to Egypt rose in importance alongside Amon and other Egyptian gods. Most notable was Apedemak, a warrior god with a lion's head. The many lion temples associated with him (as many as forty-six have been identified) reflect the great importance of this Kushite god. Such gods likely represented local deities who gradually rose to take their place alongside the highest Egyptian gods. However, some scholars have speculated about Iranian or Indian influences (via the Indian Ocean–Red Sea trade link) in the non-Egyptian elements of the Kushite cult.

In sum, we find many evidences of numerous neolithic and early iron-age African cultures above the equator in the first millennium B.C. However, urban, literate civilization and large-scale empires were made possible only in the north, with the Punic empire of Carthage, and in the east, with the Egyptian and Kushite kingdoms, through sustained contact with the main kingdoms and cultures of the ancient world.

Portfolio II: Hinduism

The term "Hinduism" is simply our modern word for the majority of the diverse religious traditions of India taken as a whole. Until the word was coined in the nineteenth century, it (like "Buddhism") was not even a concept in the West, let alone in India itself. In contemporary usage, however, it has become a catch-all term used for all the Indian religious communities that look upon the texts of the Vedas (see Chapter 1) as eternal, perfect truth.

The historical beginnings of the varied Hindu traditions can be traced to the ancient Aryan migrations into south Asia in the second millenium before our common era. This was the age in which the Vedic hymns were composed. In them we find a pantheon of gods not unlike that found among other Indo-European peoples, the Greeks, and the Romans. Centered on a sacrificial cult of these gods, Vedic religion became more and more the preserve of the Brahmin priestly class of early Indian society. The Brahmins gradually elaborated a cult characterized by complex rituals of sacrifice, involved purificatory rules, and increasingly fixed distinctions of birth upon which the later caste system was based. These developments are mirrored in the later Vedic, or Brahmanical, texts (ca. 1000–500 B.C.) that provide commentary on and instructions for ritual use of the Vedic hymns.

After about 700 B.C., new developments set in. North India produced a series of religious reformers, most of whom championed knowledge and ascetic discipline rather than purity and ritual action. Some of these reformers broke with the Vedic tradition. Of these, Siddhartha Gautama (the Buddha; born ca. 563) and Mahavira Vardhamana (founder of the Jain tradition; born ca. 550) were the two most famous. Other thinkers reinterpreted the older sacrifice as an inner activity and deepened its spiritual dimensions. They further tried to link or to identify Transcendence, or Ultimate Being *(Brahman)* with the inmost self *(atman)*. Their thinking is represented especially in the Upanishads, which many Hindus consider the most sublime philosophical texts in the Indian tradition.

First developed so long ago, such notions have been part of the complex but logically compelling vision of existence that lies behind the myriad forms of religious life known to us as "Hinduism." In this vision, the immortal part of each human being, the *atman*, is enmeshed in existence, but not ultimately of it. The nature of existence is *samsara*—unending becoming and change, a ceaseless round of cause and effect determined by the inescapable consequences of *karma*, or "action." The doctrine of *karma* is a kind of moral as well as physical economy in which every act has unavoidable results; so long as mental or physical action occurs, becoming and life go on repeatedly. Birth determines one's place and duties in the traditional Indian caste system. Caste is the most visible and concrete reminder of the pervasiveness of the Hindu concept of absolute causality that keeps us enmeshed in existence. The final goal is to transcend at some point in this or another lifetime the endless round of rebirth, or *samsara*, in which we are all caught. Release, or *moksha*, is the only way out of this otherwise endless becoming and rebirth. *Moksha* may be gained through knowledge, action, or devotion.

On the popular level, the period after about 500 B.C. is most notable in Indian religious life for two developments. Both took place alongside the ever deeper intrenchment in society of caste distinctions and a supporting ethic of obligations and privileges. The first was the elaboration of ascetic traditions of inner quest and self-realization, such as that of yoga. The second was the rise of devotional worship of specific gods and goddesses who are seen by their worshipers as identical with the Ultimate—in other words, as supreme deities for those who serve them. The latter development was of particular importance for popular religion in India. Evident in the famous and beloved Hindu devotional text, the *Bhagavad Gita*, it reached its highest level after A.D. 500 in the myriad movements of fervent, loving devotionalism, or *bhakti*, many of which remain important today. A striking aspect of Hindu piety has been its willingness to accomodate the focus on one "chosen deity" who is worshiped as supreme to a worldview that holds that the Divine can and does take many forms. Thus most Hindus worship one deity, but they do so in the awareness that faith in other deities can also lead one to the Ultimate.

The period between about 500 B.C. and A.D. 1000

saw the rise of two gods in particular, Vishnu and Shiva, to special prominence as the primary forms in which the supreme Lord is worshiped. Along with the mother-goddess figure, who takes various names and forms (Kali, Durga, for example), Vishnu and Shiva have remained to the present day the most important manifestations of the divine in India. Their followers are known as Vaishnavas and Shaivas, respectively. Countless differing traditions of devotion are practiced among Vaishnavas and Shaivas, as well as other groups. However, a few recurring phenomena and ideas can suggest something of Indian religiousness in practice.

Hindu practice is characterized especially by temple worship (puja), in which offerings of flowers, food, and the like are brought by the worshipers. The temple images are especially sought out by the faithful for the blessing that the sight of them brings. Recitation of sacred texts, many of which are vernacular hymns of praise to a particular deity, are another important part of Hindu devotionalism. Mantras, or special recitative texts from the Vedas, are also used by many Hindus in their original Sanskrit form. These texts are thought to have extraordinary power. A prominent feature of Hindu life is preoccupation with purity and pollution, most evident in the food taboos associated with caste groupings.

The ascetic tendency in India is also highly developed. Although they are influential, only a tiny minority relative to the great masses of Indians take up a life of full renunciation. In this life, the ascetic worshiper does not settle in one place, take on possessions, or perform regular worship. He or she rather wanders about in search of teachers and devotes himself or herself to meditation and self-realization. Even though the majority of Hindus have families and work at their salvation through merit gained by puja and moral living, the ascetic ideal has an important place in the overall Indian worldview. This ideal is seen even by householders as valid and worthy of respect; it stands as a constant reminder of the deeper reality beyond the everyday world and any individual life.

II-2 A Hindu Ascetic in Nepal. *The* sadhu, *or ascetic, shown here is a devotee, of Shiva. He is mediating and fasting in observance of the annual celebration of Shivaratri, the holy night of Shiva. Shiva in his ascetic manifestation is the model for the ascetic life of the* sadhu. *[Judith Aronson/Peter Arnold, Inc.]*

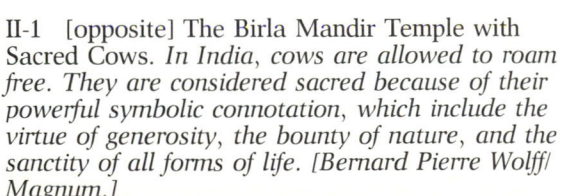

II-1 [opposite] The Birla Mandir Temple with Sacred Cows. *In India, cows are allowed to roam free. They are considered sacred because of their powerful symbolic connotation, which include the virtue of generosity, the bounty of nature, and the sanctity of all forms of life. [Bernard Pierre Wolff/ Magnum.]*

II-3 Purification Rituals in the Waters of the Holy Ganges. *Purification rituals are part of the obligatory daily rituals of all "twice-born" Hindus. The morning rituals performed by the women here in the Ganges include greeting the sun with recitation and prayer and purification by bathing. [Ian Berry/Magnum.]*

C-11

II-4 Garlanded Statue of Hanuman in a Mysore Temple. *This statue of the monkey-god Hanuman in a niche of the Chamundi Hill Temple has been draped with yellow garlands by worshippers at the shrine. Hanuman, known as "the beautiful one," is a famous figure in the great epic of the* Ramayana. *As a monkey servant and friend of Lord Rama, he used his miraculous powers to help his master regain his abducted wife, Sita, from Sri Lanka, where she was held hostage by the demon king, Ravana. As a folk deity, he is worshipped for his magical powers, especially against evil spirits. He is also a model of devotion to Lord Rama.* [Bernard Pierre Wolff/Magnum.]

II-5 Krishna Holding up Govardhana. *The beloved cycle of Krishna myths is popular not only among worshipers of Lord Krishna but most Indians. In this Bikaner painting of circa 1690, we see him using the entire mountain of Govardhana as an umbrella to protect his homeland and sacred territory of Brindavan from the deluge sent down by the great god Indra. Indra appears on his elephant in the upper right hand distance. The women gathered around Lord Krishna are the cowherdesses, or gopis, famous from other tale of the Dark Lord.* [Scala/Art Resource.]

II-6　Krishna Dancing with the Gopis. *This seven-teenth-century opaque watercolor with gold depicts one of the most frequent motifs of Indian art, namely the play and dancing of Lord Krishna with the cowherdesses of Brindavan. He lures them away from their homes to sport with him in the moonlight as his consorts. This sexual motif expresses the ideas of the intense love between Krishna and his devotees and the consequent willingness of the latter to forsake all else for their Lord. [Philadelphia Museum of Art, Gift of Mr. and Mrs. Lessing J. Rosenwald.]*

II-7　Lord Vishnu Re-clining on the Serpent of Eternity, Ananta. *Here Krishna, in his form as Lord Vishnu, is depicted in the act of creation of the world, which emerges in the form of the four-faced god Brahma from the lotus blossom that in turn arises from Vishnu's navel. On the left, Krishna's consort, Radha (or Lakshmi), serves her Lord. The serpent, Ananta (which means "without end," or eternal), rests upon the cosmic waters that ex-isted before creation. [Michael Holford.]*

II-8, II-9   Kajuraho, Temple of Kandariyo Mahadeva.
This famous eleventh-century Hindu temple sacred to the worship of Shiva as supreme Lord is built in the form of a mountain. All the way up to its main spire, or shikara its exterior teems with subsidiary peaks or "spires" and is literally covered with images of mythical and royal figures, as seen in the detail photograph. The interior takes the form of a cave/womb sanctuary in which the image of Shiva is kept. [Frontal view: Borromeo, EPA/Art Resource. Detail of facade: Scala/Art Resource.]

II-10 Shiva Nataraja, "Dancing Shiva." *This magnificent tenth-century Chola bronze statue from South India shows Shiva dancing upon the body of a fallen demon. The Lord of Dancers bearing the emblems of creation and destruction that signify his mythic role, is dancing the world in and out of existence, defeating death, and transcending time. [Borromeo, EPA/Art Resource.]*

II-11 "Kali Killing the Ashuras." *This eighteenth-century painting imaginatively portrays the Goddess, Kali, riding her tiger as she destroys with her trident the larger of two demons, or ashuras. The depiction of Kali garlanded with bodies and in a hideous manifestation belies the fact that she is fervently worshipped by her devotees as mother goddess. Like Shiva, her horrific form is part of her power to destroy demons and evil and hence can comfort as well as inspire fear and awe. [Cleveland Museum of Art, Edward L. Whittemore Fund.]*

II-12 Rama Destroys the Ten-headed Demon King, Ravana. *In another episode from the* Ramayana *epic cycle, Ravana, the king of Sri Lanka, is finally destroyed by Rama's arrow after the rescue of Sita. This death scene is told in great detail in the great epic of the* Ramayana. *[Bury Peerless.]*

The First Iranian Empire
(550–330 B.C.)

The Land

Iran is the name given to the huge expanse of southwest Asia that lies between the Caspian and the Arabian seas; it is bounded by Transoxiana to the northeast, the Indus valley to the southeast, the Tigris-Euphrates basin to the southwest, and Armenia and the Caucasus to the northwest. The region is dominated by the vast expanse of the high central Iranian plateau at its center. It is cut off on all sides by mighty mountain ranges, principally the Hindu Kush, the Sulaiman chain, the Zagros, and the Elburz. In its central reaches, it contains two large, empty, and uninhabitable salt deserts whose desolation is a more formidable barrier to travel than most of the great mountain chains themselves.

Population in Iran early clustered in the plains, the lower mountain reaches, and the many fertile oases, wherever rainfall or ground water was plentiful and communication with outside areas easiest. Foremost among these areas have been Persis, Media, Hyrcania, and Parthia. The great trade routes of Asian history have put Iran at the heart of east–west interchange. But these routes and the subsequent location of major cities and towns have been determined more by the mountain passes and traversable stretches of the Iranian plateau than by the distances involved.

The Ancient Iranian Background

The oldest texts in ancient Persian dialects show that the Aryan peoples who settled on the Iranian plateau itself, perhaps around 1100 B.C., were related to the Vedic or Indo-Aryans of north India. Presumably, both were pastoralists, horse-breeding peoples who had come originally from the Eurasian or Central Asian steppes. The most prominent of the ancient Iranian peoples were the Medes and the Persians. By the eighth century B.C., they had spread around the deserts to settle and control the western and southwestern areas of Iran to which they gave their names, Media and Persis (later Fars), respectively.

The Medes developed a tribal confederacy in western Iran. By the end of the seventh century B.C., with the Neo-Babylonians, they were able to defeat the mighty Assyrians and break their hold on the Fertile Crescent. The rise of Persian power in the seventh and sixth centuries B.C. led to the founding of the Achaemenid Empire. Many of the institutions that developed (such as the satrapy system of provincial administra-

tion) were likely continuations of Median practices, which had in turn been drawn from Babylonian and Assyrian models in many instances.

Ancient Iranian Religion

We know more about the religious tradition of ancient Iran than about other aspects of its culture, because our only preimperial texts are religious ones. These suggest that the old Iranian culture and religion were similar to those of the Vedic Aryans. The importance of water and fire, the role of sacrifice, the centrality of the cow, and the names and traits of particular divine beings and religious concepts all have their counterparts in Vedic texts. The emphasis was on moral order, or the "Right"—that is, *asha* or *arta* (equivalent to the Vedic *rta*—see Chapter 1). The supreme heavenly deity was Ahura (the equivalent of the Vedic *Varuna*) Mazda, the "Wise Lord." These facts also reflect the kinship of Vedic and Iranian tradition. Still, the Iranian religion of the early second millennium was far from monolithic. Cultural variations in ancient Iran among the southeast (Sistan), the northeast (Parthia, Herat, and Bactria), the west (Media), and the southwest (Persis) were substantial.

Zoroaster

The first person who stands out in Iranian history was not Cyrus, founder of the Achaemenid Empire, but Zarathushtra, the great prophet-reformer of Iranian religion. He is commonly known in the West by the Greek version of his name, Zoroaster. Although some scholars date his life to before 1000 B.C., according to the most common reckoning he lived from 628 to 551 B.C. in northeastern Iran. Not unlike the Hebrew prophets, the Buddha, and Confucius, Zoroaster preached a message of moral reform in an age when materialism, political opportunism, and ethical indifference were common. He found a royal protector in an eastern Iranian tribal leader said to have been converted to Zoroaster's ideas about 588 B.C.

In Zoroaster's hymns, we glimpse the values of a peasant-pastoralist society that was growing up along with early urban trade centers in northeast Iran. These values contrasted with those of the nomadic warrior peoples of the steppes. For example, Zoroaster called for a reform of traditional animal sacrifices (especially those involving the particularly sacred cow and ox) to make them more humane to the victim.

Zoroaster himself was trained as a priest in the old Iranian tradition, but his hymns, or *Gathas*, reflect the new religious vision he championed. This vision

A Hymn of Zoroaster about the Twin Spirits of Good and Evil

The focus of Zoroaster's reform was on the supremacy of Ahura Mazda (the "Wise Lord") over all the deities of the Iranian pantheon. He is pictured in the hymns, or Gathas, as the greatest of the ahuras, *the divinities associated with the good. The world is seen in terms of a moral dualism of good and evil, which is represented on the divine plane in the twin spirits created by Ahura Mazda and given the freedom to choose the Truth or the Lie. As the following selection shows, the "Most Holy Spirit" chose truth ("Righteousness"), and the "evil spirit" chose the evil of the Lie. Similarly, humans can choose with which side—the good spirit and the* ahuras, *or the evil spirit and the* daevas *("the false gods")—they will ally themselves. The struggle on the divine level between the gods is mirrored in the struggle on the human level between the righteous and the evildoers, as the hymn here emphasizes. This selection is from* Yasna *("Worship") section 30 of the main Zoroastrian holy book, the* Avesta. *It makes vivid the dualistic bent of Zoroastrianism.*

YASNA 30

Now will I speak to those who will hear
Of the things which the initiate should remember:
The praises and prayer of the Good Mind to the
    Lord
And the joy which he shall see in the light who has
    remembered them well.

Hear with your ears that which is the sovereign
    good;
With a clear mind look upon the two sides
Between which each man must choose for himself,
Watchful beforehand that the great test may be
    accomplished in our favour.

Now at the beginning the twin spirits have declared
    their nature,
The better and the evil,
In thought and word and deed. And between the
    two
The wise ones choose well, not so the foolish.

And when these two spirits came together,
In the beginning they established life and non-life,
And that at the last the worst existence should be
    for the wicked,
But for the righteous one the Best Mind.

Of these two spirits, the evil one chose to do the
    worst things;
But the Most Holy Spirit, clothed in the most
    steadfast heavens,
Joined himself unto Righteousness;
And thus did all those who delight to please the
    Wise Lord by honest deeds.

Between the two, the *false gods* also did not choose
    rightly,

For while they pondered they were beset by error,
So that they chose the Worst Mind.
Then did they hasten to join themselves unto Fury,
That they might by it deprave the existence of man.

And to him came *Devotion*, together with
    Dominion, Good
    Mind and *Righteousness:*
She gave endurance of body and the breath of life,
That he may be thine apart from them,
As the first by the retributions through the metal.

And when their punishment shall come to these
    sinners,
Then, O Wise One, shall thy Dominion, with the
    Good Mind,
Be granted to those who have delivered Evil into
    the hands of Righteousness, O Lord!

And may we be those that renew this existence!
O Wise One, and you other Lords, and
    Righteousness, bring your alliance,
That thoughts may gather where wisdom is faint.

Then shall Evil cease to flourish,
While those who have acquired good fame
Shall reap the promised reward
In the blessed dwelling of the Good Mind, of the
    Wise One, and of Righteousness.

If you, O men, understand the commandments
    which the Wise One has given,
Well-being and suffering—long torment for the
    wicked and salvation for the righteous—
All shall hereafter be for the best. ❏

From Jacques Duchesne-Guillemin (trans.), *The Hymns of Zarathushtra*, trans. from the French by M. Henning (Boston: Beacon, 1963), pp. 103, 105, 107.

stemmed from his passionate sense of personal encounter with Ahura Mazda as the most powerful of deities. He reinterpreted the old sacrificial fire as the symbol of the supreme Lord. He called on people to abandon worship of and sacrifice to all lesser deities, or *daevas*, whom he identified as demons rather than gods. He tried to reform the morality of his people by calling on them to turn from the "Lie" *(druj)* to the "Truth" *(asha)*. He warned of a "final reckoning," when the good will be rewarded with "future glory" and the wicked punished with "long-lasting darkness, ill food, and wailing."

By the mid-fourth century B.C., the Zoroastrian reform had spread into western as well as eastern Iran. The quasi-monotheistic worship of Ahura Mazda, the "Wise Lord," was rapidly accommodated to the veneration of older Iranian gods by the interpretation of these deities as secondary gods or even different manifestations of the Wise Lord himself. What role the Iranian priestly clan known as the *Magi* played in these developments is not clear. They may have integrated Zoroastrian ideas and texts into their older, polytheistic tradition, becoming thereby architects of a reformed tradition. Certainly the name *magi* was later used for the priests of the tradition that we refer to as Zoroastrian.

Zoroastrianism probably influenced not only the Jewish, Christian, and Muslim ideas of the messiah, angels, and devils, the last judgment, and an afterlife, but certain Buddhist concepts as well. Zoroastrianism was wiped out as a major force by Islam in the seventh and eighth centuries A.D. However, its tradition continues in the faith and practice of the Parsis, a community today of perhaps 100,000 people, most of whom live in western India.

The Achaemenid Empire

In October A.D. 1971, the Iranian king Muhammad Reza Shah presided over a lavish pageant amidst the ruins of the ancient Persian imperial city of Persepolis. This extravagant celebration commemorated the twenty-five-hundredth anniversary of the establishment under Cyrus the Great of "the imperial glory of Iran." The shah felt he had recreated this traditional Iranian ideal since the 1950s in his modern secularist regime. Although the Iranian revolution of 1978 thwarted his attempts to kindle a secular Iranian nationalism, modern Iran does have an undeniably dual heritage: that of the rich Iranian Islamic culture of recent centuries; and that of the far older, Indo-Iranian, Zoroastrian, and imperial culture of pre-Islamic Iran.

MAP 7-2   THE ACHAEMENID EMPIRE   *The empire created by Cyrus had fullest extent under Darius when Persia attacked Greece in 490 B.C. It reached from India to the Aegean—and even into Europe—including the lands formerly ruled by Egyptians, Hittites, Babylonians, and Assyrians.*

The latter culture had its beginning with the Persian dynasty of the Achaemenids.

The rise of Iran as a world power and a major civilization is usually dated from the reign of Cyrus the Great (559–530 B.C.), the ruling prince of the Achaemenid clan. His regional power in southwestern Iran (Persis) went back at least to his grandfather, Cyrus I. The empire that he founded was anticipated in many ways by the sizable but loosely controlled empire of his predecessors, the Medes, in Anatolia and western Iran. According to Babylonian and Greek sources, Cyrus defeated the last Median king about 650 B.C. Then he moved swiftly westward, winning northern Assyria and Cilicia and subduing the Anatolian kingdom of Lydia, near the Aegean coast of Asia Minor. The Lydian capital, Sardis, became a provincial capital of the growing Persian state (and the base for diplomatic intrigue against the Hellenic *poleis*). Next, Cyrus turned to Babylon and, in less than three weeks, he defeated the last Babylonian king.

This event, in 539 B.C., symbolically marks the beginning of the Achaemenid Empire, for it joined for the first time under one rule the Mesopotamian and Iranian spheres—a unity that would last for centuries. One of its immediate repercussions was the end of the Babylonian Exile of the Jews (see Chapter 2). Cyrus also extended Achaemenid rule in the east before being killed in battle with steppe tribes of Ekbatana (later Hamadan).

Better to administer the new empire, Cyrus had moved his capital to the old Median capital. He and his successors, in what was really a tribal confedera-tion, adopted and continued Median administrative practice; and many Medes were highly placed in the new state. Thus, it is not surprising that the Achaemenid rulers are referred to in the Bible and other sources as the "Medes and Persians." What the Medes had set in motion, Cyrus and his heirs consolidated and expanded, so that the new Iranian Empire became the most powerful the world had ever seen.

After the brief reign of Cambyses (529–522 B.C.), Darius I won the contest for succession. His reign (521–486 B.C.) was one of prosperity, in which the imperial borders reached their greatest extent—from Egypt in the west to southern Russia and Sogdiana (Transoxiana) in the north and the Indus valley in the east. The next five rulers (486–359 B.C.) fared less well, and after 478 B.C., the Persians were militarily inferior to the Greeks. The former managed to keep their divided enemy at bay by clever diplomacy, but Greek cultural influence steadily grew in Anatolia. Repeated rebellions by Egypt, internal succession struggles, renewed conflict with Scythian tribes on the steppe borders, and less enlightened leadership plagued Achaemenid rule in this era. Much might have been recouped by the able, energetic Artaxerxes III (reigned 359–338 B.C.), had he not been poisoned in a palace coup just as Philip of Macedon was unifying the Greeks. When Philip's son Alexander succeeded him, the days of the Achaemenid Empire were numbered.

The Achaemenid State

Perhaps the greatest achievement of the Achaemenids was the relative stability of their rule. They

Inscription of Darius I

The Achaemenids, like other ancient rulers before them, used public inscriptions to underscore their victories and other accomplishments. One of the best of our sources for Darius' reign in particular comes from the monumental rock reliefs and inscriptions that he had put up on a giant cliff at Behistun, a site between Hamadan and Mesopotamia, directly on the major east–west trade road. The inscription that follows reflects the Achaemenid ruler's sense of his own special relationship to Ahura Mazda and his role as a defender of the Right.

Darius the king says: By the will of Ahuramazdā I am king. Ahuramazdā delivered the kingship to me.

Darius the king says: These are the countries which came to me. By the will of Ahuramazdā I have become king over them: Persis, . . .

[There follows a list of satrapies.]

Darius the king says: These are the countries which came to me. By the will of Ahuramazdā they became my subjects, they bore me tribute. Day and night they did what I told them.

Darius the king says: Among these countries, whatever man was loyal I treated well, (but) whomever was unruly I punished well. By the will of Ahuramazdā these countries behaved according to my law. They did as I told them.

Darius the king says: Ahuramazdā delivered this kingship to me. Ahuramazdā bore me aid until I had secured this empire. By the will of Ahuramazdā I hold this empire. ❏

From William W. Malandra, *An Introduction to Ancient Iranian Religion* (Minneapolis: University of Minnesota Press, 1983), p. 48

Darius on the throne. This relief from the treasury at Persepolis depicts Darius I granting audience to a Median nobleman. Note the incense burners before the king and the noble's gesture of respect. The sceptre and lotus blossom held by Darius symbolize his kingship; his son and heir Xerxes stands behind him. [Bettmann Archive.]

justified their title of *Shahanshah*, "king of kings," as a universal sovereignty entrusted to them by Ahura Mazda. Their inscriptions reflect their sense that their justice and uprightness earned them this trust; their elaborate court ceremony and impressive architectural monuments underscored it. They acted as priests and sacrificers in the court rituals and symbolized their role as cosmic ruler by burning a special royal fire throughout each reign. The talents and evident charisma of their early leaders strengthened the force of their claim to special, divinely sanctioned royal status among their subject peoples. Yet alongside this, they were tolerant of diversity in ways earlier empires had not been. In part, the sheer size of their realms demanded this. Even Darius' conversion to Zoroastrianism did not bring forced conformity or conversion, as his lenient treatment of the Jews vividly shows.

The Achaemenids operated a powerful army, but their rule was not simply a military despotism. Much of their success lay in their administrative abilities and their willingness to learn and to borrow from predecessors like the Medes and conquered peoples like the Babylonians. Most of their leaders showed themselves adept at conciliation and sought to establish what has been termed a *pax Achaemenica*.[3] They were able to maintain continuity even while their state evolved from the relatively simple tribal confederation to a sophisticated monarchy. The state of Cyrus, with its largely Iranian troops and tribute system of revenue, was replaced by a monarchy supported by a noble class, professional armies (led by loyal Persian elite troops), an administrative system of provinces ruled by governors called satraps, and fixed-yield levies of revenue.

The excellence of their administrative skills can also be seen in their communication and propaganda systems. A courier system linked the far-flung imperial outposts with the heartlands over a system of well-kept highways, which also served to move troops at maximum speed. The greatest of these was the highway from Sardis to Susa that Herodotus called "the King's Road." A network of observers and royal inspectors kept the court abreast of activities in diverse places. An efficient chancery with large archives and numerous scribes served many administrative needs. The bureaucratic adoption of Aramaic, which had become the common language of the Near East under the Assyrians, helped link east and west. Royal proclamations were rapidly and widely distributed, often in multilingual form for different regions.

Little is known of the actual judicial system, but Achaemenid inscriptions reflect a strong emphasis on universal justice and the rule of law throughout the empire.

The choice of strategically located capitals in Western Iran, such as Ekbatana and Susa, was important to central control of the empire. In general, however, the Achaemenids moved the court as needed to one or another of their palaces, whether in Babylon or the Iranian highlands, and never fixed on a single capital.

[3] Richard N. Frye, *The Heritage of Persia* (New York and Toronto, 1966), p. 110.

PEOPLES	
CA. 2000–1000 B.C.	Indo-Iranian (Aryan) tribes move south into the Punjab of India and the Iranian Plateau
835 B.C.	Assyrian text mentions kingdom of Medes
CA. 700–600 B.C.	Medes and Persians are settled in west and southwest Iran
RELIGION	
CA. 628–551 B.C. (or before 1000? B.C.)	Zoroaster (Zarathushtra), probably in east/northeast Iran (perhaps originally in Herat?)
EMPIRES, RULERS	
559–530 B.C.	Reign of Cyrus the Great as Persian Achaemenid ruler
539–330 B.C.	Achaemenid Empire
331–330 B.C.	Alexander (d. 323) conquers Achaemenid empire
312–CA. 125 B.C.	Seleucid rule in part of old Achaemenid realm
CA. 248 B.C.– A.D. 224	Parthian empire of the Arsacids in Iran, Babylonia

The ruins of the famous royal complex at Persepolis, sacked and burned by Alexander the Great in 330 B.C. The first restoration work took place in this century. [Scala/Art resource.]

The satrapy divisions usually followed those of the previous states. The satraps were powerful princes in their own right. Although some revolted on occasion, the centralized power of the "king of kings" held together the diverse provinces and tribute-paying states.

The empire's overall stability for over two centuries testifies to the quality of the *pax Achaemenica*. The cosmopolitan basis for the coming hellenization of western Asia in the wake of Alexander's conquests was already in place.

INDIA

The First Indian Empire (321–185 B.C.)

True empire in the Indian subcontinent came only after the oriental campaigns of Alexander the Great, who conquered the Achaemenid provinces of Gandhara and the Indus valley in 327 B.C. Alexander himself made little or no impact on the subcontinent save in the extreme northwestern area of Gandhara. Here, his passage opened the way for the increased Greek and Indian cultural interpenetration that developed under the Mauryan emperors of India.

The Political Background

The basis for empire in northern India was the rise of regional states and commercial towns between the seventh and fourth centuries B.C. The most powerful of the states were the monarchies that clustered on the Ganges plains. North and northwest of the plains, in the Himalayan foothills and in the Punjab and beyond, tribal republics were more common. From two of these republics came the Buddha and Mahavira (see Chapter 2), although both spent much of their lives in the states of Kosala and Magadha, the two most powerful Ganges monarchies. In their lifetimes, Magadha emerged as the strongest state in India under Bimbisara (d. 493 B.C.).

Bimbisara was, as far as we know, the first king to build a centralized state (possibly on the Achaemenid model) strong enough for imperial expansion. He emphasized good roads, able administrators, and fair agricultural taxes. His son annexed Kosala, so that Magadha controlled the Ganges trade. Therefore, Magadha remained preeminent in the Ganges basin even under several less competent successors. A new dynasty, the Nandas, replaced the last of these as rulers of Magadha; their imperial hopes were soon dashed by the rise of the Mauryan clan.

The Mauryans

The first true Indian empire was established by Chandragupta Maurya (reigned CA. 321–297 B.C.). He seized Magadha and the Ganges basin in about 324 and made Pataliputra (the modern Patna) his capital. He next marched westward into the vacuum created by Alexander the Great's departure (326 B.C.) and brought the Indus region and much of west-central India under his control. A treaty with the invading Seleucus, Alexander's successor in Bactria, added Gandhara and Arachosia to his empire in the northwest. The Greek sources say that the treaty (303 B.C.) included a marriage alliance, possibly of a Seleucid woman to Chandragupta. If such a marriage did occur, Greek blood may flow in Indian veins to this day. Certainly there was much Seleucid-Mauryan contact thereafter.

MAP 7-3 SOUTHWEST ASIA AND INDIA IN MAURYAN TIMES. *Showing not only major cities, and regions of greater Iran and the Indian subcontinent but also the neighboring eastern Mediterranean world. While the Mediterranean was closely tied to Iran from Archaemenid times onwards, it is less often recognized how many and varied were its contacts with India in the wake of the conquests of Alexander the Great.*

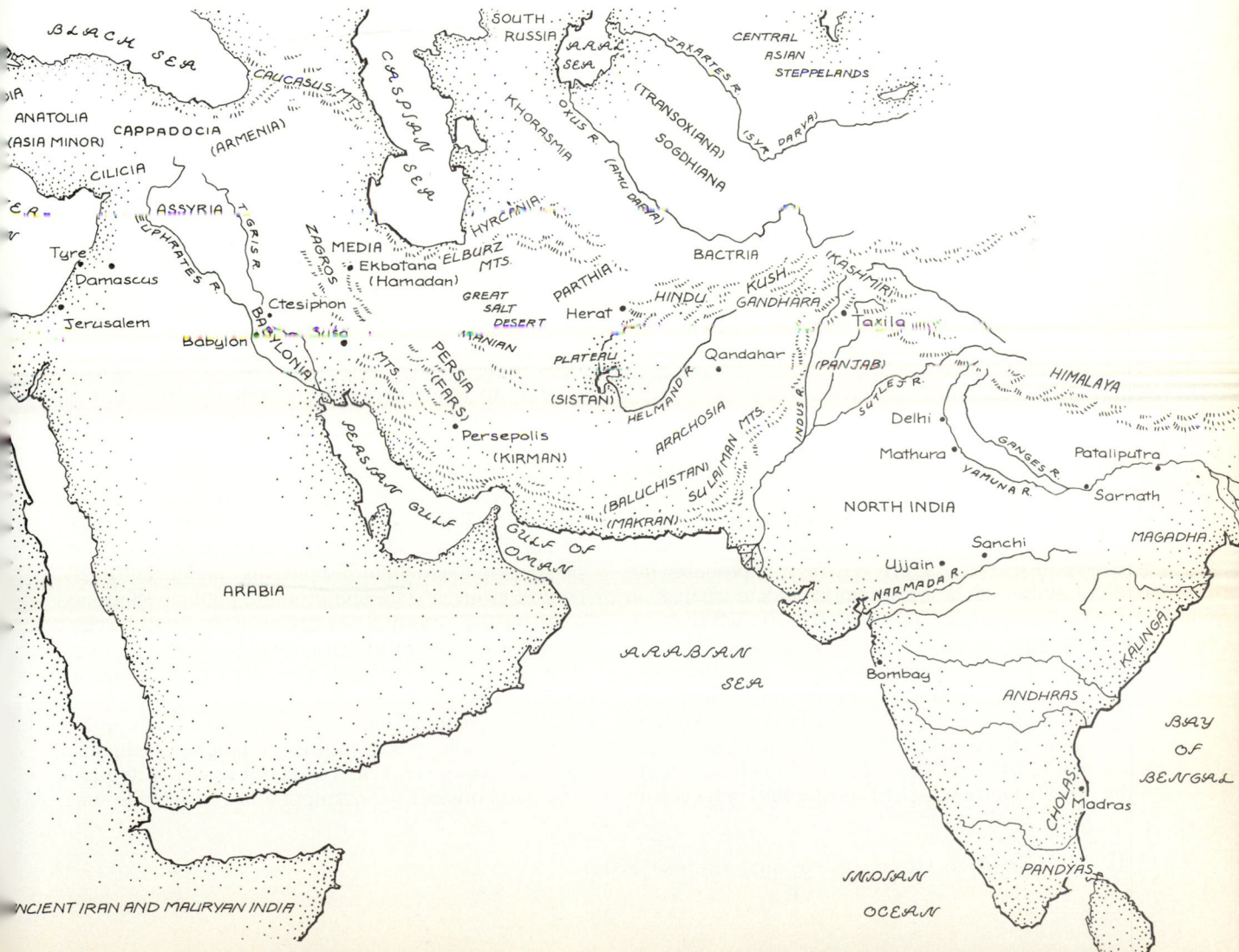

The Lion Capital of Sarnath. This famous Ashokan column capital was taken by India as its state seal after independence in 1947. It reflects both Persian and Greek influences. Originally, the capital stood atop a mighty pillar some fifty feet high and the lions supported a hugh stone wheel, the Buddhist "wheel of the Dharma," the symbol of universal law [Lauros/Giraudon.]

Chandragupta ranks as the first great Indian empire builder, although his fame is rivaled by that of his Brahman minister Kautilya. Known as the "Indian Machiavelli," Kautilya may have been the real architect of Mauryan rule. However, he was probably not the real author of the most famous Indian treatise on the art of government, the *Arthashastra*, which is ascribed to him.

Chandragupta's son and successor, Bindusara (reigned CA. 297–272 B.C.), was not long in taking up his father's imperial aspirations. He moved swiftly to conquer the Deccan, the great plateau that covers central India, dividing the far south (Tamilnad) from north India. Like his father, he had substantial contacts with the Seleucid Greeks, including Antiochus I of Syria, from whom he is said to have requested wine, figs, and a philosopher for his court!

ASHOKA. The third and greatest Mauryan emperor, Ashoka (reigned CA. 272–232 B.C.), left us numerous rock inscriptions. These are the first significant written sources in Indian history after the Indus culture. From his edicts, we can piece together much of his reign and glimpse something of the man behind the royal name as well. In his first years as king, he continued the imperial tradition by conquering Kalinga, the last independent kingdom in north India and the Deccan. He thus extended Mauryan control over the whole subcontinent except the far south.

Apparently revolted by the bloody Kalinga conquest, Ashoka underwent a religious conversion. Thereafter, he pursued the Buddhist "Middle Path" as the right course of conduct not only in personal but also in state relations. Accordingly, he forsook war, hunting, and animal flesh. Above all, he championed nonviolence *(ahimsa)*, summing up his new course in the ideal of "conquest by righteousness *(dharma)*." This is not to say that all warfare ceased however much the king may have abhorred bloodshed, but he did abandon further conquest. He also believed that by moral example he could win over others to humanitarian values. Within his realm, he looked on all his subjects as, in the words of one edict, his "children."

Ashoka's edicts show that he pursued the laity's norm of the Buddhist *dharma*, striving to attain heaven by the merit of good actions. He was not an exclusivist about his Buddhist faith, stressing tolerance for all traditions. However, he apparently sent out envoys to spread the Buddhist teaching, possibly even as far as Seleucid Macedonia in the west. Tradition has it that he was responsible for the more successful missionary work that brought the Buddhist *dharma* to Lanka (Sri Lanka, formerly Ceylon). Certainly the king of Lanka at the time was in friendly contact with Ashoka. Although Ashoka's edicts do not mention it, tradition also has it that a great Buddhist council was held at Pataliputra during Ashoka's reign (250 B.C.?). It is clear that he sought to raise standards of morality in all phases of life in his realm. For example, he appointed "*dharma* officials" under centralized control to investigate and promote public welfare and to foster just, moral government at the local level.

Ashoka evidently did ease some of the previous burdens of government and instituted many beneficial public works. However, by the end of his reign, the size of his empire had strained the limits of effective administration. His rejection of military campaigns may also have weakened imperial power in the long run, and bureaucratic corruption increased with time.

The Edicts of Ashoka

In the first of the two following excerpts from Ashokan edicts, we see the monarch's explanation of his change of heart and conversion to nonviolence after the Kalinga war and a statement of his determination to follow dharma. *"The Beloved of the Gods" was the common royal epithet used by Ashoka for himself. The second excerpt is from the end of Ashoka's reign and speaks of his efforts to better his and other people's lives by rule according to the dictates of* dharma.

FROM THE THIRTEENTH ROCK EDICT

When the king, Beloved of the Gods and of Gracious Mien, had been consecrated eight years Kalinga was conquered, 150,000 people were deported, 100,000 were killed, and many times that number died. But after the conquest of Kalinga, the Beloved of the Gods began to follow Righteousness [*dharma*], to love Righteousness, and to give instruction in Righteousness. Now the Beloved of the Gods regrets the conquest of Kalinga, for when an independent country is conquered people are killed, they die, or are deported, and that the Beloved of the Gods finds very painful and grievous. . . . The Beloved of the Gods will forgive as far as he can, and he even conciliates the forest tribes of his dominions; but he warns them that there is power even in the remorse of the Beloved of the Gods, and he tells them to reform, lest they be killed.

For all beings the Beloved of the Gods desires security, self-control, calm of mind, and gentleness. The Beloved of the Gods considers that the greatest victory is the victory of Righteousness; and this he has won here [in India] and even five hundred leagues beyond his frontiers in the realm of the Greek king Antiochus, and beyond Antiochus among the four kings Ptolemy, Antigonus, Magas, and Alexander. Even where the envoys of the Beloved of the Gods have not been sent men hear of the way in which he follows and teaches Righteousness, and they too follow it and will follow it. Thus he achieves a universal conquest, and conquest always gives a feeling of pleasure; yet it is but a slight pleasure, for the Beloved of the Gods only looks on that which concerns the next life as of great importance. . . .

FROM THE SEVENTH PILLAR EDICT

In the past kings sought to make the people progress in Righteousness, but they did not progress. . . . And I asked myself how I might uplift them through progress in Righteousness. . . . Thus I decided to have them instructed in Righteousness, and to issue ordinances of Righteousness, so that by hearing them the people might conform, advance in the progress of Righteousness, and themselves make great progress. . . . For that purpose many officials are employed among the people to instruct them in Righteousness and to explain it to them. . . .

Moreover I have had banyan trees planted on the roads to give shade to man and beast; I have planted mango groves, and I have had ponds dug and shelters erected along the roads at every eight kos. Everywhere I have had wells dug for the benefit of man and beast. But this benefit is but small, for in many ways the kings of olden time have worked for the welfare of the world; but what I have done has been done that men may conform to Righteousness. . . .

. . . I have enforced the law against killing certain animals and many others, but the greatest progress of Righteousness among men comes from exhortation in favor of noninjury to life and abstention from killing living beings.

I have done this that it may endure . . . as long as the moon and sun, and that my sons and my great-grandsons may support it; for by supporting it they will gain both this world and the next. ❑

From W. T. de Bary et al. (comps.), *Sources of Indian Tradition* (New York: Columbia University Press, 1958), pp. 146–147, 152–153.

After his death, local dynasties soon seized power from his heirs in many areas.

Ashoka's enduring influence is hard to assess, but he did provide the ideal of kingship for later Hindu and Buddhist thought—the *chakravartin*, or universal monarch who rules with righteousness, justice, and wisdom. His name lives on as a symbol of enlightened, compassionate rule that has had few if any equals in history East or West.

THE MAURYAN STATE. Mauryan bureaucracy was marked by centralization, standardization, and efficiency in long-distance communications, civil and military organization, tax collection, and information gathering (by a secret service). The fundamental unit of government, as before and ever after, was the village, with its headman and village council. Various numbers of villages formed districts within the larger provincial unit. The provinces were largely controlled through governors sent out from the capital. Some local rulers were confirmed in these positions also, much as with the Achaemenids (who very likely provided the model for much of Mauryan imperialism). The reputed pageantry and royal ceremonial of the Mauryan court must also have enhanced royal authority.

The administration of the empire depended primarily on the king himself, who did, however, have an advisory council to assist him. Each of the three great Mauryan kings was associated with one of the "new" religious movements of the age: Chandragupta with the Jains; his son with the ascetic tradition of the group known as the Ajivikas; and Ashoka with the Buddhists. Such links must have strengthened the Mauryan, especially the Ashokan, claims to righteous leadership.

Revenues came primarily from taxing the produce of the land, which was regarded as the king's property. Urban trade and production were also taxed heavily. The Mauryan economic system also involved slavery, although most of it was domestic labor, often a kind of temporary indentured service.

THE MAURYAN LEGACY. An imperial ideal and a strengthened Buddhist movement were not the Mauryans' only gifts to Indian culture. They left behind new cosmopolitan traditions of external relations and internal communication that encouraged cultural development and discouraged provincialism. The many contacts of the Mauryans with the West reflect their international perspective, as do the Ashokan edicts, which were executed in various languages and scripts. Writing and reading must have been common by this time (perhaps as a result of Buddhist monastic schooling?), or the edicts themselves would have had no purpose. The Mauryans' excellent road system facilitated internal and external contacts on an unprecedented scale, above all west to Herat and northwest to Bactria. These would later be the routes for Buddhism's spread to Central Asia and China, as well as for successive invaders of the subcontinent moving in the opposite direction.

This era also saw the flourishing of true cities across the empire: Pataliputra, Varanasi (Banaras), Ayodhya, Prayag (modern Allahabad), Ujjain, Taxila, and Qandahar. These remained centers for arts, crafts, industry, literature, and education. The architecture of the Mauryan capital, Pataliputra, has not survived intact because of its basic wood and brick construction. But Greek travelers such as Megasthenes reported that its glories surpassed those of the Achaemenid palaces. Certainly the stone building and sculpture of the Ashokan period reflect sophisticated aesthetics and technique, as well as strong Persian and Greek influences.

The Consolidation of Indian Civilization (CA. 200 B.C.–A.D. 300)

In the post-Mauryan period, the history of northwest and northern India was dominated by the influx of a variety of foreign peoples whom we shall consider in the last section of this chapter. In the rest of the subcontinent, indigenous Indian dynasties held sway. These dynasties often controlled substantial regional empires that became centers for developing Indian cultural styles. In this period, a general pattern of regional and local political autonomy arose that would be broken only by the Gupta Empire (A.D. 320–CA. 550; see Chapter 11). Religiously and culturally, the centuries between the Mauryan and the Gupta eras saw the consolidation of patterns and styles that helped to shape Indian and, through the diffusion of Buddhism, Asian civilization.

The Economic Base

Although agriculture remained, commerce flourished as the basis of the economy amidst the post-Mauryan political fragmentation. India's merchant classes prospered, as their patronage of Buddhist and Jain buildings shows. The fine Mauryan road system provided a base for trade across the length and breadth of India. Chinese and Roman demand for Indian luxury goods—jewels and semiprecious stones, sandalwood and teak, cotton and silk textiles, spices, exotic animals, and slaves—made India a center of world trade. Considerable wealth flowed in, as shown by hoards of Roman gold coins and the remains of Roman trading communities in the Tamil south. Within India, guild organizations flourished and provided technical education in skilled crafts. They were important targets of investment not only by the merchant class but by kings as well. Coin minting greatly increased after Mauryan times, and banking was a thriving concern.[4]

High Culture

In the arts, the great achievements of these centuries were primarily Buddhist in inspiration. While northwest India saw the rise of Gandharan Buddhist art, in central India as early as the first century B.C. stone-relief sculpture had developed the basic forms of what became the classical style of Indian art. The finest surviving examples of this sculpture are the stone reliefs of the great Buddhist stupas (shrines) at Bharhut and Sañchi.

Language and literature in this period rested on the sophisticated Sanskrit grammar of Panini (CA. 300 B.C.?), which remains the unsurpassed standard today. Two masterpieces of Sanskrit culture, the epics of the *Mahabharata* and the *Ramayana*, had probably taken their general shape by A.D. 200. The first of these is a composite work concerned largely with the nature of *dharma* (the moral and cosmic Law; see Chapter 2).

[4] Romila Thapar, *A History of India*, vol. 1 (Harmondsworth, 1966), pp. 105–118.

Included in its earlier, narrative portions are systematic treatments of *dharma* such as the Bhagavad Gita, or "Song of the Blessed Lord," the most famous and influential of all Indian religious texts. Evidence of the rise of devotional cults is seen in the importance of Krishna in the *Mahabharata* (especially in the Gita) and Rama in the *Ramayana*. Both are major incarnations, or *avataras*, of Vishnu.

Religion and Society

The post-Mauryan period saw Buddhist monasticism and lay devotionalism thrive throughout the subcontinent. However, the dominance of the Brahmans in ritual matters and Vedic learning also continued. It was also a period of diffusion for popular devotional cults of particular gods, above all Shiva and Vishnu, which were to be the mainstays of all later "Hindu" religious life. The parallel development in Buddhist tradition was the rise, along with Mahayana thought (see Chapter 11), of a cult of the person of the Buddha. It focused on pilgrimages to sites where his relics were deposited or to places associated with his life. Toward the end of this age, Buddhism in its Mahayana form began to spread from India over the trade routes to Central Asia, and eventually to China and Japan.

THE HINDU TRADITION. What we now call *Hinduism* emerged in this era. The major developments that were shaping a "Hindu" tradition were

Stupa and rock-cut shrine. Figure A shows the great Stupa at Sanchi, an outstanding example of early Buddhist relic mounds. The mound, seated on an Ashokan foundation, was added to over the centuries. Its most notable art work is the magnificent carvings on the stone railings and gateways, one of which is shown in Figure B. Sanchi is located in north-central India. [American Institute of Indian Studies/Bettmann Archive.]

INDIA FROM THE SIXTH CENTURY B.C. TO THE END OF MAURYAN RULE

CA. 600–400 B.C.	Late Upanishadic age: Local/regional kingdoms and tribal republics along the Ganges, in Himalayan foothills, Panjab and northwest India
CA. 540–CA. 468 B.C.	Vardhamana Mahavira, Jain founder
CA. 537–CA. 486 B.C.	Siddhartha Gautama, the Buddha
CA. 550–324 B.C.	Regional empire of Maghadan kings
330–325 B.C.	Alexander campaigns in Indus valley, Soghdiana, Bactria, and Panjab
324–CA. 185 B.C.	Mauryan empire controls most of northern India and the Deccan
CA. 272–232 B.C.	Reign of the Mauryan emperor Ashoka

(1) the consolidation of the caste system, Brahman ascendancy, and the "high" culture of Sanskrit language and learning; (2) the increasing dominance of theistic devotionalism (especially the cults of Vishnu and Shiva); and (3) the intellectual reconciliation of these developments with the older ascetic and speculative traditions going back to the Upanishadic age. These social and religious developments would continue and solidify in the Gupta era and later times.

THE BUDDHIST TRADITION. Indian Buddhist monastic communities prospered in this period under mercantile and royal patronage—especially in or near urban centers—a trait they shared with the Jains. Merchants found both traditions attractive and strongly supported Jain and Buddhist monasteries, presumably for the merit to be gained.

Buddhist lay devotion was a prominent part of Indian religious life, especially in the Ganges basin. However, it was a very different tradition from the Buddhism of the theological texts, which focuses on the quest for *nirvana* and the "extraordinary norm" (see Chapter 2). The Buddha and the Buddhist saints were naturally identified with popular Indian deities and Buddhist worship was easily assimilated to common Indian patterns of theistic piety. Consequently, popular Buddhist practice was indistinguishable from countless other devotional cults that were coming to dominate the Indian scene. One reason that Buddhist tradition remained only one among many Indian religious paths was its absorption into the religious diversity that then and now typifies the "Hindu" religious scene.

The entrance to one of the many early Buddhist shrines, or chaitva-halls, *that were cut into the cliffs along the adjoining monastaries (viharas). Most of these rock-cut shrines are found in vertical cliffs not far from modern Bombay. [Bettmann Archive.]*

GREEK AND ASIAN DYNASTIES

The Seleucids

We have seen that the successors of Alexander the Great in the Achaemenid lands, the Greek general Seleucus and his heirs, soon lost Arachosia and Gandhara to the Maurans. They did, however, rule most of the former Achaemenid domains from about 312 to 246 B.C., and lesser portions until about 125 B.C. Alexander's policies of Greco-Persian fusion—the appointment of Iranians and Greeks as satraps, as well as large-scale Greek and Persian intermarriage—helped make the Seleucid rule of many eastern areas more viable. The new "cities"—or, more accurately, military colonies—that Alexander left behind provided bases for Seleucid control. As a foreign minority, the Seleucids had ultimately to maintain their power with mercenary troops. It was, however, the leaders of their own troops and satrapies whose imperial aspirations gradually whittled away at Seleucid rule. Always at war, neither Seleucus (reigned 311–281 B.C.; see Chapter 4) nor even the greatest of his successors, Antiochus the Great (reigned 223–187 B.C.), ever secured lasting rule on the scale of the Achaemenids.

In the end, Alexander's policy of linking Hellenes with Iranians in political power, marriage, and culture bore fruit more lasting than empire. The Seleucid emphasis on the founding and cultivation of Greek-style cities stimulated the hellenization process. During the third century B.C., Hellenistic culture and law became new ideals among the upper classes and intelligentsia of the Seleucid realms. The Seleucids did not encourage cultural mixing as had Alexander, but they did

The Buddha's Nirvana. A late second or third-century A.D. Gandharan relief which has much the style of contemporary Roman stone carvings. Here the Indian-Buddhist concept does not mesh well with the realistic Roman style and craftsmanship. Note the emotions of the bystanders at their loss of the Lord Buddha; these would not appear in native Indian style. [Art Resource/Giraudon.]

welcome into the ruling classes those non-Hellenes willing to become hellenized. Aramaic continued to be the common language from Syria to the Hindu Kush (although it was in decline in eastern Iran). Local social and cultural forms were by no means displaced, but Greek culture did penetrate.

Zoroastrian and related Iranian religious traditions declined with the loss of their imperial-cult status. The many syncretistic cults of the Mediterranean Hellenistic world made inroads even in the east in Seleucid and Parthian times. The later Parthians probably laid the groundwork for the still later revival of the Zoroastrian tradition. Mystery and savior cults were becoming more popular in East and West. The new urban centers of the Hellenistic Age may have provided an environment in which the individual necessarily had less rootedness in the established traditions of culture and religious life. This would have enhanced the attractiveness of the focus on individual salvation common to many lesser Hellenistic cults. This was especially true of emerging traditions like the Christian, Mahayana Buddhist, Hindu devotionalist, and Manichaean that came to dominate Eurasia over the next few centuries.

The Indo-Greeks

The extreme extent of Hellenization in the east was realized not by the Seleucids, but by another line of Alexandrine successors, the Indo-Greeks of Bactria.[5] About 246 B.C., Bactria's Greek satrap broke away from the Seleucids. His successor, Euthydemus (reigned CA. 235–CA. 200 B.C.), managed to extend his sway north and southwest; he withstood a Seleucid attempt at reconquest by Antiochus the Great in 208 B.C. His son Demetrius exploited the growing Mauryan weakness. By 175 B.C. he had crossed the Hindu Kush to conquer Arachosia; then he moved up the Indus valley to take Gandhara. Demetrius and his successor, Menander, made Taxila their capital and were powerful enough to control other parts of north India. Both were thoroughly "Indianized" in their orientation. Most of the Indo-Greeks were very Indian, even in language and religion, as their coins and inscriptions show.

[5] In *The Indo-Greeks* (Oxford, 1957), A. K. Narian argues for *Indo-Greeks* as the appropriate term for these kings, who are usually called *Greco-Bactrians* or *Euthydemids*.

Before their demise at the hands of invading steppe peoples (CA. 130–100 B.C.), these Indo-Greeks left their mark on civilization in all the areas around their Bactrian center. Bactria was a crucial area of transmission, if not a major source, of the later Greco-Buddhist art of Gandhara, one of history's remarkable examples of cross-cultural influence. The Indo-Greeks probably also played a role in the early spread of Buddhism from India to Central Asia. The most famous of the Bactrian rulers, Menander, or Milinda (reigned CA. 155–130 B.C.?), is depicted as a Buddhist convert in a later Buddhist text, *The Questions of King Milinda.*

The Steppe Peoples

When we come to the Parthians, who succeeded the Seleucids in Iran, and to the steppe dynasties who succeeded the Indo-Greeks in Bactria and north India, separation of Iranian from Indian history is misleading. Both north India and the Iranian plateau were dominated from about 250 B.C. to A.D. 300 by Iranian tribal peoples originally from the Central Asian steppes. Although commonly ignored, they and other nomadic steppe peoples were the main force in Eurasian history alongside the great sedentary civilizations of the eastern Mediterranean, Mesopotamia, India, and China. These Indo-Iranian incursions were not the first (or the last) such invasions. Yet there is more tangible historical evidence of their penetration of northeastern Iran and northwest India than exists for any earlier Indo-Aryan migrations.

The Parthians

The Parni, said to be related to the Scythians, were probably the major group of Iranian steppe peoples who had first settled in the area south of the Aral Sea and Oxus. In late Achaemenid times, they moved south into Parthia and gradually adopted its dialect. Henceforth, we can call them Parthians. The independent control of Parthia by their dynastic family (the Arsacids) dates from about 247 B.C. Shortly afterward, they crossed the Elburz and began to extend their power onto the Iranian plateau. For decades only a regional power, the Parthians emerged under Mithradates I (CA. 171–138 B.C.) as a new imperial force in Eurasia. They were recognized as the true successors of the Achaemenids in Iran.

Facing weak Seleucid and Indo-Greek opposition, by CA. 140 B.C. Mithradates was able to secure a sizable empire. It covered the Iranian plateau and reached from Mesopotamia perhaps to Arachosia. Its center thereafter was his new winter capital at Ctesiphon, on the Tigris. The exact imperial borders and spheres of influence varied over time. But from the victory over the Romans at Carrhae in 53 B.C. (see Chapter 6) until their fall in A.D. 233, the Parthians were the

major power of Eurasia alongside Rome. In the end, the pressure of the Kushan empire in the east and, above all, the constant Roman wars of their last century weakened them sufficiently for a new Persian dynasty to replace them.

It is not easy to measure Parthian rule, despite its duration and successes, because of the scarcity and the bias of the available sources. For much of their long reign, the Parthians were under great pressure on all fronts, in Armenia, in Mesopotamia, and along their Indian and Central Asian frontiers. Yet, during their rule, trade in and around their domains apparently increased. In particular, there is evidence of vigorous commerce north over the Caucasus, on the "silk road" to China, and along the Indian Ocean coast (the ancient Arab's "monsoon route," used for the spice trade with the Indies).

Culturally, the Parthians were oriented toward the Hellenistic world of their Seleucid predecessors until the mid-first century A.D., after which they seem to have undergone a kind of Iranian revival. They then replaced Greek on their coins with Parthian and Aramaic, and they gave their cities their older Iranian names again. Their formerly Hellenic tastes in art turned to Iranian motifs like the hunt, the battle, and the feast. In late Parthian times the Iranian national epic took its lasting shape. Similarly, the worship of Ahura Mazda was preserved among the Magi despite the success of other Eastern and Western cults and the common assimilation of Greek gods to Iranian ones. Yet the Parthians seem to have tolerated religious diversity. In their era, a huge variety of religious cults and cultural traditions rubbed shoulders with one another and vied for supremacy in different contexts.

The Sakas and Kushans

The successors of the Indo-Greeks were steppe peoples even closer to their nomadic past than the Parthians. These peoples are often ignored by modern historians because they impinge on but do not figure centrally in Chinese, Iranian, or Indian history in our period. However, they played a major political and cultural role for several centuries, especially in the Indo-Iranian region. They reflect the cosmopolitan nature of the world of Central Asia, eastern Iran, and northwest India at this time.

Beginning about 130 B.C., Scythian (Saka) tribes from beyond the Jaxartes River (Syr Darya) overran northeast Iran, taking Sogdiana's Hellenic cities and then Bactria. Thus ended the Indo-Greek heyday, although the last Greek petty ruler lasted in the upper Indus valley until about 50 B.C. One group of Sakas soon extended their domain from Bactria into north India, as far as Mathura. Another went southwest into Herat and Sistan, where they encroached on the Parthians. In northwest India, the Sakas were, in turn,

312–CA. 125 B.C.	Seleucid rule in part of old Achaemenid realm
312–246 B.C.	Height of Seleucid imperial strength
CA. 248 B.C.–A.D. 224	Parthian empire of the Arsacids in Iran, Babylonia
246–CA. 50 B.C.	Indo-Greek ("Graeco-Bactrian," "Euthydemid") rulers of region from modern Afghanistan to Oxus
CA. 155–130 B.C.?	Reign of Indo-Greek ruler Menander (Milinda)
247 B.C.–A.D. 223	Parthian Arsacid Empire
CA. 171–138 B.C.	Reign of Arsacid king Mithradates I
CA. 140 B.C.–CA. A.D. 100	Movements west and south of Yüeh Chih (including Kushans) and Sythians (Sakas), into Sogdiana, then Bactria, then northwest India
CA. A.D. 50–CA. 250	Height of Kushan power in Oxus to Ganges region
CA. 78 [or 148?]	Accession of King Kanishka to Kushan throne in Taxila

Standing Buddha. This Gandharan-school statue of the Buddha from the second century (A.D.) reflects the marriage of Greco-Roman statuary styles with the Indian Buddhist content. Although the head of this example has been recut in modern times, the elongated ears and sign of wisdom on the forehead (both are identifying marks of the Buddha) are typical of Gandharan sculptures. [Otto E. Nelson/The Asia Society.]

defeated by invading Iranians known as the *Pahlavas*, who went on to rule in northwest India in the first century A.D.[6] Pahlava rule did not, however, wipe out the Sakas, for we find Saka dynasties ruling in parts of northwest and west India through the fourth century A.D.

The Sakas had been displaced earlier in Sogdiana by another steppe people, known from Chinese sources as the Yüeh Chih. They may have been driven from western China by the building of the Great Wall of China and/or drought in the steppes. These peoples, under the leadership of the Kushan tribe, next drove the Sakas out of Bactria. About a hundred years later, in the mid-first century A.D., they swept over the

[6] Tradition gives one of their rulers, Gondophares, the role of host to Saint Thomas, who is said to have brought Christianity to India. But since Gondophares probably ruled in the early to mid-first century A.D., this may be a confused report. Even if traditions of Thomas' mission to India are correct, some connect him instead with south India.

mountains into northwest India. Here they ended Pahlava rule and founded a long-lived Indian Kushan dynasty, which controlled a relatively stable empire from the upper Oxus regions over Bactria, Gandhara, and Arachosia, across the Punjab, and over the Ganges plains as far as Varanasi (Banaras). Their greatest ruler, Kanishka, reigned either at the end of the first century or the middle of the second A.D. He was the greatest patron of Buddhism since Ashoka. In their heyday (CA. the first to the third centuries A.D.), the power of the Kushans in Central Asia facilitated the missionary activity that carried Buddhism across the steppes and into China. A lasting Kushan contribution was the school of Greco-Buddhist art fostered in Gandhara by Kanishka and his successors and carried on by a later Kushan dynasty for another five hundred years.

Africa, Iran, and India before A.D. 200 in World Perspective

By the second century A.D. in Africa and in the Indo-Iranian world, we can see the development of imperial governments whose power and influence far surpassed that of any before them. In and of themselves, such empires are not the measure of progress in what we call "civilization"—that is, citied, literate culture; technological sophistication; specialized division of labor; and complex social and political structures. Yet they are indices of the security and wealth necessary to progress. This was clearly the case in the empires of the Achaemenids and Mauryans and, to a more limited degree, in that of the Kushites, and also the Carthaginians. In this respect, developments in these Afro-Asian areas paralleled those in the wider world, where the Greek, Hellenistic, and Roman empires, like the Han empire of China, provided contexts in which civilization could flourish, grow, and spread afield.

Except in the African centers of culture, this was also an era in which ultimately influential, lasting religious traditions grew up and came of age. Not all met with the same long-term success or positive response outside their homeland. The Christian, Buddhist, Confucian, and even Judaic and Hindu traditions spread abroad and took root in cultures outside their places of origin. By contrast, the Zoroastrian tradition, like the Jain in India, never had great appeal outside of its homeland, although its adherents would much later carry it with them to western India, where they continue today as the influential but small community of Parsees.

In this period, another important and portentous element for the history of civilization was the increased cross-cultural contact symbolized by the Hellenizing conquests of Alexander the Great. The central Asian reaches of Iran and India especially provided the great meeting ground of Iranian, Indian, Greek, and steppe-people's languages, customs, ideas, arts, and religious practices. In later centuries, the Iranian and Indian cultures continued to develop their own distinctive and largely independent forms, and central Asia

remained a fragmented but fertile cultural melting pot. Yet the age we have briefly surveyed here set in motion cross-cultural interchanges that would continue apace in later centuries.

This matter of interchange is important for Africa, where, like Europe, the greater part of the huge continent was visibly less developed than the central axis of cited, literate culture that ran from the Mediterranean to China over roughly the region of the original river-valley cradles of civilization. This "lagging" had little to do with the character of the peoples of either sub-Saharan Africa or Europe, but was due primarily to their relative isolation from substantial, sustained interchange with the expanding older centers of civilization. In this period, we see in Rome, Iran, or India, if less so in China, increased contacts with other cultures and increased influences from abroad. These contacts and influences were manifested in new peoples, governmental structures, technological innovations, specialized skills and arts, and ethico-religious ideas. Those areas of Africa and Europe that were in sufficiently constant intercourse with the Mediterranean and western Asian civilizations of the day were precisely those in which civilization as we understand it developed first.

Suggested Readings

AFRICA

P. BOHANNAN AND P. CURTIN, *Africa and Africans*, rev. ed. (1971). Interesting topical treatment of various sectors of society, institutions, and history.

P. CURTIN, S. FEIERMANN, L. THOMPSON, AND J. VANSINA, *African History* (1978). Probably the best survey history. The relevant portions here are Chapters 1, 2, 4, 8, and 9.

J. D. FAGE, *A History of Africa* (1978). Chapters 1 and 2, on origins of society and on Africa and the ancient Mediterranean world, are relevant.

R. W. JULY, *Precolonial Africa: An Economic and Social History* (1975). Good chapters on the environment and various kinds of peoples and their livelihoods.

J. KI-ZERBO, *Methodology and African Prehistory*. Vol. I of *UNESCO General History of Africa* (1981). Useful summary and interpretive articles treat diverse topics, including sources, languages, geography, and prehistory of the various regions.

G. MOKHTAR, *Ancient Civilizations of Africa*. Vol. II of *UNESCO General History of Africa* (1981). Relevant chapters are 8–16 on Nubia, Meroe, and Aksum; 17–20 on the Saharan region in ancient times; and 22–29 on the early history of the various regions of the African subcontinent.

IRAN

M. BOYCE, *Zoroastrians: Their Religious Beliefs and Practices* (1979). The most recent survey, organized historically and based on extensive research and experience.

J. M. Cook, *The Persian Empire* (1983). A recent, solid survey of the Achaemenid period.

W. D. Davies and L. Finkelstein, ed. *The Cambridge History of Judaism*, Vol. 1 (Introduction; The Persian Period). Good articles on Iran and Iranian religion as well as on Judaism.

J. Duchesne-Guillemin, trans., *The Hymns of Zarathustra*, trans. by M. Henning (1952, 1963). The best introduction to the original texts of the Zoroastrian hymns.

R. N. Frye, *The Heritage of Persia* (1963, 1966). A first-rate survey of Iranian history to Islamic times that is readable but scholarly.

W. W. Malandra, trans. and ed., *An Introduction to Ancient Iranian Religion: Readings from the Avesta and Achaemenid Inscriptions* (1983). Helpful especially for texts of inscriptions relevant to religion.

INDIA

W. T. de Bary et al., comp., *Sources of Indian Tradition*. 1958. 2nd ed., 2 vols. Vol. I: *From the Beginning to 1800*, ed. and rev. Ainslie T. Embree. (1988). Excellent selections from a wide variety of Indian texts, with good introductions to chapters and individual selections.

A. L. Basham, ed., *A Cultural History of India* (1975). A fine collection of historical-survey essays by a variety of scholars. See Part I, "The Ancient Heritage" (Chapters 2–16).

———, *The Wonder That Was India*, rev. ed. (1963). Excellent material on Mauryan religion, society, culture, and history.

B. Rowland, *The Art and Architecture of India: Buddhist/Hindu/Jain*, 3rd rev. ed. (1970). The standard work, lucid and easy to read. Relevant here is Part Three, "Romano-Indian Art in North-West India and Central Asia."

V. A. Smith, *The Oxford History of India*, 4th rev. ed. Percival Spear et al. (1981), pp. 71–163. Perhaps the most readable survey history. Includes useful reference chronologies.

R. Thapar, *Asoka and the Decline of the Mauryas* (1973). The standard treatment of Ashoka's reign.

———, *A History of India.* Part I (1966), pp. 50–108. Contains three chapters on the period from CA. 600 B.C. to A.D. 200 that provide a basic survey.

GREEK AND ASIAN DYNASTIES

A. K. Narain, *The Indo-Greeks* (1957. Reprinted with corrections, Oxford, 1962). The most comprehensive history of the complex history of the various kings and kingdoms.

F. E. Peters, *The Harvest of Hellenism* (1970), pp. 222–308. Helpful chapters on the various Greek rulers of the eastern world, from Seleucus to the last Indo-Greeks.

J. W. Sedlar, *India and the Greek World: A Study in the Transmission of Culture* (1980). A basic work that provides a good overview.

8 China's First Empire (221 B.C.–A.D.220)

One hallmark of Chinese history is the striking continuity of culture, language, and geography. The Shang and Chou dynasties were centered along the Yellow River or its tributary, the Wei. The capitals of China's first empire were in exactly the same areas. And north China would remain China's political center down through history to the present. It was as though Western civilization had progressed from Thebes on the Nile to Athens on the Nile, to Rome on the Nile, and then, in time, to Paris, London, and Berlin on the Nile. And as though each of these centers of culture spoke Egyptian and used a single writing system based on Egyptian hieroglyphics.

But geographical, ethnic, and linguistic continuity did not mean that China was unchanging. One of the key turning points in Chinese history was the third century B.C. when the old, quasi-feudal, Chou multistate system gave way to a centralized bureaucratic government that built an empire stretching from the steppe in the north to Vietnam in the south.

What we refer to as China's first empire was composed of three segments:

256–206 B.C.	Ch'in dynasty
206 B.C.–A.D. 8	Former Han dynasty
A.D. 25–220	Later Han dynasty

The Ch'in dynasty is dated from 256 B.C., the year in which it overthrew the previous Chou dynasty. It went on to unify China in 221 B.C. The Western word *China* is derived from the name of this dynasty. In reshaping China, the Ch'in developed such momentum that it became overextended and collapsed a single generation after the unification. The Ch'in was followed by the two Han dynasties, each lasting about two hundred years. They both used the same dynastic name of

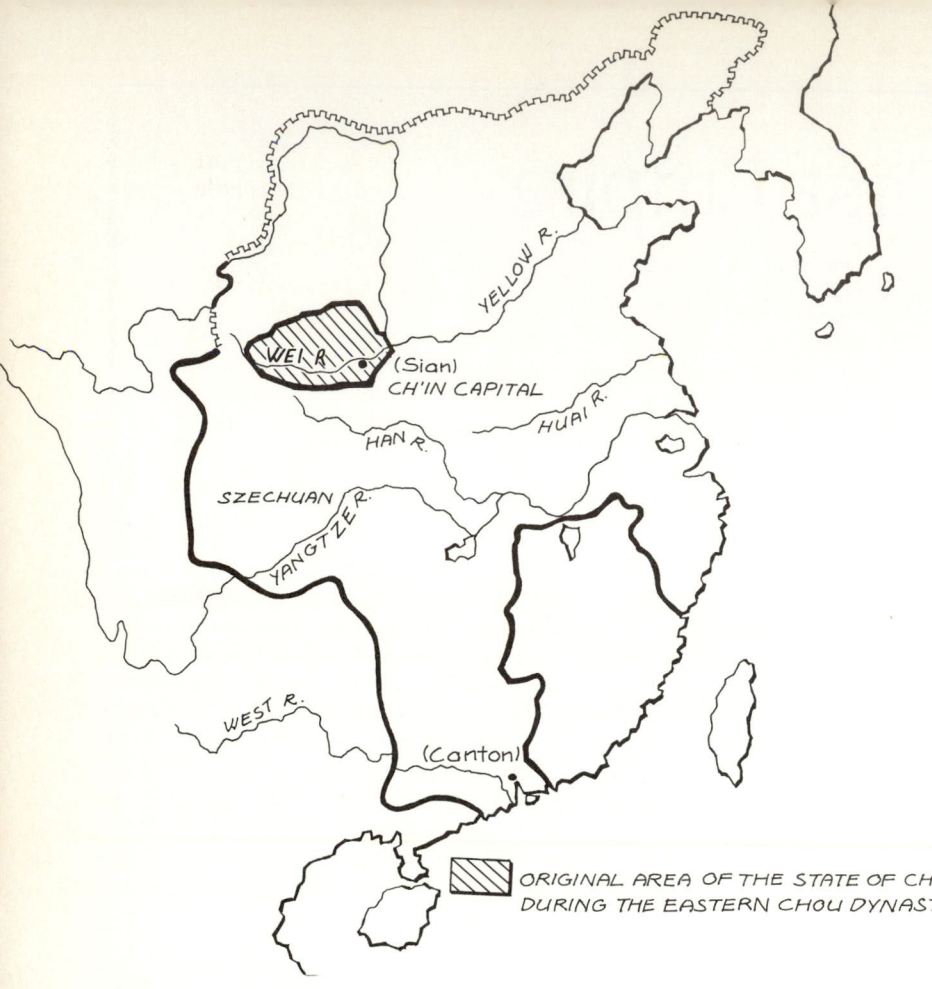

ORIGINAL AREA OF THE STATE OF CH'IN
DURING THE EASTERN CHOU DYNASTY

MAP 8-1   THE UNIFICATION
OF CHINA BY THE CH'IN
STATE   *Between* 221 *and* 206 B.C.
the Ch'in state expanded and unified China.

Han because the Later Han was founded by a descendant of the Former Han. Historians usually treat each of the Han as a separate period of rule, although, as they were almost back to back, they shared many institutions and cultural traits. So deep was the impression left by these two dynasties on the Chinese that even today they call themselves—in contrast to Mongols, Manchus, Tibetans, and other minorities—the "Han people," and their ideographs, "Han writing."

The Ch'in Unification of China

Of the territorial states of the late Chou era none was more innovative and ruthless than Ch'in. Its location on the Wei River in northwest China—the same area from which the Chou had launched their expansion a millennium earlier—gave it strategic advantages: it controlled the passes leading out onto the Yellow River plain and so was easy to defend and was a secure base from which to launch attacks on other states. From the late fourth century B.C., the Ch'in conquered a part of Szechwan and thus controlled two of the most fertile regions of ancient China. It welcomed Legalist administrators, who developed policies for enriching the

country and strengthening its military. Despite its harsh laws, farmers moved to Ch'in from other areas, attracted by the order and stability of its society. Its armies had been forged by centuries of warfare against the nomadic raiders by whose lands it was half encircled. To counter these raiders, it adopted nomadic skills, developing cavalry in the fourth century. Other states regarded the Ch'in as tough, crude, and brutal but recognized its formidable strengths.

In 246 B.C., the man who would unify China succeeded to the Ch'in throne at the age of thirteen. He grew to be vigorous, ambitious, intelligent, and decisive. He is famous as a Legalist autocrat; but he was also well liked by his ministers, whose advice he usually followed. In 232 B.C., at the age of twenty-seven, he began the campaigns that destroyed the six remaining territorial states. On completing his conquests in 221 B.C., he adopted the glorious title we translate as "emperor"—a combination of ideographs hitherto used only for gods or mythic heroes—to raise himself above the kings of the former territorial states. He is known to history as the First Ch'in Emperor. Then, aided by officials of great talent, he set about applying to all of China the reforms that had been tried and found effective in his own realm. His accomplishments in the eleven years before his death in 210 B.C. were stupendous.

Having conquered the civilized world of north China and the Yangtze River basin, the First Emperor sent his armies to conquer new lands. They reached the northern edge of the Red River basin in what is now Vietnam. They occupied China's southeastern coast and the area about the present-day city of Canton. In the north and the northwest, the emperor's armies fought against the Hsiung Nu, Altaic-speaking Hunnish nomads organized in a tribal confederation. During the late Chou, northern border states had built long walls to protect settled lands from incursions by horse-riding raiders. The Ch'in emperor had these joined into a single Great Wall that extended fourteen hundred miles from the Pacific Ocean into central Asia. (By way of comparison, Hadrian's Wall in England was seventy-three miles long.) Its construction cost the lives of vast numbers of conscripted laborers—by some accounts, one hundred thousand; by others, as many as one million.

The most significant Ch'in reform, carried out by the Legalist minister, Li Ssu, extended the Ch'in system of bureaucratic government to the entire empire. Li Ssu divided China into forty prefectures, which were further subdivided into counties. The county heads were responsible to prefects, who, in turn, were responsible to the central government. Officials were chosen by ability. Bureaucratic administration was impersonal, based on laws to which all were subject. No one, for example, escaped Ch'in taxation. This kind of bureaucratic centralism broke sharply with the old Chou pattern of establishing dependent principalities for members of a ruler's family. Furthermore, to ensure the smooth functioning of local government offices, the former aristocracies of the territorial states were removed from their lands and resettled in the Ch'in capital, near present-day Sian. They were housed in mansions on one side of the river, from which they could gaze across at the enormous palace of the First Emperor.

Other reforms further unified the First Emperor's vast domain. Roads were built radiating out from the capital city. The emperor decreed a system of uniform weights and measures. He unified the Chinese writing system, establishing standard ideographs to replace the great variety that had hitherto prevailed. He established uniform axle lengths for carts. Even ideas did not escape the drive toward uniformity. Following the precepts of Legalism, the emperor and his advisers launched a campaign for which they subsequently have been execrated throughout Chinese history. They collected and burned the books of other schools such as Confucianism and were said to have buried alive several hundred scholars opposed to the Legalist philosophy. Only useful books on agriculture, medicine, or Legalist teachings were spared.

But the Ch'in had changed too much too quickly to pay for the roads, canals, and the Great Wall. Taxes burdened the people. Commoners hated conscription and labor service and nobles resented their loss of status. Merchants were exploited, and scholars, except for Legalists, were oppressed. A Chinese historian wrote afterward: "The condemned were an innumerable multitude; those who had been tortured and mutilated formed a long procession on the roads. From the princes and ministers down to the humblest people

The Great Wall of China was originally built during the Ch'in dynasty (256–206 B.C.), *but what we see today is the wall as it was completely rebuilt during the Ming dynasty* (A.D. 1368–1644). *(Photo Researchers.)*

The army of life-size terra-cotta soldiers found in the tomb of the first emperor of the Ch'in dynasty (256–206 B.C.) (Liu Entai.)

Chinese archaeologists restoring warriors from the tomb of the Ch'in emperor. (Liu Entai.)

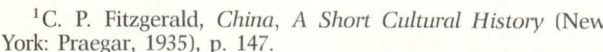

everyone was terrified and in fear of their lives."[1] When the First Emperor died in 210 B.C., intrigues broke out at court and rebellions arose in the land. At the end, the Ch'in was destroyed by the domino effect of its own legal codes. When the generals sent to quell a rebellion were defeated, they joined the rebellion rather than return to the capital and incur the severe punishment decreed for failure. The dynasty collapsed in 206 B.C.

In 1974, a farmer digging a well near Sian discovered the army of eight thousand life-sized terra-cotta horses and soldiers that guarded the tomb of the First Emperor. The historical record tells us that in the tomb itself, under a mountain of earth, is a replica of his capital, a relief model of the Chinese world with quicksilver rivers, other warriors with chariots of bronze, and the remains of horses, noblemen, and criminals sacrificed to accompany in death the emperor whose dynasty was to have lasted for ten thousand generations.

[1]C. P. Fitzgerald, *China, A Short Cultural History* (New York: Praegar, 1935), p. 147.

The Former Han Dynasty
(206 B.C.–A.D. 8)

The Dynastic Cycle

Historians of China have seen a pattern in every dynasty of long duration. They call it the *dynastic cycle*. The cycle begins with internal wars that eventually lead to the military unification of China. The fact of unification is proof that the unifier has been given the mandate of heaven. Strong and vigorous, the first ruler, in the process of consolidating his political power, restores peace and order to China. Economic growth follows, almost automatically. The peak of the cycle is marked by public works, further energetic reforms, and aggressive military expansion. During this phase, China appears invincible. But then the cycle turns downward. The costs of expansion, coupled with an increasing opulence at the court, place a heavy burden on tax revenues just as they are beginning to decline. The vigor of the monarchs wanes. Intrigues develop at the court. The central controls loosen, and provincial governors and military commanders gain autonomy. Finally, canals and other public works fall into disrepair, floods and pestilence occur, rebellions break out, and eventually the dynasty collapses. In the view of Confucian historians, the last emperors are not only politically weak but morally culpable as well.

The Early Years of the Former Han Dynasty

The first sixty years of the Han may be thought of as the early phase of its dynastic cycle. Of the several rebel generals who emerged after the collapse of the Ch'in, one gained control of the Wei basin and went on to unify China. He became the first emperor of the Han dynasty and is known by his posthumous title of Kao Tzu. He rose from plebeian origins to become emperor; only once again would this occur in Chinese history. Kao Tzu built his capital at Ch'ang-an, not far from the former capitals of the Western Chou and the Ch'in. It took many years for the early Han emperors to consolidate their power because they consciously avoided actions that would remind the populace of the hated Ch'in despotism. They made punishments less severe and reduced taxes. Good government prevailed, the economy rebounded, granaries were filled, and vast cash reserves were accumulated. Later historians often singled out the early Han rulers as model sage emperors.

MAP 8-2   THE HAN EMPIRE 206 B.C.–A.D. 220   *At the peak of the Han expansion, the Han armies advanced far out into the steppe north of the Great Wall and west into Central Asia: The silk road to Rome passed through the Tarim Basin and the Kushan Empire.*

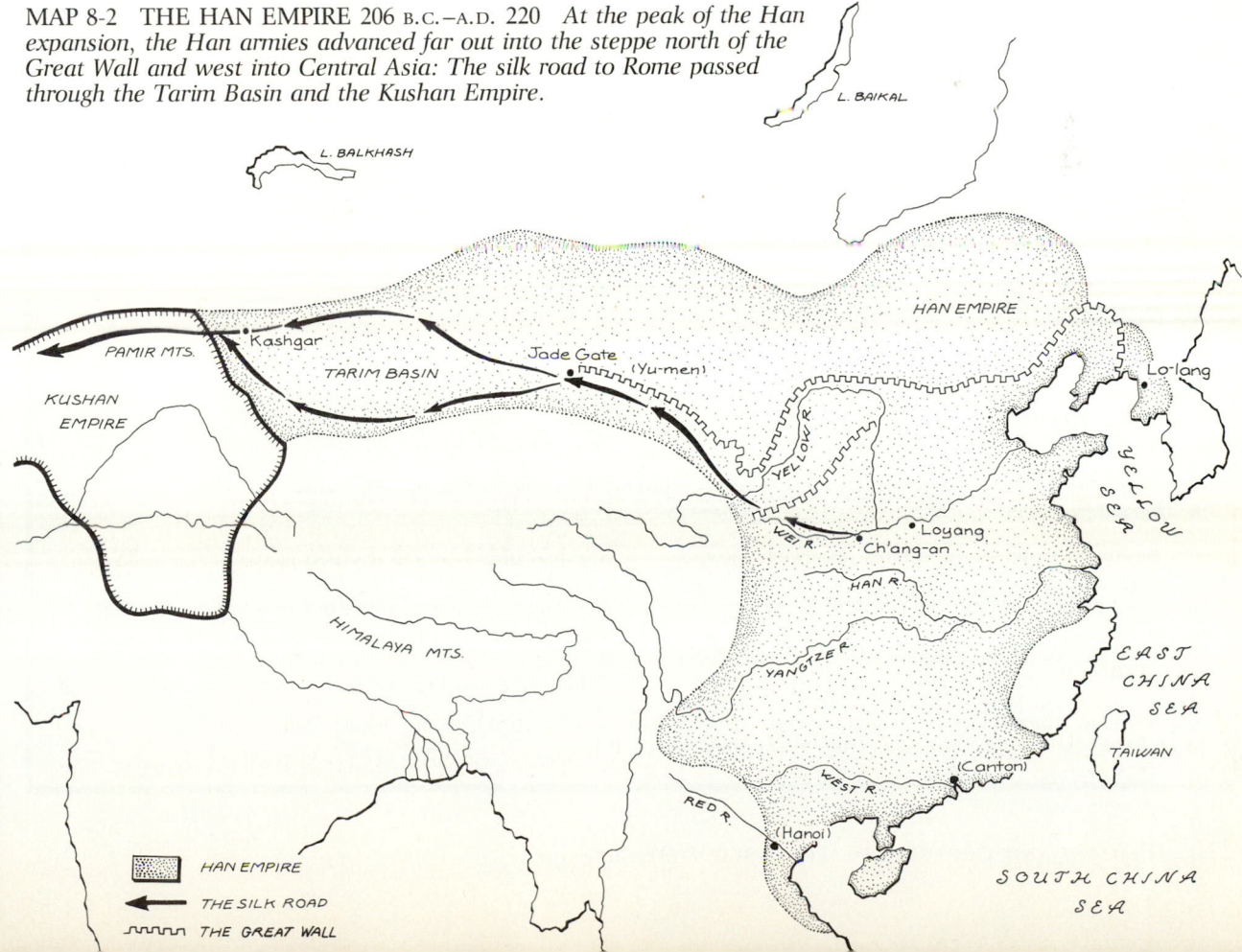

Han Wu Ti

The second phase of the dynastic cycle began with the rule of Wu Ti (the "martial emperor"), who came to the throne in 141 B.C. at the age of sixteen and remained there for fifty-four years, the second longest rule in all Chinese history. Wu Ti was daring, vigorous, and intelligent but also superstitious, suspicious, and vengeful. He wielded tremendous personal authority.

Building on the prosperity achieved by his predecessors, Wu Ti initiated new economic policies. A canal was built from the Yellow River to the capital in northwest China, linking the two major economic regions of north China. "Ever-level granaries" were established throughout the country so that bumper crops could be bought and then sold in time of scarcity. To increase revenues, taxes were levied on merchants, the currency was debased, and some offices were sold. Wu Ti also moved against merchants who had built fortunes in untaxed commodities by reestablishing government monopolies—a practice of the Ch'in—on copper coins, salt, iron, and liquor. For fear of Wu Ti, no one spoke out against the monopolies, but a few years after his death, a famous debate was held at the court. Known after the title of the chronicle as the "Salt and Iron Debate," it was frequently cited thereafter in China, and in Japan and Korea as well. On one side, quasi-Legalist officials argued that the state should enjoy the profits from the sale of salt and iron. On the other side, Confucians argued that the moral purity of officials would be sullied by dealings with merchants. The Confucian scholars who compiled the chronicle made themselves the winner in the debate; but state monopolies became a regular part of Chinese government finance.

Wu Ti also aggressively expanded Chinese borders—a policy that would characterize every strong dynasty. His armies swept south into what is today northern Vietnam and northeast across Manchuria to establish a commandery in north Korea that would last until A.D. 313.

The principal threat to the Han was from the Hsiung Nu empire to the north. Their mounted archers could raid China and flee before an army could be sent against them. To combat them, Wu Ti employed the entire repertoire of policies that would become standard thereafter. When possible he "used the barbarian to control the barbarian," making allies of border nomads against those more distant. Allies were permitted to trade with Chinese merchants; they were awarded titles and honors; and their kings were sent Chinese princesses as brides. When this method did not work, he used force. Between 129 and 119 B.C., Wu Ti sent several armies of over 100,000 troops into the steppe, destroying Hsiung Nu power south of the Gobi Desert in southern Mongolia. To establish a strategic line of defense aimed at the heart of the Hsiung Nu empire further to the west, Wu Ti then sent 700,000 Chinese colonists to the arid Kansu panhandle and

Chinese Women among the Nomads

About the year 105 B.C., Wu Ti sent a Chinese lady, Hsi-chün, to be the wife of a nomad king of the Wu-sun people of central Asia. When she got there, she found her husband to be old and decrepit. He saw her only once or twice a year, when they drank a cup of wine together. They could not converse, as they had no language in common.

My people have married me
In a far corner of Earth;
Sent me away to a strange land,
To the king of the Wu-sun.
A tent is my house,
Of felt are my walls;

Raw flesh my food
With mare's milk to drink.
Always thinking of my own country,
My heart sad within.
Would I were a yellow stork
And could fly to my old home!

Centuries later, the T'ang poet Tu Fu visited the village of another woman sent out to be the wife of a nomad king.

Ten thousand ranges and valleys approach the Ching Gate
And the village in which the Lady of Light was born and bred.
She went out from the purple palace into the desert-land;

She has now become a green grave in the yellow dusk.
Her face!—Can you picture a wind of the spring?
Her spirit by moonlight returns with a tinkling Song of the Tartars on her jade guitar,
Telling her eternal sorrow.   ❑

Arthur Waley, *Chinese Poems* (London, George Allen and Unwin, 1946), p. 43; Witter Bynner and Kiang Kang-hsi, *The Jade Mountain* (New York, Alfred Knopf, 1929), p. 157.

The Position of Women

In the teachings of Confucius, a woman first obeyed her parents, then her husband, and finally her son—as the new family head. Descent was traced through the male line. A woman left her family and her ancestors at marriage to join those of her husband. A millennium before footbinding began in China, Fu Hsüan (A.D. 217–278) wrote this lament.

WOMAN

How sad it is to be a woman!
Nothing on earth is held so cheap.
Boys stand leaning at the door
Like Gods fallen out of Heaven.
Their hearts brave the Four Oceans,
The wind and dust of a thousand miles.
No one is glad when a girl is born:
By *her* the family sets no store.
When she grows up, she hides in her room
Afraid to look a man in the face.
No one cries when she leaves her home—
Sudden as clouds when the rain stops.
She bows her head and composes her face,
Her teeth are pressed on her red lips:

She bows and kneels countless times.
She must humble herself even to the servants.
His love is distant as the stars in Heaven,
Yet the sunflower bends towards the sun.
Their hearts more sundered than water and fire—
A hundred evils are heaped upon her.
Her face will follow the year's changes:
Her lord will find new pleasures.
They that were once like substance and shadow
Are now as far as Hu from Ch'in [two distant places]
Yet Hu and Ch'in shall sooner meet
Than they whose parting is like Ts'an and Ch'en [two stars]. ❑

Arthur Waley, *Chinese Poems* (1946), pp. 84–85.

---

extended the Great Wall to the Jade Gate outpost at the eastern end of the Tarim basin. From this outpost, Chinese influence was extended over the rim oases of Central Asia, establishing the Silk Road that linked Ch'ang-an with Rome.

Government during the Former Han

As a token of how different they were from the Ch'in dynasty, the early Han emperors set up some Chou-like principalities: small, semiautonomous states with independent lords. But these were closely superintended and then, curtailed after several generations. So basically, despite its repudiation of the Ch'in and all its works, the Han continued the Ch'in form of centralized bureaucratic administration. Officials were organized by grades and were paid salaries in grain, plus cash or silk. They were recruited by sponsorship or recommendation: provincial officials had the duty of recommending promising candidates. A school was established at Ch'ang-an that was said to have thirty thousand students by the Later Han. The bureaucracy grew until, by the first century B.C., there were more than 130,000 officials—perhaps not too many for a population that, by that time, had reached sixty million.

During the course of the Han dynasty, this "Legalist" structure of government became partially Confucianized. It did not happen overnight. The first emperor, Kao Tzu, despised Confucians as bookish pedants—he once urinated in the hat of a scholar. But in time, Confucian ideas proved useful. The mandate of heaven provided an ethical justification for dynastic rule. A respect for old records and the written word fitted in well with the vast bookkeeping that the empire entailed. The Confucian classics gradually were accepted as the standard for education. Confucianism was seen as shaping moral men, who as officials would be upright, even in the absence of external constraints. For Confucius had taught the transformation of self through ethical cultivation and had presented a vision of benevolent government by men who were virtuous as well as talented. No one attempted to replace laws with a code of etiquette, but increasingly laws were interpreted and applied by men with a Confucian education.

The court during the Han dynasty exhibited features that would appear in later dynasties as well. The emperor was all-powerful. He was the "son of heaven." When he was an adult and strong, his will was paramount. But when he was weak or still a child, others ruled in his name. Four contenders for this role appeared and reappeared through Chinese history. One was the officials. They had, after all, been selected to govern; they staffed the apparatus of government; and their influence was considerable. Apart from the emperor himself, they were usually the most powerful men in China. Yet the position of court officials was often precarious. Few officials escaped being removed from office or banished once or twice during their careers. Of the seven prime ministers who served Wu Ti, five were executed by his order.

A second contender for power was the empress

dowager. Of the emperor's many wives, she was the one whose child had been named as the heir to the throne. On Kao Tzu's death in 195 B.C., for example, the Empress Lu became the regent for her child, the new emperor. Aided by members of her family, she seized control of the court and murdered a rival, and when her son was about to come of age, she had him killed and a younger son made the heir in order to continue her rule as regent. When she died in 180 B.C., loyal adherents of the imperial family who had opposed her rule massacred the members of her family.

The third group of contenders for power at the court were eunuchs. Mostly from families of low social status, they were brought to the court as boys, castrated, and assigned to serve in the emperor's harem. They were thus in contact with the future emperor from the day he was born; they became his childhood confidants; and they often continued to advise him after he had gained the throne. Emperors found eunuchs useful as a counterweight to officials. But in the eyes of the scholars who wrote China's history, the eunuchs were greedy half-men, given to evil intrigues.

The fourth group of contenders were military commanders. Dynasties were founded by military figures—generals or rebels. In the later phase of most dynasties, regional military commanders often became semi-independent rulers. A few even usurped the position of the emperor. Yet they were less powerful at the Chinese court than they were, for example, in imperial Rome. This was partly because the military constituted a separate category, lower in prestige than the better educated civil officials. It was also partly because the court took great pains to prevent them from establishing a base of personal power. An appointment to command a Han army was given only for a specific campaign, and commanders were appointed in pairs so that each would check the other.

Another characteristic of government during the Han and subsequent dynasties was that its functions were limited. It collected taxes, maintained military forces, administered laws, supported the imperial household, and carried out public works that were beyond the powers of local jurisdictions. But government in a district that remained orderly and paid its taxes was left largely in the hands of local notables and large landowners. This pattern was not, to be sure, unique to China. Most premodern governments, even those that were bureaucratic, floated on top of local society and lacked the means to reach down and interfere in the everyday lives of their subjects.

Decline and Usurpation

During the last decade of Wu Ti's rule in the early first century A.D., military expenses ran ahead of revenues. His successor cut back on military costs, eased economic controls, and reduced taxes. But over the next several generations, large landowners began to use their growing influence in provincial politics to avoid paying taxes. State revenues declined. The tax burden on smaller landowners and free peasants grew heavier. In 22 B.C., rebellions broke out in several parts of the empire. At the court, too, a decline had set in. There had been a succession of weak emperors. Intrigues, nepotism, and factional struggles grew apace. Even officials began to sense that the dynasty no longer had the approval of heaven. The dynastic cycle approached its end.

Many at the court urged Wang Mang, the regent for the infant emperor and the nephew of an empress, to become the emperor and begin a new dynasty. Wang Mang refused several times—to demonstrate his lack of eagerness—and then accepted in A.D. 8. He drew up a program of sweeping reforms based on ancient texts. He was a Confucian, yet he relied on new institutional arrangements, rather than moral reform, to produce a better society. He revived ancient titles, expanded state monopolies, abolished private slavery (about 1 per cent of the population), made loans to poor peasants, and then moved to confiscate large private estates.

These reforms, however, alienated many. Merchants disliked the monopolies. Large landowners resisted the expropriation of their lands. Nature also conspired to bring down Wang Mang: the Yellow River overflowed its banks and changed its course, destroying the northern Chinese irrigation system. Several years of poor harvests produced famines. The Hsiung Nu overran China's northern borders. In A.D. 18, the Red Eyebrows, a peasant secret society, rose in rebellion. In A.D. 23, rebels attacked Ch'ang-an, and Wang Mang was killed and eaten by rebel troops. Wang Mang had tried to found a new dynasty from within a decrepit court without having an independent military base. The attempt was futile. Internal wars continued in China for two more years until a large landowner, who had become the leader of a rebel army, emerged triumphant in A.D. 25. Because he was from a branch line of the imperial family, his new dynasty was viewed as a restoration of the Han.

The Later Han (A.D. 25–220) and Its Aftermath

The First Century

The founder of the Later Han moved his capital east to Loyang. Under the first emperor and his two successors, there was a return to strong central government and a laissez-faire economy. Agriculture and population recovered from the devastation caused by war. By the end of the first century A.D., China was as prosperous as it had been during the good years of the Former Han. The shift from pacification and recuperation to military expansion came earlier than during the previous dynasty. Even during the reign of the first emperor, south China and Vietnam were retaken. Dissension within the Hsiung Nu confederation enabled the Chinese to secure an alliance with some of the southern tribes in A.D. 50, and in A.D. 89, Chinese armies crossed the Gobi Desert and defeated the northern Hsiung Nu. This defeat sparked the migrations, some historians say, that brought the Hsiung Nu to the southern Russian steppes and then, in the fifth century A.D., to Europe, where they were known as the Huns of Attila. In A.D. 97, a Chinese general led an army as far west as the shores of the Caspian Sea. The expansion to inner Asia, coupled with more lenient government policies toward merchants, facilitated the camel caravans that carried Chinese silk across the Tarim basin to Iran, Palestine, and Rome.

Decline during the Second Century

Until A.D. 88, the emperors of the Later Han were vigorous; afterward they were ineffective and short-lived. Empresses plotted to advance the fortunes of their families. Emperors turned for help to palace eunuchs, whose power at times surpassed that of officials. In A.D. 159, a conspiracy of eunuchs in the service of an emperor slaughtered the family of a scheming empress dowager and ruled at the court. When officials and students protested against the eunuch dictatorship, over a hundred were killed and over a thousand were tortured or imprisoned. In another incident in A.D. 190, a general deposed one emperor, installed another, killed the empress dowager, and massacred most of the eunuchs at the court.

In the countryside, large landowners, who had been powerful from the start of the dynasty, grew more so. They harbored private armies. Farmers on the estates of the mighty were reduced to serfs. The landowners used their influence to avoid taxes. Great numbers of free farmers fled south to avoid taxes. The remaining freeholders paid ever heavier taxes and labor services. Many peasants turned to neo-Taoist religious movements: the Yellow Turbans in the east and the Five Pecks of Rice Band in Szechwan.

In A.D. 184, rebellions organized by members of the religious sects broke out against the government. Religion provided the ideology and organization to channel their discontents. Han generals suppressed the rebellions but stayed on to rule in the provinces they had pacified. In 220 A.D., they deposed the last Han emperor.

The Aftermath of Empire

For more than three and a half centuries after the fall of the Han, China was disunited. For several gen-

A green-glazed pottery model of a Later Han Dynasty watch tower. Note the resemblence to later Chinese Buddhist pagodas. (W.R. Nelson Trust.)

erations, it was divided into three kingdoms, whose heroic warriors and scheming statesmen were made famous by wandering storytellers. These figures later peopled the *Tales of the Three Kingdoms*, a great romantic epic of Chinese literature.

Chinese history during the post-Han centuries had two characteristics. The first was the dominant role played by the great aristocratic landowning families. With vast estates, huge numbers of serfs, fortified manor houses, and private armies, they were beyond the control of most governments. Because they took over many of the functions of local government, some historians describe post-Han China as having reverted to the quasi-feudalism of the Chou. The second characteristic of these centuries was that north and south China developed in quite different ways.

In the south, there followed a succession of ever weaker dynasties with capitals at Nanking. The entire period of Chinese history from A.D. 220 to 589 is called the Six Dynasties era after these Nanking-centered states. The main developments in the south were (1) the continuing economic growth of south China and the emergence of Nanking as a thriving center of commerce; (2) the ongoing absorption of the tribal peoples of south China into Chinese society and culture; (3) large-scale immigrations of Chinese fleeing the north; and (4) the spread of Buddhism and its penetration to the heart of Chinese culture. Although called dynasties, these six southern states were in fact short-lived kingdoms, plagued by intrigues, usurpations, and coups d'état, frequently at war with northern states, and in constant fear of their own generals.

In the north, state formation depended on the interaction of nomads and Chinese. During the Han dynasty, Chinese invasions of the steppe had led to the incorporation of semi-Sinicized Hsiung Nu as the northernmost tier of the Chinese defense system—just as Germanic tribes had acted as the teeth and claws of the late Roman Empire. But as the Chinese state weakened, the highly mobile nomads broke loose, joined with other tribes, and began to invade China. The short-lived states that they formed are usually referred to as the *Sixteen Kingdoms*. One kingdom was founded by invaders of Tibetan stock. Most spoke Altaic languages: the Hsien Pi (proto-Mongols), the

Toba (proto-Turks), and the Juan Juan (who would later appear in eastern Europe as the Avars). But differences of language and stock were less important than these tribes' similarities:

1. All began as steppe nomads with a way of life different from that of agricultural China.
2. After forming states, all became at least partially Sinicized. Chinese from great families, which had preserved the Han traditions, served as their tutors and administrators.
3. Wars were endemic. Some were fought between northern courts and conservative steppe tribes that resisted Sinicization.
4. Buddhism was powerful in the north as in the south. As a universal religion, it acted as a bridge between "barbarians" and Chinese—just as Christianity was a unifying force in post-Roman Europe. The crude tribes were especially attracted to its magical side. Usually Buddhism was made the state religion. Of the northern states, the most durable was the Northern Wei (A.D. 386–534), famed for its Buddhist sculpture.

Han Thought and Religion

Poems describe the splendor of Ch'ang-an and Loyang: broad boulevards, tiled gateways, open courtyards, watchtowers, and imposing walls. Most splendid of all were the palaces of the emperors, with

Court figures painted on ceramic tile in a Han dynasty tomb. (Museum of Fine Arts, Boston.)

their audience halls, vast chambers, harem quarters, and parks containing artificial lakes and rare animals and birds. But today little remains of the grandeur of the Han. Whereas Roman ruins abound in Italy and circle the Mediterranean, in China nothing remains aboveground. Only from the pottery, bronzes, musical instruments, gold and silver jewelry, lacquerware, and clay figurines that were buried in tombs do we gain an inkling of the rich material culture of the Han period. And only from painting on the walls of tombs do we know of its art.

But there is a wealth of written records that convey the sophistication and depth of Han culture. Perhaps the two most important areas were philosophy and history.

Han Confucianism

A major accomplishment of the early Han was the recovery of texts that had been lost during the Ch'in persecution of scholars. Some were retrieved from the walls of houses where they had been hidden; others were reproduced from memory by scholars. Debate arose regarding the relative authenticity of the old and new texts—a controversy that has continued until modern times. In 51 B.C. and again in A.D. 79, councils were held to determine the true meaning of the Confucian classics. In A.D. 175, an approved, official version of the texts was inscribed on stone tablets. In about A.D. 100, the first dictionary was compiled. Containing about nine thousand characters, it helped promote a uniform system of writing. In Han times, as today, Chinese from the north could not converse with Chinese from the southeastern coast. But a common written language bridged differences of pronunciation, contributing to Chinese unity.

It was also in Han times that scholars began writing commentaries on the classics, a major activity for scholars throughout Chinese history. Scholars learned the classics by heart and used classical allusions in their writing.

Beyond the advances in scholarship, Han philosophers also extended Chou Confucianism by adding to it the teachings of cosmological naturalism. Chou Confucianists had assumed that the moral force of a virtuous emperor would not only order society but also harmonize nature. Han Confucianists explained why. Tung Chung-shu (CA. 179–104 B.C.), for example, held that all nature was a single, interrelated system. Just as summer always follows spring, so does one color, one virtue, one planet, one element, one number, and one officer of the court always take precedence over another. All reflect the systematic workings of *yang* and *yin* and the five elements. And just as one dresses appropriately to the season, so was it important for the emperor to choose policies appropriate to the se-

quences inherent in nature. If he is moral, if he acts in accord with Heaven's natural system, then all will go well. But if he acts inappropriately, then Heaven will send a portent as a warning—a blue dog, a rat holding its tail in its mouth, an eclipse, or a comet. If the portent is not heeded, wonders and then misfortunes will follow. If was the Confucian scholars, of course, who claimed to understand nature's messages and advised the emperor.

It is easy to criticize Han philosophy as pseudo-scientific, or as a mechanistic view of nature. But it represented a new effort of the Chinese mind to encompass and comprehend the interrelationships of the natural world. Spurring an interest in nature, this effort led to inventions like the seismograph and to advances in astronomy, music, and medicine. It was also during the Han that the Chinese invented paper, the

A Chinese seismograph. The suspended weight swings in the direction of the earthquake. This moves a lever and a dragon drops a ball into the mouth of one of the four waiting ceramic frogs. [New York Public Library.]

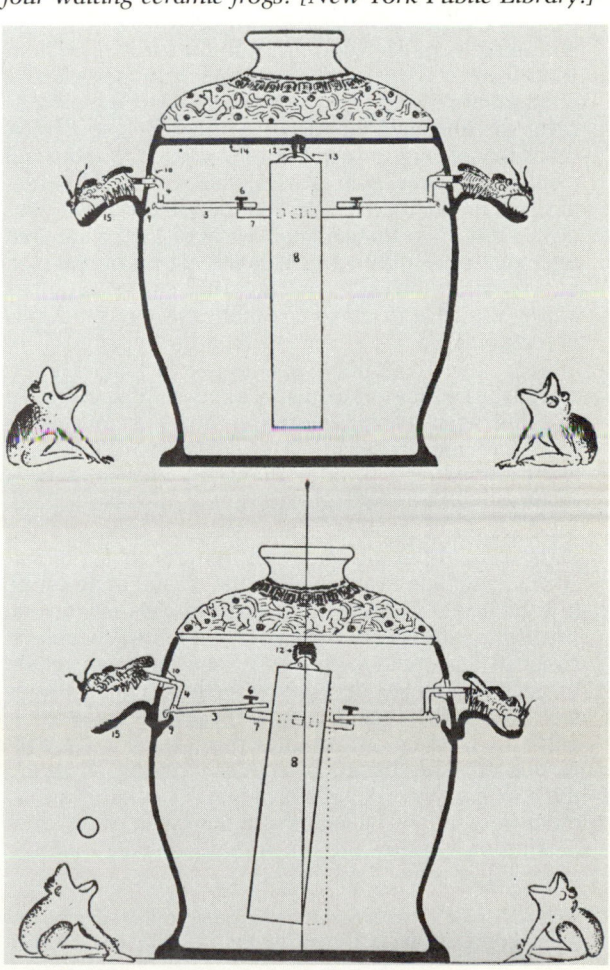

wheelbarrow, the stern-post rudder, and the compass (known as the "south-pointing chariot").

History

The Chinese were the greatest historians of the premodern world. They wrote more history than anyone else, and what they wrote was usually more accurate. Apart from the *Spring and Autumn Annals* and the scholarship of Confucius himself, history writing in China began during the Han dynasty. Why the Chinese were so history-minded has been variously explained: because the Chinese tradition is this-worldly; because Confucianists were scholarly and their veneration for the classics carried over to the written word; because history was seen as a lessonbook (the Chinese called it a mirror) for statesmen, and thus a necessity

Ssu-ma Ch'ien on the Wealthy

More than half of the chapters in Ssu-ma Ch'ien's Historical Records *(early first century* B.C.*) were biographies of extraordinary men and women. He wrote of scholars, wandering knights, diviners, harsh officials and reasonable officials, wits and humorists, doctors, and money-makers. The following is his description of the vibrant economic life of Han cities and his judgments regarding the wealthy.*

Anyone who in the market towns or great cities manages in the course of a year to sell the following items: a thousand brewings of liquor; a thousand jars of pickles and sauces; a thousand jars of sirups; a thousand slaughtered cattle, sheep, and swine; a thousand *chung* of grain; a thousand cartloads or a thousand boat-lengths of firewood and stubble for fuel; a thousand logs of timber; ten thousand bamboo poles; a hundred horse carriages; a thousand two-wheeled ox carts; a thousand lacquered wooden vessels; brass utensils weighing thirty thousand catties; a thousand piculs of plain wooden vessels, iron vessels, or gardenia and madder dyes; two hundred horses; five hundred cattle; two thousand sheep or swine; a hundred male or female slaves; a thousand catties of tendons, horns, or cinnabar; thirty thousand catties of silken fabric, raw silk, or other fine fabrics; a thousand rolls of embroidered or patterned silk; a thousand piculs of fabrics made of vegetable fiber or raw or tanned hides; a thousand pecks of lacquer; a thousand jars of leaven or salted bean relish; a thousand catties of globefish or mullet; a thousand piculs of dried fish; thirty thousand catties of salted fish; three thousand piculs of jujubes or chestnuts; a thousand skins of fox or sable; a thousand piculs of lamb or sheep skins; a thousand felt mats; or a thousand *chung* of fruits or vegetables—such a man may live as well as the master of an estate of a thousand chariots. The same applies for anyone who has a thousand strings of cash [i.e., a million cash] to lend out on interest. Such loans are made through a moneylender, but a greedy merchant who is too anxious for a quick return will only manage to revolve his working capital three times while a less avaricious merchant has revolved his five times. These are the principal ways of making money. There are various other occupations which bring in less than twenty percent profit, but they are not what I would call sources of wealth.

Thrift and hard work are without doubt the proper way to gain a livelihood. And yet it will be found that rich men have invariably employed some unusual scheme or method to get to the top. Plowing the fields is a rather crude way to make a living, and yet Ch'in Yang did so well at it that he became the richest man in his province. Robbing graves is a criminal offense, but T'ien Shu got his start by doing it. Gambling is a wicked pastime, but Huan Fa used it to acquire a fortune. Most fine young men would despise the thought of traveling around peddling goods, yet Yung Lo-ch'eng got rich that way. Many people would consider trading in fats a disgraceful line of business, but Yung Po made a thousand catties of gold at it. Vending sirups is a pretty occupation, but the Chang family acquired ten million cash that way. It takes little skill to sharpen knives, but because the Chih family didn't mind doing it, they could eat the best of everything. Dealing in dried sheep stomachs seems like an insignificant enough trade, but thanks to it the Cho family went around with a mounted retinue. The calling of a horse doctor is a rather ignominious profession, but it enabled Chang Li to own a house so large that he had to strike a bell to summon the servants. All of these men got where they did because of their devotion and singleness of purpose.

From this we may see that there is no fixed road to wealth, and money has no permanent master. It finds its way to the man of ability like the spokes of a wheel converging upon the hub, and from the hands of the worthless it falls like shattered tiles. A family with a thousand catties of gold may stand side by side with the lord of a city; the man with a hundred million cash may enjoy the pleasures of a king. Rich men such as these deserve to be called the "untitled nobility," do they not? ❑

Records of the Grand Historian of China, trans. from the *Shih chi* of Ssu-ma Ch'ien by Burton Watson (New York: Columbia University Press, 1961), pp. 494–495, 499.

The Castration of Ssu-ma Ch'ien

Why did the historian Ssu-ma Ch'ien let himself be castrated? When he incurred the wrath of the Emperor Wu Ti for defending a general defeated by the Hsiung Nu and was condemned to suffer this shame in 98 B.C., why did he not choose an honorable suicide? Read his explanation.

A man has only one death. That death may be as weighty as Mount T'ai, or it may be as light as a goose feather. It all depends upon the way he uses it. . . . It is the nature of every man to love life and hate death, to think of his relatives and look after his wife and children. Only when a man is moved by higher principles is this not so. Then there are things which he must do. . . . The brave man does not always die for honor, while even the coward may fulfill his duty. Each takes a different way to exert himself. Though I might be weak and cowardly and seek shamefully to prolong my life, yet I know full well the difference between what ought to be followed and what rejected. How could I bring myself to sink into the shame of ropes and bonds? If even the lowest slave and scullery maid can bear to commit suicide, why should not one like myself be able to do what has to be done? But the reason I have not refused to bear these ills and have continued to live, dwelling among this filth, is that I grieve that I have things in my heart that I have not been able to express

fully, and I am shamed to think that after I am gone my writings will not be known to posterity.

I too have ventured not to be modest but have entrusted myself to my useless writings. I have gathered up and brought together the old traditions of the world which were scattered and lost. I have examined the deeds and events of the past and investigated the principles behind their success and failure, their rise and decay, in one hundred and thirty chapters. I wished to examine into all that concerns heaven and man, to penetrate the changes of the past and present, completing all as the work of one family. But before I had finished my rough manuscript, I met with this calamity. It is because I regretted that it had not been completed that I submitted to the extreme penalty without rancor. When I have truly completed this work, I shall deposit it in some safe place. If it may be handed down to men who will appreciate it and penetrate to the villages and great cities, then though I should suffer a thousand mutilations, what regret would I have? ❑

W. T. de Bary, W. T. Chan, and B. Watson (eds.), *Sources of Chinese Tradition* (New York: Columbia University Press, 1960), pp. 272–273.

---

for the literate men who operated the centralized Chinese state.

The practice of using actual documents and first-hand accounts of events began with Ssu-ma Ch'ien (d. 85 B.C.), who set out to write a history of the known world from the most ancient times down to the age of the Emperor Wu Ti. His *Historical Records* consisted of 130 substantial chapters (in over 700,000 characters) divided into "Basic Annals"; "Chronological Tables"; "Treatises" on rites, music, astronomy, the calendar, and so on; "Hereditary Houses"; and 70 chapters of "Biographies," including descriptions of foreign peoples.

A second great work, *The Book of the Han*, was written by Pan Ku (d. A.D. 92). It applied the analytical schema of Ssu-ma Ch'ien to a single dynasty, the Former Han, and established the pattern by which each dynasty wrote the history of its predecessor.

Neo-Taoism

As the Han dynasty waned, the effort to realize the Confucian ethic in the sociopolitical order became more and more difficult. Some scholars abandoned Confucianism altogether in favor of Neo-Taoism, or "mysterious learning," as it was called at the time. A

few wrote commentaries on the classical Taoist texts that had been handed down from the Chou. The *Chuang Tzu* was especially popular. Other scholars, defining the natural as the pleasurable, withdrew from society to engage in witty "pure conversations." They discussed poetry and philosophy, played the lute, and drank wine. The most famous were the Seven Sages of the Bamboo Grove of the third century A.D. One sage was always accompanied by a servant carrying a jug of wine and a spade—the one for his pleasure, the other to dig his grave should he die. Another wore no clothes at home. When criticized, he replied that the cosmos was his home, and his house his clothes. "Why are you in my pants?" he asked a discomfited visitor. Still another took a boat to visit a friend on a snowy night, but on arriving at his friend's door, turned around and went home. When pressed for an explanation, he said that it had been his pleasure to go, and that when the impulse died, it was his pleasure to return. This story reveals a scorn for convention coupled with an admiration for an inner spontaneity, however eccentric.

Another concern of what is called Neo-Taoism was immortality. Some sought it in dietary restrictions and Yoga-like meditation; some, in sexual abstinence or orgies. Others, seeking elixirs to prolong life, dabbled

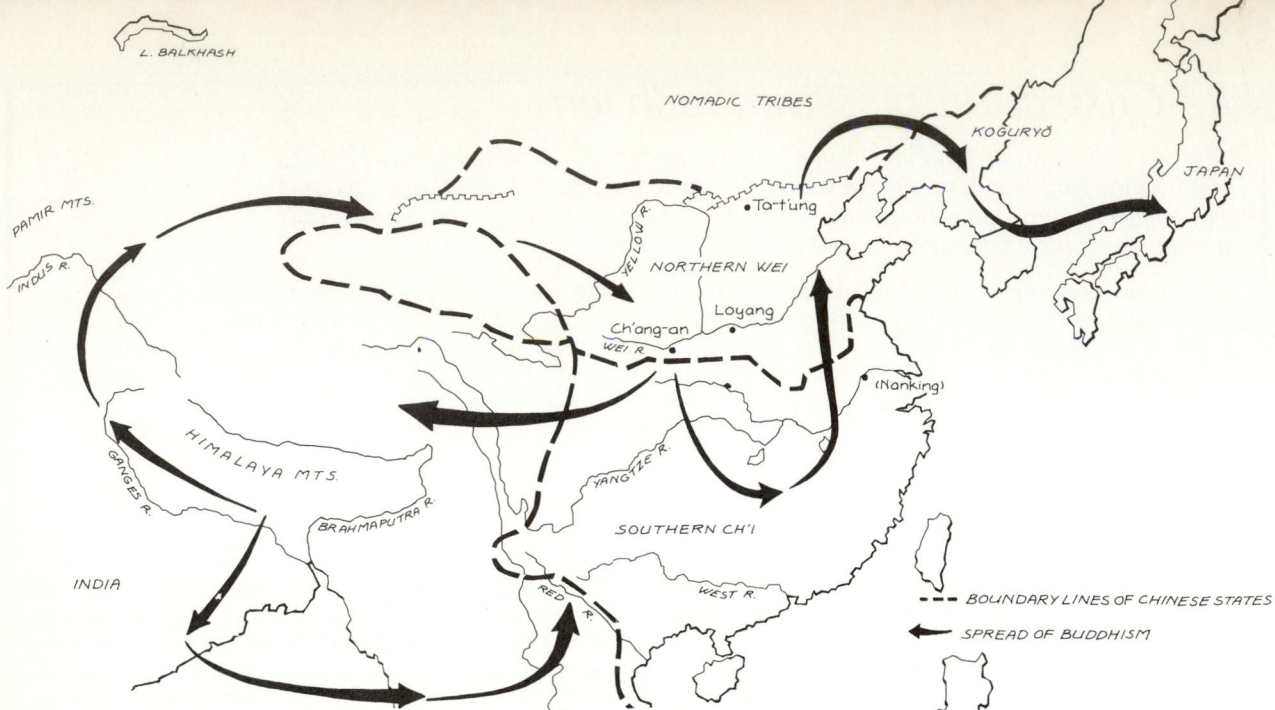

MAP 8-3   THE SPREAD OF BUDDHISM AND CHINESE STATES IN A.D. 500
Buddhism originated in a Himalayan state in northwest India. It spread in one wave south in India and on to southeast Asia as far as Java. But it also spread into northwest India, Afghanistan, Central Asia, and then to China, Korea, and Japan.

in alchemy, and although no magical elixir was ever found, the schools of alchemy to which the search gave rise are credited with the discovery of medicines, dyes, glazes, and gunpowder.

Meanwhile among the common people, there arose popular religious cults that, because they included the Taoist classics among their sacred texts, are also called Neo-Taoist. Like most folk religions, these contained an amalgam of beliefs, practices, and superstitions. They had a pantheon of gods and immortals and taught that the good or evil done in this life would be recompensed in the innumerable heavens or hells of an afterlife. This movement or cult had priests, shamans who practiced faith healing, seers, and sorceresses. For a time, it also had a hierarchical church organization, but this was smashed when the Yellow Turbans and Five Pecks of Rice rebellions were suppressed at the end of the second century A.D. Local Taoist temples and monasteries, however, continued down to modern times. With many Buddhist accretions, they furnished the religious beliefs of the bulk of the Chinese population. Even today, these sects continue in Taiwan and in Chinese communities in Southeast Asia.

Buddhism

Central Asian missionaries, following the trade routes east, brought Buddhism to China in the first century A.D. It was at first viewed as a new Taoist sect. This is not surprising because early translators used Taoist terms to render Buddhist concepts. *Nirvana*, for example, was translated as "not doing" (*wu-wei*). In the second century B.C., this led to the very Chinese view that Lao-tzu had gone to India, where the Buddha had become his disciple, and that Buddhism was the Indian form of Taoism.

Then, as the Han sociopolitical order collapsed in the third century A.D., Buddhism spread rapidly—parallel, perhaps, to the spread of Christianity at the end of the Roman Empire. Though an alien religion in China, Buddhism had some advantages over Taoism:

1. It was a doctrine of personal salvation, offering several routes to that goal;
2. It contained high standards of personal ethics;
3. It had systematic philosophies, and during its early centuries in China, it continued to receive inspiration from India;
4. It drew on the Indian tradition of meditative practices and psychologies, which were the most sophisticated in the world.

By the fifth century A.D., Buddhism had spread over all of China. Occasionally it was persecuted by Taoist emperors—in the north between A.D. 446 and 452, and again between A.D. 574 and 578. But most courts supported Buddhism. The "Bodhisattva Emperor" Wu of the southern Liang dynasty three times gave himself to a monastery and had to be ransomed back by his disgusted courtiers. Temples and monasteries abounded in both the north and the south. There were communities of women as well as of men. Chinese artists produced Buddhist painting and sculpture of surpassing beauty, and thousands of monk-scholars labored to translate sutras and philosophical treatises. Chinese monks went on pilgrimages to India. The record left by Fa Hsien, who traveled to India overland and back by sea between A.D. 399 and 413, became a prime source of Indian history. The T'ang monk Hsuan Tsang went to India from 629 until 645. Several centuries later, his pilgrimage was novelized as *Monkey*, in which faith, magic, and adventure are joined together.

A comparison of Indian and Chinese Buddhism highlights some distinctive features of its spread. Buddhism in India had begun as a reform movement. Forget speculative philosophies and elaborate metaphysics, taught the Buddha, and concentrate on simple truths: Life is suffering, the cause of suffering is desire, death does not end the endless cycle of birth and rebirth; only the attainment of *nirvana* releases one from the "wheel of karma." Thus, in this most otherworldly of the world's religions, all of the cosmic drama of salvation is compressed into the single figure of the Buddha meditating under the Bodhi tree. Over the centuries, however, Indian Buddhism developed contending philosophies and conflicting sects and, having become virtually indistinguishable from Hinduism, was reabsorbed after A.D. 1000.

In China, there were a number of sects with different doctrinal positions. But the Chinese genius was more syncretic. It took in the sutras and meditative practices of early Buddhism. It took in the Mahayana philosophies that depicted a succession of Buddhas, cosmic and historical, past and future, all embodying a

The Peach Blossom Spring

The poet Ta'o Ch'ien wrote in A.D. 380 of a lost village without taxes and untouched by the barbarian invasions and wars of the post-Han era. The simplicity and naturalness of his utopian vision was in accord, perhaps, with certain strains of Neo-Taoist thought. It struck a chord in the hearts of Chinese, and then Koreans and Japanese, inspiring a spate of paintings, poetry, and essays.

During the T'ai-yuan period of the Ch'in dynasty a fisherman of Wuling once rowed upstream, unmindful of the distance he had gone, when he suddenly came to a grove of peach trees in bloom. For several hundred paces on both banks of the stream there was no other kind of tree. The wild flowers growing under them were fresh and lovely, and fallen petals covered the ground—it made a great impression on the fisherman. He went on for a way with the idea of finding out how far the grove extended. It came to an end at the foot of a mountain whence issued the spring that supplied the stream. There was a small opening in the mountain and it seemed as though light was coming through it. The fisherman left his boat and entered the cave, which at first was extremely narrow, barely admitting his body; after a few dozen steps it suddenly opened out onto a broad and level plain where well-built houses were surrounded by rich fields and pretty ponds. Mulberry, bamboo and other trees and plants grew there, and criss-cross paths skirted the fields. The sounds of cocks crowing and dogs barking could be heard from one courtyard to the next. Men and women were coming and going about their work in the fields. The clothes they wore were like those of ordinary people. Old men and boys were carefree and happy.

When they caught sight of the fisherman, they asked in surprise how he had got there. The fisherman told the whole story, and was invited to go to their house, where he was served wine while they killed a chicken for a feast. When the other villagers heard about the fisherman's arrival they all came to pay him a visit. They told him that their ancestors had fled the disorders of Ch'in times and, having taken refuge here with wives and children and neighbors, had never ventured out again; consequently they had lost all contact with the outside world. They asked what the present ruling dynasty was, for they had never heard of the Han, let alone the Wei and the Chin. They sighed unhappily as the fisherman enumerated the dynasties one by one and recounted the vicissitudes of each. The visitors all asked him to come to their houses in turn, and at every house he had wine and food. He stayed several days. As he was about to go away, the people said, "There's no need to mention our existence to outsiders."

After the fisherman had gone out and recovered his boat, he carefully marked the route. On reaching the city, he reported what he had found to the magistrate, who at once sent a man to follow him back to the place. They proceeded according to the marks he had made, but went astray and were unable to find the cave again. ❑

J. R. Hightower, *The Poetry of Ta'o Ch'ien* (Oxford: Clarendon Press, 1970), pp. 254–255.

single ultimate reality. It also took in the sutras and practices of Buddhist devotional sects. And then, in the T'ien-t'ai sect, the Chinese joined together these various elements as different levels of a single truth. So the monastic routine of a T'ien-tai monk would include reading sutras, sitting in meditation, and also practicing devotional exercises.

Socially, too, Buddhism adapted to China. Ancestor worship demanded that there be heirs to perform the sacrifices. In the absence of progeny, ancestors might become "hungry ghosts." Hence, the first son would marry and have a family, and the second son would become a monk. The practice also arose of holding Buddhist masses for dead ancestors. Still another difference between China and India was the more extensive regulation of Buddhism by the state in China. Just as Buddhism was not to injure the family, so Buddhism was not to reduce the taxes paid on land. As a result, limits were placed on the number of monasteries, nunneries, and monastic lands, and the requirement was made that the state must give its permission before men or women abandoned the world to enter a religious establishment. The regulations, to be sure, were not always enforced.

China's First Empire in World Perspective

Were there world-historical forces that produced at roughly the same time great empires in China, India, and the Mediterranean? Certainly there were similar features in these empires. All three came after revolutions in thought. The Han built on Chou thought (it would be hard to imagine the Han bureaucratic state without Legalism and Confucianism), just as Rome used Greek thought, and the Mauryan empire Buddhist thought. In each case, the conception of universal political authority sustaining the empire derived from the earlier philosophies. All three were Iron Age empires, joining their respective technologies with new organizational techniques to create superb military forces.

The differences between the empires are also instructive. Contrast China and Rome. In China, the pervasive culture and the only higher culture in the area was Chinese—even before the first empire arose. This culture had been slowly spreading for centuries and in places outran the polity. Even the culture of the Ch'u peoples south of the Yangtse, though viewed as "semibarbarian" by northern Chinese, was only a variation of the higher culture. Thus cultural unity had paved the way for political unity.

In contrast, the polyglot empire of Rome encompassed quite different peoples, including older civilizations. The genius of Rome, in fact, was to fashion a government and a set of laws that could contain its cultural diversity. Geographically, however, Rome had an easier time of it, for the Mediterranean offered direct access to most parts of the empire and was a thoroughfare for commerce. China, in contrast, was largely landlocked. It was composed of several regional economic units, each of which, located in a segment of a river basin separated from the others by natural barriers, looked inward. It was the genius of Chinese administration to overcome physical and spatial barriers and to integrate the country politically.

A second difference was that government in Han China was more orderly, more complex, and more competent. Government officials controlled the military almost until the end, whereas in latter Roman times, emperor after emperor was set on the throne by the army or the Praetorian Guard. The Roman empire was in no sense a dynasty.

A third salient difference was in the military dynamics of the two empires. Roman power was built over centuries. Its history is the story of one state growing in power by steady increments, imposing its will on others, and gradually piecing together an empire. Not until the early centuries A.D. was the whole empire in place. China, in contrast, remained a multistate system right up to 232 B.C. and then, in a sudden surge, was unified by one state in eleven years. The greater dynamism of China during the first empire can be explained, perhaps, by the greater military challenge it faced across its northern border: an immense Hunnish nomadic empire. Since the threat was more serious than that posed to Rome by any European barbarian enemy, the Chinese response was correspondingly massive.

Suggested Readings

D. BODDE, *China's First Unifier* (1938). A study of the Ch'in unification of China, viewed through the Legalist philosopher and statesman Li Ssu.

T. T. CH'U, *Law and Society in Traditional China* (1961). Treats the sweep of Chinese history from 202 B.C. to 1911.

T. T. CH'U, *Han Social Structure* (1972).

J. K. FAIRBANK, E. O. REISCHAUER, AND A. M. CRAIG, *East Asia: Tradition and Transformation* (1989). A widely read single-volume history covering China, Japan, and other countries in East Asia from antiquity to recent times.

J. GERNET, *A History of Chinese Civilization* (1982). An excellent survey of Chinese history.

C. Y. HSU, *Ancient China in Transition* (1965). On social mobility during the Eastern Chou era.

C. Y. Hsu, *Han Agriculture* (1980). A study of the agrarian economy of China during the Han dynasty.

M. Loewe, *Everyday Life in Early Imperial China* (1968). A social history of the Han dynasty.

J. Needham, *The Shorter Science and Civilization in China* (1978). An abridgement of the multivolume work on the same subject with the same title—minus *Shorter*—by the same author.

C. Schirokauer, *A Brief History of Chinese and Japanese Civilizations* (1978). A standard text, especially good on literature and art.

M. Sullivan, *The Arts of China* (1967). An excellent survey history of Chinese art.

D. Twitchett and M. Loewe (eds.), *The Ch'in and Han Empires*, 221 b.c.–a.d. 220 (1986). (Volume 1 of *The Cambridge History of China*.)

Z. S. Wang, *Han Civilization* (1982).

B. Watson, *Ssu-ma Ch'ien, Grand Historian of China* (1958). A study of China's premier historian.

B. Watson, *Records of the Grand Historian of China*, vols. 1 and 2 (1961). Selections from the *Shih-chi* by Ssu-ma Ch'ien.

B. Watson, *The Columbia Book of Chinese Poetry* (1986).

A. Wright, *Buddhism in Chinese History* (1959).

Y. S. Yu, *Trade and Expansion in Han China* (1967). A study of economic relations between the Chinese and their neighbors.

Consolidation and Interaction of World Civilizations

BETWEEN 500 and 1500, the major civilizations of the world shaped themselves politically and culturally in new and lasting ways.

Surviving barbarian attacks and the threat of political fragmentation, a succession of Chinese dynasties not only maintained political unity, but during the T'ang dynasty (618–907), attained a true pan-China empire, the likes of which would never be known in Western Europe. In achieving this, the Chinese were aided by a universal philosophical system, Confucianism, which supported secular political power, and by a common written language and the technology to print it, which ensured cultural unity across China's vast regions. Even its dense population, close to fifty million in the year 750, encouraged unity and provided a base for communication, trade, and a stable empire. The Chinese government evolved in this period from aristocratic bureaucracy toward political absolutism. The Mongols took Peking in 1227. Kublai Khan made it his capital in 1264 and accelerated the development of absolutism that had begun in the previous Sung dynasty. Chinese culture, which had managed to absorb the foreign influences of Buddhism, became increasingly conservative and inward-looking.

In Japan, political consolidation began in this period under the Yamato "kings" in the fifth and sixth centuries, a ruling group that had evolved from tribal regional aristocracies. As in early China, an indigenous religious system was part and parcel of their daily lives, aristocratic status, and political authority. From the seventh century, these kings reached out and took in the Chinese model of centralized government. During the Nara and Heian periods — roughly the eighth to twelfth centuries — every aspect of court life was reshaped by Chinese culture and the Buddhist tradition that was also imported from China. Yet the Japanese preserved a separate identity, partly because their language was so different from Chinese and partly because Buddhism tolerated the indigenous Shinto religion in a way that Christianity in Europe did not tolerate Celtic and Germanic cults. During the early ninth century, *samurai* ("those who serve") warriors developed in local areas. Like the knights of feudal Europe, they were responsible for maintaining the local order. During the Kamakura and Ashikaga periods — roughly, the thirteenth to fifteenth centuries — confederations of samurai swept aside the Chinese-type court and established a distinctively Japanese form of government: military rule by shogun. These same centuries were Japan's age of faith, centering on Pure Land and Zen Buddhism.

In Africa, this period witnessed the rise of regional empires. Outside of Islamic north Africa and Egypt, the most prominent ones were those in the western and central Sudan. Most notable was that of ancient Ghana, whose heyday was the late tenth and most of the eleventh century. However, the Kushite empire of Aksum, in the Ethiopian highlands, remained a major power even through the sixth century A.D.; and it survived right through this age as the proud, culturally and religiously distinctive Christian state of Abyssinia, or Ethiopia. Also of note was the remarkable regional culture of Great Zimbabwe, a southeastern African kingdom that held sway in the Zambezi-Limpopo area between about 1000 and 1500. In central and southern Africa, this age is most notable as the key time of the slow but momentous diffusion of Bantu-speaking peoples from northwestern central Africa over most of the African subcontinent. In west and north Africa, the centuries-old trans-Saharan trade routes saw increased commercial traffic, as well as new interchanges in people and ideas.

The gradual penetration of Islamic religion and culture across the Sahara into the Sudanic regions was one prominent feature of the period after 1000. In the same era, east Africa was undergoing even more pronounced Islamization in the development of Swahili civilization. It was also entering ever more prominently into the international trade network of the southern seas, which reached across the Indian Ocean all the way to Indonesia and China. By 1500, much of Africa was firmly caught up in the events and interrelations of the larger global community.

In Iran, a state religion of Zoroastrian orthodoxy and official use of the Middle Persian dialect assisted political centralization during the reign of the Sasanid kings (224–651). The Sasanids further strengthened their rule by international trade and government monopolies on industries like silk and glass. However, their centuries-long conflict with their chief rival, the Byzantine Empire, and the growth of regional nobles' strength so weakened the Sasanid rule that they proved easy prey to the Arab armies of Islam that finally destroyed them. The Persian language and culture developed and nourished under the Sasanids persisted, however, and ultimately greatly enriched the literature, art and architecture, and religious sensibilities of Islamic civilization.

In India, the incursions of Hun peoples in the first half of the sixth century brought to an end the great classical era of Gupta culture and empire. The subsequent millennium saw the caste system solidify, establishing hierarchical divisions within Indian society based on rules regulating the groups with whom one could eat, marry, and work. During these centuries, Hindu tradition gained the general shape it has today. Politically, the end of Gupta empire led to the ascendancy of regional kingdoms. The arrival of Muslim Turks and Afghans after 1000 in north India brought an Islamic political and cultural presence on a scale unknown before. By 1500, Islam was an important part of the Indian scene, putting its architectural as well as its religious and political marks on Indian society.

In the seventh century, the new faith and culture of Islam emerged in Arabia, and in the next two centuries took a variety of forms from Spain to Iran. Muhammad, the proclaimed last in a line of monotheistic prophets, preached a fervent crusade against perceived idolatry, immorality, and injustice in his homeland of western Arabia. Bound by a new supratribal allegiance, his Arab successors carried his crusade abroad, sweeping over most of the Byzantine realms, all of the Persian empire, and into Spain, Central Asia, and the Indus valley within a century. Muslim traders and mystical ("Sufi") brotherhoods spread Muslim faith and culture well beyond the political boundaries of Islam. The influx of Turkish and Mongol peoples in later centuries expanded the political and military presence of Islam still further. Although split into factions, the Islamic community of faith generally opted for unity rather than division and never experienced the regional and sectarian fragmentation that Christendom suffered. Only the Mongol invasions of the thirteenth and fourteenth centuries brought shattering disruption to political order in the Islamic heartlands.

Western Europe survived barbarian and Muslim invasions to create a Christian empire under Carolingian and Merovingian rulers, most notably during the reign of Charlemagne (768–814). Toward the end of this period, Western Europe became through the Crusades an aggressor itself in Byzantium and the Near East. From the start, there was competition between Western rulers and the Christian churches. In the West, the Christian church never became the docile friend of kings and emperors that some Asian and Near Eastern religions were and Orthodox Christianity inclined also to be in the Byzantine Empire. In the West, emperor and pope struggled with each other repeatedly, occasionally to the death. During the twelfth and thirteenth centuries, "national" monarchies emerged in northern Europe, ending any possibility of a unified European empire. Europe henceforth developed as a collection of nation-states that remained politically and culturally diverse and highly competitive.

229

□

EUROPE	NEAR EAST/INDIA
500 A.D.	
511 Death of Clovis, Frankish ruler of Gaul *529* Benedict of Nursia founds Benedictine Order *590–604* Pontificate of Gregory I, "the Great" *768–814* Charles the Great (Charlemagne)	*529* Justinian's *Corpus Juris Civilis* *531–579* Reign of Chosroes Anosharvian *ca. 570–632* Muhammad *622* The Hijra *616–657* Reign of Harsha; neo-Gupta revival in India *651* Death of last Sasanid ruler *ca. 710* first Muslim invasion of India *661–750* Umayyad dynasty; continued expansion of Islam *680* Death of Al-Husayn at Karbala; second civil war begins *730* Iconoclastic Controversy, Byzantine Empire *750–1258* Abbasid Dynasty *786–809* Caliph Harun Al-Rashid reigned
800	
ca. 800–1000 Invasions of England and the Carolingian Empire (Vikings, Magyars, and Muslims) *843* Treaty of Verdun divides Carolingian Empire *910* Cluny Monastery founded *1019–1054* Yaroslav the Wise reigned; peak of Kievan Russia *1054* Schism between Latin and Greek churches *1066* Norman Conquest of England *1073–1085* Investiture Controversy *1096–1270* The Crusades	*800–1200* Period of "feudal" overlordship in India *900–1100* Golden Age of Muslim learning *945–1055* Buyid rule in Baghdad *994–1186* Ghaznavid rule in N.W. India, Afghanistan, and Iran *1055–1194* Seljuk rule in Baghdad *1071* Seljuk Turks capture Jerusalem *1081–1118* Byzantine Emperor Alexius Comnenus reigns *ca. 1000–1300* Turko-Afghan raids into India
1100	
1154–1158 Frederick Barbarosa invades Italy *1182–1226* St. Francis of Assisi *1198–1216* Pontificate of Innocent III *ca. 1100–1300* Growth of trade and towns *1215* Magna Carta granted *ca. 1225–1274* St. Thomas Aquinas *1265–1321* Dante Alighieri	*1174–1193* Saladin reigns *1192* Muslim conquerors end Buddhism in India *1206–1526* Delhi Sultanate in India; Indian culture divided into Hindu and Muslim *ca. 1220* Mongol invasions of Iran, Iraq, Syria, India *1258* Hulagu Khan, Mongol leader conquers Baghdad *1260–1335* Il-Khans rule Iran
1500	
1337 Hundred Years War begins *ca. 1340–1400* Geoffrey Chaucer *1347–1349* The Black Death *1375–1527* The Italian Renaissance *1485* The Battle of Bosworth Field; accession of Henry Tudor to the throne of England *1492* Columbus' first voyage to the New World	*1366–1405* Timur (Tamerlame) reigns *1405–1494* Timurids rule in Transoxiana and Iran *1453* Byzantine Empire falls to the Ottoman Turks, with capture of Constantinople

EAST ASIA	AFRICA	THE AMERICAS
589–618 Sui dynasty reunifies China 607 Japan begins embassies to China 618–907 T'ang dynasty in China 701–762 Li Po, T'ang poet 710–784 Nara court, Japan's first permanent capital 712 Records of Ancient Matters, in Japan 713–756 Emperor Hsuan Tsung reigns in China 755 An Lu-shan Rebellion in China 794–1185 Heian (Kyoto) court in Japan	ca. 500 States of Takrur and Ghana founded ca. 500–700 Political and commercial ascendancy of Aksum (Ethiopia) ca. 600–1500 Extensive slave trade from Sub-Saharan Africa to Mediterranean ca. 700–800 Ghanians begin to supply gold to Mediterranean ca. 700–900 States of Gao and Kanem ca. 800 Appearance of the Kanuri people around Lake Chad	ca. 600–1000 Tiahuanaco civilization in South America
856–1086 Fujiwara dominate at Heian court 960–1279 Sung dynasty in China ca. 1000 Pillow Book by Sei Shōnagon and Tale of Genji by Murasaki Shikibu 1037–1101 Su Tung-p'o, Sung poet	ca. 800–900 Decline of Aksum ca. 900–1100 Kingdom of Ghana; capital city, Kumbi Saleh ca. 1000–1100 Islam penetrates sub-Sahara Africa 1000–1500 "Great Zimbabwe" center of Bantu Kingdom in southeast Africa	800 City of Machu Picchu, Peru 800–1000 "Time of Troubles" in MesoAmerica ca. 900 Second Pueblo Period in American Southwest ca. 1000–1300 Toltic Hegemony in Mexico
1130–1200 Chu Hsi, Sung philosopher 1165–1227 Genghis Khan begins Mongol empire 1185–1333 Kamakura shogunate in Japan 1274, 1281 Mongol invasions of Japan 1279–1368 Mongol (Yuan) dynasty in China	ca. 1100–1897 Kingdom of Benin in tropical rain forest region 1194–1221 Kanem Empire achieves greatest expansion 1203 Kingdom of Ghana falls to Sosso people ca. 1230–1450 Kingdom of Mali 1230–1255 King Sundiata, 1st ruler of Mali Empire; Walata and Timbuktu become centers of trade and culture	ca. 1000–1500 Inca civilization in South America 1100 Third Pueblo Period in American Southwest
1336–1467 Ashikaga shogunate in Kyoto 1368–1644 Ming dynasty in China 1405–1433 Voyages of Cheng Ho to India and Africa 1467–1568 Warring States Era in Japan 1472–1529 Wang Yang-ming, Ming philosopher	1307–1332 Mansa Musa, greatest king of Mali; 1324, makes pilgrimage to Mecca 1490s Europeans establish trading posts on west African coast; slave trade begins mid-1400s Decline of Mali Empire; creation of Songhai Empire 1468 Sonni Ali captures Timbuktu 1476–1507 King Mai Ali of Bornu reigns; Bornu becomes most powerful state in central Sudan 1493–1528 Songhai ruler, Askia Muhammed reigns; consolidates Songhai Empire; 1497, makes pilgrimage to Mecca	ca. 1325 Aztecs arrive in Valley of Mexico 1369 City of Tenochtitlan founded on island in Lake Tezcoco

A rice-paddy scene south of the Yangtze. A farmer and his wife use their legs and feet to work the square-pallet chain pump. At left a boy drives a large water buffalo to turn a larger water-pumping device. Boy in the background fishes. [Bradly Smith/Laurie Platt Winfrey Inc.]

9 Imperial China (589–1368)

If Chinese dynasties from the late sixth to the mid-fourteenth centuries were given numbers like those of ancient Egypt, the Sui and T'ang dynasties would be called the Second Empire; the Sung, the Third; and the Yuan, the Fourth. This would be unfortunate, as each of these dynasties has a distinct personality. The T'ang (618–907) is everyone's favorite dynasty: open, cosmopolitan, expansionist, exuberant, and creative. It was the example of T'ang China that decisively influenced the formation of states and the high cultures in Japan, Korea, and Vietnam. Poetry during the T'ang reached a peak never attained in China before and never equaled since. The Sung (960–1279) rivaled the T'ang in the arts; it was China's great age of painting and was the most significant period for philosophy since the Chou, when Chinese philosophy began. Although not militarily strong, the Sung dynasty also witnessed an important commercial revolution. The Yuan (1279–1368) was a short dynasty of rule by Mongols during which China became the most important unit in the largest empire the world had yet seen.

The Reestablishment of Empire: The Sui (589–618) and T'ang (618–907) Dynasties

In the period corresponding to the European early middle ages, the most notable feature of Chinese history was the reunification of China, the recreation of a centralized bureaucratic empire consciously modeled on the earlier Han dynasty (206 B.C.–A.D. 220). The process of reunification, as usual, began in the north. The first steps were taken by the Northern Wei (386–534), the most enduring of the northern Sino-Turkic states. It moved its court south to Loyang, made Chinese the language of the court, and adopted Chinese

A Sui Dynasty A.D. *589–618 sculpture of the historical Buddha. [Fogg Art Museum, Harvard University.]*

emperors, the officials, and the military commanders of these kingdoms all came from the same stratum of aristocratic families, the social distance between them was small, and the throne was often usurped.

The Sui Dynasty

The general of mixed Chinese-Turkic ancestry, Sui Wen-ti, who came to power in 581 and began the Sui dynasty (589–618) was no exception to this rule. But he displayed great talent, unified the north, restored the tax base, reestablished a centralized bureaucratic government, and went on to conquer south China and unify the country. During his reign, all went well. Huge palaces were built in his Wei valley capital. The Great Wall was rebuilt. The Grand Canal was constructed, linking the Yellow and Yangtze rivers. This canal enabled the northern conquerors to tap the wealth of central China. Peace was maintained with the Turkic tribes along China's northern borders. Eastern Turkic khans (chiefs) were sent Chinese princesses as brides.

The early years of the Second Sui emperor were also constructive, but then, Chinese attempts to meddle in steppe politics led to hostilities and wars. The hardships and loss of Chinese lives in campaigns against Korea and along China's northern border produced rising discontent. Natural disasters occurred. The court became bankrupt and demoralized. Rebellions broke out, and once again, there was a free-for-all among the armies of aristocratic military commanders. The winner, and the founder of the T'ang dynasty, was a relative of the Sui empress and a Sino-barbarian aristocrat of the same social background as those who had ruled before him.

Chinese historians often compare the short Sui dynasty with that of the Ch'in (256–206 B.C.). Each brought all of China under a single government after centuries of disunity. Each did too much, fell, and was replaced by a long dynasty. The T'ang built on the foundations that had been laid by the Sui, just as the Han had built on those of the Ch'in.

The T'ang Dynasty

The first T'ang emperor took over the Sui capital, renamed it Ch'ang-an, and made it his own. Within a decade or so, the T'ang dynasty had extended its authority over all of China; frugality was practiced in government; tax revenues were adequate to government needs; and Chinese armies had begun the campaigns that would push Chinese borders out further than ever before. Confucian scholars were employed at the court, Buddhist temples and monasteries flourished, and peace and order prevailed in the land. The years from 624 to 755 were the good years of the dynasty.

dress and surnames. It also used the leverage of its nomadic cavalry to impose a new land tax, mobilizing resources for state use. The Northern Wei was followed by several short-lived kingdoms. Because the

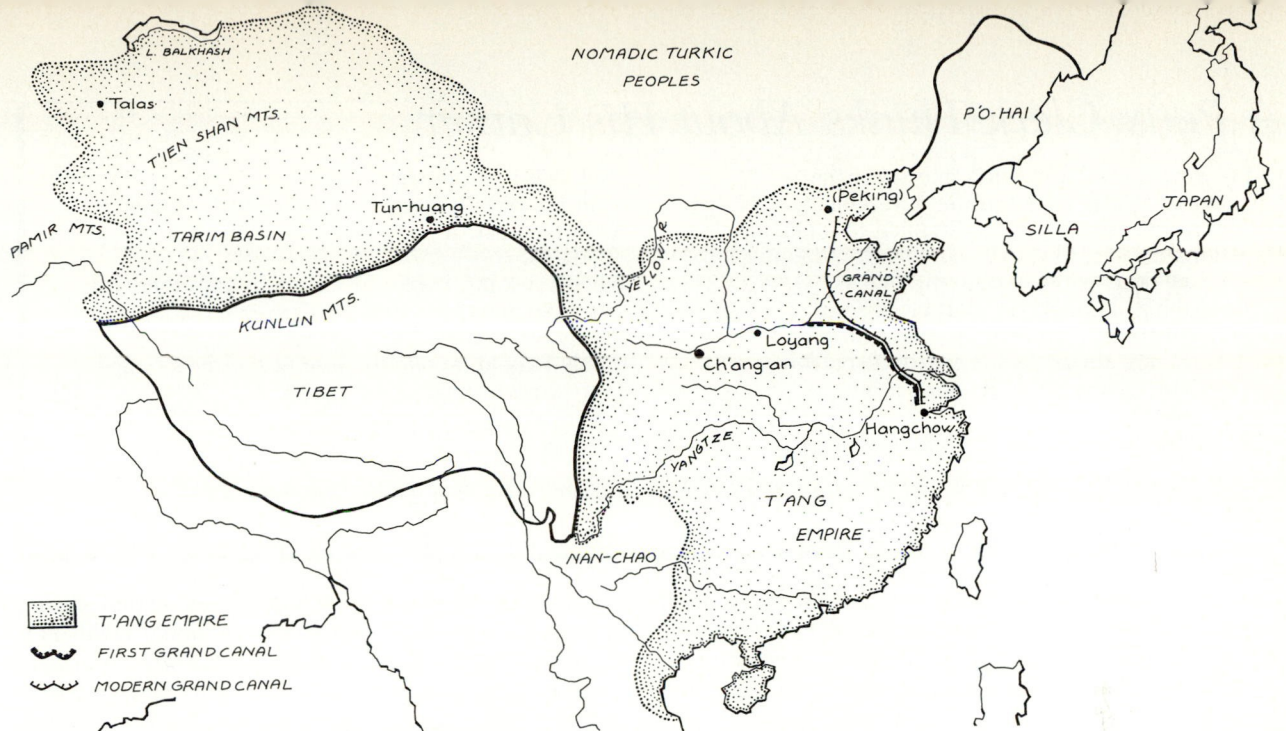

MAP 9-1   THE T'ANG EMPIRE AT ITS PEAK DURING THE EIGHTH CEN-
TURY   *The T'ang Expansion into Central Asia reopened trade routes to the Middle
East and Europe. Students from P'o-Hai, Silla (Korea) and Japan studied in the T'ang
capital of Ch'ang-an, and then returned, carrying with them T'ang books and technology.*

GOVERNMENT. The first T'ang emperor had been
a provincial governor under the Sui before he became
a rebel general. Many of those whom he appointed to
posts in the new T'ang administration were former Sui
officials who had served with him. In building the new
administration, he and his successors had to reconcile
two conflicting sets of interests. On the one hand, the
emperor wanted a bureaucratic government in which
authority was centralized in his own person. On the
other hand, he had to make concessions to the aristocrats—the dominant elements in Chinese society since
the late Han—who staffed his government and continued to dominate early T'ang society.

The degree to which political authority was centralized was apparent in the formal organization of the
bureaucracy, at right.

At the highest level were three organs: Military Affairs, the Censorate, and the Council of State. Military
Affairs supervised the T'ang armies, with the emperor,
in effect, the commander-in-chief. The Censorate had
watchdog functions: It reported instances of misgovernment directly to the emperor and could also remon-
strate with the emperor when his behavior was improper. The Council of State was the most important
body. It met daily with the emperor and was made up
of the heads of the Secretariat, which drafted policies;
the Chancellery, which reviewed them; and State Af-

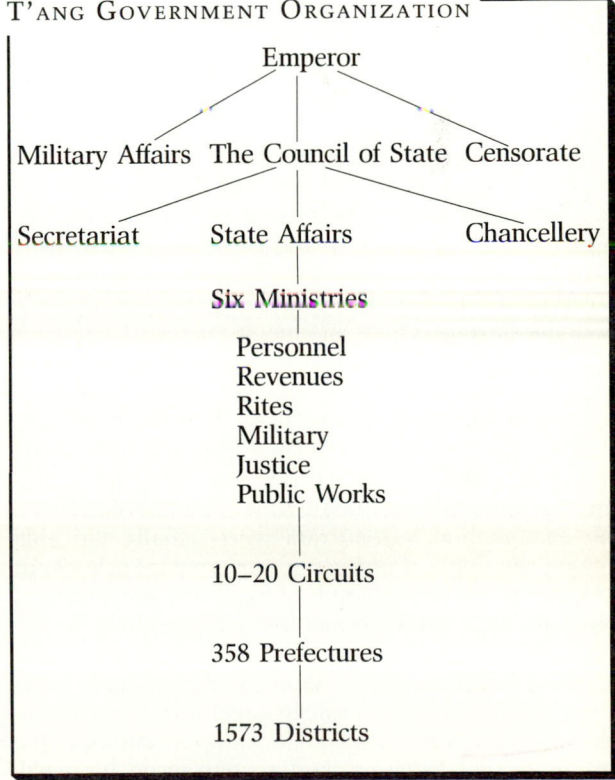

T'ANG GOVERNMENT ORGANIZATION

Emperor

Military Affairs   The Council of State   Censorate

Secretariat   State Affairs   Chancellery

Six Ministries

Personnel
Revenues
Rites
Military
Justice
Public Works

10–20 Circuits

358 Prefectures

1573 Districts

A Petty Clerk Thinks About His Career

I'm not so poor at reports and decisions—
Why can't I get ahead in the government?
The rating officials are determined to make life
  hard.
All they do is try to expose my faults.
Everything, I guess, is a matter of Fate;
Still, I'll try the exam again this year.
A blind boy aiming at the eye of a sparrow
Might just accidentally manage a hit.

In vain I slaved to understand the Three Histories;

Uselessly I pored over the Five Classics.
Until I'm old I'll go on checking census figures;
As in the past, a petty clerk scribbling in tax
  ledgers.
When I ask the Book of Changes it says there's
  trouble ahead;
All my life is ruled by evil stars.
If only I could be like the tree at the river's edge
Every year turning green again! ❑

Cold Mountains: 100 Poems by Han-shan, trans. by B. Watson (New York, Grove Press, 1962), pp. 37, 48.

---

fairs, which carried them out. Beneath State Affairs were the Six Ministries, which continued as the core of the central government down to the twentieth century; beneath these were the several levels of local administration.

Concessions to the interests of the aristocratic families were embodied in the tax system. All land was declared to be the property of the emperor, and was then redistributed to able-bodied cultivators, who paid taxes in labor and grain. Since all able-bodied adult males received an equal allotment of land (women and children got less), the land tax system was called the "Equal Field System." But the system was not egalitarian. Aristocrats enjoyed special exemptions and grants of "rank" and "office" lands that, in effect, confirmed their estate holdings.

Aristocrats were also favored in the recruiting of officials. Most officials were either recommended for posts or received posts because their fathers had been high officials. They were drawn almost exclusively from the aristocracy, at first from the northwestern aristocratic families that had supported the dynasty from the start, and then, in time, from the aristocracies of other areas. Only a tiny per cent were recruited by examinations. Those who passed the examinations had the highest prestige and were more likely to have brilliant careers. But as only well-to-do families could afford the years of study needed to master the Confucian classics and pass the rigorous examinations, even the examination bureaucrats were usually the able among the noble. Entrance to government schools at Ch'ang-an and the secondary capital at Loyang was restricted to the sons of nobles and officials.

THE EMPRESS WU. Women of the inner court also continued to play a role in government. For example, Wu Chao (626—CA. 706), a young concubine of the strong second emperor, had so entranced his weak heir by her charms that when he succeeded to the throne, she was recalled from the nunnery to which all the former wives of deceased emperors were routinely consigned and was installed at the court. She poisoned or otherwise removed her rivals and became his empress. She also murdered or exiled the statesmen who opposed her growing influence. When the emperor suffered a stroke in 660, she completely dominated the court. After his death in 683, she ruled for seven years as regent and then, deposing her son, became emperor herself, the only woman in Chinese history to hold the title. She moved the court to Loyang in her native area and proclaimed a new dynasty. A fervent Buddhist with an interest in magic, she saw herself as the incarnation of the Buddha Maitreya and built temples throughout the land. She patronized the White Horse Monastery, appointing one of her favorites as its abbot. Her sexual appetites were said to have been prodigious. She ruled China until 705, when at the age of eighty she lost her hold and was deposed.

After Empress Wu, no woman would ever become emperor again; yet, remarkably enough, her machinations do not appear to have seriously weakened the court. So highly centralized was power during these early years of the dynasty that the ill effects of her intrigues could be absorbed without provinces' breaking away or military commanders' becoming autonomous. In fact, a by-product of her struggle for power may have been a stronger central government, for, to overcome the old northwest China aristocrats, she turned not to members of her family but to the products of the examination system and to a group known as the Scholars of the North Gate. This policy broadened the base of government by bringing in aristocrats from other regions of China. The dynamism of a young dynasty may also explain why her rule coincided with the maximal geographical expansion of T'ang military power.

THE CH'ANG-AN OF EMPEROR HSUAN-TSUNG.

Only a few years after Empress Wu was deposed—years filled with tawdry intrigues— Hsuan-tsung came to the throne. In reaction to Empress Wu, he appointed special government commissions headed by distinguished aristocrats to superintend the reform of government finances. Examination bureaucrats lost ground during his reign. The Grand Canal was repaired and extended. A new census extended the tax rolls. Wealth and prosperity returned to the court. Hsuan-tsung's reign (713–756) was also the most brilliant culturally. Years later, while in exile, Li Po wrote a poem in which memories of youthful exhilaration merged with the glory of the capital of Hsuan-tsung:

Long ago, among the flowers and willows,
We sat drinking together at Ch'ang-an.
The Five Barons and Seven Grandees were of our
  company,
But when some wild stroke was afoot
It was we who led it, yet boisterous though we were
In the arts and graces of life we could hold our own
With any dandy in the town—
In the days when there was youth in your cheeks
And I was still not old.
We galloped to the brothels, cracking our gilded whips,
We sent in our writings to the palace of the Unicorn,
Girls sang to us and danced hour by hour on tortoise-
  shell mats.
We thought, you and I, that it would be always like
  this.
How should we know the grasses would stir and dust
  rise on the wind?
Suddenly foreign horsemen were at the Hsien-ku Pass
Just when the blossom at the palace of Ch'in was
  opening on the sunny boughs. . . .[1]

Ch'ang-an was an imperial city, an administrative city that lived on taxes. It was designed to exhibit the power of the emperor and the majesty of his court. At the far north of the city, the palace faced south. The placement was traditional: Confucius, speaking of Shun, said he had only "to hold himself in a respectful posture and to face due south." In front of the palace was a complex of government offices, from which an imposing 500-foot-wide avenue led to the main southern gate. The city was laid out on a north-south, east-west grid, which one T'ang poet compared to a chessboard. Each block of the city was administered as a ward with interior streets and gates that were locked at night. Enclosed by great walls, the area of the city was 30 square miles. Its population was 1,960,186—half within the walls, the other half in suburbs—the

largest city in the world. (The population of China in the year 750 was about 50 million—less than 5 per cent of its population today.) Ch'ang-an was also a trade center from which caravans set out across central Asia. Merchants from India, Iran, Syria, and Arabia hawked the wares of the Near East and all of Asia in its two government-controlled markets.

THE T'ANG EMPIRE.

A Chinese dynasty is like an accordion, first expanding into the territories of its barbarian neighbors and then contracting back to its original densely populated core area. The principal threats to the T'ang state were from Tibetans in the west, Turks in the northwest and north, and Khitan Mongols in Manchuria.

Toward these peoples, the T'ang employed a four-tier policy. When nothing else would work, the T'ang sent armies. But armies were expensive, and using them against nomads was like sweeping back an ocean tide with a broom. A victory might dissolve a confederation, but a decade or two later, it would reappear under a new tribal leader. For example, in 630, T'ang armies defeated the eastern Turks' in 648, they took the Tarim basin, opening trade routes to western Asia for almost a century; and in 657, they defeated the western Turks and extended Chinese influence across the Pamir Mountains to petty states near Samarkand. By 698, however, the Turks were back invading northeast China, and between 711 and 736, they were in control of all of the steppe from the Oxus River to China's northern frontier.

Chinese efforts against Tibet were much the same. From 670, Tibet expanded and threatened China. In 679, it was defeated. In 714, it rose again; wars were fought from 727 to 729; and a settlement was reached in 730. But wars broke out anew. In 752, Tibet entered an alliance with the state of Nan Chao in Yunnan. In 763, Tibetan forces captured and looted Ch'ang-an. They were driven out, but the point is that even during the good years of the T'ang, no final victory was possible.

The human costs of sending armies far afield was detailed in a poem by Li Po:

Last year we were fighting at the source of the Sang-
  kan;
This year we are fighting on the Onion River road.
We have washed our swords in the surf of Parthian
  seas;
We have pastured our horses among the snows of the
  T'ien Shan,
The King's armies have grown grey and old
Fighting ten thousand leagues away from home.
The Huns have no trade but battle and carnage;
They have no fields or ploughlands,

---

[1] Arthur Waley, *The Poetry and Career of Li Po* (New York: Macmillan, 1950), pp. 87–88.

A bearded "barbarian" groom tends the charger of the second T'ang emperor (reigned 626–649). This stone relief was found on the Emperor's tomb. Note the stirrup, a Chinese invention of the fourth century A.D. *[University of Pennsylvania Museum.]*

But only wastes where white bones lie among yellow
   sands.
Where the House of Ch'in built the great wall that was
   to keep away the Tartars.
There, in its turn, the House of Han lit beacons of
   war.
The beacons are always alight, fighting and marching
   never stop.
Men die in the field, slashing sword to sword;
The horses of the conquered neigh piteously to
   Heaven.
Crows and hawks peck for human guts,
Carry them in their beaks and hang them on the
   branches of withered trees.
Captains and soldiers are smeared on the bushes and
   grass;

The General schemed in vain.
Know therefore that the sword is a cursed thing
Which the wise man uses only if he must.[2]

    The second tier of Chinese defenses was to use nomads against other nomads. The critical development for the T'ang was the rise to power of the Uighur Turks. From 744 to 840, the Uighurs controlled Central Asia and were staunch allies of the T'ang. Without their support, the T'ang dynasty would not have survived as long as it did.
    A third tier was the defenses along China's borders, including the Great Wall. At mid-dynasty, whole fron-

[2]Waley, pp. 34–35.

tier provinces in the north and the northwest were put under military commanders who, in time, came to control the provinces' civil governments as well. The bulk of the T'ang military was in such frontier commands. At times, they were as much a threat to the T'ang as to the enemy.

Diplomacy is always cheaper than war. The fourth line of defense was to bring the potential enemy into the empire as a tributary. The T'ang defined the position of "tributary" with great elasticity. It included principalities truly dependent on China; central Asian states conquered by China; enemy states such as Tibet or the Thai state of Nan Chao in Yunnan when they were not actually at war with China; the Korean state Silla, which had unified the peninsula with T'ang aid but had then fought T'ang armies to a standstill when they attempted to impose Chinese hegemony; and wholly independent states such as Japan. All sent embassies bearing gifts to the T'ang court, which housed and fed them and sent costly gifts in return.

For some countries, these embassies had a special significance. As the only "developed nation" in eastern Asia, China was a model for countries still in the throes of forming a state. An embassy gained access to the entire range of T'ang culture and technology: its

philosophy and writing, governmental and land systems, Buddhism and the arts, architecture and medicine. In 640 there were eight thousand Koreans, mostly students, in Ch'ang-an. Never again would China exert such an influence, for never again would its neighbors be at that formative stage of development.

REBELLION AND DECLINE. From the mid-eighth century, signs of decline began to appear. China's frontiers started to contract. Tribes in Manchuria became unruly. Tibetans threatened China's western border. In 751, an overextended T'ang army led by a Korean general was defeated by Arabs near Samarkand in western Asia, shutting down China's caravan trade with the West for more than five centuries. And then, in 755, a Sogdian general, An Lu-shan, who commanded three Chinese provinces on the northeastern frontier, led his 160,000 troops in a rebellion that swept across north China, capturing Loyang and then Ch'ang-an. The emperor fled to Szechwan.

The event contained an element of romance. Ten years earlier, the emperor Hsuan-tsung had taken a young woman, Yang Kuei Fei, from the harem of his son (he gave his son another in exchange). So infatuated was he that he neglected not only the other "three

Pottery figures of court ladies playing polo, seventh century, T'ang dynasty. After the T'ang, for over a millennium, participation in athletic contests was considered unfeminine. [W.R. Nelson Trust.]

thousand beauties of his inner chambers" but the business of government as well. For a while his neglect did not matter because he had an able chief minister, but when the minister died, he appointed his concubine's second cousin to the post, initiating a train of events that resulted in rebellion. En route to Szechwan, his soldiers, blaming Yang Kuei Fei for their plight, strangled her. The event was later immortalized in a poem that described her "snow-white skin," "flowery face," and "moth eyebrows," as well as the "eternal sorrow" of the emperor, who, in fact, was seventy-two at the time.

After a decade of wars and much devastation, a new emperor restored the dynasty with the help of the Uighur Turks—who looted Ch'ang-an as a part of their reward. The recovery and the century of relative peace and prosperity that followed illustrate the resilience of T'ang institutions. China was smaller, but military governors maintained the diminished frontiers. Provincial governors were more autonomous, but taxes were still sent to the capital. Occasional rebellions were suppressed by imperial armies, sometimes led by eunuchs. Most of the emperors were weak, but three times strong emperors appeared, and reforms were carried out. Edwin O. Reischauer, after translating the diary of a Japanese monk who studied in China during the early ninth century, commented that the "picture of government in operation" that emerges "is amazing for the ninth century, even in China":

The remarkable degree of centralized control still existing, the meticulous attention to written instructions from higher authorities, and the tremendous amount of paper work involved in even the smallest matters of administration are all the more striking just because this was a period of dynastic decline.[3]

Of the reforms of this era, none was more important than that of the land system. The official census, on which land allotments and taxes were based, showed a drop in population from fifty-three million before the An Lu-shan rebellion to seventeen million afterward. Unable to put people back on the registers, the government abandoned the equal field system and replaced it with a tax collected twice a year. The new system, begun in 780, lasted until the sixteenth century. Under it, a fixed quota of taxes was levied on each province. After the An Lu-shan rebellion, government revenues from salt and iron surpassed those from land.

During the second half of the ninth century, the government weakened further. Most provinces were autonomous, often under military commanders, and re-

[3]E. O. Reischauer, *Ennin's Travels in T'ang China* (New York: Ronald Press, 1955), p. 7.

sisted central control. Wars were fought with the state of Nan Chao in the southwest. Bandits appeared. Droughts led to peasant uprisings. By the 880s, warlords had carved all of China into independent kingdoms, and in 907, the T'ang dynasty fell. But within half a century, a new dynasty arose. The fall of the T'ang did not lead to centuries of division of the kind that had followed the Han. Something had changed within China.

T'ANG CULTURE. The creativity of the T'ang period arose from the juxtaposition and interaction of cosmopolitan, medieval Buddhist and secular elements. The rise of each of these cultural spheres was rooted in the wealth and the social order of the recreated empire.

T'ang culture was cosmopolitan not just because of its broad contacts with other cultures and peoples but because of its openness to them. Buddhist pilgrims to India and a flow of Indian art and philosophies to China were a part of it. The voluptuousness of Indian painting and sculpture, for example, helped shape the T'ang representation of the bodhisattva. Commercial contacts were widespread. Foreign goods were vended in Ch'ang-an marketplaces. Communities of central and west Asians were established in the capital, and Arab and Iranian quarters grew up in the seaports of southeast China. Merchants brought their religions with them. Nestorian Christianity, Zoroastrianism, Manichaeism, Judaism, and Islam entered China at this time. Most would be swept away in the persecutions of the ninth century, but Islam and a few small pockets of Judaism survived until the twentieth century.

Central Asian music and musical instruments entered along the trade routes and became so popular as almost to displace the native tradition. T'ang ladies adopted foreign hairstyles. Foreign dramas and acrobatic performances by west Asians could be seen in the streets of the capital. Even among the pottery figurines customarily placed in tombs, there were representations of west Asian traders and central Asian grooms—along with those of horses, camels, and court ladies that today are so avidly sought by collectors and museums around the world. And in T'ang poetry, too, what was foreign was not shunned but judged on its own merits, or even presented as exotically attractive. Of a gallant of Ch'ang-an, Li Po wrote:

A young man of Five Barrows suburb east of the
  Golden Market,
Silver saddle and white horse cross through wind of
  spring.
When fallen flowers are trampled all under, where is it
  he will roam?

With a laugh he enters the tavern of a lovely Turkish wench.[4]

Later in the dynasty, another poet wrote of service on the frontier:

A Tartar horn tugs at the north wind,
Thistle Gate shines whiter than the stream.
The sky swallows the road to Kokonor.
On the Great Wall, a thousand miles of moonlight.[5]

The T'ang dynasty, though slightly less an age of faith than the preceding Six Dynasties, was the golden age of Buddhism in China nonetheless. Patronized by emperors and aristocrats, the Buddhist establishment acquired vast landholdings and great wealth. Temples and monasteries were constructed throughout China. To gain even an inkling of the beauty and sophistication of the temple architecture, the wooden sculpture, or the paintings on the temple walls, one must see Hōryūji or the ancient temples of Nara in Japan, for little of note has survived in China. The single exception is the Caves of the Thousand Buddhas at Tunhuang in China's far northwest, which were sealed during the eleventh century for protection from Tibetan raiders and were not rediscovered until the start of the twentieth century. They were found to contain stone sculptures, Buddhist frescoes, and thousands of manuscripts in Chinese and central Asian languages.

Only during the T'ang did China have a "church" establishment that was at all comparable to that of medieval Europe, and even then it was subservient to the far stronger T'ang state. Buddhist wealth and learning brought with it secular functions. T'ang temples served as schools, inns, or even bathhouses. They lent money. Priests performed funerals and dispensed medicines. Occasionally, the state moved to recapture the revenues monopolized by temples. The severest persecution, which marked a turn in the fortunes of Buddhism in China, occurred in 841–845, when an ardent Taoist emperor confiscated millions of acres of tax-exempt lands, put back on the tax registers 260,000 monks and nuns, and destroyed 4,600 monasteries and 40,000 shrines.

During the early T'ang, the principal Buddhist sect was the T'ien-t'ai, but after the mid-ninth century suppression, other sects came to the fore:

1. One devotional sect focused on Maitreya, a Buddha of the future, who will appear and create a par-

This pottery figurine from a mid-T'ang dynasty tomb depicts a Bactrian camel from west-central Asia. [Asian Art Museum of San Francisco.]

adise on earth. Maitreya (*Mi Lo* in Chinese and *Miroku* in Japanese) was a cosmic messiah, not a human figure. The messianic teachings of the sect often furnished the ideology for popular uprisings and rebellions like the White Lotus, which claimed that it was renewing the world in anticipation of Maitreya's coming.

2. Another devotional or faith sect worshiped the Amitabha (*A Mi T'o* in Chinese, *Amida* in Japanese) Buddha, the Lord of the Western Paradise or Pure Land. This sect taught that in the early centuries after the death of the historical Buddha, his teachings had been transmitted properly and people could obtain enlightenment by their own efforts, but that at present, the Buddha's teachings had become so distorted that only by reliance on Amitabha could humans obtain salvation. All who called on Amitabha with a pure heart and perfect faith would be saved. Developing a congregational form of worship, this sect became the largest in China and deeply influenced Chinese popular religion.

[4]S. Owen, *The Great Age of Chinese Poetry: The High T'ang* (New Haven, Conn.: Yale University Press, 1980), p. 130.
[5]A. C. Graham, *Poems of the Late T'ang* (Baltimore: Penguin, 1965), p. 9.

Stone sculpture of a Bodhisattva reflecting the full-bodied, almost voluptuous, T'ang ideal of beauty. [Bettman Archive.]

3. A third sect, and the most influential among the Chinese elites, was known in China, where it began, as *Ch'an* and is better known in the West by its Japanese name, *Zen.* Zen had no cosmic Buddhas. It taught that the historical Buddha was only a man and exhorted each person to attain enlightenment by his or her own efforts. Although its monks were often the most learned in China, Zen was anti-intellectual in its emphasis on direct intuition into one's own Buddha-nature. Enlightenment was to be obtained by a regimen of physical labor and meditation. To jolt the monk into enlightenment—after he had been readied by long hours of meditation—some Zen sects used little problems not answerable by normal ratiocination: "What was your face before you were conceived?" "If all things return to the One, what does the One return to?" "From the top of a hundred-foot pole, how do you step forward?" The psychological state of the adept attempting to deal with these problems is compared to that of "a rat pursued into a blocked pipe" or "a mosquito biting an iron ball." The discipline of meditation, combined with a Zen view of nature, profoundly influenced the arts in China, and subsequently in Korea and Japan as well.

A third characteristic of T'ang culture was the reappearance within it of secular scholarship and letters. The reestablishment of centralized bureaucratic government stimulated the tradition of learning that had been partially interrupted after the fall of the Han dynasty in the third century A.D. There emerged a scholarly-bureaucratic complex. Most men of letters, whether historians, essayists, artists, or poets, were

The T'ang poet Li Po, as imagined by the great Sung artist Liang K'ai [Tokyo National Museum.]

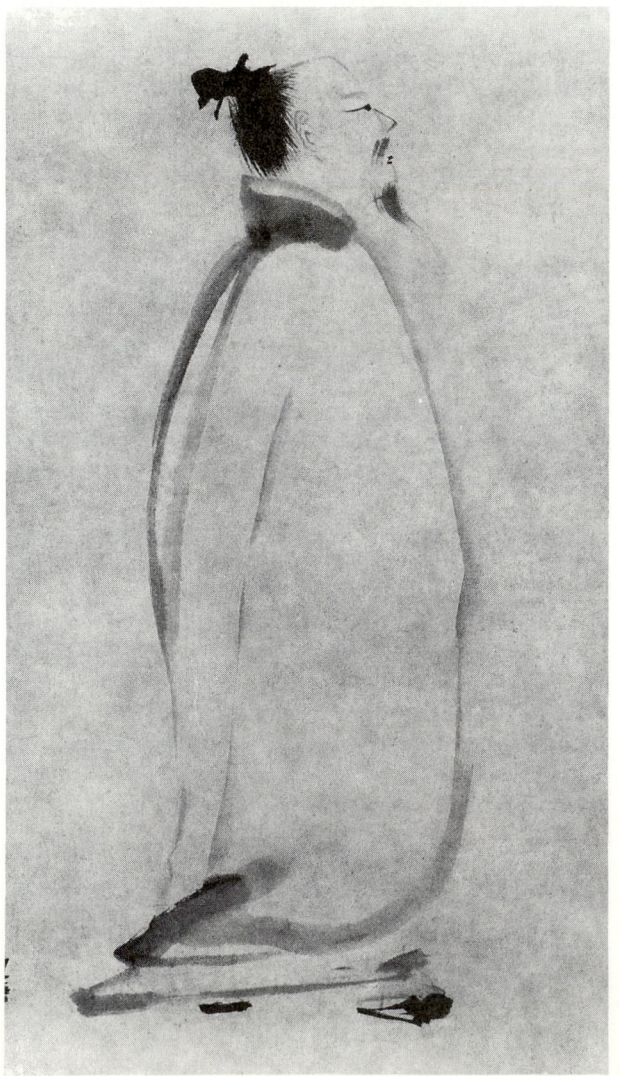

Poems by Li Po

THE RIVER MERCHANT'S WIFE:
A LETTER

While my hair was still cut straight across my
    forehead
I played about the front gate, pulling flowers.
You came by on bamboo stilts, playing horse,
You walked about my seat, playing with blue plums.
And we went on living in the village of Chokan:
Two small people, without dislike or suspicion.

At fourteen I married My Lord you.
I never laughed, being bashful.
Lowering my head, I looked at the wall.
Called to, a thousand times, I never looked back.

At fifteen I stopped scowling,
I desired my dust to be mingled with yours
Forever and forever and forever.
Why should I climb the look out?

At sixteen you departed,
You went into far Ku-to-yen, by the river of swirling
    eddies,
And you have been gone five months.
The monkeys make sorrowful noise overhead.

You dragged your feet when you went out.
By the gate now, the moss is grown, the different
    mosses,
Too deep to clear them away!
The leaves fall early this autumn, in wind.
The paired butterflies are already yellow with
    August
Over the grass in the West garden;
They hurt me. I grow older.
If you are coming down through the narrows of the
    river Kiang,
Please let me know beforehand,
And I will come out to meet you,   ❑
            As far as Cho-fu-Sa.

Ezra Pound, Personae (New York: New Directions 1926), pp. 130–131.

also officials, and most high-ranking officials painted or wrote poems. An anthology of T'ang poetry compiled during the Ming period contained 48,900 poems by almost 2,300 authors. This secular stream of T'ang culture was not ideologically anti-Buddhist. Officials were often privately sympathetic to Buddhism. But as men involved in the affairs of government, officials became increasingly this-worldly in their values.

Court historians of the T'ang revived the Han practice of writing an official history of the previous dynasty. For the first time, scholars wrote comprehensive institutional histories and regional and local gazetteers. They compiled dictionaries and wrote commentaries on the Confucian classics. Other scholars wrote ghost stories or tales of adventure, using the literary language. (Buddhist sermons, in contrast, were often written in the vernacular.) More paintings were Buddhist than secular, but Chinese landscape painting had its origins during the T'ang. But nowhere was the growth of a secular culture more evident than in poetry, the greatest achievement of T'ang letters.

Whether Li Po (701–762) can be called wholly secular is questionable. He might better be called Taoist. But he clearly was not Buddhist. Born in Szechwan, he was exceptional among T'ang poets in never having sat for the civil service examinations, though he briefly held an official post at Ch'ang-an, given in recognition of his poetry. Large and muscular, he was a swordsman and a carouser. Of the twenty thousand poems he is said to have composed, eighteen hundred have survived, and a fair number have titles like "Bring on the Wine" or "Drinking Alone in the Moonlight." According to legend, he drowned while drunkenly attempting to embrace the reflection of the moon in a lake. His poetry is clear, powerful, passionate, and always sensitive to beauty. It also contains a sense of fantasy, as when he climbed a mountain and saw a star-goddess, "stepping in emptiness, pacing pure ether, her rainbow robes trailed broad sashes." Li Po, nearer to heaven than to earth, looked down below where

Far and wide Tartar troops were speeding,
And flowing blood mired the wild grasses
Where wolves and jackals all wore officials' caps.[6]

Life is brief and the universe is large, but this view did not lead Li Po to renounce the world. His Taoism was not of the quietistic strain close to Buddhism. Rather, he exulted, identifying with the primal flux of *yin* and *yang*:

I'll wrap this Mighty Mudball of a world all
    up in a bag
And be wild and free like Chaos itself![7]

[6]Owen, p. 134.
[7]Owen, p. 125.

Tu Fu (712–770), an equally famous T'ang poet, was from a literary family. He failed the metropolitan examination at the age of twenty-three and spent years in wandering and poverty. At thirty-nine, he received an official appointment after presenting his poetry to the court. Four years later, he was appointed to a military post. He fell into rebel hands during the An Lu-shan rebellion, escaped, and was reappointed to a civil post. But he was then dismissed and suffered further hardships. His poetry is less lyrical and more allusive than Li Po's. It also reflects more compassion for human suffering: for the mother whose sons have been conscripted and sent to war; for brothers scattered by war; for his own family, to whom he returned after having been given up for dead. Like Li Po, he felt that humans are short-lived and that nature endures. Visiting the ruins of the palace of the second T'ang emperor, he saw "Grey rats scuttling over ancient tiles" and "in its shadowed chambers ghost fires green." "Its lovely ladies are the brown soil" and only "tomb horses of stone remain." But his response to this sad scene was to

Sing wildly, let the tears cover your open hands.
Then go every onward and on the road of your travels,
Meet none who prolong their fated years.[8]

His response was unlike that of Li Po. It was close to Stoicism but it was equally un-Buddhist.

The Transition to Late Imperial China: The Sung Dynasty (960–1279)

Most traditional Chinese history was written in terms of the dynastic cycle, and for good reason: the pattern of rise and fall, of expansion and contraction, within each dynasty cannot be denied. Certainly, the Sung can be viewed from this perspective. It reunified China in 960, establishing its capital at Kaifeng on the Yellow River. Mobilizing its resources effectively, it ruled for 170 years. This period is called the Northern Sung. Then it weakened. In 1127, it lost the north, but continued to rule the south for another 150 years from a new capital at Hangchow in east central China. The Southern Sung fell before the Mongol onslaught in 1279.

But there is more to Chinese history than the inner logic of the dynastic cycle. Longer-term changes that cut across dynastic lines were ultimately more important. One such set of changes began during the late T'ang period and continued on into the Sung period,

MAP 9-2 *During the Northern Sung the Mongol Liao dynasty ruled only the extreme northern edge of China. But during the Southern Sung, half of China was ruled by the Manchurian Chin dynasty.*

THE NORTHERN SUNG AND LIAO EMPIRES—CA. A.D. 1050

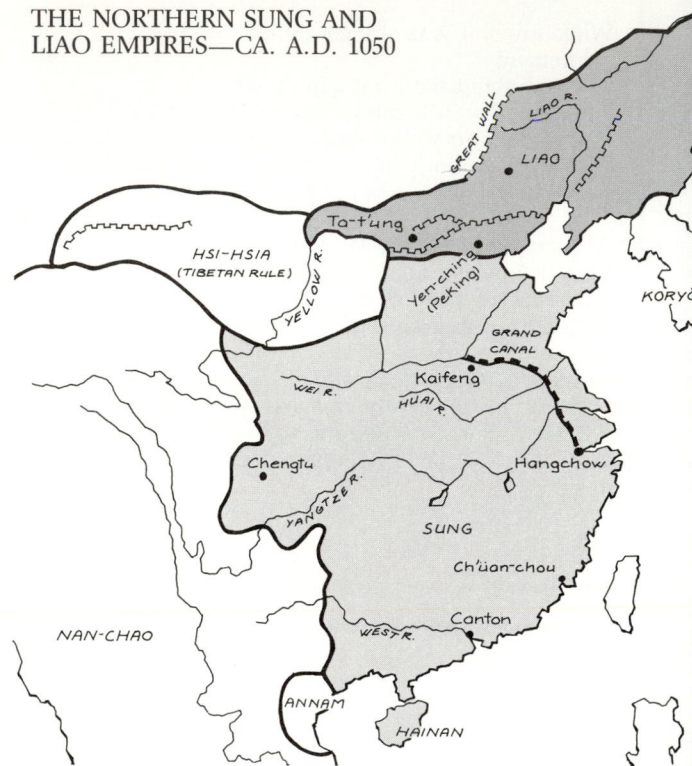

THE SOUTHERN SUNG AND CHIN EMPIRES—CA. A.D. 1150

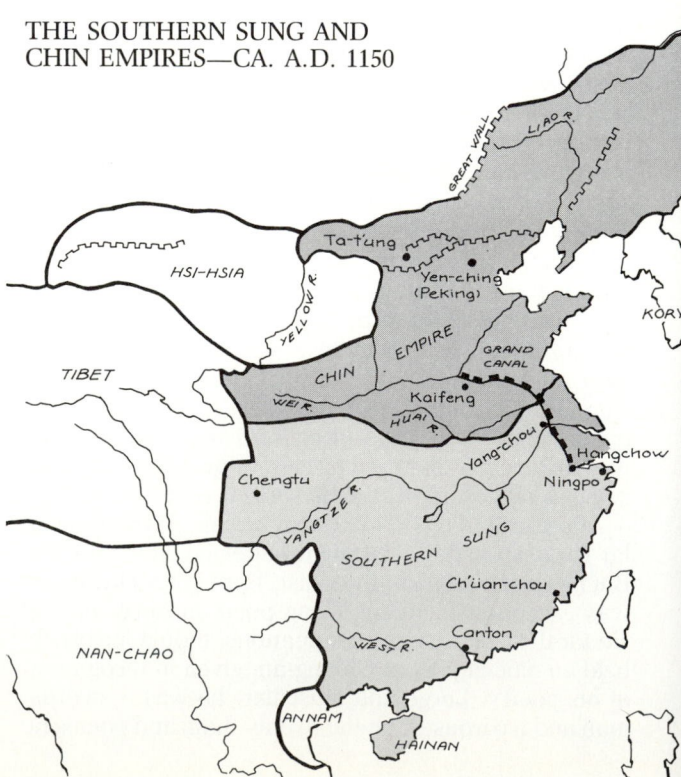

[8] Owen, pp. 223–224.

affecting its economy, society, state, and culture. Taken together, these changes help to explain why China after the T'ang did not relapse into centuries of disunity as it had after the Han, and why China would never again experience more than brief intervals of disunity. In this section, we will skip over emperors and empresses, eunuchs and generals, and focus instead on more fundamental transformations.

The Agricultural Revolution of the Sung: From Serfs to Free Farmers

Local society in China during the Sui and the T'ang periods had been dominated by landed aristocrats. The tillers of their lands were little more than serfs. Labor service was the heaviest tax, and whether performed on the office or rank lands of aristocrats or on other government lands, it created conditions of social subordination.

The aristocracy weakened, however, over the course of the T'ang and after its fall. Estates became smaller as they were divided among male children at each change of generation. Drawn to the capital, the aristocracy became less a landed, and more a metropolitan, elite. And after the fall of the T'ang, the aristocratic estates were often seized by warlords. As the aristocracy declined, the claims of those who worked the soil grew stronger, aided by changes in the land and tax systems. With the collapse of the equal field system (described earlier), farmers gained the right to buy and sell land. The ownership of land as private property gave the cultivators greater independence. They could now move about as they pleased. Taxes paid in grain gave way during the Sung to taxes in money. The commutation of the labor tax to a money tax gave the farmers more control over their own time. And conscription, the cruelest and heaviest labor tax of all, disappeared as the conscript armies of the early and middle T'ang gave way to professional armies.

Changes in technology also benefited the cultivator. New strains of an early-ripening rice permitted double cropping. In the Yangtze region, extensive water-control projects were carried out, and more fertilizers were used. New commercial crops were developed. Tea, which had been introduced during the Six Dynasties as a medicine and had been drunk by monks during the T'ang, became widely cultivated, and cotton also became a common crop. Because taxes paid in money tended to become fixed, much of the increased productivity accrued to the cultivator. Of course, not all benefited equally; there were landlords and landless tenants as well as independent small farmers.

The disappearance of the aristocrats also increased the authority of the district magistrate, who no longer had to contend with the aristocrats' interference in local affairs. The Sung magistrate became the sole representative of imperial authority in local society. But there were too many villages in his district for him to be involved regularly in their internal governance. As long as taxes were paid and order was maintained, the affairs of the village were left in the hands of the village elites. So the Sung farmer enjoyed not only a rising income and more freedom, but also a substantial measure of self-government.

One other development that began during the Sung— and became vastly more important later on—was the appearance of a scholar-gentry class. The typical gentry family contained at least one member who had passed the provincial civil-service examination and lived in the district seats or market towns. Socially and culturally, these gentry were closer to magistrates than to villagers. But they usually owned land in the villages and thus shared some interests with the local landholders. Though much less powerful than the former aristocrats, they took a hand in local affairs and at times functioned as a buffer between the village and the magistrate's office.

The Commercial Revolution of the Sung

Stimulated by changes in the countryside, and contributing to them as well, were demographic shifts, innovative technologies, the growth of cities, the spread of money, and rising trade. These developments varied by region, but overall the Sung economy reached a new level of prosperity.

THE EMERGENCE OF THE YANGTZE BASIN. Till late in the T'ang, north China had been the most populous and productive region. But from the late ninth century, the center of gravity of China's population, agricultural production, and culture shifted to the lower and eastern Yangtze region. Between 800 and 1100, the population of the region tripled as China's total population increased to about 100 million. Its rice paddies yielded more per acre than the wheat or millet fields of the north, making rice the tax base of the empire. Its wealth led to the establishment of so many schools that regional quotas for the examination system were set by the government to prevent the Yangtze region from dominating all of China. The Northern Sung capital itself was kept in the north for strategic reasons, but it was situated at Kaifeng, further east than Loyang, at the point where the Grand Canal, which carried tax rice from the south, joined the Yellow River.

NEW TECHNOLOGY. During the Northern Sung, there developed in north China a coal and ironsmelting industry that provided China with better tools and weapons. Using coke and bellows to heat furnaces to the temperatures required for carbonized steel, it was the most advanced in the world.

Printing began in China with the use of carved seals. The earliest woodblock texts, mostly on Buddhist subjects, appeared in the seventh century. By the tenth century, a complete edition of the classics had been published, and by the mid-Sung, books printed with movable type were fairly common.

Other advances during the Sung were the abacus, the use of gunpowder in grenades and projectiles, and improvements in textiles and porcelains.

THE RISE OF A MONEY ECONOMY. Exchange during the T'ang had been based on silk. Coins had been issued, but their circulation was limited. During the Northern Sung, large amounts of copper cash were coined, but the demand rose more rapidly than the supply. Coins were made with holes in the center, and 1,000 on a string constituted the usual unit for large transactions. Beginning in the Southern Sung, silver was minted to complement copper cash, ten times as much silver in the late twelfth century as in the early eleventh century. Letters of credit were used by merchants, and various kinds of paper money also were issued. The penetration of money into the village economy was such that by 1065, tax receipts paid in money had risen to thirty-eight million strings of cash—in comparison with a mere two million in mid-T'ang.

TRADE. The demand for money was spurred by the growth of trade. One may distinguish between trade within economic regions, trade between regions, and foreign trade. During the T'ang, most cities had been administrative, supported by taxes from the countryside. Official salaries and government expenditures created a demand for services and commercial products, making the cities into islands of commerce in a noncommercial hinterland. In most of China's seven or eight economic regions, this pattern continued during the Sung, but in the capital, and especially in the economically advanced regions along the Yangtze, cities became the hubs of regional commercial networks, with district seats or market towns serving as secondary centers for the local markets beneath them.

As this transition occurred, cities with more than 100,000 households almost quadrupled in number. The Northern Sung capital at Kaifeng is recorded as having had 260,000 households—probably more than one million inhabitants—and the Southern Sung capital at Hangchow had 391,000 households. Compare these to the capitals of backward Europe: London during the Northern Sung had a population of about 18,000; Rome during the Southern Sung had 35,000; and Paris even a century later had fewer than 60,000.

Furthermore, these Sung capitals, unlike Ch'ang-an with its walled wards that closed at night, were open within and spread beyond their outer walls. As in Chinese cities today, their main avenues were lined with shops. Merchant guilds replaced government officials as the managers of marketplaces. Growing wealth also led to a taste for luxury and an increasingly secular lifestyle. Restaurants, theaters, wine shops, and brothels abounded. Entertainment quarters with fortune tellers, jugglers, chess masters, acrobats, and puppeteers sprang up. These had not been absent from Ch'ang-an, but the numbers increased, and now they catered to traders and rich merchants as well as to officials.

Trade between regions during the Sung was mainly limited to luxury goods like silk, lacquerware, medicinal herbs and porcelains. Only where transport was cheap—along rivers, canals, or the coast—was interregional trade in bulk commodities economical, and even then, it was usually carried on only to make up for specific shortages.

Foreign trade also reached new heights during the Sung. In the north, Chinese traders bought horses from Tibetan, Turkic, and Mongol border states, and sold silks and tea. Along the coast, Chinese merchants took over the port trade that during the T'ang had been in the hands of Korean, Arab, and Irani merchants. The new hegemony of Chinese merchants was based on improved ships using both sail and oars and equipped with watertight compartments and better rudders. Chinese captains, navigating with the aid of the compass, came to dominate the sea routes from Japan in the north to Sumatra in the south. The content of the overseas trade reflected China's advanced economy: It imported raw materials and exported finished goods. Porcelains were sent to Southeast Asia, and then were carried by Arab ships to medieval trading centers on the Persian Gulf and down the coast of East Africa as far south as Zanzibar.

Government: From Aristocracy to Autocracy

The millennium of late imperial China after the T'ang is often spoken of as the age of autocracy or as China's age of absolute monarchy. Earlier emperors, as we have noted, were often personally powerful, but beginning with the Sung, changes occurred that made it easier for emperors to be autocrats.

One change was that Sung emperors had direct personal control over more offices than had their T'ang predecessors. For example, the Board of Academicians, an advisory office, presented the emperor with policy options separate from those presented by the Secretariat-Chancellery. The emperor could thus use the one against the other and prevent bureaucrats in the Secretariat-Chancellery from dominating the government.

A second change was that the central government was better funded than it had been previously. Revenues in 1100 were three times the peak revenues of the

T'ang, partly because of the growth of population and agricultural wealth, and partly because of the establishment of government monopolies on salt, wine, and tea, and because of various duties, fees, and taxes levied on domestic and foreign trade. During the Northern Sung, these commercial revenues rivaled the land tax; during the Southern Sung, they surpassed it. Confucian officials would continue to stress the primacy of land, but throughout late imperial China, commerce became a vital source of revenues.

A third change that strengthened the emperors was the disappearance of the aristocracy. During the T'ang, the emperor had come from the same Sino-Turkic aristocracy of northwest China as most of his principal ministers, and he was, essentially, the organ of a state that ruled on behalf of this aristocracy. Aristocrats monopolized the high posts of government. They married among themselves and with the imperial family. They called the emperor the Son of Heaven, but they knew he was one of them. During the Sung, in contrast, government officials were commoners, mostly products of the examination system. They were separated from the emperor by an enormous social gulf and saw him as a person apart.

The Sung examination system was larger than that of the T'ang, if smaller than in later dynasties. Whereas only 10 per cent of officials had been recruited by examination during the T'ang, the Sung figure rose to over 50 per cent, and these included the most important officials. The first examination was given at regional centers. The applicant took the examination in a walled cubicle under close supervision. To ensure impartiality, his answers were recopied by clerks and his name was replaced by a number before his examination was sent to the officials who would grade it. Of those who sat for the examination, only a tiny percentage passed. The second hurdle was the metropolitan examination at the national capital, where the precautions were equally elaborate. Only one in five, or about two hundred a year, passed. The average successful applicant was in his mid-thirties. The final hurdle was the palace examination, which rejected a few and assigned a ranking to the others.

To pass the examinations, the candidate had to memorize the Confucian classics, interpret selected passages, write in the literary style, compose poems on themes given by the examiners, and propose solutions to contemporary problems in terms of Confucian philosophy. The quality of the officials produced by the Sung system was impressive. A parallel might be drawn with nineteenth-century Britain, where students in the classics at Oxford and Cambridge went on to become generalist bureaucrats. The Chinese examination system that flourished during the Sung continued, with some interruptions, into the twentieth century. The continuity of Chinese government during this millennium rested on the examination elite, with its common culture and values.

The social base for this examination meritocracy was triangular, consisting of land, education, and office. Without wealth, the years of study needed to pass the examinations could not be afforded. Such an education was far beyond the means of a poor peasant or a city-dweller. Without education, official position was out of reach. And without office, family wealth could not be preserved. The Chinese pattern of inheritance, as noted earlier, led to the division of property at each change of generation. Some families were successful in passing the civil service examinations for several generations running. More often, the sons of well-to-do officials did not study as hard as those with bare means. The adage "shirt sleeves to shirt sleeves in three generations" is not inappropriate to the Sung and later dynasties. As China had an extended-family or clan system, a wealthy official often provided education for the bright children of poor relations.

How the merchants related to this system is less clear. They had wealth but were despised by scholar-officials as grubby profitseekers and were barred from taking the examinations. Some merchants avoided the system altogether—a thorough education in the Confucian classics did little to fit a merchant's son for a career in commerce. Others bought land for status and security, and their sons or grandsons became eligible. Similarly, a small peasant might build up his holdings, become a landlord, and educate a son or grandson. The system was steeply hierarchical, but it was not closed nor did it produce a new, self-perpetuating aristocracy.

Sung Culture

As society and government changed during the T'ang–Sung transition, so too did culture. Sung culture retained some of the energy of the T'ang while becoming more intensely and perhaps more narrowly Chinese. The preconditions for the rich Sung culture were a rising economy, an increase in the number of schools and higher literacy, and the spread of printing. Sung culture was less aristocratic, less cosmopolitan, and more closely associated with the officials and the scholar-gentry, who were both its practitioners and its patrons. It also was less Buddhist than had been the T'ang. Only the Zen (Ch'an) sect kept its vitality, and many Confucians were outspokenly anti-Buddhist and anti-Taoist. In sum, the secular culture of officials that had been a sidestream in the T'ang broadened and became the mainstream during the Sung.

Chinese consider the Sung dynasty as the peak of their traditional culture. It was, for example, China's greatest age of pottery and porcelains. High-firing techniques were developed, and kilns were established in every area. There was a rich variety of beautiful

An early Sung dynasty winepot. [The Metropolitan Museum of Art, Gift of Mrs. Samuel T. Peters, 1926.]

Grotto Academy, and his writings were widely distributed. Before the end of the Sung, his interpretation of Confucianism had become the orthodoxy required for the civil service examinations, and it remained so until the twentieth century.

If we search in other traditions for comparable figures, we might pick Saint Thomas Aquinas (1224–1274) of medieval Europe or the Islamic theologian al-Ghazali (1058–1111), each of whom produced a new synthesis or worldview that lasted for centuries. Aquinas joined Aristotle and Latin theology just as Chu Hsi joined Confucian philosophy and Buddhism. Because Chu Hsi used terms such as the "great ultimate" and because he emphasized a Zen-like meditation called "quiet sitting," some contemporary critics said his Neo-Confucian philosophy was a Buddhist wolf in the clothing of a Confucian sheep. This was unfair. Whereas Aquinas would make philosophy serve religion, Chu Hsi made religion serve philosophy. In his hands, the great ultimate (also known as principle or *li*) lost its otherworldly character and became a constituent of all things in the universe. We might better characterize it as innerworldly.

Later critics often argued that Chu Hsi's teachings encouraged metaphysical speculation at the expense of practical ethics. Chu Hsi's followers replied that, on the contrary, his teachings gave practical ethics a sys-

The Sung dynasty philosopher Chu Hsi (1130–1200), whose Neo-Confucian ideas remained central down to the twentieth century. [National Palace Museum, Taiwan, R.O.C.]

glazes. The shapes were restrained and harmonious. Sung pottery, like nothing produced in the world before, made ceramics a major art form in East Asia. It was also an age of great historians. Ssu-ma Kuang (1019–1086) wrote *A Comprehensive Mirror for Aid in Government*, which treated not a single dynasty but all Chinese history. His work was more sophisticated than previous histories in that it included a discussion of documentary sources and an explanation of why he chose to rely on one source rather than another. The greatest achievements of the Sung, however, were in philosophy, poetry, and painting.

PHILOSOPHY. The Sung was second only to the Chou as a creative age in philosophy. A series of original thinkers culminated in the towering figure of Chu Hsi (1130–1200). Chu Hsi studied Taoism and Buddhism in his youth, along with Confucianism. A brilliant student, he passed the metropolitan examination at the age of eighteen. During his thirties, he focused attention on Confucianism, deepening and making more systematic its social and political ethics by joining to it certain Buddhist metaphysical elements. Chu Hsi became famous as a teacher at the White Deer

tematic underpinning and positively contributed to individual moral responsibility. What was discovered within by Neo-Confucian quiet sitting was just those positive ethical truths enunciated by Confucius over a thousand years earlier. The new metaphysics did not change the Confucian social philosophy.

Because Chu Hsi's teachings became a new orthodoxy that lasted until the twentieth century, historians argue, probably correctly, that it was one source of stability in late imperial China. Like the examination system, the imperial institution, the scholar-gentry class, and the land system, it contributed to continuity and impeded change. Some scholars go further and say that the emergence of the Chu Hsi orthodoxy stifled intellectual creativity. This probably is an overstatement. The need to interpret Confucianism in terms of Chu Hsi's ideas on the civil service examinations did channelize Chinese thought, but there were always other contending schools.

POETRY. Sung poets were in awe of those of the T'ang. Yet Sung poets were also among China's best. A Japanese authority on Chinese literature, wrote:

Su Tung-p'o Imagined on a Wet Day, Wearing a Rain Hat and Clogs

After Su's death, a disciple wrote:

When with tall hat and firm baton he stood in
    council,
The crowds were awed at the dignity of the
    statesman in him.
But when in cloth cap he strolled with cane and
    sandals,
He greeted little children with gentle smiles.

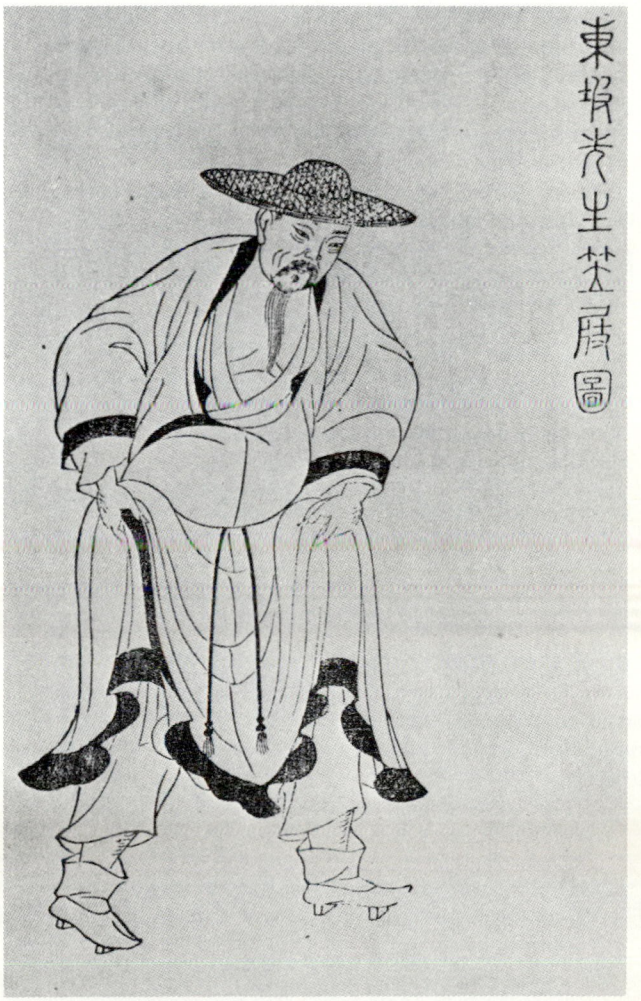

Kōjirō Yoshikawa, *An Introduction to Sung Poetry*, trans. by Burton Watson (Cambridge: Harvard University Press, Harvard-Yenching Institute Monograph Series, 1967), pp. 65 oppos., 122.

T'ang poetry could be likened to wine, and Sung poetry to tea. Wine has great power to stimulate, but one cannot drink it constantly. Tea is less stimulating, bringing to the drinker a quieter pleasure, but one which can be enjoyed more continuously.[9]

The most famous poet of the Northern Sung was Su Tung-p'o (1037–1101), a man who participated in the full range of the culture of his age: He was a painter and calligrapher, particularly knowledgeable about inks; he practiced Zen and wrote commentaries on the Confucian classics; he superintended engineering projects; and he was a connoisseur of cooking and wine. His life was shaped by politics. He was a conservative, believing in a limited role for government and social control through morality. (The other faction in the Sung bureaucracy was the reformers, who stressed law and an expanded government role.)

Passing the metropolitan examination, Su rose through a succession of posts to become the governor of a province—a position of immense power. While considering death sentences, which could not be carried over into the new year, he wrote:

New Year's Eve—you'd think I could go home early
But official business keeps me.
I hold the brush and face them with tears:
Pitiful convicts in chains,
Little men who tried to fill their bellies,
Fell into the law's net, don't understand disgrace.
And I? In love with a meager stipend
I hold on to my job and miss the chance to retire.
Do not ask who is foolish or wise;
All of us alike scheme for a meal.
The ancients would have freed them a while at
    New Year's—
Would I dare do likewise? I am silent with shame.[10]

Eight years later, when the reformers came to power, Su himself was arrested and spent one hundred days in prison, awaiting execution on a charge of slandering the emperor. Instead, he was released and sent into exile. He wrote, "Out the gate, I do a dance, wind blows in my face; our galloping horses race along as magpies cheer."[11] Arriving at his place of exile, he reflected:

Between heaven and earth I live,
One ant on a giant grindstone,
Trying in my petty way to walk to the right
While the turning of the mill wheel takes me
    endlessly left.

[9]Kōjirō Yoshikawa, *An Introduction to Sung Poetry*, trans. by Burton Watson (Cambridge: Harvard University Press, Harvard-Yenching Institute Monograph Series, 1967), p. 37.
[10]Yoshikawa, p. 119.
[11]Yoshikawa, p. 117.

Though I go the way of benevolence and duty,
I can't escape from hunger and cold. . . . [12]

But exile was soon turned to art. He farmed a plot of land at the "eastern slope" from which he took his literary name, Tung-p'o. Of his work there, he wrote:

A good farmer hates to wear out the land;
I'm lucky this plot was ten years fallow.
It's too soon to count on mulberries;
My best bet is a crop of wheat.
I planted seed and within the month
Dirt on the rows was showing green.
An old farmer warned me,
Don't let seedlings shoot up too fast!
If you want plenty of dumpling flour
Turn a cow or sheep in here to graze.
Good advice—I bowed my thanks;
I won't forget you when my belly's full.[13]

After 1086, the conservatives regained control of the government, and Su resumed his official career. In 1094, another shift occurred and Su was again sent into exile on the distant southern island of Hainan. After still another shift, Su was on his way back to the capital when he died in 1101.

PAINTING. In the West, penmanship and painting are quite separate, one merely a skill and the other esteemed as an art. In China, calligraphy and painting were equally appreciated and were seen as related. A scholar spent his life with brush in hand. The same qualities of line, balance, and strength needed for calligraphy carried over to painting. Chinese calligraphy is immensely pleasing even to the untutored Western eye, and it is not difficult to distinguish between the elegant strokes of Hui-neng, the last emperor of the Northern Sung, and the powerful brushwork of the Zen monk Chang Chi-chih.

Sung painting was various—of birds or flowers; of fish or insects; of horses, monkeys, or water buffalo; of scholars, emperors, Buddhas, or Taoist immortals. But its crowning achievement was landscapes. These are quite different from Western paintings. Each stroke of the brush on silk or paper was final. Mistakes could not be covered up. Each element of a painting is presented in its most pleasing aspect; the painting is not constrained by single-point perspective. Paintings have no single source of illumination with light and shadow, but an overall diffusion of light. Space is an integral part of the painting. A typical painting might have craggy rocks or twisted pine trees in the foreground, then mist or clouds or rain to create distance,

[12]Yoshikawa, p. 105.
[13]Yoshikawa, pp. 119–120.

Is the enlightened man depicted in this painting meditating or dozing? Zen paintings often have a touch of humorous ambiguity. Note the bold calligraphic brushwork in this Southern Sung or Yuan dynasty painting in the style of the Zen monk Shih Ko. [Tokyo National Museum.]

and in the background the outlines of mountains or cliffs fading into space. If the painting contains human figures at all, they are small in a natural universe that is very large. Chinese painting thus reflects the same world view as Chinese philosophy or poetry. The goal of the painter was to grasp the inner reality of the scene and not to be bound up in surface details.

In paintings by monks or masters of the Zen school, the presentation of an intuitive vision of an inner reality became even more pronounced. Paintings of Bodhidharma, the legendary founder of the Zen sect, are often dominated by a single powerful downstroke of the brush, defining the edge of his robe. Paintings of patriarchs tearing up sutras or sweeping dust with a broom from the mirror of the mind are almost as calligraphic as paintings of bamboo. A Northern Sung painting in the style of Shih K'o shows the figure of a monk or sage who is dozing or meditating. A Zen "broken ink" landscape might contain rocks, water, mountains, and clouds, each represented by a few explosive strokes of the brush.

China in the Mongol World Empire: The Yuan Dynasty (1279–1368)

The Mongols created the greatest empire in the history of the world. It extended from the Caspian Sea to the Pacific Ocean, from Russia, Siberia, and Korea in the north to Persia and Burma in the south. Invasion fleets were even sent to Java and Japan, though without success. Mongol rule in China is one chapter of this larger story.

The Rise of the Mongol Empire

The Mongols, a nomadic people, lived to the north of China on grasslands where they raised horses and herded sheep. They lived in felt tents called yurts—they sometimes called themselves "the people of the felt-tents." Women performed much of the work and were freer and more easygoing than women in China. Families belonged to clans, and related clans to tribes. Tribes would gather during the annual migration from the summer plains to winter pasturage. Chiefs were elected, most often from noble lineages, for their courage, military prowess, judgment, and leadership. Like Manchu or Turkic, the Mongol tongue was Altaic.

The Mongols believed in nature deities and in the sky god above all others. Sky blue was their sacred color. They communicated with their gods through religious specialists called *shamans*. They traded and warred with settled peoples on the borders of their vast domain.

The founder of the Mongol Empire, Temujin, was born in 1167, the son of a tribal chief. While he was still a child, his father was poisoned. He fled and after wandering for some years, returned to the tribe, avenged his father, and in time became chief himself. Through his wife's tribe, he became part of an alliance

The world conqueror, Genghis Khan (1167–1227). [National Palace Museum, Taiwan, R.O.C.]

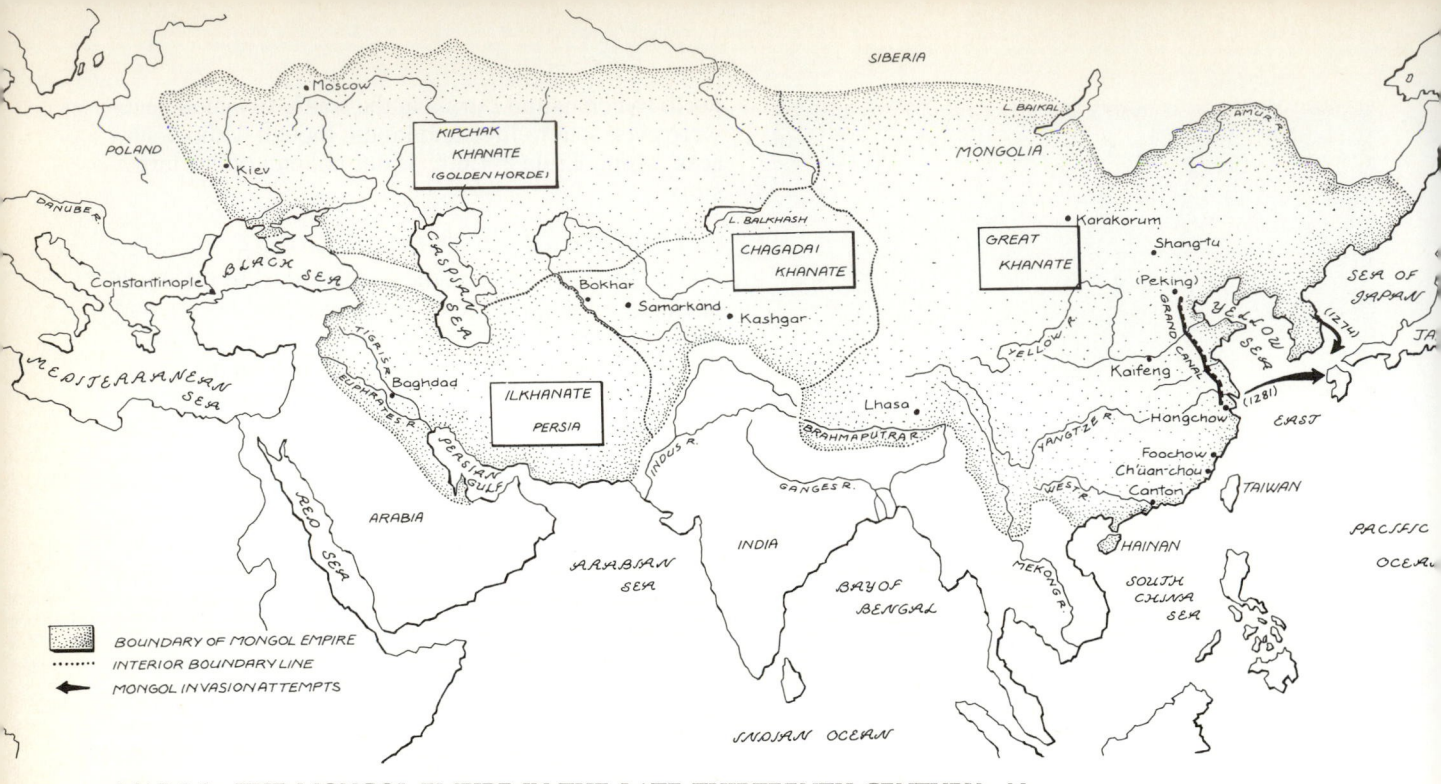

MAP 9-3   THE MONGOL EMPIRE IN THE LATE THIRTEENTH CENTURY   *Note the four khanates: the Golden Horde in Russia, the Ilkhanate in Persia, Chagadai in Central Asia, and the Great Khanate extending from Mongolia to Southern China.*

with the Ch'in empire that ruled north China. By the time he was forty, he had united all Mongol tribes and had been elected their great khan, or ruler. It is by the title *Genghis* (also spelled *Jenghiz* or *Chinggis*) *Khan* that he is known to history. Genghis possessed an extraordinary charisma, and his sons and grandsons also became wise and talented leaders. Why the Mongol tribes, almost untouched by the higher civilizations of the world, should have produced such leaders at this point in history is difficult to explain.

A second conundrum is how the Mongols, who numbered only about a million and a half, created the army that conquered vastly denser populations. Part of the answer is institutional. Genghis organized his armies into "myriads" of 10,000 troops, with decimal subdivisions of 1,000, 100, and 10. Elaborate signals were devised so that, in battle, even large units could be manipulated like the fingers of a hand. Mongol tactics were superb: units would retreat, turn, flank, and destroy their enemies. The historical record makes amply clear that Genghis' nomadic cavalry had a paralytic effect on all they encountered. Peerless horsemen, the Mongols fought with a compound bow, short enough to be used from the saddle yet more powerful than the English longbow.

They were astonishingly mobile. Each man carried his own supplies. Trailing remounts, they covered vast distances quickly. In 1241, for example, a Mongol army had reached Hungary, Poland, and the shore of the Adriatic and was poised for a further advance into Western Europe. But when word arrived of the death of the great khan, the army turned and galloped back to Mongolia to help choose his successor.

When this army encountered walled cities, it learned the use of siege weapons from the enemies it had conquered. Chinese engineers were used in campaigns in Persia. The Mongols also used terror as a weapon. Inhabitants of cities that refused to surrender in the Near East and China were put to the sword. Large areas in north China and Szechwan were devastated and depopulated in the process of conquest. Descriptions of the Mongols by those whom they conquered dwell on their physical toughness and pitiless cruelty.

But the Mongols had strengths that went beyond the strictly military. Genghis opened his armies to recruits from the Uighur Turks, the Manchus, and other nomadic peoples. As long as they complied with the military discipline demanded of his forces, they could participate in his triumphs. In 1206, Genghis promulgated laws designed to prevent the normal wrangling and warring between tribes that would undermine his empire. Genghis also obtained thousands of pledges of personal loyalty from his followers, and he appointed these "vassals" to command his armies and staff his government. This policy gave to his forces an inner coherence that countered the divisive effect of tribal loyalties.

The Mongol conquests were all the more impressive in that, unlike the earlier Arab expansion, they lacked the unifying force of religious zeal. To be sure, at an assembly of chiefs in 1206, an influential shaman revealed that it was the sky god's will that Genghis conquer the world. Yet other unabashedly frank words attributed to Genghis may reveal a truer image of what lay behind the Mongol drive to conquest: "Man's highest joy is in victory: to conquer one's enemies, to pursue them, to deprive them of their possessions, to make their beloved weep, to ride on their horses, and to embrace their wives and daughters."[14]

Genghis divided his far-flung empire among his four sons. Trade and communications were maintained between the parts, but over several generations, each of the four khanates became independent. The khanate of Chagatai was in central Asia and remained purely nomadic. A second khanate of the Golden Horde ruled Russia from the lower Volga. The third was in Persia. The fourth, led by those who succeeded Genghis as great khans, centered first in Mongolia and then in China.

Mongol Rule in China

The standard theory used in explaining Chinese history is the dynastic cycle. A second theory explains Chinese history in terms of the interaction between the settled people of China and the nomads of the steppe. When strong states emerged in China, their wealth and population enabled them to expand militarily onto the steppe. But when China was weak, as was more often the case, the steppe peoples overran China. To review briefly:

1. During the Han dynasty (206 B.C.–A.D. 220) the most pressing problem in foreign relations was the Hsiung Nu empire to the north.
2. During the centuries that followed the Han, various nomadic peoples invaded and ruled north China.
3. The energy and institutions of these Sino-Turkic rulers of the northern dynasties shaped China's reunification during the Sui (581–618) and T'ang (618–907) dynasties. The Uighur Turks also played a major role in T'ang defense policy.
4. Northern border states became even more important during the Sung. The Northern Sung (960–1126) bought peace with payments of gold and sil-

[14]J. K. Fairbank, E. O. Reischauer, and A. M. Craig, *East Asia, Tradition and Transformation* (Boston: Houghton Mifflin, 1973), p. 164.

ver to the Liao. The Southern Sung (1126–1279), for all of its cultural brilliance, was little more than a tributary state of the Chin dynasty, which had expanded into northern China.

From the very start of the Mongol pursuit of world hegemony, China was a target because of its riches. But Genghis proceeded cautiously, determined to leave no enemy at his back. He first disposed of the Tibetan state to the northwest of China and then of the Manchu state of Chin that ruled north China. Mongol forces took Peking in 1227, the year Genghis died. They went on to take Loyang and the southern reaches of the Yellow River in 1234, and all of north China by 1241. During this time, the Mongols were interested mainly in loot. Only later did Chinese advisers persuade them that more wealth could be obtained by taxation.

Kublai, a grandson of Genghis, was chosen as the great khan in 1260. In 1264, he moved his capital from Karakorum in Mongolia to Peking. It was only in 1271 that he adopted a Chinese dynastic name, the Yuan, and, as a Chinese dynasty, went to war with the Southern Sung. Once the decision was made, the Mongols swept across south China. The last Sung stronghold fell in 1279.

Kublai Khan's rule in Peking reflected the mixture of cultural elements in Mongol China. From Peking, Kublai could rule as a Chinese emperor, which would not have been possible in Karakorum. He adopted the Chinese custom of hereditary succession. He rebuilt Peking as a walled city in the Chinese style. But Peking was far to the north of any previous Chinese capital, away from centers of wealth and population; to provision it, the Grand Canal had to be extended. From Peking, Kublai could look out onto Manchuria and Mongolia and maintain ties with the other khanates. The city proper was for the Mongols. It was known to the West as *Cambulac*, "the city (*balya*) of the khan." Chinese were segregated in an adjoining walled city. The palace of the khan was designed by an Arab architect; its rooms were central Asian in style. Kublai also maintained a summer palace at Shangtu (the "Xanadu" of Samuel Taylor Coleridge's poem) in Inner Mongolia, where he could hawk and ride and hunt in Mongol style.

Early Mongol rule in north China was rapacious and exploitative, but it later shifted toward Chinese forms of government and taxation, especially in the south and at the local level. Because it was a foreign military occupation, civil administration was highly centralized. Under the emperor was a Central Secretariat, and beneath it were ten "Moving Secretariats," which became the provinces of later dynasties. These highly centralized institutions and the arbitrary style of

Kublai Khan, wearing ermine coat, with Mongol warriors at the hunt. Note camel caravan in hills at rear. [National Palace Museum, Taiwan, R.O.C.]

Mongol decision making accelerated the trend toward absolutism that had started during the previous dynasty.

About 400,000 Mongols lived in China during the Yuan period. For such a tiny minority to control the Chinese majority, it had to stay separate. One measure was to make military service a monopoly of Mongols and their nomadic allies. Garrisons were established throughout China, with a strategic reserve on the steppe. Military officers were always regarded as more important than civil officials. A second measure was to use ethnic classifications in appointing civil officials. The highest category was the Mongols, who held the top civil and military posts. The second category included Persians, Turks, and other non-Chinese, who were given high civil posts. The third category was the northern Chinese, who included Manchus and other border peoples, and the fourth was the southern Chinese. Even when the examination system was sporadically revived after 1315, the Mongols and their allies took an easier examination; their quota was as large as that for Chinese; and they were appointed to the higher offices.

The effect of this segregated system was that most Chinese had contact only with other Chinese in low-level posts, and they did not learn Mongolian. The Mongols, concentrated in Peking or in garrisons, spoke Mongolian among themselves and usually did not bother to learn Chinese. A few exceptions wrote poetry in Chinese and painted in the Chinese style. Communication was through interpreters. When a Chinese district magistrate sent a query to the court, the ruling was made in Mongolian. (The Mongols had borrowed the alphabet of the Uighurs to transcribe their tongue.) A word-for-word translation in Chinese was written below the Mongolian and passed back down to the magistrate. As the two languages are syntactically very different, the resulting Chinese was grotesque.

Foreign Contacts and Chinese Culture

Diplomacy and trade within the greater Mongol Empire brought China into contact with other higher civilizations for the first time since the T'ang period. Persia and the Arab world were especially important. Merchants, missionaries, and diplomats voyaged from the Persian Gulf and across the Indian Ocean to seaports in south China. The Arab communities in Canton and other ports were larger than during the Sung. Camel caravans carrying silks and ceramics left Peking to pass through the central Asian oases and on to Baghdad. Although the Mongols did not favor Chinese merchants and most trade was in other hands, Chinese trade also expanded. Chinese communities became established in Tabriz, the center of trading in west Asia, and in Moscow and Novgorod. It was dur-

ing this period that knowledge of printing, gunpowder, and Chinese medicine spread to west Asia. Chinese ceramics influenced those of Persia as Chinese painting influenced Persian miniatures.

In Europe, firsthand knowledge of China was transmitted by the Venetian trader Marco Polo, who had served Kublai as an official between 1275 and 1292. His book, *A Description of the World*, was translated into most European languages. Many readers doubted that a land of such wealth and culture could exist so far from Europe, but the book excited an interest in geography. When Christopher Columbus set sail in 1492, his goal was to reach Polo's Zipangu (Japan).

Other cultural contacts were fostered by the Mongol toleration or encouragement of religion. Nestorian Christianity, spreading from Persia to Central Asia, reentered China during the Mongol era. Churches were built in the main cities. The mother of Kublai Khan was a Christian of this sect. Also, several papal missions were sent from Rome to the Mongol court. An archbishopric was established in Peking; a church was built, sermons were preached in Turkish or Mongolian, and choirboys sang hymns. Kublai sent the father and the uncle of Marco Polo with a letter to the pope asking for a hundred intelligent men acquainted with the seven arts.

Tibetan Buddhism with its magical doctrines and elaborate rites was the religion most favored by the Mongols. But Chinese Buddhism also flourished. Priests and monks of all religions were given tax exemptions. It is estimated that half a million Chinese became Buddhist monks during the Mongol century. The foreign religion that made the greatest gains was Islam, which became permanently established in central Asia and western China. Mosques were built in Peking, in the Islamic areas, and in southeastern port cities. Even Confucianism was regarded as a religion by the Mongols, its teachers being exempted from taxes. But as the scholar-gentry rarely obtained important offices, they saw the Mongol era as a time of hardship.

Despite these wide contacts with other peoples and religions, the high culture of China appears to have been influenced almost not at all—partly because China had little to learn from other areas, and partly because the centers of Chinese culture were in the south, the last area to be conquered and the area least affected by Mongol rule. Also, in reaction to the Mongol conquest, Chinese culture became conservative and turned in on itself. Scholars wrote poetry in the style of the Sung. New styles of painting developed, but the developments were from within the Chinese tradition, and the greatest Yuan paintings continued the style of the Sung. Yuan historians wrote the official history of the dynasties that preceded it. The head of the court bureau of historiography was a Mongol, but the histories produced by his Chinese staff were in the traditional mold. As the dynasty waned, unemployed scholars wrote essays expressing loyalty toward the Sung and satirizing the Mongols. Their writings were not censored: The Mongols either could not read them, did not read them, or did not care.

Marco Polo Describes the City of Hangchow

Marco Polo was a Venetian. In 1300, Venice had a population of more than 100,000 and was one of the wealthiest Mediterranean city-states. But Polo was nonetheless unprepared for what he saw in China. Commenting on Hangchow, China's capital during the Southern Sung, he first noted its size (ten or twelve times greater than that of Venice), then its many canals and bridges, its streets "paved with stones and bricks," and its location between "a lake of fresh and very clear water" and "a river of great magnitude." He spoke of "the prodigious concourse of people" frequenting its ten great marketplaces and of its "capacious warehouses . . . built of stone for the accommodation of merchants who arrive from India and other parts." He then described the life of its people:

Each of the ten market-squares is surrounded with high dwelling-houses, in the lower part of which are shops, where every kind of manufacture is carried on, and every article of trade is sold; such, amongst others, as spices, drugs, trinkets, and pearls. In certain shops nothing is vended but the wine of the country, which they are continually brewing, and serve out fresh to their customers at a moderate price. The streets connected with the market-squares are numerous, and in some of them are many cold baths, attended by servants of both sexes, to perform the offices of ablution for the men and women who frequent them, and who from their childhood have been accustomed at all times to wash in cold water, which they reckon highly conducive to health. At these bathing places, however, they have apartments provided with warm water, for the use of strangers, who from not being habituated to it, cannot bear the shock of the cold. All are in the daily practice of washing their persons, and especially before their meals.

In other streets are the habitations of the courtesans, who are here in such numbers as I dare not venture to report; and not only near the squares, which is the situation usually appropriated for their residence, but in every part of the city they are to be found, adorned with much finery, highly perfumed, occupying well-furnished houses, and attended by many female domestics. These women are accomplished, and are perfect in the arts of blandishment and dalliance, which they accompany with expressions adapted to every description of person, insomuch that strangers who have once become so enchanted by their meretricious arts, that they can never divest themselves of the impression. Thus intoxicated with sensual pleasures, when they return to their homes they report that they have been in Kin-sai [Hangchow], or the celestial city, and pant for the time when they may be enabled to revisit paradise. . . .

The inhabitants of the city are idolaters, and they use paper money as currency. The men as well as the women have fair complexions, and are handsome. The greater part of them are always clothed in silk, in consequence of the vast quantity of that material produced in the territory of Kin-sai, exclusively of what the merchants import from other provinces. Amongst the handicraft trades exercised in the place, there are twelve considered to be superior to the rest, as being more generally useful; for each of which there are a thousand workshops, and each shop furnishes employment for ten, fifteen, or twenty workmen, and in a few instances as many as forty, under their respective masters. . . .

The natural disposition of the native inhabitants of Kin-sai is pacific, and by the example of their former kings, who were themselves unwarlike, they have been accustomed to habits of tranquility. The management of arms is unknown to them, nor do they keep any in their houses. Contentious broils are never heard among them. They conduct their mercantile and manufacturing concerns with perfect candour and probity. They are friendly towards each other, and persons who inhabit the same street, both men and women, from the mere circumstance of neighbourhood, appear like one family. In their domestic manners they are free from jealousy or suspicion of their wives, to whom great respect is shown, and any man would be accounted infamous who should presume to use indecent expressions to a married woman. To strangers also, who visit their city in the way of commerce, they give proofs of cordiality, inviting them freely to their houses, showing them hospitable attention, and furnishing them with the best advice and assistance in their mercantile transactions. On the other hand, they dislike the sight of soldiery, not excepting the guards of the grand khan, as they preserve the recollection that by them they were deprived of the government of their native kings and rulers. ❑

The Travels of Marco Polo (London: J. M. Dent, 1908), pp. 290–301.

The major contribution to Chinese arts during the Yuan was by dramatists, who combined poetic arias with vaudeville theater to produce a new operatic drama. Performed by traveling troupes, the operas used few stage props. They relied for effect on makeup, costumes, pantomime, and stylized gestures. The women's roles were usually played by men. Except for the arias—the highlights of the performance—the dramas used vernacular Chinese, appealing to a popular audience. The unemployed scholars who wrote the scripts drew on the entire repertoire of the Sung storyteller. Among the stock figures in the operas were a Robin Hood–like bandit, a famous detective-judge, the T'ang monk who traveled to India, warriors and statesmen of the Three Kingdoms, and romantic heroes, villains, and ghosts. Justice always triumphed and the dramas usually ended happily. In several famous plays, the hero gets the girl, despite objections by her parents and seemingly insurmountable obstacles, by passing the civil service examinations in first place. As the examinations were not in effect during most of the Yuan, this resolution of the hero's predicament is one that looked back to the Sung pattern of government. Yuan drama continued almost unchanged in later dynasties, and during the nineteenth century, it merged with a form of southern Chinese theater to become today's Peking Opera.

The Last Years of the Yuan

Despite the Mongol military domination of China and the highly centralized institutions of the Mongol court, the Yuan was the shortest of China's major dynasties. Little more than a century elapsed between Kublai's move to Peking in 1264 and the dynasty's collapse in 1368. The rule of Kublai and his successor had been effective, but a decline set in from the start of the fourteenth century. By then, the Mongol Empire as a whole no longer lent strength to its parts. The khanates became separated by religion and culture as well as by distance. Even tribesmen in Mongolia rebelled now and then against the great khans in Peking who, in their eyes, had become too Chinese. The court at Peking, too, had never really gained legitimacy. Some Chinese officials served it loyally to the end, but most Chinese saw the government as carpetbaggers and saw Mongol rule as a military occupation. When succession disputes, bureaucratic factionalism, and pitched battles between Mongol generals broke out, the Chinese showed little inclination to rally in support of the dynasty.

Problems also arose in the countryside. Taxes were heavy and some local officials were corrupt. The government issued excessive paper money and then refused to accept it in payment for taxes. The Yellow River changed its course, flooding the canals that carried grain to the capital. At great cost and suffering, a labor force of 150,000 workers and 20,000 soldiers rerouted the river to the south of the Shantung peninsula. Further natural disasters during the 1350s led to popular uprisings. The White Lotus sect preached the coming of Maitreya. Regional military commanders, suppressing the rebellions, became independent of central control. Warlords arose. The warlord who ruled Szechwan was infamous for his cruelty. Important economic regions were devastated and, in part, depopulated by rebellions. At the end, a rebel army threatened Peking, and the last Mongol emperor and his court fled on horses to Shangtu, and when that fell, they fled still deeper into the plains of Mongolia.

Imperial China in World Perspective

Rough parallels between China and Europe persisted until the sixth century A.D. Both saw the rise and fall of great empires. At first glance, the three and one half centuries that followed the Han dynasty appear remarkably similar to the comparable period after the collapse of the Roman Empire: Central authority broke down, private armies arose, and aristocratic estates were established. Barbarian tribes, once allied to the empires, invaded and pillaged large areas. Otherworldly religions entered to challenge earlier official worldviews. In China, Neo-Taoism and then Buddhism challenged Confucianism, just as Christianity challenged Roman conceptions of the sociopolitical order.

But then, from the late sixth century A.D., a fundamental divergence occurred. Europe tailed off into centuries of feudal disunity and backwardness. A ghost of empire lingered in the European memory. But the reality, even after centuries had passed, was that tiny areas like France (one seventeenth the size of China), Italy (one thirty-second), or Germany (one twenty-seventh) found it difficult to establish an internal unity, much less re-create a pan-European or pan-Mediterranean empire. This pattern of separate little states has persisted in Europe until today. In contrast, China, which is about the size of Europe and geographically no more natural a political unit, put a unified empire back together again, attaining a new level of wealth, power, and culture, and unified rule has continued down to the present in China. What is the explanation?

One reason the empire was reconstituted in China was that the victory of Buddhism in China was less complete than that of Christianity in Europe. Confucianism survived within the aristocratic families and at the courts of the Six Dynasties, and the idea of a united empire was integral to it. It is difficult even to think of Confucianism apart from the idea of a universal ruler, aided by men of virtue and ability, ruling "all under Heaven" according to Heaven's mandate. In contrast, the Roman conception of political order was not maintained as an independent doctrine. And empire was not a vital element in Christian thought—except perhaps in Byzantium, where the empire lasted longer than in Western Europe. The notion of a "Christian king" did appear in the West, but basically, the kingdom sought by Jesus was not of this world.

A second consideration was China's greater cultural homogeneity. It had a common written language that was fairly close to all varieties of spoken Chinese. Even barbarian conquerors were rapidly Sinicized. In contrast, after Rome, the Mediterranean fell apart into its component cultures. Latin became the universal language of the Western church, but for most Christians it was a foreign language, a part of the mystery of the Mass, and even in Italy it became an artificial language, separate from the living tongue. The European languages and cultures were divisive forces.

A third factor was the combination in the post-Han northern Chinese states of economic strength based on Chinese agriculture with the military striking force of a nomadic cavalry. There was nothing like it in Europe. It was by such a northern state that China was reunified in A.D. 589.

A fourth and perhaps critical factor was China's greater population density. The province (called a *circuit* at the time) of Hopei had a registered population of 10,559,728 during the eighth century A.D. Hopei was about one third the size of France, which in the eleventh century had a population of about two million. That is to say, even comparing China with France three centuries later, China's population density was fifteen times greater. (This comparison, it should be noted, is with a nonrice-producing area of China. Rice paddy areas were even more densely populated.) The far higher population density resulted in a different kind of history.

This explains why the Chinese could absorb barbarian conquerors so much more quickly than could Europe. It provided a larger agricultural surplus to the northern kingdoms than was enjoyed by comparable kingdoms in Europe. A denser population also meant better communications and a better base for commerce. To be sure, the centuries that followed the Han saw a decline in commerce and in cities. In some areas, money went out of use to be replaced by barter or the use of silk as currency. But the economic level remained higher than in early medieval Europe.

Several of the factors that explain the Sui-T'ang regeneration of a unified empire apply equally well or better to the Sung and subsequent dynasties. As schools were established and literacy rose, Confucianism and the ideal of a unified China became more widely accepted. Chinese culture was more homoge-neous and less open to outside influences in the tenth century than it had been four centuries earlier. The population was denser, with the Yangtze basin emerging as a new center of gravity.

The same cyclic regeneration of centralized bureaucratic governments—even under outside conquerors—can also be analyzed in terms of the interests it served. For the military figure who established the dynasty, the bureaucratic state was a huge tax machine that supported his armies and bestowed on him revenues beyond the imaginings of contemporary European monarchs. Government by civilian officials also offered some promise for the security of his progeny by acting as a counterweight against other military figures. For the scholar-gentry class, service to the state was the means to maintain family wealth, power, and status. Nothing was better. For merchants, a strong state was not an unmixed blessing. It might tax their profits or establish monopolies on the commodities they traded. But it also provided order and stability. More often than not, commerce expanded during such periods. For farmers, the picture was also unclear. Taxation was often exploitative, but orderly exploitation was usually preferable to rapacious warlords, bandits, or maurauding armies.

Comparisons across continents are difficult, but it seems likely that T'ang and Sung China had longer stretches of good government than any other part of the contemporary world. Not until the nineteenth century would comparable bureaucracies of talent and virtue begin to appear in the West.

Suggested Readings

GENERAL

J. CAHILL, *Chinese Painting* (1960). An excellent survey.

C. O. HUCKER, *China's Imperial Past* (1975). A superb overview of Chinese traditional history and culture by a Ming specialist.

F. A. KIERMAN, JR., AND J. K. FAIRBANK (eds)., *Chinese Ways in Warfare* (1974). Chapters by different authors on the Chinese military experience from the Chou to the Ming.

SUI AND T'ANG

P. B. EBREY, *The Aristocratic Families of Early Imperial China* (1978).

S. OWEN, *The Great Age of Chinese Poetry: The High T'ang* (1980).

E. G. PULLEYBLANK, *The Background of the Rebellion of An Lu-shan* (1955). A study of the 755 rebellion that weakened the central authority of the T'ang dynasty.

E. O. REISCHAUER, *Ennin's Travels in T'ang China* (1955). China as seen through the eyes of a ninth-century Japanese Marco Polo.

E. H. SCHAFER, *The Golden Peaches of Samarkand* (1963). A study of T'ang imagery.

D. TWITCHETT (ed.), *Sui and T'ang China, 589–906,*

Part 1 (1984). (Part 2, also in *The Cambridge History of China*, is forthcoming.)

G. W. WANG, *The Structure of Power in North China during the Five Dynasties* (1963). A study of the interim period between the T'ang and the Sung dynasties.

A. F. WRIGHT, *The Sui Dynasty* (1978).

SUNG

J. GERNET, *Daily Life in China on the Eve of the Mongol Invasion* (1962).

J. W. HAEGER (ed.), *Crisis and Prosperity in Sung China* (1975).

R. HYMES, *Statesmen and Gentlemen* (1987). On the transformation of officials into a local gentry elite during the twelfth and thirteenth centuries.

J. T. C. LIU AND P. J. GOLAS (eds.), *Change in Sung China: Innovation or Renovation?* (1969).

M. ROSSABI, *China Among Equals* (1983). A study of the Liao, Ch'in, and Sung empires and their relations.

K. YOSHIKAWA, *An Introduction to Sung Poetry*, trans. by B. Watson (1967).

YUAN

T. T. ALLSEN, *Mongol Imperialism* (1987).

J. W. DARDESS, *Conquerors and Confucians: Aspects of Political Change in Late Yuan China* (1973).

H. FRANKE AND D. TWITCHETT (eds.), *Alien Regimes and Border States*, 710–1368 (to appear soon as Volume 6 of *The Cambridge History of China*).

J. D. LANGLOIS, *China Under Mongol Rule* (1981).

R. LATHAM (trans.), *Travels of Marco Polo* (1958).

H. D. MARTIN, *The Rise of Chingis Khan and His Conquest of North China* (1981).

10 Japan: Its Early History to 1467

Japanese history has three main turning points, each marked by a major influx of an outside culture and each followed by a massive restructuring of Japanese institutions. The first turning point was in the third century B.C., when an Old Stone Age Japan became an agricultural, metalworking society, similar to those on the Korean peninsula or in northeastern Asia. This era lasted until A.D. 600. The second turning point came during the seventh century, when whole complexes of Chinese culture entered Japan directly. Absorbing these, archaic Japan made the leap to a higher historical civilization, associated with the writing system, technologies, and philosophies of China, and with Chinese forms of Buddhism. Japan would remain a part of this civilization until the third turning point, in the nineteenth century, when it encountered the West.

Japanese Origins

The antiquity of humans in Japan is hotly debated. During the ice ages, Japan was connected by land bridges to Asia. Woolly mammoths entered the northern island of Hokkaido and elephants, sabre-toothed tigers, giant elks, and other continental fauna entered the lower islands. Did not humans enter as well? Because Japan's acid volcanic soil eats up bones, there are no early skeletal remains. The earliest evidence of human habitation are finely shaped stone tools dating from about 30,000 B.C. Then, from about 10,000 B.C., there is Jōmon or "cord-pattern" pottery, the oldest in the world. Archeologists are baffled by its appearance in an Old Stone Age hunting, gathering, and fishing society—when in all other early societies pottery developed along with agriculture as an aspect of New Stone Age culture.

Along with cord-patterned pots, the hunting and gathering Jōmon people produced mysterious figurines. Is this a female deity? Why are the eyes slitted like snow goggles? [Otto E. Nelson.]

The Yayoi Revolution

After 8,000 years of Jōmon culture, the second phase of Japanese prehistory began in about 300 B.C. It is called the Yayoi culture after a place name in Tokyo where its distinctive hard, white pottery was first unearthed. There is no greater break in the entire Japanese record than that between the Jōmon and the Yayoi. For at the beginning of the third century B.C., the agricultural revolution, the bronze revolution, and the iron revolution—which in the Near East, India, and China had been separated by thousands of years, and each of which singly had wrought profound transformations—burst in upon Japan simultaneously.

The new technologies were brought to Japan by peoples moving across the Tsushima Straits from the Korean peninsula. It is uncertain whether these immigrants came as a trickle and were absorbed, or whether they came as a torrent that swept away the indigenous Jōmon people. The early Yayoi migrants, using the same seacraft by which they had crossed from Korea, spread along the coasts of northern Kyushu and western Honshu. Yayoi culture rapidly replaced Jōmon culture as far east in Japan as the present-day city of Nagoya. After that, the Yayoi culture diffused overland into eastern Japan more slowly and with greater difficulty. Conditions were less favorable for agriculture, and a mixed agricultural-hunting economy lasted longer.

The early "frontier settlements" of the Yayoi people were located next to their fields. Their agriculture was primitive. By the first century A.D., the Yayoi population had expanded to the point where wars were fought for the best land. Excavations reveal extensive stone-axe industries, and several skulls pierced by bronze and iron arrowheads have been found. An early Chinese chronicle describes Japan as made up of "more than one hundred countries" with wars and conflicts raging on all sides. During these wars, villages were relocated in defensible positions on low hills away from the fields. From these wars emerged a more peaceful order of regional states and a ruling class of aristocratic warriors. Late Yayoi excavations reveal villages once again located by fields and far fewer stone axes.

During the third century A.D., a temporary hegemony was achieved over a number of such regional states—or, more accurately, regional tribal confederations—by a queen named Pimiko. In the Chinese chronicle, Pimiko is described as a shaman who "occupied herself with magic and sorcery, bewitching the people." She was mature but unmarried. "After she became the ruler, there were few who saw her. She had one thousand women as attendants, but only one man. He served her food and drink and acted as a medium of communication. She resided in a palace surrounded by towers and stockades with armed guards in a state of constant vigilance."[1]

After Pimiko, references to Japan disappeared from the Chinese dynastic histories for a century and a half.

Tomb Culture and the Yamato State

Emerging directly from the Yayoi culture was a period, A.D. 300–600, characterized by giant tomb mounds, which remain even today, dotting the landscape of western Japan. The early tombs—like those in Korea—were circular mounds of earth built atop megalithic burial chambers. Later tombs were sometimes keyhole-shaped. The tombs were surrounded by moats and adorned with clay cylinders and statues of warriors, scribes, musicians, houses, boats, and the like. Early tombs, like the Yayoi graves that preceded them, contained mirrors, jewels, and other ceremonial objects. From the fifth century A.D., these objects were replaced by armor, swords, spears, and military trappings. The change reflected a new wave of continental

[1]L. C. Goodrich and R. Tsunoda (trans.), *Japan in the Chinese Dynastic Histories* (South Pasadena, Calif.: Perkins Asiatic Monographs, 1951), p. 13.

Late Yayoi Japan as Presented in Chinese Histories

Weapons are spears, shields, swords, and wooden bows. . . . The arrows are sometimes tipped with bone. The men all tattoo their faces and adorn their bodies with designs. The position and size of pattern indicate the difference of rank. . . . The men's clothing is fastened breadth-wise and consists of one piece of cloth. The women tie their hair in bows, and their clothing, like our gown of one single piece of cloth, is put on by slipping it over the head. They use pink and scarlet to smear their bodies, as rice powder is used in China. . . .

The women outnumber the men, and the men of importance have four or five spouses; the rest have two or three. The women are faithful and not jealous. There is no theft, and litigation is infrequent. When men break a law, their wives and children are confiscated; when the offense is serious, the offender's family is extirpated. At death mourning lasts for more than ten days, during which time members of the family weep and lament, without much drinking and eating; while their friends sing and dance. . . .

When the lowly meet men of importance on the road, they stop and withdraw to the roadside. In conveying messages to them or addressing them, they either squat or kneel, with both hands on the ground. This is the way they show respect. When responding, they say "ah," which corresponds to the affirmative "yes. . . . "

When they go on voyages across the sea to visit China, they always select a man who does not arrange his hair, does not rid himself of fleas, lets his clothing [get as] dirty as it will, does not eat meat, and does not approach women. This man behaves like a mourner and is known as the fortune keeper. When the voyage turns out propitious, they all lavish on him slaves and other valuables. In case there is disease or mishap, they kill him, saying that he was not scrupulous in his duties. ❑

L. C. Goodrich and R. Tsunoda (trans.) *Japan in the Chinese Dynastic Histories* (South Pasadena, Calif: Perkins Asiatic Monographs, 1951), pp. 1, 2, 11, 13.

A clay statue of a warrior in armor from an ancient tomb. [Tokyo National Museum.]

influences. The flow of people and culture from Korea to Japan that had began with Yayoi was continuous into historical times.

Japan reappears in the Chinese chronicles in the fifth century A.D. This period was also covered in the earliest Japanese accounts of its own history, the *Records of Ancient Matters (Kojiki)* and the *Records of Japan (Nihongi)* compiled in 712 and 720. These records dovetail with the evidence of the tombs. The picture that emerges is of regional aristocracies under the loose hegemony of the Yamato "great kings." Historians use the geographical label "Yamato" since the courts of the great kings were located on the Yamato plain, near present-day Osaka. This was the richest agricultural region of ancient Japan. The Yamato rulers also held lands and granaries throughout Japan. The tomb of the great king Nintoku is 486 meters long and 36 meters high, with twice the volume of the Great Pyramid of Egypt. By the fifth century A.D., the great kings possessed sufficient authority to commandeer the labor for such a project.

The great kings awarded Korean-type titles to court and regional aristocrats, titles that implied a national hierarchy centering on the Yamato court. These regional rulers had the same kind of political authority

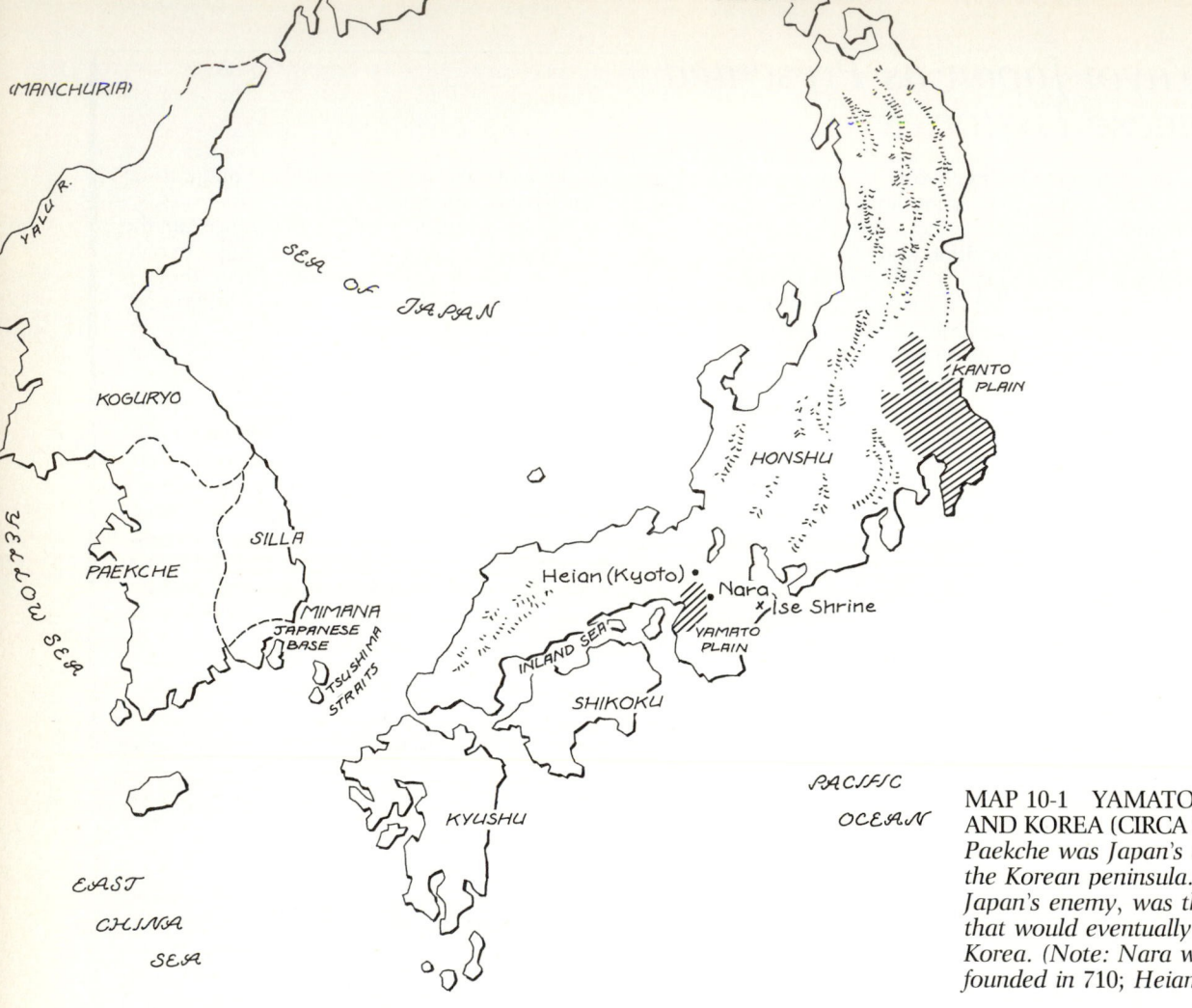

MAP 10-1   YAMATO JAPAN AND KOREA (CIRCA 500 A.D.) *Paekche was Japan's ally on the Korean peninsula. Silla, Japan's enemy, was the state that would eventually unify Korea. (Note: Nara was founded in 710; Heian in 794.)*

over their populations as is substantiated by the spread of tomb mounds to other parts of Japan.

The basic social unit of Yamato aristocratic society was the extended family (*uji*), closer in size to a Scottish clan than to a modern household. Attached to these aristocratic families were groups of specialist workers called *be*. This word was of Korean origin and was originally used to designate potters, scribes, or others with special skills who had immigrated from Korea. It was then extended to include similar groups of indigenous workers and groups of peasants as well. Yamato society had a small class of slaves, possibly captured in wars. There were also large numbers of peasants who were neither slaves nor members of aristocratic clans or specialized workers' groups.

What little is known of Yamato politics suggests that the court was the scene of incessant struggles for power between aristocratic families. There were also continuing efforts by the court to maintain control over outlying regions. Though marriage alliances were established and titles awarded, rebellions were not infre-

quent during the fifth and sixth centuries. Finally, there were constant wars with "barbarian tribes" in southern Kyushu and eastern Honshu on the frontiers of "civilized" Japan.

The Yamato Court and Korea

During the era of the Yamato court, a three-cornered military balance had emerged on the Korean peninsula between the states of Paekche in the southwest, Silla in the east, and Koguryo in the north. Japan was an ally of Paekche. Japan may also have maintained a trading base or military colony on the southern rim of Korea.

The Paekche connection was of vital importance to the Yamato court, enabling the court to expand its power within Japan. Imports of iron weapons and tools gave it military strength. The migration to Japan of Korean potters, weavers, scribes, metalworkers, and other artisans increased its wealth and influence. The significance of the immigrants from Korea can be gauged by the fact that many became established as noble families. Paekche also served as a conduit for elements of Chinese culture. Chinese writing was adopted for the transcription of Japanese names during the fifth or sixth century. Confucianism entered in 513, when Paekche sent a "scholar of the Five Classics." Buddhism first arrived in 538, when the Paekche king sent a Buddha image, sutras, and possibly a priest.

Eventually the political balance on the peninsula shifted against Japan. In 532, Paekche joined Silla in attacking Japan's southern rim colony, and by 562, Japan had been driven from Korea. But the severance of ties with Korea was less of a loss than it would have been earlier, for by this time, Japan had succeeded in establishing direct relations with China.

Religion in Early Japan

The indigenous religion of Yamato Japan was an animistic worship of the forces of nature. This was later given the name of *Shinto*, or "the way of the gods" to distinguish it from Buddhism. In all likelihood, Shinto entered Japan from the continent as a part of Yayoi culture. The underlying forces of nature might be embodied in a waterfall, a twisted tree, a strangely shaped boulder, a mountain, or in a great leader who would be worshiped as a deity after his death. Mount Fuji was holy not as the abode of a god but because the mountain itself was an upwelling of a vital natural force. Even today in Japan, a gnarled tree trunk may be circled with a straw rope and set aside as an object of veneration. The sensitivity to nature and natural beauty that pervades Japanese art and poetry owes much to Shinto. Throughout the historical period, most villages had shamans, or religious specialists who, by entering a trance, could contact directly the inner forces of nature and gain the power to foretell the future or heal sickness. The queen Pimiko was such a shaman. The sorceress is a stock figure in tales of ancient or medieval Japan. And more often than not, women, receiving the command of a god, have

Darkness and the Cave of High Heaven

The younger brother of the sun goddess was a mischief maker. Eventually the gods drove him out of heaven. On one occasion, he knocked a hole in the roof of a weaving hall and dropped in a dappled pony that he had skinned alive. One weaving maiden was so startled that she struck her genitals with the shuttle she was using and died.

The Sun Goddess, terrified at the sight, opened the door of the heavenly rock cave, and hid herself inside. Then the Plain of High Heaven was shrouded in darkness, as was the Central Land of Reed Plains [Japan]. An endless night prevailed. The cries of the myriad gods were like the buzzing of summer flies, and myriad calamities arose.

The eight hundred myriad gods assembled in the bed of the Quiet River of Heaven. They asked one god to think of a plan. They assembled the long-singing birds of eternal night and made them sing. They took hard rocks from the bed of the river and iron from the Heavenly Metal Mountain and called in a smith to make a mirror. They asked the Jewel Ancestor God to make a string of 500 curved jewels eight feet long. They asked other gods to remove the shoulder blade of a male deer and to obtain cherry wood from Mount Kagu, and to perform a divination. They uprooted a sacred tree, attaching the string of curved jewels to its upper branches, hanging the large mirror from its middle branches, and suspending offerings of white and blue cloth from its lower branches.

One god held these objects as grand offerings and another intoned sacred words. The Heavenly Hand-Strong-Male God stood hidden beside the door. A goddess bound up her sleeves with clubmoss from Mount Kagu, made a herb band from the spindle-tree, and bound together leaves of bamboo-grass to hold in her hands. Then she placed a wooden box facedown before the rock cave, stamped on it until it resounded, and, as if possessed, she exposed her breasts and pushed her shirt-band down to her genitals. The Plain of High Heaven shook as the myriad gods broke into laughter.

The Sun Goddess, thinking this strange, opened slightly the rock-cave door and said from within: "Since I have hidden myself I thought that the Plain of Heaven and the Central Land of the Reed Plains would all be in darkness. Why is it that the goddess makes merry and the myriad gods all laugh?"

The goddess replied: "We rejoice and are glad because there is here a god greater than you." While she spoke two other gods brought out the mirror and held it up before the Sun Goddess.

The Sun Goddess, thinking this stranger and stranger, came out the door and peered into the mirror. Then the Hand-Strong-Male God seized her hand and pulled her out. Another god drew a rope behind her and said: "You may not go back further than this."

So when the Sun Goddess had come forth, the Plain of High Heaven and the Central Land of the Reed Plains once again naturally shone in brightness. ❑

From the *Records of Ancient Matters* (Kojiki).

founded the "new" religions in this tradition, even down into the nineteenth and twentieth centuries.

A second aspect of early Shinto was its connection with the state and the ruling posttribal aristocracy. The more potent forces of nature such as the sea, the sun, the moon, the wind, and thunder and lightning became personified as deities. Each clan, or extended family, had its own myth centering on a nature deity (*kami*) that it claimed as its original ancestor. Aristocratic families possessed genealogies tracing their descent from the deity. A genealogy was a patent of nobility and a claim to political authority. The head of a clan was also its chief priest, who made sacrifices to its deity. When Japan was unified by the Yamato court, the myths of the several clans apparently were joined into a national composite myth. The deity of the Yamato great kings was the sun goddess, so she became the chief deity while other gods assumed lesser positions appropriate to the status of their clan.

The *Records of Ancient Matters* and *Records of Japan* tell of the creation of Japan, of the deeds and misdeeds of gods on the "plain of high heaven," and of their occasional adventures on earth or in the underworld. In mid-volume, the stories of the gods, interspersed with the genealogies of noble families, give way to stories of early emperors and early Japanese history. The Japanese emperors, the oldest royal family in the world, were viewed as the lineal descendants of the sun goddess and themselves as "living gods." And the Great Shrine of the Sun Goddess at Ise has always been the most important in Japan.

Nara and Heian Japan

The second major turning point in Japanese history was its adoption of the higher civilization of China. This is a prime example of the worldwide process by which the heartland civilizations (described in Chapter 2) spread into outlying areas. The process in Japan occurred from the seventh through the twelfth century and can best be understood in terms of three stages. The first stage was learning about China. The second stage, mostly during the eighth and ninth centuries, saw the implantation in Japan of Chinese T'ang-type institutions. The third involved the further transformation of these institutions to better fit them to conditions in Japan. By the twelfth century, this creative reworking of Chinese elements led to a distinctive Japanese culture, quite unlike that of China, yet equally unlike that of the earlier Yamato court.

The Seventh Century

The official embassies to China that began in A.D. 607, included traders, students, and Buddhist monks as well as representatives of the Yamato great kings.

Like Third-World students who study abroad today, Japanese who studied in China played key roles in their government when they returned. They brought back with them a quickening flow of technology, art, Buddhism, and knowledge of T'ang legal and governmental systems. But the difficulties of mastering Chinese and comprehending its philosophical culture were enormous for the Yamato Japanese. Large-scale institutional changes using the T'ang model actually began in the 680s with the Emperor Temmu and his successor, the Empress Jitō.

Temmu's life illustrates the interplay between court politics and the adoption of Chinese institutions. He came to the throne by leading an alliance of eastern clans in rebellion against the previous great king, his brother. The *Records of Japan* describe him as "walking like a tiger through the eastern lands." He then used Chinese systems to consolidate his power. He promulgated a Chinese-type law code, which greatly

Prince Shōtoku (574–622) *and two of his sons. Prince Shōtoku was a Buddhist and reformer who began sending regular embassies to China in 607. [Bettmann Archive.]*

augmented the powers of the ruler. He styled himself as the *"heavenly emperor"* (*tennō*), which thereafter replaced the earlier title of *great king*. He rewarded his supporters with new court ranks and with positions in a new court government, both derived from the T'ang example. He extended the authority of the court and increased its revenues by a survey of agricultural lands and a census of their population. In short, although the admiration for Chinese things must have been enormous, much of the borrowing was dictated by specific, immediate, and practical Japanese concerns.

Nara and Early Heian Court Government

Until the eighth century, the capital was usually moved each time an emperor died. Then, in 710, a new capital, intended to be permanent, was established at Nara. It was laid out on a checkerboard grid like the Chinese capital at Ch'ang-an. But then it was moved again—some say to escape the meddling in politics of powerful Buddhist temples. A final move occurred in 794 to Heian (later Kyoto) on the plain north of Nara. This site remained the capital until the move to Tokyo in 1869. Even today, Kyoto's regular geometry reflects the Chinese concepts of city planning.

The superimposition of a Chinese-type capital on a still backward Japan produced as stark a contrast as any in history. In the villages, peasants—who worshiped the forces in mountains and trees—lived in pit dwellings and either planted in crude paddy fields or used slash-and-burn techniques of dry land farming. In the capital stood pillared palaces in which dwelt the emperor and nobles, descended from the gods on high. They drank wine, wore silk, and enjoyed the paintings, perfumes, and pottery of the T'ang. Clustered about the capital were Buddhist temples, more numerous than in Nara, with soaring pagodas and sweeping tile roofs. With what awe must a peasant have viewed the city and its inhabitants!

The emperors at the Nara and Heian courts were both Confucian rulers with the majesty accorded by Chinese law and Shinto rulers descended from the Sun Goddess. Protected by an aura of the sacred, their lineage was never usurped. All Japanese history constitutes a single dynasty—though a few emperors were killed and replaced by other family members.

Beneath the emperor, the same modified Chinese pattern prevailed. Like the T'ang, Japan had a Council of State, but it was more powerful than that of China. It was the office from which leading clans manipulated the authority of an emperor who usually reigned but did not rule. Beneath this council were eight ministries—two more than in China. One of the two was a Secretariat and the other the Imperial Household Ministry. Size affected function: Where T'ang China had a population of sixty million, Nara Japan had only five

8000–300 B.C.	Jōmon Culture
Early Continental Influences	
300 B.C.–A.D. 300	Yayoi Culture
A.D. 300–680	Tomb Culture and the Yamato State
A.D. 680–850	The Chinese T'ang Pattern in Nara and Early Heian Japan

million. There were fewer people to govern in Japan; there were no external enemies to speak of; and much of local rule, in the Yamato tradition, was in the hands of local clans. Consequently, more of the business of court government was with the court itself. Of the six thousand persons in the central ministries, more than four thousand were concerned in one way or another with the imperial house itself. The Imperial Household Ministry had an official staff of 1,296, whereas the Treasury had only 305 and Military Affairs only 198.

Under the central court government were 66 provinces, which were further subdivided into districts and villages. In pre-Nara times, the regions were governed by largely autonomous regional clans; but under the new system, provincial governors were sent out from the capital. The old regional aristocrats were reduced to filling the lesser posts of district magistrates. The new system substantially increased the power of the central aristocracy.

In other respects, Japanese court government was unlike that of China. There were no eunuchs. There was little tension between the emperor and the bureaucracy—the main struggles were between clans. The T'ang movement from aristocracy toward meritocracy was also absent in Japan. Apart from clerks and monastics, only aristocrats were educated, only they took civil service examinations, and only they were appointed to important official posts. And even then, family counted more than grades.

Land and Taxes

The last Japanese embassy to China was in 838. By that time, the frenetic borrowing of Chinese culture had already slowed. The Japanese had taken in all they needed—or, perhaps, all they could handle—and were sufficiently self-confident to use Chinese ideas in innovative and flexible ways. The 350 years that followed until the end of the twelfth century were a time of assimilation and evolutionary change. Nowhere was this more evident than in the system of taxation.

The land system of Nara and early Heian Japan was the "equal field system" of the early T'ang. All land belonged to the emperor; it was redistributed every six years, and taxes were levied on people, not land. Those receiving land were liable for three taxes: a light tax in grain, a light tax in cloth, and a heavy labor tax. The system was complex, requiring land surveys, the redrawing of boundaries, and elaborate land and population registers. Even in China, with its sophisticated bureaucracy, this system broke down. In the case of Japan, the marvel is that it could be carried out at all. The evidence of old registers and recent aerial photographs suggests that it was—at least, in western Japan. Its implementation speaks of the immense energy and ability of the early Japanese, who so quickly absorbed so much of Chinese administrative technique.

Of course, as put into effect, the system was even less equal than in China. Imperial princes and high nobles received thousands or hundreds of units of rank lands, office lands, and merit lands, along with the labor to work them; local officials got much less, and the cultivators did the work.

In history, when changes are legislated or imposed from above, the results tend to be uniform. But when changes occur willy-nilly within a social system, the results are usually messy and difficult to comprehend. The evolution of the land system and taxation in late Heian Japan was of the second type.

One big change was from the equal field system to one of tax quotas payable in grain. First, the redistribution of land broke down and land holdings became hereditary. Officials discovered that peasants would not care for land they did not own. Second, the main tax of labor service was converted to a grain tax. Officials found it more efficient to hire workers and pay them in grain than to use the labor of peasants who had no incentive to work. Third, the taxes levied on provinces and districts were made over into fixed quotas. Court officials could not maintain the elaborate records needed for the equal field system. The court gave each governor a quota and he, in turn, gave one to each district magistrate. Any amount collected over the quota, they kept. The district magistrates, and other local notables and military families associated with them, gradually created a new local ruling class.

Another big change, one that affected about half of the land in late Heian Japan, was the conversion of tax-paying lands to tax-free estates. Nobles and powerful temples in Kyoto did not want to pay taxes, so they used their influence at the court to obtain *immunities*—exemptions from taxation for their lands. From the ninth century, many cultivators began to commend their small holdings to such nobles, judging that they would be better off as serfs on tax-free estates than as free farmers subject to taxation. Because of the random pattern of commendation, the typical estate in Japan was of scattered parcels of land, unlike the unified estates of Europe. The Japanese estates were managed by stewards, appointed from among the local notables. They took a share of the surplus grain for themselves, and forwarded the rest to the noble owner in Kyoto. The stewards, thus, were from the same stratum of local society as those who collected the tax quotas. Like district magistrates, they had a vital interest in upholding the local order.

The Rise of the Samurai

During the Nara period Japan experimented with a military system based on conscription. One third of all able-bodied men between the ages of twenty-one and sixty were taken. Conscript armies, however, proved inefficient, so in 792 the court abolished conscription and began a new system relying on local mounted warriors. Some were stationed in the capital and some in the provinces. They were official troops whose taxes were remitted in exchange for military service. The Japanese verb "to serve" is *samurau*, so those who served became *samurai*—the noun form of the verb. Then, from the mid-Heian period, the officially recruited local warriors were replaced by nonofficial private bands of local warriors. These constituted the military of Japan for the next half millennium or so, until the foot-soldier revolution of the fifteenth and sixteenth centuries.

Being a samurai was expensive. Horses, armor, and weapons were costly, and if they were to be used effectively, long training was required. The primary weapon was the bow and arrow, used from the saddle. Most samurai were from well-to-do local families, such as those of district magistrates or notables, or were from military families supported by the local elites or by temples or shrines. Their initial function was to preserve local order and, possibly, to help with tax collection. But at times, even early on, they contributed to disorder. From the second half of the ninth century, there are accounts of district magistrates leading local forces against provincial governors—doubtless in connection with tax disputes.

From the early tenth century, regional military coalitions or confederations began to form. They first break into history in 939, when a regional military leader, a descendant of an emperor, became involved in a tax dispute. He captured several provinces, called himself the new emperor, and appointed a government of civil and military officials. The Kyoto court responded by recruiting another military band as its champion. The rebellion was quelled, and the rebel leader died in battle. That the Kyoto court could summon a military band points up the connections that enabled it to manipulate local military leaders and maintain its political control of Japan.

The rebellion of 939 was the first of a number of conflicts between regional military bands. Many wars were fought in eastern Japan—the wild east of those days. The east was more militarized because it was the headquarters for the periodic campaigns against the tribal peoples to the north. By the middle of the twelfth century, local and regional military bands were to be found in every part of Japan.

Late Heian Court Government

Even during the Nara period, much of the elaborate apparatus of Chinese government was of little use. By the early Heian period the actual functions of government were taken over by three new offices outside the Chinese system:

1. *Audit officers.* A newly appointed provincial governor had to report on the accounts of his predecessor. Agreement was rare. So from the end of the Nara period, audit officers were sent to examine the books. By early Heian times, these auditors had come to superintend the collection of taxes and most other capital–province relationships. They tried to halt the erosion of tax revenues. But as the quota and estate systems developed, this office had less and less to do.
2. *Bureau of Archivists.* This bureau was established in 810 to record and preserve imperial decrees. Eventually it took over the executive function at the Heian court, drafting imperial decrees and attending to all aspects of the emperor's life.
3. *Police Commissioners.* Established in the second decade of the ninth century to enforce laws and prosecute criminals, the commissioners eventually became responsible for all law and order in the capital. They absorbed military functions as well as those of the Ministry of Justice and the Bureau of Impeachment.

While new institutions were evolving, there also occurred shifts in the control of the court. The key figure remained the emperor, who had the power of appointments. Until the early Heian—say, the mid-ninth century—some emperors actually ruled, or, more often, shared power with nobles of leading clans. From 856, the northern branch of the Fujiwara clan became preeminent, and from 986 to 1086, its stranglehold on the court was absolute. The administrative offices of the Fujiwara house were almost more powerful than those of the central government, and all key government posts were monopolized by members of the Fujiwara family. The Fujiwara controlled the court by marrying their daughters to the emperor, forcing the emperor to retire after a son was born, and then ruling as regents in place of the new infant emperor. At times, they even ruled as regents for adult emperors.

Fujiwara Michinaga's words were no empty boast when he said, "As for this world, I think it is mine, nor is there a flaw in the full moon."

Fujiwara rule gave way, during the second half of the eleventh century, to rule by retired emperors. The imperial family and lesser noble houses had long resented Fujiwara domination. Disputes within the Fujiwara house itself enabled an emperor to regain control. Imperial control of government was reasserted by Emperor Shirakawa, who reigned from 1072 to 1086 and, abdicating at the age of thirty-three, ruled for forty-three years as retired emperor. After his death, other retired emperors continued in the same pattern until 1156.

Ex-Emperor Shirakawa set up offices in his quarters not unlike the administrative offices of the Fujiwara family. He employed talented nobles of lesser families, and sought to reduce the number of estates by trying to confiscate those of the Fujiwara. He failed and ended, instead, by garnering huge estates for the imperial family. He developed strong ties to regional military leaders. His sense of his own power was reflected in his words—more a lament than a boast: "The only things that do not submit to my will are the waters of the Kamo River, the roll of the dice, and the soldier-monks [of the Tendai temple on Mount Hiei to the northeast of Kyoto]." But Shirakawa's powers were exercised in a capital city that was increasingly isolated from the changes in outlying regions. Even the city itself was plagued by fires, banditry, and a sense of impending catastrophe.

A momentous change occurred in 1156. The death of the ruling retired emperor precipitated a struggle for power between another retired emperor and the reigning emperor. Each called in a military confederation for backing. The House of Taira defeated the armies of the Minamoto. Taira Kiyomori had come to Kyoto to uphold an emperor, but finding himself in charge, he stayed to rule. His pattern of rule was quite Japanese: Court nobles kept their Chinese court offices; the reigning emperor, who had been supported by Kiyomori, retired and took control of the offices of the retired emperor and of the estates of the imperial family, which they managed; the head of the Fujiwara family kept the post of regent, while Taira Kiyomori married his daughter to the new emperor, and when a

WHO WAS IN CHARGE AT THE NARA AND HEIAN COURTS

710–856	Emperors or combinations of nobles
856–1086	Fujiwara nobles
1086–1156	Retired emperors
1156–1180	The military house of Taira

In the Heiji War of 1156, regional samurai bands became involved in Kyoto court politics. A scroll painting of the burning of the Sanjō Palace. [Museum of Fine Arts, Boston. Fenollosa-Weld Collection.]

son was born, Kiyomori forced the emperor to retire and ruled as the maternal grandfather of the infant emperor.

Aristocratic Culture and Buddhism in Nara and Heian Japan

If culture could be put on a scale and weighed like sugar or flour, we would conclude that the culture of Nara and early Heian Japan was overwhelmingly one of Shinto religious practices and village folkways, an extension of the culture of the late Yamato period. The aristocracy was small and was encapsulated in the routine of court life, just as the Buddhist monks were contained within the rounds of their monastic life. The early Heian aristocracy comprised one tenth of one per cent of Japan's population. Most of the court culture had only recently been imported from China. There had not been time for the commoners to ape their betters, or for the powerful force of the indigenous culture to reshape that of the elite.

The resulting cultural gap helps to explain why the aristocrats, in so far as we can tell from literature, found the commoners to be odd, incomprehensible, and, indeed, hardly human. The writings of the courtiers reflect little sympathy for the suffering and hardships of the people—except in Chinese-type poetry, where such feelings were deemed appropriate. When the fictional Prince Genji stoops to an affair with an impoverished woman, she is inevitably a princess. Sei Shōnagon was not atypical as a writer: She was offended by the vulgarity of mendicant nuns, laughed at an illiterate old man whose house had burned down,

and found lacking in charm the eating habits of carpenters, who wolfed down their food a bowl at a time.

Heian high culture resembled a hothouse plant. It was protected by the political influence of the court. It was nourished by the flow of tax revenues and income from estates. Under these conditions, the aristocrats of the never-never land of Prince Genji indulged in a unique way of life, and created canons of elegance and taste that are striking even today. The speed with which T'ang culture was assimilated and reworked was amazing. A few centuries after Mediterranean culture was introduced into northern Europe, there had appeared nothing even remotely comparable to the *Tale of Genji* or the *Pillow Book*.

The Chinese Tradition in Japan

Education at the Nara and Heian courts was largely a matter of reading Chinese books and acquiring the skills needed to compose poetry and prose in Chinese. These were enormous tasks not only because there was no prior tradition of scholarship in Japan but because the two languages were so dissimilar. To master written Chinese and use it for everyday written communications was as daunting a challenge for the Nara Japanese as it would have been for any European of the same century, but the challenge was successfully met. From the Nara period until the nineteenth century, most philosophical and legal writings, and most of the histories, essays, and religious texts in Japan, were written in Chinese. From a Chinese perspective, the writings may leave something to be desired. It would be astonishing if this were not the case, for the soul of language is the music of the spoken tongue. But the Japanese writers were competent, and

The Development of Japanese Writing

No two languages could be more different than Chinese and Japanese. Chinese is nonsyllabic, uninflected, and tonal. Japanese is polysyllabic, highly inflected, and atonal. To adopt Chinese writing for use in Japanese was thus no easy task. What the Japanese did at first—when they were not simply learning to write in Chinese—was to use certain Chinese ideographs as a phonetic script. For example, in the Man'yōshū, the eighth-century poetic anthology, shira-nami (white wave) was written with 之 for shi, 良 for ra, 奈 for na, and 美 for mi. Over several centuries, these phonetic ideographs evolved into a uniquely Japanese phonetic script:

	Original Chinese Ideograph	Simplified Ideograph	Phonetic Script (*kana*)
shi	之	亾	し
ra	良	戾	ら
na	奈	夵	な
mi	美	乄	み

It is apparent in the above examples how the original ideograph was first simplified according to the rules of calligraphy and was then further simplified into a phonetic script. In modern Japanese, unmodified Chinese ideographs are used for nouns and verb stems, and the phonetic script is used for inflections and particles.

学生 は 図書館 へ 行きました。

Students/as for/library/to/went.
(The students went to the library.)

In the above sentence, the Chinese ideographs are the forms with many strokes, and the phonetic script is shown in the simpler, cursive forms. ❑

---

the feelings and ideas that they expressed were authentic—when not copybook exercises in the style of a Chinese master. In 883, when Sugawara Michizane wrote a poem on the death of his son, he quite naturally wrote it in Chinese. The poem began:

> Since Amaro died I cannot sleep at night;
> if I do, I meet him in dreams and tears come
> coursing down.
> Last summer he was over three feet tall;
> this year he would have been seven years old.
> He was diligent and wanted to know how to
> be a good son,
> read his books and recited by heart the "Poem
> on the Capital."[2]

The capital referred to was Ch'ang-an, and the poem, one "used in Japan as a text for little boys learning to read Chinese."

Not only were Japanese writings in Chinese a vital

[2]H. Sato and B. Watson (trans.), *From the Country of Eight Islands* (1981), p. 121.

part of the Japanese cultural tradition, but the original Chinese works themselves also became a part of the same tradition. The late T'ang poet Po Chu-i was early appreciated and widely read, and later, Tu Fu and Li Po were also read and admired. As in China itself, Chinese history was read, and its stock figures were among the heroes and villains of the Japanese historical consciousness. Chinese history became the mirror in which Japan saw itself—despite the differences in the two societies. Buddhist stories and the books of Confucianism also became Japanese classics, continuously accessible and consulted over the centuries for their wisdom and philosophy. The parallel might be the Bible, Plato, and Aristotle in England.

The Birth of Japanese Literature

Stimulated by Chinese models, the Japanese began to compose poetry in their native tongue. The first major anthology was the *Collection of Ten Thousand Leaves* (*Man'yōshū*), compiled in about 760. It contained 4,516 poems. The sentiments in the poems are fresh, sometimes simple and straightforward, but

Aristocratic Taste at the Fujiwara Court:
Sei Shōnagon Records Her Likes and Dislikes

Elegant Things:
A white coat worn over a violet waistcoat.
Duck eggs.
Shaved ice mixed with liana syrup and put in a new silver bowl.
A rosary of rock crystal.
Snow on wistaria or plum blossoms.
A pretty child eating strawberries.

Pleasing Things:
Someone has torn up a letter and thrown it away. Picking up the pieces, one finds that many of them can be fitted together.

A person in whose company one feels awkward asks one to supply the opening or closing line of a poem. If one happens to recall it, one is very pleased. Yet often on such occasions one completely forgets something that one would normally know.

Entering the Empress's room and finding that ladies-in-waiting are crowded round her in a tight group, I go next to a pillar which is some distance from where she is sitting. What a delight it is when Her Majesty summons me to her side so that all the others have to make way!

Hateful Things:
A lover who is leaving at dawn announces that he has to find his fan and his paper. "I know I put them somewhere last night," he says. Since it is pitch dark, he gropes about the room, bumping into the furniture and muttering, "Strange! Where on earth can they be?" Finally he discovers the objects. He thrusts the paper into the breast of his robe with a great rustling sound; then he snaps open his fan and busily fans away with it. Only now is he ready to take his leave. What charmless behavior! "Hateful" is an understatement.

A good lover will behave as elegantly at dawn as at any other time. He drags himself out of bed with a look of dismay on his face. The lady urges him on: "Come, my friend, it's getting light. You don't want anyone to find you here." He gives a deep sigh, as if to say that the night has not been nearly long enough and that it is agony to leave. Once up, he does not

often sophisticated. They reveal a deep sensitivity to nature and strong human relationships between husband and wife, parents and children. They also display a love for the land of Japan and links to a Shinto past.

An early obstacle to the development of a Japanese poetic tradition was the difficulty of transcribing Japanese sounds. In the *Ten Thousand Leaves*, Chinese characters were used as phonetic symbols. But there was no standardization, and the work soon became unintelligible. In 951, when an empress wished to read it, a committee of poets deciphered the work and put it into *kana*, the new syllabic script or alphabet that had developed during the ninth century. A second major anthology was the *Collection of Ancient and Modern Times*, compiled in 905. It was written entirely in *kana*.

The invention of *kana* opened the gate to the most

brilliant developments of the Heian period. Most of the new works and certainly the greatest were by women, as most men were busy writing Chinese. One genre of writing was the diary or travel diary. An outstanding example of this genre was the *Izumi Shikibu Diary*, in which Izumi Shikibu reveals her tempestuous loves through a record of poetic exchanges.

The greatest works of the Heian period were by Sei Shōnagon and Murasaki Shikibu. Both were daughters of provincial officials serving at the Heian court. The *Pillow Book* of Sei Shōnagon contains sharp, satirical, amusing essays and literary jottings that reveal the demanding aristocratic taste of the early-eleventh-century Heian court—for which, as Sir George Sansom said, "religion became an art and art a religion."[3]

[3]G. Sansom, *Japan, A Short Cultural History* (New York: Appleton-Century-Crofts, 1962), p. 239.

instantly pull on his trousers. Instead he comes close to the lady and whispers whatever was left unsaid during the night. Even when he is dressed, he still lingers, vaguely pretending to be fastening his sash.

Presently he raises the lattice, and the two lovers stand together by the side door while he tells her how he dreads the coming day, which will keep them apart; then he slips away. The lady watches him go, and this moment of parting will remain among her most charming memories.

In Spring It Is the Dawn:
In spring it is the dawn that is most beautiful. As the light creeps over the hills, their outlines are dyed a faint red and wisps of purplish cloud trail over them.

In summer the nights. Not only when the moon shines, but on dark nights too, as the fireflies flit to and fro, and even when it rains, how beautiful it is!

In autumn the evenings, when the glittering sun sinks close to the edge of the hills and the crows fly back to their nests in threes and fours and twos; more charming still is a file of wild geese, like specks in the distant sky. When the sun has set, one's heart is moved by the sound of the wind and the hum of the insects.

In winter the early mornings. It is beautiful indeed when snow has fallen during the night, but splendid too when the ground is white with frost; or even when there is no snow or frost, but it is simply very cold and the attendants hurry from room to room stirring up the fires and bringing charcoal, how well this fits the season's mood! But as noon approaches and the cold wears off, no one bothers to keep the braziers alight, and soon nothing remains but piles of white ashes.

Things That Have Lost Their Power:
A large tree that has been blown down in a gale and lies on its side with its roots in the air.

The retreating figure of a sumō wrestler who has been defeated in a match.

A woman, who is angry with her husband about some trifling matter, leaves home and goes somewhere to hide. She is certain that he will rush about looking for her; but he does nothing of the kind and shows the most infuriating indifference. Since she cannot stay away for ever, she swallows her pride and returns. ❑

I. Morris (trans.), *The Pillow Book of Sei Shōnagon*, (New York: Columbia U. P., 1967), pp. 49, 216–217, 29–30, 1, 132.

The *Tale of Genji*, written by Murasaki Shikibu in about 1010, was the world's first novel. Emerging out of a short tradition of lesser works in which prose was a setting for poetry, *Genji* is a work of sensitivity, originality, and precise psychological delineation of character, for which there was no Chinese model. It tells of the life, loves, and sorrows of Prince Genji, the son of an imperial concubine, and, after his death, of his son Kaoru. The novel spans three quarters of a century and is historical in nature, though the court society it describes is more emperor-centered than the Fujiwara age in which Murasaki lived. Perhaps the book may be seen as having had a "definite and serious purpose." In one passage, Genji first twits a court lady whom he finds reading an extravagant romance; she is "hardly able to lift her eyes from the book in front of her." But then Genji relents and says:

I think far better of this art than I have led you to suppose. Even its practical value is immense. Without it what should we know of how people lived in the past, from the Age of the Gods down to the present day? For history books such as the *Chronicles of Japan* show us only one small corner of life; whereas these diaries and romances, which I see piled around you contain, I am sure, the most minute information about all sorts of people's private affairs.[4]

Nara and Heian Buddhism

The Six Sects of the Nara period each represented a separate philosophical doctrine within Mahayana

[4]R. Tsunoda, W. T. deBary, and D. Keene (eds.), *Sources of the Japanese Tradition* (New York: Columbia University Press, 1958), p. 181.

Buddhism. Their monks trained as religious specialists in monastic communities set apart from the larger society. They studied, read sutras, copied texts, meditated, and joined in rituals. The typical monastery was a self-contained community with a Golden Hall for worship, a pagoda that housed a relic or sutra, a belfry that rang the hours of the monastic regimen, a lecture hall, a refectory, and dormitories with monks' cells.

As in China, monasteries and temples were involved with the state. Tax revenues were assigned for their support. Monks prayed for rain in time of drought. In 741, temples were established in every province to protect the state by reading sutras. Monks prayed for the health of the emperor. The Temple of the Healing Buddha (Yakushiji) was built by an emperor when his consort fell ill. In China, in order to protect tax revenues and the family, laws were enacted to limit the number of monks and nuns. In Nara

Japan, where Buddhism spread only slowly outside the capital area, the same laws took on a prescriptive force. The figure that had been a limit in China became a goal in Japan. Thus the involvement of the state was the same as in China, but its role was far more supportive.

Japan in the seventh and eighth centuries was also far less developed culturally than China. The Japanese came to Buddhism not from the philosophical perspectives of Confucianism or Taoism, but from the magic and mystery of Shinto. The appeal of Buddhism to the early Japanese was, consequently, in its colorful and elaborate rituals; in the gods, demons, and angels of the Mahayana pantheon; and, above all, in the beauty of Buddhist art. The philosophy took longer to establish itself. The speed with which the Japanese mastered the construction of temples with elaborate wooden brackets and gracefully arching tile roofs, as well as

The Hōryūji Temple built by Prince Shōtoku in 607, contains the oldest wooden buildings in the world. They are the best surviving examples of Chinese Buddhist architecture. [Japan Information Center.]

the loveliness of Nara Buddhist sculpture, wall paintings, and lacquer temple altars, was no less an achievement than the establishment of a political system based on the T'ang codes.

Japan's cultural identity was also different. In China, Buddhism was always viewed as Indian and alien. Its earliest Buddha statues, like those of northwestern India, looked Greek. That Buddhism was part of a non-Chinese culture was one factor leading to the Chinese persecution of Buddhists during the ninth century. In contrast, Japan's cultural identity or cultural self-consciousness took shape only during the Nara and early Heian periods. One element in that identity was the imperial cult derived from Shinto. But as a religion, Shinto was no match for Buddhism. The Japanese were aware that Buddhism was foreign, but it was no more so than Confucianism and all of the rest of the T'ang culture that had helped shape the major portion of the Japanese identity, so there was no particular bias against it. Consequently, Buddhism entered deeply into Japanese culture and retained its vitality longer. It was not until the seventeenth or eighteenth centuries that Japanese elites became so Confucian as to be anti-Buddhist.

In 794, the court moved to Heian. Buddhist temples soon became as entrenched in the new capital as they had been in Nara. The two great new Buddhist sects of the Heian era were Tendai and Shingon.

Saichō (767–822) had founded a temple on Mount Hiei to the northwest of Kyoto in 785. He went to China as a student monk in 804 and returned the following year with the teachings of the Tendai sect (*T'ien T'ai* in Chinese; see Chapter 9). He spread in Japan the doctrine that salvation was not solely for monastic specialists but could be attained by all who led a life of contemplation and moral purity. He was a religious reformer who instituted strict monastic rules and a twelve-year training curriculum for novice monks at his mountain monastery. Over the next few centuries, the sect grew until thousands of temples had been built on Mount Hiei, and it remained a center of Japanese Buddhism until it was destroyed in the wars of the sixteenth century. Many later Japanese sects emerged from within the Tendai fold, stressing one or another doctrine within its syncretic teachings.

The Shingon sect was begun by Kūkai (774–835). He studied Confucianism, Taoism, and Buddhism at the court university. Deciding that Buddhism was superior, he became a monk at the age of eighteen. In 804, he went to China with Saichō. He returned two years later bearing the Shingon doctrines and founded a monastery on Mount Kōya to the south of the Nara plain and far from the new capital. Kūkai was an extraordinary figure. He was a bridge builder, a poet, an artist, and one of the three great calligraphers of his age. He is sometimes credited with inventing the *kana* syllabary and with introducing tea into Japan. Shingon doctrines center on an eternal and cosmic Buddha, of whom all other Buddhas are manifestations. *Shingon* means "true word" or "mantra," a verbal formula with mystical powers. It is sometimes called *esoteric Buddhism* because it had secret teachings that were passed from master to disciple. In China, Shingon died out as a sect in the persecutions of the mid-ninth century, but it was tremendously successful in Japan. Its doctrines even spread to the Tendai center on Mount Hiei. Part of the appeal was in its air of mystery and its complex rituals involving signs, the manipulation of religious objects, and mandalas—maps of the cosmic Buddhist universe.

During the later Heian period, Buddhism began to be assimilated. In village culture, many Buddhist elements were taken into folk religion. In Japanese high culture, Shinto was almost absorbed by Buddhism. Shinto deities came to be seen as the local manifestations of universal Buddhas. The cosmic or "Great Sun Buddha" of the Shingon sect, for example, was easily identified with the sun goddess. Often, great Buddhist temples had smaller Shinto shrines on their grounds. The job of the Buddha was to watch over Japan, whereas the shrine deity had the lesser task of guarding the temple itself. Not till the mid-nineteenth century was Shinto disentangled from Buddhism, and then for political ends.

Japan's Early Feudal Age

The year 1185, or 1156 if we include Taira rule in Kyoto, marked another major turning point in Japanese history. It began the shift from centuries of rule by a civil aristocracy to centuries of rule by one that was military. It saw the formation of the *bakufu* (tent government), a completely non-Chinese type of government. It saw the emergence of the *shogun* as the *de facto* ruler of Japan, though in theory he was a military official of the emperor. It marked the beginning of new cultural forms, and initiated changes in family and social organization.

The Rise of Minamoto Yoritomo

The seizure of Kyoto by Taira Kiyomori's military band in 1156 fell far short of being a national military hegemony, for other bands still flourished elsewhere in Japan. In the decades after Kiyomori's victory, the Taira embraced the elegant lifestyle of the Kyoto court while ties to their base area along the Inland Sea weakened. They assumed that their tutelage over the court would be as enduring as had been that of the Fujiwara. In the meantime, the Minamoto were rebuilding their strength in eastern Japan. In 1180, Minamoto Yoritomo responded to a call to arms by a disaf-

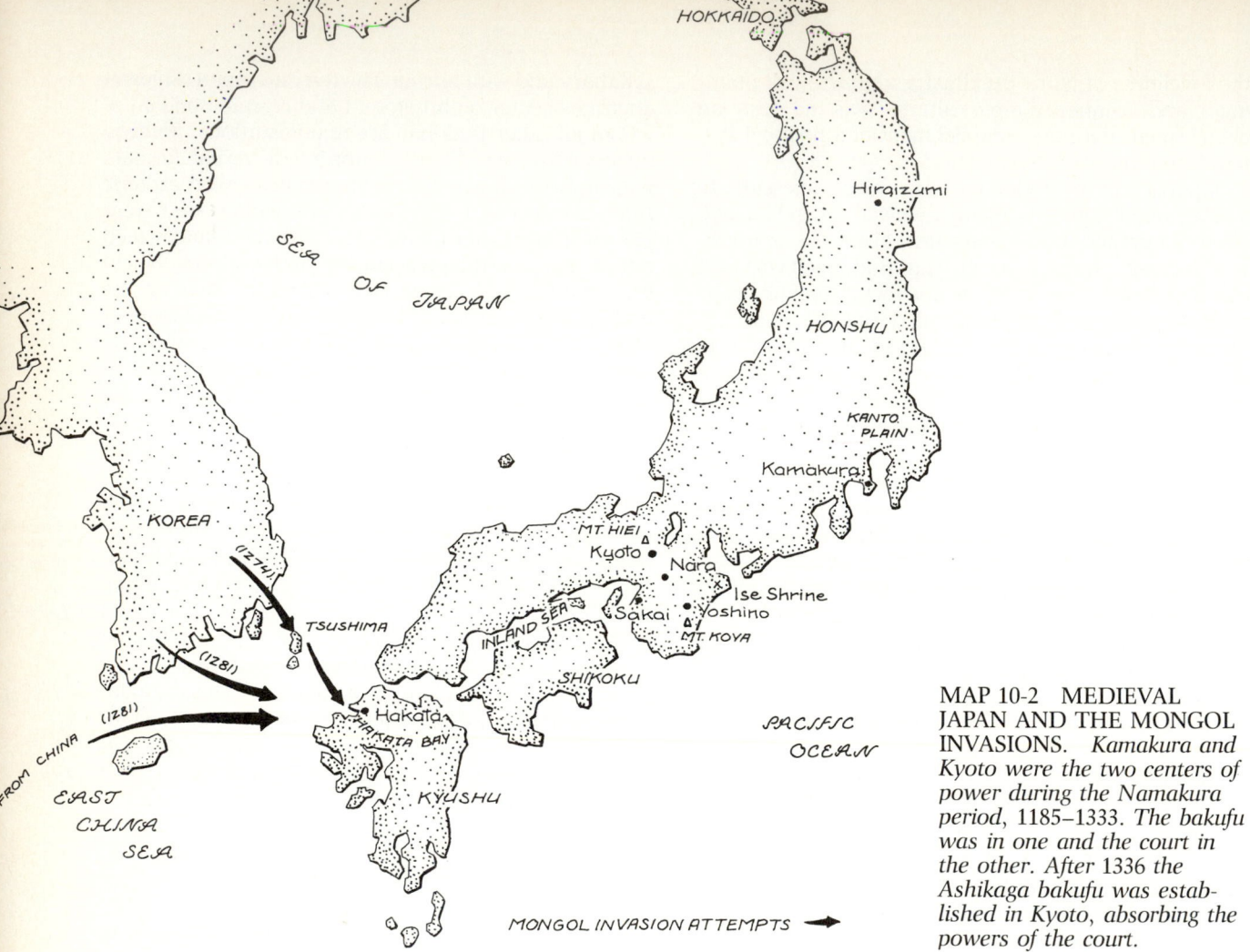

MAP 10-2 MEDIEVAL
JAPAN AND THE MONGOL
INVASIONS. *Kamakura and
Kyoto were the two centers of
power during the Namakura
period, 1185–1333. The bakufu
was in one and the court in
the other. After 1336 the
Ashikaga bakufu was established in Kyoto, absorbing the
powers of the court.*

fected prince, seized control of eastern Japan (the rich Kanto plain), and began the war that ended in 1185 with the downfall of the Taira.

Yoritomo's victory in 1185 was national, for his armies had ranged over most of Japan. After his victory, warriors from every area vied to become his vassals. Wary of the blandishments of Kyoto that had weakened the Taira forces, Yoritomo set up his headquarters at Kamakura. It was thirty miles south of present-day Tokyo, at the edge of his base of power in eastern Japan. He called his government the *bakufu* (literally, "tent government") in contrast to the civil government in Kyoto. Like the house government of the Fujiwara or the "cloister government" of the retired emperors, the offices he established were few and practical: one to deal with his samurai retainers, one to administer and execute his policies, and one to hear legal suits. Each office was staffed by vassals. The decisions of these offices, built up into a body of customary law, were codified in 1232 as the Jōei Code. Yoritomo also appointed military governors in each

province and military stewards on the former estates of the Taira and others who had fought against him. These appointments carried the right to some of the income from the land. The rest of the income, as earlier, went to Kyoto as taxes or as revenues to the noble owners of the estates.

The Question of Feudalism

Scholars often contend that Yoritomo's rule marks the start of feudalism in Japan. Feudalism may be defined in terms of three criteria: lord–vassal relationships, fiefs given in return for military service, and a warrior ethic. Do these apply to Kamakura Japan?

Certainly, the mounted warriors who made up the armies of Yoritomo were his vassals, not his kin. The Minamoto and Taira houses were originally clans or extended families, very much like the Fujiwara or the earlier Yamato nobility. Yoritomo's brothers were among his generals. But after he came to power, he favored his vassals over his kin, and the lateral ties of blood gave way to the vertical and political lord–

vassal bond. On the question of fiefs, the answer is ambiguous. Kamakura vassals received rights to income from land in exchange for military service. But the income was usually a slice of the surplus from the estates of Kyoto nonmilitary aristocrats. Fiefs, as such, did not appear until the late fifteenth century.

However, there is no ambiguity regarding the warrior ethic, which had been developing among regional military bands for several centuries before 1185. The samurai prized martial qualities such as bravery, cunning, physical strength, and endurance. They gave their swords names. Their sports were hunting, hawking, and archery—loosing their arrows at the target while riding at full tilt. If the military tales of the period are to be believed, their combat was often individual, and before engaging in battle, warriors would call out their pedigrees. That is to say, warriors thought of themselves as a military aristocracy that practiced "the way of the bow and arrow," "the way of the bow and horse," "the way of the warriors," and so on. In the *Tale of Heike*, a military romance recounting the struggle between the Taira and the Minamoto, a Taira general asks a vassal from eastern Japan:

"Sanemori, in the eight eastern provinces are there many men who are as mighty archers as you are?"

"Do you then consider me a mighty archer?" asked Sanemori with a scornful smile. "I can only draw an arrow thirteen handbreadths long. In the eastern provinces there are any number of warriors who can do so. There is one famed archer who never draws a shaft less than fifteen handbreadths long. So mighty is his bow that four or five ordinary men must pull together to bend it. When he shoots, his arrow can easily pierce two or three suits of armor at once. Even a warrior from a small estate has at least five hundred soldiers. They are bold horsemen who never fall, nor do they let their horses stumble on the roughest road. When they fight, they do not care if even their parents or children are killed; they ride on over their bodies and continue the battle.

"The warriors of the western province are quite different. If their parents are killed, they retire from the battle and perform Buddhist rites to console the souls of the dead. Only after the mourning is over will they fight again. If their children are slain, their grief is so deep that they cease fighting altogether. When their rations have given out, they plant rice in the fields and go out to fight only after reaping it. They dislike the heat of summer. They grumble at the severe cold of winter. This is not the way of the soldiers of the eastern provinces."[5]

The Taira soldiers, according to the story, "heard his words and trembled."

The Kamakura military band thus pretty well fits our definition of feudalism. Nonetheless, qualifications

are in order, since Kamakura warrior bands were only a part of the total society. One qualification is that Kamakura Japan still had two political centers. The bakufu had military authority, but the Kyoto court continued the late Heian pattern of civil rule. It appointed civil governors; it received tax revenues; and it controlled the region about Kyoto. Noble families, retired emperors, and the great Buddhist temples—in control of vast estates—also contributed to Kyoto's ongoing power; and it also remained the fount of rank and honors. After his victory in 1185, Yoritomo asked the emperor for the title of *barbarian-quelling generalissimo* (*Sei i tai shōgun*, conventionally shortened to *shōgun*). He was refused, and only after the retired emperor died in 1192 did Yoritomo get the title to match his power. Yoritomo's request for the title was partly justified by the fact that he was a Minamoto offshoot of the imperial line.

The small size of Yoritomo's vassal band is an even more telling argument against viewing Japan as fully feudal at this time. Numbering about two thousand before 1221 and three thousand thereafter, most of the band were concentrated in eastern Japan. But even if as many as half were distributed about the rest of the country as military governors and stewards, there would only have been one hundred in a region the size of Massachusetts, as Japan in 1180 was about fifteen times larger than that state. Given the difficulties of transportation and communications, how could so few control such a large area? The answer is that they did not have to.

The local social order of the late Heian era continued into the Kamakura period. Governors, district magistrates, local notables—including many warriors who were not members of Yoritomo's band—were in place and continued to function more or less as they had earlier. To gain an influence on the local scene, the newly appointed Kamakura vassals had to win the cooperation of these local figures. In short, even if the Kamakura vassals themselves can be called "feudal," they were no more than a thin skim on the surface of a society constructed according to older principles.

Kamakura Rule After Yoritomo

As soon as Yoritomo died in 1199, his widow and her Hōjō kinsmen moved to usurp the power of the Minamoto house. The widow, having taken holy orders after her husband's death, was known as the Nun Shōgun. One of her sons was pushed aside. The other became shōgun but was murdered in 1219. After that, the Hōjō ruled as regents for a puppet shōgun, just as the Fujiwara had been regents for figurehead emperors. The Kyoto court tried to take advantage of the usurpation to lead an armed uprising against Kamakura in 1221, but the rebellion was quickly suppressed. New military stewards were then placed on

---

[5] H. Kitagawa and B. Tsuchida (trans.), *The Tale of Heike* (Tokyo, Tokyo University Press, 1975), p. 330.

Mongol invaders battling with intrepid samurai horseman. Note the bomb bursting in air at the upper right of this late thirteenth century Japanese scroll painting. [Tokyo National Museum.]

the lands of those who had joined in the uprising. Any society based on personal bonds faces the problem of how to transfer loyalty from one generation to another. In 1221, the Kamakura vassals fought for the Hōjō, despite the Hōjō usurpation of the Minamoto rule. Loyalty to the institution of the bakufu, which guaranteed their landed interests, had replaced personal loyalty.

In 1266, Kublai Khan (see Chapter 9) sent envoys demanding that Japan submit to his rule. Korea had been subjugated in 1258, and his army looked outward across the Tsushima Straits. The Kyoto court was terrified, but the Hōjō at Kamakura refused. The first Mongol invasion fleet arrived with 30,000 troops in 1274, but was destroyed by a typhoon. The Mongols again sent envoys. This time, they were beheaded. A second invasion force arrived in 1281, two years after Kublai had completed his conquest of south China. Carrying 140,000 troops, it was an amphibious operation on a scale never before seen in world history. With gunpowder bombs and phalanxes of archers protected by a forward wall of soldiers carrying overlapping shields, the Mongol forces were formidable.

The Japanese tactics of fierce individual combat were not appropriate to their foe. But a wall of stone had been erected along the curved shoreline of Hakata Bay in northwest Kyushu, and the Mongols were held off for two months until again *kamikaze*, or "divine winds," sank a portion of their fleet and forced the rest to withdraw. Preparations for a third expedition ended with Kublai's death in 1294.

The burden of repelling the Mongols fell on Kamakura's vassals in Kyushu. Non-Kamakura warriors of Kyushu also were mobilized to fight under the command of military governors. But as no land was taken, unlike in 1221, there were few rewards for those who had fought, and dissatisfaction was rife. Even temples and shrines demanded rewards, claiming that their prayers had brought about the divine winds.

Women in Warrior Society

The Nun Shōgun was one of a long line of important women in Japan. Historians no longer speak of an early matriarchal age. But the central figure of Japanese mythology was the sun goddess, who ruled the Plain of High Heaven. In the late Yayoi age the shaman ruler Pimiko was probably not an exceptional figure; she was followed by the empresses of the Yamato and Nara courts, and they, in turn, by the great women writers of the Heian period. During the era of the Kamakura bakufu, there was only one Nun Shōgun, but the daughters of warrior families, as well as the sons, often trained in archery and other military arts. Women also occasionally inherited the position of military steward. As long as society was stable, women fared relatively well. But as fighting became more common in the fourteenth century, their position began to decline, and as warfare became endemic in the fifteenth, their status plummeted. It was at this time that multigeniture gave way to male primogeniture to protect the military fief—the warrior's reward for serving his lord in battle, and the lord's guarantee that his warriors would continue their service.

The Ashikaga Era

At times, formal political institutions seem rocklike in their stability and history unfolds within the framework that they provide. Then, almost as if a kaleidoscope had been shaken, the old institutions collapse and are swept away. In their place appear new institutions and new patterns of personal relations which, often enough, had begun to take shape within the confines of the old. It is not easy to explain the timing of such upheavals, but they are easy to recognize. One occurred in Japan between 1331 and 1336.

Various tensions developed within late Kamakura society. The patrimony of a warrior was divided among his children. Over several generations, vassals became poorer, often falling into debt. High-ranking vassals of Kamakura were dissatisfied with the Hōjō monopolization of key bakufu posts. In the meantime, the ties of vassals to Kamakura were weakening, while the ties to other warriors within their region were growing stronger. New regional bands were ready to emerge.

The precipitating event was a revolt in 1331 by an emperor who thought emperors should actually rule. Kamakura sent Ashikaga Takauji, the head of a branch family of the Minamoto line, to put down the revolt. Instead, he joined it, giving a clear signal to other regional lords, who threw off Kamakura's control. The Hōjō bakufu in Kamakura collapsed.

What emerged out of the dust and confusion of the period 1331–1336 was a regional multistate system centering on Kyoto. Each region was based on a warrior band about the size of the band that had brought Yorimoto to power a century and a half earlier. In the central Kyoto region, Ashikaga Takauji (1305–1358) established his bakufu. Its offices were simple and functional: a samurai office for police and military matters, an administrative office for financial matters, a documents office for land records, and a judicial board to settle disputes. The offices were staffed by Takauji's vassals, with the most trusted vassals holding the highest posts. They were lords (now called *daimyo*) in their own right who also, usually, held appointments as military governors in the provinces surrounding Kyoto. The bakufu also appointed vassals to watch over its interests in the far north, in eastern Japan, and in Kyushu.

Government in the outlying regions was more diverse. Some lords held several provinces, some only one. Some had integrated most of the warriors in their areas into their bands. Others had several unassimilated military bands in their territories, forcing them to rely more on the authority of Kyoto. Formally, all regional lords or *daimyo* were the vassals of the shōgun. But the relationship was often nominal. Sometimes the regional lords lived on their lands; sometimes they lived in Kyoto.

The relationship between the Kyoto bakufu and the regional lords fluctuated during the period from 1336 to 1467. At times, able lords made their regions into virtually independent states. At other times, the Kyoto

GOVERNMENT BY MILITARY HOUSES

1156–1180	Taira rule in Kyoto
1185–1333	The Kamakura Bakufu
1185	Founded by Minamoto Yoritomo
1219	Usurped by Hōjō
1221	Armed uprising by Kyoto court
1232	Formation of Jōei Legal Code
1274 and 1281	Invasion by Mongols
1336–1467	The Ashikaga Bakufu
1336	Begun by Ashikaga Takauji
1392	End of Southern Court
1467	Start of warring states

bakufu became stronger. The third shōgun, for example, tightened his grip on the Kyoto court. He even relinquished the military post of shōgun—to his son in 1394—in order to take the highest civil post of grand minister of state. He improved relations with the great Buddhist temples and Shinto shrines and established ties with Ming China. Most significant were his military campaigns, which dented the autonomy of regional lords outside of the inner Kyoto circle.

But the institution of vassalage in Japan's early feudal society contained a contradiction that even the third shōgun could not overcome. He had to rely on his vassals. To strengthen them for his campaigns, he gave them the authority to levy taxes; to unify in their own hands all judicial, administrative, and military authority in their regions; and to take on unaffiliated warriors as their direct vassals. But in doing so, he left problems for his successors. As ties of personal loyalty wore thin, local warrior bands began to form in the interstices of the Ashikaga regional states.

Agriculture, Commerce, and Medieval Guilds

Population figures for medieval Japan are rough estimations, but recent scholarship suggests six million for the year 1200 and twelve million for 1600. Much of the increase occurred during the Kamakura and Ashikaga periods when the country was fairly peaceful. The increase was brought about by land reclamation and improvements in agricultural technology: Iron-edged tools became available to all. New strains of rice were developed. Irrigation and diking improved. Double cropping began: vegetables in dry fields during fall and winter, and rice in irrigated paddies during the spring and summer.

In the Nara and early Heian periods, the economy was almost exclusively agricultural. Japan had no money, no commerce, and no cities—apart from Nara, which developed into a temple town living on assigned revenues, and Kyoto, where taxes were consumed. Following the example of China, the government had established a mint, but little money actually circulated. Taxes were paid in grain and labor. Commercial transactions were largely barter, with silk or grain as the medium of exchange. Artisans produced for the noble households or temples to which they were attached. Peasants were economically self-sufficient.

From the late Heian period, partly as a side effect of fixed tax quotas, more of the growing agricultural surplus stayed in local hands. This trend accelerated during the Kamakura and Ashikaga periods, when there was a transfer of income from the court aristocrats to the warrior class. As this occurred, artisans detached themselves from noble households and began to produce for the market. Military equipment was an early staple of commerce, but gradually *sake*, lumber, paper, vegetable oils, salt, and products of the sea also became commercialized. A demand for copper coins appeared, and as they were no longer minted in Japan, they were imported in increasingly huge quantities from China.

During the Kamakura period, independent merchants handling the products of artisans appeared as well. Some trade networks spread over all Japan. More often, artisan and merchant guilds, not unlike those of medieval Europe, paid a fee in exchange for monopoly rights in a given area. Early Kyoto guilds paid fees to powerful nobles or temples, and later to the Ashikaga bakufu. In outlying areas, guild privileges were obtained from the regional feudal lords. From the Kamakura period on, markets were held periodically in many parts of Japan—by a river or at a crossroads. Some place names in Japan today reveal such an origin. Yokkaichi, today an industrial city, means "fourth-day market." It began as a place where markets were held on the fourth, fourteenth, and twenty-fourth days of each month. During the fourteenth and fifteenth centuries, such markets were held with increasing frequency until, eventually, permanent towns were established.

Buddhism and Medieval Culture

The Nara and Heian periods are often referred to as Japan's classical age. The period that followed—say, from 1200 to 1600—is often called medieval. It was medieval in the root sense of the word in that it lay between the other two major spans of premodern Japanese history. It was also medieval in that it shared some characteristics that we label *medieval* in Europe and China. However, there is an important difference. Medieval Japan was a direct outgrowth of classical Japan; one can even say that there was some overlap during the early Kamakura. In contrast, Europe was torn by barbarian invasions, and there was a millennium separating the classical culture of Rome and high medieval culture. Even to have a Charlemagne, Europe had to wait for half a millennium. In China, the

Nobles in ox-drawn carriages and commoners on foot attend a sermon by the Pure Land monk Ippen (1239–1289). [Tokyo National Museum.]

era of political disunity and barbarian invasions lasted only four hundred years, and it was during these years that its medieval Buddhist culture blossomed.

The results of historical continuity are visible in every branch of Japanese culture. The native poetic tradition continued with great vigor. In 1205, the compilation of the *New Collection from Ancient and Modern Times* (*Shinkokinshū*) was ordered by the same emperor who began the 1221 rebellion against Kamakura. The flat *Yamato-e* style of painting that had reached a peak in the *Genji Scrolls* continued into the medieval era with scrolls on historical and religious themes or fairy-tale adventures. Artisan production continued without a break. The same techniques of lacquerwork with inlaid mother-of-pearl that had been used for, say, a cosmetic box for a Heian court lady were now applied to produce saddles for Kamakura warriors. In short, just as Heian estates continued on into the Kamakura era, and just as the authority of the court continued, so did Heian culture extend into medieval Japan.

Nonetheless, medieval Japanese culture had some distinctly new characteristics. First, as the leadership of the society shifted from court aristocrats to military aristocrats, changes occurred in the literature. The medieval military tales were as different from the *Tale of Genji* as the armor of the mounted warrior was from the no less colorful silken robes of the court nobility. Second, a new wave of culture entered from China. If the Nara and Heian had been shaped by T'ang culture, medieval Japan—though not its institutions—was shaped by Sung culture. This link is immediately apparent in the ink paintings of medieval Japan. Third, and most important, the medieval centuries were Japan's age of Buddhist faith. A religious revolution occurred during the Kamakura period and deepened during the Ashikaga. It fundamentally influenced the arts of Japan.

Japanese Pietism: Pure Land and Nichiren Buddhism

Among the doctrines of the Heian Tendai sect was the belief that the true teachings of the historical Buddha had been lost and that salvation could be had only by calling on the name of Amida, a cosmic Buddha who ruled over the Western Paradise (or Pure Land). During the tenth and eleventh centuries, itinerant preachers began to spread Pure Land doctrines and practices beyond the narrow circles of Kyoto. Kūya (903–972), the "saint of the marketplace," for example, preached not only in Kyoto and throughout the provinces, but even to the aboriginal Ainu in northernmost Japan. The doctrine that the world had fallen on evil times and that only faith would suffice was given credence by earthquakes, epidemics, fires, and ban-

The mid-Heian monk Kūya (903–972) preached Pure Land doctrines in Kyoto and throughout Japan. Little Buddhas emerge from his mouth. [Sekai Bunka Photo.]

ditry in the capital, as well as wars throughout the land. The deepening Buddhist coloration of the age can be read in the opening lines of the thirteenth century *Tale of the House of Taira*, written just two centuries after the *Tale of Genji* and the *Pillow Book:*

The sound of the bell of Jetavana echoes the impermanence of all things. The hue of the flowers of the teak-tree declares that they who flourish must be brought low. Yea, the proud ones are but for a moment, like an evening dream in springtime. The mighty are destroyed at the last, they are but as the dust before the wind.[6]

In the early Kamakura era, two figures stand out as religious geniuses who experienced the truth of Buddhism within themselves. Hōnen (1133–1212) was perhaps the first to say that the invocation of the name of Amida alone was enough for salvation and that only faith rather than works or rituals counted. These claims brought Hōnen into conflict with the older Buddhist establishment and marked the emergence of Pure Land as a separate sect. Hōnen was followed by Shin-

[6]A. L. Sadler (trans.), *The Tenfoot Square Hut and Tales of the Heike* (Rutland, Vt., and Tokyo: Charles E. Tuttle, 1972), p. 22.

ran (1173–1262), who taught that even a single invocation in praise of Amida, if done with perfect faith, was sufficient for salvation. But perfect faith was not solely the result of human effort: It was a gift from Amida. Pride was an obstacle to purity of heart. One of Shinran's most famous sayings is "If even a good man can be reborn in the Pure Land, how much more so a wicked man."[7]

Shinran's emphasis on faith alone led him to break many of the monastic rules of earlier Buddhism: he ate meat; he married a nun, and thereafter, the Pure Land sect had a married clergy; and he taught that all occupations were equally "heavenly" if performed with a pure heart. Exiled from Kyoto, he traveled about Japan establishing "True Pure Land" congregations. (When the Jesuits arrived in Japan in the sixteenth century, they called this sect "the devil's Christianity.")

Because of a line of distinguished teachers after Shinran, because of its doctrinal simplicity, and because of its reliance on the practice of piety, Pure Land Buddhism became the dominant form of Buddhism in Japan and remains so today. It was also the only sect in medieval Japan—apart from the Tendai sect on Mount Hiei—to develop political and military power. As a religion of faith, it developed a strong church as a protection for the saved while they were still in this world. As peasants became militarized during the fifteenth century, some Pure Land village congregations created self-defense forces. At times, they rebelled against feudal lords. In one instance, Pure Land armies ruled the province of Kaga for over a century. These congregations were smashed during the late sixteenth century, and the sect was depoliticized.

A second devotional sect was founded by Nichiren (1222–1282), who believed that the Lotus Sutra perfectly embodied the teachings of the Buddha. He instructed his adherents to chant, over and over, "Praise to the Lotus Sutra of the Wondrous Law," usually to the accompaniment of rapid drumbeats. Like the repetition of "Praise to the Amida Buddha" in the Pure Land sect or comparable verbal formulas in other religions around the world, the chanting optimally induced a state of religious rapture. The concern with an internal spiritual transformation was common to both the devotional and the meditative sects of Buddhism. Nichiren was remarkable for a Buddhist in being both intolerant and nationalistic. He blamed the ills of his age on rival sects and asserted that only his sect could protect Japan. He predicted the Mongol invasions, and his sect claimed credit for the "divine winds" that sank the Mongol fleets. Even his adopted Buddhist name, the Sun Lotus, combined the term for the rising sun of Japan with that of the flower that had become the symbol of Buddhism.

[7]Tsunoda, deBary, and Keene, p. 217.

A landscape by the Zen monk Sesshū (1420–1506). *[Tokyo National Museum.]*

Zen Buddhism

Meditation had long been a part of Japanese monastic practice. Zen meditation and doctrines were introduced by monks returning from study in Sung China. Eisai (1141–1215) transposed to Japan the Rinzai sect in 1191 and Dōgen (1200–1253) the Sōtō sect in 1227. Eisai's sect was patronized by the Hōjō rulers in Kamakura and the Ashikaga in Kyoto. Dōgen established his sect on Japan's western coast, far from centers of political power.

Zen in Japan was a religion of paradox. Its monks were learned, yet it stressed a return to ignorance, to the uncluttered "original mind," attained in a flash of intuitive understanding. Zen was punctiliously traditional, the most Chinese of Japanese medieval sects. The authority of the Zen master over his pupil-monks was absolute. Yet Zen was also iconoclastic. Its sages

Hakuin's Enlightenment

Hakuin (1686–1769) was a poet, a painter, and a Zen master. He wrote in colloquial Japanese as well as in Chinese. He illustrated the continuing power of the Zen tradition in postmedieval times. In an autobiographical account of his spiritual quest, he first told of his disappointments and failures, but then wrote:

In the spring of my twenty-fourth year, I was painfully struggling at the Eiganji in the province of Echigo. I slept neither day nor night, forgetting either to eat or sleep. A great doubt suddenly possessed me, and I felt as if frozen to death in the midst of an icy field extending thousands of *li*. A sense of an extraordinary purity permeated my bosom. I could not move. I was virtually senseless. What remained was only "*Mu*." Although I heard the master's lectures in the Lecture Hall, it was as though I were listening to his discourse from some sixty or seventy steps outside the Hall, or as if I were floating in the air. This condition lasted for several days until one night I heard the striking of a temple bell. All at once a transformation came over me, as though a layer of ice were smashed or a tower of jade pulled down. Instantly I came to my senses. . . . Former doubts were completely dissolved, like ice which had melted away. "How marvelous! How marvelous!" I cried out aloud. There was no cycle of birth and death from which I had to escape, no enlightenment for which I had to seek.

But Hakuin's teacher did not accept this as adequate. Hakuin's quest continued. Eight years later:

At the age of thirty-two I settled in this dilapidated temple [Shōinji]. In a dream one night my mother handed me a purple silk robe. When I lifted it I felt great weights in both sleeves. Examining it, I found in each sleeve an old mirror about five or six inches in diameter. The reflection of the right-hand mirror penetrated deep into my heart. My own mind, as well as mountains and rivers, the entire earth, became serene and bottomless. The left-hand mirror had no luster on its entire surface. Its face was like that of a new iron pan not yet touched by fire. Suddenly I became aware that the luster on the left-hand mirror surpassed that of the right by a million times. After this incident, the vision of all things was like looking at my own face. For the first time I realized the meaning of the words, "The eyes of the Tathā-gata behold the Buddha-nature." ❑

W. T. deBary (ed.), *The Buddhist Tradition in India, China, and Japan* (New York: Modern Library, 1972), pp. 384, 387–388.

A Zen garden outside the Abbot's Hall at Daitokuji in Kyoto—a "dry landscape" in which sand represents the sea and rocks represent mountains. [Japan Information Service.]

The Arts and Zen Buddhism

Zen Buddhism in Japan developed a theory of art that influenced every department of medieval culture. Put simply, it is, first, that intuitive action is better than conscious, purposive action. The best painter is one so skilled that he no longer needs to think of technique but paints as a natural act. Substitute a sword for a brush, and the same theory applies to the warrior. A swordsman who has to stop to consider his next move is at a disadvantage in battle. But to this concern with direct, intuitive action is added the Zen distinction between the deluded mind and the "original mind." The latter is also referred to as the "no mind," or the mind in the enlightened state. The highest intuitive action proceeds from such a state of being. This theory was applied, in time, to the performance of the actor, to the skill of the potter, to archery, to flower arrangement, and to the tea ceremony. Compare the following two passages, one by Seami (1363–1443), the author of many Nō plays, and the other by Takuan Sōhō (1573–1645), a famous Zen master of the early Tokugawa era (see Chapter 18).

Sometimes spectators of the Nō say, "The moments of 'no-action' are the most enjoyable." This is an art which the actor keeps secret. Dancing and singing, movements and the different types of miming are all acts performed by the body. Moments of "no-action" occur in between. When we examine why such moments without actions are enjoyable, we find that it is due to the underlying spiritual strength of the actor which unremittingly holds the attention. He does not relax the tension when the dancing or singing come to an end or at intervals between the dialogue and the different types of miming, but maintains an unwavering inner strength. This feeling of inner strength will faintly reveal itself and bring enjoyment. However, it is undesirable for the actor to permit this inner strength to become obvious to the audience. If it is obvious, it becomes an act, and is no longer "no-action." The actions before and after an interval of "no-action" must be linked by entering the state of mindlessness in which one conceals even from oneself one's intent. This, then, is the faculty of moving audiences, by linking all the artistic powers with one mind.

Where should a swordsman fix his mind? If he puts his mind on the physical movement of his opponent, it will be seized by the movement; if he places it on the sword of his opponent, it will be arrested by the sword; if he focuses his mind on the thought of striking his opponent, it will be carried away by the very thought; if the mind stays on his own sword, it will be captured by his sword; if he centers it on the thought of not being killed by his opponent, his mind will be overtaken by this very thought; if he keeps his mind firmly on his own or on his opponent's posture, likewise, it will be blocked by them. Thus the mind should not be fixed anywhere. ❑

R. Tsunoda, W. T. deBary, and D. Keene, *Sources of Japanese Tradition* (New York: Columbia U. P. 1958), p. 291.
W. T. deBary (ed.), *The Buddhist Tradition* (New York: Modern Library, 1972), p. 377.

were depicted in paintings as tearing up sutras to make the point that it is religious experience and not words that count. And within a rigidly structured monastic regimen, a vital give-and-take occurred as monks tested their understanding—gained through long hours of meditation—in encounters with their master. Buddhism stressed compassion for all sentient beings, yet in Japan, Zen was particularly involved with the samurai whose duty it was to fight and kill. Many of Japan's military saw the severe discipline of Zen as ideal training for single-minded attention to duty; a few Hōjō and Ashikaga rulers even practiced Zen themselves.

The most remarkable aspect of Zen was its influence on the arts of medieval Japan. The most beautiful gardens, for example, were in Zen temples. Many were designed by Zen masters. The most famous, at Ryōanji, consists of fifteen rocks set in white sand. Others only slightly less austere contain moss, shrubs, trees, ponds, and streams. With these elements and within a small compass, rocks become cliffs, raked sand becomes rivers or the sea, and a little world of nature emerges. If a garden may be said to possess philosophic stillness, the Zen gardens of Daitokuji and other Kyoto temples have it.

Zen monks such as Josetsu, Shūbun, and Sesshū certainly number among the masters of ink painting in East Asia. One painting by Josetsu shows a man trying to catch a catfish with a gourd. Like the sound of one hand clapping, the impossibility of catching a catfish with a gourd presents as art the kind of logical conundrum used to expound Zen teachings. Sesshū painted

"Broken ink" style painting by the Zen monk Sesshū (1420–1506). [Tokyo National Museum.]

parallels elsewhere in East Asia. The play was performed on an almost square, bare wooden stage (often outdoors) by male actors wearing robes of great beauty and carved, painted masks of enigmatic expressions. Many such masks and robes number among Japan's National Treasures. The chorus was chanted to the accompaniment of flute and drums. The language was poetic. The action was slow and highly stylized: Circling about the stage could represent a journey, and a motion of the hand, the reading of a letter. The artistic theory of the Nō was pure Zen, though some Nō plays also drew on Pure Land doctrines for their content. At a critical juncture in most plays, the protagonist is possessed by the spirit of another and performs a dance. Spirit possession was a commonplace of Japanese folk religion and also occurs in the *Tale of Genji.* Several plays were shown in a single performance; comic skits called Crazy Words were usually interspersed between them to break the tension.

Nō plays reveal a medley of themes present in medieval Japanese culture. Some pivot on incidents in the struggle between the Taira and the Minamoto. Some are religious: A cormorant fisher is saved from the king of hell for having given lodging to a priest. Some plays pick up incidents from the *Tale of Genji* or the Heian court: The famous Heian beauty and poet Ono no Komachi is possessed by the spirit of a lover she had spurned; their conflict is left to be resolved in a Buddhist afterlife. Some plays are close to fairy tales: A fisherman takes the feather robe of an angel, but when she begins to sicken and grow wan, he returns the robe and she dances for him a dance that is only performed in heaven. Some plays have Chinese themes: A traveler dreams an entire lifetime on a magical pillow while waiting for a bowl of millet to cook. Another play reflects the Japanese ambivalence toward China: Po Chu-i, the T'ang poet most famous in Japan, rows a boat over the seas and comes to the shores of Japan, where he is met by fishermen who turn him back in the name of Japanese poetry. One fisherman speaks:

You in China make your poems and odes out of the Scriptures of India; and we have made our "uta" out of the poems and odes of China. Since then our poetry is a blend of three lands, we have named it Yamato, the great blend, and all our songs "Yamato uta."[8]

At the end, the fisherman is transformed into the Shinto god of Japanese poetry and performs the "Sea Green Dance."

in both the broken-ink style, in which splashlike brush strokes represent an entire mountain landscape, and in a more usual calligraphic style. Because the artist's creativity itself was seen as grounded in his experience of meditation, a painting of a waterfall or a crow on a leafless branch in winter was viewed as no less religious than a painting of the mythic Zen founder Bodhidharma.

Nō Plays

Another fascinating product of Ashikaga culture was the Nō play, a kind of mystery drama with no

---

[8] A. Waley (trans.), *The Nō Plays of Japan* (New York: Grove Press, 1957), p. 252.

Early Japanese History in World Perspective

During the first millennium A.D., the major development in world history was the spread of the civilizations that had risen out of the earlier philosophical and religious revolutions. In the West, the process began with the spread of civilization from Greece to Rome, continued with the rise of Christianity and its diffusion within the late Roman Empire, and entered a third phase when the countries of northern Europe became civilized by borrowing Mediterranean culture. The spread was slow because Rome was no longer a vital center. By contrast, in East Asia the spread of civilization from its Chinese heartland was more rapid because in the early seventh century, the T'ang empire had been reestablished—more vital, more exuberant, and more powerful than ever before. Within the East Asian culture zone, and apart from post-T'ang China itself, there were three major developing areas: Vietnam, Korea, and Japan.

All three used Chinese writing for most of their history, combined indigenous and Chinese elements to create distinctive cultures and national identities, and in premodern times built independent states. The contrast between these countries and other areas around China is interesting. Vietnam, Korea, and Japan were more Chinese in their culture than Tibet, Mongolia, or Manchuria. Yet in the modern era, the latter areas have been swallowed up by China, whereas Korea, Vietnam, and Japan have preserved their independence. These three nations used Chinese culture to forge self-identities that could resist Chinese domination—just as Third-World nations today borrow Western systems and ideas to build states that are politically anti-Western.

For all their political independence, Vietnam and Korea were nonetheless too close to China to avoid its imprint. The cultural flow was too constant. Often, there was not time for a borrowed element to evolve freely. Japan, in contrast—because it was bigger, more populous, and more distant—became the major variant to the Chinese pattern within East Asian civilization. It reflected, often brilliantly, the potentials of East Asian culture in a non-Chinese milieu.

Of particular interest to Western students are the striking parallels that developed between Japan and northwestern Europe. Both had centuries of feudalism: serfs on the estates of nobles; castles and mounted warriors, who wore armor and fought in the service of their lord; cultures in which the glorification of valor and military prowess conflicted with the gentler virtues of their religions; merchant guilds and decentralized political economies. These parallels should not be surprising since both Japan and northwestern Europe began as backward tribal or posttribal societies onto which "heartland cultures" were grafted during the first millennium A.D.

Suggested Readings

R. BORGEN, *Sugawara no Michizane and the Early Heian Court* (1986). A study of a famous courtier and poet.

D. BROWN AND E. ISHIDA, (eds.), *The Future and the Past* (1979). A translation of a history of Japan written in 1219.

M. COLLCUTT, *Five Mountains* (1980). A study of the monastic organization of medieval Zen.

P. DUUS, *Feudalism in Japan* (1969). An easy survey of the subject.

W. W. FARRIS, *Population, Disease, and Land in Early Japan*, 645–900 (1985). An innovative reinterpretation of early history.

J. W. HALL, *Government and Local Power in Japan, 500–1700: A Study Based on Bizen Province* (1966). The best book on Japanese history to 1700.

J. W. HALL AND J. P. MASS (eds.), *Medieval Japan* (1974). A collection of topical essays on medieval history.

J. W. HALL AND T. TOYODA, *Japan in the Muromachi Age* (1977). Another collection of essays.

D. KEENE (ed.), *Anthology of Japanese Literature from the Earliest Era to the Mid-nineteenth Century* (1955).

D. KEENE (ed.), *Twenty Plays of the Nō Theatre* (1970).

J. M. KITAGAWA, *Religion in Japanese History* (1966). A survey of religion in premodern Japan.

I. H. LEVY, *The Ten Thousand Leaves* (1981). A fine translation of Japan's earliest collection of poetry.

J. P. MASS, *The Development of Kamakura Rule*, 1180–1250 (1979).

J. P. MASS AND W. HAUSER (eds.), *The Bakufu in Japanese History* (1985). Topics in bakufu history from the twelfth to the nineteenth century.

I. MORRIS, *The World of the Shining Prince: Court Life in Ancient Japan* (1964). A study of the court during the age in which *The Tale of Genji* was written.

I. MORRIS (trans.), *The Pillow Book of Sei Shōnagon* (1967). Observations about Heian court life by the Jane Austen of ancient Japan.

S. MURASAKI, *The Tale of Genji*, trans. by E. G. Seidensticker (1976). The world's first novel and the greatest work of Japanese fiction.

S. MURASAKI, *The Tale of Genji*, trans. by A. Waley (1952).

R. J. PEARSON et al. (eds.), *Windows on the Japanese Past: Studies in Archeology and Prehistory* (1986).

D. L. PHILIPPI (trans.), *Kojiki* (1968). Japan's ancient myths.

E. O. REISCHAUER, *Japan: The Story of a Nation* (1989). A masterful introduction to Japan.

E. O. Reischauer and A. M. Craig, *Japan: Tradition and Transformation* (1989). A widely used text.

D. T. Suzuki, *Zen and Japanese Culture* (1959).

R. Tsunoda, W. T. deBary, and D. Keene (comps.), *Sources of the Japanese Tradition* (1958). A collection of original religious, political, and philosophical writings from each period of Japanese history. The best reader.

H. P. Varley, *Imperial Restoration in Medieval Japan* (1971). A study of the 1331 attempt by an emperor to restore imperial power.

A. Waley (trans.), *The Nō Plays of Japan* (1957). Medieval dramas.

A fifth-century A.D. *standing Buddha from the sculptural workshops of Mathura in north India.* [Bettmann Archive.]

Portfolio III: Buddhism

Buddhism, along with Jainism and Upanishadic Hinduism, arose out of the spiritual ferment of Vedic India during the centuries after 700 B.C. Buddhism shares a kinship with these other religions much like the relationship found further west between Judaism, Christianity, and Islam.

Siddhartha Gautama was born about 566 B.C., a prince in a petty kingdom near what is now the border of India and Nepal. He was reared amid luxury and comforts, married at sixteen, and had a child. According to legend, when at age 29 he saw an old man, a sick man, and a corpse, he suddenly realized that all humans would suffer the same fate. Gautama renounced his wealth and family and entered the life of a wandering ascetic. He visited famous teachers, practiced extremes of ascetic self-deprivation, and finally discovered the "middle path." At the age of 35, he attained *nirvana*, becoming the *Buddha*, or the "enlightened one." In early Buddhism all of the cosmic drama of religious self-transformation is compressed into the human figure of Gautama meditating under the Bodhi tree. The rest of his 80 years the Buddha spent teaching others the truths he had learned. Even during his lifetime communities of Buddhist monks and nuns (the *sangha*) developed, with a tradition of support for the monks by lay adherents.

Basic to the Buddha's understanding of the human condition were the "four noble truths:" (1) that all life is suffering—an endless karmic chain of births and rebirths; (2) that the cause of the suffering is desire—it is desire that binds humans to the wheel of *karma*; (3) that escape from the suffering and endless rebirths can only come by the cessation of desire and the attainment of *nirvana*; and, (4) that the path to nirvana is eight-fold. The eight-fold path requires; right views, thought, speech, actions, living, efforts, mindfulness, and meditation.

Ethical living combined with long periods of meditation may lead to an inner spiritual awakening or realization. Progress in the inner spiritual life may lead, eventually, to enlightenment, to liberation or release from the trammels of karmic causation. Because the goal of Buddhism is for all humans to become Bud-

dhas, some have called Buddhism the most otherworldly of the great world religions. Even for the historical Buddha the way was not easy and one lifetime was not enough. (While meditating prior to achieving enlightenment, he recalled events from his former lives. The stories of these earlier lives are told in the Jataka tales.) For others, even with the Buddha's teachings in hand, the way was hard. Monks and nuns might meditate for years and attain an inner spiritual awakening, but only a few would gain the complete release required for Buddhahood. Most could only hope for a rebirth in a higher spiritual state, to begin again closer, as it were, to the goal. For lay people the stress was on ethical living in human socity. The Buddha condemned the caste system that flourished in the India of his day. He held that poverty was a cause of immorality, and that it was futile to attempt to suppress crime with punishments. He identified with all humanity, saying "He who attends on the sick attends on me."

Buddhism spread rapidly along the Ganges River and through northern India. In the time of King Ashoka (272-232 B.C.) of the Mauryas, it spread to southern India and Ceylon. This was its great missionary age. Eventually, however, Buddhism in India was re-Hinduized: It developed schools of metaphysics and a pantheon of gods and cosmic Buddhas. It developed devotional sects. Buddhism's meditative techniques helped shape Hindu yogic exercises. As these changes occurred, Buddhism in India lost its character as a reform movement, its *raison d'etre*, and was reabsorbed into Hinduism between A.D. 500 and 1500.

India apart, two major currents of Buddhism spread out over Asia. One known as the "Way of the Elders" (*Theravada*) swept through Southeast Asia. Its teachings were close to early Indian Buddhism and it was influenced as well by other strands of Indian culture. Scenes from the great Indian epic, the *Mahabharata*, adorn the inner walls of Thai temples. Buddhism remains today the predominant religion in Burma, Thailand, Cambodia, Laos, and Vietnam, although it must contest with more recent secular ideologies. In Thailand alone it remains the state religion:

Thai kings rule as Buddhist monarchs; Thai boys spend short periods as Buddhist monks; and temples (*wats*) continue as centers of village life. Before the spread of Islam, Buddhism also flourished in what is today Malaysia and Indonesia. The temple of Borobudur in central Java remains one of the great monuments of world Buddhism; it represents in stone the Buddhist spiritual universe.

The second major current, known to its adherents as the "Greater Vehicle" (*Mahayana*) spread through northwest India to Afghanistan and Central Asia, and then to China, Korea, and Japan. This current carried with it many doctrines. One key doctrine contained the ideal of the *bodhisattva*, a being who had gone all the way to the final goal of nirvana, but held off in order to help others attain salvation. One such *bodhisattva*, who became elevated to the status of a cosmic Buddha ruling over the Western Paradise (or Pure Land), was Amitabha (or Amida). Devotion to this Buddha and to others figured prominently in East Asian Buddhism.

Another doctrine, that of the Ch'an (in China) or Zen (in Japan) sect, stressed meditation and perhaps was closer to the teachings of the historical Buddha. Buddhism in Afghanistan and Central Asia eventually gave way to Islam. In China Buddhism was weakened by the great persecution of 845. In all of East Asia there were tensions between Buddhism and the more worldly teachings of Confucius. During the modern century the struggle, as in other parts of the world, has been between religion and modern secular doctrines.

III-1 Siddhartha Gautama at Age 29. *Gautama at age 29, having renounced all worldly attachments, cuts his hair in the forest prior to setting off on his spiritual quest. Scenes from the life of the Buddha are as common in Buddhist art as those of Jesus in Christian art. This is an early nineteenth century Bangkok temple mural. [Luca Invernizzi Tettoni/Art Resource.]*

III-2   Fasting Buddha. *Before Gautama arrived at the "middle path," he practiced severe austerites for six years. According to a description in an ancient text: "My limbs became like some withered creepers with knotted joints; my buttocks like a buffalo's hoof . . . my ribs like rafters of a dilipated shed; the pupils of my eyes appeared sunk deep in their sockets as water appears shining at the bottom of a deep well. . . ." This (fourth to second century B.C.) statue of the Buddha from Gandhara (in present-day Pakistan) reflects the Greek influence on early Buddhist sculpture. [Borromeo, EPA/Art Resource.]*

III-3 Colossal Statue of Buddha. *A 175-feet-tall statue of the Buddha was carved in a cliff in the Bamian Valley of Afghanistan during second to fifth century* A.D. *It is comparable to the Lungmen Buddhas in China or the Great Buddhas of Japan.* [SEF/Art Resource.]

III-4 Buddha with Aureole. *This Buddhist sanctuary mural at Miran on the Silk Road through Central Asia shows both Indian and Greek influences.* [Borromeo, EPA/Art Resource.]

III-5   Buddha on a Throne. *This fifth-to-sixth century painting is on the walls of a cave in Ajanta, India. The Buddha, seated on a lotus throne, teaches his disciples. The lotus, like the Buddha, emerges from the floating world of mud and water, but is not defiled by it. [Borromeo, EPA/Art Resource.]*

III-6   Thai Buddha in Bronze. *This walking Buddha is from the fourteenth century. Buddhism remains the predominant religion in Thailand today. [Luca Invernizzi Tettoni/Art Resource.]*

III-7 Barbarian Royalty Worshipping the Buddha. *This Sung or Yuan dynasty Chinese painting depicts the peoples known to China in the thirteenth century. That all came from afar to worship suggests the universality of his teachings. [Cleveland Museum of Art, Gift of Mr. and Mrs. Severance A. Millikin, 57.358.]*

III-8 Bodhisattva Kneeling in Attitude of Worship. *This polychrome bodhisattva is from a cave temple at Tunhuang in western China. This example of T'ang dynasty sculpture expresses Buddhist piety. [Arthur M. Sackler Museum, Harvard University, Cambridge, Massachusetts, First Fogg China Expedition, 1923.]*

III-9   Zen Patriarch. *The Indian Bodhidharma, the first patriarch of the Zen sect, as depicted by Itō Jakuchū (1716–1800). Bodhidharma's face reflects the fierce insight gained by years of meditation. The strong brushstrokes in his robe, however, are the focus of the painting. [Reproduced by Courtesy of the Trustees of the British Museum.]*

III-10   Zen Monks in Japan. *These Zen monks in a meditation hall are in training to become priests. Many in postwar Japan have tried Zen meditation; few have been able to integrate it with the demands of modern life. [Elliott Erwitt/Magnum.]*

III-11   Cremation Rites for a Thai Queen. *The cremation rites for a Thai Queen Rambhao Barni are conducted at the Temple of the Emerald Buddha in Bangkok in 1985. [Luca Invernizzi Tettoni/Art Resource.]*

11 Africa, Iran, and India Before Islam

In this chapter, we look at civilization in sub-Saharan Africa and in south and southwest Asia before the penetration of Islam ushered in new eras and major parts of each of these regions were changed and linked culturally and religiously in new ways. The coming of Islamic civilization—with Muslim conquerors or, much more often, with Muslim traders and religious brotherhoods—took place at very different times and with differing consequences in each of these three major cultural areas.

In Africa, with the exception of north Africa, Egypt, and the east African coast, Islam as a religious tradition and sociopolitical order had its major impact only after (and sometimes long after) A.D. 1000. By contrast, in Iran, the presence of Islam in government and public life was significant from the early years of the Arab conquests in the mid-seventh century, although conversion of the masses took considerably longer. In northwest India, Arab armies penetrated the Indus region as early as 711 and the Muslims controlled the Punjab from around 1000. The establishment of the so-called Delhi Sultanate in 1205 marked the permanent arrival of Muslim ruling dynasties in the Indian heartlands. Similarly, Sufi brotherhoods made significant converts in India from about the thirteenth century. However, in earlier trading communities on the coasts of Gujarat and south India, Muslim settlers and converts provided the nuclei of Muslim communities that grew up within the larger Hindu society.

Different kinds of change had occurred in each of these vast regions in the centuries before the coming of Islam. In sub-Saharan Africa in the first millennium A.D., major movements of peoples and major changes in basic forms of subsistence were still occurring. It was an era when African peoples lived in many very different types of sociopolitical communities. Many of these still were pre- or early Iron-Age cultures, and very few were large enough or complex enough in organization and administration to be called states. Nonetheless, as we shall see, some sizable regional states and empires did emerge.

Iran presents another contrast. From the breakdown of Parthian rule at the beginning of the third century A.D. to the coming of Islam in the seventh, there existed a period of relative political stability under a single long-lived dynasty of Persian imperial rulers known as the Sasanids. It was a time of recovery of vitality for Zoroastrian traditions. Yet there was also entrenchment of a social and political system heavily balanced in favor of a small ruling nobility and a foreign policy centered on constant competition with the Byzantine empire. This competition finally exhausted its resources much as it did those of Byzantium. Both were ripe for defeat at the hands of the unleashed energies of the Arabs under the flag of Islam.

India experienced a similarly spectacular revival of empire under the Gupta kings, who presided over a cultural florescence of unprecedented magnificence. Then incursions of new waves of steppe peoples from about 500 on brought an era of political fragmentation. Nevertheless, regional empires emerged that lasted until the thirteenth century, when Muslim power in the north under the Delhi sultans began to forge new patterns of power and culture north and south.

For all these reasons, our attempt to trace Afro-Asian civilizations up to the coming of Islam will necessarily cover different chronological ground and focus on different kinds of change. However, in all three areas we shall see how culture, trade, and communications made great strides, even if at different stages of development, in diverse forms, and at varying paces.

AFRICA

Nilotic Africa and the Ethiopian Highlands

We begin with the African story where we left off in Chapter 7, in the upper Nile regions of the eastern Sudan. Here, the Kushite empire was apparently brought to an end about A.D. 330 by a new power to the south: the newly Christianized state of Aksum, which centered in the northern Ethiopian, or Abyssinian, highlands where the Blue Nile rises. With the ascendancy of the kingdom of Aksum, the Nubian regions of the Nile sank into two centuries of relative obscurity, until the rise of new Christian Nubian states in the mid-sixth century.

The Aksumite Empire

The peoples of Aksum were the product of a cultural and genetic mixing of African Kushitic speakers with Semitic speakers from Yemenite south Arabia. This mixing occurred after south Arabians infiltrated and settled on the Ethiopian plateau around 500 B.C. It gave to Aksum and later to Ethiopia their Semitic speech and script, which are closely related to South Arabian. Greek and Roman sources attest to the existence of an Aksumite kingdom from at least the first century A.D. By this time, the kingdom, through its chief port of Adulis, had already become the major ivory and elephant market of northeast Africa. Adulis had been important in Ptolemaic times, when it was captured by Egypt and used as a conduit for Egyptian influence in the highlands. After Egypt fell to the Romans, Aksum and its major port became an important cosmopolitan commercial center.

In the first two centuries A.D., their location on the Red Sea gave the Aksumites a strategic seat astride the increasingly important Indian Ocean trade routes. These trade routes linked India and the East Indies, Iran, Arabia, and the east African coast with the Roman Mediterranean. A further basis of Aksum's power was its key location for controlling trade between the African interior and the extra-African world, from Rome to southeast Asia—notably that centered on exports of ivory, but also of elephants, obsidian, slaves, gold dust, and other inland products.

By the third century A.D., Aksum was one of the most impressive states of its age in the African or west Asian world, as the remains of the imposing stone buildings and monuments of its major cities—Aksum, Adulis, and Matara—attest. A work attributed to the prophet Mani, CA. A.D. 216–277, describes Aksum as one of the four greatest empires in the world. From the late second century on, the Aksumites often held tributary territories across the Red Sea in South Arabia. They also gained control of all northern Ethiopia and conquered Meroitic Kush. Thus by the third and fourth century, they held sway over some of the most fertile cultivated regions of the ancient world: their own plateau, the rich Yemenite highlands of South Arabia, and much of the eastern Sudan across the upper Nile as far as the Sahara.

The resulting empire was ruled by a king of kings in Aksum through tribute-paying vassal kings in the other subject states. By the sixth century, the Aksumite king was even appointing south Arabian kings himself. The minting of its own coinage in gold, silver, and copper (it was the first tropical African state to do so) was an

A Giant Stela at Aksum. *Dating probably from the first century* A.D., *this giant carved monolith is the only one of seven giant stelae, one of which reached a height of 33 meters, that once stood in Aksum amidst numerous smaller monoliths. While the exact purpose of the stelae is not known, the generally accepted explanation is that they were commemorative funerary monuments. The immense engineering feat involved in such monouments suggests how sophisticated Aksumite engineering was.*

A Sixth-Century Account of Aksumite Trade

The following document is taken from a description of a trading voyage to Sri Lanka in A.D. *625 by a Greek-speaking monk and former merchant from Alexandria, known as Cosmas Indicopleustes. In the excerpt below, he describes what he had heard of Aksumite trading practices, including those involved with procuring gold from the interior.*

The region which produces frankincense is situated at the projecting parts of Ethiopia, and lies inland, but is washed by the ocean on the other side. Hence the inhabitants of Barbaria, being near at hand, go up into the interior and, engaging in traffic with the natives, bring back from them any kinds of spices, frankincense, cassia, calamus, and many other articles of merchandise, which they afterwards send by sea to Adule, to the country of the Homerites, to Further India, and to Persia. This very fact you will find mentioned in the Book of Kings, where it is recorded that the Queen of Sheba, that is, of the Homerite country, whom afterwards our Lord in the Gospels calls the Queen of the South, brought to Solomon spices from this very Barbaria, which lay near Sheba on the other side of the sea, together with bars of ebony, and apes and gold from Ethiopia, which, though separated from Sheba by the Arabian Gulf, lay in its vicinity. We can see again from the words of the Lord that he calls these places the ends of the earth, saying: *The Queen of the South shall rise up in judgement with this generation and shall condemn it, for she came from the ends of the earth to hear the wisdom of Solomon,* Matt. xii. 42. For the Homerites are not far distant from Barbaria, as the sea which lies between them can be crossed in a couple of days, and then beyond Barbaria is the ocean, which is there called Zingion. The country known as that of Sasu is itself near the ocean, just as the ocean is near the frankincense country, in which there are many gold mines. The king of the Axumites accordingly, every other year, through the governor of Agau, sends thither special agents to bargain for the gold, and these are accompanied by many other traders—upwards, say, of 500—bound on the same errand as themselves. They take along with them to the mining district oxen, lumps of salt, and iron, and when they reach its neighbourhood they make a halt at a certain spot and form an encampment, which they fence round with a great hedge of thorns. Within this they live, and having slaughtered the oxen, cut them in pieces, and lay the pieces on the top of the thorns, along with the lumps of salt and the iron. Then come the natives bringing gold in nuggets like peas, called *tancharas*, and lay one or two or more of these upon what pleases them—the pieces of flesh or the salt or the iron, and then they retire to some distance off. Then the owner of the meat approaches, and if he is satisfied he takes the gold away, and upon seeing this its owner comes and takes the flesh or the salt or the iron. If, however, he is not satisfied, he leaves the gold, when the native seeing that he has not taken it, comes and either puts down more gold, or takes up what he had laid down, and goes away. Such is the mode in which business is transacted with the people of that country, because their language is different and interpreters are hardly to be found. . . .   ❑

J. W. McCrindle, trans., *The Christian Topography of Cosmas, an Egyptian Monk* (London, 1897), as cited in G. S. P. Freeman-Grenville, ed., *The East African Coast,* 2nd ed. (London, 1975), pp. 6–7.

index and symbol of Aksum's political as well as economic power. As a state, it enjoyed a long-lived economic prosperity. Goods of the Roman-Byzantine world and India and Sri Lanka, as well as of neighboring Meroe, flowed into Aksum. In addition to trade, vast herds and good agricultural produce gave a firm base to Aksumite prosperity.

In religion, the pre-Christian paganism of Aksum resembled the pre-Islamic paganism of south Arabia with its various gods and goddesses who were closely tied to natural phenomena such as the sun, moon, and stars, and who were served with animal sacrifices. Evidence of Jewish, Meroitic, and even Buddhist minorities living in the major cities of Aksum has also been found—an index of the cosmopolitanism of the society and of its involvement with the larger Indian Ocean, west Asian, and south Asian worlds beyond the Red Sea.

In an inscription of the powerful fourth-century ruler, King Ezana, we read of his conversion to Christianity, which led to the Christianizing of the kingdom as a whole. The conversion of Ezana and his realm was the work of Frumentius, a Syrian bishop of Aksum who also served as secretary and treasurer to the king. Subsequently, under Alexandrian influence, the Ethiopian church became Monophysite in doctrine (i.e., adhered to the dogma of the single, unitary nature of Christ; see Chapter 6). This did not cut off Aksumite trading relations with Byzantium, however much Constantinople may have persecuted Monophysites at home. In the fifth century A.D., the native language of Ge'ez began to replace Greek in the liturgy; this proved to be a major step in the unique development of the Ethiopic or Abyssinian Christian church over the succeeding centuries.

The Isolation of Christian Ethiopia

Aksumite trade continued to thrive through the sixth century, despite the decay of Rome. Strong enough at times to extend to the Yemen, Aksumite power was eclipsed in the end by the rise of Arab Islamic power. Nevertheless, the Aksumite state continued to exist long after its power had diminished. Having sheltered a refugee group of Muhammad's earliest Meccan converts, the Aksumites enjoyed relatively cordial relations with the new Muslim domains to the north in Egypt and across the Red Sea in the peninsula. But Aksum ceased to be a center of foreign trade and became more and more isolated. Its center of gravity shifted southward from the coast to the more rugged parts of the plateau. Here a Monophysite, Ge'ez-speaking culture emerged in the area of modern Ethiopia and lasted in relative isolation down to modern times, surrounded largely by Muslim peoples and Islamic states.

Ethiopia's northern neighbors, the Christian states of Maqurra and Alwa, also survived for centuries in the former Meroitic lands of the Nilotic Sudan under treaty relations with Muslim Egypt. However, incursions of the Muslim Mamluk rulers of Egypt in the fourteenth and fifteenth centuries and Arab migration from about 1300 led ultimately to the Islamization and conversion of the whole Nubian region. Ethiopia was left as the sole predominantly Christian state in Africa.

The Western and Central Sudan

In Chapter 7, we noted the apparent movements of neolithic peoples southward from the Saharan regions into the western and central Sudan and ultimately into the forests of the African equatorial regions. The rainforests were inhospitable to cows and horses, largely because of the animals' inability to survive the sleeping sickness (*trypanosomiasis*) carried by the tsetse fly. But the agriculturalists who brought their cereal grains and stone tools found particularly good conditions in the savannah just north of the west African forests. By the first or second century A.D., settled agriculture, now augmented by the use of iron tools, had become the way of life of most of the inhabitants of these western Sudanic lands. Agriculture had even made considerable progress in the forest regions farther south. The savannah areas seem to have experienced a substantial population explosion in the first few centuries A.D., especially in the areas close to the major water sup-

NILOTIC AFRICA AND THE
ETHIOPIAN HIGHLANDS

CA. 500 B.C.	Yemenites (South Arabians) enter and settle on the Ethiopian plateau
30 B.C.	Egypt becomes part of Roman empire of Octavian
CA. A.D. 1–100	Earliest mention (in Latin and Greek writers) of the kingdom of Aksum on Ethiopian plateau
CA. A.D. 330	Fall of Kushite empire to Elzana of Aksum
CA. A.D. 200–400	Heyday of Aksumite Ethiopia
CA. A.D. 500–600	Christianizing of the major Nubian states of Maqurra and Alwa
A.D. 652	Maqurra and Alwa make peace with Arab Muslim armies from Egypt

MAP 11-1 AFRICA: SAHARAN AND WEST AFRICAN TRADE ROUTES. *Showing some of the major north-south routes of the transSaharan caravan traffic and their linkage with Egypt and with sudanic and forest West Africa.*

⇒ BANTU MIGRATIONS
- - -→ TRADE ROUTES
· · · · · · · LIMIT OF RAINFOREST

plies: along the Senegal river, around the great northern bend in the Niger river, and in the Lake Chad basin. Villages, and gradually some chiefdoms consisting of several villages, remained normally the largest political units during this period. As time went on, their growth and development provided the basis (and the need) for the eventual development of larger political units that we call true states in these areas of the western Sudan.

Trans-Saharan Trade

Another element that eventually promoted or at least accompanied the rise of larger political units in the western and central Sudan was the trans-Saharan commercial trade. As we saw earlier, contacts between the Sudanic regions and the Mediterranean were maintained throughout the first millennium B.C. over the trans-Saharan trading routes. The trans-Saharan trade became, however, much more viable with the introduction from the east (probably through north Africa) of the domesticated camel (actually the one-humped Arab camel, or dromedary), sometime around the beginning of the Christian era. By the early Christian centuries, the west African settled communities were able to develop trading centers of considerable importance on their northern peripheries, in the sahel near the edge of the true desert. The salt of the desert, so badly needed in the settled savannah, and the gold of west Africa, coveted in the north, were the prime commodities exchanged. However, many other items were also traded, including cola nuts, slaves, dates, and gum from west Africa, and horses, cattle, millet, leather, cloth, and weapons from the north.

Towns such as Awdaghast, Walata, Timbuktu, Gao, Tadmekka, and Agades have been the most famous southern terminals for this trade over the centuries. These centers allowed the largely Berber middlemen who plied the trade routes across the ever dangerous Sahara to traverse the desert via oasis stations between them and the north African coastal regions or even Egypt. Thus, some of the main routes ran as follows: (1) from the first three towns just mentioned to the major desert salt-producing center of Taghaza and thence to Morocco; (2) from Timbuktu, as from Gao over the desert direct to Morocco; and (3) from Tadmekka and Agades to the desert market town of Ghat in the north-central Sahara and on to the coasts of Libyan north Africa. Other lines went up from the region of Lake Chad; one route stretched as far east as Egypt itself, passing through the mountain massifs of the central Sahara such as that of the Tassili and Ahaggar. A typical full crossing could easily take two to three months, so this was not an easy means of transporting goods.

The Rise of States

Smaller stateless societies predominated throughout sub-Saharan Africa during most of African history. Even as late as 1880, as many as 25 per cent of all west Africans probably belonged to stateless societies. Yet because of the absence of historical records of most local cultures and regional chiefdoms, we must necessarily focus here on the rise of identifiable states—that is, larger, more complex sociopolitical entities. This is not to say that there was no "culture" in early or even in contemporary stateless tribal societies or other small communities. In Chapter 7, we noted the impressive achievements of the Nok culture, which likely was not developed under the auspices of any state organization. However, it is only very recent history of, say, the past two to five centuries, to which local or tribal oral traditions can give us valuable access. We have no other ways of identifying or tracing the development of small, stateless societies that have left no written documents, monuments, or other decipherable artifacts of their history. At least we have for them nothing comparable to the sources available for the larger societies—with known rulers, fighting forces, and towns or cities—that left their own records or were documented by outsiders.

The first millennium A.D. saw the growth of settled agricultural populations and the development and expansion of trans-Saharan trade. These developments coincided with the rise of several sizable states in the western and central Sudan, significantly in the sahel border region between the desert and the savannah. The most important states were located in the following regions: (1) Takrur on the Senegal river, from perhaps the fifth century, if not earlier; (2) Ghana, between the northern bends of the Senegal and the Niger, from the fifth or sixth century; (3) Gao, on the Niger southeast of the bend, from before the eighth century; and (4) Kanem, northeast of Lake Chad, from the eighth or ninth century. While the origins and even the full extent of major states in these regions are shrouded in obscurity, each represents only the first of a series of large political entities in its region. All continued to figure prominently in subsequent west African history.

The states developed by the Fulbe people of Takrur and the Soninke people of Ghana depended early on their ability to draw gold for the Saharan trade with Morocco from the savannah region of Bambuhu (or Bambuk), west of the upper Senegal. Of all the sub-Saharan kingdoms of the late first millennium, Ghana was the most famous outside of the region, largely because of its substantial control over the gold trade. Its people built a true empire centered at its capital of Kumbi (also known as Kumbi Saleh). Inheriting his throne by matrilineal descent, the ruler was treated as a virtually semidivine ruler whose interaction with his subjects was mediated by a hierarchy of government ministers. He is described in an eleventh-century Arabic chronicle as commanding a sizable army, including horsemen and archers, and being buried with his retainers under a dome of earth and wood. In contrast to the Soninke of Ghana, the Songhai rulers of Gao had no gold trade until the fourteenth century. Unlike its western neighbors, Gao was oriented in its forest trade toward the lower, not the upper, Niger basin and in its Saharan trade toward eastern Algeria, not Morocco.

The Western and Central Sudan: Probable Dates for Founding of Regional Kingdoms

CA. 400 A.D. or earlier	Takrur (Senegal river valley)
A.D. 400–600	Ghana (in Sahel between great northern bends of the Senegal and Niger rivers)
CA. A.D. 700–800 or earlier	Gao (on the Niger river southeast of great bend)
CA. A.D. 700–900	Kanem (northeast of Lake Chad)

All of these states were built upon an agricultural base and settled populations. By contrast, the initial power of Kanem, on the northwest side of Lake Chad, originated in the borderlands of the central Sudan and the southern Sahara. Here the first state formation was a nomadic federation of black tribal peoples that persisted long enough for the separate tribes to merge and form a single people, the Kanuri. They then moved south to take over the sedentary societies of Kanem proper, just east of Lake Chad, and, later, Bornu, west of Lake Chad. By the thirteenth century, the Kanuri had themselves become sedentary; their kingdom controlled the southern terminus of perhaps the best trans-Saharan route—that running north via good watering stations to the oasis region of Fezzan in modern central Libya and thence to the Mediterranean.

Central, South, and East Africa

In the African subcontinent—that is, in central, south, and east Africa, or south of a line from roughly the Niger delta and Cameroon across to southern Somalia on the east coast—the time when human prehistory shades into history fell relatively late. Of the period before A.D. 1000, we have very little firm indigenous evidence and few outside written sources to help us write the history of the subcontinent. Some relatively certain facts and reasonable hypotheses have, however, emerged from a combination of linguistic, archaeological, and other research in this region.

The Khoisan Peoples

In the subcontinent, we find alongside the Bantu-speaking majority two smaller groups, the Khoikhoi and San peoples, both of whom are brown-skinned, usually rather short, with "peppercorn" rather than frizzy hair. Formerly and incorrectly distinguished racially, the San (long known in the West as Bushmen) and the Khoikhoi (the Hottentots of European usage) are two interrelated groups distinguished linguistically from Bantu and other language groups of Africa. Collectively, they and their language group are commonly known as *Khoisan*. The two groups are distinguished from each other more by their livelihood and distribution than any other characteristics.[1]

The San are likely the direct descendants of the Neolithic peoples of the south who have been traditionally hunter-gatherers as well as the authors of the striking prehistoric rock paintings of southern Africa. They do not form a single cultural group, but have de-

veloped linguistically and culturally diverse subgroups in different locales across southern Africa. Today they survive most prominently in the Kalahari region.

The more homogeneous Khoikhoi were sheep- and cattle-herding pastoralists who were also quite scattered across the south, yet who spoke closely related Khoisan tongues. Their ancestors probably originated in northern Botswana. They were hunters who relatively late—probably between A.D. 700 and 1000—learned animal herding from their Bantu-speaking south African neighbors. Thus, they became primarily pastoralists and soon expanded over the best pasturelands of western south Africa, as far south as the Cape of Good Hope. Here they flourished as pastoralist clans, sometimes united loosely as a tribe under a particularly strong chief, until their tragic encounter with the invading Dutch colonists in the mid-seventeenth century, which resulted in their demise as a distinct people.

The Bantu Migrations and Diffusion

In the African subcontinent, the vast majority of the peoples speak one of more than four hundred languages that belong to a single language group known as *Bantu*. All of these languages are as closely related as are the Germanic or Romance tongues of Europe. Although the place of origin and routes of diffusion of Bantu tongues have long been debated, today there is increasing consensus that the location of the proto-Bantu language must have been in the region south of the Benue river, in eastern Nigeria and modern Cameroon. Thence, in the course of the later centuries B.C. and the first millennium A.D., migrations of Bantu-speaking peoples must have taken their versions of this language in two basic directions: (1) south into the lower Zaïre (Congo) basin and ultimately to the southern edge of the equatorial forest in present-day northern Katanga; and (2) east around the equatorial forests into the lakes of highland east Africa.

In all these regions, Bantu tongues developed and multiplied in contact with other languages. Likewise, Bantu speakers intermixed and adapted in diverse ways, as the wide variety of physical types among Bantu peoples today demonstrates. Further migrations, some as early as the fourth century A.D. and others as late as the twelfth or thirteenth century, dispersed Bantu peoples even more widely, into south-central Africa, coastal east Africa, and south Africa. One result of this dispersion was the early civilization of Great Zimbabwe near the Zambezi river (treated in Chapter 15). The notion, however, that the Bantu or the Khoikhoi only arrived in south Africa at about the same time as the first European settlers is a fabrication used today to justify apartheid.

How the Bantu peoples managed to impose their languages upon the earlier cultures of these regions

---

[1] On the vexed problem of distinguishing San and Khoikhoi, see Richard Elphick, *Kraal and Castle: Khoikhoi and the Founding of White South Africa* (New Haven and London: 1977), pp. xxi–xxii, 3–42.

remains unexplained. The idea that they brought the knowledge of iron smelting with them and used it to dominate other peoples is not borne out by linguistic or other studies. The proto-Bantu had apparently been fishermen and hunters who also cultivated yams, date palms, and some cereals. They also raised goats and possibly sheep and some cattle, but they did not bring cattle with them in their migrations. Most of the migrating Bantu peoples seem to have been mainly cereal or grain agriculturists whose basic political and social unit was the village. Perhaps they had unusually strong social cohesion that allowed them to absorb other peoples; there is no evidence that they were military conquerors. Perhaps the Bantu brought diseases with them against which the aboriginals of the forests and the southern savannah had no immunities, much as later the European newcomers to the Cape brought the ravages of smallpox to the susceptible Khoikhoi.

In any case, their cultures became in time so fully interwoven with those of the peoples they settled among that the answers to these questions may never be known. For example, Bantu-Arab mixing on the eastern coasts produced the Swahili culture, which we shall encounter in Chapter 15. We find Bantu peoples as slash-and-burn farmers in the Zaïre river savannah, as cattle herders in the east African high plains, as perennial floodplain cultivators on the Zambezi river, and as terracing and irrigating farmers among the highland Kikuyu and Chagga peoples.

East Africa

The history of east Africa along the coast before Islam differed from that of the inland highlands. Long-distance travel was easy and common along the seashore, but less so inland.

The coast had had maritime contact with India, Arabia, and the Mediterranean via the Indian Ocean and Red Sea trade routes from at least as early as the second century B.C. By contrast, the direct contacts of the inland regions with any but adjacent areas of Africa itself were very limited or nonexistent until after A.D. 1000. Regional coastal trade is, however, also ancient. Both forms of sea trade remained important and interdependent over the centuries, since the Indian Ocean trade depended on the monsoon winds and could use only the northernmost coastal trading harbors of east Africa for round-trip voyages in the same year. The monsoon winds blow from the northeast and thus could carry sailing ships south from Iran, Arabia, and India only from December to March; they blow from the southwest only from April to August, when ships could sail from Africa northeast. Local coastal shipping thus had to haul cargoes from farther south than Zanzibar and then transfer them to other ships for the annual round-trip voyages to Arabia and beyond.

Long-distance trade came into its own in Islamic times—about the ninth century—as an Arab monopoly. However, long before the coming of Islam, trade was apparently largely in the hands of Arabs, many of whom had settled in the east African coastal towns and in Iran and India to handle this international commerce. We have documentation of Greco-Roman contact with these east African centers of the Red Sea and Indian Ocean trade from as early as the first century A.D. Most of the coastal trading towns were apparently independent, although Rhapta, the one town mentioned in the earliest Greek source, *The Periplus*, was a dependency of a south Arabian state.

The overseas trade was, however, evidently even more international than the earliest surviving sources indicate. Today, the language of Madagascar—Malagasy, an imported Malayo-Polynesian language—points graphically to the antiquity of substantial contact with the East Indies via the coastal trading routes of Asia's ancient southern rim. Evidence of an Indonesian migration even before the beginning of our era is seen in the fact that bananas, coconut palms, and other food crops indigenous to Southeast Asia spread across the entire African continent as staple foods. Further, as a result of the early regular commercial ties to distant lands of Asia, extra-African ethnic and cultural mixing has long been the rule for the east African coast; even today, its linguistic and cultural traditions are rich and varied (see Chapters 15, 22).

Other African imports included such items as Persian Gulf pottery, Chinese porcelain, and cotton cloth. The major African export good around which the east coast trade revolved was ivory, which was in perennial demand from Greece to India and, from the tenth century, even China. The slave trade was another major business. Slaves were procured, often inland, in east Africa and exported to the Arab and Persian world, as well as to India or China. Gold, that perennial lure of outsiders to Africa, became important only in Islamic times, from about the tenth century onward, as we shall see in Chapter 15. Wood and food grains must also have been shipped abroad.

The history of inland east Africa south of Ethiopia is much more difficult to trace than that of the coast, again because of the absence of written sources and the immense difficulty of access until relatively recent times. We can, however, use linguistic clues and other evidence to note some key developments that underlay more recent history in the highlands. These regions had early seen diffusion of peoples from the north, and changing conditions of subsistence over the centuries have continued to propel movements of small groups into new areas.

Of the early migrants from the north, first came Kushitic speakers, likely cattle herders and grain cultivators. Perhaps as early as 2000 B.C., they pushed from their homeland on the Ethiopian plateau south down the Rift valley as far as the southern end of Lake Tanganyika. They apparently displaced Neolithic hunter-gatherers who may have been related to the Khoisan minorities of modern east and south Africa. While Kushitic languages are spoken from east of Lake Rudolph northward in abundance, farther south only isolated remnants of Kushitic-speakers remain today, these largely in the Rift Valley in Tanzania.

Later, Nilotic peoples moved from the southwestern side of the Ethiopian plateau west over the upper Nile valley by about A.D. 1000. Then they pushed east and south, following the older Kushite paths, to spread over the Rift valley area by the fifteenth century and subsequently much of the east African highlands of modern-day Uganda, Kenya, and Tanzania. Here they all but completely supplanted their Kushite predecessors. Two of these Nilotic peoples were the Lwo and Maasai. The Lwo spread far and wide over a nine-hundred-mile-long swath of modern Uganda and parts of southern Sudan and western Kenya. They did so over a long period of time and mixed readily with various other peoples, absorbing new cultural elements and adapting to new situations wherever they went. The Maasai, on the other hand, are cattle pastoralists fiercely proud of their separate language, way of life, and cultural traditions. These features distinguish them sharply from the farming or hunting peoples whose settlements abut their pasturages at the top of the southern Rift valley in Kenya and Tanzania. Here, southwest and west of both Mt. Kenya and Mt. Kilomanjaro, the Maasai have concentrated and remained.

These migrations from the north and those of the

Bantu peoples from the west, who also entered the eastern highlands over many centuries, have made these highland regions a kind of melting pot of Kushitic, Nilotic, Bantu, and Khoisan groups. Their characteristics are visible in today's populations, with their immense diversity of languages and cultures. As much as any part of Africa, here we see the radical diversity of peoples and cultures of the entire continent mirrored in the heritages of a single major region.

IRAN

The Parthians

Parthian Arsacid rule (CA. 247 B.C.–A.D. 223) continued the Iranian imperial tradition begun by the Achaemenids (see Chapter 7). The relative Parthian tolerance of religious diversity was paralleled by the growth of regionalism in political and cultural affairs. A growing nobility built strong local power bases and became the backbone of the military power of the realm. Aramaic, the common language of the empire, gradually lost ground to regional Iranian tongues after the second century B.C.. The Parthian dialect and Greek became widely influential but could not replace Aramaic.

Despite their general religious tolerance, the Parthians still upheld such Zoroastrian traditions as the maintenance of a royal sacred fire at a shrine in their Parthian homeland and the inclusion of priestly advisers on the emperor's council. The last century or so of their rule saw increased emphasis on Iranian as opposed to foreign traditions in religious and cultural affairs. This was perhaps in reaction to the almost constant warfare with the Romans on their west flank and the Kushan threat in the east. By this time, Christianity and Buddhism were making sufficient converts in western and eastern border areas to threaten Zoroastrian tradition directly for the first time. This threat may have stimulated Parthian attempts to collect the largely oral Zoroastrian textual heritage. In this and other ways, Parthian rule laid the groundwork for the nationalistic emphases of the next few centuries, despite later Sasanid efforts to portray this era as one of decline in native Iranian traditions.

The Sasanid Empire
(A.D. 224–651)

The Sasanids were a Persian dynasty, like the Achaemenids. Claiming to be the latter's rightful heirs, the Sasanids put themselves forward as champions of Iranian legitimacy and tried to brand the Parthians as outside invaders who followed Greek and other foreign ways. Much of the lasting bad reputation of the Parthians stems from the fact that they are still known only through hostile sources.

The first Sasanid king, Ardashir (reigned A.D. 224–CA. 239), was a Persian warrior noble who had a priestly family background. The Sasanid name came from his grandfather, Sasan. Ardashir and his son, Shapur I (reigned CA. 239–272), built a strong internal administration and extended the empire abroad. While still his father's field general, Shapur took Bactria from the Kushans, thereby greatly expanding the Sasanid realm. Under his long rule, the empire grew significantly, not only in the east, but also beyond the Caucasus in the north and into Syria, Armenia, and parts of Anatolia in the west. Shapur inflicted humiliating defeats on three Roman emperors, even capturing one of them, Valerian. Thus, he could justifiably claim to be a restorer of Iranian glory and a "king of

kings," or *shahanshah*. He also centralized and rationalized taxation, the civil ministries, and the military, although neither he nor his successors could fully counterbalance the growing power of the nobility.

With the shift of the Roman Empire east to Byzantium at the beginning of the fourth century A.D., the stage of imperial conflict for the next 350 years was set: Byzantium (Constantinople) on the Bosporus and Ctesiphon on the Tigris were to be the seats of the two mightiest thrones of Eurasia until the coming of the Arabs. Each from time to time won victories over the other, and each championed a different religious orthodoxy, but neither could ever completely conquer the other. In the sixth century, each produced their greatest emperors: the Byzantine Justinian (reigned 527–565) and the Sasanid Chosroes Anosharvan ("Chosroes of the Immortal Soul," reigned 531–579). Yet, less than a century after their deaths, the new Arab power defeated one empire and destroyed the other. Byzantium survived with much reduced territory for another eight hundred years, but the Sasanid imperial order was swept away with the last of its rulers in 651. Memory of the Sasanids did not, however, entirely die. Chosroes, for example, became a legendary model of greatness for Persians and a symbol of imperial splendor even among the Arabs.

Society and Economy

Sasanid society was largely like that of earlier times. At all levels, the extended family was (as it is even today in Iran) the basic social unit. Zoroastrian orthodoxy recognized four classes: priests, warriors,

The palace of the Sasanid Shahanshahs at Ctesiphon. Built by Shapur I in the capital that the Sasanids inherited from the Arsacids, the imperial palace is only partially preserved. The gigantic, four storyed structure is said to have greatly impressed the Arab invaders in the seventh century. The massive open-vaulted hall or bay was a feature of Persian architecture which would be used later in Iranian mosques. [Bettmann Archive.]

scribes, and peasants. The great divide was between the royal house, the priesthood, and the warrior nobility on the one hand, and the common people of the cities (artisans, traders, and so on) and the rural peasantry on the other.

As before, the basis of the economy remained agriculture. The long-term trend was toward the concentration of land ownership among an ever-richer minority of the royalty, the nobility, and the priesthood. The growth of great estates was similar to that in Roman domains and was no less responsible for an increased imbalance between the rich few and the impoverished many. More and more small farmers were reduced to serfdom in the latter half of this era. The burden of land taxation, like that of conscript labor work and army duty, hit hardest those least able to afford it. It was not without eventual popular reaction, as the Mazdakite movement, which is discussed later, shows.

The Sasanids also closely oversaw and heavily taxed the lucrative caravan trade that traversed their territory, as well as export and import trade by sea. Silk and glass production increased under government monopoly, and the state controlled mining. The many urban centers of the empire and the foreign trade relied on a money system. It was from Jewish bankers in Babylonia and their Persian counterparts that Europe and the rest of the world got the use of bills of exchange (the very word *check* comes from a Pahlavi word).[2]

Sasanid aristocratic culture drew on diverse traditions, from Roman, Hellenistic, and Bactrian-Indian to Achaemenid and other native Iranian ones. Its heyday was the reign of Chosroes. Iranian legendary history and courtly literature were popular, as were translations of Indian narrative literature. Indian influences— not only religious ones, as in the case of Buddhist ideas, but also artistic and especially scientific ones— were especially strong. Indian medicine and mathematics were particularly well received. Hellenistic culture also was revived in the academy at Jundishapur in Khuzistan, where refugee scholars from Byzantium came to teach medicine and philosophy after Justinian closed the Greek academies in the west.

Religion

THE ZOROASTRIAN REVIVAL. Religion played a significant role in Sasanid life not only at the popular level but even in affairs of state. The Sasanids institutionalized Zoroastrian ritual and theology as state orthodoxy. Although they actually were simply continu-

The luxury art of the Sasanids was the culmination of the long development of earlier Iranian traditions. It was consciously Iranian and oriental, rather than Greco-Roman, although Western influence was inevitable. A popular motif was the hunt, always a favorite pastime of Persian aristocrats. The stylized figures shown at the bottom of this silver bowl are typical of the Sasanid style. [Bettmann Archive.]

ing the Arsacid patronage of Zoroastrian worship, the Sasanids claimed to be restoring the true faith after centuries of neglect. The initial architect of this propaganda and the Zoroastrian revival was the first chief priest of the empire, Tosar (or Tansar). Under Ardashir, Tosar instituted a state church organization and began the fixation of an authoritative, written canon of the Avesta, the scriptural texts that include the hymns of Zarathushtra. He may also have been the one to institute a calendar reform and to ban all images in the temples of the land, replacing them with the sacred altar fires of Zoroastrian tradition.

The greatest figure in Sasanid religious history was Tosar's successor, Kartir, or Kirdir, who served as chief priest to Shapur I and his three successors (CA. 239–293). Although his zealotry was at first kept in check by the religiously tolerant and eclectic Shapur, Kirdir gained greater power and influence after Shapur's death. He is the one figure other than a Sasanid king for whom we have personal inscriptions in the rock reliefs of the dynasty. He seems to have made numerous efforts to convert not only pagans, but also Christians, Buddhists, and other followers of foreign traditions. His chief opponents were, however, the Manichaeans, whom he considered Zoroas-

[2]R. Girshman, *Iran* (Harmondsworth, U.K., 1954), pp. 341–346. "Pahlavi" is the name of the middle Persian language that gradually replaced Aramaic as the Iranian *lingua franca* in Sasanid times.

On the Propagation of Mazda-Worship

The following excerpts are from an inscription of Kirdir, the second high priest to serve under the Sasanids. Here he proclaims his successful efforts to consolidate and spread the worship of Ahura Mazda. The time of the inscription is the reign of Vahram II, 276–293. The yazads *are beneficent divine beings, the* devs *the evil minions of the "Evil Spirit," Ahriman.*

And I was made Mobad and Judge of the whole empire, and I was made Master of Ceremonials and Warden of the Fires of Anahid-Ardashir and Anahid the Lady at Istakhr. And I was styled 'Kirder by whom Vahram's soul is saved, Mobad of Ohrmazd'. And in every province and place of the whole empire the service of Ohrmazd and the yazads was exalted, and the Mazda-worshipping religion and its priests received much honour in the land. And the yazads, and water and fire and cattle, were greatly contented, and Ahriman and the devs suffered great blows and harm. And the creed of Ahriman and the devs was driven out of the land and deprived of credence. And Jews and Buddhists and Brahmans and Aramaic and Greek-speaking Christians and Baptisers and Manichaeans were assailed in the land. And images were overthrown, and the dens of demons were (thus) destroyed, and the places and abodes of the yazads (i.e. fire temples) were established. . . . And from the first I, Kirder, underwent much toil and trouble for the yazads and the rulers, and for my own soul's sake.

And I caused many fires and priestly colleges to flourish in Iran, and also in non-Iranian lands. There were fires and priests in the non-Iranian lands which were reached by the armies of the King of kings. The provincial capital Antioch and the province of Syria, and the districts dependent on Syria; the provincial capital Tarsus and the province of Cilicia, and the districts dependent on Cilicia; the provincial capital Caesarea and the province Cappadocia, and the districts dependent on Cappadocia, up to Pontus, and the province of Armenia, and Georgia and Albania and Balasagan, up to the 'Gate of the Alans'—these were plundered and burnt and laid waste by Shabuhr, King of kings, with his armies. There too, at the command of the King of kings, I reduced to order the priests and fires which were in those lands. And I did not allow harm to be done them, or captives made. And whoever had thus been made captive, him indeed I took and sent back to his own land. And I made the Mazda-worshipping religion and its good priests esteemed and honoured in the land. . . . ❑

Mary Boyce, ed. and trans., *Textual Sources for the Study of Zoroastrianism* (Manchester: University Press, 1984), pp. 112–113.

---

trian heretics, much as they were regarded by Christian groups as Christian heretics.

MANICHAEISM. Mani (A.D. 216–277) was born of a noble Parthian family but was raised in Babylonia. A cosmopolitan who spoke Aramaic, Persian, and Greek and had traveled to India, Mani preached a message similar to, but at crucial points radically divergent from, its Zoroastrian, Judaic, and Christian forerunners. It centered on a radically dualistic and moralistic view of reality, in which good and evil, spirit and matter, always warred. His preaching was avowedly missionary, presenting itself as the culmination and restoration of the original unity of Zoroastrian, Christian, and Buddhist teachings. Mani may have been the first person in history consciously to "found" a new religious tradition or to create a "scripture" for his followers. He called his new system "Justice," although it has been known to outsiders as Manichaeism. Mani's movement proved a popular one; its popularity probably contributed to Kirdir's and later attempts to establish a Zoroastrian "orthodoxy" and scriptural canon.[3]

[3]W. C. Smith, *The Meaning and End of Religion* (New York, 1962), pp. 92–98.

Kirdir eventually won his struggle against Mani and had him executed as a heretic in 277. But Mani's movement was destined to have great consequences. It spread westward to challenge the young Christian church (Saint Augustine was once a Manichaean) and eastward along the silk route to coexist in central Asia with Nestorian Christian and Mahayana Buddhist communities as a third major universalistic tradition until after the coming of Islam. Its ideas figured even centuries later in both Christian and Islamic heresies. Its adherents probably carried the Western planetary calendar to China, where in some areas it was used for centuries.

ZOROASTRIAN ORTHODOXY. Kartir had firmly grounded Zoroastrian orthodoxy despite the persistence of such challenges to it as that of Mani. This orthodoxy became the backbone of Sasanid culture. Soon the Sasanids' Persian dialect, *Pahlavi*, became the official imperial language, displacing Parthian (although many Parthian words entered the Persian language). Eventually, the Zoroastrian sacred texts were set down in Pahlavi. In later Sasanid times, the priests produced many new writings, ranging from commen-

An angel from a Manichean mural of Central Asia (eighth-ninth century A.D.). Paintings such as this are an important source for our knowledge of Manichaean communities.

taries to myth, theology, and wisdom literature. Throughout Sasanid times, the priesthood grew in power as the jurists and legal interpreters as well as the liturgists and scholars of the land. With increasing endowments of new fire temples, the church establishment eventually controlled much of the wealth of Iran.

Later Sasanid Developments

Despite the high Zoroastrian moral intent of many of their rulers, the Sasanid ideal of justice did not include equal distribution of the empire's bounty. The radical inequalities between the aristocracy and the common folk in Sasanid lands erupted in conflict in one instance: the Mazdakite movement at the end of the fifth century. Its leader, Mazdak, seems to have drawn his ideas ultimately from Manichaeism. They included similar ascetic tendencies, were pessimistic about the evil state of the material world, and urged vegetarianism, tolerance, and brotherly love. Mazdak's egalitarian preaching, which included a demand for a more equal distribution of society's goods, was attractive especially to the oppressed classes, and one Sasanid ruler, Kavad I (reigned 488–531), was even sympathetic for a time to Mazdak's ideas of social justice. However, in 528, Kavad's third son, the later Chosroes Anosharvan, carried out an official massacre of Mazdak and his most important followers. Although this finished the Mazdakites, the name was still used later, in Islamic times, for various Iranian popular revolts.

INDIA

The Golden Age of the Guptas

The Gupta era has always marked for Indians the high point of their civilization. Historians have seen in it the source of the "classical" norms for Hindu religion and Indian culture, the symbolic equivalent of Periclean Athens, Augustan Rome, or Han China. The Guptas ruled at a time when the various facets of Indian life took on the recognizable patterns of a single civilization which, however diverse its parts, covered all the subcontinent. A contributing factor was the relative peace and stability that marked most of the Gupta reign.

Gupta Rule

The first Gupta king was Chandragupta (reigned A.D. 320–CA. 330; not to be confused with Chandragupta Maurya; see Chapter 7). He came to prominence first in Magadha and then the rest of the Ganges basin largely through his marriage to princess

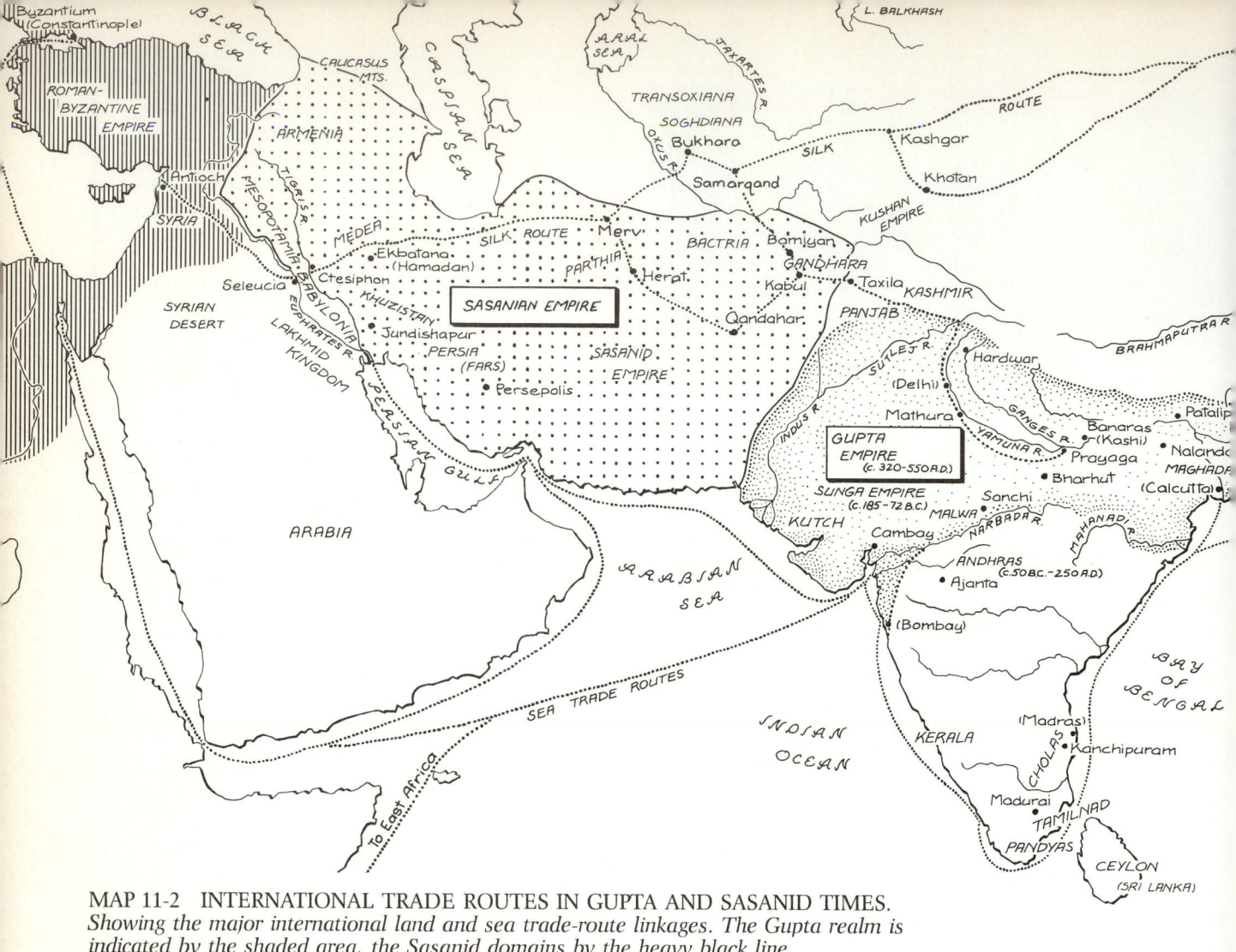

MAP 11-2 INTERNATIONAL TRADE ROUTES IN GUPTA AND SASANID TIMES.
*Showing the major international land and sea trade-route linkages. The Gupta realm is
indicated by the shaded area, the Sasanid domains by the heavy black line.*

Kumaradevi, daughter of the leader of a powerful tribe
north of the Ganges. Although their reign inaugurated
Gupta power, it was their son, Samudragupta and
especially their grandson, Chandragupta II (reigned
CA. 375–415), who turned kingdom into empire and
presided over the Gupta "golden age."

The Gupta realm became the greatest in the subcontinent, extending from the borders of the Punjab
and Kashmir south to the Narbada river in the western
Deccan and east to modern Assam. The Gupta sphere
of influence was still larger, including some of the
Kushan and Saka kingdoms of the northwest as well as
much of the eastern coast of India and possibly Ceylon
(Sri Lanka). More than the Mauryas, the Guptas were
usually ready to accept a defeated ruler as a vassal
prince rather than to try to place his kingdom under
direct central administrative control. Seated at the old
Mauryan capital of Pataliputra, Gupta splendor and
power had no rival. Under Chandragupta II, India was

arguably the most civilized and peaceful country in the
world.

Two further Gupta kings sustained this prosperity
for another half century, despite invasions by a new
wave of steppe nomads, the Huns, from about 440 on.
Various weaker kings followed until the empire collapsed around 550, but repeated Hun incursions had
already overrun western India by about 500. When
another Indian ruler did manage to break Hun control
in northwest India (530), the Guptas were too weak to
reestablish their sovereignty in the north.

Harsha, a descendant of the Guptas through his
grandmother, managed to revive some of the Gupta
splendor between 616 and 657. He ruled long and well
over a loose empire that stretched across north India.
When he died without heirs, the empire broke up
again, and the final echo of Gupta grandeur was gone.
The succeeding centuries before the arrival of Muslim
invaders in about A.D. 1000 saw several dynasties

share power in north India, but no unified rule of any duration. Outside the north, the main centers of regional empires were in the western Deccan and in Tamilnad (the extreme south), where several long-lived dynasties shared control after Gupta times. The cultural impetus of Indian civilization now shifted visibly to the Deccan and south.

Gupta Culture

With the decline of Rome in the West, from Gupta until Muslim times Indian culture experienced little new influence from outside. India's chief contacts were now with Southeast Asia and China, and most of the cultural transmission was from India eastward, not vice versa.

The Gupta period and later centuries saw massive literary and artistic productivity, of which only a few outstanding examples can be mentioned. The claim of the Gupta era to being India's golden age of culture could be sustained solely on the basis of its magnificent architecture and sculpture, the wall paintings of the Ajanta caves, and the matchless drama and verse of Kalidasa. The "Shakespeare" of Sanskrit letters, Kalidasa flourished in the time of Chandragupta II and Kumaragupta. Poetry, painting, sculpture, dance, drama, and music were popularly practiced as well as patronized in the aristocratic households of the cities that set the cultural standards.

One index of the culture was its emphasis on education, which was prominently available in Jain and Buddhist monasteries and in Brahmanical schools. Religious texts were not the only focus: Rhetoric, prose and poetic composition, grammar, logic, medicine, and metaphysics were typical subjects. Based on the

A Chinese Traveler's Report on the Gupta Realm

Fa-Hsien, a Chinese Buddhist monk, was the first of several known Chinese to travel to India to study and bring back Buddhist scriptures from the intellectual centers of Buddhist thought there. He, like later travelers of whom we know, wrote an account of his travels, first through Central Asia, then all over India, then through Ceylon and Indonesia again to China (A.D. 399–414).

On the sides of the river, both right and left, are twenty saṅghârâmas [monasteries], with perhaps 3000 priests. The law of the Buddha is progressing and flourishing. Beyond the deserts are the countries of Western India. The kings of these countries are all firm believers in the law of Buddha. They remove their caps of state when they make offerings to the priests. The members of the royal household and the chief ministers personally direct the food-giving; when the distribution of food is over, they spread a carpet on the ground opposite the chief seat (the president's seat) and sit down before it. They dare not sit on couches in the presence of the priests. The rules relating to the almsgiving of kings have been handed down from the time of Buddha till now. Southward from this is the so-called middle-country (Mâdhyadeśa). The climate of this country is warm and equable, without frost or snow. The people are very well off, without polltax or official restrictions. Only those who till the royal lands return a portion of profit of the land. If they desire to go, they go; if they like to stop, they stop. The kings govern without corporal punishment; criminals are fined, according to circumstances, lightly or heavily. Even in cases of repeated rebellion they only cut off the right hand. The king's personal attendants, who guard him on the right and left, have fixed salaries. Throughout the country the people kill no living thing nor drink wine, nor do they eat garlic or onions, with the exception of Chandâlas [outcasts] only. The Chandâlas are named "evil men" and dwell apart from others; if they enter a town or market, they sound a piece of wood in order to separate themselves; then men, knowing who they are, avoid coming in contact with them. In this country they do not keep swine nor fowls, and do not deal in cattle; they have no shambles or wine-shops in their marketplaces. In selling they use cowrie shells. The Chandâlas only hunt and sell flesh. Down from the time of Buddha's Nirvâna, the kings of these countries, the chief men and householders, have raised vihâras [monasteries] for the priests, and provided for their support by bestowing on them fields, houses, and gardens, with men and oxen. Engraved title-deeds were prepared and handed down from one reign to another; no one has ventured to withdraw them, so that till now there has been no interruption. All the resident priests having chambers (in these vihâra) have their beds, mats, food, drink, and clothes provided without stint; in all places this is the case. The priests ever engage themselves in doing meritorious works for the purpose of religious advancement (karma—building up their religious character), or in reciting the scriptures, or in meditation. ❑

From "Buddhist Country Records," in *Si-Yu-Ki: Buddhist Records of the Western World*, trans. by Samuel Beal (London, 1884; reprint, Delhi: Oriental Books Reprint Corporation, 1969), pp. xxxvii–xxxviii.

The Bodhisattva Avalokiteshvara from Ajanta. One of the magnificent murals from the Ajanta Buddhist cave shrines. The colossal figure is that of the Bodhisattva of infinite compassion. Even through the damage of centuries, this Gupta masterpiece has an aura of serene majesty. The inclined head of Avalokiteshvara as well as the tranquil face and gesturing hands embody the compassion of this figure in what is surely one of the masterpieces of world religious art. [Government of India Tourist Office.]

still older Indian number system that came later via the Arabs to the West as the "Arabic numerals," mathematics was cultivated for theoretical as well as practical purposes.

In sculpture, the superb technique and expressive serenity of Gupta style grew out of the native Mathura and Greco-Roman schools. Hindu, Jain, and Buddhists works all shared the same style and conventions. A great center for sculpture was the monastic complex at Sarnath. Even in handwork and luxury crafts, Gupta products achieved new levels of quality and were in great demand abroad: silks, muslin, linen, ivory and other carvings, bronze metalwork, gold and silver work, and cut stones, among others. In architecture, Gupta splendor is less evident, save in the culmination of cave shrine (Chaitya hall) development at Ajanta and in the earliest surviving free-standing tem-

The Durga Temple at Aihole. This Hindu temple in the southern Deccan shows how the older Chaitya-hall of the rock-cut or cave variety, such as at Ajanta, influenced the shape of free-standing temples in Gupta times. Note the small spire that became a fixture of later Indian temple architecture. [Giraudon/Art resource.]

A Lyric Poem of Kalidasa

Perhaps the greatest lyric poet as well as dramatist of Sanskrit letters, Kalidasa represents all that was refined and aesthetically sophisticated about Gupta culture. In the following poem, he paints a picture in words from an epic tale about Kumāra, the divine offspring of Shiva, and his consort, the goddess Parvati.

KUMĀRA'S FIGHT AGAINST THE DEMON TĀRAKA

A fearful flock of evil birds,
    ready for the joy of eating the army of demons,
flew over the host of the gods,
    and clouded the sun.

A wind continually fluttered their umbrellas and
    banners,
and troubled their eyes with clouds of whirling dust,
so that the trembling horses and elephants
and the great chariots could not be seen.

Suddenly monstrous serpents, as black as powdered
    soot,
scattering poison from their upraised heads,
frightful in form,
appeared in the army's path.

The sun put on a ghastly robe
of great and terrible snakes, curling together,
as if to mark his joy
at the death of the enemy demon.

And before the very disc of the sun
jackals bayed harshly together,
as though eager fiercely to lap the blood
of the king of the foes of the gods, fallen in battle.

Lighting heaven from end to end,
with flames flashing all around,
with an awful crash, rending the heart with terror,
a thunderbolt fell from a cloudless sky.

The sky poured down torrents of red-hot ashes,
with which were mixed blood and human bones,
till the flaming ends of heaven were filled with
    smoke
and bore the dull hue of the neck of an ass.

Like the thundered threat of the angry death-god
a great crash broke the walls of the ears,
a shattering sound, tearing the tops of the
    mountains,
and wholly filling the belly of heaven.

The host of the foe was jostled together.
The great elephants stumbled, the horses fell,
and all the footmen clung together in fear,
as the earth trembled and the ocean rose to shake
    the mountains.

And, before the host of the foes of the gods,
dogs lifted their muzzles to gaze on the sun,
then, howling together with cries that rent the
    eardrums,
they wretchedly slunk away.

Kumāra-sambhava, 15.14

From Louis Renou (ed.), *Hinduism* (New York: G. Braziller, 1962), pp. 181–182.

ples in India. The Hindu temple underwent its important development in post-Gupta times, in the eighth century and after.

The Consolidation of Indian Civilization (CA. A.D. 300–1000)

The Guptas' support of Brahmanic traditions and Vaishnava[4] devotionalism reflected the ascendancy of Hindu over Buddhist traditions as the mainstream of Indian religious life. In Gupta and subsequent times down to the advent of Muslim rule, Indian civilization

[4] *Vaishnava* or *Vaishnavite* means "related to Vishnu"; similarly, *Shaiva* or *Shaivite* refers to Shiva worship (compare with *Jaina/Jain* for devotees of the way of the *Jinas* such as Mahavira).

assumed its classical shape, its enduring "Hindu" forms of social, religious, and cultural life.

Society

In these centuries, the fundamentally hierarchical character of Hindu/Indian society solidified in practice and theory. The oldest manual of legal and ethical theory, the *Dharmashastra* of Manu, dates from about A.D. 200. Based on Vedic tradition, it treats the *dharma* appropriate to one's class and stage of life, rules for rites and study of the Veda, pollution and purification measures, dietary restrictions, royal duties and prerogatives, and other legal and moral questions.

In it, we find the classic statement of the four-class system of social hierarchy. This system rests on the basic principle that every person is born into a particular station in life (as a result of *karma* from earlier lives), and every station has its particular *dharma*, or appropriate duties and responsibilities, from the lowest servant to the highest prince or Brahman. The basic framework is the Brahmans' ancient division of Aryans into the four *varnas*, or classes, of *Brahman* (priest), *Kshatriya* (noble/warrior), *Vaishya* (tradesperson), and *Shudra* (servant). These divisions reflect an ancient attempt to fix the status and power of the upper three groups, especially the Brahmans, at the expense of the Shudras and the "fifth class" of non-Aryan "outcasts," who performed the most polluting jobs in society. Although class distinctions had already hardened before 500 B.C., the classes were, in practice, somewhat fluid. When the traditional occupation of a *varna* was closed to a member, he could often take up another, all theory to the contrary. When Brahmans, Vaishyas, or even Shudras gained political power as rulers (as was evidently the case with the Mauryas, for example), their family gradually became recognized as *Kshatriyas*, the appropriate class for princes.

Although the four classes, or *varnas*, provide the theoretical basis for caste relations, smaller subgroups, or *jatis*, are the units to which our English term *caste* refers. These basic divisions of all later Indian society were already the primary units of social distinction in Gupta times. *Jati* groupings are based essentially on principles of purity and pollution, which are expressed in three kinds of regulation: (1) commensality (one may take food only from or with persons of the same or a higher caste group); (2) endogamy (one may marry only within the group); and (3) trade or craft limitation (one must practice only the trade of one's group).[5]

As much as the caste system has been criticized, it has been the functional principle of Indian social organization for at least two millennia. It enabled Hindus to accommodate foreign cultural, racial, and religious communities within Indian society by treating them simply as new caste groups. It gave great stability and security to the individual and to society, as everyone could tell by dress and other marks how one should relate to a given person or group. It represented also the logical extension of the doctrine of *karma* into society (see Chapter 2), whether this doctrine be seen as a justification, a product, or a partial cause of the caste system itself.

Religion

HINDU RELIGIOUS LIFE. The growth of devotional cults of Vishnu, Shiva, and other deities unknown or unimportant in Vedic religion went on apace in Gupta and later times. The temple worship of a par-

ticular deity has ever since remained a basic form of Hindu piety. After Vishnu (especially in his form as the hero-savior Krishna) and Shiva (originally a fertility god identified with the Vedic deity Rudra), the chief focus of devotion came to be the goddess in one of her many forms, such as Parvati, Shakti, Durga, or Kali. Vishnu and Shiva, like Parvati, have many forms and names and have always been easily identified with other deities, who are then worshiped as one form of the Supreme Lord or Goddess. Older animal or nature deities were always part of popular Indian piety, presumably since Indus Valley days. Indian reverence for all forms of life and stress on *ahimsa*, or "non-injury" to living beings (see Chapter 2), is most vivid in the sacredness of the cow, which has always been both symbolically and economically a mainstay of life in India.

In the development of Hindu piety and practice, a major strand was the tradition of ardent theism known as *bhakti*, or "loving devotion." This was already evident, at the latest by A.D. 200, in the Bhagavad Gita's treatment of Krishna. Gupta and later times saw the rise, especially in the Tamil-speaking south, of schools of *bhakti* poetry and worship. The central *bhakti* strand in Hindu life derives in good part from the Tamil and other vernacular poets who first sang the praises of Shiva or Vishnu as Supreme Lord. Here, pre-Aryan religious sensibilities apparently reasserted themselves through the non-Aryan Dravidian peoples of the south. The great theologian of devotional Hinduism, Ramanuja (d. CA. 1137), would later come from this same Dravidian tradition. Of major importance also to devotional piety was the development in this era of the Puranas—epic, mythological, and devotional texts. They are still today the functional sacred scriptures of grassroots Hindu religious life (the Vedic texts remaining the special preserve of the Brahmans).

Whichever god or goddess a Hindu worships, there has never been any objection to paying homage on the proper occasion to other appropriate deities. Most Hindus view one deity as Supreme Lord but see others as manifestations of the Ultimate at lower levels. Hindu polytheism is not "idolatry," but a vivid affirmation of the infinite forms that transcendence takes in the created world. The sense of the presence of the divine in everything is evident at the popular level in the immense importance attached to sacred places in India. It is the land of religious pilgrimage *par excellence*. Sacred mountains, rivers, trees, and groves are all *tirthas*, or "river crossings" to the Divine.

The philosophical or theological articulation of Hindu polytheism and relativism found its finest form in post-Gupta formulations of Vedanta ("the End of the Veda"). This is one of the six major Hindu systems of thought based on the Vedas, especially the Upanishads. The major Vedantic thinker was Shan-

[5] A. L. Basham, *The Wonder That Was India* (New York, 1963), pp. 148–149.

बिषाू

A

kara (d. 820). He stressed a strict "nonduality" of the Ultimate, teaching that Brahman was the only Reality behind the "illusion" *(maya)* of the world of sense experience. Yet he accepted the worship of a single lesser god or goddess as appropriate for those who could not follow his "extraordinary norm"—the intellectual realization of the formless Absolute beyond all "name and form" (see Chapter 2).

Vishnu, Shiva, and Durga. Images of three of India's most important Hindu deities, seventh to eleventh centuries A.D. Figure A shows Vishnu seated upon the conquered Naga, or serpent deity. Figure B shows the goddess Durga standing on a defeated bull-headed demon. Her six arms hold weapons lent her for the battle by Shiva and Vishnu. Figure C is a magnificent South Indian bronze of Shiva. The fluid, balanced image depicts the so-called "dancing Shiva" engaged in his dance of simultaneous destruction and creation of the universe, an artistic-mythical rendering of the eternal flux of all worldly existence. [Diana L. Eck, Museum of Fine Arts Boston-Denman W. Ross Collection, W.R. Nelson Gallery of Art.]

B

C

The Lord Krishna Speaks of True Devotion

In these verses (Bhagavad Gita 9.22–34), Krishna (Vishnu) tells his friend Arjuna the "supreme secret," that pure faith in and devotion to him can save a person. This is a famous expression of the bhakti *ideal of loving devotion to one's lord.*

GOD AND THE DEVOTEE

Those persons who, meditating on Me without any thought of another god, worship Me—to them, who constantly apply themselves [to that worship], I bring attainment [of what they do not have] and preservation [of what they have attained].

Even the devotees of other divinities, who worship them, being endowed with faith—they, too, O son of Kuntī [actually] worship Me alone, though not according to the prescribed rites.

For I am the enjoyer, as also the lord of all sacrifices. But those people do not comprehend Me in My true nature and hence they fall.

Worshipers of the gods go to the gods; worshipers of the manes go to the manes; those who sacrifice to the spirits go to the spirits; and those who worship Me, come to Me.

A leaf, a flower, a fruit, or water, whoever offers to Me with devotion—that same, proffered in devotion by one whose soul is pure, I accept.

Whatever you do, whatever you eat, whatever you offer in sacrifice, whatever you give away, whatever penance you practice—that, O son of Kuntī, do you dedicate to Me.

Thus will you be freed from the good or evil fruits which constitute the bondage of actions. With your mind firmly set on the way of renunciation [of fruits], you will, becoming free, come to Me.

Even-minded am I to all beings; none is hateful nor dear to Me. Those, however, who worship Me with devotion, they abide in Me, and I also in them.

Even if a person of extremely vile conduct worships Me being devoted to none else, he is to be reckoned as righteous, for he has engaged himself in action in the right spirit.

Quickly does he become of righteous soul and obtain eternal peace. O son of Kuntī, know for certain that My devotee perishes not.

For those, O son of Prithā, who take refuge in Me, even though they be lowly born, women, vaishyas, as also shūdras—even they attain to the highest goal.

How much more, then, pious brāhmans, as also devout royal sages? Having come to this impermanent, blissless world, worship Me.

On Me fix your mind; become My devotee, My worshiper; render homage unto Me. Thus having attached yourself to Me, with Me as your goal, you shall come to Me. . . . ❑

From W. T. deBary et al., *Sources of Indian Tradition* (New York: Columbia University Press, 1958), pp. 294–296.

BUDDHIST RELIGIOUS LIFE. The major developments of these centuries were (1) the solidification of what would later become the two main strands of Buddhist tradition, the Mahayana and the Theravada, and (2) the spread of Buddhism abroad from its Indian homeland.

The Mahayana ("Great Vehicle [of salvation]") arose in the first century B.C., although Mahayana ideas had been foreshadowed in divergent schools of Buddhist thought as early as the fourth century B.C. Its proponents differentiated it sharply from the older, more conservative traditions of monk-oriented piety and thought, which they called the Hinayana ("Little Vehicle"). Mahayana speculation developed in the style of Upanishadic monism: Buddhas were viewed as manifestations of a single principle of Ultimate Reality, and the Buddha Sidhartha Gautama was held to be but one Buddha among many. In the Mahayana, the model of the Buddha's infinite compassion for all beings was paramount. The highest goal was not a *nirvana* of "selfish" extinction but the enlightened status of a *bodhisattva,* or "Buddha-to-be." The *bodhisattva* postpones individual enlightenment and vows to remain in the round of existence until he has helped all other beings achieve nirvana.

What makes it possible for the bodhisattva to offer this aid is the infinite merit gained through a long career of self-sacrifice. Salvation now becomes possible not only through one's individual efforts, but through devotion to the great Buddhas and bodhisattvas. At the popular level, this idea translated into devotional cults of the transcendent Buddha and many other Buddhas and bodhisattvas similarly conceived of as divine beings. Of such cults, one of the most important was that of the Buddha Amitabha, the personification of infinite compassion. Amitabha presides over the Western Paradise, or Pure Land, to which (through his infinite compassion) all who have faith in him have access.

The older, more conservative "Way of the Elders" (Theravada) was never the totally selfish elite tradition of the few that its Mahayana critics claimed it to be. Its focus was always the monastic community, but lay devotees were needed to support this community; and their service and gifts to the monks were a major source of merit for the laity. The emphasis on gaining merit for a better rebirth through high standards of conduct was strong for monks and laity alike. Popular lay devotion to the Buddha and pilgrimage to his relics at various *stupas* also became prominent in Theravada practice. Conversely, the Mahayana also held up monastic life as the ideal. However, one of its greatest attractions was its strong devotionalism and virtually polytheistic delight in divine Buddhas and bodhisattvas to whom the average person could pray for mercy, help, and rebirth in paradise. The basis of Theravada piety and practice was the scriptural collection of traditional teachings ascribed to the Buddha as reported by his disciples. Theravadins rejected the Mahayana claim that later texts (e.g., the Lotus Sutra) contained the highest teachings of the Buddha.

The Theravada was the form of Buddhism that India gave to Ceylon, Burma, and parts of Southeast Asia. The Mahayana was the dominant form carried

The Buddha preaching his first sermon. This seated, high-relief figure of the Buddha, found in the ruins of Sarnath, is one of the finest pieces of Gupta sculpture. Both the hand gesture, which signifies the setting in motion of the eternal Dharma, and the etherealized body and head suggest the new concept of the Buddha that emerged with the Mahayana. In Gupta times, Sarnath was a thriving monastic center as well as one of the major schools for the best sculpture of the day. [Diana L. Eck.]

INDIA FROM THE GUPTA AGE TO CA. A.D. 1000

A.D. 320–CA. 467	Gupta period
320–330	Reign of Chandragupta, first Gupta king
376–454	Reigns of Chandragupta II and Kumaragupta: Kalidasa flourishes; heyday of Gupta culture
CA. 440	Beginning of Hun invasions from Central Asia
CA. 455–467	Reign of last strong Gupta monarch, Skandagupta
399–414	Chinese Buddhist monk, Fa-Hsien, travels in India
616–657	Reign of Harsha; revival of Gupta splendor and power
820	Death of Vedantin philosopher-theologian, Shankara
550–CA. 1000	Regional Indian kingdoms in north and south; major Puranas composed; age of first great Vaishnava and Shaivite devotional poets in southern India

into central Asia and China, where it became the major form of religious practice down to the ninth century. Tantric Buddhism, an esoteric Mahayana tradition heavily influenced by Hindu Tantric speculation and ritual, entered Tibet from north India in the seventh century and became the dominant tradition there. From China, Mahayana teachings spread in the fifth to eighth centuries to fertile new fields in Korea and then Japan.

Pre-Islamic Africa, Iran, and India in World Perspective

From a European or American perspective, pre-Islamic Iran, India, and especially Africa are portrayed typically as interesting but relatively unimportant arenas of political, cultural, and religious developments. They are viewed as being on the peripheries of the late Roman and Near Eastern world of late antiquity. Such a perspective fails to recognize that the loci of major political power, cultural creativity, and religious vitality throughout most of the early centuries A.D. was not in Rome or Greece, or elsewhere in southern Europe, but in Byzantine Anatolia, Egypt, North Africa, and

The True Nature of the Buddha, According to the Lotus Sutra

The Lotus Sutra (Saddharmapundarikasutra, "Lotus of the True Dharma") is one of the best-loved sacred texts of Mahayana Buddhism. Its original Sanskrit text was translated many times into Chinese (the earliest being in A.D. 225), as well as into Tibetan and other languages. The following passage is a key one for the development of the idea of the cosmic form of the Buddha. Note that Tathagata ("Thus Gone" [i.e., having achieved release, or nirvana]) is one of the names used for a Buddha.

Fully enlightened for ever so long, the Tathagata has an endless span of life, he lasts for ever. Although the Tathagata has not entered Nirvana, he makes a show of entering Nirvana, for the sake of those who have to be educated. And even today my ancient course as a Bodhisattva is still incomplete, and my life span is not yet ended. From today onwards still twice as many hundreds of thousands of Nayutas of Kotis of aeons must elapse before my life span is complete. Although therefore I do not at present enter into Nirvana (or extinction), nevertheless I announce my Nirvana. For by this method I bring beings to maturity. Because it might be that, if I stayed here too long and could be seen too often, beings who have performed no meritorious actions, who are without merit, a poorly lot, eager for sensuous pleasures, blind, and wrapped in the net of false views, would, in the knowledge that the Tathagata stays (here all the time), get the notion that life is a mere sport, and would not conceive the notion that the (sight of the) Tathagata is hard to obtain. In the conviction that the Tathagata is always at hand they would not exert their vigour for the purpose of escaping from the triple world, and they would not conceive of the Tathagata as hard to obtain.

Hence the Tathagata, in his skill in means, has uttered to those beings the saying that "Rarely, O monks, do Tathagatas appear in the world." Because, during many hundreds of thousands of Nayutas of Kotis of aeons those beings may have the sight of a Tathagata, or they may not. And therefore, basing my statement on this fact, I say that "Rarely, O monks, do Tathagatas appear in the world." To the extent that they understand the rarity of a Tathagata's appearance, to that extent they will wonder (at his appearance), and sorrow (at his disappearance), and when they do not see the Tathagata, they will long for the sight of him. The wholesome roots, which result from their turning their attention towards the Tathagata as towards an objective basis, will for a long time tend to their weal, benefit and happiness. Considering this, the Tathagata, although he does not actually enter Nirvana, announces his entering into Nirvana, for the sake of those to be educated. And that is a discourse on Dharma by the Tathagata himself. When he utters it, there is in it no false speech on the part of the Tathagata. ❑

15, 268–272

From Edward Conze (ed.), *Buddhist Texts through the Ages* (New York and Evanston: Harper Torchbooks, 1964), pp. 142–143.

Syria-Mesopotamia. Augustine of Hippo was, after all, an African; Christian monasticism began in Egypt; and the great doctrinal councils of the Christian church were held in Asia. Our perspective must necessarily change when we give proper recognition to the overwhelming facts: the contemporaneous importance of the Aksumite empire in Ethiopia, the Sasanid imperial culture of Iran, the Zoroastrian revival, the Manichaean movement, the compilation of the Babylonian and Palestinian Tamuds, the completion of the *Mahabharata* and *Ramayana*, Gupta imperial rule, Gupta art and literature, Indian religious thought, and the spread of Mahayana Buddhism across central Asia into China and thence to Japan.

Portions of Asia and Africa were the settings for impressive and often momentous historical developments. Consequently, simplistic notions of the progressive "rise of the West" from classical antiquity to modern times do not hold very well for the first millennium A.D., especially when we take into view the coming of Islam in the seventh century. The Western world in these centuries did not appear to hold much promise as a future center of globally important political or cultural life. Instead, progressiveness and culture seemed to be best embodied in either Sasanid or Gupta culture, or, still more in East Asia. The majesty and unity of Chinese imperial power and culture under the Han dynasty (221 B.C.–A.D. 220) and its reestablishment under the Sui (589–618) and T'ang (618–907) dynasties, or the cultural, political, and religious vibrancy of the heavily Chinese-influenced Nara (710–794) and Heian (794–1180) periods in Japan cannot be underestimated.

A revised perspective would thus see a number of important centers of cultural, religious, and political traditions around the globe, both in the Asian kingdoms and also notably in the Mediterranean imperial domains of Byzantium and in Aksumite Ethiopia. This is not to say that all the political and cultural centers, let alone the important dynasties, of these centuries would long endure. The imminent coming of the last major world religious and cultural tradition—that of Islam—would affect, redefine, or even eliminate the overt presence of many of previous centers of civilization. Nevertheless, in their heydays, these civilizations were impressive achievements.

Taken as a whole, Africa, like Europe, was still a culturally diverse and largely undeveloped region except in those areas on its peripheries that were already active commercial or political participants in the larger universe. To the east, Hindu tradition and Indian culture were undergoing important developments, while Buddhism was waning in its Indian homeland even as it found new and rich fields for conquest in central Asia, China, and Japan, as well as Southeast Asia. Zoroastrian Iran appeared well on its way into a second millennium of Iranian imperial splendor under the Sasanids. Yet it would soon face the most cataclysmic changes of all the major centers of world culture in this age. Who could have suspected in the time of Chosroes Anoshirvan how radically Persian culture would be shaken, recast, and given new life in Islamic forms within three or four centuries?

Suggested Readings

AFRICA

P. BOHANNAN AND P. CURTIN, *Africa and Africans*, rev. ed. (1971). An enjoyable and enlightening discussion of African history and prehistory, and of major African institutions (e.g., arts, family life, religion).

P. CURTIN, S. FEIERMANN, L. THOMPSON, AND J. VANSINA, *African History* (1978). Probably the best survey history. The relevant portions are Chapters 1, 2, 4, 8, and 9.

T. R. H. DAVENPORT, *South Africa: A Modern History*, 3rd rev. ed. (1987). Chapter 1 gives excellent summary coverage of prehistoric south Africa, the Khoisan peoples, and the Bantu migrations.

B. DAVIDSON, *The African Past* (1967). A combination of primary-source selections and brief secondary discussions trace sympathetically the history of the diverse parts of Africa.

J. D. FAGE, *A History of Africa* (1978). A fine general history. The relevant segment here is Part I, "The Internal Development of African Society" (Chapters 1–5).

P. GARLAKE, *The Kingdoms of Africa* (1978). A lavishly illustrated set of photographic essays that provide a helpful introduction to the various historically important areas of precolonial Africa.

R. W. JULY, *Precolonial Africa: An Economic and Social History* (1975). A very readable, topically arranged study. See especially "The Savannah Farmer," "The Bantu," "Cattlemen," and "The Traders" chapters.

R. W. JULY, *A History of the African People*, 3rd ed. (1980). Part I, "Ancient Africa" covers the precolonial centuries and offers a very readable historical introduction to African civilization.

G. MOKHTAR, *Ancient Civilizations of Africa. Vol II of UNESCO General History of Africa* (1981). Relevant chapters are 8–16 on Nubia, Meroe, and Aksum; 17–20 on the Saharan region in ancient times; and 22–29 on the early history of the various regions of the Africa subcontinent.

IRAN

M. BOYCE, ed. and trans., *Textual Sources for the Study of Zoroastrianism* (1984). An extremely valuable anthology with an important introduction that includes Boyce's arguments for a revision (to sometime between 1400 and 1200 B.C.) of the dates of Zoroaster's life.

M. BOYCE, *Zoroastrians: Their Religious Beliefs and Practices* (1979). A detailed survey by the current authority on Zoroastrian religious history. See Chapters 7–9.

R. N. FRYE, *The Heritage of Persia* (1963). Still one of the best surveys. Chapter 6 deals with the Sasanid era.

R. GHIRSHMAN, *Iran* (1954 [orig. 1951]). An introductory survey—simpler and less detailed than Frye's.

R. GHIRSHMAN, *Persian Art: The Parthian and Sasanid Dynasties* (1962). Superb photographs, and a very helpful glossary of places and names. The text is minimal and less useful.

GEO WIDENGRAN, *Mani and Manichaeism* (1965). Still the standard introductory survey of Mani's life and the later spread and development of Manichaeism.

INDIA

A. L. BASHAM, *The Wonder that Was India* (1963). Still the best accessible general survey of classical Indian religion, society, literature, art, and political organization.

S. DUTT, *Buddhist Monks and Monasteries of India* (1962). The standard work. See especially Chapters 3 ("Bhakti") and 4 ("Monasteries under the Gupta Kings").

D. G. MANDELBAUM, *Society in India*, 2 vols. (1972). The first two chapters in Vol. I of this large and interesting study of caste, family, and village relations are a good introduction to the caste system.

B. ROWLAND, *The Art and Architecture of India: Buddhist/Hindu/Jain*, 3rd ed. rev. (1970). See the excellent chapters on Sungan, Andhran, and other early Buddhist art (6–8, 14), the Gupta period (15), and the Hindu Renaissance (17–19).

V. A. SMITH, *The Oxford History of India*, 4th ed. rev. (1981). See especially pp. 164–229 (covers the Gupta period and following era to the Muslim invasions).

R. THAPAR, *A History of India.* Part I (1966), pp. 109–193. Three chapters covering the rise of mercantilism, the Gupta "classical pattern," and the southern dynasties to CA. A.D. 900.

P. YOUNGER, *Introduction to Indian Religious Thought* (1972). A sensitive attempt to delineate classical concerns of Indian religious thought and culture.

The Fatiha. A fine calligraphic rendering of the opening sura, or chapter, of the Qur'an. The first five verses of the chapter are written around the circumference of the emblem, with the vertical letters extended into an arabesque design at the center. [William Graham.]

312

12 The Formation of Islamic Civilization (622–945)

Islamic civilization arose as the last great world civilization up to now, if one excepts the post-Enlightenment modern West. On the one hand, its rise is the story of the creation, spread, and elaboration of distinctive Islamic religious, social, and political institutions within an initially Arab-dominated empire. On the other, it is the story of how, in older cultural environments, Islamic ideas and institutions evolved from their Arabian beginnings into a cosmopolitan array of cultures. Each was a different, new creation of particular circumstances, yet each was identifiably part of a larger, international Islamic civilization.

The basic ideas and ideals of the Islamic worldview derived from a single, prophetic-revelatory event, Muhammad's proclamation of the Qur'an.[1] This event galvanized the Arabs into a new kind of unity—that of the community of *Muslims*, or "submitters" to God. This community subsequently spread far beyond Arabia, and Persians, Indians, and others raised it to new heights. Arab military prowess and cultural consciousness joined with a new religious orientation to effect one of the most permanent revolutions in history. But it was the peoples of the older cultural heartlands who sustained this revolution and built a new civilization. It was their acceptance of a new vision of society (and, indeed, of reality) as more compelling than any older vision—Jewish, Greek, Iranian, Christian, Buddhist—that allowed an Islamic civilization to come into being.

Origins and Early Development

The Setting

At the beginning of the seventh century A.D., the dominant Eurasian political powers, Christian Byzan-

---

[1] The common English transliteration of this Arabic word, *Koran*, is today being replaced by the more accurate *Qur'an*; similarly, *Muhammad* is preferable to *Mohammed* and *Muslim* to *Moslem*.

The Ka'ba in Mecca. The Ka'ba is viewed in Muslim tradition as the site of the first "house of God" built by Abraham and his son Ishmael at God's command. It is held to have fallen later into idolotrous use, until Mohammad's victory over the Meccans and his cleansing of the holy cubical structure (ka'ba means cube). The Ka'ba is the geographical point toward which all Muslims face when performing ritual prayer. It and the plain of Arafat outside Mecca are the two foci of the pilgrimage or Hajj that each Muslim aspires to make at once in a lifetime.

tium and Zoroastrian Iran, or Persia, had confronted one another for over four centuries. This rivalry did not, however, continue much longer. In the wake of one final, mutually exhausting conflict (608–627), a new Arab power broke in from the southern deserts to humble the one and destroy the other.

Pre-Islamic Arabia was not just the home of desert camel nomads. In the Fertile Crescent, Byzantium and Iran had managed to keep the nomads of the Syrian and northern Arabian steppe at bay with the help of small Arab client kingdoms that served as buffer states on the edge of the desert. Settled Arab kingdoms had long existed in the agriculturally rich highlands of southern Arabia, which had direct access to the inter-

national trade that moved by land and sea along its coasts (see Chapter 11). Some of these kingdoms, including a Jewish one in the sixth century, had been independent; others had been under Persian or Abyssinian domination. Farther north, astride the major trade route through the western Arabian highland of the Hijaz, the town of Mecca was a center of the caravan trade. It was also a pilgrimage center because of its famous sanctuary, the Ka'ba (or Kaaba), where many pagan Arab tribes had their gods enshrined. The settled Arabs of Mecca formed a thriving merchant republic in which older tribal values were breaking down under the strains of urban and commercial life. But neither the Meccans nor other settled Arabs were wholly cut off from the nomads who lived on herding and raids on settlements and caravans.

The Arabic language defined and linked the Arab peoples, however divided they were by religion, blood feuds, rivalry, and open conflict. From the Yemen north to Syria–Palestine and the Euphrates, the major element of culture that the Arabs shared was their highly developed poetic idiom. Traditionally, every tribe had a poet to exhort its warriors and challenge its enemies with insults before battle. Poetry contests were also held, often in conjunction with the annual trade fairs that brought diverse tribes together under a general truce.

The popular notion of Islam as a "religion of the desert" is largely untrue. Islam began in a commercial center and first flourished in an agricultural oasis. Its first converts were settled Meccan townsfolk and date farmers of Yathrib (Medina). Most of these Arabs had been pagans, but some were Jews or Christians, or were influenced by Jews or Christians, before Islam. Caravans passed north and south through Mecca, and no merchant engaged in this traffic, as Muhammad himself was, could have been ignorant of different cultures. Early Muslim leaders used the Arabs as warriors and looked to Arab cultural ideals for roots long after the locus of Islamic power had left Arabia. But the empire and culture that they built were centered in the heartlands of Eurasian urban culture and based on settled communal existence rather than desert tribal anarchy.

Muhammad and the Qur'an

Muhammad (CA. 570–632) was raised an orphan in one of the less well-to-do commercial families of the venerable Meccan tribe of Quraysh. Later, in the midst of a successful business career made possible by his marriage to Khadija, a wealthy Meccan widow, he grew increasingly troubled by the idolatry, worldliness, and lack of social conscience around him. These traits would have been equally offensive to sensitive Jewish or Christian piety and morality, about which he certainly knew something. Yet Muhammad did not find his answers in these traditions; they remained somehow foreign to mainstream Arab culture, even though some Arab tribes were Jewish or Christian.

Muhammad's discontent with the moral status quo and older religious solutions prepared the way for a sudden religious experience that changed his life when he was about forty years old. He felt himself called by the one true God to "rise and warn" his fellow Arabs about their frivolous disregard for morality and the worship and service due their creator. On repeated occasions, revelation came to him through a figure who was gradually identified as God's messenger angel, Gabriel. It took the form of a "reciting" (qur'an) of God's word—now rendered in "clear Arabic" for

THE ORIGINS AND EARLY
DEVELOPMENT OF ISLAM

CA. 570	Birth of Muhammad
622	The Hijra (*Hegira*, "emigration") of Muslims to Yathrib (henceforward *al-Madina*, "The City [of the Prophet]"); beginning of Muslim calendar
632	Death of Muhammad; Abu Bakr becomes first "Successor" (*Khalifa*, caliph) to leadership, reigns 632–634
634–644	Caliphate of Umar; rapid conquests in Egypt and Iran
644–656	Caliphate of Uthman (member of Umayyad clan); more conquests; Qur'an text established; growth of sea power
656–661	Contested Caliphate of Ali; first civil war
661–680	Caliphate of Mu'awiya; founding of Umayyad dynasty (661–750); capital moved to Damascus; more expansion
680	Second civil war begins with death of al-Husayn at Karbala

the Arabs, just as it had been given to previous prophets in Hebrew or other languages for their peoples.

The message of the Qur'an was clear: The Prophet is to warn his people against idolatrous worship of false gods and against all immorality, especially injustice to the weak and less fortunate—the poor, orphans, widows, and women in general. A judgment day at the end of time will see everyone bodily resurrected to stand alone and face eternal punishment in hellfire or eternal joy in paradise, according to how one has lived. The way to paradise lies in proper gratitude to God for the bounties of His created world, His prophetic and revelatory guidance, and His readiness to forgive the penitent. Social justice and obedient worship and service of the one Lord are demanded of every human. Everyone is to recognize his or her creatureliness and God's transcendence. The proper response is "submission" (*islam*) to God's will, becoming *muslim* ("submissive" or "surrendering") in one's worship and morality. All of creation praises and serves God by its very nature; only humans have been given a choice, either to obey or to reject Him.

In this Qur'anic message, the moral monotheism of Judaic and Christian tradition (very likely reinforced by Zoroastrian and Manichaean ideas) reached its logical conclusion in a radically theocentric vision; it demanded absolute obedience to the one Lord of the Universe. The Qur'anic revelations explicitly state that Muhammad is only the last in a long line of prophets chosen to bring God's word: Noah, Abraham, Moses, Jesus, and nonbiblical Arabian figures like Salih had been sent before on similar missions. Because the

Imru l-Qais, the Wandering Poet-Hero

With little written or visual artistic tradition, the ancient Arabs focused on the perfection of the oral word. Each tribe had a poet who in his verse extolled the greatness and prowess of his people and their ancestry and humiliated tribal enemies with satire and polemic. Such verse reinforced the cultural ideals that sprang from the life of the camel nomads of the desert: generosity and hospitality to a fault, family pride and honor, fearless audacity in love and battle, and delight in the animals and other natural beauties of the marginal desert world. In this excerpt from a famous poem of Imru l-Qais (d. CA. 540?), we see a standard beginning of the Arabic lyric ode, or qasida: *the sight of an abandoned camp that recalls some past event to the poet. There follow here boastful memories of amorous adventure and a brief segment from later in the poem about the poet's hard existence (which fell to him after his father, ruler of one of the northern desert kingdoms, banished him because he refused to give up poetry—an occupation his father felt was improper for a prince).*

Here halt, and weep, for one long-remembered love, for an old
Camp at the edge of the sands that stretch from the Brakes to Floodhead,
From Clearward to the Heights. The marks are not gone yet,
For all that's blown and blown back over them, northward, southward.
Look at the white-deer's droppings scattered in the old yards
And penfolds of the place, like black pepperseeds.

. . . .

I suffered so for love, so fast the tears ran down
Over my breast, the sword-belt there was soaked with weeping.
And yet—the happy days I had of them, of women

. . . .

One day on a sandhill back she would not do my will,
And swore an oath, and swore she meant to keep her oath.

. . . .

That night I passed the wardens who watched their tents, the men
Who would have welcomed me, for the glory of murdering me,
In an hour when Pleiades glittered in the night-heaven
Like a jewelled girdle, gem and pearl and gem;
In such an hour I came; she was all doffed for sleep
But for a shift; close by the screen of the tent she lay.
God's oath on me! she whispered, but thou hast no excuse!

And now I know that thou wilt be wild for ever.
Forth we went together; I led; she trailed behind us
A robe's embroidered hem, that tracks might tell no tales.
When we were past the fenced folkyards, then we made straight
For the heart of the waste, the waves and tumbled hillocks of sand.
I pulled her head to mine by the lovelocks, and she pressed
Against me, slender, but soft even at the ankle.
Thin-waisted she was, and white, sweetly moulded about the belly,
And the skin above her breasts shone like a polished mirror,
Or a pearl of the first water, whiteness a little gilded,
Fed of a pure pool unstirred by the feet of men

. . . .

And taking a water-skin from the house, I would strap it close
Over my shoulder—how often!—and meek to such a saddle
Crossing some hollow place like the flats of Starverib Waste
Have I heard the wolf, like a spendthrift who's gambled his darlings away,
Howl! He would howl. I would answer: It's a poor trade we follow
For profit, if thou hast kept as little as I have kept;
Whatever we get, thou and I, we bolt it; and it's gone.
A man will never be fat who thrives as we two thrive. . . . ❑

From Eric Schroeder (trans.), *Muhammad's People* (Portland, Me.: Bond Wheelwright, 1955), pp. 3–5.

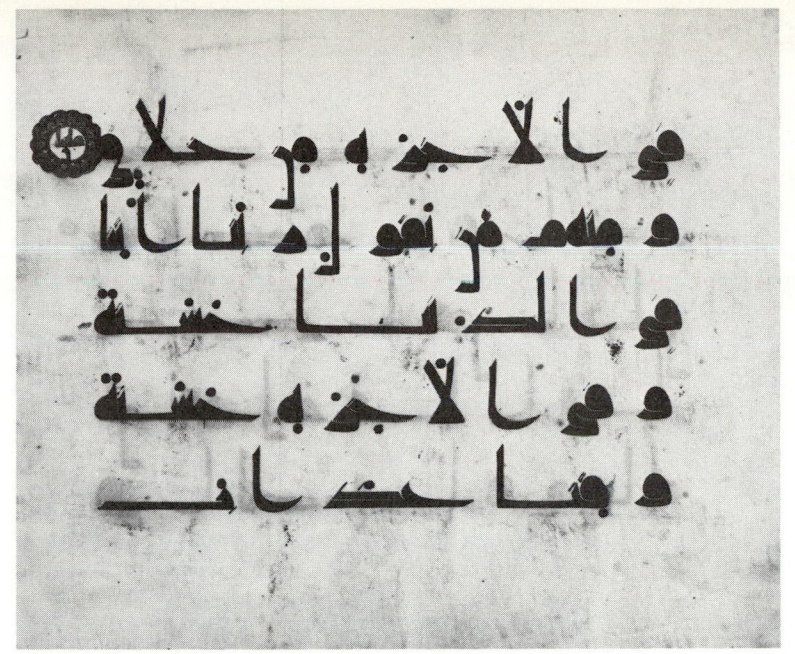

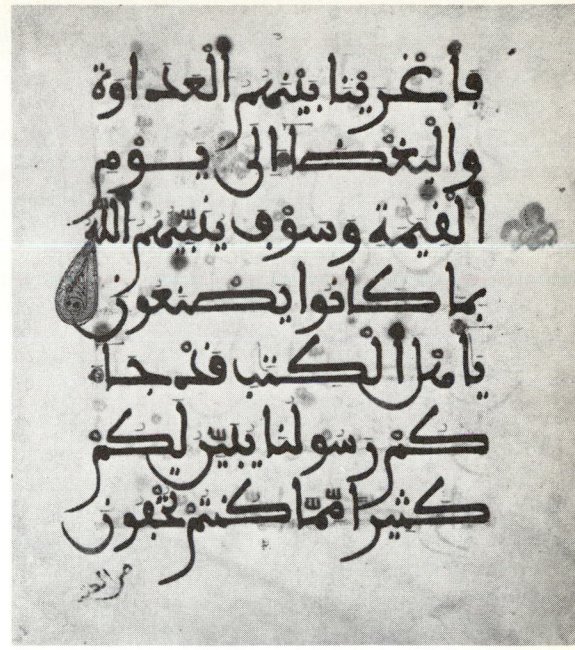

FIGURE 1   FIGURE 2

Qur'anic pages. With the Muslim aversion to images, calligraphy became a major art form in the early centuries and has continued to flourish. The Arabic script developed primarily to render the Qur'anic text as exactly as one could, and the calligraphic art developed along with it. The earliest script used widely for the Qur'an was the horizontally elongated Kufic. Figure 1 shows a page from an eighth-ninth century Qur'an written in Kufic script. The Kufic script dominated qur'anic calligraphy for three centuries. After the tenth century, other scripts began to predominate. An example of one regional script, the so-called Magribi, or North African, is shown in Figure 2. [Freer Gallery of Art.]

communities of these earlier prophets had strayed from the teachings of their scriptures or had altered them, Muhammad was given one final reiteration of God's message. Jews and Christians, like pagans, were summoned to respond to the moral imperatives of the Qur'an he recited to them.

The Prophet's preaching fell largely on deaf ears in the first years after his calling. However, a small number gradually followed the lead of his wife, Khadija, in recognizing him as a divinely chosen reformer of individual and communal life. Some prominent Meccans did join him, but the merchant aristocracy as a whole resisted. His preaching against their traditional gods and goddesses threatened not only their ancestral ways but also their Meccan pilgrimage shrine and the lucrative trade it attracted. The Muslims began to be persecuted. After the deaths of Khadija and Muhammad's uncle and protector Abu Talib, the situation worsened, and the Prophet even had to send a small band of Muslims to seek refuge in Abyssinia for a time. Then, because of his reputation as a moral and holy man, Muhammad was called to Yathrib (an agricultural oasis about 240 miles north of Mecca) as a neu-

tral arbitrator among its five quarrelsome tribes, three of which were Jewish. Having sent his Meccan followers ahead, Muhammad escaped in July 622 to Yathrib, afterward to be known as Medina (*al-Madina*, "the City [of the Prophet]"). Some dozen years later, this "emigration," or Hegira, became the starting point for the Islamic calendar. This event marked the creation of a distinctive Islamic community, or *Umma*.[2]

Muhammad quickly cemented ties between the Meccan emigrants and the Medinans, many of whom became converts. Raids on the caravans of his Meccan enemies established his leadership. They point also to the economic as well as religious dimension of the Medinan–Meccan struggle. The Jews of Medina by and large rejected his message and authority. They even had contacts with his Meccan enemies, moving

[2] The twelve-month Muslim lunar year is shorter than the Christian solar year by about eleven days, giving a difference of about three years per century. Muslim dates are reckoned from the month in 622 in which Muhammad began his Hegira [Arabic: *Hijra*]. Thus Muslims celebrated the start of their lunar year 1401 in November 1980 (A.D. 1979–1980 = A.H. [Anno Hegirae] 1400), whereas it was only 1,358 solar years from 622 to 1980.

The Qur'an, or "Recitation" of God's Word

The Qur'an has many themes, ranging from moral admonition, threats of hellfire for the ungodly, and stories of past peoples and their prophets, to praise of God, his bountiful natural world and compassion for humankind, and the joys of paradise. The following short selections touch upon (1) the qur'anic notion of revelation in both its own pages and the signs of nature; (2) praise of God the Almighty, the Creator; (3, 4) previous prophets who had testified to God's oneness and sovereignty and brought His revelations to their people.

The revelation of the Book is from God who is mighty and wise. There are signs for men of faith, in the heavens and in the earth, in your being created and in God's scattered throng of creatures—signs for people with a grasp on truth.

There are signs, too—for those with a mind to understand—in the alternation of night and day, and in the gracious rain God sends from heaven to renew the face of the parched earth, and in the veering of the winds.

These are the signs of God which truly We recite to you. Having God and His signs, in what else after that will you believe as a message?

Sura 45.1–6

He is God. There is no god but He. He knows the hidden and the evident. He is the merciful Lord of mercy.

He is God, there is no god but He. He is the King, the holy One, the Lord of peace, the Keeper of faith, the watch-Keeper, the all-strong, the ever-powerful, the Self-aware in His greatness. Glory be to God above all that idolators conceive.

Sura 59.22–23

You people of the Book, why are you so argumentative about Abraham, seeing that the Torah and the Gospel were only sent down after his time? Will you not use your reason? You are people much given to disputing about things within your comprehension: why insist on disputing about things of which you have no knowledge? Knowledge belongs to God and you lack it!

Abraham was not a Jew, nor was he a Christian. He was a man of pure worship (a *hanīf*) and a Muslim: he was not one of those pagan idolaters. The people nearest to Abraham are those who followed him and this prophet too and those who have believed. Believers are under God's care.

Sura 3.65–68

❑

From Kenneth Cragg, trans., *Readings in the Qur'ān* (London: Collins, 1988), pp. 102, 86–87, 121, 166.

Muhammad to turn on the Jews, kill or enslave some, banish others, and take their lands. Many of the continuing revelations of the Qur'an from this period pertain to communal order or to the Jews and Christians who rejected Islam.

The basic Muslim norms took shape in Medina: allegiance to the *Umma*; honesty in public and personal affairs; modesty in personal habits; abstention from alcohol and pork; fair division of inheritances; improved treatment of women, especially as to their property and other rights within marriage; careful regulation of marriage and divorce; ritual ablution before any act of worship, be it Qur'an-reciting or prayer; three (later five) daily rites of worship, facing the Meccan Ka'ba; payment of a kind of tithe to support less fortunate Muslims; daytime fasting for one month each year; and, eventually, pilgrimage to Mecca (*Hajj*) at least once in a lifetime, if one is able.

Acceptance of Islamic political authority brought a kind of tolerance. A Jewish oasis yielded to Muhammad's authority and was allowed, unlike the resistant Medinan Jews, to keep its lands, practice its faith, and receive protection in return for the payment of a head tax. This practice was followed ever after for Jews, Christians, and other "People of Scripture" who accepted Islamic rule. After long conflict, the Meccans surrendered to Muhammad, and his generosity in accepting them into the *Umma* set the pattern for the later Islamic conquests. Following an age-old practice, Muhammad cemented many of his alliances with marriage (although as long as Khadija was alive, he did not take a second wife). In the last years of the Prophet's life, the once tiny band of Muslims became the heart of an all-Arabian tribal confederation, bound together by personal allegiance to Muhammad, submission (*islam*) to God, and membership in the *Umma* of "submitters."

The Early Islamic Conquests

In 632, Muhammad died after an illness, leaving neither a son nor a named successor. The new *Umma* faced its first major crisis. A political struggle between Meccan and Medinan factions ended in a pledge of allegiance to Abu Bakr, the most senior of the early

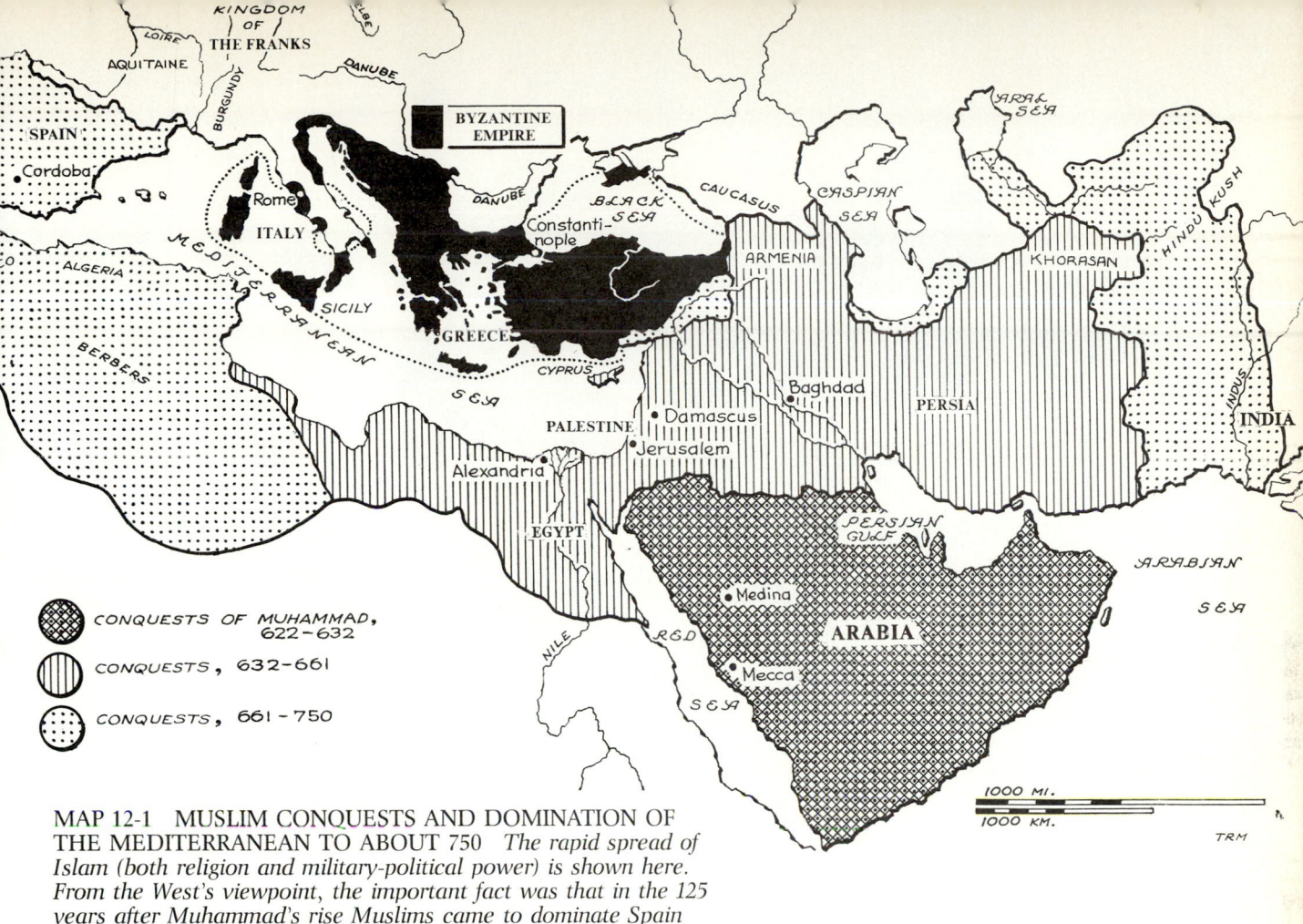

MAP 12-1   MUSLIM CONQUESTS AND DOMINATION OF
THE MEDITERRANEAN TO ABOUT 750   *The rapid spread of
Islam (both religion and military-political power) is shown here.
From the West's viewpoint, the important fact was that in the 125
years after Muhammad's rise Muslims came to dominate Spain
and all areas south and east of the Mediterranean.*

Meccan converts. Many of the naturally independent
Arab tribes renounced their allegiance to the Prophet
upon his death. Nevertheless, Abu Bakr's rule (632–
634) as Muhammad's successor, or "caliph" (Arabic,
khalifa), reestablished Medinan hegemony and at
least nominal religious conformity over the whole of
Arabia. The Arabs were forced to recognize in the
Umma a new kind of supratribal community that demanded more than allegiance to a particular leader.

The Course of Conquest

Under the next two caliphs, Umar (634–644) and
Uthman (644–656), Arab Islamic armies burst out of
the peninsula, intent on more than traditional bedouin
booty raids. In one of the most astonishing sets of military operations ever, they conquered the Byzantine
and Sasanid territories of the Fertile Crescent (by 640),
Egypt (by 642), and most of Iran (by 643). For the first
time in centuries, the lands from Egypt to Iran were
united under one rule. Finally, Arab armies swept
west over the Byzantine-controlled Libyan coast and,

in the east, pushed to the Oxus, defeating the last
Sasanid ruler by 651.

An interlude of civil war during the contested caliphate of Ali (656–661) slowed the expansion briefly.
Then, under the fifth caliph, Mu'awiya (661–680), expansion and consolidation of the new empire progressed. By 680, control of greater Iran was solidified
by permanent Arab garrisoning of Khorasan; much of
Anatolia was raided; Constantinople was besieged
(but not taken); and Armenia was brought under Islamic rule. In the Mediterranean, an Islamic fleet conquered Cyprus, plundered Sicily and Rhodes, and crippled Byzantine seapower.

Succeeding decades saw the eastern Berbers of Libyan North Africa defeated and converted in substantial
numbers, if often superficially or nominally, to Islam.
With their help, "the West" (*al-Maghrib*, modern
Morocco and Algeria), fell quickly. In 711, raids into
Spain began (the name of the Berber Muslim leader of
the first invaders, Tariq, lives on in *Gibraltar*, a corruption of *Jabal Tariq*, "Mount Tariq"). By 716, the

The Omar Mosque, or Dome of the Rock, in Jerusalem. An early example of Islamic architecture (but not a "mosque"), it dates from the seventh century, during the first wave of Arab expansion. It is built on the rock from which Muslims believe Muhammed ascended into heaven and on which Jews believe Abraham prepared to sacrifice Isaac. [Louis Goldman.]

disunited Spanish Visigoth kingdoms had fallen, and much of Iberia was under Islamic control. Pushing farther north into France, the Arabs were finally checked by a defeat at the hands of Charles Martel south of Tours (732). At the opposite end of the empire, buoyed by large-scale Arab immigration, Islamic forces consolidated their holdings as far as the Oxus river basin. In 710, Arab armies reached the Indus region of Sind. The Muslim Arabs now controlled the former Sasanid Empire and beyond. The Byzantine realm was reduced by half and Islamic power was supreme from the Atlantic to central Asia.

Factors of Success

A combination of factors contributed to this rapid expansion. Most basic was the capacity of the new Islamic vision of society and life to unite the Arabs and to attract others as well. Its corollary was the commitment among the Islamic leadership to extend "the Abode of Submission" (*Dar al-Islam*) abroad. However, too much has been made of the general Muslim zeal for martyrdom. Assurance of paradise for those engaged in *jihad*, or "struggle [in the path of God]," is less likely to have motivated the average Arab tribesman—who, at least at the beginning, was usually only nominally a Muslim—as much as promise of the booty of war.

Yet religious zeal cannot be wholly discounted, especially as time went on. The early policy of sending Qur'an-reciters among the armies' pagan tribesmen to teach the essentials of Muslim faith and practice had its effects. A major factor was certainly the leadership of the first caliphs and field generals. This leadership combined with the economic and military exhaustion of Byzantium and Iran to give Arab armies a distinct advantage. Another element was the readiness of subject populations in many areas to accept, even to welcome, Islamic rule as a relief from Byzantine or Persian oppression. Important here was the Muslim willingness to allow Christian, Jewish, and even Zoroastrian groups to continue as minorities (with their own legal systems and no military obligations) under the protection of Islamic rule. In return, they had to recognize Islamic political authority, pay a non-Muslim head tax (*jizya*), and refrain from proselytizing or interfering with Muslim religious practice.

Finally, what gave the conquests overall permanence, besides the vitality of the new faith, were the astute policies followed: relatively little bloodshed or destruction of property or economies; the adoption, with minimal changes, of existing administrative systems; the adjustment of unequal taxation; the appointment of capable governors; and the strategic siting of new Islamic garrison towns like Basra, Kufa, and Fustat (later Cairo).

Early Islamic coins. The development of early Islamic coinage reflects the evolution of Muslim self-awareness. The earliest Arab kingdom had no coinage of its own. The first Islamic caliphs and governors took over the existing Byzantine and Sasanid coinage (Figure 1: a Sasanid silver dirham with the head of the emperor), adding brief Arabic inscriptions (Figure 2), and then slightly altering previous imagery on the coins (Figure 3: "standing caliph" with sword and Arab headdress rather than Byzantine crown). It was only under Abd al-Malik, caliph from 685–705, that a reform of the coinage led to the abandonment of all imagery depicting the human form in favor of Arabic inscriptions proclaiming the basic Muslim faith (Figure 4: "There is no god but God, One, without partner"). [American Numismatic Society of New York.]

FIGURE 1

FIGURE 3

FIGURE 2

FIGURE 4

The New Islamic Order

Unlike rulers who take over an empire and continue the existing religious and cultural traditions, the Muslims brought with them a new worldview that demanded a new political, social, and cultural reality, however long it might take to effect it. Beyond the military and administrative problems they faced loomed the ultimately more important question of the nature of the Islamic state and society. Under the Prophet, a new kind of community, the *Umma*, had replaced, at least in theory and basic organization, the tribal, blood-based social and political order in Arabia. Yet, once the Arabs (most of whom became Muslims) had to rule non-Arabs and non-Muslims, new problems arose that tested the ideal of an Islamic polity. Chief among these problems were leadership and membership qualifications, social order, and religious and cultural identity.

The Caliphate

Allegiance to Muhammad had rested on his authority as a divine spokesperson and as a gifted leader. His first successors were chosen much as were Arab *shaykhs* (sheiks), or tribal chieftans, by agreement of the leaders, or elders, of the new religious "tribe" of Muslims, on the basis of superior personal qualities. Added to these qualities was now the precedence in faith conferred by piety and association with the Prophet. Their titles were "successor" (*khalifa* or caliph), "leader" (*imam*—used also for the Muslim who stands in front of Muslim worshipers to lead them in ritual prayer), and "commander (*amir*) of the faithful." These names underscored political and religious authority, both of which most Muslims were willing to recognize in the caliphs Abu Bakr and Umar, and potentially in Uthman and Ali. Unfortunately, by the time of Uthman and Ali, various dissensions had led to internal strife, then civil war. Yet the first four caliphs had all been close to Muhammad, and this closeness gave their reigns a nostalgic aura of pristine purity, especially as the later caliphal institution was based largely on sheer power and/or hereditary succession.

The nature of Islamic leadership became an issue with the first civil war (656–661) and the recognition of Mu'awiya, a kinsman of Uthman, as caliph. He founded the first dynastic caliphate, that of his Meccan clan of Umayya (661–750). Hereditary Umayyads held power until they were ousted by the Abbasid clan in 750, which based its legitimacy on descent from an uncle of the Prophet (Abbas—hence, "Abbasid"). The Umayyads had the prestige of the office held by the first four, "rightly guided" caliphs. But they also suffered by the comparison, as they were judged by many to be worldly "kings" where the earlier four had been true Muslim "successors" to Muhammad.

The Abbasids won the caliphate by open rebellion in 750, aided by their exploitation of pious dissatisfaction with Umayyad worldliness, non-Arab Muslim resentment of Arab preference (primarily in Iran), and ongoing dissension among Arab tribal factions in the garrison towns. For all their stress on the Muslim character of their caliphate, they were scarcely less worldly and continued the hereditary rule begun by the Umayyads. This they did well enough to retain control of most of the far-flung Islamic territories until 945. Thereafter, although their line continued until 1258, the caliphate was primarily a titular office representing an Islamic unity that existed politically in name only.

The Ulema

Although the caliph could exert his power, as the Abbasids did occasionally, to influence religious matters, he was never "emperor and pope rolled into one." Religious leadership in the *Umma* devolved instead on another group. The functional "successors of the Prophet" in society at large were those Muslims recognized for piety and learning and sought out as informal or even formal (as with state-appointed judges) authorities. Initially, these were the "Companions" (male and female) of Muhammad with the greatest stature in the original Medinan *Umma*—including the first four caliphs. As this generation died out, they were replaced by those younger followers most concerned with preserving, interpreting, and applying the Qur'an, and with maintaining the norms of the Prophet's *Umma*. Because the Qur'an contained very little actual legislative material, they had to draw on precedents from the practice of Medina and Mecca, as well as on oral traditions about the Prophet and Companions. In doing so, they developed an enduring pattern of education based on study under those persons highest in the chain of trustworthy Muslims linking the current age with the earliest *Umma*.

As an unofficial but generally recognized infrastructure in Islamic society, these scholars came to be known as *ulema* ("persons of right kowledge," Anglicized Arabic plural of *'alim*). Some of the most pious *ulema* refused to be judges for the Umayyads. However, their personal legal opinions and collective discussions of issues, ranging from theological doctrine to criminal punishments, established a general basis for religious and social order. By the ninth century, they had largely defined the understanding of the divine Law, or *Shari'a*, that Muslims ever after have held to be definitive for legal, social, commercial, political, ritual, and moral concerns. This understanding and the methods by which it was derived form the Muslim sci-

The ritual worship, or prayer. These illustrations show the sequence of movement prescribed for the ritual prayers that each Muslim should perform five times a day. Various words of praise, prayer, and recitation from the Qur'an accompany each position and movement. The ritual symbolizes the Muslim's complete obedience to God and recognition of God as the one, eternal, omnipotent Lord of the universe.

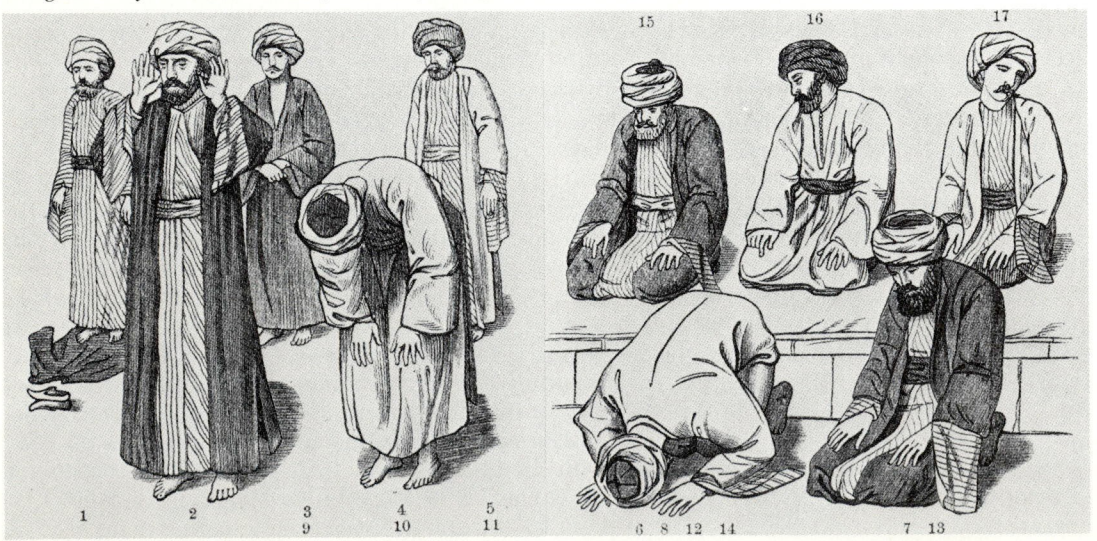

ence of jurisprudence, the core discipline of Islamic learning.

The centers of *ulema* activity were Medina, Mecca, and especially Iraq (primarily Basra and Kufa, later Baghdad), then Khorasan, Syria, North Africa and Spain, and Egypt. In Umayyad times, the *ulema* had already become the guardians of the Muslim conscience, often serving as the chief critics of caliphal rule when it departed too far from Muslim norms. In time, they became a new elite, one eventually identified with the upper class of each regional society. Caliphs and their governors regularly sought their advice, but often only for moral sanction (or legal sanction—the two are in the Muslim view the same) of a contemplated or accomplished action. Some *ulema* acquiesced in dubious sanctions and compromised themselves. Yet incorruptible *ulema* were seldom persecuted for their opinions (save when they supported sectarian rebellions), mostly because of their status and influence among rank-and-file Muslims.

Thus, without building a formal clergy, the Muslims developed a workable legal-moral system based on a formally trained if informally recognized scholarly elite and a tradition of concern with religious ideals in matters of public affairs and social order. If the caliphs and their deputies were seldom paragons of piety and often ruthless, they had at least to act with some circumspection and give compensating support for Muslim pious standards in public. Thus, the *ulema* shared the leadership in Muslim societies with the rulers, even if unequally—a pattern that has endured in Islamic states.

The Umma

A great strength of the Qur'anic message was its universalism. Although Muhammad may have conceived of his community first as an Arab one, the logical extension of the Qur'anic preaching was the acceptance into the *Umma* of anyone, of whatever race or nationality, who would submit to God and follow Muslim precepts. By the time of the first conquests, the new state was already so rooted in Muslim ideals that non-Arab converts had to be accepted, even if it meant loss of tax revenue. The social and political status of new converts was, however, clearly second to that of Arabs. Umar had organized the army register, or *diwan*, according to tribal precedence in conversion to, or (in the unique case of Christian Arab tribes) fighting for, Islam. The *diwan* served as the basis for the distribution and taxation of the new wealth, which perpetuated Arab precedence. The new garrisons, which rapidly became urban centers of Islamic rule and culture, kept the Arabs enough apart so that they were not simply absorbed into the cultural patterns or the traditions of the foreign territories. The Qur'an's centrality in Muslim life and the notion of its perfect Arabic form ensured the dominance of the Arabic language. So did the gradual implementation of Arabic in administration, where it replaced Aramaic, Greek, Middle Persian, or Coptic.

Non-Arab converts routinely attached themselves to Arab tribes as "clients." This assured protection and a place in the *diwan*, but still a permanent second-class citizenship alongside the Arabs. Although many non-Arabs, especially Persians, mastered Arabic and prospered, dissatisfaction among client Muslims was widespread and led to their participation in uprisings against caliphal authority. Persian–Arab tensions were especially strong in Umayyad and early Abbasid times. Nevertheless, a Persian cultural renaissance eventually raised the Islamicized modern Persian language to high status in Islamic culture. Consequently, it profoundly affected religion, art, and literature in much of the Islamic world.

Caliphal administration joined with the evolution of legal theory and practice and the consolidation of religious norms to give stability to the emerging Islamic society. So strong was the power of the Muslim vision of society, that when a caliph, or even a dynasty like the Umayyads, was superseded, the *Umma* and the caliphal office went on. There were, however, conflicting notions of that vision. In the course of the first three Islamic centuries, two major interpretations crystallized that reflected idealistic interpretations of the *Umma*, its leadership and membership. When neither proved viable in the practical world of society and politics, they became minority visions that continued to fire the imaginations of some but failed to win broad-based support. The third, "centrist," vision found favor with the majority; it could speak to a wide spectrum and accommodate inevitable compromises in the higher cause of Islamic unity.

THE KHARIJITES. The most radical idealists traced their political origin to the first civil war (656–661). These were the Kharijites, or "Seceders"—so named because they "seceded" from Ali's camp when, in their view, he compromised with his enemies. The Kharijite position was that the Muslim polity must be based on strict Qur'anic principles. They espoused a total egalitarianism among the faithful and held that the leadership of the *Umma* belonged to the best Muslim, whoever that might be. They took a moralistic, rigorist view of who the true members of the *Umma* were: Anyone who committed a major sin was no longer a Muslim. Extreme Kharijites called on true Muslims to join them in rebellion against the morally compromised authority of the reigning caliph. The extremist groups were constant rallying points for opposition to the Umayyads and, to a lesser degree, the Abbasids. More moderate Kharijites tempered their aversion to tolerating less-than-pious Muslims and the

The Wit and Wisdom of al-Jahiz

One of the great masters of Arabic prose, al-Jahiz (d. 869) left a number of works behind, among them his Book of Proof. *The following excerpts from this book of essays and clever sayings reflect his talent for the succinct and vivid.*

Ghailān son of Kharasha said to Ahnaf, "What will preserve the Arabs from decline?" He replied, "All will go well if they keep their swords on their shoulders and their turbans on their heads and ride horseback and do not fall a prey to the fools' sense of honour." "And what is the fools' sense of honour?" "That they regard forgiving one another as a wrong."

'Umar said, "Turbans are the crowns of the Arabs."

An Arab of the desert was asked why he did not lay aside his turban. "Surely," said he, "a thing which contains the hearing and the sight ought to be prized."

'Ali said—God be well pleased with him!—"The elegance of a man is in his bonnet, and the elegance of a woman is her boots." And Ahnaf said, "Let your shoes be fine, for shoes are to men what anklets are to women."

'Abdullah son of Ja'far said to his daughter, "O little daughter, beware of jealousy, for it is the key of divorce; and beware of chiding, for it breeds hate. Always adorn and perfume thyself, and know that the most becoming adornment is antimony and the sweetest perfume is water."

'Abdullah son of Ja'far bestowed largesse of every kind on Nusaib Abu'l-Hajīnā, who had made an ode in praise of him. "Why," they asked, "do you treat a fellow like this so handsomely—a negro and a slave?" "By God," he answered, "if his skin is black, yet his praise is white and his poem is truly Arabian. He deserves for it a greater reward than he has gotten. All he received was only some lean saddle-camels and clothes which wear out and money which is soon spent, whereas he gave an ode fresh and brilliant and praise that will never die."

Mu'āwiyah held an assembly at Kūfa to receive the oath of allegiance as Caliph. Those who swore loyalty to him were required to abjure allegiance to [the House of] 'Ali son of Abū Tālib—may God honour him! A man of the Banū Tamīm came to Mu'āwiyah, who demanded that he should repudiate 'Ali. "O Prince of the Faithful," he replied, "we will obey those of you that are living, but we will not renounce those of you that are dead." Mu'āwiyah turned to Mughīa and said, "Now, this is a man! Look after him well!"

. . . .

'Auf said on the authority of Hasan: "The feet of a son of Adam will not stir [from the place of judgment] until he be asked of three things—his youth, how he wore it away; his life, how he passed it; and his wealth, whence he got it and on what he spent it."

Yūnus son of 'Ubaid said: "I heard three sayings more than wonderful than any I have ever heard. The first is the saying of Hassān son of Abū Sinān—'Nothing is easier than abstinence from things unlawful: if aught make thee doubt, leave it alone.' The second is the saying of Ibn Sīrīn—'I have never envied any one any thing.' The third is the saying of Muwarrik al-'Ijlī—'Forty years ago I asked of God a boon which He has not granted, and I have not despaired of obtaining it.' They said to Muwarrik, 'What is it?' He replied, 'Not to meddle with that which does not concern me.'" ❑

From James Kritzeck (ed.), *Anthology of Islamic Literature* (New York: New American Library, Meridian Books, 1964), pp. 91–92.

rule of less-than-ideal caliphs, yet they retained a strong sense of the moral imperatives of Muslim personal and collective duty.

Kharijite ideals proved very attractive and influenced wider Muslim pietism in the long run. Although the movement declined in Abbasid times, even today moderate Kharijite groups survive in Muscat, Oman, and North Africa.

THE SHI'A. A second position was defined largely in terms of leadership in the *Umma*. Muhammad had no surviving sons, and his son-in-law and cousin Ali claimed the caliphate in 656, partly on the basis of his familial ties to the Prophet. His claim was contested by Mu'awiya in the first Islamic civil war. When Mu'awiya took over by default after a Kharijite mur-

dered Ali in 661, many of Ali's followers felt that Islamic affairs had gone awry. Although it is difficult to date the crystallization of the developed ideology of the "partisans of Ali" (*Shi'at Ali*, or simply the *Shi'a*, or *Shi'ites*), their roots go back to Ali's murder and especially to that of his son Husayn at Karbala, in Iraq (680).

Whereas most Muslims esteemed Ali for his closeness to Muhammad, the Shi'ites believed that he was the Prophet's appointed "successor." Ali's blood tie with Muhammad was augmented in Shi'ite thinking by belief in the Prophet's designation of him as the true *imam*, or Muslim leader, after him. Numerous rebellions in Umayyad times rallied around various figures claiming descent from such a designated and related successor, whether Ali or merely any member of

324 CONSOLIDATION AND INTERACTION OF WORLD CIVILIZATIONS

Scenes of Husayn's martyrdom from a Shi'ite Passion Play in Iran. The role of the martyrdom of al-Husayn, son of Ali and grandson of Muhammed, in Shi'ite piety can hardly be exaggerated. This event and the martyrdoms of the imams after him form the basis for the Shi'ite interpretation of history, an interpretation that stresses the suffering of the Imams and of true Muslims who follow them in this world, while promising a reward beyond the grave for the faithful. The performance of passion plays about Husayn's death is unique to Shi'ite Muslim practice. [Peter Chelkowski.]

Muhammad's clan of Hashim. Even the Abbasids based their right to the caliphate on their Hashimite blood. The major Shi'ite pretenders who emerged in the ninth and tenth centuries based their claims on both the Prophet's designation and their descent from Ali and Fatima, Muhammad's daughter. They also stressed the idea of a divinely inspired knowledge passed on by Muhammad to his designated heirs. The true Muslim was the faithful follower of the *imams*, who carried both Muhammad's blood and his mantle of spiritual authority.

When Shi'ites failed to establish a true *imam* as head of the imperial state, they interpreted this failure theologically. They saw Ali's assassination by a Kharijite, and especially the brutal massacre of Husayn and his family by Umayyad troops, as proofs of the evil nature of the rulers of this world, and as rallying points for true Muslims. The martyrdom of Ali and Husayn was extended to a line of Alid *imams* that varied among different groups of Shi'ites. True Muslims, like their *imams*, must suffer. But they would be vindicated in the end by an expected *mahdi*, or "guided one," who would usher in a messianic age and a judgment day that would see the faithful rewarded.

On several occasions in later history, Shi'ite rulers did gain control of some Islamic states. But only after 1500, in Iran, did Shi'ite tradition prevail as the majority faith in a major Muslim state. The Shi'ite vision of the true *Umma* has been a powerful one, but not one that has been able to muster sufficient consensus to dominate the larger Islamic world.

THE CENTRISTS. Kharijite and Shi'ite causes were repeatedly taken up by disaffected groups in the early and later Islamic empire. But it was a third, less sharply defined position on the nature of leadership and membership in the *Umma* that gained acceptance from most Muslims. In some ways, a compromise, it proved acceptable not only to lukewarm Muslims or simple pragmatists, but also to persons of piety as intense as that of any Kharijite or Shi'ite. We may term the proponents of this position *centrists*. To emphasize the correctness of their views, they eventually called themselves *Sunnis*—followers of the tradition (*sunna*) established by the Prophet and the Qur'an. Neither they, nor the Shi'ites, nor the Kharijites, have ever been a single sect or group; they have always encompassed a wide range of reconcilable, if not always truly compatible, ideas and groups. They have comprised the broad middle spectrum of Muslims who have tended to put communal solidarity and maintenance of the Islamic polity above purist adherence to certain theological positions. They have been inclusivist rather than exclusivist, a trait that has typified the Islamic (unlike the Christian) community through most of history.

The centrist position was simply the most workable general framework for the new Islamic state. Its basic ideas were:

1. The *Umma* is a theocratic entity, a state under divine authority mediated, first, by the Qur'an and the precedent of the Prophet and, second, by the consensus of the Muslims (in practice, the *ulema*).
2. The caliph is the absolute temporal ruler, charged with administering and defending the Abode of

680–694	Second civil war
685–705	Caliphate of Abd al-Malik; second civil war (680–694); consolidation, arabization of administration
705–715	Caliphate of al-Walid; Morocco conquered, Spain invaded; Arab armies reach the Indus
CA. 750	Introduction of paper manufacture from China through Samarqand to Islamic world
750	Abbasids seize Caliphate from Umayyads, begin new dynasty (750–1258)
756	Some Umayyads escape to Spain, found new dynasty (756–1030)
762–766	New Abbasid capital built at Baghdad

Islam and protecting Muslim norms and practice and possessing no greater authority than other Muslims in matters of faith.

3. A person who professes to be Muslim by witnessing that "There is no god but God, and Muhammad is His Messenger" should be considered a Muslim (as "only God knows what is in the heart"), and not even a mortal sin excludes such a person automatically from the *Umma*.

Under increasingly influential *ulema* leadership, these and other basic premises of Muslim community came to serve as the theological underpinnings of both the caliphal state and the emerging international Islamic social order.

The High Caliphate

The consolidation of the caliphal institution began with the victory of the Umayyad caliph Abd al-Malik in 692 in a second civil war. The succeeding century and a half marks the era of the "high caliphate," the politically strong, culturally vibrant, wealthy, and centralized institution that flourished first under the Umayyads in Damascus and then in the Abbasid capital at Baghdad.[3] The height of caliphal power and splendor came only after the final Umayyad decline, in the first century of Abbasid rule, largely during the caliphates of the fabled Harun al-Rashid (786–809) and his third son al-Ma'mun (813–833).

[3]This periodization follows that of M. G. S. Hodgson, *The Venture of Islam*, 3 vols. (Chicago, 1984), I:217–236.

The Abbasid State

The Abbasids' revolution was based on non-Arab disaffection, Khorasanian regionalism, and Shi'ite religiopolitical hopes. Their victory effectively ended Arab dominance of the empire. The shift of the imperial capital from Damascus to the new "city of peace" built at Baghdad on the Tigris (762–766) symbolized the eastward shift in cultural and political orientation under the new regime. In line with this shift, more and more Persians (albeit arabicized Persians—at least in language) entered the bureaucracy. In the Abbasid heyday under Harun, the highest caliphal advisory office, that of the vizier (Arabic, *wazir*), was dominated by the Khorasanian family of the Barmakids. Religiously, the Abbasids' disavowal of Shi'ite hopes for a divinely inspired imamate reflected their determination to gain the support of a broad spectrum of Muslims, even if they still stressed their descent from Muhammad's family.

Whereas the Umayyads had relied on their Syrian Arab forces, for their main troops the Abbasids used principally Khorasanian Arabs and Iranians and, in the provinces, regional mercenaries. Beginning in the ninth century, however, they enlisted large numbers of slave soldiers (*mamluks*), mostly Turks from the northern steppes, as their personal troops. The officers of these forces, themselves slaves, soon seized the positions of power in the central and provincial bureaucracies and the army. In a matter of years, the caliphs were dominated by their *mamluk* officers. This domination led to an increasing alienation of the Muslim populace from their own rulers. This alienation was evident in Iraq itself, where unrest with his overbearing Turkish guard led the Abbasid caliph to remove the government from Baghdad to the newly built city of Samarra sixty miles up the Tigris, where it remained from 836 to 892.

Society

The division between rulers and populace, the functionally secular state and its Muslim subjects, was ever after typical of Islamic society. However, even while the independence of more and more provincial rulers reduced the power of the Abbasid state after the mid-ninth century, such rulers generally chose to recognize caliphal authority at least in name. They thereby secured legitimacy for their rule and put themselves forward as guardians of the Islamic polity, which found its actual cohesiveness in the Muslim ideals being standardized by the *ulema*.

We must remember, however, that full conversion of the diverse populace of the Islamic Empire lagged far behind the centralization of political power and the development of Islamic socioreligious institutions. It appears that Iraq and Iran (especially Khorasan,

FIGURE 1

FIGURE 2

FIGURE 3

The congregational mosque. Three examples of the finest great mosques of the classical Islamic world. Such buildings were not only designed for worship. Their large courtyards and pillared halls were intended to hold the whole population of a given city and could be used for governmental purposes or for mustering troops in time of war. Their splendor also announced the power and wealth of Islamic rule. Figure 1 shows the mosque of Ibn Tulun, built at Cairo, 876–879, Figure 2 is the great mosque at Qayrawan, in modern Tunisia (eighth-ninth centuries). Figure 3 shows the Spanish Ummayad mosque at Cordoba, built and added to from the eighth to the tenth centuries, in a series of roofed extensions (unlike the other two, which are only partially covered). [George Gerster/William Graham/ George Holton.]

which saw early large-scale Arab Muslim immigration) were the two most important areas of the early Islamization of local elites until well into the twelfth century. They were followed by Spain, North Africa, and Syria. Conversion and fuller Islamization, when it came, meant the development of a self-confident Muslim polity no longer threatened by other religious communities or political forces and a correspondingly diminished need for centralized caliphal power.[4]

[4] Richard W. Bullet, *Conversion to Islam in the Medieval Period* (Cambridge, Mass., and London, 1979), esp. pp. 7–15, 128–138.

Decline

The eclipse of the caliphal state was foreshadowed at the very outset of Abbasid rule, when one of the last Umayyads escaped the general slaughter of his family by fleeing west to Muslim Spain. Supported by Syrian, Yemenite, and some Berber tribes, he founded a Spanish Islamic state that stood for nearly three hundred years (756–1030), producing the spectacular Moorish culture of Spain. Protected by sheer distance from Abbasid control, the Spanish Umayyads even assumed the title of caliph in 929, so strong were they, and so weak were the Abbasids by this time. In all the

The mosaic floor from the bath and pleasure hall of an Umayyad palace or hunting lodge in the desert at Khirbat al-Mafjar, in modern Israel. Both the Umayyad and Abbasid caliphs built splendid palaces in the tradition of their imperial Byzantine, Roman, and Persian predecessors. [Department of Antiquities, State of Israel.]

Abbasid provinces, regional governments were always potential bases for independent states. Besides various Kharijite states among the Berbers, the earliest separate state in North Africa was set up in 801 by the governor of Harun al-Rashid in the area of modern Tunisia. A later North African regional dynasty, the Fatimids, even conquered Egypt and set up a Shi'ite caliphate there after 969.

In the East, Iran grew ever harder for Baghdad to control. Beginning in 821 in Khorasan, Abbasid governors or rebel groups set up independent dynasties repeatedly for two centuries. Because of weakness, the caliph had commonly to recognize their *de facto* sway over various parts of the Iranian plateau. Among the longest-lived of these regional Iranian dynasties were the Samanids of Khorasan and Transoxiania, who held power at Bukhara as nominal vassals of the caliph from 875 until 999. The Samanids gave northeastern Iran a long period of economic and political security from Turkish steppe invaders. Under them, Persian poetry and Arabic scientific studies started what was to become over the next centuries a Persian Islamic cultural renaissance.

Of greatest consequence for the caliphal state was, however, the rise in the mountains south of the Caspian of a Shi'ite family, the Buyids, who took over Abbasid rule in 945. Though they kept the caliph himself "in office," he and his descendants were henceforth largely puppets in the hands of Buyid "commanders" (*amirs*, or *emirs;* later *sultans*). In 1055, the Buyids were replaced by the more famous Seljuk rulers, or *sultans.* Thus, the caliphal state broke up, even though Abbasid caliphs continued as figureheads of Muslim unity until the Mongol invaders killed the last of them in 1258.

The "Classical" Culture of Abbasid Times

The pomp and splendor of the Abbasid court were grand enough to become the stuff of Islamic legend such as we find preserved much later in the tales of *The Thousand and One Nights.* Their rich cultural legacy similarly outlived the Abbasids themselves. Their power and glory was made possible by a strong army

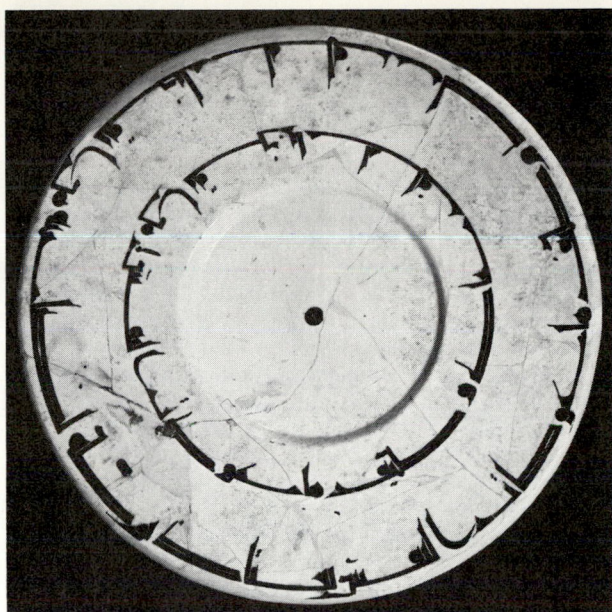

This tenth-century plate from Samarkand, decorated in Kufic script, is an example of the fine Islamic ceramic art that developed under Chinese influence beginning in early Abbasid times. [Freer Gallery of Art.]

and central government and vigorous internal and external trade. The latter may have been stimulated by the prosperous T'ang Empire of China, with which the Islamic world had much overland and sea contact. It was, for example, in the mid-eighth century that paper manufacture was introduced from China to the Islamic world through Transoxiania, at Samarkand.

Intellectual Traditions

The Abbasid heyday was marked by sophisticated tastes and an insatiable thirst for knowledge—not simply religious, but *any* knowledge. An Arab historian called Baghdad "the market to which the wares of the sciences and arts were brought, where wisdom was sought as a man seeks after his stray camels, and whose judgment of values was accepted by the whole world."[5] Older traditions continued and flourished. Contacts (primarily among intellectuals) between Muslims and Christian, Jewish, Zoroastrian, and other "protected" religious communities contributed to the cosmopolitanism of the age. Some older intellectual traditions experienced a revival in early Abbasid times, as in the case of Hellenistic learning. Philosophy, astronomy, mathematics, medicine, and other natural sciences enjoyed strong interest and support. In Islamic usage, philosophy and the sciences were subsumed under *falsafa* (from Greek *philosophia*). Is-

[5] See Oleg Grabar, *The Formation of Islamic Art* (New Haven and London, 1973), esp. pp. 1–103, 206–213.

lamic culture took over the tradition of rational inquiry from the Hellenistic world and developed as well as preserved it at a time when Europe was by comparison a cultural wasteland.

Arabic translations of Greek and Sanskrit works laid the basis for progress in astronomy and medicine. Translation reached its peak in al-Ma'mun's new academy under the guidance of a Nestorian Christian, Hunayn ibn Ishaq (d. 873), noted for his medical and Greek learning. Before, during, and after his time, there were Arabic translations of everything from Galen, Ptolemy, Euclid, Aristotle, Plato, and the Neo-Platonists to the fables that had been translated from Sanskrit originals into Middle Persian under the Sasanids. Such translations stimulated not only Arabic learning, but that of the less-advanced western European world, especially in the twelfth and thirteenth centuries.

An Egyptian crystal vase decorated with an arabesque floral design, from the early Fatimid period (late tenth century). [Freer Gallery of Art.]

The Splendor of the Abbasid Court

The following excerpts from al-Khatib's description of a visit by Byzantine ambassadors to Baghdad in 917 give some glimmer of the extravagant magnificence of the Islamic capital at the height of its opulence and power.

Then it was commanded that the ambassadors should be taken round the palace. Now there were no soldiers here, but only the eunuchs and the chamberlains and the black pages. The number of the eunuchs was seven thousand in all, four thousand of them white and three thousand black; the number of the chamberlains was also seven thousand, and the number of the black pages, other than the eunuchs, was four thousand; the flat roofs of all the palace being occupied by them, as also of the banqueting-halls. Further, the store-chambers had been opened, and the treasures therein had been set out as is customary for a bride's array; the jewels of the Caliph being arranged in trays, on steps, and covered with cloths of black brocade. When the ambassadors entered the Palace of the Tree and gazed upon the Tree, their astonishment was great. For there they saw birds fashioned out of silver and whistling with every motion, while perched on a tree of silver weighing 500 *dirhams*. Now the wonder of the ambassadors was greater at seeing these than at any of the other sights that they saw.

. . . Then at length, after the ambassadors had thus been taken round twenty-three various palaces, they were brought forth to the Court of the Ninety. Here were the pages of the Privy Chamber, full-armed, sumptuously dressed, each of admirable stature. In their hands they carried swords, small battle-axes, and maces. The ambassadors next passed down the lines formed by the black slaves; the deputy chamberlains, the soldiers, the footmen, and the sons of the chieftains, until they again came to the Presence Hall. Now there were a great number of the Slavic eunuchs in all these palaces, who during the visit were occupied in offering to all present water, cooled with snow, to drink; also sherbets and beer and some of these slaves went round with the ambassadors, to whom, as they walked or sat to take rest in some seven different places, water was thus offered, and they drank.

. . . Finally, they came again to the presence of the Caliph Muktadir, whom they found in the Palace of the Crown upon the bank of the Tigris. He was arrayed in clothes of Dabik-stuff embroidered in gold, being seated on an ebony throne overlaid with Dabik-stuff embroidered in gold likewise, and on his head was the tall bonnet called galansuwah. Suspended on the right of the throne were nine necklaces, like prayer beads and to the left were seven others, all of famous jewels, the largest of which was of such a size that its sheen eclipsed the daylight. Before the Caliph stood five of his sons, three to the right and two to the left. Then the ambassadors, with their interpreter, halted before Muktadir, and stood in the posture of humility, with their arms crossed. ❑

Oleg Grabar, *Formation of Islamic Art* (New Haven and London: Yale University Press 1973), pp. 168, 170–171.

Language and Literature

Arabic language and literature developed greatly in the wider cultural sphere of the new empire. On the secular side, there developed, largely among the secretarial class of the Abbasid bureaucracy, a significant genre of Arabic writing known as *adab*, or "manners." This genre included essays and didactic literature influenced by earlier Persian letters. As translations of different genres of writings increased the range of the original bedouin idiom, poetry was able to build on the sophisticated tradition of the Arabic ode, or *qasida*.

Grammar was central to the Qur'an interpretation that occupied the *ulema* and provided the core of an emerging curriculum of Muslim learning. A major form of Arabic writing was historical and biographical literature. It owed much to the ancient bedouin accounts of "the battle days of the Arabs." But it arose primarily to supply information about, first, the lives of the Prophet and the earliest Companions, then those of subsequent generations of Muslims. This information was crucial to judging the reliability of the "chains" of transmitters included with each traditional report, or *hadith*. The *hadith* contained words and/or deeds ascribed to Muhammad and the Companions; it became the chief source of Muslim legal and religious norms alongside the Qur'an, as well as the basic unit of history and biography. The Hadith, a collection of these reports, existed also as a separate genre that was mined by preachers and by the developing schools of legal interpretation, whose crowning glory was the work of al Shafi'i (d. 820) on the theory of legal reasoning.

Art and Architecture

In art and architecture, the Abbasid era saw the crystallization of a "classical" Islamic style by about A.D. 1000. Except for Arabic calligraphy and ceramics, there was nothing radically new about the discrete elements of Islamic art and architecture (most had clear antecedents in Greco-Roman, Byzantine, or Iranian art). What was new was the spread of such elements to new locales, generally in a movement from east (especially the Fertile Crescent) to west (Syria, Egypt, North Africa, and Spain). Sasanid stucco decoration techniques and designs turned up, for example, in Egypt and North Africa. Chronologically, urban Iraq developed an Islamic art first, then made its influence felt east and west, whether in Bukhara or in Syria and Qayrawan. Also new was the combination of discrete forms, as in the case of the colonnade (or hypostyle) mosque or the minaret tower.

The Muslims had good reason to be self-confident about their faith and culture and to want to distinguish them from others. Most monuments of the age express the distinctiveness they felt. Particular formal items, such as calligraphic motifs and inscriptions on buildings, became characteristic of Islamic architecture and defined its functions. Most striking in many ways was the avoidance of pictures or icons and overt symbols in public art. This was, of course, in line with the strong Muslim aversion both to any hint of idolatry and to the strongly iconographic traditions of Christian art. Although this iconoclasm was later eased in various strands of Islamic culture, it was a telling expression of the thrust of Muslim faith and the culture it animated. Overall, the artistic achievements of the Islamic world before the year 1000 impress us with an identifiable quality that is both distinctive and "classically" Islamic, whatever the details of a particular example.[6]

The Formation of Islamic Civilization in World Perspective

The rise of Islam as both a world religious tradition and as an international civilization is by any standard one of the great watershed events of world history. The new traditions forged first in the Arabian peninsula and then in Syria, Iraq, North Africa, Iran, and beyond were to change much of Asia and Africa and parts of Europe in major ways. Religiously, the Islamic movement was destined to become, along with the Buddhist and Christian movements, one of the three major universalist, missionary traditions of world religious history. Politically and socially, the Islamic order for government and society spread and developed in new environments far beyond even the imagination of Muhammad and his companions.

The Islamic polity was in its first three centuries the most dynamic and expansive imperial state of its day. During the same time, Chinese emperors of the T'ang were rebuilding and improving on the previous Han imperium; Charlemagne and the Carolingians were struggling to hammer out a much smaller, more homogeneous empire and a cultural renaissance in the rela-

[6]Ibid.

THE "CLASSICAL" PERIOD OF THE HIGH CALIPHATE	
786–809	Caliphate of Harun al-Rashid; apogee of caliphal power
813–833	Caliphate of al-Ma'mun; strong patronage of translations of Greek, Sanskrit, and other works into Arabic; first heavy reliance upon slave soldiers (*mamluks*)
875	Rise of Samanid power at Bukhara; patronage of Persian poetry paves way for Persian literary renaissance
909	Rise of Shi'ite Fatimid dynasty in North Africa
945–1055	Buyid amirs rules the eastern empire at Baghdad; the Abbasid caliphs continue largely as figureheads
1055	Buyid amirs replaced by Seljuk sultans as effective rulers at Baghdad and custodians of the caliphate

tively backward world of western Europe; Byzantium was struggling to survive against Islamic arms and turning inward to conserve its traditions; and post-Gupta India was divided under diverse regional kings and still subject to new forces (including those of Islam) moving into northwest India.

As different as the two were, only China compared favorably with or surpassed the Islamic world in this period in terms of political and military power, cultural unity and creativity, and cultural self-consciousness. The T'ang empire and that of the Abbasids wielded commensurate power in their heydays, although over time the Chinese held together as a centralized state much better than the Islamic did. Certainly, these were the two greatest political and cultural units in the world in their age. They each had one cultural language, although Chinese was the language of more of the masses of China's empire than was Arabic of the Islamic dominions. They also shared the central military use of nomadic cavalry as well as the adaptive ability to incorporate new peoples into their larger culture. Indeed, the great elasticity and adaptability of Islam as a religious tradition and as a social order was striking in ways that clearly give the lie to its reputation in the West today as a rigid and inflexible system of values and practices.

Nevertheless, the bases of Islamic empire were clearly different, spread as it was over vastly more culturally heterogenous and widely dispersed geographi-

Traditions from and about the Prophet

The following are the texts of three haditls, *or traditions about the words and actions of Muhammad and his companions. Such reports were transmitted from the early days of Islam after Muhammad's death, in order to instruct or regulate Muslims in the practice of their new faith. Many such reports were forged by persons who wished to lend prophetic authority to particular practices or ideas that seemed good to them, and the* ulema *developed elaborate methods of* Hadith *criticism to identify falsified or inaccurately transmitted traditions. These examples are drawn from major* Hadith *collections compiled largely in the third century of the Hijra.*

The Apostle of God passed by a pile of grain. He put his hand into the midst of it, and his fingers encountered moisture.

He exclaimed, "O merchant, what is this?"

The owner of the grain said, "It has been damaged by the rain, O Apostle of God."

Then he replied, "If that is the case, why not put the damaged grain on top of the pile so that people can see it?"

Then he concluded, "Whoever practices fraud is not one of us."

Ibn 'Umar heard a man swear, saying, "No, I swear by the Ka'bah!" Ibn 'Umar said, "Swear by none other than God. I heard the Apostle of God say, 'Whoever swears by other than God commits blasphemy and makes someone or something an associate with God.'"

When the Prophet awoke he would say, "O God, it is you who enables us to wake up in the morning and it is you who brings us into the evening. You enable us to live. You cause us to die, and at the Resurrection we go to you." When evening came he would say, "O God, it is you who brings us into the evening, and it is you who enables us to wake up in the morning. You enable us to live. You cause us to die, and with you is the issue of our life."

Ibn 'Abbās addressed the people of Al-Basrah [a city in Iraq, founded by the Muslims in 638 A.D.] at the end of Ramadān [the month of fasting], saying, "O people of Al-Basrah, do your duty and give alms after fasting." The people looked at each other.

He said, "Who is here from Medina? Come forth and teach your brothers. Should they not know that the Apostle of God prescribed as alms to be given at the end of Ramadān, a half *sā* [a cubic measure] of wheat, or a *sā* of barley, or a *sā* of dates, to be given by every person, slave and free, man and woman?" ❑

From Kenneth Cragg and Marston Speight, eds., *Islam from Within: Anthology of a Religion* (Belmont, CA: Wadsworth, 1980), pp. 84, 89, 92–93.

cal areas than that of China. Conquest initially fueled the economy of the new Islamic state, but, in the long run, trade and urban commercial centers proved to be the backbone of Islamic prosperity, as well as the chief means of dissemination of the Muslim faith to new lands. The Islamic empire was agrarian-based, yet the overall conditions for food production were not as good as those in China or western Europe. The key element that the majority of Islamic lands were (and are) lacking was abundant water, so that supporting dense populations well was difficult. This did not stop the development of impressive Islamic states, societies, and cultures, but it did set certain limits to such development.

The Islamic achievement was different from any other in this period primarily in that it resulted from an effort to build something new rather than to recapture or resuscitate previous traditions, whether of religion, society, or government. In later centuries, the early Arabic impress of Islamic culture and religion was tempered and changed by the vast numbers of Persian- and Turkish-speaking Muslims and also the many regional groups, from Urdu- or Swahili-speakers in India or Africa to Malay and Indonesian Muslims of Southeast Asia. Nevertheless, Arabic went abroad with the holy Qur'an as the sacred language of God's final revelation. Ever since, Muslims of all the world have learned little or much of Arabic and the sacred Book, but always something.

This achievement was a new historical phenomenon, at least in terms of the scale of its occurrence. Although Muslim faith can be seen as largely a reformation of Semitic monotheism, it must be seen as more fundamentally an effort to do something new. It was an attempt to subsume older traditions of Jews or Christians in a more comprehensive vision of God's plan on earth rather than an attempt to reform earlier traditions. This is not to say that Muslims did not build on previous traditions; they adopted and adapted the traditions of the many older centers of Afro-Eurasian cultures. Yet, both as a civilization and a religious tradition, Islam developed its own strikingly recognizable stamp that persisted wherever Muslims extended the *Umma.*

Suggested Readings

A. F. L. Beeston, T. M. Johnstone, R. B. Sergeant, and G. R. Smith, *Arabic Literature to the End of the Umayyad Period* (1983). The most comprehensive survey of the early Arabic historical, religious, poetic, and other literary sources.

K. Cragg and R. Marston Speight, eds., *Islam from Within: Anthology of a Religion* (1980). One of the best and most sensitive collections of selections from Islamic primary sources.

F. M. Donner, *The Early Islamic Conquests* (1981). The introduction and first chapter are especially good for an introduction to many important issues in the origin and spread of Islam.

H. A. R. Gibb, *Mohammedanism: An Historical Survey* (1970). Despite the offensive title, still the best brief introduction to Islam as a religious tradition.

H. A. R. Gibb, *Studies on the Civilization of Islam*. Ed. S. J. Shaw and W. R. Polk (1962). This volume of selected essays by Gibb has some very helpful general studies on Islamic political order and religion.

O. Grabar, *The Formation of Islamic Art* (1973). A critical and creative interpretation of major themes in the development of distinctively Islamic forms of art and architecture.

G. E. von Grunebaum, *Classical Islam: A History 600–1258*. Trans. K. Watson (1970), pp. 1–140. A competent, culturally oriented introductory survey of formative developments.

M. G. S. Hodgson, *The Classical Age of Islam. Vol. I of The Venture of Islam*. 3 vols. (1974). The most thoughtful and comprehensive attempt to deal with classical Islamic civilization as a whole and in relation to contemporaneous non-Islamic cultures.

B. Lewis, ed., *Islam and the Arab World* (1976). A large-format, heavily illustrated volume with many excellent articles on diverse aspects of Islam (not simply Arab, as the misleading title suggests) civilization through the premodern period.

F. Rahman, *Major Themes of the Qur'an* (1980). The best introduction to the basic ideas of the Qur'an and Islam, seen through the eyes of a perceptive Muslim modernist scholar.

M. A. Shaban, *Islamic History: A New Interpretation*. 2 vols. (1971–76). An influential reassessment of the course of Islamic history to A.D. 1055.

D. Sourdel, *Medieval Islam* (1979). Eng. trans. W. M. Watt (1983). A brief but masterly survey of the world of medieval Islam with emphasis on social, religious, and political institutions.

An equestrian figure of Charlemagne (or perhaps one of his sons) from the early ninth century. [Musée du Louvre, Paris. Giraudon.]

13 The Early Middle Ages in the West to 1000: The Birth of Europe

The early Middle Ages mark the birth of Europe. This was the period in which a distinctive Western European culture began to emerge. In geography, government, religion, and language, Western Europe became a land distinct from both the eastern or Byzantine world and the Arab or Muslim world. It was a period of recovery from the collapse of Roman civilization, a time of forced experimentation with new ideas and institutions. Western European culture, as we know it today, was born of a unique, inventive mix of surviving Greco-Roman, new Germanic, and evolving Christian traditions.

The early Middle Ages have been called, and not with complete fairness, a "dark age" because they lost touch with classical, especially Greek, learning and science. In this period, there were fierce invasions from the north and the east by peoples that the Romans somewhat arrogantly called barbarians. To the south, the Mediterranean was transformed by Arab dominance into an inhospitable "Muslim lake." Although Western trade with the East was by no means completely cut off, Western people became more isolated than they had been before. A Europe thus surrounded and assailed from the north, east, and south understandably became somewhat insular and even stagnant. On the other hand, being forced to manage by itself, Western Europe also learned to develop its native resources. The early Middle Ages were not without a modest renaissance of antiquity during the reign of Charlemagne. And the peculiar social and political forms of this period—manorialism and feudalism—proved to be not only successful ways to cope with unprecedented chaos on local levels but also a fertile seedbed for the growth of distinctive Western institutions.

On the Eve of the Frankish Ascendancy

Germanic and Arab Invasions

As we have already seen, by the late third century A.D., the Roman Empire had become too large for a single sovereign to govern. For this reason, Emperor Diocletian (284–305) permitted the evolution of a dual empire by establishing an eastern and a western half, each with its own emperor and, eventually, imperial bureaucracy. Emperor Constantine the Great (306–337) briefly reunited the empire by conquest and was sole emperor of the east and the west after 324. (It was redivided by his sons and subsequent successors.) In 330, Constantine created the city of Constantinople as the new administrative center of the empire and the imperial residence. Constantinople gradually became a "new Rome," replacing the old, whose internal political quarrels and geographical distance from new military fronts in Syria and along the Danube River made it less appealing. Rome and the western empire were actually on the wane in the late third and fourth centuries, well before the barbarian invasions in the west began. In 286, Milan had already replaced Rome as the imperial residence; in 402, the seat of western government was moved still again, to Ravenna. When the barbarian invasions began in the late fourth century, the West was in political disarray, and the imperial power and prestige had shifted decisively to Constantinople and the East.

GERMAN TRIBES AND THE WEST. The German tribes did not burst on the West all of a sudden. They were at first a token and benign presence. Before the great invasions from the north and the east, there had been a period of peaceful commingling of the Germanic and the Roman cultures. The Romans "imported" barbarians as domestics and soldiers before the German tribes came as conquerors. Barbarian soldiers rose to positions of high leadership and fame in Roman legions. In the late fourth century, however, this peaceful coexistence came to an end because of a great influx of Visigoths (west Goths) into the empire. They were stampeded there in 376 by the emergence of a new, violent people, the Huns, who migrated from the area of modern Mongolia. The Visigoths were a Christianized (albeit unorthodox) Germanic tribe who won from the Eastern emperor Valens rights of settlement and material assistance within the empire in exchange for their defense of the frontier as *foederati*, special allies of the emperor. When in place of promised assistance the Visigoths received harsh treatment from their new allies, they rebelled, handily defeating Roman armies under Valens at the battle of Adrianople in 378.

Salvian the Priest Compares the Romans and the Barbarians

Salvian, a Christian priest writing around 440, found the barbarians morally superior to the Romans—indeed, truer to Roman virtues than the Romans themselves, whose failings were all the more serious because they, unlike the barbarians, had knowledge of Christianity.

In what respects can our customs be preferred to those of the Goths and Vandals, or even compared with them? And first, to speak of affection and mutual charity, . . . almost all barbarians, at least those who are of one race and kin, love each other, while the Romans persecute each other. . . . The many are oppressed by the few, who regard public exactions as their own peculiar right, who carry on private traffic under the guise of collecting the taxes. . . . So the poor are despoiled, the widows sigh, the orphans are oppressed, until many of them, born of families not obscure, and liberally educated, flee to our enemies that they may no longer suffer the oppression of public persecution. They doubtless seek Roman humanity among the barbarians, because they cannot bear barbarian inhumanity among the Romans. And although they differ from the people to whom they flee in manner and in language; although they are unlike as regards the fetid odor of the barbarians' bodies and garments, yet they would rather endure a foreign civilization among the barbarians than cruel injustice among the Romans.

It is urged that if we Romans are wicked and corrupt, that the barbarians commit the same sins. . . . There is, however, this difference, that if the barbarians commit the same crimes as we, yet we sin more grievously. . . . All the barbarians . . . are pagans or heretics. The Saxon race is cruel, the Franks are faithless . . . the Huns are unchaste—in short there is vice in the life of all the barbarian peoples. But are their offenses as serious as [those of Christians]? Is the unchastity of the Hun so criminal as ours? Is the faithlessness of the Frank so blameworthy as ours? ❑

Of God's Government, in James Harvey Robinson (ed.), *Readings in European History*, Vol. 1 (Boston: Athenaeum, 1904), pp. 28–30.

After Adrianople, the Romans passively permitted settlement after settlement of barbarians within the very heart of Western Europe. Why was there so little resistance to the German tribes? The invaders found a badly overextended western empire physically weakened by decades of famine, pestilence, and overtaxation, and politically divided by ambitious military commanders. In the second half of the fourth century, the Roman will to resist had simply been sapped. The Roman Empire did not fall simply because of unprecedented moral decay and materialism, but because of a combination of political mismanagement, disease, and sheer poverty.

The late fourth and early fifth centuries saw the invasion of still other tribes: the Vandals, the Burgundians, and the Franks. In 410, Visigoths revolted under Alaric (CA. 370–410) and sacked the "eternal city" of Rome. From 451 to 453, Italy suffered the invasions of Attila the Hun (D. 453), who was known to contemporaries as the "scourge of God." In 455, the Vandals overran Rome.

By the mid-fifth century, power in Western Europe had passed decisively from the hands of the Roman emperors to those of barbarian chieftains. In 476, the traditional date for the fall of the Roman Empire, the barbarian Odoacer (CA. 434–493) deposed and replaced the Western emperor Romulus Augustulus and ruled as "king of the Romans." By the end of the fifth century, the western empire was thoroughly overrun by barbarians. The Ostrogoths settled in Italy, the Franks in northern Gaul, the Burgundians in Provence, the Visigoths in southern Gaul and Spain, the Vandals in north Africa and the Mediterranean, and the Angles and Saxons in England (see Map 13.1). Barbarians were now the western masters—but masters who were also willing to learn from the people they had conquered.

Western Europe was not transformed into a savage land. The military victories of the barbarians did not result in a great cultural defeat of the Roman Empire. The barbarians were militarily superior, but the Romans retained their cultural strength. Apart from Britain and northern Gaul, Roman language, law, and government continued to exist side by side with the new Germanic institutions. In Italy under Theodoric, Roman law gradually replaced tribal custom. Only the Vandals and the Anglo-Saxons refused to profess at least titular obedience to the emperor in Constantinople.

Behind this accommodation of cultures was the fact that the Visigoths, the Ostrogoths, and the Vandals entered the west as Christianized people. They professed, however, a religious creed that was considered heretical in the West. They were Arian Christians, that

MAP 13-1 BARBARIAN MIGRATIONS INTO THE WEST IN THE FOURTH AND FIFTH CENTURIES *The forceful intrusion of Germanic and non-Germanic barbarians into the Empire from the last quarter of the fourth century through the fifth century made for a constantly changing pattern of movement and relations. The map shows the major routes taken by the usually unwelcome newcomers and the areas most deeply affected by the main groups.*

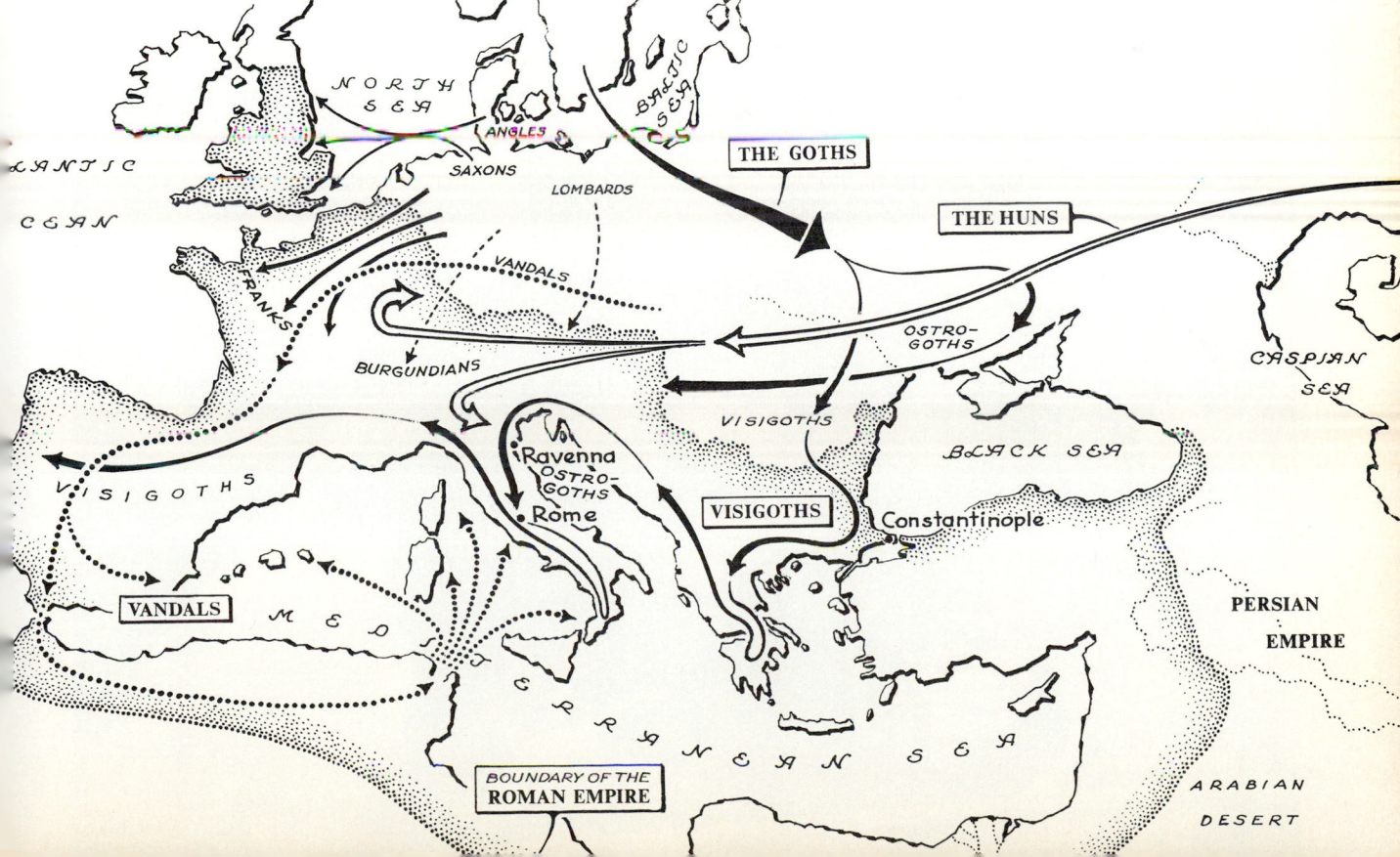

is, Christians who believed that Jesus Christ was not of one identical substance with God the Father—a point of view that had been condemned in 325 by the Council of Nicea (see Chapter 6). Later, around 500, the Franks, under their strong king, Clovis, converted to the orthodox or "Catholic" form of Christianity supported by the bishops of Rome, and they helped conquer and convert the Goths and other barbarians in Western Europe.

All things considered, rapprochement and a gradual interpenetration of two strong cultures—a creative tension—marked the period of the Germanic migrations. The stronger culture was the Roman, and it became dominant in a later fusion. Despite western military defeat, it can still be said that the Goths and the Franks became far more romanized than the Romans were germanized. Latin language, Nicene Christianity, and eventually Roman law and government were to triumph in the West during the Middle Ages.

CONTINUITY IN THE EAST. As Western Europe succumbed to the Germanic invasions, Constantinople became the sole capital of the empire, and it remained the capital until a revival of the Western empire began in the reign of Charlemagne. The Eastern empire, established in 330, was to last until May 29, 1453, when Constantinople finally fell to the Turks after centuries of unsuccessful siege.

The early Middle Ages were a period of important political and cultural achievement in the East. The

A mosaic portrait of Justinian's wife, the Empress Theodora (CA. 500-548), *from the church of St. Vitale in Ravenna. She was prominent in the heated theological controversies of the time.* [Bettmann Archive.]

Emperor Justinian (527–565) collated and revised Roman law. His *Code*, issued in 533, was the first codification of Roman law and became the foundation of most European law. Justinian was assisted by his brilliant and powerful wife, the empress Theodora. She favored the Monophysite teaching that Jesus had only one nature, a composite of both human and divine nature. Justinian did not share this view but supported

Byzantine church decoration consisted predominantly of rigidly stylized mosaics. A theme repeated endlessly in these church mosaics is that of Christ the Ruler of All. The stern, bearded judge is quite different from the gentle figure of Christ as the good shepherd. This example from about 1100 is from the Church of St. Savior in Istanbul. [AHM.]

The Dome of the Rock in Jerusalem. An early example of monumental Islamic architecture, it dates from the seventh century, during the first wave of Arab expansion, and derives its name from the rock from which Muslims believe Muhammad ascended to heaven. Jews believe the rock to be the one on which Abraham prepared to sacrifice Issac. [Israel Government Tourist Office, New York.]

southern France, and Italy, which Justinian also managed to control after decades of guerrilla warfare. But a revival and reunion of the old Roman Empire was not to be. In northern Europe the Franks were becoming the dominant western power, a power Justinian's armies were not strong enough to subdue. The appearance and the firm entrenchment of the Lombards in northern Italy three years after Justinian's death created a buffer between the Franks and imperial forces that prevented what would surely have been a fatal confrontation for the reviving empire.

Islam and Its Effects on East and West

In the south, an enemy far more dangerous than the German tribes was on the march: the faith of Islam. During the lifetime of the prophet Muhammad (570–632) and thereafter, invading Arab armies absorbed the attention and resources of the emperors in Constantinople, who found themselves in a life-and-death struggle. Unlike the comparatively mild Germanic invaders, Arab armies did not encourage a creative interpenetration of cultures, although Jews and other religious minorities were tolerated within Islam. (See Chapter 12).

By the middle of the eighth century, Muslims had conquered the southern and eastern Mediterranean coastline (territories mostly still held by Islamic states today) and occupied parts of Spain, which they controlled or strongly influenced until the fifteenth century. In addition, their armies had pushed north and east through Mesopotamia and Persia and beyond (see Map 13.1). These conquests would not have been so rapid and thorough had the contemporary Byzantine and Persian empires not been exhausted by a long period of war. The Muslims struck at the conclusion of the successful campaign of Byzantine Emperor Heraclius (D. 641) against the Persian King Chosroes II. Most of the population in the conquered area spoke Semitic language and was more easily fired by hatred of the Byzantine Greek army of occupation than it was inspired to unity by a common Christian tradition. The Christian community was itself badly divided. The Egyptian (also known as *Coptic*) and Syrian churches were Monophysitic. Heraclius' efforts to impose Greek "orthodox" beliefs on these churches only increased the enmity between Greek and Semitic Christians, many of whom leaned toward Monophysitism. Many Egyptian and Syrian Christians may have looked on Arabs as deliverers from the Byzantine conquerors.

Muslims tolerated conquered Christians, whether orthodox or Monophysite, provided they paid taxes, kept their distance, and made no efforts to proselytize Muslim communities. Always anxious to maintain the

the majority view that Jesus was of two separate natures, fully human and fully divine. Despite this theological disagreement, Justinian and Theodora succeeded in imposing an imperial theology on their subjects that made the emperor supreme in religious matters. These efforts laid the foundation for a highly successful program of state control of the Church in the east.

Justinian and Theodora did not forget the West. They took advantage of the political disunity of the German tribes and papal opposition to the Arian Ostrogoths briefly to reconquer the Western empire in the mid-sixth century. Justinian's armies overcame the Vandals in Africa in 533 and marched into Spain,

Byzantine architecture—the architecture of the Roman Empire of the East after about the fifth century and of other areas strongly influenced by Byzantium–is represented here by what are probably its two grandest remaining monuments. The first one is Emperor Justinian's Hagia Sophia (Church of the Holy Wisdom) in Constantinople, which was built between 532 *and* 537. *With its great dome,* 107 *feet in diameter, several half domes, and richly decorated interior of marbles and mosaics, it was enormously influential on subsequent church architecture. Its exterior is now much changed by minarets, tombs, and buttresses added at various times after the Turkish conquest of Constantinople in* 1453, *when the building became a mosque for nearly five hundred years. It has been a museum since* 1935. *[AHM.]*

After Hagia Sophia, the second greatest surviving example of Byzantine architecture—from a much later period of the style—is Saint Mark's in Venice. Most of the building dates from the eleventh century and was built to house the remains of the Apostle Mark, said to have been taken from Alexandria in Egypt. The building carries the characteristic rounded arches, numerous domes, and mosaics of the Byzantine style. The ornamental pointed arches and pinnacles of the facade's upper story are later additions. [Italian Government Travel Office, New York.]

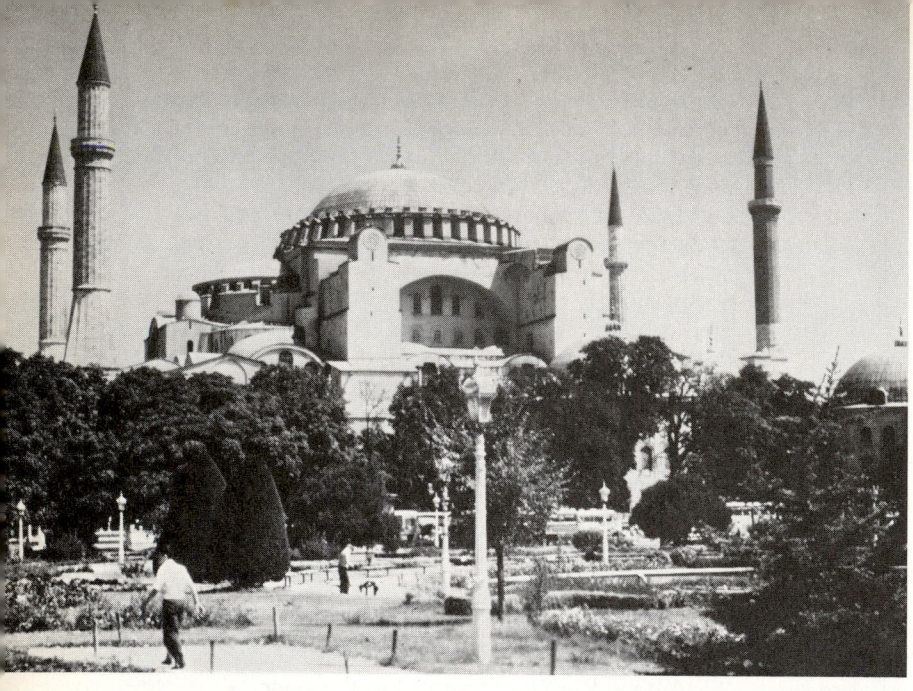

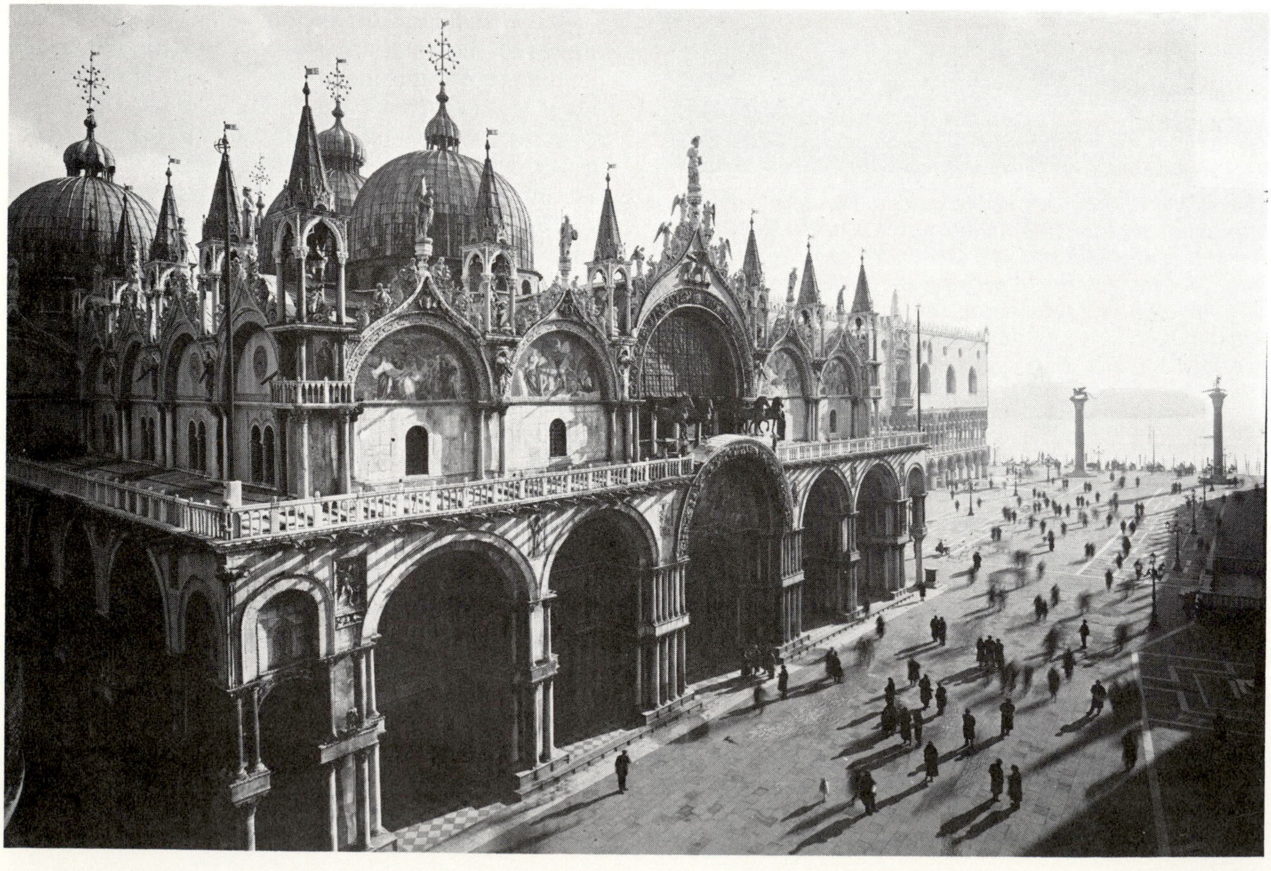

purity of their religion and culture, the Arabs forbade mixed marriages and any conscious cultural interchange. Special taxes on conquered peoples encouraged them to convert to Islam.

Assaulted on both their eastern and their western frontiers and everywhere challenged in the Mediterranean, the Europeans developed a lasting fear and suspicion of the Muslims. In the east, during the reign of the Byzantine Leo III (717–740), the Arabs were stopped after a year's siege of Constantinople (717–718). Leo and his successors in the Isaurian dynasty of Byzantine rulers created a successful defensive organization against the Arabs. It was so effective that it permitted the rulers of the following Macedonian dynasty (867–1057) to expand militarily and commercially into Muslim lands. Byzantine armies were also assisted by Muslim disunity. In 1071, the Seljuk Turks from central Asia, by way of Persia and Mesopotamia, overran Armenia at the eastern end of the empire in the first of a series of confrontations that would finally end with the fall of Constantinople in 1453 to the Seljuks' relatives, the Ottoman Turks. In 1096, the Crusaders from western Europe arrived in Constantinople in the first of a series of moves to the East that ended during the Fourth Crusade with the capture of Constantinople in 1204 and the establishment of a half century of Latin or Western rule over Byzantium.

As for the West's own dangers, the ruler of the Franks, Charles Martel, defeated a raiding party of Arabs on the western frontier of Europe near Tours (today in central France) in 732, a victory that ended any possible Arab effort to expand into Western Europe by way of Spain. From the end of the seventh century to the middle of the eleventh, the Mediterranean still remained something of a Muslim lake; although trade of the Western empire with the Orient was not cut off during these centuries, it was significantly decreased and was carried on in keen awareness of Muslim dominance.

When trade wanes, cities decline, and with them those centers for the exchange of goods and ideas that enable a society to look and live beyond itself. The Arab invasions and presence of the Mediterranean area during a crucial part of the early Middle Ages created the essential conditions for the birth of Western Europe as a distinctive cultural entity. Arab belligerency forced Western Europeans to fall back on their own distinctive resources and to develop their peculiar Germanic and Greco-Roman heritage into a unique culture. The Arabs accomplished this by diverting the attention and energies of the Eastern empire at a time of Frankish and Lombard ascendancy (thereby preventing Byzantine expansion into the West) and by greatly reducing Western navigation of the Mediterranean (thereby closing off much Eastern trade and cultural influence).

As Western shipping was reduced in the Mediterranean, coastal urban centers declined. Populations that would otherwise have been engaged in trade-related work in the cities moved in great numbers into interior regions, there to work the farms of the great landholders. The latter needed their labor and welcomed the new emigrants, who were even more in need of the employment and protection that the landholders could provide. A mild serfdom evolved both for the new landless emigrants and for the great mass of peasants on the land (perhaps 90 per cent of the population). There were free peasants, who owned their own land, and peasants who became "serfs" by surrendering their land to a more powerful landholder in exchange for assistance in time of dire need, like during periods of prolonged crop failure or foreign invasion. Basically, serfdom meant for the peasant a status of servitude to the economically and politically stronger, who provided land and dwelling in exchange for labor and goods.

As the demand for agricultural products diminished in the great urban centers and as traffic between town and country was reduced, the farming belts became regionally insular and self-contained. Production and travel adjusted to local needs, and there was little incentive for bold experimentation and exploration. The domains of the great landholders became the basic social and political units of society, and local barter economies sprang up within them. In these developments were sown the seeds of what would later come to be known as manorial and feudal society. The former was an ordering of peasant society in which land and labor were divided among lords, peasants, and serfs for the profit of some and the protection of all, whereas the latter was an ordering of aristocratic society in which a special class of warrior knights emerged as guarantors of order.

The Developing Roman Church

One institution remained firmly entrenched within the cities during the Arab invasions: the Christian church. The Church had long modeled its own structure on that of the imperial Roman administration. Like the latter, it was a centralized, hierarchical government with strategically placed "viceroys" (bishops) in European cities who looked for spiritual direction to their leader, the bishop of Rome. As the Western empire crumbled and populations emigrated to the countryside after the barbarian and Arab invasions, local bishops and cathedral chapters filled the vacuum of authority left by the removal of Roman governors. The local cathedral became the center of urban life and the local bishop the highest authority for those who remained in the cities—just as in Rome, on a larger and more fateful scale, the pope took control of the city as the Western emperors gradually departed and died out. Left to its own devices, Western Europe soon discovered that the Christian church was a rich repository of Roman administrative skills and classical culture.

The Christian church had been graced with special privileges, great lands, and wealth by Emperor Constantine and his successors. In 313, Constantine issued the Edict of Milan, giving Christians legal standing and a favored status within the empire. In 391, Emperor Theodosius I (CA. 379–395), after whose death the empire would again be divided into eastern and western parts, raised Christianity to the official religion of the empire. Both Theodosius and his predecessors acted as much for political effect as out of religious conviction; in 313, Christians composed about one fifth of the population of the empire and unquestionably composed the strongest group of the competing religions. Mithraism, the religion popular among army officers and restricted to males, was its main rival.

Challenged to become a major political force, the Church survived the period of Germanic and Arab invasions as a somewhat spiritually weakened and compromised institution, yet it was still a most potent civilizing and unifying force. It had a religious message of providential purpose and individual worth that could give solace and meaning to life at its worst. The Western church also had a ritual of baptism and a creedal confession that united people beyond the traditional barriers of social class, education, and sex. After the Germanic and Arab invasions, the Church alone possessed an effective hierarchical administration, scattered throughout the old empire, staffed by the best-educated minds in Europe, and centered in emperorless Rome. The Church also enjoyed the services of growing numbers of monks, who were not only loyal to its mission but also objects of great popular respect. Monastic culture proved again and again to be the peculiar strength of the Church during the Middle Ages.

MONASTIC CULTURE. Monks were originally hermits, who withdrew from society to pursue a more perfect way of life. They were inspired by the Christian ideal of a life of complete self-denial in imitation of Christ, who had denied himself even unto death. The popularity of monasticism began to grow as Roman persecution of Christians waned in the mid-third century. Embracing the biblical "counsels of perfection" (chastity, poverty, and obedience), the monastic life became the purest form of religious practice.

Anthony of Egypt (CA. 251–356), the father of hermit monasticism, was inspired by Jesus' command to the rich young man: "If you will be perfect, sell all that you have, give it to the poor, and follow me" (Matthew 19:21). Anthony went into the desert to pray and work,

setting an example followed by hundreds in Egypt, Syria, and Palestine in the fourth and fifth centuries. This hermit monasticism was soon joined by the development of communal monasticism. In southern Egypt in the first quarter of the fourth century, Pachomius (CA. 286–346) organized monks into a highly regimented common life. Such monastic communities grew to contain a thousand or more inhabitants, little "cities of God," separated from the collapsing Roman and the nominal Christian world. Basil the Great (329–379) popularized communal monasticism throughout the East, providing a rule that lessened the asceticism of Pachomius and directed monks beyond their enclaves of perfection into such social services as caring for orphans, widows, and the infirm in surrounding communities.

Athanasius (CA. 293–373) and Martin of Tours (CA. 315–CA. 399) introduced monasticism into the west, where the teaching of John Cassian (CA. 360–435) and Jerome (CA. 340–420) helped shape its basic values and practices. The great organizer of Western monasticism was Benedict of Nursia (CA. 480–547). In 529, Benedict founded the mother monastery of the Benedictines at Monte Cassino in Italy, the foundation on which all Western monasticism has been built. Benedict also wrote a sophisticated *Rule for Monasteries*, a comprehensive plan for every activity of the monks, even detailing how they were to sleep. The monastery was hierarchically organized and directed by an abbot, whose command was beyond question. Periods of de-

The rule of St. Benedict, followed by most medieval monasteries, required that the monks spend a third of their day at manual labor. This served to make the monastery self-sufficient and self-contained. Here monks are shown doing a variety of agricultural tasks. [Vincent Virga Archives.]

votion (about four hours each day were set aside for the "work of God," that is, regular prayers and liturgical activities) and study alternated with manual labor—a program that permitted not a moment's idleness and carefully promoted the religious, intellectual, and physical well-being of the monks.

THE DOCTRINE OF PAPAL PRIMACY.

Constantine and his successors, especially the Eastern emperors, ruled religious life with an iron hand and consistently looked on the Church as little more than a department of the state. Such "Caesaropapism"—Caesar acting as pope—involved the emperor directly in the Church's affairs, even to the point of enabling him to play the theologian and allowing him to impose conciliar solutions on doctrinal quarrels. State control of religion was the original Church–State relation in the West.

The bishops of Rome by contrast never accepted such intervention and opposed it in every way they could. In the fifth and sixth centuries, taking advantage of imperial weakness and distraction, they developed for their own defense the weaponry of the doctrine of "papal primacy." This teaching raised the Roman pontiff to an unassailable supremacy within the Church when it came to defining Church doctrine: it also put him in a position to make important secular claims. The doctrine was destined to occasion repeated conflicts between Church and State, pope and emperor, throughout the Middle Ages.

THE DIVISION OF CHRISTENDOM.

The division of Christendom into Eastern and Western churches has its roots in the early Middle Ages. From the start, there was the difference in language (Greek in the East, Latin in the West) and culture. A combination of Greek, Roman, and oriental elements had shaped Byzantine culture. The strong mystical orientation to the next world also caused the Eastern church to submit more passively than Western popes could ever do to Caesaropapism.

As in the West, Eastern church organization closely followed that of the secular state. A "patriarch" ruled over "metropolitans" and "archbishops" in the cities and provinces, and they, in turn, ruled over bishops, who stood as authorities over the local clergy.

Contrary to the evolving Western tradition of universal clerical celibacy, which Western monastic culture encouraged, the Eastern church permitted the marriage of secular priests, while strictly forbidding bishops to marry. The Eastern church also used leavened bread in the Eucharist, contrary to the Western custom of using unleavened bread. Also unliked by the West was the tendency of the Eastern church to compromise doctrinally with the politically powerful Arian and Monophysite Christians. In the background were also conflicting political claims over jurisdiction over the newly converted areas in the north Balkans.

Beyond these issues, the major factors in the religious break between East and West revolved around questions of doctrinal authority. The Eastern church

Pope Gelasius I Declares the "Weightiness" of Priestly Authority

Some see this famous letter of Pope Gelasius to Emperor Anastasius I in 494 as an extreme statement of papal supremacy. Others believe it is a balanced, moderate statement that recognizes the independence of both temporal and spiritual power and seeks their close cooperation, not the domination of Church over state.

There are two powers, august Emperor, by which this world is chiefly ruled, namely, the sacred authority of the priests and the royal power. Of these, that of the priests is the more weighty, since they have to render an account for even the kings of men in the divine judgment. You are also aware, dear son [emperor], that while you are permitted honorably to rule over humankind, yet in things divine you bow your head humbly before the leaders of the clergy and await from their hands the means of your salvation. In the reception and proper disposition of the heavenly mysteries you recognize that you should be subordinate rather than superior to the religious order, and that in these matters you depend on their judgment rather than wish to force them to follow your will. [And] if the ministers of religion, recognizing the supremacy granted you from heaven in matters affecting the public order, obey your laws, lest otherwise they obstruct the course of secular affairs . . . , with what readiness should you not yield them obedience to whom is assigned the dispensing of the sacred mysteries of religion? ❏

James Harvey Robinson (ed.), *Readings in European History*, Vol. 1 (Boston: Athenaeum, 1904), pp. 72–73.

put more stress on the authority of the Bible and of the ecumenical councils of the Church than on the counsel and decrees of the bishop of Rome. The councils and Holy Scripture were the ultimate authorities in the definition of Christian doctrine. The claims of Roman popes to a special primacy of authority on the basis of the apostle Peter's commission from Jesus in Matthew 16:18 ("Thou art Peter, and upon this rock I will build my church") were completely unacceptable to the East, where the independence and autonomy of national churches held sway. This basic issue of authority in matters of faith lay behind the mutual excommunication of Pope Nicholas I and Patriarch Photius in the ninth century and that of Pope Leo IX and Patriarch Michael Cerularius in 1054. After this time one distinguished between the Roman Catholic and the Orthodox Christian churches.

A second major issue in the separation of the two churches was the Western addition of the *filioque* clause to the Nicene-Constantinopolitan Creed—an anti-Arian move that made the Holy Spirit proceed "also from the Son" (*filioque)* as well as from the Father. This addition made clear the Western belief that Christ was "fully substantial with God the Father" and not a lesser being.

The final and most direct issue in the religious division of Christendom was the iconoclastic controversy of the first half of the eighth century. After 725, the Eastern emperor, Leo III (717–740), attempted to force Western popes to abolish the use of images in their churches. In opposing icons and images in the churches, the Eastern church was influenced by Islam. This stand met fierce official and popular resistance in the West, where images were greatly cherished.

Leo's direct challenge of the pope came almost simultaneously with still another aggressive act against the Western church: attacks by the heretofore docile Lombards of northern Italy. Assailed by both the emperor and the Lombards, the pope in Rome seemed surely doomed. But there has not been a more resilient and enterprising institution in Western history than the Roman papacy. Since the pontificate of Gregory the Great, Roman popes had eyed the Franks of northern Gaul as Europe's ascendant power and their surest protector. Imperial and Lombard aggression against the Roman pope in the first half of the eighth century provided the occasion for the most fruitful political alliance of the Middle Ages. In 754, Pope Stephen II (752–757) enlisted Pepin III and his Franks as defenders of the church against the Lombards and as a Western counterweight to the Eastern emperor. This marriage of religion and politics created a new Western church and empire: it also determined much of the course of Western history into modern times.

The Kingdom of the Franks

Merovingians and Carolingians: From Clovis to Charlemagne

A warrior chieftain, Clovis (CA. 466–511), a convert to Orthodox Christianity around 496, made the Franks and their first ruling family, the Merovingians, named for an early leader of the family Merovich, a significant force in Western Europe. Clovis and his successors subdued the pagan Burgundians and the Arian Visigoths and established within ancient Gaul the kingdom of the Franks. The Franks were a broad belt of people scattered throughout modern Belgium, the Netherlands, and western Germany, whose loyalties remained strictly tribal and local. The Merovingians attempted to govern this sprawling kingdom by pacts with landed nobility and by the creation of the royal office of count. The most persistent problem of medieval political history was the competing claims of the "one" and the "many." On the one hand, the king struggled for a centralized government and transregional loyalty, and on the other, powerful local magnates strove to preserve their regional autonomy and traditions.

The Merovingian counts were men without possessions to whom the king gave great lands in the expectation that they would be, as the landed aristocrats often were not, loyal officers of the kingdom. But like local aristocrats, the Merovingian counts also let their immediate self-interests gain the upper hand. Once established in office for a period of time, they too became territorial rulers in their own right, with the result that the Frankish kingdom progressively fragmented into independent regions and tiny principalities. This centrifugal tendency was further assisted by the Frankish custom of dividing the kingdom equally among the king's legitimate male heirs.

Rather than purchasing allegiance and unity within the kingdom, the Merovingian largess simply occasioned the rise of competing magnates and petty tyrants, who became laws unto themselves within their regions. By the seventh century, the Frankish king existed more in title than in effective executive power. Real power came to be concentrated in the office of the *mayor of the palace*, who was the spokesman at the king's court for the great landowners of the three regions into which the Frankish kingdom was divided: Neustria, Austrasia, and Burgundy. Through this office, the Carolingian dynasty rose to power.

The Carolingians (from Carolus, Charles, after Charlemagne, Charles the Great) controlled the office of the mayor of the palace from the ascent to that post of Pepin I of Austrasia (D. 639) until 751, at which time the Carolingians, with the enterprising connivance of the pope, simply expropriated the Frankish crown. Pepin II (D. 714) ruled in fact if not in title over the Frankish kingdom. His illegitimate son, Charles Martel ("the Hammer"; D. 741), created a great cavalry by bestowing lands known as *benefices* or *fiefs* on powerful nobles, who, in return, agreed to be ready to serve as the king's army. It was such an army that checked the Arab probings on the western front at Tours in 732—an important battle that helped to secure the borders of Western Europe.

The fiefs so generously bestowed by Charles Martel to create his army came in large part from landed property that he usurped from the church. His alliance with the landed aristocracy in this grand manner permitted the Carolingians to have some measure of political success where the Merovingians had failed. The Carolingians created counts almost entirely out of the landed nobility from which the Carolingians themselves had risen. The Merovingians, in contrast, had tried to compete directly with these great aristocrats by raising the landless to power. By playing to strength rather than challenging it, the Carolingians strengthened themselves, at least for the short term. Because the Church was by this time completely dependent on the protection of the Franks against the Eastern emperor and the Lombards, it gave little thought at this time to the fact that its savior had been created in part with lands to which it held claim. Later, the Franks partially compensated the Church for these lands.

THE FRANKISH CHURCH. The Church came to play a large and initially quite voluntary role in the Frankish government. By Carolingian times, monasteries were a dominant force. Their intellectual achievements made them respected repositories of culture. Their religious teaching and example imposed order on surrounding populations. Their relics and rituals made them magical shrines to which pilgrims came in great numbers. And, thanks to their many gifts and internal discipline and industry, many had become very profitable farms and landed estates, their abbots rich and powerful magnates. By Merovingian times, the higher clergy were already employed in tandem with counts as royal agents. It was the policy of the Carolingians, perfected by Charles Martel and his successor, Pepin III ("the Short"; D. 768), to use the Church to pacify conquered neighboring tribes—Frisians, Thüringians, Bavarians, and especially the Franks' archenemies, the Saxons.

Conversion to Nicene Christianity became an integral part of the successful annexation of conquered lands and people; the cavalry broke their bodies, while the clergy won their hearts and minds. The Anglo-Saxon missionary Saint Boniface (born Wynfrith; CA. 680–754) was the most important of the German clergy who served Carolingian kings in this way. Christian bishops in missionary districts and elsewhere became lords, appointed by and subject to the king—an ominous integration of secular and religious policy in which lay the seeds of the later Investiture Controversy of the eleventh and twelfth centuries.

The Church served more than Carolingian territorial expansion. Pope Zacharias (741–752) also sanctioned Pepin the Short's termination of the vestigial

A clerical scholar dictating to two of his scribes. Before the invention of the printing press at about 1450, manuscripts produced by scribes could only be duplicated, preserved, and passed on by laborious hand copying. Much of the painstaking copying was done by monks. [Bettman Archive.]

Merovingian dynasty and the Carolingian accession to outright kingship of the Franks. With the pope's public blessing, Pepin was proclaimed king by the nobility in council in 751, and the last of the Merovingians, the puppet king Childeric III, was hustled off to a monastery and dynastic oblivion. According to legend, Saint Boniface first anointed Pepin, thereby investing Frankish rule from the very start with a certain sacral character.

Zacharias' successor, Pope Stephen II (752–757), did not let Pepin forget the favor of his predecessor. Driven from Rome in 753 by the Lombards, Pope Stephen appealed directly to Pepin to cast out the invaders and to guarantee papal claims to central Italy, which was dominated at this time by the Eastern emperor. In 754, the Franks and the church formed an alliance against the Lombards and the Eastern emperor. Carolingian kings became the protectors of the Catholic church and thereby "kings by the grace of God." Pepin gained the title *patricius Romanorum*, "father-protector of the Romans," a title heretofore borne only by the representative of the Eastern emperor. In 755, the Franks defeated the Lombards and gave the pope the lands surrounding Rome, an event that created what came to be known as the *Papal States*. The lands earlier appropriated by Charles Martel and parceled out to the Frankish nobility were never returned to the Church, despite the appearance in this period of a most enterprising fraudulent document designed to win their return, the *Donation of Constantine* (written between 750 and 800), which, however, was never universally accepted in the West. This imperial parchment alleged that the Emperor Constantine had personally conveyed to the Church his palace and "all provinces and districts of the city of Rome and Italy and of the regions of the West" as permanent possessions. It was believed by many to be a genuine document until definitely exposed as a forgery in the fifteenth century by the Humanist Lorenzo Valla.

The papacy had looked to the Franks for an ally strong enough to protect it from the Eastern emperors. It is an irony of history that the Church found in the Carolingian dynasty a Western imperial government that drew almost as slight a boundary between State and Church, secular and religious policy, as did Eastern emperors. Although eminently preferable to Eastern domination, Carolingian patronage of the church proved in its own way to be no less Caesaropapist.

The False Donation of Constantine

Among the ways in which Roman ecclesiasts fought to free the Western church from political domination was to assert its own sovereign territorial and political rights. One of the most ambitious of such assertions was the so-called Donation of Constantine *(eighth century), a fraudulent document claiming papal succession to much of the old Roman Empire.*

The Emperor Caesar Flavius Constantinus in Christ Jesus . . . to the most Holy and blessed Father of fathers, Silvester, Bishop of the Roman city and Pope; and to all his successors, the pontiffs, who shall sit in the chair of blessed Peter to the end of time. . . . Grace, peace, love, joy, long-suffering, mercy . . . be with you all. . . . For we wish you to know . . . that we have forsaken the worship of idols . . . and have come to the pure Christian faith. . . .

To the holy apostles, my lords the most blessed Peter and Paul, and through them also to blessed Silvester, our father, supreme pontiff and universal pope of the city of Rome, and to the pontiffs, his successors, who to the end of the world shall sit in the seat of blessed Peter, we grant and by this present we convey our imperial Lateran palace, which is superior to and excels all palaces in the whole world; and further the diadem, which is the crown of our head; and the miter; as also the super-humeral, that is, the stole which usually surrounds our imperial neck; and the purple cloak and the scarlet tunic and all the imperial robes. . . .

And we decree that those most reverend men, the clergy of various orders serving the same most holy Roman Church, shall have that eminence, distinction, power and precedence, with which our illustrious senate is gloriously adorned; that is, they shall be made patricians and consuls. And we ordain that they shall also be adorned with other imperial dignities. Also we decree that the clergy of the sacred Roman Church shall be adorned as are the imperial officers. . . .

We convey to the oft-mentioned and most blessed Silvester, universal pope, both our palace, as preferment, and likewise all provinces, palaces and districts of the city of Rome and Italy and of the regions of the West; and, bequeathing them to the power and sway of him and the pontiffs, his successors, we do determine and decree that the same be placed at his disposal, and do lawfully grant it as a permanent possession to the holy Roman Church. ❑

Henry Bettenson (ed.), *Documents of the Christian Church* (New York: Oxford University Press, 1961), pp. 137–141.

The Reign of Charlemagne (768–814)

Charlemagne continued the role of his father, Pepin the Short, as papal protector in Italy and his policy of territorial conquest in the north. After King Desiderius and the Lombards of northern Italy were decisively defeated in 774, Charlemagne took upon himself the title "King of the Lombards" in Pavia. He widened the frontiers of his kingdom further by subjugating surrounding pagan tribes, foremost among whom were the Saxons, whom the Franks brutally Christianized and dispersed in small groups throughout Frankish lands. The Avars (a tribe related to the Huns) were practically annihilated, so that the Danubian plains were brought into the Frankish orbit. The Arabs were chased beyond the Pyrenees. By the time of his death on January 28, 814, Charlemagne's kingdom embraced modern France, Belgium, Holland, Switzerland, almost the whole of western Germany, much of Italy, a portion of Spain, and the island of Corsica—an area approximately equal to that of the modern Common Market (see Map 13.2).

THE NEW EMPIRE. Encouraged by his ambitious advisers, Charlemagne came to harbor imperial de-signs: he desired to be not only king of the Germans but a universal emperor as well. He had his sacred palace city, Aachen (in French, Aix-la-Chapelle), constructed in conscious imitation of the courts of the ancient Roman and of the contemporary Eastern emperors. Although permitted its distinctiveness, the Church was looked after by Charlemagne with a paternalism almost as great as that of any Eastern emperor. He used the Church above all to promote social stability and hierarchical order throughout the kingdom—as an aid in the creation of a great Frankish Christian empire. Frankish Christians were ceremoniously baptized, professed the Nicene Creed (with the *filioque* clause), and learned in church to revere Charlemagne.

Carolingian architecture. The cathedral church at Aachen (in modern West Germany) containing the chapel of Charlemagne. The original parts were constructed between 792 and 805. [Bildarchiv Foto Marburg.]

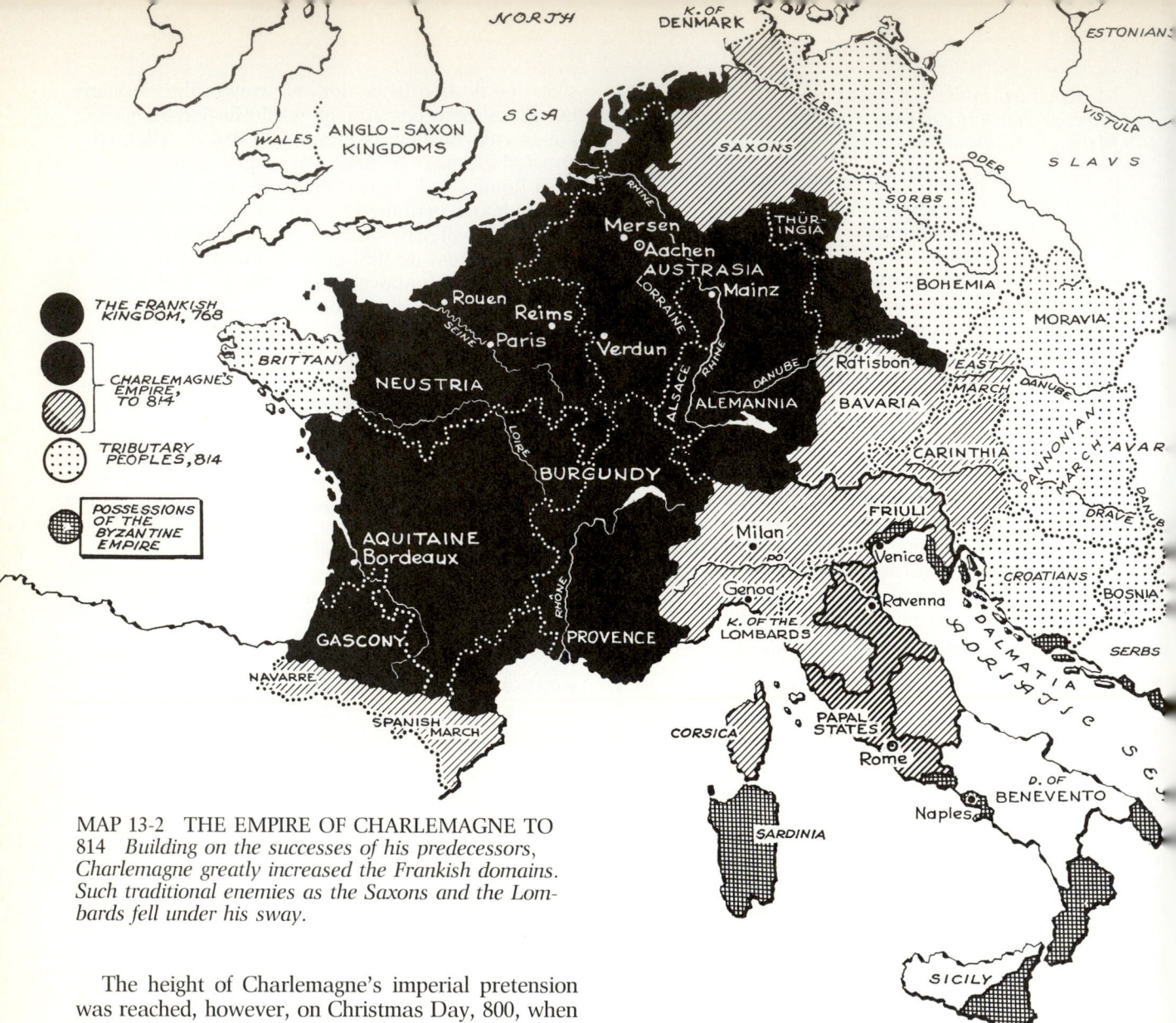

MAP 13-2   THE EMPIRE OF CHARLEMAGNE TO
814   *Building on the successes of his predecessors,
Charlemagne greatly increased the Frankish domains.
Such traditional enemies as the Saxons and the Lombards fell under his sway.*

The height of Charlemagne's imperial pretension
was reached, however, on Christmas Day, 800, when
Pope Leo III (795–816) crowned Charlemagne emperor. If the coronation benefited the Church, as it certainly did, it also served Charlemagne's imperial designs. Before Christmas Day, 800, Charlemagne had
been a minor Western potentate in the eyes of Eastern
emperors. After the coronation, Eastern emperors reluctantly recognized his new imperial dignity, and
Charlemagne even found it necessary to disclaim ambitions to rule as emperor over the East. Here began
what would come to be known as the Holy Roman
Empire, a revival, based in Germany, of the old
Roman Empire in the West.

THE NEW EMPEROR.   Charlemagne stood a ma-
jestic six feet, three and one-half inches tall—a fact
secured when his tomb was opened and exact mea-
surements were taken in 1861. He was nomadic, ever

ready for a hunt. Informal and gregarious, he insisted
on the presence of friends even when he bathed and
was widely known for his practical jokes, lusty good
humor, and warm hospitality. Aachen was a festive
palace city to which people and gifts came from all
over the world. In 802, Charlemagne even received
from the caliph of Baghdad, Harun-al-Rashid, a white
elephant, the transport of which across the Alps was
as great a wonder as the creature itself.

Charlemagne had five official wives in succession,
possessed many mistresses and concubines, and sired
numerous children. This connubial variety created
special problems. His oldest son by his first marriage,
Pepin, jealous of the attention shown by his father to

the sons of his second wife, and fearing the loss of paternal favor, joined with noble enemies in a conspiracy against his father. Pepin ended his life in confinement in a monastery after the plot was exposed.

PROBLEMS OF GOVERNMENT. Charlemagne governed his kingdom through counts, of whom there were perhaps as many as 250. They were strategically located within the administrative districts into which the kingdom was divided. In Carolingian practice, the count tended to be a local magnate, one who already possessed the armed might and the self-interest to enforce the will of a generous king. He had three main duties: to maintain a local army loyal to the king, to collect tribute and dues, and to administer justice throughout his district.

This last responsibility he undertook through a district law court known as the *mallus*. The *mallus* assessed *wergeld*, or the compensation to be paid to an injured party in a feud, the most popular way of settling grievances and ending hostilities. In very difficult cases, where guilt or innocence was unclear, recourse was often had to judicial duels or to such "divine" judgments as the length of time it took a defendant's hand to heal after immersion in boiling water. In the ordeal by water, another divine test when human judgment was stymied, a defendant was thrown with his hands and feet bound into a river or pond that was first blessed by a priest; if he floated, he was pronounced guilty, because the pure water had obviously rejected him; if, however, the water received him and he sank, then he was deemed innocent.

As in Merovingian times, many counts used their official position and new judicial powers to their own advantage, becoming little despots within their districts. As the strong were made stronger, they became more independent. They looked on the land grants with which they were paid as hereditary positions rather than generous royal donations—a development that began to fragment Charlemagne's kingdom. Charlemagne tried to supervise his overseers and improve local justice by creating special royal envoys known as *missi dominici*. These were lay and clerical agents (counts and archbishops and bishops) who made annual visits to districts other than their own. But their impact was only marginal. Permanent provincial governors, bearing the title of prefect, duke, or margrave, were created in what was still another attempt to manage the counts and to organize the outlying regions of the kingdom. But as these governors became established in their areas, they proved no less corruptible than the others.

Charlemagne never solved the problem of a loyal bureaucracy. Ecclesiastical agents proved no better than secular ones in this regard. Landowning bishops had not only the same responsibilities but also the same secular lifestyles and aspirations as the royal counts. Save for their attendance to the liturgy and to church prayers, they were largely indistinguishable from the lay nobility. Capitularies, or royal decrees, discouraged the more outrageous behavior of the clergy. But Charlemagne also sensed, rightly as the Gregorian reform of the eleventh century would prove, a danger to royal government in the emergence of a distinctive and reform-minded class of ecclesiastical landowners. Charlemagne purposefully treated his bishops as he treated his counts, that is, as vassals who served at the king's pleasure.

ALCUIN AND THE CAROLINGIAN RENAISSANCE. Charlemagne accumulated a great deal of wealth in the form of loot and land from conquered tribes. He used a substantial part of this booty to attract Europe's best scholars to Aachen, where they developed court culture and education. By making scholarship materially as well as intellectually rewarding, Charlemagne attracted such scholars as Theodulf of Orleans, Angilbert, his own biographer Einhard, and the renowned Anglo-Saxon master Alcuin of York (735–804), who, at almost fifty, became director of the king's palace school in 782. Alcuin brought classical and Christian learning to Aachen and was handsomely rewarded for his efforts with several monastic estates, including that of Saint Martin of Tours, the wealthiest in the kingdom.

Although Charlemagne also appreciated learning for its own sake, this grand palace school was not created simply for love of antiquity. Charlemagne intended it to upgrade the administrative skills of the clerics and officials who staffed the royal bureaucracy. By preparing the sons of nobles to run the religious and secular offices of the realm, court scholarship served kingdom building. The school provided basic instruction in the seven liberal arts, with special concentration on grammar, logic, and mathematics, that is, training in reading, writing, speaking, and sound reasoning—the basic tools of bureaucracy. A clearer style of handwriting—the Carolingian minuscule—and accurate Latin appeared in the official documents. Lay literacy increased. Through personal correspondence and visitations, Alcuin created a genuine, if limited, community of scholars and clerics at court and did much to infuse the highest administrative levels with a sense of comradeship and common purpose.

A modest renaissance or rebirth of antiquity occurred in the palace school as scholars collected and preserved ancient manuscripts for a more curious posterity. Alcuin worked on a correct text of the Bible and made editions of the works of Gregory the Great and the monastic *Rule* of Saint Benedict. These scholarly activities aimed at concrete reforms and served official efforts to bring uniformity to Church law and liturgy, to educate the clergy, and to improve moral life within the monasteries.

THE MANOR AND SERFDOM. The agrarian economy of the Middle Ages was organized and controlled through village farms known as *manors*. Here peasants labored as farmers in subordination to a lord, that is, a more powerful landowner who gave them land and a dwelling in exchange for their services and a portion of their crops. That part of the land farmed by the peasants for the lord was the *demense*, on average about one quarter to one third of the arable land. All crops grown there were harvested for the lord.

The peasants were treated differently according to their personal status and the size of their property, all in strict accordance with custom; indeed, a social hierarchy existed among the peasantry. When a *freeman*, that is, a peasant with his own modest allodial or hereditary property (property free from the claims of a feudal overlord) became a serf by surrendering this property to a greater landowner in exchange for his protection and assistance, the freeman received it back from the lord with a clear definition of economic and legal rights that protected the freeman's self-interest.

Although the land was no longer his property, he had full possession and use of it, and the number of services and the amount of goods to be supplied the lord were often carefully spelled out. On the other hand, peasants who entered the service of a lord without any real property to bargain with (perhaps some farm implements and a few animals) ended up as *unfree* serfs and were much more vulnerable to the lord's demands, often spending up to three days a week working the lord's fields. Truly impoverished peasants who lived and worked on the manor as serfs had the lowest status and were the least protected. Weak serfs often fled to a monastery rather than continue their servitude, and therefore this avenue of escape was eventually closed by law.

By the time of Charlemagne, the moldboard plow—which was especially needed in northern Europe where the soil was heavy—and the three-field system of land cultivation were coming into use. These developments improved agricultural productivity. Unlike the older "scratch" plow, which crisscrossed the field with only slight penetration, the moldboard cut deep into the soil and turned it to form a ridge, providing a natural drainage system for the field as well as permitting the deep planting of seeds. Unlike the earlier two-

The invention of the moldboard plow greatly improved farming. The heavy plow cut deeply into the ground and furrowed it. This illustration (CA.1340) also shows that the traction harness, which lessened the strangulating effect of the yoke on the animals, had not yet been adopted. Indeed, one of the oxen seems to be on the verge on choking. [Add. MS. 42130, f. 170. Reproduced by permission of the British Board, London.]

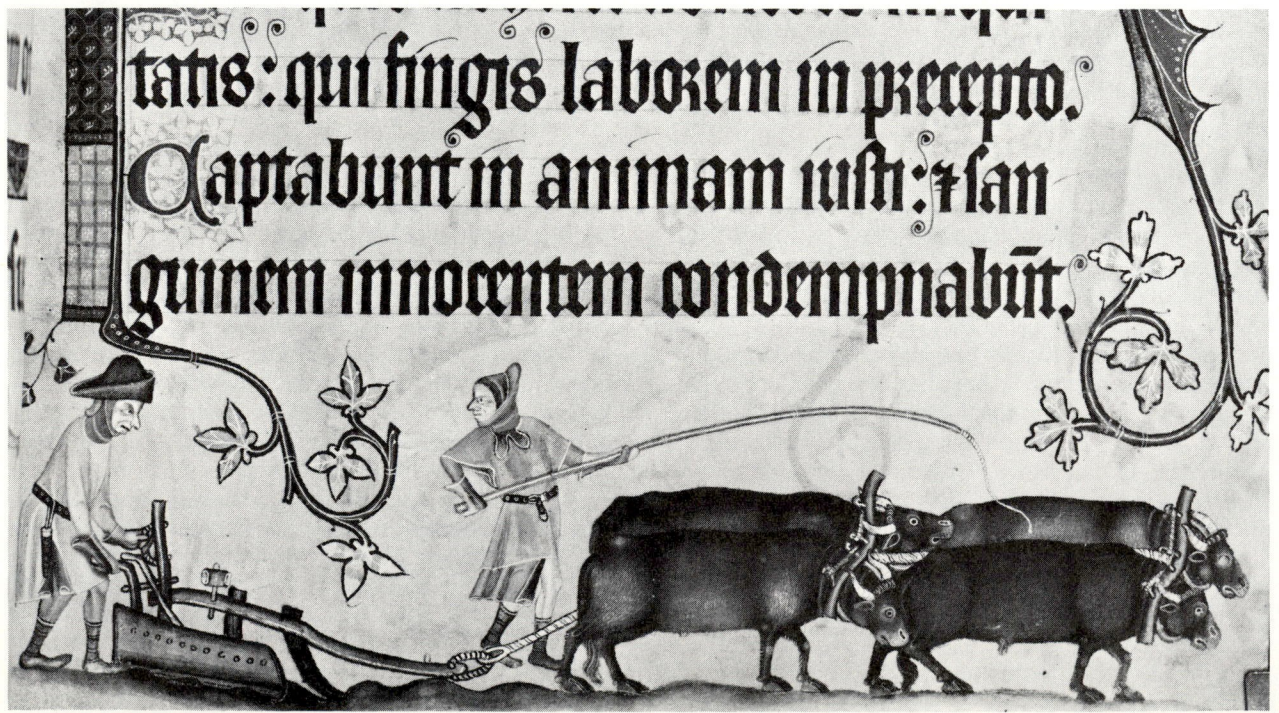

field system of crop rotation, which simply alternated fallow with planted fields each year, the three-field system increased the amount of cultivated land by leaving only one third fallow in a given year. It also better adjusted crops to seasons. In winter, one field was planted with winter crops of wheat or rye; in the summer, a second field was planted with summer crops of oats, barley, and lentils; and the third field was left fallow, to be planted in its turn with winter and summer crops.

Serfs were subject to so-called dues in kind: firewood for cutting the lord's wood, sheep for grazing their sheep on the lord's land, and the like. In this way, the lord, by furnishing shacks and small plots of land from his vast domain, created an army of servants who provided him with everything from eggs to boots. The discontent of the commoners is witnessed by the high number of recorded escapes. An astrological calendar from the period even marks the days most favorable for escaping. Escaped serfs roamed the land as beggars and vagabonds, searching for new and better masters.

RELIGION AND THE CLERGY. As owners of the churches on their lands, the lords had the right to raise chosen serfs to the post of parish priest, placing them in charge of the churches on the lords' estates. Although Church law directed the lord to set a serf free before the serf entered the clergy, lords were reluctant to do this and risk thereby a possible later challenge to their jurisdiction over the ecclesiastical property with which the serf, as priest, was invested. Lords rather preferred a "serf priest," one who not only said the mass on Sundays and holidays but who also continued to serve his lord during the week, waiting on the lord's table and tending his steeds. Like Charlemagne with his bishops, Frankish lords cultivated a docile parish clergy.

The ordinary people looked to religion for comfort and consolation. They considered baptism and confession of the Creed a surety of future salvation. They baptized their children, attended mass, tried to learn the Lord's Prayer, and received extreme unction from the priest as death approached. This was all probably done with more awe and simple faith than understanding. Religious instruction in the meaning of Christian doctrine and practice remained at a bare minimum, and the local priests on the manors were no better educated than their congregations. People understandably became particularly attached in this period to the more tangible veneration of relics and saints.

Charlemagne shared many of the religious beliefs of his ordinary subjects. He collected and venerated relics, made pilgrimages to Rome, frequented the church of Saint Mary in Aachen several times a day, and directed in his last will and testament that all but a frac-tion of his great treasure be spent to endow masses and prayers for his departed soul.

The Breakup of the Carolingian Kingdom

In the last years of his life, an ailing Charlemagne knew that his empire was ungovernable. The seeds of dissolution lay in regionalism, that is, the determination of each region, no matter how small, to look first—and often only—to its own self-interest. Despite his considerable skill and resolution, Charlemagne's realm became too fragmented among powerful regional magnates. Although they were his vassals, these same men were also landholders and lords in their own right. They knew that their sovereignty lessened as Charlemagne's increased and accordingly became reluctant royal servants. In feudal society, a direct relationship existed between physical proximity to authority and loyalty to authority. Local people obeyed local lords more readily than they obeyed a glorious but distant king. Charlemagne had been forced to recognize and even to enhance the power of regional magnates in order to win needed financial and military support. But as in the Merovingian kingdom so also in the Carolingian, the tail came increasingly to wag the dog. Charlemagne's major attempt to enforce subordination to royal dictates and a transregional discipline—through the institution of the missi dominici—proved ultimately unsuccessful.

LOUIS THE PIOUS. Carolingian kings did not give up easily. Charlemagne's only surviving son and successor was Louis the Pious (814–840), so-called because of his close alliance with the Church and his promotion of puritanical reforms. Louis had three sons by his first wife. According to Salic or Germanic law, a ruler partitioned his kingdom equally among his surviving sons. Louis, who saw himself as an emperor and no mere German king, recognized that a tripartite kingdom would hardly be an empire and acted early in his reign, in the year 817, to break this legal tradition. This he did by making his eldest son, Lothar (d. 855), coregent and sole imperial heir. To Lothar's brothers, he gave important but much lesser appanages, or assigned hereditary lands: Pepin (d. 838) became king of Aquitaine, and Louis "the German" (d. 876) became king of Bavaria, over the eastern Franks.

In 823, Louis' second wife, Judith of Bavaria, bore him still a fourth son, Charles, later called "the Bald" (d. 877). Mindful of Frankish law and custom and determined that her son should receive more than just a nominal inheritance, the queen incited the brothers Pepin and Louis to war against Lothar, who fled for refuge to the pope. More important, Judith was instrumental in persuading Louis to reverse his earlier decision and to divide the kingdom equally among his four living sons. As their stepmother and the young Charles rose in their father's favor, the three older brothers feared still further reversals, so they decided to act against their father. Supported by the pope, they joined forces and defeated their father in a battle near Colmar (833).

As the bestower of crowns upon emperors, the pope had an important stake in the preservation of the revived Western empire and the imperial title, both of which Louis' belated agreement to an equal partition of his kingdom threatened to undo. The pope condemned Louis and restored Lothar to his original inheritance. But Lothar's regained imperial dignity only stirred anew the resentments of his brothers, including his stepbrother, Charles, who resumed their war against him.

THE TREATY OF VERDUN AND ITS AFTERMATH. Peace finally came to the heirs of Louis the Pious in 843 in the Treaty of Verdun. But this agreement also brought about the disaster that Louis had originally feared: the great Carolingian empire was partitioned according to Frankish law into three equal parts, Pepin having died in 838. Lothar received a middle section, which came to be known as Lotharingia and embraced roughly modern Holland, Belgium, Switzerland, Alsace-Lorraine, and Italy. Charles the Bald received the western part of the kingdom, or roughly modern France. And Louis the German came into the eastern part, or roughly modern Germany (see Map 13.3). Although Lothar retained the imperial title, the universal empire of Charlemagne and Louis

the Pious ceased to exist after Verdun. Not until the sixteenth century, with the election in 1519 of Charles I of Spain as the Holy Roman Emperor Charles V, would the Western world again see a kingdom so vast as Charlemagne's.

The Treaty of Verdun, the oldest written document in French, proved to be only the beginning of Carolingian fragmentation. When Lothar died in 855, his middle kingdom was divided equally among his three surviving sons. This partition of the partition left the middle, or imperial, kingdom much smaller and weaker than those of Louis the German and Charles the Bald. Henceforth, Western Europe saw an eastern and a western Frankish kingdom—roughly Germany versus France—at war over the fractionalized middle kingdom, a contest that has continued into modern times.

When Charles the Bald died in 877, both the papal and the imperial thrones fell on especially hard times. Each became a pawn in the hands of powerful Italian and German magnates, respectively. Neither pope nor emperor knew dignity and power again until a new Western imperial dynasty—the Ottonians—attained dominance during the reign of Otto I (962–973). It is especially with reference to this juncture in European history—the last quarter of the ninth and the first half of the tenth century—that one may speak with some justification of a "dark age."

Simultaneously with the internal political breakdown of the empire and the papacy came new barbarian attacks, set off probably by overpopulation and famine in northern Europe. The late ninth and tenth centuries saw successive waves of Normans (Northmen), better known as Vikings, from Scandinavia;

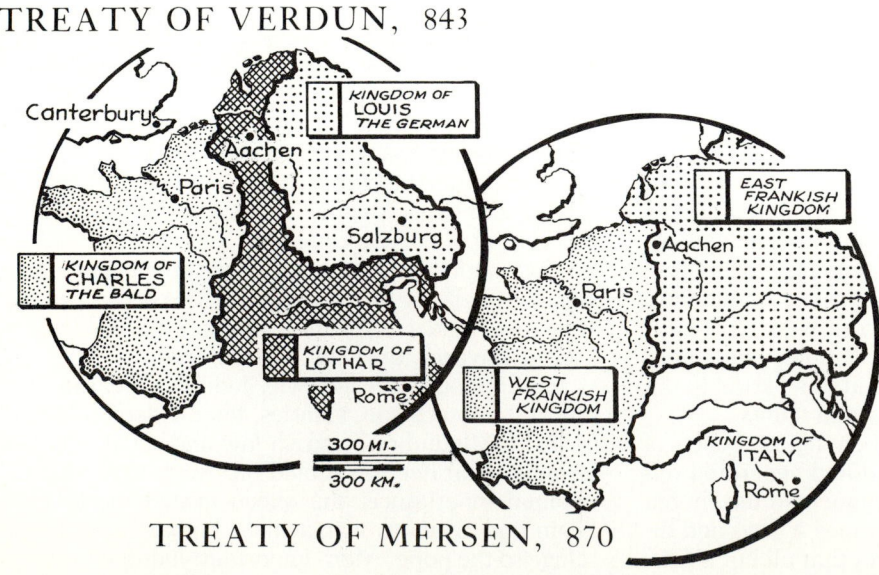

TREATY OF VERDUN, 843

TREATY OF MERSEN, 870

MAP 13-3 THE TREATIES OF VERDUN AND MERSEN *The Treaty of Verdun divided the kingdom of Louis the Pious among his three feuding children: Charles the Bald, Lothar, and Louis the German. After Lothar's death in 855 the middle kingdom was so weakened by division among his three sons that Charles the Bald and Louis the German divided it between themselves in the Treaty of Mersen in 870.*

Magyars, or Hungarians, the great horsemen from the eastern plains; and Muslims from the south (see Map 13.4). In the 880s, the Vikings penetrated to the imperial residence of Aachen and to Paris. Moving rapidly in ships and raiding coastal towns, they were almost impossible to defend against and kept western Europe on edge. The Franks built fortified towns and castles in strategic locations, which served as refuges. When they could, they bought off the invaders with outright grants of land (for example, Normandy) and payments of silver. In this period, local populations became more dependent than ever before on local strongmen for life, limb, and livelihood. This brute fact of life provided the essential precondition for the maturation of feudal society.

MAP 13-4   VIKING, MUSLIM, AND MAGYAR INVASIONS TO THE ELEVENTH CENTURY   *Western Europe was sorely beset by new waves of outsiders from the ninth to the eleventh century. From north, east, and south a stream of invading Vikings, Magyars, and Muslims brought the West at times to near collapse and of course gravely affected institutions within Europe.*

THE CAROLINGIAN DYNASTY (751–987)	
751	Pepin III "the Short" becomes king of the Franks
755	Franks drive Lombards out of central Italy; creation of Papal States
768–814	Charlemagne rules as king of the Franks
774	Charlemagne defeats Lombards in northern Italy
750–800	Donation of Constantine protests Frankish domination of Church
800	Pope Leo III crowns Charlemagne
814–840	Louis the Pious succeeds Charlemagne as "Emperor"
843	Treaty of Verdun partitions the Carolingian Empire
870	Treaty of Mersen further divides Carolingian Empire
875–950	New invasions by Vikings, Muslims, and Magyars
962	Ottonian dynasty succeeds Carolingian in Germany
987	Capetian dynasty succeeds Carolingian

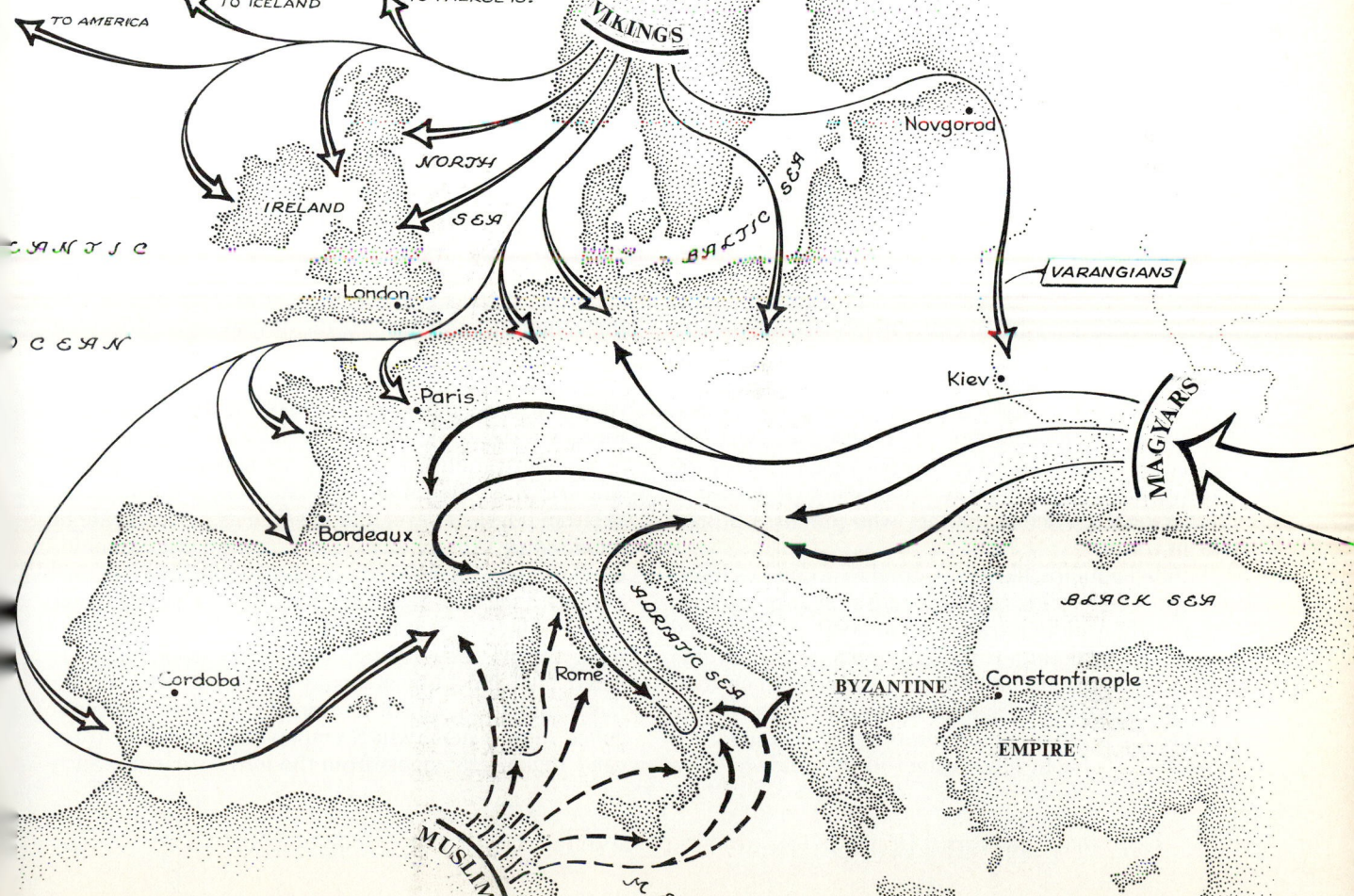

Feudal Society

A chronic absence of effective central government and the constant threat of famine, disease, and foreign invasion characterized the Middle Ages. *Feudal society* is a term used to describe the adjustment to this state of affairs as the weaker sought protection from the stronger. The term refers to the social, political, and economic system that emerged. The true lords and masters became those who could guarantee immediate protection from rapine and starvation.

A feudal society is a social order in which a regional prince or a local lord is dominant and the highest virtues are those of mutual trust and fidelity. In a feudal society, what people most need is the firm assurance that others can be depended on in time of dire need. It is above all a system of mutual rights and responsibilities.

During the early Middle Ages, the landed nobility became great lords who ruled over their domains as miniature kingdoms. They maintained their own armies and courts, regulated their area's tolls, and even minted their own coins. Large warrior groups of vassals were created by extensive bestowals of land, and they developed into a prominent professional military class with its own code of knightly conduct. In feudal society, most serfs docilely worked the land, the clergy prayed and gave counsel, and the nobility—both landed and vassal—maintained law and order by swift steed and sword.

Origins

The main features of feudal government can be found in the divisions and conflicts of Merovingian society. In the sixth and seventh centuries, there evolved the custom of individual freemen placing themselves under the protection of more powerful freemen. In this way, the latter built up armies and became local magnates, and the former solved the problem of simple survival. Freemen who so entrusted themselves to others were known as *ingenui in obsequio* ("freemen in a contractual relation of dependence"). Those who so gave themselves to the king were called *antrustiones*. All men of this type came to be described collectively as *vassi* ("those who serve"), from which evolved the term *vassalage*, meaning the placement of oneself in the personal service of another who promises protection in return.

Landed nobility, like kings, tried to acquire as many such vassals as they could, because military strength in the early Middle Ages lay in numbers. As it proved impossible to maintain these growing armies within the lord's own household, as was the original custom, or to support them by special monetary payments, the practice evolved of simply granting them land as a "tenement." Such land came to be known as a *benefice*, or a *fief*, and vassals were expected to dwell on it and maintain their steeds and other accoutrements of war in good order. Originally vassals, therefore, were little more than gangs-in-waiting.

Vassalage and the Fief

Vassalage involved "fealty" to the lord. To swear fealty was to promise to refrain from any action that might in any way threaten the lord's well-being and to perform personal services for him on his request. Chief among the expected services was military duty as a mounted knight. This could involve a variety of activities: a short or long military expedition, escort duty, standing castle guard, and/or the placement of one's own fortress at the lord's disposal, if the vassal was of such stature as to have one. Continuous bargaining and bickering occurred over the terms of service. Limitations were placed on the number of days a lord could require services from a vassal. In France in the eleventh century, about forty days of service per year were considered sufficient. It also became possible for vassals to buy their way out of military service by a monetary payment known as *scutage*. The lord, in turn, applied this payment to the hiring of mercenaries, who often proved more efficient than contract-conscious vassals. Beyond his military duty, the vassal was also expected to give the lord advice when he requested it and to sit as a member of his court when it was in session.

Beginning with the reign of Louis the Pious (814–840), bishops and abbots swore fealty and received their offices from the king as a benefice. The king formally "invested" these clerics in their offices during a special ceremony in which he presented them with a ring and a staff, the symbols of high spiritual office. Louis' predecessors had earlier confiscated Church lands with only modest and belated compensation to the Church in the form of a tithe required of all Frankish inhabitants. Long a sore point for the Church, the presumptuous practice of the lay investiture of the clergy provoked a world-shaking confrontation of Church and State in the eleventh and twelfth centuries, when reform-minded clergy rebelled against what they then believed to be involuntary clerical vassalage.

The lord's obligations to his vassals were very specific. He was, first of all, obligated to protect the vassal from physical harm and to stand as his advocate in public court. After fealty was sworn and homage paid, the lord provided for the vassal's physical maintenance by the bestowal of a benefice, or fief. The fief was simply the physical or material wherewithal to meet the vassal's military and other obligations. It could take the form of liquid wealth as well as the more common grant of real property. There were so-called money fiefs, which empowered a vassal to receive regular payments from the lord's treasury. Such

Bishop Fulbert Describes the Obligations of Vassal and Lord

Trust held the lord and vassal together. Their duties in this regard were carefully defined. Here are six general rules for vassal and lord, laid down by Bishop Fulbert of Chartres in a letter to William, Duke of Aquitaine, in 1020.

He who swears fealty to his lord ought always to have these six things in memory: what is harmless, safe, honorable, useful, easy, practicable. *Harmless*, that is to say, that he should not injure his lord in his body; *safe* that he should not injure him by betraying his secrets or the defenses upon which he relies for safety; *honorable*, that he should not injure him in his justice or in other matters that pertain to his honor; *useful*, that he should not injure him in his possessions; *easy* and *practicable*, that that good which his lord is able to do easily he make not difficult, nor that which is practicable he make not impossible to him.

That the faithful vassal should avoid these injuries is certainly proper, but not for this alone does he deserve his holding; for it is not sufficient to abstain from evil, unless what is good is done also. It remains, therefore, that in the same six things mentioned above he should faithfully counsel and aid his lord, if he wishes to be looked upon as worthy of his benefice and to be safe concerning the fealty which he has sworn.

The lord also ought to act toward his faithful vassal reciprocally in all these things. And if he does not do this, he will be justly considered guilty of bad faith, just as the former, if he should be detected in avoiding or consenting to the avoidance of his duties, would be perfidious and perjured. ❏

James Harvey Robinson (ed.), *Readings in European History*, Vol. 1 (Boston: Athenaeum, 1904). p. 184

---

fiefs were potentially quite devilish because they made it possible for one country to acquire vassals among the nobility of another. Normally, the fief consisted of a landed estate of anywhere from a few to several thousand acres. But it could also take the form of a castle.

In Carolingian times, a benefice, or fief, varied in size from one or more small villas to several *mansi*, which were agricultural holdings of twenty-five to forty-eight acres. The king's vassals are known to have received benefices of at least thirty and as many as two hundred such holdings, truly a vast estate. Royal vassalage with a benefice understandably came to be widely sought by the highest classes of Carolingian society. As a royal policy, however, it proved deadly to the king in the long run. Although Carolingian kings jealously guarded their rights over property granted in benefice to vassals, resident vassals were still free to dispose of their benefices as they pleased. Vassals of the king, strengthened by his donations, in turn created their own vassals. These, in turn, created still further vassals of their own—vassals of vassals of vassals—in a reverse pyramiding effect that had fragmented land and authority from the highest to the lowest levels by the late ninth century.

Fragmentation and Divided Loyalty

In addition to the fragmentation brought about by the multiplication of vassalage, effective occupation of the land led gradually to claims of hereditary possession. Hereditary possession became a legally recognized principle in the ninth century and laid the basis for claims to real ownership. Fiefs given as royal donations became hereditary possessions and, with the passage of time, in some instances even the real property of the possessor. Further, vassal engagements came to be multiplied in still another way as enterprising freemen sought to accumulate as much land as possible. One man actually became a vassal to several different lords. This development led in the ninth century to the concept of a "liege lord"—one master whom the vassal must obey even to the harm of the others, should a direct conflict among them arise.

The problem of loyalty was reflected not only in the literature of the period, with its praise of the virtues of honor and fidelity, but also in the ceremonial development of the very act of "commendation" by which a freeman became a vassal. In the mid-eighth century, an "oath of fealty" highlighted the ceremony. A vassal reinforced his promise of fidelity to the lord by swearing a special oath with his hand on a sacred relic or the Bible. In the tenth and eleventh centuries, paying homage to the lord involved not only the swearing of such an oath but also the placement of the vassal's hands between the lord's and the sealing of the ceremony with a kiss.

As the centuries passed, personal loyalty and service became quite secondary to the acquisition of property. The fief overshadowed fealty; the benefice became more important than vassalage; and freemen proved themselves prepared to swear allegiance to the highest bidder.

The Early Middle Ages in World Perspective

In Western Europe, the centuries between 400 and 1000 witnessed both the decline of European classical civilization and the birth of a new European civilization. Beginning with the fifth century, the barbarian invasions separated Western Europe culturally from its classical age. Continuing for centuries, this type of separation was unknown to other world cultures. Although some important works and concepts survived from antiquity in the West (due largely to the Christian church), Western civilization would for centuries be recovering its rich classical past in "renaissances" stretching into the sixteenth century. Out of the mixture of barbarian and surviving (or recovered) classical culture, Western civilization, as we know it today, was born. Aided and abetted by the Christian church, the Carolingians created a new imperial tradition. But early medieval society remained highly fragmented in the West, probably more so than anywhere else in the world, despite a certain common religious culture. Regions were organized into institutions designed primarily to ensure that all would be fed and cared for (manorialism) and that outside predators would be successfully repulsed (feudalism). It was not a time of great cultural ambition.

In China, particularly in the seventh and eighth centuries, the T'ang dynasty also searched for ways to secure Chinese borders against foreign expansion from Turkey and Tibet. As in Western Europe, religion and philosophy served and did not compete with the state (although this would change in the West after the twelfth century). Early medieval China was, however, far more cosmopolitan and politically unified than Western Europe. China was also centuries ahead in technology. Printing with movable type existed there by the tenth century, an invention the West did not see until the fifteenth century. Chinese rulers governed effectively far beyond their immediate centers of government. The T'ang dynasty held sway over their empire in a way Carolingian rulers could only dream of doing.

In Japan, the Yamato court (300–680), much like that of the Merovingians and Carolingians, struggled to unify and control the countryside. It was also aided by a religion friendly to royalty, Shinto. As in the West, a Japanese identity evolved through struggle and accommodation with outside cultures, especially with the Chinese, the dominant influence on Japan between the seventh and twelfth centuries. But foreign cultural influence, again as in the West, never managed to eradicate the indigenous culture. By the ninth century, a distinctive Sino-Japanese culture existed. But Japan, again like Western Europe, remained a fragmented land during these centuries, despite a certain alle-

giance and willingness to pay taxes to an imperial court. Throughout Japan, the basic unit of political control consisted of those same highly self-conscious and specially devoted armed knights we saw in Western Europe. A system of lordship and vassalage evolved around bands of local mounted warriors who were known as Samurai. Through this system, local order was maintained in Japan until the fifteenth century. Like the Merovingian and Carolingian courts, the Japanese court had to tolerate strong and independent regional rulers.

In the seventh century, Islam gave birth to still another powerful new international civilization, one that reached from India to Spain by 710. Consolidated by a line of successful caliphates between 750 and 945, Islam had divided by the tenth century into more exclusive (Kharijite and Shi'ite) and more inclusive (Sunni) factions. Again as in Western Europe, its central government had broken down. But the politically strong and culturally vibrant period of the high caliphate under the Umayyads and Abbasids (Islam's "classical" period) overlapped in time the Carolingian heyday, when Western Europe witnessed the birth of a new political empire and a little cultural Renaissance of its own.

Finally, in the centuries just before the awakening of Western European civilization, India enjoyed the high point of its civilization, the Gupta Age (320–467). While Western Europeans struggled for some degree of political and social order, a vocationally and socially limiting caste system neatly imposed order on Indian society from Brahmins to outcasts. Culture, religion, and politics flourished amid this unity.

All things considered, one may say that most of the world's great civilizations were reaching a peak, when that of the West was just coming to life. This may be attributed to the fact that the other world civilizations never experienced disruptions in their cultures by foreign invaders on the magnitude known in the West during the early Middle Ages.

Suggested Readings

M. BLOCH, *Feudal Society*, Vols. 1 and 2, trans. by L. A. Manyon (1971). A classic on the topic and as an example of historical study.

P. BROWN, *Augustine of Hippo: A Biography* (1967). Late antiquity seen through the biography of its greatest Christian thinker.

H. CHADWICK, *The Early Church* (1967). Among the best treatments of early Christianity.

R. H. C. DAVIS, *A History of Medieval Europe: From Constantine to St. Louis* (1972). Unsurpassed in clarity.

K. F. DREW (ed.), *The Barbarian Invasions: Catalyst of a New Order* (1970). Collection of essays that focuses the issues.

F. Dvornik, *Byzantium and the Roman Primacy* (1966).

H. Fichtenau, *The Carolingian Empire: The Age of Charlemagne*, trans. by Peter Munz (1964). Strongest on the political history of the era.

F. L. Ganshof, *Feudalism*, trans. by Philip Grierson (1964). The most profound brief analysis of the subject.

A. F. Havighurst (ed.), *The Pirenne Thesis: Analysis, Criticism, and Revision* (1958). Excerpts from the scholarly debate over the extent of Western trade in the East during the early Middle Ages.

D. Knowles, *Christian Monasticism* (1969). Sweeping survey with helpful photographs.

M. L. W. Laistner, *Thought and Letters in Western Europe, 500 to 900* (1957). Among the best surveys of early medieval intellectual history.

J. Leclercq, *The Love of Learning and the Desire for God: A Study of Monastic Culture*, trans. by Catherine Misrahi (1962). Lucid, delightful, absorbing account of the ideals of monks.

J. Leclercq, F. Vandenbroucke, and L. Bouyer, *The Spirituality of the Middle Ages* (1968). Perhaps the best survey of medieval Christianity, East and West, to the eve of the Protestant Reformation.

R. McKitternick, *The Frankish Kingdoms under the Carolingians, 751–987* (1983).

P. Munz, *The Age of Charlemagne* (1971). Penetrating social history of the period.

H. Pirenne, *A History of Europe, I: From the End of the Roman World in the West to the Beginnings of the Western States*, trans. by Bernhard Maill (1958). Comprehensive survey, with now-controversial views on the demise of Western trade and cities in the early Middle Ages.

S. Runciman, *Byzantine Civilization* (1970). Succinct, comprehensive account by a master.

P. Sawyer, *The Age of the Vikings* (1962). The best account.

O. von Simson, *Sacred Fortress: Byzantine Art and Statecraft in Ravenna* (1948).

R. W. Southern, *The Making of the Middle Ages* (1973). Originally published in 1953, but still a fresh account by an imaginative historian.

C. Stephenson, *Medieval Feudalism* (1969). Excellent short summary and introduction.

A. A. Vasiliev, *History of the Byzantine Empire 324–1453* (1952). The most comprehensive treatment in English.

H. Waddell (ed.), *The Desert Fortress* (1957).

S. F. Wemple, *Women in Frankish Society: Marriage and the Cloister 500–900* (1981). The impact of Christian marriage customs on the Franks.

L. White, Jr., *Medieval Technology and Social Change* (1962). Often fascinating account of how primitive technology changed life.

Although Gothic architecture was adopted throughout medieval Europe, it originated in France and enjoyed immense popularity there. Gothic was, in fact, often known in the Middle Ages as the "French style." Among the earliest examples of French Gothic architecture was the abbey church of Saint Denis near Paris, built by Abbot Suger between 1137–1144. This photograph shows the ribbed vaulting and pointed arches in the interior of the church. [Jean Roubier.]

358

14 The High Middle Ages (1000–1300)

The high Middle Ages mark a period of political expansion and consolidation and of intellectual flowering and synthesis. The noted medievalist Joseph Strayer has called it the age that saw "the full development of all the potentialities of medieval civilization."[1] Some even argue that as far as the development of Western institutions is concerned, this was a more creative period than the later Italian Renaissance and the German Reformation.

The high Middle Ages saw the borders of Western Europe largely secured against foreign invaders. Although there was intermittent Muslim aggression well into the sixteenth century, fear of assault from without diminished. A striking change occurred in the late eleventh and the twelfth century. Western Europe, which had for so long been the prey of foreign powers, became through the Crusades and foreign trade the feared hunter within both the Eastern and the Arab worlds.

During the high Middle Ages, "national" monarchies emerged in France, England, and Germany. Parliaments and popular assemblies representing the interests of the nobility, the clergy, and the townspeople also appeared at this time to secure local rights and customs against the claims of the developing nation-states. The foundations of modern representative institutions can be found in this period.

The high Middle Ages saw a revolution in agriculture that increased both food supplies and populations. This period witnessed a great revival of trade and commerce, the rise of towns, and the emergence of a "new rich" merchant class, the ancestors of modern capitalists. Urban culture and education flourished through the recovery of the writings of the ancient Greek philosophers, which was made possible by the

[1] *Western History in the Middle Ages—A Short History* (New York: Appleton-Century-Crofts, 1955), pp. 9, 127.

revival of Eastern trade and by way of Spanish contacts with Muslim intellectuals. Unlike the dabbling in antiquity that Carolingian times experienced, the twelfth century enjoyed a true renaissance of classical learning.

The high Middle Ages were also the time when the Latin or Western church established itself as an authority independent of monarchical secular government, thereby sowing the seeds of the distinctive Western separation of Church and State. This occurred during the Investiture Struggle of the late eleventh century and the twelfth century. In this confrontation between popes and emperors, a reformed papacy overcame its long subservience to the Carolingian and Ottonian kings. The papacy won out, however, by becoming itself a monarchy among the world's emerging monarchies, thereby preparing the way for still more dangerous confrontations between popes and emperors in the later Middle Ages.

The Revival of Empire, Church, and Towns

Otto I and the Revival of the Empire

The fortunes of both the old empire and the papacy began to revive when the Saxon Henry I ("the Fowler"; d. 936), the strongest of the German dukes, became the first non-Frankish king of Germany in 918. Henry rebuilt royal power by forcibly consolidating the duchies of Swabia, Bavaria, Saxony, Franconia, and Lotharingia. He secured imperial borders by checking the invasions of the Hungarians and the Danes. Although greatly reduced in size by comparison with Charlemagne's empire, Henry's German kingdom still placed his son and successor Otto I (936–973) in a strong territorial position.

The very able Otto maneuvered his own kin into positions of power in Bavaria, Swabia, and Franconia. He refused to treat each duchy as an independent hereditary dukedom, as was the trend among the nobility. He rather dealt with each as a subordinate member of a unified kingdom. In a truly imperial gesture in 951, Otto invaded Italy and proclaimed himself its king. In 955, he won his most magnificent victory when he defeated the Hungarians at Lechfeld, a feat comparable to Charles Martel's earlier victory over the Saracens at Tours in 732. The victory of Lechfeld secured German borders against new barbarian attack, further unified the German duchies, and earned Otto the well-deserved title "the Great."

As part of a careful rebuilding program, Otto, following the example of his predecessors, enlisted the Church. Bishops and abbots, men who possessed a sense of universal empire yet did not marry and found

competitive dynasties, were made royal princes and agents of the king. Because these clergy, as royal bureaucrats, received great landholdings and immunity from local counts and dukes, they also found such vassalage to the king very attractive.

In 961, Otto, who had long aspired to the imperial crown, responded to a call for help from Pope John XII (955–964). In recompense, Pope John crowned Otto emperor on February 2, 962. At this time, Otto also recognized the existence of the Papal States and proclaimed himself their special protector. The Church was now more than ever under royal control. Its bishops and abbots were Otto's appointees and bureaucrats, and the pope reigned in Rome only by the power of the emperor's sword. Pope John belatedly recognized the royal web in which the church had become entangled. As a countermeasure, he joined Italian opposition to the new emperor. This turnabout brought Otto's swift revenge. An ecclesiastical synod over which Otto personally presided deposed Pope John and proclaimed that henceforth no pope could take office without first swearing an oath of allegiance to the emperor. In Otto I, Western Caesaropapism reached a peak, as popes ruled at the emperor's pleasure.

Otto had shifted the royal focus from Germany to Italy. His successors became so preoccupied with running the affairs of Italy that their German base began to disintegrate, sacrificed to imperial dreams. They might have learned a lesson from the contemporary Capetian kings, the successor dynasty to the Carolingians in France, who wisely mended local fences and concentrated their limited resources on securing a tight grip on their immediate royal domain, which was never neglected for the sake of foreign adventure. The Ottonians, in contrast, reached far beyond their grasp when they tried to subdue Italy. As the briefly revived empire began to crumble in the first quarter of the eleventh century, the Church, long unhappy with Carolingian and Ottonian domination, prepared to declare its independence and exact its own vengeance.

The Reviving Catholic Church

THE CLUNY REFORM MOVEMENT. During the late ninth and early tenth centuries, the clergy had become tools of kings and magnates, and the papacy a toy of Italian nobles. The Ottonians made bishops their servile princes, and popes also served at their pleasure. A new day dawned for the Church, however, thanks not only to the failing fortunes of the empire but also to a new force for reform within the Church itself. In a great monastery in Cluny in east-central France, a reform movement appeared.

Since the fall of the Roman Empire, popular support for the Church had been especially inspired by the example of the monks. Monasteries provided an im-

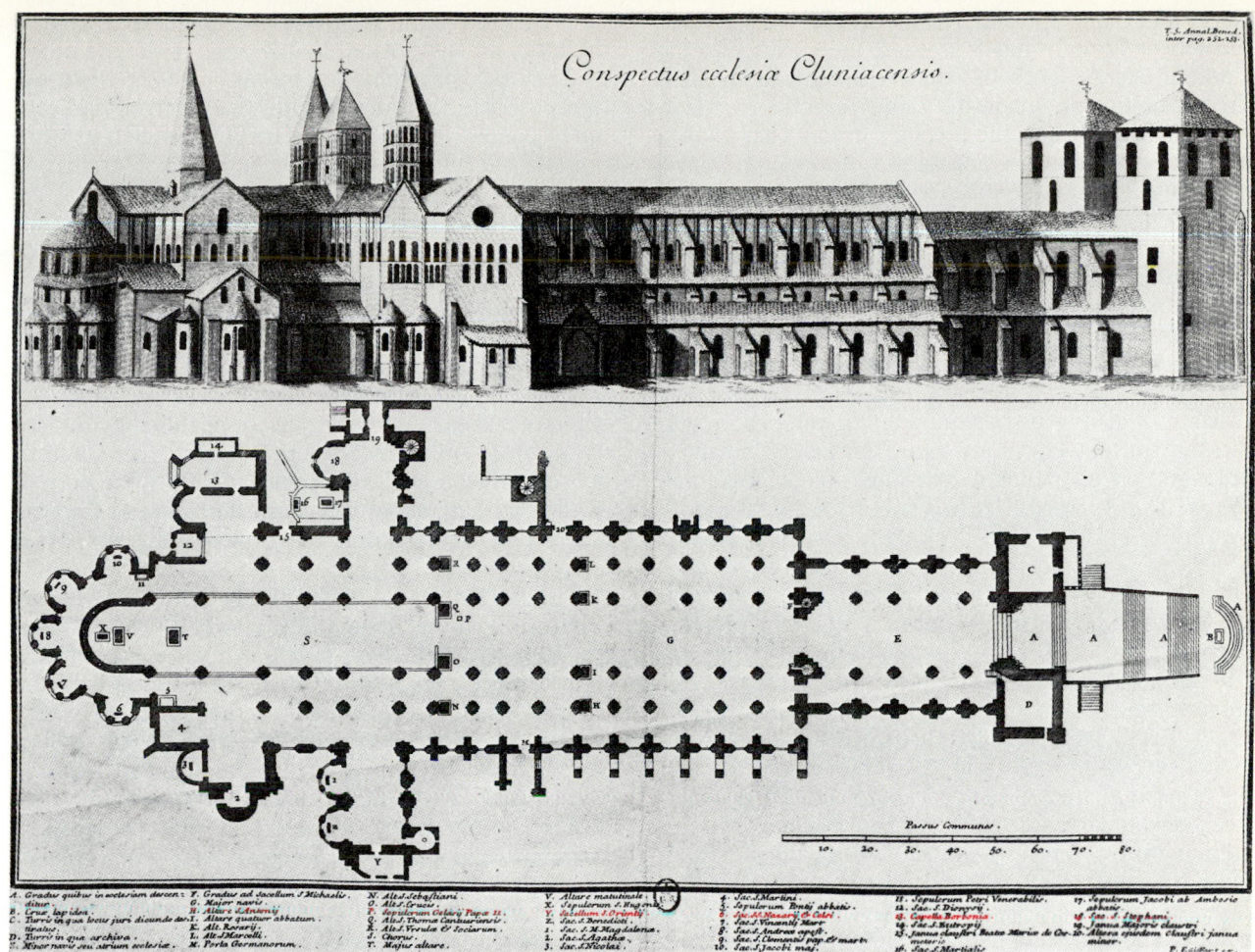

A drawing of the famous Romanesque third abbey church of St. Peter of the monastery of Cluny, France, built between 1080 and 1225, and ultimately destroyed by war and demolished between 1805 and 1823 except for one tower. When built in the twelfth century it was the largest church in Europe (555 feet long). For the next two centuries Cluny's clergy and scholars were the principal source of clerical reforms and arguments for ecclesiastical independence from secular rulers. [Giraudon.]

portant alternative style of life for the religiously earnest in an age when most people had very few options. The tenth and eleventh centuries saw an unprecedented boom in their construction. Monks remained the least secularized and most spiritual of the Church's clergy. Their cultural achievements were widely admired, their relics and rituals were considered magical, and their high religious ideals and sacrifices were imitated by the laity.

Cluny, the main source of the reform movement, was founded in 910 by William the Pious, duke of Aquitaine. A Benedictine monastery devoted to the strictest observance of Saint Benedict's *Rule for Monasteries*, it placed a special emphasis on liturgical purity. The Cluny reformers were intent on maintaining a spiritual church. They absolutely rejected the subservience of the clergy, especially that of the German bishops, to royal authority. They taught that the pope in Rome was sole ruler over all the clergy. The Cluny reformers further resented the transgression of ascetic piety by "secular" parish clergy, who maintained concubines in a relationship akin to marriage. (Later, a distinction would be formalized between the secular clergy who lived and ministered in the world [*saeculum*] and the regular clergy, monks and nuns withdrawn from the world and living according to a special rule [*regula*].)

The Cluny reformers resolved to free the clergy from both kings and "wives," to create an independent and chaste clergy. The Church alone was to be the clergy's lord and spouse. The distinctive Western separation of Church and State and the celibacy of the Catholic clergy, both of which continue today, had their definitive origins in the Cluny reform movement.

Cluny rapidly became a center from which reformers were dispatched to monasteries throughout France and Italy. It grew to embrace almost fifteen hundred dependent cloisters, each devoted to monastic and Church reform. In the last half of the eleventh century, the Cluny reformers reached the summit when the papacy embraced their reforms.

In the late ninth and early tenth centuries, the movement inspired the "Peace of God," a series of Church decrees that attempted to lessen the endemic warfare of medieval society by threatening excommunication for all who, at any time, harmed such vulnerable groups as women, peasants, merchants, and clergy. The Peace of God was subsequently reinforced by proclamations of the "Truce of God," a Church order that everyone must abstain from every form of violence and warfare during a certain part of each week (eventually from Wednesday night to Monday morning) and in all holy seasons.

Popes devoted to reforms like those urged by Cluny came to power during the reign of Emperor Henry III (1039–1056). Pope Leo IX (1049–1054) promoted regional synods in opposition to simony (that is, the selling of spiritual things, such as Church offices) and clerical concubinage. He also placed Cluniacs in key administrative posts in Rome. During the turbulent minority of Henry III's successor, Henry IV (1056–1106), reform popes began to assert themselves more openly. Pope Stephen IX (1057–1058) reigned without imperial ratification, contrary to the earlier declaration of Otto I. Pope Nicholas II (1059–1061) took the unprecedented step of establishing a College of Cardinals in 1059, and henceforth this body alone elected the pope.

THE INVESTITURE STRUGGLE: GREGORY VII AND HENRY IV. It was Pope Gregory VII (1073–1085), a fierce advocate of Cluny's reforms who had entered the papal bureaucracy a quarter century earlier during the pontificate of Leo IX, who put the Church's declaration of independence to the test. Cluniacs had repeatedly inveighed against simony. In 1075, Pope Gregory condemned under penalty of excommunication the lay investiture of clergy at any level. He had primarily in mind the emperor's well-established custom of installing bishops by presenting them with the ring and staff that symbolized episcopal office. After Gregory's ruling, bishops no more than popes were to be the creations of emperors. As popes were elected by the College of Cardinals and were not raised up by kings or nobles, so bishops would henceforth be installed in their offices by high ecclesiastical authority as empowered by the pope and none other.

Gregory's prohibition came as a jolt to royal authority. Since the days of Otto I, emperors had routinely passed out bishoprics to favored clergy. Bishops, who received royal estates, were the emperors' appointees and servants of the state. Henry IV's Carolingian and Ottonian predecessors had carefully nurtured the theocratic character of the empire in both concept and administrative bureaucracy. The church and religion were integral parts of government. Henry considered Gregory's action a direct challenge to his authority. The territorial princes, on the other hand, ever tending away from the center and eager to see the emperor weakened, were quick to see the advantages of Gregory's ruling: if the emperor did not have a bishop's ear, then a territorial prince might. In the hope of gaining an advantage over both the emperor and the clergy in their territory, the princes fully supported Gregory's edict.

The lines of battle were quickly drawn. Henry assembled his loyal German bishops at Worms in January 1076 and had them proclaim their independence from Gregory. Gregory promptly responded with the Church's heavy artillery; he excommunicated Henry and absolved all Henry's subjects from loyalty to him. The German princes were delighted by this turn of events, and Henry found himself facing a general revolt led by the duchy of Saxony. He had no recourse but to come to terms with Gregory. In a famous scene, Henry prostrated himself outside Gregory's castle retreat at Canossa on January 25, 1077. There he reportedly stood barefoot in the snow off and on for three days before the pope absolved his royal penitent. Papal power had, at this moment, reached its pinnacle. But heights are also for descending, and Gregory's grandeur, as he must surely have known when he pardoned Henry and restored him to power, was very soon to fade.

The settlement of the investiture controversy came in 1122 with the Concordat of Worms. Emperor Henry V (1106–1125) formally renounced his power to invest bishops with ring and staff. In exchange, Pope Calixtus II (1119–1124) recognized the emperor's right to be present and to invest bishops with fiefs before or after their investment with ring and staff by the Church. The old Church–State "back scratching" in this way continued, but now on very different terms. The clergy received their offices and attendant religious powers solely from ecclesiastical authority and no longer from kings and emperors. Rulers continued to bestow lands and worldly goods on high clergy in the hope of influencing them; the Concordat of Worms made the clergy more independent but not necessarily less worldly.

Pope Gregory VII Asserts the Power of the Pope

Church reformers of the high Middle Ages vigorously asserted the power of the pope within the Church and his rights against emperors and all others who might encroach on the papal sphere of jurisdiction. Here is a statement of the basic principles of the Gregorian reformers, known as the Ditatus Papae *("The Sayings of the Pope"), which is attributed to Pope Gregory VII (1073–1085).*

That the Roman Church was founded by God alone.

That the Roman Pontiff alone is rightly to be called universal.

That the Pope may depose the absent.

That for him alone it is lawful to enact new laws according to the needs of the time, to assemble together new congregations, to make an abbey of a canonry; and . . . to divide a rich bishopric and unite the poor ones.

That he alone may use the imperial insignia.

That the Pope is the only one whose feet are to be kissed by all princes.

That his name alone is to be recited in churches.

That his title is unique in the world.

That he may depose emperors.

That he may transfer bishops, if necessary, from one See to another.

That no synod may be called a general one without his order.

That no chapter or book may be regarded as canonical without his authority.

That no sentence of his may be retracted by any one; and that he, alone of all, can retract it.

That he himself may be judged by no one.

That the Roman Church has never erred, nor ever, by the witness of Scripture, shall err to all eternity.

That the Pope may absolve subjects of unjust men from their fealty. ❑

Church and State through the Centuries: A Collection of Historic Documents, trans. and ed. by S. Z. Ehler and John B. Morrall (New York: Biblo and Tannen, 1967), pp. 43–44.

The Gregorian party won the independence of the clergy at the price of encouraging the divisiveness of the political forces within the empire. The pope made himself strong by making imperial authority weak. In the end, those who profited most from the investiture controversy were the local princes.

The First Crusades

If an index of popular piety and support for the pope in the high Middle Ages is needed, the Crusades amply provide it. What the Cluny reform was to the clergy, the First Crusade to the Holy Land, proclaimed by Pope Urban II at the Council of Clermont in France in 1095, was to the laity: an outlet for the heightened religious zeal of what was Europe's most religious century prior to the Protestant Reformation. Actually, there had been an earlier Crusade of French knights, who, inspired by Pope Alexander II, had attacked Muslims in Spain in 1064. Unlike later Crusades, which were undertaken for patently mercenary as well as religious motives, the early Crusades were to a very high degree inspired by genuine religious piety and were carefully orchestrated by the revived papacy. Participants in the First Crusade to the Holy Land were promised a plenary indulgence should they die in battle, that is, a complete remission of the penance required of them for their mortal sins and hence release from suffering for them in purgatory. But this spiritual reward was only part of the crusading impulse. Other factors were the widespread popular respect for the reformed papacy and the existence of a nobility newly strengthened by the breakdown of imperial power and eager for military adventure. These elements combined to make the First Crusade a rousing success.

The Eastern emperor had petitioned both Pope Gregory VII and Pope Urban II for aid against advancing Muslim armies. The Western Crusaders did not, however, assemble for the purpose of defending Europe's borders against aggression. They freely took the offensive to rescue the holy city of Jerusalem—which had been in non-Christian hands since the seventh century—from the Seljuk Turks. To this end three great armies—tens of thousands of Crusaders—gathered in France, Germany, and Italy. Following different routes, they reassembled in Constantinople in 1097. The convergence of these spirited soldiers on the Eastern capital was a cultural shock that only deepened Eastern antipathy toward the West. The weakened Eastern emperor, Alexis I, suspected their motives, and the common people, who were forced to give them room and board, hardly considered them Chris-

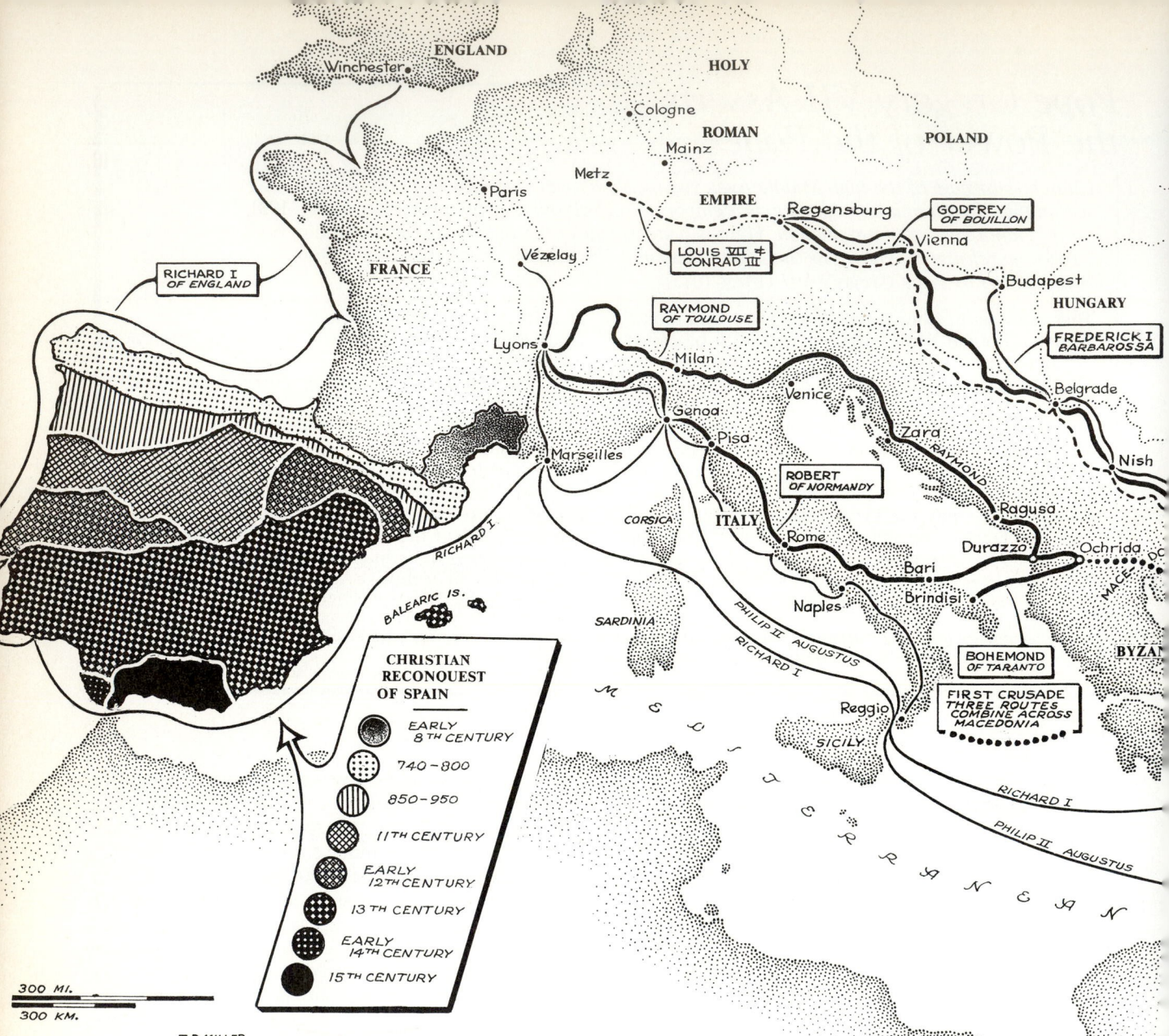

MAP 14-1 THE EARLY CRUSADES *Routes and several leaders of the crusades during the first century of the movement. Indicated names of the great nobles of the First Crusade do not exhaust the list. The even showier array of monarchs of the Second and Third still left the crusades, on balance, ineffective in achieving their ostensible goals.*

tian brothers in a common cause—especially after Rome and Constantinople had separated in 1054. Nonetheless, these fanatical Crusaders accomplished what no Eastern army had ever been able to do. They soundly defeated one Seljuk army after another in a steady advance toward Jerusalem, which fell to them on July 15, 1099.

The victorious Crusaders divided the conquered territory into the feudal states of Jerusalem, Edessa, and Antioch, which they allegedly held as fiefs from the pope. Godfrey of Bouillon, leader of the French–German army (and after him his brother Baldwin), ruled over the kingdom of Jerusalem. However, the Crusaders remained only small islands within a great sea of Muslims, who looked on the Western invaders as hardly more than savages. Native persistence finally broke the Crusaders around mid-century, and the forty-odd-year Latin presence in the East began to

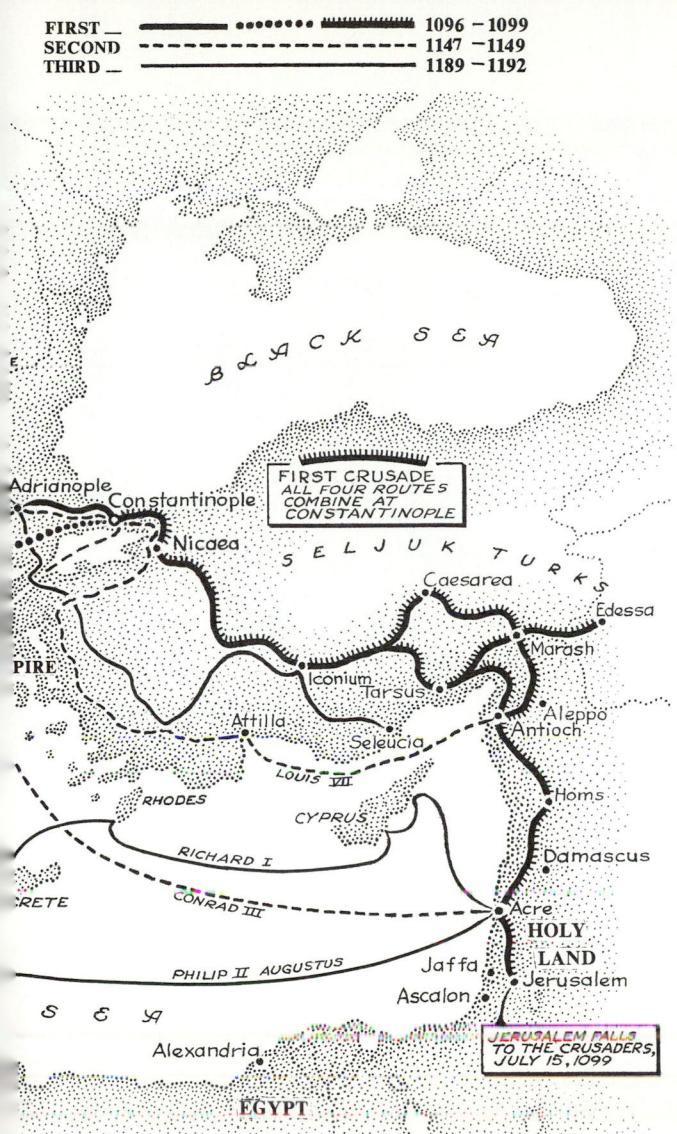

BLACK SEA

Adrianople
Constantinople
PIRE
E.

FIRST CRUSADE
ALL FOUR ROUTES
COMBINE AT
CONSTANTINOPLE

Nicaea

SELJUK TURKS

Caesarea
Edessa
Marash
Iconium
Tarsus
Aleppo
Attila
Seleucia
Antioch

LOUIS VII

RHODES
CYPRUS

Homs

RICHARD I

Damascus

CRETE
CONRAD III

Acre
HOLY
LAND
Jaffa
Jerusalem
Ascalon

PHILIP II AUGUSTUS

SEA

Alexandria

JERUSALEM FALLS
TO THE CRUSADERS,
JULY 15, 1099

EGYPT

crumble. Edessa fell to Muslim armies in 1144. A Second Crusade, preached by the eminent Bernard of Clairvaux (1091–1153), Christendom's most powerful monastic leader, attempted a rescue, but it met with dismal failure. In October 1187, Jerusalem itself was reconquered by Saladin (1138–1193), king of Egypt and Syria, and, save for a brief interlude in the thirteenth century, it remained thereafter in Islamic hands until modern times.

A Third Crusade in the twelfth century (1189–1192) attempted yet another rescue, enlisting as its leaders the most powerful Western rulers: Emperor Frederick Barbarossa; Richard the Lion-Hearted, king of England; and Philip Augustus, king of France. But the Third Crusade proved a tragicomic commentary on the passing of the original crusading spirit. Frederick Barbarossa accidentally drowned in the Saleph River while en route to the Holy Land. Richard the Lion-Hearted and Philip Augustus reached the outskirts of Jerusalem, but their intense personal rivalry shattered the Crusaders' unity and chances of victory. Philip Augustus returned to France and made war on English continental territories, and Richard fell captive to the Emperor Henry VI as he was returning to England. (Henry VI suspected Richard of plotting against him with Henry's mortal enemy, Henry the Lion, the duke of Saxony, who happened also to be Richard's brother-in-law.) The English were forced to pay a handsome ransom for their king's release. Popular resentment of taxes for this ransom became part of the background of the revolt against the English monarchy that led to the royal recognition of Magna Carta in 1215.

The long-term achievement of the first three Crusades had little to do with their original purpose. Politically and religiously, they were a failure, and the Holy Land reverted as firmly as ever to Muslim hands. These Crusades were more important for the way they stimulated Western trade with the East. The merchants of Venice, Pisa, and Genoa followed the Crusader's cross to lucrative new markets. The need to

The "Castle of the Knights" (Krak-des-Chevaliers), the most magnificent of the many crusader castles built in the Holy Land in the twelfth and thirteenth centuries and whose ruins remain in modern Syria, Lebanon, and Jordan. It is situated in northern Syria a few miles from the Lebanese border. Its defense consisted of two massive walls, one overhanging the other, divided by a great moat. The Muslims of the same period used very similar military architecture. [Arab Information Center, New York.]

The Cathedral of Pisa, Italy, built in the second half of the eleventh century. Nearby is the cathedral bell tower of 1174—the "leaning Tower of Pisa"—which has settled alarmingly out of line. [Italian Government Travel Office, New York.]

resupply the new Christian settlements in the Near East not only reopened old trade routes that had long been closed by Arab domination of the Mediterranean but also established new ones. It is a commentary on both the degeneration of the original intent of the Crusades and their true historical importance that the Fourth Crusade (1202–1204) became an enterprising commercial venture manipulated by the Venetians.

Trade and the Growth of Towns (1100–1300)

During the centuries following the collapse of the Roman Empire, Western Europe became a closed and predominantly agricultural society, with small international commerce and even less urban culture. The great seaports of Italy were the exceptions. Venice, Pisa, and Genoa continued to trade actively with Constantinople and throughout the eastern Mediterranean, including Palestine, Syria, and Egypt, during the Middle Ages. The Venetians, Europe's most sober

businessmen, jealously guarded their Eastern trade, attacking Western Christian competitors as quickly as Muslim predators. The latter were largely subdued by the success of the First Crusade, which proved a trade bonanza for Italian cities as the Mediterranean was opened to greater Western shipping. Venice, Pisa, and Genoa maintained major trading posts throughout the Mediterranean by the twelfth century. (See Map 14-2.)

THE NEW MERCHANT CLASS. The Western commercial revival attendant on these events repopulated the urban centers of the old Roman Empire and gave birth to new industries. Trade put both money and ideas into circulation. New riches, or the prospect of them, improved living conditions, raised hopes, and increased populations. In the twelfth century, Western Europe became a "boom-town." Among the most interesting creations were the traders themselves, who formed a new, distinctive social class. These prosperous merchants did not, as might first be suspected, spring from the landed nobility. They were, to the con-

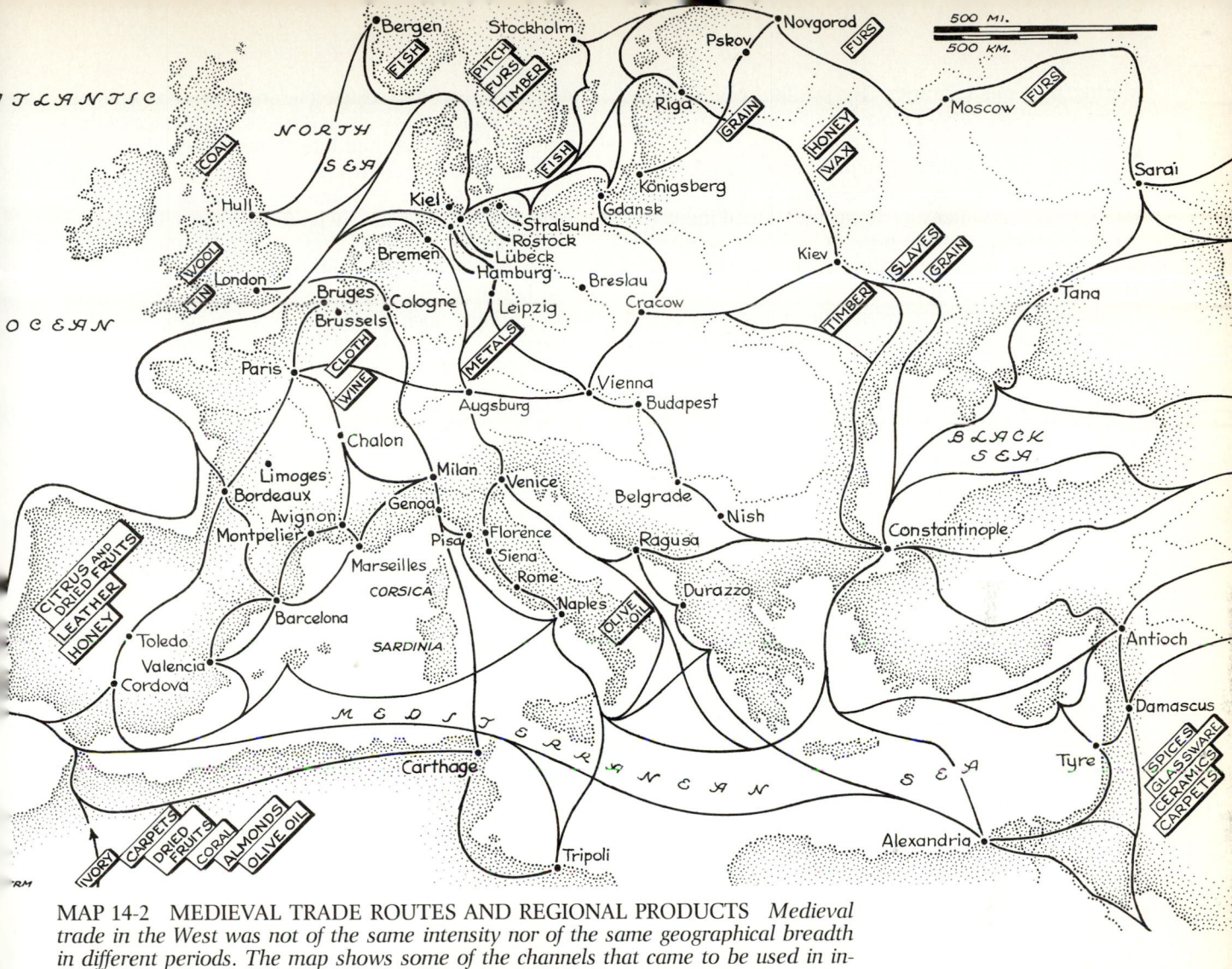

MAP 14-2 MEDIEVAL TRADE ROUTES AND REGIONAL PRODUCTS *Medieval trade in the West was not of the same intensity nor of the same geographical breadth in different periods. The map shows some of the channels that came to be used in interregional commerce. Labels tell part of what was carried in that commerce.*

trary, poor, landless adventurers who had absolutely nothing to lose and everything to gain by the risks of foreign trade. For mutual protection, they traveled together in great armed caravans, buying their products as cheaply as possible at the source and selling them as dearly as possible in Western marketplaces. They have been called the first Western capitalists, inspired by profit and devoted to little more than amassing fortunes. But their very greed and daring laid the foundations for Western urban life as we have come to know it today.

Although in power, wealth, and privilege the great merchants were destined to join and eventually eclipse the landed aristocracy, they were initially misfits in traditional medieval society. They were freemen, often possessed of great wealth, yet they neither owned land nor tilled the soil. They did not value land and farming but were persons of liquid wealth constantly on the move. Aristocrats and clergy looked down on them as degenerates, and the commoners viewed them with suspicion. They were intruders within medieval society, a new breed who did not fit into the neat hierarchy of clergy, nobility, and serfs.

Merchants fanned out from the great Flemish and Italian trading centers: Bruges, Ghent, Venice, Pisa, Genoa, Florence. Wherever they settled in large numbers, they lobbied for the degree of freedom necessary for successful commerce, opposing tolls, tariffs, and other petty restrictions that discouraged the flow of trade. This activity brought them initially into conflict with the norms of static agricultural society. But as they demonstrated the many advantages of vigorous trade, the merchants progressively won their case. They not only remodeled city government to favor their new industries and the free flow of trade but also imparted to the cities an aura of importance unknown during previous centuries. By the late Middle Ages, cities commonly saw themselves as miniature states, even self-contained Christendoms.

As they grew and became prosperous, medieval cities also became very jealous of their good fortune. They took every measure to protect skilled industries, to expand trade, and to prevent competition from the surrounding countryside. Government remained in the hands of the rich and the few—patricians, *grandi*, the "old rich"—although wealthy merchants, aspiring to the noble style of life, increasingly found their way into the inner circles of government, as money proved early that it could talk. By the thirteenth century, city councils, operating on the basis of aristocratic constitutions and composed of patricians and wealthy merchants—the old rich *and* the new rich—internally controlled city life. These oligarchies were increasingly confronted by small artisans, who demanded improved living conditions and a role in making policy. Skilled artisans formed the far greater part of the new burgher class and organized to express their will through powerful corporations or craft guilds. These were exclusive organizations for the various skilled trades; they set standards, certified craftsmen, and worked to enhance the economic well-being and political influence of their members. The high and late Middle Ages also saw a deepening conflict between craft masters, who were determined to keep their numbers at an absolute minimum, and journeymen, who found themselves frozen at the lower levels of their trade. The self-protectiveness and internal conflicts of medieval cities did not, however, prevent them from forming larger trade associations, such as the famous German Hanseatic League, or Hansa, which kept Baltic trade a German monopoly well into the fifteenth century.

CHANGES IN SOCIETY. The rise of a merchant class caused an important crack in the old social order. New-rich merchants, a class originally sprung from ordinary, landless people, broke into the aristocracy, and in doing so, they drew behind them the leadership of the new artisan class created by the urban industries that had grown up in the wake of growth of trade. In the late Middle Ages, the "middle classes" would firmly establish themselves.

Although from one perspective medieval towns

The English Nobility Imposes Restraints on King John

The gradual building of a sound English constitutional system in the Middle Ages was in danger of going awry if a monarch overstepped the fine line dividing necessary strength from outright despotism. The danger became acute under the rule of King John. The English nobility, therefore, forced the king's recognition of Magna Carta (1215), which reaffirmed the traditional rights and personal liberties of free men against royal authority. The document has remained enshrined in English law.

A free man shall not be fined for a small offense, except in proportion to the gravity of the offense: and for a great offense he shall be fined in proportion to the magnitude of the offense, saving his freehold; and a merchant in the same way, saving his merchandise; and the villein shall be fined in the same way, saving his wainage, if he shall be at our [i.e., the king's] mercy; and none of the above fines shall be imposed except by the oaths of honest men of the neighborhood. . . .

No constable or other bailiff of ours [i.e., the king] shall take anyone's grain or other chattels without immediately paying for them in money, unless he is able to obtain a postponement at the good will of the seller.

No constable shall require any knight to give money in place of his ward of a castle [i.e., standing guard] if he is willing to furnish that ward in his own person, or through another honest man if he himself is not able to do it for a reasonable cause; and if we shall lead or send him into the army he shall be free from ward in proportion to the amount of time which he has been in the army through us.

No sheriff or bailiff of ours [i.e., the king], or any one else, shall take horses or wagons of any free man, for carrying purposes, except on the permission of that free man.

Neither we nor our bailiffs will take the wood of another man for castles, or for anything else which we are doing, except by the permission of him to whom the wood belongs. . . .

No free man shall be taken, or imprisoned, or dispossessed, or outlawed, or banished, or in any way injured, nor will we go upon him, nor send upon him, except by the legal judgment of his peers, or by the law of the land.

To no one will we sell, to no one will we deny or delay, right or justice. ❑

James Harvey Robinson (ed.), *Readings in European History*, Vol. 1 (Boston: Atheneaum, 1904), pp. 236–237.

were overly self-protective and "egoistic," they also became a force for innovation and change beyond their walls. This fact is all the more remarkable when it is remembered that towns at this time contained hardly more than 5 per cent of the population. Townspeople became a major force in the breakup of feudal society, aiding both kings and the peasantry at the expense of the landed nobility. Generally speaking, towns and kings tended to ally themselves against the great feudal lords. A notable exception may be seen in England, where the towns joined the barons against the oppressive monarchy of King John (1199–1216) and became a part of the parliamentary opposition. Townspeople generally, however, found their autonomy better preserved by having one distant master rather than several nearer and factious overlords. Kings, in turn, counted on the liquid wealth and administrative skills of the town-dwellers, who began to replace the clergy and the nobility in the royal bureaucracy. Urban money made it possible for kings to hire mercenary armies and thereby to decrease their dependence on the noble cavalry—an important step in the consolidation of territories divided for centuries by feudal allegiances and customs.

From the burgher ranks, kings drew the skilled lawyers who began the long process of replacing feudal custom with centralized Roman law, and towns also often had powerful militias that could be enlisted in royal service. Kings, in return, gave towns political recognition and guaranteed their constitutions (in formal charters) against territorial magnates. This was more easily done in the stronger coastal towns than in interior areas, where urban life remained less vigorous

and territorial power was on the rise. In France, towns became integrated into the royal government. In Germany and Austria, by contrast, towns fell under ever tighter control by territorial princes. In Italy, towns uniquely grew to absorb their surrounding territory, becoming city-states.

Towns also aided the peasantry, to the detriment of the landed nobility. A popular maxim of the time in German cities was: *Stadtluft macht frei*—"City air sets one free." Cities passed legislation making serfs who spent a year and a day within their walls freemen. New urban industries provided lucky peasants vocations alternative to farming. The new money economy made it possible for serfs or their urban patrons to buy their freedom from feudal services and rents as the latter became translatable into direct money payments. A serf or his patron could simply buy up the "contract." The growth of a free peasantry became especially evident in the thirteenth century.

All of this worked against the landed nobility. As urban trade and industries put more money into circulation, its value decreased (inflation). The great landowners, whose wealth was static, found themselves confronted, on the one hand, by serfs who longed to flee to the city and, on the other, by rising prices. They were losing their cheap labor supply and facing diminished productivity; at the same time, they had to pay more for their accustomed style of life. The nobility were not disciplined people, and many fell prey to money-wise urban merchants, who beat them out of their landed wealth.

The new urban economy worked, then, to free both kings and peasants from dependence on feudal lords,

The fortified city of Carcassonne in southern France, whose defenses date from the period 1240–1285, during the reigns of Louis IX and Philip the Bold. Note the protective walls and towers. [Bildarchiv Foto Marburg.]

although this was a long and complex process. As royal authority became centralized and kings were able to hire mercenary soldiers, the noble cavalry became militarily obsolescent, at most a minor part of the king's armed forces. And as towns and urban industries grew, attracting serfs from the farms, the nobility gradually lost its once all-powerful economic base. The long-term consequence: a strengthening of monarchy.

Medieval Universities and Scholasticism

Thanks to Spanish Muslim scholars, the logical works of Aristotle, the writings of Euclid and Ptolemy, the basic works of Greek physicians and Arab mathematicians, and the larger texts of Roman law became available to Western scholars in the early twelfth century. Muslim scholars preserved these works, translated portions of the Greek ones into Latin, and wrote extensive, thought-provoking commentaries on ancient texts. This renaissance of ancient knowledge, in turn, provided the occasion for the rise of universities.

BOLOGNA AND PARIS. The first important Western university was in Bologna. It received its formal grant of rights and privileges from the emperor Frederick Barbarossa in 1158. University members, like clergy, were granted royal immunity from local jurisdiction and were viewed by local townspeople as a group apart. In Bologna, we find the first formal organizations of students and professors and the first degree programs—the institutional foundations of the modern university.

The "university" was at first simply a program of study that gave the student a license to teach others. Originally, the term *university* meant no more than a group or corporation of individuals who were united by common self-interest and for mutual protection. As the local townspeople viewed both masters and students as foreigners without civil rights, such a union was necessary. It followed the model of a medieval trade guild. Bolognese students formed such a bloc in order to guarantee fair rents and prices from the townspeople and regular and high-quality teaching from their professors. Price gouging by townspeople was met with the threat to move the university to another town—a threat that could easily be carried out because the university at this time was not a great, fixed physical plant. Professors who failed to meet student expectations were boycotted. The mobility of the first universities gave them a unique independence.

Professors also formed protective associations and established procedures and standards for certification to teach within their ranks. The first academic degree was a certificate *(licentia docendi)* given by the professors' guild, which granted graduates in the liberal arts program or in the higher professional sciences of medicine, theology, and the law "the right to teach anywhere" *(ius ubique docendi).*

Bologna was distinguished as the center for the revival of Roman law. From the seventh to the eleventh centuries, only the most rudimentary manuals of Roman law were available to be circulated. With the growth of trade and towns in the late eleventh century, Western scholars came into contact with the larger and more important parts of the Roman *Corpus Juris Civilis* of Justinian. The study and dissemination of this new material was directed by Irnerius (fl. early twelfth century). He and his students made authoritative commentaries or glosses on individual laws following their broad knowledge of the *Corpus Juris.* Around 1140, a monk named Gratian, also a resident of Bologna, created the standard legal text in church or canon law, the *Concordance of Discordant Canons,* known more commonly as Gratian's *Decretum.*

As Bologna provided the model for southern European universities and the study of law, Paris became the model for northern Europe and the study of theology. Oxford, Cambridge, and, much later, Heidelberg were among Paris's imitators. All these universities required a foundation in the liberal arts for further study in the higher sciences of medicine, theology, and law. The arts program consisted of the *trivium* (grammar, rhetoric, and logic) and the *quadrivium* (arithmetic, geometry, astronomy, and music). Before the emergence of the universities, the liberal arts had been taught in the cathedral and monastery schools, that is, schools attached to cathedrals or monasteries for the purpose of training clergy. The most famous of the cathedral schools were those of Rheims and Chartres.

The University of Paris grew institutionally out of the cathedral school of Nôtre Dame, receiving its charter in 1200 from King Philip Augustus and Pope Innocent III. Papal sanction and regulations, among them the right of the faculty to strike, were issued in 1231 in the bull *Parens scientiarum* and gave the university freedom from local church control. At this time, the University of Paris consisted of independent faculties of arts, canon law, medicine, and theology, with the masters of arts, who were grouped together in four national factions (French, Norman, English–German, and Picard), the dominant faculty.

At Paris, the college system originated. At first, colleges were no more than hospices providing room and board for poor students. But the educational life of the university rapidly expanded into these fixed buildings and began to thrive on their sure endowments. In Paris, the most famous college was the Sorbonne, founded around 1257 by Robert de Sorbon, chaplain to

The seven liberal arts of the medieval university curriculum: rhetoric, geometry, astronomy, music, natural and moral philosophy, and theology. At their feet sit the great teachers of antiquity: Cicero, Euclid, Ptolemey, Aristotle, Seneca, and Augustine. [Art Resource.]

the king, for the purpose of educating advanced theological students. In Oxford and Cambridge, the colleges became the basic unit of student life, indistinguishable from the university. By the fifteenth and sixteenth centuries, colleges had tied the universities to physical plants and fixed foundations, restricting their previous autonomy and freedom of movement.

THE CURRICULUM. Before the twelfth century the education available within the cathedral and monastic schools was quite limited. Students learned grammar, rhetoric, and elementary geometry and astronomy. They used the Latin grammars of Donatus and Priscian and studied Saint Augustine's *On Christian Doctrine*, Cassiodorus' *On Divine and Secular Learning*, and the various writings of Boethius (d. 524). Boethius was important for instruction in arithmetic and music and especially for the transmission of the small body of Aristotle's logical works known before the twelfth century. After the textual finds of the

early twelfth century, Western scholars had the whole of Aristotle's logic, the astronomy of Ptolemy, the writings of Euclid, and many Latin classics. By the mid-thirteenth century the ethical, physical, and metaphysical writings of Aristotle were in circulation in the West.

In the high Middle Ages the learning process was very basic. The student wrote commentaries on authoritative texts, especially those of Aristotle. The teachers encouraged their students not to strive independently for undiscovered truth, but to organize and harmonize the accepted truths of tradition. The basic assumption was that truth already existed. It had only to be organized and elucidated. Such conviction made logic and dialectic supreme within the liberal arts.

The Scholastic program of study, based on logic and dialectic, reigned supreme in all the faculties—in law and medicine as well as in philosophy and theology. Scholasticism was a peculiar method of study. The student read the traditional authorities in his field,

Bishop Stephen Complains about the New Scholastic Learning

Scholasticism involved an intellectual, learned approach to religion and its doctrines rather than simple, uncritical piety. Many saw in it a threat to the study of the Bible and the Church Fathers, as doctrines that should simply be believed and revered were rationally dissected for their logical meaning by allegedly presumptuous and none-too-well-trained youths. Here is a particularly graphic description of the threat, replete with classical allusion, as perceived by Stephen, Bishop of Tournai, in a letter to the pope written between 1192 and 1203.

The studies of sacred letters among us are fallen into the workshop of confusion, while both disciples applaud novelties alone and masters watch out for glory rather than learning. They everywhere compose new and recent *summulae* [little summaries] and commentaries, by which they attract, detain, and deceive their hearers, as if the works of the holy fathers were not still sufficient, who, we read, expounded Holy Scripture in the same spirit in which we believe the apostles and prophets composed it. They prepare strange and exotic courses for their banquet, when at the nuptials of the son of the king of Taurus his own flesh and blood are killed and all prepared, and the wedding guests have only to take and eat what is set before them. Contrary to the sacred canons there is public disputation over the incomprehensible deity; concerning the incarnation of the Word, verbose flesh and blood irreverently litigate. The indivisible Trinity is cut up and wrangled over . . . so that now there are as many errors as doctors, as many scandals as classrooms, as many blasphemies as squares. . . . Faculties called liberal having lost their pristine liberty are sunk in such servitude that adolescents with long hair impudently usurp their professorships, and beardless youths sit in the seat of their seniors, and those who don't yet know how to be disciples strive to be named masters. And they write their *summulae* moistened with drool and dribble but unseasoned with the salt of philosophers. Omitting the rules of the arts and discarding the authentic books of the artificers, they seize the flies of empty words in their sophisms like the claws of spiders. Philosophy cries out that her garments are torn and disordered and, modestly concealing her nudity by a few specific tatters, neither is consulted nor consoles as of old. All these things, father, call for the hand of apostolic correction. . . . ❑

Lynn Thorndike, *University Records and Life in the Middle Ages* (New York: Octagon Books, 1971), pp. 22–24.

---

formed short summaries of their teaching, disputed it by elaborating arguments pro and con, and then drew his own modest conclusions. The twelfth century saw the rise of the "summa," a summary of all that was known about a topic, and works whose sole purpose was to conciliate traditional authorities.

Society

The Order of Life

Four basic social groups were distinguished in the Middle Ages: those who fought (the landed nobility), those who prayed (the clergy), those who labored (the peasantry), and, after the revival of towns in the eleventh century, those who traded and manufactured (the townspeople). It would be false to view each of these groups as closed and homogeneous. Throughout medieval society, like tended to be attracted to like regardless of social grouping. Barons, archbishops, rich farmers, and successful merchants had far more in common with each other than they did with the middle and lower strata of their various professions.

NOBLES. As a distinctive social group, all noblemen did not begin simply as great men with large hereditary lands. Many rose from the ranks of feudal vassals or warrior knights. The successful vassal attained a special social and legal status based on his landed wealth (accumulated fiefs), his exercise of authority over others, and his distinctive social customs—all of which set him apart from others in medieval society. By the late Middle Ages there had evolved a distinguishable higher and lower nobility living in both town and country. The higher were the great landowners and territorial magnates; the lower were petty landlords, descendants from minor knights, new-rich merchants who could buy country estates, and wealthy farmers patiently risen from ancestral serfdom.

It was a special mark of the nobility that they lived on the labor of others. Basically lord of manors, the nobility of the early and high Middle Ages neither tilled the soil like the peasantry nor engaged in the commerce of merchants—activities considered beneath their dignity. The nobleman resided in a country mansion or, if he were particularly wealthy, a castle. He was drawn to the countryside as much by personal preference as by the fact that his fiefs were usually rural manors. Arms were his profession; the nobleman's sole occupation and reason for living was waging war. His fief provided the means to acquire the expensive military equipment that his rank required, and he maintained his enviable position as he had gained it, by fighting for his chief.

The nobility accordingly celebrated the physical strength, courage, and constant activity of warfare. Warring gave them both new riches and an opportunity to gain honor and glory. Knights were paid a share in the plunder of victory, and in time of war everything became fair game. Special war wagons, designed for the collection and transport of booty, followed them into battle. Periods of peace were greeted with great sadness, as they meant economic stagnation and boredom. Whereas the peasants and the townspeople counted on peace as the condition of their occupational success, the nobility despised it as unnatural to their profession. They looked down on the peasantry as cowards who ran and hid in time of war. Urban merchants, who amassed wealth by business methods strange to feudal society, were held in equal contempt, which increased as the affluence and political power of the townspeople grew. The nobility possessed as strong a sense of superiority over these "unwarlike" people as the clergy did over the general run of laity.

The nobleman nurtured his sense of distinctiveness within medieval society by the chivalric ritual of dubbing to knighthood, a ceremonial entrance into the noble class that became almost a religious sacrament. The ceremony was preceded by a bath of purification, confession, communion, and a prayer vigil. Thereafter the priest blessed the knight's standard, lance, and sword. As prayers were chanted, the priest girded the knight with his sword and presented him his shield, enlisting him as much in the defense of the church as in the service of his lord. Dubbing raised the nobleman to a state as sacred in his sphere as clerical ordination made the priest in his. This comparison is quite legitimate. The clergy and the nobility were medieval society's privileged estates. The appointment of noblemen to high ecclesiastical office and their eager participation in the church's Crusades had strong ideological and social underpinnings as well as economic and political motives.

In peacetime, the nobility had two favorite amusements: hunting and tournaments. Because of the threat to towns and villages posed by wild animals, the great hunts actually aided the physical security of

A miniature from the Codex Manesse showing lords tilting as their ladies "ooh" and "aah." [Universitatsbibliothek, Heidelberg.]

the ordinary people, while occupying the restless noblemen. However, where they could, noblemen progressively monopolized the rights to game, forbidding the commoners from hunting in the "lord's" forests. This practice built resentment among the common people to the level of revolt. Free game, fishing, and access to wood were basic demands in the petitions of grievance and the revolts of the peasantry throughout the high and later Middle Ages.

From the repeated assemblies in the courts of barons and kings, set codes of social conduct or "courtesy" developed in noble circles. With the French leading the way, mannered behavior and court etiquette became almost as important as battlefield expertise. Knights became literate gentlemen, and lyric poets sang and moralized at court. The cultivation of a code of behavior and a special literature to eulogize it was not unrelated to problems within the social life of the nobility. Noblemen were notorious philanderers; their illegitimate children mingled openly with their legitimate offspring in their houses. The advent of courtesy was, in part, an effort to reform this situation. Although the poetry of courtly love was sprinkled with frank eroticism and the beloved in these epics were married women pursued by those to whom they were not married, the love recommended by the poet was usually love at a distance, unconsummated by sexual intercourse. It was love without touching, a kind of sex without physical sex, and only as such was it considered ennobling. Court poets depicted those who did carnally consummate their illicit love as reaping at least as much suffering as joy from it.

By the fourteenth century, several factors forced the landed nobility into a steep economic and political decline from which it never recovered. These were the great population losses of the fourteenth century brought on by the Great Plague; the changes in military tactics occasioned by the use of infantry and heavy artillery during the Hundred Years' War; and the alliance of the wealthy towns with the king. Generally, one can speak of a waning of the landed nobility after the fourteenth century. Thereafter, the effective possession of land and wealth counted far more than parentage and family tree as qualification for entrance into the highest social class.

CLERGY. Unlike the nobility and the peasantry, the clergy was an open estate. Although clerical ranks reflected the social classes from which the clergy came and a definite clerical hierarchy formed, one was still a cleric by religious training and ordination, not by the circumstances of birth or military prowess. There were two basic types of clerical vocation: the regular and the secular clergy. The former were the orders of monks, who lived according to a special ascetic rule (regula) in cloisters separated from the world. They were the spiritual elite among the clergy, and theirs was not a way of life lightly entered. Canon law required that one be at least twenty-one years of age before making a final profession of the monastic vows of poverty, chastity, and obedience. Their personal sacrifices and high religious ideals made the monks much respected in high medieval society.

Although many monks (and also nuns, who increasingly embraced the vows of poverty, obedience, and chastity without a clerical rank) secluded themselves altogether, the regular clergy were never completely cut off from the secular world. They maintained frequent contact with the laity through such charitable activities as feeding the destitute and tending the sick, through liberal arts instruction in monastic schools, through special pastoral commissions from the pope, and as supplemental preachers and confessors in parish churches during Lent and other peak religious seasons. It became the special mark of the Dominican and Franciscan friars to live a common life according to a

The Stigmatization of St. Francis (early fourteenth century) by Giotto. In a vision on Mt. Alverna, St. Francis is said to have received the wounds of Christ (the stigmata) in his own body and to have borne them for almost two years before his death in 1226. The small lower panels show Francis saving the church, receiving with his followers the Franciscans' charter from the pope, and—characteristically—preaching to the birds. [Musée du Louvre, Paris. Cliché des Musées Nationaux.]

special rule, and still to be active in worldly ministry. Some monks, because of their learning and rhetorical skills, even rose to prominence as secretaries and private confessors to kings and queens.

The secular clergy were those who lived and worked directly among the laity in the world (saeculum). They formed a vast hierarchy. There were the high prelates—the wealthy cardinals, archbishops, and bishops, who were drawn almost exclusively from the nobility—the urban priests, the cathedral canons, and the court clerks; and, finally, the great

Saint Francis of Assisi Sets Out His Religious Ideals

Saint Francis of Assisi (1182–1226) was the founder of the Franciscan Order of friars. Here are some of his religious principles as stated in the definitive Rule of the Order, approved by the pope in 1223; the rule especially stresses the ideal of living in poverty.

This is the rule and way of living of the Minorite brothers, namely, to observe the holy Gospel of our Lord Jesus Christ, living in obedience, without personal possessions, and in chastity. Brother Francis promises obedience and reverence to our lord Pope Honorius, and to his successors who canonically enter upon their office, and to the Roman Church. And the other brothers shall be bound to obey Brother Francis and his successors.

I firmly command all the brothers by no means to receive coin or money, of themselves or through an intervening person. But for the needs of the sick and for clothing the other brothers, the ministers alone and the guardians shall provide through spiritual friends, as it may seem to them that necessity demands, according to time, place, and the coldness of the temperature. This one thing being always borne in mind, that, as has been said, they receive neither coin nor money.

Those brothers to whom God has given the ability to labor shall do so faithfully and devoutly, but in such manner that idleness, the enemy of the soul, being averted, they may not extinguish the spirit of holy prayer and devotion, to which other temporal things should be subservient. As a reward, moreover, for their labor, they may receive for themselves and their brothers the necessities of life, but not coin or money; and this humbly, as becomes the servants of God and the followers of most holy poverty.

The brothers shall appropriate nothing to themselves, neither a house, nor a place, nor anything; but as pilgrims and strangers in this world, in poverty and humility serving God, they shall confidently go seeking for alms. Nor need they be ashamed, for the Lord made Himself poor for us in this world. ❏

A Source Book of Medieval History, ed. by Frederic Austin Ogg (New York: Cooper Square Publishers, 1972), pp. 375–376.

mass of poor parish priests, who were neither financially nor intellectually very far above the common people they served (the basic educational requirement was an ability to say the Mass). Until the Gregorian reform in the eleventh century began to reverse the trend, parish priests lived with women in a relationship akin to marriage, and their concubines and children were accepted within the communities they served. Because of their relative poverty, it was not unusual for priests to "moonlight" as teachers, artisans, or farmers, a practice also accepted and even admired by their parishioners.

During the greater part of the Middle Ages, the clergy were the "first estate," and theology was the queen of the sciences. How did the clergy come into such prominence? It was basically popular reverence for the clergy's role as mediator between God and humanity that made this superiority possible. The priest brought the very Son of God down to earth when he celebrated the sacrament of the Eucharist; his absolution released penitents from punishment for mortal sin. Theologians elaborated the distinction between the clergy and the laity very much to the clergy's benefit. The belief in the superior status of the clergy underlay the evolution of clerical privileges and immunities in both person and property. As holy persons, the clergy could not be taxed by secular rulers without special permission from the proper ecclesiastical authorities. Clerical crimes fell under the jurisdiction of special ecclesiastical courts, not the secular courts. Because churches and monasteries were deemed holy places, they too were free from secular taxation and legal jurisdiction.

By the fourteenth century, townspeople came increasingly to resent the special immunities of the clergy. They complained that it was not proper for the clergy to have greater privileges yet far fewer responsibilities than all others who lived within the town walls. Although the separation of Church and State and the distinction between the clergy and the laity have persisted into modern times, after the fifteenth century the clergy ceased to be the superior class that they had been for so much of the Middle Ages.

PEASANTS. The largest and lowest social group in medieval society was the one on whose labor the welfare of all the others depended: the agrarian peasantry. They lived on and worked the manors of the nobility, the primitive cells of rural social life, and all were to one degree or another dependent on their lords and considered their property. The manor had originally been a plot of land within a village, ranging from twelve to seventy-five acres in size, assigned to a certain member by a settled tribe or clan. This member

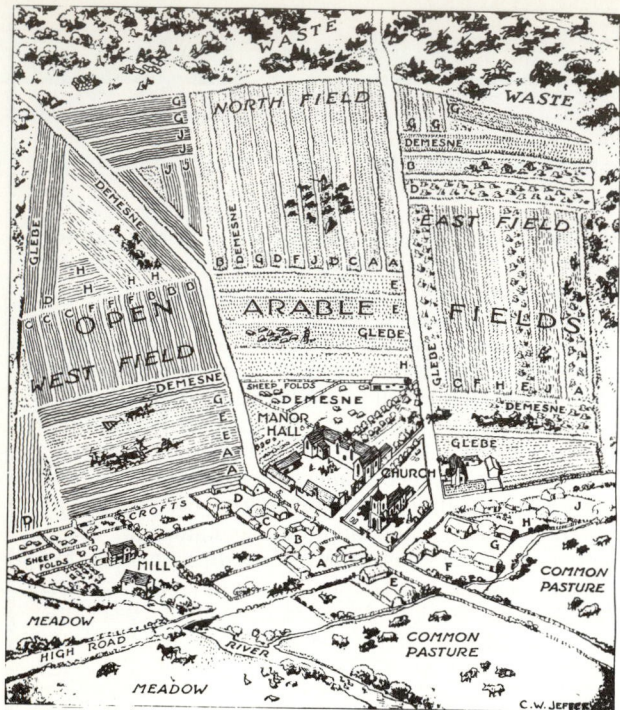

For hundreds of years and over a great part of Europe the manor was basic for much of the population. Despite regional variation and changes that came with the revival of trade and growth of towns, manors in the West had enough common features to justify this modern reconstruction of a characteristic example. Note the lord's hall and lands (demesne), the peasant village with common grounds and services for the nine families (a-j) dwelling on this manor, the church and its lands (glebe), peasant holdings in open fields, and areas for woodcutting and hunting. [The Granger Collection.]

and his family became lords of the land, and those who came to dwell there formed a smaller self-sufficient community within a larger village community. In the early Middle Ages, such a manor consisted of the dwellings of the lord and his family, the cottages of the peasant workers, agricultural sheds, and fields. The landowner or lord of the manor required a certain amount of produce (grain, eggs, and the like) and a certain number of services from the peasant families who came to dwell on and farm his land. The tenants were free to divide the labor as they wished, and what goods remained after the lord's levies were met were their own. A powerful lord might own many such manors, and kings later based their military and tax assessments on the number of manors owned by a vassal landlord.

There were both servile and free manors. The tenants of the latter had originally been freemen known as *coloni*, original inhabitants and petty landowners who

swapped their small possessions for a guarantee of security from a more powerful lord, who came in this way to possess their land. Unlike the pure serfdom of the servile manors, whose tenants had no original claim to a part of the land, the tenancy obligations on free manors tended to be limited and their rights more carefully defined. Tenants of servile manors were by comparison far more vulnerable to the whims of their landlords. These two types of manor tended, however, to merge; the most common situation was the manor on which tenants of greater and lesser degrees of servitude dwelt together, their services to the lord defined by their personal status and local custom.

Marc Bloch, the modern authority on manorial society, has vividly depicted the duties of tenancy:

On certain days the tenant brings the lord's steward perhaps a few small silver coins or, more often, sheaves of grain harvested on his fields, chickens from his farm yard, cakes of wax from his beehives or from the swarms of the neighboring forest. At other times he works on the arable or the meadows of the demesne [the lord's plot of land in the manoral fields, between one third and one half of that available]. Or else we find him carting casks of wine or sacks of grain on behalf of the master to distant residences. His is the labour which repairs the walls or moats of the castle. If the master has guests the peasant strips his own bed to provide the necessary extra bedclothes. When the hunting season comes round he feeds the pack. If war breaks out he does duty as a footsoldier or orderly, under the leadership of the reeve of the village.[2]

The lord also had the right to subject his tenants to exactions known as *banalities*. He could, for example, force them to breed their cows with his bull, and to pay for the privilege, as well as to grind their corn in his mill, bake their bread in his oven, make their wine in his wine press, buy their beer from his brewery, and even surrender to him the tongues or other choice parts of all animals slaughtered on his lands. He had the right to levy small taxes at will.

Exploited as the serfs may appear to have been from a modern point of view, their status was far from outright chattel slavery. It was to the lord's advantage to keep his serfs healthy and happy; his welfare, like theirs, depended on a successful harvest. Serfs had their own dwellings and modest strips of land and lived by the produce of their own labor and organization. They were permitted to market for their own profit what surpluses might remain after the harvest. They were free to choose their spouses within the local village, although the lord's permission was required if a wife or husband was sought from another village. And serfs were able to pass a goodly portion of their

[2] *Feudal Society*, trans. by L. A. Manyon (Chicago: University of Chicago Press, 1968), p. 250.

A woodcut showing wild animals damaging peasant crops. One of the greatest problems for peasants was how to protect their crops from stags and deer. Forbidden by law from hunting then, the peasants built fences and used clubs to drive the animals away. [Deutsche Fotothek, Dresden.]

property (their dwellings and field strips) and worldly goods on to their children.

Two basic changes occurred in the evolution of the manor from the early to the later Middle Ages. The first was the fragmentation of the manor and the rise to dominance of the single-family unit. As the lords parceled out their land to new tenants, their own plots became progressively smaller. The increase in the number of tenants and the decrease in the lord's fields brought about a corresponding reduction in the labor services exacted from the tenants. In France, by the reign of Louis IX (1226–1270), only a few days a year were required, whereas in the time of Charlemagne, peasants had worked the lord's fields several days a week. By the twelfth century, the manor was hopelessly fragmented. As the single-family unit replaced the clan as the basic nuclear group, assessments of goods and services fell on individual fields and households, no longer on manors as a whole. Family farms replaced manorial units. Children continued to live with their parents after marriage, and several generations of one family could be found within a single household, although nuclear families were also commonplace. The peasants' carefully nurtured communal life made possible a family's retention of its land and dwelling after the death of the head of the household. In this way, land and property remained in the possession of a single family from generation to generation.

The second change in the evolution of the manor was the translation of feudal dues into money pay-

ments, a change made possible by the revival of trade and the rise of the towns. This development, which was completed by the thirteenth century, permitted serfs to hold their land as rent-paying tenants and to overcome their servile status. Although tenants thereby gained greater freedom, they were not necessarily better off materially. Whereas servile workers had been able to count on the benevolent assistance of their landlords in hard times, rent-paying workers were left by and large to their own devices; their independence caused some landlords to treat them with indifference and even resentment.

Lands and properties that had been occupied by generations of peasants and recognized as their own were always under the threat of the lord's claim to a prior right of inheritance and even outright usurpation. As their demesnes declined, the lords were increasingly tempted to encroach on such traditionally common lands. The peasantry fiercely resisted such efforts, instinctively clinging to the little they had. In many regions, they successfully organized to win a role in the choice of petty rural officials. By the midfourteenth century, a declining nobility in England and France, faced with the ravages of the great plague and the Hundred Years' War, attempted to turn back the historical clock by increasing taxes on the peasantry and passing laws to restrict their migration into the cities. The peasantry responded with armed revolts in the countryside. These revolts were rural equivalents of the organization of late medieval cities in sworn communes to protect their self-interests against rulers. The revolts of the agrarian peasantry, like those of the urban proletariat, were brutally crushed. They stand out at the end of the Middle Ages as violent testimony to the breakup of medieval society. As growing national sentiment would break its political unity and heretical movements would end its nominal religious oneness, the revolts of the peasantry revealed the absence of medieval social unity.

TOWNSPEOPLE. In the eleventh century, towns and cities held only about 5 per cent of Western Europe's population. Nonetheless, one could find there the whole of medieval society: nobles visiting their townhouses, peasants living or working within the walls, resident monks and priests, university scholars, great merchants and poor journeymen, pilgrims

A medieval shoemaker. Guilds of shoemakers date back to Ancient Rome. In the Middle Ages most people wore homemade clogs or wooden shoes. Leather shoes made to order by skilled craftsmen could be quite costly and elaborate in style and were mostly for the upper classes. [Vincent Virga Archives.]

en route to shrines, and beggars passing through. By modern comparison, the great majority of medieval towns were merely small villages. Of some three thousand late medieval German towns, for example, twenty-eight hundred had populations under 1,000 and only fifteen had in excess of 10,000 inhabitants. Only London, Paris, and the great merchant capitals of Italy—Florence, Venice, and Naples—approached 100,000 by the fifteenth century.

Women appear to have slightly outnumbered men. War, the perils of long-distance travel, and illnesses resulting from immoderation in food and drink combined to reduce male ranks. The frequent remarriage of widows, whose inheritances made them attractive mates, and the church's siphoning off of an already short supply of eligible bachelors into monasteries contributed to the large number of unmarried women. Those from the upper classes entered nunneries and beguinages, and the very poor joined wandering bands of prostitutes. The great mass of lower and middle strata married women worked as virtual partners in their husbands' trade or craft. It has been speculated that the fact that unmarried women formed a large, unproductive surplus contributed to the prejudice of late medieval society against them and made them the more vulnerable targets of the great witch hunts of the fifteenth and sixteenth centuries.

The term *bourgeois* first appeared in the eleventh century to describe a new addition to the three traditional social ranks of knight (noble), cleric, and serf. The term initially designated the merchant groups, who formed new communities or "bourgs" as bases of operation in or around the old Roman towns that were governed by the landed nobility. These men, whose business was long-distance trade and commerce, were at first highly suspect within traditional medieval society. Clerics condemned the profits they gained from lending money as immoral usury, and noblemen viewed their fluid wealth and mobility as politically disruptive. The merchants in turn resented the laws and customs of feudal society that gave the nobility and the clergy special privileges. Town life was often disrupted because regional laws permitted the nobility and the clergy to live beyond the rules that governed the activities of everyone else.

Merchants especially wanted an end to the arbitrary tolls and tariffs imposed by regional magnates over the surrounding countryside. Such regulations hampered and could even bring to a standstill the flow of commerce on which both merchants and craftsmen in the growing urban export industries depended. The townspeople needed simple, uniform laws and a government sympathetic to their business interests; they wanted a government in which merchants and craftsmen had a major voice. That need created internal and external struggles with the old landed nobility. This

The vast majority of medieval women were working peasants and townswomen. This fourteenth century English manuscript shows women carrying jugs of fresh milk from the sheep pen. [Trustees of the British Museum.]

basic conflict led towns in the high and late Middle Ages to form their own independent communes and to ally themselves with kings against the nobility—developments that created a powerful challenge to feudal society.

Despite unified resistance to external domination, the medieval town was not an internally harmonious social unit. It was a collection of many selfish, competitive communities. Only families of long standing and those who owned property had the full rights of citizenship and a say in the town's government. Workers in the same trade lived together on streets that bore their name, apparently doing so as much to monitor one another's business practices as to dwell among peers. Sumptuary laws regulated not only the dress but even the architecture of the residences of the various social groups. Merchant guilds appeared in the eleventh century and were followed in the twelfth by the craft guilds (organizations of drapers, haberdashers, furriers, hosiers, goldsmiths, and so on). These organizations existed solely to advance the business interests of their members and to advance their personal well-being. They won favorable government policies and served as collection agencies for the unpaid accounts of individual members. The guilds also formed distinctive religious confraternities, close-knit associations that ministered to the needs of member families in both life and death.

The merchants and the stronger craft guilds quickly won a role in town government. "New-rich" patricians married into the old nobility and aped their social cus-toms. Sharing the power of government in the city councils, the craft guilds used their position in the most selfish way to limit their membership, to regulate their own wages favorably, and to establish exacting standards of workmanship so that their products could not be copied by others. Trademarks first appeared in the twelfth century. So rigid and exclusive did the dominant guilds become that they stifled their own creativity and inflamed the journeymen who were excluded from joining their ranks. In the fourteenth century, unrepresented artisans and craftsmen, a true urban proletariat prevented by law from either forming their own guilds or entering the existing guilds, revolted in a number of places: Florence, Paris, and the cities of Flanders. Their main opponents were the merchant and craft guilds, which had themselves risen to prominence by opposing the antiquated laws and privileges of the old nobility.

Medieval Women

The image and the reality of medieval women are two very different things. The image, both for contemporaries and for us today, was strongly influenced by male Christian clergy, whose ideal was the celibate life of chastity, poverty, and obedience. Drawing on classical, medical, philosophical, and legal traditions that predated Christianity, as well as on ancient biblical theology, Christian theologians depicted women as physically, mentally, and morally weaker than men. On the basis of such assumptions, medieval church and society sanctioned the coercive treatment of women, including corrective wife-beating. Christian clergy generally considered marriage a debased state by comparison with the religious life, and in their writings they praised virgins and celibate widows over wives. Women, as the Bible clearly taught, were the "weaker vessel." In marriage, their role was to be subject and obedient to their husbands, who, as the stronger partners, had a duty to protect and discipline them.

This image of the medieval woman suggests that she had two basic options in life: to become either a subjugated housewife or a confined nun. In reality, the vast majority of medieval women were neither.

Both within and outside Christianity this image of women—not yet to speak of the reality of their lives—was contradicted. In chivalric romances and courtly love literature of the twelfth and thirteenth centuries, as in the contemporaneous cult of the Virgin Mary, women were presented as objects of service and devotion to be praised and admired, even put on pedestals and treated as superior to men. If the Church shared traditional misogynist sentiments, it also condemned them, as in the case of the *Romance of the Rose* (late thirteenth century) and other popular "bawdy" literature. The learned churchman Peter Lombard (1100–1169) sanctioned an image of women that was often invoked in didactic Christian literature. Why, he asked, was Eve created from Adam's rib and not instead taken from his head or his feet? The answer was clear. God took Eve from Adam's side because he wanted woman neither to rule over nor to be enslaved by man, but to stand squarely at his side, as his companion and partner in mutual aid and trust. By so insisting on the spiritual equality of men and women and their shared responsibility to one another within marriage, the Church also helped to raise the dignity of women.

Women also had basic rights under secular law that prevented them from being treated as mere chattel. All the major Germanic law codes recognized the economic freedom of women, that is, their right to inherit, administer, dispose of, and confer on their children family property and wealth. They could press charges in court against men for bodily injury and rape. Depending on the country in question, punishments for rape ranged from fines, flogging, and banishment to blinding, castration, and death.

The nunnery was an option for only a very small number of unmarried women from the uppermost classes. Entrance required a dowry *(dos)* and could be almost as expensive as a wedding, although usually it was less. Within the nunnery, a woman could rise to a position of leadership as abbess or mother superior and could exercise an organizational and administrative authority denied her in much of secular life. How-

ever, the nunneries of the established religious orders were also under male supervision, so that even abbesses had finally to answer to higher male authority.

Nunneries also provided women an escape from the debilitating effects of multiple pregnancies. When, in the ninth century, under the influence of Christianity, the Carolingians made monogamous marriage their official policy (heretofore they had practiced polygyny and concubinage and had permitted divorce), it was both a boon and a burden to women. On the one hand, the selection of a wife now became a very special event. Wives gained greater dignity and legal security. On the other hand, a woman's labor as household manager and the bearer of children greatly increased. The aristocratic wife not only ran a large household but was also the agent of her husband during his absence. In addition to these responsibilities, one wife now had sole responsibility for the propagation of heirs. Such demands clearly took their toll. The mortality rates of Frankish women increased and their longevity decreased after the ninth century. The Carolingian wife also became the sole object of her husband's wrath and displeasure. Under such conditions, the cloister could serve as a welcome refuge to women. However, the number of women in cloisters was never very great. In late medieval England, for example, there are estimated to have been no more than thirty-five hundred.

The vast majority of medieval women were neither aristocratic housewives nor nuns, but working women. Every evidence suggests that they were respected and loved by their husbands, perhaps because they worked shoulder by shoulder and hour by hour with them. Between the ages of ten and fifteen, girls were apprenticed in a trade much as were boys, and they learned to be skilled workers. If they married, they either continued their particular trade, operating their bakeshops or dress shops next to their husbands' businesses, or they became assistants and partners in the shops of their husbands. Women appeared in virtually every "blue-collar" trade, from butchers to goldsmiths, although they were especially active in the food and clothing industries. Women belonged to guilds, just like men, and they became craftmasters. In the later Middle Ages, townswomen increasingly had the opportunity to go to school and to gain vernacular literacy.

It is also true that women did not have as wide a range of vocations as men. They were excluded from the learned professions of scholarship, medicine, and law. They often found their freedom of movement within a profession more carefully regulated than a man's. Usually women performed the same work as men for a wage 25 per cent lower. And, as is still true today, they filled the ranks of domestic servants in disproportionate numbers. Still, women were as prominent and as creative a part of workaday medieval society as men.

Medieval Children

Historians have found much evidence to suggest that medieval parents remained emotionally distant from their children, showing them little interest and affection. Evidence of low parental regard for children comes from a variety of sources. First, the art and sculpture of the Middle Ages rarely portray children as distinct from adults; pictorially, children and adults look alike. Then, there was high infant and child mortality, which could only have made emotional investment in children risky. How could a medieval parent, knowing that a child had a 30–50 per cent chance of dying before age five, dare become too emotionally attached?

Also, during the Middle Ages, children directly assumed adult responsibilities. The children of peasants became laborers in the fields alongside their parents as soon as they could physically manage the work. Urban artisans and burghers sent their children out of their homes to apprentice in various crafts and trades between the ages of eight and twelve. In many, perhaps most, instances a child was placed in the home of a known relative or friend, but often he or she ended up with a mere acquaintance, even a complete stranger. That children were expected to grow up fast in the Middle Ages is also suggested by the canonical ages for marriage: twelve for girls and fourteen for boys.

Infanticide is an even more striking indication of low esteem for children. The ancient Romans exposed unwanted children at birth. In this way they regulated family size, though the surviving children appear to have been given both attention and affection. The Germanic tribes of medieval Europe, by contrast, had large families but tended to neglect their children. Infanticide appears to have been directed primarily against girls. Early medieval penance books and church synods condemned the practice outright and also forbade parents to sleep with infants and small children, as this became an occasion and an excuse (alleged accidental suffocation) for killing them.

Also, among the German tribes one paid a much lower *wergild*, or fine, for injury to a child than for injury to an adult. The *wergild* for injuring a child was only one fifth that for injuring an adult. That paid for injury to a female child under fifteen was one half that for injury to a male child—a strong indication that female children were the least esteemed members of German tribal society. Mothers appear also to have nursed boys longer than they did girls, which favored boys' health and survival. However, a woman's *wergild* increased a full eightfold between infancy and her

Children watching a puppet show. [Trustees of the British Museum.]

childbearing years, at which time she had obviously become highly prized.[3]

Despite such varied evidence of parental neglect of children, there is another side to the story. Since the early Middle Ages, physicians and theologians, at least, have clearly understood childhood to be a distinct and special stage of life. Isidore of Seville (560–636), the metropolitan of Seville and a leading intellectual authority throughout the Middle Ages, carefully distinguished six ages of life, the first four of which were infancy (between one and seven years of age), childhood (seven to fourteen), adolescence, and youth.

According to the medical authorities, infancy proper extended from birth to anywhere between six months and two years (depending on the authority) and covered the period of speechlessness and suckling. The period thereafter, until age seven, was considered a higher level of infancy, marked by the beginning of a child's ability to speak and his or her weaning. At age seven, when a child could think and act decisively and speak clearly, childhood proper began. After this point, a child could be reasoned with, could profit from regular discipline, and could begin to train for a lifelong vocation. At seven a child was ready for schooling, private tutoring, or an apprenticeship in a chosen craft or trade. Until physical growth was completed, however—and that could extend to twenty-one years of age—a child or youth was legally under the guardianship of parents or a surrogate authority.

There is evidence that high infant and child mortality, rather than distancing parents from children, actually made parents look on them as all the more precious. The medical authorities of the Middle Ages were those of antiquity—Hippocrates, Galen, and Soranus of Ephesus. They dealt at length with postnatal care and childhood diseases. Both in learned and popular medicine, sensible as well as fanciful cures can be found for the leading killers of children (diarrhea, worms, pneumonia, and fever). When infants and children died, medieval parents grieved as pitiably as modern parents do. In the art and literature of the Middle Ages, we find mothers baptizing dead infants and children or carrying them to pilgrim shrines in the hope of reviving them. There are also examples of mental illness and suicide brought on by the death of a child.[4]

We also find a variety of children's toys, even devices like walkers and potty chairs, clear evidence of special attention being paid to children. The medieval authorities on child rearing widely condemned child abuse and urged moderation in the disciplining of children. In church art and drama, parents were urged to love their children as Mary loved Jesus. By the high Middle Ages, if not earlier, children were widely viewed as special creatures with their own needs and possessed of their own rights.

Politics

England and France: Hastings (1066) to Bouvines (1214)

WILLIAM THE CONQUEROR. The most important change in English political life was occasioned in 1066 by the death of the childless Anglo-Saxon ruler Edward the Confessor, so-named because of his reputation of piety. Edward's mother was a Norman princess, and this fact gave the duke of Normandy a hereditary claim to the English throne. Before his death, Edward, who was not a strong ruler, acknowledged this claim and even directed that his throne be given to William of Normandy (d. 1087). But the Anglo-Saxon assembly, which customarily bestowed the royal power, had a mind of its own and vetoed Edward's last wishes. It chose instead Harold Godwinsson. This defiant action brought the swift conquest of England by the powerful Normans. William's forces defeated Harold's army at Hastings on October 14, 1066. Within weeks of the invasion, William was crowned king of England in Westminster Abbey, both by right of heredity and by right of conquest.

The Norman king thoroughly subjected his noble vassals to the crown, yet he also consulted with them regularly about decisions of "state." The result was a unique blending of the "one" and the "many," a balance between monarchical and parliamentary elements that has ever since characterized English government.

For the purposes of administration and taxation, William commissioned a county-by-county survey of his new realm, a detailed accounting known as the *Domesday Book* (1080–1086). The title of the book reflects the thoroughness of the survey: just as none would escape the doomsday judgment of God, so none was overlooked by William's assessors.

HENRY II. William's son, Henry I (ruled 1100–1135), died without a male heir, throwing England into virtual anarchy until Henry II (1154–1189) mounted the throne as head of the new Plantagenet dynasty. Henry brought to the throne greatly expanded French holdings, partly by inheritance from his father (Burgundy and Anjou) and partly by his marriage to Eleanor of Aquitaine (1122–1204), a union that created the so-called Angevin or English-French empire. Eleanor

---

[3] David Herlihy, "Medieval Children," in *Essays on Medieval Civilization*, ed. by B. K. Lackner and K. R. Phelp (University of Texas Press, 1978), pp. 109–131.

[4] Klaus Arnold, *Kind und Gesellschaft im Mittelalter und Renaissance* (Paderborn, 1980), pp. 31, 37.

married Henry while he was still the count of Anjou and not yet king of England. The marriage occurred only eight weeks after the annulment of Eleanor's fifteen-year marriage to the ascetic French king Louis VII in March 1152. Although the annulment was granted on grounds of consanguinity (blood relationship), the true reason for the dissolution of the marriage was Louis' suspicion of infidelity (according to rumor, Eleanor had been intimate with her cousin). The annulment was very costly to Louis, who lost Aquitaine together with his wife. Eleanor bore Henry eight children, five of them sons, among them the future kings Richard the Lion-Hearted and John. Not only did England, under Henry, come to control most of the coast of France, but Henry also conquered a part of Ireland and made the king of Scotland his vassal.

The French king, Louis VII, who had lost both his wife and considerable French land to Henry, saw a mortal threat to France in this English expansion. He responded by adopting what came to be a permanent French policy of containment and expulsion of the English from their continental holdings in France—a policy that did not finally succeed until the mid-fifteenth century, when English power on the Continent collapsed at the conclusion of the Hundred Years' War.

POPULAR REBELLION AND MAGNA CARTA. As Henry II acquired new lands abroad, he became more autocratic at home. He forced his will on the clergy in the Constitutions of Clarendon (1164), measures that placed limitations on judicial appeals to Rome; subjected the clergy to the civil courts; and gave the king control over the election of bishops. The result was strong political resistance from both the nobility and the clergy. The archbishop of Canterbury, Thomas á Becket (CA. 1118–1170), once Henry's compliant chancellor, broke openly with the king and fled to Louis VII. Becket's subsequent assassination in 1170 and his canonization by Pope Alexander III at the altar in 1172 forced the king to retreat from his heavy-handed tactics, as popular resentment grew.

English resistance to the king became outright rebellion under Henry's successors, the brothers Richard the Lion-Hearted (1189–1199) and John (1199–1216). Their burdensome taxation in support of unnecessary foreign Crusades and a failing war with France left the English people little alternative. In 1209, Pope Innocent III excommunicated King John and placed England under interdict. This humiliating experience saw the king of England declare his country a fief of the pope. But it was the defeat of the English by the French at Bouvines in 1214 that proved the last straw. With the full support of the clergy and the townspeople, the English barons revolted against John. The popular rebellion ended with the king's grudging recognition of Magna Carta ("Great Charter") in 1215.

This monumental document was a victory of feudal over monarchical power in the sense that it secured the rights of the many—the nobility, the clergy, and the townspeople—over the autocratic king; it restored the internal balance of power that had been the English political experience since the Norman Conquest. The English people—at least the privileged English people—thereby preserved their right to be represented at the highest levels of government, especially in matters of taxation. The monarchy remained intact, however, and its legitimate powers and rights were duly recognized and preserved. This outcome contrasted with the experience on the Continent, where victorious nobility tended to humiliate kings and emperors and undo all efforts at centralization.

With a peculiar political genius, the English consistently refused to tolerate either the absorption of the power of the monarchy by the nobility or the abridgment of the rights of the nobility by the monarchy. Although King John continued to resist the Great Charter in every way he could, his son Henry III formally ratified it, and it has ever since remained a cornerstone of English law.

PHILIP II AUGUSTUS. During the century and a half between the Norman Conquest (1066) and Magna Carta (1215), a strong monarchy was never in question in England. The English struggle in the high Middle Ages was to secure the rights of the many, not the authority of the king. The French faced the reverse problem in this period. Powerful feudal princes dominated France for two centuries, from the beginning of the Capetian dynasty (987) until the reign of Philip II Augustus (1180–1223). During this period, the Capetian kings wisely concentrated their limited resources on securing the royal domain, their uncontested territory round about Paris known as the Île-de-France. They did not rashly challenge the more powerful nobility. Aggressively exercising their feudal rights in this area, they secured absolute obedience and a solid base of power. By the time of Philip II, Paris had become the center of French government and culture, and the Capetian dynasty a secure hereditary monarchy. Thereafter, the kings of France were in a position to impose their will on the French nobles, who were always in law, if not in political fact, the king's sworn vassals.

The Norman conquest of England helped stir France to unity and make it possible for the Capetian kings to establish a truly national monarchy. The duke of Normandy, who after 1066 was master of the whole of England, was also among the vassals of the French king in Paris. Capetian kings understandably watched with alarm as the power of their Norman vassal grew.

Philip Augustus faced, at the same time, an internal and an international struggle, and he was successful in

Beginning in the mid-twelfth century, the Gothic style evolved from Romanesque architecture. The term itself was at first pejorative: it meant "barbaric" and was applied to the new style by its critics. Gothic was also often known in the Middle Ages as the "French style" because of its unusual popularity in France. Its most distinctive visible features are its ribbed, criss-crossing vaulting, its pointed arches rather than rounded ones and its frequent exterior buttresses. The result gives an essential impression of vertical lines. The vaulting made possible more height than the Romanesque style had sought, while the extensive addition of "flying" buttresses made even greater height possible. Because walls, therefore, did not have to carry all of a structure's weight, wide expanses of windows were possible—hence the extensive use of stained glass and the characteristic color that often floods Gothic cathedrals. Use of the windows to show stories from the Bible, saints' lives, and local events was similar to earlier use of mosaics.

This diagram shows the typical vaulting arches, and buttresses of a Gothic building. [World Architecture, Trewin Copplestone, General Editor (London: Hamlyn, 1963), p. 216.]

both. His armies occupied all the English territories on the French coast, with the exception of Aquitaine. As the showdown with the English neared on the Continent, however, the Holy Roman Emperor Otto IV (1198–1215) entered the fray on the side of the English, and the French found themselves assailed from both east and west. But when the international armies finally clashed at Bouvines on July 27, 1214, in what became the first great European battle in history, the French won handily over the English and the Germans. This victory unified France around the monarchy and thereby laid the foundation for French ascendancy in the later Middle Ages. Philip Augustus also gained control of the lucrative urban industries of Flanders. The defeat so weakened Otto IV that he fell from power in Germany.

The Hohenstaufen Empire (1152–1272)

During the twelfth and thirteenth centuries, stable governments developed in both England and France. In England, Magna Carta balanced the rights of the nobility against the authority of the king, and in France, the reign of Philip II Augustus secured the authority of the king over the competitive claims of the nobility. The experience within the Holy Roman Empire, which embraced Germany, Burgundy, and northern Italy by the mid-thirteenth century, was a very different story. There, primarily because of the efforts of the Hohenstaufen dynasty to extend imperial power into southern Italy, disunity and blood feuding remained the order of the day for two centuries and left as a legacy the fragmentation of Germany until modern times.

FREDERICK I BARBAROSSA. The investiture struggle had earlier weakened imperial authority. A new day seemed to dawn for imperial power with the accession to the throne of Frederick I Barbarossa (1152–1190), the first of the Hohenstaufens, the successor dynasty within the empire to the Franks and the Ottonians. The Hohenstaufens not only reestablished imperial authority but also initiated a new phrase in the contest between popes and emperors, one that was to prove even more deadly than the investiture struggle had been. Never have kings and popes despised and persecuted one another more than during the Hohenstaufen dynasty.

As Frederick I surveyed his empire, he saw powerful feudal princes in Germany and Lombardy and a pope in Rome who believed that the emperor was his

Salisbury cathedral, built 1220–1265, an example of English Gothic. Note the flying buttresses, which permit greater height, and the soaring towers and spire. [British Tourist Authority, New York.]

creature. There existed, however, widespread disaffection with the incessant feudal strife of the princes and the turmoil caused by the theocratic pretensions of the papacy. Popular opinion was on the emperor's side. Thus, Frederick had a foundation on which to rebuild imperial authority, and he shrewdly took advantage of it. Switzerland became Frederick's base of operation. From there he attempted to hold the empire together by stressing feudal bonds.

HENRY VI AND THE SICILIAN CONNECTION. Frederick's reign ended with stalemate in Germany and defeat in Italy. Before his death in 1190, an opportunity had opened to form a new territorial base of power for future emperors when the Norman ruler of the kingdom of Sicily, William II (1166–1189) sought an alliance with Frederick that would free him to pursue a scheme to conquer Constantinople. The alliance was sealed in 1186 by a most fateful marriage between Frederick's son—the future Henry VI (1190–1197)—and Constance, heiress to the kingdom of Sicily. This alliance proved, however, to be only another well-laid political plan that went astray. The Sicilian connection became a fatal distraction for Hohenstaufen kings, leading them repeatedly to sacrifice their traditional territorial base in northern Europe to the temptation of imperialism. Equally ominous, this union of the empire with Sicily left Rome encircled, thereby ensuring the undying hostility of a papacy already thoroughly distrustful of the emperor. The marriage alliance with Sicily proved to be the first step in what soon became a fight to the death between pope and emperor.

Henry VI died in September 1197, with chaos his immediate heir. Between English intervention in its politics and the pope's deliberate efforts to sabotage the Hohenstaufen dynasty, Germany was thrown into anarchy and civil war. England gave financial support to anti-Hohenstaufen factions. Its candidate for the imperial throne, Otto of Brunswick of the rival Welf dynasty, was crowned Otto IV by his supporters in Aachen in 1198 and later won general recognition in Germany. With England supporting Otto, the French rushed in on the side of the fallen Hohenstaufen—the beginning of periodic French fishing in troubled German waters. Meanwhile, Henry VI's four-year-old son, Frederick, was safely tucked away as a ward of Pope Innocent III (1198–1215).

Hohenstaufen support remained alive in Germany, however, and Otto reigned over a very divided kingdom. In October 1209, Pope Innocent crowned him emperor. But the pope quickly changed from benefactor to mortal enemy when, after his coronation, Otto proceeded to reconquer Sicily and once again pursue an imperial policy that left Rome encircled. Within four

MAP 14-3 GERMANY AND ITALY IN THE MIDDLE AGES *Medieval Germany and Italy were divided lands. The Holy Roman Empire (Germany) embraced hundreds of independent territories that the emperor ruled only in name. The papacy controlled the Rome area and tried to enforce its will on Romagna. Under the Hohenstaufens (mid-12th to mid-13th century), internal German divisions and papal conflict reached new heights; German rulers sought to extend their power to southern Italy and Sicily.*

months of his papal coronation, Otto received a papal excommunication.

FREDERICK II. Pope Innocent, casting about for a counterweight to the treacherous Otto, joined the French, who had remained loyal to the Hohenstaufens against the English–Welf alliance. His new ally, Philip Augustus, impressed on Innocent the fact that a solution to their problems with Otto IV lay near at hand in Innocent's ward, Frederick of Sicily. Frederick, the son of the late Hohenstaufen Emperor Henry VI, was now of age and, unlike Otto, had an immediate hereditary claim to the imperial throne. In December 1212, the young Frederick, with papal, French, and German support, was crowned king of the Romans in Mainz, as Frederick II. Within a year and a half, Philip Augustus ended the Welf interregnum of Otto IV on the battlefield of Bouvines. Philip sent Frederick II Otto's fallen imperial banner from the battlefield, a bold gesture that suggests the extent to which Frederick's ascent to the throne was intended to be that of a French-papal puppet.

He soon disappointed any such hopes. Frederick was Sicilian and dreaded travel beyond the Alps. Only nine of his thirty-eight years as emperor were spent in Germany. Although Frederick continued to pursue royal policies in Germany through his representatives, he desired only one thing from the German princes, the imperial title for himself and his sons, and he was willing to give them what they wanted to secure it. His eager compliance with their demands laid the foundation for six centuries of German division. In 1220 he recognized the jurisdictional claims of the ecclesiastical princes of Germany, and in 1232 he extended the same recognition to the secular princes. The German princes were undisputed lords over their territories. Frederick's concessions have been characterized as a German equivalent to Magna Carta in the sense that they secured the rights of the German nobility. Unlike Magna Carta, however, they did so without at the same time securing the rights of monarchy. Magna Carta placed the king and the nobility (parliament) in England in a creative tension; the reign of Frederick II simply made the German nobility petty kings.

Frederick had an equally disastrous relationship with the pope, who excommunicated him no fewer than four times. The pope won the long struggle that ensued, although his victory proved in time to be a Pyrrhic one. In the contest with Frederick II, Pope Innocent IV (1243–1254) launched the church into European politics on a massive scale, and his wholesale secularization of the papacy made the Church highly vulnerable to the criticism of religious reformers and royal apologists. Innocent organized and led the German princes against Frederick. These princes—thanks to Frederick's grand concessions to them—had become a superior force and were in full control of Germany by the 1240s.

When Frederick died in 1250, the German monarchy died with him. The princes established an informal electoral college in 1257, which thereafter reigned supreme (it was formally recognized by the emperor in 1356). The "king of the Romans" became their puppet, this time with firmly attached strings; he was elected and did not rule by hereditary right. Between 1250 and 1272, the Hohenstaufen dynasty slowly faded into oblivion.

Independent princes now controlled Germany. Italy fell to local magnates. The connection between Germany and Sicily, established by Frederick I, was permanently broken. And the papal monarchy emerged as one of Europe's most formidable powers, soon to enter its most costly conflict with the French and the English.

The Rise of Russia

Early in the ninth century, missionaries from Byzantium had converted Russia to the Christianity of the Eastern Orthodox Church. This development meant that Russia would remain culturally separated from the Latin Christianity of Western Europe. Between the late ninth century and the mid-thirteenth century, the city of Kiev was the center of Russian political life. Although the city enjoyed fairly extensive trade relations with its neighbors, it failed to develop a political system that provided effective resistance to foreign domination.

The external threat to Kievan Russia came from the east when the Mongols moved across the vast Eurasian plains and into Russia as Genghis Khan built his empire. By 1240, the Mongols had conquered most of Russia and had turned its various cities and their surrounding countryside into dependent principalities from which tribute could be exacted. The portion of the Mongol Empire to which Russia thus stood in the relationship of a vassal was called the *Golden Horde*. It included the steppe, in what is now south Russia, with its largely nomadic population. This vassal relationship encouraged an Eastern orientation on the part of the Russians for over two centuries, although the connection of the Russian church to the Byzantine Empire remained important. During this period there was no single central political authority in Russia. The land was divided into numerous feudal principalities, each of which was militarily weak and subject in one degree or another to the Golden Horde.

The rise of Moscow as a relatively strong power eventually brought the feudal age of Russian history to an end. In the fourteenth century, under Grand Prince Ivan I, the city began to cooperate with its Mongol—

or as the Russians called them, Tatar—overlords in the collection of tribute. Ivan kept much of this tribute to himself and was soon called Ivan Kalita, or John of the Moneybag. When Mongol authority began to weaken, the princes of Moscow, who had become increasingly wealthy, filled the political power vacuum in the territory near the city. The princes extended their authority and that of the city by purchasing some territory, colonizing other areas, and conquering new lands. This slow extension of the principality of Moscow is usually known as *gathering the Russian land*.

In 1380, Grand Prince Dmitry of Moscow defeated the Mongols in battle. The result was not militarily decisive, but Moscow had demonstrated that the Mongol armies were not invincible. Conflict with the Mongols continued for another century before they were driven out. During these years, the princes of Moscow asserted their right to be regarded as the successors of the earlier Kievan rulers, and they also made Moscow the religious center of Russia.

France in the Thirteenth Century: The Reign of Louis IX

If Innocent III realized the fondest ambitions of medieval popes, Louis IX (1226–1270), the grandson of Philip Augustus, embodied the medieval view of the perfect ruler. His reign was a striking contrast to that of his contemporary, Frederick II of Germany. Coming to power in the wake of the French victory at Bouvines (1214), Louis inherited a unified and secure kingdom. Although he was also endowed with a moral character that far excelled that of his royal and papal contemporaries, he was also at times prey to naiveté. Not beset by the problems of sheer survival, and a reformer at heart, Louis found himself free to concentrate on what medieval people believed to be the business of civilization.

Magnanimity in politics is not always a sign of strength and Louis could be very magnanimous. Although in a position to drive the English from their French possessions during negotiations for the Treaty of Paris (1259), he refused to take such advantage. Had he done so and ruthlessly confiscated English territories on the French coast, he might have lessened, if not averted altogether, the conflict of the Hundred Years' War (CA. 1337–1453). Although he occasionally chastised popes for their crude ambitions, Louis remained neutral during the long struggle between Frederick II and the papacy, and his neutrality redounded very much to the pope's advantage. For their assis-

King Louis IX of France, shown in a thirteenth-century manuscript, riding off on a crusade with his knights and priests, as monks bless and bid him farewell. [Royal MS. 16G. VI, f. 404v. Reproduced by permission of the British Library Board, London.]

tance, both by action and by inaction, the Capetian kings of the thirteenth century became the objects of many papal favors.

Louis' greatest achievements lay at home. The efficient French bureaucracy, which his predecessors had used to exploit their subjects, became under Louis an instrument of order and fair play in local government. He sent forth royal commissioners (enquêteurs), reminiscent of Charlemagne's far less successful *missi dominici*, to monitor the royal officials responsible for local governmental administration. These royal ambassadors were received as genuine tributes of the people. Louis further abolished private wars and serfdom within his royal domain, gave his subjects the judicial right of appeal from local to higher courts, and made the tax system, by medieval standards, more equitable. The French people came to associate their king with justice, and national feeling, the glue of nationhood, grew very strong during his reign.

Respected by the kings of Europe, Louis became an arbiter among the world's powers, having far greater moral authority than the pope. During his reign, French society and culture became an example to all of Europe, a pattern that would continue into the modern period. Northern France became the showcase of monastic reform, chivalry, and Gothic art and architecture. Louis' reign also coincided with the golden age of Scholasticism, which saw the convergence of Europe's greatest thinkers on Paris, among them Saint Thomas Aquinas and Saint Bonaventure.

Louis' perfection remained, however, that of a medieval king. Like his father, Louis VIII (1223–1226), Louis was something of a religious fanatic. He sponsored the French Inquisition. He led two French Crusades against the Arabs, which were inspired by the purest religious motives but proved to be personal disasters. During the first (1248–1254), Louis was captured and had to be ransomed out of Egypt. He died of a fever during the second in 1270. It was especially for this selfless, but also quite useless, service on behalf of the Church that Louis IX later received the rare honor of sainthood.

The High Middle Ages in World Perspective

With its borders finally secured, Western Europe concentrated during the high Middle Ages on its political institutions and cultural development, something denied it during the early Middle Ages. In England and France, modern Western nations can be seen in formation. Within the empire, there was both revival (under Otto I) and total collapse (during the Hohenstaufen dynasty) of imperial rule. Everywhere, society success-

fully organized itself from noble to serf. With the flourishing of trade and the expansion of towns, a new wealthy class patronized education. Western Europe's first universities appeared and a movement called Scholasticism brought a new, and often forbidding, order to knowledge. The major disruption of the period, however, was an unprecedented conflict between former allies. The Roman Catholic church had become a monarchy in its own right, able to compete with secular states and even to dethrone (by excommunication and interdict) kings and princes. The foundation was thereby laid both for perpetual conflict between popes and rulers, which lasted well into early modern times, and for the creation of the peculiar Western separation of Church and State.

For Western Europe, the high Middle Ages were a period of clearer self-definition during which the West gained much of the shape we have come to recognize today. Other world civilizations had already become established and were beginning to depart their "classical" or "golden" periods. The best lay behind rather than before them.

Under the Sung dynasty (960–1279) before Mongol rule, China continued its technological advance. In addition to printing, the Chinese invented the abacus and gunpowder. They also enjoyed a money economy unknown in the West. But culturally, these centuries between 1000 and 1300 were closed and narrow by comparison with those of the T'ang Dynasty. Politically, the Sung was far more autocratic. In China (as also in West European lands like England and France, although not in Italy and the empire), regional aristocracies ceased to be serious obstacles to a strong centralized government.

Chinese women generally held a lower status and had fewer vocational options than in the West, as the practice of footbinding dramatically attests. As in the West, a higher degree of freedom and self-government developed in the countryside, especially by the fourteenth century, as peasants gained the right to buy and sell land and to fulfill traditional labor obligations by money payments. Intellectually, China, like the West, had a scholastic movement within its dominant philosophy; Confucianism made religious and philosophical thought more elaborate, systematic, and orthodox. Whereas Western scholasticism had the effect of making Christianity aloof, elitist, and ridiculed by its lay critics, Confucianism remained a philosophy highly adaptable and popular among laypeople.

In the late twelfth century, Japan shifted from civilian to military rule; the Kamakura Bakufu governed by mounted warriors who were paid with rights to income from land in exchange for their military services. This rise of a military aristocracy marks the beginning of Japan's "medieval," as distinct from its "classical" period. Three Mongol invasions in the thirteenth century also required a strong military. With a civilian court also in existence, Japan actually had a dual government (that is, two emperors and two courts) until the fourteenth century. However, this situation differed greatly from the deep and permanent national divisions developing at this time among the emerging states and autonomous principalities of Western Europe.

Japanese women, more like those in Western Europe than in China, traditionally played a prominent role in royal government and court culture. Nun Shogun, for example, succeeded her husband for a brief period of Kamatura rule in the late twelfth century. But the prominence of women in government would also change in Japan by the fourteenth century.

Within the many developing autonomous Islamic lands at this time, the teaching of Muhammad had created an international culture. The regular practice of religious fundamentals made it possible for Muslims to transcend their new and often very deep regional divisions. Similarly, Christianity made it possible for Englishmen, Frenchmen, Germans, and Italians to think of themselves as one people and unite in Crusades to the Holy Land. As these Crusades began in the late eleventh century, Islam too was on the march, penetrating Turkey and Afghanistan, and impinging upon India, where it gained a new challenge in Hinduism.

Suggested Readings

P. ARIÈS, *Centuries of Childhood: A Social History of Family Life*, trans. by Robert Baldick (1962). Provocative pioneer effort on the subject.

J. W. BALDWIN, *The Scholastic Culture of the Middle Ages: 1000–1300* (1971). Best brief synthesis available.

J. W. BALDWIN, *The Government of Philip Augustus* (1986). A scholarly feat.

M. W. BALDWIN (ed.), *History of the Crusades, I: The First Hundred Years* (1955). Basic historical narrative.

G. BARRACLOUGH, *The Origins of Modern Germany* (1963). Penetrating political narrative.

G. BARRACLOUGH, *The Medieval Papacy* (1968). Brief, comprehensive survey, with pictures.

M. BLOCH, *French Rural Society*, trans. by J. Sondheimer (1966). A classic by a great modern historian.

A. CAPELLANUS, *The Art of Courtly Love*, trans. by J. J. Parry (1941). Documents from the court of Marie de Champagne.

M. CLAGETT, G. POST, AND R. REYNOLDS (eds.), *Twelfth-Century Europe and the Foundations of Modern Society* (1966). Demanding but stimulating collection of essays.

F. C. COPLESTON, *Aquinas* (1965). Best introduction to Aquinas' philosophy.

F. COPLESTON, *A History of Philosophy, III/1: Ockham to the Speculative Mystics* (1963). The best introduction to Ockham and his movement.

R. H. C. DAVIS, *A History of Medieval Europe: From Constantine to St. Louis, Part 2* (1972).

G. DUBY, *Rural Economy and Country Life in the Medieval West* (1968). Slice-of-life analysis.

G. DUBY, *The Three Orders: Feudal Society Imagined*, trans. by Arthur Goldhammer (1981). Large, comprehensive, and authoritative.

R. FAWTIER, *The Capetian Kings of France: Monarchy and Nation 987–1328*, trans. by L. Butler and R. J. Adam (1972). Detailed, standard account.

E. GILSON, *Heloise and Abelard* (1968). An analysis and defense of medieval scholarly values.

C. H. HASKINS, *The Renaissance of the Twelfth Century* (1927). Still the standard account.

D. HERLIHY, *Medieval Households* (1985). Sweeping survey of Middle Ages.

C. H. HASKINS, *The Rise of Universities* (1972). A short, minor classic.

E. H. KANTOROWICZ, *The King's Two Bodies* (1957). Controversial analysis of political concepts in the high Middle Ages.

G. LEFF, *Paris and Oxford Universities in the Thirteenth and Fourteenth Centuries: An Institutional and Intellectual History* (1968). Very good on Scholastic debates.

J. LE GOFF, *The Birth of Purgatory* (1981).

R. S. LOOMIS (ed.), *The Development of Arthurian Romance* (1963). A basic study.

R. S. LOPEZ AND I. W. RAYMOND (eds.), *Medieval Trade in the Mediterranean World* (1955). An illuminating collection of sources, concentrated on southern Europe.

E. MÂLE, *The Gothic Image: Religious Art in France in the Thirteenth Century* (1913). A classic.

P. MANDONNET, *St. Dominic and His Work* (1944). For the origins of the Dominican Order.

H. E. MAYER, *The Crusades*, trans. by John Gilligham (1972). Extremely detailed, and the best one-volume account.

J. MOORMAN, *A History of the Franciscan Order* (1968). The best survey.

J. B. MORRALL, *Political Thought in Medieval Times* (1962). A readable and illuminating account.

J. T. NOONAN, *Contraception: A History of Its Treatment by the Catholic Theologians and Canonists* (1967). A fascinating account of medieval theological attitudes toward sexuality and sex-related problems.

E. PANOFSKY, *Gothic Architecture and Scholasticism* (1951). A controversial classic.

C. PETIT-DUTAILLIS, *The Feudal Monarchy in France and England from the Tenth to the Thirteenth Century*, trans. by E. D. Hunt (1964). A political narrative.

H. PIRENNE, *Medieval Cities: Their Origins and the Revival of Trade*, trans. by Frank D. Halsey (1970). A minor classic.

J. M. POWELL, *Innocent III: Vicar of Christ or Lord of the World* (1963). Excerpts from the scholarly debate over Innocent's reign.

F. W. POWICKE, *The Thirteenth Century* (1962). An outstanding treatment of English political history.

H. RASHDALL, *The Universities of Europe in the Middle Ages*, Vols. 1–3 (1936). Dated but still a standard comprehensive work.

F. RÖRIG, *The Medieval Town*, trans. by D. J. A. Matthew (1971). Excellent on northern Europe.

S. SHAHAR, *The Fourth Estate: A History of Women in the Middle Ages* (1983). Readable survey.

O. VON SIMSON, *The Gothic Cathedral* (1956).

R. W. SOUTHERN, *Medieval Humanism and Other Studies* (1970). Provocative and far-ranging essays on topics in the intellectual history of the high Middle Ages.

B. TIERNEY, *The Crisis of Church and State 1050–1300* (1964). A very useful collection of primary sources on key Church–State conflicts.

W. L. WAKEFIELD AND A. P. EVANS (eds.), *Heresies of the High Middle Ages* (1969). A major document collection.

S. WILLIAMS (ed.), *The Gregorian Epoch: Reformation, Revolution, Reaction* (1964). Variety of scholarly opinion on the significance of Pope Gregory's reign presented in debate form.

R. L. WOLFF AND H. W. HAZARD (eds.), *History of the Crusades* 1189–1311 (1962).

An allegory of the mystical life. A ceramic plate from Iran, CA. *1210, showing a man contemplating a bathing woman. What appears to be a semi-erotic painting seems to be a symbolic picture of the sufi (the man) who has abandoned his earthly desires (the riderless horse) and progressed to contemplating his immortal soul (the swimming female). [Freer Gallery of Art.]*

392

15 The Islamic Heartlands, India, and Africa (CA. 1000–1500)

By the mid-tenth century, centralized caliphal power had broken down in the Islamic world. Regional Islamic states with distinctive political and cultural configurations now dominated—a pattern that would endure to modern times. Yet Islamic lands remained part of a single larger civilization. Muslims from Córdoba in Spain could (and did) travel to Bukhara in Transoxiana or Zanzibar on the East African coast and feel much at home. Both regionalism and cosmopolitanism, diversity and unity, have characterized Islamic civilization ever since the tenth century.

In the social and religious spheres, the five hundred years between 1000 and 1500 saw the growth of a truly international Islamic community, united by shared norms of social, religious, and political order represented and maintained by the Muslim religious scholars (*ulema*). Sufism, that strand of Islam stressing personal piety and allegiance to a spiritual master, gained widespread popularity in this period, especially after 1200, through the growth of Sufi brotherhoods. These popular organizations deeply influenced Muslim life everywhere, often countering the more limiting aspects of ulema conformity. Shi'ite ideas also offered an alternative vision of society for many. Shi'ite movements loyal to Ali and his heirs repeatedly challenged but ultimately failed to displace centrist, Sunni dominance of most of the Islamic world.

Culturally, the rise of the New Persian language in the tenth century culminated thereafter in a rich new Islamic literature. A Persian renaissance fueled the spread of Persian as the major language of Islam alongside (or, in the Islamic East, even above) Arabic. The Persian-dominated Iranian and Indian Islamic world became more and more distinct from the Western Islamic lands.

Two Asian steppe peoples, the Mongols and the Turks, rose to political dominance in these centuries, but with different results. The Mongols conquered most of the Islamic heartlands. However, their culture and religion did not become dominant in the Islamic any more than in the Chinese or the Eastern Christian lands they conquered. The spread of the Turks, however, added a substantial Turkish linguistic and cultural tinge to the Islamic world. Islam impinged more and more in this age on civilization in the Indian sub-continent, Southeast Asia, and sub-Saharan Africa. Although it had not yet converted a majority in these regions, it became the major new influence in all of them.

THE ISLAMIC HEARTLANDS

Religion and Society

The notable developments of this period for the shape of Islamic society were the consolidation and institutionalization of Sunni legal and religious norms, Sufi mystical piety, and Shi'ite sectarianism.

Consolidation of Sunni Orthopraxy

The *ulema* (both Sunni and Shi'ite) gradually became an entrenched religious, social, and political elite throughout the Islamic world, especially after the breakdown of centralized power in the tenth century. Their integration into local merchant, landowning, and bureaucratic classes led to stronger identification of these groups with Islam. From the eleventh century on, the *ulema's* power and fixity as a class were expressed in the institution of the *madrasa*, or college of higher learning. On the one hand, the *madrasa* had grown up naturally as individual experts frequented a given mosque or private house and attracted students seeking to learn the Qur'an, the Hadith ("Tradition"), jurisprudence, Arabic grammar, and the like.

On the other hand, the *madrasa's* formal fixation through the endowment of buildings, scholarships, and salaried chairs was a device employed by rulers for their own as well as for pious ends. It gave them a measure of control over the *ulema* through their influence on the appointment of teachers and thus on the legal or theological slant of the curriculum. In notable contrast to the Western university with its corporate

The Sultan Hasan Madrasa *and Tomb-Mosque. This imposing Mamluk building (1356–1363) was built to house teachers and students, studying all four of the major traditions or "schools" of Islamic law. Living and teaching spaces are combined here in a building with a mosque and a tomb enclosure for the sultan. [William A. Graham.]*

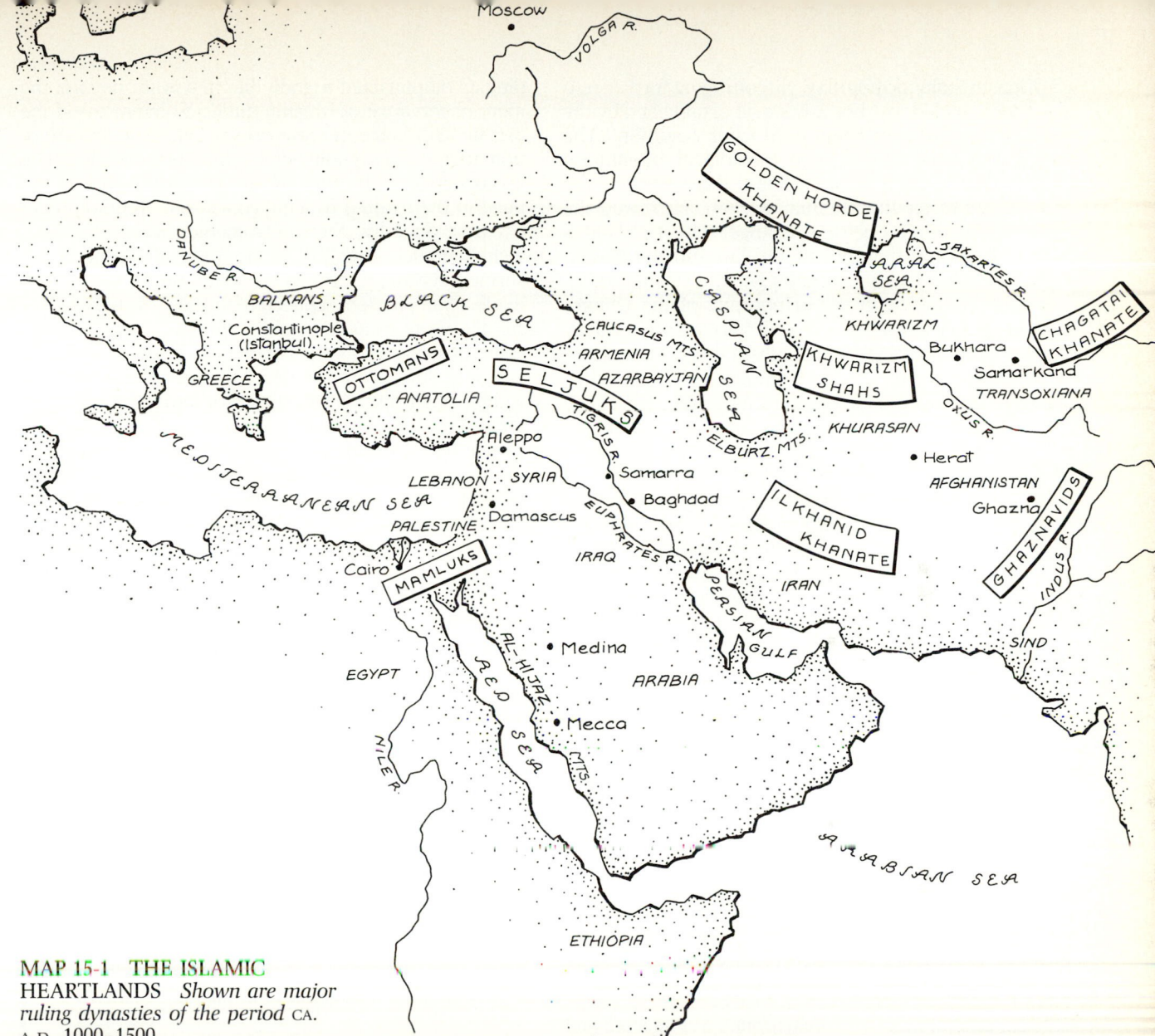

MAP 15-1   THE ISLAMIC
HEARTLANDS   *Shown are major
ruling dynasties of the period* CA.
A.D. 1000–1500.

organization and granting of institutional degrees, the *madrasa* was simply a support institution for individual teachers, who gave personal certification to students for the mastery of particular subjects. The absence of diplomas or degrees for a particular course of study indicates the personalist rather than (as in Europe) corporate nature of Muslim education.[1]

Largely outside *ulema* control, popular, "unofficial" piety flourished in local pilgrimages to saints' tombs, in folk celebrations of Muhammad's birthday and veneration of him in song and poetry, and in the ecstatic worship in song and dance of the Sufis. But the shared traditions that directed family and civil law, the daily prayer-rituals, fasting in the month of Ramadan, and the yearly Meccan pilgrimage remained the public bond among virtually all Muslims, even most Kharijites or Shi'ites. In the Christian world, dogmatic theological positions (beliefs) determined sectarian identity. In contrast, the tendency in the Islamic world, for all its many theological disputes and schools of thought, was to define Islam in terms of the things that Muslims do—hence by ortho*praxy* (practice) rather than by ortho*doxy* (beliefs). The chief arbiters of normative Sunni Islam were four mutually tolerant schools of Muslim legal interpretation (*fiqh*), not the various schools of theological interpretation.

[1]G. Makdisi, "Madrasa and University in the Middle Ages," *Studia Islamica* 31 (1970): 255–264.

A basic Sunni orthopraxy, discouraging further religious or social innovation, was well established by the year 1000 as the dominant Muslim tradition. The emergence of a conservative theological orientation tied to one of the four main Sunni legal schools, the Hanbalites (after Ibn Hanbal, d. 969), narrowed the scope for creative doctrinal change. The Hanbalites stressed reliance only on the Qur'an and the Hadith and a literalist reading of both. Thus, a certain orthodoxy was joined with the orthopraxy of the *Umma*, although there was no "church" to enforce either. Also, a growing social conservatism among the *ulema* reflected their places in regional social aristocracies. As often as not, the *ulema* were as committed to the status quo as were the rulers.

Sufi Piety and Organization

Sufi piety stresses the spiritual and mystical dimensions of Islam. The term *Sufi* apparently came from the Arabic *suf* ("wool") because of the old ascetic practice of wearing only a coarse woolen garment. Sufi simplicity and humility had roots with the Prophet and the Companions but developed as a distinctive tendency when, after about 700, various male and female pietists emphasized a godly life that went beyond the mere observance of Muslim duties. Some stressed the ascetic avoidance of temptations, others loving devotion to God. Psychologically, Sufi piety bridges the abyss between the human and the divine that is implied in the exalted Muslim concept of an omnipotent Creator. Socially, Sufi piety merges with folk piety, including such popular practices as saint veneration, shrine pilgrimage, ecstatic worship, and seasonal festivals. Sufi writers collected stories of the earlier saints, wrote treaties on the Sufi way, and composed some of the world's finest mystical poetry.

Some Sufis were revered as spiritual masters and saints. Their disciples formed brotherhoods that, from about the eleventh century, became both regional and international organizations. Each had its distinctive mystical teaching, Qur'anic interpretations, and devotional practice. These fraternal orders proved to be the chief instrument of the further spread of Muslim faith, as well as a locus of popular piety in almost all Islamic societies. Organized Sufism has always attracted members from the populace at large (in this, it differs from most monasticism), as well as those dedicated to poverty or other radical disciplines. Indeed, Sufi or-

A Muslim Description of Sufism

Writing at the end of the fourteenth century, the great historian and sociological commentator Ibn Khaldun prepared a massive "introduction" to history, the Muqaddima. *In it he described all aspects of Islamic civilization, including the various sectarian groups and schools of thought in the Islamic community. The following excerpts are taken from his long discussion of the Sufis.*

. . . The Sufi approach is based upon constant application to divine worship, complete devotion to God, aversion to the false splendour of the world, abstinence from the pleasure, property, and position to which the great mass aspire, and retirement from the world into solitude for divine worship. These things were general among the men around Muhammad and the early Muslims.

Then, worldly aspirations increased in the second [eighth] century and after. At that time, the special name of Sufis was given to those who aspired to divine worship.

. . . .

Very few people share the self-scrutiny of the Sufis, for negligence in this respect is almost universal. Pious people who do not get that far perform, at best, acts of obedience. The Sufis, however, investigate the results of acts of obedience with the help of mystical and ecstatic experience, in order to learn whether they are free from deficiency or not. Thus, it is evident that the Sufis' path in its entirety depends upon self-scrutiny with regard to what they do or do not do, and upon discussion of the various kinds of mystical and ecstatic experience that result from their exertions. This, then, crystallizes for the Sufi novice in a "station." From that station, he can progress to another, higher one.

. . . .

Thus, the Sufis had their special discipline, which is not discussed by other representatives of the religious law. As a consequence, the science of the religious law came to consist of two kinds. One is the special field of jurists and muftis. It is concerned with the general laws governing the acts of divine worship, customary actions, and mutual dealings. The other is the special field of the Sufis. It is concerned with pious exertion, self-scrutiny with regard to it, discussion of the different kinds of mystical experience to another, and the interpretation of the technical terminology of mysticism in use among them. ❑

From Ibn Khaldun, *The Muqaddimah*, trans. by Franz Rosenthal, ed. and abridged by N. J. Dawood (Princeton, N.J.: Princeton University Press, Bollingen Series, 1967), pp. 358–360.

ders became in this age one of the typical social institutions of everyday Muslim life in Islamic lands. Whether Sunni or Shi'ite, casually or seriously pious, large numbers of Muslims have ever since identified in some degree with one or another Sufi order.

Consolidation of Shi'ite Traditions

Shi'ite traditions crystallized between the tenth and twelfth centuries. Numerous states now came under Shi'ite rulers, some even before the Buyids took Baghdad in 945 (see Chapter 12). Yet the differences separating the diverse Shi'ite groups precluded a unified Shi'ism. Only the strongest Shi'ite state, that of the Fatimids, was able to establish an important empire in Egypt. And a substantial Shi'ite populace developed only in Iran, Iraq, and the lower Indus (Sind).

Two Shi'ite groups emerged as the most influential. The "Seveners," or "Isma'ilis," were those who recognized Isma'il (d. CA. 760), first son of the sixth Alid *imam*, as the seventh *imam* (rather than his brother). The Isma'ilis were esoterics, drawing on Gnostic and Neo-Platonic philosophy, knowledge of which they reserved for a spiritual elite. Isma'ili groups were often revolutionary, and three of them founded states that had substantial impact on the Islamic world. The other group, the Qarmatians of eastern Arabia, ruled or disrupted Iraq, Syria, and Arabia through much of the tenth century; the Fatimids conquered North Africa (909) and Egypt (969) and ruled as Shi'ite caliphs until 1171. The Nizari "Assassins" formed a radical theocracy in the Elburz mountains south of the Caspian Sea; they were at daggers drawn with other Shi'ite and Sunni states from 1090 to 1258.

By the eleventh century, however, most Shi'ites accepted a line of twelve *imams* (descended through another son of the sixth *imam*), the last of whom is said to have disappeared in Samarra (Iraq), in 873, into a concealment from which he will emerge as the Mahdi, or "guided one," who ushers in the messianic age and final judgment. Still today, the Shi'ite majority, the "Twelvers," focus on the martyrdom of the twelve *imams* and look for their intercession on the Day of Judgment. They have flourished best in Iran, the home of most Shi'ite thought, whatever the sect. The Buyids who took control of the Abbasid caliphate in 945 were Twelvers. So were the later Iranian Safavids, who made Twelver doctrine the "state religion" of Iran in the sixteenth century (see Chapter 22).

Unity and Diversity

The Islamic West

The western half of the Islamic world after the tenth century developed two regional foci: (1) in Spain, Moroccan North Africa, and to a lesser extent, west Africa; and (2) in Egypt, Syria–Palestine, Anatolia, and, to a lesser extent, Arabia and Libyan North Africa.

SPAIN AND NORTH AFRICA. The grandeur of Moorish Islamic culture is visible still in Córdoba's great mosque and the ruins of the legendary Alhambra castle. The *Chanson de Roland* preserves the echo of Charlemagne's retreat through the Pyrenees after he failed to check the first Umayyad ruler's growing power. That ruler, Abd al-Rahman I (ruled 756–788), founded the cosmopolitan tradition of Umayyad Spanish culture at Córdoba, which over the next two centuries was the cultural hub of the western world. Renowned for its medicine, science, literature, intellectual life, commercial activity, public baths and gardens, and courtly elegance, Córdoba reached its zenith under Abd al-Rahman III (912–961). He even assumed the title of caliph in 929. His absolutist but benevolent rule saw a largely unified and peaceful Islamic Spain. The mosque-university of Córdoba that

Stretching up 100 meters, the Giralda bell tower of the Seville cathedral was originally built as a Muslim minaret about 1190. Its upper portion was rebuilt in late-renaissance style by a Spanish Christian architect in the 1560s. [Art Resource.]

An Arab Biographer's Account of Maimonides

The following are excerpts from the section on Maimonides (Arabic: Musa ibn Maymun) in the biographical dictionary of learned men compiled by Ibn al-Qifti (d. 1248). In the first section omitted here, Ibn al-Qifti describes how the Spanish Jewish savant at first dissembled conversion to Islam when a new Berber ruler demanded the expulsion of Christians and Jews from Spain and North Africa in about 1133. He goes on to tell how Maimonides then made preparations and moved his family to the more tolerant Islamic world of Cairo, where he eventually became the court physician. The final section omitted concludes with mention of his marriage, death, and accomplishments. It was not at all unusual for Jews or Christians to hold high office under Muslim rulers in many places.

. . . This man was one of the people of Andalus, a Jew by religion. He studied philosophy in Andalus, was expert in mathematics, and devoted attention to some of the logical sciences. He studied medicine there and excelled in it. . . .

. . . After assembling his possessions in the time that was needed for this, he left Andalus and went to Egypt, accompanied by his family. He settled in the town of Fustat, among its Jews, and practiced his religion openly. He lived in a district called al-Masisa and made a living by trading in jewels and suchlike. Some people studied philosophy under him. . . .

He married in Cairo the sister of a Jewish scribe called Abu'l-Ma'ali, the secretary of the mother of Nūr al-Dīn 'Alī, known as al-Afdal, the son of Ṣalāḥ al-Dīn Yūsuf ibn Ayyūb, and he had a son by her who today is a physician in Cairo after his father. . . .

Mūsā ibn Maymūn died in Cairo in the year 605 [1208–9].[1] He ordered his heirs to carry his body, when the smell had ceased, to Lake Tiberias and bury him there, seeking to be among the graves of the ancient Israelites and their great jurists, which are there. This was done.

He was learned in the law and secrets of the Jews and compiled a commentary on the Talmud, which is a commentary and explanation of the Torah; some of the Jews approve of it. Philosophic doctrines overcame him, and he compiled a treatise denying the canonical resurrection. The leaders of the Jews held this against him, so he concealed it except from those who shared his opinion in this. He compiled an abridgement of twenty-one books of Galen, with many additions, in sixteen books. It came out very abridged and quite useless; nothing can be done with it. He edited the Kitāb al-Istikmāl [Book of Perfection] of Ibn Aflah al-Andalusī, on astronomy, and improved it, for there was some confusion in the original. He also edited the Kitāb al-Istikmāl of Ibn Hūd, on mathematics. This is a fine, comprehensive book, needing some correction. He corrected and improved it. . . .

In the latter part of his life he was troubled by a man from Andalus, a jurist called Abu'l-'Arab ibn Ma'īsha, who came to Fustat and met him. He charged him with having been a Muslim in Andalus, accused him [of apostasy] and wanted to have him punished.[2] 'Abd al-Rahīm ibn 'Alī al-Fāḍil prevented this, and said to him, "If a man is converted by force, his Islam is not legally valid." ❑

[1] In fact, he died in 1204.

[2] The penalty for apostasy was death.

From Bernard Lewis (ed. and trans.), *Islam from the Prophet Muhammad to the Capture of Constantinople*, Vol. 2 (New York: Harper and Row, 1974), pp. 189–192.

he founded was the earliest institution of its kind; it attracted students from Europe as well as from the Islamic world.

An irony of this cosmopolitan world was the rigorist conservatism that dominated both Muslim and Christian thought in Spain. From time to time, it sparked Muslim–Christian conflict—a product perhaps of the uniquely close and threatening contact of the two communities. Externally, Abd al-Rahman III checked both the new Fatimid Islamic power in the Mediterranean and the Christian kingdoms in the Spanish north, making possible this golden era of Moorish power and culture. But fragmentation into warring Muslim principalities allowed a resurgence of Spain's Christian states between about 1000 and 1085, when Toledo fell permanently back into Christian hands.

There were brief Islamic revivals in Spain and North Africa under the African reform movements of the Almoravids and Almohads. The Almoravids originated as a religious-warrior brotherhood among Berber nomads in West Africa. Having subdued virtually all of northwest Africa, in 1086 they carried their zealotry from their new capital of Marrakesh into Spain and reunited its Islamic kingdoms. Under their rule,

the arabized Christians (Mozarabs) were persecuted and many were driven out, as were some Moorish Jews. The subsequent wars in Spain with Christian rulers are best known in the West for the exploits of El Cid (d. 1099), the adventurer and mercenary who became the Spanish national hero.

A new reform movement, the Almohads, ended Almoravid rule in Morocco in 1147 and then conquered much of southern Spain. Before their demise (1225 in Spain; 1275 in Africa), they stimulated a brilliant revival of Spanish Islamic culture. In this era, paper manufacture reached Spain and then the rest of western Europe. The long westward odyssey of Indian fable literature through Iran and the Arab world ended with Spanish and Latin translations in thirteenth-century Spain. The most illustrious products of this Spanish Islamic intellectual world were a major philosopher and physician, Ibn Rushd (Averroës, d. 1198); perhaps the greatest Muslim mystical thinker, Ibn al-

Arabi (d. 1240); and the famous Arab-Jewish philosopher, Maimonides (d. 1204), who was forced to spend much of his life abroad in Cairo.

EGYPT AND THE EASTERN MEDITERRANEAN WORLD. *The Fatimids.* The major Islamic presence in the Mediterranean from the tenth to the twelfth century was that of the Shi'ite Fatimids. They began as a Tunisian dynasty, then conquered Morocco, Sicily, and Egypt (969). In Egypt, they built their new capital, Cairo (*al-Qahira*, "the Victorious"), near the original garrison town of the earliest Arab conquest. They took their name from their claim to descent from Muhammad's daughter, Fatima. Their rule as Shi'ite caliphs meant that, for a time, there were three "caliphates"— in Baghdad, Córdoba, and Cairo. The Fatimids were Isma'ilis (see the earlier discussion of "Religion and Society"). Content to rule a Sunni majority in Egypt, they sought recognition as true *imams* by other Isma'ili groups. They did win the allegiance of a Shi'ite state in Yemen and were able, for a time, to take western Arabia and most of Syria from the Buyid "guardians" of the Abbasid caliphate (see Chapter 12).

The Fatimid reign spawned two splinter groups that have played visible, if minor, roles at certain points in history. The Druze of modern Lebanon and Syria originated around 1020 with a few members of the Fatimid court who professed belief in the divinity of one of the Fatimid caliphs. The tradition they founded is too far from Islam to be considered a Muslim sect. The Isma'ili "Assassins," on the other hand, were a radical movement founded by a Fatimid defector in the Elburz mountains of Iran at the beginning of the twelfth century. The name *Assassins* comes not from the political assassinations that made them infamous but from a European corruption of the Arabic *Hashishiyyin* ("users of hashish"). A local Syrian name, it was possibly connected with the story that the assassins were manipulated with drugs to undertake their usually suicidal missions. The *Assassins* were defeated by the Mongols in the thirteenth century.

The Fatimids built the Azhar mosque in Cairo as a center of learning, a role it maintains today, although for Sunni, not (as then) Shi'ite, scholarship. Fatimid rulers treated Egypt's Coptic Christians generally as well as they did their Sunni majority. Many Copts held high offices, even that of vizier. Jews, like Copts, usually fared well under the Fatimids, except for the general persecution of Jews and Christians under the apparently deranged caliph al-Hakim (d. 1021). After 1100, the Fatimids declined, falling in 1171 to their last ruler's vizier, Salah al-Din (Saladin). A Sunni, he founded a short-lived dynasty in Egypt and Syria-Palestine. Henceforward Shi'ite Islam disappeared from Egypt.

The Mamluks. The heirs of the Fatimids and

An Egyptian bronze incense burner of Copto-Arabic origin (eight-ninth century). This nearly intact piece of fine metalwork is a reminder of the constant presence of the Coptic Christian community in Egypt throughout Islamic times and down to the present day. [Freer Gallery of Art.]

Saladin in the eastern Mediterranean were the redoubtable Mamluk *sultans* ("those with authority"). As rulers of Egypt, they styled themselves after the example of the Seljuks (see below). The Mamluks alone among major Islamic dynasties withstood the Mongol invasions that closely followed their accession. The first Mamluk sultan (1250–1257), Aybak, and his successors were Turkish and Mongol slave officers, drawn originally from the bodyguard of Saladin's dynasty. Whereas the early Mamluks were often succeeded by sons or brothers, after the 1390s succession was more often a survival of the fittest; no sultan reigned more than a few years. The Mamluk state was based on a military fief system and total control by the slave-officer elite.

The Mamluk sultan Baybars (1260–1277), who took the last Crusader fortresses, has lived on in Arab legend as a larger-than-life figure. To legitimize his rule, he revived the Abbasid caliphate after its demise in the fall of Baghdad (1258; discussed later) by installing an uncle of Baghdad's last Abbasid at Cairo. He made treaties with Constantinople and Western European sovereigns, as well as with the newly converted Muslim leader—or khan, of the "Golden Horde"—of the Mongol Tatars of southern Russia. He was the first Egyptian sultan to appoint judges from each of the four law schools to administer justice, and his public works in Cairo were numerous. He extended Mamluk rule south to Nubia and west among the Berbers. The Mamluks declined after 1300, even though the Mongols in Iran conquered only Syria and never reached

756–1021	Spanish Umayyad Dynasty
912–961	Rule of Abd al-Rahman III; height of Umayyad power and civilization
969–1171	Fatimid Shi'ite Dynasty in Egypt
CA. 1020	Origin of Druze community (Egypt/Syria)
1171	Fatimids fall to Salah al-Din (Saladin), the Ayyubid lieutenant of ruler of Aleppo
1096–1291	Major European Christian crusades into Islamic lands; some European presence in Syria–Palestine
1056–1275	Almoravid and Almohad dynasties in North Africa, West Africa, and Spain
1189	Death of Ibn Rushd (Averroës), philosopher
1204	Death of Musa ibn Maymun (Maimonides), philosopher and Jewish savant
1240	Death of Ibn al-Arabi, theosophical mystic
1250–1517	Mamluk sultanate in Egypt (claim laid to Abbasid Caliphate)
1406	Death of Ibn Khaldun, historian and social philosopher
CA. 1300	Rise of Ottoman state in western Anatolia

The tomb of Qa'it Bey, Cairo (built 1472–1474), the finest example of Mamluk architecture in Cairo. [Egyptian Tourist Authority.]

Egypt itself. The dynasty did, however, survive the Ottoman conquest of Egypt (1517); it continued to rule there as the latter dynasty's governors into the nineteenth century.

Mamluk architecture, especially that of the reigns of Baybars and the extravagant Nasir (reigned 1293–1340), much of which still graces Cairo, remains their most magnificent bequest to posterity. Calligraphy, metalwork, and mosaics were among the arts and crafts of special note. The Mamluks patronized outstanding scholars, most importantly the greatest Islamic social historian and philosopher, Ibn Khaldun (d. 1406). He was born of a Spanish Muslim family in Tunis and settled in Cairo as an adult. Mamluk scholarship excelled in several areas, notably history, biography, and the sciences of astronomy, mathematics, and medicine.

The Pre-Mongol Islamic East

We noted in Chapter 12 that the Iranian dynasties of the Samanids at Bukhara (875–999) and the Buyids at Baghdad (945–1055) were the major eastern usurpers of the previously unified Abbasid rule. Their takeovers epitomized the rise of regional states that had begun to undermine the caliphate east and west by the ninth century. Similarly, the demise of each of these dynasties reflected a second important pattern already emerging before them: namely, the ascendancy of Turkish slave-rulers (like the Mamluks later in the west) and of Turkish tribal (Turkoman) peoples. With the successors of the Samanids and the Buyids, the process begun by the use of Turkish slave troops in ninth-century Baghdad ended in the permanent presence in the Islamic world of Turks. As late converts, they became typically the most zealous of Sunni Muslims.

THE GHAZNAVIDS. The rule of the Samanids in Transoxiana was finally wiped out by a Turkoman group. But they had already lost all of eastern Iran south of the Oxus in 994 to one of their own slave governors, Subuktigin (reigned 976–997). He set up his own state in modern Afghanistan, at Ghazna, whence he and his son and successor, Mahmud of Ghazna (reigned 998–1030), launched successful campaigns against his former masters. The Ghaznavids are notable for their patronage of Persian literature and culture and their conquests in northwestern India, which began a lasting Muslim presence in India. Mahmud was their greatest ruler. His name is still known in India for his booty raids and his destruction of temples in western India. His empire at its peak stretched from western Iran to the Oxus and the Indus.

The great scientist and mathematician al-Biruni (d. 1048) and the epic poet Firdawsi (d. CA. 1020) were among the scholars and artists whom he attracted to Ghazna. Firdawsi's *Shahnama* ("The Book of Kings") is the masterpiece of Persian literature, an epic of 60,000 verses that helped fix the new Persian language and revive the pre-Islamic Iranian cultural tradition. After Mahmud, the empire began to break up, although Ghaznavids ruled at Lahore until 1186.

THE SELJUKS. The Seljuks were the first major Turkish dynasty of Islam. They were a steppe clan who settled in Transoxiana, became avid Sunnis, and ex-

EASTERN ISLAMIC LANDS

875–999	Samanid dynasty, centered at Bukhara
945–1055	Buyid Shi'ite dynasty in Baghdad, controls caliphs
994–1186	Ghaznavid dynasty in Ghazna (modern Afghanistan) and Lahore (modern Pakistan), founded by Subuktigin (r. 976–997) and his son, Mahmud of Ghazna (r. 998–1030)
1020	Death of Firdawsi, compiler of *Shahnama*
CA. 1050	Death of al-Biruni, scientist and polyglot
1055–1194	Seljuk rule in Baghdad
1063–1092	Viziership of Nizam al-Mulk
1111	Death of al-Ghazzali, theologian and scholar
1219–1222	Gengis Khan plunders eastern Iran to Indus region
1258	Hulegu Khan conquers Baghdad
1261	Mamluk–Mongol treaty halts westward Mongol movement
1260–1335	Hulegu and his Il-Khanid successors rule Iran
1379–1405	Campaigns of Timur-i Lang (Tamerlane) devastate entire Islamic East
1405–1494	Timurids, successors of Tamerlane, rule in Transoxiana and Iran
1405–1447	Shahrukh, Timurid ruler at Herat; great patronage of the arts of philosophy

tended their sway over Khorasan in the 1030s. In 1055, they took Baghdad, where the nominal Abbasid caliph was happy to greet them as his deliverers from the Shi'ite Buyids. As the new guardian of the caliphate and master of an Islamic empire, the Seljuk leader Tughril Beg (reigned 1037–1063) took the title of *sultan* ("authority") to signify his temporal power and control. He was accordingly invested by the caliph as "king of east and west." He and his first successors made various Iranian cities their capitals instead of Baghdad.

New Turkish tribes joined their ranks, and Seljuk arms extended Islamic control for the first time into the central Anatolian plateau at Byzantine expense. They even captured the Byzantine emperor in a victory in Armenia in 1071. They also conquered much of Syria and wrested Mecca and Medina from the Shi'ite Fatimids. The first Turkish rule in Asia Minor (Anatolia) dates from 1077, when the Seljuk governor there

*"Friday Mosque," Isfahan. Begun in the tenth century, it was rebuilt in classic four-*iwan *form by the Seljuk Malik Shah in 1088–1089 and remodeled by the Safavids in the fifteenth and seventeenth centuries. This view shows the large open courtyard with its ablution-pools in the center. The huge half-dome fa-cade, or* iwan, *is characteristic of Iranian mosque architecture. Here is the southern* iwan, *behind which is the original covered area built by Malik Shah. [Diane Rawson, Photo Researchers.]*

set up a separate sultanate of the Seljuks of Rum ("Rome"/i.e., Byzantium). These latter Seljuks were not displaced until after 1300 by the Ottomans, another, still greater Turkish dynasty (see Chapter 22).

The most notable figure of Seljuk rule was the vizier Nizam al-Mulk, who was the real power behind two sultans (1063–1092). In his era, new roads and inns (caravanserais) for trade and pilgrimage were built, canals were dug, mosques and other public buildings were founded (including the first great Sunni *madrasas,* the personal projects of Nizam al-Mulk), and science and culture were patronized. He supported an extremely accurate calendar reform and himself wrote a major work on the art of governing, the *Siyasatnamah.* Before his murder by an Isma'ili "Assassin" in 1092, he appointed as professor in his Baghdad *madrasa* Muhammad al-Ghazzali (d. 1111), probably the greatest of all Muslim religious thinkers and writers. He also patronized the poet and astronomer Umar Khayyam (d. 1123), whose Western fame rests on his "quatrains," or *Ruba'iyat.*

After declining fortunes in the early twelfth century, Iranian Seljuk rule crumbled and by 1194 was wholly wiped away by another Turkish slave dynasty from Khwarizm in the lower Oxus basin. By 1200, these Khwarizm Shahs had built a large if shaky empire and sphere of influence covering Iran and Transoxiana. In the same era, the Abbasid caliph at Baghdad, Nasir (reigned 1180–1225), tried to establish an independent caliphal state in Iraq. But neither his heirs nor the

Khwarizm Shahs were long to survive in the face of events already unfolding on the Asian steppes.

The Mongol Age

MONGOLS AND ILKHANIDS. The building of a vast Mongol empire spanning Asia from China to Po-

Genghis Khan addressing his new subjects from the pulpit (minbar) in a mosque in Bukhara. Miniature painting from a manuscript produced in the late fourteenth century. [The British Library.]

The Mongol Catastrophe

For the Muslim east, the sudden blitzkrieg of the Mongol hordes was an indescribable calamity. Something of the shock and despair of their reaction can be seen in the history of Ibn al-Athir (d. 1233), who lived during the time of their first onslaught. He writes in this selection about the year 1220–1221, when the Mongols ("Tartars") burst in upon the eastern lands.

I say, therefore, that this thing involves the description of the greatest catastrophe and the most dire calamity (of the like of which days and nights are innocent) which befell all men generally, and the Muslims in particular; so that, should one say that the world, since God Almighty created Adam until now, hath not been afflicted with the like therof, he would but speak the truth. For indeed history doth not contain aught which approaches or comes nigh unto it.

. . . .

. . . Now this is a thing the like of which ear hath not heard; for Alexander, concerning whom historians agree that he conquered the world, did not do so with such swiftness, but only in the space of about ten years; neither did he slay, but was satisfied that men should be subject to him. But these Tartars conquered most of the habitable globe and the best, the most flourishing and most populous part thereof, and that whereof the inhabitants were the most advanced in character and conduct, in about a year; nor did any country escape their devastations which did not fearfully expect them and dread their arrival.

Moreover they need no commissariat, nor the conveyance of supplies, for they have with them sheep, cows, horses, and the like quadrupeds, the flesh of which they eat, [needing] naught else. As for their beasts which they ride, these dig into the earth with their hoofs and eat the roots of plants, knowing naught of barley. And so, when they alight anywhere, they have need of nothing from without. As for their religion, they worship the sun when it arises, and regard nothing as unlawful, for they eat all beasts, even dogs, pigs, and the like; nor do they recognise the marriage-tie, for several men are in marital relations with one woman, and if a child is born, it knows not who is its father.

Therefore Islâm and the Muslims have been afflicted during this period with calamities wherewith no people hath been visited. These Tartars (may God confound them!) came from the East, and wrought deeds which horrify all who hear of them, and which thou shalt, please God, see set forth in full detail in their proper connection. . . . ❑

From Edward G. Browne, *A Literary History of Persia*, Vol. 2 (Cambridge: Cambridge University Press, 1902), pp. 427–430, passim.

land in the early thirteenth century proved to be momentous not only for eastern Europe and China (see Chapter 9), but also for Islamic Eurasia and India. A Khwarizm Shah massacre of Mongol ambassadors brought down the full wrath of the Great Khan, Genghis, on the hapless Islamic east. He plundered mercilessly (1219–1222) from Transoxiana and Khorasan to the Indus, razing entire cities. The death of Genghis Khan (1227) and the division of his empire into four khanates under his four sons gave the Islamic world some respite. In 1255, Hulagu Khan, a grandson of Genghis, again led a massive army across the Oxus. Constantly adding Turkish troops to his forces (Mongol armies normally included many Turks), he went from victory to victory, destroying the "Assassins" of northwestern Iran along with every other Iranian state. In 1258, when the Abbasid caliph foolishly refused to surrender, Hulagu's troops smashed Baghdad's defenses and plundered it, killing at least 80,000 men, women, and children, including the caliph and his sons.

Under the influence of his wife and many of his inner circle who were Nestorian Christians or Buddhists, Hulagu spared the Christians of Baghdad. He followed this policy in his other conquests, including the later sack of Aleppo, which, like Baghdad, resisted. When Damascus surrendered, Christians had what proved to be a vain hope of the impending fall of Mamluk Cairo and the consequent collapse of Islamic power. Hulagu's further drive west was slowed by rivalry with his kinsman Berke. A Muslim convert, Berke ruled the khanate of the "Golden Horde," the Mongol state centered in southern Russia north of the Caucasus. He was in contact with the Mamluks, and some of his Mongol troops even fought with them in their major victory over Hulagu in Palestine (1260), which stopped Mongol penetration westward. A treaty in 1261 between the Mamluk sultan and Berke established a formal alliance that confirmed the breakup of Mongol unity and of the autonomy of the four khanates: in China (the Yuan dynasty), in Iran (the Ilkhans), in Russia (the Golden Horde), and in Transoxiana (the Chagatays).

For his part, Hulagu gave allegiance to the new

The caravanserai. One of the important links in communication and commerce in the Islamic world for many centuries, the caravanserai was a building that provided shelter, food, and protection to caravans and travelers of all kinds from China to Africa. Figure above shows the exterior walls of a large Iranian caravanserai at Maragha in steppe country. In Figure below, in an Iraqui caravanserai at Feluga, north of Baghdad, we see the men and animals of a caravan taking their ease. [Bettmann Archive.]

Great Khan of China. He and his heirs ruled the old Persian Empire from Azerbaijan for some seventy-five years as the Great Khan's "viceroys" (*Il-Khans*; from which Hulagu's line is named *Ilkhanid*). Here, as elsewhere, the rule of the Mongols did not eradicate the society that they inherited. Unlike the Arabs before them, they did not convert Muslim subject populations to their own faith. Instead, both their native paganism and Buddhist and Christian leanings yielded to Muslim faith and practice, although religious tolerance remained the norm under their rule. After 1335, Ilkhanid rule fell prey to the familiar pattern of a gradual breaking away of provinces, and for fifty years, Iran was again fragmented.

TIMURIDS AND TURKOMANS This situation prepared the way for a Turko-Mongol conquest from Transoxiana, under Timur-i Lang ("Timur the Lame," or "Tamerlane"). If Genghis Khan's invasions long before had been devastating, they could not match Timur's savage campaigns between 1379 and his death in 1405. These raids were not aimed at building up a new, centralized empire so much as at sheer conquest. Timur was a Muslim convert evidently possessed of a strong sense of his role as the protector of commerce and the punisher of the injustices of regional petty tyrants and populist—often Shi'ite—extremist groups alike. Still, whatever his ends, they hardly justified his means. In successive campaigns, he swept everything before him: all of eastern Iran (1379–1385); western Iran, Armenia, the Caucasus, and upper Mesopotamia (1385–1387); central Asia from Transoxiana to the Volga and as far as Moscow (1391–1395); southwestern Iran, Mesopotamia, and Syria (1391–1393); north India (1398); and northern Syria and Anatolia (1400–1402). Timur's sole positive contributions seem to have been the buildings he sponsored at Samarkand, his capital. He left behind him death, disease, destruction, and political chaos over the entire eastern Islamic world, which did not soon recover. His was, however,

The Gur-i-Mir, the tomb of Timur in Samarkand. Built in 1490–1501 by Timur's grandson, this tile-covered structure houses the tombs of Shahrukh, Ulug Beg, and other Timurid heirs, as well as that of Timur himself. [Bettmann Archive.]

the last great steppe invasion, for firearms soon took the steppe horsemen's advantage away forever.

Timur's sons shared his conquests with varying results in Transoxiana and Iran (1405–1494). The most successful Timurid was Shahrukh (reigned 1405–1447), who ruled a united western and eastern Iran for a time. His capital, Herat, became an important center of Persian Islamic culture and Sunni piety. He patronized the famous Herat school of miniature painting as well as Persian literature and philosophy. The Timurids had to share the control of Iran with Turkoman dynasties in western Iran, once even losing Herat to one of them. They and the Turkomans were the last Sunnis to rule Iran. Both were eclipsed at the end of the fifteenth century by the rise of the militant Shi'ite dynasty of the Safavids, who ushered in a new era in the Iranian world (see Chapter 22).

The Spread of Islam Beyond the "Heartlands"

The period from roughly 1000 to 1500 saw the spread of Islam as a lasting religious, cultural, and political force into new areas. Not only Eurasia from the Caspian and Black Seas north to Moscow (under the "Golden Horde"), but also Greece and the Balkans, through the Ottoman Turks, came under the control of Islamic governments (see Chapter 22). In the African and Asian worlds, India, Southeast Asia (Malaysia and Indonesia), inland West Africa, and coastal East Africa all became major spheres of Islamic political or commercial power, or both. In all these areas, conversion to Islam and the absorption of Islamic cultural influences came most often at the hands of Sufi orders. Merchants, too, were major agents of Islamization in all these regions.

Conquest was a third (and demographically less important) means to the eventual conversion to Islam of significant groups in the areas in question. Conversion reached sometimes only ruling elites and sometimes wider circles of a population. In India, Southeast Asia, and sub-Saharan Africa, significant numbers of the populace (often the majority) retained their inherited religious practices and faith. Therefore, if we treat these regions from the standpoint of the spread of Islam, it is not because Islam was the only, or even the major, element in their civilization in this period. It is rather that the coming of Islam signaled truly epochal changes in all these areas.

INDIA

The Entrenchment of Islam

Islamic civilization in India, like earlier Indian civilization, was formed by the creative interaction of invading foreigners with indigenous peoples. Whereas the early Arab and Turkish invaders had been a foreign Muslim minority, later Indian Muslims were as much "Indian" as "Muslim." A new dimension was added thereby both to Indian and to Islamic civilization.

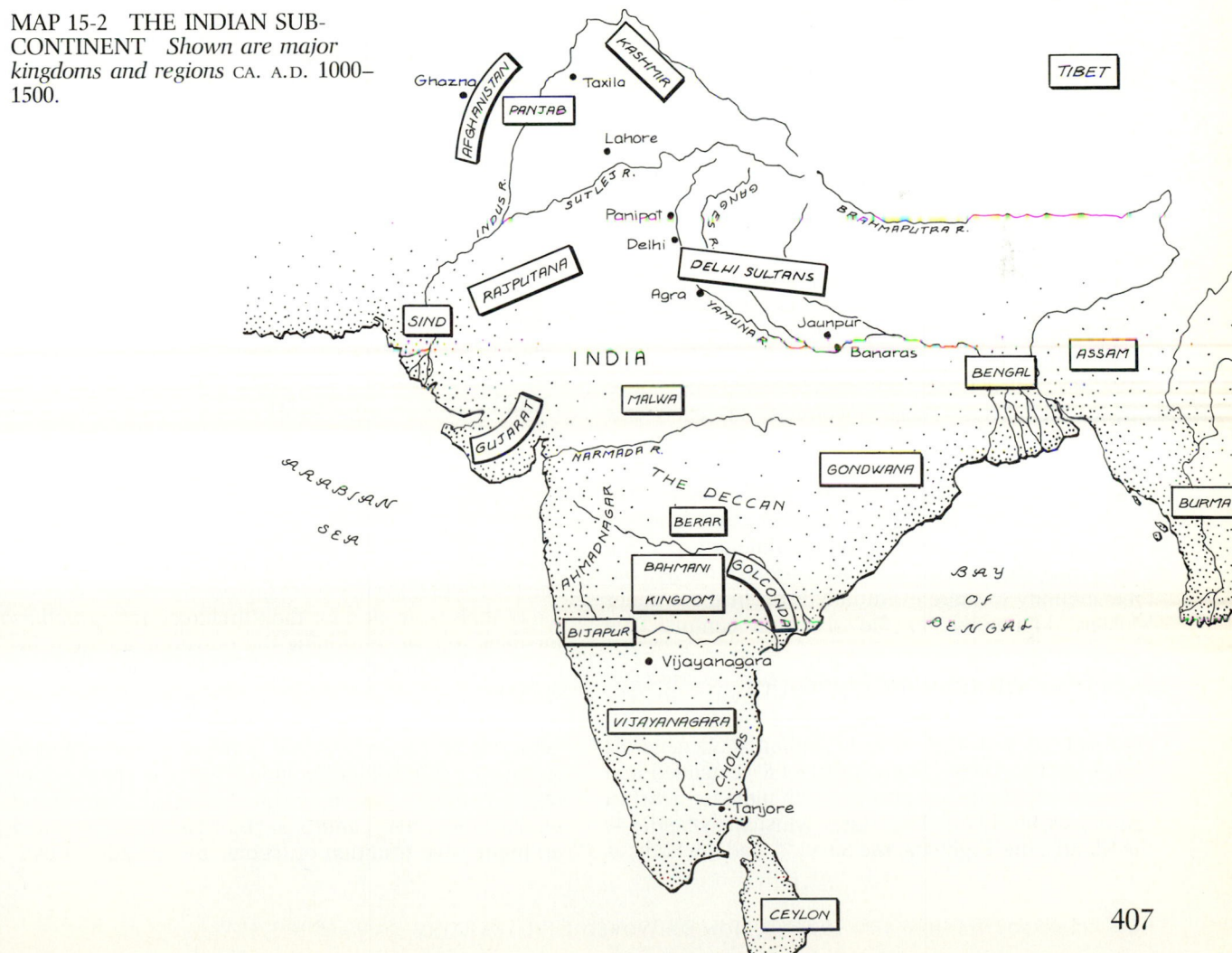

MAP 15-2   THE INDIAN SUBCONTINENT   *Shown are major kingdoms and regions* CA. A.D. 1000–1500.

The Early Spread of Islam

Well before the Ghaznavids came to the Punjab, Muslims were to be found even outside the original Arab conquest areas in Sind. Muslim merchants had settled in the port cities of Gujarat and south India to profit from internal Indian trade as well as from trade with the Indies and China. Wherever Muslim traders went, converts to Islam were attracted by business advantages as well as by the straightforward ideology and practice of Islam and its egalitarian, supposedly "classless" ethic. Sufi orders had also gained a foothold in the south, giving today's south Indian Muslims very old roots. Sufi piety also drew converts in the north, especially when the Mongol devastation of Iran in the thirteenth century sent refugees streaming over the mountains into north India. Many of these refugee converts strengthened Islamic armies and administration as well as Muslim cultural and religious life in the subcontinent.

The Muslim–Hindu Encounter

From the beginning, Muslim leaders faced the problem of ruling a country dominated by a different culture and religion. Much as early Muslim rulers in Iran had given the Zoroastrians legal status as "People of the Book" (like Christians and Jews; see Chapter 12), the first Arab conquerors in Sind (711) had treated Hindus not as pagans but as "protected peoples" under Muslim sovereignty. These precedents gave the Ghaznavids and later Muslim rulers in India a pragmatic basis for coexistence with their Hindu subjects. These precedents did not, of course, remove Hindu resistance to Muslim rule.

The chief obstacle to Islamic expansion in India was the military prowess and tradition of a Hindu warrior class that emerged after the Hun and other Asian tribal invasions of the fifth and sixth centuries. Apparently descended from such invaders and the native warrior (Kshatriya) class of Hindus, this class was known from about the mid-seventh century as *Rajputs*. Rulers and fighters of northern Hindu society, they were a large group of clans bound together by a fierce warrior ethic and a patriotism evident in their adherence to Hindu culture and strong traditionalism. They fought the Muslim invaders with great tenacity, but their inability to unite eventually brought them under Muslim domination in the sixteenth century (see Chapter 22).

Islamic States and Dynasties

After the Ghaznavids and a brief interlude of Afghan rule, a series of Turkish–Afghan slave-generals known as the "Slave Sultans of Delhi" extended and maintained Islamic power over north India for nearly a century (1206–1290). Four later Muslim dynasties—the Khaljis, the Tughluqs, the Sayyids, and the Lodis—

Building the Castle of Khawarnaq, ca. 1494. This is one of the magnificent illustrations of the Khamsa, *or "Fire Poems" of Nizami, painted by the head of the great art academy at Herat, Bihzad (died ca. 1515). It was Shahrukh's patronage that led to this flourishing school of painting. [The British Library.]*

carried on the Delhi sultanate through the fifteenth century. Their reigns were interrupted only by several years of chaos following the infamous devastation of Delhi by Timur in 1398, from which the city took decades to recover.

In the fifteenth century, the sultanate's power was limited by the rise of independent Islamic states that shared power with Rajput kingdoms in the Deccan and north India. The most important of the independent Islamic states was that of the Bahmanids in the Deccan (1347–1527). They were famous for the intellectual life of their court and for their architecture, as well as for their role in containing the powerful southern Indian Hindu state of Vijayanagar. (A Bahmani battle with the raja of Vijayanagar in 1366 was the first documented use of firearms and gunpowder in the subcontinent.) Most of the regional capitals provided fertile ground for cultural life. Jaunpur, to the north of Benares, became, for example, an asylum for artists and intellectuals after Timur's sack of Delhi and boasted an impressive tradition of Islamic architecture. Kashmir was an independent sultanate from 1346 to 1589 and a center of literary activity where Indian works were translated into Persian.

Religious and Cultural Accommodation

Except for Timur's invasion, the Delhi sultans were able to fend off the Mongol danger, much as the Mamluks did in Egypt. They thereby provided a basic political framework within which Islam could take root. Although the ruling class remained a Muslim minority of Persianized Turks and Afghans set over a Hindu majority, conversion went on at various levels of society. Some Hindu converts came from the ruling classes who served the Muslim overlords. *Ghazis* ("warriors" for Islam), like those of the same era in Anatolia, carried Islam by force of arms to pagan groups in eastern Bengal and Assam. And Sufi orders converted numerous Hindus among the lower classes. The Muslim aristocracy, at first mostly foreigners, were usually treated in Indian society as a separate caste group or groups. Similarly, when lower-class or other Hindus converted, they were assimilated into "Muslim castes," usually identified by occupation.

Persian was the language of intellectual and court life for all the Muslim dynasties of north India. However, Urdu began to develop well before 1500 as a Muslim military "camp language." It arose as increased contact between Hindus and Muslims required a shared medium of communication. Urdu is a form of Hindi (the medieval, Sanskrit-derived language of much of northern India) with many Persian words, written (like Persian) in Arabic script. Although its first literary use came before 1400, it was only much later that it replaced Persian as the major literary language of northern Indian and Deccan Muslims.

Indian Muslims were always susceptible to Hindu influence (in language, marriage customs, and caste consciousness). However, they were never utterly absorbed, as earlier invaders had been. The Muslims remained a group apart, conscious of their uniqueness

How the Hindus Differ from the Muslims

Al-Biruni (d. CA. 1050), probably the greatest scholar of medieval Islam, was born in Khwarizm in northeast Iran. Much of his later life was spent at the court of Sultan Mahmud of Ghazna, and he accompanied Mahmud on various expeditions into northwest India. He learned Sanskrit and made a deep study of India and the Hindus and wrote a "History of India." The following selections from the first pages of this work show something of the reach and sophistication of his mind.

. . . The barriers which separate Muslims and Hindus rest on different causes.

First, they differ from us in everything which other nations have in common. And here we first mention the language, although the difference of language also exists between other nations. If you want to conquer this difficulty (i.e. to learn Sanskrit), you will not find it easy, because the language is of an enormous range, both in words and inflections, something like the Arabic, calling one and the same thing by various names, both original and derived, and using one and the same word for a variety of subjects, which, in order to be properly understood, must be distinguished from each other by various qualifying epithets.

. . . .

Secondly, they totally differ from us in religion, as we believe in nothing in which they believe, and *vice versá*. On the whole, there is very little disputing about theological topics among themselves; at the utmost, they fight with words, but they will never stake their soul or body or their property on religious controversy. On the contrary, all their fanaticism is directed against those who do not belong to them—against all foreigners. They call them *mleecha*, i.e. impure, and forbid having any connection with them, be it by intermarriage or any other kind or relationship, or by sitting, eating, and drinking with them, because thereby, they think, they would be polluted. They consider as impure anything which touches the fire and the water of a foreigner; and no household can exist without these two elements. Besides, they never desire that a thing which once has been polluted should be purified and thus recovered, as, under ordinary circumstances, if anybody or anything has become unclean, he or it would strive to regain the state of purity. They are not allowed to receive anybody who does not belong to them, even if he wished it, or was inclined to their religion. This, too, renders any connection with them quite impossible, and constitutes the widest gulf between us and them.

In the third place, in all manners and usages they differ from us to such a degree as to frighten their children with us, with our dress, and our ways and customs, and as to declare us to be devil's breed, and our doings as the very opposite of all that is good and proper. By the by, we must confess, in order to be just, that a similar depreciation of foreigners not only prevails among us and the Hindus, but is common to all nations towards each other. ❏

From Edward C. Sachau, *Alberuni's India*, Vol. 1 (London: Kegan Paul, Trench, Truebner, 1910), pp. 17, 19, 20.

A dervish and a musician of Mughal times. This fine miniature watercolor is attributed to the Mughal painter Daulat and is dated about 1610. Music has traditionally played a significant role in the practice of many Sufis. [Private Collection.]

God who saves his worshipers without regard either to Hindu caste obligations or to legalistic observance of Muslim orthopraxy. The poet-saints Ramananda (d. after 1400) and Kabir (d. CA. 1518) were the two most famous of such reformers.

Other Traditions

These developments remind us that the history of India from 1000 to 1500 was not only that of the Muslims, although that is our focus here. This period was also important for the other religious communities of India. In the north, the Muslim conquests effectively ended the already greatly diminished Indian Buddhist monastic tradition. The role of the Muslim destruction of temples and monasteries in the virtual disappearance of Buddhism in this period has, however, been unduly emphasized. On the other hand, the attraction to Islam of the merchant classes, which had traditionally supported Buddhism, may have been underestimated.

Hindu religion and culture continued to flourish, even in areas of Muslim control. Both the continuing social and religious importance of the Brahmans and the popularity of *bhakti* (devotional) movements throughout India can attest the fact. In Brahmanic religious learning, it was an age of scholasticism that produced many commentaries and manuals, but few seminal works. *Bhakti* creativity was greater. The great Hindu Vaishnava Brahman, Ramanuja (d. 1137), provided a theological basis for *bhakti* devotion, reconciling its ideas with the classical Upanishadic Hindu worldview. *Bhakti* piety underlies the masterpiece of Hindu mystical love poetry, Jayadeva's *Gita Govinda* (twelfth century), which is devoted to Krishna, the most important of Vishnu's incarnations.

The south continued to be the center of Hindu cultural, political, and religious activity. Of several important dynastic states in the south in this age, the foremost was that of the Cholas (fl. CA. 900–1300). Aside from their military exploits and long political ascendency, this dynasty can claim lasting fame purely

in the Hindu world and proud to be distinct. The Muslim ruling classes saw themselves as the protectors and propagators of Islam in India. It is a measure of their sense of belonging to a larger Muslim community that, despite their independence of the rest of the Islamic world, most of the sultans of Delhi sought recognition for their rule in India from the nominal Abbasid caliphs in Baghdad or, in Mamluk times, in Cairo.

Nevertheless, reciprocal influence of Muslims and Hindus was inevitable, especially in the sphere of popular piety. Sufi devotion had an appeal similar to that of Hindu *bhakti* movements (see Chapter 11), and each at times influenced the other. Some of India's most revered Sufi and *bhakti* saints date from the fourteenth and fifteenth centuries. In this period, various theistic mystics strove to transcend the mutual antagonism and exclusivism of the more rigorous Muslims and Hindus. They typically preached devotion to a

INDIA	
CA. 900–1300	Chola dynasty in south India
1137	Death of Ramanuja
1206–1290	"Slave Sultans" of Delhi
1336–1565	Hindu dynasty of Vijayanagar
1347–1527	Muslim Bahmanid dynasty in the Deccan

Hindu Temples at Khajuraho. Here, on the central Indian plain, stand some twenty of the original eighty-five temples built by rajput princes almost 1000 years ago. The multiple spires of these spectacular structures symbolize the cosmic mountain Meru, which separated heaven and earth in Hindu mythology. In the mounting spires, the worshipper is led symbolically to union with the divine. [Diana L. Eck.]

for the school of bronze sculpture that they patronized at their capital of Tanjore. Their mightiest successor, the kingdom of Vijayanagar (1336–1565), in the fourteenth century subjugated the entire south and held out against its Muslim foes longer than had any other kingdom. Vijayanagar itself was one of India's most lavishly developed cities and a center of the cult of Shiva before its destruction by the Bahmanid sultan.

SUB-SAHARAN AFRICA

While North Africa and Egypt after 1000 were caught up in the major power struggles of the Islamic heartlands, a different situation existed in the African subcontinent, or sub-Saharan Africa. These areas developed much more strikingly according to internal African dynamics or different external influences. Nevertheless, from A.D. 1000, and largely from 1200, onward, Islam became a factor in sub-Saharan history. Thus, we allow Islamization to serve as the theme of our brief discussion of Africa in this period, even

MAP 15-3   AFRICA CA AD 1000–1500   *Shown are major cities and states referred to in the text. The circular inset provides greater detail for West Africa.*

though Islam was not in any way as important in sub-Saharan Africa as it was in North Africa and Egypt, or even India.

East Africa

The Southern Seas Trade

Along the southern rim of Asia, from the Red Sea and East Africa to Indonesia and the South China Sea, this period witnessed the gradual spread of Islamic religion and culture into new regions and among new peoples of diverse backgrounds. In port cities in Java, Sumatra, the Malaysian peninsula, South India, Gujarat, East Africa, Madagascar, and Zanzibar, Islamic traders established thriving communities. Their enclaves in these cities expanded until theirs was in many cases the dominant presence. Initially, the Muslims' economic stature attracted especially the socially and religiously mobile peoples of these cosmopolitan centers; many of them found the ideas and practices of Islam compelling as well. Typically, this first stage of conversion was followed by Islam's transmission to surrounding areas, and finally to inland centers of Hindu, Buddhist, or pagan culture and power. In this transmission, Sufi orders and their preachers and holy men played the main role. However, conquest by Muslim coastal states quickened the process later, at least in Indonesia.

The international trade network that the Muslims inherited in the southern seas went back many centuries. Before 1200, much of the trade in these waters had been dominated by Hindu or Buddhist kingdoms on the Malay Peninsula or Sumatra; Arab traders had also been active at least in the Indian Ocean. Hindu culture had been carried, along with an Indonesian language, as far as Madagascar some time in the first millennium A.D. Hindus were the chief religious group that the Muslims displaced. In the east, Islam never ousted the Indian Buddhist cultures of Burma, Thailand, and Indochina, although Muslim traders were in the port cities of all these areas. It did, however, gradually win most of Malaysia, Sumatra, Java, and the spice islands of the Moluccas—always the coastal areas first, then the inland regions.

Swahili Culture and Commerce

We saw in Chapter 11 that participation of east African port towns in the lucrative southern seas trade was ancient. Arabs, Indonesians, and at times, Indians had trafficked there for centuries. Many of them had been absorbed into what had become, from Somalia south, a predominantly Bantu-speaking east African population sometime during the first millennium A.D. From the eighth century on, Islam came along with Arab and Persian sailors and merchants to these southerly trading centers in the land of *al-Zanj*, or "the Blacks," as the Arabs called the inhabitants of Africa south of Egypt (hence "Zanzibar"). Conversion to Islam, however, went on slowly and only along the coastal perimeter. In the thirteenth century, Muslim traders from Arabia and Iran began to come in increased numbers and to dominate the coastal cities. From this time, Islamic faith and culture were influential and often predominant along the sea coast, from the port of Mogadishu south to that of Kilwa. By 1331, the traveler Ibn Battuta writes of Mogadishu as a thoroughly Islamic port and speaks of the ruler and inhabitants of Kilwa as Muslims. He also notes that there were now mosques for the faithful.[2]

By this time, a common language had developed out of the interaction of Bantu and Arabic speakers along the coast. This tongue, called *Swahili*, or *Kiswahili* (from the Arabic *sawahil*, "coastlands," a word used from ancient times for the East African coast), is Bantu in its structure, heavily Arabic in vocabulary, and written traditionally in the Arabic script, like Persian and many other languages of Islamic peoples. The

hybrid nature of this language mirrors the hybrid character of the African east-coast culture and peoples that came to be known also as Swahili.

Swahili language and culture may have developed first and most influentially in the northern towns of Manda, Lamu, and Mombasa, then further south along the coast. Today, the many coastal peoples who share them are of mixed ethnic character, joining African to Persian, Indian, Arab, and other blood. Current historical theory sees the origin of Swahili culture as basically African with a large admixture of Arab, Persian, and other extra-African elements. Nonetheless, it has ever been a source of pride for many older Swahili families to claim descent from illustrious Persian or Arab lineages of importance in Islamic history.

Swahili culture and language remained localized largely along the coast until very recent times. Likewise, the spread of Islam was largely limited to the coastal civilization and did not reach inland. The one possible exception is the Zambezi valley, where Muslim traders did penetrate some distance upriver. (This was in contrast to the lands farther north, in the Horn of Africa, where Islamic kingdoms developed in the Somali hinterland as well as on the coast.)

The height of Swahili civilization was in many ways the fourteenth and fifteenth centuries. Its centers were the harbor trading towns, most of which were on coastal islands or easily defended peninsulas. To these ports came merchants from abroad and from the African hinterlands, some to settle and stay. These towns were impressive. Beginning in the twelfth century, we can trace the development of stone-building techniques (first using coral blocks on red clay, later lime mortar). These were used for mosques, fortress-palaces, harbor fortifications, fancy private homes, and commercial buildings alike; all have their own distinctive cast that bespeaks a creative joining of African and Arabo Persian elements.

Local states had their administrative centers in these trading towns. Today, historians are recognizing that their ruling dynasties were probably African in origin with an admixture of Arab or Persian blood from immigrants. In these coastal centers, an advanced and cosmopolitan level of culture reigned; by comparison, the majority of the populace in the small villages lived in mud and sometimes stone houses. Most of the latter earned their living either by farming or fishing, the two basic occupations of the coastal peoples besides trade. Society seems to have consisted of three principal groups: the local nobility, the commoners, and resident foreigners engaged in local commerce. Slaves constituted a fourth class of people, although the extent of their local use (as opposed to their sale) is disputed.

The trade that flourished was fed mainly by inland exports of ivory. In addition, gold, slaves, turtle shells,

[2] Ibn Battuta, *Travels in Asia and Africa*, 1325–1354, trans. and selected by H. A. R. Gibb (New York: Robert M. McBride & Co., 1929), pp. 110–113.

Ibn Battuta Visits Mogadishu and Kilwa (1331)

Ibn Battuta (d. 1369 or 1377), a native of Tangier, became one of history's most famous travelers through his voluminous and entertaining writings about his long years of relentless journeying, from Africa to India and China. In the following two excerpts from his description of his trip down the east African coast in 1331, he describes first the reception of visitors at Mogadishu and then the Sultan of Kilwa.

MOGADISHU

From there [Somalia] we sailed fifteen nights and arrived at Mogadishu, which is a very large town. The people have very many camels, and slaughter many hundreds every day. They have also many sheep. The merchants are wealthy, and manufacture a material which takes its name from the town and which is exported to Egypt and elsewhere.

Among the customs of the people of this town is the following: when a ship comes into port, it is boarded from *sanbuqs*, that is to say, little boats. Each *sanbuq* carries a crowd of young men, each carrying a covered dish, containing food. Each one of them presents his dish to a merchant on board, and calls out: 'This man is my guest.' And his fellows do the same. Not one of the merchants disembarks except to go to the house of his host among the young men, save frequent visitors to the country. In such a case they go where they like. When a merchant has settled in his host's house, the latter sells for him what he has brought and makes his purchases for him. Buying anything from a merchant below its market price or selling him anything except in his host's presence is disapproved of by the people of Mogadishu. They find it of advantage to keep to this rule.

THE SULTAN OF KILWA

When I arrived, the Sultan was Abu al-Muzaffar Hasan surnamed Abu al-Mawahib [the Father of Gifts] on account of his numerous charitable gifts. He frequently makes raids into the Zanj country, attacks them and carries off booty, of which he reserves a fifth, using it in the manner prescribed by the Koran. That reserved for the kinsfolk of the Prophet is kept separate in the Treasury, and, when Sharifs come to visit him, he gives it them. They come to him from Iraq, the Hijaz, and other countries. I found several Sharifs from the Hijaz at his court, among them Muhammad ibn Jammaz, Mansur ibn Labida ibn Abi Nami and Muhamma ibn Shumaila ibn Abi Nami. At Mogadishu I saw Tabl ibn Kubaish ibn Jammaz, who also wished to visit him. This Sultan is very humble: he sits and eats with beggars, and venerates holy men and descendants of the Prophet. ❑

G. S. P. Freeman-Grenville, *The East African Coast: Select Documents*, 2nd ed. (London: Rex Collings, 1975), pp. 27–28, 31–32.

---

ambergris, leopard skins, pearls, fish, sandalwood, ebony, and local cotton cloth were among the many commodities that passed through the coastal centers. The chief imports were cloth, porcelain, glassware, china, glass beads, and glazed pottery. Certain exports tended to dominate at particular ports: cloth, sandalwood, ebony, and ivory at Mogadishu; ivory at Manda; or gold at Kilwa and, farther south still, at the port of Sofala. Cowrie shells were a common medium of payment in the inland trade, but coins minted at Mogadishu and Kilwa from the fourteenth century were increasingly used in the major trading centers. The gold trade seems to have become important only in the fifteenth century.

The decline of the original Swahili civilization in the sixteenth century can be attributed primarily to the loss of much of the trade that had originally made everything possible. The arrival of the Portuguese, and their subsequent destruction of the old oceanic trade patterns and existing Islamic city-states, seem to be the chief culprits. However, some scholars point also to decreases in rainfall or invasions of Zimba peoples from inland regions as contributing factors in the decline beginning in the sixteenth century.

Southeastern Africa: "Great Zimbabwe"

At about the same time that the trading centers of the east coast were beginning to flourish, a very different kind of African civilization was enjoying its heyday inland and farther south, in the rocky, savannah-woodland watershed between the Limpopo and Zambezi rivers, in modern southern Zimbabwe. This civilization was a purely African one sited far enough inland never to have felt the impact of Islam. It was founded in the eleventh century by the ancestors of the Bantu-speaking Shona people who still inhabit the same general area of southeastern Africa. It seems to have developed into a large and prosperous state between the late thirteenth and the late fifteenth centu-

"Great Zimbabwe," so-called because it is the most impressive of 300 such stone ruins in modern Zimbabwe and neighboring countries. These sites give clear evidence of the advanced, iron-age mining, and cattle-raising culture that flourished in this region between about A.D. 1000 and 1500. Its people are thought to have been of Bantu and Negroid stock. They apparently had a highly developed trade in gold and copper with outsiders, including Arabs on the East Coast. As yet, all too little is known about this impressive society. [Bettmann Archive.]

ries. We know it only through the archaeological remains of an estimated one hundred and fifty settlements in the Zambezi-Limpopo region.

By far the most impressive of these ruins, and the apparent capital of this ancient Shona state, is that known today as "Great Zimbabwe." This is a huge, sixty-odd-acre site encompassing two different major building complexes. One is a series of stone enclosures on a high hill; it overlooks the other—a much larger enclosure that contains numerous ruins and a large circular tower, all surrounded by a massive wall some thirty-two feet high and in places as much as seventeen feet thick. The former so-called "acropolis" complex may have contained a shrine, while the latter was apparently the royal palace and fort. The impressive stonework reflects a wealthy and sophisticated society. The artifacts found there include gold and copper ornaments, soapstone carvings, and imported beads, as well as china, glass, and porcelain of Chinese, Syrian, and Persian origins.

The state itself seems to have had some degree of control of the increasing gold trade between more inland areas and the east-coast port of Sofala. Its territory lay to the east and south of substantial gold-mining enterprises that tapped both the alluvial gold of the Zambezi tributaries and the gold-ore deposits that stretched southwest in a broad band below the middle Zambezi. We can speculate that this large settlement must have been the capital city of a prosperous empire and the residence of a ruling elite. Its wider domain was made up mostly of smaller settlements of common folk who lived on subsistence agriculture and cattle raising and whose culture was considerably different from that of the capital.

We may well speculate as to reasons for the flowering of the Zimbabwe civilization. Available evidence suggests first a general population growth and increasing economic prosperity in the Zambezi-Limpopo region prior to A.D. 1500. The specific impetus for ancient Zimbabwe may have been a significant immigration around A.D. 1000 of late-Iron-Age Shona-speakers who brought with them mining techniques and/or farming innovations along with their ancestor cults. Improved farming and animal husbandry may have led to substantial population growth. Another material cause may have been an increase in the gold trade between Sofala and the inland gold mining areas, with Great Zimbabwe being the chief beneficiary through its middle-man role. This latter hypothesis would link the flourishing of Zimbabwe to the general flourishing of the east African coast from about the thirteenth century.

None of these theories are mutually exclusive, however. Without written or new archaeological sources, we shall likely never know exactly what allowed this civilization to develop so impressively and to dominate

CA. 1000–1500	"Great Zimbabwe" civilization
CA. 1200–1400	Development of Bantu Kiswahili language
CA. 1300–1600	Height of Swahili culture

the region for nearly two hundred years. Its eventual demise is also somewhat obscure. It appears that it involved primarily a splitting up of northern and southern sectors of the state and corresponding movement of the major populations away from the environs of Great Zimbabwe, likely because of exhaustion of the farming and grazing land there. The southern successor kingdom was that known as Changamire—a state that survived to become very powerful from the late 1600s until about 1830. The northern successor state was known as the kingdom ruled by the Mwene Mutapa, or "Master Pillager"—the title by which the first Portuguese sources knew first Mutota, and then his successors, as the kings of the sixteenth-century riverine empire that stretched along the middle and lower course of the Zambezi.

West Africa

The Coming of Islam

On the other side of the subcontinent, Islam penetrated south of the Sahara not by sea, but by land—south from North Africa and Egypt across the Sahara and west from the Nile south of the Sahara. Beginning as early as about 800, Islam came chiefly with Berber traders over the desert routes (mentioned in Chapter 11) to trading towns like Awdaghast on the edge of the sahel. Thence it spread south to the Niger and beyond, and west into the Senegal basin. Another source for Muslim penetration of the central and western Sudan was Egypt and Nilotic Africa. From these eastern Islamic areas, migrating Arab tribal groups came to settle in the sub-Saharan steppeland or *sahel*. Although many more Arabs followed the Mediterranean coast from Egypt to North Africa, substantial numbers sifted westward to Lake Chad and the Niger regions, from the ninth to the sixteenth centuries and beyond.

Some Muslim conversion came quite early, virtually always through the medium of Muslim traders. The year 985 marks the first time that a royal court of west Africa officially became Muslim. This was in the kingdom of Gao, east of the Niger bend (see Chapter 11). The Gao rulers did not, however, try to convert their subjects. By contrast, the rulers of Ghana clung long to their indigenous traditions of faith; but they

kept a separate township near their capital of Kumbi (or Kumbi Saleh) for the Muslim merchants with whom they dealt extensively and the Muslim advisers who helped them govern.

From the 1030s, an overt conversion campaign was begun in coastal Mauritania and Senegal and mounted in the western sahel and Sahara by the zealous militants known as Almoravids (Arabic *al-Murabitun*, after their fortified retreat centers, or *ribats*). This movement eventually swept into Ghana's territory, taking first Awdaghast and finally Kumbi in 1076. Thereafter, the forcibly converted Soninke ruling group of Ghana spread Islam among their own populace and farther south in the savannah. Here they converted Mande-speaking traders who spread it in time south into the forests as well. Farther west, the Fulbe rulers of Takrur along the Senegal had became Muslim in the 1030s and propagated their new faith among their subjects. (The Fulbe would remain important agents of the spread of Islam as they migrated gradually into new regions as far south and east as Lake Chad over the next eight centuries.) In the region of Lake Chad, as we saw in Chapter 11, the strongest ruler was Muslim from as early as about 1100—even before the Kanuri people became fully sedentarized as the ruling group of the new kingdom of Kanem.

All in all, the spread of Islam was peaceful, gradual, and partial. Typically, it never penetrated beyond the ruling or commercial classes of a region. Even among these, it tended to coexist or blend with indigenous ideas and practices. Especially in the sub-Niger region, some major groups strongly resisted Islamization altogether—notably the Mossi kingdoms founded in the Volta region at Wagadugu around 1050 and Yatenga about 1170. Thus Islamic conversion in west Africa in general was neither rapid, forcible, nor, even by 1500, widespread.

Nevertheless, Islam and its carriers were of great moment for West African history. Agents of Islam brought, on the one hand, military and commercial developments and, on the other, the Qur'an and Arabic scholarship and literate culture. In west as in east Africa, the arrival of literate culture proved to be as important an event for subsequent African history as any other development. Many innovations, from architectural techniques to intellectual and administrative traditions, depended upon writing and literacy, which are among the most important supports of the development of large-scale complex societies and cultures.

Sahelian Empires

We noted in Chapter 11 the rise, already in the first millennium, of several substantial states just south of the Sahara proper. In the period from about 1000 to

Ghana and Its People in the Mid-Eleventh Century

The following excerpt is from the geographical work of the Spanish Muslim writer al-Bakri (d. 1094). In it, he describes with great precision some customs of the ruler and the people of the capital of Ghana as he carefully gleaned them from other Arabic sources and travelers (he never visited west Africa himself, it seems).

Ghāna is a title given to their kings; the name of the region is Awkār, and their king today, namely in the year 460/1067–8, is Tankā Manīn. . . . This Tunkā Manīn is powerful, rules an enormous kingdom, and possesses great authority.

The city of Ghāna consists of two towns situated on a plain. One of these towns, which is inhabited by Muslims, is large and possesses twelve mosques, in one of which they assemble for the Friday prayer. There are salaried imams and muezzins, as well as jurists and scholars. In the environs are wells with sweet water, from which they drink and with which they grow vegetables. The king's town is six miles distant from this one and bears the name of Al-Ghāba. Between these two towns there are continuous habitations. The houses of the inhabitants are of stone and acacia (*sunt*) wood. The king has a palace and a number of domed dwellings all surrounded with an enclosure like a city wall (*sūr*). In the king's town, and not far from his court of justice, is a mosque where the Muslims who arrive at his court (*yafid 'alayh*) pray. Around the king's town are domed buildings and groves and thickets where the sorcerers of these people, men in charge of the religious cult, live. In them too are their idols and the tombs of their kings. . . .

All of them shave their beards, and women shave their heads. The king adorns himself like a woman [wearing necklaces] round his neck and [bracelets] on his forearms, and he puts on a high cap (*tartūr*) decorated with gold and wrapped in a turban of fine cotton. He sits in audience or to hear grievances against officials (*mazālim*) in a domed pavilion around which stand ten horses covered with gold-embroidered materials. Behind the king stand ten pages holding shields and swords decorated with gold, and on his right are the sons of the [vassal] kings of his country wearing splendid garments and their hair plaited with gold. The governor of the city sits on the ground before the king and around him are ministers seated likewise. . . . When the people who profess the same religion as the king approach him they fall on their knees and sprinkle dust on their heads, for this is their way of greeting him. As for the Muslims, they greet him only by clapping their hands.

Their religion is paganism and the worship of idols (*dakākīr*). When their king dies they construct over the place where his tomb will be an enormous dome of *sāj* wood. Then they bring him on a bed covered with a few carpets and cushions and place him beside the dome. At his side they place his ornaments, his weapons, and the vessels from which he used to eat and drink, filled with various kinds of food and beverages. ❑

From J. F. P. Hopkins (trans.), N. Levtzion and J. F. P. Hopkins (eds.), *Corpus of Early Arabic Sources for West African History* (Cambridge University Press, 1981), pp. 79–80.

1500, three of these sahelian kingdoms of the western and central Sudan developed into notable and relatively long-lived empires: Ghana, Mali, and Kanem.

GHANA. Ghana was the state that established the model for later west Sudanic empire. Located far north of modern Ghana (and unrelated to it), in the sahel between the Senegal and Niger, Ghana's power was built upon a solid economic base. Tribute from the empire's many chieftaincies and taxes on royal lands and crops supplemented the two major sources of income: duties levied on all incoming and outgoing trade, including imported salt, cloth, and metal goods; and profits from control of the gold trade. Although the king and court did not convert to Islam, Muslims were used to organize and administer the government, and Muslim legists advised the ruler. Ghana's society was a stratified one, ranging from slaves at the bottom through farmers and craftsmen to a merchant class and finally the nobility of king and court. A huge, well-trained army secured the king's control of his dominions. The empire was, however, vulnerable to attack from the desert fringe, as the Almoravids proved in the late tenth century. The recurring sahelian blight of drought may also have contributed to Ghana's demise just after the peak of its power in the mid-eleventh century.

MALI. After Ghana fell to the Almoravids in the late eleventh century, it was almost two centuries before another comparable empire could be reestablished in the western sahel. With Ghana's collapse and the Almoravids' failure—largely because of their greater interest in North Africa—to build a new empire in the sahel, the western Sudan broke up into various smaller kingdoms. Only in the mid-thirteenth century was one of these kingdoms able to forge a new and lasting empire; it was based in good part on improved trade along the Niger, below it into the forests, and west into the Gambia and Senegal river basins. This empire was Mali, which arose in all likelihood with the same dominant purpose and economic base as that of Ghana earlier: monopolization of the lucrative north-south gold trade through dominating enough of the sahel to control the flow of west African gold to the trans-Saharan trade routes. Mali was, however, better able than Ghana had been to control all trade on the upper Niger and to add to it that on the Gambia to the west.

Mali's new imperial power was built largely by the efforts of one leader, the Mandinke King Sundiata (or Sunjaata; reigned 1230–1255). His royal Keita dynasty had been Muslim for a century and a half before him. Probably fueled by significant population growth in the western savannah, Malian imperial rule rested upon both strong agriculture and the great commercial skills of the Mandinke people. Sundiata and his Mandinke successors exploited both to produce an even more powerful empire than its Ghanaian predecessor. Sundiata himself extended his control far beyond the former domains of Ghana, west to the Atlantic coast and beyond Timbuktu in the east. By controlling the commercial centers of Gao, Walata, and Jenne, he was able to take the Saharan trade fully in hand. He built his capital Niani, located in the savannah well south of Ghana's capital of Kumbi, into a major city.

Sundiata's and his successor's empire encompassed ultimately three major historical regions and language groups of Sudanic west Africa: (1) the Senegal region (including Takrur) with its West Atlantic languages (such as Fulbe, Tukulor, Wolof, Serer); (2) the central-Mande states and language groups of the Soninke and Mandinke, between the Senegal and Niger; and (3) the Songhai-speaking peoples of the Niger (in the region of

Mansa Musa in Cairo

The following account is by a Damascene scholar, al-Umari (d. 1349), *who spent much of his life in Cairo. Here he describes what he learned of Mansa Musa's reception by the Mamluk sultan. The report reflects the respect commanded by Musa among the Cairenes, both for his piety and for his wealth and obvious power (he had a massive entourage with him).*

From the beginning of my coming to stay in Egypt I heard talk of the arrival of this sultan Mūsā on his Pilgrimage and found the Cairenes eager to recount what they had seen of the Africans' prodigal spending. I asked the emir Abū 'l-'Abbās Aḥmad b. al-Ḥāk the *mihmandar* and he told me of the opulence, manly virtues, and piety of this sultan. "When I went out to meet him (he said), that is, on behalf of the mighty sultan al-Malik al-Nāṣir, he did me extreme honour and treated me with the greatest courtesy. He addressed me, however, only through an interpreter despite his perfect ability to speak in the Arabic tongue. Then he forwarded to the royal treasury many loads of unworked native gold and other valuables. I tried to persuade him to go up to the Citadel to meet the sultan, but he refused persistently, saying: 'I came for the Pilgrimage and nothing else. I do not wish to mix anything else with my Pilgrimage.' He had begun to use this argument but I realized that the audience was repugnant to him because he would be obliged to kiss the ground and the sultan's hand. I continued to cajole him and he continued to make excuses but the sultan's protocol demanded that I should bring him into the royal presence, so I kept on at him till he agreed.

"When we came in the sultan's presence we said to him: 'Kiss the ground!' but he refused outright saying: 'How may this be?' Then an intelligent man who was with him whispered to him something we could not understand and he said: 'I make obeisance to God who created me!' then he prostrated himself and went forward to the sultan. The sultan half rose to greet him and sat him by his side. They conversed together for a long time, then sultan Mūsā went out. The sultan sent to him several complete suits of honour for himself, his courtiers, and all those who had come with him, and saddled and bridled horses for himself and his chief courtiers. . . . He also furnished him with accommodation and abundant supplies during his stay.

"When the time to leave for the Pilgrimage came round the sultan sent to him a large sum of money with ordinary and thoroughbred camels complete with saddles and equipment to serve as mounts for him, and purchased abundant supplies for his entourage and others who had come with him. He arranged for deposits of fodder to be placed along the road and ordered the caravan commanders to treat him with honour and respect. . . ." ❑

From J. F. P. Hopkins (trans.), N. Levtzion and J. F. P. Hopkins (eds.), *Corpus of Early Arabic Sources for West African History* (Cambridge: Cambridge University Press, 1981), pp. 269–270.

Gao). The power of the rulers of Mali was always less that of a centralized bureaucratic state than that of the center of a vast sphere of influence. In their domain, individual chieftaincies and dependencies retained much of their independence, but recognized the sovereignty of the supreme, sacred *mansa*, or "emperor," of the Malian realms.

The greatest Keita king proved to be Mansa Musa (1312–1337), whose pilgrimage through Mamluk Cairo to Mecca in 1324 became famous in Egypt. He paid out or gave away so much gold in Cairo alone that he started a massive inflation that lasted over a decade. He returned from his pilgrimage with many Muslim scholars, artists, and architects in tow to grace his court. At home, he consolidated Mali's power, securing peace for most of his reign throughout his vast dominions. Musa's claimed devoutness as a Muslim translated into a positive environment for the further spread of Islam in the empire and beyond; but not all conversions of his and later reigns survived Mali's decline in the next century. Under his rule, Timbuktu became known far and wide for its madrasas and libraries, as well as its poets, scientists, and architects. During his reign, Timbuktu became the leading intellectual center of sub-Saharan Islamic religion and culture as well as one of the major trading cities of the sahel—roles that lasted far beyond the period of Mali's imperial dominance.

Mali's dominance waned after Musa's time, most sharply in the fifteenth century. A chief cause seems to have been destructive rivalries for the succession to the *mansa*'s throne. As time went on, more and more subject dependencies became independent, and the empire shrank in extent and power. In the 1430s, Berber Tuaregs wrested control from Mali of much of its sahelian dominions, including Timbuktu and Walata. The Mossi in the south made large inroads on Malian territory in the middle of the century, and thereafter the rise of a new power in Gao signaled the end of Mali's imperial authority. It marked also the beginning of the new Songhai empire that would take its place as the major west–central Sudanic power in the sixteenth century (see Chapter 22).

KANEM. Kanem represented, as we noted in Chapter 11, a very different kind of empire. It began as a southern Saharan confederation from among the black nomadic tribes known as Zaghawah, who were spread over much of the south–central and southeastern Sahara. By the twelfth century, a Zaghawah group known as the Kanuri had apparently settled in Kanem, the sahelian and Saharan region northeast of Lake Chad, and from here they set out on military expansion. Their key leader in this, Mai Dunama Dibbalemi (reigned CA. 1221–1259), was a contemporary of

Sundiata in Mali. Like Sundiata, Dibbalemi was a Muslim—indeed, probably the first Kanuri leader to embrace Islam, although there are traditions recalling a Muslim ruler in the Kanem region as early as 1085. In any case, Islam appears to have entrenched itself among the Kanuri ruling class during Dibbalemi's reign. He and his successors expanded Kanuri power north into the desert far enough to include the Fezzan in modern Libya and northeast along the sahel-Sahara fringe toward Nilotic Africa. In both directions, the Kanuri controlled important trade routes—north to Libya and east to the Nile and Egypt.

Islam was important to some of the Kanuri rulers. Dibbalemi used it as a sanction for his rule, which otherwise had the familiar African trappings of a sacred kingship. It also provided a reason for expansion through *jihad*, or holy struggle against pagans. His reign, and that of his successors through the next two centuries, saw the mixing of Kanuri and local Kanembu peoples, primarily those known as the So. There was a corresponding transformation of the Kanuri leader from a nomadic *shaykh* to a Sudanic king and a change of the Kanembu state from a nomadic to a largely sedentary kingdom replete with quasi-feudal institutions. Like Mali to the west, Kanembu dominion was both one of direct rule over and taxation of core territories and groups as well as one of tributary influence or control of a wider region of local vassal chieftaincies. Linguistic and religious (Muslim) acculturation progressed most rapidly in the core territories.

Civil strife, largely over the succession to the kingship, weakened the Kanuri state in the later fourteenth and especially the fifteenth century. In the fifteenth century, the locus of power shifted from Kanem proper westward, to the southwest of Lake Chad. Here, at the end of the fifteenth century, in the land of Bornu, a new Kanuri empire arose almost simultaneously with that of Songhai in the western Sudan (see Chapter 22).

West African Forest Kingdoms: The Example of Benin

For most of west and central Africa, we have little or no written evidence before the sixteenth century of the many states and smaller societies that flourished in the southern reaches of the Sudanic savannahs and in the forestlands to their south. However, other kinds of evidence reveal that many states, some with distinct political, religious, and cultural traditions, had developed in the southern and coastal regions of west Africa several centuries before the first Portuguese reports in 1485. Even those states like Asante or the Yoruba kingdoms of Oyo and Ife, that reached their height only after 1500, had much earlier origins. The best-known of these forest kingdoms, Benin reflects especially in its

Benin bronze statues of a warrior and his attendant. A fine example of the renowned Benin art that flourished in the fifteenth and sixteenth century heyday of Benin power. [British Museum.]

art the great sophistication of West African culture before 1500.

THE BENIN STATE AND SOCIETY. According to linguistic evidence, the Edo-speakers of Benin have occupied the southern Nigerian region between Yorubaland and the Ibo peoples east of the lower Niger for several thousand years. Their society is characterized traditionally by three things: (1) The village is the fundamental political unit; (2) authority in the village society is built around organization of the males into age–grade units; and (3) their lineage system exhibits a strong patrilineal bias and emphasis on primogeniture.[3]

Archaeology has confirmed the local traditions that link the Edo culture of Benin closely to that of Ife, one of the two most prominent Yoruba states to the northwest of Benin. Some kind of distinct kingdom of Benin likely existed as early as the twelfth century, and traditional accounts of both Ife and Edo agree that a scion of the Ife ruling family was sent to rule in Benin around

[3] A. F. C. Ryder, *Benin and the Europeans, 1485–1897* (New York: Longman, 1969), p. 1.

1300. There are indications that the power of the king, or *oba*, at this time was sharply limited by the Edo leaders who invited the foreign ruler. These leaders were known as the *uzama*, an order of hereditary indigenous chiefs. According to tradition, the fourth Benin *oba* managed to take more control from these chiefs for himself and to institute something of the ceremonial of absolute monarchy. However, only in the fifteenth century, with King Ewuare, did this small monarchy become a royal autocracy and develop into a large state of major regional importance.

Ewuare rebuilt the capital and named it and his kingdom Edo. The capital is known today as Benin City. He seems to have set up the government under his sweeping authority, albeit an authority still exercised in light of the deliberations of a royal council. Ewuare formed this council not only from the *uzama* of the palace, but also from the towns. He also gave each of the chiefs specific administrative responsibilities and ranks in the government hierarchy. Ewuare and his successors developed a tradition of military kingship and engaged in major wars of expansion, both into Yorubaland to the west and Ibo country across the Niger River to the east. They also claimed for the office of *oba* an increasing ritual authority that presaged more radical developments in the king's role. In the seventeenth century, the *oba* would become a much less active leader who virtually withdrew into the palace; he was transformed from a military leader into a religious figure with supernatural powers. The primogeniture succession (to first-born son) of Ewuare and his successors would cease, with the new *oba* to be chosen by the *uzama* from any branch of the royal family.

BENIN ART. The lasting significance of Benin, however, lies not in its political history, but in its court art, which reached its zenith in its famous brass sculptural work. An ancient Benin tradition suggests that an Ife craftsman came to Benin at the behest of the ruler to teach the brass- and bronze-casting techniques developed first in Ife. Certainly the splendid terra-cotta, ivory, and brass statuary sculpture of the Ife–Benin civilization are among the glories of human creativity. These magnificent, initially fully realistic or naturalistic, yet later sometimes highly stylized, sculptures are by all indications wholly indigenous African products. Their artistic and technical lineage is today often traced by scholars to the sculptures of the Nok culture of ancient West Africa treated in Chapter 7.

The best of the sculptures before the sixteenth century and the coming of the Portuguese (who themselves figure in later representations) are cast brass plaques depicting legendary and historical scenes, which were mounted on the walls and columns of the

WEST AFRICA	
985	Conversion of Gao royalty to Islam
990–1076	Empire of Ghana
1076	Fall of Awdaghust to Almoravids
CA. 1230–1550	Empire of Mali, founded by Sundiata
1230–1255	Reign of Sundiata
1312–1332 or 1337	Reign of Mansa Musa
CA. 1450–1500	Rise of the Songhai empire
CA. 1100–1897	Benin state
CA. 1300	First Ife king of Benin state
1440–1475	Reign of Ewuare
CA. 1100–1500	Kanuri rule in Kanem region
1221–1259	Reign of Mai Dunama Dibbalemi
CA. 1220s–1400	Height of empire of Kanem

royal palace in Benin City. There are also brass heads, apparently of royalty, that seem to parallel the many life-size terra-cotta and brass heads found at Ife. These latter are held to represent the Oni, or religious chief of ancient Ife, or particular ancestors, who are thereby reverently remembered by their descendants.

These artistic traditions were not limited only to Ife and Benin; similar sculptures have been found both well to the north and in the Niger delta. Most spectacularly, the modern excavations east of the Niger at Igbo-Ukwu unearthed many stunning terra cottas and bronzes that, while quite distinct, belong to the same general artistic culture, which appears now to go back as early as the ninth century. These artifacts stand as a reminder of the high cultural level attained in many traditional African societies that had little or no contact with the extra-African world.

The Islamic Heartlands, India, and Africa, 1000–1500, in World Perspective

This period in both Islamic and other African and Asian territories is difficult to characterize simply. The spread of Islam to new peoples or their ruling elites has been taken as a theme of this chapter. However, we have also seen that the history of Islam in India and Africa is hardly the history of the whole. The vast conquests and movements of the Mongols and central Asian Turks across inner Asia was one of the most striking developments in world history in this period; they often had cataclysmic effects upon Chinese, south and west Asian, and eastern European societies and states. These conquests and migrations did not build lasting major states or civilizations, but they did bring destruction of existing orders. They also contributed, however unintentionally, new and often significant human resources to existing civilizations like those of China and the Islamic heartlands.

In this age, Islam became truly an international tradition of religious, political, and social values and institutions. It did so by being highly adaptable and open to "indigenization" in the seemingly hostile contexts of polytheistic Hindu or African societies. Also in this age very distinct traditions of art, language, and literature, for all their local, regional, or national diversity, became intelligible and identifiable parts of a larger whole defined by a Muslim identity. Islamic civilization had nothing of the territorial contiguousness or homogeneous linguistic and cultural traditions of either Chinese or Japanese civilization. Nevertheless, the Islamic world was an international reality in which a Muslim could travel and meet other Muslims of radically diverse backgrounds with much common ground for understanding.

Indian traditional culture was not, like the Islamic, bound up with an expanding, missionary religious tradition. Yet, in this age, Hindu kingdoms throve in Indonesia. Buddhism, even while dwindling into a small minority tradition in its Indian homeland, was expanding across much of central and east Asia, thereby solidifying its place as an international missionary tradition. Christianity, by contrast, was not rapidly expanding, in Africa, Asia, or Europe; but by 1500 its western European branch was poised on the brink of internal revolution and international proselytism that began with the voyages of discovery.

In most of Africa during this period, development went on most often without interference or great influence from abroad. Only the East African coast, Egypt, and North Africa were significantly oriented to foreign societies. However, in this age, Africa did have ever increasing and ever more significant contact and interaction with other major cultural and political regions, from Europe to China. It saw the spread of Islamic patterns to new areas, and by 1500 it witnessed the beginning of European and Christian penetration. For all its diversity, Africa's change was more an extension of previous patterns than a radical divergence—at least by comparison with the transformations brewing in Western Europe.

At the beginning of this period (1000–1500) Europe was almost a backwater of culture and power by comparison with major Islamic or Hindu states, let alone those of China and Japan. At its close, however, Euro-pean civilization was riding the crest of a cultural renaissance, enjoying economic and political growth, and starting the global exploration that would turn into a flood of imperial expansion and affect most of the rest of the globe. Neither Islamic, Indian, African, Chinese, nor Japanese culture and society were so radically changed or changing in their basic ideas and institutions as were those of Western Europe over these five hundred years.

Suggested Reading

THE ISLAMIC HEARTLANDS

J. A. BOYLE, ed., *The Cambridge History of Iran*. Vol. 5: *The Saljuq and Mongol Periods* (1968). Useful and reasonably detailed articles on political, social, religious, and cultural developments.

P. K. HITTI, *History of the Arabs*, 8th ed. (1964). Still a useful English resource, largely for factual detail. See especially Part IV, "The Arabs in Europe: Spain and Sicily."

M. G. S. HODGSON, *The Expansion of Islam in the Middle Periods*. Vol. 2 of *The Venture of Islam*. 3 vols. (1964). The strongest of Hodgson's monumental three-volume survey of Islamic civilization, and the only English work of its kind to give the period 945–1500 such broad and unified coverage.

B. LEWIS, ed., *Islam and the Arab World* (1976). A large-format, heavily illustrated volume with many excellent articles on diverse aspects of Islamic (not simply Arab, as the misleading title indicates) civilization through the premodern period.

D. MORGAN, *The Mongols* (1986). A recent and readable survey history.

J. J. SAUNDERS, *A History of Medieval Islam* (1965). A brief, simple introductory survey of Islamic history to the Mongol invasions.

D. SOURDEL, *Medieval Islam*. Trans. W. M. Watt (1983). The synthetic, interpretive chapters on Islam and the political and social orders (4, 5), and on towns and art (6) are especially helpful.

B. SPULER, *The Mongols in History*. Trans. Geoffrey Wheeler (1971). A short introductory survey of Mongol history, of which Chapters 2–5 are most relevant.

B. SPULER, *The Muslim World: A Historical Survey*. Trans. F. R. C. Bagley (1960 3 vols.). Volumes I and II are handy reference volumes offering a highly condensed chronicle of Islamic history from Muhammad through the fifteenth century.

INDIA

S. M. IKRAM, *Muslim Civilization in India* (1964). The best short survey history, covering the period 711 to 1857.

R. C. MAJUMDAR, gen. ed., *The History and Culture of the Indian People*. Vol. VI: *The Delhi Sultanate*, 3rd ed. (1980). A comprehensive political and cultural account of the period in India.

M. Mujeeb, *The Indian Muslims* (1967). The best cultural study of Islamic civilization in India as a whole, from its origins onward.

V. A. Smith, *The Oxford History of India*, 4th ed. rev. Percival Spear et al. (1981). An easy-to-read historical survey with helpful chronologies. See especially Books III–V, pp. 190–319.

AFRICA

R. E. Bradbury, *Benin Studies*. Ed. P. Morton-Williams (1973). Good material on the history of the state, village life, religion, and art.

P. Curtin, S. Feierman, L. Thompson, and J. Vansina, *African History* (1978). Chapters 4 and 5 on East Africa are especially noteworthy for the present chapter's concerns.

B. Davidson, *The African Past* (1964). A combination of primary-source selections and brief secondary-study assessments trace the history of the diverse parts of Africa.

J. D. Fage, *A History of Africa* (1978). Solid survey, with some good maps. See segments on Guinea and the impact of Islam upon Africa.

R. W. July, *A History of the African People*, 3rd ed. (1980). Part I, "Ancient Africa," covers the precolonial centuries, offering an area-by-area historical introduction to African civilization.

D. T. Niane, ed., *Africa from the Twelfth to the Sixteenth Century*. UNESCO General History of Africa, Vol. 4 (1984). Contains important, up-to-date survey articles on the topics treated here.

B. A. Ogot and J. A. Kieran, eds., *Zamani: A Survey of East African History*, 2nd rev. ed. (1974). Most helpful treatment of varied aspects of history and culture by various specialists.

A. F. C. Ryder, *Benin and the Europeans*, 1485–1897 (1969). Chapter 1, on the history of the Benin kingdom, offers a good survey.

J. S. Trimingham, *A History of Islam in West Africa* (1962). Dated, but still a fundamental survey of the topic.

The World in Transition (1500–1800)

BETWEEN 1500 and 1800, the major centers of world civilization achieved political organization and stability that in some cases endured into the present century. This period also witnessed a shift in the balance of world political and economic power toward Europe. That shift was anything but inevitable. It was the result of paths taken by Europeans and not taken by the peoples and governments of other areas of the world.

Sixteenth-century Japan was torn by wars among its various small states and regions. This civil conflict eroded the manorial social structure. The adoption of the spear in place of the sword allowed the development of foot-soldier armies that displaced the samurai. By approximately 1600, however, a new political regime was establishing itself on the basis of a "feudal" society involving complex vassal–lord relationships in many, though not all, ways similar to those in medieval Europe. Tokugawa Ieyasu established his government in Edo (now Tokyo). Through a series of land transfers and confiscations, he surrounded himself with unquestionably loyal retainers and placed those of less certain loyalty at a far geographical remove from his capital. He and his successors required vassals to send their families to live as virtual hostages near the court in Edo. Finally, Tokugawa Japan imposed on itself a policy of isolation from the rest of the world. Though stable and relatively prosperous, Japan remained separated from its neighbors and the larger world from the 1630s until the middle of the nineteenth century.

Without experiencing such civil strife, China entered on an epoch of remarkable strength, expansion, and cultural achievement. The Ming and Ch'ing dynasties ruled, and only the most minimal turmoil accompanied the transfer of power in 1644. The emperors of both dynasties governed in an absolute manner. The bureaucracy—named *mandarins* by the Jesuits, who came to China in the sixteenth century—was chosen meritocratically through a complex series of examinations and governed efficiently. The population of China expanded steadily. China experienced a second commercial revolution. Chinese shipping expanded. Although a truly national economy did not emerge, China possessed several regional economies, each as large as that of a major European national state. A banking system spread through the country to foster commerce. What did not occur in China, for all its commercial enterprise, was the development of industrialism. Nonetheless, at the end of this era, China appeared to be a very strong, stable nation. As in Japan, the tradition of Confucianism had achieved vast new influence.

In 1500, over a century of continued political and military strength lay before the Islamic world. The Ottoman Empire was at the time perhaps the most powerful military state in the world. The Safavids securely governed Iran as did the Mughals India. However, by the middle of the seventeenth century, the power of all three empires was on the wane. The growing military and naval strength of Europe defeated the Ottoman Turks at the sea battle of Lepanto in 1571 and in numerous land engagements during the seventeenth century. The final Turkish siege of Vienna failed in 1683. In Iran, the intense religiosity of the Shi'ites led to the neglect of political and military structures and, consequently, to difficulty in halting aggression from the Turks. At the same time, a distinctive mode of Shi'ite pietism arose in Iran. The Mughal Empire experienced a slow but steady decline after the late seventeenth century. By the battle of Plassey in 1757, the British East India Company had established a position of strength from which, within less than a century, Britain would come to govern the entire Indian subcontinent.

Early in the sixteenth century, Western Europe began to be divided between Protestantism and Roman Catholicism. The sectarian splintering that has resulted in hundreds of modern Protestant denominations also began at this time. Even within Catholicism, deep divisions developed between Catholics who favored traditional practices and those who championed the reforms of the Counter-Reformation and the Jesuits. A century and a half of religious war and theological conflict followed. Rulers made the most of these divisions to consolidate their territories politically. Confessionalization (that is, strict enforcement of a particular "orthodox" religious belief and practice) went hand in hand with the creation of modern Western states.

Four factors largely account for this momentous shift in the cultural balance of the world. First, the new monarchies that had arisen in the late Middle Ages, particularly in France, England, and Spain, now successfully unified their realms. Between 1500 and the middle of the eighteenth century, those monarchs learned to tame their aristocracies, to collect taxes efficiently, and to build effective armies and navies. Second, in league with the commercial sectors of their national economies, the monarchs and their bureaucrats encouraged voyages of commercial expansion and discovery. Through those voyages, Europeans penetrated markets across the globe. They also conquered and colonized the American continents and thereby europeanized two vast, rich landmasses much larger than Europe itself. Third, during the seventeenth century, European thinkers carried out new intellectual explorations that culminated in the Scientific Revolution. The new knowledge and methods of rational investigation of physical nature permitted them to develop their technological skills more fully. As a consequence, the fourth factor came into play, as Europeans, and most particularly the British, achieved an early foundation of industrial manufacturing that would permit further domination of world markets with inexpensive consumer goods. ❏

	EUROPE	NEAR EAST/INDIA
1500	*1517–1555* Protestant Reformation *1533–1584* Ivan the Terrible of Russia reigns *1540* Jesuit Order founded by Ignatius Loyola *1543–1727* The Scientific Revolution *1556–1598* Philip II of Spain reigns *1558–1603* Elizabeth I of England reigns *1562–1598* French Wars of Religion *1581* The Netherlands declares its independence from the Spanish Habsburgs *1588* Defeat of the Spanish Armada *1589–1610* Henry IV, Navarre, founds Bourbon dynasty of France	*1500–1722* Safavid Shi'ite rule in Iran *1512–1520* Ottoman ruler Selim I *1520–1566* Ottoman ruler Suleiman the Magnificent *1525–1527* Babur founds Mughal dynasty in India *1540* Hungary under Ottoman rule *1556–1605* Akbar the Great of India reigns *1571* Battle of Lepanto; Ottomans defeated *ca. 1571–1640* Safavid philosopher/writer Mullah Sadra *1588–1629* Shah Abbas I of Iran reigns
1600	*1618–1648* The Thirty Years War *1640–1688* Frederick William, the Great Elector reigns in Brandenburg-Prussia *1642–1646* Puritan Revolution in England *1643–1715* Louis XIV of France reigns *1682–1725* Peter the Great of Russia reigns *1688* The Glorious Revolution in England *1690* "Second Treatise of Civil Government," by John Locke	*1605–1657* Period of religious toleration in Mughal Empire, India *1628–1657* Shah Jahan reigns; builds Taj Mahal as mausoleum for his beloved wife *1646* Founding of Maratha empire *1648* Delhi becomes capital of Mughal Empire *1658–1707* Shah Aurangzeb, the "World Conqueror," reigns in India; end of religious toleration toward Hindus; beginning of Mughal decline *1669–1683* Last military expansion by Ottomans: 1669, seize Crete; 1670s, the Ukraine; 1683, lay siege to Vienna
1700	*1701* Act of Settlement provides for Protestant succession to English throne *1702–1713* War of Spanish Succession *1740–1748* War of Austrian Succession *1756–1763* Seven Years War *ca. 1750* Industrial Revolution begins in England *1772* First partition of Poland *1793* and *1795* Last two partitions of Poland	*1700* Sikhs and Marathas bring down Mughal empire *1708* British East India Company and New East India Company merged. *1722* Last Safavid ruler forced to abdicate *1724* Rise in the Deccan of the Islamic state of Hyderabad *1725* Nadir Shah of Afghanistan becomes ruler of Persia *1739* Persian invasion of Northern India, by Nadir Shah *1748–1761* Ahmad Shah Durrani of Afghanistan invades India *1757* British victory at Plassey, in Bengal

EAST ASIA	AFRICA	THE AMERICAS
1500–1800 Commercial revolution in Ming-Ch'ing China; trade with Europe; flourishing of the novel *1543* Portuguese arrive in Japan *1568–1600* Era of unification follows end of Warring States Era in Japan *1587* Spanish arrive in Japan *1588* Hideyoshi's sword hunt in Japan *1592–1598* Ming troops battle Hideyoshi's army in Korea	*1506* East coast of Africa under Portuguese domination *1507* Mozambique founded by Portuguese *1517* Spanish crown authorizes slave trade to its South American colonies; rapid increase in importation of slaves to the New World *1554–1659* Sa'did Sultanate in Morocco *1575* Union of Bornu and Kanem by Idris Alawma (r. 1575–1610); Kanem-Bornu state the most fully Islamic in West Africa *1591* Moroccan army defeats Songhai army; Songhai Empire collapses	*1519* Conquest of the Aztecs by Cortes; Aztec ruler, Montezuma (r. 1502–1519) killed; Tenochtitlan destroyed *1529* Mexico City becomes capital of the Viceroyalty of New Spain *1533* Pizarro begins his conquest of the Incas *1536* Spanish under Mendoza arrive in Argentina *1544* Lima becomes capital of the Viceroyalty of Peru *1584* Sir Walter Raleigh sends expedition to Roanoke Island (North Carolina)
1600 Tokugawa Ieyasu wins battle of Sekigahara, completes unification of Japan *1600–1868* Tokugawa shogunate in Edo *1630s* Seclusion adopted as national policy in Japan *1644–1694* Bashō, Japanese poet *1644–1911* Ch'ing (Manchu) dynasty in China *1661–1722* K'ang Hsi reign in China *1673–1681* Revolt of southern generals in China *1699* British East India Company arrives in China	*1600s* English, Dutch, and French enter the slave trade; slaves imported to sugar plantations in the Caribbean *1619* First African slaves in North America land in Virginia *1652* First Cape Colony settlement of Dutch East India Company *1660–1856* Omani domination of East Africa; Omani state centered in Zanzibar; 1698, takes Mozambique from Portuguese	*1607* The London company establishes Jamestown Colony (Virginia) *1608* Champlain founds Quebec
1701 Forty-seven rōnin incident in Japan *1716–1733* Reforms of Tokugawa Yoshimune in Japan *1737–1795* Reign of Ch'ien Lung in China *1742* Christianity banned in China *1784* American traders arrive in China *1787–1793* Matsudaira Sadanobu reforms in Japan *1798* White Lotus Rebellion in China	*1702* Asiento Guinea Trade Company founded for slave trade between Africa and the Americas *1700s* Trans-atlantic slave trade at its height *1741–1856* United Sultanate of Oman and Zanzibar *1754–1817* Usman Dan Fodio, founder of Sultanate in northern and central Nigeria; the Fulani become the ruling class in the region *1762* End of Funj sultanate in eastern Sudanic region	*1776–1781* The American Revolution *1783–1830* Simon Bolivar, Latin American soldier, statesman *1791* First 10 Amendments to U.S. Constitution (Bill of Rights) ratified *1791* Negro slave revolt in French Santo Domingo *1791* Canada Constitution Act divides the country into Upper and Lower Canada

Michelangelo's Pieta. This was Michelangelo's first sculpture, done when he was only eighteen in 1493–1494. Michelangelo portrayed the Madonna on a larger scale than Christ to give the effect of a mother holding her young son. The statue is now in St. Peter's in Rome. [Art Resource.]

16 The Late Middle Ages and The Renaissance in the West (1300–1527)

The late Middle Ages and the Renaissance marked a time of unprecedented calamity and of bold new beginnings in Europe. There was the Hundred Years' War between England and France (1337–1453), an exercise in seemingly willful self-destruction, which was made even more terrible in its later stages by the introduction of gunpowder and the invention of heavy artillery. There was almost universal bubonic plague, known to contemporaries as the Black Death. Between 1348 and 1350 waves of plague killed as much as one third of the population in many regions and transformed many pious Christians into believers in the omnipotence of death. There was a great schism within the Catholic church that lasted thirty-seven years (1378–1415) and saw by 1409 the election of no fewer than three competing popes and colleges of cardinals. And there was the onslaught of the Turks, who in 1453 marched seemingly invincibly through Constantinople and toward the west. As their political and religious institutions buckled; as disease, bandits, and wolves ravaged their cities in the wake of war; and as Muslim armies gathered at their borders, Europeans beheld what seemed to be the imminent total collapse of Western civilization.

But if the late Middle Ages saw unprecedented chaos, it also witnessed a rebirth that would continue into the seventeenth century. Two modern Dutch scholars have employed the same word (*Herfsttij*, "harvesttide") with different connotations to describe the period, one interpreting the word as a "waning" or "decline" (Johan Huizinga), the other as a true "harvest" (Heiko Oberman). If something was dying away, some ripe fruit and seed grain were also being gathered in. The late Middle Ages were a creative breaking up.

It was in this period that such scholars as Marsilius of Padua, William of Ockham, and Lorenzo Valla produced lasting criticisms of medieval assumptions about the nature of God, humankind, and society. It was a period in which kings worked through parliaments and clergy through councils to place lasting limits on the pope's temporal power. The principle that sovereigns (in this case, the pope) are accountable to the bodies of which they are the head was established. The arguments used by conciliarists (advocates of the judicial superiority of a Church council over a pope) to establish papal accountability to the body of the faithful provided an example for the secular sphere. National sovereigns, who also had an independent tradition of ruler accountability in Roman law, were reminded of their responsibility to the body politic.

The late Middle Ages also saw an unprecedented scholarly renaissance. Italian Humanists made a full recovery of classical knowledge and languages and set in motion educational reforms and cultural changes that would spread throughout Europe in the fifteenth and sixteenth centuries. In the process, the Italian Humanists invented, for all practical purposes, critical historical scholarship and exploited a new fifteenth-century invention, the "divine art" of printing with movable type. It was in this period that the vernacular, the local language, began to take its place alongside Latin, the international language, as a widely used literary and political language. The independent nation-states of Europe progressively superseded the universal church as the community of highest allegiance, as patriotism and incipient nationalism became a major force. Nations henceforth "transcended" themselves not by journeys to Rome but by competitive voyages to the Far East and the Americas, as the age of global exploration opened.

A time of both waning and harvest, constriction (in the form of nationalism) and expansion (in the sense of world exploration), the late Middle Ages saw medieval culture grudgingly give way to the ages of the Renaissance and the Reformation.

Political and Social Breakdown

The Hundred Years' War and the Rise of National Sentiment

From May 1337 to October 1453, England and France periodically engaged in what was for both a futile and devastating war.

CAUSES OF THE WAR. The conflict was initiated by the English king Edward III (1327–1377), who held a strong claim to the French throne as the grandson of Philip the Fair (1285–1314). When Charles VI (1322–1328), the last of Philip the Fair's surviving sons, died, Edward, who was only fifteen at the time, asserted his

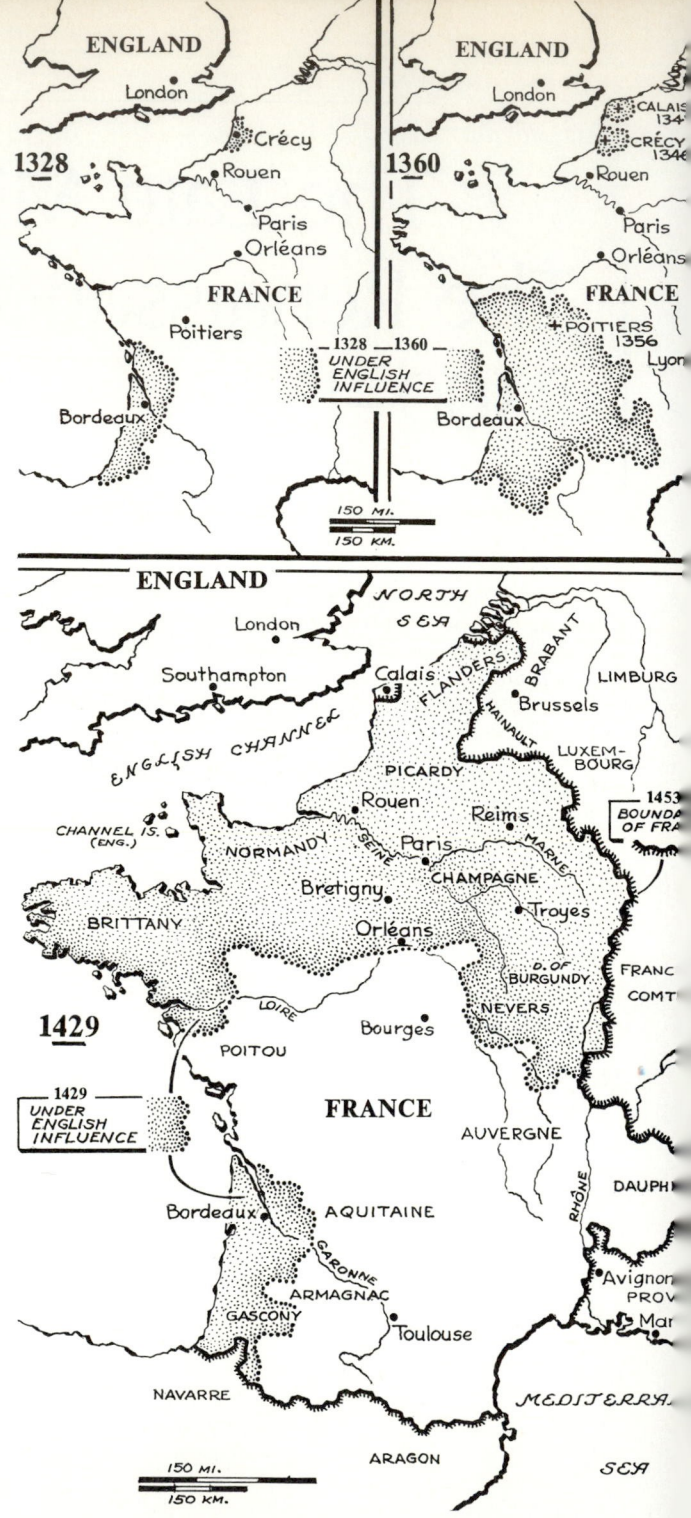

MAP 16-1   THE HUNDRED YEARS' WAR   *The Hundred Years' War went on intermittently from the late 1330s until 1453. These maps show the remarkable English territorial gains up to the sudden and decisive turning of the tide of battle in favor of the French by forces of Joan of Arc. in 1429.*

right to Capetian succession. The French barons, however, were not willing to place an English king on the French throne. They chose instead Philip VI of Valois (1328–1350), the first of a new French dynasty that was to rule into the sixteenth century.

In the background were other equally important causes. For one thing, the English king held certain French territories as fiefs from the French king. Thus he was, in law, a vassal of the French king. As Philip's vassal, Edward was, theoretically if not in fact, committed to support policies detrimental to England, if his French lord so commanded.

Still another factor that fueled the conflict was French support of the Bruces of Scotland, strong opponents of the English overlordship of Scotland who had won a victory over the English in 1314. The French and the English were also at this time quarreling over Flanders, a French fief, yet also a country whose towns were completely dependent for their livelihood on imported English wool.

Finally, there were decades of prejudice and animosity between the French and the English people, who constantly confronted one another on the high seas and in port towns. Taken together, these various factors made the Hundred Years' War a struggle to the death for national control and identity.

FRENCH WEAKNESS. Throughout the conflict, France was statistically the stronger: it had three times the population of England, was far the wealthier, and fought on its own soil. Yet, for the greater part of the conflict, until after 1415, the major battles ended in often stunning English victories. France was not as strong as it appeared. It was internally disunited by social conflict and the absence of a centralized system of taxation to fund the war. As a tool to provide him money, the king raised up a representative council of towns and nobles that came to be known in subsequent years as the *Estates General*. It convened in 1355, and although it levied taxes at the king's request, its members also used the king's plight to enhance their own regional rights and privileges. France, unlike England, still struggled in the fourteenth century to make the transition from a fragmented feudal society to a more centralized "modern" state.

Beyond this lay the clear fact of English military superiority, due to the greater discipline of its infantry and the rapid-fire and long-range capability of that ingeniously simple weapon, the English longbow, which could shoot six arrows a minute with a force sufficient to pierce an inch of wood or the armor of a knight at two hundred yards.

Finally, French weakness was related in no small degree to the comparative mediocrity of its royal leadership during the Hundred Years' War.

Progress of the War

The war had three major stages of development, each ending with a seemingly decisive victory by one or the other side.

CONFLICT DURING THE REIGN OF EDWARD III. By slapping an embargo on English wool to Flanders, Edward sparked urban rebellions by the merchants and the trade guilds. The Flemish cities, led by Ghent, revolted against the French. Having at first taken as neutral a stand as possible in the conflict, these cities, whose economies faced total collapse without imported English wool, signed a half-hearted alliance with England in January 1340, acknowledging Edward as king of France.

Edward defeated the French fleet in the first great battle of the war in the Bay of Sluys on June 23, 1340. But his subsequent effort to invade France by way of Flanders failed, largely because his allies proved undependable. As a stalemate developed, a truce was struck and was more-or-less observed until 1346. In that year, Edward attacked Normandy and won a series of easy victories that were capped by that at Crécy in August. This victory was quickly followed by the seizure of Calais, which the English held thereafter for over two hundred years. Both sides employed scorched-earth tactics and completely devastated the areas of conflict.

Exhaustion and the onset of the Black Death forced a second truce in late 1347, and the war entered a lull until 1355. On September 19, 1356, the English won their greatest victory near Poitiers, routing the noble cavalry and even taking the French king, John II the Good (1350–1364), captive back to England. After the English victory at Poitiers, there was a complete breakdown of political order in France. Disbanded soldiers from both sides became professional bandits, roaming the land, pillaging areas untouched by the war, and bringing disaster almost as great as the war itself.

Power in France lay with the privileged classes, which expressed their will through the representative assembly of the Estates General. Unlike the English Parliament, which represented the interests of a comparatively unified English nobility, the French Estates General was a many-tongued lobby, a forum for the diverse interests of the new-rich urban commercial and industrial classes, the territorial princes, and the clergy. Such a diverse body was no instrument for effective government.

On May 9, 1360, another milestone of the war was reached when England forced the Peace of Bretigny on the French. This agreement declared Edward's vassalage to the king of France ended and affirmed Edward's sovereignty over English territories in France. France also pledged to pay a ransom of three million gold crowns to win King John's release. In return, Edward renounced his claim to the French throne. Such a partition of French territorial control was completely unrealistic, and sober observers on both sides knew that it could not long continue.

FRENCH DEFEAT AND THE TREATY OF TROYES. After Edward's death, the English war effort lessened considerably, partly because of domestic problems within England. In 1396, France and England signed still another truce, this time backed up by the marriage of Richard II to the daughter of the French king, Charles VI (1380–1422). This truce lasted through the reign of Richard's successor, Henry IV of Lancaster (1399–1413). His successor, Henry V (1413–1422), reheated the war with France by taking advantage of the internal French turmoil created by the rise to power of the duchy of Burgundy under John the Fearless (1404–1419).

Henry V struck hard in Normandy, and his army routed the numerically stronger but tactically less shrewd French royal forces at Agincourt on October 25, 1415. By 1419, the Burgundians had allied with the English. With Burgundian support, France became Henry V's for the taking—at least in the short run. The Treaty of Troyes in 1420 disinherited the legitimate heir to the French throne, the dauphin (a title used by the king's oldest son), the future Charles VII, and made Henry V successor to the mad Charles VI. When Henry V and Charles VI died within months of one another in 1422, the infant Henry VI of England was proclaimed in Paris to be king of both France and England under the regency of the duke of Bedford. The dream of Edward III, the pretext for continuing the great war, was now, for the moment, realized: in 1422, an English king was the proclaimed ruler of France.

The dauphin went into retreat in Bourges, where, on the death of his father, he became Charles VII to most Frenchmen, who ignored the Treaty of Troyes.

JOAN OF ARC AND THE WAR'S CONCLUSION. Joan of Arc (1412–1431), a peasant from Domrémy, presented herself to Charles VII in March 1429. When she declared that the King of Heaven had called her to deliver besieged Orléans from the English, Charles was understandably skeptical. But the dauphin and his advisers, in retreat from what seemed to be a completely hopeless war, were desperate and were willing to try anything to reverse French fortunes on the bat-

Joan of Arc Refuses to Recant Her Beliefs

Joan of Arc, threatened with torture, refused to recant her beliefs and instead defended the instructions she received from the voices that spoke to her. Here is a part of her self-defense from the contemporary trial record.

On Wednesday, May 9th of the same year [1431], Joan was brought into the great tower of the castle of Rouen before us the said judges and in the presence of the reverend father, lord abbot of St. Cormeille de Compiegne, of masters Jean de Châtillon and Guillaume Erart, doctors of sacred theology, of André Marguerie and Nicolas de Venderes, archdeacons of the church of Rouen, of William Haiton, bachelor of theology, Aubert Morel, licentiate in canon law; Nicolas Loiseleur, canon of the cathedral of Rouen, and master Jean Massieu.

And Joan was required and admonished to speak the truth on many different points contained in her trial which she had denied or to which she had given false replies, whereas we possessed certain information, proofs, and vehement presumptions upon them. Many of the points were read and explained to her, and she was told that if she did not confess them truthfully she would be put to the torture, the instruments of which were shown to her all ready in the tower. There were also present by our instruction men ready to put her to the torture in order to restore her to the way and knowledge of truth, and by this means to procure the salvation of her body and soul which by her lying inventions she exposed to such grave perils.

To which the said Joan answered in this manner: "Truly if you were to tear me limb from limb and separate my soul from my body, I would not tell you anything more: and if I did say anything, I should afterwards declare that you had compelled me to say it by force." Then she said that on Holy Cross Day last she received comfort from St. Gabriel; she firmly believes it was St. Gabriel. She knew by her voices whether she should submit to the Church, since the clergy were pressing her hard to submit. Her voices told her that if she desired Our Lord to aid her she must wait upon Him in all her doings. She said that Our Lord has always been the master of her doings, and the Enemy never had power over them. She asked her voices if she would be burned and they answered that she must wait upon God, and He would aid her. ❑

The Trial of Jeanne D' Arc, trans. by W. P. Barrett (New York: Gotham House, 1932), pp. 303–304.

1340	English victory at Bay of Sluys
1346	English victory at Crécy and seizure of Calais
1347	Black Death strikes
1356	English victory at Poitiers
1358	*Jacquerie* disrupts France
1360	Peace of Bretigny recognizes English holdings in France
1381	English Peasants' Revolt
1415	English victory at Agincourt
1422	Treaty of Troyes proclaims Henry VI ruler of both England and France
1429	Joan of Arc leads French to victory at Orléans
1431	Joan of Arc executed as a heretic
1453	War ends; English retain only the coastal town of Calais

tlefield. Certainly the deliverance of Orléans, a city strategic to the control of the territory south of the Loire, would be a Godsend. Charles's desperation overcame his skepticism, and he gave Joan his leave to try and rescue the city.

Circumstances worked perfectly to Joan's advantage. The English force was already exhausted by its six-month siege of Orléans and actually at the point of withdrawal when Joan arrived with fresh French troops. After the English were repulsed at Orléans, there followed a succession of French victories that were popularly attributed to Joan. Joan truly deserved much of the credit, but not, however, because she was a military genius. She gave the French people and armies something that military experts could not: a unique inspiration and an almost mystical confidence in themselves as a nation. Within a few months of the liberation of Orléans, Charles VII received his crown in Rheims and ended the nine-year "disinheritance" prescribed by the Treaty of Troyes.

Charles forgot his liberator as quickly as he had embraced her. Joan was captured by the Burgundians in May 1430, and although the French king was in a position to secure her release, he did little to help her. She was turned over to the Inquisition in English-held Rouen. The Burgundians and the English wanted Joan publicly discredited, believing this would also discredit her patron, Charles VII, and might demoralize French resistance. The skilled inquisitors broke the courageous "Maid of Orléans" in ten weeks of merciless interrogation, and she was executed as a relapsed heretic on May 30, 1431. Charles reopened Joan's trial at a later date, and she was finally declared innocent of the all the charges against her on July 7, 1456, twenty-

five years after her execution. In 1920, the church declared her a saint.

Charles VII and Philip the Good made peace in 1435, and a unified France, now at peace with Burgundy, progressively forced the English back. By 1453, the date of the war's end, the English held only the coastal enclave of Calais.

During the Hundred Years' War, there were sixty-eight years of at least nominal peace and forty-four of hot war. The political and social consequences were lasting. Although the war devastated France, it also awakened the giant of French nationalism and hastened the transition in France from a feudal monarchy to a centralized state.

The Black Death

PRECONDITIONS AND CAUSES. In the late Middle Ages, nine tenths of the population were still farmers. The three-field system, in use in most areas since well before the fourteenth century, had increased the amount of arable land and thereby the food supply. The growth of cities and trade had also stimulated agricultural science and productivity. But as the food supply grew, so also did the population. It is estimated that Europe's population doubled between the years 1000 and 1300. By 1300, the balance between food supply and population was decisively tipped in favor of the latter. There were now more people than food to feed them or jobs to employ them, and the average European faced the probability of extreme hunger at least once during his or her expected thirty-five-year life span.

Famines followed the population explosion in the first half of the fourteenth century. Between 1315 and 1317, crop failures produced the greatest famine of the Middle Ages. Great suffering was inflicted on densely populated urban areas like the industrial towns of the Netherlands. Decades of overpopulation, economic depression, famine, and bad health progressively weakened Europe's population and made it highly vulnerable to the virulent bubonic plague that struck with full force in 1348. This Black Death, so called by contemporaries because of the way it discolored the body, followed the trade routes into Europe. Appearing in Sicily in late 1347, it entered Europe through the port cities of Venice, Genoa, and Pisa in 1348, and from there, it swept rapidly through Spain and southern France and into northern Europe. Areas that lay outside the major trade routes, like Bohemia, appear to have remained virtually unaffected. By the end of the fourteenth century, it is estimated that western Europe as a whole had lost as much as two fifths of its population, and a full recovery was not made until the sixteenth century. (See Map 16.2)

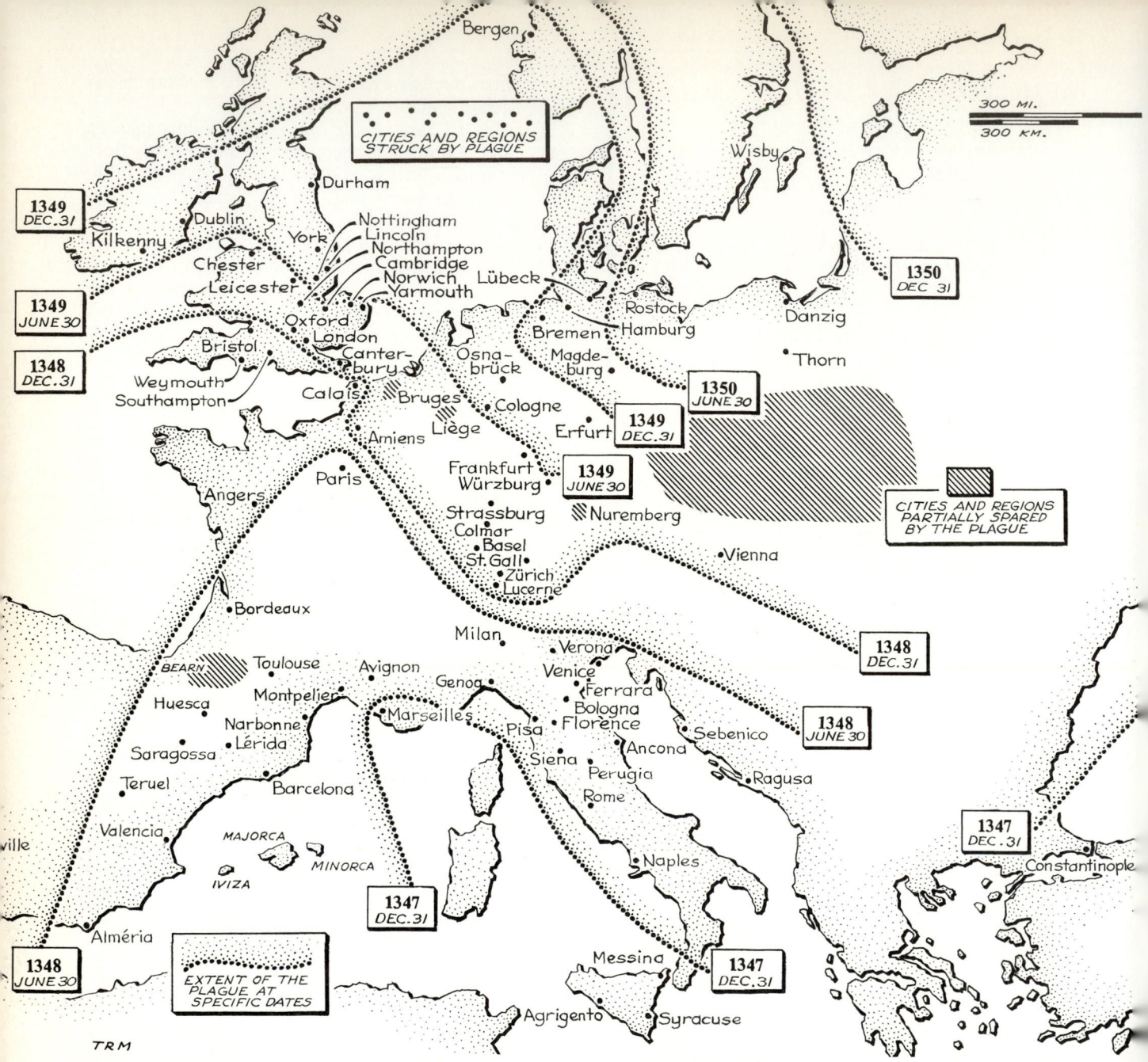

CITIES AND REGIONS
STRUCK BY PLAGUE

1349 DEC. 31

1349 JUNE 30

1348 DEC. 31

1350 DEC. 31

1350 JUNE 30

1349 DEC. 31

1349 JUNE 30

CITIES AND REGIONS
PARTIALLY SPARED
BY THE PLAGUE

1348 DEC. 31

1348 JUNE 30

1347 DEC. 31

1347 DEC. 31

1347 DEC. 31

1348 JUNE 30

EXTENT OF THE
PLAGUE AT
SPECIFIC DATES

TRM

MAP 16-2   SPREAD OF THE BLACK DEATH   *Apparently introduced by sea-borne rats from Black Sea areas where plague-infested rodents have long been known, the Black Death brought huge human, social, and economic consequences. One of the lower estimates of Europeans dying is 25,000,000. The map charts its spread in the mid-fourteenth century. Generally following trade routes, the plague reached Scandinavia by 1350, and some believe it then went on to Iceland and even Greenland. Areas off the main trade routes were largely spared.*

POPULAR REMEDIES.   In the Black Death, people confronted a catastrophe against which they had neither understanding nor defense. Never have Western people stood so helpless against the inexplicable and the uncontrollable. Contemporary physicians did not know that the disease was transmitted by rat- or human-transported fleas, and hence the most rudimentary prophylaxis was lacking. Popular wisdom held that a corruption in the atmosphere caused the disease. Some blamed poisonous fumes released by earthquakes, and many adopted aromatic amulets as a remedy. According to the contemporary observa-

Boccaccio Describes the Ravages of the Black Death in Florence

The Black Death occasioned the poet, Humanist, and storyteller Giovanni Boccaccio (1313–1375) to assemble his great collection of tales, the Decameron. *Ten congenial men and women flee Florence to escape the plague and wile away the time telling stories. In one of the stories, Boccaccio embedded a fine clinical description of plague symptoms as seen in Florence in 1348 and of the powerlessness of physicians and the lack of remedies.*

In Florence, despite all that human wisdom and forethought could devise to avert it, even as the cleansing of the city from many impurities by officials appointed for the purpose, the refusal of entrance to all sick folk, and the adoption of many precautions for the preservation of health; despite also humble supplications addressed to God, and often repeated both in public procession and otherwise, by the devout; towards the beginning of the spring of the said year (1348) the doleful effects of the pestilence began to be horribly apparent by symptoms that shewed as if miraculous.

Not such were these symptoms as in the East, where an issue of blood from the nose was a manifest sign of inevitable death; but in men and women alike it first betrayed itself by the emergence of certain tumours in the groin or the armpits, some of which grew as large as a common apple, others as an egg, some more, some less, which the common folk called gavoccioli. From the two said parts of the body this deadly gavoc-ciolo soon began to propagate and spread itself in all directions indifferently; after which the form of malady began to change, black spots or livid making their appearance in many cases on the arm or the thigh or elsewhere, now few and large, now minute and numerous. And as the gavocciolo had been and still was an infallible token of approaching death, such also were these spots on whomsoever they shewed themselves. Which maladies seemed to set entirely at naught both the art of the physician and the virtues of physic; indeed, whether it was that the disorder was of a nature to defy such treatment, or that the physicians were at fault . . . and, being in ignorance of its source, failed to apply the proper remedies; in either case, not merely were those that recovered few, but almost all died within three days of the appearance of the said symptoms, sooner or later, and in most cases without any fever or other attendant malady. ❑

The Decameron of Giovanni Boccaccio, trans. by J. M. Rigg (New York: Dutton, 1930), p. 5.

---

tions of Boccaccio, who recorded the varied reactions to the plague in the *Decameron* (1353), some sought a remedy in moderation and a temperate life; others gave themselves over entirely to their passions (sexual promiscuity among the stricken apparently ran high); and still others, "the most sound, perhaps, in judgment," chose flight and seclusion as the best medicine.

Among the most extreme social reactions were processions of flagellants. These were religious fanatics who beat their bodies in ritual penance until they bled,

A flagellant procession. Flagellants paraded from city to city, chanting songs and punishing their bodies in penance for sin. A typical flagellant parade lasted thirty-three days, one day for each year Christ lived. Note their bare backs and feet, hats with crosses, and rough penitential shirts. In their hands they carry candles and whips. [Koninlijke Bibliothek, Brussels.]

believing that such action would bring divine intervention. The Jews, who were hated by many because of centuries of Christian propaganda against them and the fact that they had become society's money lenders (a disreputable and resented profession) became scapegoats. Pogroms occurred in several cities, sometimes incited by the advent of flagellants. The terror created by the flagellants, whose dirty bodies may have actually served to transport the disease, became so socially disruptive and threatening even to established authority that the Church finally outlawed such processions.

SOCIAL AND ECONOMIC CONSEQUENCES. Among the social and economic consequences of the plague were a shrunken labor supply and the devaluation of the estates of the nobility. Villages vanished in the wake of the plague. As the number of farm laborers decreased, their wages increased, and those of skilled artisans soared. Many serfs now chose to commute their labor services by money payments, to abandon the farm altogether, and to pursue more interesting and rewarding jobs in skilled craft industries in the cities, an important new vocational option opened by the Black Death. Agricultural prices fell because of lowered demand, and the price of luxury and manufactured goods—the work of skilled artisans—rose. The noble landholders suffered the greatest decline in power from this new state of affairs. They were forced to pay more for finished products and for farm labor, and they received a smaller return on their agricultural produce. Everywhere their rents were in steady decline after the plague.

To recoup their losses, some landowners converted arable land to sheep pasture, substituting more profitable wool production for labor-intensive grain crops. Others abandoned the effort to farm their land and simply leased it to the highest bidder. Most ominously, legislation was sought to force peasants to stay on their farms and to freeze their wages at low levels, that is, to close off immediately the new economic opportunities opened for the peasantry by the demographic crisis. In France, the direct tax on the peasantry, the *taille*, was increased, and opposition to it was prominent among the grievances behind the *Jacquerie*, a great revolt of French peasants against the nobility in 1358. A Statute of Laborers was passed by the English Parliament in 1351 that limited wages to preplague levels and restricted the ability of peasants to leave the land of their traditional masters. Opposition to such legislation was also a prominent factor in the English Peasants' Revolt of 1381.

Although the plague hit urban populations especially hard, the cities and their skilled industries came, in time, to prosper from it. Cities had always been careful to protect their interests; as they grew, they passed legislation to regulate competition from rural areas and to control immigration. After the plague, their laws were progressively extended over the surrounding lands of nobles and feudal landlords, many of whom were peacefully integrated into urban life on terms very favorable to the cities.

The basic unit of urban industry was the master and his apprentices (usually one or two). Their numbers were purposely kept low and jealously guarded. As the craft of the skilled artisan was passed from master to apprentice only very slowly, the first wave of plague created a short supply of skilled labor almost overnight. But this short supply also raised the prices of available manufactured and luxury items to new heights. Ironically, the omnipresence of death whetted the appetite for the things that only skilled urban industries could produce. Expensive cloths and jewelry, furs from the north, and silks from the south were in great demand in the second half of the fourteenth century. Faced with life at its worst, people insisted on having the very best. The townspeople profited coming and going: as wealth poured into the cities and per capita income rose, the cost to urban dwellers of agricultural products from the countryside, which were now less in demand, actually declined.

The Church also profited from the plague as gifts and bequests multiplied. Although the Church, as a great landholder, also suffered losses, it had offsetting revenues from the vastly increased demand for religious services for the dead and the dying.

NEW CONFLICTS AND OPPORTUNITIES. By increasing the importance of skilled artisans, the plague contributed to new conflicts within the cities. The economic and political power of local artisans and trade guilds grew steadily in the late Middle Ages along with the demand for their goods and services. The merchant and patrician classes found it increasingly difficult to maintain their traditional dominance and grudgingly gave guild masters a voice in city government. As the guilds won political power, they encouraged restrictive legislation to protect local industries. These restrictions, in turn, brought confrontations between master artisans, who wanted to keep their numbers low and to expand their industries at a snail's pace, and the many journeymen, who were eager to rise to the rank of master. To the long-existing conflict between the guilds and the urban patriciate was now added a conflict within the guilds themselves.

Another indirect effect of the Great Plague was to assist monarchies in the development of centralized states. The plague caused the landed nobility to lose much of their economic power in the same period that the military superiority of paid professional armies over the traditional noble cavalry was being demonstrated by the Hundred Years' War. The plague also killed large numbers of clergy—perhaps one third of the German clergy fell victim to it as they heroically ministered to the sick and dying. This reduction in clerical ranks occurred in the same century in which the residence of the pope in Avignon (1309–1377) and the Great Schism (1378–1415; discussed later) were undermining the Church's popular support. After 1350, the two traditional "containers" of monarchy—the landed nobility and the Church—were on the defensive, and to no small degree as a consequence of the plague. Kings took full advantage of the new situation, as they drew on growing national sentiment to centralize their governments and economies.

Ecclesiastical Breakdown and Revival: The Late Medieval Church

During the reign of Pope Innocent III (1198–1216), papal power reached its height. Innocent elaborated the doctrine of papal plenitude of power and on that authority declared saints, disposed of benefices, and created a centralized papal monarchy with a clearly political mission.

What Innocent began, his successors perfected. The thirteenth-century papacy became a powerful political institution governed by its own law and courts, serviced by an efficient international bureaucracy, and preoccupied with secular goals.

Boniface VIII and Philip the Fair

Pope Boniface VIII (1294–1303) came to rule when England and France were maturing as nation-states. In England, a long tradition of consultation between the king and powerful members of English society evolved into formal "parliaments" during the reigns of Henry III (1216–1272) and Edward I (1272–1307), and these parliaments helped to create a unified kingdom. The reign of the French king Philip IV the Fair (1285–1314) saw France become an efficient, centralized monarchy. Boniface had the further misfortune of bringing to the papal throne memories of the way earlier popes had brought kings and emperors to their knees. He was to discover that the papal monarchy of the early thirteenth century was no match for the new political powers of the late thirteenth century.

France and England were on the brink of all-out war when Boniface became pope (1294). As both countries mobilized for war, they used the pretext of pre-

Pope Boniface VIII (1294–1303) who opposed the taxation of clergy by the kings of France and England and issued one of the strongest declarations of papal authority, the bull Unam Sanctam. *The statue is in the Museo Civico, Bologna, Italy. [Alinari/SCALA.]*

Marsilius of Padua Denies Coercive Power to the Clergy

According to Marsilius (CA. 1290–1342), a pamphleteer for the royal cause, the Bible gave the pope no right to pronounce and execute sentences on any person. The clergy held a strictly moral and spiritual rule, their judgments to be executed only in the afterlife, not in the present one. Here, on earth, they should be obedient to secular authority. Marsilius argued this point by appealing to the example of Jesus.

We now wish . . . to adduce the truths of the holy Scripture . . . which explicitly command or counsel that neither the Roman bishop called pope, nor any other bishop or priest, or deacon, has or ought to have any rulership or coercive judgment or jurisdiction over any priest or nonpriest, ruler, community, group, or individual of whatever condition. . . . Christ himself came into the world not to dominate men, nor to judge them [coercively] . . . not to wield temporal rule, but rather to be subject as regards the . . . present life; and moreover, he wanted to and did exclude himself, his apostles and disciples, and their successors, the bishops or priests, from all coercive authority or worldly rule, both by his example and by his word of counsel or command. . . . When he was brought before Pontius Pilate . . . and accused of having called himself king of the Jews, and [Pilate] asked him whether he had said this . . . [his] reply included these words . . . "My kingdom is not of this world," that is, I have not come to reign by temporal rule or dominion, in the way . . . worldly kings reign. . . . This, then, is the kingdom concerning which he came to teach and order, a kingdom which consists in the acts whereby the eternal kingdom is attained, that is, the acts of faith and the other theological virtues; not however, by coercing anyone thereto. ❑

Marsilius of Padua: The Defender of Peace: The Defensor Pacis, trans. by Alan Gewirth (New York: Harper, 1967), pp. 113–116.

---

paring for a crusade to tax the clergy heavily. Viewing English and French taxation of the clergy as an assault on traditional clerical rights, Boniface issued a bull, *Clericis Laicos*, which forbade lay taxation of the clergy without prior papal approval.

In England, Edward I retaliated by denying the clergy the right to be heard in the royal court, in effect removing from them the protection of the king. But it was Philip the Fair who struck back with a vengeance. In August 1296, he forbade the exportation of money from France to Rome, thereby denying the papacy revenues without which it could not operate. Boniface had no choice but to concede Philip the right to tax the French clergy "during an emergency."

In the year 1300, Boniface's fortunes appeared to revive. Tens of thousands of pilgrims flocked to Rome in that year for the Jubilee celebration. In a Jubilee year, all Catholics who visited Rome and there fulfilled certain conditions received a special indulgence, or remission of their sins. Heady with this display of popular religiosity, Boniface reinserted himself into international politics. Philip, seemingly spoiling for another fight with the pope, arrested Boniface's Parisian legate, Bernard Saisset, the bishop of Pamiers. Boniface demanded Saisset's unconditional release. A bull, *Ausculta Fili* ("Listen, My Son"), was sent to Philip in December 1301, pointedly informing him that "God has set popes over kings and kingdoms."

UNAM SANCTAM (1302). Philip unleashed a ruthless antipapal campaign. Boniface made a last-ditch stand against state control of national churches when on November 18, 1302, he issued the bull *Unam Sanctam*. This famous statement of papal power declared that temporal authority was "subject" to the spiritual power of the church.

After *Unam Sanctam*, the French moved against Boniface with force. An army of the king surprised the pope in mid-August 1303 at his retreat in Anagni. Boniface was badly beaten up and almost executed, before an aroused populace liberated him and returned him safely to Rome.

There was to be no papal retaliation by Boniface or his successors. Indeed, Pope Clement V (1305–1314), a former archbishop of Bordeaux, declared that *Unam Sanctam* should not be understood as in any way diminishing French royal authority. Clement established the papal court at Avignon, on the southeastern border of France, in 1309. There the papacy would remain until 1377.

After Boniface's humiliation, popes never again so seriously threatened kings and emperors, despite continuing papal excommunications and political intrigue. In the future, the relation between Church and State would tilt toward state control of religion within particular monarchies and the subordination of ecclesiastical to larger secular political purposes.

The Great Schism (1378–1417) and the Conciliar Movement to 1449

Pope Gregory XI (1370–1378) reestablished the papacy in Rome in January 1377, ending what had come to be known as the "Babylonian Captivity" of the church in Avignon, the reference being to the biblical bondage of the Israelites. The return to Rome proved to be short-lived, however. On Gregory's death on March 27, 1378, the cardinals, in Rome, elected an Italian archbishop as Pope Urban VI (1378–1389), who immediately proclaimed his intention to reform the Curia. This announcement came as an unexpected challenge to the cardinals, most of whom were French, and made them amenable to royal pressures to return the papacy to Avignon. The French king, Charles V, not wanting to surrender the benefits of a papacy located within the sphere of French influence, lent his support to a schism.

Five months after Urban's election, on September 20, 1378, thirteen cardinals, all but one of whom was French, formed their own conclave and elected a cousin of the French king as Pope Clement VII (1378–1397). They insisted, probably with some truth, that they had voted for Urban in fear of their lives, surrounded by a Roman mob that demanded the election of an Italian pope. Be that as it may, thereafter the papacy became a "two-headed thing" and a scandal to Christendom. Allegiance to the two papal courts divided along political lines: England and its allies (the Holy Roman Empire, Hungary, Bohemia, and Poland) acknowledged Urban VI, whereas France and its orbit (Naples, Scotland, Castile, and Aragon) supported Clement VII. Only the Roman line of popes, however, came to be recognized as official in subsequent Church history.

THE COUNCIL OF CONSTANCE (1414–1417).

In 1409, a council was convened in Pisa that deposed both the Roman and the Avignon popes and elected in their stead its own new pope. But to the council's consternation, neither of these accepted its action, so after 1409, Christendom confronted the spectacle of three contending popes. This intolerable situation ended when the emperor Sigismund prevailed on the Pisan pope John XXIII to summon a "legal" council of the Church in Constance in 1414, a council also recognized by the reigning Roman pope Gregory XII. Gregory, however, soon resigned his office, raising grave doubts forevermore about whether the council was truly convened with Rome's blessing and hence valid. In a famous declaration entitled *Haec Sancta*, the council fathers asserted their supremacy and proceeded to conduct the business of the church.

They also executed the Bohemian reformer Jan Hus, on July 6, 1415. Hus was the rector of the Univer-

A German portrayal of the burning of Jan Hus for heresy and the dumping of his ashes into the Rhine to prevent their becoming relics. [Vincent Virga Archives.]

sity of Prague and he had been strongly influenced in his teaching by the English reformer John Wycliffe (D. 1384). Hus advocated communion for laity with both wine and bread (traditionally only the priest received both; the laity had received only bread, indicating the clergy's spiritual superiority over them); denied the dogma of transubstantiation (that wine and bread become the true body and blood of Christ by priestly consecration); and questioned the validity of sacraments performed by priests who led immoral lives.

In November 1417, the council successfully accomplished its main business when it elected a new pope,

Martin V (1417–1431), after the three contending popes had either resigned (Gregory XIII) or were deposed (Benedict XIII and John XXIII). The council made provisions for regular meetings of Church councils, scheduling a general council of the Church for purposes of reform within five, then seven, and thereafter every ten years. Constance has remained, however, an illegitimate Church council in official eyes: nor are the schismatic popes of Avignon and Pisa recognized as legitimate (for this reason another pope could take the name John XXIII in 1958).

THE COUNCIL OF BASEL (1431–1449). Conciliar government of the church both peaked and declined during the Council of Basel. This council curtailed papal powers of appointment and taxation and directly negotiated peace with the Hussites of Bohemia, conceding the latter's demands for communion with cup as well as bread, free preaching by their ordained clergy, and like punishment of clergy and laity for the same mortal sins. The council also recognized the right of the Bohemian church to govern its own internal affairs, much as the church in France and England had long since done.

During the pontificate of Pope Eugenius IV (1431–1447), the papacy regained much of its prestige and authority and successfully challenged the Council of Basel. The notion of conciliar superiority over popes died with the collapse of the Council of Basel in 1449. A decade later, the papal bull *Execrabilis* (1460) condemned appeals to councils as "erroneous and abominable" and "completely null and void."

But the conciliar movement was not a total failure. It planted deep within the conscience of all Western peoples the conviction that the leader of an institution must be responsive to its members and that the head exists to lead and serve, not to bring disaster on, the body.

Revival of Monarchy: Nation Building in the Fifteenth Century

After 1450, there was a progressive shift from divided feudal to unified national monarchies as "sovereign" rulers emerged. This is not to say that the dynastic and chivalric ideals of feudal monarchy did not continue. Territorial princes did not pass from the scene, and representative bodies persisted and in some areas even grew in influence. But in the late fifteenth and early sixteenth centuries, the old problem of the one and the many was decided clearly in favor of the interests of monarchy.

The feudal monarchy of the high Middle Ages was characterized by the division of the basic powers of government between the king and his semiautono-

mous vassals. The nobility and the towns acted with varying degrees of unity and success through such evolving representative assemblies as the English Parliament, the French Estates General, and the Spanish Cortes to thwart the centralization of royal power. Because of the Hundred Years' War and the schism in the Church, the nobility and the clergy were in decline in the late Middle Ages. The increasingly important towns began to ally with the king. Loyal, businesswise townspeople, not the nobility and the clergy, staffed the royal offices and became the king's lawyers, bookkeepers, military tacticians, and foreign diplomats. It was this new alliance between king and town that finally broke the bonds of feudal society and made possible the rise of sovereign states.

In a sovereign state, the power of taxation, war making, and law enforcement is no longer the local right of semiautonomous vassals but is concentrated in the monarch and is exercised by his chosen agents. Taxes, wars, and laws become national rather than merely regional matters. Only as monarchs were able to act independently of the nobility and the representative assemblies could they overcome the decentralization that had been the basic obstacle to nation building.

Monarchies also began to create standing national armies in the fifteenth century. As the noble cavalry receded and the infantry and the artillery became the backbone of armies, mercenary soldiers were recruited from Switzerland and Germany to form the major part of the "king's army."

The more expensive warfare of the fifteenth and sixteenth centuries increased the need to develop new national sources of royal income. The expansion of royal revenues was especially hampered by the stubborn belief among the highest classes that they were immune from government taxation. The nobility guarded their properties and traditional rights and despised taxation as an insult and a humiliation. Royal revenues accordingly grew at the expense of those least able to resist, and least able to pay. The king had several options. As a feudal lord he could collect rents from his royal domain. He could also levy national taxes on basic food and clothing, such as the *gabelle* or salt tax in France and the *alcabala* or 10 per cent sales tax on commercial transactions in Spain. The king could also levy direct taxes on the peasantry. This he did through agreeable representative assemblies of the privileged classes in which the peasantry did not sit. The French *taille* was such a tax. Sale of public offices and issuance of high-interest government bonds appeared in the fifteenth century as innovative fund-raising devices. But kings did not levy taxes on the powerful nobility. They turned to rich nobles, as they did to the great bankers of Italy and Germany, for loans, bargaining with the privileged classes, who in many instances remained as much the kings' creditors and competitors as their subjects.

France

There were two cornerstones of French nation building in the fifteenth century. The first was the collapse of the English holdings in France following the Hundred Years' War. The second was the defeat of Charles the Bold and the duchy of Burgundy. Perhaps Europe's strongest political power in the mid-fifteenth century, Burgundy aspired to dwarf both France and the Holy Roman Empire as the leader of a dominant middle kingdom. It might have succeeded in doing so had not the continental powers joined together in opposition. When Charles the Bold died in defeat in a battle at Nancy in 1477, the dream of Burgundian empire died with him.

The dissolution of Burgundy ended its constant intrigue against the French king and left Louis XI (1461–1483) free to secure the monarchy. The newly acquired Burgundian lands and his own Angevin inheritance permitted the king to end his reign with a kingdom almost twice the size of that with which he had started. Louis successfully harnessed the nobility, expanded the trade and industry, created a national postal system, and even established a lucrative silk industry at Lyons (later transferred to Tours).

A strong nation is a two-edged sword. It was because Louis' successors inherited such a secure and efficient government that France was able to pursue Italian conquests in the 1490s and to fight a long series of losing wars with the Habsburgs in the first half of the sixteenth century. By the mid-sixteenth century, France was again a defeated nation and almost as divided internally as during the Hundred Years' War.

Spain

Spain, too, became a strong country in the late fifteenth century. Both Castile and Aragon had been poorly ruled and divided kingdoms in the mid-fifteenth century. The marriage of Isabella of Castile (1474–1504) and Ferdinand of Aragon (1479–1516) changed that situation. The two future sovereigns married in 1469, despite strong protests from neighboring Portugal and France, both of which foresaw the formidable European power such a union would create. Castile was by far the richer and more populous of the two, having an estimated five million inhabitants to Aragon's population of under one million. Castile was also distinguished by its lucrative sheep-farming industry, which was run by a government-backed organization called the *Mesta*, another example of developing centralized economic planning. Although the two kingdoms were dynastically united by the marriage of Ferdinand and Isabella in 1469, they remained constitu-

tionally separated, as each retained its respective government agencies—separate laws, armies, coinage, and taxation—and cultural traditions.

Ferdinand and Isabella could do together what neither was able to accomplish alone: subdue their realms, secure their borders, and venture abroad militarily. Townspeople allied themselves with the crown and progressively replaced the nobility within the royal administration. The crown also extended its authority over the wealthy chivalric orders, a further circumscription of the power of the nobility.

Spain had long been remarkable among European lands as a place where three religions—Islam, Judaism, and Christianity—coexisted with a certain degree of toleration. This toleration ended dramatically under Ferdinand and Isabella, who made Spain the prime example of state-controlled religion. Ferdinand and Isabella exercised almost total control over the Spanish church as they placed religion in the service of national unity. They appointed the higher clergy and the officers of the Inquisition. The Inquisition, run by Tomás de Torquemada (D. 1498), Isabella's confessor, was a key national agency established in 1479 to monitor the activity of converted Jews (*conversos*) and Muslims (*Moriscos*) in Spain. In 1492, the Jews were exiled and their properties were confiscated. In 1502, nonconverting Moors in Granada were driven into exile. Spanish spiritual life remained largely uniform and successfully controlled—a major reason for Spain's remaining a loyal Catholic country throughout the sixteenth century and providing a base of operation for the European Counter-Reformation.

Ferdinand and Isabella were rulers with wide horizons. They contracted anti-French marriage alliances that came to determine a large part of European history in the sixteenth century. In 1496, their eldest daughter, Joanna, later known as "the Mad," married Archduke Philip, the son of Emperor Maximilian I. The fruit of this union, Charles I of Spain, the first ruler over a united Spain, came by his inheritance and election as emperor Charles V in 1519 to rule over a European kingdom almost equal in size to that of Charlemagne. A second daughter, Catherine of Aragon, wed Arthur, the son of the English King Henry VII, and after Arthur's premature death, she married his brother, the future King Henry VIII. The failure of this latter marriage became the key factor in the emergence of the Anglican church and the English Reformation.

The new Spanish power was also revealed in Ferdinand and Isabella's promotion of overseas exploration. Their patronage of the Genoese adventurer Christopher Columbus (1451–1506), who discovered the islands of the Caribbean while sailing west in search of a shorter route to the spice markets of the Far East, led to the creation of the Spanish empire in Mexico and Peru, whose gold and silver mines helped

England

The last half of the fifteenth century was a period of especially difficult political trial for the English. Following the Hundred Years' War, a defeated England was subjected to internal warfare between two rival branches of the royal family, the House of York and the House of Lancaster. This conflict, known to us today as the War of the Roses (as York's symbol, according to legend, was a white rose, and Lancaster's a red rose), kept England in turmoil from 1455 to 1485.

The Lancastrian monarchy of Henry VI (1422–1461) was consistently challenged by the duke of York and his supporters in the prosperous southern towns. In 1461, Edward IV (1461–1483), son of the duke of York, successfully seized power and instituted a strong-arm rule that lasted over twenty years. Edward, assisted by loyal and able ministers, effectively bent Parliament to his will. His brother and successor was Richard III (1483–1485). During the reign of the Tudors, a tradition arose that painted Richard III as an unprincipled villain who murdered Edward's sons in the Tower of London to secure the throne. The best-known version of this characterization—unjust according to some—is found in Shakespeare's *Richard III*. Be that as it may, Richard's reign saw the growth of support for the exiled Lancastrian Henry Tudor. Henry returned to England to defeat Richard on Bosworth Field in August 1485.

Henry Tudor ruled as Henry VII (1485–1509), the first of the new Tudor dynasty that would dominate England throughout the sixteenth century. In order to bring the rival royal families together and to make the hereditary claim of his offspring to the throne uncontestable, Henry married Edward IV's daughter, Elizabeth of York. He succeeded in disciplining the English nobility through a special and much feared instrument of the royal will known as the *Court of Star Chamber*. Henry shrewdly construed legal precedents to the advantage of the crown, using English law to further his own ends. He managed to confiscate noble lands and fortunes with such success that he governed without dependence on Parliament for royal funds, always a cornerstone of strong monarchy. In these ways, Henry began to shape a monarchy that became one of early modern Europe's most exemplary governments during the reign of his granddaughter, Elizabeth I.

The Holy Roman Empire

Germany and Italy are the striking exceptions to the steady development of centralized nation-states in the last half of the fifteenth century. Unlike France, Spain, and England, the Holy Roman Empire saw the many thoroughly repulse the one. In Germany, territorial rulers and cities resisted every effort at national consolidation and unity. As in Carolingian times, rulers continued to partition their kingdoms, however small, among their sons, and by the late fifteenth century, Germany was hopelessly divided into some three hundred autonomous political entities.

The Holy Roman Emperor is shown here with the seven electors. The three ecclesiastical electors are to his right and the four secular electors to his left. Also represented here are the territorial kingdoms or principalities (dukedoms, margraviates, landgraviates, and burgraviates) and the imperial cities. [Konrad Kolbl Reprint Verlag, Grunwald bei Munchen.]

The princes and the cities did work together to create the machinery of law and order, if not of union, within the divided empire. An agreement reached between the emperor Charles IV and the major German territorial rulers in 1356, known as the *Golden Bull*, established a seven-member electoral college consisting of the archbishops of Mainz, Trier, and Cologne; the duke of Saxony; the margrave of Brandenburg; the count Palatine; and the king of Bohemia. This group also functioned as an administrative body. They elected the emperor and, in cooperation with him, provided what transregional unity and administration existed. The figure of the emperor gave the empire a single ruler in law, if not in actual fact.

In the sixteenth and seventeenth centuries, German territorial princes became virtually sovereign rulers within their various domains. Such disunity aided religious dissent and conflict. It was in the cities and territories of still-feudal, fractionalized, backward Germany that the Protestant Reformation broke out in the sixteenth century.

The Renaissance in Italy (1375–1527)

In his famous study, *Civilization of the Renaissance in Italy* (1867), Jacob Burckhardt described the Renaissance as the prototype of the modern world. He believed that it was in fourteenth- and fifteenth-century Italy, through the revival of ancient learning, that new secular and scientific values first began to supplant traditional religious beliefs. This was the period in which people began to adopt a rational, objective, and statistical approach to reality and to rediscover the importance of the individual. The result, in Burckhardt's words, was a release of the "full, whole nature of man."

Other scholars have found Burckhardt's description too modernizing an interpretation of the Renaissance and have accused him of overlooking the continuity with the Middle Ages. His critics especially stress the strongly Christian character of Humanism and the fact that earlier "renaissances" also revived the ancient classics, professed interest in Latin language and Greek science, and appreciated the worth and creativity of individuals.

Most scholars nonetheless agree that the Renaissance was a time of transition from the medieval to the modern world. Medieval Europe, especially before the twelfth century, had been a fragmented feudal society with an agriculturally based economy, its thought and culture largely dominated by the Church. Renaissance Europe, especially after the fourteenth century, was characterized by growing national consciousness and political centralization, an urban economy based on organized commerce and capitalism, and ever greater lay and secular control of thought and culture.

It was especially in Italy between the late fourteenth and the early sixteenth centuries, from roughly 1375 to 1527, the year of the sack of Rome by imperial soldiers, that the distinctive features and achievements of the Renaissance, which also deeply influenced northern Europe, are most strikingly revealed.

The Italian City-State: Social Conflict and Despotism

Italy had always had a cultural advantage over the rest of Europe because its geography made it the natural gateway between East and West. Venice, Genoa, and Pisa traded uninterruptedly with the Near East throughout the Middle Ages and maintained vibrant urban societies. During the thirteenth and fourteenth centuries, trade-rich cities expanded to become powerful city-states, dominating the political and economic life of the surrounding countryside. By the fifteenth century, the great Italian cities had become the bankers of much of Europe.

The growth of Italian cities and urban culture was also assisted by the endemic warfare between the emperor and the pope. Either of these might have successfully challenged the cities. They chose instead to weaken one another and thus strengthened the merchant oligarchies of the cities. Unlike in northern Europe, where the cities tended to be dominated by kings and princes, Italian cities were left free to expand into states. They absorbed the surrounding countryside and assimilated the area nobility in a unique urban meld of old and new rich. There were five such major, competitive states in Italy: the duchy of Milan; the republics of Florence and Venice; the Papal States; and the kingdom of Naples (see Map 16.3).

Social strife and competition for political power were so intense within the cities that, for survival's sake, most had evolved into despotisms by the fifteenth century. Venice was the notable exception. It was ruled by a successful merchant oligarchy with power located in a patrician senate of three hundred members and a ruthless judicial body, the Council of Ten, that anticipated and suppressed rival groups. Elsewhere, the new social classes and divisions within society produced by rapid urban growth fueled chronic, near-anarchic conflict.

Florence was the most striking example. There were four distinguishable social groups within the city. The first was the old rich, or *grandi*, the nobles and merchants who had traditionally ruled the city. The second group was the emergent new-rich merchant class, capitalists and bankers known as the *popolo grasso*, or "fat people." They began to challenge the old rich for political power in the late thirteenth and early fourteenth centuries. Then there were the middle-burgher ranks of guild masters, shopkeepers, and professionals, those small businessmen who, in Florence as elsewhere, tended to take the side of the new rich against the conservative policies of the old rich. Finally, there was the omnipresent *popolo minuto*, the poor masses who lived from hand to mouth: in 1457, one third of the population of Florence, about thirty thousand people, were officially listed as paupers.

These social divisions produced conflict at every level of society. In 1378, a great revolt by the poor, known as the Ciompi Revolt, established a chaotic four-year reign of power by the lower Florentine classes. True stability did not return to Florence until the ascent to power in 1434 of Cosimo de' Medici (1389–1464).

The wealthiest Florentine and an astute statesman, Cosimo controlled the city internally from behind the scenes, skillfully manipulating the constitution and influencing elections. His grandson, Lorenzo the Magnificent (1449–1492), ruled Florence in almost totalitarian fashion during the last quarter of the fifteenth century.

A terra cotta bust of Lorenzo de' Medici by the sculptor Andrea del Verrocchio (CA. 1435–1488). [National Gallery of Art, Washington; Samuel H. Kress Collection.]

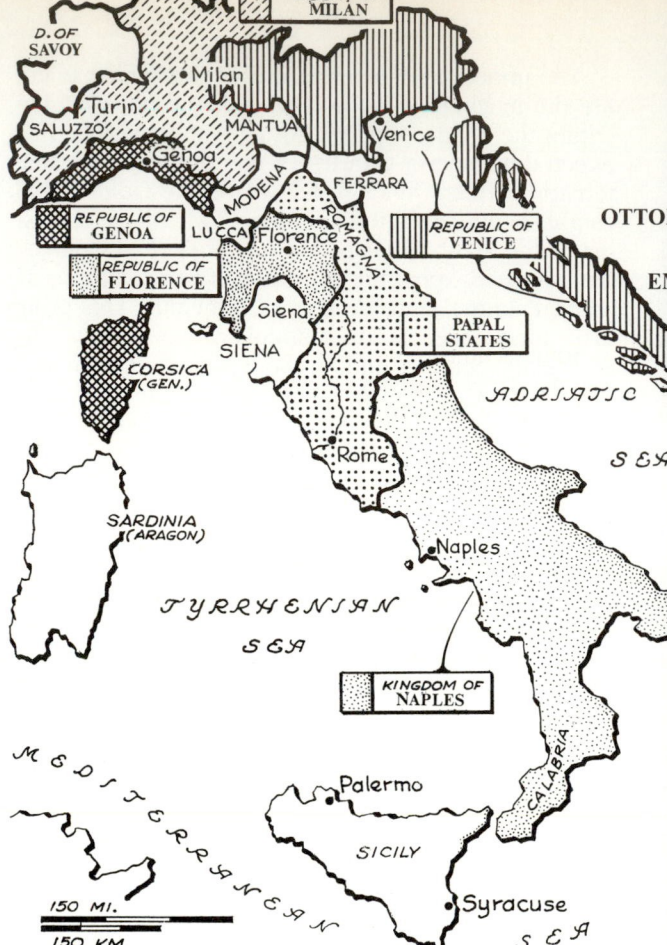

MAP 16-3   RENAISSANCE ITALY   *The city-states of Renaissance Italy were self-contained principalities whose internal strife was monitored by their despots and whose external aggression was long successfully controlled by treaty.*

Despotism was less subtle elsewhere. In order to prevent internal social conflict and foreign intrigue from paralyzing their cities, the dominant groups cooperated to install a hired strongman, known as a *podestá*, for the purpose of maintaining law and order. He held executive, military, and judicial authority, and his mandate was simple: to permit, by whatever means required, the normal flow of business. Because these despots could not depend on the divided populace, they operated through mercenary armies.

Political turbulence and warfare gave birth to diplomacy, by means of which the various city-states stayed abreast of foreign military developments and, if shrewd enough, gained power and advantage short of actually going to war. Most city-states established resident embassies in the fifteenth century. Their ambassadors not only represented them in ceremonies and as negotiators but also became their watchful eyes and ears at rival courts.

Whether within the comparatively tranquil republic of Venice, the strong-arm democracy of Florence, or the undisguised despotism of Milan, the wealthy Italian city proved a most congenial climate for an unprecedented flowering of thought and culture. Renaissance culture was promoted as vigorously by despots as by republicans and by secularized popes as enthusiastically as by the more spiritually minded.

Humanism

Some scholars describe Humanism as an unchristian philosophy that stressed the dignity of humankind and championed individualism and secular values. Others argue that the Humanists were true champions of authentic Catholic Christianity. Still others see Humanism as a form of scholarship consciously designed to promote a sense of civic responsibility and political liberty. One of the most authoritative modern commentators, Paul O. Kristeller, has accused all these views of dealing more with the secondary effects than with the essence of Humanism, which he believes, was no particular philosophy or value system but simply an educational program concentrated on rhetoric and sound scholarship for their own sake.

There is truth in each of these definitions. Humanism was the scholarly study of the Latin and Greek classics and the ancient Church Fathers both for their own sake and in the hope of a rebirth of ancient norms and values. Humanists were advocates of the *studia humanitatis*, a liberal arts program of study that embraced grammar, rhetoric, poetry, history, politics, and moral philosophy. The Florentine Leonardo Bruni (1374–1444) first gave the name *humanitas* ("humanity") to the learning that resulted from such scholarly pursuits. Bruni was a student of Manuel Chrysoloras, a Byzantine scholar who opened the world of Greek scholarship to a generation of young Italian Humanists when he taught at Florence between 1397 and 1403.

The first Humanists were orators and poets. They wrote original literature, in both the classical and the vernacular languages, inspired by the newly discovered works of the ancients, and they taught rhetoric within the universities. When Humanists were not employed as teachers of rhetoric, their talents were sought as secretaries, speech writers, and diplomats in princely and papal courts.

The study of classical and Christian antiquity existed before the Italian Renaissance. There were recoveries of ancient civilization during the Carolingian renaissance of the ninth century, within the cathedral school of Chartres in the twelfth century, during the great Aristotelian revival in Paris in the thirteenth century, and among the Augustinians in the early fourteenth century. However, these precedents only partially compare with the grand achievements of the Italian Renaissance of the late Middle Ages. The latter was more secular and lay-dominated, had broader interests, recovered more manuscripts, and possessed far superior technical skills than had been the case in the earlier "rebirths" of antiquity. Unlike their Scholastic rivals, Humanists were not content only to summarize and compare the views of recognized authorities on a question, but went directly to the original source itself and drew their own conclusions. Avidly searching out manuscript collections, Italian Humanists made the full sources of Greek and Latin antiquity available to scholars during the fourteenth and fifteenth centuries. Mastery of Latin and Greek was the surgeon's tool of the Humanist. There is a kernel of truth—but only a kernel—in the arrogant boast of the Humanists that the period between themselves and classical civilization was a "dark middle age."

PETRARCH, DANTE, AND BOCCACCIO. Francesco Petrarch (1304–1374) was the father of Humanism. He left the legal profession to pursue his love of letters and poetry. Although most of his life was spent in and around Avignon, he became caught up in Cola

Dante Aligheri as seen by his contemporary, Giotto. [The Granger Collection.]

Petrarch's Letter to Posterity

In old age, Petrarch wrote a highly personal letter to posterity in which he summarized the lessons he had learned during his lifetime. The letter also summarizes the original values of Renaissance Humanists: their suspicion of purely materialistic pleasure, the importance they attached to friendship, and their utter devotion to and love of antiquity.

I have always possessed extreme contempt for wealth; not that riches are not desirable in themselves, but because I hate the anxiety and care which are invariably associated with them . . . I have, on the contrary, led a happier existence with plain living and ordinary fare. . . .

The pleasure of dining with one's friends is so great that nothing has ever given me more delight than their unexpected arrival, nor have I ever willingly sat down to table without a companion. . . .

The greatest kings of this age have loved and courted me. . . . I have fled, however, from many . . . to whom I was greatly attached; and such was my innate longing for liberty that I studiously avoided those whose very name seemed incompatible with the freedom I loved.

I possess a well-balanced rather than a keen intellect—one prone to all kinds of good and wholesome study, but especially to moral philosophy and the art of poetry. The latter I neglected as time went on, and took delight in sacred literature. . . . Among the many subjects that interested me, I dwelt especially upon antiquity, for our own age has always repelled me, so that, had it not been for the love of those dear to me, I should have preferred to have been born in any other period than our own. In order to forget my own time, I have constantly striven to place myself in spirit in other ages, and consequently I delighted in history. . . .

If only I have lived well, it matters little to me how I have talked. Mere elegance of language can produce at best but an empty fame. ❑

Frederic A. Ogg (ed.), *A Source Book of Mediaeval History* (New York: American Book Company, 1908), pp. 470–473.

---

di Rienzo's popular revolt and two-year reign (1347–1349) in Rome as "tribune" of the Roman people. He also served the Visconti family in Milan in his later years. Petrarch celebrated ancient Rome in his *Letters to the Ancient Dead*, fancied personal letters to Cicero, Livy, Vergil, and Horace. He also wrote a Latin epic poem (*Africa*, a poetic historical tribute to the Roman general Scipio Africanus) and a set of biographies of famous Romans (*Lives of Illustrious Men*). He tirelessly collected ancient manuscripts; among his finds were some letters by Cicero. His critical textual studies, elitism, and contempt for the allegedly useless learning of the Scholastics were features that many later Humanists also shared. Petrarch's most famous contemporary work was a collection of highly introspective love sonnets to a certain Laura, a married woman whom he romantically admired from a safe distance. Medieval Christian values can be seen in his imagined dialogues with Saint Augustine and in tracts written to defend the personal immortality of the soul against the Aristotelians.

Petrarch was, however, far more secular in orientation than his famous near contemporary Dante Alighieri (1265–1321), whose *Vita Nuova* and *Divine Comedy* form, with Petrarch's sonnets, the cornerstones of Italian vernacular literature. Petrarch's student and friend Giovanni Boccaccio (1313–1375), author of the *Decameron*, one hundred bawdy tales told by three men and seven women in a country retreat from the plague that ravaged Florence in 1348, also pioneered Humanist studies. An avid collector of manuscripts, Boccaccio also assembled an encyclopedia of Greek and Roman mythology.

EDUCATIONAL REFORMS AND GOALS. Pietro Paolo Vergerio (1349–1420) left a classic summary of the Humanist concept of a liberal education:

We call those studies liberal which are worthy of a free man; those studies by which we attain and practice virtue and wisdom; that education which calls forth, trains, and develops those highest gifts of body and mind which ennoble men and which are rightly judged to rank next in dignity to virtue only, for to a vulgar temper, gain and pleasure are the one aim in existence, to a lofty nature, moral worth and fame.[1]

The ideal of a useful education and well-rounded people inspired far-reaching reforms in traditional education. Quintilian's *Education of the Orator*, the full text of which was discovered by Poggio Bracciolini (D. 1459) in 1416, became the basic classical guide for

---

[1] Cited by De Lamar Jensen, *Renaissance Europe: Age of Recovery and Reconciliation* (Lexington, Mass.: D. C. Heath, 1981), p. 111.

the Humanist revision of the traditional curriculum. The most influential Renaissance tract on education, Vergerio's *On the Morals that Befit a Free Man*, was written directly from classical models. Vittorino da Feltre (d. 1446) was a teacher who not only directed his students to a highly disciplined reading of Pliny, Ptolemy, Terence, Plautus, Livy, and Plutarch but also combined vigorous physical exercise and games with intellectual pursuits. Another educator, Guarino da Verona (d. 1460), rector of the new University of Ferrara and a student of the Greek scholar Manuel Chrysoloras, streamlined the study of classical languages and gave it systematic form. Baldassare Castiglione's famous *Book of the Courtier*, written for the cultured nobility at the court of Urbino, stressed the importance of integrating knowledge of language and history with athletic, military, and musical skills, as well as good manners and moral character.

THE FLORENTINE ACADEMY AND THE REVIVAL OF PLATONISM. Of all the important recoveries of the past made during the Italian Renaissance, none stands out more than the revival of Greek studies, especially the works of Plato, in fifteenth-century Florence. Many factors combined to bring this revival about. An important foundation was laid in 1397 when the city invited Manuel Chrysoloras to come from Constantinople and promote Greek learning. A half century later (1439), the ecumenical Council of Ferrara–Florence, having convened to negotiate the reunion of the Eastern and Western churches, opened the door for many Greek scholars and manuscripts to enter the West. After the fall of Constantinople to the Turks in 1453, Greek scholars fled to Florence for refuge. This was the background against which Platonic scholarship developed under the patronage of Cosimo de' Medici and the supervision of Marsilio Ficino (1433–1499) and Pico della Mirandola (1463–1494).

Although the thinkers of the Renaissance were interested in every variety of ancient wisdom, they seemed to be especially attracted to Platonism and those Church Fathers who had tried to synthesize Platonic philosophy and Christian teaching. In private residences, Ficino and other humanists met to discuss the works of Plato and the Neoplatonists: Plotinus, Proclus, Porphyry, and Dionysius the [Pseudo-] Areopagite. Historians have romanticized these meetings into the so-called "Florentine Academy." Ficino also edited and published the complete works of Plato.

The appeal of Platonism lay in its flattering view of human nature. Platonism distinguished between an eternal sphere of being and the perishable world in which humans actually lived. Human reason was believed to belong to the former, indeed, to have preex-

Pico della Mirandola States the Renaissance Image of Man

One of the most eloquent descriptions of the Renaissance image of mankind comes from the Italian Humanist Pico della Mirandola (1463–1494). In his famed Oration on the Dignity of Man *(CA. 1486) Pico described humans as free to become whatever they choose.*

The best of artisans [God] ordained that that creature (man) to whom He had been able to give nothing proper to himself should have joint possession of whatever had been peculiar to each of the different kinds of being. He therefore took man as a creature of indeterminate nature and, assigning him a place in the middle of the world, addressing him thus: "Neither a fixed abode nor a form that is thine alone nor any function peculiar to thyself have we given thee, Adam, to the end that according to thy longing and according to thy judgment thou mayest have and possess what abode, what form, and what functions thou thyself shalt desire. The nature of all other beings is limited and constrained within the bounds of laws prescribed by Us. Thou, constrained by no limits, in accordance with thine own free will, in whose hand We have placed thee, shall ordain for thyself the limits of thy nature. We have set thee at the world's center that thou mayest from thence more easily observe whatever is in the world. We have made thee neither of heaven nor of earth, neither mortal nor immortal, so that with freedom of choice and with honor, as though the maker and molder of thyself, thou mayest fashion thyself in whatever shape thou shalt prefer. Thou shalt have the power to degenerate into the lower forms of life, which are brutish. Thou shalt have the power, out of thy soul's judgment, to be reborn into the higher forms, which are divine." O supreme generosity of God the Father, O highest and most marvelous felicity of man! To him it is granted to have whatever he chooses, to be whatever he wills. ❑

Giovanni Pico della Mirandola, *Oration on the Dignity of Man*, in *The Renaissance Philosophy of Man*, ed. by E. Cassirer et al. (Chicago: Phoenix Books, 1961), pp. 224–225.

isted in this pristine world and to continue to commune with it, as their knowledge of mathematical and moral truth bore witness.

CRITICAL WORK OF THE HUMANISTS: LORENZO VALLA. Because they were guided by a scholarly ideal of philological accuracy and historical truthfulness, the Humanists could become critics of tradition even when that was not their intention. Dispassionate critical scholarship shook long-standing foundations, not the least of which were those of the medieval church.

The work of Lorenzo Valla (1406–1457), author of the standard Renaissance text on Latin philology, the *Elegance of the Latin Language* (1444), reveals the explosive character of the new learning. Although a good Catholic, Valla became a hero to later Protestants because of his defense of predestination against the advocates of free will and his exposé of the Donation of Constantine (see Chapter 13). The exposé of the Donation was not intended by Valla to have the devastating force that Protestants attributed to it. He only demonstrated in a careful, scholarly way what others had long suspected. Using the most rudimentary textual analysis and historical logic, Valla proved that the document contained such anachronistic terms as *fief* and made references that would have been meaningless in the fourth century. In the same dispassionate way, Valla also pointed out errors in the Latin Vulgate, then the authorized version of the Bible for the Roman Catholic church.

Such discoveries did not make Valla any less loyal to the church, nor did they prevent his faithful fulfillment of the office of Apostolic Secretary in Rome under Pope Nicholas V. Nonetheless, historical criticism of this type served those less loyal to the medieval church, and it was no accident that young Humanists formed the first identifiable group of Martin Luther's supporters (see Chapter 17).

Renaissance Art

In Renaissance Italy, as in Reformation Europe, the values and interests of the laity were no longer subordinated to those of the clergy. In education, culture, and religion, the laity assumed a leading role and established models for the clergy to imitate. This resulted in part from the Church's loss of its international power during the great crises of the late Middle Ages. But it was also encouraged by the rise of national sentiment, the creation of competent national bureaucracies staffed by laity rather than clerics, and the rapid growth of lay education during the fourteenth and fifteenth centuries. Medieval Christian values adjusted to a more this-worldly spirit. Men and women began again to appreciate and even glorify the secular world, secular learning, and purely human pursuits as ends in themselves.

This perspective on life is prominent in the painting and sculpture of the High Renaissance, the late fifteenth and early sixteenth centuries, when the art of the period reached its full maturity. In imitation of Greek and Roman art, painters and sculptors attempted to create harmonious, symmetrical, and properly proportioned figures and to portray the human form with a glorified realism. Whereas Byzantine and Gothic art had been religious and idealized in the extreme, Renaissance art, especially in the fifteenth century, became a realistic reproduction of nature and of man himself as a part of nature. Giotto (1266–1336), the father of Renaissance painting, signaled the new direction. An admirer of Saint Francis of Assisi, whose love of nature he shared, Giotto painted a more natural world than his Byzantine and Gothic predecessors. Though still filled with religious seriousness, his work was no longer quite so abstract and unnatural a depiction of the world.

Renaissance artists had the considerable advantage of new technical skills developed during the fifteenth century. In addition to the availability of oil paints, the techniques of using shading to enhance realism (*chiaroscuro*) and adjusting the size of figures so as to give the viewer a feeling of continuity with the painting (linear perspective) were perfected. Compared with their flat Byzantine and Gothic counterparts, Renaissance paintings seem filled with energy and life and stand out from the canvas in three dimensions.

Opposite: *The developing knowledge of human anatomy and physiology.*
A: *Medieval conception of the human body, from a manuscript of about* 1292, *depicting the venous system and what purport to be a few internal organs. Since post-mortems were forbidden, medieval renderings of the human body were based on a combination of speculation and animal dissection.* [The Bodleian Library, Oxford.]
B: *A chart showing the points of blood-letting, long an accepted medical practice. From the* Guidebook of the Barber Surgeons of York (*fifteenth century*), *now in the British Museum.* [Egerton MS. 2572, f. 50. Reproduced by permission of the British Library Board.]
C: *Leonardo da Vinci's drawings of the human fetus. Renaissance artists and scientists, in contrast to medieval artists, began to base their portrayal of the human body on the actual study of it.* [Bettmann Archive.]
D: *A woodcut illustration by John of Carcar from* De Humanis corporis fabrica (Structure of the Human body) (*Basel, 1543*), *by the great Flemish anatomist, Andreas Vesalius* (1514-1564), *the foundation work of modern knowledge of human anatomy.* [Bettmann Archive.]

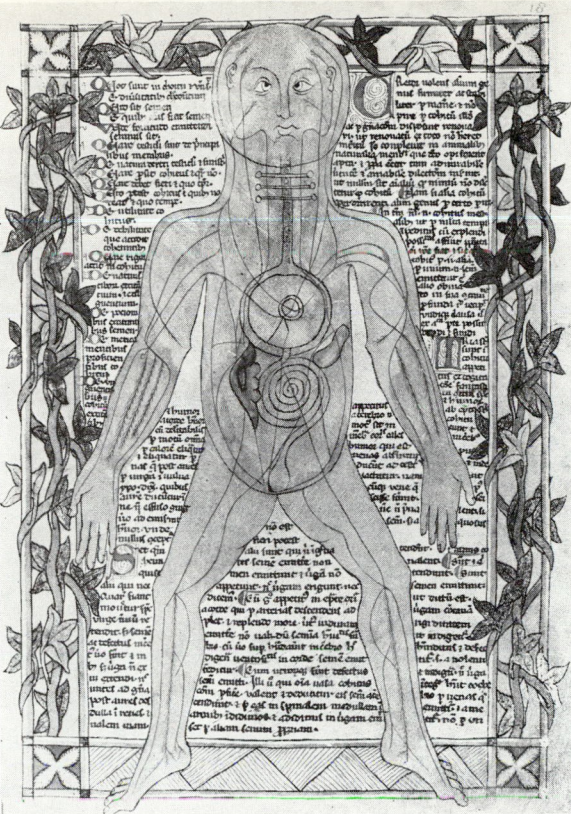

A

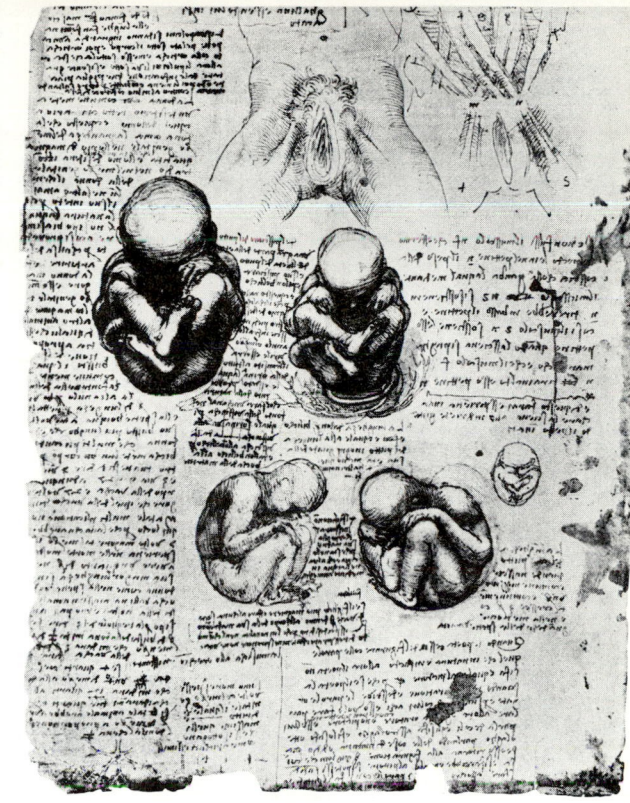

C

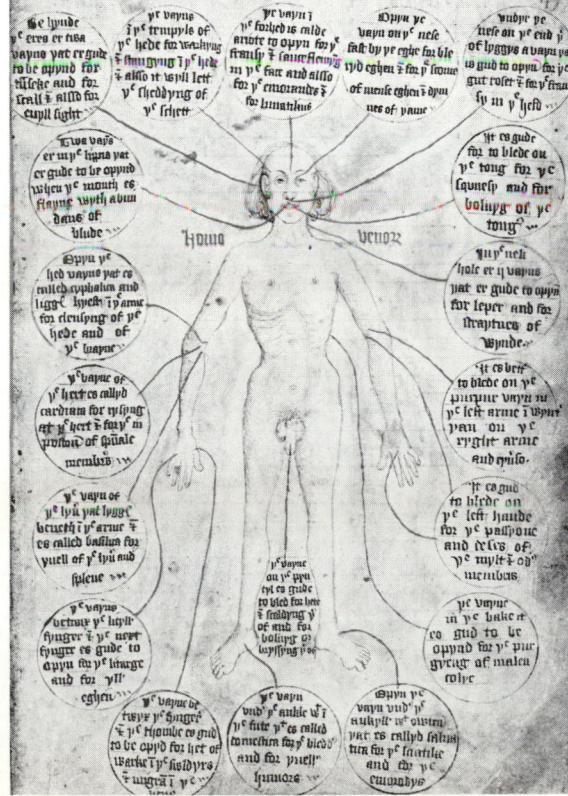

B

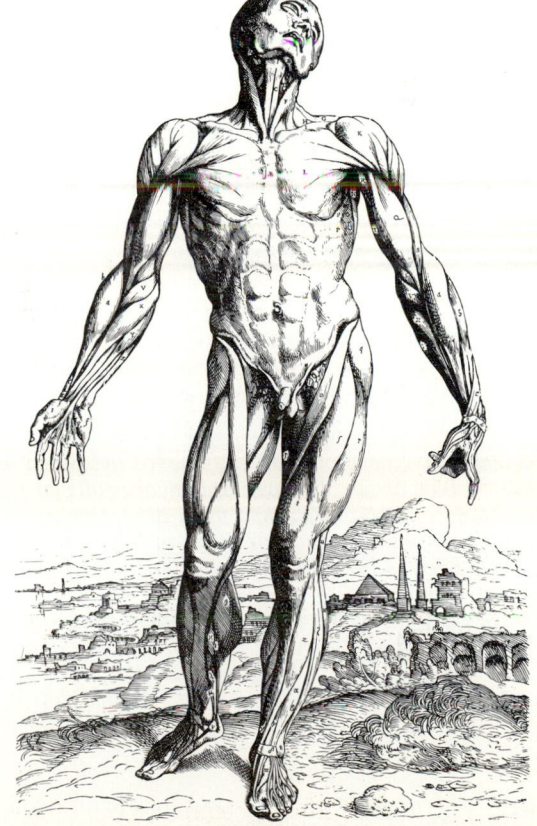

D

1378–1382	The Ciompi Revolt in Florence
1434	Medici rule in Florence established by Cosimo de' Medici
1454–1455	Treaty of Lodi allies Milan, Naples, and Florence (in effect until 1494)
1494	Charles VIII of France invades Italy
1494–1498	Savonarola controls Florence
1495	League of Venice unites Venice, Milan, the Papal States, the Holy Roman Empire, and Spain against France
1499	Louis XII invades Milan (the second French invasion of Italy)
1500	The Borgias conquer Romagna
1512–1513	The Holy League (Pope Julius II, Ferdinand of Aragon, Emperor Maximilian I, and Venice) defeat the French
1513	Machiavelli writes *The Prince*
1515	Francis I leads the third French invasion of Italy
1516	Concordat of Bologna between France and the papacy
1527	Sack of Rome by imperial soldiers

Madonna and Child, by Giotto. Giotto was the first artist to bring naturalism and realism to religious and spiritual subjects. [National Gallery of Art, Washington, D.C., Samuel H. Kress Collection.]

LEONARDO DA VINCI (1452–1519). More than any other person in the period, Leonardo exhibited the Renaissance ideal of the universal person, one who is not only a jack-of-all-trades but also a true master of many. One of the greatest painters of all time, Leonardo was also a military engineer for Ludovico il Moro in Milan, Cesare Borgia in Romagna, and the French king Francis I. Leonardo advocated scientific experimentation, dissected corpses to learn anatomy, and was an accomplished, self-taught botanist. His inventive mind foresaw such modern

Leonardo da Vinci's portrait of Ginevra de' Benci, an Italian noblewoman. The psychological acuity of Leonardo's portraits results in part from his technique. Leonardo was the first Italian to paint in oils, a medium that had been developed earlier in Northern Europe. Oils allow the artist to take more time and care and to produce colors that are more permanent and translucent. Leonardo was also the first to use light and shade effectively to bring a figure into the foreground of a painting. [National Gallery of Art, Washington, D.C., Alisa Mellon Bruce Fund.]

The School of Athens, fresco by Raphael in the Vatican in Rome, painted CA. 1510–1511. *The symmetry and organic unity of the painting, as well as its theme of antiquity, make it one of the most telling examples of Renaissance classicism.* [Bettmann Archive.]

machines as airplanes and submarines. Indeed, the variety of his interests was so great that it tended to shorten his attention span, so that he was constantly moving from one activity to another. His great skill lay in conveying inner moods through complex facial features, such as can be seen in the most famous of his paintings, the *Mona Lisa.*

RAPHAEL (1483–1520). Raphael, an unusually sensitive man whose artistic career was cut short by his premature death at thirty-seven, was apparently loved by contemporaries as much for his person as for his work. He is famous for his tender madonnas, the best known of which graces the monastery of San Sisto in Piacenza. Art historians praise his fresco *The School of Athens*, an involved portrayal of the great masters of Western philosophy, as one of the most perfect examples of Renaissance artistic theory and technique. It depicts Plato and Aristotle surrounded by the great philosophers and scientists of antiquity, who are

portrayed with the features of Raphael's famous contemporaries, including Leonardo and Michelangelo.

MICHELANGELO (1475–1564). The melancholy genius Michelangelo also excelled in a variety of arts and crafts. His eighteen-foot godlike sculpture *David*, which long stood majestically in the great square of Florence, is a perfect example of the Renaissance artist's devotion to harmony, symmetry, and proportion, as well as his extreme glorification of the human form. Four different popes commissioned works by Michelangelo, the most famous of which are the frescoes for the Sistine Chapel, painted during the pontificate of Pope Julius II (1503–1513), who also set Michelangelo to work on the pope's own magnificent tomb. The Sistine frescoes originally covered 10,000 square feet and involved 343 figures, over half of which exceeded 10 feet in height. This labor of love and piety, painted while Michelangelo was lying on his back or stooping, took four years to complete and left Michel-

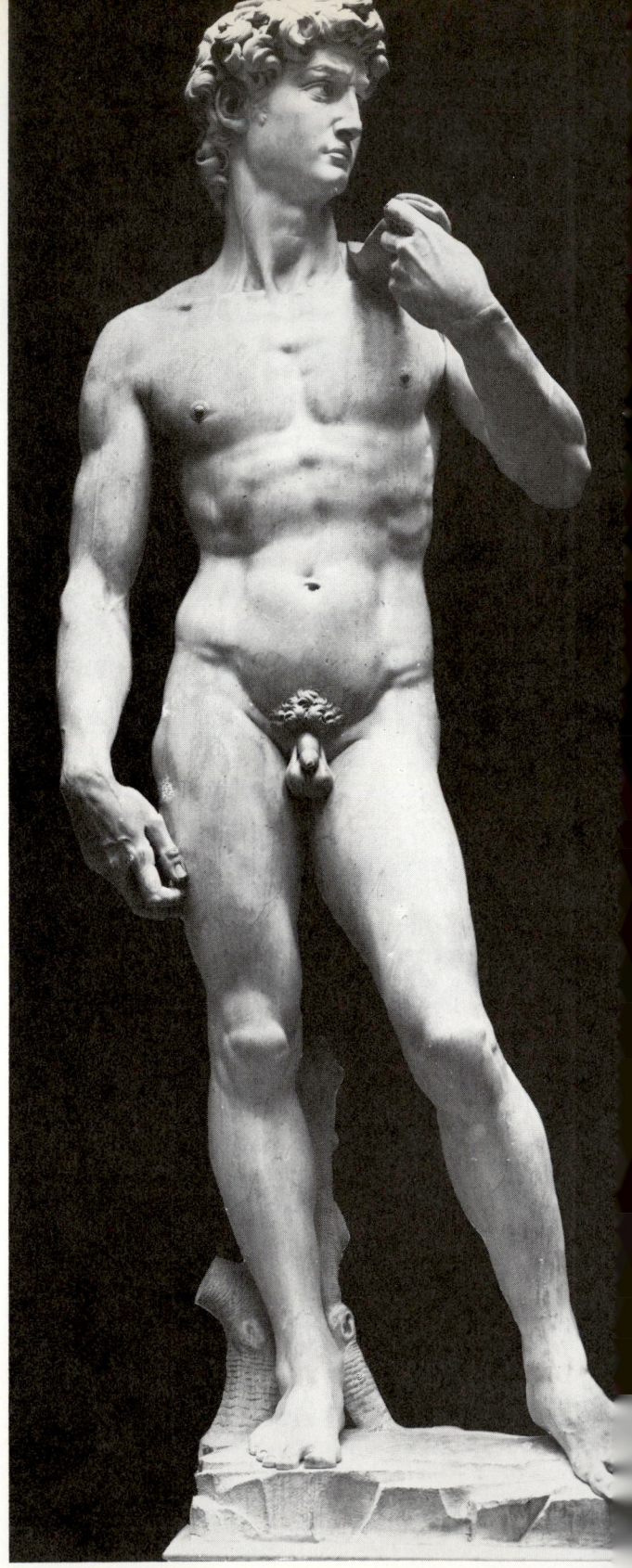

David, by Michelangelo. One of the most famous—and popular—of all the world's sculptures, it was carved in 1501–1504 and now stands in the Galleria dell' Accademia in Florence. [Alinari/SCALA.]

angelo partially crippled. A man who lived to be almost ninety, Michelangelo insisted on doing nearly everything himself and permitted his assistants only a few of the many chores involved.

His later works mark, artistically and philosophically, the passing of High Renaissance painting and the advent of a new, experimental style known as *mannerism*, which reached its peak in the late sixteenth and early seventeenth centuries. A reaction against the simplicity and symmetry of High Renaissance art, which also found expression in music and literature, mannerism made room for the strange and even the abnormal and gave freer reign to the subjectivity of the artist. It derived its name from the fact that it permitted the artist to express his own individual perceptions and feelings, to paint, compose, or write in a "mannered" or "affected" way. Tintoretto (D. 1594) and especially El Greco (D. 1614) became its supreme representatives.

Italy's Political Decline: The French Invasions (1494–1527)

The Treaty of Lodi

As a land of autonomous city-states, Italy's peace and safety from foreign invasion, especially from invasion by the Turks, had always depended on internal cooperation. Such cooperation had been maintained during the last half of the fifteenth century, thanks to a carefully constructed political alliance known as the Treaty of Lodi (1454–1455). The terms of the treaty brought Milan and Naples, long traditional enemies, into alliance with Florence. These three stood together for decades against Venice, which was frequently joined by the Papal States to create an internal balance of power that also made possible a unified front against Italy's external enemies.

The peace made possible by the Treaty of Lodi ended in 1494, when Naples, supported by Florence and the Borgia pope Alexander VI (1492–1503), prepared to attack Milan. At this point, the Milanese despot Ludovico il Moro made what proved to be a fatal response to these new political alignments: he appealed for aid to the French.

Charles VIII's March through Italy

The French king, Louis XI, had resisted the temptation to invade Italy, while nonetheless keeping French dynastic claims in Italy alive. His successor, Charles VIII (1483–1498), an eager youth in his twenties, responded to Ludovico's call with lightning speed. Within five months, he had crossed the Alps (August 1495) and raced as conqueror through Florence and the Papal States into Naples.

Charles' lightning march through Italy also struck terror in non-Italian hearts. Ferdinand of Aragon, whose native land and self-interests as king of Sicily now became vulnerable to a French–Italian axis, took the initiative to create a counteralliance: the League of Venice, formed in March 1495, with Venice, the Papal States, and the Emperor Maximilian I joining Ferdinand against the French. The stage was set for a conflict between France and Spain that would not end until 1559.

Ludovico il Moro meanwhile recognized that he had sown the wind; having desired a French invasion only so long as it weakened his enemies, he now saw Milan threatened by the whirlwind of events that he had himself created. In reaction, he joined the League of Venice, and this alliance was able to send Charles into retreat by May. Charles remained thereafter on the defensive until his death in April 1498.

Pope Alexander VI and the Borgia Family

The French returned to Italy under Charles' successor, Louis XII (1498–1515), this time assisted by a new Italian ally, the Borgia pope Alexander VI (1492–1503). Alexander, probably the most corrupt pope who ever sat on the papal throne, openly promoted the political careers of the children he had had before he became pope, Cesare and Lucrezia, as he placed the efforts of the powerful Borgia family to secure a political base in Romagna in tandem with papal policy there.

In Romagna, several principalities had fallen away from the church during the Avignon papacy, and Venice, the pope's ally within the League of Venice, continued to contest the Papal States for their loyalty. Seeing that a French alliance could give him the opportunity to reestablish control over the region, Alexander agreed to abandon the League of Venice, a withdrawal of support that made the league too weak to resist a French reconquest of Milan. In exchange, Cesare Borgia received the sister of the king of Navarre, Charlotte d' Albret, in marriage, a union that greatly enhanced Borgia military strength. Cesare also received land grants from Louis XII and the promise of French military aid in Romagna. His cunning and determination would make him the model for Machiavelli's *The Prince*.

All in all, it was a scandalous tradeoff, but one that made it possible for both the French king and the pope to realize their ambitions within Italy. Louis successfully invaded Milan in August 1499. In 1500, Louis and Ferdinand of Aragon divided Naples between them, while the pope and Cesare Borgia conquered the cities of Romagna without opposition.

Pope Julius II

Cardinal Giuliano della Rovere, a strong opponent of the Borgia family, became Pope Julius II (1503–1513). He suppressed the Borgias and placed their newly conquered lands in Romagna under papal jurisdiction. Julius came to be known as the "warrior pope" because he brought the Renaissance papacy to a peak of military prowess and diplomatic intrigue. Shocked as were other contemporaries by this thoroughly secular papacy, the Humanist Erasmus (CA. 1466–1536), who had witnessed in disbelief a bullfight in the papal palace during a visit to Rome, wrote a popular anonymous satire entitled *Julius Excluded from Heaven*. This humorous account purported to describe the pope's unsuccessful efforts to convince Saint Peter that he was worthy of admission to heaven.

Assisted by his powerful French allies, Pope Julius drove the Venetians out of Romagna in 1509, thereby ending Venetian claims in the region and fully securing the Papal States. Having realized this long-sought papal goal, Julius turned to the second major undertaking of his pontificate: ridding Italy of his former ally, the French invader. Julius, Ferdinand of Aragon, and Venice formed a second Holy League in October 1511, and within a short period, Emperor Maximilian I and the Swiss joined them. By 1512, the league had the French in full retreat, and Swiss armies soundly defeated them in 1513 at Novara.

The French invaded Italy still a third time under Louis' successor, Francis I (1515–1547). French armies massacred Swiss soldiers of the Holy League at Marignano in September 1515, revenging the earlier defeat at Novara. The victory won from the Medici pope, Leo X, the Concordat of Bologna in August 1516, an agreement that gave the French king control over the French clergy in exchange for French recognition of the pope's superiority over church councils and his right to collect taxes from the French clergy. This was an important compromise that helped keep France Catholic after the outbreak of the Protestant Reformation. But the new French entry into Italy also led to the first of four major wars with Spain in the first half of the sixteenth century: the Habsburg–Valois wars, none of which France won.

Niccolò Machiavelli

The period of foreign invasions made a shambles of Italy. The same period that saw Italy's cultural peak in the work of Leonardo, Raphael, and Michelangelo

Machiavelli Discusses the Most Important Trait for a Ruler

Machiavelli believed that the most important personality trait of a successful ruler was the ability to instill fear in his subjects.

Here the question arises; whether it is better to be loved than feared or feared than loved. The answer is that it would be desirable to be both but, since that is difficult, it is much safer to be feared than to be loved, if one must choose. For on men in general this observation may be made: they are ungrateful, fickle, and deceitful, eager to avoid dangers, and avid for gain, and while you are useful to them they are all with you, offering you their blood, their property, their lives, and their sons so long as danger is remote, as we noted above, but when it approaches they turn on you. Any prince, trusting only in their words and having no other preparations made, will fall to his ruin, for friendships that are bought at a price and not by greatness and nobility of soul are paid for indeed, but they are not owned and cannot be called upon in time of need. Men have less hesitation in offending a man who is loved than one who is feared, for love is held by a bond of obligation which, as men are wicked, is broken whenever personal advantage suggests it, but fear is accompanied by the dread of punishment which never relaxes. ❑

Niccolò Machiavelli, *The Prince* (1513), trans. and ed. by Thomas G. Bergin (New York: Appleton-Century-Crofts, 1947), p. 48.

---

also witnessed Italy's political tragedy. One who watched as French, Spanish, and Germany armies wreaked havoc on his country was Niccolò Machiavelli (1469–1527). The more he saw, the more convinced he became that Italian political unity and independence were ends that justified any means. A Humanist and a careful student of ancient Rome, Machiavelli admired the heroic acts of ancient Roman rulers, what Renaissance people called their *Virtù*. Romanticizing the old Roman citizenry, he lamented the absence of heroism among his compatriots. Such a perspective caused his interpretation of both ancient and contemporary history to be somewhat exaggerated. His Florentine contemporary, Guicciardini, a more sober historian less given to idealizing antiquity, wrote truer chronicles of Florentine and Italian history.

The juxtaposition of what Machiavelli believed the ancient Romans had been with the failure of contemporary Romans to realize such high ideals made him the famous cynic we know in the popular epithet *Machiavellian*. Only an unscrupulous strongman, he concluded, using duplicity and terror, could impose order on so divided and selfish a people.

It has been argued that Machiavelli wrote *The Prince* in 1513 as a cynical satire, not as a serious recommendation of unprincipled despotic rule. To take his advocacy of tyranny literally, it is argued, contradicts both his earlier works and his own strong family tradition of republican service. But Machiavelli seems to have been in earnest when he advised rulers to discover the advantages of fraud and brutality. He apparently hoped to see a strong ruler emerge from the restored powerful Medici family.

Whatever Machiavelli's hopes may have been, the Medicis were not destined to be Italy's deliverers. The second Medici pope, Clement VII (1523–1534), watched helplessly as Rome was sacked by the army of Emperor Charles V in 1527, also the year of Machiavelli's death.[2]

Suggested Readings

M. ASTON, *The Fifteenth Century: The Prospect of Europe* (1968). Crisp social history, with pictures.

H. BARON, *The Crisis of the Early Italian Renaissance*, Vols. 1 and 2 (1966). A major work, setting forth the civic dimension of Italian Humanism.

B. BERENSON, *Italian Painters of the Renaissance* (1901). Still incisive.

J. BURCKHARDT, *The Civilization of the Renaissance in Italy* (1867). The old classic that still has as many defenders as detractors.

W. K. FERGUSON, *The Renaissance* (1940). A brief, stimulating summary of the Renaissance in both Italy and northern Europe.

W. K. FERGUSON, *Europe in Transition* 1300–1520 (1962). A major survey that deals with the transition from medieval to Renaissance society.

F. GILBERT, *Machiavelli and Guicciardini* (1984). The two great Renaissance historians compared.

M. GILMORE, *The World of Humanism* 1453–1517 (1952). A comprehensive survey, especially strong in intellectual and cultural history.

R. S. GOTTFRIED, *The Black Death* (1983). Most up-to-date account.

[2] For the placement of the Renaissance in the West in world perspective, see the conclusion of Chapter 17.

J. R. Hale, *Renaissance Europe: The Individual and Society*, 1480–1520 (1971). A many-sided treatment of social history.

D. Hay, *Europe in the Fourteenth and Fifteenth Centuries* (1966). A many-sided treatment of political history.

J. Huizinga, *The Waning of the Middle Ages: A Study of the Forms of Life, Thought, and Art in France and the Netherlands in the Dawn of the Renaissance* (1924). A classic study of "mentality" at the end of the Middle Ages.

G. Huppert, *After the Black Death* (1986). A social historian's perspective on the transition from the Renaissance to modern times.

D. Jensen, *Renaissance Europe: Age of Recovery and Reconciliation* (1981).

R. J. Knecht, *Francis I* (1982). Up-to-date biography of the French king.

P. O. Kristeller, *Renaissance Thought: The Classic, Scholastic, and Humanist Strains* (1961). A master shows the many sides of Renaissance thought.

R. E. Lerner, *The Age of Adversity: The Fourteenth Century* (1968). A brief, comprehensive survey.

L. Martines, *Power and Imagination: City States in Renaissance Italy* (1980). Stimulating account of cultural and political history.

H. A. Miskimin, *The Economy of Early Renaissance Europe* 1300–1460 (1969). Shows the interaction of social, political, and economic change.

E. Muir, *Civic Ritual in Renaissance Venice* (1981). A study of the use of pageantry for political purposes.

H. A. Oberman, *The Harvest of Medieval Theology* (1963). A demanding synthesis and revision.

E. Perroy, *The Hundred Years War*, trans. by W. B. Wells (1965). The most comprehensive one-volume account.

Y. Renovard, *The Avignon Papacy* 1305–1403, trans. by D. Bethell (1970). Standard narrative.

Q. Skinner, *The Foundations of Modern Political Thought I: The Renaissance* (1978). A broad survey, very comprehensive.

M. Spinka, *John Hus's Concept of the Church* (1966).

J. W. Thompson, *Economic and Social History of Europe in the Later Middle Ages* 1300–1530 (1958). A bread-and-butter account.

B. Tierney, *Foundations of the Conciliar Theory* (1955). An important study showing the origins of conciliar theory in canon law.

B. Tierney, *The Crisis of Church and State* 1050–1300 (1964). Part 4 provides the major documents in the clash between Boniface VIII and Philip the Fair.

W. Ullmann, *Origins of the Great Schism* (1948). A basic study by a controversial interpreter of medieval political thought.

C. T. Wood, *Philip the Fair and Boniface VIII* (1967). Excerpts from the scholarly debate over the significance of this confrontation.

H. B. Workman, *John Wyclif*, Vols. 1 and 2 (1926). Dated but still standard.

P. Ziegler, *The Black Death* (1969). A highly readable journalistic account.

Erasmus of Rotterdam in a 1526 engraving by Albrecht Dürer. Erasmus influenced all of the reform movements of the sixteenth century. He was popularly said to have "laid the egg that Luther hatched." [National Gallery of Art, Washington, D.C.]

17 The Age of Reformation and Religious Wars

In the second decade of the sixteenth century, there began in Saxony in Germany a powerful religious movement that rapidly spread throughout northern Europe, deeply affecting society and politics as well as the spiritual lives of men and women. Attacking what they believed to be burdensome superstitions that robbed people of both their money and their peace of mind, Protestant reformers led a broad revolt against the medieval church. In a relatively short span of time, hundreds of thousands of people from all social classes set aside the beliefs of centuries and adopted a more simplified religious practice.

The Protestant Reformation challenged aspects of the Renaissance, especially its tendency to follow classical sources in glorifying human nature and its loyalty to traditional religion. Protestants were more impressed by the human potential for evil than by the inclination to do good and encouraged parents, teachers, and magistrates to be firm disciplinarians. On the other hand, Protestants also embraced many Renaissance values, especially in the sphere of educational reform and particularly with regard to training in ancient languages. Like the Italian Humanists, the Protestant reformers studied ancient languages and went directly to the original sources; only, for them, this meant the study of the Hebrew and Greek scriptures and the consequent challenge of traditional institutions founded on the authority of the Bible.

The road to the Reformation was long in preparation. As the Protestant ethic influenced an entire age, it was also itself born out of changes in European society beyond those within the purely religious and ecclesiastical spheres.

For Europe, the late fifteenth and the sixteenth centuries were a period of unprecedented territorial expansion and ideological experimentation. Permanent colonies were established within the Americas, and the exploitation of the New World's human and seem-

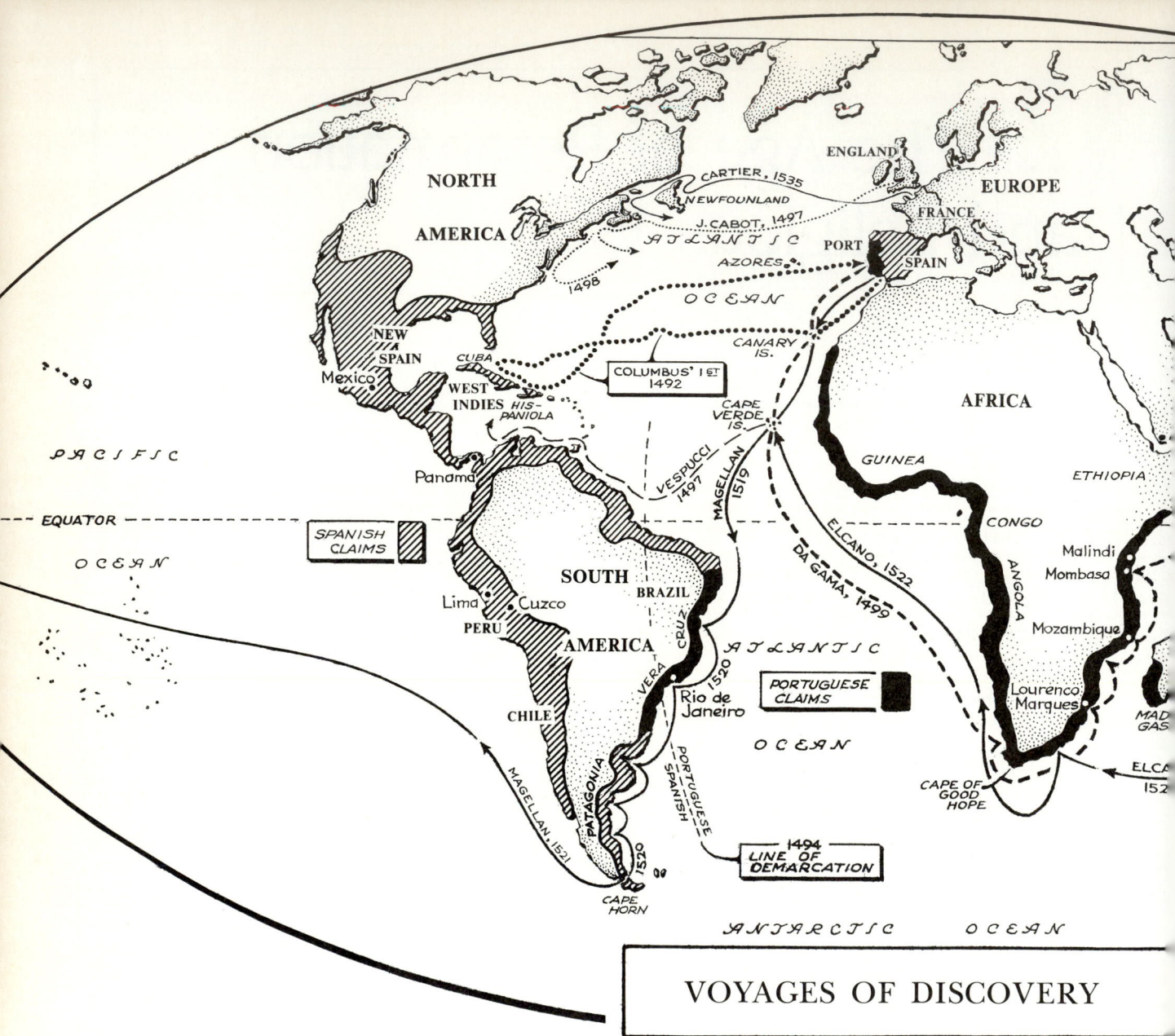

MAP 17-1 VOYAGES OF DISCOVERY   *The map dramatizes the expansion of the
area of European interest in the fifteenth and sixteenth centuries. Not until today's
"space age" has a comparable widening of horizons been possible.*

ingly endless mineral resources was begun. The American gold and silver imported into Europe spurred scientific invention and a weapons industry and touched
off an inflationary spiral that produced a revolution in
prices by the end of the sixteenth century. The new
bullion also helped to create international traffic in
African slaves, who were used in ever-increasing numbers to work the mines and the plantations of the New
World as replacements for the native Indians. This
period further saw social engineering and political
planning on a large scale as newly centralized govern-

ments developed long-range economic policies, a practice that came to be known as *mercantilism.*

The late fifteenth and the sixteenth centuries also
marked the first wide-scale use of the printing press,
an invention greatly assisted by the development of a
process of cheap paper manufacture and publishers
eager to exploit a fascinating new technology. Printing
with movable type was invented by Johann Gutenberg
(d. 1468) in the mid-fifteenth century in the German
city of Mainz. Residential colleges and universities
had greatly expanded in northern Europe during the

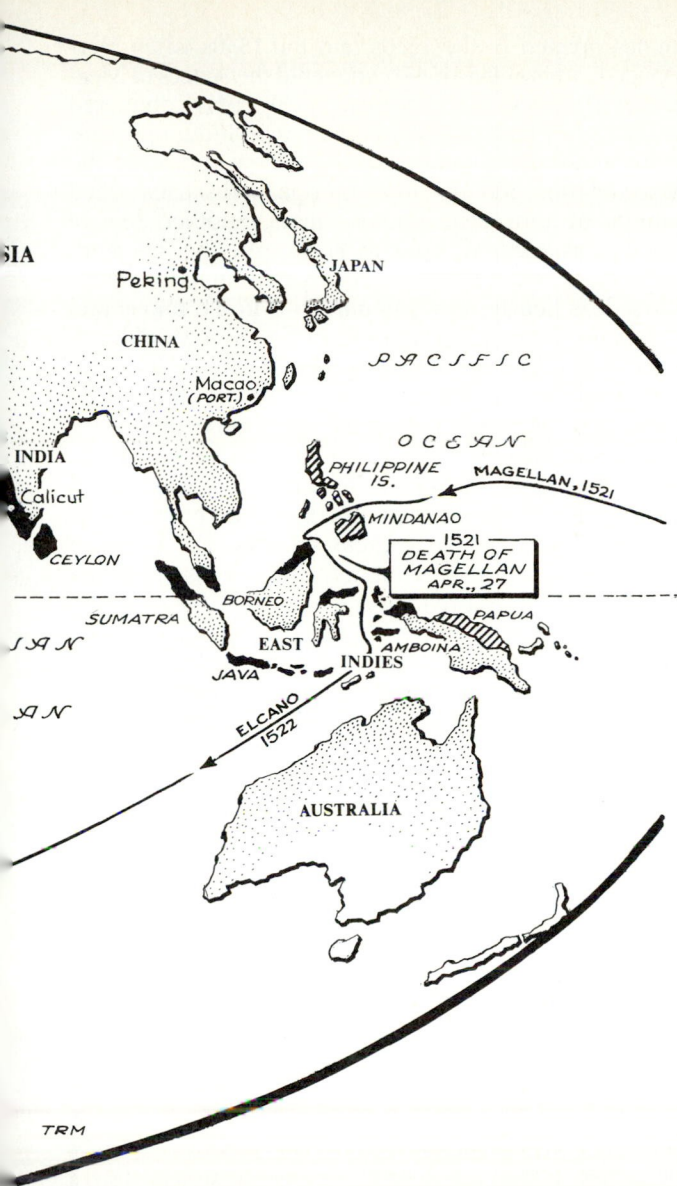

transference of commercial supremacy from the Mediterranean and the Baltic to the Atlantic seaboard. Mercenary motives, reinforced by traditional missionary ideals, inspired Prince Henry the Navigator (1394–1460) to sponsor the Portuguese exploration of the African coast. His main object was the gold trade, which for centuries had been an Arab monopoly. By the last decades of the fifteenth century, gold from Guinea entered Europe by way of Portuguese ships calling at the port cities of Lisbon and Antwerp, rather than by Arab land routes. Antwerp became the financial center of Europe, a commercial crossroads where the enterprise and derring-do of the Portuguese and the Spanish met the capital funds of the German banking houses of Fugger and Welser.

The rush for gold quickly expanded into a rush for the spice markets of India. In the fifteenth century, the diet of most Europeans was a dull combination of bread and gruel, cabbage, turnips, peas, lentils, and onions, together with what meat became available during seasonal periods of slaughter. Spices, especially pepper and cloves, were in great demand both to preserve food and to enhance its taste. Bartholomew Dias (d. 1500) opened the Portuguese empire in the East when he rounded the Cape of Good Hope at the

Model of a Portuguese caravel, a light, fast ship used extensively in trade and exploration. [National Maritime Museum, London.]

fourteenth and fifteenth centuries, creating a literate public in the cities eager to possess and read books. The new technology also made propaganda possible on a massive scale, as pamphlets could now be rapidly and inexpensively produced.

On the Eve of the Reformation

Voyages of Discovery

On the eve of the Reformation, the geographical as well as the intellectual horizons of Western people were broadening. The fifteenth century saw the beginning of Western Europe's global expansion and the

tip of Africa in 1487. A decade later, in 1498, Vasco da Gama (d. 1524) reached the coast of India. When he returned to Portugal, he brought with him a cargo worth sixty times the cost of the voyage. In subsequent years, the Portuguese established themselves firmly on the Malabar Coast with colonies in Goa and Calicut and successfully challenged the Arabs and the Venetians for control of the European spice trade.

While the Portuguese concentrated on the Indian Ocean, the Spanish set sail across the Atlantic. They did so in the hope of establishing a shorter route to the rich spice markets of the East Indies. Rather than beating the Portuguese at their own game, however, Christopher Columbus (1451–1506) discovered the Americas instead. When he reached Cuba, he actually thought he was in Japan and the South American coast beyond he believed to be the mainland of China.

Amerigo Vespucci (1451–1512) and Ferdinand Magellan (1480–1521) demonstrated that these new lands were not the outermost territory of the Far East, as Columbus died believing, but an entirely new continent that opened on the still greater Pacific Ocean. Magellan died in the Philippines.

The discovery of gold and silver in vast quantities more than compensated for the disappointment of failing to find a shorter route to the Indies. Still greater mines opened in the 1520s and the 1530s when Hernando Cortes (1485–1547) conquered the Aztecs of Mexico and Francisco Pizarro (ca. 1470–1541) conquered the Incas of Peru, enslaving the native Indian populations and forcing them to work the new mines. As the forced labor and the new European diseases killed American natives in large numbers, another item of trade was created: African slaves. In the sixteenth century, they were transported in great numbers to replace less hearty native populations in the mines and on the sugar cane plantations of the New World.

The influx of spices and precious metals into Europe was not an unmixed blessing. It contributed to a steady rise in prices during the sixteenth century that created an inflation rate estimated at 2 per cent a year. The new supply of bullion from the Americas joined with enlarged European production to increase greatly the amount of coinage in circulation, and this increase in turn fed inflation. Fortunately, the increase in prices was by and large spread over a long period of time and was not sudden. Prices doubled in Spain by mid-century, quadrupled by 1600. In Luther's Wittenberg, the cost of basic food and clothing increased almost 100 per cent between 1519 and 1540. Generally, wages and rents remained well behind the rise in prices.

The new wealth enabled governments and private

Columbus Reports His Discovery of the Entrance to Paradise

During his third voyage, Columbus reached the mouth of the Orinoco River in Venezuela. He believed he was in the East Indies, where, according to tradition, Adam and Eve had first trod the earth. Columbus believed that he had now come upon the very entrance into paradise. In October 1498, he wrote of this discovery to his patrons, Ferdinand and Isabella, monarchs of Spain.

I have already described my ideas concerning this hemisphere and its form [he believed it to be pear-shaped]. I have no doubt that if I could pass below the equinoctial line, after reaching the highest point . . . I should find a much milder temperature and a variation in the stars and in the water. Not that I suppose that elevated point to be navigable, nor even that there is water there; indeed, I believe it is impossible to ascend to it, because I am convinced that it is the spot of the earthly paradise, whither none can go but by God's permission . . . .

I do not suppose that the earthly paradise is in the form of a rugged mountain, as the descriptions of it have made it appear, but that it is on the summit of the spot, which I have described as being in the form of the stalk of a pear. The approach to it . . . must be by constant and gradual ascent, but I believe that . . . no one could ever reach the top. I think also that the water I have described may proceed from it, though it be far off, and that stopping at the place which I have just left, it forms this lake. There are great indications of this being the terrestrial paradise, for its site coincides with the opinion of the holy and wise theologians whom I have mentioned. Moreover, the other evidences agree . . . for I have never read or heard of fresh water coming in so large a quantity in close conjunction with the water of the sea. The idea is also corroborated by the blandness of the temperature. If the water of which I speak does not proceed from the earthly paradise, it seems to be a still greater wonder, for I do not believe that there is any river in the world so large or so deep. ❑

Donald Weinstein (ed.), *The Renaissance and the Reformation* 1300–1600 (New York: Free Press, 1965), pp. 138–139.

Erasmus Describes the "Philosophy of Christ"

Although Erasmus called his ideal of how people should live the "philosophy of Christ," he found it taught by classical authors as well. In this selection, he commented on its main features, with obvious polemic against the philosophy of the Scholastics.

This kind of philosophy [the philosophy of Christ] is located more truly in the disposition of the mind than in syllogisms. Here life means more than debate, inspiration is preferable to erudition, transformation [of life] a more important matter than intellectual comprehension. Only a very few can be learned, but all can be Christian, all can be devout, and—I shall boldly add—all can be theologians. Indeed, this philosophy easily penetrates into the minds of all; it is an action in special accord with human nature. What else is the philosophy of Christ, which he himself calls a rebirth, than the restoration of human nature . . . ? Although no one has taught this more perfectly . . . than Christ, nevertheless one may find in the books of the pagans very much which does agree with it. There was never so coarse a school of philosophy that taught that money rendered a man happy. Nor has there ever been one so shameless that fixed the chief good in vulgar honors and pleasures. The Stoics understood that no one was wise unless he was good. . . . According to Plato, Socrates teaches . . . that a wrong must not be repaid with a wrong, and also that since the soul is immortal, those should not be lamented who depart this life for a happier one with the assurance of having led an upright life. . . . And Aristotle has written in the *Politics* that nothing can be a delight to us . . . except virtue alone. . . . If there are things that belong particularly to Christianity in these ancient writers, let us follow them. ❑

John C. Olin (ed. and trans.), *Christian Humanism and the Reformation: Desiderius Erasmus.* (New York: Harper, 1965), pp. 100–101.

entrepreneurs to sponsor basic research and expansion in the printing, shipping, mining, textile, and weapons industries—the growth industries of the Age of Reformation. There is also evidence of mercantilism or large-scale government planning in such ventures as the French silk industry and the Hapsburg–Fugger development of mines in Austria and Hungary.

In the thirteenth and fourteenth centuries, capitalist institutions and practices had already begun to develop in the rich Italian cities. Those who owned the means of production, either privately or corporately, were clearly distinguished from the workers who operated them. Wherever possible, monopolies were created in basic goods. High interest was charged on loans—actual, if not legal, usury. And the "capitalist" virtues of thrift, industry, and orderly planning were everywhere in evidence—all intended to permit the free and efficient accumulation of wealth.

The late fifteenth and sixteenth centuries saw the maturation of such capitalism together with its peculiar social problems. The new wealth and industrial expansion raised the expectations of the poor and the ambitious and heightened the reactionary tendencies within the established and wealthy classes. This effect, in turn, greatly aggravated the traditional social divisions between the clergy and the laity, the higher and the lower clergy, the urban patriciate and the guilds, masters and journeymen, and the landed nobility and the agrarian peasantry.

The Northern Renaissance

The scholarly works of northern Humanists created a climate favorable to religious and educational reforms on the eve of the Reformation. Northern Humanism was initially stimulated by the importation of Italian learning through such varied intermediaries as students who had studied in Italy, merchants, and the Brothers of the Common Life (an influential lay religious movement that began in the Netherlands). The northern Humanists tended to come from more diverse social backgrounds and to be more devoted to religious reforms than their Italian counterparts. They were also more willing to write for lay audiences.

The most famous of the northern Humanists was Desiderius Erasmus (1466–1536), the reputed "prince of the Humanists." Erasmus gained fame as both an educational and a religious reformer. He aspired to unite the classical ideals of humanity and civic virtue with the Christian ideals of love and piety. He believed that disciplined study of the classics and the Bible, if begun early enough, was the best way to reform both individuals and society. He summarized his own beliefs with the phrase *philosophia Christi*, a simple, ethical piety in imitation of Christ. He set this ideal in starkest contrast to what he believed to be the dogmatic, ceremonial, and factious religious practice of the later Middle Ages.

To promote his own religious beliefs, Erasmus edited the works of the Church Fathers and made a Greek edition of the New Testament (1516), which became the basis for his new, more accurate Latin translation (1519), later used by Martin Luther.

These various enterprises did not please Church authorities. At one point in the mid-sixteenth century, all of Erasmus' works were placed on the *Index of Forbidden Books*. Erasmus also received Luther's unqualified condemnation for his views on the freedom of human will. Still, Erasmus' didactic and scholarly works became basic tools of reform in the hands of both Protestant and Catholic reformers.

The best known of early English Humanists was Sir Thomas More (1478–1535), a close friend of Erasmus. It was while visiting More that Erasmus wrote his most famous work, *The Praise of Folly* (1511), an amusing and profound exposé of human self-deception that was quickly translated from the original Latin into many vernacular languages. More's *Utopia* (1516), a criticism of contemporary society, still rivals the plays of Shakespeare as the most-read sixteenth-century English work. *Utopia* depicts an imaginary society based on reason and tolerance that has overcome social and political injustice by holding all property and goods in common and by requiring all to earn their bread by the sweat of their own brow.

Although More remained staunchly Catholic, Humanism in England, as in Germany, played an important role in preparing the way for the English Reformation. A circle of English Humanists, under the direction of Henry VIII's minister Thomas Cromwell, translated and disseminated late medieval criticisms of the papacy and many of Erasmus' satirical writings.

Whereas in Germany, England, and France Humanism prepared the way for Protestant reforms, in Spain it entered the service of the Catholic church. Here the key figure was Francisco Jiménez de Cisneros (1437–1517), a confessor to Queen Isabella, and after 1508 Grand Inquisitor—a position from which he was able to enforce the strictest religious orthodoxy. Jiménez was a conduit for Humanist scholarship and learning. He founded the University of Alcalá near Madrid in 1509, printed a Greek edition of the New Testament, and translated many religious tracts that aided clerical reform and control of lay religious life. His greatest achievement, taking fifteen years to complete, was the *Complutensian Polyglot Bible*, a six-volume work that placed the Hebrew, Greek, and Latin versions of the Bible in parallel columns. Such scholarly projects and internal church reforms joined with the repressive measures of Ferdinand and Isabella to keep Spain strictly Catholic throughout the Age of Reformation.

Religious Life

The Protestant Reformation could not have occurred without the monumental crises of the medieval church during the "exile" in Avignon, the Great Schism, the conciliar period, and the Renaissance papacy. The late Middle Ages were marked by independent lay and clerical efforts to reform local religious practice and by widespread experimentation with new religious forms.

On the eve of the Reformation, Rome's international network of church offices, which had unified Europe religiously during the Middle Ages, began to fall apart in many areas, hurried along by a growing sense of regional identity—incipient nationalism—and local secular administrative competence. The long-entrenched benefice system of the medieval church, which had permitted important ecclesiastical posts to be sold to the highest bidders and had left parishes without active, resident pastors, did not result in a vibrant local religious life. The substitutes hired by nonresident holders of benefices, who lived elsewhere (mostly in Rome) and milked the revenues of their offices, performed their chores mechanically and had neither firsthand knowledge of nor much sympathy with local needs and problems. Rare was the late medieval German town that did not have complaints about the maladministration, concubinage, and/or fiscalism of their clergy, especially the higher clergy (i.e., bishops, abbots, and prelates).

Communities loudly protested the financial abuses of the medieval church long before Luther published his famous summary of economic grievances in the *Address to the Christian Nobility of the German Nation* (1520). The sale of indulgences, a practice greatly expanded on the eve of the Reformation had also been repeatedly attacked before Luther.

City governments attempted to improve local religious life on the eve of the Reformation by endowing preacherships. These beneficed positions provided for well-trained and dedicated pastors and regular preaching and pastoral care, which went beyond the routine performance of the Mass and traditional religious functions. In many instances, these preacherships became platforms for Protestant preachers.

Magistrates also restricted the growth of ecclesiastical properties and clerical privileges. During the Middle Ages, special clerical rights in both property and person had come to be recognized by canon and civil law. Because they were holy places, churches and monasteries had been exempted from the taxes and laws that affected others. They were treated as special places of "sacral peace" and asylum. It was considered inappropriate for holy persons (clergy) to be burdened with such "dirty jobs" as military service, compulsory labor, standing watch at city gates, and other obligations of citizenship. Nor was it thought right that the laity, of whatever rank, should sit in judgment on those who were their shepherds and intermediaries with God. The clergy, accordingly, came to enjoy an immunity of place (which exempted ecclesiastical properties from taxes and recognized their right of asylum) and an immunity of person (which exempted the clergy from the jurisdiction of civil courts).

On the eve of the Reformation, measures were passed to restrict these privileges and to end their abuses—efforts to regulate ecclesiastical acquisition of new property, to circumvent the right of asylum in churches and monasteries (a practice that posed a threat to the normal administration of justice), and to bring the clergy under the local tax code.

The Reformation

Martin Luther and the German Reformation to 1525

Unlike France and England, late medieval Germany lacked the political unity to enforce "national" religious reforms during the late Middle Ages. There were no lasting Statutes of Provisors (1351) and *praemunire* (1353, 1365), as in England, nor a Pragmatic Sanction of Bourges (1385), as in France, limiting papal jurisdiction and taxation on a national scale. What happened on a unified national level in England and France occurred only locally and piecemeal within German territories and towns. As popular resentment of clerical immunities and ecclesiastical abuses, especially regarding the selling of indulgences, spread among German cities and towns, an unorganized "national" opposition to Rome formed. German Humanists had long given voice to such criticism, and by 1517, it was pervasive enough to provide a solid foundation for Martin Luther's reform.

Luther (1483–1546) was the son of a successful Thüringian miner. He was educated in Mansfeld, Magdeburg, where the Brothers of the Common Life were his teachers, and in Eisenach. Between 1501 and 1505, he attended the University of Erfurt. After receiving his master of arts degree in 1505, Luther registered with the Law Faculty in accordance with his parents' wishes. But he never began the study of law. To the shock and disappointment of his family, he instead entered the Order of the Hermits of Saint Augustine in Erfurt on July 17, 1505. This decision had apparently been building for some time and was resolved during a lightning storm in which a terrified Luther, crying out to Saint Anne for assistance (Saint Anne was the pa-

Martin Luther Discovers Justification by Faith Alone

Many years after the fact, Martin Luther described his discovery that God's righteousness was not an active, punishing righteousness but a passive, transforming righteousness, which made those who believed in him righteous as God himself is righteous.

Though I lived as a monk without reproach, I felt that I was a sinner before God with an extremely disturbed conscience. I could not believe that he was placated by my satisfaction. I did not love, yes, I hated the righteous God who punishes sinners, and secretly, if not blasphemously, certainly murmuring greatly, I was angry with God, and said, "As if, indeed, it is not enough, that miserable sinners, eternally lost through original sin, are crushed by every kind of calamity by the law of the decalogue, without having God add pain to pain by the gospel and also by the gospel threatening us with his righteousness and wrath!" Thus I raged with a fierce and troubled conscience. Nevertheless, I beat importunately upon Paul at that place, most ardently desiring to know what St. Paul wanted.

At last, by the mercy of God, meditating day and night, I gave heed to the context of the words, namely, "In it the righteousness of God is revealed, as it is written, 'He who through faith is righteous shall live'" [Romans 1:17]. There I began to understand that the right-eousness of God is that by which the righteous lives by a gift of God, namely by faith. And this is the meaning: the righteousness of God is revealed by the gospel, namely, the passive righteousness with which merciful God justifies us by faith, as it is written, "He who through faith is righteous shall live." Here I felt that I was altogether born again and had entered paradise itself through open gates. There a totally other face of the entire Scripture showed itself to me. Thereupon I ran through the Scriptures from memory. I also found in other terms an analogy, as, the work of God, that is, what God does in us, the power of God, with which he makes us strong, the wisdom of God, with which he makes us wise, the strength of God, the salvation of God, the glory of God.

And I extolled my sweetest word with a love as great as the hatred with which I had before hated the word "righteousness of God." Thus that place in Paul was for me truly the gate to paradise. ❑

Preface to the Complete Edition of Luther's Latin Writings (1545), in *Luther's Works*, Vol. 34, ed. by Lewis W. Spitz (Philadelphia: Muhlenberg Press, 1960), pp. 336–337.

tron saint of travelers in distress), promised to enter a monastery if he escaped death.

Ordained in 1507, Luther pursued a traditional course of study, becoming in 1509 a *baccalaureus biblicus* and *sententiarius*, that is, one thoroughly trained in the Bible and the *Sentences* of Peter Lombard. In 1510, he journeyed to Rome on the business of his order, finding there justification for the many criticisms of the Church he had heard in Germany. In 1511, he was transferred to the Augustinian monastery in Wittenberg, where he earned his doctorate in theology in 1512, thereafter becoming a leader within the monastery, the new university, and the spiritual life of the city.

THE ATTACK ON INDULGENCES. Reformation theology grew out of a problem common to many of the clergy and the laity at this time: the failure of traditional medieval religion to provide either full personal or intellectual satisfaction. Luther was especially plagued by the disproportion between his own sense of sinfulness and the perfect righteousness that medieval theology taught that God required for salvation. Traditional Church teaching and the sacrament of penance proved to be of no consolation. Luther wrote that he came to despise the phrase "righteousness of God," for it seemed to demand of him a perfection he knew neither he nor any other human being could ever achieve. His insight into the meaning of "justification by faith alone" was a gradual process that extended over several years, between 1513 and 1518. The righteousness God demands, he concluded, was not one that came from many religious works and ceremonies but was present in full measure in those who simply believed and trusted in the work of Jesus Christ, who alone was the perfect righteousness satisfying to God. To believe in Christ was to stand before God clothed in Christ's sure righteousness.

This new theology made indulgences unacceptable. An indulgence was a remission of the temporal penalty imposed by the priest on penitents as a "work of satisfaction" for their committed mortal sins. According to medieval theology, after the priest had absolved penitents of guilt for their sins, they still remained under an eternal penalty, a punishment God justly imposed on them for their sins. After absolution, however, this eternal penalty had been transformed into a temporal penalty, a manageable "work of satisfaction" that the penitent could perform here and now (for example, through prayers, fasting, almsgiving, retreats, and pilgrimages). Penitents who defaulted on such prescribed works of satisfaction could expect to suffer for them in purgatory.

At this point, indulgences came into play as an aid to a laity made genuinely anxious by the belief in a future suffering in purgatory for neglected penances or unrepented sins. In 1343, Pope Clement VI (1342–1352) had proclaimed the existence of a "treasury of merit," an infinite reservoir of good works in the Church's possession that could be dispensed at the pope's discretion. It was on the basis of this declared treasury that the Church sold "letters of indulgence," which covered the works of satisfaction owed by penitents. In 1476, Pope Sixtus IV (1471–1484) extended indulgences also to purgatory. Originally, indulgences had been given only for the true self-sacrifice of going on a crusade to the Holy Land. By Luther's time, they

Luther and the Wittenberg reformers with Elector John Frederick of Saxony (1532–1547), painted about 1543 by Lucas Cranach the Younger (1515–1586). Luther is on the far left, Philip Melanchthon in the front row on the far right. [Toledo Museum of Art, Toledo, Ohio; gift of Edward Drummond Libbey.]

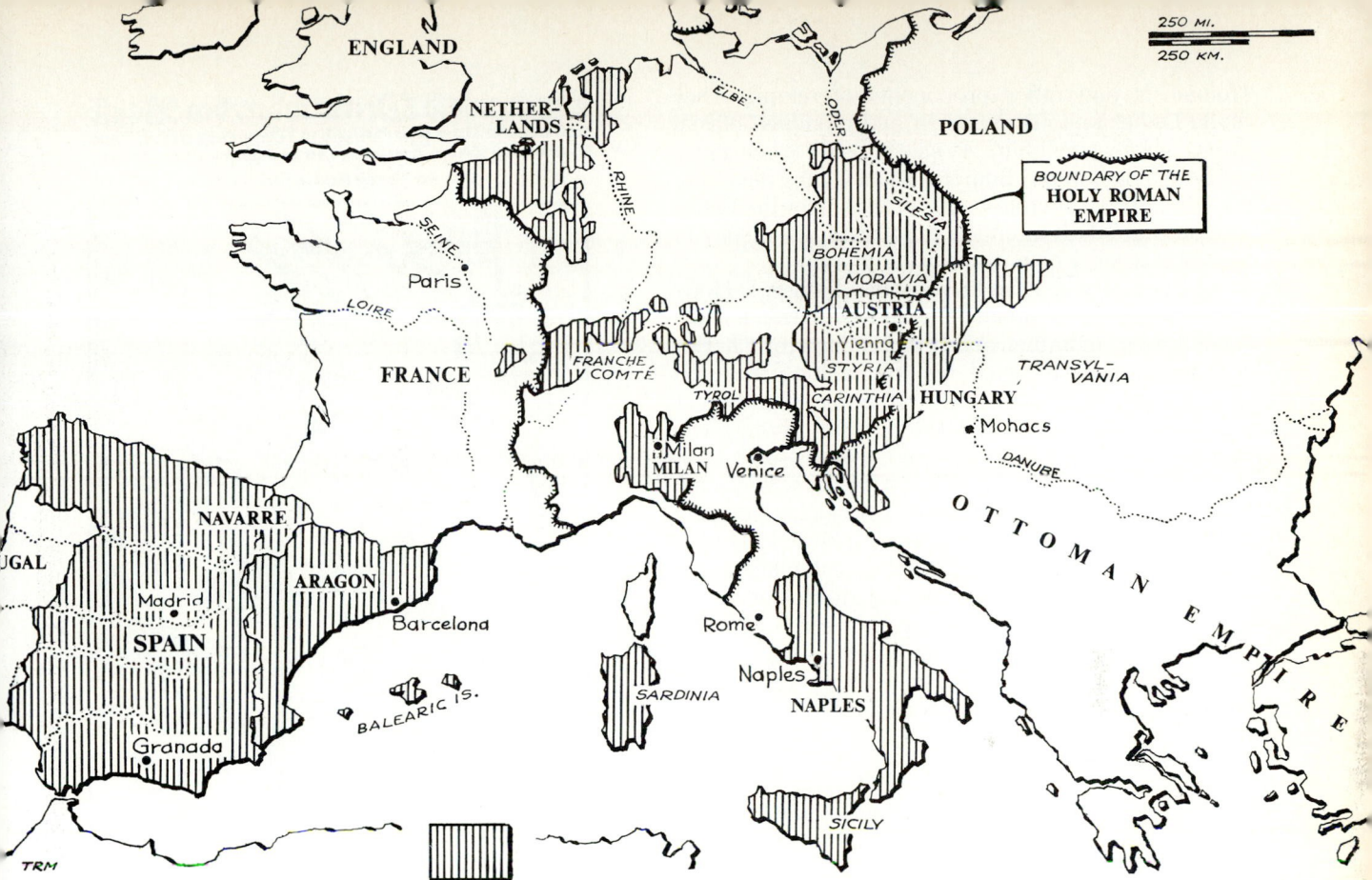

MAP 17-2   THE EMPIRE OF CHARLES V   *Dynastic marriages and simple chance concentrated into Charles's hands rule over the lands shown here, plus Spain's overseas possessions. Crowns and titles rained in on him; election in 1519 as emperor gave him new burdens and responsibilities.*

were regularly dispensed for small cash payments (very modest sums that were regarded as a good work of almsgiving) and were presented to the laity as remitting not only their own future punishments, but also those of their dead relatives presumed to be suffering in purgatory.

In 1517, a Jubilee indulgence, proclaimed during the pontificate of Pope Julius II (1503–1513) to raise funds for the rebuilding of Saint Peter's in Rome, was revived and preached on the borders of Saxony in the territories of Archbishop Albrecht of Mainz. Albrecht was much in need of revenues because of the large debts he had incurred in order to hold, contrary to church law, three ecclesiastical appointments. The selling of the indulgence was a joint venture by Albrecht, the Augsburg banking house of Fugger, and Pope Leo X (1513–1521), half the proceeds going to the pope and half to Albrecht and his creditors. The famous indulgence preacher John Tetzel (d. 1519) was enlisted to preach the indulgence in Albrecht's territories because he was a seasoned professional who knew how to stir ordinary people to action. As he exhorted on one occasion:

Don't you hear the voices of your dead parents and other relatives crying out, "Have mercy on us, for we suffer great punishment and pain. From this you could release us with a few alms. . . . We have created you, fed you, cared for you, and left you our temporal goods. Why do you treat us so cruelly and leave us to suffer in the flames, when it takes only a little to save us?"[1]

When on October 31, 1517, Luther posted his ninety-five theses against indulgences, according to tradition, on the door of Castle Church in Wittenberg, he protested especially against the impression created by Tetzel that indulgences actually remitted sins and released the dead from punishment in purgatory—claims he believed went far beyond the traditional practice and seemed to make salvation something that could be bought and sold.

ELECTION OF CHARLES V AND THE DIET OF WORMS.   The ninety-five theses were embraced by

[1] *Die Reformation in Augenzeugen Berichten,* ed. by Helmar Junghans (Düsseldorf: Karl Rauch Verlag, 1967), p. 44.

Humanists and other proponents of reform. They made Luther famous overnight and prompted official proceedings against him. As sanctions were being prepared against Luther, Emperor Maximilian I died (January 12, 1519), and this event, fortunate for the Reformation, turned all attention from heresy in Saxony to the contest for a new emperor.

The pope backed the French king, Francis I. However, Charles I of Spain, a youth of nineteen, succeeded his grandfather and became Emperor Charles V. Charles was assisted by both a long tradition of Habsburg imperial rule and a massive Fugger campaign chest, which secured the votes of the seven electors.

In the same month in which Charles was elected emperor, Luther entered a debate in Leipzig (June 27, 1519) with the Ingolstadt professor John Eck. During this contest, Luther challenged the infallibility of the pope and the inerrancy of Church councils, appealing, for the first time, to the sovereign authority of Scripture alone. All his bridges to the old Church were burned when he further defended certain teachings of Jan Hus that had been condemned by the Council of

A Catholic caricature of Martin Luther as a seven-headed demon. This picture served as the title page of a pamphlet by one of Luther's strongest Catholic critics, Johannes Cochlaeus.

A Protestant caricature of the pope as a monster with the characteristics of several beasts. Note the flag with the pope's "keys" to heaven and hell.

Constance. In 1520, Luther signaled his new direction with three famous pamphlets: the *Address to the Christian Nobility of the German Nation*, which urged the German princes to force reforms on the Roman church, especially to curtail its political and economic power in Germany; the *Babylonian Captivity of the Church*, which attacked the traditional seven sacraments, arguing that only two were proper, and which exalted the authority of Scripture, Church councils, and secular princes over that of the pope; and the eloquent *Freedom of a Christian*, which summarized the new teaching of salvation by faith alone. On June 15, 1520, the papal bull *Exsurge Domine* condemned Luther for heresy and gave him sixty days to retract. The final bull of excommunication, *Decet Pontificem Romanum*, was issued on January 3, 1521.

In April 1521, Luther presented his views before a diet of the empire in Worms, over which the newly elected Emperor Charles V presided. Ordered to recant, Luther declared that to do so would be to act against Scripture, reason, and his own conscience. On May 26, 1521, he was placed under the imperial ban and thereafter became an "outlaw" to secular as well as to religious authority. For his own protection, friends hid him in Wartburg Castle, where he spent almost a year in seclusion, from April 1521 to March 1522. During his stay, he translated the New Testament into German, using Erasmus' new Greek text, and he attempted by correspondence to oversee the first stages of the Reformation in Wittenberg.

The Reformation was greatly assisted in these early years by the emperor's war with France and the advance of the Ottoman Turks into eastern Europe. Against both adversaries Charles V, who also remained a Spanish king with dynastic responsibilities outside the empire, needed German troops, and to that end, he promoted friendly relations with the German princes. Between 1521 and 1559, Spain (the Habsburg dynasty) and France (the Valois dynasty) fought four major wars over disputed territories in Italy and along their borders. In 1526, the Turks overran Hungary at the Battle of Mohacs, while in western Europe the French-led League of Cognac formed against Charles for the second Habsburg–Valois war. Thus preoccupied, the emperor agreed through his representatives at the German Diet of Speyer in 1526 that each German territory was free to enforce the Edict of Worms (1521) against Luther "so as to be able to answer in good conscience to God and the emperor." That concession, in effect, gave the German princes territorial sovereignty in religious matters and the Reformation time to put down deep roots. Later (in 1555), such local princely control over religion would be enshrined in imperial law by the Peace of Augsburg.

THE PEASANTS' REVOLT. In its first decade, the Protestant movement suffered more from internal division than from imperial interference. By 1525, Luther had become as much an object of protest within Germany as was the pope. Original allies, sympathizers, and fellow travelers declared their independence from him.

Like the German Humanists, the German peasantry also had at first believed Luther to be an ally. The peasantry had been organized since the late fifteenth century against efforts by territorial princes to override their traditional laws and customs and to subject them to new regulations and taxes. Peasant leaders, several of whom were convinced Lutherans, saw in Luther's teaching about Christian freedom and his criticism of monastic landowners a point of view close to their own, and they openly solicited Luther's support of their political and economic rights, including their revolutionary request for release from serfdom. Luther and his followers sympathized with the peasants; indeed, for several years, Lutheran pamphleteers made *Karsthans*, the burly, honest peasant with his flail or hoe, a symbol of the simple life that God

desired all people to live. The Lutherans, however, were not social revolutionaries, and when the peasants revolted against their masters in 1524–1525, Luther not surprisingly condemned them in the strongest possible terms as "unchristian" and urged the princes to crush their revolt without mercy. Tens of thousands of peasants (estimates run between 70,000 and 100,000) had died by the time the revolt was put down.

For Luther, the freedom of the Christian was an inner release from guilt and anxiety, not a right to restructure society by violent revolution. Had Luther supported the Peasants' Revolt, he would not only have contradicted his own teaching and belief but also ended any chance of the survival of his reform beyond the 1520s.

Zwingli and the Swiss Reformation

Switzerland was a loose confederacy of thirteen autonomous cantons or states and allied areas (see Map 17.3). Some cantons (e.g., Zurich, Bern, Basel, and Schaffhausen) became Protestant, some (especially around the Lucerne heartland) remained Catholic, and a few other cantons and regions managed to effect a compromise. Among the preconditions of the Swiss Reformation were the growth of national sentiment occasioned by opposition to foreign mercenary service (providing mercenaries for Europe's warring nations was a major source of Switzerland's livelihood) and a desire for Church reform that had persisted in Switzerland since the councils of Constance (1414–1417) and Basel (1431–1449).

THE REFORMATION IN ZURICH. Ulrich Zwingli (1484–1531), the leader of the Swiss Reformation, had been humanistically educated in Bern, Vienna, and Basel. He was strongly influenced by Erasmus, whom he credited with having set him on the path to reform. An eloquent critic of mercenary service, Zwingli believed such service threatened both the political sovereignty and the moral well-being of the Swiss confederacy. By 1518, Zwingli was also widely known for opposition to the sale of indulgences and religious superstition.

In 1519, Zwingli gained the position of people's priest in Zurich, the base from which he engineered the Swiss Reformation. In March 1522, he was part of a group who defied the Lenten fast—an act of protest analogous to burning one's national flag today. Zwingli's reform guideline was very simple and very effective: whatever lacked literal support in Scripture was to be neither believed nor practiced. A disputation held on January 29, 1523, concluded with the city government's sanction of Zwingli's Scripture test. Thereafter Zurich became, to all intents and purposes, a Protestant city and the center of the Swiss Reforma-

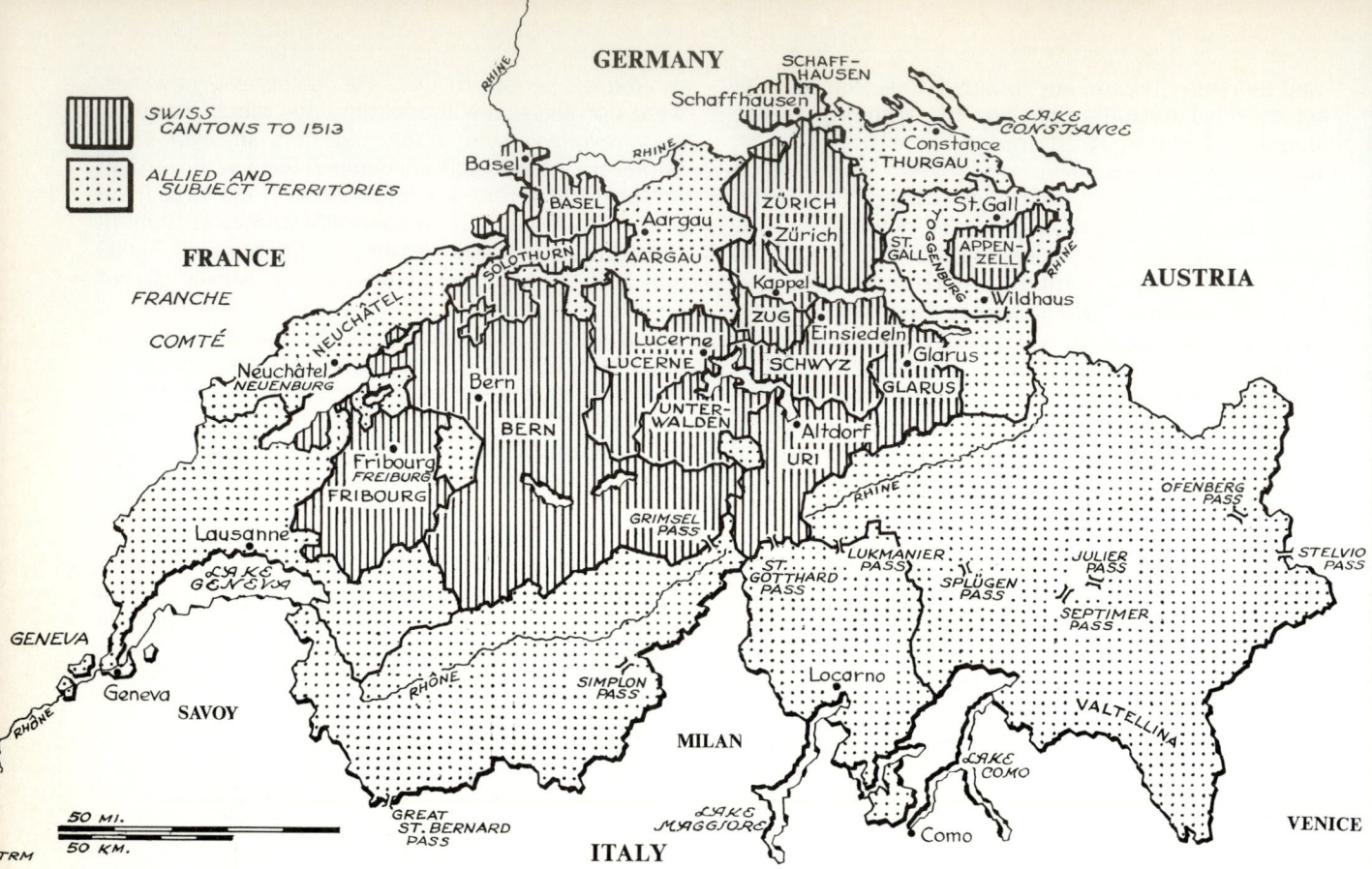

MAP 17-3 THE SWISS CONFEDERATION *While nominally still a part of the Holy
Roman Empire, Switzerland grew from a loose defensive union of the central "forest
cantons" in the thirteenth century to a fiercely independent association of regions with
different languages, histories, and finally, religions.*

tion. A harsh discipline was imposed by the new Protestant regime, making Zurich one of the first examples
of a puritanical Protestant city.

THE MARBURG COLLOQUY. Landgrave Philip
of Hesse (1504–1567) sought to unite Swiss and German Protestants in a mutual defense pact, a potentially significant political alliance. His efforts were
spoiled, however, by theological disagreements between Luther and Zwingli over the nature of Christ's
presence in the Eucharist. Zwingli maintained a symbolic interpretation of Christ's words, "This is my
body"; Christ, he argued, was only spiritually, not
bodily, present in the bread and wine of the Eucharist.
Luther, to the contrary, insisted that Christ's human
nature could share the properties of his divine nature;
hence, where Christ was spiritually present, he could
also be bodily present, for his was a special nature.

Philip of Hesse brought the two Protestant leaders
together in his castle in Marburg in early October
1529, but they were unable to work out their differences on this issue. Luther left thinking Zwingli a dan-

gerous fanatic. Although cooperation between the two
sides did not cease, the disagreement splintered the
Protestant movement theologically and politically.

Anabaptists and Radical Protestants

The moderate pace and seemingly small ethical results of the Lutheran and Zwinglian reformations discontented many people, among them some of the original coworkers of Luther and Zwingli. Many desired a
more rapid and thorough implementation of primitive
Christianity and accused the major reformers of going
only halfway. The most important of these radical
groups were the Anabaptists, the sixteenth-century
ancestors of the modern Mennonites and Amish. The
Anabaptists were especially distinguished by their rejection of infant baptism and their insistence on only
adult baptism (*anabaptism* derives from the Greek
word meaning "to rebaptize"), believing that baptism
as a consenting adult conformed to Scripture and was
more respectful of human freedom.

Anabaptists physically separated from society to
form a more perfect community in imitation of what

468   THE WORLD IN TRANSITION (1500–1800)

they believed to be the example of the first Christians. Because of the close connection between religious and civic life in this period, such separatism was viewed by the political authorities as a threat to basic social bonds.

At first, Anabaptism drew its adherents from all social classes. But as Lutherans and Zwinglians joined with Catholics in opposition to the Anabaptists, a more rural, agrarian class came to make up the great majority. In 1529, rebaptism became a capital offense throughout the Holy Roman Empire. It has been estimated that between 1525 and 1618 at least one thousand and perhaps as many as five thousand men and women were executed for rebaptising themselves as adults.

Political Consolidation of the Lutheran Reformation

THE DIET OF AUGSBURG. Charles V returned to the empire in 1530 to direct the Diet of Augsburg, a meeting of Protestant and Catholic representatives assembled for the purpose of ending the religious divisions. With its terms dictated by the Catholic emperor, the diet adjourned with a blunt order to all Lutherans to revert to Catholicism. The Reformation was by this time too firmly established for that to occur, and in February 1531, the Lutherans responded with the formation of their own defensive alliance, the Schmalkaldic League, which achieved a stalemate with the emperor, who was again distracted by renewed war with France and the Turks.

THE EXPANSION OF THE REFORMATION. In the 1530s, German Lutherans formed regional consistories, judicial bodies composed of theologians and lawyers, which oversaw and administered the new Protestant churches. These consistories replaced the old Catholic episcopates. Under the leadership of Philip Melanchthon, Luther's most admired colleague, educational reforms were enacted that provided for compulsory primary education, schools for girls, a Humanist revision of the traditional curriculum, and catechetical instruction of the laity in the new religion. These accomplishments earned Melanchthon the title "praeceptor of Germany."

The Reformation also dug in elsewhere. Introduced into Denmark by Christian II (ruled 1513–1523), Danish Lutheranism throve under Frederick I (1523–1533), who joined the Schmalkaldic League. Under Christian III (1536–1559) Lutheranism became the state religion. In Sweden, Gustavus Vasa (1523–1560), supported by a Swedish nobility greedy for Church lands, confiscated Church property and subjected the clergy to royal authority at the Diet of Vesteras (1527). In politically splintered Poland, Lutherans, Anabaptists, Calvinists, and even Antitrinitarians found

room to practice their beliefs, as Poland, primarily because of the absence of a central political authority, became a model of religious pluralism and toleration in the second half of the sixteenth century.

REACTION AGAINST PROTESTANTS: THE INTERIM. Charles V made abortive efforts in 1540–1541 to enforce a compromise agreement between Protestants and Catholics. As these and other conciliar efforts failed, he turned to a military solution. In 1547, imperial armies crushed the Protestant Schmalkaldic League.

The emperor established puppet rulers in Saxony and Hesse and issued as imperial law the *Augsburg Interim*, a new order that Protestants everywhere

MAP 17-4 THE RELIGIOUS SITUATION ABOUT 1560 *By 1560 Luther, Zwingli, and Loyola were dead, Calvin near the end of his life, the English break from Rome fully accomplished, and the last session of the Council of Trent about to assemble. Here is the religious geography of Western Europe at this time.*

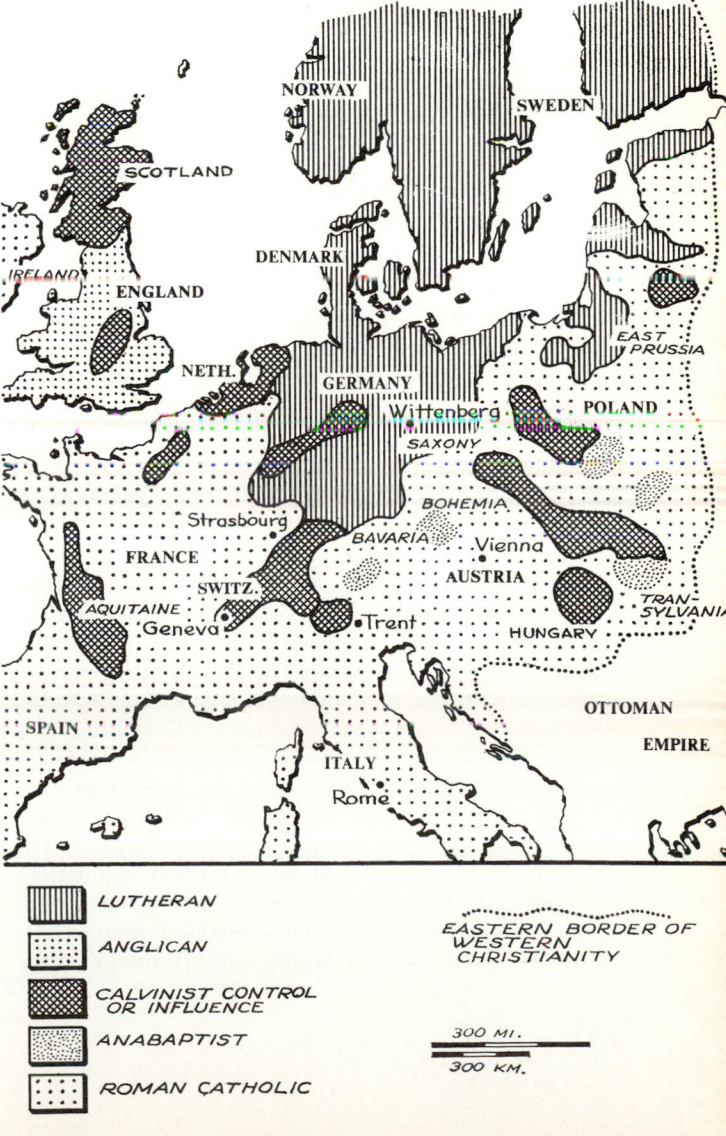

LUTHERAN

ANGLICAN

CALVINIST CONTROL OR INFLUENCE

ANABAPTIST

ROMAN CATHOLIC

EASTERN BORDER OF WESTERN CHRISTIANITY

300 MI.

300 KM.

must readopt old Catholic beliefs and practices. But the Reformation was too entrenched by 1547 to be ended even by brute force. Confronted by fierce Protestant resistance and weary from three decades of war, the emperor was forced to relent.

The Peace of Augsburg in September 1555 made the division of Christendom permanent. This agreement recognized in law what had already been well established in practice: *cuius regio, eius religio*, meaning that the ruler of a land would determine the religion of the land. Lutherans were permitted to retain all Church lands forcibly seized before 1552. Those discontented with the religion of their region were permitted to migrate to another.

Calvinism and Anabaptism were not recognized as legal forms of Christian belief and practice by the Peace of Augsburg. Anabaptists had long adjusted to such exclusion by forming their own separatist communities. Calvinists, however, were not separatists and could not choose this route; they remained determined not only to secure the right to worship publicly as they pleased but also to shape society according to their own religious convictions. While Anabaptists retreated and Lutherans enjoyed the security of an established religion, Calvinists organized to lead national revolutions throughout northern Europe in the second half of the sixteenth and the first half of the seventeenth century.

John Calvin and the Genevan Reformation

Calvinism was the religious ideology that inspired or accompanied massive political resistance in France, the Netherlands, and Scotland. It established itself within the Palatinate during the reign of Elector Frederick III (1559–1576). Believing strongly in both divine predestination and the individual's responsibility to reorder society according to God's plan, Calvinists became zealous reformers determined to transform and order society according to their religious beliefs. In a famous study, *The Protestant Ethic and the Spirit of Capitalism* (1904), the German sociologist Max Weber argued that this peculiar combination of religious confidence and self-disciplined activism produced an ethic that stimulated and reinforced emergent capitalism, bringing Calvinism and later Puritanism into close association with the development of modern capitalist societies.

POLITICAL REVOLT AND RELIGIOUS REFORM IN GENEVA. Whereas in Saxony religious reform paved the way for a political revolution against the emperor, in Geneva a political revolution against the local prince-bishop laid the foundation for the religious change. Genevans successfully revolted against the House of Savoy and their resident prince-bishop in the

The French reformer and theologian, John Calvin (1509–1564). [Musée Historique de la Réformation et Bibliothèque Calvinienne, Geneva. H. Pattusch.]

late 1520s. In late 1533, Bern dispatched Protestant reformers to Geneva. In the summer of 1535, after much internal turmoil, the Protestants triumphed, and the traditional Mass and other religious practices were removed. On May 21, 1536, the city voted officially to adopt the Reformation: "to live according to the Gospel and the Word of God . . . without . . . any more masses, statues, idols, or other papal abuses."

John Calvin (1509–1564), a reform-minded Humanist and lawyer, arrived in Geneva after these events, in July 1536. Guillaume Farel (1489–1565), the local Protestant reformer, successfully pleaded with him to stay and assist the Reformation.

Before a year had passed, Calvin had drawn up articles for the governance of the new church, as well as a catechism to guide and discipline the people, both of which were presented for approval to the city councils in early 1537. Because of the strong measures proposed to govern Geneva's moral life, the reformers were suspected by many of desiring to create a "new papacy." Both within and outside Geneva, Calvin and Farel were perceived as going too far too fast. In February 1538, the reformers were exiled from the city.

Calvin went to Strasbourg, a model Protestant city, where he became pastor to the French exiles there. During his two-year stay in Strasbourg, Calvin wrote biblical commentaries and a second edition of his masterful *Institutes of the Christian Religion*, which many consider the definitive theological statement of the Protestant faith. Calvin also married and participated in the ecumenical discussions urged on Protestants and Catholics by Charles V. Most important, he learned from the Strasbourg reformer Martin Bucer how to implement the Protestant Reformation successfully.

CALVIN'S GENEVA. In 1540, Geneva elected officials who were favorable to Calvin and invited him to return. This he did in September 1540, never to leave the city again. Within months of his arrival, new ecclesiastical ordinances were implemented that provided for cooperation between the magistrates and the clergy in matters of internal discipline. Following the Strasbourg model, the Genevan church was organized into four offices: (1) pastors, of whom there were five; (2) teachers or doctors to instruct the populace in and to defend true doctrine; (3) elders, a group of twelve laymen chosen by and from the Genevan councils and empowered to "oversee the life of everybody"; and (4) deacons to dispense church goods and services to the poor and the sick.

Calvin and his followers were motivated above all by a desire to transform society morally. Faith, Calvin taught, did not sit idly in the mind but conformed one's every action to God's law. The "elect" should live in a manifestly god-pleasing way, if they were truly God's elect. The majesty of God demanded nothing less. In the attempt to realize this goal, Calvin spared no effort. The consistory became his instrument of power. This body was composed of the elders and the pastors and was presided over by one of the four syndics. It enforced the strictest moral discipline, meting out punishments for a broad range of moral and religious transgressions—from missing church services (a fine of three sous) to fornication (six days on bread and water and a fine of sixty sous)—and, as time passed, increasingly for criticism of Calvin.

After 1555, the city's syndics were all devout Calvinists, and Geneva became home to thousands of exiled Protestants who had been driven out of France, England, and Scotland. Refugees (more than five thousand), most of them utterly loyal to Calvin, came to make up over one third of the population of Geneva. From this time until his death in 1564, Calvin's position in the city was greatly strengthened and the syndics were very cooperative.

Catholic Reform and the Counter-Reformation

SOURCES OF CATHOLIC REFORM. The Protestant Reformation did not take the medieval church completely by surprise. There were much internal criticism and many efforts at internal reform before there was a Counter-Reformation in reaction to Protestant successes. Before the Reformation, ambitious proposals had been set forth to bring about the long-demanded reform of the church in head and members. Catholic reformers were found within a variety of self-motivated lay and clerical movements. Two important organizations that brought reform-minded clergy and laity together were the Modern Devotion and the Oratory of Divine Love. The former, also known as the Brothers of the Common Life, was an organized group of laity and clergy who fostered the religious life outside formal ecclesiastical offices and apart from formal religious vows. The Oratory of Divine Love, founded in Rome in 1517, was an exclusive informal organization of earnest laity and clergy who were both learned and deeply committed to traditional religious devotion. Like Erasmus, whose religious writings the members admired, they taught that inner piety and good Christian living, not theological arguments and disputations, were the surest way to reform the church.

IGNATIUS OF LOYOLA AND THE JESUITS. Of the various reform groups, none was more instrumental in the success of the Counter-Reformation than the Society of Jesus, the new order of Jesuits, organized by Ignatius of Loyola in the 1530s and officially recognized by the Catholic church in 1540. The society grew within the space of a century from its original ten members to more than fifteen thousand scattered throughout the world, with thriving missions in India, Japan, and the Americas.

The founder of the Jesuits, Ignatius of Loyola (1491–1556), had been a dashing courtier and caballero in his youth. He began his spiritual pilgrimage in 1521 after he had been seriously wounded in the legs during a battle with the French. During a lengthy and painful convalescence, he passed the time by reading Christian classics. So impressed was he with the heroic self-sacrifice of the church's saints and their methods of overcoming mental anguish and pain that he underwent a profound religious conversion; henceforth he, too, would serve the Church as a soldier of Christ.

After recuperating, Ignatius applied the lessons he had learned during his convalescence to a program of religious and moral self-discipline that came to be embodied in the *Spiritual Exercises*. This psychologically perceptive devotional guide contained mental and emotional exercises designed to teach one absolute spiritual self-mastery over one's feelings. It taught that a person could shape his or her own behavior, even create a new religious self, through disciplined study and regular practice.

Whereas in Jesuit eyes Protestants had distinguished themselves by disobedience to Church authority and religious innovation, the exercises of Ignatius were intended to teach good Catholics to deny themselves and submit without question to higher Church authority and spiritual direction. Perfect discipline and self-control were the essential conditions of such obedience. To these was added the enthusiasm of tradi-

Ignatius of Loyola's "Rules for Thinking with the Church"

As leaders of the Counter-Reformation, the Jesuits attempted to live by and instill in others the strictest obedience to church authority. The following are some of the eighteen rules included by Ignatius in his Spiritual Exercises *to give both Jesuits and lay Catholics positive direction. These rules also indicate the Catholic reformers' refusal to compromise with Protestantism.*

In order to have the proper attitude of mind in the Church Militant we should observe the following rules:

1. Putting aside all private judgment, we should keep our minds prepared and ready to obey promptly and in all things the true spouse of Christ our Lord, our Holy Mother, the hierarchical Church.
2. To praise sacramental confession and the reception of the Most Holy Sacrament once a year, and much better once a month, and better still every week. . . .
3. To praise the frequent hearing of Mass. . . .
4. To praise highly the religious life, virginity, and continence; and also matrimony, but not as highly. . . .
5. To praise the vows of religion, obedience, poverty, chastity, and other works of perfection and supererogation. . . .
6. To praise the relics of the saints . . . [and] the stations, pilgrimages, indulgences, jubilees, Crusade indulgences, and the lighting of candles in the churches.
7. To praise the precepts concerning fasts and abstinences . . . and acts of penance. . . .

8. To praise the adornments and buildings of churches as well as sacred images. . . .
9. To praise all the precepts of the church. . . .
10. To approve and praise the directions and recommendations of our superiors as well as their personal behavior. . . .
11. To praise both positive and scholastic theology. . . .
12. We must be on our guard against making comparisons between the living and those who have already gone to their reward, for it is no small error to say, for example: "This man knows more than St. Augustine," "He is another Saint Francis, or even greater." . . .
13. If we wish to be sure that we are right in all things; we should always be ready to accept this principle: I will believe that the white that I see is black, if the hierarchical Church so defines it. For I believe that between . . . Christ our Lord and . . . His Church, there is but one spirit, which governs and directs us for the salvation of our souls. ❑

The Spiritual Exercises of St. Ignatius, trans. by Anthony Mottola (Garden City, N.Y.: Doubleday, 1964), pp. 139–141.

tional spirituality and mysticism—a potent combination that helped counter the Reformation and win many Protestants back to the Catholic fold, especially in Austria and Bavaria and along the Rhine.

THE COUNCIL OF TRENT (1545–1563). The broad success of the Reformation and the insistence of the Emperor Charles V forced Pope Paul III (1534–1549) to call a general council of the Church to define religious doctrine.

The long-delayed council met in 1545 in the city of Trent in northern Italy. There were three sessions, spread over eighteen years, from 1545 to 1563, with long interruptions due to war, plague, and imperial and papal politics. The council's most important reforms concerned internal Church discipline. Steps were taken to curtail the selling of Church offices and other religious goods. Many bishops who resided in Rome rather than within their dioceses were forced to move to their appointed seats of authority. The Council of Trent strengthened the authority of local bishops

so that they could effectively discipline popular religious practice. The Council of Trent also sought to give the parish priest a brighter image by requiring him to be neatly dressed, better educated, strictly celibate, and active among his parishioners. To this end, the council also called for the construction of a seminary in every diocese.

The English Reformation to 1553

THE KING'S AFFAIR. Although Lollardy and Humanism may be said to have prepared the soil for the seeds of Protestant reform in England, it was King Henry VIII's unhappy marriage that furnished the plough that truly broke the soil. Henry had married Catherine of Aragon (d. 1536), daughter of Ferdinand and Isabella of Spain, and the aunt of Emperor Charles V. By 1527, the union had produced no male heir to the throne and only one surviving child, a daughter, Mary Tudor. Henry was justifiably concerned about the political consequences of leaving only

By 1527, Henry, thoroughly enamored of Anne Boleyn, one of Catherine's ladies in waiting, decided to put Catherine aside and marry Anne. This he could not do in Catholic England without papal annulment of the marriage to Catherine. And therein lay a problem. The year 1527 was also the year when soldiers of the Holy Roman Empire mutinied and sacked Rome, and the reigning pope, Clement VII, was at the time a prisoner of Charles V, Catherine's nephew. Even if this had not been the case, it would have been virtually impossible for the pope to grant an annulment of the marriage. Not only had it survived for eighteen years but it had been made possible in the first place by a special papal dispensation required because Queen Catherine had previously been the wife of Henry's brother, Arthur.

After Cardinal Wolsey, Lord Chancellor of England since 1515, failed to secure the annulment, Thomas Cranmer (1489–1556) and Thomas Cromwell (1485–1540), both of whom harbored Lutheran sympathies, became the king's closest advisers. Finding the way to a papal annulment closed, Henry's new advisers struck a different course: Why not simply declare the king supreme in English spiritual affairs as he was in English temporal affairs? Then the king himself could settle the king's affair.

THE REFORMATION PARLIAMENT. In 1529, Parliament convened for what would be a seven-year session that earned it the title of "Reformation Parliament." During this period, it passed a flood of legislation that harassed and finally placed royal reins on the clergy. In January 1531, the clergy in Convocation (a legislative assembly representing the English clergy) publicly recognized Henry as head of the church in England "as far as the law of Christ allows." In 1533, Parliament passed the Submission of the Clergy, effectively placing canon law under royal control and thereby the clergy under royal jurisdiction.

In January 1533, Henry wed the pregnant Anne Boleyn, with Thomas Cranmer officiating. In 1534, Parliament ended all payments by the English clergy and laity to Rome and gave Henry sole jurisdiction over high ecclesiastical appointments. The Act of Succession in the same year made Anne Boleyn's children legitimate heirs to the throne, and the Act of Supremacy declared Henry "the only supreme head in earth of the church of England."

THE PROTESTANT REFORMATION UNDER EDWARD VI. Henry's political and domestic boldness was not carried over to the religious front, although the pope did cease to be the head of the English church and English Bibles were placed in English churches. Despite his political break with Rome, the king remained decidedly conservative in his religious

a female heir. People in this period believed it unnatural for women to rule over men: at best, a woman ruler meant a contested reign; at worst, turmoil and revolution. Henry even came to believe that his union with Catherine, who had numerous miscarriages and stillbirths, had been cursed by God, because prior to their marriage, Catherine had been the wife of his late brother, Arthur.

Hampton Court Palace, home to English royalty after it was taken over by Henry VIII from Cardinal Wolsey early in the sixteenth century. [British Tourist Authority, New York.]

beliefs, and Catholic doctrine remained prominent in a country seething with Protestant sentiment. Henry absolutely forbade the English clergy to marry and threatened any clergy who were twice caught in concubinage with execution. The Six Articles of 1539 reaffirmed transubstantiation, denied the Eucharistic cup

Thomas More Stands By His Conscience

More, loyal Catholic to the end, repudiated the Act of Supremacy as unlawful; he believed that it contradicted both the laws of England and the king's own coronation oath. More important, he believed that the act transgressed centuries of European tradition, by which he felt bound by conscience to stand, even if it meant certain death. In the following excerpt, More defended himself in a final interrogation, as reported by his prosecutors.

"Seeing that . . . ye are determined to condemn me [More said] . . . I will now in discharge of my conscience speak my mind plainly and freely. . . . Forasmuch as this indictment is grounded upon an Act of Parliament directly repugnant to the laws of God and his holy Church, the supreme government of which . . . may no temporal prince presume by any law to take upon him . . . it is . . . insufficient to charge any Christian man [who refuses to recognize this Act]."

For proof thereof, he [More] declared that this realm, being but one member and small part of the Church, might not make a particular law disagreeable with the general law of Christ's universal Catholic Church, no more than the city of London, being but one poor member in respect of the whole realm, might make a law against an Act of Parliament to bind the whole realm. So further showed he that it was contrary both to the laws and statutes of our own land . . . and also contrary to the sacred oath which the King's Highness himself and every Christian prince always with

great solemnity received at their coronations. . . .

Then . . . the Lord Chancellor . . . answered that seeing that all the bishops, universities, and best learned men of the realm had to this Act agreed, it was much marvel that he [More] alone against them all would so stiffly stick thereat. . . .

To this Sir Thomas replied . . . : "Neither as yet have I chanced upon any ancient writer or doctor that so advanceth, as your Statute doth, the supremacy of any secular and temporal prince . . . and therefore am I not bounde, my Lord, to conform my conscience to the Council of one realm against the general Council of [the whole of] Christendom. For of the foresaid holy bishops I have, for every bishop of yours, above one hundred. And for one Council or Parliament of yours (God knoweth what manner of one), I have all the Councils made these thousand years. And for this one Kingdom [of England], I have all other Christian realms." ❑

The Reformation in England: To the Accession of Elizabeth I, ed. by A. G. Dickens and Dorothy Carr (New York: St. Martin's Press, 1968), pp. 71–72.

Main Events of the English Reformation

1529	Reformation Parliament convenes
1532	Parliament passes the Submission of the Clergy, an act placing canon law and the English clergy under royal jurisdiction
1533	Henry VIII weds Anne Boleyn; Convocation proclaims marriage to Catherine of Aragon invalid
1534	Act of Succession makes Anne Boleyn's children legitimate heirs to the English throne
1534	Act of Supremacy declares Henry VIII "the only supreme head of the church of England"
1535	Thomas More executed for opposition to Acts of Succession and Supremacy
1535	Publication of Coverdale Bible
1539	Henry VIII imposes the Six Articles, condemning Protestantism and reasserting traditional doctrine
1547	Edward VI succeeds to the throne under protectorships of Somerset and Northumberland
1549	First Act of Uniformity imposes *Book of Common Prayer* on English churches
1553–1558	Mary Tudor restores Catholic doctrine
1558–1603	Elizabeth I fashions an Anglican religious settlement

to the laity, declared celibate vows inviolable, provided for private masses, and ordered the continuation of auricular confession.

Edward VI (1547–1553), Henry's son by his third wife Jane Seymour, gained the throne when he was only ten years old. Anne Boleyn had been executed in 1536 for adultery and her daughter Elizabeth declared illegitimate and thus ineligible to succeed to the English throne.

Under Edward, England fully enacted the Protestant Reformation. Henry's Six Articles and laws against heresy were repealed, and clerical marriage and communion with cup were sanctioned. In 1549, the Act of Uniformity imposed Thomas Cranmer's *Book of Common Prayer* on all English churches. Images and altars were removed from the churches in 1550. The Second Act of Uniformity, passed in 1552, imposed a revised edition of the *Book of Common Prayer* on all English churches. A forty-two-article confession of faith, also written by Thomas Cranmer, was adopted, setting forth a moderate Protestant doctrine.

All these changes were short-lived, however. In 1553, Catherine of Aragon's daughter, Mary Tudor, succeeded Edward (who had died in his teens) to the English throne and proceeded to restore Catholic doctrine and practice with a singlemindedness that rivaled that of her father. It was not until the reign of Anne Boleyn's daughter, Elizabeth (1558–1603), that a lasting religious settlement was worked out in England (to be discussed later).

The Wars of Religion

The late sixteenth century and the first half of the seventeenth century are described as an "age of religious wars" because of the bloody opposition of Protestants and Catholics across the length and breadth of Europe. In France, the Netherlands, England, and Scotland in the second half of the sixteenth century, Calvinists fought Catholic rulers for the right to form their own communities and to practice their chosen religion openly. In the first half of the seventeenth century, international armies of varying religious persuasions marched against one another in central and northern Europe during the Thirty Years' War. And by the middle of the seventeenth century, English Puritans had successfully revolted against the Stuart monarchy and the Anglican church. In the second half of the sixteenth century, the political conflict, which had previously been confined to central Europe and a struggle for Lutheran rights and freedoms, shifted to western Europe—to France, the Netherlands, England, and Scotland—and became a struggle for Calvinist recognition.

Genevan Calvinism and Tridentine Catholicism were two equally dogmatic, aggressive, and irreconcilable church systems. Calvinism adopted a presbyterian organization that magnified regional and local religious authority: boards of presbyters, or elders, representing the many individual congregations of Calvinists, directly shaped the policy of the Church at large. By contrast, the Counter-Reformation sponsored a centralized episcopal church system, hierarchically arranged from pope to parish priest, which stressed absolute obedience to the person at the top. The high clergy—the pope and his bishops—not the synods of local churches, ruled supreme. Calvinism proved attractive to proponents of political decentralization in contest with totalitarian rulers, whereas Catholicism remained congenial to the proponents of absolute monarchy determined to maintain "one king, one church, one law" throughout the land.

The French Wars of Religion (1562–1598)

Henry II died accidently during a tournament in 1559. His sickly fifteen-year-old son, Francis II, came to the throne under the regency of the queen mother, Catherine de Médicis. With the monarchy so weakened, three powerful families saw their chance to control France and began to compete for the young king's ear. They were the Bourbons, whose power lay in the south and west; the Montmorency-Châtillons, who controlled the center of France; and the Guises, who were dominant in eastern France. The Guises were far the strongest, and the name of Guise was interchangeable with militant, reactionary Catholicism. The Bourbon and Montmorency-Châtillon families, in contrast, developed strong Huguenot (as the French Protestants were called) sympathies, largely for political reasons. The Bourbon Louis I, prince of Condé (d. 1569), and

Catherine de Medicis (1519–1589). Following the death of her husband, King Henry II of France, in 1559. Catherine exercized much power during the reigns of her three sons, Francis II (1559–1560), Charles IX (1560–1574), and Henry III (1574–1589). [Bettmann Archive.]

the Montmorency-Châtillon Admiral Gaspard de Coligny (1519–1572) became the political leaders of the French Protestant resistance.

Often for quite different reasons, ambitious aristocrats and discontented townspeople joined Calvinist churches in opposition to the Guise-dominated French monarchy. In 1561, over two thousand Huguenot congregations existed throughout France, although Huguenots were a majority of the population in only two regions: Dauphiné and Languedoc. Although they made up only about one fifteenth of the population, Huguenots were in important geographic areas and were heavily represented among the more powerful segments of French society. Over two fifths of the French aristocracy became Huguenots. Many apparently hoped to establish within France a principle of territorial sovereignty akin to that secured within the Holy Roman Empire by the Peace of Augsburg (1555). In this way, Calvinism indirectly served the forces of political decentralization.

CATHERINE DE MÉDICIS AND THE GUISES. Following Francis II's death in 1560, Catherine de Médicis continued as regent for her minor son, Charles IX (1560–1574). Fearing the power and guile of the Guises, Catherine, whose first concern was always to preserve the monarchy, sought allies among the Protestants. In 1562, she granted Protestants freedom to worship publicly outside towns—although only privately within them—and to hold synods or church assemblies. In March, this royal toleration came to an abrupt end when the duke of Guise surprised a Protestant congregation at Vassy in Champagne and proceeded to massacre several score—an event that marked the beginning of the French wars of religion (March 1562).

Perpetually caught between fanatical Huguenot and Guise extremes, Queen Catherine always sought to balance the one side against the other. Like the Guises, she wanted a Catholic France; she did not, however, desire a Guise-dominated monarchy.

On August 22, 1572, four days after the Huguenot Henry of Navarre had married King Charles IX's sister, Marguerite of Valois—a sign of growing Protestant power—Coligny was struck down, although not killed, by an assassin's bullet. Catherine had apparently been a party to this Guise plot to eliminate Coligny. After its failure, she feared both the king's reaction to her complicity and the Huguenot response under a recovered Coligny. Summoning all her motherly charm and fury, Catherine convinced Charles that a Huguenot coup was afoot, inspired by Coligny, and that only the swift execution of Protestant leaders could save the crown from a Protestant attack on Paris. On the eve of Saint Bartholomew's Day, August 24, 1572, Coligny and three thousand fellow Hugue-

The massacre of Huguenots in Paris on Saint Batholomew's Day, August 24, 1572, as remembered by François Dubois, a Huguenot eyewitness. [The Granger Collection.]

nots were butchered in Paris. Within three days, an estimated twenty thousand Huguenots were executed in coordinated attacks throughout France. The event changed the nature of the struggle between Protestants and Catholics both within and beyond the borders of France. It was thereafter no longer an internal contest between Guise and Bourbon factions for French political influence, nor was it simply a Huguenot campaign to win basic religious freedoms. Henceforth, in Protestant eyes, it became an international struggle to the death for sheer survival against an adversary whose cruelty now justified any means of resistance.

THE RISE TO POWER OF HENRY OF NAVARRE. Henry III (1574–1589), who was Henry II's third son and the last to wear the French crown, found the monarchy wedged between a radical Catholic League, formed in 1576 by Henry of Guise, and vengeful Huguenots. Like the queen mother, Henry III sought to steer a middle course, and in this effort he received support from a growing body of neutral Catholics and Huguenots, who put the political survival of France above its religious unity. Such *politiques*, as they were called, were prepared to compromise religious creeds as might be required to save the nation.

In the mid-1580s the Catholic League, supported by the Spanish, became completely dominant in Paris. In what came to be known as the Day of the Barricades, Henry III attempted to rout the league with a surprise attack in 1588. The effort failed badly and the king had to flee Paris. Forced by his weakened position into guerrilla tactics, Henry successfully plotted the assassination of both the duke and the cardinal of Guise. The Catholic League reacted with a fury that matched the earlier Huguenot response to the Massacre of Saint Bartholomew's Day. The king now had only one course of action: He struck an alliance with his Protestant cousin, Henry of Navarre, in April 1589.

As the two Henrys prepared to attack the Guise stronghold of Paris, however, a fanatical Dominican friar stabbed Henry III to death. Thereupon the Bourbon Huguenot Henry of Navarre succeeded the childless Valois king to the French throne as Henry IV (1589–1610).

Henry IV came to the throne as a *politique*, weary of religious strife and prepared to place political peace above absolute religious unity. He believed that a royal policy of tolerant Catholicism would be the best way to achieve such peace. On July 25, 1593, he publicly abjured the Protestant faith and embraced the tra-

Philip II of Spain (1556–1598) at age 24, by Titian. Philip was the dominant ruler of the second half of the sixteenth century. However, he was finally denied victory over the two areas in which he most sought to impose his will, the Netherlands and England. [Museo del Prado, Madrid.]

ditional and majority religion of his country. "Paris is worth a Mass," he is reported to have said.

On April 13, 1598, a formal religious settlement was proclaimed in Henry IV's famous Edict of Nantes. This religious truce—and it was never more than that—granted the Huguenots, who by this time numbered well over one million, freedom of public worship, the right of assembly, admission to public offices and universities, and permission to maintain fortified towns. Most of the new freedoms, however, were to be exercised within their own towns and territories. As significant as it was, the edict only transformed a long hot war between irreconcilable enemies into a long cold war. To its critics, it had only created a state within a state.

Imperial Spain and the Reign of Philip II (1556–1598)

Until the English defeated his mighty Armada in 1588, no one person stood larger in the second half of the sixteenth century than Philip II of Spain. During the first half of Philip's reign, attention focused on the Mediterranean and Turkish expansion. In May 1571, a Holy League of Spain, Venice, and the pope defeated the Turks in the largest naval battle of the sixteenth century. A fleet under the command of Philip's half brother, Don John of Austria, engaged the Ottoman navy under Ali Pasha off Lepanto in the Gulf of Corinth on October 7, 1571. Before the engagement ended, thirty thousand Turks had died and over one third of the Turkish fleet was sunk or captured.

THE REVOLT IN THE NETHERLANDS. The spectacular Spanish military success in southern Europe was not repeated in northern Europe when Philip attempted to impose his will within the Netherlands and on England and France. The resistance of the Netherlands especially proved the undoing of Spanish dreams of world empire.

The Netherlands were the richest area not only of Philip's Habsburg kingdom, but of Europe as well. The merchant towns of the Netherlands were also, however, Europe's most independent; many, like magnificent Antwerp, were also Calvinist strongholds. A stubborn opposition to the Spanish overlords formed under William of Nassau, the Prince of Orange (1533–1584). Like other successful rulers in this period, William of Orange was a *politique* who placed the Netherlands' political autonomy and well-being above religious creeds. He personally passed through successive Catholic, Lutheran, and Calvinist stages.

The year 1564 saw the first fusion of political and religious opposition to Spanish rule, the result of Philip II's unwise insistence that the decrees of the Council of Trent be enforced throughout the Netherlands. A national covenant was drawn up called the *Compromise*, a solemn pledge to resist the decrees of Trent and the Inquisition.

Philip dispatched the duke of Alba to suppress the revolt. His army of ten thousand men journeyed northward from Milan in 1567 in a show of combined Spanish and papal might. A special tribunal, known to the Spanish as the Council of Troubles and among the Netherlanders as the Council of Blood, reigned over

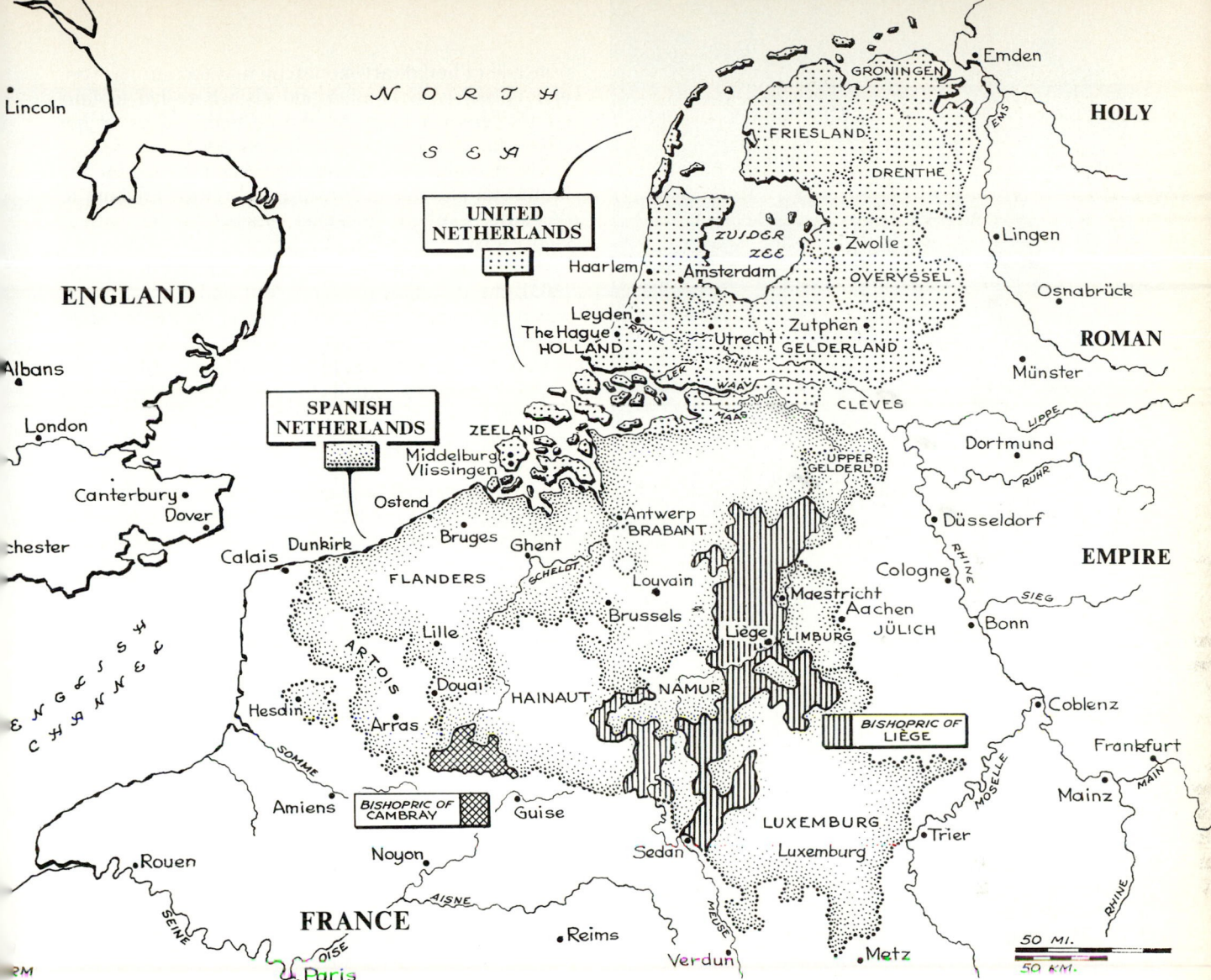

MAP 17-5 THE NETHERLANDS DURING THE REFORMATION *The northern and southern provinces of the Netherlands. The former, the United Provinces, were mostly Protestant in the second half of the sixteenth century, while the southern, the Spanish Netherlands, made peace with Spain and remained largely Catholic.*

the land. Several thousand suspected heretics were publicly executed before Alba's reign of terror ended.

William of Orange had been an exile in Germany during these turbulent years. He now emerged as the leader of a broad movement for the Netherlands' independence from Spain.

After a decade of persecution and warfare, the ten largely Catholic southern provinces (what is roughly modern Belgium) came together in 1576 with the seven largely Protestant northern provinces (what is roughly the modern Netherlands) in unified opposition to Spain. This union, known as the Pacification of Ghent,

was accomplished on November 8, 1576. It declared internal regional sovereignty in matters of religion. It was a Netherlands version of the territorial settlement of religious differences brought about in the Holy Roman Empire in 1555 by the Peace of Augsburg.

In January 1579, the southern provinces formed the Union of Arras and made peace with Spain. The northern provinces responded with the formation of the Union of Utrecht. Spanish preoccupation with France and England in the 1580s permitted the northern provinces to drive out all Spanish soldiers by 1593. In 1596, France and England formally recognized the indepen-

Elizabeth I of England painted in 1592 by Marcus Gheeraerts. Note that she is standing on a map of her kingdom. Elizabeth is considered by many to be the most successful ruler of the sixteenth century. [National Portrait Galley, London.]

principle of hereditary monarchy was too strong. Popular uprisings in London and elsewhere led to Jane Grey's removal from the throne within days of her crowning. She was eventually beheaded.

Once enthroned, Mary proceeded to repeal the Protestant statutes of Edward and return England to the strict Catholic religious practice of her father, Henry VIII.

Mary's half sister and successor, Elizabeth I (1558–1603), the daughter of Henry VIII and Anne Boleyn, was perhaps the most astute politician of the sixteenth century in both domestic and foreign policy. She repealed the anti-Protestant legislation of Mary and guided a religious settlement through Parliament that prevented England from being torn asunder by religious differences in the sixteenth century, as the Continent was.

Catholic extremists hoped to replace Elizabeth with the Catholic Mary Stuart, Queen of Scots. But Elizabeth acted swiftly against Catholic assassination plots and rarely let emotion override her political instincts.

Elizabeth dealt cautiously with the Puritans, who were Protestants working within the national church to "purify" it of every vestige of "popery" and to make its Protestant doctrine more precise. The Puritans had two special grievances: (1) the retention of Catholic ceremony and vestments within the Church of England, and (2) the continuation of the episcopal system of church governance.

Sixteenth-century Puritans were not separatists, however. They worked through Parliament to create an alternative national church of semiautonomous congregations governed by representative presbyteries (hence, Presbyterians), following the model of Calvin and Geneva. The more extreme Puritans wanted every congregation to be autonomous, a law unto itself, with neither higher episcopal nor presbyterian control. They came to be known as *Congregationalists.* Elizabeth refused to tolerate this group, whose views on independence seemed to her to be patently subversive.

DETERIORATION OF RELATIONS WITH SPAIN. A series of events led inexorably to war between England and Spain, despite the sincerest desires on the part of both Philip II and Elizabeth to avoid a direct confrontation. Following Don John's demonstration of Spain's seapower at the famous naval battle of Lepanto in 1571. England signed a mutual defense pact with France. Also in the 1570s, Elizabeth's famous seamen, John Hawkins (1532–1595) and Sir Francis Drake (1545?–1596), began to prey regularly on Spanish shipping in the Americas. Drake's circumnavigation of the glove between 1577 and 1580 was one in a series of dramatic demonstrations of English ascendancy on the high seas. In 1585, Elizabeth signed a treaty that committed English soldiers to the Nether-

dence of these provinces. Peace was not, however, concluded with Spain until 1609, when the Twelve Years' Truce gave the northern provinces their virtual independence. Full recognition came finally in the Peace of Westphalia in 1648.

England and Spain (1553–1603)

MARY I AND ELIZABETH I. Before Edward VI died in 1553, he had agreed to make the Protestant Lady Jane Grey—the teen-aged daughter of a powerful Protestant nobleman and, more important, the granddaughter on her mother's side of Henry VIII's *younger* sister Mary—his successor in place of the Catholic Mary Tudor (1553–1558). But popular support for the

lands. These events made a tinderbox of English–Spanish relations. The spark that finally touched it off was Elizabeth's reluctant execution of Mary, Queen of Scots (1542–1587) on February 18, 1587, for complicity in a plot to assassinate Elizabeth. Philip II ordered his Armada to make ready.

On May 30, 1588, a mighty fleet of 130 ships bearing twenty-five thousand sailors and soldiers under the command of the duke of Medina-Sidonia set sail for England. But the day belonged completely to the English. The invasion barges that were to transport Spanish soldiers from the galleons onto English shores were prevented from leaving Calais and Dunkirk. The swifter English and Netherlands ships, assisted by an "English wind," dispersed the waiting Spanish fleet, over one third of which never returned to Spain.

The news of the Armada's defeat gave heart to Protestant resistance everywhere. Although Spain continued to win impressive victories in the 1590s, it never fully recovered from this defeat. Spanish soldiers faced unified and inspired French, English, and Dutch armies. By the time of Philip's death on September 13, 1598, his forces had been successfully rebuffed on all fronts.

The Thirty Years' War (1618–1648)

In the second half of the sixteenth century, Germany was an almost ungovernable land of 360 autonomous political entities. The Peace of Augsburg (1555) had given each a significant degree of sovereignty within its own borders. Each levied its own tolls and tariffs and coined its own money, practices that made land travel and trade between the various regions difficult, where not impossible. In addition, many of these little "states" were filled with great power pretensions. Political decentralization and fragmentation

MAP 17-6 RELIGIOUS DIVISIONS ABOUT 1600 *By 1600 few could seriously expect Christians to return to a uniform religious allegiance. In Spain and southern Italy Catholicism remained relatively unchallenged, but note the existence of large religious minorities, both Catholic and Protestant, elsewhere.*

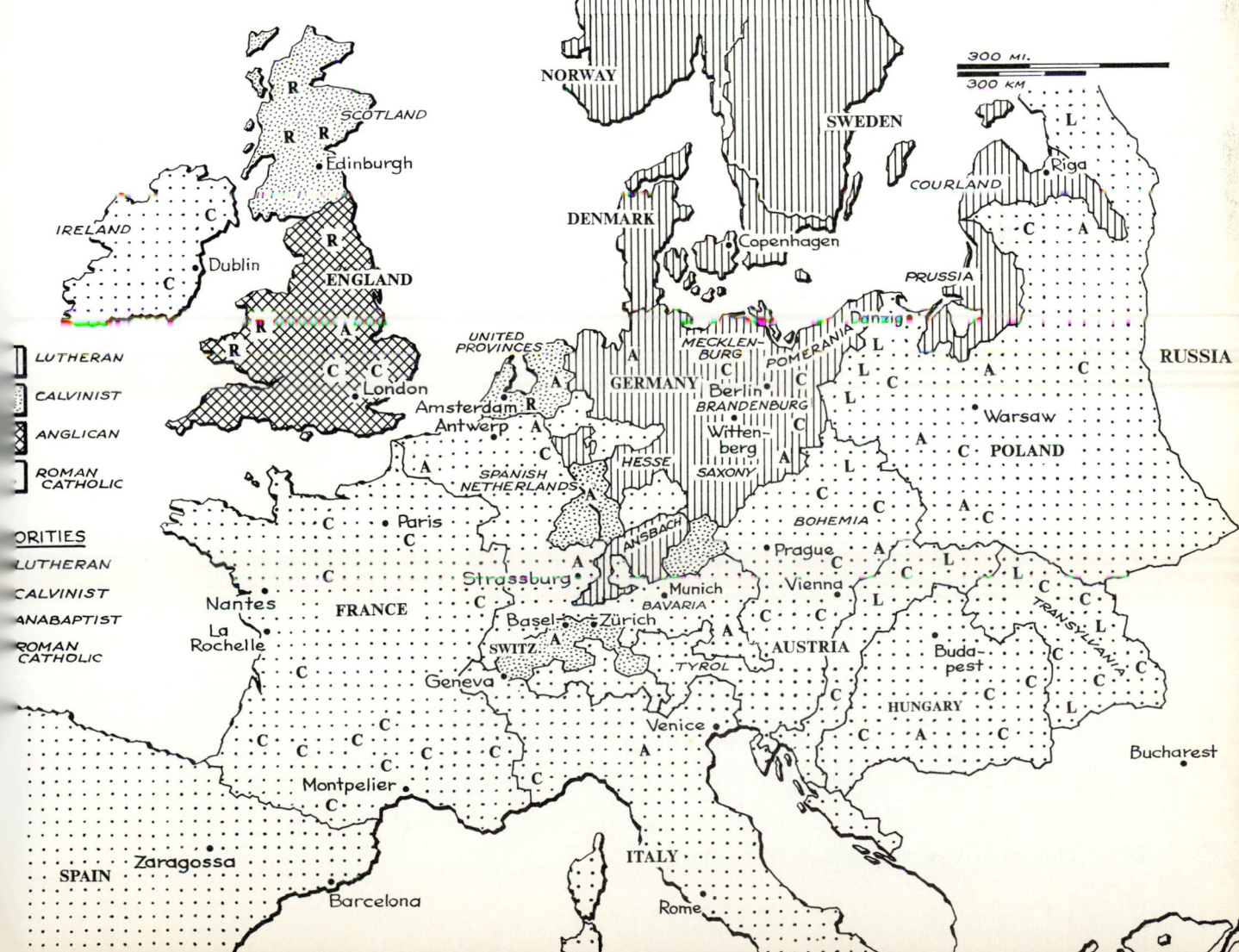

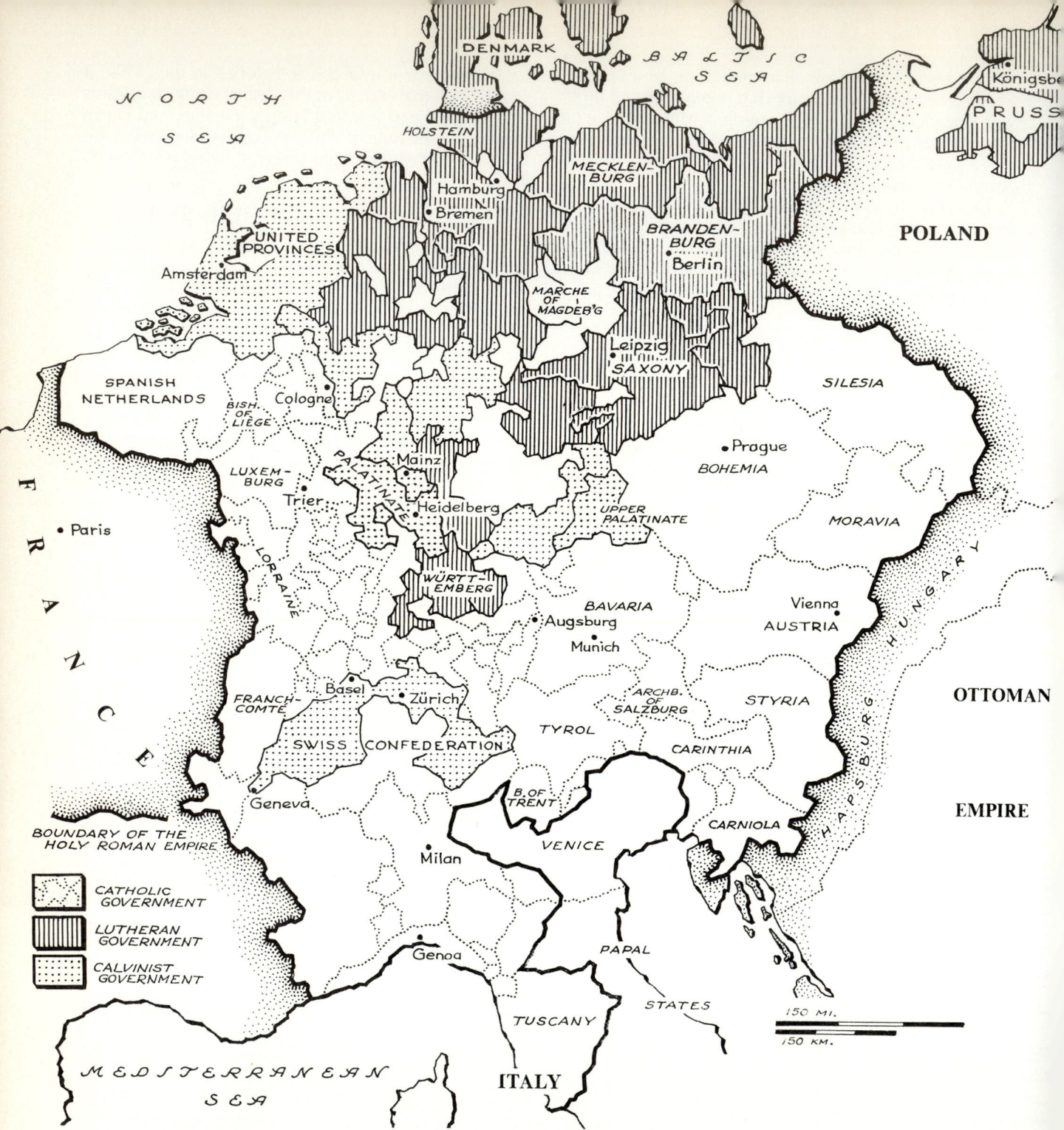

MAP 17-7 THE HOLY ROMAN EMPIRE ABOUT 1618   *On the eve of the Thirty Years' War the Empire was politically and religiously fragmented, as revealed by the somewhat simplified map. Lutherans dominated the north and Catholics the south, while Calvinists controlled the United Provinces and the Palatinate and were important in Switzerland and Brandenburg.*

characterized Germany as the seventeenth century opened; it was not a unified nation like Spain, England, or even strife-filled France.

Religious conflict accentuated the international and internal political divisions (see Map 17.7). During this period, the population within the Holy Roman Empire was about equally divided between Catholics and Protestants, the latter having perhaps a slight numerical edge by 1600. The terms of the Peace of Augsburg (1555) had attempted to freeze the territorial holdings of the Lutherans and the Catholics. In the intervening years, however, the Lutherans had gained political control in some Catholic areas, as had the Catholics in a few previously Lutheran areas. There was religious strife in the empire not only between Protestants and Catholics but also between liberal and conservative Lutherans and between Lutherans and the growing numbers of Calvinists.

As elsewhere in Europe, Calvinism was the political and religious leaven within the Holy Roman Empire. Unrecognized as a legal religion by the Peace of Augsburg, Calvinism established a strong foothold within the empire when Frederick III (1559–1576), a devout convert to Calvinism, made it the official religion of his land on becoming Elector Palatine (ruler within the Palatinate) in 1559. By 1609, Palatine Calvinists headed a Protestant defensive alliance supported by Spain's sixteenth-century enemies: England, France, and the Netherlands.

If the Calvinists were active within the Holy Roman Empire, so also were their Catholic counterparts, the Jesuits. Staunchly Catholic Bavaria, supported by Spain, became militarily and ideologically for the Counter-Reformation what the Palatinate was for Protestantism. From there, the Jesuits launched successful missions throughout the empire. In 1609, Maximilian, duke of Bavaria, organized a Catholic League to counter a new Protestant alliance that had been formed in the same year under the leadership of the Calvinist Elector Palatine, Frederick IV (1583–1610). When the league fielded a great army under the command of Count Johann von Tilly, the stage was set, both internally and internationally, for the worst of the religious wars, the Thirty Years' War.

During its course, the war drew in every major western European nation—at least diplomatically and financially if not in terms of direct military involvement. It was the worst European catastrophe since the Black Death of the fourteenth century.

The Treaty of Westphalia in 1648 brought all hostilities within the Holy Roman Empire to an end. It firmly reasserted the major feature of the religious settlement of the Peace of Augsburg (1555), as the ruler of each land was again permitted to determine the religion of his land. The treaty also gave the Calvinists their long-

sought legal recognition. The independence of the Swiss Confederacy and the United Provinces of Holland, long recognized in fact, was now proclaimed in law.

By confirming the territorial sovereignty of Germany's many political entities, the Treaty of Westphalia perpetuated German division and political weakness into the modern period. Only two German states attained any international significance during the seventeenth century: Austria and Brandenburg–Prussia. The petty regionalism within the empire also reflected on a small scale the drift of larger European politics. In the seventeenth century, distinctive nation-states, each with its own political, cultural, and religious identity, reached maturity and firmly established the competitive nationalism of the modern world.

Change and Conflict in Early Modern Society

Family Life

LATE MARRIAGES. Between 1500 and 1800, men and women married at later ages than they had done in previous centuries. Men tended to be in their mid- to late twenties rather than in their late teens and early twenties, and women in their early to mid-twenties rather than in their teens. In sixteenth-century Nuremberg, the legal minimum age for marriage without parental permission was set at twenty-five for men and twenty-three for women. The canonical or Church-sanctioned age for marriage remained fourteen for men and twelve for women, and marriage could still occur at such young ages if the parents agreed. As it had done throughout the high and later Middle Ages, the Church also recognized as valid the free, *private* exchange of vows between a man and a woman at these minimal ages. However, after the Reformation, which condemned such clandestine unions, the Church increasingly required both parental agreement and public vows in church for a fully licit marriage, a procedure it had, in fact, always preferred.

The late marriage pattern, generally observable in western Europe and England, resulted primarily from the difficulty a couple had supporting themselves as an independent family unit. Such support had become difficult because of the large population increase that occurred in the fifteenth and early sixteenth centuries, when western Europe was recovering from the great plague. Larger families meant more heirs and a greater division of resources. In Germanic and Scandinavian countries, the custom of a fair sharing of inheritance among all male children worked both to delay marriages, as more got less, and to encourage independent family units, as children did not have to remain in the family home indefinitely and live off the charity of the eldest brother after the death of their parents, as more often happened in England where primogeniture (right of the first-born son to inherit all property) remained strong. Still, it took the average couple a longer time to prepare themselves materially for marriage. Many never married. An estimated 20 per cent of all women remained spinsters in the sixteenth century. Combined with the estimated 15 per cent who were unmarried widows, this made up to a sizable unmarried female population.

Marriage tended to be "arranged" in the sense that the male heads of the two families met and discussed the terms of the marriage before they informed the prospective bride and bridegroom. However, it was rare for the two people involved not to know each other in advance or not to have a prior relationship. Parents did not force total strangers to live together, and children always had a legal right to protest and resist an unwanted marriage. A forced marriage was, by definition, invalid, and no one believed an unwanted marriage would last. The best marriage was one desired by both parties and supported by their families.

Later marriages meant marriages of shorter duration because couples who married in their thirties would not spend as much time together as couples who married in their twenties. Such marriages also contributed to more frequent remarriage because women bearing children for the first time at advanced ages had higher mortality rates than younger mothers. Later marriages also worked to slow overall population growth, although not by directly preventing older women from having as many children as younger women. Women who married later in life still had children in rapid succession, but with increased risk to health and life and hence with greater maternal mortality. As growing Church condemnation confirms, delayed marriage increased fornication. It also raised the number of illegitimate children, as is testified by the rapid growth of orphanages and foundling homes between 1600 and 1800.

FAMILY SIZE. The early modern family was conjugal or nuclear; that is, it consisted of a father and a mother and two to four children who managed to live into adulthood. The average husband and wife had six to eight children, a birth about every two years. Of these, however, an estimated one third died by age five, and one half were gone by age twenty. Rare was the family, at any social level, that did not learn first-

A sixteenth-century German family. This was a fairly comfortable household, as witnessed by the many toys and the maidservant. Note that the mother is nursing her youngest child herself. [Bildarchiv Preussicher Kulturbesitz.]

Children's Games, by Pieter Brueghel, painted in 1560. Seventy-eight different games are depicted. [Kunsthistorisches Museum, Vienna.]

hand about infant mortality and child death. The Protestant reformer Martin Luther was typical. He married late in life (at forty-two, here atypical) and fathered six children, two of whom he lost, an infant daughter at eight months and another, more painfully, at thirteen years.

BIRTH CONTROL. Artificial birth control had existed since antiquity. (The ancient Egyptians used acidic alligator dung, and the use of sponges was equally old.) The Church's frequent condemnation of *coitus interruptus* (male withdrawal before ejaculation) in the thirteenth and fourteenth centuries suggests that a "contraceptive mentality"—that is, a conscious and regular effort at birth control—may have developed in the later Middle Ages. Birth control was not, however, very effective, and for both historical and moral reasons the Church firmly opposed it. During the eleventh century the Church suppressed an extreme ascetic sect, the Cathars, that had practiced birth control, when not abstaining from sex altogether,

on the grounds that to propagate the human species was to encase immortal souls in evil matter. But the Church also turned against contraception on moral grounds. According to its most authoritative theologian, Saint Thomas Aquinas, a moral act must always aid and abet, never frustrate, the natural end of a creaturely process. In the eyes of Aquinas and his church, the natural end of sex could be only the production of children and their subsequent rearing to the glory of God within the bounds of holy matrimony and the community of the Church.

Despite the Church's official opposition on contraception, it is likely that more general Christian moral teaching actually reinforced a contraceptive mentality within the early modern family by encouraging men to be more sensitive husbands and fathers. As men identified emotionally with wives who suffered painful, debilitating, unwanted, life-threatening, serial pregnancies (the chances of dying in childbirth were about one in ten) and with hungry children in overcrowded families, Christian love may also have persuaded a father that *coitus interruptus* was a moral course of action.

WET NURSING. The church allied with the physicians of early modern Europe on another intimate family matter: the condemnation of upper-class women who put their newborn children out to wet nurses for as long as eighteen months. Wet nurses were women who had recently had a baby or were suckling a child of their own, and who, for a fee, agreed also to suckle another child. The practice appears to have greatly increased the risk of infant mortality, as an infant received a strange and shared milk supply from a woman who was usually not as healthy as its own mother and who often lived under less sanitary conditions.

But nursing a child was a chore some upper-class women, and especially their husbands, found distasteful. Among women, vanity and convenience appear to have been motives for turning to wet nurses. For husbands, even more was at stake in the practice. Because the Church forbade sexual intercourse while a woman was lactating, and sexual intercourse was believed to spoil a lactating woman's milk, (pregnancy, of course, eventually ended her milk supply), a nursing wife often became a reluctant lover. In addition, nursing had a contraceptive effect (about 75 per cent effective). There is good evidence that some women prolonged nursing their children precisely in order to delay a new pregnancy—and loving husbands understood and cooperated in this form of family planning. For other husbands, however, especially wealthy burghers and noblemen who desired an abundance of male heirs, nursing seemed to rob them of sex and offspring and to jeopardize the patrimony. Hence, their strong support of wet nursing.

LOVING FAMILIES? The early modern family had features that seem cold and unloving. Not only did parents give infants to wet nurses, but later, when the children were between the ages of eight and thirteen, parents sent them out of their houses altogether into apprenticeships or to employment in the homes and businesses of relatives, friends, or even strangers. The affective ties between spouses seem to have been as tenuous as those between parents and children. Widowers and widows sometimes remarried within a few months of their spouse's death, and marriages with extreme disparity in age—especially between older men and younger women—also suggest low affection.

Love and affection, however, are as relative to time and culture as other values. A kindness in one historical period can be a cruelty in another. "What greater love," an early modern parent would surely have asked a modern critic, "can parents have for their children than to equip them to make their way vocationally in the world?" An apprenticed child was a child

with a future. Because of primitive living conditions, contemporaries could also appreciate the purely utilitarian and humane side of marriage and wink at quick remarriages. On the other hand, marriages with extreme disparity in age were no more the norm in early modern Europe than was the practice of wet nursing, and they received just as much criticism and ridicule.

Witchcraft and Witch-Hunts

Between 1400 and 1700, courts sentenced an estimated 70,000–100,000 people to death for harmful magic (*malificium*) and diabolical witchcraft. In addition to supposedly inflicting harm on their neighbors, these witches were said to attend mass meetings known as *sabbats*, to which they were believed to fly. They were also accused of indulging in sexual orgies with the Devil, who appeared at such gatherings in animal form, most often as a he-goat. Still other charges against them were cannibalism (they were alleged to be especially fond of small Christian children) and a variety of ritual acts and practices designed to insult every Christian belief and value.

Where did such beliefs come from? Their roots were in both popular and elite cultures, especially clerical culture.

In village societies, so-called cunning folk played a positive role in helping people cope with calamity. People turned to them for help when such natural disasters as plague and famine struck or when such physical disabilities as lameness or inability to conceive offspring befell either them or their animals. The cunning folk provided consolation and gave people hope that such natural calamities might be averted or reversed by magical means.

Possession of magical powers, for good or ill, made one an important person within village society. Not surprisingly, claims to such powers seem most often to have been made by the people most in need of security and influence, namely, the old and the impoverished, especially single or widowed women. But witch beliefs in village society may also have been a way of defying urban Christian society's attempts to impose its laws and institutions on the countryside. From this perspective, village Satanism became a fanciful substitute for an impossible social revolt, a way of spurning the values of one's new masters. It is also possible, although unlikely, that witch beliefs in rural society had a foundation in local fertility cults, whose semipagan practices, designed to ensure good harvests, acquired the features of diabolical witchcraft under Church persecution.

Popular belief in magic was the essential foundation on the great witch hunts of the sixteenth and seventeenth centuries. Had ordinary people not believed that certain gifted individuals could aid or harm others

A Confession of Witchcraft

A confession of witchcraft is here exacted from a burgomaster during a witch panic in seventeenth-century Bamberg in central Germany. The account, an official transcript, accurately describes the process by which an innocent victim was brought, step by step, to confession—from the confrontation with his accusers to the application of increasingly painful tortures. By at last concurring in the accusation (albeit reluctantly and only after torture), the victims were believed by their executioners to be saving the victims' souls as they lost their bodies. Having the victims' own confession may also have helped allay the executioners' consciences.

On Wednesday, June 28, 1628, was examined without torture Johannes Junius, Burgomaster at Bamberg, on the charge of witchcraft: how and in what fashion he had fallen into that vice. Is fifty-five years old, and was born at Niederwaysich in the Wetterau. Says he is wholly innocent, knows nothing of the crime, has never in his life renounced God; says that he is wronged before God and the world, would like to hear of a single human being who has seen him at such gatherings [as the witch sabbats].

Confrontation of Dr. Georg Adam Haan. Tells him to his face that he will stake his life on it, that he saw him, Junius, a year and a half ago at a witch-gathering in the electoral council-room, where they ate and drank. Accused denies the same wholly.

Confronted with Hopffens Elsse. Tells him likewise that he was on Haupts-moor at a witch-dance; but first the holy wafer was desecrated. Junius denies. Hereupon he was told that his accomplices had confessed against him and he was given time for thought.

On Friday, June 30, 1628, the aforesaid Junius was again without torture exhorted to confess, but again confessed nothing, whereupon, . . . since he would confess nothing, he was put to the torture, and first the

Thumb-screws were applied [both hands bound together, so that the blood ran out at the nails and everywhere]. Says he has never denied God his Saviour nor suffered himself to be otherwise baptized [i.e., initiated into devilish rites]. Will again stake his life on it; feels no pain in the thumb-screws.

Leg-screws. Will confess absolutely nothing; knows nothing about it. He has never renounced God; will never do such a thing; has never been guilty of this vice; feels likewise no pain. Is stripped and examined; on his right side is found a bluish mark, like a clover leaf, is thrice pricked therein, but feels no pain and no blood flows out.

Strappado [the binding of the prisoner's hands behind the back, and pulling them up by a rope attached to a pulley, resulting in the slow dislocation of the shoulders]. Says he never renounced God; God will not forsake him; if he were such a wretch he would not let himself be so tortured; God must show some token of his innocence. He knows nothing about witchcraft. . . .

On July 5, the above named Junius is without torture, but with urgent persuasions, exhorted to confess, and at last he . . . confesses. ❑

Translations and Reprints from the Original Sources of European History, Vol. 3 (Philadelphia: University of Pennsylvania, 1912), pp. 23–24.

by magical means, and had they not been willing to make accusations, the hunts could never have occurred. But the contribution of learned society was equally great. The Christian clergy also practiced a kind of magic, that of the holy sacraments, and the exorcism of demons had been one of their traditional functions within society. Fear of demons and the Devil, which the clergy actively encouraged, allowed them to assert their moral authority over people and to enforce religious discipline and conformity.

In the late thirteenth century, the Church declared that only its priests possessed legitimate magical power. Inasmuch as such power was not human, theologians reasoned, it had to come either from God or from the Devil. If it came from God, then it was obediently confined to and exercised only on behalf of the Church. Those who practiced magic outside the Church evidently derived their power from the Devil.

From such reasoning grew accusations of "pacts" between non-Christian magicians and Satan. This made the witch hunts a life-and-death struggle against Christian society's worst heretics and foes, those who had directly sworn allegiance to the Devil himself.

The Church based its intolerance of magic outside its walls on sincere belief in and fear of the Devil. But attacking witches was also a way for established Christian society to extend its power and influence into new areas. To accuse, try, and execute witches was also a declaration of moral and political authority over a village or territory. As the "cunning folk" were local spiritual authorities, revered and feared by people, their removal became a major step in the establishment of a Christian beachhead in village society.

About 80 per cent of the victims of witch hunts were women, the vast majority between forty-five and sixty years of age and widowed. This fact has suggested to some that misogyny fueled the witch-hunts. Based in male hatred and sexual fear of women, and occurring at a time when women threatened to break out from under male control, witch hunts, it is argued, were simply woman hunts. Older women may, however, have been vulnerable for more basic social reasons. As a largely nonproductive and dependent social group, ever in need of public assistance, older and widowed women became natural targets for the peculiar "social engineering" of the witch-hunts.

It may, however, be the case that gender played a purely circumstantial role. Because of their economic straits, more women than men laid claim to the supernatural powers that made them influential in village society. For this reason, they found themselves on the front lines in disproportionate numbers when the Church declared war against all who practiced magic without its blessing. Also, the involvement of many of these women in midwifery associated them with the deaths of beloved wives and infants and thus made them targets of local resentment and accusations. Both the Church and their neighbors were prepared to think and say the worst about these women. It was a deadly combination.

Why did the witch hunts come to an end in the seventeenth century? Many factors played a role. The emergence of a new, more scientific worldview made it difficult to believe in the powers of witches. When, in the seventeenth century, mind and matter came to be viewed as two independent realities, words and thoughts lost the ability to affect things. A witch's curse was merely words. With advances in medicine and the beginning of insurance companies people learned to rely on themselves when faced with natural calamity and physical affliction and no longer searched for supernatural causes and solutions.

Witch hunts also tended to get out of hand. Accused witches sometimes alleged that important townspeople had attended sabbats; even the judges could be so accused. At this point, the trials ceased to serve the purposes of those who were conducting them. They not only became dysfunctional but threatened anarchy.

Finally, the Reformation may have contributed to an attitude of mind that put the Devil in a more manageable perspective. Protestants ridiculed the sacramental magic of the old church as superstition and directed their faith to a sovereign God absolutely supreme over time and eternity. Even the Devil served God's purposes and acted only with His permission. Ultimately, God was the only significant spiritual force in the universe. This belief made the Devil a less fearsome creature. "One little word can slay him," Luther wrote of the Devil in the great hymn of the Reformation, and he often joked outrageously about witches.

Writers and Philosophers

The end of the sixteenth century saw much weariness with religious strife and incipient unbelief as many could no longer embrace either old Catholic or new Protestant absolutes. Intellectually as well as politically, the seventeenth century would be a period of transition, one already well prepared for by the thinkers of the Renaissance, who had reacted strongly against medieval intellectual traditions.

The writers and philosophers of the late sixteenth and seventeenth centuries were aware that they lived in a period of transition. Some embraced the emerging new science wholeheartedly (Hobbes and Locke), some tried to straddle the two ages (Cervantes and Shakespeare), and still others ignored or opposed the new developments that seemed mortally to threaten traditional values (Pascal).

MIGUEL DE CERVANTES SAAVEDRA. Spanish literature of the sixteenth and seventeenth centuries was influenced by the peculiar religious and political history of Spain in this period. Spain was dominated by the Catholic church and by the aggressive piety of the Spanish rulers Charles I—who became the Holy Roman Emperor as Charles V (1516–1556)—and his son, Philip II (1556–1598). The intertwining of Catholic piety and Spanish political power underlay literary preoccupation with medieval chivalric virtues—in particular, reflected in questions of honor and loyalty.

Generally acknowledged to be the greatest Spanish writer of all time, Cervantes (1547–1616), was preoccupied in his work with the strengths and weaknesses of religious idealism. Cervantes was the son of a nomadic physician. Having received only a smattering of formal education, he educated himself by insatiable reading in vernacular literature and immersion in the "school of life." As a young man, he worked in Rome for a Spanish cardinal. In 1570, he became a soldier and was decorated for gallantry in the Battle of Lepanto (1571). He conceived and began to write his most famous work, *Don Quixote*, in 1603, while languishing in prison after conviction for theft.

The first part of *Don Quixote* appeared in 1605, and a second part followed in 1615. If, as many argue, the intent of this work was to satirize the chivalric romances so popular in Spain, Cervantes failed to conceal his deep affection for the character he had created as an object of ridicule, Don Quixote. Don Quixote, a none-too-stable middle-aged man, is driven mad by reading too many chivalric romances. He comes to believe that he is an aspirant to knighthood and must prove his worthiness. To this end, he acquires a rusty suit of armor, mounts an aged horse, and chooses for his inspiration a quite unworthy peasant girl whom he fancies to be a noble lady to whom he can, with honor, dedicate his life.

Don Quixote's foil in the story—Sancho Panza, a clever, wordly-wise peasant who serves as Don Quixote's squire—watches with bemused skepticism, but also with genuine sympathy, as his lord does battle with a windmill (which he mistakes for a dragon) and repeatedly makes a fool of himself as he gallops across the countryside. The story ends tragically with Don Quixote's humiliating defeat by a well-meaning friend, who, disguised as a knight, bests Don Quixote in combat and forces him to renounce his quest for knighthood. The humiliated Don Quixote does not, however, come to his senses as a result. He returns sadly to his village to die a shamed and broken-hearted old man.

Throughout *Don Quixote*, Cervantes juxtaposed the down-to-earth realism of Sancho Panza with the old-fashioned religious idealism of Don Quixote. The reader perceives that Cervantes really admired the one as much as the other and meant to portray both as attitudes necessary for a happy life. Cervantes wanted his readers to remember that if they are to be truly happy, men and women need dreams, even impossible ones, just as much as they need a sense of reality.

WILLIAM SHAKESPEARE. There is much less factual knowledge about William Shakespeare (1564–1616), the greatest playwright in the English language, than one would expect of such an important figure. He apparently worked as a schoolteacher for a time and in this capacity acquired his broad knowledge of Renaissance learning and literature. There is none of the Puritan distress over worldliness in his work. He took the new commercialism and the bawdy pleasures of the Elizabethan Age in stride and with amusement. In matters of politics, as in those of religion, he was very much a man of his time and not inclined to offend his queen.

That Shakespeare was interested in politics is apparent from his history plays and the references to contemporary political events that fill all his plays. He seems to have viewed government simply, however, through the character of the individual ruler, whether Richard III or Elizabeth Tudor, not in terms of ideal systems or social goals. By modern standards, he was a political conservative, accepting the social rankings and the power structure of his day and demonstrating unquestioned patriotism.

Shakespeare knew the theater as one who participated in every phase of its life—as a playwright, an actor, and a part owner of a theater. He was a member and principal dramatist of a famous company of actors known as the King's Men.

Shakespeare's work was an original synthesis of the

The English dramatist and poet, William Shakespeare. This engraving by Martin Droeshout appears on the title page of the collected edition of his plays published in 1623 and is probably as close as we shall come to knowing what he looked like.

best past and current achievements. He mastered the psychology of human motivation and passion and had a unique talent for psychological penetration.

Shakespeare wrote histories, comedies, and tragedies. The tragedies are considered his unique achievement. Four of these were written within a three-year period: *Hamlet* (1603), *Othello* (1604), *King Lear* (1605), and *Macbeth* (1606). The most original of the tragedies, *Romeo and Juliet* (1597), transformed an old popular story into a moving drama of "star-cross'd lovers." Both Romeo and Juliet, denied a marriage by their factious families, die tragic deaths. Romeo, finding Juliet and thinking her dead after she has taken a sleeping potion, poisons himself. Juliet, awakening to find Romeo dead, stabs herself to death with his dagger.

Throughout his lifetime and ever since, Shakespeare has been immensely popular with both the playgoer and the play reader. As Ben Jonson, a contemporary classical dramatist who created his own school of poets, put it in a tribute affixed to the First Folio edition of Shakespeare's plays (1623): "He was not of an age, but for all time."

Pascal Meditates on Human Beings as Thinking Creatures

Pascal was both a religious and a scientific writer. Unlike other scientific thinkers of the seventeenth century, he was not overly optimistic about the ability of science to improve the human condition. Pascal believed that science and philosophy would instead help human beings to understand their situation better. In these passages from his Pensées (Thoughts), *he discussed the uniqueness of human beings as the creatures who alone in all the universe are capable of thinking.*

339

I can well conceive a man without hands, feet, head (for it is only experience which teaches us that the head is more necessary than feet). But I cannot conceive man without thought; he would be a stone or a brute.

344

Reason commands us far more imperiously than a master; for in disobeying the one we are unfortunate, and in disobeying the other we are fools.

346

Thought constitutes the greatness of man.

347

Man is but a reed, the most feeble thing in nature; but he is a thinking reed. The entire universe need not arm itself to crush him. A vapour, a drop of water suffices to kill him. But, if the universe were to crush him, man would still be more noble than that which killed him, because he knows that he dies and the advantage which the univese has over him: the universe knows nothing of this.

All our dignity consists, then, in thought. By it we must elevate ourselves, and not by space and time which we cannot fill. Let us endeavour, then, to think well: this is the principle of morality.

348

A thinking reed—It is not from space that I must seek my dignity, but from the government of my thought. I shall have no more if I possess worlds. By space the universe encompasses and swallows me up like an atom; by thought I comprehend the world. ❑

Blaise Pascal, *Pensées and The Provincial Letters* (New York: Modern Library, 1941), pp. 115–116.

BLAISE PASCAL. Pascal (1623–1662) was a French mathematician and a physical scientist widely acclaimed by his contemporaries. Torn between the continuing dogmatism and the new skepticism of the seventeenth century, he aspired to write a work that would refute both the Jesuits, whose casuistry (i.e., confessional tactics designed to minimize and even excuse sinful acts) he considered a distortion of Christian teaching, and the skeptics, who either denied religion altogether (atheists) or accepted it only as it conformed to reason (deists). Pascal never realized such a definitive work and his views on these matters exist only in piecemeal form. He wrote against the Jesuits in his *Provincial Letters* (1656–1657), and he left behind a provocative collection of reflections on humankind and religion that was published posthumously under the title *Pensées*.

Pascal was early influenced by the Jansenists, seventeenth-century Catholic opponents of the Jesuits. The Jansenists shared with the Calvinists St. Augustine's belief in the total sinfulness of human beings, their eternal predestination by God, and their complete dependence on faith and grace for knowledge of God and salvation.

Pascal believed that reason and science, although attesting to human dignity, remained of no avail in matters of religion. Here only the reasons of the heart and a "leap of faith" could prevail. Pascal saw two essential truths in the Christian religion: that a loving God, worthy of human attainment, exists, and that human beings, because they are corrupted in nature, are utterly unworthy of God. Pascal believed that the atheists and deists of the age had spurned the lesson of reason. For him, rational analysis of the human condition attested to humankind's utter mortality and corruption and exposed the weakness of reason itself in resolving the problems of human nature and destiny. Reason should rather drive those who truly heed it to faith and dependence on divine grace.

Pascal made a famous wager with the skeptics. It is a better bet, he argued, to believe that God exists and to stake everything on his promised mercy than not to do so, because if God does exist, everything will be gained by the believer, whereas the loss incurred by having believed in God should he prove not to exist is by comparison very slight.

Pascal was convinced that belief in God measurably improved earthly life psychologically and disciplined it morally, regardless of whether or not God proved in the end to exist. He thought that great danger lay in the surrender of traditional religious values. Pascal urged his contemporaries to seek self-understanding by "learned ignorance" and to discover humankind's greatness by recognizing its misery. Thereby he hoped to counter what he believed to be the false optimism of the new rationalism and science.

BARUCH SPINOZA. The most controversial thinker of the seventeenth century was Baruch Spinoza (1632–1677), the son of a Jewish merchant of Amsterdam. Spinoza's philosophy caused his excommunication by his own synagogue in 1656. In 1670, he published his *Treatise on Religious and Political Philosophy*, a work that criticized the dogmatism of Dutch Calvinists and championed freedom of thought. During his lifetime, both Jews and Protestants attacked him as an atheist.

Spinoza's most influential writing, the *Ethics*, appeared after his death in 1677. Religious leaders universally condemned it for its apparent espousal of pantheism. God and nature were so closely identified by Spinoza that little room seemed left either for divine revelation in Scripture or for the personal immortality of the soul, denials equally repugnant to Jews and to Christians. The *Ethics* is a very complicated work, written in the spirit of the new science as a geometrical system of definitions, axioms, and propositions.

The most controversial part of the *Ethics* deals with the nature of substance and of God. According to Spinoza, there is only one substance, which is self-caused, free, and infinite, and God is that substance. From this definition, it follows that everything that exists is in God and cannot even be conceived of apart from him. Such a doctrine is not literally pantheistic, because God is still seen to be more than the created world that he, as primal substance, embraces. Nonetheless, in Spinoza's view, statements about the natural world are also statements about divine nature. Mind and matter are seen to be extensions of the infinite substance of God; what transpires in the world of humankind and nature is a necessary outpouring of the divine.

Such teaching clearly ran the danger of portraying the world as eternal and human actions as unfree and inevitable, the expression of a divine fatalism. Such points of view had been considered heresies by Jews and Christians because the views deny the creation of the world by God in time and destroy any voluntary basis for personal reward and punishment.

THOMAS HOBBES. Thomas Hobbes (1588–1679) was the most original political philosopher of the seventeenth century. Although he never broke with the Church of England, he came to share basic Calvinist beliefs, especially the low view of human nature and

the ideal of a commonwealth based on a covenant, both of which find eloquent expression in Hobbes' political philosophy.

Hobbes was an urbane and much-traveled man and one of the most enthusiastic supporters of the new scientific movement. During the 1630s, he visited Paris, where he came to know Descartes, and after the outbreak of the Puritan Revolution (see Chapter 19) in 1640, he lived as an exile in Paris until 1651. Hobbes also spent time with Galileo in Italy and took a special interest in the works of William Harvey (1578–1657). (See Chapter 23.) Harvey was a physiologist famed for the discovery of how blood circulated through the body; his scientific writings influenced Hobbes' own tracts on bodily motions.

Hobbes was driven to the vocation of political philosophy by the English Civil War. (See Chapter 19.) In 1651, his *Leviathan* appeared. Its subject was the political consequences of human passions, and its originality lay in (1) its making natural law, rather than common law (i.e., custom or precedent), the basis of all positive law, and (2) its defense of a representative theory of absolute authority against the theory of the divine right of kings. Hobbes maintained that statute law found its justification only as an expression of the law of nature and that political authority came to rulers by way of the consent of the people.

Hobbes viewed humankind and society in a thoroughly materialistic and mechanical way. Human beings are defined as a collection of material particles in motion. All their psychological processes begin with and are derived from bare sensation, and all their motivations are egoistical, intended to increase pleasure and minimize pain.

Despite this seemingly low estimate of human beings, Hobbes believed much could be accomplished by the reasoned use of science. All was contingent, however, on the correct use of that greatest of all human powers, one compounded of the powers of most people: the commonwealth, in which people are united by their consent in one all-powerful person.

The key to Hobbes' political philosophy is a brilliant myth of the original state of humankind. According to this myth, human beings in the natural state are generally inclined to a "perpetual and restless desire of power after power that ceases only in death."[2] As all people desire and in the state of nature have a natural right to everything, their equality breeds enmity, competition, and diffidence, and the desire for glory begets perpetual quarreling—"a war of every man against every man."[3]

Whereas earlier and later philosophers saw the

[2] *Leviathan Parts I and II*, ed. by H. W. Schneider (Indianapolis: Bobbs-Merrill, 1958), p. 86.

[3] Ibid., p. 106.

The famous title-page illustration for Hobbes's Leviathan. *The ruler is pictured as absolute lord of his lands, but note that he incorporates the mass of individuals whose self-interests are best served by their willing consent to accept and cooperate with him.*

original human state as a paradise from which humankind had fallen, Hobbes saw it as a corruption from which only society had delivered people. Contrary to the views of Aristotle and of Christian thinkers like Thomas Aquinas, in the view of Hobbes human beings are not by nature sociable, political animals; they are self-centered beasts, laws unto themselves, utterly without a master unless one is imposed by force.

According to Hobbes, people escape the impossible state of nature only by entering a social contract that creates a commonwealth tightly ruled by law and order. The social contract obliges every person, for the sake of peace and self-defense, to agree to set aside personal rights to all things and to be content with as much liberty against others as he or she would allow others against himself or herself.

Because words and promises are insufficient to guarantee this state, the social contract also establishes the coercive force necessary to compel compliance with the covenant. Hobbes believed that the dangers of anarchy were far greater than those of tyranny, and he conceived of the ruler as absolute and unlimited in power, once established in office. There is no room in Hobbes's political philosophy for political protest in the name of individual conscience, nor for resistance to legitimate authority by private individuals—features of the *Leviathan* criticized by his contemporary Catholics and Puritans alike.

John Locke

Locke (1632–1704) has proved to be the most influential political thinker[4] of the seventeenth century. His political philosophy came to be embodied in the Glori-

[4]Locke's scientific writings are discussed in Chapter 23.

ous Revolution of 1688–1689. Although he was not as original as Hobbes, his political writings were a major source of the later Enlightenment criticism of absolutism, and they gave inspiration to both the American and the French revolutions.

Locke read deeply in the works of Francis Bacon, René Descartes, and Isaac Newton and was a close friend of the English physicist and chemist Robert Boyle (1627–1691). Some argue that he was the first philosopher to be successful in synthesizing the rationalism of Descartes and the experimental science of Bacon, Newton, and Boyle.

Locke's two most famous works are the *Essay Concerning Human Understanding* (1690) (discussed in Chapter 23) and the *Two Treatises of Government* (1690). Locke wrote *Two Treatises of Government* against the argument that rulers were absolute in their power. Rulers, Locke argued, remain bound to the law of nature, which is the voice of reason, teaching that "all mankind [are] equal and independent, [and] no one ought to harm another in his life, health, liberty, or possessions,"[5] inasmuch as all human beings are the images and property of God. According to Locke, people enter into social contracts, empowering legislatures and monarchs to "umpire" their disputes, precisely in order to preserve their natural rights, and not to give rulers an absolute power over them.

Whenever that end [namely, the preservation of life, liberty, and property for which power is given to rulers by a commonwealth] is manifestly neglected or opposed, the trust must necessarily be forfeited and the power devolved into the hands of those that gave it, who may place it anew where they think best for their safety and security.[6]

From Locke's point of view, absolute monarchy was "inconsistent" with civil society and could be "no form of civil government at all."

Locke's main differences with Hobbes stemmed from the latter's views on the state of nature. Locke believed that the natural human state was one of perfect freedom and equality. Here the natural rights of life, liberty, and property were enjoyed, in unregulated fashion, by all. The only thing lacking in the state of nature was a single authority to give judgment when disputes inevitably arose because of the natural freedom and equality possessed by all. Contrary to the view of Hobbes, human beings in their natural state were not creatures of monomaniacal passion but were possessed of extreme goodwill and rationality. They did not surrender their natural rights unconditionally when they entered the social contract; rather, they es-

tablished a means whereby these rights could be better preserved. The state of warfare that Hobbes believed characterized the state of nature emerged for Locke only when rulers failed in their responsibility to preserve the freedoms of the state of nature and attempted to enslave people by absolute rule, that is, to remove them from their "natural" condition. Only then were the peace, goodwill, mutual assistance, and preservation in which human beings naturally live and socially ought to live undermined, and a state of war was created.

The Renaissance and Reformation in World Perspective

During the Renaissance, Western Europe recovered its classical cultural heritage, from which it had been separated for almost eight centuries. No other world civilization had known such disjunction from its cultural past. It was due to the work of Byzantine and Islamic scholars that ancient Greek science and scholarship were rediscovered in the West. In this period, Western Europe also recovered from national wars to establish permanent centralized states and regional governments. Even the great population losses of the fourteenth century were recovered by 1500. By the late fifteenth and sixteenth centuries, Europeans were in a position to venture far afield to the shores of Africa, southern and eastern Asia, and the new world of the Americas directly confronting for the first time the different civilizations of the world from Japan to Brazil.

But Western history between 1500 and 1650 was especially shaped by an unprecedented schism in Christianity, as Lutherans and other Protestant groups broke with Rome. The religious divisions contributed to both national and international warfare, which by the seventeenth century devastated the empire on a scale unseen since the Black Death.

The other world civilizations moved more slowly, maintained greater social and political unity, and remained unquestionably more tolerant of religious belief than the West. Under Mongol rule (1279–1368), China tolerated all indigenous religions as well as Islam and Eastern Christianity. No crises on the scale of those that rocked the West struck China, although plagues in 1586–1589 and 1639–1644 killed 20–30 per cent of the inhabitants in populous regions. China moved steadily from Mongol to Ming (1368–1644) to Ching (1644–1911) rule without major social and political upheaval. By Western comparison, its society was socially static, and its rulers maintained unified, even despotic, control. Whereas the West also had highly centralized and authoritarian governments between 1350 and 1650, unlike China, it also managed more

---

[5] *The Second Treatise of Government*, ed. by T. P. Peardon (Indianapolis: Bobbs-Merrill, 1952), Ch. 2, sects. 4-6, pp. 4-6.

[6] Ibid. Ch. 13, sect. 149, p. 84.

successfully to balance the interests of the one with those of the many. In the West, parliaments and estates general, representing the nobility, and lesser representative political bodies gained a permanent right to express their views forcefully to higher authority.

Although parallels may be drawn between the court culture of the Forbidden Palace in Peking and that of King Louis XIV in seventeenth-century France, Chinese government and religious philosophy (Confucianism) remained more unified and patriarchal than their counterparts in the West. There was never the degree of political dissent and readiness to fragment Chinese society in the name of religion that characterized Western society even in the West's own "age of absolutism." On the other hand, the Chinese readily tolerated other religions, as their warm embrace of Jesuit missionaries attests. There is no similar Western demonstration of tolerance for Asian religious philosophy.

Voyages of exploration also set forth from Ming China, especially between 1405 and 1433, reaching India, the Arabian gulf, and East Africa. These voyages did not, however, prove to be commercially profitable as those of the West would be, nor did they spark any notable commercial development in China. It is an open question whether this was because the Chinese were less greedy, curious, or belligerent than the Portuguese and Spanish.

Like the West in the later Middle Ages, Japan experienced its own political and social breakdown after 1467, when the Bakufu government began to collapse. Japan's old manorial society progressively fell apart, and a new military class of vassalized foot soldiers, armed with spears and muskets, replaced the mounted samurai as the new military force. In 1590, Hideyoshi (1536–1598) disarmed the peasantry and froze the social classes, thereby laying the foundation for a new social and political order in Japan. On this achievement, Tokugawa rule (1600–1850) managed to stabilize and centralize the government by 1650. Much as Western kings had to "domesticate" their powerful noblemen to succeed, Japanese emperors learned to integrate the many regional daimyo lords into imperial government. Like Louis XIV, Tokugawa emperors required these lords to live for long periods of time at court, where their wives and children also remained. As in most Western countries, the emperors of Japan thus avoided both fragmented and absolutist government.

Like the Chinese, the Japanese were also admirers of the Jesuits, who arrived in Japan with the Portuguese in 1543. The admiration was mutual, leading to 300,000 Christian converts by 1600. As in China, the Jesuits treated native religion as a handmaiden and prelude to superior Christian teaching. But the tolerance of Christianity did not last as long in Japan as in China. Christianity was banned in the late sixteenth century as part of Hideyoshi's internal unification program. With the ascent of more tolerant Confucianism over Buddhism among the Japanese ruling classes, Christianity and Western culture would again be welcomed in the nineteenth century.

During the age of Reformation in the West, absolutist Islamic military regimes formed in the Ottoman empire, among the Safavids in Iran, and among the Mughals in India. In all three cultures, religion became tightly integrated into government, so that they never knew the divisiveness and political challenge periodically prompted in the West by Christianity. In opposition to the expansive Ottomans, Shah Abbas I (1588–1629) allied with the Europeans and welcomed Dutch and English traders. Embracing Shi'ite religion and the Persian language (the rest of the Islamic world was mostly Sunni and spoke Arabic or different regional languages), Iran progressively isolated itself. Unlike the West, the Timurid empire of the Indian Mughals, particularly under Akbar the Great (1556–1605), and extending into the late seventeenth century, encouraged religious toleration even to the point of holding discussions among different faiths at the royal court. As in China and Japan, India too was prepared to live with and learn from the West.

Suggested Readings

R. H. BAINTON, *Erasmus of Christendom* (1960). Charming presentation.

C. BOXER, *Four Centuries of Portuguese Expansion 1415–1825* (1961). A comprehensive survey by a leading authority.

F. BRAUDEL, *The Mediterranean and the Mediterranean World in the Age of Philip the Second*, Vols. 1 and 2 (1976). The widely acclaimed work of a French master historian.

O. CHADWICK, *The Reformation* (1964). Among the best short histories and especially strong on theological and ecclesiastical issues.

N. COHN, *The Pursuit of the Millennium* (1957). Traces millennial speculation and activity from the Old Testament to the sixteenth century.

A. G. DICKENS, *The Counter Reformation* (1969). A brief narrative with pictures.

A. G. DICKENS, *The English Reformation* (1974). The best one-volume account.

G. DONALDSON, *The Scottish Reformation* (1960). A dependable, comprehensive narrative.

R. DUNN, *The Age of Religious Wars 1559–1689* (1979). An excellent brief survey of every major conflict.

M. DURAN, *Cervantes* (1974). Detailed biography.

J. H. ELLIOTT, *Europe Divided 1559–1598* (1968). A direct, lucid narrative account.

G. R. ELTON, *England Under the Tudors* (1955). A masterly account.

G. R. Elton, *Reformation Europe 1517–1559* (1966). Among the best short treatments and especially strong on political issues.

E. Erikson, *Young Man Luther: A Study in Psychoanalysis and History* (1962). A controversial study that has opened a new field of historiography.

H. O. Evennett, *The Spirit of the Counter Reformation* (1968). An essay on the continuity of Catholic reform and its independence from the Protestant Reformation.

J. H. Franklin (ed. and trans.), *Constitutionalism and Resistance in the Sixteenth Century: Three Treatises by Hotman, Beza, and Mornay* (1969). Three defenders of the right of people to resist tyranny.

R. Fülop-Miller, *The Jesuits: A History of the Society of Jesus*, trans. by F. S. Flint and D. F. Tait (1963). A critical survey, given to psychological analysis.

P. Geyl, *The Revolt of the Netherlands*, 1555–1609 (1958). The authoritative survey.

H. Grimm, *The Reformation Era: 1500–1650* (1973). Very good on later Lutheran developments.

J. L. Irwin (ed.), *Womanhood in Radical Protestantism, 1525–1675* (1979). A rich collection of sources.

H. Jedin, *A History of the Council of Trent*, Vols. 1 and 2 (1957–1961). Comprehensive, detailed, and authoritative.

D. Jensen, *Reformation Europe, Age of Reform and Revolution* (1981). An excellent, up-to-date survey.

T. F. Jessop, *Thomas Hobbes* (1960). A brief biographical sketch.

W. K. Jordan, *Edward VI: The Young King* (1968). The basic biography.

R. Kieckhefer, *European Witch Trials: Their Foundations in Popular and Learned Culture 1300–1500* (1976). One of the very best treatments of the subject.

R. M. Kingdon, *Transition and Revolution: Problems and Issues of European Renaissance and Reformation History* (1974). Covers politics, printing, theology, and witchcraft.

A. Kors and E. Peters (eds.), *European Witchcraft, 1100–1700* (1972).

C. Larner, *Enemies of God: The Witchhunt in Scotland* (1981). One of the most detailed and authoritative accounts of witchhunting.

P. Laslett, *Locke's Two Treatises of Government*, 2nd ed. (1970). Definitive texts with very important introductions.

A. MacFarlane, *The Family Life of Ralph Josselin: A Seventeenth Century Clergyman* (1970). Exemplary family history.

J. R. Major, *Representative Institutions in Renaissance France* (1960). An essay in French constitutional history.

G. Mattingly, *The Armada* (1959). A masterpiece and novel-like in style.

J. McNeill, *The History and Character of Calvinism* (1954). The most comprehensive account and very readable.

J. E. Neale, *The Age of Catherine de Medici* (1962). A short, concise summary.

J. Neale, *Queen Elizabeth I* (1934). A superb biography.

D. Nugent, *Ecumenism in the Age of Reformation: The Colloquy of Poissy* (1974). A study of the last ecumenical council of the sixteenth century.

S. Ozment, *The Reformation in the Cities* (1975). An essay on why people thought they wanted to be Protestants.

S. Ozment, *The Age of Reform 1250–1550: An Intellectual and Religious History of Late Medieval and Reformation Europe* (1980).

S. Ozment, *When Fathers Ruled: Family Life in Reformation Europe* (1983).

J. H. Parry, *The Age of Reconnaissance* (1964). A comprehensive account of explorations from 1450 to 1650.

T. K. Rabb (ed.), *The Thirty Years' War* (1972). Excerpts from the scholarly debate over the war's significance.

E. F. Rice, Jr., *The Foundations of Early Modern Europe 1460–1559* (1970). A broad, succinct narrative.

J. H. M. Salmon (ed.), *The French Wars of Religion: How Important Were the Religious Factors?* (1967). Scholarly debate over the relation between politics and religion.

J. J. Scarisbrick, *Henry VIII* (1968). The best account of Henry's reign.

A. Soman (ed.), *The Massacre of St. Bartholomew's Day: Reappraisals and Documents* (1974). The results of an international symposium on the anniversary of the massacre.

L. Spitz, *The Religious Renaissance of the German Humanists* (1963). Comprehensive and entertaining.

J. Stayer, *Anabaptists and the Sword* (1972). One of the most lucid and sympathetic accounts.

G. Strauss (ed. and trans.), *Manifestations of Discontent in Germany on the Eve of the Reformation* (1971). A rich collection of sources for both rural and urban scenes.

R. H. Tawney, *Religion and the Rise of Capitalism* (1947). Advances beyond Weber's arguments relating Protestantism and capitalist economic behavior.

K. Thomas, *Religion and the Decline of Magic* (1971). Something of a classic on the subject.

E. Troeltsch, *The Social Teaching of the Christian Churches*, Vols. 1 and 2, trans. by Olive Wyon (1960).

M. Weber, *The Protestant Ethic and the Spirit of Capitalism*, trans. by Talcott Parsons (1958). First appeared in 1904–1905 and has continued to stimulate debate over the relationship between religion and society.

C. V. Wedgwood, *The Thirty Years' War* (1939). The authoritative account.

C. V. Wedgwood, *William the Silent* (1944). An excellent political biography.

F. Wendel, *Calvin: The Origins and Development of His Religious Thought*, trans. by Philip Mairet (1963). The best treatment of Calvin's theology.

G. H. Williams, *The Radical Reformation* (1962). A broad survey of the varieties of dissent within Protestantism.

Portfolio IV: Christianity

The teaching of Jesus gave birth to Christianity. His simple message of faith in God and love of neighbor attracted many people whose religious needs were not adequately met by the philosophies and religions of the ancient world. In the writings of St. Paul and the teachings of the early Church, Jesus became the Christ, the son of God, the long-awaited Messiah of Jewish prophecy. According to John's gospel, Jesus was also the *Logos*, the eternal principle of all being, after which the thinkers of antiquity had quested. Christianity thus offered people something more than philosophy, Law, and ritual.

Christianity proclaimed the very Incarnation of God in man, the visible presence of eternity in time. According to early Christian teaching, the power of God's Incarnation in Jesus lived on in the preaching and sacraments of the church under the guidance of the Holy Spirit. Christian thinkers here borrowed from the popular Oriental cults of the Roman world, which had also offered their followers a sacramental participation in deity and spiritual redemption from sin. But Christianity went beyond them all when it declared the source of all being to be no longer transcendant and proclaimed the Messiah to have arrived. The Christain message was that, in Jesus, eternity had made itself accessible to every person here and now and forevermore.

The first Christians were drawn from among the rich and poor alike. People flocked to the new religion for both materialistic and deeply religious reasons. For some believers, Christianity promised a better material life. But its appeal also lay in its unique ability to impart to people a sense of spiritual self-worth regardless of their place or prospects in society. The gospel of Jesus appealed to the hopelessly poor and powerless as readily as to the socially rising and well-to-do.

In the late second century, the Romans began persecuting Christians both as "heretics" (because of their rejection of the traditional Roman gods) and as social revolutionaries. At the same time, dissenting Christians, particularly sects claiming a direct spiritual knowledge of God apart from Scripture, brought new internal divisions to the young church by advocating Christian heresies of their own. Such challenges had to be met, and by the fourth century effective weapons against both state terrorism and Christian heresy were in place: an ordained official clergy, a hierarchical church organization, orthodox creeds, and a biblical canon, the New Testament. Christianity not only gained legal status within the Roman Empire, but, by the fourth century, was the favored religion of the emperor as well.

The fortunes of Christianity after the fall of Rome (A.D. 476) is one of history's great success stories. Aided by the enterprise of its popes and the example of its monks, the church cultivated an appealing lay piety centered on the Lord's Prayer, the Apostles' Creed, veneration of the Virgin, and the sacrament of the Eucharist. Clergy became both royal teachers and bureaucrats within the kingdom of the Franks. Despite a growing schism between the Eastern (Byzantine) and Western churches, and a final split in 1054, by 1000 the Church held real economic and political power. In the eleventh century, reform-minded prelates ended secular interference in its spiritual affairs; the traditional lay practice of investing clergy in their offices was condemned under penalty of excommunication. For several centuries thereafter the church would remain a formidable international force, successfully challenging kings and emperors and inspiring crusades against the non-Christian world.

By the fifteenth century, the new states of Europe had stripped the Church of much of this political power. It would henceforth be progressively confined to its present role of spiritual and moral authority. Christianity's greatest struggles ever since have been not with kings and emperors over political power, but with materialistic philosophies and worldly ideologies over spiritual and moral hegemony within an increasingly pluralistic and secular world. Since the sixteenth century, a succession of Humanists, Skeptics, Deists, Rationalists, Marxists, Freudians, Darwinians, and Atheists have attempted to explain away some of traditional Christianity's most basic teachings.

In addition, the church has endured major internal upheaval. After the Protestant Reformation (1517–1555) made the Bible widely available to the laity, the possibilities for internal criticism of Christianity multiplied geometrically. Beginning with the split between

Lutherans and Zwinglians in the 1520s, Protestant Christians have fragmented themselves into hundreds of sects, each claiming the true interpretation of Scripture. The Roman Catholic Church, by contrast, has maintained its unity through these perilous times. However, present-day discontent with papal authority threatens the modern Catholic Church almost as seriously as the Protestant Reformation once did.

But Christianity is nothing if not resilient. It continues to possess the simple, almost magically appealing, gospel of Jesus. It finds itself within a world whose religious needs and passions still remain deep and basic.

IV-1 Nativity. *A depiction of Jesus's birth by Giotto. In the foreground are Elizabeth and her son, John, born about the same time, who would later baptise Jesus. The birth is witnessed by choirs of angels and two shepherds with their flocks. A cow and a donkey seem to be equally involved in the event. In the foreground Joseph, Mary's husband, contemplates the marvelous occurrence. [Scala Art Resource.]*

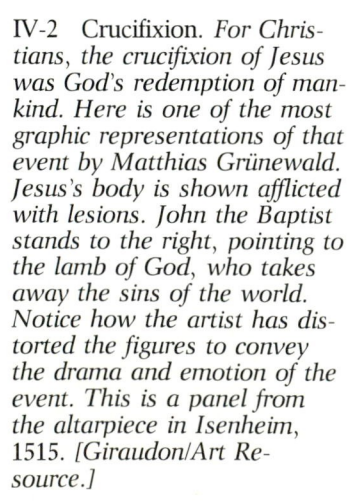

IV-2 Crucifixion. *For Christians, the crucifixion of Jesus was God's redemption of mankind. Here is one of the most graphic representations of that event by Matthias Grünewald. Jesus's body is shown afflicted with lesions. John the Baptist stands to the right, pointing to the lamb of God, who takes away the sins of the world. Notice how the artist has distorted the figures to convey the drama and emotion of the event. This is a panel from the altarpiece in Isenheim, 1515. [Giraudon/Art Resource.]*

IV-3 Crusades. *Christians briefly recaptured the Holy Land in the late eleventh and early twelfth centuries. Here the crusaders are shown besieging Antioch in 1097 en route to Jerusalem, which fell to them in 1099. The buildings within the city, however, appear to be those of a European rather than a Middle Eastern city.* [Scala/Art Resource.]

IV-4 Images of Heaven & Hell. *According to Christian teaching, man and woman were created near perfect by their Maker and lived in harmony with both God and nature. In Heaven they would return again to such harmony. After humankind's fall, however, those unredeemed by God's grace would suffer eternally in Hell. Here are imaginative portrayals of Paradise and Hell by the Dutch painter, Hieronymus Bosch (CA. 1450–1516). These are the two side panels from Bosch's triptych known as the "Garden of Delights."* [Giraudon/Art Resource.]

C-27

IV-5 Popes and the Papacy. *Raphael's portrait of the great military pope Julius II (1503–1512) at Mass. Julius secured the Papal States by successfully driving the Venetians out of Romagna in 1509 and, with the help of powerful allies, the French out of Italy in 1512. His notorious worldliness and militarism led Erasmus to make him the object of a famous satire, in which Pope Julius, clad in his papal robes, is refused entrance into heaven by St. Peter, who failed to recognize him as a Christian. [Scala/Art Resource.]*

IV-6 Popes and the Papacy. *The efforts of Pope Boniface VIII (1294–1303) to stem the rising tide of secular political power, particularly in England and France, failed. A few years after his reign, in 1309, the papacy moved to Avignon, on the southeast border of France, and was never again the powerful political force it had been in the twelfth and thirteenth centuries. [Scala/Art Resource.]*

IV-7 Gothic Cathedrals. *The interior of the Gothic Cathedral at Reims is a space designed to impress upon the worshipper the smallness of man and the soaring majesty of God. [Scala/Art Resource.]*

IV-8 Baroque Church. *Baroque art and architecture is a grandiose, three-dimensional display of life and energy, and very congenial to post-Reformation Catholicism as it set forth to reclaim the lands and people lost to the Protestant Reformation. The style is the very reverse of the new Protestant churches, which were, by comparison, remarkably subdued. This is the Baroque Altar of the chapel of St. Ignatius in Rome. [Scala/Art Resource.]*

IV-9   Early Christian Art. *The catacombs were underground tunnels where Christians buried their dead. This is a drawing on the wall of the catacomb of Priscilla in Rome. [Scala/Art Resource.]*

IV-10   Church in Roman Empire. *(Early Byzantine Empire to 600 A.D.) The power of popes in the Western Church was based on Matthew 16:19, where Jesus describes Peter, or Peter's faith, as the "rock" on which his church is to be built. This passage set Peter above the other apostles, and, by extension, Rome and its bishops above the other episcopal sees of Christendom. Here is a fourth century mosaic from the apse of S. Costanza, Rome, portraying Jesus giving of the keys to heaven to Peter. [Scala/Art Resource.]*

IV-11   Church in Roman Empire. *(Early Byzantine Empire to 600 A.D.) The old basilica of St. Peter was built during the reign of Constantine the Great (306–337). The financing of the rebuilding of this church by the selling of indulgences occasioned Martin Luther's famous protest and the eventual division of Christendom by the Protestant Reformation.* [Scala/Art Resource.]

IV-12   Church in Modern Europe. *Protestant churches generally were designed so that nothing might distract the eye and the mind from the preaching of God's word. Here for the Calvinists at worship in Lyon the preacher is absolutely at center stage. There are no decorations, paintings, statuary, or elaborate stained glass. In Zwinglian churches the walls were even whitewashed and no music or singing was permitted. Such simplicity contrasts starkly with the Baroque style of contemporary Catholic churches.* [Bibliotheque Publique et Universitaire de Geneva.]

IV-13 Church in Early Medieval Europe. *St. Jerome, seated in center, hands out copies of his Latin translation of the Bible (the Vulgate) for distribution by monks to the world. The Vulgate became Christendom's authoritative Bible until new translations from the Greek and Hebrew were adopted by Protestant Christians in the sixteenth century. This is a tenth century miniature. [Bibliotheque Nationale, Paris.]*

IV-14 Church in Early Medieval Europe. *The coronation of Charlemagne by Pope Leo III on Christmas Day 800, was an event that came to be regarded as the creation of the Holy Roman Empire, a revival of the old Roman Empire in the West. The church also gained a new importance and prestige by it. [Scala/Art Resource.]*

18 East Asia in the Late Traditional Era

One difficulty in comparing China and Japan is that although they shared so many cultural elements, they were so different in their institutions and history. Their cultural affinity is usually immediately apparent if we look at a Chinese and a Japanese painting side by side. Less visible, but no less fundamental, was a range of social values shared at least by their elites. To the extent that it was based on Confucianism, the similarity may have been the greatest in the mid-nineteenth century when Japan became more Confucian than ever before.

But the history and institutions of the two countries could not have been more different. For China, the Ming (1368–1644) and the Ch'ing (1644–1911) were just two more centralized bureaucratic states of a kind that had been in place for centuries. In the T'ang (618–907), the Chinese had discovered or rediscovered a pattern of government that worked so well that thereafter they rebuilt it each time it broke down. This pattern gives to Chinese history a cyclical cast, even though it is also replete with historical trends that cut across dynastic lines.

Japanese political history, in contrast, is longitudinal, not cyclical. Each period of Japanese history reflects a new and different configuration. The early centralized state gave way to a manorial regime, which, in turn, evolved into decentralized and then centralized feudalism. Superficially at least, Japan's history was more like that of Europe than of China. Neither Europe nor Japan ever found a pattern of rule that worked so well, and was so satisfactory to the rulers, that it was recreated, over and over again. In fact, from a Japanese or European point of view, that is not the way history works.

This chapter underlines the dynamism of both China and Japan during these late centuries. The label of "late traditional society" should not be read as "late static society." In both countries, the society became more integrated and the apparatus of government became more sophisticated than ever before. These advances shaped Chinese and Japanese response to the West during the nineteenth century. But we must also note that during these centuries, the West underwent a transformation. In fact, Greece and Rome apart, most of what seems important in Western history—the Renaissance, the Reformation, the scientific revolution, the rise of nationalism, the Industrial Revolution, the Enlightenment, and the democratic revolution—happened during the Ming and the Ch'ing dynasties in China. As we view East Asia from the perspective of Europe, it appears to have been caught in a tar pit of slow motion. But such was not the case; it was actually the West that had accelerated.

LATE IMPERIAL CHINA

The Ming (1368–1644) and Ch'ing (1644–1911) Dynasties

The Ming and the Ch'ing were China's last dynasties. The first was Chinese, the second a dynasty of conquest in which the ruling house and an important segment of the military were foreign (Manchus). They were nevertheless remarkably similar in their institutions and pattern of rule, so much so that historians sometimes speak of "Ming–Ch'ing despotism" as if it were a single system. The two dynasties are also coupled together because of certain demographic and economic trends that began during the Ming and continued through the Ch'ing.

Land and People

China's population doubled during the Ming, from about 60 million in 1368 at the start of the dynasty to about 125 million in 1644 at its end. The population then tripled during the early and middle Ch'ing dynasty, reaching about 410 million people several decades into the nineteenth century. This new density of population itself became an important factor in the growth of commerce and the new prominence of the scholar-gentry class.

Population growth was paralleled by an increase in the food supply. During the Ming, the spread of Sung agricultural technology and new strains of rice accounted for 40 per cent of the higher yields, and newly cultivated lands for the rest. During the Ch'ing, half the increased food supply was due to new lands and the other half to better seeds, fertilizers, and irrigation. New crops introduced from America during the late Ming, such as corn, sweet potatoes, and peanuts (which could be planted on dry sandy uplands and were not competitive with rice) also contributed to the

"Fishermen on Autumn River," a Ming dynasty scroll painting by Tai Ch'in (1390–1460). [Freer Gallery of Art.]

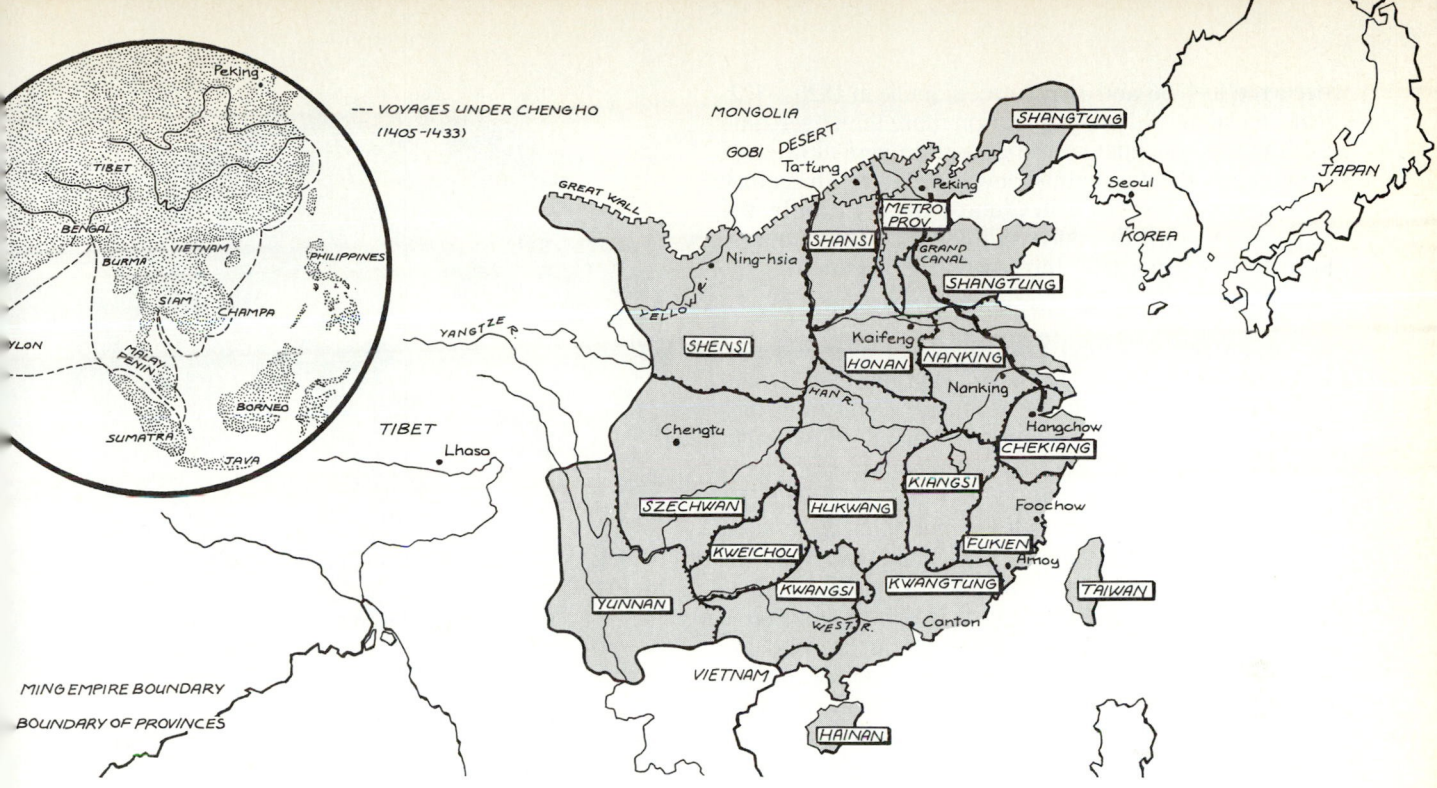

MAP 18-1   MING EMPIRE AND THE VOYAGES OF CHENG HO.   *The ships of
Cheng Ho, venturing beyond southeast Asia and India, reached the coast of East
Africa.*

increase in the food supply. By the nineteenth century, corn was grown in all parts of China.

In north China, the population had declined from 32 million to 11 million during the Mongol conquests. The Ming government acted to repopulate its open lands, resettling villages, building water control systems, and reopening the Grand Canal in 1415. The movement of people to the north continued until the nineteenth century. In the north, most farmers owned the land they worked. At times, they used hired labor. The land consisted mainly of irrigated dry fields, and the chief crops were millet, sorghum, and wheat.

South and southwest China also got migrants from the densely populated lower Yangtze region—many settling in hilly or mountainous border areas that were agriculturally marginal. The White Lotus Rebellion of 1796–1804 occurred in such an area, far from centers of governmental authority and only recently populated. The Miao Wars of the late eighteenth century were precipitated by the movement of Chinese settlers into southwestern uplands previously left to the slash-and-burn agriculture of the Miao tribes. Other Chinese crossed over to the island of Taiwan or emigrated overseas: During the Ch'ing dynasty, large Chinese mercantile communities were established in Southeast Asia.

And the Yangtze basin became even more densely populated. The Lower Yangtze region and the delta,

well supplied with waterways, had long been the rice basket of China, but from the late Ming, agricultural cash crops such as silk and cotton became predominant. Cotton was so widely grown in the delta that food had to be brought in from other areas by the early nineteenth century. In the lower Yangtze, almost half of the land was owned by absentee landlords. A typical landlord's holdings were subdivided among tenants, who paid fixed rents in kind. South China also had high levels of absentee landlordism, but far more land was owned collectively by clans, which managed the land and distributed rents among their members.

There are many unanswered questions regarding the population growth during these six centuries. Was there a decline in the death rate, and, if so, why? Or, was it simply that new lands and technology raised the limit on the number of mouths that could be fed? Did the population oblige by promptly advancing to the new limit? Certainly the Ming–Ch'ing era was the longest continuous period of good government in Chinese history. The good years of Ming rule were longer than in earlier dynasties, and the transition to Ch'ing rule was quicker and less destructive. How much did this contribute? Epidemic disease was not absent. In the great plagues of 1586–1589 and 1639–1644, as many as 20 to 30 per cent of the people died in the most populous regions of China, and in specific counties and villages, the figure was much higher. Another epidemic occurred in 1756 and a cholera epidemic in 1820–1822. The growth of China's population more than overcame such losses. Because of the growth in agriculture and population, most accounts view the eighteenth century as the most prosperous in Chinese history. But by the early decades of the nineteenth ceutury, the Chinese standard of living may have begun to decline.

China's Third Commercial Revolution

Commerce in China flourished between 300 B.C. and A.D. 220 (the late Chou through the Han dynasties) only to decline in the centuries of disunity that followed. In a boxed quotation in Chapter 8, we read Ssu-ma Chien's description of wealthy Han merchants. Between 850 and 1250 (Late T'ang through Sung), commerce again surged but then contracted during the Mongol conquest. Late Yuan warlords confiscated merchant wealth. Early Ming emperors, isolationist and agrarian in orientation, restricted the use of foreign goods, required licenses for junks, and attempted to encase foreign trade within the constraints of the tribute system. The early Ming also operated government monopolies, which stifled enterprise and depressed the southeastern coastal region by their restrictions on maritime trade and shipping. In the mid-sixteenth century commerce started to grow again, buoyed up by the surge of population and agriculture, and aided by a relaxation of government controls. If the growth during the Han and Sung dynasties may be called China's first and second commercial revolutions, then the expansion between 1500 and 1800 was the third. In some measure, this revolution was the extension to other parts of China of changes begun earlier in the Yangtze area, but it had new features as well. By the early nineteenth century, China was the most highly commercialized nonindustrial society in the world.

One stimulus to commerce was imported silver, which played the role in the Ming–Ch'ing economy that copper cash had played in the Sung dynasty. The Chinese balance of trade was favorable. Beginning in the mid-sixteenth century, silver from mines in western Japan entered China, and from the 1570s, Spanish galleons sailing from Acapulco to China via Manila brought in Mexican and Peruvian silver. In exchange, Chinese silks and porcelains were vended in the shops of Mexico City. The late Ming court also opened silver mines in Kweichow and Yunnan provinces. In the eighteenth century, copper mines were opened in South China. Also private "Shensi banks" opened branches throughout China to facilitate the transfer of funds from one area to another and extended credit for trade. Eventually they opened offices in Singapore, Japan, and Russia, as well.

As in Europe, the influx of silver and the overall increase in liquidity led to inflation and commercial

Late Ming dynasty polychrome porcelain (seventeenth century). [Asian Art Museum of San Francisco. The Avery Brundage Collection.]

growth in China. The price of land rose steadily. During the sixteenth century, the thirty or forty early Ming taxes on land that were payable in grain, labor service, and cash were consolidated into one tax payable in silver, the so-called Single Whip Reform. To obtain the silver, farmers sold their grain in the market; some switched from grain to cash crops. Moreover, by the early nineteenth century there were six times as many farm families as in the mid-fourteenth century.

Urban growth between 1500 and 1800, responding to flourishing local markets, was mainly at the level of intermediate market towns. These towns grew more rapidly than the population and provided the link between the local markets and the larger provincial capitals and cities, such as Peking, Hangchow, or Canton. The commercial integration of local, intermediate, and large cities was not entirely new, having occurred during the Sung dynasty in the lower Yangtze region. But now it spread over all of China. Interregional trade also gained. Where Sung trade between regions was mainly in luxury goods such as silk, lacquerware, porcelains, medicines, and paintings, early Ch'ing traders also dealt in staples such as grain, timber, salt, iron, and cotton. This is not to say that China developed a national economy. Seven or eight regional economies, each the size of a large European nation, were still the focus for most economic activity. However, a new level of trade developed between them, especially where water transport made such trade economical. A final feature of eighteenth century Chinese economic

Eighteenth-Century Chinese Ironworks

Some descriptions of industries in late imperial China suggest a very high level of organization and production, even if they fell short of an industrial revolution.

Their iron furnaces are seventeen or eighteen feet in height and fenced about on all sides with *yuan* trees. They are square in shape and solidly constructed of clay, with an opening at the top to allow the smoke to escape. Charcoal is put in at the bottom and ore in the middle. For every so many hundred catties of ore a certain number of catties of charcoal have to be used, a precise quantity which may not be increased or decreased. At the side more than ten persons will take it in turns to work the bellows. The fire is not put out either by day or by night. The liquid metal and the slag flow out from separate ducts at the bottom of the furnace, the liquid metal turning into iron which is cast in slabs. Every furnace has an artisan who determines the timing of the fire and who can distinguish the appearance of iron in different stages of completeness.

More than ten artisans are hired to serve each furnace. The largest numbers of men are needed for transporting timber and building the [charcoal] kilns in the Black Hills, and for opening up the seams and extracting ore from the Red Hills. The distances which the ore and charcoal have to be taken vary, but over a hundred men are required for each furnace. Thus six or seven furnaces will give employment to not less than a thousand men. Once the ore has been cast into slabs it is sometimes manufactured locally into pots and farm tools. A thousand and several hundred of men are also required for this work and for the transport [of the goods]. Thus the larger ironworks in Szechwan and the other provinces regularly have two thousand to three thousand persons, and the smaller ones with but three or four furnaces well over a thousand. ❑

M. Elvin, *The Pattern of the Chinese Past* (Stanford: Stanford U.P., 1973), p. 285.

life was the so-called "putting out" system in textiles under which merchant capitalists organized and financed each stage of production from fiber to dyed cloth.

The Political System

One might expect these massive demographic and economic changes to have produced, if not a bourgeois revolution, at least some profound change in the political superstructure of China. They did not. Government during the Ming and Ch'ing was much like that of the Sung or Yuan, only improved and made stronger. Historians sometimes describe it as the "perfected" late imperial system. This system, they argue, was able to contain and use the new economic energies that destroyed the weaker late-feudal polities of Europe. The sources of strength of the perfected Ming–Ch'ing system were the spread of education and Confucian doctrines, a stronger emperor, better government finances, more competent officials, and a larger gentry class with an expanded role in local society.

CONFUCIANISM. The role of Confucianism expanded in late imperial China. There were more schools in villages and towns than ever before. Literacy increased faster than population. Academies preparing candidates for the civil service examinations grew in number. In comparison with earlier dynasties, a larger segment of the population was inculcated with Confucian ideas and values. The Confucian view of society was patriarchal. The family, headed by the father, was the basic unit. The emperor, the son of heaven and the ruler-father of the empire, stood at its apex. In between was the district magistrate, the "father–mother official." The idea of the state as the family writ large was not just a matter of metaphor but carried with it duties and obligations that were binding at every level.

The sociopolitical philosophy was also butressed by the Neo-Confucian metaphysic. To stress the unitary nature of Ming and Ch'ing culture is not, of course, to deny the political role of different schools of Confucian thought. The vitality of late Ming thinkers was especially notable. In Europe, religious philosophies were often separate from those of the state, and a revolution in science was affecting both religious and political doctrines. In contrast, the greater unity and integration of the Chinese worldview cannot be denied.

THE EMPEROR. In Ming–Ch'ing times, the emperor was stronger than ever before. The Secretariat of high officials that had coordinated government affairs during the Sung and the Yuan was abolished by the first Ming emperor, who himself made all important and many unimportant decisions. His successors, often aided by Grand Secretaries, continued this pattern of direct, personal rule. During the late fourteenth and fifteenth centuries, the emperor was the bottleneck official, without whose active participation the business of government would bog down.

Then, during the sixteenth and early seventeenth centuries, there appeared a series of emperors who were not interested in government. One spent his days on wine, women, and sports, another on Taoist rites, and still another emperor, who never learned to write, passed his days making furniture. During this era, the emperor's authority was exercised either by Grand Secretaries or by eunuchs. But from the start of the Ch'ing, the pattern of personal government by emperors was firmly reestablished.

Emperors also wielded despotic powers at their courts. They had personal secret police and prisons, where those who gave even minor offense might be cruelly tortured. Even high officials might suffer the humiliating, and sometimes fatal, punishment of having their bared buttocks beaten with bamboo rods at court—a practice inherited from the Mongols. The dedication and loyalty even of officials who were cruelly mistreated attests to the depth of their Confucian ethical formation. One censor who had served three emperors ran afoul of a powerful eunuch. The eunuch obtained an imperial order and had the official tortured to death in 1625. In his deathbed notes to his sons, the official blamed the villain for his agonies but wrote that he welcomed death since his body belonged to his "ruler-father." An earlier mid-sixteenth century incident involved Hai Jui, the most famous censor of the Ming period:

Hai presented himself at the palace gate to submit a memorial denouncing some of the emperor's notorious idiosyncrasies. The emperor flew into a rage and ordered that Hai not be permitted to escape. "Never fear, sire," the eunuch go-between told the emperor. "He has said goodbye to his family, has brought his coffin with him, and waits at the gate!" Shih-tsung [the emperor] was so taken aback by this news that he forgave Hai for his impertinence.[1]

During the Ch'ing, the life-and-death authority of emperors did not diminish, but officials were generally better treated. As foreign rulers, the Manchu emperors took care not to alienate Chinese officials.

The Forbidden Palace of the emperors in Peking, rebuilt when the third Ming emperor moved the capital from Nanking to Peking, was an icon of the emperor's majesty. Unlike the Kremlin, which consists of an assortment of buildings inside a wall, the entire palace complex in Peking focused on the single figure of the ruler. Designed geometrically, its massive outer and inner walls and vast courtyards progress stage by stage to the raised area of the audience hall. During the T'ang, emperors had sat together with their grand councillors while discussing matters of government. In the Sung, officials stood in his presence. By the Ming, the emperor sat on an elevated dais above the officials, who knelt before him. Behind the audience hall

[1]C. O. Hucker, *China's Imperial Past* (Stanford: Stanford U.P., 1975), p. 206.

were the emperor's private chambers and his harem. In 1425, the palace had 6,300 cooks serving 10,000 persons daily. These numbers later increased. At the start of the seventeenth century, there were 9,000 palace ladies and perhaps 70,000 eunuchs. The glory of the emperor extended even to his family, whose members were awarded vast estates in north China.

THE BUREAUCRACY. A second component in the Ming–Ch'ing system was the government itself. The formal organization of offices was little different from that in the T'ang or the Sung. At the top were the military, the censorate, and the administrative branch, and beneath the administration were the six ministries and the web of provincial, prefectural, and district offices. If there was an important difference from earlier dynasties, it was that government was better financed. The productivity of China became steadily larger while the apparatus of government grew only slowly. Government finances had ups and downs, but as late as the 1580s huge surpluses were still accumulated at both the central and the provincial levels of government. These surpluses may have braked the process of dynastic decline. Only during the last fifty years of the Ming did soaring military expenses bankrupt government finances.

Then, in the second half of the seventeenth century, the Manchus reestablished a strong central government and restored the flow of taxes to levels close to those of the Ming. In fact, revenues were so ample that early in the eighteenth century, the emperors were able to freeze taxes on agriculture at the 1711 level and fix quotas for each province.

This contributed to the general prosperity of the eighteenth century and led to problems during the nineteenth century. Because agricultural productivity continued to rise, even though local officials collected some taxes outside the quotas, fixed quotas meant a decline in taxes. Both cultivators and gentry probably benefited from the new wealth, with the latter group obtaining the larger share.

If the Ming–Ch'ing system can be spoken of as "perfected," the good government it brought to China was largely a product of the ethical commitment and the exceptional ability of its officials. No officials in the world today approach in power or prestige those of the Ming and the Ch'ing. When the Portuguese arrived early in the sixteenth century, they called these officials "mandarins." (This term began as a Sanskrit word for "counselor" that became Hindi, entered Malay, and was then picked up by the Portuguese and adopted by other Europeans.) As in the Sung, the rewards of an official career were so great that the competition to enter it was intense. And as population grew and schools increased, entrance became even more competitive.

The Seven Transformations of an Examination Candidate

The Chinese civil service examination was a grueling ordeal. Like a chess tournament, it required endurance. Chinese critics said, "To pass the provincial examination a man needed the spiritual strength of a dragon-horse, the physique of a donkey, the insensitivity of a wood louse, and the endurance of a camel." The following selection is by a seventeenth-century writer who never succeeded in passing.

When he first enters the examination compound and walks along, panting under his heavy load of luggage, he is just like a beggar. Next, while undergoing the personal body search and being scolded by the clerks and shouted at by the soldiers, he is just like a prisoner. When he finally enters his cell and, along with the other candidates, stretches his neck to peer out, he is just like the larva of a bee. When the examination is finished at last and he leaves, his mind in a haze and his legs tottering, he is just like a sick bird that has been released from a cage. While he is wondering when the results will be announced and waiting to learn whether he passed or failed, so nervous that he is startled even by the rustling of the trees and the grass and is unable to sit or stand still, his restlessness is like that of a monkey on a leash. When at last the results are announced and he has definitely failed, he loses his vitality like one dead, rolls over on his side, and lies there without moving, like a poisoned fly. Then, when he pulls himself together and stands up, he is provoked by every sight and sound, gradually flings away everything within his reach, and complains of the illiteracy of the examiners. When he calms down at last, he finds everything in the room broken. At this time he is like a pigeon smashing its own precious eggs. These are the seven transformations of a candidate. ❑

I. Miyazaki, *China's Examination Hell*, trans. by C. Schirokauer (New York: Weatherhill, 1976), pp. 57–58.

After being screened at the district office, a candidate first took the county examination. If he passed, he became a member of the gentry. He gained the cap and sash of the scholar and exemption from state labor service. Even this examination required years of arduous study. About half a million passed each year. The second hurdle was the provincial examination held every third year. Only one in one hundred or more was successful. The final hurdle was the metropolitan examination, also held triennially. During the Ming,

The dilapidated remains of the examination stalls at Nanking. Doors to individual cubicles can be seen to right and left of the three-storey gate. Thousands of such cubicles made up the old examination stalls. Those who passed governed China. [Bettmann Archive.]

fewer than ninety passed each year. As in earlier dynasties, regional quotas were set to prevent the Yangtze region from dominating the officialdom.

THE GENTRY. A final component in the Ming–Ch'ing system—if not new, at least vastly more significant than in earlier dynasties—was the gentry class. It was an intermediate layer between the elite bureaucracy above and the village below. The lowest level of bureaucratic government was the office of the district magistrate. Although the population increased sixfold during the Ming and the Ch'ing, the number of district magistrates increased only from 1,171 to 1,470. Thus the average district, which had had a population of 50,000 in the early Ming and 100,000 in the late Ming, had two or three times that number by the early nineteenth century. The district magistrate came to his district as a stranger. The "law of avoidance," designed to prevent conflicts of interest, prevented him from serving in his home province. His office compound had a large staff of secretaries, advisers, specialists, clerks, and runners; but even then, he could not govern such a large population directly. To govern effectively, the magistrate had to obtain the cooperation of the local literati or gentry.

By *gentry* we do not mean a rural elite, like English squires. The Chinese gentry was largely urban, living in market towns or district seats. Socially and educationally, its members were of the same class as the magistrate—a world apart from clerks, runners, or village headmen. They usually owned land, which enabled them to avoid manual labor and to send their children to private academies. As absentee landlords—their lands were worked by sharecroppers—they were often exploitative; rebels at the end of the Ming attacked landlords as they did governmental offices. But the gentry were also local leaders. They represented community interests, which they interpreted conservatively, vis-à-vis the bureaucracy. They also performed quasi-official functions on behalf of their communities: maintaining schools and Confucian temples; repairing roads, bridges, canals, and dikes; and writing local histories.

The gentry class was the matrix from which officials arose; it was the local upholder of Confucian values. During the mid-nineteenth century, at a time of crisis, it became the sustainer of the dynasty.

THE PATTERN OF MANCHU RULE. The collapse of the Ming dynasty in 1644 and the establishment of Manchu rule was less of a break than might be imagined. First, the transition was short. Second, the Manchus, unlike the Mongols, were already partially Sinified at the time of the conquest. They had been vassals of the Chinese state during the Ming, organized by tribal units into commanderies. Even before entering China, they had had the experience of ruling over the Chinese who had settled north of the Great Wall in Manchuria.

In the late sixteenth century, an extremely able leader unified the Manchurian tribes and proclaimed a new dynasty. While still based in Mukden, the dynasty established a Confucian type of government with Six Ministries, a Censorate, and other Chinese institutions. When the Ming collapsed and rebel forces took over China, the Manchus presented themselves as the conservative upholders of the Confucian order. The Chinese gentry preferred the Manchus to Chinese rebel leaders, whom they regarded as bandits. After the Manchu conquest, a small number of scholars and officials became famous as Ming loyalists. The majority, however, shifted their loyalty and served the new dynasty. The Ch'ing as a Chinese dynasty dates from 1644, when the capital was moved from Mukden to Peking. All of south China was taken by 1659, with the aid of Ming generals who switched their allegiance to the new regime.

As the Manchus were a tiny fraction of the Chinese population, they adopted institutions to maintain themselves as an ethnically separate elite group. One was their military organization. The basic unit was the banner—the unit took the name of its flag. There were eight Manchu banners, eight Mongol, and eight Chinese. There were more companies (of 300 men each) in the Manchu banners than in either of the other two; together with their steppe allies, the Mongols, Manchus outnumbered the Chinese by more than two to one. Furthermore, the Chinese banners were mainly of Manchurian Chinese, who had been a part of the regime from its inception. Manchu garrison forces were segregated and were not under the jurisdiction of Chinese officials. They were given stipends and lands to cultivate. They were not permitted to marry Chinese, their children had to study Manchu, and they were not permitted to bind the feet of their daughters. And in 1668, north and central Manchuria were cordoned off by a willow palisade as a Manchu strategic tribal territory closed to Chinese imigrants.

In addition to the Manchu banners, there were also Chinese constabulary forces known as "armies of the green standard." Early on, the distinction between the banners and the Chinese military was critical. Later, as the dynasty became Sinicized and accepted, the ethnic basis of its military strength became less important.

The second particular feature of Manchu government was what Professor John K. Fairbank has termed "dyarchy": the appointment of two persons, one Chinese and one Manchu, to each key post in the central government. Early in the dynasty, the Chinese appointments were often bannermen or bondservants with a personal loyalty to the Manchus. At the provincial level, Chinese governors were overseen by Manchu governor-generals. Beneath the governors, most officials and virtually all district magistrates were Chinese.

Another strength of the Manchu dynasty was the long reigns of two extremely able emperors, K'ang Hsi and Ch'ien Lung. K'ang Hsi was born in 1654, ten years after the start of the dynasty. He ascended the throne at the age of seven, began to rule at thirteen, and held sway till his death in 1722. He was a man of great vigor. He rose at dawn to read memorials (official documents) before beginning his daily routine of audiences with officials. He sired thirty-six sons and twenty daughters by thirty consorts. He presided over palace examinations. Well versed in the Confucian classics, he won the support of scholars by his patronage of the *Ming History*, a new dictionary, and a five-thousand-volume encyclopedia.

K'ang Hsi also displayed an interest in Western science, which he studied with Jesuit court astronomers whom the Ch'ing had inherited from the Ming. He opened four ports to foreign trade and carried out public works, improving the dikes on the Huai and Yellow rivers and dredging the Grand Canal. On six occasions during his reign, he made tours of China's southern provinces. K'ang Hsi, in short, was a model Chinese emperor. But he was also responsible for the various policies that were aimed at preserving a separate Manchu identity. And like Kublai Khan before him, he built a summer palace on the plains of Manchuria, where he hunted, hawked, and rode horseback with the freedom of a steppe lord.

Ch'ien Lung began his reign in 1736, fourteen years after the death of his grandfather K'ang Hsi, and ruled until 1799. During his reign, the Ch'ing dynasty attained its highest level of prosperity and power. Like his grandfather K'ang Hsi, he was strong, wise, conscientious, careful, and hard-working. He visited south China on inspection tours. He patronized scholars on a grand scale: His *Four Treasures* of the classics, history, letters, and philosophy put fifteen thousand copyists to work for almost fifteen years. (But he also carried out a literary inquisition against works critical of Manchu rule.)

Only in the last years of his rule did Ch'ien Lung lose his hold and permit a court favorite to practice corruption on an almost unprecedented scale. In 1796, the White Lotus Rebellion broke out. The new emperor put down the rebellion and permitted the corrupt court favorite to take his own life. After this time, the ample financial reserves that had existed throughout the eighteenth century were never reestablished. China, nevertheless, entered the nineteenth century with its government intact and with a peaceful and stable society. There were few visible signs of what was soon to come.

The great Manchu emperor Ch'ien Lung (reigned 1736–1795). [Metropolitan Museum of Art. Rogers Fund, 1942.]

Ming–Ch'ing Foreign Relations

THE MING. Some scholars have contended that post-Sung China was not an aggressive or imperialist state. They cite its inability to resist foreign conquest, the civility, self-restraint, and gentlemanliness of its officials, and the Sung adage that good men should not be used to make soldiers just as good iron is not used to make nails. The early Ming convincingly disproves this contention. The first Ming emperor (reigned 1368–1398) oversaw the vigorous expansion of China's borders. By the year of his death, China controlled the

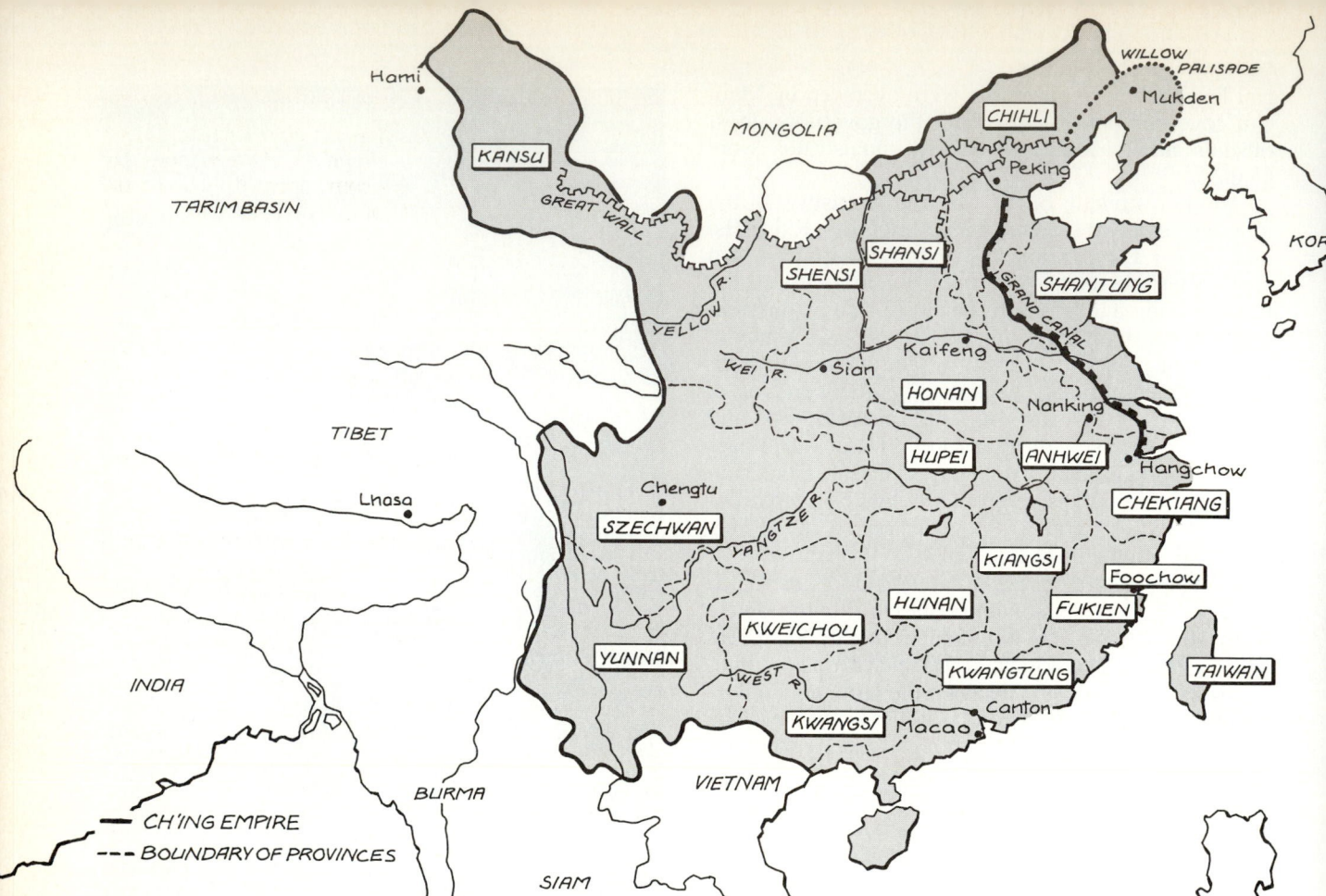

MAP 18-2 THE CH'ING EMPIRE AT ITS PEAK. *The Willow Palisade was the line of demarcation between the Manchurian homeland of the Ch'ing rulers and China. Chinese were excluded from Manchuria.*

northern steppe from Hami at the gateway of central Asia to the Sungari River in Manchuria and had regained control of the southern tier of Chinese provinces as well. The Mongols were expelled from Yunnan in 1382.

During the reign of the third Ming emperor (1402–1424), China became even more aggressive. The emperor sent troops into northern Vietnam, which for two decades became a Chinese province; eventually guerrilla attacks forced the Chinese troops to withdraw. He also personally led five expeditions into the Gobi Desert in pursuit of Mongol troops.

Whenever possible, the third emperor and his successors "managed" China's frontiers with the tribute system. In this system, the ambassadors of vassal kings acted out their political subordination to the universal ruler of the celestial kingdom. An ambassador approached the emperor respectfully, performed the kowtow (kneeling three times and bowing his head to the floor nine times) and presented his gifts. In return, the vassal kings were sent seals confirming their sta-

tus, were given permission to use the Chinese calendar and year-period names, and were appointed to the Ming nobility.

The material side of the system was notable for the benefits conferred on those willing to participate. While in Peking, the ambassadors were housed and fed in a style appropriate to their status. The gifts they received were far more valuable than those they gave. And they were permitted to trade private goods in the markets of the city. So attractive were these perquisites that some central Asian merchants invented imaginary kingdoms of which they appointed themselves the emissaries. Eventually, China had to prescribe limits to the size, frequency, and cargos of these missions.

The most far-ranging ventures of the third emperor were the maritime expeditions that sailed to Southeast Asia, India, the Arabian Gulf, and East Africa between 1405 and 1433. They were commanded by the eunuch Cheng Ho, a Muslim from Yunnan. The first of these armadas had sixty-two major ships and hundreds of smaller vessels and carried twenty-eight thousand sailors, soldiers, and merchants. Navigating by compass, the expeditions followed the sea routes of the Arab traders. It would appear that trade was not the primary purpose of the expeditions, though some eunuchs used the opportunity to make fortunes, and records show that giraffes, zebras, and other exotic items were presented at the Chinese court. Probably the expeditions were intended to make China's glory known to distant kingdoms and to enroll them in the tribute system. Cheng Ho's soldiers installed a new king in Java. They captured and brought back to China hostile kings from Borneo and Ceylon, and they signed up nineteen other states as Chinese tributaries.

The expeditions ended as suddenly as they had begun. They were costly and offered little return at a time when the dynasty was fighting in Mongolia and building the new capital at Peking. What was remarkable about these expeditions was not that they came a half century earlier than the Portuguese voyages of discovery, but that China had the necessary maritime technology and yet decided not to use it. The combination of restlessness, greed, faith, and curiosity that motivated the Portuguese was absent in China.

The chief threat to the Ming dynasty was the Mongols. In disarray after the collapse of their rule in China, the Mongols had broken into eastern, western, and southern tribes. The Chinese applied the policy of "using the barbarian to control the barbarian," and made allies of the southern tribes (those settled just north of the Great Wall) against the more fearsome grassland Mongols. This policy worked most of the time, but twice the Mongols formed confederations—pale imitations of the war machine of Genghis—strong enough to defeat Chinese armies: In the 1430s, they captured the emperor, and in 1550, they overran Peking. The Mongol forces involved in the latter attack were defeated by a Chinese army in the 1560s and signed a peace treaty in 1571.

A second foreign threat to the Ming dynasty was the Japanese and the Chinese pirates associated with them. Warrior-lords of decentralized Japan had begun raids on Korea and the northeastern Chinese coast during the thirteenth and early fourteenth centuries; they extended their activities down the coast to southeastern China and beyond during the fifteenth and sixteenth centuries. Hitherto, the seacoast had been China's most secure frontier. China built defenses and used a scorched-earth policy to make raiding less profitable, but for the most part had to put up with the depredations. The most serious threat from Japan was Hideyoshi's invasion of Korea in 1592–1598. China sent troops only after Japanese armies had occupied the entire Korean peninsula. Eventually, the Japanese troops withdrew, but only after the strain on Ming finances had severely weakened the dynasty.

THE CH'ING. The final foreign threat to the Ming was the Manchus, who, as we have seen, were the mouse that swallowed the elephant. After coming to power in 1644, the Manchu court spent decades consolidating its rule within China. The last Ming prince was pursued into Burma and killed in 1662. But then, the three Chinese generals who had conquered the south for the Manchus revolted, and their revolt was supported by a Sino-Japanese pirate state on Taiwan. The emperor K'ang Hsi suppressed the revolts by 1681—most Chinese troops in the Manchu armies remained loyal. In 1683, he took Taiwan and it became a part of China for the first time.

As always, the principal foreign threats to China, even to a Manchu dynasty, came from the north and northwest. Russia had begun expanding east across Siberia and south against the remnants of the Golden Horde during the reign of Ivan the Terrible (1533–1584). By the 1660s, Russian traders, trappers, and adventurers had reached the Amur River in northern Manchuria, where they built fortified outposts and traded with the eastern Mongols. One is reminded of the French penetration of Canada during the same decades. K'ang Hsi, acting to prevent a rapprochment between the Russians and Mongols, set up military colonies in Manchuria during the 1680s and drove the Russians from the lower Amur. This victory during the early years of the reign of Peter the Great (1682–1725) led to the 1689 Treaty of Nerchinsk. Negotiated with the assistance of Jesuit translators, this treaty excluded Russia from northern Manchuria while permitting its caravans to visit Peking.

In the west the situation was more complex, with a three-corner relationship between Russia, the Western Mongols, and Tibet. K'ang Hsi, and then Ch'ien Lung, campaigned against the Mongols, invaded Tibet, and in 1727 signed a new treaty with Russia. In the process of the campaigns, the Chinese temporarily came to control millions of square miles of new territories. Ever since, even after China's borders began to contract during the nineteenth century, the Chinese have continued to view the limits of maximal expansion under the Manchus as their legitimate borders. It is a telling comment on the Chinese concept of empire. The roots of the present contention over borders between China and the Soviet Union go back to these events during the eighteenth century.

CONTACTS WITH THE WEST. Europeans had made their way to China during the T'ang and the Yuan dynasties. But it was only in the sixteenth century, as a part of Europe's oceanic expansion, that they arrived in large numbers. Some came as missionaries of whom the most calculating, disciplined, enterprising, and successful were the Jesuits. On first arriving in Ming China, they put on the robes of the

Ch'ien Lung's Edict to King George III of England

The Chinese emperor rejected the requests of the 1793 Macartney mission for change in the restrictive "Canton system." His edict reflects the Chinese sense of their superiority to other peoples, and their belief that China was the "central kingdom" of the world.

You, O King, are so inclined toward our civilization that you have sent a special envoy across the seas to bring to our Court your memorial of congratulations on the occasion of my birthday and to present your native products as an expression of your thoughtfulness. On perusing your memorial, so simply worded and sincerely conceived, I am impressed by your genuine respectfulness and friendliness and greatly pleased. . . .

The Celestial Court has pacified and possessed the territory within the four seas. Its sole aim is to do its utmost to achieve good government and to manage political affairs, attaching no value to strange jewels and precious objects. The various articles presented by you, O King, this time are accepted by my special order to the office in charge of such functions in consideration of the offerings having come from a long distance with sincere good wishes. As a matter of fact, the virtue and prestige of the Celestial Dynasty having spread far and wide, the kings of the myriad nations come by land and sea with all sorts of precious things. Consequently there is nothing we lack, as your principal envoy and others have themselves observed. We have never set much store on strange or ingenious objects, nor do we need any more of your country's manufactures. . . .

S. Y. Teng and J. K. Fairbank, *China's Response to the West* (Cambridge: Harvard U.P., 1954), p. 19.

Buddhist monk; on learning something of the country, they switched to the gowns of the Confucian scholar. They studied Chinese and the Confucian classics and engaged in conversation with scholars. They used their knowledge of astronomy, geography, engraving, and firearms to win entry to the court at Peking and appointments in the bureau of astronomy.

When the Manchus came to power in 1644, the Jesuits kept their position. They appealed to the curiosity of the court with instruments such as telescopes, clocks, and clavichords. They tried to propagate Christianity. They attacked Taoism and Buddhism as superstitions but argued that Confucianism as a rational philosophy complemented Christianity—just as Aristotle complemented Christian theology in Europe. They handled the problem of the Confucian rites of ancestor worship by interpreting them as secular and nonantagonistic to Christianity. A few high court officials were converted. K'ang Hsi was sympathetic to the scholarly personalities of the Jesuits and appreciated the cannon they cast but was unsympathetic toward their religion: "I had asked [the Jesuit] Verbiest why God had not forgiven his son without making him die, but though he had tried to answer I had not understood him."[2]

In the meantime, their Franciscan and Dominican rivals had reported to Rome that the Jesuits condoned the Confucian rites. The debate was long and complex, but in the end, papal bulls issued in 1715 and 1742 decided against the Jesuits and forbade Chinese

[2]J. D. Spence, *Emperor of China: Self-portrait of K'ang-hsi* (New York: Alfred A. Knopf, 1974), p. 84.

Christians to participate in the family rites of ancestor worship. Thereupon the emperor banned Christianity in China, churches were seized, missionaries were forced to flee, and congregations declined.

Other Europeans came to China to trade. The Portuguese came first in the early sixteenth century but behaved badly and were expelled. They returned in mid-century and were permitted to trade on a tiny peninsula at Macao that was walled off from China. They were followed by Dutch from the East Indies (Indonesia), by the British East India Company in 1699, and by Americans in 1784.

At first, the Westerners mingled with ships from Southeast Asia in a fairly open multiport pattern of trade. Then, during the early eighteenth century, the more restrictive "Canton system" evolved. Westerners could trade only at Canton. They were barred from entering the city proper but were assigned land outside its walls along the river. They could not bring their wives to China. They were subject to the harsh dispositions of Chinese law. They were under the control of official merchant guilds. But the trade was profitable to both sides.

The British East India Company developed a triangular commerce between China, India, and Britain that enabled the English to drink tea and wear silk. Private fortunes were built. For China, this trade produced an influx of specie, and the Chinese officials in charge grew immensely wealthy. Chafing under the various restrictions, the British government in 1793 sent the Macartney mission to China to negotiate the opening of other ports, fixed tariffs, representation at Peking, and so on. The emperor Ch'ien Lung graciously permitted Macartney to present his gifts—which the Chinese described as tribute, even though Macartney refused to perform the kowtow—but he turned down Macartney's requests. Western trade remained encapsulated at Canton, distant from Peking and little noted elsewhere in China.

M'ing–Ch'ing Culture

One thing that can be said of Ming–Ch'ing culture, like population or agricultural productivity, is that there was more of it. Whether considering gentry, scholar officials, or a professionalized class of literati, their numbers and works were far greater than in previous dynasties. Even local literary figures or philosophers were likely to publish their collected works, or have them published by admiring disciples. Bookstores came of age in the Ming, selling the Confucian classics, commentaries on them, collections of T'ang and Sung poetry, and also colored prints, novels, erotica, and collections of model answers for the civil service examinations.

Chinese culture had begun to turn inward during the Sung in reaction to Buddhism. This tendency was accelerated further by the Chinese antipathy to Mongol rule and continued into the Ming and Ch'ing, when Chinese culture became virtually impervious to outside influences. Even works on mathematics and science translated into Chinese by the Jesuits left few traces in Chinese scholarly writings. Chinese cultural self-sufficiency, of course, reflected a tradition and a social order that had stood the test of time, but it also indicated a closed system of ideas, with weaknesses that would become apparent in the nineteenth century. Orthodox thought during these five centuries was Chu Hsi Neo-Confucianism. From the mid to the late Ming, some perturbations were caused by the Zen-like teachings of the philosopher Wang Yang-ming (1472–1529), whose activism caused him to be jailed, beaten, and exiled at one point in an otherwise illustrious official career.

Several other original thinkers' refusal to accept bureaucratic posts under the Ch'ing won them plaudits during the anti-Manchu nationalism of the early twentieth century, but they had only a limited influence on their own times. The most interesting was Ku Yen-wu, who wrote on both philology and statecraft. He used philology and historical phonetics to get at the original meanings of the classics and contrasted their practical ethics with the "empty words" of Wang Yang-ming. Ku's successors extended his philological studies, developing empirical methods for textual studies, but lost sight of their implications for politics. The Manchus clamped down on unorthodox thought, and the seventeenth-century burst of creativity guttered out into a narrow, bookish, conservative scholasticism. Not until the very end of the nineteenth century did thinkers draw from these studies the kind of radical inferences that philological studies of the Bible had produced in Europe.

Ming and Ch'ing Chinese esteemed most highly, and not without reason, the traditional categories of high culture: painting, calligraphy, poetry, and philosophy. Porcelains of great beauty were also produced. In the early Ming, the blue-on-white predominated. During the later Ming and Ch'ing, more decorative wares with enamel painted over the glaze became more prevalent. The pottery industry of Europe began during the sixteenth century as an attempt to imitate these wares, and down to the present, the Chinese influence has remained absolutely dominant. Chinese today, however, see the novel as the characteristic cultural achievement of the Ming and Ch'ing.

The novel in China grew out of plot-books used by earlier storytellers. Like stories, novels consisted of episodes strung together, and chapters in early novels often ended with an encouragement to the reader not to miss the next exciting development. Ming and Ch'ing novels were usually written by scholars who had failed

LATE IMPERIAL CHINA

Ming Dynasty 1368–1644

1368–1398	Reign of first Ming emperor; Chinese armies invade Manchuria, Mongolia and eastern Central Asia.
1405–1433	Voyage of Cheng Ho to India and Africa
1415	Grand Canal reopened
1402–1424	Reign of third Ming emperor; Chinese armies invade Vietnam and Mongolia.
1472–1529	Wang Yang-ming, philosopher
1592–1598	Chinese army battles Japanese army in Korea.

Ch'ing (Manchu) Dynasty 1644–1911

1668	Manchuria closed to Chinese immigrants (by Willow Palisade)
1661–1722	Reign of K'ang Hsi
1681	Suppression of revolts by Chinese generals
1683	Taiwan captured
1689	China and Russia sign Treaty of Nerchinsk
1736–1795	Reign of Ch'ien Lung
1793	Macartney mission

the examinations—which may account for their caustic comments on officials. As most novels were written in colloquial Chinese, which was not quite respectable, their authors wrote under pseudonyms.

Two collections of lively short stories are available in English: *Stories from a Ming Collection* and *The Courtesan's Jewel Box*. Many stories (though not those in the two collections mentioned) were pornographic. In fact, the Ming may have invented the humorous pornographic novel. One example has been translated, *The Before Midnight Scholar*. This genre was suppressed in China during the Ch'ing and was

A Star in Heaven

The Scholars is the story of Fan Chin—thin and sallow with grizzled beard and thread-bare linen gown—who finally passes the county examination at the age of fifty-four. On his return home, he is given a feast and advice by his domineering father-in-law, Butcher Hu. But when he asks Hu for money to travel to the provincial examination:

Butcher Hu spat in his face, and poured out a torrent of abuse. "Don't be a fool!" he roared. "Just passing one examination has turned your head completely—you're like a toad trying to swallow a swan! And I hear that you scraped through not because of your essay, but because the examiner pitied you for being so old. Now, like a fool, you want to pass the higher examination and become an official. But do you know who those officials are? They are all stars in heaven! Look at the Chang family in the city. All those officials have pots of money, dignified faces and big ears. But your mouth sticks out and you've a chin like an ape's. You should piss on the ground and look at your face in the puddle! You look like a monkey, yet you want to become an official. Come off it!"

Fan Chin takes the examination anyway. When he returns home, he discovers that his family has been hungry for two days. Fan goes to the market to sell a chicken. In the meantime, heralds on horseback arrive to proclaim he has passed the provincial examination. Returning home, Fan sees the posted announcement and falls into a dead faint. When revived, he begins ranting incoherently. A herald suggests that Butcher Hu, whom Fan fears, bring him to his senses with a slap. Butcher Hu demurs:

"He may be my son-in-law," he said, "but he's an official now—one of the stars in heaven. How can you hit one of the stars in heaven? I've heard that whoever hits the stars in heaven will be carried away by the King of Hell, given a hundred strokes with an iron rod, and shut up in the eighteenth hell, never to become a human being again. I daren't do a thing like that."

Eventually Butcher Hu slaps him, and Fan recovers in time to receive a visit from a member of the local gentry, who is wearing "an official's gauze cap, sunflower-coloured gown, gilt belt and black shoes." "Sir," he says to Fan, "although we live in the same district I have never been able to call on you." After paying his respects, the visitor presents Fan with fifty taels of silver and a more appropriate house. Soon others give him land, goods, money, rice, and servants. The chapter ends with the maids cleaning up under the supervision of Fan Chin's wife after several days of feasting. Fan Chin's mother enters the courtyard:

"You must be very careful," the old lady warned them. "These things don't belong to us, so don't break them."

"How can you say they don't belong to you, madam?" they asked. "They are all yours."

"No, no, these aren't ours," she protested with a smile.

"Oh yes, they are," the maids cried. "Not only these things, but all of us servants and this house belong to you."

When the old lady heard this, she picked up the fine porcelain and the cups and chopsticks inlaid with silver, and examined them carefully one by one. "All mine!" she crowed. Screaming with laughter she fell backwards, choked, and lost consciousness.

But to know what became of the old lady, you must read the next chapter. ❑

C. T. Wu, *The Scholars*, (Peking: Foreign Language Press, 1957), pp. 65–76.

A scholar seated under a tree. Ming dynasty ink painting on silk by Wu Wei (1479–1508). [Museum of Fine Arts, Boston.]

only rediscovered in Japanese collections in the twentieth century.

Short descriptions of several major novels may convey something of their flavor:

1. *The Romance of the Three Kingdoms* was published in 1522. It tells of the political and military struggles in China in the aftermath of the Han dynasty. Like Shakespeare, the author, whose identity is uncertain, used a historical setting to create a dramatic world in which the outcome of events is determined by human character. More than twenty editions had appeared by the end of the Ming, and the novel was also extremely popular in Japan and Korea.

2. *All Men Are Brothers* (also translated as *The Water Margin*) tells of 108 bandit heroes who flee government repression during the late northern Sung, establish a hideout on a mountain amid marshes, and in Robin Hood-like fashion avenge the wrongs perpetrated by corrupt officials. Separate episodes tell why each had to leave society and of their many daring and funny adventures. Of all Chinese novels, this was the most popular. It was officially banned as subversive during the Ch'ing but was widely read nonetheless.

3. *The Golden Lotus* is a pornographic novel about the sexual adventures of an urban merchant. It gives vivid descriptions of individual women and satirical descriptions of venal officials and greedy monks. In the end, the hero dies of his excesses and his family—children and all six wives—disintegrates. The early English translation of this novel had long passages in Latin to protect those whose minds were not disciplined by the study of that language. Despite its literary merits, the book, like all of its genre, is proscribed in China today. Copies in universities are kept under lock and key.

4. *The Dream of the Red Chamber* (also translated as *The Story of the Stone*) is generally considered China's greatest novel. It tells the story of a youth growing up in a wealthy but declining family during the early Ch'ing. Critics praise its subtlety and psychological insight. Anthropologists mine it for information on the Chinese extended family and for its depiction of social relations. Like other Ming and Ch'ing novels, it was recognized as a respectable work of art only during the twentieth century, after Western novels entered China.

5. *The Scholars* is a social satire of the early Ch'ing that pokes fun at scholars and officials.

JAPAN

The two segments of late traditional Japan could not be more different. The Warring States era (1467–1600) saw the unleashing of internal wars and anarchy that scourged the old society from the bottom up. Within the space of a century, all vestiges of the old manorial or estate system had been scrapped and almost all of the Ashikaga lords had been overthrown. The Tokugawa era (1600–1868) that followed saw Japan reunited and stable, with a stronger government than ever before. During the Tokugawa era, Japanese culture was brilliantly transformed, preparing it for the challenge it would face during the mid-nineteenth century.

The Warring States Era (1467–1600)

War is the universal solvent of old institutions. Nowhere in history was this clearer than in Japan between 1467 and 1600. In 1467, a succession dispute arose over who would be the next Ashikaga shōgun. The dispute led to an outbreak of war between two territorial lords who were important supporters of the bakufu. Other lords used the opportunity to gain territory at the expense of weaker neighbors, and wars raged throughout Japan for eleven years. Most of Kyoto was destroyed in the fighting, and the authority of the Ashikaga bakufu came to an end. This first war ended in 1477, but after a pause, the fighting resumed and continued for more than a century.

The War of All Against All

Even before 1467, the Ashikaga equilibrium had been precarious. The regional daimyo lords had relied on their relationship to the bakufu to hold their stronger vassals in check, while relying on these vassals to preserve their independence against strong neighbors. The collapse of bakufu authority after 1467 pulled the linchpin from the system. It left the regional lords standing alone, removing the last barrier to wars between them.

The regional lords, however, were too weak to stand alone. A region was a hodge-podge of competing jurisdictions. Lands might be "public," or in estates, and some were starting to look like private fiefs. Revenues might be paid to nobles in Kyoto, to regional lords, or to samurai vassals. Most regions contained military bands that were not the vassals of the daimyo. Several daimyo had lands in the territories of other lords. Occasionally, vassals were militarily more powerful than their daimyo lords. Some local vassals commanded bands of village warriors. Once the regional daimyo were forced to stand alone, they became prey to the stronger among their vassals as well as to neighboring states.

By the end of the sixteenth century, all Ashikaga daimyo had fallen—with one exception in remote southern Kyushu. In their place emerged hundreds of little "warring states daimyo," each with his own warrior band. In one prefecture along the Inland Sea, the remains of two hundred hillside castles of such daimyo have been identified. The constant wars between these men were not unlike those of the early feudal era in Europe.

The Japanese term for "survival of the fittest"—"the strong eat and the weak become the meat"—is often applied to this century of warfare. Of the daimyo bands, the most efficient in revamping their domain for military ends survived. The less ruthless, who tried to preserve old ways, were defeated and absorbed. It was an age, as one Warring States general put it, "when only muscle counts." Another said, "The warrior doesn't care if he's called a dog or beast, the main thing is winning."[3] Early in this period, when there were hundreds of small states, castles were built on a bluff above a river or on a mountain side with natural defenses against a surprise attack. Inuyama Castle, today a thirty-minute streetcar ride from Nagoya, is the most impressive surviving example of such a castle.

As fighting continued, hundreds of local states gave way to tens of regional states. The castles of such regional states were often located on a plain, and as castle towns grew up around them, merchants flocked to supply the needs of their growing soldiery. Eventually, alliances of these regional states fought it out, until in the late sixteenth century all of Japan was brought under the hegemony of a single lord. Oda Nobunaga (1534–1582) completed the initial unification of central Honshu and would have finished the job had he not been assassinated by a treacherous vassal in 1582. Toyotomi Hideyoshi (1536–1598), who had begun life as a lowly foot soldier, completed the unification in 1590. After his death, his vassal generals once again went to war, and it was only with the victory of Tokugawa Ieyasu (1542–1616) at the Battle of Sekigahara in 1600 that unification was finally conclusive. Ieyasu's unification of 1600 superficially resembled that of the Minamoto in 1185 but, in fact, was radically different, being based on a sweeping transformation of Japan's society.

The Foot Soldier Revolution

During the Warring States period, the foot soldier replaced the aristocratic mounted warrior as the backbone of Japanese military forces. Soldiers were still called *samurai*. They were still the vassals of daimyo or, sometimes, the vassals of vassals of daimyo. But their numbers, social status, and techniques of warfare changed dramatically. As a result, Japanese society became something very different from what it had been only a century earlier.

The changes began on the land. Ashikaga daimyo had diverted more and more land revenues for their own use, but Warring States daimyo took them all. Public lands and estates, including those of the imperial house, were seized and converted into fiefs. Sol-

[3] G. Elison and B. L. Smith (eds.), *Warlords, Artists, and Commoners* (Honolulu: Hawaii U.P., 1981), p. 57.

diers were paid stipends from the revenues of the daimyo's lands, and important vassals—usually the officers or commanders of the daimyo's army—were awarded fiefs of their own. The governance of fiefs was essentially private, in the hands of the fief holder.

Inheritance patterns changed to fit the new circumstances. Multigeniture—the division of a warrior's rights to revenues from land among his children—was not appropriate to a society with a hereditary military class. It had impoverished the Kamakura vassals. And so to protect the integrity of the warrior's household economy, multigeniture had begun to give way to a pattern of single inheritance during the Ashikaga period. After 1467, single inheritance became universal. As the fief was often passed to the most able son and not necessarily to the eldest, the pattern is usually called *unigeniture* and not *primogeniture*.

With larger revenues, Warring States daimyo built larger armies. They recruited mainly from the peasantry. Some of the new soldiers moved to the castle town of the daimyo. Others lived on the land or even remained in their village, farming in peace and fighting in war. The growth of the military class had begun earlier. Accounts of twelfth-century battles tell of fighting by tens of hundreds of warriors, sometimes more. Scroll paintings of the Heiji wars corroborate these figures. By the fourteenth century, battles involved thousands or tens of thousands of troops. By the late sixteenth century, hundreds of thousands were deployed in major campaigns. Screen paintings show massed troops in fixed emplacements with officers riding about on horseback. Of course, special cavalry strike forces were still used.

In the mid-fourteenth century, a new weapon was developed: a thrusting spear with a thick haft and a heavy chisel-like blade. Held in both hands, it could penetrate medieval armor as a sword could not. It could also be swung about like a quarterstaff. It was used by soldiers positioned at intervals of three feet, in a pincushion tactic that impaled charging cavalry. The weapon spelled the end of the aristocratic warrior in Japan, just as the pikes used by Swiss soldiers ended knighthood in northern Europe in the fifteenth century. This spear spread rapidly after 1467 to become the principal weapon of Warring States Japan. It was not accidental that its spread coincided with the recruitment of peasant soldiers, for it could be used effectively with only short training. By the early sixteenth century, it was every warrior's dream to be the "number one spearsman" of his lord. Even generals trained in its use. One famous general wrote that "one hundred spearsmen are more effective than ten thousand swords."

A second change in military technology was the introduction of the musket by the Portuguese in the mid-sixteenth century. It was quickly adopted by Warring States generals. Its superiority was proved in the Battle of Nagashino in 1575, in which Oda Nobunaga and

The "White Heron" Castle in Himeji, Japan. Begun during the Warring States period, it was completed shortly after 1600. [*Sekai Bunka Photo*]

Tokugawa Ieyasu used spear platoons and musket platoons against the cavalry of Takeda Katsuyori. Massing three thousand muskets behind a bamboo barrier-fence and firing in volleys, Nobunaga decimated the forces of his enemy and went on to complete his work of unifying central Japan. As individual combat gave way to mass armies, warfare became pitiless, cruel, and bloody.

How, then, shall we characterize the society that emerged from the crucible of the Warring States? Does the word *feudal* apply, with its suggestion of lords and vassals and manorial life on the fiefs of aristocratic warriors? In some respects, it does: By the late sixteenth century, all warriors in Japan were part of a pyramid of vassals and lords headed by a single over-lord; warriors of rank held fiefs and vassals of their own.

In other respects, Japan was more like postfeudal Europe. First, most of the military class were soldiers, not aristocrats. Even though they were called *samurai* and were vassals, they were something new. They were not given fiefs but were paid with stipends of so many bales of rice. Second, in contrast, say, to feudal England, where the military class was about one quarter of one per cent of the population, in mid-sixteenth century Japan it may have reached 7 or 8 per cent. It was more of a size with the mercenary armies of Europe during the fifteenth or sixteenth centuries. Third, the recruitment of village warriors added significantly to the power of Warring States daimyo but gave rise to problems as well. Taxes became harder to collect. Local samurai were often involved in uprisings. When organized by Pure Land Buddhist congregations, these uprisings sometimes involved whole provinces. Again, the parallels with postfeudal Europe seem closer. Fourth, even in a feudal society, not everything is feudal. The commercial growth of the Kamakura and Ashikaga periods continued on through the dark decades of the era of Warring States.

Foreign Relations and Trade

Japanese pirate-traders plied the seas of East Asia during the fifteenth and sixteenth centuries. Anxious to halt their depredations, the Ming emperor invited the third Ashikaga shōgun to trade with China. An agreement was reached in 1404. The shōgun was appointed as the "King of Japan." During the next century and a half, periodic "tribute missions" were sent to China. The opening of official trade channels did not, however, put an end to piracy. It stopped only after Japan was reunified at the close of the sixteenth century.

The content of the trade reflected the progress of Japanese crafts. Early Japanese exports to China were raw materials—such as raw copper, sulphur, or silver—but by the sixteenth century, manufactured goods were rising in importance and included swords,

spears, wine bottles, folding fans, picture scrolls, screen paintings, ink slabs, and the like. In exchange, Japan received copper cash, porcelains, paintings, books, and medicines.

After establishing his hegemony over Japan, Hideyoshi permitted only ships with his vermilion seal to trade with China, a policy continued by the Tokugawa. Between 1604 and 1635, over 350 ships went to China in this "vermilion-seal trade." Then, in 1635, the imposition of seclusion ended Japan's foreign trade altogether: Japanese were prohibited from leaving Japan; the construction of large ships was prohibited; trade with the continent was limited to a small Chinese community of merchants in Nagasaki, and to illegal trading with China through the Ryukyu Islands and with Korea through the Tsushima Islands.

Overlapping Japan's maritime expansion in the seas of East Asia was the arrival of Portuguese, Spanish, and then other, European ships. In 1493, after Columbus discovered the New World, the pope had awarded Spain all newly discovered lands to the west and Portugal the lands to the east. Portuguese pirate-traders made their way to Goa in India, to Malacca, and to Macao in China, and arrived in Japan in 1543. Spanish galleons came in 1587 via Mexico and the Philippines. These eastern and western waves of European expansion were followed by the Dutch and the English after the turn of the century.

The Portuguese, from a tiny country with a population of a million and a half, were motivated by a desire for booty and profits and by religious zeal. Their ships were superior. Taking advantage of the Chinese ban on maritime commerce, they became important as shippers. They carried Southeast Asian goods and Japanese silver to China and Chinese silk to Japan, and they used their profits to buy Southeast Asian spices for the European market. The Portuguese, initially at least, found it easier to trade with the daimyo of a disunited Japan than to deal with the authorities of a united China. A few Kyushu daimyo, thinking to attract Portuguese traders, even converted to Christianity.

Traders brought with them Jesuit missionaries. The Society of Jesus had been founded in 1540 to act as soldiers in the pope's campaign against the Reformation. Only nine years later, Saint Francis Xavier arrived in Japan. He soon wrote back that the Japanese were "the best [people] who have yet been discovered." Another Jesuit wrote that the Japanese "are all white, courteous, and highly civilized, so much so that they surpass all other known races of the world." The Japanese, for their part, also appeared to admire the Jesuits for their asceticism, devoutness, and learning.

As they had attempted to convert scholar-officials in China, so the Jesuits in Japan directed their efforts toward the samurai. Moving to Kyoto, they won the favor of Nobunaga, who was engaged in campaigns against warrior monks on Mount Hiei and against Pure Land strongholds in Osaka. For a time, Portuguese and Christian objects became fashionable. Painters produced "Southern Barbarian screens" that depicted the "black ships" of the Portuguese. Christian symbols were used on lacquer boxes and saddles. Nobunaga himself occasionally wore Portuguese clothes and a cross and said he might become a Christian if only the Jesuits would drop their insistence on monogamy. Christian converts increased from a very small number in the early years to 130,000 in 1579, and to an estimated 300,000 in 1600. That is to say, a higher percentage of the Japanese population in the late sixteenth century was more Christian than it is today.

It is difficult to explain why Christianity met with greater success in Japan than in other Asian lands.

The Portuguese in Japan. The Portuguese were among the first Europeans to reach Japan, arriving in 1543 from India and the East Indies. [Sekai Bunka Photo.]

When first introduced, it was seen as a new Buddhist sect. There seemed little difference to the Japanese between the cosmic Buddha of Shingon and the Christian God, between the paradise of Amida and the Christian heaven, or between prayers to Kannon—the female bodhisattva of mercy—and to the Virgin Mary. They also noted the theological similarity between the pietism of the Pure Land sect and that of Christianity. To Japanese ears, the passage in Romans 10:13, "whosoever shall call upon the name of the Lord shall be saved," was reminiscent of the Pure Land practice of invoking the name of Amida. The Jesuits, too, noted these parallels and felt that the Buddhist sects had been established in Japan by the devil to test them. Xavier, who, despite his admirable personal characteristics was narrow-minded, referred to the historical Buddha and Amida as "two demons." Although this intolerance gave rise to certain tensions and animosities, Christianity spread, and to no small measure because of the personal example of the Jesuits.

The fortunes of Christianity began to decline in 1597, when Hideyoshi banned Christianity and had six Spanish Franciscans and twenty Japanese converts crucified in Nagasaki. Hideyoshi was aware of Spanish colonialism in the Philippines, and it was said that a Spanish pilot had boasted that merchants and priests represented the first step toward the conquest of Japan. Sporadic persecutions continued until 1614, when Tokugawa Ieyasu began a serious movement to extirpate the foreign religion. Faced with torture, some Christians recanted. Over three thousand remained steadfast and became martyrs.

The last resistance was an uprising near Nagasaki in 1637–1638 in which thirty-seven thousand Christians died. After that, Christianity survived in Japan only as a hidden religion with secret rites and devotions to "Maria-Kannon"—the mother of Jesus represented or disguised as the Buddhist goddess of mercy holding a child in her arms. A few of these "hidden Christians" reemerged in the later nineteenth century. Otherwise, apart from muskets and techniques of castle building, all that remained of the Portuguese influence were certain loan words that became a permanent part of the Japanese language: *pan* for bread,

birōdo for velvet, *kasutera* for sponge cake, *karuta* for playing cards, and *tempura* for that familiar Japanese dish.

Tokugawa Japan (1600–1868)

Political Engineering and Economic Growth during the Seventeenth Century

From 1467 to 1590, for more than a century, Japan's energies were absorbed in ever bigger wars. But after the unifications of 1590 and 1600, the goal of Japan's leaders changed to the creation of a peaceful, stable, orderly society. Like a great tanker that requires many times its own length to come about, Japan made this transition only slowly. Many of the values and habits of mind of the Warring States era continued on into the seventeenth century. By the middle or late seventeenth century, however, its society and political system had been radically reengineered. Vigorous economic and demographic growth had also occurred. This combination of political and economic change made the seventeenth century a period of great dynamism.

HIDEYOSHI'S RULE. One pressing problem faced by Japan's unifiers was how to cope with an armed peasantry. In war, village warriors fought for their lord: Their advantage to the lord was greater than their cost. In peace, only the cost remained: Their resistance to taxation and the threat of local uprisings. Accordingly, in the summer of 1588, Hideyoshi ordered a "sword hunt" to disarm the peasants. Records of the weaponry collected remain for only one county of thirty-four hundred households in Kaga, a domain on the Sea of Japan: 1,073 swords, 1,540 short swords, 700 daggers, 160 spears, 500 suits of armor, and other miscellaneous items. Once the hunt was completed, the 5 per cent of the population who remained samurai could use their monopoly on weapons to control the other 95 per cent.

After the sword hunt, Hideyoshi attempted to create social stability by freezing the social classes. Samurai were prohibited from quitting the service of their lord. Peasants were barred from abandoning their fields to become townspeople. This policy was continued by the Tokugawa after 1600, and by and large, it was successful. Samurai, farmers, and townspeople tended to marry within their respective classes, and each class developed a unique cultural character. The authorities even attempted to dictate the lifestyles of the various classes with sumptuary legislation prescribing who could ride in palanquins, who could wear silk, or who would be permitted to build fancy gates in front of their houses.

WARRING STATES JAPAN 1467–1600

1543	Portuguese arrive in Japan
1575	Battle of Nagashino
1587	Spanish arrive in Japan
1588	Hideyoshi's Sword Hunt
1590	Hideyoshi unifies Japan
1592–1598	Hideyoshi sends army to Korea, battles Chinese troops
1597	Hideyoshi bans Christianity

But to grasp the class structure of Tokugawa society, it is important to note the vast range of social gradations within each class. A farmer who was a landlord and a district official was a more important figure than most lower samurai and lived in a different social world from a landless "water-drinking" peasant too poor to buy tea. A townsman could be the head of a great wholesale house, or a humble street peddler or clog mender. A samurai could be an elder, a key decision maker of his domain, with an income of thousands of bushels of rice and several hundred vassals of his own, or an impecunious foot soldier who stood guard at the castle gate.

Once the peasantry was disarmed, Hideyoshi ordered cadastral surveys on his own lands and on those of his vassals. The surveys defined each parcel of land by location, size, quality of soil, product, and the name of the cultivator. For the first time, an attempt was made to standardize the rods used to measure land and the boxes used to measure rice. For these standards to take hold took time, but they marked the beginning of the detailed record keeping that was so notable during the Tokugawa era. Hideyoshi's survey laid the foundations for a systematic land tax. Based on this system, domains and fiefs were henceforth ranked in terms of their assessed yield.

THE ESTABLISHMENT OF TOKUGAWA RULE. Bedazzled by his own power and military successes, and against all the evidence of Warring States Japan, Hideyoshi assumed that his vassals would honor their sworn oaths of loyalty to his heir. Hideyoshi was especially trustful of his great ally Tokugawa Ieyasu, whose domains were greater than his own. His trust was misplaced. After his death in 1598, Hideyoshi's former vassals, paying little attention to his heir, broke apart into two opposing camps and fought a great battle in 1600 in which the alliance headed by Tokugawa Ieyasu emerged victorious. Ieyasu was wise, he was effective in maintaining alliances, and he was a master strategist, but it was his patience that won the day. In comparing the three unifiers, the Japanese tell the story that when a cuckoo failed to sing, Nobunaga said, "I'll kill it if it doesn't sing"; Hideyoshi said, "I'll make it sing"; and Ieyasu sat down and said, "I'll wait until it sings."

Like the Minamoto of twelfth-century Kamakura, Ieyasu spurned the Kyoto court and established his headquarters in Edo (today's Tokyo) in the center of his military holdings in eastern Japan. He took the title of shōgun in 1603 and called his government the bakufu. In his capital, he built a great castle, surrounding it with massive fortifications of stone and concentric moats. The inner portion of these moats and stone walls remain today as the Imperial Palace. Ieyasu then used his military power to reorganize Japan.

Ieyasu's first move was to confiscate the lands of his defeated enemies and to reward his vassals and allies. During the first quarter of the seventeenth century, the bakufu confiscated the domains of 150 daimyo, some of former enemies and some for infractions of the Tokugawa legal code, and transferred 229 daimyo from one domain to another. The transfers completed the work of Hideyoshi's sword hunt by severing long-standing ties between daimyo and their disarmed former village retainers. When a daimyo was transferred to a new fief, he of course took his samurai retainers with him. During the second quarter of the seventeenth century, transfers and confiscations came to a halt and the system settled down.

The reshuffling of domains had not been random. The configuration that emerged was, first, of a huge central Tokugawa domain. It contained the following: most of the domains of "house daimyo"—those who had been Tokugawa vassals before 1600; the fiefs of the 5000 Tokugawa bannermen (upper samurai); and the lands that furnished the stipends of the other 17,000 Tokugawa direct retainers (middle and lower samurai). Then, strategically placed around the Tokugawa heartland were the domains of the "related daimyo." These domains had been founded by the second and third sons of early shōguns, and furnished successors to the main Tokugawa line when a shōgun had no heir. Beyond the related daimyo was a second tier of "outside daimyo" who had fought as allies of Tokugawa Ieyasu in 1600 but became his vassals only after the battle was over.

Finally, at the antipodes of the system were those outside daimyo who had been permitted to survive despite having fought against the Tokugawa in 1600. Their domains were drastically reduced. They remained the "enemies" within the system, though they had submitted and become Tokugawa vassals after 1600. Thus, the entire arrangement constituted a defensive system, with the staunchest Tokugawa supporters nearest to the center.

In addition to strategic emplacements, the Tokugawa established other controls. Legal codes were promulgated to regulate the imperial court, the temples and shrines, and the daimyo. Military houses were enjoined to use men of ability and to practice frugality. They were prohibited from engaging in drinking parties, wanton revelry, sexual indulgence, habitual gambling, or the ostentatious display of wealth. Only with bakufu consent could daimyo marry or repair their castles.

A second control was a hostage system, firmly established by 1642, that required the wives and children of daimyo to reside permanently in Edo and the daimyo themselves to spend every second year in Edo. Like the policy of Louis XIV at Versailles, this requirement transformed feudal lords into courtiers. The pa-

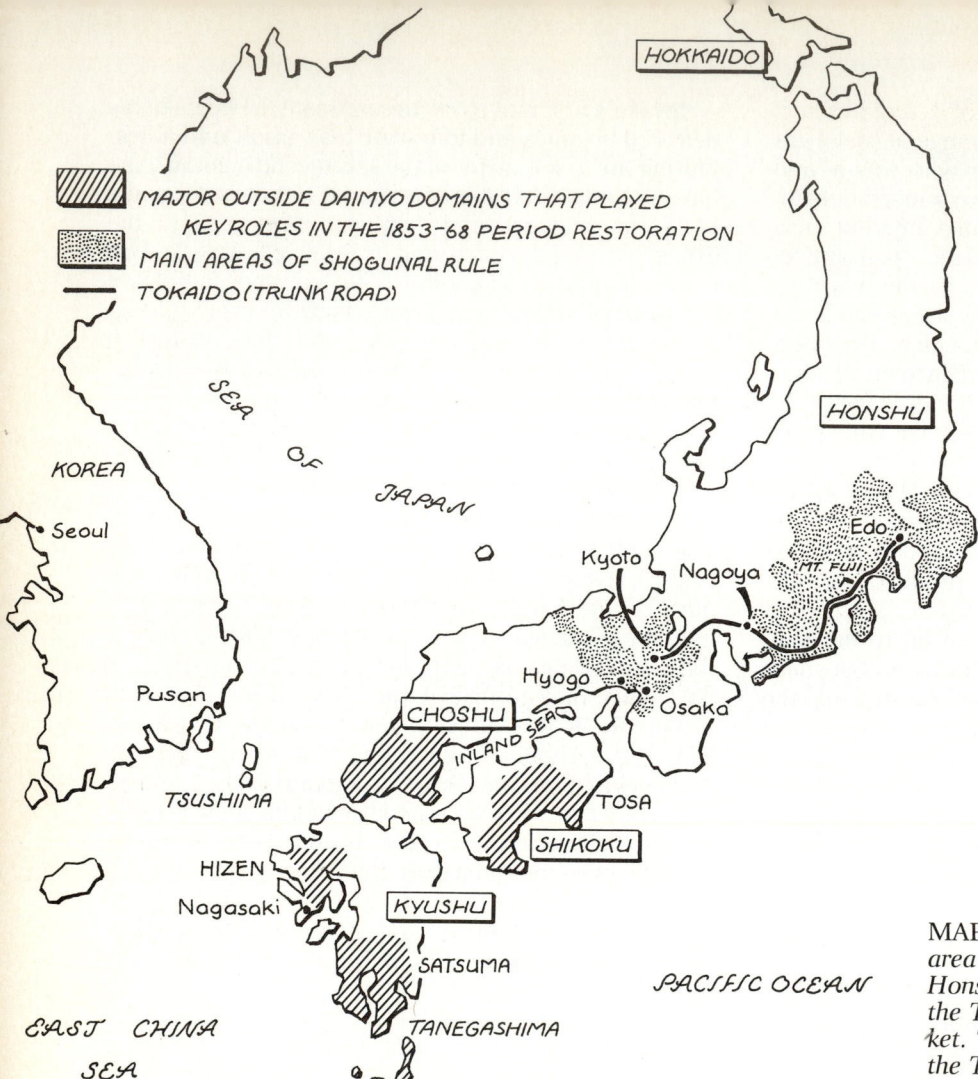

MAP 18-3 TOKUGAWA JAPAN *The area between Edo and Osaka in central Honshu was both the political base of the Tokugawa bakufu and its rice basket. The domains that would overthrow the Tokugawa bakufu were mostly in outlying areas of southwestern Japan.*

latial Edo compounds of the daimyo contained hundreds or thousands of retainers and servants and occupied a large portion of the city.

A third key control, established during the 1630s, was the national policy of seclusion. Except for small Chinese and Dutch trading contingents at Nagasaki, no foreigners were permitted to enter Japan, and on pain of death, no Japanese was allowed to go abroad. Nor could oceangoing ships be built. This policy was strictly enforced until 1854. Like the case of a watch, seclusion enclosed the workings of the entire system. Cut off from the world, the Japanese turned inward.

An interesting parallel can be drawn between Europe and Tokugawa Japan. Between the fifteenth and eighteenth centuries, France moved from a late feudal pattern toward ever greater centralization, whereas Germany moved toward a decentralized order of many independent states. In Japan, these two tendencies were delicately balanced. On the one hand, representing the forces of centralization, was the bakufu, which governed its own domain and also administered the controls over the whole system. Its offices were staffed by its vassals—its highest councils by house daimyo and high-ranking bannermen, and lesser posts by lower-ranking vassals of ability. The pool of rank was always larger than that of the posts available.

On the other hand, representing decentralization, were the domains of the 260 or so daimyo. Except for the house daimyo, these were excluded from service in the bakufu. Their domain governments, like miniature bakufu, were staffed by their samurai vassals. Each domain had its own autonomous military, finances, judiciary, schools, paper money, and so on. This balance between centralization and decentralization has led Japanese scholars to label the Tokugawa polity the "bakufu–domain system."

THE SEVENTEENTH-CENTURY ECONOMY. The political dynamism of the period from Hideyoshi through the first century of Tokugawa rule was

A daimyo seated in a palanquin and surrounded by his samurai retainers.

matched by economic growth. By the late sixteenth century, there existed a backlog of agricultural techniques, the spread of which had been impeded by regionalism and wars: methods of water control and irrigation that made double-cropping easier; better tools; new seed strains; the use of bony fish or of nightsoil from cities as fertilizers; and so on. During the seventeenth century, these techniques were widely applied. Resources no longer needed for war were applied to land reclamation. The result was a doubling of agricultural production, as well as a doubling of population from about twelve million in 1600 to twenty-four million in 1700. Agricultural by-products—cotton, silk, indigo, lumber, dyes, *sake*, and so on—also grew, especially in central Japan and along the shores of the Inland Sea.

Peace also sustained growth in Japan's commercial economy. The merchants in Warring States Japan—like geese who lay golden eggs—had always been at risk. They had to pay for security; they operated within cramped regional economies. On coming to power, Nobunaga and Hideyoshi knew that political unification alone was not enough. They recognized that prosperity would make their rule easier and, acknowledging the enterprise of the merchants, they abolished the medieval guilds and freed Japan's central markets from monopolistic restrictions. The result was a burgeoning of trade and the formation of a national market network atop the domain economies. As this network expanded during the seventeenth century, economic functions became more differentiated and more efficient. The economic chain that began with a local buyer might extend to a merchant house in a regional port, to coastal shippers, to warehousers in Osaka or Edo, and then to great wholesale houses.

Seclusion brought foreign trade to an end—with the exception of the Dutch and Chinese depots at Nagasaki and some smuggling trade with China via the Ryukyu Islands and with Korea via the Tsushima Islands. We would expect the cut in trade to dampen Japan's commercial economy, but instead, it continued to grow for the remainder of the seventeenth century.

To explain this growth, we must look at the tax system and the pattern of consumption in the castle towns and Edo. Tokugawa tax policy was based on land, not commerce. Taxes took about one third of the peasant's production. It was a heavier tax rate than in neighboring China and bespeaks the effective grasp the military class had on Japanese society. Most taxes were paid in grain. Even as late as the mid-nineteenth century, only a third was collected in money payments. Thus, the 87 per cent of the population who lived in the countryside paid almost one third of the country's wealth to the 5 per cent in the military class. The remaining 8 per cent of townspeople also lived off the tax flow by providing goods and services for samurai. This distribution of benefits was mirrored in the three-area city planning common to all castle towns: a large parklike area with castle, trees, stone walls, and moats for the daimyo and his government; an extensive samurai quarter; and a meaner townspeople's quarter.

And just as the castle towns were the consumption centers of the regional tax economies, so was Edo the national consumption center and a super-castle town. It had the same three-area layout, though on a far grander scale. When the great daimyo of Kaga, from a domain on the Japan Sea, was in attendance at Edo, he was served by eight thousand samurai. When he returned to his domain, four thousand stayed on to manage the Kaga estates in Edo: 267 acres of houses and gardens, barracks, schools, warehouses, and so on. One of these estates, with its magnificent red gate still intact, is today the main campus of Tokyo University. Other daimyo had establishments proportional to their domains. By 1700, Edo had a population of about a million.

To support their Edo establishments, the daimyo sold tax rice in Osaka. Called the "kitchen of Japan," Osaka became the redistribution center from which competing fleets of coastal shippers brought to Edo food, clothing, lumber, oil, and other supplies. By 1700, Osaka's population was about 400,000. Kyoto, rebuilt after its destruction in the early Warring States period, was almost as big. It continued as a center of handicraft production. It also was the location of the "captive" imperial court, which, after suffering penury during the Warring States era, was given support lands equivalent in revenues to those of a small daimyo.

The system of alternate-year attendance at Edo also contributed to the development of overland transportation. The most traveled grand trunk road was the Tōkaidō Road between Edo and Kyoto. The artist Hiroshige made a series of woodblock prints that depicted the scenery at its fifty-three poststations. The poststations had official inns for traveling daimyo and requisitioned supplies and horses as a tax obligation from adjacent villages. These stations often grew into thriving local towns.

The growth and the national integration of the economy produced a new richness and diversity in urban life. Townsmen governed their districts. Samurai city managers watched over the city as a whole. Official services were provided by schools, police, and

The commercial district of Osaka, the "kitchen" of Tokugawa Japan. Warehouses bear the crests of their merchant houses. Ships (upper right) loaded with rice, cotton goods, sake, etc. are about to depart for Edo (Tokyo). Their captains vied with one another to arrive first and get the best price.

"Laundry on a Snowy Day," a woodblock by Suzuki Harunobu (1725–1770). [Tokyo National Museum.]

companies of firefighters—a proverb of the time was, "Fires are the flowers of Edo." But there were also servants, cooks, messengers, restaurant owners, priests, doctors, teachers, sword sharpeners, book lenders, instructors in the martial arts, prostitutes, and bath house attendants. In the world of the popular arts, there were woodblock printers and artists, book publishers, puppeteers, acrobatic troupes, storytellers, and Kabuki and Nō actors. Merchant establishments included money changers, pawnbrokers, peddlers, small shops, single-price retail establishments like the House of Mitsui, and great wholesale merchants. Merchant households furnished the raw materials for the personae of Edo fiction: the skinflint merchant who pinches every penny, the profligate son who runs through an inheritance to an inevitable bankruptcy, an erring wife, or the clerk involved in a hopeless affair with a prostitute.

The Eighteenth and Early Nineteenth Centuries

By the late seventeenth century, the political engineering of the Tokugawa state was complete. Few major new laws were enacted, and few major changes were made in the governing institutions. From the early eighteenth century, dynamic economic growth gave way to slower growth within a high-level equilibrium. A stable status quo emerged in the society. In the words of some historians, it had become "frozen," "unchanging," or "strangely preserved." Yet changes of a different kind were under way.

THE FORTY-SEVEN RŌNIN. The eighteenth century began with high drama. In the spring of 1701, a daimyo on duty at Edo Castle drew his sword and slightly wounded a bakufu official who had insulted him. Even to unsheath a sword within the castle was punishable by death. On the same day, the daimyo was ordered to commit *harakiri* (literally, to cut his stomach), and his domain was confiscated. Fearing an attempt at revenge, the bakufu police kept an eye on the daimyo's retainers—now *rōnin*, or "masterless samurai." The retainers dissembled, working at lowly jobs, staying at home with their families, or leading lives of drunkenness and debauchery.

Twenty-one months later, on a snowy night in January, forty-seven of the retainers gathered in Edo, attacked the residence of the bakufu official, took his head, and then surrendered to the authorities. Their act struck the imagination of the citizenry of Edo and was widely acclaimed. But the bakufu council, after deliberating for two months, ordered all forty-seven to commit *harakiri*. Embodying as it did the perennial theme of duty versus human feelings, the incident was quickly taken up by writers of Kabuki drama and puppet theater and to this day, has been reworked into novels, movies, and television scripts. Just as in Western theater there have been different Hamlets, so have there been many characterizations of Ōishi Kuranosuke, the leader of the band of forty-seven.

Viewed historically, two points may be noted about the incident. First, in a similar situation, the more practical samurai of the Warring States period would have forgotten their former lord and rushed to find a new one. Loyalty was highly valued because disloyalty was a live option. But this was no longer true in the Tokugawa era. With the authority of the daimyo backed by that of the shōgun, there was no room for disloyalty. So loyalty became deeply internalized and was viewed almost as a religious obligation. It was also easier for Tokugawa samurai to be loyal unto death because, for the most part, there was so little likelihood in an era of peace that such a loyalty would be called for. In any case, in 1701, it was this Tokugawa species of absolute loyalty that moved the forty-seven *rōnin*.

Second, the incident tells something of the state in Tokugawa Japan. The 1615 "Laws for the Military Houses" contains the passage: "Law is the basis of the social order. Reason may be violated in the name of law, but law may not be violated in the name of reason. Those who break laws deserve heavy punishments."[4] One Tokugawa law forbade private vendettas. So, despite the moral purity of their act, which was recognized by all, even by those who condemned them to death, the forty-seven "virtuous warriors" had to die. The state was above ethics. Their death sentence was a bureaucratic necessity.

CYCLES OF REFORM. Most political history of late Tokugawa Japan is written in terms of alternating cycles of laxity and reform. Even during the mid-seventeenth century, the expenses of the bakufu and daimyo states were often greater than their income. In part, the reason was structural: Taxes were based on agriculture in an economy that was becoming commercial. In part, it was simple mathematics: after the samurai were paid their stipends, not enough was left for the expenses of domain government and the costs of the Edo establishments. In part, it was the toll of extraordinary costs, such as a bakufu levy, the wedding of a daimyo's daughter, or the rebuilding of a castle after a fire. In part, it was a taste for luxury among daimyo and retainers of rank.

Over the years, a familiar pattern emerged. To make ends meet, domains would borrow from merchants. Then, as finances became even more difficult, a reformist clique of officials would appear, take power, retrench the domain's finances, eliminate extravagance, and return the domain to a more frugal and austere way of life. Debts would be repaid or repudiated. Reforms usually depressed the local merchant economy. But no one likes to practice frugality forever. So, after some of the goals of the reform had been achieved, a new clique would take over the government and a new round of spending would begin. The bakufu carried out three great reforms:

1716–1733	Tokugawa Yoshimume	17 years
1787–1793	Matsudaira Sadanobu	6 years
1841–1843	Mizuno Tadakuni	2 years

The first two were of long duration and successful; the third was not. Its failure set the stage for the ineffective response of the bakufu to the West in the mid-nineteenth century. Reforms were also carried out by daimyo domains. Some were successful, enabling them to respond more effectively to the new political crisis of the mid-nineteenth century.

---

[4] R. Tsunoda, W. T. deBary, and D. Keene (eds.), *Sources of the Japanese Tradition* (New York: Columbia U.P., 1958), p. 336.

BUREAUCRATIZATION. The balance between centralization and decentralization lasted, surprisingly, until the end of the Tokugawa era. Not a single domain ever tried to overthrow the bakufu hegemony. Nor did the bakufu ever try to extend its control over the domains. But what occurred both within the bakufu and within each domain during the eighteenth and early nineteenth centuries was the steady growth of bureaucracy. One development was the extension of public authority into areas that had been private. In 1600, most samurai fiefs were run by their samurai fiefholders. They collected the taxes, often at a heavier rate than that set by the domain, and appointed fief stewards to oversee the fiefs. By 1850, however, all but the largest of samurai fiefs were administered by district officials. They collected the standard domain tax and forwarded to the samurai his income. In periods of retrenchment, samurai were often paid only half the usual amount.

A second development was the proliferation of administrative codes and government by paperwork. Domain archives (which survived the struggles of the restoration period and the bombings of World War II) house room after room of records of every imaginable kind, mostly from the late eighteenth and early nineteenth centuries: records of births, adoptions, name changes, samurai ranks, fief registers, stipend registers, land and tax registers, records of court proceedings, historical records, and so on. Administrative codes for the bakufu exchequer, for example, grew from a single page during the seventeenth century to forty pages in the late Tokugawa. They define among other things an elaborate structure of offices and suboffices, their jurisdictional boundaries, and detailed instructions about how many copies of each document should be made and to which offices they should be forwarded.

Of course, there were limits to bureaucratization as well. Only samurai could aspire to official posts. They came to the office wearing their two swords. Decision-making posts were limited to upper-ranking samurai. In periods of financial crises—endemic in the late Tokugawa—a demand arose for men of ability, and middle- or lower-middle-ranking samurai joined domain decision making by becoming staff assistants to bureaucrats of rank.

THE LATER TOKUGAWA ECONOMY. After 1700, the economy appears to have approached the limit of expansion within the available technology. The population, an important index, reached twenty-six million early in the eighteenth century and was at the same figure in the mid-nineteenth century—a period during which the population of China more than doubled. Within this constant figure were various smaller

The bridal procession of Yohime, the twenty-first daughter of the eleventh Togugawa shogun, approaches the Edo mansion of the Kaga daimyo. The red gate (upper right) was built in 1827 for this occasion. The eleventh shogun had 28 sons and 27 daughters by his more than 40 concubines. Of his children, 13 sons and 12 daughters survived to maturity. This woodblock print by Kunisada is a "national treasure."

movements. Population declined during epidemics in the 1750s and the 1760s, and during famines in the 1780s. The northeast was especially hard hit and never fully recovered. Southwestern Japan along the Inland Sea gained in population. Central Japan stayed even; it was more urban, and like most premodern cities, Tokugawa cities had higher death rates.

After 1700, taxes became stabilized and land surveys were few. But evidence suggests little increase in grain production and only slow growth in agricultural by-products. Some families made conscious efforts to limit their size in order to raise their standard of living. Contraception and abortion were commonplace, and infanticide (euphemistically called *mabiki*, the term for thinning out rice shoots in a paddy) was practiced in hard times. But periodic shortages of food, disease, and late marriages among the poor were more important. A study of one rural village showed the daughters of poor farmers marrying at twenty-two and having an average of 4.6 children, whereas for the daughters of rich farmers the figures were nineteen and 6.2. A study of another domain showed a decline in the size of the average farm household from 7 to 4.25 members.

Over the course of the Tokugawa, some farmers remained independent, but others became landlords or tenants. About a quarter of all cultivated lands were worked by tenants by the mid-nineteenth century. Most landlords were small, were residents in their villages, and often were village leaders. They were not at all like the Chinese gentry. The misery of the lower stratum of rural society contributed to an increase in peasant uprisings during the late eighteenth and early nineteenth centuries. Authorities had no difficulty in quelling them, though some involved thousands of protestors and were locally destructive. But no uprising even remotely approached those of the late Manchu dynasty.

Commerce grew slowly during the late Tokugawa. In the early eighteenth century, it was reencased within guilds. Merchants paid set fees, usually not especially high, in return for monopoly privileges in central marketplaces. Guilds were also reestablished in the domains, and some domains established domain-run monopolies on products such as wax, paper, indigo, or sugar. The problem facing domain leaders was how to share in the profits without injuring the competitive standing of the domain's exports. Most late Tokugawa commercial growth was in countryside industries—*sake*, soy sauce, dyes, silks, or cotton—and was especially prominent in central and western

Japan. Some were organized and financed by city merchants under the putting-out system. Others competed with city merchants, shipping directly to the end markets to circumvent monopoly controls. The expansion of labor in such rural industries may explain the population shrinkage in late Tokugawa cities.

The largest question about the Tokugawa economy concerns its relation to Japan's amazing industrialization, which began later in the nineteenth century. Some scholars have asked whether Japan did not have a "running start." Others have stressed Japanese backwardness in comparison with European late-developers. The question is still not resolved.

Tokugawa Culture

If *The Tale of Genji* represents the classical culture of the aristocratic Heian court, and if Nō drama or an ink painting by Sesshū represents the austere samurai culture of medieval Japan, then a satire by Saikaku, a drama by Chikamatsu, or a woodblock print of a beauty by Utamaro may be taken to represent the new urban culture of the Tokugawa era. In such works, one discerns a new secular consciousness, an exquisite taste put to plebeian ends, occasional vulgarities, and a sense of humor not often encountered in the earlier Japanese tradition.

But there was more to Tokugawa culture than the arts and literature of the townspeople. Two hundred and fifty years of peace and prosperity provided a base for a culture more complex than ever before and for a broader popular participation in cultural life. In the villages, Buddhism became more deeply rooted, new folk religions proliferated, and by the early nineteenth century, well-to-do farmers were mostly able to read and write. The aristocratic culture of the ranking samurai houses also remained vigorous. Nō plays continued to be staged. The medieval tradition of black ink paintings was continued by the Kanō school and other artists.

The Ashikaga tradition of restraint, simplicity, and naturalness in architecture was extended. The imperial villa in Katsura outside of Kyoto has its roots in medieval Zen architecture and yet to this day provides the inspiration for architects in Japan. The gilded and colored screen paintings that had surged in popularity during Hideyoshi's rule developed further, culminating in the powerful works of Ogata Kōrin (1658–1716).

Zen Buddhism, having declined during the Warring States period, was revitalized by the monk Hakuin (1686–1769). One of the great cultural figures of the Tokugawa era, Hakuin was also a writer, a painter, a calligrapher, and a sculptor. His autobiographical writings have been translated as *The Embossed Tea Kettle*.

Some scholars have argued that Tokugawa culture had a double structure. On the one hand were the samurai, serious and high minded, who produced a vast body of Chinese-style paintings, poetry, and philosophical treatises. On the other hand was the urban culture of the townspeople: lowbrow, irreverent, secular, satirical, and often even scatological. The samurai esteemed Sung-style paintings of mountains or waterfalls, often adorned with quotations from the Confucian classics or T'ang poetry. The prints of the townspeople depicted pretty girls, actors, courtesans, or scenes from everyday life. Samurai moralists saw money as the root of evil. Merchants saw it as their goal in life; in Osaka, they even held an "abacus festival," at which their adding machines were consecrated to the gods of wealth and commerce.

In poetry, too, a double structure appeared. Bashō (1644–1694) was born a samurai but gave up his warrior status to live as a wandering poet. He is famous for his travel journal *The Narrow Road of Oku* and especially for his *haiku*, little word-picture poems:

A woman smoking. One of a series of ten woodblock prints of women's physiognomies by the artist Kitagawa Utamaro (1753–1806).

Such stillness—
The cries of the cicadas
Sink into the rocks.[5]

A crow perches
On a leafless branch
An autumn evening.

Or, on visiting a battlefield of the past, he wrote:

The summer grass
All that is left
Of a warrior's dream.

Contrast Bashō's sense of the transience of life with the sly humor of the townsman:

From a mountain temple
The snores of a monk and
the voice of the cuckoo.

Showing a love-letter
to her mother
From a man she doesn't love.[6]

Even the most virtuous woman
will undo her sash
For a flea.

This is not to say, of course, that townspeople did not write proper *haiku* as well.

LITERATURE AND DRAMA. Is cultural creativity more likely during periods of economic growth and political change or during periods of stability? The greatest works of literature and philosophy of Tokugawa Japan were produced between 1650 and 1725—just as the initial political transformation was being completed but the economy was still growing and the society still not set in its ways.

One of the major literary figures and certainly the most entertaining was Ihara Saikaku (1642–1693), who is generally credited with having re-created the Japanese novel. Saikaku was born as the heir to an Osaka merchant house. He was raised to be its master, but after his wife died, he let the head clerk manage the business and devoted himself to poetry, the theater, and the pleasure quarters. At the age of forty, he wrote and illustrated *The Life of an Amorous Man*, the story of a modern and bawdy Prince Genji who cuts a swathe through bath house girls, shrine maid-ens, courtesans, and boy actors. The overnight success of the work led to a sequel, *The Life of an Amorous Woman*, the tale of a woman undone by passion and of her downward spiral through the minutely graded circles of the Osaka demimonde. Saikaku also wrote more than twenty other works, including *The Japanese Family Storehouse*, which humorously chronicles the contradictions between the pursuit of wealth and the pursuit of pleasure.

A second major figure of Osaka culture at the turn of the century was the dramatist Chikamatsu Monzaemon (1653–1724). Born a samurai in Echizen province, Chikamatsu entered the service of a court aristocrat in Kyoto and then, in 1705, moved to Osaka to write for both the Kabuki and the puppet theater. Kabuki had begun early in the seventeenth century as suggestive skits and erotic dances performed by troupes of actresses. In 1629, the bakufu forbade women to perform on the stage. By the 1660s, Kabuki had evolved into a more serious drama with male actors playing both male and female roles. Actors entered the stage on a raised runway or "flower path" through the audience. Famous actors took great liberties in interpreting plays, to roars of approval from the audience. There was a ready market for woodblock prints of actors in their most famous roles—like posters of pop musicians today, but done with incomparable greater artistry.

The three main types of Kabuki plays were dance pieces, which were influenced by the tradition of the Nō; domestic dramas; and historical pieces. Chikamatsu wrote all three. In contrast to Saikaku's protagonists, the men and women in Chikamatsu's dramas struggle to fulfill the duties and obligations of their stations in life. Only when their passions become uncontrollable—generally the case, do the plays end in tragedy. The emotional intensity of the ending is heightened by the restraint shown by the actors before they reach their breaking point. In some plays, the hero and heroine leave duty behind and set out on a flight to death. Another favorite ending is the double suicide, in which the unfortunate lovers choose union in the next world. Indeed, this ending was banned by bakufu authorities when the excessive popularity of the drama led to its imitation in real life.

It is interesting to compare Kabuki and Nō. Nō is like early Greek drama in that the chorus provides the narrative line. In Nō, the stylization of action is extreme. In Kabuki, as in Elizabethan drama, the actors declaim their lines in the dramatic realism demanded by the commoner theatergoers of seventeenth-century Japan. But to convey the illusion of realism required some deviation from it. As Chikamatsu himself noted about Kabuki: "Many things are said by the female characters which real women could not utter.

[5]D. Keene (ed.), *Anthology of Japanese Literature* (New York: Grove Press, 1955), p. 371.

[6]R. H. Blyth, *Japanese Humor* (Tokyo: Japanese Travel Bureau, 1957), p. 141.

A Kabuki theater in Edo, early eighteenth century. Actors perform on the stage. Samurai and commoners watch from below. Others talk, eat, and watch the performance from an expensive loge area (lower left).

. . . It is because they say what could not come from a real woman's lips that their true emotions are disclosed." For him, "Art is something that lies in the slender margin between the real and the unreal."[7] Yet, for all that, Chikamatsu was concerned with the refinements of his craft and the balance between emo-

tional expressiveness and unspoken restraints; he never talked of the mysterious "no mind" as the key to an actor's power. His dramas are a world removed from the religiosity of the medieval Nō.

In the early eighteenth century, Kabuki was displaced in popularity by the puppet theater (Bunraku). Many of Chikamatsu's plays were written for this genre. The word *puppet* does not do justice to the half-life-sized human figures, which rival Nō masks in their

[7] R. Tsunoda, etc. (eds.), *Sources of the Japanese Tradition* (1958), p. 448.

artistry. Manipulated by a team of three, a puppet can not only kneel and bow or engage in swordplay, but it can also mimic brushing a tear from the eye with its kimono sleeve or threading a needle. In the late eighteenth century, the puppet theater, in turn, declined, and as the center of culture shifted from Osaka to Edo, Kabuki again blossomed as Japan's premier form of drama.

CONFUCIAN THOUGHT. The most important change in Tokugawa intellectual life was the setting aside of the religious worldview of Buddhism by the ruling elite in favor of the more secular worldview of Confucianism. Had this not occurred, Japan would not have been able to adopt the secular culture of the nineteenth-century West. But the change occurred slowly. During the seventeenth century, samurai were enjoined never to forget the arts of war and to be ever ready to die for their lord. One samurai in his deathbed poem lamented dying on *tatami*—with his boots off, as it were. In this period, most samurai were illiterate. They saw book learning as unmanly. Nakae Tōju (1608–1648), a samurai and a Confucian scholar, recounted that as a youth he swaggered around with his friends during the day and studied secretly at night so as not to be thought a sissy. Schools, too, were slow in getting started. One Japanese professor has noted that in 1687 only four domains had schools, and in 1715, only ten.

The great figures of Tokugawa Confucianism lived during the same years as Saikaku and Chikamatsu, in the late seventeenth and early eighteenth centuries. They are great because they succeeded in adapting Chinese Confucianism to fit Japanese society. One problem, for example, was that in the political philosophy of Chinese Confucianism, there was no place for a shōgun, whereas in the Japanese tradition of sun-line emperors, there was no room for the mandate of Heaven. Most Tokugawa thinkers handled this discrepancy by saying that Heaven gave the emperor its mandate and that the emperor then entrusted political authority to the shōgun. One philosopher suggested that the divine emperor acted for Heaven and gave the mandate to the shōgun. Neither solution was very comfortable, for, in fact, the emperor was as much a puppet as those in the Osaka theater.

Another problem was the difference between China's centralized bureaucratic government and Japan's "feudal" system of lord–vassal relationships. Samurai loyalty was clearly not that of a scholar-official to the Chinese emperor. Some Japanese Confucianists solved this problem rather elegantly by saying that it was China that had deviated from the feudal society of the Chou sages, whereas in Japan, Tokugawa Ieyasu had re-created just such a society.

A third problem concerned the "central flowery kingdom" and the barbarians around it. No philosopher could quite bring himself to say that Japan was the real middle kingdom and China the barbarian, but some argued that centrality was relative, and still others suggested that China under barbarian Manchu rule had lost its claim to universality. There was, furthermore, an entire range of comparable problems having to do with Shinto and with Japanese family practices. Suffice it to say that by the early eighteenth century, these problems had been addressed, and a revised Confucianism acceptable for use in Japan had come into being.

Another point to note is the continuing intellectual vitality of Japanese thought—Confucian and otherwise—into the mid-nineteenth century. This vitality is partly explained by the disputes among different schools of Confucianism and partly, perhaps, by Japan's lack of an examination system. The best energies of its samurai youth were not channeled into writing the conventional and sterile "eight-legged essay" that was required for the Chinese examination system. Official preferment—within the constraints of Japan's

A mother nurses her child within a mosquito net. The father sits on the edge of the floor mats. Beyond the opened sliding wall panels can be seen the veranda and then the garden. By the Edo artist Suzuki Harunobu (1725–1770).

hereditary system—was more likely to be obtained by writing a proposal for domain reforms, though this could sometimes lead to punishments as well.

The intellectual vitality was also a result of the rapid expansion of schools from the early eighteenth century. By the early nineteenth century, every domain had its own official schools on their Edo estates. Commoner schools (*terakoya*), in which reading, writing, and the rudiments of Confucianism were taught, grew apace. And in the first half of the nineteenth century, private academies also appeared throughout the country. It is estimated that by the mid-nineteenth century about 40 to 50 per cent of the male and 15 to 20 per cent of the female populations were literate—a far higher rate than in most of the world, and on a par with some European late developers.

OTHER DEVELOPMENTS IN THOUGHT. For Tokugawa scholars, the intellectual problem of how to deal with China was vexing. Their response was usually ambivalent. They praised China as the teacher country and respected its creative tradition. They studied its history, philosophy, and literature, and began a tradition of scholarship on China that has remained powerful to this day. But at the same time, they grappled with the problem of retaining a separate Japanese identity. Most scholars dealt with this problem by adapting Confucianism to fit Japan. But two schools—never in the mainstream of Tokugawa thought but growing in importance during the eighteenth and early nineteenth centuries—arrived at more radical positions. The schools of National Studies and Dutch studies were diametrically opposed in most respects but alike in criticizing the Chinese influence on Japanese life and culture.

National Studies began as philological studies of ancient Japanese texts. One source of its inspiration was Shinto. Another was the Neo-Confucian school of Ancient Learning. Just as the School of Ancient Learning had sought to discover the original, true meanings of the Chinese classics before they were contaminated by Sung metaphysics, so the scholars in the National Studies tradition tried to find in the Japanese classics the original true character of Japan before it had been contaminated by Chinese ideas. On studying the *Record of Ancient Matters*, *The Collection of Myriad Leaves*, or *The Tale of Genji*, they found that the early Japanese spirit was free, spontaneous, clean, lofty, and honest,—in contrast to the Chinese spirit, which they characterized as rigid, cramped, and artificial. Some writings of this school appear to borrow the anti-Confucian logic of Taoism.

A second characteristic of National Studies was its reaffirmation of Japan's emperor institution. Motoori Norinaga (1730–1801) wrote of Shinto creationism as the "right way":

A mother bathing her son, woodblock print by Kitagawa Utamaro (1753–1806). [Nelson-Atkins Gallery of Art.]

Heaven and Earth, all the gods and all phenomena, were brought into existence by the creative spirits of two deities. . . . This . . . is a miraculously divine act the reason for which is beyond the comprehension of the human intellect.

But in foreign countries where the Right Way has not been transmitted, this act of divine creativity is not known. Men there have tried to explain the principle of Heaven and earth and all phenomena by such theories as in the yin and yang, the hexagrams of the Book of Changes, and the Five Elements. But all of these are fallacious theories stemming from the assumptions of the human intellect and they in no wise represent the true principle.

The "special dispensation of our Imperial Land" means that ours is the native land of the Heaven-Shining Goddess who casts her light over all countries in the four seas. Thus our country is the source and fountainhead of all other countries, and in all matters it excels all the others.[8]

[8]Tsunoda, deBary, and Keene, pp. 521, 523.

Hirata Atsutane's Views on Morality

The ancient Japanese all constantly and correctly practiced what the Chinese called humanity, righteousness, the five cardinal virtues and the rest, without having any need to name them or to teach them. There was thus no necessity for anything to be especially constituted as a Way. This is the essentially Japanese quality of Japan, and one where we may see a magnificent example of Japan's superiority to all other countries of the world. In China, as I have already had frequent occasions to mention, there were evil customs from the very outset, and human behavior, far from being proper, was extremely licentious. That is the reason why so many sages appeared in ancient times to guide and instruct the Chinese. ❑

Tsunoda, deBary, and Keene, p. 548.

National Studies became quite influential during the late Tokugawa era. It had a small but not unimportant influence on the Meiji Restoration. Its doctrines continued thereafter as one strain of modern Japanese ultranationalism. Its most enduring achievement was in Japanese linguistics. Even today, scholars admire Motoori's philology. And in an age when the prestige of things Chinese was overwhelming, Motoori helped redress the balance by appreciating and giving a name to the aesthetic sensibility found in the Japanese classics. The word he used was *mono no aware*, which means, literally, "the poignancy of things."

But National Studies had several weaknesses that prevented it from becoming the mainstream of Japanese thought. First, even the most refined sensibility is no substitute for philosophy. In its celebration of the primitive, National Studies ran headlong into the greater rationality of Confucian thought. Second, National Studies was chiefly literary, and apart from its enthusiasm for the divine emperor, it had little to offer politically in an age when political philosophy was central in both the domain and the bakufu schools.

A second development was Dutch studies. After Christianity had been proscribed and the policy of seclusion adopted, all Western books were banned in Japan. Some knowledge of Dutch was maintained among the official interpreters who dealt with the Dutch at Nagasaki. The ban on Western books (except for those propagating Christianity) was ended in 1720 by the shōgun Tokugawa Yoshimune, following the advice of a scholar whom he had appointed to reform the Japanese calendar.

During the remainder of the eighteenth century, a school of "Dutch medicine" became established in Japan. Japanese pioneers early recognized that Western anatomy texts were superior to Chinese. The first Japanese dissection of a corpse occurred in 1754. In 1774, a Dutch translation of a German anatomy text was translated into Japanese. By the middle of the nineteenth century, there were schools of Dutch studies in the main cities of Japan, and instruction was available in some domains as well. Fukuzawa Yukichi, who studied Dutch and Dutch science during the mid-1850s at a school begun in 1838 in Osaka, wrote in his *Autobiography* of the hostility of his fellow students toward Chinese learning:

Though we often had discussions on many subjects, we seldom touched upon political subjects as most of us were students of medicine. Of course, we were all for free intercourse with Western countries, but there were few among us who took a serious interest in that problem. The only subject that bore our constant attack was Chinese medicine. And by hating Chinese medicine so thoroughly, we came to dislike everything that had any connection with Chinese culture. Our general opinion was that we should rid our country of the influences of the Chinese altogether. Whenever we met a young student of Chinese literature, we simply felt sorry for him. Particularly were the students of Chinese medicine the butt of our ridicule.[9]

Medicine was the primary occupation of those who studied Dutch. But some knowledge of Western astronomy, geography, botany, physics, chemistry, and arts also entered Japan. Works on science occasionally influenced other thinkers as well. Yamagata Bantō (1748–1821) was a rich and scholarly Osaka merchant who produced a rationalistic philosophy based on a synthesis of Neo-Confucianism and Western science. After studying a work on astronomy, he wrote in 1820 that conditions on other planets "varied only according to their size and their proximity to the sun." Bantō also speculated that

"grass and trees will appear, insects will develop; if there are insects, fish, shellfish, animals and birds will not be absent, and finally there will be people too."

Bantō qualified his argument with the naturalistic supposition that Mercury and Venus would probably lack human life, "since these two planets are near to the sun and too hot." He contrasted his rational argu-

---

[9]E. Kiyooka (trans.), *The Autobiography of Fukuzawa Yukichi* (New York: Columbia U.P., 1966), p. 91.

1600	Tokugawa Ieyasu reunifies Japan
1615	"Laws of Military Houses" issued
1639	Seclusion policy adopted
1642	Edo hostage system in place
1644–1694	Bashō, poet
1653–1724	Chikamatsu Monzaemon, dramatist
1701	The forty-seven rōnin avenge their lord
1853–1854	Commodore Matthew Perry visits Japan

ments regarding evolution with the "slapdash" arguments of Buddhists and Shintoists.[10]

From the late eighteenth century, the Japanese began to be aware of the West, and especially of Russia, as a threat to Japan. In 1791, a concerned Japanese wrote *A Discussion of the Military Problems of a Maritime Nation*, advocating a strong navy and coastal defenses. During the early nineteenth century, such concerns mounted. A sudden expansion in Dutch studies occurred after Commodore Matthew Perry's visits to Japan in 1853 and 1854. During the 1860s, Dutch studies became Western studies, as English, French, German, and Russian were added to the languages studied at the bakufu Institute for the Investigation of Barbarian Books. In sum, Dutch studies was not a major influence on Tokugawa thought. It cannot begin to compare with Neo-Confucianism. But it laid a foundation on which the Japanese built quickly when the need arose.

Late Traditional East Asia in World Perspective

The history of late traditional East Asia underlines the exceptional nature of the European development from commerce to industry. The arguments and counterarguments as to why this development did not occur in China or Japan are illuminating. One often cited argument is that East Asia lacked the Protestant ethic that inspired Western capitalism. The counterargument is that all East Asian nations have strong family-centered ethics with an emphasis on frugality, hard work, and saving. If the problem is as deeply rooted as a religious ethic, why have parts of East Asia been able to achieve explosive economic growth during the past few decades?

[10] M. Jansen (ed.), *Changing Japanese Attitudes Toward Modernization* (Princeton: Princeton U.P., 1965), p. 144.

Another argument stresses the absence of a scientific revolution in premodern East Asia. The counterargument is that science made only a minimal contribution to England's early industrialization. Some scholars argue that in China merchant capital, instead of being put into industry, was invested in land, which was honorable and secure from rapacious officials. But this argument applies to the Ch'ing less well than the Ming, and does not apply to Japan, where merchants could not buy land at all.

Still another argument stresses incentives and rewards. In England, the self-educated technicians who invented the water loom and the steam engine reaped enormous rewards and honors. In China, wealth and prestige were reserved largely for officials and gentry, who were literary or political in orientation and who despised those who worked with their hands. There were no patent laws for the protection of inventors. But other scholars counter, asking whether the Ming and Ch'ing were so different from past dynasties when the Chinese had been brilliantly inventive. Whatever the explanation, all agree that substantial commercial growth in both China and Japan did not lead to an indigenous breakthrough to machine industry.

A second point of comparison concerns bureaucracy. Bureaucracy does for administration what the assembly line does for manufacturing. It breaks complex tasks into simple ones to achieve huge gains in efficiency. In the West, bureaucracies appeared only in recent centuries. They strengthened first, monarchies and then, nation-states against landed aristocracies. They are viewed as a sign of modernity, as the triumph of ability over hereditary privilege. In some respects, Chinese bureaucracy was similar; it was reasonably efficient and it strengthened the central state. Would-be officials in nineteenth-century Britain studied the Greek and Roman classics while those of China studied the Confucian classics. But in other regards the Western historian of Chinese bureaucracy feels as if he has passed through Alice's looking glass: What was recent in the West had flourished for over a thousand years in China. Chinese officials themselves were a segment of a landed gentry class in a country from which hereditary aristocracies had long since disappeared. Moreover, while Chinese officials were certainly men of talent, they would become a major obstacle to modernity.

A final point to note is the difference between Chinese and Japanese attitudes toward outside civilizations. When the Jesuits tried to introduce science, the Chinese response was occasional curiosity and massive indifference. A few Jesuits were appointed as interpreters and court astronomers, or were used to cast cannon. The Chinese lack of interest in outside cultures may be explained by the coherence of its core institutions of government—the emperor, bureaucracy, examination system, gentry, and Confucian schools—that had been in place for centuries. Having proved their worth, they were so deeply rooted and internalized as to approximate a closed system, impervious to outside influences. In contrast, the Tokugawa Japanese, despite a national policy of seclusion, reached out for Dutch science as they earlier had reached out for Chinese Neo-Confucianism. This difference would shape the respective responses of China and Japan to the West in the mid-nineteenth century.

Suggested Readings

CHINA

D. BODDE AND C. MORRIS, *Law in Imperial China* (1967). Focuses on the Ch'ing dynasty (1644–1911).

M. ELVIN, *The Pattern of the Chinese Past: A Social and Economic Interpretation* (1973). A controversial but stimulating interpretation of Chinese economic history in terms of technology. It brings in earlier periods as well as the Ming, Ch'ing, and modern China.

J. K. FAIRBANK (ed.), *The Chinese World Order: Traditional China's Foreign Relations* (1968). An examination of the Chinese tribute system and its varying applications.

C. O. HUCKER, *The Traditional Chinese State in Ming Times, 1368–1644* (1961).

C. O. HUCKER (ed.), *Chinese Government in Ming Times: Seven Studies* (1969).

H. L. KAHN, *Monarchy in the Emperor's Eyes: Image and Reality in the Ch'ien-lung Reign* (1971). A study of the Chinese court during the mid-Ch'ing period.

F. MICHAEL, *The Origin of the Manchu Rule in China: Frontier and Bureaucracy as Interacting Forces in the Chinese Empire* (1942).

F. MOTE AND D. TWITCHETT (eds.), *The Ming Dynasty 1368–1644, Part 1 of The Cambridge History of China, Vol. 7* (1987).

S. NAQUIN AND E. S. RAWSKI, *Chinese Society in the Eighteenth Century* (1987).

J. B. PARSONS, *The Peasant Rebellions of the Late Ming Dynasty* (1970).

P. C. PERDUE, *Exhausting the Earth, State and Peasant in Hunan, 1500–1850* (1987).

D. H. PERKINS, *Agricultural Development in China, 1368–1968* (1969).

M. RICCI, *China in the Sixteenth Century: The Journals of Matthew Ricci, 1583–1610* (1953).

W. ROWE, *Hankow* (1984). A study of a city in late imperial China.

G. W. SKINNER, *The City in Late Imperial China* (1977).

J. D. SPENCE, *Ts'ao Yin and the K'ang-hsi Emperor: Bondservant and Master* (1966). An excellent study of the early Ch'ing court.

J. D. SPENCE, *Emperor of China: A Self-Portrait of K'ang-hsi* (1974). The title of this very readable book does not adequately convey the extent of the author's contribution to this study of the early Ch'ing emperor.

F. WAKEMAN, *The Great Enterprise (1985)*. On the founding of the Manchu dynasty.

JAPAN

M. E. BERRY, *Hideyoshi* (1982). A study of the sixteenth-century unifier of Japan.

H. BOLITHO, *Treasures Among Men: The Fudai Daimyo in Tokugawa Japan* (1974).

C. R. BOXER, *The Christian Century in Japan, 1549–1650* (1951).

M. CHIKAMATSU (D. Keene, trans.), *Major plays of Chikamatsu* (1961).

R. P. DORE, *Education in Tokugawa Japan* (1965).

C. J. DUNN, *Everyday Life in Traditional Japan* (1969). A descriptive study of Tokugawa society.

G. S. ELISON, *Deus Destroyed: The Image of Christianity in Early Modern Japan* (1973). A study of the persecutions of Christianity during the early Tokugawa period.

J. W. HALL AND M. JANSEN (eds.), *Studies in the Institutional History of Early Modern Japan* (1968). A collection of articles on Tokugawa institutions.

J. W. HALL, K. NAGAHARA, AND K. YAMAMURA (eds.), *Japan Before Tokugawa* (1981).

H. S. HIBBETT, *The Floating World in Japanese Fiction* (1959). A study of early Tokugawa literature.

D. KEENE (trans.), *Chūshingura, The Treasury of Loyal Retainers* (1971). The puppet play about the forty-seven *rōnin*.

M. MARUYAMA (M. Hane, trans.), *Studies in the Intellectual History of Tokugawa Japan* (1974).

K. W. NAKAI, *Shōgunal Politics* (1988). A brilliant study of Arai Hakuseki's conceptualization of Tokugawa government.

P. NOSCO, (ed.) *Confucianism and Tokugawa Culture* (1984). A collection of essays.

H. OOMS, *Tokugawa Ideology* (1985). A study of seventeenth-century Confucianism.

I. SAIKAKU, (G. W. Sargent, Trans.), *The Japanese Family Storehouse* (1959).

G. B. SANSOM, *The Western World and Japan* (1950).

C. D. SHELDON, *The Rise of the Merchant Class in Tokugawa Japan* (1958).

T. C. SMITH, *The Agrarian Origins of Modern Japan* (1959). On the evolution of farming and rural social organization in Tokugawa Japan.

R. P. TOBY, *State and Diplomacy in Early Modern Japan: Asia in the Development of the Tokugawa Bakufu* (1984).

C. TOTMAN, *Tokugawa Ieyasu: Shōgun* (1983).

H. P. VARLEY, *The Ōnin War: History of Its Origins and Background with a Selective Translation of the Chronicle of Ōnin* (1967).

K. YAMAMURA AND S. B. HANLEY, *Economic and Demographic Change in Preindustrial Japan, 1600–1868* (1977).

Louis XIV (1643–1715) was the dominant ruler of his age. During his reign, France was superior to any other nation in the efficiency of its bureaucracy, the strength of its armed forces, and the cohesion of its sense of nationhood. [Bettmann Archive.]

19 European State Building in the Seventeenth and Eighteenth Centuries

During the seventeenth and early eighteenth centuries, five major states consolidated their positions in Europe and would dominate its politics until at least World War I. They were Great Britain, France, Austria, Prussia, and Russia. Through their military strength, their economic development, and in some cases their colonial empires, they would directly and indirectly touch virtually every world civilization during the modern period. Within Europe, these nations established their dominance at the expense of Spain, the United Netherlands, Poland, Sweden, and the Ottoman Empire. Equally essential to their rise was the weakness of the Holy Roman Empire after the Treaty of Westphalia (1648).

The successful competitors for power on the European scene and eventually on the world scene were those states that, in differing fashions, created strong central political authorities. There were essentially two models for effective political consolidation. The first was that of England, which by the close of the seventeenth century maintained a government with a limited monarchy and a strong Parliament. This political structure and the political theory associated with it would in time exert profound influence in the British North American colonies and elsewhere in the world where Britain came to govern. The other model was that of the French absolute monarchy, most fully perfected under Louis XIV. French absolutism involved, in addition to a strong monarchy, the building of a standing army, the organizing of an efficient tax structure to support the army, and the establishing of a bureaucracy to collect the taxes. Both the English and the French models also required that the major political classes of the country, especially the nobles, be made loyal to the central government. Finally, both models required that the Church stand in a position subordinate to that of the state.

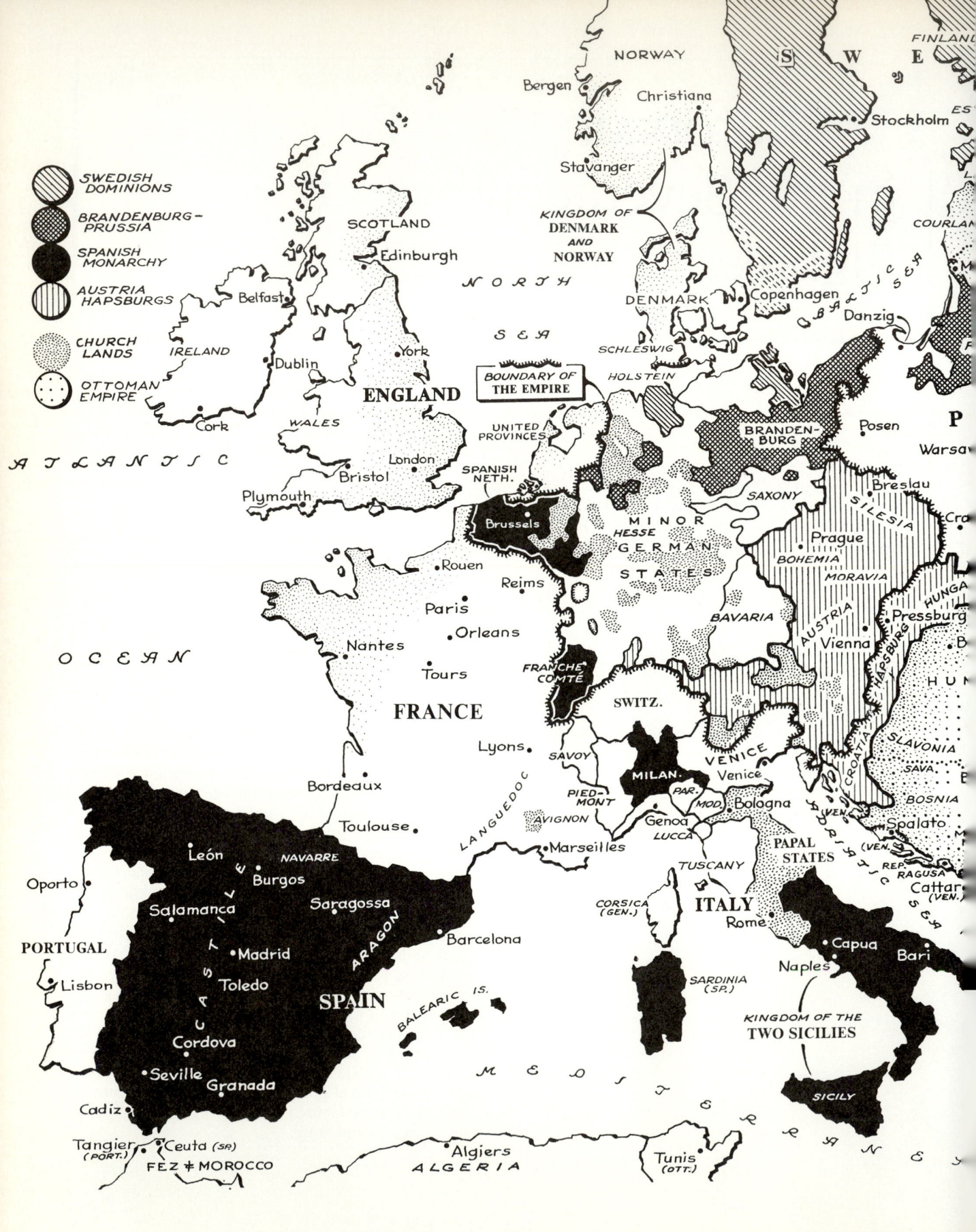

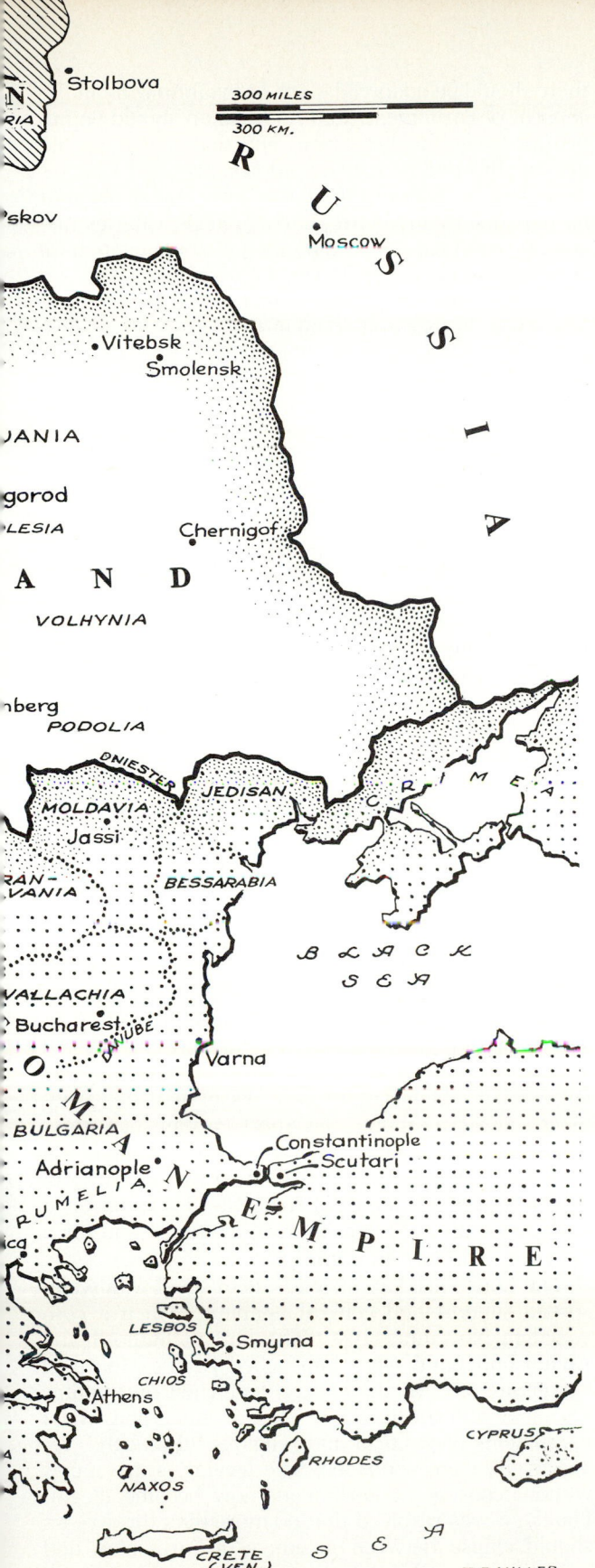

Stolbova

300 MILES

300 KM.

R U S S I A

Moscow

•Vitebsk
Smolensk
•Pskov

Chernigof

JANIA

gorod

LESIA

VOLHYNIA

nberg
PODOLIA

DNIESTER

MOLDAVIA   JEDISAN   C R I M E A
Jassi

RAN-
VANIA   BESSARABIA

B L A C K
S E A

VALLACHIA

Bucharest
DANUBE   Varna

O   M

BULGARIA   A   N

Adrianople   E   M   P   I   R   E
RUMELIA
ca

LESBOS   Smyrna

CHIOS
Athens

Constantinople
Scutari

CYPRUS

RHODES

NAXOS

CRETE   S   E   A
(VEN.)
                    T R MILLER

Constitutional Crisis and Settlement in Stuart England

Between 1603 and 1715, England experienced the most tumultuous years of its long history. In this period, Puritan resistance to the Elizabethan religious settlement merged with fierce parliamentary opposition to the aspirations toward absolute monarchy of the Stuart kings. During these years, no fewer than three foreigners occupied the English throne, and between 1649 and 1660 England was without a king altogether. Yet, by the end of this century of crisis, England provided a model to Europe of limited monarchy, parliamentary government, and measured religious toleration.

James I

The first of England's foreign monarchs was James VI of Scotland (the son of Mary Stuart, Queen of Scots), who in 1603 succeeded the childless Elizabeth as James I of England. This first Stuart king inherited not only the crown but also a royal debt of almost one-half million pounds, a fiercely divided church, and a Parliament already restive over the extent of his predecessor's claims to royal authority. Under James, each of these problems worsened.

Royal debts, his own extravagance, and an inflation he could not control made it necessary for James I to be constantly in quest of additional revenues. These he sought largely by levying—solely on the authority of ill-defined privileges claimed to be attached to the office of king—new custom duties known as *impositions*. Parliament resented such independent efforts to raise revenues as an affront to its power, and the result was a long and divisive struggle between the king and Parliament.

As the distance between king and Parliament widened, the religious problems also worsened. Since the days of Elizabeth, the Puritans had sought to eliminate elaborate religious ceremonies and to replace the hierarchical episcopal system of church governance with a more representative presbyterian form like that of the Calvinist churches on the Continent. In January 1604, to the dismay of the Puritans, the king firmly declared his intention to maintain and even enhance the Anglican episcopacy.

James' pro-Spanish foreign policy also displeased the English. In 1604, he concluded a much needed peace with Spain, England's chief adversary during the

MAP 19-1   EUROPE IN 1648   *At the end of the Thirty Years War Spain still had extensive possessions. Austria and Brandenburg-Prussia were prominent, the independence of the United Provinces and Switzerland was recognized, and Sweden held important river mouths in north Germany.*

second half of the sixteenth century. His subjects viewed this peace as a sign of pro-Catholic sentiment. James further increased suspicions when he attempted, unsuccessfully, to relax the penal laws against Catholics.

Charles I

Charles I (1625–1649) flew even more brazenly in the face of Parliament and the Puritans than had his father. Unable to gain adequate funds from Parliament for the Spanish war begun in 1624, Charles, like his father, resorted to extraparliamentary measures, among them new tariffs, duties, and taxes.

When Parliament met in 1628, its members were furious. Taxes were being illegally collected for a war that was going badly for England and that now, through royal blundering, involved France as well as Spain. Parliament expressed its displeasure by making the king's request for new funds conditional on his recognition of the Petition of Right. This major document of constitutional freedom declared that henceforth

Charles I (1625–1649) and his family. Both children in this painting became king. The future Charles II (1660–1685) is clasping his father's knee: the future James II (1685–1688) is in the arms of his mother, Queen Henrietta Marie, the daughter of Henry IV of France. [Metropolitan Museum of Art.]

there should be no forced loans or taxation without the consent of Parliament, that no freeman should be imprisoned without due cause, and that troops should not be billeted in private homes. Though Charles agreed to the petition, there was little confidence that he would keep his word. Early in 1629, Charles dissolved Parliament and did not recall it again until 1640, when war with Scotland forced him to do so.

To conserve his limited resources, Charles made peace with France and Spain in 1629 and 1630, respectively. His chief minister, Thomas Wentworth (after 1640, earl of Stafford), instituted a policy known as *thorough*, that is, strict efficiency and administrative centralization in government. This policy aimed at absolute royal control of England and required for its success the king's ability to operate independently of Parliament. Every legal fund-raising device was exploited to the full. Neglected laws suddenly were enforced, and existing taxes were extended into new areas.

Charles had neither the royal bureaucracy nor the standing army to rule as an absolute monarch. This became abundantly clear when he and his religious minister, William Laud (1573–1645; after 1633, the archbishop of Canterbury), provoked a war with Scotland. They tried to impose the English episcopal system and a prayer book almost identical to the Anglican *Book of Common Prayer* on the Scots as they had done throughout England. From his position within the Court of High Commission, Laud had already radicalized the Puritans by denying them the right to publish and preach.

Facing resistance from the Scots, Charles was forced to seek financial assistance from a Parliament that opposed his policies almost as much as they did the foreign invaders. Parliament refused even to consider funds for war until the king agreed to redress a long list of political and religious grievances. The result was the king's immediate dissolution of Parliament—hence its name, the Short Parliament (April–May 1640). When the Presbyterian Scots invaded England and defeated an English army at the battle of Newburn in the summer of 1640, Charles reconvened Parliament, this time on the latter's terms and for a long and most fateful duration.

The Long Parliament (1640–1660) acted with widespread support and general unanimity when it convened in November 1640. The earl of Stafford and Archbishop Laud were impeached by the House of Commons and eventually executed. The Court of Star Chamber and the Court of High Commission, royal instruments of political and religious "thorough," respectively, were abolished. The levying of new taxes without consent of Parliament now became illegal. Finally, it was resolved that no more than three years should elapse between meetings of Parliament and

Parliament Attacks Charles I's Royal Abuses of His Subjects

The tension between King Charles I (1625–1649) and Parliament had very few causes that did not go back to earlier reigns. The Petition of Right can, therefore, be seen as a general catalog of reasons for opposing arbitrary royal power. Specifically, angered by Charles and his levying of new taxes and other revenue-gathering devices, his coercion of freemen, and his quartering of troops in transit in private homes, Parliament refused to grant the king any funds until he rescinded such practices by recognizing the Petition of Right (June 7, 1628). Here is the Petition and the king's reply.

[The Lords Spiritual and Temporal, and Commons in Parliament assembled] do humbly pray your Most Excellent Majesty, that no man hereafter be compelled to make or yield any gift, loan, benevolence, tax, or such like charge, without common consent by Act of Parliament; and that none be called to make answer, or take such oath, or to give attendance, or be confined, or otherwise molested or disquieted concerning the same, or for refusal thereof; and that no freeman, in any such manner as is before-mentioned, be imprisoned or detained; and that your Majesty will be pleased to remove the said soldiers and mariners [who have been quartered in private homes], and that your people may not be so burdened in time to come; and that the foresaid commissions for proceeding by martial law, may be revoked and annulled; and that here-

after no commissions of like nature may issue forth to any person or persons whatsoever, to be executed as aforesaid, lest by colour of them any of your Majesty's subjects be destroyed or put to death, contrary to the laws and franchise of the land.

All which they most humbly pray of your Most Excellent Majesty, as their rights and liberties according to the laws and statutes of this realm.

[The King's reply: The King willeth that right be done according to the laws and customs of the realm; and that the statutes be put in due execution, that his subjects may have no cause to complain of any wrong or oppressions, contrary to their just rights and liberties, to the preservation whereof he holds himself as well obliged as of his prerogative.] ❑

The Constitutional Documents of the Puritan Revolution, ed. by Samuel R. Gardiner (Oxford, England: Clarendon Press, 1889), pp. 4–5.

---

that the Parliament could not be dissolved without its own consent.

There remained division within Parliament over the precise direction of religious reform. Both moderate Puritans (the Presbyterians) and extreme Puritans (the Independents) wanted the complete abolition of the episcopal system and the *Book of Common Prayer*. The majority of Presbyterians sought to reshape England religiously along Calvinist lines, with local congregations subject to higher representative governing bodies (presbyteries). Independents wanted every congregation to be its own final authority. There were also a considerable number of conservatives in both houses who were determined to preserve the English church in its current form.

The division within Parliament was further intensified in October 1641, when a rebellion erupted in Ireland requiring an army to suppress it. Puritan leaders argued that Charles could not be trusted with an army and that Parliament should become the commander-in-chief of English armed forces. Parliamentary conservatives, on the other hand, were appalled by such bold departure from tradition.

Charles saw the division within Parliament as a chance to regain power. In January 1642, he invaded

Parliament with his soldiers. Shocked by the king's action, a majority of the House of Commons passed the Militia Ordinance, a measure that gave Parliament control of the army. The die was now cast. For the next four years (1642–1646), civil war engulfed England.

Oliver Cromwell and the Puritan Republic

Two factors led finally to Parliament's victory. The first was an alliance with Scotland in 1643. The second was the reorganization of the parliamentary army under Oliver Cromwell (1599–1658), a middle-aged country squire of iron discipline and strong Independent religious sentiment. The allies won the Battle of Marston Moor in 1644, the largest engagement of the war; and in June 1645, Cromwell's New Model Army, which fought with a disciplined fanaticism, decisively defeated the king at Naseby.

Charles tried in subsequent years to regain power over Parliament, but it was not to be. On January 30, 1649, after trial by a special court, Parliament executed Charles as a public criminal and thereafter abolished the monarchy, the House of Lords, and the Anglican church.

The execution of Charles I, January 30, 1649. The king's portrait is on the upper left. Cromwell's on the upper right. [National Galleries of Scotland.]

From 1649 to 1660, England was officially a Puritan republic. During this period, Cromwell's army conquered Ireland and Scotland, creating the single political entity of Great Britain. Cromwell, however, was a military man and no politician. When in 1653 the House of Commons entertained a motion to disband the expensive army of fifty thousand men, Cromwell responded by marching in and disbanding Parliament. He ruled thereafter as Lord Protector.

But his military dictatorship proved no more effective than Charles' rule had been and became just as harsh and hated. Cromwell's great army and foreign adventures inflated his budget to three times that of Charles'. Trade and commerce suffered throughout England, as near chaos reigned in many places. Puritan prohibitions of such pastimes as theatergoing, dancing, and drunkenness were widely resented. Cromwell's treatment of Anglicans came to be just as intolerant as Charles' treatment of Puritans had been. In the name of religious liberty, political liberty had been lost. By the time of Cromwell's death in 1658, a majority of the English were ready to end the Puritan experiment and return to the traditional institutions of government.

Charles II and the Restoration of the Monarchy

The Stuart monarchy was restored in 1660 when Charles II (1660–1685), son of Charles I, returned to England amid great rejoicing. A man of considerable charm and political skills, Charles set a refreshing new tone after eleven years of somber Puritanism. His restoration returned England to the status quo of 1642, as once again a hereditary monarch sat on the throne and the Anglican church was religiously supreme.

Because of his secret Catholic sympathies, the king favored a policy of religious toleration. He wanted to allow all persons outside the Church of England, Catholics as well as Puritans, to worship freely as long as they remained loyal to the throne. But the ultraroyalist Anglicans in Parliament decided otherwise. They did not believe that patriotism and religion could be separated. Between 1661 and 1665, through a series of laws known as the Clarendon Code, Parliament excluded Roman Catholics, Presbyterians, and Independents from the religious and political life of the nation.

In 1670, England and France formally allied against the Dutch (a commercial competitor) in the Treaty of Dover. In an attempt to unite the English people behind the war with Holland, and as a sign of good faith to the French king Louis XIV, Charles issued a Declaration of Indulgence in 1672, suspending all laws against Roman Catholics and Protestant nonconformists. But again, the conservative Tory Parliament proved less generous than the king and refused to grant money for the war until Charles rescinded the measure. After Charles withdrew the declaration, Parliament passed the Test Act, which required all officials of the crown, civil and military, to swear an oath against the doctrine of transubstantiation—a requirement that no loyal Roman Catholic could honestly meet. The Test Act was aimed in large measure at the king's brother, James, duke of York, heir to the throne and a recent, devout convert to Catholicism.

James II and the "Glorious Revolution"

James II (1685–1688) came to the throne demanding the repeal of the Test Act. When Parliament balked, he dissolved it and proceeded openly to appoint known Catholics to high positions in both his court and the army. In 1687, James suspended all religious tests and permitted free worship. In June 1688, James went so far as to imprison seven Anglican bishops who had refused to publicize his suspension of laws against Catholics.

But the direct stimulus for parliamentary action against the king came on June 20, 1688, when James' second wife, a Catholic, gave birth to a son, a male Catholic heir to the English throne. The English had hoped that James would die without a male heir and that the throne would revert to his Protestant eldest daughter, Mary. She was the wife of William III of Orange, *stadholder* of the Netherlands, great-grandson of William the Silent, and the leader of European opposition to Louis XIV's imperial designs. Within days of the birth of a Catholic male heir, Whig and Tory nobles formed a coalition and invited Orange to invade England to preserve "traditional liberties," that is, the Anglican church and parliamentary government.

William of Orange arrived with his army in November 1688 and was received without opposition by the English people. In the face of sure defeat, James fled to France and the protection of Louis XIV. With James gone, Parliament declared the throne vacant and on its own authority proclaimed William and Mary the new monarchs in 1689, completing a successful bloodless "Glorious Revolution" of 1688. William and Mary, in turn, recognized a Bill of Rights that limited the powers of the monarchy and guaranteed the civil liberties of the English privileged classes. Henceforth, England's monarchs would rule by the consent of Parliament and be subject to law. The Bill of Rights also pointedly prohibited Roman Catholics from occupying the English throne. The Toleration Act of 1689 permitted worship by all Protestants and outlawed Roman Catholics and antitrinitarians (those who denied the Christian doctrine of the Trinity).

The final measure closing the century of strife was the Act of Settlement in 1701. This bill provided for the

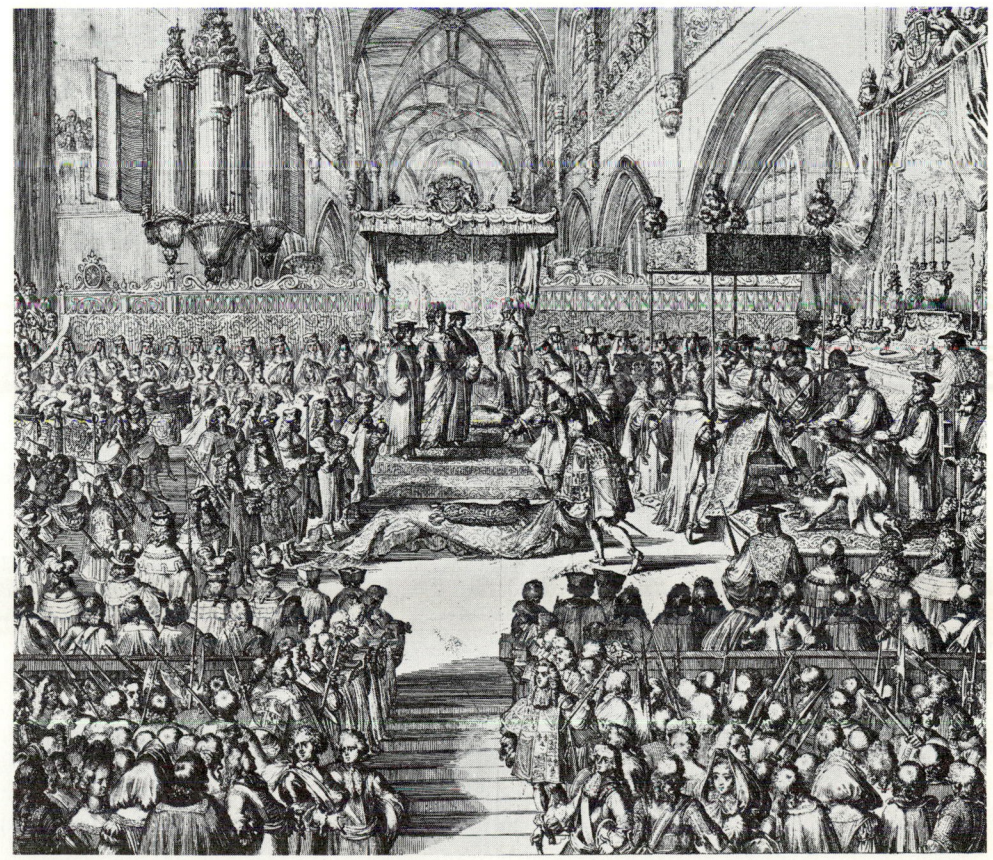

The coronation of William III and Mary II, April 11, 1689. Although Mary was the daughter of James II and William's mother was the daughter of Charles I, their rule was based on the consent of Parliament, and their powers, although great, were limited by law. [The Mansell Collection.]

1603	James VI of Scotland becomes James I of England
1604	Hampton Court Conference
1611	Publication of the Authorized or King James Version of the English Bible
1625	Charles I becomes English monarch
1628	Petition of Right
1629	Charles I dissolves Parliament and embarks on eleven years of personal rule
1640	April–May, Short Parliament; November, Long Parliament convenes
1641	Great Remonstrance
1642	Outbreak of the Civil War
1645	Charles I defeated at Naseby
1648	Pride's Purge
1649	Charles I executed
1649–1660	Various attempts at a Puritan Commonwealth
1660	Charles II restored to the English throne
1670	Secret Treaty of Dover between France and England
1672	Parliament passes the Test Act
1685	James II becomes king of England
1688	Glorious Revolution
1689	William and Mary come to the throne of England
1701	Act of Settlement provides for Hanoverian Succession
1702–1715	Reign of Queen Anne, the last of the Stuarts

English crown to go to the Protestant House of Hanover in Germany if Queen Anne (ruled 1702–1714), the second daughter of James II and the last of the Stuart monarchs, was not survived by her children. Consequently, in 1714, the Elector of Hanover became King George I of England, the third foreign monarch to occupy the English throne in just over a century.

The World of Louis XIV

King by Divine Right

Seventeenth-century France saw both representative government and religious pluralism crushed by the absolute monarchy and the closed Catholic state of Louis XIV (1643–1715). An aggressive ruler who sought glory (*"la gloire"*) in foreign wars, Louis subjected his subjects at home to "one king, one law, one faith."

Thanks to the foresight of Cardinal Mazarin (1602–1661), Louis XIV was well prepared to rule France. The rebellions against the crown he had witnessed in his youth made him loathe "kings of straw." Indoctrinated with a strong sense of the grandeur of his crown, he never missed an opportunity to impress it on the French people.

An important theorist for Louis' concept of royal authority was his tutor Bishop Jacques-Bénigne Bossuet (1627–1704). An ardent champion of the Gallican Liberties—the traditional rights of the French king and church in matters of ecclesiastical appointments and taxation—Bossuet defended what he called the "divine right of kings." He cited the Old Testament example of rulers divinely appointed by and answerable only to God. As medieval popes had insisted that only God could judge a pope, so Bossuet argued that none save God could sit in judgment on the king. Although kings remained duty-bound to reflect God's will in their rule—and in this sense Bossuet considered them always subject to a higher authority—as God's regents on earth they could not be bound to the dictates of mere princes and parliaments. Such were among the assumptions that lay behind Louis XIV's alleged declaration: *"L'état, c'est moi"* ("I am the state").

Versailles

The palace court at Versailles on the outskirts of Paris became Louis' permanent residence after 1682 and was a true temple to royalty, architecturally designed and artistically decorated to proclaim the glory of the Sun King, as Louis was known. A spectacular estate with magnificent fountains and acres of orange groves, it became home to thousands of aristocrats, royal officials, and servants. Although its physical maintenance and new additions, which continued throughout Louis' lifetime, consumed over half his annual revenues, Versailles paid political dividends well worth the investment.

Life at court was organized around the king's daily routine. His rising and dressing were a time of rare intimacy, when nobles, who entered their names on waiting lists to be in attendance, whispered their special requests in Louis' ear.

After the morning mass, which Louis always observed, there followed long hours in council with the chief ministers, assemblies from which the nobility was carefully excluded. Louis' ministers and councilors were hand-picked townsmen, servants who owed everything they had to the king's favor and were for

Cardinal Richelieu, who held France together during the reign of Louis XIII (1610–43) and laid the foundations for French political and military dominance during the reign of Louis XIV. Here in the mastermind behind French political power in the seventeenth century, in the striking triple portrait by the Flemish-French painter Philippe de Champaigne (1602–1674). [Reproduced by courtesy of the Trustees, The National Gallery, London.]

that reason inclined to serve faithfully and without question. There were three main councils: the Council of State, a small group of four or five who met thrice weekly to rule on all matters of state, but especially on foreign affairs and war policy; the Council of Dispatches, which regularly assessed the reports from the

Bishop Bossuet Defends the Divine Right of Kings

The revolutions of the seventeenth century caused many to fear anarchy far more than tyranny, among them the influential French bishop Jacques Bénigne Bossuet (1627–1704), the leader of French Catholicism in the second half of the seventeenth century. Louis XIV made him court preacher and tutor to his son, for whom Bossuet wrote a celebrated Universal History. *In the following excerpt, Bossuet defended the divine right and absolute power of kings, whom he depicted as embracing in their person the whole body of the state and the will of the people they governed and, as such, as being immune from judgment by any mere mortal.*

The royal power is absolute. . . . The prince need render account of his acts to no one. "I counsel thee to keep the king's commandment, and that in regard of the oath of God. Be not hasty to go out of his sight; stand not on an evil thing for he doeth whatsoever pleaseth him. Where the word of a king is, there is power: and who may say unto him, What doest thou? Whoso keepeth the commandment shall feel no evil thing" [Eccles. 8:2–5]. Without this absolute authority the king could neither do good nor repress evil. It is necessary that his power be such that no one can hope to escape him, and finally, the only protection of individuals against the public authority should be their innocence. This confirms the teaching of St. Paul: "Wilt thou then not be afraid of the power? Do that which is good" [Rom. 13:3].

God is infinite, God is all. The prince, as prince, is not regarded as a private person: he is a public personage, all the state is in him; the will of all the people is included in his. As all perfection and all strength are united in God, so all the power of individuals is united in the person of the prince. What grandeur that a single man should embody so much! . . .

Behold an immense people united in a single person; behold this holy power, paternal and absolute; behold the secret cause which governs the whole body of the state, contained in a single head: you see the image of God in the king, and you have the idea of royal majesty. God is holiness itself, goodness itself, and power itself. In these things lies the majesty of God. In the image of these things lies the majesty of the prince. ❑

From *Politics Drawn from the Very Words of Holy Scripture*, in James Harvey Robinson (ed.), *Readings in European History*, Vol. 2 (Boston: Ginn and Co., 1906), pp. 275–276.

Versailles as it appeared in 1668 in a painting by Pierre Patel the Elder (1605–1676). The central building is the hunting lodge built for Louis XIII earlier in the century, and some of the first expansion undertaken by Louis XIV appears as wings. The painting is in the Versailles museum. [Cliché des Musées Nationaux, Paris.]

intendants in the towns and provinces, a boring business that the king often left to his ministers; and finally, the Council of Finances, which handled matters of taxation and commerce.

The afternoons were spent hunting, riding, or strolling about the lush gardens. Evenings were given over to planned entertainment in the large salons (plays, concerts, gambling, and the like), followed by supper at 10:00 P.M.

Even the king's retirement was a part of the day's spectacle. Fortunate nobles were permitted briefly to hold his night candle as they accompanied him to his bed.

All this ritual and play served the political purpose of keeping an impoverished nobility, barred by law from high government positions, busy and dependent so that they had little time to plot revolt. The dress codes and the high-stakes gaming at court contributed to the indebtedness and dependency of the nobility on the king. Court life was a carefully planned and successfully executed domestication of the nobility.

Revocation of the Edict of Nantes

Louis believed that political unity required religious conformity. Since 1598, when the Edict of Nantes was proclaimed, a cold war had existed between the great Catholic majority (nine tenths of the French population remained Catholic) and the Protestant minority. Despite their respectable numbers, about 1.75 million by the 1660s, the Huguenots were in decline in the second half of the seventeenth century. Following the Peace of Nijmegen in 1678–1679, which halted for the moment Louis' aggression in Europe, Louis launched a methodical government campaign against the French Huguenots in a determined effort to unify France religiously. He hounded the Huguenots out of public life, banned them from government office, and excluded them from such professions as printing and medicine. Subsidies and selective taxation also became weapons to encourage their conversion to Catholicism. In 1681, Louis further bullied the Huguenots by quartering his troops in their towns. The final stage of the persecu-

Louis XIV Revokes the Edict of Nantes

Believing that a country could not be under one king and one law unless it was also under one religious system, Louis XIV stunned much of Europe in October 1685 by revoking the Edict of Nantes, which had protected the religious freedoms and civil rights of French Protestants since 1598.

Art. 1. Know that we . . . with our certain knowledge, full power and royal authority, have by this present, perpetual and irrevocable edict, suppressed and revoked the edict of the aforesaid king our grandfather, given at Nantes in the month of April, 1598, in all its extent . . . together with all the concessions made by [this] and other edicts, declarations, and decrees, to the people of the so-called Reformed religion, of whatever nature they be . . . and in consequence we desire . . . that all the temples of the people of the aforesaid so-called Reformed religion situated in our kingdom . . . should be demolished forthwith.

Art. 2. We forbid our subjects of the so-called Reformed religion to assemble any more for public worship of the above-mentioned religion . . .

Art. 3. We likewise forbid all lords, of whatever rank they may be, to carry out heretical services in houses and fiefs . . . the penalty for . . . the said worship being confiscation of their body and possessions.

Art. 4. We order all ministers of the aforesaid so-called Reformed religion who do not wish to be converted and to embrace the Catholic, Apostolic, and Roman religion, to depart from our kingdom and the lands subject to us within fifteen days from the publication of our present edict . . . on pain of the galleys.

Art. 5. We desire that those among the said [Reformed] ministers who shall be converted [to the Catholic religion] shall continue to enjoy during their life, and their wives shall enjoy after their death as long as they remain widows, the same exemptions from taxation and billeting of soldiers, which they enjoyed while they fulfilled the function of ministers. . . .

Art. 8. With regard to children who shall be born to those of the aforesaid so-called Reformed religion, we desire that they be baptized by their parish priests. We command the fathers and mothers to send them to the churches for that purpose, on penalty of a fine of 500 livres or more if they fail to do so; and afterwards, the children shall be brought up in the Catholic, Apostolic, and Roman religion. . . .

Art. 10. All our subjects of the so-called Reformed religion, with their wives and children, are to be strongly and repeatedly prohibited from leaving our aforesaid kingdom . . . or of taking out . . . their possessions and effects. . . .

The members of the so-called Reformed religion, while awaiting God's pleasure to enlighten them like the others, can live in the towns and districts of our kingdom . . . and continue their occupation there, and enjoy their possessions . . . on condition . . . that they do not make public profession of [their religion] ❏

Church and State Through the Centuries: A Collection of Historic Documents, trans. and ed. by S. Z. Ehler and John B. Morrall (New York: Biblo and Tannen, 1967), pp. 209–213.

tion came in October 1685, when Louis revoked the Edict of Nantes (see Chapter 17). In practical terms, the revocation meant the closing of Protestant churches and schools, the exile of Protestant ministers, the placement of nonconverting members of the laity in galleys as slaves, and the ceremonial baptism of Protestant children by Catholic priests.

The revocation of the Edict of Nantes became the major blunder of Louis' reign. Thereafter, he was viewed throughout Protestant Europe as a new Philip II intent on a Catholic reconquest of the whole of Europe, who must be resisted at all costs. Internally, the revocation of the Edict of Nantes led to the voluntary emigration of over a quarter million French, who formed new communities and joined the French resistance movement in England, Germany, Holland, and the New World.

War Abroad

War was the normal state for seventeenth-century rulers and for none more so than for Louis XIV, who would confess on his deathbed that he had "loved war too much." Periods of peace became opportunities for the discontented in town and countryside to plot against the king; war served national unity as well as "glory." By the 1660s, France was superior to any other nation in administrative bureaucracy, armed forces, and national unity. It had a population of nineteen million, prosperous farms, vigorous trade, and much taxable wealth. By every external measure, Louis was in a position to dominate Europe.

THE WAR OF DEVOLUTION. Louis' first great foreign adventure was the War of Devolution (1667–

1668). It was fought, as still a later and greater war would be, over Louis' claim to a Spanish inheritance through his wife, Marie Thérèse (1638–1683). According to the terms of the Treaty of the Pyrenees (1659), Marie had renounced her claim to the Spanish succession on condition that a 500,000-crown dowry be paid to Louis within eighteen months of the marriage, a condition that was not met. When Philip IV of Spain died in September 1665, he left all his lands to his sickly four-year-old son by a second marriage, Charles II (1665–1700), and explicitly excluded his daughter Marie from any share. Louis had always harbored the hope of turning the marriage to territorial gain and argued even before Philip's death that Marie was entitled to a portion of the inheritance.

Louis had a legal argument on his side, which gave the war its name. He maintained that because in certain regions of Brabant and Flanders, which were part of the Spanish inheritance, property "devolved" to the children of a first marriage rather than to those of a second, Marie had a higher claim than Charles II to these regions. The argument was not accepted—such regional laws could hardly bind the king of Spain—but Louis was not deterred from moving his armies into Flanders and the Franche-Comté in 1667. In response to this aggression, England, Sweden, and the United Provinces of Holland formed the Triple Alliance, a force sufficient to bring Louis to peace terms in the Treaty of Aix-la-Chapelle (1668).

INVASION OF THE NETHERLANDS. In 1670, England and France became allies against the Dutch, and the Triple Alliance crumbled. This left Louis in a stronger position to invade the Netherlands for a second time, which he did in 1672.

Louis' successful invasion brought the twenty-seven-year-old Prince of Orange, after 1689 King William III of England, to power. Orange was the great-grandson of William the Silent, who had repulsed Philip II and dashed Spanish hopes of dominating the Netherlands in the sixteenth century.

Orange, an unpretentious Calvinist in almost every way Louis' opposite, galvanized the seven provinces into a fierce fighting unit. In 1673, he united the Holy Roman Empire, Spain, Lorraine, and Brandenburg in an alliance against Louis, who was now seen by his enemies to be "the Christian Turk," a menace to the whole of western Europe, Catholic and Protestant alike. The Peace of Nimwegen, signed with different parties in successive years (1678, 1679), ended the hostilities of this second war.

THE LEAGUE OF AUGSBURG. Between the Treaty of Nimwegen and the renewal of full-scale war in 1689, Louis restlessly probed his perimeters. In 1681, his army conquered the free city of Strasbourg, setting off the formation of new defensive coalitions against Louis. The League of Augsburg, created in 1686 to resist French expansion into Germany, grew by 1689 to include Spain; Sweden; the United Provinces; the electorates of Bavaria, Saxony, and the Palatinate; and the England of William and Mary. It also had the support of Emperor Leopold. That year saw the beginning of the Nine Years' War (1689–1697) between France and the League of Augsburg. For the third time, stalemate and exhaustion forced the combatants into an interim settlement. The Peace of Ryswick in September 1697 became a personal triumph for William, now William III of England, and Emperor Leopold, as it secured Holland's borders and thwarted French expansion into Germany. During this same period, England and France fought for control of North America in what came to be known as King William's War (1689–1697).

WAR OF THE SPANISH SUCCESSION. After Ryswick, Louis, who seemed to thrive on partial success, made still a fourth attempt to realize his grand design of French European domination, this time assisted by an unforeseen turn of events. On November 1, 1700, Charles II of Spain, known as "the Sufferer" because of his genetic deformities and lingering illness, died. There had been negotiations before his death to arrange a partition of the inheritance in order to maintain the existing balance of power. But Charles foiled them by leaving everything to Philip of Anjou, Louis' grandson, who became Philip V of Spain. At a stroke, the Spanish inheritance seemed to be France's.

In September 1701, the Grand Alliance of England, Holland, and the Holy Roman Emperor formed against Louis in The Hague. Its intent was to preserve the balance of power by securing Flanders once and for all as a neutral barrier between Holland and France and by gaining for the emperor his fair share of the Spanish inheritance. After the formation of the alliance, Louis increased the stakes of battle by recognizing James Edward Stuart, the exiled son of James II of England as James III, king of England.

Once again, total war enveloped western Europe as the twelve-year War of the Spanish Succession (1702–1714) began. France, for the first time, went to war with inadequate finances, a poorly equipped army, and mediocre military leadership. The English had advanced weaponry (flintlock rifles, paper cartridges, and ring bayonets) and superior tactics (thin, maneuverable troop columns rather than the traditional deep ones). John Churchill, the duke of Marlborough, who succeeded William of Orange as leader of the alliance, bested Louis' soldiers in every major engagement. Marlborough routed French armies at Blenheim in August 1704 and on the plain of Ramillies in 1706—

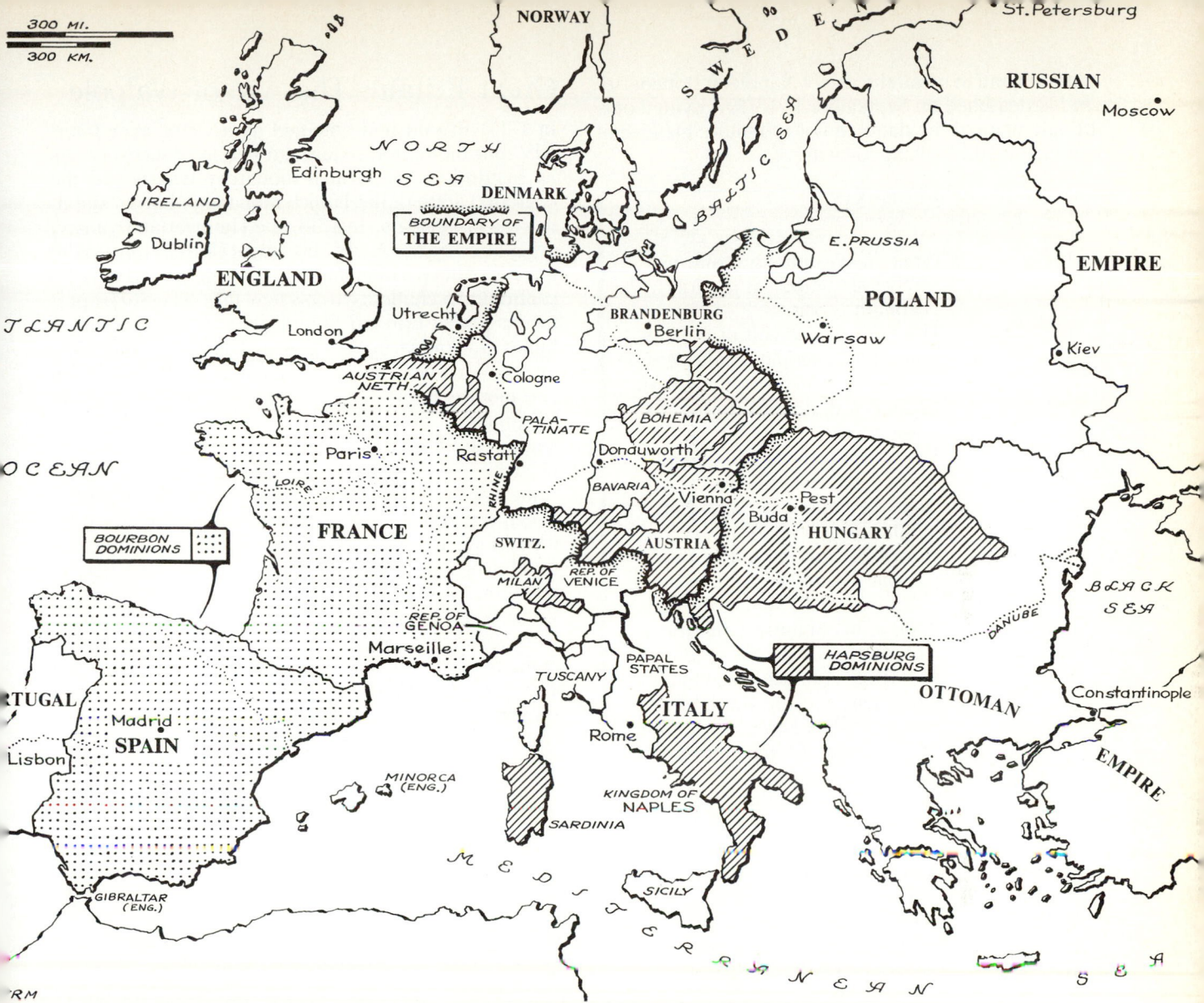

MAP 19-2 EUROPE IN 1714 *The War of the Spanish Succession ended in the year before the death of the aged Louis XIV. By then France and Spain, although not united, were ruled by members of the Bourbon family, and Spain had lost her non-Iberian possessions. Austria had continued to grow.*

two decisive battles of the war. In 1708–1709, famine, revolts, and uncollectable taxes tore France apart internally. Despair pervaded the French court, and Louis wondered aloud how God could forsake one who had done so much for him.

Though ready to make peace in 1709, Louis could not bring himself to accept the stiff terms of the alliance, which included the demand that he transfer all Spanish possessions to the emperor's grandson Charles and remove Philip V from Madrid. An immediate result of this failure to come to terms was a clash of forces at Malplaquet (September 1709), which left

carnage on the battlefield unsurpassed until modern times.

France finally signed an armistice with England at Utrecht in July 1712, and hostilities were concluded with Holland and the emperor in the Treaty of Rastadt in March 1714. These agreements confirmed Philip V as king of Spain and gave England Gibraltar, which made England thereafter a Mediterranean power.

Politically, the eighteenth century would belong to England as the sixteenth had belonged to Spain and the seventeenth to France. Although France remained intact and quite strong, the realization of Louis XIV's ambition had to await the rise of Napoleon Bonaparte. On his deathbed on September 1, 1715, a dying Louis fittingly warned the dauphin not to imitate his love of buildings and his liking for war.

THE REIGN OF LOUIS XIV (1643–1715)

1648	Peace of Westphalia reaffirms religious pluralism in Holy Roman Empire
1649–1652	The Fronde, a revolt of nobility and townspeople against confiscatory policies of the crown
1653	Jansenism declared a heresy by the pope
1659	Treaty of Pyrenees ends hostilities between France and Spain
1660	Louis XIV enforces papal ban on Jansenists
1667–1668	War of Devolution fought over Louis' claims to lands in Brabant and Flanders by virtue of his Spanish inheritance through his wife
1668	The Triple Alliance (England, Sweden, and the United Provinces) repels Louis' army from Flanders and forces the Treaty of Aix-la-Chapelle
1670	Treaty of Dover brings French and English together against the Netherlands
1672	France invades the United Provinces
1678–1679	Peace of Nimwegen ends French wars in United Provinces
1685	Louis XIV revokes Edict of Nantes
1689–1697	Nine Years' War between France and League of Augsburg, a Europe-wide alliance against Louis XIV
1697	Peace of Ryswick ends French expansion into Holland and Germany
1702–1714	England, Holland, and the Holy Roman Emperor resist Louis' claim to the Spanish throne in the War of the Spanish Succession
1712	Treaty of Utrecht between England and France
1714	Treaty of Rastadt between Spain and France

Great Britain: The Age of Walpole

In 1713, Britain had emerged as a victor over Louis XIV, but the nation required a period of recovery. As an institution, the British monarchy was not in the degraded state of the French monarchy, but its stability was not certain. In 1714, the Hanoverian dynasty, designated by the Act of Settlement (1701), came to the throne. Almost immediately, George I (1714–1727) confronted a challenge to his new title. The Stuart pretender James Edward Stuart (1688–1766), the son of James II, landed in Scotland in December 1715. His forces marched southward but met defeat less than two months later.

Although militarily successful against the pretender, the new dynasty and its supporters saw the need for consolidation. The closing years of Queen Anne's reign (1702–1714) had seen sharp clashes between the political factions of Whigs and Tories over the coming Treaty of Utrecht. The Tories had urged a rapid peace settlement and after 1710 had opened negotiations with France. During the same period, the Whigs were seeking favor from the Elector of Hanover, who would soon be their monarch. His concern for his domains in Hanover made him unsympathetic to the Tory peace policy. In the final months of Anne's reign, some Tories, fearing loss of power under the waiting Hanoverian dynasty, opened channels of communication with the Stuart pretender; and a few even rallied to his losing cause.

Under these circumstances, it was little wonder that George I, on his arrival in Britain, clearly favored the Whigs and proceeded with caution. Previously, the differences between the Whigs and the Tories had been vaguely related to principle. However, after the Hanoverian accession and the eventual Whig success in achieving the firm confidence of George I, the chief difference for almost forty years between the Whigs and the Tories was that one group did have access to public office and patronage and the other did not. This early Hanoverian proscription of Tories from public life was one of the most prominent features of the age.

The political situation after 1715 had at first remained in a state of flux until Robert Walpole (1676–1745) took over the helm of government after a financial scandal had raised questions about the integrity of the previous ministers. George I gave Walpole his full confidence. For this reason, Walpole has often been regarded as the first prime minister of Great Britain and the originator of the cabinet system of government. However, unlike a modern prime minister, he was not chosen by the majority of the House of Commons. His power largely depended on the goodwill of George I and later of George II (1727–1760). Walpole generally demanded that all of the ministers in the cabinet agree on policy, but he could not prevent frequent public differences on policy.

The real source of Walpole's power was the combination of the personal support of the king, Walpole's ability to handle the House of Commons, and his iron-fisted control of government patronage. To oppose Walpole on either minor or more substantial matters was to risk the almost certain loss of government patronage for oneself, one's family, or one's friends. Through the skillful use of patronage, Walpole bought support for himself and his policies from people who wanted to receive jobs, appointments, favors, and government contracts. Such corruption supplied the glue of political loyalty.

Walpole's favorite slogan was *quieta non movere* (roughly, "let sleeping dogs lie"). To that end, he pursued a policy of peace abroad and promotion of the status quo at home. In this regard, he and Cardinal Fleury were much alike. The structure of the eighteenth-century British House of Commons aided Walpole in his pacific policies. It was neither a democratic nor a representative body. Each of the counties elected two members. But if the more powerful landed families in a county agreed on the candidates, there was no contest. Other members were elected from units called boroughs, of which there were a considerable variety. There were many more borough seats than county seats. A few were large enough for elections to be relatively democratic. However, most boroughs had a very small number of electors. Through proper electoral management, which involved favors to the electors, the House of Commons could be controlled.

The structure of Parliament and the manner in which it was elected meant that the government of England was dominated by the owners of property and by especially wealthy nobles. They did not pretend to represent people and districts or to be responsive to what would later be called public opinion. They regarded themselves as representing various economic and social interests, such as the West Indian interest, the merchant interest, or the landed interest. These owners of property were suspicious of an administrative bureaucracy controlled by the crown or its ministers. For this reason, they or their agents served as local government administrators, judges, militia commanders, and tax collectors. In this sense, the British nobility and other substantial landowners actually did govern the nation. And because they regarded the Parliament as the political sovereign, there was no absence of central political authority and direction. Con-

Lady Mary Wortley Montagu Gives Advice on Election to Parliament

In this letter of 1714, Lady Mary Wortley Montagu discussed with her husband the various paths that he might follow to gain election to the British House of Commons. Note the emphasis she placed on knowing the right people and on having large amounts of money to spend on voters. Eventually her husband was elected to Parliament in a borough that was controlled through government patronage.

You seem not to have received my letters, or not to have understood them: you had been chose undoubtedly at York, if you had declared in time; but there is not any gentleman or tradesman disengaged at this time; they are treating every night. Lord Carlisle and the Thompsons have given their interest to Mr. Jenkins. I agree with you of the necessity of your standing this Parliament, which, perhaps, may be more considerable than any that are to follow it; but, as you proceed, 'tis my opinion, you will spend your money and not be chose. I believe there is hardly a borough unengaged. I expect every letter should tell me you are sure of some place; and, as far as I can perceive you are sure of none. As it has been managed, perhaps it will be the best way to deposit a certain sum in some friend's hands, and buy some little Cornish borough: it would, undoubtedly, look better to be chose for a considerable town; but I take it to be now too late. If you have any thoughts of Newark, it will be absolutely necessary for you to enquire after Lord Lexington's interest; and your best way to apply yourself to Lord Holdernesse, who is both a Whig and an honest man. He is now in town, and you may enquire of him if Brigadier Sutton stands there; and if not, try to engage him for you. Lord Lexington is so ill at the Bath, that it is a doubt if he will live 'till the elections; and if he dies, one of his heiresses, and the whole interest of his estate, will probably fall on Lord Holdernesse.

'Tis a surprize to me, that you cannot make sure of some borough, when a number of your friends bring in so many Parliament-men without trouble or expense. 'Tis too late to mention it now, but you might have applied to Lady Winchester, as Sir Joseph Jekyl did last year, and by her interest the Duke of Bolton brought him in, for nothing; I am sure she would be more zealous to serve me, than Lady Jekyl. ❏

Lord Wharncliffe (Ed.), *Letters and Works of Lady Mary Wortley Montagu*, 3rd ed., Vol. 1 (London, 1861), p. 211.

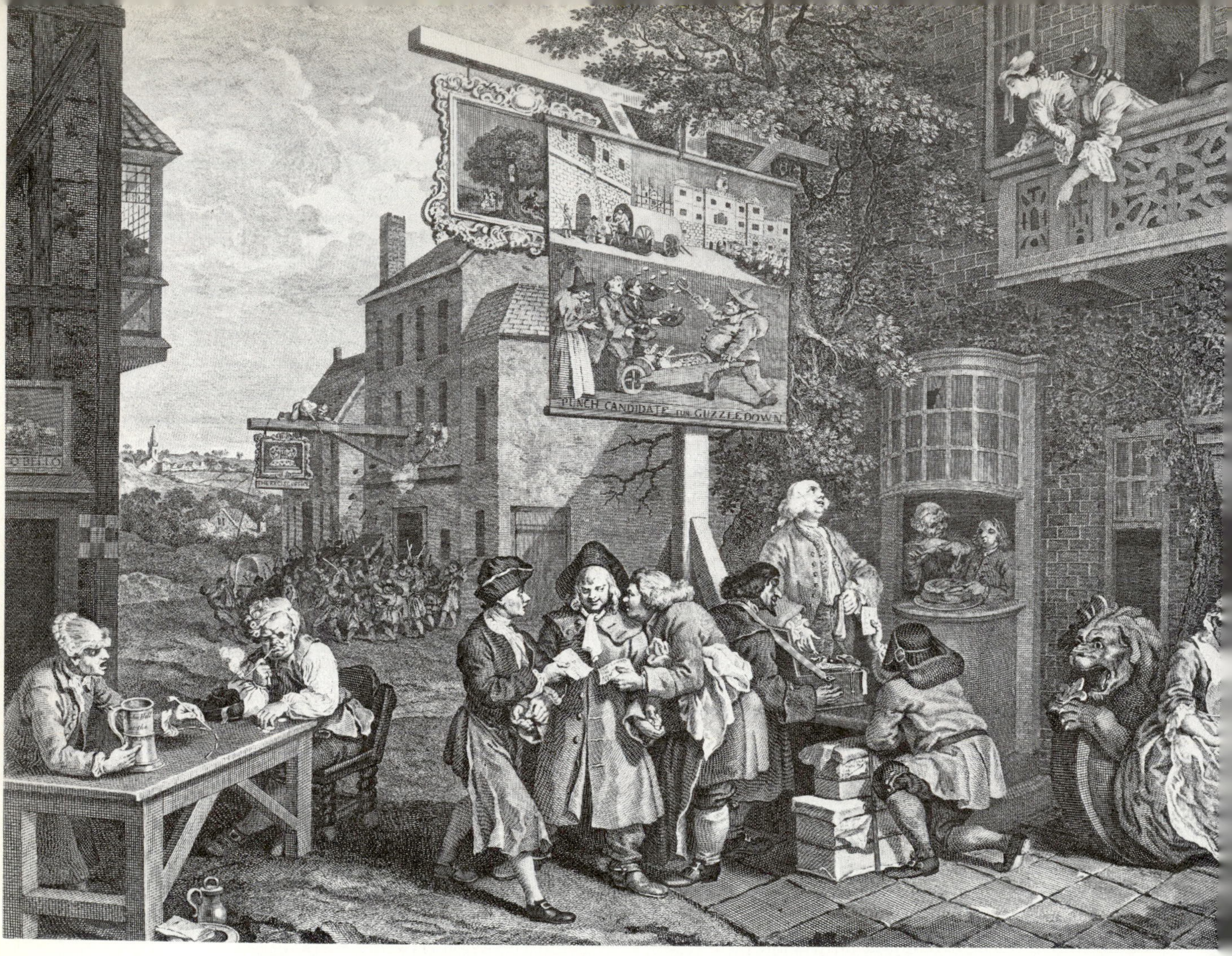
PUNCH CANDIDATE FOR GUZZLEDOWN

LIBERTY AND LOYALTY

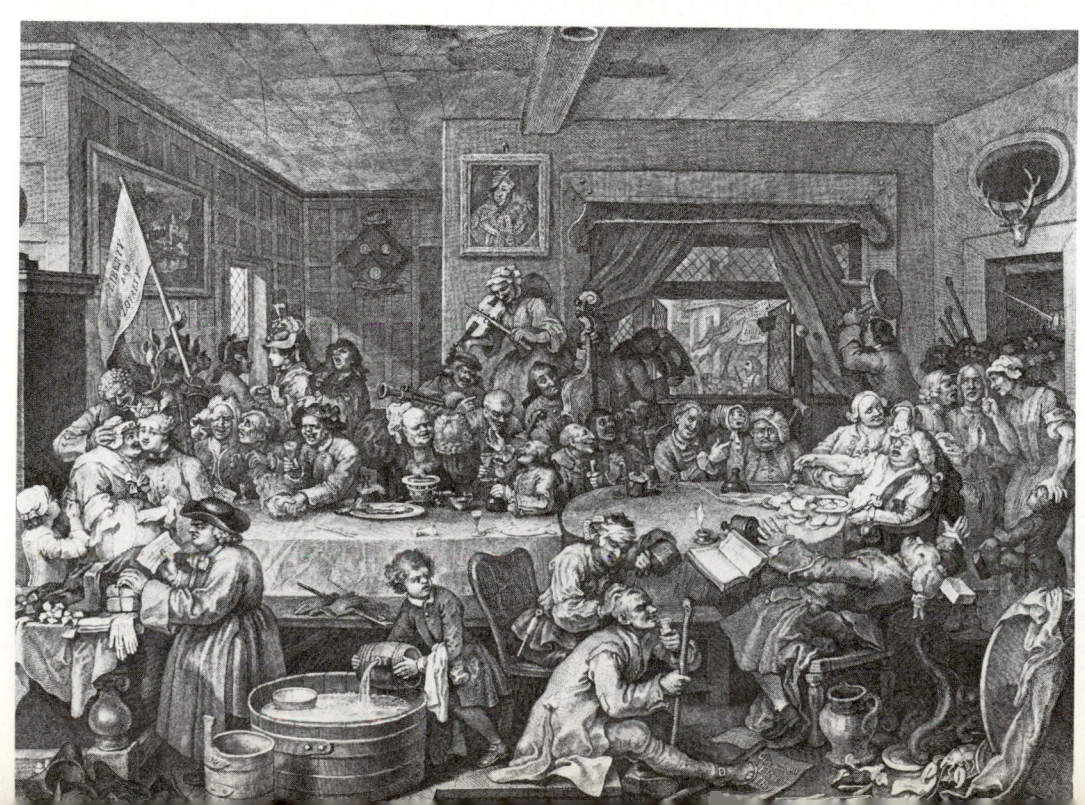

A series of four Hogarth etchings satirizing the notoriously corrupt English electoral system, Hogarth shows the voters going to the polls after having been bribed and intoxicated with free gin. (Note that voting was in public. The secret ballot was not introduced in England until 1872.) The fourth etching, Chairing the Member, shows the triumphal procession of the winner, which is clearly turning into a brawl. [Metropolitan Museum of Art.]

sequently, the supremacy of Parliament provided Britain with the kind of unity that elsewhere in Europe was sought through the institutions of absolutism.

British political life was genuinely more free than that on the Continent. There were real limits to the power of Robert Walpole. Parliament could not be wholly unresponsive to popular political pressure. Even with the extensive use of patronage, many members of Parliament maintained independent views. Newspapers and public debate flourished. Free speech could be exercised, as could freedom of association. There was no large standing army. Tories barred from political office and Whig enemies of Walpole could and did voice their opposition to his policies, as would not have been possible on the Continent.

Walpole's ascendancy, which lasted until 1742, did little to raise the level of British political morality, but it brought the nation a kind of stability that it had not enjoyed for well over a century. Its foreign trade grew steadily and spread from New England to India. Agriculture improved its productivity. All forms of economic enterprise seemed to prosper. The navy became stronger. As a result of this political stability and economic growth, Great Britain became a European power of the first order and stood at the beginning of its era as a world power. Its government and economy during the next generation became a model for all progressive Europeans.

Central and Eastern Europe

The political situation in central and eastern Europe was rather different from that in the west. Except for the cities on the Baltic, the economy was agrarian. There were fewer cities and many more large estates populated by serfs. The states in this region did not possess overseas empires. Changes in the power structure normally involved changes in borders, or at least in the prince who ruled a particular area. Military conflicts took place at home rather than overseas. The political structure of this region, which lay largely east of the Elbe River, was very "soft." The almost constant warfare of the seventeenth century had led to a habit of temporary and shifting political loyalties. The princes and aristocracies of small states and principalities were unwilling to subordinate themselves voluntarily to a central monarchical authority. Consequently, the political life of the region and the kind of state that emerged there were different from those of western Europe.

Beginning in the last half of the seventeenth century, eastern and central Europe began to assume the political and social contours that would characterize it for the next two hundred years. After the Peace of Westphalia (1648), the Austrian Habsburgs recognized the basic weakness of the position of the Holy Roman Emperor and began a new consolidation of their power. At the same time, the state of Prussia began to emerge as a factor in north German politics and as a major challenger to Habsburg domination of Germany. Most important, Russia at the opening of the eighteenth century rose to the status of a military power of the first order.

The Habsburg Empire and the Pragmatic Sanction

The close of the Thirty Years' War marked a fundamental turning point in the history of the Austrian Habsburgs. Previously, in alliance with the Spanish branch of the family, they had hoped to dominate all of Germany politically and to bring it back to the Catholic fold. They had failed to achieve either goal, and the decline of Spanish power meant that in future diplomatic relations the Austrian Habsburgs were very much on their own.

After 1648, the Habsburg family retained firm hold on the title of Holy Roman Emperor, but the effectiveness of the title depended less on force of arms than on the cooperation that the emperor could elicit from the various political bodies in the empire. These included large units (such as Saxony, Hanover, Bavaria, and Bradenburg) and also scores of small cities, bishoprics, principalities, and territories of independent knights. While establishing a new kind of position among the German states, the Habsburgs began to consolidate their power and influence within their hereditary possessions. These included, first, the Crown of Saint Wenceslas encompassing the kingdom of Bohemia (in modern Czechoslovakia) and the Duchies of Moravia and Silesia and, second, the Crown of Saint Stephen, which ruled Hungary, Croatia, and Transylvania. In the middle of the seventeenth century, much of Hungary remained occupied by the Turks and was liberated only at the end of the century.

In the early eighteenth century, the family further extended its domains, receiving the former Spanish (thereafter Austrian) Netherlands, Lombardy in northern Italy, and the Kingdom of Naples in southern Italy through the Treaty of Utrecht in 1713. The Kingdom of Naples was lost relatively quickly and played no considerable role in the Habsburg fortunes. During the eighteenth and nineteenth centuries, Habsburgs' power and influence in Europe would be based primarily on their territories located outside Germany.

In the second half of the seventeenth century and later, the Habsburgs confronted immense problems in these hereditary territories. In each, they ruled by virtue of a different title and had to gain the cooperation of the local nobility. The most difficult province was Hungary, where the Magyar nobility seemed ever

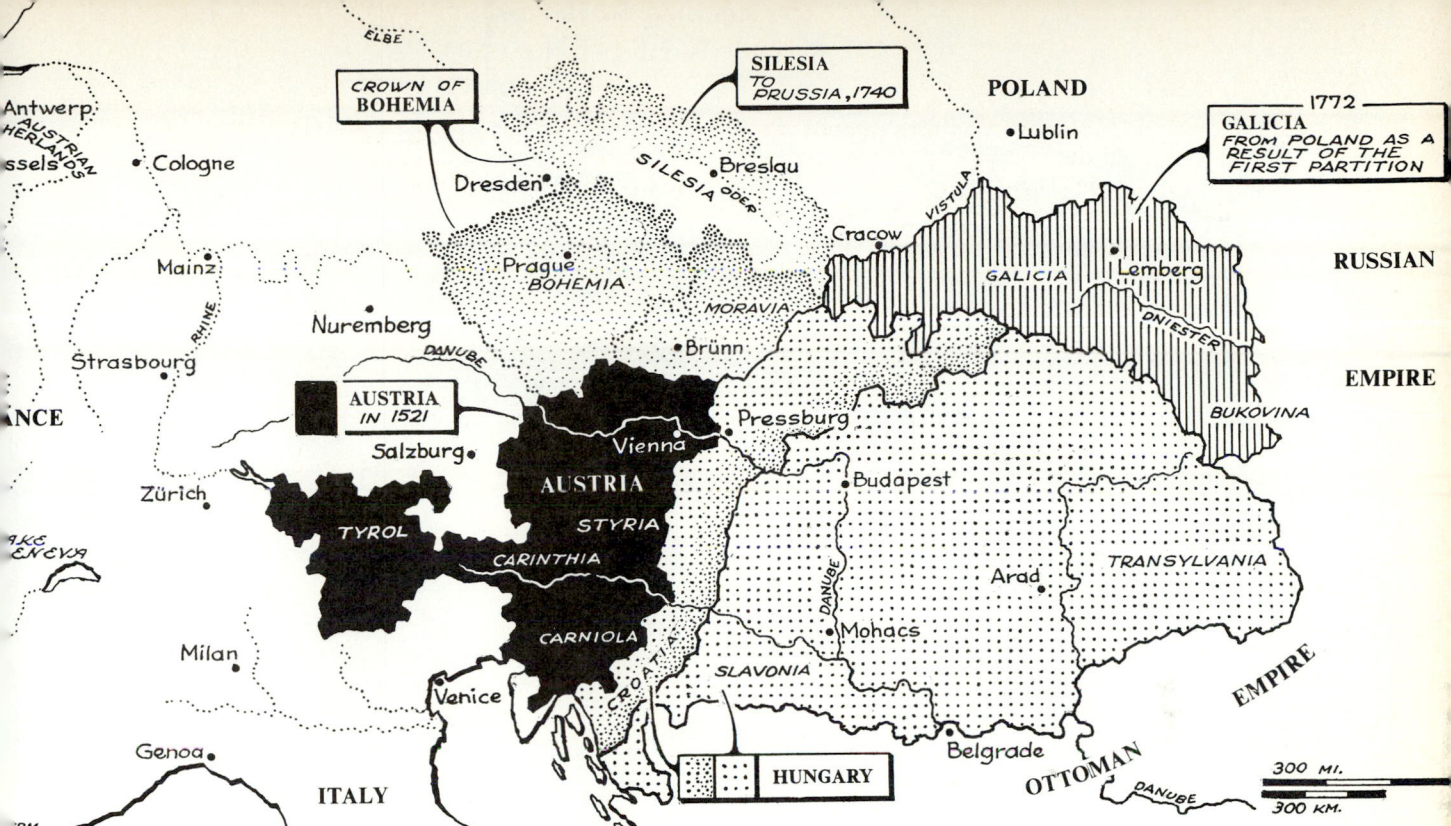

MAP 19-3 THE AUSTRIAN HABSBURG EMPIRE, 1521–1772 *The Empire had three main units—Austria, Bohemia, Hungary. Expansion was mainly eastward: east Hungary from the Ottomans (17th century) and Galicia from Poland (1772). Meantime, Silesia was lost, but Habsburgs retained German influence as Holy Roman Emperors.*

ready to rebel. There was almost no common basis for political unity among peoples of such diverse languages, customs, and geography. Even the Habsburg zeal for Roman Catholicism no longer proved a bond for unity as they continued to confront the equally zealous Calvinism of the Magyar nobles. Over the years, the Habsburgs established various central councils to chart common policies for their far-flung domains. Virtually all of these bodies dealt with only a portion of the Habsburgs' holdings. Repeatedly, they found themselves compelled to bargain with nobles in one part of Europe in order to maintain their position in another.

Despite all these internal difficulties, Leopold I (1657–1705) rallied his domains to resist the advances of the Turks and to resist the aggression of Louis XIV. He achieved Ottoman recognition of his sovereignty over Hungary in 1699 and suppressed the long rebellion of his new Magyar subjects between 1703 and 1711. He also extended his territorial holdings over much of what is today Yugoslavia and western Romania. These southeastward extensions allowed the Habsburgs to hope to develop Mediterranean trade through the port of Trieste. The expansion at the cost of the Ottoman Empire also helped the Habsburgs to

compensate for their loss of domination over the Holy Roman Empire. Strength in the East gave them greater political leverage in Germany. Leopold was succeeded by Joseph I (1705–1711), who continued his policies.

When Charles VI (1711–1740) succeeded Joseph, he added a new problem to the old chronic one of territorial diversity. He had no male heir, and there was only the weakest of precedents for a female ruler of the Habsburg domains. Charles feared that on his death the Austrian Habsburg lands might fall prey to the surrounding powers, as had those of the Spanish Habsburgs in 1700. He was determined to prevent that disaster and to provide his domains with the semblance of legal unity. To those ends, he devoted most of his reign to seeking the approval of his family, the estates of his realms, and the major foreign powers for a document called the *Pragmatic Sanction*.

This instrument provided the legal basis for a single line of inheritance within the Habsburg dynasty through Charles VI's daughter Maria Theresa (1740–1780). Other members of the Habsburg family recognized her as the rightful heir. The nobles of the various Habsburg domains did likewise, after extracting various concessions from Charles. Consequently, when Charles VI died in October 1740, he believed that he

A contemporary Dutch print views the 1683 Turkish siege of Vienna from the hills west of the city. The scene shows the Turkish forces deciding to give up the summer-long attack; their commanders, lower left, are just beginning their flight back toward the Ottoman homelands. Polish and other Christian aid for the beleaguered Habsburg forces had arrived, and the battle was clearly going against the Turks. Thanks to Leopold I, never again did the weakening Ottoman Empire penetrate so far west.

Note the Danube River toward the top, the zig-zag fortifications outside the walls, and bursts of artillery fire at several points. Most details inside the walled city are omitted, but the central cathedral and the imperial palace, toward the bottom, are shown.

One unforseen social result of the siege was the boost given to coffee drinking by the Viennese discovery of coffee beans in Turkish camps around the city. [The Granger Collection.]

had secured legal unity for the Habsburg Empire and a safe succession for his daughter. He had indeed established a permanent line of succession and the basis for future legal bonds within the Habsburg holdings, but he failed to protect his daughter from foreign aggression, either through the Pragmatic Sanction or, more

important, by leaving her a strong army and a filled treasury. Less than two months after his death, the fragility of the foreign agreements became all too apparent. In December 1740, Frederick II of Prussia invaded the Habsburg province of Silesia. Maria Theresa would now have to fight to defend her inheritance.

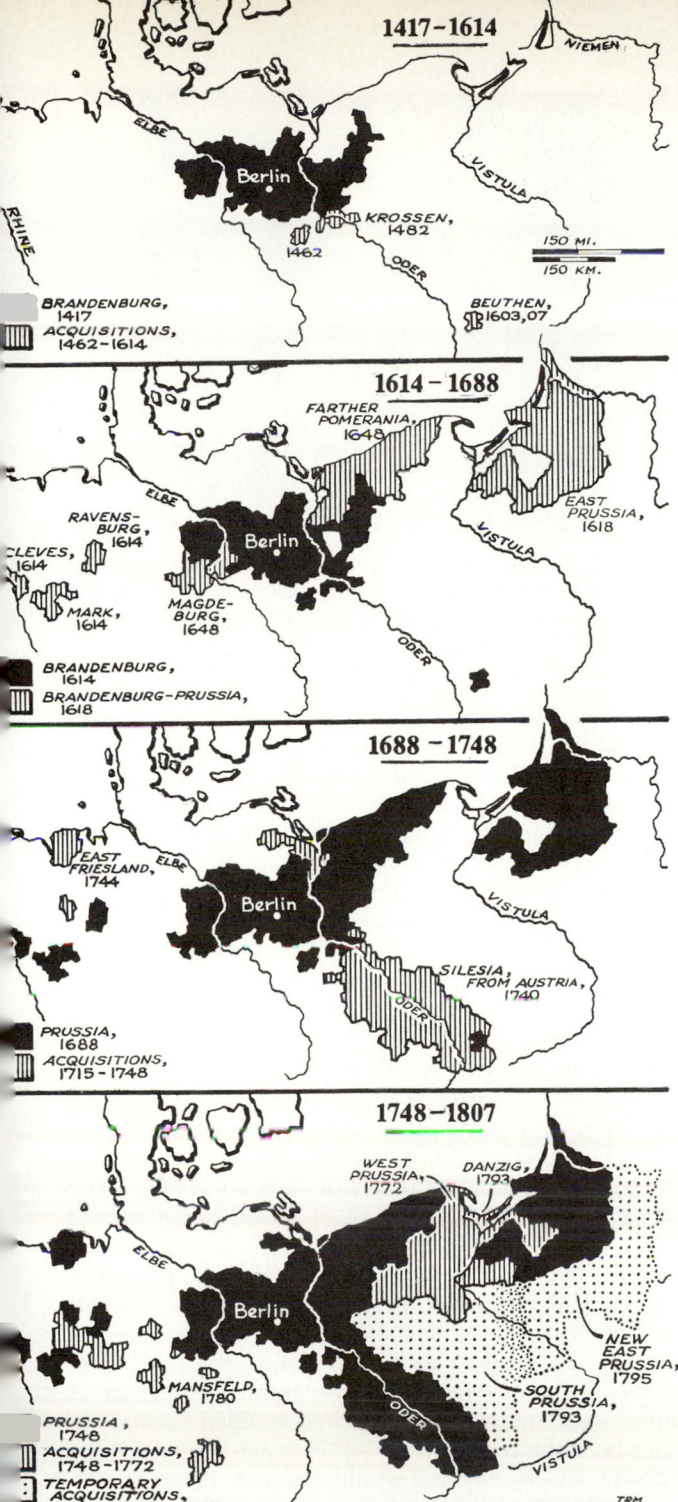

Prussia and the Hohenzollerns

The rise of Prussia occurred within the German power vacuum created by the Peace of Westphalia. It is the story of the extraordinary Hohenzollern family, which had ruled the German territory of Brandenburg since 1417. Through inheritance, the family had acquired the Duchy of Cleves and the counties of Mark and Ravensburg in 1609, the Duchy of East Prussia in 1618, and the Duchy of Pomerania in 1637. Except for Pomerania, none of these lands was contiguous with Brandenburg. East Prussia lay inside Poland and outside the authority of the Holy Roman Emperor. All of the territories lacked good natural resources, and many of them were devastated during the Thirty Years' War. At Westphalia, the Hohenzollerns lost part of Pomerania to Sweden but were compensated by receiving three more bishoprics and the promise of the archbishopric of Magdeburg when it became vacant, as it did in 1680. By the late seventeenth century, the scattered Hohenzollern holdings represented a block of territory within the Holy Roman Empire second in size only to that of the Habsburgs.

The person who began to forge these areas and nobles into a modern state was Frederick William (1640–1688), who became known as the Great Elector. He established himself and his successors as the central uniting power by breaking the medieval parliaments or estates, organizing a royal bureaucracy, and establishing a strong army.

Between 1655 and 1660, Sweden and Poland engaged in a war that endangered the Great Elector's holdings in Pomerania and East Prussia. Frederick William had neither an adequate army nor the tax revenues to confront this foreign threat. In 1655, the Brandenburg estates refused to grant him new taxes; however, he proceeded to collect the required taxes by military force. In 1659, a different grant of taxes, originally made in 1653, elapsed; Frederick William continued to collect them as well as those he had imposed by his own authority. He used the money to build up an army, which allowed him to continue to enforce his will without the approval of the nobility. Similar processes of threats and coercion took place against the nobles in his other territories.

However, there was a political and social tradeoff between the elector and his various nobles. These *Junkers*, or German noble landlords, were allowed almost complete control over the serfs on their estates. In exchange for their obedience to the Hohenzollerns, the *Junkers* received the right to demand obedience from their serfs. Frederick William also tended to choose as the local administrators of the tax structure men who would normally have been members of the noble branch of the old parliament. In this fashion, he co-opted potential opponents into his service. The taxes

MAP 19-4 EXPANSION OF BRANDENBURG-PRUSSIA *Seventeenth-century Brandenburg-Prussia expanded mainly by acquiring dynastic titles in geographically separated lands. Eighteenth-century expansion occurred through aggression to the east: Silesia seized in 1740 and various parts of Poland in 1772, 1793, and 1795.*

fell most heavily on the backs of the peasants and the urban classes. As the years passed, sons of *Junkers* increasingly dominated the army officer corps, and this practice became even more pronounced during the eighteenth century. All officials and army officers took an oath of loyalty directly to the elector. The army and the elector thus came to embody the otherwise absent unity of the state. The existence of the army made Prussia a valuable potential ally and a state with which other powers needed to curry favor.

Yet even with the considerable accomplishments of the Great Elector, the house of Hohenzollern did not possess a crown. The achievement of a royal title was one of the few state-building accomplishments of Frederick I (1688–1713). This son of the Great Elector was the least "Prussian" of his family during these crucial years. He built palaces, founded Halle University (1694), patronized the arts, and lived luxuriously. However, in 1700, at the outbreak of the War of the Spanish Succession, he put his army at the disposal of the Habsburg Holy Roman Emperor Leopold I. In exchange for this loyal service, the emperor permitted Frederick to assume the title of "King of Prussia." Thereafter, Frederick became Frederick I, and he passed the much-desired royal title to his son Frederick William I in 1713.

Frederick William I (1713–1740) was both the most eccentric personality to rule the Hohenzollern domains and one of its most effective monarchs. Frederick William organized the bureaucracy along the lines of military discipline. The discipline that Frederick William applied to the army was little less than fanati-

Frederick William I ruthlessly forged the Prussian army into a major instrument of state. But he also attempted to avoid using his valuable troops in battle. [The Granger Collection.]

cal. During his reign, the size of the military force grew from about thirty-nine thousand in 1713 to over eighty thousand in 1740. It was the third or fourth largest army in Europe, whereas Prussia ranked thirteenth in size of population. Separate laws applied to the army and to civilians. Laws, customs, and royal attention made the officer corps the highest social class of the state. Military service attracted the sons of *Junkers*. In this fashion, the army, the *Junker* nobility, and the monarchy became forged into a single political entity. Military priorities and values dominated Prussian government, society, and daily life as in no other state in Europe. It has often been said that whereas other nations possessed armies, the Prussian army possessed its nation.

Although Frederick William I built the best army in Europe, he followed a policy of avoiding conflict. The army was for him a symbol of Prussian power and unity, not an instrument to be used for foreign adventures or aggression. At his death in 1740, he passed to his son Frederick II (1740–1786; Frederick the Great) this superb military machine, but he could not pass to his son the wisdom to refrain from using it. Almost immediately on coming to the throne, Frederick II upset the Pragmatic Sanction and invaded Silesia. He thus crystallized the Austrian–Prussian rivalry for the control of Germany that would dominate central European affairs for over a century.

The Entry of Russia into the European Political Arena

Though ripe with consequences for the future, the rise of Prussia and the new consolidation of Austrian

---

AUSTRIA AND PRUSSIA IN THE LATE SEVENTEENTH AND EARLY EIGHTEENTH CENTURIES

1640–1688	Reign of Frederick William, the Great Elector
1657–1705	Leopold I rules Austria and resists the Turkish invasions
1683	Turkish siege of Vienna
1688–1713	Reign of Frederick I of Prussia
1699	Peace Treaty between Turks and Habsburgs
1711–1740	Charles VI rules Austria and secures agreement to the Pragmatic Sanction
1713–1740	Frederick William I builds up the military power of Prussia
1740	Maria Theresa succeeds to the Habsburg throne
	Frederick II violates the Pragmatic Sanction by invading Silesia

Habsburg domains seemed to many at the time only one more shift in the long-troubled German scene. However, the emergence of Russia as an active European power constituted a wholly new factor in European politics. Previously Russia had been considered a part of Europe only by courtesy. Geographically and politically, it lay on the periphery of Europe. Hemmed in by Sweden on the Baltic and by the Ottoman Empire on the Black Sea, the country had no warm-water ports. Its chief outlet to the west was Archangel on the White Sea, which was open to ships during only part of the year. There was little trade. What Russia did possess was a vast reserve of largely undeveloped natural and human resources.

Years of Turmoil

The reign of Ivan the Terrible, which had begun so well and closed so frighteningly, was followed by a period of anarchy and civil war known as the *Time of Troubles*. In 1613, hoping to resolve the tension and end the uncertainty an assembly of nobles elected as tsar a seventeen-year-old boy named Michael Romanov (1613–1654). Thus began the dynasty that in spite of palace revolutions, military conspiracies, assassinations, and family strife ruled Russia until 1917.

Michael Romanov and his two successors, Alexis I (1654–1676) and Theodore III (1676–1682), brought stability and bureaucratic centralization to Russia. However, Russia remained militarily weak and financially impoverished. The bureaucracy after these years of turmoil still remained largely controlled by the boyars (aristocrats). This administrative apparatus was only barely capable of putting down a revolt of peasants and Cossacks under Stepan Razin in 1670–1671. Furthermore, the government and the tsars faced the danger of mutiny from the *streltsy*, or guards of the Moscow garrison.

Peter the Great

In 1682 another boy—ten years old at the time—ascended the fragile Russian throne as coruler with his half brother. His name was Peter (1682–1725), and Russia would never be the same after him. He and his ill half brother, Ivan V, had come to power on the shoulders of the *streltsy*, who expected rewards from the persons they favored. Much violence and bloodshed had surrounded the disputed succession. Matters became even more confused when the boys' sister, Sophia, was named regent. Peter's followers overthrew her in 1689. From that date onward, Peter ruled personally, although in theory he shared the crown with Ivan, until Ivan died in 1696. The dangers and turmoil of his youth convinced Peter of two things. First, the power of the tsar must be made secure from the jealousy of the boyars and the greed of the *streltsy*. Second, the military power of Russia must be increased.

Peter I, who became Peter the Great, was fascinated by western Europe, particularly its military resources. He was an imitator of the first order. The products and workers from the West who had filtered into Russia impressed and intrigued him. In 1697, he made a famous visit in rather weak disguises throughout western Europe. There he dined and talked with the great and the powerful, who considered this almost seven-foot-tall ruler both crude and rude. His happiest moments on the trip were spent inspecting shipyards, docks, and the manufacture of military hardware. He returned to Moscow determined by whatever means necessary to copy what he had seen abroad, for he knew that warfare would be necessary to make Russia a great power. The tsar's drive toward westernization, though unsystematic, had four general areas of concern: taming the boyars and the *streltsy*, achieving secular control of the Church, reorganizing the internal administration, and developing the economy. Peter pursued each of these goals with violence and ruthlessness.

He made a sustained attack on the Russian boyars. In 1698, immediately on his return from abroad, he personally shaved the long beards of the court boyars and sheared off the customary long, hand-covering sleeves of their shirts and coats, which had made them the butt of jokes throughout Europe. More important, he demanded that the nobles provide his state with their services.

In 1722, Peter published a Table of Ranks, which henceforth equated a person's social position and privileges with his rank in the bureaucracy or the army rather than with his position in the nobility. However, unlike the case in Prussia, the Russian nobility never became perfectly loyal to the state. They repeatedly sought to reassert their independence and their control of the Russian imperial court.

The *streltsy* fared less well than the boyars. In 1698, they had rebelled while Peter was on his European tour. When he returned and put down the revolt of these Moscow troops, he directed massive violence and brutality against both leaders and followers. There were private tortures and public executions, in which Peter's own ministers took part. Almost twelve hundred of the rebels were put to death, and their corpses long remained on public display to discourage future disloyalty.

Peter dealt with the potential political independence of the Russian Orthodox Church with similar ruthlessness. Here again, Peter had to confront a problem that had arisen in the turbulent decades that had preceded his reign. The Russian church had long opposed the scientific as well as the theological

Bishop Burnet Looks Over a Foreign Visitor

In 1697 and 1698, Peter the Great of Russia toured western Europe to discover how Russia must change its society and economy in order to become a great power. As this description by Bishop Gilbert Burnet in England indicates, the west Europeans found the tsar a curious person in his own right.

He came this winter over to England, and stayed some months among us. . . . I had good interpreters, so I had much free discourse with him; he is a man of a very hot temper, soon inflamed, and very brutal in his passion; he raises his natural heat, by drinking much brandy, . . . he is subject to convulsive motions all over his body, and his head seems to be affected with these; he wants not capacity, and has a larger measure of knowledge, than might be expected from his education, which was very indifferent; a want of judgment, with an instability of temper, appear in him too often and too evidently; he is mechanically turned, and seems designed by nature rather to be a ship-carpen-

ter, than a great prince. This was his chief study and exercise, while he stayed here: he wrought much with his own hands, and made all about him work at the models of ships. . . . He was . . . resolved to encourage learning, and to polish his people, by sending some of them to travel in other countries, and to draw strangers to come and live among them. . . . After I had seen him often, and had conversed much with him, I could not but adore the depth of the providence of God, that had raised up such a furious man to so absolute an authority over so great a part of the world. ❏

Bishop Burnet's History of His Own Time, Vol. 4 (Oxford, England: Clarendon Press, 1823), pp. 396–397.

---

thought of the West. In the mid-seventeenth century, a reformist movement led by Patriarch Nikon arose in the church. In 1667, certain changes had been introduced into the texts and the ritual of the Church. These reforms caused great unrest because the Russian

church had always claimed to be the protector of the ritual. The Old Believers, a group of Russian Christians who strongly opposed these changes, were condemned by the hierarchy, but they persisted in their opposition. Late in the century, thousands of them

Peter the Great (1682–1725) studying ship building in Holland. In 1697, the Tsar visited western Europe incognito to study the skills that he considered necessary for Russia to build a strong, modern state. [The Bettmann Archive.]

committed suicide rather than submit to the new rituals. The Old Believers' movement represented a rejection of change and innovation; its presence discouraged the Church hierarchy from making any further substantial moves toward modern thought.

In the future, Peter wanted to avoid two kinds of difficulties with the Russian church. First, the clergy must not constitute a group within the state that would oppose change and westernization. Second, the hierarchy of the Church must not be permitted to reform liturgy, ritual, or doctrine in a way that might again give rise to discontent such as that of the Old Believers. Consequently, in 1721, Peter simply abolished the position of patriarch of the Russian church. In its place he established a synod headed by a layman to rule the Church in accordance with secular requirements. So far as transforming a traditional institution was concerned, this action toward the Church was the most radical policy of Peter's reign. It produced still further futile opposition from the Old Believers, who saw the tsar as leading the Church into new heresy.

In his reorganization of domestic administration, Peter looked to institutions then used in Sweden. These were "colleges," or bureaus, composed of several persons rather than departments headed by a single minister. These colleges, which he imposed on Russia, were to look after matters such as the collection of taxes, foreign affairs, war, and economic matters. This new organization was an attempt to breathe life into the generally stagnant and inefficient administration of the country. In 1711, he created a central senate of nine members who were to direct the Moscow government when the tsar was away with the army. The purpose of these and other local administrative reforms was to establish a bureaucracy that could collect and spend tax revenues to support an efficient army.

The economic development advocated by Peter the Great was closely related to his military needs. He encouraged the establishment of an iron industry in the Ural Mountains, and by mid-century Russia had become the largest iron producer in Europe. He sent prominent young Russians abroad to acquire technical and organizational skills. He attempted to attract west European craftsmen to live and work in Russia. Except for the striking growth of the iron industry, which later languished, all these efforts had only marginal success.

The goal of these internal reforms and political departures was to support a policy of warfare. Peter was determined to secure warm-water ports that would allow Russia to trade with the West and to have a greater impact on European affairs. This policy led him into wars with the Ottoman Empire and with Sweden. His armies commenced fighting the Turks in 1695 and captured Azov on the Black Sea in 1696. It was a temporary victory, for in 1711 he was compelled to return the port.

Peter had more success against Sweden, where the inconsistency and irrationality of Charles XII were no small aid. In 1700, Russia moved against the Swedish territory on the Baltic. The Swedish king's failure to follow up his victory at Narva in 1700 allowed Peter to regroup his forces and hoard his resources. In 1709, when Charles XII returned to fight Russia again, Peter was ready, and the Battle of Poltava sealed the fate of Sweden. In 1721, at the Peace of Nystad, which ended the Great Northern War, the Russian conquest of Estonia, Livonia, and part of Finland was confirmed. Henceforth, Russia possessed warm-water ports and a permanent influence on European affairs.

At one point, the domestic and foreign policies of Peter the Great literally intersected. This was at the spot on the Gulf of Finland where Peter founded his new capital city of Saint Petersburg (now Leningrad). There he built government structures and compelled his boyars to construct town houses. In this fashion he imitated those west European monarchs who had cop-

RISE OF RUSSIAN POWER

1533–1584	Reign of Ivan the Terrible
1584–1613	Time of Troubles
1613	Michael Romanov becomes tsar
1682	Peter the Great becomes tsar as a boy
1689	Peter assumes personal rule
1696	Russia captures Azov on the Black Sea from the Turks
1697	European tour of Peter the Great
1698	Peter returns to Russia to put down the revolt of the *streltsy*
1700	The Great Northern War opens between Russia and Sweden; Russia defeated at Narva by the Swedish Army of Charles XII
1703	Saint Petersburg founded
1709	Russia defeats Sweden at the Battle of Poltava
1718	Charles XII of Sweden dies
1718	Son of Peter the Great dies under mysterious circumstances in prison
1721	Peace of Nystad ends the Great Northern War
1721	Peter establishes a synod for the Russian church
1722	Peter issues the Table of Ranks
1725	Peter dies leaving an uncertain succession

Peter the Great built St. Petersburg on the Gulf of Finland in recently conquered territory to provide Russia with better contact with Western Europe. This is an eighteenth-century view of the city. [John R. Freeman.]

ied Louis XIV by constructing smaller versions of Versailles. However, the founding of Saint Petersburg went beyond the construction of a central court. It symbolized a new Western orientation of Russia and Peter's determination to hold his position on the Baltic coast. He had begun the construction of the city and had moved the capital there in 1703, even before his victory over Sweden was assured.

Despite his notable success on the Baltic, Peter's reign ended with a great question mark. He had long quarreled with his only son, Alexis. Peter was jealous of the young man and fearful that he might undertake sedition. In 1718, Peter had his son imprisoned, and during this imprisonment the presumed successor to the throne died mysteriously. Thereafter, Peter claimed for himself the right of naming a successor, but he could never bring himself to designate the person either orally or in writing. Consequently, when he died in 1725, there was no firmer policy on the succession to the throne than when he had acceded to the title. For over thirty years, once again soldiers and nobles would determine who ruled Russia. Peter had laid the foundations of a modern Russia, but he had failed to lay the foundations of a stable state.

Eighteenth-Century European States in World Perspective

By the second quarter of the eighteenth century, the major European powers were not yet nation-states in which the citizens felt themselves united by a shared sense of community, culture, language, and history.

They were still monarchies in which the personality of the ruler and the personal relationships of the great noble families exercised considerable influence over public affairs.

These European states displayed certain problems that also characterized the governments of China and Japan during the same epochs. In particular, like in Japan, the problem of a balance between centralization and decentralization arose in virtually all the European states. In France, Russia, and Prussia the forces of centralization proved quite strong. In Austria, the forces of decentralization were very powerful. England achieved a rather delicate balance. Furthermore, as in Tokugawa Japan, European states of the eighteenth century generally saw an increase in legal codification and in the growth of bureaucracy. Only in Prussia did the level of military influence on society resemble to any degree that of Japan.

The role of the personality of the central monarchs bore some resemblance to the activities of certain of the Chinese Manchu emperors, such as Ch'ien Lung. Louis XIV and Peter the Great had no less influence on their nations than did that great Manchu emperor. And like him, they were interested in hunting and sport as well as in military strength and innovation. However, although European rulers were developing systems of state bureaucracy, none of them achieved so brilliant a group of trained civil servants as those who administered China.

The European states that had emerged by the early eighteenth century, as will be seen in the next chapter, were developing dynamic economies. France and England established far-flung commercial empires. These, in turn, gave rise to fierce commercial rivalries. The drive for empire and commercial supremacy propelled these states into contact with Africa, Latin America, India, China, and Japan. Spain had long exploited Latin America as its own monopoly. That arrangement would be challenged in the eighteenth century by England. Both France and England would fight for commercial supremacy in India and by the middle of the century England would in effect conquer India. The slave trade between Africa and the New World continued to flourish throughout the eighteenth century. European merchants and navies would also seek to penetrate East Asia.

Consequently, by the end of the eighteenth century the European states that just two centuries before had only started to settle the Americas and to engage in very limited long-range trade had made their power and influence felt throughout the world. Beginning in the early eighteenth century, the political power of the European states became linked to a qualitatively different economic base than ever seen anywhere else in the world. That combination opened the way for a temporary European domination of the world that began in the mid-eighteenth century and that came to a close in the middle of the twentieth century.

Suggested Readings

M. S. Anderson, *Europe in the Eighteenth Century, 1713–1783* (1961). The best one-volume introduction.

T. M. Barker, *Army, Aristocracy, Monarchy: Essays in War, Society and Government in Austria, 1618–1780* (1982). Examines the intricate power relationships among these major institutions.

R. Bonney, *Political Change in France under Richelieu and Mazarin 1624–1661* (1978). An important examination of the emergence of French absolutism.

F. L. Carsten, *The Origins of Prussia* (1954). Discusses the groundwork laid by the Great Elector in the seventeenth century.

A. Cobban, *A History of Modern France*, 2nd ed., Vol. 1, (1961). A lively and opinionated survey.

L. Colley, *In Defiance of Oligarchy: The Tory Party, 1714–60* (1982). An important study that challenges much conventional opinion about eighteenth-century British politics.

P. Dukes, *The Making of Russian Absolutism: 1613–1801* (1982). An overview based on recent scholarship.

R. J. W. Evans, *The Making of the Habsburg Monarchy, 1550–1700: An Interpretation* (1979). Places much emphasis on intellectual factors and the role of religion.

F. Ford, *Robe and Sword: The Regrouping of the French Aristocracy after Louis XIV* (1953). An important book for political, social, and intellectual history.

P. Gourbert, *Louis XIV and Twenty Million Frenchmen* (1966). A fine overview of seventeenth-century French social structure.

R. Hatten (ed.), *Louis XIV and Europe* (1976). Covers foreign policy.

C. Hill, *The Century of Revolution, 1603–1714*, 2nd. ed. (1980). An influential survey.

J. M. Hittle, *The Service City: State and Townsmen in Russia, 1600–1800* (1979). Examines the relationship of cities in Russia to the growing power of the central government.

H. C. Johnson, *Frederick the Great and His Officials* (1975). An excellent recent examination of the Prussian administration.

R. A. Kann and Z. V. David, *The Peoples of the Eastern Habsburg Lands, 1526–1918* (1984). The best overview of the subject.

J. P. Kenyon, *Stuart England* (1978). A useful survey.

R. K. Massie, *Peter the Great: His Life and His World* (1980). A good popular biography.

J. Morrill (ed.), *Reactions to the English Civil War, 1642–1649* (1980). A valuable set of essays.

L. B. Namier and J. Brooke, *The History of Parliament: The House of Commons, 1754–1790*, 3 vols. (1964). A detailed examination of the unreformed British House of Commons and electoral system.

L. J. Oliva (ed.), *Russia and the West from Peter the Great to Khrushchev* (1965). An anthology of articles tracing an important and ambiguous subject.

J. B. Owen, *The Eighteenth Century* (1974). An excellent introduction to England in the period.

J. H. Plumb, *Sir Robert Walpole*, 2 vols. (1956, 1961). A masterful biography ranging across the sweep of European politics.

J. H. Plumb, *The Growth of Political Stability in England, 1675–1725* (1969). An important interpretive work.

J. G. A. Pocock (ed.), *Three British Revolutions: 1641, 1688, 1776* (1980). An important collection of essays.

N. V. Riasanovsky, *The Image of Peter the Great in Russian History and Thought* (1985). Examines the ongoing legacy of Peter in Russian history.

P. Roberts, *The Quest for Security, 1715–1740* (1947). Very good on the diplomatic problems of the period.

H. Rosenberg, *Bureaucracy, Aristocracy, and Autocracy: The Prussian Experience, 1660–1815* (1960). Emphasizes the organization of Prussian administration.

C. Russell, *Parliaments and English Politics, 1621–1629* (1979). The most recent coverage of the beginning of the clash of Parliament and Charles I.

G. Treasure, *Seventeenth-Century France* (1966). Sweeping survey.

D. Underdown, *Revel, Riot, and Rebellion: Popular Politics and Culture in England, 1603–1660* (1985). An examination of the social implications of the struggle between the crown and Parliament.

E. N. Williams, *The Ancien Régime in Europe* (1972). A state-by-state survey of very high quality.

A. M. Wilson, *French Foreign Policy During the Administration of Cardinal Fleury, 1726–1743*.

J. B. Wolf, *Louis XIV* (1968). Authoritative and readable.

Throughout Europe in the eighteenth century, the aristocracy dominated both society and government. This portrait of an English nobleman, Lord Willoughby de Brooke, and his family captures the elegance and luxury of aristocratic life. [Michael Holford.]

20 European Society Under the Old Regime

During the French Revolution (1789) and the turmoil spawned by that upheaval, it became customary to refer to the patterns of social, political, and economic relationships that had existed in France before 1789 as the *ancien régime*, or the "old regime." The term has come to be applied generally to the life and institutions of prerevolutionary Europe. Politically, the term indicated the rule of theoretically absolute monarchies with growing bureaucracies and aristocratically led armies. Economically, the old regime was characterized by scarcity of food, the predominance of agriculture, slow transport, a low level of iron production, rather unsophisticated financial institutions, and in some cases competitive commercial overseas empires. Socially, prerevolutionary Europe was based on aristocratic elites possessing a wide variety of inherited legal privileges, established Roman Catholic and Protestant churches intimately related to the state and the aristocracy, an urban labor force usually organized into guilds, and a rural peasantry subject to high taxes and feudal dues.

Eighteenth-century society was traditional. The past weighed more heavily on people's minds than did the future. Few persons outside the government bureaucracies and the movement for reform known as the *Enlightenment* considered change or innovation desirable. This was especially true of social relationships. Both nobles and peasants, for very different reasons, repeatedly called for the restoration of traditional or customary rights. The nobles asserted what they considered their ancient rights against the intrusion of the expanding monarchical bureaucracies. The peasants, in petitions and revolts, called for the revival or the maintenance of the customary manorial rights that provided them access to particular lands, courts, or grievance procedures.

With the exception of the early industrial development in Britain, the eighteenth-century economy was

A mid-eighteenth-century rural laborer's hut far to the east in Austria. Painted by
Franz Edmund Weirotter (1730-1771), the scene is probably a realistic view of the
wretched housing endured by many. [Charles Farrell Collection.]

also quite traditional. The quality and quantity of the harvest remained the single most important fact of life for the overwhelming majority of the population and the gravest concern of the governments.

Closely related to this traditional social and economic outlook was the hierarchical structure of the society. The medieval sense of rank and degree not only persisted but became more rigid in the course of the century. In several continental cities, "sumptuary laws" regulating the dress of the different classes remained on the books. These laws forbade persons in one class or occupation to wear clothes like those worn by people in a socially higher position. The point of such laws, which were largely ineffective in the eighteenth century, was to make the social hierarchy actually visible. Rather than by such legislation, the hierarchy was really enforced through the corporate nature of social relationships.

Each state or society was considered a community of numerous smaller communities. People in eighteenth-century Europe did not enjoy what Americans regard as individual rights. A person enjoyed such rights and privileges as were guaranteed to the particular communities or groups of which she or he was a part. The "community" might include the village, the municipality, the nobility, the church, the guild, or the parish. In turn, each of these bodies enjoyed certain privileges, some of which were great and some small. The privileges might involve exemption from taxation or from some especially humiliating punishment, the right to practice a trade or craft, the right of one's children to pursue a particular occupation, or, in the case of the Church, the right to collect the tithe.

Tradition, hierarchy, corporateness, and privilege were the chief social characteristics of the old regime. Yet it was by no means a static society. Factors of change and innovation were fermenting in its midst. There was a strong demand for the colonies in the Americas for European goods and manufactures. Merchants in seaports and other cities were expanding their businesses. By preparing their states for war, the various governments put new demands on the resources and the economic organizations of their nations. Perhaps most important, the population of Europe grew rapidly. The old regime itself fostered the changes that eventually transformed it into a very different kind of society.

Family Structures and the Family Economy

In preindustrial Europe, the household was the basic unit of production and consumption. That is to say, only the most limited number of productive establishments employed more than a handful of people not belonging to the family of the owner. Those very few establishments employing significant numbers of wage earners who were not members of the owner's family were located in cities. But the overwhelming majority of Europeans lived in rural areas. There, as well as in small towns and cities, the household mode of organization predominated on farms, in artisans' workshops, and in small merchants' shops. With that mode of economic organization there developed what is known as the *family economy*.

Households

What was a household in preindustrial Europe of the old regime? There were two basic models, one characterizing northwestern Europe and the other eastern Europe. In the northwestern part of the continent, the household almost invariably consisted of a married couple, their children through their early teenage years, and their servants. Except for the relatively few very wealthy people, households were quite small, rarely consisting of more than five or six members. Furthermore, in these households, more than two generations of a family rarely lived under the same roof. High mortality and late marriage prevented families of three generations. In other words, grandparents rarely lived in the same household as their grandchildren. In this regard, the family structure of northwestern Europe was nuclear rather than extended. That is to say, these families consisted of parents and children rather than of several generations under the same roof.

This particular characteristic of the northwestern European household is one of the most major discoveries of recent research into family history. Previously it had been assumed that before industrialization the European family lived in extended familial settings with several generations inhabiting a household. Recent demographic investigation has sharply reversed this picture. Children lived with their parents only until their early teens. Then they normally left home, usually to enter the work force of young servants who lived and worked in a household other than that of their parents. A child of a skilled artisan might remain with his or her parents in order to acquire the valuable skill, but only rarely would more than one of the children do so because their labor would be more valuable and remunerative elsewhere.

These young men and women who had left home would eventually marry, and they would then begin to form an independent household of their own. This practice of moving away from home is known as *neolocalism*. The effort to acquire the economic resources needed to establish a household meant the age of marriage would be relatively late. For men it was over twenty-six, and for women over twenty-three. At the time of marriage, the couple usually quickly began a family. It was not unusual for the marriage to occur at the end of a long courtship when the woman was already pregnant. Family and community pressures

seem more often than not to have compelled the man to marry the woman, but in any case premarital sexual relations were not rare, though illegitimate births were not common. The new couple would soon employ a servant, who with their growing children would undertake whatever form of livelihood the household used to support itself.

Servant in this context is a word that may seem confusing. It does not refer to someone looking after the needs of wealthy people. Rather, in preindustrial Europe, a servant was a person—either male or female—who was hired, often under a clear contract, to work for the head of the household in exchange for room, board, and wages. The servant was usually young and by no means necessarily of a social position lower than that of his or her employer. Normally, the servant was an integral part of the household and took meals with the family. Young men and women became servants when their labor was no longer needed in their parents' household or when they could earn more money for their family outside the parental household. Being a servant for several years—often as many as eight or ten—was a means of acquiring the productive skills and the monetary saving necessary for young people to begin their own household. This period of working as a servant between leaving home and beginning a new household accounts in a large measure for the late age of marriage in northwestern Europe.

As one moved toward the eastern areas of the continent, the structure of the household and the pattern of marriage changed. In Russia and elsewhere in eastern Europe, marrying involved not starting a new household but continuing in and expanding one already established. Consequently, marriage occurred quite early, before the age of twenty for both men and women. Children were born to parents of a much younger age. Quite often, especially among Russian serfs, wives were older than their husbands. Eastern European households tended to be quite large in comparison with those in the West. Often the Russian household in the countryside had more than nine and possibly more than twenty members with three or perhaps even four generations of the same family living together. Early marriage made this situation more likely.

The landholding pattern in eastern Europe accounts, at least in part, for these patterns of marriage and the family. The lords of the manor who owned land wanted to ensure that it would be cultivated so that they could receive their rents. To that end, for example, in Poland, landlords might forbid marriage between their own serfs and those from another estate. They might also require widows and widowers to remarry so there would be adequate labor for a particular plot of land. Polish landlords also frowned on the hiring of free laborers—the equivalent of servants in the West—to aid land cultivation. The landlords preferred other serfs to be used. This practice inhibited the possible formation of independent households. In Russia, landlords ordered the families of young people in their villages to arrange marriages within a short, set period of time. These lords discouraged single-generation family households because the death or serious illness of a person in such a household might mean that the land assigned to that household would go out of cultivation.

The Family Economy

In both northwestern and eastern Europe, most Europeans worked within the context of the *family economy*. That is to say, the household was the fundamental unit of production and consumption. People thought and worked in terms of sustaining the economic life of the family, and family members saw themselves as working together in an interdependent rather than an independent or individualistic manner. The goal of the family household was to produce or to secure through wages enough food to support its members. In the countryside, that effort virtually always involved farming. In cities and towns, artisan production or working for another person was the usual pattern. Almost everyone lived within a household of some kind because it was virtually impossible for ordinary people to support themselves independently. Indeed, except for members of religious orders, people living outside a household were viewed with great suspicion. It was assumed that they were potentially criminal or disruptive or, at the very minimum, potentially dependent on the charity of others.

Marriage and the family within this economy meant that all members of the household had to work. On a farm, much of the effort went directly into raising food or producing other agricultural goods that could be exchanged for food. In the countryside of western Europe, however, very few people had enough land to support their household from farming alone. For this reason, one or more family members might work elsewhere and send wages home. For example, the father or older children might work as a harvest picker or might fish or might engage in some other kind of labor, either in the local neighborhood or perhaps many miles from home. If the father were such a migrant worker, the burden of the farm work would fall on his wife and their younger children. This was not an uncommon pattern. Within this family economy, all of the goods and income produced went to the benefit of the household rather than to the individual family member. Depending on their ages and skills, everyone in the family worked. The very necessity of survival in the face of poor harvests or economic slumps meant that no one could be idle.

The family economy also dominated the life of skilled urban artisans. The father was usually the chief craftsman. He generally had one or more servants in his employ, but he would expect his children to work in the enterprise also. His eldest child was usually trained in the trade. His wife often contributed to his business by selling the wares, or she might have opened a small shop of her own. Wives of merchants also often ran their husbands' businesses, especially when the husband traveled to purchase new goods. In any case, everyone in the family was involved. If business was poor, family members would look for employment elsewhere, not to support themselves but to support the survival of the family unit.

In western Europe, the death of a father often brought disaster to the economy of the household. The ongoing economic life of the family usually depended on his land or his skills. The widow might take on the farm or the business, or her children might do so. The widow usually sought to remarry quickly in order to have the labor and skills of a male once more in the household and to prevent herself from falling into a state of dependence. The high mortality rate of the time meant that there were many households in which there were stepchildren and reconstituted second family groups. But in some cases, because of the advanced age of the widow or economic hard times, the household simply dissolved. The widow became dependent on charity or relatives, and the children became similarly dependent or moved earlier than they would otherwise have done into the work force of servants. In other cases, the situation could be so desperate that they would resort to crime or to begging. The personal, emotional, and economic vulnerability of the family economy cannot be overemphasized.

In eastern Europe, the family economy was also in place, but in the context of serfdom and landlord domination. Peasants clearly thought in terms of their families and of expanding the land available for cultivation. In some measure, the village structure may have mitigated the pressures of the family economy, as did the multigenerational family. There also, dependence on the available land was the chief fact of life, and there were many fewer artisan and merchant households. There was also far less mobility than in western Europe.

Women and the Family Economy

The family economy established many of the chief constraints on the lives and the personal experiences of women in preindustrial society. Most of the historical research that has been undertaken on this subject relates to western Europe. There, a woman's life experience was, in large measure, the function of her capacity to establish and maintain a household. For women, marriage was an institution of economic ne-

Servant girls making butter and cheese on a family farm. The farmer's wife, at left, is supervising their labor. Being a servant was a way for young people to acquire the skills and savings needed to start a household of their own when they married. [Bildarchiv Preussischer Kulturbesitz.]

cessity as well as one that fulfilled sexual and psychological needs. A woman outside a household situation lived in a highly vulnerable and precarious position. Unless she were an aristocrat or a member of a religious order, she probably could not support herself by her own efforts alone. Consequently, much of a woman's life was devoted first to aiding the maintenance of her parents' household and then to devising some means of assuring having her own household to live in as an adult. In most cases, the bearing and rearing of children were subordinate to these goals.

As a child, certainly by the age of seven, a girl was expected to begin to make contributions to the household work. On a farm, this might have meant looking after chickens or watering animals or carrying food to adult men and women working the land. In an urban artisan's household, she would do some form of light work, perhaps involving cleaning or carrying and later sewing or weaving. The girl would remain in her parents' home as long as she made a real contribution to the family enterprise or as long as her labor elsewhere was not more valuable and remunerative to the family. An artisan's daughter might not leave home until mar-

riage because she could learn increasingly valuable skills associated with the trade.

The situation was quite different for the much larger number of girls growing up on farms. There, the girl's parents and brothers could often do all the necessary farm work, and her labor at home quickly became of little value to the family. She would then leave home, usually between the age of twelve and fourteen. She might take up residence on another farm, but more likely, she would migrate to a nearby town or city. She would rarely travel more than thirty miles from her parents' household, and would then normally become a servant, once again living in a household, but this time in the household of an employer.

Having migrated from home, the young woman's chief goal was to accumulate sufficient capital for a dowry. Her savings would make her eligible for marriage because they would allow her to make the necessary contribution to form a household with her husband. The dowry would thus permit her to become an economic partner in the context of the family economy. It must be emphasized that marriage within the family economy was a joint economic undertaking, and that

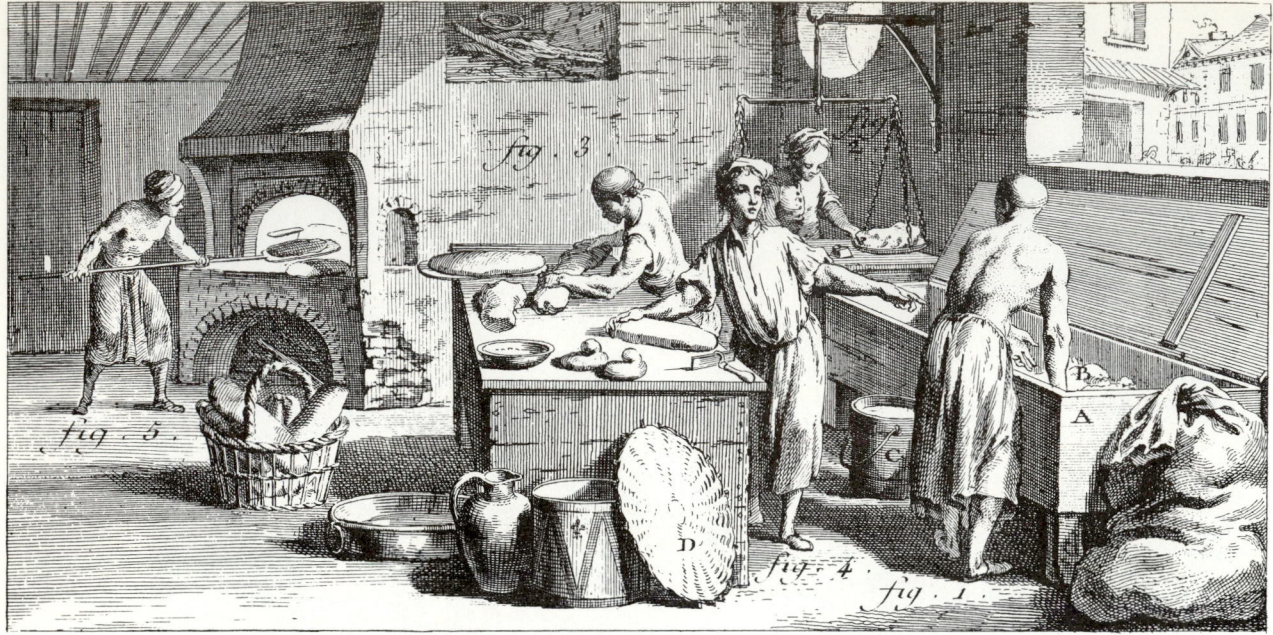

Bread was the single most important foodstuff in the eighteenth century, and its relative availability and price were constant social, economic, and political problems. This etching of an urban bakery from the Encyclopedia *illustrates, from right to left, kneading the dough, weighing and shaping of the loaves, and baking the bread. [The Granger Collection.]*

the wife was expected to make an immediate contribution of capital for the establishment of the household. A young woman might well work for ten years or more to accumulate a dowry. This practice meant that marriage was usually postponed until her mid- to late twenties.

Within the marriage, the necessity of earning enough money or producing enough farm goods to ensure an adequate food supply was always the dominant concern. Domestic duties, childbearing, and child rearing were subordinate to the economic situation. Consequently, the number of children might very well have been limited, usually through the practice of *coitus interruptus* or withdrawal of the male prior to ejaculation. Young children were often placed with wet nurses so that the mother could continue to make her economic contribution to the household. The wet nurse, in turn, was making such a contribution to her own household. The child would be fully reintegrated into its family when it was weaned and would be expected to aid the family at a very early age.

The kind of work a married woman did differed markedly between city and country and was in many ways a function of the husband's occupation. If the peasant household possessed enough land to support itself, the wife spent much of her time quite literally carrying things for her husband—water, food, seed, harvested grain, and the like. But there were few such adequate landholdings. If the husband had to do work other than farming, such as fishing or migrant labor, the wife actually might have been in charge of the farm, doing the ploughing, planting, and harvesting. In the city, the wife of an artisan or merchant often acted somewhat in the capacity of a business manager. She might well have been in charge of the household finances, and she actively participated in the trade or manufacturing enterprise. When her husband died, she might have taken over the business, perhaps hiring an artisan.

Finally, if economic disaster struck the family, more often than not it was the wife who organized what Olwen Hufton has called the "economy of expedients,"[1] within which family members might be sent off to find work elsewhere or even to beg in the streets.

In all phases of life within the family economy, women led active, often decisive roles. Industriousness rather than idleness was their lot in life. Finding a functional place in the household was essential to their well-being, but once that place had been found, their function was essential to the ongoing well-being of the household.

[1] Olwen Hufton, "Women and the Family Economy in Eighteenth-Century France," *French Historical Studies*, 9 (1975):19.

Working women in eighteenth-century France: They are crushing clay shards as a first step in making glass. It was common for the wives and daughters of artisans to help with the family trade. [New York Public Library.]

Children and the World of the Family Economy

Under the social and medical conditions of the day, the birth of a child was a time of grave danger to both mother and the infant. Both mother and child were immediately exposed to the possible contraction of contagious diseases. Puerperal fever was frequent, as well as other infections from unsterilized medical instruments. By no means were all midwives skillful practitioners of their profession. Furthermore, the immense poverty and the wretched housing conditions of the vast majority of Europe's population endangered the lives of the newborn child and the mother. For large numbers of women, childbirth constituted a time of great fearfulness of personal vulnerability.

Assuming that both mother and child survived, the mother might nurse the infant, but quite often the child would be sent a wet nurse. Convenience may have led to this practice among the wealthy, but economic necessity dictated it for the poor. The structures and customs of the family economy did not permit a woman the time away from work to devote herself entirely to rearing a child. The wet-nursing industry was quite well organized, and children born in cities might be transported to wet nurses in the country, where they would remain for months or even years.

However, throughout Europe the birth of a child was not always a welcome event. The child might be illegitimate or it might represent still one more economic burden on an already hard-pressed household. Through at least the end of the seventeenth century, and to a lesser degree beyond it, various forms of infanticide were practiced, especially among the poor.

The infant might be smothered or left exposed to the elements. These practices were one result of both the ignorance and the prejudice surrounding contraception. Though many married couples seem to have succeeded in limiting their families, young men and women who were unmarried and whose sexual relationships may have been the result of a fleeting acquaintance were less fortunate. Numerous young women, especially among servants, found themselves pregnant and without husbands. This situation and the consequent birth of illegitimate children seem to have become much more frequent over the course of the eighteenth century. The reasons for this development remain uncertain, but it probably arose from the more frequent migration of young people from their homes and the disturbance of traditional village life through enclosures (to be discussed later), the commercialization of agriculture, wars, and the late-century revolutions.

The late seventeenth and the early eighteenth centuries saw a new interest in preserving the lives of abandoned children. Large foundling hospitals were established in all the major nations. Hospitals created to care for abandoned children had existed before, but these years saw an expansion in their size and numbers. These hospitals, two of the most famous of which were the Paris Foundling Hospital (1670) and the London Foundling Hospital (1739), cared for thousands of European children. The demands on their resources vastly increased in the course of the eighteenth century. For example, early in the century, the average number of children admitted to the Paris Foundling Hospital was approximately 1,700 annually. But in the peak year of 1772, that number rose to 7,676 children.

A Lottery Is Provided for Admission of Children to the London Foundling Hospital

The London Foundling Hospital was established in 1739. The institution soon found that the demand for admission was greater than the facilities available. In 1742, its officers adopted the following policy for admitting children. The goal of the lottery was to ensure fairness. This system continued in use until 1756, when new funds allowed for the expansion of the hospital.

That all the Women who bring any Children be let into the Court Room as they come, and there set on Benches to be placed round the Room. . . . That as many white Balls as there shall be Children to be taken in, and with five red Balls for every Twenty Children who are to be taken in and so in Proportion for any greater or lesser number, and as many black Balls as with the white and red shall be Equal to the number of Women present, shall be put into a Bag or Box and drawn out by the Women who bring the Children. That each Woman who draws a white Ball shall be carried with her Child into the Inspecting Room in order to have the Child examined. That each Woman who draws a red Ball be carried with her Child into another Room there to remain till the Examination of the Children, whose Nurses drew white Balls is ended. That each Woman who draws a black Ball shall be immediately turned out of the Hospital with her Child. If on such Examination any of those Children are rejected but not so many as there be red Balls drawn, there shall be a second Drawing of Lotts by putting into the Bag or Box as many white Balls as there are Children wanting to make up the number ordered to be taken in, And as many black Balls as with the white will be equal to the whole number of red Balls drawn in the first Drawing. And the children whose Nurses draw those white Balls to be taken in if duly qualified, and so on till the whole number be compleated. . . . The Lotts to be drawn in the Court Room in the presence of all the Women to prevent all Suspicion of Fraud or Partiality. ❑

Minutes of the Foundling Hospital's General Committee, as quoted in Ruth K. McClure, *Coram's Children: The London Foundling Hospital in the Eighteenth Century* (New Haven: Yale University Press, 1981), pp. 77–78.

Not all of those children came from Paris. Many had been brought to the city from the provinces, where local foundling homes and hospitals were also overburdened. The London Foundling Hospital lacked the income to deal with all of the children brought to it and, in the middle of the eighteenth century, found itself compelled to choose children for admission by a lottery system.

Sadness and tragedy surrounded almost every aspect of abandoned children. The overwhelming majority of them were illegitimate infants drawn from across the social spectrum, but a substantial portion seem to have been left with the foundling hospitals because their parents were encountering difficult economic times. There existed a quite close relationship between rising Paris food prices and increasing numbers of abandoned children. Parents would sometimes leave personal tokens or saints' medals on the abandoned baby in the vain hope that at some future time they might be able to reclaim the child. The number of children so reclaimed was negligible. Leaving a child at a foundling hospital did not guarantee its survival. Again, to cite the situation in Paris, only about 10 per cent of all abandoned children lived to the age of ten years.

Despite all of these perils of early childhood, children did grow up and come of age across Europe. The world of the child may not have received the kind of attention that it does today, but in the course of the eighteenth century the seeds of that modern sensibility were sown. Particularly among the upper classes, new interest arose in the education of children. As economic skills became more demanding, literacy became more valuable, and there was a marked improvement in literacy during the century. However, in most areas education remained firmly in the hands of the churches. The overwhelming majority of the European population remained illiterate. It was not until the late nineteenth century that the world of childhood and the process of education became inextricably linked. Then children would be reared to become members of a national citizenry. In the old regime, they were reared to make their contribution to the economy of their parents' family and then to set up their own household.

The Land and Its Tillers

Land constituted the economic basis of eighteenth-century life. Well over three fourths of all Europeans

A hospital in Hamburg, 1746. The patients are crowded together in one room, regardless of their illness or state of health. Note the wigged doctor performing an amputation in the foreground. [Germanisches National-museum, Nuremberg.]

lived in the country, and few of these people ever traveled more than a few miles from their birthplace. With the exception of the nobility and the wealthier nonaristocratic landowners, the dwellers on the land were poor, and by any modern standard their lives were difficult. They lived in various modes of economic and social dependency, exploitation, and vulnerability.

Peasants and Serfs

The major forms of rural social dependency related directly to the land. Those who worked the land were subject to immense influence and in some cases direct control by the landowners. This situation prevailed in differing degrees for free peasants, such as English tenants and most French cultivators, and for the serfs of Germany, Austria, and Russia, who were legally bound to a particular plot of land and a particular lord. In all cases, the class that owned most of the land also controlled the local government and the courts.

The intensity of landlord power increased as one moved from west to east. In France, the situation differed somewhat from province to province. Most French peasants owned some land, but there were a few serfs. However, nearly all peasants were subject to certain feudal dues, called *banalités*, that included required use-for-payment of the lord or seigneur's mill to grind grain and his oven to bake bread. The seigneur could also require a certain number of days each year of the peasant's labor. This practice of forced labor was termed the *corvée*. Because even landowning French peasants rarely possessed enough land to support their families, they were also subject to feudal dues attached to the plots of land they rented.

Agriculture, basic to society, is illustrated in this plate from the French Encyclopedia. New machinery, such as the plows shown at the bottom, helped to increase yield from the land and thus the food supply for Europe.

Eighteenth-century France had some of the best roads in the world, but they were often built with forced labor. French peasants were required to work part of each year on such projects. This system, called the corvée, was not abolished until the French Revolution. This painting, Construction of the Major Road by Joseph Vernet, is the Louvre. [Giraudon.]

In Prussia and Austria, despite attempts by the monarchies late in the century to improve the lot of the serfs, the landlords continued to exercise almost complete control over them. In many of the Habsburg lands, law and custom required the serfs to provide service, or *robot*, to the lords. Moreover, throughout continental Europe, in addition to these feudal services, the burden of state taxation fell on the tillers of the soil. Many peasants, serfs, and other agricultural laborers were forced to undertake supplemental work to raise the cash required to pay the tax collector. Through various legal privileges and the ability to demand further concessions from the monarchs, the landlords escaped the payment of numerous taxes. They also presided over the manorial courts.

The condition of the serfs was the worst in Russia. The Russian custom of reckoning one's wealth by the number of "souls" (that is, male serfs) owned rather than by the acreage possessed reveals the contrast. The serfs were, in effect, regarded merely as economic commodities. Their services were attached to an individual lord rather than to a particular plot of land. Russian landlords could demand as many as six days a week of labor, and like Prussian and Austrian landlords they enjoyed the right to punish their serfs. On their own authority alone they could even exile a serf

to Siberia. The serfs had no legal recourse against the orders and whims of their lords. There was actually little difference between Russian serfdom and slavery.

The Russian monarchy itself contributed to the degradation of the serfs. Peter the Great gave whole villages to favored nobles. Later in the century, Catherine the Great (1762–1796) confirmed the authority of the nobles over their serfs in exchange for the political cooperation of the landowners. The situation in Russia led to considerable unrest. There were well over fifty peasant revolts between 1762 and 1769. These culminated between 1773 and 1775 in Pugachev's rebellion, during which all of southern Russia experienced intense unrest. Emelyan Pugachev (1726–1775) promised the serfs land of their own and freedom from their lords. The rebellion was brutally suppressed. Thereafter, any thought of liberalizing or improving the condition of the serfs was set aside for a generation.

Pugachev's was the greatest rebellion in Russian history and the largest peasant uprising of the eighteenth century. Smaller peasant revolts or disturbances occurred outside Russia. Rebellions took place in Bohemia in 1775, in Transylvania in 1784, in Moravia in 1786, and in Austria in 1789. Revolts in western Europe were almost nonexistent, but England experienced numerous local enclosure riots. Rural rebellions

Поддинное изображенiе
бунтовщика и обманщика
ЕМЕЛЬКИ ПУГАЧЕВА.

Wahre Abbildung
des Rebellen und Betrügers
IEMELKA PUGATSCEW.

Emelyan Pugachev (1726-1775) led the largest peasant revolt in Russian history. Here he is shown in chains. An inscription in Russian and German emphasizes the evil of revolution and insurrection. [Bildarchiv Preussicher Kulturbesitz.]

became. Failure of the harvest meant not only hardship but actual death from either outright starvation or protracted debility. Quite often, people living in the countryside encountered more difficulty finding food than did city dwellers, whose local government usually stored reserve supplies of grain.

Poor harvest also played havoc with prices. Smaller supplies or larger demand raised grain prices. Even small increases in the cost of food could exert heavy pressure on peasant or artisan families. If prices increased sharply, many of those families fell back on poor relief from their local municipality or county or the church. What made the situation of food supply and prices so difficult was the peasants' sense of helplessness before the whims of nature and the marketplace.

Over the course of the century, historians now believe, there occurred a slow but steady inflation of bread prices, spurred largely by population growth. This inflation put pressure on all of the poor. The prices rose faster than urban wages and brought no appreciable advantage to the very small peasant producer. On the other hand, the rise in grain prices benefited landowners and those wealthier peasants who had surplus grain to sell.

The increasing price of grain presented landlords with an opportunity to improve their incomes and lifestyle. To those ends, they began a series of innovations in farm production that are known as the *agricultural revolution*. This movement began during the sixteenth and seventeenth centuries in the Low Countries, where the pressures of the growing population and the shortage of land required changes in cultivation. Dutch landlords and farmers devised better ways to build dykes and to drain land so that they could farm more extensive areas. They also experimented with new crops, such as clover and turnips, that would increase the supply of animal fodder and restore the soil. These improvements became so famous that early in the seventeenth century Cornelius Vermuyden, a Dutch drainage engineer, was hired in England to drain thousands of acres of land around Cambridge.

The methods that the Dutch farmers had pioneered were extensively adopted in England during the early eighteenth century. The major agricultural innovations undertaken by the English included new methods of farming, new crops, and new modes of landholding, all of which eventually led to greater productivity. This advance in food production was necessary for the development of an industrial society. It ensured adequate food for people living in cities and freed agricultural labor for industrial production. The changing modes of agriculture sponsored by the landlords undermined the assumptions of traditional peasant production. Farming now took place not only for the local

were violent, but the peasants and serfs normally directed their wrath against property rather than persons. The rebels usually sought to reassert traditional or customary rights against practices that they perceived as innovations. Their targets were carefully chosen and included unfair pricing, onerous new or increased feudal dues, changes in methods of payment or land use, unjust officials, or extraordinarily brutal overseers and landlords. In this respect, the peasant revolts were quite conservative in nature.

The Revolution in Agriculture

Even more basic than the social dependency of peasants and small tenant farmers was their dependency on the productiveness of nature. The quantity and quality of the annual grain harvest was the most fundamental fact in their lives. On the Continent, bread was the primary component of the diet of the lower classes. The food supply was never certain, and the farther east one traveled, the more uncertain it

Turgot Describes the Results of Poor Harvests in France

Failure of the grain crop and other plantings could bring both hunger and social disruption during the eighteenth century. Anne Robert Jacques Turgot (1727–1781), who later became finance minister of France, emphasized the role of private charity and government policy in relieving the suffering. His description, written in 1769, also provides a brief survey of the diet of the French peasant.

Everyone has heard of the terrible dearth that has just afflicted this generality [a local administrative district]. The harvest of 1769 in every respect proved to be one of the worst in the memory of man. The dearths of 1709 and 1739 were incomparably less cruel. To the loss of the greatest part of the rye was added the total loss of the chestnuts, of the buckwheat, and of the Spanish wheat—cheap food stuffs with which the peasant sustained himself habitually a great part of the year, reserving as much as he could of his corn [grain], in order to sell it to the inhabitants of the towns. . . . The people could exist only by exhausting their resources, by selling at a miserable price their articles of furniture and even their clothes. Many of the inhabitants have been obliged to disperse themselves through other provinces to seek work or to beg, leaving their wives and children to the charity of the parishes. It has been necessary for the public authority to require the proprietors and inhabitants in better circumstances in each parish to assess themselves for the relief of the poor people; nearly a fourth of the population is dependent upon charitable contributions. After these melancholy sufferings which the province has already undergone, and with the reduced condition in which it was left by the dearth of last year, even had the harvest of the present year been a good one, the poverty of the inhabitants would have necessitated the greatest efforts to be made for their relief. But we have now to add the dismal fact of our harvest being again deficient. . . .   ❑

W. W. Stephens (ed.), *The Life and Writings of Turgot* (London: Longmans, Green, 1895), p. 50.

food supply but also to assure the landlord a handsome profit.

Many of the agriculture innovations, which were adopted only very slowly, were incompatible with the existing organization of land in Britain. Small cultivators who lived in village communities still farmed most of the soil. Each farmer tilled an assortment of unconnected strips. The two- or three-field systems of rotation left large portions of land annually fallow and unproductive. Animals grazed on the common land in the summer and on the stubble of the harvest in the winter. Until at least the middle of the eighteenth century the decisions about what crops would be planted were made communally. The entire system discouraged improvement and favored the poorer farmers, who needed the common land and stubble fields for their animals. The village method provided little possibility of expanding the pasture land to raise more animals that would, in turn, produce more manure, which could be used for fertilizer. Thus, the methods of traditional production aimed at a steady but not a growing supply of food.

In 1700, approximately half the arable land in Britain was farmed by this open-field method. By the second half of the century, the rising price of wheat encouraged landlords to consolidate or enclose their lands to increase production. The enclosures were intended to use land more rationally and to achieve greater commercial profits. The process involved the fencing of common lands, the reclamation of previously untilled waste, and the transformation of strips into block fields. These procedures brought turmoil to the economic and social life of the countryside. Riots often ensued. Because many British farmers either owned their strips or rented them in a manner that amounted to ownership, the larger landlords had usually to resort to parliamentary acts to legalize the enclosure of the land, which they owned but rented to the farmers. Because the large landowners controlled Parliament, there was little difficulty in passing such measures. Between 1761 and 1792, almost 500,000 acres were enclosed through parliamentary act, as compared with 75,000 acres between 1727 and 1760. In 1801, a general enclosure act streamlined the process.

The enclosures were at the time and have remained among historians a very controversial topic. They permitted the extension of both farming and innovation. In that regard, they increased food production on larger agricultural units. At the same time, they disrupted the small traditional communities. They forced off the land some independent farmers, who had needed the common pasturage, and very poor cottagers, who had lived on the reclaimed waste land. However, the enclosures did not depopulate the countryside. In some counties where the enclosures took place, the population increased. New soil had come into production, and services subsidiary to farming also expanded.

Improving agriculture tended to characterize farm production west of the Elbe. Dutch farming was quite efficient. In France, despite the efforts of the government to improve agriculture, enclosures were restricted. Yet there was much discussion in France about improving agricultural methods. These new procedures benefited the ruling classes because better agriculture increased their incomes and assured a larger food supply, which tended to discourage social unrest.

In Prussia, Austria, Poland, and Russia, only very limited agricultural improvement took place. Nothing in the relationship of the serfs to their lords encouraged innovation. In eastern Europe, the chief method of increasing production was to extend farming to previously untilled lands. The management of farms was usually under the direction of the landlords or their agents rather than of the villages. By extending tillage, the great landlords sought to squeeze more labor from their serfs rather than greater productivity from the soil. As in the West, the goal was increased profits for the landlords. But on the whole, east European landlords were much less ambitious and successful. The only significant nutritional gain achieved through their efforts was the introduction of maize and the potato. Livestock production did not increase significantly.

Population Expansion

The assault on human dependence on nature through improved farming was both a cause and a result of an immense expansion in the population of Europe. The population explosion with which the entire world must today contend seems to have had its origins in the eighteenth century. Before this time, Europe's population had experienced dramatic increases, but plagues, wars, or harvest failures had in time decimated the increase. Beginning in the second quarter of the eighteenth century, the population began to grow without decimation.

Exact figures are lacking, but the best estimates suggest that in 1700 Europe's population, excluding the European provinces of the Ottoman Empire, stood between 100 million and 120 million people. By 1800, the figures had risen to almost 190 million, and by 1850 to 260 million. The population of England and Wales rose from 6 million in 1750 to over 10 million in 1800. France grew from 18 million in 1715 to approximately 26 million in 1789. Russia's population increased from 19 million in 1722 to 29 million in 1766. Such extraordinary, sustained growth put new demands on all resources and considerable pressure on existing social organization.

The population expansion occurred across the Continent in both the country and the cities. Only a limited consensus exists about the causes of this growth. There was a clear decline in the death rate. There were fewer wars and somewhat fewer epidemics in the eighteenth century. Hygiene and sanitation also improved. Better medical knowledge and techniques were once thought to have contributed to the decline in deaths. This factor is now discounted because the more important medical advances came after the initial population explosion or would not have contributed directly to it. Rather, changes in the food supply itself may have provided the chief factor that allowed the population growth to be sustained. The improved and expanding grain production made one contribution. Another and even more important modification was the cultivation of the potato. This tuber was a product of the New World and came into widespread European production during the eighteenth century. On a single acre, enough potatoes could be raised to feed one peasant's family for an entire year. With this more certain food supply, more children could be reared, and more could survive.

The Eighteenth-Century Industrial Revolution

An Event in World History

The second half of the eighteenth century witnessed the beginning of the industrialization of the European economy. This development, more than any other single factor, distinguished Europe and eventually North America from the rest of the world for the next two centuries. The consumer products of the slowly industrializing businesses gave Europeans vast amounts of new goods to sell throughout the world and thus encouraged more international trade in which Western nations supplied the finished goods in exchange for raw materials. As a consequence, other areas of the globe became economically dependent upon the European and American demand for their own prosperity. The wealth achieved through this uneven commerce allowed Europeans to continue to dominate world markets for almost two centuries.

Furthermore, by the early nineteenth century iron and steel production and the new technologies of manufacture allowed European states and later the United States to build more powerful military forces, especially navies, than those controlled by Africa, Latin America, or Asia. In that regard, both the economic and military dominance of the West arose directly from the industrial achievement.

Much of the history of the non-Western world from the middle of the eighteenth century to the present can be understood in terms of how the nonindustrialized nations initially reacted to the penetration of their world by Europeans and Americans made wealthy and

Richard Arkwright's spinning machine which ran by water power. Cotton spinning and weaving were the classic industries of the early industrial era. [Science Museum, London. Copyright Crown.]

powerful through industrialized economies. Africa and Latin America became generally dependent economies. Japan, by the middle of the nineteenth century, decided it must imitate the European pattern and did so quite successfully. China did not make that decision and for some time became indirectly ruled by Europeans. The Chinese revolutions of the twentieth century have largely represented efforts to achieve real self-direction. Southeast Asia and the Middle East became drawn into the network of resource supply to the West; they could achieve movement toward economic independence only through imitation or, like Arab nations in the early 1970s, by refusing to supply oil to the West. Whatever the strategy, obviously the process of industrialization that commenced in very small factories in eighteenth-century Europe has changed the world more than any other single development in the last two centuries.

The European Industrial Revolution of the eighteenth century constituted the achievement of sustained economic growth. Previously, production had been limited. The economy of a province or a country might grow, but it soon reached a plateau. However, since the late eighteenth century the economy of Europe has managed to expand relatively uninterruptedly. Depressions and recessions have been temporary, and even during such economic downturns the Western economy has continued to grow.

At considerable social cost and dislocation, industrialism made possible more goods and services than ever before in human history. Industrialism in Europe eventually overcame the economy of scarcity. The new means of production demanded new kinds of skills, new discipline in work, and a large labor force. The goods produced both met immediate consumer demand and created new demands. In the long run, industrialism clearly raised the standard of living; the poverty that had been experienced by the overwhelming majority of Europeans who lived during the eighteenth century and earlier was overcome. Industrialization provided human beings greater control over the forces of nature than they had ever known before.

The wealth produced by industrialism upset the political and social structures of the old regime and led to reforms. The economic elite of the emerging industrial society would eventually challenge the political dominance of the aristocracy. At the same time, the industrializing process also undermined traditional communities and along with the growth of cities displaced many people. These processes that first occurred in Europe repeated themselves virtually everywhere that industrialization occurred in the next two centuries.

Industrial Leadership of Great Britain

Great Britain was the home of the Industrial Revolution and, until the middle of the nineteenth century, maintained the industrial leadership of Europe and the world. Several factors contributed to the early start in Britain. The nation constituted the single largest free-trade area in Europe. The British possessed good roads and waterways without tolls or other internal trade barriers. The country was endowed with rich deposits of coal and iron ore. The political structure was stable, and property was absolutely secure. Taxation was not especially heavy. In addition to the existing domestic consumer demand, the British economy also benefited from demand from the colonies in North America.

Finally, British society was relatively mobile by the standards of the time. Persons who had money or could earn money could rise socially. The British aristocracy would receive into its midst people who had amassed very large fortunes. No one of these factors preordained the British advance toward industrialism. However, the combination of them plus the progressive state of British agriculture provided the nation with the marginal advantage in the creation of a new mode of economic production.

While this economic development was occurring, people did not call it a *revolution*. That term came to be applied to the British economic phenomena only after the French Revolution. Then, continental writers observed that what had taken place in Britain was the economic equivalent of the political events in France; hence the concept of an *industrial* revolution. It was revolutionary less in its speed, which was on the whole rather slow, than in its implications for the future of European society.

NEW METHODS OF TEXTILE PRODUCTION. Although eighteenth-century society was primarily devoted to agriculture, manufacturing permeated the countryside. The same peasants who tilled the land in spring and summer often spun thread or wove textiles in the winter. Under what is termed the *domestic* or *putting-out system*, agents of urban textile merchants took wool or other unfinished fibers to the homes of peasants, who spun it into thread. The agent then transported the thread to other peasants, who wove it into the finished product. The merchant sold the wares. In literally thousands of peasant cottages from Ireland to Austria, there stood either a spinning wheel or a handloom. Sometimes the spinners or weavers owned their own equipment, but more often than not, by the middle of the century the merchant capitalist owned the machinery as well as the raw material.

What must be kept constantly in mind is the rather surprising fact that eighteenth-century industrial development took place within a rural setting. The peasant family living in a one- or two-room cottage was the basic unit of production rather than the factory. The family economy, rather than the industrial factory economy, characterized the century.

The domestic system of textile production was a basic feature of this family economy. However, by mid-century a series of production bottlenecks had developed within the domestic system. The demand for cotton textiles was growing more rapidly than production. This demand arose particularly in Great Britain, where there existed a large domestic demand for cotton textiles from the growing population. There was a similar foreign demand on British production from its colonies in North America. It was in response to this consumer demand for cotton textiles that the most famous inventions of the Industrial Revolution were devised.

Cotton textile weavers had the technical capacity to produce the quantity of fabric that was in demand. However, the spinners did not possess the equipment to produce as much thread as the weavers needed and could use. This imbalance had been created during the 1730s by James Kay's invention of the flying shuttle, which increased the productivity of the weavers. Thereafter, various groups of manufacturers and merchants offered prizes for the invention of a machine to eliminate this bottleneck. About 1765, James Hargreaves (d. 1778) invented the spinning jenny. Initially, this machine allowed 16 spindles of thread to be spun, but by the close of the century its capacity had been increased to as many as 120 spindles.

The spinning jenny broke the bottleneck between the productive capacity of the spinners and the weavers, but it was still a piece of machinery that was used in the cottage. The invention that took cotton textile manufacture out of the home and put it into the factory was Richard Arkwright's (1732–1792) water frame, patented in 1769. It was a water-powered device designed to permit the production of a purely cotton fabric rather than a cotton fabric containing linen fiber for durability. Eventually Arkwright lost his patent rights, and other manufacturers were able to use his invention freely. As a result, numerous factories sprang up in the countryside near streams that provided the necessary waterpower. From the 1780s onward, the cotton industry could meet an ever-expanding demand. In the last two decades of the century, cotton output increased by 800 per cent over the production of 1780. By 1815 cotton composed 40 per cent of the value of British domestic exports, and by 1830 just over 50 per cent.

Manchester's Calico Printers Protest the Use of New Machinery

The introduction of the new machines associated with the Industrial Revolution stirred much protest. Machine labor was replacing human labor; machines were duplicating the skills of laborers. This situation could mean the loss of jobs. It also brought about the loss of status for workers whose chief means of livelihood lay in their possession of those displaced and now mechanized skills. The following letter was sent anonymously to a Manchester manufacturer by English workers. It indicates the outrage of those workers, the modes of intimidation they were willing to use as threats, and their own economic fears.

Mr. Taylor If you dont discharge James Hobson from the House of Correction we will burn your House about your Ears for we have sworn to stand by one another and you must immediately give over any more Mashen Work for we are determined there shall be no more of them made use of in the Trade and it will be madness for you to contend with the Trade as we are combined by Oath to fix Prices we can afford to pay him a Guinea Week and not hurt the fund if you was to keep him there till Dumsday therefore mind you comply with the above or by God we will keep our Words with you we will make some rare Bunfires in this Countey and at your Peril to call any more Meetings mind that we will make the Mosney Pepel shake in their Shoes we are determined to destroy all Sorts of Masheens for Printing in the Kingdom for there is more hands then is work for so no more from the ingerd Gurnemen Rember we are a great number sworn nor you must not advertise the Men that you say run away from you when your il Usage was the Cause of their going we will punish you for that our Meetings are legal for we want nothing but what is honest and to work for selvs and familers and you want to starve us but it is better for you and a few more which we have marked to die then such a Number of Pore Men and their famerles to be starved. ❑

London Gazette, 1786, p. 36, as reprinted in Douglas Hay (ed.), *Albion's Fatal Tree* (New York: Pantheon Books, 1975), p. 318.

THE STEAM ENGINE. The new technology in textile manufacture vastly increased cotton production and revolutionized a major consumer industry. But the invention that more than any other permitted industrialization to grow on itself and to expand into one area of production after another was the steam engine. This machine provided for the first time in human history a steady and essentially unlimited source of inanimate power. Unlike engines powered by water or the wind, the steam engine, driven by the burning of coal, was a portable source of industrial power that did not fail or falter as the seasons of the year changed. Unlike human power or animal power, the steam engine depended on mineral energy that did not tire over the course of a day. Finally, the steam engine could be applied to a very large number of industrial and, eventually, transportation uses.

The first practical engine using steam power had been the invention of Thomas Newcomen in the early eighteenth century. The piston of this device was moved when the steam that had been induced into the cylinder condensed, causing the piston to fall. The Newcomen machine was very large. It was inefficient in its use of energy because both the condenser and the cylinder were heated, and it was practically untransportable. Despite these problems, English mine operators employed the Newcomen machines to pump water out of coal and tin mines. By the third quarter of the eighteenth century, almost a hundred Newcomen machines were operating in the mining districts of England.

During the 1760s, James Watt, a Scottish engineer and machine maker, began to experiment with a model of a Newcomen machine at the University of Glasgow. He gradually understood that if the condenser were separated from the piston and the cylinder, much greater efficiency would result. In 1769, he patented his new invention, but transforming his idea into application presented difficulties. His design required exceedingly precise metalwork. Watt soon found a partner in Matthew Boulton, a toy manufacturer in Birmingham, the city with the most skilled metalworkers in Britain. Watt and Boulton, in turn, consulted with John Wilkinson, a cannon manufacturer, to find ways to drill the precise metal cylinders required by Watt's design. In 1776, the Watt steam engine found its first commercial application pumping water from mines in Cornwall.

The use of the steam engine spread slowly because until 1800 Watt retained the exclusive patent rights. He was also reluctant to make further changes in his invention that would permit the engine to operate

This landscape painting by an unknown comtemporary British artist portrays the pit-head of an eighteenth-century coal mine in England. The machinery on the left included a steam engine that powered equipment either to bring the mined coal to the surface or to pump water from the mine. [Walker Art Gallery, Liverpool.]

more rapidly. Boulton eventually persuaded him to make modifications and improvements. These allowed the engines to be used not only for pumping but also for running cotton mills. By the early nineteenth century, the steam engine had become the prime mover for all industry. With its application to ships and then to wagons on iron rails, the steam engine also revolutionized transportation.

IRON PRODUCTION. The manufacture of high-quality iron has been basic to modern industrial development. It constitutes the chief element of all heavy industry and land or sea transport. Iron has also been the material out of which most productive machinery itself has been manufactured. During the early eighteenth century, British ironmakers produced somewhat less than twenty-five thousand tons annually. Three factors held back the production of the metal. Charcoal rather than coke was used to smelt the ore. Charcoal, which is derived from wood, was becoming a scarce commodity, and it did not burn at as high a temperature as coke, which is derived from coal. Until the perfection of the steam engine, insufficient blasts could be achieved in the furnaces. Finally, the demand

for iron was limited. The elimination of the first two problems eliminated the third.

In the course of the century, British ironmakers began to use coke, and the steam engine provided new power for the blast furnaces. Coke was an abundant fuel because of Britain's large coal deposits. The existence of the steam engine both improved iron production and increased the demand for iron.

In 1784, Henry Cort (1740–1800) introduced a new puddling process, that is, a new method for melting and stirring the molten ore. Cort's process allowed more slag (the impurities that bubbled to the top of the

MAJOR INVENTIONS IN THE
TEXTILE-MANUFACTURING REVOLUTION

1733	James Kay's flying shuttle
1765	James Hargreaves' spinning jenny (patent 1770)
1769	James Watt's steam engine patent
1769	Richard Arkwright's waterframe patent
1787	Edmund Cartwright's power loom

Throughout most of the eighteenth century industrial manufacture took place in relatively small workshops such as the lead-casting shop illustrated in this print from the French Encyclopedia. *Very large factories arose only in the late eighteenth century and early nineteenth.*

molten metal) to be removed and a purer iron to be produced. Cort also developed a rolling mill that continuously shaped the still-molten metal into bars, rails, or other forms. Previously, the metal had been pounded into these forms.

All of these innovations achieved a better, more versatile product at a lower cost. The demand for iron grew as its price became lower. By the early years of the nineteenth century, British iron production amounted to over a million tons annually. The lower cost of iron, in turn, lowered the cost of steam engines and allowed them to be used more widely.

The Aristocracy

Despite the emerging Industrial Revolution, the eighteenth century remained the age of the aristocracy. The nobility of every country was the single wealthiest sector of the population; possessed the widest degree of social, political, and economic power; and set the tone of polite society. Land continued to provide the aristocracy with its largest source of income, but the role of the aristocrat was not limited to the estate. The influence of aristocrats was felt in every area of life. To be an aristocrat was a matter of birth and legal privilege. This much they had in common across the Continent. In almost every other respect, they differed markedly from country to country.

Great Britain

The smallest, wealthiest, best-defined, and most socially responsible aristocracy resided in Great Britain. It consisted of about four hundred families, whose eldest male member sat in the House of Lords. Through the corruptions of the electoral system, these families also controlled a large number of seats in the House of Commons. The estates of the British nobility ranged from a few thousand to fifty thousand acres, from which they received rents. The nobles owned approximately one fourth of all the arable land in the country. Increasingly, the money of the aristocracy was being invested in commerce, canals, urban real estate, mines, and sometimes industrial ventures. Because only the eldest son inherited the title and the land, younger sons moved into commerce, the army, the professions, and the Church. The British landowners in the House of Commons levied taxes in Parliament and also paid taxes. They had almost no significant legal privileges, but their direct or indirect control of local government gave them immense political power and social influence. The aristocracy quite simply dominated the society and the politics of the English counties.

France

The situation of the continental nobilities was less clear-cut. In France, the nobility was theoretically di-

The brothers Adam dominated British decorative taste in the late eighteenth century. About 1770, Robert Adam planned this elegant drawing room for London house of the Earls of Home. [The Courtauld Institute of Art and Country Life, *London.]*

vided between nobles of the sword and those of the robe. The former families enjoyed privileges deriving from military service; the latter had either gained their titles by serving in the bureaucracy or had purchased them. The two groups had frequently quarreled in the past but tended to cooperate during the eighteenth century to defend their common privileges.

The French nobility were also divided between those who held office or favor with the royal court at Versailles and those who did not. The court nobility reaped the immense wealth that could be gained from holding high offices. The noble hold on such offices intensified over the course of the century. By the late 1780s, appointments to the Church, the army, and the bureaucracy, as well as other profitable positions, tended to go to the nobles already established in court circles. Whereas these well-connected aristocrats were quite rich, other nobles who lived in the provinces were often rather poor. These *hobereaux*, as the poverty-stricken nobles were called, were sometimes little or no better off than wealthy peasants.

Despite differences in rank, origin, and wealth, all French aristocrats enjoyed certain hereditary privileges that set them apart from the rest of society. They were exempt from many taxes. For example, most French nobles did not pay the *taille*, which was the basic land tax of the old regime. The nobles were technically liable for payment of the *vingtième*, or the "twentieth," which resembled an income tax. However, by virtue of protests and legal procedures, the nobility rarely felt the entire weight of this tax. The nobles were not liable for the royal *corvées*, or labor donations, which fell on the peasants. In addition to these exemptions, the approximately 400,000 French nobles could collect feudal dues from their tenants and enjoyed hunting and fishing privileges denied their tenants.

Eastern Europe

East of the Elbe River, the character of the nobility became even more complicated and repressive. In Poland, there were thousands of nobles, or *szlachta*, who after 1741 were entirely exempt from taxes. Until 1768, these Polish aristocrats possessed the right of life and death over their serfs. Most of the Polish nobility were relatively poor. The political power of the fragile Polish state resided in the few very rich nobles.

In Austria and Hungary, the nobility continued to

possess broad judicial powers over the peasantry through manorial courts.

In Prussia, after the accession of Frederick the Great in 1740, the position of the *Junker* nobles became much stronger. Frederick's various wars required the support of his nobles. He drew his officers almost wholly from the *Junker* class. The bureaucracy was also increasingly composed of nobles. As in other parts of eastern Europe, the Prussian nobles enjoyed extensive judicial authority over the serfs.

Russia

In Russia, the eighteenth century saw what amounted to the creation of the nobility. Peter the Great's linking of required state service to particular noble social status through the Table of Ranks (1722) established among Russian nobles a self-conscious class identity by arousing a shared determination to resist compulsory state service. In 1736, Empress Ann reduced such service to a period of twenty-five years. In 1762, Peter III removed the liability for compulsory service entirely from the greatest nobles. In 1785, in the Charter of the Nobility, Catherine the Great granted an explicit legal definition of noble rights and privileges in exchange for assurances of voluntary state service from the nobility. The noble privileges included the right of transmitting noble status to one's wife and children, the judicial protection of noble rights and property, considerable power over the serfs, and exemption from personal taxes.

The Russian Charter of the Nobility constituted one aspect of the broader European-wide development termed the *aristocratic resurgence*. Throughout the century, the various nobilities felt their social position and privileges threatened by the expanding power of the monarchies and the growing wealth of merchants, bankers, and other commercial groups. All nobilities attempted to preserve their exclusiveness by making entry into their ranks and institutions more difficult. They also pushed for exclusively noble appointments to the officer corps of the armies, the bureaucracies, the government ministries, and the Church. In that manner, the nobles hoped to control the power of the monarchies.

On a third level, the nobles attempted to use the authority of existing aristocratically controlled institutions against the power of the monarchies. These institutions included the British Parliament and on the Continent the French courts, or *parlements*; the local aristocratic estates; and the provincial diets. Economically, the aristocratic resurgence took the form of pressing the peasantry for higher rents or collecting long-forgotten feudal dues. There was a general tendency for the nobility to shore up its position by various appeals to traditional and often ancient privileges that had lapsed over the course of time. To contempo-

raries, this aristocratic challenge to the monarchies and to the rising commercial classes constituted one of the most fundamental political facts of the day.

Cities

Patterns of Preindustrial Urbanization

Remarkable changes occurred in the pattern of city growth between 1500 and 1800. In 1500, within Europe (excluding Hungary and Russia) there were approximately 156 cities with a population greater than 10,000. Only 4 of those cities, Paris, Milan, Venice, and Naples, had populations larger than 100,000. By 1800, there existed approximately 363 cities of 10,000 or more inhabitants, and 17 of those had populations larger than 100,000. The percentage of the European population living in urban areas had risen from just over 5 per cent to just over 9 per cent. There had also occurred a major shift in urban concentration from southern, Mediterranean Europe to the north.

These raw figures conceal significant changes that took place in how cities grew and how population distributed itself. A major time of urban development was the sixteenth century. This development was followed by a leveling off and even a decline in the seventeenth. New growth began in the early eighteenth century and became much accelerated in the late eighteenth and the early nineteenth centuries. Between 1500 and 1750, the major urban expansion took place within already-established and generally already-large cities. It was not a period of the emergence and growth of new cities. After 1750, the pattern changed with the birth of new cities and the rapid growth of already-existing smaller cities.

In particular, between 1600 and 1750, the urban areas that displayed the most growth and vigor were capitals and ports. This situation reflects the success of monarchical state building during those years and the consequent burgeoning of bureaucracies, armies, courts, and other groups related to the process of government who lived in the capitals. The growth of port cities, in turn, reflects the expansion of European overseas trade and most especially that of the Atlantic routes. With the exception of Lyons, France, significant growth did not take place in the cases of industrial cities. Furthermore, between 1600 and 1750, cities with populations of less than 40,000 inhabitants declined. These included older landlocked trading centers, medieval industrial cities, and ecclesiastical centers. They contributed less to the new political regimes, and the expansion of the putting-out system transferred much production that had once occurred in medieval cities into the countryside. Rural labor was cheaper than urban labor, and cities with concentra-

The port of Bristol in southwestern England, c. 1735. Bristol was the third busiest port in eighteenth-century Britain after London and Liverpool. [City of Bristol Museum.]

tions of labor declined as the site of production was moved from the urban workshop into the country.

In the middle of the eighteenth century, a new pattern emerged. The rate of growth of existing large cities declined. New cities began to emerge and existing smaller cities began to grow. Several factors were at work in the process, which Jan De Vries has termed "an urban growth from below."[2] First, there was the general overall population increase. Second, the early stages of the Industrial Revolution, particularly in Britain, occurred in the countryside and tended to aid the growth of smaller towns and cities located nearby the factories. Factory organization itself fostered new concentrations of population. But cities also grew where there was little industrialization. The reason for this growth would seem to have been the new prosperity of European agriculture. Greater agricultural production aided the growth of nearby market towns and other urban centers that served agriculture or allowed more

[2] De Vries, "Patterns of Urbanization in Pre-Industrial Europe, 1500–1800," in H. Schnal, ed., *Patterns of European Urbanization Since 1500* (London: Croom Helm, 1981), p. 103.

prosperous farmers to have access to the consumer goods and recreation they wanted. This new pattern of urban growth—new cities and the expansion of smaller existing cities—would continue into the nineteenth century.

Urban Classes

Social divisions were as marked in the cities of the eighteenth century as they were in the industrial centers of the nineteenth. At the top of the urban social structure stood a generally small group of nobles, large merchants, bankers, financiers, clergy, and government officials. These men (and they were always men) controlled the political and economic affairs of the town. Normally they constituted a self-appointed and self-electing oligarchy who governed the city through its corporation or city council. These rights of self-government had generally been granted by some form of royal charter that gave the city corporation its authority and the power to select its own members. In a few cities on the Continent, artisan guilds controlled the corporations, but more generally the councils were under the influence of the local nobility and the wealthiest commercial people.

THE MIDDLE CLASS. Another group in the city were the prosperous but not immensely wealthy merchants, tradesmen, bankers, and professional people. These were the most dynamic element of the urban population and constituted the persons traditionally regarded as the middle class, or *bourgeoisie*. The concept of the middle class was much less clear-cut than that of the nobility. They had less wealth than most nobles but more than urban artisans. The middle-class people lived in the cities and towns, and their sources of income had little or nothing to do with the land. The middle class normally stood on the side of reform, change, and economic growth. The middle-class commercial figures—traders, bankers, manufacturers, and lawyers—often found their pursuit of both profit and prestige blocked by the privileges of the nobility and its social exclusiveness. The bourgeoisie also wanted more rational regulations for trade and commerce, as did some of the more progressive aristocrats.

During the eighteenth century, the middle class and the aristocracy frequently collided. The former often imitated the lifestyle of the latter, and the nobles were increasingly embracing the commercial spirit of the middle class. The bourgeoisie was not rising to challenge the nobility; both were seeking to add new dimensions to their existing power and prestige. However, tradition and political connection gave the advantage to the nobility. Consequently, as the century passed, members of the middle class felt and voiced increasing resentment of the aristocracy. That resentment became more bitter as the wealth and the

In the late eighteenth-century Vienna, prostitutes had to appear before courts, as in this print, where they were ordered to have their hair shorn and were made to sweep the streets. [Österreichische Nationalbibliothek, Vienna.]

numbers of the bourgeoisie increased and the aristocratic control of political and ecclesiastical power became tighter. The growing influence of the nobility seemed to mean that the middle class would continue to be excluded from the political decisions of the day.

On the other hand, the middle class in the cities tended to fear the lower urban classes as much as they resented the nobility. The lower orders constituted a potentially violent element in the society, a potential threat to property, and, in their poverty, a drain on national resources. However, the lower orders were much more varied than either the city aristocracy or the middle class cared to admit.

ARTISANS. The segment of the urban population that suffered from both the grasping of the middle class and the local nobility was made up of the shopkeepers, the artisans, and the wage earners. These people constituted the single largest group in any city. The lives and experience of this class were very diverse. They included grocers, butchers, fishmongers, carpenters, cabinetmakers, smiths, printers, handloom weavers,

and tailors, to give but a few examples. They had their own culture, values, and institutions. Like the peasants of the countryside, they were in many respects very conservative. Their economic position was highly vulnerable. If a poor harvest raised the price of food, their own businesses suffered.

The entire life of these artisans and shopkeepers centered on their work. They usually lived near or at their place of employment. Most of them worked in shops with fewer than a half dozen other craftsmen. Their primary institution had historically been the guild, but by the eighteenth century the guilds rarely possessed the influence of their predecessors in medieval or early modern Europe.

Nevertheless, the guilds were not to be ignored. They played a conservative role. They did not seek economic growth or innovation. They attempted to preserve the jobs and the skills of their members. The guilds still were able in many countries to determine who might and might not pursue a particular craft. They attempted to prevent too many people from learning a particular skill. The guilds also provided a framework for social and economic advancement. A boy might at an early age become an apprentice to learn a craft or trade. After several years, he would be made a journeyman. Still later, if successful and sufficiently competent, he might become a master. The artisan could also receive certain social benefits from the guilds. These might include aid for his family during sickness or the promise of admission for his son. The guilds constituted the chief protection for artisans against the operation of the commercial market. They were particularly strong in central Europe.

The European *Ancien Régime* in World Perspective

This chapter opened by describing eighteenth-century European society as traditional, hierarchical, corporate, and privileged. These features had characterized Europe and much of the rest of the world for centuries. In virtually every society on the globe at the opening of the eighteenth century, there existed situations of marked social dependence and of discrepancies between great wealth and poverty. All societies also confronted the grave problems of scarce food supplies.

The eighteenth century witnessed important changes in all these societies. The population explosion was a global event not limited to Europe. Its exact causes still remain uncertain, but in each case, whether in Europe or China, an improved food supply that was achieved through expanded acreage and new crops helped support the new population. In China, new lands once thought to be marginal were settled. There was new farming in Europe, but there was also emigration to the New World where vast expanses of land were settled. In contrast to Europe, the farmland of China continued to be cultivated by clans or communities. But in all cases, the vast expanding population created pressures on all the existing social structures.

Another striking similarity between China and Europe is apparent in the growth of commerce during the eighteenth century. In both cultures, banking was improved and a more certain money supply established. Agriculture became more commercialized with more money payments. There was a similar expansion of cities in China. In the eighteenth century, Chinese trade expanded within Asia as well as within a larger world market. However, industrialization did not occur in China or anywhere else in the world except Europe.

Eighteenth-century Japan stood, of course, in marked contrast to both Europe and China. Tokugawa rule had achieved remarkable stability, but the nation had chosen not to enter the world-trading network except as a depot for Dutch and Chinese goods. The population grew less rapidly than in Europe or China, and the general economy seems to have grown very slowly. Like the situation in many European cities, guilds held strong control of manufacture. In all these respects, Japan in the eighteenth century stood as a nation that sought to spurn innovation and to preserve stable tradition.

Throughout the eighteenth century, Africa continued to supply slave labor to both North and South America. That trade drew Africa deeply into the transatlantic economy, about which more will be said in the next chapter.

Latin America remained at least in theory the monopolized preserve of Spain. But that situation could not survive the expansion of the British economy and the determination of Britain to enter the Latin American market. At the same time, British forces moved swiftly into mid-eighteenth-century India to establish a hegemony that would last almost two centuries.

Seen in this world context, European society stood on the brink of a new era in which the social, economic, and political relationships of centuries would be destroyed. The European manifestation of the commercial spirit and values of the marketplace clashed with the traditional values and practices of the peasants and the guilds. That commercial spirit proved to be a major vehicle of social change; and by the early nineteenth century, it led increasingly to a conception of human beings as individuals rather than as members of communities.

The expansion of the European population provided a further stimulus for change and a challenge to tradition, hierarchy, and corporateness. The traditional economic and social organization had presupposed a stable or declining population. The additional numbers of people meant that new ways had to be devised to solve old problems. The social hierarchy had to accommodate itself to more people. Corporate groups, such as the guilds, had to confront the existence of an expanded labor force. New wealth meant that birth would eventually become less and less a determining factor in social relationships, except in regard to the social roles assigned to the two sexes.

Finally, the conflicting political ambitions of the monarchies, the nobilities, and the middle class generated innovation. The monarchies wanted to make their nations rich enough to wage war. The nobilities wished to reassert their privileges. The middle class, in all of its diversity, was growing wealthier from trade, commerce, and the practice of the professions. Its members wanted social prestige and influence equal to their wealth.

All of these factors meant that the society of the eighteenth century stood at the close of one era of European history and at the opening of another. However, as these social and economic changes became connected to the world economy, the transformation of Europe led to the transformation of much of the non-European world. For the first time in the history of the world, major changes in one region literally left no corner of the globe politically or economically untouched. By the close of the eighteenth century, a movement toward world interconnectedness and interdependence that had no real precedent in terms of depth and extent had begun, and it has not yet ended.

Suggested Readings

C. B. A. Behrens, *The Ancien Régime* (1967). A brief account of life in France with excellent illustrations.

I. T. Berend and G. Ranki, *The European Periphery and Industrialization*, 1780–1914 (1982). Examines the experience of eastern and Mediterranean Europe.

J. Blum, *Lord and Peasant in Russia from the Ninth to the Nineteenth Century* (1961). A thorough and wide-ranging discussion.

J. Blum, *The End of the Old Order in Rural Europe* (1978). The most comprehensive treatment of life in rural Europe, especially central and eastern, from the early eighteenth through the mid-nineteenth centuries.

F. Braudel, *Capitalism and Material Life*, 1400–1800 (1974). An investigation of the physical resources and human organization of preindustrial Europe.

F. Braudel, *The Structures of Everyday Life: The Limits of the Possible*, trans. by M. Kochan (1982). A magisterial survey by the most important social historian of our time.

J. Cannon, *Aristocratic Century: The Peerage of Eighteenth-Century England* (1985). A useful treatment based on the most recent research.

G. Chaussinand-Nogaret, *The French Nobility in the Eighteenth Century* (1985). Suggests that culture not class was the decisive element in late eighteenth-century French society.

P. Deane, *The First Industrial Revolution*, 2nd ed. (1979). A well-balanced and systematic treatment.

J. De Vries, *The Economy of Europe in an Age of Crisis*, 1600–1750 (1976). An excellent overview that sets forth the main issues.

J. De Vries, *European Urbanization* 1500–1800 (1984). The most important and far-ranging of recent treatments of the subject.

P. Earle (ed.), *Essays in European Economic History*, 1500–1800 (1974). A useful collection of articles that cover most of the major states of Western Europe.

M. W. Flinn, *The European Demographic System*, 1500–1820 (1981). A major summary.

F. Ford, *Robe and Sword: The Regrouping of the French Aristocracy after Louis XIV* (1953). An important treatment of the growing social tensions within the French nobility during the eighteenth century.

R. Forster, *The Nobility of Toulouse in the Eighteenth Century* (1960). A local study that displays the variety of noble economic activity.

R. Forster and E. Forster, *European Society in the Eighteenth Century* (1969). An excellent collection of documents.

R. Forster and O. Ranum, *Deviants and Abandoned in French Society* (1978). This and the following volume contain important essays from the French journal *Annales*.

R. Forster and O. Ranum, *Medicine and Society in France* (1980).

D. V. Glass and D. E. C. Eversley (eds.), *Population in History: Essays in Historical Demography* (1965). Fundamental for an understanding of the eighteenth-century increase in population.

A. Goodwin (ed.), *The European Nobility in the Eighteenth Century* (1953). Essays on the nobility in each state.

P. Goubert, *The Ancien Régime: French Society*, 1600–1750, trans. by Steve Cox (1974). A superb account of the peasant social order.

H. J. Habakkuk and M. Postan (eds.), *The Cambridge Economic History of Europe* (1965). Separate chapters by different authors on major topics.

D. Hay et al., *Albion's Fatal Tree: Crime and Society in Eighteenth-Century England* (1976). Separate essays on a previously little-explored subject.

O. H. Hufton, *The Poor of Eighteenth-Century France*, 1750–1789 (1975). A brilliant study of poverty and the family economy.

C. Jones, *Charity and Bienfaisance: The Treatment of the Poor in the Montpellier Region*, 1740–1815 (1982). An important local French study.

E. L. Jones, *Agriculture and Economic Growth in England*, 1650–1815 (1968). A good introduction to an important subject.

H. Kamen, *European Society*, 1500–1700 (1985). The best one-volume treatment.

P. Laslett, *The World We Have Lost* (1965). Examination of English life and society before the coming of industrialism.

J. Lough, *An Introduction to Eighteenth-Century France* (1960). A systematic survey with good quotations (in French) from contemporaries.

R. K. McClure, *Coram's Children: The London Foundling Hospital in the Eighteenth Century* (1981). A moving work that deals with the plight of all concerned with the problem.

N. McKenderick (ed.), *The Birth of a Consumer Society: The Commercialization of Eighteenth-Century England* (1982). Deals with several aspects of the impact of commercialization.

S. Pollard, *The Genesis of Modern Management: A Study of the Industrial Revolution in Great Britain* (1965). Treats the issue of industrialization from the standpoint of factory owners.

S. Pollard, *Peaceful Conquest: The Industrialization of Europe*, 1760–1970 (1981). A useful survey.

S. Pollard and C. Holmes, *Documents of European Economic History: The Process of Industrialization*, 1750–1870 (1968). A very useful collection.

A. Ribeiro, *Dress in Eighteenth-Century Europe*, 1715–1789 (1985). An interesting examination of the social implication of style in clothing.

G. Rudé, *The Crowd in History* 1730–1848 (1964). A pioneering study.

G. Rudé, *Europe in the Eighteenth Century* (1972). A survey with emphasis on social history.

G. Rudé, *Paris and London in the Eighteenth Century* (1973).

H. Schmal (ed.), *Patterns of European Urbanization Since 1500* (1981). Major revisionist essays.

L. Stone, *The Family, Sex and Marriage in England 1500–1800* (1977). A pioneering study of a subject receiving new interest from historians.

L. Stone, *An Open Elite?* (1985). Raises important questions about the traditional view of open access to social mobility in England.

T. Tackett, *Priest and Parish in Eighteenth-Century France: A Social and Political Study of the Curés in a Diocese of Dauphiné, 1750–1791* (1977). A very important local study that displays the role of the Church in the fabric of social life in the old regime.

L. A. Tilly and J. W. Scott, *Women, Work, and Family* (1978). An excellent survey of the issues in western Europe.

R. Wall (ed.), *Family Forms in Historic Europe* (1983). Essays that cover the entire continent.

C. Wilson, *England's Apprenticeship, 1603–1763* (1965). A broad survey of English economic life on the eve of industrialism.

E. A. Wrigley and R. S. Schofield, *The Population History of England, 1541–1871: A Reconstruction* (1982). One of the most ambitious demographic studies ever undertaken.

COMMON SENSE;

ADDRESSED TO THE

INHABITANTS

OF

AMERICA,

On the following interesting

SUBJECTS.

I. Of the Origin and Design of Government in general, with concise Remarks on the English Constitution.

II. Of Monarchy and Hereditary Succession.

III. Thoughts on the present State of American Affairs.

IV. Of the present Ability of America, with some miscellaneous Reflections.

Man knows no Master save creating HEAVEN,
Or those whom choice and common good ordain.

THOMSON.

PHILADELPHIA;

Printed, and Sold, by R. BELL, in Third-Street.

MDCCLXXVI.

Common Sense, *written by Tom Paine, was the most important political pamphlet published during 1776 when the American colonies were deciding to make a final break with Great Britian.* [The Granger Collection.]

21 Empire, War, and Colonial Rebellion

Since the Renaissance, European contacts with the rest of the world have gone through four distinct stages. The first was that of the discovery, exploration, initial conquest, and settlement of the New World. The second era was one of colonial trade rivalry among Spain, France, and Great Britain. The Anglo-French side of the contest has often been compared to a second Hundred Years' War. During this second period, which may be said to have closed during the 1820s, both the British colonies of the North American seaboard and the Spanish colonies of Central and South America emancipated themselves from European control. These two eras will constitute the primary subject of this chapter, with the liberation of Latin America being treated in Chapter 25.

The third stage of European contact with the non-European world occurred in the nineteenth century, when new formal empires involving the European administration of indigenous peoples were carved out in Africa and Asia. The last period of European empire came in the present century, with the decolonialization of peoples who had previously been under European colonial rule.

During these four and a half centuries before decolonialization, Europeans exerted political dominance over much of the rest of the world that was far disproportional to the geographical size or population of Europe. Europeans frequently treated other peoples as social, intellectual, and economic inferiors. They ravaged existing cultures because of greed, religious zeal, or political ambition. These actions are major facts of European history and significant factors in the contemporary relationship of Europe and its former colonies. In turn, these actions constitute even larger elements in the experiences of those non-European cultures who were the objects of European ambition. What allowed the Europeans to exert such domination for so long over so much of the world was not any innate cultural superiority but a technological supremacy closely related to naval power and gunpowder. Ships and guns allowed the Europeans to exercise their will almost anywhere they chose.

Eighteenth-Century Empires

Navies and merchant shipping were the keystones of the mercantile empires of the eighteenth century. These empires were meant to bring profit to a nation rather than to provide areas for settlement. The Treaty of Utrecht (1713) established the boundaries of empire during the first half of the century. Except for Brazil, which was governed by Portugal, Spain controlled all of mainland South America, and in North America, it controlled Florida, Mexico, and California. The Spanish also governed the island of Cuba and half of Hispaniola. The British Empire consisted of the colonies along the North Atlantic seaboard, Nova Scotia, Newfoundland, Jamaica, and Barbados. Britain also possessed a few trading stations on the Indian subcontinent. The French domains covered the Saint Lawrence River valley; the Ohio and Mississippi River valleys; the West Indian islands of Saint Domingue, Guadeloupe, and Martinique; and stations in India. The Dutch controlled Surinam, or Dutch Guiana, in South America; various trading stations in Ceylon and Bengal; and, most important, the trade with Java in what is now Indonesia.

All of these powers also possessed numerous smaller islands in the Caribbean. As far as eighteenth-century developments were concerned, the major rivalries existed among the Spanish, the French, and the British.

Mercantile Empires

To the extent that any formal economic theory lay behind the conduct of these empires, it was mercantilism, that practical creed of hardheaded businessmen. Initially, the fundamental point of this outlook was the necessity of acquiring a favorable trade balance of gold and silver bullion. Such bullion was regarded as the measure of a country's wealth, and a nation was truly wealthy only if it amassed more bullion than its rivals. By the late seventeenth century, mercantilist thinking, as developed by writers such as Thomas Mun in *England's Treasure by Foreign Trade* (1664), had come to regard general foreign trade and the level of domestic industry as the true indications of a nation's prosperity. But from beginning to end, the economic well-being of the home country was the first concern of mercantilist writers. Colonies were to provide markets and natural resources for the industries of the home country. In turn, the home country was to furnish military security and political administration for the colonies. For decades, both sides assumed that the colonies were the inferior partner in the relationship.

The mercantilist statesmen and traders regarded the world as an arena of scarce resources and economic limitation. They assumed that one national economy could grow only at the expense of others. The home country and its colonies were to trade only with each other. To that end, they attempted to forge trade-tight systems of national commerce through navigation laws, tariffs, bounties to encourage production, and prohibitions against trading with the subjects of other monarchs. National monopoly was the ruling principle.

Mercantilist ideas had always been neater on paper than in practice. By the early eighteenth century, mercantilist assumptions were held only in the vaguest manner. They stood too far removed from the economic realities of the colonies and perhaps from human nature. The colonial and home markets simply failed to mesh. Spain could not produce sufficient goods for South America. Economic production in the British North American colonies challenged English manufacturing and led to British attempts to limit certain colonial industries, such as iron and hat making. Colonists of different countries wished to trade with each other. English colonists could buy sugar more cheaply from the French West Indies than from English suppliers. The traders and merchants of one nation always hoped to break the monopoly of another. For all these reasons, the eighteenth century became the "golden age of smugglers."[1] The governments could not control the activities of all their subjects. Clashes among colonists could and did bring about conflict between governments.

The Colonial Era of Latin America

The Spanish Empire

Columbus' voyage of 1492 marked, unknowingly to those who undertook and financed it, the beginning of more than three centuries of Spanish conquest, exploitation, and administration of a vast American empire. That imperial venture, which created the largest and longest lived of all the great mercantile trading blocs, produced important results for the cultures of both the European and the American continents. The gold and silver extracted from its American possessions financed much of the Spanish role in the Counter Reformation and contributed to European inflation in the sixteenth century. In large expanses of both South and North America, Spanish government set an imprint of

---

[1] Walter Dorn, *Competition for Empire*, 1740–1763 (New York: Harper, 1940), p. 266.

Pyramid of the Sun and "Camino de los Muertos. Teotihuacan." [*Art Resource.*]

Roman Catholicism, economic dependence, and hierarchical social structure that has endured to the present day. Spanish economic and social influences came to dominate because the early explorers conquered the existing Indian civilizations and imposed their own.

Native Americans before the Spanish Conquest

It is generally believed that human beings first came to populate the American continents by immigrating across the Bering Straits into Alaska. This movement probably occurred at least 20,000 years ago. Thereafter, human populations spread slowly southward, with evidence of human population in Peru by 13,000 B.C. and in Chile by 7000 B.C. Consequently, by the time of the Spanish discovery of America there had been sufficient time for several whole civilizations to have risen and fallen before any Westerners had knowledge of these peoples.

VANISHED CIVILIZATIONS OF MESOAMERICA. *Mesoamerica* is the term used by anthropologists and archaeologists to distinguish the civilizations that flourished in what is today southern Mexico and Guatemala. Regarded as having originated about 2500 B.C., these civilizations evolved through various stages and included a variety of different native peoples.

These cultures shared, to a greater or lesser degree, several common characteristics. They practiced the chinampa method of cultivation, involving the draining of swamps and the using of silt dredged from the bottom of the lakes. Maize, squash, and beans were the mainstays of their diet. Certain classes among them ate or drank chocolate. They wrote with hieroglyphics, many of which have still not been deciphered. These peoples built large ceremonial pyramids and practiced human sacrifices for religious purposes. Large courts were constructed for playing their common ball game. These vanished civilizations also carried out very sophisticated modes of sculpture and painting. They had developed rather sophisticated calendars. Generally speaking, however, they did not achieve significant mastery of metallurgy.

OLMEC CIVILIZATION. The earliest of the formal Mesoamerican cultures was the Olmec civilization, which had established itself by about 1200 B.C. in the Los Tuxtlas region of Veracruz, along the Gulf Coast. This culture has left a large body of archeological evidence, including gigantic portrait sculptures of their kings. These massive objects, which weigh many tons, were not discovered until the 1860s. These statues were carved from basalt rock transported probably on river rafts many miles from where they were even-

Olmec Head. Monument 17, excavated at San Lorenzo. Colossal head carved of basalt. Believed to be a portrait of an Olmec ruler. Olmec Culture, 1500 to 300 B.C. Height 5½'. Now in the Museo Nacional de Antropologia, Mexico City. [Government of Mexico.]

tually displayed. The economic basis of the civilization was a network of long-term trade relations in luxury goods as well as in products for everyday life. The major Olmec sites were La Vena, San Lorenzo, and Tres Zapotes.

Like all Mesoamerican cultures, that of the Olmecs was overwhelmingly devoted to agriculture. Its people lived on farms and developed no real urban life. Political structures were not very sophisticated; religion and economics apparently provided the major social bonds. By the fourth century B.C., the Olmec civilization had vanished for reasons that have not really been ascertained. Its peoples dispersed into other areas of Mesoamerica.

THE MAYAS. Mayan civilization flourished in the Yucatan Peninsula and Guatemala by A.D. 300. It lasted until approximately A.D. 900, leaving some of the most impressive architectural and sculptural re-

mains in the world. Their accomplishments are all the more impressive because they were carried out in the midst of a tropical forest that, after the collapse of the Mayas, overgrew their great temples and ceremonial centers. One of the most important of such centers was Tikal. Virtually all of these centers possessed one of the large ball game courts; some possessed several. The centers where the Maya built their pyramids were not cities in any European or modern sense. They seem to have been used almost exclusively as ceremonial centers, with only a few very wealthy members of the elite classes making their homes there. In that regard, it is thought that Mayan society was very hierarchical and stratified.

The Mayans made major achievements in astronomy, mathematics, and writing. They produced complicated and sophisticated calendars that were very important for a people dependent upon agriculture. Probably only a few powerful persons could actually use these calendars. The Mayas also constructed very elaborate tombs for their leaders and other members of the elite classes.

It was once thought that the Mayas were a very peaceful people, but that image has been abandoned. Anthropologists now believe that the Mayas were a people almost obsessed by warfare and conflict. Their paintings and carvings illustrate a vast number of rituals involving the use of blood and human sacrifice. One of the major challenges now confronting scholars of the Mayas is to reconcile the people's enormous cultural accomplishments with the presence of other practices that seem at odds with their art, science, and architecture.

Mayan civilization came to an end about A.D. 900. Scholars have only been able to speculate as to the causes of their demise. Clearly, too great a strain was put on their natural resources, but why this occurred is a matter of mystery. Indeed, it seems that they continued their programs of building almost to the very end. It has been suggested that the religious building became more extensive when the culture experienced a long lack of rainfall and that, as a consequence, continuing construction itself was one of the causes of new strains on resources.

URBAN LIFE AT TEOTIHUACAN. The city of Teotihuacan had a population of over 100,000. It dominated central Mexico for several centuries, beginning in the second century B.C. Teotihuacan was a major urban center by any of the standards of the great world civilizations. There was a large center of population whose people tilled a large surrounding region. The city also participated in long-range trade, including with the Mayas. Major civic and ceremonial buildings included the structures later named by the Aztecs as the Pyramid of the Sun and the Pyramid of the Moon.

A Maya pyramid in the Yucatan, Mexico. Although the Maya strongly influenced Aztec culture, Maya civilization had decayed centuries before the Spanish conquest of Mexico. [George Holton.]

These structures were connected by a grand avenue. The buildings were decorated with very skilled sculptures that illustrated the mythology of the people.

Poorer farmers in Teotihuacan lived in homes constructed of wood, whereas those of the wealthy citizens were of stone. Many of the better buildings contained complicated drainage systems. On the interiors of some buildings were paintings and murals. There were at least two thousand structures, some of which had as many as fifty to one hundred rooms.

The city was primarily dependent upon agriculture for its economic life; over half the population left it daily to till outlying land. Nevertheless, there were other means of livelihood. Major trade was conducted in obsidian tools, pottery, and weaving.

Significant urban life in Teotihuacan came to an end sometime during the middle of the seventh century A.D. As with many of the other early civilizations in Mesoamerica, the reason remains a mystery. What does seem certain is that a fire of unknown origin swept across the city. This fire undoubtedly destroyed the homes of the vast majority of the population. That destruction, in turn, probably thoroughly disrupted the social structure that supported the wealthy elite. In any case, the city never regained its status and in a few

decades seems to have disappeared as a force in Mesoamerican culture. However, the site of the city, with its great ruins, continued to fascinate the native peoples of Mesoamerica. Generations up to the time of the Spanish conquest made pilgrimages to the ruined city.

Early Spanish Conquest

THE AZTECS AND CONQUEST. After the fall of Teotihuacan, the history of Mesoamerican civilizations becomes quite confused. The major people to dominate central Mexico were the Toltecs, about whom the historical record is most uncertain. The reason for this uncertainty is that the later Aztecs destroyed all the historical records and replaced them with their own accounts of the Toltecs.

The forebears to the Aztecs whom the Spanish encountered in the early sixteenth century had arrived in the valley of Mexico early in the twelfth century. They had been forced by other tribes to live on marginal land as a subservient people. Over the years, the Aztecs became highly skilled in military matters. In 1428, under the leadership of a new chief named Itzcoatl, they allied with two other tribes and rebelled against their rulers in Atzcapotzalco. That rebellion opened a period of Aztec conquest that reached its climax just after 1500. Their last ruler in this age of conquest was Montezuma.

Aztec civilization was centered at Tenochtitlan (near present-day Mexico City), which before its conquest was laid out along three lakes. This nonfarming population may have numbered as many as 200,000. The entire society was extremely hierarchical, and was governed in a thoroughly—and indeed frightening—authoritarian manner. They had created the most powerful empire ever to exist in Mesoamerica.

The Aztecs governed a large number of smaller tribes in a particularly harsh manner. Not surprisingly, the Aztecs demanded payment of labor and tribute from the conquered tribes. This tribute included not only agricultural produce but also gold, jade, and even exotic birds. However, they also demanded and received thousands of captives each year, who they sacrificed to their gods. The Aztecs believed that the gods had literally to be fed with human bodies to guarantee continuing sunshine and soil fertility. These policies meant that the Aztecs were surrounded by various "allied" tribes who felt no loyalty; rather, they felt a terror from which they wished to be liberated.

In 1519, Hernán Cortés landed on the coast of Mexico with a force of about six hundred men and a few horses. He opened communication with tribes nearby and then with Montezuma. The Aztec chief initially believed Cortés to be a god. Aztec religion contained the legend of a priest named Quetzalcoatl, who had

A sixteenth-century Aztec depiction of the Spanish conquest of Mexico. [Bettmann Archive.]

been driven away four centuries earlier and had promised to return in the very year in which Cortés arrived. Montezuma initially attempted to appease Cortés with gifts of gold, but these only whetted the appetites of the Spanish. After several weeks of negotiations and the forging of alliances with subject tribes, Cortés' forces marched on Tenochtitlan and conquered it. Cortés imprisoned Montezuma, who later died under unexplained circumstances. The Aztecs—under a new leader, Cuauhtemoc—attempted to drive the Spanish out, but the Aztecs were defeated by late 1521 after great loss of life. Cortés proclaimed the Aztec Empire to be New Spain.

THE CONQUEST OF THE INCAS. The second great native American civilization to experience Spanish conquest was that of the Incas. Located in the highlands of Peru, the Incas were simply the most recent Indian rulers of the region. Like the Aztecs, they had commenced their own conquests in the early fifteenth century. By the early sixteenth century, the Incas ruled several million native Americans. They were not so numerous a people as the Aztecs, nor did they possess so large a military organization. Instead, they compelled conquered tribes to fight for them by richly rewarding successful warriors and by treating well the conquered tribes who aided them. The Incas also required the conquered peoples to speak Quechua, their own unwritten language. A relatively large bureaucracy helped them to make use of forced labor to build

An Aztec calendar stone. This monumental sculpture, weighing several tons, depicts the Aztec year, which consisted of thirteen months, each of twenty days, plus five "empty days" to make up a 365-day year. [Bettmann Archive.]

roads, to farm land, and to construct their great cities, such as Cuzco and Machu Picchu. By the time the Spanish arrived, the Incas, whose chief was Atahualpa, were engaged in civil war among their own political elite.

The Incas had undertaken major agricultural development and enjoyed a more varied diet than any of the other native peoples in the Americas. In particular, they are credited with developing the potato, a food that would have an impact on the diet of both the Americas and Europe in later centuries. The high mountainous land they cultivated presented many difficulties. Chief among these was the securing of adequate water supplies. The Incas devised major irrigation systems by using extensive canals and river dams. They made use of guano (dried bat droppings) to fertilize their crops and domesticated the llama and alpaca.

Inca society, like that of other native Americans, was extremely hierarchical. The ruler lived in great luxury, surrounded by wives, concubines, an extended family, and guards. He governed in a virtually despotic manner. Young aristocratic Incas went through a number of initiation rites before they were permitted to undertake public duties. Much of the public life of these officials involved impressing the peoples of subject tribes into labor. In addition to labor, local communities had to give their governors hand-crafted goods, food, and other locally produced goods, such as rope. To obtain an obedient population, the Inca administrators sometimes moved an entire village to a different location where there could be no possibility of rebellion.

The Inca economy and political administration were linked by a remarkable system of roads that amazed all of the Spanish who saw them. Connecting the great Inca cities, this transport system included bridges that crossed vast gorges and rivers.

In 1531, largely inspired by Cortés' example in Mexico, Francisco Pizarro sailed from Panama and landed on the western coast of the South American continent to undertake a campaign against the Inca Empire, about which he knew relatively little. His force included about two hundred men armed with guns and swords and equipped with horses, the military power of which the Incas did not understand. In late 1531, Pizarro lured Atahualpa into a conference, where he captured the chief and killed several thousand Indians in the process. The imprisoned Atahualpa then attempted to ransom himself by having a vast hoard of gold transported from all over Peru to Pizarro. Needless to say, Pizarro refused to release his captive. After finding he could not use Atahualpa as a puppet ruler, Pizarro had him publicly executed in 1533. Further Indian insurrections took place, with some Inca factions seeking to ally themselves with the Spanish against other factions. The Spanish conquerors also fought among themselves, and effective royal control was not established until the late 1560s.

The conquests of Mexico and Peru stand among the most dramatic and brutal stories in modern world history. One civilization armed with advanced weapons subdued, in a remarkably brief time, two advanced powerful peoples. But beyond the drama and bloodshed, these conquests, along with lesser ones of smaller groups of Indians, marked a fundamental turning point in the development of world civilizations. Never again in the Americas would native American peoples and their values be able to produce any significant impact or influence. The Spanish and the native Americans did make certain accommodations to each other, but there was never any doubt about which culture had the upper hand.

The Economy of Exploitation

There were three major components in the colonial economy of Latin America: mining, agriculture, and shipping. Each of them involved either labor or servitude or a relationship of dependence of the New World economy on that of Spain.

The early *conquistadores* ("conquerors") were primarily interested in gold, but by the middle of the sixteenth century, silver mining provided the chief source of metallic wealth. The great mining centers were Potosí in Peru and somewhat smaller sites in northern Mexico. The Spanish crown was particularly interested in mining because it received one fifth (the *quinto*) of all mining revenues. For this reason, the crown maintained a monopoly over the production and sale of mercury, which was required in the silver-mining process. Silver mining flourished in terms of extracting wealth for the Spanish until the early seventeenth century, when the industry underwent a recession because of lack of new investment and the increasing costs involved in deeper mines. Nonetheless, silver never lost predominance during the colonial era, and its production by forced labor for the benefit of Spaniards and the Spanish crown epitomized the wholly extractive economy that stood at the foundation of colonial life.

The major rural and agricultural institution of the Spanish colonies was the *haciendas*. These were large landed estates owned by persons originally born in Spain (*peninsulares*) or persons of Spanish descent born in America (*creoles*). The establishment of haciendas represented the transfer of the principle of the large unit of privately owned land, which was characteristic of Europe and especially of Spain, to the New World setting. Such estates would become one of the most important features of Latin American life and, in the century after independence, one of the most con-

A Contemporary Describes Forced Indian Labor at Potosí

The Potosí range in Peru was the site of the great silver-mining industry in the Spanish Empire. The vast amount of wealth contained in the region became legendary almost as soon as mining commenced there in the 1540s. Indians, most of whom were forced laborers working under the mita *system of conscription, did virtually all of the work underground. This description, written by a Spanish friar in the early seventeenth century, portrays both the large size of the enterprise and the harsh conditions that the Indians endured. At any one time, only one third of the 13,300 conscripted Indians were employed. The labor force was changed every four months.*

According to His Majesty's warrant, the mine owners on this massive range have a right to the mita [conscripted labor] of 13,300 Indians in the working and exploitation of the mines, both those which have been discovered, those now discovered, and those which shall be discovered. It is the duty of the Corregidor [municipal governor] of Potosí to have them rounded up and to see that they come in from all the provinces between Cuzco over the whole of El Collao and as far as the frontiers of Tarija and Tomina. . . .

. . . The mita Indians go up every Monday morning to the locality of Guayna Potosí which is at the foot of the range; the Corregidor arrives with all the provincial captains or chiefs who have charge of the Indians assigned them, and he there checks off and reports to each mine and smelter owner the number of Indians assigned him for his mine or smelter; that keeps him busy till 1 P.M., by which time the Indians are already turned over to these mine and smelter owners.

After each has eaten his ration, they climb up the hill, each to his mine, and go in, staying there from that hour until Saturday evening without coming out of the mine; their wives bring them food, but they stay constantly underground, excavating and carrying out the ore from which they get the silver. They all have tallow candles, lighted day and night; that is the light they work with, for as they are underground, they have need of it all the time. . . .

These Indians have different functions in the handling of the silver ore; some break it up with bar or pick, and dig down in, following the vein in the mine; others bring it up; others up above keep separating the good and the poor in piles; others are occupied in taking it down from the range to the mills on herds of llamas; every day they bring up more than 8,000 of these native beasts of burden for this task. These teamsters who carry the metal do not belong to the mita, but are mingados—hired. ❏

Antonio Vázquez de Espinosa, *Compendium and Description of the Indies* (CA 1620), trans. by Charles Upson Clark (Washington, D.C.: Smithsonian Institution Press, 1968), p. 62, quoted in Helen Delpar (ed.), *The Borzoi Reader in Latin American History* (New York: Alfred A. Knopf, 1972), pp. 92–93.

troversial. Laborers on the hacienda usually stood in some relation of formal servitude to the owner. They were rarely free to move from the services of one landowner to another. There were two major products of the hacienda economy: foodstuffs for mining areas and urban centers and leather goods used in vast quantities on mining machinery. Both farming and ranching thus stood subordinate to the mine economy. However, like mining, the agricultural economy was wholly commercial in nature.

In the West Indies, the basic agricultural unit was the plantation. On Cuba, Hispaniola, Puerto Rico, and other islands, the labor of black slaves from Africa produced sugar to supply what seemed to be the insatiable demand for the product in Europe.

The final major area of economic activity in the Spanish colonies was the variety of service occupations pursued in the cities. These included the governmental bureaucracy, the legal profession, and shipping. These practitioners were either *peninsulares* or *creoles*, with the former more often than not dominating. The rules they enforced, interpreted, or shipped by were those set by institutions of the Spanish government to realize the goals of a competitive mercantile empire.

All of this extractive and exploitative economic activity required labor, and the Spanish in the New World had decided very early that the Indian population would supply the labor. A series of social devices was used to draw Indians into the economic life imposed by the Spanish.

The first of these was the *encomienda*. This was a formal grant of the right to the labor of a specific number of Indians for a particular period of time. An *encomienda* usually involved a few hundred Indians but might grant the right to the labor of several thousand. *Encomienda* as an institution persisted in some parts of Latin America well into the seventeenth century but generally stood in decline by the middle of the sixteenth. The Spanish monarchs feared that the holders

In this sixteenth-century German print, Spaniards torture and kill the Indians of the New World. Illustrations such as this helped propagate the "Black Legend" of Spanish atrocities in the Americas. [Bettmann Archive.]

of *encomienda* were attempting to become a powerful independent nobility in the New World. The Spanish government was also persuaded by appeals on humanitarian grounds against this particular kind of exploitation of the Indians. The land grants that led to the establishment of haciendas were one means whereby the crown continued to use the resources of the New World for patronage without directly impinging on the Indians.

The passing of the *encomienda* led to a new arrangement of labor servitude, the *repartimiento*. This device required adult male Indians to devote so many days of labor annually to Spanish economic enterprises. In the mines of Peru, the *repartimiento* was known as the *mita*, and in some cases, Indians did not survive their days of labor rotation. The actual limitation of labor time led some Spanish managers to use their workers in an extremely harsh manner, under the assumption that more fresh workers would soon be appearing on the scene.

The eventual shortage of workers and the crown's pressure against extreme versions of forced labor led to the use of free labor. Here again, however, the freedom was more in appearance, and dependence and subservience were the reality. Free Indian laborers were required to purchase goods from the landowner or mine owner. They became indebted and were never able to pay off the debt. This situation was known as *debt peonage* and continued in different forms in Latin America long after the wars of liberation.

Black slavery was the final mode of forced or sub-

servient labor in the New World. Both the Spanish and the Portuguese had used African slaves in Europe. They were used throughout Latin America at one time or another, but the sugar plantations of the West Indies were the major center of slavery.

The conquest and the economy of exploitation and forced labor (and the introduction of European diseases) produced extraordinary demographic consequences for the Indian population. By the early seventeenth century, the Indians were dying off in huge numbers. Estimates of the Pre-Columbian population

The fortress of El Morro in the harbor of San Juan, Puerto Rico. This massive citadel protected the Spanish treasure fleets that carried gold and silver each year to Spain from the mines of Mexico and Peru. [Commonwealth of Puerto Rico.]

of America have generated major controversies. Conservative estimates put the Indian population at the time of Columbus' discovery at well over fifty million. In New Spain (Mexico) alone, the decline in population was probably from approximately twenty-five million to less than two million. Whatever the exact figures, there was and is no doubt that the Indian population encountered by the *conquistadores* largely vanished and, with it, the easy supply of labor that they had exploited.

The Church in Spanish America

Roman Catholic priests accompanied the earliest explorers and the conquerors of the Indians. Because of internal reforms within the Spanish church at the turn of the sixteenth century, these first clergy tended to be imbued with many of the social and religious ideals of Christian Humanism. They believed that they could foster Erasmus' concept of the "philosophy of Christ" in the New World. Consequently these missionary priests were filled with zeal not only to convert the Indians to Christianity but also to bring to them learning and civilization of a European kind.

A very real tension existed between the early Spanish conquerors and the mendicant friars who sought to minister to the Indians. Without conquest, the church could not convert the Indians, but the priests often deplored the harsh labor conditions imposed on the native peoples. During the first three quarters of a century of Spanish domination, priests were among the most eloquent and persuasive defenders of the rights of Indians.

By far the most effective and outspoken of these clerics was Bartolomé de Las Casas, a Dominican. He contended that conquest was not necessary for conversion. One result of his campaign was new royal regulation of conquest after 1550. Another result of his criticism was the emergence of the "Black Legend," which portrayed all Spanish treatment of Indians as unprincipled and inhumane. Advocates of this position drew heavily on Las Casas' writings. Although substantially true, the "Black Legend" nonetheless somewhat exaggerated the case against Spain. Many of the Indian rulers of other tribes had also been exceedingly cruel, as witnessed by the Aztec demands for human sacrifice.

By the end of the sixteenth century, the Church in Spanish America had become largely an institution upholding the colonial status quo. On numerous occasions, individual priests did defend the communal rights of Indian tribes, but the colonial church also prospered as the Spanish elite prospered. The Church became a great landowner through crown grants and through bequests from Catholics who died in the New World. The monasteries took on an economic as well as a spiritual life of their own. Whatever its concern for the spiritual welfare of the Indians, the Church remained one of the indications that Spanish America was a conquered world. And those who spoke for the Church did not challenge Spanish domination or any but the most extreme modes of Spanish economic exploitation. By the end of the colonial era in the late eighteenth century, the Roman Catholic church had become one of the single most conservative forces in Latin America.

The Spanish Colonial System

Spanish control of its American empire involved a system of government and a system of monopolistic trade regulation. Both were more rigid in appearance than in practice. Actual government was often informal, and the trade monopoly was often breached.

Because Queen Isabella had commissioned Columbus, the technical legal link between the New World and Spain was the crown of Castille. Its powers both at home and in America were subject to few limitations. Government of America was assigned to the Council of the Indies, which, in conjunction with the monarch, nominated the persons who served as viceroys of New Spain and Peru. These viceroys served as the chief executives in the New World and carried out the laws promulgated by the Council of the Indies. Within each of the viceroyalties was established a number of subordinate judicial councils known as *audiencias*. There were also a variety of local officers, the most important of which were the *corregidores*, who presided over municipal councils. All of these offices provided the monarchy with a vast array of patronage, usually bestowed on persons born in Spain. Virtually all political power flowed from the top of this political structure downward; in effect, there was little or no substantial local initiative or self-government.

The colonial political structures existed, in large measure, to support the commercial goals of Spain. The Casa de Contratación (House of Trade) in Seville regulated all trade with the New World. Cádiz was the only port to be used for the American trade. The Casa de Contratación was the single most influential institution of the Spanish Empire, and its members worked closely with the Consulado (Merchant Guild) of Seville and other groups involved with the American commerce in Cádiz.

A crucial change occurred in the Spanish colonial system during the eighteenth century. The War of the Spanish Succession and the Treaty of Utrecht replaced the Spanish Habsburgs with the Bourbons of France on the Spanish throne. Philip V (1700–1746) and his successors brought with them to Spain the administrative skills and expectations that had been forged by the bureaucrats of Louis XIV. The Bourbon Spanish monarchy was determined to reassert the imperial trade monopoly, which had decayed under the last Spanish

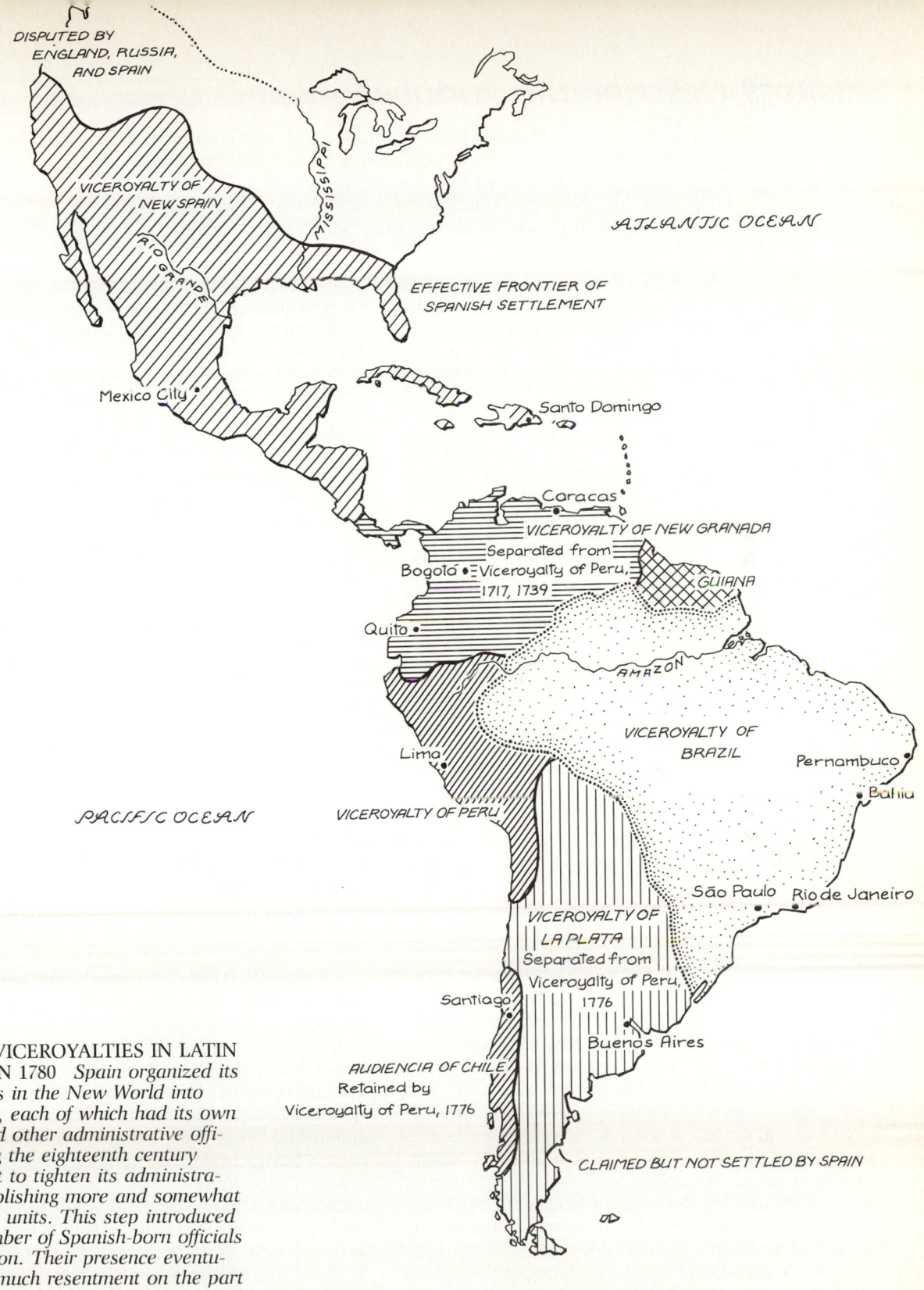

Map 21-1 VICEROYALTIES IN LATIN AMERICA IN 1780 *Spain organized its vast holdings in the New World into viceroyalties, each of which had its own governor and other administrative officials. During the eighteenth century Spain sought to tighten its administration by establishing more and somewhat smaller such units. This step introduced a larger number of Spanish-born officials into the region. Their presence eventually caused much resentment on the part of the persons born in Spanish America but who found themselves governed by foreign officials.*

Labels on map:

DISPUTED BY ENGLAND, RUSSIA, AND SPAIN

VICEROYALTY OF NEW SPAIN

RIO GRANDE

MISSISSIPPI

ATLANTIC OCEAN

EFFECTIVE FRONTIER OF SPANISH SETTLEMENT

Mexico City

Santo Domingo

Caracas

VICEROYALTY OF NEW GRANADA

Bogotá • Separated from Viceroyalty of Peru, 1717, 1739

GUIANA

Quito •

AMAZON

VICEROYALTY OF BRAZIL

Lima •

Pernambuco

Bahia

PACIFIC OCEAN

VICEROYALTY OF PERU

São Paulo

Rio de Janeiro

VICEROYALTY OF LA PLATA Separated from Viceroyalty of Peru, 1776

Santiago

Buenos Aires

AUDIENCIA OF CHILE Retained by Viceroyalty of Peru, 1776

CLAIMED BUT NOT SETTLED BY SPAIN

Visitors Describe the Portobello Fair

The Spanish attempted to restrict all trade within their Latin American empire to a few designated ports. The most famous of these was Portobello Fair on the Isthmus of Panama. In the 1730s, two visitors saw the event and described it. Note the wide variety of goods traded and the vast distances over which products had to be transported. This fair was the chief means of facilitating trade between the western coast of South America and Spain.

The town of Portobello, so thinly inhabited, by reason of its noxious air, the scarcity of provisions, and the soil, becomes, at the time of the [Spanish] galleons one of the most populous places in all South America. . . .

The ships are no sooner moored in the harbour, than the first work is, to erect, in the square, a tent made of the ship's sails, for receiving its cargo; at which the proprietors of the goods are present, in order to find their bales, by the marks which distinguish them. These bales are drawn on sledges, to their respective places by the crew of every ship, and the money given them is proportionally divided.

Whilst the seamen and European traders are thus employed, the land is covered with droves of mules from Panama, each drove consisting of above an hundred, loaded with chests of gold and silver, on account of the merchants of Peru. Some unload them at the exchange, others in the middle of the square; yet, amidst the hurry and confusion of such crowds, no theft, loss, or disturbance, is ever known. He who has seen this place during the tiempo muerto, or dead time, solitary, poor, and a perpetual silence reigning everywhere; the harbour quite empty, and every place wearing a melancholy aspect; must be filled with astonishment at the sudden change, to see the bustling multitudes, every house crowded, the square and streets encumbered with bales and chests of gold and silver of all kinds; the harbour full of ships and vessels, some bringing by the way of Río de Chape the goods of Peru, such as cacao, quinquina, or Jesuit's bark, Vicuña wool, and bezoar stones; others coming from Carthagena, loaded with provisions; and thus a spot, at all times detested for its deleterious qualities, becomes the staple of the riches of the old and new world, and the scene of one of the most considerable branches of commerce in the whole earth.

The ships being unloaded, and the merchants of Peru, together with the president of Panama, arrived, the fair comes under deliberation. And for this purpose the deputies of the several parties repair on board the commodore of the galleons, where, in the presence of the commodore, and the president of Panama, . . . the prices of the several kinds of merchandizes are settled. . . . The purchases and sales, as likewise the exchanges of money, are transacted by brokers, both from Spain and Peru. After this, every one begins to dispose of his goods; the Spanish brokers embarking their chests of money, and those of Peru sending away the goods they have purchased, in vessels called chatas and bongos, up the river Chagres. And thus the fair of Porto Bello ends. ❑

George Juan and Antonio de Ulloa, *A Voyage to South America* (London, 1772), Vol. 1, pp. 103–110, quoted in Benjamin Keen (ed.), *Readings in Latin-American Civilization* 1492 *to the Present* (New York: Houghton Mifflin, 1955), pp. 107–108.

Habsburgs, and thus to improve the domestic economy and revive the role of Spain in European affairs.

Under Philip V, attempts were made to suppress smuggling by the use of coastal patrol vessels in American waters. An incident arising from this policy (to be discussed later in this chapter) eventually led to war with England. In 1739, Philip established the viceroyalty of New Granada in what is today Venezuela, Colombia, and Ecuador. The purpose of this new administrative unit was to increase direct royal government in the area. During the reign of Ferdinand VI (1746–1759), the great mid-century wars exposed the vulnerability of the empire to naval attack and economic penetration. As an ally of France, Spain emerged as one of the defeated powers in 1763. Government circles were convinced that some changes in the colonial system had to be undertaken.

Charles III (1759–1788) made the most important strides toward imperial reform. What this reform meant was an attempt to reassert Spanish peninsular control of the empire. Like his two Bourbon predecessors, Charles III put more emphasis on royal ministers than on councils. Consequently, the role of both the Council of the Indies and the Casa de Contratación diminished. After 1765, Charles abolished the monopolies of Seville and Cádiz and permitted other Spanish commercial centers to trade with America. He also opened more South American and Caribbean ports to trade and authorized some commerce between ports in America. In 1776, he organized a fourth viceroyalty in the region of the Río de la Plata, which included much of present-day Argentina, Uruguay, Paraguay, and Bolivia. While in one sense somewhat freeing trade with and in America, Charles III attempted to increase the efficiency of tax collection and to eliminate bureaucratic corruption. To achieve those ends, he introduced the institution of the *intendent* into the Spanish Empire. These were royal bureaucrats loyal only to the crown.

These late-eighteenth-century Bourbon reforms helped to stimulate the imperial economy. Trade expanded and was somewhat more varied. But first and foremost, these reforms were attempts to bring the empire back under direct Spanish control. *Peninsulares* entered the New World in large numbers to fill new posts. Expanding trade brought more Spanish merchants to Latin America. The export orientation of the economy remained, and economic life was still organized to the benefit of Spain. A major result of these policies was to make the creoles feel that they were second-class subjects. In time, their resentment provided a major source of the discontent leading to the wars of independence in the early nineteenth century. Finally, it should be observed that the new imperial policies of Charles III were the Spanish equivalent to the new colonial directions undertaken by the British government in 1763, which, as will be seen in a later section, led to the American Revolution.

Colonial Brazil

In 1494, by the Treaty of Tordesillas, the pope had divided the seaborne empires of Spain and Portugal by drawing a line west of the Cape Verde Islands. In 1500, a Portuguese explorer landed on the coast of South America. The landmass of what is present-day Brazil extended east of the papal line of division, and thus Portugal gained a major hold on the South American continent.

Portugal had fewer human and material resources to devote to its New World empire than did Spain. The crown granted captaincies to private persons that permitted them to attempt to exploit the region. By the middle of the sixteenth century, sugar production had gained preeminence. The cane was raised on large estates (*fazendas*) that used African slave labor. Although some minerals were discovered and some cattle raised, sugar—and with it, slavery—dominated the colonial economy of Brazil. Nowhere, except perhaps in the West Indies, was slavery so important, and the institution persisted in Brazil until 1888.

As in the Spanish empire, the Church established itself as a major institution. Similarly, the Portuguese crown attempted to establish a strong mercantile network around Brazilian trade. There was perhaps less resentment of the Portuguese government in Brazil than of the Spanish administrators in the Spanish empire. The Portuguese were less efficient. Moreover, the Portuguese government condoned policies of driving Indian tribes into the back country, as well as of tribal extermination. Throughout the eighteenth century, the Portuguese government also favored the continued importation of slaves.

Brazil constituted a large area of South America outside Spanish control and open to potential penetration by other European powers. Although some commercial rivalry did take place there, its riches and trade were relatively small compared to those of the

The eighteenth-century City Hall of Buenos Aires. Buenos Aires became the capital of the Viceroyalty of Rio de la Plata in 1776. [*Jacques Jangoux, Peter Arnold.*]

A sugar mill in the French West Indies. Like all Caribbean plantations, it was worked by slaves from Africa. Europeans had developed an insatiable demand for sugar, and the profits from sugar growing were immense. [Library of Congress.]

West Indies, which became the cockpit of conflict during the eighteenth century.

Rivalry and Conflict in the West Indies

The Spanish Empire stood on the defensive throughout the century. It was a sprawling expanse of territory over which the Spanish government wished to maintain a commercial monopoly without possessing the capacity to do so. Spanish colonists looked to illegal imports from French and British traders to supply needed goods. Both France and Britain assumed a very aggressive stance toward the Spanish Empire because they viewed it as a vast potential market and a major source of gold. Their rivalry for intrusion into the mainland Spanish American markets was duplicated by their conflicts in the West Indies.

The heart of the eighteenth-century colonial rivalry was the West Indies. These islands, close to the American continents, constituted the jewels of empire. Here the colonial powers pursued their greedy ambitions in close proximity to each other. The West Indies raised tobacco, cotton, indigo, coffee, and sugar, for which there existed strong markets in Europe. Sugar, in particular, had become a product of standard consumption rather than a luxury. It was used in coffee, tea, and cocoa; for making candy and preserving fruits; and

in the brewing industry. There seemed no limit to its uses. Sugar was also important to the domestic economy of Europe. Sugar refining had become a major industry in France. Tobacco, as well, figured prominently in the re-export industry. Large quantities of tobacco were shipped from Scotland to the Continent.

The institution of slavery was basic to the economy of the West Indies as well as to that of South America and the British colonies on the south Atlantic seaboard of North America. Hundreds of thousands of slaves were imported into the Americas during the eighteenth century. Planters could not attract sufficient quantities of free labor to these areas, and they became wholly dependent on slaves. Slavery and the slave trade touched most of the economy of the transatlantic world. Cities such as Newport, Rhode Island; Liverpool, England; and Nantes, France, enjoyed prosperity that rested almost entirely on the slave trade. All of the shippers who handled cotton, tobacco, and sugar depended on slavery, though they might not have had direct contact with the institution.

There was a general triangle of trade that consisted of carrying goods to Africa to be exchanged for slaves, who were then taken to the West Indies, where they were traded for sugar and other tropical produce, which were then shipped to Europe. Not all ships necessarily covered all three legs of the triangle. Another major trade pattern existed between New England and the West Indies: New England fish or ship stores were traded for sugar.

Within the rich commerce and agriculture of the West Indies, there existed three varieties of colonial rivalry. Producers of different nations were intensely jealous of each other. The quantity of sugar produced had expanded so as to depress the price in Europe. Consequently, one group of planters hoped not to conquer the lands of their competitors but to destroy the productive capacity of those islands. There was a second form of rivalry among shippers in the Caribbean. Every captain hoped to transport as much sugar as possible to Europe. Finally, the West Indies, possessions of France and Britain provided excellent bases for penetration of the trade of the Spanish Empire. Many French and British ship captains in the West Indies were admitted smugglers, and some were little better than pirates.

The close interrelationship of the West Indies and the European economies meant that significant numbers of British, French, and Spanish subjects had an interest in the area. This West India Interest, as it was called in England, consisted of absentee plantation owners, shippers, insurers, merchants, bankers, owners of domestic industries dependent on West Indian products, and all of those involved in the slave trade. In Great Britain, it was an articulate and well-organized pressure group. In 1739, the West India Interest, along with the political enemies of Robert Walpole, succeeded in driving Britain into a war with Spain, the War of Jenkins' Ear.

The Treaty of Utrecht (1713) included two special privileges for Great Britain in regard to the Spanish Empire. The British received a thirty-year *asiento*, or contract, to furnish slaves to the Spanish. Britain also gained the right to send one ship each year to the trading fair at Portobello. These two privileges allowed British traders and smugglers potential inroads into the Spanish market. Little but friction arose from these rights. The annual ship to Portobello was often supplied with additional goods during the night as it lay in port. Much to the chagrin of the British, the Spanish government under the Bourbons took its own alleged trading monopoly seriously and maintained coastal patrols, which boarded and searched English vessels to look for contraband.

On a French West Indian plantation slaves pick cotton on the right while other slaves on the left remove the seeds from the fiber. [The Granger Collection.]

In 1731, during one such boarding operation, there was a fight, and an English captain named Robert Jenkins had his ear cut off by the Spaniards. Thereafter, he carried about his severed ear preserved in a jar of brandy. This incident was of little importance until 1738, when Jenkins appeared before the British Parliament, reportedly brandishing his ear as an example of Spanish atrocities to British merchants in the West Indies. The British merchant and West Indies' interests put great pressure on Parliament to do something about Spanish intervention in their trade. Robert Walpole attempted to reach a solution through negotiations. However, Parliament—and especially the members who believed that the war would drive Walpole from office—refused all accommodation. In late 1739, Great Britain went to war with Spain.

At the outbreak of hostilities, the French, under the administration of Cardinal Fleury, stood ready to profit from the British–Spanish conflict. They expected to see British trade harmed and eventually to receive Spanish commercial favors for aid. None of the major European powers except Britain had any standing grudge against France. The years of Fleury's cautious policy were about to pay off. Then, quite literally overnight, the situation on the Continent changed.

Mid-Century Wars

The War of the Austrian Succession (1740–1748)

In December 1740, after possessing the throne of Prussia for less than seven months, Frederick II ordered his troops to occupy the Austrian province of Silesia. The invasion shattered the provisions of the Pragmatic Sanction and upset the continental balance of power as established by the Treaty of Utrecht (see Chapter 19). The young king of Prussia had treated the House of Habsburg simply as another German state rather than as the leading state of the region. The province of Silesia itself rounded out Prussia's possessions, and Frederick was determined to keep his ill-gotten prize.

The seizure of Silesia could have marked the opening of a general hunting season on Habsburg holdings and the beginning of revolts by Habsburg subjects. Instead, it provided the occasion for new political allegiances. Maria Theresa of Austria achieved these new loyalties, especially between herself and the Magyars of Hungary, not merely through heroism but more specifically by granting new privileges to the nobles of the various Habsburg realms. The empress recognized Hungary as the most important of her crowns and promised the Magyars considerable local autonomy. In this fashion, she preserved the Habsburg state, but at great cost to the power of the central monarchy.

The war over the Austrian succession and the British–Spanish commercial conflict could have remained separate disputes. What ultimately united them was the role of France. A group of aggressive court aristocrats compelled the elderly Cardinal Fleury to abandon his planned naval attack on British trade and to support the Prussian aggression against Austria, the traditional enemy of France.

This proved to be one of the most fateful decisions in French history. In the first place, aid to Prussia consolidated a new and powerful German state that could and indeed later did, endanger France. Second, the French move against Austria brought Great Britain into the continental war, as Britain sought to assure that the Low Countries remained in the friendly hands of Austria. In 1744, the British–French conflict expanded beyond the Continent, as France decided to support Spain against Britain in the New World. As a result, French military and economic resources became badly divided.

By 1748, the war had become a military stalemate for all concerned. France had done well on the continent, but Britain had achieved victories overseas. Consequently, the war was brought to a close in 1748 by the Treaty of Aix-la-Chapelle. This treaty in effect restored the conditions that had existed before the war, with the exception that Prussia retained Silesia. Spain renewed with Great Britain the *asiento* agreement on the slave trade. All observers believed that the treaty constituted a truce rather than a permanent peace.

The Seven Years' War (1756–1763)

Before the rivalries again erupted into war, a dramatic shift of alliances took place. In 1756, Prussia and Great Britain signed the Convention of Westminster. This was a defensive alliance aimed at preventing the entry of foreign troops into the Germanies. Frederick feared invasions by both Russia and France. The convention meant that Great Britain, the ally of Austria since the wars of Louis XIV, had now joined forces with Austria's major eighteenth-century enemy. Later in 1756, Austria achieved a defensive alliance with France. In this manner, the traditional European alliances of the past century were reversed.

Although the Treaty of Aix-la-Chapelle brought peace to Europe, conflict between France and Great Britain continued unofficially on the colonial front. There were continuous clashes between English and French settlers in the Ohio River valley and in upper New England. These were the prelude to what is known in American history as the French and Indian War. Once again, however, the factor that opened a general European war that extended into a colonial theater was the action of the king of Prussia.

Maria Theresa of Austria (seated right) and her husband, Emperor Francis I (seated left), with their large family. Her son and successor, Joseph II, is the tall adolescent near her. The artist was Martin Meytens (1695–1770), court painter in Vienna. [Kunsthistorisches Museum, Vienna.]

In August 1756, Frederick II invaded the kingdom of Saxony. This attack was in Frederick's mind a preemptive strike against a conspiracy on the part of Saxony, Austria, and France to undermine and destroy Prussian power. In the spring of 1757, France and Austria made a new alliance dedicated to the destruction of Prussia. They were eventually joined by Sweden, Russia, and the smaller German states. Two factors, in addition to Frederick's strong leadership (it was after this war that he came to be called Frederick the Great), saved Prussia. First, Britain furnished considerable financial aid. Second, in 1762, Empress Elizabeth of Russia died. Her successor was Tsar Peter III (he also died in the same year), whose admiration for Frederick knew almost no bounds. Peter immediately made peace with Prussia, thus relieving the country of one enemy and allowing it to hold its own against Austria and France. The treaty of Hubertusburg of 1763 closed the continental conflict with no significant changes in prewar borders.

The survival of Prussia was less impressive to the rest of Europe than were the victories of Great Britain in every theater of conflict. The architect of victory was William Pitt the Elder (1708–1778). Pitt had a long career as a critic of the government, but during the 1750s he gained the confidence of the London merchant interest. Once war had commenced again, these groups clamored for his appointment to the cabinet. In 1757, he was named the secretary of state in charge of the war.

Although Pitt had previously criticized British involvement with the continent, once in office he reversed himself and pumped huge financial subsidies to Frederick the Great. But North America was Pitt's real concern. Put quite simply, he wanted all of North America east of the Mississippi for Great Britain, and that was exactly what he won as he directed unprecedented resources into the overseas colonial conflict. The French government was unwilling and unable to direct similar resources against the English in America. In September 1759, on the Plains of Abraham overlooking the valley of the Saint Lawrence River at Quebec City, the British army under General James Wolfe defeated the French under Lieutenant General

Louis Joseph Montcalm. The French empire in Canada was coming to an end.

However, Pitt's colonial vision extended beyond the Saint Lawrence valley and the Great Lakes basin. The major islands of the French West Indies fell to the British fleets. On the Indian subcontinent, the British forces under the command of Robert Clive defeated the French in 1757 at the Battle of Plassey. This victory opened the way for the eventual conquest of Bengal and later of all India by the British East India Company. Never had any other European power experienced such a complete worldwide military victory.

The Treaty of Paris of 1763 reflected somewhat less of a victory than Britain had won on the battlefield. Pitt was no longer in office. George III (1760–1820) had succeeded to the British throne in 1760. Having quarreled with Pitt, he replaced him with the Earl of Bute. The new minister was responsible for the peace settlement, in which Britain received all of Canada, the Ohio River valley, and the eastern half of the Mississippi River valley. Britain partially surrendered the conquest in India by giving France footholds at Pondicherry and Chandernagore. The sugar islands of Guadeloupe and Martinique were restored to the French.

The Seven Years' War had been a vast worldwide conflict. Tens of thousands of soldiers had been killed

Frederick the Great of Prussia in his later years. His face shows the strain that his ambitious wars had brought to him and to his nation. Yet he did succeed in making Prussia a major power. [Culver Pictures.]

The Battle of the Plains of Abraham, 1759. The British victory at Quebec meant the end of French rule in Canada. [Courtesy of the Trustees, National Maritime Museum, Greenwich, England.]

The English factory at Surat in India, owned and operated by the East India Company. Here Indian goods were purchased and stored until British ships arrived to take them to Britain. [The Mansell Collection.]

or wounded in major battles around the globe. At great internal sacrifice, Prussia had permanently wrested Silesia from Austria and had turned the Holy Roman Empire into an empty shell. Habsburg power now depended largely on the Hungarian domains. France, though still possessing sources of colonial income, was no longer a great colonial power. The Spanish Empire remained largely intact, but the British were still determined to penetrate its markets. On the Indian subcontinent, the British East India Company was in a position to continue to press against the decaying indigenous governments and to impose its own authority. The results of that situation would be felt until the middle of the twentieth century. From this time until World War II, Great Britain assumed the status of a world power.

CONFLICTS OF THE MID-EIGHTEENTH CENTURY

1713	Treaty of Utrecht
1739	Outbreak of the War of Jenkins' Ear between England and Spain
1740	War of the Austrian succession commences
1748	Treaty of Aix-la-Chapelle
1756	Convention of Westminster between England and Prussia
	Seven Years' War opens
1757	Battle of Plassey
1759	British forces capture Quebec
1763	Teary of Hubertusburg
	Treaty of Paris

The American Revolution and Europe

Events in the British Colonies

The revolt of the British colonies in North America was an event in transatlantic and European history. It erupted from problems of revenue collection common to all the major powers after the Seven Years' War.

The War of the American Revolution was a continuation of the conflict between France and Great Britain. The French support of the Americans deepened the existing financial and administrative difficulties of the French monarchy.

After the Treaty of Paris of 1763, the British government faced three imperial problems. The first was the sheer cost of empire, which the British felt they could no longer carry alone. The national debt had risen considerably, as had taxation. The American colonies had been the chief beneficiaries of the conflict. It made rational sense that they should henceforth bear part of the cost of their protection and administration. The second problem was the vast expanse of new territory in North America that the British had to organize. This included all the land from the mouth of the Saint Lawrence River to the Mississippi River, with its French settlers and, more importantly, its Indian possessors.

COLONISTS RESIST TAXATION. As the British ministers pursued solutions to these difficulties, a third and more serious issue arose. The British colonists in North America resisted taxation and were suspicious of the imperial policies toward the western lands. Consequently, the British had to search for new ways to exert their authority over the colonies. The Americans became increasingly resistant because their economy had outgrown the framework of mercantilism, because the removal of the French relieved them of dependence on the British army, and because they believed that their liberty was in danger.

The British drive for revenue commenced in 1764 with the passage of the Sugar Act under the ministry of George Grenville (1712–1770). The measure attempted to produce more revenue from imports into the colonies by the rigorous collection of what was actually a lower tax. Smugglers who violated the law were to be tried in admiralty courts without juries. The next year, Parliament passed the Stamp Act, which put a tax on legal documents and certain other items such as newspapers. The British considered these taxes legal because the decision to collect them had been approved by Parliament. The taxes seemed just because the money was to be spent in the colonies. The Americans responded that they had the right to tax themselves and that they were not represented in Parliament. The colonists quite simply argued that there should be no taxation without representation. Moreover, because the king had granted most of the colonial charters, the Americans claimed that their legal connection to Britain was through the monarch rather than through the Parliament. The expenditure in the colonies of the revenue levied by Parliament did not reassure the colonists. They feared that if colonial government were financed from outside, they would lose control over their government. In October 1765, the Stamp Act Congress met in America and drew up a protest to the crown. There was much disorder in the colonies, particularly in Massachusetts. The colonists agreed to refuse to import British goods. In 1766, Parliament repealed the Stamp Act, but through the Declaratory Act, it said that Parliament had the power to legislate for the colonies.

The Stamp Act crisis set the pattern for the next ten years. Parliament, under the leadership of a royal minister, would approve a piece of revenue or administrative legislation. The Americans would then resist by reasoned argument, economic pressure, and violence. Then the British would repeal the legislation, and the process would begin again. Each time, tempers on both sides became more frayed and positions more irreconcilable. In 1767, Charles Townshend (1725–1767), as Chancellor of the Exchequer, led Parliament to pass a series of revenue acts relating to colonial imports. The colonists again resisted. The ministry sent over its own customs agents to administer the laws. To protect these new officers, the British sent troops to Boston in 1768. The obvious tensions resulted, and in March 1770, the Boston Massacre, in which British troops killed five citizens, took place. That same year, Parliament repealed all of the Townshend duties except for the one on tea.

In May 1773, Parliament passed a new law relating to the sale of tea by the East India Company. The measure permitted the direct importation of tea into the American colonies. It actually lowered the price of tea while retaining the tax imposed without the colonists' consent. In some cities, the colonists refused to permit the unloading of the tea; in Boston, a shipload of tea was thrown into the harbor. The British ministry of Lord North (1732–1792) was determined to assert the authority of Parliament over the resistant colonies. During 1774, Parliament passed a series of laws known in American history as the Intolerable Acts. These measures closed the port of Boston, reorganized the government of Massachusetts, allowed troops to be quartered in private homes, and removed the trials of royal customs officials to England. The same year, Parliament approved the Quebec Act for the future administration of that province. It extended the boundaries of Quebec to include the Ohio River valley. The Americans regarded the Quebec Act as an attempt to prevent the extension of their mode of self-government westward beyond the Appalachian Mountains.

During these years, committees of correspondence, composed of citizens critical of Britain, had been established throughout the colonies. They made the various sections of the eastern seaboard aware of common problems and aided united action. In September 1774, these committees organized the gathering of the First Continental Congress in Philadelphia. This body

This view of the "Boston Massacre" of March 5, 1770 by Paul Revere owes more to propaganda than fact. There was no order to fire and the innocent citizens portrayed here were really an angry, violent mob. [Library of Congress.]

hoped to persuade Parliament to restore self-government in the colonies and to abandon its attempt at direct supervision of colonial affairs. However, conciliation was not forthcoming. By April 1775, the battles of Lexington and Concord had been fought. In June, the colonists suffered defeat at the Battle of Bunker Hill. Despite the defeat, the colonial assemblies soon began to meet under their own authority rather than under that of the king.

DECLARATION OF INDEPENDENCE. The Second Continental Congress gathered in May 1775. It still sought conciliation with Britain, but the pressure of events led that assembly to begin to conduct the government of the colonies. By August 1775, George III had declared the colonies in rebellion. During the winter, Thomas Paine's (1737–1809) pamphlet *Com-*

mon Sense galvanized public opinion in favor of separation from Great Britain. A colonial army and navy were organized. In April 1776, the Continental Congress opened American ports to the trade of all nations. And on July 4, 1776, the Continental Congress adopted the Declaration of Independence. Thereafter, the War of the American Revolution continued until 1781, when the forces of George Washington defeated those of Lord Cornwallis at Yorktown. However, early in 1778, the war had widened into a European conflict when Benjamin Franklin (1706–1790) persuaded the French government to support the rebellion. In 1779, the Spanish also came to the aid of the colonies. The 1783 Treaty of Paris concluded the conflict, and the thirteen American colonies had established their independence.

This series of events is generally familiar to Ameri-

"The Horse America throwing his Master," a cartoon mocking George III over the rebellion of the American colonies. [Library of Congress.]

can readers. The relationship of the American Revolution to European affairs and the European roots of the American revolutionary ideals are less familiar.

The political theory of the American Declaration of Independence derived from the writings of seventeenth-century English Whig theorists, such as John Locke, and eighteenth-century Scottish moral philosophers, such as Francis Hutcheson. Their political ideas had in large measure arisen out of the struggle of seventeenth-century English aristocrats and gentry against the absolutism of the Stuart monarchs. The American colonists looked to the English Revolution of 1688 as having established many of their own fundamental political liberties as well as those of the English. The colonists claimed that, through the measures imposed from 1763 to 1776, George III and the British Parliament had attacked those liberties and dissolved the bonds of moral and political allegiance that had formerly united the two peoples. Consequently, the colonists employed a theory that had developed to justify an aristocratic rebellion in order to support their own popular revolution.

These Whig political ideas were only a part of the English ideological heritage that affected the Americans. Throughout the eighteenth century, they had become familiar with a series of British political writers called the *Commonwealthmen*. These writers held republican political ideas and had their intellectual roots in the most radical thought of the Puritan revolution. During the early eighteenth century, these writers had relentlessly criticized the government patronage and parliamentary management of Robert Walpole and his successors. They argued that such government was corrupt and that it undermined liberty. They regarded much parliamentary taxation as simply a means of financing political corruption. They also attacked standing armies, which they considered instruments of tyranny. In Great Britain, this political tradition had only a marginal impact. The writers were largely ignored because most British subjects regarded themselves as the freest people in the world. However, over three thousand miles away in the colonies, these radical books and pamphlets were read widely and were often accepted at face value. The events in Great Britain following the accession of King George III made many colonists believe that the worst fears of the Commonwealthmen were coming true.

Events in Great Britain

George III (1760–1820) believed that his two immediate royal predecessors had been improperly bullied and controlled by their ministers. The new king intended to rule through Parliament, but was determined to have ministers of his own choice. This attitude led the monarch to quarrel with William Pitt, who eventually resigned. In Pitt's place, the king appointed the Earl of Bute. Between 1761 and 1770, George tried one minister after another, but each failed to gain sufficient support from the various factions in the House of Commons. Finally, in 1770, he turned to Lord North (1732–1792), who remained the king's first minister until 1782. In these actions, George III ignored the influence of the great Whig families who had dominated British politics since 1715. They and other political figures, in turn, accused the king of attempting to impose a tyranny.

THE CHALLENGE OF JOHN WILKES. Then, in 1763, began the affair of John Wilkes (1725–1797). This London political radical and member of Parliament published a newspaper called the *North Briton*. In issue Number 45 of this paper, Wilkes strongly criticized Lord Bute's handling of the peace negotiations with France. Wilkes was arrested under the authority of a general warrant issued by the secretary of state. He pled the privileges of a member of Parliament and was released. The courts also later ruled that the vague kind of general warrant by which he had been arrested was illegal. However, the House of Commons ruled that issue number 45 was a libel and expelled Wilkes from the Commons. He soon fled the country and was outlawed. Throughout these procedures, there was very widespread support for Wilkes, and many popular demonstrations were held in his cause.

In 1768, Wilkes returned to England and again stood for election to Parliament. He won the election, but again the House of Commons refused to seat him. He was elected three more times. After the fourth election, the House of Commons simply ignored the election results and seated the government-supported candidate. As earlier in the decade, large popular demonstrations of shopkeepers, artisans, and small-property owners supported Wilkes. He also received aid from some aristocratic politicians who wished to humiliate George III. Wilkes himself contended during all of his troubles that his cause was the cause of English liberty. "Wilkes and Liberty" became the slogan of all political radicals and many noble opponents of the monarch. Wilkes was finally seated in 1774, after having become the lord mayor of London.

The American colonists followed the developments of the 1760s very closely. The events in Britain confirmed their fears about a monarchical and parliamentary conspiracy against liberty. That same monarch and Parliament were attempting to overturn the traditional relationship of Great Britain to its colonies by imposing parliamentary taxes. The same government had then landed troops in Boston, changed the government of Massachusetts, and undermined the traditional right of jury trial. All of these events fulfilled too exactly the portrait of political tyranny that had developed over the years in the minds of articulate colonists.

MOVEMENT FOR PARLIAMENTARY REFORM. The political influences between America and Britain operated both ways. The colonial demand for no taxation without representation and the criticism of the adequacy of the British system of representation struck at the core of the eighteenth-century British political structure. Colonial arguments could be adopted by British subjects at home who were no more directly

A satirical etching of John Wilkes by William Hogarth. It suggests an unattractive personality and questions the sincerity of Wilke's calls for liberty. [Charles Farrell Collection.]

represented in the House of Commons than were the Americans. Both the colonial leaders and John Wilkes were appealing over the heads of legally constituted political authorities to popular opinion and popular demonstrations. Both were protesting the power of a largely self-selected aristocratic political body.

By the close of the 1770s, there was much resentment in Britain about the mismanagement of the war, the high taxes, and Lord North's ministry. In northern England in 1778, Christopher Wyvil (1740–1822), a landowner and retired clergyman, organized the Yorkshire Association Movement. Property owners or free-holders of Yorkshire met in a mass meeting to demand rather moderate changes in the corrupt system of parliamentary elections. They organized corresponding societies elsewhere. The movement collapsed during the early 1780s because its supporters, unlike Wilkes and the American rebels, were not willing to appeal for broad popular support.

Parliament was not insensitive to the demands of

the Association Movement. In April 1780, the House of Commons passed a resolution that called for lessening the power of the crown. In 1782, Parliament adopted a measure for "economical" reform, which abolished some patronage at the disposal of the monarch. However, these actions did not prevent George III from appointing a minister of his own choice. In 1783, because of shifts in Parliament, Lord North had to form a ministry with Charles James Fox (1749–1806), a long-time critic of George III. The monarch was most unhappy with the arrangement. In 1783, he approached William Pitt the Younger (1759–1806), son of the victorious war minister, to manage the House of Commons. During the election of 1784, Pitt received immense patronage support from the crown and constructed a House of Commons favorable to the king. Thereafter, Pitt sought to formulate trade policies that would give his ministry broad popularity. He attempted one measure of modest parliamentary reform in 1785. When it failed, the young prime minister, who had been only twenty-four at the time of his appointment, abandoned the cause of reform.

EVENTS IN BRITAIN AND AMERICA
RELATING TO THE AMERICAN
REVOLUTION

1760	George III ascends the English throne
1763	Treaty of Paris concludes the Seven Years' War
	John Wilkes publishes issue Number 45 of *The North Briton*
1764	Sugar Act
1765	Stamp Act
1766	Stamp Act repealed and Declaratory Act passed
1767	Townshend Acts
1768	Parliament refuses to seat John Wilkes after his election
1770	Lord North becomes George III's chief minister
	Boston Massacre
1773	Boston Tea Party
1774	Intolerable Acts
	First Continental Congress
1775	Second Continental Congress
1776	Declaration of Independence
1778	France enters the war on the side of America
	Yorkshire Association Movement founded
1781	British forces surrender at Yorktown
1783	Treaty of Paris concludes War of the American Revolution

By the mid-1780s, George III had achieved a part of what he had sought beginning in 1761. He had reasserted the influence of the monarchy in political affairs. However, it proved a temporary victory because his own mental illness, which would finally require a regency, weakened the royal power. The cost of his years of dominance had been very high. On both sides of the Atlantic, the issue of popular sovereignty had been raised and widely discussed. The American colonies had been lost.

Eighteenth-Century Empire in World Perspective

The colonial conflicts of the eighteenth century produced enormous and enduring results in world history. European commerce dominated the world for the next two centuries. Europeans and their colonists came to extract labor and other natural resources from virtually all other continents of the world. All of this was made possible by the European military, especially through naval dominance.

The mid-century wars among European powers resulted in a new balance of power on the Continent and on the high seas. Great Britain gained a world empire, and Prussia was recognized as a great power. With the surrender of Canada, France retreated from North America and thus opened the way for a continent largely dominated by the English language and Protestant religion. By contrast, Latin America would be dominated by the Spanish language and Roman Catholicism. For many years, West Africa would continue to furnish slaves to the economies of both Americas. On the subcontinent of Asia, the foundations were laid for almost two centuries of British dominance of India.

The Seven Years' War also produced extraordinary long-term political results that certainly none of the colonial powers had contemplated. Every major European government began a search for increased revenue because of the costliness of the conflict. The English pursuit of revenue led to the conflict with their North American colonists and eventual revolution. Simultaneously, the Spanish government, which had been on the losing side of the conflict, attempted to regain tighter control and thus greater income from its vast Latin American Empire. By the early nineteenth century, the result of that effort would be growing resentments that contributed to the Latin American Wars of Independence. The French government also looked to greater revenues that set the stage for conflict between the monarchy and the aristocracy. The French revenue problem became worse when France aided the American colonists in an ongoing effort to disrupt British trade. Thereafter, the French monarchy and aristocracy were set on a collision course that resulted in revolution. In Eastern Europe, the search for new revenues fostered the policies associated with Enlightened Absolutism, which is discussed in the next chapter.

In the case of the American colonies, outposts founded to serve the economic requirements of Britain and Europe repaid the debt by serving as laboratories for new political ideas and institutions. The ideas had generally been developed in Europe, but America was the place where most of them were initially put into practice. America served for a time as an experimental station for the advanced political ideas of Europe. Soon the ideas would find their way back to the lands of their origins and also into the early nineteenth-century republics of Latin America.

Suggested Readings

B. BAILYN, *The Ideological Origins of the American Revolution* (1967). An important work illustrating the role of English radical thought in the perceptions of the American colonists.

C. BECKER, *The Declaration of Independence: A Study in the History of Political Ideas* (1922). An examination of the political and imperial theory of the Declaration.

J. BREWER, *Party Ideology and Popular Politics at the Accession of George III* (1976). An important series of essays on popular radicalism.

J. BROOKE, *King George III* (1972). The best biography.

H. BUTTERFIELD, *George III, Lord North, and the People*, 1779–1780 (1949). Explores the domestic unrest in Britain during the American Revolution.

M. D. COE, *The Maya* (1986). A fine introduction.

G. A. COLLIER, R. I. ROSALDO, J. D. WIRTH, *The Inca and Aztec States* 1400–1800 (1982). An important collection of advanced essays.

N. DAVIES, *The Aztecs: A History* (1973). A useful overview.

D. B. DAVIS, *The Problem of Slavery in Western Culture* (1966). A brilliant and far-ranging discussion.

D. B. DAVIS, *The Problem of Slavery in the Age of Revolution*, 1770–1823 (1975). A major work for both European and American history.

W. DORN, *Competition for Empire*, 1740–1763 (1940). Still one of the best accounts of the mid-century struggle.

C. GIBSON, *The Aztecs Under Spanish Rule: A History of the Indians of the Valley of Mexico* (1964). An exceedingly interesting book.

C. GIBSON, *Spain in America* (1966). A splendidly clear and balanced discussion.

L. H. GIPSON, *The British Empire before the American Revolution*, 13 vols. (1936–1967). A magisterial account of the mid-century wars from an imperial viewpoint.

L. HANKE, *Bartolomé de Las Casas: An Interpretation of His Life and Writings* (1951). A classic work.

F. KATZ, *The Ancient American Civilizations* (1972). An excellent introduction.

B. KEEN AND M. WASSERMAN, *A Short History of Latin America* (1984). A good survey with very helpful bibliographical guides.

J. LOCKHARDT AND S. B. SCHWARTZ, *Early Latin America: A History of Colonial Spanish America and Brazil* (1983). The new standard work.

R. LODGE, *Great Britain and Prussia in the Eighteenth Century* (1923). The standard account.

M. E. MILLER, *The Art of Mesoamerica from Olmec to Aztec* (1986). A splendid introduction.

E. MORGAN AND H. MORGAN, *The Stamp Act Crisis* (1953). A lively account of the incident from the viewpoint of both the colonies and England.

J. B. OWEN, *The Eighteenth Century* (1974). A survey of British politics.

R. PARES, *War and Trade in the West Indies* (1936). Relates the West Indies to Britain's larger commercial and naval concerns.

R. PARES, *King George III and the Politicians* (1953). An important analysis of the constitutional and political structures.

J. H. PARRY, *Trade and Dominion: The European Overseas Empires in the Eighteenth Century* (1971). A comprehensive account with attention to the European impact on the rest of the world.

C. D. RICE, *The Rise and Fall of Black Slavery* (1975). An excellent survey of the subject with careful attention to the numerous historiographical controversies.

C. G. ROBERTSON. *Chatham and the British Empire* (1948). A brief study.

G. RUDÉ, *Wilkes and Political Liberty* (1962). A close analysis of popular political behavior.

S. J. AND B. H. STEIN, *The Colonial Heritage of Latin America: Essays on Economic Dependence in Perspective* (1970). An important work emphasizing the long-range impact of the colonial economy.

P. D. G. THOMAS, *British Politics and the Stamp Act Crisis: The First Phase of the American Revolution*, 1763–1767 (1975). An interesting work from the British point of view.

J. S. WATSON, *The Reign of George III*; 1760–1815 (1960). Covers the British domestic political scene in a traditional manner.

M. P. WEAVER, *The Aztecs, Mayas, and Their Predecessors: Archaelology of Mesoamerica* (1981). A standard textbook.

G. WILLS. *Inventing America: Jefferson's Declaration of Independence* (1978). An important study that challenges much of the analysis in the Becker volume noted above.

G. S. WOOD, *The Creation of the American Republic*, 1776–1787 (1969). A far-ranging work dealing with Anglo-American political thought.

One of the many superb multicolor paintings that grace the best examples of Safavid manuscripts of the Shah-namah, the Iranian national epic. Here an angel is seen rescuing the hero Khosrow Parviz from a blind canyon. The painting is attributed to Muzaffar Ali, ca. 1530–1535, of Tabriz. [The Metropolitan Museum of Art, Gift of Arthur A. Houghton, Jr. 1970.]

612

22 The Last Great Islamic Empires and Early European Intrusion in Asia and Africa (1500–1800)

The century and a half from 1500 to 1650 produced a magnificent blossoming of Islamic culture and political power. In this period, the creation of three mighty, absolutist empires and a number of strong regional Islamic states marked the culmination of a long process in Islamic history. During this time, the ideal of a universal Muslim caliphate gave way to the reality of numerous largely secular, albeit distinctively "Islamic," sultanates. The simultaneous growth of the mighty Ottoman, Safavid, and Mughal empires was in many ways the global climax of Islamic culture and power. By about 1600, the Ottoman Turks controlled Asia Minor, the Fertile Crescent, the Balkans, Crimean Europe, the Islamic Mediterranean, and Arabia; the Persian Safavids ruled all of Iran; and the Timurid rulers known as the Mughals governed most of the Indian subcontinent. Around them were arrayed the Muslim khanates of Central Asia and Russia, the sultanates of Southeast Asia and East Africa, the Sharifian state of Morocco, and the Islamic regional empires of the Sudan.

Thus, in 1600, Islamic civilization as a whole appeared as strong and vital as that of Western Europe, China, or Japan. Yet hard on the heels of this time of Islamic prosperity and power, a disastrous decline occurred in Islamic military preeminence as well as in basic economic and political independence. By the late seventeenth century, Islamic power almost everywhere was in retreat before the rising tide of Western European economic and military imperialism.

Throughout the period from 1500 to 1800, Islamic religion was spreading significantly while Islamic commercial, political, and military power was steadily being displaced by an economically and technologically superior European West. A keynote of the age was the growing domination of the world's seas by the

613

Europeans. This domination allowed them to contain as well as to bypass the major Islamic lands in their quest for commercial empires. Western industrial development joined vast European economic wealth and political stability by the late 1700s, giving the West global military and political supremacy for the first time. Before 1800 the Europeans were able to bring only minor Islamic states under colonial administrations. However, they laid the groundwork for extending such control by gaining important footholds in Africa, India, and Southeast Asia. The age of the last great Muslim empires was the beginning of the first great modern European empires.

In this chapter, we shall focus first upon the apogee and subsequent decline of global Islamic power in the three great empires of the period. We then turn to look briefly at the important, but smaller and less widely influential, Islamic political and cultural centers of central Asia and the coastlands of southern Asia, the Indies, and east Africa. In the latter areas, we will note the intrusion of European military and commercial power into a virtual Muslim monopoly on maritime trade. Next, we move on to the vast continent of Africa, where a variety of changes can be observed. Here we shall focus selectively on areas north of the forest where Islam was still spreading and on those regions of the African subcontinent where a new European presence was beginning to change the economic and political landscape. The European presence would be most strongly felt after 1800 (see Chapter 31), but its potential force could already be seen in such arenas as the Atlantic African slave trade.

MAP 22-1 SIXTEENTH-CENTURY ISLAMIC EMPIRES *Major Islamic Dynasties in the Central Islamic Lands,* CA. 1600.

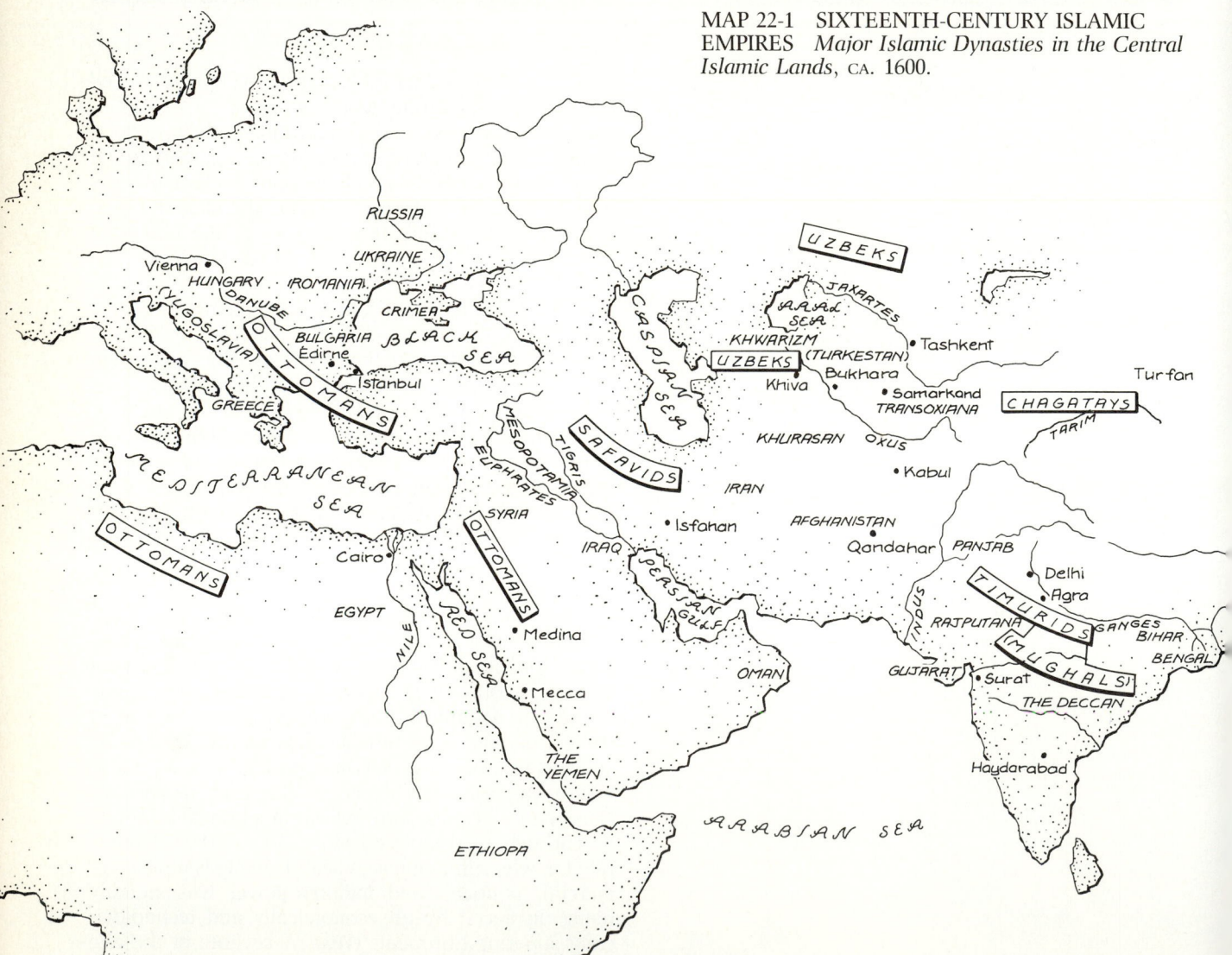

The Ottoman Empire

Origins and Early Growth

The Ottomans were a Turkish dynasty that rose to prominence as one of various groups of Anatolian *ghazis*, or frontier warriors dedicated to extending Muslim rule by *jihad*, or "struggle" in God's cause.[1] Having come to Anatolia (Asia Minor) in Seljuk times (1055–1194), the Ottomans had formed a military state along the Byzantine–Seljuk frontier in western Anatolia even before 1300. In the fourteenth century, several vigorous leaders expanded their initial domains east over central Anatolia and west across the Dardanelles into Byzantine territory, over both Macedonia and modern Bulgaria.

By 1400, the center of Ottoman rule had shifted from Anatolia to a new capital at Edirne in the Balkan peninsula. Ottoman control then extended as far as the Danube in the northwest, and over western and central Anatolia in the east. Only the completely encircled tip of Balkan Europe, on which sat Constantinople, formed an alien pocket within these dominions. The Byzantine capital had been the object of repeated sieges long before Ottoman times. The Ottomans made several further attempts before it fell to Sultan Mehmed (Turkish for "Muhammad") "the Conqueror" (ruled 1451–1481) in 1453. Constantinople, renamed Istanbul (its local dialect name), now replaced Edirne as the Ottoman capital. After hundreds of years, proud Byzantium was no more, although under the Ottomans, the Christian patriarch continued to preside in Istanbul over the eastern Church.

By 1512, Ottoman rule was secure in virtually all of southeastern Europe and north of the Black Sea in most of the Ukraine. Under Selim I (1512–1520) and Süleyman "the Lawmaker" (known in the West as "the Magnificent"; ruled 1520–1566), this rule was greatly expanded and consolidated. Selim established the Ottoman state as a major Asian as well as European empire by subjugating the Egyptian Mamluks (1517) and annexing not only Syria-Palestine and Egypt, but also most of North Africa. The Yemen and western Arabia, including the sacred precincts of Mecca and Medina, now came under Ottoman rule. Selim also met and nullified the Shi'ite threat from Iran in the east (to be discussed later). Süleyman extended Ottoman control farther eastward, over Kurdistan and

[1] The Ottomans, sometimes called *Osmanlis*, are named after Osman, also rendered *Othman* or *Uthman*, a *ghazi* said to have founded the dynasty when he set up a border state about 1288 on the Byzantine frontier in northwest Anatolia.

Georgia (in the Caucasus), as well as Mesopotamia and Iraq. He also advanced Ottoman borders much farther into eastern Europe. Having won much of Hungary and having nearly taken Vienna by siege in 1526–1529, Süleyman was able by battle and treaty to bring virtually all of Hungary under direct Ottoman rule in the 1540s.

The Ottoman ruler could now claim to be the true heir of the Abbasids and caliph for all Muslims. This claim was symbolized best in his name, where "protector of the Sacred Places [Mecca and Medina]" was added to that of emperor (*padishah*). At this point, Ottoman military might was unmatched by any state in the world, with the possible exception of China.

The Ottoman State

The entire Ottoman state was organized as one vast military institution. All members, whatever their function, held military ranks under the hereditary leadership of the Ottoman sovereign. The so-called ruling

Suleyman the Lawgiver (reigned 1520–1566). Known as "Suleman the Magnificent," this astute and capable Ottoman Sultan can be compared to other great rulers of the sixteenth century, such as the Timurid Akbar in India and Elizabeth I of England. [Bettmann Archive.]

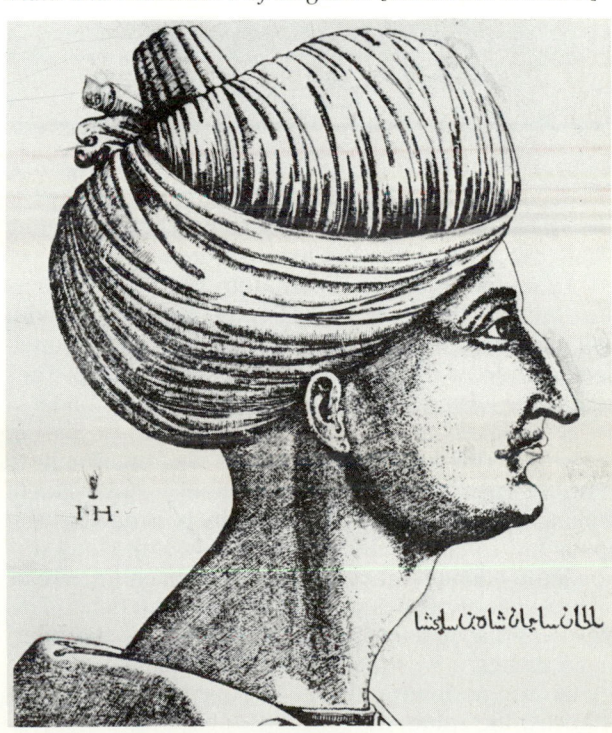

A Habsburg Ambassador on Süleyman's Entourage

The following excerpt is from a description of a 1555 visit to the Ottoman court by a European, Ghislain de Busbecq. His Turkish Letters *were written for publication in Europe, where their great praise for Süleyman and the Turks did much to enhance the Turks' reputation among western Europeans.*

The Sultan's head-quarters were crowded by numerous attendants, including many high officials. All the cavalry of the guard were there . . . , and a large number of Janissaries.

. . . .

Now come with me and cast your eye over the immense crowd of turbaned heads, wrapped in countless folds of the whitest silk, and bright raiment of every kind and hue, and everywhere the brilliance of gold, silver, purple, silk, and satin. A detailed description would be a lengthy task, and no mere words could give an adequate idea of the novelty of the sight. A more beautiful spectacle was never presented to my gaze. Yet amid all this luxury there was a great simplicity and economy. The dress of all has the same form whatever the wearer's rank; and no edgings or useless trimmings are sewn on, as is the custom with us, costing a large sum of money and worn out in three days. Their most beautiful garments of silk or satin, even if they are embroidered, as they usually are, cost only a ducat to make.

The Turks were quite as much astonished at our manner of dress as we at theirs. They wear long robes which reach almost to their ankles, and are not only more imposing but seem to add to the stature; our dress, on the other hand, is so short and tight that it discloses the forms of the body, which would be better hidden, and is thus anything but becoming, and besides, for some reason or other, it takes away from a man's height and gives him a stunted appearance.

What struck me as particularly praiseworthy in that great multitude was the silence and good discipline. There were none of the cries and murmurs which usually proceed from a motley concourse, and there was no crowding. Each man kept his appointed place in the quietest manner possible. The officers, namely, generals, colonels, captains, and lieutenants—to all of whom the Turks themselves give the title of Aga—were seated; the common soldiers stood up. The most remarkable body of men were several thousand Janissaries, who stood in a long line apart from the rest and so motionless that, as they were at some distance from me, I was for a while doubtful whether they were living men or statues, until, being advised to follow the usual custom of saluting them, I saw them all bow their heads in answer to my salutation. On our departure from that part of the field, we saw another very pleasing sight, namely, the Sultan's bodyguard returning home mounted on horses, which were not only very fine and tall but splendidly groomed and caparisoned. ❑

The Turkish Letters of Ogier Ghiselin de Busbecq, trans. by Edward E. Foster (Oxford: Clarendon Press, 1927), pp. 58–62, passim, cited in W. H. McNeill and M. R. Waldman, *The Islamic World* (New York: Oxford University Press, 1973), pp. 346–348.

institution included the emperor, his grand vizier and privy council, and the officers and standing "army" of the state. The civil bureaucracy as well as the fighting army came under the "ruling institution."

Alongside the ruling institution was the "religious institution," by means of which the Ottomans gradually coopted the legal-religious and educational-intellectual role of the Muslim scholars, or *ulema*. They made the *ulema* an arm of the government under a single religious authority, the Grand Mufti or Shaykh of Islam. This branch of the state was open only to Muslim men. Although the religious establishment upheld the supremacy of the divinely ordained religious law (*Shari'a*), the functional law of the land was the state administrative law, a situation characteristic of most Islamic states well before Ottoman times. This law was the practical code established by the ruler, even though it was theoretically governed by the religious law as interpreted by the *ulema*. In many instances, the sultan did formally apply traditional religious norms. But the conformity of administrative regulations with these norms was otherwise either a necessary pious fiction or a natural result of the Muslim faith of the administrator or ruler. This held also for Safavid Iran and Mughal India.

The Ottomans sought to keep their military leadership from becoming only a landed aristocracy (who could threaten the central power) by the control of land-revenue grants and the use of slave soldiers. The army had been based originally on the provincial cavalry, whose officers were supported out of the taxes on land grants in lieu of cash wages. But even as early as 1400, the cavalry-gentry's preeminence had been replaced by specialized infantry troops. Equipped with firearms, they were made up of well-trained and well-paid slave soldiers whose loyalty was to the emperor alone.

To sustain the high quality of their slave troops, the Ottomans developed a unique institution: the provincial slave levy, or *devshirme*. This institution selected

The heart of the Ottoman Empire, the Topkapi Palace and government complex seen from the Galata side of the Golden Horn, the harbor of Istanbul. The great dome of the Hagia Sophia, built by Justinian and turned into a mosque after 1453, is at the far right of this French engraving. [New York Public Library.]

young Christian (and some Jewish) boys from the provincial peasantry to be raised as Muslims; they were trained to serve both in the army and the bureaucracy at all levels, from provincial officer to grand vizier. How high slave soldiers could rise is exemplified by Sinan, the most famous imperial architect (d. 1578), who had been a *devshirme* recruit. The most famous slave corps was the Janissaries, the elite infantry troops of the empire. Muslim boys were not allowed into the slave corps, although some parents tried to buy them a place in what was the most promising career in the empire. Until 1572, marriage was forbidden to the slave soldiers, which further ensured loyalty and prevented hereditary claims on their offices.

The Imperial Decline

The reign of Süleyman proved to be the peak of Ottoman prestige and power. Further territorial gains were made in the seventeenth century, and the Ottoman state long remained a major force in European as well as Asian politics. However, beginning with the reign of Süleyman's weak son, Selim II (1566–1574), the empire began to falter, plagued ever more by military corruption, governmental decentralization, maritime setbacks, commercial and agricultural failures, and cultural and religious stagnation.

The seventeenth century saw a seesaw battle between the forces of decline and rejuvenation. It began on a sour note with the loss of Süleyman's conquests in

Georgia, Azerbaijan, and Mesopotamia to the Persian Safavids (1603). The Janissaries, once the backbone of Ottoman central administration and military strength, became increasingly independent of imperial control. By 1600, Muslims were allowed into the Janissary corps, marriage was possible, the *devshirme* had lapsed, and corruption was rife among the no-longer-

Janissaries marshalling Devshirme *recruits. From a Habsburg drawing. [New York Public Library.]*

understood the rural Christian population); and partly to the ruthless administration of a class of Greek Christians who gained high offices in the Balkans under the "ruling institution" in the late seventeenth and the eighteenth centuries. The long-term result of the deteriorating condition of the Christians was that they looked as never before to the Christian kingdoms of Europe and Russia for eventual liberation.

After the failure in 1683 of a second siege of Vienna, the Ottomans soon were driven out of Hungary and Belgrade and never again posed a serious threat to Europe. A second major European defeat came in 1718 at the hands of the Habsburgs. After several victories of Mahmud I (ruled 1730–1754) at the expense of the divided European powers, a crushing third European defeat by Russia cost the Ottomans the Crimea. This made the tsar the formal protector of the Orthodox Christians of the Islamic empire (1774). From this time forward, the Ottomans were prey to the West, never regaining any real strength before their final demise in 1918.

Outflanked by the rising power of Russia to their north and by growing European seapower to the south and west, the Ottomans found themselves blocked in the east by their implacable Shi'ite foes in Iran. There was no way for them to sustain the level of external trade needed to support their expensive wars. Ultimately, their dependence on an agricultural economy

Astronomers at work in the observatory of Takiyyuddin (1580). Takiyyuddin was one of the most famous Ottoman astronomers. Muslim scientists were always especially interested in astronomy and astrology. [New York Public Library.]

elite troops. Murad IV (ruled 1623–1640) introduced various reforms and ruled with an iron hand, but his death brought a relapse in central authority. Not even the Köprülüs, father and son, two efficient and capable viziers (1656–1676), could do more than effect a brief renewal of strong administrative control and military success. Thereafter, the decay of the central institutions set in anew.

Up to the seventeenth century, the large Christian subject population had been generally well treated (especially by comparison with the treatment of Jews in Christian lands). In the course of this century, however, they came under increasing burdens of taxation and other discriminatory treatment. This was due partly to increasing religious conservatism among the state *ulema*; partly to the end of the *devshirme* (which had placed men in power who came from among and

THE OTTOMAN EMPIRE	
CA. 1280	Foundation of early Ottoman principality in Anatolia
1451–1481	Rule of Sultan Mehmed "the Conqueror"
1453	Fall of Constantinople to Mehmed the Conqueror
1512–1520	Rule of Selim I
1517	Ottoman conquest of Egypt, assumption of claim to Abbasid Caliphal succession from Mamluks
1520–1556	Rule of Süleyman "the Lawmaker"
1578	Death of Ottoman master architect, Sinan
1656–1676	Governance of Köprülüs as viziers
1774	Loss of Crimea to Russia; Tsar becomes formal protector of Ottoman Orthodox Christian population
1798	Napoleon invades Ottoman Egypt
1918	End of empire

proved insufficient to face the rising commercial and industrial powers of Europe.

The Safavid Shi'ite Empire

Origins

As we noted in Chapter 15, the Safavid dynasty radically changed Iranian history after 1500. It had begun in the fourteenth century with the hereditary Turkish spiritual leaders of a Sufi order, or *tariqa*, in the northwest Iranian province of Azerbaijan. In the fifteenth century, the order developed a militant Shi'ite ideol-ogy, and by the 1480s, its members were operating as *ghazis*, or border raiders, against Christians in the southern Caucasus. The Safavid spiritual masters (*shaykhs, or pirs*) of the order claimed descent from the seventh *imam* of the Twelver Shia (see Chapter 15), which made them the focus of Shi'ite religious allegiance. Many adherents were won to the order from among the Turkoman tribesmen of eastern Anatolia, northern Syria, and northwestern Iran. These mounted warriors were called *Kizilbash* ("Red Heads") because of their distinctive uniform hats with red patches, which signaled their allegiance to their Safavid master.

Two Kinds of Drunkenness. This illustration from a splendid Safavid manuscript of the Diwan *of poetry by Hafiz was painted by Sultan Muhammad, perhaps the greatest Safavid artist. Here the comedy of drunkenness on wine (from the jars in the window below that containing the artist himself) mixes with the sublime drunkenness of mystical ecstasy, seen in the angels on the roof and perhaps in the ecstatic dance of the dervishes on the lawn below (early sixteenth century). [Fogg Art Museum.]*

The growing strength of the Safavids brought about conflict with the dominant Sunni Turkoman groups in the region. The Safavids emerged victorious in 1501 under the leadership of the young Safavid master-designate Isma'il. Recognized as a divinely appointed representative of the "hidden" *Imam* (see Chapter 12), Isma'il extended his sovereignty over the southern Caucasus, Azerbaijan, the Tigris–Euphrates valley, and all of western Iran by 1506. By 1512, the Safavids, in league with Babur, the Timurid ruler of Kabul, had taken from the Uzbek Turks all of eastern Iran between the Oxus River and the Arabian Sea. A strong central rule now united traditional Iranian lands for the first time since the heyday of the Abbasid caliphate. Shi'ite conformity, which demanded at least the formal cursing of the first three caliphs (as usurpers of Ali's office), was enforced everywhere.

In the west, however, the better-armed Ottoman army of Selim I soundly defeated the Kizilbash forces of the Safavids in 1514. This marked the beginning of an extended series of Ottoman–Safavid conflicts over

A view across the central court and ablution pool to the main iwan *of the "King's Mosque," the Masjid-i Shah, a major landmark of Isfahan built for Shah Abbas between 1612 and 1630. Turquoise-tiled buildings such as this made the Safavid capital of Shah Abbas a legend in its own time as a beauty spot · high on the central Iranian plateau. [Wheeler M. Thackston, Jr.]*

Portrait of the Safavid artist Riza-i Abbasi, by one of his pupils, Mu'in Musaffar (dated 1676). This is a good example of the superior line-drawings of this period in Iran. [Princeton University Library.]

the next two centuries. This defeat gave the Ottomans control of the Fertile Crescent and forced the Safavids to move their capital and their focus eastward—out of the extreme western parts of Iran (Azerbaijan), where they had first come to power.

Shah Abbas I

Isma'il's less able successor, Tahmasp I (ruled 1524–1576), lost territory to Süleyman. Meanwhile, the greatest Safavid ruler, Shah Abbas I (ruled 1588–1629), not only pushed the Ottomans out of Azerbaijan and Iraq but also turned back new Uzbek invasions in Khorasan. He also sought alliances with the Ottomans' European enemies. This tactic used by several Safavid rulers shows the deep division that the new militant Persian Shi'ism had brought into the Islamic world. Abbas also broke the century-long Portuguese monopoly on trade along Persian shores and opened up trade with the commercial companies of the English and the Dutch. While the European military ventures of Shah Abbas did not produce real results, his commercial enterprises did, and his reign brought considerable prosperity to Iran—symbolized by the magnificent capital that he built at Isfahan.

The Safavid Decline

After Shah Abbas, with the exception of two periods (1642–1666, and 1694–1722), the empire went slowly into eclipse. The chief causes of its decline were (1) continued pressure from Ottoman and Uzbek armies, (2) the growing concentration of wealth at the center and the corresponding economic decline in the empire as a whole, and (3) the increasing power and religious bigotry of the more conservative Shi'ite *ulema*. The conservative *ulema* not only introduced a Shi'ite legalism but also emphasized their own authority as interpreters of the law over the authority of the Safavid monarch. They also persecuted religious minorities and encouraged hatred of Sunni Muslims.

One result of the Shi'ite exclusivism was a series of tribal revolts among the Sunni Afghans. In the end, an Afghan leader took Qandahar (in modern Afghani-

stan) and then went on to defeat the imperial armies, to capture Isfahan, and to force the abdication of the last Safavid shah in 1722. Some Safavid princes managed to retake control of western Iran for a while, but the empire's greatness was past. A revived, but officially Sunni, monarchy under the talented Kizilbash tribal leader Nadir Shah (ruled 1736–1747) and several successors reestablished much of the lost territories of

Shah Abbas I

This description of the greatest Safavid ruler was written by a Carmelite missionary sent by the pope to the shah's court in 1604.

. . . The king, Shah 'Abbâs . . . is sturdy and healthy, accustomed to much exercise and toil: many times he goes about on foot, and recently he had been forty days on pilgrimage, which he made on foot the whole time. He has extraordinary strength, and with his scimitar can cut a man in two and a sheep with its wool on at a single blow—and the Persian sheep are of large size. He has done many other feats and has found no one to come up to him in them. In his food he is frugal, as also in his dress, and this to set an example to his subjects; and so in public he eats little else than rice, and that cooked in water only. . . . But in private he eats what he likes. He is sagacious in mind, likes fame and to be esteemed: he is courteous in dealing with everyone and at the same time very serious. For he will go through the public streets, eat from what they are selling there and other things, speak at ease freely with the lower classes, cause his subjects to remain sitting while he himself is standing, or will sit down beside this man and that. He says that is how to be a king, and that the king of Spain and other Christians do not get any pleasure out of ruling, because

they are obliged to comport themselves with so much pomp and majesty as they do. He causes foreigners to sit down beside him and to eat at his table. With that and accompanying all such condescension he requires that people shall not want in respect towards him and, should anyone fail in this regard, he will punish the individual severely. So the more he demonstrates kindliness to his subjects and the more familiarly he talks with them, they tremble before him, even the greatest among them, for, while joking, he will have their heads cut off. He is very strict in executing justice and pays no regard to his own favourites in this respect; but rather is the stricter with them in order to set an example for others. So he has no private friends, nor anyone who has influence with him. . . .

. . . While we were at his Court, he caused the bellies of two of his favourites to be ripped open, because they had behaved improperly to an ordinary woman. From this it comes about that in his country there are so very few murderers and robbers. In all the time I was at Isfahan, i.e. 4 months, there was never a case of homicide. ❑

From H. G. Chick (comp.), *A Chronicle of the Carmelites in Persia and the Papal Mission of the* 17th *and* 18th *Centuries* (London: Eyre and Spottiswoode, 1939), pp. 155–161, passim; reprinted in W. H. McNeill and M. R. Waldman, *The Islamic World* (New York: Oxford University Press, 1973), pp. 377–378.

Iran. However, Nadir Shah's military ventures, which included an invasion of north India and the conquest of Delhi, sapped the empire. After his autocratic and despotic reign, Iran could not regain stability for another half century.

The lasting legacies of Safavid rule were the firmly Shi'ite character of the whole Iranian region and the Persian culture that was established largely under their patronage in literature, theology, philosophy, painting, and architecture. The Safavid age saw the emergence of a distinctively Shi'ite piety. It focused on a commemoration of the suffering of the *imams* and loyalty to the qualified Shi'ite *ulema*, who (through their knowledge of the Qur'an and the traditions from Muhammad and the *imams*) alone provided guidance in the absence of the hidden *imam* (see Chapter 12).

The Empire of the Indian Timurids, or "Mughals"

Origins

Invaders from the northwest, in the age-old pattern of Indian history, set in motion a new era in the subcontinent: They ended the political fragmentation that had made the Delhi sultanate only one among many Indian states by the early sixteenth century. These invaders were the Chaghatay Turks descended from Timur (Tamerlane) and known to history, not entirely correctly, as the *Mughals* (a Persianate form of *Mongol*). They had originated beyond the Oxus River and ruled in Kabul after being driven out of Transoxiana by the Uzbek Turks. In 1525–1527, the founder of the Mughal dynasty, Babur, marched on India, defeated and replaced the last sultan of Delhi, and then defeated a Rajput confederacy. When he died in 1530, he ruled an empire stretching from the Oxus to Bihar, and the Himalaya to the Deccan. Akbar "the Great" (ruled 1556–1605), however, was the real founder of the Mughal Empire and the greatest ruler of India since Ashoka. Indeed, in an age of great monarchs—such as Elizabeth I, Charles V, and Süleyman the Magnificent— Akbar could vie for the title of "greatest" among all of them.

Akbar's Reign

Akbar would be important only for his conquests, which added all of north India and the northern Deccan to the Mughal dominions. Even more significant, however, were his administrative and economic reforms, his cultural patronage, and his religious tolerance. He completely reorganized the central and provincial governments and rationalized the tax system. His marriages with Rajput princesses and his appointment of Hindus to positions of power did much to ease

Akbar the Great. A contemporary Indian artist's depiction of Akbar overseeing one of his many massive building projects, probably at his new palace and government complex of Fathepur Sikri, near Agra. [Bettmann Archive.]

Muslim–Hindu tensions. So did his cancellation of the poll tax on non-Muslims (1564) and his official moves to negate the power of the more literalist, "hardline" *ulema*. Under his leadership, the Mughal Empire became a truly Indian empire.

Akbar was a religious eclectic who showed not only tolerance to all faiths but also unusual interest in different religious traditions. He frequently brought together representatives of all faiths—Jain and Buddhist monks, Brahmans, *ulema*, Parsis (Zoroastrians), and Jesuits—to discuss matters of religion. These debates took place in a hall built specially for them in Akbar's magnificent palace complex outside the Mughal capital, Agra. Akbar tried to promulgate among his court intimates a new monotheistic creed that subsumed Muslim, Hindu, and other viewpoints. He did not,

Some Reforms of Akbar

Akbar was certainly one of history's great rulers, but some of his fame is surely due to the laudatory quality of the voluminous Persian chronicle of his reign written by Abu'l-Fazl (d. 1602). The often exaggerated praise was, however, a convention of such Persian works. It would not have hidden from its readers Abu'l Fazl's message about the state-craft and significant achievements of his ruler.

One of the glorious boons by His Majesty the Shâhinshâh which shone forth in this auspicious year was the abolition of enslavement. The victorious troops which came into the wide territories of India used in their tyranny to make prisoners of the wives and children and other relatives of the people of India, and used to enjoy them or sell them. His Majesty the Shâhinshâh, out of his thorough recognition of and worship of God, and from his abundant foresight and right thinking gave orders that no soldier of the victorious armies should in any part of his dominions act in this manner. Although a number of savage natures who were ignorant of the world should make their fastnesses a subject of pride and come forth to do battle, and then be defeated by virtue of the emperor's daily increasing empire, still their families must be protected from the onset of the world-conquering armies. No soldier, high or low, was to enslave them, but was to permit them to go freely to their homes and relations. It was for excellent reasons that His Majesty gave his attention to this subject, for although the binding, killing or striking the haughty and the chastising the stiff-necked are part of the struggle for empire—and this is a point about which both sound jurists and innovators are agreed—yet it is outside of the canons of justice to regard the chastisement of women and innocent children as the chastisement of the contumacious. If the husbands have taken the path of insolence, how is it the fault of the wives, and if the fathers have chosen the road of opposition what fault have the children committed? Moreover the wives and innocent children of such factions are not munitions of war! In addition to these sound reasons there was the fact that many covetous and blindhearted persons from vain imaginings or unjust thoughts, or merely out of cupidity attacked villages and estates and plundered them, and when questioned about it said a thousand things and behaved with neglect and indifference. But when final orders were passed for the abolition of this practice, no tribe was afterwards oppressed by wicked persons on suspicion of sedition. As the purposes of the Shâhinshâh were entirely right and just, the blissful result ensued that the wild and rebellious inhabitants of portions of India placed the ring of devotion in the ear of obedience, and became the materials of world-empire. Both was religion set in order, for its essence is the distribution of justice, and things temporal were regulated, for their perfection lies in the obedience of mankind. ❑

From Abul-I-Fazl ibn Mubarak, *The Akbarnämä*, trans. by H. Beveridge (Calcutta: The Asiatic Society, 1905–1939); reprinted in W. H. McNeill and M. R. Waldman, *The Islamic World* (New York: Oxford University Press, 1973), pp. 360–361.

however, try to spread his ideas widely, and they died with him.

The Last Great Mughals

None of Akbar's three successors, Jahangir (1605–1627), Shah Jahan (1628–1658), or Awrangzeb (1658–1707), matched Akbar. The reigns of Jahangir and Shah Jahan were a golden age of Mughal culture, notably in architecture and painting. But economically there was progressive decline under the burdens of new building and military campaigns and erosion of Akbar's administrative and tax reforms. Jahangir set a fateful precedent in permitting English merchants to establish a trading post, or "factory," at Surat on the western coast in Gujarat. He also lost Qandahar to

The pillared hall of the public audience chamber (Divan-i Amm) of Akbar. An elegant example of the red sandstone architecture of Akbar's time. [Wheeler M. Thackston, Jr.]

the Iranian Shah Abbas II (1662) and made few territorial gains anywhere. Shah Jahan was able to conquer the three major successor states of the Bahmanid sultanate of the Deccan (see Chapter 15) and to bring the Deccan wholly under Mughal control. However, his less successful efforts to regain Qandahar and the old Timurid homelands of the Oxus region further strained the Mughal economy. No less a burden on the treasury were his elaborate building projects, the most magnificent of which was the Taj Mahal, the unparalleled tomb that he built for his beloved consort, Mumtaz.

With Shah Jahan, religious toleration also took a noticeable step backward; under his son, Awrangzeb, a narrow religious fanaticism almost completely reversed Akbar's earlier policies. The resulting internal disorder and instability hastened the end of Mughal power in India. Awrangzeb persecuted non-Muslims, destroying Hindu temples, reimposing the poll tax (1679), and wholly alienating the Rajput leaders, whose forbears Akbar had so carefully cultivated. His intransigent policies coincided with the spread of the militant reformism of the Sikh movement throughout the Punjab and the rise of the Hindu Maratha nation in western India.

Sikhs and Marathas

In the late sixteenth and early seventeenth centuries, the Sikhs, who trace their origins to the irenic teachings of Guru Nanak (d. 1538), had developed into a distinctive religious movement. Explicitly neither Muslim nor Hindu, they had their own scripture, ritual, and moralistic, reformist ideals. Angered by their rejection of Islam, Awrangzeb earned the Mughals the lasting enmity of the Sikhs by persecution that culminated in the martyrdom of their ninth leader, or guru,

Teg Bahadur, in 1675. Thereafter, the tenth and last Sikh guru, Gobind Singh (d. 1708), developed the Sikhs into a formidable military force. Awrangzeb and his successors had to contend with repeated Sikh uprisings ever after.

The Hindu Marathas, led by the charismatic Shivaji (d. 1680), rose in religious and nationalistic fervor to found their own regional empire about 1646. On Shivaji's death, the Maratha state stretched down the mountainous western coast and its army was the most disciplined force in India. Despite Awrangzeb's subsequent defeat of the Marathas and his conquest of the entire south of India, the Marathas continued to fight him. After his death, they were able to bring about a confederation of almost all the Deccan states under their leadership. While formally acknowledging Mughal sovereignty, the Marathas actually controlled far more of India after about 1740 than did the Mughals.

Final Decline

In addition to the Rajput, Sikh, and Maratha wars, a number of factors sealed the fate of the once great Mughal empire in the decades following the death of Awrangzeb in 1707. These were the rise in the Deccan of the powerful Islamic state of Hyderabad in 1724; the Persian invasion of north India by Nadir Shah in 1739; the invasions (1748–1761) by the Afghan tribal leader Ahmad Shah Durrani, "founder of modern Afghanistan"; and the British victories over Bengali forces at Plassey in Bengal (1757) and over the French on the southeast coast (1740–1763). By 1819, the dominance of the British East India Company had utterly eclipsed Mughal as it did Maratha and almost all regional Indian power, even though the Mughal line came to an official end only in 1858.

Guru Arjun's Faith

These lines are from the pen of the fifth guru of the Sikh community, Arjun (d. 1606). In them, he repeated the teaching of Kabir, a fifteenth-century Indian saint whose teachings are included with those of Guru Nanak and other religious poets in the Sikh holy scripture, the Adi Granth. This teaching focuses on the error of clinging to a doctrinaire communalist faith, be it that of the Hindus or of the Muslims.

I practice not fasting, nor observe the [month of] Ramazan:
I serve Him who will preserve me at the last hour.
The one Lord of the earth is my God,
Who judgeth both Hindus and Muslims.
I go not on a pilgrimage to Mecca, nor worship at Hindu places of Pilgrimage.
I serve the one God and no other.
I neither worship as the Hindus, nor pray as the Muslims.

I take the Formless God into my heart, and there make obeisance unto Him.
I am neither a Hindu nor a Muslim.
The soul and the body belong to God whether He be called Allāh or Rām.
Kabīr hath delivered this lecture.
When I meet a true guru or pīr, I recognize my own Master. ❑

From Max Arthur Macauliffe, *The Sikh Religion*, 6 vols. (Oxford: Clarendon Press, 1909), p. 422.

The Taj Mahal. Probably the most beautiful tomb in the world, the Taj was built (1631–1653) by Shah Jahan for his beloved wife Mumtaz Mahal on the south bank of the Jamuna River at Agra, the Mughal capital. It remains the jewel of Mughal architecture. [Art Resource.]

Religious Developments

The period from about 1500 to 1650 was one of major importance for religious life in India. Akbar's eclecticism mirrored in many ways the atmosphere of the sixteenth century in India. During that period, a number of religious figures preached a spiritually or mystically oriented piety that transcended the legalism of both the *ulema* and the Brahmans and commonly rejected all caste distinctions. In these ideas, we can see both Muslim Sufi and Hindu *bhakti* influences at work. We mentioned in Chapter 15 two forerunners of such reformers, Ramananda and Kabir. Guru Nanak, the spiritual father of the Sikh movement, took up Kabir's ideas and preached faith and devotion to one loving and merciful God. He opposed narrow alle-

The prayer-court of the Badshahi Mosque in Lahore (present-day Pakistan). Built by Awrangzeb in 1637, this great congregational mosque still serves as a major site of worship, especially during the two great Muslim feasts— that which ends the annual month of fasting and that which accompanies the yearly pilgrimage rites in Mecca. [UPI.]

giance to particular creeds or rites and taking pride in external religious observance. Nanak's hymns of praise contain both Hindu and Muslim ideas and imagery. Dadu (d. 1603), the father of the modern Dadu Panth, preached a similar message. He was born a Muslim but, like Kabir and Nanak, strove to get people to go beyond either Muslim or Hindu allegiance to a more spiritual love and service of God.

On the Hindu side, there was an upsurge of *bhakti* devotionalism that amounted to a Hindu revival. It was epitomized by the Bengali Krishna devotee Chaitanya (d. CA. 1533), who stressed total devotion to Lord Krishna. The forebears of today's Hare Krishna devotees, his followers spread widely his ecstatic public praise of God and his message of the equality of all in God's sight. The other major figure in Hindu devotionalism in this era was Tulasidas (d. 1623), whose Hindi retelling of the story of the Sanskrit *Ramayana* remains among the most popular works of Indian literature. Tulasidas used the story of Rama's adventures to present *bhakti* ideas that remain as alive in everyday Hindu life today as do his verses.

Muslim eclectic tendencies came primarily from the Sufis. By 1500, numerous Sufi retreat centers had been established in diverse parts of India. The Chishtiya Sufi order especially had already won many converts to Islam. The Sufis' enthusiastic forms of worship and their inclination to play down the externals of religion proved particularly congenial to Indian sensibilities. The Sufis were, however, often decried and opposed by the more puritanical of the *ulema*, many of whom held powerful positions as royal advisers and judges responsible for upholding the religious law. Akbar made every effort to keep puritan bigotry among the *ulema* in check. He finally named himself the supreme spiritual authority in the empire, secured *ulema* sanc-

INDIA	
	The Mughal Empire
1525–1527	Rule of Babur, founder
1556–1605	Rule of Akbar "the Great"
1605–1627	Rule of Jahangir
1628–1658	Rule of Shah Jahan, builder of the Taj Mahal
1658–1707	Rule of Awrangzeb
	Sikhs and Marathas
1538	Death of Guru Nanak, founder of Sikh religious tradition
1708	Death of tenth and last Sikh guru, Gobind Singh
1646	Founding of Maratha Empire
1680	Death of Maratha leader, Shivaji
1724	Rise of Hyderabad state

tion of this action, and then ordered that toleration be the law of the land.

After Akbar's death, the inevitable reaction set in. It was summed up in the work of the Indian leader of the central Asian Sufi order of the Naqshbandiya, Ahmad Sirhindi (d. 1624). He sought to purge Sufism of its extreme tendencies and of all popular practices not sanctioned by the schools of law. He crusaded against any practices that smacked of Hindu influence and also against tolerant treatment of the Hindus themselves. His spirit, unfortunately, eventually won the day, especially under the harsh, reactionary policies of Awrangzeb. The many possibilities for Hindu–Muslim rapprochement that had emerged in Akbar's time now vanished.

ISLAMIC ASIA

Central Asia: Islamization and Isolation

The solid footing of Islam in central Asia can be traced to the post-Timur era of the fifteenth century. Even in the preceding century, as the peoples of western central Asia had begun to shift from nomadic to settled existence, the familiar pattern of Islamic diffusion from trading and urban centers to the land had set in. Islamization by Sunni Sufis, traders, and tribal rulers went on apace thereafter, even as far as western China and Mongolia. It was slowed in the late sixteenth century by the conversion of the tribes of Mongolia proper to the Buddhism of the Tibetan lamas.

Thus, in the period after 1500, the Safavid Shi'ite realm was bounded by Sunni states in India, Afghanistan, Anatolia, Mesopotamia, Transoxiana, and western Turkestan (Khwarizm, the region between the Aral and Caspian seas). In these last two areas, the most important states were those founded by Uzbek and Chaghatay Turks, both of whom were ruled by Muslim descendants of Genghis Khan.

The Uzbeks and Chaghatays

In the fifteenth century, Timur's heirs had ruled Transoxiana and most of Iran (see Chapter 15). To the north, above the Jaxartes River (Syr Darya) and the Aral Sea, a new steppe khanate had been formed by

A lone worshipper turns toward Mecca alongside one of the many domed tombs built by Timur and his successors across Turkestan. The building of separate tomb buildings throughout the eastern Islamic lands goes back to the Seljuks. [Bettmann Archive.]

the unification in 1428 of assorted clans of Turks and Mongols known as the Uzbeks. In time, an Uzbek leader who was descended from Genghis Khan—Muhammad Shaybani (d. 1510)—invaded Transoxiana (1495–1500). There he founded a new Uzbek (or Shaybanid) Islamic empire that replaced Timurid rule. Soon after, he confirmed the Uzbek hold on the region by defeating the Chaghatay Timurid prince Babur when the latter tried to take Transoxiana for himself. (This defeat drove Babur south to rule in Kabul and thus led indirectly to his founding Timurid Mughal rule in Delhi, as described earlier.) Muhammad's line continued Uzbek rule in Transoxiana at Bukhara into the eighteenth century, while another Uzbek line broke away and ruled the independent

khanate of Khiva in western Turkestan from 1512 to 1872.

Of the other central Asian Islamic states after 1500, the most significant was that of the Chaghatay Turks in the Tarim basin area. The Chaghatays had been the successors of Genghis Khan in the whole region from the Aral Sea and the Oxus River to Yuan China. After 1350, internal anarchy and Timur had broken up their khanate. From about 1514, a revived Chaghatay state flourished in eastern Turkestan—the Tarim basin and the territory north of it, between Tashkent in the west and the Turfan oasis in the east. Although the Chaghatay rulers lasted until 1678 in one part of the Tarim basin, their real power was lost after about 1555 to various Khoja princes. These princes were Sunni zealots who claimed to be *Sharifs* (descendants of the Prophet); they gained a substantial following in their efforts to spread Islam and Muslim rule. They were *ghazi* warriors much like the early Ottomans in Anatolia or the Almoravids of North Africa and Spain. Some of them were popularly ascribed miraculous powers and venerated posthumously as local saints.

Consequences of the Shi'ite Rift

On the face of it, the Ottoman, Mughal, Safavid, and central Asian Islamic states had much in common. All were Muslim in faith and culture; all shared similar systems of taxation and law; in all four regions, the common language of cultured Muslims was Persian; and in all four areas, Turkish rulers were predominant. Yet the deep religious division between the Shi'ite Safavids and all their Sunni neighbors proved stronger than what they shared. The result was a serious geographical division that isolated central Asian Muslims in particular.

Shi'ite–Sunni political competition was sharpened by Safavid militancy, to which the Sunni states responded in kind. Attempts to form alliances with non-Muslim states, previously unheard of in the Islamic world, became a commonplace of Shi'ite political strategy. The Sunnis also resorted to such tactics; the Ottomans, for example, made common cause with Protestants against their Catholic Habsburg enemies. Although trade went on in spite of the political situation, the international flow of Islamic commerce was hurt by the presence of a militant Shi'ite state astride the major overland trade routes of the larger Islamic world.

The Safavid Shi'ite schism also ruptured the shared cultural traditions of the "abode of Islam." This rupture is especially reflected in the fate of Persian literary culture. Because of its ever stronger association with Shi'ite religious ideas after the rise of the Safavids, Persian made little progress as a potential *lingua franca* (common tongue) alongside—let alone above—Arabic in Sunni lands. Outside Iran, it was destined to

Bukhara. A modern view of the remains of the madrassa first built in the early fifteenth century by Shahrukh's son Ulug Beg and later restored by the Uzbeks in the late sixteenth century. The Arg, or citadel of Bukhara, is visible in the right background. Islamic religious schools may go back to the eleventh century in Bukhara; some think that Bukhara may even be the original home of the madrassa institution. [Bettmann Archive.]

Two wandering dervishes of Central Asia, from a nineteenth-century European engraving. Sufis such as these two were always recognizable by their patched cloaks. The patches were collected from spiritual masters, or pirs, under whom such Sufis studied the mystical path.

remain only a language of high culture and bureaucracy. In India, Urdu became the common Muslim idiom, and in Ottoman and central Asian lands, one or another Turkic tongue was spoken in everyday life. The Persian classics continued to inspire Persian learning among educated Sunnis everywhere, but the later, Safavid Persian literature was largely ignored.

Central Asia was ultimately the Islamic region most decisively affected by the Shi'ite presence in Iran. Combined with the growing pressure of Christian Russian power from the west, the militant Shi'ism of Iran worked to isolate central Asia from the rest of the Muslim world. Political and economic relations with other Islamic lands became increasingly difficult after 1500, as did religious and cultural interchange. However healthy Islam remained in this region, its contact with the original Islamic heartlands (and even with India) shrank. Contact now came primarily through small numbers of pilgrims, members of Sufi orders, *ulema*, and students. Occasionally, traders traversed the Shi'ite empire or the natural barriers that separated central Asian Sunnis from Ottoman or Mughal

CENTRAL ASIA

1428–CA. 1750	Uzbek state in Bukhara
1514–1678	Revived Chaghatay state in eastern Turkestan

Sunnis. Thus the world of central Asian Islam developed in considerable isolation, destined to be a large but peripheral area to the Islamic mainstream community.

Power Shifts in the Southern Seas

Control of the Southern Seas

The Portuguese arrived on the East African coast in 1498 (see Chapter 17). In the following three centuries, the history of the lands along the trade routes of the southern Asian seas was bound up closely not only with Islam but also with the rising power of Christian Western Europe. The key attraction for outside powers in these diverse lands was their commercial and strategic potential. Because neither geography nor history produced the conditions necessary for the rise of a major power in the southern seas, outside maritime domination was the one identifiable pattern there.

In the sixteenth century, the Europeans began to compete with and to displace by armed force the Muslims who, by 1500, had come to dominate the maritime southern rim of Asia. The keys to European success were the national support systems for their naval and commercial ventures and, at least for a time, their superior warships. Nowhere was this more evident than along the west coast of India. Here the Portuguese managed to carve out a major power base in the early years of the sixteenth century at the expense of the Muslim traders and sailors who dominated the India maritime scene. They did so by force of superior naval power, cunning exploitation of indigenous rivalries, and brutal terrorization of all who opposed their objectives.

However, in the southern seas trade centers, Islamization continued apace, even in the face of Christian proselytizing and growing European political and commercial dominance. The Muslims, unlike the European Christians, never kept aloof from the native populations and were largely assimilated everywhere. They rarely abandoned their faith, which proved generally attractive to new peoples they encountered. The result was usually an Islamicized and racially mixed population. European gunboat imperialism had considerable military and economic success, often at the expense of Islamic states. However, European culture and Christian missionary work made remarkably little headway in areas where Islam had first gotten a foothold. From East Africa to the Pacific, all along the trade routes, only in the northern Philippines did a substantial population become largely Christian.

The Indies: Acheh

As we have seen, the history of the Indonesian archipelago has always revolved around the international demand for its spices, peppers, and other produce. By the fifteenth century, the coastal Islamic states were centered on the trading ports of the Malaysian peninsula, the north shores of Sumatra and Java, and in the Moluccas, or "Spice Islands." The last great Hindu kingdom of inland Java was defeated by an Islamic coalition of states in the early 1500s. Several substantial Islamic sultanates arose in the sixteenth and seventeenth centuries, even as Europeans were carving out an economic empire in the region. The most powerful and extensive of these Islamic states was that of Acheh, on northwestern Sumatra (CA. 1524–1910).

In the early years of its existence, Acheh provided the only counterweight to the Portuguese presence across the straits in Malacca (Malaysia). Although the Acheh sultans were never able to drive the better-armed invaders out, neither could the Portuguese subdue them. In the fight with the Portuguese, Acheh called for and received at least token help from the Ottomans in the form of artillery and some logistical support. This reflected the Ottomans' awareness of the Portuguese (and European) threat in the southern

---

THE SOUTHERN SEAS

	Arrival of the Portuguese
1498	The Portuguese (under Vasco da Gama) come to the East African coast and to the west coast of India
1500–1512	The Portuguese establish bases on west Indian coast (Cochin, Goa), replace Muslims as Indian Ocean power, and conquer Malacca (on Malaysian coast)
	Indonesian Archipelago
early 1500s	Muslim sultanates replace Hindu states in Java, Sumatra
1524–1910	State of Acheh in northwest Sumatra
1873–1910	War between Holland and Acheh
1600s	Major increase in Islamization and connected spread of Malay language in the archipelago
1641	Dutch conquest of Malacca
CA. 1800	Dutch replace Muslim states as main archipelago power
	East Africa
1698	Omani forces take Mombasa, oust Portuguese from East Africa north of the port of Mozambique
1741–1856	Long-lived united sultanate of Oman and Zanzibar

A late-sixteenth-century German engraving showing the marketplace at Goa, India. Goa was occupied by the Portuguese in 1510 and remained under Portuguese rule until 1962. [Bettmann Archive.]

seas. Despite Portuguese control of Indies commerce, Acheh managed to dominate the pepper trade of Sumatra and to thrive to the end of the sixteenth century. At its height, in the first half of the seventeenth century, the sultanate controlled both coasts of Sumatra and substantial parts of the Malay peninsula. Meanwhile, also in the seventeenth century, the Dutch replaced the Portuguese in the business of milking the Indies of their wealth, and by the eighteenth, they were doing it just as ruthlessly and more efficiently. In the early twentieth century, the Dutch finally won full control in the region, but after nearly forty years of intermittent war with Acheh (1873–1910).

East Africa: The Omanis of Zanzibar

At the other end of the southern trade route, in east Africa, the Islamic commercial monopoly was disrupted even more severely by the arrival of the Portuguese. There, as everywhere, the latter saw the "Moors" as their implacable enemies. Many Portuguese viewed colonial conquests not only as commercial wars but also as crusades. The initial Portuguese

A Portuguese Treaty with a Defeated African King

Resistance to the Portuguese depredations along the East African coast gave the Portuguese an excuse to march with African mercenaries on the inland kingdom of the ruler, or monomotapa, *Manura, in 1628–1629. After his defeat, he was forced to convert to Christianity and to sign a new treaty with the Portuguese, from which the following excerpts are taken.*

First that this kingdom is delivered to him [i.e., to Manura] in the name of the king of Portugal, our lord, of whom he shall acknowledge himself to be a vassal. . . .

That he, the said king, shall allow all the religious of whatever order who may be in his *zimbahe* to build churches and in all the other lands in his dominions. . . .

That ambassadors who come to speak to him shall enter his *zimbahe* shod and covered, with their arms in their belts, as they speak to the king of Portugal, and he shall give them a chair on which to seat themselves without clapping their hands; and other Portuguese shall speak to him in the manner of ambassadors, and shall be given a *kaross* to sit upon. . . .

He shall make his lands free to the Portuguese. . . .

Throughout all his kingdom he shall allow as many mines to be sought for and opened as the Portuguese like. . . .

Within a year he shall expel all the Moors [i.e., Swahili and Arab traders from the coastal towns] from his kingdom, and those who shall be found there afterward shall be killed by the Portuguese, and their property shall be seized for the king of Portugal. . . . ❑

From G. M. Theal, *Records of South-eastern Africa* (1900), Vol. 5, p. 290; reprinted in Basil Davidson, *The African Past* (New York: Grosset and Dunlap, The Universal Library, 1967), pp. 164–166.

Slave dealing in the streets of Zanzibar. Slaving was part of East African trade for centuries. [Bettmann Archive.]

victories led to the submission of many small Islamic coastal states. However, there was no concerted effort to spread Christianity beyond the fortified settlements established in places like Sofala, Zanzibar, Mozambique, and Mombasa. Thus, the cultural and religious consequences of the Portuguese presence were slight.

What the Portuguese did bring to the east coast was widespread economic decline. When the Africans inland refused to cooperate with them, the formerly heavy gold trade up the Zambezi from Sofala dried up. The Portuguese militant presence sharply reduced Muslim coastal shipping from India and Arabia. Ottoman efforts in the late sixteenth century failed to defeat the Portuguese. But after 1660, the strong eastern Arabian state of Oman raided the African coast with impunity and, in 1698, took Mombasa and ejected the Portuguese everywhere north of Mozambique.

Oman's African power was centered in Zanzibar.

Its control of the ivory and slave trade along the coast seems to have fueled a substantial recovery of east coast prosperity by the later eighteenth century. Zanzibar itself benefited from the introduction of clove cultivation from Mauritius in the 1830s. Cloves became its staple export thereafter. (The clove plantations would come to be the basis of a new, devastating slave trade interior to East Africa, which flourished into the late nineteenth century even as the external trade was crushed.) Omani domination of the east coast continued with some lapses until 1856. Thereafter, Zanzibar and its holdings on the coast became independent under a separate branch of the ruling family in Oman. Zanzibar passed eventually to the British when they, the Germans, and the Italians divided up East Africa in the late 1880s. Still, the Arab and Islamic imprint on the whole coast has survived down to the present.

AFRICA

In the sixteenth, seventeenth, and eighteenth centuries, east Africa was not the only region of Africa affected by the major changes occurring in the Islamic and European Christian worlds. If many parts of the continent continued to be little influenced by outsiders or their affairs, many others could not escape the repercussions of new developments in the Islamic and European-American worlds—and the changing power balance between them.

Along the southern shores of the Mediterranean, the key new factor was the Ottoman Turks' imperial expansion into Egypt and North Africa. In the sub-Saharan Sudanic lands, the attraction of Islam as a religious and social ideology was still growing, especially among ruling elites. Islamic influences from North Africa and the Middle East and also Muslim conversion played increasing social and political roles in Sudanic regions east and west. The Islamic tradition

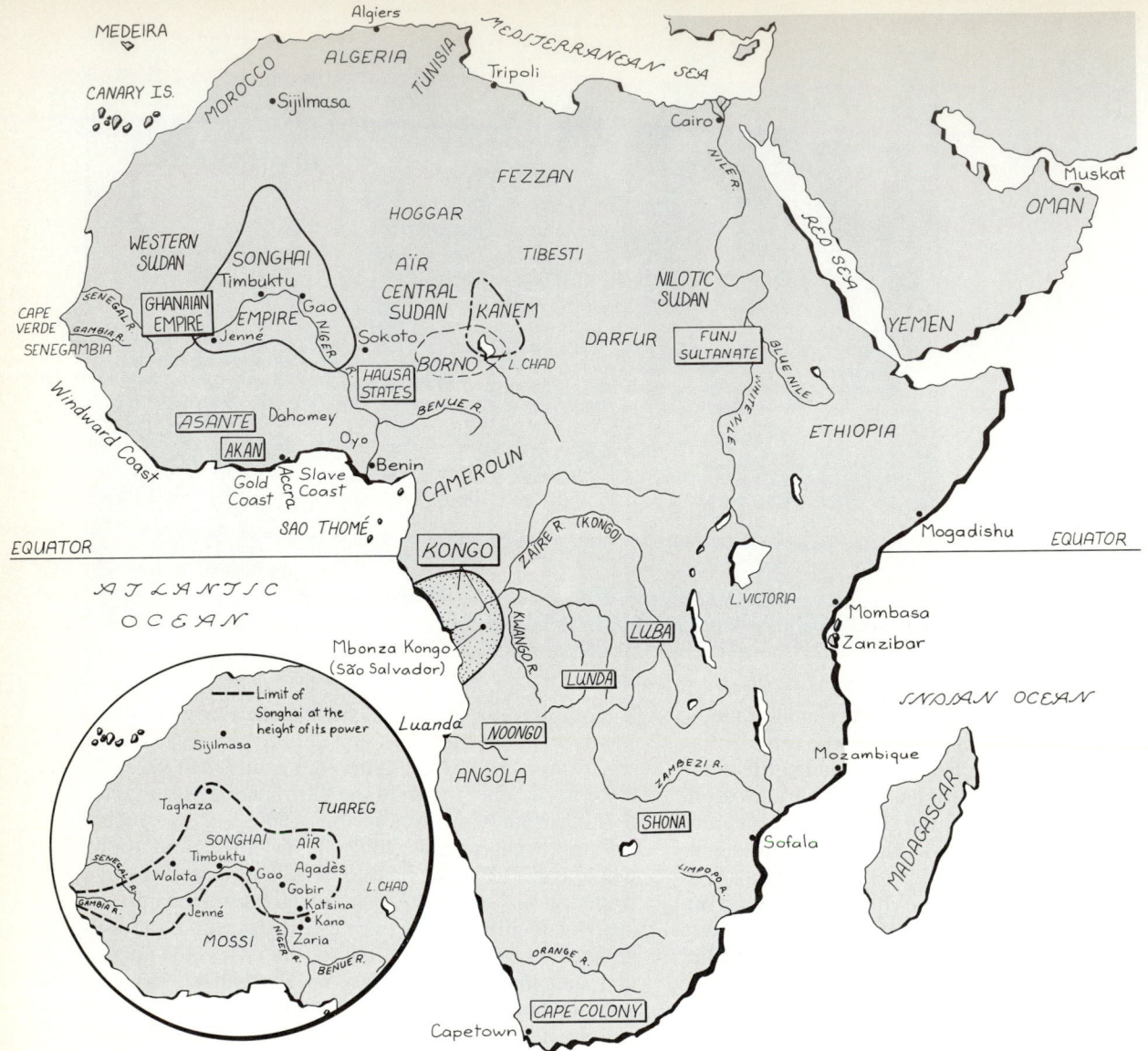

MAP 22-2 AFRICA *Important towns, regions, peoples, and states after* CA. 1500. *The inset shows empire of the Songhai at its largest extent.*

provided a common thread of experience and a shared arena of expression for very diverse groups in societies spread over a vast area from Egypt to Senegambia. The masses of Africans from the Sahara south clung largely to their older traditions. Only in central and southern Africa and in the West African forests was the Islamic presence missing as a visible agent of change.

Along the Atlantic and Indian-Ocean coasts of Africa, the key new development was the intrusion of the newly potent nations of Christian Europe. This intrusion appeared in the form of, first, the Portuguese, and

then of the Dutch and other Europeans, who came by sea in search of commerce and eventually global spheres of influence. If the European voyages of discovery of the fifteenth and sixteenth centuries proved to be portentous for world historical developments generally, they were especially so for African affairs. These voyages presaged African involvement in an expanding global trading system dominated by Europeans. It was to be a system that in general exploited rather than profited African development, as the infamous Atlantic slave trade and the South African experience indicate most vividly.

North Africa and Egypt

A feisty regionalism continued to be characteristic of the lands north of the Sahara and along the lower Nile. Still, from the sixteenth century on, all these areas felt the pressure of Ottoman and European naval rivalry in the Mediterranean. Morocco was the only fully independent North African sultanate. It was ruled by a long series of *Sharifs* (leaders claiming descent from Muhammad's family). The most important *Sharifian* dynasties were the Sa'dids (1554–1659). At least one major reason for their success as a separate state was the impetus for Arab and Berber unity provided by the new marauding and crusading spirit of the Portuguese and Spanish. No single power in North Africa—Christian or Islamic—proved capable of long controlling the states, city-states, and tribal groups of the re-gion. Even the nominally Ottoman domains from Egypt to Algeria were effectively independent by 1800.

In the seventeenth and eighteenth centuries, Istanbul's direct rule of Egypt had already passed to Egyptian governors descended from the former ruling Mamluks. Even though very weak in the eighteenth century, they survived until the rise of Muhammad Ali in the wake of the French invasion of 1800 (see Chapter 31). The Mediterranean coastlands between Egypt and Morocco were officially Ottoman provinces, or regencies, whether under local governors or Ottoman military deputies drawn from Janissary ranks. Nevertheless, by the eighteenth century, the Regency of Algiers to the east of Morocco was a separate, locally run principality existing primarily on piracy. The Regency of Tripoli was in the hands of a family of hereditary, effectively independent rulers. In Tunisia, a Janis-

Muslim Reform in Songhai

Around 1500, Askia Muhammad al-Turi, the first Muslim among the rulers of Songhai, wrote to the North African Muslim theologian Muhammad al-Maghili (d. 1504) with a series of questions about proper Muslim practices. The excerpts are from the seventh question of al-Turi and the answers given by al-Maghili.

FROM AL-TURI'S SEVENTH QUESTION:
Among the people [of the Songhay Empire, said Askia Muhammad], there are some who claim knowledge of the supernatural through sand divining and the like, or through the disposition of the stars . . . [while] some assert that they can write (talismans) to bring good fortune . . . or to ward off bad fortune. . . . Some defraud in weights and measures. . . .

One of their evil practices [continued Askia Muhammad] is the free mixing of men and women in the markets and streets and the failure of women to veil themselves . . . [while] among the people of Djenné it is an established custom for a girl not to cover any part of her body as long as she remains a virgin . . . and all the most beautiful girls walk about naked among people. . . .

So give us legal ruling concerning these people and their ilk, and may God Most High reward you!

FROM AL-MAGHILI'S ANSWER:
The answer—and God it is who directs to the right course—is that everything you have mentioned concerning people's behavior in some parts of this country is gross error. It is the bounden duty of the commander of the Muslims and all other believers who have the power [replied al-Maghili] to change every one of these evil practices.

As for any who claims knowledge of the supernatu-ral in the ways you have mentioned . . . he is a liar and an unbeliever. . . . Such people must be forced to renounce it by the sword. Then whoever renounces such deeds should be left in peace, but whoever persists should be killed with the sword as an unbeliever; his body should not be washed or shrouded, and he should not be buried in a Muslim graveyard. . . .

As for defrauding in weights and measures [continued al-Maghili] it is forbidden (*haram*) according to the Qur'an, the Sunna and the concensus of opinion of the learned men of the Muslim community. It is the bounden duty of the commander of the Muslims to appoint a trustworthy man in charge of the markets, and to safeguard people's means of subsistence. He should standardize all the scales in each province. . . . Similarly, all measures both large and small must be recti-fied so that they conform to a uniform standard. . . .

Now, what you mentioned about the free mixing of men and women and leaving the pudenda uncovered is one of the greatest abominations. The commander of the Muslims must exert himself to prevent all these things. . . . He should appoint trustworthy men to watch over this by day and night, in secret and in the open. This is not to be considered as spying on the Muslims; it is only a way of caring for them and curb-ing evildoers, especially when corruption becomes widespread in the land as it has done in Timbuktu and Djenné and so on. ❑

Translated by J. O. Hunwick (1963); reprinted in Basil Davidson, *The African Past* (New York: Grosset and Dunlap, The Universal Library, 1967), pp. 86–88.

sary state operated with virtual independence of its nominal Ottoman overlords.

The Sudan

The Songhai Empire

On the other side of the Sahara, a new Songhai empire dominated the political history of the western Sudan from the end of the fifteenth century until its downfall before the Sa'did Moroccans a hundred years later. The Songhai state in its early years was arguably the most powerful state in Africa. We saw earlier (Chapter 15) that a Songhai monarchy centered at Gao near the great bend of the Niger had flourished from as early as the eleventh century. Conquered in 1325 by Mansa Musa of Mali, the Songhai peoples had thrown off their Mali overlords in 1375. About a century later, they reemerged in a powerful state organized under the capable rule and military leadership of first Sonni Ali (ruled 1464–1492) and then Askia Muhammad al-Turi (or "Toure," from the French spelling; ruled 1493–1528). These leaders took Timbuktu from the Tuareg Berbers and built an empire that stretched westward nearly to the Atlantic, northwest into the Sahara, and east into the central Sudan. Taking advantage of their control of access to the gold and other desirable commodities of west Africa, they emulated their Ghanaian predecessors in cultivating and expanding the ancient caravan trade across the Sahara to the North African coasts of Libya and Tunisia. This provided their major source of wealth.

Although Sonni Ali still held to the traditional African religious practices and faith of his people, Muhammad al-Turi was a Muslim. Indeed, he came of the same Mande stock that had founded the Islamic empire of Mali, which he used as his model for building up the Songhai state. In Muhammad's reign, Muslim scholars from the Arab world came in substantial numbers to the Songhai cities of Gao, Timbuktu, and Jenne. He also replaced native Songhais with Arab Muslim immigrants as government officials in an apparently successful effort to strengthen his centralized power. Taking his Islam seriously, Muhammad made a triumphal pilgrimage to Mecca much like Mansa Musa before him. At Mecca, he was hailed as "Caliph of the western Sahara." Nevertheless, in the end his reforms were not sufficient to Islamize the various peoples of the empire or to ensure a strong central state under less able successors after his death.

In 1591, a motley but well-armed military force sent by the Sa'dids of Morocco used superior gunpowder weapons and internal divisions in the empire to defeat the Songhai. However, the Moroccans failed to profit from the formerly Songhai-controlled gold trade as they had hoped. Their victory destroyed the stability of the region on which regular trade and Songhai prosperity had been largely based. Consequently, the Songhai Empire was destroyed, and their state was reduced to its original holdings in the Niger valley, only one among many competitors.

Kanem-Bornu and Hausaland

With the loss of the strong central Songhai state, trade as well as political security in the western Sudan fell off. Power shifted eastward to the central Sudan. Here another great Islamic state arose in the Kanem and Bornu regions around Lake Chad. We saw in Chapter 15 that a Kanuri state of Kanem-Bornu had been in existence and that some of its peoples had been Muslim since at least the early twelfth century. It had also long been a major conduit for West African trans-Saharan trade with Egypt and the Libyan coast (Tripoli).

After the state had expanded to include Bornu and then had been reduced to rule only in Bornu, acquisition of firearms and Turkish military instructors near the end of the sixteenth century enabled Idris Alawma (ruled CA. 1575–1610) to form a renewed union of Kanem and Bornu. He set up the most fully Islamic state yet in West Africa and extended his rule even into Hausa territory to the west. Basing its prosperity on the trans-Saharan trade, his regional empire survived nearly a century. It was finally broken up by a long famine, repeated Tuareg attacks, lack of strong leadership, and loss of trade control to smaller, better organized Hausa states. The ruling dynasty held out until 1846. But by the end of the seventeenth century, its power had been sharply reduced by the growing Hausa states to the west. (The Hausa states of what is now northern Nigeria had first become important in the late fifteenth century. Their real power was to come only in the nineteenth century with their unification into several Islamic states under the Fulbe ("Fulani") sultanate of Sokoto. (See Chapter 31.)

The Eastern Sudan and Ethiopia

The often embattled Abyssinian state continued to survive after 1500 as a Christian enclave in the Ethiopian highlands, despite inroads made on its southern flanks by Somali and other Muslim groups. To the north and west, Islam spread in the upper Nile region throughout the territory of modern Sudan. The Islamization of this Nilotic eastern region was carried out by Muslim religious figures, often trained in Cairo, who combined Sufi teachings with the legal training and expertise of the ulema. Their work went on under the long-lived Funj sultanate that replaced the Alwa state (see Chapter 15). It flourished in the region between the Blue and White Niles and to the north along the main Nile from just after 1500 until 1762. The Funj were originally cattle nomads who apparently adopted

Western Sudan	
1374	Songhai state set up in Gao after throwing off Malian rule
1464–1591	Songhai empire
1464–1492	Reign of Sonni Ali
1493–1528	Reign of Askia Muhammad al-Turi
Central Sudan	
1575–1846	Kanem-Bornu state
1575–1619	Reign of Idris Alawma, major architect of Islamic state of Kanem-Bornu
Eastern Sudan	
CA. 1500–1762	Sultanate of the Funj between Blue and White Nile

Islam in the first decades after setting up their settled kingdom. In the course of the late sixteenth and the seventeenth centuries, with the influx of Arabic-speaking Nubians from the north, the Funj developed an Islamic society whose Arabized character was unique in sub-Saharan Africa. A much reduced Funj state held out until an Ottoman–Egyptian invasion in 1821.

West Africa

Along the coasts of West and Central Africa, many changes portentous for African history as a whole occurred between 1500 and 1800. Those wrought by the burgeoning Atlantic trade in slaves are the most famous. Of comparable African internal importance are those changes connected with the west African gold and other commodities and the importation and spread in west and central Africa of food crops such as maize, peanuts, squash, sweet potatoes, cocoa, and cassava (manioc) from the Americas. In general, the gradual involvement of these and other regions of Africa in the emerging global economic system were the key developments that laid the groundwork for the eventual colonial domination of Africa by the Europeans. For our purposes, two brief examples must suffice.

Senegambia

In West Africa, Senegambia was one of the earliest regions affected by European trade. This region takes its name from its major rivers, the Gambia and Senegal. Its inland regions had long been involved, especially in the heydays of the empires of Ghana and Mali,

in the trans-Saharan trade. This had meant important contact with Islamic states and culture. With the coming of the European maritime powers, Senegambia's involvement in the new Atlantic trade, as in the older desert trade, was primarily in gold and in goods such as salt, cotton goods, hides, and copper. The Wolof and other Senegambian states also provided slaves to the coast for European purchase: of all African slaves exported in the sixteenth century, as much as a third came from Senegambia. Thereafter, however, other trade increasingly accompanied slaving.

Despite continuing to supply similar levels of slaves for export, this region was eclipsed in slaving importance by the huge numbers of slaves exported from the rest of West Africa, from the Windward Coast east to Cameroon. Over time, Portuguese-African mulattos and the British came to control the Gambia river trade, while the French won the Senegal river markets.

The Gold Coast

Of all the West African coastal districts, the one most affected by the arrival of international maritime trade was that known as the Gold Coast. The name derives from its rise to importance in this period as the outlet region for the newer west African gold fields of Akan. Here, beginning with the Portuguese at Elmina in 1481, but primarily after 1600, European states and companies built numerous coastal forts to protect their trade from each other's and pirates' raids and to serve as depots for inland goods. The gold, kola-nuts, and other coastal trade seems to have stimulated the formation of larger states, as larger units could better handle and control the overland commerce. The growth of Akan forest states near the coast and the Gonja state just north of the forest provide instances of this.

The intensive contact of the Gold Coast with Europeans also led to the importation and spread of American crops, notably maize and cassava, into the tropical forests of this region. The success of these crops here as elsewhere in west and central Africa brought change. It likely contributed to substantial population growth in the sixteenth and seventeenth centuries, especially in the Akan region. The Gold Coast escaped the ravages of the slave trade for some decades; it was even an importer of slaves until long after 1500. However, slaves finally came to be big business in the late seventeenth century, especially in the Accra region.

Central Africa

Prior to 1500, the vast central area of the subcontinent had been largely cut off from international trade and contact by its own geographical barriers: There were

Affonso I of Kongo Writes to the King of Portugal

Affonso, the Christian African king of Kongo, wrote a number of letters to the Portuguese monarch about the Portuguese presence in his dominions. The one reproduced here was written in 1526. It complains of the effects of slaving on the Kongo people and economy.

Sir, Your Highness [of Portugal] should know how our Kingdom is being lost in so many ways that it is convenient to provide for the necessary remedy, since this is caused by the excessive freedom given by your factors and officials to the men and merchants who are allowed to come to this Kingdom to set up shops with goods and many things which have been prohibited by us, and which they spread throughout our Kingdoms and Domains in such an abundance that many of our vassals, whom we had in obedience, do not comply because they have the things in greater abundance than we ourselves; and it was with these things that we had them content and subjected under our vassalage and jurisdiction, so it is doing a great harm not only to the service of God, but the security and peace of our Kingdoms and State as well.

And we cannot reckon how great the damage is, since the mentioned merchants are taking every day our natives, sons of the land and the sons of our noblemen and vassals and our relatives, because the thieves and men of bad conscience grab them wishing to have the things and wares of this Kingdom which they are ambitious of; they grab them and get them to be sold; and so great, Sir, is the corruption and licentiousness that our country is being completely depopulated, and Your Highness should not agree with this nor accept it as in your service. And to avoid it we need from those [your] Kingdoms no more than some priests and a few people to teach in schools, and no other goods except wine and flour for the holy sacrament. That is why we beg of Your Highness to help and assist us in this matter, commanding your factors that they should not send here either merchants or wares, because it is *our will that in these Kingdoms there should not be any trade of slaves nor outlet for them.** Concerning what is referred above, again we beg of Your Highness to agree with it, since otherwise we cannot remedy such an obvious damage. Pray Our Lord in His mercy to have Your Highness under His guard and let you do for ever the things of His service. I kiss your hands many times. . . . ❑

*Emphasis in the original.

Basil Davidson, *The African Past* (New York: Grosset and Dunlap, 1967), pp. 191–193.

swamps in the north, coastal rainforests to the west, highlands to the east, and deserts in the south. Regional interaction in movements of peoples and in trade and culture had been the norm. Peoples such as the Lunda and Luba, on the southern savannah below the tropical rainforest, were able to carve out sizable kingdoms by about the fifteenth century, and they expanded their control over neighboring areas into the eighteenth century.

The coming of the Portuguese and their maritime trade to the western coastal regions began to change the regional isolation of the Central African lands, albeit only very slowly. The Portuguese came looking for a new source of gold and silver, but found none. Instead, they exported such goods as ivory and palm cloth. Ultimately, their main business came to be exporting human beings for foreign slavery. These slaves were taken first for gang labor to the Portuguese sugar plantation venture on São Thomé island in the Gulf of Guinea. Then, in vast numbers, people were sent as slaves to perform similar plantation labor in Brazil. In the 1640s, the Dutch briefly succeeded the Portuguese as the major suppliers of African slaves to English and French plantations in the Caribbean. Until then, however, the Portuguese were the European presence in central Africa.

The Kongo Kingdom

The major African state with which the Portuguese dealt after coming to Central Africa in 1483 was that of Kongo. Dating from probably the fourteenth century, the Kongo kingdom was located on a fertile, well-watered plateau in the region south of the lower Zaire river valley between the coast and the Kwango river in the east. Here, astride the border between forest and grassland, the Kongo kings had built up a central government based on a pyramid structure of tax or tribute collection balanced by rewards given to those who were faithful in paying their taxes. Kongo society was dominated by the king, whose authority was tied to acceptance of him as a kind of spiritual spokesman of the gods or ancestors. By 1600, the Kongo state was half the size of England and alongside farming boasted a rather high state of craft specialization in weaving and pottery, salt production, fishing, and metal-working.

The Portuguese brought Mediterranean goods, pre-eminently luxury textiles from North Africa, to use in the Kongo tribute-reward system and to trade for African goods. Amidst the rather hard agrarian life of most of the Kongo peoples, such luxury goods helped raise the prestige and wealth of the ruler and his elites. However, because the greatest central African resource turned out to be its peoples, rather than gold or minerals, slaves became the central form of export commodity that could be used for obtaining foreign luxury goods. Meanwhile, imports such as fine clothing, tobacco, and alcohol did nothing to replace the labor pool lost to slavery.

At first, the Portuguese put time and effort into education and Christian proselytizing, but later the need for more slaves led to a focus upon exploiting the human resources of Central Africa. Regional rulers sought to procure slaves from neighboring kingdoms, as did Portuguese traders who went inland themselves. As the demand grew, more and more local rulers used attacks on neighboring groups to garner slaves for the Portuguese traders.

The Kongo ruler Affonso I (reigned CA. 1506–1543), a convinced Christian convert, began by welcoming Jesuit missionaries and supporting conversion. But in time he broke with the Jesuits and began to stress traditional practices, even though he himself remained a Christian. Affonso did much to consolidate the government, but he had constant difficulty in curbing the more exploitative slaving practices as well as the more independent-minded provincial governors. The latter often dealt directly with the Portuguese, undermining royal authority. Affonso's successor, Diogo, moved finally to restrict Portuguese activity to Mpinda harbor and the Kongo capital of Mbanza Kongo (São Salvador). A few years later, Portuguese attempts to designate the Kongo royal successor led to a bloody uprising against the foreigners that in turn led to a Portuguese boycott on trade with the kingdom.

A short while after this, a series of disastrous internal wars waged by rebellious warriors known as the Jaga effectively shattered the power of the Kongo state. Slavery apparently contributed significantly to the factionalism in the provinces and the unrest that fueled the Jaga wars. Their aftermath saw increased roles for Portuguese independent traders and adventurers, who subsequently carried on trading outside of government channels and tried to control and manipulate the Kongo kings. A period of renewed strong leadership after the 1570s still did not stop the processes of fragmentation that led to the breakup of the kingdom a century later.

Kongo did, however, enjoy renewed vigor in the

CENTRAL AFRICA

1300s	Kongo kingdom founded
1483	Portuguese come to Central African coast
CA. 1506–1543	Reign of Affonso I as king of Kongo
1571	Angola becomes Portuguese proprietary colony

seventeenth century. Maize and then cassava were introduced and began slowly to become part of the staple diet of the populace. The Kongo kings, all descended from Affonso, ruled as divine-right monarchs set at the apex of a complex social and political pyramid that rose from district headmen through provincial governors to the court nobility and the king. Royal power came to depend upon a royal guard of musket-armed hired soldiers from tribes of the Stanley Pool area. The financial base of the kingdom rested on tribute from officials holding positions at the king's pleasure and on taxes and tolls on commerce. Christianity, the state religion, was accommodated to traditional religion in areas involving the ancestor cult, talismanic magic, and sorcery. Kongo sculpture, iron and copper technology, and dance and music flourished. Styles persisted down to colonial times.

Angola

To the south, in Portuguese Angola, the experience was still worse than in Kongo. The Ndongo kingdom among the Mbundu people flourished during the sixteenth century. In 1571, a Portuguese decision to turn Angola into a proprietary colony (the first white colonial enterprise in black Africa) set in motion the colonizing and "civilizing" efforts that ended in failure. By the end of the century, Angola was exporting thousands of slaves yearly through the port of Luanda. In less than a century, the hinterland had been plundered and depopulated. New internal trade in salt and the eventual spread of American food crops such as maize and cassava did produce some positive changes in the interior, but in the coastal region among the western Mbundu, the Portuguese arrival led to catastrophe.

The Atlantic Slave Trade

Virtually every premodern state in history depended upon slavery to some extent. The Mediterranean and African worlds were no exception, from the days of ancient Greece and Egypt to at least the nineteenth century. Islamic states of southwest Asia and north Africa had long imported slaves from East Africa and the Sudanic regions below the Sahara, although larger numbers probably came from eastern Europe and central Asia. The latter was the source for most of the slave-soldier dynasties that came to rule many Islamic states from India to North Africa (note that our word *slave* derives from the Arabic for *Slav*). Internal slavery in sub-Saharan Africa was also very ancient and of various kinds. As in the Islamic world, most forms of slavery were not as dehumanizing as the chattel slavery that predominated in the Americas, in which the slaves were typically treated as mere commodities.

Both Mediterranean Christian and Islamic peoples were using slaves—mostly Greeks, Bulgarians, Turkish prisoners of war, and Black Sea Tartars, but also Africans—well before the voyages of discovery opened up sub-Saharan sources for slaves for the new European colonies overseas. Europeans had built up sugar-cane plantations on Cyprus soon after Muslim forces drove them out of "the Holy Land" in the thirteenth century. This industry subsequently spread westward to Crete and Sicily, and in the fifteenth century, to the Portuguese Atlantic islands of Madeira, and then São Thomé. Slaves were used for the labor-intensive process of sugar production. The Portuguese in particular developed and employed widely the plantation system of slave labor as they began their expansion into the Atlantic and beyond.

The Atlantic System

The African slave trade across the Atlantic must be seen as a part of the larger commercial system of Atlantic trade between Europe, Africa, and European colonies in South America, the Caribbean, and North America. This system exploited New World products like tobacco, sugar, coffee, precious metals, cotton, and indigo. These were very labor-intensive crops. The trade system provided markets in Africa for European products such as textiles, liquor, guns, metal goods, and beads; it yielded African gold, ivory, wood, palm oil, gum, and other products, as well as slaves. In South America, Mexico, and then the Caribbean and North America, slave labor served as the means to the end of large-scale production.

When native American peoples, the prime candidates for colonial slave labor, were decimated by European conquest and European diseases, or proved unsatisfactory as plantation laborers, the entrepreneurs looked elsewhere. First the Portuguese, and then the Spanish, Dutch, French, and English (others would follow, including Americans) turned to west, central, and, to a lesser degree, southeast Africa for an ample, cheap, and quality supply of slave labor.

Thus began the Atlantic slave trade—not so much from racist principles (although these allowed its easy justification), but from colonial economic needs (or greed) and the willingness to exploit any available weaker peoples to serve the interests of the stronger. Gold and the search for a sea route to Asia may have brought the first European ships to Africa, but slaves were the main commodity for which they returned. Slaving was an important part of the massive new overseas trade that largely financed European economic development and its industrial revolution. The success of this overseas trade propelled Europe into world dominance by the nineteenth century.

The African Trade

With the exception of the Portuguese in central Africa, the European slave-traders generally obtained their human cargoes from private or government-sponsored African middlemen at coastal forts or simply at anchorages along the coast. This situation was the result of both the African desire to control inland trade and the immense European vulnerability to disease in the equatorial regions (a new European arrival stood less than a fifty per cent chance of surviving a year on the tropical African coast). Thus, African states and tribes were typically the suppliers of slaves to the coast. This was the basis of the system of European forts, built mostly between 1640 and 1750, that dominated the Gold Coast. Hence, the actual capture or procurement of slaves, as well as the often difficult and dangerous task of marching them to the coast, was left largely to African middlemen. These were generally wealthy merchants who could mount slaving expeditions inland or African kingdoms that sought to profit from the trade. The media of exchange were varied, but then usually involved mixed-good barter ranging from gold dust or firearms to beads and spirits.

Specific data on the African sources for slaves is scarce. The chief west and central African slaving regions provided different numbers of slaves, and the total number of slaves exported varied sharply in different periods. Thus, between 1526 and 1550 the major sources of the slaves exported by Europeans were the Kongo–Angola region (34 per cent), the Guinea coast of Cape Verde (25.6 per cent), and Senegambia (23.5 per cent).[2] By contrast, between 1761 and 1810, the French drew some 52 per cent of their slaves from Angola and 24 per cent from the Bight of Benin, but only 4.8 per cent from Senegambia, while the British relied most heavily on the Bight of Biafra and Central Africa.[3] Suppliers naturally went where population density and the presence of active African merchant or state suppliers promised the best numbers and prices.

[2]Philip Curtin, *The Atlantic Slave Trade: A Census* (Madison: Univ. of Wisconsin Press, 1969), p. 101.
[3]Curtin, p. 101; James A. Rawley, *The Transatlantic Slave Trade: A History* (New York and London: W. W. Norton, 1981), p. 129; Curtin, p. 129.

A slaver sights a British cruiser. Both European and Arab slave ships, like this East African sailing dhow had good reason to fear British warships, once Britain determined to eradicate the slave trade. Some slaver captains tried to dispose of the evidence of their trade by drowning their human cargo on the spot. [Bettmann Archive.]

The Extent of the Trade

The overall figures on African slaves exported between 1451 and 1870 are still debated. A major unknown variable concerns the numbers of slaves who died under the brutal conditions of the Atlantic crossing. Thus, the most reliable estimates pertain only to those slaves who actually landed abroad (see table). The latter totaled over eleven million souls. To assess the numbers lost by African societies, one would have to account not only for the slaves who died on the Atlantic, but also for those who died even before reaching the ships. The former have been estimated by scholars at over a million; the latter number cannot be determined. In any case, we can surmise that, at a minimum, well over twelve million persons were lost by Africa through the Atlantic trade. This number does not count those who were sold in the trans-Saharan and east African slave trade, which continued as before, albeit still not anywhere near levels reached in the Atlantic trade.

The figures in our table do not tell us very much beyond the vast numbers involved. Portuguese, French, English, and Spanish colonies were clearly major consumers involved in slavery. Yet only the Portuguese, French, and English were primary carriers of slaves; Spanish America depended on others for its supplies until the Spanish exploitation of Cuba in the nineteenth century. We can see that two-fifths of all slaves taken by Europeans were landed in Portuguese Brazil. We can also see how relatively small the North American share of the slave totals was, which is especially striking in view of the immense and long-term impact of slavery on American society.

However, we cannot see other things that reflect the many variables that make generalizations about the slave trade risky. For example, although the Portuguese were principal carriers throughout the trade, they had a virtual monopoly until the Dutch broke it in the 1640s and briefly were the chief carriers. The French and English came into the trade only in the late seventeenth century; yet in the eighteenth, the time of

ESTIMATED SLAVE IMPORTS INTO THE AMERICAS BY REGION, 1451–1870

British North America	523,000
Spanish America	1,687,000
British Caribbean	2,443,000
French Caribbean	1,655,000
Dutch Caribbean	500,000
Danish Caribbean	50,000
Brazil (Portuguese)	4,190,000
Old World	297,000
Total:	11,345,000

[Figures as calculated by James A. Rawley, *The Transatlantic Slave Trade: A History* (New York and London: W. W. Norton, 1981), p. 428, based upon his and other more recent revisions of the careful but older estimates of Philip D. Curtin, for which see the latter's *The Atlantic Slave Trade: A Census* (Madison: Univ. of Wisconsin Press, 1969), esp. pp. 266, 268.]

the greatest shipments, they carried almost half the total number transported over the entire century. Americans, too, were latecomers, but avid slavers who managed to make considerable profits before and even after both Britain and America outlawed slaving in 1807.

Taken as a whole, the slave trade varied in extent quite sharply from period to period. Its peak came in the eighteenth century and its demise only after substantial continued success in the nineteenth. Specifically, only about 3 per cent of the total trade came before 1600, and only about 14 per cent between 1600 and 1700. On the other hand, the period 1701–1810 accounted for over 60 per cent of the total, and even the final half century of slaving down to 1870 accounted for over 20 per cent of the total. Despite major European moves to abolish slaving in the early 1800s, the Portuguese still transported over a million slaves to Brazil between 1811 and 1870. In fact, the total number of slaves landed in the Americas in these final years of the trade exceeded that for the entire seventeenth century.[4]

Impact of the Slave Trade

The tendency of modern scholarship has been probably to overemphasize the importance for internal African history of the coming of the maritime European powers in general and the Atlantic slave trade in particular. In any event, the effects of the slave trade on Africa are not easy to assess. For example, we do not even know for certain if the Atlantic trade brought net population loss or gain to Africa; the wide and rapid spread of maize and cassava cultivation after their importation from the Americas may have fueled African population increases that offset the human loss through slaving. We know, however, that slaving took away large numbers of the strongest young African men in many areas. We do not know if more slaves were captured as by-products of local wars or as the result of pure slave-raiding. Nor do we know if slaving inhibited development of trade or perhaps stimulated it, since commerce in a range of African products, from ivory to wood and hides, accompanied that in slaves. We cannot determine with certainty the numerical extent of the slave trade, let alone its economic and social impact, which could only be assessed relative to presently unknown levels of African populations over the four centuries in question. Nor do we know if other exchanges, such as that of diseases, may have been of greater overall significance, for Africa or the Americas, than was slaving.

Most important—as we have stressed—the impact was so different in different places and times that even accurate general statistics inevitably mislead us about

[4]Rawley, p. 429; Curtin, p. 268.

particular situations. For some areas, slavery stimulated commerce and even political change, while for others it was a catastrophe. In a few cases, kingdoms such as that of Dahomey (the present Republic of Benin) seem to have sought and derived immense economic profit for a time by making slaving a state monopoly. In other cases, kingdoms such as that of Benin sought to stay almost completely out of slaving altogether. In many instances, including the rise of Asante power or the fall of the Yoruba Oyo empire, it now seems that increased slaving was largely a result, not a cause, of regional instability and change: Increased warfare meant increased prisoners to be enslaved and a surplus to be sold off.

Generally, the external slave trade often measurably changed patterns of life and balances of power in the main affected areas, whether by stimulating trade or warfare (or at least raiding for new supplies) or by disrupting previous market and political structures. There had been substantial internal trade in slaves in most of Africa, as well as some export trade through North Africa to the Islamic and European Mediterranean and through east Africa to the Islamic heartlands. Nevertheless, the scale of the eventual Atlantic demand was unprecedented and hence hit many native societies hard.

If the overseas slave trade did not substantially and irrevocably change a region, at the least it encouraged a siphoning off into ultimately counterproductive or destructive directions of much indigenous energy. This, in turn, meant the inhibition of true economic development, especially in central and in coastal west Africa. The Atlantic slave trade must by any standard be described as one of the major tragic by-products of modern European involvement in the African continent.

Southern Africa

The Portuguese in Southeast Africa

The Portuguese arrival on the southeastern coast of Africa in the first years of the sixteenth century was catastrophic for the east African coastal economy. With determination, they destroyed Swahili control of both the inland gold trade and the multifaceted overseas trade. Their chief object was to obtain gold from interior southeast Africa in the Zambezi region. However, because the gold production of the entire region was small, and because of the repeated difficulties they encountered in trying to control it, the Portuguese derived little lasting profit from the enterprise. When they encountered difficulties in sustaining the Zambezi gold trade by trying simply to take the place of the Swahili merchants on the coast, the Portuguese established fortified posts up the Zambezi and eventually got involved in the regional politics of the Shona peoples who controlled the region. This proved disastrous for stability in the area and led to ongoing strife between the invaders and the Shona kingdoms. In the 1690s, the Changamire Shona dynasty conquered the northern Shona territory and permanently pushed the Portuguese out of the gold country.

All along the Zambezi, however, a lasting and destablizing consequence of Portuguese intrusion was the creation of quasi-tribal chiefdoms. These were led by mixed-blood Portuguese landholders, or *prazeros*, who were descended from the first Portuguese estate-holders along the Zambezi. These estate-holders had obtained and built up huge estate communities. The descendants eventually formed a few clan-like groups of mixed-blood members (from unions with Africans, Indian immigrants, or other estate families). By the end of the eighteenth century, they controlled vast land holdings, commanded military troops (often largely made up of slaves), and were a disruptive force in the region, since they were too strong for either the Portuguese or regional African rulers to control. They serve, however, as a reminder of how diverse the peoples of modern Africa are.

South Africa: The Cape Colony

In South Africa, the Dutch planted the first European colonials almost inadvertently. Yet, the consequences of their action were to be far graver and farther reaching than almost any other European incursion onto African soil. The first Cape settlement was built in 1652 by the Dutch East India Company simply to provide a resupply point and waystation for Dutch vessels on their way back and forth between Holland and the East Indies. Despite original Company intentions, the support station grew gradually into what became by century's end a settler community larger than the Company station itself (the population of the colony in 1662, including slaves, was 394; in 1714, it reached 3,878).[5] These settlers were the forebears of the Afrikaners of modern South Africa.

Once the Company station became a settlers' colony as well, many of the less powerful pastoralist Khoikhoi people of the region were gradually incorporated into the new colonial economy. The local Khoikhoi (see Chapter 15) were almost exclusively pastoralists; they had neither traditions of strong political organization nor an economic base beyond their herds. At first, they bartered livestock freely to Dutch ships and then to the Company settlement for iron, copper, and tobacco. However, as Company employees were released from service, they sought to estab-

lish farms and become suppliers of the Cape station. Initially, they looked to the rich soils of the southwestern Cape and soon began to displace the Khoikhoi there. Conflicts and even armed struggle ensued; the results were the consolidation of European landholdings and a breakdown of Khoikhoi unity and, eventually, of society itself. Dutch military success led to even greater Dutch control of the Khoikhoi by the 1670s. Treated as free persons, many Khoikhoi drifted into the service of the Company and individual Europeans, so that they as a group became the chief source of wage-labor for the colonials—labor in increasingly greater demand as the colony's size and economy grew.

The other way that the colony met its labor need was through the importation of large numbers of slaves to the colony. Coming from all along the southern-seas trade routes, including India, East Africa, and Madagascar, they made possible a profitable agricultural industry as well as a comfortable domestic existence for the European colonists. The slave institution set the tone for relations between the emergent, and ostensibly "white," Afrikaner population and "coloreds" of any race, free or not (all of whom could eventually be easily identified with slave peoples in the colony).

After the first settlers spread out around the Company station, nomadic white livestock farmers, or *Trekboers*, moved still more widely afield, leaving the richer, but limited, farming lands of the coastal peninsula for the drier tableland farther inland. There they contested still wider groups of Khoikhoi cattle herders for the best grazing lands. To this end, they developed military techniques, preeminently that of the "commando," a collective civilian punitive raid, to secure their way of life by force where necessary. Again, the Khoikhoi were the losers. By the end of the seventeenth century, they were stripped almost completely of their own pasturages; most of their chiefdoms were shattered in the warfare; and their way of life was destroyed. More and more Khoikhoi took up employment in the colonial economy, now among the Trekboers as well as the settled colonists. Others moved north to join with other refugees from the Cape society (e.g., slaves, mixed-bloods, and some freedmen) to form raiding bands operating along the frontiers of Trekboer territory close to the Orange river. The disintegration of Khoikhoi society continued apace in the eighteenth century, fueled most sharply by three devastating epidemics of smallpox—a European import against which this previously isolated group had virtually no immunity.

The Cape society in this period was thus a diverse one. The Dutch officials of the Company (including imported Dutch Reformed ministers), the emerging Afrikaners (both settled colonists and Trekboers), the

[5]R. Elphick and H. Giliomee, *The Shaping of South African Society*, 1652–1820 (Cape Town and London: Longman, 1979), p. 4.

1652	First Cape Colony settlement of Dutch East India Company
1795	British replace Dutch as masters of Cape Colony

Khoikhoi, and the slaves of diverse nationality played differing roles in the emerging new society radiating out from Capetown. Intermarriage and cohabitation of masters and slaves added to the complexity of the emerging society, despite laws designed to keep such mixing in check. Accommodation of the non-white minority groups within the Cape society went on apace; the slow emergence of *Afrikaans*, a new vernacular language of the colonial society, shows that the Dutch immigrants themselves were also subject to acculturation processes. By the time of English domination after 1795, the social and political foundations—and the bases of the *Apartheid* doctrine—of modern South Africa were firmly laid.

The Last Islamic Empires and European Intrusion in Asia and Africa in World Perspective

The period from 1500 to 1800 in Islamic, south Asian, and African lands can be characterized in various ways. Here we have focused on only two dominant motifs of the age in these areas: (1) the striking cultural and political blossoming of Islamic societies and their ensuing sharp decline, and (2) the radically new kinds of European intrusion upon the societies of the Islamic heartlands and of Africa, India, and Southeast Asia. We have stressed these two trends largely because in the sixteenth and seventeenth centuries, Japan and China were not subject to much influence from either the powerful Islamic empires or from the burgeoning commercial and political imperialism of Western European nation-states.

The Islamic vitality in the first half of this period was exemplified in the three mighty empires and prosperous societies of the Ottomans, Safavids, and Mughals. All three built new and vast bureaucracies, using Islamic ideology but even more their own imperial vigor to legitimize their rule. They built up arguably the greatest cities in the world of their time and patronized the arts to stimulate important new traditions of Islamic literature, calligraphy, painting, and architecture. Yet for all this vitality, these were profoundly conservative societies. Much like those of China and Japan, they did not undergo the kind of generative changes in material and intellectual life that

the Western world was experiencing in the same period. There was no compelling challenge to traditional Islamic ideals of societal organization and human responsibility, even though several Islamic movements of the eighteenth century did raise calls for communal and personal reform.

As one historian has put it, the striking growth of Islamic societies and cultures in this age was "not one of *origination*, . . . but rather one of *culmination* in a culture long already mature."[6] Even in their heydays, these empires produced much scientific work, but no scientific revolution; much art, architecture, and literature of high quality, but none that departed radically in conception or inspiration from previous traditions; political consolidation and also expansion, but no conquest of significant new markets or territories; commercial prosperity, but no beginnings of a real commercial or industrial revolution. Furthermore, by the latter half of this period, all were in sharp economic, political, and military decline, even if intellectual and artistic vigor held on.

Thus, it is not surprising that European expansionism impinged fatefully in these three centuries upon Africa, India, Indonesia, and the heartland cultures of the Islamic world, rather than the reverse. Neither the great imperial Islamic states, the smaller Islamic sultanates and amirates, the diverse Hindu kingdoms, nor the varied African states (let alone the smaller societies of Africa, the Americas, and the South Pacific) fared very well in their encounters with Europeans in this age. The ensuing colonialism of the nineteenth century went hand in hand with the relentless advance of Western industrial, commercial, and military power that would hold sway globally until the middle of the twentieth century.

Suggested Readings

ISLAMIC EMPIRES, KHANATES, AND SULTANATES

A. L. BASHAM, ed., *A Cultural History of India* (1975). Part II, the "Age of Muslim Dominance," is of greatest relevance here.

M. A. COOK, ed., *A History of the Ottoman Empire to 1730* (1976). Articles from *The Cambridge History of Islam* and *The New Cambridge Modern History*, with a brief introduction by Cook.

G. HAMBLY, *Central Asia* (1966). Excellent survey chapters (9–13) on the Chagatay and Uzbek (Shaybanid) Turks.

M. G. S. HODGSON, *The Gunpowder Empires and Modern Times*. Vol. 3 of *The Venture of Islam*. 3 vols. (1974). Less ample than vols. 1 and 2 of Hodgson's

[6]Marshall G. S. Hodgson, *The Venture of Islam* (Chicago: University of Chicago Press, 1974), vol. 3, p. 15.

monumental history, but a thoughtful survey of the great post-1500 empires.

P. M. HOLT et al., *The Cambridge History of Islam*. 2 vols. (1970). A traditional, somewhat compartmentalized history useful for reference. Vol. II includes chapters on India, Southeast Asia, and Africa in the post-1500 period.

S. M. IKRAM, *Muslim Civilization in India* (1964). Still the best short survey history, covering the period 711 to 1857.

H. INALCIK, *The Ottoman Empire: The Classical Age 1300–1600* (1973). An excellent, if dated, survey with solid treatment of Ottoman social, religious, and political institutions.

R. C. MAJUMDAR, gen. ed., *The History and Culture of the Indian People*. Vol. VII: *The Mughal Empire* (1974). A thorough and readable political and cultural history of the period in India.

M. MUJEEB, *The Indian Muslims* (1967). The best cultural study of Islamic civilization in India as a whole, from its origins onward.

S. A. A. RIZVI, *The Wonder That Was India*. Vol. II (1987). A sequel to Basham's original *The Wonder That Was India;* treats Mughal life, culture, and history from 1200 to 1700.

F. ROBINSON, *Atlas of the Islamic World since 1500* (1982). Brief historical essays, color illustrations, and chronological tables, as well as maps, make this a refreshing general reference work.

S. J. SHAW, *Empire of the Gazis: The Rise and Decline of the Ottoman Empire*, 1280–1808. Vol. I of *History of the Ottoman Empire and Modern Turkey* (1976). A solid historical survey with excellent bibliographic essays for each chapter and a good index.

V. A. SMITH, *The Oxford History of India.* 4th ed. rev. Percival Spear et al. (1981). An easy-to-read historical survey with considerable detail on the period 1526–1818 in Books VI and VII.

J. O. VOLL, *Islam: Continuity and Change in the Modern World* (1982). Chapter 3 provides an excellent overview of eighteenth-century revival and reform movements in diverse Islamic lands.

AFRICA

D. BIRMINGHAM, *Central Africa to* 1870 (1981). Chapters from the *Cambridge History of Africa* that give a brief and lucid overview of developments in this region.

P. BOHANNAN AND P. CURTIN, *Africa and Africans*. Rev. ed. (1971). Very accessible, topical approach to diverse aspects of African history, culture, society, politics, and economic institutions.

M. CRATON, ed., *Roots and Branches: Current Directions in Slave Studies* (1979). Diverse articles by scholars such as Curtin and Lovejoy; note especially those on the European plantation system by S. M. Greenfield.

P. D. CURTIN, *The Atlantic Slave Trade: A Census* (1969). Still a basic work, and useful for an overview of the trade, even though figures in many areas have since been refined or amended by other work.

P. D. CURTIN, *Economic Change in Precolonial Africa: Senegambia on the Eve of the Slave Trade* (1975). The chapter on slave trading is an illuminating treatment of the topic with respect to one area of Africa.

P. D. CURTIN, S. FEIERMANN, L. THOMPSON, AND J. VANSINA, *African History* (1978). A masterly survey. The relevant portions here are Chapters 6–9.

R. ELPHICK, *Kraal and Castle: Khoikhoi and the Founding of White South Africa* (1977). An incisive, informative interpretation of the history of the Khoikhoi and their fateful interaction with European colonization.

R. ELPHICK, AND H. GILIOMEE, *The Shaping of South African Society*, 1652–1820 (1979). A superb, synthetic history of this crucial period.

J. D. FAGE, *A History of Africa* (1978). Still a readable survey history.

H. A. GEMERY AND J. S. HOGENDORN, eds., *The Uncommon Market: Essays in the Economic History of the Atlantic Slave Trade* (1979). Useful statistics on trans-Saharan and particular African regions of the Atlantic slave trade.

R. W. JULY, *A History of the African People*, 3rd ed. (1980). Chapters 3–6 treat Africa before about 1800 area by area; Chapter 7 deals with "The Coming of Europe."

R. W. JULY, *Precolonial Africa: An Economic and Social History* (1975). Chapter 10 gives an interesting overall picture of slaving in African history.

I. M. LEWIS, ed., *Islam in Tropical Africa* (1966), pp. 4–96. Lewis' introduction to this volume is one of the best brief summaries of the role of Islam in west Africa and the Sudan.

J. A. RAWLEY, *The Transatlantic Slave Trade: A History* (1981). Impressively documented, detailed, and well-presented survey history of the Atlantic trade; little focus on African dimensions.

A. F. C. RYDER, *Benin and the Europeans: 1485–1897* (1969). A basic study.

M. WILSON AND L. THOMPSON, eds., *The Oxford History of South Africa*. Vol. I: *South Africa to* 1870 (1969). Relatively detailed, if occasionally dated, treatment of the region.

Enlightenment and Revolution in the West

BETWEEN approximately 1750 and 1850, certain extraordinary changes occurred in Western civilization. Although of immediate significance primarily for the nations of Europe and the Americas, these developments produced in the long run an immense impact throughout the world. No other civilizations ultimately escaped the influence of the European intellectual ferment and political turmoil of these years. Most of the intellectual, political, economic, and social characteristics associated with the *modern* world came into being during this era. Europe became the great exporter of ideas and technologies that in time transformed one area after another of the human experience.

Intellectually, the ideals of reform and of challenge to traditional cultural authority captured the imagination of numerous writers. That movement, known as the *Enlightenment,* drew confidence from the scientific worldview that had emerged during the seventeenth century. Its exponents urged the application of the spirit of critical rationalism in one area of social and political life after another. They posed serious historical and moral questions to the Christian faith. They contended that laws of society and economics could be discovered and could then be used to improve the human condition. They embraced the idea of economic growth and development. They called for political reform and more efficient modes of government. They upheld the standard of rationality in order to cast doubt on traditional modes of thought and behavior that seemed to them less than rational. As a result of their labors in Europe and eventually throughout the world, the idea of change that has played so important a role in modern life came to have a generally positive value attached to it for the first time.

For many people, however, change seemed to come too rapidly and violently when revolution erupted in France in 1789. Commencing as an aristocratic revolt against the monarchy, the revolution rapidly spread to every corner of French political and social life. The rights of man and citizen displaced those of the monarchy, the aristocracy, and the Church. By 1792, the revolution had become a genuinely popular movement and had established a French republic whose armies challenged the other major European monarchies. The reign of terror that saw the execution of the French king unloosed domestic violence unlike anything witnessed in Europe since the age of the religious wars. By the end of the 1790s, to restore order, French political leaders turned themselves over to the leadership of Napoleon. Thereafter, for more than a decade, his armies overturned the institutions of the old regime across the continent. Only in 1815, after the battle of Waterloo, was the power of France and Napoleon finally contained.

644

The French Revolution in one way or another served as a model for virtually all later popular revolutions. It unleashed new forces and political creeds in one area of the world after another. The French Revolution, with its broad popular base, brought *the people* to the forefront of world political history. In the early revolutionary goals of establishing a legal framework of limited monarchical power, of securing citizen rights, and of making possible relatively free economic activity, the supporters of the revolution spawned the political creed of *liberalism*. The wars of the French Revolution and of Napoleon, stretching from 1792 to 1815, awakened the political force of *nationalism,* which has proved to be the single most powerful ideology of the modern world. Loyalty to the nation defined in terms of a common language, history, and culture replaced loyalty to dynasties. As a political ideology, nationalism could be used both to liberate a people from the domination of another nation and to justify wars of aggression. And nationalism was put to both uses in Europe and throughout the rest of the world in the two centuries following the revolution in France. Nationalism became a kind of secular religion that aroused a degree of loyalty and personal self-sacrifice previously called forth only by the great religious traditions.

Finally, between 1750 and 1850, Europe became not only an exporter of reform and revolution but also of manufactured commodities. The technology and the society associated with industrialism took root throughout the western portion of the continent. Europeans achieved a productive capacity that, in cooperation with their naval power, permitted them to dominate the markets of the world. Thereafter, to be strong, independent, and modern seemed to mean to become industrialized and to imitate the manufacturing techniques of Europe and later of the United States.

But industrialism and its society fostered immense social problems, dislocations, and injustices. The major intellectual and political response was *socialism,* several varieties of which emerged from the European social and economic turmoil of the 1830s and 1840s. History eventually proved the most important of these to be that espoused by Karl Marx, whose *Communist Manifesto* appeared in 1848.

Remarkable ironies are attached to the European achievements of the late eighteenth and the early nineteenth centuries. Enlightenment, revolution, and industrialism contributed to an awakening of European power that permitted the continent to dominate the world for a time at the end of the nineteenth century. Yet those same movements fostered various intellectual critiques, political ideas, and economic skills that twentieth-century non-European peoples would turn against their temporary European masters. It is for that reason that the age of enlightenment and revolution in the West was of such significance not simply in the history of Europe but in the history of the entire modern world.   ❑

	EUROPE	NEAR EAST/INDIA
1750	1762–1796 Catherine II, "the Great" reigns in Russia 1772 First Partition of Poland 1789 French Revolution begins 1793 and 1795 Last partitions of Poland 1804–1814 Napoleon's Empire 1830–1848 Louis Philippe reigns in France 1832 First British Reform Act 1837–1901 Queen Victoria of England 1848 Revolutions across Europe	1757 British victory at Plassey, in Bengal 1761 English oust French from India 1772–1784 Warren Hastings' administration in India 1772–1833 Ram Mohan Roy, Hindu reformer in India 1794–1925 Qajar shahs in Iran 1805–1849 Muhammad Ali reigns in Egypt 1835 Introduction of English education in India ca. 1839–1880 Tanzimat reforms, Ottoman Empire 1839–1897 Muslim intellectual, Jamal al-Din Al-Afghani 1845–1905 Muhammad Abduh
1850	1852–1870 The Second French Empire, under Napoleon III 1854–1856 The Crimean War 1861 Italy unified 1861 Emancipation of Russian serfs 1866 Austro-Prussian War; creation of Dual Monarchy of Austria-Hungary in 1867 1870–1871 Franco-Prussian War; German Empire proclaimed in 1871 1873 Three Emperors League 1882 Triple Alliance 1890 Bismarck dismissed by Kaiser Wilhelm II	1857–1858 Sepoy Rebellion: India placed directly under the authority of the British government in 1858 1869 Suez Canal completed; 1875, British purchase controlling interest 1869–1948 Mohandas (Mahatma) Gandhi 1876–1949 Muhammad Ali Jinnah, "founder of Pakistan" 1882 English occupation of Egypt 1886 India National Congress formed 1889–1964 Jawaharlal Nehru 1899 Ottoman sultan Abdulhamid II grants concession to Kaiser Wilhelm II to extend railway to Baghdad ("Berlin-to-Baghdad" Railway)
1900	1902 Ententé Cordial 1905 January 22, "Bloody Sunday" 1905 Revolution in Russia 1914–1918 World War I 1917 Bolsheviks seize power in Russia 1919 Versailles Settlement 1922 Mussolini and Fascists seize power in Italy 1925 Locarno Pact 1933 Hitler comes to power in Germany 1936 Outbreak of the Spanish Civil War 1938 Munich Conference 1939 Invasion of Poland; World War II begins	1908 "Young Turk" Revolt 1922 End of British occupation of Egypt 1922–1938 Mustafa Kemal, "Atatürk," founder and first president of the Turkish state 1924–1934 Reforms of Atatürk 1928 The Muslim Brotherhood founded by Hasan al-Banna

EAST ASIA	AFRICA	THE AMERICAS
1787–1793 Matsudaira Sadanobu's reforms in Japan *1789* White Lotus Rebellion in China *1823–1901* Li Hung-chang, powerful Chinese Governor-General *1835–1908* Empress Dowager Tz'u-hsi *1839–1842* Opium War; *1842*, Treaty of Nanking grants Hong Kong to the British and allows them to trade in China *1844* Similar treaties made between China and France and the U.S.	*1754–1817* Usman Dan Fodio, founder of Sultanate in northern and central Nigeria *1762* End of Funj sultanate in eastern Sudanic region *1804* Fulani Jihad into Hausa lands *1806* British take Cape Colony from the Dutch *1817–1828* Zulu chief Shaka reigns *1830–1847* French invasion of Algeria *1830s* Dutch settlers, the Boers, expand northward from Cape Colony *1848–1885* Sudanese Madhi, Muhammad Ahmad	*1789* United States Constitution *1791* Negro slave revolt in French Santo Domingo *1791* Canada Constitutional Act divides the country into Upper and Lower Canada *1804* Haitian independence *1808–1824* Wars of independence in Latin America *1847* Mexican War
1850–1873 Taiping and other rebellions *1853–1854* Commodore Perry "opens" Japan to the West, ending seclusion policy *1859* French seize Saigon *1860s* Establishment of Treaty Ports in China *1864* French protectorate over Cambodia *1868* Meiji Restoration in Japan *1870s* Civilization and Enlightenment movement in Japan *1870s–1800s* Self-Strengthening movement in China *1889* Meiji Constitution in Japan *1894–1895* Sino-Japanese War; Japan gets Taiwan as colony *1898–1900* Boxer Rebellion in China	*1856–1884* King Mutasa of Buganda reigns *1870* British protectorate in Zanzibar *1879–1880* Henry M. Stanley gains the Congo for Leopold of Belgium *1880s* Mahdist revival and uprising in Sudan *1880* French protectorate in Tunisia and the Ivory Coast *1884–1885* International Conference in Berlin to prepare rules for further acquisition of African territory; the Congo Free State declared. *1884* German Southwest Africa *1885* British control Nigeria and British East Africa *1894* The French annex Dahoney *1899* German East Africa; British in Sudan *1899–1902* The Boer War	*1854* Kansas-Nebraska Act *1856* Dred Scott Decision *1859* Raid on Harper's Ferry *1860* Abraham Lincoln elected President of the U.S. *1861–1865* U.S. Civil War *1862–1867* French invasion of Mexico *1863* Emancipation Proclamation in U.S. *1865–1877* Reconstruction *1865–1870* Paraguayan War *1879–1880* Argentinian conquest of the desert *1880s* Slavery eliminated in Cuba and Brazil *1898* Spanish American War
1904–1905 Russo-Japanese War *1910* Japan annexes Korea *1911* Republican Revolution begins in China; Ch'ing dynasty overthrown *1916–1928* Warlord Era in China *1919* May 4th Movement in China *1925* Universal manhood suffrage in Japan *1928–1937* Nationalist government in China at Nanking *1931* Japan occupies Manchuria *1937–1945* Japan at war with China	*1900* Nigeria a British Crown Colony *1907* Orange Free State and the Transvaal join with Natal and Cape Colony to form the Union of South Africa *1911* Liberia becomes a virtual U.S. protectorate *1914* Ethiopia the only independent state in Africa *1935* Mussolini invades Ethiopia	*1901* Theodore Roosevelt elected President of U.S. *1910–1917* Mexican Revolution *1912* Woodrow Wilson elected President of U.S. *1917* U.S. enters World War II *1929* Wall Street Crash; the Great Depression begins *1930–1945* Vargas dictatorship in Brazil *1932* Franklin Delano Roosevelt elected President of the U.S. *1938* Nationalization of Mexican oil

Denis Diderot (1713–1784), above, and Jean d' Alembert (1717–1783), below, surrounded by the principal contributors to the Encyclopedia. *Because it contained the most advanced critique of ideas in religion, government, and philosophy, the* Encyclopedia *was bitterly attacked by the Church and condemned by the state. [Giraudon/Art Resource.]*

23 The Age of European Enlightenment

During the eighteenth century, the conviction began to spread throughout the literate sectors of European society that change and reform were both possible and desirable. This attitude is now commonplace, but it came into its own only after 1700. It represents one of the primary intellectual inheritances from that age. The movement of people and ideas that fostered such thinking is called the *Enlightenment*. Its leading voices combined confidence in the human mind inspired by the Scientific Revolution and faith in the power of rational criticism to challenge the intellectual authority of tradition and the Christian past. Its writers stood convinced that human beings could comprehend the operation of physical nature and mold it to the ends of material and moral improvement. The rationality of the physical universe became a standard against which the customs and traditions of society could be measured and criticized. Such criticism penetrated every corner of contemporary society, politics, and religious opinion. As a result, the spirit of innovation and improvement came to characterize modern European and Western society. This outlook would become perhaps the most important European cultural export to the rest of the world.

The Scientific Revolution

The sixteenth and seventeenth centuries witnessed a sweeping change in the scientific view of the universe. An earth-centered picture of the universe gave way to one in which the earth was only another planet orbiting about the sun. The sun itself became one of millions of stars. This transformation of humankind's perception of its place in the larger scheme of things led to a vast rethinking of moral and religious matters as well as of scientific theory. At the same time, the new scientific concepts and the methods of their construction became so impressive and so influential that subse-

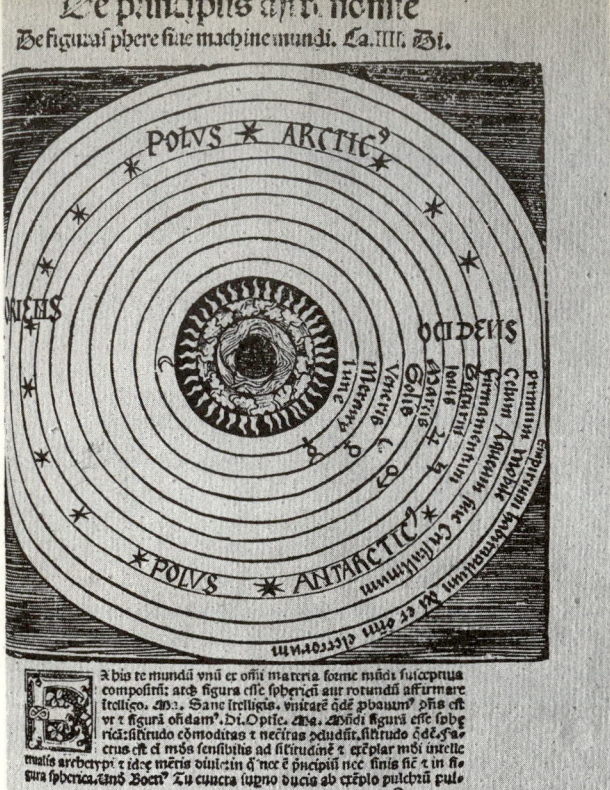

View of the universe as describe by Claudius Ptolemy in the second century A.D. Ptolemy's view, which put the earth unmoving in the center with the other heavenly objects circling it (the sun being in the fourth circle), dominated astronomy until the sixteenth century. The illustration is from a book by Gregor Reisch, Margarita Philosophica (1515). [The British Library, London.]

quent knowledge in the Western world has been deemed correct only as it has approximated knowledge as defined by science.

The process by which this new view of the universe and of scientific knowledge came to be established is normally termed the *Scientific Revolution*. However, care must be taken in the use of this metaphor. The word *revolution* normally denotes fairly rapid changes in the political world, involving large numbers of people. The Scientific Revolution was not rapid, nor did it involve more than a few hundred human beings. It was a complex movement with many false starts and many brilliant people with wrong as well as useful ideas. However, the ultimate result of this transformation of thought revolutionized the manner in which Europeans thought about physical nature and themselves. This new outlook would later be exported to every other major world civilization.

Nicolaus Copernicus

Copernicus (1473–1543) was a Polish astronomer who enjoyed a very high reputation throughout his life.

He had been educated in Italy and corresponded with other astronomers throughout Europe. However, he had not been known for strikingly original or unorthodox thought. In 1543, the year of his death, Copernicus published *On the Revolutions of the Heavenly Spheres*. Because he died near the time of publication, the fortunes of his work are not the story of one person's crusade for progressive science. Copernicus' book was "a revolution-making rather than a revolutionary text."[1]

At the time of Copernicus, the standard explanation of the earth and the heavens was that associated with Ptolemy and his work entitled the *Almagest* (A.D. 150). There was not just one Ptolemaic system; rather, several versions had been developed over the centuries by commentators on the original book. Most of these systems assumed that the earth was the center of the universe. Above the earth lay a series of crystalline spheres, one of which contained the moon, another the sun, and still others the planets and the stars. This was the astronomy found in such works as Dante's *Divine Comedy*. At the outer regions of these spheres lay the realm of God and the angels. Aristotelian physics provided the intellectual underpinnings of the Ptolemaic systems. The earth had to be the center because of its heaviness. The stars and the other heavenly bodies had to be enclosed in the crystalline spheres so that they could move. Nothing could move unless something was actually moving it. The state of rest was natural; motion was the condition that required explanation.

Numerous problems were associated with this system, and these had long been recognized. The most important was the observed motions of the planets. Planets could be seen moving in noncircular patterns around the earth. At certain times, the planets actually appeared to be going backward. The Ptolemaic systems explained that these strange motions occurred primarily through *epicycles*. The planets were said to make a second revolution in an orbit tangent to their primary orbit around the earth. The epicycle was compared with a jewel on a ring. Other intellectual but nonobservational difficulties related to the immense speed at which the spheres had to move around the earth. To say the least, the Ptolemaic systems were cluttered. However, they were effective explanations as long as one assumed Aristotelian physics and the Christian belief that the earth rested at the center of the created universe.

Copernicus' *On the Revolutions of the Heavenly Spheres* challenged this picture in the most conservative manner possible. It suggested that if the earth were assumed to move about the sun in a circle, many

[1] Thomas S. Kuhn, *The Copernican Revolution: Planetary Astronomy in the Development of Western Thought* (New York: Vintage, 1959), p. 135.

of the difficulties with the Ptolemaic systems would disappear or become simpler. Although not wholly eliminated, the number of epicycles would be somewhat fewer. The motive behind this shift away from an earth-centered universe was to find a solution to the problems of planetary motion. By allowing the earth to move around the sun, Copernicus was able to construct a more mathematically elegant basis for astronomy. He had been discontented with the traditional system because it was mathematically clumsy and inconsistent. The primary appeal of his new system was its mathematical aesthetics: with the sun at the center of the universe, mathematical astronomy would make more sense. A change in the conception of the position of the earth meant that the planets were actually moving in circular orbits and only seemed to be doing otherwise because of the position of the observers on earth.

Except for the modification in the position of the earth, most of the other parts of Copernicus' book were Ptolemaic. The path of the planets remained circular. Genuine epicycles still existed in the heavens. His system was no more accurate than the existing ones for predicting the location of the planets. He had employed no new evidence. The major impact of his work was to provide another way of confronting some of the difficulties inherent in Ptolemaic astronomy. This work did not immediately replace the old astronomy, but it did allow other people who were also discontent with the Ptolemaic systems to think in new directions.

Copernicus' concern about mathematics provided an example of the single most important factor in the developing new science. The key to the future development of the Copernican revolution lay in the fusion of mathematical astronomy with further empirical data and observation, and mathematics became the model to which the new scientific thought would conform. The new empirical evidence helped to persuade the learned public.

Tycho Brahe and Johannes Kepler

The next major step toward the conception of a sun-centered system was taken by Tycho Brahe (1546–1601). He actually spent most of his life opposing Copernicus and advocating a different kind of earth-centered system. He suggested that the moon and the sun revolved around the earth and that the other plan-

Two seventeenth-century armillary spheres, astronomical devices composed of rings that represent the orbits of important celestial bodies. The top one was built on the Copernican model, the bottom sphere reflects the much more complicated Ptolemaic universe. [Museum of the History of Science, Oxford, England.]

Copernicus Ascribes Movement to the Earth

Copernicus published De Revolutionibus Orbium Caelestium (On the Revolutions of the Heavenly Spheres) in 1543. In his preface, which was addressed to Pope Paul III, he explained what had led him to think that the earth moved around the sun and what he thought were some of the scientific consequences of the new theory. The reader should note how important Copernicus considered the opinions of the ancient writers who had also ascribed motion to the earth. This is a good example of the manner in which familiarity with the ancients gave many Renaissance writers the self-confidence to criticize medieval ideas.

I may well presume, most Holy Father, that certain people, as soon as they hear that in this book about the Revolutions of the Spheres of the Universe I ascribe movement to the earthly globe, will cry out that, holding such views, I should at once be hissed off the stage. . . .

So I should like your Holiness to know that I was induced to think of a method of computing the motions of the spheres by nothing else than the knowledge that the Mathematicians [who had previously considered the problem] are inconsistent in these investigations.

For, first, the mathematicians are so unsure of the movements of the Sun and Moon that they cannot even explain or observe the constant length of the seasonal year. Secondly, in determining the motions of these and of the other five planets, they use neither the same principles and hypotheses nor the same demonstrations of the apparent motions and revolutions. . . . Nor have they been able thereby to discern or deduce the principal thing—namely the shape of the Universe and the unchangeable symmetry of its parts. . . .

I pondered long upon this uncertainty of mathematical tradition in establishing the motions of the system of the spheres. At last I began to chafe that philosophers could by no means agree on any one certain theory of the mechanism of the Universe, wrought for us by a supremely good and orderly Creator. . . . I therefore took pains to read again the works of all the philosophers on whom I could lay hand to seek out whether any of them had ever supposed that the motions of the spheres were other than those demanded by the [Ptolemaic] mathematical schools. I found first in Cicero that Hicetas [of Syracuse, fifth century B.C.] had realized that the Earth moved. Afterwards I found in Plutarch that certain others had held the like opinion. . . .

Thus assuming motions, which in my work I ascribe to the Earth, by long and frequent observations I have at last discovered that, if the motions of the rest of the planets be brought into relation with the circulation of the Earth and be reckoned in proportion to the circles of each planet, not only do their phenomena presently ensue, but the orders and magnitudes of all stars and spheres, nay the heavens themselves, become so bound together that nothing in any part thereof could be moved from its place without producing confusion of all the other parts of the Universe as a whole. ❑

As quoted in Thomas S. Kuhn, *The Copernican Revolution: Planetary Astronomy in the Development of Western Thought* (New York: Vintage Books, 1959), pp. 137–139, 141–142.

---

ets revolved around the sun. However, in attacking Copernicus, he gave the latter's ideas more publicity. More important, this Danish astronomer's major weapon against Copernican astronomy was a series of new naked-eye astronomical observations. Brahe constructed the most accurate tables of observations that had been drawn up for centuries.

When Brahe died, these tables came into the possession of Johannes Kepler (1571–1630), a German astronomer. Kepler was a convinced Copernican, but his reasons for taking that position were not scientific. Kepler was deeply influenced by Renaissance Neoplatonists, who following upon the Greek philosopher Plato's association of knowledge with light, honored the sun. These Neoplatonists were also determined to discover mathematical harmonies that would support a sun-centered universe. After much work, Kepler discovered that to keep the sun at the center of things, he must abandon the Copernican concept of circular orbits. The mathematical relationships that emerged from a consideration of Brahe's observations suggested that the orbits of the planets were elliptical. Kepler published his findings in 1609 in a book entitled *On the Motion of Mars.* He had solved the problem of planetary orbits by using Copernicus' sun-centered universe and Brahe's empirical data.

Kepler had, however, also defined a new problem. None of the available theories could explain why the planetary orbits were elliptical. That solution awaited the work of Sir Isaac Newton.

Galileo Galilei

From Copernicus to Brahe to Kepler, there had been little new information about the heavens that might not have been known to Ptolemy. However, in the same year that Kepler published his volume on Mars, an Italian scientist named Galileo Galilei (1564–1642) first turned a telescope on the heavens. Through that recently invented instrument, he saw stars where none had been known to exist, mountains on the moon, spots moving across the sun, and moons orbiting Jupiter. The heavens were far more complex than anyone had formerly suspected. None of these discoveries proved that the earth orbited the sun, but they did suggest the complete inadequacy of the Ptolemaic system. It simply could not accommodate itself to all of these new phenomena. Some of Galileo's colleagues at the university of Padua were so unnerved that they refused to look through the telescope, since it revealed the heavens to be different from the teachings of the Church and from Ptolemaic theories.

Galielo publicized his findings and arguments for the Copernican system in numerous works, the most famous of which was his *Dialogues on the Two Chief Systems of the World* (1632). This book brought down on him the condemnation of the Roman Catholic church. He was compelled to recant his opinions. However, he is reputed to have muttered after the recantation, "E pur si muove" ("It [the earth] still moves").

Galileo's discoveries and his popularization of the Copernican system were of secondary importance in his life work. His most important achievement was to articulate the concept of a universe totally subject to mathematical laws. More than any other writer of the century, he argued that nature in its most minute details displayed mathematical regularity. Copernicus had thought that the heavens conformed to mathematical regularity; Galileo saw this regularity throughout all physical nature. He believed that the smallest atom behaved with the same mathematical precision as the largest heavenly sphere.

Galileo stood as one of the foremost champions of the application of mathematics to scientific investigation and of the goal of reducing phenomena to mathematical formulae. However, earlier in the century the English philosopher Francis Bacon had advocated a method based solely on empiricism. As the century passed, both empirical induction and mathematical analysis proved fundamental to scientific investigation.

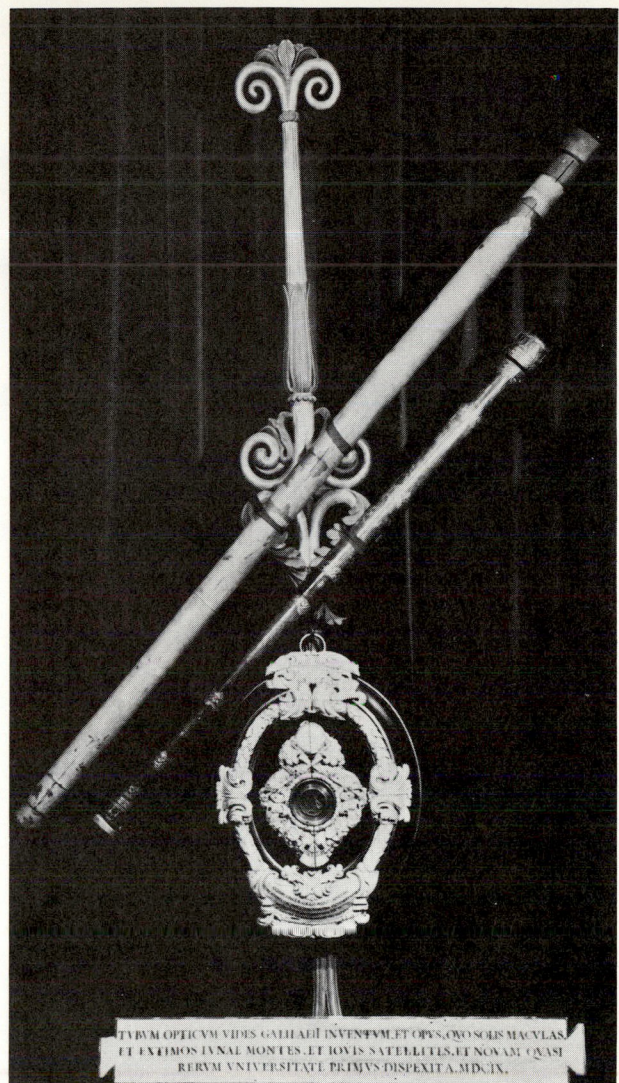

Galileo, working at first from others' suggestions, effectively invented the telescope. This is his 1609 instrument. His observations of the physical features on earth's moon and of the cyclical phases of the planet Venus and his discovery of the most prominent moons of the planet Jupiter were the first major astronomical observations since antiquity and had revolutionary intellectual and theological implications. [Istituto e Museo de Storia della Scienza, Florence.]

Francis Bacon

Bacon (1561–1626) has been regarded as the father of empiricism and of experimentation in science. Much of this reputation is unearned. Bacon was not a scientist except in the most amateur fashion. The accomplishment of this Englishman was setting a tone and helping to create a climate in which other scientists worked. In books such as *The Advancement of Learning* (1605), the *Novum Organum* (1620), and the *New Atlantis* (1627), Bacon attacked the Scholastic belief that most truth had already been discovered and only required explanation, as well as the Scholastic reverence for intellectual authority in general. He believed that Scholastic thinkers paid too much attention to tradition and to knowledge achieved by the ancients. He urged contemporaries to strike out on their own in search of a new understanding of nature. He wanted seventeenth-century Europeans to have confidence in themselves and their own abilities rather than in the people and methods of the past.

Bacon was one of the first major European writers to champion the desirability of innovation and change. Most of the people in Bacon's day, including the intellectuals, thought that the best era of human history lay in antiquity. Bacon dissented vigorously from that point of view. He looked to a future of material improvement achieved through the empirical examination of nature. His own theory of induction from empirical evidence was quite unsystematic, but his insistence on appeal to experience influenced others whose methods were more productive. His great achievement was persuading increasing numbers of thinkers that scientific thought must conform to empirical experience.

Isaac Newton

Isaac Newton (1642–1727) drew on the work of his predecessors and his own brilliance to solve the major remaining problem of planetary motion and to establish a basis for physics that endured more than two centuries. The question that continued to perplex seventeenth-century scientists who accepted the theories of Copernicus, Kepler, and Galileo was how the planets and other heavenly bodies moved in an orderly fashion. The Ptolemaic and Aristotelian answer had been the crystalline spheres and a universe arranged in the order of the heaviness of its parts. Numerous unsatisfactory theories had been set forth to deal with the question.

In 1687, Newton published *The Mathematical Principles of Natural Philosophy*, better known by its Latin title of *Principia Mathematica*. Much of the research and thinking for this great work had taken place more than fifteen years earlier. Newton was heavily indebted to the work of Galileo and particularly to the latter's view that inertia could exist in either a state of motion or a state of rest. Galileo's mathematical bias permeated Newton's thought. Newton reasoned that the planets and all other physical objects in the universe moved through mutual attraction. Every object in the universe affected every other object through gravity. The attraction of gravity explained why the planets moved in an orderly rather than a chaotic manner. He had found that "the force of gravity towards the whole planet did arise from and was compounded of the forces of gravity towards all its parts, and towards every one part was in the inverse propor-

This eighteenth-century engraving pays homage to Isaac Newton. Newton was a major intellectual influence on the Enlightenment. This engraving is in the collection of the British Museum. [British Museum.]

tion of the squares of the distances from the part."[2] Newton demonstrated this relationship mathematically. He made no attempt to explain the nature of gravity itself.

Newton was a mathematical genius, but he also upheld the importance of empirical data and observation. He believed, in good Baconian fashion, that one must observe phenomena before attempting to explain them. The final test of any theory or hypothesis for him was whether it described what could actually be observed.

With the work of Newton, the natural universe became a realm of law and regularity. Spirits and divinities were no longer necessary to explain its operation— a point of view that also contributed to skepticism about witchcraft and an end to witch hunts. Thus the Scientific Revolution liberated human beings from the

[2] Quoted in A. Rupert Hall, *From Galileo to Newton*, 1630–1720 (London: Fontana, 1970), p. 300

fear of a chaotic or haphazard universe. Most of the scientists were very devout people. They saw the new picture of physical nature as suggesting a new picture of God. The Creator of this rational, lawful nature must also be rational. To study nature was to come to a better understanding of that Creator. Science and religious faith were not only compatible but mutually supporting.

This reconciliation of faith and science allowed the new physics and astronomy to spread rapidly. At the very time when Europeans were finally tiring of the wars of religion, the new science provided the basis for a view of God that might lead away from irrational disputes and wars over religious doctrine. Faith in a rational God encouraged faith in the rationality of human beings and in their capacity to improve their lot once liberated from the traditions of the past. The Scientific Revolution provided the model for the desirability of change and of criticism of inherited views. Yet, at the same time, the new science caused some people to feel that the mystery had been driven from the universe and that the rational Creator was less loving and less near to humankind than the God of earlier ages.

John Locke

John Locke (1632–1704) attempted to achieve for philosophy a lawful picture of the human mind similar to that which Newton had presented of nature. Locke's three most famous works were the *Essay Concerning Human Understanding* (1690), *Two Treatises of Government*, and his *Letter Concerning Toleration* (1689). Each of these sounded philosophical themes that later writers of the Enlightenment found welcome. No other philosopher had so profound an impact on European and American thought during the eighteenth century.

In the *Essay Concerning Human Understanding*, Locke envisioned the human mind as being blank at the time of an individual's birth. In Locke's view, contrary to that of much medieval philosophy, there were

John Locke Explains the Sources of Human Knowledge

An Essay Concerning Human Understanding (1690) *may be the most influential philosophical work ever written in English. Locke's most fundamental idea, which is explicated in the passage below, is that human knowledge is grounded in the experiences of the senses and in the reflection of the mind on those experiences. He rejected any belief in innate ideas. His emphasis on experience led to the wider belief that human beings are creatures of their environment. After Locke, numerous writers argued that human beings could be improved if the environment in which they lived were reformed.*

Let us then suppose the mind to be, as we say, white paper void of all characters, without any ideas. How comes it to be furnished? Whence comes it by that vast store which the busy and boundless fancy of man has painted on it with an almost endless variety? Whence has it all the materials of reason and knowledge? To this I answer, in one word, from experience; in that all our knowledge is founded, and from that it ultimately derives itself. Our observation, employed either about external sensible objects, or about the internal operations of our minds perceived and reflected on by ourselves, is that which supplies our understanding with all the materials of thinking. These two are the fountains of knowledge, from whence all the ideas we have, or can naturally have, do spring.

First, our senses, conversant about particular sensible objects, do convey into the mind several distinct perceptions of things, according to those various ways wherein those objects do affect them. And thus we come by those ideas we have of yellow, white, heat, cold, soft, hard, bitter, sweet, and all those which we call sensible qualities. . . . This great source of most of the ideas we have, depending wholly upon our senses, and derived by them to the understanding, I call SENSATION.

Secondly, the other fountain from which experience furnisheth the understanding with ideas is the perception of the operations of our own minds within us, as it is employed about the ideas it has got. . . . And such are perception, thinking, doubting, believing, reasoning, knowing, willing, and all the different actings of our own minds. . . . I call this REFLECTION, the ideas it affords being such only as the mind gets by reflecting on its own operations within itself. . . . These two, I say, viz. external material things as the objects of SENSATION, and the operations of our own minds within as the objects of REFLECTION, are to me the only originals from whence all our ideas take their beginnings. . . .

The understanding seems to me not to have the least glimmering of any ideas which it doth not receive from one of these two. ❑

John Locke, *An Essay Concerning Human Understanding*, Vol. 1 (London: Everyman's Library, 1961), pp. 77–78.

no innate ideas (i.e., ideas existing in people from birth); all knowledge is derived from actual sense experience. Each individual mind grew through experience as it confronted the world of sensation. Human ideas are either simple (that is, passive receptions from daily experience) or complex (that is, products of sustained mental exercise). What people know is not the external world in itself but the results of the interaction of their minds with the outside world. In this regard, Locke's thinking represented an early form of behaviorism. The significant conclusion that followed from Locke's philosophy was that human nature is changeable and can be molded by modification of the surrounding physical and social environment. Locke also, in effect, rejected the Christian view of humankind as creatures permanently flawed by original sin. Human beings need not wait for the grace of God or other divine aid to better their lives. They could take charge of their own destiny.

Locke wrote *Two Treatises of Government* during the reign of Charles II. Locke directed them against the argument that rulers are absolute in their power. Rulers, he argued, remain bound to the law of nature. That law is the voice of reason, teaching that human beings are equal and independent and that they should not harm one another or disturb one another's property because all human beings are the images and property of God. According to Locke, people enter into political contracts, empowering legislatures and monarchs to judge their disputes in order to preserve their natural rights (which included the possession of property) but not to give rulers an absolute power over them. Locke also contended that under certain circumstances a monarch could be seen as having violated the trust that had been placed in him; the ruler could then be overthrown. The latter argument reappeared in the American Declaration of Independence. But in eighteenth-century Europe, it was Locke's argument against absolutism and in favor of limited government rather than his argument justifying revolution that exercised much influence. Like his philosophy, it opened a wider arena for individual action.

Locke's *Letter on Toleration* contended that each person was responsible for his own religious salvation. By contrast, governments existed to protect property and the civil order. Consequently, matters only became confused when governments undertook to legislate on religion and require conformity to a single church. Yet Locke himself drew the line in England against toleration of Roman Catholics and Unitarians. However, during the eighteenth century, the logic of his argument was extended to advocate toleration for persons following those faiths as well.

The young Voltaire (1694–1778). *Philosopher, dramatist, poet, historian, scientist—Voltaire was the most famous and influential of the eighteenth-century* philosophes. *[Bulloz.]*

Stages of the Enlightenment

The movement that came to be known as the Enlightenment evolved over the course of the eighteenth century and involved a number of writers living at different times in various countries. Its early exponents, known as the *philosophes*, popularized the rationalism and scientific ideas of the seventeenth century. They worked to expose contemporary social and political abuses and argued that reform was necessary and possible. The advancement of their cause and ideas was anything but steady. They confronted the obstacles of vested interests, political oppression, and religious condemnation. Yet by the mid-century they had brought enlightened ideas to the European public in a variety of formats. The *philosophes'*, "family" had come into being. They corresponded with each other, wrote for each other as well as for the general public, and defended each other against the political and religious authorities.

By the second half of the century, they were sufficiently safe from persecution to quarrel among themselves on occasion. They had stopped talking in generalities, and their major advocates were addressing themselves to specific abuses. Their books and articles had become more specialized and more practical. They had become more concerned with politics than with religion. Having convinced Europeans that change was a good idea, they began to suggest exactly what changes were most desirable. They had become honored figures.

Voltaire

One of the earliest and by far the most influential of the *philosophes* was François Marie Arouet, known to posterity as Voltaire (1694–1778). During the 1720s, Voltaire had offended the French authorities by certain of his writings, and he was arrested and put in prison for a brief time.

Later Voltaire went to England, where he visited in the best literary circles, observed the tolerant intellectual and religious climate, felt free in the atmosphere of moderate politics, and admired the science and the economic prosperity. In 1733, he published *Letters on the English*, which appeared in French the next year. The book praised the virtues of the English and indirectly criticized the abuses of French society. In 1738, he published *Elements of the Philosophy of Newton*, which popularized the thought of the great scientist. Both works were well received and gave Voltaire a reputation as an important writer.

Thereafter, Voltaire lived part of the time in France and part near Geneva, just across the French border, where the royal authorities could not bother him. He wrote essays, history, plays, stories, and letters that made him the literary dictator of Europe. He brought the bitter venom of his satire and sarcasm against one evil after another in French and European life. His most famous satire is *Candide* (1759), in which he attacked war, religious persecution, and what he regarded as unwarranted optimism about the human condition. Like most *philosophes*, Voltaire believed that improvement of human society was necessary and possible. But he was never certain that reform, if achieved, would be permanent. The optimism of the Enlightenment constituted a tempered hopefulness rather than a glib certainty. Pessimism provided an undercurrent to most of the works of the period.

Voltaire Attacks Religious Fanaticism

The chief complaint of the philosophes against Christianity was that it bred a fanaticism that led people to commit crimes in the name of religion. In this passage from his Philosophical Dictionary *(1764), Voltaire directly reminded his readers of the intolerance of the Reformation era and indirectly referred to examples of contemporary religious excesses. He argued that the philosophical spirit can overcome fanaticism and foster toleration and more humane religious behavior. In a manner that shocked many of his contemporaries, he praised the virtues of Confucianism over those of Christianity.*

Fanaticism is to superstition what delirium is to fever and rage to anger. The man visited by ecstasies and visions, who takes dreams for realities and his fancies for prophecies, is an enthusiast; the man who supports his madness with murder is a fanatic. . . .

The most detestable example of fanaticism was that of the burghers of Paris who on St. Bartholomew's Night [1572] went about assassinating and butchering all their fellow citizens who did not go to mass, throwing them out of windows, cutting them in pieces.

Once fanaticism has corrupted a mind, the malady is almost incurable. . . .

The only remedy for this epidemic malady is the philosophical spirit which, spread gradually, at last tames men's habits and prevents the disease from starting; for once the disease has made any progress, one must flee and wait for the air to clear itself. Laws and religion are not strong enough against the spiritual pest; religion, far from being healthy food for infected brains, turns to poison in them. . . .

Even the law is impotent against these attacks of rage; it is like reading a court decree to a raving maniac. These fellows are certain that the holy spirit with which they are filled is above the law, that their enthusiasm is the only law they must obey.

What can we say to a man who tells you that he would rather obey God than men, and that therefore he is sure to go to heaven for butchering you?

Ordinarily fanatics are guided by rascals, who put the dagger into their hands; these latter resemble that Old Man of the Mountain who is supposed to have made imbeciles taste the joys of paradise and who promised them an enternity of the pleasures of which he had given them a foretaste, on condition that they assassinated all those he would name to them. There is only one religion in the world that has never been sullied by fanaticism, that of the Chinese men of letters. The schools of philosophy were not only free from this pest, they were its remedy; for the effect of philosophy is to make the soul tranquil, and fanaticism is incompatible with tranquility. If our holy religion has so often been corrupted by this infernal delirium, it is the madness of men which is at fault. ❑

Voltaire, *Philosophical Dictionary*, trans. by P. Gay (New York: Harcourt, Brace, and World, 1962), pp. 267–269.

The title page of the first volume of the Encyclopedia. *The early volumes of the text received the approval of the royal censor, as noted on the last line, but when it became evident that the work challenged many widely held religious and political views, this approval was withdrawn, although the volumes were eventually published outside France.* [*The Mansell Collection.*]

The Encyclopedia

The mid-century witnessed the publication of one of the greatest monuments of the Enlightenment. Under the heroic leadership of Denis Diderot (1713–1784), and Jean le Rond d'Alembert (1717–1783), the first volume of the *Encyclopedia* appeared in 1751. The project reached completion in 1772, numbering seventeen volumes of text and eleven of plates. The *Encyclopedia* was the product of the collective effort of more than one hundred authors, and its editors had at one time or another solicited articles from all the major French *philosophes*. The project reached fruition only after numerous attempts to censor it and to halt its publication. The *Encyclopedia* set forth the most advanced critical ideas in religion, government, and philosophy. This criticism often had to be hidden in obscure articles or under the cover of irony. The articles represented a collective plea for freedom of expression. However, the large volumes also provided important information on manufacturing, canal building, ship construction, and improved agriculture.

Between fourteen and sixteen thousand copies of various editions of the *Encyclopedia* were sold before 1789. The project had been designed to secularize learning and to undermine the intellectual assumptions remaining from the Middle Ages and the Reformation. The articles on politics, ethics, and society ignored concerns about divine law and concentrated on humanity and its immediate well-being. The encyclopedists looked to antiquity rather than to the Christian centuries for their intellectual and ethical models. The future welfare of humankind lay not in pleasing God or following divine commandments but rather in harnessing the power of the earth and its resources and in living at peace with one's fellow human beings. The good life lay here and now and was to be achieved through the application of reason to human relationships.

Denis Diderot, the principal editor of the Encyclopedia. [*The Granger Collection.*]

With the publication of the *Encyclopedia*, enlightened thought became more fully diffused over the Continent. Enlightened ideas penetrated German and Russian intellectual and political circles. The *philosophes* of the latter part of the century turned from championing the general cause of reform and discussed specific areas of practical application.

The Enlightenment and Religion

Throughout the century, in the eyes of the *philosophes* the chief enemy of the improvement of humankind and the enjoyment of happiness was the existence and influence of ecclesiastical institutions. The hatred of the *philosophes* for the Church and Christianity was summed up in Voltaire's cry of "Crush the Infamous Thing." Almost all varieties of Christianity, but especially Roman Catholicism, invited the criticism of the *philosophes*. Intellectually, the churches perpetuated a religious rather than a scientific view of humankind and physical nature. The clergy taught that human beings were basically sinful and that they required divine grace to become worthy creatures. The doctrine of original sin in either its Catholic or its Protestant formulation suggested that meaningful improvement in human nature on earth was impossible. Religious concerns turned human interest away from this world to the world to come. In the view of the *philosophes*, the concept of predestination suggested that the condition of the human soul after death had little or no relationship to virtuous living during this life. Through disagreements over obscure doctrines, the various churches favored the politics of intolerance and bigotry that in the past had caused human suffering, torture, and war.

Deism

The *philosophes* believed that religion should be reasonable and should lead to moral behavior. The Newtonian worldview had convinced many writers that nature was rational. Therefore, the God who had created nature must also be rational, and the religion through which that God was worshiped should be rational. Moreover, Lockean philosophy, which limited human knowledge to empirical experience, raised the question whether such a thing as divine revelation to humankind was, after all, possible. These considerations gave rise to a movement for enlightened religion known as *deism*.

The title of one of its earliest expositions, *Christianity Not Mysterious* (1696) by John Toland, indicates the general tenor of this religious outlook. Toland and later writers wished to consider religion a natural and rational, rather than a supernatural and mystical, phenomenon. In this respect, the deists made a departure from the general piety of Newton and Locke, both of whom regarded themselves as distinctly Christian. Newton had believed that God might interfere with the natural order, whereas the deists regarded God as resembling a divine watchmaker who had set the mechanism of nature to work and had then departed from the scene.

There were two major points in the deists' creed. The first was a belief in the existence of God. They thought that this belief could be empirically deduced from the contemplation of nature. Joseph Addison's poem on the spacious firmament (1712), illustrates this idea:

> The spacious firmament on high,
> With all the blue ethereal sky,
> And spangled heav'n, a shining frame,
> Their great Original proclaim:
> Th' unwearied Sun, from day to day,
> Does his Creator's power display,
> And publishes to every land
> The work of an Almighty hand.

Because nature provided evidence of a rational God, that deity must also favor rational morality. Consequently, the second point in the deists' creed was a belief in life after death, when rewards and punishments would be meted out according to the virtue of the life a person led on this earth.

Deism was empirical, tolerant, reasonable, and capable of encouraging virtuous living. It was the major positive religious component of the Enlightenment. Voltaire declared:

The great name of Deist, which is not sufficiently revered, is the only name one ought to take. The only gospel one ought to read is the great book of Nature, written by the hand of God and sealed with his seal. The only religion that ought to be professed is the religion of worshiping God and being a good man.[3]

If such a faith became widely accepted, the fanaticism and rivalry of the various Christian sects might be overcome. Religious conflict and persecutions encouraged by the fulsome zeal would end. There would also be little or no necessity for a priestly class to forment fanaticism, denominational hatred, and bigotry.

Toleration

A primary social condition for such a life was the establishment of religious toleration. Again, Voltaire took the lead in championing this cause. In 1762, the Roman Catholic political authorities in Toulouse ordered the execution of a Huguenot named Jean Calas.

[3] Quoted in J. H. Randall, *The Making of the Modern Mind*, rev. ed. (New York: Houghton Mifflin, 1940), p. 292.

He stood accused of having murdered his son to prevent him from converting to Roman Catholicism. Calas had been viciously tortured and publicly strangled without ever having confessed his guilt. The confession would not have saved his life, but it would have given the Catholics good propaganda to use against Protestants.

Voltaire learned of the case only after Calas' death. He made the dead man's cause his own. In 1763, he published a *Treatise on Tolerance* and hounded the authorities for a new investigation. Finally, in 1765, the judicial decision against the unfortunate man was reversed. For Voltaire, the case illustrated the fruits of religious fanaticism and the need for rational reform of judicial processes. Somewhat later in the century, the German playwright and critic Gotthold Lessing (1729–1781) wrote *Nathan the Wise* (1779) as a plea for toleration not only of different Christian sects but also of religious faiths other than Christianity. All of these calls for toleration stated, in effect, that life on earth and human relationships should not be subordinated to religion. Secular values and considerations were more important than religious ones.

The Enlightenment and Society

Although the *philosophes* wrote much on religion, humanity was the center of their interest. As one writer in the *Encyclopedia* observed, "Man is the unique point to which we must refer everything, if we wish to interest and please amongst considerations the most arid and details the most dry."[4] The *philosophes* believed that the application of human reason to society would reveal laws in human relationships similar to those found in physical nature. Although the term did not appear until later, the idea of social science originated with the Enlightenment. The purpose of discovering social laws was the removal of the inhumanity that existed through ignorance of them.

Adam Smith

The most important Enlightenment exposition of economics was Adam Smith's (1723–1790) *Inquiry into the Nature and Causes of the Wealth of Nations* (1776). Smith, who was for a time a professor at Glasgow, urged that the mercantile system of England—including the navigation acts, the bounties, most tariffs, special trading monopolies, and the domestic regulation of labor and manufacture—be abolished. Smith believed that these modes of economic regulation by the state interfered with the natural system of economic liberty. They were intended to preserve the

[4]Quoted in F. L. Baumer, *Main Currents of Western Thought*, 4th ed. (New Haven, Conn.: Yale University Press, 1978), p. 374.

Adam Smith (1723–1790) *wrote the most important Enlightenment exposition of economics* Inquiry into the Nature and Causes of the Wealth of Nations *in 1776.* [*Culver Pictures.*]

wealth of the nation, to capture wealth from other nations, and to assure a maximum amount of work for the laborers of the country. However, Smith regarded such regulations as preventing the wealth and production of the country from expanding. He wanted to encourage economic growth and a consumer-oriented economy. The means to those ends was the unleashing of individuals to pursue their own selfish economic interest. The free pursuit of economic self-interest would ensure economic expansion as each person sought enrichment by meeting the demands of the marketplace. Consumers would find their wants met as manufacturers and merchants sought their business.

Smith's book challenged the concept of scarce goods and resources that lay behind mercantilism and the policies of the guilds. Smith saw the realm of nature as a boundless expanse of water, air, soil, and minerals. The physical resources of the earth seemed to demand exploitation for the enrichment and comfort of humankind. In effect, Smith was saying that the nations and peoples of Europe need not be poor. The idea of the infinite use of nature's goods for the material benefit of humankind—a concept that has dominated Western life until recent years—stemmed directly from the Enlightenment. When Smith wrote, the population of the world was smaller, its people were poorer, and the quantity of undeveloped resources per capita was much greater. For people of the eighteenth century, it was in the uninhibited exploitation of natural resources that the true improvement of the human condition seemed to lie.

Smith is usually regarded as the founder of *laissez-faire* economic thought and policy, which has argued in favor of a very limited role for the government in economic life and regulation. However, *The Wealth of Nations* was a very complex book. Smith was no simple dogmatist. For example, he was not opposed to all government activity touching on the economy. The state should provide schools, armies, navies, and roads. It should also undertake certain commercial ventures, such as the opening of dangerous new trade routes that were economically desirable but the expense or risk of which discouraged private enterprise. His reasonable tone and recognition of the complexity of social and economic life displayed a very important point about the *philosophes*. Most of them were much less rigid and doctrinaire than any brief summary of their thought may tend to suggest. They recognized the passions of humanity as well as its reason. They adopted reason and nature as tools of criticism through which they might create a climate of opinion that would allow the fully developed human personality to flourish.

Montesquieu and The Spirit of the Laws

Charles Louis de Secondat, Baron de Montesquieu (1689–1755) was a French noble of the robe, and a lawyer. He also belonged to the Bordeaux Academy of Science, before which he presented papers on scientific topics.

Montesquieu's *The Spirit of the Laws* (1748) may well have been the single most influential book of the century. It is a work that exhibits the internal tensions of the Enlightenment. Montesquieu pursued an empirical method, taking illustrative examples from the political experience of both ancient and modern nations. From these, he concluded that there could be no single set of political laws that applied to all peoples at all times and in all places. Rather, there existed a large number of political variables, and the good political life depended on the relationship of those variables. Whether a monarchy or a republic was the best form of government was a matter of the size of the political unit and its population, its social and religious cus-

Charles de Secondat Baron de Montesquieu (1689–1744) was the author of The Spirit of the Laws, *which may well have been the most influential political work of the eighteenth century. [Bulloz.]*

toms, its economic structure, its traditions, and its climate. Only a careful examination and evaluation of these elements could reveal what mode of government would prove most beneficial to a particular people. A century later, such speculations would have been classified as sociology.

So far as France was concerned, Montesquieu had some rather definite ideas. He believed in monarchical government, but with a monarchy whose power was tempered and limited by various sets of intermediary institutions. The latter included the aristocracy, the towns, and the other corporate bodies that enjoyed particular liberties that the monarch must respect. These corporate bodies might be said to represent various segments of the general population and thus of public opinion. In France, he regarded the aristocratic courts, or *parlements*, as the major example of an intermediary association. Their role was to limit the power of the monarchy and thus to preserve the liberty of the subjects. In championing these aristocratic bodies and the general role of the aristocracy, Montesquieu was a political conservative. However, he adopted that stance in the hope of achieving reform, for in his opinion it was the oppressive and inefficient absolutism of the monarchy that accounted for the degradation of French life.

One of Montesquieu's most influential ideas was that of division of power within any government. For his model of a government with power wisely separated among different branches, he took contemporary Great Britain. There he believed he had found a system in which executive power resided in the king, legislative power in the Parliament, and judicial power in the courts. He thought any two branches could check and balance the power of the other. His perception of the eighteenth-century British constitution was incorrect, because he failed to see how patronage and electoral corruption allowed a handful of powerful aristocrats to dominate the government. Moreover, he was also unaware of the emerging cabinet system, which meant that the executive power was slowly becoming a creature of the Parliament. Nevertheless, the analysis illustrated Montesquieu's strong sense of the need to limit the exercise of power through constitutionalism and the formation of law by legislatures rather than by monarchs. In this manner, although Montesquieu set out to defend the political privileges of the French aristocracy, his ideas had a profound and still-lasting effect on the liberal democracies of the next two centuries.

Jean-Jacques Rousseau (1712–1778). His writings raised some of the most profound social and ethical questions of the Enlightenment. [Metropolitan Museum of Art.]

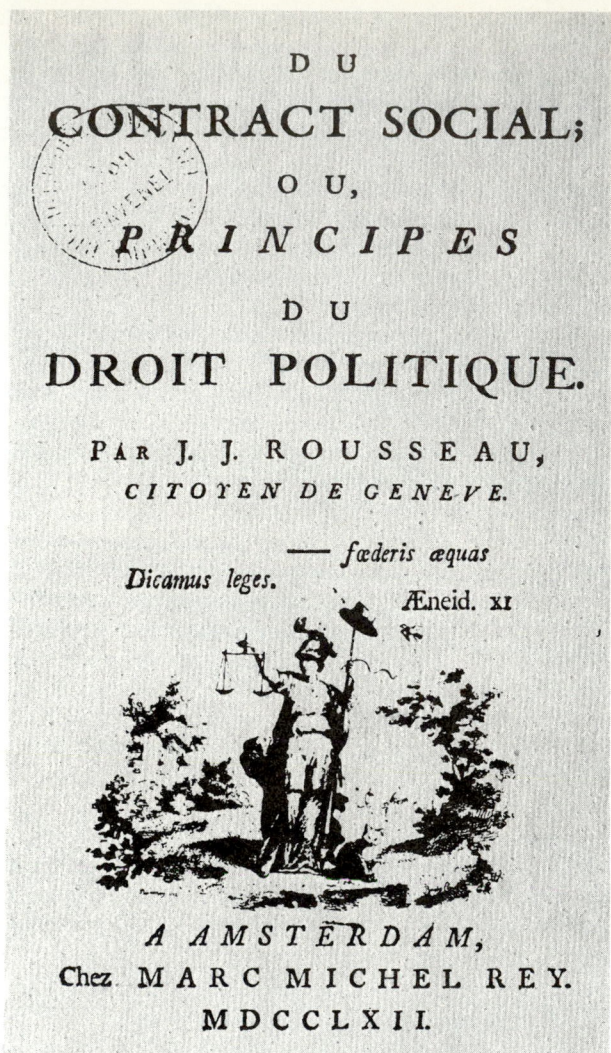

Rousseau's Social Contract (1762) *challenged the political thought of an aristocratic age by calling for radical political equality. Note that, like many other unorthodox works, it was published in relatively free Amsterdam. [The Granger Collection.]*

Rousseau

Jean-Jacques Rousseau (1712–1778) held a view of political power quite different from Montesquieu's.

Rousseau was a strange, isolated genius who never felt particularly comfortable with the other *philosophes*. Yet perhaps more than any other writer of the mid-eighteenth century, he transcended the thought and values of his own time. Rousseau had a deep antipathy toward the world and the society in which he lived. It seemed impossible for human beings living according to contemporary commercial values to achieve moral, virtuous, or sincere lives. In 1750, in his

Rousseau Argues That Inequality Is Not Natural

Jean-Jacques Rousseau was one of the first writers to assert the social equality of human beings. He argued, as in this 1755 passage, that inequality had developed through the ages and was not "natural." He directly questioned the sanctity of property based on the assumed natural inequality of human beings.

I have endeavoured to trace the origin and progress of inequality, and the institution and abuse of political societies, as far as these are capable of being deduced from the nature of man merely by the light of reason, and independently of those sacred dogmas which give the sanction if divine right to sovereign authority. It follows from this survey that, as there is hardly any inequality in the state of nature, all the inequality which now prevails owes its strength and growth to the development of our faculties and the advance of the human mind, and becomes at last permanent and legitimate by the establishment of property and laws.

Secondly, it follows that moral inequality, authorized by positive right alone, clashes with natural right, whenever it is not proportionate to physical inequality—a distinction which sufficiently determines what we think of that species of inequality which prevails in all civilized countries; since it is plainly contrary to the law of nature, however defined, that children should command old men, fools wise men, and that the privileged few should gorge themselves with superfluities while the starving multitude are in want of the bare necessities of life. ❑

Jean-Jacques Rousseau, *The Social Contract and Discourses*, trans. by G. D. H. Cole (New York: Dutton, 1950), pp. 271–272.

Discourse on the Moral Effects of the Arts and Sciences, he contended that the process of civilization and enlightenment had corrupted human nature. Human beings in the state of nature had been more dignified. In 1755, in a *Discourse on the Origin of Inequality*, Rousseau blamed much of the evil in the world on maldistribution of property.

In both works, Rousseau brilliantly and directly challenged the social fabric of the day. He drew into question the concepts of material and intellectual progress and the morality of a society in which commerce and industry were regarded as the most important of human activities. He felt that the real purpose of society was to nurture better people. In this respect, Rousseau's vision of reform was much more radical than that of other contemporary writers.

Rousseau carried these same concerns into his political thought. His most extensive discussion of politics appeared in *The Social Contract* (1762). Although the book attracted rather little immediate attention, by the end of the century it was widely read in France. *The Social Contract*, as compared to Montesquieu's *Spirit of the Laws*, is a very abstract book. It does not propose specific reforms but outlines the kind of political structure that Rousseau believed would overcome the evils of contemporary politics and society.

In the tradition of John Locke, most eighteenth-century political thinkers regarded human beings as individuals and society as a collection of such independent individuals pursuing personal, selfish goals. These writers wished to liberate these individuals from the undue bonds of government. Rousseau picked up the stick from the other end. His book opens with the declaration, "All men are born free, but everywhere they are in chains."[5] The rest of the volume constitutes a *defense* of the chains of a properly organized society over its members. Rousseau suggested that society is more important than its individual members, because they are what they are only because of their relationship to the larger community. Independent human beings living alone can achieve very little. Through their relationship to the larger community, they become moral creatures capable of significant action. The question then becomes what kind of community allows people to behave morally. In his two previous discourses, Rousseau had explained that contemporary European society was not such a community. It was merely an aggregate of competing individuals whose chief social goal was to preserve selfish independence in spite of all potential social bonds and obligations.

Rousseau sought to project the vision of a society in which each person could maintain personal freedom while at the same time behaving as a loyal member of the larger community. To that end, Rousseau drew on the traditions of Plato and Calvin to define freedom as obedience to law. In his case, the law to be obeyed was that created by the general will. This concept normally indicated the will of the majority of voting citizens who acted with adequate information and under

[5] Jean-Jacques Rousseau, *The Social Contract and Discourses*, trans. by G. D. H. Cole (New York: Dutton, 1950), p. 3.

the influence of virtuous customs and morals. Such democratic participation in decision making would bind the individual citizen to the community. Rousseau believed that the general will must always be right and that to obey the general will was to be free. This argument led him to the notorious conclusion that under certain circumstances some people must be forced to be free. Rousseau's politics thus constituted a justification for radical direct democracy and for collective action against individual citizens.

Rousseau had in effect launched an assault on the eighteenth-century cult of the individual and the fruits of selfishness. He stood at odds with the commercial spirit that was transforming the society in which he lived. Rousseau would have disapproved of the main thrust of Adam Smith's *Wealth of Nations*, which he may or may not have read, and would no doubt have preferred a study on the virtue of nations. Smith wanted people to be prosperous; Rousseau wanted them to be good even if being good meant that they might remain economically poor. He saw human beings not as independent individuals but as creatures enmeshed in necessary social relationships. He believed that loyalty to the community should be encouraged. As one device to that end, he suggested a civic religion based on the creed of deism. Such a shared tolerant religious faith would provide unity for the society. Rousseau's chief intellectual inspiration arose from his study of Plato and the ancient Greek *polis*. Especially in Sparta he thought he had discovered human beings dwelling in a moral society inspired by a common purpose. He hoped that modern human beings might also create such a moral commonwealth in which virtuous living would become subordinate to commercial profit.

Enlightened Absolutism

Most of the *philosophes* favored neither Montesquieu's reformed and revived aristocracy nor Rousseau's democracy as a solution to contemporary political problems. Like other thoughtful people of the day in other stations and occupations, they looked to the existing monarchies. The *philosophes* hoped in particular that the French monarchy might assert really effective power over the aristocracy and the Church to bring about significant reform. Voltaire was a very strong monarchist. He and others—such as Diderot, who visited Catherine II of Russia, did not wish to limit the power of monarchs but sought to redirect that power toward the rationalization of economic and political structures and the liberation of intellectual life. Most *philosophes* were not opposed to power if they could find a way of using it for their own purposes.

During the last third of the century, it seemed to some observers that several European rulers had actually embraced many of the reforms set forth by the *philosophes*. *Enlightened absolutism* is the term used to describe this phenomenon. The phrase indicates monarchical government dedicated to the rational strengthening of the central absolutist administration at the cost of other lesser centers of political power. The monarchs most closely associated with it— Frederick II of Prussia, Joseph II of Austria, and Catherine II of Russia—often found that the political and social realities of their realms caused them to moderate the degree of both enlightenment and absolutism in their policies. Frederick II corresponded with the *philosophes*, for a time provided Voltaire with a place at his court, and even wrote history and political tracts. Catherine II, who was a master of what would later be called public relations, consciously sought to create the image of being enlightened. She read the works of the *philosophes*, became a friend of Diderot and Voltaire, and made frequent references to their ideas, all in the hope that her nation might seem more modern and Western. Joseph II continued numerous initiatives begun by his mother, Maria Theresa, and imposed a series of religious, legal, and social reforms that contemporaries believed he had derived from suggestions of the *philosophes*.

Despite such appearances, the relationship between these rulers and the writers of the Enlightenment was rather more complicated. They did wish to see their subjects enjoy better health, somewhat more accessible education, the benefits of a more rational

MAJOR PUBLICATION DATES OF
THE ENLIGHTENMENT

1687	Newton's *Principia Mathematica*
1690	Locke's *Essay Concerning Human Understanding*
1696	Toland's *Christianity Not Mysterious*
1733	Voltaire's *Letters on the English*
1738	Voltaire's *Elements of the Philosophy of Newton*
1748	Montesquieu's *Spirit of the Laws*
1750	Rousseau's *Discourse on the Moral Effects of the Arts and Sciences*
1751	First volume of the *Encyclopedia* edited by Diderot
1755	Rousseau's *Discourse on the Origin of Inequality*
1762	Rousseau's *Social Contract*
1763	Voltaire's *Treatise on Toleration*
1776	Smith's *Wealth of Nations*
1779	Lessing's *Nathan the Wise*

political administration, and economic prosperity. In many of these policies, they were more advanced than the rulers of Western Europe. However, the humanitarian and liberating zeal of the Enlightenment directed only part of their policies. Frederick II, Joseph II, and Catherine II were also determined that their nations would play major diplomatic and military roles in Europe. In no small measure, they sought the rational economic and social integration of their realms so they could achieve military strength. All of the states of Europe had emerged from the Seven Years' War understanding that they would require stronger armed forces in future conflicts and looking for new sources of taxation to finance their armies. The search for new revenues and further internal political support for their rule was an additional factor that led these central and eastern European monarchs to make "enlightened" reforms. Consequently, they and their advisers used rationality to pursue many goals admired by the *philosophes* but also to further what the *philosophes* considered irrational militarism.

The most extensive political, religious, and social programs associated with enlightened absolutism were carried out by Joseph II of Austria and Catherine the Great of Russia.

Joseph II of Austria

No eighteenth-century ruler so embodied rational, impersonal force as the emperor Joseph II of Austria. He was the son of Maria Theresa and co-ruler with her from 1765 to 1780. During the next ten years he ruled alone. He has been aptly described as "an imperial puritan and a good deal of a prig."[6] During much of his life, he slept on straw and ate little but beef. He prided himself on a narrow, passionless rationality, which he sought to impose by his own will on the various Habsburg domains. Despite his eccentricities and the coldness of his personality, Joseph II genuinely and sincerely wished to improve the lot of his people. He was much less a political opportunist and cynic than either Frederick the Great of Prussia or Catherine the Great of Russia. The ultimate result of his well-intentioned efforts was a series of aristocratic and peasant rebellions extending from Hungary to the Austrian Netherlands.

As explained in Chapter 19, of all the rising states of the eighteenth century, Austria was the most diverse in its people and problems. Robert Palmer likened it to "a vast holding company."[7] The Habsburgs never succeeded in creating either a unified administrative structure or a strong aristocratic loyalty. The price of

[6] R. J. White, *Europe in the Eighteenth Century* (New York: St. Martin's, 1965), p. 214.

[7] Robert R. Palmer, *The Age of the Democratic Revolution*, Vol. 1 (Princeton, N.J.: Princeton University Press, 1959), p. 103.

the preservation of the monarchy during the War of the Austrian Succession (1740–1748) had been guarantees of considerable aristocratic independence, especially in Hungary.

However, during and after the conflict, Maria Theresa had taken major steps to strengthen the power of her crown in other of her realms. In Austria and Bohemia, through major administrative reorganization, she imposed a much more efficient system of tax collection that extracted funds even from the clergy and the nobles, and she established several central councils to deal with governmental problems. Her government became, in that regard, more bureaucratic than that of previous Habsburg rulers. She was particularly concerned about bringing all educational institutions into the service of the crown so that she could have a sufficiently large group of educated persons to serve as her officials, and she expanded primary education on the local level.

Maria Theresa was also quite concerned about the welfare of the peasants and serfs. The extension of the authority of the royal bureaucracy over that of the local nobilities was of some assistance to the peasants, as were the empress' decrees limiting the amount of labor, or *robot*, that could be demanded from the peasantry by the landowners. This concern was not particularly humanitarian; rather, it arose from her desire to assure a good military recruitment pool in the population. In all these policies and in her general desire to stimulate prosperity and military strength by royal initiative, Maria Theresa anticipated the policies of her son.

However, Joseph II was more determined, and his projected reforms were more wide-ranging than his mother's. He was ambitious to extend the borders of his territories in the direction of Poland, Bavaria, and the Ottoman Empire. But his greatest ambition lay in changing the authority of the Habsburg emperor over his various realms. He sought to overcome the pluralism of the Habsburg holdings by increasing the power of the central monarchy in areas of political and social life where Maria Theresa had wisely chosen not to exert authority. In particular, Joseph sought to lessen the very considerable autonomy enjoyed by Hungary. To that end, he refused to have himself crowned king of Hungary and even had the Crown of Saint Stephen sent to the Imperial Treasury in Vienna. By that means, he avoided having to guarantee existing or new Hungarian privileges at the time of his coronation. He reorganized local government in Hungary so as to increase the authority of his own officials, and he also required the use of the German language in all governmental matters. But eventually, in 1790, Joseph had to rescind most of the imperial centralizing measures he had attempted to impose on Hungary, as the Magyar nobility resisted one measure after another.

Another target of Joseph's assertion of royal absolutism was the Church. In October 1781, Joseph issued a Toleration Patent (decree) that extended freedom of worship to Lutherans, Calvinists, and the Greek Orthodox. They were permitted to have their own places of worship, to sponsor schools, to enter skilled trades, and to hold academic appointments and positions in the public service. From 1781 through 1789, Joseph also issued a series of patents and other enactments that relieved the Jews in his realms of certain taxes and signs of personal degradation. He also extended to them the right of private worship. Although the Jews benefited from these actions, they still did not enjoy general legal rights equal to those of other Habsburg subjects.

Joseph also sought to bring the various institutions of the Roman Catholic church directly under the control of royal authority. He forbade direct communication between the bishops of his realms and the pope. He regarded orders of monks and nuns as generally unproductive. Consequently, he dissolved over six hundred monasteries and confiscated their lands, although he excepted certain orders that ran schools or hospitals. He dissolved the traditional Roman Catholic seminaries, which he believed taught priests too great a loyalty to the papacy and too little concern for duties to their future parishioners. Having dissolved the existing seminaries, he chose to sponsor eight general seminaries for the training of priests, with an emphasis on parish duties. In effect, Joseph's policies made Roman Catholic priests the employees of the state and brought the influence of the Roman Catholic church as an independent institution in Habsburg lands to a close. In many respects, the ecclesiastical policies of Joseph II, known as *Josephinism*, prefigured those of the French Revolution.

In his policies toward serfdom and the land, Joseph II again pursued policies initiated by Maria Theresa to more far-reaching ends. Over the years of his reign, Joseph II introduced a series of reforms that touched the very heart of the rural social structure. He abolished the legal status of serfdom defined in terms of servitude to another person. He gave peasants a much wider arena of personal freedom. They could marry without approval of the landlord, and they could also engage in skilled work or have their children trained in such skills without permission of the landlord. The procedures of the manorial courts were reformed, and avenues of appeal to royal officials were opened. Joseph also encouraged landlords to change land leases so that it would be easier for peasants to inherit them or to transfer them to another peasant without bringing into doubt the landlord's title of ownership. In all of these actions, Joseph believed that the lessening of traditional burdens would make the peasant tillers of the land more productive and industrious.

Near the end of his reign, Joseph proposed a new and daring system of land taxation. He decreed in 1789 that all proprietors of the land were to be taxed, regardless of social status. No longer were the peasants alone to bear the burden of taxation. He abolished *robot* (the services due a landlord from peasants) and commuted it into a monetary tax, only part of which would in the future go to the landlord while the remainder would revert to the state. The decree was made, but resistance from the nobles led to a delay in its implementation. Then, in 1790, Joseph died, and the decree never went into effect. However, it and others of his measures had stirred up turmoil throughout the Habsburg realms. Peasants revolted over disagreements about the interpretation of their newly granted rights. The nobles of the various realms protested the taxation scheme. The Hungarian Magyars resisted Joseph's centralization measures and compelled him to rescind them.

On Joseph's death, the crown went to his brother Leopold II (1790–1792). Although quite sympathetic to Joseph's goals, Leopold found himself compelled to repeal many of the most controversial decrees, such as that in regard to taxation.

Catherine the Great of Russia

Joseph II never grasped the practical necessity of cultivating political support for his policies. Catherine II (1762–1796), who had been born a German princess but who became empress of Russia, understood only too well the fragility of the Romanov dynasty's base of power.

After the death of Peter the Great in 1725, the court nobles and the army had repeatedly determined the Russian succession. As a result, the crown fell primarily into the hands of people with little talent. Peter's wife, Catherine I, ruled for two years (1725–1727) and was succeeded for three years by Peter's grandson Peter II. In 1730, the crown devolved on Anna, who was a niece of Peter the Great. During 1740 and 1741, a child named Ivan VI, who was less than a year old, was the nominal ruler. Finally, in 1741, Peter the Great's daughter Elizabeth came to the throne. She held the title of empress until 1762, but her reign was not notable for new political departures or sound administration. Her court was a shambles of political and romantic intrigue. Needless to say, much of the power possessed by the tsar at the opening of the century had vanished.

At her death in 1762, Elizabeth was succeeded by Peter III, one of her nephews. He was a weak ruler whom many contemporaries considered mad. He immediately exempted the nobles from compulsory military service and then made rapid peace with Frederick the Great, for whom he held unbounded admiration. That decision probably saved Prussia from military defeat. The one positive feature of this unbalanced creature's life was his marriage in 1745 to a young German princess born in Pomerania. This was the future Catherine the Great, who for almost twenty years lived in misery and frequent danger at the court of Elizabeth. During that time she befriended important nobles and read widely in the books of the *philosophes.* She was a shrewd person whose experience in a court crawling with rumors, intrigue, and conspiracy had taught her how to survive. She had neither love nor loyalty for her demented husband. After a few months of rule, Peter II was deposed and murdered with the approval, if not the aid, of Catherine. On his deposition she was immediately proclaimed empress.

Catherine's familiarity with the Enlightenment and the general culture of Western Europe convinced her that Russia was very backward and that it must make major reforms if it were to remain a great power. She understood that any major reform must have a wide base of political and social support. Such was especially the case because she herself had assumed the throne through a palace coup.

Consequently, in 1767, Catherine summoned a Legislative Commission to advise her on revisions in the law and government of Russia. There were over five hundred delegates drawn from all sectors of Russian life. Before the commission convened, Catherine issued a set of *Instructions,* partly written by herself. They contained numerous ideas drawn from the political writings of the *philosophes.* The commission considered the *Instructions* as well as other ideas and complaints raised by its members. The revision of Russian law, however, did not occur for more than a half century. In 1768, Catherine dismissed the commission before several of its key committees had reported. Yet the meeting had not been useless, for a vast amount of information had been gathered about the conditions of local administration and economic life throughout the realm. The inconclusive debates and the absence of programs from the delegates themselves suggested that most Russians saw no alternative to an autocratic monarchy. For her part, it was clear that Catherine had no intention of departing from absolutism.

Catherine proceeded to carry out limited reforms on her own authority. She gave strong support to the rights and local power of the nobility. In 1777, she reorganized local government to solve problems brought to light by the Legislative Commission. She put most local offices into the hands of nobles rather than creating a royal bureaucracy. In 1785, Catherine issued the Charter of the Nobility, which guaranteed many noble rights and privileges. In part, the empress had no choice but to favor the nobles. They had the capacity to topple her from the throne. There were too few educated subjects in her realm to establish an independent

MAP 23-1 EXPANSION OF RUSSIA, 1689–1796 *The overriding territorial aim of Peter the Great in the first quarter and of Catherine the Great in the last half of the eighteenth century was the securing of northern and southern navigable-water outlets for the vast Russian Empire. Hence Peter's push to the Baltic Sea and Catherine's to the Black Sea. Catherine also managed to acquire large areas of Poland through the partitions of that country.*

bureaucracy, and the treasury could not afford an army strictly loyal to the crown. So Catherine wisely made a virtue of necessity. She strengthened the stability of her crown by making convenient friends with her nobles.

Part and parcel of Catherine's program was a continuation of the economic development begun under Peter the Great. She attempted to suppress internal barriers to trade. Exports of grain, flax, furs, and naval stores grew dramatically. She also favored the expansion of the small Russian middle class. Russian trade required such a vital urban class. And through all of these departures, Catherine attempted to maintain ties of friendship and correspondence with the *philosophes*. She knew that if she treated them kindly, they would be sufficiently flattered and would give her a progressive reputation throughout Europe.

The limited administrative reforms and the policy of economic growth had a counterpart in the diplomatic sphere. The Russian drive for warm-water ports continued. This goal required warfare with the Turks. In 1769, as a result of a minor Russian incursion, the Ottoman Empire declared war on Russia. The Russians

Empress Catherine the Great of Russia cultivated the friendship of the philosophes *but pursued many policies of which they disapproved, including warfare and censorship. [John R. Freeman.]*

responded in a series of strikingly successful military moves. During 1769 and 1770, the Russian fleet sailed all the way from the Baltic Sea into the eastern Mediterranean. The Russian army won several major victories that by 1771 gave Russia control of Ottoman provinces on the Danube River and the Crimean coast of the Black Sea. The conflict dragged on until 1774, when it was closed by the Treaty of Kuchuk-Kainardji. This treaty gave Russia a direct outlet on the Black Sea, free navigation rights in its waters, and free access through the Bosphorus. Moreover, the province of the Crimea became an independent state, which Catherine painlessly annexed in 1783.

The Partition of Poland

These military successes obviously brought the empress much domestic political support. However, they made the other states of eastern Europe uneasy. These anxieties were overcome by a division of Polish territory known as the First Partition of Poland. The Russian victories along the Danube River were most unwelcome to Austria, which also harbored ambitions of territorial expansion in that direction. At the same time, the Ottoman Empire was pressing Prussia for aid against Russia. Frederick the Great made a proposal to Russia and Austria that would give each something it wanted, prevent conflict among the powers, and

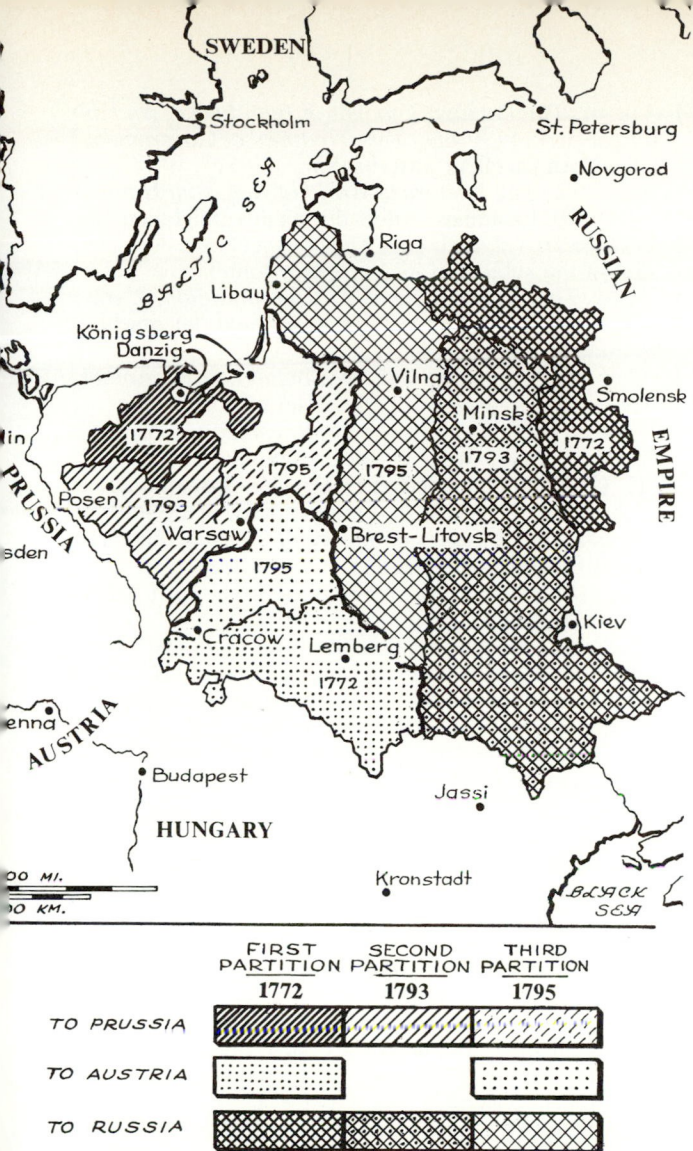

In September 1772, the helpless Polish aristocracy, paying the price for the maintenance of their internal liberties, ratified this seizure of their territory. The Polish state had lost approximately one third of its territory. That loss was not necessarily fatal to the continued existence of Poland, and a considerable national political revival took place after the partition. Real attempts were made to adjust the Polish political structures to the realities of the time. These proved to be too little and too late. The political and military strength of Poland could not match that of its stronger, more ambitious neighbors.

There were two additional partitions of Poland by Russia and Prussia, and one more by Austria. These occurred in 1793 and 1795 and removed Poland from the map of Europe. Each time, the great powers contended that they were saving themselves, and by implication the rest of Europe, from Polish anarchy. The fact of the matter was that the political weakness of Poland made the country and its resources a rich field for plunderous aggression. The last two partitions took place during the French Revolution. The three eastern European absolute monarchies objected to certain reforms undertaken by the Polish nobles for fear that even minor Polish reform might endanger the stability of their own societies.

The Enlightenment Heritage in World Perspective

No other movement of European thought produced so widespread influence over so long a time as the Scientific Revolution and Enlightenment. There exists a direct line of intellectual descent from those movements to the science and social criticism of the present day. Wherever modern science and technology are pursued and their effects felt, the spirit of the Enlightenment persists. From the eighteenth century to the present, the *philosophes* provided a pattern for the behavior of intellectuals who wished to criticize societies in order to move them in a more rational, scientific, and secular direction.

The Enlightenment *philosophes* believed human beings were more than creatures of reason. They thought the emotions and passions were also important. However, more than any other previous group of writers, they used reason as a weapon for reform and as a device to stir people to more productive economic life. In the two centuries since the Enlightenment, such a use of critical reason has become a mark of reforming and progressive social and intellectual movements. The *philosophes* first used reason against Christianity, but reason came to be used against other of the world religions as well.

MAP 23-2 PARTITIONS OF POLAND, 1772–1793–1795 *The callous eradication of Poland from the map displayed eighteenth-century power politics at its most extreme. Poland, without strong central governmental institutions, fell victim of those states in central and eastern Europe that had developed such institutions.*

save appearances. After long, complicated, secret negotiations, the three powers agreed that Russia would abandon the conquered Danubian provinces. In compensation, Russia received a large portion of Polish territory with almost two million inhabitants. As a reward for remaining neutral, Prussia annexed most of the territory between East Prussia and Prussia proper. This land allowed Frederick to unite two previously separate sections of his realm. Finally, Austria took Galicia, with its important salt mines, and other Polish territory with over two and one-half million inhabitants.

The heritage of the Enlightenment has been more complex than was its political impact in the eighteenth century. One strand of Enlightenment political thought contributed to constitutionalism and modes of government in which the power and authority of the central government stands sharply circumscribed. Montesquieu, for example, influenced the Constitution of the United States and the numerous constitutions which the U.S. document itself later influenced.

Another strand of Enlightenment political thought, found in Voltaire, contributed to the growth of strong central governments as was the case with enlightened absolutism. Advocates of this method of government believed that a single monarch or strong central bureaucracy through reason could come to a proper understanding of particular political or social problems and then impose a rational solution.

Still another strand of political thought, arising from Rousseau's writing, led to the socialist concern with inequality of property distribution. Consequently, in the modern world, liberal, socialist, and authoritarian governments partake of the Enlightenment heritage.

Suggested Readings

R. P. BARTLETT, *Human Capital: The Settlement of Foreigners in Russia. 1762–1804* (1979). Examines Catherine's policy of attracting farmers and skilled workers to Russia.

C. BECKER, *The Heavenly City of the Eighteenth Century Philosophers* (1932). An influential but very controversial discussion.

P. P. BERNARD, *Joseph II* (1968). A brief biography.

T. BESTERMANN, *Voltaire* (1969). A biography by the editor of Voltaire's letters.

D. D. BIEN, *The Calas Affair: Persecution, Toleration, and Heresy in Eighteenth-Century Toulouse* (1960). The standard treatment of the famous case.

E. CASSIRER, *The Philosophy of the Enlightenment* (1951). A brilliant but difficult work by one of the great philosophers of the twentieth century.

H. CHISICK, *The Limits of Reform in the Enlightenment: Attitudes toward the Education of the Lower Classes in Eighteenth-Century France* (1981). An attempt to examine the impact of the Enlightenment on nonelite classes.

G. R. CRAGG, *The Church and the Age of Reason* (1961). A general survey of eighteenth-century religious life.

R. DARNTON, *The Business of Enlightenment: A Publishing History of the Encyclopedia, 1775–1800* (1979). A wide-ranging examination of the printing and dispersion of the *Encyclopedia.*

R. DARNTON, *The Literary Underground of the Old Regime* (1982). Essays on the world of printers, publishers, and booksellers.

J. DUNN, *The Political Thought of John Locke; An Historical Account of the "Two Treatises of Government"* (1969). An excellent introduction.

P. FUSSELL, *The Rhetorical World of Augustan Humanism* (1969). Examines writers during the Enlightenment.

J. GAGLIARDO, *Enlightened Despotism* (1967). A discussion of the subject in its European context.

P. GAY, *The Enlightenment: An Interpretation,* 2 vols. (1966, 1969). The most important and far-reaching treatment.

P. GAY, *The Enlightenment: A Comprehensive Anthology* (1973). A large, well-edited set of documents.

L. GERSHOY, *From Despotism to Revolution, 1763–1793* (1944). A sound treatment of the political background.

C. C. GILLISPIE, *Science and Polity in France at the End of the Old Regime* (1980). A major survey of the subject.

N. HAMPSON, *A Cultural History of the Enlightenment* (1969). A useful introduction.

P. HAZARD, *The European Mind: The Critical Years, 1680–1715* (1935).

P. HAZARD, *European Thought in the Eighteenth Century from Montesquieu to Lessing* (1946). These two volumes portray the century as the turning point for the emergence of the modern mind in Europe.

M. C. JACOB, *The Newtonians and the English Revolution* (1976). A controversial book that attempts to relate science and politics.

M. C. JACOB, *The Radical Enlightenment: Pantheists, Freemasons, and Republicans* (1981). A treatment of frequently ignored figures in the age of the Enlightenment.

H. C. JOHNSON, *Frederick the Great and His Officials* (1975). An examination of the administrative apparatus of enlightened absolutism.

R. KREISER, *Miracles, Convulsions, and Ecclesiatical Politics in Early Eighteenth-Century Paris* (1978). An important study of the kind of religious life that the *philosophes* opposed.

L. KRIEGER, *Kings and Philosophers, 1689–1789* (1970). A survey that relates the social and political thought of the Enlightenment writers to their immediate political setting.

T. S. KUHN, *The Copernican Revolution* (1957). The most influential treatment.

P. LASLETT, *Locke's Two Treatises of Government,* 2nd ed. (1970). Definitive texts with very important introductions.

C. A. MACARTNEY, *The Habsburg Empire, 1790–1918* (1971). Provides useful coverage of major mid-eighteenth-century developments.

I. DE MADARIAGA, *Russia in the Age of Catherine the Great* (1981). The best discussion in English.

F. MANUEL, *The Eighteenth Century Confronts the Gods* (1959). A broad examination of the *philosophes'* treatment of Christian and pagan religion.

R. R. PALMER, *Catholics and Unbelievers in Eighteenth-Century France* (1939). A discussion of the opponents of the *philosophes.*

G. RITTER, *Frederick the Great* (trans. 1968). A useful biography.

R. O. Rockwood (ed.), *Carl Becker's Heavenly City Revisited* (1958). Important essays qualifying Becker's thesis.

J. N. Shklar, *Men and Citizens, a Study of Rousseau's Social Theory* (1969). A thoughtful and provocative overview of Rousseau's political thought.

R. E. Sullivan, *John Toland and the Deist Controversy: A Study in Adaptation* (1982). An important and informative discussion.

R. S. Westfall, *Never at Rest: A Biography of Isaac Newton* (1981). A very important major study.

A. M. Wilson, *Diderot* (1972). A splendid biography of the person behind the project for the *Encyclopedia* and other major Enlightenment publications.

Napoleon in his study. This portrait was painted by Jacques-Louis David (1748–1825) in 1812 at the height of Napoleon's power, when he was about to invade Russia. [National Gallery of Art.]

24 The French Revolution and the Wars of Napoleon

In the spring of 1789, the long-festering conflict between the French monarchy and the aristocracy erupted into a new political crisis. This dispute, unlike earlier ones, quickly outgrew the issues of its origins and produced the wider disruption of the French Revolution. The quarrel that began as a struggle between the most exclusive elements of the political nation soon involved all sectors of French society and eventually every major state in Europe. Before the turmoil settled, small-town provincial lawyers and Parisian street orators exercised more influence over the fate of the Continent than did aristocrats, royal ministers, or monarchs. Armies commanded by persons of low birth and filled by conscripted village youths emerged victorious over forces composed of professional soldiers and directed by officers of noble birth. By the turn of the century under the leadership of Napoleon Bonaparte, the armies of France began to move across the continent. They overturned the governments and social structures of the Old Regime and replaced them with the structures and laws growing out of the French Revolutionary experience.

Although the French Revolution constituted one of the turning points in modern European history, it originated from the basic tensions and problems that characterized practically all late-eighteenth-century states. From the Seven Years' War (1756–1763) onward, the French monarchy was unable to handle its finances on a sound basis. It emerged from the conflict both defeated and in debt. The French support of the American revolt against Great Britain further deepened the financial difficulties of the government. On the eve of the French Revolution, the interest and payments on the royal debt amounted to just over one half of the entire budget. Given the economic vitality of the nation, this debt was neither overly large nor disproportionate to the debts of other European powers. The problem lay with the inability of the royal government

673

The Third Estate of a French City Petitions the King

The cahiers de doléances *were the lists of grievances brought to Versailles in 1789 by members of the Estates General. This particular* cahier *originated in Dourdan, a city of central France, and reflects the complaints of the Third Estate. The first two articles refer to the organization of the Estates General. The other articles ask that the king grant various forms of equality before the law and in matters of taxation. These demands for equality appeared in practically all the* cahiers *of the Third Estate.*

The order of the third estate of the City . . . of Dourdan . . . supplicates [the king] to accept the grievances, complaints, and remonstrances which it is permitted to bring to the foot of the throne, and to see therein only the expression of its zeal and the homage of its obedience.

It wishes:

1. That his subjects of the third estate, equal by such status to all other citizens, present themselves before the common father without other distinction which might degrade them.

2. That all the orders, already united by duty and a common desire to contribute equally to the needs of the State, also deliberate in common concerning its needs.

3. That no citizen lose his liberty except according to law; that, consequently, no one be arrested by virtue of special orders, or, if imperative circumstances necessitate such orders, that the prisoner be handed over to regular courts of justice within forty-eight hours at the latest.

. . . .

12. That every tax, direct or indirect, be granted only for a limited time, and that every collection beyond such term be regarded as peculation, and punished as such.

. . . .

15. That every personal tax be abolished; that thus the *capitation* [a poll tax] and the *taille* [tax from which nobility and clergy were exempt] and its accessories be merged with the *vingtiémes* [an income tax] in a tax on land and real or nominal property.

16. That such tax be borne equally, without distinction, by all classes of citizens and by all kinds of property, even feudal . . . rights.

17. That the tax substituted for the *corvée* be borne by all classes of citizens equally and without distinction. That said tax, at present beyond the capacity of those who pay it and the needs to which it is destined, be reduced by at least one-half. ☐

John Hall Stewart. *A Documentary Survey of the French Revolution* (New York: Macmillan, 1951), pp. 76–77.

---

to tap the wealth of the French nation through taxes to service and repay the debt. Paradoxically, France was a rich nation with an impoverished government.

Between 1786 and 1788, Louis XVI (1774–1792) appointed several different ministers to deal with the financial crisis. Their goal was to find ways to persuade the French nobles and the Church to pay more taxes. In every instance, they failed: The nobility held firm, as did the Church. As these negotiations dragged on, the *Parlement* of Paris took the position that it lacked authority to authorize new taxes and said that only the Estates General could do so. The Estates General had not met since 1614. As these unfruitful discussions dragged on in Paris, local aristocratic *Parlements* and estates in the provinces began to demand a restoration of the privileges they had lost in the era of Richelieu and Louis XIV. Consequently, in July 1788, under these pressures Louis XVI agreed to convene the Estates General the next year.

The Revolutions of 1789

The Estates General Becomes the National Assembly

The aristocratic triumph proved to be quite brief. It unloosened social and political forces that neither the nobles nor the monarchy could control. The new difficulties arose from clashes among the groups represented in the Estates General. The body was composed of three divisions: the First Estate of the clergy, the Second Estate of the nobility, and the Third Estate that represented everyone else in the kingdom. During the widespread public discussions preceding the meeting of the Estates General, it became clear that the Third Estate, which included all the professional, commercial, and middle-class groups of the country, would not permit the monarchy and the aristocracy to decide the future course of the nation. Their spirit was

This French cartoon of 1789 shows a peasant carrying a priest and a nobleman on his back. The peasantry could least afford to pay but was most heavily taxed, while the clergy and aristocracy were largely tax exempt. [Giraudon.]

best displayed in a pamphlet published during 1789, in which the Abbé Sieyès (1748–1836) declared, "What is the Third Estate? Everything. What has it been in the political order up to the present? Nothing. What does it ask? To become something."[1]

The split between the aristocracy and the Third Estate occurred before the Estates General gathered. Debate over the proper organization of the body drew the lines of basic disagreement. Members of the aristocracy demanded an equal number of representatives for each estate. In September 1788, the *Parlement* of Paris ruled that voting in the Estates General should be conducted by order rather than by head, that is, that each estate, or order, should have one vote, rather than that each member should have one vote. That procedure would ensure that the aristocratic First and Second Estates could always outvote the Third. Both moves on the part of the aristocracy unmasked its alleged concern for French liberty and exposed it as a

[1] Quoted in Leo Gershoy, *The French Revolution and Napoleon* (New York: Appleton-Century-Crofts, 1964), p. 102.

group determined to maintain its privileges. Representatives of the Third Estate denounced the arrogant claims of the aristocracy. The royal council eventually decided that the cause of the monarchy and fiscal reform would best be served by a strengthening of the Third Estate, and in December 1788, the council announced that the Third Estate would elect twice as many representatives as either the nobles or the clergy. This so-called doubling of the Third Estate meant that it could easily dominate the Estates General if voting were allowed by head rather than by order. It was properly assumed that some liberal nobles and clergy would support the Third Estate. The method of voting was settled by the king only after the Estates General had gathered at Versailles in May 1789.

The complaints and demands of the representatives could not be discussed until the questions of organization and voting had been decided. From the beginning, the Third Estate, whose members consisted largely of local government officials, professional men, and lawyers, refused to sit as a separate order as the king desired. For several weeks, there was a standoff. Then, on June 1, the Third Estate invited the clergy and the nobles to join them in organizing a new legislative body. A few members of the lower clergy did so. On June 17, that body declared itself the National Assembly.

Three days later, finding themselves accidentally locked out of their usual meeting place, the National Assembly moved to a nearby tennis court, where its members took an oath to continue to sit until they had given France a constitution. This was the famous Tennis Court Oath. Louis XVI ordered the National Assembly to desist from their actions, but shortly afterward, a majority of the clergy and a large group of nobles joined the assembly. On June 27, the king capitulated and formally requested the First and Second Estates to meet with the National Assembly, where voting would occur by head rather than by order. Even had nothing further occurred, the government of France would have been transformed. Government by the privileged orders had come to an end, for the National Assembly, which renamed itself the National Constituent Assembly, was composed of persons from all three orders who possessed shared liberal goals for the administrative, constitutional, and economic reform of the country. The revolution in the governing of France had commenced.

Fall of the Bastille

Two new forces soon intruded on the scene. The first was Louis XVI himself, who attempted to regain the initiative by mustering royal troops in the vicinity of Versailles and Paris. It appeared that he might have

This well-known painting by Jacques Louis David (1748–1825) portrays the Tennis Court Oath, June 20. In the center foreground members of the three Estates join hands as equals. The presiding officer leading the oath is Jean Sylvain Bailly, soon to become mayor of Paris. The painting is in the Musée Carnavalet in Paris. [French Embassy Press and Information Division, New York.]

been contemplating the disruption of the National Constituent Assembly. Such was the advice of Queen Marie Antoinette, his brothers, and the most conservative nobles, with whom he had begun to consult. These actions marked the beginning of a steady, and consistently poorly executed, royal attempt to undermine the assembly and halt the revolution. Most of the National Constituent Assembly wished to create some form of constitutional monarchy, but from the start, Louis' refusal to cooperate thwarted that effort. The king fatally decided to throw his lot in with the aristocracy against the nation.

The second new factor to impose itself on the events at the court at Versailles was the populace of Paris. The mustering of royal troops created anxiety in the city, where throughout the winter and spring of 1789 there had been several bread riots. The Parisians who had elected their representatives to the Third Estate had continued to meet after the elections. By June, they were organizing a citizen militia and collecting arms.

On July 14, somewhat more than eight hundred people, most of whom were small shopkeepers, tradespeople, artisans, and wage earners, marched to the Bastille in search of weapons for the militia. This great fortress, with ten-foot-thick walls, had once held political prisoners. Through miscalculations and ineptitude on the part of the governor of the fortress, the troops in the Bastille fired into the crowd, killing ninety-eight people and wounding many others.

Thereafter, the crowd stormed the fortress and eventually gained entrance. They released the seven prisoners, none of whom were there for political reasons, and killed several troops and the governor. They found no weapons.

On July 15, the militia of Paris, by then called the National Guard, offered its command to Lafayette. The hero of the American Revolution gave the guard a new insignia in the design of the red and blue stripes of the city of Paris separated by the white stripe of the king. This emblem became the revolutionary cockade worn by the soldiers and eventually the flag of revolutionary France.

The attack on the Bastille marked the first of many crucial *journées*, or days when the populace of Paris would redirect the course of the revolution. The fall of the fortress signaled that the political future of the nation would not be decided solely by the National Constituent Assembly. As the news of the taking of the Bastille spread, similar disturbances took place in the provincial cities. A few days later, Louis XVI again bowed to the force of events and personally visited Paris from Versailles, wearing the revolutionary cockade and recognizing the organized electors as the legitimate government of the city. The king also recognized the National Guard. The citizens of Paris were, for the time being, satisfied.

The Great Fear and the Surrender of Feudal Privileges

Simultaneously with the popular urban disturbances, a movement known as the *Great Fear* swept across much of the French countryside. Rumors had spread that royal troops would be sent into the rural districts. The result was an intensification of the peasant disturbances that had begun during the spring. The Great Fear witnessed the burning of chateaux, the destruction of records and documents, and the refusal by peasants to pay feudal dues. The peasants were determined to take possession of food supplies and land that they considered rightfully theirs. They were reclaiming rights and property that they had lost through the aristocratic resurgence of the last quarter-century, as well as venting their general anger against the injustices of rural life.

On the night of August 4, 1789, aristocrats in the National Constituent Assembly attempted to halt the spreading disorder in the countryside. By prearrangement, a number of liberal nobles and churchmen rose in the assembly and renounced their feudal rights, dues, and tithes. In a scene of great emotion, hunting and fishing rights, judicial authority, and special exemptions were surrendered. In a sense, these nobles gave up what they had already lost and what they could not have regained without civil war in the rural

areas. Later they would also, in many cases, receive compensation for their losses. Nonetheless, after the night of August 4, all French citizens were subject to the same and equal laws.

The Declaration of the Rights of Man and Citizen

In late August 1789, the National Constituent Assembly decided that before writing a new constitution, it should set forth a statement of broad political principles. On August 27, the assembly issued the Declaration of the Rights of Man and Citizen. This declaration drew together much of the political language of the Enlightenment and was also influenced by the Declaration of Rights adopted by Virginia in America in June 1776. The French declaration proclaimed that all men were "born and remain free and equal in rights." The natural rights so proclaimed were "liberty, property, security, and resistance to oppression." Governments existed to protect those rights. All political sovereignty resided in the nation and its representatives. All citizens were to be equal before the law and were to be "equally admissible to all public dignities, offices and employments, according to their capacity, and with no other distinction than that of their virtues and talents." There were to be due process of law and presumption of innocence until proof of guilt. Freedom of religion was affirmed. Taxation was to be apportioned equally according to capacity to pay. Property constituted "an inviolable and sacred right."[2]

Although these statements were rather abstract, almost all of them were directed against specific abuses of the old aristocratic and absolutist regime. If any two principles of the future governed the declaration, they were civic equality and protection of property. The Declaration of the Rights of Man and Citizen has often been considered the death certificate of the old regime.

Louis XVI stalled before ratifying both the declaration and the aristocratic renunciation of feudalism. The longer he hesitated, the larger the existing suspicions grew that he might again try to resort to the use of troops. Moreover, bread continued to be in short supply. On October 5, a crowd of several thousand Parisian women marched to Versailles, demanding more bread. This was but one of several occasions when women played a major role in the actions of the Parisian crowd. On this day, they milled about the palace, and many stayed the night. Under this pressure, the king agreed to sanction the decrees of the assembly. The next day, he and his family appeared on a balcony before the crowd. The Parisians were deeply

[2] Quoted in Georges Lefebvre, *The Coming of the French Revolution*, trans. by R. R. Palmer (Princeton, N.J.: Princeton University Press, 1967), pp. 221–223.

A contemporary depiction of the march of the women of Paris to Versailles in October 1789. They returned to the city accompanied by Louis XVI and the royal family. [The Granger Collection.]

suspicious of the monarch and believed that he must be kept under the watchful eye of the people. Consequently they demanded that Louis and his family return to Paris. The monarch had no real choice in the matter. On October 6, 1789, his carriage followed the crowd into the city, where he and his family settled in the palace of the Tuileries. The National Constituent Assembly soon followed. Thereafter, both Paris and France remained relatively stable and peaceful until the summer of 1792.

The Reconstruction of France

Once established in Paris, the National Constituent Assembly set about reorganizing France. In government, it pursued a policy of constitutional monarchy; in administration, rationalism; in economics, unregulated freedom; and in religion, anticlericalism. Throughout its proceedings, the Assembly was determined to protect property and to limit the impact on national life

of small-property owners as well as of the unpropertied elements of the nation. While championing civic equality before the law, the Assembly spurned social equality and extensive democracy. In all these areas, the Assembly charted a general course that, to a greater or lesser degree, nineteenth-century liberals across Europe and in other areas of the world would follow.

Political Reorganization

The Constitution of 1791, the product of the National Constituent Assembly's deliberations, established a constitutional monarchy. There was a unicameral Legislative Assembly in which powers of war and peace were vested. The monarch could delay but not halt legislation. The system of voting for members of the assembly divided citizens into active and passive categories. Only active citizens—that is, men paying annual taxes equal to three days of local labor wages—could vote. Active citizens chose other electors who

In this French cartoon of 1790, rats and flames consume the symbols of aristocratic privilege. The abolition of titles of nobility and of feudal dues was a major step toward the Revolution's goal of establishing the equality of all citizens before the law. [Editorial Photocolor Archives.]

L'ABOLITION DES TITRES DE NOBLESSE
par le Decret de l'Assemblee Nationale en juin 1790.

Des Aristocrates l'engeance est allarmée
Grands titres, vains honneurs, vous n'êtes que fumée
Qui se seroit douté d'un tel evenement.
C'est ainsi que chez nous la pluie abat le vent.

actually voted for members of the legislature. Only about fifty thousand citizens of the French nation of twenty-six million could qualify as electors or members of the Legislative Assembly.

In reconstructing the local and judicial administration, the National Constituent Assembly adhered to the rational spirit of the Enlightenment. It abolished the ancient French Provinces, such as Burgundy, and replaced them with eighty-three departments (*départements*) of generally equal size named after rivers, mountains, and other geographical features. All of the ancient judicial courts, including the seigneurial courts and the *parlements*, were also abolished. In their place were established uniform courts with elected judges and prosecutors. Legal procedures were simplified, and the most degrading punishments were removed from the books.

Economic Policy

In economic matters, the National Constituent Assembly suppressed the guilds and liberated the grain trade. The assembly established the metric system to provide the nation with uniform weights and measures. These policies of economic freedom and uniformity disappointed both peasants and urban workers caught in the cycle of inflation. By the decrees of 1790, the Assembly placed the burden of proof on the peasants to rid themselves of the residual feudal dues for which compensation was to be paid. On June 14, 1791, the Assembly enacted the Chapelier Law forbidding worker associations, thereby crushing the attempts of urban workers to protect their wages. Peasants and workers were henceforth to be left to the freedom and mercy of the marketplace.

The original royal debt remained, and various revised taxes adopted by the Assembly proved insufficient. Consequently, the National Constituent Assembly decided to pay the debt by confiscating and then selling the lands of the Roman Catholic church in France. Having made this decision late in 1789, the Assembly authorized the issuance of *assignats*, or government bonds, the value of which was guaranteed by the revenue to be generated from the sale of Church property. When the assignats began to circulate as currency, the Assembly issued ever larger quantities of them to liquidate the national debate. However, within a few months, the value of *assignats* began to fall. Inflation increased and put new stress on the lives of the urban poor.

The Civil Constitution of the Clergy

The confiscation of Church lands required an ecclesiastical reconstruction. In July 1790, the National Constituent Assembly issued the Civil Constitution of the Clergy, which transformed the Roman Catholic church in France into a branch of the secular state.

This legislation reduced the number of bishoprics from 139 to 83 and brought the borders of the dioceses into conformity with those of the new departments. It also provided for the election of priests and bishops, who henceforth became salaried employees of the state. The Assembly consulted neither the pope nor the French clergy about these broad changes. The king approved the measure only with the greatest reluctance.

Creating the Civil Constitution of the Clergy was the major blunder of the National Constituent Assembly. The measure created immense opposition within the French church, even from bishops who had long championed Gallican liberties over papal domination. In the face of this resistance, the Assembly unwisely ruled that all clergy must take an oath to support the Civil Constitution. Only seven bishops and about half the clergy did so. In reprisal, the assembly designated the clergy who had not taken the oath as "refractory" and removed them from their clerical functions.

Further reaction was swift. Refractory priests attempted to celebrate Mass. In February 1791, the pope condemned not only the Civil Constitution of the Clergy but also the Declaration of the Rights of Man and Citizen. That condemnation marked the opening of a Roman Catholic offensive against liberalism and the revolution that continued throughout the nineteenth century. Within France itself, the pope's action created a crisis of conscience and political loyalty for all sincere Catholics. Religious devotion and revolutionary loyalty became incompatible for many people. French citizens were divided between those who supported the constitutional priests and those who resorted to the refractory clergy. Louis XVI and his family favored the latter.

Counterrevolutionary Activity

As the revolution continued, a considerable number of aristocrats, known as *émigrés*, left France and settled just outside its borders, were they sought to foment counterrevolution. Among the most important of their number was the king's younger brother, the Count of Artois (1757–1836). In the summer of 1791, his agents and the queen persuaded Louis XVI to flee the country. The escape failed when Louis, along with his family, was stopped at the town of Varennes. On June 24, a company of soldiers escorted the royal family back to Paris. Thereafter, the leaders of the National Constituent Assembly knew that the chief counterrevolutionary sat on the French throne.

Two months later, on August 27, 1791, under pressure from a group of *émigrés*, Emperor Leopold II of Austria, who was the brother of Marie Antoinette, and Frederick William II, the king of Prussia, issued the Declaration of Pillnitz. The two monarchs promised to intervene in France to protect the royal family and to preserve the monarchy *if* the other major European powers agreed. The latter provision rendered the statement meaningless because, at the time, Great Britain would not have given its consent. However, the declaration was not so read in France, where the revolutionaries saw the nation surrounded by aristocratic and monarchical foes.

The National Constituent Assembly drew to a close in September 1791. One of its last acts was the passage of a measure that forbade any of its own members to sit in the Legislative Assembly then being elected. This new body met on October 1 and had to confront the immense problems that had emerged during the earlier part of the year.

A Second Revolution

End of the Monarchy

The issues of the Civil Constitution of the Clergy and the untrustworthiness of Louis XVI undermined the unity of the revolution. Much factionalism displayed itself throughout the short life of the Legislative Assembly (1791–1792).

Since the earliest days of the revolution, various clubs of politically like-minded persons had organized themselves in Paris. The best organized was the *Jacobins*, whose name derived from the fact that the group met in a Dominican monastery of an order called Jacobins. The Paris club was linked to other local clubs in the provinces.

In the Legislative Assembly, a group of Jacobins known as the *Girondists* (because many of them came from the department of the Gironde) assumed leadership.[3] Pursuing a firm policy of opposing counterrevolution, they led the Legislative Assembly on April 20, 1792, to declare war on Austria, by this time governed by Francis II (1792–1835) and allied to Prussia.

The war radicalized the revolution and led to what is usually called the *second revolution*, which overthrew the constitutional monarchy and established a republic. The war initially went very poorly, and the revolution seemed in danger. Late in July, under radical working-class pressure, the government of the city of Paris passed from the elected council to a committee, or commune, of representatives from the sections (municipal wards) of Paris. On August 10, 1792, a very large Parisian crowd invaded the Tuileries palace and forced Louis XVI and Marie Antoinette to take refuge in the Legislative Assembly itself. A struggle occurred between the crowd and the royal Swiss guards, after which several hundred guards and a large number of

[3] The Girondists are also frequently called the *Brissotins* after Jacques-Pierre Brissot (1754–1793), who was their chief representative in early 1792.

Parisian citizens lay dead. Thereafter, the royal family was imprisoned in comfortable quarters, but the king was allowed to perform none of his political functions.

The Convention and the Role of the Sans-culottes

Early in September, the Parisian crowd again made its will felt. During the first week of the month, in what are known as the *September Massacres*, the Paris Commune summarily executed or murdered about twelve hundred people who were in the city jails. Many of these people were aristocrats or priests, but the majority were simply common criminals. The crowd had assumed that the prisoners were all counterrevolutionaries. The Paris Commune then compelled the Legislative Assembly to call for the election, by universal manhood suffrage, of a new assembly to write a democratic constitution. That body, called the *Convention* after its American counterpart of 1787, met on September 21, 1792. The previous day, the French army had halted the Prussian advance at the battle of Valmy in eastern France. The victory of democratic forces at home had been confirmed by victory on the battlefield.

As its first act, the Convention declared France a republic, that is, a nation governed by an elected assembly without a king. The second revolution had been the work of Jacobins more radical than the Girondists and of the people of Paris known as the *sans-culottes*. The name of the latter means "without breeches," and was derived from the long trousers that, as working people, they wore instead of aristocratic knee breeches. The sans-culottes were shopkeepers, artisans, wage earners, and, in a few cases, factory workers. The persistent food shortages and the revolutionary inflation had made their difficult lives even more burdensome. The politics of the old regime had ignored them, and the policies of the National Constituent Assembly had left them victims of unregulated economic liberty. However, the nation required their labor and their lives if the war was to succeed. From the summer of 1792 until the summer of 1794, their attitudes, desires, and ideals were the primary factors in the internal development of the revolution.

The sans-culottes generally knew what they wanted. The Parisian tradespeople and artisans sought immediate relief from food shortages and rising prices through the vehicle of price controls. They believed that all people had a right to subsistence and profoundly resented most forms of social inequality. This attitude led them to intense hostility toward the aristocracy and toward the original leaders of the revolution, whom they believed simply wanted to take over the social privileges of the aristocracy. Their hatred of inequality did not go so far as for them to de-

A Pamphleteer Describes a Sans-culotte

This pamphlet is a 1793 description of a sans-culotte, written either by one or by a sympathizer. It describes the sans-culotte as a hardworking, useful, patriotic citizen who bravely sacrifices himself to the war effort. It contrasts those virtues to the lazy and unproductive luxury of the noble and the personally self-interested plottings of the politician.

A *sans-culotte* you rogues? He is someone who always goes on foot, who has no millions as you would all like to have, no *chateaux*, no valets to serve him, and who lives simply with his wife and children, if he has any, on a fourth or fifth storey.

He is useful, because he knows how to work in the field, to forge iron, to use a saw, to use a file, to roof a house, to make shoes, and to shed his last drop of blood for the safety of the Republic.

And because he works, you are sure not to meet his person in the Café de Chartres, or in the gaming houses where others conspire and game; nor at the National theatre . . . nor in the literary clubs. . . .

In the evening he goes to his section, not powdered or perfumed, or smartly booted in the hope of catching the eye of the citizenesses in the galleries, but ready to support good proposals with all his might, and to crush those which come from the abominable faction of politicians.

Finally, a *sans-culotte* always has his sabre sharp, to cut off the ears of all enemies of the Revolution; sometimes he even goes out with his pike; but at the first sound of the drum he is ready to leave for the Vendée, for the army of the Alps or for the army of the North. . . . ❑

"Reply to an Impertinent Question: What Is a *Sans-culotte?*" April 1793. Reprinted in Walter Markov and Albert Soboul (eds.), *Die Sansculotten von Paris*, and republished trans. by Clive Emsley in Merryn Williams (ed.), *Revolutions: 1775–1830* (Baltimore: Penguin Books, in association with The Open University, 1971), pp. 100–101.

mand the abolition of property. Rather, they advocated a community of relatively small property owners. In politics, they were antimonarchical, strongly republican, and suspicious even of representative government.

Marie Antionette on the way to her execution in October 1793, sketched from life by David, as she passed his window. [Bettmann Archives.]

The goals of the sans-culottes were not wholly compatible with those of the Jacobins. The latter were republicans who sought representative government. Jacobin hatred of the aristocracy did not extend to a general suspicion of wealth. Basically, the Jacobins favored an unregulated economy. However, from the time of Louis XVI's flight to Varennes onward, the more extreme Jacobins began to cooperate with leaders of the Parisian sans-culottes and the Paris Commune for the overthrow of the monarchy. Once the Convention began its deliberations, these advanced Jacobins, known as the *Mountain* because of their seats high in the assembly hall, worked with sans-culottes to carry the revolution forward and to win the war. This willingness to cooperate with the forces of the popular revolution separated the Mountain from the Girondists, who were also members of the Jacobin Club.

By the spring of 1793, several issues had brought the Mountain and its sans-culottes allies to domination of the Convention and the revolution. In December 1792, Louis XVI was put on trial as mere "Citizen Capet." (Capet was the family name of extremely distant forebears of the royal family.) The Girondists looked for some way to spare his life, but the Mountain defeated the effort. Louis was convicted, by a very narrow majority, of conspiring against the liberty of the people and the security of the state. He was condemned to death and was beheaded on January 21,

1793. The next month, the Convention declared war on Great Britain, Holland, and Spain. Soon thereafter, the Prussians renewed their offensive and drove the French out of Belgium. To make matters worse, General Dumouriez, the Girondist victor of Valmy, deserted to the enemy. Finally, in March 1793, a royalist revolt led by aristocratic officers and priests erupted in the Vendée in western France and roused much popular support. Consequently, the revolution found itself at war with most of Europe and much of the French nation. The Girondists had led the country into the war but had proved themselves incapable either of winning it or of suppressing the enemies of the revolution at home. The Mountain stood ready to take up the task.

The Reign of Terror

The Republic Defended

In April 1793, the Convention established a Committee of General Security and a Committee of Public Safety to perform the executive duties of the government. The latter committee became more important and eventually enjoyed almost dictatorial power. The most prominent leaders of the Committee of Public Safety were Jacques Danton (1759–1794), who had provided heroic leadership in September 1792; Maximilien Robespierre (1758–1794), who became for a time the single most powerful member of the committee; and Lazare Carnot (1753–1823), who was in charge of the military. All of these men and the other figures on the committee were strong republicans, associated with the Mountain in opposing the weak policies of the Girondists. They conceived of their task as saving the revolution from mortal enemies at home and abroad. They generally enjoyed a working political relationship with the sans-culottes of Paris, but this was an alliance of expediency on the part of the committee.

The major problem was to wage the war and to secure domestic support for the effort. In early June 1793, the Parisian sans-culottes invaded the Convention and successfully demanded the expulsion of the Girondist members. That action further radicalized the Convention and gave the Mountain complete control. On June 22, the Convention approved a fully democratic constitution but suspended its operation until the conclusion of the war emergency. On August 23, Carnot began a mobilization for victory by issuing a *levée en masse*, or general military requisition of population, which conscripted males into the army and directed economic production for military purposes. On September 17, a maximum on prices was established in accord with sans-culottes' demands. During these same months, the armies of the revolution also successfully crushed many of the counterrevolutionary disturbances in the provinces.

Never before had Europe seen a nation organized in this way nor one defended by a citizen army. Other events within France astounded Europeans even more. The Reign of Terror had begun. Those months of quasi-judicial executions and murders stretching from the autumn of 1793 to the midsummer of 1794 are probably the most famous or infamous period of the revolution. They can be understood only in the context of the war, on the one hand, and the revolutionary expectations of the Convention and the sans-culottes, on the other.

The Republic of Virtue

The presence of armies closing in on the nation created a situation in which it was relatively easy to dispense with legal due process. However, the people who sat in the Convention and composed the Committee of Public Safety also believed that they had made a new departure in world history. They had established a republic in which civic virtue rather than aristocratic and monarchical corruption might flourish.

The most dramatic departure of the republic of virtue, and one that illustrates the imposition of political values that would justify the Terror, was an attempt by the Convention to dechristianize France. In October 1793, the Convention proclaimed a new calendar dating from the first day of the French Republic. There were twelve months of thirty days with names associated with the seasons and climate. Every tenth day, rather than every seventh, was a holiday. Many of the most important events of the next few years became known by their dates on the revolutionary calendar.[4] In November 1793, the convention decreed the Cathedral of Notre-Dame to be a Temple of Reason. The legislature then sent trusted members, known as *deputies on mission*, into the provinces to enforce dechristianization by closing churches, persecuting clergy and believers, and occasionally forcing priests to marry. Needless to say, this religious policy roused much opposition and deeply separated the French provinces from the revolutionary government in Paris.

During the crucial months of late 1793 and early 1794, the person who emerged as the chief figure on the Committee of Public Safety was Robespierre. He was a complex person who has remained controversial to the present day. He was utterly selfless and from the earliest days of the revolution had favored a republic. The Jacobin Club provided his primary forum and

---

[4]From summer to spring, the months on the revolutionary calendar were Messidor, Thermidor, Fructidor, Vendémiaire, Brumaire, Frimaire, Nivôse, Pluviôse, Ventôse, Germinal, Floréal, and Prairial.

Although many of the victims of the Reign of Terror were executed by other methods, the guillotine became the symbol of those frightening months in 1793 and 1794. Here prisoners are being prepared for decapitation, as the heads of those already executed are displayed to the crowd. [*Bettmann Archives.*]

base of power. A shrewd and sensitive politician, he had opposed the war in 1792 believing it to be a measure that might aid the monarchy. He largely depended on the support of the sans-culottes of Paris, but continued to dress as he had prior to the revolution and opposed dechristianization as a political blunder. For him, the republic of virtue meant wholehearted support of republican government and the renunciation of selfish gains from political life. He once told the Convention

If the mainspring of popular government in peacetime is virtue, amid revolution it is at the same time virtue and *terror:* virtue, without which terror is fatal; terror, without which virtue is impotent. Terror is nothing but prompt, severe, inflexible justice; it is therefore an emanation of virtue.[5]

He and his supporters were among the first apostles of secular ideologies who in the name of humanity would bring so much suffering to European and world politics of the left and the right in the next two centuries.

Progress of the Terror

The Reign of Terror manifested itself through a series of revolutionary tribunals established by the Convention during the summer of 1793. The tribunals were to try the enemies of the republic, but the definition of *enemy* remained uncertain and shifted as the months

[5]Quoted in Richard T. Bienvenu, *The Ninth of Thermidor: The Fall of Robespierre* (New York: Oxford University Press, 1968), p. 38.

passed. The enemies included those who might aid other European powers, those who endangered republican virtue, and finally good republicans who opposed the policies of the dominant faction of the government. In a very real sense, the Terror of the revolutionary tribunals systematized and channeled the popular resentment that had manifested itself in the September Massacres of 1792. The first victims were Marie Antoinette, other members of the royal family, and some aristocrats, who were executed in October 1793. They were followed by certain Girondist politicians who had been prominent in the Legislative Assembly.

By the early months of 1794, the Terror had moved to the provinces, where the deputies on mission presided over the summary execution of thousands of people who had allegedly supported internal opposition to the revolution. In Paris during the late winter of 1794, Robespierre turned the Terror against republican political figures of the left and right. On March 24, he secured the execution of certain extreme sans-culottes leaders. Shortly thereafter, he moved against more conservative republicans, including Danton. In this fashion, Robespierre exterminated the leadership from both groups that might have threatened his own position. Finally, on June 10, he secured passage of the Law of 22 Prairial, which permitted the revolutionary tribunal to convict suspects without hearing substantial evidence.

In May 1794, at the height of his power, Robespierre, considering the worship of reason too abstract for most citizens, abolished it and established the Cult of the Supreme Being. He did not long preside over this new religion. On June 26, he made an ill-tempered

The Festival of the Supreme Being took place in Paris in June 1794. It was one of the chief displays of the civic religion of the French Revolution. The painting is by P. A. de Machy. [Musée Carnavalet, Paris. Giraudon.]

speech in the Convention, declaring the existence of a conspiracy among other leaders of the government against him and the revolution. Such accusations against unnamed persons had usually preceded his earlier attacks. On July 27—the Ninth of Thermidor—by prearrangement, members of the Convention shouted him down when he rose to speak. That night, Robespierre was arrested; the next day, he was executed. Robespierre had destroyed rivals without creating supporters. In that regard, he was the selfless creator of his own destruction.

The Reign of Terror soon ended, having claimed over twenty-five thousand victims. The largest number of executions had involved peasants and sans-culottes who had joined rebellions against the revolutionary government. By the late summer of 1794, those provincial uprisings had been crushed, and the war against foreign enemies was also going well. Those factors, combined with the feeling in Paris that the revolution had consumed enough of its own children, brought the Terror to an end.

The Thermidorian Reaction

The End of the Terror and the Establishment of the Directory

The tempering of the revolution, called the *Thermidorian Reaction*, began in July 1794. It consisted of the destruction of the machinery of terror, including the repeal of the notorious Law of 22 Prairial, and the institution of a new constitutional regime. The influence of generally wealthy middle-class and professional people replaced that of the sans-culottes. Many of the people responsible for the Terror were removed from public life. The Paris Jacobin Club was closed, and provincial Jacobin clubs were forbidden to correspond with each other.

The Thermidorian Reaction also involved still further political reconstruction. In place of the fully democratic constitution of 1793, which had never gone into effect, the Convention issued the Constitution of the Year III. It was a conservative document that provided for a bicameral legislative government heavily favoring property owners. The executive body consisting of a five-person Directory was elected by the upper legislative house known as the Council of Elders.

By the Treaty of Basel of March 1795, the Convention concluded peace with Prussia and Spain. With the war effort succeeding, the Convention severed its ties with the sans-culottes. True to their belief in an unregulated economy, the Thermidorians repealed the ceiling on prices. When food riots resulted during the winter of 1794–1795, the Convention put them down to prove that the era of the sans-culottes *journées* had come to a close. On October 5, 1795—13 Vendemiaire—the sections of Paris rebelled against the Convention. For the first time in the history of the rev-

1789

May 5	The Estates General opens at Versailles
June 17	The Third Estate declares itself the National Assembly
June 20	The National Assembly takes the Tennis Court Oath
July 14	Fall of the Bastille in the city of Paris
Late July	The Great Fear spreads in the countryside
August 4	The nobles surrender their feudal rights in a meeting of the National Constituent Assembly
August 27	Declaration of the Rights of Man and Citizen
October 5–6	Parisian women march to Versailles and force Louis XVI and his family to return to Paris

1790

July 12	Civil Constitution of the Clergy adopted
July 14	A new constitution is accepted by the king

1791

June 20–24	Louis XVI and his family attempt to flee France and are stopped at Varennes
August 27	The Declaration of Pillnitz
October 1	The Legislative Assembly meets

1792

April 20	France declares war on Austria
August 10	The Tuileries palace is stormed, and Louis XVI takes refuge with the Legislative Assembly
September 2–7	The September Massacres
September 20	France wins the battle of Valmy
September 21	The Convention meets, and the monarchy is abolished

1793

January 21	Louis XVI is executed
February 1	France declares war on Great Britain
March	Counterrevolution breaks out in the Vendée
April	The Committee of Public Safety is formed
June 22	The Constitution of 1793 is adopted but not put into operation
July	Robespierre enters the Committee of Public Safety
August 23	*Levée en masse* proclaimed
September 17	Maximum prices set on food and other commodities
October 16	Queen Marie Antoinette is executed
November 10	The Cult of Reason is proclaimed. The revolutionary calender beginning on September 22, 1792, is adopted

1794

March 24	Execution of the Hébertist leaders of the sans-culottes
April 6	Execution of Danton
May 7	Cult of the Supreme Being proclaimed
June 8	Robespierre leads the celebration of the Festival of the Supreme Being
June 10	The Law of 22 Prairial is adopted
July 27	The Ninth of Thermidor and the fall of Robespierre
July 28	Robespierre is executed

1795

August 22	The Constitution of the Year III is adopted, establishing the Directory

olution, artillery was turned against the people of Paris. A general named Napoleon Bonaparte (1769–1821) commanded the cannon, and with what he termed a "whiff of grapeshot" he dispersed the crowd. Other enemies of the Directory would be more difficult to disperse.

The Rise of Napoleon Bonaparte

The chief danger to the Directory came from the royalists, who hoped to restore the Bourbon monarchy by legal means. The spring elections of 1797 turned out most of the incumbents and replaced them with a majority of constitutional monarchists and their sympathizers. To prevent an end to the republic and a peaceful restoration of monarchy, the antimonarchist Directory staged a coup d'état on 18 Fructidor (September 4, 1797). They put their own supporters into the legislature, imposed censorship, and exiled some of their enemies. Napoleon Bonaparte, the general in charge of the Italian campaign, had made these changes possible by sending one of his military subordinates to Paris to guarantee the success of the coup.

Napoleon Bonaparte was born in 1769 to a poor family of lesser nobles at Ajaccio, Corsica. Because France had annexed Corsica in the previous year, he went to French schools, pursued a military career, and in 1785 obtained a commission as a French artillery officer. He strongly favored the revolution and was a fiery Jacobin. In 1793, he played a leading role in recovering the port of Toulon from the British. In reward for his service, the government appointed him a brigadier general. His radical associations threatened his career during the Thermidorian Reaction, but his defense of the new regime on 13 Vendémiaire restored him to favor and won him another promotion and a command in Italy.

By 1795, French arms and diplomacy had shattered the enemy coalition, but France's annexation of Belgium guaranteed continued fighting with Britain and Austria. The attack on Italy aimed at depriving Austria of the provinces of Lombardy and Venetia. In a series of lightning victories, Bonaparte crushed the Austrian and Sardinian armies. On his own initiative, and in many ways contrary to the wishes of the government in Paris, he concluded the Treaty of Campo Formio in October 1797. The treaty took Austria out of the war and crowned Napoleon's campaign and independent policy with success. Before long, all of Italy and Switzerland had fallen under French domination.

In November 1797, the triumphant Bonaparte returned to Paris to be hailed as a hero and to confront France's only remaining enemy, Britain. He judged it impossible to cross the channel and invade England at that time. Instead, he chose to capture Egypt from the Ottoman Empire. By this strategy, he hoped to drive the British fleet from the Mediterranean, cut off British communication with India, damage British trade, and threaten the British Empire. But the invasion of Egypt was a failure. Admiral Horatio Nelson (1758–1805) destroyed the French fleet at Aboukir on August 1, 1798. The French army could then neither accomplish anything of importance in the Near East nor get home. To make matters worse, the situation in Europe was deteriorating. The French invasion of Egypt had alarmed Russia, which had its own ambitions in the Near East. The Russians, the Austrians, and the Ottomans soon joined Britain to form the Second Coalition. In 1799, the Russian and Austrian armies defeated the French in Italy and Switzerland and threatened to invade France.

Economic troubles and the dangerous international situation eroded the already fragile support of the Directory. Certain of the Directors believed the problems required a more vigorous executive body who could operate independent of the whims of the electorate. Having heard of the diplomatic misfortunes, Napoleon left Egypt, abandoning his doomed army, and returned to France in October 1799. On 19 Brumaire (November 10, 1799) his troops drove out the legislators and permitted a new coup d'état.

A new constitution provided that executive authority be divided among three consuls. Bonaparte quickly ignored these rules and issued the Constitution of the Year VII in December 1799. Behind a screen of universal manhood suffrage that suggested democratic principles, a complicated system of checks and balances that appealed to republican theory, and a Council of State that evoked memories of Louis XIV, the constitution in fact established the rule of one man, the First Consul, Bonaparte.

The Consulate in France (1799–1804)

The establishment of the Consulate, in effect, closed the revolution in France. The leading elements of the Third Estate—that is, officials, landowners, doctors, lawyers, and financiers—had achieved most of their goals by 1799. They had abolished hereditary privilege, and the careers thus opened to talent allowed them to achieve the wealth and status they sought. The peasants were also satisfied. They had acquired the land they had always wanted and had destroyed oppressive feudal privileges as well. The newly established dominant classes were profoundly conservative. They had little or no desire to share their recently won privileges with the lower social orders. Bonaparte seemed just the person to give them security. When he submitted his constitution to the voters in a largely rigged plebiscite, they approved it by 3,011,077 votes to 1,567.

Bonaparte quickly justified the public's confidence by setting about achieving peace with France's enemies. Russia had already quarreled with its allies and left the Second Coalition. A campaign in Italy brought another victory over Austria at Marengo in 1800. The Treaty of Lunéville early in 1801 took Austria out of the war and confirmed the earlier settlement of Campo Formio. Britain was now alone and, in 1802, concluded the Treaty of Amiens, which brought peace to Europe. Bonaparte was equally effective in restoring peace and order at home. He employed generosity, flattery, and bribery to win over some of his enemies. He issued a general amnesty and employed in his own service persons from all political factions. He required only that they be loyal to him.

On the other hand, Bonaparte was ruthless and efficient in suppressing opposition. He established a highly centralized administration in which all departments were managed by prefects directly responsible to the central government in Paris. He employed secret police. He stamped out, once and for all, the royalist rebellion in the west and made the rule of Paris effective in Brittany and the Vendée for the first time in many years. Nor was he above using or even inventing opportunities to destroy his enemies. When a plot on his life surfaced in 1804, he used the event as an excuse to attack the Jacobins, even though the bombing was the work of royalists.

In 1804, his forces invaded the sovereignty of Baden to seize the Bourbon duke of Enghien. The duke was accused of participation in a royalist plot and put to death, even though Bonaparte knew him to be innocent. The action was a flagrant violation of international law and of due process, and it helped to provoke foreign opposition. On the other hand, it was popular with the former Jacobins, for it seemed to preclude the possibility of a Bourbon restoration. The person who killed a Bourbon was hardly likely to restore the royal family. The execution seems to have put an end to royalist plots.

A major obstacle to internal peace was the hostility of French Catholics. Bonaparte regarded religion as a political matter. He approved its role in preserving an orderly society but was suspicious of any such power independent of the state. In 1801, Napoleon concluded a concordat with Pope Pius VII, to the shock and dismay of his anticlerical supporters. It gave Napoleon what he most wanted. Both the refractory clergy and those who had accepted the revolution were forced to resign. Their replacements received their spiritual investiture from the pope, but the state named the bishops and paid their salaries and the salary of one priest in each parish. In return, the Church gave up its claims to its confiscated property. The concordat declared that "Roman Catholicism is the religion of the great majority of French citizens." This was merely a statement of fact and fell far short of what the pope had wanted—religious dominance for the Roman Catholic church. The clergy had to swear an oath of loyalty to the state, and the Organic Articles of 1802, which were actually distinct from the concordat, established the supremacy of State over Church. Similar laws were applied to the Protestant and Jewish religious communities as well, reducing still further the privileged position of the Catholic church.

This French allegory of 1799 portrays Napoleon as the First Consul saving France from discord and ignorance. [Bibliotheque Nationale.]

Napoleon Makes Peace with the Papacy

In 1801, Napoleon concluded a concordat with Pope Pius VII. This document was the cornerstone of Napoleonic religious policy. The concordat, which was announced on April 8, 1802, allowed the Roman Catholic church to function freely in France only within the limits of Church support for the government as indicated in the oath included in Article 6.

The government of the French Republic recognizes that the Roman, catholic and apostolic religion is the religion of the great majority of French citizens.

His Holiness likewise recognizes that this same religion has derived and in this moment again expects the greatest benefit and grandeur from the establishment of the catholic worship in France and from the personal profession of it which the consuls of the Republic make.

In consequence, after this mutual recognition, as well for the benefit of religion as for the maintenance of internal tranquility, they have agreed as follows:

1. The catholic, apostolic and Roman religion shall be freely exercised in France: its worship shall be public, and in conformity with the police regulations which the government shall deem necessary for the public tranquility.

. . . .

4. The First Consul of the Republic shall make appointments, within the three months which shall follow the publication of the bull of His Holiness, to the archbishoprics and bishoprics of the new circumscription. His Holiness shall confer the canonical institution, following the forms established in relation to France before the change of government.

. . . .

6. Before entering upon their functions, the bishops shall take directly, at the hands of the First Consul, the oath of fidelity which was in use before the change of government, expressed in the following terms:

"I swear and promise to God, upon the holy scriptures, to remain in obedience and fidelity to the government established by the constitution of the French Republic. I also promise not to have any intercourse, nor to assist by any counsel, nor to support any league, either within or without, which is inimical to the public tranquility; and if, within my diocese or elsewhere, I learn that anything to the prejudice of the state is being contrived, I will make it known to the government." ❑

Frank Maloy Anderson (ed. and trans.), *The Constitutions and Other Select Documents Illustrative of the History of France 1789–1907*, 2nd ed., rev. and enlarged (Minneapolis: H. W. Wilson, 1908), pp. 296–297.

Peace and efficient administration brought prosperity and security to the French and gratitude and popularity to Bonaparte. In 1802, a plebiscite appointed him consul for life, and he soon produced still another new constitution, which granted him what amounted to full power. The years of the Consulate were employed in reforming and establishing the basic laws and institutions of France. The settlement imposed by Napoleon was an ambiguous combination of liberal principles derived from the Enlightenment and the early years of the revolution and conservative principles and practices going back to the old regime or adapted to the conservative spirit that had triumphed at Thermidor. This was especially true of the Civil Code of 1804, usually called the Napoleonic Code. However, these laws stopped far short of the full equality advocated by liberal rationalists. Fathers were granted extensive control over their children and men over their wives. Labor unions were still forbidden, and the rights of workers were inferior to those of their employers.

In 1804, Bonaparte seized on the bomb attack on his life to make himself emperor. He argued that the establishment of a dynasty would make the new regime secure and make further attempts on his life useless. Another new constitution was promulgated in which Napoleon Bonaparte was called Emperor of the French, instead of First Consul of the Republic. This constitution was also overwhelmingly ratified in a plebiscite organized by the government.

To conclude the drama, Napoleon invited the pope to Notre Dame to take part in the coronation. But at the last minute, the pope agreed that Napoleon should actually crown himself. The emperor had no intention of allowing anyone to think that his power and authority depended on the approval of the Church. Henceforth he was called Napoleon I.

Napoleon's Empire (1804–1814)

In the decade between his coronation as emperor and his final defeat at Waterloo (1815), Napoleon conquered most of Europe in a series of military cam-

British Admiral Horatio Nelson (1758–1805) *was the brilliant naval strategist in the wars against Napoleonic France. His last battle, in which he was killed, was a stunning victory over the combined French and Spanish fleets off Trafalgar on the coast of Spain, October* 21, 1805, *and ended any possible sea threat to England. The painting is by Lemuel Francis Abbott and is in the National Portrait Gallery, London. [The Granger Collection.]*

The Treaty of Amiens with Britain (1802) was doomed to be merely a truce. Napoleon's unlimited ambitions shattered any hope that it might last. He sent an army to restore the rebellious island of Haiti to French rule. This move aroused British fears that he was planning the renewal of a French empire in America, because Spain had restored Louisiana to France in 1800. More serious were his interventions in the Dutch Republic, Italy, Malta, and Switzerland, and his role in the reorganization of Germany. The Treaty of Campo Formio had required a redistribution of territories along the Rhine River, and the petty princes of the region engaged in a shameful scramble to enlarge their holdings. Among the results were the reduction of Austrian influence in Germany and the emergence of a smaller number of larger German states in the west, all dependent on Napoleon.

The British found all of these developments alarming enough to justify an ultimatum. When Napoleon ignored it, Britain declared war in May 1803. William Pitt the Younger returned to office as prime minister in 1804 and began to construct the Third Coalition. By August 1805, he had persuaded Russia and Austria to move once again against French aggression. A great naval victory soon raised the fortunes of the allies. On October 21, 1805, the British admiral Horatio, Lord Nelson, destroyed the combined French and Spanish fleets at the Battle of Trafalgar just off the Spanish coast. Nelson died in the battle, but the British lost no ships. The victory of Trafalgar put an end to all French hope of an invasion of Britain and guaranteed British control of the sea for the rest of the war.

On land, the story was very different. Even before Trafalgar, Napoleon had marched to the Danube River to attack his continental enemies. In mid-October, he forced a large Austrian army to surrender at Ulm and soon occupied Vienna. On December 2, 1805, in perhaps his greatest victory, Napoleon defeated the combined Austrian and Russian forces at Austerlitz. The Treaty of Pressburg, which followed, won major concessions from Austria. The Austrians withdrew from Italy and left Napoleon in control of everything north of Rome. He was recognized as king of Italy.

Extensive changes also came about in Germany. In July 1806, Napoleon orgainzed the Confederation of the Rhine, which included most of the western German princes. The withdrawal of these princes from the Holy Roman Empire led Francis II of Austria to dissolve that ancient political body and henceforth to call himself only emperor of Austria.

Prussia, which had carefully remained neutral up to this point, was now provoked into war against France. The famous Prussian army was quickly crushed at the battles of Jena and Auerstädt on October 14, 1806. Two weeks later, Napoleon was in Berlin. There, on November 21, he issued the Berlin Decrees forbidding

paigns that astonished the world. France's victories changed the map of Europe, put an end to the old regime and its feudal trappings in western Europe, and forced the eastern European states to reorganize themselves to resist Napoleon's armies. Everywhere, Napoleon's advance unleashed the powerful force of nationalism. The militarily mobilized French nation, one of the achievements of the revolution, was Napoleon's weapon. He could put as many as 700,000 men under arms at one time, risk as many as 100,000 troops in a single battle, endure heavy losses, and come back to fight again. He could conscript citizen soldiers in unprecedented numbers, thanks to their loyalty to the nation and to their remarkable leader. No single enemy could match such resources, and even coalitions were unsuccessful until Napoleon at last overreached himself and made mistakes that led to his own defeat.

Napoleon on the field of Austerlitz. Austerlitz is considered Napoleon's most brilliant victory: 73,000 French crushed an Austro-Russian army of 86,000 under the command of the Tsar and the Emperor of Austria. [Library of Congress.]

his allies to import British goods. On June 13, 1807, Napoleon defeated the Russians at Friedland and was able to occupy Königsberg, the capital of East Prussia. The French emperor was master of all Germany.

Unable to fight another battle and unwilling to retreat into Russia, Tsar Alexander I (1801–1825) was ready to make peace. He and Napoleon met on a raft in the middle of the Niemen River while the two armies and the nervous king of Prussia watched from the bank. On July 7, 1807, they signed the Treaty of Tilsit, which confirmed France's gains. Moreover, the Prussian state was reduced to half its size and was saved from extinction only by the support of Alexander. Prussia openly and Russia secretly became allies of Napoleon in his war against Britain.

After the Treaty of Tilsit, Napoleon knew that he must defeat the British before he could feel safe. Unable to compete with the British navy, he continued the economic warfare begun by the Berlin Decree. His plan was to cut off all British trade with the European continent. In this manner, he hoped to cripple the commercial and financial power on which Britain depended, to cause domestic unrest and revolution, and thus to drive the British from the war. The Milan Decree of 1807 attempted to stop neutral nations from trading with Britain. For a time, it appeared that this Continental System might work. British exports dropped, and riots broke out in England. But in the end, the system failed and may even have contributed significantly to Napoleon's defeat.

The British economy survived because of its access to the growing markets of North and South America and of the eastern Mediterranean, all assured by the British control of the seas. At the same time, the Continental System did great harm to the European economies. The system was meant not only to hurt Britain but also to help France economically. Napoleon resisted advice to turn his empire into a free-trade area. Such a policy would have been both popular and helpful. Instead, his tariff policies favored France, increased the resentment of foreign merchants, and made them less willing to enforce the system and more ready to engage in smuggling. It was in part to prevent smuggling that Napoleon invaded Spain in 1808, and the resulting peninsular campaign in Spain and Portugal helped to bring on his ruin.

The Wars of Liberation

In Spain more than elsewhere in Europe, national resistance to France had deep social roots. Spain had achieved political unity as early as the sixteenth century. The Spanish peasants were devoted to the ruling dynasty and especially to the Roman Catholic church. France and Spain had been allies since 1796. In 1807, however, a French army came into the Iberian Peninsula to force Portugal to abandon its traditional alliance with Britain. The army stayed in Spain to protect lines of supply and communication. When a revolt broke out in Madrid in 1808, Napoleon used it as a pretext to depose the Spanish Bourbon dynasty and to

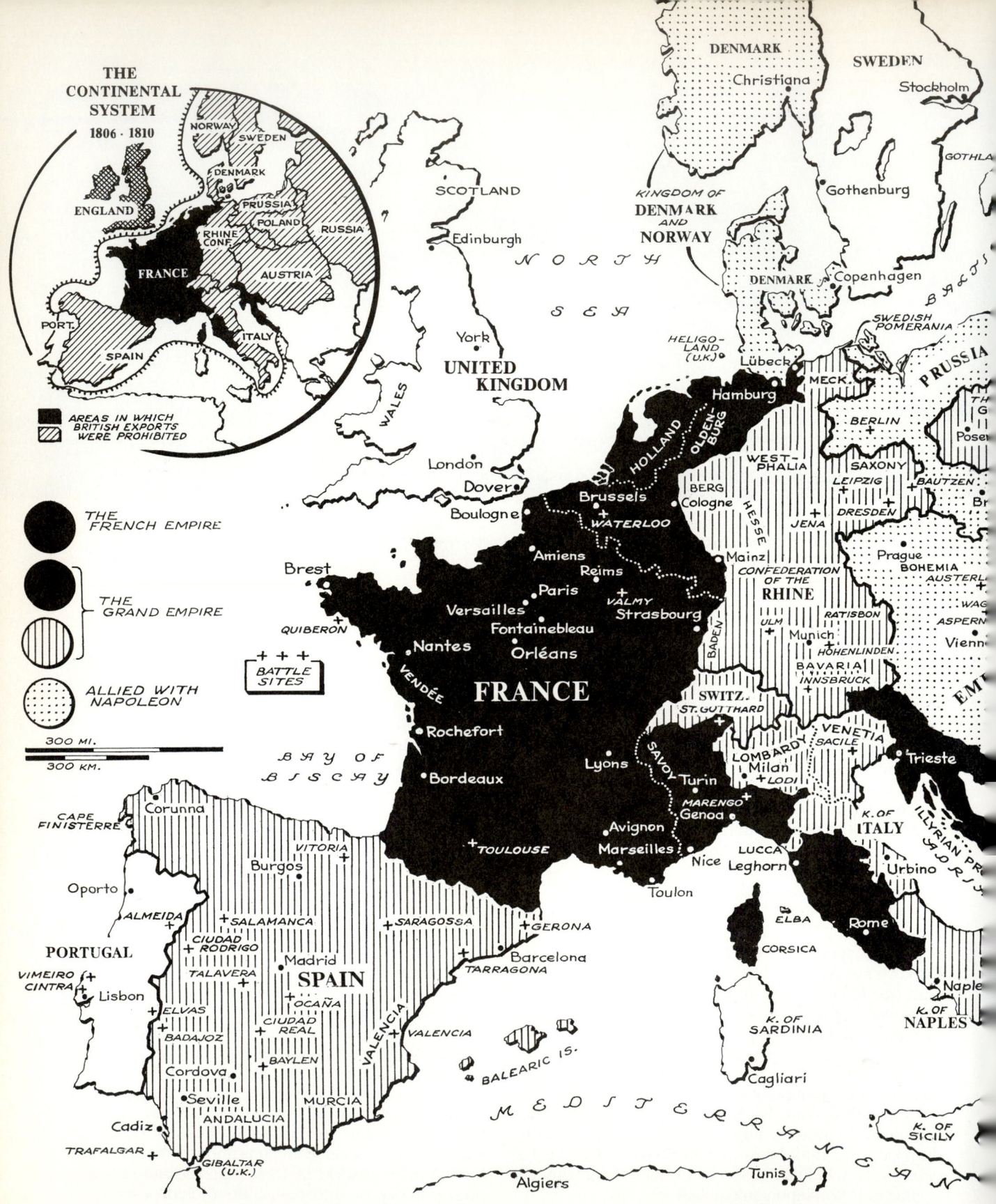

THE
CONTINENTAL
SYSTEM
1806 · 1810

NORWAY
SWEDEN
DENMARK
ENGLAND
PRUSSIA
POLAND
RHINE
CONF.
RUSSIA
FRANCE
AUSTRIA
PORT.
ITALY
SPAIN

AREAS IN WHICH
BRITISH EXPORTS
WERE PROHIBITED

THE
FRENCH EMPIRE

THE
GRAND EMPIRE

ALLIED WITH
NAPOLEON

300 MI.
300 KM.

DENMARK
Christiana
SWEDEN
Stockholm
GOTHLA
Gothenburg
KINGDOM OF
DENMARK
AND
NORWAY
DENMARK
Copenhagen
BALTI
SWEDISH
POMERANIA
PRUSSIA
HELIGO-
LAND
(U.K.)
Lübeck
MECK.
THE
G
Poser
Hamburg
BERLIN
SAXONY
Br
OLDEN-
BURG
WEST-
PHALIA
LEIPZIG
BAUTZEN
HOLLAND
BERG
Cologne
HESSE
JENA
DRESDEN
Mainz
CONFEDERATION
OF THE
Prague
BOHEMIA
AUSTERL
RHINE
WAG
ULM
RATISBON
ASPERN
Munich
BAVARIA
HÖHENLINDEN
INNSBRUCK
Vienn
EM
SWITZ.
VENETIA
ST. GOTTHARD
SACILE
LOMBARD
Trieste
Milan
K. OF
ILLYRIAN PR
Turin
LODI
ITALY
MARENGO
Genoa
Urbino
LUCCA
Leghorn
ELBA
Rome
CORSICA
Naple
K. OF
K. OF
SARDINIA
NAPLES
Cagliari
K. OF
SICILY

SCOTLAND
Edinburgh
NORTH
SEA
York
UNITED
KINGDOM
London
Dover
Boulogne
Brussels
WATERLOO
WALES
Amiens
Reims
VALMY
Paris
Strasbourg
Versailles
Fontainebleau
Brest
Orléans
QUIBERON
Nantes
BATTLE
SITES
VENDÉE
FRANCE
Rochefort
BAY OF
Lyons
BISCAY
SAVOY
Bordeaux
Avignon
Marseilles
TOULOUSE
Nice
Toulon

CAPE
FINISTERRE
Corunna
VITORIA
Burgos
Oporto
ALMEIDA
SALAMANCA
SARAGOSSA
GERONA
CIUDAD
RODRIGO
Barcelona
PORTUGAL
TALAVERA
Madrid
TARRAGONA
VIMEIRO
SPAIN
CINTRA
Lisbon
OCAÑA
VALENCIA
ELVAS
CIUDAD
REAL
VALENCIA
BADAJOZ
BAYLEN
BALEARIC IS.
Cordova
Seville
MURCIA
ANDALUCIA
Cadiz
TRAFALGAR
GIBALTAR
(U.K.)
MEDITERRANEAN
Algiers
Tunis

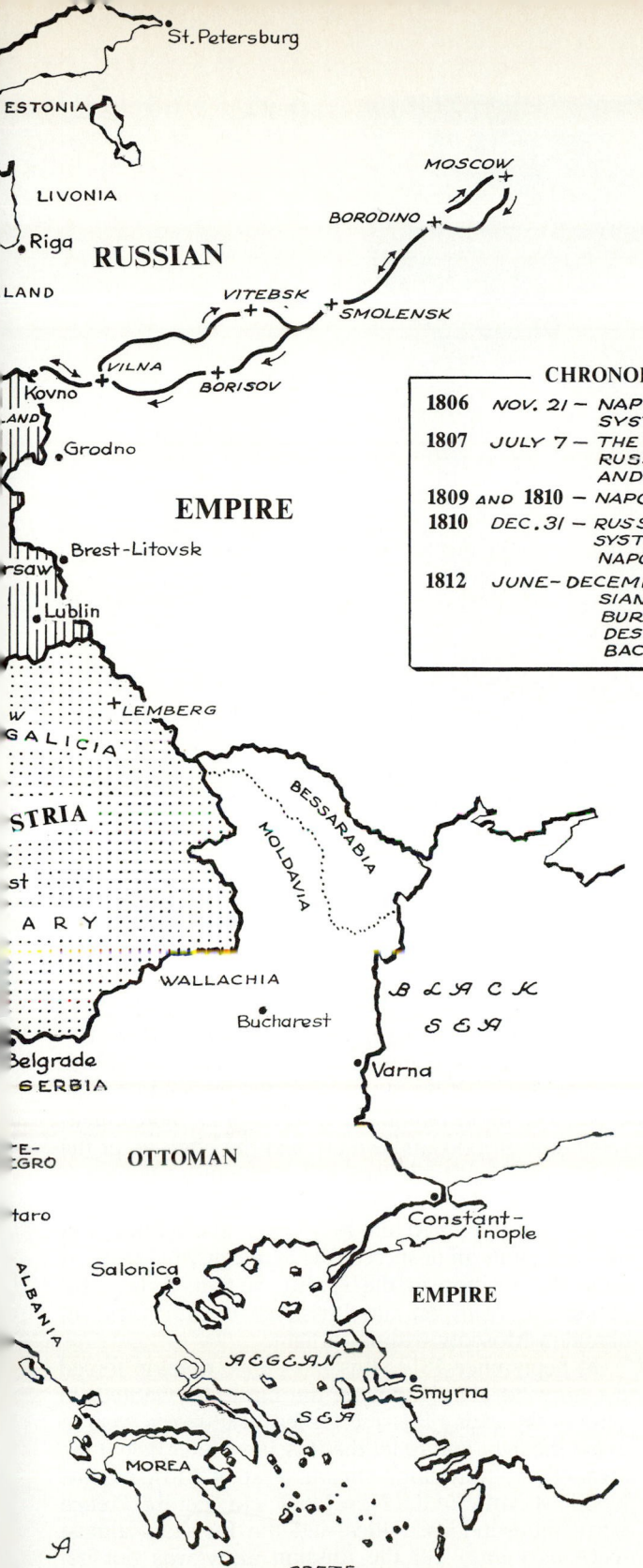

MAP 24-1 NAPOLEONIC EUROPE IN LATE
1812 *By mid-1812 the areas shown in black were incorporated into France, and most of the rest of Europe
was directly controlled by or allied with Napoleon. But
Russia had withdrawn from the failing Continental System, and the decline of Napoleon was about to begin.*

CHRONOLOGY

1806 NOV. 21 — NAPOLEON ESTABLISHES THE CONTINENTAL
SYSTEM PROHIBITING ALL TRADE WITH ENGLAND.

1807 JULY 7 — THE PEACE CONFERENCE AT TILSIT RESULTS IN
RUSSIA JOINING THE CONTINENTAL SYSTEM
AND BECOMING AN ALLY OF NAPOLEON.

1809 AND **1810** — NAPOLEON AT THE PEAK OF HIS POWER.

1810 DEC. 31 — RUSSIA WITHDRAWS FROM THE CONTINENTAL
SYSTEM AND RESUMES RELATIONS WITH BRITAIN.
NAPOLEON PLANS TO CRUSH RUSSIA MILITARILY.

1812 JUNE–DECEMBER — NAPOLEON INVADES RUSSIA. THE RUS-
SIANS ADOPT A SCORCHED-EARTH POLICY AND
BURN MOSCOW. THE THWARTED NAPOLEON
DESERTS HIS DWINDLING ARMY AND RUSHES
BACK TO PARIS.

---

place his brother Joseph on the Spanish throne. Attacks on the privileges of the Church increased public
outrage. Many members of the upper classes were
prepared to collaborate with Napoleon, but the peasants, urged on by the lower clergy and the monks, rose
in a general rebellion.

Napoleon faced a new kind of warfare not vulnerable to his usual tactics. Guerrilla bands cut lines of
communication, killed stragglers, destroyed isolated
units, and then disappeared into the mountains. The
British landed an army under Sir Arthur Wellesley
(1769–1852), later the duke of Wellington, to support
the Spanish insurgents. Thus began the long peninsular campaign that would drain French strength from
elsewhere in Europe and play a critical role in Napoleon's eventual defeat.

The French troubles in Spain encouraged the Austrians to renew the war in 1809. Since their defeat at
Austerlitz, they had sought a war of revenge. The Austrians counted on Napoleon's distraction in Spain,
French war weariness, and aid from other German
princes. However, Napoleon was fully in command in
France; and the German princes did not move. The
French army marched swiftly into Austria and won the
battle of Wagram. The resulting Peace of Schönbrunn
deprived Austria of much territory and three and a half
million subjects. Another spoil of victory was the Austrian Archduchess Marie Louise, daughter of the emperor. Napoleon's wife, Josephine de Beauharnais,
was forty-six and had borne him no children. His dynastic ambitions, as well as the desire for a marriage

Goya's "Barbarians" portrays the brutality of the guerrilla warfare waged against Napolean's armies in Spain. [Metropolitan Museum of Art.]

matching his new position as master of Europe, led him to divorce his wife and to marry the eighteen-year-old Austrian princess. Napoleon had also considered the sister of Tsar Alexander, but had received a polite rebuff.

The failure of Napoleon's marriage negotiations with Russia emphasized the shakiness of the Franco-Russian alliance concluded at Tilsit. The alliance was unpopular with Russian nobles because of the liberal politics of France and because of the prohibition of the Continental System on timber sales to Britain. Only French aid in gaining Constantinople could justify the alliance in their eyes, but Napoleon gave them no help against the Ottoman Empire. The organization of the Grand Duchy of Warsaw as a Napoleonic satellite on the Russian doorstep and its enlargement in 1809 after the battle of Wagram angered Alexander I. Napoleon's annexation of Holland in violation of the Treaty of Tilsit, his recognition of the French Marshal Bernadotte as King Charles XIV of Sweden, and his marriage to an Austrian princess further disturbed the tsar. At the end of 1810, Russia withdrew from the Continental System and began to prepare for war.

Napoleon was determined to put an end to the Russian military threat. He amassed an army of over 600,000 men, including a core of French and over 400,000 other soldiers drawn from the rest of his em-

pire. He intended the usual short campaign crowned by a decisive battle, but the Russians disappointed him by retreating before his advance. His vast superiority in numbers—the Russians had only about 160,000 troops—made it foolish for them to risk a battle. Instead, they followed a "scorched-earth" policy, destroying all food and supplies as they retreated. The so-called Grand Army of Napoleon could not live off the country, and the expanse of Russia made supply lines too long to maintain. Terrible rains, fierce heat, shortages of food and water, and the courage of the Russian rear guard defending their country against the invader eroded the morale of Napoleon's army. Napoleon's advisers urged him to abandon the venture, but he feared that an unsuccessful campaign would undermine his position in the empire and in France. He pinned his faith on the Russians' unwillingness to abandon Moscow without a fight.

In September 1812, Russian public opinion forced the army to give Napoleon the battle he wanted, in spite of the canny Russian General Kutuzov's wish to avoid the fight and to let the Russian winter defeat the invader. At Borodino, not far west of Moscow, the bloodiest battle of the Napoleonic era cost the French thirty thousand casualties and the Russians almost twice as many. Yet the Russian army was not destroyed. Napoleon had won nothing substantial, and

Arthur Wellesley, the duke of Wellington, first led troops against Napoleon in Spain and later defeated him at the battle of Waterloo, June 18, 1815. Wellington lived to become prime minister and elder statesman of Britain. The portrait is by the celebrated Spanish painter Francisco Goya (1746–1828). [The Granger Collection.]

the battle was regarded as a defeat for him. Fires, set by the Russians, soon engulfed Moscow and left Napoleon far from home with a badly diminished army lacking adequate supplies as winter came to a vast country whose people hated the invader. Napoleon, after capturing the burned city, addressed several peace offers to Alexander, but the tsar ignored them. By October, what was left of the Grand Army was forced to retreat. By December, Napoleon realized that the Russian fiasco would encourage plots against him at home. He returned to Paris, leaving the remnants of his army to struggle westward. Perhaps only as many as 100,000 lived to tell the tale of their terrible ordeal. Even as the news of the disaster reached the West, the total defeat of Napoleon was far from certain. He was able to put down his opponents in Paris and to raise another army of 350,000 men.

In 1813, patriotic pressure and national ambition brought together the last and most powerful coalition against Napoleon. The Russians drove westward and were joined by Prussia and then Austria. All were assisted by vast amounts of British money. From the west, Wellington marched his peninsular army into France. Napoleon's new army was inexperienced and poorly equipped. His generals had lost confidence and were tired. The emperor himself was worn out and sick. Still, he was able to wage a skillful campaign in central Europe and to defeat the allies at Dresden. In October, however, he met the combined armies of the enemy at Leipzig, in what the Germans called the Battle of the Nations, and was decisively defeated. At the end of March 1814, the allied army marched into Paris, and a few days later, Napoleon abdicated and went into exile on the island of Elba off the coast of northern Italy.

The Congress of Vienna and the European Settlement

Fear of Napoleon and hostility to his ambitions had held the victorious coalition together. As soon as he was removed, all allies began to pursue their own separate ambitions. The key person in achieving eventual agreement among the allies was Robert Stewart Viscount Castlereagh (1769–1822), the British foreign secretary. Even before the victorious armies had entered Paris, he brought about the signing of the Treaty of Chaumont on March 9, 1814. It provided for the restoration of the Bourbon dynasty to the French throne and the contraction of France to its frontiers of 1792. Even more important was the agreement by Britain, Austria, Russia, and Prussia to form a Quadruple Alliance for twenty years to guarantee the peace terms and to act together to preserve whatever settlement they later agreed on. Remaining problems—and there were many—and final details were left for a conference to be held at Vienna.

The Congress of Vienna assembled in September 1814 but did not conclude its work until November 1815. Although a glittering array of heads of state attended the gathering, the four great powers conducted the important work of the conference. The only full session of the Congress met to ratify the arrangements made by the big four. The easiest problem facing the great powers was France. All the victors agreed that no single state should be allowed to dominate Europe, and all were determined to see that France should be prevented from doing so again. The restoration of the French Bourbon monarchy, which was again popular, and a nonvindictive boundary settlement kept France calm and satisfied.

EUROPE, 1815
AFTER THE
CONGRESS OF VIENNA

NORWAY AND SWEDEN 1814

Bergen
Christiania
Stockholm

SCOTLAND
Edinburgh
Belfast
IRELAND
Dublin
Liverpool
Manchester
London

UNITED KINGDOM

NORTH SEA

DENMARK

SCHLESWIG
HOLSTEIN

BOUNDARY OF THE GERMAN CONFEDERATION

PRUSSIA

Danzig

EAST PRUSSIA

(FORMER DUTCH REP.)
(FORMER AUSTR. NETHS.)
K. OF THE NETHERLANDS

HANOVER

Berlin

Cologne

Wars
K. OF POLAN (RUSS.)

Breslau
Cracow

ATLANTIC

Brest
Rouen
Brussels
Rennes
Paris
Reims
Orléans
Strassburg

LORRAINE
ALSACE

Prague
BOHEMIA
MORAVIA

OCEAN

Nantes

FRANCE

Berne
SWITZ.

BAVARIA
Munich

AUSTRIA
Vienna

AUSTRIAN

HUNGARY
Budapest

EMPIRE

Lyons

SAVOY

TYROL

Trieste
Agram

Bordeaux

LOM-
BARDY

VENETIA

CROATS

Montpelier

PIEDMONT

PAR.
MOD.

Bologna

BOSNIA
Belgrad

Marseilles

NICE

LUCCA

Sarajevo
MONTE NEGR

Oviedo

ANDORRA

TUSCANY

STATES
OF THE
CHURCH

ITALY

Burgos

ELBA

PORTUGAL

Madrid

Barcelona

KINGDOM OF
SARDINIA

CORSICA
(FR.)

Rome

Lisbon

SPAIN

Valencia

BALEARIC IS.
(SP.)

SARDINIA

Naples

Cordova

Seville

Cosenza

KINGDOM OF THE
TWO SICILIES

Tangier

GIBRALTAR (U.K.)
Ceuta (SP.)

THE BARBARY STATES

SICILY

MEDITE

Algiers

Tunis

Fez
MOROCCO

ALGERIA
TURK TO 1830

TUNISIA
(TURK.)

MALTA
(U.K.)

T R MILLER

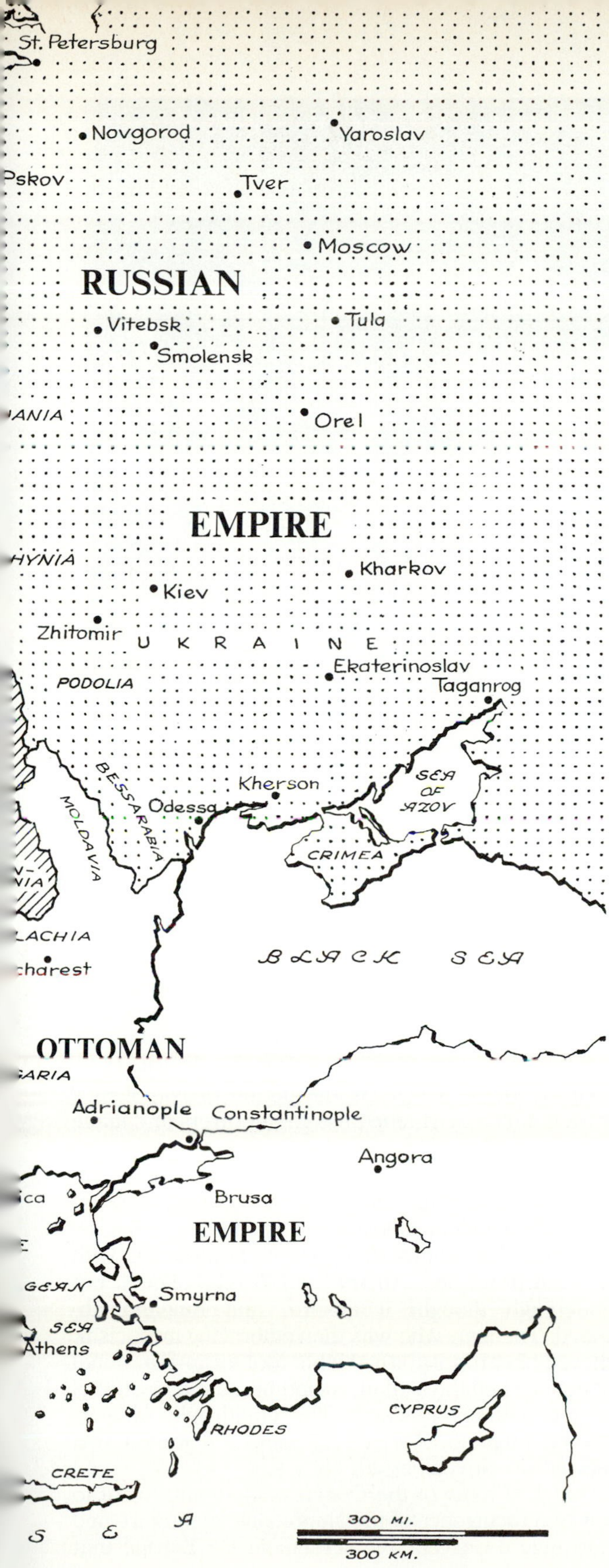

The map shows territories with labels:

St. Petersburg

Novgorod · Yaroslav

Pskov · Tver

· Moscow

RUSSIAN

Vitebsk · · Tula

Smolensk

·ANIA · Orel

EMPIRE

HYNIA

· Kiev · Kharkov

Zhitomir U K R A I N E

PODOLIA · Ekaterinoslav

Taganrog

Odessa Kherson SEA OF AZOV

BESSARABIA

MOLDAVIA

CRIMEA

·VIA

LACHIA

charest B L A C K S E A

OTTOMAN

GARIA

Adrianople Constantinople

Angora

·ica · Brusa

EMPIRE

GEAN

· Smyrna

SEA

Athens

CYPRUS

RHODES

CRETE

S E A

300 MI.

300 KM.

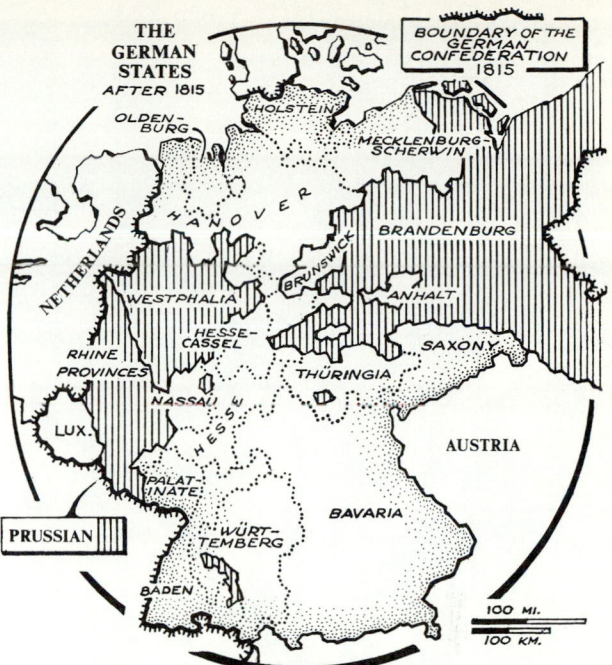

THE GERMAN STATES AFTER 1815

BOUNDARY OF THE GERMAN CONFEDERATION 1815

HOLSTEIN

OLDEN-BURG

MECKLENBURG-SCHERWIN

HANOVER

BRANDENBURG

NETHERLANDS

WESTPHALIA

BRUNSWICK

ANHALT

RHINE PROVINCES

HESSE-CASSEL

SAXONY

THURINGIA

NASSAU

LUX.

HESSE

AUSTRIA

PALAT-INATE

BAVARIA

BADEN

WÜRT-TEMBERG

PRUSSIAN

100 MI.

100 KM.

MAP 24-2   EUROPE 1815, AFTER THE CONGRESS OF VIENNA   *The Congress of Vienna achieved the post-Napoleonic territorial adjustments shown on the map. The most notable arrangements dealt with areas along France's borders (Netherlands, Prussia, Switzerland, and Piedmont) and in Poland and northern Italy.*

In addition, the powers constructed a series of states to serve as barriers to any new French expansion. They established the kingdom of the Netherlands, including Belgium in the north and added Genoa to Piedmont in the south. Prussia, whose power was increased by accessions in eastern Europe, was given important new territories in the west along the Rhine River to deter French aggression in that area. Austria was given full control of northern Italy to prevent a repetition of Napoleon's conquests there. As for the rest of Germany, most of Napoleon's arrangements were left untouched. The venerable Holy Roman Empire, which had been dissolved in 1806, was not revived. In all these areas, the Congress established the rule of legitimate monarchs and rejected any hint of the republican and democratic politics that had flowed from the French Revolution.

On these matters, agreement was not difficult, but the settlement of eastern Europe sharply divided the victors. Alexander I of Russia wanted all Poland under his rule. Prussia was willing if it received all of Saxony. But Austria was unwilling to surrender its share of Poland or to see the growth of Prussian power and the penetration of Russia deeper into central Europe. The Polish–Saxon question brought the Congress to a

The leading figures of the Congress of Vienna. Talleyrand has his arm on the table at right, and Metternich stands toward the left. The actual work of the Congress took place in small meetings, with only a few of these statesmen present. The artist was Isabey. [Austrian Information Service, New York.]

standstill and almost brought on a new war among the victors, but defeated France provided a way out. The wily Talleyrand, now representing France at Vienna, suggested that the weight of France added to that of Britain and Austria might bring Alexander to his senses. When news of a secret treaty among the three leaked out, the tsar agreed to become ruler of a smaller Poland, and Frederick William III of Prussia agreed to accept only part of Saxony. Thereafter, France was included as a fifth great power in all deliberations.

Unity among the victors was further restored by Napoleon's return from Elba on March 1, 1815. The French army was still loyal to the former emperor, and many of the French thought that their fortunes might be safer under his rule than under that of the restored Bourbons. The coalition seemed to be dissolving in Vienna. Napoleon seized the opportunity, escaped to France, and was soon restored to power. He promised a liberal constitution and a peaceful foreign policy. The allies were not convinced. They declared Napoleon an outlaw (a new device under international law) and sent their armies to crush him. Wellington, with the crucial help of the Prussians under Field Marshal von Blücher, defeated Napoleon at Waterloo in Belgium on June 18, 1815. Napoleon again abdicated and was sent into exile on Saint Helena, a tiny Atlantic island off the coast of Africa, where he died in 1821.

The Hundred Days, as the period of Napoleon's return is called, frightened the great powers and made the peace settlement harsher for France. In addition to some minor territorial adjustments, the victors imposed a war indemnity and an army of occupation on France. Alexander proposed a Holy Alliance, whereby the monarchs promised to act in accordance with Christian principles. Austria and Prussia signed; but Castlereagh thought it absurd, and England abstained. The tsar, who was then embracing mysticism, believed his proposal a valuable tool for international relations. The Holy Alliance soon became a symbol of extreme political reaction. The Quadruple Alliance between England, Austria, Prussia, and Russia was renewed on November 20, 1815.

The chief aims of the Congress of Vienna were to prevent a recurrence of the Napoleonic nightmare and to arrange an acceptable settlement for Europe that

1797	Napoleon concludes the Treaty of Campo Formio
1798	Nelson defeats the French navy in the harbor of Abukir
1799	Consulate established
1801	Concordat between France and the papacy
1802	Treaty of Amiens
1803	War renewed between France and Britain
1804	Execution of duke of Enghien
	Napoleonic Civil Code issued
	Napoleon crowned as emperor
1805	Nelson defeats French fleet at Trafalgar (October 21)
	Austerlitz (December 2)
1806	Jena
	Continental System established by Berlin Decrees
1807	Friedland
	Treaty of Tilsit
1808	Beginning of Spanish resistance to Napoleonic domination
1809	Wagram
	Napoleon marries Archduchess Marie Louise of Austria
	Invasion of Russia and French defeat at Borodino
1813	Leipzig (Battle of the Nations)
1814	Treaty of Chaumont (March) establishes Quadruple Alliance
	Congress of Vienna convenes (September)
1815	Napoleon returns from Elba (March 1)
	Waterloo (June 18)
	Holy Alliance formed at Congress of Vienna (September 26)
	Quadruple Alliance renewed at Congress of Vienna (November 20)
1821	Napoleon dies on Saint Helena

might produce lasting peace. It was remarkably successful in achieving these goals. France accepted the new situation without undue resentment. The victorious powers settled difficult problems in a reasonable way. They established a legalistic balance of power and methods for adjusting to change. The work of the Congress has been criticized for failing to recognize and provide for the great forces that would stir the nineteenth century—nationalism and democracy—but such criticism is inappropriate. The settlement, like all such agreements, was aimed at solving past ills, and in that it succeeded. If the powers failed to anticipate future problems or to yield to forces of which they disapproved, they were more than human to have done so. Perhaps it was unusual enough to produce a settlement that remained essentially intact for almost half a century and that allowed Europe to suffer no general war for nearly one hundred years.

The French Revolution in World Perspective

The French Revolution was the first of the vast popular political upheavals that have marked the last two centuries of world history. The events in France established a pattern that to a greater or lesser extent have marked other revolutions. These included a political crisis instigated by relatively conservative portions of the population. That crisis, in turn, became exploited by more extreme parties and, finally, for a time genuinely radical elements came to the fore. After the radical phase, there followed during the Thermidorian Reaction a reassertion of conservative forces very different from those that began the crisis. Finally, a single strong, caesarlike political leader emerged who imposed a largely authoritarian regime. During all of these political transformations, foreign wars and fears associated with those wars created further crises.

The French Revolution also opened a new epoch in world history by bringing the "people," including both men and women, to the fore of political action. Popular leaders and their followers who would have had little or no political standing in the *ancien régime* came to make major decisions that affected France and Europe. Since then, one of the persistent elements in world political history has been the emergence of political leaders from relatively obscure social backgrounds.

The era of the French Revolution also demonstrated for the first time the power of a nation mobilized for war when united behind a popular political ideology. Previously, Europe and much of the rest of the world had seen wars carried out by mercenary armies. From the wars of the French Revolution and Napoleon onward, citizen armies created by volunteers or government conscription would determine the military destiny of nations. The power of nationalism as carried out by the citizen armies of France had now been demonstrated.

Finally, throughout the French Revolution the social question loomed very large. Initially, this issue had involved the social and political ambitions of the middle class. But from the early 1790s onward, the demands for political and social equality on the part of the lower urban classes came directly to the fore. Before the nineteenth century was half over, the question of social revolution would begin to press against the demands for political revolution.

The patterns of liberal political ideology, nationalism, military success, and radical social visions of the French revolutionary experience would feed later nineteenth-century political and social ideologies. They would fire the Latin American Wars of Independence during the early nineteenth century. The ideal of a powerful united nation stirred the nationalists of both Italy and Germany. At the opening of the twentieth century, those ideas would inspire political and social revolution in Asia. In the late twentieth century, the goals of the Declaration of the Rights of Man and Citizen, in a somewhat transformed manner, would inspire the resistance to colonialism in Asia and the Middle East and to apartheid in South Africa. Perhaps the key feature of all these movements for which the French Revolution provided the first example was that of secular, nonreligious, political, and cultural values providing the binding force for a vast social movement.

Suggested Readings

J. F. BERNARD, *Talleyrand: A Biography* (1973). A useful account.

D. G. CHANDLER, *The Campaigns of Napoleon* (1966). A good military study.

K. CLARK, *The Romantic Rebellion* (1973). A useful discussion that combines both art and literature.

R. COBB, *The Police and the People: French Popular Protest*, 1789–1820 (1970). An interesting and imaginative treatment of the question of social control during the revolution.

A. COBBAN, *Aspects of the French Revolution* (1970). Essays on numerous subjects.

O. CONNELLY, *Napoleon's Satellite Kingdoms* (1965). The rule of Napoleon and his family in Europe.

H. C. DEUTSCH, *The Genesis of Napoleon's Imperialism*, 1801–1805 (1938). Basic for foreign policy.

W. DOYLE, *Origins of the French Revolution* (1980). An outstanding summary of recent historiographical interpretations.

J. EGRET, *The French Pre-Revolution*, 1787–88 (1978). A useful survey of the coming crisis for the monarchy.

K. EPSTEIN, *The Genesis of German Conservatism* (1966). A major study of antiliberal force in Germany before and during the revolution.

A. FORREST, *The French Revolution and the Poor* (1981). A study that expands consideration of the revolution beyond the standard social boundaries.

P. GEYL, *Napoleon: For and Against* (1949). A fine survey of the historical debate.

M. GLOVER, *The Peninsular War*, 1807–1814: *A Concise Military History* (1974). An interesting account of the military campaign that so drained Napoleon's resources in western Europe.

J. GODECHOT, *The Taking of the Bastille*, July 14, 1789 (1970). The best modern discussion of the subject and one that places the fall of the Bastille in the context of crowd behavior in the eighteenth century.

J. GODECHOT, *The Counter-Revolution: Doctrine and Action*, 1789–1804 (1971). An examination of opposition to the revolution.

A. GOODWIN, *The Friends of Liberty: The English Democratic Movement in the Age of the French Revolution* (1979). A major work that explores the impact of the French Revolution on English radicalism.

D. M. GREER, *The Incidence of the Terror during the French Revolution: A Statistical Interpretation* (1935). A study of what people in which regions became the victims of the Terror.

N. HAMPSON, *A Social History of the French Revolution* (1963). A clear account with much interesting detail.

E. HECKSCHER, *The Continental System: An Economic Interpretation* (1922). Napoleon's commercial policy.

J. C. HEROLD, *The Age of Napoleon* (1968). A lively, readable account.

R. HOLTMAN, *The Napoleonic Revolution* (1950). Good on domestic policy.

D. JOHNSON (ed.), *French Society and the Revolution* (1976). A useful collection of important essays on the social history of the revolution.

M. KENNEDY, *The Jacobin Clubs in the French Revolution: The First Years* (1982). A careful scrutiny of the organizations chiefly responsible for the radicalizing of the revolution.

H. KISSINGER, *A World Restored: Metternich, Castlereagh and the Problems of Peace*, 1812–1822 (1957). A provocative study by an author who became an American Secretary of State.

G. LEFEBVRE, *The Coming of the French Revolution* (trans. 1947). An examination of the crisis of the French monarchy and the events of 1789.

G. LEFEBVRE, *The French Revolution*, 2 vols. (1962–1964). A major study by one of the most important modern writers on the subject.

G. LEFEBVRE, *Napoleon*, 2 vols., trans. by H. Stockhold (1969). The fullest and finest biography.

F. MARKHAM, *Napoleon and the Awakening of Europe* (1954). Emphasizes the growth of nationalism.

F. MARKHAM, *Napoleon* (1963). A good biography strong on military questions.

H. NICOLSON, *The Congress of Vienna* (1946). A good, readable account.

R. R. PALMER, *Twelve Who Ruled: The Committee of Public Safety During the Terror* (1941). A clear narrative and analysis of the policies and problems of the committee.

R. R. PALMER, *The Age of the Democratic Revolution: A Political History of Europe and America*, 1760–1800, 2 vols. (1959, 1964). An impressive survey of the political turmoil in the transatlantic world.

G. Rudé, *The Crowd in the French Revolution* (1959). Examines who composed the revolutionary crowds and why.

A. Soboul, *The Parisian Sans-Culottes and the French Revolution*, 1793–94 (1964). The best work on the subject.

A. Soboul, *The French Revolution* (trans. 1975). An important work by a Marxist scholar.

T. Tackett, *Religion, Revolution, and Regional Culture in Eighteenth-Century France: The Ecclesiastical Oath of* 1791. (1986). The most important study of this topic.

J. M. Thompson, *Robespierre*, 2 vols. (1935). The best biography.

J. M. Thompson, *Napoleon Bonaparte: His Rise and Fall* (1952). A sound biography.

C. Tilly, *The Vendée* (1964). A significant sociological investigation.

M. Walzer (ed.), *Regicide and Revolution: Speeches at the Trial of Louis XVI* (1974). An important and exceedingly interesting collection of documents with a useful introduction.

This famous French painting, Liberty Leading the People, by Delacroix, symbolizes the militant spirit in which the liberals of 1830 confronted the forces of political reaction. [Bettmann Archive.]

25 Europe and Latin America in 1815–1850: Political Reform, Economic Advance, and Social Unrest

The defeat of Napoleon and the diplomatic settlement of the Congress of Vienna restored a conservative political and social order in Europe. Legitimate monarchies, landed aristocracies, and established churches constituted the major pillars of conservatism. The institutions themselves were ancient, but the self-conscious alliance of throne, land, and altar was new. Throughout the eighteenth century, these groups had been in frequent conflict. Only the upheavals of the French Revolution and the Napoleonic era transformed them into natural, if sometimes reluctant, allies. They retained their former arrogance but neither their former privileges nor their old confidence. They knew they could be toppled by the political groups who hated them. They understood that revolution in one country could spill over into another. The conservatives regarded themselves as surrounded by enemies and as standing permanently on the defensive against the forces of liberalism, nationalism, and popular sovereignty. These potential sources of unrest had to be confronted both at home and abroad.

The Conservative International Order

The Congress System

At the Congress of Vienna, the major powers—Russia, Austria, Prussia, and Great Britain—had agreed to consult with each other from time to time on matters affecting Europe as a whole. The vehicle for this consultation was a series of postwar congresses. Later, as differences arose among the powers, the consultations became more informal. This mode of working out issues of foreign policy was known as the *Con-*

Prince Klemens von Metternich (1773–1859). Foreign Minister and Chancellor of Austria, was the leading European statesman between 1815 and 1848. [Culver Pictures.]

cert of Europe. It meant that no one nation could take a major action in international affairs without the assent of others. The major goal of the Concert of Europe was to maintain the balance of power against new French aggression and against the military might of Russia. The Concert of Europe continued to function on large and small issues until the third quarter of the century.

The first congress occurred in 1818 at Aix-la-Chapelle, located in present-day West Germany. As a result of this congress, the four major powers removed their troops from France, which had paid its war reparations, and readmitted that nation to good standing among the European nations. Despite unanimity on these decisions, problems did arise during the conference. Tsar Alexander I, displaying his full reactionary colors, suggested that the Quadruple Alliance agree to uphold the borders and existing governments of all European countries. Castlereagh, representing Britain, flatly rejected the proposal. He contended that the Quadruple Alliance was intended only to prevent future French aggression.

The Spanish Revolution of 1820

These disagreements appeared somewhat academic in 1818. But two years later, a series of revolutions commenced in southern Europe. The Spanish rebelled against Ferdinand VII (1814–1833). When placed on his throne at the time of Napoleon's downfall, this Bourbon monarch had promised to govern according to a written constitution. Once securely in power, Ferdinand simply ignored that pledge. He dissolved the parliament (the *Cortes*) and ruled alone. In 1820, a group of army officers about to be sent to suppress revolution in Spain's Latin American colonies rebelled. In March, Ferdinand once again announced that he would abide by the provisions of the constitution. For the time being, the revolution had succeeded. Almost at the same time, in July 1820, the revolutionary spirit erupted in Naples, where the King of the Two Sicilies very quickly accepted a constitution. There were other, lesser revolts in Italy, but none of them succeeded.

These events frightened the watchful Klemens von

Metternich, the Austrian foreign minister. Italian disturbances were especially troubling to him. Austria hoped to dominate the peninsula to provide a buffer against the spread of revolution on its own southern flank. The other powers were divided on the best course of action. Britain opposed joint intervention in either Italy or Spain. Metternich turned to Prussia and Russia for support. The three eastern powers, along with unofficial delegations from Britain and France, met in Italy at the Congress of Troppau in late October 1820. The members of the Holy Alliance, led by Alexander of Russia, issued the Protocol of Troppau. This declaration asserted that stable governments might intervene to restore order in countries experiencing revolution. Yet even Russia hesitated to authorize Austrian intervention in Italian affairs. That decision was finally reached in January 1821 at the Congress of Laibach, located in present-day Yugoslavia. Shortly thereafter, Austrian troops marched into Naples and restored the King of the Two Sicilies to unconstitutional government.

The final postwar congress took place in October 1822 in Italy at Verona. Its primary purpose was to resolve the situation in Spain. Once again, Britain balked at joint action. Shortly before the meeting, Castlereagh had committed suicide. George Canning (1770–1827), the new foreign minister, was much less sympathetic to Metternich's goals. At Verona, Britain, in effect, withdrew from continental affairs. Austria, Prussia, and Russia agreed to support French intervention in Spain. In April 1823, the French army crossed the Pyrenees and within a few months suppressed the Spanish revolution. Liberals and revolutionaries were tortured, executed, and driven from the country. The intervention in Spain in 1823 was one of the most bloody examples of reactionary politics during the entire century.

There was a second diplomatic result of the Congress of Verona and the Spanish intervention. George Canning was much more interested in the fate of British commerce and trade than Castlereagh had been. Consequently, Canning sought to prevent the politics of European reaction from being extended to the Spanish colonies then revolting in Latin America. He intended to use those South American revolutions as the occasion for British penetration of the old Spanish trading monopoly in that area. To that end, the British foreign minister supported the American Monroe Doctrine in 1823, prohibiting further colonization and intervention by European powers in the Americas. Britain soon recognized the Spanish colonies as independent states. Through the rest of the century, British commercial interests dominated Latin America. In this fashion, Canning may be said to have brought to a successful conclusion the War of Jenkins' Ear (1739).

The Latin American situation that Canning used so astutely to British advantage was itself closely related to the years of European political turmoil.

The Wars of Independence in Latin America

The wars of the French Revolution and more particularly those of Napoleon sparked movements for independence from European domination throughout Latin America. In less than two decades, between 1804 and 1824, France was driven from Haiti, Portugal lost control of Brazil, and Spain came to control only Cuba and Puerto Rico. Three centuries of Iberian colonial government over the South American continent came to an end.

Haiti achieved independence in 1804, following a slave revolt that commenced in 1794 led by Toussaint L'Ouverture and Jean-Jacques Dessalines. Such a revolution involving the popular uprising of a repressed social group was the great exception in the Latin American drive for liberty from European masters. Generally speaking, on the South American continent, the Creole elite, composed of Spanish merchants, landowners, and professional persons born in America, led the movements against Spain and Portugal. Very few Indians, blacks, mestizos, mulattos, or

Toussaint L'Ouverture (1743–1803) began the revolt against France which led to Haitian independence in 1804. [Bettmann Archive.]

slaves became involved or benefited from the end of Iberian rule. Indeed, the example of the Haitian slave revolt haunted the Creoles, and they were determined that any drive for political independence from Spain and Portugal should not cause social disruption or the loss of their existing social and economic privileges. In this respect, the Creole revolutionaries were not unlike American revolutionaries in the southern colonies who wanted to reject British rule but keep their slaves, or French revolutionaries who wanted to depose the king but not to extend liberty to the French working class.

CREOLE DISCONTENT. There were several sources of Creole discontent with Spanish colonial government. (The Brazilian situation will be discussed separately.) Some of the Creole complaints against Spain resembled those of the American colonists against Great Britain. Latin American merchants wanted to trade more freely within the region and throughout the North American and European markets. They wanted commercial regulations that would benefit them rather than Spain. The late-eighteenth-century Bourbon imperial reforms, though liberating

trade, had done so in a manner detrimental to Latin American exports. Creoles also feared that Spanish imperial regulations might attempt to make changes in landholding, access to army officer commissions, local government, and the treatment of slaves and Indians. The Creoles deeply resented the favors granted to persons born in Spain and the clear discrimination against themselves in matters of appointments and patronage in the colonial government, church, and army.

Creole leaders had read the Enlightenment *philosophes* and regarded their reforms as potentially beneficial to the region. They were also well aware of the events and the political philosophy of the American Revolution. But something more than reform programs and revolutionary example was required to transform Creole discontent into revolt against the Spanish government. That transforming event occurred in Europe when Napoleon toppled the Portuguese monarchy in 1807 and the Spanish government in 1808 and placed his own brother on those thrones. The Portuguese royal family fled to Brazil and established its government there. But the Bourbon monarchy of Spain stood, for the time being, wholly van-

José de San Martín led the forces which liberated Argentina, Chile, and Peru from Spanish rule. San Martín was a monarchist who believed that the newly-independent Latin American states were not ready to become republics. [Bettmann Archive.]

quished. That situation created an imperial political vacuum throughout Spanish Latin America and provided both the opportunity and the necessity for action by Creole leaders.

The Creole elite feared that a liberal Napoleonic monarchy in Spain would attempt to impose reforms in Latin America that would harm their economic and social interests. They also feared that a Spanish monarchy controlled by France would attempt to drain the region of the wealth and resources needed for Napoleon's wars. To protect their interests and to seize the opportunity to take over direction of their own political destiny, between 1808 and 1810 various Creole juntas, or political committees, claimed the right to govern different regions of Latin America. Many of them quite insincerely declared that they were ruling in the name of the deposed Spanish monarch Ferdinand VII. After the establishment of these local juntas, the Spanish would not again directly govern the continent; after ten years of politically and economically exhausting warfare, they were required to make Latin American independence permanent.

SAN MARTÍN IN RÍO DE LA PLATA. The vast size of Latin America, its geographical barriers, and its distinct regional differences meant that there would be several different paths to independence. The first region to assert itself was the Río de la Plata, or modern Argentina. The center of revolt was Buenos Aires, whose citizens, as early as 1806, had fought off a British invasion against the Spanish commercial monopoly and thus had learned that they could look to themselves rather than Spain for effective political and military action. In 1810, the junta in Buenos Aires not only thrust off Spanish authority but also sent forces against both Paraguay and Uruguay in the cause of liberation from Spain and control by their own region. The armies were defeated, but Spanish control was lost in the two areas. Paraguay asserted its own independence. Uruguay was eventually absorbed by Brazil.

The Buenos Aires government was not discouraged by these early defeats and remained determined to liberate Peru, the greatest stronghold of royalist power. By 1814, José de San Martín had become the leading general of the Río de la Plata forces. He organized a disciplined army and led his forces in a daring march over the Andes Mountains. By early 1817, he had occupied Santiago in Chile, where the Chilean independence leader Bernardo O'Higgins was established as supreme dictator. From Santiago, San Martín oversaw the construction and organization of a naval force that, in 1820, he employed to carry his army by sea to an assault on Peru. The next year, San Martín drove royalist forces from the city of Lima and took for himself the title of Protector of Peru.

SIMÓN BOLÍVAR'S LIBERATION OF VENEZUELA. While the army of San Martín had been liberating the southern portion of the continent, Simón Bolívar had been pursuing a similar task in the north. Bolívar had been involved in the organization of a liberating junta in Caracas, Venezuela, in 1810. He was a firm advocate of both independence and republican modes of government. Between 1811 and 1814, civil war took place throughout Venezuela as both royalists, on the one hand, and slaves and *llaneros* (Venezuelan cowboys), on the other, challenged the authority of the republican government. Bolívar had to go into exile first in Colombia and then in Jamaica. In 1816, with help from Haiti, he launched a new invasion against Venezuela. He first captured Bogotá, capital of New Granada (including modern Colombia, Bolivia, and Ecuador), to secure a base for attack on Venezuela. The tactic worked. By the summer of 1821, Bolívar's forces had captured Caracas, and he had been named president.

Simón Bolívar, the first president of what is now Venezuela, Colombia, and Ecuador. [Bettmann Archive.]

Bolívar Denounces Spanish Rule in Latin America

In September 1815, Simón Bolívar published a long statement, often called The Jamaica Letter, *in which he explained the political and economic difficulties under which the Creole elite of the Spanish Empire had lived. Earlier in the letter, he defined* Americans *as referring to those persons in Latin America who were neither Indian nor European by birth. He also implicitly excluded black slaves. Consequently his attack on Spain was voiced on behalf of the white population of the South American continent who had been born there and who demanded rights of political participation and economic freedom.*

The role of the inhabitants of the American hemisphere has for centuries been purely passive. Politically they were non-existent. We are still in a position lower than slavery, and therefore it is more difficult for us to rise to the enjoyment of freedom. . . .

. . . We have been harassed by a conduct which has not only deprived us of our rights but has kept us in a sort of permanent infancy with regard to public affairs. If we could at least have managed our domestic affairs and our internal administration, we could have acquainted ourselves with the processes and mechanics of public affairs. . . .

Americans today, and perhaps to a greater extent than ever before, who live within the Spanish system occupy a position in society no better than that of serfs destined for labor, or at best they have no more status than that of mere consumers. Yet even this status is surrounded with galling restrictions, such as being forbidden to grow European crops, or to store products which are royal monopolies, or to establish factories of a type the [Spanish] Peninsula itself does not possess. To this add the exclusive trading privileges, even in articles of prime necessity, and the barriers between American provinces, designed to prevent all exchange of trade, traffic, and understanding. In short, do you wish to know what our future held?—simply the cultivation of the fields of indigo, grain, coffee, sugar cane, cacao, and cotton; cattle raising on the broad plains; hunting wild game in the jungles; digging in the earth to mine its gold—but even these limitations could never satisfy the greed of Spain.

So negative was our existence that I can find nothing comparable in any other civilized society, examine as I may the entire history of time and the politics of all nations. Is it not an outrage and a violation of human rights to expect a land so splendidly endowed, so vast, rich, and populous, to remain merely passive?

As I have just explained, we were cut off and, as it were, removed from the world in relation to the science of government and administration of the state. We were never viceroys or governors, save in the rarest of instances; seldom archbishops and bishops; diplomats never; as military men, only subordinates; as nobles, without royal privileges. In brief, we were neither magistrates nor financiers and seldom merchants. . . .   ❑

Harold A. Bierck, Jr. (ed.), *Selected Writings of Bolívar*, Vol. 1 (New York: The Colonial Press, 1951), pp. 110–112.

A year later, in July 1822, the armies of Bolívar and San Martín joined as they moved to liberate Quito. At a famous meeting of the two liberators in Guayaquil, a sharp disagreement occurred about the future political structure of Latin America. San Martín believed that monarchies were required; Bolívar maintained his republicanism. Not long after the meeting, San Martín quietly retired from public life and went into exile in Europe. Meanwhile, Bolívar purposefully allowed the political situation in Peru to fall into confusion, and in 1823, he sent in troops to establish his control. On December 9, 1824, at the battle of Ayacucho, the Spanish royalist forces suffered a major defeat at the hands of the liberating army. The battle marked the conclusion of the Spanish effort to retain their American empire. That final Spanish retreat left Latin Americans to confront directly the kind of political questions that had so profoundly divided San Martín and Bolívar.

INDEPENDENCE IN NEW SPAIN. The drive for independence in New Spain (present-day Mexico) illustrates better than that of any other region the socially conservative outcome of the Latin American colonial revolutions. As elsewhere, a local governing junta was organized. But before it had undertaken any significant measures, a Creole priest, Miguel Hidalgo y Costilla, issued a call for rebellion to the Indians in his parish. They and other repressed groups of black and mestizo urban and rural workers responded. Father Hidalgo set forth a program of social change, including hints of changes in landholding. Soon he stood at the head of a rather unorganized group of eighty-thousand followers who captured several major cities

Father Miguel Hidalgo y Costilla was executed in 1811 for leading the first organized revolt against Spanish rule in Mexico. [Bettmann Archive.]

general Agustín de Iturbide, who in 1821 declared Mexico independent of Spain. Shortly thereafter, Iturbide was declared emperor. His own regime did not last long, but an independent Mexico, governed by persons determined to resist any significant social reform, had been created.

BRAZILIAN INDEPENDENCE. Brazilian independence, in contrast to that of Spanish Latin America, came relatively simply and peacefully. As already noted, the Portuguese royal family took refuge in Brazil in 1807. The prince regent João addressed many of the local complaints, equivalent to those of the Spanish Creoles, by measures such as the expansion of trade. In 1815, he made Brazil a kingdom, which meant that it was no longer to be regarded merely as a colony of Portugal. Then, in 1820, a revolution occurred in Portugal, and its leaders demanded João's return to Lisbon. They also demanded the return of Brazil to colonial status. João left his son Dom Pedro as regent in Brazil and encouraged him to be sympathetic to the political aspirations of the Brazilians. In September 1822, Dom Pedro embraced the cause of Brazilian independence against the recolonializing efforts of Brazil. By the end of the year, he had become emperor of an independent Brazil, which maintained that form of government until 1889.

Father José María Morelos led the Mexican revolution against Spain from 1811, when Hidalgo was executed, until his own death in 1815. [Bettmann Archive.]

and then marched on Mexico City. Hidalgo's forces and the royalist army that opposed them committed numerous atrocities. In July 1811, the revolutionary priest was captured and executed. Leadership then fell to José María Morelos y Pavón, a mestizo priest. Far more radical than Hidalgo, he called for an end to forced labor and substantial land reforms before his execution in 1815. These five years of popular uprising that ended with Morelos' death had resulted in thousands of other fatalities.

The popular uprising and demand for fundamental social reform united all conservative political groups in Mexico whether they were Creole or Spanish. They were unwilling to undertake any kind of reform that might cause loss of their privileges. In 1820, they found their recently achieved security challenged from an unexpected source. As already explained, the revolution in Spain had forced Ferdinand VII to accept a liberal constitution. Conservative Mexicans feared that the new liberal monarchy would attempt to impose liberal reforms on Mexico. Therefore, for the most conservative of reasons, they rallied to a former royalist

The era of the wars of independence left Latin America liberated from direct colonial control but economically exhausted. The new republics felt themselves to be very weak and vulnerable and looked to Britain for protection and for markets and capital investment.

The most disadvantaged citizens received only the most marginal improvement as a result of independence. Caste distinctions and most racial distinctions were removed from the law, but the societies themselves remained very conscious of class and racial divisions. The Indian populations were not incorporated into political life. Landowners replaced urban colonial officials as the major governing section in the nations. Very considerable portions of the population of each republic felt little or no loyalty to the new regimes, which more often than not functioned almost entirely in the interests of the Creole elites that had brought them into being.

Liberalism in the Early Nineteenth Century

The nineteenth century is frequently considered the great age of *isms*. Throughout the Western world, secular ideologies began to take hold of the popular and learned imagination in opposition to the political and social status quo. These included liberalism, nationalism, socialism, and communism. In time, these ideologies born in Europe spread across the globe, assuming somewhat different identities in their various new cultural settings.

The first and earliest of these ideologies was liberalism, the values of which derived from the English constitutional experience, the political thought of the Enlightenment, and the early policies of the French Revolution. Nineteenth-century liberal goals included government restrained by law, ministries responsible to parliamentary legislative bodies rather than to a monarch, written constitutions, protection of property rights, limited government activity in regard to the economy, and self-determination for national groups. The goals and values of European liberals reappeared throughout the late-nineteenth century on one continent after another as non-European political and economic leaders sought to modernize their nations and to free them from the bonds of traditional institutions and traditional social elites.

It is important to understand that the word *liberal* for twentieth-century Americans carries with it meanings and connotations that have little or nothing to do with its significance for nineteenth-century Europeans. European conservatives of the last century saw liber-

als as more radical than they actually were; present-day Americans often think of them as being more conservative than they were. Furthermore, in present-day American political rhetoric the term *liberal* has virtually no relationship to its nineteenth-century counterpart.

Liberal Goals and Their Circumstances

POLITICS. Liberals derived their political ideas from the writers of the Enlightenment, the example of English liberties, and the so-called principles of 1789 as embodied in the French Declaration of the Rights of Man and Citizen. Liberal political figures sought to establish a framework of legal equality, religious toleration, and freedom of the press. Their general goal was a political structure that would limit the arbitrary power of the government against the persons and property of individual citizens. They generally believed that the legitimacy of government emanated from the freely given consent of the governed. The popular basis of such government was to be expressed through elected representative or parliamentary bodies. Most important, free government required that state or crown ministers be responsible to the representatives rather than to the monarch.

These goals may seem very limited, and they were. However, such responsible government existed in none of the major European countries in 1815. Even in Great Britain, the cabinet ministers were at least as responsible to the monarch as to the House of Commons. The kinds of people who espoused these changes in government tended to be those who were excluded from the existing political processes but whose wealth and education made them feel that such exclusion was unjustified. Liberals were often academics, members of the learned professions, and people involved in the rapidly expanding commercial and manufacturing segments of the economy. They believed in and were products of the career open to talent. The existing monarchical and aristocratic regimes often failed to recognize sufficiently their new status and to provide for their economic and professional interests.

Although the liberals wanted broader political participation, they were *not* advocates of democracy. Second only to their hostility to the privileged aristocracies was their general contempt for the lower, unpropertied classes. Liberals transformed the eighteenth-century concept of aristocratic liberty into a new concept of privilege based on wealth and property instead of on birth. By the middle of the century, this widely shared attitude meant that throughout Europe, liberals had separated themselves from both the rural and the urban working class.

ECONOMICS. The economic goals of the liberals also furthered that important future split in European politics and society. Here, the Enlightenment and the economic thought deriving from Adam Smith set the pattern. The manufacturers of Great Britain, the landed and manufacturing middle class of France, and the commercial interests of Germany and Italy sought the removal of the economic restraints associated with mercantilism. They wanted to be able to manufacture and sell goods freely. To that end, they favored the general removal of internal barriers to trade and of international tariffs. Economic liberals opposed the old paternalistic legislation that established wages and labor practices by government regulation or by guild privileges. Labor was simply one more commodity to be bought and sold freely. Liberals sought an economic structure in which people were at liberty to use whatever talents and property they possessed to enrich themselves. By this means, the liberals contended, there would be more goods and more services for everyone at lower prices. Such a system of economic liberty was to provide the basis for material progress.

NATIONALISM. Another major ingredient of liberalism, as it developed in Germany, Italy, and the Habsburg Empire, was nationalism. The idea of nationhood was not necessarily or logically linked to liberalism. There were conservative nationalists. However, liberalism and nationalism were often complementary. Behind the concept of a people joined naturally together by the bonds of common language, customs, culture, and history lurked the idea of popular sovereignty. The idea of the career open to talent could be applied to suppressed national groups who were not permitted to realize their cultural or political potential. The efficient government and administration required by commerce and industry would mean the replacement of the petty dynasties of the small German and Italian states with larger political units. Moreover, nationalist groups in one country could gain the sympathy of liberals in other nations by espousing the cause of representative government and political liberty.

Russia: The Decembrist Revolt of 1825 and the Autocracy of Nicholas I

During the mid-1820s, Russia took the lead in suppressing both liberal and nationalistic tendencies within its domains. In the process of driving Napoleon's army across Europe, and then of occupying defeated France, many officers in the Russian army were introduced to the ideas of the French Revolution and the Enlightenment. They realized how economically backward and politically stifled their own nation remained. Under these conditions, groups within the army officer corps formed secret societies. One such reformist coterie was the Southern Society. Led by an officer named Paul Pestel, these men sought a representative government and the abolition of serfdom. Pestel himself favored democracy and a moderately independent Poland. The Northern Society was a second, more moderate, group. It favored constitutional monarchy and the abolition of serfdom but protection for the interests of the aristocracy. Both societies were very small; there was much friction between them. They agreed only that there must be a change in the government of Russia. Sometime during 1825, they seem to have decided to carry out a coup d'état in 1826.

Other events intervened. In late November 1825, Tsar Alexander I suddenly and unexpectedly died. His death created two crises. The first was a dynastic one. Alexander had no direct heir. His brother Constantine stood next in line to the throne. However, Constantine, who was then the commander of Russian forces in occupied Poland, had married a woman who was not of royal blood. He had thus excluded himself from the throne and was more than willing to renounce any claim. Through a series of secret instructions made public only after his death, Alexander had named his younger brother, Nicholas (1825–1855), as the new tsar. Once Alexander was dead, the legality of these instructions became uncertain. Constantine acknowledged Nicholas as tsar, and Nicholas acknowledged Constantine. This family muddle continued for about three weeks—during which Russia actually had no ruler, to the astonishment of all Europe. Then, during the early days of December, the army command reported to Nicholas the existence of a conspiracy among certain officers. Able to wait no longer for the working out of legal niceties, Nicholas had himself declared tsar, much to the delight of the by-now-exasperated Constantine.

The second crisis now proceeded to unfold. There was a plot devised by a number of junior officers intent on rallying the troops under their command to the cause of reform. On December 26, 1825, the army was to take the oath of allegiance to Nicholas, who was less popular than Constantine and was regarded as more conservative. Nearly all of the regiments did so. But the Moscow regiment, whose chief officers, surprisingly, were not secret society members, marched into the Senate Square in Saint Petersburg and refused to swear allegiance. Rather, they called for Constantine and a constitution. Attempts to settle the situation peacefully failed. Late in the afternoon, Nicholas ordered the cavalry and the artillery to attack the insurgents. Over sixty people were killed. Early in 1826, Nicholas himself presided over the commission that

ПОЛЯРНАЯ ЗВѢЗДА

25 Іюля 1826 года.

The five Decembrists who were executed by Czar Nicholas I. Although a total failure, the Decembrist revolt came to symbolize the yearnings of all Russian liberals in the nineteenth century for a constitutional government. [Fotomas Index. John R. Freeman & Co. Ltd.]

investigated the Decembrist Revolt and the secret army societies. Five of the plotters were executed, and over one hundred other officers were exiled to Siberia.

The immediate result of the revolt was the crushing of liberalism as even a moderate political influence in Russia. Nicholas I was determined that never again would his power come under question. He eventually epitomized the most extreme form of nineteenth-century autocracy.

Nicholas I also manifested extreme conservatism in foreign affairs. Russia under Nicholas became the gendarme of Europe, ever ready to provide troops to suppress liberal and nationalist movements.

Revolution in France (1830)

In 1824, Louis XVIII, the Bourbon monarch restored to the throne by the Congress of Vienna, died.

He was succeeded by his brother, the count of Artois, who became Charles X (1824–1830). The new king, who had been the chief leader of the ultraroyalists at the time of the restoration, considered himself a monarch by divine right.

Charles' first action was to have the Chamber of Deputies in 1824 and 1825 provide for the indemnification of aristocrats who had lost their lands in the revolution. The existing land settlement was confirmed. However, by lowering the interest rates on government bonds, the Chamber created a fund from which the survivors of the *émigrés* who had forfeited land would be paid an annual sum of money. The middle-class bondholders, who lost income, naturally resented this measure. Another measure restored the rule of primogeniture, whereby only the eldest son of an aristocrat inherited the family domains. Charles X supported the Roman Catholic church by a law punishing sacrilege with sentences of imprisonment or death. Liberals disapproved of all of these measures.

The results of the elections of 1827 compelled Charles X to appease the liberals, who in conjunction with more moderate royalists could muster a majority in the Chamber of Deputies. Charles appointed a less conservative ministry. Laws directed against the press and those allowing the government to dominate education were eased. Yet the liberals, who wanted a genuinely constitutional regime, remained unsatisfied. In 1829, the king decided that his policy of accommodation had failed. He dismissed his ministers and in their place appointed an ultraroyalist ministry headed by the Prince de Polignac (1780–1847). The opposition was now forced to the desperate action of opening negotiations with the liberal Orléanist branch of the royal family.

In 1830, Charles X called for new elections, in which the liberals scored a stunning victory. He might have relented and tried to accommodate the new Chamber of Deputies. Instead, the king and his ministers decided to attempt a royalist seizure of power. In June and July 1830, Polignac had sent a naval expedition against Algeria. On July 9, reports of its victory reached Paris. The foundation of a French empire in North Africa had been laid. On July 25, 1830, under the euphoria of this foreign diversion, Charles X issued the Four Ordinances, which amounted to a royal coup d'état. The ordinances restricted freedom of the press, dissolved the recently elected Chamber of Deputies, restricted the franchise to the wealthiest people in the country, and called for new elections under the new royalist franchise.

The Four Ordinances provoked swift and decisive popular political reactions. Liberal newspapers called on the nation to reject the monarch's actions. The laboring populace of Paris, burdened since 1827 by an

A French Physician Describes a Working-class Slum in Lille

The work of medical doctors frequently carried them into working-class areas of industrial cities rarely visited by other members of the middle class. Louis Villermé was such a French physician. He wrote extensive descriptions of the slums and the general living conditions of industrial workers. The passage quoted below describes a particularly notorious section of Lille, a major cotton-manufacturing town in northern France.

The poorest live in the cellars and attics. These cellars . . . open onto the streets or courtyards, and one enters them by a stairway which is very often at once the door and the window. . . . Commonly the height of the ceiling is six or six and a half feet at the highest point, and they are only ten to fourteen or fifteen feet wide.

It is in these somber and sad dwellings that a large number of workers eat, sleep, and even work. The light of day comes an hour later for them than for others, and the night an hour earlier.

Their furnishings normally consist, along with the tools of their profession, of a sort of cupboard or a plank on which to deposit food, a stove . . . a few pots, a little table, two or three poor chairs, and a dirty pallet of which the only pieces are a straw mattress and scraps of a blanket. . . .

In their obscure cellars, in their rooms, which one would take for cellars, the air is never renewed, it is infected; the walls are plastered with garbage. . . . If a bed exists, it is a few dirty, greasy planks; it is damp and putrescent straw; it is a coarse cloth whose color and fabric are hidden by a layer of grime; it is a blanket that resembles a sieve. . . . The furniture is dislocated, worm-eaten, covered with filth. Utensils are thrown in disorder all over the dwelling. The windows, always closed, are covered by paper and glass, but so black, so smoke-encrusted, that the light is unable to penetrate . . . everywhere are piles of garbage, of ashes, of debris from vegetables picked up from the streets, of rotten straw; of animal nests of all sorts; thus, the air is unbreathable. One is exhausted, in these hovels, by a stale, nauseating, somewhat piquante odor, odor of filth, odor of garbage. . . .

And the poor themselves, what are they like in the middle of such a slum? Their clothing is in shreds, without substance, consumed, covered, no less than their hair, which knows no comb, with dust from the workshops. And their skin? . . . It is painted, it is hidden, if you wish, by indistinguishable deposits of diverse exudations. ❑

Louis Réné Villermé, *Tableau de l'état physique et moral des employés dans les manufactures de coton, de laine et de soie* (Paris, 1840), as quoted and trans. in William H. Sewell, Jr., *Work and Revolution in France: The Language of Labor from the Old Regime to* 1848 (Cambridge: Cambridge University Press, 1980), p. 224.

---

economic downturn, took to the streets and erected barricades. The king called out troops, and over eighteen hundred people died during the ensuing battles in the city. On August 2, Charles X abdicated and left France for exile in England. The liberals in the Chamber of Deputies named a new ministry composed of constitutional monarchists. They proclaimed Louis Philippe (1830–1848), the duke of Orléans, the new monarch. The July Days had brought to a final close the rule of the Bourbon dynasty in France.

Politically, the July Monarchy, as it was called, was more liberal than the Bourbon restoration government. Louis Philippe was called the king of the French rather than of France. The tricolor flag of the revolution replaced the white flag of the Bourbons. The Charter, or constitution, was regarded as a right of the people rather than a concession of the monarch. Catholicism became the religion of the majority of the people rather than the official religion. Censorship was abolished. The franchise became somewhat wider but remained on the whole restricted. The king had to cooperate with the Chamber of Deputies; he could not dispense with laws on his own authority.

Socially, however, the Revolution of 1830 proved quite conservative. The hereditary peerage was abolished in 1831, but the everyday economic, political, and social influence of the landed oligarchy continued. Money was the path to power and influence in the government. There was much corruption. Most important, the liberal monarchy displayed little or no sympathy for the lower and working classes.

The Great Reform Bill in Britain (1832)

The revolutionary year of 1830 saw in Great Britain the election of a House of Commons that debated the first major bill to reform Parliament. The death of George IV (1820–1830) and the accession of William IV (1830–1837) required the calling of an election. It was once believed that the July revolution in France had influenced the British elections in the summer of

The first meeting of the reformed House of Commons in 1833, painted by G. Hayter. Most seats were still filled by the gentry and the wealthy. But the elimination of rotten boroughs and the election of members from the new urban centers began to transform the House of Commons into a representative national body. [National Portrait Gallery, London.]

1830. This theory has been shown to be incorrect through a close analysis of the time and character of the individual county and borough elections. The passage of the Great Reform Bill, which became law in 1832, was the result of a series of events very different from those that occurred on the Continent. In Britain, the forces of conservatism and reform made accommodations with each other.

English determination to maintain the union with Ireland caused the first step in the reform process. England's relationship to Ireland was not unlike that of Russia's to Poland or Austria's to its several national groups. In 1800, fearful that Irish nationalists might again rebel as they had in 1798 and perhaps turn Ireland into a base for a French invasion, William Pitt the Younger had persuaded Parliament to enact the Act of Union between England and Ireland. Ireland now sent one hundred members to the House of Commons. However, because of the religious scruples of King George III, Pitt was unable to secure the passage of a law to permit Roman Catholics to sit in the House of Commons. Consequently, only Protestant Irishmen, who usually had close ties to England, could be elected to represent overwhelmingly Catholic Ireland.

During the 1820s, under the leadership of Daniel O'Connell (1775–1847), Irish nationalists organized the Catholic Association to agitate for Catholic emancipation, as the movement for legal rights for Roman Catholics was known. In 1828, O'Connell secured his own election to Parliament, where he could not legally take his seat. The British ministry of the duke of Wellington realized that henceforth an entirely Catholic delegation might be elected from Ireland. If they were not seated, civil war might erupt across the Irish Sea. Consequently, in 1829, Wellington and Robert Peel steered the Catholic Emancipation Act through Parliament. Roman Catholics could now become Members of Parliament. This measure, together with the repeal in 1828 of restrictions against Protestant nonconformists, meant that the Anglican monopoly on British political life was over.

Catholic emancipation was a liberal measure that was passed for the conservative purpose of preserving order in Ireland. It included a provision raising the franchise in Ireland so that only the wealthier Irish could vote. Nonetheless, this measure alienated many of Wellington's Anglican Tory supporters in the House of Commons. In the election of 1830, a large number of supporters of parliamentary reform were returned to Parliament. Even some Tories believed that parliamentary reform was necessary because they had concluded that Catholic emancipation could have been passed only by a corrupt House of Commons. The Wellington ministry soon fell. The Tories were badly divided. Consequently, King William IV turned to the Whigs under the leadership of Earl Grey (1764–1845) to form a government.

The Whig ministry soon presented the House of Commons with a major reform bill that had two broad goals. The first was to abolish "rotten" boroughs, which had small numbers of voters, and to replace them with representatives for the previously unrepresented manufacturing districts and cities. Second, the number of voters in England and Wales was increased by about 50 per cent through a series of new franchises. In 1831, the House of Commons narrowly defeated the bill. Grey called for a new election, in which a majority in favor of the bill was returned to the Commons. The House of Commons passed the reform bill, but the House of Lords rejected it. Mass meetings were held throughout the country. Riots broke out in several cities. Finally, William IV agreed to create enough new peers to give a third reform bill a majority in the House of Lords. Under this pressure, the House of Lords yielded, and in 1832 the measure became law.

The Great Reform Bill expanded the size of the English electorate, but it was not a democratic measure. The number of voters was increased by over 200,000 persons, or by almost 50 per cent. However, the basis of voting remained a property qualification. Some working-class voters actually were disenfranchised because of the abolition of certain old franchise rights. New urban boroughs were created to allow the growing cities to have a voice in the House of Commons. Yet the passage of the reform act did not, as it was once thought, constitute the triumph of the middle-class interest in England. For every new urban electoral district, a new rural district was also drawn. It was expected that the aristocracy would dominate the rural elections.

Toward an Industrial Society

By 1830, Europe was headed toward an industrial society. Only Great Britain had already attained that status, but the pounding of new machinery and the grinding of railway engines soon began to echo across the entire continent. Further urbanization, the disintegration of traditional social bonds and work habits, and eventually class conflict accompanied the economic development. However, what characterized the second quarter of the century was not the triumph of industrialism but the final gasps of those economic

An 1837 view of one of the first French railways, the line between Paris and the suburb of St. Germain. The line was built by Baron James de Rothschild, of the famous Jewish banking family. [Mary Evans Picture Library.]

groups that opposed it. Intellectually, the period saw the formulation of the major creeds supporting and criticizing the new society. These were years of uncertainty for almost everyone. Even the most confident businessman knew that the trade cycle might bankrupt him in a matter of weeks. For the industrial workers and the artisans, unemployment became a haunting and recurring problem. For the peasants, the question was sufficiency of food. It was a period of self-conscious transition that culminated in 1848 with a continent-wide outbreak of revolution. People knew that one mode of life was passing, but they were uncertain what would replace it.

Proletarianization of Factory Workers and Urban Artisans

During the century both artisans and factory workers underwent a process of *proletarianization*. This term is used to indicate the entry of workers into a wage economy and their gradual loss of significant ownership of the means of production, such as tools and equipment, and of control over the conduct of their own trades. The process occurred rapidly wherever the factory system arose. The factory owner provided the financial capital to construct the factory, to purchase the machinery, and to secure the raw materials. The factory workers contributed their labor for a wage. Those workers also submitted to various kinds of factory discipline. This discipline meant that, in large measure, work conditions became determined by the demands for smooth operation of the machines. Closing of factory gates to late workers, fines for such lateness, dismissal for drunkenness, and public scolding of faulty laborers constituted attempts to create human discipline that would match the regularity of the cables, wheels, and pistons. The factory worker also had no direct say in regard to the quality of the product or its price. It should be noted that for all the difficulties of factory conditions, the situation was often better than for the textile workers who resisted the factory mode of production. In particular, English handloom weavers, who continued to work in their homes, experienced decades of declining trade and growing poverty in their unsuccessful competition with power looms.

Urban artisans in the nineteenth century experienced proletarianization more slowly than factory workers, and machinery had little to do with the process. The emergence of factories in and of itself did not harm urban artisans. Many even prospered from the development. For example, the construction and maintenance of the new machines generated major demand for metalworkers, who consequently prospered. The actual erection of factories and the expansion of cities benefited all craftsmen in the building trades, such as carpenters, roofers, joiners, and masons. The lower prices for machine-made textiles aided artisans involved in the making of clothing, such as tailors and hatters, by reducing the costs of their raw materials. Where the urban artisans encountered difficulty and where they found their skills and livelihood threatened was in the organization of production.

In the eighteenth century, a European town or city work place had usually consisted of a few artisans laboring for a master, first in the capacity of apprentices and then as journeymen, according to established guild regulations and practices. The master owned the workshop and the larger equipment, and the apprentices and journeymen owned their tools. The journeyman could well expect to become a master. This guild system had allowed very considerable worker control over labor recruitment and training, pace of production, quality of product, and price.

In the nineteenth century, the situation of the urban artisan underwent very considerable change. It became increasingly difficult for artisans to continue to exercise corporate or guild direction and control over their trades. The legislation of the French Revolution had outlawed such organizations in France. Across Europe, political and economic liberals disapproved of labor and guild organizations and attempted to make them illegal.

Other destructive forces were also at work. The masters often found themselves under increased competitive pressure from larger, more heavily capitalized establishments or from the possibility of the introduction of machine production into a previously craft-dominated industry. In many workshops, masters began to follow a practice, known in France as *confection*, whereby goods such as shoes, clothing, and furniture were produced in standard sizes and styles rather than by special orders for individual customers. The result of this practice was to increase the division of labor in the workshop. Each artisan produced a smaller part of the more-or-less uniform final product. Consequently, less skill was required of each artisan, and the particular skills possessed by a worker became less valuable. Masters also attempted to increase production and reduce their costs by lowering the wages paid for piecework. Those attempts often led to work stoppages or strikes. Migrants from the countryside or small towns into the cities created, in some cases, a surplus of relatively unskilled workers who were willing to work for lower wages or under less favorable and protected conditions than traditional artisans. The dilution of skills and possible lower wages, caused not by machinery but by changes in the organization of artisan production, made it much more difficult for urban journeymen ever to hope to become masters with their own workshops, in which they would be in charge. Increasingly, these artisans became lifetime wage laborers whose skills were simply bought and sold in the marketplace.

Family Structures and the Industrial Revolution

It is more difficult to write in generalities about the European family structure in the age of early industrialism than under the old regime. The reason is that industrialism developed at very different rates across the continent and because the impact of industrialism cannot be separated from that of migration and urbanization. Furthermore, industrialism did not touch all families directly. In that regard, the structures and customs of many peasant families changed relatively little in the early and even in the later nineteenth century. Yet the process of factory expansion, proletarianization, and the growth of commercial and service sectors related to industrialism did change the structures of

Child laborers. Concern about the plight of child labor in England only became acute in the 1830s when whole families ceased to work in the mills together, and children had to toil without their parents being present. [The Mansell Collection.]

much family life and the character of gender roles within families. Much more is known about the relationships of the new industry to the family in Great Britain than elsewhere. It would seem that many of the British developments foreshadowed those in other countries as the factory system spread.

Contrary to the opinion once held, the adoption of new machinery and factory production in and of itself did not destroy the working-class family. Before the late-eighteenth-century revolution in textile production in England, the individual family involved in textiles was the chief unit of production. The earliest textile inventions, such as the spinning jenny, did not change that situation. The new machine was simply brought into the home. It was the mechanization of weaving that led to the major change. The father who became a machine weaver was employed in a factory. His work was thus separated from his home. However, the structure of early English factories allowed him to preserve many of his traditional family roles as they had existed before the factory system.

In the domestic system of the family economy, the father and mother had worked with their children in textile production as a family unit. They had trained and disciplined the children within the home setting. Their home life and their economic life were largely the same. In the early factories, the father was permitted to employ his wife and children as his assistants. The tasks of education and discipline were not removed from the work place nor from the institution of the family. Parental training and discipline were thus transferred from the home into the early factory. In some cases, in both Britain and France, whole families would move near a new factory so that the family as a unit could work there.

A major shift in this family and factory structure began in the mid-1820s in England and had been more or less completed by the mid-1830s. As spinning and weaving were put under one roof, the size of factories and of the machinery became larger. These newer machines required fewer skilled operators but many relatively unskilled attendants. The machine tending became the work of unmarried women and children, whom factory owners found would accept lower wages and were less likely than adult men to attempt any form of worker or union organization. However, factory wages for skilled adult males became sufficiently high to allow some fathers to remove their children from the factory and to send them to school. The children who were now working in the factories as assistants were often the children of the economically depressed handloom weavers. The wives of the skilled operatives also tended no longer to be working in the factories. Consequently, the original links of the family in the British textile factory that had existed for well over a quarter century largely disappeared.

It was at this point in the 1830s that much concern about the plight of child labor came to dominate workers' attention. They were concerned about the treatment of factory children because discipline was no longer being exercised by parents over their own children in the factories. The English Factory Act of 1833, passed to protect children by limiting their workday to eight hours and requiring two hours of education paid for by the factory owner, further divided work and home life. The workday for adult males remained twelve hours. Children often worked in relays of four or six hours. Consequently, the parental link was thoroughly broken. The education requirement began the process of removing nurturing and training from the home and family and setting them into a school, where a teacher rather than the parents was in charge of education.

After this act was passed, many of the working-class demands for shorter workdays for adults related to the desire to reunite, in some manner, the workday of adults with that of their children, or at least to allow adults to spend more hours with their children. In 1847, Parliament mandated a ten-hour day. By present standards this was very long, but at that time it allowed parents and children more hours together as a domestic unit because their relationship as a work or production unit had ceased wherever the factory system prevailed. By the middle of the 1840s, in the lives of industrial workers the role of men as breadwinners and men as fathers and husbands had become distinct in the British textile industry.

What occurred in Britain presents a general pattern for what would happen elsewhere with the spread of industrial capitalism and of public education. The European family was in the process of passing from the chief unit of both production and consumption to becoming the chief unit of consumption alone. This development did not mean the end of the family as an economic unit. However, parents and children now came to depend on sharing of wages often derived from several sources rather than on sharing of work in the home or in the factory.

And ultimately the wage economy meant that families were somewhat less closely bound together than in the past. Because wages could be sent over long distances to parents, children might now move farther away from home. Once they moved far away, the economic link was, in time, often broken. On the other hand, when a family settled in an industrial city, the wage economy might, in that or the next generation, actually discourage children from leaving home as early as they had in the past. Children could find wage employment in the same city and then live at home until they had accumulated enough savings to marry and begin their own household. That situation meant that children often remained with their parents to a later age than in the past.

Women in the Early Industrial Revolution

The industrial economy ultimately produced an immense impact on the home and the family life of women. First, it took virtually all productive work out of the home and put it elsewhere and allowed many families to live from the wages of the male spouse. That transformation prepared the way for a new concept of gender-determined roles in the home and in domestic life generally. Women came to be associated with domestic duties such as housekeeping, food preparation, child rearing and nurturing, and household management. The man came to be associated almost exclusively with breadwinning. Children were reared to match these expected gender patterns. Previously, this domestic division of labor had prevailed among the relatively small middle class and gentry class. During the nineteenth century, it came to characterize the working class as well. Second, industrialization created for many young women new modes of employment that allowed them to earn enough money to marry or, if necessary, to support themselves independently. Third, industrialism, though fostering more employment for women, lowered the skills required of employed women.

Because the early Industrial Revolution had begun in textile production, women and their labor were deeply involved from the very start. While both spinning and weaving were still domestic industries, women usually worked in all stages of production. Hand spinning was virtually always a woman's task. When spinning was moved into factories and involved large machines, women tended to be displaced by men. The higher wages commanded by male cotton-factory workers allowed many women to stop work or to work only to supplement their husbands' wages.

With the next generation of machines in the 1820s, unmarried women rapidly became employed in the factories. However, in the factories their jobs tended to require less skill than those they had previously exercised in the home production of textiles. The jobs also required less skill than most work done by men. Tending a machine required less skill than actually spinning or weaving or acting as foreman. There was thus a certain paradox in the impact of the factory on women. Many new jobs were opened to women, but the level of skills was lowered. Moreover, almost always, the women in the factories were young single women or widows. On marriage or perhaps the birth of the first child, the women usually found that their husband earned enough money for them to leave the

Women Industrial Workers Explain Their Economic Situation

In 1832, there was much discussion in the British press about factory legislation. Most of that discussion was concerned with the employment of children, but the Examiner *newspaper made the suggestion that any factory laws should not only address the problem of child labor but also in time eliminate women from employment in factories. That article provoked the following remarkable letter in response. This letter to the editor, composed by or on behalf of women factory workers, eloquently stated the very real necessity of such employment for women and the very unattractive alternatives. Their emphasis on not having a male to support them is an indication that the overwhelming majority of women in factories were either unmarried or widowed. No legislation excluding women from factories was passed, though later legislation, in effect, sharply reduced female employment in the mines.*

Sir,

Living as we do, in the densely populated manufacturing districts of Lancashire, and most of us belonging to that class of females who earn their bread either directly or indirectly by manufactories, we have looked with no little anxiety for your opinion on the Factory Bill. . . . You are for doing away with our services in manufactories altogether. So much the better, if you had pointed out any other more eligible and practical employment for the surplus female labour, that will want other channels for a subsistence. If our competition were withdrawn, and short hours substituted, we have no doubt but the effects would be as you have stated, "not to lower wages, as the male branch of the family would be enabled to earn as much as the whole had done," but for the thousands of females who are employed in manufactories, who have no legitimate claim on any male relative for employment or support, and who have, through a variety of circumstance, been early thrown on their own resources for a livelihood, what is to become of them?

In this neighbourhood, hand-loom has been almost totally superseded by power-loom weaving, and no inconsiderable number of females, who must depend on their own exertions, or their parishes for support, have been forced, of necessity into the manufactories, from their total inability to earn a livelihood at home.

It is a lamentable fact, that, in these parts of the country, there is scarcely any other mode of employment for female industry, if we except servitude and dressmaking. Of the former of these, there is no chance of employment for one-twentieth of the candidates that would rush into the field, to say nothing of lowering the wages of our sisters of the same craft; and of the latter, galling as some of the hardships of manufactories are (of which the indelicacy of mixing with the men is not the least), yet there are few women who have been so employed, that would change conditions with the ill-used genteel little slaves, who have to lose sleep and health, in catering to the whims and frivolities of the butter-flies of fashion.

We see no way of escape from starvation, but to accept the very tempting offers of the newspapers, held out as baits to us, fairly to ship ourselves off to Van Dieman's Land [Tasmania] on the very delicate errand of husband hunting, and having safely arrived at the "Land of Goshen," jump ashore, with a "Who wants me?" Now, then, as we are a class of society who will be materially affected by any alteration of the present laws, we put it seriously to you, whether, as you have deprived us of our means of earning bread, you are not bound to point out a more eligible and suitable employment for us?

Waiting with all humility, for your answer to our request, we have the honour to subscribe ourselves, the constant readers of the *Examiner*,

THE FEMALE OPERATIVES
OF TODMORDEN ❑

The Examiner, February 26, 1832, as quoted in Ivy Pinchbeck, *Women Workers and the Industrial Revolution*, 1750–1850 (New York: Augustus M. Kelley, 1969), pp. 199–200.

factory. Or they found themselves unwanted by the factory owners, who disliked employing married women because of the likelihood of pregnancy, the influence of their husbands, and the duties of child rearing.

In Britain and elsewhere by mid-century, industrial factory work accounted for less than half of all employment for women. The largest group of employed women in France continued to work on the land. In England, they were domestic servants. Domestic industries such as lacemaking, glove making, garment making, and other kinds of needlework employed a vast number of women. In almost all such cases, their conditions of labor were harsh, whether they worked in their homes or in sweated workshops. Generally, it cannot be overemphasized that all work by women commanded low wages and involved low skills. They had virtually no effective modes of protecting themselves from exploitation. The charwoman, in that regard, was a common sight across the continent and symbolized the plight of working women.

One of the most serious problems facing women in the work force was the uncertainty of employment. Because they virtually always found themselves in the least skilled jobs and trades, security of employment was never certain. Much of their work was seasonal. This was one reason that so many working-class women feared that at one time or another in their lives they might be compelled to turn to prostitution. On the other hand, cities and the more complex economy did allow a greater variety of jobs. Movement to cities and entrance into the wage economy also gave women wider opportunities for marriages. Cohabitation before marriage seems not to have been uncommon. Parents had less to do with arranging marriages than in the past. Marriage also now generally meant that a woman would leave the work force to live on her husband's earnings. If all went well, that arrangement might improve the woman's situation, but if the husband became ill or died, or if the husband deserted his wife, she would find herself again required to enter the market for unskilled labor at a much advanced age.

Despite all of these changes, many of the traditional practices associated with the family economy survived into the industrial era. As a young woman came of age, both family needs and her desire to marry still directed what she would do with her life. The most likely early occupation for a young woman was domestic service. A girl born in the country normally migrated to a nearby town or city for such employment, often living initially with a relative. As in the past, she would attempt to earn enough in wages to give her a dowry, so that she might marry and establish her own household. If she became a factory worker, she would probably live in a supervised dormitory. Such dormitories were one of the ways that factory owners attracted young women into their employ by convincing parents that they would be safe. The life of young women in the cities seems to have been more precarious than earlier. There seem to have been fewer family and community ties. There were also perhaps more available young men. These men, who worked for wages rather than in the older apprenticeship structures, were more mobile, so that relationships between men and women seem to have been more fleeting. In any case, illegitimate births increased. That is to say, fewer women who became pregnant before marriage found the father willing to marry them.

Marriage in the wage industrial economy was also different in certain respects from earlier marriages. Marriage still involved the starting of a separate household, but the structure of gender relationships within the household was different. Marriage was less an economic partnership. The husband's wages might well be able to support the entire family. The wage economy and the industrialization separating work place and home made it very difficult for women to combine domestic duties with work. When married women worked, it was usually in the nonindustrial sector of the economy. More often than not, children were sent to work rather than the wife. This may provide one explanation for the increase of fertility within marriages, as children in the wage economy tended to be an economic asset. Married women worked outside the home only when family needs or illness or the death of a spouse really required them to do so. As Louise Tilly and Joan Scott wrote,

Most women resolved the conflict between home and work by withdrawing from permanent employment, becoming temporary workers when their family need for their wages outweighed the advantages of their remaining at home and fulfilling economically important, but unpaid, domestic responsibilities.[1]

In the home, working-class women were by no means idle. Their domestic duties were an essential factor in the family wage economy. If work took place elsewhere, someone had to be directly in charge of maintaining the home front. Homemaking came to the fore when a life at home had to be organized that was separate from the place of work. Wives were primarily concerned with food and cooking, but they often also were in charge of the family's finances. The role of the mother expanded when the children still living at home became wage earners. She was now providing home support for her entire wage-earning family. She created the environment to which the family members returned after work. The longer period of home life of working children may also have increased and strengthened familial bonds of affection between those children and their hardworking, homebound mothers.

The Marxist Critique of the Industrial Order

Karl Marx was born in 1818 in the Rhineland. His Jewish middle-class parents sent him to the University of Berlin, where he became deeply involved in radical politics. During 1842 and 1843, he edited the radical *Rheinische Zeitung* (*Rhineland Gazette*). Soon the German authorities drove him from his native land. He lived as an exile in Paris, then in Brussels, and finally, after 1849, in London.

In 1844, Marx met Friedrich Engels (1820–1895), another young middle-class German, whose father

---

[1] Louise A. Tilly and Joan W. Scott, *Women, Work, and Family* (New York: Holt, Rinehart and Winston, 1978), p. 136.

owned a textile factory in Manchester, England. The next year, Engels published *The Condition of the Working Class in England*, which presented a devastating picture of industrial life. The two men became fast friends. Late in 1847, they were asked to write a pamphlet for a newly organized and ultimately short-lived secret Communist League. *The Communist Manifesto*, published in German, appeared early in 1848. Marx, Engels, and the league had adopted the name *communist* because the term was much more self-consciously radical than *socialist*. Communism implied the outright abolition of private property rather than some less extensive rearrangement of society. The *Manifesto* itself was a work of less than fifty pages. It would become the most influential political document of modern European history, but that development lay in the future. At the time, it was simply one more political tract. Moreover, neither Marx nor his thought had any effect on the revolutionary events of 1848.

In *The Communist Manifesto*, Marx and Engels contended that human history must be understood rationally and as a whole: It is the record of humankind's coming to grips with physical nature to produce the goods necessary for survival. That basic productive process determines the structures, values, and ideas of a society. Historically, the organization of the means of production has always involved conflict between the classes who owned and controlled the means of production and those classes who worked for them. That necessary conflict has provided the engine for historical development; it is not an accidental by-product of mismanagement or bad intentions. Consequently, piecemeal reforms cannot eliminate the social and economic evils that are inherent in the very structures of production. What is required is a radical social transformation. Such a revolution will occur as the inevitable outcome of the development of capitalism.

In Marx's and Engels' eyes, during the nineteenth century the class conflict that had characterized previous Western history had become simplified into a struggle between the bourgeoisie and the proletariat, or between the middle class and the workers. The character of capitalism ensured the sharpening of the struggle. Capitalist production and competition would steadily increase the size of the unpropertied proletariat. Large-scale mechanical production crushed both traditional and smaller industrial producers into the ranks of the proletariat. As the business structures grew larger and larger, smaller middle-class units would be squeezed out by the competitive pressures. Competition among the few remaining giant concerns would lead to more intense suffering on the part of the proletariat. As the workers suffered increasingly from the competition among the ever-enlarging firms, they would eventually begin to foment revolution and fi-

The socialist philosophy of Karl Marx eventually triumphed over most alternative versions of socialism in Europe—even though varying interpretations, criticisms, and revisions continue today. [Bettmann Archive.]

nally overthrow the few remaining owners of the means of production. For a time, the workers would organize the means of production through a dictatorship of the proletariat, which would eventually give way to a propertyless and classless communist society.

This proletarian revolution was inevitable, according to Marx and Engels. The structure of capitalism required competition and consolidation of enterprise. Although the class conflict involved in the contemporary process resembled that of the past, it differed in one major respect. The struggle between the capitalistic bourgeoisie and the industrial proletariat would culminate in a wholly new society that would be free of class conflict. The victorious proletariat, by its very nature, could not be a new oppressor class: "The proletarian movement is the self-conscious, independent movement of the immense majority, in the interest of the immense majority."[2] The result of the proletarian

[2]Robert C. Tucker (ed.), *The Marx–Engels Reader* (New York: W. E. Norton, 1972), p. 353.

A painting by Gabé of the capture of the Pantheon in Paris by government troops during the June days in 1848. The rebellion of the Parisian workers and unemployed against the conservative National Assembly was brutally suppressed. [Bulloz.]

victory would be "an association, in which the free development of each is the condition for the free development of all."[3] The victory of the proletariat over the bourgeoisie represented the culmination of human history. For the first time in human history, one group of people would not be oppressing another.

Marx's analysis was conditioned by his own economic environment. The 1840s had been a period of much unemployment and deprivation. However, capitalism did not collapse as he predicted, nor did the middle class during the rest of the century become proletarianized. Rather, more and more people came to benefit from the industrial system. Nonetheless, within a generation, Marxism had captured the imagination of many socialists and large segments of the working class. The doctrines were based on the empirical evidence of hard economic fact. This scientific aspect of Marxism helped the ideology as science became more influential during the second half of the century. Marx had made the ultimate victory of socialism seem certain. His writings had also portrayed for the first time the actual magnitude of the revolutionary transformation. His works also suggested that the path to socialism lay with revolution rather than with reform.

1848: Year of Revolutions

In 1848, a series of liberal and nationalistic revolutions spread across the Continent. No single factor caused this general revolutionary ground swell; rather, a

number of similar conditions existed in several countries. Severe food shortages had prevailed since 1846 due to poor harvests. The commercial and industrial economy was also in a period of downturn with widespread unemployment. However, the dynamic force for change in 1848 originated not with the working classes but with the political liberals, who were generally drawn from the middle classes. Throughout the Continent, liberals were pushing for their program of more representative governments, civil liberty, and unregulated economic life.

To put additional pressure on their governments, the liberals began to appeal for the support of the urban working classes. The goals of the two groups were quite different. The working classes sought improved employment and better working conditions rather than political reform for its own sake. The liberals refused to follow political revolution with social reform and thus isolated themselves from their temporary working-class allies. Once separated from potential mass support, the liberal revolutions became an easy prey to the armies of the reactionary governments. As a result, without exception the revolutions of 1848 failed to establish genuinely liberal or national states.

France: The Second Republic and Louis Napoleon

Early in 1848, liberal political opponents of the regime of Louis Philippe had organized a series of political banquets to criticize the government. On February 21, 1848, the government forbade further banquets. During the next several days, crowds erected barri-

[3] Ibid, p. 353.

De Tocqueville Analyzes the June Revolution in Paris

Alexis de Tocqueville (1805–1859) was a French liberal politician, historian, and political scientist and also a keen social observer. By the time of the 1848 uprising in Paris, he had lived two years in the United States in the 1830s; Democracy in America is still an important analysis of our early institutions. In this passage from his memoirs, he described the manner in which the conflict of the June Days of 1848 in Paris differed from earlier political upheavals in France. He understood that what had occurred was a mode of class warfare and that it might characterize European political life for many decades to come.

I come at last to the insurrection of June. . . .

What distinguished it also, among all the events of this kind which have succeeded one another in France for sixty years, is that it did not aim at changing the form of government, but at altering the order of society. . . . It was not, strictly speaking, a political struggle, in the sense which until then we have given to the word, but a combat of class against class, a sort of Servile War. It represented the facts of the Revolution of February in the same manner as the theories of Socialism represented its ideas; or rather it issued naturally from these ideas, as a son does from his mother. We beheld in it nothing more than a blind and rude, but powerful, effort on the part of the workmen to escape from the necessities of their condition, which had been depicted to them as one of unlawful oppression, and to open up by main force a road towards that imaginary comfort with which they had been deluded. It was this mixture of greed and false theory which first gave birth to the insurrection and then made it so formidable. These poor people had been told that the wealth of the rich was in some way the produce of a theft practised upon themselves. They had been assured that the inequality of fortunes was as opposed to morality and the welfare of society as it was to nature. Prompted by their needs and their passions, many had believed this obscure and erroneous notion of right, which, mingled with brute force, imparted to the latter an energy, a tenacity and a power which it would never have possessed unaided.

It must be observed that this formidable insurrection was not the enterprise of a certain number of conspirators, but the revolt of one whole section of the population against another. ❏

Alexis de Tocqueville, *Recollections*, trans. by A. T. de Mattos (New York: Macmillan, 1896), pp. 187–188.

cades in Paris and numerous clashes occurred between the citizenry and the municipal guards. On February 24, 1848, Louis Philippe abdicated and fled to England.

The liberal opposition organized a provisional government. It soon found itself confronted by working-class groups seeking social as well as political revolution. Under working-class pressure, the provisional government organized national workshops to provide work and relief for thousands of unemployed workers.

The election held on April 23 produced a National Assembly dominated by moderates and conservatives. This assembly had little sympathy for the very expensive national workshops, which they thought were socialistic. Throughout May, government troops and the Parisian crowd of unemployed workers and artisans clashed. By late June, barricades again appeared in Paris. On June 24, the government ordered troops to move into the city to destroy the barricades and to quell potential disturbances. During the next several days, more than three thousand persons died in street fighting.

The so-called June days confirmed the political predominance of conservative property owners in French life. Their search for social order received further confirmation late in 1848 with the election to the presidency of Louis Napoleon Bonaparte (1808–1873), a nephew of the great emperor. This election of the "Little Napoleon" doomed the Second Republic. Louis Napoleon was the first of the modern dictators who, by playing on unstable politics and social insecurity, had so changed European life. For three years, he quarreled with the National Assembly. On December 2, 1851, the anniversary of the great Napoleon's victory at Austerlitz, Louis Napoleon seized personal power in a military coup. In a plebiscite of December 21, 1851, over 7.5 million voters supported his actions with only 600,000 disapproving. A year later, in December 1852, France was proclaimed an empire. Louis Napoleon became Emperor Louis Napoleon. He was designated Napoleon III in deference to the first Napoleon's deceased young son.

The Habsburg Empire: Nationalism Resisted

The events of February 1848 in Paris immediately reverberated throughout the Habsburg domains, which were susceptible to revolutionary challenge on every score. Its government rejected liberal institutions. Its geographical borders ignored the principle of nationalism. Its society perpetuated serfdom. In 1848, the regime confronted major rebellions in Vienna, Prague, Hungary, and Italy.

The Habsburg troubles commenced on March 3, 1848, when Louis Kossuth (1802–1894), a Magyar nationalist, attacked Austrian domination of Hungary. Shortly thereafter, student riots broke out in Vienna. After the army failed to restore order, Metternich resigned as chancellor and fled the country. On May 17, the emperor fled Vienna and established his court at Innsbruck.

Even more than urban disturbances, the Habsburg government feared a potential uprising of the serfs in the countryside. Almost immediately after the Vienna uprising, the imperial government emancipated the serfs in large areas of Austria. The Hungarian Diet also abolished serfdom in March 1848. These actions successfully smothered the most serious potential threat to order in the Empire.

In each section of the empire, the Habsburg government confronted revolution initially with political concessions that were later repudiated after military actions. In Hungary, the emperor had approved a series of liberal laws in March 1848. However, by January 1849, the army had occupied Budapest and restored its own mode of government. Similarly, in March 1848, Czech nationalists in Bohemia and Moravia attempted to form an autonomous Slavic state. They met defeat by the middle of June. Also in March 1848, Italian nationalists carried out a revolution against the Habsburgs in Milan. King Charles Albert of Piedmont (1831–1849) supported them and commenced a war against Austria. In early July, the Habsburg army defeated Piedmont and suppressed the revolution. The imperial Habsburg government had survived its gravest internal challenge because of the divisions among its enemies and its own willingness to use military force with a vengeance.

Italy: Republicanism Defeated

The defeat of Piedmont was a sharp disappointment to Italian nationalists who hoped to unify the peninsula. Liberal and nationalist hopes then shifted to the pope. Pius IX (1846–1878) had a liberal reputation. He had reformed the administration of the Papal States. Nationalists believed that some form of a united Italian state might emerge under his leadership.

In November 1848, political disturbances erupted in Rome, forcing the pope to appoint a radical ministry. Shortly thereafter, Pius IX fled to Naples for refuge. In February 1849, the radicals proclaimed the Roman Republic. The next month, radicals in Piedmont forced Charles Albert to renew the patriotic war against Austria. After the rapid defeat of Piedmont, Charles Albert abdicated in favor of his son Victor Emmanuel II (1849–1878). In early June, France sent an army into the Italian peninsula to prevent the emergence of a strong unified state on its southern border. French troops then attacked Rome, overthrew the republic, and in early July restored the pope. French troops remained in Rome until 1870 to protect the pope. Piux IX returned, having renounced his previous liberalism. Leadership promoting Italian unification would have to come from another direction.

Germany: Liberalism Frustrated

In Germany, the major revolution occurred in Prussia on March 15, 1848. Frederick William IV (1840–1861) found himself forced to call a constituent assembly to write a constitution and to appoint a moderately liberal cabinet. In time, the king and his advisers decided to ignore the assembly. In April 1849, Frederick

In this Dutch lithograph Pope Pius IX (1846–1878) is pictured as a vicious reactionary hiding behind a mask of Jesus. After 1848 the pope, who had once been thought liberal, followed a strongly reactionary policy [John R. Freeman.]

William dissolved the assembly and proclaimed his own conservative constitution.

Elsewhere in Germany, liberals began to move to unify the nation. On May 18, 1848, representatives from all the German states gathered in Saint Paul's Church in Frankfurt to revise the organization of the German Confederation. The Frankfurt Parliament intended to write a moderately liberal constitution. However, it quickly lost the support of German workers and artisans by refusing to restore the economic protection once afforded by the guilds. As if to demonstrate its disaffection from workers, in September 1848 the Frankfurt Parliament called in troops of the German Confederation to suppress a radical insurrection in the city. The liberals in the parliament wanted nothing to do with workers who erected barricades and threatened the safety of property.

The Frankfurt Parliament floundered on the issue of

THE REVOLUTIONARY CRISIS OF 1848–1851

1848

February 22–24	Revolution in Paris forces the abdication of Louis Philippe
February 26	National workshops established in Paris
March 3	Kossuth attacks the Habsburg domination of Hungary
March 13	Revolution in Vienna
March 15	The Habsburg emperor accepts the Hungarian March Laws
	Revolution in Berlin
March 18	Frederick William IV of Prussia promises a constitution
	Revolution in Milan
March 22	Piedmont declares war on Austria
April 23	Election of the French National Assembly
May 15	Worker protests in Paris lead the National Assembly to close the national workshops
May 17	Habsburg Emperor Ferdinand flees from Vienna to Innsbruck
May 18	The Frankfurt Assembly gathers to prepare a German constitution
June 17	A Czech revolution in Prague is suppressed
June 23–26	A workers' insurrection in Paris is suppressed by the troops of the National Assembly
July 24	Austria defeats Piedmont
November 16	Revolution in Rome
November 25	Pope Pius IX flees Rome
December 2	Habsburg Emperor Ferdinand abdicates and Franz Joseph becomes emperor

December 10	Louis Napoleon is elected president of the Second French Republic

1849

January 5	Austrian troops occupy Budapest
February 2	The Roman Republic is proclaimed
March 12	War is resumed between Piedmont and Austria
March 23	Piedmond is defeated, and Charles Albert abdicates the crown of Piedmont in favor of Victor Emmanuel II
March 27	The Frankfurt Parliament completes a constitution for Germany
March 28	The Frankfurt Parliament elects Frederick William IV of Prussia to be emperor of Germany
April 21	Frederick William IV of Prussia rejects the crown offered by the Frankfurt Parliament
June 18	The remaining members of the Frankfurt Parliament are dispersed by troops
July 3	Collapse of the Roman Republic after invasion by French troops
August 9–13	The Hungarian forces finally are defeated by Austria aided by the troops of Russia

1851

December 2	Coup de'état of Louis Napoleon

unification as well as on the social question. Members differed over the inclusion of Austria in the projected united Germany. The large German (*grossdeutsch*) solution favored inclusion, whereas the small German (*kleindeutsch*) solution advocated exclusion. The latter formula prevailed because Austria rejected the whole notion of German unification, which raised too many other nationality problems within the Habsburg domains. Consequently, the Frankfurt Parliament looked to Prussian leadership. This tactic also failed because Frederick William IV refused to accept the crown of a united Germany from the liberal parliament. On his refusal in the spring of 1849, the Frankfurt Parliament began to dissolve. Not long afterward, troops drove off the remaining members. In many respects, German liberalism never overcame the failures of the Frankfurt Parliament.

The turmoil of 1848 through 1850 brought to a close the era of liberal revolution that had begun in 1789. Liberals and nationalists had discovered that rational argument and small insurrections would not help them to achieve their goals. The working class also adopted new tactics and organization. The era of the riot and urban insurrection was coming to a close. In the future, workers would turn to trade unions and political parties to achieve their political and social goals. Finally, after the revolutions of 1848, the political initiative in Europe passed for a time to the conservative political groups.

Early Nineteenth-Century Europe in World Perspective

The first half of the nineteenth century witnessed three major developments in Europe that would profoundly affect the entire world. First, the modern industrial economy with its capacity for mass production permanently established itself in European life. This achievement allowed Europeans for many decades a disproportional economic and military influence throughout the world. At the same time, the social dislocation fostered by industrialization and rapid urbanization in Europe provided an example of the kind of social problems that would repeat themselves elsewhere when other nations far away from Europe sought to become more industrialized. Family and community life in the non-European world would experience similar pressures in the late nineteenth and twentieth centuries as predominantly agricultural economies made the difficult transition to industrialized ones.

Second, during the first half of the century, Europeans developed political ideologies that eventually spread over most of the globe, although in all cases adapted to special local circumstances. The ideas associated with liberalism would come to be used against traditional forms of government elsewhere in the world. Nationalism would be used to unite previously disparate peoples. In the non-European world, nationalism would often most forcefully display itself in the twentieth century as an ideological weapon used against European rulers and administrators of non-European peoples. Marxism, originating in a protest against European industrial conditions, would spread round the world during the twentieth century as various poor and relatively underdeveloped nations sought to reject the dominance of wealthy, industrialized nations.

Third, the defeat of liberal political forces in 1848 and the triumph of conservative powers produced another very important effect on the world scene. Within a very few years Japan would emerge from its centuries of self-imposed isolation. After the Meiji Restoration, the new leaders of Japan looked to European examples of successful modern nations. The nation they would most clearly copy was Germany, and the Germany they emulated was the conservative, militaristic Germany that emerged after the defeat of the liberals of 1848.

Finally, outside Europe, the independence of Latin America represented the retreat of European government and direct administration from an entire continent. There would be many forms of indirect influence, but the South American continent for the first time since its discovery would be working out its own destiny. Yet the Latin American experience represented the only major ejection of a European power by non-Europeans. Americans and European immigrants were spreading across the North American continent, displacing and often eradicating native peoples in the process. The French conquest of North Africa, the Dutch expansion in southern Africa, the ongoing British domination of India, and the British penetration of Chinese markets foreshadowed the European drive toward imperialism and colonial conquest that would mark the second half of the nineteenth century.

Suggested Readings

S. AVINERI, *The Social and Political Thought of Karl Marx* (1969). An advanced treatment.

I. BERLIN, *Karl Marx: His Life and Environment* (1948). An excellent introduction.

S. G. CHECKLAND, *The Rise of Industrial Society in England*, 1815–1885 (1964). Strong on economic institutions.

G. D. H. COLE, *A History of Socialist Thought*, 5 vols. (1953–1960). An essential work that spans the entire nineteenth century.

W. Coleman, *Death Is a Social Disease: Public Health and Political Economy in Early Industrial France* (1982). One of the first works in English to study this problem.

I. Deak, *The Lawful Revolution: Louis Kossuth and the Hungarians*, 1848–1849 (1979). The most significant study of the topic in English.

G. Duveau, *The Making of a Revolution* (trans. 1968). A lively book that explores the attitudes of the various French social classes.

T. Hamerow, *Restoration, Revolution, and Reaction: Economics and Politics in Germany*, 1815–1871 (1958). Traces the forces that worked toward the failure of revolution in Germany.

G. Himmelfarb. *The Idea of Poverty: England in the Early Industrial Age* (1984). A major work covering the subject from the time of Adam Smith through 1850.

E. J. Hobsbawm, *The Age of Revolution*, 1789–1848 (1962). A very comprehensive survey emphasizing the social ramifications of the liberal democratic and industrial revolutions.

W. W. Kaufmann, *British Policy and the Independence of Latin America*, 1802–1828 (1951). A standard discussion of an important relationship.

K. Kolakowski, *Main Currents of Marxism: Its Rise, Growth, and Dissolution*, 3 vols. (1978). A very important and comprehensive survey.

D. Landes, *The Unbound Prometheus: Technological Change and Industrial Development in Western Europe from 1750 to the Present* (1969). The best one-volume treatment of technological development in a broad social and economic context.

W. L. Langer, *Political and Social Upheaval*, 1832–1852 (1969). A remarkably thorough survey strong in both social and intellectual history as well as political narrative.

J. Lynch, *The Spanish American Revolutions*, 1808–1826 (1973). An excellent one-volume treatment.

T. W. Margadant, *French Peasants in Revolt: The Insurrection of 1851* (1979). A study of the rural resistance to Louis Napoleon.

G. Masur, *Simon Bolívar* (1969). The standard biography in English.

J. M. Merriman, *The Agony of the Republic: The Repression of the Left in Revolutionary France*, 1848–1851 (1978). A major study of the manner in which the Second French Republic and popular support for it were suppressed.

J. M. Merriman (ed.), *Consciousness and Class Experience in Nineteenth-Century Europe* (1979). A collection of important revisionist essays in social and intellectual history covering topics across the Continent.

T. O. Ott, *The Haitian Revolution*, 1789–1804 (1973). An account that clearly relates the events in Haiti to those in France.

H. Perkin, *The Origins of Modern English Society*, 1780–1880 (1969). A provocative attempt to look at the society as a whole.

I. Pinchbeck, *Women Workers and the Industrial Revolution*, 1750–1850 (1930, reprinted 1969). A pioneering study that remains of great value.

D. Roberts, *Paternalism in Early Victorian England* (1979). An interesting study of the paternalistic response to early nineteenth-century social problems.

P. Robertson, *Revolutions of 1848: A Social History* (1952). Covers the developments of each nation.

P. Robertson, *An Experience of Women: Pattern and Change in Nineteenth-Century Europe* (1982). A useful survey.

W. H. Sewell, Jr., *Work and Revolution in France: The Language of Labor from the Old Regime to 1848* (1980). A very fine analysis of French artisans.

N. Smelzer, *Social Change in the Industrial Revolution: An Application of Theory to the British Cotton Industry* (1959). Important sections on the working-class family.

P. Stearns, *Eighteen Forty-Eight: The Tide of Revolution in Europe* (1974). A good discussion of the social background.

G. D. Sussman, *Selling Mother's Milk: The Wetnursing Business in France*, 1715–1914 (1982). An examination of an important subject in the history of the family and of women.

A. J. Taylor (Ed.), *The Standard of Living in Britain in the Industrial Revolution* (1975). A collection of major articles on the impact of industrialism.

E. P. Thompson, *The Making of the English Working Class* (1964). An important, influential, and controversial work.

L. A. Tilly and J. W. Scott, *Women, Work, and Family* (1978). A useful and sensitive survey.

A. B. Ulam, *Russia's Failed Revolutionaries* (1981). Contains a useful discussion of the Decembrists as a background for other nineteenth-century Russian revolutionary activity.

A. S. Wohl, *Endangered Lives: Public Health in Victorian Britain* (1983). An important and wide-ranging examination of the health problems created by urbanization and industrialization.

Toward the Modern World

ETWEEN approximately 1850 and 1945, the European nations achieved and exercised an unprecedented measure of political, economic, and military power across the globe. The century may quite properly be regarded as the European era of world history. But no less impressive than the vastness of this influence was its brevity. By 1945, much of Europe, from Britain to the Soviet Union, literally lay in ruins. Within a few years, the United States and the Soviet Union would emerge as superpowers with whom no European state could compete. Furthermore, nations throughout Asia, Africa, and Latin America that had once experienced direct or indirect European rule thrust off their colonial status. Both the rise and the decline of European world dominance fostered violence, warfare, and human exploitation all over the world.

In 1850, the major European states were recovering from the shock of the revolutions of 1848. Neither Germany nor Italy was united. British imperial influence lay at a relatively low ebb. The United States stood on the brink of a great sectional crisis that would result in the American Civil War. Japan still stood isolated from the rest of the world. China had already encountered immense pressures from Western nations and in particular from Britain, but the Ch'ing dynasty still held autonomous control. The British East India Company governed the Indian subcontinent. Except in the south, the African continent had not yet been seriously penetrated by Europeans. The Ottoman Empire continued to play its role as the ''sick man'' of European diplomacy.

The half century after 1850 witnessed momentous changes in this picture. Italy and Germany were united by the military forces and the skillful diplomats of the conservative monarchies of Piedmont and Prussia. As a major new political and economic power in central Europe, Germany loomed as a potential rival to Great Britain, France, and Russia. For a time, shrewd diplomacy and a series of complex alliances contained that rivalry. At the same time, while sorting out the new power relationships on the continent, the nations of Europe exported potential conflicts overseas. The result of this externalized rivalry was a period of imperialist ventures. By the turn of the century, these had resulted in the reduction of Latin America to the status of economic dependency; in the extensive penetration of China by European merchants, administrators, and missionaries; and in the outright partition of Africa into areas directly governed by Europeans. After the Indian mutiny in 1857, Britain directly administered India. European influence had reached its zenith.

What permitted this unprecedented situation to arise was the economic and technological base of late-nineteenth-century European civilization. Europeans possessed the productive capacity to dominate world markets. Their banks controlled or influenced vast amounts of capital throughout the world economy. Their military technology, especially their navies, allowed Europeans to back up economic power with armed force. While this vast European power emerged, other centers of world civilization, for quite independent reasons, found themselves particularly vulnerable because of internal political decay and the less advanced technology at their disposal.

There was one great and important exception to this general situation of European domination. That was Japan. Beginning in the 1860s, the Japanese emerged from two centuries of self-imposed isolation as their leaders determined to retain national autonomy. To that end, they set out to imitate the technological and, to some extent, the political structures of Europe. The Japanese effort proved immensely successful. By 1905, they had defeated Russia. Twenty years later, they stood as a major naval rival of the United States and Great Britain. By 1941, they directly, if ultimately unsuccessfully, challenged the United States in the Pacific after transforming themselves into an Asian colonial power.

In 1914, the more general situation of European dominance came to an abrupt end when war broke out among the major states of Europe. That conflict may be regarded as the central event of the twentieth century; its effects continue to influence the world today. The Austro-Hungarian monarchy collapsed. In Germany, a republic replaced the monarchy. The imperial government of Russia was replaced by the revolutionary government of the Bolsheviks. Social turmoil and economic dislocation accompanied the political revolutions. The victorious nations of Britain, France, and Italy had been bled white of manpower, and much of their wealth had been exhausted by wartime expenditures. The military and financial participation of the United States blocked the establishment of later independent economic policy by the European powers.

Ongoing nationalistic resentments fostered by the Paris Peace Settlement of 1919, in combination with the political and economic pressures of the 1920s, created conditions from which the authoritarian movements of Italian Fascism and German Nazism arose. By 1939, the aggression of Germany and the hesitant response of the other major powers had led again to the outbreak of war in Europe. From that conflict, Europe failed to emerge as the dominant political or economic force in the world.

Two other developments also contributed to the end of the European era of world history. First, the principle of national self-determination applied to Europeans in the 1919 settlement was adopted by colonial peoples seeking to assert their own right to national independence. The most important early example of this policy was that of the Congress Party movement in British India. Second, the demand for self-determination soon became linked to a critique of the foreign capitalist domination of colonial economic life. The latter development flowed directly from the spread of communist ideas throughout the colonial world after the Russian Revolution. In this respect, the ideologies of nationalism and revolutionary socialism developed by Europeans in the nineteenth century to solve certain problems in their own political and economic life were turned against them as peoples in Asia, Africa, and Latin America sought to solve their own political and social problems of the mid-twentieth century. ❏

EUROPE	NEAR EAST/INDIA

	EUROPE	NEAR EAST/INDIA
1750	*1762–1796* Catherine II, "the Great" reigns in Russia *1772* First Partition of Poland *1789* French Revolution begins *1793* and *1795* Last partitions of Poland *1804–1814* Napolean's Empire *1830–1848* Louis Phillippe reigns in France *1832* First British Reform Act *1837–1901* Queen Victoria of England *1848* Revolutions across Europe	*1757* British victory at Plassey, in Bengal *1761* English oust French from India *1772–1784* Warren Hastings' administration in India *1772–1833* Ram Mohan Roy, Hindu reformer in India *1794–1925* Qajar shahs in Iran *1805–1849* Muhammad Ali reigns in Egypt *1835* Introduction of English education in India *ca. 1839–1880* Tanzimat reforms, Ottoman Empire *1839–1897* Muslim intellectual, Jamal al-Din Al-Afghani *1845–1905* Muhammad Abduh
1850	*1852–1870* The Second French Empire, under Napoleon III *1854–1856* The Crimean War *1861* Italy unified *1861* Emancipation of Russian serfs *1866* Austro-Prussian War; creation of Dual Monarchy of Austria-Hungary in 1867 *1870–1871* Franco-Prussian War; German Empire proclaimed in 1871 *1873* Three Emperors League *1882* Triple Alliance *1890* Bismarck dismissed by Kaiser Wilhelm II	*1857–1858* Sepoy Rebellion: India placed directly under the authority of the British government in 1858 *1869* Suez Canal completed; 1875, British purchase controlling interest *1869–1948* Mohandas (Mahatma) Gandhi *1876–1949* Muhammad Ali Jinnah, "founder of Pakistan" *1882* English occupation of Egypt *1886* India National Congress formed *1889–1964* Jawaharlal Nehru *1899* Ottoman sultan Abdulhamid II grants concession to Kaiser Wilhelm II to extend railway to Baghdad ("Berlin-to-Baghdad" Railway)
1900 **1940**	*1902* Ententé Cordial *1905* January 22, "Bloody Sunday" *1905* Revolution in Russia *1914–1918* World War I *1917* Bolsheviks seize power in Russia *1919* Versailles Settlement *1922* Mussolini and Fascists seize power in Italy *1925* Locarno Pact *1933* Hitler comes to power in Germany *1936* Outbreak of the Spanish Civil War *1938* Munich Conference *1939* Invasion of Poland; World War II begins	*1908* "Young Turk" Revolt *1922* End of British occupation of Egypt *1922–1938* Mustafa Kemal, "Atatürk," founder and first president of the Turkish state *1924–1934* Reforms of Atatürk *1928* The Muslim Brotherhood founded by Hasan al-Banna

EAST ASIA	AFRICA	THE AMERICAS
1787–1793 Matsudaira Sadanobu's reforms in Japan *1789* White Lotus Rebellion in China *1823–1901* Li Hung-chang, powerful Chinese Governor-General *1835–1908* Empress Dowager Tz'u-hsi *1839–1842* Opium War; 1842, Treaty of Nanking grants Hong Kong to the British and allows them to trade in China *1844* Similar treaties made between China and France and the U.S.	*1754–1817* Usman Dan Fodio, founder of Sultanate in northern and central Nigeria *1762* End of Funj sultanate in eastern Sudanic region *1804* Fulani Jihad into Hausa lands *1806* British take Cape Colony from the Dutch *1817–1828* Zulu chief Shaka reigns *1830–1847* French invasion of Algeria *1830s* Dutch settlers, the Boers, expand northward from Cape Colony *1848–1885* Sudanese Madhi, Muhammad Ahmad	*1789* United States Constitution *1791* Negro slave revolt in French Santo Domingo *1791* Canada Constitutional Act divides the country into Upper and Lower Canada *1804* Haitian independence *1808–1824* Wars of independence in Latin America *1847* Mexican War
1850–1873 Taiping and other rebellions *1853–1854* Commodore Perry "opens" Japan to the West, ending seclusion policy *1859* French seize Saigon *1860s* Establishment of Treaty Ports in China *1864* French protectorate over Cambodia *1868* Meiji Restoration in Japan *1870s* Civilization and Enlightenment movement in Japan *1870s–1800s* Self-Strengthening movement in China *1889* Meiji Constitution in Japan *1894–1895* Sino-Japanese War; Japan gets Taiwan as colony *1898–1900* Boxer Rebellion in China	*1856–1884* King Mutasa of Buganda reigns *1870* British protectorate in Zanzibar *1879–1880* Henry M. Stanley gains the Congo for Leopold of Belgium *1880s* Mahdist revival and uprising in Sudan *1880* French protectorate in Tunisia and the Ivory Coast *1884–1885* International Conference in Berlin to prepare rules for further acquisition of African territory; the Congo free State declared. *1884* German Southwest Africa *1885* British control Nigeria and British East Africa *1894* The French annex Dahoney *1899* German East Africa; British in Sudan *1899–1902* The Boer War	*1854* Kansas-Nebraska Act *1856* Dred Scott Decision *1859* Raid on Harper's Ferry *1860* Abraham Lincoln elected President of the U.S. *1861–1865* U.S. Civil War *1862–1867* French invasion of Mexico *1863* Emancipation Proclamation in U.S. *1865–1877* Reconstruction *1865–1870* Paraguayan War *1879–1880* Argentinian conquest of the desert *1880s* Slavery eliminated in Cuba and Brazil *1898* Spanish American War
1904–1905 Russo-Japanese War *1910* Japan annexes Korea *1911* Republican Revolution begins in China; Ch'ing dynasty overthrown *1916–1928* Warlord Era in China *1919* May 4th Movement in China *1925* Universal manhood suffrage in Japan *1928–1937* Nationalist government in China at Nanking *1931* Japan occupies Manchuria *1937–1945* Japan at war with China	*1900* Nigeria a British Crown Colony *1907* Orange Free State and the Transvaal join with Natal and Cape Colony to form the Union of South Africa *1911* Liberia becomes a virtual U.S. protectorate *1914* Ethiopia the only independent state in Africa *1935* Mussolini invades Ethiopia	*1901* Theodore Roosevelt elected President of U.S. *1910–1917* Mexican Revolution *1912* Woodrow Wilson elected President of U.S. *1917* U.S. enters World War II *1929* Wall Street Crash; the Great Depression begins *1930–1945* Vargas dictatorship in Brazil *1932* Franklin Delano Roosevelt elected President of the U.S. *1938* Nationalization of Mexican oil

After his appointment as prime minister in 1862, Bismarck used the Prussian army to forge a united German Empire, which he dominated for two decades. "Bismarck Towers" such as this one in Hamburg, were erected as monuments to his leadership. [Bildarchiv Preussischer Kulturbesitz.]

26 The Age of European Nation-States

The revolutions of 1848 collapsed in defeat for both liberalism and nationalism. Throughout the early 1850s, authoritarian regimes entrenched themselves across the Continent. Yet only a quarter century later, many of the major goals of early-nineteenth-century liberals and nationalists stood accomplished. Italy and Germany were each at long last united under constitutional monarchies. The Habsburg emperor had accepted constitutional government; the Hungarian Magyars had attained recognition of their liberties. In Russia, the serfs had been emancipated. France was again a republic. Liberalism and even democracy flourished in Great Britain.

The Crimean War (1854–1856)

As has so often been true in modern European history, the impetus for change originated in war. The Crimean War (1854–1856), so named after the Black Sea peninsula on which it was fought, originated from a long-standing rivalry between Russia and the Ottoman Empire. Russia wanted to extend its influence over the Ottoman provinces of Moldavia and Walachia (now in Romania). The Empire's giving Roman Catholic France, instead of Orthodox Russia, the right to protect Christian shrines in the Holy Land provided the pretext for Russian aggression in 1853. The next year, France and Great Britain supported the Ottoman Empire to protect their naval and commercial interests in the eastern Mediterranean. Austria and Prussia remained neutral. The war quickly bogged down on both sides. Eventually in March 1856, a peace conference in Paris concluded a treaty highly unfavorable to Russia.

The Crimean War shattered the image of an invincible Russia that had prevailed across Europe since the close of the Napoleonic wars. It also shattered the

733

Florence Nightingale (1820–1910) organized hospitals for English troops during the Crimean War and left an indelible influence on nursing as a profession. [The Granger Collection.]

Giuseppe Mazzini supported Italian unification with pen and sword. His books and articles were widely read in nationalist circles. He also led guerilla bands against the princes of the Italian peninsula before unification. [The Granger Collection.]

power of the Concert of Europe to deal with international relations on the Continent. As historian Gordon Craig has commented, "After 1856 there were no more powers willing to fight to overthrow the existing order than there were to take up arms to defend it."[1] The major European powers were no longer willing to cooperate to maintain the existing borders between themselves and their neighbors. For the next twenty-five years, instability prevailed in European affairs, allowing a largely unchecked adventurism in foreign policy.

Italian Unification

Italian nationalists had long wanted the small absolutist principalities of the peninsula united into a single state, but there had been little agreement on the means to that end. Romantic republicans, such as Giuseppe Mazzini (1805–1872) and Giuseppe Garibaldi (1807–1882), sought to drive out the Austrians by popular military force and then to establish a republican government. They not only failed in this policy, but had frightened more moderate Italians in the process. The person who eventually achieved the goal of unification was Count Camillo Cavour (1810–1861), the moderately liberal prime minister of Piedmont.

[1]*The New Cambridge Modern History*, Vol. 10 (Cambridge: Cambridge University Press, 1967), p. 273.

Cavour was the progressive prime minister of the Kingdom of Piedmont. He was determined to make the idea of a united Italy respectable and acceptable to the rest of Europe. [Culver Pictures.]

Piedmont (officially styled the Kingdom of Sardinia), in northwestern Italy, was the most independent state on the peninsula. It had unsuccessfully fought against Austria in 1848 and 1849. Following the second defeat, Charles Albert abdicated in favor of his son, Victor Emmanuel II. In 1852, the new monarch chose as his prime minister Count Camillo Cavour, a moderate liberal and strong monarchist who rejected republicanism.

Cavour believed that if Italians proved themselves to be efficient and economically progressive, the great powers might decide that Italy could govern itself. He worked for free trade, railway construction, credit expansion, and agricultural improvement. He also fostered the Nationalist Society, which established chapters in other Italian states to press for unification

under the leadership of Piedmont. Cavour furthermore believed that Italy could be unified only with the aid of France.

Cavour joined the French and British side in the Crimean War in order to be able to raise the question of Italian unification at the peace conference. There, he gained no specific rewards, but did achieve the sympathy of Napoleon III of France. In 1858, Cavour and the French Emperor met at Plombières and plotted a war in Italy that would permit their two nations to intervene against Austria.

During the winter and spring of 1859, tension grew between Austria and Piedmont as the latter mobilized its army. In late April, war erupted. On June 4, the Austrians were defeated at Magenta, and on June 24, at Solferino. Elsewhere in Italy, popular revolutions

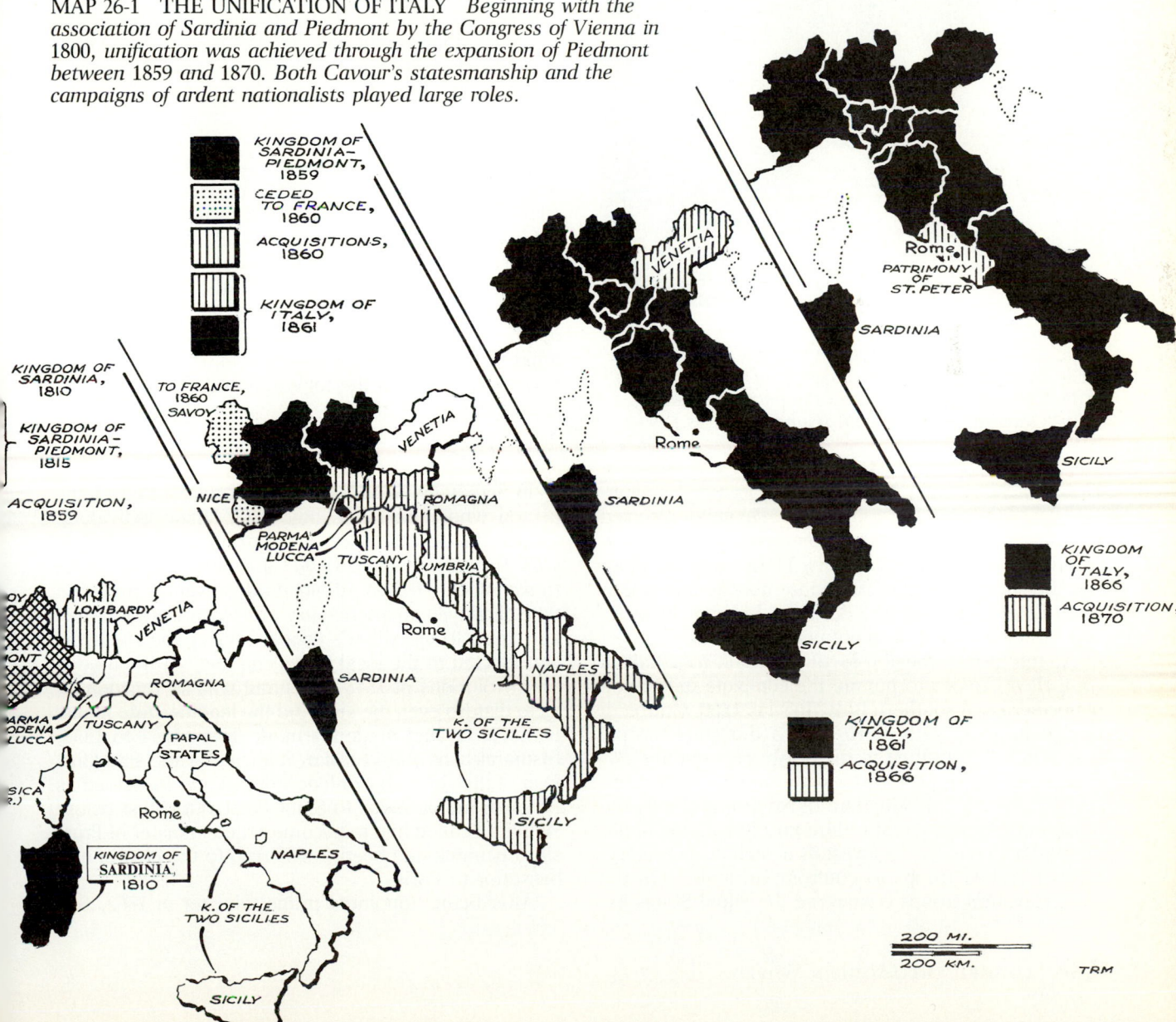

MAP 26-1   THE UNIFICATION OF ITALY   *Beginning with the association of Sardinia and Piedmont by the Congress of Vienna in 1800, unification was achieved through the expansion of Piedmont between 1859 and 1870. Both Cavour's statesmanship and the campaigns of ardent nationalists played large roles.*

Garibaldi represented the popular forces of romantic Italian nationalism. The landing of his Redshirts on Sicily and their subsequent invasion of southern Italy in 1860 forced Cavour to unite the entire peninsula sooner than he had intended. [Culver Pictures.]

cept for the area around Rome, which remained under the direct control of the pope. Garibaldi's nationalism won out over his republicanism, and he unhappily accepted the Piedmontese domination. In late 1860, the southern Italian state joined the northern union forged by Piedmont.

In March 1861, Victor Emmanuel II was proclaimed king of Italy. Three months later, Cavour died. The new state was governed by the conservative constitution promulgated in 1848 by Charles Albert at the time of his first war with Austria. The Veneto came under the new government in 1866 as a result of the war between Austria and Prussia, and Rome in 1870 as a result of the Franco-Prussian War.

German Unification

The construction of a united German nation was the single most important political development in Europe between 1848 and 1914. Germany was united by the conservative army, monarchy, and prime minister of Prussia, among whose chief motives was his wish to outflank the Prussian liberals.

In 1858, Frederick William IV was adjudged insane, and his brother William assumed the regency. William I (1861–1888), who became king in his own right in 1861, regarded the Prussian army as his first concern. In 1860, his war minister and chief of staff proposed to enlarge the army and to increase the period of conscription from two to three years. The Prussian Parliament, created by the Constitution of 1850, refused to approve the necessary taxes. A deadlock continued for two years between the monarch and the Parliament dominated by liberals.

Bismarck

In September 1862, William I turned for help to the person who, more than any other single individual, shaped the next thirty years of European history: Otto von Bismarck (1815–1898). Bismarck came from *Junker* stock. He had attended the university and for a time displayed an interest in German unification. Then he retired to his father's estate. During the 1840s, he was elected to the local provincial diet. At the time of the revolutions of 1848, his stand was so reactionary as to disturb even the king and the leading state ministers. Yet he had made his mark. From 1851 to 1859, Bismarck was the Prussian minister in the Frankfurt Diet of the German Confederation. Later he served as Prussian ambassador to Saint Petersburg. Just before William I called him to become prime minister of Prussia, Bismarck had been transferred to the post of ambassador to Paris.

After being appointed prime minister in 1862, Bis-

put the Austrians into retreat. Fearing too extensive a Piedmontese victory, Napoleon III concluded a separate peace on July 11 at Villafranca. Piedmont received Lombardy, but the Veneto remained under Austrian control. Cavour felt betrayed by France, but nonetheless the war had driven Austria from most of northern Italy. Later that summer, Parma, Modena, Tuscany, and Romagna voted to unify with Piedmont.

At this point, the forces of romantic nationalism compelled Cavour to pursue the complete unification of northern and southern Italy. In May 1860, Garibaldi landed in Sicily with more than a thousand troops, who had been outfitted in the north. He captured Palermo and prepared to attack the mainland. By September, the city and kingdom of Naples, probably the most corrupt example of Italian absolutism, lay under Garibaldi's control. To forestall a republican victory, Cavour rushed troops to confront Garibaldi. On the way, Cavour's troops conquered the Papal States ex-

Cavour Explains Why Piedmont Should Enter the Crimean War

As prime minister of Piedmont, Cavour attempted to prove that the Italians were capable of progressive government. In 1855, he urged entry into the Crimean War so that the other Europeans would consider Piedmont a military power. Earlier politics in Italy had been characterized by petty absolute princes and romantic nationalist conspiracies, both of which Cavour scorned. He understood that in the nineteenth century, a nation must possess good government, economic prosperity, and a strong army.

The experience of recent years and previous centuries has proved (at least in my opinion) how little Italy has benefited by conspiracies, revolutions and disorderly uprisings. Far from helping her, they have been a tremendous calamity for this beautiful part of Europe. And not only, gentlemen, because individual people so often suffered from them, not only because revolutions became the cause or pretext for repression, but above all because continual conspiracies, repeated revolutions and disorderly uprisings damaged the esteem and, up to a certain point, the sympathy that other European peoples cherished for Italy.

Now, gentlemen, I believe that the principal condition for the improvement of Italy's fate, the condition that stands out above all others, is to lift up her reputation once more, so to act that all the peoples of the world, those governing and those governed, may do justice to her qualities. And for this two things are necesary: first, to prove to Europe that Italy has sufficient civic sense to govern herself freely and according to law, and that she is in a condition to adopt the very best forms of government; second, to prove that her military valor is as great as that of her ancestors.

You [the Parliament of Piedmont] have done Italy one service by your conduct over the last seven years. You have shown Europe in the most luminous way that Italians are capable of governing themselves with wisdom, prudence, and trustworthiness. But it still remains for you to do Italy an equal, if not a greater, service; it is our country's task to prove that Italy's sons can fight valiantly on battlefields where glory is to be won. And I am sure, gentlemen, that the laurels that our soldiers will win in Eastern Europe will help the future state of Italy more than all that has been done by those people who hoped to regenerate her by rhetorical speeches and writings. ❑

Denis Mack Smith (ed. and trans.), *The Making of Italy*, 1796–1870 (New York: Walker and Company, 1968), pp. 199–200.

---

marck immediately moved against the liberal Parliament. He contended that in the absence of new levies, the Prussian constitution permitted the government to carry out its functions on the basis of previously granted taxes. Therefore, taxes could be collected and spent despite the parliamentary refusal to vote them. The army and most of the bureaucracy supported this interpretation of the constitution. However, in 1863, new elections sustained the liberal majority in the Parliament. Bismarck had to find some way to attract popular support away from the liberals and toward the monarchy and the army. To that end, Bismarck set about uniting Germany through the conservative institutions of Prussia. The tactic amounted to diverting public attention from domestic matters to foreign affairs.

Bismarck pursued a *kleindeutsch*, or small German, solution to the question of unification. Austria was to be ultimately excluded from German affairs when an opportunity presented itself. To achieve that end, Bismarck undertook two brief wars.

In 1864, he entered a war with Denmark over the question of the duchies of Schleswig and Holstein,

Bismarck dominated European diplomacy and German politics until his forced retirement in 1890. [Culver Pictures.]

MAP 26-2 THE UNIFICATION OF GERMANY *Under Bismarck's leadership, and with the strong support of its royal house, Prussia used most of the available diplomatic and military means, on both the German and international stages, to force the unification of German states into a strong national entity.*

areas that had long been administered by the Danes. The Austrians joined in this war, helped defeat Denmark, and then with Prussia undertook the joint administration of the two Duchies. Thereafter, Bismarck concluded various alliances with France and Italy to gain these nations' support in case of a war between Prussia and Austria. In the summer of 1866, Bismarck undertook a war against Austria on the grounds of a dispute over the administration of Schleswig and Holstein. The Seven Weeks' War led to the decisive defeat of Austria at Königgrätz. The Prussian defeat of Austria and the consequent Treaty of Prague excluded the Habsburgs from German affairs. Prussia became the only major power among the German states.

In 1867, the states of Hanover, Hesse, and Nassau, as well as the city of Frankfurt, all of which had supported Austria during the war, were incorporated into Prussia, and their ruling dynasties were deposed. Prussia and these newly incorporated territories, plus Schleswig and Holstein and the rest of the German states north of the Main River, constituted the North German Confederation. Prussia was the undisputed leader of this confederation. The constitution of the confederation, which after 1871 became the governing document of the German Empire, possessed some of the appearances but none of the substance of liberalism. Bismarck provided for a lower legislative house, or Reichstag, to be chosen by universal manhood suffrage. He had little fear of this broad franchise because he sensed that the peasants would tend to vote conservatively. The Reichstag had little real power, and its members knew that the army would always support the king and his ministers. Germany was, in effect, a military monarchy.

1854	Crimean War opens
1855	Cavour leads Piedmont into the war on the side of France and England
1856	Treaty of Paris concludes Crimean War
	July 20, secret conference between Louis Napoleon and Cavour at Plombières
1859	War of Piedmont and France against Austria
1860	Garibaldi lands his forces in Sicily and invades southern Italy
1861	March 17, Proclamation of the Kingdom of Italy
	June 6, death of Cavour
1862	Bismarck becomes prime minister of Prussia
1864	Danish–Prussian War
1866	Austro–Prussian War
	The Veneto ceded to Italy
1867	North German Confederation formed
1870	June 19–July 12, crisis over Hohenzollern candidacy for the Spanish throne
	July 13, Bismarck publishes edited press dispatch
	July 19, France declares war on Prussia
	September 1, France defeated at Sedan and Napoleon III captured
	September 4, French Republic proclaimed
	October 2, Italian state annexes Rome
1871	January 18, Proclamation of the German Empire at Versailles
	March 18–May 28, Paris Commune
	May 10, Treaty of Frankfurt between France and Germany

The Franco-Prussian War and the German Empire (1870–1871)

Bismarck now awaited an opportunity to complete unification by bringing the states of southern Germany into the confederation. The occasion arose as a result of complex diplomacy surrounding the possibility of a cousin of William I of Prussia becoming monarch of Spain. France was, of course, opposed to the idea of a second bordering state ruled by Hohenzollern. Bismarck personally edited a press dispatch surrounding these negotiations to make it appear that William I had insulted the French ambassador, even though such had not been the case. Bismarck intended to goad France into a declaration of war.

The French government of Napoleon III quickly fell for Bismarck's bait, and on July 19, the French declared war. The French emperor thought a victory over the German Confederation would give his regime a new and stronger popular base. Once the war began, the states of southern Germany honored treaties of support for Prussia. On September 1, at the Battle of Sedan, the Germans not only defeated the French army but also captured Napoleon III. By late September, Paris stood besieged. It finally capitulated on January 28, 1871. Ten days earlier, in the Hall of Mirrors at the Palace of Versailles, the German Empire had been declared. During the war, the states of South Germany had joined the North German Confederation, and their princes had requested William I to accept the imperial title. They, in turn, retained their positions as heads of their respective states within the new federation. From the peace settlement with France, Germany received the additional territory of Alsace and part of Lorraine.

France: From Liberal Empire to the Third Republic

The reign of Emperor Napoleon III (1851–1870) is traditionally divided into the years of the authoritarian empire and those of the liberal empire. After his coup in December 1851, Napoleon III kept a close rein on the legislature, strictly controlled the press, and made life difficult for political dissidents. His support came from property owners, the French Catholic church, and businessmen.

From the late 1850s onward, Napoleon III became somewhat less authoritarian. All of his moves toward moderate liberalism were closely related to problems in foreign policy. He lost control of the diplomacy of Italian unification. Between 1861 and 1867, he supported a military expedition against Mexico led by Archduke Maximilian of Austria (see Chapter 30). The venture ended in defeat and the execution of the archduke. His liberal concessions, such as the relaxation of the press laws, were attempts to compensate for an increasingly unsuccessful foreign policy. The war of 1870 against Germany was simply Napoleon III's last and most disastrous attempt to shore up French foreign policy and to secure domestic popularity.

Shortly after the news of the Sedan disaster reached Paris, a French republic was proclaimed, and a Government of National Defense was established. Paris itself was soon under Prussian siege. During the siege of Paris, the French government was transferred to Bordeaux. Paris finally surrendered in January 1871, but the rest of France had been ready to sue for peace before the capital surrendered.

From September 1870 to January 1871, Paris was besieged by the Germans and cut off from the rest of France. This photo shows the escape from the city of Leon Gambetta (1838–1882), the Minister of War in the Government of National Defense. Gambetta left Paris to organize French resistance to the Germans. [Bildarchiv Preussicher Kulturbesitz.]

The Paris Commune

The division between the provinces and Paris became even more decided after the fighting stopped. Monarchists dominated the New National Assembly, elected in February 1871, and sitting in session at Versailles. Under the leadership of Adolphe Thiers (1797–1877), the assembly negotiated a peace settlement that required paying a large indemnity to Germany and that surrendered Alsace-Lorraine to Germany.

The city of Paris resented this settlement. On March 26, 1871, the Parisians elected a new municipal government, called the Paris Commune. It intended to administer the city of Paris separately from the rest of the country. Political radicals of all stripes participated in the Paris Commune at one time or another. The National Assembly moved rapidly against the commune; by early April, its army had besieged Paris. In early May, the troops of the Assembly moved against

Paris, and on May 21, the day on which the formal treaty with Prussia was signed, the National Assembly forces broke through the city's defenses. During the next seven days, the troops restored order to Paris and in the process killed about twenty thousand inhabitants. The communards also claimed their own victims as well.

The Third Republic

The National Assembly had put down the Paris Commune directly, but it backed into a republican form of government indirectly and much against its will. Monarchists, who constituted its majority, stood divided in loyalty between the House of Bourbon and the House of Orléans. While they quarreled, time passed and events marched on. The monarchists elected as president Marshal MacMahon (1808–1893), whom they expected to prepare the way for an eventual restoration of the monarchy. In 1875, unable to find a candidate for the throne, the National Assembly decided to adopt a law that provided for a chamber of deputies elected by universal manhood suffrage, a senate chosen indirectly, and a president elected by the two legislative houses. This relatively simple republican system had resulted from the bickering and frustration of the monarchists.

The siege of Paris during the Franco-Prussian War led to extreme food shortages. Animals in the zoo, and dogs and cats were butchered to feed the hungry citizens. This sketch, made early in 1871, was published in London newspapers after being sent from Paris by balloon post. [The Granger Collection.]

Captain Alfred Dreyfus was falsely accused of passing French military secrets to Germany. His several trials during the 1890s became the occasion for major clashes, with strong anti-Semitic overtones, between the political left and right in the Third French Republic. [Culver Pictures.]

THE DREYFUS AFFAIR. The greatest trauma of the republic occurred over the Dreyfus affair. On December 22, 1894, a French military court found Captain Alfred Dreyfus (1859–1935) guilty of passing secret information to the German army. The evidence supporting his guilt was flimsy at best and was later revealed to have been forged. Someone in the officer corps had been passing documents to the Germans, and it suited the army investigators to accuse Dreyfus, who was Jewish. However, after Dreyfus had been sent to Devil's Island, secrets continued to flow to the German army. In 1896, a new head of French counter-intelligence reexamined the Dreyfus file and found evidence of forgery. A different officer was implicated, but a military court quickly acquitted him of all charges. The officer who had discovered the forgeries was transferred to a distant post.

By then, the matter had become one of widespread and sometimes near-hysterical public debate. The army, the French Catholic church, political conservatives, and vehemently anti-Semitic newspapers repeatedly contended that Dreyfus was guilty. Such anti-Dreyfus opinion was quite powerful at the beginning of the affair. In 1898, however, the novelist Emile Zola published a newspaper article entitled *"J'accuse"* ("I

Accuse"), in which he contended that the army had consciously denied due process to Dreyfus and had plotted to suppress evidence and to forge other evidence. Zola was convicted of libel and received a one-year prison sentence, which he avoided only by leaving France for exile in England.

Zola was only one of numerous liberals, radicals, and socialists who had begun to demand a new trial for Dreyfus. Although these forces of the political left had come to Dreyfus' support rather slowly, they soon realized that his cause could aid their own public image. They portrayed the conservative institutions of the nation as having denied Dreyfus the rights belonging to any citizen of the republic. They also claimed, and quite properly so, that Dreyfus had been singled out so that the guilty persons, who were still in the army, could be protected. In August 1898, further evidence of forged material came to light. The officer responsible for those forgeries committed suicide in jail. A new military trial took place, but Dreyfus was again found guilty by officers who refused to admit the original mistake. The president of France immediately pardoned the captain, and eventually, in 1906, a civilian court set aside the results of both previous military trials.

The Dreyfus case divided France as no issue had done since the Paris Commune. By its conclusion, the conservative political forces of the nation stood on the defensive. They had for a number of years allowed themselves to persecute an innocent person and to manufacture false evidence against him to protect themselves from disclosure. They had also embraced a strongly anti-Semitic posture. On the political left, radicals, republicans, and socialists developed an informal alliance that outlived the fight over the Dreyfus case itself. These groups realized that republican institutions must be preserved in a conscious fashion if the political left was to achieve its goals. Outside political circles, ever larger numbers of French citizens understood that their rights and liberties were safer under a republican than under some alternative mode of conservative government. The divisions, suspicions, and hopes growing out of the Dreyfus affair would continue to mark and to divide the Third French Republic until its defeat by Germany in 1940. The anti-Semitism associated with the attack on Dreyfus would more fully manifest itself in the Vichy regime during World War II.

The Habsburg Empire: Formation of the Dual Monarchy

In the age of national states, liberal institutions, and industrialism, the Habsburg domains remained primarily dynastic, absolutist, and agrarian. The re-

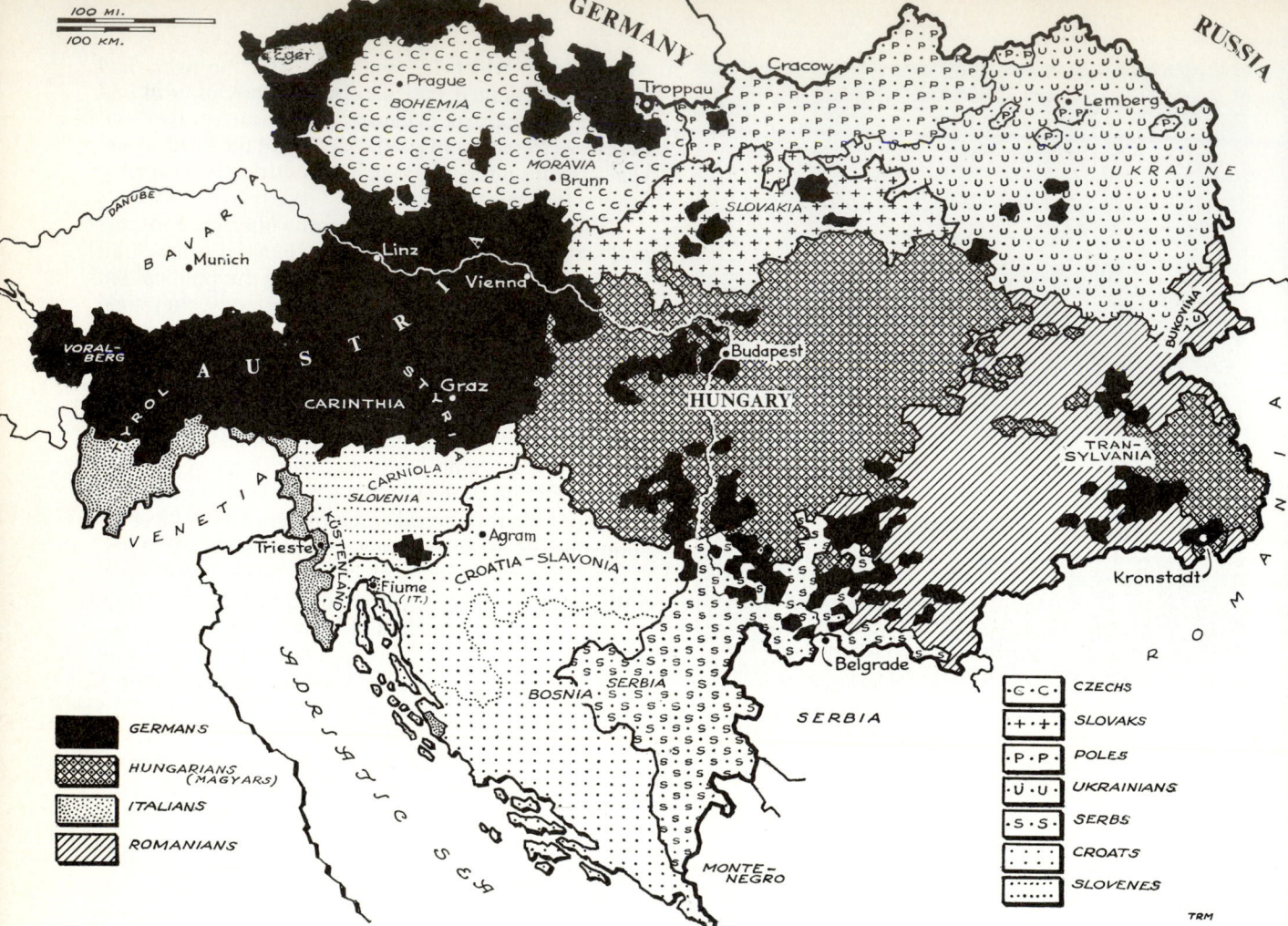

MAP 26-3   NATIONALITIES WITHIN THE HABSBURG EMPIRE *The patchwork appearance reflects the unusual problem of the numerous ethnic groups that the Habsburgs could not, of course, meld into a modern national state. Only the Magyars were recognized in 1867, leaving nationalist Czechs, Slovaks, and the others chronically dissatisfied.*

sponse to the revolts at the end of the 1840s had been the reassertion of absolutism.

During the 1850s, Emperor Francis Joseph and his ministers attempted to impose a centralized administration on the multinational empire. The system amounted to a military and bureaucratic government dominated by German-speaking Austrians. In particular, it divided Hungary, which had been so revolutionary in 1848, into military districts.

The Austrian defeat in 1859 at the hands of France and Piedmont and the subsequent loss of territory in Italy suggested the necessity for new structures of domestic government. Chief among these was a bicameral parliament, or *Reichsrat*. But one plan after another dealing with the nationality problem failed to

reconcile the Magyar nobility of Hungary to the Habsburg government.

The Austrian military collapse at the hands of Prussia in 1866 and the consequent exclusion of Austria from German affairs compelled Francis Joseph to come to terms with the Magyars. The subsequent *Ausgleich*, or Compromise, of 1867 transformed the Habsburg Empire into a dual monarchy. Francis Joseph was separately crowned king of Hungary in Budapest. Except for the common monarch, Austria and Hungary became almost separate states.

Many of the other national groups within the empire—including the Czechs, the Ruthenians, the Romanians, and the Serbo-Croations—opposed the Compromise because it permitted the German-speaking Austrians and the Hungarian Magyars to dominate all other nationalities in their respective states. The Czechs of Bohemia were the most vocal group. For over twenty years, they were conciliated by an extension of generous Austrian patronage and admission to the Austrian bureaucracy. By the turn of the century, the Czechs had become more vocal. They and German-speaking groups in the Austrian Reichsrat pursued a course of parliamentary disruption after the turn of the century rather than permitting a compromise on issues of language. The emperor ruled thereafter by imperial decree with the support of the bureaucracy. Constitutionalism was dead in Austria. It flourished in Hungary, only because the Magyars used it to dominate competing national groups.

Russia: Emancipation and Revolutionary Stirrings

Reforms of Alexander II

The defeat in the Crimean War and the humiliation of the Treaty of Paris compelled the Russian government to reconsider its domestic situation. Nicholas I had died in 1855 during the conflict. Because of extensive travel in Russia and an early introduction to government procedures, Nicholas' son Alexander II (1855–1881) was quite familiar with the chief difficulties facing the nation. The debacle of the war had created a situation in which reform was both necessary and possible. Alexander II took advantage of this turn of events to institute the most extensive restructuring of Russian society and administration since Peter the Great. Like Peter, Alexander imposed his reforms from the top.

In March 1856, at the conclusion of the Crimean War, Alexander II announced his intention to abolish serfdom. He had decided that only abolition of the institution would permit Russia to organize its human and natural resources so as to maintain its status as a great power. Serfdom had become economically inefficient; the threat of large or small revolts of serfs was always present; the serfs recruited into the army had performed poorly in the Crimean conflict; and the moral opinion of the day had come increasingly to condemn serfdom. For over five years, government commissions wrestled over the way to implement the tsar's desire. Finally, in February 1861, against much opposition from the nobility and the landlords, Alexander II promulgated the long statute ending serfdom in Russia.

The procedures of emancipation were so complicated and the immediate benefits so limited that many serfs believed that real emancipation was still to come. They received the personal rights to marry without their landlord's permission as well as to purchase and sell property freely, engage in court actions, and pursue trades. But they did not receive free title to their land. They had to pay for their frequently-too-small allotments of land over a period of forty-nine years. The redemption payments, which included interest to the government, led to almost unending difficulty and resentment. With the widespread unrest in the nation following the defeat of Russia by Japan in 1905, the tsarist government grudgingly completed the process of emancipation by canceling the remaining debts.

The abolition of serfdom required the reorganization of both local government and the judicial system. Village elders soon replaced landlords in settling family quarrels, imposing fines, and collecting taxes. In 1864, local nobles were authorized to form local

The harsh treatment of Russian serfs by their landlords was frequently criticized in the rest of Europe. This French cartoon of 1854 portrays Russian landlords using bundles of their serfs as stakes in a card game. [The Granger Collection.]

zemstvos, or councils, to oversee matters such as road or bridge repairs and education. Inadequate funding meant that the local governments never became vigorous. Also, in 1864, Alexander II promulgated a new statute on the judiciary that for the first time introduced principles of Western European legal systems into Russia. These included equality before the law, impartial hearings, uniform procedures, judicial independence, and trial by jury. The new system was far from perfect, but it marked real improvement in regard to efficiency and relative lack of corruption.

Revolutionaries

The tsarist regime had long had its critics. One of the most prominent was Alexander Herzen (1812–1870), who lived in exile. From London, he published a newspaper called *The Bell*, in which he set forth reformist positions. The initial reforms of Alexander II had raised great hopes among Russian students and intellectuals, but they soon became discontented with the limited character of the restructuring. Drawing on the ideas of Herzen and other radicals, these students formed a revolutionary movement known as *Populism*. They sought a social revolution based on the communal life of the Russian peasants. The chief radical society was called *Land and Freedom*. In the early 1870s, hundreds of young Russians, both men and women, took their revolutionary message into the countryside. They intended to live with the peasants, to gain their trust, and to teach them about the peasant role in the coming revolution. The bewildered and distrustful peasants turned most of the youths over to the police. In the winter of 1877–1878, almost two hundred students were tried. Most were acquitted or given very light sentences, because they had been held for months in preventive detention and because the court believed that a display of mercy might lessen public sympathy for the young revolutionaries. The court even suggested that the tsar might wish to pardon those students given heavier sentences. The tsar refused and let it become known that he favored heavy penalties for all persons involved in revolutionary activity.

Thereafter, the revolutionaries decided that the tsarist regime must be attacked directly. They adopted a policy of terrorism. In January 1878, Vera Zasulich attempted to assassinate the military governor of Saint Petersburg. At her trial, the jury acquitted her because the governor she had shot had a special reputation for brutality and because some people at the time believed that Zasulich had a personal rather than a political grievance against her victim. Nonetheless, the verdict further encouraged the terrorists.

In 1879, Land and Freedom split into two groups. One held to the idea of educating the peasants, and it soon dissolved. The other, known as *People's Will*,

Even after emancipation, the life of Russian peasants was difficult. They attempted to secure a livelihood partly from farming and partly from small handcraft industries, such as those seen in this picture of a Russian village in the late nineteenth century. [Culver Pictures.]

was dedicated to the overthrow of the autocracy. Its members decided to assassinate the tsar himself. Several assassination attempts failed, but on March 1, 1881, a bomb hurled by a member of People's Will killed Tsar Alexander II. Four men and two women were sentenced to death for the deed. All of them had been willing to die for their cause. The emergence of such dedicated revolutionary opposition constituted as much a part of the reign of Alexander II as did his reforms, for the limited character of those reforms convinced many people from various walks of life that the autocracy could never truly redirect Russian society.

Alexander III, whose reign (1881–1894) further underscored that pessimistic conviction, possessed all the autocratic and repressive characteristics of his grandfather Nicholas I and none of the enlightened qualities of his father. Some slight attention was directed toward the improvement of life in Russian factories, but primarily Alexander III sought to roll back the reforms of the third quarter of the century. He favored centralized bureaucracy over the new limited modes of self-government. He strengthened the secret police and increased press censorship. In effect, he confirmed all the evils that the revolutionaries saw inherent in autocratic government. His son, Nicholas II, who became tsar in 1894, would discover that autocracy could not survive the pressures of the twentieth century.

George Kennan Describes Siberian Exile in Alexander III's Russia

Under Alexander III, the police-state character of the Russian monarchy intensified. Exile was the most extreme form of punishment short of death. In effect, it robbed the person exiled not only of legal rights but almost of his or her identity, as pointed out in this account by a noted American observer (and distant relative of the well-known diplomat and historian of Soviet Russia) who spent long periods in Siberia in the 1860s and 1880s. It should be noted that he was not the person of the same name who has been an important figure in mid-twentieth-century American foreign policy.

Exile by administrative process means the banishment of an obnoxious person from one part of the empire to another without the observance of any of the legal formalities that, in most civilized countries, precede the deprivation of rights and the restriction of personal liberty. The obnoxious person may not be guilty of any crime, and may not have rendered himself unamenable in any way to the laws of the state, but if, in the opinion of the local authorities, his presence in a particular place is "prejudicial to public order," or "incompatible with public tranquillity," he may be arrested without a warrant, may be held from two weeks to two years in prison, and may then be removed by force to any other place within the limits of the empire and there be put under police surveillance for a period of from one year to ten years. He may or may not be informed of the reasons for this summary proceeding, but in either case he is perfectly helpless. He cannot examine the witnesses upon whose testimony his presence is declared to be "prejudicial to public order." He cannot summon friends to prove his loyalty and good character, without great risk of bringing upon them the same calamity that has befallen him. He has no right to demand a trial, or even a hearing. He cannot sue out a writ of habeas corpus. He cannot appeal to his fellow-citizens through the press. His communications with the world are so suddenly severed that sometimes even his own relatives do not know what has happened to him. He is literally and absolutely without any means whatever of self-defense. ❑

George Kennan, *Siberia and the Exile System*, Vol. 1 (London: Century Co., 1891), pp. 242–243.

Great Britain: Toward Democracy

While the continental nations became unified and struggled toward internal political restructuring, Great Britain continued to symbolize the confident liberal state. A large body of shared ideas emphasizing competition and individualism was accepted by the members of all classes. Even the leaders of trade unions during these years asked for little more than to receive a portion of the fruits of prosperity and to prove their own social respectability. Parliament itself continued to provide an institution that permitted the absorption of new groups and interests into the existing political processes.

The most important example of the opening of parliamentary processes was the Second Reform Act passed in 1867. The prosperity and the social respectability of the working classes had convinced many politicians that the workers truly deserved the vote. In 1866, Lord John Russell's Liberal ministry introduced a reform bill that was defeated by a coalition of traditional Conservatives and antidemocratic liberals. Russell resigned and the Tory Lord Derby replaced him. Then to the surprise of everyone, the Conservative ministry, led in the House of Commons by Benjamin Disraeli (1804–1881), introduced its own reform bill in 1867. When that measure was finally passed, the number of voters had been increased from approximately 1,430,000 to 2,470,000. Britain had taken a major step toward democracy. Disraeli thought that eventually significant portions of the working class would support Conservative candidates who proved themselves responsive to social issues. He also thought that the growing suburban middle class would become more conservative.

Gladstone and Disraeli

The immediate election of 1868, however, dashed Disraeli's hopes. William Gladstone (1809–1898) became the new prime minister. His ministry of 1868–1874 witnessed the culmination of classical British liberalism. Gladstone introduced competitive examinations into the civil service, abolished the purchase of army officers' commissions, and introduced the secret ballot. He opened Oxford and Cambridge Universities to students of all religious denominations and, by the Education Act of 1870, led the British government to assume responsibility for establishing and running elementary schools. Previously these had been supported by the various churches.

Gladstone Praises the Education Act of 1870

The British Education Act of 1870 marked the creation of the first national system of schools in Britain. Prime Minister Gladstone and others admired the measure because it still permitted private religious schools, because it was relatively inexpensive, and because it depended largely on the initiative of local government. In other words, it permitted the liberty and the low taxes that liberals prized.

The great object of all was to make education universal and effective. This was to be done, and doing it we sought, and I think reason and common sense required us to seek, to turn to account for that purpose the vast machinery of education already existing in the country, which had been devised and mainly provided by the Christian philanthropy and the voluntary action of the people. That was the second condition under which the Act was framed. The third was, and I think it was not less wise than the two former, that we should endeavour to separate the action of the State in the matter of education, and the application of State funds, in which I include funds raised by rate [taxes], from all subjects on which, unhappily, religious differences prevail. Those, I may say, were three of the principles of the measure; and the fourth principle, not less important than the others, was this: that we should trust for the attainment of these great objects, as little as possible to the central Government, and as much as possible to the local authorities and the self-governing power of the people. And let me say in passing, that in my opinion if there be one portion of our institutions more precious in my view than another, it is that portion in which the people are locally organized for the purposes of acquiring the habits and instincts of political action, and applying their own free consciences and free understandings to dealing with the affairs of the community. ❑

A. T. Bassett (ed.), *Gladstone's Speeches* (London: Methuen, 1916), pp. 412–413.

The liberal policy of creating popular support for the nation through the extension of political liberty and the reform of abuses had its conservative counterpart in concern about social reform. Disraeli succeeded Gladstone as prime minister in 1874 when the election produced sharp divisions among Liberal Party voters over matters of liquor regulation, religion, and education. Whereas Gladstone looked to individualism, free trade, and competition to solve social problems, Disraeli believed that the working classes of the country must confront those matters through paternalistic legislation. Disraeli believed in state action to protect weak groups of citizens. In his view, such paternalistic legislation would alleviate class antagonism. His most important measures were the Public Health Act of 1875 that consolidated and extended previous sanitary legislation and the Artisans Dwelling Act of 1875 through which the government became actively involved in providing housing for the working class.

The Irish Question

In 1880, a second Gladstone ministry took office as an agricultural depression and unpopular foreign policy undermined Disraeli's popularity. In 1884, with Conservative cooperation, a third reform act was passed, extending the vote to most male farm workers. However, the major issue of the decade was Ireland. From the late 1860s onward, Irish nationalists had sought to achieve home rule for Ireland, by which they meant more Irish control of local government. During his first ministry, Gladstone had addressed the Irish question through two major pieces of legislation. In 1869, he carried a measure to disestablish the Church of Ireland, which was the Irish branch of the Anglican church. Henceforth, Irish Roman Catholics would not pay taxes to support the hated Protestant church, to which only a small fraction of the population belonged. Second, in 1870, the Liberal ministry sponsored a land act that provided compensation to evicted Irish tenants and loans for tenants who wished to purchase their land.

The leader of the Irish movement for a just land settlement and for home rule was Charles Stewart Parnell (1846–1891). In 1881, the second Gladstone ministry passed another Irish land act, which provided further guarantees of tenant rights. This measure only partly satisfied Irish opinion, because it was accompanied by a Coercion Act intended to restore law and order to Ireland.

By 1885, Parnell had organized eighty-five Irish members of the House of Commons into a tightly disciplined party that often voted as a bloc. They pursued disruptive tactics to gain attention for the cause of home rule. They bargained with the two English political parties. In the election of 1885, the Irish Party emerged with the balance of power between the English Liberals and Conservatives. The Irish could decide which party would take office. In December 1885, Gladstone announced support of home rule for Ireland. Parnell gave his votes to the formation of a Liberal ministry. However, the issue split the Liberal

A House of Commons debate: Gladstone, standing on the right, is attacking Disraeli, who is sitting with legs crossed and arms folded. [Mary Evans Picture Library.]

Party. In 1886, a group of Liberals known as the Liberal Unionists joined with the Conservatives to defeat Gladstone's Home Rule Bill. Gladstone called for a new election, in which the Liberals were defeated. They remained a permanently divided party.

The new Conservative ministry of Lord Salisbury (1830–1903) attempted to reconcile the Irish to English government through public works and administrative reform. The policy, which was tied to further coercion, had only marginal success. In 1892, Gladstone returned to power. A second Home Rule Bill passed the House of Commons but was defeated in the House of Lords. There the Irish question stood until after the turn of the century. The Conservatives sponsored a land act in 1903 that carried out the final transfer of land to tenant ownership. Ireland became a country of

small farms. In 1912, a Liberal ministry passed the third Home Rule Bill. Under the provisions of the House of Lords Act of 1911, which curbed the power of that body, the bill had to pass the Commons three times over a Lords veto to become law. The third pas-

Charles Stewart Parnell, shown here in an 1880 Vanity Fair drawing by Theobald Chartran, was the leader of the Irish members of Parliament during the Home Rule crisis of the 1880s. [The Granger Collection.]

sage occurred in the summer of 1914, and the implementation of the Home Rule provisions of the bill was suspended for the duration of World War I.

The Irish question affected British politics in a manner not unlike that of the Austrian nationalities problem. Normal British domestic issues could not be adequately addressed because of the political divisions created by Ireland. The split of the Liberal Party proved especially harmful to the cause of further social and political reform. The people who could agree on matters of reform could not agree on Ireland, and the latter problem seemed more important. As the two traditional parties failed to deal with the social questions, by the turn of the century a newly organized Labour Party began to fill the vacuum.

The Age of European Nation-States in World Perspective

The movement toward strong, centralized national states in Europe during the nineteenth century had its counterparts elsewhere in the world. In Asia during this same period, Japan entered upon its course of modernization by seeking to imitate the military and economic power of the European states. In Latin America, the last half of the nineteenth century witnessed one of the most successful and stable periods for the various governments of that region. They established centralized regimes based upon relatively prosperous economies.

In the United States, the crisis of the Civil War reflected the assertion of the power of the central federal government over that of the individual states. The role of warfare in the forging of a single American nation was similar to the effect of military force employed in the unifications of Italy and Germany and the suppression of the Paris Commune.

In the cases of Italy and Germany, the triumph of nationalism was regarded as a positive achievement by many people. However, the last half of the century also saw various national and ethnic groups use the power of a national state to repress or dominate other groups. These included the Austrian and Hungarian treatment of the smaller subject nationalities as well as the Irish problem for the British government.

Elsewhere around the globe, strong national governments similarly repressed weak groups. In Latin America, the native Americans failed to gain rights. In the United States, the westward movement also brought warfare against native Americans; and the legislation of the late century saw the segregation of American blacks. In Canada, those persons who were English-speaking fared better than the citizens of French-speaking Canada. In that sense, throughout the world nationalism involved the extension of liberty to some peoples and the exclusion from liberty of others. In almost all cases, the repression of some groups generated social and political problems that would haunt the twentieth century.

Finally, the emergence of these strong European nation-states set the stage for the transfer of their rivalry from Europe to other areas of the globe. The militarily and economically strong states of Europe would soon turn to foreign adventures that would subjugate vast areas of Africa and Asia. The experience of this imperialism led many of the colonialized peoples to realize that only the development of strong nationalistic movements could eventually lead to an end of such subjugation by the militarily stronger Europeans. Consequently, during the first quarter of the twentieth century the nationalistic principle that less than fifty years earlier had stirred European politics began to influence the politics of the peoples upon whom Europeans had imposed their government and administration.

Suggested Readings

M. BENTLEY, *Politics without Democracy*, 1815–1914 (1984). A well-informed survey of British development.

G. F. A. BEST, *Mid-Victorian Britain* (1972). A good book on the social structure.

R. BLAKE, *Disraeli* (1967). The best biography.

J. BLUM, *Lord and Peasant in Russia from the Ninth to the Nineteenth Century* (1961). A clear discussion of emancipation in the later chapters.

W. L. BURN, *The Age of Equipoise* (1964). A thoughtful and convincing discussion of Victorian social stability.

M. BURNS, *Rural Society and French Politics: Boulangism and the Dreyfus Affair*, 1886–1900 (1984). An examination of the subject from the rural perspective.

G. CHAPMAN, *The Dreyfus Affair: A Reassessment* (1955). A detached treatment of a subject that still provokes strong feelings.

G. CRAIG, *Germany*, 1866–1945 (1978). An excellent new survey.

S. EDWARDS, *The Paris Commune of* 1871 (1971). A useful examination of a complex subject.

I. V. HULL, *The Entourage of Kaiser Wilhelm II*, 1888–1918 (1982). An important discussion of the scandals of the German court.

R. A. KANN, *The Multinational Empire*, 2 vols. (1950). The basic treatment of the nationality problem of Austria-Hungary.

G. KITSON CLARK, *The Making of Victorian England* (1962). The best introduction.

R. R. LOCKE, *French Legitimists and the Politics of Moral Order in the Early Third Republic* (1974). An excellent study of the social and intellectual roots of monarchist support.

P. MAGNUS, *Gladstone: A Biography* (1955). A readable biography.

A. J. MAY, *The Habsburg Monarchy*, 1867–1914 (1951). Narrates in considerable detail and with much sympathy the fate of the dual monarchy.

W. N. MEDLICOTT, *Bismarck and Modern Germany* (1965). An excellent brief biography.

W. E. MOSSE, *Alexander II and the Modernization of Russia* (1958). A brief biography.

N. M. NAIMARK, *Terrorists and Social Democrats: The Russian Revolutionary Movement under Alexander III* (1983). Based on the most recent research.

C. C. O'BRIEN, *Parnell and His Party* (1957). An excellent treatment of the Irish question.

O. PFLANZE, *Bismarck and the Development of Germany* (1963). Carries the story through the achievement of unification.

A. PLESSIS, *The Rise and Fall of the Second Empire*, 1852–1871 (1985). A useful survey of France under Napoleon III.

N. RICH, *The Age of Nationalism and Reform*, rev. ed. (1976). A sound volume based on recent research.

R. SHANNON, *Gladstone: 1809–1865* (1982). Best coverage of his early career.

D. M. SMITH, *Cavour and Garibaldi in 1860: A Study in Political Conflict* (1954). Explores the two key personalities in Italian unification.

D. M. SMITH, *The Making of Italy*, 1796–1870 (1968). A narrative that incorporates the major documents.

D. M. SMITH, *Cavour* (1984). An excellent biography.

A. J. P. TAYLOR, *The Habsburg Monarchy*, 1809–1918 (1941). An opinionated but highly readable work.

D. THOMPSON, *Democracy in France Since 1870*, rev. ed. (1969). A clear guide to a complex problem.

J. M. THOMSON, *Louis Napoleon and the Second Empire* (1954). A straightforward account.

R. TOMBS, *The War against Paris*, 1871 (1981). Examines the role of the army in suppressing the Commune.

A. B. ULAM, *Russia's Failed Revolutionaries* (1981). A recent study of revolutionary societies and activities prior to the Revolution of 1917.

F. VENTURI, *The Roots of Revolution* (trans. 1960). A major treatment of late nineteenth-century revolutionary movement.

H. S. WATSON, *The Russian Empire*, 1801–1917 (1967). A far-ranging narrative.

H. U. WEHLER, *The German Empire*, 1871–1918 (1985). An important, controversial work.

A. J. WHYTE, *The Evolution of Modern Italy* (1965). An interesting survey of the Italian problem in nineteenth-century diplomacy.

R. WILLIAMS, *The World of Napoleon III*, rev. ed. (1965). Examines the cultural setting.

C. B. WOODHAM-SMITH, *The Reason Why* (1953). A lively account of the Crimean War and the charge of the Light Brigade.

T. ZELDIN, *The Political System of Napoleon III* (1958). An examination of the local sources of political support for Louis Napoleon.

T. ZELDIN, *France: 1848–1945*, 2 vols. (1973, 1977). Emphasizes the social developments.

R. E. ZELNICK, *Labor and Society in Tsarist Russia: The Factory Workers of St. Petersburg*, 1855–1870 (1971). An important volume that considers the early stages of the Russian industrial labor force in the era of serf emancipation.

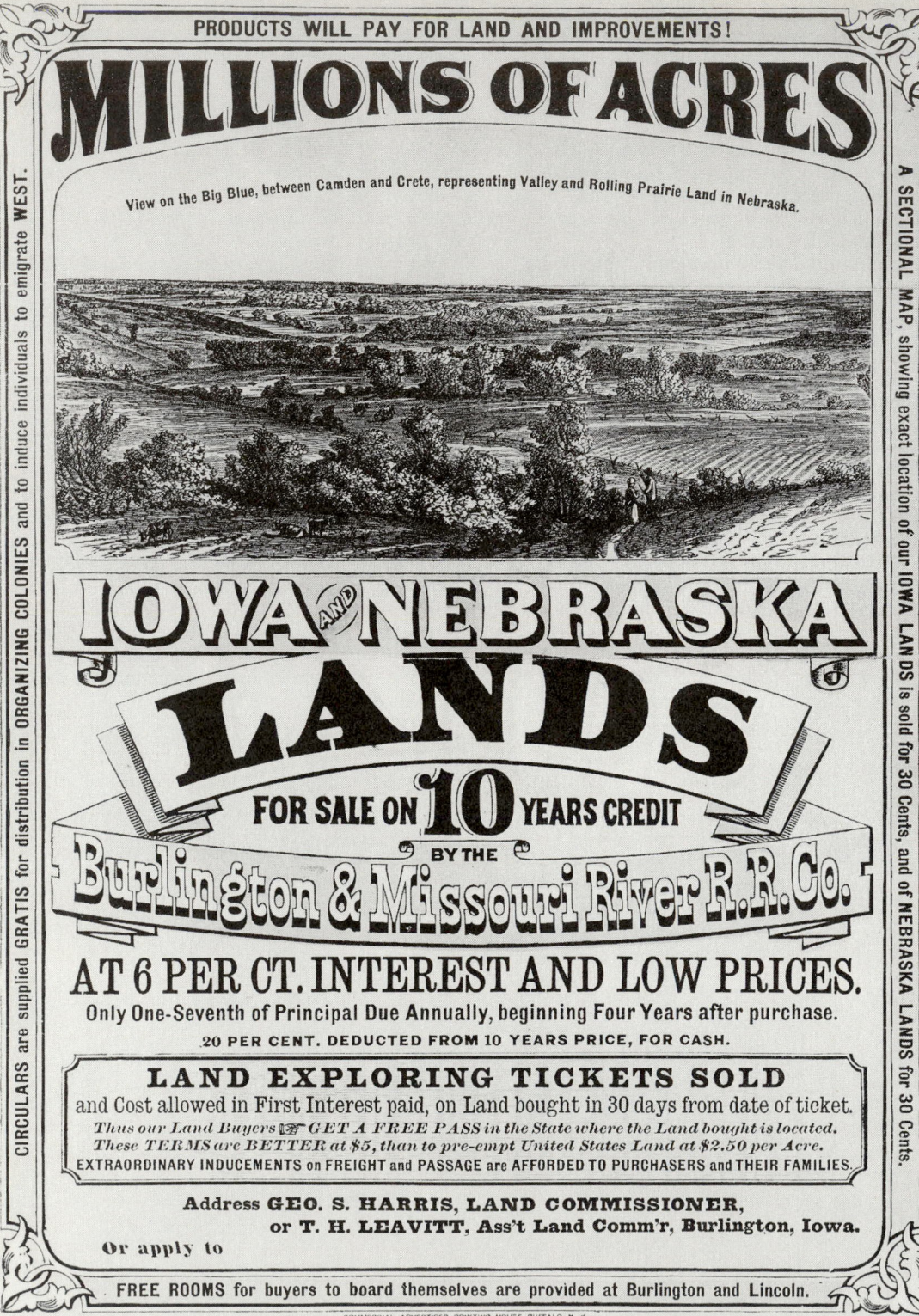

Millions of acres—Iowa and Nebraska Lands for sale on 10 years credit, by the Burlington and Missouri River R.R. Co. (Library of Congress.)

27 North America in the Nineteenth Century

Having achieved their independence from Great Britain at the conclusion of the Revolutionary War in 1783, the former English North American colonies that had become the United States set upon what the eighteenth century regarded as a radical political experiment that made them unique among nations of the world. During the nineteenth century, the states spread an English-speaking civilization across the North American continent and laid the industrial foundations that by the close of the nineteenth century made the United States a player in world affairs. The new nation debated over the institution of slavery and eventually abolished it after fighting a civil war; removed the native American population wherever it interfered with white settlement; absorbed the influx of millions of European, Asian, and Hispanic immigrants; and transformed itself from a primarily rural nation to a major industrial power that still possessed an enormous agricultural sector.

To the north, Canada remained for almost a century longer very largely under British domination. It emerged as a unified, self-governing nation by a very different path. However, like its southern neighbor it conquered an entire continent.

Experimental Political Structures

When the Continental Congress declared independence in 1776, there existed no national government that commanded real respect or power. During the Revolutionary War and for several years afterward, the nation was governed under the Articles of Confederation, which provided only a feeble central government. In 1787, dissatisfaction with this situation, concern about political stability, and apprehension about the role of the United States in European affairs led to the gathering of the Constitutional Convention in Phil-

George Washington presided over the Constitutional Convention that met in Philadelphia. The ratification of that document started the United States on a bold republican experience without modern precedent. [Library of Congress.]

adelphia. George Washington chaired the convention, the sessions of which were held in secret.

The Constitution and Bill of Rights

After long debates, the Convention proposed a constitution to provide for a federal system of government whereby political authority was divided between a central federal government and the several states. The federal government received certain major powers, including those of levying taxes, declaring war, printing money, overseeing interstate commerce, undertaking debt, and conducting foreign policy. Other crucial political and administrative powers were retained by the states, which could levy their own taxes and arrange for their own constitutions. This federal arrangement permitted the establishment of a strong central government; at the same time, the arrangement recognized the diversity of local needs and concerns. By the middle of 1788, conventions of elected delegates in nine states had ratified the new constitution, thus establishing it as the national framework of government. Still, the subsequent acceptance by the conventions in New York and Virginia, which occurred later in 1788, were required to allow the new union really to work.

The Constitutional Convention had left two major issues in this federal structure unresolved. The first was the extent of the power of the central government over citizens. The adoption in 1791 of the first ten amendments to the Constitution, which became known as the Bill of Rights, clarified this question. These amendments guaranteed certain rights to citizens, including the rights of free speech, assembly, and religion, as well as the rights to bear arms and to secure a speedy trial. The second unresolved issue was whether the power of the federal government or the states should predominate if they clashed. That issue would not ultimately be resolved until the conclusion of the Civil War (1861–1865) when the power of the federal Union generally stood supreme over that of the individual states.

The Constitution divided the authority of the federal government among three branches of government in the manner that Montesquieu and other eighteenth-century enlightenment writers praised in their works of political theory. The president was elected indirectly by an electoral college. Regardless of population, each state was permitted two senators to be elected by their respective state legislatures. A broader electorate of property owners, that excluded all women, all slaves, and many poor free males, chose the members of the House of Representatives, where the size of each state delegation depended upon the population of the state. The president appointed the justices of the Supreme Court with the advice and consent of the Senate. Even though by later standards this system excluded many people, in 1788 it permitted wider popular participation than any other political system in the world and was regarded as extremely radical.

Leadership and Political Participation

Much of the debate of the early years of the American republic involved questions relating to the degree of popular influence on the government. Under the leadership of George Washington, who was chosen as the first president, the American government took a very cautious attitude toward the French Revolution. Many Americans thought the young North American Republic should attempt to aid the French Republic. However, Washington and others—though sympathetic to the spread of greater freedom in France—feared the excesses of the revolution. They also realized that to support France would bring America directly into conflict with Great Britain and other European powers that opposed the revolution. Indeed,

Washington's general attitude toward American involvement in world affairs was that of avoiding any kind of entangling alliances. Many later American presidents continued to follow this view, and for almost a century the United States played at best a modest role in world politics.

Within the United States, however, a strong debate continued over political participation. Those who generally wished to limit it became known as the Federalists. Those who wished to expand political participation were known as Democratic Republicans; their leader was Thomas Jefferson. His election as president in 1800 was itself considered a revolutionary development because of his known sympathy for "the people" and for the French revolution. However, the major expansion of political participation, which involved extending the franchise to white males without regard to property, occurred during the 1820s as state governments changed the basis of voting. Andrew Jackson was the national political figure who most benefited from these reforms. The term *Jacksonian democracy* indicated a greater appreciation by the federal government for the so-called common man as opposed to the wealthy and holders of large property. Another key element of the Jacksonian democratic phenomenon was the growing impact of the Western frontier on American politics. Jackson's presidency (1829–1837) and that of his successor Martin Van Buren (1837–1841) also saw the emergence of strictly

A two party system emerged very early in the history of the United States. Very harsh partisan clashes occurred during the administration of Thomas Jefferson. This anti-Jeffersonian political cartoon of 1807 depicts Washington as possessing conservative political virtues and Jefferson as associated with dangerous and anti-religious thinkers. [New-York Historical Society.]

Andrew Jackson came to symbolize two elements of the political life of his day. The first was democracy and the extension of the vote to a broad electorate. The second was the preservation of the Union associated with his firm stand at the time of the Nullification Crisis. [Tennessee State Library and Archives.]

disciplined political parties that tended to provide stability to the American political scene during the mid-century.

Testing the New Republic

Toward Sectional Conflict

The original thirteen American states that stretched along the Atlantic seaboard already displayed numerous differences in social and economic life. There were more cities in the North, as well as a predominately white population. The South was more rural and was characterized by its institution of black slavery. There were other economic differences: The northern states were more commercial and were soon industrially oriented, whereas the South remained primarily agricultural.

Sectional differences had arisen in the Constitutional Convention itself over the question of slavery. In particular, there was debate over what proportion of the slave population would be counted toward the composition of the House of Representatives. The issue was resolved by a compromise that allowed the southern slave-holding states to count three-fifths of their slaves in the calculation of their population for purposes of representation in Congress. Furthermore, the Constitution forbade any federal attempt to prevent the importation of slaves before 1808. During the twenty years between the adoption of the Constitution and the possibility of halting the slave trade, thousands of slaves were imported into the United States.

The first real strains of sectionalism in the early years of the republic arose as a result of Thomas Jefferson's determination to maintain American neutrality during the Napoleonic wars. The legislation supporting this policy sharply curtailed New England trade. During the succeeding administration of James Madison, whose policies resulted in the War of 1812 with Great Britain and further strains on New England commerce, certain New England Federalists called for secession. A similar incident occurred during Jackson's presidency, when the state of South Carolina attempted to nullify a federal tariff. Again there were calls for secession.

The pressures that gave rise to the most serious sectionalism arose as Americans began to move across the continent. In 1803, Jefferson completed the Louisiana Purchase, which more than doubled the size of the United States and allowed for a westward movement as far as the Rockies. Americans moved west quite rapidly. As they did, there developed certain differences that caused social and political strains.

The Ordinance of 1787, passed by Congress under the Articles of Confederation, had prohibited slavery in the Northwest Territory that stretched from the Appalachians to the Mississippi northward. Territory south of the Ohio River was open to slavery, and there it spread. By 1820, the number of slave and free states were evenly divided; this meant that there was also an equal number of senators in Congress from slave and free states. That year, Missouri was admitted as a slave state and Maine as a free one. It was also decided that in the future no slave states would be carved out of land north of the southern border of Missouri. For the time being, this compromise ended Congressional debate over slavery. Nonetheless, the economies of the north and south were developing in very different directions.

NORTHERN ECONOMIC DEVELOPMENT. Family farms, free labor, commerce, and early industrialization in textiles characterized the economy of the northern states. The northern farmers tended primarily to produce foodstuffs that supplied their own needs and those of their local communities. The farms were

This painting of the farm of Henry Z. Van Reed presents an idealized version of northern agriculture. [Abby Aldrich Rockefeller Folk Art Center, Williamsburg, Virginia.]

relatively small and worked by families. Farm labor was free. Similarly, free laborers worked in the towns, on the ships, and in the factories of the North. The political spokesmen for the North tended to favor tariffs to protect the young industries from cheaper competition abroad.

The North was the site of the earliest textile factories in the United States. Samuel Slater had established the first of these in Rhode Island in 1790. He had learned how to manufacture textiles in the new mills of industrializing Great Britain. His transfer of that textile technology to America provides an important example of the manner in which British and European advances were transported across the Atlantic to the United States. Much of the early industrialization of the United States depended upon such technological transfers. By the second decade of the nineteenth century, there were hundreds of cotton factories in the North. These mills used cotton that was produced in the South, but they could use only a relatively small

proportion of southern cotton. The rest of that cotton had to be sold overseas. The largest market for that U.S. cotton was in England, where the textile industry was growing.

The most famous factory experiment in the United States was attempted by the Lowell system in Lowell, Massachusetts. The owners of the factory placed the entire system of processing textiles—from the carding of the cotton or wool through the weaving of the final product—under one roof. This resulted in the mass production of textiles. Through this system, textiles were manufactured more cheaply than they could be produced by women in their own homes. As had occurred in England, textile manufacture slowly moved from the home to the factory.

One of the most interesting and important features of the Lowell system was the manner in which it employed young women. Because of a shortage of labor in the United States, the nation was a land of high wages. However, American parents were quite hesitant to allow their daughters to leave home to work in the factories and to live alone. To overcome these fears, the owners of the Lowell mills established factory communities nearby, where the women could live and be carefully supervised. The company's boarding houses were regarded as comfortable; they offered recreation, opportunities to pursue hobbies, and the availability of books. Some women published a magazine known as the *Lowell Offering*. Nonetheless, even at the Lowell mills the work day was as long as thirteen hours. Many women and children in other locations worked under much less carefully supervised conditions.

The Lowell mills were not the norm. In New England and in cities throughout the North, a labor force developed that was sharply divided along class lines. There were some early attempts at labor unions in crafts such as printing, hat making, and tailoring. In 1834, even the Lowell mills encountered a major strike. Other strikes occurred as owners introduced more efficient machinery or lowered wages at times of economic downturn. Nonetheless, virtually all of these early labor organizations collapsed during periods of major economic downturn.

During the second quarter of the century, there were major innovations in transportation that led to the fuller integration of different parts of the northern economy. Canals were built to link the major rivers and the Great Lakes. The most famous of these was the Erie Canal, which connected the Hudson River to the Great Lakes. In turn, there were canals from the Great Lakes that led to the Ohio River. In addition to the canals, major efforts had to be undertaken to make the Ohio, Mississippi, and Missouri rivers navigable. Snags and logs that caused shipping wrecks had to be removed. The clearing of the rivers allowed the use of steamboats to transport goods.

But by the late 1840s, in America as in Europe, the major transportation innovation came to be the railroad. Most of the railways linked the Northeast and the West. These rail lines allowed the commercial agriculture of the Midwest to grow. In turn, its products came to be sold in the Northeast and to be exported from northern ports. Hence, the development of east–

Lowell, Massachusetts was the setting of textile mills that were constructed to constitute a community setting. The building with the cupola and that with the dormers and chimneys was a mill. The two buildings that look almost like individual residences were the housing for the girls who worked in the mills. [Museum of American Textile History.]

During the second quarter of the nineteenth century, canals such as the Erie Canal pictured here, helped to link the Northwest and the East. Canals also ran north and south between the Great Lakes and the Ohio River. [New-York Historical Society.]

west railways undermined the older river-based trade routes along the Ohio and down the Mississippi. Few major lines ran north and south, so former section links based on the rivers weakened. The building of the early railways also aided the development of the coal and iron industries in the North. The further expansion of railways at mid-century became one of the factors that caused new sectional tensions, as it became clear the railways could open for settlement vast territories, and thus could open for national debate the future of slavery. That prospect sharpened the sectional debate and in the end led to civil war.

THE SOUTHERN ECONOMY. The American South in the first half of the nineteenth century remained overwhelmingly rural. Two factors characterized its economy: dependence on cotton and dependence on slavery. In those respects, the southern economy resembled the economies of many Latin American countries, such as Brazil with its dependence on coffee, which were based on a single crop or natural resource and on slave labor. The South had to export goods either to the North or the Europe to maintain its standard of living. It should also be noted that the expansion of the textile industry in Great Britain was a force behind much of the expansion of cotton growing in the American South.

The invention of the cotton gin by Eli Whitney in 1793 had allowed cotton cultivation to expand. It was now profitable to grow short staple cotton in moderately warm areas. Previously, the South had produced only the long staple cotton that could be grown along the very warm coastlines. Prices were kept high as the world demand for cotton increased because the industrial revolution in textiles led to greater production. Growing consumer demand and the expansion in world population kept the demand steady. For those reasons, population expanded steadily westward from the long settled coastal regions toward the rich Mississippi delta in the early years of the century. The South

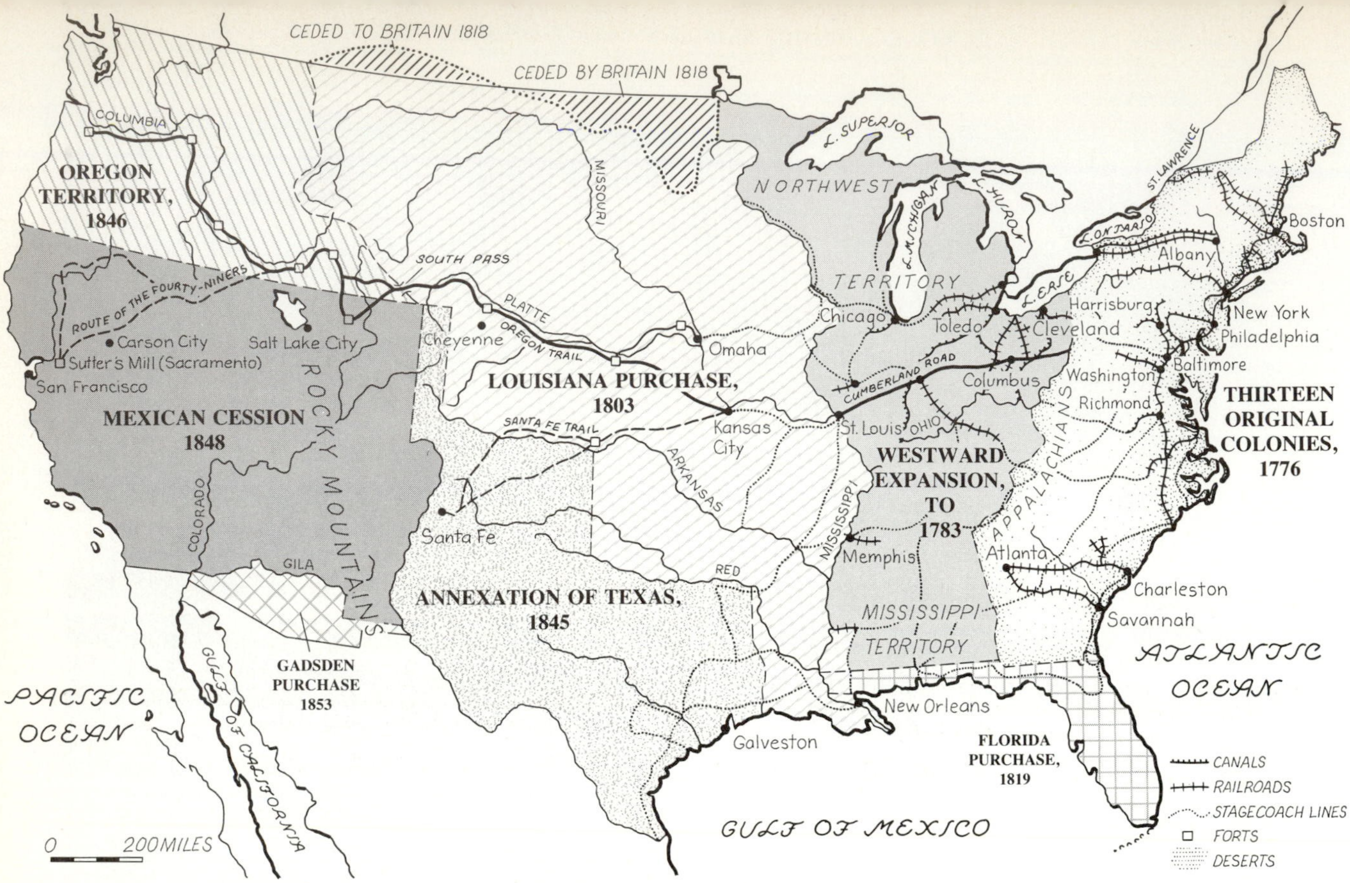

MAP 27-1   NINETEENTH-CENTURY NORTH AMERICA   *During the nineteenth century the United States expanded across the entire North American Continent. The revolutionary settlement had provided most of the land east of the Mississipi. The single largest addition thereafter was the Louisiana Purchase of 1803. The annexation of Texas and later the Mexican Cession following the Mexican War, added the major southwestern territories. The borders of the Oregon Territory were settled through long, difficult negotiations with Great Britain.*

Much of mid-nineteenth century American political life occurred in relatively small open-air settings such as this portrayal of stump speaking by the Missouri artist George Caleb Bingham. [Boatmen's National Bank of St. Louis.]

Slaves returning from the cotton fields in South Carolina (New-York Historical Society.)

profited from growing the cotton; New England from shipping it; and other parts of the North from supplying the manufacturing needs of the South. There was virtually no incentive for the South to diversify its agriculture.

SLAVERY. Slavery had once existed in the North, but it was being abolished there by the early nineteenth century; it had never been fundamental to the northern economy. But in the South, the institution of slavery continued, receiving a new lease on life with the expansion of the cotton empire in the early nineteenth century. Never did a majority of southern families own slaves, and only a relatively small minority of slave owners possessed more than a few slaves. However, slavery survived because no one could devise a way politically or socially acceptable to white southerners to abolish it—and because in point of fact it was economically viable. No less important was the strong commitment to the protection of private property, which included slaves throughout American society in both the North and the South.

But what was the life of an American slave like? First, all American slaves were black. They were the descendants of Africans who had been forcibly captured and sold in West Africa, though some came from either Central or East Africa. The slaves were then shipped in the most wretched of conditions to the United States. Second, slaves were regarded as chattel property, that is, they could be sold, given away, or even gambled away as any other piece of property. They also could be, and were, treated badly by some masters without recourse to law or constitutional protections. State laws protected them from certain forms of extreme violence, but the laws were not always enforced. Whipping and beating were permitted.

The standard of living of slaves was generally very low. One factor that led owners to maintain a minimal standard of living was the desire to see their slave investments reproduce themselves. Nonetheless, slaves suffered from numerous diseases associated with inadequate diet, poor sanitation, and bad housing.

Slaves worked primarily in the fields, where they plowed, hoed, and harvested cotton, rice, tobacco, or corn. They were usually organized into workgangs supervised by white overseers. This work was, like all farming, seasonal; but in major planting or harvest seasons labor would persist from sunrise to sunset. Children would work in the fields as helpers. Older or more privileged slaves might work in the house, cleaning or tending kitchens or aiding in child rearing.

Recent scholarship has emphasized the manner in which the slave communities helped to preserve the family life and inner personalities of the slaves. Some elements of African culture persisted in the slave communities. African legends were passed on orally. Religion proved extraordinarily important. Slaves also adopted for their own cultural needs the Old Testament stories of the Jews' liberation from Egypt.

Officially, the marriages and family lives of slaves had no legal recognition. White masters and their sons often sexually exploited black slave women. Because slaves were property, they could be sold for profit or moved when the owner moved from one region to another. Consequently, families could be, and were, separated by sale or perhaps at the time of an owner's death. Many young children were reared and cared for by other slaves to whom they were not related. In a world of white dominance, the institutions, customs, and religions of the slave community stood as the only means whereby the black slave could protect the autonomy of his or her own personality.

The Path to Civil War

Clearly by 1840 or so, two very different cultures and economies had developed in the American North and South. Yet the Union persisted and was valued by the leaders and most of the citizens of both sections. Furthermore, so long as there existed an even balance of slave and nonslave votes in the United States Senate, the South felt reasonably secure in the Union. The politics of compromise had repeatedly prevented the disruption of the Union, despite the deep-seated differences of the various regions.

In the late 1840s, two developments upset the political compromise that had maintained both the Union and southern slavery. First, in 1847 the United States defeated Mexico in a brief war and by treaty the next year gained new territory in the southwest and California, in addition to Texas, which had been annexed in 1845. During the same decade, the United States acquired the vast Oregon territory in the northwest. The acquisition of these new territories reopened the question of the expansion of slavery. Second, during the 1830s a militant antislavery movement emerged in the North. Its leaders and followers refused to accept what they regarded as the moral compromise of living in a nation that tolerated slavery. Abolitionists, such as William Lloyd Garrison, editor of *The Liberator*, con-

William Lloyd Garrison Launches The Liberator

William Lloyd Garrison (1805–1879) became perhaps the most famous and among the most extreme advocates of the complete abolition of slavery. He was the editor of the Boston-based The Liberator, *the major abolitionist newspaper. In his first editorial, he rejected the position of gradual emancipation of slavery and called for total emancipation. When he wrote this editorial in 1831, his position was a rather isolated one. By the 1850s, it had become much more widespread. He based much of his argument on the extension of the view of liberty enunciated in the American Declaration of Independence of 1776.*

Assenting to the "self-evident truth" maintained in the American Declaration of Independence, "that all men are created equal, and endowed by their Creator with certain inalienable rights—among which are life, liberty and the pursuit of happiness," I shall strenuously contend for the immediate enfranchisement of our slave population. In Park-Street Church, on the Fourth of July, 1819, in an address on slavery, I unreflectingly assented to the popular but pernicious doctrine of *gradual* abolition. I seize this opportunity to make a full and unequivocal recantation, and thus publicly to ask pardon of my God, of my country, and of my brethren the poor slaves, for having uttered a sentiment so full of timidity, injustice, and absurdity. . . .

I am aware, that many object to the severity of my language; but is there not cause for severity? I *will be* as harsh as truth, and as uncompromising as justice. On this subject, I do not wish to think, or speak, or write, with moderation. No! No! Tell a man whose house is on fire, to give a moderate alarm; tell him to moderately rescue his wife from the hands of the ravisher; tell the mother to gradually extricate her babe from the fire into which it has fallen;—but urge me not to use moderation in a cause like the present. I am in earnest—I will not equivocate—I will not excuse—I will not retreat a single inch—AND I WILL BE HEARD. The apathy of the people is enough to make every statue leap from its pedestal, and to hasten the resurrection of the dead.

It is pretended, that I am retarding the cause of emancipation by the coarseness of my invective, and the precipitancy of my measures. *The charge is not true.* On this question my influence,—humble as it is,—is felt at this moment to be a considerable extent, and shall be felt in coming years—not perniciously, but beneficially—not as a curse, but as a blessing; and posterity will bear testimony that I was right. ❑

William Lloyd Garrison, *The Liberator*, January 1, 1831, as quoted in Henry Steele Commager, ed., *Documents of American History*, Eighth Edition (New York: Appleton-Century-Crofts, 1968), 1:278.

Black Americans contributed to the activities of the abolitionist movement. Harriet Tubman, standing on the far left, was an escaped slave. She is here pictured with other former slaves whom she helped to free. [Smith College, Sophia Smith Collection.]

demned the Union and the Constitution as structures that simply perpetuated slavery. For abolitionists, there was little or no role for compromise in the moral political arena. The antislavery movement gained new adherents during the 1840s as the question of extending slavery into the new territories came to the fore.

Leaders in both the North and South saw their sectional interests threatened as the debate raged. In particular, the South feared that the changing climate of national debate and the opening of territories where slavery might be prohibited would give the South a minority status in the Union and thus eventually overturn the political and social culture of the South. The Compromise of 1850, which actually involved a number of separate legislative measures, seemed for a time to put matters to rest. It restored political calm and stability, and reassured the South.

Nonetheless, during the 1850s a number of crises occurred that led various political groups to take more extreme positions. Northern abolitionists resented the enforcement of the federal Fugitive Slave Law that required the return of escaped slaves to their owners. One reason for the hostile reaction was that the law deprived escaped slaves of virtually any recourse to the courts for protection or hearing of their cases. During the same years, the South became more economically dependent upon the manufactures and trading interests of the North. Southerners began to fear that there existed a northern conspiracy to dominate the South economically and politically.

In 1854, the introduction of the Kansas–Nebraska Bill renewed the new national debate over slavery and galvanized the antislavery forces. The principle of the bill introduced by Stephen A. Douglas was that of popular sovereignty. The people of each new territory would decide whether slavery was to be permitted within its borders. Douglas was thus willing to see the Missouri Compromise repealed. In 1854, the Republican Party was organized largely in opposition to the Kansas–Nebraska Bill. The new party provided a major political vehicle for the forces of antislavery. Furthermore, the principle of popular sovereignty meant that every newly organized territory became the site for a major local debate over slavery. Not everyone, however, was willing to take merely political action. For example, John Brown went to Kansas, where there already existed armed conflict, and carried out virtual guerrilla warfare against slaveholding settlers. During 1854, civil war was occurring in "Bleeding Kansas."

In 1856, in the Dred Scott decision the Supreme Court effectively repealed the Missouri Compromise and ruled that Congress could not legislate the issue of slavery. Radical antislavery northerners saw the decision as raising the most serious question about the morality of the Union itself. Thereafter, the question of slavery dominated all national political debate. The Republican party had become the party that opposed slavery, although it did not necessarily favor outright abolition. In 1858, Abraham Lincoln ran against Stephen Douglas for the U.S. Senate in Illinois. Lincoln

John Brown's raid on Harper's Ferry was a key factor in leading many Southerners to believe there existed a northern conspiracy against their sectional interests. [Boston Atheneaum.]

lost the Senate race, but in the debates leading up to the election he made a national reputation for himself. In 1860, Lincoln received the nomination for the presidency on the Republican ticket.

Other events had made that election crucial. In 1859, John Brown had carried out a raid on the federal arsenal at Harpers Ferry, West Virginia. He was captured, tried, and hanged. The raid led to further sectional polarization. The South feared more than ever a northern antislavery conspiracy. Northern radicals feared that the South now had control of the federal government and would use that power to protect slavery. No less important was the emergence of radical southerners who feared a northern attempt to attack the institution of slavery. In that regard, throughout the late 1850s the politics of both the North and South became radicalized.

The Civil War and Reconstruction

The election of 1860 saw the victory of Abraham Lincoln. Neither he nor the Republican Party had campaigned for the abolition of slavery. Nonetheless,

Southerners perceived his election as the victory of a party and a president dedicated to the eradication of slavery. Beginning in December 1860, southern states with South Carolina in the lead began to secede and formed the Confederate States of America. In the weeks after the election, various attempts at political compromise to maintain the Union failed. Almost immediately after Lincoln's inauguration in March 1860, the issue of the federal resupply of Fort Sumter in Charleston Harbor arose. When Lincoln ordered the fort to be resupplied in order to indicate his determination to preserve the federal Union, Confederate forces fired on the fort. With this act, the most destructive war in United States history commenced.

The Civil War lasted almost exactly four years. The nation that emerged from the violence was very differ-

The election of Lincoln in 1860 brought about the secession crisis that led directly to the Civil War. Here Lincoln is portrayed as he was elected, without his later more famous beard which he grew only after the election. [Library of Congress.]

The battle of Gettysburg was the largest military engagement in the Western world between the close of the Napoleonic Wars and the outbreak of World War I. [Library of Congress.]

Lincoln States the Ideals of American Liberty at Gettysburg

The battle of Gettysburg in 1863 was the largest battle of the American Civil War and marked the farthest intrusion of Confederate forces into the North. The Union had won the battle after great losses to both sides. A few months later, President Lincoln journeyed to Gettysburg to participate in the dedication of a military cemetery. There he delivered one of his very few public speeches during the war. In it, he set forth what he considered to be the ideals of democratic government that he had come to believe constituted the goals for which the Union stood and fought.

Four score and seven years ago our fathers brought forth on this continent, a new nation, conceived in Liberty, and dedicated to the proposition that all men are created equal.

Now we are engaged in a great civil war, testing whether that nation or any nation so conceived and so dedicated, can long endure. We are met on a great battlefield of that war. We have come to dedicate a portion of that field, as a final resting place for those who here gave their lives that that nation might live. It is altogether fitting and proper that we should do this.

But, in a larger sense, we cannot dedicate—we cannot consecrate—we cannot hallow—this ground. The brave men, living and dead, who struggled here, have consecrated it, far above our poor power to add or detract. The world will little note, nor long remember what we say here, but it can never forget what they did here. It is for us the living, rather, to be dedicated here to the unfinished work which they who fought here have thus far so nobly advanced. It is rather for us to be here dedicated to the great task remaining before us—that from these honored dead we take increased devotion to that cause for which they gave the last full measure of devotion—that we here highly resolve that these dead shall not have died in vain—that this nation, under God, shall have a new birth of freedom—and that government of the people, by the people, for the people, shall not perish from the earth. ❏

Abraham Lincoln, *The Gettysburg Address*, November 19, 1863, as quoted in Henry Steele Commager, *Documents of American History*, Eighth Edition (New York: Appleton-Century-Crofts, 1968), 1:428–429.

ent from that which had entered it. In 1863, two years after Alexander II ended Russian serfdom, Lincoln emancipated the slaves in the rebelling states. By the time of the defeat of the Confederacy in 1865, southern lands were occupied by a northern army, its farms were often out of production, its transportation in a state of disruption, and many of its chief cities in ruins. Because of the defeat, southern political leaders had virtually no impact on the immediate postwar decisions. A series of constitutional amendments (the Thirteenth, Fourteenth, and Fifteenth) largely recast the character of the Union. The Thirteenth abolished slavery. The Fourteenth and Fifteenth established broad patterns of civil rights and suffrage, and prohibited much political activity by those persons who had taken up arms against the Union. Through these amendments, the issues of slavery and the relative roles of the state and federal governments were settled.

The Civil War and the reconstruction era that followed did overturn the antebellum social and political structures in the American South. The slaves were freed and for a time participated broadly and actively in the politics of the southern states. For over ten years, federal troops occupied parts of the South. Many of the antebellum southern leaders left political life. Economically, the South remained generally rural and still dependent on cotton. Many of the freed slaves and poor whites who tilled the land remained hopelessly in debt to wealthier landowners. Although there

were attempts to bring manufacturing into the South, these were met with very limited success. Prevalent racism also acted as a block to free economic development.

For the rest of the century, the South remained in a relationship to the North that resembled the relationship of a colonial dependency to an overseeing foreign power. More than ever, the goods and services that the South needed had to be paid for by exporting cotton or other raw materials or partially finished goods to the North, according to the economic rules set by northern manufacturers and financiers. Throughout the South, especially in the rural areas, poverty was the way of life for hundreds of thousands of Americans.

Within the context of world history, the American Civil War is important for several reasons. It was the greatest war that occurred anywhere in the world between the defeat of Napoleon and the onset of World War I in 1914. It represented the triumph of the same kind of central or centralizing political authority that during the same decade was triumphing in Italy, Germany, and France. It resulted in the establishment of a continent-wide free labor market, even though in many parts of the South freed blacks lived in a situation of great poverty and economic dependence not unlike that of the rural classes of Latin America. The free labor market purged of slavery helped to permit the opening of the entire North American continent to economic development. The solution by war of the long-

During the Reconstruction Era freedmen dominated certain southern legislatures such as that of South Carolina here portrayed from a contemporary newspaper. [Bettmann Archive.]

One of the key features of segregation were separate schools for black and white Americans. Here a group of black school children in Hampton, Virginia salute the flag around the turn of the century. [Library of Congress.]

standing debate over slavery and the union also allowed American political and economic interests to develop without the distraction of the debate over states rights and the moral concern of the debate over slavery. Thereafter, free labor would become the American norm. Consequently, the debates over the role of industrial labor in the United States came to resemble those in Europe.

Dashed Hopes of Equality

The single most visible result of the Civil War was the end of slavery in the South and the promise of equality. However, the fruits of liberty for blacks in the quarter century following the war proved to be quite temporary. During the same era, the liberty of native Americans became even more curtailed.

The Emergence of Segregation of Black Americans

Throughout the decade of Reconstruction, black Americans played an important role in southern political life. Freedmen, as former slaves were called, voted, held office, and owned property. Furthermore, they assumed a larger active role in the economic life of the South. These years proved to be a false spring of political liberty for blacks.

In 1876, the election for the presidency was disputed. Rutherford B. Hayes was elected only after a series of secret political compromises were reached in Washington, whereby southern leaders agreed to allow Hayes' election in return for certain actions on the part of his administration. The latter included the removal of the last federal troops from the South. In return for this action, conservative southern politicians promised to protect the freedmen. Those promises were not kept. Simultaneously, within the North, concern for the fate of the freedmen diminished in the wake of economic growth and the emergence of urban social stresses. Northerners who had wanted to end slavery retreated from the promise of extending full civil rights to free blacks. Racism came into the ascendent.

Within the states of the old Confederacy, the border states, and to a lesser extent, elsewhere, a system of legalized discrimination against blacks slowly arose in the form of segregation. Through laws passed by city councils and state legislatures, virtually all areas of social life became divided into black and white spheres. Race defined nearly all the institutions to which persons did or did not have access. Restaurants, hospitals, prisons, churches, trains, street cars, beaches, drinking fountains, Bibles used in courtrooms, and even burial grounds were divided according to race. The 1896 Supreme Court decision of *Plessy v. Ferguson* declared these arrangements to be constitutional. That decision remained in force until 1954.

Within this segregated world, American blacks were subject to all manner of discrimination simply on the basis of the color of their skin. Furthermore, Southern states passed legislation that legalized poll taxes and literacy tests; these deprived blacks of their rights to vote. American blacks were also subject to simple intimidation and terrorism. Toward the end of the nineteenth and well into the twentieth century, waves

The United States Supreme Court Declares Segregation Constitutional

In 1896, in the decision of Plessy v. Ferguson, *the Supreme Court of the United States declared segregation of the races to be constitutional. The court had ruled legal a Louisiana statute that segregated passenger railway cars. The argument that the court set forth was based on the principle of "separate but equal," whereby it held that separate facilities, if equal, did not imply the inferiority of the black race. Behind this argument lay the idea that racial hierarchy was a fundamental part of human nature and that legislation could not make equal what nature had made unequal. Upon this decision rested the legality of various modes of segregation for over half a century.*

We consider the underlying fallacy of the plaintiff's argument to consist in the assumption that the enforced separation of the two races stamps the colored race with a badge of inferiority. If this be so, it is not by reason of anything found in the act, but solely because the colored race chooses to put that construction upon it. The argument necessarily assumes that if, as has been more than once the case, and is not unlikely to be so again, the colored race should become the dominant power in the state legislature, and should enact a law in precisely simpler terms, it would thereby relegate the white race to an inferior position. We imagine that the white race, at least, would not acquiesce in this assumption. The argument also assumes that social prejudice may be overcome by legislation, and that equal rights cannot be secured to the Negro except by an enforced commingling of the two races. We cannot accept this proposition. If the two races are to meet on terms of social equality, it must be the result of natural affinities, a mutual appreciation of each other's merits and a voluntary consent of individuals. . . . Legislation is powerless to eradicate racial instincts or to abolish distinctions based upon physical differences, and the attempt to do so can only result in accentuating the difficulties of the present situation. If the civil and political right of both races be equal, one cannot be inferior to the other civilly or politically. If one race be inferior to the other socially, the Constitution of the United States cannot put them upon the same plane. ❑

Plessy v. Ferguson, 1896, as quoted in Henry Steele Commager, Documents of American History, Eighth Edition (New York: Appleton-Century-Crofts, 1968), 1:629.

of lynchings spread across the South. The overwhelming majority of victims were blacks.

During the last quarter of the nineteenth century, many black leaders, Booker T. Washington (1856–1915) being the most prominent, argued that their fellow blacks should wait for better times, submit to the discrimination, and practice economic virtues, such as hard work and thrift, that might lead them out of poverty. Drawing upon the ideas of European economic liberalism that admonished against government action, they contended that by behaving in a careful, deferential manner blacks might eventually convince the dominant whites of their worthiness for political activity. More than a generation would pass before different black voices made themselves felt.

After the turn of the century, W. E. B. DuBois (1868–1963), who had been educated at Harvard and also in Berlin, urged more direct claims to political rights and the establishment of a well-educated black

Booker T. Washington was a major black American leader who argued that his fellow blacks should accomodate themselves to the situation of segregation and then seek to earn fuller rights. [Library of Congress.]

W. E. B. Dubois was one of the major black American leaders to challenge the position of Booker T. Washington and to call for full equality with white Americans. [Schomburg Center, New York Public Library.]

leadership group. He understood that racism in the forms of riots, lynchings, and segregation were continuing to spread and had penetrated the North as well as the South. Deference had led to nothing but ongoing discrimination and unacceptable behavior toward blacks. In 1909, DuBois and others undertook to organize the National Association for the Advancement of Colored People. In time, that organization would spearhead much of the effort of black Americans toward greater equality, but almost half a century would pass before segregation was declared illegal.

The Experience of Native Americans

Throughout the early decades of the nineteenth century, those native Americans who had originally lived east of the Mississippi—including the Cherokees, Creeks, and Seminoles—were pushed further and further west. These dislocations were not the results of voluntary movements, but were forced removals, some of the most extensive of which occurred under Andrew Jackson's presidency (1829–1837). The experience of these tribes of native Americans at the hands of the federal government became known as the "Trail of Tears." By the close of the Civil War, it is estimated

Native American leaders were frequently brought from the West to Washington to negotiate over the fate of their tribes. Here they are pictured during the administration of Rutherford B. Hayes on a tour of the Corcoran Galley of Art, Washington, D.C. [National Anthropological Museum, Smithsonian Institution.]

that there were more than three hundred thousand native Americans, the vast majority of whom lived west of the Mississippi. Most of these people were indigenous to the region; others lived there as a result of the forced marches.

During the Civil War, the federal army moved against Indians as well as the South. Hundreds of native Americans were killed; many were executed. The virtual end of their way of life took place between 1865 and the close of the century; ongoing warfare occurred over these years between native Americans and the U.S. Army. The building of the transcontinental railways opened the plains and the northwest to white settlement. The buffalo and other food supplies of the native Americans were destroyed. The army suppressed native American resistance. There were native American victories, such as the Battle of the Little Big Horn of 1876 in which Major General George Custer and his force of over two hundred soldiers were killed by the Sioux. But such victories were rare and ultimately futile as the technologically better-armed troops of the U.S. Army put down Indian opposition. In some cases, such as the infamous attack on Sioux Indians at Wounded Knee in 1890, the army simply massacred innocent native American women and children.

The federal policy against Native Americans was not unlike that of the southern states against blacks.

Both policies were fundamentally antidemocratic and calculated to make social and economic life safe and profitable for white Americans. In 1867, the federal government began a policy of placing native Americans on reservations. As the conquest of the Great Plains continued, the reservation system spread. The land assigned to native Americans was almost invariably of poor quality and far removed from areas that white Americans wished to develop. White Americans approached both native Americans and black Americans with the idea of "civilizing" them. This attitude paralleled that of the Europeans who were contemporaneously carrying out imperial ventures in Africa and Asia.

European Immigration

The very conditions that made American life so difficult for blacks and native Americans turned the United States into a land of vast opportunity for white European immigrants. These immigrants faced religious and ethnic discrimination in the United States as well as frequent poverty; however, for many of them and their children the social and economic structures of the United States allowed for assimilation and remarkable upward social mobility. This was especially true of those immigrants who arrived between approximately 1840 and 1890 and who came mostly from

European immigrants on their way to the United States, 1906. Between 1846 and 1932, over 50 million Europeans immigrated to the United States, Canada, South America, Australia, and South Africa. [Library of Congress.]

northern and western Europe. This was the great period of German, English, Welsh, Scottish, and Irish immigration. Of these, the Irish undoubtedly encountered the most difficulties and resistance.

Toward the end of the century and well into the next, millions of immigrants arrived from Italy, Spain, Portugal, Greece, Poland, Russia, and other eastern European countries. Most of these peoples left economically depressed parts of Europe. Most came on their own small resources. There were, however, instances of American companies sending ships to Italy to bring over immigrants to work in American factories and mines. The late-century immigration from eastern and southern Europe is sometimes known as the New Immigration. Around the turn of the century, these immigrants were perceived as being fundamentally different from those who had come in the middle of the nineteenth century and in the two decades after the Civil War.

These new immigrants generally came to work in the growing industrial cities. They were perceived and treated as being of a lower class and as being inherently more difficult to assimilate. Being Roman Catholic, Russian Orthodox, Greek Orthodox, and Jewish, they encountered much prejudice. The same kind of racial theory that spread through Europe during these years was present in the United States. Therefore, these new immigrants were often regarded as being from less desirable racial stocks. As a result of all these factors, turn-of-the-century immigrants often encountered very serious experiences of prejudice and endured lives of enormous poverty. They also often settled into communities with other people of their own ethnic background. What ultimately held them together were various kinds of private organizations such as churches and synagogues, clubs, newspapers in their own languages, and social agencies they organized for themselves.

Although none of these immigrants faced quite so pervasive a system of legal discrimination as did American blacks, the Jews encountered restricted covenants on real estate, obstacles in joining private clubs, and quotas for admission to many schools and universities. Asian immigrants to the west coast of the United States faced similar prejudice.

The New Industrial Economy

The full industrialization of the United States followed a pattern not unlike that experienced by nineteenth-century Europe. The first industry to become thoroughly mechanized was textile manufacture. Thereafter, growth occurred in the iron and steel industries. However, in America as in Europe, it was the building of the railways that spurred the most intense indus-

Pittsburgh became the chief center of American iron and steel manufacturing. Here workers are seen in the process of cleaning the gigantic machinery used to produce steel. [Library of Congress.]

trial growth. The number of railway miles increased from approximately fifty thousand in the mid-1860s to almost two hundred thousand by the close of the century. Much of the construction was made possible by vast European investments in the United States. The building of the railways created enormous demand for iron, steel, coal, and lumber. The railways also stimulated settlement and vastly expanded markets. Railway builders developed land in the process. The railways also did much to knit together the far-flung parts of the United States.

The Control of Business: Cartels and Trusts

The building of the railways and the other economic developments in the iron industry and in the financial markets initially led to stiff competition. The result was overproduction and very low or even nonexistent profits. The world of the manufacturer became extraordinarily uncertain from the 1880s onward. The eventual response of the growing industrial sector was to seek ways to curb or even to abolish competition. The goal was to seek a level of production that would assure profits. In other words, it was business itself that sought to avoid the perils and pitfalls of the free market.

Various devices were used to control the possible danger and turmoil of the free market. One way around competition was to establish cartels and trusts. These represented ways of organizing whole industries under a single company or group of companies that might divide the market in their own self-interests. Cartels were voluntary arrangements among a group of companies. The trust was the organization of a market for a particular industrial or consumer product under a single company. The most famous of these were associated with Andrew Carnegie's steel company, John D. Rockefeller's Standard Oil business, and J. P. Morgan's financial empire. It often seemed that some of the great companies were as powerful or more powerful than the government, and that they functioned in a manner contrary to the public interest.

The Organization of Labor: Unions

The expansion of industrialism also led to various attempts to organize the labor market through labor unions. In America as in Europe, workers faced great resistance from employers and from nonindustrialists who feared that labor unions in some manner might lead to socialism. Another difficulty arose from the social situation of the labor force itself. White laborers would not organize alongside blacks. Different ethnic minorities would not cooperate. The ongoing flood of immigration meant the presence of a supply of workers willing to work for low wages. The owners of businesses more often than not could divide and conquer the sprawling, ethnically mixed, labor force.

Samuel Gompers was one of the founders of the American Federation of Labor. His own craft had been that of a cigar maker. [National Archives.]

The impact of European immigration into the United States is vividly portrayed on this strike ballot that was printed in English, Serbo-Croation, Hungarian, Italian, Slovak, and Polish. [William Cahn, A Pictorial History of American Labor, Crown Publishers.]

  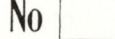

BALLOT

IRON & STEEL WORKERS

The Union Committees are now seeking to get higher wages, shorter hours and better working conditions from the steel companies. Are you willing to back them up to the extent of stopping work should the companies refuse to concede these demands?

TAJNO GLASANJE

Odbor junije sada traži da se dobije bolja plaća, kraći radni satovi i bolji uvjeti za rad od kompanija čelika. Dali ste voljni isti do skrajnosti podupreti da se prestane sa radom ako bi kompanija odbila da udovolji zahtevima?

SZAVAZZON!

Az Union Bizottsága, az Acél Társaságoktól való— magasabb fizetés, rövidebb munka idő és jobb munka feltételek—elnyerése után törekszik. Akar ezek után törekedni? s a végsőkig kitarta—ni? és ha a társaságok ezen kivánalmaknak nem tesznek eleget a munkát beszüntetni?

VOTAZIONE.

I comitati dell'Unione stanno cercando di ottenere paghe piu' alte, ore di lavoro piu' brevi, e migliori condizioni di lavoro. Desiderate voi assecondarli, anche quando dovesse essere necessario di fermare il lavoro se le Compagnie rifiutassero di accettare le demande?

HLÁSOVACI LÍSTOK

Výbor uniový chce dosiahnuť podvýšenie mzdy, menej hodín robiť a lepšie robotnícke položenie od oceliarskych spoločností. Ste vy ochotní ich podporovať do krajnosti; až do zástavenia práce, v páde by spoločnosť odoprela žiadosťučiniť tým požiadavkám.

BALOT

Komitet Unii stara się obecnie o uzyskanie od Stalowych Kompanij większej płacy, krótszych godzin i lepszych warunków pracy. Czy jesteś gotów poprzeć nas aż do możliwości wstrzymania pracy na wypadek, gdyby Kompanie odmówiły naszym żądaniom?

VOTE YES OR NO.   Mark X in square indicating how you vote

Yes ☒   No ☐

National Committee for Organizing Iron and Steel Workers
WM. Z. FOSTER, Secy-Treas.   303 Magee Bldg., Pittsburgh, Pa.

The first effort at labor organization occurred in the 1870s with the National Labor Union and railroad unions. These were followed in the same decade by the Knights of Labor, which survived into the 1880s but which were not particularly successful. In 1881, the American Federation of Labor (AFL) was founded. Based on policies of economic realism, it did not seek to transform the life of workers in a radical fashion but rather concentrated on higher wages and better working conditions. The AFL concentrated its organizing efforts among skilled workers. It did not seek to organize whole industries. Among its most effective leaders was Samuel Gompers (1850–1924). Other unions such as the United Mine Workers and the Railway Brotherhoods grew and organized workers by industry.

Throughout the nineteenth century, the federal and state governments made virtually no efforts to aid workers when they were unemployed. The industrialization of the United States—again, like that of Europe—saw major periods of business crisis or downturn. Serious depressions occurred in both the 1870s and the 1890s. There was no government relief. What little relief there was came from local authorities and private charities. Such would continue to be the case until the Great Depression of the 1930s.

On the contrary, federal and state governments attempted to curb labor organizations and to break strikes. The economic turmoil of the 1880s and 1890s spawned a number of major strikes with very considerable violence. Perhaps the most famous of these incidents was the breaking of the Pullman strike in Chicago in 1894 by federal troops. The major goal of labor for some years thereafter was the recognition of the full legal rights to organize. Although the Clayton Act of 1914 moved in that direction, the clear right to organize with the protection of the federal government was achieved only through the New Deal legislation.

In 1894 *federal troops were called in to escort trains out of the Chicago stock-yards during a strike. [Library of Congress.]*

Farmers Adrift in the World Market

Farmers, too, felt themselves the victims of the power of big business. At the same time, the opening of the plains, the use of new farm machinery, and specialization in crop cultivation led to great increases in agricultural production. American farmers entered a rapidly changing world market for farm commodities. The expansion of agriculture in the United States, across Canada, and throughout Latin America was tied to the new railway transportation. It enabled an enormous new quantity of grain to be brought onto the world market. These quantities were also unregulated and unpredictable. Consequently, prices received by farmers fell precipitously. Farmers were dependent upon banks for loans to finance their crops and to buy new machinery. They required the railways to carry their harvest and herds to market. Farmers found themselves hard-pressed and often saw themselves as the victims of the business and financial institutions of the eastern cities.

Farmers responded to this situation politically and economically. To protect their economic interests, farmers in the latter part of the nineteenth century organized themselves into farmers' cooperatives. By these means, they could attempt to work with each other to maximize their economic security. They hoped to eliminate the middle man, whom they believed put them at a competitive disadvantage. This tactic worked usually only where the particular crop was a relatively small one, such as fruit, but did not work with crops, such as wheat and corn, that were raised in large quantities across the nation. The National Farmers Alliance and Industrial Union was the most powerful of the farm organizations. It operated various stores and marketing agencies and allowed farmers to purchase expensive equipment that they would then share on a cooperative basis. The Alliance also had an extensive program of publications for farmers and the wider public. The Alliance had become politically active by the latter part of the 1880s.

Politically, farmers, along with other groups who believed the political system was dominated by big business, organized themselves into the Peoples Party. Often known as the Populist Movement, this organization in 1892 ran a candidate for the presidency. The Populists hoped to impress upon the country the importance of agriculture, the moral superiority of working the land, and the evils of cities and high finance. Like other third parties, the Peoples Party failed to capture the presidency; but the two major parties began to respond to the pressure of Populism. In 1896, the great Populist orator William Jennings Bryan (1860–1925) captured the Democratic Party Convention and received the nomination for president. He lost the election to William McKinley (1843–1891). Nonetheless, with Bryan's nomination the Populist movement finally touched one of the major parties and thus injected the concerns of the Populists into the wider political debate of the nation.

Large-scale farm machinery, such as seen in this 1911 Kansas scene, allowed American farmers to cultivate the great plains and to compete in the world market. However, participation in that market meant their economic wellbeing could be harmed by developments thousands of miles away on the farms of Argentina or Russia. [Library of Congress.]

The Populist Party Demands Reform

The Populist Party Platform of 1892 set forth a vast list of corrupt practices in American political and social life. It portrayed a nation in which agents of great wealth controlled the political system. It also called for major social reform and recognition of the rights of workers. The platform also condemned the failures of the two major parties—the Republicans and the Democrats—to address the key issues of the day.

The conditions which surround us best justify our co-operation; we meet in the midst of a nation brought to the verge of moral, political, and material ruin. Corruption dominates the ballot-box, the Legislature, the Congress, and touches even the ermine of the bench. The people are demoralized; most of the States have been compelled to isolate the voters at the polling places to prevent universal intimidation and bribery. The newspapers are largely subsidized or muzzled, public opinion silenced, business prostrated, homes covered with mortgages, labor impoverished, and the land concentrating in the hands of capitalists. The urban workmen are denied the right to organize for self-protection, imported pauperized labor beats down their wages, a hireling standing army, unrecognized by our laws, is established to shoot them down, and they are rapidly degenerating into European conditions. The fruits of the toil of millions are boldly stolen to build up colossal fortunes for a few, unprecedented in the history of mankind; and the possessors of these, in turn, despise the Republic and endanger liberty. From the same prolific womb of governmental injustice we breed the two great classes—traps and millionaires. . . .

We have witnessed for more than a quarter of a century the struggles of the two great political parties for power and plunder, while grievous wrongs have been inflicted upon the suffering people. We charge that the controlling influences dominating both these parties have permitted the existing dreadful conditions to develop without serious effort to prevent or restrain them. Neither do they promise us any substantial reform. . . .

Assembled on the anniversary of the birthday of the nation, and filled with the spirit of the grand general and chief who established our independence, we seek to restore the government of the Republic to the hands of the "plain people," with which class it originated. ❏

Platform of the Populist Party, 1892, as quoted in Henry Steele Commager, *Documents of American History*, Eighth Edition (New York: Appleton-Century-Crofts, 1968), 1:593–594.

The Progressives

During the last quarter of the nineteenth century, much of the political power in the United States lay outside of the federal government. The states retained enormous influence. The great trusts and banking interests also exerted much power. The federal government was simply not the center of American life.

Fighting Political Corruption

The organization of politics during the last quarter of the century, especially in cities, often lay in the hands of political bosses. Boss politics was deeply dependent upon elaborate forms of patronage at every level of government. As the patronage in the forms of jobs, contracts, licenses, favors, and sometimes actual services was distributed, the boss expected and received political support. Government was thus seen as a vehicle for distributing spoils. The point of boss politics was not merely venality; it was also a way, however crude and unattractive, of organizing the disorderly social and economic forces of the great cities. It was a way of managing cities that were growing as never before with highly diverse populations.

The politics of patronage was not confined to the cities. It permeated state and federal government as well. All of the presidents of the latter part of the century functioned in large measure as the orchestrators of federal patronage. The Pendleton Act of 1883 established merit selection of many civil service jobs, but many thousands of appointments lay outside its jurisdiction.

Toward the close of the century, reform-minded political figures began to emerge in major American cities and within some state governments. These reformers feared that people such as themselves from the white upper-middle classes might soon lose political and social influence. They were also fearful of more radical figures, such as those politicians to whom the depressed farmers of the South and Midwest were turning. Though reformers, they were not always liberal by our contemporary standards. For example, progressives in the South were often at the forefront of disenfranchising blacks and poor whites through the imposition of literacy tests and similar devices.

Deeply disturbed by the corruption of much of political life, these progressive reformers found the urban environment with its slums and unacceptable picture of disorder. They wanted to see more efficient government. They also wanted to see the government at the center of American life as a direct agent of change and reform. With a goal of less corrupt and more efficient government, the progressive era lasted from approximately 1890 through 1914.

The progressives were far more concerned with domestic policy than foreign policy. They began to work on the local level, especially in the cities, before they launched into national politics. The disorder and extreme disparity of wealth and poverty in the cities especially disturbed the progressives. Urban reformers believed that the politics of bosses and patronage robbed cities of the money needed to make them livable places. In place of patronage, they demanded social services and municipal services to clean up the cities. They repeatedly attacked special interests who stood in the way of public good and reform. Progressive mayors worked for lower utility rates and lower street car fares. They also attacked police graft.

Social Reform

It was not only politicians who joined the progressive crusade. Churches began to address themselves to the question of social reform. It was in this era that the "Social Gospel" was first preached, with its message that Christianity involved civic action. Young men and women began to work in settlement houses in the slums. The most famous of these was Chicago's Hull House, led by Jane Addams (1860–1935). Other young persons from the middle class became active in housing and health reform, education, and charities. They conducted extensive surveys of the poorest parts of the great cities. All of these people believed that the urban environment could be cleaned up and social order made to prevail. Their vision of such social order was very much that of the white middle class.

Beginning in the mid-nineties, progressivism had begun to have an impact on state governments. There the impulse toward reform involved various attempts to protect whole classes of persons who were perceived as unable to protect themselves against exploitation. These particularly included children and women working under unwholesome conditions for exceedingly low wages. Other aspects of progressivism at the state level involved the introduction of state civil service requirements and the regulation of railways. Virtually all of these reformers partook of the cult of science that was so influential in the late nineteenth century. They believed that the problems of society

These people lived in a New York slum in an inner court on Baxter Street. Similar slums existed not only in major U.S. cities but in most of the major cities of Europe. [Library of Congress.]

This picture taken in 1902 shows women working in the National Cash Register Company in Dayton, Ohio. Women had also actively entered similar factory workshops in Europe. [Library of Congress.]

were susceptible to solutions of scientific, rational management. The general idea was to substitute a general public interest in place of special interests.

The Progressive Presidency

ROOSEVELT. Political assassination brought the first national progressive to the presidency. Theodore Roosevelt became president in 1901 upon the death of William McKinley. Roosevelt had been Police Commissioner of New York City and later a reforming governor of New York. Roosevelt, in effect, created the modern American presidency. He saw the office as a position that could be transformed into the center of American political life. By force of personality and intelligence, he began to make the presidency the most important and powerful branch of government. As president, he began to set the agenda for national affairs and to define the problems that the federal government was to address. He surrounded himself with stronger advisers and cabinet members than had most of his predecessors. He used his own knowledge of

party patronage to outdo the bosses at their own game.

So far as domestic policy was concerned, Roosevelt regarded his most important challenge as that of controlling the powerful business trusts. He was determined that no centers of economic power would, through their organization, be stronger than the federal government. He successfully moved against some of the most powerful financiers in the country, such as J. P. Morgan and John D. Rockefeller. Through legislation associated with the term *Square Deal*, Roosevelt attempted to assert the public interest over that of the various powerful special interests. He was not opposed to big business in and of itself, but he wanted such business and other large powerful institutions to operate according to rules established by the government for the public good.

In 1902, Roosevelt brought the moral power of the presidency to the aid of mine workers who were on strike. He appointed a commission to arbitrate the dispute. This action represented a major intrusion of the federal government into the economic system. It also

Theodore Roosevelt was a great outdoorsman who advocated the leading of the strenuous life. Political cartoonists often drew him in that character; here he is portrayed attacking the great trusts. [Library of Congress.]

represented a reverse of the policies that had prevailed a decade earlier when the government had intruded in order to break strikes with federal troops. In this and other instances, Roosevelt sought to make the presidency and the federal government appear to be the guarantor of fairness in economic relations. It was in a like spirit that he fostered the passage of the Pure Food and Drug Act and the Meat Packing Act in 1906, which protected the public against adulterated foodstuffs. Here again, the regulatory principle came to the fore. Another area in which he affirmed the public interest over that of the special interests was in his conservation policies, whereby millions of acres of national forests came under the care of the federal government.

Roosevelt was associated with a vigorous foreign policy that had roots in the administration of McKinley. In 1898, McKinley had led the nation into the Spanish-American War. Through this conflict, the United States had emerged on the world scene as an imperial power. The fruits of the very brief war against Spain had been American control of Cuba, Puerto Rico, Guam, and the Philippines. Roosevelt, who had been Assistant Secretary of the Navy at the start of the conflict, led a unit of troops known as Rough Riders in the war. He continued to believe that the United States had to play a role as a major world power, and he sent the naval fleet around the world. In Latin America, he sent a naval fleet to assure the success of

the Panamanian revolt of 1903 against Colombia. Then he quickly signed a treaty with the new Panamanian government that allowed the United States to construct and control a canal across the Isthmus of Panama.

Roosevelt remained president until 1909 when he was succeeded by William Howard Taft (1857–1930), his hand-picked successor. Taft disappointed Roosevelt, and in 1912 the election was a three-way contest between Taft, Roosevelt (running as a third-party candidate), and Woodrow Wilson. The Democrat Wilson won and brought a different concept of progressivism to the White House.

WILSON. Woodrow Wilson (1856–1924) was a former president of Princeton University and a reforming governor of New Jersey, where he had battled the bosses. While still an academic, he had criticized the weak presidency of the last quarter of the nineteenth century. Wilson, like Roosevelt, accepted a modern industrialized nation. However, he differed from Roosevelt on one major issue: Wilson disliked bigness almost in and of itself. He believed in economic competition in which the weak would receive protection from the government. Wilson termed his attitude and policy the *New Freedom*. Although he had pressed this idea during the campaign, once in office he followed a policy of moderate regulation of business.

Wilson also had a somewhat different view of the presidency. He saw the office as responsible for leading Congress to legislative decisions. He was the first American president since John Adams to deliver the State of the Union address in person. He presented Congress with a vast agenda of legislation and then worked carefully with the Democratic leadership to see that it was passed. Among the most significant of his measures was the establishment of the Federal Reserve System.

Wilson had long seen his real goals in terms of domestic reform. However, war had broken out in Europe in the late summer of 1914. Wilson was reelected in 1916 on the slogan "He Kept Us Out of War!" However, six months after the election he led the nation into participation in the European conflict. All of the expertise that he and other progressives had brought to the task of efficient domestic government was then turned to making the nation an effective military force. Those two impulses, the first toward domestic reform, the second toward a strong international role, had long marked the progressive movement. Those two impulses would shape the American history in the years after the war.

The manner in which domestic reformers so quickly and effectively turned to the military effort illustrates one of the many paradoxes of Progressivism. Fundamentally, Progressivism was an attempt by political

Woodrow Wilson had served as President of Princeton University and Governor of New Jersey before his election to the presidency. [Library of Congress.]

figures on various levels of the political process to have government bring order to the society that urbanization and industrialism had created in America. However, that goal led to strange mixes of political attitudes and policies. For example, Roosevelt was a progressive at home and a strong imperialist abroad, whose thought was deeply influenced by racial thinking. Wilson was an advocate of a new mode of economic freedom, but he reimposed segregation within the civil service.

The Canadian Experience

Under the Treaty of Paris of 1763, all of Canada came under the control of Great Britain. Canada then, as now, included both an English-speaking and a French-speaking population. The latter was concentrated primarily in the province of Quebec. The Quebec Act of 1774, which had so disturbed the English colonists along the Atlantic seaboard, extended toleration to the Roman Catholic church in Canada and made it the established Church in Quebec itself. During the American Revolution, approximately thirty thousand English loyalists fled the colonies and settled in Canada. They thus established a larger English presence and were strongly committed to loyalty to the British crown.

The tension between the French and English populations led, in part, to the Constitutional Act of 1791 that divided the colony into Upper Canada (which was primarily English in ethnic composition) and Lower Canada (which was primarily French). Each section had its own legislature with a governor-general who presided over the two provinces on behalf of the British crown. The maritime provinces of Newfoundland, Nova Scotia, New Brunswick, Cape Breton Island, and Prince Edward Island remained small separate colonies.

During the late eighteenth and early nineteenth centuries, relations with the United States were often tense. There were local disputes over the fur trade and fear that the growing United States would dominate

Canada. That apprehension, along with the Anglo-French ethnic divisions, came to constitute two of the major themes of Canadian history in the nineteenth century and later.

By the late 1830s, the situation of colonial governance in Canada was beginning to generate considerable internal pressure. Tension arose between the power of long-established families with powerful economic interests in both Upper and Lower Canada and new settlers who hoped to achieve prosperity for themselves. There were quarrels over the power of the British Crown in local affairs. In 1837, rebellions occurred in both Upper and Lower Canada. Although there were relatively few casualties, the British realized that some action had to be taken.

The Road to Self-Government

The British government, operating in the more liberal political climate following the first Reform Act, was determined to avoid the kind of alienation of Canadians that had occurred with their other North American colonies a half century earlier. Consequently, the British government sent the Earl of Durham to Canada with extensive powers to make reforms. In 1839, he published his *Report on the Affairs of British North America*. In this famous document, Durham advocated responsible government for Canada. He contended that all of the Canadian provinces should be united into a single political unit. He thought that such political unification would eventually lead to a thoroughly English culture throughout Canada and thus would enable the region to overcome the widespread French influence in Quebec. He furthermore believed that most Canadian affairs should be in the hands of a Canadian legislature and that only issues such as foreign policy should remain under British control. In effect, Durham wanted Canadians generally to govern themselves in the hope that by giving political autonomy to the country, English culture would dominate. Durham's policy was carried out in the Canada Act of 1840 that gave the nation a single legislature composed of two houses.

The Canadian example that followed from the Durham Report established the political pattern that the British government would, to a greater or lesser extent, follow with other of its English-speaking colonies during the course of the nineteenth century. Britain sought to foster responsible self-government in Australia, New Zealand, and South Africa. In that respect, the Canadian experience had a considerable impact throughout the world. But, throughout the nineteenth century and well into the twentieth, the British government, like other Western imperial powers, also generally believed that nonwhite peoples, such as those of India, were not ready for responsible self-government and required direct British colonial administration.

J. A. MacDonald was the most important political leader in Canada during the second half of the nineteenth century. [The Bettmann Archive.]

Keeping a Distinctive Culture

Canadians did learn to exercise self-government, but distinct English and French cultures continued to exist. Within the legislature, there were almost always tradeoffs between the eastern and western sections of the nation. Furthermore, during the American Civil War fears arose in Canada that once the North won, the American republic might seek to invade Canada or otherwise dominate it. One response to this fear was an attempt to form a union among the maritime provinces in 1862. Those discussions in time led to broader considerations of the desirability for a stronger federation among all the parts of Canada.

The result of those debates and discussions was the British North America Act of 1867, passed by the British Parliament. It created a Canadian federation. But in establishing this new government, Canadians hoped to avoid what they regarded as flaws in the constitution of the United States that the Civil War had revealed. The Canadian system of government was to be federal, but with much less emphasis on states' rights, because of the disruption that those rights had created in the United States. Canadians established a parliamentary mode of government, but also quite consciously chose to retain the presence of the British monarchy in the person of the governor-general as head of state. The person who was most responsible for establishing this new government and who led it for most of the period between 1867 and 1891 was John A. MacDonald (1815–1891).

Like settlers in the United States, Canadians during the later part of the nineteenth century pressed westward. The St. Lawrence River had determined the corridor of settlement in eastern Canada. Initially, the far western portions of Canada had been explored and exploited by fur traders and the Hudson Bay Company. The path for the later settlement of the prairie lands of the west and the mountains of the far Canadian West was provided by the construction of the Canadian Pacific Railway, completed in 1885. The railroad crossed the continent as a kind of spine along which settlements grew. In turn, the Canadian economy became highly integrated with that of the United States. This situation, which has continued to the present day, created fears of being dominated economically by the powerful industrial economy of Canada's southern neighbor.

As Canadians established a nation that stretched across a continent and demonstrated their capacity for stable self-government, the domination of Britain diminished. The link with the British Crown remained and would continue to do so until 1982; however, Canada established a largely independent foreign policy by the close of the century. The role of the governor-general became increasingly ceremonial as real political power resided in the Canadian political parties and parliamentary system. It supported Great Britain in the Boer War, World War I, and World War II; but in each case its participation was that of an ally and not of a colony.

The Canadian experience of movement from colony to self-governing nation was thus quite different from that of the United States. Throughout the process, the British government and its representatives were actively involved. Furthermore, the presence of a strong and continuing French culture in which the Roman Catholic church played a major role led to very real cultural differences between French-speaking Canada and the expanding English-speaking portion of the nation. English-speaking Canadians dominated both political and economic life. French-speaking Canadians virtually always felt that they were in the position of second-class citizenship.

The Development of the United States and Canada in World Perspective

In 1800, the United States remained a nation of people living chiefly along the eastern seaboard. Only a rela-

SIGNIFICANT DATES IN NORTH AMERICAN HISTORY

1787	Constitutional Convention in Philadelphia
1789	George Washington becomes president
1791	Adoption of the Bill of Rights
1801	Thomas Jefferson becomes president
1803	Louisiana Purchase
1820	Missouri Compromise
1829	Andrew Jackson becomes president
1831	William Lloyd Garrison publishes *The Liberator*
1839	Lord Durham's Report on Canada
1846	Outbreak of Mexican War
1850	Compromise of 1850
1854	Kansas–Nebraska Act
1856	Dred Scott Decision
1861–1865	United States Civil War
1863	Emancipation Proclamation
1867	British North American Act creates a Canadian confederation
1877	Federal Troops removed from the Southern States
1881	American Federation of Labor founded
1896	Supreme Court upholds segregation in *Plessy v. Ferguson*
1898	Spanish-American War
1901	Theodore Roosevelt becomes president
1913	Woodrow Wilson becomes president
1917	United States enters World War I

tively few people had dared to move beyond the Appalachian mountains. In the course of a century, a unique, if often troubled, civilization dominated by the English language and Protestant religion had spread over three thousand miles to the Pacific Coast. This phenomenon represented the conquest of a continent. Indigenous people were swept aside, and natural barriers were overcome. A whole continent with its generally untapped resources was brought into the world economy. The foundations were thus established for the greatest industrial power of the mid- and late-twentieth century.

This experience of continental expansion was profoundly difficult. It involved long, heated debates over the nature of freedom and slavery. Eventually, slavery was abolished as it was in Latin America and as was serfdom in Russia. But even American slavery had existed in a larger nation where free labor predominated. Furthermore, unlike almost every other major nation of the nineteenth century, the United States did not experience the problem of having to liberate people from the land or of having to divide large landed estates into smaller ones. The United States was rich in land, and the federal government from the time of the Revolution to the end of the century had sought ways of making small parcels of land available to individual owners.

Similarly, Canadians established a nation that stretched across the entire North American continent. As in the United States, the construction of a railway system proved key to national development. Canadians did not have to confront the problem of slavery, nor was the conflict with native peoples as full of warfare as that of the United States. However, the ethnic divisions between French-speaking and English-speaking Canadians proved an ongoing source of political and social dispute.

As the political experiment of the American republic unfolded, a different political experiment took place in Canada. There, through the various legislative acts carried out in Great Britain on Canada's behalf, there emerged a modified parliamentary system. This would be copied in many of the other British English-speaking colonies during the nineteenth century. And in the twentieth century when the British government after 1945 retreated from empire, similar modified parliamentary systems would be established in the new nations of Africa and Asia. In that respect, Canada had been the great laboratory for liberal parliamentary government that appeared one place or another during the twentieth century in Latin America, Africa, and Asia.

The industrial experience of the United States largely paralleled that of Europe. Textile manufacturing developed first, and was then followed by iron and steel. The railways in America, as in Europe, provided a major spur to economic development. Like those of Europe, the cities of America were centers of immigration from the surrounding countryside; but they were also magnets that attracted millions of immigrants from other parts of the world. In this respect, the United States resembled nations of Latin America, such as Argentina.

By the turn of the century, the economic and political energy of the United States allowed it to play a new role on the world stage. In the Spanish-American War of 1898, the United States would emerge as an imperial power. In the First World War, it would emerge as one of the dominant players on the world scene. Such dominance would hardly have been imaginable to the Americans of 1800. What they did share with their successors in 1900 was a commitment to an ongoing debate over the nature and extent of liberty and to the importance of liberty for the nation and the larger world. The character of that debate may often have been imperfect, but the commitment to the importance of the questions was never in doubt; nor would it be during the history of the United States in the twentieth century.

Suggested Readings

S. AHLSTROM, *A Religious History of the American People* (1972). The major survey.

L. BANNER, *Women in Modern America: A Brief History* (1984). An excellent introductory survey.

L. BANNING, *The Jeffersonian Persuasion: Evolution of a Party Ideology* (1978). A useful introduction.

J. BLASSINGAME, *The Slave Community* (1975). Emphasizes the manner in which slaves shaped their own community.

J. B. BREBNER, *Canada: A Modern History* (1970). A survey.

A. D. CHANDLER, JR., *The Visible Hand: Managerial Revolution in American Business* (1977). The best discussion of the innovative role of American business.

J. M. COOPER, JR., *The Warrior and the Priest: Woodrow Wilson and Theodore Roosevelt* (1983). An interesting dual biography.

N. F. COTT, *The Bonds of Womanhood: "Woman's Sphere" in New England 1780–1835* (1977). A key work to the self-defined role of women in the early years of the American republic.

N. F. COTT, *The Grounding of Modern Feminism* (1987). The most important recent treatment of the subject.

D. G. CREIGHTON, *John A. McDonald* (1952, 1955). A major biography of the first Canadian prime minister.

D. B. DAVIS, *The Problem of Slavery in the Age of Revolution, 1770–1823* (1975). A transatlantic perspective on the issue.

M. DUBERMAN, ed., *The Anti-Slavery Vanguard* (1965). Important essays.

T. DUBLIN, *Women at Work: The Transformation of Work and Community in Lowell, Massachusetts, 1826–1860* (1979). The best work on this important local setting of American industrialism.

D. FEHRENBACHER, *The Dred Scott Case* (1978). A brilliant study that goes far beyond the subject of the title.

E. FONER, *Reconstruction: America's Unfinished Revolution, 1863–1877* (1988). An outstanding account that pays close attention to the role of blacks in Reconstruction.

E. D. GENOVESE, *Roll Jordan Roll* (1974). The best overview of American slavery.

H. GUTMAN, *The Black Family in Slavery and Freedom, 1750–1925* A major, pioneering survey.

R. HOFSTADTER, *The Age of Reform: From Bryan to F.D.R.* (1955). The classic treatment of the Progressive era.

A. M. KRAUT, *The Huddled Masses: The Immigrant in American Society*, 1880–1921 (1982). A recent introduction.

T. J. LEARS AND R. W. FOX (eds.), *The Culture of Consumption* (1983). Essays on changes in taste and consumer activity.

F. McDONALD, *We the People: The Economic Origins of the Constitution* (1958). A standard work.

M. E. McGERR, *The Decline of Popular Politics: The American North*, 1865–1928 (1986). Examines the decline in popular political participation.

K. W. McNAUGHT, *Pelican History of Canada* (1982). A brief overview.

J. M. McPHERSON, *The Abolitionist Legacy: From Reconstruction to the N.A.A.C.P.* (1975). A survey of the history of Black Americans.

J. M. McPHERSON, *The Battle Cry of Freedom: The Civil War Era* (1988). An excellent one-volume treatment.

F. MERK, *History of the Westward Movement* (1978). A broad survey of all the major topics.

D. MONTGOMERY, *Workers' Control in America: Studies in the History of Work, Technology, and Labor Struggles* (1979). Essays on the role of American labor in determining the character of the workplace.

D. NELSON, *Managers and Workers: Origins of the New Factory System in the United States*, 1880–1920 (1975). A major examination of the transformation of American industry.

D. M. POTTER, *The Impending Crisis*, 1848–1861 (1976). The best one-volume treatment of the coming of the Civil War.

R. V. REMINI, *Andrew Jackson and the Course of American Democracy* (1984). Biographical introduction to Jacksonian Democracy.

M. J. SCHIESL, *The Politics of Efficiency: Municipal Administration and Reform in America* (1977). Relates the attack on boss-dominated politics.

C. P. STACEY, *Canada and the Age of Conflict* (1977, 1981). A study of Canadian foreign relations.

J. C. A. STAGG, *Mr. Madison's War: Politics, Diplomacy, and Warfare in the Early Republic*, 1783–1830 (1983). A recent introduction to the diplomacy of the period.

B. F. THOMAS, *Abraham Lincoln* (1952). Generally regarded as the best biography.

A. TRACHTENBERG, *The Incorporation of America: Culture and Society in the Gilded Ages* (1982). Examines the manner in which corporate organization affected various aspects of American life outside the realm of business.

J. D. UNRUH, JR., *The Overland Emigrants and the Trans-Mississippi West*, 1840–1860 (1979). A good introduction.

R. M. UTLEY, *The Indian Frontier and the American West*, 1846–1890 (1984). A broad survey of the pressures of white civilization against Native Americans.

S. WILENTZ, *Chants Democratic: New York City and the Rise of the American Working Class*, 1788–1850 (1984). An important examination of labor history and politics.

G. S. WOOD, *The creation of the American Republic*, 1776–1787 (1969). A major study of the influences of the writing of the Constitution.

C. V. WOODWARD, *Origins of the New South* (1951). The major interpretation of the South after Reconstruction.

C. V. WOODWARD, *The Strange History of Jim Crow* (1966). The clearest discussion of the imposition of segregation.

G. WRIGHT, *The Political Economy of the Cotton South* (1978). Clearly presents the intricacies of the southern rural economy.

The Eiffel Tower under construction, March 1889. Built entirely of iron by the French engineer Gustave Eiffel (steel was still too expensive), the tower was a symbol not only of Paris, but of the new industrial age. It was the centerpiece of the great Exhibition of 1889 that was held in Paris to celebrate the one hundredth anniversary of the French Revolution. [Library of Congress.]

782

28 The Building of European Supremacy: Society and Politics to World War I

Between 1860 and 1914, European political, economic, and social life assumed many of the features characteristic of our world today. Nation-states with large electorates, political parties, centralized bureaucracies, and universal military service emerged. Business adopted large-scale corporate structures, and the labor force organized itself into trade unions. Large numbers of white-collar workers appeared. Urban life came to predominate throughout Western Europe. Socialism became a major ingredient in the political life of all nations. The foundations of the welfare state and of vast military establishments were laid. Taxation increased accordingly.

During this half century, the extensive spread of industrialism created an unparalleled productive capacity in Europe. The age of the automobile, the airplane, the bicycle, the refrigerated ship, the telephone, the radio, the typewriter, and the electric light bulb dawned. The world's economies, based on the gold standard, became increasingly interdependent. European goods flowed into markets all over the globe. In turn, foreign products, raw materials, and foodstuffs were imported.

Europe had also quietly become dependent on the resources and markets of the rest of the world. Changes in the weather conditions in Kansas, Argentina, or New Zealand might now affect the European economy. However, prior to World War I, the dependence was concealed by Europe's industrial, military, and financial supremacy. At the time, people rather assumed that such supremacy was a natural situation, but the twentieth century would reveal it to have been quite temporary. Nevertheless, while that condition prevailed, Europeans were able to dominate most of the other peoples of the earth and to display the most extreme self-confidence.

The Middle Classes in Ascendancy

The sixty years before World War I were definitively the age of the middle classes, most especially in Western Europe. The Great Exhibition of 1851 held in the Crystal Palace in London had displayed the products and the new material life they had forged. Thereafter, the middle classes became the arbiter of much consumer taste and the defender of the status quo. After the revolutions of 1848, the middle classes ceased to be a revolutionary group. Most of their political goals had been attained, even if imperfectly. Once the question of social equality had been raised, large and small property owners across the Continent moved to protect what they possessed. In the late-century drive toward protective tariffs, new business organization, militarism, and empire, the upper levels of the middle class often joined political forces with the aristocracy and other groups, such as the Church and landowners, from traditionally conservative social and political backgrounds.

The middle classes, which had never been perfectly homogeneous, now became even more diverse. Their most prosperous members were the owners and managers of great businesses and banks. They lived in a splendor that rivaled and sometimes excelled that of the aristocracy. Some, such as W. H. Smith, the owner of railway newsstands in England, were made members of the House of Lords. The Krupp family of Germany were pillars of the state and received visits from the German emperor and his court. Only a few hundred families acquired such wealth. Beneath them were the comfortable small entrepreneurs and professional people, whose incomes permitted private homes, large quantities of furniture, pianos, pictures, books, journals, education for their children, and vacations. There were also the shopkeepers, the schoolteachers, the librarians, and others who had either a bit of property or a skill derived from education that provided respectable, nonmanual employment.

Finally, there was a wholly new element, namely the white-collar workers. These included secretaries, retail clerks, and lower-level bureaucrats in business and government. The white-collar labor force was often working class in its origins and might even have belonged to unions, but its aspirations for lifestyle were middle class. This lower-middle-class or petty-bourgeois element in society consciously sought to set itself off from the lifestyle of the working class. People from the lower middle class actively pursued educational opportunities and chances for even the slightest career advancement for themselves and their children. They also tended to spend a considerable portion of their disposable income on consumer goods, such as stylish clothing and furniture, that were distinctively middle-class in appearance.

Significant tensions began to exist among the various strata of middle-class society during the latter part of the century. The small businessmen and shopkeepers, whose numbers rose steadily until shortly after 1900, often resented the power of the great capitalists. The little people of the middle class feared being edged out of the marketplace by large companies, with whom they could not hope to compete. The shopkeeping class always had to work very hard simply to maintain their lifestyle and were often dependent on banks for commercial credit. Department stores and mail-order catalogs endangered their livelihood. There is also good reason to believe that the learned professions were becoming overcrowded. To be a professional person no longer ensured a sound income. The new white-collar work force had just attained respectability and a non-working-class status. They profoundly feared slipping back to their social origins.

Before World War I, these social groups were reasonably secure but remained quite apprehensive: they feared that the business cycle might turn against them; that their small supplementary incomes from stocks, bonds, or interest from savings might disappear; that somehow the socialists might confiscate their property. After World War I, many of those fears were realized. The profound insecurity that the middle classes then experienced became one of the most significant factors of twentieth-century political life.

Middle-class people lived in every community in Western Europe. But nowhere did they exert their influence and set the social and economic tenor of the day as they did in the cities.

Late-Nineteenth-Century Urban Life

Europe became more urbanized than ever in the sixty years before World War I. Migration within the Continent and Great Britain continued to move toward the cities. In France, the percentage of the urban population within the whole population rose between 1850 and 1911 from approximately 25 per cent to 44 per cent, and in Germany the shift was from 30 per cent to 60 per cent. In other countries of Western Europe by 1900, similar proportions of national populations lived in urban areas. The rural migrants to the cities were largely uprooted from traditional social ties. They often confronted poor housing, social anonymity, and potential unemployment because they rarely possessed skills that would make them easily employable. The difficulties that peoples from different ethnic backgrounds had in mixing socially and the competition for too few jobs generated new varieties of urban political and social discontent, such as were experienced by the

The elegance of Bon Marché, *one of the great Parisian department stores, is depicted in this print from the 1890s.* Bon Marché *was one of the first department stores in Paris and still exists. Built of wrought iron and marble, illuminated by huge glass domes, equipped with the newly invented electric lighting, it was a place for the middle classes to promenade as well as to shop. One nineteenth-century writer called these stores "cathedrals of commerce." [Mary Evans Picture Library.]*

thousands of Russian Jews who migrated to Western Europe. Much of the political anti-Semitism of the latter part of the century had its social roots in these problems of urban migration.

The Redesign of Cities

The inward urban migration placed new social and economic demands on already-strained city resources and gradually produced significant transformations in the patterns of urban living. The central portions of many major European cities were redesigned during the second half of the century. Previously, the central areas of cities had been places where large numbers of people from all social classes both lived and worked. From the middle of the century onward, they became transformed into districts where relatively few people resided and where businesses, government offices, large retail stores, and theaters were located. Commerce, trade, government, and leisure activities now dominated central cities.

The commercial development of the central portion of cities, the clearing of slums, and the building of railways into cities displaced large numbers of people who had previously lived in city centers. These developments also raised the price of centrally located urban land and of the rents charged on buildings located in the center of cities. Consequently, both the middle classes and the working class began to seek housing elsewhere. The middle classes looked for neighborhoods removed from urban congestion. The working class was in search of affordable housing. As a result, outside the urban center proper, there arose in virtually all countries suburbs that housed the families whose breadwinner worked in the central city or in factories located within the city limits. The expansion of railways with cheap workday fares and the introduction of mechanical and later electric tramways allowed tens of thousands of workers from all classes to move daily between the city and the outlying suburbs. For hundreds of thousands of Europeans, home and work became physically separated as never before.

This remarkable social change and the values it reflected became embodied in the new designs of many European cities. The most famous and extensive transformation of a major city occurred in Paris. Like so many other European cities, Paris had expanded from the Middle Ages onward with little or no design or planning. Great public buildings and squalid hovels stood near each other. The Seine River was little more than an open sewer. The streets were narrow, crooked, and crowded. It was impossible to cross easily from one part of Paris to another either on foot or by carriage. In 1850, there did not even exist a fully correct map of the city. Of more concern to the government of Napoleon III, those streets had for sixty years provided the battleground for urban insurrections that had, on numerous occasions, most recently in 1848, toppled French governments.

Napoleon III personally determined that Paris must be redesigned. He wished the city to be beautiful and to reflect the achievements of his regime and of modern technology. The person whom he put in charge of the rebuilding program was Georges Haussmann. As prefect of the Seine from 1853 to 1870, Haussmann oversaw a vast urban reconstruction program. Whole districts were destroyed to open the way for the broad boulevards and streets that became the hallmark of modern Paris. Much, though by no means all, of the purpose of this street planning was political. The wide vistas were not only beautiful but also allowed for the quick deployment of troops to put down riots. The eradication of the many small streets and alleys removed areas where barricades could be and had been erected. The project was political in another sense as well. In addition to the new boulevards, there were also constructed or completed parks, such as the Bois de Boulogne, and major public buildings, such as the Paris Opera. These projects, along with the demolition and street building, created a vast number of public jobs for thousands of people. Many other laborers found employment in the private construction that paralleled the public action.

The Franco-Prussian War ended the Second Empire, and the Paris Commune brought destruction to parts of the city. Further rebuilding and redesign took place under the Third Republic. There was much private construction of department stores, office complexes, and largely middle-class apartment buildings. By the late 1870s, mechanical trams were operating in Paris. After long debate, a subway system (the "Métro") was begun in 1895, long after that of London (1863). New railway stations were also erected near the close of the century. This transport linked the refurbished central city to the suburbs. In 1889, the Eiffel Tower was built, originally as a temporary structure for the international trade exposition of that year.

After the street fighting of the revolutions of 1848, the old fortifications of Vienna were torn down. In their place arose broad boulevards lined with fine buildings. The new streets were handsome—and were also better suited for rapid movement of troops against possible insurrection. This is an early photograph of a portion of the Ringstrasse, the street replaced the walls. [Austrian Information Service, New York.]

Not all the new structures of Paris bespoke the impact of middle-class commerce and the reign of iron and steel. Between 1873 and 1914, the French Roman Catholic church oversaw the construction of the Basilica of the Sacred Heart high atop Montmartre as an act of national penance for the sins that had led to French defeat in the Franco-Prussian War. Those two landmarks—the Eiffel Tower and the Basilica of the Sacred Heart—visibly symbolized the social and political divisions between liberals and conservatives in the Third Republic.

There were other important urban transformations in Europe during the second half of the nineteenth century. They also involved battles over social and political symbols. For example, in Manchester, the English city most associated with the harshness of the Industrial Revolution in textiles, the city fathers built a great town hall according to a neo-Gothic medieval design. They wanted to remind citizens of the power and pride of the medieval city merchants, whom they regarded as their cultural and economic forebears.

The situation was somewhat reversed in Vienna, from which the politically conservative Habsburg court governed its troubled multinational empire. But political liberals gained control of the Vienna city council in the early part of the second half of the century. They employed Camillo Sitte and Otto Wagner to redesign the central area of the city. The old medieval fortifications were removed, and in their place were constructed the great boulevards of the Ringstrasse. These new streets allowed the emperor and the army to exercise control over potential political disturbances. Yet those same boulevards allowed magnificent views of the parliament building, the university, and the city hall, which stood as symbols in the heart of Habsburg Vienna of the aspirations and values of the middle classes. As historian Carl Schorske observed, the Ringstrasse "embodied in stone and space a cluster of social values."[1] And beyond those civic buildings rose new structures devoted to shopping, commerce, and the leisured occupations of the middle classes. Such was the case in one city after another across Europe as the values of business, commerce, and material progress captured the urban civic imagination.

Urban Sanitation and Housing

The efforts of governments and of the increasingly conservative middle classes to maintain public order after 1848 led to a growing concern with the problems of public health and housing for the poor. There arose a widespread feeling that only when the health and housing of the working class were improved would the

health of the middle classes also be secure and the political order stable.

These concerns first manifested themselves as a result of the great cholera epidemics of the 1830s and 1840s, during which thousands of Europeans, especially those in cities, had died from this disease of Asian origin, previously unknown in Europe. Cholera, unlike many other common deadly diseases of the day that touched only the poor, struck persons from all classes and thus generated much middle-class demand for a solution. Before the development of the bacterial theory of disease, which was achieved only late in the century, physicians and sanitary reformers believed that cholera and other diseases were spread through infection from miasmas in the air. The miasmas, the presence of which was noted by their foul odors, were believed to arise from filth. The way to get rid of the dangerous, foul-smelling air was to clean up the cities.

The proposed solution to the health hazard was cleanliness, to be achieved through new water and sewer systems. The construction of these new facilities proceeded very slowly. They were usually first begun in capital cities and then much later in provincial cities. Some major urban areas did not have good water systems until after the turn of the century. Nonetheless, the building of these systems constituted one of the major health and engineering achievements of the second half of the nineteenth century. The sewer system of Paris became one of the most famous parts of Haussmann's rebuilding program. In London, the construction of the Albert Embankment along the Thames involved not only large sewers discharging into the river but gas mains and water pipes as well, encased in thick walls of granite and concrete, the latter being one of the new building materials of the day. Wherever these sanitary reforms were undertaken, considerable decreases in the mortality rate resulted.

This concern with public health led to a considerable expansion of governmental power on various levels. In Britain, the Public Health Act of 1848; in France the Melun Act of 1851; and various laws in the still-disunited German states, as well as later legislation, introduced new restraints on private life and enterprise. This legislation allowed medical officers and building inspectors to enter homes and other structures in the name of public health. Private property could be condemned for posing health hazards. Private land could be excavated for the construction of the sewers and water mains required to protect the public. New building regulations put restraints on the activities of private contractors.

When the bacterial theory of disease had become fully accepted at the close of the century, the necessity of cleanliness assumed an ever greater role in public life. The discoveries of Louis Pasteur in France, Robert Koch in Germany, and Joseph Lister in Britain paved

[1] Carl E. Schorske, *Fin-de-Siecle Vienna: Politics and Culture* (New York: Knopf, 1980), p. 62.

The first subway in the world was built in London between 1860 and 1863. However, subways did not become truly practicable until electricity replaced steam power. The great age of subway building began with the second London subway, opened in 1890. Within the next thirty years many of the great cities of Europe and America had subway systems. This print shows construction work on the London Underground. The Houses of Parliament are in the background. [Mary Evans Picture Library.]

the way for the slow acceptance of the use of antiseptics in the practice of medicine and in public health policy. Thereafter, throughout Europe, issues related to the maintenance of public health and the physical well-being of national populations repeatedly opened the way for new modes of government intervention in the lives of citizens and expanded to vast new dimensions the social role of medical and scientific experts and governmental bureaucracies.

The information about working-class living conditions brought to light by the sanitary reformers also led to heated debates over the housing problem. The wretched dwellings of the poor were themselves a cause of poor sanitation and thus became one of the newly perceived health hazards. Furthermore, middle-class reformers and bureaucrats found themselves shocked by the domestic arrangements of the poor, whose large families might live in a single room lacking all forms of personal privacy. A single toilet facility might be furnished for a whole block of tenements. After the revolutions of 1848, the overcrowding in housing and the social discontent that it generated also appeared as a political danger that demanded remedy.

Middle-class reformers thus turned to housing reform as a solution to the medical, moral, and political dangers posed by slums. They praised the home, as it was understood by the middle class, as a remedy for these dangers. Proper, decent housing would foster a good home life, which would, in turn, lead to a healthy, moral, and politically stable population. As A. V. Huber, one of the early German housing reformers, declared, "Certainly it would not be too much to say that the home is the communal embodiment of family life. Thus the purity of the dwelling is almost as important for the family as is the cleanliness of the

The building of sewers for the disposal of urban waste was one of the great accomplishments of nineteenth-century sanitary engineering. This picture was made inside one of the sewers of Paris. [French Cultural Services, New York.]

body for the individual. Good or bad housing is a question of life and death if ever there was one."[2] Later advocates of housing reform, such as Jules Simon in France, saw good housing as leading to good family life and then to strong national patriotism on the part of the well-housed family. It was widely believed that if the poor and the working class could enjoy adequate, respectable, cheap housing, much social and political discontent would be overcome. It was also believed that the personal saving and investment required for owning a home would lead the working class to adopt the thrifty habits of the middle classes.

The first attacks on the housing problem came from private philanthropy. Companies that operated on a very low margin of profit or that loaned money for housing construction at low interest rates encouraged the building of housing for the poor. Some major industrial companies undertook similar housing programs. They tended to favor the construction of small individual houses or cottages that would ensure for the working class the kind of detached dwellings associated with the middle classes. Model housing projects

---

[2] Quoted in Nicholas Bullock and James Read, *The Movement for Housing Reform in Germany and France, 1840–1914* (Cambridge: Cambridge University Press, 1985), p. 42.

and industrial communities were constructed by industrial firms, such as the German Krupp armament concern, in all the major European nations. All of them were seeking to ensure a contented, healthy, and stable work force. These early private efforts to address the housing problem reflected the usual liberal tendency to favor private rather than governmental enterprise.

By the mid-1880s, as a result of record-breaking migration into the cities of Europe, the housing issue had come to the fore as a political question. Some form of governmental action seemed inescapable. The actual policies differed markedly in each country, but all were quite hesitant. In England, the first steps toward public housing came in the form of an act of 1885 that lowered interest rates for the construction of cheap housing. A few years later, local town councils, especially that of London, began to construct public housing. In Germany, action came somewhat later in the century, primarily through the initiative of local municipalities. In 1894, France passed legislation making credit available on an easier basis for the housing of the poor, and the terms of this legislation were somewhat expanded after the turn of the century. No government had undertaken really large-scale housing experiments before World War I. Most legislation, though not all, was permissive in nature and facilitated the construction of cheap housing by the private sector.

By 1914, the housing problem stood fully recognized if not adequately addressed. What had been recognized was the necessity for planning and action. The middle-class housing reformers had, moreover, defined the terms of the debate and of future planning. The values and the character of the middle-class family house and home had become the ideal. The goal of housing reform across Western Europe came to be that of a dwelling, whether in the form of a detached house or some kind of affordable city apartment with several rooms, a private entrance, and separate toilet facilities that would allow the working class to enjoy a family life more or less along the lines of the middle classes.

GROWTH OF MAJOR EUROPEAN CITIES (FIGURES IN THOUSANDS)			
	1850	*1880*	*1910*
Berlin	419	1,122	2,071
Birmingham	233	437	840
Frankfurt	65	137	415
London	2,685	4,470	7,256
Madrid	281	398	600
Paris	1,053	2,269	2,888
Vienna	444	1,104	2,031

Varieties of Late-Nineteenth-Century Women's Experience

The complexities of general European society reflected themselves in the variety of social experiences encountered by women. The lives of women in the various social ranks partook of the general lifestyle of those particular classes. Yet, within each of those social ranks, the experience of women was distinct from that of men. Women remained, generally speaking, in positions of economic dependence and legal inferiority, whatever their social class.

The pattern of gender-defined social roles that had begun to develop in the early nineteenth century in the industrialized sections of Western Europe spread during the later part of the century wherever industrialism and urbanization came to dominate, and especially wherever middle-class values predominated. Men worked as the chief family wage earner. Young women in the working class and the lower middle class still spent part of their youth working to support themselves and to accumulate enough money to marry. After these women married, they tended to work at home. Such was the expected social pattern for late-nineteenth-century women. Problems arose as the lives of many women did not or could not conform to this pattern. There was little or no provision for women who did not marry or who had to support themselves independently.

New Employment Patterns for Women

During the decades of the second half of the nineteenth century, two major developments affected the economic lives of women. The first was an explosion in the variety of available jobs. The second was a significant withdrawal of married women from the work force. These two seemingly contradictory situations require some explanation.

The expansion of governmental bureaucracies, the emergence of corporations and other large-scale businesses, the new and growing demand for schoolteachers resulting from compulsory education laws, and the vast expansion of retail stores of all kinds opened many new employment opportunities for women. Technological inventions and innovations such as the typewriter and eventually the telephone exchange fostered female employment. Women by the thousands became secretaries and clerks for governments and for private businesses. Still more thousands became shop assistants. These new jobs did mean new and often somewhat better employment opportunities for women, but these new jobs still required relatively low levels of skill and involved minimal training. They were occupied primarily by unmarried women or widows. Schoolteaching also became rapidly identified as a female occupation, but women very rarely entered the university world or the learned professions. They were even more rarely to be found in major positions of private or public management.

Furthermore, employers continued to pay women low wages because they assumed, quite often knowing better, that a woman did not need to support herself independently but could expect additional financial support from her father or from her husband. Consequently, a woman who did need to support herself independently was almost always unable to find a job paying an adequate income or a position that paid as well as one held by a man, who was supporting himself independently.

Most of the women in this new service work force were young and unmarried. At the time of marriage, or certainly after the birth of her first child, a woman normally withdrew from the labor force. She either did not work or she worked at some occupation that could be pursued in the home. Such withdrawal in and of itself was not new by the latter part of the century, but the extent of it was much more significant. The kinds of industrial occupations that women had filled in the middle of the nineteenth century, especially textile and garment making, were shrinking. There were consequently fewer opportunities for employment in those industries for either married or unmarried women. Employers in offices and retail stores seem to have preferred young, unmarried women whose family responsibilities would not interfere with their work. The shrinkage in the number of children being born meant that fewer married women were needed to look after other women's children.

The real wages paid to male workers increased during this period, so that there was a somewhat reduced need for the supplementary wages of their wives. Also, men tended to live longer as a result of improving health conditions, and their wives had to enter the work force less frequently in emergencies. The smaller size of families also lowered the need for supplementary wages. Working children stayed longer at home and continued to contribute to the family's wage pool. Finally, the cultural dominance of the middle class, with its generally idle wives, established a pattern of social expectations according to which the more prosperous a working-class family became, the less involved in employment its women were supposed to be. Indeed, the less income-producing work a wife did, the more prosperous and stable the family was considered.

Yet behind these generalities stands a vast variety of different social and economic experiences encountered by women. As might be expected, the chief determinant of those individual experiences was social class.

Women working in the Cadbury candy factory in England. In the late nineteenth century, although most working women were domestic servants, for the first time many women began to work in factories and stores. [Cadbury Limited, Bournville, England.]

Working-class Women

Although the textile industry and garment making were much less dominant than earlier in the century, they continued to employ large numbers of women. The situation of women in the German clothing-making trades illustrates the kind of vulnerable economic situation that they could encounter as a result of their limited skills and the organization of the trade. The system of manufacturing mass-made clothes of uniform sizes in Germany was quite complex. It was designed to require minimal capital investment on the part of the manufacturers and to protect them from significant risk. A major manufacturer would arrange for the production of clothing through a putting-out system. He would purchase the material and then put it out for tailoring. The clothing was produced not in a factory but usually in numerous, independently owned, small sweatshops or by workers in their homes. In Berlin in 1896 there were over eighty thousand garment workers, mostly women, who were so employed. When business was good and the demand strong, there was much employment for these women. But as the seasons shifted or business became poor, these workers became unemployed as less and less work was put out for production. In effect, the workers who actually sewed the clothing carried much of the risk of the enterprise. Some women did work in factories, but they, too, were subject to loss of work. Furthermore, women in the clothing trade were nearly always in positions less skilled than those of the male tailors or the male middlemen who owned the workshops.

In a very real sense, the expectation of separate social and economic spheres for men and women and the definition of the chief work of women as pertaining to the home contributed mightily to the exploitation of women workers outside the home. Because their wages were regarded merely as supplementing their husbands', they became particularly vulnerable to economic exploitation. The entire German putting-out system for clothing production and similar systems of clothing production elsewhere depended on this situation. What was regarded as an adequate wage for a woman was always seen in terms of a wage supplementary to the husband's. Consequently, women were nearly always treated as casual workers everywhere in Europe.

Prostitution

One of the major but little recognized social facts of most large and small nineteenth-century cities was the presence of a very considerable surplus of women workers whose social situation did not allow them to conform to those normal expectations of working only for wages supplementary to a father's or a husband's. There were almost always many more women seeking employment than there were jobs. The economic vulnerability of women and the consequent poverty encountered by many of them was one of the chief causes of prostitution. In any major late-nineteenth-century European city, there were thousands of prostitutes. The presence of prostitution was, of course, not new. It had always been one way for very poor women to find some income, but in the late nineteenth century it seems to have been quite closely related to the difficulty encountered by very poor women who were attempting to make their way in an overcrowded female labor force. On the Continent, prostitution was generally legalized and was subject to governmental and municipal regulations. Those regulations were, it should be noted, passed and enforced by male legislatures and councils and were enforced by male police and physicians. In Great Britain, prostitution received only minimal regulation.

Numerous myths and much misunderstanding have surrounded the subject of prostitution. The most recent studies of the subject in England emphasize that most prostitutes were active on the streets for a very few years, generally from their late teens to about age twenty-five. They tended to be very poor women who had recently migrated from nearby rural areas. Others were born in the towns where they became prostitutes. Certain cities—such as towns with large army garrisons, naval port cities, or cities with large transient populations such as London—fostered the presence of considerable numbers of prostitutes. There seem to have been many fewer prostitutes in manufacturing towns, where there were more opportunities for steady employment and where community life was more stable.

Women who became prostitutes tended to have minimal skills and education and to have come from families of unskilled workers. Many had been servants. They also tended to be from broken homes or to be orphaned. Contrary to many sensational late-century newspaper accounts, there seem to have been very few child prostitutes. Furthermore, rarely were these women seduced into their occupations by middle-class employers or middle-class clients. The customers of poor working-class prostitutes seem to have been primarily working-class men. Women remained prostitutes for relatively few years. Thereafter they seem to have moved back into the regular work force or to have married.

Women of the Middle Class

It is difficult to communicate the vast social gap that lay between the experience of poor working-class women whose economic situation led them into prostitution or into the sweated textile trades and those of their middle-class counterparts. Middle-class women participated as their fathers' and husbands' incomes permitted in the vast expansion of consumerism and domestic comfort that marked the end of the nineteenth century and the early twentieth century. Their homes were filled with manufactured items, including clothing, china, furniture, carpets, drapery, wallpaper, and prints. They enjoyed all the improvements of sanitation and electricity. They could command the services of numerous domestic servants. They moved into the fashionable new houses being constructed in the rapidly expanding suburbs.

For the middle classes, the gender distinction between work and family had become complete and constituted the model for all other social groups. Middle-class women, if at all possible, did not work. More than any other group of women, they became limited to the role of wife and mother. That situation allowed them to enjoy much domestic luxury and comfort, but it also no less markedly circumscribed what they might do with their lives, their talents, their ambitions, and their intelligence. Middle-class women became, in large measure, the product of a particular understanding of social life. The home and its occupants were to have lives very different from the life of business and the marketplace. The home was not only to be distinct from the world of work and business, but it was also to be a private refuge from that life. This view was set forth in scores of women's journals across Europe.

As studies of the lives of middle-class women in northern France have suggested, this image of the middle-class home and of the role of women in the home is quite different from the one that had existed earlier in the nineteenth century. During the first half of the century, the spouse of a middle-class husband might very well contribute directly to the business, handling accounts or correspondence. These women also frequently had little to do with rearing their children; they left that task first to nurses and later to governesses. This situation was very different later in the century. The reasons for the change are not certain, but it would appear that men began to insist on doing business with other men. Magazines and books directed toward women began to praise motherhood, domesticity, religion, and charity as the proper work of women.

For these middle-class French women, as well as for middle-class women elsewhere, the home came to be praised as the center of virtue, of children, and of the proper life for women. Marriages were usually arranged for some kind of family economic benefit. Romantic marriage was presented as a danger to social stability. Most middle-class women in northern France married by the age of twenty-one. Children were expected to follow very soon after marriage. Quite often a child was born within the first year, and the rearing and nurturing of that child and of later children was the chief task in life for the woman. Such a woman would have had no experience of or training for any role other than that of a dutiful daughter, wife, and mother.

Within the home, a middle-class woman performed major roles. She was largely in charge of the household. She oversaw virtually all domestic management and child care. She was in a very real sense in charge of the home as a major unit of consumption. It was for this reason that so much advertising was directed toward women. But all of this domestic activity occurred within the limits of the approved middle-class lifestyle and set relatively strict limits on a woman's initiative. She and

The Virtues of a French Middle-class Lady Praised

One of the chief social roles assigned to middle-class French women was that of chari-table activity. This obituary of Mme. Émile Delesalle from a Roman Catholic church paper of the late nineteenth century describes the work of this woman among the poor. It is a very revealing document because it clearly shows the class divisions that existed in the giving of charity. It also is a document that instructed its women readers through the kind of virtues praised. Note the emphasis on home life, spirituality, and instruc-tion of children in charitable acts.

The poor were the object of her affectionate interest, especially the shameful poor, the fallen people. She sought them out and helped them with perfect discre-tion which doubled the value of her benevolent inter-est. To those whom she could approach without fear of bruising their dignity, she brought, along with alms to assure their existence, consolation of the most serious sort—she raised their courage and their hopes. To others, each Sunday, she opened all the doors of her home, above all when her children were still young. In making them distribute these alms with her, she hoped to initiate them early into practices of charity.

In the last years of her life the St. Gabriel Orphan-age gained her interest. Not only did she accomplish a great deal with her generosity, but she also took on the task of maintaining the clothes of her dear orphans in good order and in good repair. When she appeared in the courtyard of the establishment at recreation time, all her protégés surrounded her and lavished her with manifestations of their profound respect and affection-ate gratitude. ❑

Annales de l'archiconfrérie des mères chrétiennes, as quoted and trans. in Bonnie G. Smith, *Ladies of the Leisure Class: The Bourgeoises of Northern France in the Nineteenth Century* (Princeton, N.J.: Princeton University Press, 1981), pp. 147–148.

her conspicuous idleness served to symbolize first her father's and then her husband's worldly success.

This cult of domesticity in France and elsewhere assigned to women very firm religious duties. The Roman Catholic church strongly supported these do-mestic and religious roles for French women. Frequent attendance at mass and religious instruction of their children were part of this role. Women were charged with observing meatless Fridays and with participating in religious observances. Prayer was a major part of their lives and daily rituals. Those portions of the Christian religion that stressed meekness and passiv-ity became a major part of the mind set of these middle-class French women. In other countries as well, religion and religious activities became part of the expected work of women. For this reason, women were regarded by political liberals as especially sus-ceptible to the influence of priests. This close associa-tion between religion and a strict domestic life for women was one of the reasons that as time passed, there often arose tension between feminism and reli-gious authorities.

Another important role for these middle-class women was the administration of charity. Women were judged especially prepared to carry out charita-ble roles because of their supposed innate spirituality and their capacity to instill domestic and personal dis-cipline. Middle-class women were often in charge of clubs for poor youth, societies to protect poor young women, schools for infants, and societies for visiting the poor. Women were supposed to be particularly in-terested in the problems of poor women, their families, and their children. Quite often, charity from middle-class women required the poor recipient to indicate in some manner the possession of a good character. By the end of the century, middle-class women who were attempting to expand their spheres of activity became social workers either for the Church, for private chari-ties, or for the government. It was a vocation that was a natural extension of the roles socially assigned to them.

The world of the middle-class wife and her family is now understood to have been much more complicated than was once thought. Not all such women or their families conformed to the stereotypes. First, recent studies have suggested that the middle classes of the nineteenth century enjoyed sexual relations within marriage far more fully than was once thought. Dia-ries, letters, and even early medical and sociological sex surveys indicate that sexual enjoyment rather than sexual repression was fundamental to middle-class marriages. Much of the inhibition about sexuality stemmed from the actual dangers of childbirth rather than from any dislike or disapproval of sexuality.

Second, one of the major changes in this regard dur-ing the second half of the century was the acceptance of small family size among the middle classes. The fertility rate in France dropped throughout the nineteenth century. It began to fall in England steadily from the 1870s onward. Middle-class married couples seem to have begun to make conscious decisions to limit the size of their families. During the last decades of the century, various new contraceptive devices such as rubber condoms became available and were used by middle-class families. One of the chief reasons for this change was the apparently conscious decision made by couples to maintain a relatively high level of material consumption by rearing fewer children. Children had become much more expensive to rear, and at the same time, more material comforts had become available. The presence of fewer children in the middle-class household probably meant that more attention was focused on the child and that mothers and their children became emotionally closer.

The Rise of Feminism

As can be seen from the previous discussion, liberal society and its values neither automatically nor inevitably improved the lot of women. Divorce was difficult everywhere. Most property laws until well into the second half of the century favored husbands or gave them virtually complete control over their wives' property. In France, for example, the major political legislation of the revolution and the Napoleonic Code excluded women from voting and made them subject to their husbands. There was a general apprehension among male political liberals that granting the vote to women would benefit political conservatives because it was widely assumed that women were unduly controlled by Roman Catholic priests. There was a similar apprehension about the alleged influence of the Anglican clergy over women in England. Consequently, anticlerical liberals had difficulty working with feminists.

Those few women who pioneered female entry into the professions, activity on government commissions and school boards, or dispersal of birth control information faced grave social obstacles, personal humiliation, and often outright bigotry. These women and their male supporters were challenging that clear separation of life into male and female spheres that had emerged in middle-class European social life during the nineteenth century. Women themselves were often hesitant to support feminist causes, because females had been so thoroughly acculturated into the recently stereotyped roles. Many women as well as men saw a real conflict between family responsibilities and feminism.

But there was another important reason for the frequent absence of support for feminist causes by women. Issues of gender constituted only one of several priorities in the minds and social concerns of women. Some women were very sensitive to their class and economic interests. Others subordinated feminist issues to national unity and nationalistic patriotism. Still others would not support particular feminist organizations because of differences over tactics. The various social and tactical differences among women led quite often to sharp divisions within the feminists' own ranks. Except in England, it was often difficult for working-class and middle-class women to cooperate. Roman Catholic feminists were uncomfortable with radical secularist feminists. There were other disagreements about which goals for improvement in women's legal and social conditions were most important.

Liberal society and law had set up many obstacles to women's developing their lives fully, and the necessity of working within the political structures of liberal states raised many of the issues that divided women. However, the intellectual and political tools for feminists' social and political criticisms were also present in the ideology of liberal society. The rationalism and the penchant for self-criticism that have characterized modern Western society manifested themselves in the movement to emancipate women. As early as 1792 in Britain, Mary Wollstonecraft (1759–1797), in *The Vindication of the Rights of Woman*, had applied the revolutionary doctrines of the rights of man to the predicament of the members of her own sex. John Stuart Mill (1806–1873), in conjunction with his wife Harriet Taylor, had applied the logic of liberal freedom to the position of women in *The Subjection of Women* (1869).

The arguments for utility and efficiency so dear to middle-class liberals could be used to expose the human and social waste implicit in the inferior role assigned to women. Furthermore, the socialist criticism of capitalist society often, though by no means always, included a harsh indictment of the social and economic position to which women had been relegated. Yet, the very fact that the earliest statements of feminism arose from critics of the existing order and were often associated with people who had unorthodox opinions about sexuality, family life, and property hardened resistance to the feminist message. This seems to have been especially true on the Continent, where feminists were never able to stir up massive public support or demonstrations as they were in Great Britain and the United States.

Much of the discussion of the social position of women remained merely theory and talk. Some women did gain meaningful employment in the professions, but their numbers were quite small. Women did not rise rapidly through the work force. However, to some extent, theory was transformed into practice, or at least into protest, as far as political life was concerned. The political tactics used by men to expand the electoral franchise and to influence the governing process earlier in the century could be and were used by

An English Feminist Defends the Cause of the Female Franchise

Frances Power Cobbe wrote widely on numerous religious and social issues of the second half of the century. She had been a feminist since early adulthood. In this letter to an English feminist magazine in 1884, she explained why women should seek the vote. More important, she attempted to refute the argument that possession of the franchise would in some manner make women less womanly.

If I may presume to offer an old woman's counsel to the younger workers in our cause, it would be that they should adopt the point of view—that it is before all things our *duty* to obtain the franchise. If we undertake the work in this spirit, and with the object of using the power it confers, whenever we gain it, for the promotion of justice and mercy and the kingdom of God upon earth, we shall carry on all our agitation in a corresponding manner, firmly and bravely, and also calmly and with generous good temper. And when our opponents come to understand that this is the motive underlying our efforts, they, on their part, will cease to feel bitterly and scornfully toward us, even when they think we are altogether mistaken. . . .

The idea that the possession of political rights will destroy "womanliness," absurd as it may seem to us, is very deeply rooted in the minds of men; and when

they oppose our demands, it is only just to give them credit for doing so on grounds which we should recognize as valid, if *their premises were true*. It is not so much that our opponents (at least the better part of them) despise women, as that they really prize what women now are in the home and in society so highly that they cannot bear to risk losing it by any serious change in their condition. These fears are futile and faithless, but there is nothing in them to affront us. To remove them, we must not use violent words, for every such violent word confirms their fears; but, on the contrary, show the world that while the revolutions wrought by men have been full of bitterness and rancor and stormy passions, if not of bloodshed, we women will at least strive to accomplish our great emancipation calmly and by persuasion and reason. ❑

Letter to the *Woman's Tribune*, May 1, 1884, quoted in Frances Power Cobbe, *Life of Frances Power Cobbe by Herself* (Boston: Houghton, Mifflin, 1894).

In 1911 Mrs. Emmeline Pankhurst led major demonstrations of British suffragettes in favor of the vote for women. Several ended in violence. Here Mrs. Pankhurst is literally being carried off to jail. [Culver Pictures.]

women later in the century to pursue the same goal. The claims to political participation set forth by the respectable, prosperous, and educated working class applied equally well to respectable, prosperous, and educated women. Nonetheless, virtually everywhere, the feminist cause was badly divided.

The most advanced women's movement in Europe was in Great Britain. There Millicent Fawcett (1847–1929) led the moderate National Union of Women's Suffrage Societies. Her view was that Parliament would grant women the vote only when convinced that women would be respectable and responsible in their political activity. In 1908, this organization could rally almost half a million women in London. Fawcett was the wife of a former liberal party Cabinet minister and economist. Her tactics were those of English liberals.

Emmeline Pankhurst (1858–1928) led a different and much more radical branch of British feminists. Pankhurst's husband, who had died near the close of the century, had been active in labor and Irish nationalist politics. Irish nationalists had developed numerous disruptive political tactics. Early labor politicians had also sometimes had confrontations with police over the right to hold meetings. In 1903, Pankhurst and her daughters, Christabel and Sylvia, founded the Women's Social and Political Union. For several years, they and their followers, known derisively as *suffragettes*, lobbied publicly and privately for the extension of the vote to women. By 1910, having failed to move the government, they turned to the violent tactics of arson, window breaking, and sabotage of postal boxes. They marched en masse on Parliament. The Liberal government of Henry Asquith imprisoned many of the women and force-fed those who went on hunger strikes in jail. The government refused to extend the franchise. Only in 1918 did some British women receive the vote as a result of their contribution to the war effort.

How advanced the British women's movement was can be seen by the contrast in France and Germany. In France, Hubertine Auclert (1848–1914) had begun campaigning for the vote in the 1880s. She stood virtually alone. During the 1890s, the National Council of French Women (CNFF) was organized among upper-middle-class women, but it did not support the idea of the vote for women until after the turn of the century. French Roman Catholic feminists such as Marie Mauguet (1844–1928) supported the franchise also. But almost all French feminists rejected any form of violence. They also were never able to organize mass rallies. The leaders of French feminism believed that the vote could be achieved through careful legalism. In 1919, the French Chamber of Deputies passed a bill granting the vote to women, but in 1922 the French Senate defeated the bill. It was not until after World War II that French women received the right to vote.

In Germany, the situation of feminist awareness and action was even more underdeveloped. German law actually forbade German women from political activity. Because no group in the German Empire enjoyed extensive political rights, women were not certain that they would benefit from demanding them. Any such demand would be regarded as subversive not only of the political state but also of German society. In 1894, the Union of German Women's Organizations (BDFK) was founded. By 1902, it was supporting a call for the right to vote. But the union was largely concerned with improvement of women's social conditions, access to education, and other protections. The group also worked to see that women might be admitted to political or civic activity on the municipal level. This work usually included education, child welfare, charity, and public health. The German Social Democratic Party supported women's suffrage, but this position made the demand all the more suspect in the eyes of the German authorities and especially in the view of German Roman Catholics. Women received the vote in Germany only in 1918, when the constitution of the Weimar Republic was promulgated after German defeat in war and revolution at home.

Throughout Europe in the years before World War I, the demands for women's rights were raised widely and vocally. But the extent of their success and their tactics tended in very large measure to reflect the political and class structures of the individual nations. Before World War I, only in Norway (1907) could women vote on national issues.

Labor, Socialism, and Politics to World War I

The Working Classes

The late-century industrial expansion wrought further changes in the life of the labor force. In all industrializing continental countries, the numbers of the urban proletariat rose. Proportionally, there were many fewer artisans and highly skilled workers. For the first time, factory wage earners came to predominate. The increasingly mechanized factories often required less highly technical skills from their operatives. There also occurred considerable growth in the very unskilled work associated with shipping, transportation, and building. Work assumed a more impersonal character. Factories were located in cities, and almost all links between factory or day-labor employment and home life dissolved. Large corporate enterprise meant less personal contact between employers and their workers. During the latter years of the nineteenth century, a few big businesses attempted to provide some security for their employees through company housing and pension plans. Although these efforts were in a few cases pioneering, they could not prove adequate for the mass of labor force.

TRADE UNIONISM. Workers still had to look to themselves for the improvement of their situation. However, after 1848, European workers ceased taking to the streets to voice their grievances in the form of riots. They also stopped trying to revive the paternal guilds and similar institutions of the past. After mid-century, the labor force accepted the fact of modern industrial production and its general downgrading of skills and attempted to receive more benefits from that system. Workers turned to new institutions and ideologies. Chief among these were trade unions, democratic political parties, and socialism.

Trade unionism came of age as legal protections were extended to unions throughout the second half of the century. Unions became fully legal in Great Britain in 1871 and were allowed to picket in 1875. In France, Napoleon III had first used troops against strikes, but as his political power waned, he allowed weak labor associations in 1868. The Third French Republic fully legalized unions in 1884. After 1890, they could function in Germany with little disturbance. Initially, most trade unions entered the political process in a rather marginal fashion. As long as the representatives of the

The Krupp works at Essen, Germany, was one of the largest military factories in Europe. This photograph was taken in the gun shop. The massive production of such arms meant that in the early twentieth century Europeans would be able to turn on themselves more sheer physically destructive force than at any previous time in history. [Culver Pictures.]

traditional governing classes looked after labor interests, members of the working class rarely sought office themselves.

The mid-century organizational efforts of the unions were directed toward skilled workers. The goal was the immediate improvement of wages and working conditions. By the close of the century, industrial unions for unskilled workers were being organized. They were very large and included thousands of workers. They confronted extensive opposition from employers, and long strikes were frequently required to bring about employer acceptance. In the prewar decade, there were an exceedingly large number of strikes throughout Europe as the unions attempted to raise wages to keep up with inflation. However, despite the advances of unions and the growth of their membership in 1910 to approximately 3 million in Britain, 2 million in Germany, and 977,000 in France, they never included a majority of the industrial labor force. What the unions did represent was a new collective fashion in which workers could associate to confront the economic difficulties of their lives and to attain better security.

DEMOCRACY AND POLITICAL PARTIES. The democratic franchise provided workers with direct po-

litical influence, which meant that they could no longer be ignored. With the exception of Russia, all the major European states adopted broad-based, if not perfectly democratic, electoral systems. Great Britain passed its second voting-reform act in 1867 and its third in 1884. Bismarck brought universal manhood suffrage to the German Empire in 1871. The French Chamber of Deputies was democratically elected. Universal manhood suffrage was adopted in Switzerland in 1879, in Spain in 1890, in Belgium in 1893, in the Netherlands in 1896, and in Norway in 1898. Italy finally fell into line in 1912. Democracy brought new modes of popular pressure to bear on all governments. It meant that discontented groups could now voice their grievances and advocate their programs within the institutions of government rather than from the outside.

The advent of democracy witnessed the formation for the first time in Europe of organized mass political parties, which had existed throughout the nineteenth century in the United States. In the liberal European states with narrow electoral bases, most voters had been people of property who knew what they had at stake in politics. Organization had been minimal. The new expansion of the electorate brought into the political processes many people whose level of political consciousness, awareness, and interest was quite low.

This electorate had to be organized and taught the nature of power and influence in the liberal democratic state. The organized political party—with its workers, newspapers, offices, social life, and discipline—was the vehicle that mobilized the new voters. The largest single group in these mass electorates was the working class. The democratization of politics presented the socialists with opportunities and required the traditional ruling class to vie with the socialists for the support of the new voters.

Marx and the First International

Karl Marx himself made considerable accommodation to the new practical realities that developed during the third quarter of the century. He did not abandon the revolutionary doctrines of *The Communist Manifesto*, and in *Capital* (Vol. 1, 1867), he continued to predict the disintegration of capitalism. His private thoughts, as revealed in his letters, also remained quite revolutionary, but his practical, public political activity reflected a somewhat different approach.

In 1864, a group of British and French trade unionists founded the International Working Men's Association. Known as the First International, it encompassed in its membership a vast array of radical political types, including socialists, anarchists, and Polish nationalists. The First International allowed Marx, who was by then quite active in the London radical community, to write its inaugural address. In it, he urged radical social change and the economic emancipation of the working class, but he also supported and approved efforts by workers and trade unions to reform the conditions of labor within the existing political and economic processes. He urged revolution but tempered the means. Privately, he often criticized such reformist activity, but those writings were not made public until near the end of the century, and after his death.

During the late 1860s, the First International gathered statistics, kept labor groups informed of mutual problems, provided a forum for the debate of socialist doctrine, and extravagantly proclaimed its own size and influence. From these debates and activities, Marxism emerged as the single most important strand of socialism. In 1872, Marx and his supporters drove the anarchists out of the First International. Marx was determined to preserve the role of the state against the anarchist attack on authority and large political organizations. Through the meetings and discussions of the First International, German socialists became deeply impressed by Marx's thought. Because, as will be seen, they became the most important socialist party in Europe, they became the chief channel for the preservation and development of Marxist thought.

The First International proved to be a very fragile structure. The events surrounding the Paris Commune presented the final blow to its existence. Few socialists and only one real Marxist were involved in the commune. However, Marx, in a major pamphlet, glorified the commune as a genuine proletarian uprising. British trade unionists, who in 1871 were finally receiving new legal protection, wanted no connection with the crimes of the Parisians. The French authorities used the uprising as an occasion to suppress socialist activity. Throughout Europe, the events in Paris cast a pall over socialism. The First International held its last European congress in 1873. Its offices were then transferred to the United States, where it was dissolved in 1876. Thereafter, the fate of socialism and the labor movement depended largely on the economic and political conditions of the individual European countries.

Great Britain: The Labour Party and Fabianism

Neither Marxism nor any other form of socialism made significant progress in Great Britain, the most advanced industrial society of the day. There trade unions grew steadily and the members normally supported Liberal Party candidates. The "new unionism" of the late 1880s and the 1890s organized the dock workers, the gas workers, and similar unskilled groups. Employer resistance to unions heightened class antagonism. In 1892, Keir Hardie became the first independent working man to be elected to Parliament. The next year the small, socialist Independent Labour Party was founded, but it remained ineffective.

Until 1901, general political activity on the part of labor remained quite limited. In that year, however, a decision by the House of Lords removed the legal protection previously accorded union funds. The Trades Union Congress responded by launching the Labour Party. In the election of 1906, the fledgling party sent twenty-nine members to Parliament. Their goals as trade unionists did not yet encompass socialism. Along with this new political departure, the British labor movement became more militant. There were scores of strikes before the war, as workers fought for wages to meet the rising cost of living. The government took a larger role than ever before in mediating these strikes, which in 1911 and 1912 involved the railways, the docks, and the mines.

British socialism itself remained primarily the preserve of intellectuals. The socialists who exerted the most influence were from the Fabian Society, founded in 1884. The society took its name from Q. Fabius Maximus, the Roman general who defeated Hannibal by waiting a very long time before attacking. Through its name, the society intended to indicate a gradualist approach to major social reform. Its leading members were Sydney (1859–1947) and Beatrice (1858–1943) Webb, H. G. Wells (1866–1946), and George Bernard Shaw (1856–1950). Many of the Fabians were civil servants who believed that the problems of industry, the

approximately forty members to the Chamber of Deputies by the early 1890s.

At the turn of the century, the two major factions of French socialism were led by Jean Jaurés (1859–1914) and Jules Guesde (1845–1922). Jaurés believed that socialists should cooperate with radical middle-class ministries to ensure the enactment of needed social legislation. Guesde opposed this policy, arguing that socialists could not, with integrity, support a bourgeois cabinet that they were theoretically dedicated to overthrow. The quarrel came to a head as a by-product of the Dreyfus affair (see Chapter 26). In 1899, as a means of uniting all supporters of Dreyfus, Prime Minister René Waldeck-Rousseau (1846–1904) appointed the socialist Alexander Millerand to the Cabinet. By 1904, the issue of "opportunism," as such Cabinet par-

Under a Dutch banner calling for the proletariat of all lands to unite, a congress of the Second Socialist International meets in Amsterdam in 1904 to debate ideology and tactics. [International Instituut voor Sociale Geschiedenis, Amsterdam.]

Beatrice and Sidney Webb, a photograph from the late 1920s. These most influential British Fabian Socialists wrote many books on governmental and economic matters, served on special parliamentary commissions, and agitated for the enactment of socialist policies. [Radio Times Hulton Picture Library.]

expansion of ownership, and the state direction of production could be achieved gradually, peacefully, and democratically. They sought to educate the country to the rational wisdom of socialism. They were particularly interested in modes of collective ownership on the municipal level, or so-called gas-and-water socialism.

France: "Opportunism" Rejected

French socialism gradually revived after the suppression of the Paris Commune. The institutions of the Third Republic provided a framework for legal activity. The major problem for French socialists was their own internal division rather than government opposition. There were no fewer than five separate parties, plus other independent socialists. They managed to elect

ticipation by socialists was termed, came to be debated at the Amsterdam Congress of the Second International. This organization had been founded in 1889 in a new effort to unify the various national socialist parties and trade unions. The Amsterdam Congress condemned "opportunism" in France and ordered the French socialist to form a single party. Jaurés, believing socialist unity the most important issue in France, accepted the decision. French socialists began to work together, and by 1914, the recently united Socialist Party was the second largest group in the Chamber of Deputies. Socialist Party members would not again serve in a French Cabinet until the Popular Front Government of 1936.

Germany: Social Democrats and Revisionism

The judgment rendered by the Second International against French socialist participation in bourgeois ministries reflected a policy of permanent hostility to nonsocialist governments previously adopted by the German Social Democratic Party (SPD). The organizational success of this party, more than any other single factor, kept Marxist socialism alive into the latter part of the century.

The SPD was founded in 1875, but its forging experience was twelve years of persecution by Otto von Bismarck, who believed socialism would undermine German politics and society. In 1878, there was an attempt to assassinate William I. Bismarck blamed the socialists, who were not involved, and steered a number of antisocialist laws through the *Reichstag*. These measures suppressed the organization, meetings, newspapers, and other public activities of the SPD. The measures failed, however, and the SPD from the 1880s steadily polled more and more votes in elections to the *Reichstag*.

Having failed in his efforts at repression, Bismarck undertook a program of social welfare legislation in hopes of separating German workers from socialist loyalties. These measures allowed for health insurance, accident insurance, and old age and disability pensions. The German state itself was organizing a system of social security that did not require any change in the system of property holding or politics.

In 1890, after forcing Bismarck's resignation, Emperor William II (1888–1918) allowed the antisocialist legislation to expire the next year. The SPD then had to decide how to operate as a legalized party. Their new direction was announced in the Erfurt Program of 1891. In good Marxist fashion, the program declared the imminent doom of capitalism and the necessity of socialist ownership of the means of production. However, these goals were to be achieved by legal political participation rather than by revolutionary activity. Because by its very nature capitalism must fail, the

Edward Bernstein, here shown late in life, was the father of democratic socialism in Europe. His theories sharply divided the German socialist camp at the turn of the century. [The Granger Collection.]

immediate task of socialists was to work for the improvement of workers' lives rather than for the revolution, which was inevitable. In theory, the SPD was vehemently hostile to the German Empire, but in practice the party functioned within its institutions.

This situation of the SPD, however, generated the most important internal socialist challenge to the orthodox Marxist analysis of capitalism and the socialist revolution. Eduard Bernstein (1850–1932) was the author of what was regarded as this socialist heresy. Bernstein, who was familiar with the British Fabians, questioned whether Marx and his later orthodox followers had been correct in their pessimistic appraisal of capitalism and the necessity of revolution. In *Evolutionary Socialism* (1899), Bernstein pointed to the rising standard of living in Europe, the ongoing power of the middle class, and the opening of the franchise to the working class. He argued that what was required to realize a humane socialist society was not revolution but more democracy and social reform. Bernstein's doctrines, known as revisionism, were widely debated among German socialists, and were finally condemned as theory, though the party actually pursued a peaceful, reformist program. His critics argued that evolution toward social democracy might be possible in liberal, parliamentary Britain, but not in authoritarian, militaristic Germany with its basically powerless *Reichstag*. Therefore, the German SPD continued to advocate a program of revolution.

The German debate over revisionism became very important for the later history of Marxist socialism on the world scene. The German SPD was, as noted, the most successful of all prewar socialist parties. Its rejection of an ideology of reform socialism in favor of an ideology of revolutionary socialism influenced all socialists who looked to the German example for direction. Most significant, Lenin adopted this position, as did the other leaders of the Russian revolution. Thereafter, wherever Soviet Marxism was influential the goal of its efforts would be revolution rather than reform.

Russia: Industrial Development and the Birth of Bolshevism

During the last two decades of the nineteenth century, Alexander II and, after him, Nicholas II, were determined that Russia should become an industrial power. They favored the growth of heavy industries such as railways, iron, and steel. There was also significant growth in the textile manufacturing, which still constituted the single largest industry. A small but significant industrial proletariat arose. At the turn of the century, there were approximately three million factory workers in Russia. Their working and living conditions were very bad by any standard.

New political departures accompanied the economic development. In 1901, the Social Revolutionary Party was founded. It opposed industrialism and looked to the communal life of rural Russia as a model for the economic future. In 1903, the Constitutional Democratic Party, or Cadets, was formed. Liberal in outlook, they were drawn from people who participated in the *zemstvos* (local governments). They wanted a parliamentary regime with responsible ministries, civil liberties, and economic progress. The Cadets hoped to model themselves on the liberal parties of Western Europe.

LENIN'S EARLY THOUGHT AND CAREER. The situation for Russian socialists differed radically from that in other major European countries. Russia had no representative political institutions and only a small working class. The compromises and accommodations achieved elsewhere were meaningless in Russia, where socialism in both theory and practice had to be revolutionary. The Russian Social Democratic Party had been established in 1898, but the repressive policies of the tsarist regime meant that the party had to function in exile. It was Marxist, and its members greatly admired the German Social Democratic Party.

The leading late-nineteenth-century Russian Marxist was Gregory Plekhanov (1857–1918), who wrote from his exile in Switzerland. At the turn of the century, his chief disciple was Vladimir Illich Ulyanov (1870–1924), who later took the name of Lenin. The future leader of the Communist Revolution had been born in 1870 as the son of a high bureaucrat. His older brother, while a student in Saint Petersburg, had become involved in radical politics. He was arrested for participating in a plot against Alexander III and was executed in 1887. In 1893, Lenin moved to Saint Petersburg, where he studied to become a lawyer. Soon he, too, was drawn to the revolutionary groups among the factory workers. He was arrested in 1895 and exiled to Siberia. In 1900, after his release, Lenin left Russia for the West. He spent most of the next seventeen years in Switzerland.

Once in Switzerland, Lenin became deeply involved in the organizational and policy disputes of the exiled Russian Social Democrats. They all considered themselves Marxists, but held differing positions on the proper nature of a Marxist revolution in primarily rural Russia and on the structure of their own party. Unlike the backward-looking Social Revolutionaries, the Social Democrats were modernizers who favored further industrial development. The majority believed that Russia must develop a large proletariat before the revolution could come. This same majority hoped to mold a mass political party like the German SPD.

Lenin dissented from both positions. In *What Is to Be Done?* (1902), he condemned any accommodation. He also criticized a trade unionism that settled for short-term gains rather than true revolutionary change for the working class. Lenin further rejected the concept of a mass party composed of workers. Revolutionary consciousness would not arise spontaneously from the working class. It must be carried to them by "people who make revolutionary activity their profession."[3] Only a small, elite party would possess the proper dedication to revolution and would be able to resist penetration by police spies. The guiding principle of that party should be "the strictest secrecy, the strictest selection of members, and the training of professional revolutionaries."[4]

In 1903, at the London Congress of the Russian Social Democratic Party, Lenin forced a split in the party ranks. During much of the congress, Lenin and his followers lost votes on various questions put before the body. But near the close, Lenin's group mustered a very slim majority. Thereafter, Lenin's faction as-

[3] Quoted in Albert Fried and Ronald Sanders (eds.), *Socialist Thought: A Documentary History* (Garden City, N.Y.: Anchor Doubleday, 1964), p. 459.

[4] Ibid., p. 468.

Lenin Argues for the Necessity of a Secret and Elite Party of Professional Revolutionaries

Social democratic parties in Western Europe had mass memberships and generally democratic structures of organization. In this passage from What Is to Be Done? *(1902), Lenin explained why the autocratic political conditions of Russia demanded a different kind of organization for the Russian Social Democratic Party. Lenin's ideas became the guiding principles of Bolshevik organization.*

I assert that it is far more difficult [for government police] to unearth a dozen wise men than a hundred fools. This position I will defend, no matter how much you instigate the masses against me for my "antidemocratic" views, etc. As I have stated repeatedly, by "wise men," in connection with organisation, I mean *professional revolutionaries*, irrespective of whether they have developed from among students or working men. I assert: (1) that no revolutionary movement can endure without a stable organisation of leaders maintaining continuity; (2) that the broader the popular mass drawn spontaneously into the struggle, which forms the basis of the movement and participates in it, the more urgent the need for such an organisation, and the more solid this organisation must be. . . ; (3) that such an organisation must consist chiefly of people professionally engaged in revolutionary activity; (4) that in an autocratic state [such as Russia], the more we *confine* the membership of such an organisation to people who are professionally engaged in revolutionary activity and who have been professionally trained in the art of combating the political police, the more difficult will it be to unearth the organisation; and (5) the *greater* will be the number of people from the working class and from other social classes who will be able to join the movement and perform active work in it. . . .

The only serious organisation principle for the active workers of our movement should be the strictest secrecy, the strictest selection of members, and the training of professional revolutionaries. ❑

Albert Fried and Ronald Sanders (eds.), *Socialist Thought: A Documentary History* (Garden City, N.Y.: Anchor Doubleday, 1964), pp. 460, 468.

sumed the name *Bolsheviks*, meaning "majority," and the other, more moderate, democratic revolutionary faction became known as the *Mensheviks*, or "minority." There was, of course, a considerable public relations advantage to the name *Bolshevik*. (In 1912, the Bolsheviks organized separately from other Social Democrats.) In 1905, Lenin complemented his organizational theory with a program for revolution in Russia: his *Two Tactics of Social Democracy in the Bourgeois-Democratic Revolution* urged that the socialist revolution unite the proletariat and the peasants. Lenin grasped better than any other revolutionary the profound discontent in the Russian countryside. He knew that an alliance of workers and peasants in rebellion probably could not be suppressed. Lenin's two principles of an elite party and a dual social revolution allowed the Bolsheviks, in late 1917, to capture the leadership of the Russian Revolution and to transform the political face of the modern world.

THE REVOLUTION OF 1905 AND ITS AFTERMATH. The quarrels among the Russian socialists and supporters of Lenin's doctrines had no immediate influence on events in their country itself. Industrialization proceeded and continued to stir resentment in many sectors. In 1904, Russia went to war with Japan, partly in expectation that public opinion would rally to the tsar. However, the result was Russian defeat and political crisis. The Japanese captured Port Arthur on the eastern coast of Russia, early in 1905. A few days later, on January 22, a priest named Father Gapon led several hundred workers to present a petition to the tsar for the improvement of industrial life. As the petitioners approached the Winter Palace in Saint Petersburg, the tsar's troops opened fire. About one hundred people were shot down in cold blood, and many more were wounded.

During the next ten months, revolutionary disturbances spread throughout Russia: sailors mutinied; peasant revolts erupted; and property was attacked. The uncle of Nicholas II was assassinated. Liberal Constitutional Democrat leaders from the *zemstvos* demanded political reform. Student strikes occurred in the universities. Social Revolutionaries and Social Democrats were active among urban working groups. In early October 1905, strikes broke out in Saint Petersburg, and for all practical purposes, worker groups, called *soviets*, controlled the city. Nicholas II issued the October Manifesto, which promised Russia constitutional government.

Early in 1906, Nicholas II announced the election of a parliament, the Duma, with two chambers. However, he reserved for himself ministerial appointments, financial policy, military matters, and foreign affairs. Nicholas named as his chief minister P. A. Stolypin (1862–1911). Neither the Tsar nor his minister was sympathetic to the idea or the functioning of the Duma. It would meet, disagreements would occur, and then it would be dismissed. In 1906, however, the government and the Duma canceled any redemptive payments that the peasants still owed to the government from the emancipation of the serfs in 1861. However, thereafter Stolypin pursued a repressive policy toward any rural discontent.

After Stolypin's assassination in 1911 by a Social Revolutionary, Nicholas II failed to find another strong minister. His government simply muddled along. But the life of his court became surrounded by scandal concerning the influence of Grigori Rasputin (1871?–1916), who claimed power to heal the tsar's hemophilic son, the heir to the throne. The undue influence of this strange and uncouth man, the continued social discontent, and the conservative resistance to any further liberal reforms rendered the position and policy of the tsar uncertain after 1911.

MAJOR DATES IN THE DEVELOPMENT OF EUROPEAN SOCIALISM

1864	International Working Men's Association (the First International) founded
1875	German Social Democratic Party founded
1876	First International dissolved
1878	German antisocialist laws passed
1884	British Fabian Society founded
1889	Second International founded
1891	German antisocialist laws permitted to expire
	German Social Democratic Party's Erfurt Program
1895	French Confédération Générale du Travail founded
1899	Eduard Bernstein's *Evolutionary Socialism*
1902	Formation of the British Labour Party Lenin's *What Is to Be Done?*
1903	Bolshevik–Menshevik split
1904	"Opportunism" debated at the Amsterdam Congress of the Second International

On "Bloody Sunday," January 22, 1905, troops of Tsar Nicholas II fired on a procession of workers who sought to present a petition at the Winter Palace in St. Petersburg. After this day there was little chance that the Russian working class could be reconciled with the existing government. [Soviet Life from Sovfoto.]

Grigori Rasputin was the sinister Russian monk who claimed the power to heal the ill son of Tsar Nicholas II and acquired great influence at court. His presence alienated many politically important persons from support of Nicholas. Rasputin was finally assassinated by a group of Russian noblemen. [The Granger Collection.]

The Building of European Supremacy in World Perspective

Between 1850 and 1914, Europe had more influence throughout the world than ever before or since. Its industrial base was more advanced than that of any other region including the still developing United States. Its wealth allowed European banks to exercise vast influence over the world. Europeans financed the building of railways in Africa, Latin America, Asia, as well as North America. Financial power brought political influence. The armaments industry gave European armies and navies a predominant power that they turned against peoples of Africa and Asia through various imperial ventures.

During these years, European culture also probably was most influential. Many capital cities in Latin America, especially in Buenos Aires, adopted European styles for their architecture. Paris became synonymous with high fashion. Paris, London, and Vienna were world intellectual centers.

The nation that most clearly understood the nature of European power and that sought to imitate it was Japan. Its administrators and intellectuals after the Meiji restoration came to Europe to study the new technology, political structures, and military organiza-

tions. The Japanese proved sufficiently successful to defeat Russia in 1905.

By contrast, China, India, the countries of the Middle East, and Africa found themselves overwhelmed by the economic and military power of Europe. In time, however, the peoples of those lands, who were dominated by the European powers, came to embrace the ideologies of revolutionary protest—most particularly those of socialism. As people from the colonial world came to work or study in Europe, they learned the kinds of ideas and criticisms that were most effective against European and Western culture. Carrying those ideas home, they adapted them to their particular circumstances, and then turned them against their colonial governors.

The self-confident Europeans eventually turned their military power against each other in 1914. The results of that conflict destroyed the late-nineteenth-century European self-confidence. At home, the Bolsheviks brought revolution to Russia. Abroad after the war, anticolonial movements began to grow, especially in India, in a manner that most Europeans in 1900 could not have imagined. In turn, those movements found many sympathetic supporters in Europe because of the spread of socialist ideas regarding social justice and public policy.

Suggested Readings

J. ALBISETTI, *Secondary School Reform in Imperial Germany* (1983). Examines the relationship between politics and education.

J. A. BANKS, *Prosperity and Parenthood: A Study of Family Planning among the Victorian Middle Classes* (1954). Probably the most sensitive and sensible study of the subject.

J. H. BATES, *St. Petersburg: Industrialization and Change* (1976). Impact of industrialization on the major city of imperial Russia.

G. BEHLMER, *Child Abuse and Moral Reform in England, 1870–1908* (1982). An important study of changes in the treatment of children.

L. R. BERLANSTEIN, *The Working People of Paris, 1871–1914* (1985). Interesting and comprehensive.

D. BLACKBOURN AND G. ELEY, *The Peculiarities of German History: Bourgeois Society and Politics in Nineteenth-Century Germany* (1985). An important and probing study.

P. BRANCA, *Silent Sisterhood: Middle Class Women in the Victorian Home* (1975). A well-researched work.

N. BULLOCK AND J. READ, *The Movement for Housing Reform in Germany and France, 1840–1914* (1985). An important and wide-ranging study of the housing problem.

R. J. EVANS AND W. R. LEE, *The German Family: Essays on the Social History of the Family in Nineteenth and Twentieth-Century Germany* (1981). Very useful.

W. H. Fraser, *The Coming of the Mass Market*, 1850–1914 (1981). Exploration of the expansion of consumer society.

P. Gay, *The Dilemma of Democratic Socialism: Eduard Bernstein's Challenge to Marx* (1952). A clear presentation of the problems raised by Bernstein's revisionism.

P. Gay, *The Bourgeois Experience: Victoria to Freud*, Vol. 1, *Education of the Senses* (1984). Vol. 2, *The Tender Passion* (1986). A major study of middle-class sexuality.

H. Goldberg, *A Life of Jean Jaurès* (1962). A splendid biography that explains the problems of the French socialists.

D. F. Good, *The Economic Rise of the Hapsburg Empire*, 1750–1914 (1985). The best available study.

O. J. Hale, *The Great Illusion*, 1901–1914 (1971). An excellent treatment.

S. C. Hause, *Women's Suffrage and Social Politics in the French Third Republic* (1984). A wide-ranging examination of the question.

E. J. Hobsbawm, *The Age of Capital* (1975). Explores the consolidation of middle-class life after 1850.

L. Holcombe, *Wives and Property: Reform of the Married Women's Property Law in Nineteenth-Century England* (1983). The standard work on the subject.

K. H. Jarausch, *Students, Society, and Politics in Imperial Germany: The Rise of Academic Illiberalism* (1982). The reaction of the academic community to the threat of socialism.

P. Joyce, *Work, Society, and Politics: The Culture of the Factory in Later Victorian England* (1980). Explores what actually happened in factories.

S. Kern, *The Culture of Time and Space*, 1880–1918 (1983). A lively discussion of the impact of the new technology.

D. I. Kertzer, *Family Life in Central Italy*, 1880–1910: *Sharecropping, Wage Labor, and Coresidence* (1984). One of the few studies of rural family life.

L. Kolakowski, *Main Currents of Marxism: Its Rise, Growth, and Dissolution*, 3 vols. (1978). The relevant sections on the last years of the nineteenth century and the early years of the twentieth are especially good.

D. Landes, *The Unbound Prometheus: Technological Change and Industrial Development in Western Europe from 1750 to the Present* (1969). Includes excellent discussions of late-century development.

A. H. McBriar, *Fabian Socialism and English Politics*, 1884–1918 (1962). The standard discussion.

A. MacLaren, *Sexuality and Social Order: The Debate over the Fertility of Women and Workers in France*, 1770–1920 (1983). Examines the debate over birth control in France.

A. J. Mayer, *The Persistence of the Old Regime in Europe to the Great War* (1981). An interesting and very controversial book which argues that less political and social change occurred in the nineteenth century than has usually been thought.

R. A. Nye, *Crime, Madness, and Politics in Modern France: The Medical Concept of National Decline* (1984). Relevant to issues of family and women.

D. Owen, *The Government of Victorian London*, 1855–1889 (1982). A study of how one city met the problems of urban development.

H. Pelling, *The Origins of the Labour Party*, 1880–1900 (1965). Examines the sources of the party in the activities of British socialists and trade unionists.

D. H. Pinkney, *Napoleon III and the Rebuilding of Paris* (1958). A classic study.

F. K. Prochaska, *Women and Philanthropy in Nineteenth-Century England* (1980). Studies the role of women in charity.

J. Rendall, *The Origins of Modern Feminism: Women in Britain, France and the United States*, 1780–1860 (1985). An exceedingly well-informed introduction.

H. Rogger, *Russia in the Age of Modernization and Revolution*, 1881–1917 (1983). The best synthesis of the period.

C. E. Schorske, *German Social Democracy*, 1905–1917 (1955). A brilliant study of the difficulties of the Social Democrats under the empire.

J. Scott, *The Glassworkers of Carmaux: French Craftsmen and Political Action in a Nineteenth-Century City* (1974). A classic analysis of the manner in which highly skilled craftsmen confronted and were eventually defeated by the mechanization of their industry.

M. Segalen, *Love and Power in the Peasant Family: Rural France in the Nineteenth Century* (1983). A pioneering work.

A. L. Shapiro, *Housing the Poor of Paris*, 1850–1902 (1985). Examines what happened to working-class housing at the time of the remodeling of Paris.

B. G. Smith, *Ladies of the Leisure Class: The Bourgeoises of Northern France in the Nineteenth Century* (1981). Emphasizes the importance of the reproductive role of women.

R. A. Soloway, *Birth Control and the Population Question in England*, 1877–1930 (1982). An important book that should be read with MacLaren (listed above).

N. Stone, *Europe Transformed* (1984). A sweeping survey that emphasizes the difficulties of late nineteenth-century liberalism.

A. B. Ulam, *The Bolsheviks: The Intellectual and Political History of the Triumph of Communism in Russia* (1965). Early chapters discuss prewar developments and the formation of Lenin's doctrines.

M. Vicinus, *Suffer and Be Still: Women in the Victorian Age* (1972). A series of excellent essays on Victorian women.

M. Vicinus (ed.), *A Widening Sphere: Changing Roles of Victorian Women* (1980). Examines late-century developments.

J. R. Walkowitz, *Prostitution and Victorian Society: Women, Class, and the State* (1980). A work of great insight and sensitivity.

E. Weber, *Peasants into Frenchmen: The Modernization of Rural France*, 1870–1914 (1976). An important and fascinating work on the transformation of French peasants into self-conscious citizens of the nation state.

M. J. Wiener, *English Culture and the Decline of the Industrial Spirit*, 1850–1980 (1981). The best study of the problem.

Charles Darwin (1809–1882). In two works of seminal importance, The Origin of Species (1859) *and* The Descent of Man (1871), *Darwin enunciated the theory of evolution by natural selection and applied that theory to human beings. The result was a storm of controversy that affected not only biology, but also religion, philosophy, sociology, and even politics. [National Portrait Gallery, London.]*

29 The Birth of Contemporary Western Thought

During the same period that the modern nation-state developed and the second Industrial Revolution laid the foundations for the modern material lifestyle, the ideas and concepts that have marked European thought for much of the present century took shape. Many of the traditional intellectual signposts disappeared. The death of God was proclaimed. Christianity had undergone the most severe attack in its history. The picture of the physical world that had dominated since Newton underwent major modification. The work of Darwin and Freud challenged the special place that Western thinkers had assigned to humankind. The value long ascribed to rationality was questioned. The political and humanitarian ideals of liberalism and socialism gave way for a time to new, aggressive nationalism. At the turn of the century, European intellectuals were more daring than ever before, but they were also probably less certain and less optimistic.

Science at Mid-Century

In about 1850, Voltaire would still have felt at home in a general discussion of scientific concepts. The basic Newtonian picture of physical nature that he had popularized still prevailed. Scientists continued to believe that nature operated as a vast machine according to mechanical principles. During the first half of the century, scientists extended mechanistic explanation into several important areas. John Dalton (1766–1844) formulated the modern theory of chemical composition. However, at mid-century and long thereafter, atoms and molecules were thought to resemble billiard balls. During the 1840s, several independent researchers arrived at the concept of the conservation of energy, according to which energy is never lost in the universe but is simply transformed from one form to another. The principles of mechanism were extended to geology through the work of Charles Lyell (1797–1875), whose *Principles of Geology* (1830) postulated that various changes in geological formation were the result of the mechanistic operation of natural causes over great spans of time.

At mid-century, the physical world was thus regarded as rational, mechanical, and dependable. Its laws could be ascertained objectively through experiment and observation. Scientific theory purportedly described physical nature as it really existed. Moreover, almost all scientists also believed, like Newton and the deists of the eighteenth century, that their knowledge of nature demonstrated the existence of a God or a Supreme Being.

Darwin and Natural Selection

In 1859, Charles Darwin (1809–1882) published *The Origin of Species*, which carried the mechanical interpretation of physical nature into the world of living things. The book proved to be one of the seminal works of Western thought and earned Darwin the honor of being regarded as the Newton of biology. Both Darwin and his book have been much misunderstood. He did not originate the concept of evolution, which had been discussed widely before he wrote. What he and Alfred Russel Wallace (1823–1913) did,

working independently, was to formulate the principle of natural selection, which explained how species had changed or evolved over time. Earlier writers had believed that evolution might occur; Darwin and Wallace explained how it *could* occur.

Drawing on Malthus, the two scientists contended that more seeds and living organisms come into existence than can survive in their environment. Those organisms possessing some marginal advantage in the struggle for existence live long enough to propagate their kind. This principle of survival of the fittest Darwin called *natural selection*. The principle was naturalistic and mechanical. Its operation required no guiding mind behind the development and change in organic nature. What neither Darwin nor anyone else in his day could explain was the origin of those chance variations that provided some living things with the marginal chance for survival. Only when the work on heredity by the Austrian monk Gregor Mendel (1822–1884) received public attention after 1900, several years following his death, did the mystery of those variations begin to be unraveled.

Darwin's and Wallace's theory represented the triumph of naturalistic explanation, which removed the idea of purpose from organic nature. Eyes were not made for seeing according to the rational wisdom and

Darwin Defends a Mechanistic View of Nature

In the closing paragraphs of The Origin of Species, *Charles Darwin contrasted the view of nature he championed with that of his opponents. He argued that interpreting the development of organic nature through mechanistic laws actually suggested a nobler concept of nature than interpreting its development in terms of some form of divine creation.*

Authors of the highest eminence seem to be fully satisfied with the view that each species has been independently created. To my mind it accords better with what we know of the laws impressed on matter by the Creator, that the production and extinction of the past and present inhabitants of the world should have been due to secondary causes, like those determining the birth and death of the individual. When I view all beings not as special creations, but as the lineal descendants of some few beings which lived long before the first bed of the Cambrian [geological] system was deposited, they seem to me to become ennobled. . . .

It is interesting to contemplate a tangled bank, clothed with many plants of many kinds, with birds singing on the bushes, with various insects flitting about, and with worms crawling through the damp earth, and to reflect that these elaborately constructed forms, so different from each other, and dependent upon each other in so complex a manner, have all been

produced by laws acting around us. These laws, taken in the largest sense, being Growth with Reproduction; Inheritance which is almost implied by reproduction; Variability from the indirect and direct action of the conditions of life, and from use and disuse: a Ration of Increase so high as to lead to a Struggle for Life, and as a consequence to Natural Selection, entailing Divergence of Character and the Extinction of less-improved forms. Thus, from the war of nature, from famine and death, the most exalted object which we are capable of conceiving, namely the production of the higher animals, directly follows. There is grandeur in this view of life, with its several powers, having been originally breathed by the Creator into a few forms or into one; and that, whilst this planet has gone cycling on according to the fixed law of gravity, from so simple a beginning endless forms most beautiful and most wonderful have been, and are being evolved. ❏

Charles Darwin, *The Origin of Species and The Descent of Man*, 6th ed. (New York: Modern Library, n.d.), pp. 373–374.

purpose of God, but had developed mechanistically over the course of time. In this manner, the theory of evolution through natural selection not only contradicted the biblical narrative of the Creation, but also undermined the deistic argument for the existence of God from the design of the universe. Moreover, Darwin's work undermined the whole concept of fixity in nature or the universe at large. The world was a realm of flux and change. The fact that physical and organic nature might be constantly changing allowed people in the late nineteenth century to believe that society, values, customs, and beliefs should also change.

In 1871, Darwin carried his work a step further. In *The Descent of Man*, he applied the principle of evolution by natural selection to human beings. Darwin was hardly the first person to treat human beings as animals, but his arguments brought greater plausibility to that point of view. He contended that humankind's moral nature and religious sentiments, as well as its physical frame, had developed naturalistically in response largely to the requirements of survival. Neither the origin nor the character of humankind on earth required the existence of a God for their explanation.

Not since Copernicus had removed the earth from the center of the universe had the pride of Western human beings received so sharp a blow. Darwin's theory of evolution by natural selection was very controversial from the moment of the publication of the *Origin of Species*. It encountered criticism from both the religious and the scientific communities. By the end of the century, the concept of evolution was widely accepted by scientists, but not yet Darwin's mechanism of natural selection. The acceptance of the latter within the scientific community really dates from the 1920s and 1930s, when Darwin's theory became combined with the insights of modern genetics.

The Prestige of Science

The prestige of Darwin's achievement, progress in medicine, and the links of science to the technology of the second Industrial Revolution made the general European public aware of science as never before. Scientific knowledge and theories became models for thought in other fields, even before the impact of Darwinian thought.

Auguste Comte and Intellectual Development

The French philosopher Auguste Comte (1798–1857), a late child of the Enlightenment and a onetime follower of Saint-Simon, developed a philosophy of human intellectual development that culminated in a science. In *The Positive Philosophy* (1830–1842), Comte argued that human thought had gone through

Auguste Comte was the founder of Positivism. He urged that all knowledge be modeled on empirical science. Because he wanted the understanding of human society to assume a scientific character, he is often regarded as the founder of sociology. [French Cultural Services, New York.]

three stages of development. In the theological stage, physical nature was explained in terms of the action of divinities or spirits. In the second or metaphysical stage, abstract principles became regarded as the operative agencies of nature. In the final or positive stage, explanations of nature became a matter of exact descriptions of phenomena, without recourse to an unobservable operative principle. Physical science had, in Comte's view, entered the positive stage, and similar thinking should penetrate other areas of analysis. In particular, Comte thought that positive laws of social behavior could be discovered in the same fashion as laws of physical nature. For this reason, he is generally regarded as the father of sociology. Works like Comte's helped to convince learned Europeans that genuine knowledge in any area must resemble scientific knowledge. This belief had its roots in the Enlightenment and continues to permeate Western thought to the present day.

Theories of ethics were modeled on science during the last half of the century. The concept of the struggle for survival was widely applied to human social relationships. The phrase "survival of the fittest" predated Darwin and reflected the competitive outlook of classical economics. Darwin's use of the phrase gave it the prestige associated with advanced science.

Herbert Spencer and Social Darwinism

The most famous advocate of evolutionary ethics was Herbert Spencer (1820–1903), the British philosopher. Spencer, a strong individualist, believed that human society progressed through competition. If the weak received too much protection, the rest of humankind was the loser. In Spencer's work, struggle against one's fellow human beings became a kind of ethical imperative. The concept could be applied to justify the avoidance of aiding the poor and the working class or to justify the domination of colonial peoples or to urge aggressively competitive relationships among nations. Evolutionary ethics and similar concepts, all of which are usually termed *social Darwinism*, often came very close to saying that might makes right.

Interestingly enough, one of the chief opponents of such thinking was Thomas Henry Huxley, the great defender of Darwin. In 1893, Huxley declared that the physical cosmic process of evolution was at odds with the process of human ethical development. The struggle in nature held no ethical implications except to demonstrate how human beings should not behave.

Scientists and their admirers enjoyed a supreme confidence during the last half of the century. They genuinely believed that they had, for all intents and purposes, discovered all of the principles that might be discovered. The issues for science in the future would be the extension of acknowledged principles and the refinement of measurement. However, the turn of the century held an unanticipated future for science. That confident, self-satisfied world of late-nineteenth-century science and scientism vanished. A much more complicated picture of nature developed, as will be seen later in this chapter.

Christianity and the Church under Siege

The nineteenth century was one of the most difficult periods in the history of the organized Christian churches. Many European intellectuals left the faith. The secular, liberal nation-states attacked the political and social influence of the Church. The expansion of population and the growth of cities challenged its organizational capacity to meet the modern age. Yet during all of this turmoil, the Protestant and Catholic churches still made considerable headway at the popular level.

The Intellectual Attack

The intellectual attack on Christianity arose on the grounds of its historical credibility, its scientific accuracy, and its pronounced morality. The *philosophes* of the Enlightenment had delighted in pointing out contradictions in the Bible. The historical scholarship of the nineteenth century brought new issues to the fore.

In 1835, David Friederich Strauss (1808–1874) published a *Life of Jesus* in which he questioned whether the Bible provided any genuine historical evidence about Jesus. Strauss contended that the story of Jesus was a myth that had arisen from the particular social

and intellectual conditions of first-century Palestine. Jesus' character and life represented the aspirations of the people of that time and place rather than events that had occurred. Other skeptical lives of Jesus were written and published elsewhere.

During the second half of the century, scholars such as Julius Wellhausen (1844–1918) in Germany, Ernst Renan (1823–1892) in France, and William Robertson Smith (1847–1894) in Great Britain contended that the books of the Bible had been written and revised with the problems of Jewish society and politics in the minds of human authors. They were not inspired books but had, like the Homeric epics, been written by normal human beings in a primitive society. This questioning of the historical validity of the Bible caused more literate men and women to lose faith in Christianity than any other single cause.

The march of science also undermined Christianity. This blow was particularly cruel because many eighteenth-century writers had led Christians to believe that the scientific examination of nature provided a strong buttress for their faith. William Paley's (1743–1805) *Natural Theology* (1802) and books by numerous scientists had enshrined this belief. But the geology of Charles Lyell (1797–1875) suggested that the earth was much older than the biblical records contended. By appealing to natural causes to explain floods, mountains, and valleys, Lyell removed the miraculous hand of God from the physical development of the earth. Darwin's theory cast doubt on the doctrine of the Creation. His ideas and those of other writers suggested that the moral nature of humankind could be explained without appeal to the role of God. Finally, anthropologists, psychologists, and sociologists suggested that religion itself and religious sentiments were just one more set of natural phenomena.

Other intellectuals questioned the morality of Christianity. The old issue of immoral biblical stories was again raised. Much more important, the moral character of the Old Testament God came under fire. His cruelty and unpredictability did not fit well with the progressive, tolerant, rational values of liberals. They also wondered about the morality of the New Testament God, who would sacrifice for His own satisfaction the only perfect being ever to walk the earth. Many of the clergy began to ask themselves if they could honestly preach doctrines they felt to be immoral.

During the last quarter of the century, this moral attack on Christianity came from another direction. Writers like Friedrich Nietzsche (1844–1900) in Germany portrayed Christianity as a religion of sheep that glorified weakness rather than the strength that life required. Christianity demanded a useless and debilitating sacrifice of the flesh and spirit rather than full-blooded heroic living and daring. Nietzsche once ob-

Matthew Arnold Contemplates the Loss of Intellectual Certainties

In this poem, written in 1867, Matthew Arnold (1822–1888) portrayed a man and a woman looking across the waters of the English Channel on a moonlit night. The speaker in the poem notes that Sophocles, the ancient Greek dramatist, had drawn lessons about the misery of life from the ebb and flow of the Aegean Sea. The speaker then compares the movement of the sea to the withdrawal of the Christian faith from the lives of nineteenth-century men and women. Finally, he says that the world that seems so beautiful is really a place where there can be no certainty, love, light, or peace. This pessimism reflects the state of mind of many writers who were no longer sure of the truth of the Christian faith.

DOVER BEACH

The sea is calm to-night.
The tide is full, the moon lies fair
Upon the Straits;—on the French coast the light
Gleams and is gone; the cliffs of England stand,
Glimmering and vast, out in the tranquil bay.

Come to the window, sweet is the night air!
Only, from the long line of spray
Where the sea meets the moon-blanch'd land,
Listen! you hear the grating roar
Of pebbles which the waves draw back, and fling,
At their return, up the high strand,
Begin, and cease, and then again begin,
With tremulous cadence slow, and bring
The eternal note of sadness in.

Sophocles long ago
Heard it on the Aegean, and it brought
Into his mind the turbid ebb and flow
Of human misery; we

Find also in the sound a thought,
Hearing it by this distant northern sea.

The Sea of Faith
Was once, too, at the full, and round earth's shore
Lay like the folds of a bright girdle furl'd.
But now I only hear
Its melancholy, long, withdrawing roar,
Retreating, to the breath
Of the night-wind, down the vast edges drear
And naked shingles of the world.

Ah, love, let us be true
To one another! for the world, which seems
To lie before us like a land of dreams,
So various, so beautiful, so new,
Hath really neither joy, nor love, nor light,
Nor certitude, nor peace, nor help for pain;
And we are here as on a darkling plain
Swept with confused alarms of struggle and flight,
Where ignorant armies clash by night! ❑

In Donald J. Gray and G. B. Tennyson, *Victorian Literature: Poetry* (New York: Macmillan, 1976), pp. 479–480.

served, "War and courage have accomplished more great things than love of neighbor."[1]

These widespread skeptical intellectual currents seem to have directly influenced only the upper levels of educated society. Yet they created a climate in which Christianity lost much of its intellectual respectability. Fewer educated people joined the clergy. More and more people found that they could lead their lives with little or no reference to Christianity. The secularism of everyday life proved as harmful to the faith as the direct attacks. This situation especially prevailed in the cities, which were growing faster than the capacity of the churches to meet the challenge. There was not even enough room in the existing urban churches for the potential worshipers to sit. Whole generations of the urban poor grew up with little or no experience of the Church as an institution or of Christianity as a religious faith.

Conflict of Church and State

The secular state of the nineteenth century clashed with both the Protestant and the Roman Catholic churches. Liberals generally disliked the dogma and the political privileges of the established churches. National states were often suspicious of the supranational character of the Roman Catholic church. However, the primary area of conflict between the state and the churches was the expanding systems of education. The churches feared that future generations would emerge from the schools without the rudiments of religious teaching. The advocates of secular education feared the production of future generations more

[1] Walter Kaufmann (ed. and trans.), *The Portable Nietzsche* (New York: Viking, 1967), p. 159.

loyal to religion or the Church than to the nation. From 1870 through the turn of the century, the issue of religious education was heatedly debated in every major country.

GREAT BRITAIN. In Great Britain, the Education Act of 1870 provided for the construction of state-supported school-board schools, whereas earlier the government had given small grants to religious schools. The new schools were to be built in areas where the religious denominations failed to provide satisfactory education. There was rivalry not only between the Anglican church and the state but also between the Anglican church and the Nonconformist denominations, that is, those Christian denominations that were not part of the Church of England. There was intense local hostility among all these groups. The churches of all denominations had to oppose improvements in education because these increased the costs of their own schools. In the Education Act of 1902, the government decided to provide state support for both religious and nonreligious schools but imposed the same educational standards on each.

FRANCE. The British conflict was relatively calm compared with that in France, where there existed a dual system of Catholic and public schools. Under the Falloux Law of 1850, the local priest provided religious education in the public schools. The very conservative French Catholic church and the Third French Republic were mutually hostile to each other. Between 1878 and 1886, the government passed a series of educational laws sponsored by Jules Ferry (1832–1893). The Ferry Laws replaced religious instruction in the public schools with civic training. Members of religious orders were no longer permitted to teach in the public schools, the number of which was to be expanded. After the Dreyfus affair, the French Catholic church again paid a price for its reactionary politics. The Radical government of Waldeck-Rousseau, drawn from pro-Dreyfus groups, suppressed the religious orders. In 1905, the Napoleonic Concordat was terminated, and Church and State were totally separated.

GERMANY AND THE *KULTURKAMPF*. The most extreme example of Church–State conflict occurred in Germany during the 1870s. At the time of unification, the German Catholic hierarchy had wanted freedom for the churches guaranteed in the constitution. Bismarck left the matter to the discretion of each federal state, but he soon felt the activity of the Roman Catholic church and the Catholic Center Party to be a threat to the political unity of the new state. Through administrative orders in 1870 and 1871, Bismarck removed both Catholic and Protestant clergy from overseeing local education and set education under state direc-

tion. The secularization of education was merely the beginning of a concerted attack on the independence of the Catholic church in Germany.

The "May Laws" of 1873, which applied to Prussia and not the entire German Empire, required priests to be educated in German schools and universities and to pass state-administered examinations. The state could veto the appointments of priests. The disciplinary power of the pope and the Church over the clergy was abolished and transferred to the state. When the bishops and many of the clergy refused to obey these laws, Bismarck used the police against them. In 1876, he had either arrested or driven from Prussia all the Catholic bishops. In the end, Bismarck's *Kulturkampf* ("cultural struggle") against the Catholic church failed. Not for the first time, Christian martyrs aided resistance to persecution. By the close of the decade, the chancellor had abandoned his attack. He had gained state control of education and civil laws governing marriage only at the price of lingering Catholic resentment against the German state. The *Kulturkampf* was probably the greatest blunder of Bismarck's career.

Areas of Religious Revival

The successful German Catholic resistance to the intrusions of the secular state illustrates the continuing vitality of Christianity during this period of intellectual and political hardship. In Great Britain, both the Anglican church and the Nonconformist denominations experienced considerable growth in membership. Vast sums of money were raised for new churches and schools. In Ireland, the 1870s saw a widespread Catholic devotional revival. Priests in France after the defeat by Prussia organized special pilgrimages by train for thousands of penitents who believed that France had been defeated because of their sins. The cult of the miracle of Lourdes originated during these years. There were efforts by churches of all denominations to give more attention to the urban poor.

In effect, the last half of the nineteenth century witnessed the final great effort to Christianize Europe. It was well organized, well led, and well financed. It failed not from want of effort but because the population had simply outstripped the resources of the churches. This persistent liveliness of the church accounts in part for the intense hostility of its enemies.

The Roman Catholic Church and the Modern World

Perhaps the most striking feature of this religious revival amidst turmoil and persecution was the resilience of the papacy. The brief hope for a liberal pontificate from Pope Pius IX (1846–1878) vanished on the night in 1848 when he fled the turmoil in Rome. In the 1860s, Pius IX, embittered by the mode of Italian unification, launched a counteroffensive against liberalism, in thought and deed. In 1864, he issued the *Syllabus of Errors*, which condemned all the major tenets of political liberalism and modern thought. He set the Roman Catholic church squarely against the worlds of contemporary science, philosophy, and politics. In 1869, the pope called into session the First Vatican Council. The next year, through the political manipulations of the pontiff and against much opposition from numerous members, the council promulgated the dogma of the infallibility of the pope when speaking officially on matters of faith and morals. No earlier pope had gone so far. The First Vatican Council came to a close in 1870, when Italian troops invaded Rome at the outbreak of the Franco-Prussian War.

Pius IX died in 1878 and was succeeded by Leo XIII (1878–1903). The new pope, who was sixty-eight years old at the time of his election, sought to make accommodation with the modern age and to address the great social questions. He looked to the philosophical tradition of Thomas Aquinas to reconcile the claims of faith and reason. His encyclicals of 1885 and 1890 per-

Pope Leo XIII led the Roman Catholic Church toward a limited recognition of the social and political problems brought on by industrial democracy. His encyclical Rerum Novarum *was the major statement of the Church on social justice [Culver Pictures.]*

The shrine at Lourdes, in southwestern France, where, it is believed, the Virgin Mary appeared to a young girl, Bernadette Soubirous, in 1858. Millions of pilgrims visit the shrine each year seeking miraculous cures. [Ullstein Bilderdienst.]

mitted Catholics to participate in the politics of liberal states.

Leo XIII's most important pronouncement on public issues was the encyclical *Rerum Novarum* (1891). In that document, Leo XIII defended private property, religious education, and religious control of the marriage laws, and he condemned socialism and Marxism. However, he also declared that employers should treat their employees justly, pay them proper wages, and permit them to organize labor unions. He supported laws and regulations to protect the conditions of labor. The pope urged that modern society be organized according to corporate groups, including people from various classes, which might cooperate according to Christian principles. The corporate society, derivative of medieval social organization, was to be an alternative to both socialism and competitive capitalism. On the basis of Leo XIII's pronouncements, democratic Catholic parties and Catholic trade unions were founded throughout Europe.

The emphasis of Pius X, who reigned from 1903 to 1914 and who has been proclaimed a saint, was intellectually reactionary. He hoped to restore traditional devotional life. Between 1903 and 1907 he condemned Catholic Modernism, a movement of modern biblical criticism within the Church, and in 1910 he required an anti-Modernist oath from all priests. By these actions, Pius X set the Church squarely against the intellectual

Leo XIII Considers the Social Question in European Politics

In his 1891 *encyclical* Rerum Novarum, *Pope Leo XIII addressed the social question in European politics. It was the answer of the Catholic church to secular calls for social reforms. The pope denied the socialist claim that class conflict was the natural state of affairs. He urged employers to seek just and peaceful relations with workers.*

The great mistake that is made in the matter now under consideration is to possess oneself of the idea that class is naturally hostile to class; that rich and poor are intended by Nature to live at war with one another. So irrational and so false is this view that the exact contrary is the truth. . . . Each requires the other; capital cannot do without labour, nor labour without capital. Mutual agreement results in pleasantness and good order; perpetual conflict necessarily produces confusion and outrage. Now, in preventing such strife as this, and in making it impossible, the efficacy of Christianity is marvellous and manifold. . . . Religion teaches the labouring man and the workman to carry out honestly and well all equitable agreements freely made; never to injure capital, or to outrage the person of an employer; never to employ violence in representing his own cause, or to engage in riot or disorder; and to have nothing to do with men of evil principles, who work upon the people with artful promises and raise foolish hopes which usually end in disaster and in repentance when too late. Religion teaches the rich man and the employer that their work people are not their slaves; that they must respect in every man his dignity as a man and as a Christian; that labour is nothing to be ashamed of, if we listen to right reason and to Christian philosophy, but is an honourable employment, enabling a man to sustain his life in an upright and creditable way; and that it is shameful and inhuman to treat men like chattels to make money by, or to look upon them merely as so much muscle or physical power. Thus, again, Religion teaches that, as among the workman's concerns are Religion herself and things spiritual and mental, the employer is bound to see that he has time for the duties of piety; that he be not exposed to corrupting influences and dangerous occasions; and that he be not led away to neglect his home and family or to squander his wages. Then, again, the employer must never tax his work people beyond their strength, nor employ them in work unsuited to their sex or age. His great and principal obligation is to give every one that which is just. ❑

F. S. Nitti, *Catholic Socialism*, trans. by Mary Mackintosh (London: S. Sonnenschein, 1895), p. 409.

currents of the day, and the struggle between Catholicism and modern thought continued. Although Pius X did not strongly support the social policy of Leo XIII, the Catholic church continued to permit its members active participation in social and political movements.

Toward a Twentieth-Century Frame of Mind

World War I is often regarded as the point of departure into the contemporary world. Although this view is possibly true of political and social developments, it is an incorrect assessment of intellectual history. The last quarter of the nineteenth century and the first decade of the twentieth century constituted the crucible of contemporary Western and European thought. During this period, the kind of fundamental reassessment that Darwin's work had previously made necessary in biology and in understanding the place of human beings in nature became writ large in other areas of thinking. Philosophers, scientists, psychologists, and artists began to portray physical reality, human nature, and human society in ways quite different from those of the past. Their new concepts challenged the major presuppositions of mid-nineteenth-century science, rationalism, liberalism, and bourgeois morality.

Science: The Revolution in Physics

The modifications in the scientific worldview originated within the scientific community itself. By the late 1870s, considerable discontent existed over the excessive realism of mid-century science. It was thought that many scientists believed that their mechanistic models, solid atoms, and theories about absolute time and space actually described the real universe. In 1833, Ernst Mach (1838–1916) published *The Science of Mechanics*, in which he urged that the concepts of science be considered descriptive not of the physical world but of the sensations experienced by the scientific observer. Science could describe only the sensations, not the physical world that underlay the sensations. In line with Mach, the French scientist and mathematician Henri Poincaré (1854–1912) urged that the concepts and theories of scientists be regarded as hypothetical constructs of the human mind rather than as descriptions of the true state of nature. In 1911, Hans Vaihinger (1852–1933) suggested that the con-

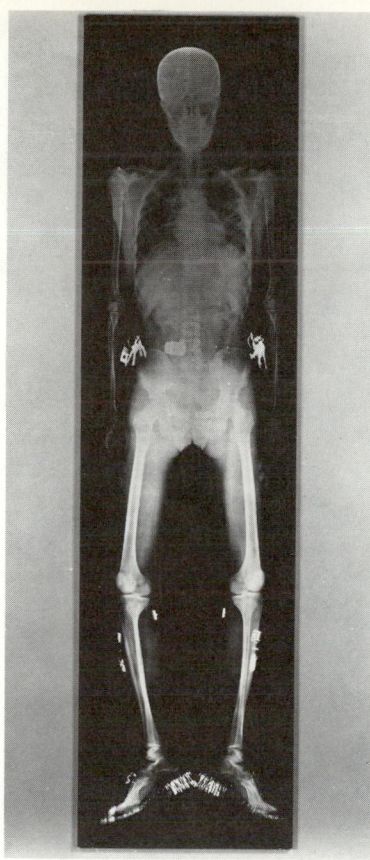

In an early demonstration Roentgen took an X ray of the entire body of a male subject. Note the buckle of his belt, the keys he had attached to the belt, and tacks in the soles and heels of his shoes. [Deutsches Museum, Munich.]

cepts of science be considered "as if" descriptions of the physical world. By World War I, few scientists believed any longer that they could portray the "truth" about physical reality. Rather, they saw themselves as recording the observations of instruments and as setting forth useful hypothetical or symbolic models of nature.

New discoveries in the laboratory paralleled the philosophical challenge to nineteenth-century science. With those discoveries, the comfortable world of supposedly "complete" nineteenth-century physics vanished forever. In December 1895, Wilhelm Roentgen (1845–1923) published a paper on his discovery of X rays, a form of energy that penetrated various opaque materials. The publication of his paper was followed within a matter of months by major steps in the exploration of radioactivity. In 1896, Henri Becquerel (1852–1908), through a series of experiments following on Roentgen's work, found that uranium emitted a similar form of energy. The next year, J. J.

Thomson (1856–1940), working in the Cavendish Laboratory of Cambridge University, formulated the theory of the electron. The interior world of the atom had become a new area for human exploration. In 1902, Ernest Rutherford (1871–1937), who had been Thomson's assistant, explained the cause of radiation through the disintegration of the atoms of radioactive materials. Shortly thereafter, he speculated on the immense store of energy present in the atom.

The discovery of radioactivity and discontent with the existing mechanical models led to revolutionary theories in physics. In 1900, Max Planck (1858–1947) pioneered the articulation of the quantum theory of energy, according to which energy is a series of discrete quantities or packets rather than a continuous stream. In 1905, Albert Einstein (1879–1955) published his first epoch-making papers on relativity. He contended that time and space exist not separately but rather as a combined continuum. Moreover, the measurement of space and time depend on the observer as well as on the entities being measured. In 1927, Werner Heisenberg (1901–1976) set forth the uncertainty

The German physicist Albert Einstein (1879–1955). Einstein's theory of relativity, published in 1905, set the fundamental theory of physics in a new direction. [Brundy Library.]

1830	Lyell's *Principles of Geology*
1830–1842	Comte's *The Positive Philosophy*
1853–1854	Gobineau's *Essay on the Inequality of the Human Races*
1859	Darwin's *The Origin of Species*
1865	Bernard's *An Introduction to the Study of Experimental Medicine*
1871	Darwin's *The Descent of Man*
1872	Nietzsche's *The Birth of Tragedy*
1883	Mach's *The Science of Mechanics*
	Nietzsche's *Thus Spake Zarathustra*
1896	Herzl's *The Jewish State*
1899	Chamberlain's *The Foundations of the Nineteenth Century*
1900	Freud's *The Interpretation of Dreams*
1905	Weber's *The Protestant Ethic and the Spirit of Capitalism*
1907	Bergson's *Creative Evolution*
1908	Sorel's *Reflections on Violence*

The British scientist Ernest Rutherford was one of the first persons to explore the internal structure of the atom. The portrait is a 1932 painting by Oswald Birley. [Culver Pictures.]

principle, according to which the behavior of subatomic particles is a matter of statistical probability rather than of exactly determinable cause and effect. So much that only fifty years earlier had seemed certain and unquestionable about the physical universe had now once again become problematical.

Nineteenth-century popularizers of science had urged its importance as a path to rational living and decision making. By the early twentieth century, the developments in the scientific world itself had dashed such optimistic hopes. The mathematical complexity of twentieth-century physics meant that despite valiant efforts, science would rarely again be successfully popularized. However, at the same time, through applied technology and further research in physics and medicine, science affected daily living more than ever before in human history. Consequently, nonscientists in legal, business, and public life have been called on to make decisions involving technological matters that they rarely can or do understand in depth or detail. By the middle of this century, some writers—such as the English essayist, novelist, and physicist, C. P. Snow

Marie Curie (1867–1934), who was born in Poland but worked most of her life in France, was one of the leading figures in the turn-of-the-century advance of physics and chemistry. She is credited with the discovery of radium. [The Granger Collection.]

(1905–1980)—spoke of the emergence of "two cultures," one of the scientists and one of literary persons. The problem was establishing ways in which they could communicate meaningfully with each other to address the major problems of human life.

Philosophy: Revolt against Reason

Within philosophical circles, the adequacy of rational thinking to address the human situation was being questioned.

FRIEDRICH NIETZSCHE. No late-nineteenth-century writer better exemplified this new attitude than the German philosopher Friedrich Nietzsche (1844–1900), who had been educated as a classical philologist rather than as an academic philosopher. His books remained unpopular until late in his life, when his brilliance had deteriorated into an almost totally silent insanity. He was a person wholly at odds with the predominant values of the age. At one time or another, he attacked Christianity, democracy, nationalism, rationality, science, and progress. He sought less to change values than to probe the very sources of values in the human mind and character. He wanted not only to tear away the masks of respectable life but also to explore the ways in which human beings made such masks.

His first important work was *The Birth of Tragedy* (1872), in which he urged that the nonrational aspects of human nature were as important and noble as the rational characteristics. Here and elsewhere, he insisted on the positive function of instinct and ecstasy in human life. To limit human activity to strictly rational behavior was to impoverish human life and experience. In this work, Nietzsche regarded Socrates as one of the major contributors to Western decadence because of the Greek philosopher's appeal for rationality in human affairs. In Nietzsche's view, the strength for the heroic life and the highest artistic achievement arose from sources beyond rationality.

In later works, such as the prose poem *Thus Spake Zarathustra* (1883), Nietzsche criticized democracy and Christianity. Both would lead only to the mediocrity of sheepish masses. He announced the death of God and proclaimed the coming of the Overman (*Übermensch*), who would embody heroism and greatness. This latter term was frequently interpreted as some mode of superman or superrace, but such was not Nietzsche's intention. He was highly critical of contemporary racism and anti-Semitism. What he sought was a return to the heroism that he associated with Greek life in the Homeric age. He thought that the values of Christianity and of bourgeois morality prevented humankind from achieving life on a heroic level. Those moralities forbade too much of human nature from fulfilling and expressing itself.

Friedrich Nietzsche became the most influential German philosopher of the late nineteenth century. His books challenged existing morality and demanded a revaluation of values. He has exerted a vast influence on twentieth-century literature and philosophy. [New York Public Library Picture Collection.]

Two of Nietzsche's most profound works were *Beyond Good and Evil* (1886) and *The Genealogy of Morals* (1887). Both are difficult books. Much of the former is written in brief, ambiguous aphorisms. Nietzsche sought to discover not what is good and what is evil but the social and psychological sources of the judgment of good and evil. He declared, "There are no moral phenomena at all, but only a moral interpretation of phenomena."[2] He dared to raise the question of whether morality itself was valuable: "We need a critique of moral values; the value of these values themselves must first be called in question."[3] In Nietzsche's view, morality was a human convention that had no independent existence apart from humankind. For Nietzsche, this discovery did not condemn morality but liberated human beings to create life-affirming instead of life-denying values. Christianity, utilitarian-

[2] Walter Kaufmann (ed. and trans.), *The Basic Writings of Nietzsche* (New York: The Modern Library, 1968). p. 275.
[3] Ibid, p. 456.

ism, and middle-class respectability could, in good conscience, be abandoned, and human beings could, if they so willed, create a new moral order for themselves that would glorify pride, assertiveness, and strength rather than meekness, humility, and weakness.

What Nietzsche said about morality was indicative of what other philosophers were saying about similar objects. There was a growing tendency to see all conceptual categories as useful creations rather than exact descriptions.

WILLIAM JAMES. The American philosopher William James (1842–1910) was one of the most influential figures to question the adequacy of nineteenth-century rationalism and science. He and his philosophy of pragmatism were very influential in Europe. James suggested that the truth of an idea or a description depended primarily on how well it worked. Knowledge was less an instrument for knowing than for acting.

HENRI BERGSON. The most important European philosopher to pursue such lines of thought was the Frenchman Henri Bergson (1859–1941). His most significant works were *Time and Free Will* (1889), *Creative Evolution* (1907), and *Two Sources of Morality and Religion* (1932). Bergson glorified instinct, will, and subjectivism. He regarded human beings as dwelling in a world of becoming, where the only certain thing was their sense of themselves. The world was permeated with a great vital force in which all things participated to a greater or lesser degree. The evolutionary nature of the universe meant that both the knower and the object of knowledge were constantly changing. What Bergson did was to set down much of the thought of earlier mystics in the language of evolutionary science.

The Birth of Psychoanalysis

A determination to probe beneath surface or public appearances united the major figures of late-nineteenth-century science, art, and philosophy. They sought to discern the various undercurrents, tensions, and complexities that lay beneath the smooth, calm surfaces of hard atoms, respectable families, rationality, and social relationships. Their theories and discoveries meant that articulate, educated Europeans could never again view the surface of life with smugness or complacency or even with much confidence. No single intellectual development more clearly and stunningly exemplified this trend than the emergence of psychoanalysis through the work of Sigmund Freud.

Freud was born in 1856 into an Austrian Jewish family that shortly thereafter settled in Vienna. He originally planned to become a lawyer but soon moved to the study of physiology and then to medicine. In 1886, he opened his medical practice in Vienna, where he continued to live until driven out by the Nazis in 1938, a year before his death. All of Freud's research and writing was done from the base of his medical practice. His earliest medical interests had been psychic disorders, to which he sought to apply the critical method of science. In late 1885, he had studied for a few months in Paris with Jean-Martin Charcot, who used hypnosis to treat cases of hysteria. In Vienna, he collaborated with another physician, Josef Breuer (1842–1925), and in 1895, they published *Studies in Hysteria*.

In the mid-1890s, Freud changed the technique of his investigations. He abandoned hypnosis and allowed his patients to talk freely and spontaneously about themselves. Repeatedly, he found that they associated their particular neurotic symptoms with experiences related to earlier experiences, going back to childhood. He also noticed that sexual matters were significant in his patients' problems. For a time, he thought that perhaps some sexual incident during childhood accounted for the illness of his patients. However, by 1897, he had privately rejected this theory. In its place, he formulated a theory of infantile sexuality, according to which sexual drives and energy exist in infants and do not simply emerge at puberty. In Freud's view, human beings are creatures of sexuality from birth through adulthood. He thus questioned in the most radical manner the concept of childhood innocence. He also portrayed the little-discussed or little-acknowledged matter of sex as one of the bases of mental order and disorder.

During the same decade, Freud was also examining the psychic phenomena of dreams. Romantic writers had taken dreams very seriously, but no one had examined dreams scientifically. As a good rationalist, Freud believed that there must exist a reasonable, scientific explanation for the irrational contents of dreams. That examination led him to a reconsideration of the general nature of the human mind. He came to the conclusion that during dreams, unconscious wishes, desires, and drives that were excluded from everyday conscious life and experience enjoyed relatively free play in the mind. He argued, "The dream is the (disguised) fulfillment of a (suppressed, repressed) wish."[4] During the waking hours, the mind repressed or censored those wishes, which were as important to one's psychological makeup as conscious thought. In fact, those unconscious drives and desires contributed to conscious behavior. Freud developed these concepts and related them to his idea of infantile sexuality in *The Interpretation of Dreams*, published in 1900. It was his most important book.

[4] *The Basic Writings of Sigmund Freud*, trans. by A. A. Brill (New York: The Modern Library, 1938), p. 235.

The Viennese physician Sigmund Freud (1856–1939) revolutionized the concept of human nature in the Western world. After his books, European thinkers have had to see rationality as only one aspect of human nature. [Bettmann Archive.]

In later books and essays, Freud continued to urge the significance of the role played by the human unconscious. He portrayed a new internal organization of the mind. That inner realm was the arena for struggle and conflict among entities that he termed the *id*, the *ego*, and the *superego*. The first of these consisted of amoral, irrational, driving instincts for sexual gratification, aggression, and general physical and sensual pleasure. The superego constituted the external moral imperatives and expectations imposed on the personality by its society and culture. The ego stood as the mediator between the impulses of the id and the asceticism of the superego. The ego allowed the personality to cope with the inner and outer demands of its existence. Consequently, everyday behavior displayed the activity of the personality as its inner drives were partially repressed through the ego's coping with the external moral expectations as interpreted by the superego. It has been a grave misreading of Freud to see him as urging humankind to thrust off all repression. He believed that excessive repression could lead to mental disorder but that a certain degree of repression of sexuality and aggression was necessary for civilized living and the survival of humankind.

Freud's work led to nothing less than a revolution in the understanding of human nature. As his views gained adherents just before and after World War I, new dimensions of human life became widely recognized. Human beings were seen as attaining rationality rather than merely exercising it. Civilization itself came to be regarded as a product of repressed or sublimated aggressions and sexual drive.

Freud stands as a son of the Enlightenment. Like the *philosophes*, he was a realist who wanted human beings to live free of fear and illusions by rationally understanding themselves and their world. He saw the personalities of human beings as being determined by finite physical and mental forces in a finite world. He was hostile to religion and spoke of it as an illusion. Freud, like the writers of the eighteenth century, wished to see civilization and humane behavior prevail. However, more fully than those predecessors, he understood the immense sacrifice of instinctual drives required for civilized behavior. He understood how many previously unsuspected obstacles lay in the way of rationality. Freud believed that the sacrifice and struggle were worthwhile, but he was pessimistic about the future of civilization in the West.

Freud's work marked the beginning of the psychoanalytic movement. By 1910, he had gathered around him a small but highly able group of disciples. Several of his early followers soon moved toward theories of which the master disapproved. The most important of these dissenters was Carl Jung (1875–1961). He was a Swiss whom for many years Freud regarded as his most distinguished and promising student. Before World War I, the two men had, however, come to a parting of the ways. Jung had begun to question the primacy of sexual drives in forming human personality and in contributing to mental disorder. He also put much less faith in the guiding light of reason. Jung believed that the human subconscious contained inherited memories from previous generations of human beings. These collective memories, as well as the personal experience of a person, constituted his or her soul. Jung regarded human beings in the twentieth century as alienated from these useful collective memories. One of this more famous books is entitled *Modern Man in Search of a Soul* (1933). Here and elsewhere, Jung's thought tended toward mysticism and toward ascribing positive values to religion. Freud was highly critical of most of Jung's work.

By the 1920s, psychoanalysis had become even more fragmented as a movement. Nonetheless, in its several varieties, the movement touched not only psychology but also sociology, anthropology, religious studies, and literary theory. It has been probably the single most important set of ideas whereby men and women in the twentieth century have come to study themselves and their civilization.

Retreat from Rationalism in Politics

Both nineteenth-century liberals and nineteenth-century socialists agreed that society and politics could be guided according to rational principles. Rational analysis could discern the problems of society and prepare solutions. They generally felt that once given the vote, individuals would behave in their own rational political self-interest. Improvement of society and the human condition was possible through education. By the close of the century, these views were under attack in both theory and practice. Political scientists and sociologists painted politics as frequently irrational. Racial theorists questioned whether rationality and education could affect human society at all.

FROM INDIVIDUALISM TO COLLECTIVE ACTIVITY. During this period, however, one major social theorist stayed profoundly impressed by the role of reason in human society. The German sociologist Max Weber (1864–1920) regarded the emergence of rationalization throughout society as the major development of human history. Such rationalization displayed itself in both the development of scientific knowledge and the rise of bureaucratic organization. Weber saw bureaucratization as the most fundamental feature of modern social life. He used this view to oppose Marx's concept of the development of capitalism as the driving force in modern society. Bureaucratization involved the extreme division of labor as each individual person began to fit himself or herself into a particular small role in a much larger organization. Furthermore, Weber believed that in modern society, people derived their own self-images and senses of personal worth from their positions in these organizations. Weber also contended again, in contrast to Marx, that noneconomic factors might account for major developments in human history. For example, in his most famous essay, *The Protestant Ethic and the Spirit of Capitalism* (1905), Weber traced much of the rational character of capitalist enterprise to the ascetic religious doctrines of Puritanism. The Puritans, in his opinion, had accumulated wealth and had worked for worldly success less for its own sake than to furnish themselves the assurance that they stood among the elect of God.

In his emphasis on the individual and on the dominant role of rationality, Weber differed from many contemporary social scientists, such as Gustave Le-Bon, Émile Durkheim, and Georges Sorel in France; Vilfredo Pareto in Italy; and Graham Wallas in England. LeBon (1841–1931) was a psychologist who explored the activity of crowds and mobs. He believed that in crowd situations, rational behavior was abandoned. Sorel (1847–1922) argued in *Reflections on Violence* (1908) that people did not pursue rationally perceived goals but were led to action by collectively shared ideals. Durkheim (1858–1917) and Wallas (1858–1932) became deeply interested in the necessity of shared values and activities in a society. These elements, rather than a logical analysis of the social situation, bound human beings together. Instinct, habit, and affections instead of reason directed human social behavior. Besides playing down the function of reason in society, all of these theorists emphasized the role of collective groups in politics rather than that of the individual formerly championed by the liberals.

Max Weber was one of the most influential writers contributing to sociology and economics in the late nineteenth and twentieth centuries. [The Granger Collection.]

RACIAL THEORY AND ANTI-SEMITISM. The same tendencies to question or even to deny the constructive activity of reason in human affairs and to sacrifice the individual to the group manifested themselves in theories of race. Racial thinking had long existed in Europe. Renaissance explorers had displayed considerable prejudice against nonwhite peoples. Since at least the eighteenth century, biologists and anthropologists had classified human beings according to the color of their skin, their language, and their stage of civilization. Late-eighteenth-century linguistic scholars had observed similarities between many of the European languages and Sanskrit. They then postulated the existence of an ancient race called the *Aryans*, who had spoken the original language from which the rest derived. During the Romantic period, writers had called the different cultures of Europe *races*. The debates over slavery in the European colonies and the United States had given further opportunity for the development of racial theory. However, in the late nineteenth century, the concept of race emerged as a single dominant explanation of the history and the character of large groups of people.

Arthur de Gobineau (1816–1882), a reactionary French diplomat, enunciated the first important theory of race as the major determinant of human history. In his four-volume *Essay on the Inequality of the Human Races* (1853–1854), Gobineau portrayed the troubles of Western civilization as being the result of the long degeneration of the original white Aryan race. It had unwisely intermarried with the inferior yellow and black races, thus diluting the qualities of greatness and ability that originally existed in its blood. Gobineau was deeply pessimistic because he saw no way to reverse the degeneration that had taken place.

Gobineau's essay remained relatively obscure for many years. In the meantime, a growing literature by anthropologists and explorers helped to spread racial thinking. In the wake of Darwin's theory, the concept of survival of the fittest was applied to races and nations. The recognition of the animal nature of humankind made the racial idea all the more persuasive. At the close of the century, Houston Stewart Chamberlain (1855–1927), an Englishman who settled in Germany, drew together these strands of racial thought into the two volumes of his *Foundations of the Nineteenth Century* (1899). He championed the concept of biological determinism through race, but he was somewhat more optimistic than Gobineau. Chamberlain believed that through genetics, the human race could be improved and even that a superior race could be developed. Chamberlain added another element. He pointed to the Jews as the major enemy of European racial regeneration. Chamberlain's book and the lesser works on which it drew aided the spread of anti-Semitism in European political life. Also in Germany, the writings of Paul de Lagarde and Julius Langbehn emphasized the supposed racial and cultural dangers posed by the Jews to traditional German national life.

Political and racial anti-Semitism, which have cast such dark shadows across the twentieth century, emerged in part from this atmosphere of racial thought and the retreat from rationality in politics. Religious anti-Semitism dated from at least the Middle Ages. Since the French Revolution, Western European Jews had gradually gained entry into the civil life of Britain, France, and Germany. Popular anti-Semitism continued to exist as the Jewish community was identified with money and banking interests. During the last third of the century, as finance capitalism changed the economic structure of Europe, people pressured by the changes became hostile toward the Jewish community. This was especially true of the socially and economically insecure middle class. In Vienna, Mayor Karl Lueger (1844–1910) used such anti-Semitism as a major attraction to his successful Christian Socialist Party. In Germany, the ultraconservative Lutheran chaplain Adolf Stoecker (1835–1909) revived anti-Semitism. The Dreyfus affair in France allowed a new flowering of hatred toward the Jews.

H. S. Chamberlain Exalts the Role of Race

Houston Stewart Chamberlain's Foundations of the Nineteenth Century (1899) *was one of the most influential works of the day to argue for the primary role of race in history. Chamberlain believed that most people in the world were racially mixed and that this mixture weakened those human characteristics most needed for physical and moral strength. However, as demonstrated in the passage below, he also believed that those persons who were assured of their racial purity could act with the most extreme self-confidence and arrogance. Chamberlain's views later had a major influence on the Nazi Party in Germany and on others who wished to prove their alleged racial superiority for political purposes.*

Nothing is so convincing as the consciousness of the possession of Race. The man who belongs to a distinct, pure race, never loses the sense of it. The guardian angel of his lineage is ever at his side, supporting him where he loses his foothold, warning him like the Socratic Daemon where he is in danger of going astray, compelling obedience, and forcing him to undertakings which deeming them impossible, he would never have dared to attempt. Weak and erring like all that is human, a man of this stamp recognises himself, as others recognise him, by the sureness of his character, and by the fact that his actions are marked by a certain simple and peculiar greatness, which finds its explanation in his distinctly typical and super-personal qualities. Race lifts a man above himself; it endows him with extraordinary—I might almost say supernatural—powers, so entirely does it distinguish him from the individual who springs from the chaotic jumble of peoples drawn from all parts of the world: and should this man of pure origin be perchance gifted above his fellows, then the fact of Race strengthens and elevates him on every hand, and he becomes a genius towering over the rest of mankind, not because he has been thrown upon the earth like a flaming meteor by a freak of nature, but because he soars heavenward like some strong and stately tree, nourished by thousands and thousands of roots—no solitary individual, but the living sum of untold souls striving for the same goal. ❑

Houston Stewart Chamberlain, *Foundations of the Nineteenth Century*, Vol. 1, trans. by John Lees (London: John Lane Limited, 1912), p. 269.

To this already ugly atmosphere, racial thought contributed the belief that no matter to what extent Jews assimilated themselves and their families into the culture of their country, their Jewishness—and thus their alleged danger to the society—would remain. The problem of race was not in the character but in the blood of the Jew. An important Jewish response to this new, rabid outbreak of anti-Semitism was the launching in 1896 of the Zionist movement to found a separate Jewish state. Its founder was the Austro-Hungarian Theodor Herzl (1860–1904). The conviction in 1894 of Captain Dreyfus in France and the election of Karl Lueger in 1895 as mayor of Vienna, as well as his personal experiences of discrimination, convinced Herzl that liberal politics and the institutions of the liberal state could not protect the Jews in Europe or ensure that they would be treated justly. In 1896, Herzl published *The Jewish State*, in which he called for the organization of a separate state in which the Jews of the world might be assured of those rights and liberties that they should be enjoying in the liberal states of Europe. Furthermore, Herzl followed the tactics of late-century mass democratic politics by particularly directing his appeal to the economically poor Jews who lived in the ghettos of eastern Europe and the slums of western Europe. The original call to Zionism thus combined a rejection of the anti-Semitism of Europe and a desire to establish some of the ideals of both liberalism and socialism in a state outside Europe.

Racial thinking and revived anti-Semitism were part of a wider late-century movement toward aggressive nationalism. Previously, nationalism had been a movement among European literary figures and liberals. The former had sought to develop what they regarded as the historically distinct qualities of particular national or ethnic literatures. The liberal nationalists had hoped to redraw the map of Europe to reflect ethnic boundaries. The drive for the unification of Italy and Germany had been major causes, as had been the liberation of Poland from foreign domination. The various national groups of the Habsburg Empire had also sought emancipation from Austrian domination.

From the 1870s onward, however, nationalism became a movement with mass support, well-financed organizations, and political parties. Nationalists tended to redefine nationality in terms of race and blood. The new nationalism opposed the internationalism of both liberalism and socialism. The ideal of nationality was used to overcome the pluralism of class, religion, and geography. The nation and its duties replaced religion in the lives of many secularized people. It sometimes became a secular religion in the hands of state schoolteachers, who were replacing the clergy as the instructors of youth. Nationalism of this aggressive, racist variety would prove to be the most powerful ideology of the early twentieth century.

Intellectual Change in World Perspective

The remarkable scientific achievements of the European intellectual community during the second half of the nineteenth century proved to be very exportable. The results of this cultural export were quite mixed.

Racism and social Darwinism came to undergird much of the ideology of imperialism. Racial thinking allowed Europeans to believe that they were in some manner inherently superior to other peoples and cultures. The concept of survival of the fittest provided for many Europeans a pattern for their relations with the rest of the world. In both Europe and the United States, persons of the nonwhite races were regarded as inferior. State governments in the southern portion of the United States enacted segregation laws based in part on racial thinking. In the opinion of certain scientific writers, non-European peoples stood on a lower level of the evolutionary ladder. Consequently, European states conquered and administered large portions of Africa and Asia, justifying this action partly on the grounds that the native peoples were less fit then Europeans to govern themselves. Racial thinking of this kind informed the minds of virtually all colonial administrators of the imperial powers.

At the same time, the technology and scientific theories that had made the Second Industrial Revolution possible also provided the technological superiority that allowed Europe and the United States to dominate so much of the world between 1850 and 1945. That technological domination gave plausibility to the conclusions of racial thinking. However, that science and technology could be copied and eventually turned against its originators. Japan after the Meiji restoration successfully set out to copy the science as well as the political administration associated with modern Western thought. In doing so, it succeeded in defending itself against the intrusions of the West and defeated a major Western power, Russia, in war.

China, at the same time, failed to embrace modern science and technology and fell victim to both the Western powers and Japan. However, after those humiliations, at the turn of the century China began to abandon its dedication to Confucian education. Reforming leaders embraced a vast spectrum of Western ideas, including social Darwinism and socialism. By the end of World War I, a strong sense of nationalism also permeated China. These ideas eventually became linked to Marxism in China, combining both a concern for social reform and a belief that Marxism was a form of scientific socialism.

The emergence of a strong industrialized Japan and of a China stirred by nationalism and Marxist revolution thus illustrates the double influence of late nineteenth-century Western ideas. Those scientific and political ideas first led to the degradation of those Asian peoples. In turn, other Western ideas, along with long-standing Asian ideas and values, provided the technological and ideological basis for national revivals leading those nations to challenge Western imperialism.

Suggested Readings

R. ARON, *Main Currents in Sociological Thought*, 2 vols. (1965, 1967). An introduction to the founders of the science.

S. AVINERI, *The Making of Modern Zionism: The Intellectual Origins of the Jewish State* (1981). An excellent introduction to the development of Zionist thought.

S. BARROWS, *Distorting Mirrors: Visions of the Crowd in Late Nineteenth-Century France* (1981). An important and imaginative examination of crowd psychology as it related to social tension in France.

F. L. BAUMER, *Religion and the Rise of Scepticism* (1960). Traces the development of religious doubt from the seventeenth to the twentieth centuries.

F. L. BAUMER, *Modern European Thought: Continuity and Change in Ideas*, 1600–1950 (1977). The best work on the subject for this period.

M. D. BIDDIS, *Father of Racist Ideology: The Social and Political Thought of Count Gobineau* (1970). Sets the subject in the more general context of nineteenth-century thought.

P. BOWLER, *The Eclipse of Darwinism: Anti-Darwinian Evolution Theories in the Decades Around 1900* (1983). A major study of the fate of Darwinian theory in the nineteenth-century scientific community.

P. BOWLER, *Evolution: The History of an Idea* (1984). An outstanding survey of the subject.

J. W. BURROW, *Evolution and Society: A Study in Victorian Social Theory* (1966). An important study of evolutionary sociology.

O. CHADWICK, *The Secularization of the European Mind in the Nineteenth Century* (1975). The best treatment available.

D. G. CHARLTON, *Positivist Thought in France During the Second Empire*, 1852–1870 (1959), and *Secular Religions in France*, 1815–1870 (1963). Two clear introductions to important subjects.

C. M. CIPOLLA, *Literacy and Development in the West* (1969). Traces the explosion of literacy in the past two centuries.

A. DANTO, *Nietzsche as Philosopher* (1965). A very helpful and well-organized introduction.

P. GAY, *Freud, Jews, and Other Germans: Masters and Victims in Modernist Culture* (1978). A collection of wide-ranging essays on German intellectual and cultural life.

P. GAY, *Freud: A Life for Our Time* (1988). A major new biography.

C. C. GILLISPIE, *Genesis and Geology* (1951). An excellent discussion of the impact of modern geological theory during the early nineteenth century.

C. C. GILLISPIE, *The Edge of Objectivity* (1960). One of the best one-volume treatments of modern scientific ideas.

J. C. GREENE, *The Death of Adam: Evolution and Its Impact on Western Thought* (1959). Emphasizes pre-Darwinian thought.

H. S. HUGHES, *Consciousness and Society: The Reorientation of European Social Thought*, 1890–1930 (1958). A wide-ranging discussion of the revolt against positivism.

W. IRVINE, *Apes, Angels, and Victorians* (1955). A lively and sound account of Darwin and Huxley.

W. A. KAUFMANN, *Nietzsche: Philosopher, Psychologist, Antichrist*, rev. ed. (1968). An exposition of Nietzsche's thought and its sources.

E. MAYR, *The Growth of Biological Thought: Diversity, Evolution, and Inheritance* (1982). A major survey by a scientist of note.

J. MOORE, *The Post-Darwinian Controversies: A Study of the Protestant Struggle to Come to Terms with Darwin in Great Britain and America*, 1870–1900 (1979). A major examination of the impact of Darwinian thought on both science and religion.

J. MORRELL AND A. THACKRAY, *Gentlemen of Science: Early Years of the British Association for the Advancement of Science* (1981). An important study that examines the role of science in early and mid-nineteenth-century Britain.

G. L. MOSSE, *Toward the Final Solution: A History of European Racism* (1978). A sound introduction.

R. PASCAL, *From Naturalism to Expressionism: German Literature and Society*, 1880–1918 (1973). A helpful survey.

L. POLIAKOV, *The Aryan Myth: A History of Racist and Nationalist Ideas in Europe* (1971). The best introduction to the problem.

P. G. J. PULZER, *The Rise of Political Anti-Semitism in Germany and Austria* (1964). A sound discussion of anti-Semitism in the world of central European politics.

C. E. SCHORSKE, *Fin de Siècle Vienna: Politics and Culture* (1980). Major essays on the explosively creative intellectual climate of Vienna.

F. STERN, *The Politics of Cultural Despair: A Study in the Rise of the German Ideology* (1965). An important examination of antimodern and anti-Semitic thought in imperial Germany.

F. M. TURNER, *The Greek Heritage in Victorian Britain* (1981). An examination of the role of Greek antiquity in Victorian thought.

J. P. VON ARX, *Progress and Pessimism: Religion, Politics, and History in Late Nineteenth Century Britain* (1985). A major study that casts much new light on the nineteenth-century view of progress.

R. WILLIAMS, *The Long Revolution* (1961). Explores the impact of literacy and popular publishing on English culture.

R. WOLLHEIM, *Sigmund Freud* (1971). An excellent introduction to Freud's intellectual development and his major concepts.

Eva Peron (1919–1952). Her enormous popularity among the Argentine masses helped buttress the power of her husband, the dictator Juan Peron. She became a cult figure to many Argentines after her death in 1952. [UPI.]

30 Latin America: From Independence to the 1940s

By the mid-eighteen-twenties, Latin Americans had driven out their colonial rulers and had broken the colonial trade monopolies, but the Latin American wars of independence had not been popular, grass-roots movements. They had originated with the Creole elite, who were seeking to resist the possible imposition of European liberalism on the region as a result of the policies of Napoleon or, later, of Spanish liberals. In that respect, the wars of independence had been fought to break the colonial trade monopolies and to preserve as much of the existing social structure as possible.

Independence without Revolution

Independence from colonial government created several sources of discontent. There was much disagreement about the character of the future government even among those persons who had most wanted to oust the Spanish. Certain institutions, such as the Roman Catholic church, that had enjoyed a very privileged status in the colonial period had to find ways to maintain those privileges under new governments. Indian communities, which had also been somewhat protected by paternalistic colonial policies, found themselves subject to new kinds of exploitation once they were made equal citizens in the eyes of the law. Major disagreements arose between the elites of different regions of the new nations. The agricultural hinterlands resented the predominance of the port cities, whose merchants set the terms of trade. Investors or merchants from one Latin American nation found themselves in conflict with those of another over transport tariffs on rivers or mining regulations.

Absence of Social Change

Yet, no matter what the actual or potential conflict among various groups in the literate political and eco-

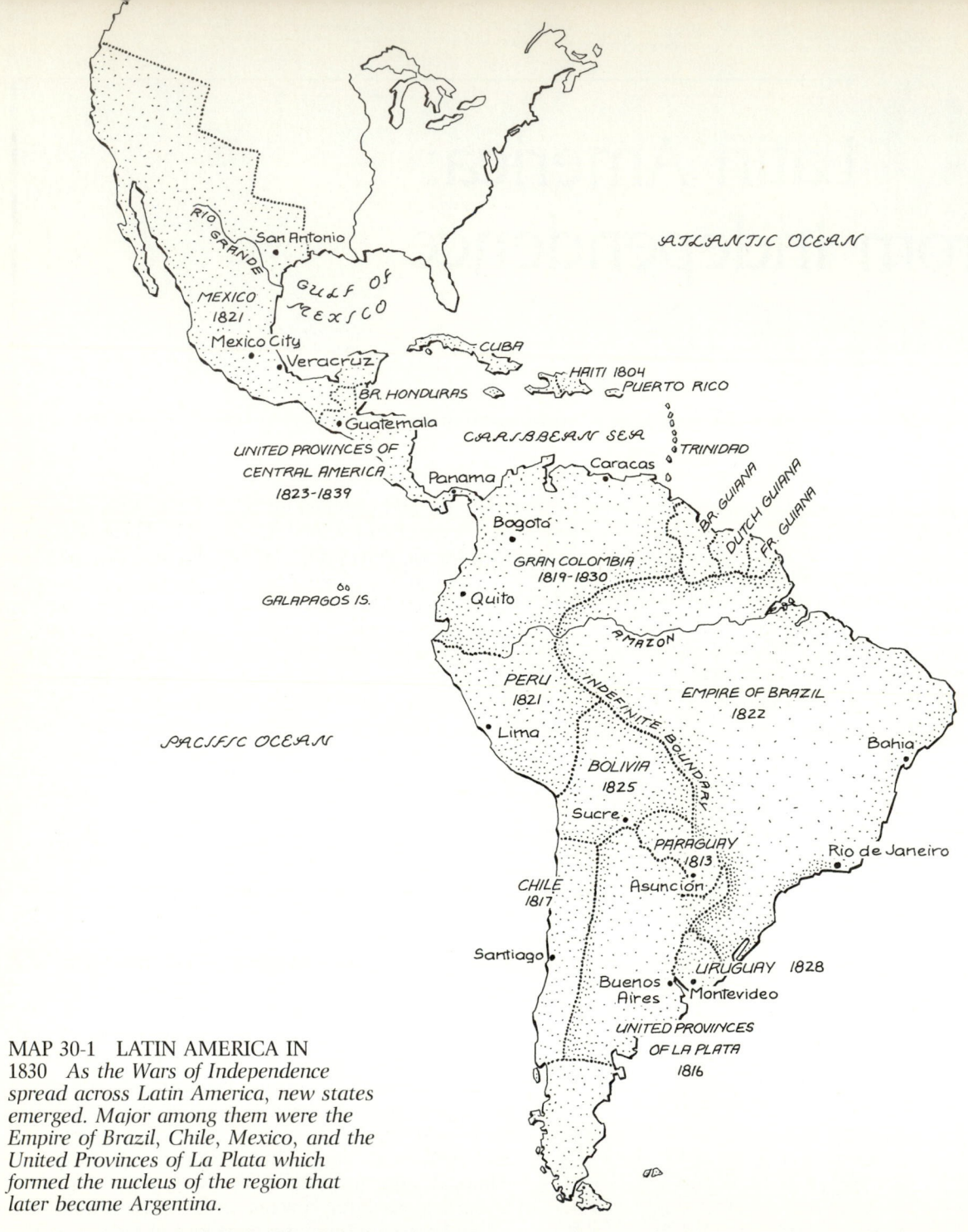

MAP 30-1 LATIN AMERICA IN
1830 *As the Wars of Independence
spread across Latin America, new states
emerged. Major among them were the
Empire of Brazil, Chile, Mexico, and the
United Provinces of La Plata which
formed the nucleus of the region that
later became Argentina.*

nomic elites might be, they stood united in their opposition to any substantial social reform. The Creole victors in the wars of independence granted equal legal and civil rights to all persons, and except for Brazil, the independent states had abolished slavery by 1855. However, equality before the law did not extend to the right to vote, which depended on a property qualification. Nor did civic equality liberate peasants from dependence on and often subservience to their landlords. The racial codes of the colonial empires disappeared, but not the racial prejudice that lay behind them. Although mestizos, mulattos, and even Indians who achieved economic success were assimilated into the higher ranks of the social structure, persons of white or nearly white complexion tended to constitute the elite of Latin America. Most important, no major changes in landholding accompanied the wars of independence; and protection of the interests of existing or of new landholders was a major goal of the ruling classes of all the newly independent nations.

With the exception of Mexico in 1910, no Latin American nation, from the wars of independence until the 1950s, experienced a fundamental revolution that overthrew the social and economic structures that dated from the colonial period. The absence of such social revolution, which would necessarily have involved changes in landholding, is perhaps the single most important factor in Latin American history during the first century of independence. The rise and fall of political regimes represented quarrels among the elite and did not substantially change the structures or expectations of everyday life for the overwhelming majority of the population.

Control of the Land

Most Latin Americans during the nineteenth century lived in the countryside. Agriculture continued to be dominated by large haciendas, or plantations. The landowners virtually ruled these estates as small domains. They were very nearly a law unto themselves. The size and extent of the latifundia (the large rural estates) actually grew during the nineteenth century. Confiscation of Church lands and conquest of Indian territories opened the way for the extension of existing estates or the establishment of new ones. Such estates might include tens of thousands of acres. These lands were tilled in a labor-intensive manner. Little machinery was available; virtually none was manufactured in Latin America. The produce of the land was generally intended for the export market.

Landowners constituted a society of their own. Their families intermarried. They sometimes formed friendships or family alliances with members of the wealthy urban classes who were involved in export commerce or the legal profession. Younger sons might enter the army or the Church. The landowners served in the various postindependence national parliaments or congresses. Their wealth, their literacy, and their connections made the landowners the rulers of the countryside. They also were assured that the army would protect them from any potential social uprising.

The landowners lived well and comfortably, though often on very isolated estates. The majority of persons dwelling in the countryside experienced conditions of immense social and economic dependence. In Brazil, slavery continued to exist until 1888. Although it has been argued that slavery in the context of a Roman Catholic country was more paternalistic and less harsh than elsewhere, there is little substantial evidence to support that contention. In other rural areas, many people lived in situations not very much different from slavery. Debt peonage was widespread and often

A Chilean cattle estate. The great landowners of Latin America ruled their huge estates as small domains. [Magnum, Sergio Larrain.]

tied a peasant to the land in a manner not dissimilar to European serfdom. A peon would become indebted to his landlord and could never get out from under the burden of debt. Later in the nineteenth century, as new lands were opened, they generally were organized as large holdings with tenants rather than as small landholdings with independent farmers. Poor roads and very limited railways made internal travel difficult and kept many people on the land. The exceedingly limited effort toward even primary education left millions of Latin American peasants ignorant, lacking any significant technological skills, and incapable of improving their condition or of protesting or escaping their bondage to the land and its owners.

The second half of the nineteenth century witnessed a remarkable growth in Latin American urban life. There was some movement from the countryside to the city, and there was a major influx of European immigrants. Throughout this period, there arose a political and social trade-off between the urban and rural elites. Each more-or-less permitted the other to pursue its economic self-interest, to profit from the commodity export economy through commerce or production, and to repress any discontent from the lower social orders.

An Argentine cattle ranch. The export and consumption of beef have been central to the Argentine economy since the nineteenth century. [Magnum, Erich Hartmann.]

Submissive Political Philosophies

The political philosophies embraced by the educated and propertied Latin American elites also discouraged any major challenge to the social order. The concepts of European liberalism, which flourished in Latin America immediately after independence, supported the establishment of republican government. The voting franchise was based on property ownership. Economic liberalism and the direct need for British investment aid led to the championing of the doctrines of free trade. Latin America was to produce raw materials and to import manufactured goods from Europe, and especially from Britain. Because of this policy, liberals supported new land development in Latin America and the confiscation of land owned by the Church and the Indian communities, which did not exploit it in a progressive manner. Consequently, Latin American liberals championed the extension of great landed estates and all the forms of social dependence associated with those rural units of production. For most of the nineteenth century, the landed sector of the economy dominated because the cheap imports from abroad discouraged Latin American attempts at industrialism.

During the second half of the century, the political ideas stemming from the French positivist philosopher Auguste Comte (1798–1857) swept across Latin America in a manner that never occurred in Europe. Comte and his followers, as explained in Chapter 29, had advocated the cult of science and technological progress. This highly undemocratic outlook, which became especially popular among military officers, suggested that either technocrats or dictatorial governments were the best vehicles for achieving modernization. The great slogan of Latin American positivism, emblazoned on the flag of the Brazilian republic, was "Order and Progress." Social or political groups that created disorder or that challenged the existing social order were to be regarded by definition as unprogressive.

Finally, the late-nineteenth-century European theories of "scientific" racism were used to preserve the Latin American social status quo and the dominance of persons of white or more nearly white complexions. Racial theory could be used to account for the economic backwardness of the region on the basis of the vast population of nonwhite persons or persons with nonwhite blood in their veins. This explanation, of course, shifted responsibility for the economic difficulties of Latin America away from the governing elites, most of whose members were white, and toward Indians, blacks, mestizos, and mulattos, who had long lived in situations of social dependence or repression.

The Economy of Dependence

The wars of independence destroyed the Spanish and Portuguese colonial trade monopolies. Where previously only a few dozen ships called annually at any particular port, hundreds laden with goods from all over the world could now drop anchor. Consequently,

Latin America had many new trading partners. However, the colonial situation of heavy dependence on non-Latin American economies did not change. The economic demands, policies, and goals of other nations continued for well over a century to shape Latin American economic life in the most fundamental manner.

New Exploitation of Resources

The wars of independence sharply disrupted the Latin American economy. Many Spanish merchants and other members of the urban colonial commercial establishment emigrated. Mining operations in both Mexico and Peru had been devastated by the wars. Mines were flooded; machinery was in disrepair; labor was in short supply. Agricultural production was in a state of disruption. Between 1825 and 1850, the new nations attempted to set their economic houses in order, but with rather mixed results. There was wholly inadequate capital financing. Virtually no domestic industries existed to manufacture heavy equipment or to build ships. Both to restore old industries, such as mining, and to utilize modern modes of transport, such as steamships and railroads, Latin Americans had to turn to the more advanced industrial economies of Europe and North America. For many decades, the British were the major foreign power exercising economic influence over Latin America. More than any other nation, the British had sought to break the old colonial monopoly. Once it was gone, they moved rapidly to establish their dominance.

To pay for needed imports and foreign services, Latin American nations turned to the production of agricultural commodities for which there was great European demand. This shift meant that the rural areas of Latin America and the commercial centers serving agriculture came to have much more political and economic importance than did many of the old colonial urban centers. The production of wheat, beef, hides, hemp, coffee, cocoa, and other foodstuffs for the export market also raised the value of land and put pressure on governments to expand into previously unsettled territory and to confiscate the lands of the Church. The vast amounts of land available meant that increases in production occurred through bringing new regions into cultivation rather than by farming existing areas more efficiently. The wealth that could be accumulated through land speculation and land development was so considerable that little incentive existed for alternative investments in manufacturing. It would also have been very difficult, if not impossible, for new Latin American industries to compete with the very cheap goods imported from abroad. The quarter century after independence also witnessed the revival of the mining industry in Mexico, Peru, and Chile through the use of foreign capital.

After 1850, the Latin American republics became, relatively speaking, more prosperous. Chile exported copper and nitrates as well as wheat. Peru exported guano all over the world to be used as fertilizer. Coffee was on its way to becoming king in Venezuela, Brazil, Colombia, and Central America. Sugar continued to be produced in the West Indies. Argentina supplied hides and tallow. But this very limited prosperity and recovery was based on the export of agricultural commodities or extracted minerals and the importation of finished goods from abroad. There were three broad varieties of Latin American exports. First, there were foodstuffs raised in Latin America that were more-or-less like those that could be raised in Europe. Chief among these were wheat and beef products. Second, there were distinctly tropical products, such as bananas, sugar, and coffee. Third, there were metals; minerals, such as nitrates; and later oil.

Both the trading patterns for these goods and the internal improvements in Latin American production deeply and inextricably linked the economy of the region to Europe and, after the turn of the century, to the United States. Europeans and North Americans not only provided capital but also supplied the technological and managerial skills for the building of bridges, roads, railroads, steam lines, and new mines. Most of the transport system was constructed to service the existing export economy rather than to foster the development of alternative forms of domestic economic development. Furthermore, every time the economy of Europe or the United States suffered a major crisis, the impact spilled over into Latin America. The region could exercise no substantial control over its own economic destiny.

Increased Foreign Ownership and Influence

During the second half of the nineteenth century, the relative prosperity of the export sector increased the situation of dependence. The growing European demand generated by spreading industrialism gave Latin Americans a false sense of the long-term security of that market. The vast profits to be made through mining and agricultural exports continued to discourage investment in local industry except as it served the export economy. Land still remained the most favored form of domestic investment. By late in the century, the wealthy classes in Latin America were prosperous, but they had, in effect, lost control and even ownership of some of the most valuable sectors of their economy. For example, in 1901, British and other foreign investors owned approximately 80 per cent of the Chilean nitrate industry. Most of the steamship lines and railroads were also owned and operated by Europeans or North Americans.

U.S. influence and Investments in Latin America grew rapidly after 1900 and surpassed those of Britain by the 1920s. As this cartoon illustrates, the U.S. tended to regard its southern neighbors as at best junior and dependent partners. [Bettmann Archive.]

Foreign ownership was not the only indication of economic dependence. Foreign powers had real economic interests in the region and used their influence to protect those interests. Britain was the dominant power until the turn of the century. Its ambassadors and military and naval officers were frequently involved directly or indirectly in the domestic political affairs of the Latin American nations. From the Spanish American War of 1898 onward, the United States began to exercise more direct influence in the region. In 1903, the United States actively participated in the rebellion of Panama from Colombia to facilitate the future building of the Panama Canal. There were numerous other instances of U.S. military intervention in the Caribbean and in Central America. By the 1920s, U.S. investments had become dominant as a result of two decades of "Dollar Diplomacy." The role of the United States was and has continued to be controversial, but from a structural standpoint, it was just one more example of a dominant foreign power treating Latin America as a very junior and dependent trading partner.

The interventions of the United States demonstrated one cost in the early twentieth century of being a dependent economy. More important, however, were the fundamental shifts in world trade occasioned by World War I and continued through the 1920s. First, the overall amount of trade carried on by European countries decreased. This situation had been worsened during the war by the division of the traditional trading partners into two warring camps. Second, during the 1920s, world prices of agricultural commodities dropped steadily. Latin American nations had to produce more goods to pay for their imports, and no easy or rapid adjustment was possible. Third, various synthetic products manufactured in Europe or North America replaced the natural products long supplied by Latin American producers. Most important among these products were synthetic nitrates. Finally, petroleum began to replace other natural products as an absolute percentage of world trade. This shift meant that petroleum-exporting countries, such as Mexico, gained a greater share of income.

Economic Crises and New Directions

The onset of the Great Depression in 1929 turned the difficult economic conditions of the 1920s into a genuine crisis. There was a virtual collapse in commodity prices. The economic decline in Europe and the United States also meant that fewer Latin American products were in demand. The republics of Latin America could not repay the debts owed to foreign banks, and a number of them suspended interest payments. Those decisions, in turn, worsened the economic crisis in the more developed creditor nations. The Depression led eventually to the beginning of a new economic era in Latin America. The new era, which really began after 1945 and the conclusion of World War II, was marked by strong economic nationalism and a determination to create sectors of the various national economies that were not wholly dependent on events and wealth outside Latin America. The success of these various drives toward economic independence has been quite mixed, but they date only from the turmoil of the Depression.

Where did industrialism fit into this general picture of a dependent economy, or what is sometimes termed a *neo-colonial economy?* The brief answer is, almost always, on the periphery of the export sector. Until the 1940s, major industrialization did not occur in Latin America. There were, however, some significant developments before that time. Before World War I, some light manufacturing was done in connection with preparing exports, such as beef processing in Argentina. There was also some domestic production of light manufactured goods, such as textiles. With the Depression, however, it became necessary to substitute domestically manufactured goods for those traditionally imported from abroad. Various nations pursued different policies of what was called *import substitution,* but all of these policies were undertaken because of the collapse of the export economy rather than because of any independent decision to industrialize. In that regard, the effort to industrialize was itself a result of the situation of dependence.

By the mid-1940s, there were three major varieties of manufacturing in Latin America. First, there were industries that, as in the past, transformed raw materials for export. These included sugar and other food processing, tin and copper mining, and petroleum refining. Second, there were industries addressing local demands, such as power plants, textiles, foundries, machine shops, and food companies. Third, there were industries depending generally on the transformation of imported materials. These were basically assembly plants whose owners could take advantage of inexpensive labor. None of this manufacturing was particularly sophisticated, and none of it involved heavy industry. Not until the 1950s would significant steel production, for example, occur in the region.

The Search for Political Stability

The new states of independent Latin America, unlike the British colonies of North America, had little or no experience in self-government. The Spanish Empire had been ruled directly by the monarchy and by Spanish-born monarchical bureaucrats. This monarchical heritage survived in two forms. First, there were many traditionalists and conservatives who favored the establishment of monarchies in Latin America, including José de San Martín. Monarchy was briefly established in Mexico. In Brazil, an emperor from the Portuguese royal family governed until 1888. The second heritage of the colonial monarchy was the proclivity of the Latin American political elites to tolerate or actively to support very strong executives in nations that possessed republican constitutions.

Few of these republican constitutions proved lasting or established a stable political life. They were frequently suspended or rewritten so that a strong leader could consolidate his own power. Such figures, who appeared throughout Latin America during the nineteenth century, were called *caudillos*. They usually came from the ranks of the army officer corps or enjoyed very strong ties with the army. Whatever constitutional justification they provided for themselves, the real basis of their rule was force and repression. *Caudillos* might support conservative causes such as protection of the Church or strong central government, or they might pursue liberal policies such as the confiscation of Church land, the extension of landed estates, and the development of education.

Initially, such dictatorial government was accepted simply to ensure political stability when republican regimes floundered. The early years of independence saw major conflicts among the regions of the various states. A national *caudillo* might reach some kind of compromise with various regional *caudillos* whereby the latter retained much local control. The repressive policies of these strongmen were another reason that they encountered little opposition. Later in the century, the new relative prosperity of expanding economies quieted potential discontent. The dictators became more skilled at both repression and patronage. The political and social elites also rallied to their support when, around the turn of the century, the young labor movement called strikes.

Even when the *caudillo* was forced from office and parliamentary government was more-or-less restored, the regimes were not genuinely liberal and were never democratic. Parliamentary governments usually ruled by courtesy of the military and in the economic interest of the existing elites. Whatever the shifts in government during the nineteenth and the early twentieth centuries, the life of the overwhelming mass of the population changed very little. Except for the Mexican Revolution of 1910, Latin American politics was run by the elite and for the elite.

Three National Histories

Three Latin American nations possess over fifty per cent of the land, people, and wealth of the continent. They are Argentina, Mexico, and Brazil. Their national histories may serve to illustrate in some detail the more general themes of Latin American history.

Argentina

Argentine history from independence to World War II can be divided into three general eras. From the rebellion against Spain in 1810 until mid-century, the question of which region of the nation would dominate political and economic life relegated most other issues to the background. From 1853 until 1916, Argentina experienced extraordinary economic expansion and large-scale immigration from Europe, which transformed its society and its position in the world. From 1916 to 1943, Argentines struggled over their unsuccessful attempt to establish a democratic state and the ramifications of an economy that was not really under national control.

BUENOS AIRES VS. THE PROVINCES. In 1810, the junta in Buenos Aires had overturned Spanish government in the viceroyalty of Río de la Plata. In the years that followed, the other regions of the viceroyalty refused to accept the leadership of the province and city of Buenos Aires. Consequently, Paraguay, Uruguay, and Upper Peru (Bolivia) went their separate ways. Divisions and conflicts between Buenos Aires and the remaining provinces dominated the first seventy years of Argentine history. It was the story of *porteños*, as the inhabitants of Buenos Aires were called, versus provincials. Eventually, Buenos Aires established its primacy because of its capacity to dominate trade on the Río de la Plata and its control of the international customhouse, which assured revenue.

Between 1821 and 1827, Bernardino Rivadavia (1780–1845) worked to create a liberal political state, but was unable to overcome the centrifugal forces of regionalism. His major accomplishment was a commercial treaty in 1823 that established Great Britain as a dominant trading partner. Thus began a deep intermeshing of trade and finance between the two nations that would continue for well over a century. After Rivadavia's resignation in 1827 came the classical period of *caudillo* rule in Argentina. The strongman of the province of Buenos Aires was Juan Manuel de Rosas (1793–1877). In 1831, he negotiated the Pact of the Littoral, whereby Buenos Aires was put in charge of foreign relations, trade, and the customhouse, while the other provinces were left to govern all local matters. Within Buenos Aires, Rosas set up what amounted to dictatorial rule. He tolerated no dissent, no civil liberties, and no political power distinct from his own. One of his devices was the secret *Mazorca* (ear of corn) association, which terrorized his opponents. His major policies were expansion of trade and agriculture, suppression of the Indians, and nationalism.

EXPANSION AND GROWTH OF THE REPUBLIC. Rosas' success in strengthening Buenos Aires bred resentment in other provinces. In 1852, Justo José de Urquiza (1800–1870), the *caudillo* of the state of Entre Rios, overthrew Rosas. The next year, a federal constitution was promulgated for the Argentine Republic. Buenos Aires remained aloof until military forces of the republic conquered the province in 1859. Disputes continued. In 1880, the city of Buenos Aires was made a distinct federal province, separate from its rich hinterland. Provincials had hoped that this arrangement would lessen the influence of the city. They were disappointed because the economic prosperity of the end of the century simply gave the capital new prominence.

The Argentine economy was overwhelmingly agricultural, the chief exports at mid-century being hides, tallow, and beef products. Internal transportation was very poor, and except along the coast, the country was sparsely populated. Technological factors changed this situation during the last quarter of the century. In 1876, the first refrigerator ship, *La Frigiorique*, steamed into the port of Buenos Aires. Henceforth, it would be possible to transport large quantities of Argentine beef to Europe. Furthermore, at about the same time, it became clear that wheat farming could be extended throughout the pampas. In 1879 and 1880, a govern-

Juan Manuel de Rosas (1793–1877), caudillo of Buenos Aires from 1827 to 1852. [Bettmann Archive.]

ment army under General (and later President) Julio Roca carried out a major campaign against the Indian population known as the *Conquest of the Desert*. The British soon began to construct and manage railways to carry wheat from the interior to the coast, where it would be loaded on British and other foreign steamships. Government policy made the purchase of land by wealthy Argentines very simple and cheap. They, in turn, rented the land to tenants. In this manner, the predominance both of large landowners and of foreign business interests continued throughout the most significant economic transformation in Argentine history.

The development of the pampas and the vastly increased production of beef and wheat made Argentina one of the wealthiest nations of Latin America. It became a major agricultural rival of the United States. The opening of land even under the condition of tenant farming encouraged hundreds of thousands of Europeans, particularly from Spain and Italy, to emigrate to Argentina. The immigrants expanded the farming population and also provided workers for the food-processing, service, and transportation industries located in Buenos Aires. The new economic life and the thousands of new citizens had, by 1900, turned Argentina into a nation very different from the kind it had been only a quarter century earlier. It had become much more urbanized and industrialized. There were more people who had reason to be politically discon-

A Priest Praises the Overthrow of Rosas

Juan Manuel de Rosas was one of the most famous and infamous Latin American caudillos. He was, as governor of the province of Buenos Aires, the major figure in the early decades of the independent Argentine Republic. His regime brought stability, but he very freely used devices of political terrorism. He was overthrown militarily in 1852 by forces of several Argentine provinces led by Justo José de Urquiza. Below are excerpts of a sermon preached at a service of thanksgiving in Buenos Aires. The priest used the occasion to compare Rosas with the Roman Emperor Nero and Urquiza with George Washington. The rhetoric is exaggerated, but the tyranny of Rosas was real. The sermon was reported by an English sea captain who witnessed the service.

. . . if it was praiseworthy in the Romans gratefully to acknowledge, and joyfully to give thanks to their gods for a deliverance from the tyranny of Nero, is it not equally so in us Argentines to offer to the true God the incense of our praise for liberating us from the despotism of Rosas—that tyrant, that wild beast, that scandal of our nation, that shame upon humanity, that scourge of society and of religion, that minotaur, more thirsty for blood than him of Crete who fed on human victims? . . .

. . . answer for me, ye numerous auditors who listen to me. Speak, yet many widows, whose hearts, as ye listen to my words, are broken with sorrow—let the tears speak with which you have been fed till the present day. Speak, yet fathers, who still pour out your grief in sighs upon your children's tombs. Speak, yet numerous orphans, who, while embracing with kisses the fathers of your love, have suddenly beheld them expire beneath the point of the dagger! Do thou, O city of Buenos Aires—do thou speak: speak every province, speak every town, speak every family of the Republic! . . .

And is it not right that we should be thankful to the Almighty for the benefits received at his hands? We have attained our liberty. Oh! incomparable good! Oh! gift of inestimable value! And to whom shall we give thanks, if not to Thee, O Father of mercies? . . . But likewise to thy name, O great Urquiza! to thee, whose name will be immortal: to thee our gratitude will be eternal, and the echo of our acknowledgements will be heard, even to the ends of the earth. The heart of every Argentine will be a temple from which thou wilt receive the sweet incense of our affection; and tradition will forever transmit to our descendants the name of him who has restored us to our liberties. Most excellent sir, we salute thee as the morning star of the happy day of freedom that has dawned upon our country. We acclaim thee as our Washington! The Washington of the Argentine Republic! ❑

Charles S. Stewart, *Brazil and La Plata: The Personal Record of a Cruise* (1856), quoted in N. Andrew N. Cleven, *Readings in Hispanic American History* (New York: Ginn and Company, 1927), pp. 493–496.

tented. And the children of the nineteenth-century immigrants often became some of the strongest Argentine nationalists during the twentieth century.

The prosperity of economic expansion quieted most political opposition for some time. The conservative landed oligarchy continued to govern under a series of presidents who sought to perpetuate a strong export economy. Like similar groups elsewhere, in Latin America they ignored the social questions raised by urbanization and industrialization. A problem of more immediate danger, they also ignored the political aspirations of the urban middle and professional classes, which wanted a greater share in political life and an end to political corruption. In 1890, these groups had founded the Radical Party, which for many years achieved few successes. However, in 1912, the conservative government passed the Sáenz Peña Law that expanded the franchise and provided for the secret ballot.

Four years later, Hipólito Irigoyen (1850–1933), leader of the Radical Party since 1892, was elected president. Without significant support in the legislature, his presidency brought fewer changes than might have been expected. He continued the policy of neutrality in World War I so Argentina could trade with both sides. Nonetheless, the war put great pressure on the economy, and much labor agitation resulted. Though at an earlier time sympathetic toward labor, Irigoyen as president used troops against strikers. The most violent labor clash occurred in January 1919, when troops quelled a general strike in Buenos Aires during what became known as the *Semana Tragica* or Tragic Week. Thereafter, the Radical Party attempted to consolidate support among conservatives and pursued policies that benefited landowners and urban businessmen. This direction was possible because of the close relationship between agricultural producers and processors and because both the landed and the middle classes wanted to resist concessions to the working classes.

Juan and Eva Peron riding through Buenos Aires after his inauguration as president for a second term in 1952. [UPI.]

THE MILITARY IN ASCENDENCE. By the end of the 1920s, the one-time reformist Radical Party had become corrupt and directionless in its policies. The worldwide depression hurt exports. In 1930, the military staged a coup against the aged Irigoyen, who, having left office in 1922, had returned to the presidency in 1928. The officers eventually turned power back to very conservative civilians, and Argentina remained heavily dependent on the British export market. At about the same time, United States' interests began to establish plants in Argentina so that even more economic activity passed from Argentine control.

In 1943, the military again seized control of the government. They had lost patience with politicians more interested in patronage than in patriotism. Many of the officers were children of immigrants and were fiercely nationalistic. Some officers had either traveled or studied in Europe and had become deeply impressed by both the Fascist and Nazi movements and their rejection of European liberal politics. The military also shared the Fascist and Nazi hostility to Britain. The officers contended that the government must address the social question, industrialize, and liberate itself from foreign economic control.

These were the political goals that, by 1946, gave rise to the Perónist movement. Juan Perón (1895–1974) had been one of the colonels involved in the 1943 coup. He was married to the actress Eva Duarte. What Perón understood better than his fellow officers was the political power that could be exerted by appeals to the Argentine working class and in particular the working class of Buenos Aires. In 1945, he had been arrested by other military leaders, but he was freed the next year when it became clear that he alone could silence trade-union and other working-class discontent. In 1946, he made himself the voice of working-class democracy, even though after his election to the presidency, he created a very authoritarian regime that addressed industrial problems in only a marginal fashion. He became the most famous of the postwar Latin American dictators, but his power and appeal were rooted in the corruption and aimlessness of Argentine politics during the depression. More than anyone else, he stood as the twentieth-century embodiment of the *caudillo.*

Mexico

The heritage of Mexican independence was a combination of the thwarted social revolution led by Father Hidalgo and José María Morelos between 1811 and 1815 and the conservative political coup carried out in 1820 by the Creole elite against a potentially liberal Spanish crown. For the first century of independence, conservative forces held sway, but in 1910, the Mexican people launched the most far-reaching revolution in Latin American history.

Antonio López de Santa Anna (1795–1863) *dominated Mexican politics from the 1820s until his exile in 1855.* [Bettmann Archive.]

TURMOIL FOLLOWS INDEPENDENCE. The years from 1820 to 1876 can only be described as a time of political turmoil, economic floundering, and national humiliation. Newly independent Mexico attempted no liberal political experiments. Its first ruler was Agustín de Iturbide, who governed until 1822 as an emperor. After this unsuccessful effort to adopt monarchical rule, Mexico found itself governed by a succession of presidents, most of whom were *caudillos* from the army or were dependent on the army for support. The strongest of these figures was Antonio López de Santa Anna (1795–1863), a general and a political opportunist always willing to modify his principles and policies simply to attain or to retain power. Usually he supported conservative political and social interests. He ruled repressively and in a thoroughly dictatorial manner. On more than one occasion, he was driven from office, but he inevitably returned until sent into a final exile in 1855.

The mid-century movement against Santa Anna's autocracy was called *La Reforma*. In theory, its supporters were liberal, but Mexican liberalism amounted to little more than policies of anticlericalism and confiscation of Church lands. Having deposed Santa Anna, the leaders of the reform movement passed the Ley Juárez of 1855 and the Ley Lerdo of 1856, named for Benito Juárez, the justice minister, and Sebastián Lerdo, the treasury minister, respectively. This legislation was intended to break up large landed estates, particularly those owned by the Church. However, the actual content of the laws permitted existing large landowners to purchase more land cheaply and thus made great estates even larger. The legislative attack on privileges of the Church led to further civil war between 1857 and 1860. In January 1861, Juárez (1806–1872) entered the capital of Mexico City as the temporary victor.

The political instability was matched by economic stagnation. After 1820, many Spanish officials and merchants fled Mexico, taking with them large quantities of gold and silver. The mines that had produced Mexico's colonial wealth were in poor condition. There was insufficient investment capital or technological knowledge to put them in good repair. The inefficiencies of the hacienda system left farming in a backward condition. Cheap imports of manufactured goods spelled the end of domestic industries. Transportation was primitive. The government remedy for this condition was massive foreign borrowing. Payment of interest became one of the largest portions of the national budget.

FOREIGN INTERVENTION. Political weakness and economic disarray invited foreign intervention. The territorial ambitions of the United States impinged on Mexico in two ways. In 1823, the Mexican government allowed Stephen F. Austin to begin the colonization of Texas. During the next decade, the policies of Santa Anna stirred resentment among the Texas settlers, and in 1835, Texans rebelled. The next year, Santa Anna destroyed the defenders of the Alamo but later the same year experienced decisive defeat at the battle of San Jacinto. Texas stood as an independent republic that within a few years would be annexed by the United States. A series of border clashes between Mexican and U.S. forces provided President James Polk with the opportunity to launch war against Mexico in 1846. Through the treaty of Guadalupe Hidalgo (1848), the United States gained a vast portion of Mexican territory.

Further foreign intervention occurred as a direct result of Juárez's liberal victory in 1861. Mexican conservatives and representatives of the Church invited the Austrian Habsburg Archduke Maximilian to become the emperor of Mexico. Napoleon III of France, who portrayed himself as a defender of the Roman

Emperor Maximillian of Mexico (1832–1867). *Although well meaning, Maximillian was out of his depth in Mexico. His empire depended on French troops, and it collapsed when they were withdrawn in 1867. [Bettmann Archive.]*

Catholic Church, provided support for this imperial venture. In May 1862, French troops invaded Mexico, and two years later, Maximilian became emperor. By 1867, Juárez had organized strong resistance forces. He captured the unhappy emperor and executed him. The Mexicans had been victorious, but their vulnerability to foreign powers had again been exposed.

DÍAZ AND DICTATORSHIP. Once restored to office, the liberal leaders continued their measures against the Church but failed to rally significant popular support. Consequently, in 1876, Porfirio Díaz (1830–1915), a liberal general, led a revolt on the grounds that he was restoring a true republic. With the exception of four years in the 1880s when a surrogate was in office, Díaz remained president through numerous corrupt elections until 1911. Díaz initially maintained what became one of the most successful dicta-

torships in Latin American history by giving almost every political sector something it wanted. He allowed landowners to purchase public land cheaply; he favored the army, whose support he required; and he made peace with the Church by leaving many anticlerical measures unenforced. Later, he freely used repression against opponents and bribery with supporters.

Wealthy Mexicans grew even richer under Díaz, and the nation as a whole became a respectable member of the international financial community. Foreign companies, especially from the United States, invested heavily in what, by 1900, appeared to be a thoroughly stable country. Yet there were also problems that could not be indefinitely ignored. The peasants remained very hungry for land and resentful of the ever-growing power of the landlords. There also existed real hunger for food because food production actually declined during the Díaz regime. There were labor unrest and strikes in the textile and mining industries. Like other Latin American rulers and governments in

Porfirio Díaz (1830–1915). *From 1876 to 1911, Díaz ran one of the most successful dictatorships in Latin American history. [Brown Brothers.]*

Europe and the United States, Díaz used military force against workers.

REVOLUTION. In 1908, the elderly Díaz announced that he would not seek reelection. Though he later changed his mind and was reelected in 1910, his first announcement spurred much public discussion of Mexico's political and social future. In 1910, Díaz stood opposed by Francisco Madero (d. 1913), a wealthy landowner and moderate liberal. Madero's campaign slogan was "Effective Suffrage—No Reelection," which ironically Díaz had coined two generations earlier. Madero was defeated by Díaz, but he then led an insurrection that drove the dictator from office and into European exile by May 1911. Shortly thereafter, Madero was elected president, but he was not in control of the revolution that his actions had unleashed. Far more radical leaders emerged, calling for social change. Pancho Villa (1874–1923) in the north and Emiliano Zapata (1879–1919) in the south rallied mass followings of peasants who demanded fundamental structural changes in rural landholding. In late 1911, Zapata proclaimed his Plan of Ayala,

Emiliano Zapata (1879–1919) led a peasant revolution which eventually led to major land reform in Mexico. [Brown Brothers.]

Emiliano Zapata Issues the Plan of Ayala

By November 1911, the Díaz regime had fallen in Mexico, and Francisco Madero was attempting to establish a moderately liberal government. He was confronted by a major popular peasant revolution led in the valley of Morelos by Emiliano Zapata. On November 28, the rebel leader set forth his opposition to Madero and announced sweeping goals of land reform. Zapata never took dominant control of the Mexican Revolution, but the radical economic demands of his Plan of Ayala would influence the course of Mexican social development for the next thirty years.

. . . be it known: that the lands, woods, and water usurped by the hacendados [great landowners] . . . henceforth belong to the towns or citizens in possession of the deeds concerning these properties of which they were despoiled through the devious action of our oppressors. The possession of said properties shall be kept at all costs, arms in hand. The usurpers who think they have a right to said goods may state their claims before special tribunals to be established upon the triumph of the Revolution.

. . . the immense majority of Mexico's villages and citizens own only the ground on which they stand. They suffer the horrors of poverty without being able to better their social status in any respect, or without being able to dedicate themselves to industry or agriculture due to the fact that the lands, woods, and water are monopolized by a few. For this reason, through prior compensation, one-third of such monopolies will be expropriated from their powerful owners in order that the villages and citizens of Mexico may obtain *ejidos* [agricultural communities], colonies, town sites, and rural properties for sowing or tilling, and in order that the welfare and prosperity of the Mexican people will be promoted in every way.

The property of those hacendados . . . who directly or indirectly oppose the present plan shall be nationalized, and two-thirds of their remaining property shall be designated for war indemnities—pensions for the widows and orphans of the victims that succumb in the struggle for this plan. ❑

Quoted in James W. Wilkie and Albert L. Michaels, ed., *Revolution in Mexico: Years of Upheaval*, 1910–1940 (New York: Alfred A. Knopf, 1969), p. 46.

Women troops in the Mexican Civil War, which raged from 1911 to the 1920s. [Bettmann Archive.]

which, in effect, set forth a program of large-scale peasant confiscation of land.

Madero found himself squeezed between the conservative supporters of the deposed Díaz and the radical peasant revolutionaries. No one trusted him, and in early 1913, General Victoriano Huerta with the help of the United States overthrew Madero, who was assassinated not long thereafter. Huerta attempted unsuccessfully to quash the peasant rebellion. In the meantime, Venustiano Carranza (1859–1920), a wealthy landowner, joined Villa's cause and soon put himself at the head of a large Constitutionalist Army. In April 1914, President Woodrow Wilson of the United States sent marines to Veracruz to establish Carranza in power. The leader very shrewdly denounced the United States for this action, thus casting himself in the role of patriot and nationalist, and the marines departed in late 1914. Carranza made another skillful move by addressing himself to the concerns of urban industrial workers as well as to the land hunger of the rural peasants. In that manner, he succeeded in edging out both Villa and Zapata as the chief leader of the revolution.

By 1917, after a civil war among revolutionaries and between revolutionaries and conservatives that had involved immense loss of life and property damage, Carranza's forces were sufficiently confident of their position to write a constitution. That document—the Constitution of 1917—was a program for future reform and ongoing social revolution. Perhaps its two most famous provisions were Articles 27 and 123. The former made the government on behalf of the nation the owner of water and mineral rights and other property rights of the subsoil. This article abrogated all prerevolutionary contracts with foreign companies in regard to oil and minerals. Article 123 guaranteed certain rights for the organization of labor. Many years

would pass before all of the provisions of the constitution could be enforced, but from 1917 onward, the document provided the ongoing goals of the revolution and the ideals toward which Mexican governments were expected to strive.

The years immediately after 1917 witnessed both confusion and consolidation. In 1919, Zapata was lured into an ambush and killed. Carranza, who had shared few of Zapata's goals and had frequently opposed him, was assassinated in 1920. Three years later, Villa was also assassinated. Other military leaders drawn from Carranza's revolutionary Constitutionalist Army served as presidents during the 1920s. They moved very cautiously and were hesitant to press land redistribution too quickly. There was much opposition from the Roman Catholic church, which at one point suspended all services for over two years. In 1929, Plutarco Elías Calles (1877–1945) organized the PRI, the Institutional Revolutionary Party, the most important political force in the nation from that time to the present day.

In 1934, Lázaro Cárdenas (1895–1970) was elected president. More than any of the other leaders to emerge from the revolution, he moved directly to fulfill the promises and programs of 1917. He instituted major land reform, and tens of millions of acres of land were being turned over to peasant villages. In 1938, he expropriated the oil industry. Mexico was then the world's third largest producer of petroleum. His nationalization policy established PeMex, which remains the Mexican national oil company. Cárdenas left other mineral industries in private and generally foreign hands.

With the election of Manuel Ávila Camacho (1897–1955) in 1940, the era of revolutionary politics came to an end. Thereafter, the major issues in Mexico were those generally associated with postwar economic development. But unlike other Latin American nations, Mexico, because of its revolution, could confront those issues with democratic concerns and a sense of collective social responsibility no matter how imperfectly they might be realized.

Brazil

Postcolonial Brazil, the largest in area of all the Latin American countries, differed in several important respects from other liberated nations in the region. Its language and colonial heritage were Portuguese. For the first sixty-seven years of its independence, Brazil retained a relatively stable monarchical government. Most distinctively, the institution of slavery persisted in Brazil until 1888.

Brazil had moved directly from the status of a part of the Portuguese monarchy to that of an independent empire in 1822. The first emperor, Pedro I—while serving as royal regent for his father, the king of Portugal—had put himself at the head of the independence movement. Although he granted the nation a constitution in 1823, Pedro I was unable to consolidate his position. His rather high-handed rule and his patronage of Portuguese courtiers rather than Brazilians led to his forced abdication in 1830. However, after a decade of political uncertainty, his fifteen-year-old son, also named Pedro, became emperor in 1840. As Pedro II (1825–1891), he governed Brazil for almost half a century. The second emperor made very wise and shrewd use of patronage. He established a reputation as a constitutional monarch by, at one time or another, asking leaders of both the conservative and liberal political parties to form ministries. Consequently, Brazil enjoyed remarkable political stability.

THE SLAVERY ISSUE. The great divisive issue in Brazil's social and political life was slavery. Sugar production had been the mainstay of the colonial economy and maintained that position until the middle of the nineteenth century. Most of the sugar plantations were located in the coastal provinces of the northeast. Their owners were very conservative and resistant to changes in production. The soil exhaustion and the general inefficiency of farming methods made the cheap labor of slaves necessary for profits. In about 1850, a key shift began to occur within Brazilian agriculture as the cultivation of coffee began in the southern provinces. Coffee would soon become the most important product of the nation. Its producers also used slave labor, but the profits were much larger than those associated with sugar. Coffee planters also tended to see themselves as being on the side of economic progress. Although they wanted to continue the slave system, a transition to free labor would be easier for coffee planters than for sugar planters. In that respect, some form of emancipation was less unthinka-

Emperor Pedro II of Brazil. During his long reign from 1830 to 1889, Brazil enjoyed remarkable political stability. [Bettmann Archive.]

ble for persons investing in coffee than for those who had invested in sugar.

As early as 1826, the Brazilian government had made a treaty with Great Britain, agreeing to the suppression of the slave trade that provided new slaves to the plantations. For many years, Brazil refused to honor these treaty provisions and encountered much pressure from the British government, which, since 1807, had been committed to using its navy to suppress the international slave trade. However, by 1850, Brazil had halted virtually all importation of slaves. This situation put the sugar planters sharply on the defensive and freed the capital once spent on slaves for investments in coffee. The end of slave importation also spelled the eventual demise of the institution because the birth rate among slaves was too low for the slave population to reproduce itself. But the long-term eventuality of the end of slavery and its actual abolition were two very different matters.

The Paraguayan War of 1865–1870 postponed consideration of the slave question. This conflict pitted Brazil, Argentina, and Uruguay, on one side, against

Emancipation of Slaves in Brazil

Slavery came under sharp attack within Brazil from the middle of the nineteenth century onward. The first major attempt to emancipate slaves occurred in 1871. This law attempted gradual emancipation by liberating the children of slaves. Note, however, the manner in which the interests of slaveowners remained protected by the provision allowing children of slaves to remain in servitude until the age of twenty-one. Discontent with the Law of 1871 and further growth of the abolitionist movement led to the final emancipation of slaves in Brazil by the legislation of 1888.

Provisions of the Law of 1871

The Princess Imperial, Regent, in the name of His Majesty Emperor Senhor D. Pedro II, makes known to all the subjects of the Empire, that the General Assembly has decreed, and that she has sanctioned, the following Law:

Article I. The children of women slaves that may be born in the Empire from the date of this Law shall be considered to be free.

1. The said minors shall remain with and be under the dominion of the owners of the mother, who shall be obliged to rear and take care of them until such children shall have completed the age of eight years.

On the child of the slave attaining this age, the owner of its mother shall have the option either of receiving from the State the indemnification of 600 dollars, or of making use of the services of the minor until he shall have completed the age of twenty-one years. . . .

The declaration of the owner must be made within thirty days, counting from the day on which the minor shall complete the age of eight years; and should he not do so within that time it will be understood that he embraces the option of making use of the service of the minor.

The Abolition of Slavery in Brazil (1888)

The Princess Imperial, Regent, in the name of His Majesty the Emperor Dom Pedro II, makes known to all subjects of the Empire that the General Assembly has decreed, and she has approved the following Law:—

Art. 1. From the date of this Law slavery is declared abolished in Brazil.

2. All contrary provisions are revoked. She orders, therefore, all the authorities to whom belong the knowledge and execution of the said Law to execute it, and cause it to be fully and exactly executed and observed. ❑

British and Foreign State Papers, 1871–1872, LXII (London: William Ridgway, 1877), 616, quoted in E. Bradford Burns, ed., *A Documentary History of Brazil* (New York: Alfred A. Knopf, 1966), 257–258.
British and Foreign State Papers, 1887–1888, LXXIX (London: Harrison and Sons, n.d.), 259, quoted in E. Bradford Burns, ed., *A Documentary History of Brazil* (New York: Alfred A. Knopf, 1966), 278.

Paraguay on the other. The war originated in border disputes and in larger commercial conflicts about ongoing Paraguayan access to the ports on the lower Plate River, in particular Montevideo. The dictator of Paraguay, Francisco Solano López (1827–1870), was regarded as troublesome by the governments of his nation's three antagonists. The initial conflict dragged itself into a long, destructive struggle because López mobilized his entire country into a war of attrition. He refused to surrender. His death in battle in 1870 finally ended the war, but only after more than half (and perhaps a larger portion) of the adult male population of Paraguay had been killed. The victorious powers installed a friendly government in Paraguay, which sold off state lands to foreign speculators.

The end of the war allowed the slavery question to return to the forefront of Brazilian politics. The abolition of slavery in the United States left Brazil and the Spanish colonies of Puerto Rico and Cuba as the only slave-holding countries in the hemisphere. The em-peror was opposed to slavery but favored gradual emancipation. The Rio Branco Law of 1871 set the stage for such emancipation by freeing slaves owned by the crown and by decreeing legal freedom for future children of slaves. The law actually had little effect because under its provisions, the children of slaves might be required to work on plantations until the age of twenty-one. However, throughout the 1870s and 1880s, the abolition movement grew in Brazil. Public figures from across the entire political spectrum called for an end to slavery. Abolitionists helped slaves to escape. The army, many of whose officers held political views associated with positivism, resented having to enforce laws protecting slavery. In 1888, Pedro II was in Europe for medical treatment, and his daughter Isabel Christina was regent. She was in favor of abolition rather than gradual emancipation. When Parliament in that year abolished slavery without any form of compensation to the slave owners, she signed the law. Slavery thus came to an end in Brazil.

A REPUBLIC REPLACES MONARCHY. The abolition of slavery brought to a head other issues that, in 1889, caused the collapse of monarchical government. Planters who received no financial compensation for their slaves were resentful. Roman Catholic church leaders were disaffected by numerous disputes that they had carried out with the emperor over education. Pedro II was unwell, and his daughter was unpopular and distrusted. The officer corps of the army had been dissatisfied with what it regarded as insufficient political influence since its victory in the Paraguayan War. In November 1889, the army toppled the monarchy and sent Pedro II into exile in France.

The Brazilian republic lasted from 1891 to 1930. Like the monarchy, it was dominated by a very small group of wealthy persons. The political arrangement that allowed the republic to function smoothly was an agreement among the state governors. The presidents were to be chosen alternately from the states of São Paulo and Minas Gerais. In turn, the other governors were permitted considerable local political latitude. Fixed elections and patronage kept the system in operation. As literacy replaced property as the qualification for voting, very few people were able to vote and there was consequently little organized opposition.

From the 1890s onward, the coffee industry dominated both the political and economic life of the nation. Around the turn of the century, Brazil produced over three fourths of the world's coffee. The success of coffee led almost inevitably to overproduction. To meet the problems of overproduction, the government of the republic devised policies for maintaining high prices. This stabilization required very large government loans from foreign banks. It also meant that world coffee prices remained sufficiently high to encourage competition from other Latin American producers, which, in turn, led to the necessity of further price supports in Brazil.

The end of slavery, the expansion of coffee production, and the beginning of a slow growth of urban industry attracted foreign immigrants to Brazil. They tended to settle in the cities and constituted the core of the early industrial labor force.

Brazilian coffee being loaded onto a British ship. From the 1890s onward, the coffee industry dominated both the political and economic life of Brazil. [Bettmann Archive.]

ECONOMIC PROBLEMS AND MILITARY COUPS. In Brazil, as elsewhere, World War I caused major economic disruption. Urban labor discontent appeared. There was a general strike in São Paulo in 1917, with the inevitable military action against the strikers. The failure to address urban and industrial social problems and the political corruption of the republic spurred an attempted military coup in 1922, followed by another in 1924. Both revolts failed to bring down the republic, but they illustrate the profound discontent with a political structure designed primarily to protect the producers of a single agricultural commodity.

If coffee had ruled as "king" of the Brazilian republic, the collapse of that economic monarchy ended the republic. As a result of the commodity crisis of 1929, coffee prices hit record lows; currency exchange rates fell in a similar manner; and foreign loans were unavailable. The economic structure of the republic lay in a shambles. In October 1930, a military coup installed Getúlio Vargas (1883–1954), the defeated presidential candidate, in the presidency. Vargas governed Brazil until 1945.

Vargas and his supporters attempted to address several immediate national problems. They sought to lessen dependence on coffee by providing aid and planning for industries that would produce domestically goods that had previously been imported from abroad. The policy was quite successful, and by the mid-1930s

Getulio Vargas (1883–1954), dictator of Brazil from 1930 to 1945. Although politically repressive, Vargas' government made Brazil the leading economic power in Latin America. [Bettmann Archive.]

domestic manufacturing was on the increase. In the Constitution of 1934, Vargas established a legal framework for labor relations. The structures were quite paternalistic, but there were real gains in the form of an eight-hour day and a minimum wage. The constitution also asserted government responsibility to protect mineral and water rights.

These measures represented the early Vargas regime, which in the Brazilian context appeared liberal and certainly marked a departure from government policy dominated by the coffee oligarchy. However, in the late 1930s, Vargas confronted major political opposition from both the Brazilian Communist Party (founded in 1922) and a new right-wing movement called *Integralism*. In 1937, confronted by this opposition, Vargas assumed personal dictatorial power. His regime thereafter took on a distinctly repressive character, and he claimed to have established an *estado novo* ("new state").

Like the European dictators of the same era, Vargas used censorship, secret police, and torture against his opponents. He also used his newly assumed power to pursue a state-directed policy of economic develop-

ment. In 1940, he announced a Five-Year Plan. Under its provisions, the government founded the Brazilian steel industry and established a petroleum exploration company. The state also set forth a new and very progressive labor code. Siding with the Allies in World War II, Brazil built up large reserves of foreign currency through the export of foodstuffs. All of this economic activity and imposed political stability allowed the government to secure foreign loans for still further economic development. By the end of the war, Brazil was well on its way to becoming the major Latin American industrial power.

In 1945, fearing that Vargas was about to move toward the political left, the military removed him from office and established a more democratic structure of government, but one that they clearly controlled. The new regime continued the general policy of economic development through foreign-financed industrialization. The state, however, assumed a much smaller role. When in 1950 Vargas was elected president, his return to office was an anticlimax. He was by then an elderly man, well past his prime. When it was discovered that without being aware of it, he had appointed many corrupt officials, he took his own life in 1954. Thereafter, Brazil would continue to oscillate between military governments and civilian governments that remained in office by the grace of the army.

Latin American History in World Perspective

Ever since the early nineteenth century, the region of Spanish- and Portuguese-speaking America stretching from the Rio Grande to Cape Horn has posed a paradox. Languages, religion, economic ties, and many political institutions render the area a definite part of the Western world. Yet the economics, politics, and social life of Latin America have developed very differently from other parts of the West. In terms of economic development, a region exceedingly rich in natural resources, possessing gold, silver, nitrates, and oil, has been plagued with extreme poverty. As other Western nations have moved toward liberal democracy and social equality, the states of Latin America have millions of citizens living in situations of marked inequality and social dependence. For over a century and a half, the political life of Latin America has been characterized by uncertain democracy, authoritarian regimes, and a general tendency toward instability. Three major explanations have been set forth to account for these difficulties, which have led to so much tragedy and human suffering.

The first and most widely accepted view contends that after the wars of independence the new states of

MAP 30-2 CONTEMPORARY CENTRAL AND SOUTH AMERICA *During the past decade certain states in Latin America have witnessed major movements toward redemocritization. These particularly include Argentina and Brazil. A popular referendum condemned the military government in Chile. A new popular political opposition scored heavily in the Mexican elections. However, Cuba continues to have a Marxist government, and civil war still divides Nicaragua.*

Latin America remained economically and culturally dependent. In effect, it is argued, that colonial framework was never really abolished. Under Spanish and Portuguese rule, Latin America experienced the extraction and export of its wealth for the benefit of those powers. After independence, the Creole elite turned toward foreign investors, first British and then American, to finance economic development and to provide the technology needed for mining, transport, and industry. As a result, Latin America became dependent on wealthy foreign powers for investment and for markets.

A second explanation of Latin American development since independence emphasizes the Iberian heritage. Advocates of this interpretation contend that Latin America should be viewed as a region on the periphery of the Western world in the same manner that Spain, Portugal, and Italy lie on the Mediterranean periphery of Europe. All of these Latin nations, dominated by Roman Catholicism, have displayed similar characteristics of unstable governments. They have often tended toward some version of dictatorship, uneven development, anticlericalism, and social cleavage between urban and rural areas and between wealthy middle-class or landed elites and poor peasant populations. If Latin America is viewed in this Iberian-Mediterranean context, its character is less puzzling than when it is viewed in the context of northern Europe.

A third explanation emphasizes conscious political, economic, and cultural decisions taken by the Latin American Creole elite in the years following independence. This explanation contends that the elite, including the army officers who won the wars, sought to enrich themselves and to maintain their positions at the cost of all other segments of the population. These officers, landowners, and urban middle-class leaders aligned their various national economies with the industrializing regions of Europe and North America. They also adopted the liberal political and economic ideologies of Europe to justify unlimited exploitation of economic resources on the basis of individualistic enterprise. They embraced European concepts of progress in order to dismiss the legitimacy of the culture and the communal values of the Indians or the peasants.

None of these interpretations actually excludes the others. To come to a satisfactory understanding of the region and its past, it seems to be necessary to draw on the aid of all three viewpoints.

Suggested Readings

S. ARROM, *The Women of Mexico City*, 1790–1857 (1985). A pioneering study.

H. BERNSTEIN, *Modern and Contemporary Latin America* (1952). Provides excellent, detailed narratives of the political development of the major states during the nineteenth and early twentieth centuries.

L. BETHEL, ed., *The Cambridge History of Latin America*, 5 vols. (1988). The single most authoritative and up-to-date coverage.

E. B. BURNS, *A History of Brazil* (1970). The most useful one-volume treatment.

E. B. BURNS, *The Poverty of Progress: Latin America in the Nineteenth Century* (1980). Argues that the elites suppressed alternative modes of cultural and economic development.

R. CONRAD, *The Destruction of Brazilian Slavery*, 1850–1888 (1973). A good survey of the most important problem in Brazil in the second half of the nineteenth century.

R. CONRAD, *World of Sorrow: The African Slave Trade to Brazil* (1986). An excellent survey of the subject.

C. C. CUMBERLAND, *Mexico: The Struggle for Modernity* (1968). A useful introduction.

E. V. DA COSTA, *The Brazilian Empire: Myths and Histories* (1985). Essays that provide a thorough introduction to Brazil during the period of the empire.

H. S. FERNS, *Britain and Argentina in the Nineteenth Century* (1968). Explains clearly the intermeshing of the two economies.

C. FURTADO, *Economic Development of Latin America: Historical Background and Contemporary Problems*, 2nd ed. (1976). An excellent volume in its clarity and its appreciation of long-term historical factors.

R. GRAHAM, *Britain and the Onset of Modernization in Brazil* (1968). Another study of British economic dominance.

C. H. HARING, *Empire in Brazil: A New World Experiment with Monarchy* (1958). The standard treatment.

J. HEMMING, *Amazon Frontier: The Defeat of the Brazilian Indians* (1987). A brilliant survey of the experience of native Americans in modern Brazil.

R. A. HUMPHREYS, *Latin America and the Second World War*, 2 vols. (1981–1982). The standard work on the topic.

B. KEEN AND M. VASSERMAN, *A Short History of Latin America*, 2nd ed. (1984). The best one-volume text with excellent bibliographies.

P. F. KLARÉN AND T. J. BOSSERT, *Promise of Development: Theories of Change in Latin America* (1986). A collection of important essays.

A. KNIGHT, *The Mexican Revolution*, 2 vols. (1986). The best treatment of the subject.

S. MAINWARING, *The Catholic Church and Politics in Brazil*, 1916–1985 (1986). An examination of a key institution in Brazilian life.

J. L. MECHAM, *Church and State in Latin America: A History of Political-Ecclesiastical Relations*, rev. ed. (1966). A standard volume on a major Latin American political issue.

M. MÖRNER, *Adventurers and Proletarians: The Story of Migrants in Latin America* (1985). Examines immigration to Latin America and migration within it.

R. E. POPPINO, *Brazil: The Land and People*, 2nd ed.

(1973). A thoughtful volume with fine bibliographical aids.

DAVID ROCK, *Politics in Argentina, 1890–1930: The Rise and Fall of Radicalism* (1975). The major discussion of the Argentine Radical Party.

J. R. SCOBIE, *Argentina: A City and a Nation*, 2nd ed. (1971). Clarifies the various struggles between the port city of Buenos Aires and the inland provinces.

S. J. AND B. H. STEIN, *The Colonial Heritage of Latin America: Essays on Economic Dependence in Perspective* (1970). A major statement of the dependence interpretation.

D. TAMARIN, *The Argentine Labor Movement, 1930–1945: A Study in the Origins of Perónism* (1985). A useful introduction to a complex subject.

H. J. WIARDA, *Politics and Social Change in Latin America: The Distinct Tradition* (1974). Excellent essays that stress the ongoing role of Iberian traditions.

J. D. WIRTH, ed., *Latin America Oil Companies and the Politics of Energy* (1985). A series of case studies.

J. WOMACK, *Zapata and the Mexican Revolution* (1968). The major volume on the subject.

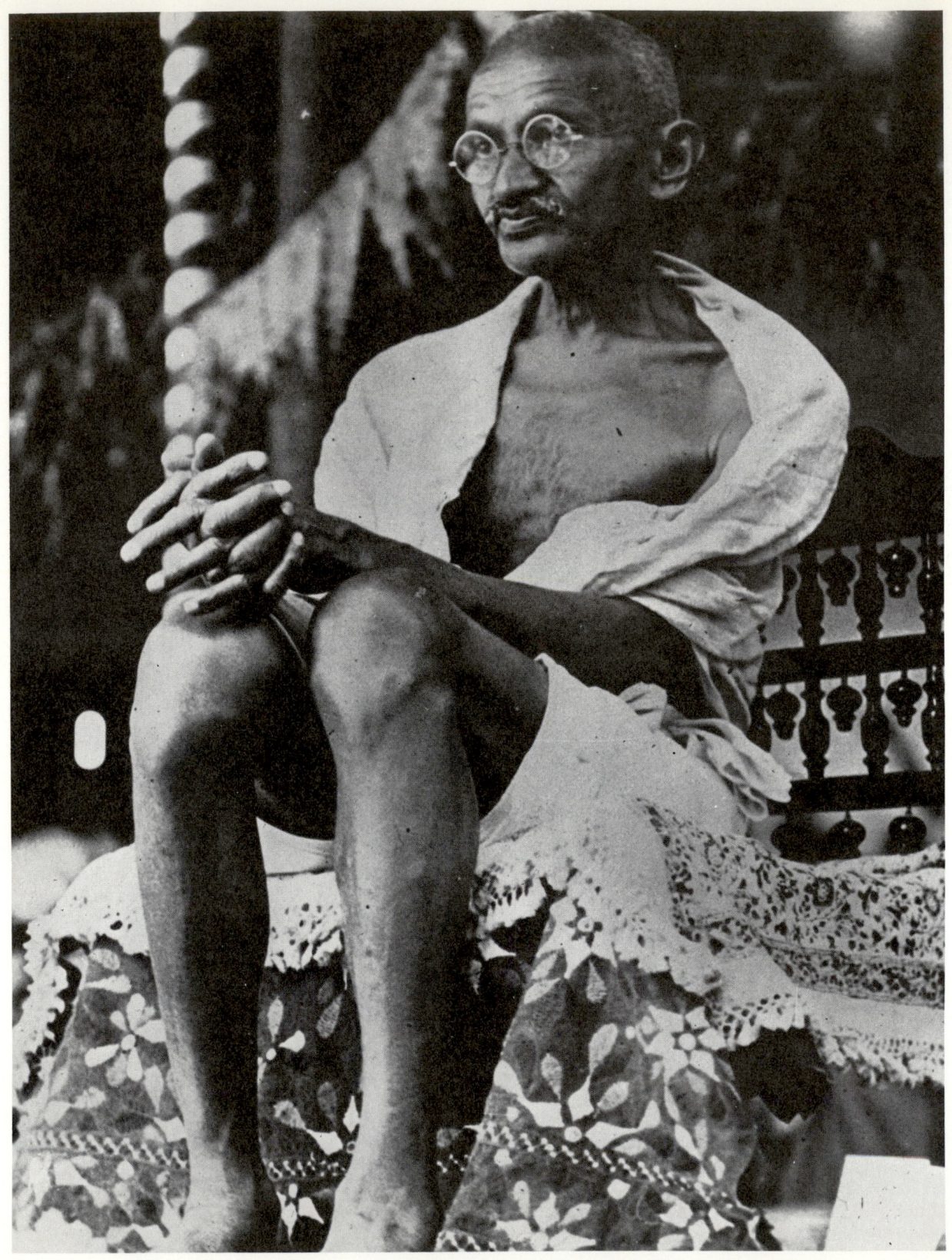

The "Great Soul," "Mahatma" Mohandas K. Gandhi, father of the modern state of India. [UPI.]

31 India, the Islamic Heartlands, and Africa: The Encounter with Western Modernity (1800–1945)

The encroachment of the European nations on the rest of the world from the late fifteenth century onward brought radical, often devastating changes. By the twentieth century, these changes had become major elements in the history of every non-European continent, whether the Americas, Australia, Asia, or Africa. Certainly they have been a dubious blessing in much of the world. The spiritual and material disruptions occasioned in the West by the Renaissance, the Reformation, the Enlightenment, and the Industrial and Scientific Revolutions have had a revolutionary effect when they have impinged on the Afro-Asian-Indian world.

Although every advanced society in any age has presumably viewed its culture as "modern," the dominance of the West in recent centuries has led it to develop a very specific and novel concept of "modernity." Western modernity is a special set of ideas and institutions that evolved in Europe between the Renaissance and the early twentieth century and then gradually was exported to or imposed on other societies around the globe. Thus, "the impact of modernity," means the effect on traditional cultures of the introduction of social, economic, technological, scientific, and ideological forms of "modern" Western civilization.

The encounter with Western culture has been of such massive consequence that we often speak of non-Western peoples as passive recipients of Western modernity. As a result, our view of the world often reflects a simplistic dualism that enhances our own Western self-esteem as the active, creative, dominant force in recent history.[1] On the one side is the "modern" West; on the other, the "backward" Orient, as though all of

---

[1] See the exaggerated and careless, but still telling and important, book of Edward W. Said, *Orientalism* (New York: Pantheon, 1978).

the world outside Europe, North America, and maybe Russia were some monolithic, archaic "East." Our popular stereotypes of the Arab, the African, the Indian, the Chinese, and so on reinforce our sense of being the true "moderns" of our age.

As parochial as such chauvinistic generalizations are, there is yet a certain grim historical accuracy in the impotence of many non-Western cultures before the sheer technological power of Western "modernity" and its agents. The impact of the West on traditional societies is a major element in the recent history of African, Asian, and Indian civilizations. Not all non-Western societies have had equal success, either in recovering or reasserting their precolonial independence and identity, or in responding creatively to the ongoing challenges of Western-style modernity. The spectrum is quite broad, ranging from the largely suc-cessful responses of Japan or China to the painful experiences of most African societies, with India, Iran, and the Middle East somewhere in between.

Nevertheless, in all of these "Third World" areas, Western modernity entered cultures that had long-developed social, religious, and political traditions of their own. Such traditions did not simply melt away at the arrival of the Westerners and their powerful new traditions. There has been considerable continuity with the past in Islamic, Hindu, and other regions of the Third World, even after the onslaught of the West in the past two hundred years. Much of the history of the twentieth-century Asian and African societies hit hardest by the new "modernity" has been shaped by their peoples' realization of the importance of their own traditions.

THE INDIAN EXPERIENCE

British Ascendancy under the British East India Company

Preceded by the Portuguese and the Dutch in the development of the Southern Seas trade in the sixteenth and seventeenth centuries, the British battled with France for India in the eighteenth. In the nineteenth century, the British eventually won the greatest European colonial empire in the Afro-Asian world. The jewel in the crown of that empire was India, the major traditional civilization of Africa and Asia to come almost completely under direct European colonial rule.

The Company Era

The British East India Company had won the first British charter for trade with the Indies in 1600 and established its first Indian trading post, or "factory," on the west coast in 1608. After a century and a half of ups and downs, the company ensured its supremacy among European powers in India with military victories over the Indian ruler of Bengal in 1757 and over the French in 1761. This supremacy was made possible by the steady disintegration of the Mughal Empire after Awrangzeb's death (1705) and by a timely defeat in 1778 of the Marathas (see Chapter 22), whom the British could not finally subjugate until 1818. The rapacity of its own fortune-hunting officers brought the East India Company to the brink of ruin in 1772, but a parliamentary reform act of 1773 addressed the major abuses. This was the first step in shifting the regula-tion of Indian affairs to the crown, a gradual process that ended in a total takeover in 1858.

A high point in the company's rule was the enlightened administration of Warren Hastings, governor-general from 1772 to 1784. He knew Indian culture and society well enough to avoid disruptive or oppressive policies. Although he had the company's interests always in view, he saw that simply bleeding India was not in anyone's long-run interest. His successors, even when well intentioned, were not generally as astute. The company's rule over more and more of India down to the Sepoy "mutiny" of 1857–1858 was progressive only by comparison; other European nations in their foreign colonies were usually irresponsible as well as despotic. The British, like the others, were out to make a profit. Indian interests were secondary to this purpose, however nobly the British might have felt about a tutelary "responsibility" for India.

After 1818, they replaced the Mughals as the effective imperial power, or *raj*, in most of India. Thereafter, until the end of East India Company control and nominal Mughal rule in 1858, the British pursued a policy of consolidating their power through treaties and eventually even the direct annexation of regional Indian states.

British–Indian Relations

The impact of British ideas and ways of doing things was limited to a small but influential Indian elite. It was felt in both their business and political life and their manners and customs, although British cul-

Portfolio V: Islam

The Islamic tradition is one of the youngest of the major traditions of world religion. Since its inception during the lifetime of the Prophet Muhammad (died A.D. 632), it has grown, like the Christian and Buddhist traditions, into a worldwide community not limited by national boundaries or defined in racial or ethnic terms. It began among the Arabs, but spread widely. Islam's historical heartlands are those Arabic-, Turkic-, and Persian-speaking lands of the Near East between the Nile and the Oxus rivers. However, today more than half of its faithful live in Asia east of Karachi, Pakistan. Indeed, more Muslims live in subSaharan Africa than in all of the Arab lands. Also, today in America and Europe, Muslims are taking their place as a visible and significant religious minority.

The central vision of Muslims is one of a human society built upon the collective piety of individuals faithful to God. It focuses upon a human community of worshipers who recognize the absolute sovereignty and oneness of God and strive to do His will. That divine will is held to be found first in His revealed word, the Qur'an; then as elaborated and specified in the actions and words of His final prophet, Muhammad; and finally as interpreted and extended in the scriptural exegesis and legal traditions of the Muslim community over the past thirteen and one-half centuries.

The Muslim vision thus centers on one God who has guided humankind throughout history by means of prophets or apostles and repeated revelations. God is the Creator of all, and in the end all will return to God just as all came from Him. His majesty would seem to make him a distant, threatening deity of absolute justice, and there is an element of this in the Muslim understanding of the wide chasm between the human and the Divine. Still, there is an immanent as well as transcendent side to the Divine in the Muslim view. Indeed, Muslims have given us some of the greatest images of God's closeness to His faithful worshiper—images that have a special place in the thought of the Muslim mystics, who are known as Sufis.

Muslims understand God's word in the Qur'an and the elaboration of that word by tradition to be a complete prescription for human life. Thus Islamic law is not law in the Western sense of civil, criminal, or international systems. Rather, it is a comprehensive set of standards for moral, ritual, social, political, economic, aesthetic, and even hygenic and dietary dimensions of life. By being faithful to God's law, the Muslim hopes to gain salvation on the Last Day, when human history shall end, and all of God's creatures who have ever lived will be resurrected and called to account for their thoughts and actions during their lives on earth. Some will be saved, but others will be eternally damned.

Thus *Islam*, which means "submission [to God]", has been given as a name to the religiously defined system of life that Muslims have sought to institute wherever they have lived their lives. Muslims have striven to organize their societies and political realities around the ideals represented in the traditional picture of the Prophet's community in Medina and Mecca. This necessitated compromise in which power was given to temporal rulers and accepted by Muslim religious leaders so long as those rulers protected God's law, the *Shari'ah*. The ideal of a single international Muslim community, or *ummah*, has never been fully realized politically, even in the heyday of the Umayyad or Abbasid empires. But it remains an ideal. Many movements of reform over the centuries have called for greater adherence to rigorous interpretations of Islamic law and greater dominance of piety and religious values in government as well as individual life.

The major sectarian, or minority, groups among Muslims are those of the Shi'ites, who have held out for an ideal of a temporal ruler who is also the spiritual heir of Muhammad and God's designated deputy on earth. Most Shi'ites, notably those of Iran, hold that after eleven designated blood descendents of the Prophet had failed to be recognized by the majority of Muslims as the rightful *Imam*, the twelfth disappeared and remains to this day physically absent from the world, although not dead. He will come again at the end of time to vindicate his faithful followers and set things right. A smaller number of Shi'ites disagree with these "twelver" Shi'ites about the rightful successor to the sixth Imam; known as "Seveners," they recognize a different line of succession beginning with the seventh Imam, Isma'il. One of these "Sevener," or "Isma'ili," groups, recognizes in the contemporary Aga Khan the living Imam of the present day and follows his guidance.

Muslim piety takes many forms. The common duties of Muslims are central for Muslims everywhere: faith in God and trust in His Prophet; regular performance of ritual worship (*Salat*); fasting during daylight hours for thirty days in Ramadan (the ninth month of the lunar year); giving of one's wealth to the needy (*zakat*); and at least once in a lifetime, if able, making the pilgrimage to Mecca and its environs (*Hajj*). Other, more regional or popular but ubiquitous practices are also important. Celebration of the Prophet's birthday indicates the exalted popular status of Muhammad, even though any divine status for him is strongly rejected theologically. Recitation of the Qur'an permeates all Muslim practice, from daily worship to celebrations of all kinds. Visitation of saint's tombs is a prominent form of popular devotion. Sufi practices of chanting or even ecstatic dancing are also practiced by Muslims around the world.

Muslims vary enormously in their physical environment, language, ethnic background, and cultural allegiances; yet all are united as part of, first, a great historical tradition of culture and religion, and, second, a larger community of the faithful that transcends national and other boundaries. What binds them now as in the past are not political allegiances but religious affinities and a shared heritage of religious faith and culture. How these allegiances and sensibilites will fare in the face of the global challenges of the coming decades will be one of the important factors in shaping the world of the twenty-first century.

V-1 Revealing God's Word. *The Angel Gabriel (Arabic: Jibril), is depicted in a fourteenth-century Arabic manuscript painting. According to Muslim tradition, it was Gabriel who brought Muhammad God's Word. He is said to have recited this Word to the Prophet so that the latter might learn it and recite it to his followers. Hence the name of the sacred text that emerged over the years of Muhammad's prophetic career:* al-Qur'an, *"the Reciting." [Reproduced by Courtesy of the Trustees of the British Museum.]*

V-2 Page from an Eighth or Ninth Century Qur'an. *Here is a fine example from a Qur'an written in the angular shapes of the early Kufic script. The passage shown is the end of the 38th and the title and beginning of the 39th sura of the Qur'an. The final words of 38 (before the gold illumination of the title of 39) have reference to the Qur'an itself: ". . . it [the Qur'anic revelation] is but a Reminder [Warning] for created beings. And ye shall know at a later point its message [as true]." The first line and a half of sura 39 contains the famous invocation, or Basmallah, "In the name of God the Merciful, the Compassionate." [Freer Gallery of Art, Smithsonian Institution.]*

V-3 A Western Qur'an Page. *One can easily see the sharp contrast in script styles between the previous Kufic Qur'an page and this page from a Spanish or North African Qur'an of the twelfth century. Both contain the Basmallah at the start of sura 39, just after the illuminated title. Here the Basmallah takes up exactly the first line of the text after the gold of the title. The sura goes on to speak of the revelation of the Qur'an itself as being from God and containing the Truth for humankind. [The Metropolitan Museum of Art, Rogers Fund, 1942.]*

V-4   The Dome of the Rock. *The unique structure of the Dome of the Rock stands atop Temple Mount in Jerusalem, one of the three holiest cities in Islamdom. This earliest of Muslim edifices, built in 692, is not a mosque or a tomb, but essentially a monument proclaiming Muslim presence. It is also a splendid covering for the huge rock outcrop that popular lore marks as the spot from which Muhammad ascended to heaven in Gabriel's company—an experience Muslims interpret variously as a vision or a physical journey. [Scala/Art Resource.]*

V-5   The Ibn Tulun Mosque. *Built in 876–879, this mosque was named after a Turkish slave who became governor of Egypt. Its ziggurat-style minaret, restored in the thirteenth century, betrays Mesopotamian influence, probably from the early giant mosque at Samarra, in Iraq. Its huge courtyard and columned arcades follow the classic form of congregational mosques, which are built to accommodate large numbers of worshipers for the Friday service. [William Graham.]*

The manuscript contains Arabic and Uighur Turkish text surrounding the illustration.

V-6 Muhammad and Moses. *An illuminated page from a fifteenth century Uighur Turkish manuscript of the* Book of the Ascension (Mirâj Nâmeh) *shows a scene from folk traditions about the miraculous ascension vision/experience of Muhammad. In it, we see Muhammad met Moses to discuss the number of times per day that God has set for the Muslims to perform the salat, or ritual worship. All the prophets, but especially Muhammad, play a large role in Muslim piety and popular lore. [Bibliotheque Nationale, Paris.]*

V-7 A Qadi Hears a Case. *The divine law, or Shari'a, is that by which all Muslims are enjoined to live, and by which they try to regulate their individual and collective lives. Muslims have a right to have disputes settled by an arbiter of the Shari'a. Here we see a husband complaining about his wife before the state-appointed judge, or qadi. The wife, backed up by two other women, points an accusing finger at the husband. In such cases, the first duty of the qadi, who should be a learned person of faith, is to try to effect a reconciliation before the husband divorces his wife, or the wife herself seeks a divorce. [Bibliotheque Nationale, Paris.]*

C-37

V-9 and V-10 To the Greater Glory of God. *Because of Muslim aversion to images in religious settings, calligraphy (usually of Qur'anic passages) and abstract design have been the chief forms of religious ornamentation in Islamic architecture. Nowhere are the glories of Islamic mosque decoration more vividly seen than the Safavid mosques of Isfahan. In plate V-9 (below), we see an interior shot of the Shaykh Lutfullah mosque. It shows the mihrah, or wall niche marking the direction of Mecca, toward which Muslims are to face when they perform the ritual worship of salat. This mihrah is decorated at its top with the stalactite-like scallops known as muqarnas and with vivid floral art designs in and around it, interspersed with the white-on-dark blue panels of magnificent ornamental Qur'anic calligraphy across the wall. Plate V-10 (upper right) offers a closeup view of the breathtaking ceramic-tiled dome of the Emperor's Mosque, or Masjid-i Shah, which stands at the end of the famous formal square of Isfahan. The lower panels and middle band of white designs on the dome are in fact not designs but again words of the Qur'an in varying styles of Arabic calligraphy. [SEF/Art Resource.]*

V-8 Worldly and Spiritual Drunkenness. *This painting of the great sixteenth-century Safavid Iranian court painter, Sultan Muhammad, is from an illustrated copy of the Diwan, or collected works of the lyric and mystical poet Hafiz. Hafiz appears himself as the drunken figure in the right upper window. The entire picture is a play upon the worldly drunkenness depicted in the wine debauchery of the painting and the spiritual drunkenness of the Sufi, or mystic, who seeks the ecstatic inebriation of union with God. The music and dance of the sufis—those drunk with spiritual experience—is seen in the garden. On the roof angels also drink—a visual reference to the line of Hafiz at the top: "The angel of mercy took the cup of revelry." [Courtesy of the Metropolitan Museum of Art and the Arthur M. Sackler Museum, Harvard University. Promised Gift of Mr. and Mrs. Stuart Cary Welch, 1988.]*

V-11   Friday Congregational Worship. *Every Friday at the noon hour of daily worship, Muslims are enjoined to gather in as large a congregation as possible to worship together and listen to a weekly preaching in the major mosque in every town or city. Here, at the Friday Mosque in Mopti, Mali, West African Muslims are seen in the midst of the worship rites, some standing, some prostrating themselves against the dramatic backdrop of the mud walls and minarets of the mosque. [George Gerster/ Comstock Photography.]*

V-12   The Holy House of God. *At Mecca, within the precincts of the Holy Mosque, once each year in the month of pilgrimage, Muslim men and women circumambulate (walk around) and pray around "the holy House of God", the Ka'ba. The Ka'ba is but a simple cubic structure of stone which for Muslims has associations with the prophets Adam, Abraham, and Muhammad as the place which each was commanded by God to purify and dedicate to His worship alone. In every year since Muhammad performed the first modern pilgrimage rites there, Muslims have gathered from far-flung places to worship. [Aramco World Magazine.]*

V-13   The Holy Mosque of Mecca. *This modern, Saudi-built mosque surrounds the most holy spot in the world for Muslims, the square rock building of the Ka'ba and its encircling area. This is the one spot in the world in which the lines of worshippers gathered for any of the daily prayer rites are circular, since every Muslim worshipper faces the Ka'ba when he or she prays. Thus it is emblematic of the unity of Muslims around the world. [Aramco World Magazine.]*

An Indian artist's miniature painting of Colonel Taylor, the East India Company Agent at the Mughal court, riding in ceremonial procession on a royal elephant. [New York Public Library.]

tural imperialism was never a major East India Company policy. Hastings's genuine interest in and openness to Indians and their culture were not wholly isolated phenomena. Some of the British mixed with and even intermarried with Indians. The company prohibited or actively opposed Christian missionary activity in India, until forced by British public pressure in the nineteenth century to reverse its policy. Yet Christian values, like British humanitarian and liberal political ideals, stimulated some of the brightest Indian minds. The most influential of these was Ram Mohan Roy (1772–1833), a Bengali Hindu. He rose to the top of the native ranks of East India Company service and became a strong voice for reform of Hindu life and practice. He was a scholar who studied the Christian scriptures and was influenced by them in his own Hindu reform efforts.

Only after the advent of the British crown *raj* in 1858 did a stricter social segregation of white rulers from Indians set in. Still, much more than their Mughal predecessors, the British overlords treated Indians all too often as backward heathens in need of the "civilizing" influences of their "enlightened" culture, education, and religion. This attitude was epitomized in the immensely influential introduction of English education in 1835.

Many Indians desired to acquire British ways and to participate in the business and administrative life of their land. Yet, the majority still recognized their ultimate subordination to foreign masters. The depth of distrust and animosity felt by most Indians (even some who had profited enormously from British rule) toward their foreign rulers was reached in mid-century. It was reflected in the "mutiny" of 1857–1858 among the

Macaulay Writes on Indian Education

The momentous decision in 1835 to introduce and encourage English-language study and the British school curriculum in Indian schools was hotly disputed by the English and the Indians alike. In the end, it bred a new generation of elite Indian spokespersons for their nation, as well as a class of bureaucrats for the British raj. *It also worked to the advantage of Hindus at the expense of the Muslims, as the latter tended to reject English schooling and thus lost considerable power in the long run. Here some of the thinking of the "Anglicists," whose view won the day over the "Orientalists," is seen in Thomas Babington Macaulay's famous position paper—as are some British prejudices about the superiority of Western culture to Sanskrit (or any other) culture.*

We now come to the gist of the matter. We have a fund to be employed as government shall direct for the intellectual improvement of the people of this country. The simple question is, what is the most useful way of employing it?

All parties seem to be agreed on one point, that the dialects commonly spoken among the natives of this part of India contain neither literary nor scientific information, and are, moreover, so poor and rude that, until they are enriched from some other quarter, it will not be easy to translate any valuable work into them. It seems to be admitted on all sides that the intellectual improvement of those classes of the people who have the means of pursuing higher studies can at present be effected only by means of some language not vernacular amongst them.

What then shall that language be? One-half of the committee maintain that it should be the English. The other half strongly recommend the Arabic and Sanscrit. The whole question seems to me to be, which language is the best worth knowing?

. . . .

To sum up what I have said, I think it clear that we are free to employ our funds as we choose; that we ought to employ them in teaching what is best worth knowing; that English is better worth knowing than Sanscrit or Arabic; that the natives are desirous to be taught English, and are not desirous to be taught Sanscrit or Arabic; that neither as the languages of law, nor as the languages of religion, have the Sanscrit and Arabic any peculiar claim to our engagement; that it is possible to make natives of this country thoroughly good English scholars; and that to this end our efforts ought to be directed.

In one point I fully agree with the gentlemen to whose general views I am opposed. I feel with them, that it is impossible for us, with our limited means, to attempt to educate the body of the people. We must at present do our best to form a class who may be interpreters between us and the millions whom we govern; a class of persons, Indian in blood and color, but English in taste, in opinions, in morals, and in intellect. To that class we may leave it to refine the vernacular dialects of the country, to enrich those dialects with terms of science borrowed from the Western nomenclature, and to render them by degrees fit vehicles for conveying knowledge to the great mass of the population. ❑

From Wm. Theodore deBary et al., *Sources of Indian Tradition* (New York: Columbia University Press, 1958), pp. 596, 601.

largely lower-class Hindu and Muslim Indian troops, or Sepoys, who made up the bulk of the East India Company's armies in the subcontinent. Not yet a nationalistic revolution, this revolt was more an uprising against foreign domination than treason, although there was not enough unified Indian feeling to bring it to victory. Still, it presaged the rise of such feeling.

From British Crown *Raj* to Independence

The Sepoy Rebellion of 1857–1858 was put down only with British reinforcements. It had numerous consequences beyond the ensuing transfer of the administration of India from the East India Company to the British Parliament. The bloody conflict had involved such atrocities on both sides that mutual fear and hatred ran at a much higher level in subsequent decades. The British, feeling the danger of the old system of a largely native Indian army under British officers, now tried to maintain at least a 1 to 3 ratio of British to Indian soldiers under arms. This policy placed a huge economic burden on India, as one third of its total annual revenues now went to pay for its own military occupation.

The Burden of Crown Rule

Mass unemployment resulted when Britain sent its cheap machine-produced goods to be paid for in Indian natural products. This destroyed Indian craft industries wholesale and forced new multitudes into poverty

A European rendering of the infamous "Cawnpore Massacre." After the British garrison surrendered to the Maratha leader Nana Sahib in June, 1857, he broke his word and murdered his prisoners, who included 125 women and children. This was only one of many tragic excesses committed by both sides during the frenzy of the 1857–1858 "mutiny," but it became a focal point of British anger and determination to reassert total dominance in India. [New York Public Library.]

or onto the land. The burden on the Indian peasantry became much worse as the result of a commercial policy that avoided the industrialization that might have provided work for the unemployed masses. British disruption of the ancient economic balance in the countryside as much as natural failure of the rains brought widespread famine in the 1870s. During the Civil War in the United States, so much cotton had been demanded of India that there was a shift to cotton farming; when famine struck, much less food was available than otherwise. Many peasants lost their hereditary lands because of other British agrarian policies. This forced thousands to become indentured servants sent as a work force for British dominions in South Africa.

The entire state of mind of the British in India was poisoned by the Sepoy Rebellion. "Cantonments" that segregated white masters from "untrustworthy" natives now became the rule in each Indian town or city. Despite noble royal statements of just intentions and nominal opening of the civil service to Indian candidates, the crown *raj* fostered anything but equality between Indian and Britisher. One bright spot, however, was the five-year sojourn of the marquess of Ripon (1880–1884) as viceroy of India. He fought to erase legal racial discrimination by allowing Indian judges to try British as well as Indian citizens. His efforts earned him the hatred of most of his compatriots in India, but he was a shining example to emerging Indian leaders of the best that British egalitarianism could produce. Although his British foes managed, by public outcry and agitation, to dilute his measures, in doing so they unwittingly gave Indians a model for political agitation of their own.[2]

[2] Stanley Wolpert, *A New History of India*, 2nd ed. (New York: Oxford University Press, 1982), pp. 256-257.

Indian Resistance

Indians were not long in taking up political activism. The Indian National Congress was formed in 1885 specifically to reform traditional Hindu and Muslim practices that were out of line with the liberal consciences of Indian modernists. They also wanted to change British Indian policies that were equally out of line with British democratic ideals. Other Indians took a harder line and agitated for the rejection of British rule altogether. The traditionally regionalist Indians had come only slowly to national consciousness, but with the all-India National Congress now functioning, nationalist feelings spread over the subcontinent in a few decades. Heavy-handed and erratic British policies fanned the flames of a growing desire for nationhood and independence.

The major obstacles to Indian independence other than Britain itself remained the Indians' own internal divisions. The many diverse langauge groups and the many tiny princely states of the subcontinent were by no means the only nor even the critical divisions politically. In the three quarters of a century before Indian independence and the partition of India and Pakistan in 1947, three major divergent groups dominanted India's political life.

The first group were those in the National Congress organization who sought to work in varying degrees with the British on gradual reform and progress toward Indian self-governance, or *swaraj*. Such Indians were epitomized by G. K. Gokhale (1866–1915), the champion of moderate and deliberate, peaceful work toward self-determination; later, the spiritual and political genius, Mohandas K. Gandhi (1869–1948); and still later, his follower and eventual first president of

An early twentieth-century photograph of British officers and their Indian troops. Note the elephants used to transport the artillery. [Bettmann Archive.]

India, Jawaharlal Nehru (1889–1964). Gandhi was the principal Indian leader after World War I. He directed the all-India drive that finally forced the British to leave India to the Indians. Himself an English-trained lawyer, Gandhi drew not only on his own native Hindu (and Jain and Buddhist) heritage, but also on that of Western liberal and Christian thinkers like Henry David Thoreau and Leo Tolstoy. In the end, Gandhi became a world figure as well as an Indian leader of the twentieth century.

The second group were the militant Hindu nationalists, whose leader, the extremist B. G. Tilak (1856–1920), stressed the use of Indian languages and a revival of Hindu culture and learning. He also subscribed to an anti-Muslim, Hindu communalist vision of Indian "self-governance." Where earlier in the nineteenth century, foreign ideas had stimulated a Hindu renaissance and various reform movements, the Hindu extremists now looked to a return to traditional Indian values and self-sufficiency. Although their movement dissipated in the course of the common war effort after 1914, their religiopolitical ideas proved influential ever after in Indian political life.

The third group were the Muslims, who had been slower than the Hindus to take up British ideas and education and, as a minority whose leaders had once ruled most of India, were generally more resistant to

Nehru and Jinnah, photographed during pre-partition discussions. The two leaders and their respective peoples were not long to walk a common or congenial path as they led the new states of India and Pakistan to separate rather than shared independence in the subcontinent. [Bettmann Archive.]

Gandhi on Passive Resistance and Swaraj

Gandhi's powerful thinking and prose were already evident in his Hind Swarāj, *or* Indian Home Rule *of 1909. This work was to remain his basic manifesto ever after. The following excerpts reflect important points in his philosophy. Swadeshi refers to reliance only on what one produces at home (rather than on foreign goods).*

Passive resistance is a method of securing rights by personal suffering; it is the reverse of resistance by arms. When I refuse to do a thing that is repugnant to my conscience, I use soul-force. For instance, the government of the day has passed a law which is applicable to me. I do not like it. If by using violence I force the government to repeal the law, I am employing what may be termed body-force. If I do not obey the law and accept the penalty for its breach, I use soul-force. It involves sacrifice of self.

Everybody admits that sacrifice of self is infinitely superior to sacrifice of others. Moreover, if this kind of force is used in a cause that is unjust, only the person using it suffers. He does not make others suffer for his mistakes. . . .

. . . The real meaning of the statement that we are a law-abiding nation is that we are passive resisters. When we do not like certain laws, we do not break the heads of law-givers but we suffer and do not submit to the laws. . . .

If man will only realize that it is unmanly to obey laws that are unjust, no man's tyranny will enslave him. This is the key to self-rule or home-rule.

. . . .

Let each do his duty. If I do my duty, that is, serve myself, I shall be able to serve others. Before I leave you, I will take the liberty of repeating:

1. Real home-rule is self-rule or self-control.
2. The way to it is passive resistance: that is soul-force or love-force.
3. In order to exert this force, Swadeshi in every sense is necessary.
4. What we want to do should be done, not because we object to the English or because we want to retaliate, but because it is our duty to do so. Thus, supposing that the English remove the salt-tax, restore our money, give the highest posts to Indians, withdraw the English troops, we shall certainly not use their machine-made goods, nor use the English language, nor many of their industries. It is worth noting that these things are, in their nature, harmful; hence we do not want them. I bear no enmity towards the English but do towards their civilization.

In my opinion, we have used the term *Swarāj* without understanding its real significance. I have endeavored to explain it as I understand it, and my conscience testifies that my life henceforth is dedicated to its attainment. ❏

From Wm. Theodore deBary et al., *Sources of Indian Tradition* (New York: Columbia University Press, 1958), pp. 811–813, 819.

---

change. Because of the prominence of Muslims in the Sepoy Rebellion, the British were much less inclined to foster Muslims' advancement than that of Hindus after 1848. The one man who did the most to win back respect and a voice for the Muslims in India was Sayyid Ahmad Khan (1817–1898), himself a longtime supporter of modernist ideas and of cooperation with the British, however sharply he criticized their mistakes in India. His opposition to Muslim participation in the National Congress foreshadowed the future trend in Hindu–Muslim relations.

Hindu–Muslim Friction

In the twentieth century, the rift between Muslims and Hindus in the subcontinent only grew wider, despite periods of cooperation against the common British enemy. In the end, the great Indo-Muslim poet, thinker, and "spiritual father of Pakistan," Muhammad Iqbal (1873–1938), and the "founder of Pakistan," Muhammad Ali Jinnah (1876–1949), led Muslims to separatism. In different ways, they succeeded when coexistence with Hindus floundered and Muslim fears of loss of communal identity and rights grew.

The independence of India and Pakistan from West-

INDIA

1772–1784	Administration of Warren Hastings
1772–1833	Ram Mohan Roy, Hindu reformer
1817–1898	Sayyid Ahmed Khan, Muslim reformer
1835	Introduction of English education
1857–1858	Sepoy "mutiny"; direct crown rule of the British colony
1885	Indian National Congress formed
1869–1948	Mohandas K. Gandhi
1889–1964	Jawaharlal Nehru
1873–1938	Muhammad Iqbal
1876–1949	Muhammad Ali Jinnah
1947	Independence and partition

ern domination was bought with a great deal of blood. Blood was spilled both in the long battle with the British and in Hindu-Muslim or other internal Indian communal violence such as accompanied partition in 1947 and the subsequent Kashmir dispute between India and Pakistan. Still, the victory of 1947 gave Indians at last a sense of participation in the world of nations on their own terms instead of on those dictated by a foreign power. The British influence was in some ways a sad one, but in other respects, also a good one. The legacy of administrative and political unity and egalitarian and democratic ideals were key elements in driving out the British themselves.

THE ISLAMIC EXPERIENCE

Islamic Responses to Decline

The eighteenth century saw the breakup of the great Muslim empires and the increasing ascendency of the West. Consequently, the diverse Islamic peoples and states were thrust from previous positions of global power into what became, by the nineteenth century, a pitched struggle for survival. Although, as we have seen in the Indian case, much of the eclipse of Islamic political preeminence was due to the rise of the modern West, much of it was also the result of internal problems.

By the eighteenth century, all of the largest Muslim empires—Mughal, Ottoman, Safavid, and central Asian—had degenerated politically, militarily, economically, and culturally from their sixteenth- and seventeenth-century heydays. Entrenched hereditary elites of landed gentry, palace guards, military castes, local princes, urban craft guilds, or even *ulema* or Sufi orders now predominated in ever more decentralized states subject to ever greater economic and political instability. A conservative, legalistic temper held sway among the *ulema*. At least in Sunni lands, they were now commonly state functionaries rather than the generally antigovernment voices of Muslim conscience that they once had been.

The Sufi orders were sometimes the voices of religious conscience raised against *ulema* conformism and governmental neglect of Islam. Yet, Sufism was also increasingly identified with popular piety in local areas, where Islamic and pre- or non-Islamic practices were commonly integrated. Many of the Sufi orders had become closely linked with particular interest groups (e.g., the Ottoman guilds and the Janissaries); they had degenerated into institutions perpetuating rather crass cults of personality, esotericism, or authoritarian religious discipline centered on Sufi masters.

During the eighteenth century, a variety of reform movements sought to revive Islam as a comprehensive way of life purified of many of the more unhappy developments in Islamic societies during the preceding centuries. Most of these movements combined an emphasis on inner piety with a puritanical stress on external practice.

The most famous of these movements was that of the Wahhabis, the followers of Ibn Abd al-Wahhab (1703–1792) in Arabia. On the one hand, it sought to combat excesses of popular and Sufi piety, such as saint worship, visitations to saints' tombs, and faith in the intercession of Sufi masters and saints. On the other, it sought to break the stranglehold of conformist legal and religious interpretation among the *ulema* in favor of the exercise of independent judgment about such matters. The only authorities were to be the Qur'an and the traditions of the Prophet, not the scholastic edifices of the traditional schools of legal and theological interpretation. Allied with a local Arab prince, Sa'ud, the Wahhabi movement swept much of the Arabian peninsula. It was crushed in the early nineteenth century by Egyptian military forces acting for the Ottoman regime. Still, the movement did not die; it finally saw victory in Arabia through a descendant of Sa'ud at the beginning of the twentieth century.

Similar types of fundamentalist and militant pietist response to Islamic decadence and decline can be seen in other, often related Muslim reform movements: in the eighteenth century that of Usman Dan Fodio in Africa (to be discussed later) and in the present day that of the Muslim Brotherhood in modern Egypt (see Chapter 37). The call is for a pristine Islam divested of the authoritarianism of medieval legal schools, *ulema* theological conformity, and degenerate Sufi orders, as well as the excesses of popular piety and Sufi esotericism. This has remained a strong rallying cry for various movements on the modern Islamic scene, from Africa to Indonesia.

The Encroachment of the West

The internal decline of Islamic societies was only one source of ferment. From the late 1700s until World War II, the political fortunes of Arab, Turkish, Persian, Indian, Southeast Asian, and African Islamic states were largely dictated from outside by the commercial and military-political rivalries of Britain, Russia, Germany, and France. Throughout this period, such rivalries succeeded one another as mainsprings of diplomatic and commercial developments in the Islamic world.

In the Ottoman Empire, as in Iran, Mughal India, and Africa, capitulations were ultimately used by Western governments for their own economic and political advantage. These "capitulations" were treaty "chapters" granting commercial concessions, special protection, and "extraterritorial" legal status to various European merchant enclaves abroad. Such concessions (the earliest going back to the sixteenth century) had originally been reciprocal and had served the commercial purposes of Muslim rulers as well as Western traders. They eventually provided Western powers with pretexts for direct intervention in Ottoman as well as in Iranian, Indian, and African affairs. Internal disunity was exemplified by the virtual independence of most Ottoman provincial rulers, or *pashas*. Together with increasing economic straits everywhere in the agrarian societies of Asia and Africa, this disunity made it easy for the rapidly mechanizing, militarizing, and industrializing Western powers to step in and take control almost at will. Repeated Ottoman diplomatic and military defeats made the once-great imperial power "the sick man of Europe" after 1800.

The event that symbolized the onset of European domination of the Islamic heartlands of the Ottoman-

Iqbal on Islam and National States

In the two excerpts that follow, Muhammad Iqbal's views on the nature of Islam as a tradition of faith and a community in relation to modern national states emerge. Most of Iqbal's writing was poetic and much less concrete or political than these passages. His political ideas reflect his personal faith and his hopes for the future of the Muslim world.

Is religion a private affair? Is it possible to retain Islam as an ethical ideal and to reject it as a polity? . . . The nature of the Prophet's religious experience, as disclosed in the Qur'an . . . is creative of a social order. Its immediate outcome is the fundamentals of a polity with implicit legal concepts whose civic significance cannot be belittled because their origin is revelational. The religious ideal of Islam, therefore, is organically related to the social order which it has created. The rejection of the one will inevitably involve the rejection of the other. Therefore, the construction of a polity on national (that is, all-India lines), if it means a displacement of the Islamic principle of solidarity, is simply unthinkable to a Muslim. . . . The Muslim demand for the creation of a Muslim India within India is, therefore, perfectly justified. . . . Personally I would go further. . . . I would like to see the Punjab, North-West Frontier Province, Sind, and Baluchistan, amalgamated into a single state. . . . The formation of a consolidated North-West Indian Muslim State appears to me to be the final destiny of the Muslims at least of North-West India. . . .

The truth is that Islam is not a church. It is a state conceived as a contractual organism. . . . and animated by an ethical ideal which regards man not as an earth-rooted creature, defined by this or that portion of the earth, but as a spiritual being understood in terms of a social mechanism, and possessing rights and duties as a living factor in that mechanism. . . .

. . . .

An international ideal . . . forming the very essence of Islam has been hitherto overshadowed or rather displaced by Arabian Imperialism of the earlier centuries of Islam. . . . [However] For the present every Muslim nation must sink into her own deeper self, temporarily focus her vision on herself alone, until all are strong and powerful enough to form a living family of republics. . . . It seems to me that God is slowly bringing home to us the truth that Islam is neither Nationalism nor Imperialism but a League of Nations which recognize artificial boundaries and racial distinctions for facility of reference only and not for restricting the social horizon of its members. . . . The race idea which appears to be working in modern Islam with greater force than ever may ultimately wipe off the broad human outlook which Muslim people have imbibed from their religion.

. . . The modern Muslim in Turkey, Egypt and Persia is led to seek fresh sources of energy in the creation of new loyalties, such as patriotism and nationalism. . . . The modern Muslim fondly hopes to unlock fresh sources of energy by narrowing down his thought and emotion. . . . Both nationalism and atheistic socialism, at least in the present state of human adjustments, must draw upon the psychological forces of hate, suspicion and resentment which tend to impoverish the soul of man and close up his hidden sources of spiritual energy.   ❏

From Kenneth Cragg and R. Marston Speight, eds., *Islam from Within* (Belmont, Calif.: Wadsworth, 1980), pp. 213, 214.

The French in Egypt. Napoleon views the royal sarcophagus in one of the great pyramid tombs at Giza.

Turkish, Arab, and Persian spheres was the invasion in 1798 of Egypt by Napoleon Bonaparte. This venture failed when the French were forced by Britain, Russia, and the Ottomans to evacuate Egypt in 1801. It nevertheless heralded a new era of European imperialism and, ultimately, colonialism. By this date, the British had already wrested control over India and the Persian Gulf from the French; now they were preeminent among European powers in the eastern Mediterranean. The French were to continue to contest British ascendancy in the larger Middle Eastern area until the disastrous Franco-German war of 1870. However, the Russians presented the most serious nineteenth-century challenge to the British colonial empire.

Russia had already won control of the Black Sea from the Ottomans. Russia also sought to gain as much territory and influence in the Iranian and central Asian regions as possible. Afghanistan, an independent kingdom established by Ahmad Shah Durrani (ruled 1737–1773), served as a buffer state protecting British India from Russian penetration southwestward. Yet in the Iranian and Ottoman spheres, these two rivals still struggled for supremacy. France was also involved: In 1852 it was in conflict with Russia over Ottoman recognition of the French protectorship of the Holy Land; and subsequently France was allied with Britain and the Ottomans against the tsar in the Crimean War of 1854–1856 (see Chapter 27).

The Western Impact

Beyond the overt political and commercial impact, the imposition of Western political ideology, culture, and technology proved to be a critical factor for change in Islamic societies. Outside of India, this imposition proved greatest in Egypt, Lebanon, and Anatolia (modern Turkey), as we shall see. Of all the Islamic states, including those in Africa and India, the ones that were the least and last affected by the impact of Western "modernity" were Iran, Afghanistan, and the central Asian khanates. The Iranian case deserves at least brief attention.

The rulers of Iran from 1794 to 1925 were the Qajar shahs, a Turkoman dynasty whose absolutist reign was not unlike that of the Safavids. However, the Qajars (themselves formerly among the "Red Hats" supporting the Safavids; see Chapter 22) did not make religious claims, as had the Safavids, to descent from the Shi'ite *imams*. Under Qajar rule, the religious leaders, or *ulema*, of the Shi'ite Iranian community were not part of the state structure as they had been under the Safavid regime. As the guardians of law and faith, they were often the chief critics of the government (not least for its every attempt to admit foreign, "Western" influences) and exponents of the people's grievances against it. A prime example of *ulema* power was the tobacco boycott introduced in 1891 by a decree of the leading authority of the Shi'ite *ulema*. This popular action was supported also by modernist-nationalist opponents of the Qajar regime. It was successful enough to force the Qajar shah to rescind the fifty-year tobacco sales monopoly that he had granted in 1890 to a British corporation.

Subject as it was to the machinations of outsiders like Russia, Britain, and France, Iran inevitably felt the impact of Western ideas about education, science, law, and government. This occurred especially in the latter half of the century, when younger Iranian intellectuals began to warm to Western liberalism on economic, social, and political issues. As in other Islamic countries, the seeds of a new, secular nationalism now were being sown where, previously, sectarian or communalist religious sentiments had held sway. An uneasy alliance of Iranian modernists with conservative *ulema* proved, on occasion, an effective counterforce to Qajar absolutism, as in the tobacco boycott and in a short-lived constitutional reform in 1906–1908. Yet it did not bridge the inherent ideological divisions of the two groups.

Islamic Responses to Encroachment

As the Iranian case shows, the encroachment of the West on the Islamic world in the nineteenth and twentieth centuries elicited varied responses. Every people or state had a different experience according to its particular circumstances and history. Yet, we can point to at least three typical Islamic reactions to Western "modernity": (1) wholesale emulation and adoption of Western ideas and institutions; (2) integrative attempts to join Western innovations with traditional Islamic institutions; and (3) conservative or fundamentalist rejection of everything Western in favor of either the status quo or a return to a purified Islamic community, or *Umma*.

Emulation of the West

The first of these reactions is exemplified in the career of the virtually independent Ottoman viceroy Muhammad Ali, pasha of Egypt from 1805–1849. He set out to rejuvenate the failing Egyptian agriculture, to introduce modern mechanized industry in Egypt, to modernize its army along European lines and with European help, and to introduce European education and culture in government schools. Although ultimately unsuccessful in bringing Egypt to a position of power alongside the European states of his day, Muhammad Ali did set his country on the path to becoming a distinct modern national state. Hence, he is rightly called "the father of modern Egypt." Although his successors' financial and political catastrophes led even to British occupation and effective rule (1882–1922), Muhammad Ali's policies had set Egypt irrevocably on a path that would bring more "Westernizing" (and inevitable countermovements) in the future.

Similar efforts to appropriate Western "progress" in wholesale fashion were made by several Ottoman sultans and viziers after the devastating defeat of the Turks by Russia in 1774. Most notable among these were the reforms of Selim III (ruled 1762–1808), Mahmud II (ruled 1808–1839), and those of the so-called Tanzimat, or beneficial "legislation," era from about

Muhammed Ali Pasha. [New York Public Library.]

1839 to 1880. Selim made serious efforts at economic as well as administrative and military reform. He brought European officers in to train new military corps that were to supplant the Janissaries. Mahmud's reforms were much like those of Muhammad Ali, his contemporary and sometime ally, sometime enemy. Most important were his destruction of the conservative power of the Janissary corps, his tax and bureaucratic reforms, and his encouragement of Western military and educational methods among the Ottoman elites. Like Selim and Muhammad Ali, he was not so much interested in European enlightenment ideas of citizen rights and equity as in a stronger, more modern central government.

Several liberal Ottoman ministers of state continued Selim's and Mahmud's efforts, the Tanzimat reforms. They were aimed still more directly at legal, penal, tax, military, minority-rights, educational, and governmental reforms that would bring the Ottoman state into line with ideals espoused by the European states. They would also give less cause for Europe's intervention in Ottoman affairs and would regenerate confidence in the state at home.

The First Ottoman Parliament

Under pressure from the Western powers, the long-standing Ottoman reform movement and the young Ottoman liberals, the wily Sultan Abdulhamid II promulgated a new constitution late in 1876 and allowed a general election—the first in Ottoman or Islamic history—to produce a modest parliament. The Parliament met in the spring of 1877 and again the next winter, but the Sultan dissolved it himself in February 1878. It was to be thirty years before it would meet again. Like earlier Tanzimat reforms, the new constitution and its parliament were doomed by the continuing absolute power (and in Abdulhamid's case, the despotism) of the sultan. The following description of the first Parliament is by the Daily News *correspondent in Istanbul, Edwin Pears.*

It was the first time that representatives from such distant places as Baghdad, Albania, Armenia and Syria met together. Their discussions were singularly full of interest and even surprises. Though most of the members spoke of serious grievances which required redress in their own district, they were surprised to learn that their own constituencies were not alone as spheres of misgovernment. When the members for Jerusalem, Baghdad, Erzerum and Salonika met together, they found that the administration throughout all the country was corrupt, and they set themselves honestly to discuss their grievances and the changes in the system which were necessary to secure a remedy. Amongst the deputies were several able and thoughtful men. They had no traditions of parliamentary government, and some of the speeches were banal, speeches which would have been brought to an end by the Speaker had they been delivered in the Legislative Chamber either of England, America, or a British colony. They often had a tendency to personalities unconnected with public affairs, but more usually they attacked this pasha or that for abuses, for receiving bribes and refusing to do what was right unless he was paid for it. Had the Sultan been as wise as his sycophants represented him to be, he would have seen the value of such statements and would have allowed the deliberations of the Chamber to continue. There were at first absolutely no attacks whatever upon him, though many of his Ministers were personally charged with specific irregularities and misconduct. The discussions were a revelation to Turkish subjects. They showed that the government from one end of the country to the other required radical reform. The Chamber had at its head a President, Ahmed Vefyk, who had been Ambassador of Turkey at the Court of Napoleon III, was an excellent French scholar, and in education was no doubt the superior of nearly all the deputies. But in public and private life he had become despotic, and his superior, school-masterly manner as Chairman of the House was arrogant and sometimes amusing. He frequently stopped deputies in the midst of speeches, telling them that they knew nothing about the subject and were talking nonsense. Dr. Washburn, the President of Robert College, was present when a white-turbanned deputy, who was making a long and prosy statement, was suddenly pulled up by a stentorian shout from the President of "Shut up, you donkey!" . . . The orator sat down as if he were shot.

Meantime the accusations brought by members against the corruption of individual Ministers became more serious and definite in form. The claim that certain of the Ministers should be brought before the Chamber in order to answer charges against them was naturally opposed by the accused Ministers and was distasteful to Abdul Hamid. The hostility between the Chamber and the pashas became serious, and various correspondents predicted that within a short time the Chamber would upset the rule of the pashas, or the pashas would get rid of the Chamber. ❑

From Sir Edwin Pears, *Life of Abdul Hamid* (London: 1917), pp. 49–51; reprinted in Bernard Lewis, *The Emergence of Modern Turkey*, 2nd ed. (Oxford: Oxford University Press, 1968), pp. 168–169.

The nineteenth-century Ottoman reforms failed to save the empire or truly revive it as an economically sound, culturally vibrant, or militarily and politically powerful state. Nevertheless, they paved the way for the rise of Turkish nationalism later seen in the "Young Turk" revolution of 1908 and especially in the nationalist revolution of the 1920s that produced modern Turkey. (Ironically, this development simultaneously frustrated similar nationalist aspirations among old Ottoman minorities like the Greeks, the Armenians, and the Kurds.)

The creation of the modern Turkish republic out of the ashes of the Ottoman state after World War I was the most extreme effort consciously to modernize and nationalize an Islamic state on a Western model. This state was largely the child of Mustafa Kemal, known as "Atatürk" ("father of the Turks"), its founder and first president (1922–1938). Atatürk's major reforms ranged from the introduction of a European-style civil code as the law of the land to the abolition of the formal institution of the caliphate, Sufi orders, Arabic script, and the Arabic call to prayer. Here we have a truly radical attempt to secularize an Islamic state and to separate religious from political and social institu-

The first Ottoman Parliament in session, 1877, from the Illustrated London News of April 14, 1877. [New York Public Library.]

tions decisively. Nothing quite like it has ever been tried before or since.

The "Father of the Turks," Mustafa Kemal.

Integration of Western Ideas

The attempt to join modernization with traditional Islamic institutions and ideas is exemplified in the thought of famous Muslim intellectuals such as Jamal al-Din al-Afghani (1839–1897), Muhammad Abduh (1845–1905), and Muhammad Iqbal (1876–1938). These thinkers argued to some degree for a progressive Islam rather than a materialist Western secularism as the best answer to life in the modern world.

Afghani is best known for his emphasis on the unity of the Islamic world, or "pan-Islamism," and on a populist, constitutionalist approach to political order. His ideas influenced political activist movements in Egypt, Iran, Ottoman Turkey, and elsewhere.

His Egyptian disciple, Muhammad Abduh, worked especially to modernize Muslim education. He argued that a firm, revealed Qur'anic base could be combined harmoniously with modern science and its open questioning of reality. Through his efforts as Grand Mufti and head of state education, he was able to introduce substantial modernist reforms. These reforms affected even the curriculum of the most venerable traditionalist institution of higher learning in the Islamic world, the great Azhar school in Cairo, where Abduh was ostracized by its more traditional leaders.

Muhammad Iqbal was the most celebrated Indian Muslim thinker of the present century (already discussed in the section on India). He went even farther in his emotional, sometimes contradictory, poetic arguments for a modernist revival of Muslim faith focused on purifying and uplifting the individual self above enslavement either to reason or to traditionalist conformity. Often credited with the original idea of a separate Muslim state in the Indian subcontinent, Iqbal still felt that Islam was essentially nonexclusivist and supranationalist. He participated in major political discussions about the future of India. Although his poetry and essays excited Muslim fervor and dynamism, it is difficult to say how great his actual impact on Islamic political and social life really was.

Purification of Islam

A third kind of Muslim reaction to Western domination has focused on recourse to Islamic values and

The Azhar Mosque and University, Cairo. The oldest madrasa, or institution of Islamic higher learning, it was founded in 969 under the Shi'ite Fatimid dynasty. Reorganized in this century into a university structure, the Azhar is still the premier place to study in the entire Islamic world for Muslims who wish to train as legal and religious scholars, or ulema. [Egyptian Ministry of Tour.]

Hasan al-Banna's Call for a Return to Muslim Principles

In 1928 al-Banna' founded the Muslim Brotherhood, an Egyptian reform movement that urged a return to a more truly Islamic order. The Brotherhood became a powerful religiopolitical force in Egypt. Its implication in political assassinations led to al-Banna's assassination in 1949, but the group has lived on to the present day, despite suppression in Egypt and elsewhere. Here al-Banna' lists some of his basic principles:

When we observe the evolution in the political, social, and moral spheres of the lives of nations and peoples, we note that the Islamic world—and, naturally, in the forefront, the Arab world—gives to its rebirth an Islamic flavor. This trend is ever-increasing. Until recently, writers, intellectuals, scholars, and governments glorified the principles of European civilization, gave themselves a Western tint, and adopted a European style and manner; today, on the contrary, the wind has changed, and reserve and distrust have taken their place. Voices are raised proclaiming the necessity for a return to the principles, teachings, and ways of Islam, and, taking into account the situation, for initiating the reconciliation of modern life with these principles, as a prelude to a final "Islamization." . . .

. . . our intention is to demonstrate to the West two points:

1. Demonstration of the excellence of Islamic principles of collective organization, and their superiority over everything known to man until now, these principles being:
   a. Brotherly love: condemnation of hatred and fanaticism.
   b. Peace: error is committed by the misguided thinking on the legitimacy of the Holy War.
   c. Liberty: error is committed by those who suspect Islam of tolerating slavery and interfering with liberty.
   d. Social justice: obvious character of the Islamic theory of power and class structure.
   e. Happiness: manifest error in the appreciation of the reality of abstinence.
   f. Family: matters concerning the rights of women, number of wives, and repudiation.
   g. Work and profit: matters concerning the different kinds of profit, and error in the appreciation of the fact of relying on God.
   h. Knowledge: error is committed by those who accuse Islam of encouraging ignorance and apathy.
   i. Organization and determination of duties: error is committed by those who see in the nature of Islam a source of imperfection and indolence.
   j. Piety: the reality of faith, and the merit and reward attached to it.

2. Demonstration of the following facts:
   a. For the good of man in general, Muslims must move toward a return to their religion.
   b. Islam will find in this return her principal strength on earth.
   c. Far from receiving impetus from a blind fanaticism, this movement will be inspired by a strong regard for the values of Islam which correspond fully to what modern thought has discovered as most noble, sound, and tested in society. It is God who says what is true and who shows the way. ❑

From Kemal H. Karpat, ed., *Political and Social Thought in the Contemporary Middle East* (New York: Praeger, 1968), pp. 118, 121–122; reprinted in John J. Donohue and John L. Esposito, eds., *Islam in Transition: Muslim Perspectives* (New York, Oxford: Oxford University Press, 1982), pp. 78, 82–83.

ideals to the exclusion of "outside" forces. This approach has involved either the kind of reformist fundamentalism already seen in Wahhabism or the kind of conservatism often associated with Sunni or Shi'ite "establishment" *ulema*, as in the case of Iran. The conservative spirit itself has often been the target of fundamentalist reformers who see in it the worst legacy of medieval Islam. Still it has sometimes served to legitimize fundamentalist reforms once they have been effected. Both conservative and fundamentalist Muslim thinkers share at least the conviction that it is within, not outside of, the Islamic tradition that answers to the questions facing Muslims in the modern world are to be found.

Traditionalist conservatism is much harder to pin down as the ethos of a particular movement than is reformist fundamentalism. Whereas Muslim fundamentalism focuses on Qur'an and Prophetic example as the sole authorities for Islamic life, Muslim conservatism commonly champions those forms of Islamic life and thought embodied in traditional law, theology, and even Sufism. It is seen in the legalistic tendencies that have often resurfaced when Islamic norms have been threatened by the breakdown of traditional society and the rise of secularism. Although such conservatism has often been associated with the most reactionary forces in Islamic society, it has often also served to preserve basic Muslim values while allowing for gradual change in a way that reformist fundamentalism could not accept.

Nationalism

Although not merely a response to Western encroachment, nationalist movements in the entire Islamic world have been either largely stimulated by Western models or else produced in direct reaction to Western imperialist exploitation and colonial occupation. The nationalistic responses to Western domination discussed in the case of India have had their analogues in the Islamic heartlands. Whether secularist, as in Turkey in the 1920s, or fundamentalist, as in Libya in the 1970s, nationalism has been distinctly a product of the last century or so. As an Afro-Asian phenomenon, it will be seen again in the next section and in Chapter 37.

ISLAMIC LANDS	
1703–1792	Ibn Abd al-Wahhab
1798	Invasion of Egypt by Napoleon Bonaparte
1737–1773	Rule of Ahmad Shah Durrani, founder of modern Afghanistan
1794–1925	Qajar shahs of Iran
1805–1849	Rule of Muhammad Ali in Egypt
CA. 1839–1880	Era of the Tanzimat reforms of the Ottoman Empire
1839–1897	Jamal Al-Din Al-Afghani
1845–1905	Muhammad Abduh
1882–1922	British occupation of Egypt
1908	"Young Turk" revolution
1922–1938	Mustafa Kemal, "Atatürk" in power

THE AFRICAN EXPERIENCE

The century and a half between 1800 and 1945 saw striking change in virtually every part of Africa, but nowhere were the changes more radical than in sub-Saharan Africa. North Africa and Egypt were more closely bound up in the politics of the Ottoman Empire and Europe throughout this period. With the important exception of South Africa below the Transvaal, tropical and southern Africa came under major influence and finally control from outside only after 1880. Before this time, internal developments—first, in demographic and power shifts and then in the rise of important Islamic reform movements—overshadowed the slowly increasing European presence in the continent.

New States and Power Centers

Southern Africa

In the south, below the Limpopo river, the first quarter of the nineteenth century saw devastating internal warfare, depopulation, and forced migrations of large numbers of Bantu peoples in what is known as the *mfecane*, or "crushing" era. Likely brought on by a population explosion and perhaps fueled by increasing economic competition in the preceding decades, the *mfecane* was marked by the rapid rise of sizable military states among the northern Nguni-speaking Bantu.

Moshoeshoe, king and founder of Basutoland. Not all of the Bantu peoples followed the militaristic example of Shaka. Moshoeshoe, prince of a subtribe of the Sotho Bantus, fought off Zulu attacks and led his people to a mountain stronghold in southern Africa, where, through diplomacy and determination, he founded a small nation that has endured to the present day. Basutoland became a British protectorate until 1966, when it achieved independence as the Kingdom of Lesotho under Moshoeshoe's great-grandson, King Moshoeshoe II. [New York Public Library.]

Zulu warriors with shields and "knob-kerry" staffs. These twentieth-century Zulu men suggest the kind of fighters whom the Nguni leader Shaka moulded into a formidable war machine in the 1820s.

Its result was a lengthy period of perpetual warfare and chaos, widespread depopulation by death and emigration, and the creation of new, multitribal, multilingual Bantu states in the regions of modern Zimbabwe, Mozambique, Malawi, Zambia, and Tanzania.

The Nguni warrior-king Dingiswayo formed the first of the new military states between CA. 1800 and 1818. The second and most important state of all was formed by his major successor, Shaka, leader of the Nguni-speaking Zulu nation and kingdom (CA. 1818–1828). Shaka's radical and brutal military tactics of total war led to the Zulu conquest of a vast dominion in southeast Africa and the virtual depopulation of a huge area covering some 15,000 square miles. Refugees from Shaka's "total war" zone fled north into Sotho-speaking Bantu territory, or fled south to put increasing pressure on the southern Nguni peoples. Virtual chaos ensued, both north and south of Zululand and even in the high veld above the Orange river, where severe depopulation also resulted from the troubles.

The net result beyond widespread suffering and death was the creation of many new states of diverse kinds. Some people tried to imitate the unique military state of Shaka; others fled to areas like the southern mountain region known today as Lesotho; others even went west into the Kalahari and built up new, largely defensive states. The most famous of these was the Sotho kingdom of King Mosheshwe, which survived as long as he lived (from the 1820s until 1870). Not only was Mosheshwe able to defend his people from the

SOUTHERN AFRICA

1800–1825	Time of the *mfecane* among the Bantu of southeastern southern Africa
CA.1800–1818	Dingiswayo, Nguni Zulu king, forms new military state
CA.1818–1828	Shaka's reign as head of the Nguni state; major warfare, destruction, and expansion
1806	British take Cape Colony from the Dutch
CA. 1825–1870	Sotho kingdom of King Mosheshwe in Lesotho region
1836–1854	The Great Trek of Boers into Natal and north onto the high veld beyond the Orange
1843	British annexation of Natal province
1852–1860	Creation of the Orange Free State and South African Republic

Zulu, but he was also able to hold off the Afrikaners, missionaries, and British. After his death, these latter groups soon became the chief predators upon his territory and sources of pressure for his kingdom of Lesotho.

The new state-building spawned by the *mfecane* was destined to be cut off and nullified eventually by Boer expansion and British annexation of the Natal province (1843). These developments harked back to the Great Trek of Boer *voortrekers*, a migration of about six thousand Afrikaners between 1835 and 1841 from the eastern Cape Colony northeastward into the more fertile regions of southern Africa, Natal, and especially the high veld above the Orange river. The result of these migrations was the creation after 1850 of the Afrikaner republics of the Orange Free State between the Orange and Vaal rivers and the South African Republic north of the Vaal.

East and Central Africa

Farther north in East and East Central Africa, increasing external trade was the basis for the formation of several strong states. In the Lakes region, peoples such as the Nyamwezi to the east of Lake Tanganyika and the Baganda west of Lake Victoria gained regional power from as early as the late eighteenth century through trade with the Arab–Swahili east coast and the states of the eastern Congo to the west. The chief traffic in this east–west commerce across Central Africa involved slaves, ivory, copper, and, from the outside, Indian cloth, firearms, and other manufactured goods.

West Africa

In West Africa, the slave trade was only slowly curtailed. But European demand for palm oil and gum arabic did gain sharply in relative importance by the 1820s. In the first half of the century, the Fulbe (or Fulani) and other *jihad* movements shattered the stability of the western savannah and forest regions from modern Senegal and Ghana through southern Nigeria. Protracted wars and dislocation resulted. Out of this, regional kingdoms such as those of Asante and Dahomey (modern Benin) emerged and flourished before finally succumbing to internal dissension and the active and dominant presence of Britain and France in the latter part of the century.

Islamic Reform Movements

The expansive vitality of Islam was one of the significant agents of change in sub-Saharan Africa before the European rush for colonies in the 1880s. It has remained a factor on the wider African scene ever since.

In 1800, Islam was already a long-established tradition from West Africa across the Sudan to the Red Sea and along the East African coast, as well as over all of Arabic-speaking North Africa. It had long been widespread in the southern Sahara and northern Sahel and was common among merchant classes such as the Jakhanke in various parts of west Africa. Islam was officially the law of the land in states such as the sultanate of Zanzibar on the east coast, and the waning Funj sultanate on the Blue Nile in the eastern Sudan. Even so, in many "Islamic" states in Africa the rural populace were still semipagan, if not wholly so; and often even the ruling and urban elites of the towns were only nominally Muslim.

The nineteenth century is notable for the number and strength of a series of militant Islamic revivalist and reform movements of *jihad*, or holy struggle. Aimed at a more truly Muslim society and wider allegiance to Muslim values, these movements both fixed and spread Islam as a lasting part of the African scene. The West African *jihad* movements began in the seventeenth century in the southwest Sahara to the north of Fuuta Tooro and Wolof states of Senegal. They eventually spread. The *jihad* movements flourished especially in the eighteenth century among the widely dispersed peoples. These movements originated with the activities of militant, reformist Sufi brotherhoods that

This famous picture of the massacre of General Gordon and his garrison at Khartoum by the fanatical troops of the Mahdi does not conform entirely to the facts. Gordan exceeded his mandate as governor-general of the Sudan, which was explicitly to extricate the Egyptians, both troops and civilians. Instead, his erratic actions led to his being cut off from Egypt. Public opinion in Britain forced the sending of a relief force, which arrived two days after the fall of Khartoum and Gordon's death, which the Mahdi had unsuccessfully ordered his troops to prevent. [Bettmann Archive.]

Usman Dan Fodio on Evil and Good Government

Following in the tradition of the Wahhabis in Arabia and virtually all previous Islamic reform movements, Dan Fodio stressed adherence to Muslim norms as expressed in the Shari'a, the divine law. In the two excerpts that follow, he enumerated some of the evils of the previous Hausa rulers and their "law," then listed five principles of proper Islamic government.

One of the ways of their government [that is, of the Hausa or Habe kings] is succession to the emirate by hereditary right and by force to the exclusion of consultation. And one of the ways of their government is the building of their sovereignty upon three things: the people's persons, their honour, and their possessions; and whomsoever they wish to kill or exile or violate his honour or devour his wealth they do so in pursuit of their lusts, without any right in the Shari'a. One of the ways of their government is their imposing on the people monies not laid down by the Shari'a, being those which they call *janghali* and *kurdin ghari* and *kurdin salla*. One of the ways of their governments is their intentionally eating whatever food they wish, whether it is religiously permitted or forbidden, and wearing whatever clothes they wish, whether religiously permitted or forbidden, and drinking what beverages [ta'am] they wish, whether religiously permitted or forbidden, and riding whatever riding beasts they wish, whether religiously permitted or forbidden, and taking what women they wish without marriage contract, and living in decorated palaces, whether religiously permitted or forbidden, and spreading soft (decorated) carpets as they wish, whether religiously permitted or forbidden.

. . . .

And I say—and help is with God—the foundations of government are five things: the first is that authority shall not be given to one who seeks it. The second is the necessity for consultation. The third is the abandoning of harshness. The fourth is justice. The fifth is good works. And as for its ministers, they are four. (The First) is a trustworthy wazir to wake the ruler if he sleeps, to make him see if he is blind, and to remind him if he forgets, and the greatest misfortune for the government and the subjects is that they should be denied honest wazirs. And among the conditions pertaining to the wazir is that he should be steadfast in compassion to the people, and merciful towards them. The second of the ministers of government is a judge whom the blame of a blamer cannot overtake concerning the affairs of God. The third is a chief of police who shall obtain justice for the weak from the strong. The fourth is a tax collector who shall discharge his duties and not oppress the subjects. . . . ❑

From translation of Usman Dan Fodio's *Kitab al-Farq* by M. Hiskett, *Bulletin of the School of Oriental and African Studies* (London: 1960), Part 3, p. 558; reprinted in Basil Davidson, *The African Past* (New York: Grosset and Dunlap, Universal Library, 1964/1967), pp. 323–325.

had penetrated West Africa from the north, especially through Mauritania.

The most important of these movements came just after the turn of the nineteenth century and was led by a Fulbe Muslim scholar from Hausa territory in the central sahel. Usman Dan Fodio (1754–1817) was influenced by the reformist ideas that spread throughout the Muslim world in the eighteenth century, from India to Saudi Arabia and Africa. Shortly after 1804, he gathered an immense army of fervent supporters and conquered most of the Hausa lands of modern northern and central Nigeria, bringing an explicitly Islamic order to the area. Dan Fodio left behind an impressive sultanate centered on the new capital of Sokoto and governed by one of his sons, Muhammad Bello, until 1837. In his wake, the Fulbe became the ruling class in the Hausa regions, and Islam spread into the countryside, where it still predominates today.

Other nineteenth-century reform movements had similar success both in gaining at least ephemeral political power and in spreading a fundamentalist, reformist Islamic message among the masses. Most notable alongside several West African *jihads* were the Sanusi reform and missionary movement of Libya and the eastern Sahara (after about 1840) and the famous Mahdist uprising of the eastern Sudan (1880s and

CENTRAL SUDAN

1754–1817	Uthman Dan Fodio, Fulbe leader of major Islamic *jihad*
1810	Dan Fodio founds Islamic sultanate in lands of former Hausa states of north and central Nigeria
1817–1837	Reign at Sokoto of Muhammad Bello, son of Dan Fodio

1890s). The Libyan movement took hold to such a degree that it still could provide the focus for resistance to the Italian invasion of 1911. The Sudanese Mahdi, Muhammad Ahmad (1848–1885), condemned the widespread corruption of basic Muslim ideals and declared himself the awaited deliverer, or Mahdi, in 1881. He led the northern Sudan in rebellion against Ottoman-Egyptian control, defeating even the British forces from Egypt under Charles George Gordon at Khartoum. His successor governed the Sudan until the British finally destroyed the young Islamic state in 1899.

Increasing European Involvement

Although Muslim reform movements did help to spread and entrench Islam in important parts of Africa, it was not the only important nineteenth-century development in the continent. Another key development was the eventual domination of Africa's politics and economy by white Christian Europe. Before the mid-1800s, the actual penetration of white outsiders had been largely limited to coastal areas, although their slave trade had had significant effects even in inland areas (see Chapter 22). This changed drastically as, first, trading companies, explorers, and missionaries, and finally, colonial troops and governments moved into Africa. Ironically, the gradual elimination of the slave trade (primarily through Britian's efforts) increased European exploration of the "Dark Continent," and the growth of Western Christian missionary enterprise—all ushered in a fierce European imperialism followed by overt colonialism. Both were to have vastly more disastrous consequences than slaving for Africa's diverse peoples and subsequent history.

Exploration

The nineteenth-century European—mainly English, French, and German—explorers gradually uncovered for Westerners the great "secrets" of Africa: the sources and courses of the Niger, the Nile, the Zambezi, and Congo rivers; natural wonders such as Mount Kilimanjaro and Lake Tanganyika; and fabled places like Timbuktu, the once great Berber trading gateway and the center of Islamic learning in the western Sahara and the Sudan. The history of European exploration is one of fortune hunting, self-promotion, violence, and mistakes. But it is also one of patience and perseverance, bravery, and dedication.

The explorers' main importance for Africa lay in their stimulation of European interest and their opening of the way for traders, missionaries, and finally soldiers and governors from the Christian West. One of the greatest explorers was Dr. David Livingston (d.

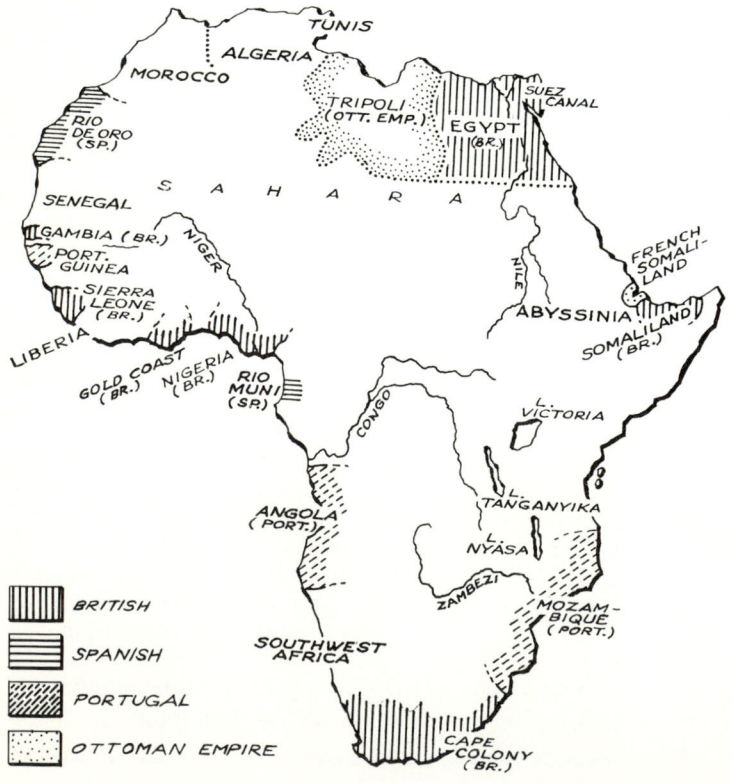

MAP 31-1   IMPERIAL EXPANSION IN AFRICA UP TO 1880   *A comparison of this map with that of 31-2 shows how rapidly the situation in Africa changed after 1880.*

Henry Stanley (left) and David Livingston (right). Stanley, the American journalist-adventurer, and Livingston, the British missionary doctor, reflect two different faces of Western interest and involvement in Africa in the nineteenth century. [Brown Brothers.]

1873). Not an adventurer with an eye to commercial gain, Livingston was a missionary in love with and dedicated to Africa and her peoples as were few other Westerners before or after him.

Christian Missions

The latter part of the nineteenth century saw a mounting influx of Christian missionaries, both Protestant and Catholic (by 1900, perhaps as many as ten thousand altogether). These vied—sometimes with one another, sometimes with Muslim traders and teachers—for the souls of Africans. Part of the motivation for coming to Africa was to eradicate the remaining slave trade, especially that in east Africa run by Arabs from Zanzibar.

The missionaries came to know the African peoples far better than did the explorers. Their accounts of Africa contained, to be sure, chauvinistic and misleading descriptions of the "degraded" state of African culture and religion, but they did bring some knowledge of and interest in Africa to Europe. Their translation work and mission schools also brought alphabetic culture and some literacy to the African tribal world. Their settlements, often in remote areas, did provide convenient pretexts for European intervention in the affairs of African tribes and states. Yet the missionaries to Africa were more often idealists than opportunists. A great many died—as many as half of those who went into the tropical regions where indigenous diseases such as malaria, yellow fever, and sleeping sickness were often too much for the newcomers.

Justifiable charges of paternalistic and imperialistic motives and actions can be leveled against these modern crusaders. However, it must be said that they did try to bring medicine and education to Africans. They did plant the seeds—sometimes intentionally, sometimes inadvertently—of African Christian churches such as the one that is today a leader of the resistance to the racist policies of South Africa (see Chapter 37). The mission effort has continued even to the present day.

The Colonial "Scramble for Africa"

Before 1850, the only significant conflict between Europeans and Africans over the attempts to take African territory for themselves was in South Africa and Algeria. In South Africa, as we have noted, the Boers came into conflict with Bantu tribes after leaving the British-ruled Cape Colony on their Great Trek to find new lands. The French invaded Algeria without cause in 1830, settled Europeans on the choice farmlands, and waged war on native resistance fighters. Over most of the continent, however, the European presence was felt with real force only from the 1880s. Yet by World War I, virtually all of Africa (the only exceptions being Ethiopia and Liberia) was divided rather

A contemporary view of the fall of Algiers to the French in 1830. The French conquest and "pacification" of Algeria took some seventeen years (1830–1847). More than a century later, the French were again involved in a protracted struggle in Algeria (1955–1962). While the first conflict had ended in French victory and colonial rule, the second ended in Algerian independence and the departure of most of the one million Europeans whose ancestors had settled there since 1830. [New York Public Library.]

arbitrarily into a patchwork of large territories ruled directly or indirectly by European colonial administrations (see Chapter 33).

This foreign takeover of Africa was supported by mounting European popular as well as commercial interest in Africa. Both factors were fueled by the public-ity given African exploration and missionary work. What made the takeover possible was the superior economic, technological, and military power that the West commanded. In particular, European technical expertise did much to open up the interior of the continent in the last few decades before World War I.

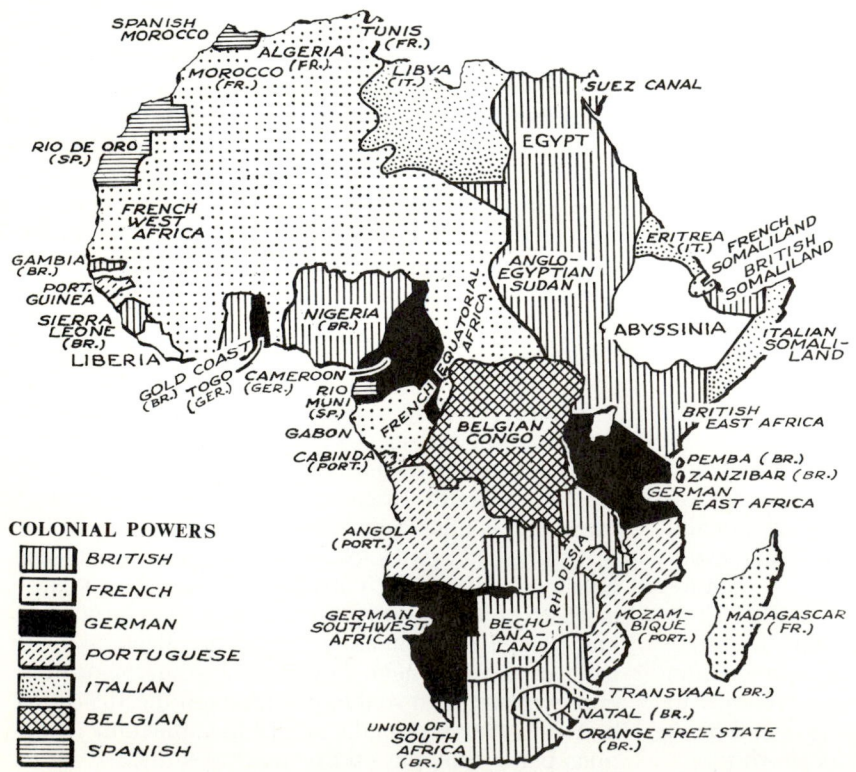

MAP 31-2   PARTITION OF AFRICA, 1880–1914   *Before 1880 European presence in Africa was largely the remains of early exploration by old imperialists and did not penetrate the heart of the continent. By 1914 the occupying powers included most large European states; only Liberia, and Abyssinia remained independent.*

The Uganda Railway, near Mombasa. The railroad was one of the greatest factors in much of Africa, not least Uganda and Nigeria, in opening the continent up both to colonial domination and to commerce, development, and the communication that also helped make national-state movements possible later on. Its true socio-economic impact has yet to be fully assessed for the whole of the continent. [Brown Brothers.]

Except for the Nile and the Niger, all of the great African rivers have impassible waterfalls only a short way inland from the sea, where the coastal plains rise sharply to the largely highland interior of the continent. The steamboat above such falls and the railroad around them (or where no navigable rivers ran) provided viable means of penetrating the African interior. This access made the riches of Africa feasible for commercial and colonial purposes. Consequently, the European desire for the industrial markets and the natural resources of Africa—together with intra-European competition for power and prestige—pushed one European state after another to lay claim to whatever segments of Africa they could take over.

The British and the French were the vanguard of the European nations that sought to include African lands in their imperial domains. The British had the largest involvement. On one axis, it ranged from their ever-increasing South African holdings (begun with the Cape Colony taken from the Dutch in 1806) to their effective protectorate in Egypt (from 1882). On another axis, it extended from West African trading interests (and ultimately protectorate rule, as in the Niger districts after 1885) to a Zanzibar-based sphere of influence in East Africa in the 1870s (and finally a protectorate for Zanizibar in 1890).

The British long resisted African colonial involvement and then chose "indirect" as preferable to "direct" colonial administration. In the end, their rule was only slightly more enlightened than that of the French, who began early to carve out a colonial empire under "direct" French control. The French had long had government-supported trading outposts in Senegal and other parts of West Africa. After a long, bitter struggle (1830–1847), they conquered Algeria, creating the first major European colony in Africa. In addition, Tunisia and the Ivory Coast became French protectorates in the 1880s; Dahomey was bloodily annexed in 1894; and the colony of Equatorial Africa was proclaimed in 1910.

Beginning in the mid-1880s, the major European powers began to work to gain each other's agreement to their claims on particular segments of Africa. Leopold of Belgium and Otto von Bismarck in Germany established their own claims to parts of South, Central, and East Africa. France and England set about consolidating their African interests. Italy, too, eventually tried to take African colonial territory in Eritrea, Somaliland, Ethiopia, and Libya. Only the Italian design on Ethiopia was thwarted, when Ethiopia used its newly modernized army to defeat an Italian invasion in 1896. This failure the Italians recouped only in 1935 by a second invasion. The "scramble for Africa" was largely over by the outbreak of World War I, which caused Germany to lose its African colonies but did not bring independence to these former possessions.

1830	French invasion of Algeria
1870	British protectorate in Zanzibar
CA. 1880	French protectorate in Tunisia and Ivory Coast
1880s–1890s	Mahdist uprising in eastern Sudan
1882	British protectorate in Egypt
1894	The French annex Dahomey
1910	French colony of Equatorial Africa

Independence had to wait for another world war and changed attitudes about colonial power, as well as changed balances of world power (see Chapter 37).

European colonial rule in Africa is one of the uglier chapters of modern history. If German, French, Belgian, Portuguese, and Boer rule was notoriously brutal and produced the worse atrocities, British sway had its own share of misrule and exploitation as well. The paternalistic attitudes of late-nineteenth-century Europe and America amounted in the end to sheer racism when applied in Africa. The regions with large-scale white settlement produced the worst exploitation at the expense of vastly greater native populations. But everywhere, white minorities exercised disproportionate power over the lives of black or brown majorities. The worst legacy of the European presence remains the white racist state of modern South Africa, but no Western nation has the right to a clear conscience about its involvement in Africa.

African Resistance to Colonialism: The Rise of Nationalism

African states were not, however, simply passive objects of European manipulation and conquest. Many astute native rulers sought, by diplomacy, trade leverage, and warfare, to use the European presence to their own advantage. Some, like the Bagandan king Mutesa in the 1870s (in what is today Uganda), were remarkably successful for some time. Direct armed resistance was in every case (even Ethiopia's) doomed because of European technological superiority. Nevertheless, such resistance was widespread, whether in the Hehe people's fight against German troops in Tanganyika or the Asante's battle against British forces, both in the 1890s. Armed resistance to colonial domination continued in the twentieth century in many places. In the end, it was less this resistance than other factors that brought an end to most foreign rule on African soil.

The most prominent of these factors was the rise of various kinds of nationalism across the African continent, especially after World War I. However little the colonial partition of Africa reflected native linguistic, racial, or cultural divisions, its divisions had consider-

An African Ruler Rejects a German Demand for Submission

The German commander in southern Tanganyika (modern Tanzania), Hermann von Wissmann, directed an offensive in 1890 aimed at building a German colonial empire on the east African coast and inland. When Macemba, chief of the Yao people, received an ultimatum from von Wissmann to surrender, he sent back the following reply. It expresses with dignity and power common African feelings about invaders from Europe.

I have listened to your words but can find no reason why I should obey you—I would rather die first. I have no relations with you and cannot bring it to my mind that you have given me so much as a pesa [fraction of a rupee] or the quarter of a pesa or a needle or a thread. I look for some reason why I should obey you and find not the smallest. If it should be friendship that you desire, then I am ready for, today and always; but to be your subject, that I cannot be. . . . If it should be war you desire, then I am ready, but never to be your subject. . . . I do not fall at your feet, for you are God's creature just as I am. . . . I am sultan here in my land. You are sultan there in yours. Yet listen, I do not say to you that you should obey me; for I know that you are a free man. . . . As for me, I will not come to you, and if you are strong enough, then come and fetch me. . . . ❑

Trans. by Basil Davidson, from F. F. Müller, *Deutschland-Zanzibar-Ostafrica* (Berlin, 1959), p. 455; reprinted in Basil Davidson, *The African Past* (New York: Grosset and Dunlap, Universal Library, 1964/1967), pp. 357–358.

Mutesa of Buganda and his court. Noted for his cunning and diplomatic skill and for his autocratic and often cruel conduct, Mutesa was one of the few African rulers who was able for a long time (1856–1884) to maintain a powerful and successful army and court, which enabled him to deal effectively with Egyptian and British efforts to encroach on his sphere of influence. [Brown Brothers.]

able influence on both nationalist movements and the eventual shape of African states. The "national" consciousness of the diverse peoples of a given colonial unit was fueled by common opposition to foreign rule. It was also fed by the use of a common European tongue and through the assimilation of European thought and culture by a growing educated native elite. Such elites were typically educated in mission schools and sometimes foreign universities. Their ranks gradually increased in the early decades of this century. From them came the leaders of Africa's nationalist movements between the two world wars and of Africa's new independent nations after World War II.

The severest indigenous critique of the Western treatment of Africa could be delivered by calling on Western religious and political ideals themselves. The African leaders of the twentieth century learned well from the West and used their learning to help end Western domination. The process culminated in the creation of over forty self-governing African nations after 1945 (see Chapter 37). African independence

Jomo Kenyatta upon his release from British imprisonment in 1961. Kenyatta emerged as a major spokesman for native Kenyan interests in the 1940s. Incorrectly sentenced in 1953 for his supposed role in the bloody Mau Mau uprising, Kenyatta became the first prime minister of independent Kenya in 1963. [Magnum.]

movements were eventually based on modern nationalist models from Europe and America, rather than ancient ones of native tradition. The nationalist and independence movements typically sought to eject the colonial intruders and not to return to an earlier status quo. Their aim was to take over and to run for themselves the Western institutions that had been introduced by colonialism. This legacy from the West is still visible today.

India, the Islamic Heartlands, and Africa, 1800–1945, in World Perspective

The century and a half following the French Revolution in Europe was a bleak one for the fortunes of the Indian subcontinent, the African continent, and the societies of the Islamic world in general. For centuries these civilizations balanced equal advances and setbacks in material and intellectual culture, commercial development, and political stability among the major cultural regions of the world. Suddenly, the European sector of the global community in this period came to dominate in crushing fashion not only the diverse parts of the Islamic heartlands, Africa, and India, but also the rest of the world, even including east Asia.

The Middle East, Africa, Iran, central Asia, India, and Indonesia, along with Central and South America—what is today referred to as "the third world" of "developing nations"—were the areas of the world most drastically affected by European imperialism and colonialism. Regardless of indigenous developments in these regions, the overarching and decisive development of this era was this new and unprecedented domination of the world's economy, intellectual life, and political and military history by one region of the global community. Certainly, the histories of the less "developed" nations of the world in this age have their own internal dynamics; in fact, numerous smaller African or South American societies were not directly affected by the global trend of radical Western dominance. Still, we can neither deny nor ignore the often sordid and ugly, if sometimes impressive, advance of Western economic, technological, intellectual, and military dominance in world affairs. This development spans roughly the period from the late eighteenth century to World War II. Today, we recognize that this dominance was by no means synonymous with "progress," as Westerners have often liked to think. Yet, we have to see it still as the hallmark of the age in most of Asia, Africa, and South America.

What should not, however, be ignored, is the striking vitality of so many of the cultures and traditions that bore the brunt of the Western onslaught. Arab, Iranian, Indian, African, and other encounters with Western material and intellectual domination were diverse and produced different responses and initiatives. The varied responses to these encounters have borne full fruit in political, economic, or intellectual independence only in the decades since 1945; however, most of them began long before this time, some even well before 1800. For example, modern Islamic reform and resurgence began in the eighteenth century, although it has become a major factor globally only in recent years. Indian national, as opposed to regional, consciousness received its major impetus from the British colonial experience, even if it has taken concrete form only after the Second World War.

Certainly one result of the imperial–colonial experience has been the sharpening in recent times of cultural self-consciousness and ultimately self-confidence among those peoples most negatively affected by Western dominance. It may well be that for the Third-World nations, the imperial–colonial experiences will prove to be not only ones of misery and reversal, but also transitions to positive development and resurgence—despite the looming economic, educational, and demographic problems.

Suggested Readings

INDIA

A. AHMAD, *Islamic Modernism in India and Pakistan*, 1857–1964 (1967). The standard survey of Muslim thinkers and movements in India in the period.

S. N. HAY, ed., "Modern India and Pakistan," Part VI of Wm. Theodore de Bary et al., eds., *Sources of Indian Tradition*, 2nd ed. (1988). A superb selection of primary-source documents with brief introductions and helpful notes.

D. KOPF, *British Orientalism and the Bengal Renaissance: The Dynamics of Indian Modernization*, 1773–1835 (1969). An intriguing study of British–Indian interchange and mutual influence in the heyday of the East India Company.

W. C. SMITH, *Modern Islam in India: A Social Analysis* (1943). A Marxist critique. Still the best survey and analysis of Indian Muslim thought from Sayyid Ahmad Khan to the early 1940s.

P. SPEAR, *The Oxford History of Modern India*, 1740–1947 (1965). Still a helpful quick reference tool.

M. N. SRINIVAS, *Social Change in Modern India* (1966). An older but highly influential treatment of topics such as "sanskritization," "westernization," and "secularization."

S. WOLPERT, *A New History of India*, 2nd ed. (1982). Chapters 14–25. A solid survey and useful quick reference source.

CENTRAL ISLAMIC LANDS

K. CRAGG, *Counsels in Contemporary Islam* (1965). A brief survey of intellectual trends in the modern Islamic world in the nineteenth and twentieth centuries.

J. J. DONAHUE AND J. L. ESPOSITO, eds. *Islam in Transition: Muslim Perspectives* (1982). An interesting selection of primary-source materials on Islamic thinking in this century.

D. F. EICKELMAN, *Knowledge and Power in Morocco: The Education of a Twentieth-Century Notable* (1985). A fascinating study of traditional Islamic education and society in the twentieth century through a social biography of a Moroccan religious scholar and judge.

M. G. S. HODGSON, *The Venture of Islam*. Vol. 3: *The Gunpowder Empires and Modern Times* (1974). While less ample than his first two volumes, this volume still provides a solid interpretative introduction.

A. HOURANI, *Arabic Thought in the Liberal Age*, 1798–1939. (1967). The standard work, by which all subsequent scholarship on the topic is judged.

N. R. KEDDI, *An Islamic Response to Imperialism* (1968). A brief study of al-Afghani, the great Muslim reformer, with translations of a number of his writings.

M. H. KERR, *Islamic Reform: The Political and Legal Theories of Muhammad 'Abduh and Rashid Rida* (1966). A fine study of two major Muslim reformers in the colonial period in Egypt.

B. LEWIS, *The Emergence of Modern Turkey*, 2nd ed. (1968). A concise but thorough history of the creation of the Turkish state, including nineteenth-century background.

E. MORTIMER, *Faith and Power: The Politics of Islam* (1982). A fine survey of contemporary Islamic countries by a knowledgeable and thoughtful journalist.

F. RAHMAN, *Islam* (1966). Chapters 12 and 13. These two chapters from a fine introductory survey of Islam by a major modern Muslim historian and thinker deal with reform movements and other modern developments in the Islamic world

J. C. B. RICHMOND, *Egypt*, 1798–1952: *Her Advance towards a Modern Identity* (1977). A basic history, with focus on political change.

S. J. SHAW AND E. K. SHAW, *History of the Ottoman Empire and Modern Turkey*. Vol. II: *Reform, Revolution, and Republic: The Rise of Modern Turkey*, 1808–1975 (1977). Detailed and careful analytic and survey history of the modern period.

W. C. SMITH, *Islam in Modern History* (1957). Dated, but still the most penetrating analysis of the dilemmas facing Muslim individuals and states in the twentieth century.

J. O. VOLL, *Islam: Continuity and Change in the Modern World* (1982). Chapters 1–6. A recent interpretive survey of the Islamic world since the eighteenth century. Its emphasis on eighteenth-century reform movements is especially noteworthy.

AFRICA

A. A. BOAHEN, *Africa under Colonial Domination, 1880–1935*. Vol. VII of the UNESCO *General History of Africa* (1985). Excellent chapters on various regions of Africa in the period. Chapters 3–10 detail African resistance to European colonial intrusion in diverse regions.

W. CARTEY AND M. KILSON, eds., *The Africa Reader: Colonial Africa* (1970). Original source materials give vivid picture of African resistance to colonial powers, adaptation to foreign rule, and the emergence of the African masses as a political force.

P. CURTIN, S. FEIERMANN, L. THOMPSON, AND J. VANSINA. *African History* (1978). The relevant portions here are Chapters 10–20.

B. DAVIDSON, *The African Genius: An Introduction to African Social and Cultural History* (1969). A sensitive analysis of Africa from the standpoint of African rather than European thought and action. Especially interesting are African responses to imperial and colonial penetration.

J. D. FAGE, *A History of Africa* (1978). The relevant chapters, which give a particularly clear overview of the colonial period, are 12–16.

D. FODE AND P. M. KABERRY, eds., *West African Kingdoms in the Nineteenth Century* (1967). Very useful treatments of the different west African states, such as Benin, Asante, and Gonja.

B. FREUND, *The Making of Contemporary Africa: The Development of African Society since* 1800 (1984). A refreshingly direct synthetic discussion and survey that takes an avowedly but not reductive materialist approach to interpretation.

R. HALLETT, *Africa since* 1875: *A Modern History* (1974). Detailed survey of modern African history from the outset of the colonial period.

R. W. JULY, *A History of the African People*, 3rd. ed. (1980). The strongest portions of the book are those on the nineteenth and twentieth centuries.

M. A. KLEIN, *Islam and Imperialism in Senegal: Sine-Saloum*, 1847–1914 (1968). A first-rate study of the shift in the Serer states of Senegal from traditional authority to that of the colonial French.

B. A. OGOT AND J. A. KIERAN, eds., *Zamani: A Survey of East African History*, 2nd rev. ed. (1974). Good material on nineteenth century and colonial period in the various regions.

Women textile workers at a turn-of-the century silk weaving mill. A company officer, at center, is visiting the shop floor. Behind him is a supervisor, wearing a Meiji-style mustache. Women constituted more than half of Japan's industrial labor force well into the twentieth century. They worked a span of years after leaving primary school and before marrying. Their hours were long, their dormitories crowded, and they often contracted tuberculosis. Using mechanically reeled silk thread, their product was superior. (Keystone View Company.)

32 Modern East Asia

From the mid-nineteenth century, the West was the expanding, aggressive, imperialistic force in world history. Its industrial goods and gunboats reached every part of the globe. It believed in free trade and had the military might to impose it on others. It was the trigger for change throughout the world. But the response to the Western impact varied immensely according to the internal array of forces in each country. From this perspective, Japan and China were both relatively successful in their responses, for although each was subject to "unequal treaties," neither became a colony.

The two countries were also similar in that their governing elites were educated in Confucianism. Unlike the otherworldly religions of Buddhism, Islam, or Christianity, Confucianism was just secular enough to crumble in the face of the more powerful secularism of nineteenth-century science and the doctrines associated with it. In both Japan and China, though much more rapidly in Japan, the leading intellectuals abandoned Confucianism in favor of Western secular doctrines. To be sure, many Confucian values, deeply embedded in the societies, survived the philosophies of which they had once been a part. In fact, one of the "breakdown products" of the Confucian sociopolitical identity was a strong new nationalism in both China and Japan.

But there the similarities end. In most other respects, modern Japan and China could hardly be more different. Perhaps this difference was only to be expected, given the pattern of recurrent dynasties in China's premodern history and the pattern of feudal evolution in Japan's.

The coming of Commodore Matthew Perry in 1853–1854 immediately set in motion a political change within Japan. In fifteen years, the old Tokugawa regime had collapsed, and the Japanese set about building a modern state. Economic growth followed. By the turn of the century, Japan had defeated China and was about to defeat imperial Russia in a war. Sustained economic growth continued during the early twentieth century. After the Great Depression, Japan, like Italy and Germany, became a militarist state and was eventually defeated in World War II. But Japan reemerged after the war more stable, more productive, and with a stronger parliamentary government than ever before.

The Chinese polity, in contrast, easily weathered the Opium War, an event of considerably greater magnitude than Perry's visit to Japan. The hold of tradition in China was remarkable, as was the effectiveness of traditional remedies in dealing with its political ills. Only in its relations with the Western powers did traditional patterns not work. In one sense, the strength of tradition was China's weakness, for it took seventy years after the Opium War to overthrow the dynasty. Only then was China willing to begin the modernization that Japan had started in 1868, and even then it was unsuccessful. Along with warlordism and the other problems that had accompanied the dissolution of past dynasties, new ills arose from the rending of the very fabric of the dynastic pattern. To these was added the unprecedented experience of being confronted by nations more powerful than itself. That China in some sense "failed" during this modern century is not a Western view imposed on China; it was the view held by the Chinese themselves.

MODERN CHINA (1839–1949)

China's modern century was not the century in which it became modern as much as it was the century in which it encountered the modern West. Its first phase, from the Opium War (1839–1842) to the fall of the Ch'ing or Manchu dynasty (1911), was remarkably little affected by Western impact. Indeed, it was only during the decade before 1911 that the Confucian tradition began to be discarded in favor of new ideas from the West. The second phase of China's modern history, from 1911 to the establishment of a Communist state in 1949, was a time of turmoil and suffering. The fighting incidental to the collapse of the dynasty gave way to decades of warlord rule, to partial military unification and continual military campaigns, to war with Japan, and then, while most countries were returning to peace, to four bitter years of civil war.

The Close of Manchu Rule

The Opium War

The eighteenth-century three-country trade—British goods to India, Indian cotton to China, and Chinese tea to Britain—was in China's favor. The silver flowing into China spurred the further monetization of Chinese markets. Then the British replaced cotton with Indian opium. Within a few decades after the turn of the century, the balance of trade was reversed, and silver began to flow out of China.

A crisis arose in the 1830s when the British East India Company lost its monopoly on British trade with China. The opium trade became wide open. To check the evil of opium and the outflow of specie, the Chinese government banned opium in 1836, closing the dens where it was smoked and executing Chinese dealers. In 1839, the government sent Imperial Commissioner Lin Tse-hsu to Canton to superintend the ban. He continued the crackdown on Chinese dealers and destroyed over twenty thousand chests—a six-month supply—of opium belonging to foreign merchants. This action set the stage for a confrontation between the Chinese and British.

War broke out in November 1839 when Chinese war junks clashed with a British merchantman. The following June, a British fleet of sixteen warships arrived at Canton, and for the next two years, the British bombarded forts, fought battles, seized cities, and attempted negotiations. The Chinese troops, with their antiquated weapons and old-style cannon, were ineffective. The war was finally ended in August 1842 by the Treaty of Nanking, the first of the "unequal treaties."

The treaty not only ended the "tribute system" but provided Britain with a superb deep-water port at Hong Kong, a huge indemnity, and the opening of five ports: Canton, Shanghai, Amoy, Ningpo, and Foochow. British merchants and their families were permitted to reside in the ports and to engage in trade; Britain could appoint a consul for each city; and British residents gained extraterritoriality, under which they were subject to British and not Chinese law. The treaty also contained a "most-favored-nation" clause, a provision that any further rights gained by any other nation would automatically accrue to Britain as well. The treaty with Britain was followed in 1844 by similar treaties with the United States and France. The American treaty permitted churches in treaty ports, and the French treaty permitted the propagation of Catholicism.

After the signing of the British treaty, Chinese im-

Commissioner Lin Urges Morality on Queen Victoria

In 1839 the British in China argued for free trade and protection for the legal right of their citizens. The Chinese position was that behind such lofty arguments, the British were pushing opium.

A communication: magnificently our great Emperor soothes and pacifies China and the foreign countries, regarding all with the same kindness. If there is profit, then he shares it with the peoples of the world; if there is harm, then he removes it on behalf of the world. This is because he takes the mind of heaven and earth as his mind.

The kings of your honorable country by a tradition handed down from generation to generation have always been noted for their politeness and submissiveness. We have read your successive tributary memorials saying, "In general our countrymen who go to trade in China have always received His Majesty the Emperor's gracious treatment and equal justice," and so on. Privately we are delighted with the way in which the honorable rulers of your country deeply understand the grand principles and are grateful for the Celestial grace. For this reason the Celestial Court in soothing those from afar has redoubled its polite and kind treatment. The profit from trade has been enjoyed by them continuously for two hundred years. This is the source from which your country has become known for its wealth. But after a long period of commercial intercourse, there appear among the crowd of barbarians both good persons and bad, unevenly. Consequently there are those who smuggle opium to seduce the Chinese people and so cause the spread of the poison to all provinces. Such persons who only care to profit themselves, and disregard their harm to others, are not tolerated by the laws of heaven and are unanimously hated by human beings. His Majesty the Emperor, upon hearing of this, is in a towering rage. . . .

We find that your country is sixty or seventy thousand li [three li make one mile, ordinarily] from China. Yet there are barbarian ships that strive to come here for trade for the purpose of making a great profit. The wealth of China is used to profit the barbarians. That is to say, the great profit made by barbarians is all taken from the rightful share of China. By what right do they then in return use the poisonous drug to injure the Chinese people? Even though the barbarians may not necessarily intend to do us harm, yet in coveting profit to an extreme, they have no regard for injuring others. Let us ask, where is your conscience? I have heard that the smoking of opium is very strictly forbidden by your country; that is because the harm caused by opium is clearly understood. Since it is not permitted to do harm to your own country, then even less should you let it be passed on to the harm of other countries—how much less to China!

Suppose there were people from another country who carried opium for sale to England and seduced your people into buying and smoking it; certainly your honorable ruler would deeply hate it and be bitterly aroused. We have heard heretofore that your honorable ruler is kind and benevolent. Naturally you would not wish to give unto others what you yourself do not want.

Now we have set up regulations governing the Chinese people. He who sells opium shall receive the death penalty and he who smokes it also the death penalty. Now consider this: if the barbarians do not bring opium, then how can the Chinese people resell it, and how can they smoke it? The fact is that the wicked barbarians beguile the Chinese people into a death trap. How then can we grant life only to those barbarians? He who takes the life of even one person still has to atone for it with his own life; yet is the harm done by opium limited to the taking of one life only? Therefore in the new regulations, in regard to those barbarians who bring opium to China, the penalty is fixed at decapitation or strangulation. This is what is called getting rid of a harmful thing on behalf of mankind.

[However] All those who within the period of the coming one year (from England) or six months (from India) bring opium to China by mistake, but who voluntarily confess and completely surrender their opium, shall be exempt from their punishment. This may be called the height of kindness and the perfection of justice. ❑

S. Y. Teng and J. K. Fairbank, *China's Response to the West* (Cambridge: Harvard U.P., 1954), pp. 24–27.

ports of opium rose from thirty thousand chests to a peak of eighty-seven thousand in 1879. Thereafter, imports declined to 50,000 chests in 1906, and ended during World War I. But other kinds of trade did not grow as much as had been hoped, and Western merchants blamed the lack of growth on artificial restraints imposed by Chinese officials. Western merchants also complained that, despite the treaties, Canton remained closed to trade. The Chinese authorities, for their part, were incensed by the export of coolies to work under harsh conditions on plantations in Cuba and Peru. A second war broke out in 1856, which continued sporadically until Lord Elgin, the British commander, captured Peking in 1860. The war

The Opium War, 1840. *Armed Chinese junks were no match for British warships. The war ended in 1842 with the Treaty of Nanking.*

resulted in a new set of conventions and treaties that provided for indemnities, the opening of eleven new ports, the stationing of foreign diplomats in Peking, the propagation of Christianity anywhere in China, and the legalization of the opium trade.

While the British fought China for trading rights, the Russians were encroaching on China's northern frontier. During the 1850s, Russia established settlements along the Amur River. In 1858, China signed a treaty ceding the north bank of the Amur to Russia, and in 1860, China signed another treaty giving Russia the Maritime Province between the Ussuri River and the Pacific. These lands are disputed by China even today.

The Taiping Rebellion

Far more immediate a threat to Manchu rule than foreign gunboats and unequal treaties were the Taiping, Nien, and Muslim rebellions that convulsed China between 1850 and 1873. The torment and suffering that they caused were of a magnitude unparalleled in world history. Estimates of those killed during the twenty years of the Taiping Rebellion range from twenty to thirty million. If one adds in losses due to other rebellions, droughts, and floods, China's population dropped by sixty million and did not recover to prerebellion levels until almost the end of the dynasty in 1911.

The Taipings were begun by Hung Hsiu-ch'uan, a schoolteacher from a poor family in a minority Hakka group in the southern province of Kwangtung. Hung had four times failed to pass the civil service examinations. He became ill and saw visions. Influenced by Protestant tracts that he had picked up in Canton, Hung announced that he was the younger brother of Jesus and that God had told him to rid China of evil

demons—including Manchus, Confucians, Taoists, and Buddhists. He formed an Association of God Worshipers. He used the old Shang term for "Deity Above" to translate "God." His followers cut off their queues as a sign of resistance to the Manchus, who called them "long-haired rebels." The Taipings began by attacking local Confucian temples, arousing the opposition of the gentry. The Taipings were soon joined by peasants, coal miners, charcoal workers, and unemployed transport workers. Hung proclaimed the Heavenly Kingdom of Great Peace in 1851 and two years later took Nanking and made it his capital. The fighting spread until the Taipings controlled most of the Yangtze basin; their expeditions eventually entered sixteen of the eighteen Chinese provinces. By this time, their army numbered almost a million.

The Taiping ideology joined Old Testament Christianity with an ancient text often used by reformers, the *Chou Rites*. The puritanical ethics of the Taipings came from the former, and the notion of sharing property equally came from the latter. The Taipings prohibited opium, tobacco, alcohol, gambling, adultery, prostitution, and footbinding. They upheld filial piety. They maintained that women were men's equals and appointed them to administrative and military posts. In short, like earlier rebels, the Taipings combined moral reform, religious fervor, and a vision of a transformed egalitarian society.

The weaknesses of the movement were several. Most Taiping leaders were too poorly educated to govern effectively, and the Taipings could not draw on the gentry. When the Taiping area was divided into kingdoms, dissension broke out. The Taipings failed to cultivate the secret societies, which were also anti-Manchu. They also failed to cultivate Westerners, who had been neutral before the 1860 treaty settlements

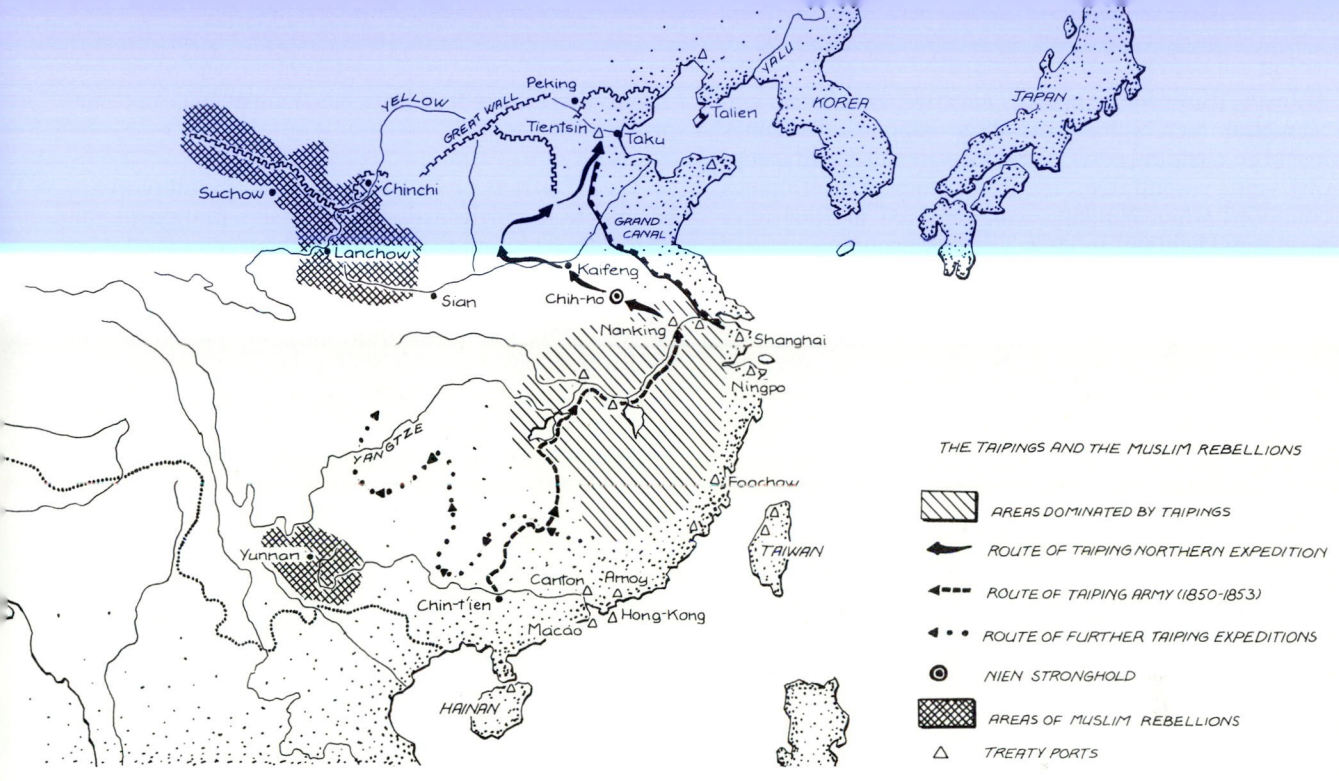

MAP 32-1 THE TAIPING, NIEN, AND MUSLIM REBELLIONS. *Between* 1850 and
*1873 China was wracked by rebellions that almost ended the Manchu dynasty. The
dynasty was saved by Chinese "gentry armies."*

and aided the Manchus thereafter. Also, many Taiping ideals were honored in the breach; for example, land was not redistributed, and although Taiping teachings emphasized frugality and the sanctity of monogamous marriage, Hung lived with many concubines in the midst of luxury.

The other rebellions were of lesser note but longer duration. The Nien were located to the north of the Taipings along the Huai River. They began as bandits who lived in walled villages, were organized in secret societies, and lived by raiding the surrounding countryside. Eventually they built an army, collected taxes, and ruled an area of 100,000 square miles. The Ch'ing court feared that the Nien would join forces with the Taipings. An even longer revolt was of Muslims against Chinese in the southwest and the northwest. One rebel set up an Islamic kingdom with himself as sultan. Like the Taiping Rebellion, these various rebellions took advantage of the weakened state of the dynasty. They occurred in areas where officials were few and Ch'ing military units absent.

Against the rebellions, the Manchu Banners and the Chinese Army of the Green Standard proved helpless: the one was useful only for defense, the other only against civilians. The first effective step was taken against the rebellions when, in 1852, the court sent

Tseng Kuo-fan (1811–1872) to Hunan Province in south-central China to organize a local army. Tseng was a product of the Confucian examination system and had served in Peking. He saw the Manchu government, of which he was an elite member, as the upholder of morality and the social order, and Chinese rebels as would-be destroyers of that order. Arriving in Hunan, he recruited members of the gentry as officers. They were from the class that, since the late Ming, had been growing in importance and performing many local government functions, in some cases organizing local militia. Not only were they Confucian, but as landlords they had the most to lose from rebel rule. They recruited soldiers from their local areas. At first Tseng's "Hunan Braves" held their ground; then they went on the offensive, stopping the Taipings' advance.

Until 1860, the Ch'ing court was dominated by Manchu conservatives who limited Tseng's role and dragged their feet in upholding the treaties. In 1860, the conservatives lost their footing when the British and the French occupied Peking. A reform government replaced the conservatives, began internal changes, adopted a policy of cooperation with the Western powers, and put Tseng in charge of suppressing the rebellions. Tseng appointed other able officials to raise regional armies. Li Hung-chang (1823–1901), with his

Anhwei Army, was especially effective. Foreigners and Shanghai merchants gave their support. Revenues from the customs service and foreign ships and weapons were essential to Tseng's armies. The Taipings collapsed when Nanking was captured in 1864 after protracted fighting. In 1865, Tseng was put in charge of the campaign against the Nien. Li Hung-chang and his Anhwei Army continued the campaign in 1866 and, using arms from the newly built Shanghai arsenal, closed in on the rebels in 1868. Five years later, the Muslim rebellion was also suppressed. Scholar-officials, relying on local gentry, had saved the dynasty.

Self-strengthening and Decline (1874–1895)

The two decades after the suppression of the mid-century rebellions illustrate the dictum that there is no single "correct" view of history. In comparison, for example, with the late Sung or the late Ming, the last decades of the nineteenth century look good. In view of China's advanced stage of administrative decentralization, the Chinese resiliency and capacity to rebuild after unprecedented destruction was impressive. Even on its borders, the dynasty was able to maintain or regain some territories while losing others. But if we ask instead how effective China's response was to the West, or if we compare China's progress with that of Japan, then China during the same decades looks almost moribund. Historians often call these years the period of "self-strengthening" after a catchphrase in vogue at the time. This term is not inappropriate, as the list of new initiatives taken during the period is long. Yet, since the firepower of Western naval forces doubled each decade, the forces that China faced at the end of the century were vastly more formidable than those of the Opium War. Despite self-strengthening, China was relatively weaker at the end of the period than at the start.

In 1895, Li Hung-chang met with Itō Hirobumi of Japan to negotiate a peace treaty after China's defeat in the Sino-Japanese War. Itō asked with uncharacteristic bluntness: "Ten years ago when I was at Tientsin, I talked about reform with the Grand Secretary (Li). Why is it that up to now not a single thing has been changed or reformed?" Li replied: "Affairs in my country have been so confined by tradition that I could not accomplish what I desired . . . Now in the twinkling of an eye ten years have gone by, and everything is still the same. I am even more regretful. I am ashamed of having excessive wishes and lacking the power to fulfill them. . . ." Itō responded: "The providence of heaven has no affection, except for the virtuous."[1] Considering that Li was the single most powerful figure in China

[1] S. Y. Teng, and J. K. Fairbank, p. 126.

during these decades, Itō's puzzlement was not surprising.

THE COURT AT PEKING. China's inability to act effectively is partly explained by the situation at the court. Prince Kung (1833–1898) and the empress dowager (1835–1908) were coregents for the young emperor. For a Manchu noble, Prince Kung was a man of ideas. After signing the treaties of 1860, he established in 1861 a new office directly under the Grand Council to handle the court's relations with foreign diplomats in Peking. The following year, he established a school to train Chinese in foreign languages. Over time, however, his position at the court grew weaker. Outmaneuvered by the empress dowager, he was ousted in 1884.

The empress dowager was the daughter of a Manchu official. She had become an imperial concubine and had produced the only male child of the former emperor. She was educated, clever, petty, strong-willed, and narrow-minded. She did not oppose change, except by circumstance, nor did she favor it. She had no conception of what was needed to reform China. Her single goal was to gather political power into her own hands. She did this by forging a political machine of conservative bureaucrats, military commanders, and eunuchs, and by maintaining a balance

The Empress Dowager Tz'u-hsi (1835–1908), who manipulated the levers of power at the Manchu court in Peking. [Bettmann Archive.]

between the court and the regional strength of the powerful governor-generals. The result was a court just able to survive, too weak to govern effectively, and not inclined to do more than approve of initiatives taken at the provincial level.

REGIONAL GOVERNMENTS. The most vital figures during these decades were a handful of governors-general whose names are legend: Tseng Kuo-fan, Li Hung-chang, Tso Tsung-t'ang, and Chang Chih-tung. Each had a staff of two or three hundred and an army, and was in charge of two or three provinces. They were loyal to the dynasty that they had restored in the face of almost certain collapse, and in return for their allegiance, they were allowed great autonomy and independence of action.

The first task confronting these regional leaders was reconstruction. In the rebellions, the mulberry trees on which the silkworms fed had been destroyed in central China, irrigation systems had been destroyed in the northwest, and millions were hungry or homeless. The leaders' response to these ills was massive and effective. Just as they had mobilized the gentry to suppress the rebellions, now they obtained their cooperation in rebuilding. They set up refugee centers and soup kitchens, reduced taxes in the devastated Yangtze valley, reclaimed lands gone to waste, began water control projects, and built granaries. By the early 1890s, a considerable measure of well-being had been restored to China's late dynastic society.

A second task facing the regional leaders was self-strengthening—the adoption of Western arms and technology. The governors-general, responsible for China's defenses, were keenly aware of China's weakness. To strengthen China, they built arsenals and shipyards during the 1860s and 1870s, and during the 1870s and 1880s, they began commercial ventures as well. The China Merchants Steam Navigation Company was established in 1872, the Kaiping Coal Mine in 1876, and then a telegraph company, short stretches of railways, and cotton mills. The formula applied in running these enterprises was "official supervision and merchant operation." The major decisions were made by scholar-officials like Tseng, but day-to-day operations were left to the merchants. This division of labor led to contradictions. The Steam Navigation Company, for example, was partly funded by the government because private capital was inadequate.

Li Hung-chang awarded the company a monopoly on shipments of the rice paid in taxes and official cargos to Tientsin and won for the company tariff concessions as well. For a time, these advantages enabled the company to compete successfully with foreign lines. But Li also used company ships to transport his troops; he took company funds to reward his political followers; and he interfered in the company by hiring

Li Hung-chang (1823–1901) was one of the most powerful political figures of late nineteenth-century China. [Bettmann Archive.]

and firing managers. Under these conditions, both investors and managers took their profits quickly and did not reinvest in the line. Soon British lines once again dominated shipping in China's domestic waters.

TREATY PORTS. Conditions in the treaty ports, of which there were fourteen by the 1860s, were different from the rest of China. The ports were little islands of privilege where foreigners lived in mansions staffed with servants, raced horses at the track, participated in amateur theatricals, drank (in Shanghai, at the longest bar in the world), and went to church on Sunday. But the ports were also islands of security, under the rule of foreign consuls, where capital was safe from confiscation, trade was free, and "squeeze" (extortion by officials) was the exception and not the rule. Foreign companies quite naturally located in the ports. The Hong Kong and Shanghai Bank, for example, was funded in 1865 by British interests to finance international trade and to make loans to Chinese firms and banks. Chinese merchants were also attracted by these conditions and located their businesses on rented lands in the foreign concessions. Joint ventures, such as steamboats on the Yangtze, were also begun by Chinese and foreign merchants. Well into the twentieth century, the foreign concessions (treaty port lands leased in perpetuity by foreigners) remained the vital sector of China's modern economy.

The effects of the treaty ports and of Western imperialism on China were mainly negative. Under the low tariffs mandated by the treaties, Chinese industries had little protection from imports. Native cotton spinning was almost destroyed by imports of yarn—though the cloth woven from the yarn remained competitive with foreign cloth. Chinese tea lost ground to Indian tea and Chinese silk to Japanese silk, as these countries developed products of standard quality and China did not. China found few products to export: pig bristles, soybeans, and vegetable oils. The level of foreign trade stayed low, and China's interior markets were affected only slightly.

By the 1870s, the foreign powers had reached an accommodation with China. They counted on the court to uphold the treaties, and in return, they became a prop for the dynasty during its final decades. By the turn of the century, for example, the court's revenues from customs fees were larger than from any other source, including the land tax. The fees were collected by the Maritime Customs Service, a notably efficient and honest treaty-port institution headed by an Irishman, Robert Hart, who saw himself as serving the Chinese government. In 1895, the Maritime Customs Service had 700 Western and 3,500 Chinese employees.

THE BORDERLANDS. China's other foreign relations concerned fringe lands inhabited by non-Chinese but which China claimed by right of past conquest or as tributaries.

In the north and northwest, China confronted imperial Russia. Both countries had been expanding onto the steppe since the seventeenth century. Both had firearms. Caught in a pincers between them, the once proud, powerful, and independent nomadic tribes gradually were rendered impotent. Conservatives at the Manchu court ordered Tso Tsung-t'ang, who had suppressed Muslim rebels within China, to suppress a Muslim leader who had founded an independent state in Chinese Turkestan (the Tarim basin, the area of the old Silk Road). Tso led his army across three thousand miles of deserts, and by 1878 had reconquered the area, which was subsequently renamed Sinkiang, or the "New Territories." A treaty signed with Russia in 1881 also restored most of the Ili region in western Mongolia to Chinese control. These victories strengthened court conservatives who wished to take a stronger stance toward the West.

To the south was Vietnam, which had wrested its independence from China in 935 and periodically had repelled Chinese invasions thereafter. It saw itself as an independent and separate state, but it used the Chinese writing system, modeled its laws and government on those of China, and traded with China within the framework of the tribute system. China, in contrast,

saw Vietnam simply as a tributary that could be aided or punished as necessary.

During the 1840s, the government in Vietnam began a suppression of Christianity in which thousands were killed, including French and Vietnamese priests. The French responded by seizing Saigon and the three provinces surrounding it in 1859, establishing a protectorate over Cambodia in 1864, and seizing Hanoi in 1882. In 1883, China, flush with confidence after its victory in central Asia, sent in troops to aid its tributary. The result was a two-year war in which French warships ranged the coast of China, attacking shore batteries and sinking ships. In 1885, China signed a treaty abandoning its claims to Vietnam. France joined its several protectorates and colonies together to form French Indochina. Newly founded Cantonese newspapers contributed to a rising Chinese nationalism with inflammatory articles on the French aggression.

A third area of contention was Korea, strategically located between Russia, China, and Japan. Korea's policy of seclusion, almost as total as that of Tokugawa Japan, had won it the name of the *Hermit Kingdom*. Its only foreign ties had been its tribute rela-

The Japanese and Chinese delegations meet to negotiate peace after China's defeat in the Sino-Japanese War of 1894–1895. Note that while the Chinese delegates are wearing traditional mandarin robes, the Japanese have adopted Western garb.

tions with China and its trade and occasional diplomatic missions to Japan. In 1876, Japan "opened" Korea to international relations, using much the same tactics that Perry had used twenty-two years earlier in Japan. Japan then contended with China for influence in Korea's internal politics. Conservatives and moderate reformers in Korea looked to China for support. The radical reformers, weaker and fewer in number, looked to Japan, arguing that only a sweeping change such as had occurred in Japan would enable Korea to survive.

In 1893, a popular religious sect unleashed a rebellion against the weak and corrupt government in Seoul. When the Korean government requested Chinese help in suppressing the rebellion, China sent troops, but Japan sent more troops, and in 1894, war broke out. China and the Western powers expected an easy Chinese victory, but they had not understood the changes occurring within Japan. Japan won handily. Neither the Chinese fleet nor the Chinese armies were a match for the discipline and the superior tactics of the Japanese units. The defeat by Japan sent reverberations throughout China, convincing many for the first time of the need for change.

From Dynasty to Warlordism (1895–1926)

China was ruled by officials who had spent the early portion of their lives mastering the Confucian classics and the historical and literary tradition that had developed from these classics. This intellectual formation was highly resistant to change. For most officials, living in China's interior, the foreign crises of the nineteenth century were "coastal phenomena," which, like bee stings, were painful for a time but were then put out of mind. Few officials realized the magnitude of the foreign threat.

China's defeat in 1895 by Japan, another Asian nation and one for which China had had little regard, came as a shock. The response within China was a new wave of reform proposals. The most influential thinker was K'ang Yu-wei (1858–1927), who described China as "enfeebled" and "soundly asleep atop a pile of kindling." For this state of affairs, K'ang blamed the "conservatives." They did not understand, K'ang argued, that Confucius himself had been a reformer and not simply a transmitter of past wisdom. Confucius had invented the idea of a golden age in the past in order to persuade the rulers of his own age to adopt his ideas. All of history, K'ang continued, was evolutionary—a march forward from absolute monarchy to constitutional monarchy to democracy. Actually, K'ang was not well versed in Western ideas; he

An American view of the "Open Door." The combination of high self-esteem and anti-foreignism at the turn of the century was not a Chinese monopoly. [Bettman Archive.]

equated the somewhat mystical Confucian virtue of humanity (*jen*) with electricity and ether. Nonetheless, his reinterpretation of the essentials of Confucianism removed a major barrier to the entry of Western ideas into China.

In 1898, the emperor himself became sympathetic to K'ang's ideas and, on June 11, launched "one hundred days of reform." He took as his models not past Chinese monarchs, but Peter the Great and the Japanese Meiji Emperor. Edicts were issued for sweeping reforms of China's schools, railroads, police, laws, military services, bureaucracy, post offices, and examination system. But the orders were implemented in only one province; conservative resistance was nationwide. Even at the court, after the one hundred days the empress dowager regained control and ended the reforms. K'ang and most of his associates fled to Japan. One reformer who remained behind was executed.

The response of the Western powers to China's 1895 defeat was what has been described as "carving up the melon." Each nation tried to define a sphere of interest, which usually consisted of a leasehold along with railway rights and special commercial privileges.

Liang Ch'i-ch'ao Urges the Chinese to Reform (1896)

Next to K'ang Yu-wei, Liang Ch'i-ch'ao (1873–1929) was the most influential thinker of late Ch'ing China.

On the *Harm of not Reforming.* Now here is a big mansion which has lasted a thousand years. The tiles and bricks are decayed and the beams and rafters are broken. It is still a magnificently big thing, but when wind and rain suddenly come up, its fall is foredoomed. Yet the people in the house are still happily playing or soundly sleeping and as indifferent as if they have seen or heard nothing. Even some who have noted the danger know only how to weep bitterly, folding their arms and waiting for death without thinking of any remedy. Sometimes there are people a little better off who try to repair the cracks, seal up the leaks, and patch up the ant holes in order to be able to go on living there in peace, even temporarily, in the hope that something better may turn up. These three types of people use their minds differently, but when a hurricane comes they will die together. . . . A nation is also like this. . . .

India is one of the oldest countries on the great earth. She followed tradition without change; she has been rendered a colony of England. Turkey's territory occupied three continents and had an established state for a thousand years; yet, because of observing the old ways without change, she has been dominated by six large countries, which have divided her territory. . . . The Moslems in central Asia have usually been well known for their bravery and skill in warfare, and yet they observe the old ways without changing. The Russians are swallowing them like a whale and nibbling them as silkworms eat mulberry leaves, almost in their entirety.

The age of China as a country is equal to that of India and the fertility of her land is superior to that of Turkey, but her conformity to the defective ways which have accumulated and her incapacity to stand up and reform make her also like a brother of these two countries. . . . Whenever there is a flood or drought, communications are severed, there is no way to transport famine relief, the dead are abandoned to fill the ditches or are disregarded, and nine out of ten houses are emptied. . . . The members of secret societies are scattered over the whole country, waiting for the chance to move. Industry is not developed, commerce is not discussed, the native goods daily become less salable. . . . "Leakage" [i.e., squeeze] becomes more serious day by day and our financial sources are almost dried up. Schools are not well-run and students, apart from the "eight-legged" essays, do not know how to do a thing. The good ones are working on small researches, flowery writing, and miscellaneous trifles. Tell them about the vast oceans, they open their eyes wide and disbelieve it. ❑

S. Y. Teng and J. K. Fairbank, *China's Response to the West* (Cambridge: Harvard U.P., 1954), pp. 155–156.

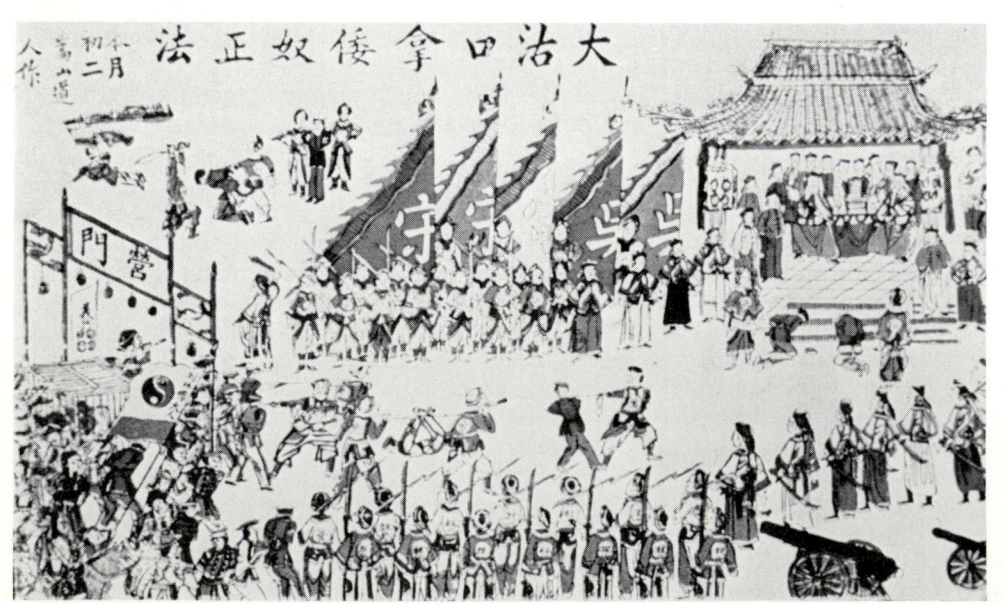

The secret society of the Boxers embodied the virulent anti-foreignism of the Chinese response to Western imperialism. Here Boxers seize (at center of picture), judge (upper right), and execute (upper left) foreigners in 1899.

Russia gained a leasehold at Port Arthur in the area that it had denied to Japan in 1895, Germany one in Shantung. Britain got the New Territories adjoining Kowloon at Hong Kong. A host of new ports and cities were opened to foreign trade. The United States, busy acquiring the Philippines and Guam, was in a weaker position in China. So it enunciated an "open-door" policy: equal commercial opportunities for all powers and the preservation of the territorial integrity of China.

There was in China at this time a religious society known as the Boxers. The Chinese name translates more literally as the "Righteous and Harmonious Fists." The Boxers had rituals, spells, and amulets that they believed made them impervious to bullets. They rebelled first in Shantung in 1898, and, gaining court support, entered Peking in 1900. The court declared war on the treaty powers, and there followed a two-month siege of the foreign legation quarter. Support for the rebellion was fueled by pent-up resentments against decades of foreign encroachments. Eventually, an international force captured Peking, won a huge indemnity, and obtained the right to maintain permanent military forces in the capital. In the aftermath of the Boxer Rebellion, the Russians occupied Manchuria.

The defeat of the Boxers convinced even conservative Chinese leaders of the futility of clinging to old ways. A more powerful reform movement began, with the empress dowager herself positioned in its vanguard. But as the movement gained momentum, the dynasty could not stay far enough in front and eventually was overrun.

Educational reforms began in 1901. Women, for the first time, were admitted as students to newly formed schools. In place of Confucianism, the instructors taught science, mathematics, geography, and an anti-imperialist version of Chinese history that fanned the flames of nationalism. Western doctrines such as classical economics, liberalism, socialism, anarchism, and social Darwinism were also introduced into China. Most entered via translations from Japanese, and in the process, the modern vocabulary coined by Japanese scholars was implanted in China. By 1906, there were eight thousand Chinese students in Japan, which had become a hotbed of Chinese reformist and revolutionary societies.

Military reforms were begun by Yuan Shih-k'ai (1859–1916), whose New Army drew on Japanese and Western models. Young men from gentry families, spurred by patriotism, broke with the traditional Chinese animus against military careers and joined the New Army as officers. Their loyalty was to their commanders and to their country, not to the dynasty.

Political reforms began with a modification of the examination system to accommodate the learning at the new schools. Then, in 1905 the examination system was abolished altogether. Henceforth, officials were to be recruited from the graduates of the schools and those who had studied abroad. Provincial assemblies were formed in 1909 and a consultative assembly with some elected members was established in Peking in 1910. These representative bodies were intended to gather the new gentry nationalism in support of the court, but they turned into forums for the expression of interests at odds with those of the dynasty.

In sum, during the first decade of the twentieth century, the three vital components of the imperial system—Confucian education, the bureaucracy, and the gentry—had been discarded or changed in ways that even a few decades earlier would have been unimaginable.

These changes sparked the 1911 revolution. It began with an uprising in Szechwan province against a government plan to nationalize the main railways. The players were: (1) gentry who stood to lose their investments in the railways; (2) Ch'ing military com-

Sun Yat-Sen (1866–1925), *father of China's 1911 republican revolution.*

manders, who broke with Peking, declaring their provinces independent; (3) Sun Yat-sen (1866–1925), a republican revolutionary. Born a peasant, he had learned English and became a Christian in Hawaii; then studied medicine in Canton and Hong Kong. He organized the Revolutionary Alliance in Tokyo in 1905, and was associated with the Nationalist Party (Kuomintang) formed in 1912; (4) Yuan Shih-k'ai, who was called on by the court to preserve the dynasty. Instead, he arranged for the last child emperor to abdicate, for Sun to step aside, and for himself to become president of the new Republic of China.

The Nationalists won the election called in 1913. Yuan thereupon had their leader assassinated, crushed the military-governors who supported them, and forced Sun Yat-sen and other revolutionaries to flee again to Japan. Yuan emerged as the uncontested ruler of China. Mistaking the temper of the times, he proclaimed a new dynasty with himself as emperor. The idea of another dynasty, however, met implacable opposition from all quarters, forcing Yuan to abandon the attempt. He died three months later in June 1916. After Yuan, China fell into the hands of warlord armies. The years until the late twenties were a time of agony, frustration, and travail for the Chinese people. Yet they also were years of intense intellectual ferment.

Cultural and Ideological Ferment: The May Fourth Movement

In the century after the Opium War, China's leading thinkers responded to the challenge of the West in terms of four successive modes of thought:

1. During the 1840s and the 1850s, and into the 1860s, the key event in China was the Taiping Rebellion. The success of gentry Confucianism in putting down the rebellion and in reestablishing the social order afterward underlined for most Chinese the effectiveness, vitality, and validity of traditional doctrines.

2. From the 1860s to the 1890s, the dominant intellectual modality was "ti–yung reformism." The essence (ti) was to remain Chinese, but useful contrivances (yung) could be borrowed from the West. This formula enabled a restabilized China to borrow and reform in small ways and to build arsenals and a few railroads, while remaining Chinese at the core. It was the ideology of the "self-strengthening" movement.

3. Then, during the decade or so after the turn of the century (the last decade of the Manchu dynasty), the ti–yung distinction broke down. It was seen as inadequate. The ti itself was reinterpreted. The dominant view was that of K'ang Yu-wei, who argued that Confucius had been a reformer and that Confucianism,

properly understood, was a philosophy of change. This kind of thought was behind the rash of reforms of 1900–1911.

4. The fourth stage was a period of freedom and vigorous experimentation with new doctrines that began in 1914 and extended into the 1920s. It is called the *May Fourth Movement* after an incident in Peking in 1919 in which thousands of students protested the settlement at Versailles that awarded former German possessions in Shantung to Japan. The powerful nationalism that led the students to demonstrate in the streets changed the complexion of Chinese thought. Instead of appealing to tradition, leading thinkers began to judge ideas in terms of their value in solving China's problems. It was also not accidental that this era of intellectual excitement corresponded almost exactly with the period of warlord rule, for it afforded a breathing space between the ideological constraints of the old dynasty and those of the nationalist and Communist eras that would follow.

Scholars who returned from abroad during the last years of Manchu rule often located in the safety of the treaty ports. During the May Fourth era, however, the center of advanced thought was Peking. Ts'ai Yuan-p'ei (1867–1940), who had been minister of education under the republic, became the chancellor of Peking University, and Ch'en Tu-hsiu (1880–1939) became his dean of letters. Both men had had a classical education and had passed the traditional examinations. Ts'ai then joined the party of Sun Yat-sen and went to study in Germany. After the fall of Yuan Shih-k'ai, he made Peking University into a haven for scholars who had returned from study in Japan or the West.

Ch'en Tu-hsiu had studied in Japan and France. In 1915, he launched *New Youth*, a magazine that played a role in the intellectual revolution of early twentieth-century China comparable to the *cahiers* in the French Revolution or the pamphlets of Thomas Paine in the American Revolution. In his magazine, Ch'en placed the blame for Chinese ills on the teachings of Confucius. He called for a generation of progressive, cosmopolitan, and scientific youth who would uphold the values of liberty, equality, and fraternity.

The greatest modern Chinese writer was Lu Hsun (1881–1936). Like most other leading intellectuals of the period, he had been born in a scholar-official family. He went to Japan for eight years to study medicine, but switched in mid-course to literature. His first work, *A Madman's Diary*, appeared in *New Youth* in 1918. Its protagonist is a pathetic figure, whose madness took the form of a belief that people ate people. Lu Hsun's message was that only the vision of a madman could truly comprehend an abnormal and inhumane society.

As the May Fourth Movement developed, ideas

Ch'en Tu-hsiu's "Call to Youth" in 1915

Struggle, natural selection, and organic process are the images of Ch'en Tu-hsiu. How different from those of Confucianism!

The Chinese compliment others by saying, "He acts like an old man although still young." Englishmen and Americans encourage one another by saying, "Keep young while growing old." Such is one respect in which the different ways of thought of the East and West are manifested. Youth is like early spring, like the rising sun, like trees and grass in bud, like a newly sharpened blade. It is the most valuable period of life. The function of youth in society is the same as that of a fresh and vital cell in a human body. In the processes of metabolism, the old and the rotten are incessantly eliminated to be replaced by the fresh and living. . . . According to this standard, then, is the society of our nation flourishing, or is it about to perish? I cannot bear to answer. As for those old and rotten elements, I shall leave them to the process of natural selection. . . . I only, with tears, place my plea before the young and vital youth, in the hope that they will achieve self-awareness, and begin to struggle.

What is the struggle? It is to exert one's intellect, discard resolutely the old and the rotten, regard them as enemies and as the flood or savage beasts, keep away from their neighborhood and refuse to be contaminated by their poisonous germs. Alas! Do these words really fit the youth of our country? I have seen that, out of every ten youths who are young in age, five are old in physique; and out of every ten who are young in both age and physique, nine are old in mentality. Those with shining hair, smooth countenance, a straight back and a wide chest are indeed magnificent youths! Yet if you ask what thoughts and aims are entertained in their heads, then they all turn out to be the same as the old and rotten, like moles from the same hill. . . . It is the old and rotten air that fills society everywhere. One cannot even find a bit of fresh and vital air to comfort those of us who are suffocating in despair. ❑

S. Y. Teng and J. K. Fairbank, *China's Response to the West* Cambridge: Harvard U.P., (1954), pp. 240–241.

---

propounded in Peking quickly spread to the rest of China, especially to its urban centers. Protest demonstrations against imperialist privilege broke out in Shanghai, Wuhan, and Canton, as they had in the capital. Nationalism and anti-imperialist sentiment were stronger than liberalism, though there were few thinkers who did not speak of democracy. Only members of an older generation of reformers, such as K'ang Yu-wei or Liang Ch'i-ch'ao, came full circle and, appalled by the slaughter of World War I and what they saw as Western materialism, advocated a return to traditional Chinese philosophies.

At the onset of China's intellectual revolution, Marxism had small appeal. Marx's critique of capitalist society did not fit Chinese conditions. The anarchism of Peter Kropotkin, who taught that mutual aid was as much a part of evolution as the struggle for survival, was more popular. But after the Russian Revolution of 1917, Marxism-Leninism entered China. The Leninist definition of imperialism as the last crisis stage of capitalism had an immediate appeal, for it put the blame for China's ills on the West and offered "feudal" China the possibility of leapfrogging over capitalism to socialism. As early as 1919, an entire issue of *New Youth* was devoted to Marxism. Marxist study groups formed in Peking and other cities. In 1919, a student from Hunan, Mao Tse-tung, who had worked in the Peking University library, returned to Changsha to form a study group. Ch'en Tu-hsiu was converted to

Marxism in 1920. Instructed in organizational techniques by a Comintern agent, Ch'en and others formed the Chinese Communist Party in Shanghai in 1921; Chou En-lai formed a similar group in Paris during the same year. The numbers involved were small but grew steadily.

Nationalist China

The Kuomintang Unification of China and the Nanking Decade (1927–1937)

Sun Yat-sen had fled to Japan during the 1913–1916 rule by Yuan Shih-k'ai. He returned to Canton in 1916, but despite his immense personal attractiveness as a leader, he was a poor organizer, and his Kuomintang (KMT), or Nationalist Party, made little headway. For a time in 1922, he was driven out of Canton by a local warlord. From 1923, Sun began to receive Soviet advice and support. With the help of Comintern agents like Michael Borodin, he reorganized his party on the Leninist model, with an executive committee on top of a national party congress, and below this, provincial and county organizations and local party cells.

Since 1905 Sun had enunciated his "three principles of the people": nationality, livelihood, and rights. Sun's earlier nationalism had been directed against Manchu rule; it was now redirected against Western imperialism. The principle of people's livelihood was defined in terms of equalizing landholdings and nationalizing major industries. By "people's rights," Sun meant democracy, though he argued that full democracy must be preceded by a preparatory period of tutelage under a single party dictatorship. Sun sent his loyal lieutenant Chiang Kai-shek (1887–1975) to the Soviet Union for study. Chiang returned after four months with a cadre of Russian advisers and established a military academy at Whampoa to the south of Canton in 1924. The cadets of Whampoa were to form a "party army." Sun died in 1925. By 1926, the Whampoa Academy had graduated several thousand officers, and the KMT army numbered almost 100,000. The KMT had grown to become the major political force in China, with 200,000 members; its leadership was divided between a left and a right wing.

The growth of the party was spurred on by changes occurring within Chinese society. Industries arose in the cities. Labor unions were organized in tobacco and textile factories. New ventures were begun outside the treaty ports, and chambers of commerce were established even in medium-sized towns. Entrepreneurs, merchants, officials, journalists, and the employees of foreign firms formed a new and politically conscious middle class.

The quicksilver element in cities was the several million students at government, Catholic, and Protestant schools. In May 1925, students demonstrated against the treatment of workers in foreign-owned factories at Shanghai. Police in the international settlement fired on the demonstrators, killing thirteen and wounding fifty. The incident further inflamed national and anti-imperialist feelings. Strikes and boycotts of foreign goods were called throughout China. Those in Hong Kong lasted for fifteen months.

Under these conditions, the Chinese Communist Party (CCP) also grew, and in 1926, it had about twenty thousand members. The party was influential in student organizations, labor unions, and even within the Kuomintang. By an earlier agreement, Sun had permitted CCP members to join the KMT as individuals but had enjoined them from organizing CCP cells within the KMT. Moscow approved of this policy. It felt that the CCP was too small to accomplish anything on its own, and that by working within the KMT, its members could join in the "bourgeois, national, democratic struggle" against "imperialism and feudal warlordism." Chou En-lai, for example, became deputy head of the Political Education Department of the Whampoa Academy.

By 1926, the KMT had established a base in the area around Canton, and Chiang Kai-shek felt ready to march north against the warlord domains. He worried about the growing Communist strength, however, and before setting off, he ousted the Soviet advisers and CCP members from the KMT offices in Canton.

Chiang Kai-shek (1887–1975).

The march north began in July. By the spring of 1927, Chiang's army had reached the Yangtze, defeating, and often absorbing, warlord armies as it advanced.

After entering Shanghai in April 1927, Chiang carried out a sweeping purge of the CCP—against its members in the KMT, against its party organization, and against the labor unions that it had come to dominate. Large numbers were killed. The CCP responded by trying to gain control of the KMT left wing, which had established a government at Wuhan, and by armed uprisings. Both attempts failed. The surviving CCP members fled to the mountainous border region of Hunan and Kiangsi to the southwest and established the "Kiangsi Soviet." The left wing of the KMT, disenchanted with the Communists, rejoined the right wing at Nanking, China's new capital. Chiang's army continued north, took Peking, and gained the nominal submission of most northern Chinese warlords during 1928. By this time, most foreign powers had recognized the Nanking regime as the government of China.

Chiang Kai-shek was the key figure in the Nanking government. By training and temperament he believed

Lu Hsun

Like Chen Tu-hsiu and other writers of the May Fourth Movement, Lu Hsun saw China's old society as rotten and corrupt. Only after a radical reform, he felt, would the Chinese be able to realize their human potential.

ON EXPRESSING AN OPINION:

I dreamed I was in the classroom of a primary school preparing to write an essay, and asked the teacher how to express an opinion.

"That's hard!" Glancing sideways at me over his glasses, he said: "Let me tell you a story—

"When a son is born to a family, the whole household is delighted. When he is one month old they carry him out to display him to the guests—usually expecting some compliments, of course.

"One says: 'This child will be rich.' Then he is heartily thanked.

"One says: 'This child will be an official.' Then some compliments are made him in return.

"One says: 'This child will die.' Then he is thoroughly beaten by the whole family.

"That the child will die is inevitable, while to say that he will be rich or a high official may be a lie. Yet the lie is rewarded, whereas the statement of the inevitable gains a beating. You. . . . "

"I don't want to tell lies, sir, neither do I want to be beaten. So what should I say?"

"In that case, say: 'Aha! Just look at this child! My word. . . . Oh, my! Oho! Hehe! He, hehehehehe!' "

ODD FANCIES:

Downstairs a man is on his deathbed, next door they have the gramophone on; in the house opposite they are playing with children. Upstairs two people are laughing wildly, and there is the sound of gambling. In the boat on the river a woman is wailing for her dead mother.

Men cannot communicate their grief or joy—all I feel is that they are noisy.

Every woman is born with the instincts of a mother and daughter. There is no such thing as wifely instincts.

Wifely instincts come through the force of circumstances, and are simply the combination of the instincts of mother and daughter.

The sight of women's short sleeves at once makes them think of bare arms, of the naked body, the genitals, copulation, promiscuity, and bastards.

This is the sole respect in which the Chinese have a lively imagination. ❑

Selected Works of Lu Hsun (Peking: Foreign Languages Press, 1956–60), Vol. 1, p. 345, Vol. 2, pp. 338–339.

---

in military force. He was unimaginative, strict, feared more than loved, and, in the midst of considerable corruption, incorruptible. Chiang venerated Sun Yat-sen and his three "people's principles." The grandeur of Sun's tomb in Nanking surpassed that of the Ming emperors. But where Sun, as a revolutionary, had looked back to the zeal of the Taiping rebels, Chiang, trying to consolidate his rule over provincial warlords, looked back to Tseng Kuo-fan, who had put down the rebels and restabilized China. Like Tseng, Chiang was conservative and, though a Methodist, often appealed to Confucian values. The New Life Movement begun by Chiang in 1934 was an attempt to revitalize these values.

Chiang's power rested on the army, the party, and the government bureaucracy. The army was dominated by the Whampoa clique, which was personally loyal to Chiang, and by officers trained in Japan. After 1927, Soviet military advisers were replaced by German advisers. They reorganized Chiang's army along German lines with a general staff system. The larger part of KMT revenues went to the military, which was expanded into a modernized force of three hundred thousand. Whampoa graduates also controlled the secret military police and used it against Communists and any others who opposed the government. The Kuomintang was a dictatorship under a central committee. Chiang became president of the party in 1938.

The densely populated central and lower Yangtze provinces were the area of Kuomintang strength. The party, however, was unable to control the outlying areas occupied by warlords, Communists, and Japanese. Some gains were made during the Nanking decade: Chiang's armies defeated the northern warlords in 1930, put down a rebellion in Fukien in 1934, and extended their control over southern and southwestern China two years later. But some areas remained under the sway of warlords until 1949. In 1931, Chiang launched a series of campaigns against the Kiangsi Soviet. In 1934, the Communists were forced to abandon their mountain base and flee to the southwest and then north to Shensi province in northwest China. Of the ninety thousand troops that set out on this epic "Long March" of six thousand miles, only twenty thousand survived. It was during this march that Mao Tse-tung wrested control of the CCP from the

Moscow-trained, urban-oriented leaders and established his unorthodox view that a revolutionary Leninist party could base itself on the peasantry.

The Japanese had held special rights in Manchuria since the Russo-Japanese War of 1905. When Chiang's march north and the rise of Chinese nationalism threatened the Japanese position, field-grade officers of Japan's Kwantung Army engineered a military coup in 1931 and, in 1932, proclaimed the independence of Manchukuo, their puppet state. In the years that followed, Japanese forces moved south as far as the Great Wall. Chinese nationalism demanded that Chiang resist. Chiang, well aware of the disparity between his armies and those of Japan, said that the internal unification of China must take precedence over war against a foreign power. But on a visit to Sian in 1936, Chiang was imprisoned by a northern warlord until he agreed to join with the CCP in a united front against Japan. In the following year, however, a full-scale war with Japan broke out, and China's situation again changed.

War and Revolution (1937–1949)

In 1937, the Kuomintang controlled the larger part of China and was recognized nationally and interna-

tionally as its government, whereas the CCP survivors of the Long March had just begun to rebuild their strength in the arid lands of Shensi, an area too remote for Chiang's army to penetrate. But by 1949, CCP forces had conquered China, including border areas never under KMT rule, and Chiang and the KMT had been forced to flee to Taiwan. What happened?

The war with Japan was the key event. It began in July 1937 as an unplanned clash at Peking and then spread. Battlefield victories soon convinced the Japanese military leaders to abandon negotiations in favor of a knockout blow. Peking and Tientsin fell within a month, Shanghai was attacked in August, and Nanking fell in December. During the following year, the Japanese took Canton and Wuhan and set up puppet regimes in Peking and Nanking. In 1940, frustrated by trying to work with Chiang, the leader of the left wing of the KMT and many of his associates joined the Japanese puppet government. Japan proclaimed its "New Order in East Asia," which was to replace the system of unequal treaties. It expected Chiang to recognize his situation as hopeless and to submit. Instead, in 1938, he relocated his capital in Chungking, far to the west behind the gorges of the Yangtze. He was joined by thousands of Chinese, students and professors, factory

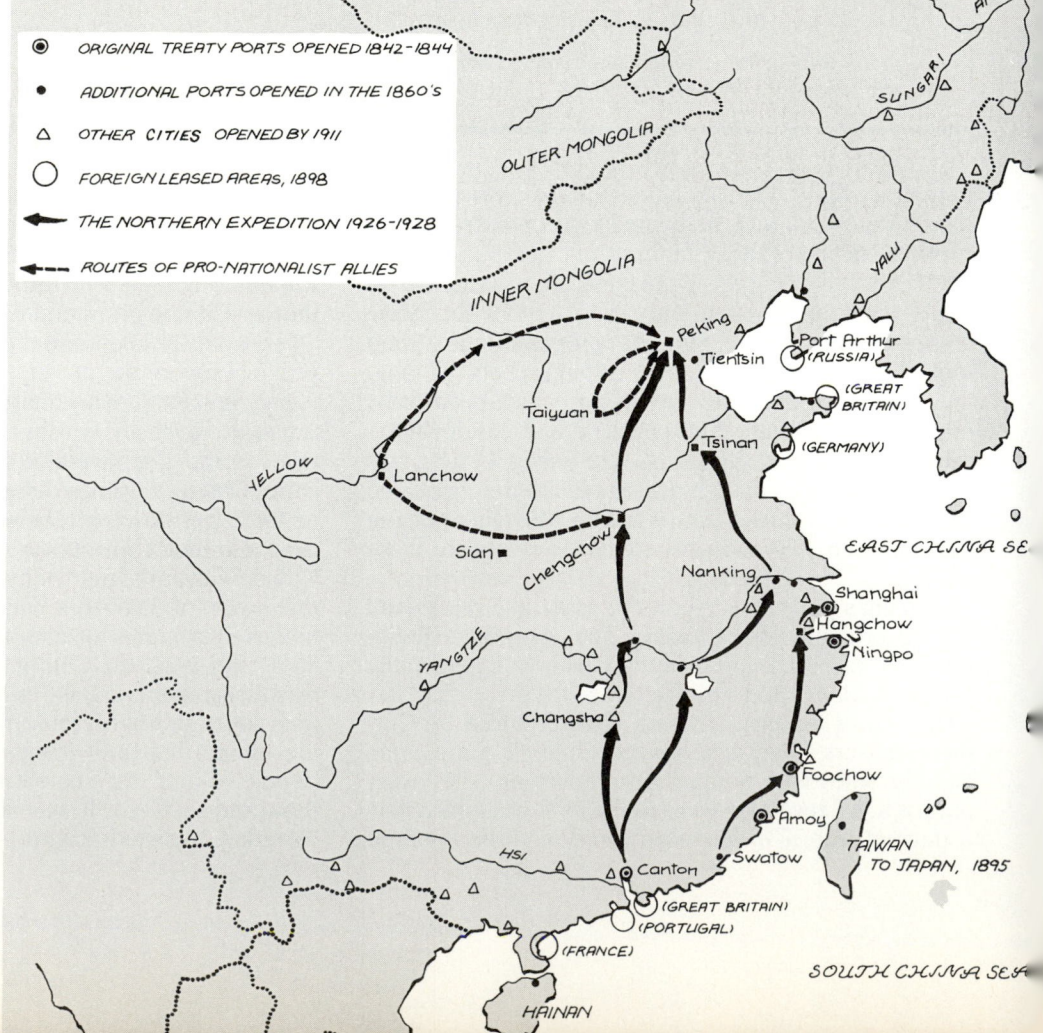

MAP 32-2 THE NORTHERN EXPEDITIONS OF THE KUOMINTANG *These expeditions 1926–1928 unified most of China under the Nationalist (Kuomintang) government of Chiang Kai-shek, inaugurating the Nanking decade. Warlord armies continued to hold power on the periphery.*

managers and workers, who moved from occupied to free China.

Chiang's stubborn resistance to the Japanese occupation won admiration from all sides. But the area occupied by the Japanese included just those eastern cities, railways, and densely populated Yangtze valley territories that had constituted the KMT base. The withdrawal to Chungking cut the KMT off from the majority of the Chinese population; programs for modernization came to an end; and the KMT's former tax revenues were lost. Inflation increased geometrically, reducing the real income of officials, teachers, and soldiers alike. By the end of World War II and during the early postwar years, salaries were paid in large packages of almost worthless money, which was immediately spent for goods that would at least have real value. This inflation produced demoralization and exacerbated the corruption that was already widespread.

The United States sent advisers and military equipment to strengthen Chiang's forces after the start of the Pacific War. The advisers, however, were frustrated by Chiang, who wanted not to fight the Japanese but to husband his forces for the anticipated postwar confrontation with the Communists. Within his own army, a gap appeared between officers and men. Conditions in the camps were primitive, food poor, and medical supplies inadequate. The young saw conscription almost as a sentence of death. Chiang's unwillingness to commit his troops against the Japanese also meant that the surge of anti-Japanese patriotism was not converted to popular support for the KMT.

For the Communists, the Japanese occupation was an opportunity. Headquartered at Yenan, they consolidated their base in Shensi province. They began campaigns to promote literacy and production drives to promote self-sufficiency. Soldiers farmed so as not to burden the peasants. The CCP abandoned its earlier policy of expropriating lands in favor of reductions in rents and interest. (This change led to the American view that the CCP were not Communists but agrarian reformers, despite their protests to the contrary.) They took only those provincial and county offices needed to ensure their control and shared the rest with the KMT and other parties. They expanded village councils to include tenants and other previously excluded strata. But while compromising with other political and social groups, they acted to strengthen their party internally.

Party membership expanded from 40,000 in 1937 to 1.2 million in 1945. Schools were established in Yenan to train party cadres. Even as the party expanded, orthodoxy was maintained by a rectification campaign begun in 1942. Those tainted by liberalism, individualism, or other impure tendencies were criticized and made to confess their failings and repent at public meetings. Mao's thought was supreme. To the Chi-

Mao Tse-tung as a young revolutionary.

nese at large, Mao represented himself as the successor to Sun Yat-sen, but within the Communist Party, he presented himself as a theoretician in the line of Marx, Engels, Lenin, and Stalin.

Whereas the Kuomintang ruled through officials and often in cooperation with local landlords, the Communists learned to operate at the grass-roots level. They infiltrated Japanese-controlled areas and also penetrated some KMT organizations and military units. CCP armies were built up from 90,000 in 1937 to 900,000 in 1945. These were supplemented by a rural people's militia and by guerrilla forces in nineteen mountainous "base areas." By most accounts, the Yenan leadership and its party, army, and mass organizations possessed a cohesion, determination, and high morale that were lacking in Chungking.

But the strength of the Chinese Communists as of 1945 should not be overstated. Most Chinese villagers were influenced by neither the CCP nor the KMT, and though intellectuals in free China had become disaffected with the KMT, most did not positively support the CCP. When the war in the Pacific ended in 1945, it was not clear what would happen in China. The Soviet

Snow, by Mao Tse-tung

The following poem was written in the winter of 1944–1945, before the end of World War II and the outbreak of the Chinese Civil War.

The northern scene:
A thousand leagues locked in ice,
A myriad leagues of fluttering snow.
On either side of the Great Wall
Only one vastness to be seen.
Up and down this broad river
Torrents flatten and stiffen.
The mountains are dancing silver serpents
And hills, like waxen elephants, plod on the plain,
Challenging heaven with their heights.
A sunny day is needed
For seeing them, with added elegance,
In red and white.

Such is the beauty of these mountains and rivers
That has been admired by unnumbered heroes—
The great emperors of Ch'in and Han
Lacking literary brilliance,
Those of T'ang and Sung
Having but few romantic inclinations,
And the prodigious Gengis Khan
Knowing only how to bend his bow and shoot at
    vultures.
All are past and gone!
For men of vision
We must seek among the present generation.   ❏

J. Ch'en, *Mao and the Chinese Revolution* (London: Oxford U.P., 1965) p. 340.

Union allowed CCP cadres to enter Manchuria, which it had seized during the last few days of the war, and blocked the entry of Kuomintang troops until the following year. But even the Soviet Union recognized the KMT as the government of China and stripped the

KMT officials fleeing Shanghai for Taiwan early in 1949 before the victorious communist advance.

MODERN CHINA

	The Close of Manchu Rule
1839–1842	Opium War
1850–1873	Taiping and other rebellions
1870s–1880s	Self-strengthening movement
1894–1895	Sino-Japanese War
1898	One hundred days of reform
1898–1900	Boxer Rebellion
1911	Republican revolution over-throws the Ch'ing dynasty
	Warlordism
1912–1916	Yuan Shih-k'ai president of Republic of China
1916–1928	Warlord era
1919	May Fourth incident
	Nationalist China
1924	Founding of Whampoa Military Academy
1926–1928	March north and Kuomintang reunification of China
1928–1937	Nanking decade
1934–1935	Chinese Communists' long march to Yenan
1937–1945	War with Japan
1945–1949	Civil war and the establishment of the People's Republic of China

equipment from Japanese factories in Manchuria in the expectation of a KMT victory in the postwar struggle. The Allies directed Japanese armies to surrender to the KMT forces in 1945. The United States flew Chiang's troops from Chungking to key eastern cities. Chiang's armies were by then three times the size of the Communists' and far better equipped.

A civil war broke out immediately. Both sides knew that the earlier united front had been a sham. Efforts by U.S. General George Marshall to mediate were futile. Until the summer of 1947, KMT armies were victorious—even capturing Yenan. But the tide turned in July as CCP armies went on the offensive in north China. They captured American military equipment left by the KMT forces, and by October 1948, the KMT forces had been driven from Manchuria. In January of 1949, Peking and Tientsin fell. By late spring, CCP armies had crossed the Yangtze, taking Nanking and Shanghai. A few months later, all of China was in Communist hands. Many Chinese fled with Chiang to Taiwan or escaped to Hong Kong: these included not only KMT officials and generals but entrepreneurs and academics as well. Not a few subsequently made their way to the United States.

In China, apprehension was mixed with anticipation. The disciplined, well-behaved soldiers of the "People's Liberation Army" were certainly a contrast to those of the KMT. As villages were liberated, lands were taken from landlords and given to the landless. In the cities, crowds gave every indication of welcoming the CCP troops as liberators. The feeling was widespread that the future of China was once again in the hands of the Chinese.

MODERN JAPAN (1853–1945)

The Overthrow of the Tokugawa Bakufu (1853–1868)

From the seventeenth century into the nineteenth, the natural isolation of island Japan was augmented by its policy of seclusion, making Japan into a little world of its own. The 260-odd domains were the states of the world, the bakufu in Edo was its hegemon, and the imperial court in Kyoto provided a sacerdotal or religious sanction for the bakufu–domain system. Then, at mid-century, the American ships of Commodore Perry came and forced Japan to sign a Treaty of Friendship, opening itself to foreign intercourse. Fourteen years later, the entire bakufu–domain system collapsed, and a new group of unusually talented leaders seized power. Seclusion, like the case of a watch, had been necessary to preserve the Tokugawa political mechanism. With the case removed, the jolt of the foreign intrusion caused the inner workings to fly apart.

It was surprising how little changed during the early years after Perry. The bakufu attended to its affairs and the domains to theirs. The daimyo continued to spend every other year living in Edo. Political action consisted mainly of daimyo cliques trying to influence bakufu policy. The break came in 1858 when the bakufu, ignoring the imperial court's disapproval, was persuaded to sign a commercial treaty with the United States. In reaction, the daimyo, who wanted a voice in national policy making, criticized the arbitrary decision as contravening the hallowed policy of seclusion. Younger samurai, frustrated by their exclusion from power, reacted by starting a movement to "honor the emperor." The bakufu, in turn, responded with a purge: Dissident daimyo were forced into retirement, while samurai critics were executed or imprisoned. The purge was effective until 1860 when the head of the bakufu council was himself assassinated by an extremist samurai. His successors lacked the nerve to continue his tough policies, thus opening the way for a new kind of politics between 1861 and 1868.

In 1861, two domains, Chōshū and Satsuma, emerged to mediate, to heal the breach that had opened between the bakufu and the court. The first to come forth was the domain of Chōshū: Its officials traveled between Kyoto and Edo, proposing a policy that leaned toward the bakufu but made concessions to the court. Next the domain of Satsuma sallied forth with a policy that made further concessions and ousted Chōshū as "the friend of the court." In response, the moderate reformist government of Chōshū adopted the proemperor policy of its extremist faction and, in turn, ousted Satsuma. Beaten in the diplomatic game, Satsuma seized the court in 1863 in a military coup, and the Chōshū radicals returned disgruntled to their domain.

Several points may be noted about the 1861–1863 diplomatic phase of domain action: (1) Even after 250 years of bakufu rule, several domains were still viable, autonomous units that were capable of action when the opportunity occurred. (2) The two domains that acted first and most of the others that followed were large domains with a numerous samurai class— Chōshū had ten thousand samurai families and substantial financial resources. (3) Both Satsuma and Chōshū had fought against the Tokugawa in 1600 and remembered an earlier independence. (4) By the 1861–

彼理像

美辣水師提督マッナウ。セ。

其和政治筆

盛頗燚駿

孔無墨利加

アーナホル
ボーフスアダナン
アーダムス像

Commodore Perry of the "North American Republic," with Adams, his second-in-command. After two centuries of seclusion, contact with foreigners was unsettling for the Japanese.

1863 period, politics was no longer in the hands of daimyo and their high-ranking advisers. In both Satsuma and Chōshū, the new politics had opened decision making to middle-ranking samurai officials in a way that would have been impossible before 1853.

The 1863 Satsuma coup at the Kyoto court initiated a military phase of politics in which war would determine every turning point. Events were complicated, for besides the court and the bakufu, there were more than 260 domains—somewhat like a circus with too

A Samurai on His Execution

Rai Mikisaburo joined the movement to "honor the emperor" in 1858, becoming a critic of the bakufu. Caught in the 1858 purge, he was arrested and sent to Edo early in 1859 and was executed later in the same year.

CROSSING HAKONE PASS
That other time, spirits so high I seemed to soar
  over the clouds,
racing east on a fast horse, never even noticing
  mountains.
Today on an anxious road, spring rain cold,
a criminal's cage to rock my dreams, I cross
  Hakone Pass.

IN PRISON
I wanted to drive back the clouds, with these hands
  sweep clear the evil stars,
but the ground gave way beneath my feet, I plunged
  to Edo Prison.
Idiot frogs fret at the bottom of their well;
the brilliance of the great moon falters on the
  horizon.
I wait the death sentence, no news from home;
in dreams, the ring of swords: I slash at sea
  monsters.
When the wind and rain of many years have
  cloaked my stone in moss,
who will remember this mad man of Japan? ❏

B. Watson (trans.), *Japanese Literature in Chinese*, (New York: Columbia U.P., 1975–1976), vol. 2, pp. 68–69.

many rings and sideshows. But most domains were too small to carry weight in national politics. Hereditary daimyo, for example, were influential mainly as bakufu officials. Of the larger domains, some were insolvent and others too closely associated with the bakufu to act independently. As long as Satsuma and Chōshū remained enemies, politics stalemated and the bakufu continued as hegemon. But when the two domains became allies in 1866, the bakufu was overthrown in less than two years.

One movement contributing to this process was for a "union of court and camp"; daimyo who earlier had criticized the bakufu campaigned for a new counciliar rule in which they would participate together with the emperor. The movement came to nothing, but it led daimyo to withdraw support that might otherwise have gone to the bakufu. A second feature of these years was a strong antiforeignism. Extremists assassinated foreigners as well as bakufu officials; one of their slogans was "expel the barbarians." Early on, Chōshū and Satsuma fired on foreign ships. But when Western gunboats bombarded those domains in retaliation, they immediately dropped their xenophobic slogan, and set about buying rifles and gunboats.

A third aspect of the military phase of politics from 1863 to 1868 was the formation of new rifle units, mostly commanded by lower samurai. These units transformed the nature of political power in Japan. For example, Chōshū troops armed with Spencers and Minies—mostly surplus left over from the U.S. Civil War—defeated a traditionally armed bakufu army in mid-1866 with a numbing force.

A fourth development was a cultural shift in the Japanese view of themselves. During the Tokugawa era, the Japanese saw themselves as civilized Confucians and most of the rest of the world as barbarians. But in the face of Western gunboats, this view seemed hollow. In 1866, Fukuzawa Yukichi, a student of Western studies and a bakufu translator, introduced a Western theory of stages of history: The West, with its technology, science, and humane laws, was seen as "civilized and enlightened"; China, Japan, and countries like Turkey were seen as half-civilized; and other areas were seen as barbarian. This theory stood the traditional view almost on its head. Fukuzawa argued, furthermore, that technology was not detachable but grew out of the Western legal, political, economic, and educational systems. James Watt had invented the steam engine, Fukuzawa suggested, because inventions were protected by patents and inventors were rewarded with profits and honors. He went on to argue that Western systems required political freedoms and a citizenry with a spirit of independence. Fukuzawa's writings became immensely influential after the Restoration, eventually sparking the "Civilization and Enlightenment Movement" of the 1870s.

In this woodblock print of 1861 an American sailor tries his hand against a Yokohama sumo wrestler. The official record of Perry's mission to Japan several years earlier tells of similar experiment with an opposite outcome. Historical truth often depends on who is telling the story.

Building the Meiji State (1868–1890)

Most attempts by non-Western nations to build modern states have occurred during the twentieth century. The idea of a "developing nation" did not exist in the mid-nineteenth century. Yet Japan after the 1868 Meiji Restoration was a developing nation. (The years from 1868 to 1912 are referred to as the Meiji period, after the name of the then-reigning emperor.) It was committed to progress, by which it meant achieving wealth and power of the kind possessed by Western industrial nations. In retrospect, we are aware that Japan had important assets that contributed to the attainment of these goals. But it also had liabilities and these loomed large in the eyes of the Meiji leaders. There was no blueprint for progress. The government faced

A Japanese View of the Inventiveness of the West

Serious Japanese thinkers reacted to their country's weakness with proposals to adopt Western science and industry. But the "Civilization and Enlightenment Movement" of the 1870s had its lighter side as well. In 1871, the novelist Kanagaki Robun wrote a satire about a man with an umbrella, a watch, and eau de cologne on his hair, who was eating and drinking in a new beef restaurant. Before the Restoration, Buddhism had banned beef eating as a defilement. The comic hero, however, wonders, "Why we in Japan haven't eaten such a clean thing before." He then goes on to rhapsodize about Western inventions.

In the West they're free of superstitions. There it's the custom to do everything scientifically, and that's why they've invented amazing things like the steamship and the steam engine. Did you know that they engrave the plates for printing newspapers with telegraphic needles? And that they bring down wind from the sky with balloons? Aren't they wonderful inventions! Of course, there are good reasons behind these inventions. If you look at a map of the world you'll see some countries marked "tropical," which means that's where the sun shines closest. The people in those countries are all burnt black by the sun. The king of that part of the world tried all kinds of schemes before he hit on what is called a balloon. That's a big round bag they fill with air high up in the sky. They bring the bag down and open it, causing the cooling air inside the bag to spread out all over the country. That's a great invention. On the other hand, in Russia, which is a cold country where the snow falls even in summer and the ice is so thick that people can't move, they invented the steam engine. You've got to admire them for it. I understand that they modeled the steam engine after the flaming chariot of hell, but anyway, what they do is to load a crowd of people on a wagon and light a fire in a pipe underneath. They keep feeding the fire inside the pipe with coal, so that the people riding on top can travel a great distance completely oblivious to the cold. Those people in the West can think up inventions like that, one after the other. . . . You say you must be going? Well, good-bye. Waitress! Another small bottle of sake. And some pickled onions to go with it! ❑

D. Keene (ed. and trans.), *Modern Japanese Literature* (New York: Grove Press, 1956), pp. 32–33.

tough decisions as it advanced by trial and error. It also demanded that the Japanese people make sacrifices for the sake of the future.

The announcement of the restoration of rule by an emperor was made on January 3, 1868. In the battles that followed, Chōshū and Satsuma troops defeated those of the bakufu. In May, Edo surrendered to the imperial forces. Within months Edo castle became the imperial palace and Edo was renamed Tokyo, the "eastern capital." A year later, the last bakufu hold-outs surrendered in Hokkaido. At the start, the Meiji government was no more than a small group of samurai leaders from Chōshū, Satsuma, and other domains associated with them. These men controlled the youthful emperor through a handful of Kyoto nobles. They controlled their own domains through domain officials and the samurai commanders of the domain armies. They have been described, only half humorously, as twelve bureaucrats looking for a bureaucracy. But such a description belittles the vision with which they defined the goals of the new government.

Ōkubo Toshimichi (1830–1878), Satsuma samurai and most important leader during the first Meiji decade.

Centralization of Power

Their immediate goal was to centralize political power. What this entailed, concretely, was using the leverage of the Chōshū and Satsuma domain armies to destroy the domains. This was a ticklish operation since many in these armies were loyal to their domain rather than to the young samurai leaders, who had left the domains to form the new central government. Nevertheless, by 1871 the young leaders succeeded in replacing the domains with prefectures controlled from Tokyo. To ensure a complete break with the past, each new prefectural governor was chosen from samurai of other regions. The first governor of the Chōshū area, for example, was a samurai of the former Tokugawa domain.

Having centralized political authority, in 1871 about half of the most important Meiji leaders went abroad for a year and a half—ostensibly to revise the unequal treaties but in fact to study the West. They traveled in the United States and Europe, visiting parliaments, schools, and factories. On their return to Japan in 1873, they discovered that the stay-at-home officials were planning to go to war with Korea. They quickly quashed the plan, insisting that the highest priority be given to domestic development.

The second goal or task of the Meiji leaders was to stabilize government revenues that, because the land tax was collected mostly in grain, fluctuated with the price of rice. The government converted the grain tax to a money tax, shifting the burden of fluctuations onto the shoulders of the nation's farmers. But a third of the revenues still went to pay for samurai stipends, so in 1873 the government raised a conscript army and subsequently abolished the samurai class. The samurai were paid off in government bonds; but as the bonds fell during the inflation of the 1870s, most former samurai became impoverished. What had begun as a reform of government finance ended as a social revolution.

Some samurai rose up in rebellion. Those in the domains that had carried out the Restoration were particularly indignant at their treatment. The last and greatest uprising was in 1877 by Satsuma samurai led by Saigō Takamori (1827–1877), who had broken with the government over the issue of Korea. When the uprising was suppressed in 1878, the Meiji government became militarily secure.

Political Parties

Other samurai opposed the government by forming political parties and campaigning for popular rights, elections, and a constitution. They drew heavily on liberal Western models that had become widely known through "civilization-and-enlightenment" thought. National assemblies, they argued, were the means by which advanced societies tapped the energies of their peoples. Parties in a national assembly would unite the emperor and the people, thereby curbing the arbitrary actions of the Satsuma-Chōshū clique. Samurai were the mainstay of the early party movement, despite its doctrines proclaiming all classes to be equal. During the mid-1870s, there was some movement between the parties and the rebellions. But as the rebellions ended, the people's rights movement became more stable.

Then, with the government's formation of prefectural assemblies in 1878, what had been, in fact, unofficial pressure groups became true political parties. Many farmers joined, wanting their taxes cut; the poor joined, hoping to improve their condition. The parties were given another boost after a political crisis in 1881, when the government promised a constitution and a national assembly within ten years. During the 1880s, the parties had ups and downs. When poorer peasant members rebelled, the parties dissolved for a time to dissociate themselves from the uprisings. But as the date for national elections approached, the parties regained strength, and the ties between party notables and local men of influence grew closer.

The Constitution

The government viewed the party movement with distaste but was not sure how to counter it. Itō Hirobumi (1841–1909), originally from Chōshū, went abroad to shop for a constitution that would serve the needs of the Meiji government. He found principles to his liking in Germany, and brought home a German jurist to help adapt the conservative Prussian constitution of 1850 to Japanese uses. As promulgated in 1889, the Meiji Constitution was notable for the extensive powers granted to the emperor and for the severely limited powers it granted to the lower house in the Diet (the English term for Japan's bicameral national assembly).

The emperor was sovereign. According to the constitution, he was "sacred and inviolable," and in Itō's commentaries, the sacredness was defined in Shinto terms. As in Prussia, the emperor was given direct command of the armed forces. Yamagata Aritomo (1838–1922) had set up a German-type general staff system in 1878. The emperor had the right to name the prime minister and to appoint the Cabinet. He could dissolve the lower house of the Diet and issue imperial ordinances when the Diet was not in session. The Imperial Household Ministry, which was outside the Cabinet, administered the great wealth given to the imperial family during the 1880s—so that the emperor would never have to ask the Diet for funds. In every case, it was intended and understood that the Meiji leaders would act for the emperor in all of these matters. Finally, the constitution itself was presented as a gift from the emperor to his subjects.

Itō Hirobumi at the time of the writing of the Meiji Constitution, of which he was the author.

Itō, born a lowly foot soldier in Chōshū, began in the new nobility as a count and ended as a prince. In 1885, Itō established a cabinet system. He became the first prime minister, followed by Kuroda Kiyotaka (1840–1900) of Satsuma, and then by Yamagata Aritomo of Chōshū. In 1887, Itō established a Privy Council, with himself as its head, to approve of the constitution he had written. In 1888, laws were passed and civil service examinations instituted to insulate the imperial bureaucracy from the tawdry concerns of politicians. By this time, the bureaucracy, which had begun as a loose collection of men of ability and of their protégés, had become highly systematized. Detailed administrative laws defined their functions and governed their behavior. They were well paid. In 1890, there were twenty-nine thousand officials; by 1908, there were seventy-two thousand.

The Growth of a Modern Economy

The late Tokugawa economy was backward and not markedly different from the economies of other East Asian countries. Almost 80 per cent of the population lived in the countryside at close to a subsistence level. Sophisticated but labor-intensive paddy-field techniques were used in farming. Taxes were high, as much as 35 per cent of the product, and two-thirds of the land tax was paid in kind. That is to say, money had only partially penetrated the rural economy. Japan had not developed factory production with machinery, steam power, or large aggregates of capital.

Early Meiji reforms unshackled the late Tokugawa economy. Occupations were freed, which meant that farmers could trade and samurai could farm. Barriers on roads were abolished, as were the monopolistic guilds that had restricted access to the central markets. The abolition of domains threw open regional economies that had been partially self-enclosed. Most large merchant houses were too closely tied to daimyo finances and went bankrupt, but there rose a groundswell of new commercial ventures and of traditional agriculturally based industries. Silk was the wonder crop. The government introduced mechanical reeling, which enabled Japan to win markets previously held by the hand-reeled silk of China. About two-thirds of Japanese silk production was exported, and not until the 1930s did cotton become more important. Silk production rose from 2.3 million pounds in the post-Restoration era to 16 million at the turn of the century and then to 93 million in 1929.

A parallel unshackling occurred on the land. The land tax reform of the 1870s, although initially lowering taxes only slightly, created a powerful incentive for growth by giving farmers a clear title to their land and by fixing the tax in money. The freedom to buy and sell

The lower house of the Diet, in contrast, was given only the authority to approve budgets and pass laws, and both of these powers were hedged. In the case of budgets, the constitution provided that the previous year's budget would remain in effect if a new budget was not approved. In the case of laws, the appointive House of Peers, the upper house of the Diet, had to approve for any bill to become law. Furthermore, to ensure that the parties themselves would represent the stable and responsible elements of Japanese society, the vote was given only to adult males paying fifteen yen or more in taxes. In 1890, this was about 5 per cent of the adult male population. In sum, Itō's intention was not to create a parliamentary system, but a constitutional system that contained, as one of its parts, a parliament.

During the 1880s, the government also created a range of institutions designed to limit the future influence of the political parties. In 1884, it created a new nobility, honorable and conservative, with which to stock the future House of Peers. The nobility was composed of ex-nobles and the Meiji leaders themselves.

land led to a rise in tenancy from perhaps 25 per cent in 1868 to about 44 per cent at the turn of the century. There also appeared progressive landlords who bought fertilizer and farm equipment. Rice production rose from 149 million bushels a year during 1880–1884 to 316 million during 1935–1937. More food, combined with a drop in the death rate—the result of better hygiene—led to population growth: from about 30 million in 1868 to 45 million in 1900 to 73 million in 1940. Because, at the same time, the farm population remained constant, labor was available for factory and other urban jobs.

The First Phase: Model Industries

The modern sector of the economy was the government's greatest concern. It developed in four phases. The first was the era of model industries, which lasted until 1881. With military strength as one of its major goals, the Meiji government expanded the arsenals and the shipyards that it had inherited from the Tokugawa. It also built telegraph lines; made a start on railroads; developed coal and copper mines; and established factories for textiles, cement, glass, tools, and other products. Every new industry begun during the 1870s was the work of the government; many were initiated by the Ministry of Industry, which was set up in 1870 under Itō Hirobumi. The quantitative output of these early industries was insignificant, however. Essentially they were pilot-plant operations that doubled as "schools" for technologists and labor.

Just as important to later economic development were a variety of other new institutions: banks, post offices, ports, roads, commercial laws, a system of primary and secondary schools, a government university, and so on. These were patterned after European and American examples, though the pattern was often altered to fit Japan's needs; for example, Tokyo Imperial University had a faculty of agriculture earlier than any university in Europe.

The Second Phase: 1880s–1890s

More substantial growth in the modern sector took place during the 1880s and 1890s. It was marked by the appearance of what would later become the great industrial combines known as *zaibatsu*. Accumulating capital was the greatest problem for would-be entrepreneurs. Iwasaki Yatarō (1834–1885) used political connections. After the Restoration, he gained control of the ships that he had managed as a samurai official for the Tosa domain. He then acquired government ships that had been used to transport troops during the 1874 Taiwan Expedition and the 1877 Satsuma Rebellion. From these beginnings, he built a shipping line to compete with foreign companies, started a bank, and invested in the enterprises that later became the Mitsubishi combine.

Shibusawa Eiichi (1840–1931) was another maverick entrepreneur. Born into a peasant family that produced indigo, he became a merchant, joined the pro-emperor movement, and then switched sides and

At the turn of the century more than half of Japanese factory labor was female. The mechanical reeling of the silk filament from the cocoon gave Japan a superior product. The women worked long hours, ate poor food, and slept in crowded dormitories. Many contracted tuberculosis.

Woodblock print of the horse-drawn streetcars, which began to operate in Tokyo in 1882. Streetcars took business away from the jinrikshas, the chairs pulled by their human drivers, which had been invented in Japan only a decade or so earlier.

became a bakufu retainer. After 1868, he entered the Finance Ministry. In 1873, he made the so-called heavenly descent from government to private business. Founding the First Bank, he showed a talent for beginning new industries with other people's money. His initial success was the Osaka Cotton Spinning Mill, established as a joint stock company in 1880. The investors profited hugely, and money poured in to found new mills; by 1896, the production of yarn had reached 17 million pounds, and by 1913, over ten times that amount. After the turn of the century, cotton cloth replaced yarn as the focus of growth: Production rose more than 100-fold, from 22 million square yards in 1900 to 2,710 million in 1936.

Another area of growth was in the railroad industry. Before railroads, most of Japan's commerce was carried on by coastal shipping. It cost as much during the early Meiji period to transport goods fifty miles overland as it did to ship them to Europe. Railroads gave Japan an internal circulatory system, opening up hitherto isolated regions. In 1872, Japan had 18 miles of track, in 1894, 2,100 miles, and in 1934, 14,500 miles.

Cotton textiles and railroads were followed during the 1890s by cement, bricks, matches, glass, beer, chemicals, and other private industries. One can only admire the foresight, vigor, and daring of those who pioneered in these products. At the same time, the role of government in creating a favorable climate for growth should not be forgotten: The society and the polity were stable, the yen was sound, capital was safe, and taxes on industry were extremely low. In every respect, the conditions enjoyed by Japan's budding entrepreneurs differed from those of neighboring China.

The Third Phase: 1905–1929

Economic growth continued after the Russo-Japanese War ended in 1905 and spurted ahead during World War I. Light industries and textiles were central, but iron and steel, shipping, coal mining, electrical power, and chemicals also grew. An economic slump followed the war and the economy grew only slowly during the twenties. One factor was renewed competition from a Europe at peace. Another was the great earthquake that destroyed Tokyo in 1923. Tokyo was rebuilt with loans but these led to inflation. Agricultural productivity also leveled off during the twenties: It became cheaper to import foodstuffs from the colonies than to invest in new agricultural technology at home.

By the twenties, Japanese society, especially in the cities, was becoming modern. The Japanese ate better, were healthier, and lived longer. Personal savings rose with the standard of living. Even workers opened postal saving accounts, drank beer, went to movies, and read newspapers. In 1890, 31 per cent of girls and 64 per cent of boys went to primary schools; by 1905, the figures were 90 per cent and 96 per cent; and in 1925, primary school education was universal. Viewed

The Cultural Revolution of Meiji Japan: Westerners' Views

While the political parties prepared for constitutional government and the government built dikes to contain the parties, Japan's society and culture were being transformed.

ON JAPANESE STUDENTS IN 1868

What a sight for a schoolmaster! . . . They are all dressed in the native costume of loose coats, with long and bag-like sleeves; kilts, like petticoats, open at the upper side; with shaven midscalps, and top-knots like gun-hammers. Men and boys carry slates and copy books in their hands, and common cheap glass ink bottles slung by pieces of twine to their girdles. Hands and faces are smeared with the black fluid; but, strangest of all, each has two of the murderous-looking swords, one long and the other short, stuck in his belt. Symbols of the soldier rather than the scholar are these; but the samurai are both.

ON JAPAN DURING THE 1870s

To understand the situation you have to realize that less than ten years ago the Japanese were living under conditions like those of our chivalric age and the feudal system of the Middle Ages, with its monasteries, guilds, Church universal, and so on; but that betwixt night and morning, one might almost say, and with one great leap, Japan is trying to traverse the stages of five centuries of European development, and to assimilate in the twinkling of an eye all the latest achievements of western civilization. The country is thus undergoing an immense cultural revolution—for the term "evolution" is inapplicable to a change so rapid and so fundamental. I feel myself lucky to be an eyewitness of so interesting an experiment.

LOOKING BACK FROM THE 1890s

If one considers the comparative precocity of the Japanese youth, as well as the wild and lawless traditions which students of twenty years ago had inherited from their predecessors, and adds thereto the further consideration that twenty years ago parental authority was at its lowest in Japan, for the reason that the go-ahead sons were conscious of knowing a great deal more than their old-fashioned, old world parents, . . . it will not be wondered at that in those early days strikes sometimes took place which bore a striking testimony to the power of organization which is innate in the Japanese. . . . But I am talking of events which took place many years ago. Things are very much changed now. . . . The go-ahead student of twenty years ago is the go-ahead parent of today, and has succeeded in reestablishing over his children that parental authority which for the time slipped from the grasp of his old world father. ❑

W. E. Griffis, *The Mikado's Empire* (New York: Harper and brothers, 1896), p. 370. E. Baelz, *Awakening Japan: The Diary of a German Doctor* (New York: Viking Press, 1932), p. 16. A. Lloyd, *Everyday Japan* (New York: Cassell and Co., 1909), pp. 272–273.

---

positively, Japan had done what no other non-Western nation had even attempted: It had achieved universal literacy. Nevertheless, there remained an immense educational and social gap between the masses with only a primary school education and the 3 per cent who attended university. This gap was the basic weakness in the political democracy of the twenties. Still, more primary school graduates went on to middle and higher schools, and a growing number entered new technical colleges. These changes would continue into the thirties and the war years.

The Fourth Phase: Depression and Recovery

A Japanese bank crisis in 1927, followed by the worldwide Great Depression in 1929, plunged Japan into several years of unemployment and suffering. The distress was particularly acute in the rice-producing regions of the northeast. The political consequences of the Depression years were enormous. Yet Japan recovered by 1935, more rapidly than any other industrial nation.

The recovery was fueled by an export boom and by military procurements at home. During the 1930s, the production of pig iron, raw steel, and chemicals doubled. For the first time, Japan was able to construct complete electric-power stations and became self-sufficient in machine tools and scientific instruments. Shipbuilding forged ahead; by 1937, Japan had a merchant fleet of 4.5 million tons, the third largest and certainly the newest in the world. Despite continued growth in cotton cloth during the 1930s, textiles slipped relative to the products of heavy industry. The quality of Japan's manufacturers also rose. The outcry in the West against Japanese exports at this time was not so much because of volume—a modest 3.6 per cent of world exports in 1936—but because for the first time, Japanese products had become competitive in terms of quality.

The Politics of Imperial Japan (1890–1945)

Parliaments began in the West and generally have worked better in the West than in the rest of the world. For Japan to establish a constitution during the nineteenth century was a bold experiment. Even so cautious a constitution as that of Meiji had no precedent outside the West at the time; most Western observers were skeptical of its chances for success. How are we now, in retrospect, to view the Japanese political experience after 1890?

One view is that because Japanese society was not ready for constitutional government, the militarism of the thirties was inevitable. From the perspective of an ideal democracy, Japanese society certainly had many weaknesses: a small middle class, weak trade unions, an independent military under the emperor, a strong emperor-centered nationalism, and so on. But these weaknesses, other historians note, did not prevent the Diet from growing in importance, nor block the transfer of power from the bureaucratic Meiji leaders to the political party leaders. The transfer fell short of full parliamentary government. However, had it not been derailed by the Great Depression and other events, the advance toward parliamentary government might well have continued.

From Confrontation to the Founding of the Seiyūkai (1890–1900)

Two political histories of Japan under the Meiji Constitution are possible. One is a history of what the government, what the executive state, did. It includes the drawing up of budgets, the building of Japan's military forces, the engagement in wars, the extension of the banking system, the establishment of new universities, the reforming of the tax system, and so on—all of those enterprises that a modernizing state must carry out. The other is a history of politics, of the struggles between different groups and bodies for power.

In 1890 the Meiji leaders, now called *oligarchs*—the few who rule—saw the cabinet as "transcendental," as serving the emperor and nation above the ruck of politics. They viewed the political parties as noisy, ineffective, irresponsible supporters of partisan interests. They saw the lower house of the Diet as a safety valve, a place where the parties could let off steam without seriously affecting the business of government. But the oligarchs had miscalculated in giving the lower house the power to approve the budget.

The first act of the parties in the new Diet of 1890 was to slash the government's budget. Prime Minister Yamagata was furious but had to make concessions to get part of the cut restored. This pattern of applying pressure to the annual budget continued for ten years.

The previous year's budget was never enough. The government tried to intimidate and bribe the parties, but failed. It even formed a government party and tried to win elections by enlisting the police and local officials for campaign support. But the opposing political parties maintained their control of the lower house. They were well organized in the prefectures where assemblies had begun in 1878. They also had the support of the voters, mostly well-to-do landowners who opposed the government's heavy land tax.

Unable to either coerce or defeat the opposing parties, and determined that the Meiji constitution not fail, in 1900 Itō Hirobumi formed a new party. The Seiyūkai was composed of ex-bureaucrats and of politicians from the Liberal Party that a Tosa samurai, Itagaki Taisuke (1837–1919), had formed in 1881. For most of the next twenty years the Seiyūkai controlled the lower house and provided parliamentary support for successive governments. This was a satisfactory arrangement for both sides. Itō and subsequent prime ministers got the Diet support necessary for the government to function smoothly. Itō had found a way to make the constitution work. The arrangement gave party politicians cabinet posts. From inside the government, they obtained legislation favorable to their party's interests and their influence grew steadily greater.

The Golden Years of Meiji

The years before and after the turn of the century represented the culmination of what the government had striven for since 1868. Economic development was under way. Revision of the unequal treaties was obtained in two steps: Japan got rid of extraterritoriality in 1899 (by a treaty signed in 1894) and regained control of its own tariffs in 1911. However, it was events in the international arena that won Japan recognition as a world power.

The first event was a war with China in 1894–1895 over conflicting interests in Korea. Western observers expected China to win, but the Japanese, using modern naval tactics, sank the Chinese fleet and also won on land. From its victory, Japan secured Taiwan, the Pescadores Islands, the Kwantung Peninsula in south Manchuria, an indemnity, and a treaty giving it the same privileges in China as those enjoyed by the Western powers. Russia, however, had its own expansionist plans and, obtaining French and German support, forced Japan to give up the Kwantung Peninsula, which included Port Arthur. Three years later, Russia took Kwantung for itself.

The second event was Japan's participation in 1900 in the international force that relieved the Boxers' siege of the foreign legations in Peking. The Japanese troops were notable for their numbers and discipline.

A third development was the Anglo-Japanese Alli-

An early session of the Diet.

ance of 1902. For Britain, this alliance ensured Japanese support for its East Asian interests and warded off the likelihood of a Russian–Japanese agreement over spheres of influence in northeast Asia. The alli-

ance ensured Japan the leeway to fight Russia without fear that a third party would intervene.

The fourth event was a war with Russia that began in 1904 when Japanese torpedo boats launched a sur-

Japanese troops take the fort at Port Arthur in 1904 in a major battle of the Russo-Japanese War. 15,000 thousand Japanese were killed in this battle, ten times the losses of the Russians.

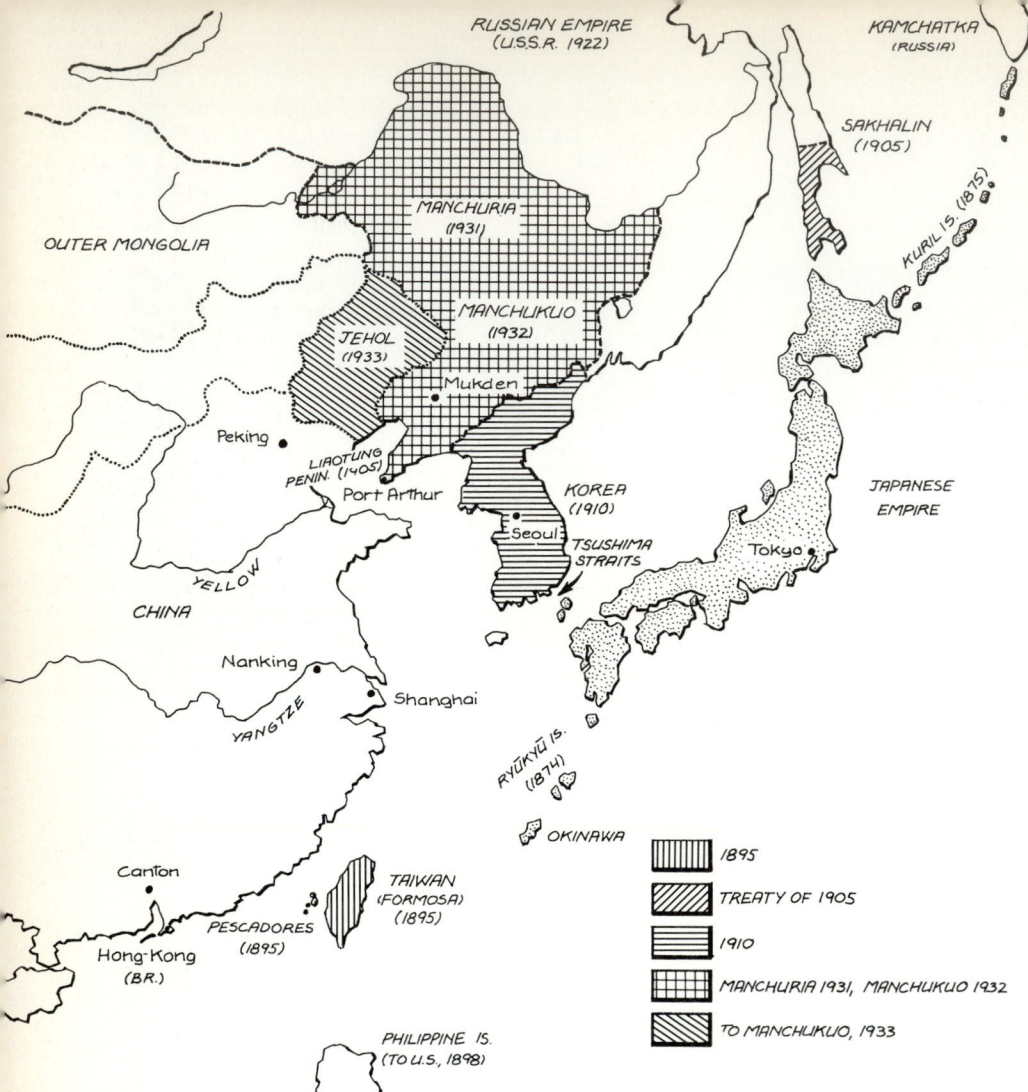

RUSSIAN EMPIRE
(U.S.S.R. 1922)

KAMCHATKA
(RUSSIA)

OUTER MONGOLIA

SAKHALIN
(1905)

MANCHURIA
(1931)

KURIL IS. (1875)

JEHOL
(1933)

MANCHUKUO
(1932)

Mukden

Peking

LIAOTUNG
PENIN. (1905)

Port Arthur

KOREA
(1910)

JAPANESE
EMPIRE

Seoul

TSUSHIMA
STRAITS

Tokyo

YELLOW

CHINA

Nanking

Shanghai

YANGTZE

RYŪKYŪ IS.
(1874)

OKINAWA

Canton

TAIWAN
(FORMOSA)
(1895)

PESCADORES
(1895)

Hong Kong
(B.R.)

PHILIPPINE IS.
(TO U.S., 1898)

1895

TREATY OF 1905

1910

MANCHURIA 1931, MANCHUKUO 1932

TO MANCHUKUO, 1933

MAP 32-3   FORMATION OF
JAPANESE EMPIRE   *The Japanese Empire grew in three
stages: the Sino-Japanese War
of 1894–1895, the Russo-Japanese War of 1904–1905, and by
Japanese conquests in Manchuria and northern China after
1931.*

prise attack on the Russian fleet at Port Arthur. On
land, Japanese armies drove the Russians from their
railway zones in Manchuria and seized Mukden in
March 1905. The Russians sent their Baltic fleet to join
the battle, but it was annihilated by Admiral Tōgō at
the Straits of Tsushima. After months of war, both
countries were worn out, and Russia was plagued by
revolution. On U.S. President Theodore Roosevelt's
initiative, a peace treaty was signed at Portsmouth,
New Hampshire. It gave Japan the Russian lease in
the Kwantung Peninsula, the Russian railway in south
Manchuria, the southern half of Sakhalin, and a recognition of Japan's "paramount interest" in Korea. Japan's formal annexation of Korea occurred in 1910.

It is ironic that Japan, a country still not free of the
system of unequal treaties, should itself have joined
the imperialist scramble for colonies. Certainly, Japan's desire for colonies is not to be explained by Japanese tradition, which, with the exception of Hideyoshi,

had rarely looked to foreign expansion. Nor is it to be
explained by Japan's economy, which was just beginning to build its modern industries and was far from
able to export capital. The explanation is simpler:
Japan wanted equality with the great Western powers,
and military power and colonies were the best credentials. Enthusiasm for empire was shared by political
party leaders, most liberal thinkers, and conservative
leaders alike.

The Rise of the Parties to Power

The founding of the Seiyūkai by Itō in 1900 ended a
decade of confrontation between the Diet and the government. The aging oligarch Itō soon found intolerable
the day-to-day experience of dealing with party politicians, who, unlike the bureaucrats, neither obeyed
him nor paid him the simple respect that he thought his
due. He relinquished the presidency of the party to the
noble Saionji Kinmochi (1849–1940) in 1903. Saionji

904   TOWARD THE MODERN WORLD

also found it too much to bear and passed the post to Hara Takashi (1856–1921) in 1905. With Hara, the office found the man.

Hara was an outsider. Born a generation after the founding fathers of the Meiji state and in a politically unimportant northeastern domain, he began his political career as a newspaper reporter. He then entered the Foreign Office, eventually becoming ambassador to Korea, and then, in turn, an editor, a bank official, a company president, and a Diet member. He helped Itō to found the Seiyūkai. The most able politician in Japan, he was painstaking, patient, paternalistic, and perspicacious. His goals for Japan centered on the expansion of national wealth and power and were no different from those of Itō or Yamagata. But he felt that they should be achieved by party government, not oligarchic rule, and worked unceasingly to expand the power of his party. The years between 1905 and 1921 were marked by the struggle between these two alternative conceptions of government.

The struggle can be represented as a rising curve of party strength and a descending curve of oligarchic influence. The rising curve was composed of two vectors: a buildup of the Seiyūkai party machine that enabled it to win elections and maintain itself as the majority (or plurality) party in the Diet, and the strengthening of the Diet vis-à-vis other elites within the government in Tokyo. For the former, Hara obtained campaign funds from industrialists and other moneyed interests. He also promoted pork barrel legislation in the Diet: Local constituencies that supported Seiyūkai candidates got new schools, bridges, dams, roads, or even railroad lines. Seiyūkai politicians established ties with local notables, who brokered the votes of their communities. On the three occasions when he served as home minister, Hara was even willing to call on the police and local officials to aid Seiyūkai election campaigns.

In coopting other governmental elites, the Seiyūkai was less successful. The party steadily increased its representation in the Cabinet. It gained some patronage appointments in the central bureaucracy and in the newly formed colonial bureaucracy, though most bureaucrats remained professionals and resisted the intrusion of outside political appointees. Some career bureaucrats, however, developed working relations with the party and became partly politicized. In the House of Peers, and in the Privy Council, which ratified treaties, the Seiyūkai was less successful. A few peers were appointed through its influence, and at times, it was allied with a faction in the Peers, but by and large, these remained independent bodies. As for penetrating the military services, the Seiyūkai had no success at all. At most, it exercised some control over the military budget in time of peace.

The descending curve of weakening oligarchic control reflected the aging of the "men of Meiji." In 1900, Itō was the last oligarch to become prime minister. From 1901 to 1912, Katsura Tarō (1847–1913), a Chōshū general and Yamagata's protégé, and Saionji, Itō's protégé, took turns in the post. Both had Seiyūkai support. Toward the end of the period, Katsura began to resent the fact that he, a grown man, had to go to Yamagata for every important decision. The oligarchs were also weakened by changes within the elites. A younger generation of officers in the military services chafed at the continuing domination by the old Satsuma and Chōshū cliques. In the civil bureaucracy, younger officials who had graduated from the Law Faculty of Tokyo Imperial University were achieving positions of responsibility. Proud of their ability, they saw the bureaucracy as an independent service and resisted oligarchic control almost as much as they resisted that of the parties.

The oligarchs did, however, maintain their power to act for the emperor in appointing prime ministers. With the deaths of Itō in 1909, Yamagata in 1922, and Matsukata in 1924, this vital function was taken over by Saionji and, later, by ex-prime ministers.

As the rising and descending curves crossed, the political parties advanced. Several turning points were critical. One came in 1912. When the army's demands for a larger budget were refused, it withdrew its minister, causing Saionji's cabinet to collapse. Katsura formed a new cabinet and tried to govern using imperial decrees in place of Diet support. This infuriated the parties and even the Seiyūkai withdrew its support. Massive popular demonstrations broke out, a movement was organized for the "Protection of the Constitution," and party orators shouted "Destroy the Sat-Chō leaders and "off with Katsura's head." Katsura tried to counter the popular forces aligned against him by forming a second political party, parallel to the Seiyūkai. The party would go on to become politically important during the 1920s. But it did not save Katsura, who was forced to resign in 1913. The lower house had defeated an oligarchic prime minister.

A second turning point came in 1918, when Hara finally became prime minister. It was the first time that a politician who was not a Meiji founding father or a protégé of one had obtained the post. He enacted reforms but did nothing to remedy the parliamentary shortcomings of the Meiji Constitution.

A third development was the wave of liberalism that began during World War I and culminated in the period of party governments from 1924 to 1932. Joining the Allies in World War I, Japan had been influenced by democratic currents of thought from England and America. Scholars discussed revising the Meiji Consti-

Natsume Sōseki on the Costs of Rapid Modernization

Natsume Sōseki (1867–1916) was one of the earliest of a series of great novelists to create a new literature in Japan after the turn of the century. Sōseki could often be humorous. One of his early works, I Am a Cat, *looked at a Tokyo household from a feline perspective. He advocated ethical individualism as superior to state morality. He also wrote of human isolation in a changing society and of the dark side of human nature.*

MY INDIVIDUALISM

Let us set aside the question of the bragging about the new teachings acquired from the West, which are only superficially mastered. Let us suppose that in forty or fifty years after the Restoration, by the power of education, by really applying ourselves to study, we can move from teaching A to teaching B and even advance to C—without the slightest vulgar fame-seeking, without the slightest sense of vainglory. Let us further suppose that we pass, in a natural orderly fashion, from stage to stage and that we ultimately attain the extreme of differentiation in our internally developed enlightenment that the West attained after more than a hundred years. If, then, by our physical and mental exertions, and by ignoring the difficulties and suffering involved in our precipitous advance, we end by passing through, in merely one-half the time it took the more prosperous Westerners to reach their stage of specialization, to our stage of internally developed enlightenment, the consequences will be serious indeed. At the same time we will be able to boast of this fantastic acquisition of knowledge, the inevitable result will be a nervous collapse from which we will not be able to recover.

PASSERS-BY

This is what your brother said. He suffers because nothing he does appears to him as either an end or a means. He is perpetually uneasy and cannot relax. He cannot sleep and so gets out of bed. But when he is awake, he cannot stay still, so he begins to walk. As he walks, he finds that he has to begin running. Once he has begun running, he cannot stop. To have to keep on running is bad enough, but he feels compelled to increase his speed with every step he takes. When he imagines what the end of all this will be, he is so frightened that he breaks out in a cold sweat. And the fear becomes unbearable.

I was surprised when I heard your brother's explanation. I myself have never experienced uneasiness of this kind. And so, though I could comprehend what he was saying, I could feel no sympathy for him. I was like a man who tries to imagine what it is like to have a splitting headache though he has never had one. I tried to think for a while. And my wandering mind hit upon this thing called "man's fate"; it was a rather vague concept in my mind, but I was happy to have found something consoling to say to your brother.

"This uneasiness of yours is no more than the uneasiness that all men experience. All you have to do is to realize that there is no need for you alone to worry so much about it. What I mean to say is that it is our fate to wander blindly through life."

Not only were my words vague in meaning but they lacked sincerity. Your brother gave me one shrewd, contemptuous glance; that was all my remarks deserved. He then said:

"You know, our uneasiness comes from this thing called scientific progress. Science does not know where to stop and does not permit us to stop either. From walking to rickshaws, from rickshaws to horsedrawn cabs, from cabs to trains, from trains to automobiles, from automobiles to airships, from airships to airplanes—when will we ever be allowed to stop and rest? Where will it finally take us? It is really frightening."

"Yes, it is frightening," I said.

Your brother smiled.

"You say so, but you don't really mean it. You aren't really frightened. This fear that you say you feel, it is only of the theoretical kind. My fear is different from yours. I feel in my heart. It is an alive, pulsating kind of fear." ❑

M. Kōsaka, *Japanese Thought in the Meiji Era* (Tokyo: Pan-Pacific Press, 1958), pp. 447–448.
E. McClellan, "An Introduction to Sōseki," *Harvard Journal of Asiatic Studies*, Vol. 22 (December 1959), pp. 205–206.

tution. Labor unions were organized, at first liberal and often Christian, and later Marxist. A social movement was launched to improve conditions in Japan's industrial slums and to pass social and labor legislation. Japan's second political party, the Kenseikai, which had been out of power since 1916, grew steadily more liberal and adopted several of the new social causes as its own, such as universal manhood suffrage. When Hara cut the tax qualification for voting from ten to three yen, the Kenseikai criticized the change as insufficient and the Seiyūkai as the perpetrator of class despotism.

Modern girls stroll on a Tokyo street during the 1920s.

When nonparty cabinets were formed between 1922 and 1924, the Kenseikai began the Second Movement for the Protection of the Constitution. It was joined by liberal factions of the Seiyūkai, and the party elements in this movement went on to form a coalition government in 1924. This coalition opened an eight-year period in which the presidents of one or another of the two major parties were appointed as prime ministers.

Dreams of Wealth

Arthur Lloyd, long a teacher in Japan, wrote of the changing ethos among his students after 1905.

The Russo-Japanese war put a stop for a while to all political strife. Since the conclusion of peace there has come over Japan a great wave of money-making, which has swept off with it Tory and Liberal alike, and turned all the intellectual classes into the votaries of Daikoku, the god of the money-bags. . . . A dozen years ago I could always lay my hand on half a score of my students whose dream it was to be Cabinet Ministers and thrill audiences of intelligent legislators with their persuasive rhetoric. Six years ago the dream was of conning-towers and bridges, of ramparts and batteries; to-day they say that their country demands from them another kind of sacrifice. It demands that they shall make themselves rich, and they take most kindly to the sacrifice.   ❑

A. Lloyd, *Everyday Japan* (1909), p. 98.

The coalition Cabinet (1924–1926) of Katō Kōmei is considered the peak of parliamentary practice in prewar Japan. Born in 1860, Katō graduated from Tokyo Imperial University at the age of twenty-one and entered the Mitsubishi firm. He married the boss's daughter, spent some time in England, and entered the Foreign Ministry, becoming foreign minister at forty. For a country that esteemed age, his rise was meteoric. He subsequently became a Diet member, a newspaper president, and an ambassador to England, and from 1914, he served as president of the Dōshikai and then, the Kenseikai. Blunt, cold, and haughty, Katō was widely respected if not liked. He was also an Anglophile who understood and supported a British style of government. His ministry passed universal manhood suffrage, increased academic appointments to the House of Peers, and cut military funds from 42 per cent of the 1922 budget to 29 per cent in 1925. He also enacted socialist and labor legislation. The parliamentary socialist movement was, in effect, legalized, and revolutionary socialism was outlawed. Katō's cabinet brought Japan close to a true parliamentary government, which though not mandated by the Meiji Constitution had not been banned either.

Militarism and War (1927–1945)

The future of Japan's parliamentary coalition seemed assured during the mid-1920s. The economy was growing; the society was stable; the party leaders were experienced. Japan's international position was secure within the multilateral treaty system established among the Great Powers at the Washington Naval Conference of 1924. By a decade later, however, the party leaders had lost the gains of thirty-five years. And by 1945, Japan had been defeated in a devastating war and was occupied by foreign troops for the first time in its history. How did this come about? Simply put, a small shift in the balance of power among the governmental elites established by the Meiji Constitution had produced a major change in Japan's foreign policy. The parties had been the aggressive elite between 1890 and 1926 and had advanced their influence by forcing the other elites to compromise. From the late 1920s, the military became the aggressive elite and did the same. Beginning in 1932, military men replaced party presidents as prime ministers. In 1937, Japan went to war with China; and by the end of 1941, Japan was allied with Germany and Italy and had gone to war with the United States.

From their inception, the military services in Japan had been separate and had been constructed on different principles from Japan's civilian society. Soldiers were not samurai. The rifle companies of Satsuma and Chōshū had broken decisively with that tradition, and universal conscription had put the new military on a changed footing. But the armed services had their own schools, which inculcated the values of discipline, bravery, loyalty, and obedience. The military saw themselves as the true heirs of those who had founded the modern Japanese state and the true guardians of Japanese tradition. They contrasted their loyalty to the emperor and their concern for all Japanese with the pandering to special interests by the political parties.

They resented their diminished national stature during the 1920s, when military budgets were cut and the prestige of a military career had declined to the point where officers wore civilian clothes when off-base. In particular, the fleet wing of the navy resented the decision of moderate admirals to accept a formula at the London Naval Conference of the Great Power in 1930 that would weaken Japan's naval strength. But even during the liberal 1920s, there had been no change in the constitutional position of the services. The general staffs remained directly responsible to the emperor. With the passing of the Meiji oligarchs, this meant that they were responsible to no one but themselves.

A CRISIS IN MANCHURIA. The new multilateral treaties (the 1924 Washington Conference and the 1930 London Conference) that replaced the earlier system of bilateral treaties (such as the Anglo-Japanese Alliance) recognized the existing colonies of the victors of World War I but opposed new colonial ventures. The Western treaty powers were especially strong in support of the "open door" in China, by which they also meant Manchuria. Japan's position in Manchuria was ambiguous. Because Japan maintained its interests through a tame Chinese warlord, Manchuria was not, strictly speaking, a colony. But because Japan had gained its special position in Manchuria at the cost of 100,000 lives in the 1905 Russo-Japanese War, it saw its position as similar to that of the Western nations in their colonies.

From the late 1920s, the Kuomintang unification of China and the blossoming of Chinese nationalism threatened Japan's special position. Japanese army units tried to block the march north and murdered the Manchurian warlord when he showed signs of independence. In this crisis, the party government in Tokyo equivocated, hoping to preserve a status quo that was crumbling before its eyes. The army saw Manchuria as a buffer between the Soviet Union and the Japanese colony of Korea and was unwilling to make any concessions. So, in 1931, the army provoked a crisis, took Manchuria over, and proclaimed it an independent state in 1932. When the League of Nations condemned Japan for violating the "open door," Japan promptly withdrew from the league in 1933.

THE GREAT DEPRESSION. Just as the crisis in China had called into question Japan's place in the in-

The Great Depression in Japan. A village council in northeastern Japan discussing how to survive without having to sell their daughters into prostitution.

ternational political order, so did the Great Depression cast doubts on the international economic order and on the *zaibatsu*. The *zaibatsu* were seen as rich and profiteering in a country full of suffering and want. They were seen as the backers of the "established parties." Rural Japan was hardest hit by the Depression. The real income of farmers fell by about a third between 1926 and 1931 and recovered only slowly. Our images of the Depression in Japan come primarily from the northeast, where a crop failure in 1931 led to famine; children turned to begging for food from passing trains and tenant farmers were forced to eat the inner bark of pine trees or to dig up the roots of wild plants. Urban workers suffered, too. The value of Japanese exports dropped 50 per cent between 1929 and 1931. The workers' real income dropped from an index of 100 in 1929 to 69 in 1931. Unemployment rose to three million, and many returned to the villages to add to the misery of the farm economy. Only the salaried middle class was better off as prices dropped.

Japan's government acted effectively to counter the Depression, as noted earlier. Going off the gold standard led to an export boom; and Japan came out of the Depression faster than any other nation. By 1936, Japan's heavy industries were growing apace, and real wages were up. The recovery came too late to help the political parties, however. By 1936, political trends that had begun during the worst years of the Depression had become irreversible.

The Depression galvanized both the political left and the political right. The main body of the left was made up of moderates who won eight Diet seats in 1928, eighteen in 1936, and thirty-seven in 1937. They would reemerge as an even stronger force after World War II. The extreme left was led by intellectuals and divided among many little Marxist parties. The right wing in pre–World War II Japan is harder to characterize, for there was no single ideology. Most Japanese were imbued with an emperor-centered nationalism. Their constant support of the major political parties did not conflict with a deeper loyalty to the nation.

THE RADICAL RIGHT AND THE MILITARY. During the 1930s, however, there appeared a new array of right-wing organizations that aimed at changing the status quo. Ultranationalists used Shinto myths and Confucian values to oppose the liberal Westernization of Japan's urban society. Some bureaucrats looked to the example of Nazi Germany and argued for government by civil and military officials without the participation of party politicians. Field-grade officers in the services envisioned a "defense state" that would be guided by themselves. They argued for military expansion and a colonial empire that would be protected from the uncertainties of the world economy. Young officers of the revolutionary right advocated "direct action" against the elites of the parliamentary coalition. Indeed, young officers in this camp called for a second restoration of imperial power.

It was the last group which precipitated political change. On May 15, 1932, a group of junior army and navy officers attacked the Seiyūkai offices, the Bank of Japan, the Tokyo police headquarters, and murdered Prime Minister Inukai. This attack occurred at the

Young officers and men of the "Imperial Way Faction" attempting a coup d'etat in Tokyo in February 1936. The words on the banner say, "Honor the emperor. Strike down the evil men."

peak of right-wing agitation and the pit of the Depression. Saionji decided that it would be unwise to appoint another party president and chose a moderate admiral. For the next four years, cabinets were led by moderate military men, with party participation. It was no more than a holding pattern—not what the parties wanted and not what the radical young officers wanted either.

During 1936 and 1937, Japanese politics were buffeted by cross-currents but continued to drift to the right. In the election of February 1936, the Minseitō overturned the Seiyūkai-dominated Diet. It used as its slogan "What shall it be, parliamentary government or Fascism?" A week later, young officers responded with an attempted coup d'état in Tokyo. Leading fourteen hundred soldiers, they attacked government offices; killed cabinet ministers, though missing the prime minister; and for three days, occupied the Diet, the Army Ministry, the general staff headquarters, and other government buildings. They wanted their army superiors to form a new government. Saionji and other men about the emperor stood firm; the navy opposed the rebellion; and within three days, it was suppressed. It was the last "direct action" by the radical

right in prewar Japan. The ringleaders were quickly tried and executed, and generals sympathetic to them were retired. The officers in charge of the purge within the army were tough-minded elitist technocrats, who even during the budget cuts of the 1920s had advocated the further modernization of Japan's weaponry. They included General Tōjō Hideki (1884–1948), who would lead Japan into World War II.

Their reassertion of control over the radical young officers did not mean a withdrawal from politics. On the contrary, the services interfered more than ever in the formation of cabinets, blocking whenever possible the appointment of party politicians or liberal bureaucrats. As a result, from 1936 on, moderates gave way to prime ministers who were more outspokenly militaristic.

Opposition to militarism remained substantial nonetheless. In the 1937 election, a prime minister who had been a general and whose political slogan was "Respect the gods and honor the emperor" tried to win control of the Diet by throwing government support to the Shōwakai, a Nazi-like party. It won only forty Diet seats, whereas the two major centrist parties, which had joined in opposition to the government, won 354. The results made clear that the Japanese people were more level-headed than their leaders. But the victory of the centrist parties proved a hollow one, for whereas a peacetime government could not rule without the Diet, the Diet could not oppose a government in wartime, and by summer, Japan was at war in China.

THE ROAD TO PEARL HARBOR. Between the outbreak of the war with China and the World War II campaign in the Pacific, there were three critical junctures. The first was the decision in January 1938 to strike a knockout blow at the Nationalist Party government in Nanking (the Kuomintang). The war had begun as an unplanned skirmish between Chinese and Japanese troops in the Peking area but had quickly spread. The Army's leaders themselves disagreed on whether to continue. Most held that the only threat to Japanese interests in Korea and Manchuria was the Soviet Union, and that a long war in China was unnecessary and foolish. But as the Japanese armies advanced, others on the general staff argued that the only way to stop the war was to convince the Nationalists that fighting was hopeless. The general staff got its way, and the army quickly occupied most of the cities and railroads of eastern China. When Chiang Kai-shek refused to give in, a stalemate ensued that lasted until 1945. China was never a major theater of the war in the Pacific.

The second critical decision was the signing of the Tripartite Pact with Germany and Italy in September 1940. Japan had long admired Germany. In 1936, it had joined Germany in the Anti-Comintern Pact directed against international communism. It also wanted an alliance with Germany against the Soviet Union. Germany insisted, however, that any alliance also be directed against the United States and Britain, to which the Japanese would not agree. The Japanese navy, especially, saw the American Pacific fleet as its only potential enemy and was not willing to risk being dragged into a German war. When Japanese troops battled Russian troops in an undeclared mini-war from May to September 1939 on the Mongolian border, sentiment rose in favor of an alliance with Germany, but then Germany "betrayed" Japan by signing a non-aggression pact with the Soviet Union. For a time, Japan decided to improve its relations with the United States, but America insisted that Japan get out of China. By the late spring of 1940, German victories in Europe—the fall of Britain appeared imminent—again led military leaders in Japan to favor an alliance with Germany.

When Japan signed the Tripartite Pact, it had three objectives: to isolate the United States, to inherit the Southeast Asian colonies of the countries defeated by Germany in Europe, and to improve its relations with

Tōjō Hideki (1884–1948), *prime minister at the time of the attack on Pearl Harbor in* 1941 *and one of the chief figures in the rise of Japanese militarism.*

the Soviet Union through the good offices of Germany. The last objective was reached when Japan signed a neutrality pact with the Soviet Union in April 1941. Two months later, Germany attacked the Soviet Union, giving its ally Japan little notice. It compounded this second "betrayal" by asking Japan to attack the Soviet Union in the east. Japan waited and watched. When the German advance was stopped short of Moscow, Japan decided to honor the neutrality pact and turn south. This decision marked, in effect, the end of Japan's participation in the Axis. Thereafter, it fought its own war in Asia. Yet instead of deflecting American criticism as intended, the pact, by linking Japan to Germany, led to a hardening of America's position on China.

The third and fatal decision was to go to war with the United States. In June 1940, following Germany's defeat of France, Japanese troops had moved into northern French Indochina. The United States retaliated by placing limits on strategic exports to Japan. In July 1941, Japanese troops took southern Indochina, and the United States put an embargo on all exports to

AFGHANISTAN

OUTER
MONGOLIA

SOVIET UNION

L. BALKASH

Irkutsk

L. BAIKAL

Chita

TRANS–SIBERIAN
R.R.

SINKIANG

Karachi

TIBET C H I N A

NEPAL

Bombay

INDIA
(U.K.)

Calcutta

Sadiya

LEDO
ROAD

NANKING

Peiping

Yenan

MANCHOUKUO

Kirin

Mukden

Vladivostok

SAKHALIN

KARAFUTO

KURILE IS.

ETORFU

HOKKAIDO

JAPAN

HONSHU

SOVIET UNION
ENTERS WAR,
8/9/1945

KOREA
(OCC.
8/16/45)

Chungking

BURMA
ROAD

Hankow

Hiroshima 8/6/45

Tokyo

1930

JAPANESE
EMPIRE

1946

JAPANESE
SURRENDER,
9/2/1945

JAPANES
EMPIRE
DEC. 6
1941

Lashio

BURMA
(U.K.)

Kunming

1944–
1945

ATOMIC
BOMBINGS

Nagasaki
8/9/45

RYUKYU IS.

Rangoon

CEYLON

Hanoi

Canton

TAIWAN

Hong Kong

OKINAWA
4/1/45

BONIN IS.

IWO JIMA
3/16/45

P A C I F I C

SIAM

Bangkok

FRENCH
INDOCHINA

PHILIPPINES

LUZON
6/30/45

Manila, 2/24/45

CORREGIDOR

MINDORO
12/15/44

O C E A N

MARIANAS
IS.

Saigon

MALAYA

SAIPAN
6/15/44

I N D I A N

SUMATRA

Singapore
(U.K.)

NETHERLANDS

BORNEO

LEYTE 10/20/44

MINDANAO

GUAM 7/21/44

YAP

PALAU
9/15/44

ENIWE
2/17/4

JAVA

O C E A N

E A S T   I N D I E S

CELEBES

TRUK

Hollandia
4/22/44

ADMIRALTY
2/29/44 IS.

BISMARCK
ARCH.

SOLOMON
IS.

NEW GUINEA

PAPUA

Lae

Darwin

Port
Moresby

C O R A L

GUADAL–
CANAL
8/7/42

AUSTRALIA

S E A

Brisbane

Sydney

ALLIED S

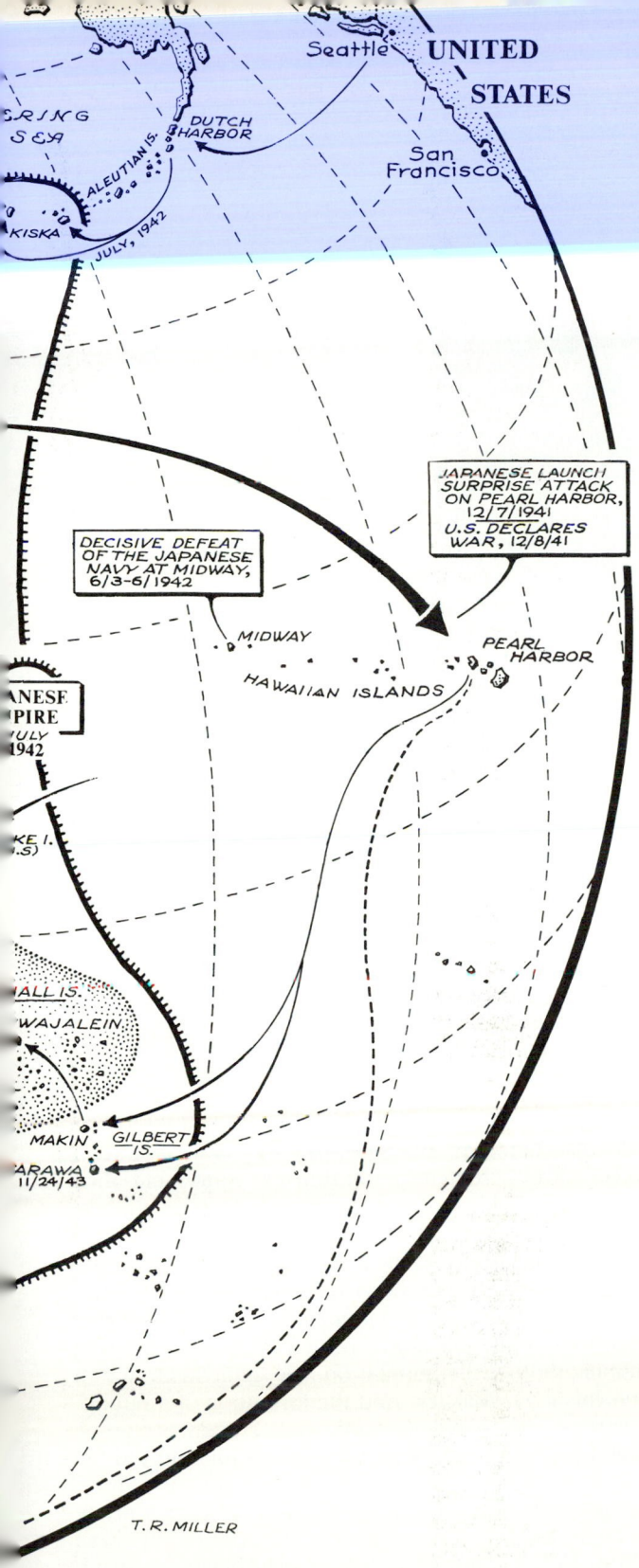

On the map:

- RING SEA (BERING SEA)
- Seattle **UNITED STATES**
- DUTCH HARBOR
- ALEUTIAN IS.
- San Francisco
- KISKA JULY, 1942
- **JAPANESE LAUNCH SURPRISE ATTACK ON PEARL HARBOR, 12/7/1941 U.S. DECLARES WAR, 12/8/41**
- **DECISIVE DEFEAT OF THE JAPANESE NAVY AT MIDWAY, 6/3–6/1942**
- MIDWAY
- PEARL HARBOR
- HAWAIIAN ISLANDS
- [JAPA]NESE [EM]PIRE [J]ULY 1942
- [WA]KE I. (U.S.)
- [MARSH]ALL IS. WAJALEIN
- MAKIN GILBERT IS.
- TARAWA 11/24/43
- T. R. MILLER

MAP 32-4 WORLD WAR II IN THE PACIFIC *As in Europe, the Pacific war was a problem in Allied recapture of areas that had been quickly taken earlier by the enemy. The enormous area represented by the map shows the initial expansion of Japanese holdings to cover half the Pacific and its islands, as well as huge sections of eastern Asia, and the long struggle to push the Japanese back to their homeland and defeat them by the summer of 1945.*

Japan, cutting Japanese oil imports by 90 per cent and producing the "crisis of the dwindling stockpile." The navy's general staff argued that reserves would last only two years; after that, the navy would lose its capability to fight. The general staff thus pressed for the capture of the oil-rich Dutch East Indies. But it felt it could not move against Dutch and British colonies in Southeast Asia without involving the United States. The navy proposed a preemptive strike against the United States, and on December 7, 1941, it bombed Pearl Harbor. This decision wagered Japan's land-based airpower, shorter supply lines, and what it saw as greater willpower against American productivity. At the Imperial Conference where the decision was taken, the navy's chief of staff compared the attack to a dangerous operation that might save the life of a critically ill patient.

THE PACIFIC WAR. Until the middle of 1942, Japanese victories were stunning. The Peal Harbor attack by naval planes was tactically brilliant: Much of the American Pacific fleet was sunk, though the aircraft carriers escaped. An equally effective blow was carried out against American airpower in the Philippines. Japanese armies swept through all of Southeast Asia. By the summer of 1942, the Japanese Empire stretched from the western Aleutian Islands south almost to Australia, and from Burma east to the Gilbert Islands in the mid-Pacific.

The tide turned at the Battle of Midway in June 1942. A month earlier, both sides had suffered equal losses in the Battle of the Coral Sea, but greater U.S. ship production made such tradeoffs unprofitable for Japan. At Midway, American planes destroyed four Japanese aircraft carriers. During the following years, U.S. submarines sank most Japanese shipping, isolating Japan from its empire. Two great island-hopping offensives brought the Allied forces within bomber range of Japan. Air raids reduced Japanese cities to ashes and industrial areas to concrete rubble and twisted girders. Atomic bombs were dropped on Hiroshima and Nagasaki on August 6 and 9, 1945. The Soviet Union attacked Japanese forces in Manchuria on August 8. The Allies' plan to invade Japan in the autumn proved unnecessary, for Japan surrendered on August 15, 1945.

Surrender: Japanese leaders aboard the U.S.S. Missouri in Tokyo Bay, September 1, 1945. [Bettmann Archive.]

Japanese Militarism and German Naziism

Some of the salient features of Japanese militarism may be revealed by a comparison with Nazi Germany. Both countries were late developers with elitest, academic bureaucracies and strong military traditions. Both had authoritarian family systems. The parliamentary systems of both were more shallowly rooted than those of England, France, or the United States. Both were stricken by the Great Depression and sought a solution in territorial expansion, justifying it in terms of being have-not nations. Both persecuted socialists and then liberals. Both were modern enough in their military services, schools, governments, and communications to implement authoritarian regimes, while their values were not modern enough or democratic enough to resist their antiparliamentary forces.

But the differences between Japan and Germany were also striking. Despite the contrast between its small educated elite and the rest of the population with only a middle school education, and despite the cultural split between the more traditional rural areas and the Westernized cities, Japan was more homogenous than Germany. It had no Catholic-Protestant split. It had no powerful Junker class, nor was its socialist movement a serious contender for political power. The political process during the 1930s was also quite different. In Germany the parliament ruled, so

that to come to power the Nazis had to win an election. They were helped by the combination of the Great Depression and a runaway inflation that destroyed the German middle class and the centrist parties along with it. But in Japan's constitutional system, the Diet was weaker. Control of the government was taken away from the Seiyūkai and Minseitō even while they continued to win elections. A part of their strength at the polls derived from the fact that Japan did not suffer from inflation and its middle class was not hurt by the Depression.

The process by which the two countries went to war was also different. In Germany, the Nazis rose as a mass party, created a totalitarian state, and then made war. The authority of the party lasted until Hitler died in a Berlin bunker. But in Japan there was neither a mass party nor a single group of leaders in continuous control of the government. And it was not the totalitarian state that made war as much as it was war that made the state totalitarian. The spiritual mobilization of the population, the implementation of controls over industry, and the formation of a nationalism was so intense that university students could be mobilized as suicide (*kamikaze*) pilots all followed the outbreak of hostilities.

The Allies depicted General Tōjō, who was prime minister and his own army minister, as the Japanese Hitler. Yet, when American planes began to bomb Japan in 1944, the elder statesmen close to the emperor removed Tōjō from office and appointed a series

	Overthrow of Tokugawa Bakufu
1853–1854	Perry obtains Treaty of Friend-ship
1858	Bakufu signs commercial treaty
1861–1863	Chōshū and Satsuma mediate
1866	Chōshū defeats bakufu army
1868	Meiji Restoration
	Nation-Building
1868–1871	Shaping a new state
1871–1873	Iwakura mission
1873–1878	Social revolution from above
1877–1878	Satsuma rebellion
1881	Promise of constitution
1889	Meiji Constitution promul-gated
1890	First Diet session
	Imperial Japan
1894–95	Sino-Japanese War
1900	Seiyūkai formed
1904–05	Russo-Japanese War
1910	Korea annexed
	Era of Party Government
1918	Hara becomes prime minister
1925	Katō becomes prime minister
1925	Universal Manhood Suffrage passed
	Militarism
1931	Japan takes Manchuria
1937	War with China
1941	Japan attacks Pearl Harbor
1945	Japan surrenders

coveted the material well-being and military power that science and industry produced in the West. They did not, to be sure, wish to become Western, for that would have denied their own cultural identity. In practice, however, it was difficult to separate what was modern from what was merely recent-Western.

We note three stages in Japan's development as the world's first non-Western modernizer. First, even prior to its contact with the modern West, it had some of the *preconditions* needed to adopt modern technology: a fairly high level of literacy, an ethic of duty and hard work, a market economy, a shift from religious to secular thought, an adequate development of bureaucracy, and political orientations in some respect resembling nationalism. These preconditions were not sufficient to produce an indigenous modernization, but they proved adequate as a base for an "external modernization."

Second, after 1868 Japan *Westernized*. The Meiji leaders introduced a wide range of new institutions: post office, banks, custom houses, hospitals, police forces, joint stock companies, universities with faculties of science and engineering, and so on. Japanese thinkers also brought in modern ideas and values: Spencer and Guizot, Turgenev and Tolstoi, Adam Smith and Marx. Japanese painters began painting in oils; Japanese writers began experimenting with new forms.

Third, little by little Japan began to *assimilate* the ideas and institutions it had borrowed from the West. The *zaibatsu* combines were modern with the most recent technologies, yet their business organizations were unlike those of the West. The spare beauty of traditional architecture was transferred to the glass, steel, concrete, and stone of the modern. A new literature, completely Japanese yet also completely modern, appeared.

Because modernization in Japan—as analyzed in terms of the above three stages—has gone further than in any other non-Western country, it becomes a useful model. We look at India or the Islamic world and note the absence of comparable preconditions. Even after colonialism had ended, countries in these areas faced a difficult task: to create the necessary preconditions while at the same time borrowing the new technologies. The difficulty explains their limited success. In Africa the dearth of preconditions was even more pronounced.

In comparison to most of the non-Western world, the Chinese tradition was advanced. It had, like Japan, many of the preconditions for modernization: a high level of literacy, a belief in education as the means for getting ahead, the ingredients for shaping a modern nationalism, a family system that adapted well to small enterprises, and a market economy. But when it came to borrowing Western ideas and institu-

of ever-more-moderate prime ministers. The military, to be sure, continued to prosecute the war. Even after the devastation of the atomic bombs, the Imperial Conference on August 14, 1945, was split three to three over the Allied ultimatum of unconditional surrender. The emperor, saying that the unendurable must be endured, broke the deadlock. It was the only important decision that he had ever been allowed to make.

Modern East Asia in World Perspective

From the late nineteenth century, most countries in the world have attempted to become modern. They have

tions, the government by Confucian literati that had long been China's outstanding asset became its greatest liability. It took decades to topple the dynasty and to advance beyond Confucian ideas.

Then, in the maelstrom of the May Fourth Movement, intellectual changes occurred at a furious pace. But no doctrine became strong enough to provide for a stable polity—a condition for modernization. Nationalism was the common denominator of most Chinese thought. The Kuomintang drew on it at the Whampoa Academy, during the march north, and in founding the Nanking government. Yet other groups also appealed to nationalism and eventually the Chinese Communist Party (CCP) won out.

We are tempted to view the CCP cadres as a new class of literati operating the machinery of a monolithic, centralized state, with the teachings of Marx and Lenin substituted for those of Confucius and local party organization replacing the earlier gentry. But this interpretation is too simple. Communism stresses science, materialism, and class conflict. It broke with the Chinese past.

Communism in China was also modified. Marx had predicted that Socialist revolutions would break out in advanced economies where the contradictions of capitalism were sharpest. Lenin shifted the emphasis from spontaneous revolutions to the disciplined revolutionary party, the vanguard of the proletariat. He thereby changed Communism into what it has been ever since: a movement best able to seize power in backward nations. Mao Tse-tung only slightly modified Lenin's ideas in admitting progressive peasants to the proletariat. But he was more original in practice. In the absence of an industrial proletariat, Mao came to power using soldiers from China's villages and sophisticated techniques of political organization and indoctrination. Despite its low level of technology, the People's Liberation Army, the Communist equivalent of a "citizen's army," was formidable in the field. It was also modern in the sense that it did not loot and despoil the areas it occupied.

However, the organizational techniques that were so effective for the party and army were less so for economic development. Mass mobilization was no substitute for individual incentives. Consequently, modernization in China proceeded unevenly.

Suggested Readings

CHINA

P. M. COBLE, *The Shanghai Capitalists and the Nationalist Government*, 1927–1937 (1980).

L. E. EASTMAN, *The Abortive Revolution: China Under Nationalist Rule*, 1927–1937 (1974).

L. E. EASTMAN, *Seeds of Destruction: Nationalist China in War and Revolution*, 1937–1949 (1984).

M. ELVIN AND G. W. SKINNER, *The Chinese City Between Two Worlds* (1974). A study of the late Ch'ing and the Republican eras.

J. W. ESHERICK, *The Origins of the Boxer Rebellion* (1987).

J. K. FAIRBANK AND D. TWITCHETT (general eds.), *The Cambridge History of China*. Like the premodern volumes in the same series, the volumes on modern China represent a survey of what is known. Vols. 10–13 have been published, and the others will be available soon. The series is superb. Each volume contains a comprehensive bibliography.

P. A. KUHN, *Rebellion and Its Enemies in Late Imperial China; Militarization and Social Structure*, 1796–1864 (1980). A study of how the Confucian gentry saved the Manchu dynasty after the Taiping Rebellion.

J. LEVENSON, *Liang Ch'i-ch'ao and the Mind of Modern China* (1953). A classic study of a major Chinese reformer and thinker.

C. HAO, *Chinese Intellectuals in Crisis: Search for Order and Meaning*, 1890–1911 (1987).

LU HSUN, *Selected Works* (1960). Novels, stories, and other writings by modern China's greatest writer.

E. O. REISCHAUER, J. K. FAIRBANK, AND A. M. CRAIG, *East Asia: Tradition and Transformation* (1989). The most widely read text on East Asian history. Contains ample chapters on Japan, Korea, and Vietnam, as well as China.

H. Z. SCHIFFRIN, *Sun Yat-sen, Reluctant Revolutionary* (1980). A biography.

B. I. SCHWARTZ, *Chinese Communism and the Rise of Mao* (1951). A classic study of Mao, his thought, and the Chinese Communist Party prior to 1949.

B. I. SCHWARTZ, *In Search of Wealth and Power: Yen Fu and the West* (1964). Study of a late-nineteenth-century thinker who introduced Western ideas into China.

J. D. SPENCE, *The Gate of Heavenly Peace: The Chinese and Their Revolution*, 1895–1980 (1981). Historical reflections on twentieth-century China.

S. Y. TENG AND J. K. FAIRBANK, *China's Response to the West* (1954). Translations from Chinese thinkers and political figures, with commentaries.

T. H. WHITE AND A. JACOBY, *Thunder Out of China* (1946). A view of China during World War II by two who were there.

JAPAN

G. C. ALLEN, *A Short Economic History of Modern Japan* (1958).

W. G. BEASLEY, *Japanese Imperialism*, 1894–1945 (1987).

G. M. BERGER, *Parties out of Power in Japan*, 1931–1941 (1977). An analysis of the condition of political parties during the militarist era.

A. M. CRAIG, *Chōshū in the Meiji Restoration* (1961). A study of the Chōshū domain during the period from 1840 to 1868.

P. DUUS, *Party Rivalry and Political Change in Taisho Japan* (1968). A study of political change in Japan during the 1910s and 1920s.

P. DUUS (ed.), *The Cambridge History of Japan, Vol. 6: The Twentieth Century* (1988).

Y. Fukuzawa, *Autobiography* (1966). Japan's leading nineteenth-century thinker tells of his life and of the birth of modern Japan.

Carol N. Gluck, *Japan's Modern Myths: Ideology in the Late Meiji Period* (1988).

A. Gordon, *The Evolution of Labor Relations in Japan: Heavy Industry, 853–1955* (1985).

T. R. H. Havens, *The Valley of Darkness: The Japanese People and World War II* (1978).

A. Iriye, *After Imperialism: The Search for a New Order in the Far East, 1921–1931* (1965). (See also other works by the same author.)

D. Keene (ed.), *Modern Japanese Literature, An Anthology* (1960). A collection of modern Japanese short stories and excerpts from novels.

J. W. Morley (ed.), *The China Quagmire* (1983). A study of Japan's expansion on the continent between 1933 and 1941. (See also other works on diplomatic history by the same author.)

R. H. Myers and M. R. Peattie (eds.), *The Japanese Colonial Empire, 1895–1945* (1984).

T. Najita, *Hara Kei in the Politics of Compromise, 1905–1915* (1967). A study of one of Japan's greatest party leaders.

K. Ohkawa and H. Rosovsky, *Japanese Economic Growth: Trend Acceleration in the Twentieth Century* (1973).

R. H. Spector, *Eagle Against the Sun: The American War with Japan* (1985).

*Bismarck and the young Kaiser William II in 1888. The two disagreed over many is-
sues, and in 1890 William dismissed the aged chancellor. [German Information Center.]*

33 Imperialism, Alliances, and World War I

During the second half of the nineteenth century, and especially after 1870, European influence and control over the rest of the world grew to an unprecedented degree. North and South America, as well as Australia and New Zealand, became almost integral parts of the European world as the great streams of European immigrants populated them. Until the nineteenth century, Asia (with the significant exception of India) and most of Africa had gone their own ways, having little contact with Europe. But the latter part of that century brought the partition of Africa among a number of European nations as well as the establishment of European economic and political power from the eastern to the western borders of Asia. By the next century, this growth of European dominance had brought every part of the globe into a single world economy and had made events in any corner of the world significant thousands of miles away.

Expansion of European Power and the "New Imperialism"

The explosive developments in nineteenth-century science, technology, industry, agriculture, transportation, communication, and military weapons provided the chief sources of European power. They made it possible for a small number of Europeans (or Americans) to impose their will on other peoples many times their number by force or by the threat of force. Institutional as well as material advantages allowed Westerners to have their way. The growth of national states that commanded the loyalty, service, and resources of their inhabitants to a degree previously unknown was a Western phenomenon. It permitted the European nations to deploy their resources in the most effective way. The Europeans also possessed another, less tangible weapon: a sense of superiority of their civiliza-

919

1880

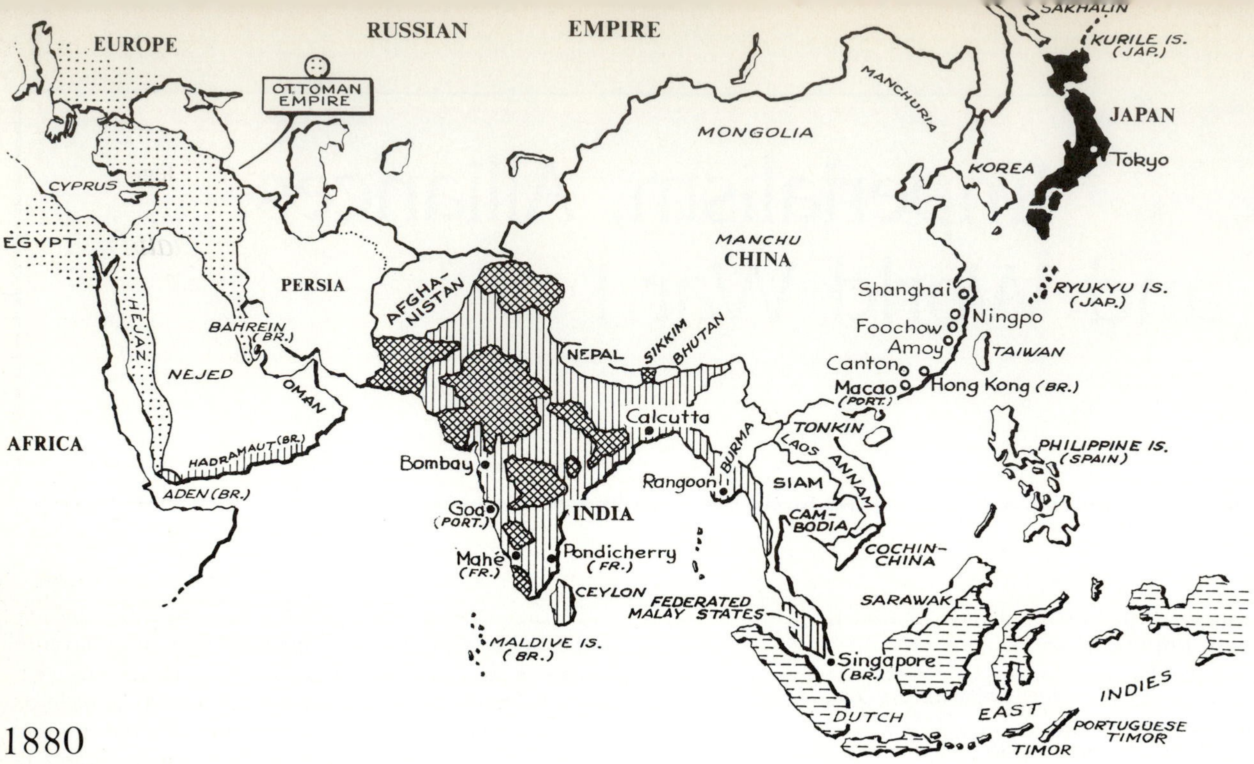

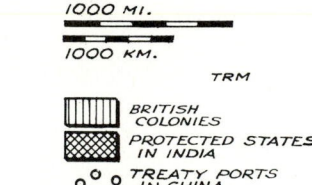

MAP 33-1 ASIA 1880–1914 *As in Africa, the decades before World War I saw imperialism spread widely and rapidly in Asia. Two new powers, Japan and the United States joined the British, French, and Dutch in extending control both to islands and to mainland and in exploiting an enfeebled China.*

1914

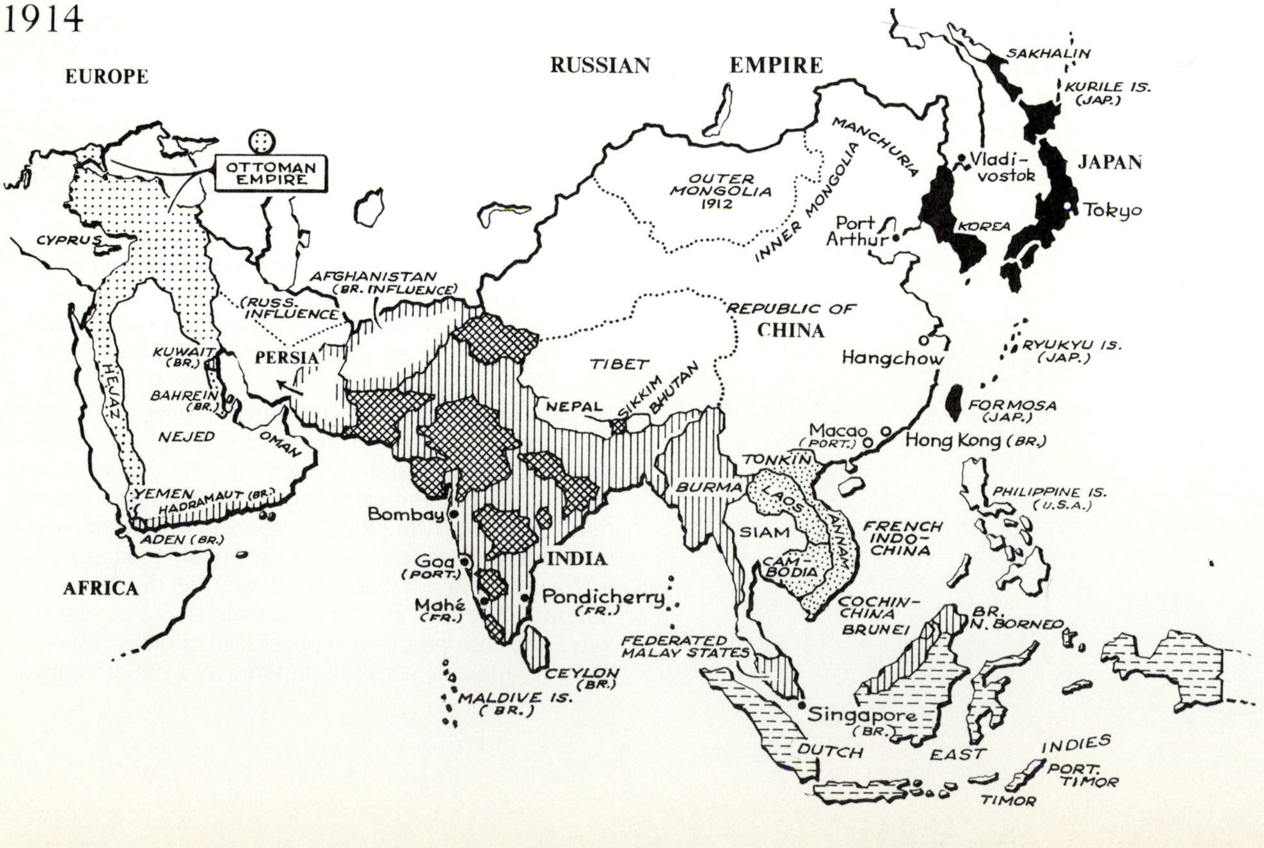

tion and way of life. This gave them a confidence that often took the form of an unpleasant arrogance and that fostered the expansionist mood.

The expansion of European influence was not anything new. Spain, Portugal, France, and Britain had controlled territories overseas for centuries, but by the mid-nineteenth century only Great Britain retained extensive holdings. The first half of the century was generally a period of hostility to colonial expansion. Even the British had been sobered by their loss of the American colonies. The French acquired Algeria and part of Indochina, and the British made some additional gains in territories adjacent to their holdings in Canada, India, Australia, and New Zealand. For the most part, however, the doctrine of free trade was dominant, and it opposed the idea of political interference in other lands.

In the last third of the century, however, the European states swiftly spread their control over perhaps 10 million square miles and 150 million people, about a fifth of the world's land area and a tenth of its population. The movement has been called the *New Imperialism.*

The New Imperialism

Imperialism is a word that has come to be used so loosely as almost to be deprived of meaning. It may be useful to offer a definition that might be widely accepted: "The policy of extending a nation's authority by territorial acquisition or by the establishment of economic and political hegemony over other nations."[1] Previous imperialisms had taken the form either of seizing land and settling it with the conqueror's people or of establishing trading centers to exploit the resources of the dominated area. The New Imperialism did not completely abandon these devices, but it introduced new ones.

The usual pattern of the New Imperialism was for the European nation to invest capital in the "backward" country—to build productive enterprises and improved means of transportation, to employ great numbers of natives in the process—and thereby to transform the entire economy and culture of the dominated area. To guarantee their investments, the European states would make favorable arrangements with the local government either by enriching the rulers or by threatening them. If these arrangements proved inadequate, the dominant power established different degrees of political control. These ranged from full annexation as a colony to protectorate status (whereby the local ruler was controlled by the dominant European state and maintained by its military power), to "spheres-of-influence" status (whereby the European state received special commercial and legal privileges without direct political involvement).

Motives for the New Imperialism: The Economic Interpretation

There has been considerable debate about the motives for the New Imperialism, and after more than a century there is still no agreement. The most widespread interpretation has been economic, most typically in the form given by the English radical economist J. A. Hobson and later adapted by Lenin. As Lenin put it, "Imperialism is the monopoly stage of capitalism,"[2] the last stage of a dying capitalist system. According to this interpretation, competition inevitably leads to the elimination of inefficient capitalists and, therefore, to monopoly. Powerful industrial and financial capitalists soon run out of profitable areas of investment in their own countries and persuade their governments to gain colonies in "backward" countries. Here they can find higher profits from their investments, new markets for their products, and safe sources of the needed raw materials.

The facts of the matter do not support this viewpoint. The European powers did export considerable amounts of capital in the form of investments abroad, but not in such a manner as to fit the model of Hobson and Lenin. Britain, for example, made heavier investments abroad before 1875 than during the next two decades. Only a very small percentage of British and European investments overseas, moreover, went to the new colonial areas. Most went into Europe itself or into older, well-established areas like the United States, Canada, Australia, and New Zealand. Even when investments were made in the new areas, they were not necessarily put into colonies held by the investing country.

The facts are equally discouraging for those who emphasize the need for markets and raw materials. Colonies were not usually important markets for the great imperial nations, and all were forced to rely on areas that they did not control as sources of vital raw materials. It is not even clear that control of the new colonies was particularly profitable. Some individuals and companies, of course, were able to make great profits from particular colonial ventures, but such people were able to influence national policy only occasionally. Economic motives certainly played a part, but a full understanding of the New Imperialism requires a search for further motives as well.

[1]*American Heritage Dictionary of the English Language* (New York: Houghton Mifflin, 1969), p. 660.

[2]V. I. Lenin, *Imperialism, the Highest Stage of Capitalism* (New York: International Publishers, 1939), p. 88.

Cultural, Religious, and Social Interpretations

Advocates of imperialism put forth various justifications for their practices. Some argued that it was the responsibility of the advanced European nations to bring the benefits of their higher culture and superior civilization to the people of "backward" lands. Few people were influenced by such arrogant arguments, though many shared the intellectual assumptions. Religious groups argued for the responsibility of Western nations to bring the benefits of Christianity to the heathen with more extensive efforts and aid from their governments. Some politicians and diplomats argued for imperialism as a tool of social policy. In Germany, for instance, some people suggested that imperial expansion might serve to deflect public interest away from domestic politics and social reform. But Germany acquired only a few colonies, and such considerations played little if any role. Another common and apparently plausible justification was that colonies would provide a good place to settle surplus population. In fact, most European emigrants went to areas not controlled by their countries, chiefly to North and South America and Australia.

Strategic and Political Interpretations: The Scramble for Africa

Strategic and political considerations seem to have been more important in bringing on the New Imperialism. The scramble for Africa in the 1880s is one example. Britain was the only great power with extensive overseas holdings on the eve of the scramble. The completion of the Suez Canal in 1869 made Egypt an area of vital interest to the British because it sat astride the shortest route to India. Under Disraeli, Britain purchased a major, but not a controlling, interest in the canal in 1875. When Egypt's stability was threatened by internal troubles in the 1880s, the British moved in and established a protectorate. Then, to protect Egypt, they advanced into the Sudan.

France became involved in Africa in 1830 by sending

In this picture based on his own sketch, Henry M. Stanley (1841–1904), arrives at an African village. Stanley was an explorer-adventurer sent in 1871 by the New York Herald to what was then called "darkest Africa" to find the supposedly lost missionary, David Livingston. The travels of these two men in Africa exemplify the motives that led westerners to explore the African interior. [Radio Times Hulton Picture Library.]

Kipling Advises the Americans: The Responsibility for Empire

After the Spanish-American War in 1898, the U.S. acquired control of the Philippine Islands. The poet Rudyard Kipling, a defender of British Imperialism, urged the Americans to take up the work of empire, too.

THE WHITE MAN'S BURDEN
1899
(The United States and the Philippine Islands)

Take up the White Man's burden—
    Send forth the best ye breed—
Go bind your sons to exile
    To serve your captives' need;
To wait in heavy harness
    On fluttered folk and wild—
Your new-caught, sullen peoples,
    Half devil and half child.

Take up the White Man's burden—
    The savage wars of peace—
Fill full the mouth of Famine
    And bid the sickness cease;
And when your goal is nearest
    The end for others sought,
Watch Sloth and heathen Folly
    Bring all your hope to nought.

Take up the White Man's burden—
    And reap his old reward:
The blame of those ye better,
    The hate of those ye guard—
The cry of hosts ye humour
    (Ah, slowly!) toward the light:—
"Why brought ye us from bondage,
    "Our loved Egyptian night?"

Take up the White Man's burden—
    In patience to abide,

To veil the threat of terror
    And check the show of pride;
By open speech and simple,
    An hundred times made plain,
To seek another's profit,
    And work another's gain.

Take up the White Man's burden—
    No tawdry rule of kings,
But toil of serf and sweeper—
    The tale of common things.
The ports ye shall not enter,
    The roads ye shall not tread,
Go make them with your living,
    And mark them with your dead!

Take up the White Man's burden—
    Ye dare not stoop to less—
Nor call too loud on Freedom
    To cloak your weariness;
By all ye cry or whisper,
    By all ye leave or do,
The silent, sullen peoples
    Shall weigh your Gods and you.

Take up the White Man's burden—
    Have done with childish days—
The lightly proffered laurel,
    The easy, ungrudged praise.
Comes now, to search your manhood
    Through all the thankless years,
Cold-edged with dear-bought wisdom,
    The judgment of your peers!

❑

"The White Man's Burden (1899)," from *Rudyard Kipling's Verse: Definitive Edition* (New York: Doubleday, 1940) pp. 321–323.

a naval expedition to Algeria to attack the pirates based there. Before long, French settlers arrived and established a colony. By 1882 France was in full control of Algeria, and at about the same time, to prevent Tunisia from falling into Italy's hands, France took over that area of North Africa also. Soon lesser states like Belgium, Portugal, Spain, and Italy were scrambling for African colonies. By the 1890s, their intervention had compelled Britain to expand northward from the Cape of Good Hope into what is now Zimbabwe. Britain may have had significant strategic reasons for protecting the Suez and Cape routes to India, but France and the smaller European nations did not have

such reasons. Their motives were political as well as economic, for they equated status as a great power (Britain stood as the chief model) with the possession of colonies. They therefore sought colonies as evidence of their own importance.

Bismarck appears to have pursued an imperial policy, however brief, from coldly political motives. In 1884 and 1885, Germany declared protectorates over Southwest Africa, Togoland, the Cameroons, and East Africa. None of these places was particularly valuable or of intrinsic strategic importance. He acquired colonies chiefly to improve Germany's diplomatic position in Europe, and tried to turn France from hostility against Germany by diverting the French toward colonial interests. At the same time, German colonies in Africa could be used as a subtle weapon with which to persuade the British to be reasonable.

The Irrational Element

Germany's annexations started a wild scramble by the other European powers to establish claims on what was left of Africa. By 1890, almost all of the continent was parceled out. Great powers and small expanded into areas neither profitable nor strategic for reasons less calculating and rational than Bismarck's. "Empire in the modern period," D. K. Fieldhouse observed, "was the product of European power: its reward was power or the sense of power."[3]

Such motives were not new. They had been well understood by the Athenian spokesman at Melos in 416 B.C., whose words were reported by Thucydides: "Of the gods we believe and of men we know clearly that by a necessity of their nature where they have the power they rule."

In Asia the emergence of Japan as a great power in touch with the rest of the world frightened the other powers interested in China. The Russians were building a railroad across Siberia to Vladivostok and were afraid of any power that might threaten Manchuria. Together with France and Germany, they applied diplomatic pressure that forced Japan out of the Liaotung Peninsula and its harbor, Port Arthur; all pressed feverishly for concessions in China. Fearing that China, its markets, and its investment opportunities would soon be closed to its citizens, the United States in 1899 proposed the "Open Door Policy." This policy opposed foreign annexations in China and allowed entrepreneurs of all nations to trade there on equal terms. The support of Britain helped win acceptance of the policy by all the powers except Russia.

The United States had only recently emerged as a force in international affairs. Victory in the Spanish-American War of 1898 brought the United States an informal protectorate over Cuba and the annexation of Puerto Rico; it thus drove Spain completely out of the Western Hemisphere. The Americans also purchased the Philippine Islands and Guam, and Germany acquired the other Spanish islands in the Pacific. The Americans and the Germans also divided Samoa between them. What was left of the Pacific islands was soon taken by France and England. Hawaii had been under American influence for some time and had been asking for annexation, which was accomplished in 1898. This outburst of activity after the Spanish war made the United States an imperial and Pacific power.

Soon after the turn of the century, most of the world

---

[3] D. K. Fieldhouse, *The Colonial Empires* (New York: Delacorte, 1966), p. 393.

had come under the control of the industrialized Western nations. The one remaining area of great vulnerability was the Ottoman Empire, but its fate was closely tied up with European developments and must be treated in that context.

Emergence of the German Empire

Formation of the Triple Alliance (1873–1890)

Prussia's victories over Austria and France and its creation of a large, powerful German Empire in 1871 revolutionized European diplomacy. The sudden appearance of a vast new political unit that brought together the majority of the German people to form a nation of great and growing population, wealth, industrial capacity, and military power posed new problems.

The balance of power created at the Congress of Vienna was altered radically. Britain retained its position and so did Russia, even though it was somewhat weakened by the Crimean War. Austria, however, had fallen quite a distance, and its position was destined to deteriorate further as the forces of nationalism threatened to disintegrate the Austro-Hungarian Empire. French power and prestige were badly damaged by the Franco-Prussian War and the German annexation of Alsace-Lorraine. The weakened French were afraid of their powerful new neighbor. At the same time, they were resentful of the defeat, the loss of territory and population, and the loss of their traditional position of dominance in western Europe.

Until 1890, Bismarck continued to guide German policy. He insisted after 1871 that Germany was a satisfied power and wanted no further territorial gains, and he meant it. He only wanted to consolidate the new international situation by avoiding a new war that might undo his achievement. Aware of French resentment, he tried to assuage it by friendly relations and by supporting French colonial aspirations in order to turn French attention away from European discontents. At the same time, he prepared for the worst. If France could not be conciliated, it must be isolated. The kernel of Bismarck's policy was to prevent an alliance between France and any other European power—especially Austria or Russia—that would threaten Germany with a war on two fronts.

WAR IN THE BALKANS. Bismarck's first move was to establish the Three Emperors' League in 1873. It brought together the three great conservative empires of Germany, Austria, and Russia. The league soon collapsed as a result of the Russo-Turkish War, which broke out in 1875 because of an uprising in the

Ottoman Balkan provinces of Bosnia and Herzegovina. The tottering Ottoman Empire was held together chiefly by the competing aims of those powers who awaited its demise. The weakness of the Ottoman Empire encouraged Serbia and Montenegro to come to the aid of their fellow Slavs. Soon the rebellion spread to Bulgaria.

Then Russia entered the fray and turned the situation into a major international crisis. The Russians hoped to pursue their traditional policy of expansion at Ottoman expense and especially hoped to achieve their most cherished goal: control of Constantinople and the Dardanelles. The Russian intervention also reflected the influence of the Pan-Slavic movement, which sought to bring together all the Slavic peoples, even those under Austrian or Ottoman rule, under the protection of Holy Mother Russia.

The Ottoman Empire was weak, and before long it was forced to ask for peace. The Treaty of San Stefano of March 1878 was a Russian triumph. The Slavic states in the Balkans were freed of Ottoman rule, and Russia itself obtained territorial gains and a heavy monetary indemnity. But the Russian victory was not lasting. The other great powers were alarmed by the terms of the settlement. Austria feared that the great Slavic victory and the powerful increase in Russian influence in the Balkans would cause dangerous shock waves in its own Balkan provinces. The British were alarmed by the damage the Russian victory would do to the European balance of power and especially by the thought of possible Russian control of the Dardanelles. Disraeli was determined to resist, and British public opinion supported him. A music-hall song that became popular gave the language a new word for superpatriotism: *jingoism*.

> We don't want to fight,
> But by jingo if we do,
> We've got the men,
> We've got the ships,
> We've got the money too!

THE CONGRESS OF BERLIN. Even before the Treaty of San Stefano, Disraeli sent a fleet to Constantinople. After the magnitude of Russia's appetite was known, Britain and Austria forced Russia to agree to an international conference at which the provisions of the treaty would be reviewed by the other great powers. The resulting Congress of Berlin met in June and July of 1878 under the presidency of Bismarck.

The decisions of the Congress were a blow to Russian ambitions. Bulgaria was reduced in size by two thirds and was deprived of access to the Aegean Sea. Austria-Hungary was given Bosnia and Herzegovina to "occupy and administer," although those provinces remained formally under Ottoman rule. Britain received Cyprus, and France gained permission to expand into Tunisia. These privileges were compensation for the gains that Russia was permitted to keep. Germany asked for nothing but got little credit from Russia for its restraint. The Russians were bitterly disappointed, and the Three Emperors' League was dead.

The major trouble spot now was in the south Slavic states of Serbia and Montenegro. They deeply resented the Austrian occupation of Bosnia and Herzegovina, as did many of the natives of those provinces. The south Slavic question, no less than the estrangement between Russia and Germany, was a threat to the peace of Europe.

GERMAN ALLIANCES WITH RUSSIA AND AUSTRIA. For the moment, Bismarck could ignore the Balkans, but he could not ignore the breach in his eastern alliance system. With Russia alienated, he turned to Austria and concluded a secret treaty in 1879. The resulting Dual Alliance provided that if either Germany or Austria were attacked by Russia, the ally would help the attacked party. If the signatory countries were attacked by someone else, each promised at least to maintain neutrality. The treaty was for five years and was renewed regularly until 1918. As the central point in German policy, it was criticized at the time, and some have judged it mistaken in retrospect. It appeared to tie the German fortunes to those of the troubled Austro-Hungarian Empire and in that way to borrow trouble. At the same time, by isolating the Russians, it pushed them in the direction of seeking alliances in the West.

Bismarck was fully aware of these dangers but discounted them with good reason. At no time did he allow his Austrian alliance to drag Germany into Austria's Balkan quarrels. He made it clear to the Austrians that the alliance was purely defensive and that Germany would never be a party to an attack on Russia.

Bismarck expected the news of the Austro-German negotiations to frighten Russia into seeking closer relations with Germany, and he was right. Russian diplomats soon approached him, and by 1881 he had concluded a renewal of the Three Emperors' League on a firmer basis. Though it did not put an end to such conflicts, it was a significant step toward peace.

THE TRIPLE ALLIANCE. In 1882, Italy, ambitious for colonial expansion and annoyed by the French preemption of Tunisia, asked to join the Dual Alliance. At this point, Bismarck's policy was a complete success. He was allied with three of the great powers and friendly with the other, Great Britain, which held aloof from all alliances. France was isolated and no threat. Although the Three Emperors' League was allowed to

	GREAT BRITAIN	FRANCE	ITALY	RUSSIA	BELGIUM	ROMANIA	GREECE
POPULATION (TOTAL)	OVERSEAS EMP. 390 MILLION / 45 000 000	OVERSEAS EMP. 58 MILLION / 40 000 000	OVERSEAS EMP. 2 MILLION / 35 000 000	164 000 000	7 500 000	7 500 000	5 000 000
SOLDIERS POTENTIALLY AVAILABLE	711 000	1 250 000	750 000	1 200 000	180 000	420 000	120 000
MILITARY EXPENDITURES 1913–1914 (MILLIONS OF $)	250 000 000	185 000 000	50 000 000	335 000 000	13 750 000	15 000 000	3 750 000
BATTLESHIPS IN SERVICE OR BEING BUILT	64	28	14	16			
CRUISERS	121	34	22	14			
SUBMARINES	64	73	12	29			
MERCHANT SHIPS MILLIONS OF TONS	20 000 000	2 000 000	1 750 000	750 000			

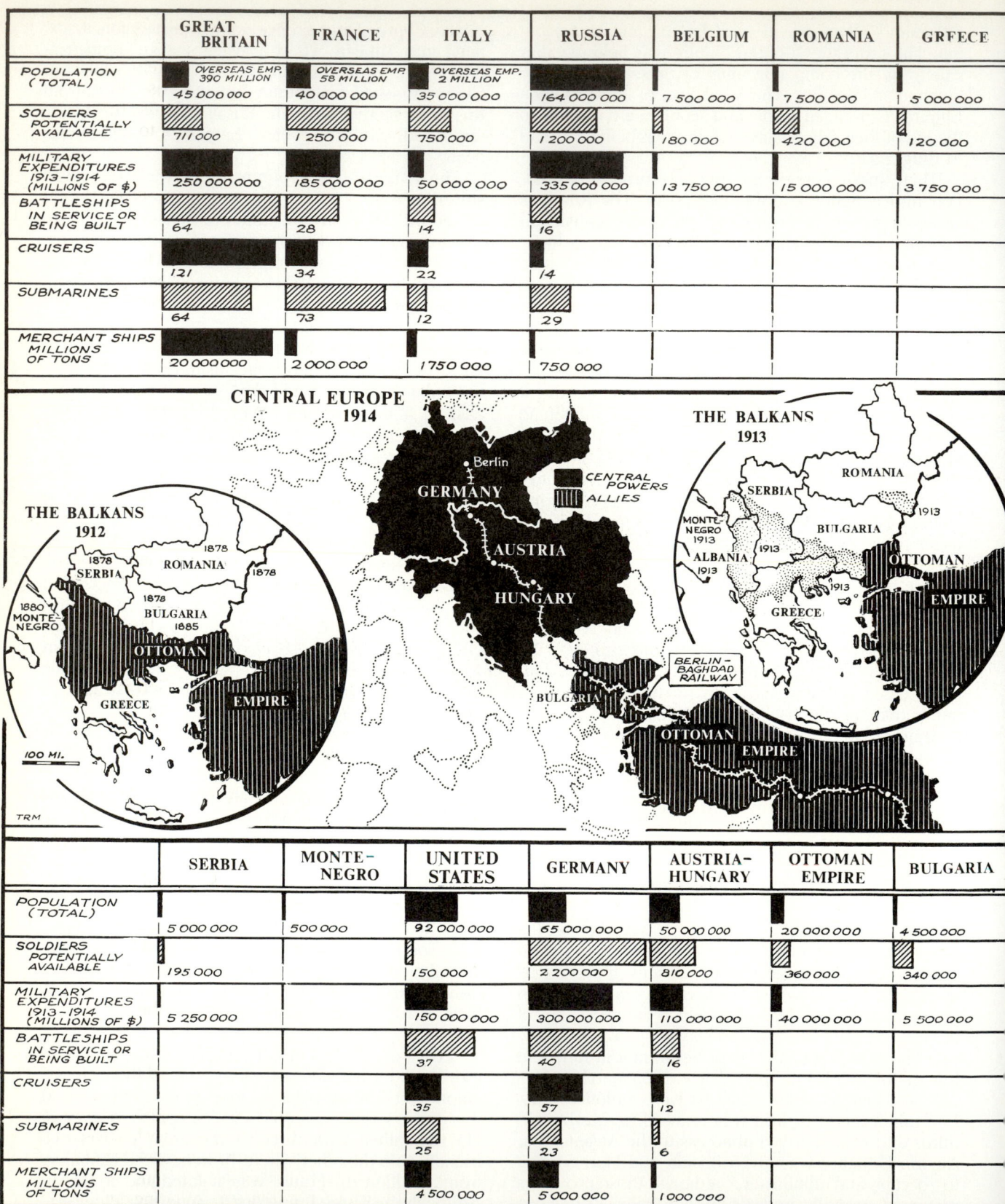

CENTRAL EUROPE 1914

CENTRAL POWERS
ALLIES

Berlin

GERMANY

AUSTRIA

HUNGARY

BULGARIA

OTTOMAN EMPIRE

THE BALKANS 1912

1878
1878
SERBIA
ROMANIA
1878
1880 MONTE-NEGRO
BULGARIA 1885
OTTOMAN
GREECE
EMPIRE

100 MI.

TRM

THE BALKANS 1913

ROMANIA

SERBIA

MONTE-NEGRO 1913

ALBANIA 1913

BULGARIA

1913

GREECE

OTTOMAN EMPIRE

1913

BERLIN – BAGHDAD RAILWAY

	SERBIA	MONTE-NEGRO	UNITED STATES	GERMANY	AUSTRIA-HUNGARY	OTTOMAN EMPIRE	BULGARIA
POPULATION (TOTAL)	5 000 000	500 000	92 000 000	65 000 000	50 000 000	20 000 000	4 500 000
SOLDIERS POTENTIALLY AVAILABLE	195 000		150 000	2 200 000	810 000	360 000	340 000
MILITARY EXPENDITURES 1913–1914 (MILLIONS OF $)	5 250 000		150 000 000	300 000 000	110 000 000	40 000 000	5 500 000
BATTLESHIPS IN SERVICE OR BEING BUILT			37	40	16		
CRUISERS			35	57	12		
SUBMARINES			25	23	6		
MERCHANT SHIPS MILLIONS OF TONS			4 500 000	5 000 000	1 000 000		

OPPOSITE: MAP 33-2 THE BALKANS 1912–1913 *Two maps show the Balkans before and after the two Balkan wars; note the Ottoman retreat. In the center we see the geographical relationship of the Central Powers and their Bulgarian and Turkish allies. Tables give relative strength of World War I combatants.*

lapse, the Triple Alliance (Germany, Austria, and Italy) was renewed for another five years. To restore German relations with Russia, Bismarck negotiated the Reinsurance Treaty in 1887, in which both powers promised to remain neutral if either was attacked. All seemed smooth, but a change in the German monarchy soon overturned everything.

In 1888, William II (1888–1918) came to the German throne. Like many Germans of his generation, William II was filled with a sense of Germany's destiny as the leading power of Europe. To achieve a "place in the sun," he and his contemporaries wanted a navy and colonies like Britain's. These aims, of course, ran counter to Bismarck's limited continental policy. In 1890, William used a disagreement over domestic policy to dismiss Bismarck.

During Bismarck's time, Germany was a force for European peace and was increasingly understood to be so. This position would not, of course, have been possible without its great military power. But it also required the leadership of a statesman who was willing and able to exercise restraint and who could make a realistic estimate of what his country needed and what was possible.

Forging of the Triple Entente (1890–1907)

FRANCO-RUSSIAN ALLIANCE. Almost immediately after Bismarck's retirement, his system of alliances collapsed. His successor was General Leo von Caprivi (1831–1899), who refused the Russian request to renew the Reinsurance Treaty. Political isolation and the need for foreign capital unexpectedly drove the Russians toward France. The French, who were even more isolated, were glad to encourage their investors to pour capital into Russia if it would help produce an alliance and security against Germany. In 1894, the Franco-Russian alliance against Germany was signed.

BRITAIN AND GERMANY. Britain now became the key to the international situation. Colonial rivalries pitted the British against the Russians in Central Asia and against the French in Africa. Traditionally, Britain had also opposed Russian control of Constantinople and the Dardanelles and French control of the Low Countries. There was no reason to think that Britain would soon become friendly to its traditional rivals or abandon its accustomed friendliness toward the Germans. Yet, within a decade of William II's accession, Germany had become the enemy in the minds of the British. The problem lay in the foreign and naval policies of the German emperor and his ministers.

At first, Germany tried to win the British over to the Triple Alliance, but when Britain clung to its policy of "splendid isolation," German policy took a different tack. The idea was to demonstrate Germany's worthiness as an ally by withdrawing support and even making trouble for Britain.

The Germans began to exert pressure against Britain in Africa by barring British attempts to build a railroad from Capetown to Cairo. They also openly sympathized with the Boers of South Africa in their resistance to British expansion. In 1896, William insulted the British by sending a congratulatory telegram to Paul Kruger (1825–1904), president of the Transvaal, for repulsing a British raid "without having to appeal to friendly powers for assistance."

In 1898, William's dream of a German navy began to achieve reality with the passage of a naval law providing for nineteen battleships. In 1900, a second law doubled that figure. The architect of the new navy was Admiral Alfred von Tirpitz (1849–1930), who openly proclaimed that Germany's naval policy was aimed at Britain. His "risk" theory argued that Germany could build a fleet strong enough, not to defeat the British, but to do sufficient damage to make the British navy inferior to that of other powers like France or the United States. The threat posed by the German navy did more to antagonize British opinion than anything else. As the German navy grew and German policies seemed to become more threatening, the British were alarmed enough to abandon their traditional attitudes and policies.

THE ENTENTE CORDIALE. The first breach in Britain's isolation came in 1902, when an alliance was concluded with Japan to relieve the pressure of defending British interests in the Far East against Russia. Next Britain abandoned its traditional antagonism toward France and in 1904 concluded a series of agreements with the French, collectively called the *Entente Cordiale*. It was not a formal treaty and had no military provisions, but it settled all outstanding colonial differences between the two nations. The Entente Cordiale was a long step toward aligning the British with Germany's great potential enemy.

Britain's new relationship with France was surprising. But in 1904, hardly anyone believed that the British whale and the Russian bear would ever come together. The Russo-Japanese war of 1904–1905 made such a development seem even less likely because Britain was allied with Russia's enemy. But Britain had behaved with restraint, and the Russians were chastened by their unexpected and humiliating defeat. The defeat had also led to the Russian Revolution of 1905. Although the revolution was put down, it left Russia weak and reduced British apprehensions in that direction. At the same time, the British were concerned that Russia might again drift into the German orbit.

THE FIRST MOROCCAN CRISIS. At this point, Germany decided to test the new understanding between Britain and France and to press for colonial gains. In March 1905, Emperor William II landed at Tangier, challenged the French protectorate there in a speech in favor of Moroccan independence—and by implication asserted Germany's right to participate in Morocco's destiny. Germany's chancellor, Prince Bernhard von Bülow (1849–1929), intended to show France how weak it was and how little it could expect from Britain and at the same time he hoped to gain significant colonial concessions for Germany.

The Germans might well have achieved their aims and driven a wedge between France and Britain. However, they pushed too far and demanded an international conference to show their power more dramatically. The conference met in 1906 at Algeciras in Spain. Austria sided with its German ally, but Spain, Italy, and the United States voted with Britain and France. The Germans had overplayed their hand, receiving trivial concessions, and the French were confirmed in their position in Morocco. German bullying had, moreover, driven Britain and France closer together. In the face of a possible German attack on France, Sir Edward Grey, the British foreign secretary, without making a firm commitment, authorized conversations between the British and the French general staffs. Their agreements became morally binding as the years passed. By 1914, French and British military and naval plans were so mutually dependent that they were effectively, if not formally, allies.

BRITISH AGREEMENT WITH RUSSIA. Britain's fear of Germany and its closer relations with France made it desirable for Britain to become more friendly with France's ally, Russia. With French support, the British made overtures to the Russians and in 1907 concluded an agreement with them much like the Entente Cordiale with France. It settled Russo-British quarrels in Central Asia and opened the door for wider cooperation. The Triple Entente, an informal but powerful association of Britain, France, and Russia, was now ranged against the Triple Alliance. Because Italy was unreliable, Germany and Austria-Hungary stood surrounded by two great land powers and Great Britain.

William II and his ministers had turned Bismarck's nightmare of the prospect of a two-front war with France and Russia into a reality and had made it more horrible by adding Britain to the hostile coalition. Bismarck's alliance system had been intended to maintain peace, but the new one increased the risk of war and made the Balkans a likely spot for it to break out. Bismarck's diplomacy had left France isolated and impotent; the new arrangement found France associated with the two greatest powers in Europe apart from Germany. The Germans could rely only on Austria, and such was the condition of that troubled empire that it was less likely to provide aid than to need it.

World War I

The Road to War (1908–1914)

The situation in the Balkans in the first decade of this century was exceedingly complicated. The weak Ottoman Empire controlled the central strip running west from Constantinople to the Adriatic. North and south of it were the independent states of Romania, Serbia, and Greece, as well as Bulgaria, technically still part of the empire but legally autonomous and practically independent. The Austro-Hungarian Empire included Croatia and Slovenia and since 1878 had "occupied and administered" Bosnia and Herzegovina.

With the exception of the Greeks and the Romanians, most of the inhabitants of the Balkans spoke variants of the same Slavic language and felt a cultural and historical kinship with one another. For centuries they had been ruled by Austrians, Hungarians, or Turks, and the growing nationalism that characterized late-nineteenth-century Europe made many of them eager for liberty. The more radical among them longed for a union of the south Slavic, or Yugoslav, peoples in a single nation. They looked to independent Serbia as the center of the new nation and hoped to detach all the Slavic provinces (especially Bosnia, which bordered on Serbia) from Austria. In this regard, Serbia was to unite the Slavs at the expense of Austria, as Piedmont had united the Italians and Prussia the Germans.

In 1908, a group of modernizing reformers called the *Young Turks* brought about a revolution in the Ottoman Empire. Their actions threatened to revive the life of the empire and to interfere with the plans of the European jackals preparing to pounce on the Ottoman corpse. These events brought on the first of a series of Balkan crises that would eventually lead to war.

THE BOSNIAN CRISIS. In 1908, the Austrian and Russian governments decided to act quickly before Turkey became strong enough to resist. They struck a bargain in which it was agreed that they would call an international conference where each of them would support the other's demands. Russia would agree to the Austrian annexation of Bosnia and Herzegovina, and Austria would support Russia's request to open the Dardanelles to Russian warships.

Austria, however, declared the annexation before any conference was called. The British, ever concerned about their own position in the Mediterranean, refused to agree to the Russian demand. The Russians, feeling betrayed by the British, were humiliated and furious. Their "little brothers," the Serbs, were frustrated and angered by the loss of Bosnia, which they had hoped one day to include in an independent south Slavic nation led by Serbia. The Russians were too weak to do anything but accept the new situation. The Germans had not been warned in advance of Austria's plans and were unhappy because the action threatened their relations with Russia. But Germany felt so dependent on the Dual Alliance that it assured Austria of its support. Austria had been given a free hand, and to an extent German policy was being made in Vienna. It was a dangerous precedent. At the same time, the failure of Britain and France to support Russia strained the Triple Entente and made it harder for them to oppose Russian interests again in the future if they were to retain Russian friendship.

THE SECOND MOROCCAN CRISIS. The second Moroccan crisis, in 1911, emphasized the French and British need for mutual support. When France sent in an army to put down a rebellion, Germany took the opportunity to "protect German interests" in Morocco as a means of extorting colonial concessions in the French Congo. To add force to their demands, the Germans sent the gunboat *Panther* to the port of Agadir, allegedly to protect German citizens there. Once again, as in 1905, the Germans went too far. The *Panther*'s visit to Agadir provoked a strong reaction in Britain. For some time, Anglo-German relations had been growing worse, chiefly because of the intensification of the naval race. But negotiations failed to persuade William II and Tirpitz to slow down naval construction.

In this atmosphere, the British heard of the *Panther*'s arrival in Morocco. They wrongly believed that the Germans meant to turn Agadir into a naval base on the Atlantic. The crisis passed when France yielded some insignificant bits of the Congo and Germany withdrew from Morocco. The main result was to increase British fear and hostility and to draw the Britons closer to France. Specific military plans were formulated for a British expeditionary force to defend France in case of German attack. The British and French navies agreed to cooperate. If France were attacked by Germany, Britain had to defend the French, for its own security was inextricably tied up with that of France.

WAR IN THE BALKANS. After the second Moroc-

can crisis, Italy feared that the recognition of the French protectorate in Morocco would encourage France to move into Libya. Consequently, in 1911, Italy attacked the Ottoman Empire to anticipate the French, defeated the faltering Turks, and obtained Libya and the Dodecanese Islands. The Italian victory encouraged the Balkan states to try their luck. In 1912, Bulgaria, Greece, Montenegro, and Serbia joined an attack on the Ottoman Empire and won easily. After this First Balkan War, the victors fell out among themselves. The Serbs and the Bulgarians quarreled about the division of Macedonia, and in 1913 a Second Balkan War erupted. This time, Turkey and Romania joined the other states against Bulgaria and stripped away much of what the Bulgarians had gained since 1878.

The alarmed Austrians were determined to limit Serbian gains and especially to prevent the Serbs from gaining a port on the Adriatic. An international conference sponsored by Britain in early 1913 resolved the

"The Mailed Fist of the Kaiser Strikes Agadir." This cartoon refers to the dispatch of the German gunboat Panther to Agadir in Morocco in 1911. The Germans were trying to press the French to make colonial concessions and, perhaps, to break up the Entente between the French and the British. The result, instead, was the second Moroccan crisis, which drew the Entente closer together and helped bring on World War I.

1871	The end of the Franco-Prussian War; creation of the German Empire; German annexation of Alsace-Lorraine
1873	The Three Emperors' League (Germany, Russia, and Austria-Hungary)
1875	The Russo-Turkish War
1878	The Congress of Berlin
1879	The Dual Alliance between Germany and Austria
1881	The Three Emperors' League is renewed
1882	Italy joins Germany and Austria in the Triple Alliance
1888	William II becomes the German emperor
1890	Bismarck is dismissed
1894	The Franco-Russian alliance
1898	Germany begins to build a battleship navy
1902	The British alliance with Japan
1904	The Entente Cordiale between Britain and France
1904–1905	The Russo-Japanese War
1905	The first Moroccan crisis
1907	The British agreement with Russia
1908–1909	The Bosnian crisis
1911	The second Moroccan crisis; Italy attacks Turkey
1912–1913	The First and Second Balkan Wars
1914	Outbreak of World War I

foundly influenced behavior in the final crisis of 1914. The Russians had once again, as in 1908, been embarrassed by their passivity, and their allies were more reluctant to restrain them again. The Austrians were embarrassed by what had resulted from accepting an international conference and were determined not to repeat the experience. They had seen that better results might be obtained from a threat of direct force; they and their German allies did not miss the lesson.

Sarajevo and the Outbreak of War (June–August 1914)

THE ASSASSINATION. On June 28, 1914, a young Bosnian nationalist shot and killed the Austrian Archduke Francis Ferdinand, heir to the throne, and his wife as they drove in an open car through the Bosnian capital of Sarajevo. The assassin was a member of a conspiracy hatched by a political terrorist society called *Union or Death*, better known as the *Black Hand*. A major participant in the planning and preparation of the crime was the chief of intelligence of the Serbian army's general staff. Even though his role was not actually known at the time, it was generally believed that Serbian officials were involved. The glee of the Serbian press lent support to that belief.

GERMANY AND AUSTRIA'S RESPONSE. News of the assassination produced outrage and condemnation everywhere. To those Austrians who had long favored an attack on Serbia as a solution to the empire's Slavic problem, the opportunity seemed irresistible. But it was never easy for the Dual Monarchy to make a decision. Conrad von Hötzendorf, chief of the Austrian general staff, urged an attack as he had often done before. Count Stefan Tisza, speaking for Hungary, resisted. Leopold Berchtold, the Austro-Hungarian foreign minister, felt the need for strong action, but he knew that German support would be required in the likely event that Russia should decide to intervene to protect Serbia. He also knew that nothing could be done without Tisza's approval and that only German support could persuade the Hungarians to accept the policy of war. The question of peace or war, therefore, had to be answered in Berlin.

William II and Chancellor Theobald von Bethmann-Hollweg (1856–1921) readily promised German support for an attack on Serbia. It has often been said that they gave the Austrians a "blank check," but their message was firmer than that. They urged the Austrians to move swiftly while the other powers were still angry at Serbia. They also made the Austrians feel that a failure to act would be taken as evidence of Austria-Hungary's weakness and uselessness as an ally. Therefore, the Austrians never wavered in their determination to make war on Serbia. They hoped, with the protection of Germany, to fight a limited war

matter in Austria's favor and called for an independent kingdom of Albania. But Austria felt humiliated by the public airing of Serbian demands. Then, for some time, the Serbs defied the powers and continued to occupy parts of Albania. Under Austrian pressure they withdrew, but in September 1913, after the Second Balkan War, the Serbs reoccupied sections of Albania. In mid-October Austria unilaterally issued an ultimatum to Serbia, and the latter country again withdrew its forces from Albania. During this crisis, many people in Austria had wanted an all-out attack on Serbia to remove its threat once and for all from the empire. At the same time, Pan-Slavic sentiment in Russia pressed Czar Nicholas II to take a firm stand. But Russia once again let Austria have its way in its confrontation with Serbia.

The lessons learned from this crisis of 1913 pro-

Moments after the assassination of Archduke Ferdinand and his wife the police captured one of the assassins in Sarajevo. [The Granger Collection.]

The Austrian Ambassador Gets a "Blank Check" from the Kaiser

At a meeting at Potsdam on July 5, 1914, the Austrian ambassador received from the Kaiser assurance that Germany would support Austria in the Balkans, even at the risk of war.

After lunch, when I [the Austro-Hungarian Ambassador] again called attention to the seriousness of the situation, the Kaiser authorised me to inform our gracious Majesty that we might in this case, as in all others, rely upon Germany's full support. He must, as he said before, first hear what the Imperial Chancellor has to say, but he did not doubt in the least that Herr von Bethmann-Hollweg would agree with him. Especially as far as our action against Serbia was concerned. But it was his (Kaiser Wilhelm's) opinion that this action must not be delayed. Russia's attitude will no doubt be hostile, but for this he had been for years prepared, and should a war between Austria-Hungary and Russia be unavoidable, we might be convinced that Germany, our old faithful ally, would stand at our side. Russia at the present time was in no way prepared for war, and would think twice before it appealed to arms. But it will certainly set other powers on the Triple Alliance and add fuel to the fire in the Balkans. He understands perfectly well that His Apostolic Majesty [Francis Joseph] in his well-known love of peace would be reluctant to march into Serbia; but if we had really recognised the necessity of warlike action against Serbia, he (Kaiser Wilhelm) would regret if we did not make use of the present moment, which is all in our favour. ❏

Outbreak of the World War: German Documents Collected by Karl Kautsky, ed. by Max Montgelas and Walther Schücking (New York: Carnegie Endowment for International Peace, 1924), p. 76.

that would not bring on a general European conflict. However, they were prepared to risk even the latter. The Germans also knew that they risked a general war, but they hoped to "localize" the fight between Austria and Serbia.

These calculations proved to be incorrect. Bethmann-Hollweg hoped that the Austrians would strike swiftly and present the powers with a *fait accompli* while the outrage of the assassination was still fresh. He also hoped that German support would deter Russian involvement. Failing that, he was prepared for a continental war that would bring rapid victory over France and allow a full-scale attack on the Russians, who were always slow to bring their strength into action. All of this policy depended on British neutrality, and the German chancellor convinced himself that the British could be persuaded to stand aloof.

However, the Austrians were slow to act. They did not even deliver their deliberately unacceptable ultimatum to Serbia until July 24, when the general hostility toward Serbia had begun to subside. Serbia further embarrassed the Austrians by returning so soft and conciliatory an answer that the mercurial German emperor thought it removed all reason for war. But the Austrians were determined not to turn back. On July 28, the Austrians declared war on Serbia, even though they could not put an army into the field until mid-August.

THE TRIPLE ENTENTE'S RESPONSE. The Russians, previously so often forced to back off, angrily responded to the Austrian demands on Serbia. The most conservative elements of the Russian government opposed war, fearing that it would bring on revolution as it had in 1905. But nationalists, Pan-Slavs, and most of the politically conscious classes in general demanded action. The government responded by ordering partial mobilization, against Austria only. This policy was militarily impossible, but its intention was the diplomatic one of putting pressure on Austria to hold back its attack on Serbia.

Mobilization of any kind, however, was a dangerous political weapon because it was generally understood to be equivalent to an act of war. It was especially alarming to General Helmuth von Moltke (1848–1916), head of the German general staff. The possibility that the Russians might start mobilization before the Germans could move would upset the delicate timing of Germany's only battle plan: The Schlieffen Plan required an attack on France first, and would put Germany in great danger. From this point on, Moltke pressed for German mobilization and war. The pressure of military necessity mounted until it became irresistible.

The western European powers were not eager for war. France's president and prime minister were on their way back from a visit to Russia when the crisis flared up again on July 24. The Austrians had, in fact, timed their ultimatum precisely so that these two men would be at sea at the crucial moment. Had they been at their desks, they might have attempted to restrain the Russians. But the French ambassador to Russia gave the Russians the same assurances that Germany had given its ally. The British worked hard to avoid trouble by traditional means: a conference of the powers. Austria, still smarting from its humiliation after the London Conference of 1913, would not hear of it. The Germans privately supported the Austrians but publicly took on a conciliatory tone in the hope of keeping the British neutral.

Soon, however, Bethmann-Hollweg came to realize what he should have known from the first: If Germany attacked France, Britain must fight. Until July 30, his public appeals to Austria for restraint were a sham. Thereafter, he sincerely tried to persuade the Austrians to negotiate and to avoid a general war, but it was too late. While Bethmann-Hollweg was urging restraint on the Austrians, Moltke was pressing them to act. The Austrians wondered who was in charge in Berlin, but they could not turn back without losing their own self-respect and the respect of the Germans.

On July 30, Austria ordered mobilization against Russia. Bethmann-Hollweg resisted the enormous pressure to mobilize, not because he had any further hope of avoiding war but because he wanted Russia to mobilize against Germany first and appear to be the aggressor. Only in that way could he win the support of the German nation for war, especially the pacifistic Social Democrats. His luck was good this time. The news of Russian general mobilization came only minutes before Germany would have mobilized in any case. The Schlieffen Plan went into effect. The Germans invaded Luxembourg on August 1 and Belgium on August 3. The latter invasion violated the treaty of 1839 in which the British had guaranteed Belgian neutrality. This factor undermined the considerable sentiment in Britain for neutrality and united the nation against Germany. Germany then invaded France, and on August 4 Britain declared war on Germany.

The Great War had begun. As Sir Edward Grey, the British foreign secretary, put it, the lights were going out all over Europe. They would come on again, but Europe would never be the same.

Strategies and Stalemate (1914–1917)

Throughout Europe, jubilation greeted the outbreak of war. No general war had been fought since Napoleon, and the horrors of modern warfare were not yet understood. The dominant memory was of Bismarck's swift and decisive campaigns, in which costs and casualties were light and the rewards great.

Both sides expected to take the offensive, force a

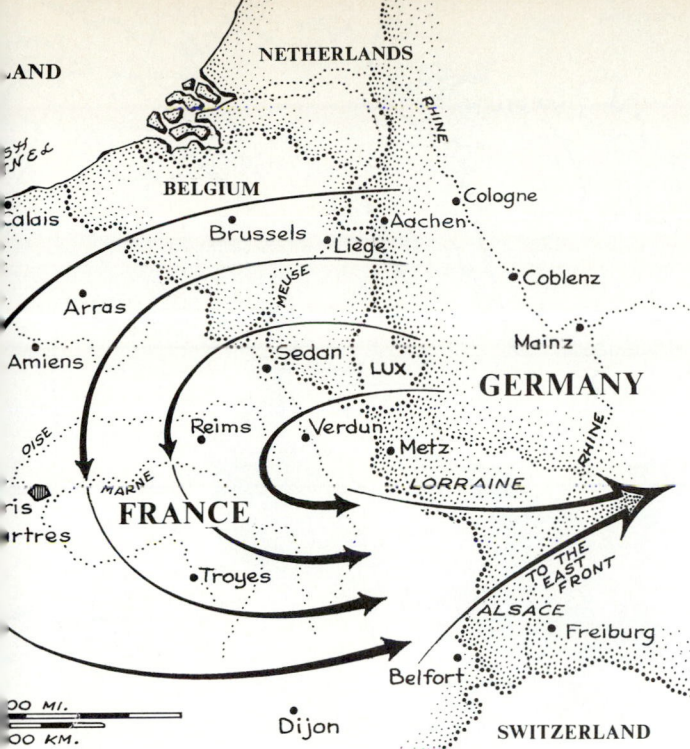

MAP 33-3 THE SCHLIEFFEN PLAN OF 1905 *Germany's grand strategy for quickly winning the war against France in 1914 is shown by the wheeling arrows on the map. The crushing blows at France were, in the original plan, to be followed by the release of troops for use against Russia on Germany's Eastern front. But the plan was not adequately implemented, and the war on the Western front became a long contest in place.*

battle on favorable ground, and win a quick victory. The Triple Entente powers—or the Allies, as they came to be called—held superiority in numbers and financial resources as well as command of the sea. Germany and Austria, the Central Powers, had the advantages of internal lines of communication and of having launched their attack first.

After 1905, Germany's only war plan was the one developed by Count Alfred von Schlieffen (1833–1913), chief of the German general staff from 1891 to 1906. It aimed at going around the French defenses by sweeping through Belgium to the Channel, then wheeling to the south and east to envelop the French and to crush them against the German fortresses in Lorraine. In the east, the Germans planned to stand on the defensive against Russia until France had been crushed, a task they thought would take only six weeks.

The apparent risk, besides the violation of Belgian neutrality and the consequent alienation of Britain, lay in weakening the German defenses against a direct attack across the frontier. Yet Schlieffen is said to have uttered the dying words, "It must come to a fight. Only make the right wing strong." The execution of his plan, however, was left to Helmuth von Moltke, the nephew

of Bismarck's most effective general. The younger Moltke was a gloomy and nervous man who lacked the talent of his illustrious uncle and the theoretical daring of Schlieffen. He added divisions to the left wing and even weakened the Russian front for the same purpose. The consequence of this hesitant strategy was the failure of the Schlieffen Plan by a narrow margin.

THE WAR IN THE WEST. The French had also put their faith in the offensive, but with less reason than the Germans. They badly underestimated the numbers and the effectiveness of the German reserves and set too much store by the importance of the courage and spirit of their troops. These proved insufficient against modern weapons, especially against the machine gun. The French offensive on Germany's western frontier failed totally. In a sense, this defeat was better than a partial success because it released troops for use against the main German army. As a result, the French and the British were able to stop the Germans at the Battle of the Marne in September 1914.

Thereafter, the nature of the war in the west changed completely and became one of position instead of movement. Both sides dug in behind a wall of trenches protected by barbed wire that stretched from the North Sea to Switzerland. Strategically placed machine-gun nests made assaults difficult and dangerous. Both sides, nonetheless, attempted massive attacks prepared for by artillery barrages of unprecedented and horrible force and duration. Still, the defense was always able to recover and to bring up reserves fast enough to prevent a breakthrough.

THE WAR IN THE EAST. In the east, the war began auspiciously for the Allies. The Russians advanced into Austrian territory and inflicted heavy casualties, but Russian incompetence and German energy soon reversed the situation. A junior German officer, Erich Ludendorff (1865–1937), under the command of the elderly General Paul von Hindenburg (1847–1934), destroyed or captured an entire army at the Battle of Tannenberg; he also defeated the Russians at the Masurian Lakes. In 1915, the Central Powers pressed their advantage in the east and drove into the Baltic states and western Russia, inflicting over two million casualties in a single year. Russian confidence was badly shaken, but the Russian army stayed in the field.

As the battle lines hardened, both sides sought new allies. Turkey (because of its hostility to Russia) and Bulgaria (the enemy of Serbia) joined the Central Powers.

Italy seemed an especially valuable prize, and both sides bid for Italian support with promises of a division of the spoils of victory. Because what the Italians wanted most was held by Austria, the Allies were able to make the more attractive promises. In a secret

WORLD WAR I IN EUROPE

T. R. MILLER

Legend:
- TRIPLE ENTENTE
- ALLIES OF THE TRIPLE ENTENTE
- CENTRAL POWERS
- ALLIES OF THE CENTRAL POWERS

WESTERN FRONT — SEE INSET

ITALIAN FRONT

BALKAN FRONT

BATTLELINE DEC., 1917

FARTHEST RUSSIAN ADVANCE 1914

BATTLELINE MAY, 1915

BRUSILOV'S OFFENSIVE AUG., 1916

250 MI.
250 KM.

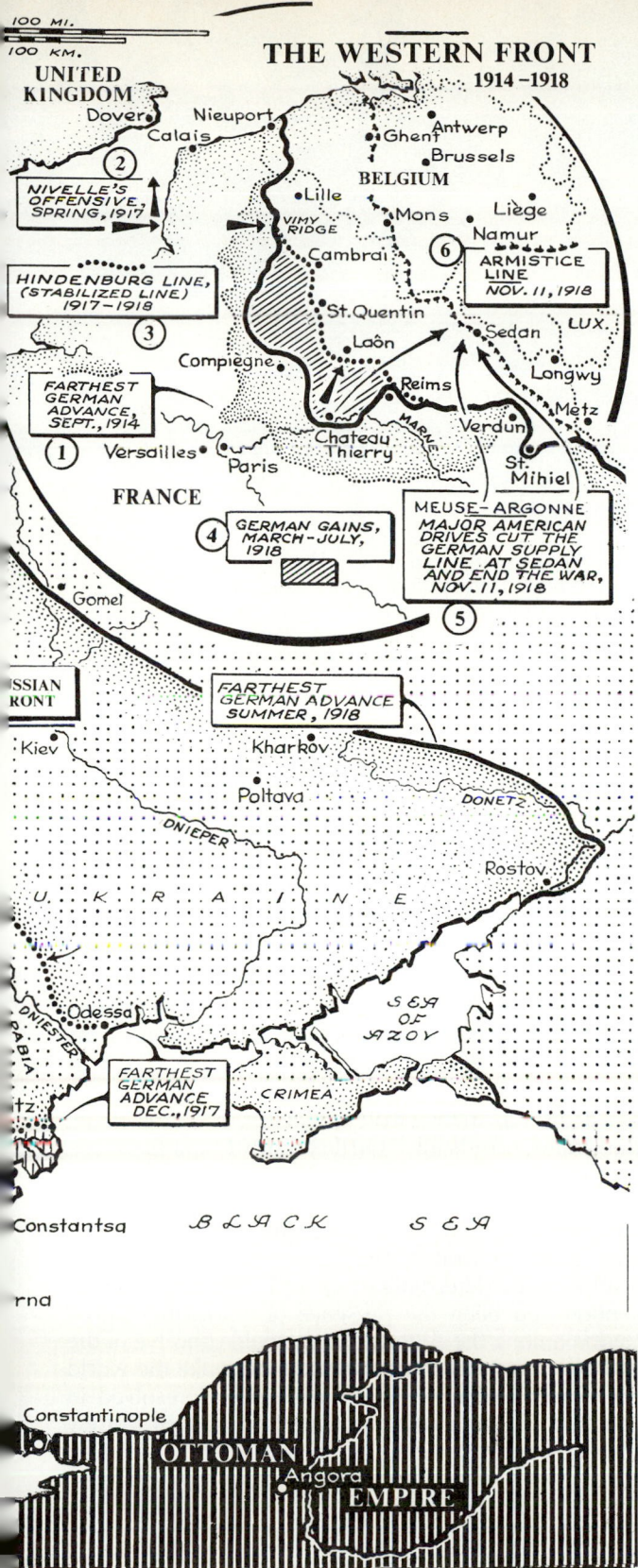

THE WESTERN FRONT
1914–1918

100 MI.

100 KM.

UNITED KINGDOM

Dover
Calais
Nieuport
Ghent
Antwerp
Brussels
BELGIUM
Lille
Mons
Liège
Namur
VIMY RIDGE
Cambrai
St.Quentin
Laôn
Sedan
LUX.
Compiegne
Reims
Longwy
Metz
Verdun
Chateau Thierry
St. Mihiel
Versailles
Paris
FRANCE

② NIVELLE'S OFFENSIVE, SPRING, 1917

③ HINDENBURG LINE (STABILIZED LINE) 1917–1918

① FARTHEST GERMAN ADVANCE SEPT., 1914

④ GERMAN GAINS, MARCH–JULY, 1918

⑥ ARMISTICE LINE NOV. 11, 1918

⑤ MEUSE–ARGONNE MAJOR AMERICAN DRIVES CUT THE GERMAN SUPPLY LINE AT SEDAN AND END THE WAR, NOV. 11, 1918

FARTHEST GERMAN ADVANCE SUMMER, 1918

Gomel
Kiev
Kharkov
Poltava
Rostov
DNIEPER
DONETZ
U K R A I N E
Odessa
DNIESTER
SSIAN RONT

FARTHEST GERMAN ADVANCE DEC., 1917

CRIMEA
SEA OF AZOV
Constantsa
B L A C K S E A
rna

Constantinople
OTTOMAN EMPIRE
Angora

MAP 33-4   WORLD WAR I IN EUROPE   *Despite the importance of military action in the Far East, in the Arab world, and at sea, the main theaters of activity in World War I were in the European areas shown here. The crucial Western front is seen in somewhat greater detail in the inset map.*

treaty of 1915, the Allies agreed to deliver to Italy most of *Italia Irredenta* (i.e., the Trentino, the South Tyrol, Trieste, and some of the Dalmatian Islands) after victory. By the spring of 1915, Italy was engaging Austrian armies. Although the Italian campaign drained the strength of the Central Powers to a degree, the alliance with Italy generally proved a disappointment to the Allies. It never produced significant results. Romania joined the Allies in 1916 but was quickly defeated and driven from the war.

In the Far East, Japan honored its alliance with Britain and entered the war. The Japanese quickly overran the German colonies in China and the Pacific and used the opportunity to improve their own position against China.

In 1915, the Allies undertook to break the deadlock in the fighting by going around it. The idea came chiefly from Winston Churchill (1874–1965), First Lord of the British Admiralty. He proposed an attack on the Dardanelles and the swift capture of Constantinople. This policy would knock Turkey from the war, bring help to the Balkan front, and ease communication with Russia. Success depended on timing, speed, and daring leadership, but all of these were lacking. The execution of the attack was inept and overly cautious. Troops were landed, and as resistance continued, the Allied commitment increased. Before the campaign was abandoned, the Allies lost almost 150,000 men and diverted three times that number from more useful occupation.

RETURN TO THE WEST. Both sides turned back to the west in 1916. General Erich von Falkenhayn (1861–1922), who had succeeded Moltke in September 1914, sought success by an attack on the French stronghold of Verdun. The commander of Verdun, Henri Pétain (1856–1951), became a national hero. "They shall not pass" became a slogan of national defiance. The Allies tried to end the impasse by launching a major offensive along the River Somme in July. Once again, the superiority of the defense was demonstrated. Enormous casualties on both sides brought no result. On all fronts, the losses were great and the results meager. The war on land dragged on with no end in sight.

THE WAR AT SEA. As the war continued, control of the sea became more important. The British ignored the distinction between war supplies (which were contraband according to international law) and food or other peaceful cargo, which was not subject to seizure. They imposed a strict blockade meant to starve out the enemy, regardless of international law. The Germans responded with submarine warfare meant to destroy British shipping and to starve the British. They declared the waters around the British Isles a war zone, where even neutral ships would not be safe. Both policies were unwelcome to neutrals, and especially to the United States, which conducted extensive trade in the Atlantic, but the sinking of neutral ships by German submarines was both more dramatic and more offensive.

In 1915, the British liner *Lusitania* was torpedoed by a German submarine. Among the 1,200 drowned were 118 Americans. President Woodrow Wilson (1856–1924) warned Germany that a repetition would not be accepted, and the Germans desisted for the time being rather than further anger the United States. This development gave the Allies a considerable ad-

This scene of trench warfare on the western front in World War I characterizes the twentieth century's first great international conflict. The trenches were defended by barbed wire and machine guns, which gave the defense the advantage in this war. The masks worn by these French soldiers were a defense against poison gas. [Collection Viollet.]

The tank was invented during World War I. It gave its crew armored protection, could cross many obstacles, and permitted a commander to advance fire power with some impunity closer to an enemy force than was possible by the traditional infantry charge. This photograph shows a light tank crossing an obstacle in a British military experiment. [Bettmann Archive.]

vantage. The German fleet that had cost so much money and had caused so much trouble played no significant part in the war. The only battle it fought was at Jutland in the spring of 1916. The battle resulted in a standoff and confirmed British domination of the surface of the sea.

AMERICA ENTERS THE WAR. In December 1916, President Woodrow Wilson of the United States intervened in an attempt to bring about a negotiated peace. But neither side was willing to renounce war aims that its opponent found unacceptable. The war seemed likely to continue until one or both sides reached exhaustion. Two events early in 1917 changed the situation radically. On February 1, the Germans announced the resumption of unrestricted submarine warfare, which led the United States to break off diplomatic relations. On April 6, the United States declared war on the Central Powers.

One of the deterrents to an earlier American intervention had been the presence of autocratic czarist Russia among the Allies. Wilson could conceive of the war only as an idealistic crusade "to make the world safe for democracy." That problem was resolved in March of 1917 by a revolution in Russia that overthrew the czarist government.

The Russian Revolution

The March Revolution in Russia was neither planned nor led by any political faction. It was the result of the collapse of the monarchy's ability to govern. Military and domestic failures produced massive casualties, widespread hunger, strikes by workers, and disorganization in the army. The peasant discontent that had plagued the countryside before 1914 did not subside during the conflict. In 1916, the tsar adjourned the Duma and proceeded to rule alone. All political factions were in one way or another discontented.

In early March 1917, strikes and worker demonstrations erupted in Petrograd, as Saint Petersburg had been renamed. The ill-disciplined troops in the city refused to fire on the demonstrators, and the tsar abdicated on March 15. The government of Russia fell into the hands of members of the reconvened Duma, who soon constructed a provisional government composed chiefly of Constitutional Democrats with Western sympathies. At the same time, the various socialists, including both Social Revolutionaries and Social Democrats of the Menshevik wing, began to organize the workers into councils called soviets. Initially, they allowed the provisional government to function without actually supporting it. But they became estranged as the Cadets failed to control the army or to purge "reactionaries" from the government.

In this climate, the provisional government made the important decision to remain loyal to the existing Russian alliances and to continue the war against Germany. The fate of the provisional government was sealed by the collapse of the new offensive in the summer of 1917. Disillusionment with the war, shortages of food and other necessities at home, and the growing demand by the peasants for land reform undermined the government—even after its leadership had been taken over by the moderate socialist Alexander Kerensky (1881–1970).

Ever since April, the Bolshevik wing of the Social Democratic Party had been working against the provisional government. The Germans, in their most successful attempt at subversion, had rushed the brilliant Bolshevik leader V. I. Lenin in a sealed train from his exile in Switzerland across Germany to Petrograd in the hope that he would cause trouble for the revolutionary government. The Bolsheviks soon gained control of the soviets, or councils of workers and soldiers. They demanded that all political power go to the soviets. The failure of the summer offensive encouraged them to attempt a coup, but the effort was premature and a failure. Lenin fled to Finland, and his chief collaborator, Leon Trotsky (1877–1940), was imprisoned.

The failure of a right-wing counter coup gave the Bolsheviks another chance. Trotsky, released from prison, led the powerful Petrograd Soviet. Lenin returned in October, insisted to his doubting colleagues that the time was ripe to take power, and by the extraordinary force of his personality persuaded them to act. Trotsky organized the coup that took place on November 6 and that concluded with an armed assault on the provisional government. The Bolsheviks, almost as much to their own astonishment as to that of the rest of the world, had come to rule Russia.

The victors moved to fulfill their promises and to assure their own security. The provisional government had decreed an election for late November to select a Constituent Assembly. The Social Revolutionaries

Field guns, under a red banner, in Petrograd (formerly St. Petersburg) during the Russian Revolution in March 1917. [The Granger Collection.]

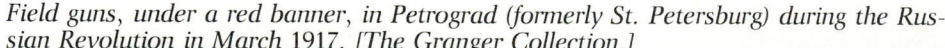

won a large majority over the Bolsheviks. When the assembly gathered in January, it met for only a day before the Red Army, controlled by the Bolsheviks, dispersed it. All other political parties also ceased to function in any meaningful fashion. In November and January the Bolshevik government promulgated decrees that nationalized the land and turned it over to its peasant proprietors. Factory workers were put in charge of their plants. Banks were taken from their owners and seized for the state, and the debt of the tsarist government was repudiated. Property of the Church reverted to the state.

The Bolshevik government also took Russia out of the war, which they believed benefited only capitalism. They signed an armistice with Germany in December 1917. On March 3, 1918, they accepted the Treaty of Brest-Litovsk, by which Russia yielded Poland, the Baltic states, and the Ukraine. Some territory in the Transcaucasus region went to Turkey. In addition, the Bolsheviks agreed to pay a heavy war indemnity. These terms were a terribly high price to pay for peace, but Lenin had no choice. Russia was incapable of renewing the war effort, and the Bolsheviks needed time to impose their rule on a devastated and chaotic Russia.

Until 1921, the New Bolshevik government confronted major domestic resistance. A civil war erupted between the "Red" Russians supporting the revolution and the "White" Russians, who opposed the Bolshevik triumph. In the summer of 1918, the tsar and his family were murdered. Loyal army officers continued to fight the revolution and eventually received aid from the Allied armies. However, under the leadership of Trotsky, the Red Army eventually overcame the domestic opposition. By 1921, Lenin and his supporters were in firm control.

The End of World War I

The Military Resolution

The internal collapse of Russia and the later Treaty of Brest-Litovsk brought Germany to the peak of its success. The Germans controlled eastern Europe and its resources, especially food. By 1918 they were free to concentrate their forces on the western front. This turn of events would probably have been decisive had it not been balanced by American intervention. Still, American troops would not arrive in significant numbers for about a year, and both sides tried to win the

Lenin Establishes His Dictatorship

After the Bolshevik coup in October, elections for the Constituent Assembly were held in November. The results gave a majority to the Social Revolutionary Party and embarrassed the Bolsheviks. Using his control of the Red Army, Lenin closed the Constituent Assembly in January 1918, after it had met for only one day, and established the rule of a revolutionary elite and his own dictatorship. Here is the crucial Bolshevik decree.

. . . The Constituent Assembly, elected on the basis of lists drawn up prior to the October Revolution, was an expression of the old relation of political forces which existed when power was held by the compromisers and the Cadets. When the people at that time voted for the candidates for the Socialist-Revolutionary Party, they were not in a position to choose between the Right Socialist-Revolutionaries, the supporters of the bourgeoisie, and the Left Socialist-Revolutionaries, the supporters of Socialism. Thus the Constituent Assembly, which was to have been the crown of the bourgeois parliamentary republic, could not become an obstacle in the path of the October Revolution and the Soviet power.

The October Revolution, by giving the power to the Soviets, and through the Soviets to the toiling and exploited classes, aroused the desperate resistance of the exploiters, and in the crushing of this resistance it fully revealed itself as the beginning of the socialist revolu-

tion . . . the majority in the Constituent Assembly which met on January 5 was secured by the party of the Right Socialist-Revolutionaries, the party of Kerensky, Avksentyev and Chernov. Naturally, this party refused to discuss the absolutely clear, precise and unambiguous proposal of the supreme organ of Soviet power, the Central Executive Committee of the Soviets, to recognize the program of the Soviet power, to recognize the "Declaration of Rights of the Toiling and Exploited People," to recognize the October Revolution and the Soviet power. . . .

The Right Socialist-Revolutionary and Menshevik parties are in fact waging outside the walls of the Constituent Assembly a most desperate struggle against the Soviet power. . . .

Accordingly, the Central Executive Committee resolves: The Constituent Assembly is hereby dissolved. ❑

R. V. Daniels (Ed.), *A Documentary History of Communism*, Vol. 1 (New York: Random House, 1960), pp. 133–135.

war in 1917. An Allied attempt to break through in the west failed disastrously, bringing heavy losses to the British and the French and causing a mutiny in the French army. The Austrians, supported by the Germans, defeated the Italians at Caporetto and threatened to overrun Italy, but they were checked with the aid of Allied troops. The deadlock continued, but time was running out for the Central Powers.

In 1918 the Germans, persuaded chiefly by Ludendorff—by then Quartermaster-General, second in command to Hindenburg, but the real leader of the army—decided to gamble everything on one last offensive. The German army pushed forward and even reached the Marne again but got no farther. They had no more reserves, and the entire nation was exhausted. The Allies, on the other hand, were bolstered by the arrival of American troops in ever-increasing numbers. They were able to launch a counteroffensive that proved to be irresistible. As the Austrian fronts in the Balkans and Italy collapsed, the German high command knew that the end was imminent.

Ludendorff was determined that peace should be made before the German army could be thoroughly defeated in the field and that the responsibility should fall on civilians. For some time, he had been the effective ruler of Germany under the aegis of the emperor. He now allowed a new government to be established on democratic principles and to seek peace immediately. The new government, under Prince Max of Baden, asked for peace on the basis of the Fourteen Points that President Wilson had declared as the American war aims. These were idealistic principles, including self-determination for nationalities, open diplomacy, freedom of the seas, disarmament, and establishment of a league of nations to keep the peace. Wilson insisted that he would deal only with a democratic German government because he wanted to be sure that he was dealing with the German people and not merely their rulers.

The disintegration of the German army forced William II to abdicate on November 9, 1918. The majority branch of the Social Democratic Party proclaimed a republic to prevent the establishment of a soviet government under the control of their radical, Leninist wing, which had earlier broken away as the Independent Socialist Party. Two days later, this republican, socialist-led government signed the armistice that ended the war by accepting German defeat. At the time of the armistice, the German people were, in general, unaware that their army had been defeated in the field and was crumbling. No foreign soldier stood on German soil. It appeared to many Germans that they could expect a negotiated and mild settlement. The real peace was quite different and embittered the German people, many of whom came to believe that Germany had not been defeated but had been tricked by the enemy and betrayed—even stabbed in the back—by republicans and socialists at home.

The victors rejoiced, but they also had much to mourn. The casualties on all sides came to about ten million dead and twice as many wounded. The economic and financial resources of the European states were badly strained. The victorious Allies, formerly creditors to the world, became debtors to the new American colossus, itself barely touched by the calamities of war.

The old international order, moreover, was dead. Russia was ruled by a Bolshevik dictatorship that preached world revolution and the overthrow of capitalism everywhere. Germany was in chaos. Austria-Hungary had disintegrated into a swarm of small national states competing for the remains of the ancient empire. These kinds of change stirred the colonial territories ruled by the European powers; overseas empires would never again be as secure as they had seemed before the war. Europe was no longer the center of the world, free to interfere when it wished or to ignore the outer regions if it chose. Its easy confidence in material and moral progress was shattered by the brutal reality of four years of horrible war. The memory of that war lived on to shake the nerve of the victorious Western powers as they confronted the new conditions of the postwar world.

The Settlement at Paris

THE PEACEMAKERS. The representatives of the victorious states gathered at Versailles and other Parisian suburbs in the first half of 1919. Wilson speaking for the United States, David Lloyd George (1863–1945) for Britain, Georges Clemenceau (1841–1929) for France, and Vittorio Emanuele Orlando (1860–1952) for Italy made up the Big Four. Japan, now recognized for the first time as a great power, also had an important part in the discussions.

Wilson's idealism came into conflict with the more practical war aims of the victorious powers and with many of the secret treaties that had been made before and during the war. The British and French people had been told that Germany would be made to pay for the war. Russia had been promised control of Constantinople in return for recognition of the French claim to Alsace-Lorraine and British control of Egypt. Romania had been promised Transylvania at the expense of Hungary. Some of the agreements contradicted others: Italy and Serbia had competing claims to the islands and shore of the Adriatic. During the war, the British had encouraged Arab hopes of an independent Arab state carved out of the Ottoman Empire; those plans conflicted with the Balfour Declaration (1917), in which the British seemed to accept Zionist ideology and to promise the Jews a national home in Palestine. Both of these plans stood in conflict with an Anglo-

The Big Three at Versailles. Georges Clemenceau, French Prime Minister (left), American President Woodrow Wilson (center), and British Prime Minister David Lloyd George (right) tip their hats to the crowd after signing the Treaty of Versailles on June 28, 1919. [Culver Pictures.]

French agreement to divide the Near East between the two Western powers.

The continuing national goals of the victors presented further obstacles to an idealistic "peace without victors." France was keenly conscious of its numerical inferiority to Germany and of the low birth rate that would keep it inferior. Naturally, France was eager to achieve a settlement that would permanently weaken Germany and preserve French political and military superiority. Italy continued to seek the acquisition of *Italia Irredenta* (unredeemed Italy); Britain continued to look to its imperial interests; Japan pursued its own advantage in Asia; and the United States insisted on freedom of the seas, which favored American commerce, and on its right to maintain the Monroe Doctrine.

Finally, the peacemakers of 1919 faced a world still in turmoil. The greatest immediate threat appeared to be posed by the spread of Bolshevism. While Lenin and his colleagues were distracted by civil war, the Allies landed small armies at several places in Russia in the hope of overthrowing the Bolshevik regime. The revolution seemed likely to spread as Communist governments were established in Bavaria and Hungary. Berlin also experienced a dangerous Communist uprising led by the "Spartacus group" (Communist extremists). The Allies were sufficiently worried by these developments to allow and to support suppression of these Communist movements by right-wing military forces. They even allowed an army of German volunteers to operate against the Bolsheviks in the Baltic states.

The fear of the spread of Communism played a part in the thinking of the diplomats at Versailles, but it was far from dominant. The Germans kept playing on such fears as a way of getting better terms, but the Allies, and especially the French, would not hear of it. Fear of Germany remained the chief concern for France; attention to interests that were more traditional and more immediate governed the policies of the other Allies.

THE PEACE. The Paris settlement consisted of five separate treaties between the victors and the defeated powers. Formal sessions began on January 18, 1919, and the last treaty was signed on August 10, 1920. The notion of "a peace without victors" became a mockery when the Soviet Union (as Russia was now called) and Germany were excluded from the peace conference. The Germans were simply presented with a treaty and compelled to accept it in a manner that fully justified their complaint that the treaty had not been negotiated but dictated. The principle of national self-determination was violated many times, as was unavoidable. Nevertheless, the diplomats of the small nations were angered by their exclusion from decisions. The undeserved adulation accorded Wilson on his arrival gradually turned into equally undeserved

OPPOSITE: MAP 33-5   WORLD WAR I PEACE SETTLEMENT   *The map of central and Eastern Europe, as well as that of the Middle East, underwent drastic revision after World War I. The enormous geographical losses suffered by Germany, Austria-Hungary, the Ottoman Empire, Bulgaria, and Russia were the other side of the coin represented by gains for France, Italy, Greece, and Romania and the appearance, or reappearance, of at least eight new independent states from Finland in the north to Yugoslavia in the south. The mandate system for former Ottoman territories outside Turkey proper laid foundations for several new, mostly Arab, states in the Middle East.*

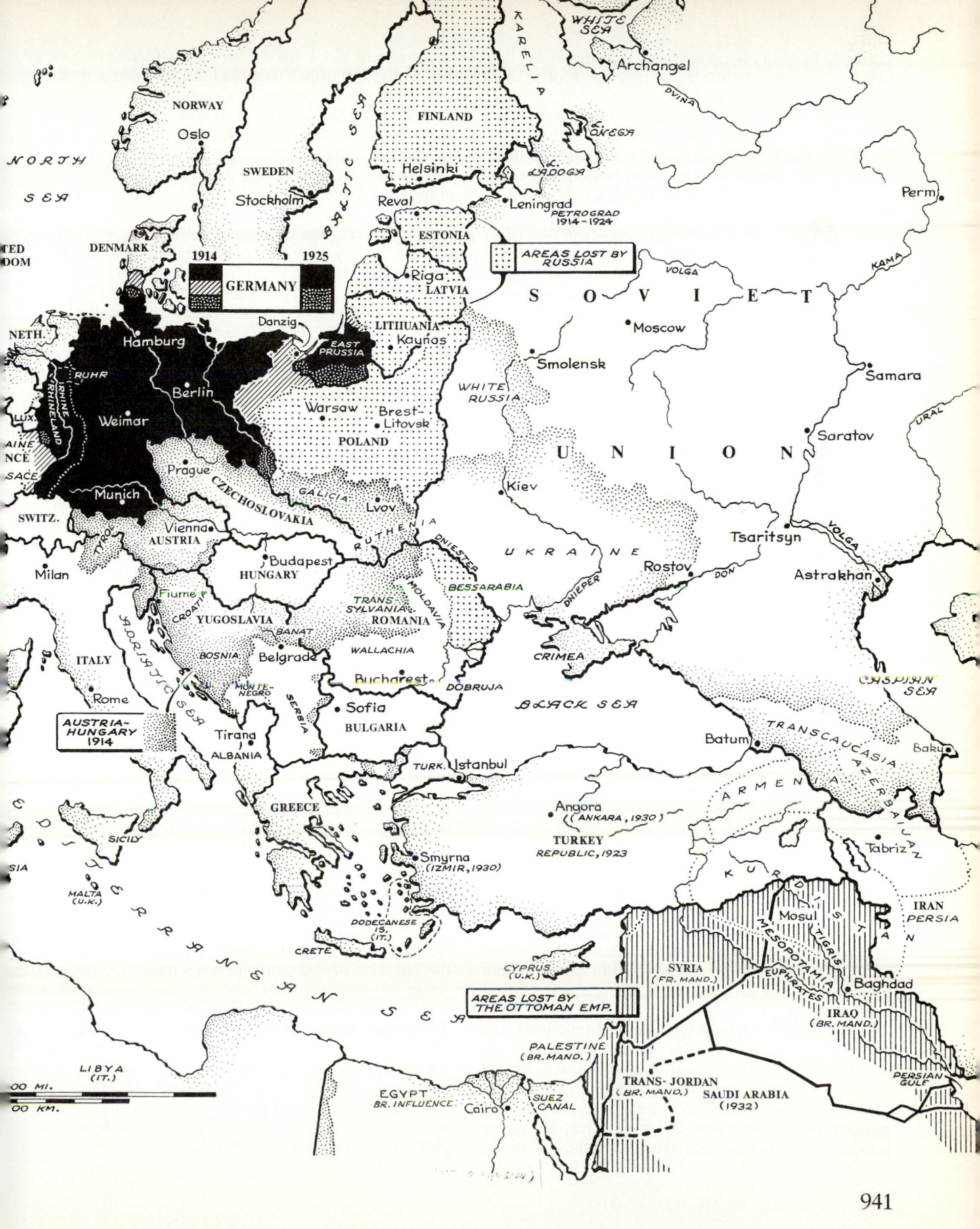

NORTH SEA

NORWAY
Oslo

SWEDEN
Stockholm

DENMARK

NETH.

LUX.

AINE
NCE

SACE

SWITZ.

Milan

ITALY

Rome

MALTA
(U.K.)

LIBYA
(IT.)

BALTIC SEA

FINLAND
Helsinki

Reval

ESTONIA

Riga
LATVIA

LITHUANIA
Kaunas

1914		1925
	GERMANY	

Danzig

EAST
PRUSSIA

Hamburg

RUHR
RHINELAND

Berlin

Weimar

Warsaw

Brest-
Litovsk

POLAND

Munich

CZECHOSLOVAKIA

GALICIA

Lvov

Prague

RUTHENIA

Vienna
AUSTRIA

TYROL

AUSTRIA-
HUNGARY
1914

Budapest
HUNGARY

Fiume

CROATIA

YUGOSLAVIA

BANAT

TRANS-
SYLVANIA

MOLDAVIA

ROMANIA

WALLACHIA

BESSARABIA

DNIESTER

BOSNIA

Belgrade

SERBIA

MONTE-
NEGRO

Tirana

ALBANIA

Bucharest

DOBRUJA

Sofia

BULGARIA

GREECE

SICILY

ADRIATIC SEA

MEDITERRANEAN SEA

OO MI.
OO KM.

TURK. Istanbul

Angora
((ANKARA, 1930)

TURKEY
REPUBLIC, 1923

Smyrna
(IZMIR, 1930)

DODECANESE
IS.
(IT.)

CRETE

CYPRUS
(U.K.)

PALESTINE
(BR. MAND.)

EGYPT
BR. INFLUENCE

Cairo

SUEZ
CANAL

WHITE
SEA

Archangel

DVINA

L. ONEGA

ÖNEGA

KARELIA

L. LADOGA

Leningrad
PETROGRAD
1914-1924

Perm

VOLGA

KAMA

SOVIET

Moscow

Smolensk

Samara

WHITE
RUSSIA

U N I O N

Kiev

Saratov

URAL

Tsaritsyn

Astrakhan

UKRAINE

DNIEPER

DON

Rostov

VOLGA

BLACK SEA

CRIMEA

CASPIAN
SEA

TRANSCAUCASIA

Batum

ARMENIA

AZERBAIJAN

Baku

KURDISTAN

Tabriz

IRAN
PERSIA

Mosul

MESOPOTAMIA

TIGRIS

EUPHRATES

Baghdad

SYRIA
(FR. MAND.)

IRAQ
(BR. MAND.)

PERSIAN
GULF

AREAS LOST BY
RUSSIA

AREAS LOST BY
THE OTTOMAN EMP.

TRANS-JORDAN
(BR. MAND.)

SAUDI ARABIA
(1932)

941

scorn. He had not abandoned his ideals lightly but had merely given way to the irresistible force of reality.

THE LEAGUE OF NATIONS. Wilson was able to make unpalatable concessions without abandoning his ideals because he put great faith in a new instrument for peace and justice, the League of Nations. Its covenant was an essential part of the peace treaty. The league was not intended as an international government but as a body of sovereign states who agreed to pursue some common practices and to consult in the common interest, especially when war threatened. In that case, the members promised to submit the matter to arbitration or to an international court or to the League Council. Refusal to abide by this agreement would justify league intervention in the form of economic and even military sanctions.

But the league was unlikely to be effective because it had no armed forces at its disposal. Any action required the unanimous consent of its council, consisting of Britain, France, Italy, the United States, and Japan, as well as four other states that had temporary seats. The Covenant of the League bound its members to "respect and preserve" the territorial integrity of all its members; this was generally seen as a device to ensure the security of the victorious powers. The exclusion from the League Assembly of Germany and the Soviet Union further undermined the league's claim to evenhandedness.

COLONIES. Another provision of the covenant dealt with colonial areas. These were to be placed under the "tutelage" of one of the great powers under league supervision and encouraged to advance toward independence. Because there were no teeth in this provision, very little advance was made. Provisions for disarmament were doomed to be equally ineffective. Members of the league remained fully sovereign and continued to pursue their own national interests.

GERMANY. In the west, the main territorial issue was the fate of Germany. Although a united Germany was less than fifty years old, no one seems to have thought of undoing Bismarck's work and dividing it into its component parts. The French would have liked to detach the Rhineland and set it up as a separate buffer state, but Lloyd George and Wilson would not permit that. Still, they could not ignore France's need for protection against a resurgent Germany. France received Alsace-Lorraine and the right to work the coal mines of the Saar for fifteen years. Germany west of the Rhine, and fifty kilometers east of it, was to be a demilitarized zone; and Allied troops on the west bank could stay there for fifteen years. In addition to this physical barrier to a new German attack, the treaty provided that Britain and the United States would guarantee to aid France if it were attacked by Germany. Such an attack was made more unlikely by the permanent disarmament of Germany. Its army was limited to 100,000 men on long-term service; its fleet was all but eliminated; and it was forbidden to have war planes, submarines, tanks, heavy artillery, or poison gas. As long as these provisions were observed, France would be safe.

THE EAST. The settlement in the east ratified the collapse of the great defeated empires that had ruled it for centuries. Germany's frontier was moved far to the west, excluding much of Silesia and most of Prussia. What was left of East Prussia was cut off from the rest of Germany by a corridor carved out to give the revived state of Poland access to the sea. The Austro-Hungarian Empire disappeared entirely, giving way to many smaller successor states. Most of its German-speaking people were gathered in the small Republic of Austria, cut off from the Germans of Bohemia and forbidden to unite themselves with Germany. The Magyars occupied the much-reduced kingdom of Hungary.

The Czechs of Bohemia and Moravia joined with the Slovaks and Ruthenians to the east to form Czechoslovakia, and this new state also included several million unhappy Germans. The southern Slavs were united in the kingdom of Serbs, Croats, and Slovenes, or Yugoslavia. Italy gained the Trentino and Trieste. Romania was enlarged by receiving Transylvania from Hungary and Bessarabia from Russia. Bulgaria was diminished by the loss of territory to Greece and Yugoslavia. Russia lost vast territories in the west. Finland, Estonia, Latvia, and Lithuania became independent states, and a good part of Poland was carved out of formerly Russian soil.

The old Ottoman Empire disappeared. The new republic of Turkey was limited to little more than Constantinople and Asia Minor. The former Ottoman territories of Palestine and Iraq came under British control and Syria and Lebanon under French control as mandates of the League of Nations. Germany's former colonies in Africa were divided among Britain, France, and South Africa. The German Pacific possessions went to Australia, New Zealand, and Japan.

In theory, the mandate system was meant to have the "advanced nations" govern the former colonies in the interests of the native peoples until they became ready to govern themselves. For this purpose they were divided into three categories—A, B, and C—in descending order of their readiness for independence. In practice, most mandated territories were treated as colonies by the powers under whose "tutelage" they came. Not even one Class A mandate had achieved full independence twenty years after the signing of the treaty. The legacy of colonialism was to remain a problem even after World War II.

REPARATIONS. Perhaps the most debated part of the peace settlement dealt with reparations for the damage done by Germany during the war. Before the armistice, the Germans promised to pay compensation "for all damages done to the civilian population of the Allies and their property." The Americans judged that the amount would be between $15 billion and $25 billion and that Germany would be able to pay that amount. However, France and Britain, worried about repaying their war debts to the United States, were eager to have Germany pay the full cost of the war, including pensions to survivors and dependents. There was general agreement that Germany could not afford to pay such a sum, whatever it might be, and no sum was fixed at the conference. In the meantime Germany was to pay $5 billion annually until 1921. At that time, a final figure would be set, which Germany would have to pay in thirty years. The French did not regret the outcome. Either Germany would pay and be bled into impotence, or Germany would refuse to pay and justify French intervention.

To justify these huge reparation payments, the Allies inserted the notorious Clause 231 into the treaty:

The Allied and Associated Governments affirm, and Germany accepts, the responsibility of Germany and her allies for causing all the loss and damage to which the Allied and Associated Governments and their nationals have been subjected as a consequence of the war imposed upon them by aggression of Germany and her allies.

The Germans, of course, did not believe that they were solely responsible for the war. They bitterly resented the charge. They had suffered the loss of vast territories containing millions of Germans and great quantities of badly needed natural resources; they were presented with an astronomical and apparently unlimited reparations bill. To add insult to injury, they were required to admit to a war guilt that they did not feel. Finally, to heap insult on insult, they were required to accept the entire treaty as it was written by the victors, without any opportunity for negotiation. German's Prime Minister Philipp Scheidemann (1865–1939) spoke of the treaty as the imprisonment of the German people and asked, "What hand would not wither that binds itself and us in these fetters?" But there was no choice. The Social Democrats and the Catholic Center Party formed a new government, and their representatives signed the treaty. These were the parties that formed the backbone of the Weimar government that ruled Germany until 1933, and they never overcame the stigma of accepting the Treaty of Versailles.

Evaluation of the Peace

Few peace settlements have undergone more severe attacks than the one negotiated in Paris in 1919. It was natural that the defeated powers should have objected to it, but the peace soon came under bitter criticism in the victorious countries as well. Many of the French thought that it failed to provide adequate security for France, because it tied that security to promises of aid from the unreliable Anglo-Saxon countries. In England and the United States, a wave of bitter criticism arose in liberal quarters because the treaty seemed to violate the idealistic and liberal aims and principles that the Western leaders had professed. It was not a peace without victors. It did not put an end to imperialism, but attempted to promote the national interests of the winning nations. It violated the principles of national self-determination by leaving significant pockets of minorities outside the borders of their national homelands.

The most influential critic was John Maynard Keynes (1883–1946), a brilliant British economist who took part in the peace conference. When he saw the

This British cartoon points out the supposedly devastating effect on postwar Germany of the heavy reparations payments demanded by the Allies. The caption reads: "Perhaps it would gee-up better if we let it touch earth." [New York Public Library Picture Collection.]

direction it was taking, he resigned in disgust and wrote a book called *The Economic Consequences of the Peace* (1920). It was a scathing attack, especially on reparations and the other economic aspects of the peace. It was also a skillful assault on the negotiators and particularly on Wilson, who was depicted as a fool and a hypocrite. Keynes argued that the Treaty of Versailles was both immoral and unworkable. He called it a Carthaginian peace, referring to the utter destruction of Carthage by Rome after the Third Punic War. He argued that such a peace would bring economic ruin and war to Europe unless it were repudiated. Keynes had a great effect on the British, who were already suspicious of France and glad of an excuse to withdraw from continental affairs. The decent and respectable position came to be one that aimed at revision of the treaty in favor of Germany.

Even more important was the book's influence in the United States. It fed the traditional tendency toward isolationism and gave powerful weapons to Wilson's enemies. Wilson's own political mistakes helped prevent American ratification of the treaty. Consequently, America was out of the League of Nations and not bound to defend France. Britain, therefore, was also free from its obligation to France. France was left to protect itself without adequate means to do so for long.

Many of the attacks on the Treaty of Versailles are unjustified. It was not a Carthaginian peace. Germany was neither dismembered nor ruined. Reparations could be and were scaled down, and until the great world depression of the 1930s, the Germans recovered a high level of prosperity. Complaints against the peace should also be measured against the peace that the victorious Germans had imposed on Russia at Brest-Litovsk and the plans they had made for a European settlement in case of victory. Both were far more severe than anything enacted at Versailles. The attempt at achieving self-determination for nationalities was less than perfect, but it was the best solution Europe had ever accomplished in that direction.

The peace, nevertheless, was unsatisfactory in important ways. The elimination of the Austro-Hungarian Empire, however inevitable that might seem, created a number of serious problems. Economically it was disastrous, for it separated raw materials from manufacturing areas and producers from their markets by new boundaries and tariff walls. In hard times, this separation created friction and hostility that aggravated other quarrels also created by the peace treaties. Poland contained unhappy German minorities. Czechoslovakia was a collection of nationalities that did not find it easy to live together as a nation. Disputes over territories in eastern Europe promoted further tension. The peace was inadequate on another level, as well. It rested on a victory that Germany did

not admit. The Germans believed that they had been cheated rather than defeated. At the same time, the high moral principles proclaimed by the Allies undercut the validity of the peace, for it plainly fell far short of those principles.

Finally, the great weakness of the peace was its failure to accept reality. Germany and Russia must inevitably play an important part in European affairs, yet they were excluded from the settlement and from the League of Nations. Given the many discontented parties, the peace was not self-enforcing; yet no satisfactory machinery for enforcing it was established. The league was never a serious force for this purpose. It was left to France, with no guarantee of support from Britain and no hope of help from the United States, to defend the new arrangements. Finland, the Baltic states, Poland, Romania, Czechoslovakia, and Yugoslavia were created as a barrier to the westward expansion of Russian Communism and as a threat in the rear to deter German revival. Most of these states, however, would have to rely on France in case of danger. France was simply not strong enough for the task if Germany were to rearm.

The tragedy of the Treaty of Versailles was that it was neither conciliatory enough to remove the desire for change, even at the cost of war, nor harsh enough to make another war impossible. The only hope for a lasting peace required the enforcement of the disarmament of Germany while the more obnoxious clauses of the peace treaty were revised. Such a policy required continued attention to the problem, unity among the victors, and far-sighted leadership; but none of these was present in adequate supply during the next two decades.

Imperialism and World War I in World Perspective

The outburst of European imperialism in the last part of the nineteenth century brought the Western countries into contact with almost all the inhabited areas of the world and intensified their activity in places where they had already been interested. The growth of industry, increased ease of transportation and communication, and the growth of a world economic system all tended to bring previously remote and isolated places into the orbit of the West. By the time of the outbreak of the war, European nations had divided all of Africa among themselves for exploitation in one way or another. The vast subcontinent of India had long been a British colony. The desirable parts of China were very much under European control for commercial purposes. Indo-China was under French rule. The islands of the Pacific had been divided among the powers.

Much of the Middle East was under the nominal control of the Ottoman Empire, which was in its death throes and under European influence. The Monroe Doctrine made Latin America a protectorate of the United States. Japan, pushed out of its isolation, had itself become an imperial power at the expense of China and Korea.

But the world created by the New Imperialism did not last long. What began as yet another Balkan War involving the European powers became a world war that had a profound influence on much of the rest of the world. As the terrible war of 1914–1918 dragged on, the real motives that had driven the European powers to fight gave way to public affirmations of the principles of nationalism and self-determination. The peoples under colonial rule took the public statements, and sometimes private promises, seriously and sought to win their independence and nationhood. For the most part, they were disappointed by the peace settlement. The establishment of the League of Nations and the system of mandates in place of the previous system of open colonial rule did not seem to change much. The British Empire inherited vast territories from the defeated German and the defunct Ottoman Empire and was larger than ever. The French retained and expanded their holdings in Africa, the Pacific, and the Middle East. The Americans added to the islands they controlled in the Pacific. Japanese imperial ambitions were rewarded at the expense of China.

A glance at the new map of the world could give the impression that the old imperial nations, especially Britain and France, were more powerful than ever. However, that impression would be superficial and misleading. The great Western European powers had paid an enormous price in lives, money, and will for their victory in the war. Colonial peoples pressed for the rights that were proclaimed as universal by the West but denied to their colonies; influential minorities in the countries that ruled them sympathized with colonial aspirations for independence. Tension between colonies and their ruling nations was a cause of instability in the world created by the Paris treaties of 1919.

Suggested Readings

L. ALBERTINI, *The Origins of the War of 1914*, 3 vols. (1952, 1957). Discursive but invaluable.

M. BALFOUR, *The Kaiser and His Times* (1972). A fine biography of William II.

V. R. BERGHAHN, *Germany and the Approach of War in 1914* (1973). A work similar in spirit to Fischer's [see below] but stressing the importance of Germany's naval program.

R. BOSWORTH, *Italy and the Approach of the First World War* (1983). A fine analysis of Italian policy.

V. DEDIJER, *The Road to Sarajevo* (1966). The fullest account of the assassination that provoked World War I and its Balkan background.

S. B. FAY, *The Origins of the World War*, 2 vols. (1928). The best and most influential of the revisionist accounts.

M. FERRO, *The Great War*, 1914–1918 (1973). A solid account of the course of World War I.

D. K. FIELDHOUSE, *The Colonial Experience: A Comparative Study from the Eighteenth Century* (1966). An excellent recent study.

F. FISCHER, *Germany's Aims in the First World War* (1967). An influential interpretation that stirred a great controversy in Germany and around the world by emphasizing Germany's role in bringing on the war.

F. FISCHER, *War of Illusions* (1975). A long and diffuse book that tries to connect German responsibility for the war with internal social, economic, and political developments.

I. GEISS, *July 1914* (1967). A valuable collection of documents by a student of Fritz Fischer's. The emphasis is on German documents and responsibility.

O. J. HALE, *The Great Illusion* 1900–1914 (1971). A fine survey of the period, especially good on public opinion.

J. JOLL, *The Origins of the First World War* (1984). A brief but thoughtful analysis.

P. KENNEDY, *The Rise of the Anglo-German Antagonism 1860–1914* (1980). An unusual and thorough analysis of the political, economic, and cultural roots of important diplomatic developments.

J. M. KEYNES, *The Economic Consequences of the Peace* (1920). The famous and influential attack on the Versailles Treaty.

L. LAFORE, *The Long Fuse* (1965). A readable account of the origins of World War I that focuses on the problem of Austria-Hungary.

W. L. LANGER, *The Diplomacy of Imperialism* (1935). A continuation of the previous study for the years 1890–1902.

W. L. LANGER, *European Alliances and Alignments*, 2nd ed. (1966). A splendid diplomatic history of the years 1871–1890.

B. H. LIDDELL HART, *The Real War* 1914–1918 (1964). A fine short account by an outstanding military historian.

D. C. B. LIEVEN, *Russia and the Origins of the First World War* (1983). A good account of the forces that shaped Russian policy.

E. MANTOUX, *The Carthaginian Peace* (1952). A vigorous attack on Keynes' view [see Keynes, above].

J. STEINBERG, *Yesterday's Deterrent* (1965). An excellent study of Germany's naval policy and its consequences.

Z. STEINER, *Britain and the Origins of the First World War* (1977). A perceptive and informed account of the way British foreign policy was made in the years before the war.

A. J. P. TAYLOR, *The Struggle for Mastery in Europe*, 1848–1918 (1954). Clever but controversial.

L. C. F. TURNER, *Origins of the First World War* (1970). Especially good on the significance of Russia and its military plans.

The Nazi party used massive political rallies such as this one, in Berlin in 1937, to display its power and whip up enthusiasm. [United Press International Photo.]

34 Depression, European Dictators, and the American New Deal

Throughout the Western world, pursuit of experimentation in politics and economic life marked the two decades that followed the conclusion of the Paris Settlement. Two broad factors accounted for these experiments. First, the turmoil of the war, the Russian Revolution, and the peace treaty had transformed the political face of Europe. New political regimes studded the map of Europe in the wake of the collapse of the monarchies of Germany, Austria-Hungary, and Russia. These new governments immediately faced the problems of postwar reconstruction, economic dislocation, and nationalistic resentments. Virtually all of these nations also confronted large groups in their populations that questioned the legitimacy of their governments.

Second, beginning in the early twenties, a major economic downturn that became known as the Great Depression began to spread across the world. It occurred through the combination of financial turmoil in the more advanced industrial nations and a collapse of commodity prices in the commodity-exporting countries. In the face of the postwar political instability and the later economic crisis, governments contrived various political and economic responses. In Europe, these often involved the establishment of authoritarian political regimes. In the United States, the response to the Depression led to a much increased role of the federal government in the life of the nation.

Demands for Revision of Versailles

The Paris settlement fostered both resentment and discontent in numerous European countries. Those resentments counted among the chief political factors in Europe for the next two decades. Germany had been humiliated. The arrangements for reparations led to seemingly endless haggling over payments. Various national groups in the successor states of the Austro-Hungarian Empire in eastern Europe felt that injustice had been done in their particular cases of self-determination. There were demands for further border adjustments. On the other side, the victorious powers, and especially France, often believed that the provisions of the treaty were being inadequately enforced. Consequently, throughout the 1920s and into the 1930s demands either to revise or to enforce the Paris treaties contributed to domestic political turmoil across the Continent. All too many political figures were willing to fish in these troubled international waters for a large catch of domestic votes.

Toward the Great Depression in Europe

Three factors combined to bring about the intense severity and the extended length of the Great Depression. There was a financial crisis that stemmed directly from the war and the peace settlement. To this was added a crisis in the production and distribution of goods in the world market. These two problems became intertwined in 1929, and as far as Europe was concerned, they reached the breaking point in 1931. Finally, both of these difficulties became worse than might have occurred because of the absence of strong economic leadership and responsibility on the part of any major Western European country or the United States.

The Financial Tailspin

As one of the chief victors in the war, France was determined to collect reparations from Germany. The United States was no less determined to receive repayments of the wartime loans extended to its allies. The European allies also owed to each other various debts. It soon became apparent that German reparations were to provide the means of repaying the American and other allied debts. Most of the money that the Allies collected from each other also went to the United States.

The quest for payment of German reparations caused one of the major diplomatic crises of the 1920s; the crisis itself resulted in further economic upheaval. In early 1923, the Allies, and France in particular, declared Germany to be in technical default of its reparations payments. On January 11, to ensure receipt of the hard-won reparations, the French government ordered its troops to occupy the Ruhr mining and manufacturing district. The response of the Weimar Republic was to order passive resistance that amounted to the calling of a general strike in the largest industrial region of the nation. Confronted with this tactic, the French government sent French civilians to run the

In January 1923 French troops occupied the Ruhr in Germany because of alleged defaults in the delivery of reparations to France. [The Granger Collection.]

German mines and railroads. France got its way. The Germans paid, but France confronted a great price for its victory. The English were alienated by the French heavy-handedness and took no part in the occupation. Britain became more suspicious of France and more sympathetic to Germany. The cost of the Ruhr occupation, moreover, vastly increased French as well as German inflation and damaged the French economy.

The political and economic turmoil of the Ruhr invasion led to international attempts to ease the German payment of reparations. The most famous of these was the Dawes Plan of 1924 and the Young Plan of 1929, both devised by Americans. At the same time, large amounts of American investment capital was pouring into Europe. However, by 1928 this lending decreased as American money became diverted into the booming New York stock market. The crash of Wall Street in October 1929—the result of virtually unregulated financial speculation—saw the loss of large amounts of money. There followed a sharp reduction of credit in the United States as numerous banks failed. Thereafter, little American capital was available for investment in Europe.

As the credit for Europe began to run out, a major financial crisis struck the continent. In May 1931, the Kreditanstalt collapsed. The Kreditanstalt was a primary lending institution and major bank for much of central and eastern Europe. The German banking system consequently came under severe pressure and was saved only through government guarantees. As the German difficulties increased, U.S. president Herbert Hoover announced in June 1931 a one-year moratorium on all payments of international debts. The Hoover moratorium was a prelude to the end of reparations. The Lausanne Conference of the summer of 1932 brought, in effect, the era of reparations to a close. The next year, the debts owed to the United States were settled either through small token payments or simply through default.

Problems in Agricultural Commodities

The 1920s witnessed a contraction in the market demand for European goods relative to the Continent's productive capacity. Part of this problem originated within Europe and part outside. In both instances, the difficulty arose from agriculture. Better methods of farming, improved strains of wheat, expanded tillage, and more extensive transport facilities all over the globe vastly increased the quantity of grain produced. World wheat prices fell to record lows. While this development helped consumers, it decreased the income of European farmers. At the same time, higher industrial wages raised the cost of the industrial goods used by the farmer or peasant. Consequently, they also had great difficulty paying off their mortgages and normal annual operation debts. These problems were especially acute in central and eastern Europe and played a part in farmers' disillusionment with liberal politics. For example, in Germany, farmers provided the National Socialist Workers Party (Nazis) with a major source of political support.

Outside Europe, similar problems affected other producers of agricultural commodities. The prices they received for their products plummeted. Government-held reserves accumulated to record levels. This glut of major world commodities involved the supplies of wheat, sugar, coffee, rubber, wool, and lard. The people who produced these goods in underdeveloped nations could no longer make enough money to buy finished goods from industrial Europe. As world credit collapsed, the economic position of these commodity producers became all the worse. Commodity production had simply outstripped world demand.

The result of the collapse in the agricultural sector of the world economy and the financial turmoil was stagnation and depression for European industry. Coal, iron, and textiles had depended largely on international markets. Unemployment spread from these industries to those producing finished consumer goods. Persistent unemployment in Great Britain and, to a lesser extent, in Germany during the 1920s had created "soft" domestic markets. The policies of reduced spending with which the governments confronted the Depression further weakened domestic demand. By the early 1930s, the Depression was feeding on itself.

Depression and Government Policy

The Depression did not mean absolute economic decline or total unemployment. However, the economic downturn did spread potential as well as actual insecurity. People in nearly all walks of life feared the loss of their own economic security and lifestyles. The Depression also frustrated normal social and economic expectations. Even the employed often seemed to make no progress; and their anxieties created a major source of social discontent.

The governments of the late 1920s and the early 1930s were not particularly well fitted in either structure or ideology to confront these problems. The electorates demanded some action. In large measure, the government response depended on the severity of the Depression in a particular country and on the self-confidence of the nation's political system.

Great Britain and France undertook rather moderate political experiments. In 1924, the Labour Party in Great Britain established itself as a viable governing party by forming a government briefly. It again formed a ministry in 1929. Under the pressure of the Depression and at the urging of King George V, the Labour prime minister Ramsay MacDonald organized a National Government, which was a coalition of the Labour, Conservative, and Liberal Parties. It remained in power until 1935, when a Conservative ministry led by Stanley Baldwin replaced it.

The most important French political experiment was the Popular Front Ministry that came to office in 1936. It was composed of Socialists, Radicals, and Communists—the first time that Socialists and Communists had cooperated in a ministry. The Popular Front addressed a number of major labor problems in the French economy. By 1938, various changes in the Cabinet in effect brought the Popular Front to an end.

The political changes in Britain and France were significant only to their respective national histories and societies. But the political experiments of the 1920s and 1930s that reshaped world history and civilization involved the establishment of a Fascist regime in Italy, a Nazi dictatorship in Germany, and a Soviet government in Russia.

The Fascist Experiment in Italy

From the Italian Fascist movement of Benito Mussolini (1883–1945) was derived the general term of *fascist*, which has frequently been used to describe the various right-wing dictatorships that arose between the wars.

The exact meaning of *fascism* as a political term remains much disputed among both historians and political scientists. However, a certain consensus does exist. The governments regarded as fascist were antidemocratic, anti-Marxist, antiparliamentary, and frequently anti-Semitic. They hoped to hold back the spread of Bolshevism, which seemed at the time a very real threat. They sought a world that would be safe for the middle class, small businesses, owners of moderate amounts of property, and small farmers. The fascist regimes rejected the political inheritance of the French Revolution and of nineteenth-century liberalism. Their adherents believed that normal parliamentary politics and parties sacrificed national honor and greatness to petty party disputes. They wanted to overcome the class conflict of Marxism and the party conflict of liberalism by consolidating the various groups and classes within the nation for great national purposes. As Mussolini declared in 1931, "The fascist conception of the state is all-embracing, and outside of the state no human or spiritual values can exist, let alone be desirable."[1] The fascist governments were usually single-party dictatorships characterized by terrorism and police surveillance. These dictatorships were rooted in the base of mass political parties.

The Rise of Mussolini

The Italian *Fasci di Combattimento* ("Band of Combat") was founded in 1919 in Milan. Its members came largely from among Italian war veterans who felt that the sacrifies of World War I had been in vain. They resented the failure of Italy to gain the city of Fiume, toward the northern end of the Adriatic Sea, at the Paris conference. They feared socialism, inflation, and labor unrest.

Their leader, Benito Mussolini, had been born the son of a blacksmith. For a time, he had been a schoolteacher, then a day laborer. He became active in Italian socialist politics and by 1912 had become editor of the socialist newspaper *Avanti*. In 1914, Mussolini broke with the socialists and supported Italian entry into the war on the side of the Allies. His interventionist position lost him the editorship of *Avanti*. He then established his own paper, *Il Popolo d'Italia*. Later he served in the army and was wounded. In 1919, although of some prewar political stature, Mussolini was simply one of many Italian politicians. His *Fasci* organization was, for its part, simply one of numerous small political groups in a country characterized by such entities. As a politician, Mussolini was an opportunist par excellence. He proved capable of changing his ideas and principles to suit every new occasion. Action for him was always more important than thought or rational justification. His one real rule was that of political survival.

Postwar Italian politics was a muddle. During the conflict, the Italian Parliament had for all intents and purposes ceased to function. It had been quite willing to allow the ministers to rule by decree. However, the parliamentary system as it then existed had begun to prove quite unsatisfactory to large sectors of the citizenry. Many Italians besides those in Mussolini's band of followers felt that Italy had emerged from the war as less than a victorious nation, had not been treated as a great power at the peace conference, and had not received the territories it deserved. The main spokesman for this discontent was the extreme nationalist poet and novelist Gabriele D'Annunzio (1863–1938). In 1919, he successfully led a force of patriotic Italians in an assault on Fiume. Troops of the Italian government, enforcing the terms of the Versailles Treaty, eventually drove him out. D'Annunzio had provided the example of the political use of a nongovernmental military force. The action of the government in removing him from Fiume gave the parliamentary ministry a somewhat less than patriotic appearance.

Between 1919 and 1921, Italy also experienced considerable internal social turmoil. Numerous industrial strikes occurred, and workers occupied factories. Peasants seized uncultivated land from large estates. Parliamentary and constitutional government seemed incapable of dealing with this unrest. The Socialist Party had captured a plurality of seats in the Chamber of Deputies during the 1919 election. A new Catholic Popular Party had also done quite well. Both appealed to the working and agrarian classes. However, neither party would cooperate with the other, and parliamentary deadlock resulted. Under these conditions, many Italians honestly—and still others conveniently—believed that there existed the danger of a communist revolution.

Initially, Mussolini was uncertain of the direction of the political winds. He first supported the factory occupations and land seizures. However, never one to be concerned with consistency, he soon reversed himself. He had discovered that large numbers of both upper-class and middle-class Italians who were pressured by inflation and who feared property loss had no sympathy for the workers or the peasants. They wanted order rather than some vague social justice that might harm their own interests. Consequently, Mussolini and his Fascists took direct action in the face of the government inaction. They formed local squads of terrorists who disrupted Socialist Party meetings, mugged Socialist leaders, and terrorized Socialist supporters. They attacked strikers and farm workers and protected strikebreakers. Conservative land and factory owners were grateful. The officers and institutions of the law simply ignored the crimes of the Fascist squads. By early 1922, the Fascists had turned their intimidation through arson, beatings, and murder against local officials in cities such as Ferrara, Ravenna, and Milan. They controlled the local government in many parts of northern Italy.

In 1921, Mussolini and thirty-four of his followers

---

[1] Quoted in Denis Mack Smith, *Italy: A Modern History* (Ann Arbor: University of Michigan Press, 1959), p. 412.

Mussolini Heaps Contempt on Political Liberalism

The political tactics of the Italian Fascists wholly disregarded the liberal belief in the rule of law and the consent of the governed. In 1923, Mussolini explained why the Fascists so hated and repudiated these liberal principles. The reader should note his emphasis on the idea of the twentieth century as a new historical epoch requiring a new kind of politics and his undisguised praise of force in politics.

Liberalism is not the last word, nor does it represent the definitive formula on the subject of the art of government. . . . Liberalism is the product and the technique of the 19th Century. . . . It does not follow that the Liberal scheme of government, good for the 19th century, for a century, that is, dominated by two such phenomena as the growth of capitalism and the strengthening of the sentiment of nationalism, should be adapted to the 20th Century, which announces itself already with characteristics sufficiently different from those that marked the preceding century . . .

I challenge Liberal gentlemen to tell me if ever in history there has been a government that was based solely on popular consent and that renounced all use of force whatsoever. A government so constructed there has never been and never will be. Consent is an ever-changing thing like the shifting sand on the sea coast. It can never be permanent. It can never be complete. . . . If it be accepted as an axiom that any system of government whatever creates malcontents, how are you going to prevent this discontent from overflowing and constituting a menace to the stability of the State? You will prevent it by force. By the assembling of the greatest force possible. By the inexorable use of this force whenever it is necessary. Take away from any government whatsoever force—and by force is meant physical, armed force—and leave it only its immortal principles, and that government will be at the mercy of the first organized group that decides to overthrow it. Fascism now throws these lifeless theories out to rot. . . . The truth evident now to all who are not warped by [liberal] dogmatism is that men have tired of liberty. They have made an orgy of it. Liberty is today no longer the chaste and austere virgin for whom the generations of the first half of the last century fought and died. For the gallant, restless and bitter youth who face the dawn of a new history there are other words that exercise a far greater fascination, and those words are: order, hierarchy, discipline . . .

Know then, once and for all, that Fascism knows no idols and worships no fetishes. It has already stepped over, and if it be necessary it will turn tranquilly and step again over, the more or less putrescent corpse of the Goddess of Liberty. ❑

Benito Mussolini, "Force and Consent" (1923), as cited and translated in Jonathan F. Scott and Alexander Baltzly, *Readings in European History Since* 1814 (New York: F. S. Crofts, 1931), pp. 680–682.

A scene from the Fascist march on Rome in October 1922. When it was clear the king would not authorize force against them, the marchers, in their characteristic black shirts, posed for a friendly photographer. [United Press International Photo.]

had been elected to the Chamber of Deputies. Their importance grew as the local Fascists gained more direct power. The Fascist movement now had hundreds of thousands of supporters. In October 1922, the Fascists, dressed in their characteristic black shirts, began a march on Rome. King Victor Emmanuel III (1900–1946), because of both personal and political fear, refused to sign a decree that would have authorized the use of the army against the marchers. Probably no other single decision so ensured a Fascist seizure of power. The Cabinet resigned in protest. On October 29, the monarch telegraphed Mussolini in Milan and asked him to become prime minister. The next day, Mussolini arrived in Rome by sleeping car and, as head of the government, greeted his followers when they entered the city.

Technically, Mussolini had come into office by legal means. The monarch did possess the power to appoint the prime minister. However, Mussolini had no majority or even near majority in the Chamber of Deputies. Behind the legal facade of his assumption of power lay the months of terrorist disruption and intimidation and the threat of the Fascists' October march itself.

The Fascists in Power

Mussolini had not really expected to be appointed prime minister. He moved cautiously to shore up his support and to consolidate his power. His success was the result of the impotence of his rivals, his own effective use of his office, his power over the masses, and his sheer ruthlessness. On November 23, 1922, the

Mussolini was a powerful public orator. His gestures, which often appear comic in hindsight, were part of a public image designed to make him appear at all times a leader. [Culver Pictures.]

king and the Parliament granted Mussolini dictatorial authority for one year to bring order to the lower levels of the government. Wherever possible, Mussolini appointed Fascists to office. Late in 1924, under Mussolini's guidance, the Parliament changed the election law. Previously, parties had been represented in the Chamber of Deputies in proportion to the popular vote cast for them. According to the new election law, the party that gained the largest popular vote (with a minimum of at least 25 per cent) received two thirds of the seats in the chamber. Coalition government, with all its compromises and hesitant policies, would no longer be necessary. In the election of 1924, the Fascists won a great victory and complete control of the Chamber of Deputies. They used that majority to end legitimate parliamentary life. A series of laws passed in 1925 and 1926 permitted Mussolini, in effect, to rule by decree. In 1926, all other political parties were dissolved. By the close of that year, Italy had been transformed into a single-party, dictatorial state.

The Italian dictator made one important domestic departure that brought him significant political dividends. Through the Lateran Accord of February 1929, the Roman Catholic church and the Italian state made peace with each other. Ever since the armies of Italian unification had seized papal lands in the 1860s, the Church had been hostile to the state. The popes had remained virtual prisoners in the Vatican after 1870. The agreement of 1929 recognized the pope as the temporal ruler of Vatican City. The Italian government agreed to pay an indemnity to the papacy for confiscated land. The state also recognized Catholicism as the religion of the nation, exempted Church property from taxes, and allowed Church law to govern the institution of marriage. The Lateran Accord brought further respectability to Mussolini's authoritarian regime.

German Democracy and Dictatorship

The Weimar Republic

The German Weimar Republic was born from the defeat of the imperial army, the revolution of 1918 against the Hohenzollerns, and the hopes of German Liberals and Social Democrats. Its name derived from the city in which its constitution was written and promulgated in August 1919. While the constitution was being debated, the republic, headed by the Social Democrats, accepted the humiliating terms of the Versailles Treaty. Although its officials had signed only under the threat of an Allied invasion, the republic was nevertheless permanently associated with the national disgrace and the economic burdens of the treaty.

Throughout the 1920s, the government of the republic was required to fulfill the economic and military provisions imposed by the Paris settlement. It became all too easy for nationalists and military figures whose policies had brought on the tragedy and defeat of the war to blame the young republic and the socialists for the results of the conflict. In Germany, more than in other countries, the desire to revise the treaty was closely related to a desire to change the mode of domestic government.

The Weimar Constitution was a highly enlightened document. It guaranteed civil liberties and provided for direct election, by universal suffrage, of the *Reichstag* and the president. However, it also contained certain crucial structural flaws that allowed the eventual overthrow of its institutions. Within the *Reichstag*, a complicated system of proportional representation was adopted. This system made it relatively easy for very small political parties to gain seats in the *Reichstag* and resulted in shifting party combinations that led to considerable instability. Ministers were technically responsible to the *Reichstag*, but the president appointed and removed the chancellor, the head of the cabinet. Perhaps most important, Article 48 allowed the president, in times of emergency, to rule by decree. In this manner, the constitution permitted the possibility of presidential dictatorship.

A number of major and minor humiliations as well as considerable economic instability impinged on the new government. In March 1920, the right-wing Kapp *Putsch*, or armed insurrection, erupted in Berlin. Led by a conservative civil servant and supported by army officers, the attempted coup failed. But the collapse occurred only after government officials had fled the city and German workers had carried out a general strike. The same month, a series of strikes took place in the Ruhr mining district. The government sent in troops. Such extremism from both the left and the right would haunt the republic for all its days. In May 1921, the Allies presented a reparations bill for 132 billion gold marks. The German republican government accepted this preposterous demand only after new Allied threats of occupation. Throughout the early 1920s, there were numerous assassinations or attempted assassinations of important republican leaders. Violence was the hallmark of the first five years of the republic.

INVASION OF THE RUHR AND INFLATION. Inflation brought the major crisis of this period. The financing of the war and the continued postwar deficit spending generated an immense rise in prices. Consequently, the value of German currency fell. By early 1921, the German mark traded against the American dollar at a ratio of 64 to 1, compared with a ratio of 4.2 to 1 in 1914. The German financial community contended that the value of the currency could not be sta-

In 1923 German inflation became so extreme that eventually money was not worth the paper on which it was printed. In this photograph poor citizens sell tin cans to raise money. [The Granger Collection.]

bilized until the reparations issue had been solved. In the meantime, the printing presses kept pouring forth paper money, which was used to redeem government bonds as they fell due.

The French invasion of the Ruhr in January 1923, to secure the payment of reparations, and the German response of economic passive resistance produced cataclysmic inflation. The Weimar government paid subsidies to the Ruhr labor force, who had laid down their tools. Unemployment soon spread from the Ruhr to other parts of the country, creating a new drain on the treasury and also reducing tax revenues. The printing presses by this point had difficulty providing enough paper currency to keep up with the daily rise in prices. Money was literally not worth the paper it was printed on. Stores were unwilling to exchange goods for the worthless currency, and farmers withheld produce from the market.

The moral and social values of thrift and prudence were thoroughly undermined. The security of middle-class savings, pensions, and insurance policies was wiped out, as were investments in government bonds. Simultaneously, debts and mortgages could be paid off. Speculators in land, real estate, and industry made great fortunes. Union contracts generally allowed workers to keep up with rising prices. Thus inflation was not a disaster to everyone. However, to the middle class and the lower middle class the inflation was still one more traumatic experience coming hard on the heels of the military defeat and the peace treaty. Only when the social and economic upheaval of these months is grasped can the later German desire for order and security at almost any cost be comprehended.

HITLER'S EARLY CAREER. Late in 1923, Adolf Hitler (1889–1945) made his first major appearance on the German political scene. In 1889, he had been born the son of a minor Austrian customs official. By 1907, he had gone to Vienna, where his hopes of becoming an artist were soon dashed. He lived off money sent by his widowed mother and later off his Austrian orphan's allowance. He also painted postcards for further income and later found work as a day laborer. In Vienna, he became acquainted with Mayor Karl Lueger's Christian Social Party, which prospered on an ideology of anti-Semitism and from the social anxieties of the lower middle class. Hitler's own relatively precarious situation and his own social observations taught him how desperately the lower middle class feared slipping into a working-class condition. He also absorbed the rabid German nationalism and extreme anti-Semitism that flourished in Vienna. He came to hate Marxism, which he associated with Jews. During World War I, Hitler fought in the German army, was wounded, was promoted to the rank of corporal, and was awarded the Iron Cross for bravery. The war gave him his first sense of purpose.

After the conflict, Hitler settled in Munich. In the new surroundings, he became associated with a small nationalistic, anti-Semitic political party that in 1920 adopted the name of National Socialist German Workers Party, better known simply as the Nazis. The same year, the group began to parade under a red banner with a black swastika. It issued a platform, or program, of Twenty-five Points. Among other things, these called for the repudiation of the Versailles Treaty, the unification of Austria and Germany, the exclusion of Jews from German citizenship, agrarian reform, the prohibition of land speculation, the confiscation of war profits, state administration of the giant cartels, and the replacement of department stores with small retail shops. Originally, the Nazis had called for a broad program of nationalization of industry in an attempt to compete directly with the Marxist political parties for the vote of the workers. As the tactic failed, the Nazis redefined the meaning of the word *socialist* in the party name so that it suggested a *nationalistic* outlook. In 1922, Hitler said:

Whoever is prepared to make the national cause his own to such an extent that he knows no higher ideal than the welfare of his nation; whoever has understood our great national anthem, *Deutschland, Deutschland, über Alles* ["Germany, Germany, over All"], to mean that nothing in the wide world surpasses in his eyes this Germany, people and land, land and people—that man is a Socialist.[2]

[2]Alan Bullock, *Hitler: A Study in Tyranny*, rev. ed. (New York: Harper & Row, 1962), p. 76.

This definition, of course, had nothing to do with traditional German socialism. The "socialism" that Hitler and the Nazis had in mind was not state ownership of the means of production but the subordination of all economic enterprise to the welfare of the nation. It often implied protection for very small economic enterprise. Increasingly, over the years, the Nazis discovered that their social appeal was to the lower middle class, which found itself squeezed between well-organized big business and socialist labor unions or political parties. The Nazis tailored their message to this very troubled economic group.

Soon after the promulgation of the Twenty-five Points, the Stormtroopers, or SA (*Sturm Abteilung*), were organized under the leadership of Captain Ernst Roehm. It was a paramilitary organization that initially provided its members with food and uniforms and later in the decade with wages. In the mid-1920s, the SA adopted its famous brown-shirted uniform. The Stormtroopers were the chief Nazi instrument for terror and intimidation before the party came into control of the government. They were a law unto themselves. The organization constituted a means of preserving military discipline and values outside the small army permitted by the Paris settlement. The existence of such a private party army was a sign of the potential for violence in the Weimar Republic and the widespread contempt for the law and the institutions of the republic.

The social and economic turmoil following the French occupation of the Ruhr and the German inflation provided the fledgling party with an opportunity for direct action against the Weimar Republic, which at that point seemed incapable of providing military or economic security to the nation. By this time, because of his immense oratorical skills and organizational abilities, Hitler personally dominated the Nazi Party. On November 9, 1923, Hitler and a band of followers, accompanied by General Erich Ludendorff, attempted an unsuccessful *Putsch* at a beer hall in Munich. When the local authorities crushed the rising, sixteen Nazis were killed. Hitler and Ludendorff were arrested and tried for treason. The general was acquitted. Hitler employed the trial to make himself into a national figure. In his defense, he condemned the republic, the Versailles Treaty, the Jews, and the weakened condition of his adopted country. He was convicted and sentenced to five years in prison. He actually spent only a few months in jail before being paroled. During this time, he wrote *Mein Kampf* ("My Struggle"). Another result of the brief imprisonment was a decision on Hitler's part that in the future, he and his party must seek to seize political power by legal methods.

THE STRESEMANN YEARS. Elsewhere, the officials of the republic were attempting to repair the damage from the inflation. Gustav Stresemann (1878–1929) was primarily responsible for reconstruction of the republic and for its achievement of a sense of self-confidence. He served as chancellor only from August to November 1923, but he provided the nation with a new basis for stability. Stresemann abandoned the policy of passive resistance in the Ruhr. The country simply could not afford it. Then, with the aid of banker Hjalmar Schacht, he introduced a new German currency. The rate of exchange was one trillion of the old German marks for one new *Rentenmark*. Stresemann also moved against challenges from both the left and the right. He supported the crushing of both Hitler's abortive *Putsch* and smaller communist disturbances. In late November 1923, he resigned as chancellor and assumed the position of foreign minister, a post that he held until his death in 1929. In that office, he exercised considerable influence over the affairs of the republic.

In 1924, the Weimar Republic and the Allies agreed to a new systematization of the reparation payments. The Dawes Plan lowered the annual payments and allowed them to fluctuate according to the fortunes of the German economy. The last French troops left the Ruhr in 1925. The same year, Friedrich Ebert (1871–1925), the Social Democratic president of the republic, died. Field Marshal Paul von Hindenburg, a military hero and a conservative monarchist, was elected as his successor. He governed in strict accordance with the constitution, but his election suggested that a new conservative tenor had come to German politics. It looked as if conservative Germans had become reconciled to the republic. This conservatism was in line with the prosperity of the latter part of the decade. The new political and economic stability meant that foreign capital flowed into Germany, and employment, which had been poor throughout most of the postwar years, improved smartly. Giant industrial combines spread. The prosperity helped to establish broader acceptance and appreciation of the republic.

In foreign affairs, Stresemann pursued a conciliatory course. He was committed to a policy of fulfilling the provisions of the Versailles Treaty, even as he attempted to revise it by diplomacy. He was willing to accept the settlement in the west but was a determined, if sometimes secret, revisionist in the east. He aimed to recover German territories lost to Poland and Czechoslovakia and possibly to unite with Austria, chiefly by diplomatic means. The first step, however, was to achieve respectability and economic recovery. That goal required a policy of accommodation and "Fulfillment," for the moment at least.

LOCARNO. These developments gave rise to the Locarno Agreements of October 1925. The spirit of conciliation led politicians Austen Chamberlain for Britain and Aristide Briand for France to accept

The signing of the Locarno Agreements in October of 1925, which brought a new, if temporary, spirit of conciliation and hope to Europe. [United Press International Photo.]

Stresemann's proposal for a fresh start. France and Germany both accepted the western frontier established at Versailles as legitimate. Britain and Italy agreed to intervene against the aggressor if either side violated the frontier or if Germany sent troops into the demilitarized Rhineland. Significantly, no such agreement was made about Germany's eastern frontier, but the Germans made treaties of arbitration with Poland and Czechoslovakia, and France strengthened its ties with those countries. France supported German membership in the League of Nations and agreed to withdraw its occupation troops from the Rhineland in 1930, five years earlier than specified at Versailles.

Germany was pleased to have achieved respectability and a guarantee against another Ruhr occupation, as well as the possibility of revision in the east. Britain was pleased to be allowed to play a more evenhanded role. Italy was glad to be recognized as a great power. The French were happy, too, because the Germans voluntarily accepted the permanence of their western frontier, which was also guaranteed by Britain and Italy, and France maintained its allies in the east.

The Locarno Agreements brought a new spirit of hope to Europe. Germany's entry into the League of Nations was greeted with enthusiasm. Chamberlain, Briand, and Stresemann jointly received the Nobel Peace Prize in 1926. The spirit of Locarno was carried even further when the leading European states, Japan, and the United States signed the Kellogg–Briand Pact in 1928, renouncing "war as an instrument of national policy." The joy and optimism were not justified. France had merely recognized its inability to coerce Germany without help. Britain had shown its unwillingness to uphold the settlement in the east. Austen Chamberlain declared that no British government ever would "risk the bones of a British grenadier" for the Polish corridor. Germany was by no means reconciled to the eastern settlement. It maintained clandestine military connections with the Soviet Union and planned to continue to press for revision.

In both France and Germany, moreover, the conciliatory politicians represented only a part of the nation. In Germany, especially, most people continued to reject Versailles and regarded Locarno as only an extension of it. When the Dawes Plan ran out in 1929, it was replaced by the Young Plan, which lowered the reparation payments, put a term on how long they must be made, and removed Germany entirely from outside supervision and control. The intensity of the outcry in Germany against the continuation of any reparations showed how far the Germans were from accepting their situation. In spite of these problems, major war was by no means inevitable. Europe, aided by American loans, was returning to prosperity. German leaders like Stresemann would certainly have continued to press for change, but there is little reason to think that they would have resorted to force, much less to a general war. Continued prosperity and diplomatic success might have won the loyalty of the German people for the Weimar Republic and moderate revisionism, but the Great Depression of the 1930s brought new forces to power.

Depression and Political Deadlock

The outflow of foreign, and especially American, capital from Germany commencing in 1928 undermined the economic prosperity of the Weimar Republic. The resulting economic crisis brought parliamentary government to an end. In 1928, a coalition of center parties and the Social Democrats governed. All went reasonably well until the Depression struck. Then the coalition partners differed sharply on economic policy. The Social Democrats wanted no reduction in social and unemployment insurance. The more conservative parties, remembering the inflation of 1923, insisted on a balanced budget. The coalition dissolved in March 1930. To resolve the parliamentary deadlock in the *Reichstag*, President von Hindenburg appointed Heinrich Brüning (1885–1970) as chancellor. Lacking a majority in the *Reichstag*, the new chancellor governed through emergency presidential decrees as authorized by Article 48 of the constitution. The party divisions in the *Reichstag* prevented the overriding of the decrees. In this manner, the Weimar Republic was transformed into a presidential dictatorship.

German unemployment rose from 2,258,000 in March 1930 to over 6,000,000 in March 1932. There had been persistent unemployment during the 1920s, but nothing of such magnitude or duration. The economic downturn and the parliamentary deadlock worked to the advantage of the more extreme political parties. In the election of 1928, the Nazis had won only 12 seats in the *Reichstag*, and the Communists had won 54 seats. Two years later, after the election of 1930, the Nazis held 107 seats and the Communists 77.

The power of the Nazis in the streets was also on the rise. The unemployment fed thousands of men into the Stormtroopers, which had 100,000 members in 1930 and almost 1 million in 1933. The SA freely and viciously attacked Communists and Social Democrats. For the Nazis, politics meant the capture of power through the instruments of terror and intimidation as well as by legal elections. Anything resembling decency and civility in political life vanished. The Nazis held rallies that resembled secular religious revivals. They paraded through the streets and the countryside. They gained powerful supporters and sympathizers in the business, military, and newspaper communities. Some intellectuals were also sympathetic. The Nazis were able to transform this discipline and enthusiasm born of economic despair and nationalistic frustration into impressive electoral results.

Hitler and President von Hindenburg riding together in 1933 shortly after the aged president had appointed Hitler chancellor. After von Hindenburg's death the next year, Hitler combined the powers of president with those of chancellor. [Culver Pictures.]

Hitler Comes to Power

For two years, Brüning continued to govern through the confidence of Hindenburg. The economy did not improve, and the political situation deteriorated. In 1932, the eighty-three-year-old president stood for re-election. Hitler ran against him and forced a runoff. In the first election, the Nazi leader garnered 30.1 per cent of the vote, and he gained 36.8 per cent in the second. Although Hindenburg was returned to office, the results of the poll convinced him that Brüning no longer commanded sufficient confidence from conservative German voters. On May 30, 1932, he dismissed Brüning, and on the next day, he appointed Franz von Papen (1878–1969) in his place. The new chancellor was one of a small group of extremely conservative advisers on whom the aged Hindenburg had become increasingly dependent. Others included the president's son and several military figures. With the continued paralysis in the *Reichstag*, their influence over the president amounted to virtual control of the government. Consequently, the crucial decisions of the next several months were made by only a handful of people.

Papen and the circle around the president wanted to find some way to draw the Nazis into cooperation with them without giving any effective power to Hitler. The government needed the popular support on the right that only the Nazis seemed able to generate. The Hindenburg circle decided to convince Hitler that the Nazis could not come to power on their own. Papen removed the ban on Nazi meetings that Brüning had imposed and then called a *Reichstag* election for July 1932. The Nazis won 230 seats and polled 37.2 per cent of the vote. As the price for his entry into the Cabinet, Hitler demanded appointment as chancellor. Hindenburg refused. Another election was called in November, partly as a means of wearing down the Nazis' financial resources. It was successful in that regard. The number of Nazi seats fell to 196, and their percentage of the popular vote dipped to 33.1 per cent. The advisers around Hindenburg still refused to appoint Hitler to office.

In early December 1932, Papen resigned, and Kurt von Schleicher (1882–1934) became chancellor. There now existed much fear of civil war between groups on the left and the right. Schleicher decided to attempt the construction of a broad-based coalition of conservative groups and trade unionists. The prospect of such a coalition, including groups from the political left, frightened the Hindenburg circle even more than the prospect of Hitler. They did not trust Schleicher's motives, which have never been very clear. Consequently, they persuaded Hindenburg to appoint Hitler as chancellor. To control him and to see that he did little mischief, Papen was named vice-chancellor, and other traditional conservatives were appointed to the Cabinet. On January 30, 1933, Adolf Hitler became the chancellor of Germany.

Much credit was once given to German big business

for the rise of Hitler. However, little evidence exists that business money financed the Nazis in a fashion that made any crucial difference to their success or failure. Hitler's supporters were frequently suspicious of business and giant capitalism. They wanted a simpler world and one in which small property would be safe from both socialism and large-scaled capitalist consolidation. These people looked to Hitler and the Nazis rather than to the Social Democrats because the latter, though concerned with social issues, never appeared sufficiently nationalistic. The Nazis won out over other conservative nationalistic parties because, unlike the latter, they did address themselves to the problem of lower-middle class social insecurity.

Hitler's Consolidation of Power

Once in office, Hitler moved with almost lightning speed to consolidate his control. This process had three facets: the capture of full legal authority, the crushing of alternative political groups, and the purging of rivals within the Nazi Party itself.

On February 27, 1933, a mentally ill Dutch communist set fire to the *Reichstag* building in Berlin. The Nazis quickly turned the incident to their own advantage by claiming that the fire proved the existence of an immediate communist threat against the government. To the public, it seemed plausible that the communists might attempt some action against the state now that the Nazis were in power. Under Article 48, Hitler made the Emergency Decree suspending civil liberties and proceeded to arrest communists or alleged communists. This decree was not revoked for as long as Hitler ruled Germany.

In early March, another *Reichstag* election took place. The Nazis still received only 43.9 per cent of the vote. However, the arrest of the newly elected Communist deputies and the political fear aroused by the fire meant that Hitler could control the *Reichstag*. On March 23, 1933, the *Reichstag* passed an Enabling Act that permitted Hitler to rule by decree. Thereafter, there were no legal limits on his exercise of power. The Weimar Constitution was never formally repealed or amended. It had simply been supplanted by the February Emergency Decree and March Enabling Act.

Perhaps better than anyone else, Hitler understood that he and his party had not inevitably come to power. All of his potential opponents had stood divided between 1929 and 1933. He intended to prevent them from regrouping. In a series of complex moves, Hitler outlawed or undermined various German institutions that might have served as rallying points for opposition. In early May 1933, the offices, banks, and newspapers of the free trade unions were seized, and their leaders were arrested. The Nazi Party itself, rather than any government agency, undertook this action. In late June and early July, all of the other German political parties were outlawed. By July 14, 1933, the National Socialists were the only legal party in Germany. During the same months, the Nazis had moved against the governments of the individual federal states in Germany. By the close of 1933, all major institutions of potential opposition had been eliminated.

The final element in Hitler's consolidation of power involved the Nazi Party itself. By late 1933, the SA, or Stormtroopers, consisted of approximately one million active members and a larger number of reserves. The commander of this party army was Ernst Roehm, a possible rival to Hitler himself. The German army officer corps, on whom Hitler depended to rebuild the na-

Hermann Göring (1893–1946), *Hitler's second in command, with other Nazi officers,*
[United Press International Photo.]

tional army, were jealous of the SA leadership. Consequently, to protect his own position and to shore up support with the regular army, on June 30, 1934, Hitler personally ordered the murder of key SA officers, including Roehm. Others killed between June 30 and July 2 included the former chancellor General Kurt von Schleicher and his wife. The exact number of victims purged is unknown, but it has been estimated to have exceeded one hundred persons. The German army, which was the only institution in the nation that might have prevented the murders, did nothing. A month later, on August 2, 1934, President Hindenburg died. Thereafter, the offices of chancellor and president were combined. Hitler was now the sole ruler of Germany and of the Nazi Party.

The Police State

Terror and intimidation had been a major factor in the Nazi march to office. As Hitler consolidated his power, he oversaw the organization of a police state. The chief vehicle of police surveillance was the SS (*Schutzstaffel*), or security units, commanded by Hein-

Jews being interrogated in Berlin in 1933. The Nazi accession to power led immediately to the issuance of anti-Jewish laws and to a government-sponsored boycott of Jewish businesses. During the early days of the boycott, Jews frequently were interrogated, detained, and even arrested. [Wide World Photos.]

The Nazis Pass Their Racial Legislation

Anti-Semitism had been a fundamental tenet of the Nazi Party and became a major policy of the Nazi government. This comprehensive legislation of September 15, 1935, carried anti-Semitism into all areas of public life and into some of the most personal areas of private life as well. It was characteristically titled the "Law for the Protection of German Blood and Honor." Hardly any aspect of Nazi thought and action was as shocking to the non-German world as was this policy toward the Jews.

Imbued with the knowledge that the purity of German blood is the necessary prerequisite for the existence of the German nation, and inspired by an inflexible will to maintain the existence of the German nation for all future times, the Reichstag has unanimously adopted the following law, which is now enacted:

Article I: (1) Any marriages between Jews and citizens of German or kindred blood are herewith forbidden. Marriages entered into despite this law are invalid, even if they are arranged abroad as a means of circumventing this law.

(2) Annulment proceedings for marriages may be initiated only by the Public Prosecutor.

Article II: Extramarital relations between Jews and citizens of German or kindred blood are herewith forbidden.

Article III: Jews are forbidden to employ as servants to their households female subjects of German or kindred blood who are under the age of forty-five years.

Article IV: (1) Jews are prohibited from displaying the Reich and national flag and from showing the national colors.

(2) However, they may display the Jewish colors. The exercise of this right is under state protection.

Article V: (1) Anyone who acts contrary to the prohibition noted in Article I renders himself liable to penal servitude.

(2) The man who acts contrary to the prohibition of Article II will be punished by sentence to either a jail or penitentiary.

(3) Anyone who acts contrary to the provisions of Articles III and IV will be punished with a jail sentence up to a year and with a fine, or with one of these penalties.

Article VI: The Reich Minister of Interior, in conjunction with the Deputy to the Führer and the Reich Minister of Justice, will issue the required legal and administrative decrees for the implementation and amplification of this law.

Article VII: This law shall go into effect on the day following its promulgation, with the exception of Article III, which shall go into effect on January 1, 1936. ❑

Louis L. Snyder (ed. and trans.), *Documents of German History* (New Brunswick, N.J.: Rutgers University Press, 1958), pp. 427–428.

During the night of November 9, 1938, all across Germany the windows of Jewish businesses were smashed in a vicious outburst of anti-Semitism. This photograph was made in Berlin the following day. The Nazis then confiscated the insurance money and refused to allow compensation. [The Granger Collection.]

rich Himmler (1900–1945). This group had originated in the mid-1920s as a bodyguard for Hitler and had become a more elite paramilitary organization than the larger SA. In 1933, the SS was composed of approximately fifty-two thousand members. It was the instrument that carried out the blood purges of the party in 1934. By 1936, Himmler had become head of all police matters in Germany and stood second only to Hitler in power and influence.

The police character of the Nazi regime was all-pervasive, but the people who most consistently experienced the terror of the police state were the German Jews. Anti-Semitism had been a key plank of the Nazi program. It was anti-Semitism based on biological racial theories stemming from late-nineteenth-century thought rather than from religious discrimination. Prior to World War II, the Nazi attack on the Jews went through three stages of increasing intensity. In 1933, shortly after assuming power, the Nazis excluded Jews from offices in the civil service. For a time, they also attempted to enforce boycotts of Jewish shops and businesses. The boycotts won relatively little public support. In 1935, a series of measures known as the *Nuremberg Laws* robbed German Jews of their citizenship. All persons with at least three Jewish grandparents were defined as Jews. The professions and the major occupations were closed to Jews. Marriage and sexual intercourse between Jews and non-Jews were prohibited. Legal exclusion and humiliation of the Jews became the order of the day.

The persecution of the Jews increased again in 1938. Business careers were forbidden. In November 1938, under orders from the Nazi Party, thousands of Jewish stores and synagogues were burned or other-

wise destroyed. The Jewish community itself was required to pay for the damage that occurred on *Kristallnacht* because the government confiscated the insurance money. In all manner of other ways, large and petty, the German Jews were harassed. This persecution allowed the Nazis to inculcate the rest of the population with the concept of a master race of pure German "Aryans" and also to display their own contempt for civil liberties. After the war broke out, Hitler decided in 1942 to destroy the Jews in Europe. It is thought that over six million Jews, mostly from east European nations, died as a result of that staggering decision, unprecedented in its scope and implementation.

The Soviet Experiment

The political right had no monopoly on authoritarianism between the wars. The consolidation of the Bolshevik Revolution in Russia established the most extensive and durable of all twentieth-century authoritarian governments. However, the dictatorships of the left and the right did differ from each other. Unlike the Italian Fascists or the German National Socialists, the Bolsheviks had seized power illegally through revolution. For several years, they confronted effective opposition, and their leaders long felt insecure about their hold on the country. The Communist Party was not a mass party nor a nationalistic one. Its early membership rarely exceeded more than 1 per cent of the Russian population. The Bolsheviks confronted a much less industrialized economy than existed in Italy or Germany. They believed in and practiced the collectivization of economic life attacked by the right-wing dictatorships. The Marxist-Leninist ideology was far more all-encompassing than the nationalism of the Fascists and the racism of the Nazis. Communism was an exportable commodity. The communists regarded their government and their revolution not as local events in a national history but as an epoch-making event in the history of the world and the development of humanity.

War Communism

Within the Soviet Union, the Red Army under the organizational genius of Leon Trotsky had suppressed internal and foreign military opposition to the new government. Within months of the revolution, a new secret police, known as *Cheka*, appeared. Throughout the civil war, Lenin had declared that the Bolshevik Party, as the vanguard of the revolution, was imposing the dictatorship of the proletariat. Political and economic administration became highly centralized. All major decisions flowed from the top in a nondemocratic manner. Under the economic policy of "War Communism," the revolutionary government confis-

Lenin and Trotsky (saluting) in Red Square in Moscow in 1919, from a documentary film made by Herman Axelbank. Trotsky's organizational skill was largely responsible for the Red Army's victory in the Russian Civil War of 1918–1920. By 1921, as a result of war, revolution, and civil war, the Russian economy had all but collapsed. [United Press International Photo.]

cated and then operated the banks, the transport facilities, and heavy industry. The state also forcibly requisitioned grain produced by the peasants and shipped it from the countryside to feed the army and the workers in the cities. The fact of the civil war permitted suppression of possible resistance to this economic policy.

"War Communism" aided the victory of the Red Army over its opponents. The revolution had survived and triumphed. However, the policy generated domestic opposition to the Bolsheviks, who in 1920 numbered only about 600,000 members. The alliance of workers and peasants forged by the slogan of "Peace, Bread, and Land" had begun to come apart at the seams. Many Russians were no longer willing to make the sacrifices demanded by the central party bureaucrats. In 1920 and 1921, major strikes occurred in numerous factories. Peasants were discontented and resisted the requisition of grain. In March 1921, the navy mutinied at Kronstadt. The Red Army crushed the rebellion with grave loss of life. Each of these incidents suggested that the proletariat itself was opposing the dictatorship of the proletariat. Also, by late 1920, it had become clear that further revolution would not sweep across the rest of Europe. For the time being, the Soviet Union would constitute a vast island of revolutionary socialism in the larger sea of worldwide capitalism.

The New Economic Policy

Under these difficult conditions, Lenin made a crucial strategic retreat. In March 1921, following the Kronstadt mutiny, he outlined the New Economic Policy, normally referred to as *NEP*. Apart from what he termed "the commanding heights" of banking, heavy industry, transportation, and international commerce, there was to be considerable private economic enterprise. In particular, peasants were to be permitted to farm for a profit. They would pay taxes like other citizens, but they could sell their surplus grain on the open market. The NEP was in line with Lenin's earlier conviction that the Russian peasantry held the key to the success of revolution in the nation. After 1921, the countryside did become more stable, and a secure food supply seemed assured for the cities. Similar free enterprise flourished within light industry and domestic retail trade. By 1927, industrial production had reached its 1913 level. The revolution seemed to have transformed Russia into a land of small family farms and small, privately owned shops and businesses.

Stalin Versus Trotsky

The New Economic Policy had caused sharp disputes within the Politburo, the highest governing committee of the Communist Party. The partial return to capitalism seemed to some members nothing less than a betrayal of sound Marxist principles. These frictions increased as Lenin's firm hand disappeared. In 1922, he suffered a stroke that broke his health. He returned to work but never again dominated party affairs. In 1924, Lenin died. As the power vacuum developed, an intense struggle for future leadership of the party commenced. Two factions emerged. One was led by Trot-

The youthful Stalin, possibly a tsarist police photo. As he worked his way up the Bolshevik political hierarchy, Stalin became a master of the details of its bureaucracy, experience that eventually helped him to oust and destroy his opponents, real and fancied, in the politburo. [The Granger Collection.]

sky; the other by Joseph Stalin (1879–1953), who had become general secretary of the party in 1922. Shortly before his death, Lenin had criticized both men. He was especially harsh toward Stalin. However, the general secretary's base of power lay with the party membership and with the daily management of party affairs. Consequently, he was able to withstand the posthumous strictures of Lenin.

The issue between the two factions was power within the party, but the struggle was fought out over the question of Russia's path toward industrialization and the future of the communist revolutionary movement. Trotsky, speaking for what became known as the left wing, urged rapid industrialization financed through the expropriation of farm production. Agriculture should be collectivized, and the peasants should be made to pay for industrialization. Trotsky further argued that the revolution in Russia could succeed only if new revolutions took place elsewhere in the world. Russia needed the skills and wealth of other nations to build its own economy. As Trotsky's influence within the party began to wane, he also demanded that party members be permitted to criticize

the policies of the government and the party. However, Trotsky was very much a latecomer to the advocacy of open discussion. When in control of the Red Army, he had been known as an unflinching disciplinarian.

A right-wing faction opposed Trotsky. Its chief ideological voice was that of Nikolai Bukharin (1888–1938), the editor of *Pravda*, the official party paper. Stalin was the major political manipulator. In the mid-1920s, this group pressed for the continuation of Lenin's NEP and a policy of relatively slow industrialization. Stalin emerged as the victor in these intraparty rivalries.

Stalin had been born in 1879 into a very poor family. Unlike the other early Bolshevik leaders, he had not spent a long period of exile in Western Europe. He was much less an intellectual and internationalist. He was also much more brutal. His handling of various recalcitrant national groups within Russia after the revolution had shocked even Lenin. Stalin's power lay in his command of bureaucratic and administrative methods. He was neither a brilliant writer nor an effective public speaker; however, he mastered the crucial, if dull, details of party structure, including admission and promotion. That mastery meant that he could draw on the support of the lower levels of the party apparatus when he came into conflict with other leaders.

In the mid-1920s, Stalin supported Bukharin's position on economic development. In 1924, he also enunciated, in opposition to Trotsky, the doctrine of "socialism in one country." He urged that socialism could be achieved in Russia alone. Russian success did not depend on the fate of the revolution elsewhere. In this manner, Stalin nationalized the previously international scope of the Marxist revolution. Stalin cunningly used the apparatus of the party and his control over the Central Committee of the Communist Party to edge out Trotsky and his supporters. By 1927, Trotsky had been removed from all his offices, expelled from the party, and exiled to Siberia. In 1929, he was sent out of Russia and eventually took up residence in Mexico, where he was murdered in 1940, presumably by one of Stalin's agents. With the removal of Trotsky from all positions of influence, Stalin was firmly in control of the Soviet state. It remained to be seen where he would direct its course and what "socialism in one country" would mean in practice.

The Decision for Rapid Industrialization

While the capitalist economies of Western Europe floundered in the doldrums of the Depression, the Soviet Union entered on a period of tremendous industrial advance. As in similar eras of past Russian eco-

Stalin Explains the Problem of Agriculture

By the late 1920s, Stalin had changed his earlier views and had decided that the Soviet Union must industrialize rapidly. This shift meant that the agricultural sector must also be modernized in order to feed industrial workers and to pay for needed imports. Stalin saw the means to improved farming in the large-scale collectivization of agriculture and the introduction of farm machinery. When implemented, this policy led to widespread peasant resistance in the countryside.

The characteristic feature of the present state of our national economy is that we are faced by the fact of an excessive lag in the rate of development of grain farming behind the rate of development of industry, while at the same time the demand for marketable grain on the part of the growing towns and industrial areas is increasing by leaps and bounds. The task then is not to *lower* the rate of development of industry to the level of the development of grain farming . . . , but to bring the rate of development of grain farming into line with the rate of development of industry and to *raise* the rate of development of grain farming to a level that will guarantee rapid progress of the entire national economy, both industry and agriculture.

Either we accomplish this task, and thereby solve the grain problem, or we do not accomplish it, and then a rupture between the socialist town and the small-peasant countryside will be inevitable.

. . . .

What ways and means are necessary to accelerate the rate of development of agriculture in general, and of grain farming in particular?

There are three such ways, or channels:
(a) By increasing crop yields and enlarging the area sown by the individual poor and middle peasants.
(b) By further development of collective farms.
(c) By enlarging the old and establishing new state farms.

. . . .

I should like to draw your attention to the collective farms, and especially to the state farms, as levers which facilitate the reconstruction of agriculture on a new technical basis, causing a revolution in the minds of the peasants and helping them to shake off conservatism, routine. The appearance of tractors, large agricultural machines and tractor columns in our grain regions cannot but have its effect on the surrounding peasant farms. Assistance rendered the surrounding peasants in the way of seed, machines and tractors will undoubtedly be appreciated by the peasants and taken as a sign of the power and strength of the Soviet State, which is trying to lead them on to the high road of a substantial improvement of agriculture. ❏

J. Stalin, *Collected Works*, Vol. 2 (Moscow: Foreign Language Publishing House, 1952–1956), pp. 268–269, 272, 279. Originally written in 1928.

---

nomic progress, the direction and impetus came from the top. Stalin far exceeded his tsarist predecessors in the intensity of state coercion and terror he brought to the task. Russia achieved its stunning economic growth during the 1930s only at the cost of literally millions of human lives and the degradation of still other millions. Stalin's economic policy clearly proved that his earlier rivalry with Trotsky had been a matter of political power rather than one of substantial ideological difference.

Through 1928, Lenin's New Economic Policy, as championed by Bukharin with Stalin's support, had charted the course of Soviet economic development. Private ownership and enterprise were permitted to flourish in the countryside as a means of ensuring an adequate food supply for the workers in the cities. A few farmers, the *kulaks*, had become quite prosperous. They probably numbered less than 5 per cent of the rural population. During 1928 and 1929, these and other farmers withheld grain from the market because of dissatisfaction with prices. Food shortages occurred in the cities and provided a cause of potential unrest against the regime. The goals of the NEP were no longer being fulfilled.

Sometime during these troubled months, Stalin came to a momentous decision. Russia must industrialize rapidly in order to match the economic and military power of the West. Agriculture must be collectivized to produce sufficient grain for food and export and to free peasant labor for the factories. This program, which basically embraced Trotsky's earlier economic position, unleashed nothing less than a second Russian revolution. The costs and character of "socialism in one country" now became clear.

AGRICULTURAL POLICY. In 1929, Stalin ordered party agents into the countryside to confiscate any hoarded wheat. The *kulaks* bore the blame for the grain shortages. As part of the general plan to erase the private ownership of land and to collectivize farming, the government undertook a program to eliminate the *kulaks* as a class. However, the definition of a

A tractor station on a Russian collective farm. Soviet agricultural policy sought to increase the productivity of Russian farms by mechanization. Mechanization also led to increased state control, since the collectives had to rent all machinery from the state. [Sovfoto.]

kulak soon embraced anyone who opposed Stalin's policy. In the countryside, there was extensive resistance from peasants and farmers at all levels of wealth. The stubborn peasants were determined to keep their land. They wreaked their own vengeance on the policy of collectivization by slaughtering more than 100 million horses and cattle between 1929 and 1933. The situation in the countryside amounted to nothing less than open warfare. The peasant resistance caused Stalin to call a brief halt to the process in March 1930. He justified the slowdown on the grounds of "dizziness from success."

Soon thereafter, the drive to collectivize the farms was renewed with vehemence, and the costs remained very high. As many as ten million peasants were killed, and millions of others were sent forcibly to collective farms or labor camps. Initially, because of the turmoil on the land, agricultural production fell. There was famine in 1932 and 1933. Milk and meat remained in short supply because of the livestock slaughter. Yet Stalin persevered. The uprooted peasants were moved to thousand-acre collective farms. The machinery for these units was provided by the state through machine-tractor stations. In this fashion, the state retained control over major farm machines. That monopoly was a powerful weapon.

The upheaval of collectivization did change Russian farming in a very dramatic way. In 1928, approximately 98 per cent of Russian farmland consisted of small peasant holdings. Ten years later, despite all the opposition, over 90 per cent of the land had been collectivized, and the quantity of farm produce directly handled by the government had risen by 40 per cent. Those shifts in control meant that the government now had primary direction over the food supply. The farmers and peasants could no longer determine whether there would be stability or unrest in the cities. Stalin and the Communist Party had won the battle of the wheat fields, but they had not solved the problem of producing sufficient quantities of grain. That difficulty has continued to plague the Soviet Union to the present day.

THE FIVE-YEAR PLANS. The revolution in agriculture had been undertaken for the sake of industrialization. The increased grain supply was to feed the labor force and provide exports to finance the imports required for industrial development. The scope of the industrial achievement of the Soviet Union between 1928 and World War II stands as one of the most striking accomplishments of the twentieth century. Russia made a more rapid advance toward economic growth than any other nation in the Western world has ever achieved during any similar period of time. By even the conservative estimates of Western observers, Soviet industrial production rose approximately 400 per cent between 1928 and 1940. Emphasis was placed on the production of iron, steel, coal, electrical power, tractors, combines, railway cars, and other heavy machinery. Few consumer goods were produced. The labor for this development was supplied internally. Capital was raised from the export of grain, even at the cost of internal shortage. The technology was generally borrowed from already-industrialized nations.

The organizational vehicle for industrialization was a series of Five-Year Plans first begun in 1928. The State Planning Commission, or Gosplan, oversaw the program. It set goals of production and organized the economy to meet them. The task of coordinating all facets of production was immensely difficult and complicated. Deliveries of materials from mines or factories had to be assured before the next unit could carry out its part of the plan. There was many a slip between the cup and the lip. The troubles in the countryside were harmful. A vast program of propaganda was undertaken to sell the Five-Year Plans to the Russian people and to elicit cooperation. However, the industrial labor force soon became subject to regimentation similar to that being imposed on the peasants. By the close of the 1930s, the accomplishment of the three Five-Year Plans was truly impressive and probably allowed the Soviet Union to survive the German invasion. Industries that had never existed in Russia now challenged and in some cases, such as tractor production, surpassed their counterparts in the rest of the world. Large, new industrial cities had been built and populated by hundreds of thousands of people.

Many non-Russian contemporaries looked at the

By the late 1930s the cult of Stalin dominated Soviet life. Even at beach resorts his picture was always near. In this 1950 photograph swimmers in the Black Sea carry large pictures of him on small rafts. [Sovfoto.]

Soviet economic experiment quite uncritically. While the capitalist world lay in the throes of the Depression, the Soviet economy had grown at a pace never realized in the West. The American writer Lincoln Steffens reported after a trip to Russia, "I have seen the future and it works." Beatrice and Sydney Webb, the British Fabian Socialists, spoke of "a new civilization" in the Soviet Union. These and other similar writers ignored the shortages in consumer goods and the poor housing. More important, they seem to have had little idea of the social cost of the Soviet achievement. Millions of human beings had been killed and millions more uprooted. The total picture of suffering and human loss during those years will probably never be known; what is known is that the deprivation and sacrifice of Soviet citizens far exceeded anything described by Marx and Engels in relation to nineteenth-century industrialization in Western Europe.

The Purges

Stalin's decisions to industrialize rapidly and to move against the peasants did arouse internal political opposition because these were all departures from the policies of Lenin. In 1929, Stalin forced Bukharin, the fervent supporter of the NEP and his own former ally, off the Politburo. Little detailed information is known about further opposition, but it does seem to have existed among lower-level party followers of Bukharin and other previous opponents of rapid industrializa-

tion. Sometime in 1933, Stalin began to fear loss of control over the party apparatus and the emergence of possibly effective rivals. These fears were probably produced as much by his own paranoia as by real plots. Nevertheless they resulted in the Great Purges, among the most mysterious and horrendous political events of this century. The purges were not understood at the time and have not been fully comprehended either inside or outside the Soviet Union to the present day.

On December 1, 1934, Sergei Kirov (1888–1934), the popular party chief of Leningrad (formerly Saint Petersburg and Petrograd) and a member of the Politburo, was assassinated. In the wake of the shooting, thousands of people were arrested, and still larger numbers were expelled from the party and sent to labor camps. At the time, it was believed that Kirov had been murdered by opponents of the regime. Direct or indirect complicity in the crime became the normal accusation against the persons whom Stalin attacked. It now seems practically certain that Stalin himself authorized Kirov's assassination in fear of eventual rivalry with the Leningrad leader.

The purges after Kirov's death were just the beginning of a larger process. Between 1936 and 1938, a series of spectacular show trials were held in Moscow. Previous high Soviet leaders, including former members of the Politburo, publicly confessed all manner of political crimes. They were convicted and executed. It

1919	August, Constitution of the Weimar Republic promulgated
1920	Kapp *Putsch* in Berlin
1921	March, Kronstadt mutiny leads Lenin to initiate his New Economic Policy
1922	October, Fascist march on Rome leads to Mussolini's assumption of power
1923	January, Fance invades the Ruhr
	November, Hitler's Beer Hall *Putsch*
1924	Death of Lenin
1925	Locarno Agreements
1928	Kellogg–Briand Pact
	First Five-Year Plan launched in USSR
1929	January, Trotsky expelled from USSR
	February, Lateran Accord between the Vatican and the Italian state
	October, New York stock-market crash
	November, Bukharin expelled from his offices in the Soviet Union; Stalin's central position thus affirmed
1930	March, Brüning government begins in Germany
	Stalin calls for moderation in his policy of agricultural collectivization because of "dizziness from success"
	September, Nazis capture 107 seats in German *Reichstag*
1931	August, National Government formed in Britain
1932	March 13, Hindenberg defeats Hitler for German presidency
	May 31, Franz von Papen forms German Cabinet
	July 31, German *Reichstag* election
	November 6, German *Reichstag* election
	December 2, Kurt von Schleicher forms German Cabinet
1933	January 30, Hitler made German chancellor
	February 27, *Reichstag* Fire
	March 5, *Reichstag* election
	March 23, Enabling Act consolidates Nazi power
1934	June 30, Blood purge of the Nazi Party
	August 2, Death of Hindenberg
	December 1, Assassination of Kirov leads to the beginning of Stalin's purges
1936	May, Popular Front government in France
	July–August, Most famous of public purge trials in Russia

is still not certain why they made their palpably false confessions. Still other leaders and lower-level party members were tried in private and shot. Thousands of people received no trial at all. The purges touched persons in all areas of party life. There was apparently little rhyme or reason to why some were executed, others sent to labor camps, and still others left unmolested. After the civilian party members had been purged, the prosecutors turned against the army. Important officers, including heroes of the civil war, were sent to their deaths. Within the party itself, hundreds of thousands of members were expelled, and applicants for membership were removed from the rolls. The exact numbers of executions, imprisonments, and expulsions are unknown but certainly ran into the millions.

The trials and purges astonished Western observers. Nothing quite like this phenomenon had been seen before. Political murders and executions were not new, but the absurd confessions were novel. The scale of the political turmoil was also unprecedented. The Russians themselves did not believe or comprehend what was occurring. There existed no national emergency or crisis. There were only accusations of sympathy for Trotsky or of complicity in Kirov's murder or of other nameless crimes. If a rational explanation is to be sought, it probably must be found in Stalin's concern over his own power. In effect, the purges created a new party structure absolutely loyal to him. The "old Bolsheviks" of the October Revolution were among his earliest targets. They and others active in the first years of the revolution knew how far Stalin had moved from Lenin's policies. New, younger members appeared to replace all of the party members executed or expelled. The newcomers had little knowledge of old Russia or of the ideals of the original Bolsheviks. They had not been loyal to Lenin, to Trotsky, or to any Soviet leader except Stalin himself.

The Great Depression and the New Deal in the United States

The United States emerged from the First World War as a major world power. However, it retreated from that role when the Senate refused to ratify the Versailles Treaty and subsequently failed to join the League of Nations. In 1920, Warren Harding became president and urged a return to what he termed "normalcy," which meant minimal involvement abroad and conservative economic policies at home. Business interests clearly remained in the ascendent, with the federal government taking a relatively inactive role in national economic life. Indeed, inactivity of government was the virtual creed of Harding's successor, President Calvin Coolidge.

The first seven or eight years of the decade witnessed a remarkable period of American prosperity. New electrical appliances, such as the radio, phonograph, washing machine, and vacuum cleaner, appeared on the market. Large scale advertising campaigns attempted to persuade consumers to purchase such items. Real wages rose for many groups of workers. Industry grew at a robust rate. Automobile manufacturers assumed a major role in national economic life. Henry Ford's Model T exemplified the determination of the automobile industry to produce for a mass market. Increasing numbers of factories became mechanized. Engineers and efficiency experts were the heroes of the business world. For most of the 1920s, the New York stock market boomed. All of this remarkable activity stood in marked contrast to the various economic dislocations occurring in Europe.

The material prosperity appeared, however, in a sharply divided society. Segregation remained a basic fact of life for black Americans throughout the South and to a lesser degree in other areas of the country. There was a resurgence of Ku Klux Klan activity, which sought to terrorize blacks, Roman Catholics, and Jews. The Prohibition Amendment of 1919 (repealed in 1933) forbade the manufacture and transport of alcoholic beverages. In the wake of this divisive national policy, major criminal operations arose to supply liquor and to disrupt the stability of civic life. Large numbers of immigrants came from Mexico and Puerto Rico. They settled in cities where their labor was desired but where they were often not really welcomed or assimilated. Finally, the wealth of the nation was overwhelmingly concentrated in a relatively few hands.

Economic Collapse

In March 1929, Herbert Hoover assumed the presidency, the third Republican in as many elections. On October 23, 1929, the New York stock market crashed. The other financial markets also went into a tailspin. During the next year, the stock market continued to fall. The banks that had loaned people money with which to speculate in the market suffered great losses.

The financial collapse of 1929 triggered in America the Great Depression, although there were other underlying domestic causes. During the 1920s, manufacturing firms had not made sufficient capital investment. The disproportionate amount of profits going to about 5 per cent of the U.S. population had by the end of the decade begun to undermine the purchasing power of other consumers. Furthermore, agriculture had been in trouble for several years. Finally, the economic difficulties in Europe and Latin America, which predated those in the United States, meant foreigners were less able to purchase products produced in the United States.

A "Bread Line" in New York City during the Great Depression.

The most pervasive problem of the Great Depression was the spread of unemployment. Joblessness hit poor unskilled workers most rapidly, but then worked its way up the job ladder to touch factory workers and white-collar workers. As unemployment spread, small retail businesses suffered. In the major American manufacturing cities, hundreds of thousands of workers could not find jobs. In the agricultural heartland, the price of corn fell so low in some areas that it was not profitable to harvest the crop. By the early 1930s, banks across the country began to fail, and people lost their savings.

The federal government was not really equipped to address the emergency. There was no tradition of federal action to alleviate economic distress. President Hoover did undertake certain actions, including organizing a number of economic conferences in Washington and encouraging the Federal Reserve to make borrowing easier. He supported the ill-advised Hawley-Smoot Tariff Act of 1930 with which Congress had hoped to protect American industry by a high tariff barrier. But fundamentally, Hoover believed relief was a matter for local government action and for voluntary organizations. In many areas, the local relief agencies had actually run out of money by 1931.

New Role for Government

The election of 1932 was one of the most crucial in American history. Franklin Delano Roosevelt, in accepting the Democratic nomination, pledged his party to a "new deal for the American people." He overwhelmingly defeated Hoover, and quickly set about redirecting the federal policy toward the Depression.

Roosevelt had been born into a moderately wealthy New York family. A distant cousin of Theodore Roosevelt, he had been educated at Harvard College and Columbia Law School. During the First World War, he had served as Secretary of the Navy and in 1920 he had run as the Democratic vice presidential candidate. The next year, however, he was struck with polio and his legs became paralyzed. With extraordinary determination, he overcame this disability and went on to be elected governor of New York in 1928. As the newly elected president, he attempted to convey to the nation the same kind of determination and spirit of optimism that had informed his own personal struggle of the 1920s.

Roosevelt's first goal was to give the nation a sense that the federal government was acting to meet the economic challenge. The first hundred days of his administration became legendary. Coming into office at the height of the crisis in the banking system, he immediately closed all the banks, and permitted only sound institutions to reopen. Congress convened in a special session and rapidly passed a new banking act. Shortly thereafter, Congress enacted the Agricultural Adjustment Act and the Farm Credit Act to aid the farm sector of the economy. To provide jobs, Roosevelt's administration sponsored the Civilian Conservation Corps. The Federal Emergency Relief Act provided funding for state and local relief agencies. In a further effort to restore confidence, Roosevelt began making speeches to the American people; these speeches were known as his "fireside chats."

Roosevelt's most ambitious program was the National Industrial Recovery Act (NIRA), which established the National Recovery Administration (NRA). This agency attempted to foster codes written by various industries to regulate wages and prices. It was hoped that competition might be thus regulated so as to protect jobs and assure production.

The NIRA and other New Deal legislation, such as the Wagner Act of 1935 that established the National

During the Great Depression Franklin D. Roosevelt replaced Herbert Hoover as President of the United States. FDR's aggressive recovery program was intended to give American a "New Deal." [The Bettmann Archive.]

Labor Relations Board and the Fair Labor Standards Act of 1938, provided a larger role in the American economy for organized labor. It became easier for unions to organize. Union membership grew rapidly and steadily. American unionism took on a new character during these years. Previously, most unions had organized by craft and had been affiliated with the American Federation of Labor. The major union gains of the 1930s, however, occurred through the organization of whole industries composed of workers in various crafts in a single union. The most important of these were the United Mine Workers and United Automobile Workers. These new unions organized themselves into the Congress of Industrial Organizations. For many years, the CIO and the AFL were rivals. They eventually merged in the 1950s. The emergence of these new strong industrial labor organizations introduced a powerful new force into the American economic scene.

In 1935, the United States Supreme Court declared the NRA unconstitutional. Thereafter, Roosevelt pursued a course that involved somewhat less centralized economic planning. There were no fewer federal agencies; indeed their number increased, but they operated in general independence from each other.

Through New Deal legislation, the federal government was assuming a far more activist role in the economy than it had ever done before. The federal government itself was attempting to provide relief for the unemployed in the industrial sector. The major institution of the relief effort was the Works Progress Administration, created in 1935. It undertook a massive program of large public works, including the erection of numerous public buildings.

The programs of the New Deal years also involved the federal government directly in economic development rather than turning such development over to private enterprise. Through the formation of the Tennessee Valley Authority, the federal government undertook direct involvement in the economy of the four states of the Tennessee River valley. The agency built dams and then produced and sold hydroelectricity. Never had the federal government undertaken so extensive an economic role. Another major new function for the government was the decision to provide security for the elderly, through the establishment of the Social Security Administration in 1935.

Hence, in one area of American life after another, it was decided that individual voluntary effort could not provide sufficient personal economic security and that the government must act to do so. The result of all these actions was the establishment of a mixed economy in the United States—that is, an economy in which the federal government would have an ongoing active role alongside the private sector.

The New Deal changed much of the face of American life. Yet despite all of its programs and new initia-

tives, it did not solve the unemployment problem. Indeed, in the late 1930s the economy began to falter again. The event that brought the U.S. economy to a level of full employment was the entry of the nation into the World War II.

However, the New Deal did achieve the preservation of American democracy and capitalism. The experience of the United States in the era of the New Deal stood in marked contrast to the economic and political experiments taking place in Europe. Many business-people found Roosevelt far too liberal and his policies too activist. Nonetheless, the New Deal, though fostering a mixed economy, fundamentally preserved capitalism. Roosevelt and the New Deal also flourished in a democratic setting where, in contrast to that of Europe, there was a broad spectrum of political debate—much of it highly critical of the administration. The United States had demonstrated that a nation with a vast industrial economy could confront its gravest economic crisis and still preserve democracy.

The Economic and Political Crisis in World Perspective

The two decades between the great wars marked a period of immense political and economic transition round the globe. Politically many regions witnessed a time of political turmoil and economic instability followed by the establishment of militaristic authoritarian regimes. In Italy it was the Fascists; in Germany, the Nazis; in the Soviet Union, Stalin's regime. In East Asia, Japan came into the grip of a right-wing militaristic government. China saw over twenty years of civil war and revolution. Numerous countries of Latin America came under the sway of dictators or governments heavily influenced by the military. To many observers in the late 1930s, it appeared that the day of liberal parliamentary democracy might be ending. The disruptions arising from World War I and the social and economic turmoil of depression seemed to pose problems that could not be addressed by liberal governments.

The interwar period also saw a turning away from the nineteenth-century ideal of economies in which central governments assumed little responsibility. The German inflation of the early 1920s, the worldwide financial collapse of the late 1920s, the vast unemployment of the early 1930s, and the agricultural crisis of both decades roused demands for government action. One reason for these demands was quite simply that more governments throughout the world were responsible to mass democratic electorates. Governments that did not seek to address the problems were put out of office. This happened to the Republicans in the United States, the socialist and liberal parties in Germany, the left-wing parties in Japan, and various polit- ical parties in Latin America that failed to deal with the Depression. In that respect, paradoxically many democratic electorates actually turned themselves over to politically authoritarian regimes as they searched for social and economic stability. That would be an important lesson in the years after World War II. Then in response to the experience of the 1920s and 1930s, democratic governments around the globe would seek to provide economic and social security as a means of protecting democratic political structures.

It was not only economic turmoil that spawned au- thoritarianism. The interwar years also witnessed the emergence of extreme forms of nationalism in both Europe and Japan. The authoritarian governments of Germany, Italy, and Japan all had agendas of nation- alistic aggression. They were prepared to move wher- ever they saw fellow nationals living outside their bor- ders or where they could establish dominance over other peoples and thus assume the status of imperial powers. Japan moved against Manchuria and later other areas of Asia. Italy invaded Ethiopia. Germany sought union with German-speaking peoples in Aus- tria and Czechoslovakia and then sought to expand throughout eastern Europe by invading Poland. In turn, those actions challenged in various areas of the world the imperial dominance of Great Britain and the vital security interests of the United States. By the end of the 1930s, the authoritarian regimes and the liberal democracies stood on the brink of a major con- frontation.

During these years, the United States and the So- viet Union remained relatively withdrawn from the world scene. The former pursued the bold democratic experiment of the New Deal, while the latter pursued the equally bold experiment of central-government planning and repression. The aggression of other pow- ers would draw the United States and the Soviet Union directly into the world conflict. Because of their vast economic resources, they would emerge, as the two strongest postwar powers. The United States had at- tained that economic role through democracy; the So- viet Union through repression. The relative virtues of those two modes of political and social life would form the issues around which much of the postwar great power rivalry would center.

Suggested Readings

W. S. ALLEN, *The Nazi Seizure of Power: The Experi- ence of a Single German Town*, 1930–1935 (1965). A classic treatment of Nazism in a microcosmic setting.

J. BARNARD, *Walter Reuther and the Rise of the Auto Workers* (1983). A major introduction to the new Amer- ican unions of the 1930s.

K. D. BRACHER, *The German Dictatorship* (1970). A comprehensive treatment of both the origins and the functioning of the Nazi movement and government.

A. BULLOCK, *Hitler: A Study in Tyranny*, rev. ed. (1964), The best biography.

E. H. CARR, *A History of Soviet Russia*, 9 vols. (1950–19–). An extensive and important study.

S. F. COHEN, *Bukharan and the Bolshevik Revolution: A Political Biography*, 1888–1938 (1973). An interesting examination of Stalin's chief opponent on the Commu- nist right.

R. CONQUEST, *The Great Terror: Stalin's Purges of the Thirties* (1968). The best treatment of the subject to this date.

G. CRAIG, *Germany*, 1866–1945 (1978). An important survey.

R. DAHRENDORF, *Society and Democracy in Germany* (1967). An important commentary by a leading sociolo- gist.

I. DEUTSCHER, *The Prophet Armed* (1954), *The Prophet Unarmed* (1959), and *The Prophet Outcast* (1963). A major biography of Trotsky.

I. DEUTSCHER, *Stalin: A Political Biography*, 2nd ed. (1967). The best biography in English.

M. DOBB, *Soviet Economic Development since* 1917, 6th ed. (1966). A basic introduction.

E. EYCK, *A History of the Weimar Republic*, 2 vols. (trans. 1963). The story as narrated by a liberal.

M. S. FAUSOLD, *The Presidency of Herbert Hoover* (1985). An important recent treatment.

L. FISCHER, *The Life of Lenin* (1964). A sound biography by an American journalist.

P. FUSSELL, *The Great War and Modern Memory* (1975). A brilliant account of the literature arising from World War I during the 1920s.

K. GALBRAITH, *The Great Crash* (1979). A well-known account by a leading economist.

H. J. GORDON, *Hitler and the Beer Hall Putsch* (1972). An excellent account of the event and the political situ- ation in the early Weimar Republic.

N. GREENE, *From Versailles to Vichy: The Third Repub- lic*, 1919–1940 (1970). A useful introduction to a difficult subject.

H. GRUBER, *International Communism in the Era of Lenin: A Documentary History* (1967). An excellent col- lection of otherwise difficult-to-find documents.

H. HOLBORN, *A History of Modern Germany:* 1840–1945 (1969). A very comprehensive treatment.

C. KINDLEBERGER, *The World in Depression*, 1929–1939 (1973). An account by a leading economist whose analysis is comprehensible to the layperson.

D. LANDES, *The Unbound Prometheus: Technological Change and Industrial Development in Western Europe from* 1750 *to the Present* (1969). Includes an excellent analysis of both the Great Depression and the few areas of economic growth.

W. LAQUEUR AND G. L. MOSSE (EDS.), *The Great Depression* (1970). A useful collection of articles.

R. S. MCELVAINE, *The Great Depression* (1984). An excellent introduction.

C. S. Maier, *Recasting Bourgeois Europe: Stabilization in France, Germany, and Italy in the Decade after World War I* (1975). An important interpretation written from a comparative standpoint.

D. Milton, *The Politics of U.S. Labour: From the Great Depression to the New Deal* (1980). A clear presentation.

R. K. Murray, *The Harding Era* (1969). A useful overview.

E. Nolte, *Three Faces of Fascism* (1963). An important, influential, and difficult work covering France, Italy, and Germany.

R. Pipes, *The Formation of the Soviet Union*, 2nd ed. (1964). A study of internal policy with emphasis on Soviet minorities.

H. Rogger and E. Weber (eds.), *The European Right: A Historical Profile* (1965). An anthology of articles on right-wing political movements in various European countries.

A. M. Schlesinger, Jr., *The Age of Roosevelt*, 3 vols. (1957–1960). The most important overview.

D. Schoenbaum, *Hitler's Social Revolution: Class and Status in Nazi Germany* (1966). A fascinating analysis of Hitler's appeal to various social classes.

C. Seton-Watson, *Italy from Liberalism to Fascism*, 1870–1925 (1967). A useful survey.

H. Seton-Watson, *Eastern Europe Between the Wars*, 1918–1941 (1946). Somewhat dated but still a useful work.

D. Mack Smith, *Mussolini's Roman Empire* (1976). A general description of the Fascist regime in Italy.

A. Solzhenitsyn, *The Gulag Archipelago*, 3 vols. (1974–1979). A major examination of the labor camps under Stalin by one of the most important of contemporary Russian writers.

R. J. Sontag, *A Broken World*, 1919–1939 (1971). An exceptionally thoughtful and well-organized survey.

A. J. P. Taylor, *English History*, 1914–1945 (1965). Lively and opinionated.

R. Tucker, *Stalin as Revolutionary*, 1879–1929: *A Study in History and Personality* (1973). A useful and readable account of Stalin's rise to power.

H. A. Turner, Jr., *German Big Business and the Rise of Hitler* (1985). An important major study of the subject.

E. Wiskemann, *Fascism in Italy: Its Development and Influence* (1969). A comprehensive treatment.

Global Conflict and Detente

THE PEOPLE of Europe and the United States saw the great conflict of 1914–1918 as a world war. By far, the largest part of the fighting and suffering was confined to the European continent. The consequences of that war, however, affected the whole world. Though Germany and Russia lost their colonies, these and the other colonial areas remained under the control of the victorious European powers, Japan, and the United States under the guise of mandates from the new League of Nations. Advances in transportation and communication and the rapid growth of an interrelated world economy meant that both economic and political problems would not long remain isolated in a single country, or even on one continent. The failure of the League of Nations to bring international stability, widespread dissatisfaction with the peace settlement, a terrible worldwide economic depression, and the rise of fiercely nationalistic and militaristic regimes in Europe and Japan brought an end to an uneasy peace, which had lasted only two decades.

The second great upheaval of the twentieth century, the war of 1939–1945, was truly global in scope and even more devastating than the first. Heavy fighting took place in Africa, Asia, and Europe, and the people of every continent were involved. The battle casualties were great, and the assault on civilians was unprecedented. Massive aerial bombardment of cities began with the German attack on Britain in 1940 and concluded with the use of the new and terrifying atomic weapons against Japan in 1945. Hitler in Germany and Stalin in the Soviet Union made war on designated populations within their own countries; the Japanese treated the civilians of the lands they conquered with great brutality. The cost of this world war in life and property was even greater than that of the first.

After the war, the hopes of many for peace and stability in the future rested with a new international organization, the United Nations. Unlike the League of Nations, which the United States had never joined, the new organization included not only all the victorious powers but has since come to include all the nations of the world. Its success, however, required the cooperation of the great powers. However, the coalition of the victors was always tenuous because of the differences between the political and economic systems of the Western nations and those of the Soviet Union and because of the mutual suspicion between them. The Western powers' insistence on free, democratic elections in the liberated states of Eastern Europe was incompatible with the Soviet Union's desire to control the areas on its western border. Disputes over Poland, the Balkan states, and Germany led to a division of Germany and of all of Europe into east and west. Hence began a period of competition and sometimes open hostility called the *Cold War*. The division hardened with the formation of the North Atlantic Treaty Organization (NATO) in 1949 and the Warsaw Pact in 1955. Since then, the former allies have faced each other across what Winston Churchill called an "Iron Curtain" with ever-increasing collections of deadly weapons and with continuing tension, occasionally relaxed by hopes for cooperation.

The Cold War quickly spread to Asia, where the Communist Party under Mao Tse-tung gained control of China. Allying itself with the Soviet Union, China supported the Communist regime of North Korea against South Korea, which was supported by the United States and its allies. Later the same alignment appeared in Vietnam. However, by the 1960s, a split between the Chinese and the Russians became apparent, and international relations became more complex. By the 1980s, China and the United States had established reasonably friendly relations; a new Chinese regime had even begun to introduce elements of a free-market economy. This action followed similar steps in such Communist nations as Yugoslavia, Hungary, and Romania, all of them undoubtedly influenced by the remarkable success of free-market economies in the defeated nations of West Germany and Japan. Both countries had swiftly recovered from a condition of devastation and poverty to achieve unprecedented prosperity in what were widely seen as economic miracles. Similar advances took place in the other Western countries and in such Asian lands as South Korea and Taiwan. In contrast, the socialist economies of Eastern Europe and the Soviet Union were in serious trouble by the 1980s. Likewise, Mao's desperate attempts in China to produce economic progress through state control had been badly disappointing.

World War II destroyed the capacity of the European nations to maintain their colonial empires and led to the establishment of new, independent nations in Africa, Asia, and the islands of the Pacific. The withdrawal of foreign control was joyously welcomed, but independence brought new problems. Rapid growth of population; ethnic, religious, and tribal rivalries; inadequate educational systems and political experience; a shortage of technological expertise and investment capital—all of these factors often led to civil wars and to political and economic crises. A new wave of Islamic fundamentalism with serious political implications swept through the heart of the Islamic world, from North Africa to Pakistan, dividing it and threatening the stability of more moderate Islamic countries. The added problem in the Middle East of Arab-Israeli conflicts and tensions has been a further source of political and social upheaval. This instability in the so-called Third World created further tensions between the two great power blocs.

The defeat of the Axis powers in World War II had saved the world from a terrible threat to freedom and civility, but it had not, of course, produced universal peace, prosperity, and democracy. Advances in science and technology made it easier than ever for tyrants to abuse their subjects and for totalitarian regimes to stamp out freedom. The new and varied means of destruction that these advances provided also threatened the very existence of the human race. Yet the presence of such dangerous weapons seems, for forty-five years, to have helped avoid such general and terrible conflicts as the two world wars. The wonders of science and technology have also brought longer spans of life, better health, and unprecedented prosperity to people in the advanced nations and have offered the same promises to the developing countries. Both the dangers and the opportunities challenge humanity's capacity for wisdom, restraint, and patience. ❏

	EUROPE	NEAR EAST/INDIA
1940	*1944* D-Day *1945* World War II ends *1948* Berlin blockade and airlift *1949* NATO treaty; Russia detonates the atomic bomb *1953* Death of Stalin *1955* Warsaw Pact *1956* Soviets crush Hungarian rebellion *1957* European Economic Community founded *1958* Charles de Gaulle comes to power in France	*1947* Indian independence *1948* Assassination of Mahatma Gandhi *1949* State of Israel founded *1954–1970* Abdel Nasser leads Egypt *1956* Suez Crisis; Nasser nationalizes the Suez Canal *1958–1969* Dictatorship of General Ayyub Khan in Pakistan
1960	*1960* Paris Summit Conference collapses after U-2 incident *1961* Berlin Wall erected *1964* Krushchev replaced as Soviet Prime Minister by Kosygin; as Party Secretary by Brezhnev *1966* Charles de Gaulle inaugurated for second term as French president *1968* Russian invasion of Czechoslovakia	*1961* Ben Gurion forms coalition government in Israel *1964* King Sa'ud of Saudi Arabia deposed; son Faisal succesor *1966* Indira Gandhi becomes Prime Minister of India *1967* Israeli-Arab June War *1969* Golda Meir becomes Prime Minister of Israel *1969* Yasir Arafat elected Chairman of P.L.O.
1970	*1971* Women granted the right to vote in Switzerland *1972* British impose direct rule on Northern Ireland *1972* Israeli Olympic athletes killed by Arab terrorists *1974* End of military rule in Greece *1974* Portuguese dictatorship deposed; democractic reforms begin *1977* Brezhnev elected President of the USSR *1979* Margaret Thatcher becomes British prime minister	*1971* India signs treaty of friendship with USSR *1972* Bangladesh established as a sovereign state *1973* Arab oil embargo against U.S., Western Europe, and Japan *1975* Egypt reopens Suez Canal *1977* Menachem Begin becomes Prime Minister of Israel *1977* Sadat of Egypt visits Israel *1979* Egyptian-Israeli Peace Treaty *1979* Iran takes U.S. hostages *1979* Soviets invade Afghanistan
1980	*1980* Solidarity Movement in Poland; *1981*, crackdown against movement *1980* Socialist Francois Mitterand elected in France *1981* Lack of jobs; riots in Liverpool and London *1982* Spain, Portugal, and Greece apply for membership in the Common Market *1982* Christian Democrat Helmut Kohl elected in West Germany *1984–1985* Bitter strikes by miners in England *1984* Mikhail Gorbachev introduces *glasnost* in USSR.	*1980* First president elected in Iran; dismissed in 1981 *1981* Release of American hostages in Iran *1981* Assassination of Egyptian president Anwar Sadat; succeeded by Hosni Mubarak *1981* Israel begins bombing P.L.O. headquarters in Beirut *1982* Israel invades Lebanon and is condemned by the U.N. Security Council *1984* Indira Gandhi assassinated *1989* Soviets withdraw troops from Afghanistan

EAST ASIA	AFRICA	THE AMERICAS
1941 Japan attacks Pearl Harbor	*1942–1945* North African campaigns; theater of war extends from Morocco to Egypt and the Suez Canal	*1941* U.S. enters World War II
1945 Japan surrenders after U.S. atomic bombs		*1945* Death of Franklin Delano Roosevelt
1945–1949 Civil war in China	*1955–1962* Wars of independence in French Algeria	*1946* Juan Peron elected president of Argentina
1949 People's Republic of China established by Communists	*1956* Sudan gains independence from Britain and Egypt	*1954* Supreme Court outlaws segregation
1950 North Korea invades South Korea	*1956* Morocco and Tunisia gain independence from France	*1955* Juan Peron overthrown in Argentina
1952 U.S. ends occupation of Japan	*1957* Ghana an independent state under Kwame Nkrumah	*1956* Montgomery bus boycott
1953–1972 Double-digit economic growth in Japan	*1958* Guinea gains independence from France	*1959* Fidel Castro comes to power in Cuba
1955 Liberal-Democratic Party formed in Japan		
1959–1960 Sino-Soviet split		
1959–1975 Vietnam War		
1965–1976 Cultural Revolution devastates China	*1960* Belgian Congo granted independence as Zaire	*1960* John F. Kennedy elected
1968 Death of Ho Chi Minh, president of North Vietnam	*1963* Kenya becomes an independent republic	*1962* Cuban Missile Crisis
1971 Lin Piao killed in China	*1964* Zanzibar, the Congo, and Northern Rhodesia (Zambia) become independent republics	*1963* Assassination of John F. Kennedy
1972 President Nixon visits China	*1965* Revolution in Kenya	*1964* Passage of Civil Rights Act
1973 on Economic growth continues in Japan at slower pace	*1966* British Guiana becomes an independent nation, Guyana	*1965* Major increase in U.S. commitment in Vietnam
	1968 Swaziland gains independence from Britain; Equatorial Guinea from Spain	*1968* Assassination of Dr. Martin Luther King and Robert Kennedy; major campus unrest
		1968 Richard Nixon elected
1976 Death of Mao Tse-tung	*1970* Biafra surrenders to Nigerian government; civil war ends	*1970* Sálvador Allende elected president of Chile
1978–1989 New economic policies of Teng Hsiao-p'ing in China	*1970* Gambia is proclaimed a republic	*1972* Nixon visits China and USSR; is re-elected president of the U.S.
1978–1989 Vietnamese occupy Cambodia	*1974* Drought and famine throughout Africa	*1973* Watergate scandal breaks
	1974 Emperor Haile Selassie of Ethiopia is deposed	*1973* Juan Peron re-elected president of Argentina
	1974–1975 Portugal grants independence to Guinea, Angola, Mozambique, Cape Verde	*1973* Allende overthrown in Chile
	1976 Republic of Transkei, in South Africa, is proclaimed	*1974* Nixon resigns presidency
		1979 Revolution in Nicaragua and El Salvador
1980s South Korea and Taiwan achieve double-digit economic growth	*1980* Algeria helps in release of American hostages in Iran	*1980* Iran hostage crisis
1985 Great Britain agrees to return Hong Kong to China in 1997	*1980* Southern Rhodesia (Zimbabwe) gains independence from Great Britain; Marxist Robert Mugabe elected president	*1980* Election of Ronald Reagan as U.S. President
1987 Roh Tae-woo elected as president in South Korea	*1981* Relations between Libya and the U.S. seriously weakened	*1982* War between Argentina and Great Britain over Isla Malvinas (Falkland Islands)
1988 Japan's GNP becomes second largest in world	*1984* Bishop Desmond Tutu awarded Nobel Peace Prize for oppression in South Africa	*1983* Military government in Argentina overthrown; an elected civilian government restored
1988–1989 Scandals in Japan weaken Conservative Party, force resignation of Prime Ministers Takeshita and Uno	*1985* U.S. economic sanctions against South Africa result in more repression	*1983* End of Mexican oil boom
1989 Vietnam pledges to withdraw from Cambodia		*1986* Explosion of U.S. space shuttle Challenger
1989 Massive demonstrations in favor of democracy in Peking (Beijing) crushed by machine guns and tanks		*1988* Major arms agreement between U.S. and USSR

The first experimental thermonuclear device (H-Bomb) was exploded off Elugelab Island, in the Pacific, on November 1, 1952. [Los Alamos National Laboratory.]

35 World War II and the Cold War

The more idealistic survivors of the First World War, especially in the United States and Great Britain, thought of it as "the war to end all wars" and "a war to make the world safe for democracy." Only in those ways could they justify the awful slaughter, expense, and upheaval of the terrible conflict. How appalled they would have been had they known that only twenty years after the peace treaties a second great war would break out that would be more truly global than the first. In this war, the democracies would be fighting for their lives against militaristic, nationalistic, authoritarian, and totalitarian states in Europe and in Asia. Great Britain and the United States would be allied with the Communist Soviet Union in the struggle. The defeat of the militarists and dictators would not bring the longed-for peace, but a Cold War in which the European states became second-class powers, subordinate to the two new great powers, partially or fully non-European: the Soviet Union and the United States.

Again the Road to War (1933–1939)

World War I and the Versailles Treaty had only a marginal relationship to the world depression of the 1930s. But in Germany, where the reparations settlement had contributed to the vast inflation of 1923, economic and social discontent focused on the Versailles settlement as the cause of all ills. Throughout the late 1920s, Adolf Hitler and the Nazi Party had never ceased denouncing Versailles as the source of all Germany's trouble; the economic woes of the early 1930s seemed to bear them out.

Nationalism and attention to the social question, along with party discipline, had been the sources of Nazi success. They continued to influence Hitler's foreign policy after he became chancellor in early 1933.

Moreover, the Nazi destruction of the Weimar Constitution and of political opposition meant that to an extraordinary degree German foreign policy lay in Hitler's own hands. Consequently, it is important to know what his goals were and what plans he had for achieving them.

Hitler's Goals

From the first expression of his goals in *Mein Kampf* to his last days in the bunker where he died, Hitler's racial theories and goals held the central place in his thought. He meant to go far beyond Germany's 1914 boundaries, which were the limit of the vision of his predecessors. He meant to bring the entire German people (*Volk*), understood as a racial group, together into a single nation. The new Germany would include all the Germanic parts of the old Habsburg Empire, including Austria. This virile and growing nation would need more space to live (*Lebensraum*), which would be taken from the Slavs, a lesser race, fit only for servitude. The new Germany would be purified by the removal of the Jews, another inferior race in Nazi theory. The plan always required the conquest of Poland and the Ukraine as the primary areas for the settlement of Germans, and for the provision of badly needed food. However, neither *Mein Kampf* nor later statements of policy were blueprints for action. Hitler was a brilliant improviser who sought after and made good use of opportunities as they arose. But he never lost sight of his goal, which would almost certainly require a major war.

The Destruction of Versailles

When Hitler came to power, Germany was far too weak to permit the direct approach to his goals. The first problem was to shake off the fetters of Versailles and to make Germany a formidable military power. In October of 1933, Germany withdrew from an international disarmament conference and also from the League of Nations. These acts alarmed the French but were merely symbolic. In January of 1934, Germany made a nonaggression pact with Poland that was of greater concern, for it put into question France's chief means of containing the Germans. At last, in March

Hitler Describes His Goals in Foreign Policy

From his early career, Hitler had certain long-term general views and goals. They were set forth in his Mein Kampf, *which appeared in 1925, and included consolidation of the German* Volk (People), *provision of more land for the Germans, and contempt for such "races" as Slavs and Jews. Here are some of Hitler's views on land.*

The National Socialist movement must strive to eliminate the disproportion between our population and our area—viewing this latter as a source of food as well as a basis for power politics—between our historical past and the hopelessness of our present impotence. . . .

. . . .

The demand for restoration of the frontiers of 1914 is a political absurdity of such proportions and consequences as to make it seem a crime. Quite aside from the fact that the Reich's frontiers in 1914 were anything but logical. For in reality they were neither complete in the sense of embracing the people of German nationality, nor sensible with regard to geomilitary expediency. . . .

As opposed to this, we National Socialists must hold unflinchingly to our aim in foreign policy, namely, to secure for the German people the land and soil to which they are entitled on this earth. . . .

. . . The soil on which some day German generations of peasants can beget powerful sons will sanction the investment of the sons of today, and will some day acquit the responsible statesmen of blood-guilt and sacrifice of the people, even if they are persecuted by their contemporaries. . . .

Much as all of us today recognize the necessity of a reckoning with France, it would remain ineffectual in the long run if it represented the whole of our aim in foreign policy. It can and will achieve meaning only if it offers the rear cover for an enlargement of our people's living space in Europe. . . .

If we speak of soil in Europe today, we can primarily have in mind only *Russia* and her vassal border states. . . .

. . . See to it that the strength of our nation is founded, not on colonies, but on the soil of our European homeland. Never regard the Reich as secure unless for centuries to come it can give every scion of our people his own parcel of soil. Never forget that the most sacred right on this earth is a man's right to have earth to till with his own hands, and the most sacred sacrifice the blood that a man sheds for this earth. ❑

Adolf Hitler, *Mein Kampf*, trans. by Ralph Manheim (Boston: Houghton, Mifflin, 1943), pp. 646, 649, 652, 653, 656.

1935, Hitler formally renounced the disarmament provisions of the Versailles Treaty with the formation of a German air force, and soon he reinstated conscription, which aimed at an army of half a million men.

His path was made easier by growing evidence that the League of Nations was ineffective as a device for keeping the peace and that collective security was a myth. In September 1931, Japan occupied Manchuria, provoking an appeal to the League of Nations by China. The league responded by sending out a commission under the Earl of Lytton. The Lytton Report condemned the Japanese for resorting to force, but the powers were unwilling to impose sanctions. Japan withdrew from the league and kept control of Manchuria.

When Hitler announced his decision to rearm Germany, the league formally condemned that action, but it took no steps to prevent Germany's rearming. The response of France and Britain was hostile, but they felt unable to object because they had not carried out their own promises to disarm. Instead, they met with Mussolini in June 1935 to form the so-called Stresa Front, making an agreement to use force to maintain the status quo in Europe. But Britain was desperate to maintain superiority at sea. Contrary to the Stresa accords and at the expense of French security needs, Britain soon made a separate naval agreement with Hitler, allowing him to rebuild the German fleet to 35 per cent of the British navy.

Italy Attacks Ethiopia

The Italian attack on Ethiopia made the impotence of the League of Nations and the timidity of the Allies even clearer. Using a border incident as an excuse, Mussolini attacked Ethiopia in October 1935. His real intent was to avenge a humiliating defeat that the Italians had suffered in 1896, to begin the restoration of Roman imperial glory, and, perhaps, to turn the thoughts of Italians away from the corruption of the Fascist regime and their economic misery.

The League of Nations condemned Italian aggression and, for the first time, voted economic sanctions. It imposed an arms embargo that limited loans and credits to and imports from Italy. But Britain and

Italian Fascists giving Hitler their famous dagger salute during his state visit to Italy in May 1938. *The visit cemented the alliance between the German and Italian dictators.* [United Press International.]

France were afraid of alienating Mussolini, so they refused to place an embargo on oil, the one economic sanction that could have prevented Italian victory. Even more important, the British fleet did not prevent the movement of Italian troops and munitions through the Suez Canal. The results of this wavering policy were disastrous. The League of Nations and collective security were totally discredited, and Mussolini was alienated as well. He now turned to Germany, and by November 1, 1936, he could speak publicly of a Rome–Berlin "Axis."

Remilitarization of the Rhineland

No less important a result of the Ethiopian affair was its effect on Hitler's evaluation of the strength and determination of the Western powers. On March 7, 1936, he took his greatest risk yet, sending a small armed force into the demilitarized Rhineland. This was a breach not only of the Versailles Treaty but of the Locarno Agreements of 1925 as well, agreements that Germany had made voluntarily. It also removed one of the most important elements of French security. France and Britain had every right to resist. The French especially had a claim to retain the only element of security left after the failure of the Allies to guarantee its defense. Yet neither did anything but make a feeble protest with the League of Nations. British opinion would not permit any support for France. The French themselves were paralyzed by internal division and by military ideas that concentrated on defense and feared taking the offensive. Both countries were further weakened by a growing pacifism.

A Germany that was rapidly rearming and had a defensible western frontier presented a completely new problem to the Western powers. Their response was the policy of "appeasement." It was based on the assumption that Germany had real grievances, that Hitler's goals were limited and ultimately acceptable, and that the correct policy was to bring about revision by negotiation and concession before a crisis could arise and lead to war. Behind this approach was the general horror at the thought of another war. Memories of the losses in the last war were still fresh, and the advent of aerial bombardment made the thought of a new war terrifying. A firmer policy, moreover, would have required rapid rearmament. But British leaders especially were reluctant to pursue this path because of the expense and because of the widespread belief that the arms race had been a major cause of the last war. As Germany armed, the French huddled behind their newly constructed defensive wall, the Maginot Line, and the British hoped things would go well.

The Spanish Civil War

The new European alignment that found the Western democracies on one side and the fascist states on the other was made clearer by the Spanish Civil War, which broke out in July 1936. In 1931, the Spaniards had driven out their king and established a democratic republic. Elections in February 1936 brought to power a Spanish Popular Front government ranging from republicans of the left to Communists and anarchists. The defeated groups, especially the Falangists, the Spanish version of fascists, would not accept defeat at the polls. In July, General Francisco Franco (1892–1975) led an army from Spanish Morocco in rebellion against the republic.

Thus began a civil war that lasted almost three

The Spanish Civil War. Here Loyalist volunteers attack Franco's forces in the medieval Moorish fortress of the Alcazar of Toledo. Although closely besieged for ten weeks, the Alcazar held out until relieved by Franco's army in September 1936. The war itself continued with increasing savagery until Franco's victory in March 1939. [United Press International.]

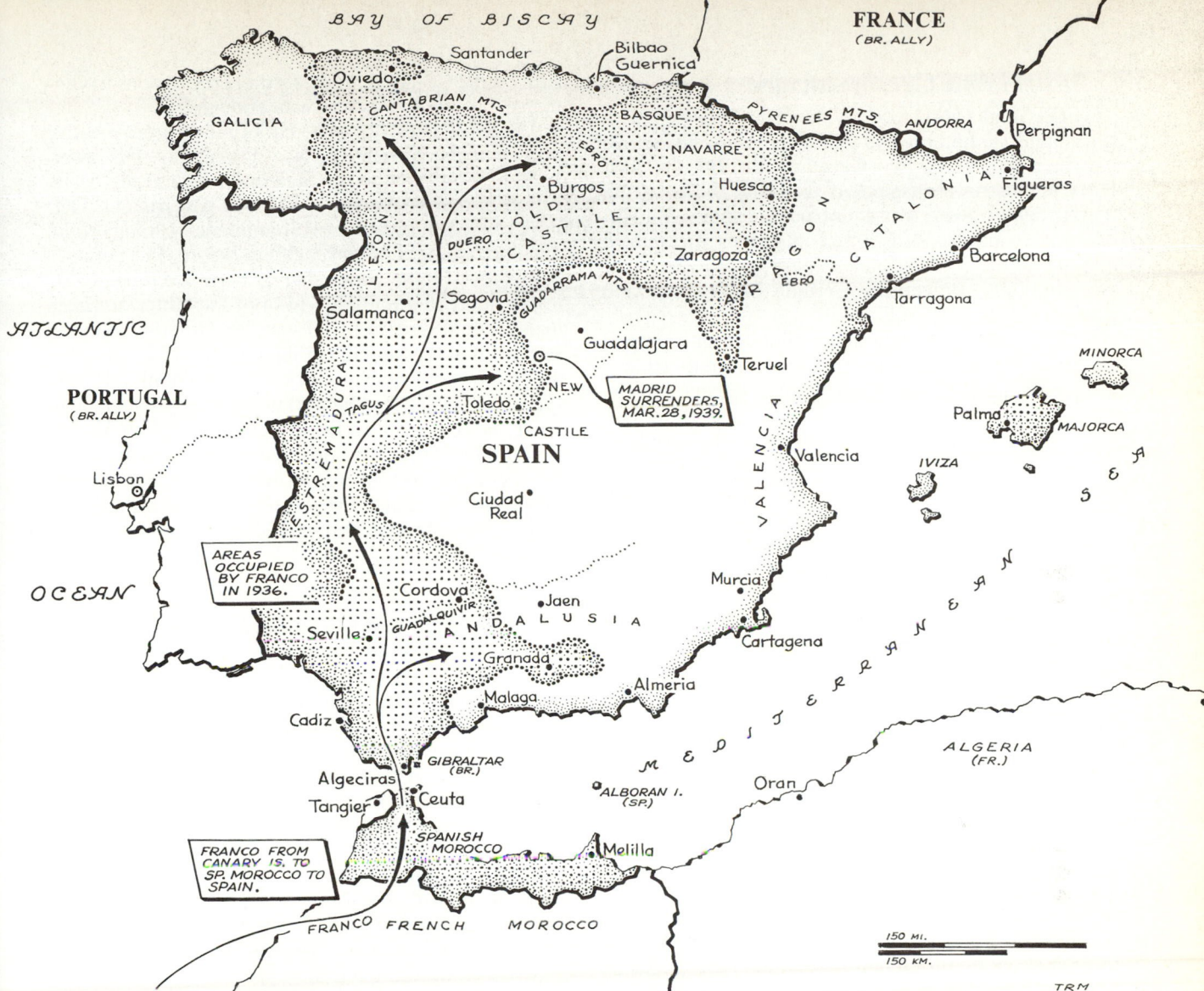

MAP 35-1 THE SPANISH CIVIL WAR 1936–1939 *The dotted area on the map shows the large portion of Spain quickly overrun by Franco's insurgent armies during the first year of the war. In the following two years, progress came more slowly for the fascists as the war became a kind of international rehearsal for the coming World War II. Madrid's fall to Franco in the spring of 1939 had been preceded by that of Barcelona a few weeks earlier.*

years, cost hundreds of thousands of lives, and provided a training ground for World War II. Germany and Italy aided Franco with troops, airplanes, and supplies. The Soviet Union sent airplanes, equipment, and advisers to the republicans. Liberals and leftists from Europe and America volunteered to fight in the republican ranks against fascism.

The civil war, fought on blatantly ideological lines, had a profound effect on world politics. It brought Germany and Italy closer together, leading to the Rome–Berlin Axis Pact. The Axis powers were joined in the same year by Japan in the Anti-Comintern Pact, osten-

sibly against Communism but really a new and powerful diplomatic alliance. Western Europe, especially France, had a great interest in preventing Spain from falling into the hands of a fascist regime closely allied with Germany and Italy. But the appeasement mentality reigned. Although international law permitted the sale of weapons and munitions to the legitimate republican government, France and Britain forbade the export of war materials to either side. The United States passed new neutrality legislation to the same end. When the city of Barcelona fell to Franco early in 1939, the fascists had won effective control of Spain.

Austria and Czechoslovakia

Hitler made good use of his new friendship with Mussolini. He had always planned to make his native Austria a part of the new Germany. In 1934, the Nazi Party in Austria assassinated the prime minister and tried to seize power. Mussolini, not yet allied with Hitler, was suspicious of German intentions. He moved an army to the Brenner Pass in the Alps between Austria and Italy, preventing German intervention and causing the coup to fail.

In 1938, the new diplomatic situation encouraged Hitler to try again. He seems to have hoped to achieve his goal by propaganda, bullying, and threats, but the Austrian Premier Kurt Schuschnigg refused to collapse. On March 9, the premier announced a plebiscite on the following Sunday, March 13, in which the Austrian people could decide the question of union with Germany for themselves. Hitler dared not let the plebiscite take place and sent his army into Austria on March 12. To his great relief, Mussolini made no objection and Hitler could march into Vienna to the cheers of his Austrian sympathizers. This peaceful outcome was fortunate for the Germans. Their army was far from ready for combat, and a high percentage of German tanks and trucks broke down along the roads of Austria.

The *Anschluss*, or union of Germany and Austria, had great strategic significance, however, especially for the position of Czechoslovakia, one of the bulwarks of French security. The union with Austria left the Czechs surrounded by Germany on three sides.

The very existence of Czechoslovakia was an affront to Hitler. It was democratic and pro-Western; it had been created as a check on Germany and was allied both to France and to the Soviet Union. It also contained about 3.5 million who lived in the Sudetenland near the German border. These Germans had been the dominant class in the old Austro-Hungarian Empire and they resented their new minority position. Supported by Hitler and led by Konrad Henlein, the chief Nazi in Czechoslovakia, they made ever-increasing demands for privileges and autonomy within the Czech state. The Czechs made many concessions, but Hitler did not want to improve the lot of the Sudeten Germans. He wanted to destroy Czechoslovakia. He told Henlein, "We must always demand so much that we can never be satisfied."[1]

The French, as had become their custom, deferred to British leadership. The British prime minister was Neville Chamberlain, a man thoroughly committed to the policy of appeasement. He was determined not to allow Britain to come close to war again. He put pressure on the Czechs to make further concessions to Germany, but no concession was enough.

On September 12, 1938, Hitler made a provocative speech at the Nuremberg Nazi Party rally. His assertions led to rioting in the Sudetenland, and the declaration of martial law by the Czech government. German intervention seemed imminent. Chamberlain, aged sixty-nine, had never flown before, but between September 15 and September 29 he made three flights to Germany in an attempt to appease Hitler at Czech expense and thus to avoid war. At Hitler's mountain retreat, Berchtesgaden, on September 15 Chamberlain accepted the separation of the Sudetenland from Czechoslovakia. And he and the French premier, Daladier, forced the Czechs to agree by threatening to desert them if they did not. A week later, Chamberlain flew yet again to Germany only to find that Hitler had raised his demands: He wanted cession of the Sudetenland in three days and immediate occupation by the German army.

Munich

Chamberlain returned to England thinking that he had failed, and France and Britain prepared for war. Almost at the last moment, Mussolini proposed a conference of Germany, Italy, France, and Britain. It met on September 29 at Munich. Hitler received almost everything he had demanded. The Sudetenland, the key to Czech security, became part of Germany, thus depriving the Czechs of any chance of self-defense. In return, the powers agreed to spare the rest of Czechoslovakia. Hitler promised, "I have no more territorial demands to make in Europe." Chamberlain returned to England with the Munich agreement and told a cheering crowd that he had brought "peace with honour. I believe it is peace for our time."

Even in the short run the appeasement of Hitler at Munich was a failure. Soon Poland and Hungary tore bits of territory from Czechoslovakia, and the Slovaks demanded autonomy. Finally, on March 15, 1939, Hitler broke his promise and occupied Prague, putting an end to Czechoslovakia and to illusions that his only goal was to restore Germans to the Reich. Munich remains an example of short-sighted policy that helped bring on a war in disadvantageous circumstances because of the very fear of war and the failure to prepare for it.

Hitler's occupation of Prague discredited appeasement in the eyes of the British people. In the summer of 1939, a Gallup Poll showed that three quarters of the British public believed it worth a war to stop Hitler. Though Chamberlain himself had not lost all faith in his policy, he felt the need to respond to public opinion, and he responded to excess.

It was apparent that Poland was the next target of German expansion. In the spring of 1939, the Germans

[1] Quoted by Alan Bullock in *Hitler, A Study in Tyranny* (New York: Harper & Row, 1962), p. 443.

Winston Churchill Warns of the Effects of the Munich Agreement

Churchill delivered his speech on the Munich agreement before the House of Commons on October 5, 1938. Following are excerpts from it.

The Chancellor of the Exchequer [Sir John Simon] said it was the first time Herr Hitler had been made to retract—I think that was the word—in any degree. We really must not waste time after all this long Debate upon the difference between the positions reached at Berchtesgaden, at Godesberg and at Munich. They can be very simply epitomized, if the House will permit me to vary the metaphor. One pound was demanded at the pistol's point. When it was given, £2 were demanded at the pistol's point. Finally, the dictator consented to take £1 17s. 6d. and the rest in promises of good will for the future. . . .

. . . .

I do not grudge our loyal, brave people, who were ready to do their duty no matter what the cost, who never flinched under the strain of last week—I do not grudge them the natural, spontaneous outbursts of joy and relief when they learned that the hard ordeal would no longer be required of them at the moment; but they should know the truth. They should know that there has been gross neglect and deficiency in our defenses; they should know that we have sustained a defeat without a war, the consequences of which will travel far with us along our road; they should know that we have passed an awful milestone in our history, when the whole equilibrium of Europe has been deranged, and that the terrible words have for the time being been pronounced against the Western democracies: "Thou art weighed in the balance and found wanting." And do not suppose that this is the end. This is only the beginning of the reckoning. This is only the first sip, the first foretaste of a bitter cup which will be proffered to us year by year unless, by a supreme recovery of moral health and martial vigor, we arise again and take our stand for freedom as in the olden time. ❑

Winston S. Churchill, *Blood, Sweat, and Tears* (New York: G. P. Putnam's Sons, 1941), pp. 56, 66.

put pressure on Poland to restore the formerly German city of Danzig and to allow a railroad and a highway through the Polish Corridor to connect East Prussia with the rest of Germany. When the Poles would not yield, the usual propaganda campaign began, and the pressure mounted. On March 31, Chamberlain announced a Franco-British guarantee of Polish independence. Hitler appears to have expected to fight a war with Poland but not with the western allies, but he did not take their guarantee seriously. He had come to hold their leaders in contempt. He knew that both countries were unprepared for war and that large segments of their populations were opposed to fighting a war to save Poland.

The Munich Conference, October 1938. The figures in front are, from left to right, Chamberlain of Great Britain, Daladier of France, Hitler of Germany, and Mussolini of Italy. [Imperial War Museum, London.]

1919	(June) The Versailles Treaty
1923	(January) France occupies the Ruhr
1925	(October) The Locarno Agreements
1931	(Spring) Onset of the Great Depression in Europe
1933	(January) Hitler comes to power
	(October) Germany withdraws from the League of Nations
1935	(March) Hitler renounces disarmament, starts an air force, and begins conscription
	(October) Mussolini attacks Ethiopia
1936	(March) Germany reoccupies and remilitarizes the Rhineland
	(July) Outbreak of the Spanish Civil War
	(October) Formation of the Rome–Berlin Axis
1938	(March) *Anschluss* with Austria
	(September) The Munich Conference and partition of Czechoslovakia
1939	(March) Hitler occupies Prague; France and Great Britain guarantee Polish independence
	(August) The Nazi–Soviet pact
	(September 1) Germany invades Poland
	(September 3) Britain and France declare war on Germany

Belief in the Polish guarantee was further undermined by the inability of France and Britain to get effective help to the Poles. An attack on Germany's western front was out of the question for the French, still dominated by the defensive mentality of the Maginot Line. The only way to defend Poland was to bring Russia into the alliance against Hitler, but a Russian alliance posed many problems. Each side was profoundly suspicious of the other. The French and the British were hostile to Russia's Communist ideology, and since Stalin's purge of the officer corps of the Red Army, they stood unconvinced of the military value of an alliance with Russia. Besides, the Russians could not help Poland without the right of transit through Romania and the right of entry into Poland. Both nations, suspicious of Russian intentions, and with good reason, refused to grant these rights. As a result, Western negotiations with Russia moved forward slowly and cautiously.

The Nazi–Soviet Pact

The Russians had at least equally good reason to hesitate. They resented being left out of the Munich agreement. They were annoyed by the low priority that the West seemed to give to negotiations with Russia compared with the urgency with which they dealt with Hitler. They feared, quite rightly, that the Western powers meant them to bear the burden of the war against Germany. As a result, they opened negotiations with Hitler, and on August 23, 1939, the world was shocked to learn of a Nazi–Soviet nonaggression

On the eve of World War II, in August 1939, the Soviet Union and Nazi Germany shocked the world by signing a non-aggression pact. For years National Socialists and Communists had been the most bitter enemies and regularly hurled insults at each other, but now they came together in a marriage of convenience. This British cartoon by David Low (1891–1963) emphasizes the ironic character of the new relationship. [Cartoon by David Low. By arrangement with the Trustees and the London Evening Standard.]

pact. Its secret provisions, which were easily guessed and soon carried out, divided Poland between the two powers and allowed Russia to take over the Baltic states and to take Bessarabia from Romania. The most bitter ideological enemies had become allies, Communist parties in the West changed their line overnight from the ardent advocacy of resistance to Hitler to a policy of peace and quiet.

The Nazi–Soviet Pact sealed the fate of Poland, and the Franco-British commitment guaranteed a general war. On September 1, 1939, the Germans invaded Poland. Two days later, Britain and France declared war on Germany. World War II had begun.

World War II (1939–1945)

World War II had a better claim to its name than its predecessor, for it was truly global. Fighting took place in Europe and Asia, the Atlantic and the Pacific oceans, the Northern and Southern hemispheres. The demand for the fullest exploitation of material and human resources for increased production, the use of blockades, and the intensive bombing of civilian targets made the war of 1939 even more "total"—that is, comprehensive and intense—than that of 1914.

The German Conquest of Europe

The German attack on Poland produced swift success. The speed of the German victory astonished everyone, not least the Russians, who hastened to collect their share of the booty before Hitler could deprive them of it. On September 17, they invaded Poland from the east, dividing the country with the Germans. They then forced the encircled Baltic countries to sign treaties with them. By 1940, Estonia, Latvia, and Lithuania were absorbed as constituent republics into the USSR (Union of Soviet Socialist Republics, or the Soviet Union). In November 1940, the Russians invaded Finland, but the Finns put up a surprisingly effective resistance. Although they were finally worn down and compelled to yield territory and bases to Russia, they

MAP 35-2   PARTITIONS OF CZECHOSLOVAKIA AND POLAND, 1938–1939   *The immediate background of World War II is found in the complex international drama unfolding on Germany's eastern frontier in 1938 and 1939. Germany's expansion inevitably meant the victimization of Austria, Czechoslovakia, and Poland. With the failure of the Western powers' appeasement policy and the signing of a German-Soviet pact, the stage for the war was set.*

retained their independence. Russian difficulties in Finland may well have encouraged Hitler to invade the Soviet Union in June 1941, just twenty-two months after the 1939 treaty.

Through the fall of 1939 and the winter of 1939–1940, the western front was quiet. The French remained quiet behind the Maginot Line while Hitler and Stalin swallowed Poland and the Baltic states. Britain hastily rearmed and reorganized the traditional naval blockade. Cynics in the West called it the phony war, or *"Sitzkrieg,"* but Hitler shattered the stillness in the spring of 1940. In April, without warning and with swift success, the Germans invaded Denmark and Norway. Hitler's northern front was secure, and he now had both air and naval bases closer to Britain. A month later, a combined land and air attack struck Belgium, the Netherlands, and Luxembourg. German air power and armored divisions were irresistible. The Dutch surrendered in a few days, and the Belgians, though aided by the French and the British, surrendered less than two weeks later. The British and French armies in Belgium were forced to flee to the English Channel to seek escape from the beaches of Dunkerque. By the heroic effort of hundreds of Britons manning small boats, over 200,000 British and 100,000 French soldiers were saved, but casualties were high and much valuable equipment was abandoned.

The Maginot Line ran from Switzerland to the Belgian frontier. Until 1936, the French had expected the Belgians to continue the fortifications along their German border. After Hitler remilitarized the Rhineland without opposition, the Belgians lost faith in their French alliance and returned to neutrality, leaving the Maginot Line exposed on the left flank. Hitler's swift advance through Belgium therefore circumvented France's main line of defense. The French army, poorly and hesitantly led by generals who lacked a proper understanding of the use of tanks and planes, quickly collapsed. Mussolini, eager to claim the spoils of victory when it was clearly safe to do so, sent an army across the French border on June 10. Less than a week later, the new French government, under the ancient hero of Verdun, Henri Philippe Pétain, asked for an armistice. In two months, Hitler had accomplished what Germany had failed to achieve in four years of bitter fighting in the previous war.

The terms of the armistice, signed June 22, 1940, allowed the Germans to occupy more than half of France, including the Atlantic and English Channel coasts. In order to prevent many of the French from fleeing to North Africa to continue the fight, and even more to prevent the French from turning their fleet over to Britain, Hitler left southern France unoccupied. Pétain set up a dictatorial regime at the resort city of Vichy and followed a policy of collaboration with the Germans in order to preserve as much autonomy as possible. Most of the French were too stunned to resist. Many thought that Hitler's victory was certain and saw no alternative to collaboration. A few, most notably General Charles de Gaulle (1890–1969), fled to Britain, where they organized the French National Committee of Liberation, or "Free French." The Vichy government controlled most of French North Africa and the navy. But the Free French began operating in central Africa and from London beamed messages of hope and defiance to their compatriots in France. As the passage of time dispelled expectations of a quick German victory, a French underground movement arose that organized many forms of resistance.

The Battle of Britain

The fall of France left Britain isolated, and Hitler expected the British to come to terms. He was prepared to allow Britain to retain its empire in return for a free hand for Germany on the Continent. If there was any chance that the British would consider such terms, that chance disappeared when Winston Churchill (1874–1965) replaced Chamberlain as prime minister in May of 1940.

One of Churchill's greatest achievements was establishing a close relationship with the American President Franklin D. Roosevelt, who found ways to help the British in spite of strong political opposition. In 1940 and 1941, before the United States was at war, America sent military supplies, traded badly needed warships for leases on British naval bases, and even convoyed ships across the Atlantic to help the British survive.

As weeks passed and Britain remained defiant, Hitler was forced to contemplate an invasion, and that required control of the air. The first strikes by the German air force (*Luftwaffe*), directed against the airfields and fighter planes in southeastern England, began in August 1940. There is reason to think that if these attacks had continued, Germany might soon have gained control of the air and, with it, the chance of a successful invasion. In early September, however, seeking revenge for some British bombing raids on German cities, the *Luftwaffe* made London its major target. For two months, London was bombed every night. Much of the city was destroyed, and about fifteen thousand people were killed, but the theories of victory through air power alone proved vain. Casualties were many times fewer than expected and morale was not shattered. In fact, the bombings brought the British people together and made them more resolute.

At the same time, the Royal Air Force (RAF) inflicted heavy losses on the *Luftwaffe*. Aided by the newly developed radar and an excellent system of communications, the Spitfire and Hurricane fighter

In May 1940 Winston Churchill replaced Neville Chamberlain as Prime Minister of Great Britain. Appeasement was dead, and David Low's cartoon celebrates the new spirit of determination and resistance Churchill inspired. The recognizable faces in the first three or four rows are those of the then leading British politicians of all parties; in the front row to the right of Churchill, who was a Conservative, are Clement Atlee and Ernest Bevin, the leaders of Labor. Chamberlain is behind Churchill. [Cartoon by David Low. By arrangement with the Trustees and the London Evening Standard.]

ALL BEHIND YOU, WINSTON

planes destroyed more than twice as many enemy planes as were lost by the RAF. Hitler had lost the Battle of Britain in the air and was forced to abandon his plans for invasion.

The German Attack on Russia

From the first, the defeat of Russia and the conquest of the Ukraine to provide *Lebenstraum* ("living room") for the German people had been a major goal for Hitler. Operation Barbarossa, the code name for the invasion of Russia, was aimed at knocking Russia out of the war before winter could set in. Success depended in part on an early start, but here Hitler's Italian alliance proved costly. Mussolini was jealous of Hitler's success and annoyed by the treatment he had received from the German dictator. Unable to make progress against the French army even while Hitler was crushing the part of it that was on his own frontier, Mussolini was not allowed any gain at the expense of France or even of French Africa.

Consequently, Mussolini launched an attack against the British in Egypt and drove them back some sixty miles. Encouraged by this success, he invaded Greece from his base in Albania (which he had seized in 1939). But in North Africa, the British counterattacked and drove the Italians back into Libya, and the Greeks themselves pushed into Albania. In March 1941, the British sent help to the Greeks, and Hitler was forced to divert his attention to the Balkans and to Africa. General Erwin Rommel (1891–1944), later to earn the title "The Desert Fox," went to Africa and soon got the British out of Libya and back into Egypt. In the Balkans, the German army swiftly occupied Yugoslavia and crushed Greek resistance, but the price was a delay of six weeks. The diversion caused by Musso-

lini's vanity proved to be costly the following winter in the Russian campaign.

Operation Barbarossa was launched against Russia on June 22, 1941, and it came very close to success. Stalin appears to have panicked. He had not fortified his frontier, nor had he issued orders for his troops to withdraw when attacked. In the first two days, some two thousand planes were destroyed on the ground. By November, Hitler had gone further into Russia than Napoleon: The German army stood at the gates of Leningrad, on the outskirts of Moscow, and on the Don River. Of the 4.5 million troops with which the Russians had begun the fighting, they had lost 2.5 million; of their 15,000 tanks, only 700 were left. Moscow was in panic, and a German victory seemed imminent.

But the Germans could not deliver the final blow. In August, there was a delay in their advance to decide on a course of action. One plan was to drive directly for Moscow and take it before winter. There is some reason to think that such a plan might have worked and brought victory, for unlike the situation in Napoleon's time, Moscow was the hub of the Russian system of transportation. Hitler, however, imposed his own view of his generals and diverted a significant part of his forces to the south. By the time he was ready to return to the offensive near Moscow, it was too late. Winter struck the German army, which was neither dressed nor equipped to face it. Given precious time, Stalin was able to restore order and to build defenses for the city. Even more important, there was time for troops to come from Siberia, where they had been placed to check a possible Japanese attack. In November and December, the Russians were able to counterattack. The *Blitzkrieg* had turned into a war of attrition, and the Germans began to have visions of Napoleon's retreat.

Hitler's Europe

The demands and distractions of war and Hitler's defeat prevented him from fully carrying out his plans. Therefore, it is hard to be sure what his intentions were, but the measures he took before his death provide indications. They give evidence of a regime probably unmatched in history for carefully planned terror and inhumanity. To accomplish his plan of giving *Lebensraum* to the Germans at the expense of people he deemed inferior, Hitler established colonies of Germans in parts of Poland, driving the local people from their land and employing them as cheap labor. He had similar plans on an even higher scale for Russia. The Russians would be driven eastward to central Asia and Siberia; they would be kept in check by frontier colonies of German war veterans, and the more desirable lands of European Russia would be settled by Germans.

Hitler's long-range plans included Germanization as well as colonization. In lands inhabited by people racially akin to the Germans, like the Scandinavian countries, the Netherlands, and Switzerland, the natives would be absorbed into the German nation. Such peoples would be reeducated and purged of dissenting elements, but there would be little or no colonization. He even had plans, only slightly realized, of adopting selected people from the lesser races into the master race. One of these plans involved bringing half a million Ukrainian girls into Germany as servants and finding German husbands for them; about fifteen thousand actually did reach Germany.

In the economic sphere, Hitler regarded the conquered lands merely as a source of plunder. From eastern Europe, he removed everything useful, including entire industries. In Russia and Poland, the Germans simply confiscated the land. In the west, the conquered countries were forced to support the occupying army at a rate several times the real cost. The Germans used the profits to buy up everything useful and desirable, stripping the conquered peoples of most necessities. The Nazis were frank about their policies. One of Hitler's high officials said, "Whether nations live in prosperity or starve to death interests me only insofar as we need them as slaves for our culture."[2]

Racism and the Holocaust

The most horrible aspect of the Nazi rule in Europe arose not from military or economic necessity but from the inhumanity and brutality inherent in Hitler's racial doctrines. He considered the Slavs *Untermenschen*, subhuman creatures like beasts who need not be thought of or treated as people. In parts of Poland the

[2] Quoted by Gordon Wright, *The Ordeal of Total War, 1939–1945* (New York: Harper & Row, 1968), p. 117.

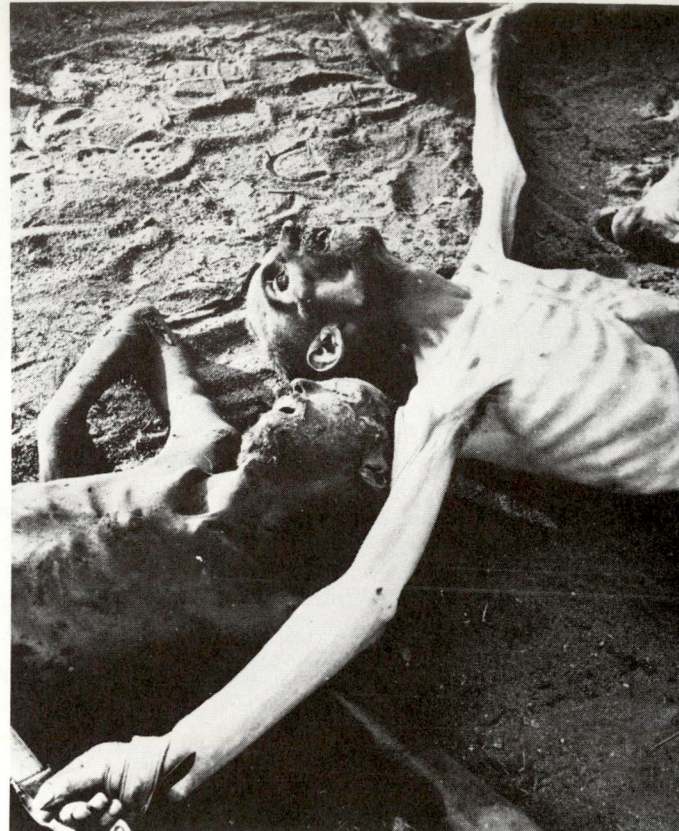

German concentration camps—the dead and the dying as found by Western armies in 1945. The Nazis set up their first concentration camps in Germany to hold the German opponents of their regime, but, after the war had begun, the new camps established in Poland were planned as part of Hitler's "final solution," the extermination of the Jews and others. Even in those camps not avowedly dedicated to extermination the conditions were brutal in the extreme, and the armies that liberated them in 1945 found scenes such as this. [United Press International Photo.]

upper and professional classes were entirely removed—either jailed, deported, or killed. Schools and churches were closed; marriage was controlled by the Nazis to keep down the Polish birth rate; and harsh living conditions were imposed. In Russia things were even worse. Hitler spoke of his Russian campaign as a war of extermination. Heinrich Himmler, head of Hitler's elite SS guard, planned the elimination of thirty million Slavs to make room for the Germans, and he formed extermination squads for the purpose. The number of Russian prisoners of war and deported civilian workers who died under Nazi rule may have reached six million.

Hitler had special plans for the Jews. He meant to make all Europe *Judenrein* ("free of Jews"). For a time

An Observer Describes the Mass Murder of Jews in the Ukraine

After World War II, some German officers and officials were put on trial at Nuremberg by the victorious powers for crimes they were charged with having committed in the course of the war. The following selections from the testimony of a German construction engineer who witnessed the mass murder of Jews at Dubno in the Ukraine on October 5, 1942, reveal the brutality with which Hitler's attempt at a "final solution of the Jewish problem" was carried out.

On October 5, 1942, when I visited the building office at Dubno, my foreman told me that in the vicinity of the site, Jews from Dubno had been shot in three large pits, each about 30 metres long and 3 metres deep. About 1,500 persons had been killed daily. All the 5,000 Jews who had still been living in Dubno before the pogrom were to be liquidated. As the shooting had taken place in his presence, he was still much upset.

Thereupon, I drove to the site accompanied by my foreman and saw near it great mounds of earth, about 30 metres long and 2 metres high. Several trucks stood in front of the mounds. Armed Ukrainian militia drove the people off the trucks under the supervision of an S.S. man. The militiamen acted as guards on the trucks and drove them to and from the pit. All these people had the regulation yellow patches on the front and back of their clothes, and thus could be recognized as Jews.

My foreman and I went directly to the pits. Nobody bothered us. Now I heard rifle shots in quick succession from behind one of the earth mounds. The people who had got off the trucks—men, women and children of all ages—had to undress upon the orders of an S.S. man, who carried a riding or dog whip. They had to put down their clothes in fixed places, sorted according to shoes, top clothing and underclothing. I saw a heap of shoes of about 800 to 1,000 pairs, great piles of underlinen and clothing.

Without screaming or weeping, these people undressed, stood around in family groups, kissed each other, said farewells, and waited for a sign from another S.S. man, who stood near the pit, also with a whip in his hand. During the fifteen minutes that I stood near I heard no complaint or plea for mercy. I watched a family of about eight persons, a man and a woman both about fifty with their children of about one, eight and ten, and two grown-up daughters of about twenty to twenty-nine. An old woman with snow-white hair was holding the one-year-old child in her arms and singing to it and tickling it. The child was cooing with delight. The couple were looking on with tears in their eyes. The father was holding the hand of a boy about ten years old and speaking to him softly; the boy was fighting his tears. The father pointed to the sky, stroked his head, and seemed to explain something to him.

At that moment the S.S. man at the pit shouted something to his comrade. The latter counted off about twenty persons and instructed them to go behind the earth mound. Among them was the family which I have mentioned. I well remember a girl, slim and with black hair, who, as she passed close to me pointed to herself and said "23." I walked around the mound and found myself confronted by a tremendous grave. People were closely wedged together and lying on top of each other so that only their heads were visible. Nearly all had blood running over their shoulders from their heads. Some of the people shot were still moving. Some were lifting their arms and turning their heads to show that they were still alive. The pit was already two-thirds full. I estimated that it already contained about 1,000 people. ❑

From the *Nuremberg Proceedings*, as quoted in Louis L. Snyder, *Documents of German History* (New Brunswick: Rutgers University Press, 1958), pp. 462–464.

he thought of sending them to the island of Madagascar, but later he arrived at the "final solution of the Jewish problem": extermination. The Nazis built extermination camps in Germany and Poland and used the latest technology to achieve the most efficient means of killing millions of men, women, and children for no other reason than their birth into the designated group. Before the war was over, six million Jews had died in what has come to be called the *Holocaust*. Only about a million remained alive, those mostly in pitiable condition.

Japan and America's Entry into the War

The sympathies of the American government were very much on the British side, and the various forms of assistance that Roosevelt gave Britain would have justified a German declaration of war. Hitler, however, held back. It is not clear that the United States government would have overcome isolationist sentiment and entered the war in the Atlantic if war had not been thrust on America in the Pacific.

Pearl Harbor, December 7, 1941. The successful Japanese attack on the American base at Pearl Harbor in Hawaii, together with simultaneous attacks on other Pacific bases, brought the United States into war against the Axis powers. This picture shows the sinking battleships Arizona, Tennessee, *and* West Virginia. *[Official United States Navy Photograph.]*

Since the Japanese conquest of Manchuria in 1931, American policy toward Japan had been suspicious and unfriendly. The outbreak of the war in Europe emboldened the Japanese to move forward more quickly in their drive to dominate Asia. They allied themselves with Germany and Italy, made a treaty of neutrality with the Soviet Union, and penetrated into Indochina at the expense of defeated France. At the same time, they continued their war in China and made plans to gain control of Malaya and the East Indies at the expense of beleaguered Britain and the conquered Netherlands. The only barrier to Japanese expansion was the United States.

The Americans had temporized, unwilling to cut off vital supplies of oil and other materials for fear of provoking a Japanese attack on Southeast Asia and Indonesia. The Japanese seizure of Indochina in July 1941 changed that policy, which had already begun to stiffen. The United States froze Japanese assets and cut off oil supplies; the British and Dutch did the same. Japanese plans for expansion could not continue without the conquest of the Indonesian oil fields and Ma-

layan rubber and tin. In October, a war faction led by General Tōjō Hideki (1885–1948) took power in Japan and decided to risk a war rather than yield.

On Sunday morning, December 7, 1941, even while Japanese representatives were discussing a settlement in Washington, Japan launched an air attack on Pearl Harbor, Hawaii, the chief American naval base in the Pacific. The next day, the United States and Britain declared war on Japan. Three days later, Germany and Italy declared war on the United States.

The Tide Turns

The potential power of the United States was enormous, but right after Pearl Harbor, America was ill prepared for war. Though conscription had been introduced in 1940, the army was tiny, inexperienced, and ill supplied. American industry was not ready for war. The Japanese swiftly captured Guam, Wake Island, and the Philippine Islands. At the same time, they attacked Hong Kong, Malaya, Burma, and Indonesia. By the spring of 1942, they controlled these places and the southwest Pacific as far as New Guinea. They were poised for an attack on Australia, and it seemed that nothing could stop them.

In the same year, the Germans advanced deeper into Russia and almost reached the Caspian Sea in their drive for Russia's oil fields. In Africa, too, Axis fortunes were high. Rommel drove the British back into Egypt toward the Suez Canal and finally was stopped at El Alamein, only seventy miles from Alexandria. Relations between the democracies and their Soviet ally were still far from close; German submarine warfare was threatening British supplies; the Allies were being thrown back on every front; and the future looked bleak.

The first good news for the Allied cause in the Pacific came in the spring of 1942. A naval battle in the Coral Sea sent many Japanese ships to the bottom and gave security to Australia. A month later, the United States defeated the Japanese in a fierce air and naval battle off Midway Island, blunting the chance of another assault on Hawaii and doing enough damage to halt the Japanese advance. Soon American Marines landed on Guadalcanal in the Solomon Islands and began in a small way to reverse the momentum of the war. The war in the Pacific was far from over, but Japan was checked sufficiently to allow the Allies to concentrate their efforts first in the West.

ALLIED LANDINGS IN AFRICA, SICILY, AND ITALY. In November 1942, an Allied force landed in French North Africa. Even before that landing, the British Field Marshal Bernard Montgomery (1887–1976), after stopping Rommel at El Alamein, had begun a drive to the west. And the American General Dwight D. Eisenhower (1890–1969) had pushed eastward through Morocco and Algeria. The two armies caught the German army between them in Tunisia and crushed it. The Suez Canal and the Mediterranean were now under Allied control, and southern Europe was exposed. In July and August 1943, the Allies took Sicily. Mussolini was driven from power, and the new government tried to make peace, but the Germans moved into Italy. The Allies landed in Italy, and Marshal Pietro Badoglio (1871–1956), the leader of the new Italian government, went over to their side, declaring war on Germany. Churchill had spoken of Italy as the "soft underbelly" of the Axis, but German resistance was tough and determined. Still, the need to defend Italy put a strain on the Germans' energy and resources and left them vulnerable on other fronts.

BATTLE OF STALINGRAD. The Russian campaign became especially demanding. In the summer of 1942, the Germans resumed the offensive on all fronts but were unable to get very far except in the south. The goal was the oil fields near the Caspian Sea, and they got as far as Stalingrad on the Volga, a key point for the protection of the flank of the German army in the

MAP 35-3 NORTH AFRICAN CAMPAIGNS, 1942–1945 *Control of North Africa was important to the Allies in order to have access to Europe from the south. The map diagrams this theater of the war from Morocco to Egypt and the Suez Canal.*

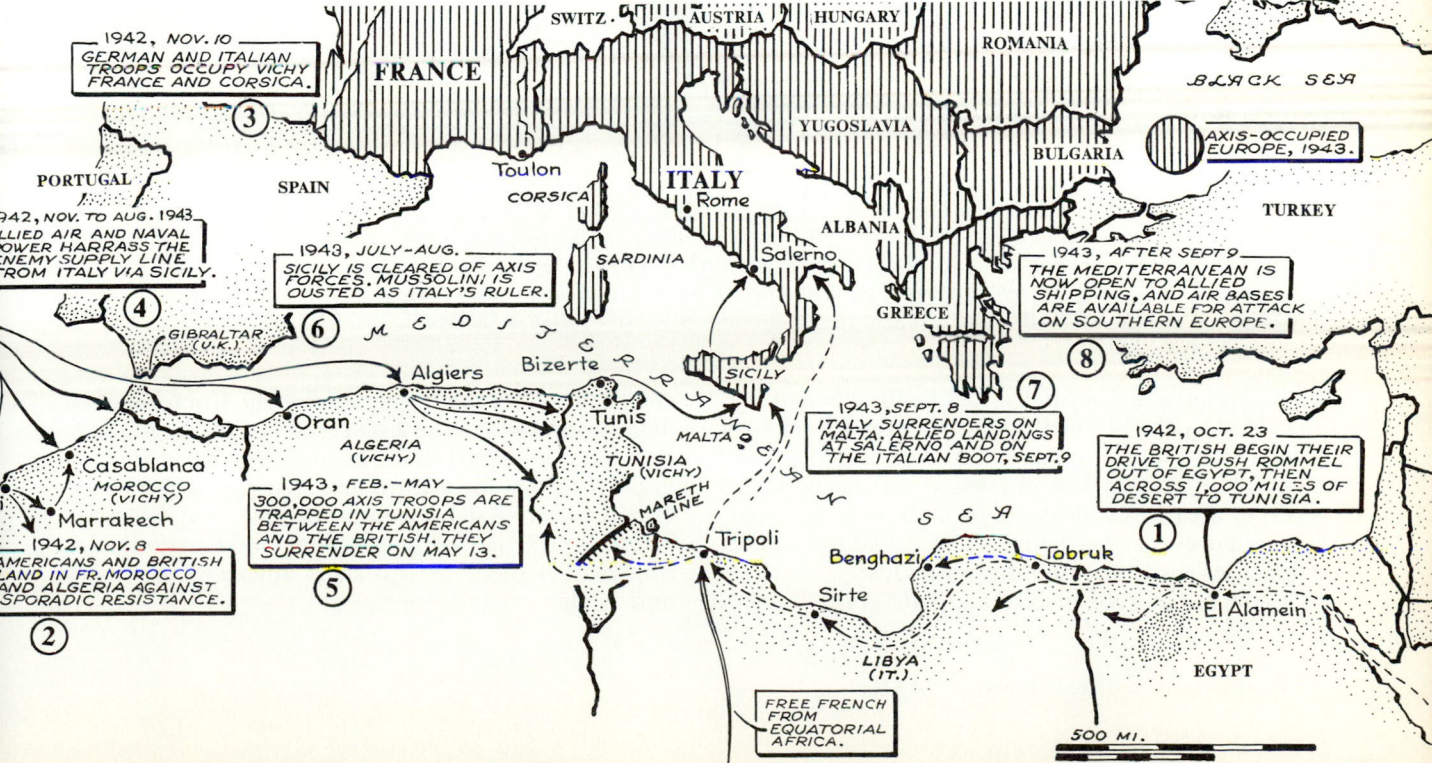

MAP 35-4 AXIS EUROPE 1941 *On the eve of the German invasion of the Soviet Union the Germany-Italy Axis bestrode most of Western Europe by annexation, occupation, or alliance—from Norway and Finland in the north to Greece in the south and from Poland to France. Britain, the Soviets, a number of insurgent groups, and, finally, America had before them the long struggle of conquering this Axis "fortress Europe."*

south. Hitler was determined to take the city and Stalin to hold it. The Battle of Stalingrad raged for months with unexampled ferocity. The Russians lost more men than the Americans lost in combat during the entire war, but their heroic defenses prevailed. Because Hitler again overruled his generals and would not allow a retreat, an entire German army was lost.

Stalingrad marked the turning point of the Russian campaign. Thereafter, material help from America and, even more, increased production from their own industry (which have been moved to or built up in the safety of the central and eastern regions of the USSR) allowed the Russians to gain and keep the offensive. As the German military and material resources dwindled, the Russians advanced westward inexorably.

STRATEGIC BOMBING. In 1943, the Allies began to gain ground in production and logistics as well. The industrial might of the United States began to come into full force. At the same time, new technology and tactics made great strides in eliminating the submarine menace. In the same year the American and British air forces began a series of massive bombardments of Germany by night and day. It does not appear that either kind of bombing had much effect on the war until 1944. Then the Americans introduced long-range fighters that could protect the bombers and allow accurate missions by day. By 1945, the Allies had cleared the skies of German planes and could bomb at will.

The Defeat of Nazi Germany

On June 6, 1944 ("D-Day"), American, British, and Canadian troops landed in force on the coast of Normandy. The German defense was strong, but the Allies were able to establish a beachhead and then to break out of it. In mid-August, the Allies landed in southern France to put more pressure on the enemy. By the beginning of September, France had been liberated.

All went smoothly until December, when the Germans launched a counterattack on the Belgian front through the Forest of Ardennes. Because the Germans were able to push forward into the Allied line, this was called the Battle of the Bulge. It brought heavy losses

and considerable alarm to the Allies. That effort, however, was the last gasp for the Germans. The Allies recovered the momentum and pushed eastward. They crossed the Rhine in March of 1945, and German resistance crumbled. This time there could be no doubt that the Germans had lost the war on the battlefield.

In the east, the Russians swept foward no less swiftly. By March 1945, they were within reach of Berlin. Because the Allies insisted on unconditional surrender, the Germans fought on until May. Hitler and his intimates committed suicide in an underground hideaway in Berlin on May 1, 1945. The Russians occupied Berlin by agreement with their Western allies. The Third Reich had lasted a dozen years instead of the millennium predicted by Hitler.

The Fall of the Japanese Empire

The war in Europe ended on May 8, 1945, and by then victory over Japan was in sight. The original Japanese attack on the United States had been a calculated risk against the odds. The longer the war lasted, the greater was the advantage to the American superiority in industrial production and human resources. Beginning in 1943, the American forces, still relatively small in number, began a campaign of "island hopping." They did not try to recapture every Pacific island held by the Japanese, but selected major bases and places strategically located along the enemy supply line.

Dresden in ruins. In February 1945, with the end of the war in sight, the Allies launched a series of air raids on the defenseless city of Dresden in Germany. The raids destroyed the heart of the city and are thought to have caused twice as many casualties as those caused by the atomic bomb dropped on Hiroshima, Japan, in August of the same year. [Bildarchiv Preussischer Kulturbesitz.]

500 MI.

500 KM.

NORTH SEA

N. IRELAND

EIRE

UNITED KINGDOM

Liverpool
Hull
Coventry
London

NORWAY
Trondheim
Stavanger
Oslo

SWEDEN
Stockholm

FINLAND
L. LADOGA
Viborg
Leningra
Helsinki
Reval
Novgor

BALTIC SEA

ESTONIA
LATVIA
Riga
Vitebsk
Smol
LITHUANIA
Memel
Kaunas
Vilna
BYELO-
RUSSIA
KAT

DENMARK
Copenhagen

(10) GERMAN SURRENDER IN REIMS, MAY 7, 1945 BERLIN, MAY 8, 1945

NETH.
Rotterdam

Hamburg
Bremen
Danzig
EAST PRUSSIA
Berlin

GREATER GERMANY

POSEN

BELG.

(5) NORMANDY INV. JUNE 6, 1944

Dunkirk

Essen
Cologne
Remagen
Torgau
Dresden
Breslau
P O L A N D
Warsaw

(8) BATTLE OF THE BULGE DEC. 1944

Reims

(9) RHINE CROSSING, MAR. 7, 1945

Cracow
Lemberg

(6) RUSSIAN FRONT JUNE 23, 1944

Paris
St. Nazaire
Orléans

Nürnberg
Strassburg
BOHEMIA
MORAVIA

DNIESTER

Tours

Munich

SLOVAKIA

FRANCE

Vichy

Vienna
AUSTRIA

HUNGARY
Budapest

Jassi
BESSARABIA

SWITZ.
TYROL

Lyons

Bordeaux

(1) AXIS TROOPS OCCUPY VICHY FRANCE, NOV. 10 AND 11, 1942

Marseilles
Toulon

Milan

Bologna

Florence

PROVENCE

A D R I A T I C   S E A

CROATIA

YUGOSLAVIA
SERBIA

Belgrade

ROMANIA
Bucharest

(7) ALLIES LAND IN PROVENCE, AUG. 15, 1944

SPAIN

Barcelona

CORSICA (VICHY)

ITALY
Rome

Anzio
Cassino
Naples
Salerno

MONTE-NEGRO

Tirana
ALBANIA

BULGARIA
Sofia
Varna

Skoplje

(TURK.)
Is

Valencia

BALEARIC IS.

SARDINIA (IT.)

(3) ALLIES INVADE SICILY & ITALY, JULY-SEPT. 1943

CALABRIA

GREECE

Salonika

AEGEAN SEA
Izmir

Algiers

Bizerte

SICILY

(4) ITALIAN SURRENDER, SEPT. 8, 1943

Athens

(2) AXIS TROOPS EVACUATED, MAY 1943

Tunis

ALGERIA (VICHY)

TUNISIA (VICHY)

MALTA (U.K.)

M E D I T E R R A N E A N   S E A

Candia

CRETE

994

MAP 35-5 **DEFEAT OF THE AXIS IN EUROPE, 1942–1945** *This is the sequel to Map 33-5. Here we see some major steps in the progress toward allied victory against Axis Europe. From the south through Italy, from the west through France, and from the east through Russia the Allies gradually conquered the continent to bring the war in Europe to a close.*

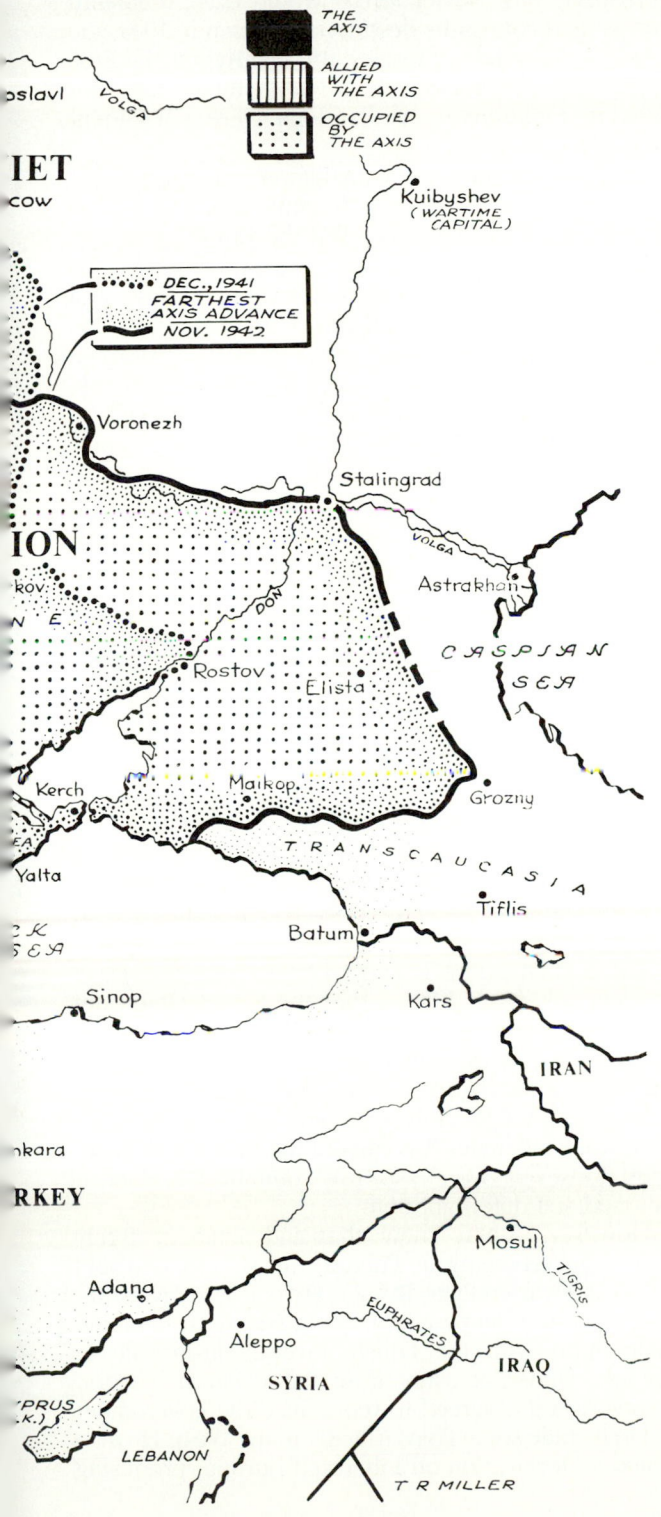

Starting from the Solomons, they moved northeast toward the Japanese homeland. From new bases, closer to Japan, the American bombers launched a terrible wave of bombings that destroyed Japanese industry and disabled the Japanese navy. But still the Japanese government, dominated by a military clique, refused to surrender.

Confronted with Japan's determination, the Americans made plans for a frontal assault on the Japanese homeland, which, they calculated, might cost a million American casualties and even greater losses for the Japanese. At this point, science and technology presented the Americans with another choice. Since early in the war, a secret program had been in progress. Its staff, made up in significant part of exiles from Hitler's Europe, was working to use atomic energy for military purposes.

On August 6, 1945, an American plane dropped an atomic bomb on the city of Hiroshima. The city was destroyed, and more than 70,000 of its 200,000 residents were killed. Two days later, the Soviet Union declared war on Japan and invaded Manchuria. The next day, a second atomic bomb fell, this time on Nagasaki. Even then, the Japanese did not yield. The Japanese Cabinet was prepared to resist further, to face an invasion rather than give up. It was only the unprecedented intervention of Emperor Hirohito that convinced the government to surrender on August 14. Even then, they made the condition that Japan could keep its emperor. The Allies had continued to insist on unconditional surrender. However, President Harry S. Truman (1884–1972), who had come to office on April 12, 1945, on the death of Franklin D. Roosevelt, accepted the condition. Peace was formally signed aboard the U.S.S. *Missouri* in Tokyo Bay on September 2, 1945.

The Cost of War

World War II was the most terrible war in history. Military deaths are estimated at some fifteen million, and at least as many civilians were killed. If deaths linked indirectly to the war are included, the figure of victims might reach as high as forty million. Most of Europe and significant parts of Asia were devastated. Yet the end of so terrible a war brought little opportunity for relaxation. The dawn of the Atomic Age that brought the dramatic end to the war made people conscious that another major war might bring an end to humanity. Everything depended on the conclusion of a stable peace, but even as the fighting came to an end, conflicts among the victors made the prospects of a lasting peace doubtful.

Preparations for Peace and the Onset of the Cold War

The split between the Soviet Union and its wartime allies should cause no surprise. As the self-proclaimed center of world Communism, the Soviet Union was openly dedicated to the overthrow of the capitalist nations, though this message was muted when the occasion demanded. On the other side, the Western allies were no less open about their hostility to Communism and its chief purveyor, the Soviet Union.

Though cooperation against a common enemy and strenuous propaganda efforts in the West helped improve Western feeling toward the Soviet ally, Stalin remained suspicious and critical of the Western war effort. Likewise, Churchill never ceased planning to contain the Soviet advance into Europe. For some time, Roosevelt seems to have been hopeful that the Allies could continue to work together after the war. But even he was losing faith as the war and his life drew to a close. Differences in historical development and ideology, as well as traditional conflicts over political power and influence, soon dashed hopes of a mutually satisfactory peace settlement and continued cooperation to uphold it.

The Atlantic Charter

In August 1941, even before the Americans were at war, Roosevelt and Churchill had met on a ship off Newfoundland and agreed to the Atlantic Charter. A broad set of principles in the spirit of Wilson's Fourteen Points, it provided a theoretical basis for the peace they sought. When Russia and the United States joined Britain in the war, the three powers entered a purely military alliance in January 1942, leaving all political questions aside. The first political conference was the meeting of foreign ministers in Moscow in October 1943. The ministers reaffirmed earlier agreements to fight on until the enemy surrendered without condition and to continue cooperating after the war in a united-nations organization.

Tehran

The first meeting of the three leaders of state took place at Tehran, the capital of Iran, in 1943. Western promises to open a second front in France the next summer (1944) and Stalin's agreement to join in the war against Japan (when Germany was defeated) created an atmosphere of goodwill in which to discuss a postwar settlement. Stalin wanted to retain what he had gained in his pact with Hitler and to dismember

Germany. Roosevelt and Churchill were conciliatory, but they made no firm commitments. The most important decision was the one that chose Europe's west coast as the point of attack instead of southern Europe, by the way of the Mediterranean. That meant, in retrospect, that Soviet forces would occupy eastern Europe and control its destiny. At Tehran in 1943, the Western allies did not foresee this clearly, for the Russians were still fighting deep within their own frontiers, and military considerations were paramount everywhere.

By 1944, the situation was different. In August, Soviet armies were in sight of Warsaw, which had risen in expectation of liberation. But the Russians halted, allowing the Polish rebels to be annihilated while they turned south into the Balkans. They gained control of Romania and Hungary, advances of which centuries of expansionist tsars had only dreamed. Alarmed by these developments, Churchill went to Moscow and met with Stalin in October. They agreed to share power in the Balkans on the basis of Soviet predominance in Romania and Bulgaria, Western predominance in Greece, and equality of influence in Yugoslavia and Hungary. These agreements were not enforceable without American approval, and the Americans were known to be hostile to such un-Wilsonian devices as "spheres of influence."

Agreement on European questions was more difficult. The three powers easily agreed on Germany's disarmament and denazification and on its division into four zones of occupation by France and the Big Three (the USSR, Britain, and the United States). Churchill, however, began to balk at Stalin's plan to dismember Germany and objected to his demand for reparations in the amount of $20 billion as well as forced labor from all the zones, with Russia to get half of everything. These matters were left undecided to fester and to cause dissension in the future.

The settlement of Eastern Europe was no less a problem. Everyone agreed that the Soviet Union deserved neighboring governments that were friendly, but the West insisted that they also be independent, autonomous, and democratic. The Western leaders, and especially Churchill, were not eager to see Eastern Europe fall under Russian domination. They, especially Roosevelt, were also truly committed to democracy and self-determination.

However, Stalin knew that independent, freely elected governments in Poland and Romania would not be safely friendly to Russia. He had already established a subservient government in Poland at Lublin in competition with the Polish government-in-exile in London. Under pressure from the Western leaders, however, Stalin agreed to reorganize the government and to include some Poles friendly to the West. He also signed a Declaration on Liberated Europe, promising

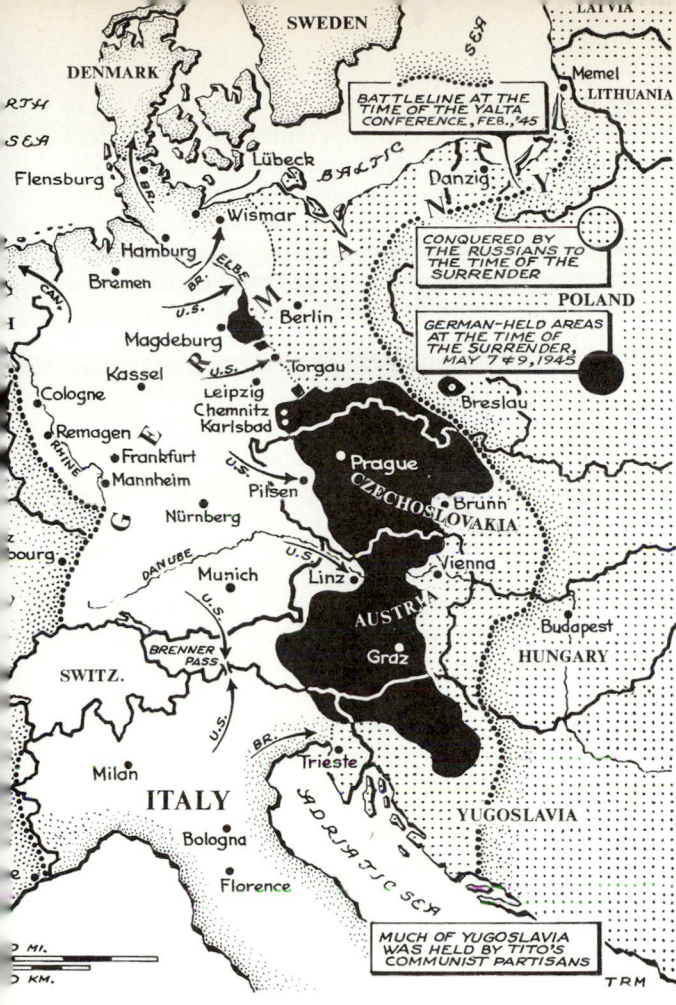

MAP 35-6 YALTA TO THE SURRENDER *"The Big Three," Roosevelt, Churchill, Stalin, met at YALTA in the Crimea in February of 1945. At the meeting concessions were made to Stalin concerning the settlement of Eastern Europe, as Roosevelt was eager to bring the Russians into the Pacific war as soon as possible. This map shows the positions held at the time of the surrender.*

Yet he appeared eager to avoid conflict before the war with Germany was over—and he probably thought it worth endorsing some meaningless principles as the price of continued harmony. In any case, he wasted little time in violating these agreements.

Yalta

The next meeting of the Big Three was at Yalta in the Crimea in February 1945. The Western armies had not yet crossed the Rhine, and the Soviet army was within a hundred miles of Berlin. The war with Japan continued, and no atomic explosion had yet taken place. Roosevelt, faced with an invasion of Japan and prospective heavy losses, was eager to bring the Russians into the Pacific war soon as possible.

As a true Wilsonian, Roosevelt also suspected Churchill's determination to maintain the British Empire and Britain's colonial advantages. The Americans thought that Churchill's plan to set up British spheres of influence in Europe would encourage the Russians to do the same and lead to friction and war. To encourage Russian participation in the war against Japan, Roosevelt and Churchill made extensive concessions to Russia in Sakhalin and the Kurile Islands, in Korea, and in Manchuria. Again in the tradition of Wilson, Roosevelt laid great stress on a united-nations organization: "Through the United Nations, he hoped to achieve a self-enforcing peace settlement that would

self-determination and free democratic elections. Stalin never was free of the fear that the Allies might still make an arrangement with Germany and betray him.

The "Big Three" met at Yalta in February 1945 to plan the final defeat of Germany and Japan and to settle the future of the post-war world. [United Press International Photo.]

not require American troops, as well as an open world without spheres of influence in which American enterprise could work freely."[3] Soviet agreement on these points seemed well worth concessions elsewhere.

Potsdam

The Big Three met for the last time in the Berlin suburb of Potsdam in July 1945. Much had changed since the last conference. Germany was defeated, and news of the successful experimental explosion of an atomic weapon reached the American president during the meetings. The cast of characters was also different: President Truman replaced Roosevelt; and Clement Attlee (1883–1967), leader of the Labour Party that had defeated Churchill's Conservatives in a general election, replaced Churchill as Britain's spokesman during the conference. Previous agreements were reaffirmed, but progress on undecided questions was slow.

Russia's western frontier was moved far into what had been Poland and included part of German East Prussia. In compensation, Poland was allowed "temporary administration" over the rest of East Prussia and Germany east of the Oder–Neisse river line, a condition that became permanent. In effect, Poland was moved about a hundred miles west, at the expense of Germany, to accommodate the Soviet Union. The Allies agreed that Germany would be divided into occupation zones until the final peace treaty was signed. As no such treaty has ever been made, Germany remains divided to this day.

A Council of Foreign Ministers was established to draft peace treaties for Germany's allies. Growing disagreements made the job difficult, and it was not until February 1947 that Italy, Romania, Hungary, Bulgaria, and Finland signed treaties. The Russians were dissatisfied with the treaty that the United States made with Japan in 1951 and signed their own agreements with the Japanese in 1956. These disagreements were foreshadowed at Potsdam.

Causes of the Cold War

Some scholars attribute the hardening of the atmosphere to the advent of Truman in place of the more sympathetic Roosevelt and to the American possession of an effective atomic bomb. The fact is that Truman was trying to carry Roosevelt's policies forward, and there is evidence that Roosevelt himself had become distressed by Soviet actions in eastern Europe. Nor did Truman use the successful test of the atomic bomb to try to keep Russia out of the Pacific. On the contrary, he worked hard to ensure Russian intervention against Japan. In part, the new coldness among the Allies arose from the mutual feeling that each had

[3] Robert O. Paxton, *Europe in the Twentieth Century* (New York: Harcourt Brace Jovanovich, 1975), p. 487.

violated previous agreements. The Russians were plainly asserting permanent control of Poland and Romania under puppet Communist governments. The United States, on the other hand, was taking a harder line on the extent of German reparations to the Soviet Union.

In retrospect, however, it appears unlikely that friendlier styles on either side could have avoided a split that rested on basic differences of ideology and interest. The Soviet Union's attempt to extend its control westward into central Europe and the Balkans and southward into the Middle East was a continuation of the policy of tsarist Russia. It had been Britain's traditional role to try to restrain Russian expansion into these areas; and it was not surprising that the United States should inherit that task as Britain's power waned. The alternative was to permit a major change in the balance of power in the world in favor of a huge, traditionally hostile nation. That nation, dedicated in its official ideology to overthrow nations like the United States, was governed by an absolute dictator who had already demonstrated many times his capacity for the most amazing deceptions and the most horrible cruelties. Few nations would be likely to take such risks.

Nevertheless, the Americans made no attempt to roll back Soviet power where it existed. This despite the fact that American military forces were the greatest in their history, their industrial power was unmatched in the world, and atomic weapons were their monopoly. In less than a year from the war's end, American forces in Europe were reduced from 3.5 million to half a million. The speed of the withdrawal was the result of pressure to "get the boys home" but was fully in accord with American plans and peacetime goals. These traditional goals were support for self-determination, autonomy, and democracy in the political area; free trade; freedom of the seas; no barriers to investment; and the Open Door in the economic sphere. These goals agreed with American principles, and they served American interests well. As the strongest, richest nation in the world—the one with the greatest industrial plant and the strongest currency—the United States would benefit handsomely if such an international order were established.

American hostility to colonial empires created tensions with France and Britain, but these were minor. The main conflict came with the Soviet Union. From the Soviet perspective, the extension of its frontiers and the domination of formerly independent states in eastern Europe were necessary for the security of the USSR as well as for a proper compensation for the fearful losses that the Russians had suffered in the war. American resistance to the new state of things could be seen as a threat to the Soviets' security and legitimate aims. American objections over Poland and

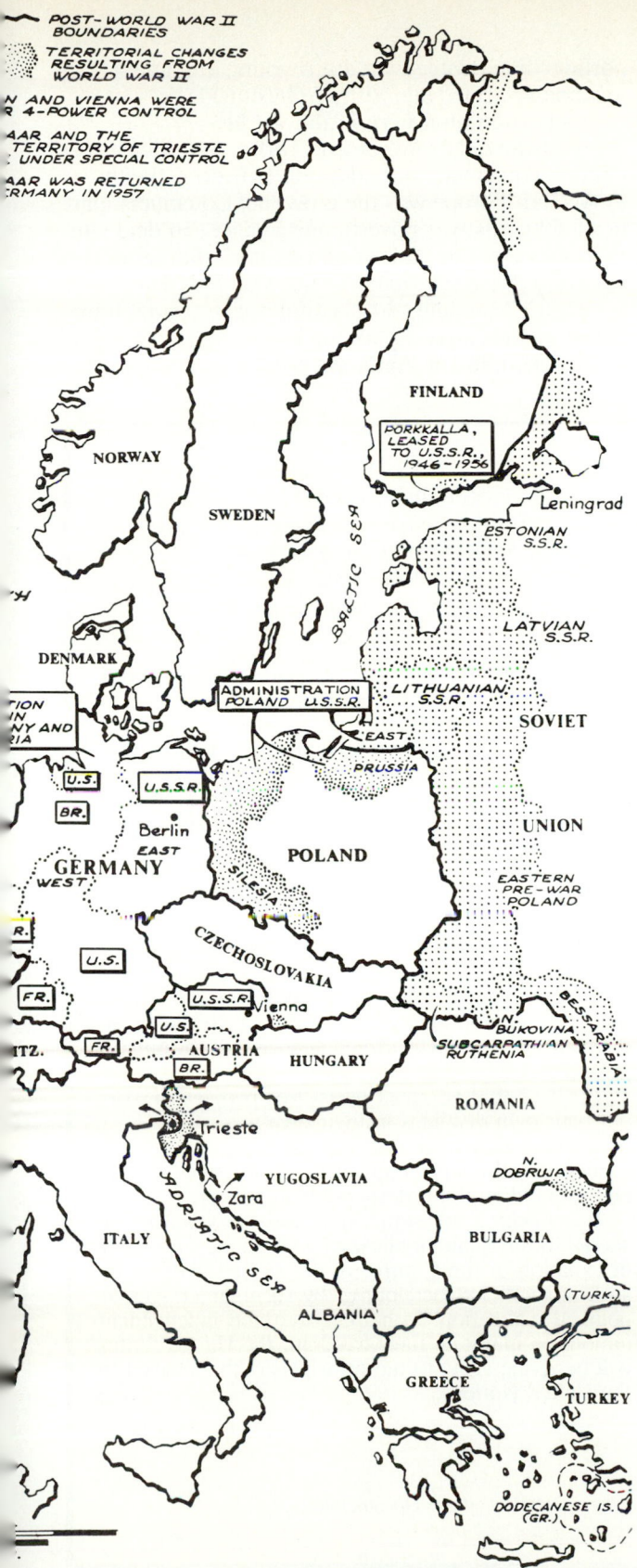

(Map legend):
POST–WORLD WAR II BOUNDARIES
TERRITORIAL CHANGES RESULTING FROM WORLD WAR II
...N AND VIENNA WERE ...R 4-POWER CONTROL
...AAR AND THE ...ERRITORY OF TRIESTE ...UNDER SPECIAL CONTROL
...AAR WAS RETURNED ...RMANY IN 1957

(Map labels): NORWAY, SWEDEN, FINLAND, PORKKALLA, LEASED TO U.S.S.R., 1946–1956, Leningrad, BALTIC SEA, ESTONIAN S.S.R., LATVIAN S.S.R., LITHUANIAN S.S.R., DENMARK, ADMINISTRATION POLAND U.S.S.R., U.S., U.S.S.R., BR., Berlin, EAST PRUSSIA, SOVIET UNION, EAST GERMANY, WEST, POLAND, SILESIA, EASTERN PRE-WAR POLAND, CZECHOSLOVAKIA, U.S., FR., U.S.S.R., Vienna, U.S., AUSTRIA, BR., HUNGARY, N. BUKOVINA, SUBCARPATHIAN RUTHENIA, BESSARABIA, ROMANIA, Trieste, YUGOSLAVIA, Zara, N. DOBRUJA, ITALY, ADRIATIC SEA, BULGARIA, ALBANIA, (TURK.), GREECE, TURKEY, DODECANESE IS. (GR.)

other states could be seen as attempts to undermine regimes friendly to Russia and to encircle the Soviet Union with hostile neighbors. Such behavior might be seen to justify Russian attempts to overthrow regimes friendly to the United States in Western Europe and elsewhere.

The growth in France and Italy of large Communist parties plainly taking orders from Moscow led the Americans to believe that Stalin was engaged in a great worldwide plot to destroy capitalism and democracy by subversion. In the absence of reliable evidence about Stalin's intentions, certainty is not possible, but most people in the West thought the suspicions plausible. Rivalry between the Soviet Union and the United States dominated international relations for the next three decades. In the flawed world of reality it is hard to see how things could have been otherwise. The important question was whether the conflict would take a diplomatic or a military form.

The Cold War

Evidence of the new mood of hostility among the former allies was not long in coming. In February 1946, both Stalin and his foreign minister, Vyacheslav Molotov, gave public speeches in which they spoke of the Western democracies as enemies. A month later Churchill gave a speech in Fulton, Missouri, in which he viewed Russian actions in eastern Europe with alarm. He spoke of an Iron Curtain that had descended on Europe, dividing a free and democratic West from an East under totalitarian rule. He warned against Communist subversion and urged Western unity and strength as a response to the new menace. In this atmosphere, difficulties grew.

The attempt to deal with the problem of atomic energy was an early victim of the Cold War. The Americans put forward a plan to place the manufacture and control of atomic weapons under international control; but the Russians balked at the proposed requirements for on-site inspection and for limits on the veto power in the United Nations. The plan fell through. The United States continued to develop its own atomic weapons in secrecy, and the Russians did the same. By 1949, with the help of information obtained by Soviet spies in Britain and the United States, the Soviet Union exploded its own atomic bomb, and the race for nuclear weapons was on.

Western resistance to what they increasingly perceived as Soviet intransigence and Communist plans for subversion and expansion took clearer form in

1947. Since 1944, civil war had been raging in Greece between the royalist government restored by Britain and insurgents supported by the Communist countries, chiefly Yugoslavia. In 1947, Britain informed the United States that it was financially no longer able to support the Greeks. On March 12, President Truman asked Congress for legislation to support Greece and also Turkey, which was under Soviet pressure to yield control of the Dardanelles. Congress voted funds to aid Greece and Turkey. But the Truman Doctrine, as enunciated in a speech of March 12, had a broader significance. The president advocated a policy of supporting "free people who are resisting attempted subjugation by armed minorities or by outside pressures," by implication anywhere in the world.

American aid to Greece and Turkey took the form of military equipment and advisers. However, the threat in Western Europe was the growth of Communist parties fed by postwar poverty and hunger. To deal with this menace, the Americans devised the European Recovery Program, named the Marshall Plan after George C. Marshall, the secretary of state who introduced it. This was a plan for broad economic aid to European states on condition only that they work to-

The Truman Doctrine

In 1947, the British informed the United States that they could no longer support the Greeks in their fight against a Communist insurrection supported from the outside. On March 12 of that year, President Truman asked Congress for legislation in support of both Greece and Turkey, which was also in danger. The spirit behind that request, which became known as the Truman Doctrine, *appears in the following selections from Truman's speech to the Congress.*

I am fully aware of the broad implications involved if the United States extends assistance to Greece and Turkey, and I shall discuss these implications with you at this time.

One of the primary objectives of the foreign policy of the United States is the creation of conditions in which we and other nations will be able to work out a way of life free from coercion. This was a fundamental issue in the war with Germany and Japan. Our victory was won over countries which sought to impose their will, and their way of life, upon other nations.

To insure the peaceful development of nations, free from coercion, the United States has taken a leading part in establishing the United Nations. The United Nations is designed to make possible lasting freedom and independence for all its members. We shall not realize our objectives, however, unless we are willing to help free peoples to maintain their free institutions and their national integrity against aggressive movements that seek to impose upon them totalitarian regimes. This is no more than a frank recognition that totalitarian regimes imposed upon free peoples, by direct or indirect aggression, undermine the foundations of international peace and hence the security of the United States.

The peoples of a number of countries of the world have recently had totalitarian regimes forced upon them against their will. The Government of the United States has made frequent protests against coercion and intimidation, in violation of the Yalta agreement, in Poland, Rumania, and Bulgaria. I must also state that in a number of other countries there have been similar developments.

At the present moment in world history nearly every nation must choose between alternative ways of life. The choice is too often not a free one.

One way of life is based upon the will of the majority, and is distinguished by free institutions, representative government, free elections, guaranties of individual liberty, freedom of speech and religion, and freedom from political oppression.

The second way of life is based upon the will of a minority forcibly imposed upon the majority. It relies upon terror and oppression, a controlled press and radio, fixed elections, and the suppression of personal freedoms.

I believe that it must be the policy of the United States to support free peoples who are resisting attempted subjugation by armed minorities or by outside pressures.

I believe that we must assist free peoples to work out their own destinies in their own way.

I believe that our help should be primarily through economic and financial aid, which is essential to economic stability and orderly political processes.

The world is not static, and the *status quo* is not sacred. But we cannot allow changes in the *status quo* in violation of the Charter of the United Nations by such methods as coercion, or by such subterfuges as political infiltration. In helping free and independent nations to maintain their freedom, the United States will be giving effect to the principles of the Charter of the United Nations. ❑

Senate Committee on Foreign Relations, *A Decade of American Foreign Policy: Basic Documents 1941–1949* (1950), pp. 1235–1237.

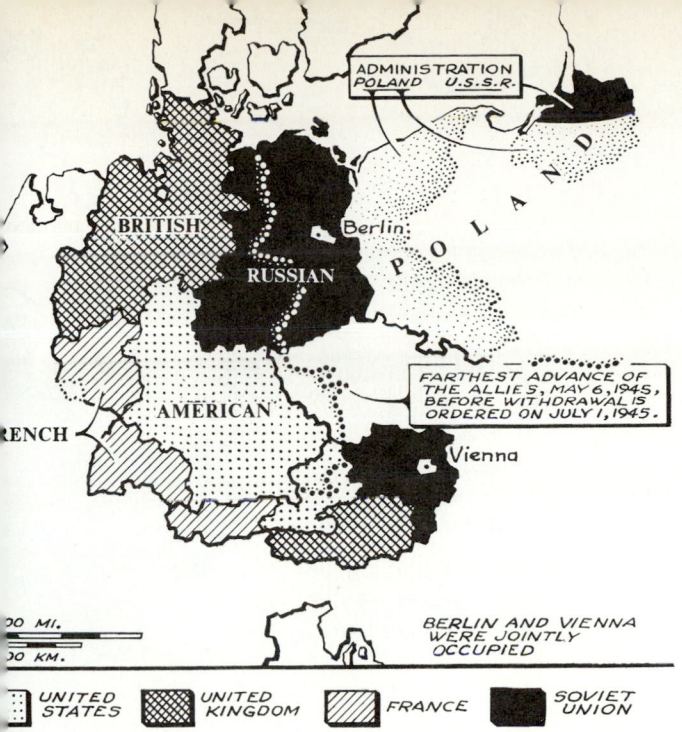

BRITISH

Berlin

RUSSIAN

P O L A N D

FARTHEST ADVANCE OF
THE ALLIES, MAY 6, 1945,
BEFORE WITHDRAWAL IS
ORDERED ON JULY 1, 1945.

AMERICAN

FRENCH

Vienna

BERLIN AND VIENNA
WERE JOINTLY
OCCUPIED

| UNITED STATES | UNITED KINGDOM | FRANCE | SOVIET UNION |

MAP 35-8 OCCUPIED GERMANY AND AUSTRIA
At the war's end, defeated Germany, including Austria, was occupied by the victorious Allies in the several zones shown here. Austria, by prompt agreement, was reerected into an independent, neutral state and no longer occupied. But the German zones have hardened into an "East" Germany (the former Soviet zone) and a "West" Germany (the former British, French, and American zones). The city of Berlin, within the Soviet zone, was similarly divided.

gether for their mutual benefit. The invitation included the Soviet Union and its satellites. Finland and Czechoslovakia were willing to participate, and Poland and Hungary showed interest. The Soviets, fearing that American economic aid would attract many satellites out of their orbits, forbade them to take part. The Marshall Plan was a great success in restoring prosperity to Western Europe and in setting the stage for Europe's unprecedented postwar economic growth. It also led to the waning of Communist strength in the West and to the establishment of solid democratic regimes.

From the Western viewpoint, this policy of "containment" was a new and successful response to the Soviet and Communist challenge. To Stalin, it may have seemed a renewal of the old Western attempt to isolate and encircle the USSR. His answer was to put an end to all multiparty governments behind the Iron Curtain and to replace them with thoroughly Communist regimes completely under his control. He also called a meeting of all Communist parties around the world at Warsaw in the autumn of 1947. There they

organized the Communist Information Bureau (Cominform), a revival of the old Comintern, dedicated to spreading revolutionary Communism throughout the world. The era of the popular front was officially over. Communist leaders in the West who favored friendship, collaboration, and reform were replaced by hardliners who attempted to sabotage the new structures.

In February 1948, a more dramatic and brutal display of Stalin's new policy took place in Prague. The Communists expelled the democratic members of what had been a coalition government and murdered Jan Masaryk, the foreign minister and son of the founder of Czechoslovakia, Thomas Masaryk. President Eduard Beneš (1884–1948) was also forced to resign, and Czechoslovakia was brought fully under Soviet rule.

These Soviet actions, especially those in Czechoslovakia, increased American determination to go ahead with its own arrangements in Germany. The Russians proceeded swiftly to dismantle German industry in the eastern zone, but the Americans acted differently. They concluded that such a policy would require the United States to support Germany for the foreseeable future. It would also cause political chaos and open the way for Communism. They preferred, therefore, to try to make Germany self-sufficient, and this meant restoring rather than destroying its industrial capacity. To the Soviets, the restoration of a powerful industrial Germany, even in the Western zones only, was frightening and unacceptable. The same difference of approach hampered agreement on reparations because the Soviets claimed the right to the industrial equipment in all the zones, and the Americans resisted their demands.

Disagreement over Germany produced the most heated of postwar debates. When the Western powers agreed to go forward with a separate constitution for the western sectors of Germany in February 1948, the Soviets walked out of the joint Allied Control Commission. In the summer of that year, the Western powers issued a new currency in their zone. Berlin, though well within the Soviet zone, was governed by all four powers. The Soviets feared the new currency that was circulating in Berlin at better rates than their own and chose to seal the city off by closing all railroads and highways to West Germany. Their purpose was to drive the Western powers out of Berlin.

The Western allies responded to the Berlin Blockade with an airlift of supplies to the city that lasted almost a year. In May 1949, the Russians were forced to back down and to open access to Berlin. The incident was decisive in greatly increasing tensions and suspicions between the opponents. It hastened the lasting separation of Germany into two states. West Germany formally became the German Federated Republic in September 1949, and the eastern region became the German Democratic Republic a month later. Ironically, Germany had been dismembered in a way no one had planned or expected.

NATO and the Warsaw Pact

Meanwhile, the nations of Western Europe had been coming closer together. The Marshall Plan encouraged international cooperation. In March 1948, Belgium, the Netherlands, Luxembourg, France, and Britain signed the Treaty of Brussels, providing for cooperation in economic and military matters. In April 1949, these nations joined with Italy, Denmark, Norway, Portugal, and Iceland to sign a treaty with Canada and the United States that formed the North Atlantic Treaty Organization (NATO). NATO committed its members to mutual assistance in case any of them was attacked. For the first time in history, the United States was committed to defend allies outside the Western Hemisphere. The NATO treaty formed the West into a bloc. A few years later, West Germany, Greece, and Turkey joined the alliance.

Soviet relations with the states of Eastern Europe were governed by a series of bilateral treaties providing for close ties and mutual assistance in case of attack. In 1949, the Council of Mutual Assistance (COMECON) was formed to integrate the economies of these states. Unlike the NATO states, the Eastern alliance system was under direct Soviet domination through local Communist parties controlled from Moscow and overawed by the presence of the Red Army. The Warsaw Pact of May 1955, which included Albania, Bulgaria, Czechoslovakia, East Germany, Hungary, Poland, Romania, and the Soviet Union, merely gave formal recognition to a system that already existed. Europe was divided into two unfriendly blocs. The Cold War had taken firm shape in Europe.

MAP 35-9   MAJOR EUROPEAN ALLIANCE SYSTEMS   *The North Atlantic Treaty Organization, which includes both Canada and the United States, stretches as far east as Turkey. By contrast, the Warsaw Pact nations are contiguous communist states of eastern Europe, with the Soviet Union, of course, as the dominant member.*

World War II and the Cold War in World Perspective

The second great war of the twentieth century (1939–1945) grew out of the unsatisfactory resolution of the first. In retrospect, the two wars appear to some people to be one continuous conflict—a kind of twentieth-century "Thirty Years' War"—with the two main periods of fighting separated by an uneasy truce. To others, that point of view seems to oversimplify and distort the situation by implying that the second war was the inevitable result of the first and its inadequate peace treaties.

The latter opinion seems more sound. Whatever the flaws of the treaties of Paris, the world suffered an even more terrible war than the first because of failures of judgment and will on the part of the victorious democratic powers. The United States, which had be-

come the wealthiest and potentially the strongest nation in the world, disarmed almost entirely and withdrew into a short-sighted and foolish isolation; it could play no important part in restraining the angry and ambitious dictators who would bring on the war. Britain and France refused to face the reality of the threat posed by the Axis powers until the most deadly war in history was required to put it down. If the victorious democracies had remained strong, responsible, and realistic, they could easily have remedied whatever injustices or mistakes arose from the treaties, without any danger to the peace.

The second war itself was plainly a world war. There is good reason to think that if the Japanese occupation of Manchuria in 1931 was not technically a part of that war, it was a significant precursor. Italy attacked the African nation of Ethiopia in 1935. Italy, Germany, and the Soviet Union intervened in the Spanish Civil War (1936–1939). Japan attacked China in 1937. All these developments revealed that aggressive forces were on the march around the globe and that the defenders of the world order lacked the will to stop them. The formation of the Axis between Germany, Italy, and Japan guaranteed that when the war came it would be fought around the world. There was fighting and suffering in Asia, Africa, the islands of the Pacific, and Europe. Men and women from all the inhabited continents took part in this war. The use of atomic weapons brought the frightful struggle to a close, but what are called conventional weapons did almost all the damage. The world reached a level of destructiveness that threatened the survival of civilization, even without the use of atomic or nuclear devices.

This war ended not with unsatisfactory peace treaties but with no treaty at all in the European area where the war had begun. The world quickly split into two unfriendly camps: the western led by the United States, and the eastern led by the Soviet Union. This division, among other things, hastened the liberation of former colonial territories. The bargaining power of these new nations was temporarily increased, as the two rival great powers tried to gain their friendship or allegiance. It has become customary to refer to these nations as "the Third World," with the Soviet Union and the United States and their respective allies being the first two. With the passage of time, the differences between these newer nations became so great as to make the name not very helpful.

One of the most surprising aspects of the second war, the treatment received by the defeated powers, was also largely the result of the emergence of the Cold War. Instead of their being held back, democratic governments were installed in them. They were taken into the Western alliance and assisted in their economic recovery to the point where Japan and Germany are among the richest nations in the world and Italy is more prosperous than it has ever been. At the same time, the ideological threat posed by Communism, very much feared soon after the war, has waned as state control of the economy has produced disastrous results around the world. Communism has been discredited, to some degree even in Communist China and the Soviet Union. So, too, has the political attraction of the Communist system declined with the knowledge of the brutalities of Stalin in the Soviet Union and Mao in China, and more recently the horrors perpetrated by Communist regimes in Cambodia and Vietnam. What remains is the enormous military power of the Soviet Union. It remains to be seen whether recent developments in that country will lead to more peaceful relations between the rivals.

Suggested Readings

A. ADAMTHWAITE, *France and the Coming of the Second World War, 1936–1939* (1977). A careful account making good use of the newly opened French archives.

A. BULLOCK, *Hitler: A Study in Tyranny*, rev. ed. (1964). A brilliant biography.

W. S. CHURCHILL, *The Second World War*, 6 vols. (1948–1954). The memoirs of the great British leader.

H. FEIS, *From Trust to Terror: The Onset of the Cold War, 1945–1950* (1970). The best general account.

H. W. GATZKE, *Stresemann and the Rearmament of Germany* (1954). An important monograph.

M. GILBERT AND R. GOTT, *The Appeasers*, rev. ed. (1963). A revealing study of British policy in the 1930s.

K. HILDEBRAND, *The Foreign Policy of the Third Reich* (1970).

M. KNOX, *Mussolini Unleashed* (1982). An outstanding study of Fascist Italy's policy and strategy in World War II.

G. KOLKO, *The Politics of War* (1968). An interesting example of the new revisionist school that finds the causes of the Cold War in economic considerations and emphasizes American responsibility.

W. L. LANGER AND S. E. GLEASON, *The Challenge of Isolation* (1952). American foreign policy in the 1930s.

B. H. LIDDELL HART, *History of the Second World War*, 2 vols. (1971). A good military history.

S. MARKS, *The Illusion of Peace* (1976). A good discussion of European international relations in the 1920s and early 1930s.

V. MASTNY, *Russia's Road to the Cold War* (1979). Written by an expert on the Soviet Union and Eastern Europe.

W. MURRAY, *The Change in the European Balance of Power 1938–1939* (1984). A brilliant study of the relationship between strategy, foreign policy, economics, and domestic politics in the years before the war.

N. RICH, *Hitler's War Aims*, 2 vols. (1973–1974).

M. SHERWIN, *A World Destroyed: The Atomic Bomb and the Grand Alliance* (1975). An analysis of the role of the atomic bomb in the years surrounding the end of World War II.

R. J. SONTAG, *A Broken World 1919–1939* (1971). An excellent survey.

A. J. P. TAYLOR, *The Origins of the Second World War* (1966). A lively, controversial, even perverse study.

H. THOMAS, *The Spanish Civil War*, 3rd ed. (1986). The best account in English.

C. THORNE, *The Approach of War 1938–1939* (1967). A careful analysis of diplomacy.

A. ULAM, *The Bolsheviks* (1968). An outstanding account of Lenin's faction and its rise to power.

G. WRIGHT, *The Ordeal of Total War 1939–1945* (1968). An excellent survey.

An antinuclear demonstration in West Germany in 1982. By the 1980s, many West Europeans felt trapped between the two nuclear superpowers, the United States and the Soviet Union. [Sygma.]

36 The West since World War II

Over forty years have passed since the conclusion of World War II and the onset of the Cold War. The rivalry between the United States and the Soviet Union as the two superpowers with nuclear arsenals has been the most fundamental political fact of life throughout this era. The East–West conflict has spilled over into one area of international relations after another, profoundly affecting domestic politics. At the same time, remarkable changes have occurred within both the Communist and non-Communist states.

Within both the world context and the more narrow Western context, the greatest change since 1945 has been the entrance of the United States into the stage as a fully active great power. The retreat from leadership that occurred in 1919 was not repeated. The decision on the part of the United States to take an activist role in world affairs has touched virtually every aspect of the postwar world. As a result of this acceptance of a leadership role, American domestic politics and its foreign policy often are intertwined.

In Western Europe, the years since World War II have witnessed a period of remarkable economic prosperity and political stability. These nations have for over three decades been moving toward extensive economic cooperation and integration.

The Soviet Union has experienced a series of changes of political and economic direction within the constraints of Communist Party rule. It has confronted an ongoing problem of agricultural production. Throughout the period, the Soviet Union has dominated both the politics and economic life of Eastern Europe.

The American Domestic Scene since World War II

Three major themes have characterized the postwar American experience. These have been an opposition to any expansion of Communism, an expansion of civil rights to blacks and other minorities at home, and a determination to achieve ongoing economic growth. Virtually all of the major postwar political debates and social divisions have arisen from one or more of these issues.

The Truman and Eisenhower Administrations

The foreign policy of President Harry Truman was directed against Communist expansion in Europe and East Asia. He enunciated the Truman Doctrine in regard to Greece and Turkey and initiated the Marshall Plan for European reconstruction. As will be discussed more fully in the next chapter, he led the United States to support the United Nations' intervention against aggression in Korea. Domestically, the Truman administration pursued what may be regarded as a continuation of the New Deal. However, he encountered very considerable opposition from conservative Re-publicans. The major achievement of those Republicans was the passage of the Taft-Hartley Act in 1947, which placed limits on various forms of labor union activity. Truman won the 1948 election over great odds. Through policies he termed the Fair Deal, Truman sought to extend economic security through actions of the federal government.

However, those efforts became quite frustrated as fear of a domestic Communist menace swept much of the country. Senator Joseph McCarthy of Wisconsin led the campaign against the perceived Communist danger within the ranks of American citizens and within agencies of the government. The patriotism and loyalty of scores of prominent Americans came under public scrutiny and question. That development, a frustration with the war in Korea, and perhaps the natural weariness of the electorate after twenty years of Democratic Party government led to the election of war hero Dwight Eisenhower (1890–1969) in 1952.

In retrospect, the Eisenhower years now seem a period of calm after the war years of the 1940s and before the turmoil of the 1960s. Eisenhower, personally popular, brought the Korean War to a conclusion. The country was generally prosperous. Homebuilding increased dramatically, and the vast interstate highway system was initiated. He was by design a less

President Dwight Eisenhower of the United States and Premier Nikita Khrushchev of the Soviet Union were the two dominant world leaders during the late 1950s. [U.S. Navy Photo from the Eisenhower Library.]

activist president than either Roosevelt or Truman had been.

Beneath the apparent quiet of the Eisenhower years, however, stirred several forces that would lead to the disruptions of the 1960s. First, during the Eisenhower administration, major foreign policy commitments were made throughout the world to oppose the advance of Communism. The honoring of those commitments led to American involvement in Vietnam; indeed, that involvement began under Eisenhower.

Civil Rights

In 1954, the United States Supreme Court in the decision of *Brown v. Board of Education of Topeka* declared unconstitutional the segregation of the black and white races. Shortly thereafter, the Court ordered the desegregation of schools. For the next ten years, the struggle over school integration and civil rights for black Americans stirred the nation. Various southern states attempted to resist school desegregation. In 1957, Eisenhower sent troops into Little Rock, Arkansas to integrate the schools, but resistance continued to appear in various forms in other southern states.

While the battle raged over the schools, an awakened civil rights movement among American blacks began to protest segregation in other areas of national life. In 1955, Reverend Martin Luther King, Jr. (1929–1968) organized a boycott in Montgomery, Alabama against segregated buses. The Montgomery bus boycott marked the beginning of the use of civil disobedience to fight racial discrimination in the United States. Drawing upon the ideas of Henry David Thoreau and the experience of Ghandi in India, the leaders of the civil rights movement went to jail rather than obey laws they believed to be unjust. The civil rights struggle continued well into the 1960s. One of its most dramatic moments was the march in 1963 on Washington by tens of thousands of supporters of civil rights legislation. The greatest achievement of the movement was the passage of the Civil Rights Act of 1964, which desegregated public accommodations, and the Voting Rights Act of 1965, which cleared the way for large numbers of blacks to vote. The results of that legislation as well as of ongoing protests in areas of housing and job discrimination brought black citizens nearer to the mainstream of American life than ever before.

However, much yet remained to be done. In 1967, major race riots occurred in several American cities. There was significant loss of life. Those riots, followed by the assassination of Martin Luther King, Jr. in 1968, greatly weakened the civil rights movement that had commenced in Montgomery. Despite new efforts to

The United States Supreme Court Declares Segregation Unconstitutional

In 1954, the United States Supreme Court in Brown v. the School Board of Topeka *reversed the decisions of* Plessy v. Ferguson *of 1896. The Court declared that separate facilities were inherently unequal. This decision was one of the major sparks to the Civil Rights Movement of the 1950s and 1960s.*

In approaching this problem, we cannot turn the clock back to 1868 when the [Fourteenth] Amendment was adopted, or even to 1896 when *Plessy v. Ferguson* was written. We must consider public education in the light of its full development and its present place in American life throughout the Nation. Only in this way can it be determined if segregation in public schools deprives these plaintiffs of the equal protection of the laws.

Today, education is perhaps the most important function of state and local governments. Compulsory school attendance laws and the great expenditures for education both demonstrate our recognition of the importance of education to our democratic society. It is required in the performance of our most basic public responsibilities, even service in the armed forces. It is the very foundation of good citizenship. Today it is a principal instrument in awakening the child to cultural values, in preparing him for later professional training, and in helping him to adjust normally to his environment. In these days, it is doubtful that any child may reasonably be expected to succeed in life if he is denied the opportunity of an education. Such an opportunity where the state has undertaken to provide it, is a right which must be made available to all on equal terms.

We come to the question presented: Does segregation of children in public schools solely on the basis of race, even though the physical facilities and other "tangible" factors may be equal, deprive the children of the minority group of equal educational opportunities? We believe that it does. . . .

We conclude that in the field of public education the doctrine of "separate but equal" has no place. Separate educational facilities are inherently unequal. ❑

Brown v. Board of Education of Topeka, 1954, as quoted in Henry Steel Commager, *Documents of American History*, Eighth Edition (New York: Appleton-Century-Crofts, 1968), 2: 607–608.

Rev. Martin Luther King stood as the foremost civil rights leader in the United States. His tactic of nonviolent resistance mobilized thousands of black Americans to demand an end to segregation. [Library of Congress.]

fight discrimination, a major national leader of the civil rights movement was missing. Not until the late 1980s did a new leader emerge in the person of the Reverend Jesse Jackson, who actively contested the Democratic Party nomination for the presidency in 1984 and 1988. Jackson raised new issues of racial equality and fostered the registration of significant numbers of black voters.

New Social Programs

The advance of the civil rights movement in the late 1950s and early 1960s represented the cutting edge of a new advance of political liberalism. In 1960, John F. Kennedy (1917–1963) narrowly won the presidential election. He saw himself as attempting to set the country moving again after the years of Eisenhower calm. Kennedy defined his goals as seeking to move toward a New Frontier. One of his goals was to enable the U.S. space program to put a man on the moon. He also attempted unsuccessfully to expand medical care under the social security program. In terms of the civil rights movement, however, he basically reacted rather than led.

Nevertheless, the reaction to Kennedy's assassination in 1963 provided the occasion for his successor, Lyndon Johnson (1908–1973), to press for activist legislation. In order to fulfill Kennedy's programs and to launch those of his own, Johnson pushed through Congress the Civil Rights Act of 1964 and the tax cut of that

year. Johnson then set forth a bold domestic program known as the War on Poverty, which established major federal programs to create jobs and provide job training. Furthermore, new entitlements were added to the social security program, including Medicare which provides medical services for the elderly. Johnson's drive for what he termed the Great Society represented the close of the era of major federal government initiatives that had commenced under Franklin Roosevelt. The liberal impulse remained alive in American politics, but by the late 1960s the electorate began a move toward a much more conservative stance.

The Vietnam War and Domestic Turmoil

Johnson's activist domestic vision very quickly was overshadowed by issues surrounding U.S. involvement in Vietnam (to be considered more fully in the next chapter). By 1965, Johnson had made the decision to send tens of thousands of Americans to Vietnam. This policy led to the longest of American wars. At home, the Vietnam involvement resulted in vast public protests over the war and more particularly over the draft. The overwhelming majority of young American men who were drafted went into the armed forces. However, very significant numbers resisted the draft. Large-scale protests involving civil disobedience, often patterned after those of the civil rights movements, erupted on college and university campuses. In some

The clash between protesting students and the Ohio National Guard at Kent State University was the most violent moment in the protests against the United States involvement in Vietnam. [Kent State University News Service.]

cases, units of the National Guard were sent to restore calm. In the case of Kent State University in Ohio in 1970, the National Guard killed four protestors. The Vietnam War divided the nation as had no conflict since the Civil War.

The national unrest led Lyndon Johnson to decide against seeking reelection in 1968. Richard Nixon led the Republicans to victory. His election marked the beginning of an era of American politics dominated by conservative policies, though some believe the nomination of Senator Barry Goldwater by the Republicans in 1964 marked that beginning. Nixon pressed his campaign on a platform of law and order. He also stressed his experience as vice president in foreign policy. In that regard, perhaps the most important act of his administration was his reestablishment of relations with the People's Republic of China after a quarter century in which there had been no diplomatic relations between the two nations. Initially, Nixon's policies toward Vietnam were no more successful than those of Johnson. Half of the war casualties occurred under his administration. Nonetheless, he concluded the war in 1972. That same year, he was reelected. Very soon thereafter, the Watergate Scandal began to unfold.

The Watergate Scandal

On the surface, the Watergate Scandal involved a burglary of the Democratic Party National headquarters by White House operatives in 1972. The deeper issues related to questions of the extent of presidential authority and the right of the government to intrude into the personal lives of citizens. In 1973, Congress established a committee to investigate the scandal. Testimony before that committee revealed that President Nixon had recorded large numbers of conversations in the White House. The Special Prosecutor, who had been appointed to investigate the charges, finally gained access to the tapes in the summer of 1974 through a decision of the Supreme Court. In the meantime, the Judiciary Committee of the House of Representatives voted three articles of impeachment against Nixon. Shortly thereafter, certain of the newly released tapes revealed that Nixon had ordered federal agencies to try to cover up White House participation in the burglary. After this revelation, Nixon became the only president in American history to resign the presidency.

Economic Growth and Changing Fiscal Policy

The Watergate Scandal further shook public confidence in the government. It had also proved a remarkable distraction from the major problems facing the country. One of the chief of these was inflation, which had resulted from fighting the war in Vietnam while pursuing the expansion of federal domestic expenditures under Johnson. The subsequent administrations of Gerald Ford (1974–1977) and Jimmy Carter (1977–1981) battled the inflation and high interest rates without any significant success. Furthermore, the Carter administration became bogged down in the Iran hostage crisis of 1980 when more than forty Americans were held hostage in Iran for over a year.

In 1980, Ronald Reagan (b. 1911) was elected presi-

President Richard Nixon, here pictured with his wife, resigned his office in 1974 after months of public testimony and acrimony over the Watergate break-in and its aftermath. [Photo: Laffont.]

dent by a large majority. He was reelected four years later. Reagan was the first fully ideological conservative to be elected in the postwar era. His goals were relatively straightforward. In foreign policy, he took a tough line toward the Soviet Union and vastly increased defense spending. For all eight years of his administration, he also sought to contain the Sandinistas in Nicaragua. At the same time, he had concluded a major missile reduction treaty with the Soviet Union by the end of his second term. In domestic policy, Reagan sought to reduce the role of the federal government in American life. The chief vehicle to this end was a major tax cut and reform of the taxation system. The consequence of the defense spending and the tax policy was the accumulation of the largest fiscal deficit in American history. However, in the process the infla-

tion came under control and the economy experienced its longest peacetime expansion in American history.

The straightforward conservatism of the Reagan administration proved offensive to numerous groups of Americans who had traditionally supported a liberal political and social agenda. Reagan's policies were regarded as being hostile to blacks and women. A number of scandals took place that involved directly or indirectly a number of high administration officials. The most important of these scandals involved the sale of military arms to Iran in exchange for the promised release of American hostages being held in Lebanon. Despite all of these difficulties during his second term, Reagan left office as probably the most popular and successful of the post-World War II American presidents.

This 1988 meeting of President Ronald Reagan, Vice-President Bush, and President Gorbachev symbolized the new co-operative relationship that has begun to develop between the United States and the Soviet Union. [Photos: Jean Louis Atlan/Sygma.]

In 1988, Vice President George Bush was elected to succeed Reagan.

All of these domestic developments provided the backdrop for the American rivalry with the Soviet Union.

Europe and the Soviet–American Rivalry

From approximately 1848 to 1948, the nation-state characterized European political life and rivalry. Generally, these countries sought to expand their political influence and economic power at each other's expense. During the same century, Europe's economic and technological supremacy allowed certain of its states to rule or administer a vast area of the globe inhabited by non-European peoples. These nation-states have obviously continued to exist, but the economic and political collapse occasioned by World War II led them to become more interrelated and interdependent. The loss of economic and military superiority

coincided with and in some cases aided the rise of nationalism throughout the colonial world. The United States and the Soviet Union—with their extensive economic resources, military forces, and nuclear capacities—have filled the power vacuum created by the European collapse.

The first round of Cold War confrontation culminated in the formation of NATO (1949) and the intervention of U.S. and United Nations' forces in Korea (1950). In 1953, Stalin died, and later that year an armistice was concluded in Korea. Both events produced hope that international tensions might lessen. In early 1955, Austria agreed to become a neutral state, and Soviet occupation forces left. Later that year, the leaders of France, Great Britain, the Soviet Union, and the United States held a summit conference at Geneva. Nuclear weapons and the future of divided Germany were the chief items on the agenda. Although there was much public display of friendliness among the participants, there were few substantial agreements on major problems. Nonetheless, the fact that world leaders were discussing problems and issues produced the so-called spirit of Geneva. This atmosphere proved to

The "spirit of Geneva" is displayed in this picture of the four major leaders who met there in the summer of 1955 for a summit conference. From left to right they are Nikolai Bulganin of the Soviet Union, Dwight Eisenhower of the United States, Edgar Faure of France, and Anthony Eden of Great Britain. [United Press International Photo.]

be short-lived, and the rivalry of power and polemics soon resumed.

The Crises of 1956

The year 1956 was one of considerable significance for both the Cold War and the recognition of the realities of European power in the postwar era.

SUEZ. In July 1956, President Gamal Abdel Nasser (1918–1970) of Egypt nationalized the Suez Canal. Great Britain and France feared that this action would close the canal to their supplies of oil in the Persian Gulf. In October 1956, war broke out between Egypt and the eight-year-old state of Israel. The British and the French seized the opportunity of this conflict to intervene. Publicly they spoke of acting to separate the combatants, but their real motive was to recapture the canal. The Anglo-French military operation was a fiasco of the first order and resulted in a humiliating diplomatic defeat. The United States refused to support the Anglo-French action. The Soviet Union protested in the most severe terms. The Anglo-French

forces had to be withdrawn, and control of the canal remained with Egypt. The Suez intervention proved that without the support of the United States the nations of Western Europe could no longer undertake meaningful military operations. They could no longer impose their will on the rest of the world. At the same time, it appeared that the United States and the Soviet Union had acted to restrain their allies from undertaking actions that might result in a wider conflict. The fact that neither of the superpowers wanted war put limitations on the actions of both Egypt and the Anglo-French forces.

POLAND. The autumn of 1956 also saw important developments in Eastern Europe. These demonstrated in a similar fashion the limitations on independent action among the Soviet bloc nations. When the prime minister of Poland died, the Polish Communist Party leaders refused to choose as his successor the person selected by Moscow. Considerable tension developed. The Soviet leaders even visited Warsaw to make their opinions known. In the end, Wladyslaw Gomulka

(1905–1982) emerged as the new Communist leader of Poland. He was the choice of the Poles, and he proved acceptable to the Soviets because he promised continued economic and military cooperation and most particularly continued Polish membership in the Warsaw Pact. Within those limits he moved to halt the collectivization of Polish agriculture and to improve the relationship between the Communist government and the Polish Roman Catholic church.

UPRISING IN HUNGARY. Hungary provided the second trouble spot for the Soviet Union. In late October, as the Polish problem was approaching a solution, demonstrations of sympathy for the Poles occurred in Budapest. The Communist government moved to stop the demonstrations, and street fighting erupted. A new ministry headed by former premier Imre Nagy (1896–1958) was installed by the Hungarian Communist Party. Nagy was a Communist who sought a more independent position for Hungary. He went much further in his demands than had Gomulka in Poland, and Nagy made direct appeals for political support from non-Communist groups in Hungary. Nagy called for the removal of Soviet troops and the ultimate neutralization of Hungary. He even went so far as to call for Hungarian withdrawal from the Warsaw Pact. These demands were wholly unacceptable to the Soviet Union. In early November, Soviet troops invaded the country; deposed Nagy, who was later executed; and imposed Janos Kadar (b. 1912) as premier.

The Suez intervention had provided an interna-

Wrecked ships were strewn throughout the Suez Canal after France, Britain, and Israel attacked Nasser's Egypt in 1956. [United Press International Photo.]

tional diversion that helped to permit free action by the Soviet Union. The Polish and Hungarian disturbances had several results. They demonstrated the limitations of independence within the Soviet bloc, but they did not bring an end to independent action. They also demonstrated that the example of Austrian neutrality would not be imitated elsewhere in Eastern Europe. Finally, the failure of the United States to take any action in the Hungarian uprising proved the hollowness of American political rhetoric about liberating the captive nations of Eastern Europe.

The Cold War Intensified

The events of 1956 brought to a close the era of fully autonomous action by the European nation-states. In very different ways and to differing degrees, the two superpowers had demonstrated the new political realities. After 1956, the Soviet Union began to talk about "peaceful coexistence" with the United States. In 1958, negotiations began between the two countries for limitations on the testing of nuclear weapons. However, in the same year the Soviet Union announced that the status of West Berlin must be changed and the Allied occupation forces must be withdrawn. The demand was refused. In 1959, tensions relaxed sufficiently for several Western leaders to visit Moscow and for Soviet Premier Nikita Khrushchev (1894–1971) to tour the United States. A summit meeting was scheduled for May 1960, and American President Dwight D. Eisenhower was to go to Moscow.

The Paris Summit Conference of 1960 proved anything but a repetition of the friendly days of 1955. Just before the gathering, the Soviet Union shot down an American U-2 aircraft that was flying reconnaissance over Soviet territory. Khrushchev demanded an apology from President Eisenhower for this air surveillance. Eisenhower accepted full responsibility for the policy but refused to issue any apology. Khrushchev then refused to take part in the summit conference just as the participants arrived in the French capital. The conference was thus aborted, and Eisenhower's proposed trip to the Soviet Union never took place.

The Soviet actions to destroy the possibility of the summit conference on the eve of its opening were not simply the result of the American spy flights. The Soviets had long been aware of the American flights but chose to protest at this time for two reasons. Khrushchev had hoped that the leaders of Britain, France, and the United States would be sufficiently divided over the future of Germany so that a united Allied front would be impossible. The divisions did not come about as he had hoped. Consequently, the conference would have been of little use to him. Second, by 1960 the Communist world itself had become split between the Soviets and the Chinese. The latter were portraying the Russians as lacking sufficient revolutionary zeal. Khrushchev's action was, in part, a response to those

Budapest, October 1956. Street battles raged for several days until Soviet tanks finally put down the Hungarian revolt. [Raymond Darolle. Sygma.]

President Kennedy Defines the Cold War Arena

This passage is from President John F. Kennedy's speech at the time of the Berlin Wall crisis of 1961. He called for a democratic challenge to communism throughout the world. The commitment to Southeast Asia would later lead to the major war in Vietnam.

The immediate threat to free men is in West Berlin. But that isolated outpost is not an isolated problem. The threat is worldwide. Our effort must be equally wide and strong, and not be obsessed by any single manufactured crisis. We face a challenge in Berlin, but there is also a challenge in Southeast Asia, where the borders are less guarded, the enemy harder to find, and the dangers of Communism less apparent to those who have so little. We face a challenge in our own hemisphere, and indeed wherever else the freedom of human beings is at stake. ❑

Public Papers of the Presidents of the United States, John F. Kennedy, January 20 to December 31, 1961, ed. by Wayne C. Gover (Washington: U.S. Government Printing Office, 1962), p. 533.

charges and proof of the hard-line attitude of the Soviet Union toward the capitalist world.

The abortive Paris conference opened the most difficult period of the Cold War. In 1961, the new U.S. president, John F. Kennedy and Premier Khrushchev met in Vienna. The conference was inconclusive, but the American president left wondering if the two nations could avoid war. Throughout 1961, thousands of refugees from East Germany were crossing the border into West Berlin. This outflow was a political embarrassment to East Germany and a detriment to its economic life. In August 1961, the East Germans erected a concrete wall along the border between East and West Berlin. Henceforth, it was possible to cross only at designated checkpoints and with proper papers. The United States protested and sent Vice President Lyndon Johnson to Berlin to reassure its citizens, but the Berlin Wall remained—and does so to the present day. The refugee stream was halted, and the United States' commitment to West Germany was brought into doubt.

A year later, the most dangerous days of the Cold War occurred during the Cuban missile crisis. The Soviet Union attempted to place missiles in Cuba, which was a nation friendly to Soviet aims lying less than a hundred miles from the United States. The United States blockaded Cuba, halted the shipment of new missiles, and demanded the removal of existing installations. After a very tense week, with numerous threats and messages between Moscow and Washington, the crisis ended and the Soviets backed down.

The Cuban missile crisis was the last major Cold War confrontation that would have involved Europe directly because there had existed the possibility of the launching of missiles into the Soviet Union over Europe or from European bases. Thereafter, the American–Soviet rivalry shifted to the war in Vietnam and the Arab–Israeli conflict in the Near East. A "hotline" communications system was installed between Moscow and Washington for more rapid and direct exchange of diplomatic messages in times of crisis.

President John F. Kennedy (1917–1963) and Premier Nikita Khrushchev (1894–1971) in Vienna in June, 1961. Secretary of State Dean Rusk (b. 1909) is on the left. The meeting between the two leaders was not a success. Kennedy considered Khrushchev a war-monger. Khrushchev felt that Kennedy was weak. [AP/Wide World Photos]

Detente and After

In 1963, the two powers concluded a Nuclear Test Ban Treaty. This agreement marked the beginning of a lessening in the tensions between the United States and the Soviet Union. The German problem somewhat subsided in the late 1960s as West Germany, under Premier Willy Brandt (b. 1913), moved to improve its relations with the Soviet Union and Eastern Europe. In 1968, the Soviet Union invaded Czechoslovakia to prevent its emergence into further independence. Although deplored by the United States, this action led to no renewal of tensions. During the presidency of Richard Nixon, the United States embarked on a policy of detente or reduction of tension with the Soviet Union. This policy involved trade agreements and mutual reduction of strategic armaments.

In 1975, President Gerald Ford attended a conference in Helsinki, Finland, that in effect recognized the Soviet sphere of influence in Eastern Europe. The Helsinki Accords also committed its signatory powers, including the Soviet Union, to recognize and protect the human rights of their citizens.

The foreign policy of President Jimmy Carter placed much stress on the observance of these human rights clauses. However, the Soviet invasion of Afghanistan in 1979, though not directly affecting Europe, hardened relations between Washington and Moscow. The United States refused to participate in the 1980 Olympic Games held in Moscow and placed an embargo on American grain being shipped to the Soviet Union. Furthermore, in 1979, President Carter signed a second Strategic Arms Limitation Treaty with the Soviet Union. The U.S. Senate refused to ratify it.

The administration of President Ronald Reagan adopted a much tougher policy and rhetoric toward the Soviet Union, although the United States relaxed the trade embargo and placed less emphasis on human rights. Initially, the Reagan administration sharply slowed arms limitation negotiations and successfully deployed a major new missile system in Europe. The United States also launched a new arms proposal, known as the Strategic Arms Defense Initiative, involving a system of highly developed technology designed to provide defense in outer space against nuclear attack (hence the name Star Wars given it by the press). The proposal has been very controversial, but it has played a major role in recent arms negotiations between the United States and the Soviet Union.

President Reagan and Mikhail S. Gorbachev (b. 1931) held a friendly summit meeting in 1985, the first East-West Summit in six years. Other meetings followed. Arms negotiations continued with very hard bargaining on both sides until, in December 1987, the United States and the Soviet Union signed a major treaty in regard to nuclear missiles. The two powers have agreed to dismantle over two thousand medium- and shorter-range missiles. The treaty also provides for mutual inspection. This action represents the most significant agreement since World War II between the two superpowers.

Retreat from Empire

Power Vacuums

At the onset of World War II, many of the nations of Europe were still imperial powers. Great Britain, France, the Netherlands, Belgium, Italy, and Portugal governed millions of non-European peoples. One of the most striking and significant postwar developments has been the decolonization of these imperial holdings and the consequent emergence of the so-called Third World political bloc.

The process of retreat from empire involved the colonial powers in three major stages of difficulties. The first was the turmoil created by nationalist movements and revolts in the colonies. The second was the injection of Cold War diplomacy and rivalries into the power vacuums formed by the European withdrawals. Finally, in recent years, the control of important natu-

---

MAJOR DATES IN THE ERA OF THE SUPERPOWERS

1948	Berlin Blockade
1949	Formation of the North Atlantic Treaty Organization
1950	Outbreak of the Korean War
1953	Death of Stalin
1956	(July) Egypt seizes the Suez Canal (October) Anglo-French attack on the Suez Canal; Hungarian Revolution
1957	Treaty of Rome establishes the European Economic Community
1958	De Gaulle comes to power in France
1960	Paris Summit Conference collapses
1962	Cuban missile crisis
1963	Russian–American Test Ban Treaty
1967	Six Days' War between Israel and Egypt
1968	Russian invasion of Czechoslovakia
1975	Helsinki Accords
1978	Camp David Accords
1979	Russian invasion of Afghanistan
1980	Socialist victory in France
1981	Military crackdown on Solidarity Movement in Poland
1985	Reagan–Gorbachev Summit
1987	Major American–Soviet Arms Limitation Treaty

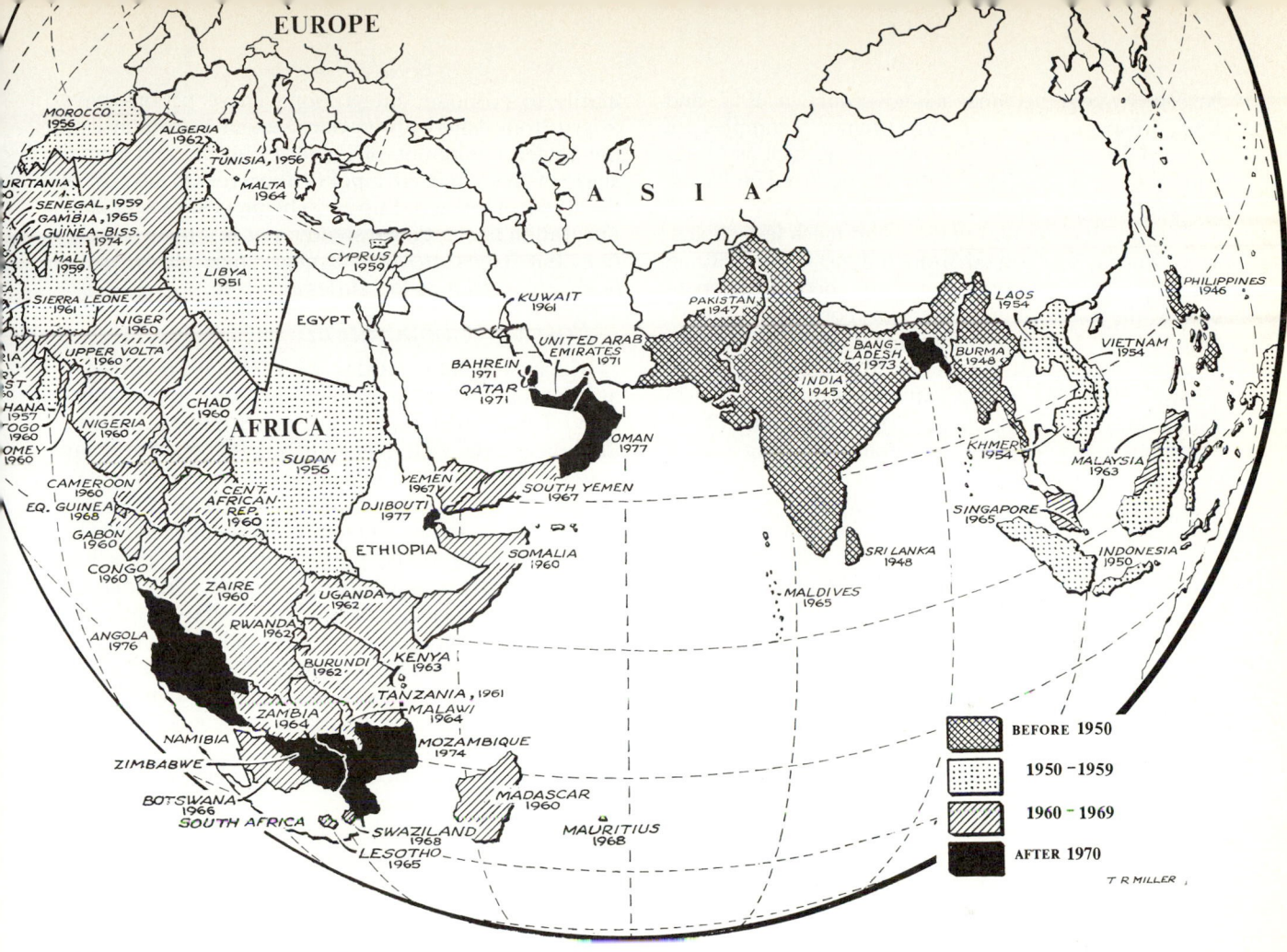

MAP 36-1   DECOLONIZATION SINCE WORLD WAR II   *The extent of the rapid retreat from imperialism on the part of the powers after World War II is graphically shown on this outline map.*

ral resources and particularly of oil by the new nations of the Third World has put considerable economic pressure on both Western Europe and the United States. This last condition may well prove one of the most important factors in world politics for the remainder of this century.

The decolonization that has occurred since 1945 has been a direct result of both the war itself and the rise of indigenous nationalist movements within the European colonial world. World War II drew the military forces of the colonial powers back to Europe. The Japanese conquests of Asia helped to turn out the European powers from that area. After the military and political dislocations of the war came the postwar economic collapse. This collapse meant that the colonial powers could no longer afford to maintain their positions abroad.

Nationalist Movements

The war aims of the Allies undermined colonialism. It was difficult to fight against tyranny in Europe while maintaining colonial dominance abroad. Moreover, the postwar policy of the United States generally opposed the continuation of European empires. Within the colonies, there had also arisen nationalist movements of varying strengths. These were often led by gifted persons who had been educated in Europe. The values and political ideologies they had learned in Europe itself helped them to present effective critiques of the colonial situation. Such leadership, as well as the frequently blatant injustice imposed on colonial peoples, paved the way for effective nationalist movements.

There was a wide variety in decolonization. Some cases were relatively systematic; in others, the European powers simply beat a hasty retreat. In 1947, Britain left India. The result of internal disputes, including religious differences, was the creation of two states, India and Pakistan. In 1948, Burma and Sri Lanka (formerly Ceylon) became independent of Britain. During the 1950s, the British attempted to prepare colonies for self-government. Ghana (formerly the Gold Coast) and

Nigeria—which became self-governing in 1957 and 1960, respectively—were the major examples of planned decolonization. In other areas, such as Malta and Cyprus, the British withdrawal occurred under the pressure of militant nationalist movements.

The smaller colonial powers had much less choice. The Dutch were forced from Indonesia in 1950. In 1960, the Belgian Congo, now Zaire, became independent in the midst of great turmoil. For a considerable time, as will be seen in the next chapter, France attempted to maintain its position in Southeast Asia but met defeat in 1954. It was similarly driven from North Africa. President De Gaulle carried out a policy of referendums on independence within remaining French colonial possessions. By the late 1960s, only Portugal remained a traditional colonial power. In 1975, it finally abandoned its African colony of Angola.

Power of Natural Resources

The retreat from empire represents a major turning point in both European and world history. European and Western influences remain active in the former colonial world. Multinational corporations can and do exert considerable power over developing economies. The trade policies of the major Western industrial nations can do likewise. However, it now seems certain that in the future, the command over natural resources possessed by some of these new nations will mean a considerable loss of independence by European and Western nations generally. At the end of the nineteenth century, the technological power of Europe allowed certain nations to become colonial powers. At the close of the twentieth century, the dependence of European industry and technology on the resources of the developing countries may very well mean that the former colonies will exert immense influence over the destiny of Europeans. The oil embargo of 1973 imposed on Europe by the oil-producing countries of the world demonstrated the potential for such powerful influence.

The rest of this century will be largely devoted to the working out of this new economic balance. Although the political power of Europe will thus be lessened, the impact of its culture and of the technology originally developed in Europe will continue to expand as nations throughout the world continue to become Westernized.

Toward Western European Unification

Since 1945, the nations of Western Europe have taken unprecedented steps toward cooperation and potential unity. The moves toward unification have related pri-marily to economic integration. These actions have arisen from American encouragement in response to the Soviet domination of Eastern Europe, and from a sense of lack of effective political power on the part of the states of Western Europe. The process of economic integration has not been steady, nor is it near completion; but it has provided a major new factor in the domestic politics of the states involved.

Postwar Cooperation

The movement toward unity could have occurred in at least three ways: politically, militarily, or economically. The economic path was taken largely because the other paths were blocked. In 1949, ten European states organized the Council of Europe, which meets in Strasbourg, France. Its organization involved foreign ministers and a Consultative Assembly elected by the parliaments of the participants. The Council of Europe was and continues to be only an advisory body. It had been hoped by some persons that the council might become a parliament of Europe, but during the early 1950s none of the major states was willing to surrender any of its sovereignty to the newly organized body. The initial failure of the council to bring about significant political cooperation meant that for the time being unity would not come about by political or parliamentary routes.

Between 1950 and 1954, there was some interest in a more thorough integration of the military forces of NATO. When the Korean War broke out, the United States began to urge the rearmament of Germany. The German forces would provide Western Europe with further protection against possible Soviet aggression while the United States was involved in Korea. France continued to fear a German army. In 1951, the French government suggested the creation of a European Defense Community that would constitute a supranational military organization. It would require a permanent British commitment of forces to the Continent to help France, in effect, counter any future German threat. The proposal continued to be considered for some time, but in 1954 the French Parliament itself vetoed the program. In 1955, Germany was permitted to rearm and to enter NATO. Supranational military organization had not been achieved.

Rather than in politics or the military, the major moves toward European cooperation and potential unity came in the economic sphere. Unlike the other two possible paths of cooperation, economic activity involved little or no immediate loss of political sovereignty. Moreover, the material benefits of combined economic activity brought new popular support to all of the governments involved.

The Marshall Plan of the United States created the Organization for European Economic Cooperation (OEEC). It was a vehicle set up to require common planning and cooperation among the participating countries and to discourage a return to the prewar economic nationalism. The OEEC and later NATO gave the countries involved new experience in working with each other and demonstrated the productivity, the efficiency, and the simple possibility of cooperative action.[1] Although neither organization provided a means of political or economic integration, the experience was most important.

Among European leaders and civil servants, there existed a large body of opinion that only through the abandonment of economic nationalism could the newly organized democratic states avoid the economic turmoil that had proved such fertile ground for dictatorship. Economic cooperation carried the possibility of greater efficiency, prosperity, and employment. The leading figures holding these opinions were Robert Schuman (1886–1963), the foreign minister of France; Konrad Adenauer (1876–1967), the chancellor of the Federal Republic of Germany; Alcide De Gasperi (1881–1954), the prime minister of Italy; and Paul-Henri Spaak (1899–1972), the prime minister of Belgium. Among major civil servants and bureaucrats, Jean Monnet (1885–1981) of France was the leading spokesman.

In 1950, Schuman proposed that the coal and steel production of Western Europe be undertaken on an integrated, cooperative basis. The next year, France, West Germany, Italy, and the "Benelux" countries (Belgium, the Netherlands, and Luxembourg) organized the European Coal and Steel Community. Its activity was limited to a single part of the economy, but that was a sector affecting almost all other industrial production. An agency called the *High Authority* administered the plan. The authority was genuinely supranational, and its members could not be removed during their appointed terms. The Coal and Steel Community prospered. By 1955, coal production had grown by 23 per cent. Iron and steel production was up by almost 150 per cent. The community both benefited from and contributed to the immense growth of material production in Western Europe during this period. Its success reduced the suspicions of government and business groups about the concept of coordination and economic integration.

The European Economic Community

It took more than the prosperity of the European Coal and Steel Community to draw European leaders toward further unity. The unsuccessful Suez intervention and the resulting diplomatic isolation of France and Britain persuaded many Europeans that only through unified action could they exert any significant influence on the two superpowers or control their own destinies. Consequently, in 1957, through the Treaty of Rome, the six members of the Coal and Steel Community agreed to form a new organization: the European Economic Community. The *Common Market*, as the EEC soon came to be called, envisioned more than a free-trade union. Its members sought to achieve the eventual elimination of tariffs, a free flow of capital and labor, and similar wage and social benefits in all the participating countries. Its chief institutions were a Council of Foreign Ministers and a High Commission composed of technocrats. The former came to be the dominant body.

The Common Market achieved a stunning degree of success during its early years. By 1968, all tariffs among the six members had been abolished well ahead of the planned schedule. Trade and labor migration among the members grew steadily. Moreover, nonmember states began to copy the community and later to seek membership. In 1959, Britain, Denmark, Norway, Sweden, Switzerland, Austria, and Portugal formed the European Free Trade Area. However, by 1961 Great Britain had decided to seek Common Market membership. Twice, in 1963 and 1967, British membership was vetoed by President de Gaulle of France. The French president felt that Britain was too closely related to the United States and its policies to support the European Economic Community wholeheartedly.

The French veto of British membership demonstrated the major difficulty confronting the Common Market during the 1960s. The Council of Ministers, representing the individual national interests of member states, came to have more influence than the High Commission. Political as well as economic factors increasingly entered into decision making. France particularly was unwilling to compromise on any matter that it regarded as pertaining to its sovereignty. On more than one occasion, President de Gaulle demanded his own policies and refused French participation under any other conditions. This attitude caused major problems over agricultural policy.

Despite the French actions, the Common Market survived and continued to prosper. In 1973, Great Britain, Ireland, and Denmark became members. Discussions continued on further steps toward integration, including proposals for a common currency. Throughout the late 1970s, however, and into the 1980s, there seemed to be a loss of momentum. Norway and Sweden, with relatively strong economies, declined to join. Although in 1982 Spain, Portugal, and Greece applied for membership and were admitted, there continued to

---

[1] The OEEC continued in existence until 1961, when it was reorganized as the Organization for Economic Cooperation and Development (OECD). Both organizations included nations not involved in the more formal moves toward unity. The OECD also included Japan and has been interested in Third World economic development.

The European Economic Community Is Established

The 1957 Treaty of Rome identified the major goals of the European Economic Community (Common Market) for the original six members.

Article 2: It shall be the aim of the Community, by establishing a Common Market and progressively approximating the economic policies of Member States, to promote throughout the Community a harmonious development of economic activities, a continuous and balanced expansion, an increased stability, an accelerated raising of the standard of living and closer relations between its Member States.

Article 3: For the purposes set out in the preceding Article, the activities of the Community shall include, under the conditions and with the timing provided for in this Treaty:

(a) the elimination, as between Member States, of customs duties and of quantitative restrictions in regard to the importation and exportation of goods, as well as of all other measures with equivalent effect;

(b) the establishment of a common customs tariff and a common commercial policy towards third countries;

(c) the abolition, as between Member States, of the obstacles to the free movement of persons, services and capital;

(d) the inauguration of a common agricultural policy;

(e) the inauguration of a common transport policy;

(f) the establishment of a system ensuring that competition shall not be distorted in the Common Market;

(g) the application of procedures which shall make it possible to co-ordinate the economic policies of Member States and to remedy disequilibria in their balances of payments;

(h) the approximation of their respective municipal law to the extent necessary for the functioning of the Common Market;

(i) the creation of a European Social Fund in order to improve the possibilities of employment for workers and to contribute to the raising of their standard of living;

(j) the establishment of a European Investment Bank intended to facilitate the economic expansion of the Community through the creation of new resources; and

(k) the association of overseas countries and territories with the Community with a view to increasing trade and to pursuing jointly their effort towards economic and social development. ❑

Treaty Establishing the European Economic Community (Brussels: Secretariat of the Interim Committee for the Common Market and Euratom, 1957), pp. 17–18.

---

be sharp disagreements and a sense of stagnation within the Community.

After a decade of disagreements and loss of direction, the leaders of the Community reached an important decision in early 1988. They set upon the year 1992 as the goal for achieving a virtual free-trade zone throughout the Community, entailing the elimination of remaining trade barriers and other restrictive trade policies. If carried to a successful conclusion, this new policy will establish all of Western Europe as a zone for free trade not unlike that existing within the United States. This new situation will create a vast new market benefiting the large companies of Western Europe. These companies will be able to compete more easily with non-European rivals.

Western European Political Development

Great Britain: Power in Decline

In July 1945, the British electorate overwhelmingly voted for a Labour Party government. For the first time, the Labour Party commanded in its own right a majority of the House of Commons. Labour Party leader Clement Attlee (1883–1967) replaced Winston Churchill as prime minister.

Attlee's ministry was socialist but clearly non-Marxist. It made a number of bold departures in both economic and social policy. The government assumed ownership of certain major industries, including the Bank of England, the airlines, public transport, coal, electricity, and steel. The ministry also undertook a major housing program. Probably its most popular accomplishment was the establishment of a major program of social welfare legislation. This involved further unemployment assistance, old-age pensions, school lunches, and, most important, free medical service to all citizens.

The progressive domestic policy of the Labour government was matched by a policy of gradual retreat of Britain on the world scene. In 1947, the enunciation of the Truman Doctrine in regard to Greece and Turkey marked Britain's admission that it could not afford to oversee the security of those areas. In the same year, Britain recognized the independence of India and Pakistan. In the postwar era, Britain was repeatedly confronted by nationalist movements within the empire.

Gradually, and usually gracefully, Britain retreated from those outposts.

In 1951, the Conservative Party, under Churchill, returned to office remaining in power until 1964. This was the longest period of continuous government by any party in modern British history. Under Churchill and then under his successors, Sir Anthony Eden (1955–1957), Harold Macmillan (1957–1963), and Sir Alec Douglas-Home (1963–1964), the Conservatives attempted to draw major differences between themselves and the Labour Party. In reality, the differences were of degree rather than of kind. The Conservative government returned the steel industry to private ownership, but it did not reestablish an economy based wholly on private enterprise. The program of national welfare and health services continued, and the Conservatives actually undertook a building program larger than that of the Labour Party.

The decline of power and prestige continued, however. From the mid-1950s onward, one part of the empire after another became independent. The Suez intervention of 1956 brought an end to independent British military intervention. Increasingly, British policy was made subservient to that of the United States as British economic power declined. However, the economy constituted the most persistent difficulty. Through the 1950s, the slogan "Export or die" was heard. Exports grew rapidly, yet more slowly than imports. Productivity remained discouragingly low. British unions were old-fashioned and less forward-looking than those on the Continent. Management was quite timid. Perhaps most important, the rate of capital investment in both privately and nationally owned industries was low.

In 1964, the Labour Party returned to office under Harold Wilson (b. 1916). For the next fifteen years, both the Labour Party and the Conservatives moved in and out of power with neither giving a fundamental direction to national policy. Then in 1979 Margaret Thatcher led the Conservative Party to a major electoral victory, the first of three to be achieved under her guidance. The first woman to be British prime minister, she is one of the most forceful personalities in modern British political history.

Within the context of the British Conservative Party, Thatcher has stood very far to the right. Her cabinet has pursued a policy of very high interest rates, sharp tax cuts, and somewhat reduced government spending. Generally, Thatcher also has taken a very hard line with the trade unions. The results of these policies, popularly known as Thatcherism, has led to mixed results. Inflation came under limited control while the rate of British unemployment in the early 1980s reached the levels of the Great Depression years. The policies pursued by the government also has involved various forms of privatization. These

Prime Minister Margaret Thatcher has led Great Britain in new more conservative directions throughout the 1980s. Her administration has been marked by a dedication to the operation of the free market. [Photos: Derek Hudson/Sygma.]

have included the sale of public housing units to their inhabitants (thus creating a new property owning group), and the sale of shares in various previously government-owned companies to the general public. Furthermore, the government through loans and other devices has attempted to foster small business ventures and a general atmosphere of free enterprise.

The Thatcher era has seen major new strains within British society. For example, in the summer of 1981 riots broke out in several of the major cities, including Liverpool and London. These disturbances erupted among the large number of jobless British youth and among the tens of thousands of nonwhite immigrants from the nation's former colonies. Some of the riots of 1981, and later ones, involved racial clashes; others involved both white and nonwhite youths jointly attacking the police, viewed in some urban areas as symbols of political repression. During 1984 and 1985, the nation was divided over a major strike by coal mine workers. Here the issue was the power of the central government over a recalcitrant labor union. The chief issue was the determination of the government to shut down inefficient mines. In the end, the Thatcher government was regarded as the victor.

Finally, over the course of the 1980s a division began to emerge between the north and the south of Britain. The southern part of the nation generally has prospered; however, northern England and Scotland continued to have stagnant economic life and an ongoing loss of industry.

In the spring of 1982, after years of fruitless negotiations over the question of legal ownership, the government of Argentina ordered the invasion of the Falkland Islands (Malvinas), located in the South Atlantic and governed by Great Britain for over a century and a half. The Argentines claimed that the dispute involved the recapture of territory held by a colonial power. The British contended that the Argentines had committed an act of international aggression, an opinion in which the government of the United States concurred. The invasion occurred on April 3. Shortly thereafter, the British dispatched a very large fleet to the South Atlantic. During the following weeks, the largest naval engagements since World War II took place between Britain and Argentina. Both forces sustained major losses before the British emerged the victors.

The election of 1983, held in the wake of the Falklands military success, proved a great victory for Thatcher. Her party retained firm control of Parliament. She achieved a third victory in 1987. In both elections, the Labour Party was badly divided between its moderate and extreme left wing. Furthermore, during the early 1980s, the Social Democrats, composed of relatively conservative Labour Party members, and the Liberal Party represented a third force in British

politics that drained votes away from Labour. However, by the end of the 1980s, the Social Democrats had failed to make a significant lasting impact on British electoral politics.

In addition to the war in the South Atlantic and the problems of having to face the gravest economic situation in the Western world, Britain has also had to confront a major internal disturbance in Northern Ireland. By the treaty of 1921, the Ulster counties have remained part of the United Kingdom while retaining a large measure of self-government. The Protestant majority used its power to discriminate systematically against the Roman Catholic minority in the province. In 1968, a Catholic civil rights movement was launched. Units of the Provisional Wing of the Irish Republican Army became active in seeking to unite Ulster with the Irish Republic. In turn, militant Protestant organizations became mobilized. The British government sent in units of the army to restore order. Soon, the British army units became the target of both groups of militant Irish. In 1972, the British suspended the Northern Irish Parliament and began to govern the province directly. Since that time, despite a series of attempts to achieve peace, Northern Ireland has remained a territory stricken with civil war and violence.

West Germany: The Economic Miracle

No country in Europe since the war has so contrasted with Britain as the Federal Republic of Germany. The nation was organized in 1949 from the three Western Allied occupation sectors. Its amazing material progress from the ruins of the conflict became known as the economic miracle of postwar Europe. Between 1948 and 1964, West German industrial production grew by 600 per cent. Unemployment became almost unknown. All of this time, the country remained the center of Cold War disputes and was occupied by thousands of foreign troops. In the midst of Cold War tensions, the Germans prospered.

The economic growth of the nation stemmed from a number of favorable factors. The Marshall Plan provided a strong impetus to recovery. The government of the republic throughout the 1950s and 1960s pursued a policy of giving private industry a relatively free hand while providing sufficient planning to avoid economic crisis. The goods produced by Germany proved attractive to the customers of other nations. *Volkswagen* became a household word throughout the world. Moreover, domestic demand was vigorous, and skilled labor and energetic management were available. Finally, Germany had very few foreign commitments or responsibilities. A relatively small portion of its national income had to be spent on defense. This situation aided capital formation.

In a very real sense, postwar West Germany indulged in economic expansion rather than in politics or

The rebuilt center of West Berlin that emerged in the 1950s and 60s. Only the ruins of the Emperor William I Memorial Church were left as a monument and a reminder of war's destruction. [United Press International Photo.]

active international policy. Unlike the Weimar Constitution, the constitution of the Federal Republic did not permit the proliferation of splinter parties. Nor did the president possess extraordinary power. The Federal Republic returned to the arena of nations very slowly. In 1949, it participated in the Marshall Plan and two years later in the European Coal and Steel Community. In 1955, the nation joined NATO, and in 1957 it was one of the charter members of the European Economic Community. The Federal Republic has been perhaps the major champion of European cooperation.

Throughout this period, political initiative lay with the Christian Democrats led by Konrad Adenauer (1876–1967). His domestic policies were relatively simple and consistent: West Germany must become genuinely democratic and economically stable and prosperous. His foreign policy was profoundly anti-Communist. Under what was known as the Hallstein Doctrine, the Federal Republic refused to have diplomatic ties with any nation, except the Soviet Union, that extended diplomatic recognition to East Germany. Adenauer's position on East Germany contributed to the Cold War climate, and it may have led the United States to overestimate the threat of communist aggression in Europe. The Hallstein Doctrine separated the Federal Republic from all the nations of Eastern Europe.

Adenauer remained in office until 1963, when he retired at the age of eighty-seven. The Christian Democrats remained in power, led first by Ludwig Erhard (1897–1977) and later by Kurt Kiesinger (b. 1904). In 1966, however, they were compelled to form a coalition with the Social Democratic Party (SDP). After the

war, this party had revived but had been unable to capture a parliamentary majority. By the early 1960s, the SDP had expanded its base beyond the working class and had become more a party of social and economic reform than a party of socialism. This shift reflected the growing prosperity of the German working class. The major leader of the SDP in the 1960s was Willy Brandt (b. 1913) the mayor of West Berlin. In 1966 he became vice-chancellor in the coalition government. In 1969, Brandt and the SDP carried the election in their own right.

The most significant departure of the SDP occurred in the area of foreign policy. While continuing to urge further Western unity through the Common Market, Brandt moved carefully but swiftly to establish better relations with Eastern Europe (a policy called *Ostpolitik*). In 1970, he met with the leadership of East Germany. Later that year, he went to Moscow to sign a treaty of cooperation. By November 1970, Brandt had completed a reconciliation treaty with Poland that

Konrad Adenauer of West Germany and Charles De Gaulle of France were the two major West European statesmen of the late 1950s and early 1960s. These two Catholic conservatives ended the old animosity between Germany and France. [United Press International Photo.]

recognized the Oder–Neisse river line as the Polish western border. A treaty with Czechoslovakia soon followed.

In 1973, both the Federal Republic of Germany and the German Democratic Republic were admitted to the United Nations. Brandt's policy of *Ostpolitik*, to a large extent, regularized the German situation, but that regularity will probably remain only as long as the two superpowers desire it. Brandt's moves were in part a subdevelopment of the policy of detente on the part of the United States and the Soviet Union. In 1974, Brandt resigned. He was succeeded by Helmut Schmidt, who continued a policy of conversations with the Communist bloc nations and Moscow. Schmidt also took a lead in asserting the necessity of close United States consultation with its West European allies on both economic and military matters.

In 1982, Helmut Kohl (b. 1930) a conservative Christian Democrat, became the West German chancellor. His first years in office were marked by a number of political and financial scandals. He also pursued a controversial policy of allowing Germany to begin to acknowledge more openly its Nazi epoch in an effort to bring about full reconciliation with Germany's allies. He visited World War I battlefields with President Mitterand of France. In 1985, he persuaded President Reagan to visit the German military cemetery at Bitburg among whose graves were those of SS officers. Kohl and his party have also generally maintained the strength of the German economy.

France: Search for Stability

France experienced the most troubled postwar domestic political scene of any major West European nation. After the defeat of 1940, a little-known general named Charles de Gaulle (1890–1970) had organized a Free French government in London. In 1944, De Gaulle presided over the provisional government in liberated France. He was an immensely proud, patriotic person who seemed to regard himself as personally embodying the spirit of France. In 1946, De Gaulle, who hated the machinations of political parties, suddenly resigned from the government, believing that the newly organized Fourth Republic, like the Third, gave far too little power to the executive. The Fourth French Republic thus lost the single strong leader it had possessed. After De Gaulle's departure, the republic returned to the rapid turnover of ministries that had characterized the Third Republic during the 1920s and 1930s.

A major source of domestic discontent related to France's colonial problems in North Africa and Indochina. By 1954, the government of Premier Mendes-France (1907–1982) had withdrawn from Indochina after a protracted war. He later granted independence to Tunisia; Morocco was also soon moving in that direction. The seemingly intractable problem lay in Algeria, which was regarded not as a colony but as part of France. An anticolonial revolt in Algeria deeply divided France.

With France on the brink of civil war over Algeria, in 1958 a group of politicians in Paris turned to De Gaulle, whom the army trusted would uphold their cause in Algeria. De Gaulle came to power and created the Fifth French Republic, giving the president extraordinary power. Having secured his own authority, De Gaulle moved to attack the Algerian problem. In the face of major domestic opposition, he made large concessions to the Algerian Liberal Movement, and by 1962 Algeria was independent.

Throughout the rest of the 1960s, De Gaulle pursued a policy of making France the leading nation in a united Europe. He presented himself as a strong nationalist, in part no doubt to heal the wounds remaining from the Algerian problem. He pursued systematically good relations with Germany but was never friendly with Great Britain. He deeply resented the influence of the United States in Western Europe.

De Gaulle wanted Europe to become a third force in the world between the superpowers. For that reason, he pushed for the development of a French nuclear capacity and refused to become a party to the 1963 Nuclear Test Ban Treaty. His withdrawal of French military forces from NATO in 1967 caused its headquarters to be moved from Paris to Brussels, but he did not take France out of the alliance itself. He was highly critical of the American involvement in Vietnam. That American intervention served to convince him even further that Europe under French leadership must prepare to fend for itself.

For ten years, De Gaulle succeeded in leading France according to his own lights. Then in 1968, he confronted domestic unrest in France. The troubles began among student groups in Paris and spread to other major sectors of French life. Hundreds of thousands of workers went on strike. Having assured himself of the support of the army, De Gaulle made a brief television speech to rally his followers. Soon they, too, came into the streets to demonstrate for De Gaulle and stability. The strikes ended and police moved against the student groups. The government itself quickly moved to improve the wages and benefits of workers. May 1968 had revealed the fragile strength of the Fifth Republic. But the economic progress of France since the war had created a large body of citizens with sufficient stake in the status quo to fear and prevent disruption.

In 1969, President de Gaulle resigned after some relatively minor constitutional changes were rejected in a referendum. His immediate successors and supporters, Georges Pompidou (1911–1974) and Valéry Giscard D'Estaing (b. 1926), set about improving the economic conditions that had fostered discontent among factory workers in 1968. They also continued to favor a strong policy for European unity. In 1973, three years after De Gaulle's death in political retirement, France permitted Great Britain to join the Common Market. Throughout the rest of the decade, the French government pursued a center-right course and emphasized technocratic solutions to French economic problems.

The presidential election of 1980 witnessed a sharp turnaround in French politics. François Mitterand (b. 1916), the Socialist Party candidate, decisively defeated Giscard d'Estaing. A few weeks later, the Socialists also captured control of the French Parliament. Giscard d'Estaing had become personally unpopular and was regarded as increasingly aloof from the French people. But no less important was Mitterand's successful effort throughout the 1970s to build a united political left. The traditional divisions within the French left wing no longer had a major influence.

The Mitterand government initially pursued a policy of active socialism in rhetoric and rather moderate policies in action. Government ownership of large industries increased. There was an unsuccessful attempt to reform the educational system to the detriment of Roman Catholic influence. In the realm of foreign policy, Mitterand pursued a strong anti-Soviet line and a moderately strong pro-American position. This stance differed from the traditional Gaullist position, which had put France on a course of independent mediation between the two superpowers. Mitterand, however, strongly supported the continuation of the independent French nuclear capability.

The French parliamentary elections of 1986 resulted in two new situations for the Fifth Republic. First, the election saw the emergence of the National Front, an extreme right-wing group led by Jean-Marie LePen. This group seemed to appeal to certain working-class voters aroused by racial and ethnic tensions resulting from the immigration of workers from North Africa into the French labor market.

Second, a coalition of traditional French conservative parties won control of the National Assembly. The French Constitution, which had been tailored by and for De Gaulle, had not envisioned a situation in which the presidency would be held by one party and the Assembly controlled by another. Through an arrangement known popularly as cohabitation, the two parties managed to handle matters of state. However, in 1987 Mitterand was elected to a new term in office. Shortly thereafter, the left-wing parties won a narrow majority in the National Assembly, and cohabitation came to an end. The main result of this election has been an apparent determination of the majority of the French electorate to pursue a middle political course and to avoid the extremes of traditional ideology.

The Soviet Union and Eastern Europe

The Soviet Union since the Death of Stalin (1953)

Many Russians had hoped that the end of World War II would signal a lessening of Stalinism. No other nation had suffered greater losses or more deprivation than the Soviet Union. Its people anticipated some immediate reward for their sacrifice and heroism. They desired a reduction in the scope of the police state and a redirection of the economy away from heavy industry to consumer products. They were disappointed. Stalin did little or nothing to modify the character of the regime he had created. The police remained ever-present. The cult of personality expanded, and the central bureaucracy continued to grow. Heavy industry was still favored over production for consumers. Agriculture continued to be troubled. Stalin's personal authority over the party and the nation remained unchallenged. In foreign policy, Stalin moved to solidify Soviet control over Eastern Europe for the purposes of both Communist expansion and Soviet national security. He attempted to impose the Soviet model on those nations. The Cold War stance of the United States simply served to confirm Stalin in his ways.

By late 1952 and early 1953, it appeared that Stalin might be ready to unloose a new series of purges. In January 1953, a group of Jewish physicians was arrested and charged with plotting the deaths of important leaders. Charges of extensive conspiracy appeared in the press. All of these developments were similar to the events that had preceded the purges of the 1930s. Then, quite suddenly, in the midst of this new furor, on March 6, 1953, Stalin died.

For a time no single leader replaced Stalin. Rather the Presidium (the renamed Politburo) pursued a policy of collective leadership. A considerable amount of reshuffling occurred among the top party leaders. Lavrenty Beria (1899–1953), the dreaded director of the secret police, was removed from his post and eventually executed. Georgy Malenkov (b. 1902) became premier, a position he held for about two years. Gradually, however, power and influence began to devolve on Nikita Khrushchev (1894–1971), who in 1953 had been named party secretary. By 1955, he had edged out Malenkov and had successfully urged the appointment of Nikolai Bulganin (1895–1975) in his place.

Three years later, Khrushchev himself became premier. His rise constituted the end of collective leadership, but at no time did he enjoy the extraordinary powers of Stalin.

The Khrushchev Years

The Krushchev era, which lasted until the autumn of 1964, witnessed a marked retreat from Stalinism, though not from extreme authoritarianism. Indeed, the political repression of Stalin had been so extensive that there was considerable room for relaxation of surveillance within the limits of tyranny. Politically, the demise of Stalinism meant shifts in leadership and party structure by means other than purges. In 1956, at the Twentieth Congress of the Communist Party, Khrushchev made a secret speech (later published outside the Soviet Union) in which he denounced Stalin and his crimes against socialist justice during the purges of the 1930s. The speech caused shock and consternation in party circles and opened the way for limited, but genuine, internal criticism of the Soviet government. Gradually, the strongest supporters of Stalinist policies were removed from the Presidium. By 1958, all of Stalin's former supporters were gone, but none had been executed.

Under Khrushchev, intellectuals were somewhat more free to express their opinions. This so-called thaw in the cultural life of the country was closely related to the premier's interest in the opinions of experts on problems of industry and agriculture. He often went outside the usual bureaucratic channels in search of information and new ideas. Novels such as Aleksandr Solzhenitsyn's (b. 1918) *One Day in the Life of Ivan Denisovich* (1963) could be published. However, Boris Pasternak (1890–1960), the author of *Dr. Zhivago*, was not permitted to accept the Nobel Prize for literature in 1958. The intellectual liberalization of Soviet life during this period should not be overestimated. It looked favorable only in comparison with what had preceded it and has continued to seem so because of the decline of such freedom of expression after Khrushchev's fall.

The economic policy also somewhat departed from the strict Stalinist mode. By 1953, the economy had recovered from the strains and destruction of the war, but consumer goods and housing still remained in very short supply. The problem of an adequate food supply also continued. Malenkov had favored improvements in meeting the demand for consumer goods; Khrushchev also favored such a departure. Khrushchev also moved in a moderate fashion to decentralize economic planning and execution. During the late 1950s, he often boasted that Soviet production of consumer goods would overtake that of the West. Steel, oil, and electric-power production continued to grow, but the consumer sector improved only marginally. The ever-growing defense budget and the space program that successfully launched the first human-engineered satellite of the earth, *Sputnik*, in 1957 made major demands on the nation's productive resources. Economically Khrushchev was attempting to move the country in too many directions at once.

Khrushchev strongly redirected Stalin's agricultural policy. He recognized that in spite of the collectivization of the 1930s the Soviet Union had not produced an agricultural system capable of feeding its own people. Administratively, Khrushchev removed many of the most restrictive regulations on private cultivation. The machine tractor stations were abandoned. Existing collective farms were further amalgamated. The government undertook an extensive "virgin lands" program to extend wheat cultivation by hundreds of thousands of acres. This policy initially increased grain production of new records. However, in a very few years the new lands became subject to erosion. The farming techniques applied had been inappropriate for the soil. The agricultural problem has simply continued to grow. Currently the Soviet Union imports vast quantities of grain from the United States and other countries. United States grain imports have constituted a major facet of the policy of detente.

Adventuresomeness also characterized Khrushchev's foreign policy. In 1956, the Soviet Union adopted the phrase "peaceful coexistence" in regard to its relationship with the United States. The policy implied no less competition with the capitalist world but suggested that war might not be the best way to pursue Communist expansion. The previous year, Khrushchev had participated in the Geneva summit meeting alongside Bulganin. Thereafter followed visits around the world, culminating with one to the United States in 1959. By the early 1960s, it had become clear that Khrushchev had made few inroads on Western policy. He was under increasing domestic pressure and also pressure from the Chinese. The militancy of the denunciation of the U-2 flight, the aborting of the Paris summit meeting, the Berlin Wall, and the Cuban missile crisis were all responses to those pressures. The last of these adventures brought a clear Soviet retreat.

By 1964, numerous high Russian leaders and many people lower in the party had concluded that Khrushchev had tried to do too much too soon and had done it too poorly. On October 16, 1964, after defeat in the Central Committee of the Communist Party, Khrushchev resigned. He was replaced by Alexei Kosygin (1904–1980) as premier and Leonid Brezhnev (1906–1982) as party secretary. The latter eventually emerged as the dominant figure. In 1977, the constitution of the Soviet Union was changed to combine the offices of president and party secretary. Brezhnev became president, and thus head of the state as well as of the party. He held more personal power than any Soviet leader since Stalin.

Brezhnev

Domestically, the Soviet government became markedly more repressive after 1964. All intellectuals had enjoyed less and less freedom and little direct access to the government leadership. In 1974, the government expelled Solzhenitsyn. Perhaps most important among recent developments, Jewish citizens of the Soviet Union have become subject to harassment. Major bureaucratic obstacles were placed in the way of the emigration of Soviet Jews to Israel. These policies suggest a return to the limitations of the Stalinist period.

The internal repression gave rise to a dissident movement. Certain Soviet citizens dared to criticize the regime in public and to carry out small demonstrations against the government. They accused the Soviet government of violating the human rights provisions of the 1975 Helsinki Accords. The dissidents included a number of prominent citizens, such as the Nobel Prize physicist Andrei Sakharov. The response of the Soviet government to the dissident movement was further repression. Prominent dissidents, such as Anatoly Shcharansky (since released), Aleksandr Ginzburg, and Vladimir Slepak, were arrested, tried on clearly trumped-up charges, and sentenced to long periods of imprisonment or internal exile in Siberia.

In foreign policy, the Brezhnev years witnessed attempts to reach accommodation with the United States while continuing to press for expanded Soviet influence and further attempts to maintain Soviet leadership of the Communist movement. During the Vietnam War, the Soviet Union pursued a policy of restrained support for North Vietnam. Under President Richard Nixon, the United States pursued a policy of detente based on arms limitation and trade agreements. Nonetheless, Soviet spending on defense, and particularly on naval expansion, continued to grow. During the Ford and Carter administrations in the United States, Soviet involvement in African affairs was troubling.

More important in leading to a cooling of relations between the superpowers was the Soviet invasion of Afghanistan in December 1979. A Soviet presence had already existed in that country, but for reasons that still remain unclear the Soviet government felt that it was required to send in troops to ensure its influence in central Asia. As noted earlier, the invasion brought a grain embargo and a boycott on participation in the Moscow Olympic Games from the United States government. The invasion also dashed any hope for U.S. Senate ratification of the arms limitation treaty signed by President Carter and President Brezhnev in 1979. The Reagan administration continued a similar policy but stiffened it by postponing arms negotiations. It did relax the grain embargo. The Afghanistan invasion also tied the hands of the Soviet government in its own sphere of influence in Eastern Europe. There seems little doubt that the Soviet hesitation to react more strongly to events in Poland, which are discussed in the next section, stemmed in part from having military resources committed to Afghanistan and from having encountered broad condemnation for the invasion from some West European Communist parties and from the governments of nations not aligned with the West.

The Gorbachev Phenomenon

Brezhnev died in 1982. Both of his immediate successors, Yuri Andropov and Constantine Chernenko, died after holding office for very short periods. In 1984, Mikhail S. Gorbachev came to power. He immediately set about making the most remarkable changes that the Soviet Union has witnessed since the 1920s.

Gorbachev stands as one of those major figures in Russian and Soviet history who have attempted to impose major reforms from above. He and his supporters have challenged the traditional role of the Communist Party bureaucracy in directing the economy and government policy. The term that has been applied to these changes is *perestroika* or restructuring. The targets of this effort have been various economic ministries that were considerably reduced in size. A larger role has been allowed for private enterprise on the local level.

Within the Soviet context, Gorbachev's approach has been genuinely radical. It has challenged centralized planning and centralized Communist Party control. He and his supporters have proved to be exceedingly critical of the corruption and inefficiencies in the economy and the party bureaucracy. Prominent figures have been put on trial for corruption. Gorbachev personally has favored smaller farms in the hope of increasing agricultural productivity. Thus far, he has made little headway in implementing this policy. Consequently, his reforms have done little to improve agricultural productivity.

Second, Gorbachev has allowed what is within the Soviet context a remarkably broad public discussion and criticism of Soviet history and government policy. This general policy has been termed *glasnost* or openness. In the summer of 1988, Gorbachev presided over a party congress that witnessed very full debates on policy. Certain figures from the 1920s purged by Stalin have once again received official public recognition for their positive contributions to Soviet history. Within factories, workers have been able to criticize party officials and the economic plans set forth by the party and the government. Intellectuals have experienced extensive possibilities of free expression. Censorship has been relaxed, and many of the dissidents have been

The Leader of the Soviet Union Calls for Change

In July 1988, the Communist Party of the Soviet Union held one of the most extraordinary conferences in its history. It was characterized by open debate and criticism of previous government and party policies. In the closing speech to the conference, Mikhail S. Gorbachev explained what he understood to be the meaning of the new atmosphere.

A major event in the history of our party has taken place.

First of all, about the atmosphere of the discussion. This was a truly open party talk about the principal things that concern today the Communists, Soviet people, an attempt to find answers to questions that worry them. . . .

The questions were posed in an acute and principled way, and at the same time there was party comradeship, one can even say benevolence with regard to each other. And this too sets an example for the whole party, for our entire society. This is how it should be among like-minded persons, people who embarked on a great cause of perestroika, renewal of society, and feel that they are backed by hundreds, thousands, millions of their comrades in the party, by all Soviet people, who followed with great interest our work. . . .

In the conditions of democritization, glasnost, the changes in the functions of party committees, the par-

ty's prestige, comrades, will undergo a serious test. This process is already under way. Let us be candid: In conditions of the command and administrative system when the party apparatus was in charge of all and everything at times it was not easy to discern where the party committee and the party secretary enjoyed genuinely the prestige of a leader and where, at best the 'prestige of office' and they were obeyed only out of necessity.

There is no doubt, comrades, that perestroika, the reform of the political system, creates a fundamentally different situation. In the new conditions the party's guiding role will be fully determined by the real prestige which every time anew will have to be proved by concrete deeds. That is why it is simply vitally important for us to overcome the slightest passiveness among party members. Each Communist must become a fighter for perestroika, for the revolutionary renewal of society. ❑

New York Times, July 2, 1988, p. 6.

---

released from prison. Another manifestation of this more open atmosphere has been a more tolerant attitude toward political demonstrations by certain national minorities. However, it is possible to overestimate the new openness. Only moderate complaints by nationalist groups have been tolerated. Furthermore, within the governing Politburo at least one major critic of Gorbachev was summarily dismissed.

Third, in foreign policy Gorbachev has made a considerable effort to win over the public opinion of Western Europe. He has traveled extensively in the West and is the first major Soviet leader to have a rather clear understanding of the value of good public relations. His negotiations with the Reagan administration led to the limitation on intermediate-range nuclear missiles. In 1988, the Soviet Union dramatically began to withdraw from its military engagement in Afghanistan and completed the withdrawal in 1989. Late in the same year, Gorbachev announced to the United Nations that there would be cutbacks in the numbers of Soviet tanks and troops stationed in Eastern Europe. Gorbachev seems to have seen a close link between these goals of foreign policy and his ongoing efforts at domestic economic and political reform.

In 1989 Gorbachev made still another foreign policy

departure within the communist world. He journeyed to China and formally healed the thirty-year breach between that country and the Soviet Union.

Perhaps the most striking aspect of the Gorbachev phenomenon has been the manner in which he has focused world attention upon himself and the changes within the Soviet Union. Virtually all of his reforms have been applauded in the Western Europe. Through his personality and his policies he has drawn leaders of Western Europe to believe a much more cooperative stance should be taken toward the Soviet Union. Many observers believe these policies mark the final end of the Cold War Era. This attitude, about which other observers voice scepticism, plus the growing economic unity of the European Economic Community have created strains within the NATO alliance. It is possible that Gorbachev's time in power will establish fundamentally new East-West relations. It is yet too early to be certain.

Polycentrism in the Communist World

Throughout the Cold War, observers in the West have concentrated their attention on the tensions between the Soviet Union and the United States. But beyond its continuing confrontation of and rivalry with

Eastern Europe has been the scene of rapid and unpredictable changes in the wake of the new policies of the Soviet Union. Here President Gorbachev is pictured with President Jarulewski of Poland where some of the most striking changes have taken place. [Photo: Bernard Bisson er Thierry Orban: Sygma.]

America, the Soviet government has also had to deal with growing tension and division within the world Communist movement. During most of the Stalin era, the Soviet Union was the center of world communism. Stalin hoped to impose his model on other parties. Immediately after the war, the Soviets attempted to construct governments in the peoples' democracies of Eastern Europe in the Stalinist mold.

Since the late 1940s, the unity of world communism, which was always more frail than Cold War rhetoric suggested, became strained and finally shattered. As early as 1948, Yugoslavia began to construct its own model for socialism independent of Moscow. From 1956 onward, the governments of Eastern Europe began to seek a freer hand in internal affairs. By the late 1950s, the monumental split between the Soviet Union and the People's Republic of China had developed. The Communist world has come to have many centers—thus the descriptive term *polycentrism*—and the Soviet Union has had to compete for leadership.

There have been three stages in postwar relations between the Soviet Union and Eastern Europe. There were the years of Stalinism, then of revolt, and finally of socialist polycentrism. These stages closely paralleled internal developments in the Soviet Union itself.

Before the death of Stalin in 1953, the so-called peoples' democracies were brought steadily into line with Soviet policy. By 1948, single-party Communist governments had been established in Bulgaria, Romania, Hungary, Yugoslavia, Albania, Czechoslovakia, Poland, and East Germany. Yugoslavia, headed by Marshal Tito (1892–1980), pursued an independent course of action and was bitterly denounced by Stalin. Elsewhere, however, Soviet troops and Stalinist party leaders prevailed. The economies of those states were made to conform to the requirements of Soviet economic recovery and growth. The Soviet Union paid low prices for its imports from Eastern Europe and demanded high prices for its exports. In this fashion and through outright reparations, it drained the resources of the region for its own uses. The Soviet Union prevented the Eastern European nations from participating in the Marshall Plan and responded with its own Council for Economic Mutual Assistance in 1949. In 1955, it organized the Warsaw Pact to confront NATO.

The Stalinist system of control was bound to generate discontent. This first manifested itself shortly after Stalin's death in 1953, when a brief revolt occurred in East Berlin. It was immediately crushed. Talk in the

Nationalist protests in the Soviet Union, such as this one among Armenians, have challenged the traditional mode of Communist Party rule in the Soviet Union. [AP LaserPhoto.]

early Eisenhower administration in America about the "liberation" of Eastern Europe may have contributed to this disturbance by raising hopes of some form of American support. Khrushchev's speech of 1956 in which he denounced Stalin sent reverberations throughout Eastern Europe as well as the Soviet Union. It was no accident that following the speech came the Polish October Revolution and the Hungarian Revolution of 1956. In the short run, the bids for independence had the most limited kind of success; however, in retrospect they can be seen as marking the close of the Stalinist period and as paving the way for the emergence of polycentrism.

During the early years of the Cold War, it was common in the West to regard the communist movement as a single monolithic structure. There was a failure to take into account the role of nationalism in Eastern Europe and the potential for division between the Soviet Union and China. The events of 1956 delineated the limits of acceptable independence for the Soviet-dominated successor states. Those nations of Eastern Europe had to remain members of the Warsaw Pact, and their leaders had to be willing to consult and cooperate with the Soviet Union. They might trade with Western Europe and the United States and even establish cultural contacts, but their chief political and economic orientation must remain with the Soviet Union.

Since 1956, within these limits considerable diversity has appeared within the Communist bloc in Eastern Europe. In Hungary, the Janos Kadar government,

which was installed by Soviet troops, pursued a program of economic growth and consumer satisfaction. He was replaced in 1988 after economic problems began to arise. Hungary is now probably the most prosperous and stable country in the region.

East Germany and Bulgaria retained the closest relationships with the Soviet Union. After the Berlin Wall crisis of 1961 and the subsequent halt in the outflow of refugees, East Germany experienced very substantial economic growth. Romania has witnessed a resurgence of limited nationalism. Under the leadership of President Nicolae Ceauşescu (b. 1918), it has maintained ties with both the Soviet Union and China. Moreover, it has also cultivated friendly relations with the United States, as witnessed by President Nixon's visit in 1969 and President Ceauşescu's visit to America in 1977. However, in all of these countries the independence achieved is extremely limited and exists within the limits of one-party government, authoritarianism, and absence of the traditional civil liberties.

THE CZECHOSLOVAKIAN CRISIS. In 1968, the Soviet Union moved to crush an experiment in developing a socialist model independent of Soviet domination. In that year, the nations of the Warsaw Pact invaded Czechoslovakia to halt the political experimentation of the Alexander Dubcek government. It was quite clear that the Soviet Union felt that it could not tolerate so liberal a Communist regime on its own borders. Dubcek was permitting in Czechoslovakia the very kind of intellectual freedom and discussion that was simultaneously being suppressed within Russia itself. At the time of the invasion, Soviet Party Chairman Brezhnev declared the right of the Soviet Union to interfere in the domestic politics of other communist countries. Such direct interference has nevertheless not occurred since 1968. Moreover, at a conference of Communist parties held in East Berlin in 1976, the Soviet Union accepted a declaration stating that there could be several paths to socialism. That policy has yet to be put to a meaningful test.

Ongoing Crisis in Poland. Such a test seems to have been occurring within Poland since the summer of 1980. After 1956, the Polish Communist Party, led by Wladyslaw Gomulka (b. 1905), made peace with the Roman Catholic church, halted land collectivization, established trade with the West, and participated in cultural exchange programs with non-communist nations. However, Poland experienced chronic economic mismanagement and persistent shortages in food and consumer goods. In 1970, food shortages led to a series of strikes, the most famous of which occurred in the shipyards of Gdansk. In December 1970, the Polish authorities broke the strike at the cost of a number of workers' lives. These events led to the departure of Gomulka. His successor was Edward Gierek (b. 1913).

In the decade after 1970, the Polish economy made very little progress. Food and other consumer goods remained in very short supply. In early July 1980, the Polish government raised meat prices. The result was hundreds of protest strikes across the country. On August 14, workers occupied the Lenin shipyard at Gdansk. The strike soon spread to other shipyards, transport facilities, and factories connected with the shipbuilding industry. Lech Walesa (b. 1944) emerged as the most important leader among the strikers. He and the other strike leaders refused to negotiate with the government through any of the traditionally government-controlled unions. The Gdansk strike ended on August 31, 1980 with the promises of the right for the workers to organize an independent union and the right of access to the media for the union (by now called Solidarity) and the Polish Roman Catholic church. Less than a week later, on September 6, Edward Gierek was dismissed as the head of the Polish Communist Party. He was replaced by Stanislaw Kania. Later in September, the Polish courts recognized Solidarity as an independent union and the state-controlled radio broadcast a Roman Catholic mass for the first time in thirty years.

During the summer of 1981, other remarkable events occurred within the governance of the Polish Communist Party. For the first time in any European communist state, secret elections for the congress of the party permitted real choices among the candidates. Poland remained a nation governed by a single

Lech Walesa, leader of the Polish Solidarity Movement, at a moment of triumph in September 1980. For a time, Solidarity seemed capable of gradually inducing the government to liberalize Poland. But in December 1981, under pressure from Moscow the Polish army took control of the country. Solidarity was suspended, and Walesa was held incommunicado for several months. [Sygma.]

party, but for the time being, real debate was permitted within the party congress.

The extraordinary Polish experiment came to a rapid close in late 1981. General Wajciech Jaruzelski (b. 1923) became head of the party and the army moved into the center of Polish events. In December 1981, martial law was declared in Poland. The government moved against Solidarity, arresting a number of its leaders.

By the late 1980s events in Poland took another turn. The government had modified martial law though Jaruzelski remained in control. However, the economic situation continued to deteriorate. During 1987 the government released the last of the Solidarity prisoners through a sweeping amnesty. In 1988 strikes again occurred, and as a result of consultations between the government and Solidarity, the union was legalized. Lech Walesa again came into the public spotlight as a kind of mediator between the government and the more independent elements of the trade union movement he had founded. On this occasion the Communist government was no longer able to control the situation.

Jaruzelski began to undertake a number of political reforms with the tacit consent of the Soviet Union. Martial law was repealed. The Communist government promised free elections in a more powerful parliament. In 1989 the Communists lost overwhelmingly to Solidarity candidates. Later in the year Jaruzelski was unable to find any Communist who could form a government that would receive the support of a majority in the parliament. Late that summer he turned to Solidarity to form a government and negotiated directly with Lech Walesa as to who would become the next prime minister. On August 24, 1989, Tadeusz Mazowiecki (b. 1927) of Solidarity became the first non-communist Prime Minister of Poland since 1945. The appointment was made with the express approval of Gorbachev. Quite significantly the Communists will continue to hold the ministries that direct the armed forces and the police. Furthermore, there were observers who believed the Communists had permitted Solidarity to come to power because the economic problems facing the country were so grave that it could not succeed and would thus lose credibility. Whatever the motives of the Polish Communist and the Soviet Union, in 1989 Poland embarked on a new political road that could have enormous implications for all of eastern Europe.

The West since 1945 in World Perspective

The history of the West since the end of World War II has been full of paradoxes. The continent of Europe, which gave birth to Western civilization and remained its center until the war, has declined in world influence. The two great nations to the extreme west and east of continental Europe have risen to predominance. Consequently, while the traditional center of Western influence exerts little power, both of the new great Western powers have come to exert more political and military power than any previous nation of continental Europe. Yet both the United States and the Soviet Union are today perceived as having wasted much of their new-found influence—the United States through its involvement in Vietnam and the Soviet Union through its involvement in Afghanistan and the stagnation of its economy.

Within continental Europe, nationalism is less powerful than at any time in the past century. Whereas after World War I the principle of national self-determination guided political developments, since 1945 Western Europe has attempted to overcome the divisions of nationalism. The most important effort has been the European Economic Community.

Western nations have discovered that they may no longer command power over other parts of the globe. The traditional European imperial nations have retreated from empire. The Soviet Union has found itself in rivalry with the People's Republic of China for leadership of the Communist world. The United States must compete with Japan in the world economy. Furthermore, the United States and the Soviet Union no longer possess a monopoly on nuclear weapons. A more integrated world economy and political system has established a more intricate web of interdependencies. Therefore, the next fifty years of world history will be more complicated and complex than the last fifty.

Suggested Readings

K. L. BAKER, R. J. DALTON, AND K. HILDEBRANDT, *Germany Transformed: Political Culture and the New Politics* (1981). Useful essays on the functioning of German democracy.

S. BEER, *Modern British Politics: Parties and Pressure Groups in the Collectivist Age* (1982). The best introduction to the subject.

C. D. BLACK AND G. DUFFY, eds., *International Arms Control Issues and Agreements* (1985). Useful essays.

E. BOTTOME, *The Balance of Terror: Nuclear Weapons and the Illusion of Security*, 1945–1985 (1986). A pessimistic evaluation.

Z. BREZEZINSKI, *The Soviet Block: Unity and Conflict* (1967). A somewhat dated discussion of Eastern Europe.

C. BURDICK, H–A. JACOBSEN, AND W. KUDSZUR (eds.) *Contemporary Germany: Politics and Culture* (1984). A collection of wide-ranging essays.

L. T. CALDWELL AND W. DIEBOLD, JR., *Soviet American Relations in the 1980's: Superpower Politics and*

East-West Trade (1980). An attempt to delineate the major problems in Soviet-American relations.

A. W. DE PORTE, *Europe Between the Superpowers: The Enduring Balance* (1979). A very important study.

R. EMERSON, *From Empire to Nation: The Rise to Self-assertion of Asian and African Peoples* (1960). An important discussion of the origins of decolonization.

M. FRANKLIN, *The Decline of Class Voting in Britain* (1986). The argument is stated in the title.

J. R. FREARS, *France in the Giscard Presidency* (1981). A survey.

D. J. GARROW, *Bearing the Cross: Martin Luther King, Jr. and the Southern Leadership Conference 1955–1968* (1986). The best work on the subject.

M. I. GOLDMAN, *Gorbachev's Challenge: Economic Reform in the Age of High Technology* (1988). A consideration of recent events in the Soviet Union with emphasis on economic structures. (1988)

M. GORBACHEV, *Perestroika: New Thinking for Our Country and the World* (1988). Gorbachev's book discussing his goals.

R. HISCOCKS, *The Adenauer Era* (1966). A treatment of postwar German political development.

S. HOFFMAN (ed.), *In Search of France* (1963). A useful collection of essays on the problems of postwar France.

D. HOLLOWAY, *The Soviet Union and the Arms Race* (1985). Excellent treatment of internal Soviet decision-making.

R. W. HULL, *The Irish Triangle: Conflict in Northern Ireland* (1976). A thoughtful and generally dispassionate treatment of a difficult problem.

P. JENKINS, *Mrs. Thatcher's Revolution: The Ending of the Socialist Era* (1988). A major examination.

D. KEARNS, *Lyndon Johnson and the American Dream* (1976). A useful biography.

W. W. KULSKI, *De Gaulle and the World: The Foreign Policy of the Fifth French Republic* (1968). A straightforward treatment of De Gaulle's drive toward French and European autonomy.

W. LEONHARD, *Three Faces of Communism* (1974). An analysis of the ideological divisions within the communist world.

R. F. LESLIE, *The History of Poland since 1863* (1981). An excellent collection of essays that provide the background for current tensions in Poland.

L. MARTIN (ed.), *Strategic Thought in the Nuclear Age* (1979). A collection of useful essays on an issue that lies at the core of the American relationship to Western Europe.

M. MCCAULEY, *The German Democratic Republic since 1945* (1983). Useful survey of East Germany.

R. MAYNE, *The Recovery of Europe, 1945–1973* (1973). A sound treatment emphasizing the movement toward economic integration.

Z. A. MEDVEDEV, *Gorbachev* (1986). The best available biography.

C. MURRAY, *Losing Ground: American Social Policy 1950–1980* (1983). A pessimistic assessment.

D. W. REINHARD, *The Republican Right since 1945* (1983) A useful overview.

D. ROBERTSON, *Class and the British Electorate* (1986). Emphasizes the decline of class voting.

R. ROSE, *Governing Without Consensus: An Irish Perspective* (1971). An excellent exploration of the origins and development of the Irish problem.

G. ROSS, *Workers and Communists in France: From Popular Front to Eurocommunism* (1982). An important issue in recent French politics.

J. RUSCOE, *The Italian Communist Party, 1976–81: On the Threshold of Government* (1982). Examines the party at the height of its influence.

A. SAMPSON, *The Changing Anatomy of Britain* (1982). An exploration of the social and political elites.

L. SCHAPIRO, *The Communist Party of the Soviet Union* (1960). A classic analysis of the most important institution of Soviet Russia.

A. M. SCHLESINGER, JR., *A Thousand Days: John F. Kennedy in the White House* (1965). A biography by an adviser and major historian.

A. M. SCHLESINGER, JR., *The Imperial Presidency* (1973). An assessment of the American presidency in the light of Vietnam.

H. SIMONIAN, *The Privileged Partnership: Franco-German Relations in the European Community (1969–1984)* (1985). An important examination of the dominant role of France and Germany in the E.E.D.

J. STEELE, *Soviet Power: The Kremlin's Foreign Policy—Brezhnev to Andropov* (1983). A broad survey.

D. STOCKMAN, *The Triumph of Politics: The Inside Story of the Reagan Revolution* (1987). A critical memoir by one of Reagan's aids.

C. TUGENHAT, *Making Sense of Europe* (1986). Evaluation of Common Market by one of its commissioners.

H. A. TURNER, JR., *The Two Germanies since 1945* (1987). The best and most recent introduction.

A. ULAM, *Expansion and Coexistence: The History of Soviet Foreign Policy, 1917–1967* (1968). The best one-volume treatment.

D. M. WILLIAMS, *French Politicians and Elections, 1951–1969* (1970). Excellent coverage of the establishment and early years of the Fifth Republic.

B. WOODWARD AND C. BERNSTEIN, *The Final Days* (1976). A discussion of the Watergate scandal by the reporters who uncovered it.

上海市人民政府

中国共产党上海市委员会

必须对爱国学潮正名!
〜苏州人民〜

声援学生爱国运动
苗苗商店退休工人

Shanghai Students and Workers with Statue of Liberty. In May 1989, student demonstrators erected a statue of liberty on the Bund, the most strategic thorough-fare in Shanghai, immediately in front of the Shanghai government offices and those of the Shanghai branch of the Chinese Communist Party. Students and workers maintained a vigil about the statue. In June the movement was smashed. Students and workers were cowed. The movement's leaders were imprisoned, executed, or fled China. (AP World Wide Photos.)

1034

37 New Departures in the World at Large

In the past half century, Europe has been eclipsed by the rise of the two superpowers. Elsewhere in the world, there has been an end of the colonial experience. This development must, however, be set within a larger historical perspective. Since the sixteenth century, the various non-European portions of the globe had been drawn steadily into the European sphere of economic and political influence. This European dominance, through the power of its economy and military forces, reached its height between approximately 1850 and 1939.

European colonialism, for all its immense impact across the world, was a relatively brief, though traumatic, episode in the long context of world history. And for that reason, the postcolonial experience may be considered still another relatively brief episode leading to new, yet-to-be-determined alignments of world cultures and political power. It would seem that today, much—perhaps most—of the direct postcolonial experience lies behind us. What we shall be witnessing in the future is the forging of the new alignments and the creation of new powers, such as that of the new economic giant of the 1980s, Japan.

Since 1945, two distinct developments have occurred in the postcolonial world. The first is the process that is generally termed *decolonization*. This word indicates the emergence of the various parts of Africa and Asia from the direct government and administration of the European powers and of Japan, and the organization of those previous colonial dependencies into independent states. The most notable examples of this development are the numerous new countries in Africa and the independence of India and Pakistan. No less significant has been the renewed autonomy of China under the revolutionary Communist government established in 1949 and the remarkable reemergence of Japan as a powerful economic force after its defeat in World War II. The process of decolonization has been an exceedingly troubled one that has resulted, in some cases, in civil wars within the new states. In other cases, as with France in Algeria and France and then the United States in Vietnam, prolonged warfare resulted.

There has been a second accompanying postwar development. Although many of the bonds of colonial rule have been broken, the emerging nations have been drawn into two new kinds of relationships with the Western powers. First, the rivalry of the United States and the Soviet Union has manifested itself in one way or another on every continent and has added to the tensions and turmoil of the era. Second, the character of the world economy, including issues of both trade and resource allocation, has inevitably led to new modes of interdependence. At present, those new relationships of interdependence remain ill defined and the source of much political friction, whether they relate to automobile production, Mideast oil, or the structure of international debt. The rhetoric of the period of decolonization is still used, but the reality it attempts to describe is very different. Those new realities and their resulting problems will probably be the main concerns of the next era of world history.

However, if we seek to understand the larger global scene, we must recognize the persistent influence of the great religions and moral traditions of humankind. In particular, Buddhist, Christian, and Islamic faith and values continue to claim the allegiance of major sectors around the world, not only in Africa and Asia, but also in Europe and the Americas.

The Postcolonial Experience of the African and Asian Worlds

Throughout Africa, the Middle East, Iran, the Indian subcontinent, and Southeast Asia, the dominant notes of postwar history have been those of independence and self-determination. Today, Africa and Asia have nearly a hundred sovereign states, whereas before 1939, they had only twelve. The rise of new nationalisms in these areas goes back to the nineteenth century, but it was only with the cataclysm of World War II that nationalistic movements emerged. Fueled by diverse grievances accumulated over many generations of foreign domination and exploitation, these movements found themselves strong enough— and their colonial masters weak (and/or receptive) enough—to win independence in country after country. Ironically, what now defined a "country" or a "nation" was, however, often less a common linguistic, racial, or other communal affinity than the often arbitrary boundaries of previous colonial administrative units. As the colonial administrations themselves had been the principal targets of nationalist agitation, preindependence boundaries naturally provided the geographical frameworks for most new nation-states.

The postwar period has seen more than forty new states created in Africa alone, as well as numerous others throughout the less developed areas of Asia. The often massive difficulties and the frequent instability these new states have suffered are clear evidence of how little the colonial European powers really did for the countries they profited from and governed for so long. Economically, few of the new nations have had the technological, commercial, and political bases for self-sufficiency; the common problem has been spiraling overpopulation, which has generally far surpassed indigenous food production or even natural resources. The less developed nations of the world have typically experienced the highest rates of population growth in the world. Latin American and the Afro-Asian "Third World" peoples (including China, but not Japan) now amount to about three quarters of the world's population (which is now approaching five billion, as compared with about two billion in 1930).

The small elites in each former colonial domain that flourished economically under foreign domination

Under British aegis, in 1979 the warring parties in Rhodesia sign both a cease-fire that ends a long, bloody guerrilla war between blacks and whites and a constitutional agreement that led to the new state of Zimbabwe.

were commonly educated abroad—usually in the universities of a colonial power. Politically, they have been often too cut off from the masses of their own people to be able to lead their new independent states well. The populist movements for independence and self-rule have foundered again and again on internal rivalries and lack of modern political experience. Class differences have often pitted one group against another within a given society. In other instances, tribal or other affinity groups have found it hard to pull together with former rival groups in new nation-states. For many of these new nations, such as the Arab, black African, Southeast Asian, and Indian nations, the price of independent nationhood has been high in blood, political strife, economic chaos, and a continuing inequity in the distribution of wealth. Even the massive oil resources of many of these lands cannot begin to provide answers to all the dilemmas that this Third World faces.

Yet, in the midst of the severe and often tragic birth and growing pains of these new nations, there have also been hopeful signs. Some of these states have made inroads on mass illiteracy, poverty, and disease. They have done so even in the face of the overriding juggernauts of runaway population growth and the escalating destruction of the natural environment through deforestation, the contamination of water resources, and the depletion of natural resources generally. Some have been able to develop their own senses of cultural, political, or religious identity in continuity with their precolonial pasts, without retreating from the realities of their modern experiences and situations. With the notable exception of the black African population of Apartheid South Africa, most African and Asian peoples can now pursue their own course into the twenty-first century. Even if that course is a difficult one, at least it is not one that they are being directly forced to run by alien colonial armies and bureaucracies.

West, East, Central, and South Africa

The rise of African nationalism can be dated generally to the period between the two world wars, when previously fragmented and regional opposition to European colonial occupation began to be replaced by larger-scale anti-imperialist movements. In World War II, the important roles that Africa was called on to play with its natural and human resources, as well as the experience of thousands of Africans abroad, proved a catalyst for African nationalism. The postwar European world was also largely disposed for the first time to give up its theories of white supremacy and its colonial empires.

Thus, the decades since World War II have seen a previously European-dominated continent become a huge array of new, independent national states. In

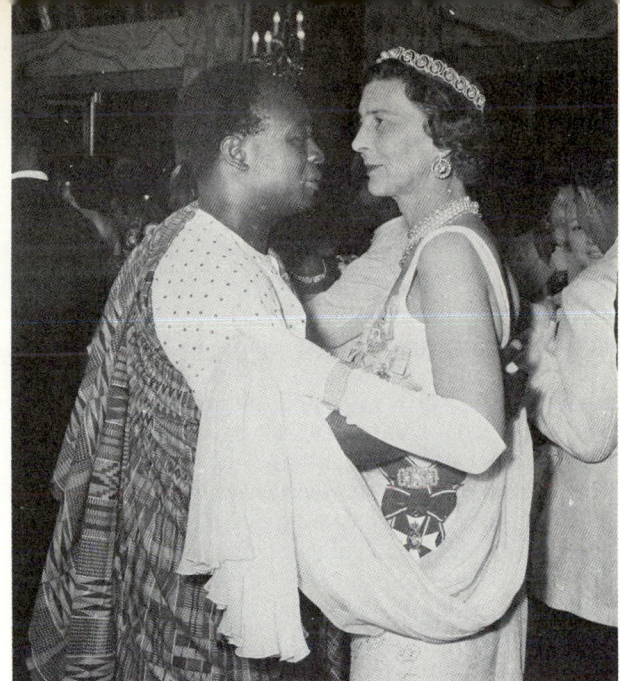

Kwame Nkrumah and the Duchess of Kent, a member of the British royal family, dancing at the state ball held to celebrate Ghana's independence on March 6, 1957. Like other nationalist rulers across Africa, Nkrumah had endured imprisonment and won a fierce internal struggle among competing native parties during the last years of colonial rule. After 1957, he became a pan-African leader in the movement to gain independence for other African states. [AP/Wide World Photos.]

1950, apart from Egypt, only Liberia, Ethiopia, and white-controlled South Africa were sovereign states. By 1980, no African state (with the exception of two tiny Spanish holdings on the Moroccan coast) was ruled by a European state, although South Africa and Namibia continued to be white-dominated. Native sons such as Kwame Nkrumah (1909–1972) in the Gold Coast (modern Ghana), Jomo Kenyatta (1893–1978) in Kenya, and Patrice Lumumba (1925–1961) in the Congo emerged as charismatic leaders who became symbols of African self-determination and freedom from foreign domination.

The African experience in these years has been often a violent one, involving both wars for freedom from foreign rule and substantial civil strife surrounding the creation of new sovereign states. The most protracted wars of liberation or independence were the guerrilla struggles fought in French Algeria from 1955 to 1962; in formerly Portuguese Angola and Mozambique from 1961 to 1975; and in Zaire (formerly the Belgian Congo), Zambia (formerly Northern Rhodesia), and Zimbabwe (formerly Southern Rhodesia) from 1960 to 1980. In most of these same countries, separatist struggles, civil wars, and border wars between new states grew out of the independence struggles. Likewise, they did so in Nigeria, Gambia, and Senegal; Morocco and the western Sahara; Libya and Chad; South African–held Namibia; Ethiopia and Eritrea; Kenya, Uganda, and Tanzania; Rawanda and Burundi; Somalia; and the Sudan. At the present time, it is impossible to say that great progress toward peace and prosperity has been made in most of these areas.

Much of the instability in Africa is a legacy of the colonial era, with its haphazard division of the continent into often arbitrary units and minimal efforts to prepare African nations for self-government. Much is also due to tribal divisions and the dire problems of overpopulation, poverty, disease, famine, lack of educational and technological expertise, and general underdevelopment that plague much of the continent. Also not to be discounted are the disruptive social changes wrought over the past several decades by the explosive growth of new urban societies at the expense of traditional agrarian life. A consequence was disruption of age-old family and tribal allegiances, religious values, and sociopolitical systems.

One of the most tragic and still potentially explosive chapters in the history of modern Africa is being written in Southern Africa. Minority white-settler governments in various parts of East and Southern Africa have tried in vain in the postwar period to put down African independence movements and even efforts at participatory multiracial states. However, only in South Africa have they managed to maintain the upper hand today.

Based on the avowedly racist principle of Apartheid ("apartness"), the Union of South Africa is still run by its 4.5 million white minority, while some 21 million blacks, 850,000 Indians, and 2.5 million "coloreds" (of mixed blood) are legally and strictly segregated. They are treated as, at best, second-class citizens and, at worst, noncitizens or even nonhumans. South Africa has seen itself increasingly isolated as the rest of Africa, including other white-run states like Rhodesia (now Zimbabwe), pass over to majority, African rule. In 1961, South Africa withdrew from the British Commonwealth of Nations. Two of its anti-Apartheid black leaders, the Zulu chief Albert Luthuli in 1960 and the Anglican bishop Desmond Tutu in 1984, have been awarded Nobel Peace Prizes for their struggles on behalf of justice in South Africa. The Union's continued existence depends chiefly on repressive measures ranging from military and police action to the creation of tiny "independent homelands," to which the ten

Desmond Tutu Speaks Out about Nelson Mandela

Nelson Mandela (1918–   ) has been imprisoned by the South African government since 1962 under life sentence for inciting strikes and leaving the country without a valid passport. In the 1950s, he emerged as one of the leaders of the black underground opposition to the Apartheid government. In the following text excerpt, 1984 Nobel Laureate Bishop Desmond Tutu, in an address at Natal University, April 28, 1980, calls for Mandela's release and for a change in attitude on the part of the government.

Blacks may not have much military power. But we have our consumer power, and South Africa still depends to a large extent on our labour. We are not yet properly organised, but the latent power is there. Banning, detentions, banishments will not stop freedom coming. They merely postpone the inevitable, and build up a legacy of bitterness and hatred, which we could well do without, as we learned from Zimbabwe. Okay—there is going to be a black Prime Minister in South Africa within five-to-ten years. The white community cannot stop that happening. What the white community still has in its power to do is to decide whether that Prime Minister is going to end up there through a process of reasoned negotiation, and discussion at a conference table, or whether he will have to do so after bitter fighting and bloodshed. I think we have a very good chance of pulling off the first alternative. And we need Nelson Mandela, because he is almost certainly going to be that first black Prime Minister. He represents all our genuine leaders, in prison and in exile. So to call for his release is really to say, please let us sit down, black and white together, each with our acknowledged leaders, and work out our common future, so that we can move into this new South Africa, which will be filled with justice, peace, love, righteousness, compassion and caring. . . .

I think we can have a new non-racial South Africa, and that we can achieve it reasonably peacefully, but that means we must negotiate and bargain at the conference table, and this can only be done by genuine and acknowledged leaders. Hence our call, Free Mandela, and start talking. ❑

From Desmond Tutu, *Crying in the Wilderness: The Struggle for Justice in South Africa.* Ed. John Webster (Grand Rapids, Mich.: William B. Eerdmans Publishing Co., 1982), pp. 96–97.

*Two leaders of black South Africa, Nelson Mandela and Bishop Desmond Tutu.
[AP/Wide World Photos, Magnum.]*

major black tribal groups are to be assigned. (The "homelands," which most blacks will never see, allow the whites to treat blacks as immigrant "foreigners" in the major parts of South Africa where most have to work.) Despite world censure and some boycotts of South African commerce and other activity abroad, the Apartheid system still stands, a vivid example in the global community of the ugliest face of Western imperialism and white racism.

The Arab World and Israel

The postwar history of the Middle East and North Africa has been dominated by four major developments: (1) the emergence of new national states and international alignments, (2) the intrusion of the Zionist state of Israel into Palestine, (3) the increase in importance of Middle Eastern oil production and reserves, and (4) a new resurgence of religious, political, and social reform movements in the name of a purified Muslim society.

Saudi Arabia, Iraq, and Egypt had already obtained sovereign-state status within a dozen years after World War I, and Lebanon and Syria were officially given theirs by France during the war. Yet it was

only in the post–World War II period that these states became truly independent of European control. Jordan (1946), Libya (1951), Morocco and Tunisia (1956), Algeria (1962), and, by 1971, the two Yemens, Oman, and the small Arabian Gulf states achieved sovereign status. Political instability has been a constant in many of the Arab states. There have been various abortive attempts at Pan-Arab alliances or federation by some of these countries. Although the Arabic language and, except in Lebanon, the Islamic faith bind these lands together, many historical and regional or nationalistic factors give each of them a distinctive character. Europe, America, and Russia have become interested parties in the oil-rich and therefore strategically important Arab world. Their often heavy-handed presence has led also to shifting external alliances that have further complicated relations among these states as a whole.

Nowhere has the presence of the superpowers and Europe been more tragically and clumsily felt than in the 1948 creation of the state of Israel. Located in the formerly British mandate territory of Palestine, Israel was declared a national homeland for the Jewish people. This event was the achievement of the world Zi-

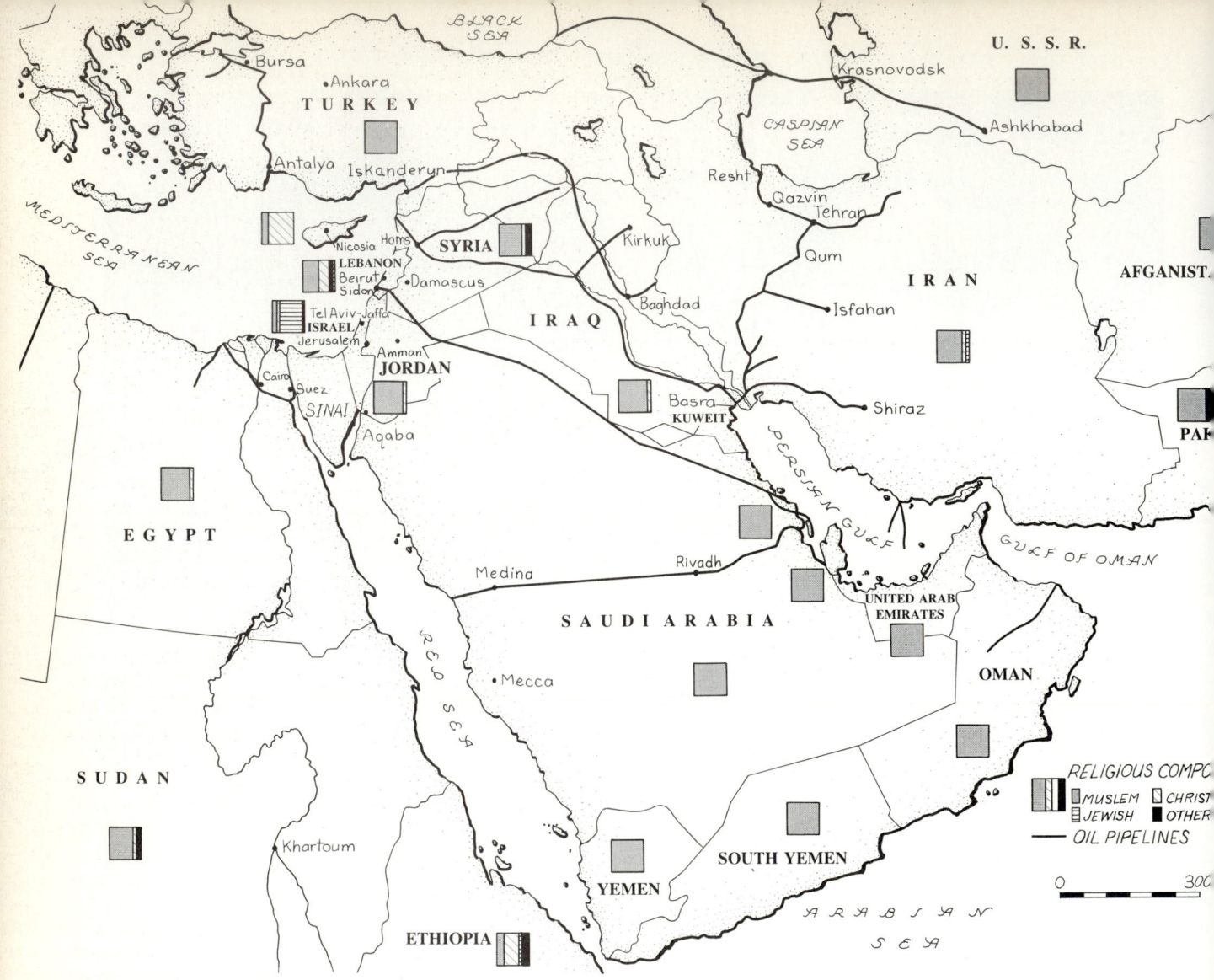

MAP 37-1   THE MODERN MIDDLE EAST   *Shown are distribution of major religious communities by countries.*

onist movement founded in 1897 by Theodor Herzl in Europe. The British Balfour Declaration of 1917 had already favored the establishment of a national homeland for the Jews in Palestine. Yet in 1920, there were only about sixty thousand Jews and ten times that number of Arabs in Palestine.

The interwar years saw increasing Jewish settlement and growing communal conflict that was rather poorly mediated by the British. With the nightmarish attempt of the Nazis to exterminate European Jewry, the Zionist movement received a tremendous boost among international Jewry and the Allied nations, who felt the need to atone for the indescribable horror of the Holocaust. However, the Palestinian Arabs did

not see why they should be displaced and persecuted to pay for Europe's sins against the Jews.

So the stage was set for conflict when Britain washed its hands of the problem and the United Nations passed a resolution calling for partition of the territory into a Jewish and an Arab state. Despite the Arab states' refusal to accept the UN resolution, the Jews in Palestine declared the independence of the new state of Israel in 1948. This declaration led to the Israeli–Arab war of 1948–1949, in which Syria, Lebanon, Jordon, Egypt, and Saudi Arabia lost even more ground to the determined Israelis than the UN resolution had called for originally.

Since that time, there has been, at best, an armed

Portfolio VI: Contemporary Religion

In the late twentieth century the major religious traditions of human civilization that we have examined over the centuries have experienced a remarkable revival and reasserted the centrality of their position in world affairs. Sometimes these revivals have stood primarily as manifestations of religious faith and practice; in other instances they have become deeply involved with politics and most especially with nationalism.

A key feature of contemporary religious life is the close proximity in which practitioners of the various major religious faiths now dwell. All of those faiths now exist in more than eighty countries. More than at any previous time in human history, each religious community exhibits a greater awareness of the beliefs and practices of other religious communities. Television and radio as well as the migration of members of religious communities into new locations account for this situation. Sometimes this new awareness has led to greater understanding; in other instances the close proximity of different religious faiths in combination with political conflict has led to sharp and deadly clashes.

No doubt the most recently visible religious movement of our era is the apparent revival of Islam. From North Africa to Iran across southern Asia through Pakistan and into Indonesia the intensity of Islamic devotion has appeared in all classes of society. Islamic fundamentalism, associated with both the Shi'ite and Sunnite branches of the faith, has arisen in protest against political and social modernization and materialism. In the Iranian revolution, Islamic fundamentalism has also been associated with a distinctly antisecular outlook. This has led to manifestations Anti-Westernism and Anti-Americanism since the West in general and the United States in particular was closely associated with secular modernization in Iran.

Hinduism has continued to dominate the Indian subcontinent. Its adherents found themselves in strong opposition to the Muslims still living in India after the partition. More recently, major hostility has erupted between Hindus and adherents of the Sikh tradition which is one of the major religions of a minority of the population of India. Despite these well known conflicts, there are also examples of cooperation between the adherents of these major faiths.

Buddhism has maintained its enormous cultural presence in East Asia. Like other religions it has sometimes been associated with resistance of modern secular forms of life and to Western influences. In Korea during the late 1980s Buddhists were deeply involved with protests against the government. In Sri Lanka Buddhist monks became closely associated with the nationalist movement. Buddhist thought has influenced thinkers throughout the world in recent decades.

Jews emerged from the experience of the Holocaust of World War II with vigorous determination never again to find themselves victimized by the forces of anti-Semitism. The state of Israel became a homeland for Jews from around the world. Both inside and outside Israel recent years have witnessed a revival of Orthodox Judaism with emphasis on strict religious observance. Yet both Reform and Conservative Judaism continue to flourish.

Christianity has seen several remarkable modes of recent revival. The Roman Catholic Pope in the last quarter century has become a world figure travelling to all continents. Roman Catholicism has also become much more pluralistic than in earlier periods. In Eastern Europe it is very conservative politically whereas in Latin America many of its priests have advocated a vaguely or sometimes specifically Marxist outlook associated with Liberation Theology. Since the 1960s there has also emerged a major ecumenical movement throughout the Christian world that has witnessed unprecedented cooperation among Christian denominations.

In the United States Protestantism has often taken very political forms in the black community and among fundamentalists. Black ministers took the lead in the civil rights struggle of the 1960s and have remained politically active. White fundamentalists clergy have frequently advocated quite conservative political agendas and turned to television to spread their message.

Virtually all of the major religions find themselves struggling with the role of women in the life of faith, teaching, and practice. The new role of women in every area of the world has led to serious controversies that remain in many cases unresolved.

In the last decade of this century, perhaps the chief characteristic of all the practitioners of the major religious faiths is a desire to return toward what they regard as the fundamentals of the faith or toward very rigorous forms of religious practice. This has led to clashes within religious communities and sometimes between religious communities. But perhaps most significant it has led to spokesmen for various religions attacking modern secular or nonreligious culture and proposing distinctly different visions of humanity based on their particular religious traditions.

VI-1   Judaism. *An on-duty Israeli soldier prays alongside Orthodox Hassidim at the Wailing Wall in Jerusalem. [James Nachtwey/ Magnum.]*

VI-2 Judaism. *Israeli West Bank settlers read the Torah. [Alon Reininger/Contact Press.]*

VI-3 Buddhism. *Politics and religion mesh as Buddhists demonstrate against the government in South Korea in 1987. [Kim Newton/Woodfin Camp.]*

VI-4 Sikhdom. *In India Sikhs demonstrate for sovereignty at the Golden Temple or Akal Takht. [Raghu Rai/Magnum.]*

VI-5 Islam. *Led by the Ayatollah Khomeini, fundamentalist Muslims came to power after the Iranian Revolution. Inspired by Khomeini, Iran waged a long and costly war with neighboring Iraq. (Here Iraqi prisoners of war are shown at Friday prayers.) [Jean Gaumy/Magnum.]*

VI-6   Islam. *Modern Islam has also become a religion associated with television as the Koran is read to a television audience in Brunei. [Philip Jones Griffiths/Magnum.]*

VI-7   Islam. *In Baghdad, as in all Muslim lands, students study the Qur'an in mosques. [Steve McCurry/Magnum.]*

VI-8 Islam. *Wherever Muslims live, they continue to observe Islamic practices. These Muslims pray in the streets of Marseille, France. [J. Pavlovsky/Sygma.]*

VI-9 Islam. *Each year millions of Muslims make the pilgrimage to Mecca to pray at the most sacred shrine of the faith. [Robert Azzi/Woodfin Camp.]*

VI-10 Christianity. *In Tulsa, Oklahoma, evangelist Oral Roberts has constructed an impressive medical center before which stands the massive Hands of Faith sculpture.* [Steve McCurry/Magnum.]

VI-11 Christianity. *Evangelism has been popular among Protestants in the United States. At the Congress of the Holy Spirit meeting in New Orleans in 1987, numerous people lie on the floor after having been "slain in the spirit." [Steve McCurry/Magnum.]*

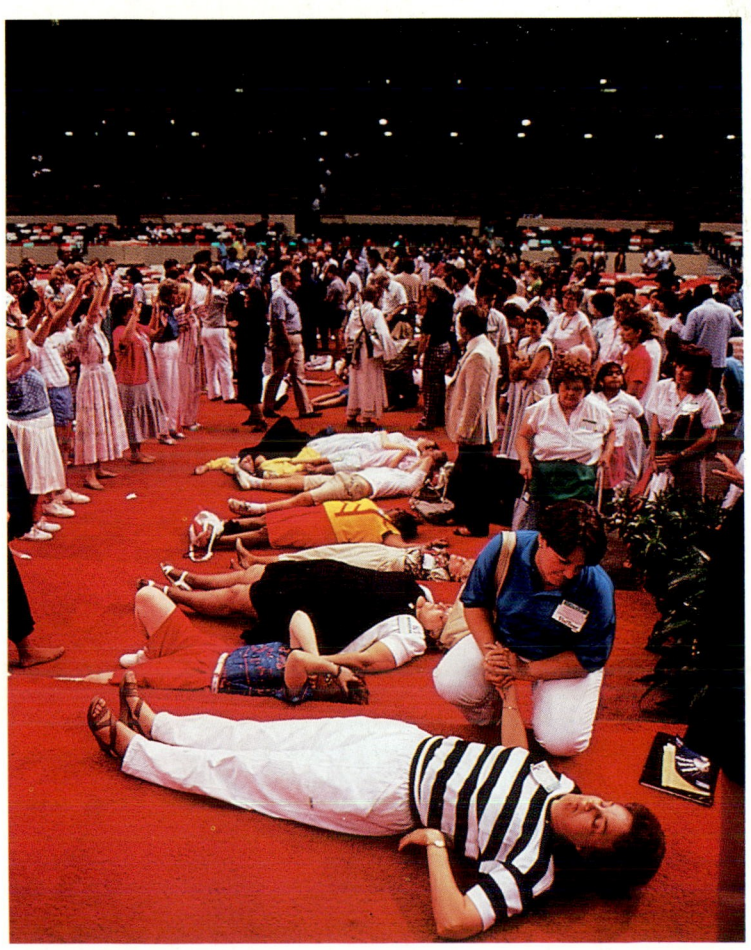

VI-12 Christianity. *Each year thousands of pilgrims visit the Roman Catholic shrine of Lourdes, France, in hope of receiving healing. [G. Rancinan/ Sygma.]*

VI-13 Christianity. *Pope John Paul II has made many overseas journeys to countries with large Catholic populations. (Here he visits Native Americans in Phoenix, Arizona in 1984.) [Kenneth Jarecke/Contact Press.]*

Palestinian youths confront Israeli troops March, 1988. The Palestinian uprising, Intifada ("shaking, tremor"), which began in December 1987, has continued for nearly two years. It marks the first widespread and sustained active resistance by West Bank Arabs to the long Israeli occupation of their territories. (Patrick Robert/SYGMA.)

truce between Israel and its neighbors and, at worst, open warfare. The most serious outbreaks occurred in 1956 over the Suez Canal, in the 1967 June War, in the October War of 1973, and in the Lebanese–Syrian conflict subsequent to the Israeli seizure of the Golan Heights (1981) and the Israeli invasions of Lebanon (1978, 1982). Even apart from overt war, bloodshed has been regular in and around Israel. The frustrations of disenfranchised and dispossessed Palestinians have been channeled repeatedly into guerrilla warfare against Israel. With mixed success, the Palestine Liberation Organization and other more radical groups have carried on a determined guerrilla battle within and along Israel's borders to the present day. It is a sad irony of history that these guerrillas have used terrorist tactics that Zionist extremists of the Stern Gang and the Irgun had employed so effectively against the British in Palestine to gain Israeli statehood originally.

Simultaneously, the corresponding frustrations of an embattled Israel have brought an increasing willingness on her part to resort to violent reprisals and preemptive military actions, both at home and abroad. Israel has responded to guerrilla attacks and civilian resistance with repressive measures against the Arab populations of the occupied territories, air and commando raids on Arab states thought to support Palestinian terrorism, and a hardline stance against negotiation over the status of the territories seized in 1967. Arab states have been equally intransigent about recognizing the legitimacy of the existence of Israel and dealing directly with her in trying to reach a long-term Middle-East solution. The notable exception was Egypt, under Gamal Abdel Nasser's successor, President Anwar Sadat (1918–1981). Sadat, in consonance with American initiatives, dealt directly with Israel between 1977 and his assassination in 1981 by Egyptian Muslim extremists.

Despite the 1978 Camp David Accords between Is-

Announcement of the historic Camp David Accords in 1978. Left to right, President Sadat of Egypt, President Carter, and Prime Minister Begin of Israel. [UPI.]

rael and Egypt, the next decade saw the bloody Israeli invasion and ensuing Lebanese war of 1982–1983, the continuing West Bank uprising of 1987–1989, and an unchanged Israeli determination to hold the West Bank and Jerusalem. These actions testify to the continuing lack of a solution to what is a tragic, debilitating, and morally as well as materially draining impasse for all the peoples of the area. In December 1988, Yassir Arafat, on behalf of the moderate wing of the Palestine Liberation Organization, moved to recognize Israel's right to exist. This offer seems to be countered by an uncompromising attitude in the Israeli government that leaves the two parties as far apart as ever.

The oil wealth of the Arab world has been another significant factor in the recent history of the region. Since Saudi Arabia's first oil production in 1939, the world demand for oil—for its industrial power and petroleum-based commodities—has grown by leaps and bounds. Especially in the past two decades, oil has become a major counter in international diplomacy; the Arab and other Third World states, such as Venezuela, Nigeria, Iran, and Indonesia, have used it as such. In the Arab countries of North Africa and especially of Arabia and the Gulf, oil production and wealth have brought about massive changes in every aspect of life. Oil has propelled formerly peripheral and virtually unknown countries of the Sahara or the Arabian deserts into major roles in the world of international banking and finance. Beyond the internal economic, social, and political consequences, one effect has been to boost the badly damaged self-confidence

of the Arab world after a century and a half of being effectively under the heel of the West.

This last effect of oil wealth should not be underestimated. It has coincided with a new round of Muslim efforts to revive pristine Muslim values and standards in order to reform present evils and failures in Muslim societies. In the spirit, and often in the footsteps, of earlier Muslim resurgences such as those of the eighteenth century in India, Arabia, and Africa, many Muslims have sought to return to the "fundamentals" of Islamic life, faith, and society. They too see this as a means of rejuvenation and defense against the encroachment of foreign, usually Western secularist, values and norms. Such fundamentalism has been seen in the Muslim Brethren movement in Egypt and elsewhere, as well as in the 1978 Iranian revolution. Whether such revivalist and fundamentalist movements can achieve lasting change in Islamic societies remains to be seen.

Iran and Central Asia

Iran had been ruled from 1925 to 1941 as a monarchy by a former army commander, Reza Khan, who had come to power by military takeover and governed under the old Persian title Shah Reza Pahlavi. He had attempted to introduce modernist economic, educational, and governmental reforms (not unlike his contemporary in Turkey, Atatürk, although his reforms were aimed at creating not a parliamentary, popularly based state, but a highly centralized monarchy). By the time Russian and British forces deposed Reza in 1941 and installed his son, Muhammad Reza, as shah, the power of the Shi'ite religious leaders, or *ulema*, had been effectively muted and a rather strong, centralized state established. The son, like his father, sought to ground the legitimacy of Pahlavi rule on the ancient, pre-Islamic imperial dynasties of greater Iran, especially that of the Achaemenids (see Chapter 7). He continued his father's basically secularist state-building from the end of World War II until 1978, with one interruption from 1951 to 1953. These two years saw Muhammad Mosaddeq come to power through a nationalist revolution, only to be overthrown in a counterrevolution that apparently had American and other outside support.

In the 1960s, Muhammed Reza Shah was finally forced by popular opposition, led by educated elites of the secular left and *ulema* of the religious right, to institute land- and other socialist or populist reforms. However, his cavalier attitude toward—and his violent repressive measures against—leftist and especially religious opposition did little to endear his regime to the Iranian masses. For all of the modernizing and the military and economic buildup that the Shah initiated, his reign failed to narrow the gap between the very wealthy elites and the very poor masses of his people. The fact that fully half of Iran's forty million inhabitants are non-Persian-speaking Turks, Kurds, Arabs, and other minorities did little to help consolidate and strengthen his nationalistic Iranian monarchy.

Finally, in 1978, religious leaders and secularist revolutionaries joined forces to end the shah's long regime with a revolution fueled largely by Shi'ite Islamic feeling and symbolism. In 1979, the constitution of a new Islamic republic was adapted under the guidance of the major Shi'ite religious leader, or *ayatollah*, Ruhollah Khomeini (Khumayni; b. 1902). Subsequent years have seen a protracted war with Iraq (halted only in 1988 by a truce agreement) and the institution of repressive and violent measures against enemies of the new regime not unlike those used under the shah. Still, the new state has survived up to now. It must face not only the same problems as the shah before it, but also the unprecedented (at least since the early Safavid rule of the sixteenth century) role of political leadership for the religious leaders of the Iranian community. No longer able to stand untainted by the dirt of politics, Khomeini and his religious cohorts must find a new formula for combining Muslim values and norms with twentieth-century *Realpolitik*.

North of Iran, forty million central Asian Muslims (over one sixth of the total population) make up the large majority of the Soviet peoples across the south-central reaches of the USSR between the Crimea and China. These people have had to hold to their religious and intellectual traditions in the face of Russian cultural, linguistic, and political imperialism, as have the thirty million or more Muslims in Chinese central Asia. In the 1980s, both Soviet and Chinese Muslims

Ayatollah Khomeini upon return from exile. This photo, taken in Teheran February 3, 1979, shows the Iranian resistance leader greeting several thousand women come to cheer him after his return to Iran two days before. Two days later, he created the Islamic Revolutionary Council to govern Iran in the wake of the flight of the Shah in mid January. (Alain Keler/SYGMA.)

appeared to be asserting themselves as Muslims. The potential importance of this movement is reflected in the 1979 Soviet invasion and occupation of Afghanistan, whose people have close ties to the Muslim peoples in the Soviet Union itself. If the fierce Afghan resistance to the occupation is any indication, the last may not have been heard of them or their coreligionists in the Soviet Union. The 1988 phased withdrawal of Soviet forces from Afghanistan looks surprisingly like the United States' withdrawal from South Vietnam in 1974. Its consequences, either for Afghanistan itself, or for its neighbors, have yet to be seen.

The Indian Subcontinent and the East Indies

At least four major nations, together containing more than half of all the Muslims in the world, have come into being since World War II. They now dominate the South and Southeast Asian world, apart from Indochina (where foreign presences—chiefly French, American, Russian, and Chinese—have been so prominent as to determine to an unusual degree the area's postwar history). These four are India, Pakistan, Indonesia, and Malaysia.

India and Pakistan were created as separate countries with the granting of independence and the agreement to a "partition" of the subcontinent by the British in 1947. Much of their subsequent history has been dominated by the rivalry and mutual antagonism of the largely Hindu Indian state and the largely Muslim Pakistani state. These rivalries were born out of the Hindu–Muslim communal violence and the disputes over Kashmir and other border areas that accompanied the partition.

The architect and first president of Pakistan, Muhammad Ali Jinnah (d. 1948), oversaw the creation of a Muslim state comprising the widely separated East and West Pakistan in the two predominantly Muslim areas of the northwest and East Bengal. The tragedy

Jawharlal Nehru Looks to the Future (1945)

Jawharlal Nehru wrote The Discovery of India *while he was imprisoned at Ahmadnagar Fort during the latter part of World War II (as he had been several times before, for his nationalist activities). The book was an attempt to probe the past and present circumstances of the vast, diverse Indian world. The following excerpt comes late in the book, where he looks ahead. His words show the dilemma and opportunity of not only India but many other new nations of the past forty years who have had to face an uncertain future with meager resources and dubious, if powerful and seductive, models among the powerful nations of the modern world.*

The world of today has achieved much, but for all its declared love for humanity, it has based itself far more on hatred and violence than on the virtues that make man human. War is the negation of truth and humanity. War may be unavoidable sometimes, but its progeny are terrible to contemplate. Not mere killing, for man must die, but the deliberate and persistent propagation of hatred and falsehood, which gradually become the normal habits of the people. It is dangerous and harmful to be guided in our life's course by hatreds and aversions, for they are wasteful of energy and limit and twist the mind and prevent it from perceiving the truth. Unhappily there is hatred in India and strong aversions, for the past pursues us and the present does not differ from it. It is not easy to forget repeated affronts to the dignity of a proud race. Yet, fortunately, Indians do not nourish hatred for long; they recover easily a more benevolent mood.

India will find herself again when freedom opens out new horizons and the future will then fascinate her far more than the immediate past of frustration and humiliation. She will go forward with confidence, rooted in herself and yet eager to learn from others and co-operate with them. Today she swings between a blind adherence to her old customs and a slavish imitation of foreign ways. In neither of these can she find relief or life or growth. It is obvious that she has to come out of her shell and take full part in the life and activities of the modern age. It should be equally obvious that there can be no real cultural or spiritual growth based on imitation. Such imitation can only be confined to a small number who cut themselves off from the masses and the springs of national life. True culture derives its inspiration from every corner of the world, but it is home-grown and has to be based on the wide mass of the people. Art and literature remain lifeless if they are continually thinking of foreign models. The day of a narrow culture confined to a small fastidious group is past. We have to think in terms of the people generally and their culture must be a continuation and development of past trends, and must also represent their new urges and creative tendencies. ❑

Robert I. Crane (ed.), *The Discovery of India*, (Garden City, NY: Doubleday, Anchor Books, 1959), pp. 414–415.

Lord Mountbatten, the last Viceroy of India, announcing Indian and Pakistani independence in August 1947. [UPI.]

of the massive displacement of Muslims from the new India and of Hindus and Sikhs from the new Pakistan (about eight million people in each case) was and still is an immense one for millions of families and individuals. The two new states have survived for over thirty-five years, albeit without resolving major differences, such as their conflicting claims to Kashmir. In 1971, the less affluent and politically disadvantaged area of East Pakistan seceded, largely as a result of Indian military intervention, and became the new Islamic nation of Bangladesh. Indian and Bangladeshi relations have been troubled by a number of disputes ever since. However, the main division in the subcontinent remains that between India and Pakistan.

Pakistan's groping efforts to create a fully Islamic society and to solve its massive economic problems have been hampered by periodic lapses from constitutional republicanism into dictatorship. Such lapses are usually punctuated by bloodshed and military coups, the most recent being that which brought the military

For most of its independent period, India has been led by prime ministers from the same family: Jawaharlal Nehru, his daughter Indira Gandhi, and after her assassination in 1985, her son Rajiv Gandhi. Nehru was the political heir of the Mahatma and led India until his death in 1964. Indira Gandhi, who was prime minister for most of the next two decades, was an astute leader, adept at both international rivalry and domestic politics. [UPI/Bettmann Newsphotos.]

leader, Zia ul-Haqq, to power in 1977. The elections of November 1988, following the death of Zia ul-Haqq in a suspicious air crash, have opened the door to the possible success of a parliamentary government's rule. The new Prime Minister, Benazir Bhutto, is the daughter of the man Zia ul-Haqq overthrew and executed. She is also the first female leader of a major Islamic state in this century. Amidst the economic and political problems facing the Pakistanis, it remains to be seen whether they can work out a system that will meet their physical needs while allowing them to remain true to their personal faith and their commitment to an identifiably Islamic society.

India, bereft of its spiritual and material father, Mohandas Gandhi, after his assassination in 1948, has been directed for most of its lifespan by the leaders of Gandhi's Congress Party. First came Gandhi's follower and cohort, Jawaharlal Nehru (1889–1964), then Nehru's daughter, Indira Gandhi (prime minister, 1966–1977, 1980–1984), who was assassinated by Sikh extremists. Both managed to steer a tricky course of neutralism in the 1950s Cold War and amidst subsequent East–West tensions. Indira Gandhi's son, Rajiv Gandhi, was elected prime minister in the wake of her death. His handling of the very thorny Sikh issue has been generally applauded. Indications that he and Prime Minister Bhutto may work concertedly to resolve some of the old India–Pakistan hostilities are especially noteworthy.

Still, India's problems remain large. The vast Indian state has been divided and administered internally largely on the basis of the linguistic affinities of particular regions. Along with the overwhelming problems of overpopulation and poverty, separatist movements based on linguistic affinity, such as that of the Tamil peoples of the south, or religious affinity, such as that of the Sikhs of the Punjab, have pulled at the unity of the Indian state. Industrialization and agricultural modernization have made great strides in recent years. Yet the neutralizing force of runaway population growth has yet to be countered effectively enough to ensure a brighter future for India.

Indonesia came into being in 1949 as a nominal republic succeeding the long Dutch and the brief Japanese colonial dominion in the East Indies. Malaya received its independence from British colonial rule in 1957 as a federation under a rotating monarch; it was later joined by the states of Sarawak and Sabah in northern Borneo, forming the federation of Malaysia. Each of these two new sovereign states faces different kinds of problems.

Indonesia, the largest Muslim country in the world (about 130 of its 150 million people are Muslim), is trying to achieve a consensus among its disparate and scattered parts. It must determine how Muslim religious faith is to be reconciled with secularist govern-ment. Malaysia's overriding problem has been the cleft between the largely Chinese and partly Indian non-Muslim minority, and the largely Muslim Malay majority. Both nations have rich cultural traditions and natural resources; it remains to be seen how each will choose to preserve these while meeting the demands of modern global politics and participation in the global economy. An important part of the future of Islam as a global religious and cultural tradition, as well as the future of these two Asian states, is at stake.

Latin America since 1945

During the last forty years, the nations of Latin America have experienced divergent paths of political and economic change. Their leaders have attempted numerous policies to remove the peoples of the continent from their state of dependence on the more developed portions of the globe. At best, these efforts have had mixed results; at worst, they have led to political repression and human tragedy.

Before World War II, the states of Latin America stood in economically dependent relationships to the United States and the countries of western Europe. Since the 1950s, a shift has occurred in those dependent relationships without any significant change in the general situation of dependency. The United States looms larger than ever before; at the same time, the Soviet Union has come to play a far larger economic and political role. In that respect, Latin America, like so many other parts of the world, has come to dwell in the shadow of the rival superpowers. And as elsewhere, Latin America has been the arena for direct confrontations between the United States and the Soviet Union.

The economic life of the region has reflected these new facts of dependence. Various attempts have been made to expand the industrial base and the agricultural production of the various national economies. Virtually all the financing has come from U.S. and West European banks or from Soviet subsidies. In the case of the former, enormous debts have been undertaken, and these debts have made the economies involved virtually prisoners to the fluctuations of world interest rates and the international banking community. Subsidies and special market arrangements with the Soviet Union have made other nations no less dependent on outside economic forces. Despite these new relationships of economic dependence, the various national economies remain overwhelmingly exporters of agricultural commodities and mineral resources.

The social structures of the Latin American nations have become more complicated since World War II. A culture of poverty continues to be the single most dominant social characteristic of the area. Even periods of economic boom, such as the one fostered in Mexico by oil production in the late 1970s, have proved brief and have almost inevitably been followed by years of decline. Migration into the cities from the countryside has caused in Latin America, as elsewhere in the developing world, tremendous urban overcrowding and slums inhabited by very poor people. In many countries, the standards of health and of nutrition have fallen. At the same time, the growth of service industries in the cities has fostered the emergence of a professional, educated middle class, often possessed of a strong desire to imitate the affluent lifestyle of their social counterparts in the United States and Western Europe. This new professional middle class has displayed little taste for radical politics, major social reform, or revolution. They and the more traditional landed and industrial elites have been willing to support military governments pledged to order and the maintenance of the status quo.

Political events in Latin America have led to the establishment of authoritarian governments of both the left and the right and to a retreat from the ideal and model of parliamentary democracy. Of the major states, only Mexico, Colombia, and Venezuela remain parliamentary states. Elsewhere, two paths of political development have been followed. In Cuba and Nicaragua, and for a short time in Chile, revolutionary socialist governments with close ties to the Soviet Union have been established. Elsewhere, often in response to the fear of revolution or Communist activity, military governments have held power for long periods, sometimes punctuated with brief interludes of civilian rule. Such has been the situation in Chile, Brazil, Argentina, Bolivia, Peru, and Uruguay. Governments of both the left and the right have pursued policies of political repression, the suspension of civil liberties, and the arrest of perceived political enemies.

These political changes have fostered new roles for two traditional Latin American institutions: the military and the Roman Catholic church. The armies of the various nations have played key political roles ever since the wars of independence. But in recent years, they have frequently assumed the direct government of nations rather than using indirect influence. In the clash between the forces of social revolution and reaction, a significant number of Roman Catholic priests and bishops have become politically active in protesting social and economic inequalities and in attacking the use of repression against opposition political forces. Certain Roman Catholic theologians have combined traditional Christian ideas of concern for the poor with Marxist ideology to formulate what has come to be known as a *liberation theology.* Generally speaking, this Latin American theological initiative has received a very critical response from Roman Catholic authorities in the Vatican.

Revolutionary Challenges

There have been three major attempts among the nations of Latin America to establish genuinely revolutionary governments pursuing major social and economic change. These occurred in Cuba in 1959, in Chile in 1970, and in Nicaragua in 1979. Each of them involved some form of Marxist political organization, and each revolutionary government has pursued a close relationship with the Soviet Union. All three revolutionary Marxist situations have achieved immense symbolic importance not only in Latin America but also anywhere the colonial influence of Europeans and the economic dominance of the United States once prevailed. The establishment of these governments has provoked active resistance and intervention on the part of the United States. It has encouraged opposition to social and political change on the part of traditional elites throughout Latin America.

THE CUBAN REVOLUTION. Cuba had remained a colony of Spain until the Spanish-American War of 1898. Thereafter, it achieved independence within a sphere of U.S. influence, which took the form of economic domination and occasional military intervention. The fluctuating governments of the island had been both ineffective and corrupt. During the 1950s, Fulgencio Batista (1901–1973), a dictator supported by the U.S. government, ruled Cuba.

Over the decades, there had been much political unrest in Cuba. During the 1940s, various university student groups led antigovernment agitation. Among the students thus politicized in those years was Fidel Castro Ruz (b. 1926), the son of a wealthy landowner. On July 26, 1953, he and others unsuccessfully attacked a government army barracks. The revolutionary movement that he came to lead in exile took its name from that date: the Twenty-sixth of July Movement. In 1956, Castro and a handful of followers set sail on a yacht from Mexico and landed in Cuba. They took refuge in the Sierra Maestra mountains, from which they organized guerrilla attacks on Batista's government and supporters. By late 1958, Castro's forces were in a position to topple Batista, who fled Cuba on New Year's Day in 1959. By the middle of the month, Castro had arrived in Havana as the revolutionary victor.

Castro undertook the most extensive political, economic, and social reconstruction seen in recent Latin American history. He rejected parliamentary democracy and chose to govern Cuba in an authoritarian manner. For approximately the first decade of the revolution, he ruled in a very personal manner; by the early 1970s, though Castro continued to dominate,

Fidel Castro, as the successful guerrilla leader, at the time of his triumph over the Batista regime in 1959. [UPI.]

executive power was vested in a council. The revolutionary government carried out major land redistribution. In some cases, groups of relatively small landowners were established. On other parts of the island, large state farms became the model.

Perhaps most interesting, the Cuban Revolution spurned an industrial economic model and concentrated on improving the agricultural sector. There was an attempt to turn toward more mixed agriculture, but in the end, the production of sugar assumed its traditionally leading role. The Cuban economy remained that of a monoculture. Throughout the 1960s, there was a concerted effort to expand sugar production. The results were disappointing, as too much was attempted too quickly by people who had had too little direct experience in raising and processing sugar cane. Even after the sugar industry became somewhat more stabilized during the 1970s, it continued to depend on large Soviet subsidies and on the Soviet-bloc nations for its market. In that respect, the Cuban economy did not escape the cycle of external dependence.

In foreign affairs, the Cuban Revolution was characterized by a sharp break with the United States and a close relationship with the Soviet Union. Very shortly after achieving power, Castro aligned himself with the Cuban Communist Party and thereafter with the Soviet bloc. The United States, under both Republican and Democratic administrations, pursued a policy of hostility toward Castro and toward the presence of a Communist state less than a hundred miles from

the Florida mainland. In 1961, the United States and Cuban exiles launched the unsuccessful Bay of Pigs invasion. The close Cuban relationship to the Soviet Union prepared the ground for the missile crisis of 1962. Thereafter followed about a decade of cool relations without overt acts of hostility. During the late 1970s and the 1980s, a dialogue of sorts was undertaken between Cuba and the United States, but formal diplomatic relations have not resumed. An atmosphere of mutual distrust continues.

Perhaps most important, ever since 1959, Cuba has served as a center for the export of Communist revolution throughout Latin America and, in the case of the sending of Cuban troops to Angola in the late 1970s, in Africa as well. A key policy of the U.S. government, pursued with differing intensities and strategies under different administrations, has been the prevention of the establishment of a second Cuba or Communist-dominated state in Latin America. That goal has led to direct and indirect intervention in other revolutionary situations and to support for authoritarian governments in Latin America dedicated to resistance to Marxist revolution.

THE CASE OF CHILE. Until the past two decades, Chile stood as the single, most-enduring model of parliamentary democracy in Latin America. It had experienced political turmoil and governments of the left and the right, but the parliamentary structures had remained in place. During the 1960s, however, as economic life became more difficult and class relation-

Castro Asserts the Necessary Marxist Character of Revolution

In a speech delivered at the University of Havana in 1967 Fidel Castro discussed the relationship of Cuban revolutionaries to the wider Marxist ideology. He asserted that the revolutionary struggle itself led to the embracing of a strict Marxism. He rejected cooperation with groups that sought reform rather than revolution even if they called themselves Communist. At the same time he opened the way for accepting into the revolutionary movement those who had finally come to accept Marxism even if that political outlook had not been their original position.

Anyone can give himself the name of "eagle" without having a single feather on his back. In the same way, there are people who call themselves communists without having a communist hair on their heads. The international communist movement, to our way of thinking, is not a church. It is not a religious sect or a Masonic lodge that obliges us to hallow any weakness, any deviation; that obliges us to follow a policy of a mutual admiration with all kinds of reformists and pseudo-revolutionaries.

Our stand regarding communist parties will be based on strictly revolutionary principles. The parties that have a line without hesitations and capitulationism, the parties that in our opinion have a consistent revolutionary line, will receive our support in all circumstances; but the parties that entrench themselves behind the name of communists or Marxists and believe themselves to have a monopoly on revolutionary sentiment—what they really monopolize is reformism—will not be treated by us as revolutionary parties. . . . For every true revolutionary, who bears within him the revolutionary spirit, revolutionary vocation, will always come to Marxism! It is impossible for a man, traveling the road of revolution, not to arrive at Marxism! And every revolutionary on the continent who is deserving of the name will arrive at the Marxist conception of society! What is important are the revolutionaries, those who are capable of making revolution and developing themselves in revolutionary theory.

Many times practice comes first and then theory. Our people too, are an example of that. Many, the immense majority of those who today proudly call themselves Marxist-Leninists, arrived at Marxism-Leninism by way of the revolutionary struggle. To exclude, to deny, to reject a priori all those who from the beginning did not call themselves communists is an act of dogmatism and unqualified sectarianism. Whoever denies that it is the road of revolution which leads the people to Marxism is no Marxist, although he may call himself a communist. ❑

Martin Kenner and James Petras, *Fidel Castro Speaks* (New York: Grove Press, 1969), p. 131.

Salvador Allende. A Marxist socialist, Allende was President of Chile from 1970 until he was overthrown and killed in a military coup in 1973. [UPI/Bettmann Newsphotos.]

ships deteriorated, Chilean politics likewise became polarized. Unemployment became rampant. There was much labor unrest and profound popular resentment of the economic domination of Chile by large U.S. corporations.

The situation came to a head in 1970 when Salvador Allende (1908–1973), the candidate of the left-wing political coalition and a Marxist, was elected president with a plurality of the votes. His coalition did not control the Chilean Congress, nor did it have the support of the military. For a few months, the center and right-wing political groups took a watch-and-wait attitude. Allende nationalized some businesses. Other policies, related to land redistribution, wage improvement, and resistance to foreign economic influence, were blocked in the Congress, and Allende had to govern by decree. By this latter device, he began to expropriate foreign property, much of which belonged to U.S. corporations. This policy frightened the Chilean owners of small and medium-sized businesses. Workers were dissatisfied with the relatively small extent of socialization touching their daily lives. Inflation ballooned. Despite the expropriation of large estates and the reorganization of agriculture, the harvests were poor.

In the autumn of 1973, Allende found himself governing a nation in turmoil without significant domestic political support and with many foreign enemies. He proved unwilling to make significant political compromises or to change the general course of his policies. In the wake of strikes and disorder, the army became very hostile. The government of the United States was deeply disturbed by the Allende experiment and by the prospect of a Marxist nation on the western coast of South America. The Nixon administration consequently actively supported the discontent within the Chilean army. In mid-September 1973, an army coup overthrew Allende, who was killed in the air-force bombing of the presidential palace. Chile's short-lived experiment in Marxist socialism came to an end.

Thereafter, Chile for fifteen years was governed by a military junta, whose most important member General Augusto Pinochet (b. 1915) served as president. The military government pursued a close relationship with the United States and a policy of strong resistance to Marxism in the hemisphere. The junta followed a policy of state-directed free-market economy. The expropriations of the Allende years were reversed. After a brief period of economic improvement, inflation and unemployment resumed. The rule of the Chilean military was marked by policies of political repression. However, in late 1988 a referendum in Chile rejected Pinochet's bid for another term as president. At that time, preparations began for a return to more nearly normal party politics. Whether that transition will be accomplished and democratic stability restored remains to be seen. If it is accomplished, it would provide a major example of what may become a major movement in the region toward redemocratization.

THE SANDINISTA REVOLUTION IN NICARAGUA. In the summer of 1979, a Marxist guerrilla force, the Sandinistas, overthrew the corrupt dictatorship of the Somoza family in Nicaragua. This family had governed the small Central American nation more or less as its own personal preserve since the 1930s, with moderate, but rarely enthusiastic, support from the United States. The Sandinistas established a collective government in Managua that has pursued a policy of social and economic reform and reconstruction. The movement epitomizes the new political and social forces in Latin America in that Roman Catholic priests have served on the leadership council. The exact direction of the revolutionary government remains somewhat unclear because it has confronted significant domestic political opposition and direct military challenge from the *contra* guerrilla movement.

The government of the United States, particularly under the Reagan administration, has taken a strongly hostile attitude toward the Sandinistas. It has attempted to provide both direct and indirect aid to the

Jubilant Sandinistas celebrating the overthrow of the Somoza dictatorship in June 1979. [UPI.]

opposition guerrilla movement and has repeatedly criticized the revolutionary government. The U.S. government has feared the spread of Marxist revolutionary activity into the other states of Central America. This fear has been confirmed by the close ties between the revolutionary government and the Soviet Union. In the eyes of the U.S. government, the Sandinista government represents in Central America a problem analogous to that of Cuba a generation ago. Clearly the revolutionary victory in Nicaragua is much less certain than that of Castro in 1959. But it remains to be seen whether the U.S. attempts to destabilize the Sandinistas will fail as in Cuba or succeed as in Chile. It also remains to be seen whether the situation in Nicaragua will become the occasion for new tensions between the United States and the Soviet Union in this hemisphere.

Pursuit of Stability under the Threat of Revolution

ARGENTINA. In 1955, the Argentine army revolted against the excesses and corruption of the Perón dictatorship, and Juan Perón went into exile. Thereafter followed two decades of economic stagnation and social unrest. Neither the army nor civilian political leaders were able to forge the kind of political coalition involving the working class that Perón had created. Nor could any of the post-Perón governments successfully address the issues of unemployment and inflation. In 1973, Perón was recalled from exile in a desperate attempt to restore the fragile stability of a generation earlier. He died about a year later.

By 1976, the army had undertaken direct rule. There was much repression of the civilian population, and thousands of citizens simply disappeared, never to be heard of again. The leading army officers played something like a game of musical chairs as members of the ever-changing junta. In April 1982, General Leopoldo Galtieri, in an effort to score some kind of political success, launched the disastrous invasion of the Islas Malvinas (Falkland Islands). Argentina was decisively defeated by Britain, and the military junta was thoroughly discredited.

In 1983, civilian rule was restored and Argentina set out on the road to redemocritization. The major political leader responsible for this achievement is President Raúl Alfonsín (b. 1927). Under his leadership, many of the former military figures responsible for the years of repression received prison sentences. Civilian courts took over the role formerly assigned to military tribunals. Alfonsin also sought to turn more real political authority over to the Argentine Congress. In all respects, Argentina has provided the most extensive example in Latin America of the restoration of democratic practices after a period of military rule. In 1989

peaceful elections led to the victory of a Peronist party candidate for the presidency. The challenge that will now face Argentina is the transition between parties.

BRAZIL. In Brazil, a similar path to direct military rule was trod. In 1950, Vargas had returned to power on the understanding that the military would remain neutral. After his suicide in 1954, the Brazilian army came to play an increasingly large role in Brazilian politics. By the spring of 1964, the military assumed the direct government of the nation and has continued to play that role to the present day. The military government has pursued a political policy of order and has used repression wherever necessary. The government has also pursued a policy of denationalized industrial development. That is to say, non-Brazilian corporations have been invited to spearhead the drive toward industrialization. In this respect, Brazil has opted for an industrial model, but for industrialism guided and dominated from the outside.

One result has been the accumulation of a massive foreign debt, the servicing and repayment of which has become perhaps the single most important national problem. At the same time, the relative success of the government's industrialization policy has made Brazil the major industrialized nation in Latin America. The great question now is the manner in which the social

Brasilia, the capital of Brazil. Built in the 1960s from an empty wilderness, Brasilia was designed as an ultramodern city, the symbol of the late-twentieth century economic development of Brazil. [Magnum.]

changes wrought by industrialism, such as growing urbanization, will receive political accommodation. In Brazil, as in Argentina, the economic and social pressures of the society have spawned conditions ripe for revolutionary agitation. It is just that possibility that has led so many citizens within both the traditional and the new professional elites to support authoritarian government. In 1985, a civilian government was restored under the watchful eye of the military.

MEXICO. Until 1959, Mexico stood as the foremost example of revolutionary change in Latin America. But since 1959, the ideology of Marxist revolution has displaced the goals of the Mexican Revolution as the agenda for social and political change in the region.

Institutionally, Mexico has undergone relatively few political changes since World War II. In theory at least, the goals of the revolution continue to be pursued by the government, which remains firmly in the control of the *Partido Revolucionario Institucional* (PRI). Yet there have been shifts under this apparently stable surface. The government has retreated from some of the aims of the revolution and appears conservative when compared to the new revolutionary states. In the early 1950s, certain large landowners were exempted from the expropriation and redistribution of land. The Mexican government has maintained open relations with Cuba and the other revolutionary regimes of Latin America but has, at the same time, resisted any intrusion of Marxist doctrines into the country. When necessary, it has arrested political malcontents.

Economically, the most important development was the brief oil boom from 1977 to 1983. Oil revenues brought immense new wealth into the nation, but the world oil glut burst that balloon. In the aftermath, what became revealed was the absence of any policy of stable growth. Like so many other states in the region, Mexico has amassed large foreign debts and, in doing so, has surrendered real economic independence.

In 1988, the PRI received a major challenge at the polls. Opposition candidates received a large proportion of the vote in a hotly contested election. Whether the election results were honestly reported may never be known. The PRI remained in power but with the knowledge that it would not be able to dominate the political scene in the manner it had for over half a century.

What is most striking about the past four decades of Latin American history is the tragic continuity of its previous history. Revolution has brought moderate social change, but at the price of continuous authoritarian government, economic stagnation, and dependence on different foreign powers. Real independence

has not been achieved. Throughout the region for much of the period, parliamentary democracy has been at best fragile; it appears to be the first element of national life to be sacrificed to the conflicting goals of socialism, economic growth, or resistance to revolution. The trend toward redemocratization of the past few years may mark a break in that previous tendency.

Postwar East Asia

Some East Asian nations became Communist but have achieved only a small improvement in the conditions of their peoples. In stark contrast are those nations that used a mixture of state guidance and market-oriented economies to make the region as a whole the most dynamic in the postwar world. Japan led the way, achieving economic growth that has often been spoken of as miraculous but that can more sensibly be described as singleminded. Japan has also developed into a robust parliamentary democracy with freedoms comparable to those of Western Europe or the United States.

Taiwan and South Korea have until recently lacked the political freedom of Japan. But despite their dictatorial governments, they have enjoyed some social and intellectual freedoms and stunning economic successes. The latter has been true in the tiny British colony of Hong Kong and the even tinier ex-British colony of Singapore. When we view the progress of these countries, it would appear that the values of the East Asian heritage—hard work, frugality, a family orientation, a thirst for education, and a concern for getting ahead—lead almost automatically to economic development if given half a chance.

China, in contrast, has achieved little per capita growth. In spite of having reunified an area roughly comparable to that of the Ch'ing Empire and of having lost the burden of the unequal treaties (from 1943 actually), China has been unable to tap the immense energies and talents of its people. Vietnam, because of endemic wars, has done worse. North Korea, where most of the industry of Japan's prewar colony was located, has done better and has become the East Germany of Asia, though its per capita product is less than half that of South Korea.

China

The story of China after 1949 might begin with the four Ma's: Malthus, Marx, Ma Yin-ch'u (Ma Yinchu), and Mao Tse-tung (Mao Zedong). Malthus said that population would expand geometrically whereas food would increase only arithmetically. Marx rejected the Malthusian hypothesis, along with classical economics, as myths of capitalism. Professor Ma Yin-ch'u (1882–1982), the chancellor of Peking University, published in 1957 *New Principles on Chinese Population*; in it he argued that unchecked population growth would impede capital accumulation and depress living standards. Mao Tse-tung, faithfully following the teachings of Marx, purged Ma and closed down population institutes at Chinese universities. There followed a population increase from 550 million in 1949, to 657 million in 1957, to over a billion during the early 1980s. To combat this crisis of overpopulation, China adopted in 1981 a policy of one child per family. It recognized that the policy ran contrary to the deep-rooted Chinese sense of family but argued that otherwise China's future would be bleak.

More mouths ate up real economic gains, however, and despite impressive gains after 1978, China in the mid-1980s was still one of the poorest countries in the world. Using the rough yardstick of gross national product divided by population, Chinese per capita product in 1986 was $260. Bangladesh ($150) was poorer; India ($270) was about the same. Other countries often regarded as poor were, statistically at least, better off: Pakistan ($320), Indonesia ($430), Zimbabwe ($510), Philippines ($570), and Thailand ($790). Taiwan, to which the Chinese Nationalists had fled in 1949, achieved substantial growth and a per capita product of $3630—fourteen times that of China. Hong Kong's 1986 per capita product ($4270) was sixteen times greater, one reason for its ambivalence about the prospect of rejoining China in 1997.

THE SOVIET PERIOD (1950–1960). The People's Republic of China was proclaimed in October 1949. The following year, the Sino-Soviet Alliance was signed. The decade that followed is often called the *Soviet period* because the Soviet model was adopted for the government, the army, the economy, and higher education.

The first step was military consolidation. Even after the republic was proclaimed, Chinese armies continued to push outward, conquering vast areas with non-Chinese populations. Tibet was invaded in 1950. Once subdued, the areas inhabited by Uighur Turks, Mongols, Tibetans, and other minorities were designated "autonomous regions." Though the regional governments were mostly composed of the minority, they were tightly controlled by the Chinese Communist Party. The regions were occupied by the Chinese army and were often settled by large numbers of Chinese immigrants, a settlement that changed their ethnic complexion. Policies toward minorities reflected changes in Peking.

Political consolidation followed. The most powerful elite was the Communist Party. Its members held the key positions in both the government and the army. Mao was both the chairman of the party and the head of state. The party expanded from 2.7 million members in 1947 to 17 million in 1961. Ultimate power in the party was exercised by the Standing Committee of the Political Bureau (Politburo) of the Central Committee. Below this were regional, provincial, and district committees with branches in every "unit": villages, factories, and schools. Every Chinese was a member of a unit. At these various levels, the party energized and policed the government's administration of its policies.

Economic reconstruction began immediately. An attempt was made to integrate the industries of Manchuria and the former treaty ports with the rest of China. Huge numbers of workers were mobilized to build new bridges, dams, roads, and railways. A major achievement of the new regime was to end fam-

Mao Tse-tung chatting with Soviet premier Nikita Khrushchev in Moscow in 1958. By this time the Sino-Soviet alliance was already beginning to fray. [UPI/Bettmann Newsphotos.]

ine in China. Before 1949 the regional economies had been sufficiently separate so that one could prosper while another starved. China's first five-year plan for economic development began in 1953. The Soviet Union sent financial aid as well as engineers and planners.

One vital change of the postwar years was the remaking of rural society. Teams of Communist cadres visited villages and held meetings at which landlords were denounced and made to confess their crimes. Some were rehabilitated, others were sent to labor camps, and hundreds of thousands—some scholars estimate several million—were killed. The landlord holdings were redistributed to the landless. The local responsibilities formerly borne by the landlord gentry were shifted to peasant associations in which the formerly landless peasants were prominent. Two years later, in 1955 and 1956, before the new landowners could entrench themselves, all lands were taken away from individual landowners and collectivized. The process reached its peak with the formation of communes in 1958. The effects on production were so disastrous, however, that the basic accounting unit was shifted back to production brigades in 1959, and two years later, to production teams of forty households. Even with these changes, the ills of low incentives and collective responsibility continued until 1978, with agricultural production only barely managing to keep up, with population growth.

During the second half of the 1950s, Sino-Soviet relations took a turn for the worse. One reason was ideological. From the start, the new government had attempted to remold the thinking of the Chinese people— the Chinese slang term for the process was *brainwashing*. It involved study and indoctrination, group pressures to produce an atmosphere of insecurity and fear, followed by confession, repentance, and reacceptance by society. The indoctrination was intended to strengthen party control. But beyond this was the optimistic belief (which some Western scholars saw as rooted in China's Confucian past) that the inculcation of correct moral doctrines could mobilize human energies on behalf of the revolution. In 1956, satisfied that even intellectuals had been adequately indoctrinated and concerned lest creativity be stifled, Mao said in a speech, "Let the hundred flowers bloom." A torrent of criticism broke forth, which extended even to the Communist Party. Then, an antirightist campaign was mounted, and many leading writers and intellectuals were purged and sent to labor camps.

In 1958, Mao took ideology a step further and abandoned a second five-year plan (and the Soviet model) in favor of a spiritual mobilization for economic development. He called it the Great Leap Forward. Mass campaigns were set to work on vast projects. Instant industries, backyard smelters, and communes were

the order of the day. The Great Leap Forward was condemned as "leftist fanaticism" by the Soviet Union, which also disapproved of Mao's view of himself, following the death of Stalin, as the foremost theoretician and exponent of world Communism. China, for its part, was embarrassed by the Soviet debunking of Stalin's cult of personality because within China, Mao was still venerated as the "great helmsman."

There were also disputes over borders. In 1960, the Soviet Union halted its economic aid and withdrew its engineers from China. This action led to a further deterioration in the relationship between the two great Communist states. Each country deployed about a million troops along its mutual border—forces that would have been used elsewhere had the relationship been amicable. The Sino-Soviet split was arguably the most important development in postwar international relations.

The years between 1960 and 1965 saw conflicting trends. The utter failure of the Great Leap Forward and the consequent widespread hunger and malnutrition led away from Mao's utopian mass line toward a more moderate economic policy. Mao retained his position as the head of the party but gave up his post as head of state to another veteran Communist bureaucrat. Yet even as the government moved toward more stable bureaucratic management, General Lin Piao (Lin Biao) reestablished within the army the party committees and procedures for ideological indoctrination that had lapsed during the late 1950s.

THE GREAT PROLETARIAN CULTURAL REVOLUTION (1965–1976). In 1965, Mao once again emerged to dominate Chinese politics. The key to the events that followed was Mao himself. Mao the revolutionary had never been able to make the transition to head of an established state. He looked at the Chinese Communist Party and the government bureaucracy and saw a new privileged elite; he looked at younger Chinese and saw a generation with no experience of revolution.

Mao feared that the Chinese revolution—his revolution—would end as a Soviet type of bureaucratic Communism run for the benefit of officials and not the people. So he called for a new revolution to create a truly egalitarian culture and urged students and teenaged youth to form Red Guards and attack the party bureaucracy. He obtained the backing of the army. Mass rallies were held. One rally in Peking was attended by millions of youths, who then made "long marches" back to their provinces to carry out Mao's program. Universities were shut down as student factions fought. Professors were beaten, imprisoned, and subjected to such extremes of humiliation that many committed suicide. Chinese with foreign experience or relatives abroad were persecuted. Homes were ran-

Protest during the Cultural Revolution against the Vietnam War. The man in the foreground wears the badge of the Central Academy of Art. [Magnum.]

1969, a new Central Committee, composed largely of military men, was established, and General Lin Piao (Lin Biao) was named as Mao's successor. Millions of students and intellectuals were sent to the countryside to work on farms. In 1970 and 1971, the revolutionary committees were reconstituted as party committees. Changes in China's foreign relations also made China's leaders want greater stability at home. China's relations with the Soviet Union had worsened to the point where in 1969, a pitched battle had broken out between Chinese and Russian troops over an island in the Ussuri River. After this encounter, bomb shelters were built in the main Chinese cities. It was just at this time that President Nixon began to withdraw United States troops from Vietnam. When he proposed a renewal of ties with China, China responded. Nixon visited Peking in 1972, and a new era of diplomatic relations began.

The second phase of the Cultural Revolution during the years between 1969 and 1976 was more moderate, but only in comparison with what had gone before. On farms and in factories, the emphasis continued to be placed on ideology, not incentives. Universities reopened, but students were selected by class background and not by examinations. In 1971, Lin Piao (Lin Biao) clashed with and attempted to kill Mao and seize the government, but his coup was foiled. He himself was killed when his plane crashed as he tried to flee to the Soviet Union. That is the official account of the events. Lin's place was taken by the so-called Gang of Four, which included Mao's wife and was abetted by the aging Mao. Class struggle was revived, and an official campaign was begun attacking the rightist "political swindlers" Lin Piao (Lin Biao) and Confucius.

CHINA AFTER MAO. Mao died in 1976. Four weeks later, the Gang of Four and other leading radicals were arrested. Teng Hsiao-p'ing (Deng Xiaoping, b. 1904), who had twice been purged for rightist tendencies during the Cultural Revolution, emerged as the central figure in Chinese politics. Teng ousted his enemies, rehabilitated those purged during the Cultural Revolution, and put his supporters in power. Portraits of Mao were removed from public places in August 1980.

After 1978, China's policies were those of Teng. He gave the Chinese people a greater measure of freedom, new material well-being, and hope for the future. In the economy, for example, new policies led to a surge in productivity. Communes were abolished and the basic accounting unit was shifted from the production team to the farm household. Grain production rose from 305 million tons in 1978 to 400 million in 1984. As one local leader commented, "When people work for themselves, they work better." Production

sacked for foreign books or works of art. Stone Buddhist sculptures that had endured since the Sung dynasty were smashed or defaced. High party officials were purged. Local party headquarters were attacked, and persons viewed as reactionaries, including some party cadres, were beaten to death. The crippled apparatus of party and government was replaced by revolutionary committees. During this early phase of the Cultural Revolution, Mao and the little red book containing his sayings were invoked almost as religious icons.

Eventually even Mao became tired of the violence and near anarchy. In 1968 and 1969, he called in the army to take over the revolutionary committees. In

Premier Chou En-lai and President Nixon eating with chopsticks in Shanghai in February 1972. Nixon's visit signaled a major change in both Chinese and American foreign policy. [UPI/Bettmann Newsphotos.]

incentives and a new market orientation enabled factories to produce more and better goods.

By the late eighties, rapid industrial growth led to overheating of the economy and inflation. Exports were expanded, and foreign investment was encouraged in New Economic Zones. Even private enterprises were permitted on a small scale. Instead of radios and bicycles—the household treasures of the 1970s—consumers during the 1980s sought color televisions, washing machines, and motorscooters. General Secretary Hu Yao-pang (Hu Yaobang), who was later demoted, supported the new realism, saying in 1985 that China "had wasted twenty years" on "radical leftist nonsense." But a month later, Teng reassured leftist critics within the army and the party that China's "ultimate goal is to implement Communism."

The same tension was apparent in China's intellectual life. Attempting to revive higher education after a generation of disruptions, universities reinstituted examinations in 1977, returned purged teachers to their

A confrontation in Peking (Beijing). In May 1989 Chinese democrat pleads with soldiers to end killings in Peking. He was pulled to safety by bystanders, and the tanks rolled on. In other instances, tanks crushed protesters. (Photo by AP Photographer Jeff Widener.) (AP World Wide Photos.)

classrooms, and sent scientists and scholars to study in Japan and the West. Official approval of attacks on the Cultural Revolution led to an outpouring of stories, plays, and reports. In *Nightmare* by Hsu Hui (Xu Hui), a mother whose son was killed during the Cultural Revolution asks, "Why? Why? Can anyone tell me why?" Liu Pin-yen (Liu Binyan) wrote of a corrupt officialdom that had "degenerated into parasitical insects that fed off the people's productivity and the socialist system."

But the new leeway to criticize the past did not extend to the post-1976 present. Writers were regularly enjoined to be "led by the Communist Party and guided by Marx-Leninism." University students spent one afternoon a week in political study groups, reading and discussing party directives or the *Selected Works of Teng Hsiao-p'ing*. When a writer in 1983 overstepped the invisible line separating what was permissible and what was not, a short campaign was launched against "spiritual pollution."

During the late eighties, the ferment that marked Eastern Europe and the Soviet Union under Gorbachev also appeared in China; it was as if a new virus had entered the communist world. China's growing contacts with the West, the ever more visible prosperity of Japan, Taiwan, and Hong Kong, and the increase in freedom within China itself led to a demand for still more freedom and political democracy. The government was divided, wanting the increases in productivity associated with greater economic freedom, yet loathe to make substantial concessions on political rights. In 1985 and 1987, it launched campaigns against "capitalist thinking" and "bourgeois democracy." But then in 1989, millions of students, workers, and ordinary Chinese from all walks of life demonstrated for democracy in Peking and dozens of other cities. Stunned, the government moved to reestablish order. Where the government would ultimately draw the line between material incentives and socialist equality, between intellectual freedom and Marxist conformity, was unclear. But the likelihood of any real alternative to the supremacy of the Communist Party seemed small. Nowhere else in the world was the fate of so many determined by the decisions of so few.

Japan

In 1945, Japan was poor, hungry, and ill clothed. Its cities were burnt out and its factories either destroyed or idle. Its shipping had been sunk, its railways were dilapidated, and trucks and cars were scarce. Yet, despite their wretched condition, the Japanese people steeled themselves for invasion and a final battle in defense of their homeland. Then, on August 15, 1945, the emperor broadcast Japan's surrender, saying that the "unendurable must be endured." After years of wartime propaganda, the Japanese reacted with shock at the fact of surrender, sadness at having lost the war, relief that the bombing was over, and apprehension about what would come next. They expected a harsh and vindictive occupation, but when they found it con-

Hiroshima after the atomic bomb.

structive, they turned to positive cooperation. Their receptivity to new democratic ideas and their repudiation of militarism led a Japanese writer to label this era "the second opening of Japan."

THE OCCUPATION. General Douglas MacArthur was the Supreme Commander for the Allied Powers in Japan. His headquarters in Tokyo was almost entirely staffed by Americans, and the occupation forces themselves were American except for British Commonwealth troops on the island of Shikoku. The chief concern of the first phase of the occupation was demilitarization and democratization. Civilians and soldiers abroad were returned to Japan and the military were demobilized. Ultranationalist organizations were dissolved and the Home Ministry was abolished. The police were decentralized and political prisoners were freed. Wartime leaders were charged with crimes against humanity—despite the absence of Dachaus in Japan—on the model of the Nuremberg trials in Germany. In addition, 210,000 officers, businessmen, teachers, and officials were removed from office for having supported the war. The thoroughness of these reforms reflected the occupation view that Japanese society had been tainted by feudal and militaristic values, and that Japan's leaders had been joined in a huge conspiracy to wage aggressive war.

As a part of democratization, women were given the vote, Shinto was disestablished as the state religion, labor unions were encouraged, and the holding companies of *zaibatsu* combines were dissolved. The old educational system, which had forced students at an early age to choose either an elite or a mass track,

was changed to a single-track system that kept open longer the option of continuing in school. The most radical undertaking, implemented like other reforms by progressive Japanese bureaucrats, was a land reform that expropriated landlord holdings and sold them to landless tenants at a fractional cost. The effect, ironically, was to create a countryside of politically conservative small farmers. Of all the occupation reforms, however, none was more important than the new constitution, written by the Government Section of MacArthur's headquarters and passed into law by the Japanese Diet. It fundamentally changed Japan's polity in four respects:

1. A British-style parliamentary state was established in which the cabinet was a committee of the majority party or coalition in the Diet. To this was added an American-style independent judiciary and a federal system of prefectures with elected governors and local leaders.

2. The rights of life, liberty, the pursuit of happiness, a free press, and free assembly were guaranteed. These were joined by newer rights, such as academic freedom, collective bargaining, sexual equality in marriage, and minimal standards of wholesome and cultural living.

3. Article 9, the no-war clause, stipulated, "The Japanese people forever renounce war as a sovereign right of the nation" and will never maintain "land, sea, and air force" or "other war potential." This article made Japan into something unique in the world: a major power without commensurate military strength.

4. The new constitution defined a new role for the

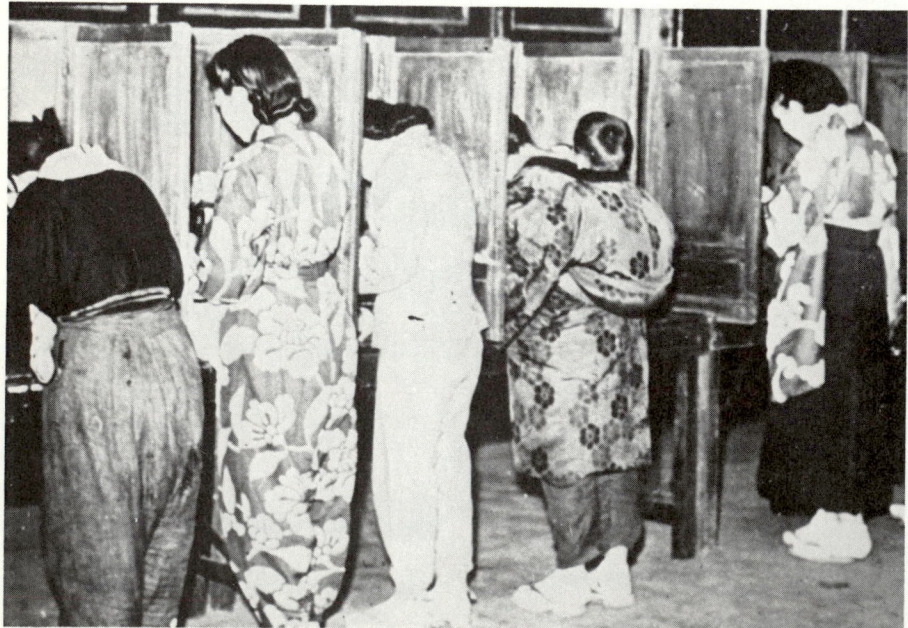

Women, newly enfranchised, voting in post-war Japan.

emperor as "the symbol of the state . . . deriving his position from the will of the people with whom resides sovereign power."

The Japanese people accepted the new constitution. Democracy was embraced with an intense if uncritical enthusiasm. The no-war clause was viewed by most as the guarantee of a peaceful future. Though it did not prevent the formation of a Self-Defense Force, it acted as a brake on military expenditures—which even forty years later were less than 1 per cent of Japan's gross national product. The Japanese had been readied for the changed position of the emperor by his speech on January 1, 1946, in which he renounced all claims to divinity. The occupation saw to it that the emperor traveled about Japan in a manner appropriate to a national symbol. No one who saw this rumpled-looking and inarticulate man suspected him of being a Shinto god. By the late 1960s the Japanese had come to feel a considerable affection for the Emperor Hirohito, who had shared in their wartime and postwar hardships; they were greatly saddened by his death in 1989.

The second phase of the occupation, during 1948 and 1949, turned to economic recovery so that democracy could take root and grow. To this end, the occupation dropped plans to deconcentrate big business further, encouraged the Japanese government to curb inflation, and cracked down on Communist unions that used strikes for political ends. The United States gave Japan $2 billion in economic aid.

The outbreak of the Korean War in 1950 marked the start of the final, quiescent phase of the occupation. The Japanese government looked to the Cabinet and the Diet, not to the occupying forces. By the time Japan regained its sovereignty in April 1952, the effect of the changeover was hardly noticeable in the daily life of the Japanese people. On the same day as the peace treaty, Japan signed a security treaty with the United States that provided for American bases and committed the United States to Japan's defense. Although politically controversial, the security treaty became the cornerstone of Japan's minimalist defense policy.

PARLIAMENTARY POLITICS. In 1945, Japan had a parliamentary potential that harked back to the rise of party power in the Diet between 1890 and 1932. It also had an authoritarian potential compounded of those factors that had led to the rise of militarism. Had it been occupied by the Soviet Union, the efficiency of its bureaucracy, its wartime economic planning, its educated and disciplined work force, and its receptivity to change at war's end would doubtless have made Japan a model Communist state. Occupied by the United States, the parliamentary potential emerged. Not surprisingly, the early postwar politics was the lin-

When the Emperor Shōwa died in 1989, nothing changed yet something was different. For older Japanese his death marked the passing of an era that had seen World War II and the postwar transformation of Japan. Here, well-wishers greet the emperor in 1985. [UPI/Bettmann Newsphotos.]

eal extension of the prewar party tradition, although within the new constitutional framework.

In 1946, the two big middle-of-the-road prewar parties resumed their contest for political power. The Minseitō became the Democratic Party (Minshutō). The Seiyūkai became the Liberal Party (Jiyūtō). The Socialist Mass Party, which had received 9 per cent of the vote in the 1937 elections, became the Japanese Socialist Party and won 26 per cent of the vote in 1947. For most of the first decade, the Liberals held power under Prime Minister Yoshida Shigeru (1878–1967). Before the war, Yoshida Shigeru had been an ardent imperialist, but he had favored close ties with Britain and the United States and had opposed the rise of militarism. After the war, he became president of the Liberal Party, cooperated closely with MacArthur, and worked to rebuild Japan's economy. He was probusiness and anti-Communist, and so autocratic in his dealings with bureaucrats and lesser politicians that he was nicknamed "one-man Yoshida."

An important turning point came in 1955, when the left and right wings of the Socialists, which had split into two parties in 1951, rejoined forces. This merger spurred the two big conservative parties to merge into a new Liberal Democratic Party (LDP). It was this party that governed Japan for the next thirty years and that remained unchallenged even during the late 1980s. Single-party rule is not usually associated with truly democratic governments. What did it mean in Japan? In the immediate postwar years, the strength of the conservatives was simply the continuation of prewar constituencies: the network of ties between local men of influence, prefectural assemblymen, and Diet politicians, and their ties to business and the bureaucracy. From the early 1960s on, the LDP became identified as the party that had produced the economic miracle and that had maintained Japan's security through close ties with the United States. It was widely recognized as more able than other parties. The Japanese people voted to keep it in power. Within the larger pattern of LDP hegemony, four trends were notable in Japanese politics:

1. From 1955 to 1960, the LDP was led by wartime figures who had resumed their political careers. It rather high-handedly modified several occupation reforms, recentralized the police, strengthened the Ministry of Education, and even considered a revision of the constitution. The opposition, led by Marxist socialists, many of whom had been persecuted during the war, branded these actions—LDP legislation was often passed by "snap votes"—as the "tyranny of the majority" and spoke of the revival of authoritarianism. Diet sessions were marked by rancor, confrontation, and even occasional violence. In 1960, however, a new prime minister decided to take a "low posture" in dealing with the opposition. He shifted the emphasis from politics to economics and drew up a plan to double national income in ten years. This plan led to a more peaceful era. In the prosperous 1970s and 1980s, confrontation declined further. The LDP not only regularly consulted opposition parties before presenting bills to the Diet but also won opposition support for most legislation.

2. Another trend was a steady decline in the LDP's popular vote: from 63.2 per cent in 1955 to 54.7 per cent in 1963, to 42.7 per cent in 1976. This decline was a result of the decreasing population of farmers, small shopkeepers, and others who traditionally voted for the LDP, and of an increase in the numbers of unionized laborers and white-collar workers, who tended to vote against it. For a while in the 1970s, the conserva-

tives faced the possibility that they would have to enter a coalition to stay in power.

3. In spite of receiving less than half of the popular vote, the LDP was able to maintain its Diet majority because its opposition became fragmented. In 1960, right-wing members broke away from the Socialist Party to form the Democratic Socialist party. In 1964, the Value Creating Society (*Sōka Gakkai*), a Nichiren Buddhist sect that grew to include about one tenth of the Japanese population, formed the Clean Government Party (*Kōmeitō*). The Japanese Communist Party gained ground as it became less militant, and during the 1970s, it received almost 10 per cent of the popular vote. The competition between opposition candidates at the polls worked to the advantage of the conservatives.

4. A final change—if not yet a trend—was the reversal in 1979 of the twenty-year decline in the LDP popular vote. It rose from 42.7 per cent in the general election of 1976 to 44.6 per cent in 1979, to 47.9 per cent in 1980, and then settled back to 45.8 per cent in 1983 and rose even further to 49.4 per cent in 1986. The LDP gains, despite a major scandal, reflected a growing conservatism. In the same socioeconomic groups, voters in their twenties were often more conservative than those in their thirties. Conservatism seemed to progress hand in hand with Japan's new prosperity.

ECONOMIC GROWTH. By one estimate, Japanese productivity in 1945 was about the same as it had been in 1918. It took a decade even to recover to prewar levels in textiles, steel, chemicals, and light industries. But then, just as growth was expected to moderate, productivity forged ahead and double-digit growth continued for almost two decades. Shipbuilding, machine tools, automobiles, and consumer electronics were followed by specialty chemicals, pharmaceuticals, scientific equipment, computer peripherals, and robots. Before the war, the phrase "made in Japan" had meant cheap, ten-cent-store goods. By the late 1970s, the names Toyota, Honda, Sony, Seiko, Suzuki, Kawasaki, and Yamaha were known throughout the world to stand for quality products. By the early 1980s, Japan was ahead of Europe in technology and was beginning to compete, one on one, with the United States in computers, advanced ceramics, and biotechnology.

Japan's extraordinary growth was the result of a combination of factors. An infrastructure of banking, marketing, and manufacturing skills had been carried over from prewar Japan. The international situation was favorable: Oil was cheap, access to raw materials and export markets was easy; and American sponsorship gained Japan early entry into the World Bank, the International Monetary Fund, and other international organizations. Japan's high rate of savings—close to

The "bullet train" that links Tokyo and Osaka at three times the speed of Amtrak.

20 per cent—contributed to reinvestment. Savings reflected an ingrained frugality ethic but were also a necessity because pensions were inadequate.

A revolution in education also aided growth. In the prewar years, education for most Japanese ended with middle school, and only a tiny fraction went to university. By the early 1980s, virtually everyone went to high school and 40 per cent went on to higher education, a larger percentage than in any European country. Moreover, with only half the population, Japan in the early 1980s was graduating more engineers than the United States—all of them employed in nonmilitary industries. This upgrading of human capital enabled Japan to tap the huge backlog of technology available in the United States. It was far cheaper to license or buy technology than to invent it. After "improvement engineering," Japan was then able to sell its products to the United States. By the late 1970s, the backlog was gone, and Japan's research expenses began to mount sharply.

Another factor was an abundance of high-quality labor. After a postwar baby boom, Japan in 1950 had a population of 83 million. It rose to 120 million by the mid-1980s and is expected to stabilize after the turn of the century. The excess of labor until the 1960s held down wages, and though wages subsequently rose, they remained slightly behind those of Japan's chief competitors. In 1945, almost 47 per cent of Japan's work force was in agriculture, but as agriculture became more efficient and excess labor was siphoned off by industry, this proportion declined to about 10 per cent in the mid-1980s. Industrial workers in Japan were more highly unionized than in the United States. The components of the national labor federations were company unions, however; although they engaged in spring offensives and marched with red flags on May Day, they took great pains not to impair their companies' productivity.

The role of government in helping developing industries with tariff protection and controls over foreign exchange was also important. It gave special depreciation allowances to industry, and low defense spending enabled it to keep corporate taxes low. The Finance Ministry and the Ministry of Trade and Industry encouraged the Bank of Japan to back private banks in refinancing Japan's industries. Particularly industries engaged in advanced technologies were the beneficiaries of cheap loans, subsidies, and the research results

COMPARISON OF GROSS NATIONAL PRODUCT

China	$ 272.0		
North Korea	20.1		
South Korea	95.7		
Taiwan	70.7		
Hong Kong	23.5		
Singapore	18.6		
Philippines	34.2		
Indonesia	76.2		
Malaysia	26.4		
India	210.0		
Pakistan	33.0		
Australia	231.0		
New Zealand	23.4	Japan	$1658
	$1134.8 billion		$1658 billion

of government laboratories. Critics who spoke of "Japan Inc." as though Japan were a single giant corporation may have overstated the case: Competition between companies in Japan was often fierce. But there is no denying that government was more supportive of business than it was regulative.

The magnitude of Japan's achievement may be grasped through a comparison of its Gross National Product (GNP) with those of other countries. To balance the two lists shown in the table, it would be necessary to add all of the countries in South America to the left-hand column.

Another comparison, easier for the inhabitants of a developed country to comprehend, is to point out that Japan in 1986 was roughly equivalent to France and West Germany combined. Of course, the yen was undervalued in 1986. As it rose during 1987 and 1988, Japan's GNP soared, becoming larger than that of the Soviet Union. And, while the U.S. GNP was larger still, the Japanese per capita product became several thousand dollars higher than that of Americans. It was especially significant that Japan's advance to a European level of well-being was based not on war and conquest but on the peaceful development of human resources in a free society.

Despite their economic strength, the Japanese continued to feel anxiety at what they saw as the precarious dependence of their economy on the vagaries of the world order. To live—let alone, prosper—they had to import foodstuffs and raw materials and export manufactured goods. Almost 80 per cent of Japan's oil came from the Near East. Trouble there or disruption of shipping lanes could be fatal to its economy. The Japanese in the late 1980s had yet to adjust to the reality that Japanese markets must be accessible to the world, if world markets were to be open to Japan. Despite a tremendously favorable balance of trade, Japanese policies continued to be self-serving. The United States sold Japan mainly food and raw materials. Even in areas where the United States was ahead in technology, it could sell to Japan only when Japan lacked competitive products. Japan was even more protectionist toward South Korea, Taiwan, and Hong Kong, which were developing a Japan-like productivity with lower labor costs. The economic question of the late 1980s was whether Japan could adjust its policies before world markets began to close to its products.

The triple engines of change in postwar Japan were occupation reforms, economic growth, and the explosive expansion of higher education. Taken together, one might expect them to have produced deep cultural strains and social dislocations. At the margin, these did occur. The growth among the urban poor of "new religions" such as the Value Creating Society was one indication. The social pressure on schoolchildren to excel was another. Tough competitive examinations were required merely to enter the better cram schools, which then prepared high school graduates for the all-important university entrance examinations. Serious magazines were filled with articles lamenting the excesses of Japan's "examination society."

Yet the ability of the society—the family, the office, the workshop, or the laboratory—to absorb the strains and to lend support to the individual was also impressive. Lifetime employment contributed to the low unemployment rate of about 2 per cent. Divorce rates were less than a third of those of the United States, homicide rates one fifth. No city was unsafe at night. There were no inner-city ghettos, no serious problems with guns or drugs. Pollution had been largely overcome—the LDP had preempted the issue to avoid attacks by opposition parties. Infant mortality was the lowest in the world and longevity the highest. By most comparative measures, the society was healthy, efficient, stable, and enjoyable.

The great tradition of Japanese culture continued in poetry, painting, the tea ceremony, flower arrange-

COMPARISON OF PER CAPITA PRODUCT

	GNP (in billions)	Population (in millions)	Per Capita GNP
France	$ 762.6	55.4	$13,770
West Germany	$ 908	61	$14,890
	$1670.6	116.4	
Japan	$1658.0	121.4	$13,660

Street scene in Shinjuku, Tokyo. Leisure in an increasingly affluent society.

ment, the Kabuki and Nō theaters. On New Year's Day, the emperor presided at a poetry contest. Masters of pottery, papermaking, or swordsmithing were honored by being designated as "Living National Treasures." In the modern arts, the prewar tradition of vigorous experiments with new or hybrid forms continued. The Japanese awareness of nature, so evident in exciting films like Kurosawa's *Rashomon* or *The Seven Samurai*, carried over to the photography in Japanese National Television dramas that rivaled those of the British Broadcasting Corporation in quality. Symphony orchestras in Japan's major cities played Mozart and Stravinsky and also native compositions with haunting passages played on the Japanese flute and zither. Clothing designers competed in New York and Paris as well as in Tokyo. College students attended rock concerts or listened to jazz and read Japanese science fiction along with the writings of contemporary novelists. The case of postwar Japan amply supports an argument for parallelism between economic and cultural dynamism.

Korea, Vietnam, and America's Wars in Asia

Korea and Vietnam, the other two countries in the East Asian zone of civilization, both became colonies. Korea was annexed by Japan in 1910; Vietnam became a part of French Indochina in 1883. In each country, colonialism engendered a powerful anticolonial nationalism. After World War II, each became divided into a Communist north and a non-Communist south, Korea immediately and Vietnam later. Each experienced civil war. The United States joined both wars to stem the spread of Communism. Never before had the United States fought in countries about which it knew so little.

Korea. On Japan's surrender in 1945, U.S. forces occupied Korea south of the thirty-eight parallel and Soviet troops occupied the north. Though there had been a promise of unification, two separate states developed. In the south, the United States sought to encourage the formation of an independent, democratic, self-governing nation. But it settled for Syngman Rhee, a skillful politician and long-term nationalist leader, who emerged to form a government that was anti-Communist and conservative. Rhee's party won the May 1948 election. At the age of seventy-three, Rhee became the first president of the Republic of Korea, and the U.S. military government formally ended. Most of the officers in Rhee's army had formerly served in the Japanese army. Rhee's conservative government was strongly supported by the million Koreans who had fled the north.

In the north, the Russians established a Communist government under Kim Il-sung. Kim, who had spent time with the Chinese Communists during the 1930s, entered the capital of Pyongyang wearing the uniform of a Soviet army major. When the south held elections in 1948, the north hurriedly followed suit. In September, the Democratic People's Republic of Korea was established. From the late 1940s, most of the officers in the North Korean army were men who had fought on the Communist side in the Chinese civil war. At the end of 1948, the Soviet Union withdrew its troops from North Korea. During 1949 and early 1950, the United States withdrew its troops from the south. The withdrawal was a part of a larger American disengagement from continental Asia after the victory of the Communists in China. The United States also dissociated itself from the Chinese Nationalist regime on Taiwan as a part of its policy of "letting the dust settle."

On June 25, 1950, North Korea invaded the south in an attempt to reunite Korea. Its armies were stronger than those of the south and would have succeeded had the United States not intervened. But the Cold War had begun in Europe. The invasion, coming four months after the signing of the Sino-Soviet Alliance, was seen by the United States not as an internal matter of Korean state politics but as an act of world Communism. (North Korean archives are closed, and it is not known whether or not the decision to invade had Chinese or Soviet approval.) The United States rushed troops from Japan to Korea, and it obtained UN backing. It also sent naval forces to the Taiwan Straits to protect the Nationalist Chinese. Over the next several years, it entered into military alliances with South Korea, Japan, the Nationalists on Taiwan, the Philippines, and the non-Communist states of Southeast

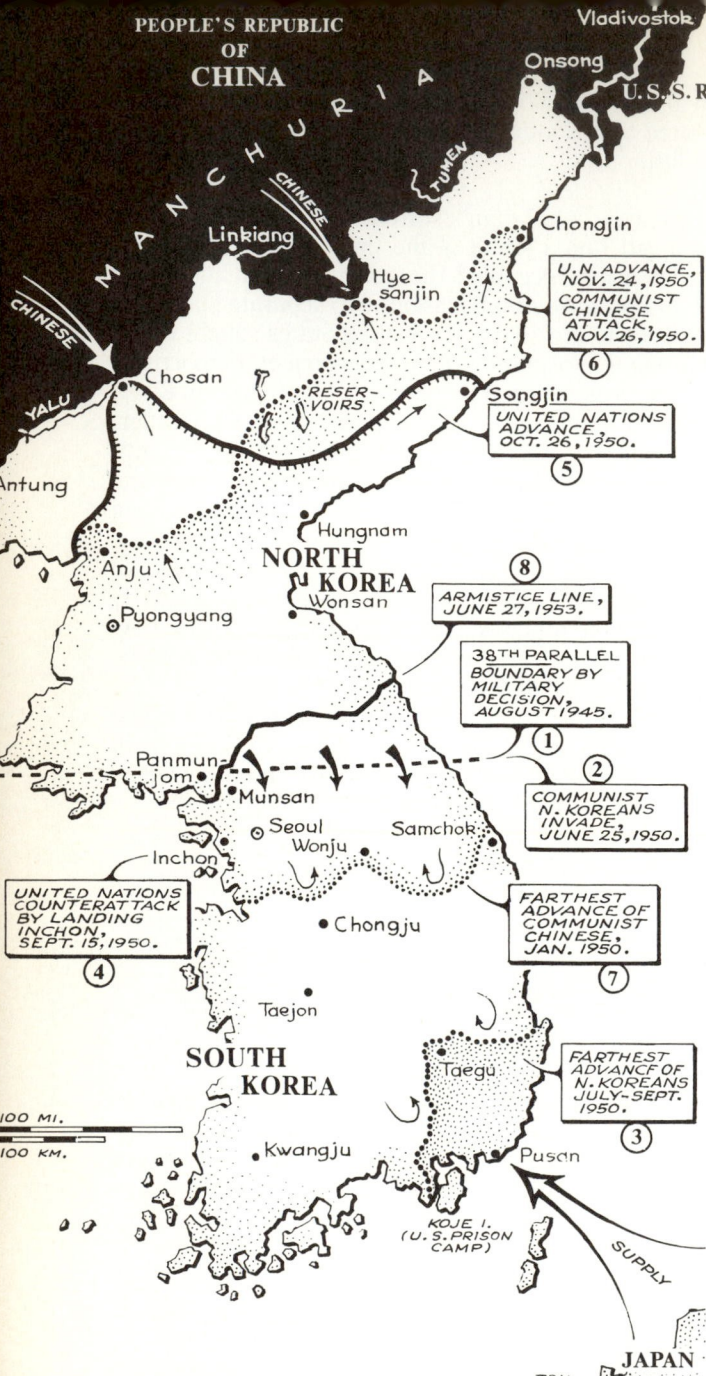

MAP 37-2 KOREA, 1950–1953 *The North Korean
invasion of South Korea in 1950 and the bitter three-
year war to repulse the invasion and stabilize a firm
boundary near the thirty-eight parallel are outlined
here. The war was a dramatic application of the American policy of "containment" of communism.*

Asia. This was a major turn in postwar American foreign policy.

During the first months of the war, the unprepared
American and South Korean forces were driven south-

ward into an area only fifty miles in diameter about
Pusan on the southeastern rim of the Korean peninsula. But then amphibious units led by the United Nations commander General Douglas MacArthur landed
at Inchon in the middle of the peninsula. They drove
back the North Korean armies beyond the thirty-eighth
parallel—almost as far north as the Yalu River. In
midwar, the American policy had shifted from the containment of Communism to a rollback. The UN forces
in Korea were one-half American and two-fifths Korean; the rest were made up of contingents from Britain, Australia, Turkey, and twelve other nations. In
the final phase of the war, it was China rather than the
Soviet Union that sent in "volunteers" to rescue the
beleaguered North Korean forces. Chinese troops
pushed the overextended UN forces back to a line
close to the thirty-eighth parallel. The war became
stalemated in 1951 and ended with an armistice on July
27, 1953. The 142,000 American casualties made the
war the fourth largest in U.S. history.

Since 1953, the border between the two Koreas has
remained closed. Each side has maintained about
600,000 troops. The north has remained a closed, authoritarian state with a planned economy, a stress on
heavy industry, collectivized agriculture, a scarcity of
consumer goods, and a totally controlled press. The
cult of personality surrounding Kim Il-sung, who in
1989 was still in power at the age of seventy-seven,
was developed to an extent unimaginable in either Stalin's Russia or Mao's China. Kim designated his son as
his political successor. Kim rules through a Marxist-
Leninist Korean Communist Party. However, the kinship terminology used to describe the fatherly leader,
the mother party, and the familial North Korean state
seem almost Confucian. In 1986, the population of
North Korea was 20 million, its GNP was about $20
billion, and its per capita product was about $1000.

Postwar South Korea, in contrast to the totalitarian
North, might be called semiauthoritarian. South Koreans could travel abroad and read foreign books and
newspapers as long as they were not Communist.
Opposition parties were active, though hobbled, and
their leaders were frequently jailed. Students were
able to mount protest demonstrations, though they
were usually blocked by the riot police. Syngman Rhee
ruled until 1960, when massive student demonstrations forced him to retire at the age of eighty-five. In
the thirty years that followed, power was held by three
generals: Park Chung-hee (1961–1979), Chun Doo-
hwan (1980–1988), and Roh Tae-woo (1988–). Park
and Chun came to power by coups d'état; then, doffing
their uniforms, they won controlled elections as civilian presidents. On coming to power, Chun had promised to step down in 1988. A free election was held
in December 1987. The leaders of the two opposition parties fought each other for the urban anti-

Opening at Soeul Olympics. Just as the 1964 Olympics in Tokyo became a symbol of Japan's reemergence in the postwar world, so did the 1988 Olympics in Soeul mark the coming of age for an industrializing Korea.

government votes, permitting Roh, the hand-picked successor of Chun, to become president. Most Koreans saw the election as the beginning of Korea's transition to democracy.

The other development in South Korea was economic growth. The GNP rose from $11.2 billion in 1960 to $27.6 billion in 1970, $60.6 billion in 1980, and $95.7 billion in 1986. With a population of 41.6 million, its per capita product in 1986 was $2300. This double-digit Japanese-type of performance was achieved by a combination of factors: a legacy of skills from the colonial era, U.S. aid after the Korean War, a consistent and determined government policy for promoting growth within a market economy, a disciplined and hard-working labor force, an educated people, and an open U.S. market for Korean exports. The results transformed Korean society, making it more prosperous than could have been imagined during the 1960s. Korean heavy industry was dominated by groups such as Hyundai or Daewoo, which resembled the Mitsui or Mitsubishi of prewar Japan.

VIETNAM. The history of Vietnam since 1945 consists of three cycles of war. The first was an anticolonial war against the French that lasted from 1946 to 1954. On one side was the Viet Minh (League for the Independence of Vietnam), headed by Ho Chi Minh (1892–1969). Ho had participated in the founding of

the French Communist Party in 1920, studied in Moscow in 1923, worked under Mikhail Borodin in Canton in 1925, and founded the Vietnamese Communist Party in 1930.

In 1941, Ho began the Viet Minh as a united-front organization to resist the Japanese. At the war's end, when he proclaimed the Democratic Republic of Vietnam, he was the preeminent nationalist leader in his country. However, his authority was contested by non-Communist nationalists and several religious sects. On the other side were the French, who from 1883 to 1940 had ruled Indochina, composed of the ethnically distinct units of Vietnam, Cambodia, and Laos. The French had been Japanese puppets from 1940 to March 1945 when they were interned. The French returned immediately after the war and forcibly occupied the country. A civil war soon broke out between the French and their Vietnamese allies, on the one hand, and the forces of Ho Chi Minh, on the other. The French tried to legitimize their rule by setting up a puppet government in 1948. The fighting continued until 1954, when the French lost a major battle at Dien Bien Phu and, with it, their willingness to continue an unpopular war.

A conference at Geneva divided the country into a Communist north and a non-Communist south. The French left Vietnam. In the south, Diem Ngo Dinh, a non-Communist nationalist who had not collaborated with the French, came to power and established the Republic of Vietnam. Much of his political support came from the 900,000 Vietnamese who had fled from the north.

The role of the United States in this struggle changed. Initially, in line with its wartime anticolonial position, the United States urged the French to reach an accommodation with Ho Chi Minh. But after the rise of Communist China and the outbreak of the Korean War, the United States came to see the French actions in Vietnam as an attempt to stem the tide of Communism. The French encouraged this view. The United States recognized the French puppet government and gave $4 billion in aid to France between 1950 and 1954. After the French withdrawal, the United States transferred its support to Diem.

A second cycle of war was fought in Vietnam between 1959 and 1975. The fighting began with guerrilla

Ho Chi Minh (1890–1969), *nationalist, communist, and father of the Vietnamese revolution.* [Magnum.]

warfare in the south. Some said it was a local response to Diem's suppression of his political enemies. Others, including North Vietnam after the war's end, said it was directed from the north. Eventually the struggle became a full-scale war between the north and the south. The north was aided by the Soviet Union and China. Unlike the Korean War, China sent no volunteers to fight in Vietnam. The south was aided by the United States. U.S. forces increased from 600 military advisers in 1961, to 16,000 troops in 1963, to 70,000 in 1965, and then rose steadily to a peak of over half a million in 1969. Despite massive aid, South Vietnam—and the United States—lost the war. The reasons for the defeat were debated long after the war ended:

1. The South Vietnamese government, all too often corrupt, inspired little loyalty in its citizens.
2. Ho Chi Minh was a national hero to most South Vietnamese as well as in the north. Even many who were anti-Communist felt pulled in two directions. South Vietnamese often viewed the United States as the successor to the French—despite its billions in aid and its total lack of colonial ambitions in Southeast Asia—and supported Communist guerrillas as the continuation of the earlier anticolonial struggle.
3. Both the Communist guerrillas in the south and the North Vietnamese troops fought better than those of South Vietnam.
4. In the jungle terrain of Vietnam, the tremendous technological edge of the United States could not be brought to bear. A greater tonnage of bombs was dropped on supply trails in Cambodia than was

MAP 37-3   VIETNAM AND ITS SOUTHEAST ASIAN NEIGHBORS.

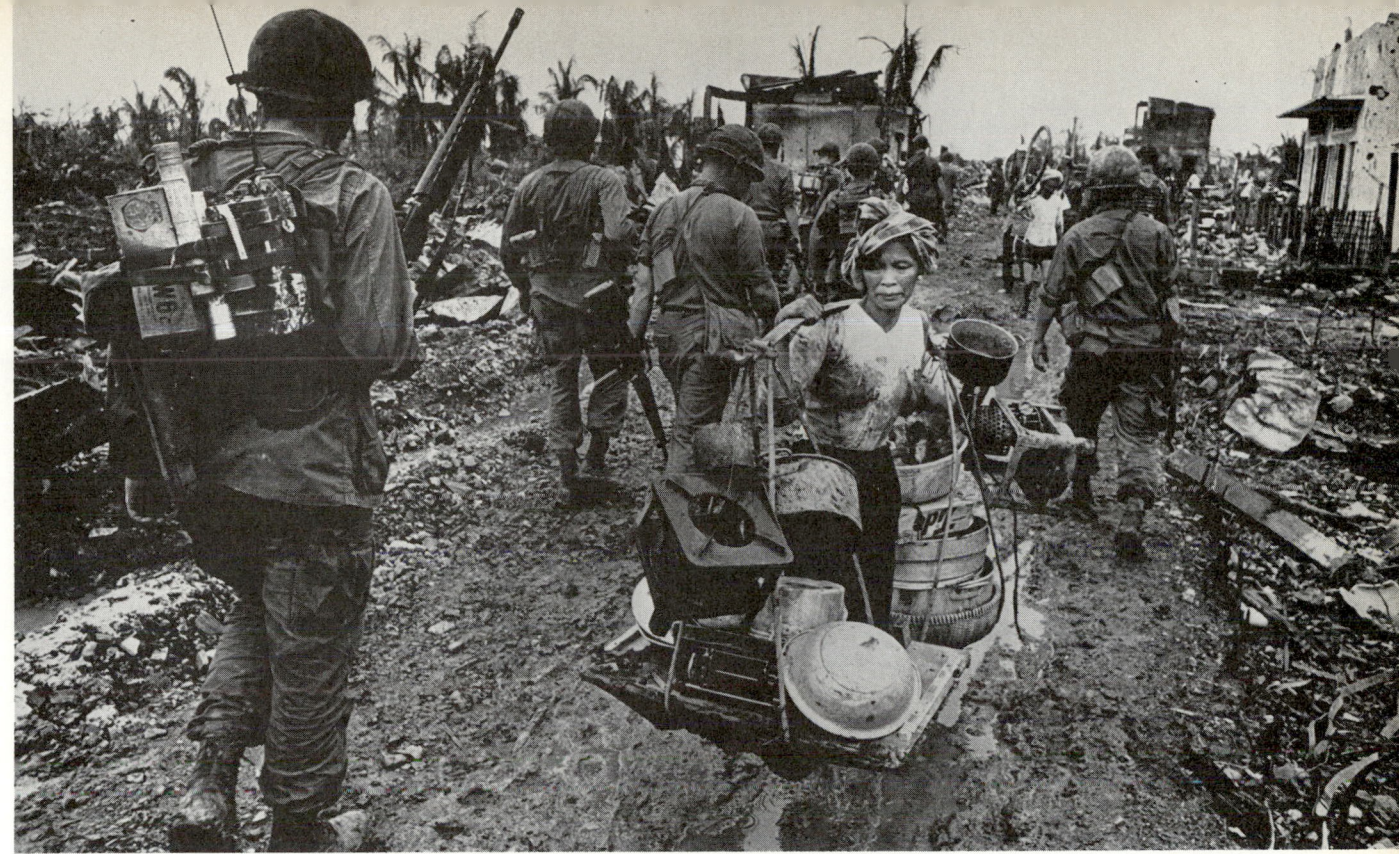

The Vietnam War. Never before had the United States fought in a country of which it knew so little. American troops were withdrawn in 1973, and Hanoi overran the South two years later. The real losers in the war were the Vietnamese people, whose land had been devastated. [Griffiths: Magnum.]

dropped on Japan in World War II, but supplies continued to flow to the south.

5. Early in the war, the U.S. action in Vietnam was seen, as in Korea, as a battle against world Communism. After the gravity of the Sino-Soviet split was understood, it became a battle to halt the spread of Chinese Communism. Yet sentiment in the United States against a cruel and remote war was so strong that it divided the country and led to a political and spiritual crisis.

Lyndon Johnson chose not to run for reelection in 1968. When Richard Nixon became president, he began slowly to withdraw American troops, calling for the "Vietnamization" of the war. In January 1973, a ceasefire was arranged in Paris. The last U.S. troops left two months later. The fighting continued. In 1975, the South Vietnamese forces collapsed, and the country was reunited under the Hanoi government in the north. Saigon was renamed Ho Chi Minh City.

In the mid-1970s, few areas were as devastated as Vietnam and its neighbors. After unifying the country, Hanoi sent many thousands of those associated with the former South Vietnamese government to labor camps, collectivized agriculture, and in 1976 began a five-year plan. Several hundred thousand Vietnamese and ethnic Chinese fled by boat or across the Chinese border for refuge.

A third cycle of war began in 1978 when Vietnam invaded Cambodia. Pol Pot, the head of the Communist Khmer Rouge, had come to power in Cambodia in 1975. In the next three years, his government evacuated cities and towns, abolished money and trade, banned Buddhism, and executed or caused to die of starvation an estimated one million persons—roughly 15 per cent of the total population. Schoolteachers and persons with education were singled out as targets.

Border incidents also broke out between Cambodian and Vietnamese troops. Vietnam was Cambodia's traditional enemy as China was Vietnam's. In 1978, Vietnam occupied Cambodia and the following year set up a puppet government. They were unable, however, to suppress the guerrilla forces of Pol Pot completely. Most Cambodians passively accepted Vietnamese rule because their fear of a return by Pol Pot was far greater than their hostility toward the Vietnamese. The costs of Vietnam's Cambodian adventure were high: It had to abandon its first five-year plan, and in the mid-1980s, its per capita product was approximately the same as that of Bangladesh.

In its international relations, Vietnam became an ally of the Soviet Union and an enemy of China. It gave the Soviets a naval base at Cam Ranh Bay in return for economic, military, and diplomatic support. Vietnam's relations with China deteriorated almost immediately after 1975. Vietnam feared that China would attempt to dominate it and resented China's invitation to Nixon in 1972, when American troops were still fighting in Vietnam. China, for its part, resented Vietnam's treatment of its ethnic Chinese and felt that Vietnam was ungrateful for the aid it had received during the war. In 1979, China decided to "teach Vietnam a lesson" and invaded its four northern provinces. Vietnam repelled the invaders, but losses were heavy on both sides. Since 1979, China has supported Pol Pot's guerrillas and has maintained pressure on Vietnam's northern border with occasional shelling and shooting. In 1985, it threatened to teach Vietnam a second lesson.

From 1988 the situation again began to change. Vietnam began economic reforms of the kind being carried out in the Soviet Union and China. China's relations with the Soviet Union improved. China's relations with Vietnam also improved, and some trade was permitted. In 1988 Vietnam withdrew some troops from Cambodia and in April 1989 announced that all troops would be withdrawn by September. These changes boded well for peace in the area. Only the future of Cambodia, where Pol Pot's guerrillas remained a potent force, remained clouded.

An Uncertain Future in World Perspective

As we close this volume, we need to point to several major elements in the contemporary world scene. First, we are struck by the remarkable elements of continuity in world history. The great religious and moral traditions with which we opened our narrative (as supplemented by the later rise of Christianity and Islam) remain forces of immense influence throughout the world despite all of the vast political, economic, and social changes that we have traced. The power of these cultural forces should not be underestimated when we look to the future. In nation after nation, various forms of religious revival or traditionalist resurgence challenge those modes of life associated with science, technology, and economic development.

Second, the new forces of science and modern technology, as they have developed for the past three centuries, touch every part of the globe. Rapid communication, the computer revolution, the advanced technology of military weapons, and new modes of manufacturing are changing and redirecting virtually all human cultures. Both the tempo and instruments of human change are more rapid than ever before in history.

Third, all world civilizations are touched today by the reality of human vulnerability. In the midst of great medical progress, a new disease, such as AIDS, raises questions for science and social values. Nations with less than stable political structures possess military weapons of enormous destructive potential. As economic growth expands into new areas of the globe, the problems of pollution and environmental damage spread. The exhaustibility of natural resources haunts one society after another.

The challenges we face are thus now global. One question that confronts all of us is how the traditions that have sustained the human experience on this planet may be drawn upon to provide wisdom, as humankind faces unprecedented challenges and by the same token unprecedented opportunities. Moreover, there arises the question of how humankind may go beyond those traditions to forge and direct its own future.

Suggested Readings

AFRICA

A. BOYD, *An Atlas of World Affairs*, 7th ed. (1983). A simple and brief, but useful, quick reference book on the current shape of world nations, alliances, and major political issues. Especially useful for keeping up with the changing political units of contemporary Africa.

B. DAVIDSON, *Let Freedom Come* (1978). A broad-ranging study of modern Africa, using incisive specific examples to support thoughtful analyses of trends and events across the continent since the nineteenth century.

B. FREUND, *The Making of Contemporary Africa: The Development of African Society since* 1800 (1984). The final three chapters give excellent treatment of decolonization after 1940, tropical Africa since independence, and southern Africa into the 1980s.

R. W. JULY, *A History of the African People*, 3rd ed. (1980). Chapters 14–22. The last part of the book provides a careful and clear survey of post-World War I history, including chapters on the various regions of the continent and on topics like nationalism.

C. M. TURNBULL, *The Lonely African* (1962). A haunting and vivid series of case studies of contemporary Africans caught in the upheavals of modernization and rapid change.

INDIA AND PAKISTAN

W. T. DE BARY et al., eds., *Sources of Indian Tradition*, 2nd ed. (1988). The final chapters offer selections from major modern Indian political and literary figures, accompanied by solid introductions.

N. MAXWELL, *India's China War* (1970). A fascinating, detailed study of the Sino-Indian border war of the early 1960s. It is illuminating especially about the intricacies of Indian politics of the time.

D. E. SMITH, *India as a Secular State* (1963). Still pertinent today for the vexed question in South Asia of how to deal with secularism and religion in the political arena.

S. WOLPERT, *A New History of India*, 3rd ed. (1988). The closing chapters of this fine survey history are particularly helpful in orienting the reader in postwar Indian history down to the mid-1980s.

ISLAM

J. J. DONOHUE AND J. L. ESPOSITO, eds., *Islam in Transition: Muslim Perspectives* (1982). Selections from Muslim writers, including many since World War II, on issues of social, political, and religious change in the Islamic world.

S. T. HUNTER, ed., *The Politics of Islamic Revivalism: Diversity and Unity* (1988). Collected papers on specific Islamic countries from North Africa to Indonesia. Helpful overview with political emphasis.

N. R. KEDDIE, *Roots of Revolution: An Interpretive History of Modern Iran* (1981). Chapters 6–9 focus on Iran from 1941 through the first years of the 1978 Revolution and provide a solid overview of history in this era.

H. MUNSON, JR., *Islam and Revolution in the Middle East* (1988). Based on numerous specific studies of recent years, this little book offers a good general picture, especially for students, of the historical and ideological background of contemporary Islamic religiopolitical movements and on the Iranian revolution in particular.

W. C. SMITH, *Islam in Modern History* (1957). Old, but still the most thoughtful and comprehensive treatment of issues facing Muslim peoples from the Arab World to Inida.

J. O. VOLL, *Islam: Continuity and Change in the Modern World* (1982). Chapters 5–8. A brief, yet detailed survey of trends and major events in recent Islamic history from Indonesia to Africa.

LATIN AMERICA

S. DE VYLDER, *Allende's Chile* (1976). A sound introduction to a difficult and controversial subject.

J. DOMÍNGUEZ, *Cuba: Order and Revolution* (1978). A useful overview.

W. LAFEBER, *The Panama Canal: The Crisis in Historical Perspective* (1981). An important and far-ranging consideration of U.S. policy in Latin America.

W. LAFEBER, *Inevitable Revolutions: The United States in Central America* (1984). Essential for understanding the background of the present tensions in the area.

O. LEWIS, *Five Families: Mexican Case Studies in the Culture of Poverty* (1959). A classic.

C. MESA-LAGO, *The Economy of Socialist Cuba* (1981). The best introduction.

A. STEPAN (ed.), *Authoritarian Brazil: Origins, Politics, and Future* (1973). A group of excellent essays.

G. WYNIA, *Argentina in the Post-War Era* (1978). The standard introduction.

CHINA

F. BUTTERFIELD, *China, Alive in the Bitter Sea* (1982). Observations about China by a Chinese-speaking *New York Times* reporter.

A. CHAN, R. MADSEN, AND J. UNGER, *Chen Village: A Recent History of a Peasant Community in Mao's China* (1984). An account of the postwar history of a Chinese village.

H. LIANG, *Son of the Revolution* (1983). An autobiographical account of a young man growing up in Mao's China.

B. LIU, *People or Monsters? and Other Stories and Reportage from China After Mao* (1983).

M. MEISNER, *Mao's China: A History of the People's Republic* (1977).

F. W. MOTE AND D. TWITCHETT (eds.), *The Cambridge History of China, Vol. 14: The People's Republic, Part I* (1987). A summary of the best recent research.

M. WOLF, *Revolution Postponed: Women in Contemporary China* (1985).

JAPAN

G. BERNSTEIN, *Haruko's World: A Japanese Farm Woman and Her Community* (1983). A study of the changing life of a village woman in postwar Japan.

H. HIBBETT (ed.), *Contemporary Japanese Literature: An Anthology of Fiction, Film, and Other Writing Since 1945* (1977). Translations of postwar short stories.

H. PATRICK AND H. ROSOVSKY, *Asia's New Giant: How the Japanese Economy Works* (1976).

E. O. REISCHAUER, *The Japanese* (1977). The best overall account of contemporary Japanese society and politics.

E. F. VOGEL, *Japan as Number One: Lessons for America* (1979). A sociological analysis of the sources of Japan's economic strength.

Index

Index